Environmental
Physiology
of the
Amphibians

Environmental Physiology of the Amphibians

Edited by
Martin E. Feder
and Warren W. Burggren

The University of Chicago Press / Chicago and London

Martin E. Feder is professor of organismal biology and
anatomy at the University of Chicago. Warren W. Burggren is
a professor in the Department of Biological Sciences at the
University of Nevada at Las Vegas.

The University of Chicago Press, Chicago 60637
The University of Chicago Press, Ltd., London
© 1992 by The University of Chicago
All rights reserved. Published 1992
Printed in the United States of America
01 00 99 98 97 96 95 94 93 92   5 4 3 2 1

ISBN (cloth): 0-226-23943-8
ISBN (paper): 0-226-23944-6

Library of Congress Cataloging-in-Publication Data

Environmental physiology of the amphibians / edited by
    Martin E. Feder and Warren W. Burggren.
        p.   cm.
    Includes bibliographical references and index.
    ISBN 0-226-23943-8. — ISBN 0-226-23944-6 (pbk.)
    1. Amphibians—Physiology.   2. Amphibians—
Ecology.   I. Feder, Martin E.   II. Burggren, Warren W.
QL669.2.E58   1992
597.6′041—dc20   91-30944
                                            CIP

⊗ The paper used in this publication meets the minimum re-
quirements of the American National Standard for Information
Sciences—Permanence of Paper for Printed Library Materials,
ANSI Z39.48-1984.

Contents

Preface

The proliferation of biological knowledge poses an enormous challenge to life scientists. The literature is so large as to defy mastery, and can necessitate specialization at the expense of breadth or a sense of general issues or priorities for a field. In no area of the life sciences is this challenge so great as in organismal biology. Organismal biologists must keep abreast of recent advances in biochemistry, molecular biology, cell biology, genetics, developmental biology, morphology, physiology, neurobiology, endocrinology, behavior, population biology, ecology, evolutionary biology, and systematics, as well as relevant advances in environmental aspects of the physical sciences. Fortunately, the incentive and rewards to organismal biologists for meeting this challenge are also large: a deepened understanding of how complex biological systems work and how they have evolved.

In many ways, the environmental physiology of amphibians is organismal biology in microcosm. The most important recent breakthroughs increasingly come from highly focused studies of particular systems or at particular levels of biological organization. As the bibliography of this volume demonstrates, the literature of even as circumscribed a field as the environmental physiology of amphibians is both already voluminous and still expanding. Yet the reason this field exists as a discrete scientific discipline is the desire of its practitioners to relate their diverse findings to the function of intact amphibians in an environmental context. To this end, a knowledge of recent progress in related disciplines is relevant, and a sense of major foci of research, research areas approaching the point of diminishing returns, and major biological questions yet to be answered is essential.

We began this project because we believed that an entire book on the environmental physiology of the amphibians could advance the study of this group. We planned this volume in hopes that it would emulate the role that John Moore's *Physiology of the Amphibia* (1964) had played in invigorating the general physiological study of amphibians more than twenty-five years ago; chapter 1 discusses this role in detail.

We immediately found the magnitude and diversity of the relevant literature to be daunting, and sought help. Recognizing that edited volumes of this nature run the risk of ratifying a particular set of research priorities or questions, we chose an ecumenical approach. We invited contributors who, although they might have strong opinions on past achievements of the field and future directions, were capable of accommodating and presenting diverse points of view on their assigned topics. These contributors were invited to become thereafter the "first among equal" authors of chapters. We corresponded with numerous additional colleagues to explain this project and invite them to supply input (literature, data on work in progress, advice, opinions, and actual assistance in writing) to the lead author of each chapter. We also encouraged the lead author of each chapter to involve as many coauthors as might be reasonable. In many cases, lead authors also corresponded with one another and circulated drafts of chapters to avoid overlap and encourage complementarity. So many colleagues became involved that we found the selection of competent but previously uninvolved reviewers to be no easy task. Nonetheless, each chapter was reviewed by at least one external reviewer and at least one editor, and several chapters passed through several rounds of revision. We are especially grateful to these reviewers for the considerable improvement they have engendered in this volume. At any rate, this volume is, to an unusual extent, a product of the entire community of those who study the environmental physiology of amphibians.

Despite this considerable collegial cooperation, each lead author faced a formidable task. Any of the chapters in this volume could well be expanded into a book in itself, and the contributors had to run a fine line between so encyclopedic a treatment that major themes would be obscured and so terse a presentation that a chapter's value as a review of the literature would be diminished. In addition, some topics were the subject of major reviews that appeared either before or during the preparation of chapters. Our editorial response to these issues was to give the lead authors free rein. Because of the role we hope this book will play as a springboard for future research, we felt it more important to encourage the particular enthusiasms of lead authors than to constrain every chapter to conform to some standard formula. Thus, some chapters present compendious tables, others are eclectic, and still others strongly advocate particular points of view or research approaches, in each case because the authors believed their approach would best serve the scientific advancement of their topic. We recognize that some heterogeneity is the result but prefer spirited heterogeneity to bland conformity.

We have designed this book so that it can be read from cover to cover to yield an overview of the environmental physiology of amphibians and a prospectus for future research. We have edited individual chapters extensively to achieve this end, and in each chapter have included extensive references to relevant material elsewhere in the volume. Moreover, each entry in the bibliography indicates all chapters in which it has been cited, in hopes that readers will be led to diverse considerations of topics.

The University of Chicago Press has played a special and commendable role in the production of this book. The press has readily accommodated components of the book that add to its scientific utility (e.g., extensive tabular material and bibliography, and its very size), and indeed made scientific utility and accessibility first among its considerations. We are especially grateful to Susan E. Abrams, Executive Editor, who not only has encouraged an emphasis on scientific utility and impact rather than on convenient publication, but also has been an articulate and effective spokesperson for the role of books in advancement of scientific disciplines.

The editing of this book was supported in part by NSF Grants DCB87-18264 (to MEF) and DCB86-08658 (to WWB). As always, Juan Markin provided advice, support, and friendship throughout the rigors of editing.

1 A Perspective on Environmental Physiology of the Amphibians

Martin E. Feder

The vertebrate class Amphibia manifests extraordinary biological diversity and evolutionary novelty. Amphibians range from the permafrost of Alaska to equatorial lowland jungles, from forest canopies to rivers below to burrows beneath the soil to caves far underground, and from deserts to mountains to ocean beaches. Amphibians include as many species as there are species of mammals, range from smaller than a fingertip to 1.5 m long, exhibit more variation in reproductive modes than any group but fishes, and sometimes travel many times their length in a single leap. Amphibians represent both the fastest known vertebrate movements and the lowest vertebrate metabolic rates. Many species are esteemed as gourmet delicacies, and some serve as Australian Aboriginal canteens, while at least one species is so toxic that touching it might be fatal. Most importantly, this abundant and successful group has persisted through eons of environmental challenges that have doomed many other kinds of organisms.

Understanding the mechanistic underpinnings of this extraordinary biological diversity and persistence has long been an attractive challenge for physiologists. Indeed, the use of amphibians in the analysis of general physiological problems predates the founding of modern physiology. As early as 1671, Malpighi used amphibians as a model for the investigation of renal structure and function. Since that time, amphibians have become standard subjects in studies of neuromuscular function, active transport, endocrinology, developmental biology, and so forth. A spectacular example was Otto Loewi's (1921) use of a perfused amphibian heart preparation in the discovery of neurotransmitters. In these and other studies, however, the choice of amphibians was primarily a matter of convenience and utility rather than an end in itself. Accordingly, the publication of John Moore's edited volume *Physiology of the Amphibia* in 1964 was a milestone for the study of amphibian physiology. Literally for the first time, enough information was assembled in one place to achieve a comprehensive overview of the basic physiology of some amphibians. What distinguished Moore's book was that its contributors analyzed these previous studies in terms of the integrated function of amphibians as entire organisms. Moore's book set the stage for an understanding of how amphibians work as amphibians. Brian Lofts (1974–1976) expanded Moore's earlier

work, editing two additional volumes that emphasize environmental aspects of reproduction as well as neural, endocrine, and immune systems, among other topics.

Moore's book came at a time when the techniques and paradigms of environmental physiology, physiological ecology, and ecological physiology were just becoming prevalent in the study of lower vertebrate tetrapods. The 1960s were a time of major revolution in the study of vertebrate physiology. Previously, vertebrate physiology had been studied largely in the experimental laboratory preparation, in which subjects were exposed to a controlled, typically univariate environment only occasionally resembling actual environments, and were specifically prevented from exercising normal behavioral responses to physiological challenges. The major objective of such studies was the enumeration and understanding of physiological mechanisms that underlie homeostasis in the sense in which it occurs in mammals. Environmental physiology, by contrast, sought to describe the environments normally encountered by free-ranging animals and the mechanisms by which matter and energy were exchanged between organisms and their environment; the implications (i.e., advantages, costs, and constraints) of these exchanges for organismal function; the suite of physiological, biochemical, morphological, and behavioral mechanisms with which animals normally responded to environmental challenges and opportunities; and the historical trajectories and processes by which these mechanisms evolved. Thus, although the integrative perspective of Moore's book was a major stepping-stone for the developing field of environmental physiology of amphibians, the book itself could present at best an incomplete or premature characterization of amphibian ecophysiology.

The twenty-five years after Moore's book appeared witnessed many important advances in the environmental physiology of amphibians. These are too numerous to list comprehensively here; indeed, this entire book is necessary to do so. As just one example, the web of complex, interrelated behaviors and processes affecting the simultaneous exchange of heat, water, and respiratory gases was yet to be described in detail in 1964. The pivotal role of anaerobiosis in support of exercise, described in chapter 12, was yet to be discovered. Beginning in the late eighteenth century, physiologists had examined individual components of gas exchange and circulatory regulation; but in 1964 no one had come to grips with amphibians' simultaneous regulation of multiple gas exchangers and perfusion thereof (described in chapters 5–7 and 16). Our understanding of the physiology of amphibians, particularly its "environmental" aspects, has undergone a major qualitative shift from its state in 1964. Curiously, however, there has been no synthetic volume to describe this advance in understanding of amphibians.

The many dramatic advances in amphibian environmental physiology have led directly to the present volume. The objectives here are

1. to present a synthetic overview of amphibian ecophysiology,
2. to review the primary data on which this synthesis is based,
3. to enumerate current trends in the field, and
4. to identify major gaps in our knowledge and productive avenues of future research.

We hope this book will define the environmental physiology of amphibians in the same way that Moore's book defined the general physiology of amphibians.

THE MYTH OF THE "TYPICAL" AMPHIBIAN

To evaluate the current state of the environmental physiology of amphibians, we must understand the intellectual context in which its scientific investigations have been carried out. Historically, the study of the environmental physiology of amphibians rested on two major but incorrect characterizations. First, amphibians incorrectly have been assumed to represent an intermediate stage in the evolution from fishes (a "primitive" stage restricted to water) to amniotes ("advanced" forms that, in invading terrestrial environments, have escaped this restriction). The second incorrect characterization shaping previous ecophysiological studies was that amphibians as a group inhabit both aquatic and aerial environments either simultaneously or during their life cycle. As the ensuing chapters will document, the second of these characterizations is inaccurate for many amphibians, and the first may be inaccurate for all Recent amphibians. Nonetheless, these characterizations are extremely widespread among students of amphibian physiology, and so have greatly influenced the nature of investigations, experimental design, and the interpretation of resultant data.

One of the goals of environmental physiology is to understand the ramifications of physiological diversity (or lack thereof) for the differential performance and reproductive success of individuals, the distribution and abundance of populations, and the evolutionary longevity of species and higher taxa (Feder et al. 1987; Pough 1989b). Obviously, success in attaining this goal necessitates the correct specification a priori of the extant physiological diversity in a subject taxon. In the eyes of most biological scientists and in most introductory accounts of the group, amphibians are typified by ranid frogs (e.g., *Rana catesbeiana*, the bullfrog; *Rana pipiens*, the leopard frog; and *Rana temporaria*, the "common frog" [Porter 1972], toads (Bufonidae: *Bufo bufo*, the common toad; *Bufo americanus*, the American toad; and *Bufo marinus*, the

marine toad), the clawed frog (Pipidae: *Xenopus laevis*), and the tiger salamander and the spotted salamander (Ambystomatidae: *Ambystoma tigrinum* and *Ambystoma maculatum*). These species have several important similarities, not all of which are biological. Most significantly, all are (or were) fairly abundant in the wild, easily captured and transported to the laboratories of experimental biologists, easily maintained in the laboratory, and amenable to experimentation. All except *Xenopus* have habits that make them conspicuous to man (at least by amphibian standards), and all except *Xenopus* have geographical ranges that overlap the largely Holarctic distribution of amphibian physiologists. Accordingly, when experimental protocols call for amphibians, these are the most likely subject species, as a glance at the bibliography of this volume will attest.

Not surprisingly, then, the explanation of amphibian environmental physiology has become heavily vested in the biological attributes that these genera share. Each of these species, however, is an extremely specialized form. None can be considered typical of amphibians, any more than could hummingbirds be considered typical of birds in general or could a champion weightlifter be considered representative of humans in general. Nonetheless, if the particular biological attributes of these unrepresentative but convenient species happen to accord with inappropriate preconceptions concerning amphibians and evolution, biologists can be misled into believing that amphibian attributes in general support these preconceptions. How representative of amphibians, then, are *Ambystoma, Bufo, Rana,* and *Xenopus?*

A BESTIARY

The objective of this section is to survey the phylogenetic, physiological, morphological, behavioral, and ecological diversity of the Amphibia. Its intent is to convey the extremes of diversity rather than to provide a comprehensive overview of the amphibians. For the latter, we refer the interested reader to the pioneering but still pertinent work of Noble (1931) and the recent works of Duellman and Trueb (1986), Halliday and Adler (1986), Pough (1989a), and Pough, Heiser, and McFarland (1989), from which the following is drawn.

HISTORICAL ASPECTS OF EVOLUTION

Early tetrapods first appear in the fossil record during the Devonian period (ca. 400 million years ago). Their probable ancestors were sarcopterygian fishes, either crossopterygians or Dipnoi (lungfishes). Several major subclasses of amphibians of uncertain relationship to living amphibians (and to one another) flourished, diversified, and then declined during the late Paleozoic. Living amphibians belong to a single subclass, the Lissamphibia, which is the only subclass to persist beyond the Jurassic period. Unfortunately, except for a similarity to branchiosaur temnospondyls, the exact relationship between the Lissamphibia and potentially ancestral groups of amphibians is unclear. The earliest fossil Lissamphibia are from the Jurassic period and already differ considerably from the other groups. The amphibians giving rise to the Lissamphibia arose as a distinct group before the groups that eventually gave rise to synapsids (the primitive reptiles that would eventually give rise to mammals) and the groups giving rise to dinosaurs and modern reptiles. Thus, the Lissamphibia cannot be considered the progenitor of any amniote; indeed, the Lissamphibia have been a separate evolutionary lineage for more than 350 million years.

The Lissamphibia comprise three extant orders. Gymnophiona, the caecilians or apodans, lack limbs and have elongated, snake- or wormlike bodies. Anura (= Salientia), frogs, toads, and the like, lack tails as adults and have four limbs, with the hindlimbs often specialized for saltatory locomotion. Caudata (= Urodela), the salamanders, have tails as adults. Although authorities can be found to support all possible relationships among these three orders, the exact relationship is obviously enigmatic and controversial. Importantly, the three orders represent three separate lines of evolution whose divergence may be more ancient than that of the archosaurs (dinosaurs and birds), mammals, chelonians (turtles and tortoises), and squamates (lizards and snakes). Each, then, constitutes a long-independent solution to a complex of environmental challenges.

DIVERSE LIFESTYLES OF AMPHIBIANS

To what extent can amphibians be viewed as evolutionary progenitors, intermediates, or transitional forms? The answer to this question depends largely on the perspective of the investigator and the context into which physiological data are placed. As an example, the absence of a complete ventricular septum in the hearts of amphibians and many reptiles has been known for centuries. From the perspective of a physiologist acquainted only with mammals, this absence is a gross circulatory defect that has been remedied fully only in the evolution of birds and mammals. From the perspective of a physiologist familiar with sarcopterygian fishes, amphibians, and reptiles, this absence is a beneficial specialization that permits the shunting of blood between the systemic circulation and that serving the air-breathing organs (see Johansen and Burggren 1985). From a similar perspective drawn from the breadth of amphibian physiology, we comment on several of the "defects" that are allegedly inherent in the physiology of amphibians, or in whose remediation amphibians allegedly represent a first step.

• Misconception: Obligate transition from aquatic to terrestrial medium. Reality: In each order of amphibians, species range from those that never leave water to those that never enter water. Some caecilians are entirely aquatic while others inhabit burrows and leaf litter; some of the latter are viviparous and thus do not enter water to breed. Some anurans (e.g., *Xenopus* and the related genus *Pipa*) are so specialized for an aquatic existence that they are nearly incapable of moving on land. By contrast, many frogs (e.g., *Eleutherodactylus coqui* [Leptodactylidae]) never enter the water. Similarly, salamanders include both strictly aquatic forms (*Amphiuma* [Amphiumidae], *Cryptobranchus* [Cryptobranchidae], *Necturus* [Proteidae], and *Siren* [Sirenidae]) and entirely terrestrial species (many plethodontid salamanders). On land, various species are diurnal, nocturnal, crepuscular, arboreal, and fossorial. Some amphibians take terrestriality to an extreme by inhabiting deserts (e.g., *Cyclorana* [Hylidae], and *Neobatrachus* [Myobatrachidae] in Australia and *Scaphiopus* [Pelobatidae] in North America).

• Misconception: Obligate link to standing water for reproduction, including egg laying and larval development. Reality: Amphibians include species whose eggs, larvae, or both exist outside of water, and direct-developing species that lack larval stages. Many frogs lay their eggs in terrestrial habitats (e.g., the frog *Agalychnis dacnicolor* [Hylidae], which lays its eggs on tree limbs above water and whose larvae fall into the water upon hatching). Others construct nests out of foam (e.g., *Physalaemus pustulosus* [Leptodactylidae]). Various frogs may deposit their eggs in special pits or folds in the dorsal skin (*Pipa* [Pipidae]), the mouth, vocal sacs (*Rhinoderma* [Rhinodermatidae]), or the stomach, and brood the eggs and/or larvae therein. In all three orders (e.g., the caecilian *Ichthyophis,* the frog *Neobatrachus,* and the urodele *Salamandra* [Salamandridae]), eggs hatch within the mother, the young consume yolk and/or maternal tissue, and partially grown young eventually emerge from the mother. Many species of terrestrial plethodontid salamanders and some leptodactylid frogs lay their eggs on land, with larval stages passing within the egg and postlarval offspring emerging from the egg. In species with larvae, some may develop on the backs of parents; some morphologically specialized anuran larvae inhabit the banks of streams above the waterline.

• Misconception: Transition from noncleidoic eggs vulnerable out of water to cleidoic eggs that resist water flux. Reality: As is obvious from the foregoing account, some amphibians lack external eggs entirely. In other cases, noncleidoic eggs clearly do well outside of water, and cleidoic eggs undergo considerable water fluxes. Some fishes and amphibians intentionally lay eggs in air above water; immersion becomes a hatching cue when water rises. In many frogs and salamanders, however, the eggs are entirely terrestrial. Amphibian eggs are clearly "open" (i.e., noncleidoic), but so are the eggs of all other tetrapods. In many reptiles with flexible-shelled eggs, uptake of water from the immediate environment is critical to successful development of the embryo and its survival thereafter. The same appears true of some direct developing amphibians. In birds, the *loss* of an appropriate amount of water through the "cleidoic" egg is essential for proper development, as is the exchange of respiratory gases.

• Misconception: Transition from branchial to pulmonary gas exchange. Reality: Amphibians in no sense represent a unique (or perhaps even a remarkable) structural innovation in the evolution of lungs. Air-breathing organs evolved independently numerous times in the bony fishes. Even an ontogenetic transition from branchial to pulmonary gas exchange does not occur in many cases. In the aquatic salamanders *Cryptobranchus* and *Necturus,* the lungs (although present) contribute negligibly to total gas exchange. By contrast, hundreds of species from five different families of urodeles never develop functional lungs as adults. A near-universal but often overlooked feature of amphibian gas exchange is reliance upon the skin. "Cutaneous" gas exchange is significant in eggs, larvae, and adults; in air and in water; and in all three orders of amphibians. Amphibians include species that lack lungs, gills, or both. With the possible exception of those few species of frogs with greatly reduced integumentary permeability, cutaneous gas exchange is the rule.

• Misconception: Improvement in integumentary impermeability. Reality: Most extant amphibians have integuments that are relatively permeable by the standards of other vertebrates or many arthropods. That a permeable integument is necessarily an impediment to a terrestrial existence is questionable on several accounts. First, as mentioned above, many amphibians with permeable skins are terrestrial, and some inhabit deserts. Second, loss of a heavily scaled (and presumably impermeable) integument is a derived condition and likely a result of natural selection, that is, an adaptation. Early tetrapods were heavily scaled, and some extant caecilians retain rudimentary scales. Possible explanations of the utility of a permeable skin reflect its use as a respiratory and osmoregulatory organ: Permeability enhances the exchange of respiratory gases, osmolytes, and water, as well as evaporative cooling. In air, cutaneous gas exchange may have little or no ventilatory cost. Amphibians can rehydrate transcutaneously, often through specialized regions of the skin. Finally, when necessary some amphibians can reduce integumental permeability through integumentary specializations, secretion of waterproofing substances, or formation of cocoons. Permeable skin may better be viewed as a specialization for the amphibian mode of life than as a design flaw.

• Misconception: Improvement from poikilothermic ectothermy to homeothermic endothermy. Reality: Even during the most strenuous of activities (escape from predators, calling), amphibians have at best modest abilities to increase body temperature through high rates of heat production. Although endothermy is clearly not their strong suit, many anurans and urodeles have the capacity for behavioral thermoregulation. At some times, many amphibians experience stable body temperatures in the field. Whether this stability in body temperature is a result of behavioral thermoregulation per se, amphibians' occupancy of microhabitats that coincidentally are thermostable, high rates of evaporative cooling in dry air, or some combination of these processes is currently a matter of controversy. At other times, many amphibians experience variable body temperatures. Some of this lability is undoubtedly due to the lack of environmental thermal heterogeneity suitable for thermoregulation. Even when the thermal environment will permit behavioral thermoregulation, however, some amphibians appear to thermoregulate imprecisely or not at all, for good reason: because the associated costs of thermoregulation (e.g., water loss, risk of predation, energetic cost of a high constant body temperature) are too high. Indeed, in part because amphibians invest so little energy in heat production and often experience low body temperatures by mammalian standards, their overall energy requirements can be spectacularly low; amphibians can tolerate prolonged starvation and persist in food-poor habitats that would be lethal to mammals.

• Misconception: Improvement in capacity for sustained locomotion. Reality: Although the frog's leap, the larva's startle response, and the salamander's tongue projection are models of intense, rapid behaviors in vertebrates, these activities are not sustainable. Many amphibians, when they do move or behave, do so at a slow, deliberate pace. To what extent are the typical behaviors of amphibians evidence for an evolutionary restriction of sustainable behavior, which amniotes have circumvented? The fastest speed (or the most intense behavior) that a moving animal can sustain is a joint function of the efficiency with which it moves and its maximum rate of aerobic metabolism. With respect to the efficiency of gait,

textbooks have long characterized amphibians as evidencing a sprawling posture that impedes locomotion. However, measurements of the cost of both ambulatory and saltatory locomotion in amphibians do not support any general inefficiency in amphibian movement (Full, Zuccarello, and Tullis 1990). With respect to aerobiosis, amphibians typically achieve only modest rates of oxygen consumption during locomotor activity and rely heavily upon anaerobic metabolism. Moreover, aspects of amphibians' muscular systems, cardiorespiratory apparatus, and metabolic enzyme profiles do not accord with sustainable activity. Male anurans, however, can sustain high rates of oxygen consumption during vigorous calling, suggesting that a modest aerobic capacity is not an obligate feature of amphibians. Finally, the notion that amphibians are handicapped by an inability to sustain locomotion or other behavior may not bear scrutiny. Just as amphibians may realize a substantial energetic savings by not thermoregulating precisely, they may minimize costs and risks of activity by being inactive. According to this perspective, modest aerobic capacities may be an outcome of evolutionary selection rather than an evolutionary constraint or impediment.

• Misconception: Inability to cope with osmoregulatory challenges. Reality: When *Physiology of the Amphibia* appeared in 1964, the limits of amphibians' adaptation to osmoregulatory challenges were known poorly or not at all. The following instances have since been studied in detail: The crab-eating frog (*Rana cancrivora*), green toad (*Bufo viridis*), and some salamanders of the genus *Ambystoma* (Ambystomatidae) and *Batrachoseps* (Plethodontidae) live in saline habits, including saline lakes and ocean beaches. "Waterproof" frogs, *Phyllomedusa sauvagei* (Hylidae) and *Chiromantis* spp. (Rhacophoridae), are uricotelic and rival desert reptiles in rates of transcutaneous water loss. The Australian desert frogs *Cyclorana* (Hylidae) and *Neobatrachus* (Myobatrachidae) surround themselves with cocoons and can store water equal to 50% of body mass in their bladders. The North American spadefoot toads, *Scaphiopus* (Pelobatidae), accumulate urea in their bladders during dehydration and use the bladders as a water store. Also poorly known in 1964 were many of the physiological, morphological, and behavioral specializations for water conservation or uptake: water-conserving postures, costal grooves and epidermal sculpturing, the "pelvic patch" for uptake of water from the soil, behavioral hydroregulation, cutaneous mucous discharge, capillary derecruitment in dry environments, and so on. Many, if not most, amphibians restrict their activities to habitats in which dehydration may be easily avoidable. However, the exceptions to this rule suggest that considerable osmoregulatory latitude is inherent in the physiology of amphibians.

Not only do the foregoing vignettes establish that the environmental physiology of the Amphibia as a group is far more diverse than that of *Rana, Bufo, Ambystoma,* and *Xenopus,* they collectively pose a major challenge to physiologists. Experimental physiology usually operates from a strong consensus as to what constitutes a normal or effective physiology. Physiologies that can potentiate high levels of performance (e.g., work, speed, endurance, courtship, reproduction, acquisition of food and water, homeostasis, all throughout a wide range of extreme environmental conditions) are ideal. The "best physiology," either as exemplified by a particular organism or by an abstract optimality model, thus becomes a ready standard for evaluating the capacity of other lesser physiologies, the extent of disease, or the physiology of a particular species or group. This physiological standard, however, may fail utterly when applied to amphibians. We contend (as did Pough [1980, 1983] originally and at greater length) that amphibians' physiological systems typically underlie a lifestyle involving modest requirements for energy, mass, and water; small size; behavioral regulation; voluntary abandonment of homeostasis when possible. These attributes, in turn, have substantial benefits in minimizing vulnerability to extinction, by enabling amphibians to survive protracted periods of starvation, unfavorable climate, and so forth. If this perception is correct, then the *absence* of many attributes associated with the physiological success of mammals may in fact be specializations for amphibians' way of life. Accordingly, in practice physiologists may find it difficult to distinguish whether a given trait whose presence in mammals would be maladaptive is actually maladaptive in amphibians, actually adaptive in the context of amphibians' lifestyles, or simply insufficiently understood. Furthermore, in making such distinctions, physiologists will need to consider long-term measurements of mass and energy balance, risk management as a life history tactic, the behavior and physiology of free-ranging individual amphibians, and other principles and practices outside the traditional scope of physiology. No uniform context of physiological investigation can be applied to animals independent of their phylogenetic status. We hope that physiologists will look upon this point as a challenge rather than as a frustration.

Finally, we urge that physiologists who study amphibians familiarize themselves with the biological diversity of the entire group. A useful starting point is the recent work *Biology of Amphibians* by William Duellman and Linda Trueb (1986), in which chapter 19 presents a classification of the entire group. *Ambystoma, Bufo, Rana,* and *Xenopus,* the amphibians of greatest convenience to physiologists, are four genera in two orders. According to Duellman and Trueb, the Amphibia include 62 extant genera comprising 350 living species in the order Caudata, 34 extant genera comprising 162 living species in the order Gymnophiona, and 301 extant genera comprising 3,438 living species in the order Anura. More than 80% of all citations in amphibian biology are to investigations of two genera, *Rana* and *Xenopus* (Wassersug and Nishikawa 1988), with most probably to no more than eight species within these genera, which account for less than 0.2% of the species diversity of amphibians. Not only does an emphasis on the species of physiological convenience grossly underrepresent the physiological diversity of the amphibians; it ignores many interesting attributes of the group that may lend insights into its physiology. We hope that physiologists will take increasing advantage of this diversity. We also warn that readers of this book will need to exercise judgment about the extent to which a literature so dominated by a few species can be generalized with respect to the Amphibia as a group. To expand the phylogenetic awareness of readers, we will routinely present the families (and, when ambiguous or potentially confusing, the orders) to which species of urodeles and anurans belong when the species are given in the text (e.g., *Bufo* [Caudata: Bufonidae], *Rana* [Caudata: Ranidae], and *Xenopus* [Caudata: Pipidae]). As a concession to the phy-

logenetic selectivity of the literature, however, we will routinely abbreviate the foregoing three genera as *B., R.,* and *X.*

THE PHYSIOLOGY OF AMPHIBIANS

"Despite the high long-term probability of extinction, every organism alive today is a link in a chain of parent-offspring relationships that extends back unbroken to the beginning of life on earth. Every organism is a part of an enormously long success story—each of its direct ancestors has been sufficiently well-adapted to its physical and biological environments to allow it to mature and reproduce successfully" (Bartholomew 1987, 14).

That amphibians have flourished in diverse environments on a geological time scale convincingly establishes their physiologies as successful in evolutionary terms. Like every other kind of organism alive today, amphibians represent a simultaneous solution to a variety of intersecting problems:

- acquiring, assimilating, and sequestering enough mass, water, and energy to grow and reproduce;
- maintaining the internal environment within reasonable limits such that growth and reproduction can be accomplished;
- avoiding abiotic and biotic hazards, defending against them, or both.

What gives organismal biology its coherence and its practitioners such stimulus is that these problems are coupled (fig. 1.1; see also Porter 1989). In isolation, a particular solution to one of these problems may well exacerbate the others. An organism that acquires mass and energy and avoids inimical environments by being very active may thereby jeopardize water, charge, and heat balance, greatly increase requirements for mass and energy, and have little discretionary mass and energy for reproduction. An organism that is impermeable to water loss may thereby impede exchange of respiratory gases, ions, and nitrogenous wastes. These examples are admittedly both hypothetical and extreme but emphasize that organisms must balance a series of simultaneous mass, heat, energy, charge, and water equations. Each of these equations is simultaneously external (i.e., between organism and environment) and internal (i.e., partitioning among "competing" sources and sinks within the organism). Also, each equation is dynamic; it may be far from equilibrium at any moment, but must balance over the life of the organism.

One sense in which amphibians are especially interesting for scientific study is that the external component of their simultaneous equations, exchange between organism and environment, is comparatively large. All other groups of vertebrates have evolved structures that resist, to a greater or lesser extent, the integumentary exchange of mass, energy, and/or water, for example, slime, scales, feathers, and hair. In general, other vertebrates have internalized their highly permeable gas exchangers to a greater extent than have amphibians. As a result, the entire skin of amphibians is a site of seemingly unbridled flux of water, energy, osmolytes, and respiratory gases. In many cases these fluxes seemingly permit only limited independence from the immediate environment. Accordingly, the internal milieu of amphibians may be far less fixed than that of many other vertebrates! The indi-

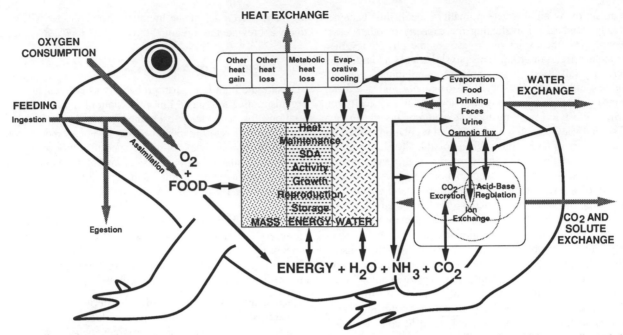

Fig. 1.1 Coupled fluxes of energy and mass. The *shaded arrows* represent the fluxes of mass (respiratory gases, organic and inorganic substances, water) and energy (heat, charge, and potential energy in mass) between organism and environment. The *solid arrows* represent the fluxes of mass and energy within an amphibian, both between various compartments and functions and as coupled with environmental fluxes.

The various fluxes and compartments of amphibians are all coupled to one another. No single flux or allocation occurs in isolation; amphibians must simultaneously solve every problem of mass and energy flux in a way that will permit successful internal homeostasis, growth, and reproduction. (After Porter 1989.)

vidual mechanistic solutions to each of these problems is, of course, a first major focus of amphibian ecophysiology and is reviewed extensively in this volume. How evolution has resulted in the simultaneous solution of these problems is a second focus, which currently eludes resolution.

A second source of general interest in the environmental physiology of amphibians is the extraordinary extent to which some amphibians temporarily depart from energy/mass balance, equilibrium, or homeostasis in the course of their lives, and the extent to which amphibians in general otherwise depart from mammalian rules for evolutionary success in vertebrates. The foundation of these features is a metabolic rate that is low by vertebrate standards, especially in urodeles (Feder 1976a; see chapter 14). Some amphibians can go for years without food and, when they do feed, can devote nearly half of what they assimilate to reproduction. Amphibians may tolerate, both on an annual and a short-term basis, excursions in body water, temperature, and osmolyte concentrations that would kill other vertebrates, especially mammals. The temporary abandonment of homeostasis enables amphibians to live in ways not permissible to mammals, and their minuscule energy requirements enable amphibians to endure protracted spells of gross environmental unfavorability. Together, these traits may underlie a profound resistance to extinction. The physiological mechanisms that underlie these extraordinary abilities of amphibians, as well as the evolutionary histories

of these traits, are unknowns whose resolution will require the combined efforts of physiologists, ecologists, and evolutionary biologists.

This is an exciting time, not just for the environmental physiology of amphibians, but for ecological and comparative physiology in general (Burggren 1990a; Calow 1987; Feder 1987a; Prosser 1986; Spotila 1989). Some of the possible "new" directions for these conjoined fields resonate strongly with the major issues in amphibian ecophysiology; for example, the assignment of priorities among interacting physiological systems (Jackson 1987a), optimization in physiology (Sibly and Calow 1986), the coupling of organism-environment fluxes (Porter 1989), and evolutionary physiology (Feder et al. 1987). Similarly, the increasing application of modern molecular techniques in organismal biology (Block 1991; Feder and Block 1991) may yield enormous benefits in our understanding of amphibian physiology (e.g., Spotila et al. 1989). The future of the study of amphibian ecophysiology, however, will also depend on a comprehensive knowledge of the field's past and the present consolidation of the field's achievements. This is above all a book of facts. The past twenty-five years have produced numerous advances in our understanding of the environmental physiology of amphibians. The hope of the editors and contributors to this volume is that it will serve as a foundation for even greater advances in the future.

Part 1
Control Systems

Traditionally, the practitioners of amphibian environmental physiology, neurobiology, and endocrinology have led separate scientific lives. They patronize different journals, attend different meetings, solicit funding from separate sources, and so on. This unfortunate separation may have been an outgrowth of the extraordinary vitality of each scientific discipline, it being nearly impossible to remain abreast of recent scientific developments *within* each of these disciplines, let alone developments in the others. Indeed, accounts of either the neurobiology of amphibians or their endocrinology could legitimately occupy entire volumes of their own (and have already done so). Not surprisingly, treatises on the environmental physiology of other groups often have not emphasized neural and endocrine functions, sometimes relegating them to separate volumes and sometimes ignoring them entirely. The approach in this volume is otherwise. A sophisticated understanding of organism-environment interactions, including the transduction of environmental stimuli, the initiation of organismal responses, and the integration of regulatory processes on both a short- and long-term basis, requires a firm grounding in modern neurobiology and endocrinology. Accordingly, this volume begins with chapters introducing each of these topics.

A comparison of chapter 2, "The Nervous System" (Wilczynski) and chapter 3, "Endocrinology" (Herman), with their counterparts in *Physiology of the Amphibia* (volume 1 in 1964, volume 2 in 1974, and volume 3 in 1976) reveals several remarkable developments. First, the revolution in molecular biology and the extraordinary advances in cell physiology have led to major qualitative changes in these fields. In chapter 3, for example, Ceil Herman discusses posttranslational processing of gene products, receptor densities, calcium-mediated signal transduction, and related topics as a matter of course; these topics are simply absent from *Physiology of the Amphibia*. Application of the techniques and results of molecular pharmacology evidently has widely and rapidly permeated the study of amphibian physiology, not only in these two chapters but in many others in the present book. Similarly, the discussion of amphibian neurobiology reflects the extraordinary advances in the neurosciences, particularly in neuroethology and neuroanatomical techniques.

Chapters 3 and 4 reveal the conservative nature of morphological and gross physiological evolution as evidenced by the nervous and endocrine systems of amphibians. Sometimes at levels of great detail, urodeles, anurans, and caecilians (when studied) share many features of nervous and endocrine function with one another and with other vertebrates. Either one must invoke a highly unlikely scenario of parallel evolution to explain these similarities, or concede that these features must have arisen before the Lissamphibia diverged from other vertebrate lineages and must have been maintained since then. However, weaving through this conservatism in the "raw materials" of the nervous and endocrine system is also considerable diversity. For example, in any given amphibian species calcium ion concentration in blood is regulated by several different hormones; however, the hypercalcemic action of prolactin in urodeles has not evolved (or has been lost) in anurans. Thus, while the basic elements of the nervous and endocrine systems are common to most amphibians, the uses to which motor output and chemical messengers are put are less predictable.

Against this mixed background of basic patterns and diversity, chapters 2 and 3 present a cohesive and detailed description of the major integrative systems of amphibians. What clearly emerges is that the study of these integrative systems has changed markedly in recent years. Rather than amphibian biologists having to settle for data generated by general physiologists attempting to elucidate general physiological principles (and often collected under convenient but quite unrealistic conditions), the studies on the endocrine and nervous systems described in chapters 2 and 3 indicate that data are being collected by environmental physiologists with the *primary* goal of understanding how these systems operate *in amphibians*.

2 The Nervous System

Walter Wilczynski

The nervous system is the interface between an animal and its environment. Through its sensory systems, the organism monitors the external world and its own internal state. The central nervous system integrates the incoming information and uses it to select and guide behavioral responses to the processed information. The reponses are finally effected through motor and neurosecretory neurons. Understanding the features of sensory systems and their interconnections with brain areas responsible for controlling visceral and somatic motor expression is a prerequisite for an environmental approach to the physiology of the nervous system, in which the basic pattern of neural organization and variation on it can be interpreted in light of life history and environmental challenges. The amphibian nervous system has provided several models for exploring these processes (Wilczynski and Ryan 1988b), particularly the visual and auditory systems of frogs and toads (Ewert 1987; Fite 1976; Roth 1987; Fritzsch et al. 1988).

The nervous system of any amphibian reflects a hierarchy of influences. First, amphibians possess a general organizational plan of sensory, motor, and integrative systems typical of all vertebrates. Variation in size, circuitry, and physiological properties occur within the bounds imposed by this phylogenetically conserved and probably developmentally constrained architecture.

Second, features that typify nearly all amphibians have taxonomically widespread influences on neural systems. Chief among these is metamorphosis, the theme of chapter 16. Except for species that lack a free-swimming larva, amphibians undergo a radical change in niche and body form that affects virtually every physiological system as they change from aquatic larvae to (in many cases) terrestrial adults. The degree of change is greatest in anurans (Wassersug 1989). In addition, temperature is an important influence on amphibians (see chapters 8 and 9). These vertebrates are ectothermic, and their small size and relatively inactive lifestyle exacerbate the influence of ambient temperature. Neural membrane properties vary with temperature, and therefore body temperature should affect neural processes, from sensory transduction and axonal transmission to the system properties of neural pattern generators.

Third, beyond the basic characters shared with all vertebrates or the general influences affecting all amphibians, neural adaptations specific to species or groups of amphibians may reflect variation in habitat or behavior. Interspecific neural variation coincident with behavior or habitat differences are particularly obvious in the visual and auditory systems (reviewed below). A facet of their behavior makes amphibians good models for investigating such meaningful variation: As a general, but not necessarily universal, rule, anurans and urodeles have specialized sensory systems for particular classes of natural behavior. Vision guides prey capture in many amphibians and urodeles, audition is the primary sensory system used during reproductive social behavior in anurans, and olfaction is of primary importance in many aspects of urodele behavior (see also chapter 15). (So little is known about neural processing in apodans that it is unclear whether this generalization holds for them.)

Since the last volume of the *Physiology of the Amphibia* appeared in the mid-1970s, appreciation of interspecific variation within amphibian nervous systems has grown. In synergy with this has been the explosion of techniques and interest affecting all of neuroscience. Consequently, investigations of the physiology of the amphibian nervous system have broadened beyond the studies of the retinotectal and peripheral auditory systems of ranid frogs that were the major areas of inquiry at that time, as well as deepened the understanding of those two systems. Research has not targeted all aspects of amphibian neural processing equally. As was true fifteen years ago, the majority of neurophysiological studies of amphibians have investigated anurans, with a large proportion of these studies, especially those concerned with interspecific variation, focusing on visual and auditory processing and the motor systems associated with them. Substantial work on vision in urodeles has also recently accumulated. By contrast, there are still virtually no physiological studies of neural processing in apodans.

The author thanks P. Grobstein for comments on the chapter. The author's research is supported by NIMH Grant R01 MH45350 and National Science Foundation Grant BNS-8606289.

GENERAL ORGANIZATION OF THE NERVOUS SYSTEM

All vertebrates, including the various amphibian groups, manifest the same general principles of neural organization (Ariëns-Kappers, Huber, and Crosby 1960; Romer 1971). Amphibians occupy a relatively simple grade of vertebrate nervous system development. Their brains are small (relative to body size) and less well differentiated into numerous, distinct nuclei than those of other tetrapods or of advanced teleosts and sharks. Their central nervous system, and especially forebrain areas, lie on a grade equivalent to squalomorph (primitive) sharks and polypteroform and sarcopterygian bony fish (Northcutt and Kicliter 1980). Amphibians differ among themselves mainly in overall brain size and the relative size of various brain divisions (fig. 2.1). Among the major amphibian groups, the anura have the most cytoarchitectonically complex nervous system.

As in all vertebrates, amphibians have a dorsally situated, segmentally organized spinal cord. Pairs of dorsal (sensory) and ventral (motor) spinal roots emanate from each functional segment to form repeating pairs of spinal nerves. The number of spinal cord segments and associated paired spinal nerves varies among amphibians, but adult anurans typically have ten or eleven segments, far fewer than adult urodeles or apodans (Ariëns-Kappers, Huber, and Crosby 1960; Duellman and Trueb 1986; Neiuwenhuys 1964). By contrast, larval anurans have many more segments than their adult counterparts (Nishikawa and Wassersug 1989). Anuran metamorphosis therefore entails a substantial loss of functional segments and spinal nerves, at least partly due to the loss of the larva's tail, and perhaps to functional reorganization and condensation of spinal segments related to the development of limbs and the drastic switch in type of locomotion that occurs when frogs metamorphose (see also chapter 16).

The paired cranial nerves, originating mainly from the brainstem, are also present in amphibians in a pattern typical of tetrapods. Nerves for the special senses are apparent (I, olfactory; II, optic; VIII, statoacoustic; anterior and posterior lateral line nerves in larvae and some adults). Motor nerves innervating the eye muscles (nerves III, IV, and VI) are also apparent. The presence of a hypoglossal nerve (XII) in amphibians has sometimes been denied (e.g., Romer 1971), but a large hypoglossal nucleus is obvious in the caudal medulla. Peripheral nerves originating from the motor neurons there innervate the complex tongue and mouth structures in many amphibians (Roth and Wake 1985a; Weerasuriya and Ewert 1981). Hypoglossal fibers exit in what is often considered the first spinal nerve (Roth 1987). A large trigeminal nerve (V), containing both motor and somatosensory components, and a small facial nerve (VII), also possibly mixed, are present. A series of nerve roots from the midcaudal medulla are regarded as homologous to cranial nerves IX and X together (Ariëns-Kappers, Huber, and Crosby 1960; Kelley et al. 1988; Roth 1987). A large component of this IX-X complex innervates the larynx (Kelley 1980; Matsushima, Satou, and Ueda 1986; Schneider 1988; Simpson, Tobias, and Kelley 1986), while other components innervate tongue protrusion muscles (Roth and Wake 1985) or contribute to the parasympathetic innervation of the viscera (Roth 1987). Axons constituting a spinal accessory nerve (XI) arise from a nucleus in the cervical spinal cord and exit with the vagus (X) nerve (Wake et al. 1988).

The major brain divisions characteristic of all vertebrates are clearly evident in amphibians (fig. 2.1). Each of these brain areas contains dozens of separate nuclei and tracts (fig. 2.2); a thorough description at that level of detail is beyond the scope of this chapter. Several fine reviews of the cytoarchitecture of various parts of the amphibian brain are available. These include Northcutt 1974 and Kicliter and Ebbesson 1976, which describe the cytoarchitecture and histochemistry of telencephalic areas; Opdam, Kemali, and Nieuwenhuys 1976, Opdam and Nieuwenhuys 1976, and Roth et al. 1988, which provide topological reconstructions of anuran and urodele brainstems; Neary and Northcutt 1983 and Wicht and Himstedt 1988, which outline the topography and connectional zonation of the diencephalon; and Roth 1987, an excellent analysis of the architecture and connections of the anuran and urodele brain. Each of these works can serve as an atlas of nuclei within the anuran or urodele central nervous system. No comparable works exist for apodans. The following descriptions are based in part on these reviews.

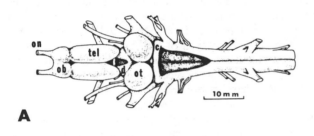

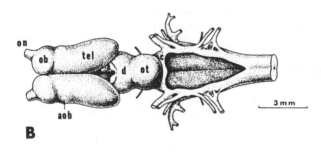

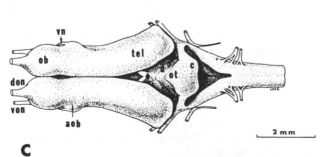

Fig. 2.1 Dorsal views of the brains of a frog, *Rana catesbeiana* (A), a salamander, *Ambystoma tigrinum* (B), and a caecilian, *Ichthyophis glutinosus* (C). Note differences in calibration bars. *aob*, accessory olfactory bulb; *c*, cerebellum; *d*, diencephalon; *don*, dorsal olfactory nerve; *ob*, olfactory bulb; *on*, olfactory nerve; *ot*, optic tectum; *tel*, telencephalon; *von*, ventral olfactory nerve. (Reprinted, by permission, from Northcutt and Kicliter 1980.)

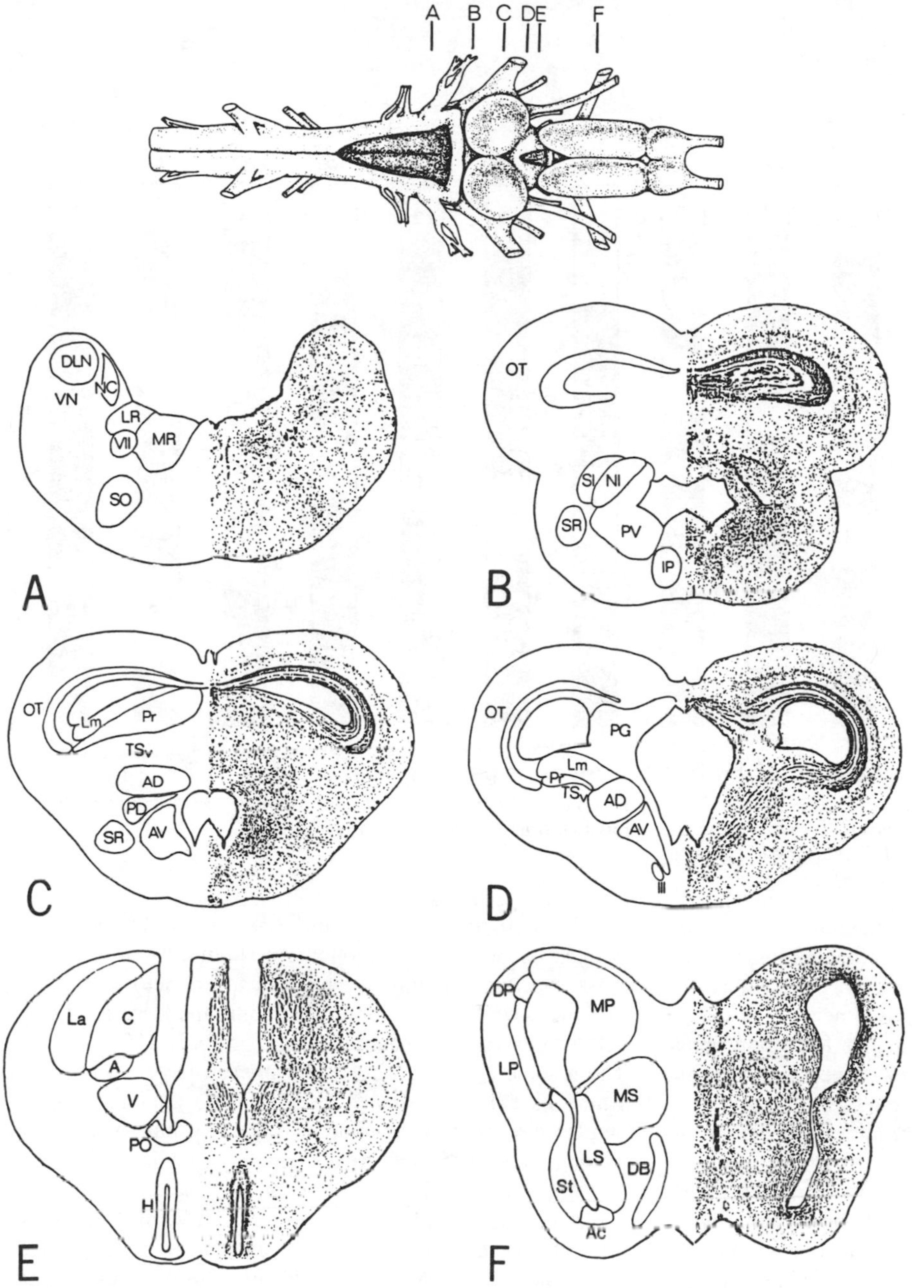

Fig. 2.2 Frontal sections through a bullfrog (*Rana catesbeiana*) brain at levels shown at top of figure. *A*, medulla; *B–C*, midbrain; *D*, rostral midbrain/caudal pretectum; *E*, diencephalon; *F*, telencephalon. See table 2.1 for abbreviations.

TABLE 2.1. List of Abbreviations Used in Figure 2.2

A, anterior thalamic nucleus	H, hypothalamus	MS, medial septum	SI, secondary isthmal nucleus
Ac, nucleus accumbens	III, oculomotor nucleus	NB, nucleus of Bellonci	SO, superior olivary nucleus
AD, anterodorsal tegmentum	IP, interpeduncular nucleus	NC, nucleus caudalis	SR, superficial reticular nucleus
AV, anteroventral tegmentum	La, anterior lateral nucleus	NI, nucleus isthmi	St, striatum
C, central thalamic nucleus	Lm, laminar nucleus of the torus	OT, optic tectum	TSv, ventral toral area
DB, diagonal band	LP, lateral pallium	PD, posterodorsal tegmentum	V, ventral thalamus
DLN, dorsolateral nucleus	LR, lateral reticular formation	PG, pretectal gray	VII, facial motor nucleus
DP, dorsal pallium	LS, lateral septum	PO, preoptic area	VN, vestibular nucleus
Ea, anterior entopeduncular nucleus	MP, medial pallium	Pr, principal nucleus of the torus	
	MR, medial reticular formation	PV, posteroventral tegmentum	

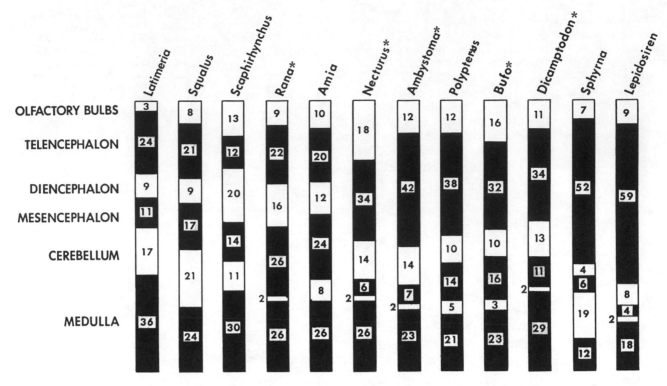

Weight of brain subdivisions as percent of total brain

Fig. 2.3 Relative size of brain divisions in various amphibians (noted by *asterisk*), as well as the coelacanth (*Latimeria*), sharks (*Squalus, Scaphirhynchus, Sphyrna*), a primitive bony fish (*Polypterus*), a holostean bony fish (*Amia*), and a lungfish (*Lepidosiren*). (Reprinted, by permission, from Northcutt, Neary, and Senn 1978.)

The most caudal brain division, the medulla, contains the primary nuclei of the auditory, vestibular, lateral line systems where present, and trigeminal somatosensory system as well as motor neurons for many of the cranial nerves. Its core is constructed by as yet ill-defined reticular formation areas. The cerebellum, apparent as a strip of tissue, lies above the medulla's rostral border. The cerebellum, which is important in motor coordination, is smaller in amphibians than in any other vertebrates save the agnathans.

The midbrain consists of a ventral portion, the tegmentum, containing reticular formation fields and some cranial nerve nuclei, and a dorsal "roof" portion, the tectum. In anurans, the visual part of the roof, the optic tectum, and the auditory portion, the torus semicircularis, expand greatly relative to their size in urodeles and apodans, and in so doing construct the large dorsal midbrain lobes characteristic of anuran brains. The optic tectum and torus semicircularis are major sensory and sensorimotor integration areas in anuran brains (reviewed below). Important visuomotor processes involved in prey capture are mediated by the tectum in anurans and urodeles (such processes are unexplored in apodans), and anatomical studies (Roth 1987; Wilczynski and Northcutt 1977, 1983a, 1983b) suggest that forebrain areas work predominantly via connections through the midbrain roof.

Although textbooks often suggest that the midbrain is the largest and in some (usually undefined) sense "highest" center in the amphibian brain, (e.g., Romer 1971; Rosenzweig and Leiman 1989), a quantitative assessment of the relative size of brain areas clearly shows otherwise (Northcutt, Neary,

and Senn 1978). The forebrain, composed of the diencephalon and telencephalon, accounts for about 40% of total brain mass in *Rana* and *Bufo* even when the olfactory bulbs are excluded, while the midbrain, including the large tecta characteristic of advanced anurans, averages only 21% (fig. 2.3). The relative size of the forebrain is even larger in urodeles, which have less expansive tecta than do anurans. For example, the forebrain (excluding olfactory bulbs) in *Ambystoma* represents 56% of total brain mass, while the midbrain accounts for only 7%.

Furthermore, neither the forebrain as a whole nor its rostral division, the telencephalon, is exclusively olfactory (Kicliter and Ebbesson 1976; Northcutt 1981). Although the olfactory system does provide an input to large areas of the telencephalon (Kemali and Guglielmotti 1987; Northcutt and Royce 1975; Scalia 1976b), substantial visual, auditory, and somatosensory information does reach various telencephalic areas via thalamic relays (Kicliter 1979; Neary 1988; Northcutt 1981). The existence of heavy nonolfactory projections to forebrain centers suggests an important role, as yet only vaguely understood, in the expression of behaviors triggered by nonolfactory cues.

The caudal portion of the forebrain, the diencephalon, contains two major regions in addition to the smaller epithalamus (the habenular nuclei) and ventral thalamic area. The first major region, the dorsal thalamus, serves as a sensory relay system transmitting nonolfactory information to the telencephalon (Neary and Northcutt 1983; Roth 1987; Wicht and Himstedt 1988). Neary and Northcutt (1983) divided the anuran dorsal thalamus into three zones, each containing several nuclei, distinguished most importantly by their efferent connections. A similar zonation probably exists in urodeles (Wicht and Himstedt 1988) but is less obvious due to the extremely poor differentiation of thalamic nuclei in those amphibians. A rostral zone (the anterior nucleus and nucleus of Bellconci) relays multimodel inputs, including visual information from direct retinothalamic projections, to pallial areas of the cerebral hemispheres (Kicliter 1979; Neary 1988; Northcutt 1981). A middle zone (central nucleus and anterior lateral nucleus) receives ascending input from the torus semicircularis and optic tectum and in turn sends ascending projections to the striatum (Neary 1988; Wilczynski and Northcutt 1983a). The posterior zone (posterior nucleus and posterior lateral nucleus, plus several smaller nuclei), by contrast, has mainly descending projections, most heavily to midbrain areas (Naujoks-Manteuffel and Manteuffel 1986; Roth 1987; Wilczynski and Northcutt 1977). This zone is a major portion of the amphibian pretectal area and is heavily interconnected with the optic tectum.

The second major diencephalic region is the hypothalamus. As in other vertebrates, the hypothalamus of amphibians is intimately connected with the pituitary gland and plays an important role in regulating endocrine and visceral functions (Jørgensen 1974a; Pasquier, Cannata, and Tramezzani 1980). Rostrally the hypothalamus meets the preoptic area, a similar endocrine and visceral control region. Significant hypothalamic and preoptic area inputs arise from the telencephalon and from portions of the rostral and middle thalamic zones (Allison and Wilczynski 1989; Kokoros and Northcutt 1977; Neary 1988; Neary and Wilczynski 1986; Ronan and Northcutt 1979; Wilczynski and Allison 1989).

Earlier controversy surrounding the assignation of homologies to the various regions of the telencephalic hemispheres has mostly given way to a consensus that at least general regions of the amphibian forebrain and telencephalons of other tetrapods are equivalent, although strict one-to-one homologies remain problematic (Northcutt and Kicliter 1980). Amphibian hemispheres are divided into a dorsal (pallial) half with medial and lateral divisions plus a dorsal transition zone, and a ventral (subpallial) half, again with medial and lateral divisions. Olfactory bulbs append rostrally to the lateral pallium. An amygdalar complex lies in the caudal telencephalon. Although mammalian and reptilian cortical areas are considered to derive from the same precursors as the amphibian pallial areas, none of the amphibian pallial divisions shows an obvious laminar cytoarchitecture. The telencephalic areas of amphibians are far less expanded and differentiated than comparable regions in amniotes, or for that matter, than in advanced fish and sharks (Northcutt 1981).

The medial pallium, the largest of the pallial regions, receives the bulk of its input from other telencephalic areas that receive olfactory input (Neary 1988; Northcutt 1981). In addition, it receives nonolfactory sensory input from the rostral thalamic zone, as noted above. This pallial division is considered homologous to the mammalian hippocampal complex or, more broadly, to the hippocampus and associated limbic cortical areas (Northcutt and Kicliter 1980). Its main targets outside the telencephalon are the preoptic area and hypothalamus (Allison and Wilczynski 1989; Ronan and Northcutt

1979). The lateral pallium receives direct projections from the olfactory bulb and as such has been homologized to mammalian olfactory cortices (Kemali and Guglielmotti 1987; Northcutt and Royce 1975; Schmidt, Naujoks-Manteuffel, and Roth 1988). Lateral pallial efferents are exclusively to other telencephalic regions (Northcutt and Kicliter 1980). The homologous relationships of the dorsal pallium remains unresolved. In the past it has been equated with all or part of mammalian neocortex, but a clear confirmation of this has remained elusive. Like the medial pallium, the dorsal pallium receives input from the rostral thalamus (Neary 1984). However, unlike the medial or lateral pallium, most of the dorsal pallium receives no olfactory input.

The medial portion of the ventral, or subpallial, division contains the septal nuclei and associated olfactory centers. Other than connections with the olfactory system (Kemali and Guglielmotti 1987; Northcutt and Royce 1975) and medial pallium (Ronan and Northcutt 1979), the pathways to and from this area are poorly understood. The lateral subpallium is occupied by the striatum and its associated anterior entopeduncular nucleus. Topographically and histochemically, this amphibian region matches the mammalian basal ganglia (Kicliter and Ebbesson 1976; Northcutt 1974). The mammalian and amphibian counterparts have some similar connections, but the mix of inputs to the amphibian striatum suggests a different functional emphasis than that seen in mammals. In amphibians, the main striatal afferents arise from middle thalamic-zone nuclei (Neary 1988; Wicht and Himstedt 1986, 1988; Wilczynski and Northcutt 1983a). In fact, the striatum is by far the major target of these relay nuclei. Although thalamic inputs to the mammalian striatum exist, they are secondary in size to massive projections from the neocortex. Such massive cortical (or pallial) inputs to the striatum are not seen in amphibians. Rather, only an input from medial pallial cells, which is relatively much smaller than the thalamic input, is seen (Neary 1988). A difference between mammals and amphibians also exists in basal ganglia efferents. The main output from the mammalian basal ganglia flows through the thalamus back to its main source of input, the neocortex, and specifically motor and premotor cortex, cortical areas that can not readily be perceived in amphibians. By contrast, the major efferents from the amphibian striatum and anterior entopeduncular nucleus target the pretectal nuclei and tegmental fields, which in turn have substantial projections to the optic tectum and torus semicircularis (Neary 1988; Wilczynski and Northcutt 1983b). Direct projections to the tectum and torus and to the medulla and spinal cord can also be seen.

The long descending efferents of the striatum are particularly noteworthy in that they do not compete with the extensive system of descending efferents from pallial or cortical areas, as in mammals. A major difference between amphibians and mammals is that the amphibian telencephalon lacks anything structurally or functionally equivalent to nonlimbic, nonolfactory areas of mammalian neocortex or to the homologous pallial expansions in reptiles and birds (even though, as noted above, the amphibian dorsal pallium has been suggested as homologous to the neocortex; for reviews of vertebrate telencephalic organization, see Ebbesson 1980 and Northcutt 1981). That is, amphibian pallial areas contain

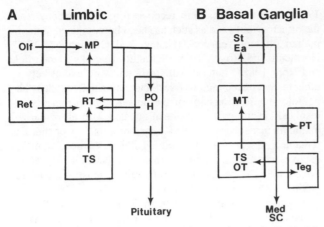

Fig. 2.4 Simplified schematic diagram of connections in the limbic (*A*) and basal ganglia (*B*) forebrain systems. *Ea,* anterior entopeduncular nucleus; *H,* hypothalamus; *Med,* medulla; *MP,* medial pallium; *MT,* middle thalamus; *Olf,* olfactory areas; *OT,* optic tectum; *PO,* preoptic area; *PT,* pretectum; *Ret,* retina; *RT,* rostral thalamus; *SC,* spinal cord; *St,* striatum; *Teg,* tegmentum; *TS,* torus semicircularis.

no unimodal sensory areas like primary sensory cortex, no areas like the motor cortices with their long, descending efferents to the brain stem and spinal cord, and nothing like the association cortices between them. Mammals use these neocortical areas for important perceptual, voluntary motor, and cognitive functions. One would therefore expect significant differences between amphibians and mammals in these domains. However, as yet no systematic investigations, or even theoretical arguments, have articulated just what those differences might be.

This complex set of amphibian forebrain connections can be conceptualized as representing two functional systems, a limbic and a basal ganglia system (fig. 2.4). In the first, multisensory input from olfactory and rostral thalamic nuclei project to the medial pallium, which then sends descending efferents to the septal nuclei, preoptic area, and hypothalamus. This system is therefore in a position to affect visceral and endocrine control systems strongly. In the second system, tectal visual and toral auditory information project via middle thalamic nuclei to the striatum, which, with the anterior entopeduncular nucleus, provides descending projections to the pretectum, tegmental and medullary reticular areas, midbrain roof, and spinal cord. These interconnected areas are all involved in the control of various behaviors effected via somatic musculature. Missing from this scheme are analogues of the expansive sensory and motor systems of the neocortex, which in mammals feed information to both systems, bridge them, and provide an independent source of afferent control to somatic and visceral areas of the brain stem and spinal cord. An important but unanswered question is whether this overall forebrain organization is characteristic of all anamniotes.

The physiological organization of these two amphibian forebrain effector systems is poorly understood. However, spinal cord and brain-stem motor systems have received considerable scrutiny, and a substantial body of work describes the physiology of the sensory systems that supply information necessary to guide all behavioral expression.

LOCOMOTOR SYSTEMS

Movement ultimately involves the activation of spinal cord motor neurons. In vertebrates, the control of this activation is conceptualized as involving a hierarchy of interacting circuits, beginning with reflex arcs within the spinal cord, and continuing with central pattern generators in the spinal cord or lower brain stem and a series of descending projections from various levels of the brain. Amphibians resemble other vertebrates in this regard (reviewed in Roberts 1989 and the following discussion). However, what is interesting about amphibians is that a metamorphic event marks a shift in locomotory behavior that is extreme in the case of anurans (see Wassersug 1989 and chapter 16 for review).

Much work on amphibian locomotion has investigated mechanisms in embryos and larvae, and most neurophysiological studies have relied on *Xenopus* or *Rana* larvae as model systems. In premetamorphic amphibians, oscillatory movements of the tail and trunk result in swimming at low or moderate speed (more so in urodeles and apodans than anurans; Wassersug 1989; chapter 16). The rhythmic movements reflect alternating ipsilateral and contralateral activation of motor neurons within spinal segments, with phase lags between segments (Stehouwer and Farel 1980). Motor neuron activation is controlled by a central pattern generator (presumably in the spinal cord) that interacts with sensory (probably proprioceptive, but possibly also cutaneous) input arriving via dorsal spinal roots (Stehouwer and Farel 1980, 1981). In experimental preparations, stimulation of a single dorsal root yields an episode of "fictive" swimming involving waves of activation along the spinal cord as the sensory input activates the central pattern generator for swimming. Cutting the dorsal roots in free-swimming larvae eliminates the normal phase relationship in the contractions of the series of spinal segments and impairs a larva's ability to control the rate of tail oscillation. The alternating limb movements characterizing walking in adult anurans appear to be similarly organized, with an intrinsic pattern generator dependent on somatosensory input for activation and coordination (Gray and Lissmann 1940, 1946).

Sensorimotor influences within the pattern-generating circuits are actually reciprocal. The activation of motor neurons results in the presynaptic inhibition of incoming sensory afferents in the same spinal segment. This centrally mediated decrease in somatosensory sensitivity may compensate for the excessive activation of somatosensory receptors caused by the movement induced when the motor neurons are firing (Stehouwer and Farel 1981).

Stimulation of visual or tactile receptors in the head can also elicit swimming movements in embryonic *Xenopus* via descending projections from the head region of the nervous system (Roberts 1989). Descending projections elaborate throughout larval life, with progressively more rostral projection sources as larval development proceeds (ten Donkelaar and de Boer–van Huizen 1982). Well before metamorphosis, larval amphibians possess a complement of spinal projections from reticular, vestibular, tegmental (including a possible red nucleus homologue), and hypothalamic areas in a pattern typical of all vertebrates (Forehand and Farel 1982b). Only one descending input has been studied physiologically or

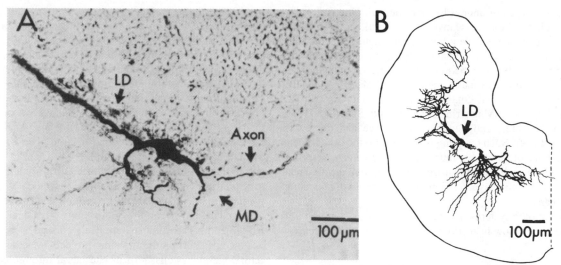

Fig. 2.5 *A*, photomicrograph of a horseradish peroxidase (HRP)–filled Mauthner cell in a bullfrog larva (*Rana catesbeiana*), showing its lateral (*LD*) and medial (*MD*) dendrites and its axon coursing toward the con-tralateral brain stem. *B*, reconstruction of the entire dendritic tree of this cell. (Reprinted, by permission, from Hackett, Cochran, and Brown 1979.)

functionally to any great extent: the Mauthner cell system (see also chapter 16).

Mauthner cells are single, large neurons located one on each side of the medullar reticular formation (fig. 2.5). They are present in most aquatic vertebrates and are always part of a stereotyped startle or escape response (see Nissanov and Eaton 1989 for a review of the neurobiology of such responses in fish and amphibian larvae). Each Mauthner cell sends a single, large-diameter, and therefore fast-conducting axon down the contralateral medulla and spinal cord, where it synapses in every spinal segment on motor neurons innervating axial muscles. Mauthner cells always receive multimodal input. In anuran larvae, Mauthner cells receive inputs at least from the inner ear and visual system (Hackett, Cochran, and Brown 1979; Rock 1980). Activation of a Mauthner cell quickly results in a large, fast contraction of axial muscles along the contralateral side of the body, yielding a contralateral turn and a tail flick that propels the larva (or fish) ballistically in an "escape" from whatever stimulus triggered the cells (Nissanov and Eaton 1989; Rock 1980).

No amniotic vertebrate has a Mauthner cell system. Most amphibians have Mauthner cells as larvae. Mauthner cells have been reported to degenerate at metamorphosis, when most amphibians prepare for a terrestrial niche (Moulton, Jurand, and Fox 1968; Stefanelli 1951). However, Will (1986) examined the medullas of several amphibian species and concluded that Mauthner cells remain postmetamorphically in those species that possess them as larvae. In terrestrial frogs such as *Rana* that lose the lateral line system at metamorphosis (see below), the dorsal branches of the large dorsolateral dendrite of the cell are reduced, presumably reflecting the loss of lateral line input to this portion of the dendrite. In *Xenopus*, which retains an adult lateral line system, these branches remain patent. In both cases, Mauthner cell axons to the spinal cord remain in the adult. The function of the adult Mauthner system remains unknown. Will (1986) suggests that in *Xenopus* it may continue to mediate some type of escape response. However, the body form and loco-motory pattern of adult anurans preclude the type of movement that Mauthner cells mediate in larvae. Therefore, there must be a significant reorganization of Mauthner cell axon terminations or their targets to allow them to trigger what must be a drastically different pattern of motor expression.

Other neural changes also occur at metamorphosis (see chapter 16). The most extreme spinal cord changes occur in anurans, as their metamorphic body changes are greater than in other amphibians. Motor neurons degenerate with loss of the tail (Forehand and Farel 1982a), and the number of spinal cord segments and nerves decreases precipitously. Wassersug (1989) has argued that metamorphosis is a time of greatly increased predation risk for anurans, given the awkwardness of the intermediate forms, and that several peripheral morphological features of anuran larvae, such as the lack of vertebrae in the tail, are adaptations to minimize the time needed for the transition to adult form. Nishikawa and Wassersug (1989) have shown that a reduced number of larval spinal cord segments and nerves is an independently derived condition in several anuran groups and have suggested that this too decreases the time necessary to complete metamorphosis.

What is most remarkable about anuran metamorphosis and central motor systems is what does not change. Many spinal cord motor and intrinsic neurons remain intact, and the descending pathways from the brain are conserved (Forehand and Farel 1982a, 1982b; ten Donkelaar and de Boer–van Huizen 1982; ten Donkelaar et al. 1981; Will 1986), even though the peripheral structures and locomotor behaviors they control differ radically in pre- and postmetamorphic anurans. A similar conservation of neural structure occurs as the head reorganizes. The larval mouth apparatus degenerates as the adult jaw emerges, while the motor neurons innervating larval muscles remain and simply make new connections with the adult jaw muscles (Barnes and Alley 1983).

More subtle changes in central motor systems also must occur during metamorphosis, although the extent of such changes is unknown. Some neural features of anurans seem related to their more derived forms of locomotion. For example, two types of anuran locomotion, jumping and swimming via hindlimb thrusts, involve the simultaneous bilateral activation of many muscle groups. Motor neurons in the adult lumbar spinal cord are synaptically coupled between segments ipsilaterally, and medial motor neurons send dendrites across the midline to make chemical and electrical dendro-dendritic synapses on contralateral motor neurons (Erulkar and Soller 1980; Magherini, Precht, and Schwindt 1976; Sonnhof, Richter, and Taughner 1977; see also review in Peterson 1989). Such coupling would ensure the synchronous contractions of hindlimb muscles. Unfortunately, it is unknown when such coupling arises during anuran development and whether similar synaptic interactions appear in nonanuran amphibians.

Other motor systems that relate to vision or audition will be discussed below in sections devoted to the various sensory systems.

VISUAL SYSTEMS

The vertebrate visual system is actually several separate systems channeling information from retinal photoreceptors to different brain areas with different functions (figs. 2.6 and 2.7). In amphibians, retinal ganglion cell axons gather to form the optic nerve (cranial nerve II). Retinal projections are reviewed in Fritzsch 1980, Roth 1987, and Scalia 1976b. Most axons cross in the optic chiasma, although nearly all retinal targets receive some uncrossed input in adult amphibians. Some axons terminate in the suprachiasmatic region of the preoptic area immediately above the chiasma. Retinal projections then reach rostral thalamic targets (the nucleus of Bellonci and anterior thalamic nucleus), the ventral thalamus (nucleus geniculatus thalami), and several pretectal nuclei. A separate fascicle of optic fibers terminates in the nucleus of the basal optic root forming the "accessory optic system." The bulk of the retinal axons innervate the optic tectum. The retinal terminations there and in the thalamic targets form retinotopic maps, thereby preserving the spatial relationships of visual stimuli in the termination patterns (fig. 2.8).

When anurans such as *Xenopus laevis* metamorphose, their eyes shift position from the sides of the larval head to a more frontal placement, creating a large zone of binocular overlap in the visual field of adults. Grobstein (1988b) suggested that this change is related to a shift from a herbivorous to a predatory carnivorous lifestyle, inasmuch as binocular overlaps may enhance depth perception and hence aid visually mediated prey capture. Before this positional shift, retinal projections are almost completely crossed, but as the shift occurs, ipsilateral retinothalamic projections arise from new retinal ganglion cells born in late larval through early postmetamorphic life (Hoskins and Grobstein 1985a, 1985b) under the influence of circulating thyroxine (Beach and Jacobson 1979a; Hoskins and Grobstein 1985c). Functionally, the change may reflect a restructuring of central visual maps to accommodate the binocular field seen by both eyes in adults.

A functionally similar restructuring occurs in optic tectum circuitry. New ipsilateral retinal projections do not reach the tectum. Rather, in adults the two tecta are linked via a pathway through a midbrain tegmentum structure, the nucleus isthmi, such that input from each eye corresponding to the same point of visual space merges in the neural map of the visual field in the tectum (Grobstein and Comer 1983; Grob-

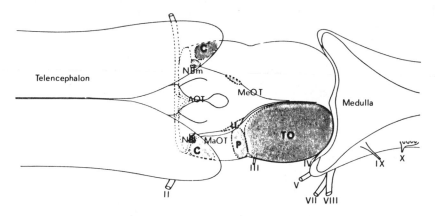

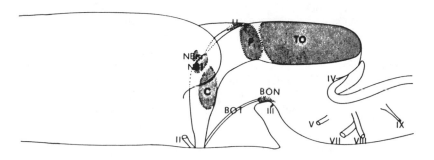

Fig. 2.6 Dorsal and lateral view of the brain of the newt *Triturus* (Salamandridae), showing location and size of retinal terminal fields. *AOT,* axial optic tract; *BON,* basal optic neuropil; *BOT,* basal optic tract; *C,* corpus geniculatum; *MaOT,* marginal optic tract; *MeOT,* medial optic tract; *NBl, NBm,* lateral and medial neuropils of Bellonci; *P,* posterior thalamic neuropil; *TO,* optic tectum; *U,* uncinate neuropil of the pretectum; *I to X,* cranial nerves. (Reprinted, by permission, from Fritzsch 1980.)

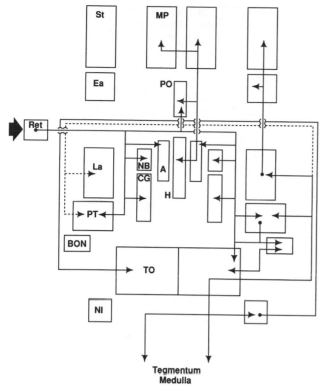

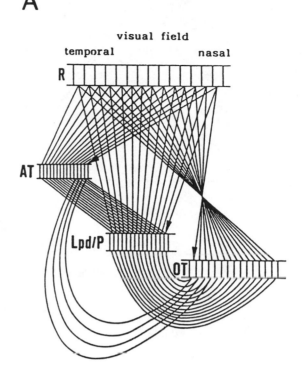

Fig. 2.7 Schematic diagram of retinal and other connections in the amphibian visual system. The anterior thalamic nucleus (*A*) receives retinal input via dendrites extending into the nucleus of Bellonci (*NB*); cells in parts of the ventral thalamus (not shown) similarly extend dendrites into the corpus geniculatum (*CG*). The projections of several rostral thalamic retinal targets to the tectum (Neary and Wilczynski 1980) are not shown. *BON*, basal optic nucleus; *Ea*, anterior entopeduncular nucleus; *H*, hypothalamus; *La*, anterior lateral nucleus; *MP*, medial pallium; *NI*, nucleus isthmi; *PO*, preoptic area; *PT*, pretectum; *Ret*, retina; *St*, striatum; *TO*, optic tectum.

stein et al. 1978; Gruberg and Lettvin 1980). The part of nucleus isthmi mediating the intertectal connections grows much more than other parts when metamorphosis occurs (Grobstein 1988b).

Prey Catching and the Tectal-Pretectal Systems

The optic tectum is critical for visually guided predation (Ewert 1987; Roth 1987). Its intrinsic organization is discussed in detail by Lázár (1984) and Roth (1987). Specializations of this part of the visual system for the control of prey catching begin with the retinal ganglion cells innervating the tectum. Lettvin et al. (1959; see also Maturana et al. 1960) divided the retinal ganglion cell axons entering the tectum into five physiological classes differing in their receptive field size, sensitivity to movement and contrast, and general response to ambient light level. Similar classes are seen in urodeles (Roth 1987). Lettvin et al. (1959) proclaimed class 2 neurons as "bug detectors" because these cells respond to small moving objects but are relatively insensitive to changes in overall light levels. Indeed, the properties of these neurons suggest that their function is to encode an environmental stimulus of crucial importance to a frog: a moving, insect-sized object.

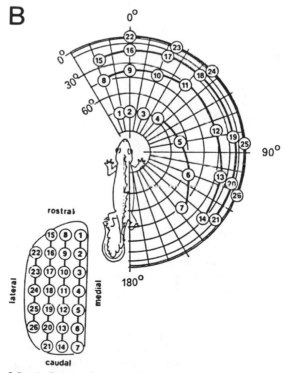

Fig. 2.8 *A*, diagram of visual field mapping from the retina (*R*) to the rostral thalamic fields (*AT*), pretectum (*Lpd/P*) and optic tectum (*OI*). (From Ewert 1987. Copyright ©1987 Cambridge University Press. Reprinted with the permission of Cambridge University Press). *B*, physiologically determined map of the visual field onto the tectum in *Triturus cristatus*. (Reprinted, by permission, from Roth 1987.)

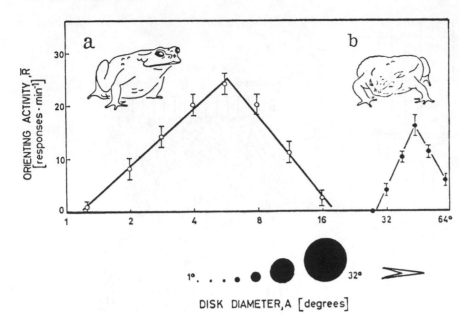

Fig. 2.9 Magnitude of orienting toward (A) and away from (B) a moving stimulus as a function of size. (From Ewert 1970. Reprinted with the permission of S. Karger, AG, Basel.)

Although it was tempting to conclude that frog prey catching is controlled entirely through peripheral specializations (Lettvin et al. 1959), subsequent work quickly established that amphibian prey-catching behavior cannot be explained on the basis of retinal response properties alone (see below). The retinal "bug detectors" bias the input to the brain to signal the presence of a potentially important object in the environment. The brain must further process this information and compare it with other incoming stimuli before deciding to enact a behavioral program.

The first investigations of central specializations found that anurans respond to moving objects in two ways (Ewert 1970; Ingle 1970), either orientation toward them if they are small or turning away from them if they are large (fig. 2.9). The two behaviors are mutually exclusive; it seems that triggering the avoidance (or "predator escape") behavior blocks the approach (or "prey orientation") response (see also chapter 13).

The mechanism for deciding which behavior to enact involves an interaction between the visual areas of the posterior thalamus, or pretectum, and the optic tectum (Ewert 1970, 1987; Finkenstädt 1980; Ingle 1970; Lara and Arbib 1985; Roth 1987). While the tectum receives all classes of retinal input, the pretectum preferentially receives input from the large-receptive field-class 3 and 4 retinal ganglion cells and is thus most sensitive to large objects (Ewert 1987; Roth 1987). Pretectal neurons send an inhibitory projection to the tectum and therefore, when activated by large objects ("predators"), turn off the orientation response (Ewert 1987). The tectum is necessary for the avoidance response as well as the orientation response, and presumably triggers avoidance when signaled by its own class 3 and 4 ganglion cell inputs (Maturana et al. 1960), which arrive as the pretectal input is shutting down the tectal neurons responsible for orientation.

The pretectum plays two additional roles in visually guided behavior. First, its inhibitory input may mediate habituation of the prey-catching response. Frogs will stop responding to an artificial prey object after repeated presentations even though the retinal ganglion "bug detectors" continue to fire. Lesions of the pretectum profoundly retard habituation (Ingle 1973). Second, the pretectum mediates the detection and avoidance of stationary barriers during visually guided movements (Ingle 1977, 1980). Such a function is an important adjunct to tectally mediated prey catching, as it allows an animal to compensate for obstacles while stalking or lunging at a prey object. The pretectum performs this function independent of its connections with the tectum. Frogs without tectums can successfully avoid obstacles when moving, but pretectal lesions alone abolish this ability.

More recently, attention has turned to the mechanism by which shape preference is constructed (reviewed in Ewert 1984, 1987; Roth 1987). Ranid frogs, such as those studied by Lettvin et al. (1959), show little shape preference for visual orientation. Not all anurans or salamanders are so undiscriminating. Many show a distinct behavioral preference for elongated objects more like worms than like bugs. Ewert first quantified this phenomenon, showing that elongation parallel to the axis of movement enhanced a stimulus's attractiveness, while elongation perpendicular to the movement actually elicited an avoidance response. Ewert established that this property emerged in a class of optic tectum neurons that he termed "T-5-2" cells.

Subsequent characterizations of tectal neuron response properties have shown them to be as complicated as the behavior they subserve. The behavioral responses amphibians make to artificial prey stimuli are preferences rather than dichotomous choices (see also chapter 13). For example, in a test situation animals will generally respond less robustly to a moving square than to a moving horizontal rectangle, but they will nevertheless respond to it. Tectal neurons show the same graded response (fig. 2.10). Moreover, in both anurans and urodeles some tectal neurons actually prefer squares to rectangles, and in some cells the preference is dependent on stimulus velocity (Himstedt and Roth 1980; Roth 1987; Roth and Jordan 1982). None of this variability appears in the re-

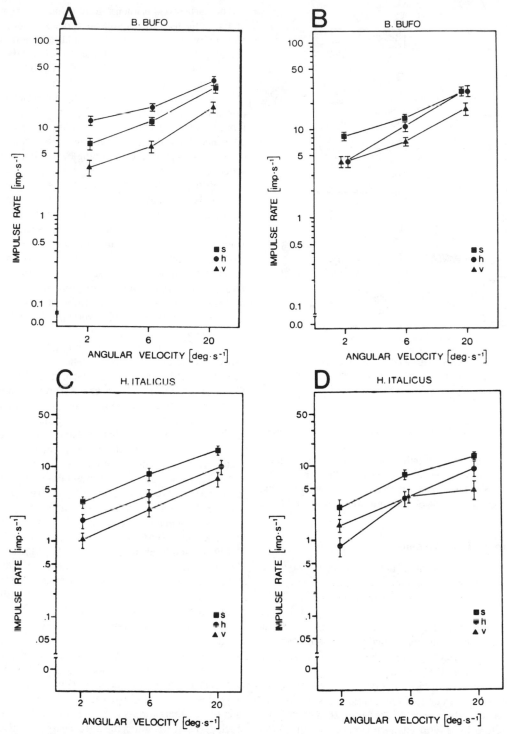

Fig. 2.10 Response magnitude as a function of stimulus velocity of a square (s), horizontal rectangle (h), and vertical rectangle (v) in two tectal neurons from the toad *Bufo bufo* (A, B) and two from the salaman-der *Hydromantes italicus* (Plethodontidae; C, D). Note the preference inversion that occurs at high velocity in B and D. (Reprinted, by permission, from Roth 1987.)

sponse properties of the retinal ganglion cell "bug detectors" feeding the tectum its information, but it appears in real bugs and worms and in the responses of amphibians to them. The tectum seems to use the size- and motion-biased iput from the retina to construct a variety of tectal feature detectors sensitive to different shapes and speeds.

Roth (1987) has suggested that the optic tectum assembles these various feature detectors into a repeating series of "recognition modules," such that each patch of the visual world is analyzed by a patch of tectal surface containing an array of cells with various shape-velocity preferences (fig. 2.11). Any prey-sized object entering that patch of visual world would

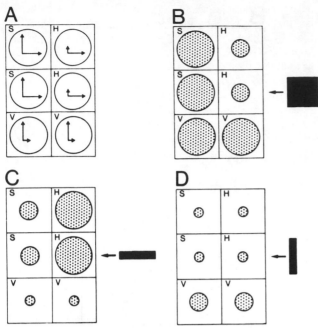

Fig. 2.11 Hypothetical "recognition module" proposed by Roth (1987) for the optic tectum. Six neurons with varying response strengths (indicated by vector *arrows*) make up the module (*A*). They respond to varying degrees (indicated by size of the circles) to moving squares and rectangles (*B–D*). Stimulus shape is coded in the pattern of activity across the six cells. (Reprinted, by permission, from Roth 1987.)

excite a bank of class 2 ganglion cells focused on it. These cells would transmit that information to a patch of tectum, where the feature detectors would respond in varying degrees depending on how well the object matched their shape and speed preference. The percept of that object would then be contained in the pattern of activation among an assembly of tectal neurons.

Integration with Motor Systems

The tectum triggers the various behavioral acts associated with prey catching, through bilateral descending efferents to reticular areas in the midbrain and medulla (Roth 1987; Rubinson 1968; Wilczynski and Northcutt 1977), and ultimately to cranial nerve nuclei and spinal cord motor neurons. Some controversy still surrounds the functional organization of these triggering pathways (Ingle 1983; Ewert 1987; Roth 1987; Grobstein 1988a, 1988b).

The controversy has arisen as an appreciation of the complexity of the motor elements of prey capture has grown (see also chapter 11 for a discussion of the biomechanics of feeding). Prey capture in several advanced urodeles and all but the most primitive anurans is highly specialized. It involves orientation toward a potential prey, locomotion toward it if necessary, and lunging at it, all of which require activation of body and limb musculature under the control of spinal cord motor neurons. It also involves mouth opening followed by tongue protraction and retraction ("snapping"), which are mediated by a large number of muscles innervated by several cranial nerve nuclei in the medulla. The muscular control of tongue protrusion and retraction in various anurans and salamanders is described by Gans and Gorniak (1982a), Matsushima, Satou, and Ueda (1985), and Roth (1987).

The earliest experiments found that electrical stimulation of the optic tectum elicited all aspects of prey capture, directed toward the point in the visual field appropriate for the stimulated area of the visual map on the tectal surface (Ewert 1970). This work concluded that the visual map on the tectal surface lies in register with a deep "motor map" consisting of command neurons. Each command neuron codes prey capture toward a point in space. When activated by the visual input terminating above it, the command neuron in turn excites medullary and spinal cord motor neurons via descending efferents to capture prey in a single, fixed action pattern–like sequence.

Grobstein (1988a, 1988c) has discussed why this most parsimonious explanation is a bad one. Prey-catching behavior varies with distance and prey elevation, neither of which are simply coded by points on the tectal surface. In addition, frogs can make an orienting turn from any posture without passing through a common intermediate position, which must mean that proprioceptive and vestibular information is taken into account in planning the movement, and that the pattern of muscle activation can take different forms even if the position of the visual stimulus remains constant (Ingle 1970; Grobstein 1988a, 1988c).

Furthermore, lesions of descending tracts can disrupt some aspects of the prey-capture sequence while leaving others intact (Ingle 1983; Kostyk and Grobstein 1982; Masino and Grobstein 1989a, 1989b). A crossed projection from the optic tectum to a column of neurons in the ventrolateral tegmentum, and from there to the spinal cord, is responsible for turning toward a prey stimulus (Masino and Grobstein 1989b). When the pathway is cut at any point while leaving direct tectal efferents to the medulla and spinal cord intact, frogs fail to turn towards a prey. Lunging and tongue snapping remain normal, except that, because no turn occurs, the behaviors are always directed forward, that is, in whatever direction the frog happened to be facing when the stimulus appeared (Kostyk and Grobstein 1982; Masino and Grobstein 1989a).

Masino and Grobstein's (1989a, 1989b) results suggest that the longer descending tectal efferents to the medulla and spinal cord are not responsible for head and body turning. Rather, these efferents may be involved in the mouth and tongue movements associated with snapping at prey. Tectobular projections terminate near brain-stem nuclei innervating tongue muscles (Ewert 1987; Roth 1987; Rubinson 1968; Satou and Ewert 1985; Wilczynski and Northcutt 1977) but apparently not on them. Satou et al. (1985) have shown that, in toads, interneurons interpose between tectal efferents and hypoglossal neurons innervating tongue muscles. The location of the interneurons (i.e., whether within the hypoglossal nucleus itself or some distance away within the medullary or even tegmental reticular formation) is unknown. The physiological interactions Satou et al. (1985) found are more complicated than simple excitation. At least two sets of interneurons are present, a low-threshold inhibitory system and a high-threshold excitatory system. Low-intensity tectal stimulation therefore inhibits tongue motor neurons, while high intensity or repetitive stimulation engages the excitatory pathway, which overrides the inhibitory input to fire the motor neurons. This pattern may be part of a mechanism that inhibits snapping until orientation movements are complete and the prey is fixated and observed for a short time. Satou et al.

(1985) also found that electrical stimulation of the tongue protractor motor neurons caused depolarization of most tongue retractor motor neurons, presumably via a reflex arc involving tongue proprioceptors. The protractor-retractor sequence is controlled by a central pattern generator, but as for the control of locomotion pattern generators (see above), sensory afferents appear to modify the final expression of the behavior (Satou et al. 1985).

Beyond this, the mechanisms for coordinating the contraction of the many muscles used during snapping remain unknown. Roth (1987) noted that in salamanders the temporal sequence of muscles contracting matches a rostral-to-caudal sequence of motor neurons for those muscles in the medulla. A tectal signal sequentially activating the motor nuclei as it travels down the tectobulbar pathway could be a simple mechanism for the gross timing of muscle contraction (Roth 1987). However, such an explanation may be inapplicable to anurans, in which the position of the functionally equivalent motor neurons is different. For example, the tongue protractor muscle in plethodontid salamanders is innervated by glossopharyngeal motor neurons located rostral to the hypoglossal motor neurons innervating the tongue retractors (Roth 1987; Roth et al. 1988). By contrast, in the toad *Bufo japonica*, both muscles are innervated by hypoglossal motor neurons, and retractor motor neurons lie rostral to protractor motor neurons (Satou et al. 1985). Given that the highly specialized tongue protrusion systems of plethodontids and anurans are independently derived, it is not surprising that the neural control mechanisms for these systems might be very different.

A distributed system for interfacing tectal visual representation with motor neurons in amphibians is now generally accepted, although disagreements remain over how many separate channels exist, how they are organized, and what type of information they actually represent. Grobstein (1988a) argues that such a system enhances behavioral flexibility by allowing input from each point in space access to an array of possible behavioral outputs. Nonretinal inputs impinging on the relay nuclei or interneurons between the tectal cells and motor neurons can select and modify whatever behavioral output is most appropriate given all sensory and motor activity occurring when a visual target appears. Grobstein (1988a) further suggests that such an arrangement is not an amphibian specialization, but rather a common solution of vertebrate nervous systems to problems of sensorimotor integration.

Tectal efferents also travel rostrally to the anterior lateral thalamic nucleus (Rubinson 1968; Wilczynski and Northcutt 1977), which in turn projects to the striatum (Wilczynski and Northcutt 1983a). Descending basal ganglia projections to the tectum, pretectum, and tegmentum complete a feedback loop (Wilczynski and Northcutt 1983b) that appears to modulate tectally mediated visual orientation. Lesions of the striatum decrease responsiveness to preylike stimuli (Patton and Grobstein 1986).

Interspecific Differences in Tectal Function

The visual pathways and basic features of retinal and tectal neuron physiology are remarkably similar among amphibians. Some interspecific differences in the retinotectal system

occur, but the relationship of most differences to habitat or life history is elusive. For example, the retinal ganglion cell receptive fields within physiological classes are generally larger in urodeles than in anurans, which is probably due to urodeles having larger, less numerous photoreceptors and ganglion cells (Roth 1987). How, or if, this affects perception and ultimately behavior is unknown.

One interspecific difference in physiological properties relates directly to behavior, however: variation in the shape preference in tectal cells (see also chapter 13). Ewert (1984, 1987) has shown that toads (*Bufo bufo*) strongly prefer elongated stimuli ("worm") to compact stimuli ("bugs") as prey objects. Accordingly, many tectal neurons respond preferentially to horizontally elongated stimuli, and in Ewert's terms act as "worm detectors." By contrast, such worm detectors are rare in the tecta of ranid frogs (Schurg-Pfeiffer and Ewert 1981). Tectal cells in *Rana temporaria* show virtually equal responses to squares and rectangles. Behaviorally, ranid frogs do not prefer rectangles to squares as prey objects in test situations.

A remarkably similar species difference occurs between two urodeles, *Salamandra salamandra* (Salamandridae), which is toadlike in its behavioral preference and tectal physiology, and *Hydromantes italicus* (Plethodontidae), which, like *Rana*, shows no behavioral preference for rectangular "worms" over squares and lacks tectal "worm detectors" (Finkenstädt and Ewert 1983; Himstedt and Roth 1980; Roth 1982, 1987). Furthermore, *Hydromantes* tectal neurons will continue to respond robustly to faster-moving stimuli than will tectal neurons in *Salamandra* (Roth 1987). The behavioral and physiological preferences reflect the natural diets of these two species (Roth 1987). *Salamandra* is a terrestrial forager with a short tongue and poorly developed tongue-protrusion apparatus. Its diet consists largely of slow-moving prey such as gastropods and some insects. By contrast, *Hydromantes* is a plenthodontid salamander, a group with sophisticated tongue-projecting mechanisms that allow them to extend the tongue rapidly over a considerable distance to catch prey on a sticky terminal pad. As might be expected, plethodontids prefer smaller, more compact prey and are able to catch more rapidly moving insects than can *Salamandra*.

Other visual functions, occasionally related in general ways to prey catching, are distributed to other brain areas. As in the pretectal-tectal system, peripheral input acts as an important biasing force for the physiological functions of these areas.

Color Coding and the Rostral Thalamus

Other retinal recipient areas may connect with the optic tectum, but not all work exclusively through it. As noted above, the pretectum's control of stationary barrier avoidance during locomotion is mediated without tectal involvement. A second independent system is composed of visual nuclei in the rostral thalamus involved in color vision and color-selective phototaxis.

Amphibian retinas contain several types of photoreceptors (Donner and Reuter 1976; fig. 2.12A). Like all vertebrates, they possess a rhodopsin-containing rod with a peak absorption of light at a wavelength of 502 nm (the "red" rod). Adult amphibians also have a rod receptor containing a pigment

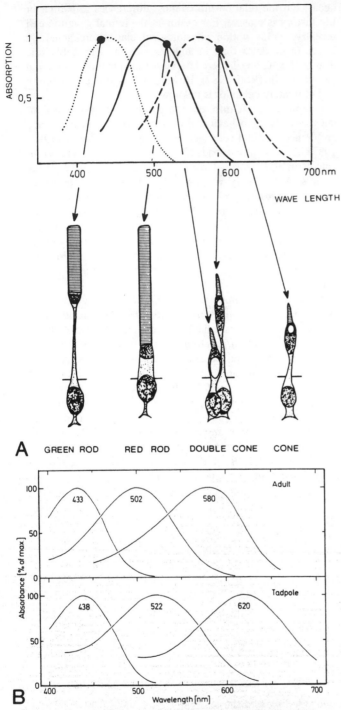

A

GREEN ROD   RED ROD   DOUBLE CONE   CONE

B

Fig. 2.12 *A,* absorption characteristics of photoreceptors in the amphibian eye. (Reprinted, by permission, from Roth 1987.) *B,* differences in the absorption peaks of the receptors in adults and tadpoles. (Reprinted, by permission, from Donner and Reuter 1976.)

cone"), and a double-cone complex containing a "principle cone" with the same pigment as the single cone and an "accessory cone" with the same pigment as the red rod.

The red rods, like rhodopsin-containing photoreceptors in other vertebrates, are presumably responsible for scotopic (low light) vision and play little role in color vision. Although four receptors with three different pigments remain (green rods, accessory cones, and the identically sensitive single and principal cones), amphibians appear to use a dichromatic mechanism for color vision in which the blue-sensitive green rods are matched against yellow-sensitive single and principal cones (Donner and Reuter 1976). The 502 nm–absorbing accessory cones apparently act only to supplement the activity of the principal cones in intermediate and low light (Backstrom and Reuter 1975). This dichromatic system is manifested in the presence of classical color-opponent receptive fields in the retinal ganglion cells (Donner and Reuter 1976; Kicliter, Kay, and Chino 1981; Reuter and Virtanen 1976). In the majority of neurons, activation of the green rods (by blue light) excites the color-opponent cells, while long-wavelength yellow light inhibits responding. This preferential blue light activation of the color system is reflected in a positive phototaxis toward blue light in adult amphibians (Fite, Soukup, and Carey 1978; Hailman and Jaeger 1978; Muntz 1962a).

The characteristics of the retinal pigments are different in larval amphibians (Donner and Reuter 1976; and see chapter 16; fig. 2.12B). In larvae, retinal is enzymatically converted to 3-dehydroretinal, which then serves as the base of the pigments (Liebman and Entine 1968); enzymatic activity ceases at metamorphosis. As a consequence, the peak absorptions of all receptor pigments in larvae are at higher wavelengths than in adults, making the color-opponent cells maximally excited by light in the yellow-green range. This shift is the apparent reason that anuran larvae show a positive phototaxis to yellow rather than blue light (Jaeger and Hailman 1976).

Jaeger and Hailman (1976) argue that the shift in pigment absorption and phototactic behavior relates to the different habitats and feeding strategies in the larval aquatic and terrestrial adult stages of anurans. Larvae live and feed in the often turbid water around aquatic vegetation, where light filtering through plants and water takes on a distinctly yellowish-green cast. Matching the pigment absorption peaks to longer wavelengths characteristic of this environment would increase the sensitivity of the visual system. In fact, the occurrence of 3-dehydroretinal-based porphyropsin rather than rhodopsin in the rod system is common among aquatic nonmammals. Secondarily, the phototaxis toward middle wavelengths might bring larvae to food and shelter. When given a choice between green plants and identical plants bleached of their green color, anuran larvae prefer the unbleached vegetation (Jaeger and Hailman 1976).

The postmetamorphic shift to shorter wavelengths and a blue phototaxis is more difficult to explain. However, Jaeger and Hailman (1976) note that visual systems all have an optimum light level where contrast sensitivity is maximized (Hailman and Jaeger 1976), and adult amphibian tectal cells and prey-catching behavior itself are both contrast-sensitive (Ewert 1984). Jaeger and Hailman (1976) speculate that the blue phototaxis causes adults to move from under thick vegetation toward more open, higher light-level areas (i.e., to

with a peak absorption at 433 nm (the "green" rod). (The names of these rods are not based on the color sensitivity, but rather on their gross appearance. The red rod responds best to yellow-green light, while the green rod responds best to blue light.) The green rod is unique to amphibians. Three cones are present, a "single cone," which maximally absorbs light with a wavelength of 580 nm (the "yellow-sensitive

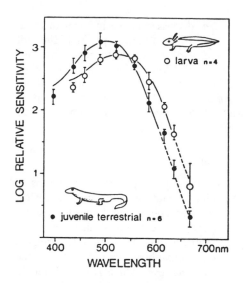 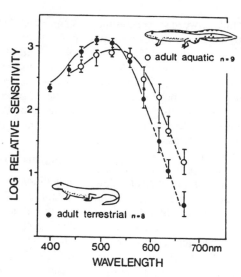

Fig. 2.13 Spectral sensitivities from electroretinograms of the eye of *Triturus vulgaris* (Salamandridae) during different life stages. (Reprinted, by permission, from Himstedt 1973.)

areas where they can see sky) during the evening to maximize the detection abilities of their tectal prey-catching systems.

Two interesting cases of lifestyle specializations are worth noting in reference to the transformations of the retinal pigments (see also chapter 16). Common newts of the genus *Triturus* (Salamandridae) have an adult aquatic stage interposed between terrestrial stages. Upon the newt's returning to an aquatic lifestyle, the enzymatic conversion of retinal to 3-dehydroretinal recommences, thereby shifting the pigment absorptions back to the longer wavelengths found in larval forms (Himstedt 1973). The conversion stops again when the newts reemerge to their second terrestrial phase. In this way, the sensitivity peaks of the receptors remain matched to the environmental spectral peaks in every life phase of this urodele (fig. 2.13).

A different pattern occurs in the anuran *Xenopus* (Pipidae), which remains aquatic throughout life. At metamorphosis, the adults switch to blue-preference phototactic behavior just as terrestrial anurans do, suggesting an equivalent shift in photoreceptor absorption (Jaeger and Hailman 1976). As the lifestyle of the Pipidae probably represents a specialized return to an aquatic niche, the metamorphic pigment change is presumably an atavism from their terrestrial ancestry. Because these creatures retain a lateral line system as adults and use this system for prey capture (see below), *Xenopus* may not need to alter the normal course of metamorphic pigment change.

Color-sensitive retinal ganglion cells project to both the rostral thalamus and the optic tectum (Himstedt, Helas, and Sommer 1981). The physiological characteristics of the rostral thalamic system strongly suggest that those nuclei or their subsequent targets are responsible for the blue-light phototactic behavior of adults (Fite, Cary, and Vicario 1977; Kicliter, Kay, and Chino 1981; Muntz 1962a, 1962b). Virtually all ganglion cells terminating in the rostral thalamus are strongly and preferentially excited by blue light, while the tectal projection contains a mixture of fibers inhibited by blue light and fibers with an on-off response, Muntz (1962a, 1962b) demonstrated that the physiological responses of the anterior thalamic system in response to color stimuli match the frog's behavioral response perfectly.

Additional details about how this thalamic blue-sensitive phototaxis system operates are lacking. However, anatomical descriptions of the connections of rostral thalamic cell populations suggest that whatever visual function is mediated there occurs relatively independently of tectal circuitry. Although retinal recipient nuclei in the rostral thalamus have some sparse efferents to the tectum, their main interconnections are with telencephalic, hypothalamic, and other dorsal thalamic nuclei (see above).

Optokinetic Responses and the Basal Optic System

Compensatory eye or head movements elicited by slowly moving backgrounds or body movements are a ubiquitous part of vertebrate vision. These movements stabilize gaze to maintain visual fixation, an important function in animals with visually guided prey capture. Optokinetic movements are the responsibility of the accessory, or basal, optic system (see Fite 1985 for review).

In amphibians, the accessory optic system is centered on the basal optic nucleus in the base of the rostral midbrain (Manteuffel, Petersen, and Himstedt 1983; Montgomery et al. 1982). This nucleus receives its own direct retinal input and is interconnected with several other small cell populations in the ventral mesencephalon and pretectum (Fite, Bengston, and Montgomery 1988; Montgomery, Fite, and Bengston 1981; Naujoks-Manteuffel and Manteuffel 1986). Pretectal nuclei also participate in optokinetic responses (Fite 1985). In anurans, this system of nuclear groups provides efferents to the motor neurons of the extraocular muscles and descending projections to the medulla and spinal cord, presumably to influence head and neck movements as well (Montgomery, Fite, and Bengston 1981). Projections from both the basal optic nucleus (Montgomery, Fite, and Bengston 1981) and pretectal optokinetic areas (Cochran, Dieringer, and Precht 1984) make monosynaptic connections on motor neurons of the extraocular muscles. Furthermore, the proportion of myelinated axons reaching the accessory optic system is higher than the proportion of myelinated axons in the optic nerve as a whole (Fite, Bengston, and Montgomery 1988). These facts suggest that the accessory optic system is constructed to provide the fastest link between sensory stimulation and motor activation of any of the functional systems associated with vision.

The physiological properties of retinal ganglion cells innervating the basal optic system are in keeping with the system's role in mediating compensatory movements to a moving visual world (fig. 2.14). Virtually all the cells are movement-sensitive and directionally selective (Cochran, Dieringer, and Precht 1984; Grubert and Grasse 1984; Katte and Hoffman 1980). Both vertical- and horizontal-movement-selective cells are apparent. The cells generally have large receptive fields and respond best to relatively slow movements. Movement-selective neurons are also found in the pretectum (Cochran, Dieringer, and Precht 1984; Katte and Hoffman 1980). These tend to be more responsive to horizontal movements than are basal optic nucleus cells. Cochran, Dieringer, and Precht (1984) argued that horizontal nystagmus is more the responsibility of the pretectal portion of the system, while vertical nystagmus is more the responsibility of the basal optic nucleus.

Interspecific variation in the optokinetic behavior exists and might be linked to feeding strategies, in that optokinetic movements allow an animal to maintain visual fixation while an object or an animal's own head and body are moving (see also chapter 13). In this regard, a comparison of *Hydro-*

mantes and *Salamandra*, discussed above in terms of tectal physiology, is interesting (Manteuffel, Kopp, and Himstedt 1986; Roth 1987). *Hydromantes* is able to compensate for movements up to $19°·s^{-1}$, while *Salamandra* can follow movements up to $3°·s^{-1}$ and follows more poorly at all velocities. *Salamandra* normally eats slow-moving gastropods and arthropods, while *Hydromantes* catches fast-moving prey via its tongue-projecting apparatus.

Nonretinal Photoreception

In addition to the eyes, amphibians possess a second visual system related to the pineal gland (reviewed in Adler 1976). The pineal lies above the diencephalon just beneath the skull. Photoreceptors are present in the gland in all amphibians, where they synapse on intrinsic pineal neurons (Hetherington 1981; Koft 1976). Anuran amphibians also possess a frontal organ, a stirnorgan or parietal eye, which is a small retina-like structure in a shallow covered pit on the head between the eyes. Photoreceptors synapse on ganglion cells whose axons form the "frontal nerve" running from the organ to the pineal gland (Adler 1976).

The frontal organ ganglion cells and the intrinsic pineal neurons make surprisingly widespread connections with virtually identical areas of the brain (Eldred, Finger, and Nolte 1980). Projections occur to parts of the amygdala, preoptic area, and ventral thalamus, and to large areas of the pretectal gray, the central gray matter of the rostral mesencephalon.

Several functions have been attributed to the frontal organ and pineal photoreceptor system (reviewed in Adler 1976). One is the control of pigmentation (see also chapters 3, 9, and 16). In larval amphibians, melanophores in the skin are under the hormonal control of the pineal gland. As with all other photoreceptors, pineal photoreceptors are most depolarized in the dark. The increased activity of darkened pineal photoreceptors stimulates the release of melatonin, which causes skin melanophores to contract, thereby causing the larva to lighten. Neither the lateral eyes nor the frontal organ plays any role in this larval response.

As development progresses, a radical change in pigmentation control ensues, so that by metamorphosis a completely different system emerges to override the pineal's control (Adler 1976). Light stimulation of the eyes, not the pineal or frontal organ, ultimately blocks the pituitary's release of melanophore-stimulating hormone (MSH). As MSH causes melanophore expansion, blocking MSH release results in a lightening of the skin. The advent of this new control system therefore means that while larvae lighten in the dark, adults lighten in the light. The neural link between the retina and the MSH-secreting cells is unknown, but direct retinopreoptic connections exist in amphibians and may provide quick access to endocrine control systems of the basal diencephalon.

Why the skin of larvae lightens in the dark is unclear. However, adult amphibians would not want to increase their contrast with their surroundings and so become more obvious to potential predators. The switch to the mature control mechanism stops potentially disadvantageous color changes and provides a mechanism by which frogs can match their skin coloration to the substrate and so remain cryptic.

A second proposed function of pineal–frontal organ photoreception is the control of circadian rhythms. Activity

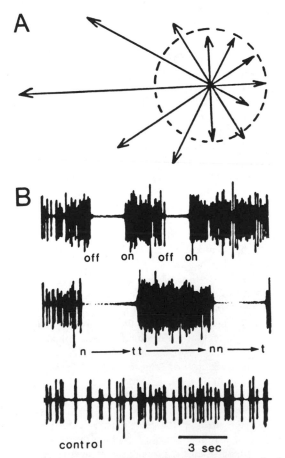

Fig. 2.14 *A,* Vector representation of direction preference of a basal optic nucleus cell. *B,* Neural response of a basal optic nucleus cell to light on and off and to nasal (*n*) to temporal (*t*) movements and vice versa. (Reprinted, by permission, from Gruberg and Grasse 1984.)

rhythms in *Rana clamitans* and *Notophthalmus viridescens* (Salamandridae; Demian and Taylor 1977) can be shifted by changes in the light cycle only if the frontal organ is intact. By contrast, light entrainment is normal when the eyes are removed. Stimulation of the frontal organ in frogs, or the pineal photoreceptors in urodeles, is thought to synchronize endogenous activity rhythms with the day-night cycle of the external world by a still unknown mechanism.

Temperature and Visual Sensitivity

The absolute sensitivity of the entire array of visual systems is limited by the characteristics of the photopigments in the visual receptors. Thermally induced random isomerization of the photopigment molecules causes electrical activity indistinguishable from that induced by light. This sets a limit on the visual system's ability to detect a discrete light signal; at very low light levels the signal is lost among the thermally induced noise (Barlow 1956; Hecht, Schlaer, and Pirenne 1942). Psychophysical experiments with humans and other primates show that the absolute detection threshold does indeed lie close to the point at which the amount of pigment bleaching by the signal equals the calculated level of spontaneous thermal isomerization (see Baylor, Nunn, and Schnapf 1984).

The amount of random isomerization increases with temperature. A series of elegant experiments on *Rana temporaria* (Aho et al. 1988; Aho et al. 1987; Donner 1989) showed that for heterothermic animals with low body temperatures like amphibians, thermal isomerization of photopigments is low and retinal ganglion cells are excited by dim flashes of light down to the low limit imposed by the thermal noise. Consequently the behavioral threshold for light detection, indicated by a frog's jumping toward a dimly lit window in a black background or snapping at a dimly lit moving target, is also extremely low. Aho et al.'s (1988) experiments show that the absolute behavioral threshold for visual detection in *Bufo bufo* and *Rana temporaria* at 15°C (room temperature during the tests) is one-eighth of the threshold for human vision (where body temperature places the receptors at 37°C; see fig. 2.15).

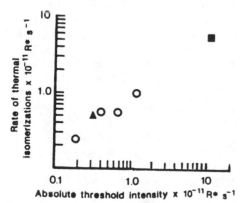

Fig. 2.15 Rate of thermal isomerization versus absolute behavioral threshold (both expressed as isomerization rate per rhodopsin molecule) for *Bufo bufo* (▲) at 15°C, *Rana temporaria* (○) at 10°, 16°, 16°, and 20°C (from left to right), and *Homo sapiens* (■) at a body temperature of 37°C. (From Aho et al. 1988. Reprinted, by permission, from *Nature* 334:348–350 copyright ©1988 Macmillan Magazines Ltd.)

In addition to illuminating a fundamental phenomenon of vision, these studies show that amphibians gain an unexpected visual advantage by virtue of their low body temperatures. Detection becomes sensitive enough to allow visually mediated foraging, predator detection, and conspecific recognition (Rand 1988) to proceed efficiently in the evening or night. Temperate zone amphibians would generally be active under more thermally favorable conditions than tropical species. An open question is whether systematic variations in species-typical behavior patterns are linked to thermal habitat characteristics.

THE AUDITORY SYSTEM

Physiological studies of the amphibian auditory system have centered on postmetamorphic anurans, although limited information is available for larvae (chapter 16). Anatomical investigations of the peripheral and, much less often, central auditory structures and connections in urodeles and apodans exist but are far fewer than comparable studies of anuran structures. The anatomical studies of nonanuran amphibians have often been undertaken as part of an inquiry into the octaval (auditory plus vestibular) and lateral line systems (e.g., Fritzsch 1988). While these studies provide valuable information on the evolution of amphibian and vertebrate auditory systems, they generally have not addressed physiological or ecological aspects of audition and therefore will not be discussed here.

By contrast, investigations of the anuran auditory system are often built around physiological, behavioral, or ecological questions, and often highlight interspecific differences. This is because audition in anurans is intimately tied into a social communication system marked by species-specific advertisement calls (see chapter 14). In most species, only males produce an advertisement call, and do so only during the breeding season (Wells 1977). Females are attracted by the call (Gerhardt 1988; Wells 1977) and may use it to select among males in a chorus in some species (Ryan 1985b, 1988a; Schwartz 1986; Sullivan and Leek 1987). Among males, the same call mediates antiphonal calling (Narins and Zelick 1988; Wells 1977) and intermale spacing (Brenowitz, Wilczynski, and Zakon 1984; Robertson 1984; Wilczynski and Brenowitz 1988), and triggers aggressive interactions (Wagner 1989; Wells 1988). Call characteristics and intermale spacing interact in complex ways to influence the overall sound field around a chorus (J. H. Fox 1988). Thus the call plays a major role in the dynamics and spatial organization of breeding aggregations. Other types of calls have been documented in some species. Most common is a release call, produced by both sexes, which signals nonreceptivity to a clasping male (McClelland and Wilczynski 1989a; Rand 1988; Wells 1977). Visual, olfactory, or tactile stimuli may play some role in anuran social behavior (Rand 1988). The overwhelming importance of acoustic signals, however, and the clear and quantifiable expressions of species differences in the signal and behavior have understandably steered neuroethologists toward the auditory system.

Peripheral Auditory Structures

Many adult anurans possess tympanic ears (fig. 2.16) that are superficially similar to those of amniotes (Jaslow, Hethering-

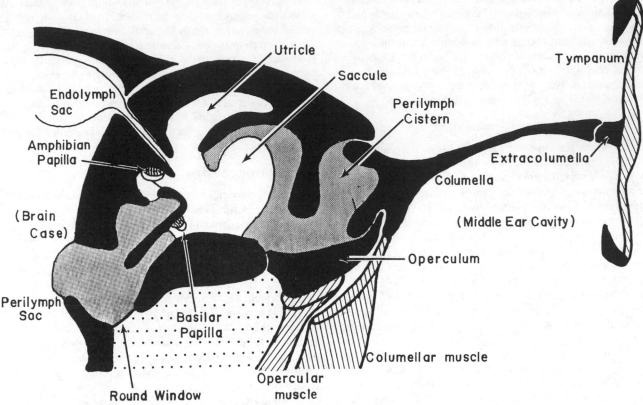

Fig. 2.16 Drawing of components of an anuran ear. (From Wilczynski and Capranica 1984. Reprinted with permission from Pergamon Press PLC.)

ton, and Lombard 1988; Wilczynski and Capranica 1984), although the anuran condition may represent an independently evolved condition (Lombard and Bolt 1979, 1988). A tympanic membrane lies on the surface of the head over a middle ear cavity. The membrane is connected by a bone, the columella and its attached extracolumella, to the oval window of the otic capsule. Airborne vibrations, detected by the tympanic membrane, can thus be coupled into the fluid of the inner ear. Eustachian tubes link the middle ear cavity with the mouth. This results in the two ears being coupled in such a way that pressure changes associated with stimulation of one ear can be passed to the other. The interaural coupling may be important during sound localization.

Anuran ears also contain an "opercularis system," composed of the operculum bone lying over part of the oval window and an opercularis muscle running from this bone to the scapula. Urodeles also have this system even though they lack a tympanic membrane. Hetherington, Jaslow, and Lombard (1986; Hetherington 1988a) have argued that this system represents a second sound or ground vibration transmission pathway to the inner ear. Several lines of evidence suggest that low-frequency sound especially can be coupled to the inner ear independent of the tympanic-columella pathway (Lombard and Straughan 1974; Narins, Ehret, and Tautz 1988; Wilczynski, Resler, and Capranica 1987). The anuran ear is also extremely sensitive to seismic vibrations (Koyama et al. 1982; Narins and Lewis 1985). It responds primarily to Rayleigh waves, the component of substrate surface waves with

a large vertical energy vector. Hetherington (1985, 1988a) demonstrated that the opercularis system is constructed so as to be particularly apt at transmitting vertically oriented ground vibrations such as those in Rayleigh waves.

In some anuran species, many or all parts of the middle ear are reduced or absent, often as a derived condition, even though many of these middle-earless frogs incorporate acoustic communication signals into their social behavior. After a careful review of middle ear variation, Jaslow, Hetherington, and Lombard (1988) could discern no single developmental, ecological, or behavioral factor that might account for the middle ear reduction.

The adult anuran condition represents a drastic change from the premetamorphic ear (Hetherington 1988b; see also chapter 16). In larvae, an otic capsule with an obvious oval window is present, but no middle ear structures are apparent. This might be expected, given that the middle ear structures are constructed to overcome the problem associated with coupling airborne sound into the fluids of the inner ear, and that frogs do not face this problem premetamorphically. Sound may couple directly from the water into the surrounding tissues in larvae. Ranid larvae manifest an additional coupling method, which disappears at metamorphosis. A "bronchial columella" stretches from the lungs to the round window of the otic capsule, which in adults serves as a pressure release for the inner ear (Witschi 1956; Hetherington 1988b). This premetamorphic columella could couple vibrations of the air-filled lungs caused by sound-induced pressure changes in the water into the inner ear. Ostariophysian fish employ an analogous apparatus, the Weberian ossicles, for sound transmission (Fay and Popper 1980). This alternative larval coupling mechanism may be restricted to ranid frogs (Hetherington 1988b).

No urodele or apodan possesses a tympanic ear as either a larva or an adult (Jaslow, Hetherington, and Lombard 1988). Adult urodeles also lack middle ear cavities. The columella can be moveable in larvae, but in adults it is fused to the skull. Few apodans have been investigated, but the adults of some species have moveable columellas attached to the skull.

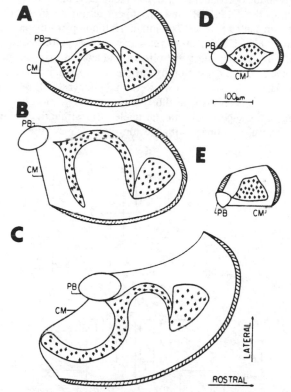

Fig. 2.17 Outlines of amphibian papillae from the relatively advanced anurans *Bombina orientalis* (Discoglossidae; *A*), *Scaphiopus couchii* (Pelobatidae; *B*), and *Kassina senegalensis* (Hyperoliidae; *C*); the urodele *Ambystoma maculatum* (Ambystomatidae; *D*); and the primitive anuran *Ascaphus truei* (Leiopelmatidae; *E*). Arrows show orientation of hair cells. *CM*, contact membrane; *PB*, amphibian papilla branch of nerve VIII. (Reprinted, by permission, from Lewis and Lombard, "The amphibian inner ear," in *The Evolution of the Amphibian Auditory System*, 93–123, copyright 1988 by John Wiley and Sons.)

The absence of tympanic membranes and the often severe reduction of other middle ear structures in these amphibians and in many species of anurans is curious in that virtually all amphibians possess qualitatively similar inner ear receptor organs.

Two auditory receptor organs, the amphibian and basilar papillae, characterize amphibians (Lewis and Lombard 1988; Wilczynski and Capranica 1984). Using two papillae to cover the frequency spectrum to which the auditory system responds is unique to amphibians. The saccule also has some auditory sensitivity along with its probable vestibular functions and role in responding to seismic vibrations (Lewis et al. 1982; Moffat and Capranica 1976a). These organs change little during development other than to add receptor cells, a process that accelerates at metamorphosis (Fritzsch, Wahnschaffe, and Bartsch 1988). Variation across species is also mainly quantitative, although a few urodele species lack a basilar papilla.

The amphibian papilla (AP) is the larger of the two auditory organs and is sensitive to sounds of lower frequency than the basilar papilla (BP) is. It contains a bank of receptor cells connected to cranial nerve VIII fibers. The receptors and their connected nerve fibers are tuned to frequencies from less than 100 Hz to about 1.2 kHz in advanced frogs. The range of receptor tuning represents a major interspecific difference, one that follows a phylogenetic pattern in anurans (Lewis 1981a, 1981b). Primitive frogs have a small AP and receptors confined to a narrow frequency range. In more advanced anurans, the amphibian papilla forms an elongated tail, which contains receptors tuned to progressively higher frequencies along its length (fig. 2.17). Urodeles and apodans all have relatively simple APs much like the most primitive anuran condition. Their tuning characteristics are unknown.

The receptor cells in anurans are arranged along the AP tonotopically (fig. 2.18), as in the mammalian cochlea (Lewis, Leverenz, and Koyama 1982; Lewis and Lombard 1988). Surprisingly, some sort of traveling wave is involved in the tonotopic organization (Hillery and Narins 1984; Lewis 1984; Lewis and Lombard 1988). Tonotopy and traveling-wave phenomena in amniotes are widely believed to be due to the properties of the moving basilar membrane on which the hair cells reside. However, amphibians have no basilar membrane; the hair cells are fixed to an apparently immobile cartilage shelf. AP tuning is probably due to a combination of tectorial membrane mechanical properties (possibly supporting the suspected traveling wave) and electrical tuning of

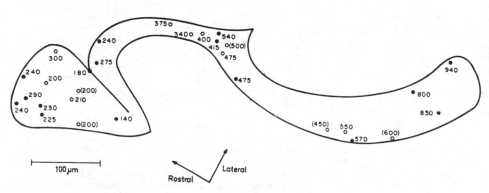

Fig. 2.18 Tonotopic organization of the bullfrog (*Rana catesbeiana*) amphibian papilla. Numbers denote best excitatory frequency of afferents. (Reprinted, by permission, from Lewis, Leverenz, and Koyama 1982.)

the hair cells themselves (Ashmore and Pitchford 1985; Capranica and Moffat 1980; Zakon and Wilczynski 1988).

The basilar papilla is a smaller patch of receptor cells lying in its own separate cartilaginous chamber. It contains fewer receptors tuned to a narrower, higher range of frequencies than the AP; in small frogs it is often well above the highest AP receptor tuning. BP tuning is species-specific (reviewed in Zakon and Wilczynski 1988). Rather than demonstrating a progressive phylogenetic pattern such as that seen in the AP, BP tuning varies (inversely) with species size and maintains a close correspondence with the spectral content of the species advertisement call (see below). BP tuning has been considered to depend mainly on the resonant properties of its composing structures (hence the inverse relationship of tuning with size; Shofner 1988; Zakon and Wilczynski 1988).

The receptors in both organs synapse on the processes of ganglion cells whose axons form cranial nerve VIII. Each afferent fiber has a V-shaped tuning curve (fig. 2.19A) typical of vertebrate ears (Wilczynski and Capranica 1984; Zakon and Wilczynski 1988). Different fibers with a wide range of thresholds can be seen tuned to any one frequency (fig. 2.19B).

One can therefore think of the anuran periphery as dividing the auditory world into a matrix of responses, with each nerve VIII fiber responding best to a particular frequency with a particular sensitivity.

Central Auditory Areas

Auditory and vestibular fibers travel in cranial nerve VIII to terminate in a set of nuclei in the ipsilateral dorsal medulla (reviewed in Fuzessery 1988 and Will and Fritzsch 1988). In anurans the two modalities terminate in separate zones within this area: vestibular fibers ventrally and auditory fibers dorsally in the dorsolateral, or dorsal medullary, nucleus (DLN). Within the DLN, BP and AP fibers terminate in separate areas in such a way as to maintain the tonotopy of the peripheral system. DLN neurons relay the auditory information bilaterally to the superior olivary nucleus, which in turn projects (mainly ipsilaterally) to the torus semicircularis via the lateral lemniscus (reviewed in Wilczynski 1988; fig. 2.20). The DLN also has direct projections to the torus. Neurons of the superficial reticular nucleus lie within the lemniscus and also connect with the torus. They may represent a

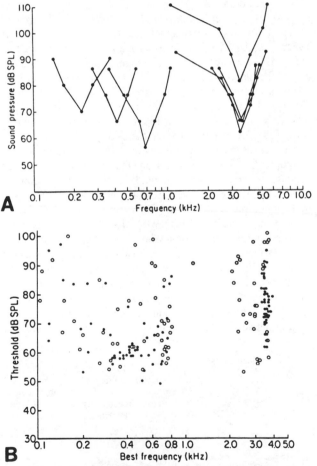

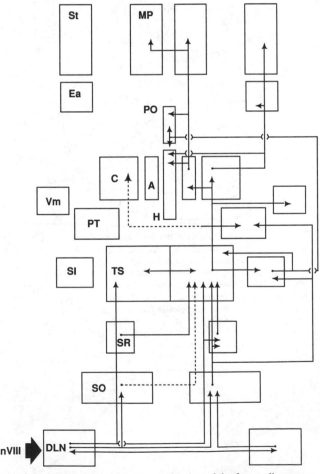

Fig. 2.19 A, Representative tuning curves of nerve VIII fibers from a single *Hyla crucifer* (Hylidae). Three curves on the left are from the amphibian papilla; three on the right from the basilar papilla. B, Scatter plot of best frequency versus threshold for nerve VIII fibers in male (●) and female (○) *H. crucifer*. Fibers above 2.0 kHz derive from the basilar papilla. (Reprinted, by permission, from Wilczynski, Zakon, and Brenowitz 1984.)

Fig. 2.20 Diagram of ascending connections of the frog auditory system. *A*, anterior thalamic nucleus; *C*, central thalamic nucleus; *DLN*, dorsolateral nucleus; *Ea*, anterior entopeduncular nucleus; *H*, hypothalamus; *MP*, medial pallium; *nVIII*, cranial nerve VIII; *PO*, preoptic area; *PT*, pretectum; *SI*, secondary isthmal nucleus; *SO*, superior olivary nucleus; *SR*, superficial reticular nucleus; *St*, striatum; *TS*, Torus semicircularis; *Vm*, ventromedial thalamic nucleus.

homologue of the mammalian nuclei of the lateral lemniscus (Rose and Wilczynski 1984). Tonotopy is preserved in each nucleus (Fuzessery 1988), and commissural connections are present at every stage. The commissural connections plus the bilateral projections of each DLN manifest themselves physiologically in the abundance of binaural neurons in each auditory nucleus. Brain-stem auditory pathways are generally similar to those in other vertebrates (Wilczynski 1988).

The connections of the torus are numerous and complex (Neary 1988; Wilczynski 1981, 1988). Descending connections from various of its component nuclei provide feedback to brain-stem auditory nuclei and reach reticular formation areas extending to the spinal cord. A particularly large projection terminates in the secondary isthmal nucleus, with which the torus is reciprocally connected (Neary 1988; Neary and Wilczynski 1986). Ascending connections terminate in many dorsal and ventral thalamic nuclei (Neary 1988). The heaviest termination is in the central thalamic nucleus, a large

component of the middle thalamic zone, which relays the input to the striatum (fig. 2.21A). A secondary projection reaches the anterior thalamic nucleus, a part of the rostral thalamic zone, which in turn projects to the medial and dorsal pallium.

These two thalamic nuclei also send surprisingly robust inputs to the preoptic area and ventral hypothalamus (fig. 2.21B); Allison and Wilczynski 1989; Hall and Feng 1987; Neary 1988; Neary and Wilczynski 1986). They are joined by a third strong auditory input from the secondary isthmal nucleus (fig. 2.21C). These inputs enable the activity of many preoptic and ventral hypothalamic neurons to be modulated by acoustic stimuli (Urano and Gorbman 1981; Wilczynski and Allison 1989).

The robust connections of the auditory system with preoptic and hypothalamic areas is one of the differences between this sensory system and the visual system, although a few cells in the tectal recipient thalamic nucleus project to the

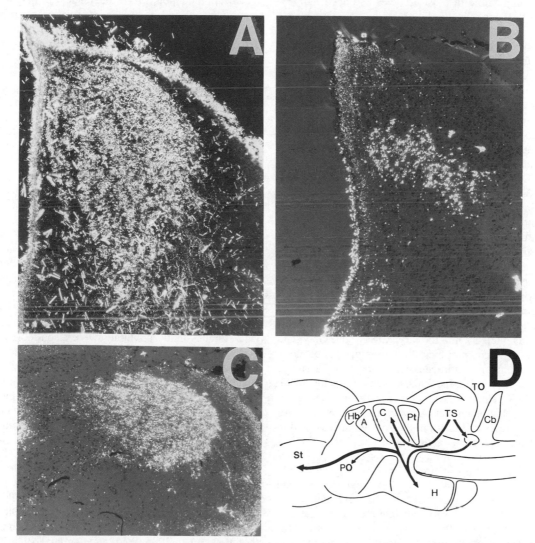

Fig. 2.21 A, Photomicrograph of horseradish peroxidase (HRP)–filled cells in the central and anterior lateral thalamic nuclei after an HRP injection in the striatum of *Rana pipiens*. B, HRP–filled cells in the central nucleus after an injection in the ventral hypothalamus. C, HRP–filled cells in the secondary isthmal nucleus after HRP injection in the ventral hypothalamus. D, Diagram of ascending auditory connections to the forebrain in ranid frogs. A, anterior thalamic nucleus; C, central thalamic nucleus; Cb, cerebellum; H, hypothalamus; Hb, habenula; PO, preoptic area; Pt, pretectum; St, striatum; TO, optic tectum; TS, torus semicircularis. (After Neary 1988.)

ventral hypothalamus (Neary 1988). Furthermore, the magnitude of these auditory-basal diencephalic connections may be a special feature of anurans (other amphibians have not been examined), and may be related to the importance of the auditory system for processing signals crucial to appropriate reproductive behavior. Reproduction and its attendant social behavior involve the coordinated expression of somatic motor acts (orientation, locomotion, maintaining particular postures) and visceral motor control (including endocrine release). Forebrain pathways in frogs are constructed so as to send auditory information to systems responsible for these two realms of expression, the striatum and basal diencephalon, in parallel (fig. 2.21D).

Vocal Production

One of the behaviors intimately tied to the auditory system is vocalization. Sound production is an integral part of the social behavior of most anurans but is apparently unimportant and perhaps impossible in most urodeles and apodans. The production of calls is sexually dimorphic in most anuran species. Males vocalize more than females, and as a correlate of this the larynx and other peripheral structures associated with sound production are also sexually dimorphic. The extensive work on the peripheral structures associated with vocalizations will not be discussed here. These structures are discussed in other contributions to this volume (e.g., chapter 14) and in Martin 1972, McClelland and Wilczynski 1989b, and the thorough reviews in Kelley 1986 and Schneider 1988.

The laryngeal muscles are innervated by motor neurons of the medulla located in the fused cranial nerve nuclei of cranial nerves IX and X (Schneider 1988; Simpson, Tobias, and Kelley 1986). Just as the laryngeal muscles are sexually dimorphic (Sassoon and Kelley 1986; Schneider 1988; McClelland and Wilczynski 1989b), so is the cranial nerve nucleus containing their motor neurons (Gorlick and Kelley 1987; Hannigan and Kelley 1981). In *Xenopus laevis,* females have about 60% of the neurons contained in the male nucleus. This sexual dimorphism arises only after metamorphosis (Gorlick and Kelley 1987). An equal number of nucleus IX-X neurons appear in males and females during the neurogenic period of larval development, so that at metamorphosis this nucleus, like the larynx (Sassoon, Gray, and Kelley 1987), is monomorphic. Within six months of metamorphosis, circulating androgens cause the male larynx to grow relatively larger than the female larynx. Coincident with this, male IX-X neurons remain numerous, while female IX-X neurons decrease in number. Apparently, the lack of appropriate targets causes cell death in the female nucleus, and in this way steroid hormones acting on a peripheral structure dictate a change in the central nervous system (see Purves 1988 for a review of trophic effects on nervous systems).

The motor neurons innervating laryngeal muscles are controlled by the pretrigeminal nucleus (Schmidt 1973, 1974b), also called the dorsal tegmental area of the medulla (Wetzel, Haerter, and Kelley 1985), a nucleus beneath the cerebellum. This area, possibly in concert with other reticular zones involved in respiration (see chapter 7), acts as a central pattern generator for call production (Schmidt 1974a). The call pattern generator acts as a slightly variable oscillator with an intrinsic refractory period that limits the call rate or the ability of a frog to answer a calling conspecific (Moore et al. 1989; Zelick and Narins 1985). Once stimulated, the brainstem area can generate calling sequences without peripheral proprioceptive feedback (Schmidt 1974a). In fact, the pattern-generating circuitry may be much less sensitive to proprioceptive feedback than the central pattern generators for locomotion or tongue snapping (see above). Complete deafferentiation of the brain stem has no effect on neural correlates of calling (Schmidt 1974a), and, in fact, laryngeal muscles lack proprioceptors (Schneider 1988).

Descending projections from the anterior preoptic area provide a major input to the pretrigeminal nucleus (Wetzel, Haerter, and Kelley 1985). Early ablation (Aronson and Noble 1945) and later stimulation (Schmidt 1984b; Wada and Gorbman 1977) experiments showed that the preoptic area facilitates calling. However, behavioral (Ryan 1986b) and neural (Schmidt 1988) studies show that calling can proceed without preoptic involvement. The preoptic area's role in normal vocal production is therefore unclear. It may integrate an array of neural and endocrine information to modulate the expression of several reproductive behaviors including vocalization. The striatum also sends a small projection to the pretrigeminal nucleus (Wetzel, Haerter, and Kelley 1985). The function of this recently discovered pathway has not been explored.

Input from the auditory system and the influence of circulating androgens interact at each point of the descending vocal control system prior to the laryngeal motor neurons. Neurons in the striatum (Mudry and Capranica 1980), preoptic area (Urano and Gorbman 1981), and pretrigeminal nucleus (Aitken and Capranica 1984) respond to auditory stimulation. In fact, the detection of conspecific calls is a major influence on an anuran's calling behavior (reviewed in Narins and Zelick 1988 and Wells 1988).

Walkowiak (1988c) showed that at least two distinct auditory inputs influence the vocal system in *Bombina bombina* (Discoglossidae). One, a narrowly tuned call recognition system, appears to act at higher levels in the vocal control pathway to stimulate calling. A second, very short latency, broadly tuned (and hence relatively nonspecific) input acts at lower levels to increase the duration of the refractory period via a stimulus-induced inhibition (see also Moore et al. 1989; Zelick 1986). The result is a common behavior in anurans: antiphonal calling (reviewed in Narins and Zelick 1988), in which a male answers a conspecific's call, but with a delay so as to reduce acoustic interference. The physiological characteristics of the separate channels (Walkowiak 1988c) suggest that frogs would be relatively selective in initiating vocalization to a sound, but would adjust their call rate, even when spontaneously calling, to avoid any loud, repetitive noise (such as, for example, heterospecific calls). However, this has not been investigated.

Androgen receptors are located at each level of the descending vocal control pathway (Kelley 1980, 1981), and circulating androgens must be present for males to produce calls (Mendonça et al. 1985; Wada and Gorbman 1977; Wetzel and Kelley 1983). Preliminary studies (Wilczynski et al. 1989) suggest that the androgens may exert their priming effect by increasing the number of postsynaptic dopamine receptors on forebrain neurons. Nongonadal hormones such as vasotocin and prostaglandin also influence calling and reproductive behavior (Diakow and Nemiroff 1981; Diakow and Raimondi 1981).

Auditory, vocal, and hormonal systems are intertwined in other ways. Sex steroid receptors are also found in the torus semicircularis, and estrogen treatment increases auditory activity there (Yovanof and Feng 1983). Thalamic auditory nuclei provide a major input to endocrine control areas of the ventral hypothalamus (Neary 1988; Neary and Wilczynski 1986), and Brzoska and Obert (1980) showed that exposure to conspecific mating calls influences sex steroid production. These studies suggest complicated interactions among these three systems as they participate in anuran reproductive behavior.

Functional Specializations: Acoustic Communication

The specialization of the anuran auditory system for processing acoustic communication signals seen in the anatomy of forebrain pathways is also evident in several aspects of auditory physiology (Capranica and Moffatt 1983). As is the visual system, the auditory system is constructed so that peripheral physiology biases input to the central areas, where additional manipulations hone the feature-detection abilities of the system.

Peripheral specialization is most apparent in the tuning of the BP. The advertisement call of a majority of frog species has a spectral composition with an energy peak matching the best frequency of BP afferents (reviewed in Zakon and Wilczynski 1988). Many calls also contain energy overlapping the tuning of the AP, but for many frogs the BP is the only organ capable of responding to call frequencies. The match between call and BP tuning even extends to the population level in *Acris crepitans* (Hylidae; fig. 2.22), where small changes in the dominant frequency of the call are matched by coincident changes in BP tuning (Capranica, Frishkopf, and Nevo 1973; Keddy-Hector, Wilczynski, and Ryan 1989; Ryan and Wilczynski 1988). These small changes are enough to bias a female's mate choice toward her own population.

Similar interspecific tuning differences in the AP directly

correlated with call differences are not always discernible (e.g., Walkowiak, Capranica, and Schneider 1981; Zelick and Narins 1982). All anurans have an AP regardless of whether their call frequencies stimulate it, and the AP characteristics of AP-stimulators and non-AP-stimulators do not seem different.

In two cases, however, AP physiology is related to call processing. Capranica (see Capranica and Moffat 1983) discovered that the call of the bullfrog (*Rana catesbeiana*) stimulates both the BP and the low-frequency portion of the AP. Stimulating the midfrequency AP fibers blocks one behavioral response to the call (antiphonal calling). Physiologically, stimulation of the AP with midfrequency sound inhibits responding in low-frequency fibers. Two-tone suppression is a general feature of vertebrate audition. It is present in all anurans, including *Hyla cinerea* (Hylidae; Ehret, Moffat, and Capranica 1983), where call energy stimulates the midfrequency AP region, and in *Hyla crucifer* (Wilczynski, Zakon, and Brenowitz 1984), where the call only stimulates the BP. Nevertheless, in bullfrogs, two-tone suppression provides a simple mechanism to prevent males from responding to broadband noise as though it were a conspecific call.

A second specialization was found by Narins and Capranica (1976) in *Eleutherodactylus coqui* (Leptodactylidae). One call note (the "co") triggers aggressive responses in males. Narins and Capranica found more AP units tuned to the co frequency in males than in females, perhaps providing males with more sensitivity or more resolving power in this important frequency region.

In anurans in general, the phylogenetic pattern of AP development may profoundly affect speciation (Ryan 1986c, 1988a). At each grade of AP development, anuran species diversity increases dramatically. Ryan argued that one explanation may be that the characteristics of the AP control the number of species possible by controlling the number of different frequency bands available for advertisement calls.

As in the visual system, peripheral responses alone are insufficient to explain the discrimination shown by many anuran species, especially those whose calls stimulate both papillae or those using temporal cues like amplitude modulation (AM). These additional discriminations require central processing of the incoming information (reviewed in Walkowiak 1988b).

For frogs with call recognition based on coactivation of both papillae (e.g., *Rana catesbeiana*, *R. pipiens*, *Hyla cinerea*), central processing involves a convergence of inputs from the two organs. AP and BP representations remain separate through the medulla, although central inhibitory mechanisms sharpen frequency selectivity there (Fuzessery 1988). Beginning in the torus, and much more often in the thalamus, neurons that respond to stimulation from either papilla emerge (reviewed in Fuzessery 1988). In the thalamus, many show a nonlinear increase in their activity (fig. 2.23) when the papillae are stimulated together (Hall and Feng 1987; Mudry and Capranica 1987; Mudry, Constantine-Paton, and Capranica 1977).

The midbrain and thalamus are also the levels at which temporal selectivity emerges (Hall and Feng 1987; Walkowiak 1988a). The peripheral auditory system allows indiscriminate, unmodified passage of temporal patterns below

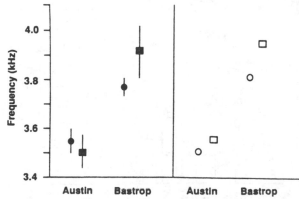

Fig. 2.22 Dominant frequency of the call (*circles*) and best frequency of the basilar papilla (*squares*) in two populations of *Acris crepitans* (Anura: Hylidae), uncorrected (*left*) and corrected (*right*) for body size. (Reprinted, by permission, from Ryan and Wilczynski 1988. Copyright 1988 by the AAAS.)

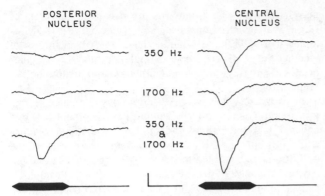

Fig. 2.23 Nonlinear summation of auditory activity in two thalamic nuclei in *Rana pipiens*. Evoked potentials to a 350-Hz and a 1,700-Hz tone alone and to the tones presented together are shown. (Reprinted, by permission, from Hall and Feng 1987.)

repetition rates of several hundred hertz. In the torus, neurons tuned to particular rates of AM emerge. Rose, Brenowitz, and Capranica (1985) found that the distribution of AM-tuned units in *Hyla versicolor* and *H. chrysoscelis* was centered at the modulation rate typical of each species' call (fig. 2.24), as are temporally tuned toral neurons in different species of *Bufo* (Rose and Capranica 1984). In the thalamus (Hall and Feng 1987) and torus (Diekamp and Gerhardt 1988) are feature-detecting neurons sensitive to variables such as signal duration. The construction of call-feature detectors at toral and thalamic levels is significant, given that at this point information begins to be shunted to somatomotor and visceromotor control centers of the forebrain.

Just as the tectum constructs an array of shape detectors associated with potential prey objects from biased peripheral input, the frog auditory system constructs an array of feature detectors for various spectral and temporal characteristics of potential communication signals. These auditory detectors form a distributed recognition system where temporal and spectral features are represented among separate neurons and in distinct parts of the thalamus (Hall and Feng 1987).

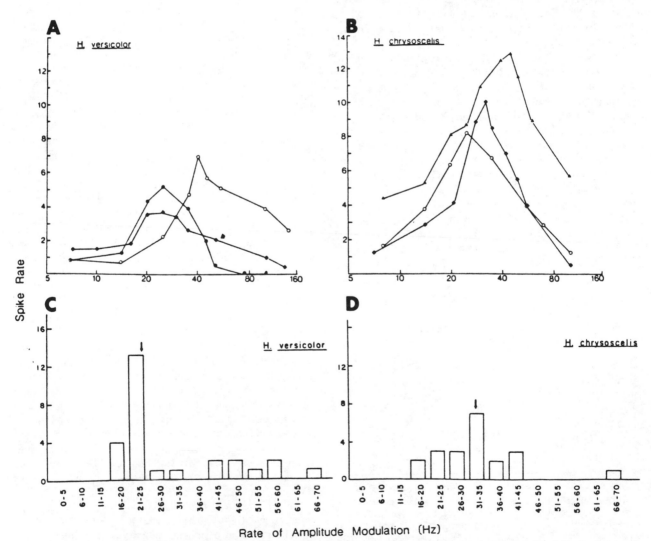

Fig. 2.24 *A, B,* temporally tuned units in the torus semicircularis of *Hyla versicolor* and *H. chrysoscelis* (Anura: Hylidae). *C, D,* distributions of best amplitude modulation rates of toral cells in the two species; *arrows* mark the mean modulation rate of the species' advertisement calls. (Reprinted, by permission, from Rose, Brenowitz, and Capranica 1985.)

Functional Specializations: Sound Localization

Communication signals are of little use if they cannot be localized. For amphibians, sound localization is a problem because their head size is extremely small relative to the wavelength of the sounds to which they are sensitive, making interaural time and intensity cues usually used for sound localization negligibly small. To overcome this problem, the peripheral auditory system is structured in an unusual way to turn each ear into a highly directional sound receiver.

Eggermont (1988) has presented the most thorough analysis of anuran sound localization. As suggested by Rheinlaender, Walkowiak, and Gerhardt (1981) and by Feng (1980), the first step in organizing the ear as a directional receiver is to construct the tympanic membrane as a pressure gradient receiver by allowing sound to impinge on both its outer and inner surfaces. The large eustachian tubes ensure a ready pathway from the contralateral ear or other source entering the mouth (Feng and Shofner 1981; Fletcher and Thwaites 1979; Narins, Ehret, and Tautz 1988; Rheinlaender, Walkowiak, and Gerhardt 1981). Because the phase of sound in the inner and outer paths will vary depending on the source location, the tympanic membrane's vibration will be highly directional. This is the same principle by which insect ears and commercial directional microphones work.

Eggermont's (1988) careful analysis shows, however, that the pressure gradient arrangement alone does not fully account for the directional characteristics of the ear (see also Barrett 1981; Wilczynski, Resler, and Capranica 1981a). In addition, a second extratympanic route to the inner ear such as that shown by several researchers (Lombard and Straughan 1974; Wilczynski, Resler, and Capranica 1987) that arrives in parallel with the tympanic-columella path must be invoked. The final directional output of the ear seen in the physiological properties of the nerve VIII afferents appears to derive from an interaction of these two pathways (Eggermont 1988; Wilczynski, Resler, and Capranica 1987). Binaural processing in the central auditory areas further sharpens the directional acuity by comparing the inputs from the two highly directional ears (Feng 1981).

Eggermont's (1988) formulation, and indeed all previous models of anuran sound localization, holds only for frogs with tympanic membranes. Many anuran species, however, and all nonanuran amphibians, lack tympanic membranes and often all semblance of a middle ear (Jaslow, Hetherington, and Lombard 1988). How sound localization is achieved in these amphibians is unknown.

Environmental Influences on Audition

Several environmental factors affect a communication system like the one used by frogs. One is ambient noise. Noise from heterospecifics, conspecifics, and abiotic sources degrades the performance of any auditory system by masking its ability to detect a signal (Megela and Capranica 1982; Simmons 1988).

Anurans attempt to compensate for some sources of biotic noise by adjusting their calling behavior to avoid overlap with potential noise emissions. At the species level, sympatric species avoid heterospecific calls by subdividing the acoustic habitat spectrally, placing call energy in different frequency bands (Drewry and Rand 1983; Narins and Zelick 1988). The

band pass characteristics of nerve VIII afferents and the noise rejection achieved by matching the call frequencies with papilla tuning helps filter out sound from other frogs. AM can be added to the call, after which temporarily tuned cells in the torus will selectively respond to the modulated signal, but not to unmodulated background noise (Capranica and Rose 1983). Lewis and Lombard (1988) have argued that receiver directionality is also an effective noise-reduction mechanism when used to focus reception on an important target. Finally, the timing of the breeding season may be staggered so that the peak calling of one species does not overlap with another (Drewry and Rand 1983).

Obviously, conspecifics cannot avoid each others' calls in the same way. Many frogs call antiphonally, however, which prevents an overlap and consequent jamming or smearing of the signal at a receiving individual (Narins and Zelick 1988).

Compensating for general, broadband environmental noise is more difficult. In theory, animals could match call frequencies to troughs in the ambient spectrum where noise is minimal. However, this phenomenon has not been demonstrated in frogs. For discussions of the effects of noise and other aspects of habitat acoustics on acoustic communication, see Brenowitz 1986 and Narins and Zelick 1988.

Temperature is a second environmental factor affecting both call production and auditory processing (see also chapters 8 and 14). Ideally, the effects of temperature should vary in concert to maintain sensitivity and recognition. For temporal processing this seems to be the case. The AM rate of a call, for example, increases with temperature. The temporal tuning of toral neurons increases similarly (fig. 2.25; Breno-

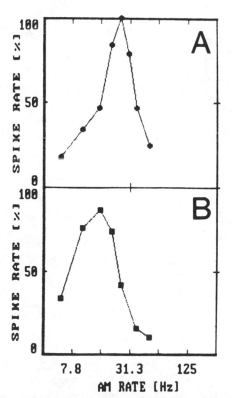

Fig. 2.25 Temporal tuning curves for a *Hyla versicolor* toral cell taken at 21.8°C (*A*) and 13.6°C (*B*). (Reprinted, by permission, from Walkowiak, "Central temporal coding," in *The Evolution of the Amphibian Auditory System*, 275–294, copyright 1988 by John Wiley and Sons.)

witz, Rose, and Capranica 1985; Walkowiak 1988a), which probably accounts for the fact that behavioral preference for AM rate is temperature-compensated in such a way as to match a species' preference at a given temperature to the AM rate produced at that same temperature (Gerhardt 1978).

Temperature compensation in the spectral domain is more complicated. The frequency characteristics of the call, AP tuning, and BP tuning all react differently to temperature changes. Call frequencies increase only slightly with increasing temperature (Walkowiak 1988b; Zweifel 1968). This increase may be due more to temperature effects on calling energetics than on the vocal production structures per se, as increasing air pressure through the larynx increases both amplitude and pitch of a signal (Martin 1972). In comparison, AP tuning increases to a much greater extent than the call, while BP tuning is not affected by temperature changes at all (fig. 2.26A, B). Large temperature-dependent shifts in behavioral preference for calls with dominant frequencies in the AP range have been demonstrated (Gerhardt and Mudry 1980). Changes in preference for frequencies in the BP range have not been investigated. The different responses of the or-

gans to temperature changes reflects their different tuning mechanisms (reviewed in Zakon and Wilczynski 1988). The electrical membrane filters implicated in AP tuning are highly susceptible to temperature shifts, but simple mechanical resonators like BP receptors are not. The result is that, when call spectral features change with temperature, the AP overcompensates while the BP does not compensate at all. The implications of this spectral compensation problem for the evolution of call characteristics have not been explored. It suggests, however, that anuran species that breed in temperate zones, where temperature fluctuations are great, would be better served by basing call recognition on temporal features for which temperature compensation is more reliable (Zakon and Wilczynski 1988).

The sensitivity of the auditory system also increases with temperature (Walkowiak 1988a). Again, the AP is more affected than the BP (fig. 2.26C, D). Because many frogs use perceived amplitude as a distance cue to regulate intermale spacing (Brenowitz, Wilczynski, and Zakon 1984; Robertson 1984; Wilczynski and Brenowitz 1988), temperature changes should cause changes in the spatial organization of a chorus,

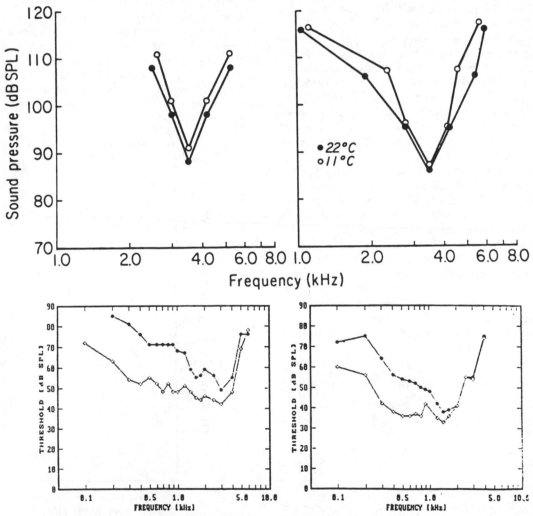

Fig. 2.26 A, B, basilar papilla tuning curves from two *Hyla crucifer* individuals taken at 22°C and 11°C. (Reprinted, by permission, from Wilczynski, Zakon, and Brenowitz 1984). C, D, multiunit audiograms taken from the torus of *Hyla arborea* (C) and *Rana temporaria* (D) at 20°C (○) and 5°C (●). (Reprinted, by permission, from Walkowiak, "Neuroethology of anuran call recognition," in *The Evolution of the Amphibian Auditory System*, 485–509, copyright 1988 by John Wiley and Sons.)

as equal-amplitude calls should be perceived as louder at higher temperatures, especially if call frequencies fall in the AP range. This has not been tested.

Finally, environmental or other selective forces acting on body size will coincidentally cause changes in the auditory system. Because the resonant properties of the ear, and hence much of its tuning, are determined by physical properties such as mass and stiffness that increase with size, the overall frequency response of the ear decreases with increasing body size. This is apparent during postmetamorphic growth (Shofner 1988) and may also occur among populations where geographic variation in body size due to increasing xeric conditions (Nevo and Capranica 1985; Wilczynski and Ryan 1987) or altitudinal changes (Drewry and Rand 1983; Narins and Smith 1986) occur. The BP is most affected, as its tuning is largely derived from its resonant properties (Zakon and Wilczynski 1988). Generally, these shifts pose no problem as far as communication is concerned, as the structures of the larynx also change with body size, thereby changing call characteristics in the same direction (e.g., McClelland, Wilczynski, and Ryan 1988a, 1988b).

One situation where a problem may arise, however, is where body size differences between males and females occur. A sex difference in BP tuning occurs in three different anuran species in which females are larger than males and consequently have a BP tuned to lower frequencies (Narins and Capranica 1976; Wilczynski, Zakon, and Brenowitz 1984; Wilczynski and Ryan 1988a). Male *Hyla crucifer* (Hylidae), which produce an extremely narrow-band call, have adjusted their vocal system so that the dominant frequency of the call matches the female BP tuning rather than their own (Wilczynski, Zakon, and Brenowitz 1984). This deprives males of a great deal of sensitivity to their own call, but maximizes the detectability of their call by females (Wilczynski 1986). *Acris crepitans* (Hylidae), which produce a very broad-band call, reach a different compromise solution. The call dominant frequency lies between the male and female tuning, insuring that each sex has relatively equal sensitivity to the call (Wilczynski and Ryan 1988a).

Across species one also sees a general trend of decreasing BP tuning with increasing body size (Zakon and Wilczynski 1988). However, body size alone is not the only factor dictating tuning. One important example of this is the frog *Physalaemus pustulosus* (Leptodactylidae), where intense sexual selection for low-frequency calls has resulted in a frog with call characteristics and BP tuning much lower than would be expected for its size (Ryan 1986b). Even between populations of a single species, call and tuning differences are not solely explicable from allometric considerations (Keddy-Hector, Wilczynski, and Ryan 1989; Ryan and Wilczynski 1988). Thus while selection on body size can have a strong impact on auditory functions, its influence can be mitigated.

OTHER SENSORY SYSTEMS

Fewer physiological studies of other amphibian sensory systems have been undertaken. Nevertheless, such systems will be outlined briefly, as behavioral or anatomical investigations often suggest that other systems are important participants in amphibian behavior.

Lateral Line Systems

Rows of hair cell receptors on the head and body (fig. 2.27) form the amphibian lateral line system (Wahnschaffe, Fritzsch, and Himstedt 1985). One portion is a mechanoreceptive system, where the receptors respond to the deformation of overlying cupulae caused by water movement (Elepfandt and Wiedemer 1987; Görner, Moller, and Weber 1984; Münz, Claas, and Fritzsch 1984). The properties of these receptors are quite similar to auditory receptors, although they respond to water vibrations at frequencies usually much lower than those to which auditory receptors are sensitive (Elepfandt, Seiler, and Aicher 1985; Münz, Claas, and Fritzsch 1984). A second portion consists of electroreceptors sensitive to the presence of electrical fields in the water surrounding the animal (Fritzsch and Wahnschaffe 1983; Münz, Claas, and Fritzsch 1982; Wahnschaffe, Fritzsch, and Himstedt 1985). The receptors of both systems synapse on lateral line afferents that transmit the mechanoreceptive and electroreceptive information via special cranial nerves to nuclei in the medulla associated with, but separate from, auditory and vestibular nuclei (Fritzsch 1981; Fritzsch, Wahnschaffe, and Bartsch 1988). Lateral line information ascends to the torus semicircularis in parallel with auditory fibers and eventually occupies its own lateral toral zone (Fritzsch, Nikundiwe, and Will 1984; Lowe 1986; Plassmann 1980; Will 1988). Projections beyond the midbrain are as yet poorly understood. Electroreceptive information reaches the striatum, but its route there is unknown (Northcutt and Plassmann 1989).

Stimulation of the mechanoreceptive system in adult *Xenopus laevis* by water waves results in the animal orienting toward the source of the waves, approaching it quickly, and performing stereotyped prey-capture behaviors (e.g., see Elepfandt 1982; Görner, Moller, and Weber 1984). The toral lateral line area is necessary for the accuracy of this orientation (Elepfandt 1988a). Lesion studies suggest that the lateral line representation there takes the form of a space map like the somatosensory system rather than a frequency map like the auditory system (see above; Elepfandt 1988b). Elepfandt's (1988a, 1988b) studies also suggest that access to the ventrolateral tegmentum is necessary for turning to be triggered by the lateral line stimulation, just as in the case of visually triggered turning (see above). However, the optic tectum is not necessary for proper lateral line–triggered orientation, meaning that the toral lateral line area has an independent interface with the descending motor control systems. The same holds true for tactually elicited prey capture (Comer and Grobstein 1981a; see below).

Lateral line systems are invariably associated with an aquatic habitat. As such the mechanoreceptive lateral line system is universally present in larval amphibians (reviewed in Fritzsch, Wahnschaffe, and Bartsch 1988). Electroreception is found in larval urodeles and apodans but appears to be lacking in anuran larvae. Whether these systems are retained postmetamorphically depends in part on whether the adults remain in an aquatic niche. Neotenic urodeles and apodans that remain aquatic have both lateral line subsystems as adults. Aquatic anurans like the Pipidae have well-developed mechanoreceptive receptors, but electroreception cannot be demonstrated. Because it is not clear whether anuran larvae are electroreceptive as well as mechanore-

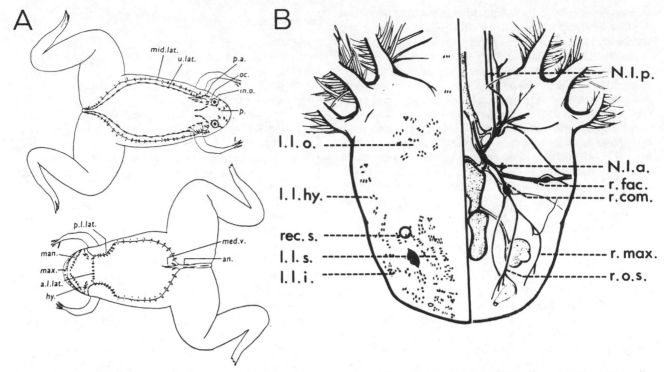

Fig. 2.27 *A*, lateral line receptors in *Xenopus laevis*. (Reprinted, by permission, from Russell 1976.) *B*, lateral line system in *Ambystoma mexicanum*. *Left*, position of electroreceptive (*black*) and mechanoreceptive (*gray*) organs. *Right*, Schematic showing, in *black*, lateral line nerves and ganglia for the head (*Nla*) and body (*Nlp*). *llhy*, hyomandibu- lar lateral lines; *lli*, infraorbital lateral lines; *llo*, orbital lateral lines; *lls*, supraorbital lateral lines; *rcom*, ramus communicans; *rfac*, ramus fa- cialis; *rmax*, ramus maxillaris; *ros*, ramus ophthalmicus. (Reprinted, by permission, from Münz, Claas, and Fritzsch 1984.)

ceptive, it is not clear whether the adult pipid condition represents a selective loss of electroreception or a simple postmetamorphic retention of the (electroreceptor-less) pre- metamorphic condition.

The profound nature of the metamorphic change in animals with terrestrial adult stages cannot be minimized. Unlike metamorphic changes in the visual and auditory systems, the lateral line change can involve the total loss of a functioning sensory system (Fritzsch, Wahnschaffe, and Bartsch 1988). Furthermore, because the larval lateral line presumably inter- faces with its own central processing network (Jacoby and Rubinson 1983), fundamental changes in the central nervous system probably occur once peripheral receptors disappear. Even more curious are those amphibians that return to aqua- ticism either during some life stage like the newt *Triturus* (Salamandridae) or during the breeding season like the anu- ran *Bombina* (Discoglossidae; Fritzsch, Nikundiwe, and Will 1984; Fritzsch, Wahnschaffe, and Bartsch 1988). In these species functional lateral line systems reemerge as the aquatic niche is entered. Exploring how the nervous system accom- modates such radical changes over the life of an organism could provide valuable insights into neural development, gene expression, and evolution.

Olfaction

Amphibians possess both main and accessory (vomeronasal) olfactory systems (Scalia 1976b). Separate olfactory bulbs re- ceive input from epithelia associated with each system and distribute the olfactory information to many areas of the am- phibian forebrain (Kemali and Guglielmotti 1987; Northcutt and Royce 1975; Schmidt, Naujoks-Manteuffel, and Roth 1988). The main olfactory bulb projects most heavily to the lateral pallium and septal region. The major output of the accessory bulb is to the lateral amygdala. The targets of both olfactory bulbs are heavily interconnected with the visceral and endocrine control regions of the preoptic area and hypo- thalamus (Allison and Wilczynski 1989; Neary 1988; Wil- czynski and Allison 1989).

The presence of a vomeronasal system is often an indica- tion of the use of olfactory signals, or pheromones, for intra- specific communication. Chemical signals associated with courtship or territoriality have been repeatedly demonstrated in adult urodeles (e.g., Dawley 1984; Horne and Jaeger 1988; Parzefall, Durand, and Richard 1980), but not in adult anu- rans. However, anuran larvae do produce an alarm phero- mone (Hews and Blaustein 1985), and kin recognition and its manifestation in selective aggregation (reviewed in Waldman 1988) may be under olfactory control (Blaustein and O'Hara 1982). Whether similar functions carry over postmetamor- phically has not been examined. Two different instances of olfactory sensitivity have been demonstrated in adult anurans. Olfactory cues may be involved in homing toward ponds in anurans (Grubb 1976) as well as urodeles (McGregor and Teska 1989). Second, odors increase feeding behavior in both anurans and urodeles (Luthardt and Roth 1983; Roth 1976, 1987; Shinn and Dole 1978). In fact, urodeles will seek and attack prey based on olfactory cues alone.

How each or both of the olfactory systems participate in any of these behaviors is unknown. The neural mechanisms of olfactory-mediated behavior is a major unexplored area of amphibian neuroethology.

Amphibians also possess a terminal nerve associated with the olfactory nerves (Muske and Moore 1988; Wirsig and Getchell 1986). As in all other vertebrates, terminal nerve fiber endings are present in the olfactory mucosa, their cell bodies are embedded in the olfactory nerves, and the central processes terminate in septal and preoptic areas. The terminal nerve neurons contain, and are assumed to secrete, gonadotropin-releasing hormone (GnRH) (see chapters 3 and 15). The function of the terminal nerve is unknown. However, its projections to brain areas associated with reproduction and the presence of GnRH within it have led to speculation that it influences reproductive physiology or behavior in response to pheromonal cues (Demski and Northcutt 1983).

Somatosensory System

Frog skin contains thermal, nociceptive, and mechanosensitive receptors. Their basic physiological properties have been thoroughly reviewed (Catton 1976; Spray 1976). Of particular interest is a large set of "dome-shaped" mechanoreceptors (Holloway, Ramsundar, and Wright 1976). These receptors respond with a single discharge to the onset of a displacement of the skin. Maintained deformation does not result in additional firing, but rhythmic deformations produce rhythmic discharges phase-locked to the stimulation. This is interesting because one type of tactile communication in frogs involves just such rhythmic vibrations. In many species, when a male or unresponsive female is clasped by another male, the clasped frog produces a release call (Rand 1988; Wells 1977). Although in *Rana* the call is clearly audible, in some *Bufo* species the "call" is little more than a vibration of trunk muscles. In both *Rana* and *Bufo*, and in other frogs as well, the tactilely received trunk vibration is thought to play a major role in communicating nonreceptivity.

The domelike receptors are far more sensitive to deformations immediately above them than to stimulation of the surrounding skin (Holloway, Ramsundar, and Wright 1976), giving them an acute ability to localize slight, abrupt pressures to the body. Comer and Grobstein (1981c) showed that such tactile stimulation can elicit orientation and prey catching in ranid frogs. The lateral torus, where somatosensory fibers terminate in a topographic map of the contralateral half of the body (fig. 2.28), is the center for tactilely elicited prey catching (Comer and Grobstein 1981a, 1981b). Such prey catching can occur in the absence of an optic tectum (Comer and Grobstein 1978), which suggested to Comer and Grobstein (1981a, 1981b) that this region of the brain has a parallel access to the motor control areas triggered by the tectum during visually guided prey catching.

Somatosensory information ascends from the spinal cord and via a separate dorsal column system to the medullar and midbrain reticular areas, the cerebellum, pretectum, and ventral thalamus as well as to the lateral torus (Ebbesson 1976; Neary and Wilczynski 1977). These other somatosensory pathways have not been investigated physiologically or behaviorally. Ascending pathways from the spinal cord change substantially at metamorphosis in anurans, much more so than the descending pathways (Forehand and Farel 1982b), but the lack of physiological and behavioral data means that the functional significance of the changes remains obscure.

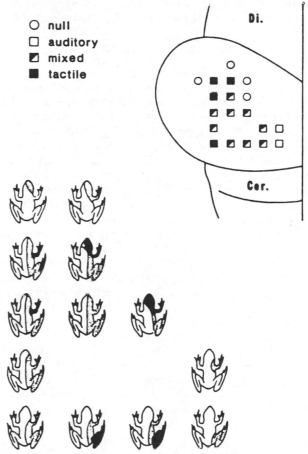

Fig. 2.28 Modality and somatotopic organization of the *Rana pipiens* torus. *Frog outlines* show receptive fields of mixed and tactile units diagrammed in brain outline at upper right; *black areas* indicate maximum response; *shaded areas* indicate total extent of receptive field. *Cer*, cerebellum; *Di*, diencephalon. (Reprinted, by permission, from Comer and Grobstein 1981b.)

GENERAL PRINCIPLES OF NEURAL ORGANIZATION

Each sensory system is a reflection of the general rules by which amphibian neural systems are organized and operate. Several of these principles have implications for neural processing and evolution in vertebrates in general.

Peripheral Bias

In each system, physiological properties of peripheral sensory structures are biased toward the detection and discrimination of stimuli important for the triggering of some class of natural behavior. Peripheral biases in response properties are seen in all vertebrate sensory systems, but nowhere are they seen as clearly as in amphibians. The peripheral bias does not mean that frogs see only small, moving insects or hear only their own calls, just that these important stimuli are given a privileged status of increased sensitivity mediated by a special receptor class. This allows perception of important key stimuli to rise above the noise of extraneous visual, auditory, or other sensory input activating the sense organs and entering the central nervous system. However, peripheral sense organs cannot be made too specific, and therefore too restrictive, in their response properties if an animal is to respond effectively to the highly variable stimuli it encounters in the unpredictable real world (Wilczynski and Capranica 1984).

Central Sharpening and Distributed Representation

Central neural systems sharpen the information and construct more specific feature detectors whose characteristics more closely resemble the animal's behavioral discriminations (Walkowiak 1988a). However, the coding of any object, or percept, seems to be the responsibility of assemblies of neurons rather than a single pontifical neuron (cf. Heiligenberg, Baker, and Matsubara 1978; Rose, Kawasaki, and Heiligenberg 1988). This distributed representation is seen in the recognition modules hypothesized for tectal recognition (Roth 1987) and in the separate coding of spectral and temporal aspects of calls (Hall and Feng 1987). On a broader scale, different functions associated with a sensory system are distributed to different central systems so that, for example, the optic tectum is not responsible for all visually mediated behavior.

Motor commands seem to be similarly distributed among several pathways, although the representation of information in motor systems is much less understood than it is in sensory systems (Grobstein 1988a, 1988c). A distributed motor arrangement enhances flexibility. It allows independent modulation of various parts of a behavioral sequence such as prey catching, which normally includes orientation with eye fixation and accommodation, stalking or lunging, and a complex activation of jaw and tongue movements. In a distributed command structure, the accessory optic system could modulate fixation and the pretectal area could modify stalking to compensate for stationary barriers without mutual interference. Further, distributed representation allows all or some parts of a programmed sequence to be appropriately activated by different sensory systems for different reasons. For example, visual, lateral line, or tactile stimuli could activate the entire prey-catching sequence for feeding, while audition might enact only the orientation part during mate recognition.

The organization of the forebrain also reflects a distribution of effector systems. Visceromotor and somatomotor centers lie in different systems. Each sensory system interfaces with these systems in a different way. Olfactory input is far more heavily connected to limbic than basal ganglia centers, while the tectal visual system has the opposite pattern. Auditory information makes a virtually equal contribution to each. The differences reflect the specialized use to which each sensory system is put. The reproductive social behavior dependent on acoustic signals requires the coordinated expression of both somatomotor (basal ganglia) and visceromotor (limbic/basal diencephalic) systems, while opportunistic visually guided prey catching probably requires little acute limbic involvement. Just as in the case of peripheral biasing, the central processing patterns are common features of nervous systems. The amphibian nervous system manifests them in an exceedingly clear way, however, and the specific patterns seen reflect the specialized way amphibians use their sensory systems.

Changes with Metamorphosis

Extensive changes in the properties of amphibian neural systems occur with the advent of metamorphosis (Hughes 1976; chapter 16). Among sensory systems, these changes often involve reorganization of the periphery to maintain the efficient neural coupling to the drastically different habitats occupied by larval and adult amphibians. In fact, peripheral metamorphic changes may be more dramatic than central ones. The magnitude of the change varies with each system. It can be as subtle as the visual system's change in receptor absorption or as profound as the total loss of the lateral line system. Changes in the brain's effector systems also occur. As for sensory systems, peripheral changes are much more apparent than are central reorganizations. Nevertheless, it seems as though something must be changing in the way that central neurons within both motor and sensory systems interact to accommodate the radical transformations that metamorphosis engenders in virtually every behavioral and physiological process, from color changes in the skin to feeding and breathing. So little work has been done on the more subtle aspects of the functional organization of either larval or adult amphibian brains that these neural changes cannot even be imagined.

Interspecific Differences

Large-scale structural variation in neural systems most often reflects broad phylogenetic trends rather than obvious species-specific adaptations. One sees such trends in the developmental grades of the amphibian papilla or the generally smaller size and increased density of anuran as compared to urodele photoreceptors. These changes have physiological consequences (greater frequency range and smaller visual receptive fields respectively), but the consequences cannot readily be explained by group differences in habitat or life history. Similarly, anatomical differences in the brains of anurans and nonanuran amphibians are mainly a reflection of the greater expansion and differentiation of all central areas in anurans. The circuitry of neural systems within the brain is poorly understood in urodeles, and not at all in apodans, but comparisons that can be made suggest that the basic wiring of the central nervous system pathways is very conservative.

Where one sees most interspecific variation is in the physiological properties of neurons within these very conservative neural systems. This physiological variation appears to be due more to such things as changes in the mechanical properties of peripheral transduction mechanisms, cellular aspects of receptors and other neurons, and, perhaps, local circuit organization within a brain region rather than to more fundamental changes in nervous system pathways. This variation often starts at the periphery, where receptors bias input to the brain in species-specific ways. For example, all anurans have a basilar papilla whose afferents travel in cranial nerve VIII to terminate in the dorsolateral nucleus and so feed into a standard set of ascending auditory pathways. However, the tuning of the BP receptors shifts among species so that the physiological properties of high-frequency neurons shift throughout the entire system. In other cases, central rather than peripheral physiological changes occur. This is seen among temporally tuned cells in the torus or the shape-specific cells in the tectum; in both cases species differences occur in the midbrain, where no species differences in these properties are apparent in the periphery.

Direct links to behaviors with such importance to an organism's survival and the clear cases of parallel physiological changes in certain species of urodeles and anurans (Roth 1987) suggest that interspecific physiological changes might reflect the work of natural and sexual selection. While adaptive hypotheses are easy to generate, unequivocal proof of the adaptive value of neural characters is difficult to demonstrate. Nevertheless, adaptations seem to be reflected more in the physiological properties of neural systems than in the anatomical composition of their pathways.

This may be a fundamental characteristic not only of the evolution of the amphibian nervous system, but of vertebrate brain evolution in general. Structurally, vertebrate nervous systems are rather conservative in their overall organization. Homologues of most of the neural structures seen in amphibians can be identified in other vertebrates, and the pathways interconnecting them are often similar across vertebrate classes. While circuitry differences can certainly be found, most of the anatomical variance among vertebrate groups is either quantitative or reflects the way in which brain areas are subdivided into functional divisions and local circuits within these divisions are constructed (Wilczynski 1988). These local circuits, in concert with changes in neurons themselves, can yield the physiological variation apparent even at the species level within the anatomically conservative systems composing the vertebrate nervous system. In amphibians, many neural systems have close, specialized links with specific natural behaviors. Because of this, amphibians offer an excellent model for exploring the covariation of neurophysiological and behavioral traits, the change in each under different environmental conditions and selective regimes, and therefore, the evolution of vertebrate nervous systems.

3 Endocrinology

CEIL A. HERMAN

Amphibians inhabit diverse environments. Endocrine regulation is extremely sensitive in responding to environmental change. This chapter will discuss the role of endocrine systems in the regulation of selected physiological processes in amphibians and will focus on relationships between regulatory processes and the environment. Studies examining seasonal endocrine changes with respect to naturally occurring environmental variables such as temperature, humidity, and photoperiod and studies examining effects of laboratory acclimation will be discussed.

General reviews of the literature by Gorbman (1964, 1987) and Hanke (1974, 1978) discuss morphology as well as function of the endocrine glands. More recent works on comparative morphology include reviews of hypothalamic-releasing hormones (Peter 1987), pituitary (Schreibman 1987), pineal (Korf and Oksche 1987), thyroid (Dent 1987), parathyroid (Clark, Kaul, and Roth 1986), ultimobranchial body (Robertson 1987b), gastrointestinal hormones (Vigna 1987), pancreatic islets (Gapp 1986; Epple and Brinn 1987), adrenal (interrenal) (Chester-Jones and Phillips 1987), ovary (Dodd 1987), and testes (Nagahama 1987). Accordingly, this chapter will instead focus on current research on selected topics. Readers should refer to the above works for comprehensive reviews and the older literature.

In examining physiological processes, the chapter departs from the conventional approach of discussing the function of endocrine glands one gland at a time. Because regulation is integrative and involves the interplay of many hormones, this chapter will instead focus on selected *processes* relevant to environmental adaptation in anurans and urodeles. These are (1) the response of the integument to changes in the environment, (2) maintenance of calcium homeostasis, (3) metabolism and physiological adjustments to stress, (4) cardiovascular regulation, (5) the role of the thyroid in adult amphibians, and (6) reproduction and sexual behavior. Other chapters discuss hormonal regulation of ion and water balance (chapters 5 and 6), growth (chapter 15), development (chapter 16), and reproduction (chapter 15). Unfortunately, the only literature for caecilians is primarily morphological and will not be discussed.

For each exemplary process, the following questions will be addressed: (1) What hormones regulate the process? (2) How is the production of these hormones controlled? (3) How do these hormones act at the cellular level? and (4) What is the interaction between the production/effects of these hormones and seasonal or other environmental factors? Major recent advances are in purification and structural analysis of hormones, development of homologous radioimmunoassays and immunohistochemical methods for hormone and receptor localization, and regulatory control of hormone production. These advances have allowed comparative endocrinology to develop significantly and have resulted in further understanding of the evolution of hormone structure and function.

HORMONAL REGULATION OF THE INTEGUMENT
Color Adaptation

Introduction   The ability to change skin color is advantageous to an organism, both in providing protective coloration and in temperature regulation (see chapter 9). The target cell for color change is the chromatophore (Bagnara and Hadley 1973; Bagnara 1976; Sawyer *et al.* 1983). In amphibians, the three distinct types of chromatophores in the integument are melanophores, iridophores, and xanthophores or erythrophores organized in a dermal chromatophore unit as shown in figure 3.1. These three chromatophores are morphologically and functionally distinct, and all migrate from their origin in the neural crest to populate the integument (Bagnara 1983, 1987).

Research in this field has investigated structural changes in the melanophores, which contain melanin in subcellular organelles (melanosomes). Melanophores vary in location, morphology, and function. Dermal melanophores are stellate and participate in rapid color adjustments (physiological color change). This response is transitory and reversible, involving either dispersion (causing darkening) or aggregation

The author of this chapter would like to thank Drs. Joseph Bagnara, Roger deRoos, Robert Dores, Eugenia Farrar, and Peter Herman for their careful reading and helpful comments concerning this manuscript. Thanks are also due to Matt Chiono, Scott Heller, and Cindy Guiterrez-Barraza for their help with all the time-consuming jobs needed in the completion of this manuscript. The preparation of this manuscript was supported by National Science Foundation Grant DCB-8702228.

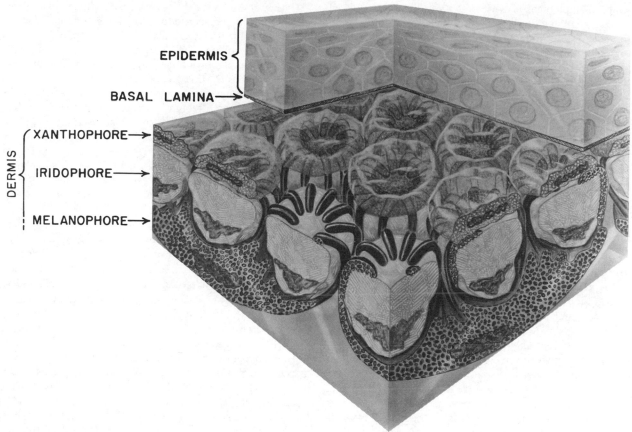

EPIDERMIS {

BASAL LAMINA →

XANTHOPHORE →

IRIDOPHORE →

MELANOPHORE →

DERMIS

Fig. 3.1 Schematic representation of the dermal chromatophore unit of anurans, showing adaptation to a dark background. (Adapted from Bagnara, Taylor, and Hadley 1968.)

(causing lightening) of the melanosomes. Epidermal melanophores involved in morphological color change are long and slender. Morphological color change, a response to long-term exposure to dark background, is considerably slower than physiological color change and involves both the synthesis of melanin and its deposition in adjacent epidermal cells (epidermal melanophore unit). In contrast, adaptation to light background results in a loss of melanin. Recently a melanization-inhibiting factor (MIF) has been shown to participate in amphibian pattern formation and to inhibit melanization of *Xenopus laevis* neural crest cells (Fukuzawa and Ide 1988; Fukuzawa and Bagnara 1989).

While melanophores play the major role in darkening and lightening of amphibian integument, two other chromatophore cell types also participate. In iridophores, the surface of subcellular organelles reflect light. These organelles (reflecting platelets) contain crystalline purines. Iridophores appear metallic in reflected light or colored in transmitted light. The third type of chromatophore is xanthophores, which contain red, orange, or yellow pigments composed of pteridines or carotenoids. Pteridines are stored in subcellular organelles, the pterisomes, while the fat-soluble carotenoids are stored as fat or oil droplets.

α-Melanocyte-Stimulating Hormone The primary hormone controlling color change in amphibians is α-melanocyte-stimulating hormone (α-MSH), a tridecapeptide synthesized and released from the pars intermedia (reviewed by Sawyer et al. 1983; Dores 1990). This hormone is one of a group of peptide hormones cleaved from a common precursor, proopiomelanocortin, which contains the other structurally related peptides γ-MSH, β-MSH, and adrenocorticotropic hormone (ACTH). Of these, α-MSH is the only peptide that regulates color adaptation in vertebrates at physiological levels. α-MSH (maximum response at 10^{-10} M *in vitro*) is more potent than β-MSH in *Rana pipiens*, *R. catesbeiana*, and *R. berlandieri* (Castrucci, Hadley and Hruby 1984). Although α-MSH is considered a pituitary peptide, melanotropic compounds also occur in amphibian brain, including the hypothalamus (Jégou et al. 1983).

In amphibian development, the larvae acquire the ability to adapt to background color during the secondary phase. Until this time, the larvae will remain dark regardless of the background (primary phase). The biosynthesis of α-MSH in *Xenopus laevis* first appears at developmental stage 37–38 (Nieuwkoop and Faber 1967), just before the animal's ability to adapt to the environmental background (Verburg–van Kemenade et al. 1984). Processing of proopiomelanocortin is developmentally regulated. Corticotropic cells of the anterior pituitary of *Ambystoma tigrinum* (Caudata: Ambystomatidae) produce both ACTH (1–39) and α-MSH before and immediately after metamorphosis. However, at sexual maturity ACTH (1–39) is the major product with only trace amounts of α-MSH (Dores et al. 1989).

Only in amphibians is α-MSH stored as the nonacetylated ACTH (1–13) amide. This occurs in anuran (*X. laevis, Rana ridibunda*: Martens, Jenks, and van Overbeeke 1981; Martens et al. 1983) and larval urodele amphibians (*Ambystoma tigrinum*: Dores, Schenk, and Rothenberg 1987). N-acylated β-endorphin-related peptides also result from posttranslational processing of proopiomelanocortin in the posterior pituitary of *X. laevis* (Dores and Rothenberg 1987). α-MSH is acetylated as a cosecretory or postsecretory processing event before entering the circulation (Jenks et al. 1985).

Primary control of release of stored α-MSH is inhibitory (Etkin 1962; Hadley, Davis, and Morgan 1977). Central nervous system regulation of α-MSH production has been reviewed by Barnawell (1982). Hypothalamic catecholaminergic neurons innervate the pars intermedia. These inhibit α-MSH secretion by release of dopamine. Mechanisms of action of other catecholamines are species-specific. Stimulation of β-receptors results in adenosine 3', 5' cyclic monophosphate (cyclic AMP) elevation and release of MSH in *R. pipiens* (Bower, Hadley, and Hruby 1974) and *R. ridibunda* (Tonon et al. 1983). In the pars intermedia of *X. laevis*, α-agonists, including norepinephrine and epinephrine, inhibit release of α-MSH through dopamine D-2 receptors. β-adrenergic receptors are absent in this species; however, cyclic AMP participates in α-MSH release (Verburg–van Kemenade, Jenks, and van Overbeeke 1986). Release or inhibition of release of MSH is dependent on the amount of light reaching the upper retina. On a dark background, little light reaches the upper-retina, and MSH is released. MSH is inhibited if the animal is on a light background (reviewed by Hadley 1988b).

Other hormones, including thyrotropin-releasing hormone (TRH) and thyroid-stimulating hormone (TSH), directly affect α-MSH release (Tonon et al. 1980; Tonon et al. 1985). Although TRH releases α-MSH, it does not act through the production of thyroxine (T_4), since perfusion of the frog neurointermediate lobe with T_4 does not modulate α-MSH release (Leroux et al. 1983). In addition, γ-aminobutyric acid (GABA) inhibits the secretion of α-MSH, at least in *X. laevis*, via specific GABA receptors (Verburg–van Kemenade et al. 1987).

Many changes result from α-MSH stimulation of melanophores, iridophores, and xanthophores (Bagnara 1976). At physiological concentrations, the action of α-MSH on the target dermal melanophore is to disperse melanosomes to the periphery of the cell. In the absence of α-MSH, the melanosomes are punctate in the central (perinuclear) portion of the melanophore. In addition, α-MSH causes morphological color change by stimulating melanin synthesis in the epidermal melanophores, mitosis of existing melanophores, and differentiation of latent chromatoblasts. Short periods of α-MSH exposure result in physiological color change, while long periods result in morphological color change (Bagnara 1987).

α-MSH also affects iridophores. In normal larvae and intact adults, iridophores are punctate due to concentration of reflecting platelets toward the center of the cell, a state that reverses in the absence of a pituitary. Dispersion of melanosomes is accompanied by aggregation of reflecting platelets in iridophores. The same structural sites on the α-MSH molecule seem involved in both functions.

During physiological color change, xanthophores of some species expand in response to α-MSH and contract in its absence. Hypophysectomized larvae have lower pteridine levels in their xanthophores, while administration of α-MSH restores these levels to normal. However, normal adult frogs given exogenous α-MSH do not show changes.

Signal transduction and generation of cyclic AMP by the dermal melanophore require calcium, but hormone binding and pigment migration do not (reviewed by Hadley 1988b), nor does the action of α-MSH on the epidermal melanophore (Ferroni and Castrucci 1987). Cyclic AMP is necessary for melanosome dispersal (Sawyer et al. 1983). Other stimulators of cyclic AMP in the absence of calcium, including β-agonistic catecholamines and prostaglandins (PGE_2, $PGF_{2\alpha}$, PGE_1), mimic this effect. In addition, dibutyryl cyclic AMP and the phosphodiesterase inhibitor theophylline can cause darkening (van de Veerdonk and Brouwer 1973; Veseley and Hadley 1979). Cyclic AMP also causes aggregation of reflecting platelets in iridophores. The effects of α-MSH on these two chromatophores are opposite, yet they probably contain identical receptor sites. The different response is due to cell-specific interactions occurring distal to cyclic AMP production (Bagnara 1976).

Cyclic AMP also participates in the activation of tyrosinase and subsequent melanin synthesis in epidermal melanophores in murine melanoma cells; probably the same applies to amphibians (Hadley 1988b). The mechanism of paling is less clear and may be associated with decreases in cyclic AMP levels or generation of guanosine 3', 5' cyclic monophosphate (cyclic GMP); however, this has not been associated with physiological stimulation (Novales 1983).

Recent structural studies have examined α-MSH to determine the active portion of the molecule. The central tetrapeptide sequence, amino acids 6 through 9, is the minimal chain length for biological activity. Amino acids at positions 4, 10, and 12 are also important in determining biopotency (Hruby et al. 1987). A superpotent analogue, with norleucine substituted at position 4 and phenylalanine substituted at position 7, has been used for comparative darkening studies in *Rana pipiens, R. catesbeiana, Xenopus laevis, Bufo alvarius*, and *B. cognatus* (Hadley et al. 1985). This compound causes prolonged darkening that persists for 6 weeks. In contrast, the native hormone darkens for 2 days (Hadley et al. 1981). This analogue may bind more strongly to the α-MSH receptor or resist inactivation by serum enzymes. The first possibility is more likely. Inactivation does not seem to be carried out to a large extent, since α-MSH is more potent *in vivo* than *in vitro* despite the fact that it is inactivated in 30 min when incubated with plasma (Castrucci, Hadley, and Hruby 1984).

Melatonin Lightening of the integument of amphibians is due to melatonin, a hormone found in pineal, brain, and retina (Baker, Quay, and Axelrod 1965; Pang, Shiu, and Tse 1985) of amphibians. Melatonin aggregates the melanin granules in dermal melanophores (see reviews by Heward and Hadley 1975; Ralph 1983). The discovery of melatonin in beef pineal glands and its identification as N-acetyl-5-methoxytryptamine used *R. pipiens* skin as a bioassay (Lerner et al. 1958).

Larval amphibians can lighten when maintained in darkness. The suggested mechanism is pineal release of melatonin, which causes contraction of dermal melanophores but does not affect epidermal melanophores or iridophores. Even blinded larvae pale when in darkness (Bagnara 1960). Pinealectomy abolishes the blanching reaction. In secondary stage larvae, the blanching is probably due to elimination of α-MSH production combined with the direct action of melatonin. In *R. pipiens* larvae, melatonin lightens at 5×10^{-11} M. Melatonin receptors are associated with dermal melanophores, suggesting this tissue is a target (Heward and Hadley 1975). The methoxy group on the fifth carbon and the N-acetyl group are important for biological activity. That adult amphibians do not respond to administration of melatonin by lightening suggests that melatonin is not involved in physiological color change in adults.

Another role for melatonin is regulation of eye pigmentation. *Rana tigrina regulosa* exhibits a diurnal rhythm of melatonin in the retina, with peak levels in the dark period, suggesting that environmental light controls synthesis and secretion (Pang, Shiu, and Tse 1985).

Temperature and photoperiod affect melatonin concentrations in *Rana perezi* (Delgado and Vivien-Roels 1989). Day-night melatonin rhythm in plasma, eye, and pineal occurs in July with long photoperiod and high temperature. Decrease in temperature abolishes the rhythm, which does not occur in February under short photoperiod and low temperature. Ocular melatonin and circulating levels are correlated, suggesting that melatonin may be released into the circulation from the eyes.

Catecholamines Catecholamines cause blanching, in part due to the inhibition of α-MSH release. In addition, catecholamines have direct effects through stimulation of adrenergic receptors (reviewed by Bagnara 1976; Hadley 1988b). The distribution of α- and β-receptors on the chromatophores can account for species differences in response to α-MSH. In *R. pipiens*, for example, epinephrine and norepinephrine lighten the α-MSH–darkened skin, while in *Xenopus laevis* and *Scaphiopus* (Anura: Pelobatidae) β-receptors predominate, resulting in catecholamine-induced darkening. Even within a species, the effects can differ depending on α- and β-receptor distribution. Thus, northern *R. pipiens* containing α-receptors on melanophores and iridophores lighten in response to norepinephrine, while southern frogs of the same or related species darken due to the predominance of β-receptors (Hadley and Goldman 1970).

Catecholamines may be important in early stages of background adaptation (van Zoest et al. 1989). During adaptation to a dark background, plasma levels of MSH remain low for 24 h in *X. laevis*. Experiments with epinephrine and norepinephrine as β-agonists and with propranolol as a β-receptor antagonist suggest a β-adrenergic mechanism of pigment dispersion during early stages of dark background adaptation. Plasma MSH levels decreased rapidly following transfer from dark to light backgrounds in this study.

Melanocyte-Concentrating Hormone The physiological actions of melanocyte-concentrating hormone (MCH; see reviews by Castrucci et al. 1988; Hadley, Castrucci, and Hruby 1988) to lighten fish suggested that it might also lighten amphibian integument. However, in *R. pipiens* and *Anolis carolinensis* (a lizard), MCH causes darkening, although it is only 1/600 as potent as α-MSH (Wilkes et al. 1984). MCH, like α-MSH, induces dispersion of melanin in cultured melanophores of bullfrog larvae, but causes contraction of iridophore cell bodies (Ide, Kawazoe, and Kawauchi 1985). Since its biological potency is low when compared with α-MSH, since melanophores have no receptors for MCH, and since it has not been found in the circulation of amphibians, the physiological significance of it as a second darkening hormone is not clear in the amphibian.

Summary of Endocrine Control of Color Adaptation and Directions for Future Research Following early research that established basic histology, physiology, and biochemistry of the chromatophores, recent research has focused on structural requirements for hormone activity and mechanisms of release of α-MSH. In particular, the role of the melanophore in physiological and morphological color change has been investigated. Further work is needed on the regulation of iridophores and xanthophores. The role of calcium and cyclic AMP needs further elucidation, particularly in iridophores that show an opposite response to the melanophores. Beyond the generation of the intracellular messenger, the mechanism for aggregation or dispersion of melanosomes needs further clarification.

Many questions remain unresolved about the hormonal control of paling in amphibians. For example, are hormones involved or is paling a simple chromatophore response to the absence of MSH? Why does melatonin cause lightening in larval amphibians but not in adults? Do the different effects of catecholamines depend on α- and β-receptor predominance? The physiological importance of MCH in amphibians remains to be determined.

Hormonal Regulation of Molting

Introduction Molting or shedding of the outer keratinized epidermal tissue occurs in aquatic and terrestrial urodeles and anurans (see Larsen 1976; Budtz 1979; chapter 3). The first stage, which involves differentiation of the keratinized layer of the epidermis, is more or less independent of hormones. This upper layer (stratum corneum) separates from the underlying layer. Mucus is secreted beneath the replaced stratum corneum and lubricates the process. The separated stratum corneum (slough) is eaten, and a period between molts (intermolt) follows. Intermolt durations are species-specific. Both the shedding of the slough and the intermolt frequency are under endocrine control.

In the laboratory, environmental conditions affect molting frequency. Molt frequency increases with temperature (Stefano and Donoso 1964). At low temperatures (5° to 7°C), however, infrequent molting still occurs (Larsen 1976). Photoperiod is less important. *Bufo regularis* in total darkness molt less frequently than animals on a photoperiod (Taylor and Ewer 1956). The relationship of food to molting is variable and unclear. Molting is less frequent in adult animals than in juveniles (Jørgensen and Larsen 1961).

Under natural conditions, molting frequency is more difficult to assess. Larsen (1976) concluded that the molting interval is 6 to 11 days in natural populations of adult toads (*B. bufo*) and 4 to 7 days in juveniles.

Endocrine Regulation of Molting Interestingly, hormonal control of molting in amphibians differs in anurans and urodeles. In urodeles, T_4 regulates molting rhythm (reviewed in

Larsen 1976). Because thyroid hormones are involved in metamorphosis and molting in urodeles starts at metamorphosis, it was assumed that thyroid hormones also control molting in anurans. In toads, however, removal of the pars distalis or ectopic transplantation reduces intermolt periods. The new strata cornea are not shed, but rather accumulate (Houssay 1949; Jørgensen and Larsen 1961; Budtz 1979). Injections of ACTH or corticosterone produce shedding (Jørgensen and Larsen 1964; Stefano and Donoso 1964), but formation of new strata cornea is still abnormal. Administration of ACTH or corticosterone to intact toads does not elicit molting, suggesting that a cyclic fall and rise in ACTH secretion is necessary. In *B. bufo* with the pars distalis removed or transplanted and cortisol pellets implanted, the epidermis maintains normal appearance but does not molt. When the cortisol implants were removed, the toads showed loosened strata cornea typical of hypophysectomy. When the cortisol pellets were reinserted, all five toads molted within 6 to 7 h. For the next 2 months, these toads did not molt (Jørgensen 1988a).

The frequency of epidermal differentiation determines the molting rhythm in toads. The absence of adrenocortical hormone increases replacement of the stratum corneum, but not shedding (Jørgensen and Larsen 1961; Budtz 1979). Large doses of cortisol increase the molt interval in animals with the pars distalis removed or transplanted (Jørgensen 1988a). A temporary decrease in ACTH is not necessary for molting. The integration of replacement and shedding of the stratum corneum may be under hormonal control, but where the hormones act remains to be elucidated.

Other hormones may also affect molting in toads. Exogenous T_4 increases molting frequency, but the absence of thyroid hormones does not affect molting (Jørgensen, Larsen, and Rosenkilde 1965; Rosenkilde 1982).

Summary of Endocrine Control of Molting and Directions for Future Research

Although the hormones involved in molting in toads and urodeles have been investigated, recent work is scant. A direction for future research is elucidation of the mechanisms of hormones involved in molting. Protein synthesis is implicated in urodele molting, because inhibitors of T_4-induced protein delay molting a few hours in hypophysectomized *Notophthalmus viridescens* (Caudata: Salamandridae; Butterstein and Osborn 1968).

Studies of molting have emphasized too few species to represent the diversity of amphibians. For example, molting in *Rana temporaria* and *Xenopus laevis* is not as well defined as in the more thoroughly studied toads. These nonbufonid species often shed the skin in flakes rather than as a slough (reviewed by Larsen 1976). Neither corticotropin, frog pituitary extract, T_4, nor prolactin induces molting in these frogs. The hormonal control of molting in these and other species deserves further study.

A poorly understood modification of the molting cycle is cocoon formation. Amphibians from arid environments have evolved behavioral and physiological mechanisms to prevent water loss (see chapters 6 and 10). Slowing water loss by a cutaneous barrier is accomplished by epidermal cocoon formation (Ruibal and Hillman 1981; McClanahan, Ruibal, and Shoemaker 1983). Formation of cocoons occurs when shedding ceases and the slough accumulates. The stratum corneum layers are interspersed with mucoid material. Since this

effect is similar to the accumulation of strata in the hypophysectomized animal, hormones are probably involved. This phenomenon deserves more attention.

The biological importance of molting is a mystery. Molting yields profound changes in integument, ion and water balance, and vulnerability to predators. The slough may have some food value (see chapter 13), or molting may remove waste.

HORMONAL REGULATION OF CALCIUM HOMEOSTASIS

Introduction Calcium homeostasis is important because of its widespread involvement in biochemical and physiological processes and its role as a major component of bone. Regulation of calcium metabolism is the subject of many recent reviews (Pang, Kenny, and Oguro 1980; Barlet 1982; Feinblatt 1982; Clark 1983; Bentley 1984; Oguro and Sasayama 1985). Some amphibians are perfect subjects for these studies because they represent transition from aquatic to terrestrial habitats (but see chapter 1). Calcium from fresh water can be exchanged through gill and skin epithelium (Baldwin and Bentley 1980, 1981a, 1981b; chapter 5). Because calcium concentrations are low in fresh water, calcium regulation is especially problematic.

In mammals, important target organs for the hormones that control calcium homeostasis include the bone, small intestine, and kidney. Amphibian bone is also a target organ; however, involvement of small intestine and kidney in amphibian calcium homeostasis is less clear (Bentley 1984). Amphibians differ from mammals in their sites of calcium storage. Calcium may be stored under the dermis (reviewed in Bentley 1984). Larval anurans also store calcium carbonate in paravertebral lime sacs from which it is reabsorbed during metamorphosis (Pilkington and Simkiss 1966; see also chapter 16).

Amphibian species differ in calcium homeostasis. As a rule, however, the primary hormones of calcium metabolism in amphibians include the hypercalcemic hormones, parathyroid hormone (PTH) from the parathyroid glands, and, in some species, prolactin from the pars distalis. 1,25-dihydroxy vitamin D_3 is hypercalcemic in *Bufo marinus* (Bentley 1983) and is synthesized by *Rana catesbeiana* kidney (Baksi, Galli-Gallardo, and Pang 1977). Calcitonin from the ultimobranchial glands may cause hypocalcemia (Barlet 1982).

Parathyroid Hormone The Amphibia represent the first evolutionary appearance of parathyroid glands, which occur in both larval and adult anurans and in many urodeles. They develop from pharyngeal pouches, lie adjacent to the hypoglossal nerve and external jugular vein, and are structurally different from the glands of other vertebrates (see reviews by Clark 1983; Clark, Kaul, and Roth 1986). Parathyroid glands of *R. pipiens* show seasonal degeneration in winter (Cortelyou, Hibner-Owerko, and Mulloy 1960; Cortelyou and McWhinnie 1967).

Removal of the parathyroid glands in most adult and larval anurans results in hypocalcemia (Cortelyou and McWhinnie 1967; Sasayama and Oguro 1975; Robertson 1977; Wittle and Dent 1979; Pang 1981; see also chapter 16). This hypocalcemia is typically short-lasting, and calcium levels begin to rise within 1 or 2 weeks, but remain subnormal through 29 weeks (Cortelyou, Hibner-Owerko, and Mulloy 1960; fig. 3.2). Seasonal changes in plasma ionic calcium occur in

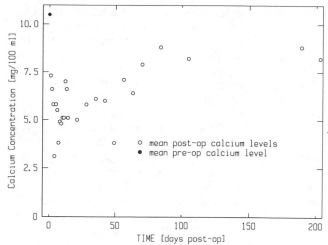

Fig. 3.2 Distribution of blood calcium values obtained from whole blood samples of normal and parathyroidectomized *Rana pipiens*. Blood calcium decreases during the first postoperative week, followed by a gradual rise, which remains subnormal through 29 weeks. (Redrawn from Cortelyou, Hibner-Owerko, and Mulloy 1960.)

parathyroidectomized *R. pipiens,* with maximal depression in October (D. R. Robertson 1986). Hypocalcemia results from parathyroidectomy in some (Oguro and Uchiyama 1975; Oguro and Sasayama 1978) but not all urodeles (Oguro 1973; Oguro and Uchiyama 1975). Injections of bovine PTH cause hypercalcemia in some (Cortelyou 1967; Cortelyou and McWhinnie 1967) but not all species (*B. marinus;* Bentley 1983).

The kidney is an important target organ for PTH action in mammals. However, urinary calcium in amphibians does not change after parathyroidectomy (*R. pipiens:* Sasayama and Clark 1984; *Notophthalmus viridescens;* Wittle and Dent 1979). In mammalian kidney, PTH stimulates adenylate cyclase with resultant cyclic AMP production. PTH does not stimulate adenylate cyclase from kidney membranes of *R. catesbeiana* and *R. pipiens* (Dousa 1974), but does so in membrane from *R. esculenta;* however, the stimulation is considerably lower than in rat or chicken kidney membranes (Helwig and Pang 1987). These differences may reflect different incubation conditions. In the *R. esculenta* study, some stimulation occurs in the presence of a guanyl nucleotide analogue. Thus, the principal targets of PTH in amphibians appear to be bone and the paravertebral sacs (Bentley 1984).

Vitamin D Following parathyroidectomy, calcium levels begin to rise toward normal, suggesting either regeneration of the glandular tissue or other hypercalcemic hormones in amphibians. Active vitamin D_3 is synthesized in amphibian kidney, which converts 25-hydroxy vitamin D_3 to the active 1,25-dihydroxy vitamin D_3 (Baksi, Galli-Gallardo, and Pang 1977; Baksi et al. 1978). Vitamin D_3 is hypercalcemic in amphibians, increasing calcium absorption from the intestine and mobilizing calcium from bone and paravertebral sacs (Robertson 1975; Bentley 1983). In addition, synthesis of vitamin D_3–dependent calcium-binding proteins in frog retina (Schreiner, Jande, and Lawson 1985) and bullfrog cerebellum (Gona et al. 1986) suggests additional target tissues.

Prolactin Prolactin is a hypercalcemic hormone in many aquatic urodeles and larval anurans. In adult *Necturus macu-*

losus (Caudata: Proteidae; Oguro and Uchiyama 1975; Pang 1981) and in larval *R. catesbeiana* (Uchiyama and Pang 1981; Sasayama and Oguro 1982a), hypophysectomy causes hypocalcemia, and prolactin restores calcium levels to normal. An exception is *Notophthalmus viridescens,* in which prolactin does not elevate calcium levels following parathyroidectomy, and hypophysectomy causes hyponatremia but not hypocalcemia (Wittle 1984). The involvement of prolactin in calcium homeostasis in primitive urodeles and larval amphibians is of evolutionary interest, because fish, which lack parathyroids, also use prolactin as a hypercalcemic hormone (Clark 1983). This condition has been superseded in the more advanced amphibians, which have evolved an endocrine gland working in conjunction with the pituitary to maintain calcium levels (Pang, Kenny, and Oguro 1980).

Calcitonin The site of calcitonin production in amphibians is the ultimobranchial glands. These structures, located lateral to the glottis, have a follicular structure similar to the thyroid gland (Robertson 1968). These glands are larger in winter than in summer (Robertson 1971). Robertson (1987b) reviewed morphological and histochemical work on these glands, and the calcitonin secretory cells have been described (Treilhou-Lahille et al. 1984; Robertson 1988). Calcitonin-like material is present in plasma of *R. pipiens* (Robertson 1981; Oguro et al. 1981). Calcitonin levels vary seasonally, peaking in October (Robertson 1987a). Plasma calcium levels show an annual cycle with maximum calcium levels attained in October–November (fig. 3.3). Removal of the ultimobranchial glands does not affect this cycle.

Despite the correlations in structure of the ultimobranchial glands and the plasma calcitonin levels, proving that calcitonin has a physiological role in amphibians has been difficult. Removal of the ultimobranchial glands in *R. pipiens* causes a small (10%) increase in plasma calcium, with a larger increase if the frogs are kept in a high calcium environment (Robertson 1969, 1970; Sasayama and Oguro 1976). The physiological significance of these observations is not clear. In addition, administration of calcitonin to amphibians yields conflicting results. Some of these problems may stem from the use of heterologous hormone. For example, bovine cal-

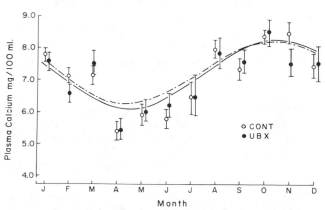

Fig. 3.3 Annual plasma calcium concentration in sham control (CONT) and ultimobranchialectomized (UBX) adult male frogs (*Rana pipiens*). Both groups display a significant ($p = .001$) minimum in April–June, while the maximum plasma calcium levels are obtained in October–November. Each point is mean ± SD ($N = 15$ to 30 frogs). (Reprinted, by permission, from Robertson 1977.)

citonin (Boschwitz and Bern 1971), but not salmon calcitonin (Bentley 1983), decreases calcium levels in *B. marinus*. However, salmon calcitonin causes hypocalcemia and hypophosphatemia in *Rana tigrina* (Srivastav and Rani 1989). Hypercalcemia follows on day 10, suggesting enhanced secretion of the parathyroid glands. Even studies with frog calcitonin have not given clear answers. Intact *R. nigromaculata* do not respond to frog calcitonin; however, if three of the four parathyroid glands are removed, hypocalcemia follows calcitonin administration (Oguro and Sasayama 1985).

In the urodeles *Onychodactylus japonicus* and *Hynobius nigrescens* (both Hynobiidae), hypocalcemic potency of the ultimobranchial glands is low (Oguro, Tarui, and Sasayama 1983). Eel calcitonin reduces calcium influx in *Ambystoma mexicanum* (Caudata: Ambystomatidae) but does not affect plasma calcium, sodium, potassium, or magnesium (Kingsbury and Fenwick 1989).

Despite the problems involved in demonstrating effects in intact animals, calcitonin clearly affects target tissues. Calcitonin blocks bone reabsorption (Robertson 1969, 1971), stimulates the small intestine to increase calcium transport (Robertson 1978), inhibits PTH mobilization of calcium stores (Robertson 1977), and affects calcium accretion into paravertebral lime sacs (Robertson 1969; Sasayama and Oguro 1985). Calcitonin may not affect the kidney, since salmon calcitonin does not cause hypercalciuria (Bentley 1983); however, these experiments used heterologous hormones. If calcitonin has a physiologically important hypocalcemic role in amphibians, it may be apparent only in the absence of PTH control of calcium homeostasis.

Summary of Endocrine Regulation of Calcium Homeostasis and Directions for Future Research

Amphibians, often confronted with low levels of environmental calcium, have evolved mechanisms to regulate calcium levels and achieve homeostasis. They share some target organs with mammals, but they have other target tissues for calcium storage. PTH, calcitonin, and vitamin D_3 perform functions similar to those in mammals, but in some species there is also pituitary involvement.

The literature on calcium homeostasis in amphibians contains conflicting data suggesting species differences in the involvement of these hormones in regulation. Further clarification of the actions and mechanisms of these hormones will be aided by the availability of homologous hormones. This is particularly true in resolving the physiological importance of calcitonin in the amphibian.

HORMONAL CONTROL OF GLUCOSE LEVELS

Introduction Environmental factors profoundly affect metabolism and its regulation in amphibians. The general areas of metabolism and energetics are very broad topics that are discussed in chapters 4, 12, and 14 of this volume. Metabolism in larval amphibians is discussed in chapter 16.

This section focuses on regulation of blood glucose levels and involvement of this process in adaptation to stress. Hormones that regulate circulating glucose levels in amphibians are extremely important for reasons relating to the environmental physiology of the animals. Adult amphibians are carnivorous, with low dietary intake of carbohydrates. In ad-

dition, amphibians must adapt to food scarcity and caloric restriction, especially during hibernation (chapter 10) and metamorphic climax (chapter 16). During fasts, amphibians deplete glycogen and fat stores, but presumably gluconeogenesis maintains blood glucose at nonfasting levels by catabolizing tissue protein. Sympathetic neurotransmitter release stimulates anaerobic glycolysis, which can sustain animals with low metabolic rates for long periods.

While studies in the literature on amphibian blood glucose levels are plentiful, their interpretation is difficult. Factors such as the feeding history and age of the animals are important. Methods of blood collection can often elevate blood glucose. Some amphibians have low or undetectable blood glucose levels, suggesting that blood glucose may not be continually required for central nervous system function (deRoos and Parker 1982). Stored liver glycogen and triglycerides provide energy for metabolism. Blood glucose, other metabolites, and tissue energy stores show seasonal fluctuations, as do the regulatory hormones (for reviews see Hanke and Neumann 1972; Hanke 1974; Gapp 1986).

Insulin Insulin is produced by the endocrine pancreas in amphibians and is regulated by plasma glucose levels in a manner similar to mammalian insulin (Penhos and Ramey 1973; Gapp 1986). Insulin has recently been characterized from *Xenopus laevis* (Shuldiner et al. 1989) and *Rana catesbeiana* (Hulsebus, Farrar, and Tabataba in press). *X. laevis* has two forms of insulin, which are more similar to bird and mammalian insulin than to fish and reptilian insulin (Shuldiner et al. 1989). *R. catesbeiana* insulin is similar to *Xenopus* insulin II, but has a two–amino-acid extension at the A1 position (Hulsebus, Farrar, and Tabataba in press). Insulin receptors in frog brain and liver have basic features typical of other vertebrate insulin receptors. This suggests that the insulin receptor is conserved evolutionarily (Hart et al. 1987).

Insulin lowers blood glucose in amphibians in a dose-dependent manner (Hanke and Neumann 1972; deRoos and Parker 1982; deRoos and Rumpf 1987). Bullfrogs (*R. catesbeiana*) experience no adverse symptoms following doses of 5 or 15 IU of insulin, although glucose levels decline 80% within 12 h. Glucose levels require at least 3 days to return to initial values. Plasma alanine and lactate also decline in response to insulin followed by surges in some animals (deRoos and Rumpf 1987). Thus, stable blood glucose may not be as important in amphibians as it is in mammals.

Studies of the axolotl, *Ambystoma mexicanum*, demonstrated that the mechanism of action of insulin is to counteract the effects of glucagon or epinephrine on hepatic glycogenolysis by stimulating phosphodiesterase, which metabolizes cyclic AMP generated in response to stimulation by these hormones (Janssens and Maher 1986). Insulin also decreases glutamate-pyruvate transaminase (GPT) and glutamate-oxaloacetate transaminase (GOT) activities in liver from *Amphiuma means* (Caudata: Amphiumidae), while glucagon increases these enzyme activities (Brown, Fleming, and Balls 1975).

Insulin levels vary seasonally (Schlaghecke and Blum 1981). In cold-adapted summer frogs (*R. temporaria*), insulin lowers plasma free fatty acids by stimulating reesterification. This action is presumably of value in deposition of fat stores before hibernation. Serum and pancreatic insulin are low dur-

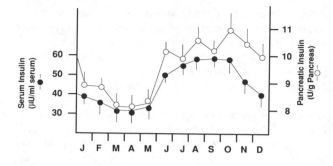

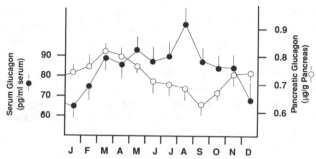

Fig. 3.4 Seasonal changes in serum and pancreatic concentrations of insulin and glucagon in the frog *Rana esculenta*. (Reprinted, by permission, from Schlaghecke and Blum 1981.)

ing hibernation in *R. esculenta* (Schlaghecke and Blum 1981; fig. 3.4).

Glucagon Glucagon is produced by α-cells of the amphibian endocrine pancreas under regulatory control by blood glucose levels (see review in Gapp 1986). Glucagon stimulates hyperglycemia in amphibians (Farrar and Frye 1977; Farrar and Frye 1979b; Gapp 1986). Endogenous glucagon levels are high in winter *R. pipiens* (Schlaghecke and Blum 1981), presumably to mobilize energy stores. However, exogenous hormone has more effect in summer and autumn (Farrar and Frye 1977). Glucagon regulates hepatic glycogenolysis via the generation of cyclic AMP in *Ambystoma mexicanum* (Janssens and Maher 1986). Glucagon also increases gluconeogenesis from pyruvate and alanine in conjunction with increased tissue levels of GOT, GPT, and fructose-1,6-diphosphate (Brown, Fleming, and Balls 1975). Mammalian glucagon has no effect on plasma free fatty acids in *R. temporaria* but decreases circulating cholesterol and stimulates ketogenesis by liver in *Bufo marinus* (Gapp 1986).

Catecholamines Two cell types found in amphibian adrenal medullary chromaffin tissue produce epinephrine and norepinephrine and release these hormones into the circulation upon stimulation of the sympathetic nervous system (Azuma, Binia, and Visscher 1965; Herman 1977; Mastrolia 1985). Epinephrine is the more potent stimulator of liver and muscle glycogenolysis, resulting in hyperglycemia. The mechanism of epinephrine action involves β-receptor stimulation, resulting in elevated cyclic AMP and glycogen phosphorylase activity in anurans (Herman and Brown 1983; Janssens, Caine, and Dixon 1983, 1985) and urodeles (Brown, Fleming, and Balls 1975).

In stress, the sympathetic nervous system stimulates synthesis and release of neurotransmitters and circulating catecholamines, resulting in rapid physiological adjustments. Administration of exogenous catecholamines can also induce one such adjustment, the elevation of plasma glucose (Herman 1977; Farrar and Frye 1977, 1979a). Epinephrine also increases circulating lactate, presumably due to muscle glycogenolysis (Farrar and Frye 1979a, 1979b; MbangKollo and deRoos 1983). This effect is more pronounced in the autumn, suggesting a role for epinephrine in preparation for hibernation (Farrar and Frye 1977; chapter 10).

The proposed roles of the catecholamines in elevating glucose levels during stress need reevaluation. Handling increases plasma lactate and hematocrit but not plasma glucose, suggesting that rapid adjustments of plasma glucose result from nervous system activation rather than corticosteroid or catecholamine release, unless stress is severe (MbangKollo and deRoos 1983). The primary function of catecholamines may be in cardiovascular rather than in metabolic regulation, as discussed below in the context of the cardiovascular system (see also Chan 1985).

Glucocorticoids A hypothalamic-pituitary-adrenocortical (interrenal) axis is present in anuran amphibians (Hanke 1978, 1990; Ball 1981; Hanke and Master 1985). Immunocytochemical techniques show an ACTH-like peptide in brain of several species (Doerr-Schott 1976; Campantico, Guastalla, and Patriarca 1985). ACTH is released following stimulation by corticotropin-releasing hormone (CRH) from the hypothalamus (Ball 1981). Both mammalian ACTH and extracts of anuran pituitaries stimulate corticosterone and aldosterone secretion from the adrenal glands (Leboulenger et al. 1978). Furthermore, incubations of adrenal tissue of *Xenopus laevis* with post- and preoptic hypothalamus, as well as pars distalis tissue, releases aldosterone. However, only pars distalis tissue stimulates corticosterone (Thurmond, Kloas, and Hanke 1986b). Cyclic AMP is the second messenger for ACTH action on adrenal production of corticosterone and aldosterone in *Rana berlandieri* (Chavin, Honn, and Clifford 1978a).

Other regulators may include arginine vasotocin and angiotensin II (Hanke and Maser 1985), and vasoactive intestinal peptide (Leboulenger et al. 1983; Leboulenger et al. 1984). Prostaglandins also stimulate the adrenal cortex to produce corticosterone and aldosterone (Chavin, Honn, and Clifford 1978b; Perroteau et al. 1984; Delarue et al. 1986). The effects of prostaglandins, however, are not correlated with cyclic AMP production (Chavin, Honn, and Clifford 1978b). The cholinergic nervous system may also participate, and acetylcholine releases steroids from isolated frog adrenal tissue through stimulation of muscarinic receptors (Benyamina et al. 1987).

Atrial natriuretic factor (ANF), a family of peptides localized in secretory vesicles of cardiocytes in vertebrates (Chapeau et al. 1985), has recently been characterized in atrium and ventricle of *Rana ridibunda*. It is biochemically and immunologically similar to mammalian ANF (Netchitaïlo et al. 1986; Netchitaïlo, Feuilloley, Lihrmann, Gutkowska, Leboulenger, Cantin, Pelletier, and Vaudry 1988; Netchitaïlo, Feuilloley, Pelletier, DeLean, Ong, Cantin, Gutkowska, Leboulenger, and Vaudry 1988). ANF inhibits ACTH and angiotensin II stimulated corticosteroid production from perfused frog adrenal slices, with aldosterone production more suppressed than corticosterone secretion. ANF-like immuno-reactive fibers occur near the adrenal cells, suggesting that this regulator may have a role in the production of corticosteroids in amphibians (Lihrmann et al. 1988).

The target organs producing glucocorticoids are the adrenal glands, which lack mammalian zonation (Hanke 1974, 1978). Either two separate cell types (Varma 1977) or one cell type (Hanke and Maser 1985) produce corticosterone and aldosterone, the major corticosteroids (Carstensen, Burgers, and Li 1961; Leboulenger et al. 1978; Leboulenger et al. 1982). The ratio of corticosterone to aldosterone following stimulation by mammalian ACTH varies, depending on the species (Johnson et al. 1967; Dupont et al. 1976).

Both seasonal and daily fluctuations occur in circulating corticosteroid levels. These fluctuations vary considerably among species. *Bufo americanus* exhibits daily surges at 1730 before locomotory activity, and a circannual rhythm that peaks in spring and autumn (Pancak and Taylor 1983). *Xenopus laevis* has maximal corticosteroid levels in the morning from 0900 to 1200 and low levels at night (Thurmond, Kloas, and Hanke 1986a). Corticosteroid levels of *Rana esculenta* vary seasonally, with peaks in May and June coinciding with spawning (Delarue et al. 1979). In addition, levels of both corticosterone and aldosterone are greater at night despite the animals' diurnal peak in activity and feeding (Delarue et al. 1979; Leboulenger et al. 1982). Although corticosterone is associated with reproductive activity in anurans, it inhibits sexual behavior in newts (Salamandridae; Moore and Miller 1984).

Glucocorticoid receptors vary in *X. laevis* liver with respect to sex, time of day, and season (Lange and Hanke 1988). ^{3}H dexamethasone binding capacity is three times higher in females than in males. In males, binding capacity is highest in June–July and October–November, while females exhibit maximum binding capacity in August. Binding is maximum at 0600 and 1800, 9 h after the maximum serum level of corticosterone.

ACTH or corticosterone increases blood glucose (Hanke 1978; Broughton and deRoos 1984; Hanke and Maser 1985), while aldosterone either increases (*Rana temporaria;* Hanke 1978) or does not increase (*R. catesbeiana;* Broughton and deRoos 1984) blood glucose. Glucocorticoids appear to stimulate gluconeogenesis (Hanke 1978; Rosenthal and deRoos 1985) in some but not in all species (*Bufo marinus;* Janssens 1970).

In addition to a direct effect on gluconeogenesis, glucocorticoids affect protein catabolism to provide substrates for gluconeogenesis. In *R. catesbeiana,* mammalian ACTH increases glucose, urea, and alanine levels, suggesting that amino acids are a substrate for gluconeogenesis (Rosenthal and deRoos 1985). The hyperglycemia develops slowly, suggesting that protein catabolism and enzyme activation are necessary before glucose release. Aldosterone-stimulated increases in glucose may be due to gluconeogenesis as well, because aldosterone increases urea levels in *R. pipiens,* although the increase only occurs in spring and summer (Jungreis and Johnston 1979).

Amphibians rapidly release corticosterone when stressed (Maser, Hittler, and Hanke 1980), but hours elapse before effects occur (Hanke 1978; MbangKollo and deRoos 1983;

Rosenthal and deRoos 1985), suggesting that these hormones do not participate in the immediate response to stress. Plasma glucose levels are elevated for several days following surgical stress, which may indicate a role for glucocorticoids in prolonged stress (Herman 1977; deRoos and Parker 1982; MbangKollo and deRoos 1983; Rosenthal and deRoos 1985).

Summary of Hormonal Effects on Carbohydrate Metabolism and Directions for Future Research Insulin is probably responsible for hypoglycemia in amphibians, although its importance has been questioned. Clarification of this issue requires characterization of amphibian insulins and the eventual availability of homologous hormone.

The hyperglycemic hormones in mammals, which include glucagon, epinephrine, and glucocorticoids, also are hyperglycemic in amphibians. However, the extent to which glucose is important in amphibians with normally low circulating glucose levels is not clear. In addition, the hyperglycemic responses of both epinephrine and glucocorticoids may be involved to only a limited extent in the response of the amphibian to stress. Further research is necessary to elucidate the physiological roles of these hormones.

CARDIOVASCULAR REGULATION

Introduction Recent advances in the regulatory control of the cardiovascular system in amphibians have focused on endocrine regulation by recently discovered hormones including prostaglandins, leukotrienes, and calcitonin gene-related peptide as well as by long-recognized hormones including catecholamines, arginine vasotocin, PTH, and angiotensin II. Chapters 5 and 7 also discuss regulation of the cardiovascular system.

Catecholamines Although epinephrine has metabolic effects, its primary physiological role may be cardiovascular (Chan 1985). Epinephrine and norepinephrine both increase blood pressure and reflexly decrease heart rate in cannulated bullfrogs (*Rana catesbeiana;* Herman and Sandoval 1983). Isoproterenol, a β-adrenergic agonist with no vascular effects, increases heart rate. However, in isolated perfused bullfrog hearts, epinephrine increases heart rate through activation of the β-receptors (Erlij, Certrangolo, and Valdez 1965; Stene-Larsen and Helle 1978; Kimmel 1990). These effects on blood pressure diminish at low environmental temperatures (5°C, Herman and Mata 1985; 12°C, Herman, Robleto, Mata, and Heller 1986), and the β-receptor–mediated stimulation of heart rate disappears.

Parathyroid Hormone PTH, long associated with calcium homeostasis, has cardiovascular effects. Bovine-PTH (b-PTH 1-34) causes hypotension and vasodilation in terrestrial vertebrates. The hypotensive effects of PTH appear to be direct and cannot be ascribed to release of neurotransmitters or receptor modification (Pang, Yang, Oguro, Phillips, and Yee 1980). PTH is vasodilatory in both kidney and hindlimb perfusions in *R. catesbeiana* (Chiu, Uchiyama, and Pang 1983).

PTH also exerts positive chronotropic and inotropic effects on isolated bullfrog atria, and propanolol does not block these effects (Furspan et al. 1984). Modification of arginine in PTH decreases the chronotropic and inotropic effects, and oxidation with hydrogen peroxide and modification of arginine abolishes the effects (Sham, Kenny, and Pang 1984). Despite the reported effect on adult bullfrog atria, b-PTH does not affect atria from *R. catesbeiana* larvae or *Necturus maculosus*. In the trout, b-PTH is also ineffective (Furspan et al. 1984). The cardiac effects of PTH may therefore be correlated with a terrestrial environment.

Angiotensin II   A renin-angiotensin system is present in all vertebrates studied except cyclostomes and elasmobranchs (Nishimura 1980; Wilson 1984). Reported effects are both osmoregulatory and cardiovascular (see review in Wilson 1984). Angiotensin of *R. catesbeiana* is (Asp[1], Val[5], Asn[9]) angiotensin I. The decapeptide is converted *in vivo* to angiotensin II (Hasegawa et al. 1983). Renin is present in kidneys of several amphibian species (Grill, Granger, and Thurau 1972) and has been localized histochemically in the juxtaglomerular cells of *Bufo bufo* (Lamers et al. 1985).

Angiotensin increases blood pressure in amphibians (Carroll and Opdyke 1982; Harper and Stephens 1985). Native angiotensin I (AI) and II (AII) both increase bullfrog blood pressure. (Sar[1], Ile[8]) AII reduces these responses, and the AI response is blocked by captopril, an angiotensin-converting enzyme inhibitor. The α-adrenergic antagonist phenoxybenzamine reduces both the AI and AII responses by 40%, suggesting that a portion of the response is not catecholamine-mediated. AI stimulates the release of epinephrine and norepinephrine in *R. catesbeiana* (Carroll and Opdyke 1982). Amphibians therefore appear to be intermediate between agnathans and elasmobranchs, in which the entire AII response is inhibited by α-antagonists, and mammals, in which only about 10% of the response is inhibited (Carroll and Opdyke 1982).

Arginine Vasotocin   Arginine vasotocin (AVT) is present in neurohypophyseal extracts of amphibians (Sawyer, Munsick, and van Dyke 1961; reviewed by Acher 1990). Chapters 5 and 6 discuss the effects of AVT on water balance. AVT also has cardiovascular effects in amphibians. It causes antidiuresis and pressor responses in *R. catesbeiana* and *Necturus maculosus* (Uchiyama and Pang 1985). The synthetic AVT antagonistic analogue KB IV-24 inhibits the vasopressor and antidiuretic response completely in *Necturus*, while in *R. catesbeiana* it inhibits only the vasopressor response completely and the antidiuretic response partially (Uchiyama and Pang 1985).

AVT has positive chronotropic effects in atrial preparations from *Bufo melanostictus*, *Rana tigrina*, *Xenopus laevis*, and *Triturus* (Caudata: Salamandridae). The atria of *R. tigrina* are most responsive, and those of *Triturus* are least responsive (Chiu, Lim, and Pang 1988). Positive chronotropic responses also occur in all atrial preparations, with *X. laevis* most responsive and *B. melanostictus* least responsive. The mechanism of action is not known, although the effects cannot be abolished with a β-adrenergic blocker.

Prostaglandins and Leukotrienes   Prostaglandins and leukotrienes, termed *eicosanoids*, are hormones derived from fatty acid substrates located in phospholipids of cell membranes. Produced by cells and tissues rather than endocrine organs, they diffuse to their targets. Both prostaglandins and leukotrienes occur in amphibians. Frog tissues, including heart, produce prostaglandins (Flitney and Singh 1980; Ghiara, Parente, and Piomelli 1984; Herman, Hamberg, and Granström 1987; Herman 1990), and frog white cells produce leukotrienes (Green et al. 1987).

Prostaglandins increase ($PGF_{2\alpha}$, $PGF_{1\alpha}$, TXB_2, PGD_1, and PGD_2) or decrease (PGE_1, PGE_2, PGE_3, PGI_2, PGA_1, PGA_2) blood pressure in cannulated bullfrogs, *Rana catesbeiana* (Leffler, Hanson, and Schneider 1980; Herman, McCloskey, and Doolittle 1982). The most potent hypertensive prostaglandin is $PGF_{2\alpha}$, and the most potent hypotensive compound is PGI_2. These effects decrease when bullfrogs are acclimated to 5°C. The twenty carbon fatty acid prostaglandin precursors, arachidonic acid, eicosatrienoic acid, and eicosapentaenoic acid, all are hypotensive in the warm-acclimated bullfrog and hypertensive in the cold-acclimated bullfrog. This suggests that prostaglandin synthesis differs depending on the acclimation temperature of the animal (Herman, Robleto, Mata, and Lujan 1986).

Whether prostaglandins increase or decrease blood pressure, they always increase heart rate *in vivo* (Herman, McCloskey, and Doolittle 1982). The effects of $PGF_{2\alpha}$ and PGI_2 on heart rate are abolished in cold-acclimated bullfrogs at 5°C (Herman, Robleto, Mata, and Lujan 1986).

The sulfidopeptide leukotrienes LTC_4, LTD_4, and LTE_4 decrease blood pressure in warm-acclimated cannulated bullfrogs and increase heart rate (Herman, Robleto, Reitmeyer, Martinez, and Herman 1988; Robleto, Reitmeyer, and Herman 1988; Herman, Charlton, and Cranfill 1991). As with prostaglandin effects, the response of cold-acclimated bullfrogs to leukotrienes is lower than that of warm-acclimated animals (Herman, Charlton, and Cranfill 1991). In isolated bullfrog heart, they have positive inotropic effects and do not affect heart rate (Herman, Heller, Canavan, and Herman 1988; Herman, Heller, and Herman 1990), suggesting that the effect *in vivo* is due to reflex regulation of the heart in response to hypotension. Leukotriene C_4 receptors have been characterized in bullfrog ventricle membranes and are similar to their mammalian counterpart, suggesting that these receptors have been conserved (Chiono, Heller, Andazola, and Herman 1991).

Calcitonin Gene-Related Peptide   Calcitonin gene-related peptide (CGRP), a thirty-seven–amino-acid peptide, is a recently discovered product of the calcitonin gene (Amara et al. 1982). CGRP is found in brain and spinal cord extracts of *Rana catesbeiana*. It exerts a vasorelaxant effect on the femoral artery by inhibiting the mobilization of intracellular calcium (Kline et al. 1988).

Summary of Endocrine Control of Cardiovascular System and Directions for Future Research   The hormones discussed above have cardiovascular effects in amphibians when administered exogenously. However, their endogenous regulation needs clarification. In addition, interactions between and among hormones need further study. While little has been done on environmental effects on cardiovascular regulation, studies suggest that the response of the amphibian to cardiovascular hormones is blunted at low environmental temperatures. This may be of no importance to the animal, because blood pressure and heart rate are lower at these temperatures. However, it is important to understand how the animal regulates the cardiovascular system at low temperatures (chapter 10).

While some hormones discussed in this section have been studied with respect to cardiovascular activity in a variety of amphibians, others have been studied in only one species. This is in part because the reports of some of these hormones are still very recent. In some cases, where more than one species has been examined, the response is species-specific. For example, PTH affects anurans but not urodeles. Further work is necessary to delineate the mechanisms of action of these regulatory compounds.

ROLES OF THYROID HORMONES IN ADULT AMPHIBIANS

Introduction An important endocrine regulatory process involves control of growth and development in amphibians. This topic is discussed in detail in chapter 16. A complicated interplay of hormones is involved (Etkin 1964; Frieden 1967; Dodd and Dodd 1976; Rosenkilde 1979; Dickhoff and Darling 1983; Norris 1983; Dent 1988; Eales 1990). The thyroid has important roles in larval amphibians, but less is known of the role of the thyroid hormones triiodothyronine (T_3) and thyroxine (T_4) in adult amphibians. A brief discussion of this problem follows.

Thyroid Hormones Hypothalamic extracts of amphibians contain TRH (Ball 1981), which also releases prolactin (Kuhn et al. 1985) and TSH (Darras and Kuhn 1982; Jacobs, Michielsen, and Kuhn 1988). TRH is also produced outside the nervous system. Immunoreactive TRH circulates in the blood of *Rana pipiens* at high concentrations (227 ng·ml^{-1}; Jackson and Reichlin 1979). The levels are too high to originate solely from the brain, and the skin is a source of TRH. However, Etkin and Gona (1968) and Gona and Gona (1974) have questioned the role of TRH in release of thyroid hormones in amphibians.

Gonadotropin-releasing hormone (GnRH) is more potent than TRH in increasing plasma T_4 levels in *Rana ridibunda* in November (Jacobs et al. 1988). In February, however, fewer than half of the *R. temporaria* were responsive to GnRH. Removal of the pituitary abolishes the effect of GnRH, suggesting that GnRH control of thyroid hormone production is via the pituitary. These reported effects of GnRH may be species-specific or temperature-dependent.

The hypothalamo-hypophyseal-thyroid axis in frogs varies seasonally. Levels of TRH in the hypothalamus of *R. pipiens* are lower in spring than in autumn or winter (Jackson, Saperstein, and Reichlin 1977). Pituitary thyrotrophs and follicular cells of the thyroid show parallel seasonal variation (Rosenkilde 1979).

At the level of the thyroid, seasonal effects also occur but vary among species. At cold temperatures, iodine uptake by the thyroid both decreases (*Bufo bufo;* Egeberg and Rosenkilde 1965) and increases (*R. temporaria;* Ceusters, Darras, and Kuhn 1978). Thyroid content of T_3 and T_4 is low during winter in *R. ridibunda,* and the levels increase rapidly after hibernation to maximum values in May and June (Kuhn, Darras, and Verlinden 1985). Plasma levels of T_3 are low in December and March. Plasma T_4 concentrations are low in winter, followed by a biphasic pattern. Thyroid glands activate at the end of hibernation and reach full size before reproduction. During reproduction they are resistant to TSH stimu-

lation, but afterwards a second reactivation occurs (Kuhn, Darras, and Verlinden 1985). These seasonal patterns differ somewhat among different species. *B. bufo* have higher plasma T_4 during hibernation and spring breeding periods than in summer and autumn (Rosenkilde 1982). *Ambystoma tigrinum* also have low T_4 levels in summer and autumn, which suggests that the thyroid hormone levels may be inversely related to environmental temperature (Norris et al. 1977).

The role of the thyroid in adult amphibians is far from clear. The adult thyroid gland can synthesize T_3 and T_4 (Ceusters, Darras, and Kuhn 1978). TSH is present in bullfrog (*R. catesbeiana*) pituitary gland (MacKenzie, Licht, and Papkoff 1978), but thyroid glands are less active in adults. Thyroid hormone levels in the blood of adult amphibians vary tremendously (see review in Stieff and Kaltenbach 1986). T_4 is also present within the plasma and nuclei of adult red blood cells (RBCs) of *R. pipiens, R. catesbeiana, Bufo marinus, Xenopus laevis,* and *Notophthalmus viridescens,* which suggests that thyroid hormone may be of some physiological importance in adult amphibians.

The documentation of glandular activity and circulating levels in adults does not clarify the potential roles of thyroid hormones. Following metamorphosis, T_4 is unable to promote growth in *X. laevis* but does increase mobilization of energy stores. T_4-treated animals have smaller fat bodies and livers than the control groups (Nybroe, Rosenkilde, and Ryttersgaard 1985). Increased oxygen consumption of *R. tigrina* liver occurs in response to T_4 administration in frogs acclimated at 25°C but not at 15°C (Packard and Packard 1975).

A possible explanation for the lack of effect of thyroid hormones may be due to thyroid hormone receptor number in the adult. While larvae have thyroid hormone nuclear receptors in liver (Galton 1980), tail fins (Suzuki and Kikuyama 1983), and RBCs (Galton 1984) and have a T_4 monoiodinating system before metamorphic climax (Galton and Munck 1981), the adult differs with respect to receptors in hepatic nuclei and RBCs. Adult frog liver nuclei have two sets of T_3 binding sites comparable with those described in larvae; however, the number of binding sites is low compared to that of larvae. Receptor number in RBCs is also lower in the adult frogs and *Necturus.* Low receptor number may account for lack of response of adults to thyroid hormones (fig. 3.5; Galton 1985).

Summary of Endocrine Control of Growth and Directions for Future Research The presence of the hypothalamo-hypophyseal-thyroid axis hormones in adult amphibians, the seasonal variation in these hormones, and the measurement of circulating thyroid hormones in blood suggest that these hormones may function in adult amphibians. The mere presence of hormones does not necessarily imply physiological action, however, and the low receptor numbers may prevent physiological responses. Further studies are necessary to clarify the roles of T_3 and T_4 in adult amphibians.

REPRODUCTIVE BIOLOGY

Introduction Reproductive endocrinology of amphibians is an important research area discussed in chapter 15. Several excellent reviews also discuss the relationship between environment and endocrine regulation of reproduction (Licht

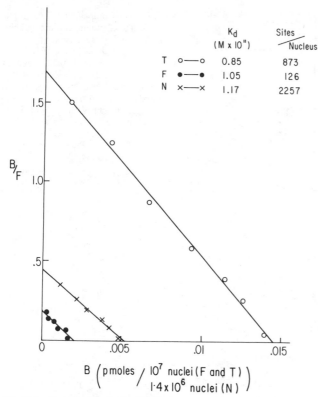

	K_d $(M \times 10^{11})$	Sites / Nucleus
T o—o	0.85	873
F •—•	1.05	126
N x—x	1.17	2257

Fig. 3.5 Scatchard analysis of T_3 binding to red blood cell (RBC) nuclei of anuran larva (T), adult frog (F, *Rana catesbeiana*), and *Necturus* (N, Caudata: Proteidae). Each tube contained RBC (frog and larva 1×10^6; *Necturus* 1.4×10^6) in 2 ml of amphibian Ringer's solution, pH 7.5. The incubation was continued for 20 h at 21°C. B = pmol bound T_3/tube; F = pmol free T_3·ml^{-1} incubation medium. (Reprinted, by permission, from Galton 1985.)

1979, 1983, 1986; Rastogi and Iela 1980; Lofts 1984; Moore and Deviche 1988; King and Millar 1990). These reviews clearly show considerable species differences in patterns of reproductive activity, annual hormonal cycles, circulating levels, and gonadal steroid hormone production, which are dependent on the life history of the animal in many ways. A possible explanation for differences in reported hormonal levels is that gonadotropin and gonadal steroid levels taken at the time of capture are considerably higher than in captive animals (Licht et al. 1983). This section will briefly summarize the recent work on hormonal control of reproduction and reproductive behavior.

Gonadotropin-Releasing Hormone Control of amphibian reproduction is by GnRH from the hypothalamus. Recent immunohistochemical studies correlate the localization of immunoreactive GnRH with seasonal changes (*Bufo japonicus;* Jokura and Urano 1985; *Taricha granulosa* [Caudata: Salamandridae]: Zoeller and Moore 1985); however, the correlations are highly species-specific. Median eminences of *B. japonicus* show weak GnRH immunoreactivity during migration, and greater amounts in both spring and autumn (Jokura and Urano 1985). GnRH concentrations in the infundibulum and rostral hypothalamus of *T. granulosa* are positively correlated throughout the reproductive cycle, while levels in the ventral preoptic area fluctuate independent of the other two areas. However, all three areas have undetectable GnRH levels in March and April. These low levels are pres-

ent before the end of the breeding season and before the decrease in plasma androgen and may trigger the end of reproductive activity (Zoeller and Moore 1985).

A negative feedback system controls release of GnRH from the hypothalamus. Seasonal changes in gonadotropins and steroid levels in bullfrogs do not exhibit a negative feedback relationship, however, since both levels become elevated simultaneously (Licht et al. 1983). Dihydroxytestosterone may affect the hypothalamus negatively and the pituitary positively, while estrogen has only negative feedback activity (McCreery and Licht 1984).

Unlike many other vertebrates, amphibians have multiple forms of GnRH, including forms that are identical to the mammalian and salmonid form (King and Miller 1980; Sherwood, Zoeller, and Moore 1986; fig. 3.6). The role of these multiple forms of GnRH is not clear. The GnRH receptors on amphibian pituitaries may be less specific than their counterparts in other vertebrates (Licht, Porter, and Miller 1987).

Another possible explanation for the presence of different forms of GnRH is that, in amphibians, GnRH has roles other than the regulation of gonadotropin release by the pituitary. GnRH may serve as a neurotransmitter, having been isolated from frog sympathetic ganglia (Jan and Jan 1981). GnRH has also been implicated in control of reproductive behavior in *Taricha granulosa* (Moore, Muske, and Propper 1987). The isolation of immunoreactive GnRH from testes, which undergo seasonal changes in concentration (Fasano et al. 1988), and from the nervus terminalis associated with the olfactory system of three amphibians (Muske and Moore 1987) also suggests other roles for GnRH.

In addition to its stimulatory effects on gonadotropin release by the pituitary, GnRH stimulates T_4 release in *Rana ridibunda* and *R. esculenta*. Neither testosterone nor T_4 increase in hypophysectomized frogs. In sham-operated animals, the increase in plasma testosterone is more prolonged than the increase in T_4. The effect is seasonal and species-dependent. In February, only a minority of *R. temporaria* may respond to GnRH. Perhaps GnRH once controlled the thyroid and gonad, as is true in fish. The pars distalis appears to be involved in GnRH-mediated release of T_4. GnRH may act as a neurotransmitter or stimulate the thyrotrophs directly (Jacobs et al. 1988).

The Gonadotropins: FSH and LH Two types of gonadotropins, luteinizing hormone (LH) and follicle-stimulating hormone (FSH), are present in all vertebrates except the Squamata (Licht 1979). These hormones show species differences and distinct isoelectric profiles (Tanaka et al. 1985; reviewed by Ishii 1990). The hormones in amphibians have structural similarities to mammalian gonadotropins. As in mammals, however, these hormones contain α- and β-subunits, with the β-subunit responsible for the unique properties of the molecules. Release of the gonadotropins in amphibians is continuous rather than pulsatile, however, as in mammals (Hubbard and Licht 1986).

The specificity of biological action of LH and FSH in mammalian systems is not necessarily true of amphibians. Both hormones stimulate some physiological responses equally, including testes/ovarian growth, spermiation, and estrogen secretion. However, LH and not FSH is required for ovulation, androgen secretion, and ovarian progesterone secretion (Licht 1986).

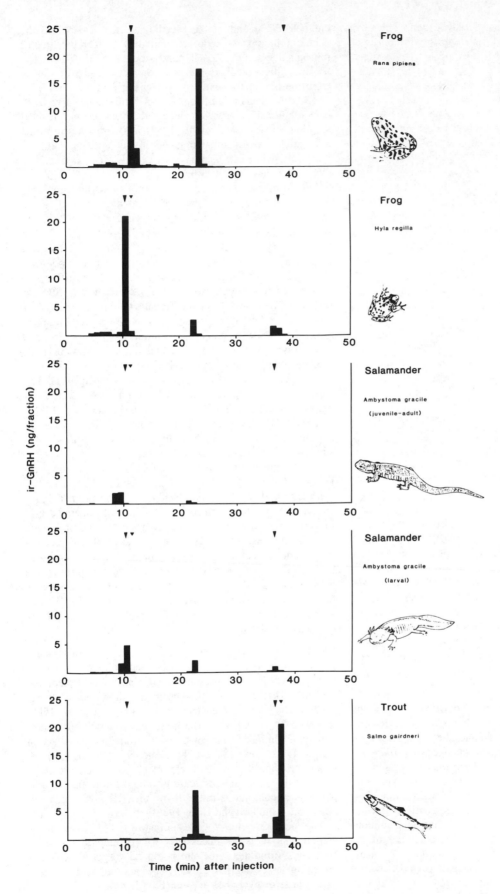

Fig. 3.6 Comparison of the high-performance liquid chromatography pattern of frog, salamander, and trout brain immunoreactive GnRH. Synthetic mammalian GnRH eluted at 11–12 min and salmon GnRH at 36–39 min. Each extract is compared to standards run on the same day. (Reprinted, by permission, from Sherwood, Zoeller, Moore 1986.)

While amphibians have distinct LH, FSH, and TSH molecules, the LH of bullfrogs can stimulate the thyroid of reptiles and birds, suggesting that it may have been an evolutionary precursor to reptile and bird TSH (MacKenzie and Licht 1984). As might be expected, LH and FSH in female bullfrogs show seasonal fluctuations with a pattern that follows that of the gonadal steroids. Levels are low from August to April, then become high during the breeding season (Licht et al. 1983). Testicular LH and FSH receptor characteristics adapt to environmental temperature. In the newt *Cynops pyrrhogaster* (Caudata: Salamandridae), which spawns in the spring when water temperatures are 15° to 20°C, kinetic parameters of binding of radioiodinated FSH to testes receptors have been reported (Ishii and Kubokawa 1985). The rate constant of association between hormone and receptor (k^+) determines the speed of binding of the hormone and is related to the latent time of response to the hormone. In these studies, k^+ decreases with decreasing temperature. Change with temperature is less for the newt than for rat testes membranes, however, indicating that the retardation in hormonal response is less in a poikilothermic animal. The equilibrium constant of association (K_a) expresses the maximum concentration of the hormone-receptor complex, which is related to the maximum hormonal response. The highest K_a for newt testicular membranes is at 18°C, the spawning temperature, and decreases at temperatures above and below 18°C. Rat membranes have a K_a that is highest at 38°C. In addition, the formation of the hormone-receptor complex is thermodynamically identical in rat, newt, and turtle at the physiological temperature of each species.

Testicular Steroid Hormones Amphibian testes produce androgens under hypothalamic-hypophyseal control, and testicular binding sites for LH and FSH are present (Ishii and Kubokawa 1985). In addition, local concentrations of estradiol inhibit, and testosterone and dihydrotestosterone enhance, LH-stimulated testicular androgen production (Pierantoni et al. 1986; Fasano et al. 1989).

Plasma androgen concentrations have been reported for many species (reviewed by d'Istria et al. 1985; Moore and Deviche 1988). Figure 3.7 shows seasonal variations in plasma androgen levels in several anuran and urodele species. In general, circulating testosterone is higher in urodeles than in anurans. Dihydrotestosterone (DHT) may also be high. Although both androgens are generally equal in concentration, DHT levels are higher than testosterone levels in *R. catesbeiana*. These levels change with the season and are coordinated with the spermatogenic cycle (Licht, Ryan, and Barnes 1985). Androgen levels are low in the summer during proliferation of secondary spermatogonia and spermatocyte formation. As the environmental temperature decreases, androgen levels increase and spermatid formation begins.

Androgens also aid in the development of seasonal thumb pads in males, and act on the skin to increase epidermal thickness and glandular epithelial height. Receptors have been localized at these targets (reviewed by Ho et al. 1985).

The brain is a target for androgens in amphibians and carries out extensive metabolism (reviewed by Callard 1985). Aromatase converts testosterone to estrogen and is high in the hypothalamic or limbic system. 5α-reductase converts testosterone to dihydrotestosterone. Estrogen mimics the effect of

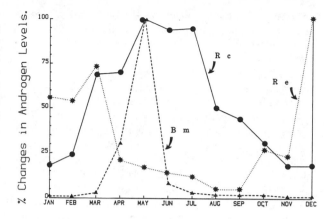

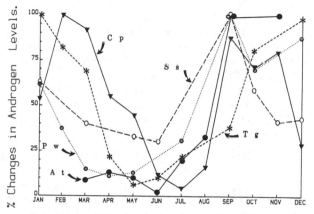

Fig. 3.7 Seasonal variations in plasma androgen concentrations in anurans (*top*) and urodeles (*bottom*). Data represent plasma concentrations of testoterone (*B.m.* and *R.e.*), dihydrotestosterone (*R.c.*), or total androgen immunoreactivity (other species). Percentage of androgen was calculated from maximum values (ng·ml⁻¹) for each species. *R.c., Rana catesbeiana*, 27; *R.e., Rana esculenta*, 19; *B.m., Bufo mauritanicus*, 595; *C.p., Cynops pyrrhogaster* 65; *S.s., Salamandra salamandra*, 107; *P.w., Pleurodeles waltl*, 58; *A.t., Ambystoma tigrinum*, 39; *T.g., Taricha granulosa*, 38. (Reprinted, by permission, from Moore and Deviche 1988.)

androgens on sexual behavior of frogs when placed directly on the brain. Inhibition of aromatization blocks androgen-induced clasping in frogs.

Androgens have a role in reproductive behavior of amphibians (Deviche and Moore 1988). In general, castration eliminates sexual behavior and androgen treatment restores it, with some exceptions. Circulating androgens are not correlated with sexual activity in the newt (Moore and Muller 1977). Testosterone also fails to stimulate calling behavior in castrated male *Pachymedusa dacnicolor* (Anura: Hylidae; Rastogi et al. 1986). The behavioral effects of testosterone are mediated by testosterone, not by enzymatic conversion to estradiol or DHT (Deviche and Moore 1988).

Ovarian Steroid Hormones The amphibian ovary produces steroid hormones in response to LH, a sensitivity that is acquired after metamorphosis (Hsu et al. 1989). Seasonal hormonal cycles are present in many female anurans, including *Rana catesbeiana* (Licht et al. 1983), *R. esculenta* (Pierantoni et al. 1984), and *Pachymedusa dacnicolor* (Iela et al. 1986). Plasma 17β-estradiol, androstenedione, testosterone, and progesterone are correlated with ovarian changes in *R. esculenta* (Pierantoni et al. 1984). Female *R. catesbeiana* have higher testosterone levels than do males, and plasma testosterone but not estrogen is correlated with ovarian growth (Licht et al. 1983).

In urodeles, uptake of tritiated estradiol has been observed in the müllerian duct of *Pleurodeles waltl* and brain of *Triturus cristatus* (both Caudata: Salamandridae; Ho et al. 1985). The liver of several amphibian species has both cytosolic and nuclear estrogen receptors (see Paolucci and Botte 1988 for review). Estrogen receptors in female *R. esculenta* have a high and specific affinity for estradiol and diethylstilbestrol, with less binding to estrone and estriol. Chemical characterization indicates that the molecular weight is 48,000. K_d values obtained from Scatchard plots indicate that these values are unchanged throughout the annual cycle. Filled and unfilled receptors were found throughout the cycle, but the numbers increase during vitellogenesis.

Estrogen binding is affected by temperature. At 4°C, binding is low in the nuclear extract for the first 4 h of incubation, after which it stabilizes with the cytosolic binding for 36 h. In contrast, at 20°C, binding is higher in the nuclear extract than in the cytosolic, and both decrease at 4 h. At 37°C, the maximum value is at 10 min for both nuclear and cytosolic fractions, and rapid decrease occurs so that no binding is detectable at 4 h (Paolucci and Botte 1988).

Arginine Vasotocin and Reproductive Behavior AVT is present in the neurohypophysis of amphibians (Sawyer, Munsick, and van Dyke 1961) and in serum of *Rana ridibunda* (Nouwen and Kuhn 1983). AVT affects both water balance and blood pressure (Sawyer and Pang 1987; Chiu, Lim, and Pang 1988). AVT also affects sexual behavior (Deviche and Moore 1988). Intercranial administration of AVT to male rough-skinned newts, *Taricha granulosa,* stimulates male sexual behavior. Immunoreactive AVT localizes in the dorsal preoptic area and the optic tectum (Zoeller and Moore 1986). Optic tectum AVT increases in the spring in correlation with sexual activity, suggesting that the AVT in this area might be important in sexual behavior. In contrast, the immunoreactive (ir) AVT levels in the dorsal preoptic area are high in summer and decline in autumn, with fluctuations in winter and spring. Sexually responsive males have higher concentrations of irAVT in the dorsal preoptic area, optic tectum, ventral infundibular nucleus, and cerebrospinal fluid than do nonresponsive males (Zoeller and Moore 1988). Different areas of the brain are associated with AVT regulation of reproductive behavior and hydromineral balance. Dehydrated males have lower concentrations of irAVT in the ventral preoptic area (Zoeller and Moore 1988).

Another behavior under endocrine control is mating call phonotaxis (see chapters 2 and 14). Gravid *Bufo marinus* females move toward conspecific mating calls (Schmidt 1984a). Human chorionic gonadotropin induces this behavior, as do $PGF_{2\alpha}$ and AVT following progesterone priming. The human chorionic gonadotropin–induced phonotaxis terminates with indomethacin, which inhibits prostaglandin synthesis. Prostaglandins also stimulate female reproductive behavior in *Xenopus laevis* (Kelley, Bockman, and Weintraub 1987).

Summary of Endocrine Control of Reproductive Biology and Directions for Future Research The hypothalamo-hypophyseal-gonadal axis is involved in control of amphibian reproduction as it is in other vertebrates. Amphibian reproduction is extremely sensitive to environmental conditions, including photoperiod, temperature, and humidity. The many studies that examine changes in hormonal levels with respect to environmental conditions establish the extreme diversity of hormonal regulation found in amphibians.

Major advancement has been made in this field with the clarification of structures of homologous hormones involved in reproduction. More research is necessary to elucidate the roles of the multiple forms of GnRH. The mechanisms involved in hormonal control of reproduction are also important and fascinating topics for future research.

GENERAL CONCLUSIONS

The endocrinology of the Amphibia is an exciting and rapidly progressing field. Recent years have seen the characterization of homologous hormones with subsequent development of radioimmunoassays for the measurements of plasma and tissue levels. Histochemical procedures have allowed the localization of hormone production and receptors. New regulatory compounds such as prostaglandins, leukotrienes, calcitonin gene-related peptide, and many other peptide hormones are beginning to be understood with respect to hormonal effect.

The study of amphibian endocrinology is important in understanding comparative endocrinology in general. In addition, hormonal processes are sensitive to environmental regulation. Much more information is needed about regulatory controls of hormone and receptor production, as well as information concerning transduction mechanisms at the target tissues. In many cases, information is only known for one or a few amphibian species. To understand the comparative endocrinology of amphibians, a wider range of amphibian species, from aquatic to terrestrial, requires investigation.

Part 2
Exchange of Gases, Osmolytes, Water, and Heat

Environmental physiologists have long recognized that the exchanges of energy, ions, water, and respiratory gases are inextricably linked. Understandably, however, the traditional experimental program in environmental physiology typically has been to limit investigation to one particular system at a time (e.g., the respiratory system) and to explore a particular problem within that system (e.g., ventilatory responses to hypoxia). While an experimentalist might have realized, for example, that changes in lung ventilation would alter the rate of water and heat transfer from an animal and would elicit acid-base adjustments due to changes in CO_2 elimination, rarely would experiments be designed specifically to account for these and other factors. This highly focused, unidimensional approach was appropriate for a field still in a relatively young and exploratory phase. At the time, investigators were describing the basic diversity in amphibian physiology, frequently with respect to unusual species occurring in extreme environments. (Moreover, even though authors in this section argue that a more synthetic approach is of increasing value, unidimensional studies of the majority of amphibian species that are yet unexamined will continue to yield valuable data.) Also, the analytical tools and concepts necessary for a multivariate approach (e.g., the relationship between ion fluxes and acid-base regulation and their joint effects on metabolism; coupled equations for heat and mass balance) were then still under development.

The approach taken in Moore's (1964) book (however enlightened for the times) manifested this tendency to reduce the physiological view of animals to their individual components. The mass transfer of heat, water, ions, and respiratory gases was treated in separate chapters, with little attempt to create (and probably little demand for) a more synthetic approach.

The logic underlying the organization of part 2 is to consider first the physical mechanisms responsible for the transfer of energy and matter between amphibians and their environments; next how animals themselves actually exchange respiratory gases, water, and various solutes (e.g., ions) with the environment; and finally how these exchanges are regulated. Because the exchange of matter is qualitatively

different in the aquatic/amphibious setting and the aerial/terrestrial setting, these nominally are discussed in separate chapters. However, as emphasized in chapter 1 and as will become obvious, all of the topics in this section are interrelated and should not be discussed in isolation from one another.

Chapter 4, "Biophysics of Heat and Mass Transfer" (Spotila, O'Connor and Bakken), begins by explicating the biophysical principles underlying the transfer of heat, water, ions, and gases between animals and environments. The pervasive theme is that heat and mass transfers cannot be treated independently and that similar if not identical theory governs each. Spotila and his colleagues indicate the promise (and pitfalls) of a rigorous quantitative approach to biophysical heat and mass transfer.

Chapter 5, "Exchange of Respiratory Gases, Ions, and Water in Amphibious and Aquatic Amphibians" (Boutilier, Stiffler, and Toews) goes beyond the component processes of mass exchange described in chapter 4 and discusses the actual exchange of respiratory gases, ions, and water in "aquatic" amphibians. Moreover, it considers phylogenetic and environmental correlates of these exchanges as well as the cellular and molecular mechanisms underlying their regulation. Many amphibians spend some, if not all, of their life in water. The physiological processes that regulate the mass transfer in water are fundamental to understanding the biology and evolution of all amphibians.

While many amphibians exploit aquatic habitats at least part of their lives, many spend some time out of water, and many are predominantly or totally terrestrial. With the transition to terrestrialism comes a different set of environmental problems and a wide variety of physiological solutions, often constrained by features retained from an aquatic existence. Chapter 6, "Exchange of Water, Ions, and Respiratory Gases in Terrestrial Amphibians" (Shoemaker and colleagues) details the highly varied adaptations for terrestrial life. Two themes predominate: the relative abundance of oxygen relative to the aquatic habitat, and the pressing need to conserve water.

The mechanisms that integrate the regulatory processes of

amphibians in both aquatic and terrestrial environments reside in the neural and endocrine systems. As in mammalian physiology, the study of neural and endocrine mechanisms of cardiorespiratory regulation in amphibians has become a field in its own right. In chapter 7, West and Van Vliet review the increasingly complex developments in this field, which suggest that the basic elements of cardiorespiratory homeostasis are common to all tetrapods. This and the other chapters in part 2 exemplify the extent to which a sophisticated understanding of neurobiology and endocrinology has become essential to the analysis of mass transfer.

Amphibians exhibit enormous variation in patterns of body temperatures in the field. Some at times are remarkably constant in temperature; others at times undergo enormous diel, intermediate, and annual fluctuation. Moreover, individual amphibians may vary between these extremes according to season and stage in their life cycle, and populations within a species may differ according to their geographic range.

Some major issues in the study of amphibian thermal biology are the explanation of this variation in pattern, from constancy to extreme fluctuation, and the determination of its implications. The several approaches to the explanation of pattern have yielded different, often contradictory results. As Chapter 4 exemplifies, those biologists who have undertaken field studies of amphibian thermoregulation have understandably emphasized the extent to which the environment may limit amphibians' opportunities for thermoregulation. Environmental limitations may be direct; an environment may lack sufficient thermal diversity for behavioral thermoregulation, or one made of heat exchange (e.g., evaporative cooling in a dry environment) may so predominate that alternative temperatures cannot be attained. Alternatively, environmental limitations may be indirect; the physical environment may be permissive of thermoregulation, but the cost of thermoregulation (in water loss, energy expenditure, or risk of predation) may be prohibitive. By contrast, as chapter 9 (Hutchison and Dupré) exemplifies, biologists who have undertaken laboratory studies of amphibian thermoregulation have understandably emphasized amphibians' obvious capacity to thermoregulate and the numerous behavioral and physiological mechanisms with which they do so.

The extent to which either view is "correct" is still unresolved. Resolution will probably require detailed, long-term field studies in which biologists assess the microhabitats that amphibians (as opposed to biologists in the field) encounter throughout their lives, and the physiological states during which amphibians encounter these microhabitats. A first step will be the acquisition of good long-term records of the body temperatures of free-ranging amphibians, and may be imminent, given the rapid development of miniature biotelemetry equipment. When such records are available, however, their interpretation will be far from simple. Might a given instance of variable body temperatures be due to an insufficiency of the organs and systems involved in thermoregulation, absence of suitable heat sources and sinks in the environment, voluntary heterothermy to reap the benefits of a high or low body temperature, abandonment of thermoregulation to save water, or temporary chance encounters with uncharacteristically extreme microclimates? Might a given instance of constant body temperature be due to precise thermoregulation, an animal's occupancy of a thermal environment that does not permit otherwise, or regulation of some other physiological variable (e.g., body water) that happens to result in a constant body temperature? Field biophysical ecology will prove especially important in evaluating whether a given microenvironment provides an amphibian with the opportunity to achieve alternative body temperatures, and laboratory studies (chapter 9) have already demonstrated that amphibians have the necessary sensors, effectors, and control systems to thermoregulate if the opportunity presents itself. Clearly, free-ranging amphibians sometimes appear to thermoregulate; but how often is "sometimes," what does the thermoregulation achieve, and what is the relationship between the frequency of successful thermoregulation and an amphibian's ability to survive and reproduce?

Whether such instances are temporary lapses in otherwise precise thermoregulation, protracted episodes of involuntary thermal conformity, or intentional bouts of heterothermy with a sound biological rationale, many amphibians clearly experience considerable variation in body temperature at some time in their lives. As chapter 8 details, such variation will usually have profound consequences for most biochemical and cellular processes as well as the organismal functions that they underlie. Thus, considerable interest has arisen in the processes that may mitigate the effects of this thermal variation: thermal acclimation on a short-term basis and the evolution of temperature-insensitive systems in the longer term. The description of both temperature effects and mitigating processes, often in encyclopedic detail, occupies a large fraction of the literature on amphibian physiology. As chapter 8 presents, however, the criteria for the evaluation of these mitigating processes vary. Some workers will accept any difference between two individuals, populations, species, and so forth, as evidence for acclimation or adaptation, while others require differences of specific magnitude, direction, and correlation with environmental variables. Thus, an analysis of this field is as much a matter of definitions as of biological data. Rome, Stevens, and John-Alder recommend a highly specific definition in chapter 8, one that excludes the bulk of previously published work. Although their definition (and its implication for the interpretation of the literature) may not receive universal acceptance, it certainly will encourage increased rigor in the evaluation of acclimatory and adaptational phenomena. Finally, Rome, Stevens, and John-Alder discuss a small number of studies that exemplify the multidisciplinary approach that is necessary if we are to increase our understanding of temperature effects and thermal adaptation. In these examples, groups of people have expended considerable effort to understand thermal effect on function in great detail at all levels of organization, from the enzyme or molecule, to the cell, the organ, the organism, and the population. In these studies, exclusion of any level or inattention to detail would have led to misleading results. By contrast, the majority of studies in the field concentrate upon a particular level or levels of organization, often in lesser detail. If the results of the few studies cited in chapter 8 can be generalized, we may know remarkably little about the adaptations of amphibians to variation in temperature despite the vast number of papers that have been published on the subject. If so, the field may need to concentrate on understanding a small number of systems very well. These considerations unfortunately diminish the value of simple descriptive studies of thermal effects and thermal compensation at "entry-level" projects for research careers and as contributions that modestly equipped and staffed laboratories can make to the primary literature.

Finally, like other kinds of organisms, amphibians will eventually confront environmental challenges to normal activity that exceed their physiological capabilities. Alternatively, amphibians will eventually encounter environmental problems whose solutions, although within the realm of physiological capability, are so costly that they are not tenable in the long run. In such circumstances, organisms often withdraw from normal activity entirely until better conditions return. This withdrawal is itself a carefully orchestrated suite of physiological adjustments with its own self-generated problems and environmental challenges. In chapter 10, Pinder, Storey, and Ultsch consider the related processes of estivation and hibernation and their ecological correlates. In some cases, estivation and hibernation include the same physiological responses that are detailed in the previous chapters,

but taken to their extremes. In other cases, estivation and hibernation involve truly novel responses; for example, the controlled freezing of an entire organism. In all cases, however, the suite of physiological responses must constitute a comprehensive solution to the interrelated problems of mass and energy balance.

One of the most exciting new trends in environmental animal physiology is the blossoming of highly integrative experimental approaches and analytical techniques. Aside from technical and technological advances, this trend is permitting ecophysiologists to make major advances in addressing both classical (but unresolved) and modern questions: How should animals prioritize competing demands for physiological regulation? Are animals optimally designed physiologically? How can we explain the evolution of complex physiological characteristics? To what extent do inherited physiological characteristics constrain the evolution of physiological novelty? Although this section emphasizes a relatively circumscribed series of topics, it can be viewed as one discrete case of the general sense in which environmental physiologists are approaching these questions.

4 Biophysics of Heat and Mass Transfer

JAMES R. SPOTILA, MICHAEL P. O'CONNOR, AND GEORGE S. BAKKEN

The usually moist skin of amphibians intimately couples them to their physical environment by the exchange of energy, water, and respiratory gases. This coupling presents amphibians with a common set of environmental challenges. Nearly all active amphibians are tied to wet habitats in both their larval and adult stages. For terrestrial forms, large increases in cutaneous evaporation as body temperatures rise tend to maintain relatively low, stable body temperatures, but may expose the animal to the risks of dehydration. Amphibians are not a uniform group of animals, however. Rather, they represent a diversity of morphological types that inhabit microhabitats ranging from aquatic systems to terrestrial forests (both tropical and temperate), grasslands, and even deserts. Frogs, salamanders, and caecilians have distinctly different body shapes and live in quite different microhabitats. They therefore face different problems in adapting to the biophysics of exchange of heat and water.

For example, although salamanders are restricted to water or relatively cool, moist microhabitats on land, frogs inhabit a wide range of microhabitats that include xerophytic open forest and brush (i.e., phyllomedusine frogs) and even deserts (i.e., Pelobatidae and Leptodactylidae). Accordingly, frogs exhibit a variety of physiological and behavioral adaptations to dehydration that include excretion of uric acid (Loveridge 1970; Shoemaker et al. 1972) and the modification of skin structure by mechanisms such as the production of a lipid barrier to skin water loss (Blaylock, Ruibal, and Platt-Aloia 1976; Withers, Hillman, and Drewes 1984), and cocoon formation (Lee and Mercer 1967; Loveridge and Crayé 1979; Mayhew 1965). Chapters 6 and 10 discuss these features in detail. In contrast, caecilians are restricted to the tropics and are either aquatic or fossorial. Little is known about their environmental physiology, but they do not appear to have any specialized structures for retarding skin water loss or for thermoregulation, and they occur in microhabitats that provide moderate temperatures and adequate moisture. Thus, the environmental physiology of amphibians is shaped by the physical environment in which they live.

Like all other animals, amphibians are affected by the laws of thermodynamics (Gates 1962). Heat exchange determines the animal's body temperature and thus affects biochemical, physiological, and behavioral processes. All amphibians are ectotherms; that is, body temperatures depend more on the thermal environment than on physiological processes, and the regulation of body temperature is primarily behavioral (see chapters 8 and 9). Amphibians, in general, have highly vascularized, moist skin surfaces that are very permeable to water and respiratory gases and offer little resistance to the evaporation of water (Spotila and Berman 1976). Evaporative water loss cools amphibians and may keep body temperatures below air temperature even when the animals are exposed to direct solar radiation (Carey 1978b; Lillywhite 1975; Lillywhite and Licht 1975; O'Connor 1989; Tracy 1975, 1976). Changes in skin structure can reduce permeability to water vapor, reducing evaporative water loss (Lillywhite and Maderson 1988), but may also reduce the capacity for oxygen and carbon dioxide exchange. Because amphibians depend on cutaneous respiration for much of their oxygen and carbon dioxide exchange, such reductions in permeability to water vapor may require changes in metabolic rate and/or changes in cardiorespiratory systems.

The physics of heat transfer between an amphibian and its environment has, until recently (O'Connor 1989; Spotila and Berman 1976; Tracy 1975, 1976; Wygoda 1984, 1988a), received little attention. The implications of the interaction of heat and mass transfer for the environmental physiology and ecology of amphibians have been discussed for salamanders by Spotila (1972) and for frogs by Tracy (1976). The aim of this chapter is to review the biophysics of exchange of heat and mass and to indicate how the physical principles governing these exchanges place constraints on the environmental physiology and ecology of amphibians.

Preparation of this chapter was supported by grants from the Department of Energy to Drexel University (DE-FG02-88ER60727) and the Savannah River Ecology Laboratory (DE-AC09-76ROO-819). We dedicate this chapter to John A. Sealander upon the occasion of his retirement from the University of Arkansas in 1988 and to David M. Gates for his pioneer research and scholarly writing that crystallized the field of biophysical ecology.

MECHANISMS OF HEAT EXCHANGE

The transfer of heat energy occurs by a variety of physical processes (Kreith 1973; Porter and Gates 1969). In the case of an amphibian underwater, the prdominant modes of energy exchange are convection and conduction, and an amphibian rarely experiences a body temperature more than 2°C different than that of the water in which it swims. Thus, heat exchange in amphibians in water has been little studied (see Erskine and Spotila 1978 for application of underwater heat transfer to biological systems). In air, an amphibian undergoes a more complex energy exchange due to additional modes of heat transfer. When amphibians emerge into the atmosphere, they are subject to evaporative water loss; the effects of wind (convection); conduction from the ground; thermal loading from direct, scattered, and diffuse solar radiation; and exchange of thermal radiation with the atmosphere and the surroundings (fig. 4.1). Detailed descriptions of animal heat energy budgets have been given by Birkebak (1966) and Porter and Gates (1969), and applied to ectothermic vertebrates by Spotila, Soule, and Gates (1972); Spotila et al. (1973); Porter et al. (1973); Tracy (1976); Porter and James (1979); Scott, Tracy, and Pettus (1982); and Christian, Tracy, and Porter (1983). Gates (1980) described biophysical ecology in detail, Tracy (1982) reviewed the application of biophysical modeling to reptiles, and Spotila and

Standora (1985) discussed heat and food energy budgets of ectothermic vertebrates.

The amphibian-environment energy interaction can be described by an energy budget equation that accounts for each mode of heat transfer between the animal and its environment. The simplest and most commonly used type of balance is the equilibrium energy balance, which assumes that the animal is at thermal equilibrium with its environment. Most studies of the thermal biology of amphibians (and of other small ectotherms) have adopted this approach. More complex models, in which the animal's body temperature approaches thermal equilibrium over time, have been used to model the thermal biology of large reptiles (Grigg, Drane, and Courtice 1979; Spotila et al. 1973; Tracy 1982; Turner and Tracy 1985, 1986). Such "transient energy balance" models have not often been used for amphibians, not only because of the increased complexity of these models, but also because amphibians are generally thought to remain close to thermal equilibrium with their environments. Aquatic amphibians are essentially at the same temperature as the water because of the rapid heat transfer in that medium and the high heat capacity of water. Conduction dominates the heat exchange of fossorial caecilians, and their body temperatures should be essentially at environmental (soil) temperature. Terrestrial frogs and salamanders, in general being small, have relatively low capacities for heat storage but can exchange heat rapidly

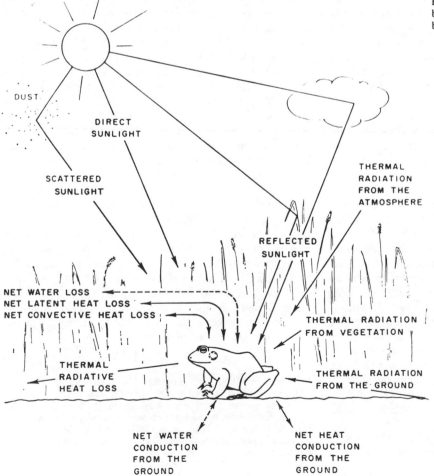

Fig. 4.1 Avenues of heat and water exchange between a frog and its environment. (Reprinted, by permission, from Tracy 1976.)

via evaporation. Thus, terrestrial amphibians are usually assumed to approach thermal equilibrium with their surroundings rapidly. Under most circumstances, then, an amphibian is thought to be near steady-state energy balance with the environment. Few studies have examined the rate of change of body temperatures in amphibians (Lillywhite 1975; Wygoda 1988a), and, to our knowledge, none have done so under natural conditions.

In steady state, no net energy flow occurs between an amphibian and its environment, so that energy flows into the animal are equal to energy flows out of the animal, or ENERGY IN = ENERGY OUT.

An amphibian receives energy in the form of solar and thermal radiation from the environment and heat from metabolic activity and, under some circumstances, from condensation. Energy leaves the animal in the form of thermal radiation to the environment, convection to the atmosphere, evaporation, and conduction to the substrate. These factors are combined into an energy budget equation following the convention of Gates (1980),

(1) $$Q_{abs} + M = R + C + \lambda E + G,$$

where

Q_{abs} = radiation absorbed
by the surface of the animal (W · m^{-2})
M = metabolic heat production (W · m^{-2})
R = radiation emitted
by the surface of the animal (W · m^{-2})
C = energy lost by convection (W · m^{-2})
λE = heat lost by evaporation
or gained by condensation (W · m^{-2})
G = heat lost by conduction
(through direct physical contact of the animal
with soil, water, or substrate; W · m^{-2})

Note that C, λE, and G may be either positive (energy flowing from the animal to the environment) or negative (energy flowing from the environment to the animal). Heat exchange via each of these pathways can be described by more detailed models of mass and energy exchange. In describing these models, we will draw heavily on engineering principles (Kreith 1973; Streeter and Wylie 1975; Tracy, Welch, and Porter 1980; White 1984) and applications of those principles to biology (Bakken and Gates 1975; Bakken, Santee, and Erskine 1985; Campbell 1977; Feder and Burggren 1985a; Gates 1962, 1980; Gates and Schmerl 1975; Mitchell 1976; Monteith 1973; Porter and Gates 1969; Porter et al. 1973; Rosenberg 1974; Spotila and Berman 1976; Tracy 1976, 1982; Vogel 1981). Most of the equations that follow (many of them developed quite some time ago) come from the engineering literature. Since it is their application to amphibians that is of interest here, we will forgo detailed citations of many of the basic principles and equations. Further, it is quite impossible to review all of the details of environment biophysics in this chapter. Interested readers should consult the above sources for the details. Among those sources, Campbell (1977) and Monteith (1973) provide quite accessible introductions to environmental biophysics. Gates (1980) is more complete but consequently more technical. Porter and Gates (1969), Porter et al. (1973), and Tracy (1982) provide

excellent introductions to the modeling of heat transfer in ectothermic animals, and Tracy (1976) gives a model of the heat and water exchanges of a leopard frog. Vogel (1981) provides a quite readable (and witty) introduction to the fluid mechanics concepts of environmental biophysics.

In the discussion that follows, we will concentrate, in many cases, on the heat exchanges of amphibians in the more complex terrestrial environment. We do not imply that the terrestrial habitat is more important than others. Rather, energy balances in other, more homogeneous environments with fewer avenues of heat exchange are regarded as simpler cases of the terrestrial energy balance.

Solar Radiation and Spectral Properties of Skin

A major potential source of heat gain for a terrestrial amphibian is the absorption of solar and thermal radiation. An animal receives radiant energy from a variety of environmental sources and presents different surface areas to each of these sources. The radiation absorbed, Q_{abs} (W·m^{-2}), by the animal over its entire surface area, A (m^2), is

(2) $$AQ_{abs} = a_S A_S S + a_s A_s s + a_r A_r r,$$

where

S = direct sunlight (W·m^{-2})
s = skylight (scattered radiation from sky or
surroundings; W·m^{-2})
r = reflected sunlight and skylight (W·m^{-2})
a = absorptance to direct (a_S), scattered (a_s), and
reflected (a_r) radiation
A_S = area exposed to direct sunlight (m^2)
A_s = area exposed to skylight (m^2)
A_r = area exposed to reflected sunlight and skylight (m^2)

The areas receiving radiation are effective rather than actual areas and are defined as follows: The area of the animal's projection on a plane normal to the sun's rays is A_S. The areas absorbing scattered and reflected radiation are based on the effective radiation area, A_e (m^2), which is the area of the animal with all concave areas filled. A_e is thus smaller than the area of the skin and can be measured with a photodermoplanimeter (Halliday and Hugo 1963). The effective area exposed to skylight (A_s) is approximately $A_e/2$. The effective area exposed to reflected sunlight (A_r) is $A_e/2$ less the surface area in contact with the ground. The effective absorptances (a_S, a_s, and a_r) are determined by both the spectral distribution of the incident radiation and the spectral absorptance ("color") of the animal. The procedure for computing effective absorptance is described by Porter and Gates (1969) and Gates (1980).

The effective absorptances of amphibians are quite variable, and accuracy requires measurement of spectral absorptance at wavelengths from 0.3 to 2.5 μm with a spectroreflectometer. Visual appearance is an unreliable guide, as near-infrared (0.7 to 2.5 μm) absorptance is quite variable. Some green frogs have very low near-infrared absorptance (Cott 1940; Schwalm, Starrett, and McDiarmid 1977). The absorptance spectrum of the salamander *Plethodon ouachitae* (Plethodontidae) is more typical (fig. 4.2). The skin is strongly absorptive (i.e., dark-colored). Absorptance decreases from 0.3 to 1.3 μm, and shows a spectral pattern typical of mela-

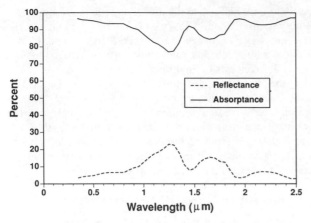

Fig. 4.2 Spectral reflectance and absorptance of the dorsal skin of a living adult salamander, *Plethodon ouachitae* (Plethodontidae), plotted as a function of wavelength.

Plethodon ouachitae (Rich Mountain Salamander)

Low Sun		High Sun	
Mean Reflectance	10.1%	Mean Reflectance	8.6%
Mean Absorptance	89.9%	Mean Absorptance	91.4%

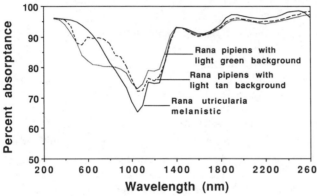

Fig. 4.3 Spectral absorptance of the dorsal skin of two color morphs of the frog *Rana pipiens* and one of *R. utricularia*, plotted as a function of wavelength. (Reprinted, by permission, from Tracy 1976.)

nin pigments. The remainder of the spectrum (1.3 to 2.5 μm) is essentially that of liquid water. Integrated against solar spectral irradiance, this absorptance spectrum gives an a_s of 0.93. Other salamanders we have measured have effective absorptances in the range from 0.71 to 0.93. Absorptance spectra for two color morphs of the frog *Rana pipiens* and for *R. utricularia* are shown in fig. 4.3. Integrated against solar spectral irradiance, these spectra give values for a_s of 0.83 to 0.87.

Thermal Radiation

Solar radiation may be avoided in deep shade or under rocks or logs, but all terrestrial amphibians exchange longwave "thermal radiation" with their surroundings. All surfaces radiate heat in proportion to the fourth power of the absolute temperature of the radiating surface and according to the emissivity (ε) of the surface. Thus,

$$(3) \qquad R = \varepsilon\sigma\,(T_r + 273.15)^4,$$

where

R = emitted thermal radiation (W · m⁻²)
ε = longwave infrared emissivity of skin
σ = the Stefan-Boltzmann constant (5.673×10^{-8} W · m⁻² · K⁻⁴)
T_r = body surface temperature (°C)

For an amphibian on land, T_r is equal to the surface temperature (T_s). For an amphibian in water $R = 0$, because thermal radiation is not propagated in water.

Due to their high water content, amphibians, like most other animals, are nearly perfect emitters and absorbers of thermal radiation with thermal absorptances of 0.95 to 1.0 (Gates 1980). Thus, an amphibian will absorb about 95 to 100% of the thermal radiation that strikes its surface. The average net heat transfer between an animal (at temperature T_r) and an enclosed environment (burrow, leaf litter, or closed forest canopy, at ambient temperature T_a) is

$$(4) \qquad R = A_R \varepsilon\sigma[(T_r + 273.15)^4 - (T_a + 273.15)^4]$$

where

$A_R = (A_s + A_r)$ area exposed to thermal radiation (W · m⁻²)
ε = longwave absorptance (≈ 0.96)
T_a = air temperature (°C)

The situation is more complex in an open habitat, where nearby surfaces are not all at the same temperature. The simplest case is an amphibian in the open, exposed to the sky and to the ground (at temperature T_g). The sky has an effective radiant temperature (T_{sk}) that depends on both the temperature of the air and the amount of moisture in the atmosphere (see Brutsaert 1975). Then

$$(5) \qquad R = \sigma\varepsilon[A_s(T_r^4 - T_{sk}^4) + A_r(T_r^4 - T_g^4)].$$

(N.B.: in this case, for the sake of clarity, we have assumed that all temperatures are expressed in °K rather than in °C).

A frog sitting in the open at night will lose heat to the night sky. The clear night sky has a radiant temperature of about 20°C below air temperature, and an overcast sky has a radiant temperature of only 5° to 10°C below air temperature (Gates 1980). Closed vegetative canopies, however, will have temperatures closer to air temperature (air temperatures near the ground below such canopies will also be warmer). On a typical summer night in the beech-maple forest alongside Douglas Lake, Michigan, the difference between ground temperature and the radiant temperature of the canopy as measured with a Barnes infrared thermometer was not more than 1.5°C (Spotila unpublished data; fig. 4.4). Other habitats may require more complex averaging (see Love 1968).

Convection

Convective heat loss is the removal of heat from a surface (e.g., skin) by a cooler fluid moving by that surface. If the fluid is warmer than the surface, the surface gains heat. Very near the surface of the animal, the velocity of the fluid varies depending on the distance from the animal (Gates 1980; Streeter and Wylie 1975; Vogel 1981). Indeed, at the skin surface, fluid velocity is assumed to be zero (the "no-slip"

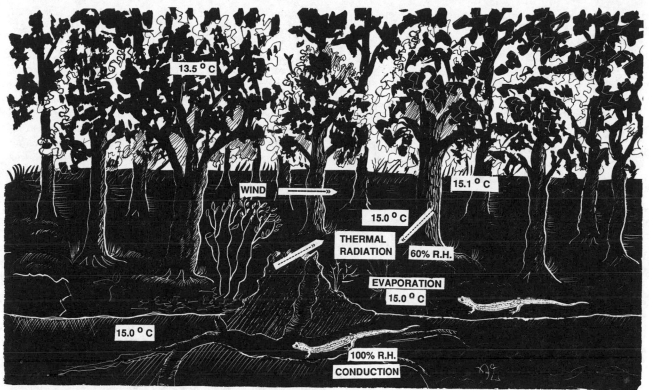

Fig. 4.4 Thermal environment in a beech-maple forest at Douglas Lake, Michigan, at 2300, 1 July 1970. Eight salamanders were active in a 2-m² area at the base of a maple tree where the temperatures were measured. The salamanders, *Plethodon cinereus* (Plethodontidae), were operating in essentially a blackbody cavity because the forest floor, herbaceous vegetation, and tree canopy were all at similar temperatures. (Drawing by A. List.)

condition). Thus, at the skin surface, heat transfer occurs by "diffusion" (i.e., conduction), and fluid mixing and mass transport become progressively more important further from the skin surface. The film of reduced fluid velocity near the surface is called a boundary layer and can be visualized by Schlieren photography (Gates 1980; Monteith 1973). Since the boundary layer is thin compared to the amphibian it surrounds, and the transfer of heat across the boundary layer is of greater interest than microscale processes within the layer, convection is often modeled as a two-step process in which heat is first conducted across an idealized, still boundary layer and then carried away by mass flow.

Diffusion across this idealized boundary layer, being the slower process, is the rate-limiting step. Factors that reduce the thickness of the boundary layer across which heat must travel by conduction or that increase the rate of conduction, then, increase rates of convective heat transfer. The rate of conduction increases when the temperature gradient across the boundary layer increases, or when the thermal conductivity of the fluid is changed. Water has a higher thermal conductivity than air, so convective heat loss will be higher in water than in air (with boundary layers of the same thickness). More viscous fluids will lead to thicker boundary layers (see Vogel 1981 for a description of the different measures of viscosity). All other things being equal, a boundary layer in water will be thinner than that in air because the dynamic viscosity of water is lower than that of air. Higher fluid velocities in the "free stream" result in thinner boundary layers.

Thus, the higher the free-stream velocity, the higher the rate of convective heat transfer. In laminar (i.e., nonturbulent) flows, increased fluid velocity leads to increased shear, thinning the boundary layer. As flow rate continues to increase, however, turbulence develops, and local eddies further thin the boundary layer (see Vogel 1981).

The geometry of the surface and the flow affect the pattern of fluid flow across the surface and therefore affect the thickness of the boundary layer. At the leading edge of a thin, flat plate, oriented parallel to fluid flow, the boundary layer is relatively thin, but it increases in thickness further back along the plate. Any bends, curves, nooks, crannies, or appendages will tend to deflect the fluid flow and alter the boundary layer thickness. Thus, the thickness of the boundary layer is not uniform over the whole organism. Calculation of a convection coefficient for an animal requires one to integrate convective heat transfer over the entire body surface area to get an average boundary layer thickness. Attempts to do so for any but the most regular and well-behaved surfaces and defined flow directions has led engineers to develop a computation-intense field known as numerical fluid mechanics. Such techniques are beyond the scope of this chapter, and the means of most biologists.

The rate of convective heat transfer, then, is affected by the rate of fluid (e.g., air, water) flow, the properties of the fluid, the size and characteristics of the surface over which the fluid flows, and the temperature difference between the surface and the fluid. The effects of these complex interactions are described by an empirical convection coefficient, h_c ($W \cdot m^{-2} \cdot {}°C^{-1}$), such that

$$(6) \qquad C = Ah_c(T_r - T_a),$$

where

A = surface area of the animal (m^2)
T_r = surface temperature of the animal (°C)
T_a = fluid temperature (°C)

The convection coefficient can be calculated for organisms with simple shapes (e.g., spheres) under constrained conditions. In practice, however, convection coefficients for biological systems are determined empirically in wind tunnels (Bakken and Gates 1975; Mitchell 1976; Spotila and Berman 1976; Tracy 1976). In many cases, convection coefficients must be approximated when they are not known. Based on the relationship between Nusselt and Reynolds numbers (in oversimplified terms, dimensionless expressions of the convection coefficient and rate of fluid flow respectively; see eqs. [21] and [22]) for airflow across an assortment of biological and geometrical shapes, Mitchell (1976) found that h_c could be approximated for terrestrial organisms by

$$(7) \qquad h_c = 6.77V^{0.6}D^{-0.4}$$

$$(8) \qquad D = (\text{volume})^{1/3}$$

where

D = the characteristic dimension of the animal (m)
V = wind speed ($m \cdot s^{-1}$)

For animals ranging from spiders to cows, Mitchell found that equations (7) and (8) provided estimates of h_c that were usually accurate to within 5%, although deviations of up to 20% occurred. For amphibians in flowing water, the coefficient in equation (7) is 811 instead of 6.77. Volume can be estimated by dividing mass by density. One would expect that the orientation of an amphibian relative to the direction of fluid flow would affect the convection coefficient. However, orientation seems to affect the convection coefficient only slightly for model leopard frogs in stereotypical sitting positions (Tracy 1976).

In the natural environment, airflow is normally turbulent, which enhances convection. Mitchell (1976) found that, for an object resting on the ground, outdoor turbulence increases h_c to 1.7 times the value given by equation (7). Note that the wind speed (V) in equation (7) is the wind speed experienced by the animal, not the wind speed measured at a reference height (commonly 1.0 or 1.5 m). The earth, like any surface, has a boundary layer, within which many terrestrial amphibians will live. The calculation of wind speed profiles in the first few meters above the ground is discussed by Rosenberg (1974), Campbell (1977), and Tracy (1982).

All of the equations for convective heat transfer presented so far have been for animals in flowing water or air, that is, for "forced" convection. Stationary animals in still water or air cannot convect heat to a nonexistent fluid flow. The variation of fluid densities with temperature, however, leads to thermally induced flows around bodies that are warmer or cooler than their environments. Take the case of an amphibian sitting in air cooler than the animal. Heat is conducted into the air around the animal, warming the air which expands and rises, carrying away the heat that had warmed it. This phenomenon is known as natural or free convection. No single relation similar to Mitchell's (equation [7]) has been developed for free convection, in part because the process is very sensitive to geometric details. Instead a series of relations exists and is discussed by Tracy and Sotherland (1979) and Gates (1980). The importance of forced convection increases from negligible at very low fluid velocities to dominant at high velocities. Gates (1980) recommends treating wind speeds of less than $0.1 \ m \cdot s^{-1}$ as producing free convection and those greater than $0.1 \ m \cdot s^{-1}$ as producing forced convection. (For detailed treatments of convection from vertebrate ectotherms see Porter and Gates 1969; Mitchell 1976; Kowalski and Mitchell 1976; Campbell 1977; Tracy and Sotherland 1979; Spotila, Weinheimer, and Paganelli 1981; Tracy 1982.)

Evaporative Heat Loss

Evaporation of water from an animal results in the loss of heat energy of $2.44 \times 10^6 \ J \cdot kg^{-1}$ at ordinary biological temperatures. This is the latent heat of vaporization of water, λ, which varies slightly with the temperature at which the evaporation takes place (skin surface temperature for an amphibian). The thermal energetics and mechanisms of evaporation from amphibians have been discussed by Spotila (1972), Tracy (1976), Spotila and Berman (1976), and O'Connor (1989). For an animal in water, no evaporation takes place, and evaporative cooling does not occur.

A plethora of terms are used to describe the wetness of air, including relative humidity, water vapor density, water vapor pressure, and water potential. The multiplicity of terms arises from the different uses of humidity, and confusion arises because the solubility of water vapor in air rises exponentially as air temperature increases. Thus, the relationships among the terms depend on air temperature. Water vapor density is descriptively named. It is the mass of water vapor in a given volume of air. Thus, its units are mass per unit volume, $kg \cdot m^{-3}$ in the SI system. Water vapor density is also called absolute humidity. Water vapor pressure is the partial pressure of water vapor in the air. It has units of pressure, $N \cdot m^{-2}$ or Pa in the SI system. A kilopascal is a pressure of 1,000 newtons per square meter (approximately 0.01 of atmospheric pressure). Conveniently, at atmospheric pressure, water vapor and dry and wet air all behave approximately as predicted for an ideal gas (Gates 1980; Rosenberg 1974). Thus, water vapor density and vapor pressure are related by the ideal gas law

$$(9) \qquad p = \frac{nRT}{V} = \rho \frac{R}{M} T,$$

where

p = pressure (Pa)
V = volume (m^3)
n = number of moles of gas in V
R = gas constant ($8.31 \ J \cdot K^{-1} \cdot mole^{-1}$)
T = absolute temperature (K)

ρ = density of gas (kg · m^{-3})
M = molecular weight of gas (kg · mole^{-1} = 0.0290 for dry air)

When applied to water vapor, the ideal gas law is usually written as

$$(10) \qquad \rho_w = \frac{e}{RT} M_w,$$

where

ρ_w = water vapor density (kg · m^{-3})
e = water vapor pressure (Pa)
M_w = molecular weight of water (0.018 kg · mole^{-1})

Thus, at constant temperature, vapor density and vapor pressure are linearly related. Recall that as air is warmed the saturation vapor density increases. The actual relationship is complicated (see List 1951; Tracy, Welch, and Porter 1980), but a useful approximation for vapor pressure between 0° and 40°C is given by (Rosenberg 1974)

$$(11) \qquad \log_{10} e_s = 0.02604 \, T_a + 2.82488,$$

where

e_s = saturation vapor pressure (Pa)
T_a = air temperature (°C)

Relative humidity is a ratio of the actual water vapor pressure to the vapor pressure in saturated air at the same temperature (e/e_s). It can be expressed either as a fraction (0–1) or as a percentage. Now, if we fix the density of water vapor in a given volume of air and warm the air, the water vapor pressure will rise (eq. [10]) while the relative humidity will fall. The relative humidity falls because saturation vapor pressure rises more rapidly than the water vapor pressure. Likewise, the saturation deficit ($e_s - e$), sometimes used as a measure of the driving force for evaporation from saturated surfaces, rises.

The last of the terms used to discuss humidity, water potential, is the one that causes the most problems for animal biologists. Although used extensively by plant physiologists, water potential has been used by animal biologists almost exclusively to describe the transfer of water between an animal and the soil or a liquid solution. Water potential is defined in terms of an equivalent hydrostatic pressure difference (pure water a fixed distance above ground at atmospheric pressure has $\Psi = 0$) and has units of pressure (Pa). A convention that causes considerable trouble because of its inconsistent use is that substances drier than pure water have negative water potentials; the drier the substance, the more negative the water potential. Thus, the water potential of a leopard frog that is nearly fully hydrated (97% of standard hydration) is −50 kPa, while that of a frog at 70% of standard hydration is −400 kPa (Tracy 1976). Confusingly, the dehydrated frog is sometimes said to have the larger water potential. To make matters worse, the negative signs are sometimes dropped as a matter of convenience. This usage is incorrect.

The concept of water potential is useful in describing many forms of water transport. Any water transport process, at equilibrium, will have equal water potentials in the two compartments between which water is being exchanged. A wide variety of driving forces can be translated into water potential (e.g., osmotic, capillary, gravitational, and static pressures), and water potential is thus most useful in describing water transport processes where several such forces are important. The water potential of vapor in air is approximated by (Tracy, Welch, and Porter 1980)

$$(12) \qquad \Psi = 4.615 \times 10^5 \, T_a \ln(\text{RH}),$$

where

Ψ = water potential (Pa)
T_a = air temperature (K)
RH = relative humidity (0–1)

Water potential is most useful in discussions of evaporation in amphibians where the aim is to discover the effects of osmolytes in the cutaneous secretions on evaporation. The water potential of pure water is nearly zero and that of 1-mol NaCl or KCl is approximately −500 Pa at 20°C. Saturated air has a water potential of nearly zero, whereas air with a relative humidity of 99.5% has a water potential of approximately −7 × 10^5 Pa at 20°C (Tracy, Welch, and Porter 1980). Thus, in most situations the humidity of the air will be more important than the osmotic composition of secretions in determining the evaporative water loss of wet-skinned animals, because unsaturated air has a much more negative water potential than body fluids with solutes at almost any physiological concentration.

For further discussion of the concepts above see Rose 1966, Rosenberg 1974, and Gates 1980. Useful tabulations of vapor densities, vapor pressures, and water potentials are contained in List 1951 and Tracy, Welch, and Porter 1980.

The processes of molecular diffusion and gross mixing of the air near the animal which are responsible for convective heat transfer also account for the transport of gases such as water vapor, carbon dioxide, and oxygen between an animal and its environment. The general form of the transport equation (sometimes known as Fick's law) is the same for all processes. For mass transport of water vapor from an amphibian with a fully wetted skin, this equation takes the form

$$(13) \qquad E_c = Ah_e(\rho_s - \text{RH}\rho_a) = A(1/r_e)(\rho_a - \text{RH}\rho_a),$$

where

E_c = rate of water transport (kg · s^{-1})
A = surface area (m^2)
h_e = mass convection coefficient (m · s^{-1})
ρ_s = saturation water vapor density at skin surface (kg · m^{-3})
ρ_a = saturation water vapor density in ambient air (kg · m^{-3})
RH = relative humidity (0–1)
r_e = external (convective) resistance to water vapor transport (s · m^{-1})

Resistance notation (resistance being the inverse of conductance, $r = 1/h$) is commonly used for mass transport and is especially convenient when several different processes operate in series (see below).

Because heat and mass (water vapor, CO_2, etc.) transfer

are all accomplished by the same mechanisms, the close relationship among the coefficients for heat and mass transport is not surprising. For heat and water vapor transfer, the relationship is known as the Lewis rule:

$$(14) \qquad r_e = 0.93 \, r_h = 0.93 \, \rho c_p / h_c$$

where

r_e = external resistance to water vapor transfer (s · m^{-1})
r_h = external resistance to heat transfer (s · m^{-1})
h_c = heat transfer (convection) coefficient (W · m^{-2} · °C^{-1})
ρ = density of air (kg · m^{-3})
c_p = specific heat of air at constant pressure (J · kg^{-1} · °C^{-1})

Strictly speaking, ρc_p varies with the temperature of the surroundings, but a constant value of 1,200 J · m^{-3} · °C^{-1} is commonly used in biological studies.

In most amphibians, the skin provides negligible resistance to evaporative water loss, and equations (13) and (14) can be used ignoring cutaneous resistance to water vapor transport. Some frogs, in fact, secrete watery mucus onto their dorsal integuments when heat-stressed, and thus circumvent any possible cutaneous resistance to the diffusion of water vapor (Lillywhite and Licht 1975). Under these conditions of negligible internal resistance to water loss, the boundary layer provides the only effective resistance (200 to 300 s · m^{-1}) to water loss. In contrast, reptiles have skin resistances ranging from 4,700 to 78,800 s · m^{-1} (Lillywhite and Maderson 1982), and bird eggs have internal resistance of 38,700 s · m^{-1} (Spotila, Weinheimer, and Paganelli 1981). Boundary layer resistance in lizards and bird eggs is on the order of the boundary layer resistance in amphibians. Thus, boundary layer resistance is of relatively little importance in comparison to the large internal resistance in reptiles (Tracy 1982).

Some frogs, for example, *Phyllomedusa* (Hylidae), have a significant resistance to water loss through their skins due to the presence of an extraepidermal lipid barrier formed from epidermal wax gland secretions, which the frogs wipe over the entire surface of the skin (Blaylock, Ruibal, and Platt-Aloia 1976). Other frogs have significant cutaneous resistances to water loss due to intercellular epidermal lipids (*Litoria* [Hylidae]; Withers, Hillman, and Drewes 1984), multiple dermal iridiophores (*Chiromantis* [Rhacophoridae]; Drewes et al. 1977), or dried mucus (*Hyperolius* [Hyperoliidae]: Geise and Linsenmair 1986; Kobelt and Linsenmair 1986; *Hyla* [Hylidae]: Wygoda 1984, 1988a). When burrowed, many desert frogs form a keratinized cocoon of stratum corneum that appears to offer a barrier to the outward movement of water (Lee and Mercer 1967; Loveridge and Crayé 1979; McClanahan, Shoemaker, and Ruibal 1976).

In amphibians with significant cutaneous resistance to water vapor transport (i.e., without fully wetted surfaces), both internal (r_i) and external (r_e) resistances must be considered when estimating evaporative water loss. These two resistances act in series, and sum to give the total resistance to water vapor transport ($r_i + r_e$), as with electrical resistances in series. Because the internal tissues are nearly saturated with water, the equation for overall water vapor transport becomes

$$(15) \qquad E_c = A \, \Delta \rho / r = A \, \frac{\rho_s(T_s) - RH \, \rho_a(T_a)}{r_i + r_e},$$

where

E_c = evaporative water loss (kg · s^{-1})
A = surface area (m^2)
$\Delta \rho$ = change in vapor density from tissues to air (kg · m^{-3})
r = total resistance to water vapor transport (s · m^{-1})
$\rho_s(T_s)$ = saturated water vapor density at tissue temperature (kg · m^{-3})
$\rho_a(T_a)$ = saturated water vapor density at air temperature (kg · m^{-3})
RH = atmospheric relative humidity (0–1)
r_i = internal (cutaneous) resistance to vapor transport (s · m^{-1})
r_e = external (boundary layer) resistance to vapor transport (s · m^{-1})

The actual process of transport of water from inside the skin to the skin surface is more complicated than indicated by a simple resistance model because body water on the inner side of the cutaneous barrier is not in the vapor phase (Zucker 1980). However, Mautz (1982) discussed the theoretical aspects of this problem and concluded that such models are appropriate for most physiological and ecological studies of water loss because they avoid an intractable thermodynamic analysis of water transport with a phase change across a permeability barrier. However, the investigator should recognize that r_i may depend upon other factors, including temperature, vapor concentration, hydration state of the skin, and regional variation in skin structure.

Traditional wisdom (Adolph 1932) asserts that atmospheric humidity never, or almost never, condenses on the skin of an amphibian because metabolism will warm the animal, raising body temperature above that of the surrounding atmosphere. Such a situation would prevent any condensation because the vapor pressure of water at the skin surface would be higher than that in the surrounding air, leading to evaporation from the skin. In some situations, however, atmospheric water could condense on the skin of an amphibian. The requisite conditions include (1) air that is locally saturated (or very nearly so) with water vapor and (2) amphibian skin that is cooler than the air surrounding it. That locally saturated atmosphere can exist in many environments is evidenced by the nocturnal formation of dew in desert habitats. Cool skin can result from two situations. First, amphibians can be cooler than their environments for a brief period of time if and when they shuttle between microhabitats (Lasiewski and Bartholomew 1969). Second, in situations with low incident thermal and solar radiation (e.g., an amphibian in the open on a clear night, especially if the ground is cool), thermal radiative exchange with the night sky can maintain body temperatures far enough below air temperatures to encourage condensation in a saturated atmosphere (Tracy 1976). To our knowledge, the occurrence and frequency of such phenomena have not been investigated.

The presence of a wet skin and the associated evaporative water loss confers some stability of body temperature upon most amphibians (Lillywhite 1975; Lillywhite and Licht

1975; O'Connor 1989; Tracy 1975, 1976, 1979a). The saturation water vapor density increases rapidly and nonlinearly with increased body temperature. Thus, at higher temperatures, a small rise in body temperature results in greatly increased evaporative water loss and evaporative cooling, slowing any further increases in body temperature. To the extent that cutaneous resistance inhibits evaporative water loss and the consequent damping of body-temperature variability, frogs with significant resistance to evaporative water loss would be predicted to have greater need and opportunities for thermoregulation (O'Connor 1989; Shoemaker et al. 1987).

Conduction

Conduction can be an important component of the heat energy budgets of amphibians because the animals often have a considerable portion of their ventral surface in contact with the ground. The process is conceptually simple. For a warm animal on a cool substrate, heat diffuses from the core of the animal to and across the skin, across the contact area between the animal and the substrate, and then away through the substrate.

Unfortunately, conduction to the substrate can be a nightmare to deal with analytically, for several reasons. First, as with convection, the geometry of the interface between the animal and the substrate is important. Furthermore, the geometry depends not only on the usual shape of the animal, but also on the animal's posture and possibly the surface characteristics of the substrate. Second, the temperature of the substrate on which the amphibian sits is modified by the very act of the amphibian sitting there (Tracy 1976). Both horizontal (along the surface of the soil) and vertical (into the soil) temperature gradients develop in the soil (Tracy 1976), and the gradients vary with time. Third, a complete evaluation requires one to consider conduction within the animal and within the soil. Neither the animal nor the soil are homogeneous bodies. Inhomogeneous animals have been assumed to be homogeneous in many studies with substantial success. The same is not necessarily true for soils. Soil conductivities and diffusivities differ depending on soil type, degree of compaction, and water content (Rosenberg 1974), and vertical (and sometimes horizontal) differences in soil thermal properties are commonplace. Fourth, conduction makes less tenable one of the common hidden assumptions of many energy balance models, radial symmetry. Most models assume that all energy gains and losses are spread equally around the skin surface (see Porter and Gates 1969; Tracy 1982). This is another simplifying assumption tolerated simply because it appears to work. A frog sitting in full sun on a cool (e.g., due to evaporative cooling) substrate causes problems for such an assumption because the frog has a warm dorsal surface and a cool ventral surface (Tracy 1976, 1982). Thus, no "core" exists. Fifth, at least one of the resistances involved, the "contact resistance" (Kreith 1973; White 1984) between the amphibian and the substrate, is difficult to evaluate. Finally, despite some simplifying assumptions, the mathematical solutions to such problems can be dauntingly complex.

Three approaches to the modeling of conduction to a substrate have been taken. The first is to assume that the major resistance to conduction is within the surface layers of the amphibian. The thermal conductivity of amphibian skin lies between 0.392 and 0.502 $W \cdot m^{-1} \cdot °C^{-1}$ (Drane 1981; Gates 1980). Since the conductivity of many wet substrates (especially wet porous soil, e.g., wet sand or clay, 1.6–2.0 $W \cdot m^{-1} \cdot °C^{-1}$) is greater than that of tissues, the rate-limiting step in conduction is usually within the tissues of the animal (Monteith 1973; Spotila, Soule, and Gates 1972; Tracy 1976). The rate of conductive heat transfer is then calculated as

$$(16) \qquad G = K_f A_g \left(\frac{T_b - T_g}{d_f} \right),$$

where

G = conduction to the substrate
K_f = conductivity of the skin ($W \cdot m^{-1} \cdot °C^{-1}$)
A_g = area of the animal in contact with the substrate (m^2)
T_b = body temperature of the animal (°C)
T_g = temperature of the substrate (°C)
d_f = thickness of the skin (m)

This method is the simplest, but the least likely to be accurate with drier, lower conductivity substrates. This method also ignores any significant effects of the animal's geometry and of conduction through the animal.

The second method still assumes that the limiting resistance is that of conduction within the animal, but abandons the thermally homogeneous model for an animal that has dorsal and ventral surfaces that may be at different temperatures and thus have conduction between them (Tracy 1976). One then computes two equilibrium energy balances, one for the dorsal surface of the animal, and another for some central plane in the animal. Conduction between the dorsum and the central plane and between the central plane and the venter are computed using "shape factors" (see Tracy 1976, 1982). Although more realistic than the first method, this method has the disadvantage of being considerably more complex.

The third method is to assume that the major resistance to heat conduction is in the substrate and then calculate a heat transfer coefficient similar to a convection coefficient based on the conductivity of the soil (Ackerman et al. 1985).

$$(17) \qquad G = H_g A_g (T_b - T_g)$$
$$(18) \qquad H_g = 2.0 k_g / D,$$

where

G = conduction to the ground (W)
H_g = thermal conductance between venter and substrate ($W \cdot m^{-2} \cdot °C^{-1}$)
A_g = skin area in contact with the ground (m^2)
T_b = body temperature (°C)
T_g = substrate temperature (°C)
k_g = thermal conductivity of the soil ($W \cdot m^{-1} \cdot °C^{-1}$)
D = characteristic dimension of the animal (m)

This method has the disadvantages of ignoring resistances to conduction within the animal and being based on soil thermal properties that are difficult to determine. None of these methods treat internal and substrate conduction in an integrated manner. Thus, the choice of a model for conductive heat exchange with the substrate should be made with care and based on where the predominant resistance to conduction is thought to lie (skin, all tissues, substrate).

Metabolism

The metabolic rates of amphibians are directly dependent upon body temperature, rising as body temperature rises (see Bennett 1978). Except in the case of actively calling anurans, however, metabolic heat production is low, both compared to that in birds and mammals and compared to the heat fluxes to and from the amphibian by conduction, convection, evaporation, and radiation. Thus, metabolism plays a very small part in the overall heat energy budget of amphibians and is usually ignored in models of amphibian body temperatures.

Integration

To examine the relative importance of different pathways of heat exchange in an ecologically meaningful context, we computed equilibrium heat flows and body temperatures for a model frog under a variety of different circumstances. We used a heat and water transfer model similar to that used by Tracy (1976) and varied four factors: (1) the kind of radiative environment (open versus shaded), (2) the wind speed (calm versus windy), (3) whether the frog was sitting on a conductive (sand) or insulating (grass) substrate, and (4) whether the frog had significant cutaneous resistance to evaporative water loss. A frog in an open, sunny habitat was assumed to receive $800 \text{ W} \cdot \text{m}^{-2}$ of solar radiation, while an animal in deep shade was assumed to receive $100 \text{ W} \cdot \text{m}^{-2}$. Wind speeds used were $0.3 \text{ m} \cdot \text{s}^{-1}$ (calm) and $2.0 \text{ m} \cdot \text{s}^{-1}$ (windy). Animals sitting on the ground (sand) were assumed to exchange heat with the ground as described by Tracy (1976). Otherwise, conduction was assumed to be negligible. "Wet-skinned" frogs were assumed to have no measurable cutaneous resistance to water vapor transport. Because of the range of cutaneous resistance values reported for frogs, we chose, as an extreme, an aquatic reptile, and assumed that a "dry-skinned" frog (one with high cutaneous resistance) lost water at the same rate as a turtle with the same surface area (Foley and Spotila 1978). In all cases, air and ground temperatures were assumed to be 25°C.

Results of the simulations are given in table 4.1. Three general patterns are discernable. (1) In wet-skinned animals not in direct contact with high-conductance substrates such as rocks or standing water (see O'Connor 1989), evaporation and solar radiation are the two most important pathways of heat exchange, each often being larger than the sum of the heat flows via convection, conduction, and thermal radiation. Concomitantly, changes in heat exchange via convection, conduction, and thermal radiation (e.g., due to changes in wind speed, or microhabitat) are usually compensated almost entirely by reciprocal changes in heat flow via evaporation. (2) Body temperatures of wet-skinned animals are lower than those of drier-skinned animals under the same conditions. (3) Body temperatures of wet-skinned animals are less perturbed by changes in the thermal environment (wind speed, conduction, solar and thermal radiation) than are the body temperatures of drier-skinned animals. Thus, "waterproof" frogs save water but are likely to have higher and more labile body temperatures (26.0° to 42.4°C under simulation conditions) than would animals without impediments to evapora-

tion (23.4° to 28.3°C) under the same conditions. Indeed, some waterproof frogs secrete watery mucus onto their skin surfaces as the frogs' body temperatures rise, thereby increasing evaporative water loss and slowing further increases in body temperature (Kaul and Shoemaker 1989; Shoemaker et al. 1987).

We also conducted a more formal sensitivity analysis of the response of amphibian body temperature to changes in the thermal environment and important morphological parameters. The analytic strategy was to choose a set of reference conditions and then, changing only one variable at a time, to examine the changes in predicted body temperature induced by specified changes in each variable (table 4.2). The same thermal model was used as in the preceding analysis. The analysis was run for an animal sitting on the sand (high conductivity) or on grass, and for animals in an open habitat where the radiative environment includes open sky, and in closed vegetative canopies, where the radiative environment includes mostly vegetation at air temperature.

As might be expected from the form of the heat transfer equations, the effect of variation in all parameters but wind speed was nearly linear regardless of the reference and increment values used (data not shown). To gauge the effect of wind speed, we show the effect of a $0.1 \text{ m} \cdot \text{s}^{-1}$ increment in wind speed at low ($0.3–0.7 \text{ m} \cdot \text{s}^{-1}$) and high ($1.5–3.0 \text{ m} \cdot \text{s}^{-1}$) wind speeds, because body temperature was more sensitive to increases in wind velocity at low than at high wind speeds.

The response of body temperature to the independent variables did not vary greatly among habitats (table 4.2). The predicted temperatures of "dry-skinned" amphibians (i.e., those having high cutaneous resistance to water vapor transport) are often two to three times as sensitive to body mass, color, and environmental variables as those of "wet-skinned" frogs. However, temperatures of wet-skinned animals were more sensitive to changes in humidity than those of dry-skinned frogs.

Equilibrium versus Transient Energy Balances

So far, although we have said a great deal about mechanisms of heat exchange and the equilibrium body temperatures of amphibians, we have said little about heat storage by the animals and how quickly the animals will reach those temperatures. To correct this situation, we need to expand the verbal model that gives rise to equation (1) from

$$\text{ENERGY IN} = \text{ENERGY OUT}$$
(equilibrium energy balance)

to

$$\text{ENERGY IN} = \text{ENERGY OUT} + \text{ENERGY STORED}$$
(transient energy balance).

These two models differ in more than just the inclusion of an extra term in the transient model. The two models make different assumptions, are solved by different methods, and provide answers to different questions. Since the purpose of modeling energy exchange is to answer questions about animals, let us start with the questions the two models answer. Equilibrium energy balances provide information about the thermal environment of the animal. The body temperatures

TABLE 4.1. Predicted Body Temperatures and Rates of Heat Exchange via Major Pathways for a 50-g Leopard Frog, *Rana pipiens*

Habitat	Wind Speed (m·s⁻¹)	On Ground	Skin	Conduction (W)	Convection (W)	Evaporation (W)	Thermal Radiation (W)	Solar Radiation (W)	Body Temperature (°C)
Open Q_t = 800 W·m⁻²	0.3	Yes	Wet	0.36	0.50	2.81	1.48	5.14	28.3
			Dry	1.29	1.78	0.02	2.05	5.14	36.8
		No	Wet	—	0.57	3.06	1.51	5.14	28.8
			Dry	—	2.62	0.06	2.42	5.14	42.4
	2.0	Yes	Wet	0.01	0.03	3.83	1.27	5.14	25.1
			Dry	0.65	2.82	0.01	1.65	5.14	31.0
		No	Wet	—	0.03	3.84	1.27	5.14	25.1
			Dry	—	3.39	0.02	1.73	5.14	32.2
Sheltered Q_t = 100 W·m⁻²	0.3	Yes	Wet	0.08	0.11	0.88	0.05	0.64	24.3
			Dry	0.22	0.31	0.02	0.13	0.64	27.1
		No	Wet	—	0.13	0.83	0.05	0.64	24.1
			Dry	—	0.47	0.02	0.20	0.64	28.1
	2.0	Yes	Wet	0.17	0.73	1.64	0.10	0.64	23.4
			Dry	0.11	0.47	0.00	0.06	0.64	26.0
		No	Wet	—	0.78	1.52	0.10	0.64	23.4
			Dry	—	0.57	0.00	0.08	0.64	26.2

Notes: Air and ground temperatures = 25°C. Relative humidity = 85%. Model similar to that of Tracy 1976.

TABLE 4.2. Sensitivity of Amphibian Body Temperature to Animal Characteristics and Environmental Factors

Variable	Reference Value	Change	Venter on Ground		Venter Not on Ground	
			Wet	Dry	Wet	Dry
Air temperature						
T_a (constant RH)	25°C	1°C	0.82	0.89	0.75	0.73
T_a (constant ρ_a)	25°C	1°C	0.35	0.85	0.31	0.66
Ground temperature	25°C	1°C	0.03	0.08	0.11	0.29
Solar radiation	500 W·m⁻²	100 W·m⁻²	0.53	1.67	0.48	1.30
Relative humidity	85%	10%	1.59	0.12	1.41	0.10
Wind speed						
Low (0.3–0.7 m·s⁻¹)	0.5 m·s⁻¹	0.1 m·s⁻¹	−0.32	−0.68	−0.29	−0.34
High (1.5–3.0 m·s⁻¹)	2.0 m·s⁻¹	0.1 m·s⁻¹	−0.03	−0.08	−0.04	−0.06
Absorptance	0.86	0.1	0.16	0.49	0.14	0.38
Mass	50 g	0.5 log units	0.26	0.60	0.20	0.68

Note: Tabulated values are predicted changes in body temperature for a 50-g leopard frog (*Rana pipiens*) in response to stated change in animal characteristic or environmental variable. Model used for predictions is similar to that of Tracy 1976.

computed from equation (1) are those the animal would come to if the animal stayed in one place for a long time and neither the environment nor the animal changed (e.g., the animal does not lose enough water to change its thermal properties). Such models are useful in describing animal body temperatures only to the extent that the amphibian does stay in one place (or similar places) long enough to approach thermal equilibrium with the environment. Since, as we argued above, many amphibians tend to approach thermal equilibrium rather quickly, equilibrium models have proved useful in calculating the body temperatures of amphibians (O'Connor 1989; Porter and Tracy 1974; Spotila 1972; Tracy 1975, 1976, 1979a).

"Transient" energy balance models, on the other hand, predict how an amphibian's body temperature will change with time. If the amphibian is already at its equilibrium body temperature, no change in body temperature is predicted. Thus, an equilibrium model is a special case of the transient model in which only the "final" (equilibrium) body temperature is predicted. The more generalized transient model predicts body temperatures of amphibians in changing microhabitats and shuttling animals (before they reach equilibrium).

Then why does anyone ever bother to solve an equilibrium energy balance? There are several answers. The first is computational convenience. The solution of an equilibrium energy balance can usually be cast as the solution of an algebraic equation. The solution of transient energy balances, on the other hand, involves the solution of a differential equation, although this fact is usually hidden in the computer program that predicts the body temperatures. If the transient balance can be stated in simple enough terms, standard solutions of the model can often be found (Gates 1980; White 1984), but the mathematics of solving transient models is, in general, more complex than that for solving equilibrium balances. Thus, if equilibrium models are sufficient, they are preferable. The second reason for solving equilibrium models is that they are useful in understanding transient energy balances. The simplest, most easily understood, and most generalizable statements of transient energy balances (and those most likely to lead to standard solutions) are stated in terms of how quickly an animal's body temperature approaches its equilibrium body temperature (Bakken and Gates 1975; White 1984). Thus, the equilibrium model is required to understand the more generalized transient model. Finally, equilibrium energy balance models can be used to describe the thermal environment. Not only is such information useful in describing what temperatures are available to the amphibian, but it may serve as a predictor of animal behavior if animals change microhabitats before unacceptable body temperatures are reached. Thus, equilibrium and transient energy balance models provide different types of information about the thermal biology of amphibians. The modeling approach chosen should be appropriate to the question being asked about the animal. If information is needed on how quickly animals change temperatures, or on how body temperatures respond to rapidly varying environments, transient energy balance models are required. On the other hand, if one needs to know what temperature an amphibian will eventually attain, and the animal is likely to come close to that temperature, equilibrium models are sufficient.

Energy Storage

The term added to an equilibrium energy balance model to convert it to a transient energy balance is an energy storage term. Conservation of energy requires that, if energy flowing into (or generated within) the animal exceeds that flowing out, the excess be stored in the animal. The storage of thermal energy results in an increase in the animal's temperature. Likewise, if energy outflow exceeds inflow, the animal cools. The rate of cooling is given by

$$(19) \qquad \Delta E = mC_p \frac{dT_b}{dt},$$

where

$$
\begin{aligned}
\Delta E &= \text{energy storage (W)} \\
m &= \text{mass (kg)} \\
C_p &= \text{specific heat } (\text{J} \cdot \text{kg}^{-1} \cdot {}^\circ\text{C}^{-1}) \\
T_b &= \text{body temperature } ({}^\circ\text{C}) \\
t &= \text{time (s)}
\end{aligned}
$$

Note that, in this formulation, C_p is an average value of specific heat over the entire body, and the entire body is assumed to change temperature at the same rate. The energy storage term introduces two variables into the energy balance: time and the mass of the animal. The importance of time was discussed above. Mass affects the convection coefficient (equations [7] and [8]) and the surface areas for various exchanges, but this is the first explicit inclusion of mass in the energy balance. That inclusion has interesting implications. For equal rates of heat storage, the rate of change in body temperature is inversely proportional to mass. Thus, larger animals can absorb larger amounts of heat for the same change in body temperature, and are said to have more thermal inertia than smaller animals (Gates 1980; McNab 1978; Spotila 1980; Turner and Tracy 1986). The importance of thermal inertia to shuttling ectotherms has been investigated for reptiles (Dreisig 1984; Fraser and Grigg 1984; Gates 1980; Grigg, Drane, and Courtice 1979; Spotila 1980; Stevenson 1985a, 1985b; Tracy, Turner, and Huey 1986; Turner and Tracy 1986), but rarely for amphibians.

Newtonian Heating and Cooling

One of the simplest and best-known solutions of a transient energy balance is that for a "Newtonian" object (or animal). A Newtonian animal is one in which two conditions are met. First, the animal must not be thermally complex; that is, one must be able to assume that body temperatures are the same anywhere in the animal. Such is rarely true in amphibians, but the inaccuracies introduced are largely confined to the very early portions of the warming or cooling curve of an animal entering a stable environment (Turner 1987). Second, the animal's heat transfer must be "linear"; that is, rates of heat transfer by processes such as convection, thermal radiation, and evaporation must be linearly related to the difference between body and environmental temperatures (Bakken et al. 1974; Gates 1980). Again, this condition is unlikely to be true in amphibians. Thermal radiation depends on the fourth power of body temperature (eq. [4]), and evaporation depends on the water vapor density at the skin surface, which is complexly related to the body temperature (eqs. [10], [11], and [13]). In each case, linearized approximations are available (Penman 1958; Tracy et al. 1984), although those approximations can result in 4–5°C errors in predicted equilibrium body temperatures (Tracy et al. 1984). Despite these problems, amphibians, like many other objects, will behave approximately as Newtonian objects, at least over a range of several degrees of body temperature. Under such circumstances, the amphibian's body temperature can be predicted by

$$(20) \qquad T_b - T_e = (T_o - T_e) \exp\left(\frac{Ah}{mC_p}\, t\right),$$

where

$$
\begin{aligned}
T_b &= \text{body temperature at time } t \ ({}^\circ\text{C}) \\
T_e &= \text{equilibrium body temperature } ({}^\circ\text{C}) \\
T_o &= \text{initial body temperature } ({}^\circ\text{C}) \\
A &= \text{body surface area (m}^2) \\
h &= \text{combined heat transfer coefficient } (\text{W} \cdot \text{m}^{-2} \cdot {}^\circ\text{C}^{-1}) \\
m &= \text{mass (kg)} \\
C_p &= \text{specific heat of tissue } (\text{J} \cdot \text{kg}^{-1} \cdot {}^\circ\text{C}^{-1}) \\
t &= \text{time (s)}
\end{aligned}
$$

The combined heat transfer coefficient (h) is analogous to the convection coefficient but includes such exchange processes as thermal radiation and conduction. Methods for estimating such combined coefficients are given in Bakken et al. 1974 and Gates 1980 (see also Bakken 1981; Bakken and Gates 1975).

Body temperatures of Newtonian animals approach equilibrium body temperatures asymptotically with time, and the rate of that approach depends on body size and the heat transfer coefficient. Care must be exercised in modeling frog body temperatures as those of a Newtonian object. Such modeling can be accurate to within 1–2°C as long as we ignore the early parts of a heating or cooling curve (i.e., things do not change too often) and the difference between body and air temperatures isn't more than 5–6°C (Tracy et al. 1984). The heat transfer coefficient really does vary significantly with temperature, however, and the size of the approximation error increases if air and body temperatures are very different, especially if the air is dry.

MECHANISMS OF MASS EXCHANGE

In many ways the exchanges of heat and mass are similar. The exchange pathways are alike. Water, respiratory gases, and solutes can be exchanged with the environment by either convection or conduction by processes that are mechanistically related to thermal convection and conduction (see Vogel 1981). We will explore an approach that takes advantage of those relationships to allow estimation of water and respiratory gas fluxes. However, amphibians have more physiological (and anatomical) control over cutaneous concentrations and tissue conductances of water, solutes, and gases than of body temperature and tissue thermal conductivity. Thus, we also examine the interaction of physiology and the biophysics of mass exchange and discuss briefly the ecological contexts of water, respiratory gas, and solute exchange.

Mass Balance: Estimates by Analogy and Dimensional Analysis

As we saw in discussing evaporative cooling, it is sometimes necessary or convenient to estimate mass transfer processes by analogy to heat transfer theory. Mass transfer to flowing fluids can be modeled by analogy to thermal convection. Such convection models can be extremely useful. They also appear to be vexing to most biologists. In order to avoid dependence on endless tables for each situation, modelers have resorted to the use of dimensional analysis and dimensionless expressions (see Rouse 1938; White 1984). Here it is our intention neither to convert biologists into users of dimensional analysis, nor even to present the subject in depth (see Campbell 1977, Gates 1980, and Vogel 1981 for more detailed presentations useful to biologists). Rather we wish to present a quite useful result that arises from such analyses.

In discussing evaporation, we presented a formula (eq. [14], known as the Lewis rule) that estimates the resistance (and thus its inverse, the conductance) to evaporation due to the boundary layer effects in terms of heat transfer properties. Specifically, resistance to the transport of water vapor into the atmosphere is calculated from the thermal convection coefficient (h_c) in air. The relationship exists because the diffusion and mixing processes that drive thermal convection and evaporation are the same. Dimensional analysis allows us to extend the analysis to the transfer of heat or any gas between an amphibian and water or air. In order to do so, we must have relationships allowing us to predict the heat transfer coefficient in water from the heat transfer coefficient in air, and to predict the gas transfer coefficient from the appropriate heat transfer coefficient. To present those relationships, we need, first, to present some artificial groups of variables all of which are dimensionless (i.e., all dimensions cancel out within the groupings so that each group appears to be a pure number). For reasons that we will not go into, but which are important to our abilities to make the analogies we are interested in, the dimensionless nature of the numbers is considered a virtue (see Kreith 1973; Rouse 1938; White 1984).

We will present all of the dimensionless groups together, and then review their use.

$$(21) \qquad \text{Re} = VD/\nu \quad \text{Reynolds number}$$

$$(22) \qquad \text{Nu} = h_c D/k \quad \text{Nusselt number}$$

$$(23) \qquad \text{Pr} = \nu/\alpha \quad \text{Prandtl number}$$

$$(24) \qquad \text{Sh} = h_j D/d \quad \text{Sherwood number}$$

$$(25) \qquad \text{Sc} = \nu/d \quad \text{Schmidt number}$$

where

$V =$ fluid velocity (m · s^{-1})
$h_c =$ convection coefficient (W · m^{-2} · °C^{-1})
$k =$ thermal conductivity of fluid (W · m^{-1} · °C^{-1})
$\alpha =$ thermal diffusity of fluid (m^2 · s^{-1})
$h_j =$ mass convection coefficient (m · s^{-1})
$d =$ molecular diffusivity of fluid (m^2 · s^{-1})

The Reynolds number (Re) is used to describe the flow characteristics of fluid flows (e.g., laminar versus turbulent; see Vogel 1981), to determine drag coefficients (Vogel 1981), and to determine heat and mass transfer coefficients (Gates 1980). Fluid flows with the same geometry and the same Re will have the same turbulence characteristics and drag and transfer coefficients. The Nusselt number (Nu) can be regarded as a dimensionless expression of the thermal convection coefficient. Similarly, the Sherwood number (Sh) can be thought of as a dimensionless mass transfer coefficient. The Prandtl and Schmidt numbers relate the diffusivities of heat and mass, respectively, to the diffusivity of fluid momentum.

These dimensionless numbers are important because they allow us to express the sameness of the processes of heat and mass transfer mathematically. The Nu depends on the Re and Pr numbers and on a few empirical coefficients that depend only on the geometry of the flow (e.g., the shape of the organism and the direction of the flow across that shape).

$$(26) \qquad \text{Nu} = a\text{Re}^b\text{Pr}^{1/3}$$

Thus, if the thermal characteristics for the fluids are known (and they are tabulated for air and water), convection coefficients in one fluid can be used to calculate convection coefficients in the other. Like the Nu number, the Sh number depends on the Re and Sc numbers and the same two empirical coefficients.

$$(27) \qquad \text{Sh} = a\text{Re}^b\text{Sc}^{1/3}$$

Since a and b are the same in equations (26) and (27), we can divide the quantities in equation (27) by those in equation (26), and rearrange to obtain

$$(28) \qquad h_j = \frac{h_c}{\rho c_p}\left(\frac{d}{\alpha}\right)^{2/3},$$

or if resistance notation is more convenient,

$$(29) \qquad r_j = \frac{\rho c_p}{h_c}\left(\frac{\alpha}{d}\right)^{2/3}.$$

Using values for water vapor at 20°C, we would predict from this relationship that the external resistance to evaporation would be 0.92 times the external resistance to heat transfer ($\rho c_p/h_c$). This estimate agrees with that we gave as the Lewis rule in equation (14). Densities (ρ) of fluids and their specific heats (c_p) are tabulated in a number of places (Gates 1980; Tracy, Welch, and Porter 1980; Weast 1987; White

1984). Thermal diffusivities often are not tabulated but are easily calculable since

$$\alpha = \frac{k}{\rho c_p}, \tag{30}$$

and thermal conductivities are tabulated. Thus, if the heat transfer convection coefficient and molecular diffusivity of a gas in a fluid are known, gas transfer convection coefficients or convective resistances can be calculated. The Lewis rule (eq. [14]) is a special case of the more general relationship (eqs. [28] and [29]).

Dimensional analysis does not solve all problems. All of the relationships given above are for forced convection, and their applicability in very slow fluid flows (in which free convection is the dominant convective mode) is dubious. Furthermore, the similarities between thermal free convection and any mass transfer analogues are to our knowledge poorly explored, although such analogies have been used successfully to model evaporation from eggs (Tracy and Sotherland 1979). Most of the constants in equations 21–25 are not, in fact, constants. Most thermal characteristics of fluids vary somewhat with temperature. Finally, these results apply only to external heat and mass transfer and not to transfer within the animal's skin and body. But, if estimates of convective transfer are required and difficult to obtain, equations (26) and (27), judiciously applied, can be quite helpful. Examples of such applications are the estimates of convective resistance or conductance to evaporative water loss provided by equation (14) and used in equations (13) and (15).

WATER BALANCE
Evaporation of Water

Although evaporative water loss (EWL) may lower and stabilize the body temperatures of amphibians, such stabilization puts certain demands on the water balance of the animal. Many frogs among those noted to bask secrete watery mucus onto their dorsal integuments when heat-stressed (Lillywhite and Licht 1975). When exposed to artificial "solar" radiation, frogs that do not secrete these substances suffer drying and necrosis of the dorsal skin and die (Lillywhite and Licht 1975). Alternatively, some anurans have complex patterns of grooves or sculpting of their skin to facilitate the transfer of water from venter to dorsum by capillary action (Lillywhite 1971b). Calculations of expected EWL (for terrestrial frogs that do not impede evaporation with lipids) under natural conditions suggest that avoidance of desiccation can restrict the time free from water sources (Dole 1965a, 1965b, 1967; Tracy 1975, 1976; Wylie 1981) or the microhabitats that frogs can use at certain times of day (O'Connor 1989). *Eleutherodactylus coqui* (Leptodactylidae) spend the entire evening in stereotypical water-conserving postures in protected microhabitats in order to prevent desiccation. If this hydroregulatory behavior is prevented, the frogs can undergo lethal dehydration before morning (Pough et al. 1983). Evaporative water loss also appears to limit the habitat use and foraging times of some salamanders (Feder 1983b; Jaeger 1978, 1980b; Keen 1979; Spotila 1972), and some salamanders are thought to compete for hydrically suitable sites (Jaeger 1981a; Keen 1982). An alternative means of avoiding

dehydration used by other anurans is to secrete wax coatings on their dorsal skins for at least part of the day, inhibiting evaporative water loss (Blaylock, Ruibal, and Platt-Aloia 1976; Shoemaker et al. 1972; Shoemaker and McClanahan 1975; Withers, Hillman, and Drewes 1984; Withers et al. 1982).

Liquid Water Uptake from the Soil

To remain hydrated in a terrestrial environment, a typical amphibian must take up water from the environment to replace water lost by evaporation. In many cases, this is done by direct absorption through the skin. The force driving this transcutaneous absorption is the water potential difference between the soil and the tissues of the amphibian:

$$\frac{dm}{dt} = \frac{A_v}{r} (\Psi_s - \Psi_a), \tag{31}$$

where

dm/dt = rate of uptake of water by amphibian ($kg \cdot s^{-1}$)
A_v = area in contact with substrate (m^2)
r = resistance to water uptake ($s \cdot m^2 \cdot Pa \cdot kg^{-1}$)
Ψ_s = water potential of soil (Pa)
Ψ_a = water potential of amphibian (Pa)

Note that the resistance terms here and in equation (32) are hydraulic resistances (i.e., resistance to mass flow of liquid water rather than resistances to water vapor diffusion as in eq. [15], thus the difference in units).

Water potential here can be thought of as the energetic potential for water absorption. Differences in solute concentration, capillary forces, and gravitational potential of the amphibian and the surrounding soil generate the water potential difference driving liquid water transport (see Gates 1980; Salisbury and Ross 1969; Tracy 1976). The water potential of a leopard frog (*Rana pipiens*) varies from -50 to -400 kPa for frogs dehydrated to 97% and 70%, respectively, of their standard masses (Tracy 1976; see eq. [33]). The water potential of substrates can range from 0 kPa for a shallow pool of rainwater on a clean rock to very large negative values in desiccated soil. These water potentials, in general, must be determined empirically. A sandy loam soil with about 1% water content by mass has a water potential of about -10 kPa. Tracy (1976) found that a 60-g leopard frog dehydrated to only 97% of standard mass could absorb water at the rate of $0.1 \ g \cdot min^{-1}$ from such a soil. A frog dehydrated to 70% of standard mass could absorb more than $1 \ g \cdot min^{-1}$. Liquid water uptake is complexly dependent on soil composition, hydration, and temperature, amphibian skin properties, and body temperature. As with conductive heat exchange with the ground, water transfer with the substrate can be difficult to model precisely. As with heat exchange, the presence of an anuran on a patch of soil leads to complex temporal and spatial changes in the water potential of the substrates immediately around the animal. Tracy (1976) found it necessary to model those changes as hemispherical gradients of water potential in the soil. Soils are rarely spatially homogeneous in their hydric properties, and their hydric characteristics vary with soil type, compaction, temperature, depth, and water content (Ackerman et al. 1985; Rose 1966; Rosenberg 1974).

Thus, the approximations inherent in any expression for water exchange must be seen as necessary, but potentially inaccurate, simplifications of complex biophysics. Water absorption by the frog creates complex transients in soil hydration and body temperature (Tracy 1976). Thus, rates of water uptake from the soil can only be approximated at this time (e.g., Tracy 1976). Finally, liquid water uptake depends on the hormonal state of the amphibian. Antidiuretic hormone (ADH) modifies both the blood flow to the ventral seat patch of anuran amphibians and the permeability to water of some of the tissues on the venter (Christensen 1974b, 1975b; Mahany and Parsons 1978). ADH also appears to alter the apparent water potential of the seat patch (Tracy and Rubink 1978).

Liquid Water Exchange in Aquatic Settings

The expression for water exchange with standing water is similar to that for exchange with soil,

$$(32) \qquad \frac{dm}{dt} = \frac{A_w}{r} (\Psi_w - \Psi_a),$$

where

dm/dt = rate of uptake of water by amphibian (kg $\cdot$ s^{-1})
A_w = area in contact with water (m^2)
r = resistance to water uptake (s $\cdot$ m^2 $\cdot$ Pa $\cdot$ kg-1)
Ψ_w = water potential of water (Pa)
Ψ_a = water potential of amphibian (Pa)

Because spatial inhomogeneities in water potential are more likely to dissipate in water than in soil, this model is somewhat easier to apply than equation (31). As with soil-water absorption, the resistance to liquid water uptake varies with the thickness of the skin, the relative perfusion of the skin (capillary recruitment), and the hormonal state of the animal (ADH; Christensen 1974, 1975; Lillywhite and Maderson 1988; Mahany and Parsons 1978). Because resistance to water uptake is under physiologic control, estimates of that resistance should be regarded as variables rather than constants. Resistances (r) in leopard frogs (*Rana pipiens*) dehydrated to 90% of their fully hydrated masses are around 4.8 $\times$ 10^7 s $\cdot$ m^2 $\cdot$ Pa $\cdot$ kg^{-1} for body temperatures between 12° and 28°C (Tracy 1976).

Tracy (1976) provides a polynomial regression relation for the water potential of a leopard frog at different levels of hydration:

$$(33) \quad \Psi_a = -2.88576 \, \vartheta^3 + 783675 \, \vartheta^2$$
$$- 712541 \, \vartheta + 2.17655 \times 10^7,$$

where

Ψ_a = water potential of the amphibian (Pa)
ϑ = 100 $\times$ ratio of dehydrated mass to fully hydrated mass

If no capillary or gravitational forces or hydrostatic pressure heads are involved (as they should not be), then the water potential of the water in which the frog sits is simply the osmotic pressure

$$(34) \qquad \Psi_w = -\pi = -iCRT,$$

where

Y_w = water potential of the water (Pa)
π = osmotic pressure (Pa)
i = isotonic coefficient
C = concentration of solute (moles of solute $\cdot$ m-3)
R = gas constant (8.31 J $\cdot$ K-1 $\cdot$ mol-1)
T = water temperature (K)

In this connection, water potential is sometimes given in J $\cdot$ kg^{-1} instead of Pa (= J $\cdot$ m^{-3}) and can be calculated by simply dividing the value from equation (34) by the density (kg $\cdot$ m^{-3}) of the solution. The isotonic coefficient describes the dissociation of ionic species. Thus, it is 1 for nondissociating compounds, between 1 and 2 for salts dissociating into two ions, and so forth.

CUTANEOUS RESPIRATION

A variety of amphibians depend heavily upon cutaneous respiration, and some, for example, plethodontid salamanders, exchange respiratory gases exclusively via the skin (Feder and Burggren 1985a). In considering the biophysics of cutaneous respiration in amphibians, one must consider three transfer processes in series. Consider a molecule of CO_2 expired to the environment. It was delivered to the skin by the blood, diffused across the skin to the skin surface, and then was transferred by convection to the free stream of the surrounding fluid. Although diffusion across the skin is usually considered the rate-limiting step for the exchange of respiratory gases, each of the processes—blood supply, cutaneous diffusion, and external convection—can be important and in some sense limiting to cutaneous respiration in amphibians (for reviews see Burggren 1988b; Feder and Burggren 1985a; Feder and Pinder 1988a, 1988b; Piiper 1988).

Cutaneous Diffusion

Respiratory gases cross from the capillaries to the skin surface by diffusion. The process can be modeled by Fick's law of diffusion:

$$(35) \qquad F_j = A \frac{D_j}{\Delta x} (C_i - C_o),$$

where

F_j = gas transfer rate of j, inner to outer skin surface (kg $\cdot$ s^{-1})
A = area (m^2)
D = diffusivity of j in skin (m^2 $\cdot$ s^{-1})
Δx = diffusion path length (thickness of skin, m)
C_i = concentration of j at inner skin surface (kg $\cdot$ m^{-3})
C_o = concentration of j at outer skin surface (kg $\cdot$ m^{-3})

The units of concentration used here are consistent with concentration terms in earlier expressions. Other units can be used, but the units of diffusivity and possibly gas transfer rate must be adjusted accordingly. Because the concentrations of respiratory gases are usually measured as partial pressures, the diffusion equation is usually recast as

$$(36) \qquad F_j = A \frac{D_j s_j}{\Delta x} (P_i - P_o),$$

where

P_i = partial pressure of j at inner skin surface (Pa)
P_o = partial pressure of j at outer skin surface (Pa)
s_j = "solubility" of j in skin (kg $\cdot$ m^{-3} $\cdot$ Pa^{-1})

Any increase in diffusive surface area, diffusivity, or tissue capacitance (s_j) or decrease in the diffusion path length will facilitate the cutaneous diffusion of respiratory gases (see Feder and Burggren 1985a for review). Thus, folds of vascularized skin or villous skin surfaces and thinning of the skin overlying the dermal capillaries all should enhance dermal diffusion. Alteration of blood flow patterns (e.g., capillary recruitment; Burggren and Feder 1986) also increases the "functional" surface area for diffusion (Feder and Burggren 1985a; Lillywhite and Maderson 1988); that is, each unit area is used more intensively. Differences in tissue capacitance (analogous to a measure of solubility in tissue) affect the relative rates of O_2 and CO_2 exchange. Although O_2 is a smaller molecule than CO_2 and therefore has a higher diffusivity, the higher tissue capacitance for CO_2 leads to higher rates of diffusion for CO_2 (Guyton 1976; West 1974, 1977). Not surprisingly, in most amphibians in which the subject has been examined, cutaneous respiration accounts for a larger proportion of CO_2 exchange than of O_2 exchange (Feder and Burggren 1985a).

Convection

Cutaneous respiration is usually thought to be limited primarily by the rate of transcutaneous diffusion of respiratory gases, but it appears that, in still waters, convective resistances to gas exchange can be significant (Burggren and Feder 1986; Feder and Pinder 1988a, 1988b; Pinder 1987b). Unfortunately, these are precisely the sorts of situations in which the analogies to forced thermal convection discussed above break down. At water velocities less than 1 cm $\cdot$ s^{-1} and at water temperatures near 5°C (simulating overwintering conditions), convective resistances may account for as much as 75% of the total resistance to gas transfer and reduce oxygen uptake to 50% of the value found at higher water velocities (Pinder 1987b). Further, bullfrogs, *Rana catesbeiana*, subjected alternately to still and moving water recruit cutaneous capillaries when in still water, presumably increasing effective diffusive area (Burggren and Feder 1986).

Blood Flow

Blood flow delivers CO_2 to the skin for transport and removes absorbed O_2. The amount of gas delivered or removed is given by

$$(37) \qquad M_j = \dot{Q}\beta_j(P_a - P_v),$$

where

M_j = gas delivered to or removed from skin (kg $\cdot$ s^{-1})
$\dot{Q}$ = blood flow (L $\cdot$ s^{-1})
β_j = blood capacitance (solubility) for gas (kg $\cdot$ L^{-1} $\cdot$ Pa^{-1})
P_a = partial pressure of gas in artery (Pa)
P_v = partial pressure of gas in vein (Pa)

The units of M_j and b_j should be set so that M_j has the same units as F_j in equations (35) and (36).

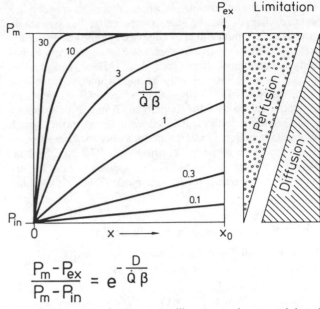

$$\frac{P_m - P_{ex}}{P_m - P_{in}} = e^{-\frac{D}{\dot{Q}\beta}}$$

Fig. 4.5 Approach of cutaneous capillary gas tensions toward that of the environment as blood travels along capillary (increasing x). The distance along the capillary before the environmental and capillary gas tensions reach steady state depends on the ratio of diffusive conductance (D) to blood carrying capacity ($Q\beta$) for a respiratory gas (see text for explanation). The relative importance of diffusion and circulatory limitation of cutaneous respiration depends on the $D/Q\beta$ ratio. (Reprinted, by permission, from Piiper 1988.)

Piiper (1988) has provided a quantitative model of respiratory gas exchange across the skin incorporating the processes of vascular supply and cutaneous diffusion, starting with a steady-state mass balance (gas supplied by the blood = gas diffusing across the skin). From this relationship, he derives a ratio $D/(\dot{Q}\beta)$, where D is the diffusive conductance of the skin to gas transport, $\dot{Q}$ is the rate of blood flow, and β is the effective solubility of the gas in blood. This ratio determines the volume of gas that diffuses across the skin as reflected in the partial pressure of the gas still remaining in the blood (fig. 4.5). For very high values of $D/(\dot{Q}\beta)$, the blood reaches equilibrium with the external environment early in its transit through the capillary, and gas transfer is limited primarily by the rate of blood flow. For low values of $D/(\dot{Q}\beta)$, the blood never approaches equilibrium with the external environment, and gas transfer is limited principally by diffusion. This model does not incorporate external resistances to transport, which can be larger than the cutaneous diffusive resistances for amphibians in still water (Feder and Pinder 1988b). Future research should include the integration of the "series resistance" representation of diffusive and convective limits on gas exchange (Feder and Pinder 1988a, 1988b) with models like Piiper's (1988), and the inclusion of realistic values for blood flow, diffusive resistance, and convection (Burggren 1988b; Feder and Pinder 1988a, 1988b) into the integrated model.

Cutaneous Respiration in Air

As mentioned above, in most amphibians the skin provides little resistance to the diffusion of water vapor (Spotila and Berman 1976; Tracy 1982). Therefore, the boundary layer provides the only significant resistance, which is small (200 to 300 s · m⁻¹). In contrast, reptiles have high skin resistances to diffusion of water vapor (4,700 to 78,800 s · m⁻¹; Lillywhite and Maderson 1982). Similarly, cutaneous exchange of respiratory gases is more prevalent and physiologically significant in amphibians than in reptiles (Feder and Burggren 1985a). While the relationship between cutaneous resistance to the diffusion of water vapor and respiratory gases has not been well explored (Lillywhite and Maderson 1988), similarities between these two diffusion processes suggest that they will be correlated. Both water vapor and respiratory gases cross lipophilic membranes primarily by diffusion rather than by following transmembranous protein channels as do most ions (Lillywhite and Maderson 1988). Furthermore, the geometry of diffusion (skin thickness, area, "functional area" due to capillary recruitment) significantly affects the diffusion of both water vapor and respiratory gases (Feder and Burggren 1985a). Some wax-covered insect eggs have high resistance to water vapor loss, however, but lower resistances to respiratory gas exchange (Buck 1962).

"Waterproof" frogs (e.g., *Phyllomedusa* [Hylidae]), inhibit evaporative water losses via the application of waxes and other lipids to their skins (Blaylock, Ruibal, and Platt-Aloia 1976; Shoemaker et al. 1972; Shoemaker and McClanahan 1975; Withers, Hillman, and Drewes 1984; Withers et al. 1982). To the extent that such waxes also interfere with cutaneous diffusion of CO_2 and O_2, these frogs may have to rely primarily on their lungs for gas exchange and/or reduce their metabolic rate to compensate for the reduction of gas transport through the skin when they apply waxes to their skins. Little data are available to indicate to what extent such lipids also interfere with the exchange of respiratory gases (Lillywhite and Maderson 1988), but in *Phyllomedusa sauvagei*, differences among individuals in cutaneous O_2 uptake and CO_2 loss were directly proportional to differences in cutaneous evaporation (Stinner and Shoemaker 1987).

In comparing the relative importance of biophysical limitations on respiratory gas exchange and evaporation, Feder (1983b) and Feder and Burggren (1985a) compare predicted and actual patterns of exchange in plethodontid (lungless) salamanders. The importance of the geometry of diffusion suggests that larger animals with lower surface-to-mass (and surface-to-metabolic rate) ratios and thicker skins would be less likely to depend on cutaneous respiration than smaller animals. Similarly, lower rates of gas exchange and less control over rates of exchange with cutaneous than with pulmonary respiration suggest that plethodontids should have low metabolic rates and be active at relatively low body temperatures (Feder and Burggren 1985a). In fact, many plethodontids are small, have low metabolic rates, and are active at relatively low body temperatures, but some plenthodontids are among the largest salamanders in the world, and some tropical, lowland plethodontids are active at relatively high body temperatures (Feder 1983b). In contrast, hydric conditions appear to significantly limit plethodontid activity times and foraging periods (see Feder 1983b for review), suggesting, circumstantially at least, that water vapor exchanges may constrain the activity and distribution of plethodontids more than gas exchange. To our knowledge, there are no similar analyses for other groups of amphibians, and no direct tests of the relative ecological importance of water and gas exchange.

Cutaneous Respiration in Water

Several environmental factors limit the availability of oxygen to aquatic organisms. First, oxygen is much less "concentrated" in water (6.6 ml O_2 · l⁻¹ H_2O at 20°C) than in air (209 ml O_2 · l⁻¹ air). Depending on temperature, carbon dioxide is 30–60 times more soluble in water than either oxygen or nitrogen. Furthermore, the solubility of all three gases decreases as water temperature increases. The solubility of oxygen in water falls from 8.0 ml O_2 · l⁻¹ at 10°C to 6.6 ml O_2 · l⁻¹ at 20°C, and 5.6 ml O_2 · l⁻¹ at 30°C. Thus, the oxygen available for transport between the environment and an aquatic amphibian's blood is likely to be lower than that for a terrestrial amphibian. Second, oxygen diffuses thousands of times more slowly in water than in air, and objects in still or slowly moving water have considerable boundary layers (Erskine and Spotila 1977; Feder and Pinder 1988b; Gates 1980) that respiratory gases cross by diffusion. Finally, because of its greater density, vastly more energy is needed to move a volume of water than to move an equal volume of air. Thus, transfer of gases between the respiratory surface and the water limits respiration to such an extent that active animals typically require some form of convective motion (fluid flow or animal movement) to bring oxygen-rich water close to the respiratory surface (Guimond and Hutchison 1973a; Rahn, Wangensteen, and Farhi 1971), or suffer a decrease in oxygen uptake in the absence of convection (Burggren and Feder 1986; Feder and Pinder 1988a, 1988b; Piiper 1988; Pinder 1987b).

The results of these limitations are evident in many amphibians. In the case of stream-dwelling amphibians, the movement of water in the stream reduces the boundary layer around the respiratory surfaces, and gills are reduced in size with short, broad filaments. Pond-dwelling larval salamanders such as *Ambystoma tigrinum* have elongate and featherlike gills that facilitate gas exchange (Noble 1931). The mudpuppy, *Necturus maculosus* (Caudata: Proteidae), lives in streams and lakes. It ventilates its gills by waving them; the frequency of waving changes with metabolic rate, oxygen content of the water, and water velocity. Other specialized adaptations increase the respiratory surfaces of aquatic amphibians. The adult male hairy frog of Cameroon, *Astylosternus robustus* (Ranidae), grows fine glandular filaments resembling hairs on its sides and hind legs. These short vascular papillae appear to act as a respiratory structure (Porter 1972). The hellbender, *Cryptobranchus alleganiensis* (Caudata: Cryptobranchidae), lives in mountain streams in the eastern United States and has highly vascularized folds of skin along the sides of its body with capillaries penetrating to the stratum corneum. This salamander carries out 90% of oxygen uptake and 97% of its carbon dioxide release through its skin. The lungs are large transparent sacs and serve primarily as hydrostatic organs. Ventilation of the skin is increased by a "rocking maneuver" in which the salamander sways from side to side (Guimond and Hutchison 1973a). Finally, the frog *Telmatobius culeus* (Leptodactylidae) lives in Lake Titicaca at 3,812 m and ranges from the surface to a depth of 281 m. Its lungs are reduced in size and are rarely ventilated, but its skin is expanded by many large folds that hang from the dorsum, sides, and hindlimbs. The folds are highly vascularized and penetrate to the outermost layers of the stratum corneum (Macedo 1960). Metabolic rate is very low, and these frogs do not surface if the water is oxygenated. In hypoxic water, they surface and breathe. If prevented from surfacing in hypoxic water, they ventilate the skin by a bobbing behavior and can survive oxygen concentrations near zero (Hutchison, Haines, and Engbretson 1976).

Exchange of Ions and Other Osmolytes

Some aspects of the cutaneous exchange of such ions as Na^+, Cl^-, HCO_3^-, NH_4^+, and H^+ are similar to the exchange of respiratory gases as discussed above. For instance, convection will affect the supply or removal of ions and osmolytes to and from the skin surface and blood flow may affect the transfer of some ions in ways similar to those described by Piiper (1988; Stiffler 1988). However, substantial differences exist between the internal transport of respiratory gases and of ions. (1) Some ions are carried by active, energy-requiring processes across membrane barriers, allowing transport of ions against concentration gradients (Krogh 1937; Prosser 1986). In other cases ions cross membranes via transmembranous protein channels (Lillywhite and Maderson 1988). Ions must cross at least two membrane barriers between the blood and the external environment, at the capillary wall and at the skin surface. In each case, different "diffusive" conductances may exist, depending on the direction of the ion transport. Furthermore, because ions may be moved against concentration gradients, any analogy between the transport of respiratory gases and ions must allow for physiological control of the "apparent concentration" of ions. Finally, the "diffusive" conductances and "apparent concentrations" of ions may vary depending on the hormonal state of the animal. (2) Transport of ions across membranes is affected by the maintenance of electroneutrality. If a cation is carried across a membrane, either an anion must accompany it, another cation must be transported across the membrane in the opposite direction, or an electrochemical potential is established. For transport purposes, the maintenance of a transmembrane electric potential is, at best, a metastable state. Thus, the maintenance of electroneutrality results in the linkage of transport of two or more ionic species. The maintenance of electroneutrality also establishes a linkage between ion transport processes and the acid-base balance of the animal (Boutilier 1988b; Stiffler 1988). (3) Chemical reactions may alter the concentrations of some ions, particularly HCO_3^- (Stiffler 1988). None of these differences are conducive to simple biophysical modeling. Thus, although biophysical concepts may be useful in describing the convective transfer of ions to or from the skin surface, ion transport remains, for now, in the realm of the physiologist (see Prosser 1973b, 1986).

BIOPHYSICS AND THE ECOLOGY OF AMPHIBIANS
Climate Space

A climate space is a diagrammatic method of describing an ectotherm's thermal environment and relating the animal's body temperature to that environment. Construction of a steady-state climate space is one of the simpler forms of biophysical analysis that can be carried out for an animal. In the case of amphibians, however, it can provide interesting insights into the biophysical constraints that the physical envi-

ronment places on the animal. Climate spaces can be used to define the boundaries of the microclimate within which an animal must remain in order to function well or survive. These boundaries are usually given in terms of absorbed radiation (Q_{abs}), air temperature (T_a), wind speed (V), and body temperature (T_b). The boundaries of the climate space are fixed in part by the interaction of the amphibian's physical properties (size, shape, absorptivity of solar radiation) and those of its environment (fig. 4.6). The left- and right-hand boundaries of the climate space in fig. 4.6 are set by the limits of what thermal conditions could be available to the animal in its environment. The radiation absorbed by an amphibian at different air temperatures on a cloudless day when body orientation provides maximum exposure to direct sunlight (line marked *full sun*) sets the right side of the climate space. Radiation absorbed by the amphibian at night from the sky, the atmosphere, and the substrate (line labeled *clear sky*) sets the boundary for the left side of the climate space. The blackbody line is a reference line indicating the amount of energy received by an amphibian in a blackbody cavity. A blackbody cavity is an enclosure that traps all radiation that enters it through a small hole or aperture so that the hole appears perfectly black to an observer on the outside. Examples of blackbody cavities in nature include caves, burrows, hollow logs and cavities under logs, rocks, other surface debris, or dense vegetative canopies. The upper and lower boundaries of the climate space are lines of equal body temperature. The upper boundary corresponds to the highest body temperature tolerated by the amphibian. Likewise, the lower boundary is set by the lowest tolerated body temperature. The criteria for what represents a maximum or minimum tolerated temperature vary depending on the investigators' preferences and the purpose of the study (see chapter 8). The criteria for the body temperatures chosen as tolerance temperatures can be physiological (lethal temperatures, temperature limits for loss of

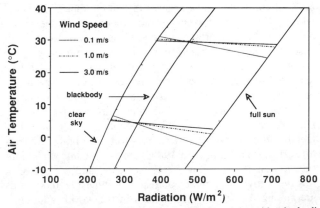

Fig. 4.6 Climate space for a plethodontid salamander with a body diameter of 0.9 cm and a skin thickness of 0.08 cm at wind speeds of 0.1, 1.0, and 3.0 m · s^{-1}. The left boundary represents the conditions of radiation and temperature the salamander encounters when exposed to a clear sky with no sun (e.g., a clear night on open ground). The right boundary represents conditions it encounters in full sun. The upper set of three lines marks the upper limit of the climate space when $T_b = 30°C$, $T_a = 30°C$, RH = 100%, and 5% of the surface of the salamander is in contact with the substrate. The lower set of three lines marks the lower limit of the climate space when $T_b = 5°C$, $T_a = 5°C$, RH = 100%, and 5% of the salamander's surface is in contact with the substrate.

muscular coordination, body temperatures at which an animal performs a certain task well, e.g., locomotion), behavioral (temperatures selected in a gradient, temperatures associated with shuttling in a shuttlebox experiment), or ecological (optimal temperatures for some ecological process).

Humidity, Conduction to the Ground, and the Climate Space A wet-skinned amphibian requires a climate space with two added axes to show the effects of relative humidity and conduction to the ground. A four-dimensional diagram on a two-dimensional page is impractical, so we have prepared four climate spaces to illustrate the effects of changes in these additional environmental parameters on the boundaries of the climate space. The climate spaces presented here are for a terrestrial salamander and are based on morphological and physiological data for *Desmognathus fuscus* and *Plethodon glutinosus* (both Plethodontidae). Figure 4.6 shows a climate space that displays the effect of wind when relative humidity (RH) is 100%, that is, when the evaporation is minimized and wind mainly affects convective heat transfer. Figure 4.7 shows the effect of wind speed at low RH, where wind affects both convective heat transfer and evaporative cooling. Figure 4.8 illustrates the effect of different RH values at a fixed wind speed. Different RH values affect evaporative cooling only. Figure 4.9 shows the effect of conduction to the ground at a fixed wind speed and RH.

We determined the upper boundary of the climate space by solving an equilibrium energy budget equation (eq. [1]) for Q_{abs} using our estimate of the upper lethal body temperatures of these salamanders (30°C, based on our unpublished data), the corresponding metabolic rate and evaporative water loss values for this temperature, and the convection coefficient for a given wind speed. This procedure was repeated for several air temperatures, and the upper lines were plotted as T_a versus Q_{abs}. Lower lines were computed for the body temperature that corresponded to the lowest limit for voluntary activity of these salamanders (5°C, based on field data) following the above procedures.

In fig. 4.6, a climate space has been computed for an ani-

mal with 5% of its surface in contact with the ground. Ground temperature is assumed to equal air temperature. The soil is assumed to be damp, allowing the animal to maintain normal hydration. The upper and lower climate space boundaries were computed for wind speeds of 0.1, 1.0, and 3.0 m · s⁻¹ with 100% RH. Increased wind speed couples the animal's body temperature more closely to air temperatures, and reduces the effect of solar heating. This results in more nearly horizontal upper and lower boundaries for the climate space. The wind has some effect on evaporation and condensation, but such effects are minimal due to the assumption of saturated air.

In fig. 4.7, the climate space is computed as in fig. 4.6, but the RH is assumed to be 25% instead of 100%. In this case wind increases both convective heat transfer and evaporative cooling. The effect of higher wind speeds is to raise both the high and low air temperature tolerance boundaries, that is, to allow the maintenance of a particular body tem-

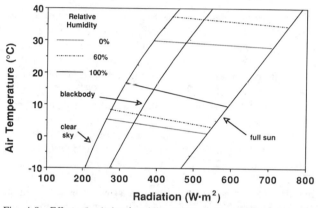

Fig. 4.8 Effect of relative humidity (RH) on the climate space of a plethodontid salamander with a body diameter of 0.9 cm and a skin thickness of 0.08 cm at a wind speed of 1.0 · ⁻¹. Upper and lower limits are presented for RH of 0%, 60%, and 100%. As RH decreases, the limits of the climate space rise. See figure 4.6 for an explanation of the climate space.

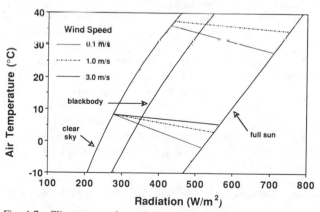

Fig. 4.7 Climate space for a plethodontid salamander with a body diameter of 0.9 cm and a skin thickness of 0.08 cm at wind speeds of 0.1, 1.0, and 3.0 m · s⁻¹. The upper set of lines marks the upper limit of the climate space when T_b = 30°C, T_a = 30°C, RH = 25%, and 5% of the surface of the salamander is in contact with the substrate. The lower set of three lines marks the lower limit of the climate space when T_b = 5°C, T_a = 5°C, RH = 25%, and 5% of the salamander's surface is in contact with the substrate.

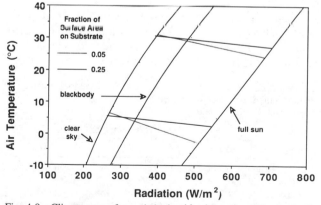

Fig. 4.9 Climate space for a plethodontid salamander with a body diameter of 0.9 cm and a skin thickness of 0.08 cm for two different amounts of conduction with a wind speed of 0.1 m/s. The lower horizontal lines of each pair are the upper and lower limits of the climate space when 5% of the salamander's surface is in contact with the substrate, and the higher horizontal lines of each pair are the upper and lower limits when 25% of the salamander's surface area is in contact with the substrate. See figure 4.6 for an explanation of the climate space.

perature at higher air temperatures (or higher radiant load). This effect is due to the increases in evaporative cooling occasioned by the higher wind speeds.

Figure 4.8 illustrates the effects of different RH values at a fixed wind speed of 1.0 m · s⁻¹. Different RH values affect evaporative cooling only. This raises both the upper and lower air temperature tolerance limits, again at the cost of higher rates of evaporative water loss. The effect is nonlinear, with a given change in RH having a greater effect at low rather than high RH and at high rather than low air temperature.

Figure 4.9 shows the effect of the animal varying conduction to the ground by changing the area in contact with the soil in the same environment as in the previous figures. Wind speed is assumed fixed at 0.1 m · s⁻¹. The upper and lower bounds of the climate space are computed for animals with 5 and 25% of their body surfaces in contact with the ground. The greater contact area makes the boundary more horizontal, indicating closer coupling of body and ground temperatures with more of the venter pressed to the ground.

Water Storage The climate space computations above assumed that the amphibian could remain fully hydrated. At high temperatures and low humidities, the rate of EWL is high and may result in rapid desiccation. The time an animal can be active in a desiccating environment is set by the tolerable body water loss. Taking the loss of 20% of body mass as water as the tolerable limit for a fully hydrated amphibian, we can compute the activity time (i.e., time to go from full hydration to maximum tolerable dehydration) from the rate of EWL in different situations (e.g., Feder 1983b; O'Connor 1989; Spotila 1972; Tracy 1975, 1976). For example, at an RH of 60% and air and body temperatures of 30°C, a salamander would lose 20% of its mass as water in 1.36 h in air moving at only 0.1 m · s⁻¹, but in just over 12 min in a wind of 3 m · s⁻¹ (table 4.3). The same humidity and wind speed in a cooler environment (5°C) are much less desiccating because the vapor density of the amphibian's skin is greatly reduced at lower temperatures (see Tracy, Welch, and Porter 1980) and thus the vapor density deficit is reduced (eqs. [13–15]).

Environmental Boundary Layer Effects The climate space is computed for the values of the environmental parameters acting directly on the animal, rather than for standardized measurements (e.g., in a Stevenson screen, the louvered box

TABLE 4.3. Evaporative Water Loss (g·h⁻¹) Predicted for a Small Plethodontid Salamander as a Function of Temperature, Wind Speed, and Relative Humidity

RH (%)	Wind Speed (m·s⁻¹)		
	0.1	1.0	3.0
Evaporative water loss for T_b = 30°C and T_a = 30°C			
100	0.000	0.000	0.000
60	0.588 (1.36)	2.100 (0.38)	3.840 (0.21)
10	1.470 (0.54)	5.238 (0.15)	9.594 (0.08)
Evaporative water loss for T_b = 5°C and T_a = 5°C			
100	0.000	0.000	0.000
60	0.132 (6.06)	0.468 (1.71)	0.858 (0.93)
10	0.330 (2.42)	1.176 (0.68)	2.154 (0.37)

Note: The number in parentheses is the time in hours for a salamander with a body diameter of 0.9 cm to lose 20% of its body mass.

commonly used to house weather instruments). The microenvironment occupied by the animal is strongly affected by the boundary layer of the surface on which the animal rests. Thus, interpreters of climate space diagrams should bear in mind that wind speed decreases rapidly near surfaces, humidity increases, and air temperature increases or decreases rapidly, depending on whether the surface is warmer or cooler than the surrounding air. Bakken and Gates (1975) found experimentally that much of the size dependence of body temperature seen when cylindrical "animals" were suspended 1 m above the ground disappeared when the cylinders rested on the ground. Amphibians should be similarly affected by variation in humidity near the ground.

Bakken (1989) found that the diameter of an arboreal perch significantly affected the equilibrium body temperatures of lizards. Similar effects might be expected for arboreal amphibians such as treefrogs. The effects of environmental boundary layers need further study, particularly the effect of humidity boundary layers on wet-skinned amphibians.

Ecological Implications The climate space delimits the thermal environment within which an amphibian must remain in order to survive (or perform well, find its "preferred" body temperatures, reproduce, etc.). Available environmental conditions at different times of day and in different microhabitats may be plotted on a climate space to determine when ectotherms can or cannot use certain microhabitats (e.g., Scott, Tracy, and Pettus 1982) or when they might use different habitats for processes with different thermal optima (see Bustard 1967). Similar approaches have been used to describe, predict, and/or understand the habitat use of amphibians (Feder 1978b; O'Connor 1989; Porter et al. 1975; Porter and Tracy 1974, 1983; Tracy 1975, 1976).

This type of analysis may also be useful in assessing the possible thermoregulatory strategies that may be available to an amphibian in the field. Laboratory studies may underestimate or overestimate the potential for an amphibian to exploit the biophysical spectrum of thermoregulation in its natural environment (see chapter 9). Only by comparing the range and phenology of available thermal microhabitats (and utilized habitats) with the other requirements and resources of the animal can we determine the utility of thermoregulation. Thus, some salamanders that select body temperatures in the laboratory may be unable to do so in the field because the thermal heterogeneity of microhabitats required for such selection is not available (Feder 1978b). Quantitative field studies are needed to understand fully the interaction of amphibians and their normal physical environment. Theoretical biophysical calculations may greatly strengthen field studies and allow the investigator to plan more effective field experiments.

Other Methods of Describing the Thermal Environment

Climate spaces, as they have been drawn classically, are not appropriate descriptors of the thermal environment for submerged amphibians. Thermal radiation is not propagated in water, so that heat is transferred primarily by conduction and convection. Solar radiation may add heat to the amphibian if it is just below the surface, but in general, an amphibian submerged more than a few centimeters below the surface is in a unithermal environment due to rapid heat transfer through the water. Even near the surface, heat will be rapidly transferred away from the animal, which will seldom be warmer than water temperature except for brief transients. This phenomenon is illustrated paradoxically by the observation that a large aggregation of dark frog larvae in shallow water may warm both themselves and the water in which they are found (Brattstrom 1962). Thus, for a strictly aquatic amphibian, a more useful approach would be a temperature-tolerance polygon like those developed for fish by Fry and his students (Brett 1952; Fry 1947; Fry, Brett, and Clawson 1942; see Prosser 1973a for discussion) because the animal is at the same temperature as the water. For an amphibian that spends part of its time above and part of it below water, however, it is a useful convention to indicate its thermal location while it is submerged as being on the blackbody line of the climate space, keeping in mind that heat transfer is by conduction and convection as opposed to thermal radiation.

A second problem with using climate spaces to characterize the environment of terrestrial amphibians is that, by focusing on the heat transfer environment, climate spaces underemphasize the importance of the hydric environment, which can influence amphibians' habitat use (Dole 1965a, 1965b; Feder 1983b; O'Connor 1989; Spotila 1972; Tracy 1975, 1976). Another approach that allows one to integrate as many factors as desired are activity isoclines (see Porter and Tracy 1974; Tracy 1975, 1976). In this approach, one computes a relevant measure of the animal's ecological function (e.g., time free from standing water, time free for foraging, availability of some resource) as it varies with two ecological variables (time of day, season, air temperature, radiation, substrate water potential) and then plots isoclines of equal levels of the ecological function. Such plots can display quite vividly the variance of biophysical constraints with time (Porter and Tracy 1974; Tracy 1975). From a strictly biophysical point of view, this approach has the disadvantage of hiding most of the mechanistic details. In so doing, however, such an approach allows the integration of a large number of biophysical factors. For example, Tracy (1975, 1976) has used such diagrams, in conjunction with an integrated model of heat and water exchange for a leopard frog (*Rana pipiens*), to explore the limits that avoidance of dehydration may place on some anurans. Porter and Tracy (1974) used similar diagrams to investigate thermal effects on predatory encounters between garter snakes (*Thamnophis*) and leopard frogs.

The thermal environment can also be viewed as an ecological resource, in the idiom of the population or community ecologists (Magnuson, Crowder, and Medvick 1979; Roughgarden, Porter, and Heckel 1981; Tracy and Christian 1986). Tracy, his students (Christian, Tracy, and Porter 1983, 1984; O'Connor 1989; Tracy and Christian 1986; Waldschmidt 1980; Waldschmidt and Tracy 1983; Zimmerman and Tracy 1989), and others (Dunham, Grant, and Overall 1989; Grant and Dunham 1988; Peterson 1987) have begun to provide the methodology for realizing such an approach. In this approach, different parts of the environment are characterized as thermally suitable, unsuitable, or suitable only for an animal that remains there only for a brief time. The approach can then examine what parts of the environment are used by the organism and what strategies the animal employs in dealing with thermally favorable and unfavorable parts of its environment.

Different areas of the environment are usually described by their operative temperature, which is a measure of the net effect of air and ground temperature, sun, and wind on a particular animal. It has been defined as the temperature of an object with all the external heat exchange properties of the animal, but no evaporation, metabolism, or thermal inertia (Bakken and Gates 1975). Such an environmental temperature has the virtue of describing the animal's thermal environment with a single temperature of relevance to the animal. Operative temperature can be measured directly using hollow copper models of the animal of interest, or computed from the heat transfer equations described earlier. For an animal with little metabolism or evaporation (e.g., a lizard or a very waterproof frog), operative temperature is the body temperature the animal would reach if it stayed in a constant environment until it came to steady state. The measurement, computation, and uses of operative temperature have been reviewed by Bakken, Santee, and Erskine (1985).

The pronounced effect of humidity on wet-skinned amphibians requires some modification of the classical definition of operative temperature. This has not been done for amphibians, although humid operative temperature indices have been prepared (Campbell 1977; Nishi and Ibamato 1969) and could be adapted for amphibian studies. Thermal models of wet-skinned amphibians can be made using agar (Spotila and Berman 1976; Tracy 1976) or plaster (O'Connor 1989).

Bioenergetics, Activity, and Water Loss

To occupy a given habitat successfully, an organism must be able to obtain sufficient energy for growth, maintenance, and reproduction. An amphibian population will not persist in a locality where its food-seeking activity is restricted to the extent that most individuals are in negative energy balance. Favorable biophysical conditions must be present during a sufficient portion of the year so that amphibians can obtain enough food to satisfy their energy requirements. If high temperatures and dry conditions or cold temperatures persist for an extended period of time, the activity of these animals will be restricted. The point may be reached where metabolic energy requirements exceed food energy intake. In addition, amphibians must remain active to locate and court mates, disperse, and so forth.

Terrestrial amphibians will be unable to remain active in areas where their daily water loss resulting from activity exceeds their daily water uptake from the soil. For example, the salamander *Plethodon caddoensis* (Plethodontidae) in the Ouachita Mountains of Arkansas has its activity curtailed by high temperatures and lack of moisture common in its habitat during the summer months. Biophysical simulations suggest that, at air temperatures of 25°C, *P. caddoensis* could be active during the day for 3 h at 65% RH, 4.5 h at 80% RH, and 7.5 h at 100% RH, assuming the soil on which the animal sat was at field moisture capacity of −3.3 kPa. The critical environmental temperature level for this species (i.e., that temperature above which "normal" activity is curtailed) is reached in early summer, and salamander activity is severely limited until ambient temperature declines in fall. The seasonal reduction in food energy intake experienced by *P. caddoensis* results in a shorter growing season and may be responsible for the small size attained by adult *P. caddoensis* as compared to *Plethodon ouachitae*, which inhabits nearby Rich Mountain and has more favorable microclimatic conditions for a greater portion of the year (Spotila 1972).

Frogs are also restricted in habitat use by their interaction with their biophysical environment. The constraints on a leopard frog, *Rana pipiens*, due to the interactions between the frog's water and thermal ecology were detailed by Tracy (1976). A frog exposed to the sun in June would have a T_b only 2.5°C higher than a frog in a fully shaded environment (because of evaporative cooling) but would have twice the rate of water loss. The cumulative water loss for a 60-g frog between 1100 and 1400 would be over 30 g. This rate of water loss would be debilitating (O'Connor 1989)—and probably lethal—unless the frog had a ready supply of water from the substrate. Dole (1965b) reported that leopard frogs on their home ranges in grassy fields in northern Michigan typically spent more than 95% of the time during fair sunny days sitting quietly on wet soil in "forms." Thus, the thermoregulatory opportunities for this frog are restricted both by the constraint that they remain on wet substrates during sunny days and by the buffering effect of evaporative heat loss on body temperature. Evaporative cooling from the surface of the frog and the wet substrate surface will tend to dampen out body temperature responses to changing thermal conditions and give the frog a relatively stable T_b. Thus, frogs found in a "prostrate basking posture" (i.e., limply flattened to the ground exposed to the sun) may be maintaining a posture that maximizes exposure to the substrate environment to maximize water uptake while minimizing the cooling and desiccating effect of the wind. Leopard frogs in northern Michigan are active throughout the day and night in summer (Dole 1965a). It is likely that they can feed and escape from predators during midday in summer, but not if these activities prevent them from taking up needed water from wet substrates.

DIRECTIONS FOR THE FUTURE

As we develop a more complete understanding of the biophysical constraints on amphibians, several exciting and important avenues of inquiry become tractable. These research possibilities can be divided into two groups. First, we need to better understand the environmental biophysics of amphibians. In particular, we need more quantitative information on the importance of various pathways of heat, water, and gas exchange in amphibians under different circumstances (e.g., on open substrate, in vegetation, in burrows, in still water) in order to understand the morphological and physiological adaptations of different amphibians to their environments. For example, although the wet skins of amphibians buffer the animals' body temperatures against changes in the thermal environment, the extent of this buffer effect, the conditions under which such buffering will be ecologically important, and the implications of such effects for an amphibian's thermal ecology are largely unknown. The extent to which adaptations to conserve water by limiting cutaneous evaporation, such as waxy or mucoid coats on the integument, interfere with cutaneous gas exchange are not well understood. Similarly, the dependence of thermal, hydric, and gas exchanges of amphibians on microhabitat characteristics (e.g., open vegetation, wet versus dry substrates, sunny versus shaded microsites, still versus moving water) have been little explored. Until we understand the thermal and hydric diversity of the environments in which amphibians are found, we will continue to have difficulty understanding processes such as behavioral thermoregulation and hydroregulation.

A second set of research directions includes the linking of amphibian biophysics to behavioral and population ecology. Biophysical models and experiments may be used to examine limitations on the bioenergetics of amphibians, including their short- and long-term habitat use (e.g., Porter and Tracy 1974). Subsequently a food energy budget analysis could be done for several points on the climate space to ascertain the amount of energy ingested, the amount assimilated, and the amount required for metabolism. These results, in turn, would give the amounts of energy available for growth and reproduction. Combining these approaches, we could determine the activity patterns for amphibians for particular locations and times of year, the potential for food intake at these locations and times, and whether or not the amphibian could remain in energy balance in a particular location. This would allow us to predict the distribution and abundance of amphibian species on several spatial scales. Biophysical models (in conjunction with behavioral and population data) may be particularly important in anticipating the effects of habitat modification and climate changes. This approach may give us a clearer understanding of the environmental physiology of amphibians than has been gained to date by laboratory experiments and field studies.

5 Exchange of Respiratory Gases, Ions, and Water in Amphibious and Aquatic Amphibians

Robert G. Boutilier, Daniel F. Stiffler, and Daniel P. Toews

Regulation of the exchanges of ions, water, and respiratory gases in aquatic amphibians is complex, owing to the numerous sites at which such transfers can occur and to the ability of many such sites to exchange materials with either air or water. Gas exchange occurs across lungs, gills, and skin, whereas ionic and aqueous transfers are restricted to the skin, gill, and renal systems. The skin and gills exchange all materials, and the high permeability of these systems means that the surrounding water is essentially an extension of the extracellular space of the animal. While this external environment can effectively receive unwanted metabolic end products (e.g., CO_2 and NH_3), it can also become a liability if its chemical composition drastically alters. Thus, amphibians require mechanisms at their epithelial surfaces that enable them to regulate, to various extents, the passage of gases, ions, and water. Whereas the epithelial surfaces of submerged amphibians continually exchange dissolved gases, water, and ions, periodic losses of ions and water occur in urination, just as periodic exchanges of gases occur when aquatic amphibians surface to breathe air. The intent of this chapter is to examine (1) the processes involved in materials transport between animal and environment, (2) the limitations that the environment poses to such transport processes, and (3) the common linkages between ionic, aqueous, and gaseous exchange.

Respiratory Gas Exchange in Amphibians

Oxygen transfer from the environment to the cell occurs as a series of discrete steps (fig. 5.1) that include ventilatory convection, diffusion across the blood-gas barrier, transport of oxygen by the blood circulation, and delivery of O_2 across the blood-cell barrier. The flow of O_2 at any one step is the product of a prevailing driving force (i.e., the O_2 partial pressure difference) and an associated conductance for O_2 (table 5.1; see also chapter 4). Conductances in air (or water) and blood are proportional to the mass flow rate of the carrier (gas, water, blood) multiplied by its O_2 capacitance ($\Delta C_{O_2}/P_{O_2}$ = the increment in concentration that occurs in the carrier per unit increase in partial pressure). The diffusing capacities of the lungs, skin, and tissues (i.e., $D_{L,S,T}$) represent transfer conductances from environmental medium to blood,

and blood to cell. Transfer equations for CO_2 movements from cell to environment follow the same principles of driving force times conductance (fig. 5.1, table 5.1). Several variables (e.g., structural properties of the exchange organs, ventilation-perfusion relationships, chemical limitations), many of which are modified in accordance with changing requirements for gas exchange, determine the conductances for O_2 or CO_2 at any one step.

Ventilatory Convection

Several recent reviews examine the mechanics of lung and gill ventilation in amphibians (Shelton, Jones, and Milsom 1986; Boutilier 1988a; Burggren 1989; Malvin 1989). Regulation of the amounts of gas exchange between animal and environment is less well known, however, due to the considerable analytical difficulties caused by periodic breathing (Shelton and Boutilier 1982; Boutilier 1984; Pinder and Burggren 1986). Clearly, nevertheless, lung ventilation is modulated to meet changing demands in the supply of O_2 or in the removal of CO_2. Much of our information on the control and coordination of breathing movements in amphibians comes from studies examining respiratory responses to experimental alterations in the inspired gases. In virtually all cases, decreases in inspired O_2 or elevations in CO_2 lead to increased pulmonary ventilation.

Hypoxia Environmental hypoxia elicits increased ventilation in a wide variety of amphibious and aquatic amphibians (e.g., *Amphiuma tridactylum* [Caudata: Amphiumidae]: Lenfant and Johansen 1967; Toews 1971; *Bufo marinus:* Boutilier and Toews 1977; *Typhlonectes compressicauda* [Gymnophiona]: Toews and Macintyre 1978; *Rana pipiens:* Pinder and Burggren 1986) as well as certain larvae (review by Feder 1984; see also chapter 16). Lung ventilation in *R. pipiens* is

The authors' works are supported by the Natural Sciences and Engineering Research Council of Canada (RGB and DPT) and the National Science Foundation of the United States (DFS). We wish to thank Juan Markin for his helpful suggestions on the first draft of this manuscript. Thanks are also extended to Dr. Alan Pinder for access to unpublished data.

TABLE 5.1   Quantitative Relationships at Each Step of Gas Exchange for Rates of O_2 Uptake ($\dot{M}o_2$) and Co_2 Production ($\dot{M}co_2$)

Gas Exchange	Transfer Equations
Ventilation/irrigation, lungs, gills, skin	$\dot{M}o_2 = \dot{V}(C_Io_2 - C_Eo_2)$
	$\dot{M}co_2 = \dot{V}(C_Eco_2 - C_Ico_2)$
Blood-gas barrier	$\dot{M}o_2 = D_L(P_Ao_2 - P_co_2)$
	$\dot{M}co_2 = D_L(P_cco_2 - P_Aco_2)$
Circulatory convection	$\dot{M}o_2 = \dot{V}_b(C_ao_2 - C_vo_2)$
	$\dot{M}co_2 = \dot{V}_b(C_vo_2 - C_aco_2)$
Blood-cell barrier	$\dot{M}o_2 = D_T(P_co_2 - P_to_2)$
	$\dot{M}co_2 = D_T(P_tco_2 - P_cco_2)$

Notes: a = arterial; A = alveolar; b = blood; c = capillary; D_L = diffusing capacity of lung; D_T = diffusing capacity of tissue; E = expired; I = inspired; t = tissue; v = venous.

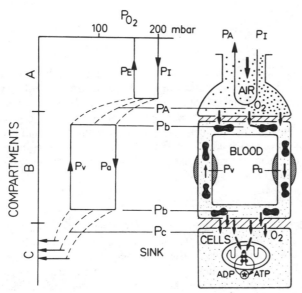

Fig. 5.1   Schematic of the respiratory system showing O_2 and CO_2 partial pressure differences at each step of gas exchange. See text for further details. *A* = alveolar; *a* = arterial; *b* = blood; *c* = cell; *E* = expired; *I* = inspired; *P* = pressure; *v* = venous. (Reprinted, by permission, from Taylor and Weibel 1981.)

proportional to the rate of O_2 consumption ($\dot{M}o_2$; fig. 5.2). A hypoxia-induced decrease in $\dot{M}o_2$ occurs largely as a result of a decline in cutaneous $\dot{M}o_2$, whereas hyperventilation maintains pulmonary O_2 uptake. During decreased O_2 availability (or increased O_2 demands due to heightened activity), pulmonary hyperventilation appears the primary way in which these animals regulate their $\dot{M}o_2$ (Pinder and Burggren 1986).

Pulmonary ventilation also increases in direct proportion to temperature and therefore resting metabolic rate in the toad *Bufo paracnemis* (Kruhoffer et al. 1987). In addition, these animals exhibit a pronounced temperature dependence in their ventilatory responses to hypoxia (fig. 5.3): the greater the temperature, the more marked the ventilatory response. Responses such as these may be related to the temperature dependence of hemoglobin O_2 affinity (see below). Large increases in ventilation also occur after "anaerobic dives" in *Xenopus laevis* (Boutilier and Shelton 1986a) as the animals repay an O_2 debt (cf. Jones 1972a), or during environmental hypoxia (Brett 1980).

Many anuran larvae (e.g., *Rana*, *Xenopus*) ventilate their lungs periodically. In normoxic conditions, pulmonary res-

piration of this sort accounts for 10 to 20% of the total O_2 consumed (Burggren and West 1982; Burggren, Feder, and Pinder 1983; Feder 1983a, 1983e; Feder and Wassersug 1984; West and Burggren 1983). In normoxic water, larvae maintain their normal aerobic metabolic rates even if prevented from surfacing to breathe air. Though aquatic gas exchange predominates in normoxic conditions in a wide temperature range (Burggren, Feder, and Pinder 1983), air breathing becomes crucial in maintaining aerobic metabolic rates during aquatic hypoxia.

Exposure of larvae to reductions in dissolved O_2 initiates increases in pulmonary ventilation (up to several breaths/minute) in proportion to the degree of hypoxia (Feder 1983a, 1983e; Wassersug and Seibert 1975; West and Burggren 1984). Though hypoxia evokes greater activity and/or movement to more oxygenated water (Feder 1983e), behavioral conditions in nature may dictate that larvae remain in secluded microhabitats that are more hypoxic than surrounding waters (e.g., Noland and Ultsch 1981). Aquatic hypoxia reduces the Po_2 gradient across the aquatic gas exchangers and hence the ability to extract dissolved oxygen. Under such adverse conditions, the animals must either reduce their aerobic metabolic rate, resort to alternate metabolic sources of energy (anaerobiosis), or surface to breathe air (i.e., at the lungs, the Po_2 gradient remains high). Breathing air in response to aquatic hypoxia enables the animal to defend its aerobic metabolic rate without having to resort to anaerobiosis and its consequent problems (Hochachka and Somero 1984). Indeed, when larvae of *Xenopus* are prevented from using their lungs to breathe air, they accumulate lactate in hypoxic water but not in normoxia (Feder and Wassersug 1984). When free to breathe air, however, lactate does not accumulate even in severe aquatic hypoxia.

Though anuran larvae can meet increased demands for O_2 through air breathing, this capacity is evidently not required when high temperatures increase the O_2 requirement. In fact, the partitioning of gas exchange between skin, gills, and lungs in *Rana berlandieri* and *R. catesbeiana* (approximately 70, 20, and 10%, respectively) does not change from 15° to 33°C (Burggren, Feder, and Pinder 1983). This contrasts with similar studies on the aquatic salamanders *Ambystoma*, *Amphiuma*, and *Siren* (Guimond and Hutchison 1976; Lenfant, Johansen, and Hansen 1970) and the aquatic frog *Xenopus laevis* (Hutchison and Miller 1979a). As pointed out by Burggren, Feder, and Pinder (1983), it is often implicitly assumed that ectotherms are facultative air-breathers at low temperatures and obligate air-breathers at high temperatures. Elevated energetic costs associated with gill ventilation and/or inadequate abilities to extract the reduced amount of dissolved O_2 at higher temperatures are commonly cited as reasons for the switch to obligate air breathing. In reality, however, these assumptions have rarely been tested in amphibians, or in bimodal breathers in general. The results of the studies on larvae suggest that neither the energetic costs of branchial ventilation nor any physical constraints on O_2 extraction should limit aquatic gas exchange at elevated temperatures (Burggren, Feder, and Pinder 1983).

Hypercapnia   Increases in arterial CO_2 tensions, whether of metabolic (McDonald, Boutilier, and Toews 1980; Boutilier, McDonald, and Toews 1980) or environmental origin (Jackson and Braun 1979; Boutilier and Shelton 1986b), increase

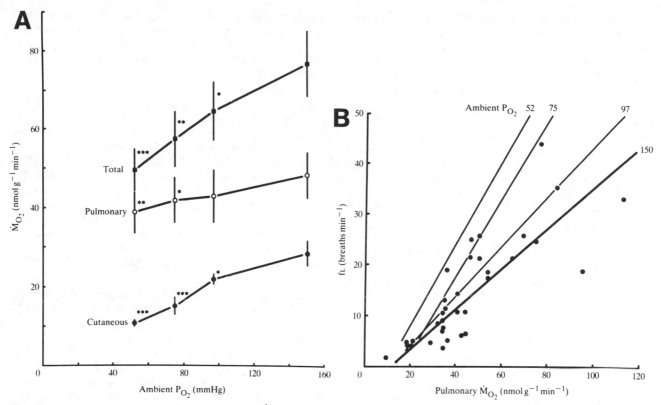

Fig. 5.2 A, partitioning of the total O_2 consumption ($\dot{M}O_2$) between pulmonary and cutaneous exchangers as a function of the ambient P_{O_2} in freely moving *Rana pipiens* at 25°C. *Asterisks* denote when values differ significantly from normoxic level. B, changes in ventilation frequency (f_L) at various ambient P_{O_2} levels, as a function of pulmonary $\dot{M}O_2$. Re-gression data for each level of P_{O_2}: 52 mm Hg, $f_L = 0.802 (\dot{M}O_2) - 8.04$, $N = 12$; 75 mm Hg, $f_L = 0.764 (\dot{M}O_2) - 13.34$, $N = 11$; 97 mm Hg, $f_L = 0.486 (\dot{M}O_2) - 5.87$, $N = 11$; 150 mm Hg, $f_L = 0.370 (\dot{M}O_2) - 2.28$, $N = 34$. (Reprinted, by permission, from Pinder and Burggren 1986, *Journal of Experimental Biology*, © Company of Biologists Ltd.)

ventilation (see also chapter 7). Addition of CO_2 to inspired air also results in hyperventilation (*Bufo:* Macintyre and Toews 1976; Boutilier et al. 1979a; R. M. Jones 1982; *Typhlonectes* [Gymnophiona]: Toews and Macintyre 1978; *R. catesbeiana:* Jackson and Braun 1979; *Xenopus:* Boutilier 1981; *Cryptobranchus* [Caudata: Cryptobranchidae]: Boutilier and Toews 1981a). The sensitivity of these ventilatory responses to hypercapnia and their impact on controlling respiratory acid-base balance (see below) can vary enormously. For instance, pulmonary ventilation of the urodele *Amphiuma tridactylum* is unresponsive to high CO_2 (Toews 1971). Other amphibians, such as *B. marinus, R. catesbeiana,* and *X. laevis,* can alter their respiratory acid-base balance through ventilation (Boutilier et al. 1979a; Jackson and Braun 1979; Boutilier and Shelton 1986a, 1986b, 1986c).

As temperatures increase from 10° to 30°C, metabolically linked increases in the rate of CO_2 elimination ($\dot{M}CO_2$) occur by pulmonary ventilation alone in *R. catesbeiana,* with cutaneous CO_2 removal constant (MacKenzie and Jackson 1978). Jackson and Braun (1979) examined the CO_2 conductance of the skin of bullfrogs exposed to either aerial or aquatic hypercapnia. In those experiments, animals could maintain a constant arterial P_{CO_2} during aquatic hypercapnia. That the lungs could eliminate metabolically produced CO_2 as well as that added via the skin clearly demonstrates that pulmonary ventilation can control acid-base balance. Similar experiments on *Xenopus* have shown a marked rise in the respiratory exchange quotient of the lung (i.e., more CO_2 is given off than O_2 taken up) when the animals confront aquatic hy-

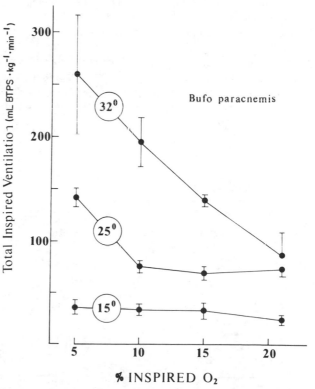

Fig. 5.3 The effect of changes in inspired O_2 concentration on total inspired ventilation (± 1, SEM) of *Bufo paracnemis* at temperatures of 15°, 25°, and 32°C. (Redrawn from Kruhoffer et al. 1987).

percapnia (Boutilier and Shelton 1986b). When, on the other hand, the same concentrations of CO_2 as were delivered to the skin are instead delivered to the lungs, arterial P_{CO_2} increases in both *Rana* (Jackson and Braun 1979) and *Xenopus* (Boutilier 1981), resulting in a respiratory acidosis. In both cases, the skin cannot eliminate CO_2 as can the lungs.

Patterns of Ventilation   Changes in ventilation as a result of hypoxia, hypercapnia, temperature, or duration of diving all are associated with a more continuous breathing pattern than normal. For example, bullfrogs exposed to aquatic hypoxia spend more time ventilating their lungs at the surface and spend less time diving (Boutilier 1990b). Because the volume of the buccal pump is relatively fixed in amphibians (West and Jones 1975a; Brett 1980; Boutilier 1984), the capacity for altering pulmonary ventilation through changes in the depth of breathing is slight. Instead, minute ventilation is primarily controlled by altering the number of breaths per unit time. Even so, some anurans adjust individual breath patterns during respiratory stress, exhibiting higher than normal pulmonary pressure cycles (Boutilier and Toews 1977; Pinder and Burggren 1986), increasing the number of inspirations per expiration (Boutilier 1984), or changing the coordination of sequences for emptying and filling the lungs (Kruhoffer et al. 1987).

Detailed measurements of the ventilatory patterns in *Xenopus laevis* reveal two distinct breathing patterns (Boutilier 1984, 1988a). In one (burst breathing), long dives are periodically interrupted by brief visits to the surface, whereupon a discrete series of lung ventilations occurs. At other times, the same animal might remain at the surface, ventilating its lungs intermittently over prolonged time (bout breathing). The minute ventilation during a breathing burst is approximately two to three times higher than that of a bout, consonant with greater requirements for O_2 uptake and CO_2 removal during activity (Boutilier 1984; Boutilier and Shelton 1986a). Control of gas exchange in both breathing styles results in large part from manipulations of the temporal pattern of lung ventilations. Animals respond to hypercapnia with a threefold increase in minute ventilation, 80% due to an in-

creased frequency of breathing (fig. 5.4a), the remainder being attributable to changes in the depth of breathing (Boutilier 1988a; fig. 5.4b). Thus, the primary output of the respiratory control system appears to be adjustment of the timing of individual breaths, rather than large alterations in the individual breaths themselves.

Behavior requirements to remain submerged and the depth of diving influence the periodicity of lung ventilation in aquatic amphibians. For instance, threats imposed at the surface will cause *X. laevis* to remain submerged (Boutilier 1984), even if anaerobiosis results (Boutilier 1988a). The depth of a dive also determines air-breathing rates, perhaps because the cost of travel to the surface increases with depth (Kramer 1988). Accordingly, with increasing depth *X. laevis* increases both the time spent replenishing the O_2 stores at the surface and the interval between visits to the air-water interface (Shannon and Kramer 1988). Bullfrog larvae also surface to breathe less frequently in deep water (Feder 1984).

Conflicts between several underwater activities (e.g., feeding, locomotion, predator avoidance, mating) and air breathing will determine time spent underwater and, therefore, the pattern of air breathing. In suspension-feeding larvae, for example, the buccopharyngeal respiratory surfaces are the site of food particle entrapment, and gill ventilation frequency decreases as the density of suspended food increases. Suspension-feeding larvae of *Xenopus* increase aerial ventilation in dense food suspensions. This increased air breathing is not due to an elevated metabolism, suggesting that the lung hyperventilation simply offsets the decreased gill ventilation in concentrated food suspensions (Feder, Seale, Boraas, Wassersug, and Gibbs 1984). If larvae in hypoxic water cannot breathe air, however, they decrease food capture while they increase gill ventilation frequency. This uncoupling of the normal regulation of food intake through buccopharyngeal ventilation may arise because of decreased mucus secretion by the gills. The reduced mucus formation would not only minimize food particle entrapment (Seale, Hoff, and Wassersug 1982) but might also facilitate greater gas exchange by decreasing the diffusion barrier, thereby increasing the diffusive conductance of the gill (Feder 1984).

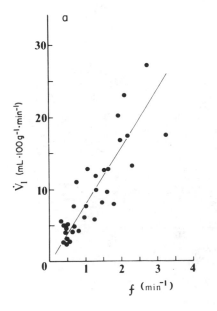

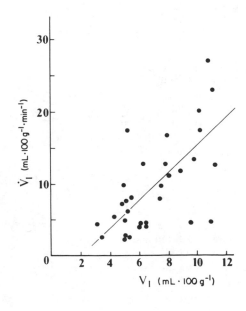

Fig. 5.4   The relationship between (*A*) minute ventilation ($\dot{V}_I$) and total respiratory frequency (*f*) and (*B*) $\dot{V}_I$ and inspiratory volume (V_I) for normocapnic and hypercapnic *Xenopus* at 25°C (*N* = 7). Hypercapnia was induced by exposing animal to 1% CO_2–99% air delivered to both aquatic and aerial compartments. Each point represents a mean value for a 1- to 2-h period of continuous ventilatory recordings as animals voluntarily dived and surfaced at a blowhole fitted with a pneumotachograph. Best fit lines were determined by least squares regression analysis. (Reprinted, by permission, from Boutilier 1988a.)

Another conflict between underwater behavior and air breathing is that of sexual display in the newt *Triturus vulgaris* (Salamandridae; Halliday and Sweatman 1976). During courtship, the male newt will forgo air breathing as long as there is opportunity to display to a female. Removal of this "stimulus" leads to an immediate resumption of its normal periodic air-breathing habit. Presumably, the resolution of these and other conflicts resides with higher brain centers that can override suprathreshold input stimuli (e.g., low P_{O_2}, high P_{CO_2}) that normally initiate air breathing (Boutilier 1989; Boutilier and Shelton 1986b; Jackson 1978b; Shelton, Jones, and Milsom 1986).

Blood-Gas Barrier

Respiratory gas exchange in some amphibians can occur simultaneously across lungs, skin, gills, and buccopharyngeal cavity. The transfer of gases at each site is dependent on variables that include surface area, capillary density, blood-gas diffusion distances, and partial pressure gradients.

Buccal Cavity and Gills   Diffusion of gases across the buccal cavity itself may be most important in terrestrial lungless salamanders, where up to 10% of the total respiratory vasculature may be in the epithelia lining the mouth (Czopek 1961; Foxon 1964). However, the epithelia of the buccal cavity in the exclusively aquatic urodele *Cryptobranchus* is also richly vascularized (R. G. Boutilier and D. P. Toews pers. observations), and these animals convect water into and out of the mouth at increased rates during respiratory stresses such as aquatic hypercapnia (Boutilier and Toews 1981a). The external gills of some neotenic salamanders simply hang in the water (e.g., *Siren* [Sirenidae]), whereas other animals actively move the gills back and forth (e.g., *Necturus* [Proteidae]). Such movements convect water over the branchial surfaces and disrupt boundary layers, effectively increasing the diffusive conductance for oxygen by raising the P_{O_2} of the water immediately adjacent to the surface of the gill (see Feder and Pinder 1988b). This may be quite important in forms such as *Ambystoma mexicanum,* where blood-to-medium diffusion distances can be in the order of 5 to 15 μm (Hackford, Gillies, and Goldblatt 1977). The extensive vascularization of the gills of such animals (see review by Malvin 1989) underscores their potential as gas exchange organs. *Necturus maculosus,* for example, can achieve up to 60% of its $\dot{M}_{O_2}$ through branchial respiration at 25°C (Guimond and Hutchison 1972, 1976). Although the internalized gills of anuran larvae are continuously ventilated at rates as high as 60–80 min^{-1} (Feder 1983a, 1983e; West and Burggren 1982), branchial respiration accounts for only 20% of the total O_2 uptake at temperatures ranging from 15° to 33°C (Burggren, Feder, and Pinder 1983). Moreover, experimental increases in water flowing over the gills have little effect on branchial O_2 uptake (Burggren and West 1982), indicating that, like skin (see below), the gills are primarily diffusion limited.

Pulmonary Gas Exchange   Amphibian species differ greatly in surface area and capillary density of their lungs, even at the macroscopic level. Lungs range from the poorly vascularized saclike organs seen in *Cryptobranchus, Necturus,* and *Telmatobius* (Anura: Leptodactylidae), to the highly vascularized and architecturally complex lungs of *Amphiuma* (Caudata: Amphiumidae) and *Siren* (Guimond and Hutchison 1973a, 1976; Hutchison, Haines, and Engbretson 1976; Ultsch 1976). The degree of complexity increases even further in aquatic anurans that typically inhabit hypoxic waters (e.g., *Xenopus laevis, Pipa pipa* [both Pipidae]), as well as in the more terrestrial bufonids (Smith and Rapson 1977; reviewed by Burggren 1989). Exposure of larval *Rana catesbeiana* to chronic hypoxia changes the morphology of the lungs; lung volume increases as does internal septation of the pulmonary surface (Burggren and Mwalukoma 1983). Blood-to-air diffusion distances are 1 to 2 μm in normoxic larvae, and these do not change with chronic hypoxia.

For the most part, the lungs of amphibians have a small dead space; during breathing, pulmonary P_{O_2} and P_{CO_2} levels differ only slightly from those of inspired gas (Boutilier and Shelton 1986b). Between breaths, diffusion gradients are large for both respiratory gases. For example, alveolar P_{O_2} not uncommonly exceeds 130 mm Hg immediately after a breath in *Amphiuma tridactylum* (Toews, Shelton, and Randall 1971) and *X. laevis* (Boutilier and Shelton 1986b). The P_{O_2} gradient from lung to pulmonary venous blood averages about 9 mm Hg in *Xenopus* (fig. 5.5), changing little as alveolar P_{O_2} fluctuates during voluntary diving and surfacing. Similarly, the P_{CO_2} gradient in the reverse direction is also constant at approximately 2 mm Hg. Even larger gradients occur in the urodele *Amphiuma tridactylum* (Toews, Shelton, and Randall 1971). Unlike the lungs of mammals, the lungs of amphibians are unlikely to reach complete blood-gas equilibration for several reasons. The blood-gas diffusion distances are comparatively large (0.7–2.3 μm; Meban 1973; Burggren and Mwalukoma 1983; Burggren 1989) and capillary densities of the lungs are relatively small (Weibel 1972) in comparison to mammals. The lungs of amphibians are also subject to great anatomical as well as physiological blood shunts (Smith and Rapson 1977; Shelton 1976, 1985; Boutilier and Shelton 1986b; Burggren 1989), both of which negate blood-gas equilibration. The incomplete blood-gas equilibration in amphibian lungs does not imply less efficiency than mammalian lungs, just difference; that is, mammalian lungs in an amphibian would be as ineffectual as amphibian lungs in a mammal.

Extrapulmonary Gas Exchange   The skin of most amphibians plays a major role in overall gas exchange, often increasing in regulatory importance as temperature, and therefore metabolic rate, decreases (see review by Feder and Burggren 1985a). Studies on the partitioning of gas exchange in anuran larvae show, however, that cutaneous respiration not only maintains a constant fraction of gas exchange but also predominates overall gas exchange at temperatures ranging from 15° to 33°C (Burggren, Feder, and Pinder 1983). In some aquatic salamanders (e.g., *Cryptobranchus alleganiensis*), virtually all O_2 uptake and CO_2 removal occurs across the skin, irrespective of temperature. The respiratory exchange ratios ($R = \dot{M}_{CO_2}/\dot{M}_{O_2}$) of the skin of these exclusively aquatic and predominantly skin-breathing animals are therefore essentially the same as the animals' metabolic respiratory quotient (RQ; i.e., 0.8–0.9). When the cutaneous exchanger is less effective in O_2 uptake, however, the exchange ratio of the skin increases to extraordinarily high values

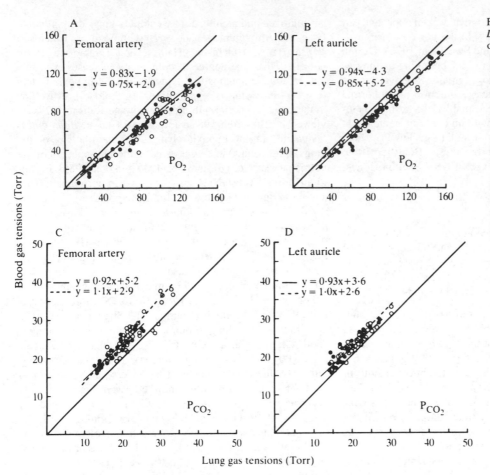

A

Femoral artery

$y = 0.83x - 1.9$
$y = 0.75x + 2.0$

P_{O_2}

B

Left auricle

$y = 0.94x - 4.3$
$y = 0.85x + 5.2$

P_{O_2}

C

Femoral artery

$y = 0.92x + 5.2$
$y = 1.1x + 2.9$

P_{CO_2}

D

Left auricle

$y = 0.93x + 3.6$
$y = 1.0x + 2.6$

P_{CO_2}

Blood gas tensions (Torr)

Lung gas tensions (Torr)

Fig. 5.5 P_{O_2} (*A, B*) and P_{CO_2} (*C, D*) relationships between simultaneous lung and blood samples taken from freely diving *Xenopus laevis* at 25°C. The blood samples were taken from the femoral artery in ten animals (*A, C*) and the left atrium in eleven animals (*B, D*) in separate series of experiments. The animals were breathing air in all experiments and were in water equilibrated with air (●) or with a 1% CO_2–99% air mixture (○). Regression equations are given (correlation coefficients between 0.91 and 0.98) and lines plotted through the points for aerated water (*solid lines*) and hypercapnic water (*dashed lines*). (Reprinted, by permission, from Boutilier and Shelton 1986b.)

(fig. 5.6), to as much as ten times the metabolic RQ of the animal. Despite its role in O_2 uptake, the skin of amphibians remains a primary site for the elimination of CO_2. Similar relationships exist for the "gill-skin" system of bimodal breathing fish (Rahn and Howell 1976).

Reliance on cutaneous surfaces for gas exchange depends on several additional factors: for example, the skin morphology, the presence of alternative exchange organs, the gas exchange medium (air or water), and the ambient O_2 and CO_2 levels (Feder and Burggren 1985a). Differences in capillary density and blood-to-medium diffusion distances may account for much of the interspecific variation in the efficacy of skin gas exchange. For instance, subepidermal capillary networks in amphibians can account for as little as 20% to as much as 96% of the total respiratory capillarization (Czopek 1965; Saint-Aubain 1982a; Feder and Burggren 1985a). In some exclusively aquatic and predominantly skin-breathing forms, such as the anuran *Telmatobius culeus* or the urodele *Cryptobranchus*, extensive folds or flaps of skin appear as specializations for increasing the cutaneous surface area. In *Cryptobranchus*, the folds of skin that run along each side of the body are extensively vascularized with capillaries that penetrate almost to the outer layer of the skin (Noble 1931; R. G. Boutilier pers. observations), acting as a crude gill. Indeed, in conditions of low oxygen, these animals sway from side to side to ventilate the skin, as does *Telmatobius* (Hutchison, Haines, and Engbretson 1976). Other species ex-

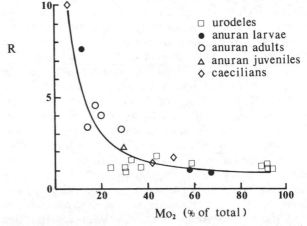

R

□ urodeles
● anuran larvae
○ anuran adults
△ anuran juveniles
◇ caecilians

$\dot{M}_{O_2}$ (% of total)

Fig. 5.6 Plot of the exchange ratio of the cutaneous exchange site ($R = \dot{M}_{CO_2}/\dot{M}_{O_2}$) as a function of the relative amount of O_2 that this system provides ($\dot{M}_{O_2}$% of total). R values were computed from tabulated data shown in Feder and Burggren 1985a, table 3, for amphibians breathing both air and water. (Original data on urodeles are from Guimond and Hutchison 1972, 1973a, 1973b, 1974; on anuran larvae are from Burggren and West 1982; on anuran adults and juveniles are from Gottlieb and Jackson 1976 and Burggren and Moalli 1984; and on caecilians are from Mendes 1945 and Sawaya 1947.)

hibit seasonal specializations that increase cutaneous surface areas. The male of the so-called hairy frog, *Astylosternus robustus* (Ranidae), develops highly vascularized dermal papillae during the breeding season, when metabolic rates and underwater activities are greatest (Noble 1931). The surface area of the tail fin of certain male newts also increases during the breeding season, presumably to facilitate increased demands for cutaneous gas exchange during underwater courtship (Czopek 1965; Halliday and Sweatman 1976).

Gas exchange across the skin is dependent on (1) the ventilation (or irrigation) of the skin with the respiratory medium, (2) the diffusion of gas through the skin, and (3) the rate at which gas is transported in the blood by convection. This area has received considerable attention as of late (Feder and Burggren 1985a; Piiper 1988; Malvin 1988), and several models of cutaneous gas exchange are available (Piiper, Gatz, and Crawford 1976; Burggren and Moalli 1984; Malvin and Hlastala 1986a, 1986b; Pinder 1987a; see also chapters 4 and 7). It is beyond the scope of this chapter to develop details of the various perfusive and diffusive resistances to skin gas exchange, though it should be recognized that debate has been extensive about the degree to which the skin of amphibians is "diffusion limited" (cf. Piiper, Gatz, and Crawford 1976). In a "diffusion-limited" gas exchanger the major limitation to O_2 uptake or CO_2 removal is the diffusion barrier between ambient medium and blood. Though the diffusive resistance of amphibian skin is often large, this does not preempt some capacity for modulating gas exchange through changes in cutaneous blood flow or skin ventilation.

In a strictly diffusion-limited system, the uptake of O_2 ($\dot{M}o_2$) can be considered to take place across a single compartment of fixed surface area (Piiper, Gatz, and Crawford 1976). In this case, cutaneous gas exchange would obey the equation

$$\dot{M}o_2 = Do_2 \times \Delta Po_2$$

where ΔPo_2 is the partial pressure gradient across the skin and Do_2 is the cutaneous diffusing capacity for O_2. Because such a model considers Do_2 to be fixed anatomically, any ability to regulate gas exchange could only occur as a result of changes in the Po_2 gradient across the skin. Changes in the number of perfused capillaries in the skin could alter the *functional* surface area as opposed to the *total* surface area of the skin (Burggren and Moalli 1984). The functional surface area is the proportion of the total area of the skin that is actually ventilated and perfused at any given time, and can change depending on whether the capillaries are open to blood flow (i.e., recruited) or closed. In this case, the surface area available for gas exchange will vary depending on the ratio of open to closed capillaries,

$$\dot{M}o_2 = (n_{open}/n_{total}) \times D_{cap} \times \Delta Po_2,$$

where n_{open} is the number of open capillaries, n_{total} is the total number of capillaries that could be recruited, and D_{cap} is the total diffusing capacity of all capillaries. In this case, the model predicts that cutaneous gas exchange can be regulated by adjusting the number of open to closed capillaries. The actual parameters involved in regulating gas exchange could include changes in capillary density, radius, or blood flow

(Malvin 1988). Indeed, Malvin has shown that even in the absence of capillary recruitment, gross changes in blood flow will have some effect on cutaneous gas exchange, despite the large but incomplete diffusion limitation. Although the exact mechanisms and adjustments are still the subject of some debate (Pinder 1987a; Piiper 1988; Malvin 1988; Burggren 1988a; Feder and Pinder 1988b), gas exchange across amphibian skin is regulated to some extent by the cutaneous microcirculation.

For example, cold submerged bullfrogs (*Rana catesbeiana*) can maintain their normoxic $\dot{M}o_2$ as aquatic Po_2 levels decrease from 140 to 80 mm Hg (Pinder 1987a; see also chapter 10). This occurs both through decreases in arterial Po_2, which helps to maintain the transcutaneous Po_2 gradient, and by increases in cutaneous diffusing capacity (fig. 5.7). These observations support the model of cutaneous gas exchange proposed by Burggren and Moalli (1984), where gas exchange is modulated through active changes in the diffusing capacity of the skin.

Earlier studies of cutaneous gas exchange in water concluded that gas flux through the amphibian skin was largely passive and poorly controlled. Such conclusions follow from studies in which the increases in cutaneous gas exchange associated with an elevated metabolism can be accounted for entirely by increases in the partial pressure gradients for O_2 and CO_2 across the skin (MacKenzie and Jackson 1978; Boutilier, McDonald, and Toews 1980; Moalli et al. 1981). However, as pointed out by Pinder (1987a), most of these studies

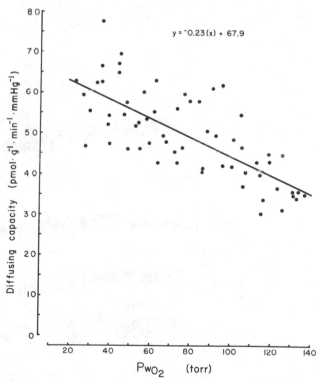

Fig. 5.7 Cutaneous diffusing capacity of submerged bullfrogs (*Rana catesbeiana*) as a function of the partial pressure of O_2 in water (P_wO_2). Points are single measurements; nine to twelve measurements taken per animal ($N = 6$). Temperature = 5°C. (Reprinted, by permission, from Pinder 1987a)

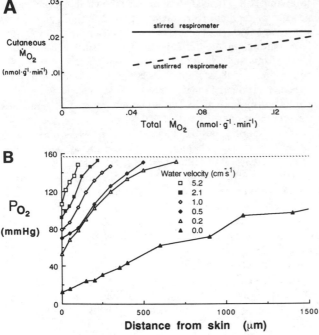

were carried out at higher temperatures, where the potential to augment cutaneous gas exchange may be severely limited. The key point in the case of the cold submerged bullfrogs (Pinder 1987a) is that adaptive regulation of Do_2 may be the most evident at temperatures at which cutaneous gas exchange alone can meet the resting gas exchange requirements. Cold normoxic animals may operate at a $\dot{M}o_2$ that is well below the maximum cutaneous $\dot{M}o_2$ possible at such temperatures. Thus, future studies of adaptive modulation of cutaneous gas exchange should focus on conditions in which the $\dot{M}o_2$ of the animal is below the maximum ceiling for cutaneous $\dot{M}o_2$. Studies should also consider whether the skin is being "ventilated," which is known to increase gas flux (fig. 5.8A) by disrupting hypoxic boundary layers (fig. 5.8B), thereby helping to maintain partial pressure gradients across the skin (Pinder and Burggren 1986; Burggren and Feder 1986; Feder and Pinder 1988b). Indeed, direct measurements of cutaneous blood flow in bullfrogs have shown that skin perfusion increases when the ambient medium is well mixed but decreases sharply when the water becomes still and boundary layers develop (fig. 5.9). Other experiments with bullfrogs have shown that the relative distribution of pulmocutaneous blood flow to skin decreases during aquatic hypoxia (fig. 5.10). This latter response can be viewed in two ways: blood may be directed toward the site of gas exchange where most O_2 is available (i.e., the lungs), or it could be related to the conservation of body O_2 stores (Shelton 1985), since O_2 gained by air breathing may be lost transcutaneously to hypoxic water (Feder and Burggren 1985a).

Losses of O_2 to hypoxic water may also occur across the gills of aquatic amphibians (Malvin 1989). However, shunting blood through nonrespiratory pathways in the gill or simply reducing gill ventilation can curtail these losses. For

Fig. 5.8   *A,* incidental effect of locomotor movements on cutaneous O_2 uptake in frogs (*Rana pipiens*) spontaneously active at 25°C. Frogs were breathing both air and water. In unstirred water, more active frogs (i.e., those with elevated total rates of O_2 consumption [$\dot{M}o_2$]) had a greater cutaneous O_2 uptake than less active frogs. In stirred water, cutaneous O_2 uptake was constant. (Reprinted, by permission, from Feder and Pinder 1988.) *B,* O_2 boundary layers, measured at a single middorsal point adjacent to the skin of a lightly sedated bullfrog (*R. catesbeiana* at various water velocities. The boundary layer is "still" water was measured after 1 h with no convection. A. W. Pinder and M. E. Feder, unpublished data.)

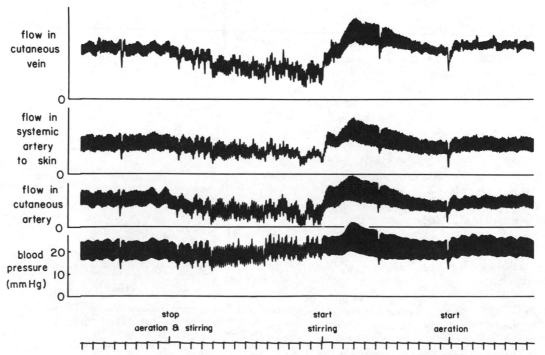

Fig. 5.9   Effect of skin ventilation on blood flow to and from the skin of *Rana catesbeiana.* Both the systemic and the cutaneous arteries supply the skin. Some (but not all) return from both supplies is via the cutaneous vein. Blood flow in all vessels decreases markedly when ventilation is stopped and increases quickly when ventilation is restored. (Reprinted, by permission, from Feder and Pinder 1988b.)

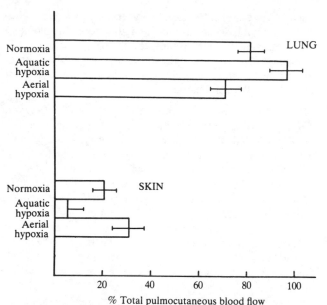

Fig. 5.10 The relative distribution to the lungs and skin of pulmocutaneous blood in conscious, unrestrained bullfrogs (*Rana catesbeiana*) 10 min into a voluntary dive. Frogs were subjected to normoxia ($Po_2 = 155$ mm Hg), aquatic hypoxia ($Po_2 = 40$ mm Hg) only, and aerial hypoxia ($Po_2 = 40$ mm Hg) only. (Reprinted, by permission, from Boutilier, Glass, and Heisler 1986.)

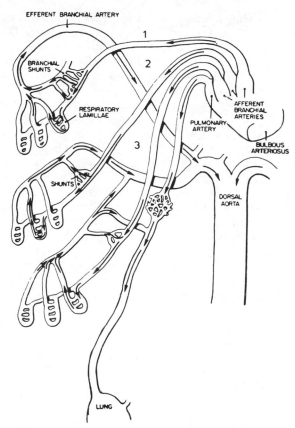

Fig. 5.11 Schematic of the vascular arrangement of the aortic arches, gills, and lung in the salamander *Ambystoma tigrinum*. (Reprinted, by permission, from Malvin and Boutilier 1985.)

example, the reflex inhibition of gill ventilation for the first 15 to 20 s following an air breath in *R. catesbeiana* larvae (West and Burggren 1983) lengthens after the animals breathe O_2 or when they are exposed to aquatic hypoxia (West and Burggren 1982). In severe aquatic hypoxia, gill ventilation ceases entirely, presumably to minimize loss of blood-borne O_2 (derived from lung gas) to hypoxic branchial water. Despite the reductions in gill ventilation frequency, larvae of *Rana* are still subject to transcutaneous O_2 losses to the surrounding water (Feder 1983e, 1984). Although adult frogs may shunt blood away from the skin (fig. 5.10), such shunting is undocumented in larvae (Burggren, Feder, and Pinder 1983). Regardless, larvae of *Rana* (Feder 1983e) and other species (Feder 1981b, 1983a) clearly cannot prevent O_2 losses across the skin and must therefore compensate for these losses by increasing aerial ventilation. As a consequence, air breathing in severe aquatic hypoxia can account for more than 100% of the total O_2 consumption (Feder 1984).

Air-breathing larvae of *Xenopus* ventilate their gills at a relatively constant frequency regardless of water Po_2 (Feder and Wassersug 1984). If they cannot surface to breathe, however, gill ventilation frequency increases in proportion to aquatic hypoxia (Feder and Wassersug 1984), as it does in the lungless larvae of *Bufo* (Feder 1983a). In severely hypoxic conditions (i.e., water $Po_2 < 20$ mm Hg), exclusively aquatic larvae cannot meet their aerobic metabolic demands, and anaerobiosis ensues.

As in anuran larvae, gill-breathing urodeles such as *Ambystoma* also risk losing O_2 to hypoxic water. The circulatory anatomy of gills of *Ambystoma* (fig. 5.11) reveals several shunt vessels, and vasoactivity of the entire branchial vasculature is controlled through adrenergic, cholinergic, and renin-angiotension systems (Malvin 1985a, 1985c). During aquatic hypoxia, blood is diverted away from gill arch I to arches II and III (fig. 5.11; Malvin 1985b), with more blood being shunted to the lung (in series with gill arch III). This not only reduces transbranchial O_2 losses to hypoxic water (i.e., gill arch I normally receives blood high in O_2), but it also facilitates aerial gas exchange (Malvin 1989). Shunting of afferent branchial blood through nonrespiratory pathways also occurs in anuran larvae (McIndoe and Smith 1984b).

Adaptive changes in cutaneous gas exchange can also occur in air. Malvin and Hlastala (1986a, 1986b) monitored inert gas washout into a ventilated capsule on the ventral surface of adult frogs (*Rana pipiens*) and showed that gas exchange increased in response to local hypoxia. Burggren and Moalli (1984), on the other hand, found that overall cutaneous CO_2 elimination of bullfrogs decreased when capillary recruitment in the skin decreased during air exposure, presumably as a water conservation mechanism. Numerous recent studies of the lungless and gill-less plethodontid salamanders indicate that they have a marked capacity for adjusting their cutaneous $\dot{M}o_2$ in response to increased activity, that is, up to ten times the standard metabolic rate (Feder 1988; Full 1986; Full et al. 1988). The plethodontid *Desmognathus quadramaculatus* evidently meets increased O_2 requirements during exercise through increases in cutaneous diffusing capacity (Feder, Full, and Piiper 1988). Chapter 6, which focuses on more terrestrial species, considers these mechanisms further.

While most recent work on cutaneous gas exchange has considered O_2 uptake, similar processes should act to modulate CO_2 elimination and should therefore participate in respiratory acid-base regulation, especially at low temperatures.

In this regard, it would be instructive to know the fate of dissolved CO_2 as it crosses the skin and enters the water. Does it remain as molecular CO_2, or is it hydrated to produce H^+ and HCO_3^-? Much will depend on whether the reaction is catalyzed. The uncatalyzed hydration of CO_2 is in the order of minutes (Kern 1960). However, externally located carbonic anhydrase (e.g., on the apical skin surface or in the mucus) would promote relatively rapid hydration. Carbonic anhydrase occurs in the skin of several amphibians (Rosen and Friedley 1973; Toews et al. 1978), but the exact location is unknown. In CO_2 excretion, the catalyzed versus uncatalyzed reaction would become increasingly important when boundary layers are large (i.e., in still water). At such times, the uncatalyzed conversion of CO_2 could decrease the transcutaneous P_{CO_2} gradient. In contrast, rapid hydration of CO_2 and the formation of H^+ and HCO_3^- would maximize the P_{CO_2} gradient from blood to water. The presence or absence of "external" carbonic anhydrase could also have important consequences for ammonia excretion and ionic exchange mechanisms through alteration of transcutaneous H^+ distribution. For example, if external carbonic anhydrase were to acidify the water immediately surrounding an ammoniotelic animal, formation of NH_4^+ would maintain the NH_3 partial pressure gradient. This would, of course, only occur as long as CO_2 excretion is greater than NH_3 excretion, and water pH is greater than the pK of the carbonic acid system; see reviews by Randall (1990) and Randall and Wright (1989).

Blood Respiratory Properties

Oxygen cascades from environment to cell in a number of well-defined steps (table 5.1). The uptake, storage, and delivery of oxygen by the circulation are influenced by blood flow, hemoglobin-O_2 (Hb-O_2) affinity, and blood O_2 carrying capacity. The number of circulating erythrocytes determines the hemoglobin concentration and therefore the blood O_2 carrying capacity. Intraerythrocytic factors (e.g., nucleotide triphosphates, pH, hemoglobin multiplicity) affect Hb-O_2 affinity, which in turn determines the PO_2 gradients between ambient medium and blood.

Hemoglobin Concentrations and Blood Oxygen Carrying Capacity
Blood O_2 capacities (C_{O_2max}), hemoglobin concentrations ([Hb]), and hematocrit (hct) vary similarly in the Urodela and in the Anura (table 5.2). These variables do not change during induced metamorphosis in the salamander *Ambystoma mexicanum*, but [Hb] and C_{O_2max} in bullfrog larvae (*Rana catesbeiana*) are approximately half those of adult frogs (Pinder and Burggren 1983). Mean cellular [Hb] (i.e., MCHC = [Hb]/hct) as well as Hb-O_2 carriage per gram of hemoglobin is comparatively low in the red blood cells of larvae (cf. table 5.2). Hb-O_2 carriage per gram of hemoglobin may vary as much within a species (i.e., *R. catesbeiana*) as among the entire class of Amphibia (table 5.2). The total O_2 store of the animal, however, will also depend on the blood volume, which is greater in aquatic species such as *Xenopus* (13.4% body mass; Emilio and Shelton 1980) and *Typhlonectes* (25% body mass; Toews and Macintyre 1978) than in semiterrestrial forms such as *R. pipiens* and *Bufo marinus* (9.5% and 7.4% body mass respectively; Thorson 1964). The high blood volumes of aquatic species also reflect high Hb-O_2 carriage and MCHC (table 5.2), all of which may facilitate prolonged breath-hold diving (Boutilier and Shelton 1986b; Toews and Macintyre 1978). High blood O_2 capacities, however, are sometimes due to abnormally high hct values obtained by blood-sampling methods other than chronic cannulation (see Boutilier and Shelton 1986; Toews and Boutilier 1986; Burggren 1987).

TABLE 5.2   Blood O_2 Capacity Relationships in the Three Orders of Amphibia

	Hct (%)	[Hb] (g · 100 ml^{-1})	C_{O_2max} (ml · 100 ml^{-1})	Reference
Urodela				
Amphiuma tridactylum	23.0	5.7	7.62	Lenfant and Johansen 1967
Necturus maculosus	19.0	4.5	6.26	Lenfant and Johansen 1967
Dicamptodon ensatus	24.2	4.4	5.25	Wood 1971
Taricha granulosa	36.7	9.5	9.70	Wood et al. 1975
Ambystoma mexicanum				
Gill form	27.7	7.5	10.04	Gahlenbeck and Bartels 1970
Metamorphosed	29.8	7.6	10.15	
Desmognathus fuscus	28.0	7.5	9.80	Gatz, Crawford, and Piiper 1974
Anura				
Rana catesbeiana				
Larva	20.9	3.7	2.91	Pinder and Burggren 1983
Adult	23.5	5.7	8.02	Lenfant and Johansen 1967
	22.2	6.3	5.84	Pinder and Burggren 1983
	23.4	5.7	7.15	Maginniss, Song, and Reeves 1980
Rana esculenta	27.3	7.8	10.43	Gahlenbeck and Bartels 1968
Xenopus laevis	28.3	8.3	9.38	Boutilier and Shelton 1986c; Bridges, Pelster, and Scheid 1985
	38.7	11.3	15.80	Jokumsen and Weber 1980
Telmatobius culeus	27.9	8.1	11.70	Hutchinson, Haines, and Engbretson 1976
Chiromantis petersi	21.1	—	7.1	Johansen et al. 1980
Apoda				
Boulengerula taitanus	40.0	10.3	14.0	Wood et al. 1975
Typhlonectes compressicauda	37.6	11.3	—	Toews and Macintyre 1978

In their recent review of red cell function in vertebrates, Wood and Lenfant (1987) point out that many ectotherms survive anemias (e.g., Flores and Frieden 1968) far more severe than endotherms can tolerate, probably because ectotherms can better reduce metabolic requirements and/or recruit anaerobic energy production (Hochachka and Somero 1984; Hochachka and Guppy 1987). This is not to say that red blood cell mass is unimportant. Indeed, the stimuli that lead to erythrocyte production in fish and mammals also evoke erythropoietic activity in amphibians. Red blood cell production increases when *Triturus cristatus* (Caudata: Salamandriadae) is made anemic by starvation, or when *Necturus* is subjected to hypoxia (Jordan 1938). Also, human urinary erythropoietin enhances uptake of ^{59}Fe in both the spleen and circulating erythrocytes of the plethodontid salamander *Desmognathus* (Gordon 1960). In addition, frogs evidently release an erythropoietic stimulating factor into the bloodstream during acute anemia, since infusion of plasma from bled frogs increases red blood cell production in normal animals (Rosse, Waldmann, and Hull 1963). As in other vertebrates, the spleen of amphibians is under nervous control (Nilsson 1978), and sympathetic stimulation in *Bufo marinus* causes the spleen to contract. The increased hct and blood [Hb] after enforced activity in both *B. marinus* and *Xenopus laevis,* when plasma catecholamine levels are markedly elevated (Boutilier, Emilio, and Shelton 1986; Boutilier and Lantz 1989; Emilio and Shelton 1980; Tufts, Mense, and Randall 1987), may result in part from mobilization of erythrocyte reserves in the spleen. Such acute mobilization in other animals (reviewed by Nikinmaa 1990) increases blood O_2 capacity in response to elevated metabolic demands.

Hematological Properties Influencing Oxygen Uptake

Within the Amphibia, cellular concentrations of hemoglobin and Hb-O_2 carrying capacities per gram of hemoglobin are remarkably stable over an enormous range of cell sizes (tables 5.2 and 5.3). By far the largest erythrocytes are those of *Amphiuma* (Caudata: Amphiumidae), the volumes of which are some thirty-five times greater than the comparatively small red blood cells (RBCs) of *Telmatobius* (Anura: Leptodactylidac). Despite such differences in size, the MCHC and milli-

liters of O_2 per gram of hemoglobin of *Amphiuma* are only slightly lower than those of *Telmatobius*. The comparatively small erythrocytes (i.e., high surface-area-to-volume ratio) of the high-altitude-dwelling frog *Telamatobius* (Hutchison, Haines, and Engbretson 1976) would seem to provide a direct correlation between RBC size and ambient O_2 availability if not for the fact that many urodeles, including *Amphiuma* (with the largest erythrocytes), also live in O_2-poor conditions.

Although RBC size in urodeles is clearly much greater than in anurans (table 5.3), no correlation is obvious between RBC size and the variables associated with O_2 capacity (table 5.2). Size, however, is probably important in determining O_2 transfer between RBC and the ambient medium. Data from reptilian, avian, and mammalian RBCs suggest advantageous effects of small erythrocyte size on O_2 transfer (Holland and Forster 1966; Yamaguchi et al. 1988). The main morphological feature determining O_2 transfer efficiency of erythrocytes is the ratio of surface area to effective diffusion path length. This ratio is approximately one-fourth of the mean cell thickness irrespective of cell size and shape (Yamaguchi et al. 1988). Differences in O_2 transfer conductances also depend on capillary hct and intracellular O_2 diffusivity (Yamaguchi et al. 1987), about which little is known, particularly for amphibians. By virtue of their RBC sizes, amphibians seem especially well suited for future studies of the relationship between RBC surface-area-to-volume ratios and kinetics of O_2 uptake.

Most amphibian erythrocytes are nucleated, which likely enables protein synthesis. Mature RBCs of *Bufo marinus* consume O_2 and evidently can increase their metabolic rate in response to certain catecholamine hormones (B. L. Tufts and R. G. Boutilier unpublished observations). Although anucleate erythrocytes are relatively rare in Amphibia and in ectotherms in general, they make up 5% of the circulating population of RBCs in several lungless urodeles (Turner 1988). In a unique case, that of the plethodontid salamander *Batrachoseps,* more than 90% of circulating erythrocytes lack a nucleus (Emmel 1924). For a lungless animal, this could facilitate O_2 uptake by increasing the RBC surface-area-to-volume ratio. Differences in hemoglobin content between nucleated and anucleate erythrocytes would have a

TABLE 5.3 Red Blood Cell Numbers and Sizes in the Three Orders of Amphibia

	RBC Count $(10^6 \cdot \mu l^{-1}$ blood)	RBC Volume (μm^3)	RBC Dimensions (μm)	Reference
Urodela				
Amphiuma means	0.03	13,857	62.5 × 36.3	Wintrobe 1933
Cryptobranchus alleganiensis	0.07	7,425	40.5 × 21.0	Wintrobe 1933
Necturus maculosus	0.02	10,070	52.8 × 28.2	Wintrobe 1933
Dicamptodon ensatus	0.05	4,938	51.4 × 29.3	Wood et al. 1975
Taricha granulosa	0.11	3,336	40.4 × 25.9	Wood et al. 1975
Anura				
Rana catesbeiana	0.44	670	24.8 × 15.3	Wintrobe 1933
Rana pipiens	0.32	768	23.8 × 16.2	Rouf 1969
Rana esculenta	0.43	659	—	Gahlenbeck and Bartels 1968
Telmatobius culeus	0.73	394	17.0 × 12.0	Hutchison, Haines, and Engbretson 1976; Ruiz, Rosenmann, and Veloso 1983
Apoda				
Boulengerula taitanus	0.68	588	22.1 × 15.6	Wood et al. 1975

minor influence on Hb-O_2 carrying capacity; that is, the condensed chromatin in nucleated amphibian erythrocytes is surrounded by nuclear hemoglobin at approximately the same concentration as found in the cytoplasm (Small and Davies 1970; Turner 1988).

Rheological Properties Influencing Circulatory Convection of Respiratory Gases

In addition to the architecture and vasomotor properties of the circulatory system (see below), the viscosity of blood plays an important role in determining the resistance to blood flow. Because changes in vascular resistance can alter perfusion of tissues and affect gas exchange efficacy, consideration of blood rheology is important. Viscosity is proportional to the concentration of RBCs. Because most of the resistance to blood flow occurs in the capillaries (where most exchange of materials occur), how RBCs in the microvasculature affect blood viscosity is important. The apparent coefficient of viscosity of blood takes into account interactions of blood cells, plasma, and blood vessel wall (Fung 1984). It can increase markedly due to (1) the presence of extraordinarily large erythrocytes (i.e., with diameters greater than those of the capillary vessel), (2) vasoconstriction of the vessel, (3) adhesion of cells to the vessel wall, and/or (4) decreased flexibility of the RBC.

The forces that oppose blood flow are the shear stresses caused by blood viscosity and turbulences (Fung 1984). Erythrocyte membranes may elongate or "shear" with no change in the surface area and without bending. Although nucleated erythrocytes exhibit limited deformation in shear stress (i.e., are less elastic than nonnucleated erythrocytes), blood viscosity decreases with increasing shear rates in nucleated erythrocytes of fish (e.g., Fletcher and Haedrich 1987). RBCs exhibiting better alignment in the direction of blood flow at high than at low shear rates might explain this change in viscosity (Gaehtgens, Schmidt, and Will 1981). Experiments on frog RBCs suspended in a dextran solution suggest a lack of orientation to flow at high shear rates (Fischer 1978). However, observations of the microvasculature of frog lung in vivo (Koyama 1985) show that RBCs orient their long axis in the direction of blood flow. Certainly, the most common orientation for mammalian erythrocytes entering a blood vessel is edge on (Fung 1981, 1984), with the axis of symmetry of the erythrocyte being perpendicular to the axis of the cylindrical microvessel.

The greater resistance to shear-induced shape changes in nucleated than in nonnucleated erythrocytes may be due to a more rigid cytoskeletal framework in the former. The more complex framework is also thought to explain the lack of the "tank-treading" mechanism in nucleated erythrocytes (Schmid-Schonbein and Gaehtgens 1981). Rotation of the membrane of the mammalian erythrocyte (i.e., tank-treading) as it passes through microvessels may reduce friction between RBC and blood vessel wall, decreasing viscous drag (Fung 1984).

Although nucleated erythrocytes resist shear stresses more than their nonnucleated counterparts, certain RBCs of amphibians exhibit remarkable "elasticity" when traversing capillaries having much smaller diameters than the cells themselves. Both frog and Amphiuma erythrocytes can pass through filters with pore diameters as small as one-quarter of the minor oval diameter of the cell (table 5.3); the value for

human erythrocytes is approximately one-third (Chein et al. 1971). The large RBCs (45–55 μm diameter) of the apodan Typhlonectes compressicauda exhibit remarkable flexibility in vivo by bending in half during transit through small skin capillaries (Toews and Macintyre 1978). Amphiuma erythrocytes traversing lung capillaries (R. G. Boutilier and D. P. Toews unpublished observations) and RBCs in capillary vessels of dog messentary (Fung 1981) deform so much that the RBCs appear to plug the vessel. Between successive "plugs," the motion of the plasma or "bolus flow" (Prothero and Burton 1961) creates eddy currents that apparently aid in convecting materials from the center of the vessel to its wall. This action is supposed to facilitate mass transfer (Fung 1984), though it appears to benefit macromolecular movements more than respiratory gases (Aroesty and Gross 1970).

Blood Oxygen Affinity Relationships

Amphibians are excellent models for studying the adaptability of Hb-O_2 affinity to environmental conditions, particularly in ontogenetic and phylogenetic comparisons (Frieden 1961; Lenfant and Johansen 1967; McCutcheon 1936; McCutcheon and Hall 1937; Moss and Ingram 1968; Riggs 1951). Differences in Hb-O_2 affinity can arise from hemoglobin heterogeneity (Aggarwal and Riggs 1969; Jokumsen and Weber 1980; Perutz and Brunori 1982; Maginniss, Song, and Reeves 1980), differences in sensitivity of hemoglobin to allosteric effectors (Bonaventura et al. 1977; Condo et al. 1989; Johansen and Lenfant 1972; Wood et al. 1975), and the intracellular concentrations of such effectors (Rapoport and Guest 1941; Hazard and Hutchison 1982).

In general, Hb-O_2 affinity in amphibians is correlated with the relative importance of water and air as respiratory media (Lenfant and Johansen 1967; McCutcheon and Hall 1937). The increase in P_{50} with ontogeny (i.e., bullfrog larvae versus adult, table 5.4) may be associated with an increased reliance on air breathing and movement onto land (see chapter 16). The lower O_2 affinity in more terrestrial forms may also reflect the increased availability of O_2 in air as well as the increased costs of locomotion on land (Johansen and Lenfant 1972; Lenfant and Johansen 1967; Wood and Lenfant 1979). Table 5.4 shows that at any given temperature and pH, the P_{50} of most water-breathing urodeles is lower than that of semiterrestrial anurans. Aquatic anurans (i.e., Xenopus and Telmatobius), on the other hand, have comparatively high Hb-O_2 affinity, as do aquatic and fossorial apodans. High Hb-O_2 affinity is evidently associated with reduced O_2 availability in the animals' environment. This reduced availability reflects the lesser quantity of O_2 in water as opposed to air, as well as the greater tendency for respiratory gases to oscillate in aquatic systems or in secluded aerial environments. This "relative hypoxia" is also consistent with the comparatively high Hb-O_2 affinity that accompanies ontogenetic development in aquatic systems (e.g., bullfrog larvae) or in utero (e.g., the apodan Typhlonectes; table 5.4). In comparison to the adult, the markedly lower P_{50} of Typhlonectes larvae assists maternal-to-fetal gas exchanges across uterine-gill membranes (Toews and Macintyre 1977); hemoglobin of fetal blood is highly saturated when maternal blood is only moderately saturated.

Adaptive explanations of interspecific differences in Hb-O_2 affinity must be carefully considered (Burggren, McMahon,

TABLE 5.4 Blood Oxygen Affinity Relationships in the Three Orders of Amphibia

	Principle Gas Exchange Organ	Temperature (°C)	Conditions of O₂ Curve Construction			Bohr Coefficient ($\Delta\log P_{50}\cdot\Delta pH^{-1}$)	Hill Coefficient	Reference
			P_{50} (mm Hg)	pH	Pco_2 (mm Hg)			
Urodela								
Cryptobranchus alleganiensis	Skin	25	23.6	7.73	7.4	−0.24	2.90	Boutilier and Toews 1981b
Necturus maculosus	Gill	20	14.5	—	6.0	−0.13	1.40	Lenfant and Johansen 1967
Ambystoma mexicanum								
Gill form	Gill	20	25.7	7.40	—	−0.14	2.00	Gahlenbeck and Bartels 1970
Metamorphosed	Lung	20	28.7	7.40	—	−0.26	3.40	Gahlenbeck and Bartels 1970
Dicamptodon ensatus								
Gill form	Gill	15	21.9	7.80	—	−0.13	2.50	Wood 1971
Metamorphosed	Lung	15	31.6	7.80	—	−0.14	2.80	Wood 1971
Amphiuma tridactylum	Lung	22	27.0	—	8.5	−0.21	1.95	Lenfant and Johansen 1967
Taricha granulosa	Lung	20	36.5	7.70	—	−0.12	2.40	Wood et al. 1975
Desmognathus fuscus	Skin	13	27.0	7.50	7.4	—	2.64	Gatz, Crawford, and Piiper 1974
Anura								
Rana catesbeiana								
Larva	Gill	23	9.4	7.70	7.0	−0.06	2.50	Pinder and Burggren 1983
Adult	Lung	22	39.0	—	10.0	−0.29	1.95	Lenfant and Johansen 1967
		23	33.0	7.70	7.0	−0.65	2.40	Pinder and Burggren 1983
		25	42.0	7.79	15.0	−0.27	2.60	Tazawa, Mochizuki, and Piiper 1979a
		25	36.6	7.83	22.1	−0.16	1.66	Maginniss, Song, and Reeves 1980
		5	13.5	8.07	22.1	−0.13	1.66	Maginniss, Song, and Reeves 1980
Rana esculenta	Lung	20	39.7	7.40	—	−0.26	—	Gahlenbeck and Bartels 1968
Rana temporaria	Lung	20.5	37.0	7.67	14.5	−0.22	1.60	Lykkeboe and Johansen 1978
Rana brevipoda	Lung	25	52.0	7.72	12.0	−0.18	2.50	Tazawa, Mochizuki, and Piiper 1979a
Bufo marinus	Lung	25	53.0	7.75	14.8	−0.23	2.78	Boutilier and Toews 1981
Xenopus laevis	Lung	25	27.0	7.60	—	−0.39	2.10	Jokumsen and Weber 1980
		25	29.6	7.73	14.5	−0.37	2.64	Boutilier 1981; Boutilier and Shelton 1986c
Telmatobius culeus	Skin	10	25.1	7.47	14.6	−0.49	2.20	Bridges, Pelster, and Scheid 1985
Chiromantis petersi	Lung	25	15.6	7.63	—	−0.30	2.00	Hutchison, Haines, and Engbretson 1976
		25	47.5	7.65	14.7	−0.35	2.60	Johansen et al. 1980
Apoda								
Typhlonectes compressicauda								
Fetal larva	Gill	30	9.3	7.60	11.4	—	—	Toews and MacIntyre 1977
Adult	Lung	30	22.2	7.62	11.4	−0.08	2.15	Toews and MacIntyre 1977
Boulengerula taitanus	Lung	25	27.0	7.60	—	−0.21	1.79	Wood et al. 1975

and Powers 1991; Seymour 1982; Wells 1990). For example, in diving *Xenopus,* the high affinity of the blood can be considered adaptive for extracting O_2 from an ever-diminishing supply in the lung; alternatively, in diving *R. catesbeiana,* the low affinity of the blood can be considered adaptive for maintaining Po_2 gradients from blood to mitochondria as blood O_2 levels fall. Phylogenetic and interspecific comparisons of Hb-O_2 affinity may be less profitable than correlating blood respiratory properties with activity metabolism, behavior, and natural habitats within a species. Indeed, intraspecific variations in O_2 equilibrium curve position (e.g., due to ontogeny, body mass, genotype, etc.) can be as great if not greater than the differences ascribed to phylogeny. In humans, for example, Wood and Lenfant (1987) point out that the P_{50} of mutant hemoglobins can range from 12 to 70 mm Hg (similar to the interspecific range in amphibians; table 5.4). Despite this, there is little effect on O_2 uptake by muscle, or even maximal O_2 uptake, since increases in hemoglobin concentration compensate for such differences in Hb-O_2 affinity (Stamatoyannopoulos, Bellingham, and Lenfant 1971). Thus, other components of the O_2 transport system (cf. fig. 5.1) can compensate for shifts in P_{50} within a species.

Analysis of the shape of the O_2 dissociation curve routinely uses a "Hill plot" (log saturation/[1 − saturation] versus log Po_2), which is linear for single hemoglobin systems. The slopes of such lines (customarily between 30 and 70% saturation) express the cooperativity coefficient (Hill's n) of the hemoglobin. As a general measure of subunit cooperativity, the higher the n value the greater the sigmoidicity. Highly sigmoid dissociation curves offer a combination of loading and unloading capacities that maximize diffusion gradients at both the sites of O_2 uptake and O_2 delivery (Boutilier and Toews 1981; Lykkeboe and Johansen 1978; Maginniss, Song, and Reeves 1980; McCutcheon and Hall 1937). Within the Urodela are the highest and lowest n values recorded (3.4 in metamorphosed *Ambystoma* and 1.4 in *Necturus*). Hill coefficients for other forms (table 5.4) show no correlation to mode of breathing or habitat.

Investigation of hemoglobin heterogeneity in amphibians (e.g., Jokumsen and Weber 1980) and associated heterophasic cooperativity in O_2 binding suggests that the parameters commonly used for describing predominantly single hemoglobin systems (i.e., Hill's n, P_{50}, Bohr coefficient) may be inappropriate for the multiple hemoglobin systems of amphibians (Maginniss, Song, and Reeves 1980). Hill plots for *Rana temporaria* and *R. catesbeiana* (Lykkeboe and Johansen 1978; Maginniss, Song, and Reeves 1980), *R. esculenta* (Barnikol and Burkhard 1979), and *Xenopus laevis* (Boutilier 1981) depart from linearity, indicating that a single n value is not adequate to describe the O_2 dissociation curve. For instance, the value of Hill's n varies substantially depending on the saturation (S) range over which it is estimated; in *R. catesbeiana* it varies from 1.66 (0.35 to 0.65 S) to 2.72 (0.50 to 0.90 S), and neither value accurately represents the experimental data (Maginniss, Song, and Reeves 1980). The CO_2 Bohr coefficient (Δlog $P_{50} \cdot \Delta pH^{-1}$), the coefficient describing the combined effects of CO_2 and protons on Hb-O_2 affinity, also changes in amphibians as a function of Hb-O_2

saturation (Lykkeboe and Johansen 1978; Maginniss, Song, and Reeves 1980). In *R. temporaria* the Bohr coefficient ranges from −0.22 at 50% Hb-O_2 saturation to −0.50 at 90% Hb-O_2 saturation (Lykkeboe and Johansen 1978), and in *R. catesbeiana* similar O_2-dependent changes occur (Maginniss, Song, and Reeves 1980). In all cases, the Bohr coefficient declines as Hb-O_2 saturation falls, and to complicate matters even further, the relationship between O_2 saturation and Bohr effect differs depending on the temperature.

The bi- or triphasic O_2 equilibrium curves and O_2-dependent Bohr effects are credited with improving both O_2 uptake and delivery. Lykkeboe and Johansen (1978) suggest that the increasing n values with increasing Hb-O_2 saturations will facilitate O_2 loading at the lungs, by maintaining a large Po_2 driving gradient. Maginniss, Song, and Reeves (1980) argue that the low n value and Bohr coefficient associated with the lower limb of the bullfrog O_2 curve favors O_2 extraction from the lung as Po_2 continues to fall throughout a dive.

Circulatory Convection

Cardiovascular Anatomy The hearts of anurans and urodeles differ markedly in anatomy. In textbooks, the so-called amphibian heart usually refers to an anuran heart with little or no mention of the interordinal variation in atrial and ventricular septation. Moreover, the literature poorly documents the cardiac anatomy of the apodans.

Figure 5.12 illustrates the heart of a typical anuran amphibian (Shelton 1976; Shelton and Boutilier 1982), showing two atrial chambers emptying into a single ventricle. In some anurans, the atria appear as simple sacs (*Rana, Bufo*), whereas in others (e.g., *Xenopus*) the atria have several fingerlike projections, the functional significance of which is presently unknown. Although the ventricular lumen lacks a septum, the ventricular myocardium has several muscular trabeculae that subcompartmentalize the ventricle along its long axis (i.e., its outflow direction). The trabeculae are considered important in compartmentalizing the atrial inflows and then channeling separate streams of oxygenated and deoxygenated blood during ventricular ejection (Shelton 1976; Johansen 1985). During ventricular diastole, oxygenated blood from the left atrium enters the ventricle and becomes entrapped by the trabeculae of the left wall. A similar process occurs on the right side of the heart with deoxygenated blood from the right atrium. From the ventricle, blood is then directed to the conus (bulbus) arteriosus, which contains a spiral valve along its longitudinal axis. This value attaches to the inner wall of the conus along one edge, with the other edge free. Separation of oxygenated and deoxygenated bloodstreams in anurans (Johansen and Ditadi 1966; Meyers and Felsher 1976; Shelton 1976; Tazawa, Mochizuki, and Piiper 1979b) means that relatively uncontaminated streams of blood must enter separate sides of the spiral valve and remain separate through the clockwise spiral in the conus arteriosus (fig. 5.12). The conus has three semilunar cusp valves that prevent reflux of blood from the pulmocutaneous and systemic circulations during diastole (Burggren 1988a).

The hearts of urodeles appear to be more simple anatomically than those of anurans; however, separation of oxygenated and deoxygenated bloodstreams is efficient (Johansen

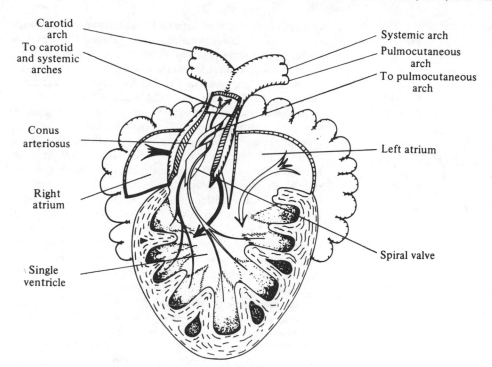

Carotid arch
To carotid and systemic arches
Conus arteriosus
Right atrium
Single ventricle

Systemic arch
Pulmocutaneous arch
To pulmocutaneous arch
Left atrium
Spiral valve

Fig. 5.12 Diagram of the heart of the anuran *Xenopus* from the ventral aspect. The ventral walls of atria, ventricle, and conus arteriosus are removed to show direction of flow streamlines necessary to account for selective distribution of blood. *Open arrows* show the flow of oxygenated blood, *filled arrows* for deoxygenated blood. (Reprinted, by permission, from Shelton and Boutilier 1982.)

1963; Toews, Shelton, and Randall 1971). Such hearts often have thin and/or fenestrated septa dividing the atria. *Siren lacertina* has a complete interatrial septum (Putnam 1977), whereas in *Necturus* (Wischnitzer 1972) and *Cryptobranchus* (Reese 1906) this structure contains perforations. The heart of *S. lacertina* has a partially septate sinus venous (Putnam 1977) whereas in *Cryptobranchus* a complete septum in the sinus venosus has been reported (Putnam and Parkerson 1978). The effective separation of oxygenated and deoxygenated blood evidently occurs as described for anurans. Using angiocardiographic techniques Johansen (1963) showed that contrast injected into the posterior vena cava of *Amphiuma tridactylum* fills the right portion of the ventricle and, upon ventricular discharge, is preferentially directed to the pulmonary arteries. When contrast is injected into the pulmonary vein, the pattern of flow is through the left side of the ventricular chamber of the systemic arterial arches (Johansen 1963) and is distinctly laminar (Johansen 1985). Detailed anatomical studies on *S. lacertina* reveal muscular trabeculae extending dorsoventrally and anteroposteriorly along the walls of the ventricle (Putnam 1977). A lack of septal organization to these trabeculae leads to marked variations in the thickness of the walls of the ventricle. However, a large and discrete mass of these trabeculae partially divides the ventricle of *Siren* into a comparatively larger right and more reduced left ventricular chamber. The alignment of this partial interventricular septum with the interatrial septum provides the appropriate anatomy for effective separation of oxygenated and deoxygenated bloodstreams (Putnam 1975, 1977), although physiological confirmation is lacking to date. Partial interventricular septation also occurs in the mudpuppy, *Necturus maculosus* (Putnam and Dunn 1978). The cardiovascular anatomy of the lungless plethodontid salamanders (Foxon

1964; Holmes 1975; Putnam and Kelly 1978) is reminiscent of that in water-breathing fish (i.e., no pulmonary vasculature and a highly reduced interatrial septum; Burggren 1988a). Although the skin is the sole organ of gas exchange, blood returning from the cutaneous circulation is not preferentially directed through the heart. Instead, the blood from the skin and internal organs is completely mixed when reaching the heart (Piiper, Gatz, and Crawford 1976).

The hearts of apodan amphibians have thin or fenestrated atrial septa, and the spiral valve can be reduced or entirely absent (Goodrich 1930). Toews and Macintyre (1978) describe completely separated atria in *Typhlonectes compressicauda*, with the left atrium receiving blood from the lungs and the right atrium receiving blood from the systemic circulation via the sinus venosus. During diastole, blood enters a completely undivided spongy ventricle and then passes into the conus arteriosus upon ventricular contraction. Unlike the typical spiral valve arrangement (e.g., fig. 5.12), the conus and truncus arteriosus of *T. compressicauda* are divided in half by a complete partition (fig. 5.13). One side is in direct communication with the pulmonary artery, which extends a small branch to the anterior portion of the lung and a larger branch posteriorly to the two major portions of the lung. The systemic side of the truncus extends anteriorly before branching posteriorly to form the systemic arch and anteriorly to form the carotid vessels. Blood samples drawn from cannulas implanted in the systemic and pulmonary outflow channels (1 cm anterior to the semilunar valves) revealed separation of oxygenated and deoxygenated blood in the absence of a spiral valve; that is, P_{O_2} differences as great as 40 mm Hg exist between pulmonary and systemic outflow channels (Toews and Macintyre 1978).

Various workers have attempted to determine the degree of

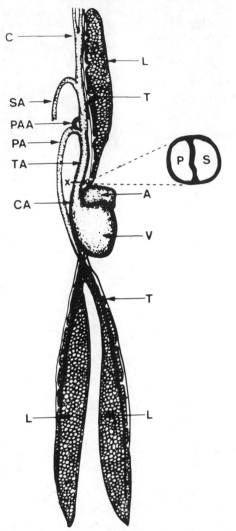

Fig. 5.13   Heart, lungs, and associated blood vessels of *Typhlonectes compressicauda*. *A*, atrium; *C*, carotid artery; *CA*, conus arteriosus; *L*, lung (note that the length of posterior lung is much reduced for convenience [scale about one-quarter]); *P*, pulmonary side of truncus; *PA*, pulmonary artery; *PAA*, anterior branch of pulmonary artery; *S*, systemic side of truncus; *SA*, systemic arch; *T*, trachea; *TA*, truncus arteriosus; *V*, ventricle. (Reprinted, by permission, from Toews and Macintyre 1978.)

central vascular admixture or "intracardiac shunt" in anurans (Johansen and Ditadi 1966; Meyers and Felsher 1976; Tazawa, Mochizuki, and Piiper 1979b) and urodeles (Johansen 1963; Toews, Shelton, and Randall 1971). Shunts are described as "left-to-right" or "right-to-left," depending on the origins of the admixture, and play an important role in determining the degree of blood O₂ saturation.

Cardiovascular Shunts and Gas Exchange   The undivided ventricle of the amphibian heart allows the relative amounts of blood flowing to the lungs and body to be adjusted over an infinitely variable range (Johansen and Ditati 1966; Shelton 1970, 1976, 1985; Shelton and Boutilier 1982). The degree of mixing between the two bloodstreams can influence the resulting blood-gas tensions (Wood 1982; Burggren 1988a). A central vascular right-to-left shunt will shunt part of the systemic venous return into pulmonary venous blood. Such "systemic venous admixture" can decrease the P_{O_2} and per-

centage of saturation of arterial blood relative to pulmonary venous blood. Thus, arterial P_{O_2} can be altered either by pulmonary gas exchange or by the degree of central vascular shunt. In fact, central shunting provides these animals with the ability to alter arterial P_{O_2} independently of ventilation (Wood and Hicks 1985; Hicks and Wood 1989).

In *Xenopus* the pulmonary venous-to-arterial P_{O_2} gradient (fig. 5.5) is larger when the P_{O_2} levels are high (i.e., during breathing) than when they are low (i.e., during a dive). Both of these differences can be attributed to right-to-left shunting. However, the larger P_{O_2} gradient at high P_{O_2} values does not necessarily mean that the shunt is greater at these levels. It may simply reflect differences in the slope of the O₂ dissociation curve at high and low P_{O_2} ranges. For example, small quantities of venous blood would produce relatively large decreases in arterial P_{O_2} when mixed with highly saturated blood of the pulmonary venous return (i.e., the flat part of the O₂ dissociation curve); the same quantity of blood would produce much less of an effect as the blood became progressively less saturated (i.e., the steep part of the O₂ dissociation curve).

Given these anatomical shunts, the arterial P_{O_2} of a mixture of pulmonary venous and mixed venous blood *in vivo* is a function of the resulting O₂ saturation (Wood 1982). This mixing *in vivo* is analogous to the *in vitro* "mixing method" for O₂ dissociation curve construction, whereby various mixtures of known volumes of oxygenated and deoxygenated whole blood are prepared for P_{O_2} measurement (Haab, Piiper, and Rahn 1960). The relationships can be modeled as in fig. 5.14 (Wood 1984; Hicks and Wood 1989), where the lung is treated as an ideal exchanger in which end capillary and alveolar P_{O_2} are in equilibrium (i.e., the "perfect" compartment). The shunt compartment on the other hand, can be treated as any quantity of blood that effectively lowers the saturation of the perfect value. As a function of the total blood flow ($\dot{Q}_t$), arterial O₂ content is affected by blood flow of the shunt ($\dot{Q}_s$), viz.,

$$\dot{Q}_s/\dot{Q}_t = (C_pO_2 - C_aO_2)/(C_pO_2 - C_vO_2),$$

where

C_pO_2 = the O₂ content of the perfect compartment

C_aO_2 = the O₂ content of the systemic arterial blood

C_vO_2 = the O₂ content of mixed venous blood

Taking the nonshunt fraction $\dot{Q}_{ns}/\dot{Q}_t$ to be equal to $1 - \dot{Q}_s/\dot{Q}_t$, the following equation expresses the impact of shunt on arterial O₂ content:

$$C_aO_2 = \dot{Q}_s/\dot{Q}_t(C_vO_2) + \dot{Q}_{ns}/\dot{Q}_t(C_pO_2).$$

As illustrated in fig. 5.14, the mixing of blood between the perfect and shunt compartments occurs in a "closed system." Because of this, O₂ content and P_{O_2} in arterial blood are related to one another such that P_{O_2} becomes the dependent variable (i.e., it becomes a function of the O₂ affinity, [Hb], and arterial O₂ content).

This simplified approach, while limited by several assumptions (see Hicks and Wood 1989), is useful for interpreting relationships between shunt patterns and blood gases. Though most experimental work in this area has concerned reptiles (see reviews by Wood and Hicks 1985; Hicks and Wood

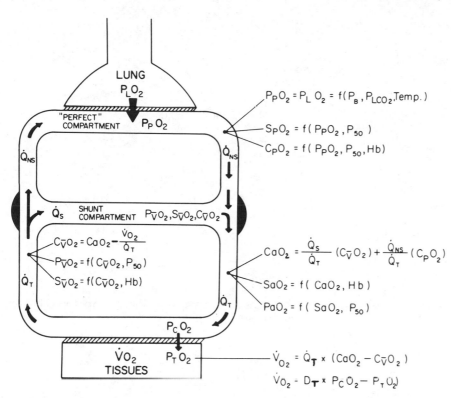

Fig. 5.14 The two-compartment O_2 transport model in animals with intracardiac shunts. Equations represent the relationships of the O_2 transport parameters that make up the various compartments. See text for further details. (Model is adapted from Rosoff et al. 1980. Reprinted, by permission, from Wood 1984.)

$$P_P O_2 = P_L O_2 = f(P_B, P_{LCO_2}, Temp.)$$

$$S_P O_2 = f(P_P O_2, P_{50})$$

$$C_P O_2 = f(P_P O_2, P_{50}, Hb)$$

$$C_{\bar{V}} O_2 = CaO_2 - \frac{\dot{V}O_2}{\dot{Q}_T}$$

$$P_{\bar{V}} O_2 = f(C_{\bar{V}} O_2, P_{50})$$

$$S_{\bar{V}} O_2 = f(C_{\bar{V}} O_2, Hb)$$

$$CaO_2 = \frac{\dot{Q}_S}{\dot{Q}_T}(C_{\bar{V}} O_2) + \frac{\dot{Q}_{NS}}{\dot{Q}_T}(C_P O_2)$$

$$SaO_2 = f(CaO_2, Hb)$$

$$PaO_2 = f(SaO_2, P_{50})$$

$$\dot{V}O_2 = \dot{Q}_T \times (CaO_2 - C_{\bar{V}} O_2)$$

$$\dot{V}O_2 = D_T \times P_C O_2 - P_T O_2)$$

1989), several studies on amphibians reveal the same general findings. The model predicts that any decrease in O_2-affinity (i.e., right-shifted O_2 dissociation curve) will increase arterial Po_2. The most common causes of changes in O_2 affinity are those resulting from changes in temperature or pH. In *Xenopus laevis* and *Bufo marinus,* for example, the rightward shift of the O_2 curves with rising temperature (fig. 5.15) evidently increases arterial Po_2 of the animals *in vivo* (Boutilier, Glass, and Heisler 1987). Increases in arterial Po_2 with temperature also occur in the toad *B. paracnemis* (Kruhøffer et al. 1987) as well as in larval *Ambystoma tigrinum* (Wood 1982). Decreases in arterial pH that occur during hypercapnia (see below) also shift the O_2 curve to the right and increase arterial Po_2 in both *Cryptobranchus* (Boutilier and Toews 1981b) and *B. marinus* (Boutilier and Heisler 1988).

A common feature of the response to both temperature change and hypercapnia is that O_2 saturation is maintained at (or near) a constant level, despite obvious changes in blood O_2 affinity (e.g., fig. 5.15). Thus, the common denominator of O_2 homeostasis in these animals may be O_2 saturation and/ or content rather than partial pressure (Wood 1982, 1984; Boutilier, Glass, and Heisler 1987). Though not directly tested in amphibians, the threshold for ventilatory responses to hypoxia is correlated with a decreased arterial saturation (independent of temperature) in the turtle *Chrysemys* (Glass, Boutilier, and Heisler 1983). Similar relationships may exist in toads (figs. 5.3 and 5.15). Further advancement in this area will require a better understanding of the receptor mechanisms involved in O_2 uptake, transport, and delivery.

Because amphibians can distribute their blood supply selectively, different regions of the O_2 store can run down at different rates between breaths. As shown below, the main O_2 stores are in the lungs and systemic venous blood (fig. 5.16). If regulation of the O_2 stores were to occur with reference to

a single receptor, for example, in the arterial blood, information would also be required about heart output as well as the levels of blood flow (or peripheral resistance) in the major divisions of the circulation. This would be a complex means of regulating the labile O_2 storage and transport systems of amphibians. Although regulation through more widespread receptor sites seems more plausible, progress in locating them has been scant (see chapter 7).

The shunt model of Wood (1982) also provides a new basis for interpreting interspecific differences in the blood O_2 affinity (cf. table 5.4). An early study by Lenfant and Johansen (1967), for example, reported a direct relationship between species' O_2 affinity and their arterial Po_2. The high O_2-affinity blood of the aquatic salamander *Necturus* was considered adaptive to an animal that would likely experience environmental hypoxia and therefore low arterial Po_2. Conversely, the lower affinity blood of the bullfrog (*Rana catesbeiana*) was considered adaptive to its semiterrestrial existence in an environment high in O_2 (Lenfant and Johansen 1967). The two-compartment model, on the other hand, predicts that a right-to-left shunt could be responsible for the low P_aO_2 of the high affinity blood of *Necturus* and for the high P_aO_2 of the low affinity blood of the bullfrog (Wood 1982).

Ventilation-Perfusion Relationships in Periodic Breathers

Transfer of gases by the blood depends not only on the cardiovascular dynamics of the circulation but also on the respiratory properties of hemoglobin. For example, the efficacy of pulmonary gas exchange is largely dependent on ventilation-perfusion matching, which can be decidedly periodic in aquatic amphibians (Shelton and Boutilier 1982). Upon surfacing to breathe, most aquatic amphibians replenish their O_2 stores by synchronizing marked increases in pulmonary perfusion with each periodic breath (cf. Shelton 1970). Because

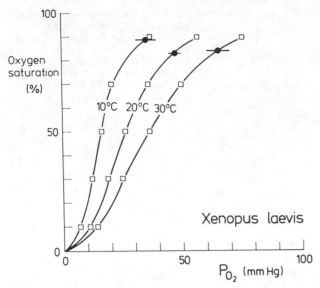

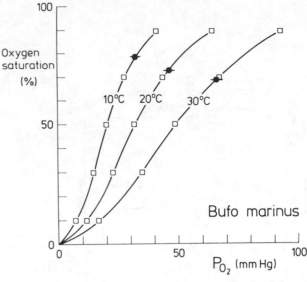

Fig. 5.15 O_2 dissociation curves for whole blood of *Xenopus laevis* and *Bufo marinus* at 10°, 20°, and 30°C. ● (±1 SEM) are *in vivo* arterial blood PO_2 values for each respective temperature. (Reprinted, by permission, from Boutilier, Glass, and Heisler 1987.)

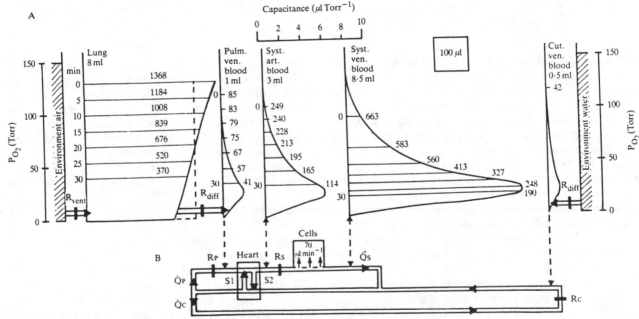

Fig. 5.16 Model of (*A*) O_2 exchange, O_2 storage, and (*B*) O_2 transport in *Xenopus laevis* (100 g at 20–25°C). In *A*, arrows indicate the direction of O_2 movement in the system, PO_2 transfer being determined by ventilation (R_{vent}), diffusion (R_{diff}), and perfusion (not shown) resistances. During dive, R_{vent} is infinite and no environmental O_2 is transferred to the lung; skin O_2 transfer is constant at 15 $\mu l \cdot min^{-1}$. O_2 stores in lung, pulmonary venous, systemic arterial, systemic venous, and cutaneous venous blood are shown as areas (note 100-μl calibration square) by plotting store capacitances against PO_2. The volumes of air and blood making up each store are also given. The reduction in O_2 content of each store (in μl; figures shown at the right of each store) during a 30-min dive is shown for 5-min intervals. The capacitance relationships for the lung are derived from calculations of $\Delta VO_2/\Delta PO_2$ based on the assumptions that PCO_2 changed by only 3 mm Hg, water vapor pressure remained constant, and the volume of N_2 in the lung was unchanged throughout the dive. If N_2 is also absorbed, there will be even more pronounced decreases in lung O_2 capacitance values as PO_2 falls. In *B*, large arrows indicate pulmonary ($\dot{Q}_p$), cutaneous ($\dot{Q}_c$), and systemic ($\dot{Q}_s$) blood flows, whose rates are determined, in a large part, by respective peripheral resistances (R_p, R_c, R_s). In the heart, arrows show right-to-left (S_1) and left-to-right (S_2) shunts. (Reprinted, by permission, from Boutilier and Shelton 1986b.)

most CO_2 is eliminated via nonpulmonary routes during dives in such animals (e.g., fig. 5.6), CO_2 that builds during a dive and is excreted upon surfacing, while significant, is not as great as the O_2 that is taken up. As a result, the CO_2:O_2 exchange ratio of the lung (R) is lower than the metabolic respiratory quotient (RQ). This condition can change, however,

if blood or tissue PCO_2 levels rise, as they do during anaerobic dives or aquatic hypercapnia (Boutilier and Shelton 1986b). At such times, the hyperventilation upon surfacing results in lung R values that are much higher than the metabolic RQ, due to the different rates at which the O_2 and CO_2 stores are adjusted during ventilation. As most of the O_2 store is located in the blood and lungs, it can readjust much faster than the CO_2 store, which must be mobilized from blood and tissues. Clearly, the increased blood flow to the lung during breathing (Boutilier, Glass, and Heisler 1986; Johansen, Lenfant, and Hanson 1970; Shelton 1970; West and Burggren 1984) will facilitate gas exchange, as will the O_2 and CO_2 carrying properties of hemoglobin. For example, the comparatively high Bohr and Haldane effect of the blood of *Xenopus* (Boutilier and Shelton 1986c), compared to that of more terrestrial anurans (Boutilier, Glass, and Heisler 1987; Tazawa, Mochizuki, and Piiper 1979a), may be an adaptation to the animals' predominantly aquatic existence and periodic nature of air breathing. The high Bohr effect facilitates O_2 delivery to the tissues during a dive, whereas the high Haldane effect means that deoxygenated blood can carry more CO_2 to the lungs during breathing (or to the skin during submergence). These biochemical adaptations appear to be evolutionarily linked to the changes in blood flow that are made possible by the undivided ventricle (cf. Shelton 1976; Shelton and Boutilier 1982). Thus, in *Xenopus,* the high Haldane effect is matched to the increased perfusion of the lungs during breathing, and the high Bohr effect to the increased movement of blood into the systemic circuit throughout a dive.

Oxygen Storage, Transport, and Delivery

An idealized model for the uptake, storage, and transport of O_2 between environment and cells (e.g., fig. 5.16), developed for the aquatic toad *Xenopus,* serves as a focal point for further discussion of the role of the circulatory system in gas exchange. Though a similar model for CO_2 elimination awaits development, many of the principal components will be the same for both respiratory gases. The model is based on a 100-g animal at 25°C during a voluntary dive (fig. 5.16). Under these conditions, pulmonary O_2 uptake is 55 $\mu l \cdot min^{-1}$, cutaneous O_2 uptake is 15 $\mu l \cdot min^{-1}$, yielding a total O_2 consumption of 70 $\mu l \cdot min^{-1}$ (all values derived from measurements made by Emilio and Shelton 1980). The primary O_2 stores are in the blood and lungs (note that for O_2, the tissue stores are negligible whereas for CO_2 they are a major component; cf. White 1989). The total blood volume of 13 ml (Emilio and Shelton 1980) can be divided into arterial and venous compartments as illustrated in fig. 5.16, whereas the volume of gas in the lung during a dive is 8 ml (Boutilier and Shelton 1986a).

The volumes of O_2 stored in the lungs and various blood compartments can be depicted graphically as joint functions of the volumes of the compartments and their respective P_{O_2} (fig. 5.16A). In this analysis, Boutilier and Shelton (1986b) derived a quantity B, which is the product of the compartment volume (V) and the capacitance for oxygen (βO_2) of the medium within:

$$B_{O_2} = V_{gas} \times \beta O_{2gas} \quad \text{or} \quad V_{blood} \times \beta O_{2blood},$$

where βO_2 is defined in units of volumes $O_2 \cdot mm \ Hg^{-1}$. Thus, the volume of O_2 (V_{O_2}) released by lowering the oxygen partial pressure from P_1 to P_2 in a compartment (e.g., the lung) is

$$V_{O_2} = V_{gas}\beta O_{2gas}(P_1 - P_2) = \beta O_{2gas}(P_1 - P_2).$$

In this analysis, the O_2 either liberated or taken up by each of the stores constitutes a change in area in fig. 5.16A (note the

100-μl O_2 calibration square). As P_{O_2} levels change, neither blood nor lung O_2 stores are of constant volume, nor is βO_{2blood} constant. The variations in the shapes of the areas representing blood O_2 stores are due to changes in blood O_2 capacitance coefficients as a function of P_{O_2} (i.e., the slope of the O_2 equilibrium curve changes with P_{O_2}; Boutilier and Shelton 1986c), the volume of blood being constant. On the other hand, apparent increases in lung O_2 volume occur at high P_{O_2} levels because lung volume declines during a dive, βO_{2gas} being constant. In fig. 5.16A, the dashed line in the lung store constitutes the line of constant O_2 volume that would occur if lung volume remained constant (at 8 ml) throughout the dive. As shown in the model, these O_2 volume relationships for the lung rest on the assumptions that P_{CO_2} changes by only 3 mm Hg (cf. Boutilier and Shelton 1986b), that the water vapor pressure of the lung remains constant, and that the volume of nitrogen in the lung is constant throughout the dive.

Lung gas P_{O_2} falls from a predive level of 130 mm Hg to an end-dive level of 40 mm Hg (Boutilier and Shelton 1986b). After a dive ends, the stores can be estimated from blood-gas O_2 equilibration data (fig. 5.5) and blood O_2 dissociation curves (Boutilier and Shelton 1986b, 1986c). The O_2 content of systemic venous blood (C_{sv}) at the start of the dive (time 0) can be calculated from the cell O_2 consumption ($\dot{V}O_{2cells}$), systemic arterial O_2 content (C_{sa}), and a systemic blood flow rate ($\dot{Q}_s$) of 14 ml $\cdot min^{-1}$ (Shelton 1970):

$$C_{sv} = C_{sa} - \dot{V}O_{2cells}/\dot{Q}_s.$$

The total amount of O_2 in the systemic venous store ($V_{O_{2svs}}$) is simply the product of the blood O_2 content (Boutilier and Shelton 1986b) and the systemic venous blood volume:

$$V_{O_{2svs}} = C \times V_{sv}.$$

Thereafter, the decline in the systemic venous blood O_2 store is the difference between the volume of O_2 consumed by the cells ($V_{O_{2cells}}$), cutaneous oxygen uptake ($V_{O_{2cut}}$) and that from stores in the lung ($V_{O_{2gas}}$), pulmonary venous blood ($V_{O_{2pv}}$), and systemic arterial blood ($V_{O_{2sa}}$), viz.:

$$\Delta V_{O_{2svs}} = V_{O_{2cells}} - V_{O_{2cut}} - \Delta V_{O_{2gas+pv+sa}}.$$

The lung of *Xenopus* is an important store from which O_2 can be "metered out" during a dive (fig. 5.16). Apart from the volume of the lungs, their comparatively small dead space (cf. Smith and Rapson 1977) means that P_{O_2} levels can increase to as much as 140 to 150 mm Hg during breathing. Thus, despite an incomplete blood-gas equilibrium (fig. 5.5), the blood leaving the lungs remains highly saturated with O_2 well into a dive.

The systemic venous blood is also an important O_2 store, especially early in a dive (fig. 5.16A). Early use of this store provides an advantage by reducing the P_{O_2} of the venous return and pulmocutaneous blood, as long as shunt 2 (S_2) remains relatively small (fig. 5.16B). Conditions such as these would facilitate continued O_2 uptake from the lungs and skin, even if blood flow to these areas (Q_p, $\dot{Q}_c$) were to decline. Cutaneous O_2 uptake could also increase under these conditions, particularly if frogs simultaneously recruit skin capillaries (Burggren and Moalli 1984). Use of the venous store in the early stages of the dive occurs by a reduction in systemic blood flow (calculated according to the model in fig. 5.16) from 14 ml $\cdot min^{-1}$ at time 0, to 6 ml $\cdot min^{-1}$ at 5 min,

4 ml · min^{-1} at 10 min, and 3 ml · min^{-1} thereafter. These changes result from increasing the systemic resistance (R_s) or decreasing cardiac output, both of which occur as part of the "diving response" of *Xenopus* (Emilio and Shelton 1972; Shelton 1970).

The model also predicts how other O_2 stores might be used during a dive. The use of any of the O_2 stores will be determined in major part by the O_2 concentration differences and the rates of blood flow to and from the store itself. For instance, an increase in pulmonary resistance (R_p) caused by lung vasoconstriction would decrease $\dot{Q}_p$ more than $\dot{Q}_s$. This in turn would increase shunt 1 (S_1), thereby conserving the stores in the pulmonary vein and lung. During this time, however, the systemic and venous blood O_2 stores would be used more rapidly than is shown (fig. 5.16A), encouraging even greater cutaneous gas exchange (see above). This would lead eventually to the lung O_2 stores being used at progressively increasing rates during the latter stages of a dive. In a highly active animal, with high pulmonary blood flow and cardiac output (cf. Emilio and Shelton 1972), the Po_2 differences between arterial and venous blood would not increase, and Po_2 levels in all parts of the O_2 storage system would move closer together than in the model. These animals can change metabolic rates, blood flow distribution, and breathing behavior throughout a breathing-diving cycle. The present model is, therefore, a single example of doubtless several and varied forms of O_2 store utilization. Further development of the model should account for more of these unsteady states and should also incorporate CO_2 storage, transport, and elimination. For the latter, knowing the tissue capacitance for CO_2 as well as for the blood, lungs, and environment is essential (see review by White 1989).

EXCHANGES OF WATER AND IONS

Because amphibians have an external surface that is highly permeable to respiratory gases, these animals face immediate and pressing problems in water and electrolyte balance. Amphibians' movements back and forth between the aquatic and terrestrial environments complicate these problems. On land, in air, they continuously face the threat of desiccation from loss of water across their skin; in fresh water they experience the opposite problems of osmotic flooding and diffusive and urinary loss of electrolytes. Thus, movement between the two environments results in contraction and concentration of body fluids in air, and expansion and dilution in water. Since physiological activities such as enzymatic reactions, nerve and muscle function, and transmembrane transport of vital materials are sensitive to ionic strength and the proper concentrations of reactants and cofactors, extreme variation of body fluid composition may impair development, growth, metabolism, behavior, and reproduction.

Amphibians have solved these problems with physiological and behavioral adaptations that limit ionic losses via skin and urine and retard, to varying extents, evaporation and osmotic uptake of water across exposed surfaces.

Exchanges of Water across the Skin

Water moves across skin in three ways: evaporation, diffusion, and osmosis (see also chapters 4 and 7). Evaporative water loss is most important in highly terrestrial species and is discussed in detail in chapter 6. Nevertheless, evaporation plays a role in semiaquatic amphibians and deserves mention in this chapter as well. Osmosis is most important to strictly aquatic species but also affects semiaquatic (and terrestrial) species when they return to water for reproduction, predation, or escape. Diffusion of water occurs when the animals are in the aquatic environment and is distinct from osmosis. Such diffusion is important in a mechanistic sense but plays no role in the animals' responses to the environment, as diffusive influx and efflux are equal but opposite, resulting in zero net flux.

Evaporative Water Loss Overton (1904) pioneered the study of water loss in amphibians, which was greatly expanded by Adolph (1932, 1933). These studies described the physical nature of water loss in this group and laid the groundwork for the modern comparative studies of today.

Early studies suggested that aquatic amphibians lose water by evaporation at higher rates than do terrestrial species (Warburg 1965). Other factors not controlled in these early studies, however, might better explain differences in evaporative water loss between species (Claussen 1969; Spight 1968). Of major importance is the body size and shape of animals. Spight (1968) compared rates of water loss among lungless salamanders that inhabit environments of variable free water content, and found that the shape and size of animals are stronger determinants of evaporation rate than habitat. Smaller animals, due to their larger surface-to-volume ratio, have greater area-specific evaporative water loss than do larger species, and slender cylindrical salamanders have higher rates than stout-bodied animals. A similar comparison of six anuran species from both aquatic and terrestrial environments found interspecific variation resulting from differences in body mass (Claussen 1969).

While aquatic and terrestrial species generally do not differ with respect to evaporative water loss, differences can occur in specific cases. The totally aquatic tailed frog, *Ascaphus truei* (Leiopelmatidae), for example, loses water evaporatively at a greater rate than does the arboreal *Hyla regilla* (Hylidae) of similar size (Claussen 1973). Similarly, the totally aquatic *Xenopus laevis* and the semiaquatic *Rana pipiens* lose water more rapidly than the terrestrial *B. marinus* and *Agalychnis dacnicolor* (Hylidae; Bentley and Yorio 1979b). After accounting for differences in surface area among the three species, *A. dacnicolor* still has by far the lowest rate of evaporation. This arboreal species was also least affected by increasing air velocity. Some specialized terrestrial amphibians have greatly reduced rates of cutaneous water loss due to unique adaptations (Drews et al. 1977; Shoemaker and McClanahan 1975), as discussed in chapter 6. Behavioral responses to dehydration include aggregation of animals to reduce the area of each exposed to the air (Alvarado 1967; Gehlbach, Kimmel, and Weems 1969; Warburg and Degani 1979).

Rehydration Following Evaporative Water Loss Bentley, Lee, and Main (1958) have suggested that terrestrial amphibians gain water more rapidly following dehydration than do aquatic species. Claussen (1969) found no consistent correlation with environment in the six anuran species he tested.

However, the extremely xeric anuran *Chiromantis petersi* (Rhacophoridae) has one of the fastest rehydration rates known (Drews et al. 1977) and terrestrial *Bufo viridis* rehydrate faster than aquatic *Rana ridibunda* (Katz and Graham 1980).

Osmosis and Diffusion Osmosis and diffusion differ fundamentally with respect to the way in which water molecules move through biological membranes. While water molecules diffuse across the lipid bilayers of such membranes one at a time and are essentially independent of each other, osmosis involves bulk movement or flow of water molecules through pores. No one has ever seen such pores, even though electron-microscopic studies have attempted to image them. The evidence that supports their existence is indirect but, when related to physicochemical principles, is quite persuasive.

Koefoed-Johnson and Ussing (1953) provided the first evidence for such pores while studying the effect of the neurohypophyseal antidiuretic hormone (ADH) on water permeability of frog skin. They measured diffusive permeability with the isotopic water tracer ^3H_2O (tritiated water or THO) and osmotic permeability by gravimetric means. The result of ADH treatment was a 10% increase in diffusive permeability but a 100% increase in osmotic permeability. To explain this difference one needs to consider the difference between diffusion (which is governed by Fick's law) and osmotic flow through channels or pores (which can be considered to be governed by Poiseuille's law). Fick's law is

$$\Delta S/\Delta t = -DA(\Delta S/\Delta x),$$

where

$\Delta S/\Delta t$ = the rate of diffusion of the solute S
D = the diffusion constant
A = the cross-sectional area through which S is diffusing
$\Delta S/\Delta x$ = the concentration gradient for S.

Poiseuille's law is

$$Q = \frac{(P_2 - P_1)r^4 \pi}{8l\eta},$$

where

Q = flow
$P_2 - P_1$ = the pressure gradient
r = the radius of the channel
l = the length of the channel
η = the viscosity of the fluid

Diffusion through pores is proportional to the second power of the radius of the pore ($A = \pi r^2$), while flow through pores is proportional to r^4. Therefore, expanding the pore radius as a result of ADH action would have a greater effect on osmotic flow than on diffusion. This not only suggests that ADH acts to expand pore radius, it indicates that water moves osmotically through epithelial cell membranes via pores. Later Andersen and Ussing (1957) expanded the evidence for osmotic movement by bulk flow through pores by demonstrating "solvent drag," in which small molecules such as acetamide and urea are accelerated when diffusing in the same direction as

the osmotic movement and retarded when diffusing against the osmotic flow. The simplest interpretation of these findings is that the diffusing molecules are convected by the movement of water through pores.

Diffusion of Water across the Skin Skin permeability is quite variable in amphibians; that is, coefficients of permeability for diffusive water movement can vary from 310×10^{-7} cm $\cdot$ sec^{-1} in *Necturus maculosus* to $1,390 \times 10^{-7}$ cm $\cdot$ sec^{-1} in *Amphiuma means* to $2,356 \times 10^{-7}$ cm $\cdot$ sec^{-1} in larval *Ambystoma tigrinum* (Bentley and Baldwin 1980). The frog *Rana pipiens* exchanges ^3H_2O at 154 μl $\cdot$ cm^{-2} $\cdot$ h^{-1} (Mahany and Parsons 1978), which ADH does not affect. In the skin of the urodele *Ambystoma tigrinum*, *in vivo* and *in vitro* diffusive water permeabilities do not differ (225–50 μl $\cdot$ cm^{-2} $\cdot$ h^{-1}), whereas in *N. maculosus* the *in vivo* value of 150 μl $\cdot$ cm^{-2} $\cdot$ h^{-1} is intermediate between *in vitro* values of 373 and 31 μl $\cdot$ cm^{-2} $\cdot$ h^{-1} in the presence and absence, respectively, of ADH (Baldwin and Bentley 1982). ADH does not increase diffusive permeability to water in *A. tigrinum* (Bentley and Baldwin 1980). Adult *A. tigrinum* are primarily terrestrial and have a higher tritiated water flux (334 μl $\cdot$ cm^{-2} $\cdot$ h^{-1}) than the aquatic larvae. The exchange of water in larval or neotenic salamanders is evidently confined to the skin, as ligation of the gills has no measurable effect (Baldwin and Bentley 1982). Circulation to the skin directly affects diffusive water movement in *R. pipiens*. For instance, cutting the sciatic nerve (which reduces sympathetic vasomotor tone to increase leg circulation) increases diffusive water exchange, while ligating the sciatic artery (to reduce circulation) decreases such exchange (Mahany and Parsons 1978).

Osmotic Movement of Water across the Skin The literature on osmotic exchange of water in amphibians is large and impressive. While diffusive water exchange is of little consequence in the physiological ecology of amphibians, osmotic water exchange is of major importance. Most amphibians spend at least a portion of their life in water, and in most cases this water is much more dilute than their extracellular fluids. Depending on the permeability of the skin to osmotic water movement, there will be varying rates of osmotic flooding of the tissues and attendant expansion and dilution of bodily fluids.

The osmotic permeability of amphibian skin is not always uniform over the body surface. While the completely aquatic species *Xenopus laevis* has similar osmotic permeability in dorsal, ventral pectoral, and ventral pelvic regions, the tree-frog *Hyla moorei* has a much greater pelvic permeability. The semiaquatic *Rana pipiens* has uniform osmotic permeability in the absence of ADH, but pelvic permeability increases when this hormone is present (Bentley and Main 1972). In general, terrestrial and semiterrestrial species have higher osmotic permeabilities than do aquatic species, which has been interpreted as an adaptation to an aquatic existence (Bentley 1969; Harlow 1977; Mullen and Alvarado 1976; Schmid 1965). Table 5.5 summarizes osmotic water fluxes for a variety of aquatic and terrestrial amphibian species. While the general trend is toward higher osmotic permeability in less aquatic species, differences in body size may also account for this trend.

TABLE 5.5 Representative Values for Osmotic Water Uptake Across Amphibian Skin in the Presence and Absence of Antidiuretic Hormone

	Control ($\mu l \cdot g^{-1} \cdot h^{-1}$)	ADH ($\mu l \cdot g^{-1} \cdot h^{-1}$)	Reference
Anura			
Terrestrial			
Bufo melanostictus	36	75*	Dicker and Elliott 1967
Aquatic			
Rana catesbeiana	0	90*	Alvarado and Johnson 1966
Rana ridibunda	40	71*	Goldenberg and Warburg 1977a
Urodela			
Terrestrial			
Aneides lugubris	12	52*	Hillman 1974
Triturus vittatus	80	190*	Warburg and Goldenberg 1978b
Salamandra salamandra	32	36	Bentley and Heller 1965
(= *maculosa*)	7	7	Warburg and Goldenberg 1978b
Taricha torosa	59	104*	Brown and Brown 1980
Aquatic			
Siren lacertina	3	3	Bentley 1973a
Amphiuma means	5	6	Bentley 1973a
Notophthalmus viridescens			
Eft	20	120*	
Newt	80	120*	P. S. Brown and S. C. Brown 1977
Ambystoma tigrinum			
Larva	13	12	Alvarado and Johnson 1965
Adult	14	14	
Necturus maculosus	10	14	Bentley and Heller 1964

*Significantly greater than control $p < .05$.

Control of Osmotic Water Movement across the Skin

The amphibian posterior pituitary, or neurohypophysis, secretes two octapeptides that are evolutionarily related to arginine vasopressin and oxytocin in mammals (Acher et al. 1964; Acher et al. 1960). These are, respectively, arginine vasotocin (AVT) and mesotocin.

While the effect of AVT (or ADH) on diffusive water permeability is usually slight or absent (see above), this hormone can stimulate osmosis in amphibians. This is particularly true of semiaquatic and terrestrial amphibians. However, purely aquatic amphibians such as larval *Ambystoma tigrinum*, *Amphiuma means* (Amphiumidae), *Siren lacertina* (Sirenidae), and *Xenopus laevis* do not increase cutaneous osmotic permeability in response to AVT (Alvarado and Johnson 1965; Bentley 1969; Yorio and Bentley 1978a). The increased osmotic permeability or hydroosmotic effect of AVT is often called the Brunn effect (Brunn 1921). Table 5.5 summarizes responses of amphibians to ADH. Mesotocin has a lesser effect on cutaneous osmotic permeability (Bentley 1969).

Although AVT undoubtedly plays a major role in controlling the osmotic permeability of the skin, other less well understood factors are at play. Neurohypophyseal hormones cannot completely reverse the effects of functional hypophysectomy on cutaneous osmosis in the toad *Bufo marinus* (Bakker and Bradshaw 1977). Midbrain lesions of the toad *B. arenarum* increase osmotic water uptake (Segura et al. 1982). Injection of the α-adrenergic antagonist phenoxybenzamine into the midbrain of this species also increases osmotic permeability and subcutaneous injection of α-agonist stimulates osmotic uptake as well (Segura, Bandsholm, and Bronstein 1982). Conversely, the β-adrenergic antagonist propranolol blocks osmotic uptake of water in the toad *B. cognatus* while the β-agonist isoproterenol stimulates it (Yokota and Hillman 1984). These findings suggest an α-adrenergic inhibition and a β-adrenergic stimulation of osmotic water uptake in at least some amphibians.

Another hormone controlling osmotic permeability is prolactin (see also chapter 16). Prolactin increases cutaneous osmotic permeability in *Xenopus laevis* larvae (Schultheiss, Hanke, and Maetz 1972), *Rana ridibunda* (Goldenberg and Warburg 1977a), and the salamandrids *Salamandra salamandra* and *Triturus vittatus* (Warburg and Goldenberg 1978b). On the other hand, prolactin in the presence of thyroxine decreases cutaneous osmotic permeability in *Notophthalmus viridescens* (Brown and Brown 1973), whereas prolactin alone decreases permeability in *Taricha torosa* (both Caudata: Salamandridae; Brown and Brown 1980). These latter authors stress that prolactin is also responsible for the "water drive" behavior that signals the return of terrestrial newts to the aquatic environment for reproduction; a reduced cutaneous osmotic permeability is obviously beneficial in the aquatic environment. Long-term treatment with prolactin not only decreases cutaneous osmotic permeability in intact (sham operated) *T. torosa* but also decreases further an already depressed osmotic permeability in hypophysectomized newts (Brown and Brown 1982). The difference between these and earlier studies may stem from the short-term prolactin treatments of the latter and the existence of ADH contaminants in many early prolactin preparations (Bern 1975).

Hormones may govern seasonal variation in osmotic permeability. Osmotic permeability of the skin of ranid frogs increases during winter (Hevesy, Hofer, and Krogh 1935;

Share and Ussing 1965). Both the increased permeability resulting from AVT (Parsons et al. 1978) and the decreased permeability resulting from prolactin (Brown, Brown, and Specker 1984) may be responsible.

Exchanges of Ions across the Skin

Amphibian skin exchanges large quantities of ions between environmental water and extracellular fluid. The great majority of the ions exchanged are Na^+ and Cl^-, and the inward movement greatly exceeds the outward movement. This net inward cutaneous flux counterbalances a urinary loss of ions (see below).

The net inward flux of ions across amphibian skin occurs against a large electrochemical gradient. This gradient arises from the high sodium concentration of amphibian extracellular fluid (approximately 100 mM in Na^+ salts; primarily NaCl) and the internal electrical potential, upwards of 100 mV positive to the bathing solution. This potential, first discovered by Du Bois–Reymond (1848), is Na^+-dependent (Galeotti 1904). To explain how such fluxes might be maintained, Huf (1936) suggested that either Cl^- or Na^+ are actively transported.

To characterize active ionic transport, Ussing (1949) developed the Ussing flux ratio equation:

$$\dot{M}_{in}/\dot{M}_{out} = (C_{out}/C_{in})e^{ZFE/RT},$$

where

$$
\begin{aligned}
\dot{M}_{in} \text{ and } \dot{M}_{out} &= \text{influx and efflux respectively} \\
C_{in} \text{ and } C_{out} &= \text{inside and outside concentrations} \\
&\quad \text{of the ions in question} \\
Z &= \text{the valence} \\
F &= \text{Faraday constant} \\
E &= \text{transepithelial potential (TEP)} \\
R &= \text{gas constant} \\
T &= \text{temperature}
\end{aligned}
$$

If the measured flux ratio agrees with the calculated flux ratio, the ion in question is distributed passively across the membrane. If the measured flux ratio disagrees with the calculated ratio, the ion must be actively transported. Experimental results demonstrate that Na^+ is the only ion that departs from the flux ratio calculation.

Later, Ussing and Zerahn (1951) developed short-circuit current measurements to provide further evidence for active transport of Na^+ with passive Cl^- movement coupled electrically. These measurements place isolated amphibian skin (usually frog skin) between two chambers with amphibian Ringer's solution on both sides. An equal and opposite potential difference provided by an external circuit is used to null the inside-positive TEP. The current required to bring the spontaneous potential difference to zero is known as the short-circuit current (SCC) and is equal to the algebraic sum of the fluxes of all ions moving across the skin. Ussing and Zerahn (1951) showed that the SCC is equivalent to the net Na^+ flux in the inward direction and that net Cl^- flux is essentially zero under these conditions. These experiments are generally interpreted to mean that Na^+ transport across amphibian skin is active and that Cl^- moves passively following the positive charge carried by Na^+.

Models of Amphibian Cutaneous NaCl Transport Ussing subsequently expanded these observations into a model of frog skin ion transport (Koefoed-Johnson and Ussing 1958). The model held that the outer surface of frog skin is permeable to Na^+ but not K^+, while the inner surface is permeable to K^+ but not Na^+; the active ion transport consists of a Na^+/K^+ exchange antiporter (Na^+K^+–ATPase) located on the inner-facing membranes of the cells with a stoichiometry estimated to range from $2Na^+:1K^+$ (Nagel 1980) to $3Na^+:2K^+$ (Nielsen 1979). Both inner and outer membranes are considered permeable to Cl^- (the outer membrane much less so), which diffuses across the skin to maintain electroneutrality. The extracellular space of frog skin (paracellular shunt) is also an important route of passive Cl^- movement (Voute and Ussing 1970).

These observations are inconsistent with the early observations of Krogh (1937, 1938), which conclusively demonstrated independent inward movement of both Na^+ and Cl^- across the skin of intact frogs. In Krogh's experiments, however, the frogs were in dilute solutions similar to natural environments. These early observations were later confirmed for a variety of anuran and urodele species (Alvarado and Kirschner 1963; Dietz, Kirschner, and Porter 1967; Garcia-Romeu, Salibian, and Pezzani-Hernandez 1969; Jørgensen, Levi, and Zerahn 1954; Salibian, Pezzani-Hernandez, and Garcia-Romeu 1968). The ability to transport cations and anions independently implies exchange of those ions for ions of like charge to maintain electroneutrality (Krogh 1937). Evidence for such ion exchange transport systems began to accumulate following the observation that Na^+ influx was equivalent to H^+ excretion in *Rana pipiens* in dilute solutions (Kirschner, Greenwald, and Kerstetter 1973). Also, Cl^- influx and base excretion are strongly correlated in *R. pipiens* (Alvarado, Poole, and Mullen 1975). Similar correlations between Na^+ uptake and H^+ excretion, and between Cl^- uptake and base excretion have also been reported for *R. esculenta* (Garcia-Romeu and Ehrenfeld, 1975a), and for isolated skin of *R. pipiens* (Alvarado, Dietz, and Mullen 1975) and of *R. esculenta* (Ehrenfeld and Garcia-Romeu 1977, 1978; Garcia-Romeu and Ehrenfeld 1975b). With these observations, a model for amphibian skin ion transport emerged that was entirely different than the earlier Koefoed-Johnson–Ussing (1958) model (Kirschner 1983). In this new model, Na^+ is transported into the cutaneous epithelial cells in exchange for H^+ (or NH_4^+) across the outward-facing membranes, while Cl^- is exchanged for HCO_3^- (or OH^-) across the same membranes. The major difference between the two models is that the Koefoed-Johnson–Ussing model holds when both surfaces of frog skin are bathed by Ringer's solution, while the Krogh-Kirschner model holds when the outer skin is bathed with more physiologically dilute solutions (Kirschner 1983).

Direct Na^+/H^+ exchange is unlikely because fluxes of Na^+ and H^+ can become uncoupled, with one or the other becoming predominant depending upon the experimental conditions (Ehrenfeld, Garcia-Romeu, and Harvey 1985). Instead of direct coupling, the Na^+ influx appears to be linked electrically to an active electrogenic efflux of H^+ across the outward-facing membranes of frog skin cells.

Our increased understanding of the structural and functional organization of amphibian skin have reconciled the two models (Larsen 1988).

Structure of Amphibian Skin Frog (*Rana pipiens*) skin is a stratified epithelium containing an inner basal lamina, a stratum germanitivum, a stratum spinosum, a stratum granulosum, and an outer stratum corneum composed of dead, cornified cells (Farquhar and Palade 1964). The cells of the outermost living layer join together with tight junctions. Numerous exocrine gland cells are scattered among the epithelial cells, but they are probably not involved in homeostatic transcutaneous exchanges of ions. The proteid urodele, *Necturus maculosus*, displays a similar integumentary organization; however, the outer layer is not cornified and has been called the stratum mucosum (Lindinger 1984). Interestingly, *N. maculosus* does not transport Na^+ and Cl^- across its skin, owing to a low permeability of the apical surfaces of the outer layer of cutaneous cells (Bentley and Yorio 1977).

The living layers of the granulosum, spinosum, and germinativum of frog skin are composed of two cell types: principal cells, which make up the vast majority and are in intracellular communication to form a functional syncytium, and mitochondria-rich cells, which are fewer and form a parallel pathway to the principal cells for ion exchange. The outward-facing membranes (apical membranes) of the mitochondria-rich cells are just below the stratum corneum at the same level as the outward-facing principal cells. The mitochondria-rich cells extend inward through the third layer of principal cells, increasing in girth from a narrow neck in the outer layer to a relatively large base in the inner layers. There are 50,000 to 100,000 mitochondria-rich cells · cm^{-2} in toad skin (Willumsen and Larsen 1985).

The high Na^+ permeability barrier described by Koefoed-Johnson and Ussing (1958) is located in the outward-facing membrane of the outer layer of living cells (Ussing and Windhager 1964). The inner layers of principal cells are not polarized with respect to membrane characteristics, as they contain Na^+-K^+-ATPase (the Na^+/K^+ exchange transport system of the inner or basolateral membrane) in the membranes facing all extracellular compartments (Mills, Ernst, and DiBona 1977). Because these cells are in intracellular communication with each other and contain the Na^+-permeable apical membranes in their outward-facing layer, they provide a large surface for the transport of Na^+ into the interstitium. In fact, the rate-limiting step in transmural transport is apical entry (Katz 1986). Both cell types have a high passive K^+ permeability in the membranes facing the intercellular spaces (Larsen 1988). However, the mitochondria-rich cells have a high passive Cl^- permeability in both outward- and inward-facing membranes (Voute and Meier 1978). This forms a transcellular shunt path for the passive movement of Cl^- that is coupled to the electrogenic portion of the Na^+/K^+ exchange. About 50% of the Na^+/K^+ exchange is electroneutral, while the other 50% produces an electrical gradient that couples Cl^- movement to Na^+ transport (Nagel 1980). When frogs are cool, these Cl^- fluxes decrease (Voute and Meier 1978) and pass primarily through the paracellular shunts described by Ussing and Windhager (1964).

The transport properties of the membranes of mitochondria-rich cells and principal cells display both similarities and differences (fig. 5.17). Both cell types have the basal Na^+/K^+ exchange pump that maintains the characteristic intracellular ratio of low $[Na^+]$ to high $[K^+]$ (table 5.6) and provides the driving force for coupling of passive Cl^- transport to active Na^+ transport. Both cell types also have an apical, amiloride-inhibitable passive Na^+ permeability and basal passive K^+ permeability in accordance with the Koefoed-Johnson–Ussing model (see above). Cuthbert (1973) estimated about 400 apical Na^+ channels · μm^{-1} of membrane surface. In addition, the principal cells have basal membrane cotransporters that carry Na^+, K^+, and Cl^- into the cells in a $1:1:2$ ratio (Ussing 1982). This transport system is primarily responsible for cell volume control; it is inhibitable with furosemide and bumetanide, which also inhibit NaCl transport in the mammalian renal ascending limbs of Henle's loops. Principal cells also have a basal Na^+/H^+ exchanger that is involved in intracellular pH regulation (Ehrenfeld and Harvey 1987), as well as apical K^+ channels that can become acti-

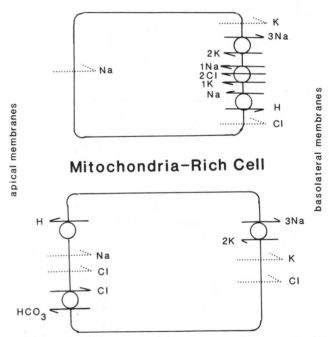

Fig. 5.17 Diagrammatic principal cell and mitochondria-rich cell with apical and basolateral pumps and passive permeabilities.

TABLE 5.6 Intracellular Ionic Concentrations of Frog Skin Epithelial Cells

	Ion	Intracellular Concentration (mM)	Reference
Principal cell	$[Na^+]$	12	Rick et al. 1978
	$[K^+]$	153	
	$[Cl^-]$	47	
Mitochondria-rich cells	$[Na^+]$	11	Rick et al. 1984
	$[K^+]$	111	
	$[Cl^-]$	12	

vated to secrete K^+ during potassium loading (Zeiske and Van Driessche 1979; Nielsen 1984). The mitochondria-rich cells, on the other hand, have apical Cl^- channels, not present in principal cells, which provide a transcellular diffusion pathway for chloride (Foskett and Ussing 1986; Katz, Van Driessche, and Scheffey 1985). Frog skin cells also possess apical Cl^-/HCO_3^- exchangers that can be blocked with 4,4'-diisothiocyanostilbene-2,2'-disulfonic acid (DIDS; Drewnowska and Biber 1988). DIDS is an inhibitor of Cl^-/HCO_3^- exchange in many epithelia.

Effects of Environmental Acidification on Ion Exchanges
Low pH in Ringer's solution bathing frog skin reduces active Na^+ transport (Schoffeniels 1955). Acid precipitation in the Northern Hemisphere has lowered the pH of many amphibian habitats (Likens and Bormann 1974). Not only does low pH inhibit active uptake of Na^+, it increases passive loss of ions (DeRuyter and Stiffler 1988; Freda and Dunson 1984; McDonald, Ozog, and Simons 1984) due to disruption of tight junctions (Freda 1986). The ionic losses associated with these changes kill animals when the pH of the environment falls below 4–5.

Effects of Cations on Na+ Transport
Copper ion (Cu^{2+}, 10^{-5} M), placed on the apical side, reduces passive chloride permeability, which increases the TEP of frog skin (Cuthbert, Painter, and Prince 1969; Ussing and Zerahn 1951) and decreases Na^+ transport. Silver ion (Ag^+, 10^{-4} M), on the other hand, decreases TEP when placed in the apical solution and may increase shunt conductance and apical membrane K^+ permeability (Curran 1972). Iron ion (Fe^{3+}, 10^{-3} M) decreases SCC and increases passive Cl^- efflux in frog skin (Biber, Mullen, and DeSimone 1980). Biber and Mullen (1980) studied the effects of monovalent cations (10^{-1} M) and found that H^+, Li^+, K^+, Rb^+, Cs^+, and choline (in decreasing order of ability) inhibit Na^+ transport in frog skin. Ionic forms of the alkaline earth elements (10^{-3} M) inhibit SCC with the order of effectiveness being $Ba^{2+} = Ca^{2+} > Sr^{2+} > Mg^{2+}$ for skin of larval bullfrogs (*Rana catesbeiana*) and $Ba^{2+} > Ca^{2+} = Mg^{2+}$ for adults (Alvarado and Cox 1985). Thus, ionic substitutions alter the ionic strength of the solutions bathing the apical membranes of the skin; this in turn alters the surface charge of these membranes, affecting electrochemical gradients that influence Na^+ movement into the cells (Alvarado and Cox 1985; Biber and Mullen 1980). Conversely, transition elemental ions, such as Co^{2+}, Cd^{2+}, and La^{3+} (10^{-3} M), stimulate Na^+ transport in adult but not larval frog skin (Alvarado and Cox 1985; Goncharevskaya, Monin, and Natochin 1986). This is postulated to result from interference with Na^+ self-inhibition (Alvarado and Cox 1985; see below).

Effects of Anions on Na+ Transport
Sulfate (59.5 mM) and gluconate (119 mM) inhibit Na^+ transport in frog skin, while Br^- and I^- have either little effect (Ferreira 1968) or act to stimulate Na^+ transport in frog skin (Biber and Mullen 1980). Once again, the effect of ionic strength on the surface charge of the apical membranes is suspected to be involved.

Chloride Exchanges
In addition to the passive transport of Cl^- that is coupled to active Na^+ transport (see above), active Cl^- transport reportedly occurs in frog skin (Zadunaisky, Candia, and Chiarandini 1963; Schneider 1975) and toad skin (Berman, Soria, and Coviello 1987). The isolated skin of the toad *Bufo arenarum*, when treated with amiloride to block Na^+ exchange across the apical membrane, responds with a reversed SCC that is energy dependent and requires Cl^- in the medium bathing the apical surface (Berman, Soria, and Coviello 1987). These observations confirm the early suggestions of Na^+-independent Cl^- transport (Krogh 1937).

Potassium Exchanges
The classic Koefoed-Johnson–Ussing model of frog skin ion transport (1958) predicts that transepithelial K^+ transport cannot occur across frog skin because of the vanishingly low permeability to K^+ in the apical membranes of the outward-facing layer of granulosa cells. Indeed, unidirectional transepithelial K^+ fluxes are very small and do not result in a net K^+ flux when frog skin is bathed with normal Ringer's solution on both sides (Varanda and Lacaz-Vieira 1979). Nevertheless, intact *Rana pipiens* excrete K^+ across their skin into dilute water and can increase the cutaneous excretion rate when K^+ is loaded (Frazier and Vanatta 1981). Studies of *R. temporaria* revealed that 10–20% of the skins examined had a significant K^+ permeability and that curtailing Na^+ uptake with Na^+-free solutions in the apical bath induces K^+ permeability in all skins (Nagel and Hirschmann 1980). Nielsen (1984) found that the skin of *R. temporaria* bathed in Na^+-gluconate (i.e., Cl^--free) Ringer's displayed an SCC that is less than the inward movement of Na^+, and only an active outward movement of K^+ can account for this difference.

Calcium Exchanges
Watlington, Burke, and Estep (1968) reported a small (<0.2 nM $\cdot$ cm^{-2} $\cdot$ h^{-1}) influx of ^{45}Ca across frog skin that was significantly greater than the efflux of this ion. However, Zadunaisky and Lande (1972) and Baldwin and Bentley (1981a, 1981b) could find no significant difference between influxes and effluxes of Ca^{2+} in *Rana pipiens*, *Ambystoma tigrinum*, or *Necturus maculosus*. Larval *R. catesbeiana*, however, appear to take up Ca^{2+} across their gills (Baldwin and Bentley 1980). Under some conditions frog skin can secrete net Ca^{2+}; however, this secretion occurs in cells of exocrine glands (Ziyadeh, Kelepouris, and Agus 1986; Ziyadeh et al. 1985) and may not be related to homeostatic ion exchanges.

Exchanges of Organic Compounds
Rana esculenta can actively transport urea inward across the skin (Svelto et al. 1982). The flux ratio ($\dot{M}_{in} / \dot{M}_{out}$) is 2.4 at 1 mM bath urea; the transport is inhibitable with phloretin, which inhibits urea transport in shark kidney and has an apparent K_m (reciprocal of the affinity) of 1.31 mM^{-1}. *R. pipiens* can absorb glucose across its skin by a phlorhizin-inhibitable mechanism (Vanatta and Frazier 1982). Phlorhizin is an inhibitor of active glucose transport.

Adaptation of Ion Transport to Environment
The analogy between active transport carrier molecules and enzymes has prompted the use of Michaelis-Menton kinetics to analyze ion transport systems in amphibian skin (Kirschner 1970). The use of such analyses to compare aquatic and terrestrial amphibian transport systems has resulted in the hypothesis that

cutaneous ion transport systems of aquatic amphibians have higher affinities (K_m^{-1}) for the transported ion than do the transport systems of terrestrial amphibians (Greenwald 1972; Mullen and Alvarado 1976). These affinities appear to be constant for a given species and are not subject to control, since salt depletion, which results in acceleration of cutaneous ion transport in *Ambystoma gracile*, does not alter the K_m. Rather, the maximal rate (V_{max}) increases (Alvarado and Dietz 1970b).

The application of Michaelis-Menton kinetics to ion transport systems is not strictly analogous to enzyme-substrate reactions, as the "affinity" of the transport system is doubtfully the true affinity of the carrier for the transported ion (Kirschner 1983). As external [Na^+] increases, apical Na^+ permeability decreases, presumably due to some interaction between Na^+ and the apical membrane. This phenomenon, termed self-inhibition, is an explanation for the Michaelis-Menton–like kinetics of epithelial transport (Lindemann 1977). Recently, Kirschner (1988) has argued that the transport of H^+ in the opposite direction might limit Na^+ influx when external [Na^+] increases. This sets up the electrical gradient that attracts Na^+ to cross apical membranes and enter into the cell's transport pool (Ehrenfeld, Garcia-Romeu, and Harvey 1985). Therefore, the "K_m" and "V_{max}" derived from kinetic analyses of Na^+ flux rates relate to the apical entry step (at least for Na^+) rather than to the "affinity" and "capacity" of the basolateral transport system for the transported ion. The analyses are still useful in a phenomenological sense to describe adaptations of amphibians to particular environments, but they are not accurate in a literal sense as descriptors of ion transport carrier kinetics.

Role of Cutaneous Ion Exchanges in Acid-Base Balance

Exchanges of Na^+ for H^+ (or NH_4^+) and Cl^- for HCO_3^- (or OH^-) suggest that these ion transport mechanisms might be involved in regulation of extracellular pH. An early observation that the skin of *Rana pipiens* acidifies the medium bathing the apical surface and alkalinizes the basal medium (Friedman et al. 1967) provides evidence for this. This same species increases cutaneous excretion of H^+ and NH_4^+ when made acidotic, and HCO_3^- when made alkalotic (Frazier and Vanatta 1980; Vanatta and Frazier 1981). *Bufo viridis* becomes acidotic when treated with amiloride, which blocks the electrically coupled Na^+/H^+ exchange (Katz 1981).

The ability of amphibians to transport Na^+ across their skin and their ability to compensate for respiratory acidosis are also related (Stiffler 1988). For example, larvae of the salamander *Ambystoma tigrinum* require NaCl in the bathing medium to compensate for a respiratory acidosis. Moreover, Na^+ influx and net uptake increases, while Cl^- influx decreases and net Cl^- loss increases, during this acid-base disturbance (Stiffler, Ryan, and Mushkot 1987). Furthermore, when larval *A. tigrinum* exercise, their rate of recovery from the associated acidosis decreases in hypoionic media (Rohrbach and Stiffler 1987). Clearly, ionoregulation and acid-base regulation are intimately related by the ionized forms of carbon dioxide and ammonia (i.e., H^+, HCO_3^-, and NH_4^+).

Metamorphosis of Ion Transport Systems

Krogh (1937) could not detect Cl^- uptake in larval *Rana esculenta* and concluded that these animals get salts from their food, unlike adults. The TEP across the skin of anurans does not appear until the larvae have almost completely metamorphosed (Taylor and Barker 1965b). Alvarado and Moody (1970) measured Na^+ and Cl^- fluxes and potential differences and found that the TEP appears at stage XXII (Taylor and Kollros 1946) in larval *R. catesbeiana*, but animals actively transport Na^+ and Cl^- as early as stage VII. This active transport is in the gills of the larvae. In larvae, gill Na^+ and Cl^- fluxes proceed independently (as in adults) with NH_4^+, K^+, and H^+ exchanging for Na^+, and base (HCO_3^-?) exchanging for Cl^- (Dietz and Alvarado 1974). When the skin is carefully removed from larvae and mounted to prevent "edge damage" (Helman and Miller 1974), a sizable TEP develops. This TEP, however, is due primarily to a high electrical resistance because the SCC (equivalent to net Na^+ flux) is very low as compared to adults (Cox and Alvarado 1979). The antibiotic nystatin, which induces cation channels in epithelial apical membranes (Lewis et al. 1977), dramatically increases the rate of Na^+ transport across larval skin (Cox and Alvarado 1983), suggesting that at least one event in the metamorphosis of transport properties in anuran skin is the appearance of apical sodium channels (Cox and Alvarado 1983). Though branchial ion transport and Na^+K^+–ATPase activity are correlated in bullfrog larvae, significant quantities of the ATPase do not appear in the skin until after metamorphosis (Boonkoom and Alvarado 1971). Increased ouabain binding to stratum spinosum and stratum germinativum cells after metamorphosis suggests an increased density of pump sites following metamorphosis (Robinson and Mills 1987a, 1987b).

Larval urodeles involve their skin in thermodynamically active ion exchanges (Alvarado and Kirschner 1963). However, larvae and adults differ. Larval *Ambystoma gracile* increase the TEP across their skin in proportion to ambient [Na^+] and independently of the anion; the TEP of adults, on the other hand, is dependent upon the anion when [Na^+] increases in the bathing solution (Alvarado and Stiffler 1970). Larval *A. tigrinum* have a lower rate of Na^+ transport than adults (Bentley and Baldwin 1980) due to an increase in amiloride-sensitive Na^+ channels in the apical membrane following metamorphosis (Cox 1986).

Control of Cutaneous Ion Transport

Cutaneous ion transport in aquatic amphibians is under a variety of control systems. These are primarily endocrine, and occasionally neural (see also chapter 16).

The neurohypophyseal octapeptide, AVT, stimulates active Na^+ transport in the skin of many amphibians. Frog skin responds to neurohypophyseal extracts with increased Na^+ transport and SCC (Ussing and Zerahn 1951). Jørgensen, Levi, and Ussing (1947), working with *Ambystoma mexicanum*, found that the pressor fraction of mammalian posterior pituitary extracts increased Na^+ influx 200%. The oxytocic fraction produced a net loss of Na^+. The skin of the salamanders *Triturus alpestris* and *T. cristatus* (Salamandridae) responds to AVT with an increased Na^+ influx (Bentley and Heller 1964). Larval and adult *Ambystoma tigrinum* (Alvarado and Johnson 1965) and *Rana catesbeiana* (Alvarado and Johnson 1966) increase Na^+ influx when treated with

AVT. The anurans *Bufo marinus, Xenopus laevis,* and *R. catesbeiana* all increase SCC in response to AVT; however, the urodeles *Amphiuma means* (Amphiumidae), *Siren lacertina* (Sirenidae), and *Necturus maculosus* (Proteidae) do not (Bentley 1969; Bentley and Yorio 1977). Arginine vasopressin (the mammalian neurohypophyseal ADH) stimulates SCC in the skin of the plethodontid salamander *Aneides lugubris* (Hillman 1974). Hypophysectomy, which removes several neurohypophyseal and adenohypophyseal hormones that may be involved in skin transport, reduces SCC in the skin of the plethodontids *Desmognathus fuscus* and *D. monticola* (Brown, Brown, and Frye 1979). However, hypophysectomy does not reduce the rate of Na^+ influx in *Ambystoma tigrinum* (Kerstetter and Kirschner 1971; Brown, Brown, and Wittig 1981).

The site of AVT action is at the apical membrane. The hormone increases the rate of uptake of Na^+ across the apical membranes of the transporting cell both during open-circuit (Cereijido and Rotunno 1971) and short-circuited (Biber and Cruz 1973) conditions. The use of fluctuation analysis shows that this increase is due to an increased density of amiloride-inhibitable Na^+ channels (Helman, Cox, and Van Driessche 1983).

Because teleost prolactin affects Na^+ balance in fish (Ensor and Ball 1972), many workers anticipated a role for this hormone in ion transport in amphibian skin. The results are conflicting and controversial. Early observations of increased SCC in amphibian skin as a result of prolactin treatment (Howard and Ensor 1975; Eddy and Allen 1979) preceded reports of prolactin decreasing SCC and/or TEP (Brown et al. 1983; Brown et al. 1985; Lodi, Biciotti, and Viotto 1982; Takada and Hara 1988). Prolactin might be involved in the metamorphosis of Na^+ transport in larval skin, as it has a stimulatory effect between stages XXII and XXV (Eddy and Allen 1979; Takada 1986) when the Na^+ channels appear (see above). Following metamorphosis, prolactin probably inhibits Na^+ transport by increasing apical resistance to Na^+ (Brown 1988).

The adenohypophysis also produces adrenocorticotropic hormone (ACTH), which significantly increases the TEP of *Notophthalmus viridescens* (Caudata: Salamandridae; Brown et al. 1983). Hypophysectomy reduces plasma Na^+, while ACTH replacement restores this ion in *N. viridescens* (Brown et al. 1983), and *Ambystoma tigrinum* (DeRuyter and Stiffler 1986). The ACTH is probably acting through interrenal steroids (see below).

Thyroid-stimulating hormone (TSH), acting through thyroid hormones, may also influence Na^+ exchanges in skin. Thyroxine can reverse the decreases in plasma $[Na^+]$ and transcutaneous TEP that follow hypophysectomy in desmognathine salamanders (Plethodontidae; Brown, Brown, and Frye 1979). Green and Matty (1963) found thyroxine stimulated increases in Na^+ transport in skin of *Bufo bufo*. However, Taylor and Barker (1967) could not confirm this.

The amphibian adrenocortical tissue is interspersed among the kidney tubules and is called interrenal tissue or the interrenal glands. The predominant amphibian interrenal steroids are aldosterone and corticosterone (Krug et al. 1983; Stiffler et al. 1986). Aldosterone stimulates Na^+ transport in the skin

of the frog (Taubenhaus, Fritz, and Morton 1956), toad (Crabbe and DeWeer 1964), and larval salamander *Ambystoma tigrinum* (Alvarado and Kirschner 1964). Aldosterone does not stimulate cutaneous Na^+ transport in all amphibians; for example, the skin of *Xenopus laevis* does not respond (Yorio and Bentley 1978b). Corticosterone also can stimulate Na^+ transport in frog skin, but is much less effective than aldosterone (Yorio and Bentley 1978a). Aldosterone may be involved further in acid-base–related alterations in skin ion transport; both respiratory acidoses and exercise-induced mixed acidoses produce elevations in aldosterone (Stiffler, Ryan, and Mushkot 1987; Rohrbach and Stiffler 1987).

Aldosterone also affects Cl^- transport, independently of its effect on Na^+ flux (Beauwens et al. 1986). The effect is to increase Cl^- permeability in the apical membranes of the mitochondria-rich cells so as to accelerate the movement of Cl^- through the transcellular shunt.

In amphibian skin, aldosterone could conceivably increase the number of Na^+ and Cl^- channels at the apical membranes, or increase the pumping rate of the Na^+/K^+ exchange pump at the basal membranes. Simultaneous microelectrode measurements of TEP and apical membrane potentials suggest that the primary effect of aldosterone is to increase apical permeability to Na^+. However, increased pumping of Na^+ across the basal membrane is an additional response to the hormone (Nagel and Crabbe 1980).

Insulin, perhaps by interacting with aldosterone, can stimulate Na^+ transport in frog skin (Herrera, Whittembury, and Planchart 1963). Prostaglandin (PGE) also can stimulate SCC in frog skin (Els and Helman 1981; Fassina, Carpendo, and Santi 1969; Gerencser 1978; Lote, Rider, and Thomas 1974). Progesterone inhibits SCC of toad skin when applied to the apical side; when applied to the basal side, a transient stimulation may result from prostaglandin release, followed by inhibition of SCC (Neuman, Quevedo, and Concha 1986). Catecholamines also stimulate cutaneous ion transport. Epinephrine increases SCC of frog skin. Initially this effect was presumed due to increased transport of Cl^- in conjunction with secretion of mucus by exocrine cells (Koefoed-Johnson and Ussing 1952). Later studies showed, however, that catecholamines can also stimulate Na^+ influx (Norris et al. 1988; Rajerison et al. 1972; Tomlinson and Wood 1976; Watlington 1968). Parathyroid hormone has been reported to stimulate Ca^{2+} transport in frog skin (Watlington, Burke, and Estep 1968).

Role of the Kidney in Ion and Water Exchanges

The paired amphibian kidney is a mesonephros, situated in a posterior dorsal location in the coelomic cavity. The functional units are glomeruli, which filter blood, and nephric tubules, which process the filtrate, reabsorb water, electrolytes, and nutrients, and secrete waste materials. The circulation to the kidney consists of arterial perfusion of the glomeruli from segmental renal arteries arising from the aorta, and renal portal venous perfusion of the peritubular capillaries. The two vascular beds are almost completely isolated from each other. Venous return to the vena cava is via renal veins that drain the two vascular beds. The tubular fluid

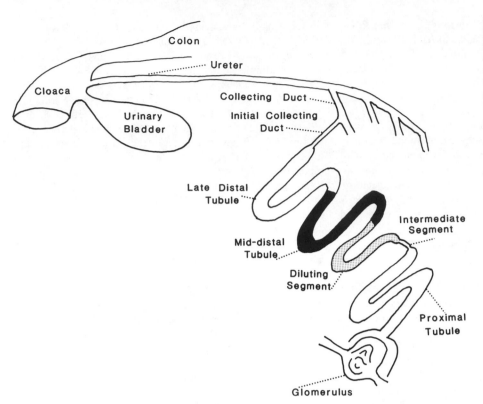

Fig. 5.18 The amphibian urinary tree. Filtrate from the glomerulus traverses the proximal tubules and the segments of the distal tubule and is drained by collecting ducts into the ureter. The two ureters empty into the cloaca, independently of the urinary bladder. The urine may then enter the bladder or pass out of the cloaca to the environment, depending upon the needs of the animal. (Distal nephron arrangement adapted from Yucha and Stoner 1986.)

proceeds through convoluted proximal tubules, through a short connecting segment, into a diluting segment, a segmented distal tubule, and collecting ducts. The collecting ducts are drained by ureters, which open into the cloaca. The urinary bladder opens off the cloaca, separately from the ureters, so that urine must traverse the cloaca in order to enter the bladder (fig. 5.18).

Glomerular Function In vertebrates the algebraic sum of the net hydrostatic and oncotic pressures exerted across the glomerular walls drives glomerular filtration. Because protein filtration is negligible, the oncotic pressure of the fluid in the nephron is assumed to be zero. The filtration pressure (P_f) is thus

$$P_f = P_g - P_t - \pi_g,$$

where

P_g = glomerular hydrostatic pressure
P_t = proximal tubular pressure
π_g = glomerular oncotic pressure

Persson (1981), working with *Amphiuma means* (Caudata: Amphiumidae), has measured glomerular hydrostatic pressure (17.3 cm H_2O) and Bowman's space pressure (6.5 cm H_2O), and calculated glomerular oncotic pressure from afferent and efferent arteriolar plasma protein concentration. Filtration pressure at the beginning of the glomerulus is 3.6 cm H_2O. By the end of the glomerulus it falls to 0.2 cm H_2O. The decrease in P_f is due to an increase in plasma protein concentration (thus oncotic pressure) resulting from filtration of plasma water as the blood passes through the glomerulus.

Single nephron glomerular filtration rates (SNGFR) are known for only a few amphibians: the SNGFR of *Amphiuma means* is 14.7 nl · min^{-1} (Persson 1981), while *Necturus maculosus* has a SNGFR of 12.9 nl · min^{-1} (Giebisch 1956). Whole-animal glomerular filtration rates (GFR) are known for a larger number of amphibian species (table 5.7). Both urine flow and GFR are quite variable in amphibians (Schmidt-Nielsen and Forster 1954), due largely to glomerular intermittency (Forster 1942). Glomerular intermittency is the variation of GFR by varying the number of filtering glomeruli.

Tubuloglomerular feedback, which regulates GFR in mammals (Navar et al. 1982), is also present in amphibians (Persson and Persson 1981). When GFR increases, flow into the distal tubule increases and is sensed by the cells of that tubule. Negative feedback on the glomerulus decreases GFR. The distal tubule cells detect the flux of Cl$^-$. As distal flow increases, so does intracellular [Cl$^-$]; furosemide, which blocks Cl$^-$ transport into cells, uncouples the feedback mechanism (Persson and Marsh 1987).

Tubular Reabsorption Amphibian nephrons reabsorb water and electrolytes along their entire length. Under normal conditions of body fluid hydration, water reabsorption in aquatic and semiaquatic amphibians can be quite low, ranging from 10 to 30% in urodeles and caecilians (Kirschner et al. 1971; Stiffler and Alvarado 1974; Stiffler, DeRuyter, and Talbot 1990), and from 20 to 60% in anurans (Carlisky et al. 1970; Long 1973; Schmidt-Nielsen and Forster 1954). This accords with the needs of aquatic animals to excrete water taken on osmotically across their permeable surfaces (Vondersaar and Stiffler 1989).

Reabsorption of electrolytes, on the other hand, is high. Among urodeles, *Amphiuma means* (Amphiumidae) reab-

TABLE 5.7   Renal Function in Aquatic and Semiaquatic Amphibians

	$\dot{V}$ (ml·g^{-1}·h^{-1})	GFR (ml·g^{-1}·h^{-1})	Urine (mM)			Reference
			[Na$^+$]	[K$^+$]	[Cl$^-$]	
Anura						
Calyptocephalella gavi	0.010	0.019				Carlisky et al. 1970
Xenopus laevis	0.024	0.030				McBean and Goldstein 1970b
			6.8	0.8		Edwards and Chan 1973
Rana pipiens	0.022	0.034				Sasayama and Clark 1984
*Rana cancrivora**	0.023	0.058				Schmidt-Nielsen and Lee 1962
Rana esculenta	0.024	0.053	2.1	1.1		Jard and Morel 1963
Urodela						
Ambystoma tigrinum						
Adult	0.009	0.018				Stiffler, Hawk, and Fowler 1980
Larva	0.009	0.013	4.6	2.2	6.2	Stiffler 1981
Ambystoma gracile, larva	0.008	0.010	10.2	3.9	6.4	Stiffler and Alvarado 1974
Dicamptodon ensatus, larva	0.004	0.006	5.3	3.6		Stiffler and Alvarado 1980
Notophthalmus viridescens	0.060	0.140				P. S. Brown and S. C. Brown 1977
Necturus maculosus, neotene	0.007	0.011	3.7	1.1	1.7	Vondersaar and Stiffler 1989
Taricha granulosa	0.029	0.049	13.2	1.3	6.6	Vondersaar and Stiffler 1989
Caeciliidae						
Typhlonectes compressicauda	0.013	0.014	4.9	0.6	2.5	Stiffler, DeRuyter, and Talbot 1990
Ichthyophis kohtaoensis	0.017	0.027	21.3	1.4	5.9	Stiffler, DeRuyter, and Talbot 1990

*Marine frog.

sorbs 90% of the filtered Na$^+$ and 75% of K$^+$ (Wiederholt, Sullivan, and Giebisch 1971). *Ambystoma gracile* reabsorbs 92% of filtered Na$^+$, 94% of Cl$^-$, and 71% of K$^+$ (Stiffler and Alvarado 1974). *Dicamptodon ensatus* (Dicamptodontidae) reabsorbs 96% of Na$^+$ and 96% of Cl$^-$ (Stiffler and Alvarado 1980). *Ambystoma tigrinum* reabsorbs 95% of Na$^+$, 71% of K$^+$, and 93% of Cl$^-$ (Stiffler 1981). The combination of relatively low fractional water reabsorption and high fractional ion reabsorption results in a large volume of dilute urine (table 5.7).

Little is known about renal reabsorption of nutrients in amphibians. *Necturus maculosus* reabsorbs glucose from proximal tubular fluid (Walker and Hudson 1937). The reabsorption can be inhibited with phlorhizin, suggesting a similarity with mammalian renal glucose transport. *Rana catesbeiana* reabsorbs all of the normally filtered glucose by a transport maximum–limited process (Forster 1942). Amino acid transport has been studied in only one species, *N. maculosus,* which reabsorbs at least nineteen amino acids in the proximal tubule (Oken and Weise 1978). Fractional reabsorption varies from 30% of filtered glutamic acid to 96% of filtered proline. Molecular weight, transport class or plasma concentration, and fractional reabsorption are not correlated (Oken and Weise 1978).

Tubular Secretion   Tubular secretion of urea occurs in several amphibian species. Marshall and Crane (1924) first reported it in the bullfrog, *Rana catesbeiana,* when they observed that urea is excreted by a saturable mechanism. Urea secretion was subsequently shown to be energy-dependent (Forster 1954) and competitive with thiourea (Schmidt-Nielsen and Schrauger 1963). *R. pipiens* also is capable of renal urea secretion (Walker and Hudson 1937). However, the secretion is much weaker than that in the bullfrog, as is only apparent when water reabsorption in the nephron is low (Long 1973).

Such weak secretion has also been observed in the frog *Leptodactylus ocellatus* (Leptodactylidae; Carlisky et al. 1970) and the salamander *Ambystoma tigrinum* (Stiffler, Hawk, and Fowler 1980). Although adult bullfrogs secrete urea, the larvae do not (Forster, Schmidt-Nielsen, and Goldstein 1963). Micropuncture experiments demonstrate that secretion takes place in both proximal and distal segments of the nephron (Walker and Hudson 1937). Urea secretion is not a general attribute of the amphibian kidney, however, as the urodele *Necturus maculosus* cannot secrete urea (Walker and Hudson 1937; Vondersaar and Stiffler 1989).

Mammalian nephrons avidly secrete paraaminohippuric acid (PAH) (Weiner 1973). The frog *R. clamitans* also secretes this compound (Schmidt-Nielsen and Forster 1954), as does the bullfrog, *R. catesbeiana* (Irish and Dantzler 1976). Irish and Dantzler showed that PAH is actively transported into proximal tubule cells across the peritubular membranes with a saturable mechanism, and diffuses into the tubular fluid across the luminal membranes. Urea may compete with PAH for the transport carrier (Forster 1954; Irish and Dantzler 1976). The situation is different in some urodeles; that is, PAH is simultaneously secreted and reabsorbed in the *Necturus* tubule (Kinter 1959). The secretory flux is competitively inhibited by Diodrast, while the reabsorptive flux is competitively inhibited by octanoate (Tanner and Kinter 1966). PAH transport takes place in the proximal tubule (Tanner 1967). The metabolic inhibitor iodoacetamide and the Na$^+$ transport inhibitor ouabain both block uptake of PAH by *N. maculosus* kidney slices, suggesting that the secretion is dependent on metabolic energy and Na$^+$ transport (Khalsa, Goldinger, and Hong 1984). Removal of Na$^+$ from the medium also inhibits PAH uptake. PAH secretion has also been observed in *A. tigrinum* (Stiffler, Hawk, and Fowler 1980), although it is not known whether simultaneous reabsorption occurs (as in *Necturus*).

Phenolsulfonphthalein (phenol red), which is secreted by the nephric tubules of mammals (Weiner 1973), is neither secreted by the tubules of *N. maculosus* nor taken up by kidney slices. Phenol red is, however, taken up by kidney slices of *R. pipiens* (Tanner, Carmines, and Kinter 1979).

Although creatinine is used extensively as a GFR marker in amphibians (Forster 1942), there is evidence for its tubular secretion (Swanson 1956). When creatinine is infused into the arterial circulation only, the clearance ratio C_{cr}/C_{inulin} is close to one. However, when creatinine is infused into both the arterial circulation and the renal portal circulation, C_{cr}/C_{inulin} averages 1.27, indicating significant creatinine secretion. This secretion is inhibitable with various metabolic inhibitors.

In addition to organic molecules, some ions are secreted by the amphibian nephron. The kidney tubules of *R. catesbeiana* and *R. pipiens* secrete NH_4^+ at the distal tubule (Walker 1940). The secretion is not transtubular, as NH_4^+ is not demonstrable in sufficient quantities in the peritubular vasculature to account for the flux into the tubules. Therefore, the ammonia must form in the tubule cells. The tubule cells probably form NH_3, which is secreted into the lumen where it combines with H^+ to form NH_4^+. Elevation of plasma $[K^+]$ leads to K^+ secretion in the distal tubules of *Amphiuma means* (Wiederholt, Sullivan, and Giebisch 1971). Potassium loading also stimulates K^+ secretion in *R. catesbeiana* (Deeds, Sullivan, and Welling 1978) and *Ambystoma tigrinum* (Stiffler et al. 1986). Secretion of H^+ occurs in the distal tubules of *R. esculenta* (Oberleithner et al. 1984) and *Amphiuma means* (Stanton et al. 1987).

Renal Ionic Transport Mechanisms   Fluid reabsorption from the proximal tubule of *Necturus maculosus* is energy-dependent and inhibitable with ouabain, which blocks active Na^+/K^+ exchange transport (Schatzmann, Windhager, and Soloman 1958). The rate of reabsorption is dependent on luminal $[Na^+]$ (Windhager et al. 1959). Early measurements of TEP across the wall of the proximal tubule averaged about 20 mV, lumen negative (Giebisch 1961; Whittembury and Windhager 1961; Wilbrandt 1938). This implies that Na^+ must be actively transported, as confirmed by Spring and Paganelli (1972), who used a silver wire, placed axially in the proximal tubule of *N. maculosus*, to voltage-clamp the epithelium in a manner analogous to the SCC measurements of Ussing and Zerahn (1951) on frog skin. Na^+ was reabsorbed in the absence of electrochemical gradients, and the rate of absorption equaled the SCC. Thus, the Na^+ flux in the proximal tubule meets the most rigorous test for active transport. Since Na^+ must cross both apical and basolateral membranes, as in skin, both steps of the reabsorption process need examination. Boron and Boulpaep (1983b) have reported an amiloride-sensitive Na^+/H^+ exchange system in the luminal membrane that may be analogous to that in skin (see above). The exit of Na^+ across the basolateral membrane probably occurs via an Na^+/K^+ exchanger as in skin; however, a second NaCl pump in parallel cannot be excluded (Giebisch, Sullivan, and Whittembury 1973).

Cl^- reabsorption in the proximal tubule was initially considered passive (Giebisch and Windhager 1963). With the advent of ion-specific microelectrodes and the ability to evaluate electrochemical gradients across the apical and basolateral membranes of proximal tubule cells, the picture has become more complex. Intracellular Cl^- activity is three times greater than predicted for passive distribution across the luminal membrane, and dependent on luminal [NaCl] (Spring and Kimura 1978). The relationship between luminal Cl^- activity and intracellular Cl^- activity is nonlinear, suggesting an interaction with the membrane. Finally, the rate of Cl^- entry is independent of luminal potential. From this evidence, Spring and Kimura suggested that Cl^- crosses the luminal membrane by a carrier-mediated process that is electroneutral. From a similar approach, Shindo and Spring (1981) concluded that Cl^- exit across the basolateral membrane is also carrier-mediated, and either Na^+- or K^+-dependent. Edelman, Bouthier, and Anagnostopoulos (1981) and Guggino et al. (1983), however, observed dependence of Cl^- extrusion on peritubular HCO_3^- and, in the latter study, Na^+, so that the basolateral exchange may be $Cl^-/Na^+ + 2HCO_3^-$.

No net reabsorption of K^+ occurs in the proximal tubules of *N. maculosus* (Khuri et al. 1963) or *Amphiuma means* (Wiederholt, Sullivan, and Giebisch 1971). Using K^+-specific microelectrodes to evaluate the electrochemical gradients across apical and basolateral membranes in proximal tubules of *N. maculosus*, Khuri et al. (1972) concluded that K^+ is in electrochemical equilibrium across both membranes.

Fluid reabsorption is isoosmotic in the amphibian proximal tubule. This reabsorption takes place via two parallel paths. The first is transcellular and requires ions and water molecules to pass across the luminal and basolateral membranes in series. The second path is between the cells and is usually termed the paracellular path. Both ions (Boulpaep 1972) and water (Tripathi and Boulpaep 1988) can move through this paracellular path between the lumen and the basolateral spaces. A complete description of the dynamics of this process is beyond the scope of this chapter; however, excellent treatments of the subject exist (Boulpaep 1972; Spring 1973; Tripathi and Boulpaep 1988).

The distal nephron comprises the distal convoluted tubule and the collecting ducts. The distal tubule consists of three segments that differ in function and morphology (Hinton et al. 1982; Stanton et al. 1984): the diluting segment (the early distal tubule), the middistal tubule, and the late distal tubule. The collecting ducts are also divided into the initial collecting ducts and collecting ducts (Stanton et al. 1984; Yucha and Stoner 1986). The cells of the diluting segment are cuboidal with central nuclei with densely packed mitochondria. The cells of the late distal tubule are also cuboidal with central nuclei but are much less densely packed with mitochondria (Hinton et al. 1982).

The TEP across the distal tubule wall changes between early and late segments. In *Bufo marinus* the TEP across the diluting segment is $+5$ mV, in *Rana pipiens* it is $+14$ mV, and in *Ambystoma tigrinum* it is $+14$ mV. The late distal tubule TEP is -41 mV in *A. tigrinum* (Stoner 1977). The diluting segments have a lumen-positive $+22$ mV potential in *Triturus alpestris* (Caudata: Salamandridae), whereas the late distal tubules of this species have lumen-negative potentials as great as -35 mV (Teulon and Anagstopoulos 1982). The early distal tubule (diluting segment) potential in *Amphiuma means* is $+8$ mV (Persson and Marsh 1987).

The diluting segment of *Ambystoma tigrinum* is impermeable to water but avidly transports NaCl by a furosemide-sensitive, amiloride-independent system. Thus, in this segment, the Na^+-K^+-$2Cl^-$ carrier rather than Na^+/H^+ exchange evidently transports Na^+. The late distal tubule is also impermeable to water and transports Na^+ via an amiloride-sensitive system (Stoner 1977). Working with *Amphiuma means* diluting segments, Oberleithner and co-workers (Oberleithner, Guggino, and Giebisch 1983a; Oberleithner, Lang, Greger, Wang, and Giebisch 1983; Oberleithner et al. 1982) demonstrated that Cl^- uptake by the luminal membrane is dependent on both Na^+ and K^+. This transport system is also furosemide sensitive and thus resembles the basolateral Na^+-K^+-$2Cl^-$ transport system involved in volume regulation in frog skin cells (see above). Oberleithner, Lang, Wang, Messner, and Deetjen (1983) have also discovered an amiloride-sensitive Na^+/H^+ exchange mechanism in the luminal membrane of the diluting segment of *A. means* during potassium loading. Potassium loading also induces a luminal membrane K^+ conductance that leads to net K^+ secretion in the diluting segment (Oberleithner, Guggino, and Giebisch 1985). In comparison to the diluting segment, the late distal tubule is poorly known. [NaCl] declines along this segment (Bott 1962; Wiederholt, Sullivan, and Giebisch, 1971). Microelectrode studies of *Necturus maculosus* late distal tubules show that Cl^- enters the tubular cells across the luminal membrane against an electrochemical gradient; the exit step is down a small electrochemical gradient and may be passive (Anagostopoulos and Planelles 1987). These authors also found that Na^+ enters the cell along a favorable electrochemical gradient and discounted the possibility of Na^+/H^+ exchange. Na^+ exits actively through the Na^+/K^+ exchange pump. K^+ enters the cell against the gradient and possibly by K^+/H^+ exchange; its basolateral exit is passive. Compared to the luminal membranes of the distal tubular cells, we know very little about the basolateral membranes. There is the usual Na^+/K^+ exchange pump characteristic of basolateral membranes of epithelia (Sullivan 1968). The peritubular membrane potential is dependent on luminal Na^+, suggesting that this exchange is electrogenic (Cohen et al. 1984).

Acid-Base Balance   The amphibian distal nephron can acidify the urine (Montgomery and Pierce 1937), and the ability to excrete ammonia (Walker 1940) can aid in excreting acid. These abilities could be the basis for a role of the kidney in acid-base balance. Unequivocal documentation of this role, however, has been elusive.

Yoshimura et al. (1961) first attempted to establish a role for such mechanisms in homeostatic adjustments to acidosis. They induced metabolic acidosis in *Rana catesbeiana* and *R. limnocharis* by HCl infusion, and used environmental hypercapnia to establish respiratory acidosis. Increased secretion of ammonia resulted from the metabolic acidosis; however, H^+ secretion was unaffected. The pH of the blood before treatment was 7.4–7.5 at 25°C, which is 0.3–0.4 pH units below normal amphibian pH at this temperature (Howell 1970). Thus, acidosis before treatment might have obscured changes due to the treatments.

Infusion of sulfate into *Bufo marinus* acidifies the urine (Long 1982). Such acidification, however, might occur in organs other than the kidneys, for example, in the bladder. Indeed, in ureteral urine of *B. marinus,* no renal responses are evident during respiratory acidosis (Tufts and Toews 1985).

Following immersion of *Ambystoma tigrinum* in either NH_4Cl or $NaHCO_3$, perfused distal tubules isolated from these animals can increase or decrease HCO_3^- absorption, respectively. The pH of the perfusate in this experiment, however, was acidotic relative to the species' normal pH (see review by Toews and Stiffler 1989).

Renal Tubular Mechanisms of Acid-Base Exchanges   The proximal tubule cannot acidify the tubular fluid (Montgomery and Pierce 1937). The enzyme carbonic anhydrase, which is closely tied to acid-base–related ionic fluxes, is present only in trace quantities in this segment (Lonnerholm and Ridderstrale 1974). Na^+/H^+ exchangers occur on both the luminal and basolateral membranes, and an outward Na^+-HCO_3^- cotransport system is present on the basolateral membranes of *Ambystoma tigrinum* (Boron and Boulpaep 1983a, 1983b). A similar Na^+-HCO_3^- cotransport mechanism occurs in *Necturus maculosus* (Lopes et al. 1987). Also, Cl_{in}^-/HCO_{3out}^- (Edelman, Bouthier, and Anagnostopoulos 1981) and $Na^+ + 2HCO_{3in}^-/Cl_{out}^-$ (Guggino et al. 1983) exchanges occur across *N. maculosus* basolateral proximal tubule cell membranes. However, these mechanisms may function in intracellular pH regulation only. Attempts to measure HCO_3^- transport across *A. tigrinum* proximal tubule walls have yielded only very small fluxes (Yucha and Stoner 1986).

Yucha and Stoner (1986) found reabsorption of HCO_3^- in the late distal tubule but not the diluting segment of the distal nephron of *A. tigrinum*. This late distal transport of HCO_3^- is Na^+-dependent and sensitive to the carbonic anhydrase inhibitor ethoxzolamide. Bicarbonate reabsorption also occurs in the initial collecting tubules (Yucha and Stoner 1987). This flux is insensitive to ethoxzolamide and Cl^- deprivation, which seems to rule out Cl^-/HCO_3^- exchange.

The plasma-to-tubular fluid pH gradient increases along the distal tubule of *Amphiuma means* (Persson and Persson 1983). Passage through isolated distal tubules of *A. means* decreases perfusate pH by about 0.3 units (Stanton et al. 1987). This acidification is amiloride-sensitive, suggesting Na^+/H^+ exchange. Stanton et al. (1987) and Stanton (1988) have proposed a model in which *A. means* has two types of cells in its distal tubules. Both type 1 and type 2 cells have the Na^+/H^+ exchanger on the luminal membrane; type 1 cells have a Na^+-HCO_3^- cotransporter on the basolateral membrane, and type 2 cells have Cl^-/HCO_3^- exchangers on both the luminal and basolateral membranes.

In diluting segments of *Rana esculenta*, Oberleithner et al. (1984) found an amiloride-inhibitable, NA^+-dependent H^+ flux on the luminal membranes. The acid-base transport properties of the basolateral membranes of this segment include a Na^+-HCO_3^- cotransporter (Wang, Dietl, and Oberleithner 1987), which removes HCO_3^- from the cell.

Hormonal Control of Renal Function

PITUITARY   Amphibian kidney function is, of necessity, very flexible. Because some amphibians are both aquatic and terrestrial, they must change their urine flow drastically when they go from one habitat to the other. When the primarily aquatic *Rana clamitans* ventures out of water, urine flow decreases by almost 50% after the first hour and to only about 15% after 5 h. The response is due both to a decrease in GFR and an increase in tubular water reabsorption (Schmidt-Nielsen and Forster 1954). Completely aquatic amphibians like *Xenopus laevis* (Funkhouser and Goldstein 1973), *Ambystoma gracile,* and larval *Dicamptodon ensatus* (Caudata: Dicamptodontidae; Stiffler and Alvarado 1974) also decrease GFR when placed in dehydrating conditions of isoosmotic mannitol or sucrose. Tubular water reabsorption increases somewhat, but not as much in *A. gracile* as in *R. clamitans.* The GRF response takes place in about 2 h.

The first efforts to account for amphibian renal responses to dehydrating conditions focused on the posterior pituitary ADH. Extracts of this gland decreased GFR and increased tubular water reabsorption in *R. catesbeiana* and *Bufo marinus,* as also occurs during dehydration (Sawyer 1951, 1957). With the identification of AVT as the active ADH in the amphibian neurohypophysis (Acher et al. 1960), efforts began to implicate this hormone in renal responses to dehydration. Uranga and Sawyer (1960) demonstrated that AVT acts similarly to neurohypophyseal extracts in *R. catesbeiana.* Similar findings followed for *R. esculenta* (Jard and Morel 1963); *Triturus alpestris* and *T. cristatus,* but not *Necturus maculo-*sus (Bentley and Heller 1964); *Ambystoma tigrinum* (Alvarado and Johnson 1965); and *Siren lacertina* and *Amphiuma means* (Bentley 1973). In a later micropuncture study, Garland, Henderson, and Brown (1975) demonstrated both tubular and glomerular responses to AVT in *N. maculosus.* Stoner (1977) has shown that the distal tubules of *Ambystoma tigrinum* do not increase osmotic permeability in response to AVT.

If a given humoral substance is a hormone, it must not only act on its presumed target in a reproducible manner, but also increase in circulating concentration in response to appropriate stimuli. Rosenbloom and Fisher (1974) showed by radioimmunoassay that AVT increases in concentration in dehydrated bullfrogs. The stimulus is apparently a decrease in extracellular volume rather than an increase in extracellular fluid concentration (Pang 1977). If AVT is the amphibian ADH, hypophysectomy should produce a diuresis. Such treatment does block the tubular (water reabsorption) response to dehydration in hyperosmotic saline but not the GFR response in larval *Ambystoma tigrinum* (Kerstetter and Kirschner 1971). Nonetheless, hypophysectomy can decrease GFR in these larvae in normal environmental conditions (Stiffler, Hawk, and Fowler 1980).

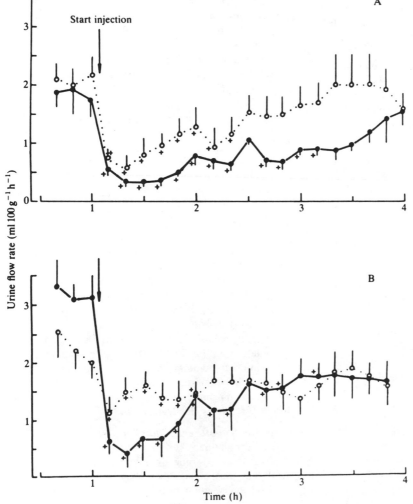

Fig. 5.19 Urine flow changes following periodic (every 10 min) bolus injections of AVT into primed (●) and unprimed (○) *Bufo marinus. A,* 10 ng · kg⁻¹ bolus injections; *B,* 100 ng · kg⁻¹ bolus injections. A *plus sign* beside the mean indicates a significant difference from the control ($p \leq 0.05$). For the 100 ng · kg⁻¹ animals, there was also a significant difference between primed and unprimed groups between 20 and 50 min after the injection of AVT. (Reprinted, by permission, from Toews, Mallet, and MacLatchy 1889.)

AVT also is a pressor in amphibians, causing a generalized vasoconstriction and increased blood pressure under some conditions. Pang, Galli-Gallarado, Collie, and Sawyer (1980) showed, however, that the pressor response requires a higher dose than the response of decreased GFR.

The methods previously used to elicit a hormonal response, especially injection or infusion of neurohypophyseal hormones into the blood, may be problematic. Hormones such as ADH and AVT are naturally released in an episodic fashion. If continuous infusions or regular injections are administered, the responding tissues rapidly become refractory to stimulation. If toad bladders are incubated with high concentrations of vasopressin, the bladders are somewhat refractory to further stimulation by lower concentrations of the hormone (Handler and Preston 1981). The isolated toad bladder responds readily to short bursts of exposure to AVT (Eggena 1987). In the same species (*Bufo marinus*), the kidney reacts to AVT by decreasing urine flow rates, primarily due to a lowered GFR (Toews, Mallet, and MacLatchy 1989). However, the response to single bolus injections of AVT dissipates after 1 h, despite the continued presence of AVT in the blood, whereas continuous infusion of AVT by osmotic pumps at levels as high as 100 ng · kg^{-1} is ineffective in lowering flow rates, suggesting that pulsatile increases in the hormone might be necessary for a more prolonged response. In toads that are "primed" or continuously infused with AVT, additional pulses of AVT reduce flow rates for 1 h, with sensitivity to the hormone decreasing with increasing (primed) concentrations of AVT (figs. 5.19 and 5.20).

The other posterior pituitary hormone in amphibians is mesotocin or 8-isoleucine-oxytocin (Acher et al. 1964). This peptide is a diuretic in *Rana catesbeiana* (Pang and Sawyer 1978), *Calyptocephalella gayi* (Anura: Leptodactylidae), and *Necturus maculosus* (Galli-Gallardo, Pang, and Oguro 1979). It also reverses the antidiuresis that follows hypophysectomy in larval *Ambystoma tigrinum* (Stiffler 1981). Mesotocin will similarly reverse the antidiuresis brought about by AVT (but not by dehydration) in *R. catesbeiana* and larval *A. tigrinum* (Pang 1977; Stiffler et al. 1982). Mesotocin is also diuretic in adult *A. tigrinum* and *Notophthalmus viridescens* (Harten-

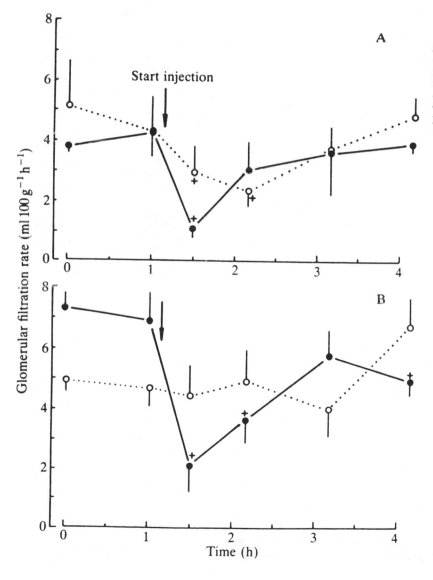

Fig. 5.20 Effect of periodic bolus injections of AVT on GFR in *Bufo marinus*. A, 10 ng · kg^{-1} injections in primed (●; $N = 9$) and unprimed (○; $N = 7$) animals. B, 100 ng · kg^{-1} injections in primed (●; $N = 10$) and unprimed (○; $N = 5$) animals. All values given as means + 1 SE. A *plus sign* beside the mean indicates a significant difference from the control ($p \leq .05$). (Reprinted, by permission, from Toews, Mallet, and MacLatchy 1989.)

stein and Stiffler 1990). Extracellular fluid (ECF) volume apparently plays a large role in triggering mesotocin responses, as volume expansion is a stronger diuretic stimulus than ECF concentration is an antidiuretic stimulus (Stiffler et al. 1982). Effective doses of oxytocin, mesotocin, and isotocin (4-ser-mesotocin) suggest that mesotocin and isotocin are both diuretic, that oxytocin is not, and that mesotocin is effective at lower doses than isotocin (Stiffler, Roach, and Pruett 1984). Recently, the supplier of the isotocin informed the authors that the isotocin used in those experiments was missing an isoleucine residue in the number 3 position, casting some doubt on the results. Although mesotocin is diuretic in several aquatic and semiaquatic amphibians, it may not be effective in terrestrial species, as it fails to produce responses in *Taricha torosa* (Brown and Brown 1980) and *T. granulosa* (both Caudata: Salamandridae; Hartenstein and Stiffler 1981).

Prolactin, an anterior pituitary hormone, appears to conserve Na+ in several species of amphibians (Pang and Sawyer 1974; Wittouck 1975; see above). A role in urinary Na+ reabsorption is therefore a possibility. In *T. torosa*, hypophysectomy does not affect urinary Na+ concentration, but injection of prolactin decreases urinary [Na+] (Brown, Brown, and Wittig 1981). As the authors point out, the decrease could result from decreased filtered load of Na+ due to decreased plasma [Na+], increased reabsorption in the bladder, or increased reabsorption in the kidney. A role for this hormone in the kidney remains an open question.

INTERRENAL STEROID HORMONES   The steroid hormone aldosterone is important in Na+, K+, and H+ balance in vertebrates and is, therefore, a candidate for a role in amphibian renal-control. Corticosterone may also be involved in electrolyte balance in amphibians (Middler et al. 1969). The drug aminoglutethimide inhibits steroid synthesis in vertebrates (Gaunt, Steinetz, and Chart 1968). When given to electrolyte-depleted *Ambystoma tigrinum*, it increases urinary [Na+] and relative Na+ clearance while it decreases urinary [K+] and relative K+ clearance; aldosterone reverses these effects (Heney and Stiffler 1983). Salt depletion stimulates aldosterone secretion and fractional reabsorption of Na+ in *A. tigrinum*, while salt loading lowers the aldosterone titer and inhibits fractional Na+ reabsorption (Stiffler et al. 1986). Potassium loading also stimulates aldosterone secretion in larval *A. tigrinum* as well as triggering net K+ secretion (Stiffler et al. 1986). Potassium loading again stimulates renal K+ secretion in the diluting segment of the distal tubule of *Amphiuma means*, accompanied by increased circulating aldosterone (Oberleithner, Lang, Greger, Wang, and Giebisch 1983). Aldosterone also stimulates H+ secretion in *Rana pipiens* diluting segment (Weigt et al. 1987).

PARATHYROID GLANDS   Studies of amphibian responses to parathyroid hormones do not accord with the mammalian responses of increased Ca2+ reabsorption and PO4^3− excretion. Parathyroidectomy reduces plasma and increases urine [Ca2+] concentration in *R. pipiens* (Cortelyou, Hibner-Owerko, and Mulloy 1960). In a subsequent study, Cortelyou (1967) observed increased Ca2+ excretion following treatment with parathyroid hormone (PTH) in the same species. Parathyroid-

ectomy decreases plasma and urinary [Ca2+] in the newt *Notophthalmus viridescens*, while PTH replacement elevates only urine [Ca2+] (Wittle and Dent 1979). Parathyroidectomy elevates both plasma and urinary [PO4^3−] in *R. pipiens* (Cortelyou 1962), while PTH injections elevate urinary [PO4^3−] (Cortelyou, Quipse, and McWhinnie 1967). PTH injections elevate plasma and urinary [PO4^3−] in *N. viridescens* (Wittle and Dent 1979). In a recent reexamination of the responses of *R. pipiens* to parathyroidectomy, Sasayama and Clark (1984) found that removal of the parathyroids increases PO4^3− reabsorption but does not affect Ca2+, Na+, or K+ excretion.

The Bladder

The urinary bladder functions primarily as a water store when water availability is low but, under most other circumstances, participates in water and ion exchange processes. The bladder is a well-vascularized baglike structure connected to a short bladder stalk that opens into the cloaca. Ureteral urine enters the cloaca from the kidney and by some unknown mechanism moves into the bladder itself. In hydrated conditions, animals will release bladder fluid at irregular intervals; for example, when hydrated the toad *Bufo marinus* will urinate about every 15 to 30 min. Urination will stop immediately if the toads are deprived of water, and kidney function (primarily glomerular filtration) will decrease (Tufts and Toews 1986).

Salamanders and aquatic anurans generally have proportionally smaller bladders than do more terrestrial species (Bentley 1966b). *Salamandra salamandra* (Caudata: Salamandridae), however, has a bladder that can contain a fluid volume up to 35% of the body mass (Bentley 1966b), and the aquatic salamander *Amphiuma tridactylum* (Amphiumidae) has a large bladder that it uses for fluid storage and/or ion exchange processes. In anurans, the bladder is expanded into a large bilobed sac that is extremely well vascularized and has an extensive lymphatic network (LeFevre 1974).

The bladder tissue in most amphibians is a "tight" epithelium and thereby is selectively permeable to ions and water. Hormones such as AVT and aldosterone can modify its permeability. Urodele and anuran bladders differ in structure; for example, Mullen et al. (1976) have shown that the bladder epithelium of *Amphiuma* has fewer mitochondria-rich cells than do other amphibians. In addition the bladders of urodeles are much less responsive to neurohypophyseal hormones (Bentley 1971b).

In the toad bladder, the epithelial lining in contact with the urine is termed the mucosal or apical membrane, and the membrane facing the capillaries is the serosal or basolateral surface. Usually three different types of epithelial cells constitute the epithelium; granular, mitochondria-rich, and goblet (mucus) cells (MacKnight, DiBona, and Leaf 1980). Transport across the epithelium is by two primary routes, either across cells, transcellularly (the pathway used by active sodium transport), or between cells, usually referred to as the paracellular pathway (the route for most passive solute movement).

Reabsorption of bladder water facilitates water balance during dehydration, a common problem for semiterrestrial species. The movement of water from the bladder mucosal to the serosal surface is most probably through pores or channels, which are permeable to water and impermeable to small ions and nonelectrolytes (Levine, Jacoby, and Finkelstein 1984a, 1984b). Antidiuretic hormones increase the water permeability of the channels and enhance the uptake of water from the bladder. Although this hydroosmotic effect of the neuropeptides has been known for some years (Bentley 1958), Eggena (1987) has recently shown that toad bladder preparations are much more responsive to episodic exposures of AVT than to prolonged exposures. Hormone release in intact animals (such as those experiencing dehydration) might occur in short bursts, thereby eliminating the potential for downregulation of the hormone receptors.

Active transport of Na$^+$ from the bladder mucosa to the serosal surface ensures that the high rates of urine flow in hydrated animals (rates are about ten times those for a freshwater fish of comparable size) will not decrease total body salt levels. Neurohypophyseal extracts stimulate active uptake (Leaf, Anderson, and Page 1958), although again, with continuous exposure to hormones, the bladder becomes refractory to further stimulation (MacKnight, DiBona, and Leaf 1980). Aldosterone, from the adrenal cortex, also stimulates sodium uptake from the toad bladder (Ludens and Fanestil 1974).

The secretion (serosal to mucosal surfaces) of solute is another important function of the bladder. The toad bladder excretes H$^+$ and ammonia when the animals are exposed to a respiratory acidosis (Frazier and Vanatta 1971). The process is the same in toad hemibladder preparations but varies in toads from different locations (Ludens and Fanestil 1972). Bladders from some toads lack carbonic anhydrase and as a result have a much lower bladder acidification rate (Ziegler, Ludens, and Fanestil 1974). The complete absence of carbonic anhydrase in these toads needs examination, as does whether the low levels of carbonic anhydrase in fact limit the acidification process.

In isolated toad bladder preparations, the acidification of bladder contents clearly occurs, with carbonic anhydrase playing a major role (Ziegler, Ludens, and Fanestil 1974). The bladder in intact *Bufo marinus* is important in the reabsorption of HCO$_3^-$ (and/or excretion of acid equivalents). Toads in which the bladder is bypassed surgically cannot elevate plasma [HCO$_3^-$] to compensate for a respiratory acidosis (Tufts and Toews 1985).

Active chloride uptake (mucosal to serosal surface) by the isolated toad bladder is quite possibly related to H$^+$ transport (Finn, Handler, and Orloff 1967; Soboslai, McTigue, and Weiner 1977). A pH gradient (more acid on the mucosal side) stimulates chloride transport from the mucosal to the serosal surface (Weiner 1980). A HCO$_3^-$ or OH$^-$ exchange process is a possible mechanism. HCO$_3^-$ excretion is possible in the toad bladder (bladder sac preparation), and the absence of serosal Cl$^-$ decreases the excretion rate (Fitzgerrel and Vanatta 1980).

K$^+$ is actively reabsorbed by toad bladder epithelial cells, and the process is not necessarily coupled to sodium transport (for review, see MacKnight, DiBona, and Leaf 1980). Toad bladders *in vitro* actively secrete Ca^{2+} (serosal to mucosal surface). Calcium in the mucosal medium is also necessary for active sodium uptake to proceed (Rosoff, Baldwin, and Bentley 1983).

The Lymphatic System

The thin-walled vessels, lymph spaces, and pulsatile hearts of the amphibian lymphatic system have intrigued physiologists for more than a century (Muller 1832) but nevertheless remain poorly understood. The lymphatics are probably major contributors to the overall water balance in many species, and this function is perhaps most critical in aquatic habitats, where the elimination of excess water is of prime importance.

The thin-walled lymph vessels arise from muscle tissue and empty into large subcutaneous lymph sacs (Conklin 1930). These sacs, which include all spaces between the skin and muscle and surrounding internal organs, are all part of the lymphatic organization (Carter 1979). Septa between the muscles and skin loosely divide the spaces into distinct sacs, and fluid can readily flow through perforations in the septa (fig. 5.21). Pulsatile lymph hearts move fluid within the spaces (Deyrup 1964). The hearts number from two to fifteen or more pairs in some species, and beat in synchrony at an average rate of 50–60 beats per minute, quite independent from the main cardiovascular heart (Conklin 1930). The volume of fluid that the lymph hearts handle is quite remarkable; Isayama (1924) has calculated that in the frog *Rana*, the lymph hearts pump fluid equal to fifty times the total plasma volume in 24 h, a rate approximately fifty times that of a mammal (Churchill, Nakazawa, and Drinker 1927). This appears to be, rather astoundingly, only that volume that has leaked from the plasma. Other fluids will most certainly enter from outside the animal via the skin. Carter (1979) suggests that the extensive fluid levels in the lymph sacs of curarized frogs (lymph heart function therefore stopped) has entered directly through the skin as opposed to moving first into the circulatory system and then into the sacs. Water influx via the skin is 2% of the body mass per hour in adult *Xenopus* and 30% in *Scaphiopus couchii* (Pelobatidae) juveniles (Ewer 1952a; Jones 1978).

Recent experiments establish the routes taken by tritiated water entering the body of *Bufo marinus* (McNeil 1989). In these studies, the femoral lymph sac, femoral artery (on the opposite leg), both ureters, and the bladder were chronically catheterized and samples taken from the various compartments at regular intervals. Tritiated water in the bathing medium moves at a higher rate into the lymph than into the plasma (fig. 5.22). Higher levels of tritiated water in the ureteral urine as compared to the plasma most probably reflect the unique arrangement of fluid movement in the posterior parts of most amphibians. Lymph from posterior lymph hearts is pumped into the posterior veins; a significant number of these supply blood to the peritubular vessels in the kidney, which originate in the renal portal vasculature. In a situation where an amphibian is in a completely hydrated condition and water is rapidly entering the body through the skin, it is possible to shunt the water through the lymphatics and hence excrete it via the kidney without diluting the arterial blood.

In general, aquatic amphibians have a more extensive net-

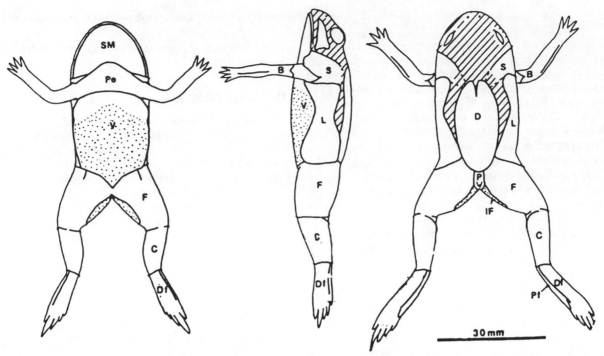

Fig. 5.21 Ventral, lateral, and dorsal views of *Neobatrachus pictus* (representative of terrestrial amphibians including *Bufo marinus*), showing subcutaneous sacs and the septa. *B*, brachial sac; *C*, crural sac; *D*, dorsal sac; *Df*, dorsal sac of foot; *F*, femoral sac; *If*, interfemoral sac; *L*, lateral sac; *P*, pubic sac; *Pe*, pectoral sac; *Pf*, plantar sac of foot; *S*, scapular sac; *SM*, submandibular sac; *V*, ventral sac. *Crosshatching* indicates areas where the skin is closely attached to the muscle, reducing lymph sac area. *Stippling* indicates myointegumental tissue fibers. (Adapted from Carter 1979.)

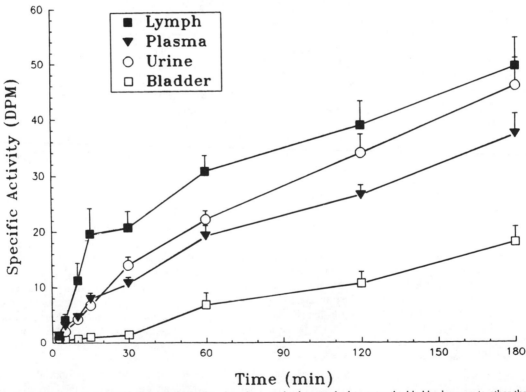

Fig. 5.22 The total specific activity of ^3H_2O in plasma, urine, lymph, and bladder fluid of the toad *Bufo marinus*. Animals were freely moving but were chronically catheterized in the femoral artery (see Boutilier et al. 1979a), in both ureters and the bladder (see Tufts and Toews 1985), and in a femoral lymph sac that was "tapped" using a thin-walled polyethylene catheter. The isotopic water that was introduced into the ambient water rapidly appeared in the lymph, and levels were higher in the lymph than the plasma at all sample times. Since the ureters were catheterized, water had to enter the bladder by a route other than the cloaca. Tritiated water was found at higher concentrations in the ureteral urine than in the plasma at most sample times. The posterior lymph hearts pump lymph into the posterior venous circulation, which supplies the renal portal veins; these in turn perfuse the renal peritubular circulation, resulting in elevated urine isotope levels. All values are expressed as a percentage of the total specific activity of the ambient water at the time the sample was collected. *DPM* = disintegrations per minute.

work of lymph sacs than do more terrestrial species. Although Deyrup (1964) and Middler, Kleeman, and Richards (1968b) suggest that the main function of the sacs is to store water during dry periods, the larger numbers of hearts and sacs in aquatic forms suggest that fluid elimination is the primary function.

To obtain samples of lymph from the lymph sacs of intact animals is exceedingly difficult. Conklin (1930), however, found that the obtainable lymph increases fourfold when lymph hearts are curarized. A reliable measure of available fluid space in the lymph sacs is elusive; the lymph volume is small in intact animals because the lymph hearts rapidly remove the fluid, and the lymph sacs expand to become edematous in curarized animals. Clearly, lymph volume is low in intact animals, and seemingly few species use this space as a water store during desiccation.

Allometry of Water and Ion Exchange

Allometric studies have informed the analysis of gas exchange (Whitford and Hutchison 1967; Ultsch 1974a; Feder 1976a) and evaporative water loss. By contrast, allometric analyses of cutaneous or renal exchanges of ions or water in aquatic amphibians are scarce.

Yokota, Benyajati, and Dantzler (1985) thoroughly reviewed the allometry of renal function in vertebrates. An allometric coefficient (i.e., b in the equation $x = A \cdot \text{mass}^b$) of 0.894 describes GFR in thirteen species of amphibians. The coefficient for anurans is 0.574, suggesting that renal filtration increases much more rapidly with size among urodeles than among anurans. Nagy and Peterson (1988) analyzed the allometry of isotopic water exchange (diffusion) in animals, although data for amphibians are sparse. However, isotopic water exchange has an allometric coefficient of 0.98 in aquatic larval amphibians; the intercept (A in the allometric equation) is 1.765 ml $\cdot$ day^{-1}. For evaporative water loss, urodeles have an allometric coefficient of 0.40 (Spight 1968). The coefficient for anurans, in the absence of air convection, is 0.25 and decreases to 0.18 at an airflow of 270 ml $\cdot$ min^{-1} (Claussen 1969).

The influx of Na$^+$ has an allometric coefficient of 0.52 in larval *Ambystoma tigrinum;* the coefficient for the efflux is 0.60 and is not significantly different than that of the influx (Stiffler 1988). Analysis of twenty-four species of amphibians from the literature yields an influx coefficient of 0.61, which is not significantly different from the coefficient for *A. tigrinum* alone.

Recently, Pruett, Hoyt, and Stiffler (1991) analyzed the allometry of water and ion fluxes for forty-one species of amphibians. The results are presented in table 5.8. When all amphibians are considered, osmotic exchange of water (J_v), urine flow ($\dot{V}$), and GFR all have allometric coefficients of 0.72 to 0.73. The intercepts for J_v and $\dot{V}$ are equal. The intercept for GFR is relatively large, which is consistent with steady-state volume maintenance and a GFR that exceeds urine flow. Similarly, Na$^+$ influx (J_in) scales to the 0.68 power in this analysis; thus these allometric relationships have coefficients between those for surface area (0.67) and metabolic rate (0.75). The allometry of ion and water flux differs, however, between anurans and urodeles and between

TABLE 5.8 Allometric Relationships for Osmotic Water Uptake (J_v), Urine Flow ($\dot{V}$), Glomerular Filtration Rate (GFR), and Sodium Influx (J_in) from Forty-one Species of Amphibians

Function Group	N	Slope	Intercept	r^2
J_v				
All amphibians[a]	23	0.72	0.046	0.71
All urodeles	11	0.45	0.085	0.71
Aquatic urodeles	9	0.52	0.058	0.84
Terrestrial urodeles	3	0.46	0.130	0.66
All anurans	10	0.97[b]	0.029	0.91
Aquatic anurans	3	0.59	0.046	0.50
Terrestrial anurans	6	0.85	0.056	0.98
$\dot{V}$				
All amphibians[a]	28	0.73	0.046	0.69
All urodeles	15	0.49	0.067	0.81
Aquatic urodeles	9	0.55	0.047	0.81
Terrestrial urodeles	6	0.49	0.088	0.43
All anurans	10	0.77	0.060	0.85
Aquatic anurans	5	0.82	0.035	0.96
Terrestrial anurans	7	0.69	0.108[b,c,d]	0.87
GFR				
All amphibians[a]	24	0.73	0.085	0.74
All urodeles	8	0.52	0.109	0.77
Aquatic urodeles	6	0.54	0.094	0.78
Terrestrial urodeles	2	Insufficient data for regression		
All anurans	14	0.64	0.187[b]	0.79
Aquatic anurans	6	0.72	0.106	0.89
Terrestrial anurans	7	0.54	0.350[b,c,d]	0.73
J_in				
All amphibians[a]	26	0.68	0.374	0.58
All urodeles	12	0.56	0.356	0.60
Aquatic urodeles	10	0.56	0.380	0.60
Terrestrial urodele	2	Insufficient data for regression		
All anurans	11	0.96[b]	0.180[b]	0.86
Aquatic anurans	4	0.86	0.160	0.86
Terrestrial anurans	7	0.87	0.338	0.93

Source: Data from Pruett, Hoyt, and Stiffler 1991.
Note: Data are not available for all parameters from all species.
[a] Includes two caecilians and one marine anuran
[b] Significantly different than urodeles; $p < .05$.
[c] Significantly different than aquatic urodeles; $p < .05$.
[d] Significantly different than aquatic anurans; $p < .05$.

aquatic and terrestrial species. The allometric coefficient for J_v of anurans is about twice that of urodeles. The allometric coefficient for $\dot{V}$ appears independent of taxa or habitat type. By contrast, terrestrial anurans have greater intercepts for $\dot{V}$ than do aquatic urodeles and anurans, suggesting that aquatic amphibians have lower osmotic permeabilities than terrestrial amphibians. The allometric coefficients for GFR do not vary by taxon or habitat type, while the intercepts for terrestrial anurans are significantly higher than for aquatic anurans and urodeles. Allometric relationships for J_in (Na$^+$) also vary among amphibians. Anurans tend to have greater allometric coefficients for Na$^+$ influx than do urodeles. Urodeles have greater intercepts than do anurans, however, suggesting that, at least for smaller aquatic amphibians, rates of cutaneous transport may be greater than in their terrestrial counterparts. Anurans also have much greater slopes for the cutaneous functions of osmotic water exchange and active ion transport than do urodeles, while both groups have about the same coefficients for renal functions. Anurans have different body shapes and differences in skin circulation patterns, and the distribution of water and ion transport intensity over different body regions may play a role in the distinctions between the two orders. For example, some anurans have greater rates of ion and/or water transport rates on their ventral surfaces (Bentley and Main 1972), while some urodeles appear to have greater blood flow to ventral skin (Stiffler 1988).

Intraspecific allometric coefficients for osmotic and ionic exchanges are available only for aquatic *Ambystoma tigrinum* (Pruett, Hoyt, and Stiffler 1991). Its coefficient for osmotic flux is 0.76, which is similar to the coefficient for amphibians in general but twice the coefficient for aquatic urodeles. GFR for aquatic *A. tigrinum* yields a coefficient of 0.54, which is the same as the value for the slope for eight aquatic urodele species reported by Pruett, Hoyt, and Stiffler (1991). Similarly, the J_{in} (Na$^+$) coefficient for aquatic *A. tigrinum* is 0.52, which is near the value of 0.56 for aquatic urodeles. Studies of the scaling of osmotic and ionic exchanges, both within and between species of amphibians, are needed to bring greater clarity to these allometric relationships.

Ammonia, Urea, and Hydrogen Ion Distribution in Amphibians

Total ammonia (Tamm; i.e., NH$_3$ plus NH$_4^+$) exists as both a respiratory gas and a weak base. With a pK of approximately 9.5, ammonium ion (NH$_4^+$) predominates at *in vivo* pH (6.5–8.0). Only a small proportion exists as nonionic gas (NH$_3$). Since biological membranes are readily permeable to NH$_3$, this substance will usually equilibrate between the intracellular and extracellular compartments, and NH$_4^+$ will be distributed within each compartment according to the pH of the respective area. Because mammals are ureotelic and have

very low levels of ammonia in their body fluids (Campbell 1973), the distribution of ammonia appears to be according to the intracellular to extracellular pH gradient (Meyer, Dudley, and Terjung 1980). With a pH$_i$-pH$_e$ gradient of 0.4–0.6 pH units, Tamm$_i$/Tamm$_e$ is about 2.5–4.0 in mammals.

The distribution of Tamm is quite different in ammoniotelic teleost fish, where body fluid ammonia levels are comparatively high. Wright, Randall, and Wood (1988) and Wright and Wood (1988) have shown that the Tamm$_i$/Tamm$_e$ in teleost muscle is about 30, and that nonionic diffusion cannot explain the distribution. They suggest that if fish membranes are significantly permeable to NH$_4^+$, then the Nernst equation best describes the distribution, which is thus in an electrochemical equilibrium across the cell membrane.

Following the above argument, Wood, Munger, and Toews (1989) hypothesized a relative reduction in cell permeability to NH$_4^+$ that may have accompanied the evolutionary transition from ammoniotelism to ureotelism in amphibians. They examined the intracellular fluid/extracellular fluid (ICF/ECF) distributions of ammonia or urea, and their possible relationships to the pH$_i$-pH$_e$ gradient in diverse amphibians: adult bullfrogs (*Rana catesbeiana*), adult marine toads (*Bufo marinus*), neotenic mudpuppies (*Necturus maculosus*), larval tiger salamanders (*Ambystoma tigrinum*), and adult South African clawed toads (*Xenopus laevis*). *Xenopus* was also subjected to salt stress to see if the short-term conversion from ammoniotelism to ureotelism modifies the pNH$_3$/pNH$_4^+$ ratio.

The results of Wood, Munger, and Toews (1989) confirm other studies in which the percentage of ammoniotelism decreases in terrestrial amphibians (Balinsky 1970; Balinsky, Cragg, and Baldwin 1961). In the aquatic *Xenopus*, the percentage of urea excretion increases when the animals are salt-stressed (fig. 5.23). While urea$_i$/urea$_e$ ratios are uniformly

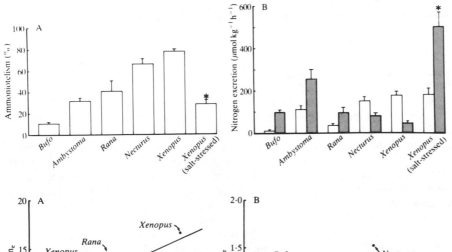

Fig. 5.23 *A*, the percentages of total N-excretion (ammonia-N + urea-N) in the form of ammonia (percentage of ammoniotelism) in five different amphibian species in fresh water and in *Xenopus* subjected to salt stress. *B*, absolute N-excretion rates as ammonia-N (*open columns*) and urea-N (*shaded columns*) in these same animals. Asterisk indicates significant difference ($p \geq .05$) from corresponding value for freshwater *Xenopus* (Reprinted, by permission, from Wood, Munger, and Toews 1989.)

Fig. 5.24 *A*, the relationship between the mean distribution ratio for ammonia between intracellular and extracellular fluids of muscle (Tamm$_i$/Tamm$_e$) and the percentage of ammoniotelism in five different amphibian species in fresh water, and in *Xenopus* subjected to salt stress. *B*, The lack of relationship between the mean distribution ratio for urea between intracellular and extracellular fluids of muscle (urea$_i$/urea$_e$) and the percentage of ammoniotelism in these same animals. (Reprinted, by permission, from Wood, Munger, and Toews 1989.)

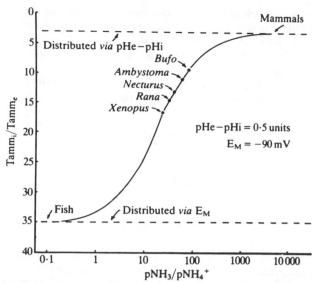

Fig. 5.25 The relationship between the distribution of ammonia at equilibrium between intracellular and extracellular compartments of muscle ($Tamm_i/Tamm_e$) and the relative permeability (pNH_3/pNH_4^+) of the cell membrane to NH_3 and NH_4 (calculated from equations from Boron and Roos 1976 and Roos and Boron 1981). The five different amphibian species in fresh water are plotted, as well as previously documented ranges for teleost fish and mammals. E_m = membrane potential. (Reprinted, by permission, from Wood, Munger, and Toews 1989.)

close to 1.0, $Tamm_i/Tamm_e$ ratios correlate directly with the ammoniotelism in each species, ranging from 9.1 (*Bufo*, 10% ammoniotelic) to 16.7% (*Xenopus*, 79% ammoniotelic). The values are midway between those for ammoniotelic fish and ureotelic mammals (figs. 5.24 and 5.25). The equilibrium distributions seem influenced by both the membrane potential and the pH_i-pH_e gradient, rather than being an exclusive function of either. These studies support an evolutionary transition in ammonia distribution accompanying the progression from ammoniotelism to ureotelism.

REGULATION OF CARBON DIOXIDE EXCRETION AND ACID-BASE BALANCE: INTERACTIONS BETWEEN GASES AND IONS

Like ammonia, carbon dioxide can exist in both ionized and un-ionized forms. In general, epithelia such as gills and skin are much more permeable to the un-ionized gaseous forms (i.e., CO_2, NH_3) than to the ionized species (HCO_3^-, NH_4^+). The intimate relationship between the ionized forms and their respective counterions, Cl^+ and Na^+ (see above and fig. 5.17), links ionic and gaseous exchange with acid-base regulation.

Most studies linking acid-base regulation to ion exchange in amphibians have been carried out *in vitro* on various tissue or organ preparations (e.g., toad bladder, frog skin, kidney). On the other hand, most *in vivo* studies of acid-base regulation through ventilatory control of CO_2 levels have not examined the relative role that transepithelial ion transfers play in the overall control process. Thus, while the lungs, kidneys, bladder, and skin are all involved in acid-base regulation, the relative contributions of each to the overall acid or base load of an intact animal is poorly understood.

In the steady state, production of acidic or alkaline metabolic end products is relatively small, and animals can maintain their acid-base balance by regulation of respiratory CO_2

losses and eliminate nonvolatile metabolic end products by ionic exchange. However, much larger perturbations of acid-base balance occur when the animals encounter acute changes in temperature or aquatic hypercapnia, or when they become extraordinarily active (see review by Toews and Boutilier 1986). At such times, one would suspect the entire arsenal of respiratory and ionic regulatory mechanisms to be set into motion. Exposure of amphibians to hypercapnia has become a commonly used tool for examining the relative contributions of respiratory and ionic mechanisms to pH regulation *in vivo*, and serves as a focus for the discussion that follows.

Hypercapnic Acidosis

Amphibious as well as exclusively aquatic species of amphibians can encounter hypercapnia in the water surrounding their highly permeable epithelial surfaces. In fact, the environments in which many aquatic amphibians reside undergo seasonal as well as daily oscillations in environmental Pco_2 (reviewed by Ultsch 1976a). In the habitats of the giant North American salamanders, *Siren lacertina*, *Amphiuma means*, and *A. tridactylum*, environmental Pco_2 may reach 60 mm Hg (Ultsch 1976a; see also chapter 10), often in association with hypoxia (Heisler et al. 1982). Amphibians may also incur rises in blood Pco_2 through various activities such as breath-holding (Boutilier and Shelton 1986a, 1986b, 1986c), exercise (Boutilier, McDonald, and Toews 1980), or emergence onto land (Lenfant and Johansen 1967).

Respiratory Responses When increases in environmental Pco_2 of 10 to 15 mm Hg are solely at the skin, as is most often the case in nature, anurans such as *Bufo marinus*, *Rana catesbeiana*, and *Xenopus laevis* can eliminate all of the added CO_2 by increasing pulmonary ventilation (Boutilier et al. 1979a; Jackson and Braun 1979; Boutilier and Shelton 1986b; Toews and Stiffler 1989). By so doing, these animals effectively offset any increases in arterial Pco_2 and therefore maintain their blood pH at a steady state. When the animals experience either greater hypercapnia at the skin or total environmental hypercapnia, however, the rise in Pco_2 causes blood pH to decline and plasma HCO_3^- to increase.

An initial CO_2 equilibration and acid-base adjustment occurs in several species upon exposure to environmental hypercapnia (fig. 5.26). The slope of the *in vivo* buffer line ($\Delta[HCO_3^-]/\Delta pH$; point A to B) varies considerably amongst the species, as does the degree of pH compensation that later ensues (point B to C). During the initial 1–2 h of hypercapnia (A to B, fig. 5.26), the rate at which Pco_2 increases is dependent upon diffusive and convective conductance of CO_2 as well as on the buffering and storage capacities of the animal. Most amphibians increase pulmonary ventilation when confronted with hypercapnic conditions. In *B. marinus*, as well as *R. catesbeiana*, the hypercapnia-induced increases in pulmonary ventilation markedly reduce the Pco_2 gradient between arterial blood and air (Boutilier et al. 1979a; Jackson and Braun 1979; Boutilier and Heisler 1988; Toews and Stiffler 1989). This increase in ventilation and the associated reduction in the blood-to-air Pco_2 gradient act to reduce the pH change that would otherwise occur. Despite increasing its rate of pulmonary ventilation in response to environmental hypercapnia, the blood-to-air Pco_2 gradient of the predominantly skin-breathing urodele *Cryptobranchus* (Cryptobranchidae)

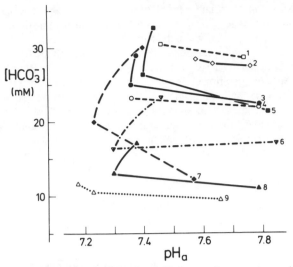

Fig. 5.26 Extracellular [HCO₃⁻] and pH changes that occur in a variety of amphibian species when exposed to hypercapnia. Except for lines 1 and 2 the time course of the changes shown involve normal (farthest right, point A) 1–2-h hypercapnia (next value left, point B) and 24-h hypercapnia (next value usually with elevated [HCO₃⁻] indicating some compensation, point C). *1, Amphiuma means,* Heisler et al. 1982; *2, Xenopus laevis,* Boutilier 1981; *3, Bufo marinus,* Boutilier et al. 1979a; *4, Siren lacertina,* Heisler et al. 1982; *5, B. marinus,* Toews and Heisler 1982; *6, Ambystoma tigrinum,* Stiffler, Tufts, and Toews 1983; *7, Typhlonectes compressicauda,* Toews and Macintyre 1978; *8, Cryptobranchus alleganiensis,* Boutilier and Toews 1981b; *9, Necturus maculosus,* Stiffler, Tufts, and Toews 1983.

is unaffected, much as in other water-breathing species (Randall et al. 1981). However, the lungs of *Cryptobranchus* are rudimentary in comparison to those of *Bufo* and *Rana* and account for only 3% of the animals' CO_2 elimination at 25°C (Guimond and Hutchison 1976) versus 20 to 25% in anurans at comparable temperatures (Hutchison, Whitford, and Kohl 1968; Smith 1974).

Obviously, the lungs can perform substantial "respiratory regulation" of acid-base balance during hypercapnia by lowering arterial P_{CO_2}. At least at 25°C, *Cryptobranchus* is unable to carry out any comparable "respiratory regulation" either through increases in ventilation or, evidently, through cutaneous gas exchange. In addition, cutaneous gas exchange is not sufficient to correct the decrease in blood pH that occurs when animals in normocapnic water breathe hypercapnic gas mixtures (Jackson and Braun 1979). Even so, the skin of *Amphiuma* can excrete all of the CO_2 added to the lung without causing any increase in ventilation (Toews 1971). Although no blood-gas or pH data are available for this particular experiment, this result may be indicative of respiratory regulation of acid-base balance by the skin of an amphibian. Most experiments on the acid-base physiology of amphibians have been performed at temperatures above 15°C, and little is known about the potential of the skin as a modulator of acid-base balance at lower temperatures (see section on gas exchange and chapter 10).

Extracellular and Intracellular pH Adjustments Upon exposure to elevated levels of CO_2, pH falls due to a shift in the equilibria of the CO_2/HCO_3^- system. As hypercapnia continues, however, other mechanisms act to compensate for the initial fall in pH. These include (1) the conversion of molecular CO_2 to HCO_3^- by nonbicarbonate buffering and (2) the accumulation of HCO_3^- through ion exchange processes (see above for mechanisms). Both of these processes act to return the pH towards its original value, thereby compensating for the original acidosis.

During hypercapnia, the CO_2/HCO_3^- buffer system, as well as nonbicarbonate buffers (NB) are set in motion (Heisler 1986):

$$B_1^- \rightleftharpoons HB_1$$
$$+$$
$$CO_2 + H_2O \rightleftharpoons H^+ + HCO_3^-$$
$$+$$
$$B_2^- \rightleftharpoons HB_2$$

Within the blood and intracellular compartments, nonbicarbonate buffers (i.e. NB_1^- and NB_2^- are in equilibrium with the CO_2/HCO_3^- system. In the absence of nonbicarbonate buffers, changes in physically dissolved CO_2 would result in dissociation of H^+ and HCO_3^- into equimolar amounts. However, when nonbicarbonate buffers are in equilibrium with the CO_2/HCO_3^- system, transfer of free H^+ to the nondissociated state allows for nonbicarbonate buffering and a rise in HCO_3^-. The changes in $[HCO_3^-]$ are equimolar to the changes in buffer ions ($-\Delta B_{total}$ or ΔHB_{total}) such that a nonbicarbonate buffer value (β_{NB}) can be determined (e.g., by CO_2 titration) according to principles defined by Van Slyke (1922) as extended by Heisler (1986):

$$\beta_{NB} = \frac{\Delta[H^+]_b}{-\Delta pH} = \frac{\Delta[HB]}{-\Delta pH} = \frac{-\Delta[B^-]}{-\Delta pH} = \frac{\Delta[HCO_3^-]}{-\Delta pH}$$

Nonbicarbonate buffer (NB) slopes determined on blood samples equilibrated at a range of P_{CO_2} *in vitro* are generally higher than the "apparent buffer slopes" that arise when the animals themselves are equilibrated to the same range of P_{CO_2}. The initial rise in plasma HCO_3^- within the first hour of CO_2 exposure is due to physicochemical actions of the extracellular nonbicarbonate buffers. The lesser buffer slope *in vivo* than *in vitro* is due to a net flux of HCO_3^- (or their functional equivalent, H^+) between extracellular, interstitial, and intracellular compartments, all of which have different nonbicarbonate buffering capacities (see Heisler 1986). This initial period of equilibration and redistribution of the CO_2/HCO_3^- system (i.e., points A to B in fig. 5.26) often precedes, by a species-specific time period (2–6 h), an additional accumulation of HCO_3^- that occurs at relatively constant P_{CO_2}, thereby partially compensating for the initial acidosis (points B to C). The source of this accumulated HCO_3^- occurs as the result of net transfers of bicarbonate-equivalent ions between the extracellular and intracellular compartments of the animals as well as between ECF and environmental water (see below). However, not all animals exhibit this secondary "compensatory" increase in plasma HCO_3^-. Studies on the urodeles *Siren* and *Amphiuma* (Heisler et al. 1982), as well as on the anuran *Xenopus* (Boutilier 1981), have shown that the initial nonbicarbonate buffering and CO_2/HCO_3^- redistribution process is the only form of pH compensation seen in the extracellular compartment. In these three animals, the respiratory acidosis will persist in this un-compensated state for as long as 36 h. Moreover, addition of HCO_3^- either to the water surrounding the animal or to the animal itself does not lead to any further compensation of blood pH in either *Siren* (Heisler et al. 1982) or *Bufo* (Bou-tilier and Heisler 1988). The lack of any compensatory rise in plasma HCO_3^- in *Siren, Amphiuma,* and *Xenopus* seem-ingly suggests that these animals do not regulate their acid-base balance very effectively. However, the intracellular pH (pH_i) levels of both the skeletal and heart muscle tissues of at least *Siren* are practically unaffected by hypercapnia, due in large measure to a marked increase in intracellular [HCO_3^-] (Heisler et al. 1982). The pH_i of the same tissues in *B. mar-inus* is similarly well defended against any large pH changes (Toews and Heisler 1982).

Toews and Stiffler (1989) have recently shown that further pH compensation during chronic hypercapnia in *B. marinus* or *Rana catesbeiana* is probably not limited by a maximum [HCO_3^-] set-point in the plasma (cf. Heisler 1986). For ex-ample, the HCO_3^- levels accumulated in the plasma of both animals over 4 days of progressive increases in environmental CO_2 (e.g., fig. 5.27 for *R. catesbeiana*) are much greater than would be predicted on the basis of earlier studies. Neverthe-less, for any given level of hypercapnia a certain HCO_3^- threshold exists (Boutilier and Heisler 1988; Heisler 1986), and the animals defend this new steady state in the same fash-ion as do normocapnic animals (Toews and Stiffler 1989).

Following the initial respiratory acidosis, many amphib-ians compensate for the decline in extracellular pH (pH_e) by increasing their plasma [HCO_3^-] at relatively constant P_{CO_2} (point B to C, figs. 5.26 and 5.27). In most amphibians, this HCO_3^- accumulation increases pH_e to a limited extent (0 to 30% compensation; fig. 5.26), the exception being the Ama-zonian apodan *Typhlonectes compressicauda* (80% compen-sation; Toews and MacIntyre 1978). Compensatory responses such as these result from net transfers of bicarbonate-equivalent ions* between extracellular and intracellular com-partments, as well as between ECF and environmental water. Mechanisms to conserve HCO_3^- exist in the skin, kidney, and bladder (see above), and some recent experiments have also shown how these systems might interact to control the acid-base balance of amphibians. For example, bladder-bypassed but otherwise intact *Bufo marinus* cannot compensate for an ongoing respiratory acidosis (Tufts and Toews 1985), dem-onstrating the importance of the urinary system in the HCO_3^- accumulation process. The inability of the skin to re-dress the loss of renal compensation suggests that cutaneous ion exchange is unimportant in this regard. This was certainly not the conclusion of recent experiments on *Ambystoma ti-*

---

*Net H^+ flux is usually determined as the difference between net ammonia flux and net bicarbonate flux (i.e., Δ ammonia $-$ Δ bicarbon-ate, signs considered). Methods used to determine H^+ movements (re-viewed by Heisler 1984, 1986) are unable to separate H^+ uptake from its functional equivalent, HCO_3^- excretion (or vice versa). Nor can the pres-ent methodology discriminate between ammonia movement in the NH_3 or NH_4^+ forms. Rather, such determinations give a valid measure of *net* acidic equivalent flux. Various *descriptive terms* to denote such H^+ movements are used interchangeably in the current literature (e.g., acidic equivalent flux, net H^+ flux, bicarbonate-equivalent flux, among others) and *should not be mistaken for* statements about *the mechanisms* in-volved in transepithelial ion transfers.

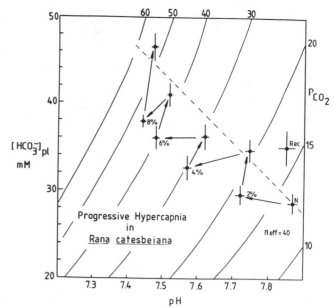

Fig. 5.27 A pH–HCO_3^- diagram showing the responses of *Rana cates-beiana* to progressive increases in environmental hypercapnia, taking place over several days. After the initial blood sampling (normal sample, *N*), the animals were exposed to 2% CO_2 with samples taken after 1 h and 24 h of equilibration. After the 24-h sample, the environmental CO_2 was increased to 4% and the same sampling procedure carried out, and so on for 6% and 8%, until a final recovery period sample was taken after 24-h reexposure to air (*Rec*). Values are means (± 1 SEM) of ten ani-mals. The β_{eff} buffer line (*broken line*) was calculated using normal and 24-h values. (Reprinted, by permission, from Toews and Stiffler 1989.)

grinum, which indicate that the epithelial surfaces play a ma-jor role in pH regulation (fig. 5.28). In these experiments, compensation of pH during hypercapnia was impossible without suitable levels of counterions in the ambient medium; when such ions are added, pH compensation occurs.

To quantify the contribution of transepithelial ion transfer processes to pH regulation *in vivo,* net bicarbonate-equivalent fluxes between the animal and its aquatic environment must be measured and related to the total changes in the body HCO_3^- pool. Recent studies on *B. marinus* (Boutilier and Heisler 1988) use a model (see Heisler 1982) in which changes in intracellular and extracellular HCO_3^- pools (i.e., $\Delta HCO_{3i,e}^-$) are compared with the amount of HCO_3^- that can be produced by nonbicarbonate buffering (ΔHCO_{3NB}^-) as well as that introduced to the body fluids by net transfer of bicarbonate-equivalent ions ($\Delta HCO_{3x \to y}^-$).

Changes in bicarbonate in the body fluid compartments (e.g., between time 1 and 2) can be estimated for the extra-cellular (e) and intracellular (i) space, viz.:

$$\Delta HCO_{3e}^- = [HCO_3^-]_{Pl,2} \times V_{e,2} - [HCO_3^-]_{Pl,1} \times V_{e,1}$$

or

$$\Delta HCO_{3i}^- = [HCO_3^-]_{i,2} \times V_{i,2} - [HCO_3^-]_{i,1} \times V_{i,1},$$

where

V = extracellular or intracellular water volumes
$[HCO_3^-]_{Pl}$ = true plasma bicarbonate concentrations

Intracellular [HCO_3^-] is generally estimated from pH_i and ar-terial P_{CO_2} (assuming arterial P_{CO_2} to be in near equilibrium

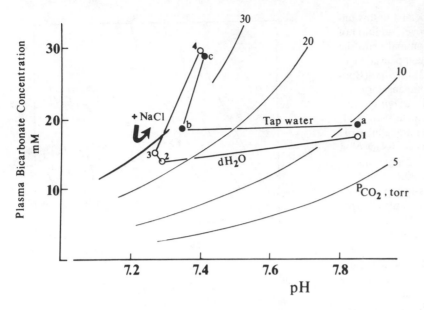

Fig. 5.28 A pH-[HCO_3^-] diagram showing differences in responses to environmental hypercapnia between *Ambystoma tigrinum* larvae immersed in tap water or running distilled water (dH_2O). Larvae in tap water: *a*, normocapnic control; *b*, 2-h hypercapnia; *c*, 24-h hypercapnia. Larvae in dH_2O: *1*, normocapnic control in tap water; *2*, 2-h hypercapnia in running dH_2O; *3*, 24-h hypercapnia in running dH_2O; *4*, an additional 24-h hypercapnia after dH_2O flow terminated and NaCl added to bath. (After Stiffler, Ryan, and Mushkot 1987.)

with intracellular P_{CO_2}; e.g., Toews and Heisler 1982). In practice, estimates of the intracellular HCO_3^- pool often rely on simplifying assumptions (e.g., that the intracellular compartment of white muscle represents the total intracellular space (cf. Heisler 1982, 1984, 1986; Boutilier and Heisler 1988).

The production of bicarbonate from nonbicarbonate buffering can be estimated for blood, viz.,

$$\Delta HCO_{3NBbl}^- = \beta_{Pl} \times \Delta pH_{Pl} \times F_{CO_2} \times V_{bl},$$

where

bl = blood

F_{CO_2} = blood total CO_2 content/plasma total CO_2

β_{Pl} = the NB value for true plasma ($\Delta[HCO_3^-]/\Delta pH$).

HCO_3^- production by nonbicarbonate buffers in the intracellular compartment can be estimated, viz.,

$$\Delta HCO_{3NBi}^- = \beta_{NBi} \times \Delta pH_i \times \left(\frac{V_{i,1} + V_{i,2}}{2}\right),$$

where β_{NBi} = the buffering capacity (i.e., $\Delta[HCO_3^-]/\Delta pH$) of the intracellular compartment, for example, white muscle.

The amount of HCO_3^- introduced to the body fluid compartments by net transfer of bicarbonate equivalents from the water to extracellular space (index "w→e") can be estimated by

$$\Delta HCO_{3w \to e}^- = -\Delta H_{e \to w}^+ + \Delta H_{e \to w, control}^+,$$

where ΔH^+ = the change in net proton equivalent transfers between animal and environment.

With the above relationships, a "balance sheet" can estimate the changes in the total HCO_3^- pool (ΔHCO_{3e+i}^-) of *Bufo marinus* during 24-h exposure to environmental hypercapnia, and can compare that estimate to the sum of the HCO_3^- produced by nonbicarbonate buffering ($\Delta HCO_{3NBbl+i}^-$) plus that taken up from the surrounding water ($\Delta HCO_{3w \to e}^-$). In the case of hypercapnic *Bufo*, $\Delta HCO_{3e+i}^- = 7.8$ mmol · kg^{-1} body water in a 24-h period, whereas $\Delta HCO_{3NBbl+i}^- + \Delta HCO_{3w \to e}^- = 6.4$ mmol · kg^{-1} body water. Boutilier and Heisler (1988)

suggest that the difference between the two is due to additional HCO_3^- production through dissolution of calcium carbonate deposits, known to occur during chronic hypercapnia in anurans (Sulze 1942; Simkiss 1968; Tufts and Toews 1985). A major limitation of this balance-sheet approach is obtaining sufficient information about the intracellular tissue compartments (see Heisler 1982, 1984, 1986; Boutilier and Heisler 1988). An additional approach models the animal as a two-compartment system surrounded by a semiclosed fluid compartment (i.e., the environmental water). In this case, temporal changes in the extracellular HCO_3^- pool (ΔHCO_{3e}^-) can be related to transfers from the environment to extracellular space (i.e., $\Delta HCO_{3w \to e}^-$), and from the extracellular to intracellular space ($\Delta HCO_{3e \to i}^-$), viz.,

$$\Delta HCO_{3e \to i}^- = \Delta HCO_{3w \to e}^- + \Delta HCO_{3NBbl}^- - \Delta HCO_{3e}^-.$$

As shown in fig. 5.29, the bulk of the rise in extracellular HCO_3^- bicarbonate during 24 h of hypercapnia in *Bufo* is due to net uptake of HCO_3^- bicarbonate from the environmental water. This can occur by numerous mechanisms, as detailed previously, acting at the skin, kidney, or bladder (note that H^+ excretion, e.g., by the skin, is equivalent to HCO_3^- uptake). The overall transmembrane transfer ($\Delta HCO_{3e \to i}^-$) is limited to transient shifts of smaller magnitude, though the initial rapid rise in extracellular HCO_3^- appears to occur at the expense of the intracellular compartment. After 8 h of hypercapnia, the contribution of HCO_3^- from the environment progressively decreases. However, the limited extracellular compensation (i.e., fig. 5.26) cannot be due to limited HCO_3^- pools in the environment, since additions of HCO_3^- to the water do not lead to greater HCO_3^- uptake (Boutilier and Heisler 1988).

Temperature

Many amphibious and aquatic amphibians habitually experience large changes in ambient temperature (see chapters 8 and 9); this leads to significant perturbations of arterial blood pH (table 5.9).

The inverse relationship between body temperature and extracellular pH (pH_e) in poikilothermic animals (Howell et al. 1970; Rahn 1967; Robin 1962) led to the formulation of two models of pH regulation (see review by Cameron 1989), constant relative alkalinity (Rahn 1967) and the alphastat hypothesis (Reeves 1972). The basis of both models was the experimental finding that pH_e changed with temperature *in vivo* ($\Delta pH_e/\Delta t$) in a manner similar to that of neutral water (i.e., $\Delta pN/\Delta t = -0.019$ units · $°C^{-1}$ from 5° to 20°C, and -0.017 units · $°C^{-1}$ from 20° to 35°C; *Handbook of Chemistry and Physics*). Rahn (1967) interpreted this to mean that extracellular pH varies with temperature by a species-specific

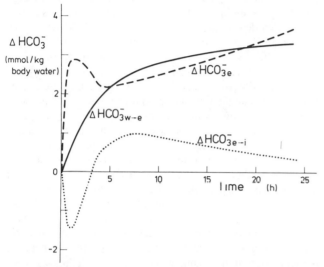

Fig. 5.29 Changes in the amount of extracellular bicarbonate (ΔHCO_{3e}^-), and cumulative net transfer of bicarbonate equivalents between environmental water and extracellular space ($\Delta HCO_{3w \to e}^-$), and between extracellular and intracellular space ($\Delta HCO_{3e \to i}^-$) of *Bufo marinus* after the onset of environmental hypercapnia (5% CO_2). See text for details of calculations. (Reprinted, by permission, from Boutilier and Heisler 1988.)

constant from the neutral pH of water; that is, the animals defend a constant relative alkalinity or constant OH^-/H^+ ratio. The fact that the pH/temperature coefficients ($\Delta pH/\Delta t$; table 5.9) were also close to the $\Delta pK/\Delta t$ of biological histidine-imidazole moieties ($\Delta pK_{im}/\Delta t = -0.018$ to 0.024 units · $°C^{-1}$, depending on ligands and steric arrangements; see Edsall and Wyman 1958), led Reeves (1972) to propose that the decreases in pH_e with increasing body temperature result from an adjustment towards a constant ionization of histidine-imidazole. He suggested further that this net charge state of imidazole is the regulated variable of temperature-dependent acid-base regulation. He termed maintenance of a constant fractional dissociation of imidazole (α_{im}) *alphastat regulation*. A central criterion of this alphastat hypothesis is that pH_e adjustments with temperature are accomplished solely through changes in ventilation and therefore Pco_2. He also postulated that plasma $[HCO_3^-]$ would remain constant because of the lack of titration of nonbicarbonate buffers and the absence of any acid-base relevant ion transfers among intracellular, extracellular, and environmental compartments (i.e., the buffer system would be closed for ionic species but open for CO_2). Malan, Wilson, and Reeves (1976) considered that this type of regulation should also apply to intracellular compartments and that histidine-imidazole protein residues might even act as intracellular sensors for regulating the ratio of CO_2 production to ventilation and therefore Pco_2 (Rahn and Reeves 1980).

For the most part, the changes in blood pH with temperature in amphibians (table 5.9) appear to occur through adjustments in arterial Pco_2. Presumably, many species accomplish this through modulation of pulmonary ventilation. The predominantly skin-breathing urodele *Cryptobranchus* (Cryptobranchidae), however, also adjusts its arterial Pco_2 so that $\Delta pH_e/\Delta t$ follows the predicted ectotherm relationship (Moalli et al. 1981). The latter might occur as a passive consequence of the corresponding changes in metabolic rate and Pco_2, together with a temperature-independent CO_2 conductance of

TABLE 5.9 Changes of Extracellular pH ($\Delta pH/\Delta t$), Pco_2 (Q_{10}) and Bicarbonate Concentration ($1/Q_{10}$) with Changes in Temperature in a Variety of Amphibians

	Temperature Range (°C)	Plasma $\Delta pH/\Delta t$	Pco_2 (Q_{10})	$[HCO_3^-]$ ($1/Q_{10}$)	Reference
Urodela					
Necturus maculosus	5–25	−0.015	1.08	1.50	Hicks and Stiffler 1984
Cryptobranchus alleganiensis	5–25	−0.017	1.89	1.10	Moalli et al. 1981
Amphiuma means	5–25	−0.018	1.46	1.17	Hicks and Stiffler 1984
Ambystoma tigrinum					
Larva	5–25	−0.013		1.22	Burggren and Wood 1981
	5–25	−0.015	1.86	1.24	Hicks and Stiffler 1984
	5–25	−0.012	1.31	1.21	Hicks and Stiffler 1980
Adults	5–25	−0.013		1.20	Burggren and Wood 1981
	5–25	−0.015	1.24	1.27	Hicks and Stiffler 1984
Anura					
Rana catesbeiana	8–30	−0.016	1.51	1.03	Reeves 1972
	10–30	−0.011	1.46	1.03	MacKenzie and Jackson 1978
	5–30	−0.013	1.58	1.08	Howell et al. 1970
Bufo marinus	10–30	−0.015	1.44	1.19	Howell et al. 1970
	10–30	−0.014	1.60	1.03	Boutilier, Glass, and Heisler 1987
Xenopus laevis	10–30	−0.016	1.71	1.05	Boutilier, Glass, and Heisler 1987

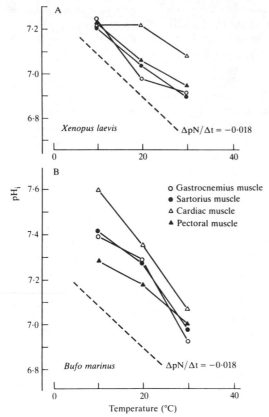

Fig. 5.30 Intracellular pH (pH$_i$) as a function of body temperature for three groups of skeletal muscle and for cardiac muscle of *Xenopus laevis* (*A*) and *Bufo marinus* (*B*). pH$_i$ was determined by the 5,5-dimethyl-2,4-oxazolidinedione (DMO) distribution technique. (Reprinted, by permission, from Boutilier, Glass, and Heisler 1987.)

the skin. The gilled urodele *Necturus,* on the other hand, regulates pH$_e$ primarily through adjustments in plasma [HCO$_3^-$] with arterial P$_{CO_2}$ changing very little (table 5.9).

While the majority of data in table 5.9 are in agreement with alphastat-type regulation, the biological importance of the hypothesis rests on the assumption that the pH of the intracellular compartments should change in a like fashion. Measurements of striated muscle pH of bullfrogs (*Rana catesbeiana*) are in general agreement with alphastat control (Malan, Wilson, and Reeves 1976), whereas recent measurements of pH$_i$ of a number of intracellular compartments of *Bufo marinus* and *Xenopus laevis* depart from the predicted pattern. Indeed, figure 5.30 suggests that pH$_i$ may change with temperature in a distinctly nonlinear fashion. This is particularly evident in the heart muscle of *X. laevis,* where pH$_i$ is constant between 10° and 20°C but falls by 0.14 pH units between 20° and 30°C. Thus, temperature-related pH$_i$ regulation is relatively independent of extracellular acid-base regulation. Moreover, regulatory patterns such as these cannot be accounted for by the alphastat model, that is, with adjustment of only organismic P$_{CO_2}$.

The active regulatory processes leading to temperature-dependent acid-base regulation must be sought in transmembrane and transepithelial ion transfer processes (see above), as occurs in other animals (Heisler 1986). To date, the studies on amphibians have been limited to descriptions of pH/temperature coefficients. More indicative features of acid-base regulation, such as compartmental buffering, ventilatory control of P$_{CO_2}$, and transmembrane and transepithelial transfers, must be examined in future studies of temperature-dependent pH regulation in these animals.

6 Exchange of Water, Ions, and Respiratory Gases in Terrestrial Amphibians

Vaughan H. Shoemaker
with
Stanley S. Hillman, Stanley D. Hillyard, Donald C. Jackson, Lon L. McClanahan, Philip C. Withers, and Mark L. Wygoda

Amphibians cannot be conveniently classified as aquatic or terrestrial. While some are virtually confined to water and others to land, most move between land and water and must cope with the challenges of each environment. This chapter thus deals with the ways in which amphibians interact with the terrestrial environment with regard to regulation of the water and electrolyte contents of their bodies, the excretion of metabolic wastes, and the exchange of respiratory gases.

Because amphibians have permeable skins, the flux of water across the integument reverses as the animal moves between terrestrial and aquatic environments. On land the magnitude of cutaneous efflux is determined both by the driving forces for evaporation and by the resistance of the integument to water loss. In this regard amphibians have evolved a wide spectrum of behavioral and physiological adaptations that permit them to exploit the terrestrial environment to varying degrees. Most require access to fresh water to replace evaporative losses. Because of the limited concentrating capacity of their kidneys, amphibians typically require more water than other terrestrial vertebrates for excretion of ions and nitrogen wastes, and are unable to rid themselves of excess solutes without access to water. However, many amphibians are unusually tolerant of water deficits and of excesses of ions and nitrogenous wastes. Thus, strict homeostasis is not required, and terrestrial amphibians can be opportunistic in obtaining water for rehydration and excretion.

In water, adult amphibians may exchange gases with both water and air, and use gills, skin, and lungs in various combinations (see also chapters 4, 5, and 16). Air-breathing terrestrial amphibians tend to rely primarily on lungs for gas exchange, but the permeable integument can contribute importantly, and in some cases exclusively, to respiratory gas transfer. Thus opportunities for gas exchange offset to some degree the liabilities of a permeable integument in terms of water balance. In both osmoregulation and gas exchange, the variety of habitats, body forms, and activities of amphibians on land is reflected in a diverse array of exchange mechanisms.

CUTANEOUS WATER EXCHANGE
Evaporative Water Losses

Rates of evaporative water loss (EWL) via the skin in amphibians are very high (with a few notable exceptions) in comparison with other terrestrial vertebrates. In at least some species, and perhaps in most, the skin itself provides absolutely no barrier (resistance) to the evaporation of water. Adolph (1932) found that skinned frogs (*Rana*) lost water at the same rate as intact ones. More recent studies have shown that a variety of amphibians lose water at the same rate as replicas made of agar or plaster that present a free water surface of the same size and shape as the live animal (Spotila and Berman 1976; Wygoda 1984). Rates of cutaneous EWL in amphibians are such that survival time on dry land in moving air would be less than 1 day, even under moderate conditions of temperature and humidity. Because amphibians lose water so rapidly by evaporation, possible modification of cutaneous water loss has been a major focus of research.

Rates of EWL are available for more than one hundred amphibian species, but a compilation of these results is of little value because the rates depend greatly on the method of measurement, which varies widely between studies. EWL can be measured either directly, by determining the mass of water vapor leaving the animal, or indirectly, by determining the change in mass of the animal. Because most amphibians lose mass quickly and usually do not urinate or defecate under dehydrating conditions, the two methods are equally reliable. The major causes of variance among techniques stem from other sources. For example, if the measurement process (e.g., weighing) disturbs an experimental subject, then higher rates will obtain because of the activity of the animal (see Heatwole et al. 1969). Animals must be undis-

When Martin Feder and Warren Burggren suggested that I write this chapter and draw on the expertise of as many amphibiologists as possible, I thought it would never work. However, Don, Lon, Mark, Phil and the two Stans proved me wrong by making enormous contributions to the preparation of this chapter. They cheerfully and promptly responded to all requests, large and small. Thanks! V.H.S.

turbed until they become quiescent in their normal posture, and repeated measurements are necessary to assure steady-state conditions.

Direct methods meet these requirements and usually involve passing dry air into a chamber containing the animal and measuring the water in the excurrent air. This can be done by collecting the water in an absorbent such as anhydrous calcium sulfate (Drierite) or by passing the air over a sensor to determine vapor density (usually from dew point or relative humidity). The use of absorbents is simple and reliable but requires no leakage of air. The use of sensors permits continuous recording of EWL so that nearly instantaneous values result and the attainment of steady state is obvious. Because only a sample of the excurrent air is required, outward air leaks do not introduce errors. However, EWL must be calculated as the product of the vapor density difference between incurrent and excurrent air and the rate of airflow into the chamber, requiring measurement of the latter.

Mass changes of the animal (the indirect method) are also possible without disturbing the animal if it is kept on a balance. A cage containing the animal may be suspended from a balance located above a desiccator (Adolph 1932; Warburg 1967). Alternatively, for studies in moving air, a mesh cage containing an animal (Buttemer 1990; Geise and Linsenmair 1986; Heatwole et al. 1969) or a paralyzed animal (Lillywhite 1971b; Wygoda 1984) may rest on top of an electronic balance in an airstream.

The major difficulties in comparing studies or interpreting their results are differences in airflow rate and body size. For a highly permeable animal, the rate of water loss is wholly or largely determined by the resistance of the boundary layer of moist air surrounding the animal (see also chapter 4). Boundary layer resistance is exhibited by a wet surface of the same geometry as the animal. The inverse of this resistance, the mass transfer coefficient (h_D) obeys the following approximate relationship for frogs (see Mitchell 1976; Tracy 1976):

$$(1) \qquad h_D = 0.3(D/L)(VL/\nu)^{0.6},$$

where

h_D = mass transfer coefficient (cm $\cdot$ s^{-1})
D = diffusivity of water vapor in air (cm $\cdot$ s^{-1})
L = snout-vent length of frog (cm)
V = wind velocity (cm $\cdot$ s^{-1})
ν = kinematic viscosity of air (cm $\cdot$ s^{-1})

Values for D and ν are available in Tracy, Welch, and Porter 1980.

Total resistance (r) to evaporation is the sum of the boundary layer resistance (r_b) and the resistance provided by the integument (r_i). EWL depends on the total resistance and the vapor density gradient (see, e.g., Spotila and Berman 1976 and chapter 4).

$$(2) \qquad EWL = \rho/(r_b + r_i)$$

where

EWL = evaporative water loss (g $\cdot$ cm^{-2} $\cdot$ s^{-1})
ρ = vapor density gradient (g $\cdot$ cm^{-3} = vapor density of water at the temperature of the evaporating surface − vapor density of water in the air
r, r_b, r_i = resistances (s $\cdot$ cm^{-1})

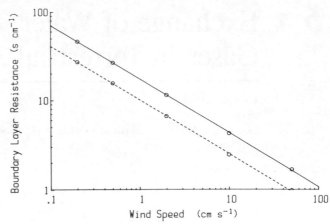

Fig. 6.1 Approximate boundary layer resistance as a function of wind speed for a 500-g frog (*solid line*) and a 5-g frog (*dashed line*). Note logarithmic scales.

The boundary layer resistance varies with both wind speed and body size (eq. [1]). Fig. 6.1 illustrates the profound effects of wind speed on r_b. This is the range of wind speeds that would apply in a typical flow-through system. An airflow of 1 l $\cdot$ min^{-1} through a chamber with a cross-sectional area of 80 cm^2 results in an air velocity of 0.2 cm $\cdot$ s^{-1}. Thus even modest differences in flow rate and chamber geometry will profoundly affect r_b and hence EWL in most amphibians, and confound the interpretation of many previous studies. Moreover, a small integumentary resistance is difficult to detect if r_b is large by comparison.

Differences in body size will of course affect mass specific rates of EWL because surface area scales allometrically with mass. Larger animals will have lower surface-specific rates of EWL for two additional reasons. First, boundary layer resistance is larger in bigger animals (eq. [1], fig. 6.1). Second, especially at low flow rates, large water losses from a large animal may increase the vapor density in the chamber and hence reduce the driving force for evaporation (eq. [2]).

Terrestrial and Aquatic Amphibians Despite these difficulties in interpreting EWL values, terrestrial existence in amphibians is not generally associated with changes in cutaneous resistance to EWL. Early studies on North American anurans (Thorson 1955) and on California salamanders (Cohen 1952) first reached this conclusion. Subsequent comparative studies (Bentley, Lee, and Main 1958; Claussen 1969; Farrell and MacMahon 1969; Ray 1958; Schmid 1965; Shoemaker and McClanahan 1980; Spight 1968) have generally failed to find interspecific differences in EWL that are not explained by differences in posture, activity, or body size (see review by Heatwole 1984). Low rates of EWL reported in some Australian and Israeli anurans (Warburg 1972) appear due to techniques that promote very large boundary layers (animals placed with moist cotton in vials within a desiccator). Bentley (1966a, 623) concluded that "the most valuable evolutionary novelty which they [amphibians] could invent to assist their survival there [in hot, dry habitats] would be a more impermeable integument. This has not occurred in the Amphibia." Although this statement holds for many, and probably most, terrestrial amphibians, exceptions among both arboreal and fossorial species are discussed below. For the majority of terrestrial species, behavioral avoidance of desiccating conditions is the key to survival.

Arboreal Frogs Exceptions to the generalization that the amphibian integument provides no resistance to water loss occur in several genera of arboreal frogs. These so-called waterproof frogs can have integumentary resistances of the same order as terrestrial reptiles (300 s · cm^{-1}) and hence lose water by evaporation at very low rates even at high wind speed and low humidity. Other aboreal forms have low but measurable skin resistances (ca. 2 s · cm^{-1}) that significantly reduce rates of dehydration, and still others have intermediate integumentary resistance (10–100 s · cm^{-1}).

Loveridge (1970) first reported such a radical departure from the usual amphibian pattern. An arboreal frog of southern Africa, *Chiromantis xerampelina* (Rhacophoridae), is often exposed during the dry season, sometimes even sitting in the sun (Poynton 1964). Loveridge placed *C. xerampelina* in dry buckets covered with mesh and weighed them at intervals. For comparison, he exposed other species of frogs (*Xenopus laevis, Rana angolensis,* and *Bufo regularis*) and one species of lizard (*Chamaeleo dilepus*) to the same conditions. *Xenopus, Rana,* and *Bufo* quickly desiccated and died, whereas *C. xerampelina* survived well and lost mass at rates comparable to the lizards (fig. 6.2). Other members of the genus *Chiromantis* are also waterproof. *Chiromantis petersi* have very low rates of EWL (Drewes et al. 1977), as do *C. rufescens* (Withers, Hillman, and Drewes 1984).

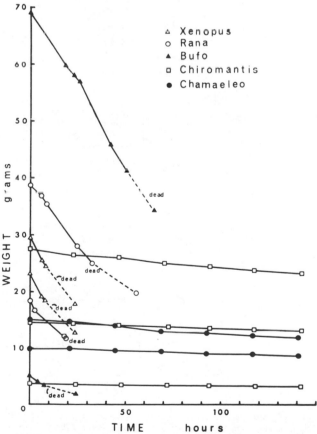

Fig. 6.2 Mass changes of frogs and lizards (*Chamaeleo*) kept without food in gauze-covered containers (25°C, 20 to 28% relative humidity). (Reprinted, by permission, from Loveridge 1970.)

Frogs of the South American genus *Phyllomedusa* (Hylidae) are also "waterproof." The rates of EWL for *P. sauvagei* are much lower than those for semiaquatic or terrestrial amphibians and are nearly as low as in the desert iguana, *Dipsosaurus dorsalis* (Shoemaker et al. 1972). Other members of the genus *Phyllomedusa* also exhibit very low rates of EWL, whereas members of the other genera in the hylid subfamily Phyllomedusinae have much higher rates (Shoemaker and McClanahan 1975).

Members of another African genus (*Hyperolius*: Hyperoliidae) exhibit low rates of water loss during the dry season and are more permeable in the rainy season. Loveridge (1976) found a twentyfold difference in EWL from wet season to dry season in *Hyperolius nasutus*. Withers, Louw, and Nicolson (1982) and Withers et al. (1982) confirmed low rates of EWL in *H. nasutus* and in three other species of *Hyperolius*. Geise and Linsenmair (1986) studied *H. viridiflavus* and found a thirtyfold difference in EWL between frogs kept under different moisture conditions. Two other species of *Hyperolius* have relatively high EWL (Withers, Hillman, and Drewes 1984). These same authors found similar diversity within the genera *Litoria* and *Hyla* (both Hylidae) in Australia. *Litoria gracilenta* and *Hyla kivuensis* have very low rates of EWL, whereas some congeners have much higher rates.

Several species of arboreal frogs (Hylidae except where noted) lose water at rates one-third to one-half those of typical amphibians. Wygoda (1984) compared water loss rates of seven species of arboreal hylids (*Hyla cinerea, H. crucifer, H. femoralis, H. gratiosa, H. triangulum, Osteopilus dominicensis, O. septentrionalis*) to those of eleven nonarboreal species in a wind tunnel system where mass loss was measured continuously (fig. 6.3). Mean area-specific water loss rates of nonarboreal species ranged from 25 to 31 mg · cm^{-2} · h^{-1}, whereas rates for arboreal species were 10 to 16 mg · cm^{-2} · h^{-1}. The difference in water loss rates reflects a much higher skin resistance in the arboreal species (1.4–2.7 s · cm^{-1}) compared to the nonarboreal species (0.05–0.07 s · cm^{-1}). In these studies, skin and boundary layer resistances were approximately equal in the arboreal species. Skin resistance in *Hyla cinerea* increases at low relative humidities (Wygoda 1988a) and results in enhanced heating and slow cooling (Wygoda 1988b, 1989b). Bentley and Yorio (1979b), also using a direct open flow system, found water loss in *Pachymedusa dacnicolor* to be one-half to one-third that of three nonarboreal species. Wygoda (1984) reached a similar conclusion for *P. dacnicolor,* as well as *Agalychnis annae* and *Rhacophorus leucomystax* (Rhacophoridae), after reanalyzing water loss rates from previous studies in terms of total resistance. Withers, Hillman, and Drewes (1984), using a direct open flow system, found total resistances of six arboreal species (*Hyla arenicolor, H. gratiosa, Agalychnis callidryas, Afrixalus fornasinii* (Hyperoliidae), *Afrixalus pygmaeus,* and *Afrixalus quadrivittatus*) to be two to three times higher than those of other anurans. However, total resistance in two other arboreal species (*Osteopilus septentrionalis* and *Litoria caerulea*) was as low as that of more typical anurans, possibly as a result of activity of the animals (Withers, Hillman, and Drewes 1984).

Litoria caerulea (Hylidae) does have a substantial resistance to cutaneous EWL of about 9 s · cm^{-1}, and a congener,

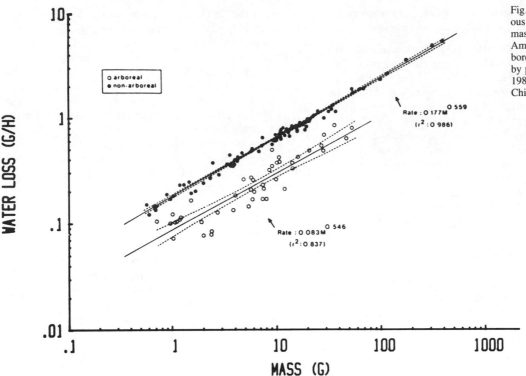

Fig. 6.3 Relation of cutaneous water loss rates to body mass for arboreal North American hylids and nonarboreal anurans. (Reprinted, by permission, from Wygoda 1984, © University of Chicago.)

L. chloris, has an even higher resistance (ca. 40 s · cm⁻¹) despite its restricted distribution in coastal rainforest (Buttemer 1990). Thus, arboreal frogs generally have some resistance to cutaneous evaporation, ranging from 2–3 s · cm⁻¹ in North American hylids to 200–300 s · cm⁻¹ in some African and South American treefrogs. Australian representatives of the genus *Litoria* have resistances ranging from 10 to 100 s · cm⁻¹ (fig. 6.4).

The mechanism by which waterproof arboreal frogs restrict EWL is well understood only for *Phyllomedusa* (Hylidae). Frogs of this genus possess a unique type of skin gland whose contents stain intensely with lipophilic dyes (Blaylock, Ruibal, and Platt-Aloia 1976). The glands are small but numerous (30/mm²). After activity, or if the animal is handled, *Phyllomedusa* exudes a waxy secretion and proceeds to wipe the entire body surface in a stereotyped fashion, using all four feet (Blaylock, Ruibal, and Platt-Aloia 1976). After the secretion dries, the skin surface is hydrophobic and has a shiny appearance. The lipid component of these secretions is heterogeneous but is predominantly wax ester with lesser amounts of free fatty acids and hydrocarbons (McClanahan, Stinner, and Shoemaker 1978). The fatty acid component of the wax is primarily oleic acid that is esterified with saturated long chain (28- to 38-carbon) alcohols.

The skins of *Chiromantis* and *Hyperolius* do not contain lipid glands, and the waterproofing mechanism is not clear. Both genera have well-developed stacked layers of iridophores that may impede water movement (Drewes et al. 1977; Kobelt and Linsenmair 1986). However, capillaries penetrate the iridophore layers, and several layers of living cells overlie them. In *Chiromantis*, as in other frogs without cocoons, the stratum corneum is only a single layer. Cross sections of this layer viewed by transmission electron microscopy reveal a

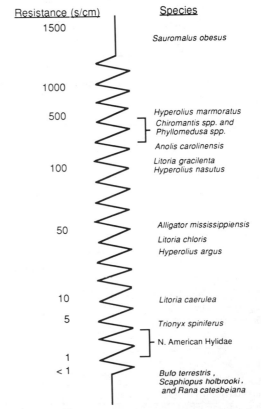

Fig. 6.4 Comparison of cutaneous resistance to evaporation for a variety of anurans and a few species of reptiles (*Trionyx, Alligator, Anolis, Sauromalus*). Scale is logarithmic. (Reprinted, by permission, from Buttemer 1990, © University of Chicago.)

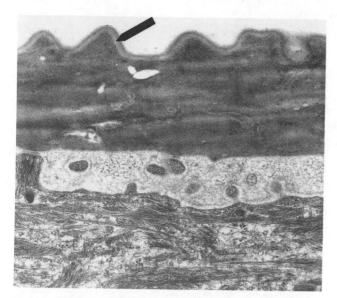

Fig. 6.5 Transmission electron micrograph of the outer portion of the dorsal skin of *Chiromantis xerampelina*. Only the light band underlying the outermost cell membrane (*arrow*) distinguishes this from comparable preparations of the ventral skin of *Chiromantis* or the skin of other frogs. (Courtesy of R. Ruibal.)

differentiated band approximately 0.2 μm thick underlying the outer cell membrane (fig. 6.5). This feature is not apparent in the ventral skin of *Chiromantis*, which is not waterproof, and is not seen in the dorsal skin of *Bufo*, *Rana*, or *Phyllomedusa* (R. Ruibal, pers. comm.). The chemical nature of this layer has not been determined but on morphological grounds seems likely to contribute to the high resistance of the skin to EWL. This resistance may be due not to a single barrier but to a series of resistances that sum to reduce EWL (Damstra 1986).

Dried mucus on the skin surface may contribute to the water loss barrier in some species. Wygoda (1988a) found that transient body temperature depressions occur in *Hyla cinerea* and attributed the depressions to the cooling effect of evaporation of water from mucus discharged onto the surface. These depressions are more frequent and intense at low than at high relative humidity, suggesting that skin resistance increases by thickening the layer of dried mucus. Dried mucus also may contribute to the waterproofing mechanism in some highly waterproof arboreal frogs (Geise and Linsenmair 1986). The waterproofing mechanism in *Hyla kivuensis* and *Chiromantis rufescens* may involve lipids, inasmuch as swabbing a patch of dorsal skin with chloroform-methanol increases EWL *in vivo* (Withers, Hillman, and Drewes 1984). However, lipids extracted from dorsal and ventral skin in *Chiromantis* or from skins of waterproof and permeable species do not differ. Similarly, no unusual aspects of cutaneous lipids account for reduced EWL in *Pachymedusa dacnicolor* (Bentley and Yorio 1979b).

Chiromantis, *Phyllomedusa*, and *Hyperolius* all inhabit semiarid regions where air temperature can exceed 40°C. In the absence of evaporative heat loss, these "waterproof" frogs would probably attain lethal body temperatures. However, under these conditions EWL increases so that evapo-

rative heat loss matches heat gain. *Phyllomedusa* and *Chiromantis* regulate body temperature precisely via controlled secretion—apparently from the mucous glands (Kaul and Shoemaker 1989; Shoemaker et al. 1987). *Hyperolius* may have a similar thermoregulatory mechanism (Geise and Linsenmair 1986), as does *Litoria chloris* and, to a lesser extent, *L. caerulea* (Buttemer 1990).

Cocoon-Forming Fossorial Amphibians Some burrowing amphibians reduce EWL by forming "cocoons" (see chapter 10). The term *cocoon* was applied in this context by Mayhew (1965), who observed spadefoot toads (*Scaphiopus couchii*: Pelobatidae) emerging from underground with fragments of skinlike material covering the back. However, *Scaphiopus* have not been observed to form an intact and functional cocoon in the sense that the term is now used. Lee and Mercer (1967) first described true cocoons in fossorial amphibians. They examined the ultrastructure of the cocoon of *Neobatrachus pictus* (Myobatrachidae) and also reported cocoon formation in three species of *Cyclorana* (Hylidae) and one species of *Limnodynastes* (Myobatrachidae). They characterized these cocoons as single layers of stratum corneum approximately 1 μm thick. It is now clear that functional cocoons comprise not one but many layers of stratum corneum, as described by McClanahan, Shoemaker, and Ruibal (1976) for South American ceratophryd frogs (Leptodactylidae). Further studies on *Neobatrachus* (P. C. Withers pers. comm.) and *Cyclorana* (van Beurden 1984) confirm this finding. Urodeles also form cocoons. Reno, Gehlbach, and Turner (1972) described a cocoon from estivating *Siren intermedia* (Sirenidae) that appears indistinguishable from the multiple layers of stratum corneum typical of anuran cocoons, although they concluded that the cocoon was formed wholly from mucus. Figure 6.6 shows a cocooned *Ceratophrys ornata*, a transmission electron micrograph of a cocoon cross section from the burrowing North American hylid *Pternohyla fodiens* (Ruibal and Hillman 1981), and a scanning electron micrograph of a cocoon from *Cyclorana*. Cocoons also occur in the African anurans *Leptopelis bocagei* (Hyperoliidae; Loveridge 1976) and *Pyxicephalus adspersus* (Ranidae; Loveridge and Crayé 1979) and in the North American hylid *Smilisca baudinii* (McDiarmid and Foster 1987). In all studies of cocoon-forming amphibians, the cocoon reduces EWL. McClanahan, Ruibal, and Shoemaker (1983) followed both EWL and cocoon thickness (number of layers) for *Lepidobatrachus llanensis* over time (fig. 6.7). At least for the first 1.5 months, the cocoon accumulates almost one layer per day, and each layer increases the cutaneous resistance to water loss by 3 s · cm⁻¹. Water losses after 1 month are less than 1 mg · g⁻¹ · h⁻¹ and presumably would be even lower in their normal subterranean environment with higher humidities and no air movement. Cocooned *Cyclorana platycephala* (van Beurden 1984) and *Pyxicephalus adspersus* (Loveridge and Crayé 1979) achieve similarly low EWL (ca. 0.5–1.0 mg · g⁻¹ · h⁻¹). Although the resistance of amphibian cocoons is most often measured in air, their main function is likely to be the prevention of water loss to dry soil (see below).

Frogs readily form cocoons in the laboratory in response to drying of the soil or gravel in which they have burrowed, and they also form cocoons in dry containers if left undis-

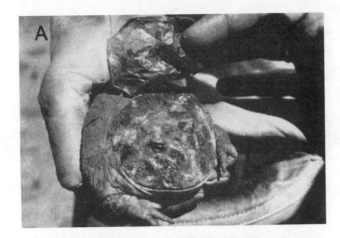

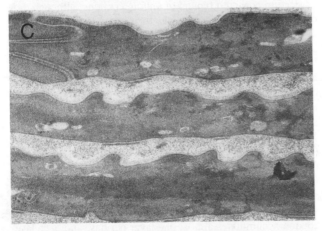

Fig. 6.6   Cocoons of fossorial amphibians. *A*, a freshly excavated *Ceratophrys ornata* with cocoon partially removed. (Reprinted, by permission, from McClanahan, Shoemaker, and Ruibal 1976.) *B*, scanning electron micrograph of a cocoon of *Cyclorana platycephala*, showing lamellar structure. (Courtesy of P. C. Withers.) *C*, transmission electron micrograph of a cross section of a cocoon of *Pternohyla fodiens*, showing only the outermost layers. (Courtesy of R. Ruibal.)

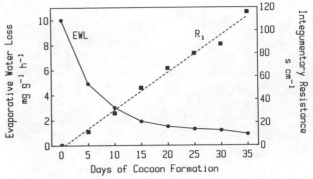

Fig. 6.7   Relationship between cocoon formation and evaporative water loss (●) and integumentary resistance (■) in *Lepidobatrachus llanensis*. (Modified from McClanahan, Ruibal, and Shoemaker 1983.)

the animals during the dry season. *Cyclorana platycephala* digs to 20–30 cm into moist soil near the base of trees or bushes, and forms a spherical chamber about twice the volume of the frog (van Beurden 1984). A cocooned specimen of *Ceratophrys ornata* was found at a depth of about 15 cm, encased in hard clay soil (McClanahan, Shoemaker, and Ruibal 1976). These few observations suggest that cocoon-forming amphibians need not find subterranean environments where soil water is available for most or all of the dry season, in contrast to forms such as spadefoot toads (see sections below on water uptake from soil and nitrogen excretion).

Water Uptake

Uptake from Soil   Soil provides a potential source of water for amphibians if the free energy of water in the soil is greater than that of an animal's body fluids. Conventionally the free energy of water is expressed as water potential, with the potential of pure water defined as zero (see chapter 4 for a detailed discussion). For soil, the primary determinant of water potential is the force with which the soil particle matrix holds the water molecules, termed the matrix or matric potential. The water potential of an animal is primarily determined by the osmotic concentration of the body fluids. Both the soil matrix and solutes reduce the free energy of water and hence the water potential. The energy gradient for water movement is from higher (less negative) water potential to lower water potential.

The ceramic plate extraction technique (Slatyer 1967) is useful in studies on soil moisture absorption by amphibians. In this technique, soil samples are saturated with water and placed on a ceramic plate, which is then sealed in a pressure vessel. Positive gas pressure (usually nitrogen) is applied to the vessel, and the water is forced from the soil, across the ceramic plate, and into a reservoir on the underside of the plate. This reservoir is connected to a tube on the outside of the pressure vessel so that one can determine when the forces retaining water in the soil have equilibrated with the gas pressure in the vessel. Soil samples that have been equilibrated are then removed and dried, and a plot of applied pressure versus the percentage of water content is made (fig. 6.8). This curve indicates the force with which various soils hold water at a given water content. This force can be expressed as atmospheres and has values ranging from zero when no pressure is applied to more negative values as more pressure is

turbed. The former situation probably reflects the natural circumstance because most of the cocoon-forming species are known to estivate below ground (see chapter 10). Most species possess well-developed metatarsal tubercles for digging, but some may use burrows constructed by other animals. However, relatively little is known of the natural history of

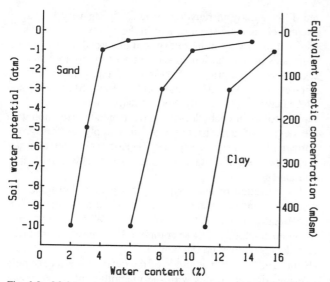

Fig. 6.8   Moisture tension for soils varying in composition. Higher proportions of clay shift the curve to the right, whereas larger particles (sand) shift the curve to the left. Scale on left shows water potential in atmospheres. Scale on right indicates osmotic concentrations of solutions of equivalent free energy of water. (Modified from Ruibal, Tevis, and Roig 1969.)

used to drive water out of the soil particle matrix. The osmotic concentration of an animal's body fluids (C) can be related to water potential (π) by the equation

$$(3) \qquad \pi = -CRT,$$

where

R = the gas constant
T = absolute temperature (°K)

A more recent technique employs the thermocouple psychrometer (Brown 1970). With this method, a thermocouple is placed in an airspace whose vapor pressure is in thermodynamic equilibrium with water molecules of a soil sample. A layer of pure water is condensed on the thermocouple, and the rate of evaporation of this water cools the thermocouple in inverse proportion to the vapor pressure of the soil. Drier soils will have a lower vapor pressure, and thus more cooling of the thermocouple junction will occur due to more rapid evaporation of the condensed water. The resulting change in current is then measured as a microvolt change in potential across a resistance. The thermocouple can be calibrated by placing it in an airspace equilibrated with solutions of known osmotic concentration, so that a potential change produced by a given soil sample can be equated directly to an osmotic concentration.

Amphibians can use soil moisture to replenish body water stores (Degani and Warburg 1980; Dole 1967; Lee 1968; Packer 1963). The lowest water potential at which water gain occurs is termed the *absorptive threshold*. The plethodontid salamander *Plenthodon cinereus* can obtain moisture from soils having a matric potential of −1 to −2 atm (Heatwole and Lim 1961). The absorptive threshold for numerous species of salamanders is about −2 atm (Spight 1967b; Spotila 1972). Xeric-adapted anurans can absorb water from soils of more negative water potential (Walker and Whitford 1970).

Scaphiopus couchii, S. multiplicatus (both Pelobatidae), and *Bufo cognatus* gain water from soil having a matric potential of −2.5 atm, while the mesic-adapted species *Hyla cinerea* (Hylidae) and *Rana pipiens* require matric potentials of −1.2 and −0.8 atm, respectively. The absorptive threshold for *Cyclorana platycephala* (Hylidae) is less than −3 atm (van Beurden 1984).

The osmolality of body fluids in hydrated amphibians is typically more than 200 mOsm (Bentley 1971a), which corresponds to a water potential of about −4.5 atm (eq. [3]). Thus for many species a large water potential gradient must exist for net soil moisture absorption. Hillyard (1976a) studied the gradient required for water uptake by placing isolated skin from *Scaphiopus couchii, B. cognatus* and *R. pipiens* between halves of a chamber, with the outer surface in contact with soil of known water potential and the inner surface at a known osmotic concentration. Inward water movement generally occurred across *S. couchii* and *B. cognatus* skin whenever a positive water potential gradient was present. With *R. pipiens* skin, however, water movement was often outward despite the presence of a water potential gradient favoring inward movement. In *S. couchii* and *B. cognatus* many more soil particles adhere to the surface of the skin than in *R. pipiens*. Since soil-bound water must move by capillarity to the surface of the skin, the surface topography of the skin of desert species may facilitate this process.

Two types of adaptations may enhance water uptake by amphibians from soil with relatively low (i.e., more negative) water potential. One is the establishment of intimate contact between the skin and soil, mentioned above. The other, apparent from equation (3), is the reduction of the animal's water potential by the accumulation of solutes. Ruibal, Tevis, and Roig (1969) estimated an absorptive threshold of −10 atm for burrowed *Scaphiopus* because they accumulate urea when burrowed in soils having very negative water potentials (see also McClanahan 1972; Shoemaker, McClanahan, and Ruibal 1969). Nevertheless, the uptake of moisture from desert soil requires that animals burrow to considerable depths, where the soil dries slowly. The relationship between soil water potential and water content is such that a small amount of soil drying in the range of body fluid water potentials results in a very large decrease in soil water potential (see fig. 6.8). The advantage of forming a cocoon to impede the outward movement of water in this situation is obvious.

Uptake from Water   Osmotic water fluxes in amphibians are typically measured as body mass changes, which include the mass of any urine produced over the test interval. The skin of amphibians behaves as a semipermeable membrane, and the osmotic flow of water is proportional to the osmotic (water potential) gradient between the bathing medium and the animal's body fluids (see also chapter 5). The proportionality "constant" is a measure of the ease with which water passes the barrier by osmosis and is termed the *hydraulic conductance* or *osmotic permeability* (see, e.g., Tracy 1976).

All amphibians examined to date take up water rapidly across the skin when in fresh water (see also chapter 5). For hydrated animals in steady state, cutaneous water influx is on the order of 500 ml · kg⁻¹ · day⁻¹ and varies with temperature, body size, and species (Shoemaker and Nagy 1977).

Large osmotic influxes burden the kidneys, which must produce an equivalent volume of dilute urine. Perhaps for this reason, osmotic influxes in aquatic amphibians tend to be lower than those found in terrestrial or semiterrestrial species. Water uptake is more rapid in two terrestrial *Bufo* species than in the aquatic *Xenopus laevis* (Ewer 1952b). Survival time in distilled water is greatest in aquatic anurans (*Rana* > *Hyla* > *Bufo*), and osmotic fluxes across isolated skin are inversely correlated with survival time (Schmid 1965). In a highly aquatic anuran genus (*Ascaphus*: Leiopelmatidae), osmotic permeability of the skin is only one-third that of *Bufo* (Mullen and Alvarado 1976). Numerous studies confirm this trend in both anurans and urodeles (see Alvarado 1979 and Bentley 1971a for reviews). The lowest rates of osmotic influx (ca. 100 ml · kg^{-1} · day^{-1}) are apparently in aquatic urodeles (Bentley 1973a). However, the aquatic newt *Notophthalmus viridescens* has a very high permeability when it returns to water following its terrestrial eft phase (P. S. Brown and S. C. Brown 1977).

Amphibians in general, and especially terrestrial and semiterrestrial anurans, can withstand large losses of body water (see below). Under these conditions, rehydration via cutaneous uptake from water can be extremely rapid. Although dehydration increases internal solute concentration, increases in osmotic influx are far greater than the increase in the water potential gradient, and hydraulic conductance can increase by an order of magnitude or more (see, e.g., Christensen 1975b).

Several studies have examined the correlation between rehydration rates and the degree of "terrestriality" among amphibians (primarily anurans). Ewer found *Bufo regularis* rehydrates much more rapidly than *X. laevis* and concluded that rapid rehydration was one "of the physiological adaptations of Anura to life on land" (1952b, 437). Thorson found that rehydration in *Rana pipiens* is more rapid than in the more aquatic *R. clamitans*, but both rehydrate much faster than a terrestrial spadefoot toad (*Scaphiopus hammondii*: Pelobatidae). Thorson concluded that "no general statement can be made that ready rehydration following desiccation is associated with terrestrialism in amphibians" (1955, 114). Bentley, Lee, and Main (1958) compared several species in two Australian genera from areas with widely differing numbers of wet days per year. Aridity of habitat and rehydration rate are correlated in one myobatrachid genus (*Neobatrachus*) but not in another (*Heleioporus*). *Heleioporus* burrows deeply in friable soil to seek moisture, whereas *Neobatrachus* burrows are shallow and in dry clay soil. As Bentley, Lee, and Main (1958, 683) state, "Rate of water uptake need not correlate with aridity of the environment if a behavior pattern is present by which risk of serious desiccation is avoided." In fact the use of deeply burrowing animals such as *Scaphiopus* to represent the extreme in aridity of habitat generally seems to confuse the issue (e.g., Claussen 1969). Hillyard (1975) has shown that dehydrated *Scaphiopus* do not take up water rapidly except immediately following emergence. The microhabitat is apparently of great importance to rates of rehydration. Eleven anuran species in Borneo have a wide range of rehydration rates despite the prevailing mesic conditions (Shoemaker and McClanahan 1980). Two terrestrial *Bufo* species and three species of arboreal *Rhacophorus* (Rhacophoridae) rehydrate rapidly. The six species of *Rana* studied differ greatly in rehydration rates, being very low in an exclusively aquatic species, and highest in two arboreal species and one living in more exposed disturbed areas. In fact, high rates of rehydration appear to occur in arboreal anurans regardless of the aridity of the climate (see Claussen 1969; Drewes et al. 1977; Main and Bentley 1964; Shoemaker and McClanahan 1975, 1980). Some salamanders also rehydrate rapidly following dehydration, and a general correlation with the degree of terrestriality may also apply in this group (Brown, Hastings, and Frye 1977). However, rates of water uptake per unit of surface area are considerably less than in anurans.

The secretion of neurohypophyseal peptide hormones increases cutaneous water uptake in dehydrated amphibians (see Bentley 1971a, 1974 for reviews). When injected into hydrated amphibians, these compounds increase water uptake and depress urine production, leading to rapid mass gain (Brunn 1921). The magnitude of the cutaneous effect of peptide injection correlates with the magnitude of the response to dehydration (Cree 1988a; Brown and Brown 1980; Brown, Hastings, and Frye 1977; Ewer 1952b; Hillyard 1975, 1976b). Dehydrated amphibians deplete stores of neurosecretory material in the posterior pituitary (Jørgensen, Wingstrand, and Rosenkilde 1956; Levinsky and Sawyer 1953) and have high levels of circulating arginine vasotocin (AVT), the primary neurohypophyseal peptide in amphibians (Nouwen and Kühn 1983; Pang 1977). However, increased cutaneous uptake is apparently not due entirely to the action of AVT for several reasons. Injections of neurohypophyseal peptides generally do not stimulate as great a response as does dehydration (Jørgensen and Rosenkilde 1956), section of the neurohypophyseal stalk does not affect the response (Jørgensen, Wingstrand, and Rosenkilde 1956), and even lesioning of the hypothalamic nuclei containing the neurosecretory cell bodies does not completely abolish the response (Bakker and Bradshaw 1977; Jørgensen, Rosenkilde, and Wingstrand 1969; Shoemaker and Waring 1968).

The nervous system has influences on cutaneous water uptake that appear to be independent of the neurohypophysis. Lesions in the midbrain greatly augment water uptake (Adolph 1934; Segura et al. 1982). Pharmacological studies using *Bufo arenarum* suggest that an α-adrenergic mechanism reduces water uptake when activated, and that α-adrenergic blockade enhances water uptake (Segura, Bandsholm, and Bronstein 1982). β-adrenergic agonists increase the permeability of anuran skin (Bastide and Jard 1968; Elliott 1968; Hillyard 1979), and their role in the cutaneous response to dehydration has recently been investigated. Propranolol, a β-adrenergic antagonist, blocks more than 60% of the response to dehydration, whereas a β-adrenergic agonist, isoproterenol, increases cutaneous uptake in hydrated toads (*B. cognatus*) by a similar amount (Yokota and Hillman 1984). Yokota and Hillman conclude that the effects of AVT and β-adrenergic agonists are independent and additive and also observed that isoproterenol, but not AVT, caused vasodilation in the ventral skin. The effects of AVT and β-adrenergic agonists are also independent and additive in their stimulatory effects on osmotic flux across isolated skin of *B. marinus* (DeSousa and Grosso 1982). Thus current evidence suggests that a β-adrenergic mechanism contributes importantly to high rates of water uptake in dehydrated anurans, and that changes in both the permeability and perfusion of the skin are involved.

Rapid water uptake ensues even if dehydrated anurans are placed in a very shallow layer of water (see, e.g., van Berkum et al. 1982) and occurs primarily through the pelvic region of the ventral skin. This region of the skin is heavily vascularized and typically thinner than the dorsal skin. Called the "seat patch" or "pelvic patch," it accounts for only 10% of the surface area but 70% of the water uptake in dehydrated *B. punctatus* (McClanahan and Baldwin 1969). The hydraulic conductance of pelvic skin is six times that of pectoral skin in dehydrated *B. marinus* (Parsons and Mobin 1989), and only pelvic skin shows dramatic increases in hydraulic conductance when treated with AVT (Bentley and Main 1972; Cree 1988b; Yorio and Bentley 1977). Christensen (1974a) found high rates of water uptake in ventral skin of *Bufo* and *Rana* but not *Xenopus*, and noted a correlation between uptake and the vascularization of the skin. Roth (1973) provides a detailed anatomical analysis of the vascular anatomy of the pelvic integument in species from various habitats. In the absence of rapid circulation, high rates of cutaneous water flux will reduce the water potential gradient and thus tend to negate the increased hydraulic conductance (Christensen 1974b, 1975a). Exchange of tritiated water across the skin of *Rana* species varies directly with blood flow (Mahany and Parsons 1978) but not with increased osmotic flux stimulated by AVT (Parsons et al. 1990). Clearly both rapid circulation and high permeability are necessary to maintain rapid osmotic uptake. Thus the relative roles of AVT and of epinephrine on skin permeability and circulation in promoting rapid rehydration merit further examination.

Uptake from the Urinary Bladder The amphibian urinary bladder, like the skin, is a widely used *in vitro* preparation for studies of sodium transport mechanisms and control of epithelial water permeability (see Bentley 1966b and chapter 5). In the living amphibian these properties of the bladder have important osmoregulatory consequences. The bladder forms during development as a ventral out-pouching of the cloaca and is thin, well vascularized, and highly distensible. A single layered epithelium overlies a thin basement layer of connective tissue. Smooth muscle fibers with cholinergic innervation are in the connective tissue layer (see Bentley 1966b; Peachey and Rasmussen 1961). In amphibians the ureters empty into the cloaca, and urine then flows into the bladder.

Because the bladder is highly distensible, its capacity is difficult to define. However, bladder volumes compiled from the literature by Bentley (1966b) are illustrative. Terrestrial and arboreal anurans (e.g., *Bufo*, *Neobatrachus*, *Cyclorana*, *Hyla*) frequently hold 25 to 50% of their standard mass (bladder empty) as dilute urine in the bladder. Bladders of terrestrial urodeles (e.g., *Salamandra* [Salamandridae] and *Ambystoma* [Ambystomatidae]) may contain 20 to 34% of standard mass. Highly aquatic anurans (e.g., *Xenopus*) and urodeles (e.g., *Triturus* [Salamandridae] and *Necturus* [Proteidae]) have very small bladder capacities (1 to 5% of standard mass). Bladder contents of anurans excavated from burrows can considerably exceed those observed in the labo-

ratory, amounting to more than 100% of standard mass in *B. cognatus* (Shoemaker, McClanahan, and Ruibal 1969) and 130% of standard mass in the Australian "water-holding" hylid frog *Cyclorana platycephala* (van Beurden 1984). This stored fluid serves as an important water reserve, especially in animals experiencing high rates of EWL or prolonged periods when water is unavailable.

Water in urine can offset EWLs (e.g., Ruibal 1962; Shoemaker 1964a). Toads that become dehydrated with urine in the bladder maintain constant plasma solute concentrations until evaporative losses exceed bladder reserves. Spadefoot toads (*Scaphiopus couchii*: Pelobatidae) also reabsorb water from the bladder but apparently do not regulate plasma concentrations as precisely as do *Bufo* species (McClanahan 1967). Even frogs with low rates of evaporation, such as the hylid *Phyllomedusa sauvagei*, store large volumes of dilute urine and reabsorb it to maintain plasma osmolality (Shoemaker and Bickler 1979). The urodele *Ambystoma tigrinum* also uses bladder stores (Alvarado 1972), and this ability is probably present in all amphibians with bladders of significant volume. An interesting and open question is whether gross water reabsorption from the bladder balances evaporative loss, or whether gross uptake exceeds loss, with the excess uptake returned to the bladder via the kidneys. AVT regulates the water permeability of the bladder as it does in the skin and also participates in the control of urine production by the kidneys (see below and chapter 5).

The adaptive value of a large bladder reserve is readily apparent. Terrestrial amphibians can tolerate the loss of body water (exclusive of bladder reserves) equivalent to about 30 to 40% of body mass. A bladder store of this same magnitude will double the survival time in a desiccating environment. The ability of the urinary bladder to reabsorb sodium may also play a significant role in water conservation (Middler, Kleeman, and Edwards 1968c). As water is withdrawn from the bladder, urinary sodium concentration does not rise (Shoemaker 1964b). Active transport of salts would permit the animal to reclaim virtually all of the bladder fluid even if it were to become isoosmotic with plasma. AVT also stimulates active sodium uptake from the bladder (Bentley 1966b). Neurohypophyseal hormones enhance movement of urea across the urinary bladder in anurans (Ackrill et al. 1970; Leaf 1967). Urea reabsorption from the bladder is important for urea accumulation in *Rana cancrivora* (Chew, Elliott, and Wong 1972). Urea analogues, but not metabolic inhibitors, reduce urea movement across the bladder of *Bufo viridis*, implying passive facilitated diffusion (Shpun and Katz 1988).

Drinking Amphibians typically do not drink but instead obtain water through the ventral skin, sometimes at high rates (see above). Frogs and salamanders dehydrated by exposure to seawater may drink, but still die of dehydration (Bentley and Schmidt-Nielsen 1971; Licht, Feder, and Bledsoe 1975). In dehydrated *Bufo marinus*, *Rana catesbeiana*, and *Xenopus laevis*, oral uptake is incidental and unimportant in rehydration (Bentley and Yorio 1979a). However, drinking may play a significant role in the water economy of the "waterproof" frog *Phyllomedusa sauvagei*. Although these animals can take up water rapidly when the ventral skin is immersed in water (Shoemaker and McClanahan 1975), they can also gain considerable water by drinking rainwater that strikes the head, either directly or by dripping from leaves (McClanahan and Shoemaker 1987). They respond to dripping water by pointing the snout upward and initiating vigorous gular "pumping" motions. Uptake by drinking can be substantial (over 20% of standard mass per hour) and would permit these arboreal animals to rehydrate without leaving the trees in search of standing water.

Behavior and Water Balance

Evaporative Water Loss   For most amphibians on land, control of EWL is primarily a matter of behavior and depends on the availability of humid and protected microhabitats. Amphibians often are both secretive and nocturnal, and little is known of their locations and activities for most of the time. The greatest gap in our understanding of the water economies of free-living amphibians derives from this fact.

An indirect approach to the assessment of interactions of water balance and behavior is to use physical and physiological data to calculate limits to behavior. Feder (1983b) used this approach to estimate the maximum time that plethodontid salamanders could forage under various combinations of relative humidity, body size, temperature, and wind speed. He assumed that the animals could forage until they lost 10% of body mass by evaporation, and found that possible foraging times ranged from almost a day for a 3-g animal in still air of high relative humidity and low temperature, to only about 10 min for a 1-g animal in moving air of moderate temperature and relative humidity (fig. 6.9). However, laboratory trials indicate that these salamanders cease foraging and retreat to water long before they approach levels of dehydration that are demonstrably deleterious (Feder and Londos 1984).

While anecdotal evidence is ample that the hydric environment dictates amphibian behavior, field studies are rare. In terrestrial salamanders, moisture conditions restrict foraging (see, e.g., Cunningham 1960; Keen 1979; Spotila 1972).

Plethodon cinereus (Plethodontidae) forage on plants only on rainy nights, forage in the leaf litter following heavy rains, are found under large objects after brief dry periods, and retreat to underground burrows when soil beneath rocks and logs dries (Jaeger 1978, 1980b). For a Puerto Rican frog, *Eleutherodactylus coqui* (Leptodactylidae), behavior and water loss are related even when humidity is high (Pough et al. 1983). In the absence of a wet substrate (leaves), animals remain in a water-conserving posture that minimizes surface exposure and avoid the exposed posture associated with calling (fig. 6.10). However, these frogs feed more on dry nights, perhaps because they are calling less. Emergence in *Leiopelma archeyi* (Leiopelmatidae) is strongly dependent on moisture conditions, and these frogs leave their daytime retreats on the forest floor only when relative humidity exceeds 87%, usually in association with recent rainfall and wet vegetation (Cree 1989). Dobkin, Gettinger, and O'Connor (1989) used radiotelemetry to follow *Bufo marinus*, studied wet plaster models to assess water loss rates in various microhabitats, and found retreat site selection and reduced activity critical in preventing desiccation during dry periods.

Water Uptake from Damp Substrates   Amphibians can locate and use moisture at the soil surface or on wet vegetation or rocks. *Rana pipiens* use morning dew on dead grass (Dole 1967), and *Leiopelma archeyi* can rehydrate while sitting on wet leaves (Cree 1989). *Bufo woodhousii* emerge from burrows in the early evening and walk over dry sand to the wet sand along a shoreline (Stille 1951). Tracks indicate the toads do not lower their pelvic skin to the substrate until they near the shore. On moist substrates frogs exhibit a "water absorption response," in which they splay the hind legs and press the ventral surface of the hind legs and abdomen to the substrate (Stille 1958; fig. 6.11). If the moist surface is not porous (leaves, stones) frogs continually shift position as if wiping up the water. Angiotensin II stimulates the water ab-

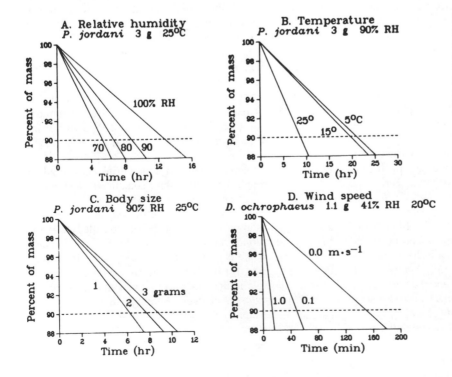

Fig. 6.9   Effect of (*A*) relative humidity, (*B*) temperature, (*C*) body size, and (*D*) wind speed on water loss and foraging time for plethodontid salamanders. The intersection of the plotted lines with the horizontal broken lines yields the time required for a salamander to lose 10% of its body mass, which may approximate the maximum duration of foraging. (Reprinted, by permission, from Feder 1983.)

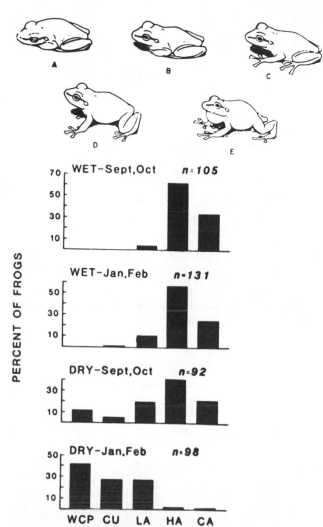

sorption response in *B. punctatus,* while toads pretreated with the competitive inhibitor saralasin behave like control animals (Hoff and Hillyard 1991). Thus regulation of behavior related to cutaneous water uptake in amphibians may resemble the control of drinking in other tetrapods.

Stille (1951) suggested that toads might be able to detect soil moisture levels with their feet and initiate the water absorption response accordingly. Desert toads, *B. punctatus,* dehydrated by as little as 1% of their standard mass show this behavior, and hydrated animals do not (Brekke, Hillyard, and Winokur 1991). On tissue paper wetted with urea solutions having concentrations of 100, 250, and 500 mM urea, dehydrated toads progressively decrease water absorption behavior. When toads' feet are covered, time spent on the 500 mM substrate increases significantly. Thus, terrestrial amphibians appear to detect highly negative water potentials, which might otherwise result in a loss of water (i.e., the "critical level" of Heatwole and Lim 1961). Pough et al. (1983) artificially moistened leaves on which frogs rested on dry nights. When leaves were moistened with distilled water, animals assumed more exposed postures, but when a carbowax solution with a low water potential was used, the frogs behaved like the untreated controls.

Bufonid toads have morphological specializations that may facilitate uptake from moist substrates. Epidermal channels, particularly in the posterior ventral skin, conduct water from the substrate to other parts of the skin (Christensen 1974a; Lillywhite and Licht 1974). Winokur and Hillyard (1985)

Fig. 6.10 *Top,* typical postures of coquís (*Eleutherodactylus coqui*) resting on leaves at night. *A,* water conserving; *B,* chin up; *C,* low alert; *D,* high alert; *E,* calling. *Bottom,* histograms indicate modal postures of coquís on nights when leaves were wet or dry in summer (September to October) and winter (January to February). *WCP,* water-conserving posture; *CU,* chin up; *LA,* low alert; *HA,* high alert; *CA,* calling. (Reprinted, by permission, from Pough et al. 1983.)

Fig. 6.11 *Hyla versicolor* in the water-conserving posture on a dry substrate (*left*) and showing the water absorption response on a wet substrate (right). (Reprinted, by permission, from Stille 1958.)

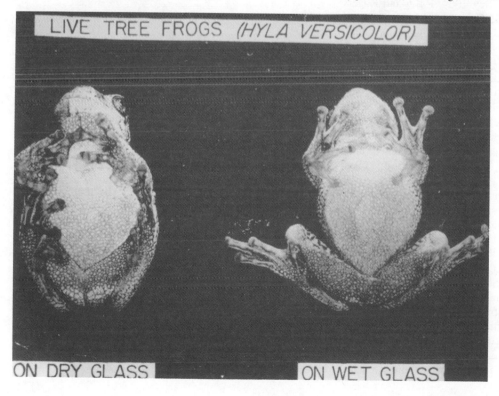

have reexamined the cutaneous attachments of the gracilis minor and an unnamed muscle that fan out across the posterior ventral skin. Electrical stimulation of these muscles produces movements of the skin that could enhance substrate contact and facilitate water absorption. Noble (1922) described these attachments in several bufonids and noted that they were more extensive in fossorial forms, although no consistent taxonomic relationship could be established.

TOLERANCE TO DEHYDRATION

When water loss exceeds water gain and bladder reserves of water are exhausted, continued survival of an amphibian on land depends upon its tolerance to dehydration. This tolerance is typically defined as the fraction of body water lost at the point that the animal loses the ability to right itself (critical activity point). Interspecific differences in dehydration tolerance are readily apparent, but other important sources of variability also determine the dehydration tolerance of a species. First, populations within a species can differ in dehydration tolerance (Ralin and Rogers 1972). Second, the rate of dehydration can influence dehydration tolerance; high rates of dehydration significantly depress estimates of a species' dehydration tolerance (see Thorson 1955). Third, dehydration tolerance characteristically declines as individuals of a species grow (Thorson 1955). Fourth, temperature can influence dehydration tolerance, with lower tolerance at both low and high temperatures (Thorson 1955).

Dehydrational stress appears to have been an important selective factor in the colonization of terrestrial environments by amphibians, as is emphasized by the positive correlation of species' dehydration tolerance and their degree of terrestriality (Alvarado 1972; Bentley, Lee, and Main 1958; Claussen 1973; Farrell and MacMahon 1969; Hillman 1980b; Krakauer 1970; Littleford, Keller, and Phillips 1947; McClanahan 1967; Main and Bentley 1964; Ralin and Rogers 1972; Ray 1958; Schmid 1965; Thorson 1955; Thorson and Svihla 1943). The combined data of these studies are illustrated in figure 6.12. Conclusions from this summary are (1) anurans are more tolerant of dehydration than urodeles, (2) dehydration tolerance is positively correlated with degree of terrestriality, and (3) tolerance is not necessarily phylogenetically conservative, as families having wide ecologic distributions also have wide ranges of dehydration tolerance.

Although species differences in dehydration tolerance and the striking tolerance to dehydration relative to other vertebrates are well known, the physiological bases for this tolerance are not well understood. The physiological processes that fail in dehydrational death may indicate the mechanisms extending tolerance in more resistant forms.

The water lost during dehydration comes from three sources: cells, plasma, and nonvascular extracellular fluid. One consequence of water loss is that the concentration of solutes in the body increases (Alvarado 1972; Degani and Warburg 1984; Hillman 1978b, 1982b; Shoemaker 1964a). This hyperosmotic stress will influence the function of all organ systems. Because some water is lost from plasma (Hillman 1978b; Hillman, Zygmunt, and Baustian 1987; Shoemaker 1964b), the cardiovascular system must deal with a hypovolemic stress. A complicating feature of this stress on the cardiovascular system is that the cellular components of blood are not lost

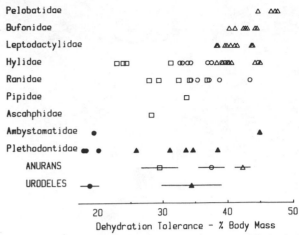

Fig. 6.12 Dehydration tolerance for amphibian species differing in degree of terrestriality. *Squares*, aquatic; *circles*, semiterrestrial; *triangles*, primarily terrestrial. Anurans are represented by *open symbols*, urodeles by *filled symbols*. Horizontal lines are 95% confidence intervals for means of all species of anurans and all species of urodeles of a particular degree of terrestriality. See text for sources.

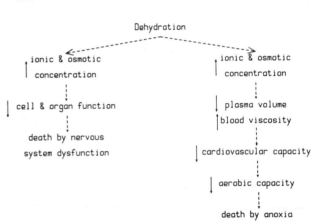

Fig. 6.13 Summary of physiological changes in amphibians resulting from dehydration.

with plasma; hence the hematocrit increases with dehydration (Hillman 1978b, 1980b; Hillman, Zygmunt, and Baustian 1987). Blood viscosity is exponentially related to hematocrit (Weathers 1976b). Consequently, the cardiovascular system must deal with hyperviscosity as well as hypovolemia.

Dehydrational death may result from osmo-ionic debilitation and/or cardiovascular collapse. The first implies an osmotic or ionic concentration limit that, when exceeded, debilitates systemic function. The second entails combined hyperosmolality, hypovolemia, and hyperviscosity, compromising cardiovascular function (fig. 6.13).

Correlations between dehydration tolerance and initial water content, initial plasma sodium concentration, and sodium tolerance sometimes suggest osmo-ionic debilitation. Initial water content has a low interspecific and intraspecific variance and does not explain interspecific differences in dehydration tolerance (Ralin and Rogers 1972; Schmid 1965; Thorson 1955; Thorson and Svihla 1943), but is positively correlated with dehydration tolerance within species (Ralin and Rogers 1972; Thorson 1955). Initial plasma sodium concentration is not correlated with interspecific differences in dehydration tolerance (Hillman 1980b), indicating that starting dehydration at a lower sodium concentration does not increase the amount of water loss that can be tolerated. However, interspecific differences in tolerance to sodium chloride loading correspond to differences in dehydration tolerance (Hillman 1978a, 1980b). The increases in plasma sodium concentration tolerated by amphibians (100 to 200 mM) are remarkable when compared to mammals, in which 20 to 40 mM increases are fatal (see Arieff, Guisado, and Lazarowitz 1977).

That cardiovascular failure contributes to dehydrational death is indicated by a precipitous decline in arterial pressure when tolerance limits are approached in *Bufo marinus* (Shoemaker 1964b) and *Scaphiopus couchii* (Pelobatidae; McClanahan 1967). Recent work has extended these observations to measurements of maximal blood flow in arteries during exercise as an animal dehydrates, to quantify how cardiovascular capacity declines during dehydration (Hillman 1987). Blood flow measurements are especially relevant because they integrate blood pressure and vascular resistance. Dehydration-tolerant *Bufo marinus* maintain greater flow than *Rana catesbeiana* under equivalent dehydrational stress because of *Bufo*'s greater ability to compensate for volume depletion, to maintain plasma volume by mobilizing extravascular reserves, and to delay the increase in hematocrit during dehydration (Hillman and Withers 1988; Hillman et al. 1985; Hillman, Zygmunt, and Baustian 1987). Whether this ability is a consequence of greater availability of interstitial fluid reserves or differential capacity to mobilize these reserves to the vascular space (Middler, Kleeman, and Edwards 1968b) is not clear. The principal cardiovascular effect of these treatments is decreased stroke volume, although heart rate also decreases in response to hyperosmolality as it does during dehydration (Hillman 1978a, 1987).

The decline in cardiovascular capacity could cause dehydrational death through an inability to support resting aerobic metabolism, forcing the animal to meet resting metabolic demands anaerobically (Hillman 1978a). Observations consistent with this are a decline in maximal aerobic capacity that intersects the resting rate of oxygen consumption at dehydrational tolerance limits (Gatten 1987; Hillman 1978a, 1987; Pough et al. 1983) and a parallel decline in aerobic and cardiovascular capacity during dehydration (Hillman 1987). Jumping performance in *Eleutherodactylus* (Anura: Leptodactylidae) is not impaired by dehydration to 75% of standard mass, but declines precipitously as the lethal limit is approached (Beauchat, Pough, and Stewart 1984).

Apparently two mechanisms are necessary to extend dehydration tolerance in amphibians: cardiovascular specialization and systemic tolerance of hyperosmolality (fig. 6.13). The principal cardiovascular adaptation appears to be a differential ability to maintain plasma volume. The fundamental adaptations to hyperosmolality are not known.

KIDNEY FUNCTION

In general, the renal excretory capacities of aquatic and terrestrial amphibians do not differ markedly (Deyrup 1964; Shoemaker and Nagy 1977; see also chapter 5). All amphibians so far examined can produce urine at rates of about 500 $ml \cdot kg^{-1} \cdot day^{-1}$ when in water and thus balance the high rates of cutaneous water influx (see above). Similarly, both aquatic and terrestrial forms can produce urine that is very dilute (<10 mM sodium) and thus conserve electrolytes while excreting excess water. Out of water, even in the absence of significant water loss, urine production declines rapidly, and in both aquatic and terrestrial forms urine production typically ceases. Thus water conservation takes precedence over renal excretion, and if water deprivation is prolonged, nitrogen wastes accumulate in the body fluids (see section on nitrogen excretion below). Frogs that excrete uric acid are exceptional in this regard and are discussed separately at the end of this section.

The rate of plasma filtration at the glomeruli (GFR), subsequent reabsorption of water and solutes in the proximal and distal tubules, and the addition of solutes by tubular secretion determine the volume and composition of the ureteral urine. In addition, the bladder may further modify the urine, primarily through reabsorption of water and salts. These processes are discussed below with particular reference to terrestrial existence in amphibians.

Glomerular Filtration Rate

Amphibians exhibit profound changes in GFR that are related to their state of water balance and rate of urine production (see Yokota, Benyajati, and Dantzler 1985 for review). Schmidt-Nielsen and Forster (1954) demonstrated a twenty-fold decline in GFR in moderately dehydrated *Rana clamitans* and corresponding changes in urine production. In *Bufo marinus* removed from water, both GFR and urine production decline within an hour, and most animals become completely anuric by 8 to 10 h (fig. 6.14; Tufts and Toews 1986). *B. marinus* reduce GFR and urine flow within 30 min of removal from water; by 2 h GFR is about 50% of control, whereas urine production is 25% of control (Bakker and Bradshaw 1977). *B. boreas* react similarly (Shoemaker and Bickler 1979). GFR in water is 63 $ml \cdot kg^{-1} \cdot h^{-1}$, and during the first 12 h out of water averages only 1.8 $ml \cdot kg^{-1} \cdot h^{-1}$. In these studies, toads were in moist air and hence did not lose water by evaporation. Thus, if dehydration is the cue for renal water conservation, the loss of only a very small fraction of body water must somehow be detected. Tufts and Toews (1986) found no change in plasma osmolality, and postulate that small changes in extracellular fluid volume due to urine production and blood sampling provide the stimulus for the response. Petriella et al. (1989) observed a very rapid reduction in urine production when toads (*Bufo arenarum*) are exposed to isoosmotic or hyperosmotic solutions even before any changes in plasma concentration could be detected. Because the response is both rapid and inhibited by guanethidine, they propose the existence of cutaneous osmotic sensors involving an adrenergic component. In any event, glomerular filtration probably ceases altogether in most amphibians out of water, and significant desiccation is not required for the response.

Postglomerular Reabsorption

When amphibians are in fresh water, half or less of the filtered water is reabsorbed (Shoemaker and Nagy 1977), and

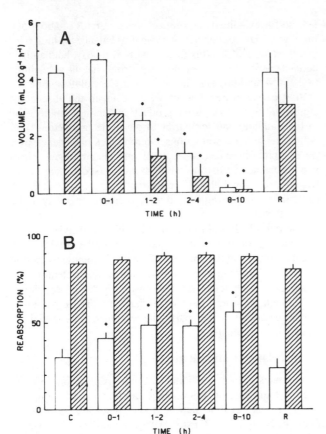

Fig. 6.14 Effect of removal from water on renal function in *Bufo marinus*. *A*, time course of changes in GFR (open) and ureterial urine flow rate (shaded). *B*, time course of changes in fractional reabsorption of water (open) and solutes (shaded). Values return to control levels (C) following rehydration (R). (Reprinted by permission, from Tufts and Toews 1986.)

fractional water reabsorption is especially low in urodeles (Kirschner et al. 1971; Stiffler and Alvarado 1974). Removal from water increases fractional reabsorption of water. For example, in *Bufo boreas* out of water for 12 h, sampling of bladder urine indicated 94% of the filtrate is reabsorbed (Shoemaker and Bickler 1979). Other studies in which bladder urine was analyzed show that increased water reabsorption makes a large contribution to the antidiuretic response in anurans (Bakker and Bradshaw 1977; Schmidt-Nielsen and Forster 1954). Tufts and Toews (1986) collected ureteral urine from *Bufo marinus*. Fractional reabsorption of water increased with water deprivation, but only to 60% in toads that were nearly anuric (fig. 6.14). Thus, reabsorption of water from the bladder apparently contributes significantly to the initial antidiuretic response to water deprivation.

For amphibians in water, fractional reabsorption of total solutes is high (ca. 90%). This value does not change appreciably as GFR and urine flow decline in animals removed from water. Moreover, bypassing the bladder has no effect on total solute clearance during antidiuresis (Bakker and Bradshaw 1977; Tufts and Toews 1986). When only sodium and chloride are considered, reabsorption may be nearly complete (95–99%), and these fractions do not change with water deprivation (Bakker and Bradshaw 1977; Garland and Henderson 1975; Shoemaker and Bickler 1979). However, the urinary bladder may participate in the final stages of urine dilution (salt reabsorption) when amphibians are in fresh water (Middler, Kleeman, and Edwards 1968c).

Uricotelic Frogs

Nearly all amphibians excrete nitrogen wastes in soluble form as ammonia or urea (see below). For these animals, excretion of nitrogen wastes requires considerable water because the kidneys of amphibians cannot produce urine that is hyperosmotic to plasma. Representatives of two of the genera of "waterproof" frogs discussed above (*Chiromantis* and *Phyllomedusa*) excrete nitrogen primarily as precipitated uric acid (Loveridge 1970; Shoemaker et al. 1972). Unlike other amphibians, these uricotelic frogs continue to produce urine and excrete nitrogen wastes when they are kept out of water (Drewes et al. 1977; Shoemaker and McClanahan 1975). In *Phyllomedusa sauvagei* deprived of water, GFR is 30 ml · kg^{-1} · h^{-1} even after 1 month. Rates of urine production are low (<2 ml · kg^{-1} · h^{-1}) even when the animals are handled frequently. When the animals are left undisturbed, urine accumulates in the bladder at only one-tenth this rate. Urine-to-plasma ratios of inulin in ureteral urine are about 10 and range from 30 to 100 in bladder urine. Thus the kidney tubules can reabsorb at least 90% of the filtered water, and the urinary bladder accounts for the final reabsorption. The kidney tubules of *P. sauvagei* actively secrete uric acid; renal clearances of this compound are far in excess of inulin clearance. Urate clearance is similar to that for para-aminohippuric acid and thus is probably about the same as renal plasma flow. Continued excretion of nitrogen of *P. sauvagei* in the absence of water uptake accompanies significant excretion of electrolytes, both in solution in the urine and coprecipitated with urate, but little expenditure of water (Shoemaker and Bickler 1979).

Control of the Antidiuretic Response

In amphibians out of water, reduction or cessation of urine production is essential to conserve water. As noted above, this response appears in all amphibians examined to date and occurs even in the absence of significant dehydration or elevation of plasma osmolality. This antidiuretic response is mediated via neurohypophyseal peptides. Brunn (1921) first demonstrated that mammalian neurohypophyseal extracts reduce urine production of frogs maintained in water. The homologous molecule in the amphibian neurohypophysis is AVT, and this exerts a strong antidiuretic effect in amphibians (reviewed by Bentley 1974; Pang 1977; Pang, Uchiyama, and Sawyer 1982; Sawyer and Pang 1975).

AVT can exert its antidiuretic effect in two ways. The first, which applies to both anurans and urodeles, is by reduction of GFR. Visual observations (Richards and Schmidt 1925) and changes in the vascular resistance of arterially perfused kidneys (Pang, Galli-Gallardo, Collie, and Sawyer 1980) indicate that the glomerular effect is due to vasoconstriction of the afferent glomerular arterioles, and that these vessels are much more sensitive to the action of AVT than are peripheral arterioles. In addition, at least in anurans, AVT increases the reabsorption of water in the renal tubules (Sawyer 1957; reviewed by Bentley 1974). Thus AVT can mimic the effects of

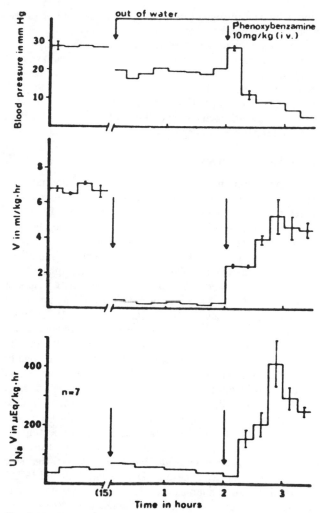

Fig. 6.15 Effect of phenoxybenzamine, an α-adrenergic antagonist, on blood pressure, urine production, and sodium excretion in dehydrated frogs (*Rana catesbeiana*). (Reprinted, by permission, from R. Gallardo, P. K. T. Pang, and W. H. Sawyer, Neural influences on bullfrog renal functions, *Proceedings of the Socitey for Experimental Biology and Medicine* 165:233–240, 1980, © by Society for Experimental Biology and Medicine.)

water deprivation on the function of amphibian kidneys in terms both of the overall effect (reduced urine production) and of the individual components (glomerular and tubular) of the antidiuretic response.

However, factors other than AVT probably participate in the antidiuretic response. Lesions at the sites of AVT production and/or release do not abolish the antidiuretic response (Bakker and Bradshaw 1977; Gallardo, Pang, and Sawyer 1980; Jørgensen, Rosenkilde, and Wingstrand 1969; Jørgensen, Wingstrand, and Rosenkilde 1956; Shoemaker and Waring 1968). Studies of bullfrogs (*Rana catesbeiana*) by Sawyer and Pang (1975) and Pang (1977) show that reduction in urine production is not always associated with increases in plasma AVT levels. These observations, together with earlier reports that catecholamines produce antidiuresis in frogs via constriction of the afferent glomerular arterioles and consequent reduction of GFR (Forster 1943; Richards and Schmidt 1925), imply a role for nervous control of renal function. The smooth muscle cells of afferent glomerular arterioles of *Bufo*

marinus are innervated by adrenergic fibers, and some fibers may innervate the distal tubule as well (Morris and Gibbins 1983). Stimulation of the renal nerve increases the vascular resistance of the isolated perfused kidney of *B. marinus*, presumably through constriction of the afferent glomerular arterioles, and this response is blocked by the α-adrenergic antagonist phenoxybenzamine (Morris 1983). Experiments by Gallardo, Pang, and Sawyer (1980) demonstrate that the antidiuretic response to water deprivation in intact bullfrogs is reversed by phenoxybenzamine, whereas administration of norepinephrine reduces urine flow and GFR while increasing the vascular resistance of the kidney (fig. 6.15). In other experiments, phenoxybenzamine was administered via the renal portal circulation at perfusion pressures that did not permit the perfusate to reach the glomeruli, and this also caused diuresis. Thus the sympathetic nervous system may influence both tubular reabsorption and glomerular filtration. The β-adrenergic agonist isoproterenol also reduces urine production in hydrated *Scaphiopus couchii* (Pelobatidae; Hillyard 1979) and *Bufo arenarum* (Segura, Bandsholm, and Bronstein 1982). The relative roles of hormonal and nervous control of urine flow rate in amphibians are presently unclear.

Another neurohypophyseal hormone, mestocin, may also regulate urine flow in amphibians. This peptide elevates GFR and urine flow even though it reduces blood pressure (Pang and Sawyer 1978). Inulin urine to plasma ratios are unaffected, indicating no tubular effect on water reabsorption. Amphibians can produce urine at extremely high rates, given a water load or during recovery from administration of AVT, and it is possible that a diuretic hormone is involved. Levels of mesotocin are higher than those of AVT in plasma of hydrated *Rana ridibunda* and are unaffected by 3 h of dehydration (Nouwen and Kühn 1983). Knowledge of circulating mesotocin levels under various hydration states would be valuable in elucidating its role in amphibian osmoregulation.

Nitrogen Excretion

Detoxification of ammonia resulting from protein metabolism was extremely important in the evolution of terrestriality in amphibians. Their aquatic ancestors could readily excrete ammonia in their aqueous environment both by diffusional exchange across skin and gills and via the urine. On land, excretion of this highly diffusible and toxic substance is more difficult because the kidneys have limited capacity to concentrate the urine, and large volumes of water are unavailable for this purpose. Consequently selection to produce and excrete a less toxic product of protein catabolism was strong. All of the terrestrial species that have been examined can produce urea, a highly soluble and relatively nontoxic end product. The most important organ in this detoxification process is the liver, and the ornithine cycle enzymes associated with urea production are located in the mitochondria and cytosol of hepatocytes. The widespread occurrence of these enzymes in aquatic and terrestrial amphibians suggests that urcotelism evolved early in the evolutionary history of this group.

Some aquatic anurans are obligatorily ammoniotelic and die when water intake is restricted (Shoemaker and McClanahan 1980). Other aquatic and some terrestrial anurans shift from ammoniotelism to ureotelism when deprived of water or acclimated to saline media (Balinsky 1970; Balinsky, Cragg, and Baldwin 1961; Shoemaker and McClanahan 1980). These accumulate urea in their body fluids as a result of increased urea production and/or decreased renal excretion (Funkhouser and Goldstein 1973; Goldstein 1972). Because many aquatic anurans can produce and store urea during water deprivation, ancestral terrestrial anurans were presumably preadapted to invade saline or terrestrial habitats with low water potentials (see below).

The production and excretion of uric acid, or urate salts, provides a mechanism for water conservation for vertebrates living in arid areas. Since urates have low solubility, they precipitate when water is reabsorbed in the kidney tubules, bladder, or cloaca. Urates thus require little water for excretion as a semisolid mass. Uricotelism in anurans occurs in several species from two unrelated families. The South American arboreal frogs *Phyllomedusa* (Hylidae) and the African frogs *Chiromantis* (Rhacophoridae) have coupled low cutaneous EWL with urate excretion to achieve the water economy necessary to survive in extremely dry habitats (Loveridge 1970; Shoemaker et al. 1972). In *Chiromantis* the activities of all five urea cycle enzymes in the liver are lower than other amphibians examined (Balinsky et al. 1976). Likewise the activities of enzymes for the catabolism of uric acid (uricase, allantoinase, and allantoicase) are much lower than those in ureotelic amphibians. The activity of the first enzyme of purine biosynthesis, phosphoribosylpyrophosphate amidotransferase, is higher than that found in ureotelic anurans and equivalent to the levels found in chicken livers. The level of this enzyme in *Phyllomedusa sauvagei* liver is three times higher than in *Chiromantis*. Urea cycle enzymes are also found in the liver of *Phyllomedusa*; however, reports conflict regarding the activity levels of these enzymes (Balinsky et al. 1976; Campbell, Vorhaben, and Smith 1984; Carlisky et al. 1968).

A key event in the evolution of uricotely was the localization in liver mitochondria of glutamine synthetase, an enzyme that catalyzes the ATP-dependent synthesis of glutamine from glutamate and ammonia (Campbell, Vorhaben, and Smith 1987). Avian and reptilian livers have high intramitochondrial activities of glutamine synthetase. Interestingly, the liver of the uricotelic frog *Phyllomedusa* has high rates of amino acid catabolism, as measured by glutamate dehydrogenase activities, whereas levels of glutamine synthetase are an order of magnitude lower than in avian and reptilian livers (Campbell, Vorhaben, and Smith 1984). Moreover, the greatest activity of this enzyme occurs in the soluble portion of liver homogenate, indicating that the enzyme occurs in the cytosol of hepatocytes, unlike in other uricotelic vertebrates (Smith and Campbell 1988). The mechanisms underlying amphibian uricotely are unclear and await further investigation.

Reed frogs (*Hyperolius*), although "waterproof," apparently do not share with *Chiromantis* and *Phyllomedusa* the ability to excrete nitrogen as uric acid. Rather they excrete nitrogen primarily as urea (Geise and Linsenmair 1986; Withers et al. 1982). However, they may store nitrogen as purines when deprived of water (Schmuck and Linsenmair 1988). They accomplish this via accelerated deposition of iridophores, which are composed primarily of guanine (80–90%), with the balance of hypoxanthine. While urea concentration in the body fluids still increases considerably, iridophores

store sufficient nitrogen (about 35% of the total) to be of osmoregulatory benefit.

Nitrogen excretory patterns are diverse in the Amphibia. Ureotelism must have evolved early, and the enzymatic mechanisms associated with the ornithine cycle are consistent throughout the ureotelic vertebrate groups. However, the differing localization of purine cycle enzymes and their activity levels suggest independent evolutions of uricotelism in specialized arboreal anuran species.

Fossorial Amphibians

Urea production and storage in body fluids is important for many desert amphibians. Numerous species of anurans, and at least some urodeles, can survive underground for many months without feeding (see also chapter 10). They burrow at the end of the rainy season and wait until rains commence the following year. As soils dry, their water potentials become very negative (see above section on water uptake from soil). Spadefoot toads (*Scaphiopus:* Pelobatidae) living in southwestern North America can produce and store up to 300 mM urea in their body fluids (McClanahan 1967, 1972; Shoemaker, McClanahan, and Ruibal 1969). These concentrations lower the water potential of the toad's body fluids, thereby preventing or slowing the cutaneous water loss of the toad to the drying soil. The rate at which these species produce and store urea is inversely proportional to the soil water potential (McClanahan 1972). Dormant toads have higher rates of urea production than nondormant toads as well as higher activities of carbamyl phosphate synthetase, an enzyme indicating ornithine cycle enzyme activities (Jones 1980a). A desert subspecies of the salamander *Ambystoma tigrinum* uses the same mechanism to survive in deserts (Delson and Whitford 1973).

Not all fossorial anurans use urea to prevent water loss to drying soils. Some form cocoons when they burrow (see above). Hence urea accumulation and storage is not necessary to prevent water loss to soils with highly negative water potentials (McClanahan, Shoemaker, and Ruibal 1976). Nevertheless, some urea production is necessary to detoxify ammonia produced from protein metabolism.

Hypersaline Environments

Balinsky (1981) lists thirteen species of urodeles representing four families and sixty-one species of anurans in ten families reported to inhabit or tolerate "brackish" water. No amphibians are truly marine, but the crab-eating frog (*Rana cancrivora*) inhabits estuaries and is exposed to high salinity (Gordon, Schmidt-Nielsen, and Kelly 1961). Relatively few species can survive well in salinities that exceed the normal osmotic concentrations (200–300 mOsm) of amphibian body fluids. In addition to *R. cancrivora*, *Bufo viridis* (Gordon 1962) and *Xenopus laevis* (Schlisio, Jürss, and Spannhof 1973) are unusually tolerant of high salinities, and most studies of this phenomenon have focused on these three species of anurans (see Balinsky 1981 and Katz 1989 for reviews). Some *Batrachoseps* (Plethodontidae) salamanders are also unusually tolerant of saline conditions and live near the tide line (Licht, Feder, and Bledsoe 1975), and *Batrachoseps attenuatus* and *B. major* can be acclimated to NaCl concentrations up to 600 mOsm (Jones and Hillman 1978).

Adult amphibians surviving in saline media increase the osmotic concentration of their body fluids to maintain a favorable but relatively small gradient for the osmotic influx of water (fig. 6.16). This is accomplished in part through increases in the sodium and chloride concentrations of the plasma, but the distinguishing characteristic of the most salt-tolerant species is the ability to accumulate high levels of urea in the body fluids (fig. 6.17). Euryhaline species approximately double the sodium and chloride concentrations of the plasma and achieve urea concentrations of 250 to 350 mM in both plasma and tissues when adapted to environmental salinities of about 800 mOsm (table 6.1). In *R. cancrivora* and *B. viridis* electrolyte levels in muscle increase much less than in plasma, but free amino acids reach levels of 150 to 200 mM in this tissue. Licht, Feder, and Bledsoe (1975) could not account for the increased osmotic concentration observed in *Batrachoseps* (subsequently classified as *B. relictus*) as electrolytes, urea, or amino acids, whereas Jones and Hillman (1978) found increases in both sodium and urea in saline-adapted *Batrachoseps attenuatus* and *B. major* that resemble the pattern for euryhaline anurans (table 6.1).

The increase in urea concentration associated with salinity tolerance is due to both urea retention and increased urea synthesis. In the short term, urea retention is associated with decreased urine production and a modest increase in the rate of urea synthesis (McBean and Goldstein 1970a, 1970b). Reabsorption of urea from the urinary bladder under the influence of neurohypophyseal hormones (Chew, Elliot, and Wong 1972; Elliot and Chew 1973) also contributes to urea retention. In *R. cancrivora*, low rates of urea loss are due to low rates of urine production, and there is no evidence for tubular reabsorption of urea (Schmidt-Nielsen and Lee 1962). In the long term, urea synthesis accelerates, and urea cycle enzymes increase (fig. 6.18). In *R. cancrivora*, the magnitude of the increase in urea cycle enzymes reflects the severity of the osmotic challenge (Balinsky, Dicker, and Elliot 1972). *Xenopus laevis* adapted to high salinity also shows elevated levels of all urea cycle enzymes except for argininosuccinate synthetase, whereas in *Bufo viridis* the only significant increase is in argininosuccinate lyase (ASL). ASL shows the highest relative increase in all three species and thus probably represents a rate-limiting step (Balinsky 1981). Increases in liver glutamate dehydrogenase also accompany acclimation of high salinities in *X. laevis* and *B. viridis*, and this probably increases the supply of ammonia for entry into the urea cycle (Lee et al. 1982).

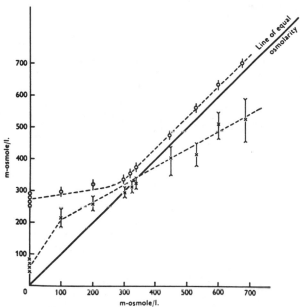

Fig. 6.16 Relations between osmotic concentration of the bathing fluid (NaCl) and that of plasma and urine in adult *Rana cancrivora*. ○, plasma; ×, urine. Each point represents mean ± 1 SE of at least five experiments. Note that plasma is always hyperosmotic to the medium. (Reprinted, by permission, from Dicker and Elliott 1970.)

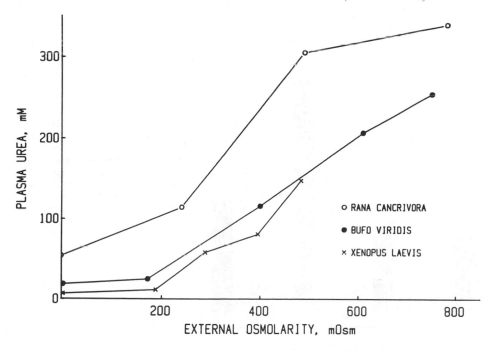

Fig. 6.17 Relations of plasma urea concentration to environmental concentration in three species of euryhaline anurans. (Reprinted, by permission, from Balinsky 1981.)

TABLE 6.1 Concentrations of Small Molecules in the Body Fluids of Some Amphibia Adapted to Media of Different Concentrations

Tissue[a]	External Medium	Internal Osmolarity	Internal Concentrations (mEq)				
			Na$^+$	K$^+$	Cl$^-$	Urea	Free Amino Acids
Xenopus laevis Plasma	Fresh water	233	120	6	120	7	
	NaCl 300 mOsm	304	120	6	120	105	
	500 mOsm	545	150	6	155	155	
Rana cancrivora Plasma	Fresh water	290	125	9	98	40	
	NaCl 250 mOsm	340	161	8	122	110	
	500 mOsm	590	174	6	155	310	
	800 mOsm	830	252	14	227	350	
Muscle	Fresh water		16	103	9	39	54
	NaCl 600 mOsm		26	127	21	300	111
	800 mOsm		32	131	17	350	151
Plasma (larva)[b] Stages XIV–XVII	Fresh water	272	153	5	99		
	NaCl 190 mOsm	339	179	6	120		
	560 mOsm	385	207	6	169		
	930 mOsm	523	265	6	253		
Stage XIX	740 mOsm	583	252	6	259		
Stage XXV	740 mOsm	813	252	10	221		
Bufo viridis Plasma	Fresh water	270	113	5	99	38	
	NaCl 380 mOsm	441	173	7	159	69	
	475 mOsm	502	207	10	196	69	
	770 mOsm	805	285	10	240	265	
Muscle	Fresh water		30	95	17	38	101
	NaCl 380 mOsm		73	105	58	90	181
	475 mOsm		77	130	66	93	186
Red cells	Fresh water		24	75		19	
	NaCl 400 mOsm		38	114		111	
Skin epithelial cells	Fresh water		6	125			
	NaCl 410 mOsm		9	205			
Batrachoseps attenuatus and *B. major* Plasma	Fresh water	339	110			48	
	NaCl 500 mOsm	673	236			218	
Ambystoma tigrinum Plasma (larva)	Fresh water		106		98		
	NaCl 280 mOsm		145		125		

Source: Reprinted, by permission, from Balinsky 1981.
[a]Refers to adult animals unless noted.
[b]Taylor and Kollros (1946) stages for *Rana pipiens*.

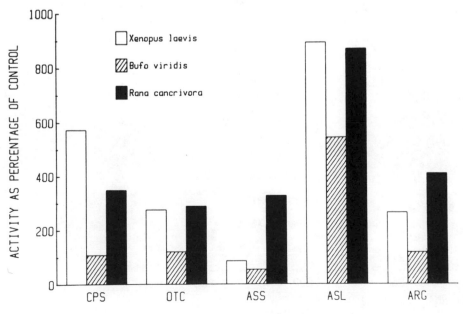

Fig. 6.18 Relative changes in hepatic urea cycle enzyme activities of three anuran species acclimated to high salinity. For *Xenopus laevis* and *Bufo viridis*, values are for animals in 600 mOsm NaCl compared to animals in tap water (Lee et al. 1982). For *Rana cancrivora*, values are for animals in 800 mOsm NaCl compared to animals in 100 mOsm NaCl (Balinsky, Dicker, and Elliot 1972). *CPS*, carbamyl phosphate synthetase; *OTC*, ornithine carbamyl transferase; *ASS*, argininosuccinate synthetase; *ASL*, argininosuccinate lyase; *ARG*, arginase.

Several features of salinity tolerance in adult amphibians resemble characteristics previously discussed in terms of terrestrial life (Katz 1989). Urea accumulation serves similar functions under burrowing and hypersaline conditions, and tolerance to greatly elevated electrolyte levels occurs in both dehydrated and saline-acclimated animals. Numerous studies of *B. viridis* illustrate the similarity of body fluid changes, dominated by greatly elevated concentrations of urea, that occur in burrowed or saline-acclimated animals (see, e.g., Degani, Silanikove, and Shkolnik 1984; Hoffman, Eliath, and Katz 1988; Katz 1973b; Katz and Gabbay 1986; Katz, Degani, and Gabbay 1984).

Larval amphibians appear generally less tolerant of saline conditions than adults, which is correlated with much lower capacities for synthesis and retention of urea (Balinsky 1981). Larvae of *X. laevis* tolerate 330 mOsm salinity, and remain slightly hyperosmotic to the environment through increased electrolyte concentrations (Seiter, Schultheiss, and Hanke 1978), and larval *Ambystoma tigrinum* show the same response when adapted to a 280 mOsm saline environment (Kirschner et al. 1971). A subspecies of *A. tigrinum* inhabiting a saline (300 mOsm) pond tolerates environments up to 350 mOsm and can accumulate urea (ca. 40 mM), although increases in sodium and chloride account for the majority of the increase in plasma osmotic concentration in saline media (Gasser and Miller 1986). Larvae of *R. cancrivora* may be unique among the Amphibia in their ability to regulate internal osmolality below that of the environment. As larvae they can live in 930 mOsm NaCl while maintaining a plasma concentration of 523 mOsm, reflecting the concentrations of sodium and chloride (~250 mM; Gordon and Tucker 1965). These remarkable animals presumably osmoregulate in the same manner as marine teleosts, by drinking the hypersaline medium and excreting excess salts via the gills.

RESPIRATORY GAS EXCHANGE

Many of the ecological, behavioral, morphological, and physiological factors that influence the exchange of water and ions in terrestrial amphibians also affect gas exchange because these basic processes are inextricably linked. This section considers mechanisms of gas exchange, both cutaneous and pulmonary, that are relevant to terrestrial amphibians. Coverage is largely restricted to species that spend most of their adult lives out of water. Discussion of this topic for aquatic and semiaquatic amphibians can be found in chapters 4, 7, and 16.

The exchange of respiratory gases in terrestrial amphibians occurs primarily across the skin and lung surfaces in a proportion that varies considerably depending on species, body size, and environmental circumstances. At one extreme are salamanders that lack lungs and therefore exchange respiratory gases exclusively across cutaneous (or more accurately, nonpulmonary) surfaces; at the other are dehydration-resistant frogs that exchange predominantly via their lungs. Between these extremes are species that may rely on both surfaces for substantial fractions of O_2 and CO_2 exchange. In these intermediate, or bimodal, breathers, the skin is more important for CO_2 loss than for O_2 uptake.

Because gas exchange involves exposing a relatively large, permeable surface to the gas phase, excessive water loss through evaporation is a potentially serious problem in the terrestrial environment. For amphibians this problem is aggravated, in most species, by reliance on moist permeable skin as a major site of respiratory exchange. Two general solutions to this problem appear in extant amphibians: (1) animals retain a permeable skin but select moist microenvironments where evaporation is minimized or remain near water so that losses can be replenished (Feder 1983b); (2) permeability of the skin to water decreases so that constant proximity to water or confinement to a moist microenvironment is not necessary. The latter solution may curtail dehydration but compromises the skin as a gas exchange organ; exchange must therefore shift to the lung. The advantage of lung exchange, with respect to water balance, is that lungs lose less water than exposed wet skin, because the lungs are internalized and exposure of their moist permeable membranes to the environment occurs only intermittently during ventilatory episodes. This solution—relatively impermeable skin and predominant pulmonary exchange—has been advantageous for exploitation of dry terrestrial environments, as evidenced by the reptiles, birds, and mammals. Terrestrial amphibians as a group may be less successful in this respect.

Despite the potential problems associated with dehydration, the terrestrial environment offers distinct advantages for respiratory gas exchange. A consideration of these advantages, in contrast to water, begins this discussion of gas exchange in terrestrial amphibians.

Air as a Respiratory Medium

One major advantage of aerial respiration is that O_2 is more abundant in air than in water. For example, a volume of air at sea level and 15°C contains thirty times as much O_2 as an equal volume of distilled water equilibrated with the same gas phase (see also chapter 4). Adding solutes to the water increases this discrepancy still further. Consequently, as Rahn (1966) discussed quantitatively, an air breather ventilates its respiratory surfaces with a much smaller volume than a water breather to obtain the same amount of O_2. This has important advantages for water retention because evaporative loss from lungs is usually a direct function of the volume of ventilated air. Because air and water hold about equal volumes of CO_2 at the same P_{CO_2}, however, reduced ventilation in air has important consequences for acid-base balance, as discussed below.

Air is also vastly less dense and less viscous than water, so that the work of moving a volume of air is far less than that required to move the same volume of water. The smaller ventilated volume contributes still further to energy savings for air breathers.

Finally, the diffusivity of gases is much higher in the gas phase than in water so that stratification of gases within the internalized gas exchanger or at the skin surface should be much less in the gas phase. Krogh's diffusion constant for O_2 at 20°C is some 2×10^5 as high in air as in water (Dejours 1981). At an exchange surface in air, the unstirred layer should as a consequence be greatly reduced in thickness compared to a surface in water, and should in fact make an inconsequential contribution to the overall resistance to gas diffusion between the environment and the animal (Feder and Pinder 1988b; Piiper 1988). This is supported by the obser-

TABLE 6.2 Physical Properties of Respiratory Gases in Water and Air and Selected Properties of Water and Air

	Water (20°C)	Air (20°C)	Air/Water (15°C)
Solubility ($\mu mol \cdot l^{-1} \cdot mm\ Hg^{-1}$)			
O_2	1.82	54.7	30
CO_2	51.4	54.7	1.06
Diffusion coefficient ($cm^2 \cdot s^{-1}$)			
O_2	2.5×10^{-5}	0.198	8×10^3
CO_2	1.8×10^{-5}	0.155	9×10^3
Krogh's constant ($nmol \cdot cm^{-1} \cdot s^{-1} \cdot mm\ Hg^{-1}$)			
O_2	4.6×10^{-5}	10.9	2×10^5
CO_2	9.3×10^{-4}	8.5	9×10^3
Viscosity (poise)	0.0114	1.80×10^{-4}	0.017
Density ($kg \cdot l^{-1}$)	0.999	1.23×10^{-3}	0.00125

Source: Dejours 1981.

vation of Gatz, Crawford, and Piiper (1974b) that blood P_{CO_2} in the lungless salamander (*Desmognathus fuscus*) is about 6 mm Hg. This is far below that expected if exchange limitation were significant in the gas phase (Rahn and Howell 1976) and accords with the "infinite pool" model for skin respiration originally proposed by Piiper and Scheid (1975) and recently revised (Piiper 1988; see also chapter 5). According to this model, the gas phase offers minimal resistance to exchange because the P_{O_2} at the skin surface approximates ambient P_{O_2}. Air convection can reduce the unstirred layer still further, although the benefits are probably insignificant in contrast to the demonstrated importance of convection in the aquatic milieu (Burggren and Feder 1986). In water, the unstirred layer can constitute a diffusive resistance to gas exchange that is equal to or even greater than that of the skin itself (Feder and Pinder 1988b).

These considerations of the physical properties of air compared to those of water help explain the great explosion of terrestrial life forms following the initial colonization of land in the Devonian period. Table 6.2 summarizes these properties in air and water.

Skin Respiration

In general, amphibians, including terrestrial and semiaquatic species, have highly permeable skin that is a major site for gas exchange. Documentation is derived from studies of both respiratory anatomy (Czopek 1965) and partitioning of gas exchange between lungs and skin in urodeles (Whitford and Hutchison 1965b) and anurans (Hutchison, Whitford, and Kohl 1968). The subject of cutaneous gas exchange in amphibians and its control has been the subject of several extensive reviews (Burggren 1988b; Feder and Burggren 1985a, 1985b; Jackson 1987b; Malvin 1988). Cutaneous exchange in aquatic and semiaquatic forms is dealt with in chapters 4, 5, 7, and 16. Here discussion is limited to amphibians in air. The lungless salamanders are emphasized because regulatory mechanisms for cutaneous gas exchange may be most evident in these animals.

Studies of gas exchange in lungless salamanders have largely addressed the extent to which this condition restricts O_2 uptake and hence aerobic metabolism under various envi-

ronmental and physiological conditions. Limitations and controls of gas exchange operating at the gas exchange surface can involve ventilation, diffusion, and perfusion. As discussed above, the physical characteristics of air are such that the ventilatory resistance to cutaneous gas exchange is small if not negligible (i.e., the P_{O_2} at the skin surface is very close to that of the ambient air). Thus the major factors affecting O_2 uptake are diffusion from the skin surface to the capillaries of the skin and convection of O_2 by the blood perfusing these capillaries.

For the diffusion step,

$$(4) \qquad \dot{M}_{O_2} = D(P_{env} - P_{blood}),$$

where

$\dot{M}_{O_2}$ = the rate of O_2 consumption
D = the diffusive conductance (= diffusing capacity)
P_{env} = the P_{O_2} in the environmental medium
P_{blood} = the P_{O_2} in the blood perfusing the skin capillaries

D is a function of the following variables (Piiper 1988):

$$(5) \qquad D = d\alpha A/x,$$

where

d = diffusivity of O_2 in the skin
α = solubility of O_2 in the skin
A = skin surface area
x = skin thickness

For the perfusion step,

$$(6) \qquad \dot{M}_{O_2} = \dot{Q}\beta(P_{ex} - P_{in}),$$

where

$\dot{Q}$ = blood flow through the skin
β = the effective solubility of O_2 in the blood (determined primarily by the concentration and O_2 binding characteristics of hemoglobin)
P_{ex} = the P_{O_2} of blood exiting skin capillaries
P_{in} = the P_{O_2} of blood entering skin capillaries

P_{in} may vary in anurans depending on the admixture of systemic and pulmocutaneous blood supply to the skin (Burggren 1988b; see chapter 5). Also, both $\dot{Q}$ and β of the blood perfusing the cutaneous capillaries may differ from that of the blood perfusing the skin in general if significant shunting of either bulk blood or red blood cells occurs. This relationship illustrates the potential for regulation of the exchange capacity of the skin via blood flow. However, if D is small relative to $\dot{Q}\beta$, the exchanger is "diffusion limited," and an increase in $\dot{Q}$ will be largely offset by a decrease in P_{ex} (see Piiper 1988).

The most obvious limitation imposed by reliance on cutaneous gas exchange is that the surface area (A) available for gas transfer is small compared to the extensive amplification of surface possible in complexly organized lungs and gills. Small amphibians, particularly those with elongate bodies, may have relatively large surface areas for gas exchange (Beckenbach 1976). However, total respiratory surface area of lungless salamanders is less than that of lunged species at body masses greater than 0.5 g, and the discrepancy increases with body size (Ultsch 1974a). A second problem is that the protective functions of the skin require a relatively thick layer between the environment and the capillaries, so that the effective diffusion distance (x) across amphibian skin, rarely less than 20 μm (Czopek 1965), is much greater than in lungs and gills, where the distance is on the order of 1 μm. Allometric changes in the spacing and radius of cutaneous capillaries, as well as in A and x, contribute to changes in diffusing capacity that make cutaneous gas exchange increasingly problematic as body size increases in terrestrial salamanders (Feder 1988).

Resting metabolic rates of salamanders are low, about 60% of the predicted value for air-breathing ectotherms, but differences between lunged and lungless salamanders are not apparent (Feder 1976a). Thus lunglessness does not appear to limit O_2 consumption in salamanders at rest under normoxic conditions. When the environmental Po_2 is reduced, however, or when metabolic demand is increased during exercise, lungless salamanders exhibit profound deficits as compared to salamanders breathing with lungs. These limitations are exaggerated at large body sizes.

Beckenbach (1976) measured O_2 uptake in a selection of plethodontid salamanders while progressively decreasing the O_2 content of ambient gas and determined the critical Po_2 or P_c (the Po_2 below which O_2 consumption is depressed). Specimens of small body mass (<4 g) had P_c values well below atmospheric Po_2, but the P_c of larger animals (about 20 g) approached the ambient level (fig. 6.19). For these larger animals exchange capacity of the body surface approaches the minimum required to supply resting O_2 demands, whereas the smaller salamanders possess considerable exchange reserve. Feder (1988) compared morphological cutaneous diffusing capacity of salamanders with resting Mo_2 as a function of body size, and also concluded that exchange capacity is far greater than resting needs in small animals but not in large ones (fig. 6.20).

Measurements of aerobic capacity during exercise are especially useful in assessing cutaneous exchange capacity in lungless salamanders. Stimulation by electrical shock (Feder 1977) or repeated overturning (Withers 1980) elevated Mo_2 up to four times resting, but large animals had lower factorial scopes. More recent studies in which plethodontid salamanders ran on an exercise wheel or a treadmill demonstrated factorial scopes of nine to eleven in *Desmognathus ochrophaeus* (Feder 1986) and up to nine in *Plethodon jordani* (Full 1986). However, the peak O_2 consumption of lungless salamanders is only a third that of anurans under comparable conditions (Full 1986) and is also less than for lunged salamanders of similar size (Full et al. 1988). Furthermore, experimental elimination of lung exchange in lunged salamanders severely reduces their maximum aerobic capacity (Feder 1988).

Reliance on the skin for gas exchange substantially reduces an amphibian's abilities to meet certain respiratory challenges, and may restrict these animals to habitats where O_2 supply is dependable and temperatures are relatively cool, and to behavioral circumstances that do not require sustained vigorous activity (Feder 1983b). Nevertheless, the lungless plethodontid salamanders are a highly successful group.

Lungless amphibians apparently have some capacity to regulate gas exchange when environmental or physiological circumstances warrant (e.g., in hypoxia or exercise). Less

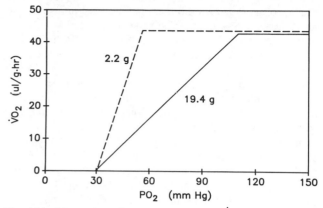

Fig. 6.19 Mean values of oxygen consumption ($\dot{V}o_2$) as a function of ambient Po_2 for two size ranges of lungless salamanders (*Desmognathus quadramaculatus*). Note that critical O_2 pressure is higher in larger animals (mean body mass = 19.4 g; N = 4) than in the smaller animals (mean body mass = 2.2 g; N = 4). (Data from Beckenbach 1976.)

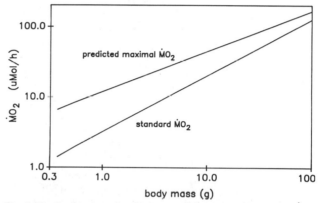

Fig. 6.20 Predicted maximal and standard oxygen consumption ($\dot{M}o_2$) as a function of body mass in lungless salamanders. Predicted $\dot{M}o_2$ is based on morphologic characteristics and represents a theoretical upper limit of exchange at a Po_2 gradient of 100 mm Hg. Measured values of Mo_{2max} approximate this predicted limit but slightly exceed it (see Feder 1988). Standard $\dot{M}o_2$ is based on measured values. Note that the predicted maximal value and the standard value converge near a body mass of 100 g. (Adapted from Feder 1988.)

clear is whether this regulation occurs at the diffusion step (eq. 4), the perfusion step (eq. 6), or both. During the 1970s and early 1980s, mathematical models, inert gas equilibration studies, morphometric analyses, and direct measurements all suggested that D is small relative to $\dot{Q}\beta$ and that cutaneous gas exchange is primarily diffusion-limited (reviewed by Feder and Burggren 1985a, 1985b). Because D is determined by variables that seemingly cannot be adjusted on a minute-to-minute basis (eq. 5), this result implies that cutaneous gas exchange is largely passive and not under physiological control. However, it seems unlikely that the metabolic responses of lungless salamanders to hypoxia and exercise could result passively from changes in Po_2 gradients. Piiper, Gatz, and Crawford (1976) estimated the normal Po_2 difference between ambient air and capillary blood to be about 100 mm Hg. This is close to the maximum difference possible, so little further exchange capacity could be achieved by this means.

It now seems likely that circulatory changes in the skin can affect both the diffusive and convective steps in gas transfer.

Studies of inert gas equilibration indicate that diffusion limitation lessens in skin-breathing salamanders during treadmill exercise (Feder, Full, and Piiper 1988). This effect could be due to capillary recruitment, which increases the area available for diffusion into the blood stream (Burggren and Moalli 1984; Burggren and Feder 1986; Malvin 1988). Moreover, changes in blood flow to the skin (rather than diffusing capacity) account for most of the change in cutaneous gas exchange in frogs (Malvin and Hlastala 1989). Pinder, Clemens, and Feder (1990, in press) developed a preparation of isolated perfused frog skin in which D, $\dot{Q}$, β, and $(P_{env} - P_{blood})$ could be controlled. This work suggests that at rest, at cool temperatures, and in normoxic conditions, O_2 uptake in skin-breathing animals is well below the maximum permitted by the diffusing capacity of the skin, and they have considerable latitude for regulating cutaneous gas exchange through changes in $\dot{Q}\beta$. At higher rates of O_2 consumption (e.g., in activity or at high temperature), O_2 demand may approach the diffusion capacity of the skin such that further increases in blood flow do not enhance gas transfer.

The interactions of ventilation, diffusion, and perfusion are complex but must be considered for a clear understanding of either the limits or regulation of gas exchange across the skin as in any respiratory surface. To choose a single variable (e.g., gas solubility in the skin, skin thickness, capillary recruitment, bulk blood flow through the skin) for study means overlooking other variables, such that the physiological relevance of the investigation may be compromised. Accordingly, the study of cutaneous gas exchange has gradually metamorphosed from a phase in which variables have been studied individually to a phase emphasizing the interaction of multiple variables and processes. Elegant models of these interactions have been developed (see, e.g., Malvin 1988; Piiper 1988) that point the way for modern studies of cutaneous gas exchange.

Because of their reliance on cutaneous gas exchange, lungless salamanders readily lose water across their skin—this is an obligatory association. The other adaptive extreme among terrestrial amphibians is illustrated by arboreal frogs inhabiting arid regions of Africa (*Chiromantis*) and South America (*Phyllomedusa*). These anurans have cutaneous resistances to evaporation that are similar to those of desert reptiles (see above). However, this permeability barrier to water also markedly limits exchange of respiratory gases; CO_2 and O_2 transit of their skin occurs at levels typical of terrestrial reptiles but far below levels typical of other anurans (Stinner and Shoemaker 1987). These exceptional animals confirm in dramatic fashion the correlation in terrestrial amphibians between cutaneous EWL and cutaneous gas exchange. These exchange processes cannot be effectively dissociated; water loss and gas exchange apparently increase and decrease together.

Lung Respiration

The lungs of terrestrial amphibians play an important, but not always dominant, role in gas exchange. The widespread use of cutaneous exchange in amphibians has reduced the reliance on lungs more than in other terrestrial vertebrate classes. This section discusses aspects of lung structure and function with emphasis on terrestrial or semiterrestrial anurans, which have been the most studied in this regard. See chapters 5, 7, and 16 for additional information on this topic.

Lung Structure In contrast to skin, with its serious limitations as a gas exchange organ, the lung has the potential for enormous adaptive capacity, as is evident from its remarkable development among the terrestrial vertebrates. Because the lung is a protected organ largely dedicated to one function, specialized structural features have evolved that amplify the surface area and minimize the distance for diffusion of gases. Among the amphibians, a considerable range of specialization occurs (for review see Burggren 1989), from simple saclike lungs, as in *Cryptobranchus alleganiensis* (Cryptobranchidae), that may serve more as buoyancy devices than gas exchangers (Guimond and Hutchison 1973a), to the complexly subdivided lungs of *Xenopus laevis*. In general, though, lung development is more modest in amphibians than in amniotes and is related more to habit and habitat than to phylogeny (Tenney 1979; Burggren 1989).

Information is available on both exchange surface area and air-to-blood diffusion distance in selected amphibians. Tenney and Tenney (1970) reported that total respiratory surface area (lungs plus skin) in both aquatic and terrestrial amphibians varies directly with body mass$^{0.98}$. This differs from the expected 0.75 exponent that is found in mammals and reptiles and that conforms to metabolic allometry. The authors' interpretation for this apparent anomaly is that the total measured respiratory surface overestimates the effective exchange surface because of the variable extent of exchange surface capillarization. Data from Czopek (1965) and Szarski (1964) on capillary morphometry in the exchange surfaces show indeed that total capillary length varies with body mass$^{0.80}$. Czopek (1965) also demonstrated with his extensive data that the importance of the lung, as represented by the percentage of total capillary length residing in that organ, increases with body size. In 0.6-g *Rana pipiens*, for example, lung capillaries are 31% of the total, whereas in a 127-g specimen, they account for 76% of the total capillary length. This accords with the increased importance of pulmonary gas exchange in bimodal amphibians as body size increases. The thickness of the pulmonary exchange barrier, the air-to-blood diffusion distance, also favors pulmonary exchange. In a representative anuran, urodele, and apodan (Pattle et al. 1977), the barrier thickness is close to 1 μm, far less than the cutaneous diffusion distance. Because of the difference in diffusion distances in the two respiratory surfaces, surface area comparisons alone may underestimate the potential importance of the lung vis-à-vis the skin. For an anuran, the diffusing capacity of the lung is estimated to be more than fifty times that of the skin (Withers and Hillman 1988) based on diffusion properties of lung (Glass, Burggren, and Johansen 1981) and skin (Ultsch 1974a). However, an important point in this regard is that the skin is always exposed to the environment for exchange, whereas the lung only participates when actively ventilated. An amphibian that does not breathe has no pulmonary gas exchange, regardless of how well developed its lungs. Consequently, morphologic considerations by themselves cannot reveal the actual functional contributions of the lung and skin.

Lung Mechanics Present-day amphibians all apparently use positive-pressure (buccal pump) breathing, similar to air-breathing fishes but distinctly different from reptiles, birds,

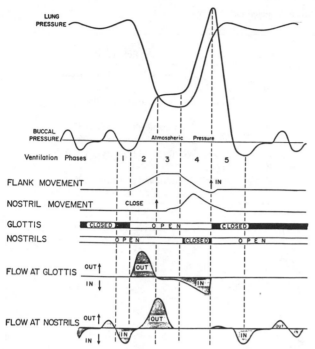

Fig. 6.21 Mechanical events during breathing in the bullfrog, *Rana catesbeiana*. Depicted are three buccal oscillations (oropharyngeal ventilations) with a lung ventilatory cycle occurring between the second and third. (Reprinted, by permission, from de Jongh and Gans 1969.)

and mammals, which use negative-pressure (aspiration) breathing. Detailed descriptions of the mechanical events occurring during breathing in anurans have been provided by de Jongh and Gans (1969) on *Rana catesbeiana*, by West and Jones (1975a) on *R. pipiens*, and by Macintyre and Toews (1976) and Jones (1982) on *Bufo marinus*. These papers also survey earlier work on the subject that was often contradictory and inconclusive. Chapter 11 summarizes biomechanical aspects of breathing.

A variety of respiratory events occur in anuran respiration, including buccal pumping or oropharyngeal ventilation, single-lung ventilations, stepwise exaggerated inflation of the lung, and stepwise deflation of the lung. The sequence of key events associated with the first two of these patterns can be seen in figure 6.21. During oropharyngeal ventilation, active elevation of the buccal cavity expels air out the nares, and passive lowering of the cavity draws air in to refill it. This is a frequent event but may not serve a significant respiratory function because of the limited surface and capillary bed that is ventilated. Periodically, the almost continuous buccal oscillations are interrupted by a lung ventilation, the effective gas exchange mechanism. A lung ventilation is a more complex sequence of events that begins with opening of the glottis (the nares are already open) and passive expiration of lung gas past the full buccal cavity. De Jongh and Gans (1969) suggest that streaming of gas limits mixing of expired pulmonary gas with O_2-rich gas in the buccal cavity, although this assertion has been questioned (Jones 1982; Shelton, Jones, and Milsom 1986; Vitalis 1988). The nares then close and the buccal pump is activated, forcing air from the buccal cavity into the lungs. The glottis then closes and the nares open (the relaxed positions for these valves), and the buccal cavity passively refills from the outside. Exaggerated infla-

tions occur infrequently (1 or 2 per hour) in *B. marinus* (Macintyre and Toews 1976) but as often as 1 per minute in *R. pipiens* (West and Jones 1975a). A series of active lung inspirations by buccal pumping, at progressively increasing pressure, inflates the lungs with relatively uncontaminated outside air. The function is uncertain but could serve to avoid the buccal cavity dead space problem associated with normal lung ventilations (Shelton, Jones, and Milsom 1986). A quite different pattern occurs in *Bufo paracnemis* (Kruhoffer et al. 1987). Periodic ventilatory episodes begin with a stepwise deflation, continue with a series of lung ventilations with equal inspiratory and expiratory volume, and conclude with a stepwise inflation. Smaller-amplitude buccal ventilations appear to occur less frequently in this species. These observations reveal a considerable diversity of respiratory pattern in these animals.

During all these breathing maneuvers, lung pressure remains above atmospheric pressure, whereas buccal pressure falls below atmospheric during its filling phases. Buccal pressure changes are considerably less during oropharyngeal ventilations than during lung ventilations, although the volume changes can be similar. This is probably due to the added work required during lung ventilations to inflate the lung/chest wall system. These inflation pressures are particularly large during the exaggerated stepwise inflations (West and Jones 1975a).

Amphibians have quite compliant lungs and chest walls so that the work required for inflation is still relatively modest (see review by Burggren 1989). Hughes and Vergara (1978) and Dupré, Taylor, and Frazier (1985) found lung compliance of frogs (*R. pipiens* and *R. catesbeiana*, respectively) to be similar to other ectothermic vertebrates but some ten times greater than lungs from similar-size mammals. This greater distensibility in the amphibian lung can be attributed to larger airspaces or alveoli (Tenney and Tenney 1970) compared to mammals. The larger-diameter airspaces reduce surface tension of the alveolar wall according to the law of Laplace. Surface tension is also reduced by the presence of surface active material (surfactant) that reduces recoil forces at the air/liquid interface in the alveoli (Hughes and Vergara 1978; Pattle et al. 1977) that would otherwise make lungs less distensible.

The above measurements of compliance were all made on lungs removed from the body cavity. If compliance is measured on lungs *in situ* within an intact chest wall, compliance is reduced to about one-third that of the isolated lung (Hughes and Vergara 1978). This accords with the generalization of Milsom (1989) that the major elastic resistance in ectothermic vertebrates resides not in the lung but in the chest wall. The opposite is generally the case in mammals.

The ventilatory mechanism of amphibians has been characterized as inefficient and unable to meet the full gas exchange requirements of the animals, particularly with respect to CO_2 loss (Gans 1970). This point of view can be challenged on several grounds, one of which relates to the metabolic cost of breathing. The cost of breathing is that portion of the total metabolic expenditure of the animal that is consumed by the respiratory pump. West and Jones (1975b) estimated the cost of breathing in the frog *R. pipiens* to be 5% of the total resting metabolic rate of the animal. This figure, although higher than in mammals, is similar to that of ecto-

TABLE 6.3   Lung Oxygen Uptake ($\dot{V}O_2$) and Carbon Dioxide Excretion ($\dot{V}CO_2$) in Selected Amphibians as a Percentage of Total Exchange (Lung plus Skin)

	Temperature (°C)	Lung $\dot{V}O_2$	Lung $\dot{V}CO_2$	Reference
Hyla versicolor	5	39	15	Hutchison, Whitford, and Kohl 1968
	25	67	16	
Bufo terrestris	5	35	22	Hutchison, Whitford, and Kohl 1968
	25	69	25	
Phyllomedusa sauvagei	24	94	86	Stinner and Shoemaker 1987
Chiromantis xerampelina	24	93	81	Stinner and Shoemaker 1987
Ambystoma tigrinum	10	31	15	Whitford and Hutchison 1965b
	25	69	29	
Taricha granulosa	10	33	13	Whitford and Hutchison 1965b
	25	68	25	

thermic vertebrates that breathe with an aspiration pump mechanism (Milsom 1989). One could argue that this is still a high cost because the need for pulmonary ventilation in the frog is lessened by its cutaneous exchange, but as discussed below, pulmonary ventilation in many amphibians increases adaptively in response to activity or altered ambient gas composition.

Lung Gas Exchange   At rest, lunged terrestrial amphibians use both lungs and skin for gas exchange, but the lungs have more importance of O_2 uptake than for CO_2 loss and assume a greater role in exchange of both gases as ambient temperature rises (table 6.3). Quantitative generalizations are difficult because of the diversity of habitats and adaptations. Included in table 6.3, for example, are the xeric-adapted frogs *Phyllomedusa sauvagei* and *Chiromantis xerampelina,* which have very low rates of cutaneous water loss and rely almost exclusively on their lungs for exchange of both respiratory gases (Stinner and Shoemaker 1987).

Accelerated metabolic rate due to elevated temperature is met principally by augmenting pulmonary exchange (Hutchison, Whitford, and Kohl 1968; MacKenzie and Jackson 1978; Pinder and Burggren 1986; Whitford and Hutchison 1965b). This is true also when metabolic rate rises at constant temperature due to spontaneous (Gottlieb and Jackson 1976) or forced (Withers and Hillman 1983) activity (see chapter 12). In the former study, pulmonary $\dot{V}O_2$ accounted for most of the increase in total $\dot{V}O_2$, whereas skin uptake changed very little (fig. 6.22). As noted above, Feder (1988) found that elimination of pulmonary exchange in lunged salamanders severely curtailed their capacity to exercise. These studies indicate that in those terrestrial amphibians that possess both pulmonary and cutaneous exchange, regulatory responses to changing metabolic demand, whether due to temperature or activity, are met principally by alterations in pulmonary, not cutaneous, exchange. The lungs, however, must be effective gas exchange structures for this to be true. Boutilier, McDonald, and Toews (1980) found that *Bufo marinus,* which possesses a well-developed lung, recovered rapidly from a bout of activity, whereas an aquatic salamander, *Cryptobranchus alleganiensis,* which has a saclike lung with little exchange capacity, recovered very slowly.

Pulmonary ventilation and gas diffusion between the lungs and the pulmonary blood are the initial steps in the transfer of O_2 between the environment and the cells. During maximal exercise in terrestrial anurans, this avenue of exchange pre-

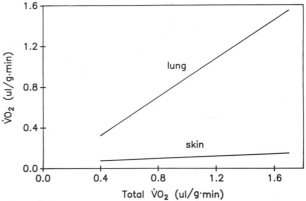

Fig. 6.22   Lung and skin oxygen consumption ($\dot{V}O_2$) as a function of total $\dot{V}O_2$ in bullfrogs, *Rana catesbeiana*. Note that increases in total oxygen demand are met principally by increases in lung uptake in this bimodally breathing amphibian. (Adapted from Gottlieb and Jackson 1976.)

dominates, and cutaneous uptake is of relatively minor importance (see chapter 12). A theoretical analysis by Withers and Hillman (1988) of the sequence of events in O_2 uptake (and the reverse flow of CO_2) during maximal exchange concluded that the pulmonary events are not primary limiting steps for O_2 delivery in this cascade. The most persuasive evidence for this conclusion is that simulated increases in alveolar ventilation and pulmonary diffusing capacity (over their observed maximal values) would have only minor effects on maximal $\dot{V}O_2$ calculated by the model. The major limiting step in the sequence, according to this analysis, is the cardiovascular system. These theoretical analyses conform closely to experimental data collected on a variety of anurans by these same authors (e.g., Hillman and Withers 1979; Withers and Hillman 1983).

Withers and Hillman further conclude, however, that the lungs are the primary limiting step for CO_2 excretion, which would appear to support the contention of Gans (1970) that the amphibian respiratory mechanism is inadequate for this function. However, a key criterion used by Withers and Hillman (1988) to evaluate limitation is the magnitude of the partial pressure difference of the gas at each step of the transport process. They assert that the higher the difference, the greater the limitation. This can largely be explained by the high CO_2 capacitance ($\Delta[CO_2]/\Delta P CO_2$) of the body fluids (much higher than O_2 capacitance) that results in small $P CO_2$ differences between arterial and venous blood and between venous blood and tissues. Most of the change in P_{CO_2} between the cells and the environment occurs between the lungs and the environment. This profile is not unique to anurans, however, but is true for air-breathing vertebrates generally, whatever the state of development of their lungs (see, e.g., Dejours 1981, 98). If indeed the lungs of anurans are limiting for CO_2 loss as this analysis concludes, this does not represent a defect peculiar to amphibian lungs but is a general phenomenon. Unlike mammals, however, anurans do exhibit limitation to CO_2 excretion, manifested by respiratory acidosis (CO_2 retention), following maximal exercise (Boutilier, McDonald, and Toews 1980).

Control of Gas Exchange

The ventilatory response of terrestrial anurans to changes in metabolic rate indicates the existence of homeostatic control of gas exchange. This conclusion is also supported by the increased ventilation that occurs when amphibians breathe hypoxic or hypercapnic gas mixtures. Documentation of these findings can be found in chapters 5, 7, and 16 and will not be repeated here.

The regulatory system underlying these ventilatory responses is not well understood, but by analogy with other vertebrates, we can surmise that specialized chemoreceptors responding to blood or tissue levels of P_{CO_2}, P_{O_2}, and pH relay information to a brain-stem integrating center, which then produces an appropriate motor output to the respiratory muscles. Shelton, Jones, and Milsom (1986) note that lung ventilation in amphibians, unlike the ventilatory cycling in fish and mammals, is less regular, and its occurrence as well as its intensity depends upon the needs of the moment; that is, amphibians are facultative breathers. From this they further suggest that respiratory events may be triggered by chemoreceptor signals.

Chemoreceptors sensitive to both CO_2 and O_2 and capable of eliciting ventilatory responses have been described in air-breathing amphibians (Jones and Milsom 1982), and are the subject of chapter 7. Receptors affected by both mechanical stretch and CO_2 level have been detected in the lungs of anurans (Kuhlmann and Fedde 1979; Milsom and Jones 1977). These receptors are activated by stretch but inhibited by CO_2. Because the central effect is to inhibit respiration, the CO_2 effect is therefore excitatory to respiration. Glomus-type receptor cells sensitive to low O_2 reside in the carotid labyrinth of anurans (S. Kobayashi 1975) and promote breathing in response to hypoxia (Ishii, Honda, and Ishii 1966; Smyth 1939). Other less-studied peripheral chemoreceptors, as well as a variety of mechanical receptors, have also been described in amphibians, but their role, and indeed the role of the receptors described above, in activating or modulating breathing is poorly understood (Shelton, Jones, and Milsom 1986). A preliminary report by Smatresk and Smits (1989) indicates the existence of brain chemoreceptors sensitive to hypercapnia and low pH in the medullary region of the toad *Bufo marinus*. These are apparently similar in location and function to previously described receptors in turtles (Hitzig and Jackson 1978) and mammals (Leusen 1954) that are regarded as having great importance in respiratory control in these animals. The various receptors, peripheral and central, are presumably

integrated in the amphibian's central nervous system to produce pulmonary ventilation appropriate to the homeostatic needs of the animal in face of changing metabolic and environmental conditions.

Environmental Conditions

Terrestrial life presents environmental challenges that are relevant to gas exchange, and that differ from the aquatic environment. The dominant challenge of dehydration and the need to adapt the respiratory exchange to meet this challenge have already been addressed. Hypoxia is probably not a major problem for terrestrial amphibians because of the relative abundance of aerial O_2 and because hypoxia is usually only encountered at high elevations where few species reside. Withers and Hillman (1983) measured maximal $\dot{V}_{O_2}$ of *Bufo cognatus* and *Rana pipiens* at varying P_{O_2} levels, induced both by low pressure and by low O_2 concentration, and found that the critical P_{O_2} was not reached until 80 mm Hg. This corresponds to an altitude of 4,500 m, above that of any known amphibian habitat (Hock 1964).

The abundance of O_2, although an immensely positive feature of the terrestrial environment, nevertheless poses a potential physiological problem because of the drastic reduction in ventilation that accompanies the transition from water breathing to air breathing (Dejours, Garey, and Rahn 1970). This reduced ventilation, which also occurs in lunged amphibians in water, results in CO_2 retention and requires adjustments in acid-base balance. These changes have been documented in various amphibians during metamorphosis from aquatic larvae to air-breathing adults (Burggren and Wood 1981; Erasmus, Howell, and Rahn 1970/71; Just, Gatz, and Crawford 1973), as discussed in chapter 16. In general, the response corresponds to what in clinical terminology is termed compensated respiratory acidosis. Blood P_{CO_2} is elevated as a consequence of reduced ventilation (respiratory acidosis), but increased $[HCO_3^-]$ accompanies this change (compensation). Thus blood pH, as observed in the bullfrog (*R. catesbeiana*), is close to the level of the aquatic larva (Erasmus, Howell, and Rahn 1970/71; Just, Gatz, and Crawford 1973). In *Ambystoma tigrinum*, the "compensation" is less complete, and the adult blood is acidotic relative to the larval blood (Burggren and Wood 1981). It is important to qualify this metaphor derived from medical terminology, however, by emphasizing that terrestrial lunged amphibians are not "fish out of water" responding to an acid-base disturbance. Instead they are adapted to this environment, and their acid-base state represents normal homeostasis.

Temperature also has an important influence on amphibian respiration in the terrestrial environment as well as in water, both because of the thermal effect on energy metabolism and because of the temperature-linked adjustments of O_2 transport and acid-base balance. In air, these changes are often more rapid and more extreme than in water. Only a brief account will be given here because these topics are dealt with extensively with respect to semiaquatic air-breathing amphibians in chapter 5. (Temperature effects are also discussed in chapters 8–10.)

As discussed above, a fall in temperature shifts the distribution of respiratory gas exchange in the direction of the cutaneous mode in bimodal terrestrial amphibians, and at very low temperature, pulmonary ventilation may not even be necessary. At high temperature, ventilation must increase to transport the additional O_2 required. At each temperature, the combined exchanges of the lungs and skin must preserve acid-base homeostasis and maintain O_2 saturation at a suitable level. Temperature has pervasive effects on both these functions. Acid-base relevant reactions in the body fluids, weak acid and base equilibria, and CO_2 solubility are all temperature-dependent, as is the affinity of hemoglobin for O_2 (e.g., Burggren and Wood 1981). The net acid-base effect is an inverse relationship between blood pH and body temperature. Although the precise details of temperature-linked acid-base regulation are still under debate (Cameron 1989; Reeves 1972), the control system is apparently based on maintenance of protein charge state within the body fluids. In most lunged terrestrial amphibians, control is complicated by the active participation of two exchangers, the lungs and the skin, each subject to physiological control, the details of which are yet to be worked out. However, cutaneous exchange alone can produce these temperature-dependent acid-base changes in the aquatic salamander *Cryptobranchus alleganiensis* (Moalli et al. 1981).

SUMMARY AND CONCLUSIONS

In moving from water to land, amphibians entered an environment where oxygen is plentiful but water is potentially scarce. Most species have retained a highly permeable integument and must have access to environments of high water potential to maintain or restore body water. Temporary excursions into drier environments are made possible by the ability to store and subsequently use large volumes of water in the urinary bladder, the ability to tolerate very large losses of body water, and use of urea instead of ammonia as the primary nitrogen waste. Reduction or cessation of urine production conserves water and permits accumulation of urea in the body fluids. The latter is useful in lowering the water potential of the animal in relation to soil or saline environments, and is enhanced by increased capacity for urea synthesis under conditions of osmotic "stress." Although most do not drink, terrestrial amphibians can absorb water rapidly through the ventral skin from water or wet substrates. These general attributes of terrestrial amphibians are more pronounced in anurans than in urodeles, but in both groups are correlated with the severity of the environments they occupy.

Arboreal amphibians have, to various degrees, increased the resistance of the skin to the evaporation of water. These resistances range from a few to several hundred seconds per centimeter, the latter rivaling those of terrestrial reptiles. A few "waterproof" anurans excrete nitrogen waste as uric acid and can thus achieve considerable independence from water.

Desert amphibians typically retreat below ground in unfavorable seasons. As the soil dries, some form "cocoons" that restrict water movement across the skin, and others accumulate high concentrations of urea.

Retention of a moist and permeable integument has allowed continued use of the skin as a major site of respiratory gas exchange in most terrestrial amphibians. Indeed, in the lungless species this surface accounts for all gas exchange. A shift to lung ventilation is apparent in many terrestrial amphibians, particularly among the anurans. A few species with low skin permeability exchange gases almost entirely via their lungs. Amphibians ventilate their lungs with a positive pressure buccal pump that is regarded as inefficient. However, based on the aerobic scope it supports, it represents a highly effective form of gas exchange, especially in comparison with the strictly skin-breathing condition. Air breathing requires less ventilation and thus leads to higher P_{CO_2}, but this is wholly or partially compensated by bicarbonate to maintain pH. In addition to dehydration, the terrestrial environment poses thermal and acid-base problems, but the evolution of solutions to these problems has permitted amphibians to exploit the enormous respiratory advantage of abundant oxygen in air.

7 Sensory Mechanisms Regulating the Cardiovascular and Respiratory Systems

NIGEL H. WEST AND BRUCE N. VAN VLIET

The primary role of the respiratory and cardiovascular systems of vertebrates is to secure adequate tissue oxygenation in the face of changing oxygen availability and tissue demands (Dejours 1979; Jones 1983; Rahn 1967). A related role is the elimination of carbon dioxide and the regulation of acid-base status. Information reaching the central nervous system concerning the mechanical or gas exchange performance of either system may result in ventilatory or cardiovascular adjustments that act to prevent tissue hypoxia (reduced O_2) or hypercapnia (elevated CO_2).

The demands placed on the cardiovascular and respiratory systems of amphibians can be diverse and extreme. Aquatic amphibians occupy environments in which Po_2 may fluctuate from near anoxia to hyperoxia on a diurnal basis due to photosynthesis and respiration of green plants (Dejours 1976). Amphibians may experience hypoxia at high altitude or may become hypercapnic for protracted periods while estivating, burrowing, or diving (Boutilier 1989; Boutilier et al. 1979a; Boutilier and Heisler 1988; Burggren 1989; see also chapters 5, 6, and 10). Activity also increases oxygen demand.

In vertebrates, the receptors monitoring ventilatory and cardiovascular function may be peripheral or central. The former group includes chemoreceptors or mechanoreceptors located on the skin, within the airways and lungs, or in the vascular system, while the latter comprises receptors located within the central nervous system itself. The peripheral receptors of nonmammalian vertebrates and their role in the control of ventilation have recently been reviewed (Jones and Milsom 1982; Shelton, Jones, and Milsom 1986). Other reviews have related the amphibian respiratory and cardiovascular systems and the gaseous environment, with the implicit assumption that receptor systems are important in providing chemical and mechanical information related to respiration (Boutilier 1988; Shelton and Boutilier 1982).

This chapter concentrates on the response characteristics of mechano- and chemoreceptors in amphibians and describes their involvement in respiratory and cardiovascular control. An analysis of the role of receptors in controlling such systems is difficult. The intermittent nature of amphibian respiration means that blood gases are seldom in a steady state (Boutilier 1988, 1989; chapter 5). Amphibians can use both air and water in gas exchange. The relative importance

of gas exchangers can change during ontogeny (Burggren and West 1982; see also chapter 16). Finally, gas transport is complex in circulations based on intracardiac shunting (Shelton 1985; Shelton and Croghan 1988). The question of how, or whether, such receptor systems are conserved during amphibian metamorphosis is an intriguing but unresolved one (Boutilier 1988; West and Burggren 1982, 1983).

In spite of these difficulties, data are now sufficient to describe the properties of some receptors and regulatory systems involved in respiratory and cardiovascular control in amphibians. Unfortunately, appropriate experiments illuminate only a few corners of this large field, inevitably emphasizing a few systems in a few species. Respiratory and cardiovascular control has been studied mainly in anurans, usually species of *Rana* or *Bufo,* which are not representative of all amphibians (see chapter 1). For example, the response characteristics of anuran pulmocutaneous baroreceptors have recently been described in enough detail to compare with mammalian baroreceptors (Van Vliet and West 1987b, 1987c), but no comparable neurophysiological information is available from urodeles, and the cardiorespiratory control systems in caecilians remain unexplored.

Although the receptors and regulatory systems in modern amphibians may well differ from those in ancestral forms, study of modern systems may elucidate the evolution of air breathing and the terrestrial habit. Such studies therefore not only have intrinsic merit but may ultimately enable us to put cardiorespiratory control mechanisms in "higher" vertebrates into an evolutionary perspective.

RECEPTOR FEEDBACK FROM THE RESPIRATORY SYSTEM
Afferent Innervation of the Airways and Lungs in Amphibians

The afferent innervation of the airways and lungs in amphibians is by the dorsal roots of the cranial nerves. Eckcr (1889, 167–175) describes the general anatomy of the cranial nerves

We wish to thank Dr. Mark Evered and Mr. Paul McCulloch for their helpful comments on drafts of the manuscript. Original research performed by us and described in this chapter was supported by operating grants to NHW from the Medical Research Council and the Natural Sciences and Engineering Research Council of Canada.

TABLE 7.1 Airway Receptors Identified by Neurophysiology in Anurans

Position of Receptive Fields	Stimulus Modality	Afferent Nerve	Possible Function	Reference[a]
External nares	Mechano	Trigeminal (V)	Induce apnea	West and Jones 1976
Olfactory epithelium	Mechano/H_2O?	Trigeminal (V) Olfactory (I)?	Induce apnea	Sakakibara 1978
Tongue (mucosa)	H_2O	Glossopharyngeal (IX)	Induce apnea?	Zotterman 1949
Tongue (mucosa)	Mechano	Glossopharyngeal (IX)	Induce apnea?	Inoue 1978
Pharynx	Mechano	Vagus (X) (carotid and aortic pharyngeal branches)		Van Vliet and West 1987a
Glottis and larynx	Mechano	Vagus (X) (rLN branch)	Induce apnea	Van Vliet and West 1986, 1987c
Larynx	Irritant	Vagus (X) (rLN branch)	Induce apnea	Van Vliet and West 1986, 1987c
Lungs	Mechano/CO_2	Vagus (X)	Drive ventilation (CO_2)	Kuhlmann and Fedde 1979
			Lung volume/ buoyancy	Taglietti and Casella 1966
			Terminate inspiration	Serbeniuk and Gurskaia 1987
			Inhibit gill ventilation (larva)	West and Burggren 1983
			Influence pulmonary systemic blood flow	Shelton 1970; West and Burggren 1984

[a]Not all references are included here. See text for details.

in the adult anuran and their relationship with other elements derived from the branchial system of the larva. Table 7.1 summarizes the distribution of receptive fields and afferent neural pathways for airway and pharyngeal receptors identified by neurophysiological techniques in anurans.

Functional Characteristics of Receptors Located in the Respiratory Tract

Narial Receptors The external nares are an important sensory site in aquatic or semiaquatic air-breathing amphibians such as *Xenopus laevis, Rana pipiens,* and *Notophthalmus meridionalis* (Caudata: Salamandridae). Sensory input from this area evokes acute responses that prevent water entering the airways (including the buccal cavity) and lungs upon submergence. They may also maintain the apnea and cardiovascular adjustments that are associated with submergence, and provide proprioceptive feedback during the ventilatory cycle.

Mechanoreceptors with receptive fields located on or around the external nares in the frog *Rana pipiens* possess afferents in the ophthalmic branch of the trigeminal (V) nerve (West and Jones 1976). The ophthalmic branch runs rostrally to the nares and parallel to the cranium between the cranium and the eyeball. Two branches divide at the anterior margin of the orbit. These eventually reach the nasal cavity and branch to innervate the mucous membrane before penetrating the skull to supply the skin in the region of the snout and the external nares (Ecker 1889). Narial mechanoreceptors are sensitive to the passage of a water meniscus across their receptive fields (West and Jones 1976). Multiunit neurograms reveal populations of rapidly and slowly adapting receptors with all units adapting to continued submergence in still water in 5 to 10 s (fig. 7.1A). Water flow causes a resumption of neural activity. In contrast, mechanoreceptors serving the dorsal skin, with afferents in the second, third, and fourth spinal nerves, do not respond to the passage of a water meniscus and respond only weakly to a sudden pressure increment of 2 cm H_2O. Thus, narial mechanoreceptors may have low stimulus thresholds relative to those of typical skin mechanoreceptors.

Presumably mechanical displacement or compression of the skin stimulates the narial mechanoreceptors. In frogs, the most sensitive rapidly adapting units of the foot, with afferents in the sciatic nerve, reach threshold when the skin is indented by 31 μm (Ogawa, Morimoto, and Yamashita 1981), while the threshold of sensitive slowly adapting units is about 19 μm (Ogawa et al. 1984). No comparable data are available for narial mechanoreceptors with trigeminal afferents.

Changing levels of sympathetic efferent activity may modulate the thresholds and sensitivity of narial mechanoreceptors during prolonged submersion (West and Jones 1976). Sympathetic trunk stimulation increases sensitivity in most classes of mechanoreceptors in frog skin, likely by the direct effect of sympathetic neurotransmitters on the receptor membranes (Calof, Jones, and Roberts 1981).

Tongue "Water Receptors" Application of distilled or tap water to the tongue elicits a "massive discharge" of slowly adapting large units in the glossopharyngeal nerve of *Rana temporaria* (Zotterman 1949). Washing the tongue with isotonic solutions containing NaCl or other salts, but not isotonic sugar solution, abolishes this activity (Koketsu 1951; Zotterman 1949). In fact, sugar solutions produce a response indistinguishable from that of water alone (Zotterman 1949). Clearly, the transduction process is not dependent on an osmotic effect but probably involves changes in the forces driving the rate of ionic diffusion when Na$^+$ is removed from the bathing solution. The receptors respond specifically to solutions containing less than 0.05% NaCl and are not mechanosensitive (Andersson and Zotterman 1950).

Stimulation by water depolarizes single frog taste cells

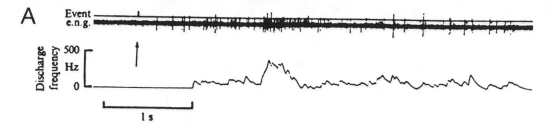

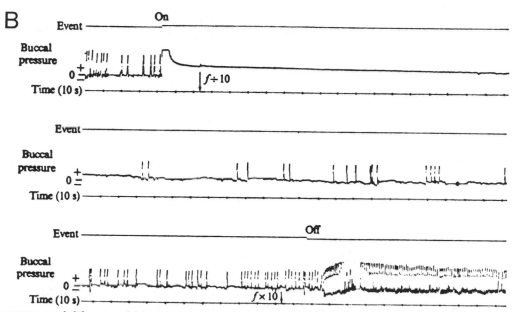

Fig. 7.1 *A*, response recorded from a narial branch of the trigeminal nerve (V) in *Rana pipiens* to the passage of a water meniscus across the nares. *Top trace*, event marker; *middle trace*, multiunit neurogram; *lower trace*, multiunit discharge frequency. *B*, ventilatory effects of bilateral electrical stimulation of the cut central ends of the ophthalmic branch of the trigeminal nerves in *Rana pipiens*. *Upper trace*, event marker; *middle trace*, buccal pressure; *lower trace*, 10-s time marker. Stimulation parameters were 100 Hz, 300 mV, 4-ms duration. Frequency was reduced to 10 Hz at the first *arrow* and restored to the initial rate at the second *arrow*. (Reprinted, by permission, from West and Jones 1976, *Journal of Experimental Biology,* © Company of Biologists, Ltd.)

after a transient hyperpolarization, and this depolarization presumably generates action potentials in glossopharyngeal axons (Akaike and Sato 1976). The removal of NaCl from Ringer's solution applied to the mucosal surface of isolated dorsal epithelium from the bullfrog tongue slowly changes the transepithelial potential and increases tissue resistance (Soeda and Sakudo 1988). The mucosa is slightly negative (−1.32 mV) relative to the grounded serosal surface when the surfaces are perfused with isotonic Ringer's solution, but becomes relatively positively charged (mean 19.4 mV) when water is applied. The addition of NaCl, but not sucrose or other sugars, to the mucosa inhibits this response, in agreement with the findings of Zotterman (1949). The slow potential change is unaffected by ouabain (which inhibits the active transport of Na$^+$), metabolic inhibitors such as dinitrophenol (DNP), or oxygen availability, suggesting that it represents a change in the passive distribution of Na$^+$ or Cl$^-$ ions across the epithelium rather than a change in the rate of active transport. The addition of Na$^+$ to the solution bathing the mucosa is more effective in reducing the potential than the addition of Cl$^-$. Thus, the transepithelial potential produced by water on the mucosal surface seemingly represents a decrease pri-

marily in passive movement of Na$^+$ across the tongue epithelium from the mucosa to the serosa.

Glottal and Pharyngeal Receptors A dense population of mechanoreceptors supplies the glottis of *Bufo marinus*. Their afferents run in the recurrent laryngeal branch of the vagus (Van Vliet and West 1987c). Many small unnamed branches of the vagus also innervate the larynx. Receptors with afferents in the recurrent laryngeal nerve respond to punctuate stimulation of the ipsilateral glottal margin, opening of the glottis, airflow through the glottis, and punctuate stimulation within the larynx (fig. 7.2). Large single units respond to punctuate stimulation with discharges as high as 180 spikes · s^{-1}. Input from these receptors probably protects the airways by inhibiting lung ventilation when prey is swallowed or during accidental entry of water into the buccal cavity. Receptors with receptive fields on the glottal margins may serve a proprioceptive function, signaling glottal closure during intermittent lung ventilation and perhaps influencing its pattern. Some afferents within the recurrent laryngeal nerve appear to be those of nociceptors and respond to cigarette smoke (fig. 7.2) or ammonia vapor blown through the open glottis. These

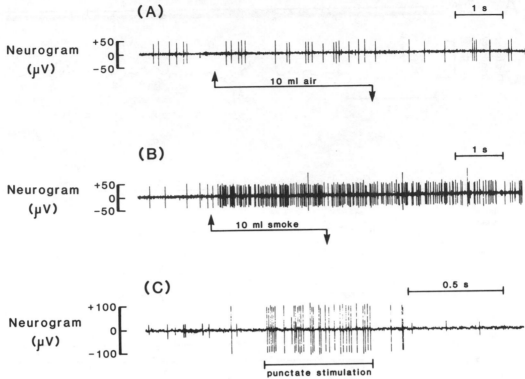

Fig. 7.2 Recordings from afferents within the recurrent laryngeal nerve with receptor endings in the region of the glottis of *Bufo marinus*. *A*, unit responding to 10 ml of air perfused through the open glottis. *B*, same unit increases activity in response to 10 ml of cigarette smoke, indicating nociceptive modality. *C*, a different unit responding to punctate stimulation of the free margin of the glottis. (Reprinted, by permission, from Van Vliet and West 1987c.)

have low signal-to-noise ratios compared to the glottal mechanoreceptors (Van Vliet and West 1987c) and may be small myelinated or non-myelinated fibers.

Mechanoreceptors with afferents in a pharyngeal branch of the vagus, the "aortic" nerve (Ishii, Ishii, and Kusakabe 1985a; Van Vliet and West 1987c; fig. 7.6, X, PH2) innervate the lining of the buccal cavity contiguous with the glottis. The receptive fields of mechanoreceptors whose afferents lie in a small vagal branch cranial to the aortic nerve surround the receptive fields of aortic nerve mechanoreceptors in a concentric fashion, centered on the glottis (Van Vliet and West 1987c). Both of these branches of the vagus also contain baroreceptive afferents (see below, "Receptor Feedback from the Cardiovascular System").

Pulmonary Stretch Receptors In common with all other air-breathing vertebrates, amphibians possess intrapulmonary stretch receptors, which report the rate of lung inflation and the resulting distension to the central nervous system via afferents in the pulmonary vagi. The pulmonary stretch receptors of anuran amphibians lie in the subepithelial connective tissue sheet of the lung walls and internal septa and, like those of mammals, are especially dense near the bronchi. The receptors themselves are free nerve endings (Gaupp 1896–1904), which frequently look like balls of thread ("clews") and less frequently are needle- or plaque-shaped (Cuccati 1888).

McKean (1969) and Milsom and Jones (1977) divided the pulmonary stretch receptor population of *Rana pipiens* into three categories on the basis of their responses to lung infla-

tion, although these almost certainly represent samples taken from a continuous spectrum of adaptation rates. Rapidly adapting "rate" receptors are sensitive to the rate of lung inflation but adapt at constant lung volume. Slowly adapting "proportional" receptors increase discharge frequency as lung volume increases on inflation, are relatively insensitive to the inflation rate, and show a slowly adapting discharge proportional to the final volume achieved. Receptors with intermediate time constants, "rate plus proportional" receptors, combine the properties of the other two groups. In the studies of McKean (1969) and Milsom and Jones (1977), "rate plus proportional" receptors predominated in the population (50–64%), while slowly adapting "proportional" receptors were the least common (12–20%).

Although the pulmonary stretch receptors respond to changes in lung volume, pulmonary volume per se obviously cannot represent their stimulus modality, for they are mechanically coupled to the "container," that is, lung tissue. Bonhoeffer and Kolitat (1958) considered discharge frequency to be linearly related to lung volume, but both Taglietti and Casella (1966) and McKean (1969) concluded that discharge frequency of pulmonary stretch receptors was not linearly related to either pulmonary volume or transpulmonary pressure, but rather to calculated pulmonary wall tension.

The time constant of an individual receptor may stem from the nature of the mechanical coupling to its environment rather than by any property of the nerve ending. In isolated lungs of *Rana temporaria*, changes in pulmonary smooth muscle contractility produced by acetylcholine or histamine produced corresponding changes in pulmonary stretch receptor excitability (Serbeniuk and Gurskaia 1986). McKean (1969) demonstrated that the three classes of response to lung inflation with volume ramps could be modeled if the receptor was linked to surrounding tissue by a dashpot (representing tissue viscosity) and a spring (representing tissue elasticity) in parallel. If the local tissue viscosity/elasticity ratio is low (short dashpot time constant or strong spring), the receptor is more rate-sensitive than if the ratio is high (long dashpot time constant or weak spring), because the region containing the receptor undergoes more deformation more rapidly during inflation.

Taglietti and Casella (1966) were convinced that the mechanical state of the lung showed a more consistent relationship with the response of the whole receptor population than with single units, and consequently neglected to perform single-unit studies. However, McKean (1969) pointed out that information relating to the rate of inflation and the inspired volume may be segregated on the basis of central synaptic connections to functionally discrete central neurons, necessitating single-unit studies. Taglietti and Casella (1968) also claimed that the frog lung contained a receptor population responding specifically to deflation in the range of volumes above the normal resting volume of the lung. However, as Jones and Milsom (1982) pointed out, it is impossible to determine in the absence of single-unit studies whether the response is derived from a population of receptors that respond solely to deflation or from conventional rate-sensitive receptors responding to lung deflation. In the absence of evidence to the contrary, the latter explanation fits the facts.

In vertebrates, the partial pressure of CO_2 in the lungs (P_{CO_2}) varies inversely with alveolar ventilation, so detection of the concentration or partial pressure of CO_2 within the lung is potentially an important sensory modality. In experiments with *Rana pipiens* in which gas flows through the lungs via cannulas implanted in their apices (unidirectionally venti-

lated), the addition of 10% CO_2 to the ventilating gas stream reduces the discharge frequency of rapidly adapting and slowly adapting receptors by about 50% and reduces discharge frequency by 20 to 30% in receptors with intermediate time constants (Milsom and Jones 1977; fig. 7.3).

In *Rana catesbeiana*, most receptors decrease discharge frequency when the lungs are ventilated with 4% CO_2, and frequency decreases further at 8% CO_2. A large group of receptors are initially refractory to the CO_2 stimulus, but respond when intrapulmonary pressure is increased tenfold, suggesting either that the two sensory modalities interact at the level of the receptor (Kuhlmann and Fedde 1979) or that CO_2 mediates changes in receptor sensitivity via changes in smooth muscle tone. In mammals, the effects of CO_2 on pulmonary stretch receptor activity can be largely secondary to such changes in bronchial muscle tone (Mitchell et al. 1980). On the other hand, hypocapnia generally stimulates peripheral nerves (Tenney and Lamb 1965). One model for this effect of CO_2 at the receptor level is that H^+ ions formed by the hydration of CO_2 in extracellular water block ion channels within the receptor membrane. For example, the delayed rectifier K^+ channel of skeletal muscle is extremely sensitive to a reduction in extracellular pH (Blatz 1984). Surprisingly, whether intrapulmonary receptors in amphibians respond to pH changes within the physiological range in pulmonary capillary blood is currently unknown. Reducing the pulmonary perfusate pH from 9.5 to 5.5 reversibly reduces inflation-related activity in the bullfrog lung (Kontani and Koshiura 1981b). In birds and reptiles (Fedde et al. 1974; Molony 1974), some pulmonary receptors are sensitive to changes in intrapulmonary CO_2 concentration but not to lung inflation within the physiological pressure range. To date, no such pulmonary receptors have been found in amphibians. The combined chemosensitivity and mechanosensitivity of pulmonary mechanoreceptors in frogs led Milsom and Jones (1977) to

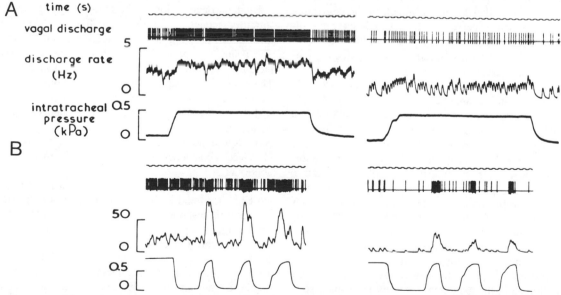

Fig. 7.3 Responses of intrapulmonary, CO_2-sensitive mechanoreceptors in *Rana pipiens* to CO_2 and lung inflation. *A*, response of a slowly adapting receptor to lung inflation with air (*left*) and air + 3% CO_2 (*right*). *B*, response of a rapidly adapting rate-sensitive receptor to lung inflation with air (*left*) and 3% CO_2 (*right*). *Upper trace* in each set is a 1-s time marker; *second trace* is a single-unit neurogram; *third trace* is discharge frequency; *lower trace* is pressure recorded from the trachea. (Reprinted, by permission, from Milsom and Jones 1977.)

suggest that these receptors may represent functional precursors of the CO_2-sensitive units found in the relatively inexpansible lungs of birds (Molony 1974; Osborne and Burger 1974) and the slowly adapting mechanosensitive units found in the relatively hypercapnic mammalian lung, which, however, are relatively insensitive to changes in P_{CO_2} above 20 mm Hg (Mitchell et al. 1980).

Functional Significance of Input from Receptors in the Airways and Lungs

Receptors Located in the Upper Airways The location and response characteristics of receptors within the upper airways and pharynx of anurans suggest that they represent successive lines of defense against the impairment of gas exchange by the incursion of water (or food). Closure of the external nares upon submergence and the resulting apnea appear to be reflex responses to water on the external nares, resulting in narial closure and apnea in both frogs and salamanders (Lombroso 1913; Spurway and Haldane 1953; West and Jones 1976; Willem 1920). For example, in restrained but conscious *Rana pipiens,* apnea does not occur until water rises to the external nares (West and Jones 1976). This does not, of course, exclude volitional narial closure as part of the normal behavioral repertoire associated with submergence.

All respiratory airflow occurs through the nares in anurans, suggesting that the mechanoreceptors with receptive fields on the external nares and trigeminal afferents (West and Jones 1976) represent the first line of defense against the entry of water into the respiratory tract, although Zotterman (1949) speculated that tongue "water receptor" input may also contribute to inhibiting ventilation.

Electrical stimulation of the central cut ends of the ophthalmic branch of the trigeminal nerves (which contain narial mechanoreceptor afferents) renders conscious *R. pipiens* apneic (fig. 7.1B). Narial closure requires a stimulating voltage higher than that producing a cessation of ventilatory movements (West and Jones 1976). Electrical stimulation of the cut central ends of either the nasal branch of the trigeminal nerves or the olfactory nerves, both of which serve the olfactory epithelium, results in apnea in anesthetized *Bufo marinus* (Sakakibara 1978), suggesting that the olfactory epithelium itself may be sensitive to water.

Involuntary submergence or injection of water into the buccal cavity, via an implanted canulla causes frogs (*R. pipiens*) in which the ophthalmic nerves are denervated to flatten and elevate the buccal floor (West and Jones 1976). This response expels some, but not all, water from the buccal cavity on submergence in denervated animals. Normally, negligible amounts of water enter the buccal cavity of semiterrestrial anurans. Neither *R. pipiens* or *B. marinus* drink in response to dehydration or immersion in hyperosmotic saline (Bentley and Yorio 1979; see chapter 6). West and Jones (1976) suggest that glossopharyngeal "water receptors" act as a backup to narial receptors. Indeed, mechanical stimulation or the application of chemical solutions or distilled water to the tongue of *Rana nigromaculata* results in a reflex discharge in the ipsilateral branch of the hypoglossal nerve (first spinal) serving the hyoglossal muscle of the buccal floor (Inoue 1978; Kumai 1981). However, the normal role of the reflex may be to trigger the retraction of the extended tongue upon contact with prey.

Ophthalmic nerve denervation itself presumably does not significantly impair normal narial closure by the destruction of motor pathways. Although electromyograms (EMGs) synchronous with narial closure are evident from the region of the nares (Jones 1970; West and Jones 1975a), this is the normal result of the action of the lower jaw muscles on the premaxilla (de Jongh and Gans 1969; Gans and Pyles 1983).

Glottal and pharyngeal mechanoreceptors with vagal afferents may inhibit ventilation if water reaches the glottis, as in aquatic birds (Bamford and Jones 1974). However, the exclusion of water from the buccal cavity in relatively terrestrial anurans like *B. marinus* suggests that the usual role of these receptors may be to inhibit ventilation during swallowing. Receptors with fields on the glottal margins may also provide proprioceptive information related to the breathing cycle by reporting glottal closure.

Intrapulmonary Receptor Input The functional role of intrapulmonary CO_2-sensitive mechanoreceptors in amphibians is far from clear, although they may be involved in the regulation of both respiratory and cardiovascular variables (Kuhlmann and Fedde 1979; Shelton 1970; West and Burggren 1983, 1984) and buoyancy in aquatic anurans (Evans and Shelton 1984; Taglietti and Casella 1966).

Sensory input from intrapulmonary stretch receptors may be important in patterning the length of inspiratory and expiratory periods in anurans, as it is in mammals (von Euler 1986). Simultaneous recordings of inspiratory motor nerve activity and mass afferent activity in the pulmonary vagus in *Rana temporaria* demonstrated that, after inspiration, vagal afferent activity adapts to a threshold level, which is associated with the start of activity in the motor nerves (Serbeniuk and Gurskaia 1987). Decreases in afferent activity of the pulmonary vagi caused by an increase in pulmonary arterial P_{CO_2} or the application of novocaine also stimulates activity in the inspiratory motor nerves, while vagotomy biases the system against expiration (Serbeniuk and Gurskaia 1987).

Bilateral denervation of the pulmonary vagi decreases inspiratory frequency and minute ventilation in *Xenopus laevis* for 4 days following denervation (Evans and Shelton 1984). The inspiratory period (TI) decreases, but inspiratory flow increases, resulting in no net change in inspiratory volume. The frequency of expiration decreases, resulting in high lung volumes and an increase in buoyancy that interferes with normal diving behavior. In spite of these changes, denervation of the pulmonary vagi does not affect the ventilatory responses to hypoxia. Minute ventilation returns to control levels 6 weeks postdenervation, but the ventilatory pattern is still abnormal.

The CO_2 sensitivity of anuran pulmonary stretch receptors led Kuhlmann and Fedde (1979) to suggest that these receptors may be responsible for mediating the reflex increase in lung ventilation that occurs in response to hypercapnia. Evidence of central (De Marneffe-Foulon 1962; Smatresk and Smits 1991) and carotid chemoreceptor (Van Vliet and West 1991) sensitivity to CO_2 in anurans demonstrates the considerable redundancy in the detection of this gas. Elsewhere in the airways, high levels of CO_2 (5.7%) delivered to the nasal mucosa result in apnea in anesthetized bullfrogs (Sakakibara 1978), perhaps as the result of the stimulation of nociceptors with axons in the olfactory and trigeminal nerves.

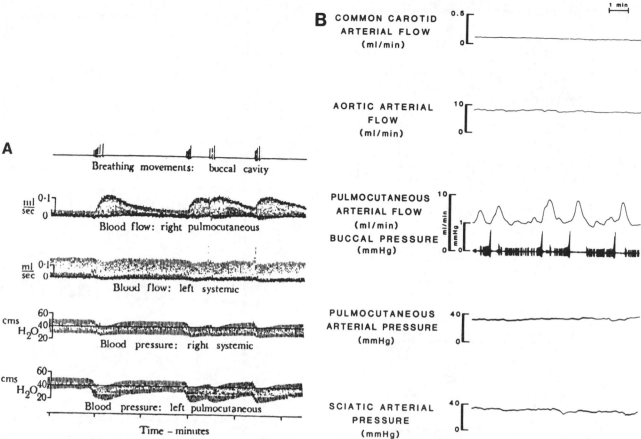

Fig. 7.4 *A,* pulsatile pressures and flows recorded from the arterial arches in anesthetized *Xenopus laevis.* Pulmocutaneous artery blood flow increases following a burst of breathing movements, without much effect on systemic flow. Pulmocutaneous pressure falls coincident with the increases in flow, suggesting that they are brought about by decreases in pulmocutaneous peripheral resistance. (Reprinted, by permission, from Shelton 1970.) *B,* mean pressures and flows recorded from the arterial arches in conscious *Bufo marinus* performing lung inflation cycles. Most of the increase in pulmocutaneous artery blood flow occurs after the lungs have been inflated, and peaks between lung ventilation cycles, when the lungs are held inflated. Lung ventilation does not influence flow in the carotid arteries or the aortae. (From N. H. West and A. Smits unpublished.)

Denervation of the pulmonary vagi does not abolish the increase in heart rate associated with lung ventilation in conscious *X. laevis* (Evans and Shelton 1984). This suggests that lung stretch receptor input is not solely responsible for the respiration-related modulation of heart rate. Segura, Bronstein, and Schmajuk (1981) demonstrated that artificial lung inflation produced tachycardia in *Bufo arenarum* and concluded that the action of a concomitant increase in pulmonary venous return on the cardiac pacemaker was partially responsible for the effect. Lung stretch receptor input in amphibians may be involved in regulating the distribution of ventricular output via the intracardiac shunt by reflexly influencing pulmonary, and perhaps systemic, flow resistance. Lung inflation produced by spontaneous breathing movements and artificial lung inflation in lightly anesthetized *X. laevis* does not significantly influence heart rate or aortic blood flow, but increases blood flow in the pulmocutaneous artery. Thus, ventricular output increases, and this increase is directed preferentially to the pulmocutaneous artery. Pulmocutaneous diastolic pressure falls coincidentally, suggesting that a decrease in pulmonary resistance causes the increase in flow (Emilio and Shelton 1972; Shelton 1970; fig. 7.4A). Experiments on conscious *B. marinus,* in which increased lung ven-

tilation stimulated by CO_2 results in a large increase in flow in the pulmocutaneous artery (but not in the common carotid artery or the aorta), support this viewpoint (N. H. West and A. Smits unpublished; fig. 7.4B).

West and Burggren (1984), using anesthetized *B. marinus,* attempted to disassociate the cardiovascular effects of lung inflation from any accompanying changes in the concentrations of intrapulmonary CO_2 and O_2 by unidirectionally ventilating the lungs. Lungs were inflated by raising the outflow resistance to gas flow. Lung inflation with air increases pulmonary artery blood flow and reduces pulmonary arterial resistance (fig. 7.5A). On the other hand, unidirectional ventilation with air + 5% CO_2 at constant lung volume decreases pulmonary arterial flow, as first noted by Smith (1978), and increases pulmonary artery resistance (fig. 7.5B). Changes in cutaneous artery blood flow and resistance, although small, are opposite to those in the pulmonary artery. Heart rate does not change.

The attendant increases in pulmocutaneous or pulmonary arterial blood flow do not appear to be a consequence of lung inflation reducing pulmonary vascular resistance mechanically. Indeed, transmural pressure gradients for collapsible intrapulmonary vessels presumably decrease as intrapulmonary

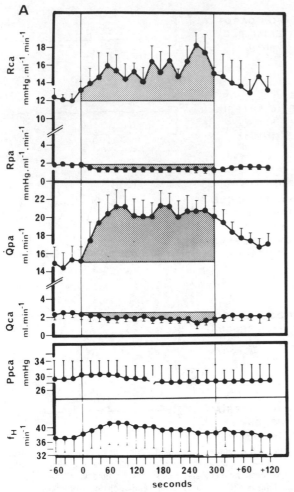

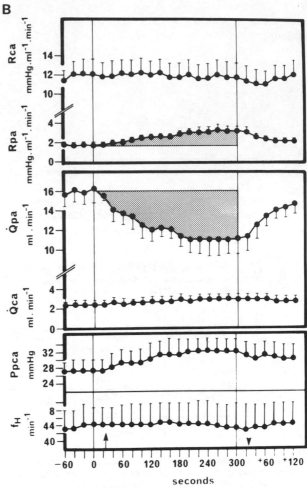

Fig. 7.5 Dissociation of the effects of lung inflation and intrapulmonary CO_2 levels on pulmonary and cutaneous artery blood flow and resistance in unidirectionally ventilated, anesthetized toads, *Bufo marinus*. *A*, Increase in intrapulmonary pressure from 0 to 3 cm H_2O with no change in intrapulmonary CO_2. *B*, intrapulmonary CO_2 changed from 0 to 5% at a constant inflating pressure of 2 cm H_2O. Test gas enters the lungs at the *arrow. Rca*, cutaneous artery resistance; *Rpa*, pulmonary artery resistance; *Qpa*, pulmonary artery blood flow; *Qca*, cutaneous artery blood flow; *Ppca*, mean pulmocutaneous artery pressure; f_H, heart rate. (Reprinted, by permission, from West and Burggren 1984.)

pressures become increasingly positive during lung inflation, promoting an increase in intrapulmonary vascular resistance. Deep anesthesia abolishes responsiveness in previously responsive preparations (Emilio and Shelton 1972; West and Burggren 1984). Atropine administration results in high constant levels of pulmocutaneous blood flow, which are unaffected by lung inflation, while acetylcholine injected into the pulmocutaneous artery reduces flow in the pulmonary artery, suggesting that pulmonary resistance is normally determined by the level of vagal efferent activity to the pulmonary vasculature (Emilio and Shelton 1972; Shelton 1970; West and Burggren 1984).

The site at which resistance is controlled is probably a vagally innervated, muscular sphincter located within the extrinsic segment of the pulmonary artery in both *R. temporaria* and the urodele *Ambystoma* (Saint-Aubain 1982b; Saint-Aubain and Wingstrand 1979). A detailed anatomical study has yet to be performed in *B. marinus,* although a sphincter has been observed in the congeneric toad *Bufo bufo* (M. L. de Saint-Aubain pers. comm.). Sectioning the pulmonary vagus in anurans permanently dilates the ipsilateral

artery, while stimulation of the distal end of the cut vagal trunk, with the cardiac vagus cut, constricts a segment of the extrinsic pulmonary artery with no apparent changes in cardiac frequency or output (Saint-Aubain and Wingstrand 1979; Luckhardt and Carlson 1921). Bilateral pulmonary vagotomy abolishes the pulmonary vasoconstriction in response to hypercapnia in *B. marinus* (Smith 1978). Emilio and Shelton (1972) suggested that pulmonary stretch receptors may represent the afferent limb of the reflex pathway. Rapid lung inflation or high static lung volumes, resulting in a high frequency of pulmonary stretch receptor traffic, would reflexly reduce pulmonary vascular resistance and increase blood flow by reducing efferent vagal tone. As West and Burggren (1984) pointed out, the CO_2 sensitivity of intrapulmonary stretch receptors would reduce afferent activity at any given lung volume if intrapulmonary CO_2 concentrations rise, increasing vascular resistance and reducing pulmonary blood flow. Such a mechanism may redistribute ventricular output away from the lungs during apnea in anurans.

Unidirectional ventilation of one lung with air + 5% CO_2 reduces vascular engorgement in *both* lungs (Smith 1978).

This finding demonstrates that the reduction in pulmonary blood flow in response to pulmonary hypercapnia is reflex and involves central contralateral connections.

Apnea results in hypercapnia in several species of anurans despite cutaneous CO_2 loss (Emilio 1974; Jones 1972a). Therefore, the dual sensitivity of intrapulmonary stretch receptors potentially allows amphibians to match pulmonary perfusion to their intermittent ventilation.

RECEPTOR FEEDBACK FROM THE CARDIOVASCULAR SYSTEM
Afferent Innervation of the Aortic Arches in Anuran Amphibians

Two types of primary afferent neurons, mechanoreceptors and chemoreceptors, contribute sensory feedback from the cardiovascular system. Table 7.2 summarizes the distribution and afferent pathways of receptors within the cardiovascular system that have been identified by neurophysiological techniques. Mechanoreceptors have sensory endings located in the walls of the vessels and provide feedback concerning the distension of the segments of the vasculature in which they reside. Because arterial blood pressure distends the walls of arteries, mechanoreceptors with endings in the walls of large arteries are referred to as arterial pressure receptors, or arterial "baroreceptors." Cardiovascular chemoreceptors provide feedback concerning the chemical composition of the arterial blood. The sensory apparatus of arterial chemoreceptors consists of the sensory nerve ending and two additional cell types, glomus and satellite cells. Together these constitute a neurite complex. The chemoreceptor neuron provides feedback, but the sensory nerve ending does not necessarily function as the chemoreceptor per se. Chemoreceptors in the

vascular system are termed peripheral arterial chemoreceptors to distinguish them from chemoreceptors in the brain stem, and the sensory fibers are referred to as chemoreceptor afferent fibers.

Comparative anatomy and homology have guided the search for arterial baroreceptors in amphibians. In 1931, Koch noted that the arterial segments containing baroreceptors in adult mammals were the adult remnants of the branchial arch arteries and were innervated by the corresponding branchial arch nerve derivatives. Koch's observation provided a rationale for the examination of many vertebrate species. The only amendment presently required is to include derivatives of the ventral aorta, such as the truncus arteriosus, because baroreceptor zones may extend from the aortic arches into their divisions of the truncus in amphibians and reptiles (fig. 7.6).

Mutatori (cited in Adams 1958) subsequently extended Koch's account of baroreceptors to include peripheral arterial chemoreceptors. The essential point is that peripheral arterial chemoreceptors usually lie near baroreceptive segments of the vasculature, and baroreceptor and chemoreceptor afferents often travel to the brain stem in the same nerve. From an anatomical standpoint, therefore, any branchial arch artery or its derivative that is in close association with either the vagus or glossopharyngeal nerve constitutes a potential baroreceptive or chemoreceptive zone. Larval amphibians have four branchial arch arteries, each closely associated with corresponding branchial arch nerves (Watteville 1875; Wyman 1852). Because adult amphibians maintain this close correspondence (Ecker 1889; Fedele 1943; Francis 1934; Kingsley 1902; Norris 1908; Saxena 1967), the search for arterial baroreceptor and chemoreceptor zones and the deduction of appropriate homologies for such regions on an anatomical basis are simplified.

TABLE 7.2 Cardiovascular Receptors in Anurans

Position of Receptors	Stimulus Modality	Afferent Nerve	Proposed Function	Reference[a]
Carotid artery or labyrinth	Chemo/O_2	Glossopharyngeal (IX)	Ventilation drive (O_2)	Ishii, Honda, and Ishii 1966
Carotid artery or labyrinth	Mechano	Glossopharyngeal (IX)	Arterial pressure regulation?	Ishii, Honda, and Ishii 1966
Carotid artery	Mechano	Vagus, carotid branch (X)[b]	Arterial pressure regulation?	Van Vliet and West 1987c
Aortic arch	Chemo/O_2	Vagus, aortic branch (X)	Ventilation drive (O_2)	Ishii, Ishii, and Kusakabe 1985a
Aortic arch	Mechano	Vagus, aortic branch (X)	Arterial pressure regulation?	Ishii, Ishii, and Kusakabe 1985a; Van Vliet and West 1987c
Pulmocutaneous artery	Mechano	Vagus, rLN branch (X)	Arterial pressure regulation	West and Van Vliet 1983; Van Vliet and West 1987b, 1987c
Pulmocutaneous artery	Chemo/O_2	Vagus, rLN branch (X)	Ventilation drive (O_2); enhance bradycardia?	Lillo 1980b; Hoffman and Cordeiro de Sousa 1982
Truncus arteriosus	Mechano	Vagus, cardiac branch (X)	None demonstrated	Downing and Torrance 1961
Truncus arteriosus	Mechano	Vagus, rLN branch (X)	None demonstrated	Van Vliet and West 1987c
Ventricle	Mechano	Vagus, cardiac branch (X)	None demonstrated	Kolatat, Kramer, and Muhl 1957; Downing and Torrance 1961; Niijima 1970
Atria	Mechano	Vagus, cardiac branch (X)	None demonstrated	Kontani and Koshiura 1983
Sinus venosus	Mechano	Vagus, cardiac branch (X)	None demonstrated	Kolatat, Kramer, and Muhl 1957; Niijima 1970

Note: Existence of pulmocutaneous arterial chemoreceptors is postulated but not proven.
[a] Not all references are included here. See text for details.
[b] Infrequent occurrence.

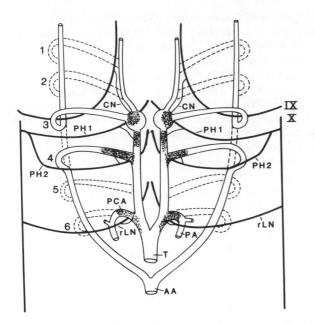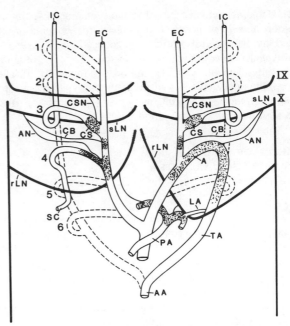

Fig. 7.6 A comparison of the visceral arch nerve supply and the location within the central arteries of major baroreceptor populations. Ventral view. *Left*, anuran circulation; *right*, mammalian circulation. *Stippled areas* represent the receptive fields of baroreceptor populations. *A*, aortic arch; *AA*, abdominal aorta; *AN*, aortic nerve; *CB*, carotid branch of superior laryngeal nerve; *CN*, carotid nerve; *CS*, carotid sinus; *CSN*, carotid sinus nerve; *EC*, external carotid artery; *IC*, internal carotid artery;

LA, ligament of ductus arteriosus; *PA*, pulmonary artery; *PCA*, pulmocutaneous artery; *PH1*, *PH2*, pharyngeal branches of the vagus; *rLN*, recurrent laryngeal nerve; *SC*, subclavian artery; *sLN*, superior laryngeal nerve; *T*, thoracic aorta; *TA*, truncus arteriosus; *IX*, glossopharyngeal nerve; *X*, vagus nerve; *arabic numerals*, visceral arches. (Reprinted, by permission, from Van Vliet and West 1987c.)

Carotid Arch   Early anatomical studies suggested the carotid labyrinth (or carotid gland, carotid body) as a prospective baroreceptive region in anurans (Ask-Upmark 1935; Boyd 1933). The anuran carotid labyrinth is a conspicuous dilation of the internal carotid artery or carotid bifurcation. The carotid labyrinth and dilation of the internal carotid artery in mammals (the carotid sinus or bulbus caroticus) are obviously similar (e.g., Boyd 1933), and indeed, the two structures may be considered developmentally homologous (Adams 1958). However, in contrast to the structure of the carotid sinus, which is simply a conducting vessel with dilated walls, the vascular structure of the labyrinth is extremely complex (Carman 1955, 1967a, 1967b; Ishida 1954; Smith, Berger, and Evans 1981).

The carotid labyrinth and adjacent carotid vasculature receive a fine branch (or several) of the glossopharyngeal nerve. This branch, referred to variously as the carotid, intercarotid, or sinus nerve (Boyd 1933; Carman 1955; Ishii and Ishii 1978; Ishii, Honda, and Ishii 1966; Ishii, Ishii, and Kusakabe 1985a; Neil, Strom, and Zotterman 1950; Rogers 1964), provides a rich afferent as well as efferent innervation of the carotid labyrinth and adjacent carotid arteries (Ishii and Ishii 1970; Rogers 1964, 1966). Afferent fibers may also reach the labyrinth via a fine pharyngeal branch of the vagus (Van Vliet and West 1987c), referred to as the *long laryngeal nerve* by Fedele (1943).

The carotid labyrinth includes chemoreceptor neurite complexes as well as free nerve endings. According to Rogers (1964, 1966), free nerve endings in the labyrinth exhibit ring, knob, and clublike terminations. Although such endings may be those of mechanoreceptors, the endings appear somewhat

simpler in structure than those characteristic of baroreceptors in most mammals (Rogers 1964).

The neurite complexes in the amphibian carotid labyrinth are similar to the chemoreceptor apparatus of birds and mammals (Ishii and Oosaki 1966, 1969; S. Kobayashi 1975). The chemoreceptor neurite complex is composed of three cell types as in other vertebrates: sensory nerve endings, glomus (type I) cells, and satellite (type II, sustentacular) cells. Glomus cells are the most conspicuous cells of the complex and are evident in light and fluorescence microspectrometry (Chowdhary 1951; De Boissezon 1939; Ishii, Honda, and Ishii 1966; Ishii and Oosaki 1969; Rogers 1966). These cells are scattered throughout the stroma of the labyrinth, appearing alone or in groups of two or three cells. They are oval and contain numerous vesicles, which may contain catecholamines (Ishii and Oosaki 1969). Glomus cells of the carotid labyrinth are closely enveloped by satellite cells, which form a thin sheath around one to three cells and are often in close apposition to smooth muscle (Kusakabe, Ishii, and Ishii 1987). Unmyelinated and myelinated nerve fibers are associated with both cell types but form specialized contacts only with the membrane of glomus cells (Ishii and Oosaki 1969; S. Kobayashi 1975). Amphibian neurite complexes do not coalesce to form discrete "bodies" of tissue, often referred to as paraganglia, or epithelioid bodies (e.g., carotid bodies in mammals and birds), although many epithelioid bodies of unknown function occur along the central aortic arches of amphibians.

Aortic Arch   The aortic arch of anurans receives a thin branch of the vagus, which has been referred to as the aortic

(Ishii, Ishii, and Kusakabe 1985a) or truncal (Fedele 1943) nerve. The aortic nerve is a pharyngeal branch of the vagus, because it innervates pharyngeal muscles and the larynx as well as the aorta (Van Vliet and West 1986). The anuran aortic nerve does not appear to be homologous with the aortic (depressor) nerve in mammals (Van Vliet and West 1986), although it contains both baroreceptor and chemoreceptor afferent fibers.

The fine structure of the aortic innervation has not received as much attention as that of the carotid labyrinth. Endings that may subserve a mechanoreceptive function are as yet unknown. However, Busch (1929) described nerves "seen to terminate in or about spherical or oval bodies" in methylene blue–stained sections of the aorta of *Rana esculenta*. Presumably, Busch's description was of the innervation of glomus cells within the aorta, which have recently been observed in the aorta of *Bufo vulgaris* (Ishii, Ishii, and Kusakabe 1985a). According to these authors, the fine structure of aortic glomus cells and their innervation are similar to those of carotid labyrinth chemoreceptor tissue. Satellite cells, although present, are poorly developed compared with those of the carotid labyrinth, because they did not completely envelope the glomus cells. As in the carotid labyrinth, the chemoreceptor neurite complexes are distributed within the stroma of the aortic wall and do not aggregate to form a discrete epithelioid body, such as the aortic body of mammals.

Pulmocutaneous Artery   The pulmocutaneous artery (PCA) is intimately associated with a long branch of the vagus, which crosses directly over its ventral surface before passing to the larynx. This conspicuous vagal branch has been strongly implicated in the reflex control of arterial pressure and, to a lesser extent, ventilation. Historically this branch has been referred to as the *laryngeal* (Ecker 1889; Ishii, Honda, and Ishii 1966; Ishii and Ishii 1978; Ishii, Ishii, and Kusakabe 1985a; Neil, Strom, and Zotterman 1950; Marshall 1928; Watteville 1875), *long laryngeal* (Fedele 1943), *superior laryngeal* (West and Van Vliet 1983), and *recurrent branch* or *ramus* of the vagus (Ecker 1889; Marshall 1928; Wyman 1852). As this nerve passes to the larynx and is truly recurrent in its path (that is, it loops about the PCA) we will refer to it as the recurrent laryngeal nerve (rLN; Van Vliet and West 1986, 1987b, 1987c). This name is consistent with that of its homologue in mammals (Watteville 1875; Wyman 1852) and distinguishes it from the laryngeal branch of the vagus that arises near the cardiac branch (Ecker 1889; Watteville 1875) or that which Volkmann (cited by Wyman 1852) described as communicating with the facial nerve.

Mechanoreceptors and chemoreceptor neurite complexes have not been described within the wall of the PCA. Although fluorescent microscopy has demonstrated neuroepithelial cells in the cutaneous and pulmonary arteries, as well as the pulmonary epithelium (Rogers and Haller 1978; D. G. Smith 1976), they are distinct from chemoreceptive glomus cells and are presumably efferent.

The Heart   A discrete cardiac branch of the vagus nerve on each side innervates the amphibian heart (Ecker 1889), Abraham (1969) has described the fine structure of the innervation of the hearts of *Rana ridibunda* and *Salamandra maculosa* (Salamandridae). Both myelinated and unmyelinated fibers richly innervate each chamber of the heart. The abundant nerve fibers and their endings arise from pre- and postganglionic parasympathetic and postganglionic sympathetic efferent nerves, as well as vagal sensory fibers. Some fibers of the atria, ventricle, and bulbus terminate in specialized ring- or disk-shaped endings. Such endings are presumed to be afferent and therefore may represent the termination of at least one form of vagal sensory fiber. More complex sensory endings typical of mammalian hearts are not apparent. The ring endings are particularly abundant in regions of the bulbus. Endings in this region therefore may constitute a depressor afferent system similar to the aortic arch baroreceptor regions of "higher" vertebrates (i.e., mammals and birds).

Functional Characteristics of Cardiovascular Mechanoreceptors

Pulmocutaneous Arterial Baroreceptors   The first evidence for baroreceptor endings in the PCA came from Neil, Strom, and Zotterman (1950), who recorded a rhythmic discharge in the rLN of *Rana temporaria* that was in phase with the T wave of the electrocardiogram. Cutting a fine branch of the rLN that passed to the PCA abolished the rhythmic activity. Arterial blood pressures were not recorded in the study, and therefore the discharge could not be related to the cardiac cycle. Several subsequent studies (Ishii and Ishii 1978; Van Vliet and West 1987b, 1987c) confirmed and extended the observations of Neil, Strom, and Zotterman (1950). Anuran PCA baroreceptors and their attendant reflex are presently the most extensively characterized of nonmammalian vertebrate baroreceptors. Therefore, the information relating to pulmocutaneous baroreceptors summarized below may not only elucidate their particular role in cardiovascular regulation, but also that of other amphibian baroreceptor populations.

According to Ishii and Ishii (1978), the receptive fields of pulmocutaneous baroreceptors in *Bufo vulgaris* are in the wall of the PCA, approximately midway between its separation from the truncus and the origin of the independent cutaneous and pulmonary arteries. Such a location is convenient for experimentation because it readily permits control of the stimulus to the baroreceptor population by isolation and cannulation (Ishii and Ishii 1978; Hoffmann and Cordeiro de Sousa 1982; West and Van Vliet 1983). In *B. marinus*, however, the receptive fields of pulmocutaneous baroreceptors lie in the wall of either the PCA or the pulmocutaneous division of the truncus arteriosus, typically within 5 mm of the point of separation of the PCA from the truncus (Van Vliet and West 1987c). Vascular isolation of the PCA may therefore exclude the receptive fields of some baroreceptors that lie within the truncus in *B. marinus*. This distribution of receptive fields is consistent with the variable success achieved in eliciting the PCA baroreflex by isolation and distension of the extratruncal segment of the PCA (West and Van Vliet 1983). Variation in the position of this receptive field in different species of anurans requires further investigation.

The conduction velocities of PCA baroreceptors in *B. marinus* range from 0.3 to 0.7 m · s^{-1}, with a mean of 0.5 m · s^{-1} (Van Vliet and West 1987c). Conduction velocities in this range suggest that the baroreceptor endings are connected to unmyelinated afferent fibers (Bishop and Heinbecker 1930). This has both anatomical and functional implications. In mammals, baroreceptor endings that connect to unmyelinated afferent fibers have a much less elaborate and conspicuous structure than those that connect to myelinated afferent fibers (Krauhs 1979). Therefore, the PCA baroreceptors may be simple nerve endings, as are some endings in the carotid labyrinth (Rogers 1964). In mammals, baroreceptors with unmyelinated afferent fibers have higher pressure thresholds and a lower range of discharge frequencies than do their myelinated counterparts (Thoren 1981). The functional properties of the baroreceptor afferents in amphibians are consistent with a slow conduction velocity and lack of myelination (Van Vliet and West 1987b). They exhibit high pressure thresholds relative to their resting arterial pressure, and a low range of discharge frequencies (see below, and also Van Vliet and West 1987b).

In anesthetized or pithed toads (*B. vulgaris* or *B. marinus*), pulmocutaneous baroreceptors discharge rhythmically, with their peak discharge frequency coinciding with the arterial systole (Ishii and Ishii 1978; Van Vliet and West 1987c). At pressures close to their threshold, a single baroreceptor spike may occur in intermittent cardiac cycles. As arterial pressures increase, the discharge becomes more regular, and additional spikes occur in each cardiac cycle. Accompanying further increases in arterial pressure are more numerous spikes in each cardiac cycle, a fall in the smallest interspike interval (increasing peak discharge frequency), earlier initiation of the discharge relative to the beginning of the systole, and extension of the discharge into diastole (fig. 7.7).

In the isolated PCA, step increases in pressure elicit a phasic discharge at 31 to 35 mm Hg pressure in single units in *B. vulgaris* (Ishii and Ishii 1978). Discharges lasting more than 10 s occur only at pressures maintained above 60 mm Hg. Pressure thresholds range from 21 to 37 mm Hg (mean 30 ± 2 mm Hg) in *B. marinus* (Van Vliet and West 1987b). Tonic firing, defined as the discharge of units in the period 45 to 60 s after a step change in pressure, occurs as long as pressures remain above 23 to 44 mm Hg (mean 36 ± 3 mm Hg; Van Vliet and West 1987b).

Pulmocutaneous baroreceptors discharge continuously only within a range of frequencies. The "minimum adapted firing frequency" is the lowest of these discharge frequencies. The adapted discharge consists of a series of almost equally spaced spikes in response to a large pressure step, for example, 60 mm Hg. In response to smaller pressure steps the discharge often adapts to a frequency at which one or several spikes drop out of the series. A similar response occurs during pres-

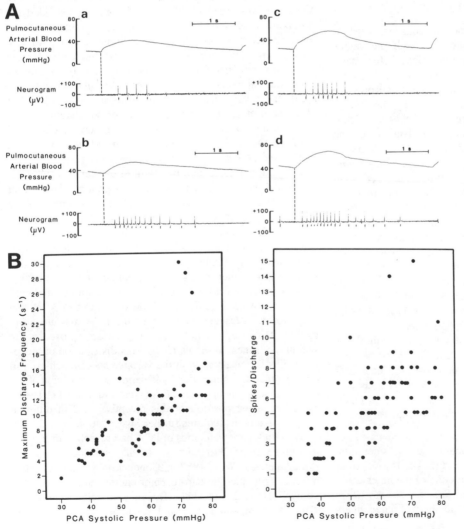

Fig. 7.7 *A*, discharge of a single pulmocutaneous artery baroreceptor related to the arterial pressure waveform in *Bufo marinus*. *a*, discharge at a control pressure of 41/20 mm Hg. *b*, lengthening of discharge by raising diastolic pressure. *c*, increased discharge frequency at increased systolic (and pulse) pressure. *d*, discharge at elevated systolic and diastolic pressure. *B*, relationship between maximum discharge frequency and the number of spikes per cardiac cycle, and systolic pressure in the pulmocutaneous artery. (Reprinted, by permission, from Van Vliet and West 1987c.)

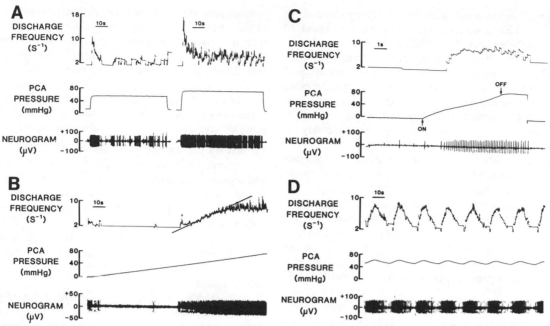

Fig. 7.8 Waveforms used to analyze pulmocutaneous arterial baroceptor response characteristics in *Bufo marinus*. *A*, pressure steps. *B*, slow pressure ramp. Line drawn on discharge frequency trace is a graphical estimation of rate of change of discharge frequency with time, used to calculate pressure sensitivity. *C*, response to infusion of physiological saline at a constant rate of 32 μl · s^{-1} (volume ramp). *D*, response to a sinusoidal pressure stimulus with a mean pressure of 55 mm Hg and a pulse pressure of 10 mm Hg. All traces are from different units. (Reprinted, by permission, from Van Vliet and West 1987b.)

sure ramps (fig. 7.8B), in which an irregular initial discharge precedes regular spikes as the pressure reaches higher values. The minimum adapted discharge frequency of PCA baroceptors ranges from 2 to 3 spikes · s^{-1} (Van Vliet and West 1987b) and may represent a limitation of the frequency-encoding mechanisms of the spike-initiating zone of the afferent fiber.

The maximum discharge frequency is the greatest frequency at which the baroreceptors discharge in response to pressure. In response to step increases in pressure to 76 mm Hg, the maximum observed phasic discharge frequency is 13.7 ± 2.6 spikes · s^{-1} in *B. marinus* (Van Vliet and West 1987c). Similar maximum discharge frequencies occur during the stimulation of pulmocutaneous baroreceptors by pressure ramps at 30 mm Hg · s^{-1}. Some pulmocutaneous baroreceptors discharge at frequencies up to 30 spikes · s^{-1} in response to large step changes in pressure and elevated circulatory pressures (Van Vliet and West 1987b, 1987c).

The pressure sensitivity of baroreceptors is defined as the rate of change of their discharge frequency with respect to pressure and has been estimated with both pressure step and pressure ramp stimulation (Van Vliet and West 1987b). With pressure ramp stimuli, the pressure sensitivity of pulmocutaneous baroreceptors range from 0.19 to 0.52 spikes · s^{-1} · mm Hg^{-1}. Pressure sensitivity increased with increasing rates of pressure rise (*dP/dt*), from 0.5 to 30 mm Hg · s^{-1} (Van Vliet and West 1987b). The dependency of the pressure sensitivity on the rate of pressure rise is also apparent when pressure undergoes step increases. The mean pressure sensitivity of the peak discharge at the onset of pressure steps is 0.51 spikes · s^{-1} mm Hg^{-1}, whereas that for the tonic discharge, 45 to 60 s after the onset of the pressure step, is 0.19 spikes · s^{-1} · mm Hg^{-1} (Van Vliet and West 1987b). These values are

in good agreement with those obtained using pressure ramp stimuli.

Rate sensitivity and adaptation are manifestations of a single property, an enhanced response to dynamic pressure stimuli. The sensitivity of pulmocutaneous baroreceptors to the rate of change of a stimulus is evident from their adaptation to a step change in pressure, their increase in pressure sensitivity with the rate of rise of pressure ramps, and the greater pressure sensitivity of their initial response to a pressure step than that 45 to 60 s later (Van Vliet and West 1987b). The frequency response of pulmocutaneous baroreceptors is evident in the increase in their mean discharge frequency with increasing frequency of sinusoidal pressure stimuli (Van Vliet and West 1987b; fig. 7.8D).

Because the pulmocutaneous baroreceptors require several seconds to adapt to a step change in pressure and can maintain a tonic discharge, they are classified as "slowly adapting mechanoreceptors." A constant stimulus may elicit only a brief discharge or single spike in rapidly adapting mechanoreceptors (Catton 1970). The significance of slow adaptation is that receptors can provide feedback on the mean arterial blood pressure. Rapidly adapting mechanoreceptors (e.g., Pacinian corpuscle) respond only briefly (e.g., a single action potential) to a constant stimulus. Although this dynamic a response would cause the receptors to discharge with the pressure pulse during each cardiac cycle, the response would be to the rate of pressure change rather than its mean level. Although the PCA baroreceptors respond best to rapidly changing pressures, they can encode the mean level of arterial pressure (Ishii and Ishii 1978; Van Vliet and West 1987b, 1987c).

The properties outlined above allow us to predict how the pulmocutaneous baroreceptors may function *in vivo*. For example, in *Bufo marinus* pressure thresholds range from about 20 mm Hg to almost 40 mm Hg, with a mean of about 30 mm Hg (Van Vliet and West 1987c). In undisturbed conscious *B. marinus*, mean systemic arterial blood pressure is typically 20 to 22 mm Hg with a systolic pressure of 30 to 32 mm Hg (Van Vliet and West 1989). In other words, the mean pressure threshold is nearly equivalent to the systolic arterial pressure of undisturbed toads. Therefore, about one-half of the PCA baroreceptor population may be at least sparsely active in undisturbed animals.

Two mechanisms determine pulmocutaneous baroreceptor feedback to the central nervous system at and near resting pressures. The first mechanism is recruitment of receptor discharge. As arterial pressure increases, more and more receptors are recruited. On the other hand, as pressures fall, the number of active receptors falls. Recruitment will depend on the distribution of thresholds in the receptor population and is probably a significant determinant of the feedback provided by the receptors at pressures between 20 to 40 mm Hg in *B. marinus*.

The second mechanism influencing pressure-related feedback is the sensitivity of those receptors operating above their pressure threshold. For phasic pressure stimuli, this amounts to an increased discharge of about 0.5 spikes $\cdot$ s^{-1} for each 1 mm Hg increment (Van Vliet and West 1987b). Although this sensitivity seems small, its magnitude is considerable relative to the maximum discharge frequency of the receptors. The receptors will develop almost 2% of their maximum discharge frequency for each 1 mm Hg increment above their threshold.

Feedback on arterial blood pressure will therefore arise from both the recruitment and the pressure sensitivity of individual baroreceptors. Because the receptor thresholds are near normal systolic arterial pressures, a fall in pressure below resting encodes largely as a reduction in active receptors, whereas an increase in pressure above resting encodes as an increase in both the number and activity of receptors operating above threshold. Therefore, PCA baroreceptors may be more capable of signaling an increase in arterial pressure above resting (e.g., during physical activity or disturbance) than a fall in arterial blood pressure below resting (e.g., during severe hemorrhage).

Aortic Baroreceptors   The aortic nerve of toads transmits the response of aortic baroreceptors (Ishii, Ishii, and Kusakabe 1985a; Van Vliet and West 1987c; B. N. Van Vliet and N. H. West unpublished). In many respects, these receptors are similar to the PCA baroreceptors. Discharge within the aortic nerve occurs spontaneously at physiological arterial pressures (25–45 mm Hg) and is rhythmic, with peak discharge frequencies during systole. At lower pressures (25–35 mm Hg), the discharge is predominantly confined to a brief period during systole. As arterial pressure increases, the discharge increases in frequency and extends into diastole. In response to step changes in pressure in the artificially perfused aorta, single units show a phasic burst of activity that adapts in a few seconds, but maintain a tonic discharge if the pressure is greater than 30 mm Hg (Ishii, Ishii, and Kusakabe 1985a).

Ishii, Ishii, and Kusakabe (1985a) distinguished a second form of pressure-sensitive aortic-discharge during distension of the aorta by step changes in perfusion pressure. This activity has relatively small spike amplitudes and pressure thresholds of more than 60 mm Hg. Although baroreceptors with such thresholds are of unlikely importance in routine pressure regulation in anurans, whose arterial blood pressure is usually well below 60 mm Hg, arterial pressures may occasionally exceed this in toads. The significance of this second form of pressure-sensitive activity remains undetermined.

Carotid Baroreceptors   Neil, Strom, and Zotterman (1950) first recorded afferent activity from the carotid branch of the glossopharyngeal nerve in *Rana temporaria*. Carotid nerve activity was synchronous with the distension of the central arteries during cardiac systole. Unfortunately, arterial blood pressures were not recorded and could not be related to the characteristics of the receptors. The rhythmic discharge depended upon adjusting the filling of the sinus venosus so that cardiac output was maximum, suggesting relatively high pressure thresholds.

Ishii, Honda, and Ishii (1966) clarified the properties of carotid baroreceptors in recordings from the carotid nerve of *Bufo vulgaris*. Raising the carotid pressure above 70 mm Hg evoked a discharge consisting of large-amplitude action potentials. The discharge adapted rapidly and completely to such step increases in pressure, and spontaneous pressure-sensitive activity did not occur at the prevailing arterial pressure (31–46 mm Hg).

The carotid baroreceptors described by Neil, Strom, and Zotterman (1950) and Ishii, Honda, and Ishii (1966) have properties that resemble those of the low-amplitude baroreceptors in the aortic nerve (Ishii, Ishii, and Kusakabe 1985a) and differ markedly from those of regular-amplitude aortic baroreceptors and PCA baroreceptors (Ishii and Ishii 1978; Ishii, Ishii, and Kusakabe 1985a; Van Vliet and West 1987b, 1987c, unpublished). The functional significance of the carotid baroreceptors is questionable because their pressure thresholds are near the upper limit of arterial pressures of toads. That the receptors adapt both quickly and completely appears to preclude a role in the regulation of arterial blood pressure, because they are unlikely to provide information related to the mean arterial pressure even if the arterial pressure achieves their high phasic pressure threshold. This conclusion is consistent with the failure of distension of the carotid labyrinth in anesthetized toads to affect either heart rate or systemic arterial blood pressure (Ishii, Honda, and Ishii 1966; Segura 1979). Possibly the high-amplitude activity arises from mechanoreceptors that are outside the cardiovascular system but are close enough to respond to movement of the vessels during large pressure steps.

Cardiac Mechanoreceptors   Mechanoreceptors are present in the heart of anurans (Downing and Torrance 1961; Kolatat, Kramer, and Muhl 1957; Kontani and Koshiura 1981a, 1983; Niijima 1970). The receptive fields of the cardiac mechanoreceptors are distributed within the sinus venosus (Kolatat, Kramer, and Muhl 1957; Niijima 1970) and truncus arteriosus ("conus"; Downing and Torrance 1961) as well as the ventricle and atria (Downing and Torrance 1961; Kolatat, Kramer, and Muhl 1957; Kontani and Koshiura 1983; Niijima 1970).

The spontaneous discharge of atrial and ventricular mechanoreceptors peaks during systole but may sustain some activity for almost the entire cardiac cycle (Kolatat, Kramer, and Muhl 1957; Kontani and Koshiura 1983). The spontaneous discharge of ventricular receptors consists of large-amplitude spikes (Kolatat, Kramer, and Muhl 1957) that probably arise from myelinated afferent fibers (Niijima 1970). Probing the cardiac chambers can activate both myelinated and nonmyelinated cardiac mechanoreceptor afferents (Niijima 1970). The activity of the unmyelinated fibers may possibly arise from ring- and disklike sensory endings (Abraham 1969). The myelinated afferent fibers have diameters of 3 to 8 μm and conduct at velocities between 6 and 16 m · s^{-1}. In both cases, the receptive fields occupy a small area (less than 6 mm^2) and are largely confined to the endocardium or sub-endocardial muscle, at least in the ventricle (Niijima 1970).

Regulation of Arterial Blood Pressure by Baroreceptors

Reflex Regulation of Blood Pressure in Urodeles and Anurans Only two studies document arterial baroreflexes in urodeles. In the first, Lutz and Wyman (1932) reported that in spinally pithed or decerebrate *Necturus* (Proteidae), electrical or mechanical stimulation of the gills or increases in branchial artery pressure inhibited the heart for several beats. The branchial arterial pressure threshold for the reflex was as low as 34 mm Hg.

In *Amphiuma* (Amphiumidae), Johansen (1963) observed that artificially increasing the pressure in the pulmonary artery depressed blood pressure in the systemic vasculature and vice versa. At a mean pulmonary arterial pressure of 33 mm Hg, a 10% increase in pulmonary artery pressure slowly decreased systemic pressure, reducing it about 10% within 1 min. Heart rate was unchanged. The depressor response therefore appeared to be mediated by changes in the vascular resistance or possibly cardiac stroke volume.

Evidence that the reflexes of anurans compensate rapidly for sudden alterations in arterial blood pressure has come from studies in which the feedback loop of the reflex remains intact; that is, the feedback loop is said to be closed. In addition to documenting neural pressure-regulating systems in anurans, such methods illustrate several properties of the reflexes. However, most details of regulatory systems have come from studies that interrupt the normal feedback loop of a baroreflex. When the feedback loop opens, no action of the reflex effectors influences the feedback received by the central nervous system, which the experimenter may control. The main advantage over closed-loop methods is that the source of the input to the receptors is known and the influence of extraneous inputs reduced. The sensitivity of a baroreflex is much greater in the open-loop than in the closed-loop configuration. Open-loop techniques have been used to localize the receptive fields of the major baroreceptor population in the arterial circulation, and to investigate the properties of baroreflexes arising from different baroreceptor populations.

Closed-Loop Studies In the bullfrog, *Rana catesbeiana*, intravascular injection of the catecholamines epinephrine and norepinephrine or the synthetic α-adrenergic agonist phenylephrine increases arterial blood pressure and cardiac interval, the time between heartbeats (Herman and Sandoval 1983; Millard and Moalli 1980). Conversely, the smooth-muscle relaxant sodium nitroprusside reduces arterial blood pressure and cardiac interval (Millard and Moalli 1980). Pretreatment with atropine abolishes changes in cardiac interval by blocking reflex adjustments of heart rate mediated by the parasympathetic nervous system (Millard and Moalli 1980). The relationship between arterial blood pressure and cardiac interval was analyzed as linear (fig. 7.9), with the slope (25 ms · mm Hg^{-1}; Millard and Moalli 1980) reflecting the sensitivity of all the systems that regulate the arterial blood pressure by control of cardiac interval.

In the toad *B. marinus* the relationship between cardiac interval and systolic arterial pressure is sigmoidal over a wide

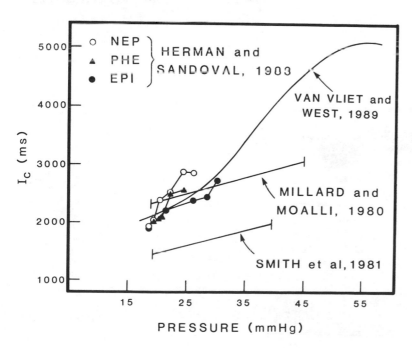

Fig. 7.9 Relationship between cardiac interval (I_c) and arterial blood pressure in *Bufo marinus* (Smith, Berger, and Evans 1981; Van Vliet and West 1989) and *Rana catesbeiana* (Herman and Sandoval 1983; Millard and Moalli 1980). Arterial blood pressure was manipulated pharmacologically except in the study of Smith, Berger, and Evans, in which cuff occlusion of the central arterial arches was used to alter arterial pressure. I_c is shown as a function of mean arterial pressure except in the study of Van Vliet and West, where it is a function of systolic pressure. *NEP*, norepinephrine; *PHE*, phenylephrine; *EPI* epinephrine. (Reprinted, by permission, from Van Vliet and West 1989.)

range of pressures (Van Vliet and West 1989; fig. 7.9). Because the relationship is nonlinear, slope is a function of pressure. The peak slope of the relationship is 140 ms · mm Hg^{-1} and occurs at 37 mm Hg systolic pressure. Analysis of the same data by linear regression yields a lower slope (79 ms · mm Hg^{-1}; Van Vliet and West 1987a, 1989).

Because resting cardiac interval differs among species and the cardiac interval–cardiac output relationship is not known in any amphibian, the regression of cardiac interval on arterial pressure conveys limited information. However, the sigmoidal relationship between cardiac interval and pressure demonstrates some features of the pressure regulating reflexes in the toad that may relate jointly to the properties of arterial baroreceptors, the central integration of baroreceptive information, and the properties of the effectors. The threshold of the relationship occurs at systolic pressures of 20 to 25 mm Hg, which is consistent with the lower range of phasic thresholds of pulmocutaneous baroreceptors (Van Vliet and West 1987b). The relationship saturates at pressures above 50 mm Hg. Because pulmocutaneous baroreceptors increase their discharge with pressure until well above 50 mm Hg (Van Vliet and West 1987b, 1987c), saturation at 50 mm Hg pressure may stem from the central integration of the reflex or a limitation of the effector limbs. At 25 to 50 mm Hg, the increase in cardiac interval is approximately proportional to systolic pressure. The peak slope occurs at 37 mm Hg, a pressure at which PCA baroreceptor recruitment is just complete (Van Vliet and West 1987b).

Pulmocutaneous Artery: Open-Loop Studies

Smith, Berger, and Evans (1981) and West and Van Vliet (1983) demonstrated a correlation between cardiac interval and arterial pressure through cuff occlusion of the central arteries. In contrast to pharmacological manipulation of arterial pressure, cuff occluders can control local pressure in baroreceptive segments of the vasculature. Cuff occlusion is therefore an open-loop technique. However, this technique relies on changes in heart rate as an index of baroreceptor activation, as do pharmacological closed-loop studies. Occlusion of the carotid arteries and aortic arch, alone or in combination, slow the heart. Thus, the vasculature containing the dominant baroreceptor population must lie either upstream in the carotid and/or aortic divisions of the truncus, or in the parallel circulation of the pulmocutaneous artery. Occlusion at the junction of the

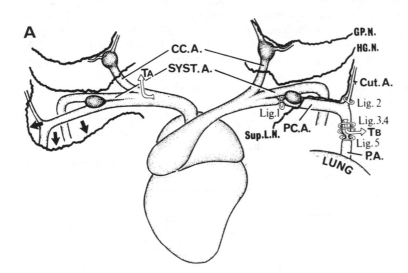

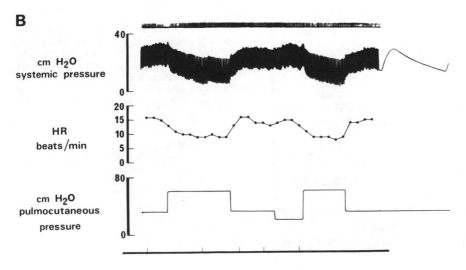

Fig. 7.10 *A*, isolated pulmocutaneous sac preparation used to investigate open-loop gain in conscious *Bufo marinus*. Ligatures 1–5 were used to form the isolated sac. *CCA*, common carotid artery; *CutA*, cutaneous artery; *GPN*, glossopharyngeal nerve; *HGN*, hypoglossal nerve; *PA*, extrinsic pulmonary artery; *PCA*, pulmocutaneous artery; *SupLN*, recurrent laryngeal nerve; *SYSTA*, systemic arches; T_A, T_B, cannulas used to record sac and systemic arterial pressures. Contralateral rLN is shown dissected away from the reflexogenic zone (*arrows*). From West and Van Vliet 1983. *B*, effects on aortic blood pressure and heart rate of pressure changes in an isolated pulmocutaneous sac. Traces, top to bottom 5-s time marker, aortic blood pressure, heart rate, pressure within the isolated sac, event marker. (Reprinted, by permission, from West and Van Vliet 1983.)

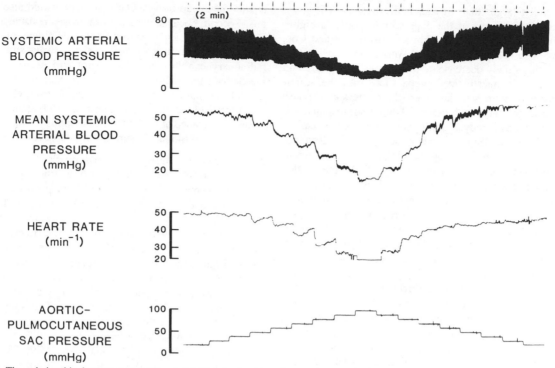

Fig. 7.11 The relationship between systemic arterial blood pressure and heart rate, and pressure in the isolated right aorta and pulmocutaneous artery in a conscious toad (*Bufo marinus*). The contralateral re-flexogenic zones had been denervated. (B.N. Van Vliet and N.H. West unpublished.)

PCA with the truncus increases heart rate, suggesting that the dominant baroreceptor population controlling heart rate is downstream in the PCA.

Distension of the vascularly isolated PCA in anesthetized (Ishii and Ishii 1978) and unanesthetized toads (Hoffmann and Cordeiro de Sousa 1982; West and Van Vliet 1983) decreases systemic blood pressure and heart rate, showing that pulmo-cutaneous baroreceptor feedback can regulate arterial blood pressure. Reductions in systemic arterial pressure could occur in the absence of changes in heart rate, suggesting that the reflex may also control the cardiac stroke volume and/or systemic vascular resistance.

West and Van Vliet (1983) studied the relationship between systemic arterial pressure and the pressure applied to the vascularly isolated PCA in unanesthetized toads (*B. marinus;* fig. 7.10). At pulmocutaneous pressures between 30 and 45 mm Hg, the maximum slope of the relationship between PCA and systemic pressure (the open-loop gain, G_o) is 0.35. In other words, an experimental increase in the isolated PCA pressure produces a decrease in systemic arterial blood pressure that is 35% of the experimental perturbation. Because $G_c = 1/(1 + 1/G_o)$ (where G_o and G_c represent open-loop and closed-loop gains, respectively), an open-loop gain of 0.35 corresponds to a closed-loop gain of 0.26. That is, pulmocutaneous baroreceptors will compensate for 26% of a perturbation in arterial blood pressure in the intact animal.

The experiments of West and Van Vliet (1983) may have underestimated open-loop gain. They used feedback from the PCA on only one side of the animal, whereas baroreceptor feedback sums bilaterally in intact animals (Hoffmann 1985; Van Vliet and West 1986). If the open-loop gain estimate

were doubled to 0.70, closed-loop gain would be 0.41. They used nonpulsatile pressures within the isolated arterial sac, but pulmocutaneous baroreceptors responded more to dynamic than static pressure stimuli (Van Vliet and West 1987b), so that a pulsatile pressure stimulus would probably have increased the gain of the PCA baroreflex. Lastly, some baroreceptive fields may have been excluded during vascular isolation of the PCA.

Recently we developed an open-loop preparation that includes the receptive fields of all pulmocutaneous barorecep-tors and aortic baroreceptors, on one side of the animal. In this aortic-pulmocutaneous preparation the reflex is potent in influencing systemic arterial pressure and heart rate (fig. 7.11). Even so, potency may have been underestimated, because we still used unilateral, nonpulsatile stimulating pressures.

Several workers have used electrical stimulation of the cut central end of the rLN to elicit the pulmocutaneous baroreflex in toads (Hoffman 1985; Hoffman and Cordeiro de Sousa 1982; Ishii and Ishii 1978; Van Vliet and West 1986; West and Van Vliet 1983). In anesthetized toads, electrical stimulation of the cut central end of the rLN typically slowly decreases systemic arterial pressure and heart rate (Van Vliet and West 1986; West and Van Vliet 1983). During continued stimulation, blood pressure and heart rate often recover and may continue to rise above control values. Stimulation within regions of the brain stem in which baroreceptor afferents are presumed to synapse on second-order neurons of the barore-flex may also evoke depressor or pressor responses (Cordeiro de Sousa and Hoffman 1981).

In conscious toads, electrical stimulation of the cut central end of the rLN elicits both pressure and depressor responses that are much larger than in anesthetized toads. The magnitude and time course of the depressor response is highly dependent upon the stimulus intensity (Hoffmann and Cordeiro de Sousa 1982; Van Vliet and West 1986). Low stimulus intensities slowly decrease systemic arterial pressure and heart rate, as in anesthetized preparations. As the stimulus intensity is increased, however, the depressor response abruptly changes. This high threshold depressor response is a prompt and intense bradycardia, hypotension, and apnea.

Although the two depressor responses may arise from the activation of the pulmocutaneous baroreflex at different intensities (Hoffmann and Cordeiro de Sousa 1982), the sudden transition between the two responses, the lack of intermediate responses, and the striking differences in their time course, intensity, and ventilatory effects all suggest a more complex mechanism. For example, the high-threshold depressor response may result from the stimulation of a second population of fibers within the rLN (Van Vliet and West 1986). The rLN contains the afferent fibers of laryngeal mechanoreceptors and nociceptors in addition to baroreceptor afferents. Stimulation of the upper airways elicits apnea (Carlson and Luckhardt 1920; Van Vliet and West 1986; West and Jones 1976; Zotterman 1949) and an intense bradycardia (Van Vliet and West 1986) in anurans, as in other vertebrates. Therefore, not all depressor responses to rLN stimulation may be due solely to baroreceptor stimulation.

Hoffman (1985) and Van Vliet and West (1986) studied the bilateral integration of depressor responses in unanesthetized toads (*Bufo paracnemis* and *B. marinus*). In both studies bilateral summation of hypotensive and bradycardic responses to rLN stimulation occurred; responses to simultaneous stimulation of left and right rLNs were greater than the responses to stimulation of either rLN alone. The results of the two studies differ in the extent of summation. Hoffman (1985) found that most animals exhibited facilitated summation of blood pressure and heart rate responses; the response to simultaneous bilateral stimulation was greater than the sum of the responses to unilateral stimulation. However, incompletely additive summation occurred when maximum unilateral stimuli were used. Van Vliet and West (1986) examined summation exclusively in low threshold depressor responses and found incompletely additive summation.

Van Vliet and West (1986) used electrical stimulation of the rLN to evaluate the role of adjustments in the systemic and pulmocutaneous vascular resistances in controlling blood pressure in *B. marinus*. An 18% reduction in the resistance of the aortic vasculature accompanied low- and high-threshold depressor responses, suggesting that the systemic vascular resistance is one effector with which the pulmocutaneous baroreflex controls the arterial blood pressure. Paradoxically, the vascular resistance of the PCA increased by 76% during low- and high-threshold depressor responses. This change in resistance probably largely reflected changes in the resistance of the pulmonary vasculature, because some 79 to 92% of pulmocutaneous blood flow passes to the pulmonary artery, with the remainder passing to the cutaneous vasculature (West and Burggren 1984).

The increase in the resistance of the PCA during depressor responses has several implications. First, an increase in the pulmonary resistance would redistribute blood flow away from the lung and towards the systemic circulation. The reduction of the aortic vascular resistance would also facilitate this. Second, because the site of increased resistance is probably in the extrinsic pulmonary artery (see "Functional Significance of Input from Receptors in the Airways and Lungs"), pulmonary capillary blood pressure will decrease. By this mechanism the pulmocutaneous baroreceptors may protect the delicate pulmonary microvasculature from elevated central arterial blood pressures. The price to be paid is that increased resistance of the PCA would oppose reductions in the central arterial blood pressure during depressor responses.

Pulmocutaneous Artery: Denervation Studies Several investigators have denervated the rLN to study the role of the pulmocutaneous baroreceptors in blood pressure regulation (Hoffmann and Cordeiro de Sousa 1982; Ishii and Ishii 1978; Smits, West, and Burggren 1986; Van Vliet and West 1987a, 1989). In anesthetized toads, severing the rLNs slightly but promptly increases arterial blood pressure (Ishii and Ishii 1978). In unanesthetized toads, bilateral denervation or local lidocaine anesthesia of the rLNs acutely increases systemic blood pressure, heart rate, and pulmonary blood flow, while the blood pressure becomes more labile. This suggests that a tonic restraint upon the cardiovascular system has been removed (Hoffmann and Cordeiro de Sousa 1982; Smits, West, and Burggren 1986; Van Vliet and West 1989). The response occurs even in undisturbed toads with systolic pressures at which approximately half the PCA baroreceptor population should be active (Van Vliet and West 1989).

Denervation of the rLNs increases the net pulmonary fluid filtration of plasma tenfold (Smits, West, and Burggren 1986). The increased filtration may arise from an increased pulmonary capillary pressure as well as an increase in capillary recruitment. Although the extent to which lymphatic drainage accommodates increases in pulmonary fluid filtration has not been investigated, the results of Smits, West, and Burggren (1986) are consistent with the PCA baroreflex providing protection for the pulmonary microcirculation in addition to a feedback regulation of central arterial blood pressure (Van Vliet and West 1986; West and Van Vliet 1983).

The elevated systemic blood pressure and heart rate that occur after rLN denervation in *Bufo marinus* require some 10 min to develop fully and subside within 2 days (Van Vliet and West 1989). However, the variability of systemic arterial blood pressure remains elevated 2 days following denervation. Two weeks after PCA baroreceptor denervation, the means and variances of arterial blood pressure and heart rate of PCA denervated toads are indistinguishable from those of sham-operated controls. However, the closed-loop control of heart rate is deficient at this time. The peak sensitivity of cardiac interval to pharmacological manipulations of arterial pressure decreases by about 50% in 16-day baroreceptor-denervated toads compared with sham-operated controls, and the maximum increase in cardiac interval at high arterial pressures decreases by about one-third (Van Vliet and West 1989). Although pulmocutaneous baroreceptors contribute to cardiovascular regulation in anurans, their involvement extends only to the short-term regulation and not the long-term maintenance of arterial blood pressure.

Aortic Baroreflex Kuno (1914) showed that stretching the aorta could evoke bradycardia in *Rana esculenta*. However, Ishii, Ishii, and Kusakabe (1985a) could not elicit a baroreflex in anesthetized *Bufo vulgaris* by distending the vascularly isolated aorta or by electrically stimulating the aortic nerve. Electrical stimulation of the aortic nerve elicited a pressor response, which was presumed to arise from recruitment of chemoreceptor afferent fibers that are also present in the aortic nerve. This chemoreflex during electrical stimulation may have masked a modest aortic baroreflex. The absence of a response to distension of the aorta (Ishii, Ishii, and Kusakabe 1985a) is curious, however, in light of the existence of aortic baroreceptors and the results of Kuno (1914). Possibly anesthesia obscured an aortic baroreflex in the study of Ishii, Ishii, and Kusakabe (1985a). Further studies are required to assess the significance of aortic baroreceptors in the regulation of arterial pressure in anurans.

Carotid Baroreflex Meyer (1927) originally suggested that the carotid labyrinth regulates arterial blood pressure. In Meyer's studies, electrical stimulation of the glossopharyngeal nerve lowered arterial blood pressure and heart rate, whereas severing the glossopharyngeal nerve increased arterial pressure.

Subsequent investigations by Ishii, Honda, and Ishii (1966) and Segura (1979) failed to demonstrate that the carotid labyrinth regulates arterial blood pressure. In the study by Ishii, Honda, and Ishii (1966), distension of the vascularly isolated carotid labyrinth affected neither arterial blood pressure nor heart rate. Distension of the carotid labyrinth by intraarterial injection of saline increased arterial blood pressure and heart rate (Segura 1979). Denervation of the carotid labyrinth did not affect these responses to saline injection, which reflect a response of the cardiac pacemaker to increased venous return (Hakumaki 1987).

Anesthesia may have obscured a carotid baroreflex in the studies of Ishii, Honda, and Ishii (1966) and Segura (1979). However, these results are consistent with the high pressure thresholds characteristic of carotid labyrinth baroreceptors.

Summary of the Role of Baroreceptors in Cardiovascular Regulation PCA baroreceptors provide the principal feedback of the arterial blood pressure to brain-stem cardiovascular centers in *B. marinus*, with a smaller contribution arising from the aortic arch. Despite its gross anatomical similarity to the carotid sinus baroreceptor zone in mammals, the participation of the carotid in the reflex regulation of arterial blood pressure in anuran amphibians is unproven.

At the arterial blood pressures (i.e., systolic pressure of about 30 mm Hg) of undisturbed toads (*B. marinus*), approximately half the arterial baroreceptors are active. As pressures rise, recruitment increases until all receptors are active. At pressures above threshold, the peak and mean discharge frequencies of the arterial baroreceptors increase with arterial blood pressure in the physiological range of arterial pressures.

The feedback provided by the arterial baroreceptors can tonically inhibit the cardiovascular system, even at the low arterial blood pressures of undisturbed toads. As pressures rise above resting, increased feedback from the arterial baroreceptors slows the heart and reduces the systemic vascular resistance (fig. 7.12). These responses partially compensate for the increase in arterial blood pressure and oppose its further elevation. In concert, these actions constitute the negative feedback regulation of arterial blood pressure by arterial baroreceptors.

An additional effector response is the increased resistance

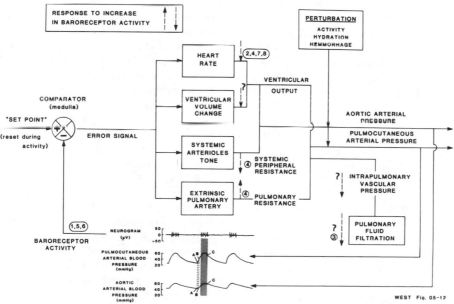

Fig. 7.12 Schematic diagram of the mechanisms participating in the baroreflex regulation of cardiovascular variables in *Bufo*. The diagram is a "classical" representation of negative feedback, which uses a hypothesized "set-point" for arterial pressure and a medullary comparator. The response of the heart and the systemic vasculature to baroreceptor stimulation is a reduction in heart rate and systemic resistance, which opposes elevations in central arterial pressure. However, PCA resistance increases, probably because of a vagally mediated constriction of the extrinsic pulmonary artery. This opposes the regulation of PCA pressure and ultimately central arterial pressure, but protects the pulmonary microcirculation from pressure elevations. Some relevant references are numbered on the diagram: *1*, Ishii, Ishii, and Kusakabe 1985a. *2*, Smith, Berger, and Evans 1981. *3*, Smits, West, and Burggren 1986. *4*, Van Vliet and West 1986. *5*, Van Vliet and West 1987c. *6*, Van Vliet and West 1987b. *7*, Van Vliet and West 1989. *8*, West and Van Vliet 1983.

of the pulmocutaneous vasculature, which probably reflects a constriction of the extrinsic pulmonary artery. This response opposes the negative feedback regulation of arterial blood pressure but may protect the pulmonary microcirculation from the deleterious effects of high central arterial blood pressures (fig. 7.12). This action is consistent with suggestions that the primary responsibility of the baroreceptors may be to protect the delicate vasculature of the gas exchanger from the elevated systemic arterial pressures that the incompletely divided circulation transmits.

The receptor and reflex properties outlined above suggest that arterial baroreflexes are more capable of counteracting increases in arterial blood pressure than decreases. Therefore, the principle role of arterial baroreflexes in anuran amphibians may be to protect the circulation by limiting rapid elevations in arterial pressure. In other words, the system may act more to protect the circulation from physically damaging pressure levels than to guard against reduced tissue perfusion.

Cardiac interval lengthens when experimental increases in arterial pressure stimulate the arterial baroreceptors (Van Vliet and West 1989; fig. 7.9). However, in undisturbed toads (*Bufo marinus*), cardiac interval and arterial blood pressure are generally reciprocally related (Van Vliet and West 1989). In nature, baroreceptive information is only one of many inputs converging on the cardiovascular centers of the medulla, which are integrated to determine cardiovascular variables such as arterial pressure and flow distribution. These inputs derive from other cardiorespiratory receptors (e.g., chemoreceptors, pulmonary stretch receptors) and also from higher integrative centers in the brain. For example, efferents from the optic tectum descend as far as the cervical medulla in anurans (Rubinson 1968). Electrical stimulation of the optic tectum produces both tachycardia and hypertension in conscious *Bufo paracnemis,* as does the presentation of visual stimuli producing prey-catching or avoidance responses (Cordeiro de Sousa and Hoffman 1985). Treadmill exercise causes a sustained increase in both arterial blood pressure and heart rate in *B. marinus* (Wahlqvist and Campbell 1988). This too, although neurogenically mediated, may be partly psychogenic in origin, because toads show similar cardiovascular changes when suspended over a moving treadmill without walking. It is unknown whether the input-output relationship of the baroreflex in anurans is reset under these circumstances or whether baroreceptive information is prevented from impinging on the cardiovascular centers.

Autonomic control of the cardiovascular system is meager in resting *Rana* and *Bufo* (Burggren and Doyle 1986c; Wahlqvist and Campbell 1988). Modest cholinergic cardioinhibition is present in *Bufo,* but no adrenergic pressor tone. Adrenergic efferents mediate the initial rapid increase in arterial blood pressure and heart rate in response to treadmill exercise and alerting stimuli (Cordeira de Sousa and Hoffmann 1985). Increases in the circulating levels of adrenaline and noradrenaline sustain tachycardia during treadmill exercise (Wahlqvist and Campbell 1988).

Several other neurohormones influence the relationship between arterial blood pressure and heart rate in anurans (see also chapter 3). Arginine vasotocin (AVT), angiotensin II (ANG II), and gonadotropin-releasing hormone (GnRH) all increase mean arterial pressure in *B. marinus;* however, only AVT infusion increases heart rate (Wilson et al. 1987). Resting arterial blood pressure rises at the beginning of the reproductive season in *Bufo* (Segura and D'Agostino 1964). GnRH levels correlate with the reproductive state (King and Millar 1979), and GnRH infusion increases plasma catecholamines in *B. marinus*. This suggests that endogenous GnRH may prepare the anuran cardiovascular system for seasonal reproductive activity (Wilson, Van Vliet, and West 1984).

Functional Characteristics of Arterial Chemoreceptors

Carotid Labyrinth Chemoreceptors The carotid labyrinth of anurans is chemoreceptive (Adams 1958; Chowdhary 1951; De Boissezon 1939) and a possible homologue of the mammalian carotid sinus (Adams 1958).

Ishii, Honda, and Ishii (1966) perfused the carotid labyrinth of *Bufo vulgaris* with either hypoxic solutions or solutions containing peripheral chemoreceptor stimulants (sodium cyanide and lobeline sulphate). This treatment increased the afferent discharge frequency of randomly firing small units recorded from the carotid nerve, a fine branch of the glossopharyngeal nerve leading from the labyrinth, which also contains baroreceptor afferents. Perfusion of the labyrinth with deoxygenated Ringer's increased lung ventilation in anesthetized toads, suggesting that hypoxemia (i.e., perfusion with hypoxic blood) and the resulting increases in carotid chemoreceptor activity are related to an increased hypoxic ventilatory drive (fig. 7.13).

Ishii and Ishii (1973) estimated the antidromic conduction velocities of chemoreceptive afferent fibers by recording evoked potentials from the carotid nerve while stimulating the cranial nerve roots entering the glossopharyngeal (jugular) ganglion, or by orthodromic stimulation of the carotid nerve while recording from the cranial nerve roots central to the ganglion. The diameter of afferent fibers may change, as may the extent of myelination central to the ganglion, while conduction is usually delayed at the bifurcation of fibers within a ganglion. Nevertheless, the velocities measured, 0.15 to 0.6 m · s^{-1}, strongly suggest that the chemoreceptor afferent fibers are nonmyelinated. By contrast, carotid baroreceptor afferents within the carotid nerve conduct at between 1 and 7 m · s^{-1}. Orthodromic stimulation showed that the thinner of two nerve roots entering the glossopharyngeal ganglion, perhaps corresponding to the mammalian cranial nerve IX root, is the main afferent chemoreceptive pathway.

Electrical stimulation of efferent fibers within the glossopharyngeal nerve of *B. marinus* markedly reduced the chemoreceptor discharge (Ishii and Ishii 1973). This is also the most obvious response to the stimulation of carotid body efferents in mammals (Neil and O'Regan 1971). Such efferent stimulation also results in the dense-cored vesicles concentrating in the peripheral regions of the glomus cells, a decrease in vesicle numbers (Kusakabe, Ishii, and Ishii 1987), vasoconstriction, and reduced perfusion within the labyrinth (Ishii and Ishii 1970). A reduction in perfusion brought about by other means enhances chemoreceptor firing, suggesting that the fall in discharge frequency results from a modulation of chemoreceptor sensitivity by efferents to the labyrinth and is not secondary to the observed reduction in blood flow.

Inhibitory fibers in the glossopharyngeal nerve trunk have been investigated by stimulating either the sympathetic trunk

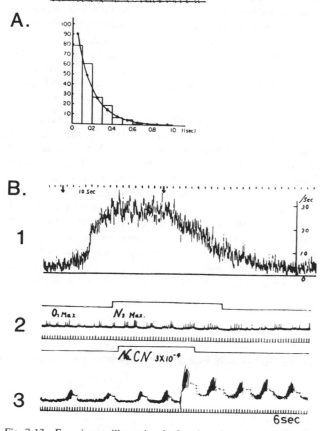

Fig. 7.13 Experiments illustrating the function of carotid labyrinth chemoreceptors in the anuran *Bufo vulgaris*. *A*, spontaneous discharge of a single chemoreceptive unit recorded from the peripheral cut end of the carotid nerve and a histogram showing the frequency distribution of interspike intervals. *B*, (1) rate meter record of chemoreceptor firing recorded from the peripheral cut end of the carotid nerve. Between the *arrows* the perfusate to the labyrinth (Ringer's solution equilibrated with 100% O_2) was replaced with Ringer's solution equilibrated with N_2. (2) change in respiration associated with the perfusion of anoxic Ringer's through the carotid labyrinth during the event marker. (3) change in respiration associated with stimulating the carotid labyrinth with NaCN. During the event marker, NaCN was added to the inflow of perfusate to the carotid labyrinth. (Reprinted, by permission, from Ishii, Honda, and Ishii 1966.)

or the cranial nerve roots adjacent to the ganglia from which the glossopharyngeal nerve is derived. Sympathetic efferents within the carotid nerve, with their origins mainly in the fourth spinal root, conduct impulses at 0.15 to 2 m · s⁻¹ (Ishii and Ishii 1973), suggesting that they may be small myelinated preganglionic fibers. Sympathetic stimulation inhibits spontaneous chemoreceptor activity in most preparations. In a few preparations stimulation of the vagal root was also effective, but only sympathetic stimulation produced vasoconstriction within the carotid labyrinth. The results imply that sympathetic efferents that join the glossopharyngeal nerve independently modulate chemoreceptor sensitivity and vasomotion within the carotid labyrinth. Atropine in the carotid labyrinth sometimes prevents the inhibition of chemoreceptor firing caused by sympathetic stimulation (Ishii and Ishii 1976), suggesting that a muscarinic synapse may lie somewhere on the efferent pathway. Preganglionic cholinergic synapses, how-

ever, are probably nicotinic. Similarly, acetylcholine in the carotid labyrinth itself increases chemoreceptor discharge, suggesting excitatory cholinergic synapses with the chemoreceptive cells within the labyrinth.

Efferent sympathetic discharges in the carotid nerve increase during spontaneous increases in respiratory activity in anesthetized toads. Similar increases occur when the contralateral carotid labyrinth is stimulated with 2,4-dinitrophenol (an uncoupler of oxidative phosphorylation, which stimulates carotid chemoreceptors in the dog and cat) or acetylcholine (Ishii and Ishii 1976). If sympathetic activity depresses chemoreceptor firing frequency, the efferent pathway within the carotid nerve may represent part of a control loop that determines chemoreceptor activity in response to hypoxemia and sympathetic tone. Changes in sympathetic tone could represent an important mechanism by which hypoxic ventilatory drive could be reset during acclimatization to altitude in amphibians, as in mammals (Lahiri et al. 1983).

Hormonal factors may also influence carotid labyrinth chemoreceptor sensitivity. Electrical stimulation of the right sympathetic nerve trunk, which innervates the heart via the right vagosympathetic nerve (Taxi 1976), increases carotid chemoreceptor discharge frequency in toads (*Bufo vulgaris*) in which the left carotid labyrinth is perfused with Ringer's solution by the heart (Ishii and Ishii 1967; Ishii, Ishii, and Honda 1966). The effect continues as long as heart rate is elevated, is resistant to hexamethonium (which blocks sympathetic efferents by blocking cholinergic synaptic transmission within the ganglion), but is abolished by passing fresh Ringer's solution through the heart. Similar increases in heart rate produced by noradrenaline perfusion reduce chemoreceptor activity, suggesting that perfusion of the labyrinth does not itself stimulate chemoreceptor activity. Indeed, in the artificially perfused labyrinth, increased perfusion reduces chemoreceptor firing, presumably by increasing oxygen availability (Ishii, Honda, and Ishii 1966).

In vitro, adrenaline and noradrenaline do not affect spontaneous chemoreceptor firing, but acetylcholine and dopamine enhance spontaneous chemoreceptor activity, as does perfusate from a heart that had been stimulated via the sympathetic nerve trunk. In the toad, as efferent sympathetic excitation to the heart increases, cardiac sympathetic nerve endings may release dopamine, which acts as an excitatory transmitter within the carotid labyrinth (Ishii and Ishii 1967). In *Bufo marinus*, however, dopamine inhibited and epinephrine stimulated chemoreceptor firing *in vivo* (Van Vliet and West 1991).

The sensitivity of carotid labyrinth chemoreceptors to changes in perfusion suggests that they may be important in both cardiovascular and respiratory regulation. In pithed *B. marinus*, chemoreceptor discharge increases during spontaneous bradycardia at a constant intrapulmonary oxygen concentration (B. N. Van Vliet and N. H. West unpublished). Interestingly, if the cardiac outflow is occluded, or if a partial atrioventricular block is produced by crushing the atrioventricular junction, chemoreceptor discharge does not increase. Discharge increases markedly when flow is resumed, suggesting that prolonged residence within the heart modifies the blood subsequently ejected to the labyrinth so as to stimulate the labyrinth chemoreceptors (B. N. Van Vliet and N. H.

West unpublished). Perhaps these treatments deplete oxygen in the blood within the heart so that the initial cardiac outflow is hypoxemic, thus stimulating the carotid chemoreceptors. Alternatively, blood that resides in the heart for a long time may accumulate cardiac metabolites capable of modulating chemoreceptor sensitivity (Ishii and Ishii 1967).

Effects of Carotid Labyrinth Denervation Denervation of the carotid labyrinth provides the most direct evidence for its contribution to hypoxic ventilatory drive in amphibians. Smyth (1939) concluded that denervation of the aortae and carotid labyrinths in *Rana esculenta* with phenol or alcohol diminishes the ventilatory response to anoxia. Ventilation also decreases if the aortae are undisturbed, suggesting that the carotid labyrinths are of primary importance to the ventilatory responses to hypoxia.

More recently, West, Topor, and Van Vliet (1987) investigated the role of the carotid labyrinth in conscious toads (*B. marinus*) by determining the relationship between respiratory activity (measured as the time integral of positive buccal pressure) and oxygen partial pressure (Po_2) of arterial blood in intact and labyrinth-denervated toads unidirectionally ventilated with normoxic and hypoxic gas mixtures. The gases contained 2% CO_2 to produce normocapnic arterial blood. Denervation of the carotid labyrinth did not reduce ventilatory sensitivity to hypoxemia. Ventilatory activity at any given arterial Po_2 is lower in denervate than in intact animals, but the proportionate increase in ventilation in response to decreased arterial Po_2 is preserved (in fact slightly increased) in denervate toads. This suggests that hypoxic sensitivity derived from the carotid labyrinth contributes to, but is not solely responsible for, the hypoxic drive to breathe in *B. marinus*.

Evans and Shelton (1984) obtained similar results in the aquatic *Xenopus laevis*. In these animals, carotid labyrinth denervation reduced minute ventilation, respiratory frequency, and inspiratory volume, but hypoxia increased ventilation to the same extent as in intact toads. Jones and Chu (1988) recently confirmed and extended these observations in *Xenopus*. In normoxia, ventilation is significantly lower in carotid labyrinth-denervated than in intact animals, indicating that the carotid labyrinth influences respiratory drive. However, a larger relative increase in ventilation in denervated animals resulted in the same minute ventilation in both groups of animals under hypoxic conditions (inspired $Po_2 = 35-65$ mm Hg).

Denervation of the carotid labyrinths may affect not only ventilation but also the cardiovascular system. Arterial Pco_2 declines in carotid labyrinth–denervated toads unidirectionally ventilated with gas mixtures containing 0 or 2% CO_2 (West, Topor, and Van Vliet 1987). This suggests that pulmonary blood flow may increase in denervated toads. As a corollary, enhanced carotid labyrinth chemoreceptor activity may reduce pulmocutaneous arterial flow, perhaps by increasing tone in the extrinsic pulmonary artery. Increasing carotid chemoreceptor input during submergence may not only contribute to bradycardia (Lillo 1980b) but also influence the distribution of ventricular output between the systemic and pulmonary circuits.

At least in terrestrial and aquatic toads, respiratory sensi-

tivity to hypoxia survives the destruction of neural pathways from chemoreceptors within the carotid labyrinth (Evans and Shelton 1984; Jones and Chu 1988; West, Topor, and Van Vliet 1987). However, as is well established in birds and mammals, resting ventilation declines when the carotid chemoreceptors are denervated. The location and nature of the other (surviving) chemoreceptive zones sensitive to hypoxia are unknown.

Aortic Chemoreceptors The prompt pressor and ventilatory responses to intra-aortic injections of lobeline sulphate or sodium cyanide in conscious *Bufo marinus* (Van Vliet and West 1986) suggest that the aortic arches contain chemoreceptors. Neurophysiological investigations have revealed aortic chemoreceptor afferents within fine pharyngeal branches of the vagus that terminate in the aortic trunk. In the toad *B. vulgaris,* randomly discharging receptors within the aorta increase firing frequency in response to sodium cyanide, perfusion with hypoxic or hypoxic-hypercapnic solutions, and also to the cessation of perfusion in the vascularly isolated aorta (Ishii, Ishii, and Kusakabe 1985a; fig. 7.14). Van

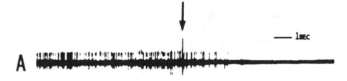

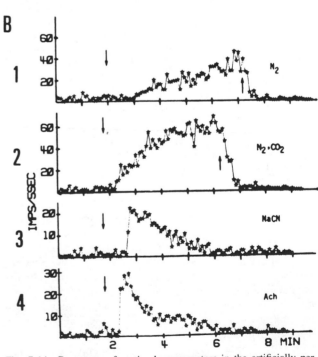

Fig. 7.14 Responses of aortic chemoreceptors in the artificially perfused aorta of the toad *Bufo vulgaris*. *A,* firing of a single chemoreceptive unit in the aorta in response to stagnant perfusate. Perfusion was restarted at the *arrow. B,* time course of response of a few chemoreceptive units to (*1*) the perfusion of N_2-saturated saline, (*2*) the perfusion of a solution saturated with 95% N_2, 5% CO_2, (*3*) the infusion of 2.5 μg sodium cyanide (NaCN), and (*4*) the infusion of 1.25 μg acetylcholine (Ach). (After Ishii, Ishii, and Kusakabe 1985a.)

A

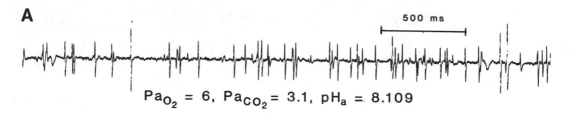

$Pa_{O_2} = 6$, $Pa_{CO_2} = 3.1$, $pH_a = 8.109$

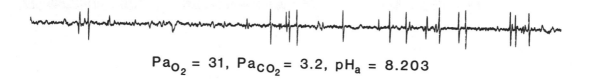

$Pa_{O_2} = 31$, $Pa_{CO_2} = 3.2$, $pH_a = 8.203$

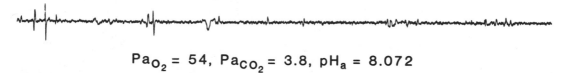

$Pa_{O_2} = 54$, $Pa_{CO_2} = 3.8$, $pH_a = 8.072$

B

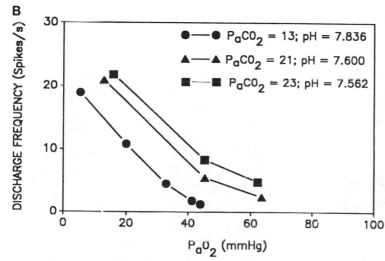

● —— ● $P_aCO_2 = 13$; pH = 7.836
▲ —— ▲ $P_aCO_2 = 21$; pH = 7.600
■ —— ■ $P_aCO_2 = 23$; pH = 7.562

Fig. 7.15 *A*, response of carotid labyrinth chemoreceptors in *Bufo marinus* to hypoxemia at a constant arterial P_{CO_2}. Arterial P_{O_2} was changed between 6 and 54 mm Hg, while arterial P_{CO_2} was held at a low constant value (3.1–3.8 mm Hg). Most chemoreceptive units fall silent at an arterial P_{O_2} of 54 mm Hg, which was found to be the threshold for the hypoxic ventilatory drive in conscious animals at a similar arterial P_{CO_2} (4.7 mm Hg; West, Topor, and Van Vliet 1987). Slow waveform is the ECG. *B*, interaction of hypoxemia and hypercapnia at the level of the carotid labyrinth chemoreceptors in *B. marinus*. In a few-fiber preparation, an increase in arterial P_{CO_2} from 13 to 23 mm Hg caused an increased rate of chemoreceptor firing at the same arterial P_{O_2}, demonstrating the CO_2 sensitivity of the receptors. (B.N. Van Vliet and N.H. West unpublished.)

Vliet and West (1987c, unpublished) have recently confirmed these results in *B. marinus*.

Although toads have both aortic and carotid chemoreceptors, no published information relates their firing frequency to the most probable stimulus, arterial P_{O_2}. Our recent studies relate carotid labyrinth chemoreceptor discharge to arterial P_{O_2} while at constant arterial P_{CO_2} (B. N. Van Vliet and N. H. West unpublished). Chemoreceptor discharge frequency increases sharply at arterial P_{O_2}'s below 50 mm Hg in these experiments (fig. 7.15A). The hypoxemic threshold for lung ventilation is 54 mm Hg in unidirectionally ventilated, conscious toads (West, Topor, and Van Vliet 1987). This suggests that input from carotid labyrinth chemoreceptors contributes to ventilatory drive under normoxic conditions and mediates at least part of the increased respiratory drive associated with hypoxia (fig. 7.16A).

In mammals, the steady-state discharge frequency of arterial chemoreceptors is a function of both the P_{O_2} and P_{CO_2} of the perfusing blood. In cats, the peripheral arterial chemoreceptors are normally silent in normoxia if arterial P_{CO_2} is below 15 to 20 mm Hg (Cunningham, Robbins, and Wolff (1986). No published studies investigate the interactions of O_2 and CO_2 stimuli in the peripheral chemoreceptors of amphibians, although in *B. marinus* an increase in arterial P_{CO_2} from 13 to 23 mm Hg doubles carotid labyrinth chemoreceptor firing frequency at arterial P_{O_2}'s from 10 to 50 mm Hg (fig. 7.15B; B. N. Van Vliet and N. H. West unpublished).

Pulmocutaneous Chemoreceptors The pulmocutaneous arteries of anurans may contain an intraarterial chemoreceptive zone. The existence of a functionally "venous" chemoreceptor would provide the central nervous system with informa-

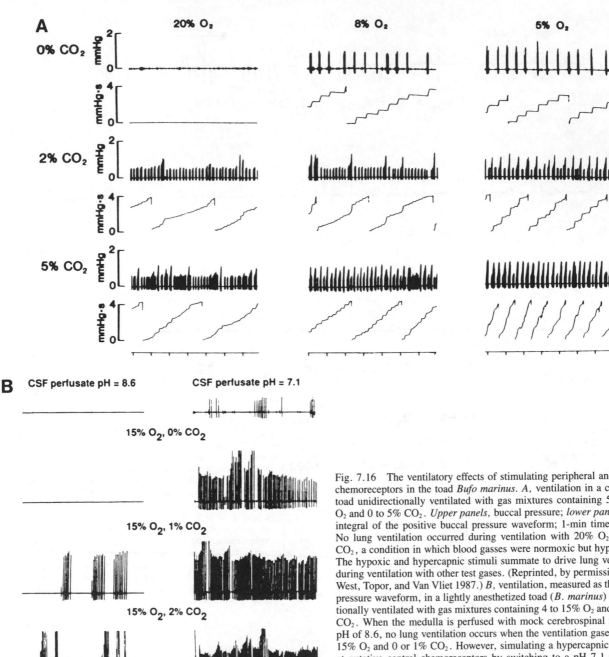

Fig. 7.16   The ventilatory effects of stimulating peripheral and central chemoreceptors in the toad *Bufo marinus*. *A,* ventilation in a conscious toad unidirectionally ventilated with gas mixtures containing 5 to 20% O_2 and 0 to 5% CO_2. *Upper panels,* buccal pressure; *lower panels,* time integral of the positive buccal pressure waveform; 1-min time marker. No lung ventilation occurred during ventilation with 20% O_2 and 0% CO_2, a condition in which blood gasses were normoxic but hypocapnic. The hypoxic and hypercapnic stimuli summate to drive lung ventilation during ventilation with other test gases. (Reprinted, by permission, from West, Topor, and Van Vliet 1987.) *B,* ventilation, measured as the buccal pressure waveform, in a lightly anesthetized toad (*B. marinus*) unidirectionally ventilated with gas mixtures containing 4 to 15% O_2 and 0 to 2% CO_2. When the medulla is perfused with mock cerebrospinal fluid at a pH of 8.6, no lung ventilation occurs when the ventilation gases contain 15% O_2 and 0 or 1% CO_2. However, simulating a hypercapnic stimulus at putative central chemoreceptors by switching to a pH 7.1 perfusate stimulates ventilation under these conditions, and increases the level of ventilation at all levels of peripheral chemoreceptor drive. This suggests that the CO_2-mediated drive to breathe has a large central component. (From N.J. Smatresk and A. Smits unpublished.)

tion related to oxygen consumption as well as to oxygen acquisition. To date, however, chemoreceptive afferents are unknown within the rLN, which innervates the pulmocutaneous artery, although it contains afferents from both pulmocutaneous baroreceptors and laryngeal receptors (Ishii and Ishii 1978; Van Vliet and West 1987b, 1987c).

The injection of sodium cyanide into the pulmocutaneous arches of lightly anesthetized bullfrogs (*Rana catesbeiana*) stimulates ventilation, or enhances bradycardia in submerged animals (Lillo 1980b). Perfusions or injections of lobeline or sodium cyanide into the pulmocutaneous arteries of con-

scious toads (*Bufo marinus*) increases arterial blood pressure and the frequency of lung ventilation (Hoffman and Cordeiro de Sousa 1982; Van Vliet and West 1986). In the latter study, however, both the increases in blood pressure and the ventilatory responses are less sustained than those produced by intra-aortic injections of the drugs (Van Vliet and West 1986), while control injection of saline increases ventilation. Thus, arousal of the animals may be at least partially responsible for the respiratory responses. Unilateral electrical stimulation of the rLN produces an initial hypotension and apnea, which give way to a pressor response at high stimulus intensities, often coincident with a restoration of ventilation (Van Vliet and West 1986). Hoffman and Cordeiro de Sousa (1982), using a different stimulation protocol, found similar increases in arterial pressure and ventilation upon rLN stimulation. These authors considered the pressor effects to have arisen from the stimulation of chemoreceptor afferents within the rLN. However, Van Vliet and West (1986) could not abolish pressor responses to lobeline or sodium cyanide by sectioning the rLN and glossopharyngeal nerve, and suggested that the pressor response may have originated from the stimulation of laryngeal afferents. A rise in arterial blood pressure often followed mechanical stimulation of the larynx, a phenomenon also noted in mammals (Tomori and Widdicombe 1969). In the absence of recordings from pulmocutaneous chemoreceptors, the role of the PCA as a chemoreceptive site in amphibians is unproven. However, Benchetrit, Armand, and Dejours (1977) concluded from respiratory responses to sodium cyanide that the pulmonary arch of the tortoise (*Testudo horsfieldi*) is the primary chemoreceptive zone, although Ishii, Ishii, and Kusakabe (1985b) later reported that baroreceptors, not chemoreceptors, predominate in this arch in the turtle *Geoclemmys reevesii*.

Many of the inconsistencies in these findings may be due to the use of different species, variability of innervation, and differences in experimental technique. The carotid, aortic, and perhaps pulmocutaneous arches of anuran amphibians contain chemoreceptive zones, but the details of their distribution and afferent innervation remain to be explored.

THE CENTRAL NERVOUS SYSTEM AS A CHEMORECEPTIVE ZONE
Central Sensitivity to Hypoxia

In mammals, increases in ventilation in response to brain hypoxia in the absence of peripheral chemoreceptor stimulation have been variously attributed to central lactic acidosis, the release of suprapontine structures from cortical inhibition, and an increased response of the sympathetic nervous system (Santiago and Edelman 1976). In teleost fish, on the other hand, the central nervous system may contain oxygen-sensitive chemoreceptors (Saunders and Sutterlin 1971; Bamford 1974). Central lactic acidosis may confer central sensitivity to hypoxia on amphibians under some circumstances, as anaerobic metabolism may be commonplace (Bennett 1978), but this hypothesis has not been tested. Indeed, any or all of the above mechanisms may bestow central hypoxic sensitivity on amphibians.

Central Sensitivity to CO_2

Varying the pH of artificial cerebrospinal fluid demonstrates intracerebral CO_2 sensitivity in turtles (Hitzig and Jackson 1978; Hitzig and Nattie 1982). Comparable data for amphibians are sparse. In decerebrate *Rana*, solutions of very low pH applied to the floor of the fourth ventricle or perfused through the spinal canal decrease the frequency of buccal cycles and increase the frequency of lung ventilation. Solutions of high pH have the opposite effect (De Marneffe-Foulon 1962). Smatresk and Smits (1991) have recently studied central ventilatory drive in lightly anesthetized toads (*Bufo marinus*), in which the lungs were unidirectionally ven-

tilated to control peripheral chemoreceptor drive (West, Topor, and Van Vliet 1987). Superfusion of the medulla at a pH of 7.6 or less stimulated ventilation regardless of ventilatory drive from peripheral chemoreceptors (fig. 7.16B). This suggests that central pH-sensitive chemoreceptors in *B. marinus* exert a dominant hypercapnic ventilatory drive, as they do in other air-breathing vertebrates.

REGULATION OF VENTILATION BY RECEPTORS
Hypoxic Ventilatory Drive

Babak (1911, cited in Smyth 1939) first demonstrated ventilatory sensitivity to hypoxia in intact, conscious amphibians. Smyth (1939) confirmed these findings in *Rana esculenta*. In the terrestrial toad *B. marinus*, progressive hypoxia increases frequency of lung ventilation in spite of the resulting respiratory alkalosis (Boutilier and Toews 1977). As hypoxia intensifies, lung inflation cycles predominate in the breathing pattern. In the aquatic toad *Xenopus laevis*, hypoxia increases minute ventilation (Brett 1980; Evans and Shelton 1984; Jones and Chu 1988). At 25°C, a fall in environmental Po_2 from 150 to between 35 and 65 mm Hg increases minute ventilation fourfold in intact *X. laevis*, largely due to an increase in the frequency of lung ventilation (Jones and Chu 1988).

Because of the complexity of the ventilatory pattern, which consists of both buccal and lung ventilatory movements (de Jongh and Gans 1969; West and Jones 1975a), comparable studies on terrestrial anurans are few. In *Bufo paracnemis* at 25°C, decreasing inspired Po_2 from 150 to 35 mm Hg (5% inspired O_2) increases minute ventilation, especially between 70 and 35 mm Hg Po_2 (Kruhoffer et al. 1987).

During air breathing, adult anurans exhibit an O_2-related respiratory drive. The replacement of inspired air with O_2 halts lung ventilation in undisturbed conscious *B. marinus* even though, as a consequence, the animals become hypercapnic (Toews and Kirby 1985). The carotid labyrinth and aortic groups of arterial chemoreceptors are active at arterial Po_2's of undisturbed *B. marinus*, suggesting that their input contributes to ventilatory drive (B. N. Van Vliet and N. H. West unpublished; West, Topor, and Van Vliet 1987; fig. 7.17). The activity of the receptors is sparse at arterial Po_2's above approximately 100 mm Hg, suggesting that breathing hyperoxic gases diminishes the hypoxic ventilatory drive.

Hypercapnic Ventilatory Drive
Urodeles Evidence for a ventilatory drive mediated by CO_2-sensitive receptors is sparse, although salamanders routinely face chronic or acute aquatic hypercapnia in some environments. For example, in southeastern North America, water hyacinths on the surface of ponds may insulate the water from normal gas exchange with air, resulting in aquatic hypercapnia (up to 60 mm Hg Pco_2) combined with hypoxia or anoxia (Ultsch and Anthony 1973; Ultsch 1973a). The most common response is to allow arterial Pco_2 and pH to vary within wide limits with little or no attempt at respiratory compensation (Boutilier and Toews 1981a; Heisler et al. 1982). For example, in *Amphiuma tridactylum* (Amphiumidae), the onset of air breathing and arterial Pco_2 are unrelated, and injections of 5 to 15% CO_2 into the lungs do not alter the time between air breaths. If aquatic Pco_2 increases from normocapnic val-

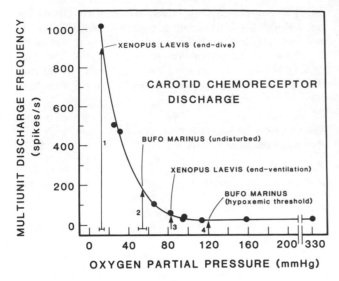

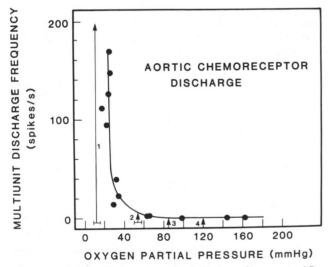

Fig. 7.17 Relationship between multiunit discharge frequency and P_{O_2} for (A) carotid labyrinth and (B) aortic chemoreceptors in *Bufo marinus* (B.N. Van Vliet and N.H. West unpublished). Arterial P_{CO_2} range in A was 15.8–17.7 mm Hg and in B 9.8–10.2 mm Hg. The *vertical lines* drawn on the response curves and labeled *1* and *4* represent end-dive and end-ventilatory arterial P_{O_2}'s, respectively, in undisturbed *Xenopus* (Brett 1980). The line labeled *2* represents the range of arterial P_{O_2}'s recorded in undisturbed *Bufo marinus*, while *3* represents the hypoxemic threshold for lung ventilation in normocapnic, unidirectionally ventilated *Bufo* (West, Topor, and Van Vliet 1987). See text for details.

ues to 80 mm Hg, arterial P_{CO_2} more than doubles while air-breathing frequency stays the same (Toews 1971). Combined aquatic hypercapnia and hypoxia doubles lung ventilation in *Siren lacertina* (Sirenidae) and *Amphiuma means,* but this response only slows the rise of arterial P_{CO_2} in hypercapnic water (Heisler et al. 1982).

In *Cryptobranchus alleganiensis* (Cryptobranchidae), the hellbender, more than 90% of O_2 and CO_2 exchanges via the skin (Guimond and Hutchison 1976). Increases in arterial P_{CO_2} due to activity increase the frequency of lung ventilation in this species, although this response does not correct the accompanying acidosis (Boutilier, McDonald, and Toews 1980). Aquatic hypercapnia increases lung ventilation, aquatic

buccal pumping, and rocking motions that ventilate the skin (Boutilier and Toews 1981a). In spite of the increases in lung ventilation, arterial P_{CO_2} increases fivefold in hypercapnia. However, a compensatory increase in arterial P_{O_2} preserves blood O_2 saturation during hypercapnia despite a CO_2-mediated depression of blood O_2 content. Thus, arterial blood oxygenation and not CO_2 may be the regulated variable. The increases in ventilation, apparently in response to CO_2, would, in this view, be attributable instead to an O_2-sensitive receptor stimulated by the CO_2-dependent Bohr shift (Boutilier and Toews 1981a). Such a mechanism may explain the respiratory CO_2 sensitivity of teleost fish (Shelton, Jones, and Milsom 1986; Smith and Jones 1982) and reflects current opinions on the relative importance of the regulation of CO_2 and O_2 in aquatic vertebrates (Dejours 1981; see also chapter 5). In the absence of any neurophysiological evidence that urodeles possess receptors that respond to O_2 content, or O_2 or CO_2 partial pressures, such analyses must remain speculative.

Anurans Anurans increase ventilation in response to hypercapnia, which adjusts arterial P_{CO_2} and pH towards normocapnic levels, provided inspired CO_2 is not elevated. For example, *Rana catesbeiana* double ventilation volume when exposed to 3% CO_2 in water, while their arterial P_{CO_2} changes by less than 2 mm Hg. Thus, the regulating systems increase lung ventilation to produce an almost isocapnic regulation of arterial P_{CO_2} (Jackson and Braun 1979).

The addition of 2% CO_2 to inspired air stimulates ventilation in *R. esculenta* (Smyth 1939). Addition of 2 to 3% CO_2 to inspired gas in *Bufo marinus* increases the frequency of buccal and lung ventilations (Jones 1982; Macintyre and Toews 1976). Arterial P_{CO_2} inevitably rises under these circumstances because the increase in ventilation does not alleviate the consequences of inspiring hypercapnic gas: arterial P_{CO_2} cannot be reduced below inspired levels. For example, in *B. marinus* breathing 5% CO_2 in air, arterial P_{CO_2} rises from 13 to 38 mm Hg despite increased lung ventilation (Boutilier et al. 1979a). This suggests that ventilatory CO_2 sensitivity in air-breathing amphibians arose to compensate for changes in the rate of endogenous metabolic CO_2 production rather than changes in environmental P_{CO_2}.

Mammals show an inverse relationship between arterial P_{CO_2} and alveolar ventilation rate so that an increase in alveolar ventilation reduces arterial P_{CO_2}, provided the rate of CO_2 production is constant (West 1984). Anurans differ from mammals in that the former routinely and frequently ventilate the buccal cavity without ventilating the lungs (de Jongh and Gans 1969; West and Jones 1975a). Buccal cavity gas is reinspired during lung ventilation, and therefore increasing the frequency of lung ventilations at the expense of buccal cycles may reduce the P_{CO_2} of gas entering the lungs (Macintyre and Toews 1976), as will more complete ventilation of the buccal cavity upon each lung ventilation. *B. marinus* breathing 2% CO_2, for example, reduce mean narial resistance during lung ventilation. By this maneuver, either a larger volume of fresh gas enters the buccal cavity or a greater proportion of total buccal gas exits during a lung ventilation cycle (R. M. Jones 1982). In either case, the buccal gas will more closely approximate the atmosphere after a subsequent inspiration. Input from CO_2-sensitive pulmonary mechanoreceptors (Milsom and Jones 1977) or narial receptors may be important in adjusting narial resistance.

Experimentally induced hypocapnia in conscious *B. marinus* decreases arterial P_{CO_2} from 11.6 mm Hg to less than 5 mm Hg. Although low-amplitude buccal ventilation continues, lung ventilation ceases in undisturbed animals, demonstrating the reliance of the central oscillator driving lung ventilation on a tonic CO_2 stimulus (West, Topor, and Van Vliet 1987; fig. 7.16A).

The marked respiratory responses of anurans to experimental changes in inspired CO_2 reflect their ability to regulate changes in arterial P_{CO_2} by this means. Therefore, changing inspired CO_2 is a useful experimental protocol. As pointed out above, however, increasing ventilation in the face of an increased inspired CO_2 is ineffective in regulating arterial P_{CO_2} but is effective in compensating for an increased rate of endogenous CO_2 production, such as occurs during activity.

Gill Ventilation and Perfusion

West and Burggren (1982, 1983) investigated the response of gill ventilation to aquatic hypoxia and hyperoxia in bullfrog (*Rana catesbeiana*) larvae. Bullfrog larvae show a strong oxygen-related ventilatory drive in air-equilibrated water. Larval *R. catesbeiana* of developmental stages XVII–XIX (Taylor and Kollros 1946) halve both gill ventilation frequency and pressure amplitude when aquatic P_{O_2}'s change from normoxic to hyperoxic (West and Burggren 1983; also see chapter 16). On the other hand, hypoxic water increases the frequency of lung ventilation (West and Burggren 1982). These results suggest a central location for hypoxia-sensitive receptors in anuran larvae, for Boutilier (1988a) states that the carotid labyrinths are not present at this stage of development. However, an equally plausible and more parsimonious explanation is that aortic chemoreceptors are functional and mediate the hypoxic drive to breathe. Alternatively, the receptors may be associated with the vasculature of gill arch 3 at this stage. Indeed, larval bullfrogs adjust branchial ventilation within 2–4 s of inspiring hypoxic or hyperoxic water; lesioning gill arch 3 eliminates this rapid response (X. Jia and W. W. Burggren unpublished).

Intrapulmonary stretch receptor input may not only match ventilation to perfusion during intermittent ventilation in adult anurans, but also coordinate gill and lung ventilation in the bimodally breathing anuran larva. In unanesthetized bullfrog larvae (stages XVII–XIX; Taylor and Kollros 1946), in which the internal gills and lungs are functional, lung ventilation inhibits gill ventilation, limiting the loss of O_2 acquired from the air to hypoxic water in contact with the gills (West and Burggren 1982). Regardless of the P_{O_2} of the inflating gas, rapid artificial lung inflation to an estimated 100% of volume immediately reduces gill ventilation, suggesting that pulmonary stretch receptor input, rather than changes in arterial or pulmonary partial pressures, mediates the effect. The addition of 5 to 20% CO_2 to N_2 inflating the lungs partially abolishes the phasic decrease in gill ventilation, implicating CO_2-sensitive pulmonary stretch receptors in the response (West and Burggren 1983). Gradwell (1970) found that the addition of debris to the inspired water flow, or stimulation of the opercular lin-

ing with a fine wire, caused hyperinspirations in bullfrog larvae. Thus, input from irritant receptors, perhaps pharyngeal mechanoreceptors, also influences the ventilatory rhythm.

The larva of the anuran *Ascaphus truei* (Leiopelmatidae) lives in well-oxygenated mountain streams and attaches to the substrate with an oral sucker. Gill ventilation continues when the sucker is attached, and the negative buccal pressures generated on inspiration are transmitted to the sucker. Buccal pressures become more negative when the water velocity over the larva increases, suggesting that receptors exist that can sense water velocity and influence the activity of the buccal pump (Gradwell 1971a).

The control of gill perfusion in amphibians has been studied most extensively in the aquatic neotenic tiger salamander *Ambystoma tigrinum*, which uses skin, gills, and lungs for gas exchange. The vasculature associated with the gas exchange organs is complex, and vascular resistance is probably under both neural and humoral control via the stimulation of adrenergic α- and β-receptors (Malvin 1985a). Ventricular blood is ejected via a bulbus arteriosus into four pairs of aortic arches. The first three are afferent branchial arteries, and the fourth is the pulmonary artery. A ductus arteriosus connects the third gill arch efferent artery with the pulmonary artery, placing the pulmonary circulation in series with the third gill and in parallel with the first two gills and the systemic circulation. Malvin (1985b) has identified several potential shunt pathways in *A. tigrinum*. These include intrabranchial shunting between respiratory lamellae and shunt pathways directly connecting afferent and efferent branchial arteries; shunting between the proximal pulmonary artery and the ductus arteriosus; and shunting between the gills and the lung. Malvin and Heisler (1988) showed that 60 to 70% of branchial blood flows through shunt vessels at the base of the gills in resting *A. tigrinum*. The shunt pathway is unresponsive to norepinephrine although the afferent branchial artery dilates, suggesting that an increase in circulating norepinephrine concentration or adrenergic efferent outflow should differentially reduce the flow resistance of the respiratory vasculature and increase the perfusion of the respiratory lamellae. Figge (1936) found that CO_2 at the gills contracts the shunt vessel and dilates the gill capillaries in *A. tigrinum*. Lung ventilation with O_2 has the opposite effect, suggesting that the shunt potentially may be reflexly controlled by peripheral or central chemoreceptor input. Larvae of *Rana temporaria* and *Bufo bufo* also possess nonrespiratory shunts in the gills, although these are not at the base of the gill arch, but within the gill lamella (Saint-Aubain 1981b).

The lung is perfused in series with gill arch 3 via the ductus arteriosus. Therefore, the circulation to the first two gill arches is functionally in parallel with that of the lung, as well as that of gill arch 3. Consequently, the ratio of resistances of the first three gill arches will influence pulmonary blood flow. In severe aquatic hypoxia, blood in shunted away from gill arch 1 and towards the other two arches, increasing flow to the lung via the ductus arteriosus (Malvin 1985b). Lung ventilation frequency increases fivefold in aquatic hypoxia, which suggests pulmonary ventilation-perfusion matching. This redistribution of blood will also reduce the O_2 lost to water from relatively highly oxygenated blood perfusing gill arch 1 (Malvin and Heisler 1988).

O_2, CO_2, and pH exert no local control on gill perfusion (Malvin 1985c), but the role of receptor input in the vascular responses of the gills described above is unknown. Reflex control may be based on input from peripheral chemoreceptors and pulmonary stretch receptors. An integrated study of the response of gill ventilation and perfusion to aquatic hypoxia in any amphibian remains lacking. Currently most information on ventilatory responses deals with anuran larvae, while knowledge of the corresponding vascular adjustments is largely derived from larval urodeles (West and Burggren 1982, 1983; Malvin 1985a, 1985b, 1985c).

Cutaneous Gas Exchange

The skin is a significant gas exchange organ in both larval and adult amphibians (Burggren and West 1982; Jackson and Braun 1979; see chapters 4–6 and 16). Cutaneous gas exchange in larval amphibians is exclusively with water, but may involve air, water, or both after metamorphosis. Skin ventilation, skin perfusion, the functional surface area for gas exchange, and the source of the blood perfusing the skin all influence cutaneous gas exchange (Feder and Burggren 1985b). Early studies on the skin-breathing salamander *Desmognathus fuscus* (Plethodontidae) and the bullfrog (*Rana catesbeiana*) concluded that cutaneous gas exchange is overwhelmingly diffusion-limited and therefore not significantly influenced by changes in skin blood flow (Gatz, Crawford, and Piiper 1975; Piiper and Scheid 1975; Piiper, Gatz, and Crawford 1976; Moalli et al. 1980). These studies assumed a single blood compartment, however, which precludes the possibility of cutaneous capillary recruitment or derecruitment. Change in the number of patent capillaries putatively alters the functional surface area for gas exchange, and therefore the diffusing capacity of the skin (Burggren and Moalli 1984; Malvin 1988). Differential vasomotion of skin capillaries may allow cardiovascular reflexes or local control mechanisms to regulate cutaneous gas exchange.

Outside the skin is an unstirred diffusion boundary layer, which may resist the diffusion of respiratory gases, especially in quiescent submerged animals. Movements of the body or water that disrupt the boundary layer may reduce diffusive resistance (Feder and Pinder 1988b). Therefore, both cutaneous perfusion and "ventilation" may control cutaneous gas exchange.

Control of Cutaneous Perfusion In anuran amphibians a cutaneous artery branches from each of the paired pulmocutaneous trunks to supply the skin with blood that is more hypoxic and hypercapnic than that in the systemic arterial circuit. The cutaneous artery in *Bufo marinus* is largely innervated by excitatory adrenergic fibers running in the pulmonary branch of the vagosympathetic trunk (D. G. Smith 1976), whereas the extrinsic pulmonary artery constricts when vagal efferents are stimulated (Saint-Aubain and Wingstrand 1979). This reciprocal innervation may represent the efferent limb of a reflex mechanism for selectively perfusing the lungs or skin from the PCA (West and Burggren 1984). Lung deflation and combined intrapulmonary hypercapnia and hypoxia (which may occur in apneic periods or diving) divert blood from the pulmonary into the cutaneous

circulation in anesthetized *B. marinus* (West and Burggren 1984). During forced diving in bullfrogs, *Rana catesbeiana*, however, cutaneous artery blood flow does not increase but falls to about a third the predive value due to the reduced cardiac output caused by diving bradycardia (Moalli et al. 1980). Boutilier, Glass, and Heisler (1986), using voluntarily diving bullfrogs, have provided evidence that pulmonary and cutaneous artery blood flow are adjusted appropriately to match O_2 availability at the lung or skin. The normal distribution of pulmocutaneous blood flow during air breathing (80% to lungs, 20% to skin) is altered by aquatic hypoxia to favor lung perfusion, or by aerial hypoxia to favor skin perfusion. Apparently, anurans can alter blood flow distribution to minimize the loss of O_2 from blood into the hypoxic medium at either the aerial or aquatic gas exchanger.

All regions of the skin of bullfrogs (*R. catesbeiana*) receive blood from both the pulmocutaneous and systemic arches, although the dorsal skin of the trunk may receive a greater proportion of pulmocutaneous flow (Moalli et al. 1980; Boutilier, Glass, and Heisler 1986). A variety of reflexes can control systemic blood flow to mammalian skin (Roddie 1983). It is unclear, however, whether reflex changes in resistance can control the proportion of cardiac output supplying amphibian skin to regulate cutaneous gas exchange. Sympathetically mediated redistribution of systemic blood away from the skin occurs in bullfrogs in which water balance is challenged by air exposure (Burggren and Moalli 1984). This at least suggests that appropriate effector mechanisms exist. In *R. pipiens*, passive lung inflation with air or O_2 in anesthetized animals, or voluntary lung ventilation upon recovery from anesthesia, decreases cutaneous gas exchange from an area supplied by the systemic circulation (Malvin and Hlastala 1986a). Lung inflation with N_2 has no effect, suggesting that increased intrapulmonary P_{O_2} rather than increased lung volume decreases systemic perfusion of the skin. Either peripheral chemoreceptor input or the direct effect of arterial P_{O_2} on the systemic vascular resistance of the skin may mediate the response. On the other hand, Malvin and Hlastala (1986b) found that change in skin blood flow are reciprocally related to changes in O_2 concentration above adjacent skin. Such responses to hypoxia and hyperoxia (see also Poczopko 1958) are probably due to the local effect of O_2 on vascular smooth muscle, because they occur in the absence of changes in arterial pressure or heart rate. Malvin and Hlastala (1986b) suggest that this mechanism may divert blood away from occluded or hypoxic skin and towards air-exposed skin. Aquatic amphibians are also subject to diurnal P_{O_2} fluctuations due to the respiratory and photosynthetic activities of aquatic plants (Dejours 1981). Cutaneous vasoconstriction may minimize O_2 loss to hypoxic water and may be particularly important when cutaneous gas exchange predominates (Burggren and West 1982; West and Burggren 1982).

Although cutaneous arterial flow falls during forced diving in *R. catesbeiana*, systemic blood flow to the skin increases markedly even though cardiac output decreases (Moalli et al. 1980). Vascular resistance must decrease in systemic cutaneous vascular beds. A reciprocal change in flow in the cutaneous arterial and systemic blood supplies to the skin may maintain its effectiveness as a gas exchanger in conditions such as prolonged diving in which the blood in both the pulmocutaneous and systemic arches is hypoxemic and hypercapnic. Blood flow falls in both the cutaneous artery and a systemic skin artery in curarized bullfrogs (*R. catesbeiana*) submerged at 5°C when aeration and stirring are halted (Feder and Pinder 1988b). Intense bradycardia occurs shortly thereafter. Thus, blood flow evidently decreases in response to decreased cardiac output rather than to increased vascular resistance brought on by aquatic hypoxia. Such intense bradycardia probably results from increasing peripheral chemoreceptor activity in the absence of ventilation (N. H. West and B. N. Van Vliet unpublished).

If systemic blood flow to the skin is reflexly controlled by changes in vascular flow resistance, this must be a complex arrangement involving the central integration of several sets of receptors. As yet undiscovered O_2 receptors may be present in the skin, but presumably blood gas tensions in cutaneous vessels are intermediate between cutaneous and systemic arterial values. They would also vary depending on the predominant local blood supply and therefore provide an unreliable controlling signal. It may be proposed that feedback from peripheral chemoreceptors (sensing arterial Po_2 and Pco_2) and CO_2-sensitive central chemoreceptors controls skin blood flow. However, the same arterial gas values could perhaps be achieved under radically different circumstances, for example, by lung ventilation or apneic submersion in hyperoxic water, which would place different requirements on the skin circulation.

"Ventilation" of the skin Amphibians that rely on the skin for gas exchange when submerged make movements of the body that may dissipate the boundary layer (Feder and Burggren 1985b; Feder and Pinder 1988b). This reduces the series resistance to the diffusion of respiratory gases across the interface between the water and skin. Skin ventilation clearly can dissipate the O_2 boundary layer, as oxygen microelectrode studies document (Pinder and Feder 1990). However, more data are needed before we can be confident of the global respiratory significance of these movements. In particular it would be useful to explore the relationship between "ventilatory" behavior and the partial pressure gradient for respiratory gases across the skin. If the surrounding water is more hypoxic than cutaneous capillary blood, for example, such movements will serve only to facilitate the movement of O_2 out of the blood into the surrounding water. The potential exists for skin ventilation to exacerbate problems in gas exchange. Presumably, under these circumstances skin ventilation should be minimized.

Dive duration is greater for *Xenopus* and *Siren* (Caudata: Sirenidae) in moving water than in still water, and *Xenopus* moves more frequently (thereby ventilating its skin) in still water than in moving water (M. E. Feder unpublished). Moreover, submerged bullfrogs, *Rana catesbeiana*, move their limbs more frequently in slow currents or still water. However, the consequences of experimental ventilation of the skin in conscious bullfrogs are ambiguous (Burggren and Feder 1986). Cutaneous O_2 uptake increases by 31% in stirred water, but pulmonary uptake also rises, so that the percentage of total O_2 consumption due to cutaneous uptake does not change.

A possible additional mechanism that can adjust diffusive resistance in still water is the recruitment of cutaneous capillaries. Burggren and Feder (1986) reported capillary recruitment in the foot web (in air) upon cessation of experimental ventilation of the rest of the skin (in water). If this reflects vasomotion in the skin as a whole under these conditions, then the results differ from those of Malvin and Hlastala (1986b) and Poczopko (1958), which suggest that skin blood flow falls in local hypoxia. Correspondingly, Feder and Pinder (1988b) reported decreases in cutaneous perfusion in submerged bullfrogs when skin ventilation ceased or when frogs stopped moving. Malvin and Hlastala (1986b) found that skin blood flow was reciprocally related to the O_2 concentration above adjacent skin, and this may explain the results of Burggren and Feder (1986). Malvin (1988) reported no correlation between capillary recruitment and gas exchange, so the functional significance of the observed changes in cutaneous perfusion is open to debate.

ROLE OF RECEPTORS IN THE CONTROL OF INTERMITTENT VENTILATION AND PERFUSION

Figure 7.18 is a schematic of the chemoreceptive control of ventilation and perfusion in an anuran. Lungs, gills, and the skin have been included, so the schematic is a composite, most accurately representing the gas exchange organs present in the metamorphosing larva. Interactions between gas exchange organs are indicated, as are the relevent references.

In many amphibians, ventilation and lung perfusion are intermittent processes intimately related to diving rather than the more familiar continuous processes of mammals. The involvement of receptor input in patterning ventilation and the accompanying cardiovascular adjustments in such a nonsteady-state system is just beginning to be understood. Until recently the threshold and sensitivity characteristics of the receptors associated with the respiratory and cardiovascular systems of amphibians were unknown. The neurophysiological evidence outlined above has been obtained only from bufonids and ranids. Any speculation, therefore, about the involvement of the receptor systems in the patterning of intermittent ventilation requires extrapolation from the limited information currently available.

Boutilier (1988a) and Shelton and Croghan (1988; fig. 7.20) have proposed plausible models for the role of receptors in the patterning of intermittent ventilation in aquatic amphibians. They propose that receptors sense the chemical and mechanical changes occurring in the respiratory and circulatory systems during both nonventilatory and ventilatory periods, and changes in receptor input terminate these periods. The relative duration of the periods primarily determines lung ventilation (Boutilier 1988a). The basic output unit of respiratory rhythm generation may be a sequence of lung ventilations (Jackson 1978b; West, Topor, and Van Vliet 1987) rather than a single inspiration, as in mammals and birds. The likely stimuli are the partial pressures of arterial gases and the chemical composition and volume of the lung contents.

In the aquatic anuran *Xenopus laevis,* arterial Po_2 falls

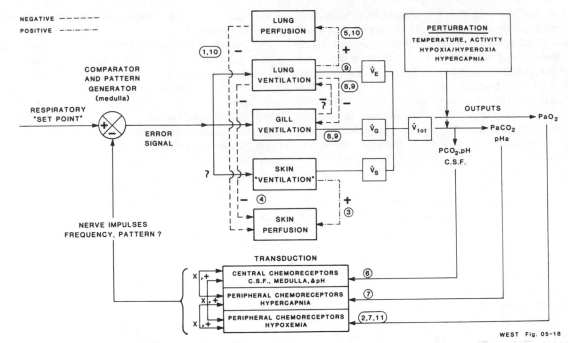

Fig. 7.18 Schematic of the chemoreceptive control of ventilation and perfusion in an anuran amphibian. Although most of the interactions illustrated have been shown in the adult, gills have been incorporated in the diagram to illustrate interactions between gas exchangers in larvae. The control system is represented by a classical negative feedback loop with a hypothesized "set point" and medullary comparator. No attempt has been made to account for the intermittency of lung ventilation. Some relevant references are numbered next to known control components or their interactions: *1*, Boutilier, Glass, and Heisler 1986. *2*, Ishii, Honda, and Ishii 1966. *3*, Malvin and Hlastala 1986b. *4*, Malvin and Hlastala 1986a. *5*, Shelton 1970. *6*, Smatresk and Smits 1991. *7*, B. N. Van Vliet and N. H. West unpublished. *8*, West and Burggren 1982. *9*, West and Burggren 1983. *10*, West and Burggren 1984. *11*, West, Topor, and Van Vliet 1987. *Question marks* indicate possible interactions or pathways. CSF = cerebrospinal fluid; $\dot{V}_E$ = minute ventilation; $\dot{V}_g$ = gill ventilation; $\dot{V}_s$ = skin ventilation.

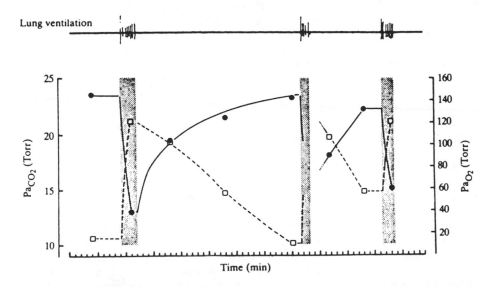

Fig. 7.19 Changes in arterial P_{O_2} ($\square$) and P_{CO_2} ($\bullet$) during voluntary diving in *Xenopus laevis* at 25°C. Intermittent periods of lung ventilation are shown in the *upper trace*, and their timing is represented by the *shaded rectangles*. (Reprinted, by permission, from Boutilier and Shelton 1986a.)

from 80–125 mm Hg on lung ventilation to 10–15 mm Hg at the end of 30-min voluntary dives (Brett 1980). Arterial P_{CO_2} rises by 6 to 8 mm Hg during apnea (fig. 7.19), with a corresponding fall in arterial pH of about 0.1 units (Boutilier 1981). If the carotid labyrinth and aortic chemoreceptors of *X. laevis* possess similar sensitivity curves to those in *Bufo marinus* (B. N. Van Vliet and N. H. West unpublished; fig. 7.17), the central nervous system must receive a progressive increase in peripheral chemoreceptor input that reports progressive hypoxemia and hypercapnia during submersion, as

well as an unknown contribution from central CO_2-sensitive chemoreceptors (De Marneffe-Foulon 1962; Smatresk and Smits 1991). Presumably, this increasing chemoreceptor input facilitates the initiation of ventilation.

In *X. laevis*, lung ventilation often continues after alveolar and arterial P_{O_2} increase maximally during breathing (Boutilier and Shelton 1986b; Shelton and Boutilier 1982). In humans, overventilation after apnea may stem from the increased sensitivity of peripheral chemoreceptors when hypoxemic (Lahiri, Maret, and Sherpa 1983). Similarly, a fall in arterial P_{O_2}

to ≤15 mm Hg during apnea may place peripheral chemo-receptors of amphibians on the most sensitive part of their response curves (B. N. Van Vliet and N. H. West unpublished; fig. 7.17). The resulting hypoxic drive at the end of apnea may be the most potent factor in determining the ensuing level of ventilation.

An alleviation of hypoxic drive from carotid labyrinth and aortic chemoreceptors is probably important in terminating the ventilatory burst and facilitating submersion. Such a reduction of input would occur if the peripheral chemoreceptors in *X. laevis* possess thresholds and sensitivities similar to those in *B. marinus* (figs. 7.15, 7.17). Shelton and Croghan (1988) have demonstrated that intermittent ventilation could be generated by means of a controller detecting only the upper and lower critical levels of blood PO_2 (fig. 7.20). In reality, the removal of CO_2 from tissue stores takes longer than the renewal of O_2 stores in *X. laevis*. Thus, although pulmonary PO_2 rises quickly at the start of a breathing burst, pulmonary PCO_2 is still falling as the breathing burst ends, suggesting that the alleviation of a CO_2-based ventilatory drive may in part terminate breathing bursts (Boutilier and Shelton 1986b). Early in submersion, arterial PCO_2 is relatively low and arterial PO_2 is relatively high. Similarly, normoxic hypocapnic or hyperoxic hypercapnic *B. marinus* become apneic (Toews and Kirby 1985; West, Topor, and Van Vliet 1987). Thus, pulmonary gas exchange during the ventilatory period probably drives the blood gases past their apneic thresholds in diving amphibians, and ventilatory drive only returns late in the submerged period as arterial PO_2 falls and arterial PCO_2 rises.

In anurans, a second factor maintaining apnea during submergence is input from narial receptors connected to afferent fibers in the trigeminal nerve (fig. 7.1A, B; West and Jones 1976). Stimulation of mechanoreceptors at the nares by water probably inhibits the increasing ventilatory drive during submersion. Because the narial mechanoreceptors in *Rana pipiens* adapt to a constant stimulus in seconds, these receptors cannot provide tonic input (West and Jones 1976). However, just as efferent sympathetic innervation may modulate cutaneous mechanoreceptor sensitivity in frog skin (Calof, Jones, and Roberts 1981), including bursts of fictive firing in the absence of a touch stimulus (Chernetski 1964; Lowenstein 1956), such efferent modulation of narial mechanoreceptor firing may occur during submersion. Narial input may be most important in maintaining apnea in escape dives in which animals submerge while still relatively hypoxic and hypercapnic.

In *X. laevis*, a ventilation-perfusion ratio of zero during submersion increases pulmonary arterial PCO_2 from about 12 to 19 mm Hg and decreases arterial PO_2 towards the mixed venous values (Shelton and Boutilier 1982; Boutilier and Shelton 1986a; fig. 7.19). Pulmonary volume also declines due to the cutaneous elimination of CO_2 (Boutilier and Shelton 1986b). Most of the increase in PCO_2 occurs early in submersion. The afferent traffic from pulmonary stretch receptors (Milsom and Jones 1977) probably declines during submersion in response to these changes. Such a progressive reduction in pulmonary afferent traffic may contribute to an increasing inspiratory drive as submergence proceeds (Serbeniuk and Gurskaia 1987). Denervation of the pulmonary vagi in *X. laevis* increases the number of inspirations in a ventilatory period, which overinflates the lungs (Evans and

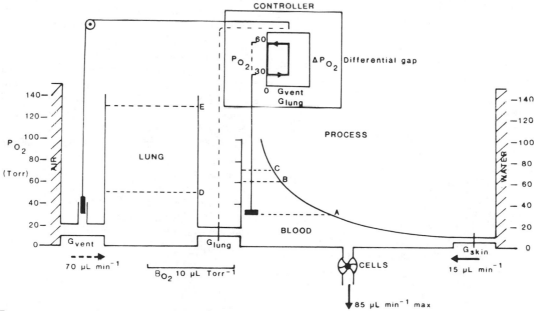

Fig. 7.20 Two-compartment model of intermittent gas exchange, storage, and use in an anuran in which the lungs and the skin are gas exchange surfaces (bimodal breather). Based on 100-g *Xenopus laevis*. Oxygen capacitance, BO_2, plotted on the abscissa, is the product of the slope of the O_2 dissociation curve for blood (modeled as a hyperbolic curve for simplicity) and blood volume. Area beneath curve at any PO_2 represents O_2 stored. Movement of O_2 from air to lung is regulated by conductance G_{vent}, from lung to blood by conductance G_{lung}, and from skin to blood by conductance G_{skin}. The controller initiates a breathing burst when blood PO_2 falls to level *A* (30 mm Hg) and ends the burst when blood PO_2 reaches level *B* (60 mm Hg). During the burst G_{lung} increases from 0 to about 1.6 μl $O_2 \cdot min^{-1} \cdot mm$ Hg^{-1}, and the lung O_2 store is also replenished (from level *D* to *E*). The blood O_2 store continues to increase (from level *B* to *C*) at the expense of the lung store after the breathing burst ends. $\dot{V}O_{2max}$ is set at 85 $\mu l \cdot min^{-1}$. (Reprinted, by permission, from Shelton and Croghan 1988.)

Shelton 1984), suggesting that pulmonary stretch receptor traffic normally inhibits ventilatory drive, and a decline in such traffic facilitates it (Serbeniuk and Gurskaia 1987).

During submergence, a decline in pulmonary afferent traffic due to low lung volume and pulmonary hypoxia and hypercapnia may divert ventricular output away from the lungs and towards the cutaneous and systemic vasculature by reflexly increasing the resistance of the extrinsic pulmonary artery (Emilio and Shelton 1972; West and Burggren 1984). Receptor input and central interactions between receptors may also influence the fall in heart rate in submerged anurans (Jones and Shelton 1964). In mammals, bradycardia results from the stimulation of peripheral chemoreceptors, receptors within the upper airways, or baroreceptors. Lung deflation and the withdrawal of pulmonary stretch receptor input facilitates the access of this input to vagal motor neurons (Lopes and Palmer 1976). In *Bufo marinus,* electrical stimulation of the rLNs (which contain axons from upper airway receptors and baroreceptors) at voltages that produce apnea likewise potentiates the resulting bradycardia (Van Vliet and West 1986). Therefore, a similar interaction may exist in anurans and may contribute to diving bradycardia. Conceivably, pulmocutaneous baroreceptor input during submersion could also contribute to shunting blood away from the lungs by increasing the pulmonary vascular resistance (Van Vliet and West 1986).

No known arterial level of P_{O_2}, P_{CO_2}, or any combination of the two reliably triggers a ventilatory period in an undisturbed submerged animal such as *X. laevis* (Boutilier 1984). In this respect, amphibians clearly do not behave like hardwired automata. Input from receptors sensing the internal and external environments is no doubt linked to ventilatory output in a probabilistic manner (Shelton and Croghan 1988). Furthermore, the termination of the submerged period involves a volitional behavioral act, surfacing, that is influenced by other behavioral priorities. For example, male newts, *Triturus vulgaris* (Salamandridae), extend submergence if potential mates are present underwater (Halliday and Sweatman 1976). On the other hand, surface threats prolong submergence in *X. laevis* (Boutilier 1984). An increase in water depth significantly lengthens nonventilatory periods in voluntarily diving *X. laevis,* implying that they load more oxygen at the surface under these circumstances (Kramer 1988; Shannon and Kramer 1988). Air breathing interacts with feeding behavior in *Ambystoma tigrinum* larvae. The larvae air-breathe frequently when feeding on pelagic prey and infrequently when feeding on benthic prey. Thus the rate of air breathing is used to regulate buoyancy and to reduce the energy cost of feeding (Lannoo and Bachmann 1984b).

The large potential for both extrapulmonary gas exchange and anaerobic metabolism in both anurans and urodeles suggests that gas exchange requirements need not be the sole, or necessarily the most important, determinant of the initiation of ventilatory periods. As in mammals, descending information from higher centers can clearly override receptor input and, in the short term at least, determine the pattern of ventilation (Boutilier 1988a).

CONCLUDING REMARKS

As do other vertebrates, amphibians possess a formidable array of neural receptors that sense respiration-related variables in both the internal and external environment. Homology has been useful in the analysis of receptors, and the comparison of response characteristics with those of more extensively studied mammalian receptors has provided a framework for experimental protocols and the analysis of results.

However, preconceptions based on mammalian systems may impede understanding the receptor-mediated control of the cardiovascular and respiratory systems in amphibians. Boutilier (1988a) makes this clear for the ventilatory control system by pointing out that earlier views of the amphibian respiratory system as ineffective were primarily founded on steady-state models of gas exchange that were themselves ineffective in analyzing intermittently ventilated systems with more than one gas exchanger. Preconceptions may also hinder understanding cardiovascular regulation in amphibians. For example, the dominant group of baroreceptors in anurans now seems homologous to those in the pulmonary artery, rather than the carotid artery, of mammals (Van Vliet and West 1987b).

Furthermore, recent work in both aquatic and terrestrial anurans demonstrates that denervation of carotid labyrinth chemoreceptors does not abolish or even reduce the ventilatory sensitivity to hypoxia (Jones and Chu 1988; West, Topor, and Van Vliet 1987). This conclusion is inconsistent with our knowledge of mammalian physiology, but accords reasonably well with the presence of chemoreceptors in the aortae (Ishii, Ishii, and Kusakabe 1985a; B. N. Van Vliet and N. H. West unpublished) and possibly the pulmocutaneous arteries (Hoffman and Cordeiro de Sousa 1982; Lillo 1980b) of anurans.

So little is known of the control of the cardiovascular and respiratory systems of amphibians that any informed experimental approach is likely to be fruitful. For example, an area of considerable potential interest is the impact of changes in temperature on receptor input and the central control systems. To date the effects of temperature on chemoreceptor thresholds or discharge rates in amphibians are unknown, and only Kruhoffer et al. (1987) have examined the effects of temperature on hypoxic ventilatory drive.

8 The Influence of Temperature and Thermal Acclimation on Physiological Function

Lawrence C. Rome, E. Don Stevens, and Henry B. John-Alder

Amphibians can undergo temperature changes of 30°C on a daily basis (Carey 1978a) and up to about 35°C on a seasonal basis. Because of its large influence on the rate of biological reactions and physiological processes, temperature can be an enormously important environmental variable (see also chapter 9). This chapter uses both integrative and comparative approaches to examine the influence of temperature and thermal acclimation on physiological function.

In many cases, temperature effects and responses have been better elucidated in groups of ectotherms other than amphibians (e.g., fish and lizards), often because other organisms were better models or simply the first to be examined. Because the basic mechanisms that underlie many physiological processes are often common to many groups, we include information on fish and lizards to clarify the physiology of amphibians.

The first section of this chapter considers the influence of temperature on physiological function, and the second considers the effects of temperature acclimation.

TEMPERATURE EFFECTS: PHYSICAL AND CHEMICAL

Temperature is a measure of the average velocity of particles (e.g., atoms and molecules). At biological temperatures (0° to 40°C) this molecular movement is primarily translational and, to a lesser extent, rotational (Hochachka and Somero 1984). The higher the temperature, the higher the average velocity of particles. Therefore, temperature influences all physical, chemical, and biological processes that are influenced by the velocity of particles. For example, particles with higher average velocities will diffuse more rapidly than those with lower average velocities (i.e., at a lower temperature).

The Q_{10} is one of several "temperature coefficients" that describe the effect of temperature on biological rate processes. The Q_{10} is the ratio of two rates at a temperature difference of 10°C:

$$Q_{10} = (R_2/R_1),$$

where

R_2 = rate at temperature $(T + 10°C)$
R_1 = rate at temperature T

When the rates are measured at temperatures that are not exactly 10°C apart,

$$Q_{10} = (R_2/R_1)^{[10/(T_2 - T_1)]}.$$

Bennett (1984) suggested a new coefficient, R_{10}, to describe the effect of temperature on variables that are not rate functions (e.g., force development during tetanic muscle contraction). Nonetheless, we will use Q_{10} even when it may be technically inappropriate because of its extensive use in other areas of biology and its widespread familiarity among biologists.

Physical processes generally have Q_{10} values in the range of 1.0 to 1.5, whereas chemical and biological processes are more temperature-sensitive and have higher Q_{10}'s (i.e., 1.8 to 4). A further generalization is that the Q_{10} of a process tends to decrease with increasing temperatures.

The mechanism by which temperature influences diverse physical, chemical, and biological processes is the subject of an enormous literature. Readers seeking an overview should consult the review in Prosser 1986. Here we illustrate the intricacy and complexity of these mechanisms in brief discussions of two biologically relevant processes, diffusion and chemical reactions. An exhaustive discussion of temperature effects is beyond the scope of this book.

Diffusion

Diffusion is one of the most important processes that govern the rates of physiological functions, and it exemplifies the low temperature sensitivity of physical processes. Figure 8.1 shows the effect of temperature on the diffusivity of a weak solution of benzoic acid in water. Throughout the temperature range illustrated, the relation between diffusivity and temperature is linear. Because the relationship has a positive intercept, the ratio of two rates 10°C apart decreases with an increase in temperature. Thus the Q_{10} is 1.41 for the temperature range 10° to 20°C, but is 1.29 for the temperature range 20° to 30°C.

Supported by NIH Grant AR38404 (LCR), Whitaker Foundation Grant (LCR), and National Science Foundation Grant DCB-8702490 (HBJ-A), NSERC (EDS).

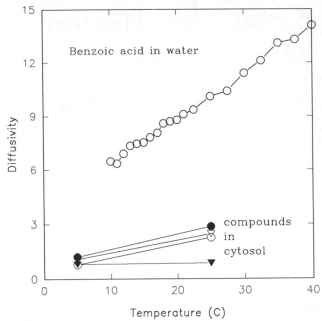

Fig. 8.1 The effect of temperature on a simple physical parameter, the diffusivity of benzoic acid in water ($\times$ 10^{-6} cm$^2 \cdot$ s^{-1}) (data from Lozar, Laguerie, and Couderc 1975). The lines at the bottom show that diffusivity of small molecules through cytosol (Sidell and Hazel 1987) is much slower than in water (cytosol data are displayed with an expanded scale in fig. 8.2).

To understand the biological significance of this phenomenon, Sidell and Hazel (1987) examined the effect of temperature on diffusivity of small biologically important molecules *in vitro* through undiluted cytosolic preparations made from homogenates of fish white muscle. Diffusion was two- to fivefold slower through cytosol than through a dilute aqueous solution (see fig. 8.1). This result is not unusual: diffusion through protein solutions is much slower than through pure water. The data are illustrated with an expanded scale in figure 8.2. Three of the four Q_{10} values (i.e., excepting that for the ATP analogue) are greater than 1.5; the corresponding value for benzoic acid in water is 1.4. The reasons for the temperature independence of diffusivity of the ATP analogue are not known. The lower diffusivity in cytosol results in large part from the greater kinematic viscosity of the medium through which the molecules are diffusing, especially at lower temperatures. Viscosity is itself an important determinant of the rate of diffusion (Mastro et al. 1984; Gershon, Porter, and Trus 1985; Wojcieszyn et al. 1981), and kinematic viscosity decreases as temperature falls. Other factors (e.g., the increase in bond strength of ionic and dipole interactions) may also influence the temperature sensitivity of diffusion (Sidell and Hazel 1987).

Because diffusivity is not the only factor governing flux, thermal effects on other factors may mitigate or exacerbate the temperature sensitivity due to diffusivity. An example of the influence of temperature concerns oxygen flux through living frog sartorius muscle (Mahler 1978; fig. 8.3). As expected, the Q_{10} for the diffusivity of oxygen is low. However, solubility is an important determinant of flux of oxygen through tissues (i.e., the flux of oxygen is proportional to the product of the solubility and diffusivity). Because the solubility of oxygen decreases with increasing temperature, the flux of oxygen is essentially independent of temperature.

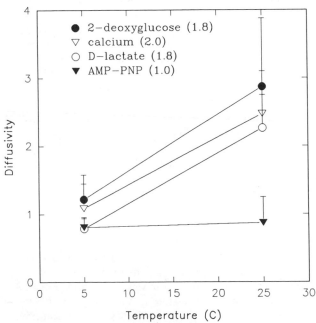

Fig. 8.2 The effect of temperature on the diffusivity ($\times$ 10^{-6} cm$^2 \cdot$ s^{-1}) of small molecules through cytosol (Sidell and Hazel 1987). Note that these values are considerably less than for diffusion through water (fig. 8.1). The Q_{10} values are indicated in parentheses. The large variation for some of these measurements is indicated by showing the SEM. The Q_{10} values are not exactly the same as those you would calculate from the data, because the Q_{10}'s were determined from paired chambers containing identical cytosolic preparations. They do not reflect exactly those calculated from mean values at each temperature (i.e., the ratio of the means is not the same as the mean of the ratios, especially when the variance of each measurement is so large).

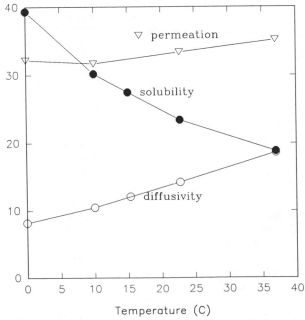

Fig. 8.3 The effect of temperature on diffusivity ($\times$ 10^{-6} cm$^2 \cdot$ s^{-1}, solubility (μl O$_2 \cdot$ cm$^{-3} \cdot$ atm^{-1}), and permeation or flux (μl O$_2 \cdot$ cm$^{-1} \cdot$ atm^{-1}) through resting, living frog muscle. (Data from Mahler 1978.)

In summary, these studies do not support the generalization that the Q_{10} of diffusion *in cells* is less than 1.5. Rather, the Q_{10} of the rate of diffusion is a function of numerous interacting processes (each with its own Q_{10}).

Chemical Reactions

The effect of temperature on the rate of chemical reactions is even more complex than that on diffusion. We must consider the effect of temperature on both the average velocity of particles and on the fraction of molecules that possess enough energy to react (i.e., the fraction having energy greater than or equal to the minimum activation energy required for the particular reaction in question). The minimum energy (activation energy) is referred to as the activation enthalpy and is calculated as

$$H = RT \frac{(d \ln k)}{dT},$$

where

R = gas constant
K = rate constant of the reaction
T = absolute temperature

In vivo, this relation is complex. Among other reasons, reaction rate depends on substrate and modulator concentrations, both of which often change with temperature (Hochachka and Somero 1984). The Q_{10} of enzyme-catalyzed reactions is usually highest at optimal substrate concentrations (i.e., where the velocity of the reaction equals V_{max}, the maximum reaction velocity) and decreases with lower sub-

strate concentrations (Hochachka and Somero 1984). Thus, many textbook examples of such Q_{10}'s are unrealistically high because they are based on data obtained *in vitro*. Maximum reaction rates are not necessarily obtained *in vivo*. A typical example (fig. 8.4) shows the effect of temperature on V_{max} of a digestive enzyme, trypsin. The Q_{10} for the temperature range 20° to 30°C is 2.0. The line for the effect of diffusivity of benzoic acid in water from figure 8.1 is included for comparison. Also shown are the temperature effects on two metabolic enzymes (these were measured as maximum specific activity rather than V_{max}, but should be comparable). The Q_{10} for both metabolic enzymes is 2.0. In summary, the Q_{10} of all three enzyme-catalyzed reactions is greater than that of strictly physical processes.

TEMPERATURE EFFECTS: PHYSIOLOGICAL RATES AS OPPOSED TO PHYSIOLOGICAL LIMITS

Inasmuch as organisms comprise numerous biochemical systems, these effects of temperature depend on numerous aspects of tissue, organ, and organismal function. Many studies of these phenomena have examined physiological limits (e.g., the high or low temperature that will kill an amphibian within a finite time). We will examine this literature at the end of this chapter. Also, a considerable literature examines the effect of temperature on rates well within the lethal limits, and we next focus on these studies. A more comprehensive review of this topic appears later in this chapter; for now we seek to illustrate the diverse effects of temperature on physiological rates.

The metabolic rate of amphibians decreases with decreasing temperature (fig. 8.5). These examples were chosen to

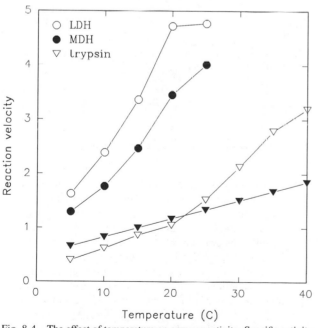

Fig. 8.4 The effect of temperature on enzyme activity. Specific activity of two amphibian metabolic enzymes (*LDH*, lactate dehydrogenase; *MDH*, malate dehydrogenase), μM product $\cdot$ min^{-1} $\cdot$ mg protein^{-1} (redrawn from Feder 1983). V_{max} of the digestive enzyme trypsin from fish, μM product $\cdot$ min^{-1} $\cdot$ mg^{-1} protein $\times$ 10^{-1} (redrawn from Stevens and McLeese 1984). ▼, diffusivity of benzoic acid in water (Fig. 8-1), where a value of 1.0 equals the diffusivity at 15°C.

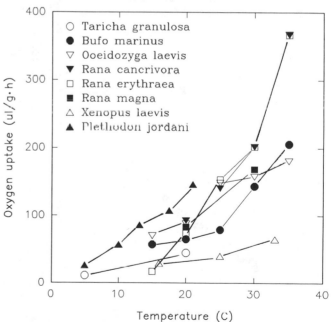

Fig. 8.5 The effect of temperature on oxygen uptake. The data shown illustrate the marked range of the effect. *T. granulosa* and *R. erythraea* (μl O$_2$ $\cdot$ g^{-1} $\cdot$ h^{-1}; Feder 1983c); *B. marinus, R. cancrivora, R. magna,* and *O. laevis* (μl O$_2$/g$^{-0.8}$ $\cdot$ h^{-1}; Feder 1982b); *X. laevis* (μl O$_2$ $\cdot$ h^{-1}; Feder 1985a); *P. jordani* (μl O$_2$ $\cdot$ h^{-1}; Feder, Gibbs, Griffith, and Tsuji 1984).

show variability in the response to temperature; all were measured by Feder and his co-workers using similar techniques and thus should be comparable. The Q_{10} is very low in some cases (Q_{10} 20°–30°C for *Xenopus laevis* is 1.6, Q_{10} 20°–30°C for *Ooeidozyga laevis* [Anura: Ranidae] is 1.8) but is very high in other cases (Q_{10} 10°–20°C for *Plethodon jordani* [Caudata: Plethodontidae] is 2.4, Q_{10} 20°–30°C for *Rana erythraea* is 2.7). Many similar values are in the literature, and in general most Q_{10} values lie in the range of 1.8 to 2.2 when measurements are made on summer-acclimated animals at temperatures at which they are normally active in the field.

The second example shows the effect of temperature on the heart rate of frogs (fig. 8.6). Included are the *in vivo* heart rates of unanesthetized frogs and larvae (*Rana temporaria*) and the *in vitro* rate of isolated frog heart. In the temperature range where the data overlap (15° to 20°C), the Q_{10} values are 1.9 for the *in vivo* frog heart rate, 1.8 for the *in vitro* frog heart rate, and 1.5 for the *in vivo* larval heart rate. However, the Q_{10} for the larval heart rate at higher temperatures (25° to 33°C) is 2.4. Clearly temperature affects heart rate. Heart rate depends on the permeability of the pacemaker cells to ions, and the effect of temperature on heart rate reflects in part the sum of its combined effect on different ions.

The third example shows the effect of temperature on a simple behavior: toads (*Bufo americanus*) catching mealworms that are presented at a fixed rate (fig. 8.7). In this case, capture rate is essentially independent of temperature. Within a fixed time period, toads were motivated and able to capture the same number of mealworms over a wide range of ambient temperatures (Stevens 1988a).

Obviously, few generalizations apply to all amphibians or to all systems. A notable exception is that an increase in temperature usually causes an increase in rate. The literature on the thermal dependence of other aspects of amphibian physi-

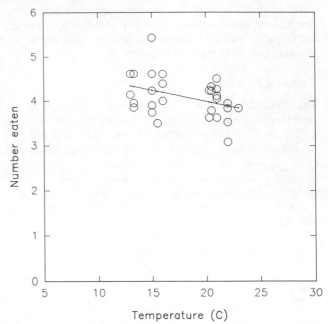

Fig. 8.7 The effect of temperature on the motivation (and/or ability) of *Bufo americanus* to capture and eat mealworms when they are presented at a constant rate (Stevens 1988a). *Line* is a simple least squares regression.

TABLE 8.1 Initial Speed ($cm \cdot s^{-1}$) of White Muscle Fiber Recruitment as a Function of Acclimation Temperature and Muscle Temperature

Acclimation Temperature	Test Temperature	
	10°C	20°C
8°C	31	44
15°C	26	46
26°C	22	43

Source: Reprinted, by permission, from Rome 1986.
Note: Mean values ($N = 6$) at 10°C are statistically different from one another; at 20°C they are not.

ology is summarized in table 8.1 and is discussed in a later section.

THE NECESSITY OF AN INTEGRATIVE VIEW

As we have seen in the previous sections, temperature influences some biological reactions strongly and others weakly. If physiological processes were simple (i.e., a single chemical reaction or physical process), then it would be simple to derive the influence of temperature on whole-animal function from the temperature dependence of suborganismal processes. Complex integrative processes such as brain function, metabolism, and locomotion, however, comprise many subprocesses with varying temperature dependencies. For example, animal locomotion is supported by muscular, neural, metabolic, and biomechanical components, each with a different temperature dependence.

To understand how temperature influences a physiological process at the level of the whole animal, it is essential to understand how molecular, cellular, and organ-level subprocesses fit together to influence performance of the whole animal. This integrative approach is necessary for several

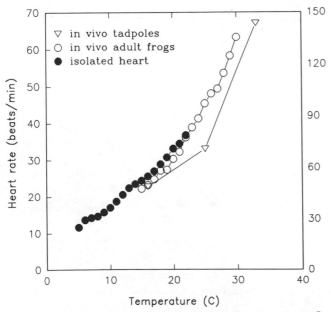

Fig. 8.6 The effect of temperature on heart rate *in vivo* in frogs (○, Harri and Talo 1975a) and larvae (▽, Feder 1985c), and on rate *in vitro* of isolated hearts of frogs (●, Harri and Talo 1975b). Scale for larval data is on the right side.

reasons. First, an integrative approach facilitates a comprehensive appreciation of the environmental challenges that animals face. It is tempting to dismiss the impact of lowering an animal's body temperature as a simple slowing of the animal's ability to perform physiological functions. Lowering of body temperature, however, presents animals with a more serious problem. The temperature dependencies of the subprocesses vary tremendously from near independence ($Q_{10} = 1$) to strong dependence ($Q_{10} > 3$). Thus, it is remarkable that an animal can perform as complex a function as coordinated locomotion over a 10° or 20°C range in body temperature. Second, erroneous conclusions can result if one simply compares the Q_{10} of cellular and biochemical processes to that of whole-animal function. For instance, in the case of locomotion, if the Q_{10} of a particular muscle function is much larger than that of locomotion, one might conclude that this muscle function does not limit locomotion. We will show later that this reasoning can be incorrect. Third, understanding a system and how temperature influences its various components can yield considerable predictive power (e.g., what is the influence of temperature on the locomotory performance of a previously unstudied organism?). Finally, by understanding the various components of the system and determining which may be limiting under different conditions, one can appreciate which functions of an animal must be altered during acclimation to improve performance.

Often, for historical or practical reasons, integrative studies of thermal effects on organismal function have emphasized certain systems and animal models but not others. For example, the most detailed studies relating thermal effects on the biochemistry and general metabolism of cells to integrated organismal function have concerned mammals and microorganisms. Thermal effects on the growth and reproduction of fish and certain invertebrates have received enormous attention, perhaps because of their economic importance. Novel adaptations to extreme thermal environments are best known in species that inhabit such environments. More is known about behavioral thermoregulation in lizards than in other ectotherms because behavioral thermoregulation was first described in this group and has been explored there most thoroughly.

Because the thermal biology of amphibians has merited relatively little attention in each of these respects, a comprehensive account integrating the effects of temperature on organismal function is currently impossible for this group. The lack of attention is itself surprising, given the interaction of heat, energy, and mass exchange in amphibians (chapter 4), which may be more complex in this group than in any other. Nonetheless, although we can review isolated studies, we cannot present a detailed system-by-system overview of thermal effects because of insufficient data. We hope the present account will stimulate further study.

A conspicuous exception to this insufficiency of data for amphibians concerns locomotion and temperature. Perhaps because of the considerable use of frog muscle in experimental preparations, much is known about the inner workings of this system. Moreover, locomotion has been a major focus for studies of behavioral energetics and activity physiology in amphibians (see chapters 11, 12, and 14). In the following section, we develop "locomotion" as an extended example of

an integrative approach to thermal effects in amphibians. We do so not because the locomotor system is more important than other systems, but because of the amount of information available for this system and the likely applicability to amphibians of information gathered on locomotion in other animals. We suggest that application of this integrative approach to other amphibian systems will be fruitful for future investigators.

ANIMAL LOCOMOTION

In this section, we first attempt to explain locomotion in terms of the temperature dependence of the standard contractile properties of isolated muscle. We show that such properties can explain only some of the thermal limitations on maximal performance but not the influence of temperature on submaximal performance. To explain the latter, we must consider the influence of temperature on muscle fiber recruitment and develop a more complex and general model in terms of the recruitment order of muscle. This theory serves as a descriptive model of both maximal and submaximal performance, and it focuses attention on aspects of locomotor physiology that may have undergone evolutionary temperature adaptation. The theory, however, fails to explain limitations on performance at extreme temperatures, which appear to involve neurological as well as less studied properties of muscle. We hope the presentation of this theory will stimulate the further research needed to resolve these issues.

The approach we use is also comparative. We develop the most general theory that explains the influence of temperature on locomotory performance of all animals and show that the influence of temperature on amphibian locomotion is a subset of this general theory. In developing this general theory, we have used information derived from amphibians as much as possible. Nonetheless, we also rely on information from other groups of ectotherms (especially fish), because they are presently better understood than amphibians. Basic neuromuscular mechanisms demonstrated in one group of ectotherms are likely to be shared by others. We are not aware of evidence to suggest otherwise, although further empirical studies would be useful in this regard.

Influence of Temperature on Muscle Mechanics

Bennett (1984) has catalogued the influence of temperature on mechanical properties of muscle from diverse vertebrates, including some amphibians. Rate functions of muscle such as the maximum speed of shortening (V_{max}; fig. 8.8), maximum power production, and rates of twitch and tetanic force generation and relaxation all have large Q_{10}'s (3–4 at low temperatures and about 1.6 at higher temperatures). Tension-generating capacities (twitch and tetanic tensions), on the other hand, are nearly independent of temperature ($Q_{10} = 1.0–1.2$) over broad temperature ranges.

These indices, as well as the energetic ones discussed below, have been used by muscle physiologists for ease of measurement. They set bounds on *in vitro* isometric and isotonic contractile performance of muscles, but they do not characterize the types of contractions that occur during locomotion. Accordingly, these measurements are "arbitrary *in vitro* measurements" and may have little to do with how muscles

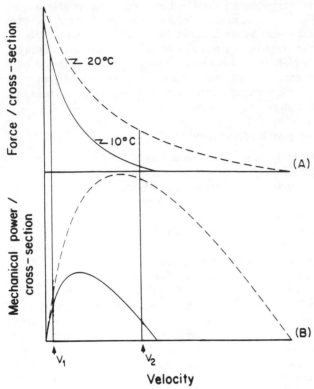

Fig. 8.8 Force and mechanical power generation as a function of muscle-shortening velocity of a muscle at two temperatures separated by 10°C. (Graphs calculated from Hill 1938.)

perform *in vivo*. For example, the velocity of shortening of frog muscle is generally measured by a release experiment, in which the muscle is tetanized and held isometric for 200–300 ms prior to shortening. During jumping at moderate temperatures, however, the frog's muscles shorten well before this time.

Influence of Temperature on Muscle Energetics

The influence of temperature on muscle energetics is less well understood. Almost all measurements have been made on isometric contractions, and very few on shortening contractions. Using heat measurements on *Rana temporaria* muscle, Hill (1938) showed that maximum efficiency (rate of mechanical work generation / rate of ATP utilization) is nearly independent of temperature but that the rate of energy utilization has a large Q_{10} (2–3). Heat and oxygen consumption measurements on muscles from *R. temporaria* and *R. pipiens* (Hill 1938; Rome and Kushmerick 1983) have shown that the energetic cost of generating isometric force (F) for a particular time interval ($\int F \cdot dt$) has a Q_{10} of 3.

The Influence of Temperature on Mechanics of Locomotion

Biomechanics Is Independent of Temperature   Aside from muscle function, locomotion involves physical processes that are essentially independent of temperature. Temperature does not influence gravity, the lever arms that muscles make around joints, the moment of inertia or mass of limbs, or the friction between foot and substrate. Thus for terrestrial animals, at least, the extramuscular mechanical system (tendon,

ligament, bones, joints, friction, gravity, etc.) is unaffected by temperature. Stride frequency and stride length are independent of muscle temperature in lizards running at a given speed (Rome 1982). Rome hypothesized that there is an optimal way to move the extramuscular mechanical system and that the neuromuscular system is able to compensate for changes in muscle properties and move this system in the same manner at different temperatures (see "Compression of Recruitment Order" below). Similar relationships should apply to terrestrial amphibians.

During aquatic locomotion, on the other hand, temperature does change some aspects of the extramuscular mechanical system. Water viscosity increases 30% with a 10°C decrease in temperature (Webb 1975), and this might be expected to cause a change in locomotory mechanics. However, because drag (frictional force of water or air that must be overcome to keep moving) is proportional to viscosity$^{-1/3}$ (Webb 1975), a 10°C decrease in temperature results in only a 10% change in drag. Numerous papers on tail beat frequency of swimming fish have shown small or negligible effects attributable to thermal effects on viscosity of the medium (Stevens 1979; Rome, Loughna, and Goldspink 1984; Sisson and Sidell 1987). No alteration in any locomotory parameter (tail height, tail beat amplitude, tail beat frequency, muscle shortening speed) occurs with temperature change in carp swimming at a given speed (Rome, Funke, and Alexander 1990). Similar relationships should apply to aquatic amphibians, including larvae.

Influence of Temperature on Locomotory Performance
Animals move in a variety of ways and use different types of contractions (i.e., lengthening and shortening). As a result, different muscle properties may be limiting in each case. Amphibians are particularly diverse in their modes of locomotion (see also chapters 11 and 12). Anurans can jump, hop, and walk. Salamanders and larval amphibians make side-to-side movements during swimming, which from a muscle viewpoint are similar to swimming in fish; adult anurans, however, employ a different swimming technique that requires simultaneous activation of both limbs. The effects of temperature have been investigated for jumping in frogs (fig. 8.9), hopping in toads (Londos and Brooks 1988), swimming in frogs (fig. 8.9) and salamanders (Else and Bennett 1988), and walking in salamanders (Else and Bennett 1988). In general, all of these forms of locomotion are subject to the same thermal constraints that are seen in other ectotherms. Amphibian locomotion is depressed and tends to have a higher thermal dependence (high Q_{10}) at low temperatures than at higher temperatures. The adaptive significance of interspecific differences in the thermal dependence of jumping is discussed later. We first explore the power of an integrative approach in explaining the mechanistic basis of thermal limitations on locomotion.

Cyclical versus "One-Shot" Locomotion   Locomotion such as running or swimming at constant speed involves continuous cyclical movements. Thus, one set of muscles must activate, shorten, and relax, followed by the same sequence in the opposite set. One property of active muscle is that it can generate far more force while being stretched than while shortening. Therefore, it is advantageous to an animal for a muscle to relax before being stretched by the shortening of

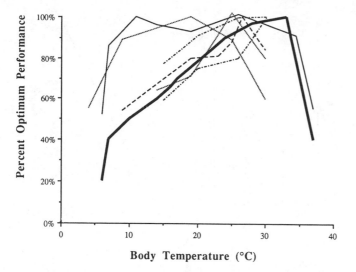

Fig. 8.9 Influence of temperature on locomotor capabilities of anuran amphibians. The curve for *Xenopus laevis* (Miller 1982) is for swimming; all others are for jumping or hopping. (Curve *a* for *Rana pipiens* is from Hirano and Rome 1984, curve *b* is from Tracy 1979b. Data for *Rana clamitans* are from Huey and Stevenson 1979. (Reprinted, by permission, from Whitehead et al. 1989, © University of Chicago.)

the opposite muscle set (either contralateral or antagonists on the same side). At some temperatures the rate of activation and relaxation of muscle may limit maximal performance, whereas at other temperatures the maximum speed of shortening of the muscle may be more important.

"One-shot" locomotion is exemplified by the frog jump. In frog jumping the muscle is activated, it generates force, and it shortens. At normal temperatures, the muscle has sufficient time to relax before the next jump. Thus, the rate of relaxation of the muscle is of little import.

Aquatic versus Terrestrial Cyclical Locomotion Aquatic and terrestrial locomotion differ in locomotory mechanics and in types of muscle contractions. The fundamental difference is in the amount of drag the animals face from the medium. During swimming, muscles must generate substantial mechanical power to overcome drag (force of drag × velocity of movement). Thus, during locomotion in the water, the muscle's ability to generate mechanical power is likely to be limiting. On land, however, the only drag is from the air, which is inconsequential at most speeds. Work, however, is required to decelerate the center of mass and limbs and subsequently to reaccelerate them. This is done by muscles first performing negative work (i.e., muscle lengthening during activation to decelerate the animal) and subsequently performing positive work to reaccelerate the animal. In negative work, the muscle, tendons, and ligaments may store energy elastically and then return it to the animal in the propulsive phase. This requires precise timing of activation and subsequent relaxation. Thus, in running, the kinetics of activation and relaxation (twitch properties) may be limiting rather than the ability to generate mechanical power.

Relation between Muscle Properties and Locomotory Performance The previous section discusses muscle properties that may limit different types of locomotion. The quantitative manner in which they influence locomotion is complex. For example, the Q_{10} of jump distance of *Rana pipiens* is 1.6 (Fig. 8.10A; Hirano and Rome 1984), whereas the Q_{10} of power generation by the muscle active during jumping is about 2.7 (fig. 8.10B). To conclude that muscle power output does not limit jump distance because it has a smaller Q_{10} would be erroneous. In fact, mechanical power production of the muscle sets maximum jump distance (fig. 8.10C). Al-

though jump distance is linearly proportional to peak mechanical power generation, the Q_{10} of actual jump distance is low because the intercept of the relationship between jump distance and temperature is large (fig. 8.10C). This intercept represents "takeoff distance," which is simply the horizontal distance the frog moves before its feet leave the ground (in turn, a function of hindlimb length, which does not change with temperature). Furthermore, by comparing isolated muscle data, Hirano and Rome (1984) were able to demonstrate that the frogs recruit all their extensor muscle fibers and that their fibers generate their maximal power during the jumps. Thus, the apparent Q_{10} for jump distance is substantially smaller than that of the muscle because of the biomechanical relationship between jump distance and power generation. Nonetheless, the low mechanical power output of muscle at cold temperatures causes maximum locomotory ability to diminish.

Mechanical power also limits swimming speed in fish, but in a different manner than in frog jumping. The mechanical power needed for swimming is proportional to speed$^{2.5}$. Thus, a large Q_{10} in mechanical power production would be necessary to yield even a small Q_{10} in maximum swim speed.

The quantitative relationship between steady locomotion in amphibians at low temperature and twitch properties of muscle is more straightforward. Because the muscle should activate and relax before the activation and shortening of opposing muscles or those in the contralateral limb, the time for activation and relaxation should limit the minimum time between alternating movements (i.e., the time for one-half cycle). If an animal tries to locomote at a higher frequency, then a muscle may not be relaxed when the opposing muscle starts to stretch it and thereby may offer too much resistance to be overcome. During swimming in the frog *Hyla crucifer*, stroke frequency below 8°C appears to be limited by the time required for contraction and relaxation (fig. 8.11; John-Alder, Barnhart, and Bennett 1989). Since the twitch properties are far more temperature-sensitive than is the limb cycling frequency (see prior discussion), at temperatures above 8°C the twitch properties no longer limit performance. At higher temperatures, the limiting properties on performance are unknown, but may be mechanical power generation as suggested for fish.

The salamander *Ambystoma tigrinum nebulosum* (Ambystomatidae) displays a similar pattern. At 20°C, the sum of

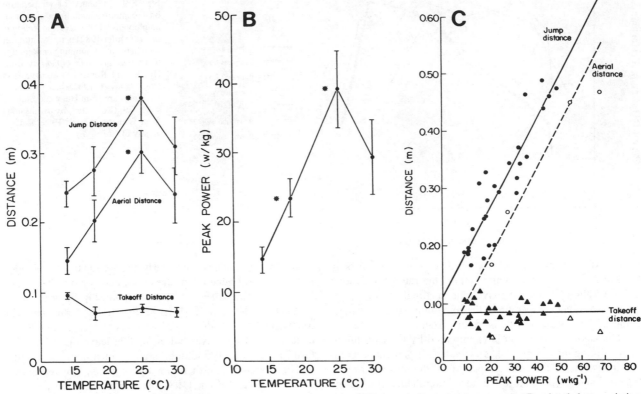

Fig. 8.10 Jump distance (*A*) and peak power output (*B*) as a function of muscle temperature. *C*, jump distance as a function of peak power output. Jump distance = aerial distance (traveled after feet leave ground) + takeoff distance (prior to leaving ground). (Reprinted, by permission, from Hirano and Rome 1984, *Journal of Experimental Biology,* © Company of Biologists Ltd.)

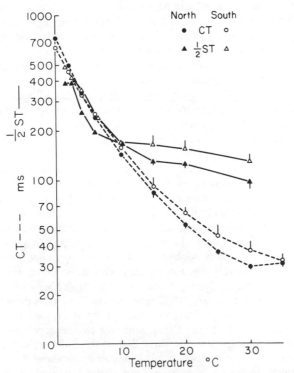

Fig. 8.11 Effects of temperature on the contraction time of fast twitch skeletal muscle (contraction time = time from the onset of force to 50% relaxation in an isometric twitch) and on the time required for the power stroke during swimming in the frog *Hyla crucifer. Open symbols* are for a southern population, and *filled symbols* for a northern population. (Reprinted, by permission, from John-Alder, Barnhart, and Bennett 1989, *Journal of Experimental Biology,* © Company of Biologists Ltd.)

time to peak tension and one-half relaxation set the stride frequency, but at 10°C the sum of the contractile times (324 ms) greatly exceeds the time for a half stride (203 ms; Else and Bennett 1987). How animals can overcome the assumed resistance to muscle lengthening is unclear, and the large discrepancy between the timing of twitch performance and limb cycling underscores the uncertainty of using *in vitro* muscle performance to explain *in vivo* function. The "arbitrary *in vitro* measurement" may not be an accurate measure of muscle function *in vivo* (i.e., twitch properties may be quite different in the isometric case, which is measured *in vitro,* than in the shortening case *in vivo*). The only way to answer these questions definitively is actually to reproduce *in vitro* the excitation pattern and length changes that the muscle undergoes *in vivo*.

Similarly in lizards at low temperatures, the time for one-half stride at maximum running speed just equals the sum of the time to peak twitch tension and time to one-half relaxation (Marsh and Bennett 1985, 1986a, 1986b; Bennett, John-Alder, and Huey 1986). These muscle properties limit the maximum stride frequency and hence burst speed (burst speed = stride frequency × stride length). Again at high temperatures, what limits maximum performance has not yet been determined.

Is Muscle Function Sufficient to Explain Locomotory Performance? Isolated muscle properties appear to explain some limitations of maximal locomotory performance at some temperatures. As the following considerations show, however, muscle performance alone is not sufficient to explain the influence of temperature on submaximal locomotory performance. For instance, the Q_{10} of the maximum speed of shortening of muscle, 2 to 3, might suggest that limb movements and stride frequency should increase similarly with temperature in animals moving at a constant speed.

These predictions are incorrect. Savannah monitor lizards (*Varanus exanthamaticus*) running at a given speed on a treadmill with muscle temperatures of 28° and 38°C have exactly the same limb movements and stride frequency at both temperatures (i.e., $Q_{10} = 1$; Rome 1982), and likewise fish swim with exactly the same movements at different temperatures (Rome, Funke, and Alexander 1990).

Difficulties in extrapolating from *in vitro* muscle function to *in vivo* locomotion may arise in part because the pattern of stimulation differs between isolated muscle and whole-animal experiments. In isolated muscle experiments, all muscle fibers are active by virtue of direct electrical stimulation. Therefore, all muscle fibers are active at each temperature (which is, of course, a necessary condition for measuring the temperature dependence of muscle). In the whole animal, however, not all the muscle fibers are active at one time and not all are identical in V_{max}. The muscle fibers are arranged into motor units stimulated through motor neurons; the nervous system controls which motor units are active. Therefore, the nervous system could recruit more muscle fibers and faster muscle fiber types at low temperatures to compensate for the influence of temperature on muscle function and to enable animals to make identical movements at varying temperatures despite these changes in muscle function (Rome 1982).

Compression of Recruitment Order   The essence of the compression of recruitment order is that motor units are recruited in the same order at low and high temperatures (first slow motor units and then fast ones). To compensate for the decrease in power production at low temperatures, animals recruit more of the motor units at a given speed (i.e., "compress" the recruitment order into a narrower range of speeds).

In most vertebrates (including amphibians), direct examination of recruitment order is problematic because "fast" and "slow" motor units intermingle. By contrast, fish provide an excellent experimental model because their different muscle fiber types, red (slow, aerobic fibers) and white (fast, anaerobic fibers), are anatomically separate (fig. 8.12). With electromyography, Rome, Loughna, and Goldspink (1984) monitored the activity of the different fiber types during

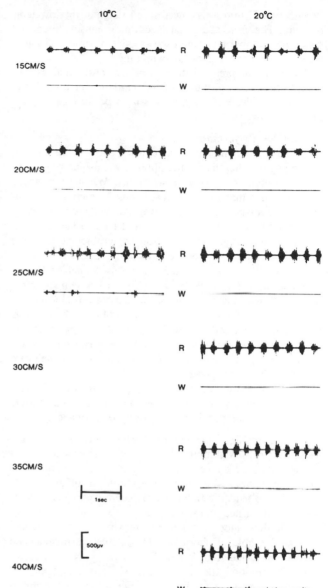

Fig. 8.13   Electromyography from red (*R*) and white (*W*) muscle of carp swimming at various speeds at 10° and 20°C. (Reprinted, by permission, from Rome, Loughna, and Goldspink 1984.)

swimming at different muscle temperatures. Recently, Jayne, Bennett, and Lauder (1990) have shown that lizards, too, compress their recruitment order. Thus, amphibians may also compress their recruitment order while locomoting with low muscle temperatures (Rome 1986, 1990).

The entire theory is best introduced by example. Figure 8.13 (Rome, Loughna, and Goldspink 1984) shows the typical results from a carp swimming at 10°C and then at 20°C. At both temperatures, only the red muscle shows electrical activity at slow swim speeds, and as speed increases, the white muscle is recruited as well. At the cooler temperature, however, the white muscle is recruited at a relatively slow speed (mean = 26 cm · s⁻¹), whereas at the warmer temperature, white muscle is not recruited until a higher speed (mean = 46 cm · s⁻¹). Thus, motor units are recruited in the same order with increasing speed regardless of temperature (i.e., recruitment order is fixed), but the order is simply

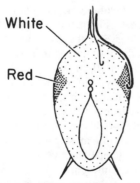

Fig. 8.12   Muscle fiber types and electromyography electrode placement in carp.

"compressed" into a narrower speed range at the low temperature. Therefore at a given speed, more muscle fibers and faster muscle fiber types are used at low temperatures to generate the power necessary for swimming.

Although compressing the recruitment order enables animals to maintain constancy of locomotion over a moderate range of speeds, low temperatures limit performance as explained below.

Sustainable Performance Anaerobic ("fast" or "white") fibers have low mitochondrial density and low capillarity. Consequently, they have little ability to consume oxygen to replenish high-energy phosphate stores. When swim speed increases such that anaerobic fibers must be recruited to generate the requisite mechanical power, the ATP used will likely be supplied anaerobically. This would lead to lactate accumulation, glycogen depletion from anaerobic muscle, and ultimately fatigue. Therefore, swimming speeds at which anaerobic fibers are recruited are not sustainable (Rome, Loughna, and Goldspink 1984, 1985). At low temperatures, the mechanical power output of the aerobic muscle fibers is depressed to only one-third to two-thirds of that which can be generated at temperatures 10°C higher. Accordingly, at low temperatures the anaerobic fibers must be recruited at a lower speed, significantly reducing the maximum sustainable swim speed at low temperatures.

Therefore, during both maximum performance and maximum sustainable performance, the properties of the muscle fibers are the major limit of locomotory performance.

Factors Limiting Locomotory Performance at Extreme Temperatures Maximum locomotory performance may suffer at extreme temperatures if any of the following occur: First, the nervous system may not recruit all of the muscle fibers due to synaptic failure in the central nervous system, spinal cord, or neuromuscular junction. Second, the velocity at which fibers shorten (V) and the maximum speed at which they are capable of shortening (V_{max}) may be mismatched (Hill 1938; Rome et al. 1988). To generate maximum power during locomotion, the muscles must shorten at the appropriate V/V_{max} (see fig. 8.8). Third, the time following the stimulus may be insufficient for complete muscle activation. Finally, the relative timing of contractions of different muscles during locomotion may be inappropriate.

At most temperatures, jumping frogs avoid these problems. As exemplified by *Rana pipiens,* frogs recruit all of their muscle fibers during maximal jumps, and the fibers generate the maximum power of which they are capable (Hirano and Rome 1984). Jump distance is linearly proportional to peak power generated and thus increases with temperature as well. Throughout a moderate temperature range, jumping performance appears to be limited solely by the maximum mechanical power output capability of the frog's muscles.

At higher temperatures (≈30°C), however, this pattern no longer holds. For instance, as muscle temperature increases between 25° and 30°C, both the peak mechanical power generated and distance jumped by *R. pipiens* decreases (fig. 8.10A, B). By contrast, in isolated frog muscle experiments the maximum mechanical power output increases in this range of temperatures. Some factor limits the power output of the muscle *in vivo* below the level it is capable of generat-

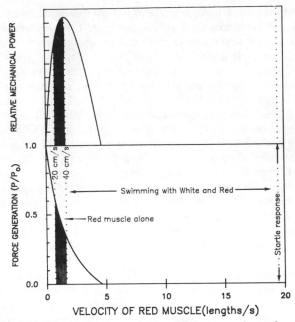

Fig. 8.14 Force and power generation of red carp muscle as a function of shortening speed determined from *in vitro* experiments. The actual shortening of the red muscle during swimming between speeds of 20 and 40 cm · s⁻¹ is superimposed (*shaded*) on the force-velocity and power-velocity curves. The red muscle cannot shorten fast enough to power the startle response. (From Rome et al. 1988. Reprinted, by permission, from *Nature* 355:824–827, Copyright © 1988 Macmillan Magazines Ltd.)

ing *in vitro.* An obvious explanation for the reduced mechanical power output at high temperatures is the inability of the nervous system to recruit all muscle fibers. A possible site of failure is the neuromuscular junction. Neuromuscular transmission is blocked only when temperature falls below 1°C for 10°C-acclimated frogs and 4°C for 25°C-acclimated frogs (Takeuchi 1958; Grainger and Goldspink 1964; Jensen 1972). Heat block of neuromuscular transmission, however, has received relatively little attention. Both mini-end-plate potentials and postjunctional depolarization in response to acetylcholine decline at high temperatures (Jensen 1972). Evidence for heat block of neuromuscular transmission has been found in Antarctic fish (Macdonald and Montgomery 1982). Failure could also occur at the synaptic connections that activate the motor neuron, but this has not been reported in amphibians.

Rome et al. (1988) have evaluated the appropriateness of V/V_{max} in carp by determining which muscle fibers are active at a given speed of locomotion, the V *in vivo*, and the V_{max} of different fiber types. Figure 8.14 shows the force-velocity curve and power curve of the carp red muscle. The shaded region represents the V of the red muscle fibers during swimming between 20 and 40 cm · s⁻¹. At 40 cm · s⁻¹ the red muscle shortens at a velocity where it is generating maximal mechanical power. If the fish tried to swim faster, the V of the muscle would have to increase and the power generated by the red muscle would actually decrease. Thus the carp must recruit its fast white muscle.

The influence of temperature on $\dot{V}/V_{max}$ is predictable. As previously discussed, the Q_{10} for V_{max} is 2 to 3, whereas V during locomotion at a given speed and the optimal V/V_{max}

are independent of temperature. It follows that animals at low temperatures must move at a lower speed, with a lower V so that the V/V_{max} does not exceed the optimal value of 0.40. For instance, at 10°, 15°, and 20°C, carp recruit their white muscle at 27, 35, and 42 cm · s^{-1}, which represent equivalent values of V/V_{max} (Rome, Funke, and Alexander 1990; Rome and Sosnicki 1990).

This principle may be very important for understanding amphibian locomotion. The V_{max} of frog (*R. pipiens*) muscle is already known at various experimental and acclimation temperatures (Rome 1983; Renaud and Stevens 1984). Still to be determined is whether the velocity of shortening of the fibers (V) *in vivo* is appropriate for maximum power generation and whether or not these "appropriate velocities" occur at the same time in different muscles. Indirect evidence suggests V/V_{max} may be optimal: Hirano and Rome (1984) concluded for frogs that each fiber must be generating maximum power during jumps, which implies that each shortens at its correct V/V_{max}. To date, however, V/V_{max} has never been adequately measured directly in an amphibian species.

Summary of the Influence of Temperature on Locomotion in Amphibians

The influence of temperature on locomotory performance is quite complex, and to understand it requires consideration of many subtle parameters. Essentially, animals move in the same manner at low temperatures as at high ones. They may compensate for diminished power output of their muscles at low temperatures by compressing their recruitment order. Maximum burst performance and maximum sustainable performance, however, remain temperature-sensitive because, at these levels, differential fiber recruitment is no longer possible, and thus performance becomes a function of the muscle properties alone. At extreme temperatures neural and *in vivo* muscle properties may limit performance below the limitation set by muscle properties determined *in vitro*.

Amphibian locomotion has not yet received the same attention as that of fish, but no doubt it will shortly. Jumping of frogs has received the most attention (see chapters 11 and 12). As described above, jumping distance is related to muscle power output and thus is quite temperature-sensitive. At high temperatures, however, the system fails for an unknown reason. This is a crucial area to explore in the future, using the important concepts of timing and V/V_{max}. In addition, the biomechanical approach (i.e., force plate and film analysis) must be used on a greater diversity of species. Hylids, for example, exhibit lower Q_{10}'s for jumping performance at intermediate temperatures than do ranids (John-Alder, Morin, and Lawler 1988).

Frog swimming has been examined to a lesser extent. It differs from fish swimming in not involving cyclical contraction and relaxation of the contralateral side. Instead, both sides contract simultaneously. However, muscle relaxation before each stroke may be crucial. In *Hyla crucifer* (Hylidae), stroke velocity (stroke length / stroke time) has a large temperature sensitivity ($Q_{10} = 10$) at low temperatures (1.5° to 6°C), and a small temperature sensitivity ($Q_{10} = 1.2$) at higher temperatures (20° to 30°C; John-Alder, Barnhart, and Bennett 1989). Stroke frequency shows a large temperature

sensitivity and at low temperature seems to be limited by the twitch contractile kinetics of the muscle. The limitation at high temperatures has not yet been determined (John-Alder, Barnhart, and Bennett 1989).

Toads and frogs also can perform short jumps (hops). Little is known about the mechanism by which they perform submaximal movements or its sensitivity to temperature (Walton and Anderson 1988).

Locomotion of salamanders running and swimming has been examined (Else and Bennett 1987), and as one might expect, this cyclical locomotion is limited at low temperatures by the twitch properties of the muscle. They may compress their recruitment order at low temperatures. Salamanders fatigue at low speeds at low temperatures (Else and Bennett 1987), as do some fish. This may reflect the early recruitment of anaerobic muscle fibers.

Swimming in salamanders and larval anurans requires cyclical activation and relaxation of the contralateral sides. From this viewpoint, this form of locomotion is more similar to that of fish than to that of adult anurans, but little is known about thermal effects on muscle function during these activities.

GENERAL EFFECTS OF TEMPERATURE ON AMPHIBIAN PHYSIOLOGY

The present section discusses general aspects of amphibian thermal physiology. Acclimation and adaptation are discussed separately in later sections. Table 8.2 exemplifies the diversity of amphibian physiological processes whose temperature dependencies have been investigated. These processes can be categorized by their biological time scales as short-term (e.g., locomotion, vocalization), intermediate (e.g., digestive and assimilation efficiencies), and long-term (e.g., growth and development). Thermal effects on short-term functions are readily measured over a broad range of temperatures, whereas studies on long-term effects present more serious logistical and interpretive problems.

Ecological implications of temperature responses differ with the time scales. Short-term responses can be important on an hourly or daily basis as an amphibian exploits the thermal variability of its environment, and laboratory simulations of rapid temperature changes can accurately reflect natural situations. Long-term responses sometimes occur only on a seasonal basis, and animals may rarely experience the conditions of thermal constancy found in experimental investigations. Some thermal responses (especially tolerance limits; see below) can change on a daily or seasonal basis (Pough 1974a; Layne and Claussen 1982) or with development (e.g., Zweifel 1977).

The experimental approach to amphibian thermal physiology is analogous to that for other ectotherms. This area is the subject of excellent reviews (Huey and Stevenson 1979; Huey 1982) and will only be summarized briefly here. The reader is referred to Huey 1982 for extensive citations. The appropriate level of biological organization at which an analysis should be directed depends on the question at hand. When the focus is on ecological issues, analyses of integrated organismal performance such as swimming velocity or predation success are more instructive than mechanistic analyses

TABLE 8.2 Some Ecologically Relevant Physiological Effects of Temperature on Amphibians

Effect	Reference
Water balance	Dinno and Nagel 1988; Segura, Varsavsky, and Petriella 1987; Brown et al. 1986; Pitkin 1978; Warburg and Degani 1979; Larionov, Medvedev, and Khramenko 1978
Digestion	Bobka, Jaeger, and McNaught 1981; Freed 1980; Gossling et al. 1980; Kharlamova 1976
Oxygen uptake	Blem, Ragan, and Scott 1986; Feder 1978b; Chitko 1977
Vision	Aho et al. 1988; Tsin and Beatty 1980; Schaeffer et al. 1978; Sillman et al. 1978; Nartsissova 1977
Hearing	Walkowiak 1980; Gerhardt 1977, 1978; Moffat and Capranica 1976b
Emergence	Smits and Crawford 1984; Degani 1982; Uwa et al. 1981; Dimmitt and Ruibal 1980a
Call	Matsui 1985; Schneider and Sofianidou 1985; Sullivan 1984a; Gayou 1984; Sullivan 1982b; Fairchild 1981; Schneider and Brzoska 1981; Gerhardt and Mudry 1980; Schneider, Tunner, and Hoedl 1979
Development	Ushakov and Pashkova 1986; Pawlowska 1985; Dettlaff 1986; Townsend and Stewart 1986b; Michael 1981; Pawlowska 1980; Moriya 1979
Metamorphosis	Schindelmeiser 1985; Pandian and Marian 1985; Eagleson and McKeown 1978b
Growth	Marian and Pandian 1985; Keen, Travis, and Julianna 1984; Degani, Goldenberg, and Warburg 1980
Regeneration	Schauble and Nentwig 1974
Mitosis	Mazin and Detlaf 1985; Speit 1980
Sex reversal	Dournon and Houillon 1985, 1984, 1983
Pathology	Juacaba et al. 1987; Zavenella 1985; Seppanen et al. 1984

of lower-level functions such as muscle contraction or evoked potentials. Obviously, a comprehensive understanding of a process can be gained only through a multifaceted investigation at multiple levels of biological organization. However, the investigator must recognize that thorough knowledge of lower-level processes may not accurately predict organismal performance, just as organismal performance may not reflect lower-level physiological capacities. A further caution is that organismal performance will be a function of both behavioral and physiological components. Experimental results may differ among labs when different techniques may measure behavioral rather than physiological limitations. For example, Tracy (1979b) reported jumping ability in *Rana pipiens* to be temperature-independent at a wide range of temperatures, while Hirano and Rome (1984) found a marked temperature dependence over the same temperature range. This discrepancy may be due to differences in the stimulatory technique (see discussion in Whitehead et al. 1989).

The rate or capacity of the physiological function under investigation is best measured at regular temperature intervals between the upper and lower tolerance limits of the animal, and a curve can be fit to the ensuing thermal response data (thermal performance curve, rate-temperature curve). Typically, the level of a function will increase with temperature in some fashion (e.g., linear or nonlinear) up to a maximal level that may be sustained in a range of relative thermal independence. Ultimately performance will decline sharply at high temperatures, often because of irreversible damage to the biological system. Parameters of interest, including thermal tolerance limits, thermal performance breadths (i.e., thermal ranges of competent performance), and thermal optima (thermal points or ranges of optimal performance), can then be extracted from the curve. (For present purposes, "optimality" is equated with the "maximal" performance level that can be attained by a function. Many authors have correctly noted that optimality is best qualified in the ecological context of the animal under investigation.) Special care must be taken to control body temperature, particularly in small animals at extreme temperatures. For example, a moist, 1-g frog moved from a 35°C cabinet to an experimental platform at 25°C will cool quickly, and reliable measurements of its body temperature may not be possible within the constraints of an experiment. In such cases, cooling (or heating) curves (Riggs 1970) can be constructed by measuring the time course of changes in body temperature of similar animals under identical conditions. Subsequent experiments must be timed carefully, and body temperatures can be estimated by interpolation.

Tolerance limits define the upper and lower bounds beyond which a physiological function fails. These limits are analogous to the well-known organismal measures of critical thermal minima (CTMin) and critical thermal maxima (CTMax) and are conceptually related to resistance adaptation (Precht et al. 1973). Tolerance limits (particularly CTMax; see below) are the most commonly measured aspect of amphibian thermal physiology (Hutchison and Maness 1979). Their proximate ecological significance is unproven (especially in adult amphibians; see below), but they can be correlated with distributional ranges (e.g., Miller and Packard 1977). Performance breadths define the range of temperatures over which some arbitrary level of performance can be attained (e.g., 80% or 95% of maximal jump distance). Performance levels should be chosen so that performance breadths will include ecologically relevant temperatures (van Berkum 1986), but this is often not possible for amphibians because of the paucity of reliable records of field body temperatures, particularly for nonbreeding amphibians. Thermal optima describe the temperature or range of temperatures over which an animal can perform best. Performance breadths and performance optima are conceptually related to capacity adaptation (Precht et al. 1973). These parameters provide analytical tools for considering the physiological significance of variability in an animal's thermal environment. As a corollary, performance breadths indicate how well an animal could function if it migrated through an environmental thermal barrier, and in this context performance breadths facilitate an interpretation of temperature as a geographical isolating mechanism (Janzen 1967; Huey 1978; Feder 1978b). The temperatures at issue are often within the normal activity range of an animal, and the ecological relevance of these parameters can be interpreted, given accurate thermal ecological data.

Parameters of thermal performance are determined from thermal performance curves and, with the exception of tolerance limits, are thus subject to the method of curve fitting (Huey and Stevenson 1979; Huey 1982). Artifactual differences in estimates of thermal performance parameters may be introduced by differences in curve fitting, but such artifacts are not likely to alter the general interpretation of data (John-

Alder, Morin, and Lawler 1988). Descriptors of thermal performance can subsequently be used for a variety of analytical purposes, although their utility as descriptors of thermal niche has recently been questioned (Whitehead et al. 1989; but see below).

In general, physiological rates and capacities in amphibians increase until high temperature becomes damaging. With the exceptions of spermiogenesis (Fraile et al. 1989) and locomotion in some cases (see other sections), there is little evidence of optimal functioning at midrange body temperatures. However, thermal performance curves differ in form among various functions. For example, the temporal qualities of frog calls (e.g., pulse frequency, rate of call repetition; Bellis 1957; Zweifel 1959, 1968a) and rates of larval development (Bachmann 1969) are linear functions of temperature, whereas locomotor performance and most in vitro muscle contractile properties (Else and Bennett 1987; John-Alder, Barnhart, and Bennett 1989) have more complex temperature dependencies. Even closely related functions can differ in thermal performance. Whereas the temporal properties of calls increase linearly with Q_{10}'s of about 2.5 (Bellis 1957; Gayou 1984), the spectral properties (e.g., dominant frequency) are much more temperature-independent, typically increasing in frequency by only 1 to 2% per degree C (Gerhardt and Mudry 1980). A second example concerns nutritional physiology. An increase in temperature usually increases digestive efficiency (e.g., Freed 1980), but it may decrease assimilation efficiency (Bobka, Jaeger, and McNaught 1981). This example underscores the requirement of an integrative approach to investigating thermal physiology: net energy gain cannot be predicted from a simple understanding of its isolated components.

Some processes improve with decreasing temperature. For example, visual sensitivity is improved by low body temperature, apparently because background thermal excitation of visual cells is reduced (Aho et al. 1988). Complementary functions of different individuals sometimes undergo parallel changes with temperature. In frogs, for example, female Hyla versicolor (Hylidae) prefer mating calls with temperature-dependent temporal properties produced by males at about the same body temperature as their own (Gerhardt 1978), and the thermal sensitivity of hearing frequency corresponds to the temperatures at which Bombina bombina (Discoglossidae) and Rana temporaria engage in mating behavior (Walkowiak 1980). However, such patterns are not universal. Temperature-induced changes in the frequency preference of female Hyla cinerea are not matched by corresponding changes in the dominant frequency of male calls (Gerhardt and Mudry 1980). In fact, female H. cinerea at about 20°C are predicted to prefer the call of H. gratiosa over that of male conspecifics. Generalities concerning temperature effects on amphibian physiology and behavior must be stated cautiously and should be interpreted with care.

Differences in the forms of thermal performance curves suggest that all systems do not share a single thermal optimum. In addition to the potential for multiple thermal optima at one point in time, there can also be temporal changes in thermal optima. Brattstrom (1979) speculated that body temperatures higher in juvenile than in adult Bufo debilis (Seymour 1972) may promote rapid feeding, accelerated digestion, and rapid fat deposition, and Lillywhite, Licht, and

Chelgren (1973) observed that young Bufo boreas bask except when food is withheld. The implication is that optimal temperatures may be higher in well-nourished and/or juvenile amphibians than in unfed adults. In contrast, however, Freed (1980) observed no differences in the basking behavior of fed and unfed Hyla cinerea, even though basking elevated body temperature from 23.9° to 28°C and clearly enhanced the rate of digestion. More intensive analysis of multiple thermal optima will be an important addition to the literature on amphibian thermal physiology, particularly in the context of ecological thermal physiology (below).

In light of the typically broad ranges of activity body temperatures (Brattstrom 1963) and the available records on low-temperature breeding (see Bachmann 1969), amphibians clearly do many things at suboptimal temperatures. Some amphibians may rarely experience body temperatures that permit high levels of performance. Indeed, normally experienced body temperatures in Limnodynastes tasmaniensis (Myobatrachidae) are below the lower bound of the 80% performance breadth for jump distance (Whitehead et al. 1989). Behavioral thermoregulation can help to ameliorate the retarding effects of low temperature on physiological processes and thus benefit the amphibian (Brattstrom 1979; chapter 9), but empirical documentation of this conjecture is badly needed.

Animals active over broad temperature ranges may experience greater selection for thermally independent performance than animals active over narrow temperature ranges (Tracy 1979b). Thus frogs, which are typically active over wider temperature ranges than lizards (compare Brattstrom 1963, 1965), should also have wider thermal performance breadths. While this hypothesis is not refuted by the available data, there is surprisingly extensive overlap between thermal performance breadths for lizard running and frog jumping, particularly for lizards and summer-breeding and/or low-latitude frogs (John-Alder, Barnhart, and Bennett 1989). For instance, sprint-running performance of lizards is characterized by 80% performance breadths of 7.9° to 16.2°C (Tracy 1979b; Bennett 1980b; Hertz, Huey, and Nevo 1983; Marsh and Bennett 1985, 1986b; van Berkum 1986; mean = 11.6°C, R. B. Huey pers. comm.), whereas values range from 10.3° to 22.0°C in frogs (mean 15.6°C). In other words, lizards can run at 80% of their maximal velocities over an average range of 11.6°C, and frogs can jump 80% of their longest distances over an average range of 15.6°C. A comparison of thermal breadths for embryonic development is more consistent with Tracy's hypothesis. Normal development occurs in most amphibians over a range of about 15°C (Bachmann 1969) versus about 6° to 10°C in reptiles (Packard and Packard 1988).

The likely importance of temperature in the ecological physiology of amphibians is summarized most dramatically by Berven, Gill, and Smith-Gill (1979) in a study on Rana clamitans. They concluded that "all of the observed variation in green frog life history characteristics, including duration of the breeding season, length of the metamorphic period, size of developing larvae at all stages, and rate of development, was interpretable as the direct effect of temperature alone" (619). Nonetheless, our knowledge of amphibian thermal ecological physiology is characterized by insufficient data, particularly for nonbreeding adult amphibians.

Correlations between amphibian behavior and environmental temperatures (e.g., Benski, Zalisko, and Larsen 1986; Bider and Morrison 1981; Cooke 1982; Gittins 1983; Gittins, Parker, and Slater 1980; Haapanen 1982; Harrison, Gittins, and Slater 1983; Hock 1967; Semlitsch 1985a; Wisniewske, Paull, and Slater 1981) clearly indicate that daily and seasonal activity patterns are at least partly cued by temperature, but few investigators have presented quantitative analyses of multiple environmental factors (e.g., Smits and Crawford 1984). Detailed long-term studies of amphibian thermal ecological physiology (e.g., Brattstrom and Warren 1955; Fitch 1956) are required for the development of an ecological context of amphibian thermal ecology and for the establishment of interpretational contexts of laboratory studies. Nonetheless, present data clearly indicate that amphibians often operate at suboptimal temperatures, perhaps because of ecological constraints (see Bachmann 1969). The interface between ecological constraints and thermal physiology has largely been a conjectural domain. For example, John-Alder, Morin, and Lawler (1988) suggested that some anurans breed late in ephemeral ponds, despite apparent disadvantages of this phenology (Wilbur and Alford 1985; Morin 1987), simply because they are physiologically unable to breed earlier. Brattstrom (1963) speculated that differences in the thermal requirements of *Hyla californiae* and *H. regilla* may create the appearance of temporal partitioning of the habitat between these asynchronously sympatric species. The interface between thermal physiology and ecology should be a fruitful area of further research on amphibians.

THERMAL ACCLIMATION

In most chemical reactions and physical processes, a measurement at a given temperature always yields the same value. Physiological measurements of amphibians at a given temperature may not give the same results each time, because such measurements are often dependent on the animal's thermal history (i.e., body temperature[s] during the time period preceding the measurements) as well. This phenomenon is thought to result from biochemical and physiological responses to continued exposure to temperature and may collectively be termed "acclimation to temperature." (Note that the temperature to which an animal is exposed before experimentation is often termed, confusingly, the "acclimation temperature.")

The term *acclimation*, however, is used in several different ways, which leads to considerable confusion. Here we compare three standard definitions of acclimation, each in widespread use, and we offer a fourth. We do so to minimize confusion and because the extant definitions can accommodate virtually any phenomenon related to thermal history as "acclimation," which consequently suffers as a useful biological concept. Our guiding principle is to consider how animals actually respond to exposure to different temperatures and how different scientists characterize these responses. We conclude this section by examining whether cold-acclimated animals can perform at low temperatures as well as warm-acclimated animals at higher temperatures.

In one sense of the word, animals exposed to low temperatures for a sufficiently long period (days to weeks) are called "cold-acclimated" animals and those exposed to warm temperatures for a sufficient period are considered "warm-acclimated." In this sense (definition 1) "acclimation" is equated with "exposure" or "thermal history," without reference to any particular changes that occur in the animal.

A more restrictive definition of acclimation (definition 2) requires that animals undergo some change in function after either cold or warm exposure. (A common practice that distinguishes between thermal history [definition 1] and its result [definition 2] is to term the temperature at which a measurement is made the "experimental temperature" [ET], the temperature to which an animal is exposed before measurement the "acclimation temperature" [AT], and any biological change related to differences in AT as "thermal acclimation.") Definition 2 requires qualification via a complex terminology (Prosser 1973a). Confusion can result when one physiological function undergoes an alteration with AT (e.g., jumping distance in frogs), whereas another related function does not (e.g., mechanical power output of isolated frog muscle). Has the animal acclimated or not? According to definition 2 the animal has undergone acclimation, even though clearly not all functions have done so.

Acclimation (in the sense of definition 2) may be of two types. In "resistance acclimation" (Precht et al. 1973), prolonged exposure to an AT induces changes in the thermal limits between which an animal can perform particular functions such as survival (lethal limits), maintenance of coordination (CTMin and CTMax), or the conduction of action potentials (cold block, heat block). In that a function either works or fails at a particular temperature, determination of resistance is often qualitative rather than quantitative. Some analyses, however, use time until death at a particular temperature as a metric of tolerance acclimation. In some animals, tolerances change upon exposure to a new AT (e.g., exposure to a cold AT may enable an animal to withstand a cooler temperature before a function fails, or exposure to a warm AT beforehand may extend the time of survival at a high temperature). The second type of acclimation, "capacity acclimation," involves quantitative change in a physiological function at temperatures within the zone of tolerance upon prolonged exposure to a new AT. For example, exposure to a cool AT might eventually increase or decrease the kinetics of enzyme function or muscle contraction at a cool but nonlethal temperature.

A more restrictive definition of acclimation (definition 3), which the International Union of Physiological Sciences recently promulgated, is that of Commission for Thermal Physiology (1987, 568) "a physiological change, occurring within the lifetime of an organism, which reduces the strain caused by experimentally induced stressful changes in particular climatic factors." In the application of this definition to capacity acclimation, not only must a physiological function change upon exposure to a new AT, but the change must tend to restore the physiological function towards its original level (i.e., the level before exposure to the AT). In the case of temperature, acclimation (according to definition 3) is the reduction of the acute thermal dependence of a particular physiological function. Definition 3 requires that acclimation always be compensatory, but not that compensation be complete.

Definition 4, as discussed below, will require that capacity acclimation be compensatory, that the compensation be complete, *and* that the physiological function under study occur at a higher rate or level after acclimation. For example, to be considered acclimation under definition 4, prolonged exposure to a cold AT, which should initially depress a physiological function (e.g., maximum sustainable speed, transit time of food in the gut), should eventually restore the physiological function to its original high (i.e., preacclimation) level or capacity. Physiological adjustments after exposure to a warm AT, however, will seldom satisfy this definition. Initial exposure to a warm AT will typically increase physiological functions. If a physiological function subsequently returns to its original (preacclimation) level, this would be tantamount to a depression in the function and would accordingly not qualify as acclimation. If the physiological function subsequently does not return to its original level, acclimation will also not have occurred according to definition 4.

Although definition 4 is the most restrictive of these definitions, we contend that it is the most objectively applied and biologically relevant of the definitions. By not taking the magnitude and direction of change into account, definition 2 may fail to exclude "acclimatory" changes that are accidental, inconsequential, or maladaptive. Definition 3 improves upon definition 2 by requiring a reduction in "strain" induced by changing temperature. In practice, however, any "acclimatory" change can in some sense be hypothesized as a reduction in strain, and falsifying the contention that a particular "acclimatory" change reduces strain can be very difficult if not impossible (Feder 1987b). Definition 4 is clear and unequivocal and readily indicates whether acclimation has occurred in any given instance. Moreover, the outcome of acclimation according to definition 4, thermal independence of biological function, is the most complete form of thermal compensation that is possible. Admittedly, complete compensation resulting in high capacity might not be adaptive in every circumstance (e.g., see chapter 10), and definition 4 is likely to apply only to acclimation to cold temperatures. We contend, however, that its advantages outweigh these drawbacks.

An Additional Definition of Thermal Acclimation to the Cold (Definition 4)

Many studies purport thermal acclimation to the cold, suggesting that acclimation is a common mechanism with which animals compensate for changes in the thermal environment. But are animals able to compensate completely, that is, show homeokinesis? Does a cold animal always perform worse than a warm one? Ectothermic animals are usually at a physiological disadvantage when acutely exposed to low temperatures (unless they simply become dormant). Definition 4 requires that thermal acclimation be complete. It must enable animals to perform at low temperatures as they do at high temperatures.

Criterion 1: Compensation Must Be Complete Although we recognize that partial compensation may be beneficial to an animal, for our present purposes we require that compensation be complete (i.e., increase performance to achieve homeokinesis). For instance, if the rate of some reaction is 2

at 20°C and on acute exposure to 10°C the reaction rate is 1, an improvement to 1.2 after 1-month exposure to 10°C does not enable the cold animal to perform as well as the warm one. Thus, although thermal acclimation occurs by definitions 1 to 3, acclimation does not occur by definition 4.

Criterion 2: Compensation Must Benefit the Animal Moreover compensation must occur at the level of the whole animal and be of some obvious benefit. A change in the reaction rate of a single enzyme in a metabolic pathway does not satisfy this definition unless the overall flux through the pathway is compensated as well. The control of metabolism is complex, and one cannot conclude that performance improves without demonstrating it physiologically at the level of the whole animal. Second, compensation of the metabolic rate must be advantageous to the animal. As discussed in a later section, the role of basal metabolism is not known, and the advantages of "positive compensation" and "negative compensation" are still under debate.

Finally, the underlying mechanisms of thermal acclimation must be identifiable (e.g., increased mechanical power per fiber plus increased number of fibers enable cold-acclimated carp to swim faster than warm-acclimated ones at low temperatures; Rome, Loughna, and Goldspink 1985).

Application of a Restrictive Definition to Thermal Acclimation of Locomotory Performance

As demonstrated above, at low temperatures the low mechanical power output of the aerobic fibers and total musculature limit maximal sustainable performance and maximal performance, respectively. To exceed these respective limits, animals must increase the mechanical power output of their aerobic fibers or total musculature, presumably either by (1) modifying the myosin of muscle so that each fiber can shorten faster and generate greater mechanical power or (2) adding more muscle (hypertrophy). Carp can do both. Following cold acclimation, the mechanical power output per gram of aerobic muscle at low temperatures increases (Johnston, Sidell, and Driedzic 1985), as does the proportion of aerobic muscle fibers (Sidell 1980). These changes increase the mechanical power output of the aerobic muscle fibers at low temperatures. Therefore at low temperatures, cold-acclimated carp can swim faster with their aerobic muscle than can warm-acclimated carp (Rome, Loughna, and Goldspink 1985). Because rapid fatigue accompanies the recruitment of the white muscles, this acclimation reduces the Q_{10} for sustainable swim speed, but it is not complete (table 8.1). If it were, then the cold-acclimated fish at 10°C should be able to swim as fast as the warm-acclimated fish at 20°C before recruitment of the white muscle. Thus, although this response satisfies definitions 1–3 of acclimation, it does not satisfy definition 4.

Amphibians are unable to acclimate in this manner. For instance, the muscle performance and locomotory performance of the salamander *Ambystoma tigrinum nebulosum* (Ambystomatidae) were unchanged by long-term exposure to cold temperatures (Else and Bennett 1987). The mechanical properties of frog (*Rana pipiens*) muscle also do not change following cold acclimation (Rome 1983; Renaud and Stevens 1984). Frogs therefore cannot exceed the limitations set by the low power output of their muscles, and cold-acclimated frogs

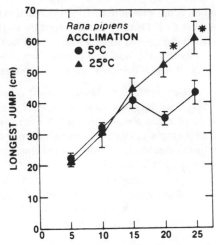

Fig. 8.15 Jump distance as a function of acclimation and test temperature. Asterisk = statistical difference between the acclimation groups. (Reprinted, by permission, from Renaud and Stevens 1983).

could jump no further at 5° to 15°C than warm-acclimated frogs (fig. 8.15; Renaud and Stevens 1983).

It is clear from this analysis that cold animals do not locomote as well as warm ones (see "Adaptation of Locomotor Performance" below).

THERMAL ACCLIMATION OF OTHER PHYSIOLOGICAL FUNCTIONS

Amphibians occur throughout the tropics and temperate regions of the world as far north as the tree line (their range extends into Alaska and northern Canada). The diversity of amphibian species is greatest in the tropics and becomes progressively more depauperate with increasing latitude (Duellman 1970). Daily and seasonal temperature changes in amphibian habitats are less in the tropics than in the temperate regions, and in general, amphibians from the tropics show less capacity for temperature acclimation than temperate ones (Feder 1978b). Most studies are on temperate species because that is the locale of most workers.

Molecular Acclimation: The Mechanistic Approach

Although our main goal is to identify acclimation that occurs and is of obvious benefit at the level of the whole animal (criterion 2), the mechanism for most forms of acclimation would be at the molecular level. Thus, evidence of thermal acclimation (or lack thereof) at the molecular level may indicate acclimation at the level of the whole animal. In the classic book *Biochemical Adaptation* (Hochachka and Somero 1984), only 6 out of the 427 references concern amphibians, and none of the 6 concern adaptations to temperature. This area is much better studied in fish and reptiles than in amphibians. Hochachka and Somero stress four major areas of study of the adaptive responses to temperature: (1) making new enzymes that are catalytically more efficient at low temperatures, to overcome the fundamental problem that the reactants have less kinetic energy at low temperatures, and vice versa at high temperatures; (2) increasing the concentration of enzymes to compensate for the decrease in kinetic energy of the reactants, and vice versa at high tem-

peratures; (3) changing concentrations of enzyme modulators so that the enzyme's affinity for its substrate is the same at all temperatures (essential in order to regulate metabolic pathways); and (4) altering the constituents of cell membranes so that they maintain their fluidity, often called homeoviscous adaptation. Below we will discuss each of these areas as they relate to amphibians.

1. Evidence for synthesis of different isozymes with greater catalytic efficiency in the cold (or lesser catalytic efficiency at high temperatures) has been sought in several studies of acclimation in amphibians (Enig, Ramsay, and Eby 1976; Tsugawa 1976, 1980; De Costa, Alonso-Bedate, and Fraile 1979, 1981; Feder 1983c) but has never been confirmed.

Most studies focus on lactic dehydrogenase (LDH), and all show that cold acclimation in frogs or salamanders results in a relative increase in cathodic or M type and a decrease in anodic or H form of the isozymes (Tsugawa 1976, 1980; De Costa, Alonso-Bedate, and Fraile 1979, 1981; Pasanen 1979). Tsugawa (1976) showed that this change appeared in cultured cell lines acclimated to different temperatures and concluded that the response was controlled at the level of the cell rather than being mediated by the central nervous system or hormones. Pasanen (1979) showed that all isoenzyme forms were present in animals in the wild in all seasons. Feder (1983c) also studied malate dehydrogenase (MDH) and isocitrate dehydrogenase (IDH) and found no evidence of new isoforms at different temperatures.

2. If new enzymes are not manufactured, then a second solution to the problem of less kinetic energy of the reactants at lower temperature is to make more of the enzymes that are present (and vice versa at high temperatures). De Costa, Alonso-Bedate, and Fraile (1979) reported such a response in larval *Discoglossus* (Discoglossidae), but the same authors observed the opposite response in adults of the same species (1981). The increase in catalase (a protective enzyme that removes hydrogen peroxide and deleterious oxidation of lipids, especially membrane phospholipids) is sufficient to result in complete thermal compensation (Gil and Barja-de-quiroga 1988). This is especially important because of the increase in double bonds in membrane phospholipids of cold-acclimated animals (Baranska and Wlodawer 1969; Lagerspetz 1977; Lagerspetz and Skytta 1979; De Costa, Alonso-Bedate, and Fraile 1979, 1981; Feder and Gibbs 1982). Studies showing no change in specific activity upon cold acclimation include those by Tsugawa (1980); De Costa, Alonso-Bedate, and Fraile (1981); and Feder (1983c).

3. A crucial feature of enzyme function is the capacity to maintain its apparent Michaelis constant (i.e., its K_m) within the range appropriate for the proper catalytic rate and at the same time maintain sufficient regulatory sensitivity. To regulate metabolism, regulatory enzymes must operate at substrate concentrations somewhat near their K_m, so that the reaction rates can be increased or decreased in response to regulatory signals (Hochachka and Somero 1984). The adaptive response that is predicted from these considerations is that the K_m of metabolic enzymes should not change markedly when temperature changes; that is, the Q_{10} of K_m should be very low. This prediction is satisfied; the Q_{10} (15° to 25°C) of LDH from the newt *Taricha granulosa* is 1.3 and that for MDH is 1.4 (Feder 1983c). One would also predict that

changes with acclimation would be small unless there are large changes in substrate concentrations. A change in K_m with acclimation suggests either that new enzymes are being made (the evidence in the literature does not support this result; see paragraph 1 above) or that the ratio of different isozymes that catalyze the same reaction is altered (supported by results in Enig, Ramsey, and Eby 1976; Tsugawa 1980; Feder 1983c; Feder and Gibbs 1982).

4. Homeoviscous acclimation has not been well characterized in amphibians. In the newt *Taricha granulosa*, cold acclimation was associated with an increase in unsaturation of double bonds from 71.9% (warm-acclimated at 20°C) to 76.0% (cold-acclimated at 5°C; Feder 1983c). Except for sphingomyelin (which was 20% greater in cold-acclimated animals) the major classes of liver phospholipids did not differ in their proportion between warm- and cold-acclimated animals. Cold acclimation of *Rana esculenta* (7°C) resulted in an increase in unsaturated fatty acids from 57.3 to 68.0% and a corresponding decrease in saturated fatty acids (Baranska and Wlodawer 1969). The increase in unsaturated fatty acids was due to a very large increase in polyenoic fatty acids (surprisingly, monoeoic acids slightly decreased). Neither the form nor the amount of Na^+-K^+-ATPase in frog skin changes (Lagerspetz and Skytta 1979; Lagerspetz and Laine 1984). However, the higher fluidity observed in membranes from cold-acclimated animals results in perfect thermal acclimation of net sodium transport across frog skin. Thus the changes in membrane phospholipids are adaptive during cold acclimation because they maintain membrane fluidity.

Acclimation at the level of the whole animal often requires acclimation at the molecular level. From the above evidence for the lack of acclimation at the molecular level, one would not predict compensatory thermal acclimation of metabolism in amphibians. Rather, the evidence at the molecular level suggests that amphibians do not compensate when placed in the cold. One would predict that in general they have lower metabolic fluxes and may show inverse compensation. Studies on thermal acclimation of metabolic rate rarely integrate results with those at the molecular level. A notable exception is the study on the newt discussed in the next section.

Acclimation of Metabolic Rate

Feder has measured the effect of acclimation temperature on routine metabolic rate in a large number of species of amphibians. Feder (1982c) summarized the results of experiments on twenty-nine species and concluded that, of seven tropical species studied (to 1982), six species showed no compensation; the other showed inverse compensation. He also concluded that all temperate zone species that have been studied show significant acclimation of metabolism. Additional studies that support his position include Burggren and Wood 1981, Feder 1983c, and Feder and Gibbs 1982. Some species show partial compensation of metabolic rate during cold acclimation: *Plethodon cinereus* (Caudata: Plethodontidae; 66%; Feder 1985b), *Xenopus* (15–22%; Tsugawa 1982). Others show inverse or no compensation during cold acclimation. For example, Feder (1986, 271) reported that in *Desmognathus* (Plethodontidae) "cold acclimated animals had a significantly greater oxygen consumption rate ($\dot{V}O_2$) than

warm acclimated animals" and that "$\dot{V}O_2$ decreased 16–28% during warm acclimation"; that is, this species shows partial compensation during both cold acclimation and warm acclimation. For the same species Feder (1985b, 241) also states, "They underwent no significant variation in $\dot{V}O_2$ during 28 days of acclimation to 5°C." Clearly the metabolic response to temperature is not simple. Acclimation of organismal metabolism requires 2 to 11 days (Dunlap 1969; Harri 1973b; Feder and Gibbs 1982; Feder 1985b). At this rate the effect is clearly too slow to compensate for changes that occur during the day. However, it is fast enough to compensate for changes that occur with weather systems that usually last 3 to 5 days.

Feder, Gibbs, Griffith, and Tsuji (1984) in a paper entitled "Thermal acclimation of metabolism in salamanders: Fact or artifact?" described many of the difficulties in demonstrating in a definitive sense that thermal acclimation actually occurs. Researchers measuring acclimation effects often neglect many "seemingly" extraneous factors that need to be controlled. These include the amount of activity, feeding, reproductive state, photoperiod, and recovery from acute exposure to a new temperature.

Fry (1947) introduced the importance of relating metabolic rate to the magnitude of activity at the time of the measurement, and most studies of thermal acclimation in fish take activity into account. In contrast, very few studies on metabolic rate in amphibians have controlled for activity, largely because it is difficult to control. Thus, almost all measures of thermal acclimation of metabolic rate in amphibians are measures of "routine" metabolic rate (i.e., during routine activity that is not controlled by the experimenter). Most investigators confined their studies to resting or inactive animals. In some instances, however, the so-called acclimation effects could be due to changes in activity rather than to acclimation of metabolic rate per se.

In one of the few studies in which activity was controlled, Feder (1986) studied metabolic rate in walking salamanders. Their maximum sustainable speed was spectacularly low (fig. 8.16). When tested at an intermediate temperature, cold-acclimated salamanders showed partial thermal acclimation in that their metabolic rate was greater than that of warm-acclimated animals during rest and at all speeds. Thus, the cost of transport was higher in the cold-acclimated animals (17.2 ml $O_2 \cdot g^{-1} \cdot km^{-1}$) than in warm-acclimated animals (14.5 ml $O_2 \cdot g^{-1} \cdot km^{-1}$). Even though the cold-acclimated animals had a higher maximum metabolic rate, their stamina was the same as that of the warm-acclimated ones. When tested at the warm temperature, the results were the opposite. That is, the metabolic rates during activity were the same, but the cold-acclimated animals had less stamina. Similar lack of correlation between changes in metabolism and those in performance have been reported (Feder 1978a; Carey 1979b; Miller and Zoghby 1983). Feder concluded his 1986 paper with the comment, "Thus, at least in salamanders, the 'adaptive significance' of thermal acclimation of metabolic rate remains to be demonstrated" (282). A similar study on a tropical salamander showed no changes in the cost of locomotion with acclimation temperature (Feder 1987b).

The importance of feeding in creating artificial evidence for thermal acclimation has also been studied (Feder, Gibbs, Griffith, and Tsuji 1984). If animals are fed before acclima-

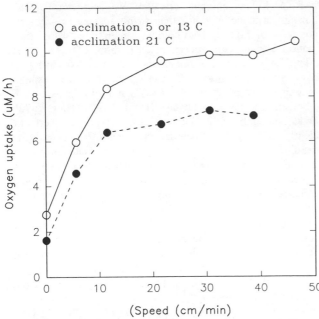

Fig. 8.16 The effect of acclimation temperature on the metabolic rate of salamanders (*Desmognathus*) walking at various speeds (Feder 1988). *Solid line* for cold-acclimated animals (5° or 13°C), *dashed line* for warm-acclimated animals (21°C). Experimental temperature was 13°C.

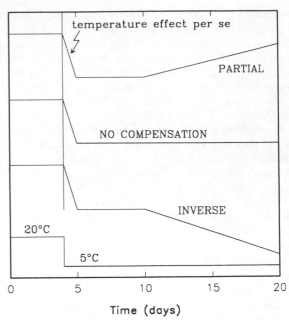

Fig. 8.17 Possible metabolic responses following exposure to a rapid step decrease in ambient temperature. The initial response is the acute effect of temperature, that is, the effect of temperature per se. The later response is the acclimation response.

tion, then digestion will cease in the animals placed in the cold (because of the effect of temperature on the rate of enzymatic digestion of food, as illustrated in fig. 8.4), whereas it will be stimulated in those placed in warmth. When both animals are placed in warmer temperatures in order to measure metabolic rate, digestion will resume in the cold-adapted group, whereas it will have been completed in the warm-acclimated group. Compensation of metabolic rate may be reported when in fact the metabolic rate of the cold-adapted group is higher not because of an acclimation effect, but rather because of specific dynamic action (SDA). No compensation would be observed when metabolic rate is measured in the cold because the contribution of digestion to total metabolism is minimal in both groups. This type of acclimation pattern (compensation when measured at warm temperatures, but no difference when measured at cold temperatures) is commonly reported in thermal acclimation of routine metabolic rate studies of amphibians. The SDA effect is substantial; metabolic rate increased 77% after feeding in salamanders and had not returned to the prefeeding level even 11 days after feeding ceased.

The third major difficulty in interpreting thermal acclimation of metabolic rate in amphibians is that all possible patterns of acclimation occur and each different pattern is claimed to be adaptive. Some of these patterns are illustrated in figure 8.17 (pattern types after Precht et al. 1973): partial compensation (type 3), no compensation (type 4), and inverse compensation (type 5). When ambient temperature suddenly decreases, then metabolic rate decreases due to the acute effect of temperature. In the top example, acclimation is evident because metabolic rate gradually increases and returns close to the previous level at the warmer temperature. It is argued that the animal changes its metabolic machinery to compensate for the cold and thus should be able to perform

as well in the cold as the warm-acclimated animal can perform at warmer temperatures. This type of acclimation satisfies criterion 1 (appreciable compensation) of definition 4. In the bottom example, others argue that acclimation is evident because metabolic rate gradually decreases even lower than that due to the effect of temperature per se. In this case it is argued that this strategy is adaptive because it conserves energy supplies at a time when food is likely to be scarce. Because the role of maintenance metabolism is not clearly understood, it cannot be rigorously argued that a change in either direction is adaptive and thus beneficial to the animal.

A plausible explanation of the direction of the response is that the animal adapts by decreasing its metabolism (inverse) if it interprets the environmental cues as indicating a long-term (e.g., seasonal) decrease in temperature. The animal thereby conserves supplies for the winter and prepares for dormancy. On the other hand, if an animal interprets the environmental cues as indicating a relatively short-term decrease in temperature, then it adjusts metabolism so as to be able to maintain the capacity to become active rapidly when warm temperatures return (partial compensation). In both cases the costs of maintenance metabolism (using energy stores) must be weighed against potential benefits. Presumably, the main benefit is the speed with which energy stores can be replenished when warm temperatures return. This hypothesis has not been rigorously tested.

Acclimation of Capacity to Capture and Eat Prey

Very few studies of complex behaviors examine the effects of acclimation on animals in the wild. The capacity of toads to capture and eat mealworms or crickets is markedly depressed when the animals are held at low (5°C) or high (30° to 35°C) temperatures, but they can capture and consume prey best

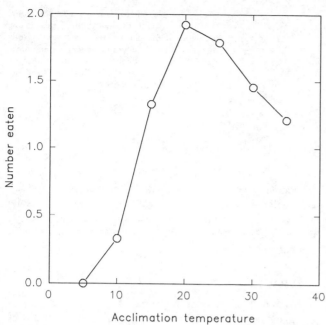

Fig. 8.18 The effect of acclimation temperature on feeding performance of toads ($N = 19$ at each temperature; Stevens 1988a). Animals were tested at their acclimation temperature. Feeding performance is the ability to capture and eat prey (mealworms) in a 2-min trial.

when held at an intermediate temperature (i.e., 20°C; fig. 8.18; Stevens 1988a, 1988c). The response is of appreciable magnitude but is not in the right direction to be compensatory. Animals might be expected to pace food intake so as not to exceed the capacity of the system to process it at the lower temperatures. However, the adaptive advantage of decreasing intake at the higher temperatures is not obvious. In addition, the underlying mechanisms are not clear. At low temperatures the rate-limiting step is digestion, and, as far as is known, no ectotherms make isozymes of digestive enzymes. As temperature decreases, the rate of digestion decreases and food is processed more slowly. The mechanism operating at the higher temperatures is not obvious, however, because the activity of all digestive enzymes continues to increase, as does gastric motility.

Acclimation of Critical Thermal Maximum

CTMax is defined as "the thermal point at which locomotory activity becomes disorganized and the animal loses its ability to escape from conditions that will promptly lead to its death" (Cowles and Bogert 1944, 277). As such, CTMax is an ecological end point, although prolonged exposure to CTMax would itself culminate in death. Criteria for the assessment of CTMax include onset of spasmodic swimming movements (Zweifel 1957), loss of righting response (Brooks and Sassman 1965), onset of spasms (Hutchison 1961), and the appearance of rigor (Pough and Wilson 1970). Death itself is an undesirable end point, at least partly because of the difficulties in judging the exact point of demise. The mechanism of death is unknown but is likely to be set by the thermal "resistance of the most sensitive essential tissue" (Brett 1956). Orr (1955) reported that the order of heat death in adult *Rana pipiens* is (1) the whole animal as an integrated organism,

(2) the muscular system, (3) heart muscle, (4) the nervous system. Carlsten et al. (1983) reported the appearance of heart lesions prior to the attainment of CTMax in *R. pipiens*, and Paulson and Hutchison (1987b) concluded that the initiation of muscle spasms at the CTMax of anurans occurs in the central nervous system.

CTMax can be altered by diverse factors, including dehydration (decreases CTMax: Claussen 1977; Pough and Wilson 1970), nutritional status (starvation decreases CTMax: Cupp 1980; Floyd 1985), photoperiod (Brattstrom 1968; Floyd 1985; Hutchison 1961; Mahoney and Hutchison 1969), hormones (melatonin decreases CTMax: Erskine and Hutchison 1982), fatigue (decreases CTMax: Burke and Pough 1976), natural daily temperature fluctuation (Pough 1974a), and season (e.g., higher CTMax in winter than in summer *Notophthalmus viridescens* (Caudata: Salamandridae): Hutchison 1961; lower CTMax in winter than in summer *Bufo viridis*: Pashkova 1985). The underlying mechanism(s) of changes in CTMax are unknown. Feder and Pough (1975a) demonstrated an increase in CTMax of *Notophthalmus viridescens* following exposure to ionizing radiation and suggested that ionizing radiation produces free radicals, which in turn stimulate radical-resistance mechanisms which are the basis of acclimation. This hypothesis merits further investigation.

An amphibian's CTMax can be changed by acclimation to heat or to cold (figs. 8.19 and 8.20), and the direction of acclimation is always compensatory. The rate of acclimation is faster for heat than for cold (Hutchison and Maness 1979), and animals collected in the spring can acclimate to CTMax more quickly than those collected in the fall (Layne and Claussen 1982). The magnitude of change in CTMax is typically much less than the change in acclimation temperature. For the data shown in figure 8.19, CTMax changes modestly

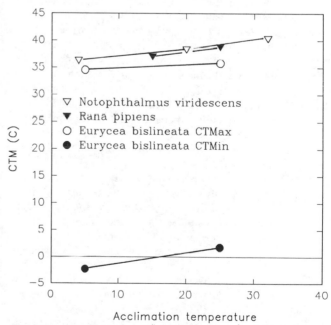

Fig. 8.19 The effect of acclimation temperature on critical thermal maxima for three amphibians. Critical thermal minima for *Eurycea bislineata* are also shown. (Data for *Notophthalmus viridescens* and *Rana pipiens* from Hutchison and Maness 1979, for *E. bislineata* from Layne and Claussen 1982.)

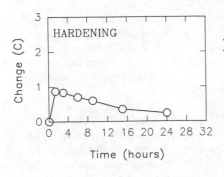 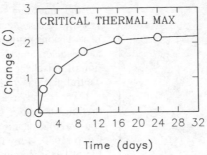

Fig. 8.20 The rate of change of heat hardening (*left*) and critical thermal maximum (*right*) in the lungless salamander *Eurycea bislineata*. Note that abscissa is in hours for hardening and days for CTMax. (Hardening data from Rutledge, Spotila, and Easton 1987; CTMax data from Rutledge, Easton, and Spotila 1987.)

(0.7° to 1.8°C) for a change of 10°C in acclimation temperature. Claussen introduced the acclimation response ratio (ARR = change in CTMax / change in acclimation temperature) to characterize the responses of amphibians, and values of ARR are typically about 0.2 (0.07 to 0.44; Claussen 1977). The utility of ARR is limited, however, as this value falsely assumes a linear relationship between change in CTMax and change in acclimation temperature. For example, the ARR for heat rigor in *Ambystoma jeffersonianum* (Caudata: Ambystomatidae) is 0.12 from 15° to 25°C and 0.06 from 5° to 25°C (Claussen 1977).

Although compensatory acclimation of CTMax is real, reproducible, and widespread among amphibians, the changes are small in magnitude, and the ecological significance of this response and the benefit to the animal are unproven.

Heat Hardening

Exposing amphibians to a temperature within 2°C of their CTMax induces the production of heat shock proteins (HSPs). These proteins are not synthesized except at very high ambient temperatures (i.e., the genes are activated only if ambient temperature is within 2°C of CTMax), and their presence is correlated with a small (less than 1.0°C) but significant increase in CTMax. This slight protection due to a preexposure of high temperatures is termed heat hardening. It has been argued that heat hardening is ecologically important during diurnal temperature fluctuations. Rutledge, Easton, and Near (n.d.) have shown that the salamander they use for the HSP and CTMax studies, *Eurycea bislineata* (Caudata: Plethodontidae), does occasionally experience very high temperatures in the field. They found many individuals in microhabitats (under sun-exposed rocks in the afternoon) with body temperatures up to 30°C.

Heat hardening does not occur in all species tested. For example, it is present in all *E. bislineata* but in only about 20% of the individuals of *Desmognathus ochrophaeus* (Plethodontidae). The kinetics of heat hardening is the same if the salamanders are exposed to 2°C less than CTMax or to CTMax briefly. Interestingly, the change in CTMax when exposed to 2°C less than CTMax is accompanied by the synthesis of HSP. However, the change in CTMax when exposed to CTMax is *not* accompanied by induction of HSP (Easton, Rutledge, and Spotila 1987).

The heat hardening response differs from acclimation of CTMax in that heat hardening is transitory: the response (i.e., the increase in CTMax) appears within 1 h of the heat exposure and gradually dissipates over a period of 24 h (Rutledge, Spotila, and Easton 1987). In contrast, the increase in CTMax with acclimation takes about 3 weeks to develop and results in twice as much protection as heat hardening (i.e., CTMax increases about 2°C with acclimation and less than 1°C with heat hardening).

THERMAL ADAPTATION

Our examination above of the thermal acclimation of various physiological systems did not provide any case that satisfies the strict criteria that definition 4 requires. Thus, we are forced to conclude that if an individual animal is acclimated to low body temperature, its physiological functions will be slower than they were at high temperatures. It is possible that different species can adapt evolutionarily to low temperatures. Unlike thermal acclimation, which occurs in an animal's lifetime, thermal adaptation involving genetic changes can occur in evolutionary time. Evolutionary thermal adaptation as the result of natural selection for physiological change might be evident in tolerance limits, physiological rates or capacities at normally experienced body temperatures, and/or acclimatory ability. Adaptive differences might be found in comparisons of high- versus low-latitude species, high- versus low-altitude species, and/or warm- versus cold-season species.

Adaptation of Tolerance Limits

Numerous authors have reported apparently adaptive differences in CTMax among species (e.g., Brattstrom 1968, 1970b; Claussen 1973), among species and among populations across geographical clines (e.g., Cupp 1980; Howard, Wallace, and Stauffer 1983; Manis and Claussen 1986; Miller and Packard 1977), over seasons (e.g., Layne and Claussen 1982; Pashkova 1985), and with daily temperature fluctuations (Pough 1974a). Snyder and Weathers (1975) compared ranges of temperature tolerance for amphibians (data from Brattstrom 1968) with predicted variation in body temperature, which was approximated from published records of variability in environmental temperatures. Collection localities ranged from 9° to 52°N latitude at altitudes less than 1,000 feet above sea level. Mean monthly temperatures decrease with increasing latitude, and the monthly minimum decreases more than the monthly maximum. Thus, variability in environmental temperature increases with latitude. Similarly, critical thermal limits generally decrease with increasing latitude, but CTMin decreases about twice as fast as CTMax. Thus, temperature-tolerance ranges of amphibians increase with increasing latitude. The slope of the relation between variation in environmental temperature and ranges of thermal tolerance is 0.93 ($r = .76$; $p < .01$). Cold tolerance is likely to have a significant impact on species distributional ranges (Brattstrom 1968).

Adaptive differences in tolerance ranges are also associated with altitudinal differences in environmental thermal variability (Brattstrom 1968). In the mountainous regions of the United States and Mexico, tolerance limits of montane species behave much like those of lower-elevation species at equivalent thermal latitudes. Biogeographically young species, however, may not show this response. For example, the montane species in the Costa Rican highlands has narrow tolerance limits much like its ancestral lowland tropical species. Adaptive differences in tolerance limits are also found along altitudinal clines among populations of a single species (Beattie 1987; Miller and Packard 1977).

Despite the striking correlation between environmental thermal variability and tolerance ranges reported by Snyder and Weathers (1975), there is little evidence that amphibians ever experience temperatures that approach CTMax. As pointed out by Feder (1982b, 23), "The evident capabilities for behavioral thermoregulation and the paucity of field body-temperature records that are at or near lethal temperatures suggest that amphibians generally do not experience extreme temperatures." It would appear that CTMax is correlated with thermal responses that have a more direct bearing on the ecology of amphibians and is not itself directly important. A possible exception to this conclusion occurs in some desert amphibians that breed in ephemeral ponds. Apparently adaptive differences in developmental high-temperature tolerance have been reported for a number of amphibians of the deserts of southwestern United States (Brown 1969; Zweifel 1968b, 1977). Brown (1967) reported a rapid developmental increase in high-temperature tolerance of late-embryonic *Scaphiopus hammondii* (Anura: Pelobatidae) from about 35°C up to 39° or 40°C, and he reported environmental temperatures as high as 39°C in ponds where this species was developing. He suggested that the rapid attainment of this high developmental tolerance limit may be biologically important in enabling developing *S. hammondii* to survive high temperatures that may be encountered during their first 24 h of development. Zweifel (1977) reached the same conclusion regarding *S. couchii*.

Adaptation of Locomotor Performance

Adaptive differences in the thermal dependence of locomotor performance have been explicitly examined in two studies of hylid frogs. In the first study, northern species of Holarctic treefrogs jumped farther at low temperatures than did southern species (fig. 8.21; John-Alder, Morin, and Lawler 1988). Moreover, the species that breed early jumped farther at low temperatures than the species that breed late. The lowest temperatures at which these hylids attained 80% of their longest jump distances are strongly correlated with their lowest reported field body temperatures, and thermal adaptation has compensated for much of the differences in the lowest temperatures at which species are active. It should be noted that this analysis is based on normalized jump distance rather than absolute distances. An analysis of absolute distances is nec-

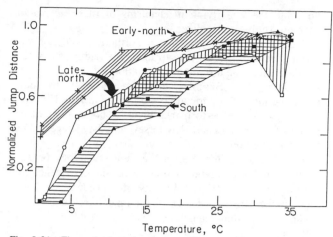

Fig. 8.21 Thermal adaptation in jump distance of treefrogs. Species means are plotted; the areas are defined by means within each group. *Diagonal striping,* early-breeding northern; *vertical striping,* later-breeding northern; *horizontal striping,* later-breeding southern. +, *Hyla crucifer;* ×, *Pseudacris triseriata* (Hylidae); ○, *H. andersonii;* □, *H. versicolor;* ●, *Acris gryllus;* ■, *H. cinerea;* ▲, *H. squirella.* (Reprinted, by permission, from John-Alder, Morin, and Lawler 1988, © University of Chicago.)

essary to prove whether, at ecologically relevant temperatures, cold-tolerant species can jump as well as warm-tolerant species. These adaptive differences in thermal physiology of locomotion may help to explain patterns of breeding phenology and geographical distribution.

Because hylids are believed to have originated in the New World tropics (Duellman 1970), physiological adaptation for low-temperature performance seems the derived condition. In hylids, at least, plasticity in the thermal sensitivity of locomotion is more evident at low than at high temperatures. As minimum field body temperature deceases, low-temperature performance improves more than high-temperature performance deteriorates. As a result, thermal performance breadths for jumping are broader in cold-adapted species than in warm-adapted congenerics, much as ranges of thermal tolerance are greater for cold-adapted, high-latitude species than for low-latitude species (Snyder and Weathers 1975). The pattern of thermal adaptation seen in hylids is fundamentally different from that of lizards. Plasticity in the thermal sensitivity of running occurs at high rather than low temperatures in lizards, and performance breadths are broadened by increases in CTMax (R. B. Huey pers. comm.). In contrast to the situation in hylids, the evolution of low preferred temperatures in lizards has resulted in reduced performance and restricted performance breadths (Huey and Bennett 1987).

Two independent lines of evidence indicate that the differences in thermal performance of hylids reflect genetic differences rather than thermal acclimation. First, thermal performance breadths and optimal temperatures do not acclimate in *Hyla regilla* (R. B. Huey pers. comm.). Second, a revised phylogeny of Holarctic hylids (Hedges 1986), which is based on electrophoretic data, groups species that are all early-breeding and cold-tolerant into an expanded genus, *Pseudacris,* and leaves the remaining summer breeders in the genus *Hyla.* The apparently adaptive shifts in thermal performance suggest corresponding changes at the level of muscle function, but the underlying mechanisms of these adaptations have not yet been elucidated.

These findings suggest that a northern population of a given species might be able to locomote better at low temperatures than can a southern population. In *Hyla crucifer* at least, John-Alder, Barnhart, and Bennett (1989) have shown this to be false. They found no differences in muscle properties or swimming performance between populations of this species from Florida and New Jersey, and they suggested that thermal inflexibility of *H. crucifer* may be at least partially responsible for differences in breeding phenology between northern and southern populations. More direct evidence concerning the thermal requirements of reproductive biology leads to the same conclusion, that temperature imposes constraints on breeding phenology (Bachmann 1969; Rühmekorf 1958a).

Adaptation of Reproduction, Growth, and Development

Adaptive features of the breeding biology of amphibians have been investigated more thoroughly than any other ecological aspect of amphibian thermal physiology. Some species change their breeding behavior as the temperatures of breeding ponds become warmer (Caldwell 1986; Seale 1982). In addition, thermal absorptivity and thermal inertia of egg masses are thought to ameliorate potentially harmful environmental temperatures (Hassinger 1970; Herreid and Kinney 1967; Ryan 1978). Although the magnitude of temperature differences between egg masses and surrounding water is modest (about 1°C), thermal tolerance ranges are most restrictive during embryonic development (e.g., Zweifel 1977), and the small temperature difference may be a significant benefit.

In a classic series of studies, Moore (1939, 1940, 1949, 1952) demonstrated that developmental temperature tolerances and developmental rates of Northern American ranids are well correlated with geographical range. In one study (Moore 1939), four species exhibited normal development over similarly broad ranges of about 22°C, but the species with the northernmost distribution limits (*Rana sylvatica*) had the lowest tolerance limits and the species with the southernmost distribution limits (*R. clamitans*) had the highest tolerance limits. Moreover, development rates were partially compensated for differences in temperatures such that development at a standardized intermediate temperature was faster in *R. sylvatica* than in *R. pipiens, R. palustris,* and *R. clamitans.* Most of the evidence of thermal adaptation in thermal requirements for development were restricted to the species level, and Moore (1949) inadvertently overstated purported interpopulational adaptive differences in the thermal requirements of *R. pipiens* by including several sibling species within *R. pipiens* (Pace 1974). More recently, Beattie (1987) reported adaptive differences of 1°C in developmental thermal tolerances of populations of *R. temporaria* that experienced a difference of 1.1°C in mean pond temperature as a result of differences in altitude. Moreover, the upland population developed 4% more quickly than the lowland population at low temperature (6°C), whereas the lowland population developed about 1% more quickly than the upland population at 16°C.

Not all ranids fit the general correlation between thermal requirements and geographical distribution. *R. septentrionalis* has a more northern distribution than would be expected on the basis of its developmental temperature requirements, and Moore (1952) attributed this paradox to competitive exclusion from a more southerly distribution by *R. catesbeiana.*

More recently, thermal requirements of North American desert anurans were investigated (Brown 1967, 1969; Zweifel 1968b, 1977). Embryonic thermal tolerances and rates of developmental increases in upper tolerance limits are highest in *Scaphiopus,* which breed in ephemeral desert ponds.

Bachmann (1969) reviewed the literature on developmental temperature requirements of amphibians. He defined the "adaptive temperature" of a species as the temperature 10°C higher than the x-intercept of the developmental rate–temperature curve for that species. The adaptive temperature is an empirical value and appears to be useful for comparative purposes. Adaptive temperatures approximate the middle of the range between developmental tolerance limits and are typically in the range of 10° to 15°C for cold-adapted species and 20° to 25°C for warm-adapted ones. Bachmann also defined a developmental constant to compare the times required for development to a standard stage at the adaptive temperature of a species. He found virtually no evidence that developmental rate is compensated for temperature at the levels of species, race, and population. McLaren and Cooley (1972) suggested that Bachmann (1969) falsely assumed developmental rate to be a linear function of temperature and thus reached a false conclusion about temperature compensation. In contrast to Bachmann and others (e.g., Herreid and Kinney 1967), McLaren and Cooley (1972) reported a close relationship between spawning temperature and their measure of developmental rate for several species of ranids. Despite evidence of some compensation for temperature (Kuramoto 1975; Moore 1939, 1949; Ruibal 1955; Volpe 1953, 1957), the magnitude of the compensation is small, and development still occurs most slowly in cold-tolerant species at ecologically relevant temperatures. The major adaptive differences in the thermal requirements of embryonic amphibians are seen in tolerance limits rather than compensation in developmental rates.

Adaptation of Metabolic Rate

Resting metabolic rates have been compared between Neotropical and temperate zone lungless salamanders of the same body size (Feder 1976b). At a constant acclimation temperature of 12°C, metabolic rate is lower in Neotropical than in temperate salamanders. The reduction in metabolic rate is thought to compensate for the higher body temperatures of Neotropical salamanders. As the purpose of having a particular resting metabolic rate is unknown, it is not clear that this apparent compensation is beneficial to the animals.

Adaptation of Acclimatory Ability

Acclimatory ability has been investigated primarily with regard to thermal tolerance limits and resting metabolic rate, and fundamentally different adaptive patterns have been described. Animals from highly variable thermal environments are surprisingly not better able to undergo acclimatory adjustments in tolerance limits than animals from more stable environments (Brattstrom 1968, 1970b). With regard to metabolic rate, however, temperate zone salamanders show much greater ability to acclimate than tropical species (Feder 1978b). As the tropical species are thought to have evolved from more temperate ancestors (Wake and Lynch 1976), the loss of acclimatory ability appears to be the derived condition. Tropical species' inability to acclimate appears to be one factor associated with their restricted altitudinal distributions (Feder 1978b; Huey 1978).

These claims of acclimation do not satisfy definition 4 and tend to be small in magnitude and of unproven benefit to the animal.

SUMMARY

It is clear that temperature has a large influence on many physiological functions and can be a keystone environmental variable for amphibians. Despite evidence of partially compensatory responses to chronic temperature change, amphibians have limited capacity for thermal acclimation. Our most restrictive criteria for assessing acclimation require that compensatory changes be both significant in magnitude and of obvious adaptive advantage. Neither of these criteria is generally met. Although an individual may have the ability to seek different microhabitats, the physiological performance of amphibians is undoubtedly constrained by environmental temperature.

Thermal adaptation occurs slowly in different populations of a given species in warm and cold habitats, and such adaptation is most often restricted to tolerance limits rather than physiological rates or capacities. Substantial thermal adaptation is not evident below the species level. Thermal adaptation of tolerance limits is commonly evident in interspecific analyses and is likely to play an important role in setting temporal and distributional limits on amphibians. Substantial adaptations have been demonstrated for locomotor performance; however, the definitive experiments have not yet been performed.

Thus, in general, the physiological rates of cold amphibians are slower than those of warm ones, regardless of how long the individuals, populations, or species have been at cool temperatures. More research in the field of temperature effects on physiological function may reveal examples that counter the general statement above. Our opinion is that both an *integrative* approach and an understanding of thermoecology are essential and represent the best way to interpret the information. Functions such as locomotion, neural function, feeding and digestion, reproduction, growth and development, circulation, respiration, and metabolism may yield the greatest insights.

9 Thermoregulation

Victor H. Hutchison and R. Keith Dupré

Temperature is the most pervasive factor in the holocoenotic environment of most organisms. Temperature affects the kinetic energy of reactants and thus almost all biochemical and physiological processes, including those underlying behavior. Temperature mediates the effects of most other environmental factors and is reciprocally influenced by these environmental factors. These basic attributes of temperature, along with the relative ease of measurement, have contributed to the development of a voluminous literature on thermal biology (see also chapter 8). Ectothermic vertebrates have been well studied, but amphibians have received far less attention than fishes or reptiles. This lack of attention may stem in part from the complexities of thermoregulation of animals with moist skin and significant cutaneous gas exchange (see chapters 4–6) and animals that are not strictly aquatic (as are most fishes) or strictly terrestrial (as are most reptiles). The conflicts of the requirements for respiration and hydroregulation with those for thermoregulation may have prevented amphibians from evolving the same degree of physiological and behavioral thermoregulatory control as seen in fishes and, particularly, reptiles.

The phylogenetic position of amphibians makes them an important group for study of the evolution of thermal control mechanisms. The limitations on physiological control of temperature in amphibians suggest that behavioral regulation of body temperature might be dominant. Enough information now exists to refute the general perception that amphibians have little ability to control body temperature. By comparison with other vertebrates, amphibians *are* poor thermoregulators (Brattstrom 1963), but they *do* thermoregulate, often by "interplaying water economy and thermoregulation to allow them to be more active longer" (Brattstrom 1979, 346).

Amphibians have the potential for thermal control through a variety of mechanisms. These include (1) changes at the organism-environment interface (e.g., reflectance of the skin, evaporation from body surfaces, vasomotor changes in peripheral circulation, thickness and other characteristics of boundary layers); (2) internal adjustments of the cardiovascular system (e.g., circulatory shunts, cardiac output); (3) changes in heat production (e.g., thyroid-induced changes in metabolism, muscular activity); (4) alteration of central and peripheral neural elements; (5) tolerance of high or low temperatures; and (6) behavioral adjustments (e.g., selection of temperatures in available microhabitats, basking, postural and orientation responses, social interactions, diel and seasonal cycles of activity). Some of these mechanisms have not been described or very well studied in amphibians; others have only limited capacities to influence amphibian thermal relations.

The mechanisms for thermal control listed in the preceding paragraph are often influenced by thermal acclimation, the short-term (i.e., hours, days, or weeks) metabolic and physiological alterations in response to a chronic shift in environmental temperature. As defined by many biologists (chapter 8), acclimation allows an animal to function more effectively at the new temperature. Thermal acclimation occurs at many levels of organization and can influence an animal's complete biochemical and physiological function. Consideration of the role of acclimation is essential in understanding the thermal relationships of amphibians.

Amphibians share with fishes and reptiles two basic physiological traits that distinguish them from the largely endothermic birds and mammals: ectothermy and a reliance upon the anaerobic generation of energy to support the occasional requirement for high levels of activity (Pough 1980, 1983; see also chapter 12). These two characteristics allow for a low energy flow and high efficiency of biomass production. The relatively narrow range of body temperature during activity of ectothermic vertebrates, accomplished primarily with behavioral and secondarily with physiological mechanisms, simplifies the integration of internal processes (Pough 1980). A knowledge of thermoregulatory mechanisms is essential for an understanding of the physiological, behavioral, and ecological interrelationships in this evolutionarily transitional group.

For convenience in organization we have divided the material in this chapter into laboratory and field studies where possible. Our division of material should not imply that field and laboratory studies are exclusive in any way. Indeed, both approaches are necessary for a full understanding of the thermal biology of organisms. As with most biological phenomena, progress in understanding thermoregulation will be made by multiple approaches. Laboratory experimentation occupies a pivotal position between natural history and theory. Controlled laboratory studies will yield details of the mechanisms as well as the limits of thermoregulatory processes. Knowledge of these mechanisms may make observations in an often bewildering natural environment more intelligible. As in most other fields of biology (Diamond 1986; Wilbur 1989), there is a need for pluralism in thermoregulatory biology.

The growth of information on thermoregulation has been rapid. The inability to keep pace with new information probably accounts, at least in part, for a "phylogenetic provincialism," where workers on one systematic group of animals are not familiar with similar studies on other groups. This particularly has been the case with ectothermic vertebrates. The literature on fishes seldom contains appropriate citations to similar work on amphibians and reptiles, and vice versa. To place current knowledge of amphibian thermoregulation in proper perspective, we have cited many works on other systematic groups, especially fishes and reptiles.

The following abbreviations are used throughout the chapter: AT, acclimation temperature; PT, preferred (= selected) temperature; T_b, body temperature.

Terminology

Few fields are so beset with semantic confusion as that of animal temperature regulation. This confusion has resulted in a literature dealing primarily with the terminology of thermoregulation (Bligh and Johnson 1973; Commission for Thermal Physiology 1987; Cowles 1940, 1962; Cowles and Bogert 1944; Fraenkel and Gunn 1940; Folk 1974, chap. 1; Fry 1947, 1958; Gunn and Cosway 1938; Hutchison 1980; Pough 1974; Pough and Gans 1982; Precht et al. 1973). Despite this attention to semantics, consistent usage of many terms in the field is elusive. We have generally followed Pough's and Gans's (1982) vocabulary, with exceptions discussed in the following paragraphs.

The confusion in the etymology of the vocabulary of thermoregulation stems from several sources. Much of the disorder may reflect the complexity and diversity observed in animal thermoregulation (Cossins and Bowler 1987). Early studies of thermoregulatory and metabolic functions in mammals and the large number of investigations of endotherms established a vocabulary subsequently applied to ectotherms, often erroneously. Additional conflict in usage of terms originates in the increasing phylogenetic provincialism of some current investigators (as mentioned above). Even between persons working with fishes and those studying amphibians and reptiles, somewhat distinct sets of definitions have evolved to describe similar thermobiological processes.

Acclimation is a "physiological change, occurring within the lifetime of an organism, which reduces the strain caused by experimentally induced stressful changes in particular climatic factors" (Commission for Thermal Physiology 1987, 568). This is definition 3 of chapter 8. In practice the term acclimation is often used to describe a functional compensation over a period of hours, days, or weeks in response to an

experimentally induced change in an environmental factor (e.g., temperature, photoperiod, water saturation deficit, etc.). Although acclimation and acclimatization are etymologically indistinguishable, there have been attempts to assign different meanings, especially for use with ectotherms (Hutchison 1976). Acclimatization has been used to describe the response to (1) two or more environmental factors (as opposed to acclimation, for a response to a single factor); (2) long-term physiological adjustments involving evolutionary changes; (3) changes in environmental factors in a natural environment; and (4) both specific and general habituation. The history of the usage of these two terms was reviewed by Folk (1974, chap. 1). The Commission for Thermal Physiology (1987, 568) defined acclimatization as "a physiological change occurring within the lifetime of an organism which reduces the strain caused by stressful changes in the natural climate (e.g., seasonal or geographical)." The commission noted that "acclimatization may also be specified as a particular phenotypic variation; therefore the usefulness of the term may be questioned." The panel of contributors to the commission's report consisted mostly of mammalian physiologists; the history of terminology for ectothermic animals may thus have been inadequately represented.

The terms poikilothermy, wide variations in T_b that result from changing environmental conditions, and homeothermy, fairly constant T_b ($\pm 2°C$ or less; Bligh and Johnson 1973), have limited use in current studies. In most cases another dichotomy, introduced by Cowles (1962), replaces poikilothermy and homeothermy, respectively: ectothermy, thermoregulation in which the main source of heat for T_b regulation is the environment, and endothermy, thermoregulation based primarily on internal metabolic heat production. These useful terms emphasize the energetics of thermoregulation. Cowles (1962) also separated ectotherms into heliotherms, those animals that gain heat mostly from basking in sunlight, and thigmotherms, those that derive heat from the conductive medium in which they live. Although these terms are useful, care should be used in their application, because an animal may use both modes of heat gain to varying degrees.

Further confusion results from the blurring of the boundaries between endotherms and ectotherms. The facultative lowering of internal heat production by endotherms during hibernation, periods of food restriction, and daily periods of inactivity is heterothermy. The facultative increase in T_b by ectotherms through an increased metabolic rate (often accompanied by a decreased heat loss) lacks a term to describe it other than facultative endothermy. The extension of heterothermy to ectotherms is not desirable (Pough and Gans 1982) because it would add to the confusion. Perhaps the terms facultative ectothermy (for heterotherms) and facultative endothermy would be more descriptive and less ambiguous.

The terms bradymetabolic, describing the "low" metabolic rates of ectotherms, and tachymetabolic, denoting the "high" metabolic rates of endotherms (Bligh and Johnson 1973), are unfortunate; the blurring of the distinction in these two terms parallels that of endotherm and ectotherm. The metabolic rates of some active reptiles, such as varanid lizards (Bartholomew 1982), overlap the resting rates of mammals. The role of insulation in the attainment of a T_b at any given metabolic rate is not included in the definition of tachy-

and bradymetabolic. All endotherms do not have high resting rates of metabolic heat production (Dawson and Grant 1980; Poczopko 1980). "Consequently, distinction between brady-metabolism and tachymetabolism does not appear to be applicable to either ectotherms or endotherms" (Pough and Gans 1982, 21).

Although not precisely defined (Precht, Laudien, and Havsteen 1973, 334), the terms *stenothermal,* for organisms that tolerate narrow ranges of environmental temperatures, and *eurythermal,* for those that tolerate wide ranges, are now well established in the literature on diverse groups of ectotherms. Thus, the use of these terms to describe animals that normally undergo limited (stenothermy) or large (eurythermy) variations in T_b (Pough and Gans 1982) should probably be avoided. The roots *eury-* and *steno-* are widely used (e.g., stenohydric, euryhaline, etc.) to denote tolerance to environmental factors, not precision of regulation.

Due to the diverse and changing biological and physical processes governing heat exchange, the *body temperature* (T_b) of an animal is not usually defined by a single measurement. The surface temperature of a frog exposed in air where water is evaporating from the skin may be quite different from the deep T_b. Thus, T_b values should always be accompanied by the process, site, duration, and time of measurement and "must be considered within the context of the methods by which they have been obtained" (Avery 1982, 97). Due to the ease of measurement, the reported "body" temperatures of amphibians are often cloacal readings and may be different from surface or deeper T_b.

The *activity temperature range,* defined as the "normal activity range" by Cowles and Bogert (1944), has been used to describe the T_b of free-ranging animals during "routine" activities (Pough and Gans 1982), but often without clear descriptions of the activities included as "routine." A *mean activity temperature* is often calculated for use in comparisons among species, since a single value is easier to use than a range.

Voluntary minimum is the lowest T_b voluntarily tolerated by a thermoregulatory animal in a laboratory apparatus such as a shuttlebox or in the field. The *voluntary maximum* denotes the highest T_b voluntarily tolerated. In practice these terms are often used for the lowest and highest temperatures, respectively, recorded from an active animal (Brattstrom 1970a). The terms *voluntary minimum* and *maximum* have their equivalents, *lower exit* and *upper exit temperatures,* for experiments in shuttleboxes or similar devices. *Upper* and *lower escape temperatures* are similar terms sometimes applied to animals under either field or laboratory conditions.

Sophisticated theoretical models have been developed to describe thermoregulatory function in endotherms (Bligh 1973). These models usually include the hypothalamus as the major integrator and the concept of a set-point, that temperature or range of temperatures at which an animal attempts to regulate T_b. This "thermostat" model has been applied to ectotherms, with the set-point as the PT (Crawford 1982; Crawshaw 1980; Heller, Crawshaw, and Hammel 1978). Four categories of thermoregulation based on set-point theory were described for endotherms (Snell and Atkins 1968) and have been applied to ectotherms: *normothermia,* set-point and attained T_b are equal; *hypothermia,* T_b is below set-point;

hyperthermia, T_b is higher than set-point; *fever,* set-point is raised and the attained T_b may or may not be raised to the same level. During fever an animal is regulating T_b, but at a higher level than during normothermia. Of these four terms, all but normothermia have the connotation of some degree of pathology in the literature on mammals. The application of these terms to ectotherms has not been consistent with the application of these definitions to endotherms. For example, *voluntary hypothermia* has been used to describe the selection of lower temperatures at night by diurnally active ectotherms (Firth and Turner 1982; Regal 1967), but this diel temperature cycle may be due to a circadian rhythm where the normally lower PTs at night are simply due to a change in the behavioral "set-point." It certainly is not a pathology.

Thermoregulation (*temperature regulation*) implies that T_b is maintained ("defended") within a given, usually narrow, range when ambient temperatures vary well beyond the regulated T_b. Animals employ both physiological and behavioral mechanisms to maintain T_b near the set-point. Typical endotherms use physiological changes predominantly (but not exclusively), while typical ectotherms use mostly behavioral methods. *Temperature conformity* implies little or no thermoregulation; T_b parallels changes in environmental temperature. Note, however, that a conformer in a constant thermal environment may undergo little change in T_b. Many species are regulators during some periods and conformers during others. For example, diurnally active ectotherms may be effective behavioral thermoregulators during the day, but typical conformers during inactive periods at night. Thus, these two terms are opposite ends of a continuum, and the precise conditions should be specified when the terms are used (Pough and Gans 1982).

Behavioral thermoregulation by an animal in a laboratory gradient, shuttlebox, or other laboratory apparatus is usually described by calculation of the resultant mean values of T_b produced by behavioral mechanisms (movement within a gradient, "escape" temperatures in a shuttlebox, postural changes, orientation in relation to a heat source, etc.). The calculated T_b produced by these behavioral changes has been called preferred (*Vorzugstemperatur, Wahltemperatur*), selected, indifferent zone, voluntary, eccritic and optimum temperature.

The terms used to define behavioral "choice" of temperature constitute a "minefield of definitions and concepts" (Fischer, Standora, and Spotila 1987, 1629). *Preferred temperature* and *selected temperature* are the most commonly used terms in the measurement of behavioral thermoregulation. There has been much debate about which of these should be used. Gunn and Cosway (1938) were among the first to question the use of *preferred,* on the grounds that the term was too anthropomorphic; others have recommended that the term not be used (Pough and Gans 1982). The perception that *preferred* is more anthropomorphic than *selected* does not match the definitions and etymology of the two words. Both *prefer* and *select* have "to choose" as a basic element of their definitions in English dictionaries. If standardization is desirable, then *preferred temperature* (= thermopreferendum) would be the best to use for the following reasons: it (1) is more often used in the biological literature; (2) has derived terms such as *preferendum* and *final thermal preferendum* in common use; (3) is often used and defined in current textbooks on comparative physiology (e.g., Schmidt-Nielsen 1983; Hainsworth 1981), the major reference volumes on thermobiology (e.g., Precht et al. 1973), and a classic work on animal behavior (Fraenkel and Gunn 1940); (4) has probable priority and earlier establishment in the literature (Herter 1926); (5) has parallel usages in terms in ecology and behavior (food preference, habitat preference, mate preference, etc.); and (6) has been approved in a glossary of terms by the Commission for Thermal Physiology of the International Union of Physiological Sciences (1987). *Preferred temperature* has also been used solely for reference to temperatures observed in laboratory gradients, and *eccritic temperature* for field measurements (Hutchison and Hill 1976; Licht et al. 1966; Lillywhite 1971a), but this restriction in usage has not gained universal acceptance.

Fry (1947, 24) defined the *final thermal preferendum* in two ways: as that temperature (1) "around which all individuals will ultimately congregate, regardless of their thermal experience before being placed in the gradient," and (2) "at which the preferred temperature is equal to the acclimation temperature." Although the term was first applied to fishes and has become entrenched in the literature on fish thermal biology, it has also been applied to other animal groups, including amphibians (e.g., Dupré and Petranka 1985; Stauffer, Gates, and Goodfellow 1983). The validity of the concept of a final thermal preferendum has been questioned (Hutchison and Spriestersbach 1986a). Despite attempts to clarify the final preferendum paradigm with standardized methods (Reynolds and Casterlin 1979) and suggestions for revision of the concept (Jobling 1981), we believe that the term itself and the concept it represents are no longer biologically sound. Animals in gradients do not usually gravitate to a single temperature. The original definition was changed to "zone of final preferendum" to accommodate the range of temperatures actually selected (see Jobling 1981 for definitions). The PT of animals varies with factors such as time of day, season, photoperiod, age, nutritional status, health (fever), aggregation and other behaviors, and so forth. In many ectotherms the range of temperatures "voluntarily" attained is quite broad, even under rigidly controlled conditions of acclimation and testing. Diel cycles of temperature selection, many (most?) of which result from endogenous circadian rhythms, are often quite pronounced in amplitude. A "zone" of temperatures large enough to accommodate the range of such diel cycles, much less the range of circannual (seasonal) cycles, would be so broad as to be meaningless. For example, the thermal preference of some Lake Erie fishes may be as much as 15° to 20°C higher in summer than in winter (Reutter and Herdendorf 1976). A distinction has been made between an *acute thermal preferendum*, measured within 2 h or less after placing an animal in a gradient, and the *final preferendum*, measured 24 to 96 h after placement in the gradient (Reynolds and Casterlin 1979). The value for an "acute" preferendum will vary widely in many animals, depending upon which 2-h period of a diel cycle is selected. An "acute" preferendum is thus nothing more than a PT attained during a 2-h period. The second definition of the final thermal preferendum, the temperature where PT is equal to AT (crossover point), is rarely constant; the crossover point obviously will change with time as PT or AT changes (Reynolds 1978). Al-

though the concept of the final thermal preferendum is thoroughly embedded in the literature, it has probably outlived its usefulness and should be abandoned.

STATISTICAL CONSIDERATIONS

Because thermoregulation is a multifaceted process, no one analytical method can encompass all ramifications (Huey 1982). What measure(s), for example, should be used to define the PT? The accumulation within a distinct zone of data points for T_b from freely moving animals in a thermal gradient or in the field is often used to describe the PT. But should the PT be defined as the mean, mode, total range, interquartile range, range of the central 68% $\pm$ SD, $\pm$95% confidence limits, and so forth, of this zone, all of which have been used? Proper use of parametric statistics usually requires that the data be normally distributed. The distribution of data from behavioral thermoregulators in both field and laboratory studies is often skewed (DeWitt and Friedman 1979). Thermal gradients or other laboratory apparatus with insufficient temperature ranges or narrow ranges of temperatures available to animals in the field during the times of measurement can produce truncated distributions at the high or low end of the thermal range. Selection by animals of relatively narrow zones of temperature with high "precision" will produce leptokurtic distribution curves; selection of relatively wide zones of temperature with low "precision" may result in platykurtic distributions. Calculations of coefficients of skewness and kurtosis may be essential in selection of appropriate statistical tests and interpretation of results.

An additional problem in statistical analyses of thermal preferences has been the incorrect assessment of the degrees of freedom in analysis of variance (ANOVA), covariance, and regression (Mathur and Silver 1980). In most such analyses sample size (N) should be the number of individuals, not the total number of observations on all individuals. If T_b is measured at smaller and smaller time intervals as independent data points, N can be increased greatly. If such an inflated N is used, very small differences in temperature may be made improperly significant. Simply by sampling at more frequent intervals, one can often obtain "significant" differences. Measurements of temperatures of a thermoregulating animal over time are not independent of preceding values. Some individuals among a sample may tend to thermoregulate at relatively high, and others at relatively low, temperatures. For these reasons the assumptions of independence implicit in many statistical analyses may be violated. With the use of one measure for each individual (N), repeated-measures methods, and proper nesting of data, such statistical problems can be reduced (Mathur and Silver 1980).

Measurement of T_b over time will often result in an inequality of T_b variances. However, in most cases ANOVA is a sufficiently robust test to overcome the minor assumption of equal variances implicit in the method (Winer 1971).

Nonparametric procedures may be appropriate for answering certain questions and analyzing certain data sets. For most studies of behavioral thermoregulation, the data are interval-scaled measurements and are inappropriate for nonparametric procedures. Information will be lost when interval measures are transformed to rank-order.

Multivariate statistics (principal components analysis and canonical correlation analysis) have been used for evaluation of thermal behavior in ectotherms (James and Porter 1979) and can be useful for studying such processes. Like some univariate methods, however, multivariate techniques are not appropriate for all biological problems (Gibson 1984). Due to the curvilinear relationship between PT and AT in many animals, linear regressions may not be appropriate to represent this interdependence.

Changes in PT during the course of the day and year can confound results, especially when one does not consider the possibility of diel and seasonal cycles in the experimental design (Hutchison and Maness 1979). Until demonstrated otherwise, such cycles should be assumed. The times of day and season at which measurements were made should be reported. Temporal differences in thermal selection are usually analyzed with a Duncan multiple range test (Duncan 1955) or, usually better, a Tukey's studentized range test (SAS Institute 1982), with both preceded by an appropriate ANOVA.

The "precision" with which vertebrate ectotherms thermoregulate has been defined in widely different ways. Examples are ranges of 50, 68, and 95% of T_b (DeWitt 1967); standard deviation of mean T_b (Withers and Campbell 1985); amplitude and period of T_b cycles (Bowker 1984); hourly variation about mean T_b (Gleeson 1981); coefficient of variation of PT (Bradshaw, Gans, and Saint Girons 1980); variance of T_b (Sievert and Hutchison 1988). Thermoregulatory precision has also been defined as the maintenance of T_b of active field animals near the mean T_b obtained in a laboratory thermal gradient (Peterson 1987); such a definition implies that the "true value" of PT is that obtained in the laboratory gradient. This definition is of accuracy, not precision.

Huey (1982) suggested that variance is a statistically inappropriate measure of precision because (1) animals (lizards) regulate T_b between upper and lower set-points, not around some mean value; and (2) variance underestimates thermoregulatory precision when set-points vary. The latter problem is also true for other measures of precision such as standard deviation and coefficient of variation. Calculation of the slope of linear regression of T_b on ambient temperature integrates both the adjustments and results of thermoregulation. A slope of 0 suggests perfect regulation; a slope of 1 indicates total conformity of T_b with ambient temperature. Limitations to this method are several (Huey 1982), and the technique does not replace the need to measure true thermoregulatory precision. The definition of variance used should be relevant to the hypothesis being tested; where T_b itself is the focus (such as studies with thermal gradients), the use of variance as a measure of precision may be appropriate.

The variance of mean selected T_b has been proposed as a standard measure of precision in ectothermic behavioral thermoregulators because (1) precision is inversely proportional to variance; (2) variance is always a positive value; (3) variance of animal T_b will usually be greater than unity; (4) variance is calculated in most statistical tests and is readily available; (5) the reciprocal of the variance is a measure of information in the system; (6) variance is independent of sample size (standard error of the mean is not, for example); (7) standard deviation also does not vary with sample size, but variance has convenient and tractable properties not shared with its square root, the standard deviation; (8) F_{max} test tables allow for convenient statistical comparisons of precision between groups (Sievert and Hutchison 1988). A standardized measure of thermoregulatory precision would allow comparisons among future studies, at least where T_b is the statistic of primary interest.

Precision is best determined on individuals, rather than on groups. Individuals within a group may thermoregulate precisely, but at different individual T_b. Thus, if all temperatures from all individuals are pooled and variance calculated, precision would be less than if based on data from each individual. However, seldom are some individuals of a species precise thermoregulators and others not. Intraspecific semblance seems to be characteristic, at least in lizards (Bowker 1984; Bowker and Johnson 1980).

To assign values for thermoregulatory precision is inappropriate without consideration of the behavior, diel and seasonal cycles, social interactions, temperature, and other environmental factors. An inactive animal will have a relatively constant T_b and therefore appear more "precise" than an active animal whose T_b changes as it moves along a thermal gradient or within a heterothermal natural environment. For example, comparisons of precision during different parts of a diel cycle would lead to the false conclusion that individuals during inactive ("sleeping") periods of a diel cycle thermoregulate more precisely than active animals.

Comparison of the precision of different individuals over time is facilitated with group variances derived from pooling all T_b data of all members of the group and determining a mean variance. Because all individuals may not thermoregulate about the same temperature, the variance will be inflated. This method provides an indicator of similarity of T_b selected by all members of the group but is valid only for comparisons during the same portion of the diel activity cycle (Sievert and Hutchison 1988, 1989).

FIELD STUDIES
Methods

Studies of amphibian T_b in the field have used methods developed mainly for reptiles. Three types of temperature-measuring devices have dominated: (1) mercury thermometers, (2) electronic thermometers (thermocouples and thermistors), and (3) radiotelemetry (Brattstrom 1970a). Early investigators employed regular laboratory mercury thermometers, usually inserted into the cloaca or lower digestive tract. Conventional mercury thermometers were not suitable for small animals. Although Cowles and Bogert (1944) used thermocouples to measure T_b in their classic study of desert reptiles enclosed in outdoor cages, the equipment then available was too cumbersome for extensive field use. These problems led to the development of the Schultheis "quick-reading" reptile thermometer, which has been used over the past 40 years for much of the work on semiaquatic and terrestrial vertebrates (Avery 1982; Bogert 1949). This small (18 cm long) mercury thermometer with a reduced bulb (7–12 mm long, 2-mm diameter) was calibrated in 0.2°C divisions with a range of 0° to 50°C. First manufactured by E. W. Schultheis and Sons of Brooklyn, New York, it is now made by Miller and Weber of Queens, New York. This thermometer has been used (some would say often misused) in a pre-ponderance of field studies on reptiles and amphibians since its introduction. The Schultheis thermometer made possible the compilations of data bases for field temperature measure-ments of many amphibians and reptiles.

Recent reductions in the size of batteries and the electronic components of thermocouple and thermistor devices and re-corders have allowed greater use of electronic thermometry in the field. In addition, the response time, accuracy, read-ability, and miniaturization of sensing probes have improved the quality of measurements.

Problems encountered in field measurement of T_b of rep-tiles (reviewed by Avery 1982) apply equally to amphibians. These include methods of location, capture, and handling. For example, transfer of heat from the captor's hand or from a surface on which the animal is placed during measurement can greatly influence the temperature recorded, especially in small individuals. Movements of the animal to escape capture and during handling, along with attendant stress, can change T_b, as can evaporative water loss due to changes in wind speed, and so forth.

Radiotelemetry can avoid many of the problems encoun-tered with mercury and electronic thermometers, but may in-troduce other difficulties. The major problem, the mass of the transmitters, is rapidly lessening as miniaturization of bat-teries (the major contributor to transmitter mass) and elec-tronics develops. However, the units (or an accompanying thermistor probe) must be surgically implanted or the entire unit fed to the animal. The former method involves surgery, stress, and the chance of infection; the latter method may interfere with normal feeding and digestion and may also elevate PT through a postprandial effect. Transmitters may not remain in the gut for sufficient periods of time. Radio-telemeters, especially the newer, smaller units, have re-stricted transmission ranges. Electronic drift may occur dur-ing use; units should be calibrated immediately before and after each use.

Published information on T_b of amphibians in the field come from a wide variety of studies, from anecdotal listings to detailed analyses of thermoregulatory behavior over time. Although random measurements of ectotherms in the field often show a unimodal distribution of T_b (Brattstrom 1963, 1970a), they should be used with caution. The introduction of the Schultheis thermometer led to an accelerated growth in publications containing measurements of T_b in a variety of ectotherms. Such field temperature records without informa-tion on the microenvironmental conditions at the time of mea-surement and, particularly, without any knowledge of the immediate past thermal or behavioral history of the animal have drawn much criticism (Avery 1982). Such an approach has been called the "grab and jab" or "noose and goose" school of thermal biology. These humorous and mildly deri-sive names are not without some justification. "Uncontrolled field methods of collecting body temperatures" and the resul-tant "accumulation of much inconclusive data" were criti-cized by Heath's study (1964, 784) of what has become known as "beer-can thermoregulation." Heath distributed water-filled metal cans in the sun and shade, then recorded air and can temperatures for 8 h during the day. The plotted distribution of can temperatures were "indistinguishable

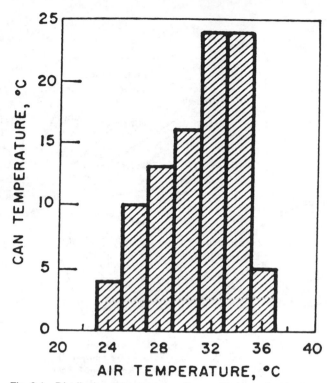

Fig. 9.1 Distribution of temperatures of water-filled beer cans in direct sunlight. Temperatures were recorded hourly with a hypodermic therm-istor probe between 1030 and 1930. The sharp break at 35°C is typical of records obtained from heliothermic lizards and has been interpreted to mean that animals at such a break actively seek shade at that temperature. The original histogram (Heath 1964) was corrected to the one shown here. (Reprinted, by permission, from Heath 1965, copyright 1965 by the AAAS.)

from that of a heliothermic reptile" (fig. 9.1). The main ques-tion posed by this study was, "Can we study a regulatory process with a method that involves no controls and no direct observation of regulation?" (Heath 1965, 1251).

Examples of behavior and microclimatic field conditions that influence T_b but are not often noted in reports are (1) time since retreat or emergence from a shelter, burrow, water, and so forth; (2) microclimate of the retreat; (3) length of time basking or in retreat; (4) whether the animal was wet or dry; (5) orientation of the animal to sun and wind; (6) posture; (7) wind speed; (8) capture and handling conditions; and (9) time of day and season, among others (fig. 9.2). A divergence of T_b from ambient temperatures alone does not establish that thermoregulation occurs. Behavioral and physiological ac-tivities other than thermoregulation may require different ranges of temperatures and may take precedence over thermal considerations alone.

Basking time or frequency of shuttling between sun and shade have been used as indicators of thermoregulation in ectotherms, often with the assumption that the longer the time spent in the sun (or under a heat lamp), the higher will be the T_b (Brattstrom 1963; Huey 1982). Such an assumption may lead to incorrect conclusions, especially in amphibians with access to moisture. Evaporation of water, especially under conditions of low humidity and wind, can lower T_b of am-phibians, even while they are receiving direct solar radiation

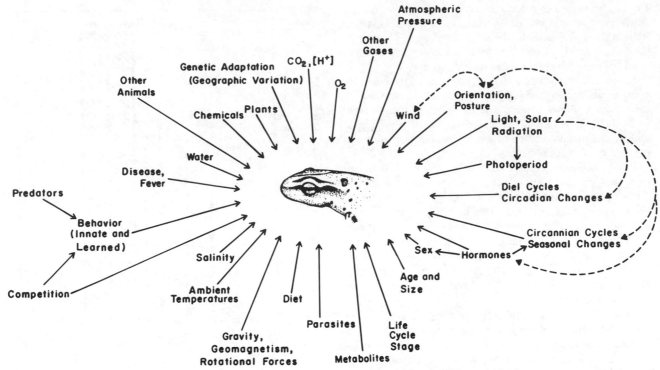

Fig. 9.2 Some factors that may influence the body temperature and thermal relations of amphibians. The quantity, quality, duration of exposure, and rate of change of the environmental factors can also influence thermal exhanges, as can the methods of measurement, acclimation, and interrelationships between controlling, directing, and lethal factors (Fry 1971). (Redrawn from Hutchison 1976.)

(Tracy 1976; see also chapters 4 and 6). Postural changes during basking may also influence T_b (Lillywhite 1970).

The range of microenvironmental conditions present in the field at any given time of day or season may not allow an animal full utilization of behavioral thermoregulation. Such conditions may lead to false conclusions about thermoregulatory abilities.

Physiological control of T_b, although secondary to behavioral control in amphibians, may depend upon temperatures other than cloacal or intestinal. Skin surface and abdominal temperatures, as well as temperatures within the central nervous system, may influence thermoregulatory behavior (discussed later in this chapter). "What is indeed the body temperature of a frog sitting on a cool grassy patch, its head exposed to the sun, and the peripheral temperature of which is influenced by the evaporation of water from the skin?" (Wieser 1973, 15).

The interpretation of T_b recorded in the field (or in the laboratory) must be within the context of the methods used to obtain them (Avery 1982). Although isolated records of T_b sometimes may be useful, especially for rare or hard-to-study species, an understanding of the thermal relations of a species will result only from full consideration of its behavior, ecology, and physiology over sufficient time periods.

Field Activity Temperatures

The T_b of an amphibian in its natural environment results from complex interactions of numerous environmental factors and internal physical changes and physiological adjustments (figs. 9.2, 9.3). Knowledge of T_b's experienced by amphibians in natural environments is valuable in ecological and biophysical modeling, energy budget compilations, experimental design, and so forth, and is essential for an understanding of environmental physiology of any species. Only when the "normal" pattern of temperature relations is identified can exceptional thermal regimes experienced by a species be described and the physiological mechanisms determined (Feder, Lynch, Shaffer, and Wake 1982). As with other animals, amphibians can escape the exigencies of climate by selection of appropriate microhabitats, employment of behavioral mechanisms, or physiological regulation.

Because T_b's of amphibians in the field have been summarized well by others, we have not included this detailed information here. Temperatures of free-living amphibians and their environments measured over many years on the University of Kansas Natural History Reservation were summarized by Fitch (1956). The first comprehensive summary of the thermal requirements of amphibians was the often cited and valuable compilation by Brattstrom (1963). This work was based on the author's approximately 6,500 temperature measurements of T_b's, air, soil, and water environments of ninety-nine species of North and Central American amphibians; previous observations of others were also included. Additional compilations of field T_b's include tropical and temperate zone salamanders (Feder, Lynch, Shaffer, and Wake 1982) and southern and central Australian anurans (Johnson 1971b).

We are beginning to understand something of the thermal ecology and physiology of salientians and salamanders, but almost nothing is known about the thermal relations of the third group of extant amphibians, the caecilians (Brattstrom 1963). This lack of information is perhaps due to their secretive behavior and largely burrowing habits, although some species are entirely aquatic. The high evaporative water loss

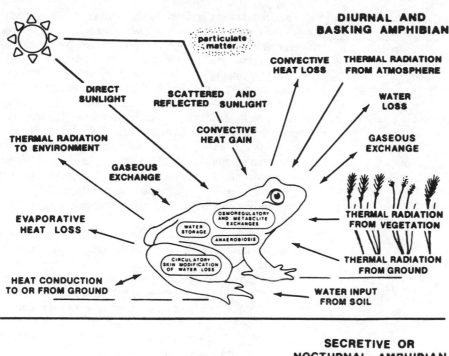

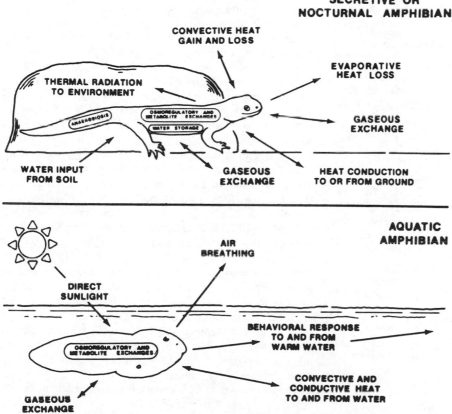

Fig. 9.3 Interactions of body and environments in a basking frog (*top*), a cryptic salamander or nocturnal anuran (*middle*), and an aquatic larval or adult amphibian (*bottom*). (Reprinted, by permission, from Brattstrom 1979.)

from the skin and high rates of cutaneous gas exchange (Steele and Louw 1988) may severely limit their thermoregulatory ability, but nothing is yet known about their capabilities for thermoregulatory behavior, in the laboratory or the field.

Overall mean field temperatures of generic or family groups reveal correlations only with general climatic distributions (table 9.1). Among North and Central American salamanders, temperate aquatic plethodontids have the lowest mean T_b (11.3°C) and cryptobranchids, amphiumids, and sirenids the highest mean field temperatures (20.1°C).

Among anuran genera the highest mean (26.5°C) is for *Gastrophryne* (Microhylidae; two species) from warm-climate terrestrial habitats; the lowest (10.0°C) is for *Ascaphus* (Leio-

TABLE 9.1 Temperatures of North and Central American Amphibians Recorded in the Field

Group	Number		Temperature (°C)	
	Species	Individuals	Range	Mean
Salamanders				
Cryptobranchids, amphiumids, sirenids	5	12	8.0–28.0	20.1
Salamandrids	4	109	4.5–28.4	16.0
Temperate ambystomatids	9	933	1.0–26.7	14.5
Tropical ambystomatids	12	56	10.5–30.0	19.0
Temperate aquatic plethodontids	9	261	2.0–22.0	11.3
Temperate terrestrial plethodontids	28	2065	−2.0–26.3	13.5
Tropical plethodontids	43	1660	1.8–30.0	14.2
Anurans				
Ascaphus	1	5	4.4–14.0	10.0
Scaphiopus	2	11	12.2–25.0	21.4
Leptodactylids	5	11	22.0–28.0	24.7
Bufo	17	474	2.2–33.7	24.0
Hylids	14	507	3.8–33.7	23.7
Gastrophryne	2	108	15.5–35.7	26.5
Rana	12	299	4.0–34.7	21.3

Sources: Based on data in Brattstrom 1963 and Feder, Lynch, Shaffer, and Wake 1982. Modified slightly from Duellman and Trueb 1986 with permission of McGraw-Hill Book Company.

pelmatidae; one species), a cool-climate aquatic resident. The lowest T_b ($-2.0°C$) for an active salamander is for *Hydromantes platycephalus* (Plethodontidae) walking on snow (Brattstrom 1963, 1970a); the highest (30°C), for the tropical *Bolitoglossa occidentalis* (Plethodontidae; Feder, Lynch, Shaffer, and Wake 1982). The highest T_b (35.7°C) for an anuran, *Gastrophryne olivacea*, was recorded by Fitch (1956) in Kansas; the lowest anuran T_b (2.2°C) listed is for *Bufo canorus* in the Sierra Nevada of California (Karlstrom 1962). The minimum activity temperature of *B. boreas halophilus* at 2,057 m at Big Bear Lake, California, was about 3°C; the lower lethal temperature was reported as −2.0°C (Mullally 1952). *Hyla regilla* (Hylidae) can swim slowly in water of nearly 0°C and have been seen swimming beneath ice in ponds; males were observed calling in water as low as 3.8°C (Cunningham and Mullally 1956). The highest measured field temperature for any amphibian is 41°C for *Phyllomedusa sauvagei* (Hylidae), an arboreal "waterproof" frog of the semiarid South American Chaco (McClanahan and Shoemaker 1987).

Altitude and Latitude

The air at higher altitudes is characterized by lower density than at lower altitudes, and by higher transmissions of solar radiation during the day and of longwave outgoing radiation at night. The air at higher altitudes is also often drier than at lower locations. Amphibians at higher altitudes may experience greater intensities of sunlight during the day and larger radiational losses of heat at night. Thus, high-altitude habitats often have wider fluctuations in substrate and air temperatures (Swan 1952).

The relationships between T_b and altitude at different latitudes are complex. Temperate zone salamanders have lower minimum T_b's than Neotropical salamanders. No latitudinal trends in maximum T_b are evident; tropical plethodontids do not have maximum T_b's higher than temperate zone species. Tropical ambystomatids and plethodontids have similar rates of decline in mean T_b with increasing elevation. At the same elevation plethodontids have significantly lower T_b's than ambystomatids (Feder and Lynch 1982). High-altitude populations of *Ambystoma tigrinum* (Ambystomatidae) choose the warmest temperatures (13° to 25°C) available in ponds (Heath 1975); this contrasts with populations of this species at lower elevations, where the salamanders move into shallow water during the day only when temperatures fall below about 15°C (Whitford and Massey 1970).

The trends seen in the influence of thermal acclimation on thermal tolerance in fifty-four species of anurans as a function of altitude and latitude do not entirely match the trends seen in T_b's of salamanders (Brattstrom 1968; Brattstrom and Lawrence 1962). These studies showed that (1) the entire thermal regime of acclimation in tropical anurans is broader than in temperate forms; (2) species with restricted ranges have relatively poor acclimatory abilities; (3) high-altitude species from the old mountains of North America are similar to temperate forms at equivalent thermal latitudes; (4) high-altitude forms from the more recent mountains of Central America are basically lowland tropical types whose physiological plasticities are limited. Other studies on the thermal tolerances of amphibians yield similar conclusions (Snyder and Weathers 1975). Comparative studies on both salamanders and anurans of behavioral thermoregulation would be helpful for a better understanding of altitudinal-latitudinal influences on thermal relations.

Bufo b. bufo from northern latitude (Norway) and high altitude (Switzerland) grow slower, mature at later age and greater body size, and attain larger maximum sizes than those from more southern latitudes and lower elevations (Germany and the Netherlands). However, when the length of seasonal activity is applied as a correction to the different populations, the toads from higher altitudes and latitudes actually grow faster, and differences in body sizes at maturity disappear. Populations from France (*B. b. spinosus*) grow faster, mature earlier, and reach larger maximal sizes than do the populations of *B. b. bufo* (Hemelaar 1988). Although temperature is probably a major determinant of growth rate and ultimate body size in altitudinal and latitudinal gradients (Berven 1982a, 1982b), genetic factors may be more important, and other factors (food quality and abundance, parasite loads, disease, etc.) are likely influences.

The daily range of T_b of montane *B. boreas boreas* is substantially greater than that of lowland *B. b. halophilus*. The montane toads are active over a wider range of T_b's than lowland toads and display greater diurnal activity, including sitting in direct sunlight (Carey 1978b). Increased diurnality, which allows attainment of a higher T_b than nocturnality, may be a behavioral feature of anurans at higher elevations. Extensive diurnal activity at high altitudes occurs in postmetamorphic *B. canorus* (Mullally and Cunningham 1956), *B. b. boreas* (Black and Black 1969; Lillywhite and Wassersug 1974), *B. spinulosus* (Pearson and Bradford 1976; Sinsch

1989), *Hyla labialis* (Valdivieso and Tamsitt 1974), and *Rana muscosa* (Bradford 1984b).

Daily activity periods may be governed by thermal conditions at different altitudes. *B. spinulosus* at 3,200 m in Mantaro Valley, central Peru, in March were active throughout 24 h (Sinsch 1989); at 4,300 m in Challapalca, south Peru, these toads were active from 0800 to 2200 (Pearson and Bradford 1976). Toads at the lower elevation apparently used heliothermic behavior during the daytime and thigmothermic regulation in the evening as the main sources of heat (Sinsch 1989). Substrate temperatures at higher elevations are apparently too low for thigmothermy to provide adequate heat for activity in the evening.

Species with extensive latitudinal ranges often have broad thermal regimes with wide tolerance ranges, but selection of appropriate microhabitats can ameliorate the diverse climatic conditions. The broad geographic distribution of *B. boreas* has been attributed to microhabitat selection, particularly to the thermal buffering provided by burrows (Smits 1984). Microhabitat use, especially the occupation of burrow retreats, can be of greater significance near the limits of a geographic range, where environmental variables approach the animal's limit of tolerance (Bider and Morrison 1981; Tester, Parker, and Siniff 1965). The period of reproduction and development is the most critical where environmental extremes are most likely to be limiting; extremes of environmental factors are more likely to occur near the geographical limits of distribution. Yet developmental stages under such regimes have received little study, with a few notable exceptions, especially Moore's (1949b) work on the *Rana pipiens* "complex" and a few other studies (e.g., Herreid and Kinney 1966, 1967).

Tolerance of broad thermal regimes may be one important aspect of the preadaptation in amphibians for range extension, island colonization, and introduction by humans, particularly into disturbed habitats. In Puerto Rico two introduced anurans, *Eleutherodactylus planirostris* (Leptodactylidae) and *E. johnstonei,* display higher thermal tolerances and behavioral selection of higher temperatures than do the native congenerics *E. cundalli* and *E. gossei.* Along with a significantly higher tolerance of water loss, the thermal relations of the introduced species allow them to occupy habitats disturbed by humans where the native species are excluded (Pough, Stewart, and Thomas 1977). The extensive natural distribution and successful introductions of the now pantropical *Bufo marinus* is probably due in no small part to the ability to function well at high temperatures (Johnson 1972; Zug and Zug 1979); the lack of adaptability to colder temperatures has clearly prevented expansion of this species into climates where the isopleth of mean minimum annual temperature is about 15°C or less (Krakauer 1970; Stuart 1951).

Although salamanders have distinct PTs when tested in laboratory gradients (table 9.2), observations of behavioral thermoregulation in the field, particularly of terrestrial forms, are uncommon (Feder and Lynch 1982). The PTs of Neotropical plethodontids determined in the laboratory were influenced by AT and feeding and were negatively correlated with the elevation of the habitat where each species was collected, but the PT was often imprecise. The inability to thermoregulate under natural conditions may result from a lack

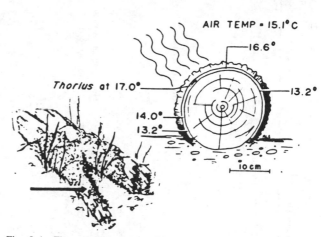

Fig. 9.4 Thermal diversity provided by a fallen log occupied by a plethodontid salamander, *Thorius narisovalis,* at 2,850 m in Oaxaca, Mexico. The salamander occupied the space beneath the rotting bark of a log in a forest clearing on an east-facing slope. Cross-section of the log shows the temperatures available in these microhabitats. The salamander occupied the highest temperature available (17°C). (Reprinted, by permission, from Feder 1982c.)

of thermal heterogeneity of available microhabitats and the restriction to moist locations by their hydric requirements. In instances where thermally diverse microhabitats are available, salamanders thermoregulate behaviorally. In a natural thermal gradient provided beneath the bark of a log exposed to sunlight, a *Thorius narisovalis* (Plethodontidae) had a T_b of 17.0°C, the warmest temperature available beneath the bark and 3.8°C warmer than the minimum temperature available (fig. 9.4). Temperatures within eleven other logs ranged up to 6.4°C between highest and lowest values; in eight of these logs salamanders were at the maximum temperature available (11.4° to 21.2°C) and in two were within 0.2°C of the warmest temperature (Feder 1982c). The limited observations of behavioral thermoregulation by amphibians, particularly salamanders in the field, may reflect more the lack of appropriate thermal diversity of the environment than lack of ability.

Basking

Amphibians can modulate T_b behaviorally by movement between microhabitats (between water and land, occupation of a burrow, etc.) and by direct exposure to sunlight. Basking behavior is apparently uncommon in salamanders but has been described in several anurans. Most of the descriptions of basking are of an anecdotal nature and are without sufficient data for proper interpretation. The first detailed analysis of basking in an anuran was Lillywhite's (1970) investigation of *Rana catesbeiana.* Additional studies have now been made on *R. catesbeiana* (Lillywhite 1975), *R. lessonae* and *R. temporaria* (Sinsch 1984), and *R. muscosa* (Bradford 1984b); the hylids *Hyla caerulea* (Brattstrom 1970a), *H. cinerea* (Freed 1980), and *H. labialis* (Valdivieso and Tamsitt 1974); the myobatrachid *Taudactylus diurnus* (Johnson 1971a); and the bufonids *Bufo boreas* (Carey 1978; Lillywhite, Licht, and Chelgren 1973), *B. debilis* (Seymour 1972), *B. punctatus* (Moore and Moore 1980), and *B. spinulosus* (Pearson and Bradford 1976; Sinsch 1989). Basking as a behavioral ther-

TABLE 9.2 Laboratory Studies on Amphibian Thermal Preferences

Species and Stage (Elevation)	N	Acclimation (°C)	Mean (°C) [Mode]	Gradient Range (°C) and Type	Time of Day or Season	Remarks (Photoperiod)	Reference
Salamanders							
Cryptobranchus alleganiensis	15	5	11.6 [7]	4–30 Lin, UL	13–17 Oct–Nov	(LD 12:12) Distribution truncated at 4° in 5° AT.	Hutchison and Hill 1976
	15	15	17.7 [15]	4–30 Lin, UL	13–17 Oct–Nov		
	15	25	21.7 [27]	4–30 Lin, UL	13–17 Oct–Nov		
Necturus maculosus	15	5	9.1 [8]	4–30 Lin, UL	13–17 Oct–Nov		Hutchison and Hill 1976
	15	15	16.1 [15]	4–30 Lin, UL	13–17 Oct–Nov		
	15	25	20.2 [15]	4–30 Lin, UL	13–17 Oct–Nov		
	10–13	15	10.4	5–35 Lin, UL	24 h Jan–Feb	(LD 12:12) Means over 24-h periods. See reference for values on 2d day of animals in gradient and for values in pronounced diel cycles.	Hutchison and Spriestersbach 1986a
	10–13	15	12.0	5–35 Lin, UL	Feb–Mar		
	10–13	15	11.7	5–35 Lin, UL	Apr–May		
	10–13	15	11.7	5–35 Lin, UL	May–Jun		
	10–13	15	13.1	5–35 Lin, UL	Jun		
	10–13	15	13.4	5–35 Lin, UL	Jul		
	10–13	15	10.1	5–35 Lin, UL	Aug		
	10–13	15	10.9	5–35 Lin, UL	Sep–Oct		
	10–13	15	9.9	5–35 Lin, UL	Nov–Dec		
Salamandra s. salamandra	6	?	18.6	9–?	?	AT conditions not given. Temperature of substrate in gradient where animal located. See reference for localities and gradient sizes. Gradients in "semidarkness."	Strübing 1954
Salamandra atra	6	?	18.5	9–? Lin, UL	?		Strübing 1954
Taricha granulosa Larvae: 10 weeks	24	Field	23	0–34 Lin, UL	?	Freshly captured.	Licht and Brown 1967
Taricha rivularis Larvae: 8 weeks	30	23	23.6	0–34	?	Not significant from AT of 10°–30°.	Licht and Brown 1967
10 weeks	24	Field	23.6 / 23.9	0–34	?	Two localities. Groups of up to 10.	

Larvae: 1–16 weeks	6–32	15 & 23	20–25	0–34	?	No effect of AT. Sample size varied. Groups in gradient.	Licht and Brown 1967
Terrestrial juveniles	14	15	21.5	0–34	?	Range of PT: 14.5°–26.0°.	
Terrestrial adults	15	15	?	0–34	?		
Aquatic adults	8	23	12.8	0–34	?		
Taricha torosa							
Larvae: 10 weeks	24	Field	18	0–34	?		Licht and Brown 1967
Triturus alpestris	9	?	22.6	9–?	?	See under *Salamandra*.	Strübing 1954
Triturus c. cristatus	6	?	20.6	9–?	?	See under *Salamandra*.	Strübing 1954
Triturus c. carnifex	2	?	19.4	9–?	?	See under *Salamandra*.	Strübing 1954
Triturus helveticus	5	?	21.2	9–?	?	See under *Salamandra*.	Strübing 1954
Triturus vulgaris	7	?	23.5	9–?	?	See under *Salamandra*.	Strübing 1954
Ambystoma jeffersonianum							
Larvae: 13–58 mm total length	5	6	8.4	?	09–16	(LD 12:12) Gradient temperatures not given. Values listed calculated from equations given. "Final" thermal preferendum given as 25.2°.	Stauffer, Gates, and Goodfellow 1983
	5	12	17.8	Lin, UL, HL	09–16		
	5	18	20.5	Lin, UL, HL	09–16		
	5	24	24.5	Lin, UL, HL	09–16		
	5	30	26.3	Lin, UL, HL	09–16		
Ambystoma maculatum:							
Larvae: 13–58 mm total length	5	6	6.7	Lin, UL, HL	09–16	"Final" thermal preferendum given as 34.6°.	
	5	12	14.2	Lin, UL, HL	09–16		
	5	18	20.8	Lin, UL, HL	09–16		
	5	24	26.6	Lin, UL, HL	09–16		
	5	30	31.5?	Lin, UL, HL	09–16		
Larvae: 9.8 mm SVL	10	5	15.5	3–36	12–24	All 10 in gradient at same time.	Keen and Schroeder 1975
14.3	10	5	17.8	3–36	12–24		
17.3	10	5	22.9	3–36	12–24		
26.0	10	5	14.5	3–36	12–24		
10.8	10	20	19.0	3–36	12–24		
15.8	10	20	25.6	3–36	12–24		
18.7	10	20	24.3	3–36	12–24		
24.7	10	20	21.3	3–36	12–24		
Ambystoma texanum							
Larvae: 11.6 mm SVL	10	5	17.8	3–36	12–24	(LD 13:11) Groups of 10 in gradient at same time.	Keen and Schroeder 1975
28.2	10	5	20.2	3–36	12–24		
13.1	10	20	20.0	3–36	12–24		
25.6	10	20	22.0	3–36	12–24		
Larvae: hatchlings	10	25	24.8 [27]	10–45	10–18	(LD 13:11) Groups of 10 in gradient at same time.	Dupré and Petranka 1985
Front limbs w/2 toes	10	25	25.3 [24]	10–45	10–18		
Rear limbs w/5 toes	10	25	25.6 [24]	10–45	10–18		
Near metamorphosis	10	25	26.5 [27]	10–45	10–18		
Ambystoma tigrinum							
Larvae: no size given	10	20	24.8 [25]	8–38	? / Jun	(LD 13:11) Tested in groups of 10. Left in gradient "2.5 hours." No PT in July group.	Lucas and Reynolds 1967
	10	20	None		Jul		

(continued)

TABLE 9.2 (continued)

Species and Stage (Elevation)	N	Acclimation (°C)	Mean (°C) [Mode]	Gradient Range (°C) and Type	Time of Day or Season	Remarks (Photoperiod)	Reference
Larvae: 1st year	13	Field	23.1–23.7 [24]	10–30	?	(LD 13.5:10.5?) Measured hourly for 18–36 h. From different elevations.	Heath 1976
1st year	4	9–11	20.3 [22]	10–30	"Summer" ?		
1st year	4	27–29	17.7 [22]	10–30	"Summer" ?		
2–4 years	15	Field	24.3–25.5 [25]	10–30	"Summer" ?		
Adults: [2,865 m]	4	Field	19.1 [19]	10–30	"Summer" ?		
[3,000 m]	5	Field	18.4 [23]	10–30	"Summer" ?		
[3,320 m]	8	Field	23.7 [26]	10–30	"Summer" ?		
Neotenic adults: [3,349 m]	3	Field	23.6	10–30	"Summer" ?		
Aneides lugubris	21	12?	15.2 [12]	12–26	?	On dry soil. Results given as % of animals at each condition.	Rosenthal 1957
	21	12?	5.5 [3.0]	2–21		Gradient of compartments. No group effect. Truncated at coldest temperatures (3°, 12°). Run singly and in groups of 2 to 4.	
Desmognathus fuscus Rich Mt., AR	9	15	23.8	0–40?	07–23.5	(LD 16:8) Groups of up to 11. Temperature recorded after 2 h in gradient.	Spotila 1972
Montgomery Co., AR	10	15	25.6	0–40?	07–23.5		Spotila 1972
Desmognathus monticola	11	15	20.3	0–40?	07–23.5		Spotila 1972
Desmognathus ochrophaeus NC	13	15	17.4	0–40?	07–23.5		Spotila 1972
TN	7	15	19.5	0–40?	07–23.5		Spotila 1972
Eurycea longicauda	16	15	21.7	0–40?	07–23.5		Spotila 1972
Eurycea lucifuga	15	5	23.3	0–40?	07–23.5		Spotila 1972
	11	15	22.2	0–40?	07–23.5		Spotila 1972
	11	25	19.3	0–40?	07–23.5		Spotila 1972
Eurycea multiplicata	5	15	18.8	0–40?	07–23.5		Spotila 1972
Plethodon caddoensis	11	5	20.8	0–40?	07–23.5		Spotila 1972
	14	15	17.7	0–40?	07–23.5		Spotila 1972
	10	25	18.8	0–40?	07–23.5		Spotila 1972
Plethodon c. cinereus	10	15	16.2	0–40?	07–23.5		Spotila 1972
Plethodon c. serratus	15	15	16.3	0–40?	07–23.5		Spotila 1972
Plethodon dorsalis	13	15	14.4	0–40?	07–23.5		Spotila 1972
Plethodon glutinosus	14	15	17.4	0–40?	07–23.5		Spotila 1972
Plethodon jordani	11	15	20.4	0–40?	07–23.5		Spotila 1972
Plethodon longicrus	7	15	21.2	0–40?	07–23.5		Spotila 1972

Species							Notes	Reference
Plethodon yonahlossee	15	5	20.2	0–40?	07–23.5			Spotila 1972
	10	15	19.3	0–40?	07–23.5			Spotila 1972
	14	25	22.4	0–40?	07–23.5			Spotila 1972
Plethodon glutinosus, AR	10	5	21.5	0–40?	07–23.5		(LD 16:8, 8:16 combined) No difference between photoperiods.	Spotila 1972
NC	10	5	21.5	0–40?	07–23.5			
AR	10	15	17.7	0–40?	07–23.5			
NC	10	15	20.2	0–40?	07–23.5			
AR	10	25	18.7	0–40?	07–23.5			
NC	10	25	19.4	0–40?	07–23.5			
Plethodon jordani	10	5	18.0	0–40?	07–23.5			Spotila 1972
	10	15	15.4	0–40?	07–23.5			Spotila 1972
	10	25	22.1	0–40?	07–23.5			
Plethodon ouachitae	10	5	18.7	0–40?	07–23.5		(LD 16:8, 8:16 combined) No difference between photoperiods.	
	10	15	20.1	0–40?	07–23.5			
	10	25	18.2	0–40?	07–23.5			
Plethodon c. cinereus	15–20	5	19.3	5–35	08.5–17.5	Jun	No diel cycles observed. Rates of acclimation.	Feder and Pough 1975b
		15	16.2	Lin, UL		Jun		
	15–20	15	21.0	Lin, UL		Aug		
	15–20	15	20.4	Lin, UL		Oct		
	15–20	25	15.9	Lin, UL		Jul		
Bolitoglossa occidentalis [1,050 m]	10	12	15.9	Varied	08.5–?		(LD 14:10) Gradient varied from 10–20 to 10–40 and influenced PT. Temperatures taken hourly.	Feder 1982c
	10	22[a]	16.7	Varied	08.5–?			
Bolitoglossa flaviventris [600 m]	5	22	20.5	Varied	08.5–?			Feder 1982
Bolitoglossa rostrata [2,850 m]	8	12	11.6	Varied	08.5–?			Feder 1982
	10	22	12.4	Varied	08.5–?			Feder 1982
Pseudoeurycea gadovii [3,250 m]	9	12	9.5	Varied	08.5–?			Feder 1982
Pseudoeurycea smithii [2,960 m]	10	12	11.5[b]	Varied	08.5–?			Feder 1982
	10	22	11.2	Varied	08.5–?			
Thorius narisovalis [2,850 m]	10	12	14.0	Varied	08.5–?			Feder 1982
Thorius pulmonaris [2,150 m]	5	12	13.7	Varied	08.5–?			Feder 1982
Frogs								
Ascaphus truei							Recorded hourly over 16–32 h. Lights on during observations. Avoided temperatures above 22°.	deVlaming and Bury 1970
Larvae: 1st year	14	5	8.6 [8]	0–26, Lin, Dark		Apr	(LD 10:14)	
	5	10	4.7 [3]	0–26, Lin, Dark		Mar	(LD 10:14)	
	15	5	7.2 [7]	0–26, Lin, Dark		Jun	(LD 16:8)	
	14	12	8.0 [6]	0–26, Lin, Dark		Jun	(LD 16:8)	

(continued)

TABLE 9.2 (continued)

Species and Stage (Elevation)	N	Acclimation (°C)	Mean (°C) [Mode]	Gradient Range (°C) and Type	Time of Day or Season	Remarks (Photoperiod)	Reference
	11	16	9.5 [8]	0–26 Lin, Dark	Jun	(LD 16:8)	
	5	11	9.7 [5]	0–26 Lin, Dark	Jun	(LD 16:8)	
Larvae: 2d year	6	5	13.1 [16]	0–26 Lin, Dark	Mar	(LD 16:8)	
	10	10	12.2 [16]	0–26 Lin, Dark	Apr	(LD 16:8)	
	6	16	15.1 [16]	0–26 Lin, Dark	Apr	(LD 16:8)	
	5	5	10.3 [13]	0–26 Lin, Dark	Mar	(LD 10:4)	
	5	10	10.6 [14]	0–26 Lin, Dark	Jun	(LD 10:14)	
	10	16	12.0 [12]	0–26 Lin, Dark	Apr	(LD 10:14)	
Alytes cisternasi	1	?	33.2	?	?	See under *Salamandra*.	Strübing 1954
Alytes obstetricans	6	?	31.5	?	?	See under *Salamandra*.	Strübing 1954
Bombina bombina	9	?	21.2	?	?	See under *Salamandra*.	Strübing 1954
Bombina v. variegata	3	?	26.2	?	?	See under *Salamandra*.	Strübing 1954
Bombina v. scabra	2	?	21.5	?	?	See under *Salamandra*.	Strübing 1954
Discoglossus p. pictus	4	?	28–34	?	?	See under *Salamandra*.	Strübing 1954
Discoglossus p. sardus	1	?	29.7	?	?	See under *Salamandra*.	Strübing 1954
Pelodytes punctatus	2	?	29.9	?	?	See under *Salamandra*.	Strübing 1954
Hyla cinerea	47	22–35	25.5	Non-Lin HL	?	(LD 12:12) Housed in cages. Heat allowed T_b of 20°–35°. Day 1 controls; day 2 experimentals. No diel cycles. Injections of bacteria produced a behavioral fever of 2°.	Kluger 1977
Hyla crucifer	6?	22	23.8	18–42	07–09	(LD 12:12) Tested individually.	Gatten and Hill 1984
	?	22	25.9	18–42	Jun–Jul	Tested in groups of 3–4. Groups significantly higher than individuals.	
Hyla regilla	2	?	31.4	?	?	See under *Salamandra*.	Strübing 1954
	5?	21.7	19–24?	4.5–27	02–21.5	(LD ?) No significance between individuals and groups of 5–10.	Claussen 1973
	10?	23.0	19–24?	4.5–27	02–21.5		
Hyla raddiana	2	?	28.7	?	?	See under *Salamandra*.	Strübing 1954
Hyla a. arborea	3	?	31.8	?	?	See under *Salamandra*.	Strübing 1954
Hyla a. meriodionalis	?	?	27.4	?	?	See under *Salamandra*.	Strübing 1954
Hyla a. meriodionalis	4	?	27.9	?	?	See under *Salamandra*.	Strübing 1954
Hyla savignyi	2	?	29.8	?	?	See under *Salamandra*.	Strübing 1954

	n	Acclim. temp (°C)	PT	Range / Method	Time	Notes	Reference
Pseudacris triseriata							
Larvae: Stage 25	10	25	23.8	10–45	10–18	(LD 13:11) Groups of 10 in gradient at same time.	Dupré and Petranka 1985
29	10	25	22.1	Lin, UL	10–18		
33–35	10	25	23.5	Lin, UL	10–18		
36–38	10	25	28.3	Lin, UL	10–18		
41–43	10	25	30.2	Lin, UL	10–18		
Rana cascadae							
Larvae: Stage 29–32	9	21	26.9	7–35	14–18	(LD 14:10) In gradient 5 h; only last hour recorded. PT of 4 stages at AT of 7° also graphed.	Wollmuth et al. 1987
39–40	9	21	28.1	Lin	Jul–Aug		
42	8	21	28.8	Lin	Jul–Aug		
43	9	21	27.3	Lin	Jul–Aug		
44–45	5	21	19.0	Lin	Jul–Aug		
46	5	21	14.5	Lin	Jul–Aug		
Adults (2 years)	5	21	16.0	Lin	Jul–Aug		
Rana catesbeiana							
Larvae: Stage 35	10	20	[24]	8–38	May	(LD 13:11) Groups of 10 in gradient at 20° and then gradient established. Data recorded each 10 min for 2.5 h. Time of day and LD not given.	Lucas and Reynolds 1967
	10	20	[28]	Lin	Jun		
	10	20	[30]	Lin	Jul		
25–26	6–9	4.4	14.9	4–38	Day	(LD 16:8) Complex interactions between AT and larval stage. Overall PT for all groups was 20.66° and a mode of 20.97°. No obvious diel cycles during photophase. Modes given for each experiment.	Hutchison and Hill 1977
25–26	6–9	15.5	20.9	Lin, UL	Mid-Jun		
25–26	6–9	26.7	25.7	Lin, UL	Mid-Jun		
25–26	6–9	35.0	20.8	Lin, UL	Mid-Jun		
35–36	6–9	4.4	10.2	Lin, UL	Mid-Jun		
35–36	6–9	15.5	20.7	Lin, UL	Mid-Jun		
35–36	6–9	26.7	20.6	Lin, UL	Mid-Jun		
35–36	6–9	35.0	22.5	Lin, UL	Mid-Jun		
39–40	6–9	4.4	19.7	Lin, UL	Mid-Jun		
39–40	6–9	15.5	19.8	Lin, UL	Mid-Jun		
39–40	6–9	26.7	19.3	Lin, UL	Mid-Jun		
39–40	6–9	35.0	23.0	Lin, UL	Mid-Jun		
41	6–9	4.4	18.9	Lin, UL	Mid-Jun		
41	6–9	15.5	20.7	Lin, UL	Mid-Jun		
41	6–9	26.7	21.6	Lin, UL	Mid-Jun		
41	6–9	35.0	21.5	Lin, UL	Mid-Jun		
43–44	6–9	4.4	20.9	Lin, UL	Mid-Jun		
43–44	6–9	15.5	21.7	Lin, UL	Mid-Jun		
43–44	6–9	26.7	23.8	Lin, UL	Mid-Jun		
43–44	6–9	35.0	25.9	Lin, UL	Mid-Jun		
35–36	9	24	24.4	Lin, UL	Mid-Jun		
41	9	24	[27]	13–41	06–21	(LD 14:10) Measured every 15 min during photophase. No difference between larvae tested individually or in groups at same or different stages.	Dupré et al. 1986
41			29.2	Lin, UL	Summer		
45–46	9	24	[31]	13–41	09–21		
45–46			31.7	Lin, UL	Summer		
26–30 (3–5 g)	8	Field	25.4	7–36	12–18	(LD 15:9?) From outdoor pool. Tested individually.	Wollmuth and Crawshaw 1988
26–30 (8–10 g)	8	10.5–24	26.2	Lin	Summer		

(continued)

TABLE 9.2   (continued)

Species and Stage (Elevation)	N	Acclimation (°C)	Mean (°C) [Mode]	Gradient Range (°C) and Type	Time of Day or Season	Remarks (Photoperiod)	Reference
31–35	8	10.5–24	25.1	Lin	Summer		
39–40	9	10.5–24	31.6	Lin	Summer		
41	17	10.5–24	31.9	Lin	Summer		
41	10	10.5–24	30.9	Lin	Summer		
42	9	10.5–24	31.6	Lin	Summer		
43	8	10.5–24	30.0	Lin	Summer		
44	7	10.5–24	16.1	Lin	Summer		
45–46	8	10.5–24	18.1	Lin	12–18	(LD ?) Acclimated for 2 weeks; values also given for 1 week.	Wollmuth and Crawshaw 1989
26–30	9	7	26.0	Lin	Summer	Seasonal variation observed in prometamorphic larvae only. No difference in feeding and fasting animals. Values are for 6th h in gradient; values also given in reference for 2d h.	
26–30	9	21	26.6	Lin	Summer		
39–40	9	7	28.7	Lin	Summer		
39–40	9	21	30.8	Lin	Summer		
41	9	7	30.6	Lin	Summer		
41	9	21	32.0	Lin	Summer		
42	7	7	28.7	Lin	Summer		
42	7	21	31.8	Lin	Summer		
45–46	7	7	20.2	Lin	Summer		
45–46	7	21	16.8	Lin	Summer		
Juveniles (20–60 g)	12	10	22.3 [21]	4–40	13–14	(LD 12:12) Individually tested. In-dwelling thermocouples.	Lillywhite 1971a
	9	25	27.6 [26]	Lin, UL, HL	13–14	(LD 8:16)	
	12	25	26.7 [28]	Lin, UL, HL	13–14	(LD 12:12)	
	12	25	27.1 [26]	Lin, UL, HL	13–14	(LD 16:8)	
	10	16–26	25.3 [26]	Lin, UL, HL	13–14	(LD 12:12) Lowest temperature during dark, highest during light.	
	137	Cycle Field	29.6 [28]	Lin, UL, HL	13–14	(LD 12:12) Fed, above unfed.	
	12	25	28.1 [17.5]	Lin, UL, HL	13–14	(LD 12:12) Fed. Significant effect of feeding.	
	11	16–26	26.6 [26]	Lin, UL, HL	13–14		
Rana esculenta	48	21	25–28 [25–28]	0–40	?	Skin temperatures. No significant difference of groups of 5 and of individuals.	Cabanac and Jeddi 1971
	9	17–18	26	0–40	?	Aquatic gradient. Spinal cord heating lowered PT.	Duclaux, Fantino, and Cabanac 1973
Rana a. arvalis	7	?	28.7	?	?	See under *Salamandra.*	Strübing 1954
	5	?	29.6	?	?	See under *Salamandra.*	Strübing 1954
Rana clamitans	1	?	29.1	?	?	See under *Salamandra.*	Strübing 1954

Species / Stage	N	AT	PT	Gradient range	Time of Day	Notes	Reference
Rana dalmatina	3	?	28.4	?	?	See under *Salamandra*.	Strübing 1954
Rana r. ridibunda	3	?	30.9	?	?	See under *Salamandra*.	Strübing 1954
Rana temporaria	5	?	29.6	?	?	See under *Salamandra*.	Strübing 1954
Rana pipiens							
Larvae: Stage 29	10	13	[20]	8–38	Jun	(LD 13:11) See under *R. catesbeiana*.	Lucas and Reynolds 1967
29	10	25 & 27	[25]	8–38	Jul		
33	10	15 & 27	[20]	8–38	Jun		
34	10	20	[23]	8–38	Apr		
37	10	20	[27]	8–38	Jun		
39	10	20	[30]	8–38	Jul		
Larvae: 40–60 mm	20	22	27.8 [28]	Shuttlebox	06–18	(LD 12:12) Tested individually over 48-h periods. Bimodal diel cycle with nocturnal and diurnal peaks (28.8°) and minima at transition from light to dark (27.4° and 27.1°).	Casterlin and Reynolds 1978
	20	22	28.1 [27]	Shuttlebox	18–06		
Rana sphenocephala							
Larvae: Stage 26	10	25	25.9	10–45	10–18	(LD 13:11) Groups of 10 in gradient at same time.	Dupré and Petranka 1985
28	10	25	17.9	10–45	10–18		
32	10	25	24.3	10–45	10–18		
38–40	10	25	28.8	10–45	10–18		
41	10	25	30.4	10–45	10–18		
42	10	25	28.5	10–45	10–18		
Adults	5	?	28.3	?	?	See under *Salamandra*. Listed in reference as *R. pipiens*.	Strübing 1954
Rana sylvatica							
Larvae: Stages 26–31?	?	?	[19–20]	6–33	?	Groups of 25–34 in gradient at same time with data taken every 5 min for 30 min.	Herreid and Kinney 1967
Hyperolius horstocki	1	?	33.1	?	?	See under *Salamandra*.	Strübing 1954
Hyperolius marmoratus	1	?	28.2	?	?	See under *Salamandra*.	Strübing 1954
Polypedates buergeri	1	?	28.7	?	?	See under *Salamandra*.	Strübing 1954
Gastrophryne carolinensis	2	?	31.6	?	?	Listed as *Microhyla*.	Strübing 1954
Chiromantis xerampelina	8	Gradient	[34], [29]	20–40	HL	Both species tested together in gradient. Bimodal distribution, see reference. "No distinct preference." About 50% were between 34° and 39°.	Shoemaker et al. 1987
Chiromantis petersi	4	Gradient	[34], [29]		HL		

Notes: Animals are adults unless otherwise noted. Larval stages of anurans have been converted where possible to Gosner (1960) stages. Sample sizes (N) are for numbers of individual animals. Some values were read from graphs and are approximate. "Time of Day" is beginning and ending times where known; "24 h" indicates temperatures were taken periodically over full 24-h periods. AT = acclimation temperature; HL = heat lamp used as heat source; LD = light and dark (photophase and scotophase, respectively) portions of a photoperiod; UL = uniform lighting over gradient. SVL = snout-vent length; Lin = Linear; PT = preferred (selected) temperature.

[a] No effect of feeding.

[b] Fed animals had increased preferred temperature of 3°–5° and declined over 14 days to prefed values.

moregulatory mechanism of anurans under field conditions was reviewed by Brattstrom (1979).

In artificial ponds in southern California, Lillywhite (1970) observed that bullfrogs (*Rana catesbeiana*) moved toward the shore as the early morning sun warmed the air and water. As temperatures increased during the day, nearly all of the frogs moved onto the bank in full sunlight; most of the frogs were exposed on the bank at the time of highest temperatures in midafternoon. A drop in temperature of the air in late afternoon was followed by movement of the frogs from shore back into the now warmer water. More frogs emerged on warm than on cool days (fig. 9.5). During the course of the day the frogs alternated movements between water and land, with exposures on the bank ranging from a few minutes to 1 h. The longer durations of exposure were only by frogs with parts of the body touching the water. Near the end of the day as air temperatures dropped, so did the T_b of the frogs. Upon the frogs' reentry into the water later in the day, the T_b increased over what it had been in air (Fig. 9.5).

Rana muscosa above 3,060 m in the Sierra Nevada of California tend to maximize T_b during the day by basking, moving between water and land, and selecting warmer microhabitats along the shoreline (Bradford 1984b). These frogs are almost exclusively diurnal, as opposed to most lowland species, which tend to be nocturnal, and rarely stay in total shade for more than 20 min. Basking frogs had a mean maximum difference of 14.4°C between T_b and shade temperature. The maximum difference recorded in an individual was

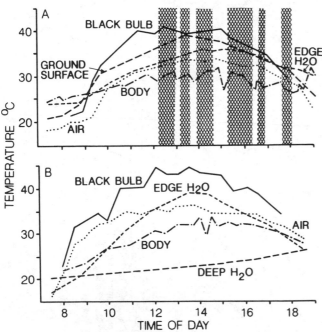

Fig. 9.5 Telemetered measurements of the body temperature of two adult bullfrogs, *Rana catesbeiana*, in a southern California pond in August. The frog in *A* (325-g female) was out of the water and sitting on the shoreline during periods indicated with *shading*. Cloud cover or convection produced the dips in black-bulb temperature. The frog in *B* (205-g female) remained in the pond but maintained a comparably uniform body temperature by shuttling between microhabitats with dissimilar temperatures (shallow, deep, or surface water). (Reprinted, by permission, from Lillywhite 1970.)

18.6°C, and the highest T_b recorded in the field was 28.4°C. At 2,650 m in the Sabana de Bogotá, Colombia, the heliothermic hylid frog *Hyla labialis* had T_b's higher than ambient air as a result of basking, even under a usual light cloud cover (fig. 9.6). The air temperature at the study locality fluctuates between 4.4°C at night and 17.2°C during the day, with a yearly mean of about 14.5°C. These frogs are both diurnal and nocturnal, but adults and subadults are more active in the morning and early afternoon; juveniles are most active at night (Valdivieso and Tamsitt 1974). These activity patterns are unlike those in most toads (Brattstrom 1979), where juveniles bask more often and have higher T_b's than adults (Seymour 1972; Lillywhite, Licht, and Chelgren 1973). *H. labialis* has a relatively narrow altitudinal distribution and a wide geographical range but differs from most lowland-derived hylids with small geographic ranges (Brattstrom 1970) by having a broad thermal tolerance but a narrow range for acute acclimation (Hutchison 1971a). The T_b's of mature *Bufo boreas boreas* are highly correlated with the extent of solar radiation, while the T_b's of *B. b. halophilus* are more correlated with air and substrate temperature (Carey 1978b). This difference suggests that toads at higher altitude employ basking behavior to a greater extent than those from lowland areas where higher ambient temperatures occur. In lowland *B. b. halophilus*, however, basking behavior is clearly a part of thermoregulatory behavior (Smits 1984).

Due to their relatively moist skin (and other factors) most anurans are apparently unable to attain a temperature differential between body and air comparable to those of reptiles, except under conditions of very high humidities. Comparison of a telemetered free-ranging toad (*B. spinulosus*) and a lizard (*Liolaemus multiformis*) at 4,300 m in the Andes of Peru showed that toads do not achieve the high T_b's characteristic of the lizard (fig. 9.7). During 9.75 h of daytime measurement the toad had an average integrated T_b of 14.7°C and the lizard 15.7°C. Although the toad did not reach a T_b as high as the lizard, by emerging sooner in the morning and by staying in contact with a warm boulder later in the day, the toad had a higher T_b than the lizard for much of the observation period (Pearson and Bradford 1976). Although many ectotherms use basking to elevate T_b to a suitable activity level, in some anurans (e.g., *Bufo woodhousii*) basking does not lead to increased activity (Hadfield 1966). *B. spinulosus* appeared to use basking as a terminal activity. Pearson and Bradford (1976) concluded that *B. spinulosus* has to balance insolation against the concomitant evaporation of body water. They estimated that the toads retreated to burrows after a length of time basking that would have reduced body mass by about 10% due to evaporation.

Sinsch (1984) studied the diurnal behavior of three species of European anurans in a habitatlike experimental environment. The northern species *Rana temporaria* shows an effective cooling behavior at high temperatures and heating behavior at low temperatures, mostly by changing microhabitat with very little basking behavior. This species tends to shift its activity to night at high temperatures and to the daytime at lower temperatures. The more southern species *R. lessonae* has a higher PT than the other species and intensive basking behavior independent of ambient temperature. Bask-

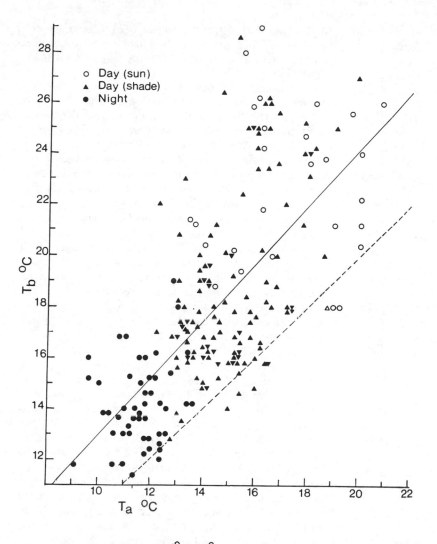

Fig. 9.6 Body temperatures of *Hyla labialis* at different air temperatures at 2,650 m in the Sabana de Bogotá, Colombia. The *dashed line* represents equality of body (T_b) and air (T_a) temperatures. The *solid line* regression is $y = 0.99 + 1.27x$. (Reprinted, by permission, from Valdivieso and Tamsitt 1974.)

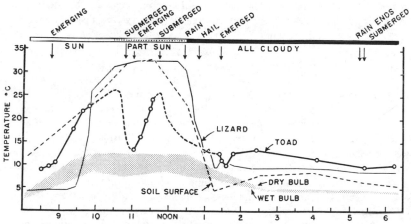

Fig. 9.7 Body temperatures of a telemetered free-ranging toad (*Bufo spinulosus*) and a lizard (*Liolaemus multiformis*) at 4,300 m in the Peruvian Andes in March. Notations on emergence and submergence at the top refer to the toad. Soil temperature was taken at a location in sunlight. (Reprinted, by permission, from Pearson and Bradford 1976.)

ing is infrequent in the closely related and more aquatic *R. ridibunda,* which thermoregulates mostly by shuttling between water and land.

Orientation and postural changes to maximize insolation during basking are common features of the thermoregulatory repertoire of diurnal lizards (Templeton 1970), snakes (Lillywhite 1987), and turtles (Hutchison 1979), but appear in-frequently in anurans. For example, random orientation to the sun occurs in *B. boreas* (Carey 1978b), *R. catesbeiana* (Lillywhite 1970), *R. muscosa* (Bradford, 1984b, fig. 6), and *Hyla labialis* (Valdivieso and Tamsitt 1974).

Although the body itself may not be oriented to receive maximum sunlight, frogs may seek out a substrate where the angle to the sun will afford maximum heat gain. Juvenile

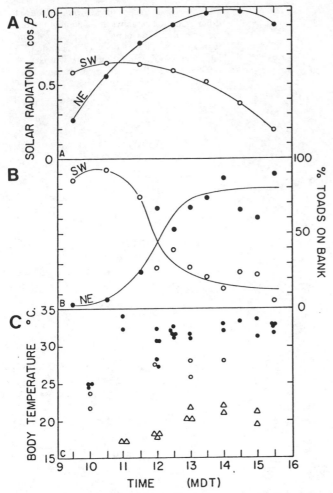

Fig. 9.8 Body temperatures (C) of juvenile green toads, *Bufo debilis*, at different times of day along a small stream in September in New Mexico in relation to solar radiation (A) falling on the southwest (SW) and northeast (NE) stream banks. The proportion of frogs on the bank is shown by B. ●, basking; ○, hopping in the sun; △, sitting in shade. The index of the intensity of solar radiation is given as the cosine of the angle made by the sun's rays with the stream bank. (Reprinted, by permission, from Seymour 1972.)

green toads (*B. debilis*) changed locations during the day to seek out moist sides of small streams that received the most direct insolation (fig. 9.8; Seymour 1972).

Postural changes to maximize solar heat gain, also especially common in some lizards, apparently have not been reported in anurans but have been observed in response to heat stress or water loss. The ventral surface of *R. catesbeiana* may be held off the ground when heat-stressed, but against the substrate when T_b is low (Lillywhite 1970). Basking frogs frequently have at least a portion of their body in direct contact with water or moist substrate. Under such conditions an anuran may be able to regulate the amount of water being absorbed and evaporation from the skin as a function of heat load, thus maintaining a fairly constant T_b. Brattstrom (1970a) observed this mechanism in the basking Australian frog *Hyla* (= *Litoria*) *caerulea*, but not in *H. chloris*, a smaller frog from less arid regions. Although most frogs bask on a moist substrate, *B. boreas* was observed basking on dry

soil (Lillywhite, Licht, and Chelgren 1973). The water storage ability of *B. boreas* may allow it to bask on dry substrates and then move to water or wet soil for rehydration (Brattstrom 1979).

Some investigators have used dry-bulb or wet-bulb air, substrate, and water temperatures as a substitute for direct measurement of T_b in amphibians in the field (Brattstrom 1963). Such environmental temperature may deviate significantly from the T_b, due to the more immediate past thermal history of the animal. Shuttling between microhabitats, basking, and other behaviors, as well as myriad influences from the physical environment, can result in major deviations of T_b from ambient temperatures. Differences can result from body-size variations, evaporation from body surfaces, and so forth, and, to a more limited extent, from physiological mechanisms such as peripheral vasomotor changes. In a study of *Hyla crucifer*, L. E. Brown and J. R. Brown (1977) observed significant differences between T_b and air and water temperatures. In the African painted reed frog, *Hyperolius marmoratus* (Hyperoliidae), nocturnal mean T_b's of males calling from elevated perches were significantly higher (3.1°C, range 0.5° to 6.0°C) than dry-bulb air temperatures, although dry-bulb air temperature and T_b were strongly positively correlated (Passmore and Malherbe 1985). The elevated T_b may have resulted from earlier basking in the sun and retention of body heat by having a very low evaporative water loss. These reed frogs have very low rates of cutaneous evaporation (Withers, Louw, and Nicolson 1982).

Although basking is usually thought to be primarily thermoregulatory, it may serve a variety of functions and serve different mechanisms in different species (Avery 1982; Hutchison 1979). Some of the more obvious functions would result from increased energy exchange at higher T_b: increased ingestion of food due to greater activity, digestion, linear growth, body mass, lipid storage, reproductive processes, and so forth. The possible significances of the relationship between PT and biological functions are discussed later in this chapter.

Aggregations and Vertical Migrations

Aggregations of amphibians, particularly of aquatic larvae, have been widely observed. These group behaviors often show diel cycles of movement from shallow water near shore to deeper water (Beiswenger 1977; Bradford 1984b; Brattstrom 1962; Griffiths 1985a; Griffiths, Getliff, and Mylotte 1988) or vertically within a water column (Anderson and Williamson 1974; Holomuzki and Collins 1983). The latter movements may result in a stratification of larvae. This aggregative behavior in larvae was reviewed by Wassersug (1973). Simple aggregations may result from taxic responses to water currents (rheotropisms), light (phototaxy), odors, oxygen concentration, temperature (thermotaxy), and so forth. Response to food concentration, predators, or metamorphic changes may also influence such assemblages (Anderson and Graham 1967; Branch and Altig 1981; Hassinger, Anderson, and Dalrymple 1970; Holomuzki 1986; Lucas and Reynolds 1967; Stangel and Semlitsch 1987). Biosocial aggregates may lead to schooling behavior (Wassersug 1973). Aggregation

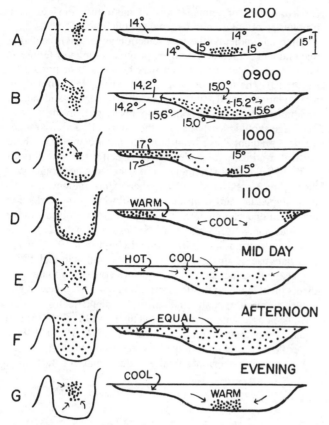

Fig. 9.9 Aggregation behavior in *Rana boylii* larvae associated with temperatures at different times of the day. Vertical section of the pond is on *right*, horizontal on *left*. Observations were made in Del Norte County, California, on 28–29 June. At 0900 larvae were concentrated on the bottom in the middle of a pond cove at an ambient temperature of 15°C (*B*). During the day they were able to exploit the changing water temperatures by movement to various microhabitats (*C–G*). By 2100 they had reaggregated in the deeper portions (*A*). (Reprinted, by permission, from Brattstrom 1962.)

behavior where no external stimuli (temperature, light, food, etc.) were apparent has often been termed *social aggregation* (Bragg 1964; Brattstrom 1962, 1970a).

Aggregations have been attributed most often to thermoregulatory behavior. Anuran and salamander larvae often congregate on warm days in the shallow portions of ponds during the morning where water temperatures are elevated by sunlight, move to deeper (cooler) water at midday or early afternoon, and move to still deeper (warmer) water at night (fig. 9.9). In some instances larvae may orient to maximize the dorsal surface area exposed to solar radiation (Brattstrom and Warren 1955). More radiant energy may be absorbed and dispersed to the surrounding water by larvae in aggregations than by isolated individuals (Brattstrom 1962; Beiswenger 1977).

Although temperature is both an important proximate factor in directive behavior (e.g., such as that leading to aggregations) and an ultimate ecological factor (e.g., behavioral thermoregulation), nonthermal components may provide the ultimate adaptive value of a response to temperature. Examples include food-resource location, predator avoidance, and diel and seasonal migrations. Nonthermal factors, particu-

larly light and photoperiod, may act as accessories to proximate factors (Reynolds 1977b).

Environmental temperatures are often so closely correlated with changes in light intensity that the effects of the two factors are difficult to separate. The diel cycles of movements of larval *Bufo americanus* in ponds are closely correlated with light; the increasing light in the morning triggers activity and the formation of aggregations, while decreasing light leads to dispersal of aggregations and inactivity. Once the larvae become active, they are attracted to particular microhabitats by both temperature and light. Although thermal gradients in the habitat are primarily responsible for directing larvae into aggregations, temperature does not act alone as a controlling factor (Beiswenger 1977).

Although the nocturnal stratification of larval *Ambystoma* (Caudata: Ambystomatidae) appears to be light-cued and correlated with the diel cycle of migration of the planktonic food (Anderson and Graham 1967), diel changes in water temperature may affect thermoregulatory behavior to produce the vertical migration patterns (Stangel and Semlitsch 1987). Branch and Altig (1981, 873) concluded that *Ambystoma* larvae "must stratify to remain in contact with the greatest concentration of the most abundant but smallest prey at a time when feeding is behaviorally most intense." However, vertical migrations of *A. talpoideum* in ponds in South Carolina are apparently not related to diel movement of prey zooplankton but are significantly influenced by the presence of a fish predator (Stangel and Semlitsch 1987).

In a study of larval *A. tigrinum* in Arizona, Holomuzki (1986) concluded that the risk from predation, particularly from predaceous diving beetles (*Dytiscus*), forces the salamanders to balance the conflicting demands of feeding and predator avoidance by altering diel patterns of movement. Temperature, although an important determinant of microhabitat use, exerts less influence than the risk of predation. In contrast, a field study of larval *Bufo bufo* in England showed no consistent relationship between larval diel migrations and predatory dytiscid beetles (Griffiths, Getliff, and Mylotte 1988).

Aggregations of larvae in warmer environments may provide an adaptive advantage through increased growth and earlier metamorphosis (Bizer 1978; Lillywhite, Licht, and Chelgren 1973; Stangel and Semlitsch 1987). Increased T_b's can lead to increased digestive rates to support greater growth rates in juveniles and increased lipid storage in adults. Temperature ranks second only to the availability of a food resource as a major external factor governing embryonic development.

Aggregations of postmetamorphic amphibians are apparently infrequently observed, except for the nonstationary groupings associated with migrations from ponds or during reproductive periods. Postmetamorphic aggregations occur in *Rana muscosa* (Bradford 1984b) and *Bufo boreas* (Black and Black 1969; Lillywhite and Wassersug 1974). Stationary aggregations of adult *B. cognatus* were implied by Bragg and Brooks (1958), but they provided no details. Since evaporation is the predominant route of water and heat loss under dry environments and because evaporation rates are higher with increased elevation, Bradford (1984b) suggested that aggregations of adult frogs served to retard the loss of both heat and water, especially by reduction of evaporation from the lateral surfaces of the aggregated animals.

Although Brattstrom (1970b) described some groupings as "thermal" aggregations, as opposed to "feeding," "metamorphosing," and "social" aggregations, such classifications are obviously not mutually exclusive. Aggregations often cannot be explained by a single factor. Although temperature is clearly operative, both directly and indirectly, proximally and ultimately, in most (perhaps all) aggregations, "it is more accurate to consider that aggregations are regulated by a complex of several factors operating simultaneously or in sequence" (Beiswenger 1977, 107).

LABORATORY STUDIES
Methods

Two basic methods, thermal gradients and shuttleboxes, are employed in laboratory studies of thermoregulatory behavior. Methods for determining PT in aquatic animals were reviewed by Fry (1958) and McCauley (1977). McCauley concluded that the designs of gradient devices have less influence on experimental results than do other variables such as physiological state, social interactions, age, season, and so forth. Laudien (1973) reviewed animal behavior leading to selection

(or avoidance) of temperatures in laboratory devices as a problem in orientation in thermal stimulus fields.

Thermal gradients (thermal selection apparatus), heated at one end and cooled at the other, provide a range of temperatures in air, water, or soil and may be vertical or horizontal (fig. 9.10). The range of temperatures available to animals in a gradient can greatly influence results (table 9.2) and should be appropriate to the hypotheses being tested. In most cases the range should clearly exceed the "normal" activity range. Vertical gradients have been used for aquatic animals, where vertical stratification is aided by the rise of warm water (Brett 1952). The vertical stratification of water in a horizontal gradient can also be used to "lengthen" the gradient; a mesh floor sloped upward from the cold end to near the surface at the warm end can change stratification from a disadvantage to an advantage (Hutchison and Spriestersbach 1986a). Baffles along the gradient (Graham and Hutchison 1979) or appropriate use of air diffusers (Crawshaw and Hammel 1974) can also counteract stratification. More complex aquatic gradients involve the controlled inflow and outflow of heated and cooled water at opposite ends of the gradient; such gradients have been used with fishes (Hill, Schnell, and Pigg 1975) and aquatic amphibians (Hutchison and Hill 1976, 1977). Where water flow is used, care must be taken to insure that animals are responding thermotactically rather than rheotactically.

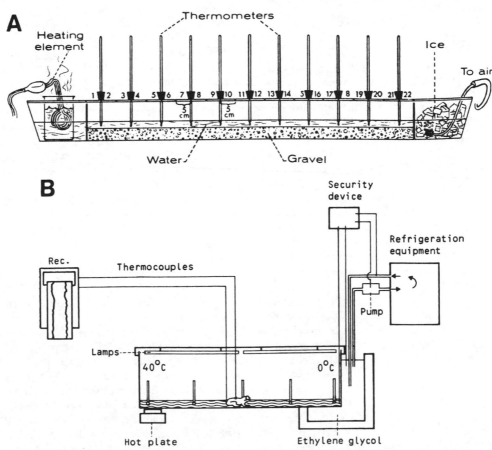

Fig. 9.10 Examples of aquatic linear thermal gradients. A, simple laboratory apparatus with mercury thermometers at equal intervals along the gradient; used to study thermal selection of amphibian larvae. (Reprinted, by permission, from Lucas and Reynolds 1967.) B, a more au-

tomated device for continuous recording of body temperature; used to study behavioral fever in frogs. (From Myhre, Cabanac, and Myhre 1977. Reprinted with the permission of Blackwell Scientific Publications Ltd.)

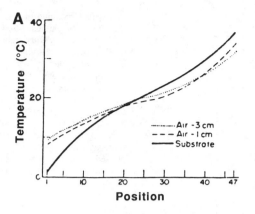

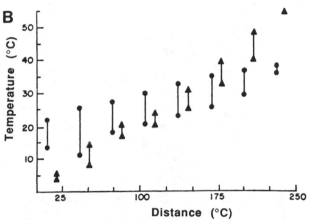

Fig. 9.11 Examples of temperature profiles of laboratory thermal gradients. *A*, graph for a terrestrial gradient with numbers on the abscissa representing positions along the gradient approximately 7 cm apart. The substrate was moist sand. (From Claussen 1973, Reprinted with permission of Pergamon Press PLC.) *B*, graph for an aquatic gradient. ●'s include ranges of vertical temperatures at the beginning of a 24-h measurement period; water, 2.4 cm deep. △, vertical ranges of temperature at the end of the 24-h period; water, 1.5 cm deep. (From Lillywhite 1971a. Reprinted with the permission of Pergamon Press PLC.)

Differences in oxygenation along aquatic gradients can be a problem; care should be taken to insure that experimental animals are responding to thermal, rather than chemosensory, stimuli.

Nonaquatic gradients are easier to construct, especially when heat-conductive metal is used as a floor. In such gradients heat gained or lost by an animal may be "thigmothermic"; air temperatures just above the gradient floor may not be a good indicator of animal temperature. Thus, except for very small animals, T_b should be recorded from indwelling thermocouple or thermistor probes or with radiotelemetry. Temperature gradients should be fairly linear (fig. 9.11); abrupt changes in the temperature profile could produce avoidance responses in experimental animals.

The use of incandescent or heat lamps as point sources of heat for the warm end of a gradient may confound results. Light, independent of air or substrate temperature, influences behavioral thermoregulation of lizards (Sievert and Hutchison 1988, 1989). Gradients with heat lamps (photothermal gradients) allow basking behavior, which may produce different results from use of thigmothermic gradients.

Because temperature and photoperiod influence PT, the acclimatization conditions and sampling period should be given. Sufficient time for the acclimation process should be allowed. Because acclimation to any new thermal (photic, hydric, etc.) environment will occur during the time in a test apparatus, the total time animals are maintained in a gradient should be stated. When transferred to a gradient or shuttlebox, many animals display increased exploratory behavior and activity or retreat to corners or shelter before showing more "normal" behaviors. Thus, a habituation period should be considered and, if used, the length reported.

Other factors may influence results obtained in gradients and should be considered in experimental design. Thigmotactic selection of corners or edges may influence distribution along thermal gradients, as will objects such as shelters. Regularly placed shelters have been employed as part of the apparatus (e.g., Feder and Pough 1975b). Thigmotactic selection can also be reduced by use of a circular apparatus (e.g., Lillywhite 1971a). Moisture and humidity differences along thermal gradients should be minimized. Amphibians are notable in their ability to respond to substrate moisture (Spotila 1972), and responses in thermal gradients may be due to both thermic and hydric drives (Bundy and Tracy 1977; Licht and Brown 1967). Some species may aggregate if more than one individual is in a gradient. Data obtained from individual measurements may differ significantly from those obtained from groups, but not in all species (table 9.2). Obviously, control experiments are necessary to determine the influences of such factors on any results obtained from gradients. At a minimum, tests should be run with the gradient apparatus where temperature is uniform throughout; such a control should determine if factors other than temperature produce a nonrandom distribution of animals in the gradient.

In linear thermal gradients animals usually have a broad range of temperatures from which to "select." A shuttlebox apparatus provides no such "choice." The apparatus consists of two chambers with a connecting window or passageway just large enough to permit passage of the experimental animal (fig. 9.12). Each chamber may be heated or cooled independently until the temperature reaches the point of escape or avoidance and the animal exists to the other side. The movement of the animal between chambers can be recorded from photocells or a treadle device in the opening between the chambers (Neill, Magnuson, and Chipman 1972). Recorders and computer data acquisition equipment can allow such devices to record unattended (fig. 9.13). Shuttleboxes can be filled with water for aquatic forms or contain air for terrestrial forms. Variations of the basic shuttlebox design include a four-chamber, two-axis model to allow simultaneous study of temperature plus an additional variable such as oxygen, salinity, and so forth (Reynolds and Casterlin 1976; Reynolds 1977a).

The shuttling of an animal from the upper to the lower limit in a shuttlebox apparatus is analogous to the maximum and minimum voluntary temperatures. This behavior is consistent with a dual-threshold thermoregulatory system, with setpoints at the upper and lower avoidance temperature (Crawford 1982). Within these thermal limits is a refractory zone

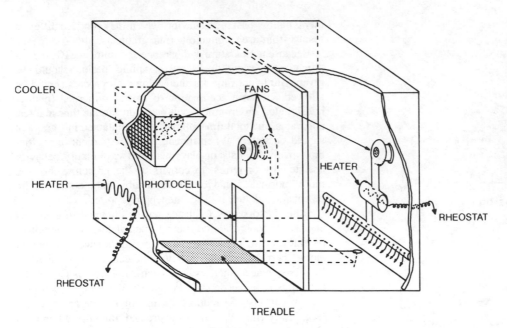

COOLER

FANS

HEATER

HEATER

PHOTOCELL

RHEOSTAT

RHEOSTAT

TREADLE

Fig. 9.12 Example of a simple shuttlebox apparatus used to study thermoregulatory behavior in a lizard. Each chamber may be heated or cooled independently until the temperature reaches the point of escape and the animal exits to the opposite compartment. Movement of the animal between chambers is recorded from the treadle device. (From Cabanac and Hammel 1971. Reprinted with the permission of Masson S.A. Paris.)

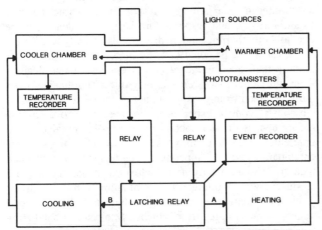

Fig. 9.13 Diagram of a shuttlebox with automatic recordings and controls. Movements of an animal between chambers are sensed by the interruption of a light beam and initiate a reversal of the heating/cooling of each chamber. The state of a bistable latching relay depends upon which light beam was last interrupted by the animal. Heating continues in the warmer chamber as long as the animal remains there. When the animal becomes too warm, it will move to the cooler chamber. This movement turns off the heaters and turns on the cooling equipment in the cool chamber. When the animal becomes too cool, it returns to the warmer chamber, thereby turning off the cooling unit and turning on the heaters. Computer data acquisition, recording, and control equipment is now available for operation of such an aparatus. (From Reynolds et al. 1976. Reprinted with the permission of Pergamon Press PLC.)

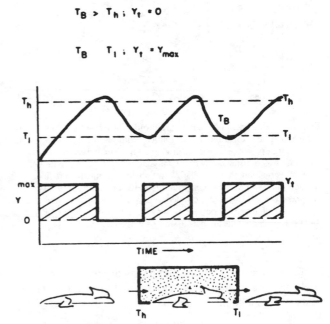

Fig. 9.14 The oscillation of body temperature (T_b) between high (T_h) and low (T_l) limits as an animal shuttles between hot and cool chambers of a shuttlebox (or between sun and shade in a natural environment), an example of a coupled on-off thermoregulatory control system. In the refractory range ($T_h - T_l$) the animal does not have to thermoregulate. The effector output (Y) is equated with heat from the sun (or heat from the test apparatus), where $Y = 0$ in the shade or lowest temperature (T_l) in test apparatus, and $Y = $ max in direct sunlight or at highest temperature (T_h) in the test apparatus. (Reprinted, by permission, from Heath 1970.)

where the "need" for thermoregulatory behavior is minimal (Berk and Heath 1975a; Dreisig 1984). The shuttling movements produce an oscillation of T_b, such as would be seen in an animal shuttling between sun and shade (fig. 9.14). The refractory zone has both ecological and physiological importance. Some lack of precision in the behavioral regulatory system is desirable; if the control is too tightly linked to temperature, an animal would oscillate rapidly between the two temperature thresholds and would spend all of its time shut-

tling. It would be an excellent thermoregulator but an ineffective animal otherwise (Heath 1970; Crawford 1982).

Do the two basic methods used in the laboratory to study behavioral thermoregulation measure somewhat different responses? Are responses in a linear gradient the results of "selection" of temperature or are they a consequence of avoidance of thermal extremes? The answers to this preference-avoidance question depend to a large extent upon the thermoregulatory models adopted by various investigators (Reynolds 1977b). The dual set-point model for behavioral thermoregulation (Heath 1970), used to explain results in a shuttlebox, may appear incompatible with the unimodal distribution of T_b obtained in a linear thermal gradient or from field measurements. However, Barber and Crawford (1977) formulated a stochastic mathematical model based on results from shuttlebox experiments; this model provided a good approximation of the distribution of T_b in a heterothermal environment. According to the model, increases in variance of the limiting temperature produce a decrease in variance of unimodal distribution of T_b in a linear gradient. As variance of the lower limiting temperature increases relative to the upper limit, the model predicts a negatively skewed distribution of temperatures, a common feature of the data obtained from linear gradients and field measurements (Crawford 1982). Such models have been applied primarily to data from fishes and lizards. The applicability of the various competing models to ectotherms in general, much less to the little-studied amphibians, awaits additional definitive study.

The laboratory study of diel and seasonal cycles of thermoregulatory abilities may be severely limited: natural cycles of environmental parameters are often very difficult to reproduce experimentally. The periods of endogenous daily cycles (circadian rhythms) and seasonal cycles (circannual or circenniel) are characterized by being "free-running" (i.e., persist in the absence of an environmental cue or zeitgeber) and relatively independent of temperature. In natural or artificial environments many stimuli may serve as zeitgebers. Photoperiod and temperature cycles often act as environmental cues to entrain rhythms. Laboratory photoperiods usually differ from natural light-dark cycles in light quality (spectral distribution), intensity, and rate of change (twilight duration of sunrise and sunset, spectral and intensity differences at different times of day, etc.). Many environmental cues can influence the period length and amplitude of endogenous rhythms. If such cues are "unnatural" in quality, quantity, duration, rate of change, and so forth, abnormal behavior of the animals may result (Griffiths 1986).

Data from Gradients and Shuttleboxes

Responses of amphibians in laboratory thermal gradients or shuttleboxes can furnish valuable predictive information on responses under field conditions. Under rigidly controlled conditions, laboratory measurements can define limits and lead to some understanding of physiological and behavioral mechanisms. However, applying laboratory results to the greater complexity of field environments should be cautious. Comparisons of amphibian PTs determined in the laboratory with mean T_b's under field conditions often show disparities (Carey 1978b; Lillywhite 1971a; Smits 1984). Such differences should be expected. Amphibians in a natural environment may be active under ambient environmental conditions where attainment of a PT is not possible; demands of feeding, reproduction, osmoregulation, predator avoidance, and so

forth, may take precedence over the maintenance of an "optimum" T_b at any given time. Many of the activities of *Bufo boreas* in the field during an annual cycle take place at T_b's different from the PTs determined in the laboratory, but foraging and retreat behaviors in spring and summer produce T_b's close to the PT (Smits 1984). Clearly, laboratory and field studies together are more likely to yield a fuller understanding of amphibian thermal responses than either alone.

Determinations of behavioral thermoregulation in amphibians are summarized in table 9.2. We caution readers in the uncritical use of this table. Diverse methods yielded the results summarized, and we were selective in the details presented. Direct comparisons of results from different studies may not be appropriate. The original references should be consulted to determine if the methods and statistical procedures used by different investigators allow meaningful comparisons.

Results of some studies were not amenable to the summary format used in table 9.2 and are thus not listed. For example, Degani (1984) studied temperature selection in larval and juvenile *Sulumandra salamandra* (Caudata: Salamandridae) from moist and xeric habitats. In a linear thermal gradient (5°–25°C), larvae from xeric areas selected higher temperatures than those from more moist habitats. After metamorphosis juveniles from xeric habitats preferred lower temperatures than those from moist locales. Results were given as percentages of animals selecting different 5°C intervals of the gradient; means or modes were not given and were not readily calculable from the data given. Rudolph (1978) measured thermal selection by larvae of plethodontid salamanders (*Typhlotriton spelaeus*, *Eurycea lucifuga*, *E. longicauda*, *E. tynerensis*, *E. multiplicata*) in a linear gradient (10°–25°C) after acclimation at 16°C, but did not report stage of development or mean PT; his graphical data indicated PT modes of about 19° to 20.5°C for all except *E. tynerensis*. The latter species was without a distinct modal distribution. The PTs of other amphibians not listed in table 9.2 include *Salamandra atra* and *Triturus alpestris* (Knapp 1974), larval *Rana temporaria* (Rühmekorf 1958b), and hydrated and dehydrated *Chiromantis xerampelina* (Anura: Rhacophoridae) and *Phyllomedusa sauvagei* (Anura: Hylidae; Shoemaker, Baker, and Loveridge 1989). Reichling (1957), using an apparatus designed by Strübing (1954), reported the PTs of nine species of central European amphibians; details of acclimation conditions or season of collection were not reported, and the data are thus not included in table 9.2. Shoemaker, Baker, and Loveridge (1989) studied the influence of water balance on thermal selection in *Chiromantis xerampelina* and *Phyllomedusa sauvagei* but gave their results as frequency distributions; their results are discussed under "Osmoregulation," below. Laboratory studies on behavioral thermoregulation were reviewed by Huey (1982) for reptiles and by Coutant (1977) and Mathur et al. (1981) for fishes.

Temperature Acclimation

The recent thermal history clearly influences PT in most ectotherms. The PT is usually positively correlated with AT, but a decrease in the PT at an AT above the preferred "optimum" is a common response in fishes (e.g., Cheetham et al. 1976), amphibians (e.g., Hutchison and Hill 1977; Lillywhite 1971a; table 9.2), and reptiles (e.g., Licht 1968; Mueller 1970; Wilhoft and Anderson 1960). Licht (1968) suggested that this "reverse" acclimation in PT results from a pathology due to prolonged exposure to high AT. Under natural conditions, animals are not normally exposed to constant high temperatures but usually experience diel cycles in both the physical environment and their own efforts at thermoregulation. However, the curvilinear relationship between AT and PT is not unlike that between PT and many physiological rates (enzyme activity, sensory sensitivity, immune responses, metabolism, etc.).

Feder and Pough (1975b) described an inverse relationship between AT and PT in the plethodontid salamander *Plethodon c. cinereus* (table 9.2). They suggested that a reduction of PT after exposure to increasing AT induces this lungless salamander to move to a cooler (and concomitantly moister) microenvironment where an obligate cutaneous gas exchange would be better served. However, not all plethodontid salamanders have such an inverse relationship between AT and PT (table 9.2). As a group, the tropical plethodontids studied by Feder (1982c) have an overall increase of PT at higher AT (PT = 0.235AT + 9.88). The temperature plethodontids investigated by Spotila (1972) had an overall decrease (PT = −0.155AT + 21.43).

Other examples of positive correlations of PT with AT are the salamanders *Necturus maculosus* (Proteidae) and *Cryptobranchus alleganiensis* (Cryptobranchidae), where each increase of 1°C in AT results in an increase in PT of 0.5° and 0.51°C, respectively (table 9.2). During development *Rana catesbeiana* has the following changes (ΔPT/ΔAT): Gosner (1960) stages 25–26, 0.48°C; stages 35–36, 0.36°C; stage 41, 0.12°C; stages 43–44, 0.19°C (calculated from data in table 9.2). Amphibians in general respond to increasing AT at temperatures below the "optimum" by elevating PT from 0.1° to 0.6°C per degree increase in AT. Above the "optimum," ΔPT/ΔAT decreases by a similar magnitude. The biological significance of these different values for ΔPT/ΔAT needs additional study; the values may be nothing more than a reflection of the net sum of the rates of biochemical and physiological systems (i.e., an overall Q_{10} effect).

Acclimation to a diel cycle of temperature may result in a PT intermediate to that of animals acclimated to a constant high and to a constant low temperature representing a "compromise" between the thermal extremes (Lillywhite 1971a). This intermediate response to cyclic AT contrasts with that observed for critical thermal maximum (CTMax), where acclimation to cycled temperatures is a response to the highest temperature experienced (e.g., Hutchison and Ferrance 1970; Seibel 1970).

The rate of PT acclimation has not been directly studied in many amphibians but appears to be more rapid and of greater magnitude than acclimation of thermal tolerance. In *Plethodon cinereus* PT acclimation was complete within 48 h after transfer from 5° to 25°C (Feder and Pough 1975b). The rate of PT acclimation in other species, in different geographic populations of the same species and at different seasons, needs study.

Exposure to an acute heat stress can also influence subsequent thermal selection in amphibians. *Necturus maculosus* exposed to the CTMax (onset of spasms as an end point) or sub-CTMax (2.75°C below CTMax) and placed in a linear thermal gradient select significantly higher temperatures than controls, followed by a gradual decline in selected T_b over 3 days. Exposure to heat stress can alter the ability to exploit available microclimates for thermoregulation and can also remove the ability to express diel cycles of T_b.

Ontogeny of Thermoregulation

Temperatures selected by amphibian larvae are not always consonant with adult PTs (table 9.2). Bullfrog larvae (*Rana catesbeiana*), approximately Gosner stage 30, select lower temperatures (Lucas and Reynolds 1967) than the PTs of recently metamorphosed and adult bullfrogs (Lillywhite 1970, 1971a). Similarly, second-year larvae of the tailed frog, *Ascaphus truei* (Leiopelmatidae), aggregate at warmer temperatures than first-year larvae (de Vlaming and Bury 1970); both PTs are lower than those of adult tailed frogs (Claussen 1973). However, some studies suggested no difference in the PT of larval and adult amphibians (Casterlin and Reynolds 1978; Licht and Brown 1967).

The failure of some investigators to recognize potential physiological differences between developmental stages (Casterlin and Reynolds 1978), or their study of very narrow ranges of developmental stages (Lucas and Reynolds 1967), obscure ontogenetic trends in behavioral thermoregulation. Not until Hutchison and Hill (1977) examined temperature selection of bullfrog larvae as a function of AT and a wide range of developmental stages did a trend toward the selection of warmer temperatures with advancing developmental stage begin to emerge. Subsequently, Floyd (1984) found that the PT of larvae of the marine toad, *Bufo marinus*, increases during development until metamorphic climax, then decreases slightly. In fact, the increase in PT with developmental stage is quite common among anuran species (Dupré et al. 1986; Dupré and Petranka 1985; Wollmuth and Crawshaw 1988; Wollmuth et al. 1987). Mean PT often increases to a maximum at or near metamorphic climax, then decreases, sometimes precipitously (Wollmuth et al. 1987). In addition to selecting progressively warmer temperatures throughout development, some anuran larvae thermoregulate more precisely with advancing development, as evidenced by a decrease in the variability about the mean PT (fig. 9.15) with increasing developmental stage (Dupré et al. 1986; Dupré and Petranka 1985).

Only Keen and Schroeder (1975) have reported a developmental shift (suggested by size) in PT of a urodele, the smallmouth salamander, *Ambystoma texanum* (Ambystomatidae), which, like most anurans, selects progressively warmer temperatures during early development but lower temperatures during late development; no clear trend was discernible for *A. maculatum*. To the contrary, Dupré and Petranka (1985) found no difference in the PT of developing *A. texanum*. Thermal preferences of larvae of the red-bellied newt, *Taricha rivularis* (Salamandridae), also do not change during development, nor are they significantly different from PTs of

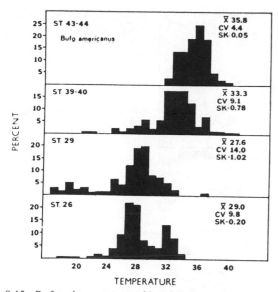

Fig. 9.15 Preferred temperatures of larval *Bufo americanus* as a function of stage of development. *st.*, stage of development; *cv*, coefficient of variation; *sk*, coefficient of skewness. Stages in original paper have been converted to those of Gosner (1960). (Reprinted, by permission, from Dupré and Petranka 1985.)

terrestrial adults (Licht and Brown 1967). Future studies of the developmental aspects of urodele behavioral thermoregulation are required to determine whether any trends exist.

Social Influences

Most laboratory studies of larval PT examined groups of individuals in a thermal gradient (table 9.2); the PT of lone animals is often not determined (e.g., Beiswenger 1978; Dupré and Petranka 1985; Licht and Brown 1967; Spotila 1972). Among larval forms, larval *Rana catesbeiana* display no differences between individuals and groups (Dupré et al. 1986). The PT of individual adults and those tested in groups do not differ in *Aneides lugubris* (Caudata: Plethodontidae; Rosenthal 1957), *Hyla regilla* (Anura: Hylidae; Claussen 1973) or *Rana esculenta* (Cabanac and Jeddi 1971). However, *H. crucifer* tested in groups of three to four had a higher mean PT (25.9°C) than those tested individually (23.8°C; Gatten and Hill 1984). More studies are needed to determine the extent and possible role of social influences on thermoregulatory behavior of both adults and larvae. Changes in social influences during different parts of the daily and seasonal activity cycles, group size, body size, and other factors need examination. Appropriate laboratory studies may provide information on the thermal aspects of aggregations and migrations of animals in the field. Social interactions clearly affect thermal distributions and behavior in other ectothermic vertebrates (Beitinger and Magnuson 1975; Regal 1971). Temperature influences selection of territories in bluegills (*Lepomis macrochirus*); subordinates are excluded from their PT by agonistic behavior of dominants (Medvick, Magnuson, and Sharr 1981). Interactions among and between species in a community can result in temperospatial partitioning of the thermal habitat and thereby govern thermoregulatory behaviors.

In the presence of a predator (bass, *Micropterus salmoides*) bluegills had significantly higher avoidance temperatures in a shuttlebox than in the absence of a predator (Fischer, Standora, and Spotila 1987). Similar studies on amphibians, especially on larval forms, would be useful.

Diel and Seasonal Cycles

Ectotherms not only thermoregulate through the behavioral exploitation of the spatial heterogeneity of heat provided by different microhabitats, but also of the temporal diversity provided by the natural daily and annual cycling of the thermal environment. Diel cycles in thermoregulatory behavior are well documented in ectothermic vertebrates, particularly in fishes and reptiles (Avery 1982; Hutchison and Maness 1979), but relatively few amphibians have been examined for such cyclic responses (table 9.2). The reported absence of diel cycles of PT or locomotor activity may result from improper sampling periods, "unnatural" conditions of experimental lighting, inadequate acclimation regimes, constraints placed on the animal by the experimental apparatus, and so forth. The diel cycles may also vary with season and not be expressed at certain times of the year. Diel cycles of PT are lacking in *Bufo boreas* (Smits 1984), *Plethodon cinereus* (Caudata: Plethodontidae; Feder and Pough 1975b), and larval *Rana cascadae* (Wollmuth et al. 1987). By contrast, the strictly aquatic salamander *Necturus maculosus* (Proteidae), acclimated to 15°C and an LD 12:12 photoperiod, exhibits significant diel and seasonal cycles of both PT and activity (Hutchison and Spriestersbach 1986b). Both activity and mean PT are highest during scotophase (fig. 9.16), as would be expected for this nocturnal species. Although this study required 4 years of observations and more than three hundred animals, it was limited by the use of only one AT and one photoperiod. The relevance of one AT and one photoperiod to the study of annual cycles is questionable. Investigations with appropriate and more natural combinations of temperature and day length (e.g., short photophase and longer scotophase at winter temperatures and the reverse for summer) for each season of the year are needed. However, the time and number of animals required for such studies are formidable (Hutchison and Spriestersbach 1986a).

The significance of diel cycles in PT in ectotherms probably rests ultimately on the optimization of the utilization of energy; an example is the bioenergetic model of thermoregulatory behavior in sockeye salmon described in the now classic work by Brett (1971). The ability of ectotherms to select environments that produce a low T_b during inactive periods or when food is scarce may be highly adaptive. Maintenance of T_b near the physiological optimum throughout each diel period, with accompanying higher metabolic rate and increased energy requirements, would be wasteful (Hutchison and Maness 1979; Pough 1980). Differences in diel cycles of PT may aid resource partitioning in the environments of co-occurring and, especially, closely related species, but apparently no such studies of amphibians are comparable to those of fishes. Differences in timing in the use of the thermal environment might result in a niche segregation that would reduce competition for energy sources (Reynolds and Casterlin 1978). Aquatic communities with two or more species of po-

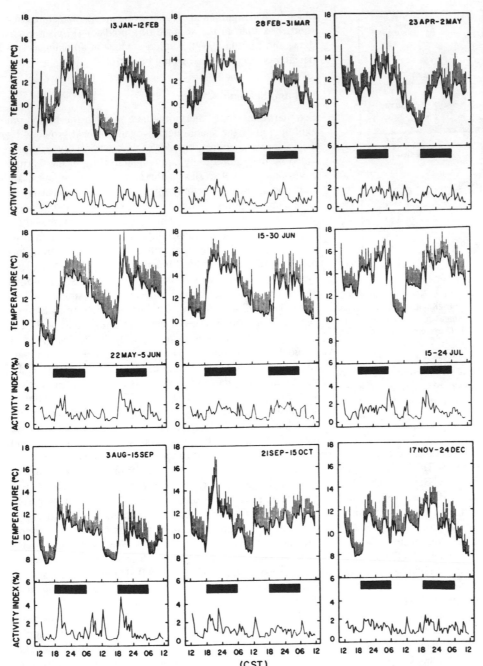

Fig. 9.16 Daily thermal selection and activity at different times of the year in the mudpuppy, *Necturus maculosus*, over 2-day periods in a linear thermal gradient after acclimatization at 15°C and a photoperiod of LD 12:12 for at least 2 weeks. (Reprinted, by permission, from Hutchison and Spriestersbach 1986a.)

tentially competing amphibian larvae might be an appropriate system in which to address such questions.

Physiological Thermoregulation

Physiological regulation of T_b among amphibians is more limited than in other ectothermic vertebrate groups. Regional endothermy of the swimming muscles in some fishes and the facultative endothermy of brooding pythons are obvious examples of physiological thermoregulation. No such specialized mechanisms for heat production occur in amphibians. Physiological thermoregulation in amphibians appears to be limited to comparatively minor cardiovascular adjustments, which may alter rates of heating and cooling. An ectotherm

with a cooling rate slower than the heating rate could presumably lengthen the time spent at a more favorable T_b. Dead animals heat and cool at the same rate. Compared with reptiles, amphibians apparently have rather limited differences between heating and cooling rates and thus less control over the underlying cardiovascular mechanisms. Thus, few such studies have examined amphibians. Heating and cooling rates are determined by exchanging animals between high and low constant temperatures and measuring the rates of change in T_b. Results of such measurements can be influenced by type of medium (water or air), saturation deficit of the air, flow of the medium, body size, location of T_b measurement, and so forth. The methods used for calculating rates in ectotherms have varied widely (e.g., the time for an animal to gain or lose 50%, or some other fraction, of the difference between initial and final T_b; the rate coefficient from Newton's law of cooling; various other time constants based on regression equations of time versus temperature change).

The strictly aquatic salamander *Amphiuma means* (Amphiumidae) has very limited capacity for physiological adjustment of heating and cooling rates. The half-times of fifteen *Amphiuma* (77–784 g) subjected to reciprocal transfers between 22.1° and 28.3°C differed by less than 7% (Bohlin and Beitinger 1979). The lack of hysteresis in heating-cooling curves contrasts with many heliothermic reptiles, in which cooling is significantly slower than heating (Bartholomew 1982).

Heating and cooling rates of bullfrogs (*R. catesbeiana*) switched between 10° and 30°C are not different in air or water; heart rate is significantly higher during heating than during cooling in water, but not in air. The difference in the heart rates in water probably results from the oxygen demands of cutaneous respiration (Tripp and Lustick 1974).

When exposed to step temperature changes from 15° to 30°C, equilibration T_b's were significantly higher in *Hyla cinerea* (26.6°C) than in *Rana sphenocephala* (18.1°C). Rates of temperature change were 2.5 times higher in *Hyla* than in *Rana*, perhaps due to a reduced skin evaporative heat loss in the treefrog (Wygoda 1988a). Wygoda (1989b, 145) suggested that the calculation of thermal time constants in anurans may "be appropriate for intraspecific comparisons of heat exchange and interspecific comparisons of cooling, but not interspecific comparisons of heating."

The core T_b and dorsal subcutaneous temperatures rise more rapidly in dead bullfrogs than in live controls when placed under a heat lamp. In live frogs the dorsal integument temperature reaches a plateau, while both the substrate and core temperatures continue to rise. A bullfrog covered with oil had a heating curve almost identical to that of a lizard (*Dipsosaurus dorsalis*). These results suggest that the requirement to maintain the skin in a state of relative hydration governs cutaneous blood circulation during basking (Lillywhite 1975). These data furnish another example of the conflict in amphibians between hydro- and thermoregulatory mechanisms under some environmental conditions.

Blood viscosity is inversely related to temperature. In *R. catesbeiana* mean viscosity decreases exponentially from 4.55 cP at 10°C to 2.55 cP at 30°C, a change of 44%. Large variations in viscosity observed between individuals are probably due to large individual-to-individual variations in hematocrit (Langille and Crisp 1980). Such a major temperature dependence of blood viscosity will significantly influence heating and cooling rates. Although active regulation of cutaneous blood flow is important in the thermoregulation of ectothermic vertebrates, differences in heating and cooling rates cannot be assumed to indicate physiological thermoregulation; such differences may result, at least in part, from temperature-induced changes in blood viscosity (Langille and Crisp 1980). In amphibians large variations in heating-cooling curves may result from wide variations in hematocrit, due in part to fairly large fluctuations in the state of body hydration. Carefully controlled *in vivo* studies are needed to assess the influences of temperature on blood viscosity, hematocrit, and cutaneous perfusion.

Although amphibians may have limited abilities to produce large hystereses in heating-cooling curves, they do have some control over blood flow to the skin and microvascular regulation of cutaneous gas exchange (Burggren 1988b; Malvin 1988). Such studies on changes in perfusion have focused largely on respiratory gas exchange; similar investigations on the role of temperature are needed. The clearance rate of inert gases from the skin, used to quantify diffusion (Feder, Full, and Piiper 1988), may allow investigations on the effects of temperature on the regional distribution of blood and the resultant heat exchange between animal and environmental medium. However, such studies will be complicated by the conflict between thermoregulatory and respiratory control mechanisms. Thus, amphibians have three major and often conflicting processes at the organism-environment interface: hydroregulation, thermoregulation, and respiratory gas exchange. The characteristics of the boundary layer of the environmental medium at this interface may significantly impact all three of these regulatory processes.

Skin Reflectance   Color in animals has three major functions: communication (usually with conspecifics), protective coloration (cryptic, aposematic, pseudoaposematic), and thermoregulation. An unambiguous definition of color is given only by a complete reflectance curve at an appropriately wide range of wavelengths within the electromagnetic spectrum. Some biologically important wavelengths, particularly within the ultraviolet and near-infrared, are not within the visual range of humans and many other animals. However, the greatest energy (about 79%) in solar radiation falls between 400 and 1,100 nm (List 1951), which includes the range of vision in humans (400 to 700 nm). Wavelengths above 1,500 nm contain only about 7 to 9% of the total energy in solar radiation; at longer wavelengths animals are close to blackbodies in absorption and emission, and "color" has little bearing on thermal exchange. Human color discrimination is often not accurate in terms of the judgment of "light" versus "dark" skin. In metachrotic chorus frogs (*Pseudacris triseriata* [Hylidae]), green frogs with a "lighter" color to the human eye actually absorb more light than brown ("darker") frogs (Hoppe 1979).

Color change as an important mechanism for thermoregulation in ectothermic vertebrates has been studied mostly in lizards (Bartholomew 1982). Very few such studies have been made on amphibians. Amphibians exposed to cold temperatures and darkness often show a darkening of the integument as a result of melanophorotropic hormone release (see chapter 3); at higher temperatures and in light the animals tend to blanch as a result of melanophore contraction (Moriya and Miyashita 1989). Gray treefrogs (*Hyla versicolor* [Hylidae]) are brown under constant light and green in constant darkness and tend to darken at colder temperatures (Edgren 1954). Green frogs (*Rana clamitans*) show a regional metachrosis of body surfaces: body parts exposed to direct sunlight are bright green; portions in the shade or under water are bronze or dark olive-green (Porter 1972). A similar regional metachrosis occurs in the leaf frog, *Agalychnis dacnicolor* (Hylidae; Iga and Bagnara 1975). The darker skin typical of cooled *Bufo boreas* absorbs about 4% more of incident solar radiation than lighter (warmer) skin (Carey 1978b). Differences in skin color are not likely to have a significant impact on the heating rate of this toad, although a lighter skin would achieve a lower temperature equilibrium between body and environment and thus contribute to the prevention of overheating. Temperature during development influences the expression of color polymorphism in the ornate chorus frog, *Pseudacris ornata* (Harkey and Semlitsch 1988).

As an adaptation to an arid environment during dry seasons in African savannas, the reed frog (*Hyperolius viridiflavus* [Hyperoliidae]) can greatly increase the number of iridophores (purine crystals; see chapter 6). These iridophores represented up to 35% of the total nitrogenous wastes during 42 days of water deprivation, and accumulated 100 to 150 μg per milligram of dry mass of the skin. As an osmoregulatory mechanism, the deposition of the osmotically inert and nontoxic purine would prevent the accumulation of lethal levels of osmolarity, if all nitrogenous wastes were in the form of urea (Schmuck and Linsenmair 1988). The deposition of the iridophores may also have a major impact on thermoregulatory abilities through a greatly increased skin reflectance and the reduction of heat load by radiation remission (Kobelt and Linsenmair 1986; Schmuck and Linsenmair 1988; Schmuck, Kobelt, and Linsenmair 1988; Withers, Louw, and Nicolson 1982). The "waterproof" frogs (*Chiromantis* [Rhacophoridae]) have a layer of dermal iridophores in which the pigment is dispersed during the hot (40°C) portion of the day to increase skin reflectance and thereby reduce radiant heat gain (Shoemaker pers. comm.). Neotropical leaf-sitting glass frogs (*Centrolenella fleischmanni, C. prosoblepon* [Centrolenidae]) and treefrogs (*Agalychnis moreletti, Pachymedusa dacnicolor* [both Hylidae]) reflect light in the near-infrared (700–900 nm). This reflectance in the infrared and the frogs' green color in visible light would tend to make them indistinguishable from their leaf backgrounds to predators with vision in the visible (human) and near-infrared portion of the spectrum. The infrared reflectance may also serve in thermoregulation (Schwalm, Starrett, and McDiarmid 1977). Skin water permeability and cutaneous chromatophore regulation in amphibians are not directly related (Tercafs 1966).

The role of skin reflectance in thermoregulatory processes in amphibians is highly complex due to likely competition with other regulatory mechanisms, particularly hydroregulation and cutaneous respiratory gas exchange. The heat resulting from an increased absorption of radiation by amphibians vaporizes water from the wet skin; in animals with relatively dry skin, such as in most reptiles, the heat gained is available for storage and thus an elevation of T_b. Amphibian T_b may thus be little influenced by increased absorption of radiation (Tracy 1976, 1979b). Absorbed radiation at the skin surface of amphibians may also directly affect cutaneous gas exchange through increased skin blood perfusion due to local heating; it may have an indirect effect through changes in the rate of water loss.

Thyroid Hormones Thyroid hormones are critical to the hypermetabolic responses of endotherms to cold. The role of thyroid hormones in the physiology of amphibians has also been appreciated, but primarily for its role in inducing metamorphosis (White and Nicoll 1981; see also chapter 16).

Thyroid hormones also appear to play a significant role in the modulation of thermoregulation in amphibians. Larvae of the leopard frog, *Rana pipiens*, immersed in 10 μg · l^{-1} L-thyroxine, selected modal temperatures of 15°–19°C (table 9.3), lower than the modal temperatures of 23°–30°C selected by untreated larvae; when thyroxine treatment was discontinued 48 h before determining thermal preferences,

TABLE 9.3   The Effect of Naturally Occurring Hormones on Temperature Selection by Amphibians

Hormone and Species	N	AT	Dose	Route	PT Control	PT Treatment	Comments	Reference
Histamine,	10–13	15	0.01 mg·kg^{-1}	Ip	12.0	10.9	Day 1	Hutchison and Spriestersbach 1986b
Necturus maculosus	10–13	15	0.1 mg·kg^{-1}	Ip	12.0	9.2	Day 1	
	10–13	15	0.5 mg·kg^{-1}	Ip	8.9	11.0	Day 2	
	10–13	15	1.0 mg·kg^{-1}	Ip	10.9	12.0	Day 1, Sep	
	10–13	15	1.0 mg·kg^{-1}	Ip	10.0	11.0	Day 1, Nov	
	10–13	5	1.0 mg·kg^{-1}	Ip	8.6	10.8	Day 1	
	10–13	5	1.0 mg·kg^{-1}	Ip	7.9	10.0	Day 2	
	10–13	15	0.25 mg·kg^{-1}	Ivent	9.7	11.8	Day 2	
Melatonin,	10	15	4 mg·kg^{-1}	Ip	13.6	9.7	Day 1	Hutchison, Black, and Erskine 1979
Necturus maculosus	10	15	4 mg·kg^{-1}	Ip	13.6	7.4	Day 2	
Neurotensin,	4–6	15	7.5 μg	Ivent	20.5	20.0	Day 1	Hutchison 1981
Necturus maculosus	4–6	15	7.5 μg	Ivent	18.3	20.9	Day 2	
Prostaglandin E$_1$								
Rana esculenta	5	20?	2.5 μg	Ivent	25–28	32–35		Myhre, Cabanac, and Myhre 1977
Necturus maculosus	9	15	2.5 μg	Ivent	12.6	17.3	Day 1	Hutchison and Erskine 1981
	9	15	2.5 μg	Ivent	11.9	16.8	Day 2	
L-thyroxine								
Rana pipiens (larvae)	15	20	10 μg·l^{-1}	Immersion	23–30	15–19		Lucas and Reynolds 1967
Xenopus laevis	13	25	2.5 × 10^{-8} M	Immersion	25.3	24.3		Dupré, Just, and Ritchart 1986
L-triiodothyronine,								
Xenopus laevis	13	25	2.5 × 10^{-8} M	Immersion	25.2	26.1		Dupré, Just, and Ritchart 1986

Note: AT = acclimation temperature; Ip = introperitoneal; Ivent = injection into third ventricle; N = sample size (individuals); PT = preferred (selected) temperature.

larvae selected a modal temperature of about 30°C (Lucas and Reynolds 1967). These findings are consistent with data from thyroxine-treated clawed frogs, *Xenopus laevis,* where immersion in 2.5 × 10⁻⁸ M L-thyroxine promoted a decrease in mean PT from 25.3°C to 24.3°C (Dupré, Just, and Ritchart 1986). A thyroxine-stimulated decline in temperature selection also occurs in other aquatic ectotherms: goldfish, *Carassius auratus,* and bluegill sunfish, *Lepomis macrochirus* (Reynolds, Casterlin, and Spieler 1982).

The precise mechanism by which thyroxine promotes the selection of lower temperatures by ectotherms is not clear. Both Lucas and Reynolds (1967) and Reynolds, Casterlin, and Spieler (1982) suggested that the thermoregulatory response might be related to a calorigenic effect of thyroid hormones; that is, thyroxine-treated amphibians select lower temperatures to facilitate loss of the additional heat produced due to thyroid hormone stimulation of metabolism.

While the importance of a calorigenic role of thyroid hormones in the maintenance of T_b of mammals and birds is well established, that thyroid hormones increase oxygen consumption in amphibians is equivocal. Thyroxine treatment has no effect on the oxygen consumption of *Bufo spinulosus* (Marusic, Martinez, and Torretti 1966). Similarly, treatment with thyroxine or propylthiouracil, a thyroid poison, does not alter oxygen consumption of metamorphosing (Parker 1967) or adult *R. pipiens* (Galton and Ingbar 1962). Neither thyroxine nor triiodothyronine affected oxygen consumption of the clawed frog, *X. laevis* (Dupré, Just, and Ritchart 1986).

Where differences in oxygen consumption of amphibians occur after thyroid hormone treatment, they are often temperature dependent. Thyroxine treatment (1 μg · 10 g⁻¹ body mass) produces a 25–50% rise in oxygen consumption of *R. pipiens* acclimated for 1–2 weeks at 20° and 25°C, but not of those acclimated at 10° or 15°C (Maher 1967). By contrast, thyroxine stimulates oxygen consumption of *Bufo woodhousii* acclimated to a wide range of temperatures (Maher 1967). Likewise, *R. pipiens* injected with 100 μg thyroxine · 100 g⁻¹ body mass · day⁻¹ for about 27 days at 18°C show a slight but nonsignificant increase in oxygen consumption, whereas oxygen consumption of thyroxine-treated frogs at 30°C increases by about 33% by day 14 and remains elevated until thyroxine treatment ceases (McNabb 1969).

Whether or not thyroid hormones are calorigenic in amphibians, these hormones are probably not the stimuli for the selection of lower temperatures associated with thyroxine treatment. Increased oxygen consumption by itself, as induced by 2,4-dinitrophenol treatment, does not significantly alter temperature selection in *X. laevis*. Further, the form of thyroid hormone makes a difference as to the behavioral thermoregulatory response of *X. laevis;* thyroxine promotes the selection of lower temperatures as previously noted (table 9.3), while the identical dose of triiodothyronine results in the selection of warmer temperatures (Dupré, Just, and Ritchart 1986), a trend more consistent with developmental changes in thermal preference discussed earlier in this chapter.

The Pineal Complex and Melatonin

The pineal complex, consisting of an extraoptic photosensitive frontal organ or stirnorgan (in some groups) and the pineal organ (epiphysis cerebri), is important in gathering and integrating photic characteristics of the environment (Ralph, Firth, and Turner 1979). In this capacity, the pineal complex has been associated with orientation to light (Adler and Taylor 1973; Hamasaki and Eder 1977; Justis and Taylor 1976; Taylor and Adler 1978) and the integration of circadian and/or seasonal rhythms (Adler 1976; Demian and Taylor 1977; Justis and Taylor 1976).

The pineal complex also influences ectotherm thermoregulation. Because ectotherms rely on environmental heat sources and sinks for regulating T_b, the ability to orient to or away from the light of the sun is an important aspect of behavioral thermoregulation in which the pineal complex plays a role. Parietalectomy (i.e., removal of the parietal eye, the reptilian counterpart to the frontal organ) of the lizard, *Anolis carolinensis* results in the selection of higher temperatures than sham-operated controls (Hutchison and Kosh 1974). Similarly, parietalectomized *Sceloporus magister* regulate T_b about 0.5°–1.5°C higher than control or sham-operated lizards. Removal of the pineal gland of the lizards *S. occidentalis* and *Crotaphytus collaris* results in lower PTs (Firth, Ralph, and Boardman 1980; Firth, Mauldin, and Ralph 1988; Stebbins 1960) as compared to sham-operated animals. Furthermore, pinealectomized *C. collaris* are less precise thermoregulators than control lizards (Firth, Ralph, and Boardman 1980).

Shielding of the frontal organ of both the leopard frog, *Rana pipiens,* and the toad *Bufo terrestris* results in an increase in time of exposure to higher light intensities and concomitant higher temperatures (Adkins 1961). In some instances, prolonged exposure following frontal organ shielding led to death due to desiccation.

Melatonin, the predominant substance associated with the pineal organ and whose levels fluctuate rhythmically with light cycle (Ralph, Firth, and Turner 1979), also modulates ectotherm thermoregulation. Exogenous melatonin influences behavioral thermoregulation by *C. collaris;* collared lizards select significantly warmer temperatures during photophase and lower temperatures during scotophase (Cothran and Hutchison 1979). Intraperitoneal injection of exogenous melatonin significantly decreases the panting threshold of the agamid lizard *Amphibolurus muricatus;* serotonin, another pineal substance, increases panting threshold (Firth and Heatwole 1976). In addition, melatonin treatment eliminates the normal diel variation in panting threshold of *A. muricatus,* with significant decreases in the normally higher photophase values (Chong, Heatwole, and Firth 1973). In the turtle *Terrapene carolina triunguis* intraperitoneal injection of either melatonin or chlorpromazine (which blocks degradation of circulating melatonin) decreases mean PT (Erskine and Hutchison 1981).

To date, studies on the role of melatonin in amphibian thermoregulation are few. As shown in figure 9.17, intraperitoneal injection of melatonin (4 mg · kg⁻¹) and chlorpromazine (25 mg · kg⁻¹) to *Necturus maculosus* (Caudata: Proteidae) decreases mean PT from about 13°–15°C to about 7°–8°C (Hutchison, Black, and Erskine 1979). Melatonin and chlorpromazine also produced dose-dependent decreases in thermal tolerance (as measured by CTMax) of *N. maculosus,* providing further support of melatonin's role in lowering PT (Erskine and Hutchison 1982). Furthermore, exogenous melatonin eliminates the typical diel cycle of temperature selection in *N. maculosus* (Hutchison, Black, and Erskine 1979;

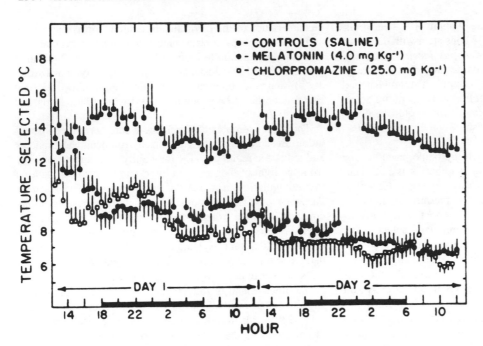

Fig. 9.17 The effect of melatonin and chlorpromazine on preferred temperatures in *Necturus maculosus*. Data are presented as mean ± 1 SE for ten animals. *Black bars* indicate the scotophase of a light-dark 12:12 photoperiod. Injections were made at 1200 each day. (Reprinted, by permission, from Hutchison, Black, and Erskine 1979.)

Hutchison and Spriestersbach 1986b), suggesting that daily fluctuations in melatonin concentration may be involved in establishing this thermoregulatory rhythmicity.

Melatonin synthesis in vertebrates is largely under photic control. Diel cycles of different photoperiods produce corresponding changes in cycles of melatonin production. In paedomorphic tiger salamanders (*Ambystoma tigrinum* [Ambystomatidae]) a T_b of 20°C causes a significant depression in plasma melatonin during the scotophase (when melatonin titers are maximum) in contrast to high melatonin titers at 10°C. Thus, environmental temperature as well as light may influence melatonin production (Gern, Norris, and Duvall 1983).

Melatonin may also affect thermoregulation through its effect on skin color. Melatonin promotes melanosome aggregation of dermal melanophores: that is, melanosomes concentrate in the center of the melanophore, resulting in a blanching of the skin (see also chapter 16). Subcutaneous injection of melatonin in the middorsum of *Chiromantis xerampelina* (Rhacophoridae) results in a blanching of the legs and lower flank (V. H. Shoemaker pers. comm.). Larval *Xenopus laevis* pinealectomized by cauterization of the diencephalic roof do not exhibit the body blanching typical of these larvae when placed in the dark (Bagnara 1960). Whether or not melatonin is important in the modulation of color for thermoregulation requires further studies.

Catecholamines The calorigenic action of catecholamines in mammals and birds is well established. However, few data exist on the role of catecholamines in ectotherm thermoregulation. Administration of norepinephrine to lateral cerebral ventricles of the monitor lizard, *Varanus albigularis albigularis,* did not effect thermoregulation (Bligh, Louw, and Young 1976). However, microinjections of norepinephrine into the anterior aspect of the nucleus preopticus periventricularis of the goldfish, *Carassius auratus,* resulted in a dose-dependent decrease in PT (Wollmuth, Crawshaw, and Panayiotides-Djaferis 1987), which is apparently mediated by both α_1- and α_2-adrenergic receptors (Wollmuth, Crawshaw, and Rausch 1988).

Catecholamines have a calorigenic effect in the frog *Rana temporaria,* where injections of 0.2 mg · kg^{-1} epinephrine and 5 mg · kg^{-1} norepinephrine significantly increase (by as much as 50%) oxygen consumption (Harri and Hedenstam 1972). Although amphibians do not possess sufficient insulation to utilize effectively additional heat production for thermoregulation, calorigenesis has been implicated in behavioral thermoregulatory responses to thyroid hormones as already mentioned (Lucas and Reynolds 1967; Reynolds, Casterlin, and Spieler 1982).

Another potential role for the catecholamines in amphibian thermoregulation is their effect on peripheral thermoreceptor activity. Sympathetic stimulation elicits a shift in the temperature-specific activity of cutaneous cold receptors of *R. pipiens,* such that maximum activity occurs at a lower temperature (Spray 1974). If activity of these thermoreceptors provides thermal cues for behavioral thermoregulation, such a decrease in static maximum temperature might be associated with a decrease in thermal preference similar to that reported for goldfish.

Catecholamines may also be important in the modulation of evaporative water loss during thermoregulatory "sweating" in amphibians. Evaporative water loss increases in a dose-dependent fashion with epinephrine administered subcutaneously in the middle of the back of *Chiromantis xerampelina,* apparently via β-adrenergic receptor mediation (Kaul and Shoemaker 1989).

Catecholamines may also modulate color change in amphibians. Subcutaneous administration of epinephrine to *C. xerampelina* resulted in skin blanching from the middorsum injection site (V. H. Shoemaker pers. comm.).

Acetylcholine Cholinergic compounds affect thermoregulation in vertebrates. Injection of the cholinomimetic compound carbachol into the lateral cerebral ventricles of the monitor lizard, *Varanus a. albigularis,* significantly increases panting threshold (Bligh, Louw, and Young 1976). Immersion of the fish *Chromus chromus* in the muscarinic cholinomimetic substance oxotremorine decreases escape temperatures from a warm tank (upper exit temperature of a dual threshold model for behavioral thermoregulation). Atropine, but not an equal concentration of scopolamine (another anticholinergic compound), blocks this response. Atropine alone produces no statistically significant rise in escape temperature (Green and Lomax 1976).

Injection of oxotremorine into the third ventricle of *Necturus maculosus* (table 9.4) produces no significant changes in mean PT (Hutchison 1981). Neither does intraventricular administration of scopolamine to *N. maculosus* have a consistent effect on behavioral thermoregulation.

Acetylcholine and related cholinergic compounds promote a dose-dependent excitation of cutaneous cold receptors in *R. pipiens* (Spray and Galansky 1975). Activity is enhanced at low doses and becomes refractory at higher concentrations, suggesting that cholinergic compounds depolarize these thermal receptors. Such an increase in the temperature-dependent activity could lead to an upward shift in static maximum temperature of the cold receptors. Assuming that cutaneous cold receptors represent the sensors defining the lower exit temperature of a dual-limit hypothesis for ectothermic behavioral thermoregulation, cholinergic substances should promote an increase in mean PT of anurans, analogous to the elevated panting threshold of *V. a. albigularis* (Bligh, Louw, and Young 1976).

TABLE 9.4   The Effect of Pharmacological Agents on Temperature Selection by Amphibians

Pharmacological Agent and Species	N	AT	Dose	Route	PT Control	PT Treatment	Comments	Reference
2,4-dinitrophenol, *Xenopus laevis*	8	25	1 μM	Immersion	25.9	25.6	Uncouples electron transport, increases O_2 consumption.	Dupré, Just, and Ritchart 1986
Chlorpromazine, *Necturus maculosus*	10	15	25 mg·kg^{-1}	Ip	13.6	8.7	Day 1, blocks melatonin break down.	Hutchison, Black, and Erskine 1979
	10	15	25 mg·kg^{-1}	Ip	13.6	7.0	Day 2.	
Oxotremorine, *Necturus maculosus*	10	15	10 μg·kg^{-1}	Ivent	15.5	15.4	Day 1, muscarinic cholinomimetic.	Hutchison 1981
	10	15	10 μg·kg^{-1}	Ivent	16.0	15.7	Day 2.	
Scopolamine, *Necturus maculosus*	10	15	10 μg·kg^{-1}	Ivent	15.8	14.6	Day 1, anticholinergic.	Hutchison 1981
	10	15	10 μg·kg^{-}	Ivent	14.6	15.2	Day 2.	
L-histidine, *Necturus maculosus*	10–13	15	500 mg·kg^{-1}	Ip	10.4	11.2	Day 1, histamine precursor.	Hutchison and Spriestersbach 1986b
	10–13	5	500 mg·kg^{-1}	Ip	9.8	12.3	Day 1.	
Cimetidine, *Necturus maculosus*	10–13	15	25.2 mg·kg^{-1}	Ip	11.7	12.6	Day 1, histamine H_2-receptor antagonist.	Hutchison and Spriestersbach 1986b
	10–13	15	0.50 mg·kg^{-1}	Ivent	11.6	12.5	Day 1.	
Pyrilamine, *Necturus maculosus*	10–13	15	5 mg·kg^{-1}	Ip	11.9	10.7	Day 2, histamine H_1-receptor antagonist.	Hutchison and Spriestersbach 1986b
	10–13	15	5 mg·kg^{-1}	Ip	13.4	11.1	Day 1.	
	10–13	15	50 mg·kg^{-1}	Ip	14.0	9.5	Day 2.	
	10–13	15	0.1 mg·kg^{-1}	Ivent	11.3	10.6	Day 2.	
Dimaprit, *Necturus maculosus*	10–13	15	0.01 mg·kg^{-1}	Ivent	11.1	10.6	Day 2, histamine H_2-agonist.	Hutchison and Spriestersbach 1986b
	10–13	15	0.10 mg·kg^{-1}	Ivent	15.4	14.2	Day 1.	
	10–13	15	0.20 mg·kg^{-1}	Ivent	12.1	9.6	Day 2.	
2-pyridylethylamine, *Necturus maculosus*	10–13	15	0.01 mg·kg^{-1}	Ivent	11.7	10.3	Day 1, histamine H_1-agonist.	Hutchison and Spriestersbach 1986b
	10–13	15	0.01 mg·kg^{-1}	Ivent	13.4	9.2	Day 2.	
	10–13	15	0.1 mg·kg^{-1}	Ivent	9.9	11.4	Day 2.	
Ethanol, *Necturus maculosus*	11	15	3 mg·kg^{-1}	Ip	12.7	12.4	Day 1, nervous system depressant.	Hutchison 1981
	11	15	3 mg·kg^{-1}	Ip	10.9	11.5	Day 2.	
Capsaicin *Necturus maculosus*	10–11	15	25 mg·kg^{-1}	Sc	14.3	11.2	Day 1, stimulates substance P secretion.	Hutchison 1981
	10–11	15	25 mg·kg^{-1}	Sc	11.1	14.2	Day 2.	
Rana esculenta	7	25	20 mg·kg^{-1}	Ip	25	3	Within 1 h.	Cormarèche-Leydier 1986
	4	25	20 mg·kg^{-1}	Ip	25	15	7–24 days after injection.	

Notes: AT = acclimation temperature; Ip = intraperitoneal; Ivent = injection into third ventricle; N sample size (individuals); PT = preferred (selected) temperature; Sc = subcutaneous.

Many cholinergic agonists and antagonists produce effects that differ from those expected from typical muscarinic and nicotinic stimulation/antagonism (Spray and Galansky 1975). These differences, along with the mixed effect of scopolamine on behavioral thermoregulation by *N. maculosus* in the absence of an influence by oxotremorine (Hutchison 1981), support the contention that fundamental differences may exist among the cholinergic receptors of vertebrates (Green and Lomax 1976).

Histamine Histamine, a putative neurotransmitter in the brains of mammals, also appears to affect thermoregulation by ectothermic vertebrates. Histamine administered in the aquarium water to the fish *Chromus chromus* significantly increases upper escape temperature (Green and Lomax 1976). Because this action is blocked by the simultaneous administration of pyrilamine, the hyperthermic response appears mediated through H_1-type histamine receptors, the specific receptors at which pyrilamine exerts its histamine-antagonistic effect. Although imidazole acetic acid, a metabolite of histamine, administered at dosages similar to those for histamine did not produce a change in upper escape temperature, a higher dosage (10 mg $\cdot$ l^{-1}) resulted in a slight (nonsignificant) increase.

Histamine also affects thermoregulation by the mudpuppy, *Necturus maculosus* (fig. 9.18). Low doses of histamine (0.01 and 0.1 mg $\cdot$ kg^{-1}) administered via intraperitoneal injection produce significantly lower PTs (table 9.3); higher dosages (0.5 and 1.0 mg $\cdot$ kg^{-1}) promote the selection of significantly higher T_b's (Hutchison and Spriestersbach 1986b). Intraperitoneal administration of pyrilamine produces a significant decrease in PT, suggesting that the behavioral hyperthermia observed following histamine administration at high doses is mediated by H_1-receptors as in *C. chromus*. Alternatively, the behavioral hypothermia ("heat seeking") exhibited by *N. maculosus* at low histamine dosages appears to be the result of stimulation of H_2-type histamine receptors.

Initially, thermoregulatory responses of both the fish and mudpuppy appear to be opposite to those of histamine-treated mammals in which H_1-receptor stimulation lowers body temperature and H_2-receptor activation promotes a hyperthermia (Dhawan, Shukla, and Srimal 1982). However, the hyperthermia of ectotherms may be the behavioral equivalent of an autonomic lowering of T_b by endotherms (Hutchison and Spriestersbach 1986a). Similarly, the behavioral response to an autonomic increase in T_b would be selection of lower temperatures. This hypothesis is supported by the observation that rats with lower T_b's will seek out heat sources if available (Pilc and Nowak 1980).

Other Pharmacological Agents Ethanol leads to a decrease in T_b of mammals (Freund 1973; Lomax et al. 1980). Similarly, administration of ethanol to the goldfish, *Carrasius auratus*, by immersion (O'Connor et al. 1988) or intracerebroventricular injection (Crawshaw, Wollmuth, and O'Connor 1989) promotes the selection of significantly lower temperatures. However, Hutchison (1981) found no significant differences in mean PTs of saline- and ethanol-injected (intraperitoneally) *Necturus maculosus* (table 9.4).

Subcutaneous administration of capsaicin to *N. maculosus* results in a significantly lower PT than that selected by saline-injected controls on the first day of application (table 9.4); however, capsaicin-treated animals select significantly higher temperatures than controls on the second day of exposure (Hutchison 1981). These data parallel observations made of capsaicin-treated mammals where an initial dose-dependent hypothermia is typically followed by hyperthermia (Obal et al. 1979; Cabanac, Cormarèche-Leydier, and Porier 1976). Intraperitoneal injection of capsaicin similarly promotes behavioral hypothermia in *Rana esculenta;* thermal preference decreases from about 25° to 3°C (Cormarèche-Leydier 1986). At 7 to 24 days after injection, *R. esculenta* select about 15°C, still significantly lower than before treatment (table 9.4). The mechanism by which capsaicin produces its ther-

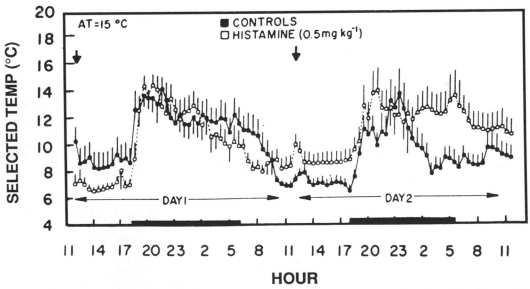

Fig. 9.18 The effect of histamine on mean PT in *Necturus maculosus*. Data are presented as mean ± 1 SE for ten animals. Injections (*vertical arrows*) were made at 1200 each day. *Black bars* indicate the scotophase of an LD 12:12 photoperiod. (From Hutchison and Spriestersbach 1986a. Reprinted with the permission of Pergamon Press PLC.)

moregulatory effects is not clear. However, capsaicin does not appear to impair the ability of *N. maculosus* to select temperatures in a heterothermal environment.

Feeding and Gastrointestinal Hormones Temperature influences several nutrient procurement processes. For example, feeding performance of adult *Bufo americanus* was tested at temperatures between 5° and 35°C in an arena with prey (mealworms) moving at a constant speed on a circular track; performance was optimal at 20°C and decreased at both higher and lower temperatures (fig. 9.19; Stevens 1988a). Temperature-dependent changes in feeding performance were much more pronounced than temperature-induced changes in metabolic rate or jumping performance (Renaud and Stevens 1983).

A behavioral increase in T_b after feeding (postprandial hyperthermia) occurs in some reptiles (Gatten 1974; Lang 1979; Lysenko and Gillis 1980; Regal 1966b; Sievert 1989), and time spent basking increases in others (Moll and Legler 1971; Regal 1966). Such a hyperthermia may facilitate digestive efficiency in lizards (Harlow, Hillman, and Hoffman 1976). Laboratory experiments by Freed (1980) showed that increased T_b in the treefrog *Hyla cinerea* (Hylidae) resulted in greater feeding and digestive rates (fig. 9.20). Postprandial thermophily has sometimes been reported where none was actually proven because investigators used (1) improper statistics, (2) inadequate sample sizes, (3) no controls, and (4) basking time alone as an indicator of T_b (Sievert 1989).

The PT increases after feeding in some of the few amphibians studied (table 9.2). Juvenile western toads, *Bufo boreas*, select temperatures of about 26°–27°C when fed as little as a single mealworm (fig. 9.21), compared with PTs of 15°–20°C by fasted toads (Lillywhite, Licht, and Chelgren 1973). Likewise, *B. boreas boreas* observed in the field increase mean PT by 0.7°C following a meal (Carey 1978b). *B. b. boreas* acclimated to 20°C in the laboratory show an even more pronounced postprandial hyperthermia, behaviorally in-

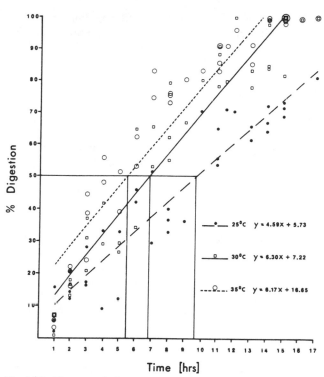

Fig. 9.20 The stomach digestion of *Hyla cinerea* as a function of time at acclimation temperatures of 25°, 30°, and 35°C. Frogs were fed houseflies. Digestion was calculated from oven dry weights of partially digested flies pumped from the stomach compared with oven dry weights of whole flies. (Reprinted, by permission, from Freed 1980.)

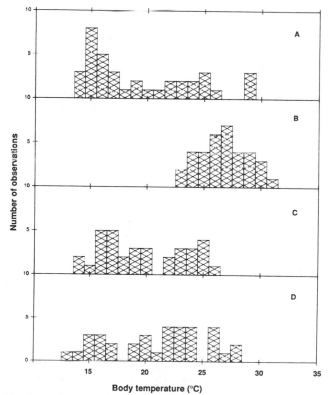

Fig. 9.21 Body temperatures of juvenile *Bufo boreas* as a function of nutritional status. *A*, fasted animals; *B*, same animals as in *A*, but 1 day following feeding; *C*, same animals as in *B*, 3 days following feeding; *D*, same animals as in *C*, 1 day following feeding of glass beads. (Redrawn from Lillywhite, Licht, and Chelgren 1973.)

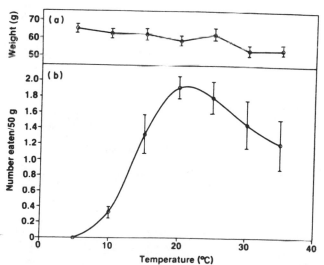

Fig. 9.19 The influence of temperature on feeding performance and body mass in *Bufo americanus*. *Vertical lines* represent ±1 SEM for nineteen toads. Animals were held at each temperature for 7 days, returned to 20°C (control) for 7 days, then exposed to a new temperature for 7 days. Photoperiod throughout was LD 12:12. (Reprinted, by permission, from Stevens 1988a.)

creasing T_b from 26.2°C to 29.3°C after feeding; *B. b. halophilus,* to the contrary, show no significant difference in PT. The PT of the plethodontid salamander *Pseudoeurycea smithii,* increases 3° to 5°C after feeding, then declines gradually over an 8–13-day period (Feder 1982c). Another plethodontid salamander, *Bolitoglossa occidentalis,* exhibits no behavioral hyperthermia following feeding. Juvenile bullfrogs also show no significant increase in T_b after feeding (Lillywhite 1971a).

Postprandial hyperthermia may facilitate digestive efficiency in lizards (Harlow, Hillman, and Hoffman 1976). In addition, increased T_b in *Hyla cinerea* increases digestive rate (fig. 9.20) and is associated with greater feeding rates; growth is greater in basking than nonbasking frogs (Freed 1980). However, assimilation efficiency (% energy content of ingested food not subsequently excreted as nitrogenous waste products or feces) is inversely related to ambient temperature in the plethodontid salamanders *Plethodon cinereus* and *P. shenandoah* (Bobka, Jaeger, and McNaught 1981). The temperature actually selected by an ectotherm following feeding will depend upon a balancing of thermally dependent changes in physiological characteristics, such as digestive efficiency and assimilation efficiency, to optimize overall performance.

The mechanism for stimulating postprandial hyperthermia has not been elucidated. However, Lillywhite, Licht, and Chelgren (1973) investigated the stimulus by force-feeding a group of juvenile *B. boreas* small glass beads instead of mealworms. Most bead-fed toads selected temperatures comparable to those selected by unfed toads. Where bead-fed toads selected warmer temperatures, the hyperthermic response was not as great, had a longer latency, and was of shorter duration than the hyperthermia exhibited by mealworm-fed toads. These data suggest that the primary stimulus for a postprandial hyperthermia is not mechanical distention of the stomach. Instead, some chemical stimulus may elicit postprandial hyperthermia, either directly from the food itself or indirectly through the secretion of gastrointestinal hormones. Hormones, many of which have potential thermo-

regulatory activity (Blatteis 1981; Brown 1981; Zetler 1982), and that are typically considered as being gastrointestinal have been identified in vertebrate brains (Blatteis 1981; Rehfeld et al. 1979; Straus and Yalow 1979). Future studies on behavioral hyperthermia after feeding might focus on the fluxes in gastrointestinal hormone concentrations following a meal and how these hormones affect thermoregulation by ectotherms.

Fever Like diverse vertebrates (Kluger 1979) and invertebrates (Cabanac and LeGuelte 1980; Reynolds, Casterlin, and Covert 1980), amphibians exhibit a behavioral fever in response to bacterial or endogenous pyrogenic agents (table 9.2). Subcutaneous injection of dead *Aeromonas hydrophila* (approximately 5×10^9 bacteria) into the green treefrog, *Hyla cinerea,* elevates mean PT more than 2°C for about 12 h (Kluger 1977). *Rana esculenta* injected intraperitoneally with pathogenic bacteria, *Mycobacterium xenopi* or *M. ranae,* also exhibit a behavioral fever with PT increasing from about 26° to about 31°C (Myhre, Cabanac, and Myhre 1977). Similar injections with bacteria that are nonpathogenic (*M. aquae*) to *R. esculenta* do not promote hyperthermia. Injection of *A. hydrophila* into larvae of the leopard frog, *R. pipiens,* and the bullfrog, *R. catesbeiana,* also elevates PTs by 2.6° and 2.7°C, respectively (Casterlin and Reynolds 1977).

Endogenous pyrogens, which may be produced in response to bacterial insult, also elicit a febrile response. *R. esculenta* injected intraperitoneally with plasma from frogs previously injected with killed *M. ranae* select warmer temperatures, elevating colonic temperature by 2.0° to 5.3°C; injection of frogs with plasma from normal untreated frogs does not affect PT. Injection of prostaglandin E_1 (PGE₁) into the diencephalon of *R. esculenta* produces (in as little as 2–3 min) a behavioral hyperthermia ranging from 5.8° to 9.7°C (Myhre, Cabanac, and Myhre 1977). Similarly, injection of PGE₁ into the third ventricle of the mudpuppy, *Necturus maculosus,* results in a relatively long-lasting behavioral fever (fig. 9.22),

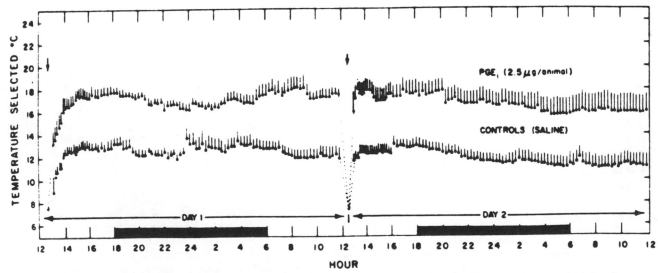

Fig. 9.22 Mean preferred temperatures of *Necturus maculosus* over a 2-day period following injection with 2.5 μg of prostaglandin E_1 in 2.5 μl saline (PGE₁) or 2.5 μl saline (control) into the third ventricle. *Vertical lines,* the SEMs of the measurements in each time period; *dashed lines,* periods of cold anesthesia. $N = 9$ on both days for experimentals; $N = 9$ on both days for controls, except $N = 8$ from 2330 to 1100 on day 1 and from 2100 to 2400 on day 2 due to mechanical malfunction. (Reprinted, by permission, from Hutchison and Erskine 1981.)

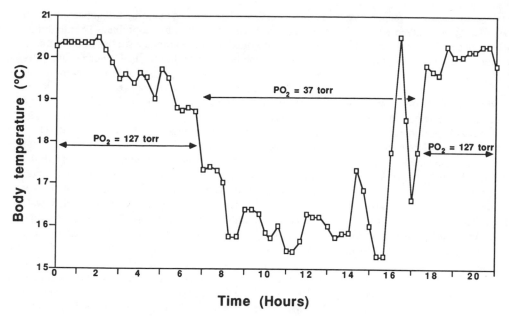

Fig. 9.23 The effect of ambient oxygen tension on preferred temperature by a typical paedomorphic tiger salamander, *Ambystoma tigrinum*. (Reprinted, by permission, from Dupré and Wood 1988.)

which is 4.7°C higher than controls on the first day after injection, and 4.9°C higher following a second injection on the second day after the initial injection (Hutchison and Erskine 1981).

Hypoxia and Hypercapnia Temperature has a profound effect on the metabolism of organisms (reflected by oxygen consumption) via a van't Hoff effect. Therefore, that oxygen availability also has an effect on thermoregulation is not surprising. Hypoxia, whether environmental (hypoxic hypoxia) or internal (anemic hypoxia), lowers T_b in virtually every animal studied. Ectotherms lower their T_b primarily by behaviorally selecting lower temperatures in a heterothermal environment. Paedomorphic tiger salamanders, *Ambystoma tigrinum*, exposed to an ambient oxygen tension of 37 mm Hg in an airtight aquatic thermal gradient, select temperatures about 2°–3°C lower than during normoxia as shown in figure 9.23 (Dupré and Wood 1988). Marine toads, *Bufo marinus*, in an airtight terrestrial gradient with free access to water, also behaviorally regulate T_b at about 29°C during normoxia, but reduce body temperature to about 18°C when ambient oxygen partial pressure (P_{O_2}) was reduced to 60 mm Hg (Riedel and Wood 1988). Anemic hypoxia will also elicit a behavioral hypothermia in amphibians. Induced anemia in *B. marinus*, brought about by an isovolumetric hemodilution to 50% of initial hematocrit, lowers PT from 24.5° to 18°C (Wood, Malvin, and Reidel 1989). However, Noland and Ultsch (1981) detected no correlation between temperature and dissolved oxygen concentration as factors influencing the distribution of larvae of the leopard frog, *R. pipiens*, and the toad *B. terrestris* in the field.

The relevance of the hypoxic hypothermia to terrestrial ectotherms has been questioned because of the extreme levels of hypoxia required to elicit the response (typically at P_{O_2}'s of 40–50 mm Hg corresponding to an altitude of about 7,000 m). Very few ectotherms occur at or above this altitude; some of those that do exist at those elevations have PTs comparable to those of low-altitude ectotherms (Hertz and Huey 1981; Pearson 1954). However, altitudinal differences

in PT may exist for some lizards (Hertz 1979; Hertz and Huey 1981). Likewise, Feder (1982c) presented data for two genera of plethodontid salamanders that suggested an altitudinal decrease in PT. *Pseudoeurycea gadovii* collected from 3,250 m had a mean PT of about 9.5°C as compared to a mean PT of 11.5°C for *P. smithii* collected from 2,960 m (table 9.2). Similarly, *Bolitoglossa rostrata* from 2,850 m and acclimated to 22°C had a PT of about 12.4°C as compared to about 16.7°C for *B. occidentalis* (from 1,050 m) and 20.5°C for *B. flaviventris* (from 600 m). Regardless of whether or not an altitudinal gradient of PT reflects the lowering of T_b common during hypoxia, the physiological benefits of a hypoxic hyperthermia accrued by a terrestrial ectotherm are no less significant than those obtained by hypoxic ectotherms from aquatic environments, where the occurrence of hypoxia may be more common (see chapters 4–6).

A similar dependence of ectothermic behavioral thermoregulation on oxygen availability is evident when PT is examined as a function of hematocrit and/or oxygen-carrying capacity. While variability between species at a given hematocrit may be significant, lizards with hematocrits lower than 16% (anemic hypoxia) have lower PTs than conspecifics with higher hematocrits (Wood, Hicks, and Dupré 1987). In the toad *Bufo marinus* PT decreases as hematocrit increases. However, surgically cannulated *B. marinus* rendered anemic by isovolumetric hemodilution with isotonic saline have a PT of 18°C as compared to the 24.5°C PT of preanemic controls (Wood, Malvin, and Riedel 1989).

Clearly, anemic hypoxia in amphibians reduces PT as in reptiles. The inverse relationship between PT and hematocrit found for untreated toads may reflect a greater significance of other physiological parameters in the nonanemic toad, such as dehydration (with subsequent hemoconcentration) or optimal hematocrit. For example, optimal hematocrit, the hematocrit providing for the greatest oxygen transport which takes into account both oxygen-carrying capacity and viscosity, varies with temperature in some ectotherms (Snyder 1971; Weathers 1976b). This characteristic is often interpreted as a response to a changing thermal regime. While modulating hematocrit in response to seasonal temperature shifts is clearly significant, PT during any given seasonal temperature profile may actually be dependent on the prevailing hematocrit; that is, an ectotherm may select a T_b that optimizes oxygen utilization to oxygen transport for a given hematocrit.

Hicks and Wood (1985; Wood and Hicks 1985) discuss in detail the physiological significance of a hypoxic hypothermia. To summarize, a lower T_b would (1) promote a leftward shift in the oxyhemoglobin equilibrium curve, thus increasing the ability of hemoglobin to take up oxygen when availability of oxygen is limited; (2) decrease critical P_{O_2}; (3) decrease the threshold P_{O_2} for hypoxic hyperventilation; and (4) generally lower metabolic rate. Of these, probably the most significant effect of a hypoxic hypothermia is the lowering of metabolic rate. By lowering T_b during hypoxia, the concomitant decrease in metabolism provides for closer matching of oxygen demand to the limited supply.

One argument against the benefits of a hypoxic hypothermia might be that a lower T_b and metabolic rate would reduce the ability of an ectotherm to escape a predator. Certainly, aerobic metabolism of an ectotherm will decrease as T_b decreases. However, during hypoxia, oxygen availability may be more limiting than temperature to sustainable aerobic metabolism. In this sense, hypothermia would be no more debilitating than hypoxia. Second, anaerobic rather than aerobic metabolism is more closely associated with escape activities. For a large number of ectotherms, anaerobic metabolism is relatively temperature-independent over the normal activity temperature range (Bennett 1980a; see also chapter 12). Therefore, a reduction of T_b may not impair an animal's ability to escape a potentially hazardous situation, although the ability to perceive the situation may not be as acute (i.e., central and/or peripheral nervous activity might be reduced). Moreover, since cooler temperatures are typical of more secluded microhabitats, movement to these areas for thermoregulation may decrease the chance of encountering predators.

Hypercapnia also elicits hypothermia in a number of mammals. In the marine toad, *Bufo marinus*, exposed to a P_{CO_2} of about 60 mm Hg, PT decreases from 29° to about 21°C (Riedel and Wood 1988). The adaptive significance of a hypercapnic hypothermia is not as clear. One possibility is that hypercapnia interferes with oxygen delivery, and the hypothermia is identical to that induced by hypoxia. Hypercapnia and its accompanying acidosis (via carbonic acid formation) both promote a rightward shift (Bohr shift) in the oxyhemoglobin equilibrium curve, a phenomenon that will facilitate oxygen unloading from hemoglobin to tissues but may compromise the ability of hemoglobin to load oxygen at the lung. Thus, lowering T_b during hypercapnia will provide for some degree of correction of hemoglobin oxygen affinity. Behavioral hypothermia during hypercapnia may also be related specifically to acid-base regulation. Rather than regulating pH of body fluids at a specific value, most ectotherms maintain a constant alkalinity; pH varies with temperature with a slope roughly parallel to the temperature-dependent neutral pH of water, about -0.014 pH units $\cdot$ °C^{-1} (Howell et al. 1970; see also chapters 5 and 6). Therefore, lowering T_b during hypercapnia would promote an increase in pH to offset the accompanying respiratory acidosis.

Osmoregulation   Few studies examine the impact of hydration state on thermoregulation by amphibians. Yet hydration often may confound thermoregulatory studies of amphibians. As many amphibians dehydrate, they engage in water-conservation behaviors such as postural reduction of surface area to minimize evaporative water loss (Beuchat, Pough, and Stewart 1984; Shoemaker 1988). In the American toad, *Bufo americanus*, postural reduction of surface area during dehydration supersedes thermoregulatory behavior (R. M. Dupré unpublished observations).

Most amphibians lose water from the skin at a rate similar to that of a free water surface of the same area, and experience a coupling of T_b with water vapor density of the surrounding air. By controlling skin resistance to regulate water loss, some amphibians can uncouple T_b from water vapor density, at least over limited ranges. In the green treefrog, *Hyla cinerea* (Hylidae), T_b is independent of water vapor density cycled hourly between 7.5 and 9.8 g $\cdot$ m^{-3} at 27°C. Under the same conditions the T_b of a toad, *Bufo valliceps*, cycled directly with changes in vapor density (Wygoda 1989a). In the "waterproof" frogs *Phyllomedusa* (Hylidae) and *Chiromantis* (Rhacophoridae), T_b is uncoupled from water vapor density over a much wider range (Shoemaker, Baker, and Loveridge 1989).

The effect of water balance on thermoregulation by amphibians has been explicitly studied in two species of "waterproof" frogs, *Chiromantis xerampelina* and *Phyllomedusa sauvagei* (Shoemaker, Baker, and Loveridge 1989). Fully hydrated *C. xerampelina* in a thermal gradient has PTs of 35° to 38°C; only 12% of total observations occur at temperatures below 30°C (fig. 9.24). In *C. xerampelina* kept without water, PT is below 30°C 28% of the time with no clear mode at higher temperatures. Hydrated *P. sauvagei* select slightly cooler temperatures (40% of observations being below 30°C), but similarly decrease PT when water is withheld, with 74% of observations occurring at temperatures below 30°C. These data are qualitatively similar to the effect of water balance on thermoregulation in several lizards (Bury and Balgooyen 1976; Crowley 1987).

Malvin, Wood, and Reidel (1989) similarly reported that the introduction of dry air into an airtight linear thermal gradient reduces temperatures selected by *Bufo marinus* from about 26° to 12°C. However, it is still not clear whether this represents a thermoregulatory response. Relative humidity is inversely related to temperature such that, if the air of the chamber is moist, the relative humidity of the cold side of the gradient would be higher than that of the warm side. Therefore, the hypothermia exhibited by *B. marinus* in response to dry air may have been an artifactual consequence of selecting a region with a more favorable vapor pressure for minimization of evaporative water loss, that is, a solely osmoregulatory response.

Hydration state influences physiological thermoregulation, especially in terrestrial amphibians (Farrell 1971; Tracy 1976). Dehydrated *C. xerampelina* and *P. sauvagei* at 40°C both allow T_b to increase beyond the temperature maintained by evaporative cooling when hydrated, a measure that spares water during water stress (Shoemaker, Baker, and Loveridge 1989). Infusion of 0.5-M NaCl beneath the dorsal skin of *C. xerampelina* increases the defended T_b at an ambient tem-

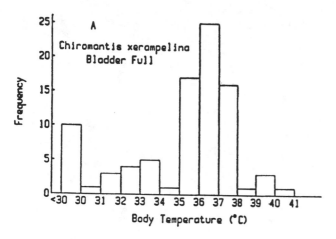

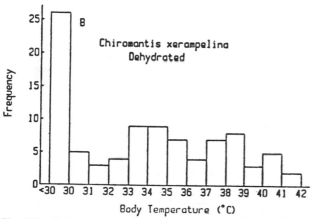

Fig. 9.24 Preferred temperatures of the "waterproof" frog *Chiromantis xerampelina* when hydrated (*A*) and dehydrated (*B*). (Reprinted, by permission, from Shoemaker, Baker, and Loveridge 1989. © University of Chicago.)

perature of 41°C, similar to that noted for dehydrated frogs. In *P. sauvagei* NaCl infusion has little effect on the T_b defended at high ambient temperatures, suggesting that the increase observed with dehydration may be predominantly influenced by decreased body fluid volume. The relative ratio of Na^+ concentration to Ca^{2+} concentration may directly affect the set-point of thermoregulation in mammals (Myers and Veale 1971; Myers and Yaksh 1971). The increase in T_b defended by *C. xerampelina* observed by Shoemaker, Baker, and Loveridge (1989) is consistent with the results of Myers and his colleagues, where a rise in the concentration of Na^+ relative to Ca^{2+} promotes an increase in T_b. While injection of a NaCl solution might be expected to increase the relative Na^+ to Ca^{2+} concentration ratio and increase PT, the relative importance of this ionic ratio in the determination of evaporative cooling thresholds has not been established.

Mucus secretion by bullfrog (*Rana catesbeiana*) skin increases dramatically as ambient temperature is raised above 28°C (Lillywhite 1971b). Although this response has been suggested primarily as a means for preventing skin desiccation, it is qualitatively similar to the enhanced evaporation noted for the "waterproof" frogs during extreme heating. When mucous gland activity is eliminated, subcutaneous temperatures increase (Lillywhite 1975). The difference be-

tween subcutaneous temperatures of these experimentally treated bullfrogs and control frogs is probably due to reduced evaporative water loss (implied passive) across visibly desiccated skin; however, the higher temperatures may be due to a reduction of evaporative cooling via a thermoregulatory effector. Future studies of mucus discharge by amphibian skin might examine this phenomenon as a potential thermoregulatory mechanism for evaporative cooling comparable to that of *C. xerampelina* and *P. sauvagei*, rather than focusing solely on its osmoregulatory role. For example, the African savanna-dwelling reed frogs, *Hyperolius viridiflavus* (Hyperoliidae), estivate in exposed positions on dry plants during the severe dry season. At elevated temperatures (40.5° to 43.9°C) this species uses skin gland secretions for evaporative cooling. Individuals can regulate the temperature at which the secretion begins within 0.1°C, thus making economical use of limited water resources (Geise and Linsenmair 1988. These authors defined the temperature at which the mucus discharge began as the "critical thermal maximum," a usage not in agreement with current practice [Hutchison 1961; 1980]).

Basking anurans increase hydration by water uptake through the ventral pelvic skin to replace water lost by mucus production. In the hylid green and golden bell frog, *Litoria aurea*, a basking species, both dehydration and exogenous arginine vasotocin (AVT) increase cutaneous water uptake and bladder water retention. The ventral skin takes up water seven times faster than through the average body surface of immersed frogs. The hydroosmotic response of the ventral pelvic skin of *L. aurea* to AVT, especially large for a semi-aquatic anuran, may be an adaptation for basking (Cree 1988b). The hydroregulatory response of the ventral skin to AVT in basking species deserves further study.

Neurophysiology of Thermoregulation The neural control of thermoregulation in amphibians has received limited attention (Boulant and Dean 1986). However, available data suggest that the neurophysiology of amphibian thermoregulation qualitatively resembles that of other vertebrate groups (primarily mammals) that have been studied more extensively. Although experimental verification is scarce for amphibians, the rostral brain stem appears to be the site for the central control of thermoregulation. This is supported by thermal stimulation of this area in ectotherms such as lizards (Hammel, Caldwell, and Abrams 1967; Myhre and Hammel 1969), turtles (Morgareidge and Hammel 1975), and fishes (Crawshaw and Hammel 1971, 1974; Hammel, Stromme, and Myhre 1969; Nelson and Prosser 1979). Warming of this region of the hypothalamus results in the selection of cooler temperatures. In addition, temperature-sensitive neurons have been identified in the preoptic region of the hypothalamus of lizards (Cabanac, Hammel, and Hardy 1967) and fish (Nelson and Prosser 1981), lending further support for the role of this region as the site for central integration of peripheral (and central) thermal input.

The role of the hypothalamus in behavioral thermoregulation by ectotherms is also supported by studies in which specific brain nuclei were ablated in lizards (Kluger, Tarr, and Heath 1973; Berk and Heath 1975b). Electrocautery of either the preoptic or posterior regions of the hypothalamus results in a virtual loss of thermoregulatory capabilities. Juvenile bullfrogs (*Rana catesbeiana*) whose hypothalamus was lesioned by electrocautery would not move when introduced within a thermal gradient (despite appearing alert), even when placed at 35°C (Lillywhite 1971a).

Extrahypothalamic warming is also effective in eliciting behavioral thermoregulatory responses by amphibians. *Rana esculenta* warmed intraabdominally by a thermode for 10 min selected ambient temperatures of 5°–6°C, as compared to about 25°C before warming (fig. 9.25); decreases in PT were proportional to the magnitude of thermode output (Cabanac and Jeddi 1971). Likewise, thermode warming of the spinal cord of *R. esculenta* stimulated a proportional reduction in PT (Duclaux, Fantino, and Cabanac 1973).

External modulation of spinal cord temperature also effects changes in the cardiovascular system that might also influence thermoregulation (Nagai and Iriki 1985, 1986). Warming of the spinal cord by passing 40°C water through a U-shaped cannula running the length of the vertebral cavity increases ventricular pressure from 28.4 to 37.3 mm Hg and pulmocutaneous blood flow from 24.5 to 29.5 ml · min⁻¹. Cooling of the spinal cord by passing 7°C water through the thermode decreased ventricular pressure from 29.3 to 24.0 mm Hg and pulmocutaneous blood flow from 22.4 to 18.5 ml · min⁻¹. Further, this response appears to be mediated via β-adrenergic receptors in that the increase in ventricular pressure and pulmocutaneous blood flow associated with spinal cord warming may be blocked by propanolol (Nagai and Iriki 1986).

Perhaps the most studied aspect of the neurophysiology of thermoregulation in amphibians is cutaneous thermosensitivity. Spray (1974) provided a comprehensive characterization of cutaneous cold receptors whose output was carried in dorsal cutaneous nerves of the bullfrog, *R. catesbeiana*, and leopard frog, *R. pipiens*. The neurons exhibited a dynamic response to specific (either warm or cold) rapid changes in temperature, a static activity at a given temperature, and specificity in modality (namely temperature), thereby meeting the criteria set forth by Hensel, Iggo, and Witt (1960) to define thermoreceptors. Sympathetic stimulation and catecholamines modulate the activity of these cold receptors

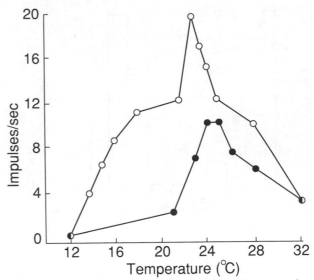

Fig. 9.26 Temperature-dependent static activity of cold receptors from dorsal cutaneous nerves of warm-acclimated (●) and cold-acclimated (○) *Rana pipiens*. Data are presented as the mean activity of five receptors; SEs are smaller than the symbols. (Reprinted, by permission, from Spray 1975.)

(Spray 1974). In addition, the range of temperatures over which activity is static and the temperature of peak activity (static maximum) shift to lower temperatures during cold acclimation, as shown in figure 9.26 (Spray 1975); however, the results may be due to higher levels of circulating catecholamines during cold acclimation rather than a true acclimation effect (Spray 1976).

The precise role of cutaneous thermoreceptors in ectothermic behavioral thermoregulation is not clear. Spray (1974) pointed out that the static maximum temperature of cutaneous cold receptors of the leopard frog (24.8°C) is comparable to the frog's mean activity temperature of 24.2°C (Brattstrom 1963) and may thus play a role in governing behavioral thermoregulation by this species. This contention is in keeping with observations that skin temperature appears to be the most important cue for behavioral thermoregulation by the lizard *Dipsosaurus dorsalis* (Barber and Crawford 1977, 1979) and for eliciting autonomic thermoregulatory responses such as panting in lizards (Dupré and Crawford 1985; Templeton 1971). Therefore, the temperature range over which static activity of cold receptors can be measured may define the range of activity temperatures of the amphibian, with static maximum temperature representing the "set-point" temperature about which the amphibian thermoregulates.

A dual-limit hypothesis (Heath 1970), in which animals cue on two thermal set-points (an upper and lower exit temperature), best describes ectotherm behavioral thermoregulation, rather than a single set-point for the regulation of T_b. From thermoregulatory behavior in *D. dorsalis*, Barber and Crawford (1977) suggested two populations of temperature receptors in lizard skin, cold receptors and warm receptors, whose static activity temperature ranges would correspond to lower and upper exit temperatures in shuttlebox experiments, respectively. Because the static maximum temperature measured by Spray (1974) for cold receptors of bullfrogs (27.5°C; *Rana catesbeiana*) is lower than the mean PT of 29.1°C

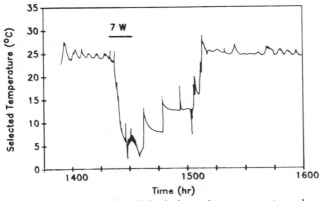

Fig. 9.25 The effect of intraabdominal warming on temperature selection by *Rana esculenta*. The *horizontal bar* represents the duration of warming at 7 W. (Reprinted, by permission, from Cabanac and Jeddi 1971.)

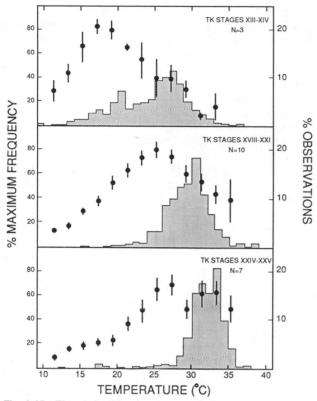

Fig. 9.27 The relationship of temperature-dependent static activity of cold-sensitive neurons to preferred temperatures (*stippled areas*) of larval *Rana catesbeiana*. Data for cold-sensitive neuron activity is presented as a mean ± 1 SE for the number of neurons indicated in each panel. *TK* = Taylor-Kollros stage of development. (Reprinted, by permission, from Dupré et al. 1986. © University of Chicago.)

(Lillywhite 1970), these receptors may serve as the lower-limit sensors of the dual-limit hypothesis. Likewise, temperatures of static activity measured in cold-sensitive neurons of bullfrog larvae were below mean PT (fig. 9.27); changes in the static activity temperature range of the cold-sensitive neurons paralleled changes in PT. The static activity temperature range of three warm-sensitive neurons is higher than both the range for static activity of the cold-sensitive neurons and the range of temperatures selected by the larvae (Dupré et al. 1986). Further investigations of the temperature-dependent activity of cold and, especially, warm receptors relative to temperature selection by ectotherms will be required to understand the role of cutaneous receptors in behavioral thermoregulation.

Behavioral thermoregulatory mechanisms are more sensitive and predominate over physiological mechanisms in vertebrates (Cabanac 1975; Crawshaw 1980; Boulant and Dean 1986). Some experimental results support a distinct anatomical and functional separation of autonomic and behavioral neuronal networks (Satinoff 1978, 1980). However, because diverse biochemical and pharmacological agents have very similar actions on thermoregulatory function in phylogenetically diverse groups, a more parsimonious conclusion would be that the neural structures of autonomic and behavioral mechanisms did not evolve separately but may differ primarily in the nature (behavioral or physiological) of effector output (Hutchison and Spriestersbach 1986b).

SIGNIFICANCE OF THERMOREGULATION

Does PT reflect the optimum temperature (the temperature for peak function) of an ectothermic organism such as an amphibian? This is a difficult question to address. An individual organism represents a phenomenal number of simultaneously occurring biophysical and biochemical reactions. The chance of each of these reactions having evolved precisely the same thermal optimum is negligible. Nonetheless, the PT might coincide with at least some optimum temperatures. This is supported by Huey (1982), who compared the temperature optima from studies of a variety of physiological processes with PTs of the lizards *Sceloporus occidentalis* and *Dipsosaurus dorsalis;* in both species the PT corresponds to the temperature range in which several measures of performance were high, despite differences in the absolute optimum temperature of each process.

Environmental temperatures at the time of reproductive activities (including male calling behavior, time of daily sexual activity, and selection of spawning site) and embryonic thermal requirements of growth and development are correlated (Brown 1975a, 1975b; Licht 1971). In fact, thermal influences on parameters such as male call qualities (Gerhardt 1978; Sullivan 1984a; Wagner 1989; see also chapter 14) may dictate when the "successful" call might be produced, or received. Regardless, it is clear that amphibian eggs are deposited in a thermal environment that optimizes growth and development.

Upon hatching from the egg, larvae represent not only developing organisms but free-living organisms that must respond to an unpredictable and potentially hostile environment. In addition, freedom from the confines of the egg allows for the behavioral exploitation of more diverse thermal habitats. Consequently, the PT of hatchling/juvenile ectotherms may be different from embryonic thermal requirements. Nonetheless, juvenile striped bass, *Morone saxatilis*, have a PT of 25°C (Mcldrin and Gift 1971), comparable to the thermal optimum for growth at 24°C (Cox and Coutant 1981). Likewise, Kellogg and Gift (1983) found that the PT of four fish species was generally less than 2°C different than the optimum temperature for growth. Juvenile *Bufo boreas* feed and grow maximally at about 27°C, which closely approximates the PT of fed toads (Lillywhite, Licht, and Chelgren 1973).

The relationship between PT and the thermal optima for growth and development of amphibian larvae is not clear. Although both growth and development rates have approximately the same thermal optimum in *Rana pipiens,* lower temperatures are generally associated with a decrease in developmental rate and a higher stage-specific growth (Smith-Gill and Berven 1979). Conversely, higher temperatures preferentially promote development with minimal growth at a given developmental stage. Thus, the developmental differences in PT discussed earlier in this review may represent a delicate balance between these potentially conflicting rate functions to maximize growth during early development and optimize size at metamorphic climax (Wilbur and Collins 1973).

One of the most evaluated aspects of amphibian biology relative to thermal effects is locomotion (see chapter 12). Locomotor performance of the leopard frog, *R. pipiens,* shows a plateau between 20° and 29°C (Putnam and Bennett 1981). Indices of jumping performance such as peak force during jump, jump distance, aerial distance, and vertical takeoff velocity of *R. pipiens* are maximal at 25°C (Hirano and Rome 1984). Both studies suggest optimum locomotor performance at temperatures approximating the mean PT for this species, 24.2°C (Brattstrom 1963). Renaud and Stevens (1983) also showed a temperature-dependent increase in jump distance of *R. pipiens* and *Bufo americanus* to 25°C; however, performance at temperatures above 25°C was not examined, preventing the estimation of a thermal optimum. Mean velocity for locomotion, mean jump frequency, mean jump length, and maximum jump length of 20°C-acclimated Woodhouse's toad, *B. w. woodhousii*, are temperature-dependent, with peaks in mean jump frequency at 20°C and longest jump length occurring at 25°C (Londos and Brooks 1988), both temperatures comparable to the range of PTs common to toads.

Swimming performance of aquatic species is also temperature-dependent (see chapter 8). The swimming velocity of the mudpuppy, *Necturus maculosus*, is greatest at 15°C (Miller 1982), which is also the PT (Hutchison and Hill 1976). The maximum swimming velocity of the clawed frog, *Xenopus laevis*, at 27°C (Miller 1982) accords well with the PT of 25.6°C (Dupré, Just, and Ritchart 1986). Swimming velocity and stroke frequency of the treefrog *Hyla crucifer* are maximal at 30°C, while stroke length is maximal at about 20°C (John-Alder, Barnhart, and Bennett 1989); these thermal optima compare favorably with a range of reported PTs, from 23.8°C (Gatten and Hill 1984) to 31.4°C (Strübing 1954).

AT influences the optimum temperature for locomotor performance. Acclimation to 30°C increases the thermal optimum of mean jump frequency in *Bufo w. woodhousii* (Londos and Brooks 1988). Also 5°C-acclimated *R. pipiens* show temperature-independence of jump distance between 15° and 25°C, as compared to the temperature-dependent increase noted for 25°C-acclimated frogs (Renaud and Stevens 1983). Although neither study provides data reflecting changes in thermal preference with temperature acclimation, the observed trends are consistent with the common finding of a higher PT for animals acclimated to higher temperatures (table 9.2).

Physiological indices such as locomotion are ultimately dependent on oxygen availability. Thus, blood-gas transport properties might also be expected to be temperature-dependent in ectotherms. Blood oxygen capacity varies with temperature such that maximum oxygen capacity occurs at temperatures comparable to the PTs of reptiles (Pough 1976). The only exceptions are the chelonians, whose oxygen capacity is maximal at temperatures significantly lower than PT. Although the temperature dependency of amphibian blood is unknown, a comparable relationship with PT likely exists.

Despite correlations between PT and the thermal optima of the physiological functions cited above, the thermal optima of all processes of an animal need not approximate PT, or even the normal activity temperature range. For example, horizontal jump distance of the nocturnal terrestrial frog, *Limnodynastes tasmaniensis* (Myobatrachidae), is greatest at temperatures between 30° and 33°C, temperatures generally avoided by the frogs in a thermal gradient and significantly

higher than the PT of about 24°C (Whitehead et al. 1989). Similarly, thermal optima for sprint performance and activity temperature range do not correspond in five species of nocturnal geckos, whose optimum temperature for sprinting is 35.2°C as compared to a PT of 31.0°C and mean activity body temperature of 28.5°C (Huey et al. 1989).

A similar disparity between PT and optimum temperature is evident for the temperature-dependent response of amphibian photoreceptors. The magnitude of the dark current of rods from the retina of *Bufo marinus* increases linearly with temperature over the range of 0°–30°C; however, peak sensitivity occurs at about 22°C (T. D. Lamb 1984). Likewise, the amplitude of saturating responses (indicative of the magnitude of the dark current) of rods from the aspartate-treated retina of the frog *Rana temporaria* increases linearly with temperature over the range of 6°–26°C, with a maximum sensitivity at about 18°C (Donner, Hemila, and Koskelainen 1988). Both temperatures at which photosensitivity is optimal are significantly lower than the respective PTs of about 29°C (Riedel and Wood 1988) and 29.6°C (Strübing 1954). This is not to imply that a complex relationship between photosensitivity and thermal preference may not exist, especially since PT likely reflects an integration of the whole of physiological responses of an organism. Indeed, the shift in spectral preference observed during amphibian development (Jaeger and Hailman 1976; see chapter 16) may be an important feature promoting the increase in PT observed during development of a variety of amphibian species, as discussed earlier in this chapter.

The benefits of a close correspondence between thermal optima for physiological responses and PT are obvious; an organism will be maximally efficient in those processes with optimum temperatures approximating PT. The significance of divergence between optimum temperatures for locomotion and PT (or mean activity temperature) is not as intuitive. Such a divergence may reflect evolutionary conservation of thermal characteristics. An alternative explanation might be that the thermal optimum represents an important emergency response system for when an ectotherm finds itself outside of its normal activity temperature range. Finally, a physiological response with an optimal temperature different from PT may simply represent an exception to the majority of the organism's physiological systems having thermal optima approximating PT. Additional studies that specifically address these hypotheses will be required to determine the relative significance of departure of thermal optima from PT.

CONCLUSIONS

The thermoregulatory "system" of an animal "borrows" its effectors from other regulatory systems; thus, by its very nature, thermoregulatory output must reflect not only an integration of thermal sensory input but the status of other systems as well. Although the competition between thermoregulatory and hydroregulatory processes in amphibians may have led to less precise control of T_b in amphibians than in reptiles (Tracy 1975, 1976, 1979), amphibians *do* have the capacity to thermoregulate, as we believe the information in this chapter shows. Although Tracy (1979) developed his hypothesis on the lesser thermoregulatory precision in amphibians from mechanistic biophysical models and some empirical data (Tracy 1975) on frogs not behaviorally thermoregulating, daily patterns of changes in T_b can clearly be attributed erroneously to thermoregulation, especially in a widely varying biophysical environment. However, evidence is now abundant that amphibians, when presented with temporal or spatial heterothermal environments, will select behaviorally a range of temperatures within which to spend a majority of their time. We now need more information on how often amphibians have an opportunity to thermoregulate under natural conditions in the field. How often do amphibians have to abandon thermoregulation in favor of hydroregulation or cutaneous respiratory gas exchange? How often do micrometeorological conditions allow thermoregulation? The paucity of data on regulatory processes in natural environments severely limits current understanding of the environmental physiology of amphibians.

Their complicated interrelationships have likely deterred the use of amphibians as thermoregulatory models. Likewise, the status of some species as intermediates between a wholly aquatic and wholly terrestrial lifestyle has probably mini-mized amphibians' use as models of thermoregulation in that investigators are often interested in thermoregulation only in an aquatic environment (where fish may be used) *or* only in a terrestrial environment (where reptiles may be used). Indeed, among studies of reptilian thermoregulation, the number dealing with aquatic and semiaquatic forms is relatively small (Avery 1982). Yet, because some amphibians are the best available models of the evolutionary transition from an aquatic to a terrestrial existence, we need to understand their thermoregulation more fully. Throughout this discussion, we have had to invoke studies of temperature regulation in either fish or reptiles to provide insight into the workings of the thermoregulatory system of amphibians. In some cases, parallels based upon data for other phylogenetic groups admittedly are speculative. Our hope is that the glaring lack of significant "real" data for amphibian thermoregulation in some sections of our discussion may serve as a catalyst to increase the awareness of and interest in the thermoregulatory physiology of this evolutionarily and ecologically significant group of vertebrates.

10 Estivation and Hibernation

ALAN W. PINDER, KENNETH B. STOREY, AND GORDON R. ULTSCH

Amphibians, despite a physiology that seemingly might restrict them to a small variety of habitats, range widely over the globe, avoiding only marine habitats and environments so extreme that little survives. Much of this extensive environmental range is due to amphibians' ability to withstand long periods with unfavorable conditions and to condense their life cycle into brief active periods when conditions are less stringent; in extreme cases, an amphibian might be active only 2 months in a year. Amphibians' main challenges to survival are starvation, cold, and drought. Associated with these challenges may be secondary problems such as hypoxic, osmotic, or ionic stresses.

The physiological problem is simple: how to survive to the next breeding or active period while conserving as many resources as possible. Because inimical environments are diverse, however, physiological solutions vary greatly. Estivation, the response to a periodically dry but relatively warm (>10°C) environment, commonly involves burrowing in moist soil, formation of a cocoon to slow water loss, and metabolic reduction to conserve fuel. Physiological responses to estivation may depend on whether the animal is normally terrestrial and buries in loose, relatively well aerated soil, or is normally aquatic and buries in the bottom of a drying pond or stream in more-compact drying mud.

Responses to seasonally cold temperatures in temperature or high-altitude environments are termed *hibernation* or overwintering. Three responses considered here are (1) submergence under water (often under ice cover), (2) hibernating on land in a burrow or hibernaculum to avoid freezing, and (3) tolerating freezing while hibernating on land. All are ways of surviving winter but have very different mechanisms and associated problems. Submergence in water prevents freezing, but may risk hypoxia. Terrestrial hibernation avoids hypoxia, but may risk freezing. Tolerating freezing of extracellular fluid is perhaps the most exotic solution and involves preventing formation of intracellular ice crystals and dehydration; death results if intracellular water freezes.

A variety of terms have been used to describe these physiological states: estivation, dormancy, brumation, cold torpor, hibernation, and overwintering. In this chapter, *estivation* will be used to denote a state of inactivity and metabolic reduction in response to lack of water or high temperatures. *Hibernation* and *overwintering* will be used to denote the various responses to cold temperatures. Although *hibernation* is also used by mammalian physiologists to describe the state of controlled torpor and reduced body temperature of small endotherms, it is derived from the Latin term for winter quarters or overwintering and has been used extensively in the literature on ectotherms. *Dormancy* and *torpor* should not be used as general terms for amphibians at cold temperatures, because many amphibians are neither dormant nor torpid but are capable of movement and responding to disturbance; some even feed during the winter. *Brumation*, derived from the Latin *bruma* (winter), is appropriate but unfamiliar to most people.

ESTIVATION

Estivation is a state of reduced metabolism seen most commonly in anurans inhabiting periodically dry habitats, in which the animal burrows into soil or mud and becomes inactive. Estivation sometimes resembles hibernation; *Scaphiopus* in a cold area "estivating" during the winter dry season may be physiologically similar to a more northern *Bufo* species that "hibernates" on land. The physiology of burrowing anurans estivating during the dry season may also resemble their physiology while buried in soil during the day in summer; diurnal "rest" may be tantamount to short-term estivation. Similarly, burrowing anurans that have not been reported to estivate may nonetheless share most or all of the physiological adaptations that make estivation possible. Metabolic reduction may be a general feature of fossorial amphibians, whether they estivate or not (Whitford 1969). For example, *Bufo marinus* have not been reported to estivate in nature, but bury themselves and enter a state of torpor typical of estivators when kept under appropriate laboratory conditions (Boutilier et al. 1979c).

Life-history Characteristics of Estivators

Estivating anurans generally inhabit desert or near-desert areas that are subject to highly variable and seasonal rainfall. Most species are highly terrestrial, but some occur in "per-

250

manent" streams or ponds in the desert and, apart from estivation, are not obviously adapted to xeric environments. *Scaphiopus* (Pelobatidae), the spadefoot toads from North America; *Cyclorana* (Hylidae), the water-holding frogs from Australia; and *Pyxicephalus* (Ranidae), the African bullfrog, are some of the best-known estivators. Many other genera have terrestrial, fossorial members, some of which may estivate: *Bufo*, throughout its worldwide distribution; *Limnodynastes, Neobatrachus, Notaden*, and *Heleioporus* (all Myobatrachidae) in Australia; and *Breviceps* (Microhylidae) in Africa. Mayhew (1968) includes an exhaustive listing of publications prior to 1968 on xeric amphibians, which includes most of the natural history literature on estivators. Other reviews of the biology of xeric amphibians are provided by Bentley (1966a). Main, Littlejohn, and Lee (1959); Main (1968); Main and Bentley (1964); and Seymour and Lee (1974) review Australian species.

In many cases, estivation is inferred from the environment in which animals are found. If they occur in areas with prolonged drought during which surface water disappears, they likely estivate during the dry part of the year. Because animals that burrow into the soil without leaving an open tunnel are very difficult to find, most putatively estivating species are poorly known during estivation. Estivation in some species (e.g., *Scaphiopus couchii* and *S. hammondii*) may be obligate, since individuals exposed to constant laboratory environments still exhibit periods when they do not feed and are less responsive than during the normal active season; animals that do not estivate but refuse to feed generally die before the next active season (Seymour 1973a).

The behavior and ecology of many desert-adapted anurans have a common pattern. Adults are highly terrestrial and return to water only to breed, sometimes not even then. They are nocturnal and fossorial, escaping heat and dehydration during the day by burrowing a short distance under the surface in soil-filled burrows. Most of a desert amphibian's life may be spent in estivation: *S. couchii, S. hammondii*, and *Pyxicephalus adspersus* commonly estivate for 7 to 10 months per year (McClanahan 1967; Ruibal, Tevis, and Roig 1969; Seymour 1973a; Loveridge and Withers 1981). They are active for relatively short periods after seasonal rains produce ephemeral pools in which they breed. Larvae develop quickly and metamorphose before the pools evaporate. Since rainfall is highly unpredictable, breeding is opportunistic, cued primarily by rainfall and secondarily by temperature, and can occur any time over several months when conditions are favorable (Main, Littlejohn, and Lee 1959; Main 1968; Mayhew 1968). Estivation has been documented only in adult anurans, although larvae of *Siren lacertina* (Caudata: Sirenidae) and *Ambystoma tigrinum* (Ambystomatidae) have been reported to estivate (Ethcridge 1986; Webb 1969). No cases of direct development are known among estivators (Main 1968). After the rains stop, adults and newly metamorphosed subadults bury themselves for the dry season, most commonly in loose or sandy soil (but in clay in *Neobatrachus* and *Cyclorana*), digging down to a moist layer, often under vegetation or surface detritus (Mayhew 1968; Ruibal, Tevis, and Roig 1969; van Beurden 1980).

A variant form of reproduction in ephemeral pools occurs in species of *Heleioporus, Crinia*, and *Pseudophryne* (all Anura: Myobatrachidae), which lay eggs on land in areas that subsequently flood. The eggs hatch upon flooding and complete larval development quickly (Main, Littlejohn, and Lee 1959). The eggs develop to the point of hatching (Gosner stages 26–28), then can slow development and reduce their rate of oxygen consumption ($\dot{V}O_2$) somewhat until floods induce hatching. The embryos can remain in this "arrested" state ($\dot{V}O_2$ decreases only slightly) for several weeks, provided the surrounding air approaches 100% humidity, and can withstand the loss of up to 90% of the water from the egg, but cannot "estivate" until the next season at this developmental stage (Martin and Cooper 1972; Bradford and Seymour 1985). Hatched larvae of *Leptodactylus* (Anura: Leptodactylidae) can similarly reduce metabolic rate and withstand extreme dehydration, but this response is insufficient to survive more than a few days without rain (Candelas et al. 1961).

A smaller group of estivating amphibians are highly aquatic, including the anurans *Xenopus* (Africa), *Lepidobatrachus, Ceratophrys* (South America, both Leptodactylidae), *Pseudophryne*, and *Hyla* (Australia, Hylidae), and the salamanders *Ambystoma, Siren*, and *Amphiuma* (North America, Amphiumidae). These animals burrow into mud as the streams and ponds in which they normally live dry up, and remain encased in hardening mud until the next rainy season. Some species are not good burrowers (e.g., *Hyla rubella*) and shelter under loose debris where the soil remains damp (Main, Littlejohn, and Lee 1959). *Ambystoma tigrinum* may estivate in other animals' burrows (e.g., deep rodent burrows) and newly metamorphosed *Ambystoma* occur in the cracks between mud cakes at the bottom of drying cattle ponds (Webb 1969). Very little is known of amphibians estivating in mud, although their problems of water balance and respiration are likely to be quite different from those of amphibians estivating in more friable and porous soils.

Cues for entering and breaking estivation are not well understood. Rain, or the lack of it, is an obvious candidate. Estivators may extend their active season if rain or high humidity continues (Bragg 1944; Mayhew 1962) and generally reappear only after a significant rain ends the dry season. Although rainfall cues emergence from the soil, *Scaphiopus* approach the surface before the rain and are only a few centimeters deep when rain does arrive (Bragg 1945; Ruibal, Tevis, and Roig 1969). Photoperiod seems another cue: Seymour (1973a) reported that toads kept in constant light would frequently come to the soil surface rather than estivate; an endogenous rhythm is also indicated because they refuse to feed during the normal period of estivation. *Pyxicephalus natalensis* kept in constant light and temperature become dormant at the normal time of year (Poynton 1964, quoted in Mayhew 1968). Temperature also is a factor: *Scaphiopus* will not respond to rain during the winter, when temperatures are too low (Mayhew 1962) and will not appear after a summer rain if the temperature is too high (Bragg 1945). *Scaphiopus* do not enter estivation as readily at 23°C as at 15°C (Seymour 1973a).

The ability to estivate during periods of adverse conditions allows some anurans to survive in truly extreme environments. Mayhew (1962) reports *Scaphiopus couchii* from a California desert with an average of less than 6 cm of rain per year, no permanent water, and occasional years with no rainfall at all. Air temperature may reach 50°C, soil surface temperature can exceed 60°C, and soil temperature is generally above 30°C even 27 cm under the surface (*Scaphiopus* probably do not burrow deeper than this during the summer). *Cyclorana platycephala* may encounter up to 5 consecutive drought years with insufficient rain to emerge from estivation, with only a small fraction of the population surviving such a long period of estivation (van Beurden 1980).

Burrow Microenvironment

Because amphibians estivate in burrows, the physiological challenges during estivation depend on the microenvironment of the burrow rather than on the surface environment. The most important physical variables are temperature, soil water tension, and concentrations of respiratory gases, which depend on burrow depth, soil type, and climate. Daily temperature fluctuations decrease with increasing depth of soil over the burrow, so that at 40 cm under the soil surface in open areas temperature shows no daily fluctuation at all (van Beurden 1980). Soil moisture tension is the affinity of soil for water, expressed as equivalence to the osmotic concentration of an aqueous solution (see also chapter 4). Soil moisture tension is a function of water content, particle size, and soil chemistry. Sandy soils do not hold water as tightly as soils with high clay and silt concentration; thus at the same water content per unit mass sand has a lower water tension than clay. Little is known about soil gas concentrations around buried amphibians. Gas concentrations depend on respiration of the estivator and other organisms in the soil and soil gas permeability.

Anurans that bury in loose soil may dig deeper as the dry season progresses and the horizon of moist soil retreats. Those that burrow into harder soils or drying mud probably cannot move to follow the moisture level. The burrow often collapses behind the animal, so the animal is completely surrounded by soil. *Scaphiopus* average about 20 cm deep in the fall, reach 50 to 70 cm in midwinter (individual toads may be much deeper), and work their way toward the surface again in the early summer (McClanahan 1967; Ruibal, Tevis, and Roig 1969; Seymour 1973b). Burrows excavated for daytime use during the summer are much more shallow, about 6 to 8 cm (Seymour 1973b). *Heleioporus, Notaden, Breviceps,* and *Pyxicephalus* may burrow to 80 to 150 cm (references in Mayhew 1968). *Cyclorana* and *Neobatrachus,* digging in harder clay soils, are generally only 2 to 30 cm below the surface (Main, Littlejohn, and Lee 1959; van Beurden 1980).

Burrow temperatures are much lower and, depending on the depth of the burrow, much less variable than surface temperatures. Burrow temperatures may still vary with season (some animals remain in estivation through 1 or more entire year) and geographic location. As van Beurden (1980) points out, the temperature regime to which an estivator is exposed is important because metabolic rate is an exponential function of temperature and metabolic rate determines the rate of fuel depletion. However, measurements of burrow temperatures are even more rare than discoveries of naturally estivating animals. *Scaphiopus couchii* will estivate at temperatures at least up to 23°C in the laboratory, but 15°C is more representative of field temperatures during estivation (Seymour 1973a). Temperatures in *Scaphiopus* burrows vary from 17°

to 22°C in fall, 5° to 15° in winter, and 24° to 25° just before emergence in June and July, with a maximum temperature of 39°C recorded in a shallow summer burrow (Ruibal 1962; Shoemaker, McClanahan, and Ruibal 1969). At the depths to which *Scaphiopus* burrows, temperature should vary seasonally but not daily. Van Beurden measured temperatures of *Cyclorana* in burrows, finding both seasonal and daily fluctuations: the average temperature of estivation was about 15°C, with daily variations of 7°. *Siren,* in drying mud, experiences 21° to 27°C (Gehlbach, Gordon, and Jordan 1973). In any case, temperatures are not likely to approach freezing as they do in terrestrial hibernation, but rapid utilization of fuel reserves due to the relatively high metabolism associated with high temperatures may be a problem.

Burrow location, whether in loose or compact soil, under vegetation, in areas with a shallow water table, and so forth, may greatly affect conditions during estivation and thus potentially affect survival. Yet the cues used to choose burrowing sites are unknown. Primarily aquatic estivators have little choice in burrow location, although stream and pond bottoms may not be entirely homogeneous. Terrestrial anurans, however, are more mobile and could perhaps search for suitable areas before digging a burrow. Burrows are nonrandomly distributed, with most areas having no burrows but with relatively high densities in other areas. For example, thirty-nine *Scaphiopus hammondii* and eight *Bufo cognatus* were found in one area 5.7 m² (Ruibal, Tevis, and Roig 1969). Unlike primarily aquatic estivators, terrestrial estivators do not bury in the bottom of their breeding ponds (Ruibal 1962). Two of the four burrowing sites for *S. hammondii* found by Ruibal, Tevis, and Roig (1969) were in the sides of ravines; the other two were relatively flat. Far fewer of two sympatric *Scaphiopus* species (*S. couchii* and *S. bombifrons*) were found at these sites; thus, the three species do not share the same estivating sites. There is no obvious way to predict what sites will yield toads; discoveries of estivating sites are rare and fortuitous. Although most *Scaphiopus* are found in sandy soil, some are found in compacted soil (Ruibal, Tevis, and Roig 1969); many are found under vegetation and surface detritus, which may keep the soil cooler and more moist (Bragg 1945; Mayhew 1965). *Cyclorana* may also take advantage of plant cover (van Beurden 1980). Careful choice of estivating site may be important only in very dry habitats. Mayhew (1962) suggests that *Scaphiopus* in extreme desert conditions burrow in dry washes and at the edges of dunes, where moist soil is closer to the surface and the probability of receiving runoff is higher.

Water Relations

Starvation and desiccation constrain prolonged survival during estivation. To survive without food, amphibians accumulate large reserves of metabolic fuels during the brief feeding period (see also chapter 15) and reduce metabolic rate to minimize energy needs during estivation. To deal with water stress, amphibians conserve water and may take up water osmotically (see also chapters 5 and 6). To these ends, some species form waterproof cocoons, and others increase osmolality of body fluids by accumulating urea. Also, the metabolic machinery of estivating species functions over a wide range of hydration levels. For example, dehydration affects muscle contraction in *S. couchii* less than in *Rana pipiens* (Hillman 1982b).

Cocoons   Many estivators form estivational "cocoons"; some cocoons may reduce evaporative water loss sufficiently for an estivating amphibian to survive on water stores and metabolically produced water alone (see also chapter 6). At least three different types of cocoon occur among amphibians: multiple layers of shed stratum corneum, a single layer of stratum corneum, and a layer of secreted mucus.

Lepidobatrachus llanensis (Leptodactylidae), aquatic anurans, bury in mud and form a cocoon of several layers of shed epithelium during the dry season in Argentina, and can survive 150 days in dry soil. The cocoon reduces evaporative water loss by about 90%. The closely related *Ceratophrys ornata* form a similar cocoon (McClanahan, Shoemaker, and Ruibal 1976). *Pyxicephalus adspersus* also form a cocoon of multiple layers of shed skin that reduces evaporative water loss by up to 95%; given the reduction in water loss and a bladder water store of 30% of body mass, these large (up to 1 kg) frogs should survive 260 days or more in dry soil (Loveridge and Withers 1981). Animals in this study became dormant in air with no possibility of water uptake from soil. *Cyclorana* spp., *Limnodynastes spenceri*, and *Neobatrachus pictus* excavated from "dry" clay have cocoons of a single layer of stratum corneum, which they shed as a single unit and reduce water loss by up to 90% (Lee and Mercer 1967). Given the reduction in water loss of cocooned frogs in a dry atmosphere, they should survive about 25 days; since such frogs normally estivate for more than 3 months, soil moisture is essential for these species to reduce water loss (Lee and Mercer 1967). *Scaphiopus* also emerge covered by a black layer of shed skin, but the resistance of this "cocoon" to water and gases is questionable (McClanahan, Shoemaker, and Ruibal 1976).

In contrast to the cocoons of anurans, which are derived from shed skin, the cocoon of *Siren intermedia* (Sirenidae) consists of layers of dried mucus covering all body openings except the mouth (Reno, Gehlbach, and Turner 1972; Gehlbach, Gordon, and Jordan 1973), similar to the estivational cocoon of the lungfish *Protopterus aethiopicus* (DeLaney, Lahiri, and Fishman 1974). It effectively slows water loss, since *Siren* in this study survived 16 weeks buried in drying clay at 25°C. The closely related *Siren lacertina*, however, form a cocoon of shed epithelium (Etheridge 1986).

Water Uptake and Storage   Some features of general amphibian water economy have been interpreted as being important in xeric habitats (see chapter 6). Amphibians have an unusually high body water content for vertebrates: about 77 to 83% of body mass is water compared to 70% for mammals or reptiles (Bentley 1966a; Main and Bentley 1964). They are generally able to withstand greater loss of body water than other vertebrate classes, both because they are normally more hydrated and because they can withstand relatively high osmotic concentrations in body fluids; many withstand a loss of 30–50% of body mass before death (Main 1968; Mayhew 1968; Schmid 1965; Thorson 1955). Most desert anurans can store large quantities of water in the bladder, up to 50% of body mass, from which they can absorb water (Bentley

1966a; Mayhew 1968; Main and Bentley 1964). Xeric amphibians sometimes rehydrate more quickly than aquatic amphibians, although differences are not large and are not evident in all studies (e.g., McClanahan 1967; Thorson 1955). Water storage and tolerance of dehydration may be essential for survival of amphibians that cocoon themselves in drying mud (see below), but for amphibians such as *Scaphiopus* or *Bufo*, these features are probably more important for short-term water balance during the active season. Similar characteristics occur in xeric-adapted species such as *Heleioporus eyrei*, which burrow but are not reported to estivate (Lee 1968; Packer 1963).

Most amphibians are often thought poorly adapted for xeric habitats because of their permeable skin (see chapter 6): amphibians that estivate do not have a significantly less permeable skin than aquatic amphibians unless they form cocoons (Thorson 1955). Yet, in conjunction with burrowing, permeable skin becomes a means of obtaining water from damp soil when water is not available to other "waterproof" vertebrates. Many estivating amphibians must be in at least slightly damp soil for most or all of estivation, not just to decrease evaporative water loss but to allow for water uptake from the soil.

Scaphiopus, Siren, and perhaps other amphibians that burrow into loose, moist, sandy soil, probably do not dehydrate until toward the end of estivation (Etheridge 1986; Shoemaker, McClanahan, and Ruibal 1969). Water tension in the soil surrounding estivating *Scaphiopus* is low (60 to 200 mOsm · l⁻¹) just after the rainy season. The toads dig deeper during the dry season, so moisture tension around them rises only slightly to 150–200 mOsm by February or March. Soil water tension is lower than that of body fluids; thus the toads absorb water osmotically. When the toads approach the surface again in spring and early summer, the soil is much drier, with a water tension of 450 to 600 mOsm · l⁻¹ (Shoemaker, McClanahan, and Ruibal 1969; Ruibal, Tevis, and Roig 1969). Thus, without an increase in body osmotic concentration during estivation, the water tension gradient would reverse and water would be lost to the soil. Osmotic concentration of plasma remains relatively constant in naturally estivating *Scaphiopus* between September and March, increasing sharply in spring concomitant with an increase in soil moisture tension (Shoemaker, McClanahan, and Ruibal 1969). Osmolality of body fluids can increase by 65% in *Pyxicephalus adspersus* and 50–100% in *S. couchii* through dehydration and urea production; in combination these effects resist water loss (Jones 1980a; Loveridge and Withers 1981; McClanahan 1967; Shoemaker, McClanahan, and Ruibal 1969). Bladder volume and length of estivation are not correlated, indicating that the bladder is not used as a simple water reservoir during estivation; cutaneous water uptake and urine formation are continuous, at least until just before emergence (Shoemaker, McClanahan, and Ruibal 1969).

Xenopus laevis (Pipidae), an aquatic anuran that estivates in drying mud, may exhibit a similar response. Balinsky et al. (1967) examined *Xenopus* estivating for an estimated 2–3 months in "fairly dry soil." Urea excretion increased greatly when the animals were placed in water, but mass did not change, indicating urea accumulation but no dehydration during estivation. *Xenopus* kept in drying mud in the lab died when the mud became dry and hard (Jokumsen and Weber 1980), suggesting that *Xenopus* cannot make itself sufficiently waterproof to withstand desiccation of surrounding soil. Water potentials (see chapter 4) around other normally aquatic amphibians that bury into the mud of pond bottoms would be of interest, especially in areas with high clay content. If mud has a high proportion of clay and silt, water potential may be very negative at the end of the dry season even if the mud is not entirely dry.

Presumably, urine production continues in animals such as *Scaphiopus* that take up water osmotically from the soil. Continued urine production permits excretion of nitrogenous wastes (thus urea retention may be a greater problem than excretion) and iono-, osmo-, and acid-base regulation. Estivators that seal themselves into waterproof cocoons probably halt glomerular filtration and urine production to prevent renal water loss. Indeed, renal shutdown occurs during acute dehydration in *Bufo marinus* and *Rana catesbeiana* (Schmidt-Nielsen and Forster 1954; Tufts and Toews 1986) but has not been examined in estivators.

Urea and Electrolyte Balance

At the biochemical level, amphibians tolerate high and variable electrolyte levels in body fluids; this tolerance is more pronounced in species that routinely experience dehydration (McClanahan 1964; Hillman 1988). Anurans appear unaffected by increases in electrolyte concentrations (Na^+ in particular) in the cerebrospinal fluid that in mammals would lead to severe nervous system dysfunction (Hillman 1988). The molecular basis of this tolerance of high ions is not yet known but could include reversible control over the numbers and activities of ion channels in excitable membranes.

Increased urea concentrations in body fluids are widely employed to resist dehydration among both salt-adapted and terrestrial amphibians (including burrowers and estivators; Shoemaker and Nagy 1977; Balinsky 1981; Katz and Gabbay 1986). Urea is also a major osmolyte in estivating lungfish and elasmobranch fishes (Janssens and Cohen 1968; DeLaney et al. 1977; Schmidt-Nielsen 1983). Plasma urea rises to 200–300 mM in *Scaphiopus couchii* during estivation, accounting for half of the plasma osmolality (McClanahan 1967). Plasma urea rises less in *Siren lacertina*, increasing from 8 to 50 mM, but also helps maintain water uptake from moist soil (Etheridge 1986). In cocooned frogs, which may not take up water osmotically from surrounding soil, urea concentrations are also lower: 35 mM in estivating *Lepidobatrachus llanensis* (McClanahan, Shoemaker, and Ruibal 1976) and 80 mM in *Pyxicephalus adspersus* (Loveridge and Withers 1981). Urea in blood, liver, and thigh muscle of estivating *Xenopus laevis* increase fifteen- to twentyfold to 30, 17, and 19 mM, respectively (Balinsky et al. 1967). In this species, blood amino acid content doubles during estivation, with only small changes in tissue amino acid content and few alterations in the composition of the amino acid pool. Differences in absolute urea concentrations are difficult to interpret because urea is produced in response to osmotic stress. The osmotic stress depends in turn on the experimental protocol used and can vary over a wide range in a single species or individual.

Urea nitrogen derives from protein catabolism, and during urea accumulation, energy metabolism partially shifts from lipid to amino acid oxidation. In water stress, the rate of urea biosynthesis increases, generally supported by increased activities of the enzymes of the urea cycle in liver (Balinsky et al. 1967; Janssens and Cohen 1968; Jones 1980a; Lee et al. 1982). For example, the activity of carbamyl phosphate synthetase in liver of newly emerged *Scaphiopus couchii* is double that in active summer animals, and enzyme activity increases fivefold in liver of water-restricted *Xenopus laevis* (Janssens and Cohen 1968; Jones 1980a).

Urea denatures proteins, and levels of urea such as occur naturally in the body fluids of many species during estivation (100–400 mM) can substantially perturb enzyme function *in vitro* (Yancey and Somero 1979, 1980). Animals that accumulate high urea contents in cellular fluids must alleviate the potentially harmful effects of urea on metabolism. Although modifications to protein structure may occur in some instances to enhance stability to urea, the primary solution to the problem, at least in elasmobranch fishes, is the introduction of one or more counteracting solutes (Hochachka and Somero 1984). Disturbances to enzyme conformation and function by urea are counterbalanced by the stabilizing actions of another class of solutes, the methylamines (Yancey and Somero 1979, 1980). These include trimethylamine N-oxide, betaine, and sarcosine. Body fluids of elasmobranchs maintain a constant 2:1 ratio of urea to methylamines, a ratio that perfectly balances the opposing effects of these compounds to permit optimal enzyme function (Yancey and Somero 1979, 1980). A system of counteracting solutes could also be the optimal choice for estivating and salt-tolerant amphibians that experience variable levels of urea in response to varying degrees of water stress. To date, however, no counteracting solute for urea has been identified in the body fluids of estivating anurans.

Energy Metabolism

Metabolic Reduction   To survive food and water deprivation during prolonged estivation and emerge with sufficient reserves to breed, estivators must conserve fuel and produce nontoxic metabolic end products. All estivators studied to date depress metabolism (fig. 10.1). O_2 uptake decreases to 30% of resting within 3 h in *Cyclorana* (van Beurden 1980), to 25% of resting after several days in *Pyxicephalus* (Loveridge and Withers 1981), and to 20% of resting after 2–3 weeks in *Scaphiopus* (Seymour 1973a). Whole-animal O_2 consumption gradually decreases to between 12 and 36% of resting levels in *Siren* over 16 weeks of estivation (Etheridge 1986; Gehlbach, Gordon, and Jordan 1973), but body mass decreases to 75% in the same time. Metabolic depression is temperature-dependent (Seymour 1973a): both the resting metabolic rate and its reduction during estivation decrease with temperature, with no depression of metabolic rate at temperatures below 6°C. Some of the reduction in metabolic rate is associated with starvation rather than with estivation per se; starved *Scaphiopus* may reduce resting metabolic rate 50% (Seymour 1973a). Some further depression may be due to decreased muscle tone: O_2 uptake in estivating *Scaphiopus* is similar to curarized *Rana pipiens* at the same temperature (Seymour 1973a).

Metabolic depression is a common response to adverse en-

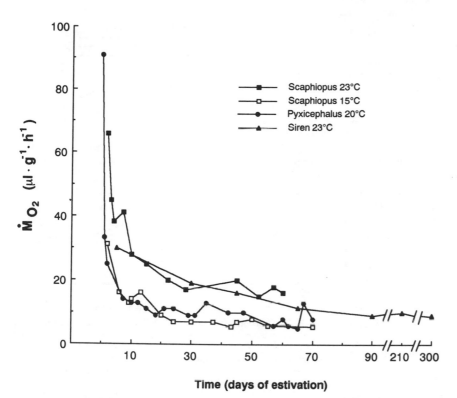

Fig. 10.1 Metabolic reduction during estivation in *Scaphiopus couchii* at 23° and 15°C, *Pyxicephalus adspersus* at 20°C, and *Siren lacertina* at 23° C. Metabolism is progressively reduced over the first 2 or 3 weeks of estivation. (Data from Seymour 1973a, Loveridge and Withers 1981, and Etheridge 1986.)

vironmental conditions throughout the animal kingdom and underlies hibernation, torpor, diapause, anaerobiosis, and anhydrobiosis as well as estivation (Hochachka and Guppy 1987; Storey 1988; Storey and Storey 1990). Recent studies have begun to analyze the molecular mechanisms involved in metabolic depression, particularly as they occur in anaerobiosis and hibernation (Storey 1985b; Storey and Storey 1990), and new research suggests that these same mechanisms underlie metabolic depression during estivation in *S. couchii* (S. P. J. Brooks and K. B. Storey unpublished data).

Broad-based regulatory mechanisms must coordinate numerous cellular processes to achieve a stable hypometabolic state. Processes that use and produce ATP, as well as passive processes in cells, must all readjust. For example, rates of ATP expenditure by active ion pumps in membranes can slow only if the counterflow of ions via passive ion channels similarly slows. To date, three regulatory mechanisms are known to participate in metabolic rate depression (Storey 1988; Storey and Storey 1990). These are (1) alteration of enzyme/protein activity states via posttranslational modifications, specifically protein phosphorylation or dephosphorylation reactions, (2) changes in the subcellular location of enzymes via reversible binding to macromolecular structures, and (3) regulation of the anabolic uses of carbohydrate via fructose-2,6-bisphosphate control over phosphofructokinase, the rate-limiting enzyme of glycolysis. The first two mechanisms are widely applicable to many metabolic processes in the cell. Indeed, control via reversible phosphorylations of proteins (often coordinated by hormone stimulation) is now known to extend to the regulatory enzymes of many metabolic pathways and also to membrane ion channel proteins (Cohen 1980; Reuter 1987). Glycolytic rate depression during anaerobiosis, for example, occurs via covalent modifications of key regulatory enzymes (glycogen phosphorylase, phosphof-

ructokinase, pyruvate kinase) that produce less active enzyme forms, dissociation of glycolytic enzymes from "glycolytic complexes" bound to subcellular structures, and a sharp drop in fructose-2,6-bisphosphate content that effectively leaves phosphofructokinase (and glycolysis in general) responsive only to adenylate (energy status) control during anoxia (Brooks and Storey 1988; Kelly and Storey 1988; Rahman and Storey 1988; Storey 1987b, 1988; Plaxton and Storey 1986). Similar mechanisms of glycolytic rate control appear during estivation in *S. couchii*, and the responses to estivation are distinctly different from those to starvation in the nonestivating toad. For example, in liver of *S. couchii* after 1 month of estivation the percentage of glycogen phosphorylase in the active a (phosphorylated) form drops by one-half (from 35 to 17%). The kinetic properties of pyruvate kinase are consistent with a covalent modification of the enzyme (K_m of phosphoenolpyruvate increased 3.5-fold, I_{50} of ATP increased 2-fold, and K_a of fructose-1,6-bisphosphate decreased 2-fold; S. P. J. Brooks and K. B. Storey unpublished data). Starvation, on the other hand, does not affect phosphorylase a content or the kinetic properties of pyruvate kinase in toad liver, although both enzymes are typically modified in mammalian liver during starvation to promote gluconeogenesis. Fructose-2,6-bisphosphate content decreases considerably in the brain, heart, and kidney of estivating toads, but decreases only in the brain of starved animals.

The biochemical triggers initiating metabolic depression during estivation are as yet unknown and, indeed, are poorly understood for virtually all forms of hypometabolism. Changes in pH have frequently been proposed as signals, since metabolic depression is typically associated with an acidosis of body fluids (DeLaney et al. 1977; Busa and Nuccitelli 1984; Hochachka and Guppy 1987). The same is true in dormant *Pyxicephalus adspersus* (blood pH is 7.4 compared to 7.9 in fed controls; Loveridge and Withers 1981), and acidosis occurs transiently during the initial hours of dormancy in *Bufo marinus* (Boutilier et al. 1979c). In both cases, however, acidosis appears to be due to a shift in the relative dependence on pulmonary versus cutaneous sites for gas exchange in the burrowed animal (see below). Overall, pH changes are a consequence of dormancy and not its cause. Acidification typically develops over the long term, whereas metabolic depression is an early response. Brooks and Storey (1989) have recently confirmed that covalent modification of regulatory enzymes during anoxia-induced metabolic depression is stimulated by O_2 lack and not by pH change. Hormonal contributions to the induction and maintenance of metabolic arrest have been implicated in both lungfish estivation and mammalian hibernation, although the experimental evidence for hormonal triggers is not always consistent and the humoral factors involved have never been isolated (Swan et al. 1981; Wang et al. 1988). A role for opiates has been suggested in mammalian hibernation (Margules, Goldman, and Finck 1979; Heller, Musacchia, and Wang 1986). Naltrexone, an opiate antagonist, can block the hypothermic response during entry into mammalian hibernation (Oeltgen et al. 1982). Opioids may also have a role in maintaining dormancy in the toad *Bufo marinus*. Burrowing leads to a 225% increase in plasma opiate content in the dormant toad, whereas naloxone injections cause a rapid arousal of burrowed animals and a rapid increase in O_2 uptake and CO_2 elimination (D. J. Randall pers. comm.).

Fuel Reserves Estivating amphibians probably maintain a wholly aerobic metabolism, even in cocoon-forming species, since the nares are always left open (Loveridge and Withers 1981). The primary metabolic fuel is lipid, as confirmed by measurements of respiratory quotients in estivating animals and by seasonal changes in body fuel reserves (Jones 1980a; Loveridge and Withers 1981; McClanahan 1967; Seymour 1973a; van Beurden 1980). The major reserves of triglyceride are in the abdominal fat bodies, but lipids are also in the liver and other organs ("carcass lipids"). Just before estivation, the fat bodies represent about 3 to 4.5% of body mass (compared to 1% or less in aquatic frogs), although they are extremely variable (Seymour 1973a; van Beurden 1980; see also chapter 15). After estivation they are much reduced (Gehlbach, Gordon, and Jordan 1973; McClanahan 1967; Seymour 1973a). Seymour (1973a) calculated that the fat bodies and carcass lipids each contribute about 50% to energy requirements during estivation in *Scaphiopus*. Loveridge and Withers (1981) estimated that 3% body mass of fat would be sufficient for 260 days of estivation in *Pyxicephalus adspersus*, about as long as water stores would last. Fat stores are sufficient for all energy requirements during estivation in *Scaphiopus* and *Siren* (McClanahan 1967; Gehlbach, Gordon, and Jordan 1973).

Van Beurden (1980) measured the major body components (carcass lipids, fat bodies, protein, and carbohydrate) in *Cyclorana platycephala* during estivation and, in combination with data on metabolic rate and temperature, generated a model of substrate use during a hypothetical long-term estivation (fig. 10.2). According to this model, some carbohydrate is used at the start of estivation, but the major energy source is fat body. Protein is used only at the end of extreme

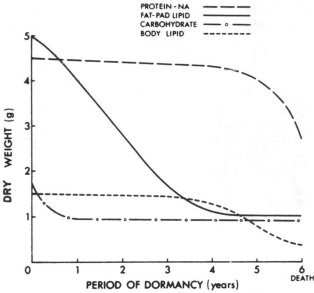

Fig. 10.2 Utilization of whole-body fuel reserves calculated for a 38-g *Cyclorana platycephala* during estivation according to the model of van Beurden (1980). The fat body is the major fuel depot, with some contribution from carbohydrates early in estivation and from body lipids and proteins when the fat body is exhausted. (Reprinted, by permission, from van Beurden 1980.)

estivation, when all other fuel sources are exhausted (this model assumes that sufficient water is available from soil moisture and that large amounts of urea are not produced for osmotic water uptake). In such extreme cases, large animals have a much better chance of surviving because they have disproportionately larger fat stores and lower metabolic rates (Etheridge 1986; Gehlbach, Gordon, and Jordan 1973; van Beurden 1980). *Scaphiopus couchii* consumes 28% of its total reserves, whereas the smaller species *S. multiplicatus* uses 51% of its total reserves (Jones 1980). Female *Scaphiopus* in extreme conditions could survive another year if they resorbed the lipid and protein in their eggs (Seymour 1973a).

For estivating *Scaphiopus* species the contributions to total energy needs average 72% from lipid oxidation, 23% from protein, and 5% from carbohydrate (Jones 1980). Urea biosynthesis during low water stress determines the percentage contribution from protein. The contribution of protein catabolism thus varies among species in proportion to the amounts of urea accumulated (higher in the burrowing toads, lower in the cocoon-forming frogs; McClanahan 1967; Loveridge and Withers 1981). Protein catabolism also varies during dormancy, rising in the later stages as water potential of the soil declines (Shoemaker, McClanahan, and Ruibal 1969). Indeed, changes in the proportions of lipid versus protein oxidation are consistent with respiratory quotients that are higher for *S. couchii* kept in dry (RQ = 0.79) versus wet (RQ = 0.71) soil, indicating elevated protein catabolism when toads are osmotically stressed (Jones 1980). The amount of protein oxidized can be considerable. To produce the urea concentrations present in the body fluids of estivating *S. couchii* would require deamination of 30% of total body protein (McClanahan 1967). Protein loss during estivation was 17% and 32% of total body protein in *S. couchii* and *S. multiplicatus*, respectively (Jones 1980).

Lipid oxidation follows the pathways typical of vertebrates; fatty acids are processed via β-oxidation reactions, and acetyl-CoA units are oxidized by the tricarboxylic acid cycle. A minor input of four carbon units is needed to balance biosynthetic drains on the intermediates of the cycle; this is typically provided from carbohydrate reserves via the carboxylation of pyruvate (or phosphoenolpyruvate) to form oxaloacetate. The use of triglycerides as the primary fuel for estivation is additionally advantageous because of the metabolic water formed during oxidation. The complete oxidation of 1 mol of palmitoyl-CoA, for example, yields 146 mol H_2O. Thus, lipid reserves are also a water reserve for animals that lack access to drinking water (Schmidt-Nielsen 1983).

Cardiorespiratory Physiology

To use fuel efficiently, estivators must remain aerobic while buried. Anaerobiosis provides only a small fraction of the energy from oxidative phosphorylation of glucose, and no energy at all from fat. During estivation, gas exchange must continue while the animal is completely encased in soil and exposed to respiratory environments quite unlike free air or water. Cocoon formation or burial may alter partitioning of gas exchange among lungs, gills (in *Siren*), and skin. Plasma volume changes secondary to dehydration or effects of changing ion and urea concentrations on hemoglobin O_2 affinity may complicate gas transport. Estivating amphibians thus must adjust for changes in metabolic rate, sites of gas exchange, plasma volume, and gas transport characteristics and viscosity of the blood.

Respiratory gas partial pressures surrounding naturally estivating amphibians are nearly unknown. In the only study to date, Seymour (1973b) measured gas partial pressures in interstitial gas around estivating *Scaphiopus* and found almost normal atmospheric values: no significant hypoxia, no hypercapnia, and little microbial respiration. Thus burial in loose porous soil may not impede respiration greatly, although surface area for cutaneous gas exchange must be reduced by contact with soil. These measurements were made at least 8 cm away from toads, so local changes in gas concentration immediately adjacent the animals might also affect cutaneous gas exchange or increase functional dead space for lung ventilation. Hypoxia and hypercapnia might be a greater problem for amphibians encased in drying mud, which is much more resistant to gas movement and probably has much higher microorganismal respiration. Whether all estivators in mud leave the burrow entrance open is uncertain, but probably a breathing channel is open to the surface as in lungfish (Smith 1931). Animal or microbial respiration could alter gas partial pressures in the burrow even with an open channel to the surface.

Most adult amphibians take up O_2 through both lungs and skin and excrete most CO_2 through the skin. Since more CO_2 is excreted through the skin than O_2 is taken up in nonestivating amphibians, decreases in cutaneous gas exchange may affect acid-base balance more than O_2 delivery. Because cutaneous gas exchange is largely diffusion-limited (Feder, Full, and Piiper 1988; Piiper, Gatz, and Crawford 1976; Pinder 1987a), anything that decreases diffusion (such as cocoons, boundary layers due to lack of convection in interstitial gas, reduction of effective surface area by contact with soil particles) will decrease cutaneous gas exchange (see

chapters 4 and 6). Dehydration during estivation may cause derecruitment of cutaneous capillaries, as occurs in *Rana catesbeiana*, *Aneides* (Caudata: Plethodontidae), and *Bufo marinus* during air exposure and dehydration, with consequent decrease in cutaneous diffusing capacity (Boutilier et al. 1979c; Brown 1972; Burggren and Moalli 1984). Physical constraints on ventilation volume or increased dead space imposed by cocoons or soil may decrease pulmonary gas exchange if the animal rebreathes at least some of its own exhaled gas. Unfortunately, only a few incomplete and contradictory observations are available to evaluate these speculations.

Scaphiopus do not ventilate their lungs during estivation; all gas exchange is apparently cutaneous, although this may change in the late stages of estivation when there are several layers of shed skin surround the animal (Seymour 1973b). This implies that blood Po_2 is probably low, because of diffusion limitation of cutaneous gas exchange. Pco_2 might be expected to rise somewhat if the lungs are not ventilated, but Withers (1978) reports no acidosis associated with estivation in *Scaphiopus*; this does not indicate whether blood is hypercapnic or whether hypercapnia is compensated. In contrast, *Pyxicephalus adspersus*, which forms a waterproof (and presumably gas-proof) cocoon, ventilates its lungs as frequently during estivation as at rest; gas exchange is thought to be almost entirely pulmonary (Loveridge and Withers 1981). Despite relative hyperventilation (since metabolic rate is greatly reduced), during estivation blood is acidotic; Loveridge and Withers (1981) interpret this as a respiratory acidosis associated with decreased cutaneous CO_2 excretion, although development of the acidosis precedes formation of the cocoon. Their analysis cannot be extended without measurement of blood Pco_2, bicarbonate, or strong ion difference. How the waterproof cocoon of *Siren*, which breathes through lungs, gills, and skin in water (Ultsch 1976b), affects pulmonary and cutaneous gas exchange is unknown. In fact nothing is known about respiratory physiology of any amphibian estivating in drying mud.

Bufo marinus exhibits many of the characteristics of an estivator in appropriate laboratory conditions. It burrows to moist soil, reduces metabolism (D. J. Randall pers. comm.), leaves its nostrils above the soil surface, and ventilates its lungs during dormancy, although at reduced rate (Boutilier et al. 1979c). Hypoventilation, along with presumably reduced cutaneous CO_2 excretion, results in a doubling of blood Pco_2. Although *Bufo marinus* can compensate for decreased cutaneous CO_2 excretion by hyperventilation, it does not do so. Instead, an increase in plasma bicarbonate completely compensates for the respiratory acidosis in the first 3 days of dormancy. The source of bicarbonate is unknown but could result from ion exchange in the urinary bladder, as in the acid-based response to environmental hypercapnia (Tufts and Toews 1985; see also chapters 5 and 6). The regulation of pulmonary ventilation apparently changes during dormancy in that hypercapnia and acidosis do not induce hyperventilation. Renal or bladder regulation of acid-base balance is less feasible for those amphibians that do not take up water from soil, because without replenishment the urine compartment is too small and too poorly buffered to affect whole-body acid-base balance significantly.

Blood properties and cardiovascular function do not vary

consistently in estivation, perhaps because of different degrees of dehydration used in various studies. Heart rate usually decreases along with metabolic rate (Gehlbach, Gordon, and Jordan 1973; Seymour 1973a; Whitford 1969), although the magnitude of depression is variable and apparently does not occur in *Pyxicephalus adspersus* (Loveridge and Withers 1981). Bradycardia is proportional to temperature, as is metabolic depression (Seymour 1973a). Blood pressure in *Scaphiopus* does not change until the animals are severely dehydrated (>35% loss of body mass). McClanahan (1967) interpreted this as preferential maintenance of plasma volume (although blood pressure can be maintained by vasoconstriction in the face of large plasma losses; A. W. Pinder and A. W. Smits unpublished). In contrast, in *P. adspersus* hemoglobin concentration increases four- to fivefold after a 20% loss of body mass (Loveridge and Withers 1981), suggesting a disproportionately large loss of fluid from plasma. No change in hemoglobin concentration or hematocrit occurs in naturally estivating *S. couchii* and *S. hammondii* (Seymour 1973b) or in *Xenopus laevis* estivating in the laboratory (Jokumsen and Weber 1980), consistent with these species' constant hydration during estivation.

An increase in O_2 affinity (i.e., a decrease in P_{50}) may be advantageous to estivating amphibians if they are in hypoxic burrows or relying on cutaneous O_2 uptake (e.g., *Scaphiopus*). Urea increases blood O_2 affinity in *X. laevis* (Jokumsen and Weber 1980). Urea may account for some of the large (35%) decrease in P_{50} observed in *Scaphiopus* blood *in vitro* (Seymour 1973b), although the P_{50} changed before the largest changes in urea occur. *In vivo* O_2 affinity is unknown in estivating anurans.

No clear pattern of cardiorespiratory function or acid-base balance has emerged from these few studies. The most complete data available are those of Boutilier et al. (1979b, 1979c) for *Bufo marinus*, but the short-term dormancy demonstrated in these toads may not be equivalent to long-term estivation. *Scaphiopus* might be similar to *Bufo marinus*, since both species burrow into porous, sandy soils, and *Scaphiopus* spp. sometimes estivate close to *Bufo* spp. (*B. cognatus* and *B. punctatus*). That *Scaphiopus* does not ventilate during estivation (Seymour 1973b), however, suggests major differences between the genera. The apparent reliance of *Scaphiopus* on cutaneous gas exchange is inconsistent with the assumed reduction of cutaneous gas exchange by dehydration and contact with soil (Boutilier et al. 1979c). *Pyxicephalus adspersus* may represent an alternative respiratory solution associated with a waterproof cocoon that restricts cutaneous gas exchange, relying more heavily on pulmonary gas exchange.

Terrestrial animals normally maintain acid-base balance by a combination of respiratory control and ion exchange mechanisms (see chapter 6). Estivators like *Scaphiopus*, which maintain osmotic water uptake but do not ventilate their lungs, may regulate acid-base balance primarily through ion exchange mechanisms. Those amphibians that form waterproof cocoons may have to rely on ventilatory adjustments. They may have difficulty maintaining acid-base balance, both because of reduction in cutaneous CO_2 excretion and because disturbances associated with hypercapnia or production of metabolic acids cannot be compensated by retention or uptake of bicarbonate equivalents by skin, kidneys, or bladder.

OVERWINTERING
Zoogeography

Amphibians are primarily a tropical and subtropical assemblage, with the exception of the salamanders, of which most genera are primarily north temperate. Most data on cold-adapted amphibians refers to far northern rather than far southern distributions, mainly because most of the habitable cold-climate land masses and most of the biologists are in the Northern Hemisphere.

Darlington (1957) has given the northern limits of ectothermic tetrapods (table 10.1). Frogs are universally the northernmost of all ectothermic tetrapods, and salamanders are second in three of four areas. *Rana temporaria* occurs well above the Arctic Circle in Europe, *R. sylvatica* crosses it in inland Alaska, and *Pseudacris triseriata* penetrates well into the Northwest Territories of Canada (fig. 10.3). The salamander *Ambystoma laterale* reaches a high latitude, but this is due to a coastal northern extension of the range (Conant 1975). The newt *Taricha granulosa* (Salamandridae) reaches southern Alaska. In Asia the salamander genus *Hynobius* (Hynobiidae) ranges as far north as the ranid frogs (Goin, Goin, and Zug 1978); *H. keyserlingi* lives where the winter temperatures fall to as low as −50°C (Berman, Leirikh, and Mikhailova 1984; Darlington 1957). This salamander, however, is exceptional because it crosses the Arctic Circle, unlike any other salamander.

Only about 10% of anuran species are north temperate (Darlington 1957), yet they occur farther north than other ectothermic tetrapods. Most northern species are from widespread genera such as *Rana*, *Hyla*, and *Bufo*. Salamanders do not extend as far north. No general ecological explanation for these observations is obvious. Generally, northern terrestrial salamanders that breed in water, such as *Ambystoma*, have a more prolonged development of both eggs and larvae at a given temperature than do anurans (Bishop 1943; Logier 1952; Oliver 1955; Wright and Wright 1949). In high northern latitudes (at least in North America), the larvae of terrestrial aquatic-breeding salamanders have not been reported to overwinter. If this is because they cannot overwinter, ambystomatid salamanders perhaps must breed early in the year to allow time for development during the short summers. The time available for development and metamorphosis of larvae might thus set the northern limit for salamanders. Larvae of *Ambystoma opacum* do overwinter, however, since this salamander lays its eggs on land in the autumn and they hatch when flooded in the winter. Also, in at least one of the southern ambystomatids, *A. talpoideum*, some of the larvae over-

TABLE 10.1 The Rank Order of Northerly Distribution of Reptiles and Amphibians in Four Major Regions of the World Listed from Northernmost to Southernmost

Northern Europe	Northern Asia	Western North America	Eastern North America
Frogs	Frogs	Frogs	Frogs
Lizards	Salamanders	Salamanders	Salamanders
Snakes	Snakes	Snakes	Snakes
Salamanders	Lizards	Lizards	Turtles
Turtles	Turtles	Turtles	Lizards
	Crocodilians	Crocodilians	Crocodilians

Source: Darlington 1957.

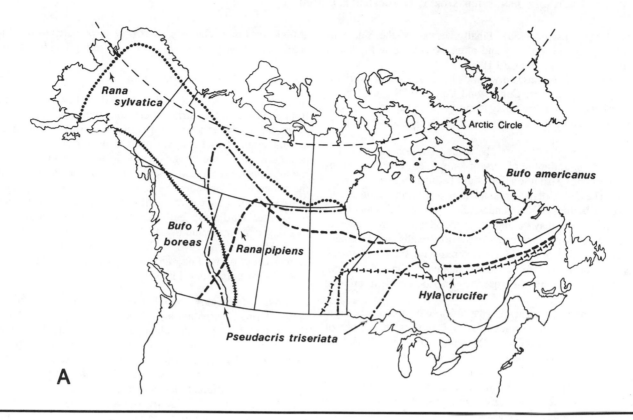

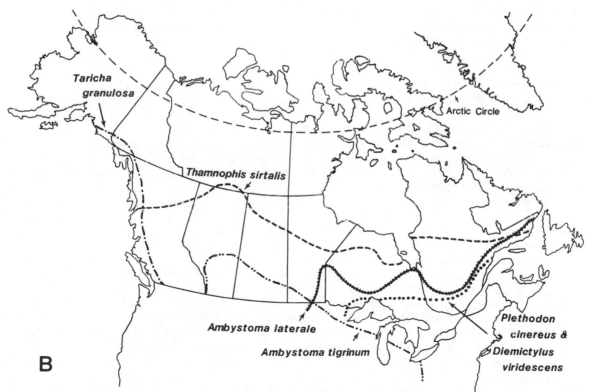

Fig. 10.3 The northern limits of distribution of some North American amphibians found in seasonally cold climates (*A*, anurans; *B*, salamanders). For comparison, the distribution of the most northerly North American snake (*Thamnophis sirtalis*) is also shown. (After Conant 1975 and Stebbins 1966.)

winter (Semlitsch 1985b). Finally, larvae of the Salamandridae in Europe and England often overwinter in the larval stage (Smith 1951; Steward 1969).

Among the anurans, only ranids have larvae that overwinter, (thirteen species; Collins and Lewis 1979), and only a few of these do so routinely. Smith (1951) reports overwintering larvae of the toad *Bufo bufo* but suggests that this is rare.

What generalizations can be made? The following are hypotheses about the life history of amphibians and their northern limits of distribution that could be investigated:

1. The ability of the larval forms to overwinter limits northern distributions of salamanders. For species with aquatic larvae, the larvae may be able to overwinter in more moderate climates because they can surface to breathe air. In colder climates, where ice becomes covered with snow and severe hypoxia or anoxia may develop, salamander larvae may not be able to overwinter because they may be unable to prolong anaerobiosis.

2. Frogs can live at high latitudes and altitudes because their larvae are more tolerant of low oxygen than those of salamanders. Bradford (1983) found complete winterkill of adult *Rana muscosa* adults in twenty-one of twenty-six high-altitude lakes in California, while at least some larvae survived in all lakes. At high latitudes, larval *R. catesbeiana* and *R. clamitans* overwinter for one to two seasons. On the other hand, overwintering of the larva of the northernmost ranid, *R. sylvatica*, is not common, at least not where it occurs with other ranids whose larvae do overwinter routinely.

3. Only larvae of thoroughly aquatic adults can overwinter. Northern *R. clamitans* and *R. catesbeiana* are primarily streamside and pondside frogs, whose larvae are slow-growing and routinely overwinter, while *R. sylvatica* is a woodland frog whose larvae do not normally overwinter. Among the more northern salamanders, *Eurycea bislineata* is a stream plethodontid with a 1- to 3-year larval period. In England, three species of newts whose adults range from primarily aquatic to primarily terrestrial have larvae that often overwinter (Smith 1951). The North American newt *Notophthalmus viridescens* (Salamandridae) is aquatic as both a larva and an adult; larvae normally metamorphose in the autumn, but they may remain as gilled forms for 1 or more years. The ambystomatids are strictly terrestrial as adults, and the larvae do not usually overwinter (except for *A. opacum*, see above; see also Whitford and Vinegar 1966 for an exceptional case of overwintering larvae of *A. maculatum*).

The ability of the larvae to overwinter is only one factor that might limit the northern distribution of amphibians. Other possibilities include food availability for either adults or the larvae, the length of the potential breeding season, and cold tolerance of the adults. Whatever the limiting factors may be, amphibians live in some very cold environments, often in large populations. While they may have to spend more than half of their lives in their winter retreats, they are able to take advantage of the high seasonal productivity of northern latitudes during the warm, albeit short, summers. This may be aided by their relatively small size (none of the largest amphibians live at high latitudes), which allows them to feed at lower food-web level both as larvae and as adults. This position in the food web is important, as they must feed at high rates in a relatively short time to prepare for the energetic challenges of overwintering and springtime breeding.

Responses to Cold and Starvation

All hibernators must deal with prolonged cold and starvation. Both aquatic and terrestrial hibernators apparently use many of the same basic strategies for winter survival, including an accumulation of fuel reserves prior to winter, a primary dependence on aerobic lipid oxidation to fuel metabolism during hibernation (as in estivation), and adjustments to cellular membranes and proteins to optimize low-temperature function. Hormones appear to coordinate metabolic adjustments for winter hardiness; biological amines (epinephrine, 5-hydroxytryptamine) and thyroid hormones appear to play key roles (Harri 1973a, 1973c). Growth hormone helps set the annual cycle of feeding, growth, and fattening (Jørgensen 1989; Wind-Larsen and Jørgensen 1987; see chapter 15).

Metabolic Reduction Metabolism does not appear to decrease during hibernation more than would be expected from the effects of temperature alone, at least in amphibians that do not freeze. The literature refers to "torpid" amphibians (e.g., Holzapfel 1937; Willis, Moyle, and Baskett 1956), but whether these frogs were just sluggish at low temperature or were in a truly different metabolic state, as suggested by Holzapfel (1937), is not clear. In contrast to repeated observations of large and rapid reductions in metabolic rate at the onset of estivation, no obvious start of hibernation or metabolic depression is distinct from the simple effect of decreasing environmental temperature. However, the Q_{10} (see chapter 8) at low temperature may be much higher than the Q_{10} within the normal temperature range for activity (Herbert and Jackson 1985; Ott, Heisler, and Ultsch 1980). Consequently, metabolism decreases greatly as temperature drops below the activity range. Inverse acclimation (decreased metabolic rate after acclimation to low temperature) sometimes occurs (Fitzpatrick and Brown 1975; Fromm and Johnson 1955; Packard 1972), although not always (Bradford 1983; Dunlap 1973; Holzman and McManus 1973). Most studies on acclimation and Q_{10} use 5°C as the lowest acclimation or measurement temperature, whereas hibernators may often be exposed to 0° to 5°C (even lower for terrestrial hibernators). If the Q_{10} is extremely large, this small temperature change may cause a significant metabolic reduction.

Fuel Reserves Starvation during overwintering may last up to 9 months. Therefore, amphibians must accumulate fuel reserves sufficient to sustain life over the winter, support vitellogenesis in females, and sustain the early spring activities of both sexes at breeding ponds. Seasonal cycles in the levels of carbohydrate, lipid, and protein reserves of frogs are well known, the liver and fat body being the primary storage sites (Brenner 1969; Byrne and White 1975; Farrar and Dupré 1983; Farrar and Frye 1979b; Milone et al. 1978; Morton 1981; Mizell 1965; Pasanen and Koskela 1974; Schlaghecke and Blum 1978a, 1978b; Smith 1950; reviewed by Fitzpatrick 1976; see also chapter 15). The general pattern is as follows: Body growth is greatest in spring and early summer, with greater conversion of food to glycogen and lipid reserves in summer and early autumn causing a large increase in the proportional size of the liver and fat body. Glycogen accumulation often accelerates during the early autumn (Jørgensen 1989; Wind-Larsen and Jørgensen 1987). Levels of both glycogen and lipid decline over the winter months, although lipid is the primary fuel. Remaining glycogen reserves in liver deplete rapidly during spring breeding (Pasanen and Koskela 1974; Storey and Storey 1987). Carbohydrates and lipids are at their lowest levels immediately after spring breeding, but increase again when feeding commences. This cycle is endogenous in *Bufo bufo;* feeding decreases in autumn even under constant light and temperature in the laboratory (Wind-Larsen and Jørgensen 1987; see also chapter 13). Administration of growth hormone extends feeding and growth for several weeks, although feeding eventually decreases (Jørgensen 1989; Wind-Larsen and Jørgensen 1987).

Species vary in the pattern of lipid and glycogen storage. The proportional masses of fat bodies are greater in the terrestrially hibernating toad species (>3% of body mass) compared to aquatically hibernating frogs (1% or less), suggesting a greater relative dependence on lipid versus carbohydrate fuels for winter survival in toads (van Beurden 1980; Jones 1980a). In contrast, liver glycogen appears to contribute more substantially to the winter fuel needs of frogs (Mizell 1965; Schlaghecke and Blum 1978b). Liver glycogen content is higher in frogs from northern populations, in accordance with the longer wintering period at high latitudes (Pasanen and Koskela 1974; Farrar and Frye 1979b). Freeze-tolerant frogs convert liver glycogen to cryoprotectant (glucose or glycerol) during freezing and reconvert it to glycogen after thawing (Storey 1987b; see below). Blood glucose is typically high during spawning and the summer months (Byrne and White 1975; Farrar and Frye 1979b; Mizell 1965), whereas plasma free fatty acids are high in both the spring and autumn (Harri 1975).

Much of the fat reserve goes into gamete production and gonad maintenance, especially in females, which may deposit most of the material in eggs during hibernation. The fat bodies are apparently essential for gonadal maintenance, since extirpation of the fat bodies causes gonadal regression in newts (Salamandridae). Autotomy of the tail in salamanders (which contains large fat stores) also can cause failure of reproduction (Fitzpatrick 1976); thus reproduction may depend on whole-body fat stores rather than on the fat bodies alone. Bradford (1983) calculates that a 20-g frog and a 5-g larva (*Rana muscosa*) would need about 2.1 and 2.5% body mass, respectively, as fat for fuel during 8 months of hibernation. Because adult frogs in Bradford's study had about 4.3% (adult males) or 5.8% (females) body mass as fat (including both fat bodies and carcass lipids), this was sufficient to support winter metabolism with one-third to one-half remaining for egg production in females. Similarly, *Desmognathus ochrophaeus* (Caudata: Plethodontidae) females use 38 mg of fat for metabolic maintenance during winter and deposit 19 mg of fat in eggs (Fitzpatrick 1976). Some amphibians (e.g., *Rana temporaria* and *Bufo bufo*) complete vitellogenesis before hibernation; only oocyte maturation occurs during hibernation (Jørgensen 1984c; Jørgensen, Hede, and Larsen 1978).

Enzyme and Protein Function Adjustments to the enzyme and protein complement of organs may adjust metabolic pro-

cesses for optimal function at low winter temperatures or reorganize metabolism for prolonged starvation.

Seasonal variation in enzyme activities of anurans is commonplace (Brachet et al. 1971; De Costa, Alonso-Bedate, and Fraile 1983; Lagerspetz, Harri, and Okslahti 1974; Nagano, Itoh, and Shukuya 1975; Pasanen 1977; Pasanen and Koskela 1974). Such changes appear to be largely geared to the yearly cycles of feeding (summer) versus starving (winter), but may also be linked to reproductive state, growth, or temperature change. Glycogen phosphorylase in liver and lipase-esterase in fat body of mature frogs are highest during spring emergence and spawning, when stored reserves must maintain high metabolic activity (Pasanen and Koskela 1974). By contrast, levels of phosphoenolpyruvate carboxykinase and glutamate-oxaloacetate transaminase in liver are highest in the summer months, probably due to the processing of dietary amino acids (Nagano, Itoh, and Shukuya 1975; Pasanen 1977). Kidney alkaline phosphatase activity is lowest in winter, in line with reduced kidney function during hibernation (Pasanen 1977).

Acclimation to low temperature (see chapter 8) can often involve changes in the activities of enzymes to maintain or enhance catalytic potential in the cold or to alter the relative activities of different metabolic pathways at low temperature (Hochachka and Somero 1984; Prosser 1973a). In some fish species, changes in isozyme or allozyme form also occur during cold acclimation (Hochachka and Somero 1984), but this is not a general mechanism of low-temperature adaptation, nor has it been reported in amphibians. Warm acclimation in March or cold acclimation in July has little effect on the activities of phosphorylase, lipase-esterase, or alkaline phosphatase in *Rana temporaria* (Pasanen 1977). Both cold acclimation and starvation modify the activities of glycolytic and gluconeogenic enzymes in liver of *R. pipiens* (Blier and Guderley 1986), indicating that both stresses contribute to metabolic reorganization during winter hardening. Cold acclimation in late summer increases the activities of regulatory enzymes of glycolysis (phosphofructokinase, pyruvate kinase), increases glycogen deposition, and decreases the activities of transaminase enzymes in liver of both fed and starved animals. Starvation, on the other hand, causes changes in enzyme activities that increase the gluconeogenic potential of liver; in particular, pyruvate kinase activity decreases and phosphoenolpyruvate carboxykinase activity increases. Starvation-associated changes are more pronounced in warm-acclimated versus cold-acclimated frogs, reflecting protein catabolism during starvation at 22°C, but not at 4°C (Blier and Guderley 1986).

Membrane Function Adjustment of membrane function by changing membrane composition is a key component of ectotherms' adaptive response to both seasonal temperature variation and laboratory temperature acclimation (Cossins 1983; Hazel 1984). "Homeoviscous adaptation" matches the physical properties of membranes to the prevailing thermal environment so that physiological processes (e.g., permeability, enzyme and transport activities, receptor and neural functions) may be temperature-compensated. Cold acclimation can modify (1) acyl chain composition (particularly, an increase in proportions of unsaturated fatty acids), (2) the distribution of fatty acids within the phospholipid molecule, and (3) the relative phospholipid composition (Hazel 1984). Studies of homeoviscous adaptation in vertebrates have largely focused on fish (Hazel 1984), but the principles also apply to amphibians, and the few studies on amphibians concur with these results. Low-temperature acclimation increases both the proportion of unsaturated fatty acids and the proportion of polyenoic fatty acids in both the neutral lipid and phospholipid fractions of liver of *Rana esculenta* (Baranska and Wlodawer 1969). Fluidity of the lipid matrix of microsomal and mitochondrial membranes from skin of *R. temporaria* is greater in preparations from 8°C-acclimated frogs than from 23°C-acclimated frogs (Lagerspetz and Laine 1984). Mitochondrial and microsomal membranes of *Hyla arenicolor* (Hylidae) liver respond to a shift in body temperature from 32° to 15°C with rapid changes in phospholipid composition. Within 1 hour the phospholipids become more unsaturated and longer in chain length and the proportion of phosphatidylethanolamine increases from less than 1% to over 10% of total phospholipid (Carey and Hazel 1984).

Overwintering Microenvironments

Although all hibernators share similar solutions to the problems of cold and prolonged starvation, the secondary problems of hypoxic, ionic, and osmotic stress are very different depending on whether the animal hibernates on land or in water. The microenvironment of the hibernaculum, if used, is also important. Northern amphibians may spend more than half of their lives hibernating, but very little is known about the microclimate of their hibernacula and even less about their wintertime behavior. A hibernaculum must not get too cold for too long or promote desiccation and must provide protection from winter predators, supply environmental cues

that appropriately trigger emergence, and maintain oxygen levels and temperatures that permit aerobic respiration.

Hibernation underwater protects animals from freezing, provided that the water is deep enough that it does not freeze to the bottom, since the freezing point of the body fluids is less than that of fresh water. Water loading and salt loss are osmotic challenges, and oxygen may be unavailable. Evidence is accumulating (see below) that amphibians, especially adults, are not very tolerant of anoxia. North temperate ponds, particularly shallow ones, frequently become severely hypoxic or anoxic during winters when the ice is covered by snow (Barica and Mathias 1979; fig. 10.4). This is unlikely to occur in running water, which usually remains well oxygenated. Upper levels of lakes and ponds are usually better oxygenated than deeper layers, but an obvious disadvantage of movement into the water column or to the surface to obtain oxygen is that it increases the risk of predation; this may be an unavoidable consequence of aquatic hibernation.

Thus, while overwintering in water may prevent freezing and certainly prevents desiccation, it does present other problems. Terrestrial overwintering probably minimizes the risk of predation and oxygen lack. The challenge is finding a hibernaculum that is moist and does not freeze. Probably more northern amphibians hibernate on land than in water, including some of the most northern (e.g., *Rana sylvatica, Hynobius, Ambystoma, Hyla, Plethodon, Taricha* [Salamandridae], *Pseudacris*, and many *Triturus* [Salamandridae]). If they hibernate far enough down into the substrate, they can remain active and feed, as is the case in at least three species of plethodontid salamanders (Ashton 1975; Ashton and Ashton 1978). Hibernation deep in the soil usually is associated with adequate soil moisture content, so freezing is likely the major problem with terrestrial overwintering. A small proportion of amphibians that overwinter on land can withstand freezing of

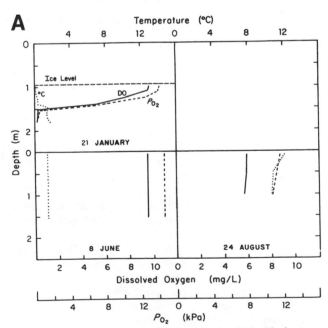

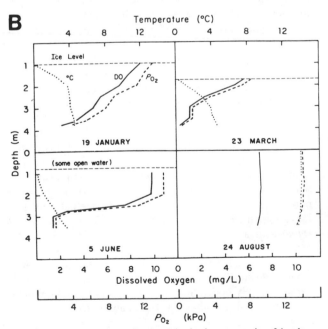

Fig. 10.4 Dissolved O₂, Po₂, and temperature in a high-altitude stream (A) and lake (B) in which adults or larvae of *Rana muscosa* were found, over the course of a year. Ice level is the lower margin of ice layer. (Reprinted, by permission, from Bradford 1983.)

extracellular water. This is effective in dealing with freezing but requires drastic changes in cell metabolism and the intracellular milieu and some means of reestablishing integrative functions upon thawing. This may be why freeze tolerance is rare among vertebrates (see below).

In widely distributed amphibian species, physiological adjustments during overwintering vary across their geographic ranges. At lower latitudes, the relatively short winters, high temperatures, and lack of protracted ice cover may not only affect the duration of hibernation but also the mode. For example, studies using drift fences indicate that *Rana clamitans* in South Carolina leave the ponds after breeding and do not return until the following breeding season, which means that they may hibernate on land (R. D. Semlitsch and J. Pechmann pers. comm.). Hibernation of this species in the northern part of its range is reported to be primarily aquatic (Logier 1952; Pope 1944). Similarly, Johnson (1987) states that *R. palustris* overwinters regularly and in large numbers in caves in Missouri, while Logier (1952) reports that they hibernate underwater in eastern Canada. Such latitudinal clines in behavior, if real rather than apparent, will have as important an effect upon the physiology of wintering as will the differences in the length and severity of the winter. Some species, for example, *Rana temporaria* and *Bufo bufo asiaticus*, seem to require exposure to low temperatures for normal gamete development (Bebak 1958; Tchau and Wang 1963) and growth cycle (e.g., *B. bufo*; Jørgensen 1986b), while some (e.g., *R. pipiens* and *R. catesbeiana*) seem not to require cold temperatures for normal growth and reproduction.

Generally, amphibians hibernate where they live; terrestrial anurans and salamanders hibernate on land; aquatic salamanders, frogs, and some larvae hibernate underwater. There are exceptions to this generalization, however, and some species may hibernate in either situation. A summary of the major groups follows.

Salamanders Three species of strictly aquatic salamanders range far enough north in North America to encounter prolonged cold. *Necturus maculosus* (Proteidae) reach southern Canada on both sides of the Great Lakes and apparently do not hibernate. They are often caught by fishers through holes in the ice, and move and feed during the winter throughout their range (Breckenridge 1944; Collins 1974; Johnson 1987; Logier 1952). *Cryptobranchus alleganiensis* (Cryptobranchidae) ranges into southern New York; little is known of its winter behavior, but it may be active all year in Kansas (Collins 1974). The northern limit of *Siren intermedia* is Illinois and Indiana, and it may overwinter on land (Cockrum 1941) or in water (Cagle and Smith 1939). Terrestrial overwintering is probably the result of pond drying, where estivation continues through the winter, rather than exit from the water. Overwintering animals are not torpid but apparently do not feed (Cagle and Smith 1939).

The Salamandridae (newts) are variable in their degree of commitment to aquatic environments, and include some whose adults are primarily terrestrial (e.g., *Salamandra* in Europe and *Taricha* in western North America) and others that are primarily aquatic (*Notophthalmus* in North America and some populations of *Triturus* in Europe; Arnold and Burton 1978; Stebbins 1966). Aquatic species tend to overwinter

in water, and they may be more or less active throughout the winter (e.g., *Notophthalmus*, Breckenridge 1944); the more terrestrial ones tend to hibernate on land. However, many of the species of salamandrids apparently can overwinter on land or in the water, depending upon local conditions (e.g., *Notophthalmus*, Logier 1952; *Triturus*, Steward 1969). Therefore winter behavior tends to resemble summer behavior in this family, in that adults of some species are truly amphibious. Late-hatching larvae that overwinter do so in water (e.g., *Salamandra salamandra* in Europe, Steward 1969).

Terrestrial salamanders overwinter on land. In general, the northern Plethodontidae move below the frost line, near streams if they are stream-edge forms such as *Eurycea bislineata* and *Desmognathus fuscus*, and into subterranean burrow systems (e.g., ant mounds) if they are woodland forms like *Plethodon cinereus*. They are intolerant of freezing and therefore must avoid temperatures below their supercooling points (e.g., *P. cinereus* and *Ambystoma laterale*, Storey and Storey 1986a, 1988). *E. bislineata* and *D. fuscus* in Ohio (Ashton 1975; Ashton and Ashton 1978) and *P. cinereus* in Indiana (Caldwell 1975; Caldwell and Jones 1973) are active and feed throughout the winter in their burrow systems, which also function as a refugium for invertebrates, including some that the salamanders eat. Winter feeding could be important in the overall energetics of the salamanders, enabling these small forms to overwinter without large energy reserves. Blanchard (1933), however, found no food in the guts of *Hemidactylium scutatum* in early spring in southern Michigan, so winter feeding may not occur in all plethodontids. Feeding while overwintering is unknown in other terrestrial salamanders (e.g., *Ambystoma* and terrestrially hibernating salamandrids).

Anurans The Bufonidae ("true" toads) and the Pelobatidae (spadefoot toads), both of which are usually terrestrial when not breeding, and certain genera of the Discoglossidae (e.g., *Bombina*, fire-bellied toads; *Alytes*, midwife toads) all apparently hibernate on land, even the decidedly aquatic *Bombina bombina* (Kowalcski 1979), although occasionally *Bufo bufo* submerge in mud during the winter. *Bufo americanus*, which range well into eastern Canada, are not freeze-tolerant (Storey and Storey 1986a), which suggests that bufonids must avoid microclimates below their supercooling points. In Minnesota, where winter temperatures of −20° to −30°C are common, *Bufo hemiophrys* move downward in the soil in response to falling soil temperatures (Breckenridge and Tester 1961). In Colorado, *Bufo boreas* hibernate in rock chambers near streams, where subsurface water flow just below the animals keeps the chamber temperature near 0°C while surface air temperatures fall as low as −31°C during hibernation (Campbell 1970).

Hibernation is terrestrial in (apparently) all northern *Hyla*, *Acris*, and *Pseudacris* (Hylidae). These frogs are not adept at digging, as they lack the keratinized structures on the hindlimbs found on toads and spadefoots. Therefore they must exploit preexisting burrows, deep crevices, or simply bury beneath leaf litter or in rotting logs. Accordingly, most of them are freeze-tolerant, although not all (e.g., *Hyla regilla*; Storey and Storey 1988).

The ranid frogs of the north usually hibernate underwater,

but some are found in other situations (the most notable exception being the wood frog, *Rana sylvatica,* which is a woodland form ranging into central Alaska). Bohnsack (1951) found a single *R. clamitans* in Michigan hibernating under 5 cm of leaf litter at least 30 m from the nearest water. Temperatures measured intermittently near the frog from mid-January through mid-April ranged from 0° to 3°C. Bohnsack (1952) also found a single *R. catesbeiana* under similar conditions in Michigan in March, and presumed it to have come from a marsh about 100 m distant. Neither animal was torpid. Both of these species hibernate underwater in northern locales, so it remains to be seen if terrestrial hibernation in these species is common but undetected, or simply the result of being caught away from water when the temperature falls rapidly.

Occasionally *R. pipiens,* which often range far from water during the nonbreeding season, overwinter on land. Rand (1950) found eight frogs in crevices about 60 m inside a cave in Indiana, and one on the floor of a nearby cave. Both caves had streams running through them, and the frogs were not dormant in either. Arnold and Burton (1978) state that the pool frog (*R. lessonae*) of Europe often hibernates on land, implying that it also hibernates underwater; terrestrial hibernation in this species is the rule in Poland (Kowaleski 1979). Some *R. temporaria* in England hibernate on land (Savage 1961; Smith 1951), although this species usually overwinters in water. Koskela and Pasanen (1974), who conducted extensive field studies of hibernation on this species in northern Finland, concluded that terrestrial hibernation was rare and resulted from the lack of suitable aquatic sites near the frogs when cold weather arrived.

The pattern for ranids thus remains somewhat inconsistent. Pond and marsh forms (as opposed to the woodland *R. sylvatica*) generally hibernate underwater, and terrestrial hibernation becomes infrequent as latitude increases. A definitive study will involve tracking individuals radioactively or radio-telemetrically tagged. Nevertheless, most ranids overwinter submerged; the question then becomes one of microenvironment, particularly with regard to P_{O_2}. While this group is commonly reported to hibernate under mud, amphibians are apparently unable to withstand severe hypoxia or anoxia even at temperatures of 1° to 5°C. One possible explanation of this apparent contradiction is that, since the frogs are not completely torpid in the field, animals collected from mud are driven there by the actions of the collector. Alternatively, the frogs are only partly buried and use buccopharyngeal respiration (Hutchison and Whitford 1966). Finally, mud burial may occur, but it need not be continuous. Since most frogs can swim slowly at low temperature (Cunjak 1986; Cunningham and Mullaly 1956), they could occasionally emerge from the mud to replenish oxygen stores from the atmosphere or from the water.

Burial in mud is not universal among frogs hibernating underwater and may not even be preferred. *Rana clamitans* kept in aquaria with a mud substrate at 5°C for 5 months made no effort to bury themselves and instead settled into depressions in the mud (Brenner 1969). Emery, Berst, and Kodaira (1972), during under-ice scuba dives in Ontario, Canada, found fifteen *R. pipiens* in small pits apparently excavated by the frogs. The frogs were usually covered dorsally with silt, but their flanks were in contact with the water, which would permit cutaneous oxygen uptake. Cunjak (1986) has also found this species wintering unburied under rubble in streams in Ontario. Breckenridge (1944) found a wintertime aggregation in Minnesota just below a dam that controlled the outflow from a lake. On a clean sand substrate where the water was not frozen because of the high flow, he found the bottom "literally paved with hundreds of closely crowded leopard frogs" that showed occasional spontaneous activity, including swimming. Mertens (1947, cited in Smith 1951) reported an analogous situation for *R. temporaria* in the Vogelsberg Mountains of Germany; the frogs were on the bottom of a clear, slowly flowing stream at about 60 cm depth and 6°C. In three collections, Mertens took a total of 600 to 900 frogs.

These observations suggest that mud burial may not be routine for frogs that overwinter in water. Respiratory advantages would certainly accrue to amphibians hibernating where water flows over them. For example, flowing water tends to be highly oxygenated, and water flowing over the body reduces the buildup of a diffusion boundary layer by inhibiting the local depletion of dissolved oxygen (Feder and Pinder 1988; Pinder and Feder 1990; see below and chapters 4 and 5). If the animal can also hide under an object while having water flow about it, these advantages can be realized with a minimal predation risk. Because buried frogs are seldom discovered, however, the possible predominance of this response may be missed by occasional occurrences of partially buried animals.

Emergence Cues

Field observations attest to preeminence of temperature as an entrance and exit cue for hibernation in northern amphibians and other ectotherms. Amphibians disappear as temperatures fall; more important, they reappear in unseasonably warm temperatures during the normal hibernation period (Koskela and Pasanen 1974; Willis, Moyle, and Baskett 1956), which rules out photoperiod as a controlling factor, at least for emergence. The nature of the hibernaculum in most species also rules out photoperiod.

Spring rains are closely associated with spring breeding migrations of amphibians, and rain is sometimes necessary for migration of terrestrial species without desiccation. Moisture may be more crucial to terrestrial salamanders than to toads or frogs. Some toads are relatively desiccation-resistant, and some frogs are highly mobile and usually not found far from water. Rain may well increase the temperature in the hibernaculum, to which the animals respond. Rain may make migration less stressful upon emergence, but moisture per se does not trigger emergence. Warm temperatures without rain bring about minor emergences in *Bufo hemiophrys* in Minnesota (Breckenridge and Tester 1961), which supports the importance of temperature as a cue. Major emergences are associated with rain, but chiefly because it eliminates the frost line in the soil. Toads emerging before the soil thaw may have hibernated in crevices and chambers similar to those described for *B. boreas* in Colorado (Campbell 1970). Animals in such hibernacula can follow a thermal gradient as a cue for emergence. *Ambystoma maculatum* migrate on warm, foggy nights in Rhode Island (Whitford and Vinegar 1966), again suggesting that temperature is an important cue and that only humidity, not rain, is important to the salamanders that breed in water. Nevertheless, the major migrations occur on rainy nights.

Heavy spring rains not only provide a temperature cue for emergence but also create vernal breeding ponds used by many species. Thus rain conveys information of importance to breeding. Whether or not the animals are genetically attuned to this information is an interesting question. Amphibians should respond only to rain at a suitable breeding temperature, because they might otherwise breed too early, resulting in freezing of the eggs. Thus, winter rains should not cause emergence. Anecdotally, this appears to be the case, but data are either scarce or lacking.

Winter Mortality

Mortality of amphibians during winter can be significant, especially in populations occupying marginal habitats. Winter mortality in terrestrial amphibians is difficult to observe directly, as dead animals are seldom found. Vernberg (1953) estimated 50% winterkill in *Plethodon cinereus* and *Eurycea bislineata* in Indiana, but this is probably an overestimate due to his methodology. Breckenridge and Tester (1961) radioactively tagged six Manitoba toads (*B. hemiophrys*) in Minnesota, five of which survived the winter; the sixth may have died from infection resulting from the tag implant. Whitford and Vinegar (1966) found greater than 90% survival of marked *Ambystoma maculatum* over one winter, and at least 76% survival over two winters. Their study was in Rhode Island, not far from the Atlantic coast, and the winters were not exceptionally cold. High winter mortality seems to be episodic rather than routine. For example, the winter of 1977/78 was one of the coldest on record in the United States, and its effects are reflected in a study by Petranka (1979) of *Plethodon dorsalis* and *P. richmondi* in central Kentucky. Temperatures were below normal by 1.2°C in December, 6.4°C in January, and 7.8°C in March. From 8 January to 12 March, temperatures were below normal 63 of 64 days, and the daily maximum temperature was above 0°C only nine times in January through February. The following spring, Petranka made eleven thorough searches of six sites that had previously yielded at least ten salamanders, and only one produced any animals. In several other likely areas, only two yielded many (twenty and twenty-three) salamanders. Sites with salamanders had rocky substrates with numerous and deep subterranean passages. Only animals that located such sites may have survived the winter. The same winter eliminated a study population of *Rana clamitans*, both adults and larvae, that had been followed for several years in the Shenandoah region of Virginia; a new population has only begun to emerge ten years later (D. Gill pers. comm.).

Winterkill of aquatic animals, usually associated with anoxia, is more directly observable and may occur frequently when ice and snow cover result in oxygen depletion from the water (Bradford 1983; Manion and Cory 1952; Smith 1951). As aquatic frogs are not freeze-tolerant, death can also occur if the entire water column freezes. Because mud is usually anoxic, regardless of the degree of oxygenation of the water

(Jørgensen and Revsbech 1985), death may result when hibernating animals are forced to retreat from encroaching ice into mud. These conditions are more likely during particularly severe winters, and they can devastate populations. Such considerations may explain why most far-northern amphibians hibernate on land or, if in water, may favor microenvironments that are not subject to long-term freezing (natural wells, springs, flowing water).

Terrestrial Hibernation

In northern or alpine climates, terrestrial hibernators must deal with subzero temperatures. Maintenance of a liquid state by deep supercooling of body fluids is not an option for amphibians. Their supercooling capacity is low (−2° to −3°C only), and with a water-permeable skin, inoculation by environmental ice can occur easily below the freezing point of body fluids (−0.5°C; Layne and Lee 1987; Lotshaw 1977; MacArthur and Dandy 1982; Schmid 1982; Storey and Storey 1986a, 1987). The useful options are (1) avoid exposure to subzero temperatures, or (2) tolerate freezing (Storey 1990). Most terrestrially hibernating amphibians use the avoidance strategy, burrowing below the frost line (Froom 1982; see above); the lethal minimum temperature for both *Bufo americanus* and *B. boreas* is −2°C, the supercooling point (Mullally 1952; Storey and Storey 1986a). Species of North American frogs that hibernate at the soil surface covered by leaf litter and snow (*Rana sylvatica, Hyla versicolor, H. crucifer,* and *Pseudacris triseriata*) have evolved the alternative solution; all tolerate the formation of ice in extracellular fluid spaces (Layne and Lee 1987; Lotshaw 1977; MacArthur and Dandy 1982; Schmid 1982; Storey 1985a, 1990; Storey and Storey 1984, 1985a, 1986a, 1990). The Siberian salamander, *Hynobius keyserlingi,* whose distribution extends well beyond the tree line, also has a well-developed capacity for survival of long-term freezing (Berman, Leirikh, and Mikhailova 1984).

How amphibians survive the winter in stable (nonfreezing), moist, well-aerated hibernacula is clear. Low temperature itself ensures a low metabolic rate, and amphibians have sufficient energy reserves stored in fat bodies and carcass lipids to survive months at low temperature without feeding. Water and O_2 are absorbed through the skin, and the bulk of CO_2 is excreted through the skin in any case. At extremes of altitude or latitude, problems with energy balance may limit distributions, more because of a short active period than extended hibernation. An unresolved problem is how amphibians can find appropriate hibernacula, especially in harsh environments that have few appropriate sites. Terrestrial hibernators may, however, face the same problems as aquatic hibernators if the hibernaculum floods during winter or if they are forced below the water table to avoid frost.

Natural freeze tolerance is well known in several invertebrate groups (many terrestrial insects, intertidal barnacles, mussels, and snails) and many types of plants (Levitt 1980; Storey and Storey 1988). Among vertebrate animals, however, only four species of frogs, one salamander species, and hatchlings of the midland painted turtle *Chrysemys picta marginata* can withstand the natural freezing of body water during winter hibernation (Berman, Leirikh, and Mikhailova

1984; Storey et al. 1988; Storey 1990); a very limited tolerance (only a few hours) has also been found for garter snakes, *Thamnophis sirtalis,* the most northerly distributed reptile in North America (Costanzo, Claussen, and Lee 1988; Storey 1990). The 1769 journal of the Arctic explorer Samuel Hearne contains perhaps the earliest description of freezing in the natural environment: "I have frequently seen frogs [*Rana sylvatica*] dug up with the moss, when pitching tents in Winter, frozen as hard as ice, in which state the legs are as easily broken off as a pipe-stem; but by wrapping them up in warm skins, and exposing them to a slow fire, they soon recover life" (1911, 368).

Early reviews of animal resistance to cold contain a number of citations that describe experimental freezing of frogs (presumably common aquatic frogs) and survival of brief exposures to $-1°$ or $-2°C$ (Duméril 1849; Holmes 1932; Smith 1958). Lotshaw (1977) reported similar survival of very brief freezing for *Rana catesbeiana.* All of these instances appear to involve freezing of only a low percentage of body water. As long as ice formation is extracellular, such freezing has the same osmotic consequences for cells as does dehydration, and amphibians are highly tolerant of wide variation in body hydration state (Balinsky 1981; Shoemaker and Nagy 1977; see also chapter 6). However, extended freezing under conditions that are natural for terrestrial hibernators (5 days at $-6°C$) kills aquatic species (*R. pipiens, R. septentrionalis*) but not *R. sylvatica, Hyla versicolor,* or *H. crucifer* (Schmid 1982). Terrestrial hibernators from milder climates (*R. aurora* and *H. regilla* from British Columbia) also cannot survive freezing (Storey and Storey 1988).

As for all freeze-tolerant animals, survival of terrestrially hibernating frogs closely matches the microenvironmental temperatures at the hibernation site. Frogs from northern populations (Ontario, Minnesota) survive freezing at $-6°$ to $-8°C$ (Schmid 1982; Storey 1985a), whereas frogs sampled in the spring from Ohio tolerate only $-3°C$ (Layne and Lee 1987). Lower temperatures are not tolerated, but such conditions rarely occur in protected hibernation sites under leaf litter and snow; even in arctic locales, temperatures are only $-5°$ to $-7°C$ (Miller and Dehlinger 1969; MacArthur and Dandy 1982; Schmid 1982). Long-term freezing is well tolerated. *R. sylvatica, H. versicolor, H. crucifer,* and *Pseudacris triseriata* can all survive at least 3 days frozen at $-3°C$ (Storey and Storey 1986a). Mature adult *R. sylvatica* and *H. versicolor* tolerate 2 weeks of freezing at $-2.5°C$, and 50% of immature adults survive 11 days at $-6°C$ (Storey 1985a; Storey and Storey 1984, 1985a). Repeated cycles of freezing and thawing are also well tolerated (Storey 1987a). Frogs of all four species retain freeze tolerance when newly emerged from hibernation in the spring, but tolerate only milder temperatures ($-2°$ to $-3°C$) and lose tolerance when feeding begins (Layne and Lee 1987; Storey and Storey 1987a). Tolerance also extends to isolated organs. Gastrocnemius muscle from *R. sylvatica* remains excitable to sciatic nerve stimulation down to the freezing point ($-3°$ to $-5°C$) and can recover excitability and contractility after freezing (Miller and Dehlinger 1969). Ventricle strips from *R. sylvatica,* but not from *R. pipiens,* recover contractility after freezing at $-5°C$ in the presence of cryoprotectant (Canty, Driedzic, and Storey 1986).

Amphibians can tolerate ice in extracellular fluid spaces only. Intracellular ice formation is always lethal, and many of the adaptations involved in freeze tolerance are those that effectively render cytoplasmic water unfreezable (Franks 1985). The basic strategy of freeze tolerance is as follows: Animals initiate extracellular freezing at high subzero temperatures ($> -10°C$) to permit a slow rate of ice formation. The withdrawal of pure water into ice raises the concentration of extracellular fluids and sets up the outward movement of water and inward movement of solutes across the cell membrane. Cells shrink and dehydrate, and extracellular ice content increases until remaining liquid compartments reach a solute concentration whose melting point is equivalent to the ambient temperature. No supercooled compartment remains, eliminating the risk of spontaneous nucleation within cells. With subsequent temperature change only minor osmotic adjustments are needed to maintain the equilibrium between ice and fluids. The biochemical adaptations that typically support freeze tolerance include (1) the control of extracellular ice: ice-nucleating proteins induce ice formation at multiple extracellular sites and at high subzero temperatures, whereas thermal hysteresis proteins inhibit the recrystallization of ice during long-term freezing; (2) the regulation of cell volume: the colligative actions of high concentrations of cryoprotectants of low molecular mass prevent cell shrinkage below a critical minimum cell volume; (3) protection of subcellular organization: trehalose and proline stabilize membrane bilayer structure against the physical stresses imposed by cell volume reduction, whereas carbohydrate cryoprotectants stabilize protein structure; and (4) viability in the frozen state: a well-developed tolerance for ischemia plus mechanisms of facultative metabolic depression support long-term survival in the frozen state (Storey and Storey 1988). Available information to date with respect to the biochemical adaptations of freeze-tolerant frogs is summarized below.

Nucleation and Ice Content   Freezing begins in peripheral areas of the frog body and progresses towards the central core. Surface moisture on the skin initiates nucleation, often with no supercooling of body fluids. Blood of *Rana sylvatica* contains a protein that nucleates at $-8°C$, but whether such a nucleator would have a physiological role is questionable (Wolanczyk, Storey, and Baust 1989). As freezing progresses, ice crystals form under the skin, between skeletal muscle fibers, and in the bladder and the abdominal cavity. Breathing, heartbeat, and blood flow gradually slow and then stop. The metabolic controls regulating the cessation of these vital signs, and their reactivation upon thawing, are not yet known. When fully frozen, blood pools in distended sinuses above the heart, suggesting that blood drains from organs during freezing, perhaps due to a progressive vasoconstriction. Freezing is a relatively slow event; for 2-g *R. sylvatica* the freezing exotherm persists for at least 3 h (fig. 10.5; Storey and Storey 1985b, 1986a), whereas maximal ice formation in 14-g frogs requires about 24 h at $-3°C$, with a halftime of 6.5 h and a linear rate of 2.9% per h (Layne and Lee 1987). Such slow rates of extracellular ice formation provide ample time for cell volume regulation, the synthesis and distribution of cryoprotectants, and the transition to an ischemic metabolic state. Measurements of the percentage of total body water as ice range from 35 to 65% for *R. sylvatica* and *Hyla versicolor* frozen at $-2°$ to $-6°C$ (Layne and Lee 1987; Schmid 1982;

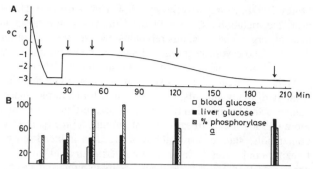

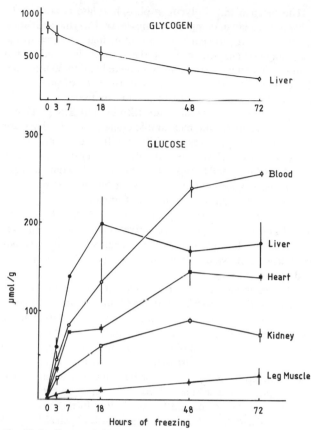

Fig. 10.5 Triggering and accumulation of glucose cryoprotectant in *Rana sylvatica*. *A,* a composite cooling and freezing curve for a typical 2-g frog held at a constant −3°C. *Arrows* indicate sampling times relative to the appearance of the freezing exotherm. (Reprinted, by permission, from Storey 1985a.) *B,* values for blood (μmol · ml⁻¹) and liver (μmol · g⁻¹) glucose contents and the percentage of liver glycogen phosphorylase in the active *a* form at these sampling times. (Reprinted, by permission, from Storey and Storey 1986b.)

Storey 1984; Storey and Storey 1985a). A limit of 65% of total body water as ice applies to most freeze-tolerant animals and represents the limits of cell shrinkage tolerated before a critical minimum cell volume is reached (Storey and Storey 1988).

Cryoprotectants Freeze-tolerant amphibians accumulate high concentrations of carbohydrate cryoprotectants of low molecular mass during freezing. In three species the cryoprotectant is glucose (*Rana sylvatica, Hyla crucifer,* and *Pseudacris triseriata*); in *Hyla versicolor* and *Hynobius keyserlingi* it is glycerol (Berman, Leirikh, and Mikhailova 1984; Storey and Storey 1986a). Average amounts are 200–300 mM in blood and organs with maximal levels as high as 550 mM glucose (9.9 g per 100 ml) or 420 mM glycerol measured in blood of freezing-exposed mature adult *R. sylvatica* and *H. versicolor,* respectively (Storey 1985a; Storey and Storey 1986a). By contrast, levels of these compounds in unfrozen control frogs are 1 to 5 mM for glucose and less than 1 mM for glycerol. Glycerol appears in the urine of *H. versicolor,* but glucose concentration is low in the urine of abdominal fluid compartments (Schmid 1982; Storey 1987b).

Synthesis of cryoprotectants uses the massive reserves of glycogen stored in liver (up to 1,000 mM as glucosyl units or 180 mg · g⁻¹; fig. 10.6; Storey and Storey 1984, 1985b). The blood rapidly distributes cryoprotectant to all organs during the early hours of freezing. Levels are highest in the central core organs (liver, heart, brain) and progressively lower at more peripheral sites, apparently reflecting circulatory changes during freezing. Species that accumulate glucose begin the process of clearing cryoprotectant immediately upon thawing, restoring the carbon as liver glycogen (Storey and Storey, 1986b; Storey 1987b). Multiple cycles of freeze/thaw produce a repeating pattern of cryoprotectant synthesis and degradation (Storey 1987b). Glycerol content in the organs of *H. versicolor,* however, not only appears to be much more evenly distributed among organs but remains high for several weeks after thawing (Schmid 1982; Storey and Storey 1985a). This species may simply maintain the inert pool of glycerol throughout the winter months.

Production of cryoprotectant by liver of freeze-tolerant frogs is triggered only in response to ice nucleation in periph-

Fig. 10.6 Course of glucose accumulation by organs of *Rana sylvatica* over 72 h of freezing at −2.5°C. Also shown is the corresponding depletion of liver glycogen reserves. (Modified from Storey and Storey 1986b.)

eral tissues. No anticipatory production of cryoprotectant occurs during autumn cold hardening, as in insects (Storey and Storey 1988). In *R. sylvatica,* glucose synthesis is underway within 5 min of the appearance of the freezing exotherm (fig. 10.5). The synthetic pathway has only three enzymatic steps (glycogen phosphorylase, phosphoglucomutase, and glucose-6-phosphatase) for the conversion of glycogen to glucose. Enzymatic controls, a rapid activation of glycogen phosphorylase and an inhibition of phosphofructokinase (preventing endogenous oxidation of hexose phosphate), channel glycogenolysis into glucose output from liver (Storey 1987a). The link between peripheral ice formation and liver glucose output is undoubtedly nervous or hormonal, probably catecholamine-mediated. Studies with isolated hepatocytes from *R. sylvatica* have shown that glucose output is highly sensitive to epinephrine stimulation (T. Mommsen and K. B. Storey unpublished data), and injection of a β-adrenergic antagonist (propranolol) blocks the freezing-induced production of glucose (K. B. Storey and J. M. Storey unpublished data). Epinephrine readily stimulates hyperglycemia in cold- (5°C), but not in warm- (25°C), acclimated *R. temporaria* (Harri and Lindgren 1972). The hyperglycemic response to adrenalin in *R. pipiens* is greatest in the autumn (Farrar and Frye 1977). Thus, the synthesis of cryoprotectant by freeze-tolerant frogs may be an exaggerated response to a normally increased sensitivity of liver to catecholamine stimulation during the winter months.

The mechanism of glycogen phosphorylase control in *R. sylvatica* has novel components, however. Enzyme activation appears to have two parts: (1) an immediate increase in the percentage of enzyme in the active *a* form, initiated within 2 min of freezing exposure and complete in 30 to 60 min, and (2) a slower rise in the total activity (*a* + *b*) of phosphorylase, first apparent after about 30 min of freezing exposure and persisting for several hours (Storey and Storey 1988). Thus, for example, the measurable content of phosphorylase is 3 units · g^{-1} wet mass and 37% *a* in liver of control (3°C) frogs but rises to 18.6 units and 80% *a* in liver of frogs frozen at −4°C (Storey and Storey 1984). Overall, the content of active phosphorylase *a* in liver can rise seven- to thirteenfold to support rates of glucose synthesis of greater than 20 μmol · g^{-1} · h^{-1} at −2.5°C (Storey and Storey 1985b, 1988). Control of glycogen phosphorylase activation in *R. sylvatica* liver is via protein phosphorylation, the mechanism somewhat modified from that typical of mammalian liver (Crerar, David, and Storey 1988).

Glucose is an unusual cryoprotectant, and recent studies have explored the protective effects of this hexose sugar compared to those of the more commonly occurring polyhydroxy alcohols such as glycerol. Glucose appears advantageous for the resumption of metabolic function after freezing. *In vitro* studies with isolated heart strips of *R. sylvatica* have shown that contractility is regained after freezing only when the tissue is frozen in the presence of the natural cryoprotectant, glucose (Canty, Driedzic, and Storey 1986). In the absence of glucose or with the substitution of glycerol, physical function is not regained after freezing. Glucose, glycerol, and dimethylsulfoxide are equally effective in the physical cryoprotection of isolated hepatocytes of *R. sylvatica*, but only glucose shows additional metabolic effects in depressing cellular functions (e.g., urea synthesis) during freezing (T. Mommsen and K. B. Storey unpublished data).

Life in the Frozen State Extracellular freezing imposes an ischemic and anoxic state on all cells of the body. Organs must rely upon their endogenous fuel and energy reserves throughout freezing and tolerate the accumulation of metabolic end products. Freezing selectively increases the activities of glycogen phosphorylase and glucose-6-phosphatase in the liver of *R. sylvatica* and phosphorylase in the liver of *H. versicolor*, as expected for cryoprotectant synthesis (fig. 10.5; Storey and Storey 1984, 1985a). However, freezing does not affect the activities of fifteen other enzymes in either liver or leg muscle (when corrected for differences in organ water contents of control versus frozen frogs).

Energy metabolism in the frozen state relies on anaerobic glycolysis with lactate and/or alanine accumulating as end products (fig. 10.7). Creatine phosphate hydrolysis or amino acid fermentation may also contribute to ATP production in some organs (Storey and Storey 1984, 1985a, 1986b). Individual organs differ both in the lactate to alanine ratio and in the net accumulation of end products during freezing, this latter suggesting organ-specific metabolic rates in the frozen state. Energy stress during freezing also differs between organs. Energy charge ([2ATP + ADP]/2[ATP + ADP + AMP]) remains consistently high in skeletal muscle over both single and multiple freezing exposures, whereas ATP levels and energy charge decrease sharply in liver while frozen (fig. 10.7;

Storey 1987b; Storey and Storey 1984, 1985a, 1986b). However, the metabolic stresses of the frozen state are not permanent; organ energy status rebounds over several days after thawing, and cryoprotectants and metabolic end products are rapidly cleared (Storey 1987b; Storey and Storey 1986b).

Metabolic depression is a key feature of the overwintering strategy of many animals, characterizing, for example, insect diapause and hibernation of mammals and turtles (Storey and Storey 1990). For a freeze-tolerant animal, a preexisting hypometabolic state or a metabolic depression induced during freezing could greatly improve long-term survival under ischemia. Indeed, winter dormancy occurs in numerous freeze-tolerant insects and marine invertebrates. Whether there is a specific metabolic depression in freeze-tolerant amphibians over and above the effects of low temperature on metabolism is not yet clear.

Aquatic Hibernators: Hypoxia and Osmotic Stress

Most amphibians have little difficulty submerging in well-aerated water for long periods at low temperatures, because they can breathe through their skins. Since the amphibians that overwinter underwater are generally aquatic, winter submergence in well-aerated water is an extension of normal diving. Most adult amphibians cannot remain submerged indefinitely at high temperatures because the diffusing capacity of the skin is insufficient to supply a relatively high metabolic rate. Cutaneous diffusing capacity remains constant as temperature and metabolic rate decrease (Jackson 1978a), so that cutaneous gas exchange is adequate for all O_2 uptake at low temperatures. CO_2 is more easily exchanged through the skin than is O_2 because it diffuses through tissues much more readily, so CO_2 excretion is not a problem. Only if the water becomes hypoxic do submerged amphibians face respiratory stress.

Anaerobiosis Unlike freeze-tolerant frogs, amphibians in severely hypoxic or anoxic water cannot rely on anaerobic energy production for long. Glycogen is rapidly depleted from the liver and heart, with a concomitant buildup of plasma and tissue lactate (Christiansen and Penney 1973). Protons (H$^+$) are produced with lactate, resulting in rapid and severe metabolic acidosis (Christiansen and Penney 1973; Pinder 1985). In *Rana pipiens* submerged in anoxic water at 5°C, plasma pH decreases almost 0.7 units within 3 days as plasma lactate concentration increased sixtyfold, and the animals became moribund and unable to move (fig. 10.8). Plasma bicarbonate buffer capacity is exhausted as bicarbonate is titrated by metabolically produced protons and excreted as CO_2. Whether depletion of cardiac glycogen and the cessation of glycolytic ATP production or acidosis per se causes death is uncertain, but in any case anaerobiosis cannot support metabolism for long enough to permit winter survival in anoxic water.

The sensitivity of frogs to anoxia is in marked contrast to turtles (*Chrysemys picta*) that submerge for the winter: *Chrysemys* can survive on anaerobiosis for several months at 3°C by reducing metabolism much more than would be expected from temperature alone. These turtles have large glycogen stores at the start of winter, and buffer huge lactic acid loads by releasing $CaCO_3$ from the shell (Herbert and Jackson 1985; Jackson and Heisler 1983; Jackson and Ultsch 1982).

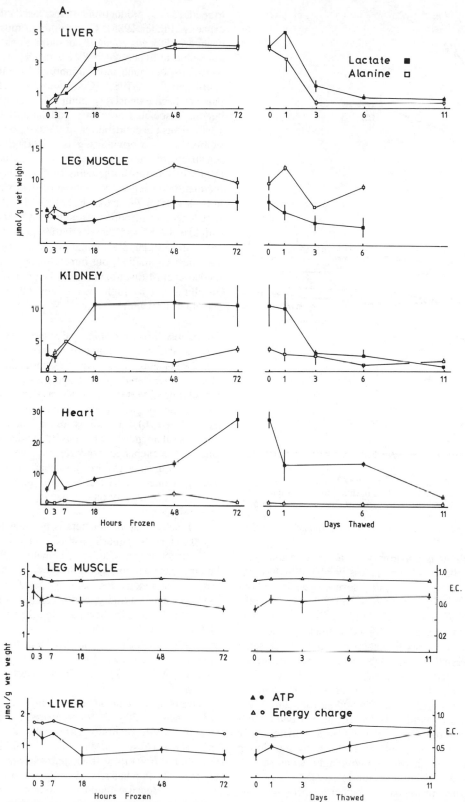

Fig. 10.7 Energy metabolism in organs of *Rana sylvatica* over a course of 3 days of freezing at −2.5°C and subsequent 11 days of thawing at 3°C. *A*, lactate and alanine accumulate as end products of anaerobic glycolysis in the ischemic state produced by extracellular freezing. Individual organs differ in total end product accumulation and in the ratio of lactate to alanine. *B*, ATP content and energy charge, [2ATP + ADP]/ 2[ATP + ADP + AMP], in liver and leg skeletal muscle. Freezing has little effect on energy status in muscle; ATP content is still 71% of control after 3 days of freezing, and energy charge decreases only fractionally. Liver shows greater energy stress, a 50% drop in ATP content and a decline in energy charge from 0.86 to 0.70, but both parameters readily recover upon thawing. (Redrawn from Storey and Storey 1986b.)

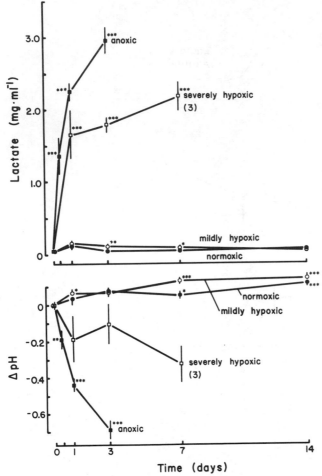

Fig. 10.8 Changes in plasma lactate concentration and pH during exposure of submerged *Rana pipiens* to various O_2 concentrations at 5°C. Po_2 of normoxic water = 150 mm Hg; mildly hypoxic = 80 mm Hg; severely hypoxic = 30 mm Hg; anoxic <9 mm Hg. (From Pinder 1985.)

Although amphibians apparently cannot reduce total metabolism greatly, they may nonetheless be able to reduce energy use enough to withstand more severe hypoxia without incurring lactic acidosis, or withstand anoxia longer than otherwise possible. *Bufo bufo* at 20°C reduce O_2 uptake to 20% of normal resting values during forced submergence with no O_2 debt, and reduce metabolic heat production by the same proportion (Leivestad 1960). Submergence also depresses metabolism in normally air-breathing *Siren* (Ultsch 1974a, 1976b). A 30% reduction of resting metabolism occurs in *Desmognathus fuscus* (Caudata: Plethodontidae) during hypoxia at 13°C (Gatz and Piiper 1979). In anoxic *Rana pipiens* at 5°C energy metabolism may decrease approximately 50% (Pinder 1985). Thus, although metabolic reduction during overwintering has not yet been convincingly demonstrated, moderate metabolic reduction occurs in closely related conditions (submergence or hypoxia at higher temperatures) and may increase tolerance to hypoxia.

Mechanisms by which overwintering frogs might regulate extracellular and intracellular pH during moderate hypoxia and lactic acidosis are unknown but are likely to resemble to those used by skin-breathing amphibians at higher temperatures. Skin ventilation is an unlikely regulatory mechanism, because blood P_{CO_2} is less than 1 mm Hg during hypoxia due

to reduced CO_2 production and increased cutaneous diffusing capacity (Pinder 1985). Compensation must involve ion exchange in kidneys, bladder, or skin. Renal compensation is negligible in hypercapnic *Bufo marinus* at 20°C; the bladder appears to be much more important in acid-base regulation (Tufts and Toews 1985). Cutaneous ion exchange in amphibians has been extensively studied (see chapter 5 for details), but the associated acid-base adjustments have not (Stiffler 1988). Thus the contribution of the skin to acid-base compensation during overwintering is unknown. The temperature sensitivity of ion-exchange mechanisms and the maximum capacity of these mechanisms to compensate for lactic acid production during winter anoxia or hypoxia is unknown. As in turtles, amphibians may be able to liberate $CaCO_3$ from the skeleton or from nodules found within endolymphatic sacs (Simkiss 1968) and thereby buffer pH (see chapters 5 and 16). Intracellular pH regulation in hibernating amphibians has not been studied, but intracellular pH may be better defended against disturbance from lactic acid buildup than extracellular pH by high intracellular buffer capacity (Toews and Boutilier 1986).

Cutaneous Oxygen Uptake Because frogs may not become hypometabolic and cannot survive on anaerobic metabolism alone, cutaneous O_2 uptake is essential for survival, at least of submerged ranid frogs. Cutaneous gas exchange is widespread among vertebrates but is usually in combination with other modes of gas exchange (lungs, gills, or both; see chapters 4–6 and 16). Exceptions are the Plethodontidae and other lungless salamanders, which as adults depend entirely on cutaneous gas exchange; however, they are a largely terrestrial group and are not exposed to aquatic hypoxia. Amphibians that overwinter underwater are thus unique among vertebrates in relying exclusively on cutaneous gas exchange under prolonged hypoxia.

O_2 uptake in skin breathers is peculiar because cutaneous gas exchange is primarily diffusion-limited (Feder, Full, and Piiper 1988; Piiper, Gatz, and Crawford 1976; Pinder 1987a; Pinder, Clemens, and Feder in press; see also chapter 6). As a result, cutaneous gas exchange is often regarded as relatively passive, auxiliary, and inflexible in regulating gas exchange and acid-base balance (Boutilier 1988b; Gottlieb and Jackson 1976; Piiper, Gatz, and Crawford 1976). Although cutaneous gas exchange may not be as flexible as pulmonary or branchial exchange; it need not be entirely passive (Burggren and Moalli 1984; Feder and Burggren 1985a; Pinder 1987a).

Because the cutaneous epithelium is relatively thick for a gas exchanger (20–50 μm compared to 0.1–2 μm in lungs and gills), diffusion limits gas exchange across the epithelium, and blood perfusing the skin does not equilibrate with external Po_2. In bullfrogs in well-aerated water at 5°C, blood returning from the skin has a Po_2 of only 30 mm Hg (Pinder 1987a; fig. 10.9). Because blood returning from the skin is mixed with deoxygenated systemic venous blood before reaching the heart, systemic arterial Po_2 is even lower, only 10 to 15 mm Hg. Because hemoglobin-O_2 affinity is high, however (P_{50} = 14 mm Hg at 5°C compared to 45 mm Hg at 25°C; Pinder and Burggren 1983), oxygenated blood draining from the skin is 70 to 80% saturated and systemic arterial blood is about 45% saturated in bullfrogs in well-aerated water at 5°C.

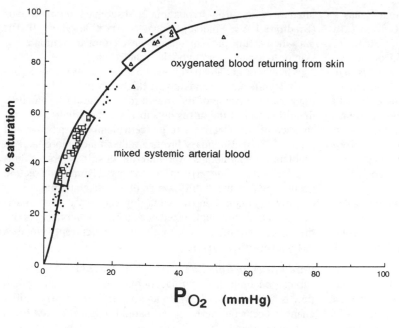

Fig. 10.9   *In vivo* hemoglobin-oxygen equilibrium curve for *Rana catesbeiana* at 5°C, noting the P_{O_2} and saturation of systemic arterial blood and venous return from the skin. Blood samples were taken from cannulated bullfrogs submerged in water of various P_{O_2}'s between 50 mm Hg and 600 mm Hg. (Pinder unpublished data.)

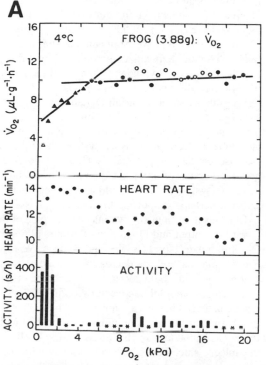

Fig. 10.10   Measurements of O_2 uptake ($\dot{V}_{O_2}$), activity, ventilation, and heart rate in a *Rana muscosa* adult (*A*) and larva (*B*) at 4°C as O_2 was depleted from a closed respirometer over the course of about 12 h. The critical P_{O_2} is that at the intersection of the two $\dot{V}_{O_2}$ regression lines. $\bigcirc$,

$\dot{V}_{O_2}$'s obtained during moderate or high locomotor activity and are not included in the calculation of critical P_{O_2}. *Asterisks* indicate zero activity over the specified range in P_{O_2}. (Reprinted, by permission, from Bradford 1983.)

Krogh's diffusion constant for CO_2 in aqueous solutions is about thirty times that for O_2; thus the P_{CO_2} gradient between blood and water is less than one-thirtieth the gradient for O_2; blood P_{CO_2} is 3 mm Hg. Bicarbonate concentration is around 21 mM, for a blood pH of about 8.0 to 8.2 at 5°C (Pinder 1985). The high hemoglobin-O_2 affinity in overwintering bullfrogs, due largely to the effect of temperature on hemoglobin-O_2 binding and less importantly on the low P_{CO_2} and high pH, clearly emphasizes loading and would seem particularly important in environments that may become hypoxic.

Blood P_{O_2} and the gradient across the skin decrease in proportion to external P_{O_2}. Bullfrogs (*Rana catesbeiana*) submerged at 5°C maintain O_2 uptake as long as water P_{O_2} remains above 80 mm Hg, in spite of the decreased P_{O_2} gradient across the skin, by an increase in cutaneous diffusing capacity (Pinder 1987a). The critical P_{O_2} is even lower in *R. muscosa*: about 30 mm Hg in adults and 15 mm Hg in larvae (Bradford 1983; fig. 10.10). Some of this difference may be related to body size (Ultsch 1973b, 1976b). Cutaneous diffusing capacity increases only as the 0.57 power of body mass (Feder 1988); if $\dot{M}O_2$ (rate of O_2 consumption) has a higher allometric coefficient (coefficients from 0.52 to 1.16 have been reported in amphibians [Bradford 1983; Hutchison, Whitford, and Kohl 1968; Whitford and Hutchison 1967]) than cutaneous diffusing capacity, $\dot{M}O_2$ in larger animals may exceed the ability of the skin to supply O_2. As a result, aerobic scope may decrease and critical PO_2 may increase with body size. Although Bradford (1983) found no allometric relationship between critical PO_2 and body mass in the limited size range of *R. muscosa*, Ultsch (1973b, 1974a, 1976b) demonstrated that large skin-breathing *Siren* (Sirenidae) have much reduced aerobic scope and higher critical PO_2's than small *Siren*. Urodeles may have lower critical PO_2's than anurans of equivalent size because they have (1) an elongated shape with more surface area per unit mass, (2) thinner cutaneous epithelium, and (3) greater cutaneous capillary density, combining to give approximately tenfold higher cutaneous diffusing capacity (Czopek 1965).

Boundary Layers Boundary layers next to the skin may potentially affect water, ion, and gas exchange in submerged amphibians (Feder and Burggren 1985a; Feder and Pinder 1988b; see also chapters 4 and 5). Diffusion boundary layers occur in any exchange between a solid body and fluid. At water velocities less than 1 cm · s⁻¹ the O_2-depleted boundary layer limits O_2 uptake of immobile bullfrogs at 5°C (Pinder and Feder 1990). The boundary layer is a significant part (35%) of the total resistance to gas exchange even at 5 cm · s⁻¹ and below 1 cm · s⁻¹ is the dominant resistance, larger than the resistance of the skin itself to O_2 diffusion (fig. 10.11). Occasional small body movements in freely moving frogs sufficiently disrupt the boundary layer to maintain O_2 uptake even in still water (Pinder and Feder 1990). Body movements

often increase during hypoxia in cold submerged amphibians (Bradford 1983; Pinder personal observations; fig. 10.10), but whether the movements are an attempt to ventilate the skin or to escape from hypoxia is uncertain.

Whether or not any particular boundary layer is physiologically significant depends on its thickness (which is proportional to the inverse of the square root of the fluid velocity), the diffusivity of the diffusing substance, and the relative resistance of other barriers (e.g., cell membranes; Feder and Pinder 1988b). Boundary layers are thus much more likely a problem for amphibians overwintering in still waters—ponds or lakes—than along rivers or streams. Natural convection occurs even in the "still" water of lakes; amphibians may conceivably choose an overwintering site partly on the basis of ventilation, although whether aquatic amphibians choose their overwintering sites according to local current velocities or O_2 levels is unknown.

Cardiovascular Function When hypoxia reduces $\dot{M}O_2$ in cold submerged bullfrogs, cardiac output decreases, and blood flow is redistributed (A. W. Pinder unpublished data). Similar changes occur during extended natural dives or forced dives in mammals and birds. Cardiovascular responses to changes in aquatic PO_2 are shown in figure 10.12. Heart rate in severe hypoxia decreases almost 50%, but blood pressure is constant (A. W. Pinder and A. W. Smits unpublished). Cardiac output falls in hypoxia, and celiacomesenteric blood flow ceases altogether in severe hypoxia. Cutaneous blood flow changes little or may slightly decrease in hypoxia.

Frogs thus appear to curtail O_2 delivery to nonessential tissues (gut and probably skeletal musculature) and to reserve the limited O_2 uptake for tissues more important for immediate survival (central nervous system, heart, and kidney). Because cardiac output and systemic blood flow decrease greatly, the ratio of oxygenated (cutaneous venous) to deoxygenated (systemic venous) blood returned to the heart increases, perhaps supporting O_2 delivery to essential tissues.

Changes in plasma volume may cause some of the changes in cardiac output and blood flow. Plasma volume varies with O_2 saturation of blood (A. W. Pinder and A. W. Smits unpublished): plasma volume decreases with decreasing O_2 saturation, and thus hematocrit increases (fig. 10.13). Mean corpuscular hemoglobin concentration is constant, indicating that hematocrit changes are not caused by red cell swelling as in hibernating turtles (Maginniss, Tapper, and Miller 1983). Increased hematocrit is also not due to red cell release from the spleen, since hematocrits of animals with the spleen ligated also increased in hypoxia. Most of the volume change occurs at arterial saturations below 45%, the arterial saturation in normoxic water at 5°C. The mechanism of plasma volume reduction during hypoxia is uncertain, but probably involves increased fluid filtration across capillaries or decreased lymphatic return of fluid to the circulatory system or both. The water permeability of individual frog mesenteric capillaries increases severalfold when perfused or superfused with anoxic saline (Tucker and Huxley 1987). In prolonged hypoxia with associated lactate production, plasma volume could also decrease due to the osmotic effect of intracellular lactate (Boutilier, Emilio, and Shelton 1986). This would decrease both plasma and extracellular fluid volumes, whereas

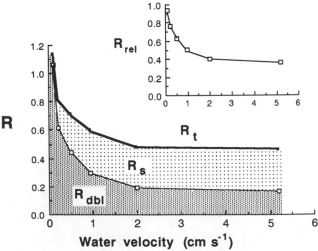

Fig. 10.11 Total resistance to cutaneous O_2 uptake (R_t, the inverse of diffusing capacity) and its components of skin resistance (R_s) and boundary layer resistance (R_{dbl}) in immobilized bullfrogs (*Rana catesbeiana*) submerged in normoxic water at 5°C as a function of water velocity (U). The relative resistance of the boundary layer (R_{rel}, the proportion of R_t made up by R_{dbl}) is graphed in the inset. The resistance of the diffusion boundary layer is a significant part (35%) of the total resistance to O_2 uptake even at the relatively high water velocity of 5 cm s⁻¹ and is the predominant component of resistance at water velocities below 1 cm s⁻¹. (From Pinder and Feder 1990.)

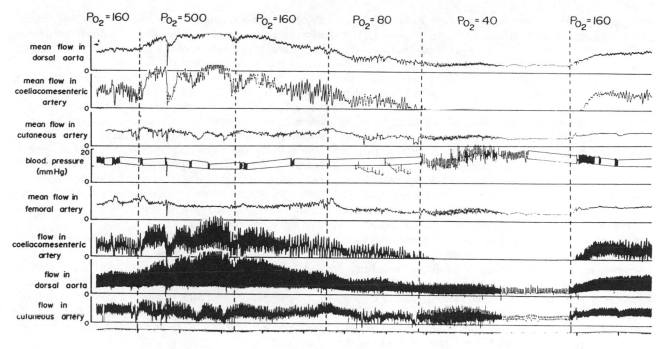

Time (hours)

Fig. 10.12 Changes in blood flow distribution and central arterial blood pressure during exposure to aquatic normoxia, hypoxia, and hyperoxia of an intact, lightly sedated bullfrog (*Rana catesbeiana*) submerged at 5°C. Blood flow was measured with pulsed-Doppler flow probes chronically implanted on the dorsal aorta as an indicator of cardiac output, the celiacomesenteric artery as a measure of blood flow to viscera, the cutaneous artery to measure blood flow to the gas exchanger, and the femo-ral artery, which carries blood both to hindlimb musculature and skin. Blood pressure remains fairly constant, with a slight decrease in hyperoxia and an increase in hypoxia (the trace is incomplete due to repeated plugging of the cannula). Transients in the pressure trace mark spontaneous movements by the frog; there was no movement until the frog was exposed to hypoxia; movements increased dramatically in more severe hypoxia. (Pinder unpublished data.)

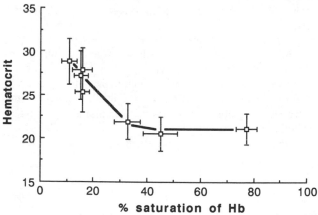

Fig. 10.13 Hematocrat as a function of arterial hemoglobin saturation in submerged bullfrogs at 10°C. A similar relationship is obtained at 5°C. Hemoglobin saturation was manipulated by placing the frog in hypoxic or hyperoxic water.

hypoxic frogs seem to have large lymph volumes (Christiansen and Penney 1973; Jørgensen, Brems, and Geckler 1978).

Reduced plasma volume must alter cardiovascular function. Because cardiac output is a function of cardiovascular filling pressure and blood volume, changes in cardiac output and blood distribution during hyperoxia and hypoxia may be due in part to blood volume changes; blood volume or cardiac output may not be sufficient to perfuse all of the body during hypoxia. Blood viscosity is a function of red cell concentra-tion and must increase as hematocrit increases, making the blood more difficult to pump. O_2 carrying capacity of blood, O_2 delivery, and perhaps diffusing capacity of capillaries are also dependent on hematocrit. Whether decreased plasma volume and increased hematocrit are adaptive for survival of hypoxia is unclear. Possible adaptive scenarios are that the increased hematocrit helps O_2 delivery to critical tissues when O_2 saturation decreases, or that increased hematocrit is associated with greater numbers of red cells in cutaneous capillaries, thus increasing cutaneous diffusing capacity.

Osmoregulation Intra- and extracellular fluid compartment volumes and osmolarity change both with hypoxia during submergence and with submergence alone (which causes hypoxemia compared to bimodally breathing amphibians). Several studies, almost all on adult aquatic ranid frogs, report a rapid increase in body mass and decrease of osmotic concentration due to osmotic water influx upon submergence without hypoxia. The amount of influx depends on the temperature: no effect occurs above 8°C, but influx increases with decreasing temperature and is about 20% of body mass at 0.5°C (Bradford 1984c; Jørgensen 1950; Miller, Standish, and Thurman 1968; Rey 1937; Schmidt-Nielsen and Forster 1954). The initial change at 4°C, consisting primarily of a water influx and resulting in dilution of ion concentrations, is complete within 1 or a few days. Ion concentrations may increase, and more water enter, during subsequent weeks or months until a new steady state is established in which Na^+ concentrations are returned to normal, but fluid volume and total extracellular Na$^+$ are both increased about 70% compared to animals at 20°C (Bradford 1984c; Jørgensen 1950; Jørgensen, Brems, and Geckler 1978). Body water content changes seasonally in *Pseudacris triseriata maculata*, but osmotic concentration decreases while body mass remains constant during acute cold exposure (MacArthur and Dandy 1982). Osmotic concentration decreases in both extra- and intracellular fluids upon cold submergence (Miller, Standish, and Thurman 1968). The immediate reason for mass increase is that urine production ceases for 12 to 18 h after transfer to cold, after which urine output rises to balance osmotic water influx (Schmidt-Nielsen and Forster 1954). Net water influx and decrease in body osmotic concentration are apparently not due to an inability of the kidney to excrete sufficient water to balance the influx or to inadequacy of cutaneous ion pumps, but indicate a change in the set-point for osmoregulation.

During aquatic hypoxia, body water increases more than in normoxic cold submergence. Christiansen and Penney (1973) noted that aquatic frogs gained 16% body mass upon submersion in anoxic water, looked bloated, and had copious lymph in the dorsal lymph sacs and other subcutaneous spaces; they concluded that accumulation of lymph was responsible for much of the body mass gain. Volumes of the intracellular, extracellular, and cardiovascular fluid compartments during aquatic hypoxia are not known, nor is whether increases in body mass during hypoxia are due to limits on renal function or to changes in renal set-point. One possible reason for lowered osmotic concentration during winter is to decrease osmotic influx of water and thus the cost of osmoregulation; requirements for higher ionic concentrations necessary for function of transport systems and excitable cells may be relaxed during winter inactivity. Problems of balancing osmotic fluid intake during hypoxia are potentially exacerbated by increased osmotic influx due to capillary recruitment (Mahany and Parsons 1978; Stiffler 1988).

DIRECTIONS FOR RESEARCH IN ESTIVATION AND HIBERNATION

Much of the foregoing discussion is a thin fabric woven from a few scattered studies, often using different species and conditions. Extensive data are available for very few species; data interpreted here as representative of common patterns of response may in fact be from different responses. Large gaps remain in our understanding.

The microenvironments surrounding amphibians during estivation or hibernation are almost entirely unknown, making realistic laboratory studies difficult to design. This is particularly true of amphibians estivating in mud or hibernating underwater. Microenvironments are likely to vary greatly both spatially and temporally; no single study can comprehensively address all possible variations even for a single species. Our present ignorance is such, however, that measuring the microenvironment surrounding a single animal through a single season of estivation or hibernation would add immensely to our knowledge.

Although metabolic reduction is potentially advantageous to both estivators and hibernators, the mechanism is not understood in amphibians. In estivators, the phenomenon is well established, but our knowledge of how it is induced is largely limited to what little is known from other vertebrates and invertebrates. Even the existence of metabolic reduction is uncertain in hibernators during environmental or freezing-associated anoxia.

As in any physiological problem, the most difficult aspect to study is the control system. Many instances of altered control are found in estivation and hibernation: in addition to metabolic reduction, ventilation and the effect of CO_2 seem to be altered in estivators. The set-point for fluid and ion balance seems to be reset in aquatic hibernators. Cardiovascular function and control seem to be drastically altered in aquatic hibernation and hypoxia due to decreased plasma volume. Internal signals for emergence from estivation or hibernation, formation of urea during estivation, or formation of cryoprotectants in freezing frogs remain undescribed. A fascinating yet entirely unstudied problem is how a frog reestablishes integrated body function after thawing.

Estivation and hibernation are a large part of the life cycle of many amphibians and are responsible for much of the success of amphibians as a group. Although there are many technical problems working with estivating or hibernating animals, research opportunities abound.

Part 3
Energetics and Locomotion

Amphibians face interrelated problems of internal control, coordination, and homeostasis as well as external environmental challenges. Solving these problems provides amphibians with an *opportunity* to exploit a given environment, and the limits to these solutions correspondingly limit the magnitude of this opportunity. What an amphibian makes of this opportunity, however, depends largely upon its ability to locate, capture, and ingest food; to convert the chemical bonds in the foodstuffs to biologically useful energy; to employ this energy in various activities (e.g., courtship, foraging, predator avoidance, care of offspring, dispersal, and migration); and to produce additional biomass. This latter complex of issues, both physiological and ecological, is an additional focus for this book, which parts 3 and 4 consider. The key themes in the present section are energy and activity.

Both energy flow and activity depend critically on the effective use of the musculoskeletal system. Fortunately for students of amphibians, amphibian muscle has long enjoyed extensive use in general physiological examinations of muscle structure and function. Unfortunately, the resulting literature has been so voluminous as to defy comprehensive overviews, is often highly specialized, and sometimes bears little relation to the physiology of amphibians as entire organisms. In Chapter 11 Carl Gans and Greet de Gueldre have undertaken the formidable task of reviewing this literature and placing it in context. The context is twofold. First, understanding locomotion, feeding, courtship, and the other roles that muscles perform will benefit from a detailed understanding of muscle structure and function itself. This understanding will need to integrate both a considerable body of now classical material on muscle physiology and biomechanics, and more modern studies drawing upon the neurosciences, biophysics, and molecular biology. Second, understanding the properties of muscle per se is not enough; one needs to understand the relationships of muscles to one another and to the skeletal and nervous systems, the patterns of neuromuscular coordination, the ultimate behaviors that the muscles underlie, and the environments in which these behaviors occur. These latter issues constitute the larger field of functional morphology, in whose development Gans has been a major figure. As Gans and de Gueldre point out, either the physiology of amphibian

muscle or the functional morphology of amphibians could well require an entire book in itself. This chapter will provide entrée to the considerable literature.

In organizing the ensuing chapters on energetics, the editors were cognizant of several important reviews that have recently appeared in print. In *Biology of Amphibians* (1986), Duellman and Trueb devote an entire chapter to food and feeding, as well as portions of several other chapters. Seale (1987) reviewed the energetics of amphibians in great detail. In light of these excellent works, the editors saw little point in retreading the ground that Duellman, Seale, and Trueb have so recently and thoroughly explored. The contributors on energetics have therefore, for the most part, prepared chapters that complement rather than duplicate these two reviews; readers are urged to consult these reviews in addition to the present volume to obtain a comprehensive overview of energy use in amphibians.

A most useful feature of the whole-organism metabolic rate is that it can serve as a general and simultaneous indicator of both the overall internal function of an organism and the effect of the environment on that function (Fry 1947). For the metabolic rate to be useful as an indicator, one must first know what rate is normal, standard, or expected for an amphibian of a given size in given circumstances (temperature, time of day, intensity of activity, sex, season, and so on). Although broadly based standards are available for other vertebrate classes (e.g., Bennett and Dawson 1976 and Andrews and Pough 1985 for reptiles), none has been available for amphibians until now. In chapter 12, Gatten, Miller, and Full summarize the extensive literature on minimum metabolic rates of amphibians and provide such a standard. With this standard as a point of departure, one can explore a host of related issues. How much energy does an amphibian require simply to stay alive, and how does this amount compare to the energy or food available in various environments? How much additional energy is required to move, capture prey, escape predators, attract mates, and so on? Given that individual amphibians must do more than just stay alive, has natural selection resulted in forms of activity that are economical or efficient? In an economic sense, what is the relationship between the rate of energy expenditure and the rate of return? What limits energy use, and through it activity? How, mechanistically, do amphibians gather and process the energy in their food? Finally, in a broadly comparative sense, what is the relationship between the magnitude of energy use and perpetuation of a group in geological time?

The contributors to chapters 12–14 approach these issues from a variety of perspectives. Since the recognition of the singular significance of anaerobic metabolism (glycolysis) to physical activity in amphibians (Bennett and Licht 1973, 1974), interest has burgeoned in the relative proportions of aerobic and anaerobic metabolism during activity in various species, the physiological underpinnings of high capacities for aerobiosis or anaerobiosis, the ecological consequences of a large aerobic or anaerobic scope, and so on. Chapter 12 reviews this large and still growing literature. A complementary perspective has been to examine the energetic cost of activity irrespective of the metabolic source of the energy. Biologists such as R. Brett, R. J. Full, C. F. Herreid, K. Schmidt-Nielsen, C. R. Taylor, and V. L. Tucker have pioneered the analysis of how the body form and size of organisms affect the cost of their locomotion. Curiously, despite amphibians' unusual modes of locomotion, these animals have seldom figured in this analysis, and chapter 12 seeks to redress this omission. In addition to reviewing the larger issues of feeding and digestion, chapter 13 exemplifies an unusual perspective for this volume: the extremely detailed study of a particular amphibian, in this case toads (*Bufo*). Particularly in the European scientific community, sensory, motor, endocrinological, nutritional, and natural historical aspects of toads have received intense scrutiny. As a result of this work, more may be known about toads than about any other kind of amphibian. Finally, whereas chapter 12 considers the energetics of amphibians engaging in stereotypical activity in the laboratory, chapter 14 considers the energetics of amphibians engaging in naturalistic behavior, often unrestrained or in the field. The study of these behaviors, chiefly foraging and courtship, is undertaken as much to clarify their ecological implications and evolutionary significance as to understand their physiological underpinnings. This chapter, more than any other in this book, exemplifies how the physiological study of amphibians can exceed the bounds of more typical physiological studies.

11 Striated Muscle: Physiology and Functional Morphology

Carl Gans and Greet de Gueldre

Amphibians have contributed enormously to our understanding of general principles of vertebrate biology, advancing areas such as development, regeneration, bioelectricity, and vision; in each, amphibian studies have led to major breakthroughs, and untold human patients have benefited from the information. Indeed, the early experiments of Galvani (1791) used anuran muscles to detect current; since then electrophysiology has relied heavily on amphibian skeletal muscles. Much of the work that led to our present level of knowledge on the process and control of muscular contraction (e.g., the difference between twitch and tonic motor fibers and units) used amphibian tissues. The sequence of discovery has generated an incredibly voluminous literature, much of which does not address issues that are intrinsically amphibian, but rather uses amphibian muscles to investigate more general topics.

Recent studies have begun to ask questions of muscular adaptation among amphibians more directly: How does a particular caecilian bite? How does a salamander ventilate? How does a frog swim? The explosion in physiological technology now is letting us answer such questions, and our increased knowledge of the connections of the nervous system (see chapter 2) has added new dimensions to the answers.

This chapter attempts more to sample than to summarize all studies in these two extensive categories. Indeed, a comprehensive summary would occupy several volumes. In this chapter we address the following kinds of questions: What does a physiological ecologist need to know about amphibian striated muscle? What are some of the techniques that permit questions to be evaluated? Is amphibian muscle unique in any of its characteristics? What aspects of amphibian muscle deserve special attention? What do we know about the ways that amphibian muscles are placed structurally and functionally to perform the roles these animals demand? How do amphibians feed and breathe, move and call?

We must stress that by far the greatest portion of what follows is derived from a relatively limited number of species (see chapter 1). This is particularly true for the anatomical, physiological, and biochemical studies of muscle as a tissue. Therefore, some caution is required in extrapolating from the present statements to amphibians as a whole. Throughout, we

have framed the chapter and selected the references to facilitate further studies.

We list at the outset some major aspects in which amphibian muscle is unique. First, it displays some patterns of motor innervation unusual among vertebrates. Next, it characteristically undergoes major changes at metamorphosis. Although Recent amphibians are highly derived, the changes that occur in amphibian muscle at metamorphosis may reflect changes involved in the shift from water to land, from fishes to tetrapods. Finally, many muscles in many (but not all) species of amphibians display a spectacular capacity for regeneration.

Several overviews of amphibian biology are excellent references: Frost (1985) for the most recent checklist of amphibian species; Duellman and Trueb (1986) for a broad yet detailed review of amphibian biology; Abbott and Brady (1964) for issues concerning amphibian muscle; Llinás and Precht (1976) and chapter 2 for a review of the anuran nervous system; Brooks (1981), Hill (1970), Hoyle (1983), Peachey (1983), and Schmalbruch (1985) for recent compendia broadly reviewing vertebrate muscles as tissues; and Jouffroy (in press) and Renous (in press) for listings of amphibian muscles (intended for publication in the *Traité de Zoologie*).

Many studies and reviews used the musculature as an approach to phylogenetic analyses (cf. Cannatella and Trueb 1988; Jones 1933; Griffiths 1963; Tyler 1971b; Wilcy 1979; this literature tends to be best reviewed in the *Zoological Record*). Table 11.1 lists a sampling of major descriptive studies on amphibian muscle. References cited there include detailed descriptions of the musculature of a particular species, and papers that consider individual muscles or groups of muscles in various families, often to determine taxonomic and phylo-

We thank Mr. J. O'Reilly for a preliminary search of the literature and H. Akster, David Carrier, Frits de Vree, Abbot S. Gaunt, Victor H. Hutchison, N. E. Kemp, Kiisa Nishikawa, James O'Reilly, Linda Trueb, and Richard Wassersug for comments on various portions of the manuscript. Sabine Renous and Françoise Jouffroy kindly sent us preprints of their chapters on amphibian muscle intended for the *Traité de Zoologie*. Ms. Katherine Vernon effectively helped with a check of the bibliography. Preparation supported by National Science Foundation Grant G-BSR-850940, a grant from the office of the vice president for research of The University of Michigan, and a travel award from the Leo Leeser Foundation.

TABLE 11.1   Descriptions of Muscle Anatomies in Various Amphibians

Order	Family	Species	Reference
		Whole body	
Amphibia			Ihle et al. 1927
Caudata			Wiedersheim 1875
Caudata	Plethodontidae	*Pseudoeurycea*	Baird 1951
Caudata	Plethodontidae	*Typhlomolge* sp.	Emerson 1905
Caudata	Salamandridae	*Salamandra maculosa*	Drüner 1902
Caudata	Salamandridae	*Salamandra* sp.	Francis 1934
Caudata	Cryptobranchidae	*Cryptobranchus*	Humphry 1871
Anura			Dugès 1834
Anura			Gaupp 1896–1904
Anura	Bufonidae	*Bufo vulgaris*	Bigalke 1926
Anura	Hemisidae	*Hemisus*	Beddard 1908b
Anura	Microhylidae	*Phrynomantis stictogaster*	Burton 1983
Anura	Microhylidae	*Breviceps verrucosus*	Beddard 1908a
Anura	Myobatrachidae	*Rheobatrachus silus*	Davies and Burton 1982
Anura	Pelobatidae	*Megalophrys*	Beddard 1907
Anura	Pipidae	*Pipa americana*	Beddard 1895a
Anura	Pipidae	*Xenopus*	Beddard 1895b
Anura	Pipidae	*Xenopus*	Deuchar 1975
Anura	Pipidae	*Xenopus*	Grobbelaar 1924
Gymnophiona			Wiedersheim 1879
Gymnophiona	Caeciliidae	*Hypogeophis rostratus*	Lawson 1965
		Axial	
Trunk muscles			
Amphibia			Nishi 1916, 1925, 1938
Caudata			Hofbauer 1934
Caudata			Naylor 1978
Anura			Dugès 1834
Anura	Leiopelmatidae	*Ascaphus truei*	Ritland 1955
Epaxial muscles			
Caudata	Sirenidae	*Siren*	Auffenberg 1959
Caudata	Amphiumidae	*Amphiuma*	Auffenberg 1959
Caudata	Proteidae	*Necturus*	Auffenberg 1959
Hypaxial muscles			
Caudata			Maurer 1891, 1895, 1911
Caudata	Limbless or nearly limbless		Auffenberg 1959, 1962
Caudata	Ambystomatidae	*Ambystoma*	Detwiler 1955
Anura			Maurer 1895
Gymnophiona			Naylor and Nussbaum 1980
Gymnophiona			Nussbaum and Naylor 1982
Cutaneous muscles			
Anura	Microhylidae		Burton 1980
Prevertebral muscles			
Amphibia			Cords 1923
		Head region	
Cranial muscles			
Amphibia			Edgeworth 1935
Caudata	Ambystomatidae	*Dicamptodon ensatus*	Eaton 1951
Mandibular muscles			
Amphibia	Recent and Paleozoic		Carroll and Holmes 1980
Amphibia			Göppert 1894
Amphibia			Kesteven 1944
Amphibia			Lubosch 1913, 1914
Amphibia			Luther 1914
Amphibia			Olson 1961
Anura	Ceratophrynidae		Limeses 1965
Anura	Pipidae	*Hymenochirus boettgeri*	Sokol 1969
Caudata	Cryptobranchidae	*Cryptobranchus japonicus*	Schumacher 1958a
Caudata	Amphiumidae	*Amphiuma tridactylum*	Erdman and Cundall 1984
Gymnophiona	Dermophiidae	*Dermophis*	De Jager 1939
Mandibular muscles, larvae			
Anura			Ramaswami 1943

TABLE 11.1 *(continued)*

Order	Family	Species	Reference
Hyoid, laryngeal, branchial muscles			
Amphibia			Edgeworth 1920, 1923, 1931
Amphibia			Chaine 1901, 1903
Caudata and Anura			Walter 1887
Caudata			Drüner 1903
Caudata			Piatt 1939, 1940
Caudata	Ambystomatidae	*Ambystoma*	Larsen and Guthrie 1975
Caudata		*Ambystoma punctatum*	Piatt 1938
Caudata	Plethodontidae		Piatt 1935
Caudata	Plethodontidae		Tanner 1952
Caudata	Cryptobranchidae	*Cryptobranchus japonicus*	Schumacher 1958b
Anura			Martin 1971
Anura	Hylidae	*Hyla arborea*	Schneider 1977
Anura	Pipidae	*Hymenochirus boettgeri*	Sokol 1969
Temporal muscle			
Caudata			Dubecq 1925
Throat muscles			
Caudata	Ambystomatidae	*Ambystoma*	Krogh and Tanner 1972
Myointegumental attachments associated with vocal sac			
Anura			Tyler 1971a, 1971b
Vocal sac muscles			
Anura	Ranidae	*Rana (Ptychadena)*	Inger 1956
Submandibular and vocal sac muscles			
Anura	Rhynophrynidae	*Rhinophrynus dorsalis*	Tyler 1974
Superficial throat muscles			
Anura	Microhylidae		Emerson 1976b
Tongue muscles			
Amphibia			Magimel-Pélonnier 1924
Anura	Australian Hylidae and Leptodactylidae		Horton 1977, 1982
Caudata			Lombard and Wake 1976, 1977, 1986
Caudata	Plethodontidae	*Bolitoglossa*	Thexton, Wake, and Wake 1977
Nasal muscles			
Caudata	Salamandridae	*Salamandrina*	Bruner 1901
Anura		*Rana* and others	Bruner 1901
Anura			Gans and Pyles 1983

Pectoral Muscles

Order	Family	Species	Reference
Primitive appendage			
Amphibia			Sewertzov 1907
Development			
Amphibia			Byrnes 1898
Caudata	Ambystomatidae	*Ambystoma*	Detwiler 1920
Pectoral muscles			
Amphibia			Fürbringer 1873, 1874
Amphibia			Perrin 1899
Amphibia			McMurrich 1903a, 1903b, 1904
Amphibia			Ribbing 1907, 1938
Amphibia			Lewis 1910
Amphibia			Anthony and Vallois 1914
Amphibia			Miner 1925
Amphibia			Howell 1936
Anura			Jones 1933
Anura		*Uperodon systoma*	Shukla and Bhati 1973
Anura	Pipidae	*Xenopus*	de Villiers 1929
	Pipidae	*Pipa*	de Villiers 1929
	Pipidae	*Hymenochirus*	de Villiers 1929
Anura	Ranidae	*Rana tigrina*	Bhati 1955
Anura	Bufonidae	*Bufo andersonii*	Bhati 1955

TABLE 11.1 (*continued*)

Order	Family	Species	Reference
Extensor muscles			
Tetrapods			Haines 1939
Pectoral muscles			
(development)			
Caudata			Rylkoff 1924
Carpal muscles			
Anura			Andersen 1978
		Pelvic Muscles	
Amphibia			Ribbing 1909, 1938
Amphibia			Perrin 1892a, 1982b
Caudata			Man 1873, 1874–75
Anura			Man 1873, 1874–75
Anura	Ranidae	*Rana tigrina*	Charan 1971
Thigh muscles			
Tetrapods			Appleton 1928
Anura			Noble 1922
Anura			Dunlap 1960
Anura		Microranid genera	Nel 1941
Limb muscles			
Caudata	Proteidae	*Necturus*	Wilder 1908
Tarsal muscles			
Anura			Andersen 1978
		Special muscles	
Eye muscles			
Amphibia			Burkard 1902
Caudata			Tretjakoff 1906
Caudata			Hilton 1956
Anura	Ranidae	*Rana*	Kilarski and Bigaj 1969
Middle ear and opercularis			
muscles			
Anura			Wever 1979, 1985
Caudata			Dunn 1922, 1941
Caudata			Monath 1965
Anura			Eiselt 1941
Integumentary muscles			
Amphibia			Cords 1922
Cutaneous pelvic patch			
Anura	Bufonidae		Winokur and Hillyard 1985, 1988
Brooding pouch muscles			
Anura	Hylidae, Hemiphractinae		
	(part)		del Pino 1980

genetic relationships. Also listed are a few papers that refer to muscles now considered to be smooth (cf. Gans and Pyles 1983).

TECHNIQUES
Analysis of Muscles

The following considerations are important in performing functional analyses of muscle: Most striated muscles act on supportive structures formed hydrostatically or on such supportive tissues as the notochord, cartilage, and bone. Characterization of portions of the muscular system hence should proceed in parallel with those of one or more skeletal preparations. Three major approaches to skeletal description facilitate comparison, namely, drying of skeletons (by dissection, maceration, and beetling), clearing (making soft tissues translucent) and staining (to show cartilage, bone, and neurons), and three-dimensional reconstruction from serial sections (the old wax-plate approach now facilitated by computer reconstruction). Muscles are defined and act by their attachment to connective tissue compartments; hence, mapping these is also useful. The mapping of muscles, using techniques described by Hildebrand (1968) and Dingerkus and Uhler (1977), provides information that indirectly reflects the developmental patterns of muscles and the way they are controlled. The placement of the cell bodies in the brain stem and spinal cord provides clues to the latter (Takei et al. 1987); hence, descriptive neuroanatomy is necessary as well.

As muscle fibers are intrinsically polarized, their positions need to be determined relative to those of the enclosing connective tissues; the changing positions of the muscles throughout the range of motion require special attention. Establishment of fiber position may require stereotactic mapping of fiber origin and insertion (Gans and de Vree 1987). Initial analyses should determine fiber length, both *in situ* and separated, as the force exerted and the muscular excursion may independently reflect pinnation and factors of equivalence (Gans and de Vree 1987). Fiber length and position may be determined by a combination of nitric acid digestion and gold staining (cf. Loeb and Gans 1986, Appendix 1, for these and subsequent techniques). One can map the distribution of motor end plates by staining fresh or formalin-fixed muscle (Karnovsky and Roots 1964); the differences in end-plate placement (noted below) deserve further attention. As the muscles generally comprise fibers of distinct types (which differ in contractile properties, discussed below), the types must be determined, usually by histochemistry. It is important to establish whether such fibers are clumped in particular zones of the muscle or distributed more or less evenly throughout its cross section. In the former case, differential activation of portions of the muscle will affect, at the least, its force resultant.

Activation of living muscle occurs via motorneurons that innervate a variable number of fibers, thus forming a motor unit. All such associated fibers have a single fiber type. The cell bodies of motor units lie in the ventral horn of the basal portion of the central nervous sytem, with those of each muscle forming a variably tight "nucleus" overlapping those of other muscles (cf. Fetcho 1987); mapping these is a problem in small species (particularly in small caudates with very large cell sizes) in which cell dimensions approach those of the ventral horn. Various techniques, for instance, retrograde transport of horseradish-peroxidase (HRP), will label the cells and indicate the motor compartments. The peripheral nerves may be stained with Sudan black B (Nishikawa 1987).

Analysis of Functional Systems

Functional analyses of amphibian motor systems may have various aims. In the present framework they attempt to test matching of morphology to environmental demands; they establish the capacity of the organism to deal with the biotope it occupies and let the investigator determine whether and which phenotypic aspect may enable or be limiting for a particular activity.

A fundamental question is the extent to which the phenotypic aspect is heritable, as selection exerts evolutionary effects mainly on heritable components. Such studies are only now in progress; they obviously require breeding experiments and longitudinal assessment of the performance of the system. A second question is whether a particular heritable component (or its performance at a given stage) has an effect on the overall fitness of the organism. Here the current performance tends to be matched to future survival or reproductive success. In any such case it is important to establish variability of the phenomenon, both within individuals and among the individuals of a population. The statistical methods of Shaffer and Lauder (1985a) have permitted quantification and comparison of motor phases and of electromyographic parameters of such aspects.

Performance can be sampled and correlated with aspects of the physiology (electromyography [EMG]) and morphology of muscle by various techniques. The overall effect of the behavior can be recorded, often with cinematographic and videographic techniques. Also, various physiological approaches allow registration of movement, pressure, and force as effected by particular muscles. Such records initially should be taken from relatively undisturbed animals and, whenever possible, in both laboratory and field situations.

Formerly, the actions of muscles were assayed by stimulat-

ing them in anesthetized specimens (Eaton 1957). Currently, the activity of twitch (or spiking) component fibers is commonly established by EMG (Loeb and Gans 1986); the activity of tonic fibers requires the different analysis mentioned below. The EMG traces are only indirectly related to the force and the work performed by the muscles, and the relation may differ with the behavior involved. Hence, it is important to test the analytical methods (such as EMG integration) and to attempt direct measurement of their correlation with performance, separately for each kind of behavior. In each case, it becomes important to compare the EMG analyses with independently derived information about the distribution of the motor units that have been sampled. Recently, it has become possible to test the mechanics of "purified" behavioral subroutines by evoking these centrally (Satou et al. 1985).

Tonic fibers produce relatively low-frequency signals that are difficult to discern because they overlap sources of noise and hence tend to be filtered out by the experimental apparatus. Such tonic fibers can be studied by denervating animals, by Fourier analysis of their signals, or by multiple stimulation approaches (Hetherington and Lombard 1983; Carrier 1989). Contractile characteristics of twitch and tonic fiber bundles are distinguishable by attaching them to a muscle lever; tonic fibers will produce characteristically slow contractions in response to potassium in the medium (Morgan and Proske 1984).

Analyses of the muscle-tendon system in mammals consider the series elasticity, both of the muscle itself and of the serially placed connective tissues. In some mammals, these systems may store energy during locomotion. Similarly, energy may be stored by deforming cartilages and bones; however, such energy storage (for instance, in the jumps of a frog) remains to be demonstrated in Amphibia.

GENERAL PROPERTIES OF STRIATED MUSCLE

The striated muscles of amphibians consist of multinuclear fibers, variable numbers of which are organized into motor units by motor neurons, the cell bodies of which lie in the ventral horn of the spinal cord (see also chapters 2 and 16). The axon of each motorneuron leaves the cord via a ventral root and generally splits before reaching its muscle. Stimulation involves parallel action of all fibers. We know little about the extent of the component muscle fibers and about their differences in various muscles. Of obvious interest are the diameter, length, and contractile properties both of the motor units and individual fibers, as well as those aspects of muscle placement that affect the forces and moments exerted on skeletal elements (Gans and Bock 1965; Gans and de Vree 1987). Contractile properties of particular interest are the unloaded velocity of shortening, and the velocity of shortening against different loads. Of similar interest are the forces generated for particular shortening velocities and excursions. How do all of these values differ among species and which of them vary with size and possibly with age? Amphibian tissues are sensitive to such environmental factors as moisture and temperature (Gatten and Clark 1989; Putnam and Bennett 1981; John-Alder, Barnhart, and Bennett 1989; chapters 5, 6, and 8); thus, experiments must take these factors into account.

Because of the recognition of the major gaps in our knowledge of these important aspects, we have assembled a preliminary set of such values in table 11.2. It should be noted

TABLE 11.2 Physiological Characteristics of the Various Muscle Types in Amphibians

		Twitch			Tonic		
	Temp.	Type 1	Type 2	Type 3	Type 4	Type 5	Note
		Fiber characteristics					
Diameter (μ)		156	95	74	83		1
		40–70	15–30		25–30		2
		100–150	55–110	40–70	35–70	35–70	7
		100–130	85–125				8
		140	70		75		11
		30–70		10–15			12
		169 ± 17.8	145 ± 17.6	76.7 ± 12.1	60.7 ± 5.4	44.0 ± 7.7	13
		<140	40–60	15–30			14
Area of cross section (μ^2)		19,262 ± 393	7,200 ± 336	4,280	5,410 ± 226		1
Myofibril cross section (μ^2)		3.3 ± 1.0	1.1 ± 0.3	0.7 ± 0.2	2.8 ± 1.2	5.4 ± 2.5	13
Threshold of motor nerve (V)			0.5 (0.3–0.7)		4.0 (1.7–5.7)		4
Latency of response (ms)			2.9 (2.2–4.3)		13.9 (8.7–18.6)		4
Nerve conduction velocity (m/s)		28–46	20–27		5–17		10
Amplitude of response (mV)			3.1 (0.5–11.5)		1.3 (0.4–4.5)		4
Resting potential (mV)			−81 (71–94)		−45 (34–55)		4
		Isometric contraction characteristics					
Twitch contraction time (ms)		29.3 ± 2.3	37.2 ± 2.0	53.8 ± 4.5			9
	20°C	25.8 ± 3.7	33.1 ± 6.0				8
		16–27	20–40				10
Half-relaxation time (ms)		34.3 ± 1.3	34.3 ± 2.5	56.2 ± 3.5			9
	20°C	42.0 ± 9.2	35.7 ± 9.4				8
Maximum tetanic tension ($kg \cdot cm^{-2}$)			2.5–3		2.5		3
		3.3 ± 0.4	3.1 ± 0.2	3.1 ± 0.3	0.15–4		9
	20°C	3.7 ± 0.5	3.2 ± 0.5				8
Tetanus/twitch		2.0 ± 0.2	3.0 ± 0.3	3.7 ± 0.3			9
	20°C	1.4	1.7				8
Fusion frequency (Hz)		33–60	33–48	23–33			9
Time-to-peak tetanic tension (ms)	20°C	120	140				8
		Isotonic contraction characteristics					
Unloaded shortening velocity Vmax (lengths·s^{-1})	5°C		1.49 (1.31–1.66)				6
	10°C		2.55 (2.38–2.81)				6
		4.35 ± 0.49	2.89 ± 0.23				8
	15°C	5.76 ± 0.34	4.44 ± 0.47				8

that the old subdivision between skeletal and branchiomeric muscles now lacks a functional corollary (cf. Gans 1990). Also, the literature often subdivides muscles into axial and appendicular. Sometimes the segmental muscles of the former category are referred to as metameric or myotomal; these terms are inappropriate.

Fiber Types

Studies in anurans led to the initial recognition that skeletal muscles comprise different motor units, each category with fibers of distinct contractile types (Sommerkamp 1928; Wachholder 1930a, 1930b; Wachholder and Ledebur 1930; Krüger 1949). The two general types of extrafusal motor units in anuran hindlimb muscle are *twitch* (phasic, fast) and *tonic* (slow; Burke and Ginsborg 1956; Kuffler and Gerard 1947; Kuffler and Vaughan Williams 1953b; Orkand 1963; Tasaki and Mitzutani 1944).

Throughout this chapter, the types of muscle fibers will be termed *twitch* or *tonic* to avoid confusion with the fiber typing now prevalent for mammals. For instance, and as detailed

below, only some of the slow fibers of amphibians twitch, whereas almost all mammalian fibers do (except for some fibers in the extraocular and ear muscles; Hess 1970; Morgan and Proske 1984). Twitch and tonic fibers also differ in their arrays of organelles and enzymic constituents; these differences make it difficult to place fibers in discrete categories.

The important discovery that amphibian muscle fibers could be broadly divided, based on their different contractile responses and correlated differences in internal structure and innervation, was later extended to reptiles, birds, and mammals (for reviews see Hess 1970; Morgan and Proske 1984; Peachey 1961, 1968). However, intrinsic differences in fiber type differentiate each of these groups (Guthe 1981). For instance, the several categories of twitch and tonic muscle tend to be confused with white and red muscle. Furthermore, the categories differ among organisms, making it essential to specify exactly the basis of muscle typing, whether anatomical, histochemical, electron-microscopical, or physiological; many papers lack this information.

Consequently, this simple division of fiber types is considered insufficient to describe the organization of amphibian

TABLE 11.2 (*continued*)

	Temp.	Twitch			Tonic		Note
		Type 1	Type 2	Type 3	Type 4	Type 5	
	20°C		5.20 (4.64–5.89)				6
		7.24 ± 0.44	6.00 ± 0.48				8
		5.2		2.2	1.10		7
	22.5°C		6.34		1.10		6
					0.11		3
Hill constants							
$a \cdot P_0$	0°C		0.22				5
	5°C		0.35 (0.30–0.45)				6
	10°C		0.35 (0.31–0.42)				6
		0.35 ± 0.15	0.26 ± 0.09				8
	15°C	0.47 ± 0.17	0.27 ± 0.09				8
	20°C		0.38 (0.27–0.47)				6
		0.48 ± 0.11	0.26 ± 0.07				8
		0.38		0.22	0.10		7
	22.5°C				0.10		6
b (lengths·s^{-1})	0°C		0.27				5
	5°C		0.52 (0.42–0.63)				6
	10°C		0.88 (0.79–1.03)				6
		1.43 ± 0.63	0.75 ± 0.27				8
	15°C	2.69 ± 0.86	1.15 ± 0.37				8
	20°C		1.97 (1.53–2.24)				6
		3.51 ± 0.68	1.53 ± 0.35				8
	22.5°C				0.11		6

[1] Asmussen and Kiessling 1970. *Rana esculenta*, sartorius, iliofibularis, and semitendinosus and other limb muscles.
[2] Engel and Irwin 1967. Frogs, several limb muscles.
[3] Floyd and Smith 1971. Frogs.
[4] Forrester and Schmidt 1970. *Rana temporaria*, rectus abdominis muscle.
[5] Hill 1938. Standard for sartorius muscle.
[6] Lännergren 1978. *Xenopus laevis*, iliofibularis muscle.
[7] Lännergren 1979. *Xenopus laevis*.
[8] Lännergren, Lindblom, and Johansson 1982. *Xenopus laevis*, iliofibularis muscle.
[9] Lännergren and Smith 1966. *Xenopus laevis*, iliofibularis muscle.
[10] Luff and Proske 1979. *Litoria aurea*, iliofibularis muscle.
[11] Putnam and Bennett 1983. *Bufo boreas, Rana pipiens, Xenopus laevis*, several hindlimb muscles.
[12] Sasaki 1974. *Rana* sp., *Bufo b. japonicus, Xenopus laevis*, tail muscles.
[13] Smith and Ovalle 1973. *Xenopus laevis*, iliofibularis muscle.
[14] Totland 1976b. *Ambystoma mexicanum* (axolotl), tail muscles.

skeletal muscle, at least that of the anurans thus far studied. Also, there are no data yet on plasticity of fibers in amphibians. Modern histochemical techniques show that each primary fiber type is subdivisible into secondary ones, which are likely to be functionally discrete. Unfortunately, the literature abounds with a confusing variety of names, a result of the apparent lack of unanimity as to whether tonic fibers have a low or a high oxidative capacity (and exacerbated by the comparison of nonhomologous muscles from misidentified species). In addition, the characterization refers almost exclusively to hindlimb muscles rather than to those of the trunk, on which emphasis has been minimal using physiological methods. Table 11.4 is an attempt to correlate the different nomenclatures and histochemical reactions into a single scheme. In the following account, fibers will be named simply twitch 1, 2, and 3 and tonic 4 and 5, in analogy to the terms of Smith and Ovalle (1973).

Amphibian twitch fibers respond to a single nerve stimulus with a propagated action potential that results in a contraction (twitch). The tension developed is independent of the strength of the stimulus and hence is termed an all-or-nothing response. Twitch fibers relax completely during sustained depolarization. In contrast, the membranes of tonic fibers are usually incapable of propagating an action potential (Burke and Ginsborg 1956; Kuffler and Gerard 1947; Kuffler and Vaughan Williams 1953a; Orkand 1963; Tasaki and Mitzutani 1944). In tonic fibers, a single nerve impulse causes only a small junction potential with very little mechanical response. Only repeated stimulation (either to the nerve, or to the muscle by direct application of depolarizing solutions containing acetylcholine or potassium) produces a slow (on the order of 1 s) graded contraction of the fiber along its entire length; this results from summation of local synaptic potentials. Unlike the rapid (on the order of milliseconds), maximal, potentially oscillating responses of twitch fibers, this contraction develops slowly and may continue without evidence of fatigue.

The membrane of tonic fibers appears to be sensitive to acetylcholine along its entire length. However, the opinion that acetylcholine receptors are distributed evenly along the entire length of tonic fibers (Kiessling 1964) is untenable because acetylcholine receptor density is greater in synaptic re-

TABLE 11.3   Details of the Ultrastructural Differences for Amphibian Fiber Types

	Twitch Fibers	Tonic Fibers
Innervation		
Number of axons	Single	Multiple
Diameter of motor axon	Coarse, thick	Thin
End-plate type	Robust en plaque	En grappe
Cholinesterase activity	High	Very low
Subsynaptic sarcolemma	Extensively folded	Lack of regular folds
Ultrastructure		
Myofibrils	Small (<1 μ); distinct, individual fibrils surrounded by sarcoplasm; *Fibrillenstruktur*	Large; irregular fibrils clump together; *Felderstruktur*
Nuclei	Internal	Subsarcolemmal
Sarcotubular system	Well-developed, regular SR and T system; regular triads	Sparse and irregular sarcoplasmic reticulum; T system virtually absent; few irregular triads
Z band	Square lattice; straight; thin	Irregular lattice; zigzag or jagged; thick
M band	Straight	Less prominent or absent
Lipid droplets	Numerous	Few
Mitochondria	Abundant	Sparse

gions (Nasledov 1969; Nasledov and Thesleff 1974; Orkand, Orkand, and Cohen 1978). Hence, activation of tonic fibers probably results in an electrotonic spread of the potential from the motor end-plate sites, similar to that in twitch fibers (but over shorter distances). The nonspiking graded potentials of tonic fibers occur at frequencies below 100 Hz; recording of these requires special EMG techniques, because the 50–60-Hz range is commonly filtered out electronically during recordings.

The two types of muscle fibers also differ in innervation and ultrastructure. Significant features of innervation include diameter of motor axons (Kuffler and Vaughan Williams 1953a, 1953b; Tasaki and Mitzutani 1944), end-plate type (Gray 1957; Günther 1949; Hess 1960; Lännergren and Smith 1966; Page 1965), cholinesterase activity (Lännergren and Smith 1966), and folding of subsarcolemmal membrane (Asmussen and Kiessling 1974; Page 1965; table 11.3). En plaque endings (corresponding to twitch fibers) generally appear long and rather uniform, running lengthwise along the muscle fiber; they occur at about the same level on adjacent fibers, thus forming bands of innervation (fig. 11.1). Long en plaque end plates are often referred to as *Endbüschel* (Tiegs 1953). En grappe endings (corresponding to tonic fibers) appear as small, irregularly spaced endings that differ in number and position on adjacent fibers (Hess 1960; fig. 11.2).

Under the light microscope, twitch fibers have an extensive and regular sarcoplasmic reticulum with abundant regular triads in each sarcomere, resulting in regularly ordered myofibrils (*Fibrillenstruktur*). Tonic fibers are irregular in striation. The actin filaments occur irregularly in relation to the myosin filaments and are surrounded by sparse sarcoplasm, so that in cross section the myofibrils are difficult to distinguish and form an irregular field (*Felderstruktur*; Krüger 1929, 1949, 1950; fig. 11.3). Significant ultrastructural differences occur in the tubular system, Z disk, M line, and number of lipid droplets and mitochondria (Hess 1960, 1967, 1970; Orkand, Orkand, and Cohen 1978; Page 1965; Peachey and Huxley 1962; Smith and Ovalle 1973; table 11.3).

In the most common view, histochemical (Asmussen and

Kiessling 1970; Ogata 1958) and combined histochemical-physiological studies (Engel and Irwin 1967; Lännergren and Smith 1966; Smith and Lännergren 1968) initially establish at least three fiber types in anuran hindlimb muscles (table 11.2; fig. 11.4). The two major fiber types are twitch and tonic. Twitch fibers stain darkly for ATPase, whereas tonic fibers have a unique histochemical profile, staining very lightly for ATPase (following alkaline preincubation) and mitochondrial oxidative enzymes (succinic dehydrogenase [SDH]) and lacking intracellular lipids (Sudan black B negative).

At least two types of twitch fibers are evident, each correlated with a particular fiber diameter (table 11.4). They differ in their twitch contraction times and resistance to fatigue. The large-diameter fibers, with few lipid droplets and oxidative enzymes, have a short twitch, develop large tension, and fatigue rapidly upon prolonged stimulation. The small-to-medium–diameter fibers, richly supplied with lipid droplets and oxidative enzymes, show a longer twitch and develop less tension but do not fatigue rapidly (Lännergren and Smith 1966). Electron microscopy supports this division of twitch fibers by demonstration of differential abundance of mitochondria (table 11.3).

Histochemically intermediate muscle types occur frequently in anurans. This, in combination with ultrastructural criteria, has led to the identification of five different kinds of anuran muscle fibers, twitch 1, 2, and 3 and tonic 4 and 5 (Smith and Ovalle 1973; Smith, Blinston, and Ovalle 1973; table 11.4). Types 1 and 2 correspond to the two fibers formerly described as twitch fibers. Twitch 3 fibers are smaller than twitch 2 fibers and have a very high content of oxidative enzymes and lipids, and a moderately developed sarcoplasmic system. The twitch 3 fibers also lack well-developed postsynaptic sarcolemmal infoldings at their nerve terminals (Becker and Lombard 1977; Bone, Ridge, and Ryan 1976). Twitch 3 fibers occur only in zones with tonic 4 and 5 fibers (Asmussen and Kiessling 1970; Becker and Lombard 1977; Smith and Ovalle 1973). Physiologically, they are slower and more fatigue-resistant than the twitch 2 fibers. Twitch 3 fibers may be involved in small movements with sustained effort.

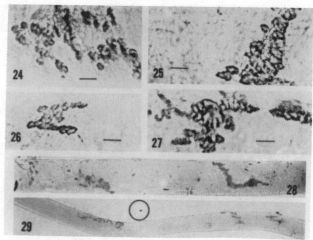

Fig. 11.2 *24–27*, en grappe endings on teased muscle fibers from the tonus bundle after glyoxal fixation and cholinesterase staining. All the endings shown are one of several on each muscle fiber. Phase-contrast microscopy at a magnification similar to that of *21* in fig. 11.1. *28–29*, teased muscle fibers from the tonus bundle, glyoxal fixation and cholinesterase staining. Three en grappe endings of varying appearance are scattered along each of the muscle fibers. (Reprinted, by permission, from Hess 1960.)

Fig. 11.1 *18*, teased muscle fibers with en plaque endings of *endbüschel* form from a portion of the iliofibularis muscle without the tonus bundle. Glyoxal fixation, cholinesterase staining. *19*, en plaque endings on teased muscle fibers from the tonus bundle at the same magnification as *18*, to compare the extent and form of the endings. The en plaque endings in the tonus bundle are more variable in form and much shorter in extent than the *Endbüschel*. *20*, a montage photograph of a single muscle fiber teased from the tonus bundle after glyoxal fixation and cholinesterase staining. At least four en grappe endings are seen scattered irregularly along the muscle fiber. *21*, teased muscle fibers with *Endbüschel* endings photographed in the phase-contrast microscope. This montage includes almost the entire extent of the *Endbüschel*. Glyoxal fixation, cholinesterase staining. (Reprinted, by permission, from Hess 1960.)

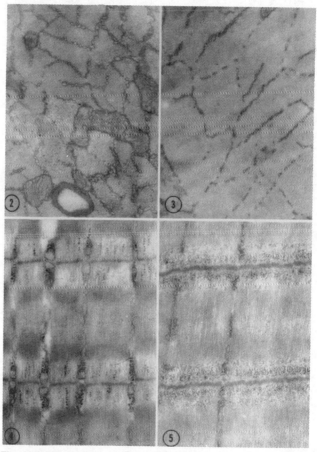

Fig. 11.3 Electron micrographs of isolated muscle fibers, magnification 25,000. *2*, transverse section of a twitch fiber (iliofibularis). *3*, transverse section of a tonic fiber (iliofibularis). *4*, longitudinal section of a twitch fiber (semitendinosus). *5*, longitudinal section of a tonic fiber (iliofibularis). (From Peachey and Huxley, reproduced from the *Journal of Cell Biology*, 1962, 13:177–180 by copyright permission of the Rockefeller University Press.)

Tonic 5 fibers represent the classical tonic type. In contrast, the tonic 4 fibers are slightly larger and characterized by a light staining for ATPase, low content of oxidative enzymes, and lipid droplets (Lännergren 1979). Tonic 4 fibers sometimes have M bands, and Z bands irregularly configured in a square lattice pattern.

Measurements of mechanical properties of isolated motor units and fibers support the division of fibers into more than three types. The contractile properties of isolated motor units (as determined by stimulation of isolated nerves) parallel the diameter and conduction velocity of their motor axons (Lännergren, Lindblom, and Johansson 1982; Luff and Proske 1979; Ridge and Thomson 1980c; Smith and Lännergren 1968). The existence of a fiber type intermediate between

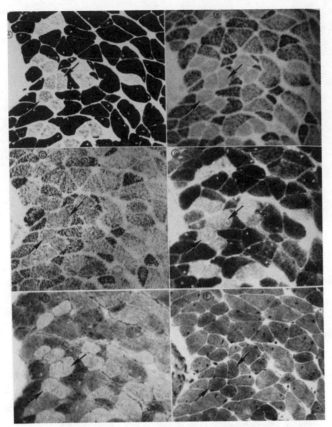

Fig. 11.4 Transverse serial sections of the ventral portion of rectus abdominis (× 225). One group of presumed tonic fibers (stained lightly with ATPase) is marked on each picture. *A*, ATPase; *B*, menadione-mediated α-glycerophosphate dehydrogenase; *C*, DPNH dehydrogenase; *D*, phosphorylase; *E*, periodic acid–Schiff; *F*, modified trichrome, showing nuclei dark. Small unstained regions in the fibers shown in *A* and *D* are nuclei. (Reprinted, by permission, from Engel and Irwin 1967.)

twitch and tonic is still controversial, however. Seemingly, such a fiber type was discovered more than 20 years ago from the ability of some tonic fibers in the rectus and iliofibularis muscles of the frog to generate a propagating action potential (Shamarina 1962). Since then, several investigators have identified fibers with similar intermediate properties (Lännergren 1979; Miledi and Uchitel 1984; Smith and Lännergren 1968; Smith, Blinston, and Ovalle 1973). The structure of these fibers corresponds to that of tonic 4 fibers. Others believe that the "intermediate" fiber is no more than the small fatigue-resistant twitch 3 fiber (Forrester and Schmidt 1970; Hess 1970; Luff and Proske 1979; Orkand 1963). This assumption rests on the observation that twitch contraction in response to nerve stimulation is fiber-length–dependent. Slow twitch fibers resembling twitch 3 appear not to give rise to an action potential in response to a single nerve impulse at a fiber length at or near the tetanic optimum, but do so after being stretched (e.g., iliofibularis muscle of *Litoria aurea* [Anura: Hylidae]; Luff and Proske 1979). Because direct stimulation docs not yield length-dependent contractions, it seems likely that the length dependence results from stretch-dependent facilitation of the neuromuscular transmission.

Fiber typing, especially in combination with physiological studies, has received much less attention in the skeletal muscle of caudates (urodeles), and the fiber types of Gymnophiona are unknown. However, the caudate fibers probably also fall into different classes (Bone, Ridge, and Ryan 1976; Mather and Hynes 1934; Totland 1976a, 1976b; Watanabe et al. 1980).

One confusing aspect is that fiber types are often characterized only as thick "white" and thin "red" in both anurans and caudates; sometimes fibers are characterized as "pink" to show an intermediate oxidative metabolism (Gradwell and Walcott 1971; Kordylewski 1986; Kordylewski and Gruszka 1986; Sasaki 1974, 1977; Sasaki and Watanabe 1983; Talesara and Mala 1978; Totland 1976a, 1976b; Watanabe and

TABLE 11.4 Summary of Nomenclature of Fiber Types

Twitch			Tonic		Reference
Type 1	Type 2	Type 3	Type 4	Type 5	
Large white	Medium	Small red			Ogata 1958
Pale fibers	Dark fibers		Clear fibers		Lännergren and Smith 1966
Large twitch	Medium twitch	Small twitch	Small-medium tonic		Engel and Irwin 1967
Mitochondrienarme Fasern	*Mäßig mitochondrienreiche Fasern*	*Mitochondrienreiche Fasern*	*Tonische Fasern*		Asmussen and Kiessling 1970
Large pale, type 1	Large dark, type 2	Small dark, type 3	Small pale, type 4	Small clear, type 5	Smith and Ovalle 1973
Inner muscle fiber	Small inner muscle fiber	Peripheral muscle fiber			Sasaki 1974, 1977
		Type 2	Type 1		Bone, Ridge, and Ryan 1976
Large-diameter fibers (white)	Medium-diameter fibers (intermediate)	Small-diameter fibers (red)			Totland 1976b
Type II white$_1$	Type II red$_{2,4}$	Type II red$_{1,3}$	Type I red/intermediate		Talesara and Mala 1978
Large fatiguable motor units	Small fatigue-resistant motor units		Slow units		Luff and Proske 1979
Fast-twitch, fast-fatiguing type 1 fibers	Slow-twitch, slow-fatiguing type 2 and type 3 fibers				Sperry 1981
Fast-twitch, glycolytic (FG), large fibers	Fast-twitch, oxidative, glycolytic (FOG), smaller fibers		Tonic, small fibers		Putnam and Bennett 1983
Thick white	Pink	Thin red			Kordylewski 1986
Type IIB	Type IIA	Type I	Tonic		Faber and Zawadowska 1988

Sasaki 1974; Watanabe et al. 1980). These terms especially pertain to the segmental trunk and tail muscles, by analogy to those of other anamniotes. Most of the thin "red" fibers have a very high oxidative capacity, raising questions as to whether they are indeed tonic, as often assumed (Fetcho 1987; Morgan and Proske 1984); after all, the latter fibers have a low oxidative capacity (Lännergren and Smith 1966). Similarly, Focant and Reznik (1980) identified "intermediate" fibers in the cruralis bundle of *Rana esculenta*, as well as tonic fibers characterized by high metabolic activity and alkaline-labile ATPase (pH 9.4).

Although red fibers may be as slow as true tonic fibers, most red fibers described thus far are not tonic. The red color of some red fibers results mainly from the abundance of blood-filled capillaries associated with small twitch fibers (resembling twitch 3; Asmussen and Kiessling 1974; see also Czopek 1963). Also, fibers of tonus bundles appear to contain more myoglobin (Asmussen and Kiessling 1974). Furthermore, the tonic fibers appear to show differences in pH stability of ATPase. Two distinct types of "slow" muscle fibers that differ in pH stability of ATPase and correlated metabolic profile have been described in seven forelimb muscles of *Rana temporaria* (Faber and Zawadowska 1988). One of these types is claimed to be tonic, the other one twitch. The ATPase of the slow-twitch type (so-called type I, table 11.4) is stable only after preincubation at pH 4.4. Also, the twitch type has a high oxidative capacity. It corresponds to the "red" fibers of fish myotomes, as well as to the twitch 3 fibers. Possibly the fiber represents the mammalian "slow-twitch oxidative" fiber (Peter et al. 1972). The tonic type contains ATPase that is stable after preincubations between pH 4.2 and 10.8, but exhibits little or no oxidative capacity.

The ultrastructure of "small red" fibers of the tail muscle of the axolotl, *Ambystoma mexicanum* (Caudata: Ambystomatidae), appears similar to twitch 3 fibers. The myofibrils of these fibers have relatively wide Z lines and distinct M bands, and their sarcoplasmic reticulum is relatively scanty; triads occur irregularly at the level of the Z lines, and mitochondria and lipid droplets are numerous (Totland 1976b). Similarly, red fibers of tail muscles of several anuran larvae possess a well-developed sarcoplasm and abundant mitochondria and lipid droplets (Sasaki 1974, 1977).

Fiber Type Distribution

The proportions of fibers of twitch and tonic types differ among the skeletal muscles of amphibians and among particular muscles of several species; these differences lack sufficient characterization, and we still know too little about their possible association with environmental or life history characteristics.

In most hindlimb muscles of several frog species, 80–90% of the cross section consists of large twitch 1 fibers, whereas the proportion of tonic fibers rarely exceeds 10% (Sperry 1981; Putnam and Bennett 1983). Exceptions are the pyriformis muscle of *Xenopus*, in which 70% are tonic fibers (Orkand, Orkand, and Cohen 1978), and the distal bundle of the cruralis (anterior head of triceps femoris) of *Rana pipiens*, in which 50% of fibers are tonic (Gilly 1975).

The postural rectus abdominis muscle contains 9% of tonic fibers comprising the superficial ventral layer in *Rana temporaria* (Forrester and Schmidt 1970), 15–25% in *R. esculenta* (Asmussen and Kiessling 1970), 14% in *Bufo americanus*, 12% in *R. pipiens*, and 6% in *Xenopus laevis* (Putnam and Bennett 1983). More than 40% of the fibers of the opercularis muscle are tonic in several species of both anurans and caudates: *Hyla* (Anura: Hylidae), 80%; *Desmognathus* (Caudata: Plethodontidae), 90%; *Ambystoma*, 45% (Becker and Lombard 1977).

The organization of fiber types also differs among muscles. In several limb muscles, the main muscle mass is composed of large twitch 1 fibers, among which twitch 2 fibers are intermingled in a mosaic pattern (e.g., in *Rana*: sartorius: Asmussen and Kiessling 1970; Engel and Irwin 1967; medial head of anconeus: Faber and Zawadowska 1988; sartorius, semimembranosus, and triceps muscles: Smith, Blinston, and Ovalle 1973; in *Litoria aurea*: sartorius: Luff and Proske 1976). In the sartorius and gracilis major of *R. pipiens* and *Xenopus laevis*, twitch 2 fibers are more abundant along the surface of the muscles (Sperry 1981). Except for the sartorius, all limb muscles having this fiber distribution may possess some tonic fibers situated at their periphery.

In several species of anurans, other limb muscles, such as the iliofibularis, semitendinosus, and gastrocnemius, share all five fiber types; however, they are segregated into separate zones. These muscles typically have a tonus bundle, surrounded by an outer mantle of twitch fibers (Hess 1960; Krüger 1949, 1950; Sommerkamp 1928). The tonus bundle lies close to the nerve supply and appears to be composed of a mixture of tonic 4 and 5 and twitch 3 fibers. The outer mantle is composed of twitch 1 and 2 fibers, with the twitch 1 fibers concentrated in the peripheral zone (Asmussen and Kiessling 1970, 1974; Engel and Irwin 1967; Lännergren and Smith 1966; Lännergren, Lindblom, and Johansson 1982; Putnam and Bennett 1983; Smith and Ovalle 1973; Smith, Blinston, and Ovalle 1973). Small limb muscles, such as the pyriformis of *Xenopus laevis*, contain fiber types 2–5 but lack twitch 1 (Orkand, Orkand, and Cohen 1978; Smith and Ovalle 1973; Smith, Blinston, and Ovalle 1973).

The fibers of the axial musculature of larval and adult amphibians also are arranged in zones. A thin outer mantle of small-diameter (red) fibers overlies the main bulk of thick-diameter (white) fibers, with which intermediate fibers are frequently intermingled (Kordylewski 1986; Kordylewski and Gruszka 1986; Sasaki 1974, 1977; Totland 1976a, 1976b; Watanabe and Sasaki 1974; Watanabe et al. 1980). In *Rana*, the tonic fibers of the rectus abdominis are confined to the ventral and medial surface; here they are mixed with thin (tonic 3) fibers. The remaining part of this axial muscle consists of twitch fibers (Asmussen and Kiessling 1970; Engel and Irwin 1967; Forrester and Schmidt 1970; Lynch 1984; Uhrik and Schmidt 1973).

The distribution and abundance of tonic fibers seems related to fiber length. Tonic fibers occur in the superficial layers of muscles or in the distal portion of muscles that contain a tonus bundle; however, such tonic fibers are reported absent in muscles in which their fiber length would be longer than 10 mm (Asmussen and Kiessling 1970; Engel and Irwin 1967). The shorter length of tonic fibers reflects a lower mean number of sarcomeres (Gregory et al. 1978). This issue deserves further study, particularly in view of recent reports suggesting that muscle fibers of lower vertebrates have a maximum length (Gans, Loeb, and de Vree 1989; Gaunt and Gans 1989).

Functional explanations for the histochemical fiber-type profile, enzymatic profile, and contractile properties are scant for any given amphibian muscle. For various species of anurans, such parameters of the propulsive muscles have been correlated with their locomotor capabilities and activity physiologies (ten hindlimb muscles, Putnam and Bennett 1983; sartorius and gracilis major muscles, Sperry 1981). Fiber composition appears similar among muscles within a given species and among amphibian species; muscles are primarily composed of large twitch 1 fibers (except for the gracilis major and sartorius of *Bufo americanus*, which contain only oxidative fibers; Sperry 1981). However, metabolic enzyme activity and contractile properties vary with the metabolic and behavioral capabilities of the organisms. Slow-moving hopper-walkers have propulsive hindlimb muscles that contract more slowly than those of rapid jumpers and strong aquatic swimmers. Walker-hoppers, such as *Bufo boreas*, rely mainly on aerobiosis and fatigue relatively slowly, whereas rapid jumpers and strong aquatic swimmers, such as *Rana pipiens* and *Xenopus laevis*, respectively, rely heavily on anaerobiosis and fatigue rapidly (Putnam and Bennett 1983).

The arrangement of fibers in the trunk musculature of anuran and caudate larvae is the same as that seen in the caudal musculature (Kordylewski 1986; Watanabe and Sasaki 1974; Watanabe et al. 1980). However, quantitative differences between basal and final parts of the tail appear to be related to functional demands. The caudal tip of *Xenopus* consists entirely of thin (red) fibers, perhaps reflecting its involvement in the continuous oscillations by which these larvae remain adrift (Wassersug and Hoff 1989). The basal part of the tail mainly consists of thick (white) fibers, allowing an occasional quick escape (Kordylewski 1986; Sasaki 1977; Watanabe and Sasaki 1974; Nishikawa and Wassersug 1988).

Growth and Metamorphosis

Among vertebrates, the anuran amphibians are proverbial in the complexity of their metamorphosis (see chapter 16). Their muscles change markedly, either continuously throughout their development or during a brief interval near metamorphosis. Early skeletal muscle differentiation involves muscle cells in various stages of development: myoblasts, early muscle cells, and myotubes with differentiating myofibrils (Hay 1963; Lewis and Hughes 1960; Muntz 1975). Myoblasts, the earliest muscle cell precursors, are characterized by abundant cytoplasm with free ribonucleoprotein granules, traces of myofilaments, and large nuclei and nucleoli, but little endoplastic reticulum. Myoblasts often appear in close association with each other (syncytia) and with adjacent developing muscle (by lateral processes). In contrast to mesenchymal cells, myoblasts contain sparse granular endoplasmic reticulum. Myoblasts fuse with each other, forming myotubes, elongate cells having a centrally placed nucleus. The earliest myofilaments may be thin or thick. Cross striations are said to appear among muscles in no specific order.

In *Xenopus*, the earliest movements produced by the developing axial muscles (the first muscles that develop) can be elicited before spontaneous movements or simple nerve function (Lewis and Hughes 1960; Muntz 1975). At this stage, myotubes contain a small number of striated myofibrils. Gap junctions then electrotonically interconnect them and provide a simple motor system at an early stage of development (free-swimming embryos). However, the structure and contractile properties of these muscles are simple compared with those of muscles that differentiate over a longer time and have nerves present before becoming functional (e.g., limb muscles).

Once myotubes reach a certain degree of differentiation, electrotonic junctions close coincidentally with arrival of outsprouting axon terminals of the motorneuron. In *Xenopus* and *Bombina* (Anura: Discoglossidae), but not in *Ambystoma*, the gap junctions persist after myotube formation (Blackshaw and Warner 1975, 1976; Hayes 1975). The target tissue promotes sprouting of nerve endings (Aguilar et al. 1973), but junctional characteristics develop only where nerve endings and muscle become closely associated. The first synaptic contacts are made by fast motor axons and appear at random on short myotubes, measuring about 200–300 μm. These first synapses seem to make the membrane refractory to further synapse formation (Aguilar et al. 1973), and this condition extends as the fibers lengthen by addition of sarcomeres at their ends (for sartorius and iliofibularis of *Hyla*, see Bennett and Pettigrew 1975). The earliest presynaptic elements begin as small enlargements at the ends of unmyelinated axons. They subsequently grow parallel to the long axis of the myotube and finally mature by forming complex terminal arborizations. The first nerve contacts generally lack acetylcholinesterase (AChE) activity, which appears gradually later in development (cutaneous pectoris of *Rana catesbeiana*: Letinsky and Decino 1980; Letinsky and Morrison-Graham 1980; see Bennett 1983 for review). For a discussion of the interaction between gap junctions and fiber types, see Nishikawa and Wassersug 1988.

Axons of several motorneurons compete for the formation of the final motor end plate. Hence, the developing motorneurons produce transient polyneuronal and overlapping innervation patterns at the site of initial contact. The iliofibularis muscle adds sarcomeres to its ends at a constant rate. In contrast, the rate of fusion of myoblasts and addition of sarcomeres during growth of the sartorius muscle becomes unequal at the two ends once the sartorius muscle is longer than about 1 mm; this results in an increasingly asymmetrical position of the first synapse. The sartorius also forms new synapses at the fast-growing pelvic end of its fibers. In this muscle, however, those synapses lying within about 12 mm of the original synapse disappear subsequently, as the refractory zone extends to the end of the fibers. Polyneuronal innervation largely disappears during and after metamorphosis (Bennett and Pettigrew 1975; Letinsky 1974; Letinsky and Morrison-Graham 1980), suggesting that innervation by more than one motorneuron may be involved in the mechanism for spacing out motor unit territories in growing muscle (fig. 11.5).

Long before metamorphic climax, larval muscles differentiate quantitatively and qualitatively. The size of some muscles increases, through increases in both number and di-

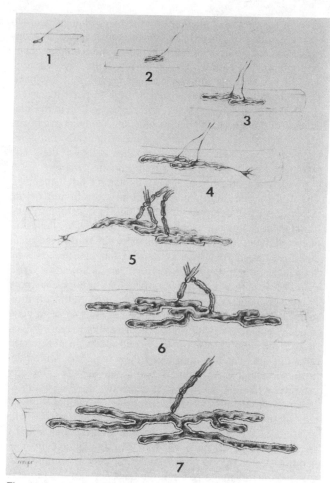

Fig. 11.5 A schematic representation of the development of a neuro-muscular junction in amphibians. *1*, initial nerve contacts are small and lack AChE activity. *2–4*, with further development the neural processes grow and junctional sites begin to have multiple innervations; patchy AChE activity gradually appears to outline some or all of the nerve terminal processes. *4–5*, growth cones and terminal processes that have extended outside the AChE-defined junctional site are often seen. *3–7*, as nerve terminal processes grow in size, the extent of multiple terminal innervation reaches a peak; thereafter the redundant innervations gradually are eliminated. A single en plaque nerve ending remains on each muscle fiber. (From Letinsky and Morrison Graham 1980. Reprinted with the permission of Chapman and Hall.)

mensions of the fibers (Alley and Cameron 1983; Kordylewski 1986; Lynch 1984). In the larvae of *Rana pipiens* the rectus abdominis forms new fibers, mainly along its medial margin (Lynch 1984). In the other axial muscles, the increase in thickness depends on the position of the fiber in the muscle. The axial musculature of *Xenopus* larvae consists of two strips of metameric muscles that continue without interruption into the tail; the fibers become thicker in the more cranial myotomes and remain thinner in the more caudal ones (Kordylewski 1986). Although it cannot be derived histochemically (e.g., the longissimus dorsi of larvae shows no affinity for Sudan black B; Kordylewski 1986; Kordylewski and Gruszka 1986; Lynch 1984; Watanabe et al. 1980), differences in fiber diameter can be used to identify larval fiber types in both anurans and caudates.

Fully differentiated adult muscle fibers are multinucleated. Multinucleation results from fusion of myoblasts (and/or pre-

cursor satellite cells) into myotubes (Allen 1978). In amphibians multinucleation seems to be coupled with metamorphosis. The axial muscles, which develop to a fully functional state and large size before the onset of metamorphosis, at first remain uninucleate (Holtfreter 1965; Lewis and Hughes 1960; Muchmore 1962, 1965; Muntz 1975). They become multinucleate at the onset of metamorphosis, possibly by accumulation and subsequent fusion with smaller satellite cells added at the ends of the growing muscle fibers (Muntz 1975).

Fiber type, determined at the time of initial fiber formation, may not be recognizable histochemically until late premetamorphic stages. The heterogeneous nature of larval muscles is well known (de Jongh 1968; Gradwell and Walcott 1971; Sasaki 1974, 1977; Watanabe and Sasaki 1974; Watanabe et al. 1980). In the larva of *Rana catesbeiana*, the interhyoideus muscle in the floor of the mouth varies regionally in percentage of fiber types; furthermore, the composition of this muscle changes during ontogeny (Gradwell and Walcott 1971). Similarly, the rectus abdominis of the larva of *R. pipiens* contains both twitch and tonic fibers, the latter being confined to the medial half of the muscle (Lynch 1984). The trunk musculature of anuran and caudate larvae also is zoned (Kordylewski 1986; Sasaki 1977; Watanabe and Sasaki 1974; Watanabe et al. 1980). As the axial musculature is the first to develop ontogenetically, the zonal arrangement may represent an archaic feature typical of primitive muscles (Kordylewski 1986) or of those that develop directly from the somites. A mosaic pattern of twitch and tonic fibers occurs in muscles that either appear early in ontogeny or are primitive characters. Nishikawa and Wassersug (1988) discuss the nature of the caudal spinal cord.

During metamorphosis some muscles degenerate, others form, and still others undergo structural changes from the larval to the mature state (Fox 1984; chapter 16). The changes correspond to major changes in the mode of life. In particular, the locomotor and feeding systems reorganize. The conversion tends to be more gradual in the former than in the latter.

Tail degeneration in metamorphosing anuran larvae includes that of the segmented musculature, apparently induced by mesenchymal macrophages (Watanabe and Sasaki 1974). The latter proliferate during metamorphosis and invade the muscle fibers during the initial stages of degeneration. Long cytoplasmic processes of the macrophages are then extruded into the muscle fibers and separate the nerves (Watanabe and Sasaki 1974). Disappearance of the Z bands precedes either fragmentation of the myofibrils or fanning out of the myofilaments without myofibrillar fragmentation. The rate of degeneration appears to be independent of fiber type. In *Xenopus*, the axial musculature remains as the longissimus dorsi (Kordylewski and Gruszka 1986).

Metamorphic remodeling of muscles that function in both the larvae and adults involves proliferative as well as degenerative processes. Both processes occur in certain jaw muscles of anurans (levator mandibulae anterior and posterior: Alley and Cameron 1983, 1984), as well as those of the trunk (rectus abdominis: Lynch 1983, 1984; Lynch and Harris 1984). During the premetamorphic phase or at the onset of metamorphic climax, new fibers arise, probably in response to hormonal changes. Satellite cells appear between the plasma and basement membranes adjacent to the large larval muscle fibers and differentiate into a population of myoblasts. The myoblasts increase in number and subsequently fuse into new myotubes, which contain early traces of myofibrils. In jaw muscles, the larval fibers degenerate as the new fibers form (Alley and Cameron 1983, 1984; de Jongh 1968; Takisawa and Sunaga 1951; Takisawa, Shimura, and Kaneko 1976). However, in the rectus abdominis the supporting fibers do not degenerate upon separation of the newly formed fibers (Lynch 1983, 1984). In this muscle, the response to metamorphic stimuli differs among the portions of muscle according to the regional variation of fiber types. Proliferation is confined to the medial half of the muscle and is coincident with degeneration of larval fibers in the lateral half. However, a second degenerative phase occurs in the remaining (medial) part of the muscle during the last stage of metamorphosis and the first postmetamorphic stage. Hence, both jaw and trunk muscles may reorganize after complete loss of larval fibers; that is, metamorphic remodeling may be associated with a complete turnover of larval muscle fibers.

Thyroid hormone may cause satellite cells to proliferate and muscle fibers to degenerate (Galton 1983). However, the tail likely degenerates at a later stage than do the rectus abdominis and jaw muscles, indicating a different response level (Lynch 1984). Denervation does not seem to play a role in fiber degeneration; the presynaptic elements of degenerating fibers and the basal laminae of fibers that have been phagocytosed remain structurally intact (Lynch 1984).

Not only the fibers, but entire muscles and the skeletal elements they connect, change at metamorphosis in association with major shifts in their roles (de Jongh 1968; Duellman and Trueb 1986; Noble 1931; Sedra 1950). Two major hypotheses bear on this issue. The first assumes that the central pattern generators and other aspects of the nervous system become modified after changes in the musculoskeleton are complete (Reilly and Lauder 1988; Shaffer and Lauder 1988); in short, shifts in activation sequence drive ontogenetic (and even phylogenetic) modification. The second assumes that the outflow characteristics of the central pattern generators are conserved; modification is assumed to result from changes in the peripheral (muscular and skeletal) structures (Lauder and Shaffer 1988, 1993; Peters and Goslow 1983; Shaffer and Lauder 1988).

The exact properties of continuously changing and displacing muscles are difficult to assess in metamorphosing larvae. Some larval fibers remain in the adult, but others change their nature and attachment (Alley and Cameron 1983, 1984). The hypothesis (Lauder and Shaffer 1988; Shaffer and Lauder 1988; Reilly and Lauder 1988) that the neuronal motor pattern remains constant and that shifts in role primarily reflect peripheral reorganization deserves further study. Thus far, the analyses have been too few and the behaviors assayed too limited to yield definitive conclusions.

The fate of the larval trigeminal motorneurons during the drastic remodeling of the jaws and turnover of the muscles during metamorphosis has been studied in the jaw muscles of *Rana pipiens* (Alley and Barnes 1983; Barnes and Alley 1983). The full complement of motorneurons apparently forms during embryogenesis; moreover, motorneurons settle along a rostrocaudal gradient within the fifth nucleus. No cells are added or deleted during subsequent larval development or at metamorphosis. Hence, during metamorphosis larval trigeminal motorneurons may be respecified by switching their nerve terminals from larval to new adult muscle fibers. The competence of the associated tissue is important.

In contrast to jaw muscles, the limbs and their muscles develop more gradually before and during metamorphosis. Mesenchymal cells of the limb bud increase in size and number and progressively differentiate into cartilage cells and myoblasts. The hindlimbs are already functional before metamorphosis and aid in propulsion of the larva (see chapter 16). The well-formed forelimbs are ready to protrude just before the onset of metamorphosis. In analogy to developing axial muscles, development of the hindlimbs of *Xenopus laevis* includes prefunctional and functional periods. During the functional premetamorphic period, muscle diameter increases by fiber hypertrophy; the rate of hyperplasia is unknown. Also in *Xenopus*, appendicular muscles become multinucleate more or less simultaneously with the appearance of multinucleation in axial muscles. Thus, limb muscles are multinucleate prior to development of myofibrils and contractility (Muntz 1975).

After metamorphosis, muscles continue to grow throughout adult life. The jaw muscles of *Bufo regularis*, which decrease in length and volume during metamorphosis, initially grow very fast but later grow at a slower rate (Sedra 1950). In contrast to mammals, postmetamorphic growth in *Bufo* occurs by a combination of hypertrophy and hyperplasia. The axial muscles (e.g., the rectus abdominis) grow primarily by fiber hypertrophy (Lynch 1984). However, significant fiber addition occurs during postmetamorphic growth in the sartorius and gracilis major of three anuran species, *Rana pipiens*, *Xenopus laevis*, and *Bufo americanus*, and is greatest in the latter. In all three species, growth is associated with a strong positive allometric increase in muscle cross section; relative abundance of fiber types remains unchanged (Sperry 1981).

Regeneration and Autotomy

Various amphibians not only show metamorphic effects but can repair accidental damage and renew organs or larger parts of the body, a phenomenon that is uncommon among other vertebrates. Regeneration proceeds in the so-called regeneration blastema and involves initial dedifferentiation and subsequent differentiation. Following amputation of a limb or a tail, muscle fibers adjacent to the wound dedifferentiate (lose myofilaments and associated membrane systems) and give rise to mesenchymal cells that divide. Later in regeneration, these cells differentiate into the muscles and other tissues forming the new part. The regeneration of muscle differs from embryonic myogenesis in the functional state of the animal and the presence of nerves. In the regenerating limb of the newt *Notophthalmus viridescens* (Salamandridae), muscle-fiber dedifferentiation is associated with loss of the cytological specializations of the neuromuscular junction and decrease of the area of contact of the axon with the muscle. In a later stage, the axons withdraw from the muscle fibers, and junctional folds disappear completely. Coincidentally, cytochemical specializations associated with the synapse are lost.

Hence, both muscle fiber and nerve must have a certain degree of specialization to maintain the neuromuscular junction (Lentz 1970).

After a nerve crush, degenerated end plates regenerate only if the nerve fiber is present. Spontaneous reinnervation occurs only at the former synaptic sites; however, implanted axons form synapses both at the site of the implant and at former sites. Axons grow back along the basement membrane, Schwann cells, and perineurium. A substrate provided by the naked basal lamina guides precise reinnervation; reinnervation proceeds in the absence of original myofibers and intact original axonal sheath cells. However, the presence of myofibers significantly increases the rate of reinnervation (Bennett 1983; cutaneous pectoris muscle of *Rana pipiens*, Kuffler 1986).

Some caudates show caudal autotomy, in that part or all of the tail can be shed and subsequently regenerated. Apparently, no equivalent regeneration occurs in anuran larvae nor has this been tested in gymnophionans. The tails of primitive plethodontids show no specializations for tail breakage (Wake and Dresner 1967). In some Salamandridae and Plethodontidae, breakage of the skin occurs one segment posterior to that of the muscles; this allows the empty skin to cover the exposed vertebra and facilitates healing and subsequent regeneration. About two-thirds of the plethodontids possess constricted-based tails associated with several anatomical features that permit and facilitate caudal autotomy. Among these are areas of weakness in the skin posterior to the first caudal segment (which is reduced in length and diameter), anterior to the first caudal segment at the attachment of the musculature to the intermyoseptal septum, and between the last caudosacral and the first caudal vertebrae (Wake 1966; Wake and Dresner 1967).

Motor Innervation and End-plate Pattern

The spinal motor outflow proceeds via the ventral spinal roots. In the axial muscles of anurans and caudates primary (large) and secondary (small) motorneurons may differ, respectively producing large and small axons and projecting to regions composed of different fiber types (Fetcho 1987). However, no topographic relationship is obvious between the position of the motorneurons in the motor column and the dorsoventral position of the associated myomeres. Similarly, the motor neurons of the various dorsal neck muscles of the leopard frog, *Rana pipiens*, do not show any positional segregation (Feng 1982). In various ranid anurans, the motorneurons lie in a small and diffuse longitudinal column in the ventral horn between the second and third spinal nerves, medial to the lateral motor column neurons that innervate the anterior extremities (Silver 1942; see also chapter 2). Motorneurons associated with the opercularis muscle are limited to the rostrolateral portions of the lateral motor column itself (Feng 1982). In *Ambystoma* the motor neurons of the appendicular muscles form distinct but overlapping pools (Stephens and Holder 1985).

In contrast, Wake et al. (1988) refer to different populations in distinct places of the anterior motor column (see also Matesz and Szekely 1978). These populations show funda-

mentally different arrangements in anurans and caudates. The motorneurons of particular anuran muscles differ in number and range of variability (Roth et al. 1988b; Sperry 1987, 1988; Sperry and Grobstein 1985; Stuesse, Cruce, and Powell 1983; Wake et al 1988; Weerasuriya and Ewert 1981). Characterization of intermuscle differences is complicated because the diameter of the spinal cord is small relative to the size of the motor neurons; however, new labeling techniques should gradually resolve these issues (cf. Matsushima, Satou, and Ueda 1987).

Muscle fibers of most vertebrates are not indefinitely long but have a terminal length; long muscles are composed of short fibers (Gans, Loeb, and de Vree 1989; Gaunt and Gans 1989). Hence, banding of the motor end-plate arrays on the surface of long muscles of larger amphibians (Asmussen and Kiessling 1974; fig. 11.6) does not represent an exceptional state, but the rule. However, the site of motor nerve endings

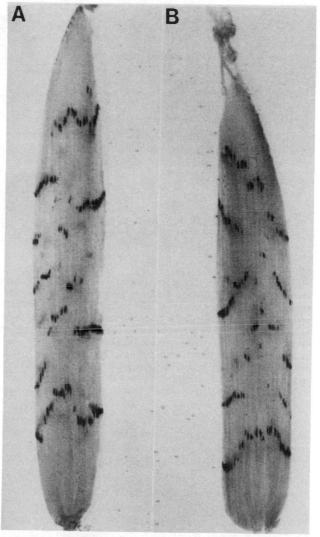

Fig. 11.6 Arrangement of motor nerve endings of the superficial fibers of the sartorius muscle of *Rana esculenta*. Acetylcholinesterase staining, magnification 4×. *A*, external side of muscle. *B*, internal side of muscle. (From Asmussen and Kiessling 1974. Reprinted with the permission of S. Karger, AG, Basel.)

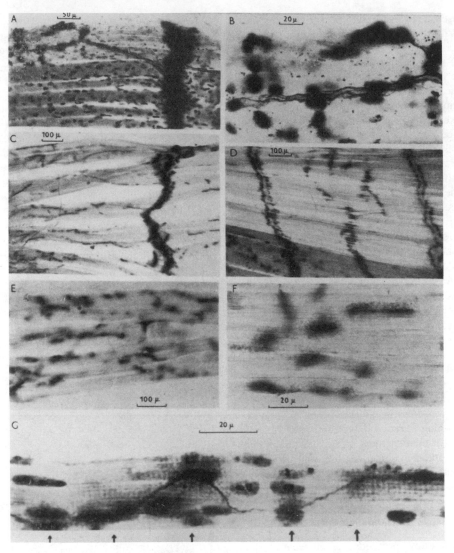

Fig. 11.7 *A*, stage 48 (Lewis and Hughes 1960). Part of abdominal muscle stained by the Bodian technique after the esterase procedure, showing the primary reaction at the septum (right) and the earliest development of the secondary pattern of innervation from a bundle of nerve fibers branching off from the septum. *B*, a more magnified view of part of *A*, showing some of the myoneural junctions of the developing secondary pattern. *C*, stage 55. Part of abdominal muscle, showing secondary pattern of motor endings along course of muscle fibers. *D*, soon after metamorphosis. Part of abdominal musculature, showing groups of motor endings running obliquely across the muscle segment and persistent esterase activity at the ends of the muscle fibers. *E*, stage 55. Part of the lateral segment of the transverse ventralis muscle, showing the profuse pattern of motor endings. *F*, a more magnified view of part of the muscle segment in *E*. *G*, stage 48. Part of the lateral segment of the transverse ventralis muscle stained by the Bodian technique after the esterase procedure, showing a single nerve fiber forming five esterase-positive junctions (*arrows*) with three muscle fibers over a total length of about 150 μm. (From Lewis and Hughes 1960. Reprinted with the permission of the Company of Biologists, Ltd.)

varies widely in both larval and adult muscles. In the main axial musculature of anuran larvae, almost all fibers have more than a single motor end plate. Also, fibers may receive axons from multiple motorneurons (Best and Bone 1973). However, the typically terminal motor innervation is unique. Axons (arising from a myoseptal plexus) form complex arborizations (basket endings) around the fiber ends, close to their insertions into myoseptal regions (Bone and Best 1973; Filogamo and Gabella 1967; Kordylewski and Gruszka 1986; Lewis 1958; Lewis and Hughes 1960; Mackay, Muir, and Peters 1960; fig. 11.7). A similar pattern of terminal innervation also occurs in axial muscles of larval and adult caudates (Best and Bone 1973; Mackay, Muir, and Peters 1960; Mather and Hines 1934; D. Carrier pers. comm.) and is common in the muscles of all groups of fishes except for the higher teleosts (Barets 1952; Best and Bone 1973; Bone 1966; Couteaux 1955). Hence, it is assumed to be a primitive state, with the double innervation pattern being more advanced (the plesiomorphic state). Terminal innervation of axial muscles appears to be rare among adult anurans (Ceccherelli 1904).

There are a few possible functional explanations for terminal innervation. Double innervation in premetamorphic axial muscle fibers may compensate for the inability of these fibers to propagate impulses over long distances. Terminal innervation is an adaptation for undulation in water (allowing tighter packing of white fibers) and correlated with the role of axial twitch fibers in rapid swimming (Best and Bone 1973). Innervation at the tips may be associated with the need of rapid transmission of signals required for rapid swimming (Lewis and Hughes 1960).

In axial muscle fibers, both polyinnervation and terminal innervation largely disappear during and immediately after metamorphosis, coincident with the advancement of muscle fiber differentiation (Lewis and Hughes 1960). Thus, nonterminal innervation is most commonly seen in postmetamorphic axial muscles. Apparently, the initially terminal motor end plates are displaced to a subterminal or equatorial position (Filogamo and Gabella 1967; also Kordylewski and Gruszka 1986, who discuss possible mechanisms for the elimination of polyinnervation and shift from terminal to nonterminal innervation).

The changes in end-plate position during ontogeny coincide with structural changes in end-plate morphology (Kordylewski and Gruszka 1986). Terminally situated end plates of axial muscle fibers of anuran larvae are simple and compact (Lewis and Hughes 1960). Their neuromuscular junction is relatively unspecialized, having a postsynaptic sarcolemma devoid of complex infoldings (Best and Bone 1973; Mackay, Muir, and Peters 1960). In caudates and postmetamorphic anurans, many end plates acquire a branched, extended form, and the junctions obtain well-defined subjunctional folds (Best and Bone 1973; Mackay, Muir, and Peters 1960). However, a few compact end plates still occur in the adult. Apparently, thick (white) fibers most frequently bear complexly branched motor end plates that lie in a nonterminal position, whereas compact termini generally lie on thin (red) fibers. Intermediate fibers apparently show intermediate types of innervation (Kordylewski and Gruszka 1986). Similarly, motor endings in the tail of Xenopus larvae are branched and more complex than those of the trunk musculature (Lewis and Hughes 1960). However, we still lack a direct correlation between fiber type and type of innervation.

The end-plate patterns also differ on various long muscles and appendicular ones. In long muscles of Xenopus larvae (external eye muscles, geniohyoideus), motor innervation is partially terminal. However, in broad muscular sheets (walls of pharyngeal, branchial, and abdominal cavities), secondary patterns of innervation rapidly replace the initial terminal innervation along the surfaces of the fibers (Lewis and Hughes 1960).

Most or all fibers from the submaxillary of Rana temporaria have numerous end plates (five to ten per fiber) that differ in size and shape even on single fibers. The electrical properties of these fibers are similar to those of twitch fibers (generating action potentials and not maintaining contracture); composite end-plate potentials indicate polyneuronal innervation. These fibers have been assumed to represent an "intermediate" type different from the tonic 4 fibers previously described (Miledi and Uchitel 1984).

Most appendicular twitch fibers are singly innervated; motor innervation is confined to about the midpoint of each fiber, a condition that is supposed to represent the normal vertebrate type of innervation (Ypey 1975, 1978). In the gastrocnemius of Rana the spatial arrangement of the single end plates is correlated with the spatial arrangement of the associated muscle fibers; end plates lie on a surface that surrounds the flat inner aponeurosis but is interrupted by the tonic bundle (Ypey 1978).

However, in analogy to axial muscles, multiterminal and/or polyneuronal innervation occurs on some twitch fibers of adult anurans. The pectoral muscle of adult Xenopus laevis contains fibers with doubly innervated end-plate sites, that is, single end-plate sites receiving two different axons (Angaut-Petit and Mallart 1979). The individual terminals of such doubly innervated end-plate sites are smaller and release less transmitter than those of singly innervated end plates. The small size may result from competition among endings for a limited available synaptic space (and hence, represent persistence of polyneuronal innervation of developing muscle), or from reciprocal interaction among closely located terminals.

Most fibers of the sartorius of Rana receive two end plates that do not show a regular position (Asmussen and Kiessling 1974; Hess 1970; Miledi and Uchitel 1984); similarly, the majority of fibers in the sartorius of Litoria aurea (Anura: Hylidae) show multiple end plates (Luff and Proske 1976). At least two end-plate regions appear on twitch 1 and twitch 2 fibers of the iliofibularis of Xenopus (Lännergren and Smith 1966; Lännergren, Lindblom, and Johansson 1982). Two or three end plates, each consisting of a relatively branching network, occur on the fibers of the pyriformis muscle of X. laevis (Orkand, Orkand, and Cohen 1978). Multiple innervation may be related to muscle fiber length (Asmussen and Kiessling 1974); possibly, mutual repulsion of nerve terminals limits the number of terminals on short fibers (Luff and Proske 1979).

The difference between tetanic tension that develops when two motor units are stimulated simultaneously, and the linear sum of their tensions when they are stimulated separately, provides physiological evidence for overlap of motor innervation (fig. 11.8). The sartorius of the frog Litoria aurea has a high proportion of polyinnervated units (Luff and Proske 1976), and almost all fibers in the extensor digitorum longus IV of Xenopus laevis are polyinnervated (Ridge and Thomson 1980c). In contrast, polyneuronal innervation is relatively uncommon in the iliofibularis muscle of L. aurea; here only 20% of the twitch motor units appear to overlap (Luff and Proske 1979).

The extent of innervational overlap between pairs of motor units has a wide range: maximally 30% of the tetanic tension of the smaller unit in the frog iliofibularis, over 60% in the sartorius, up to 80% in the extensor digitorum longus IV. The occurrence of multiple motor axons appears independent of the properties of the associated motor unit, but generally involves extensive overlap in properties between pairs of motor units. However, in the extensor digitorum longus IV some overlapping pairs show remarkably diverse twitch contraction times and tensions. In this muscle, even twitch and tonic fibers may overlap in innervation (Ridge and Thomson 1980c). Thus, individual muscle fibers of single motor units of extensor digitorum longus IV can have very dissimilar mechanical properties, determined by the combined properties of the innervating motor axons. Moreover, the efficacy of the neuromuscular transmission appears to be low at some junctions in this muscle, which may reflect the relative effect of different axons (Ridge and Thomson 1980a, 1980b).

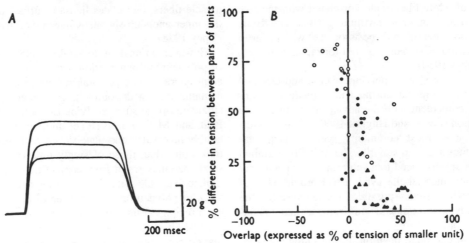

Fig. 11.8 *A*, isometric tetanic tension developed by two motor units with some muscle fibers common to both. The two lower records represent the tension for each motor unit when stimulated alone, the uppermost record the tension when the two units are stimulated together. Stimulus frequency 100 · s⁻¹ for 500-ms duration. *B*, a plot of the percentage difference in tension between pairs of motor units (the difference in tension when each unit was stimulated separately expressed as a percentage of their sum) against the amount of the overlap. The overlap is expressed as a percentage of the tension of the smaller unit in the pair. ○, smaller unit of the pair developed less than 5% of its respective whole-muscle tension. ▲, smaller unit of the pair greater than 20% of its whole-muscle tension. ●, remaining pairs of units. (Reprinted, by permission, from Luff and Proske 1976.)

As in axial muscles, end plates of twitch fibers vary in appendicular muscles. Five types of motor endings occur in fore- and hindlimb muscles of *Taricha torosa* (Caudata: Salamandridae; Mather and Hines 1934). Endings on twitch fibers that are intermingled with tonic fibers of hindlimb muscles (twitch 3 fibers) are much shorter but more branched and complex than normal en plaque endings (Asmussen and Kiessling 1974; Bone, Ridge, and Ryan 1976; Hess 1960, 1970; Lännergren and Smith 1966; Orkand, Orkand, and Cohen 1978). Adjacent fibers bearing such endings are not necessarily innervated at the same level (Asmussen and Kiessling 1974; Hess 1970).

As mentioned earlier, tonic fibers show profuse, multiterminal, polyneuronal innervation (Asmussen and Kiessling 1974; Lewis and Hughes 1960). Three widely spaced groups of en grappe motor end plates, with those of adjacent fibers scattered irregularly along the entire length of the muscle, occur on fibers of the pyriformis (Orkand, Orkand, and Cohen 1978). However, tonic fibers with four (extensor digitorum longus IV of anurans, Gray 1957) and even thirteen endings (Hess 1970) may occur. The iliofibularis muscle of anurans shows 50–95% overlap among pairs of tonic motor units; the tension developed by two of its slow motor units does not sum linearly, suggesting polyneural innervation (Luff and Proske 1979).

The wide variety of motor innervation may indicate that frog neuromuscular junctions are continuously remodeled (Kordylewski and Gruszka 1986). Such remodeling has been documented by combined light and electron microscopy for junctions on the surface of the cutaneous pectoris muscle of adult *Rana temporaria* (Anzil, Biezer, and Wernig 1984; Wernig et al. 1981; Wernig, Pécot-Dechavassine, and Stöver 1980). In this muscle, new and abandoned synaptic sites are common. By light microscopy, the new synapses appear as small, isolated rings of cholinesterase reaction product that are associated with small nerve terminals.

Nerve sprouting and new synapse formation appear ultrastructurally as local swelling of the axon at sites of contact with the muscle fiber. Synaptic vesicles occur in this part of the axon, which also lacks a Schwann cell sheath. Cholinesterase deposits appear in the synaptic cleft, but subsynaptic folds are initially absent. Acetylcholine receptors are usually present. Former synaptic sites are characterized by cholinesterase remnants that are not associated with nerve terminals. However, these areas lack acetylcholine receptors, indicating that the latter disappear from the subsynaptic membrane after nerve and Schwann cell retraction.

Sensory Innervation

As in the hindlimb muscles of most higher vertebrates, those of several anurans have muscle spindles (see also chapter 2). Their intrafusal fibers are distinctly either large or small (Brown 1971; Matthews 1964; Page 1966; Smith 1964a, 1964b). Both categories of fibers twitch, but the small ones contract more slowly. The structure of the large fibers resembles that of twitch extrafusal fibers, which have a somewhat less regularly organized sarcoplasmic reticulum; the small fibers resemble tonic 4 fibers (so-called intermediate fibers; Page 1966). Hence, no intrafusal fiber corresponds to the tonic extrafusal fiber. Moreover, muscles without tonic fibers lack small intrafusal fibers (Brown 1971). Motor innervation of intrafusal fibers is not exclusively fusimotor; collaterals of motor axons of large and small diameter innervate the respective intrafusal fibers (Katz 1949; Morgan and Proske 1984; Gray 1957; Smith 1964a). There are indications that twitch 2 motor neurons co-innervate the large intrafusal fibers, whereas tonic 4 motor neurons co-innervate the small intrafusal fibers (Smith, Blinston, and Ovalle 1973).

Thus far no urodele muscle has been shown to contain encapsulated spindles. However, fine-beaded nerve endings occur in limb muscles of newts (Salamandridae) and axolotls (Ambystomatidae); the shape of these terminals clearly differs from that of motor endings (Mather and Hines 1934). These endings respond to passive stretch; hence, they are likely to be sensory (Bone, Ridge, and Ryan 1976). Associated extrafusal muscle fibers are of small diameter, and the groupings always lie at, or close to, the outer surface of the muscle. Most of these extrafusal fibers appear to be tonic fibers (probably tonic 4); a few larger ones are twitch fibers (probably twitch 2), according to histochemical and ultrastructural criteria. Although the sensory terminals are morphologically (Katz 1961) and physiologically (Bone, Ridge, and Ryan 1976; Shepherd and Ottoson 1965) very similar to those found in anuran spindles, they never are encapsulated in connective tissue, nor do the associated muscle fibers differ from other extrafusal fibers.

Contrary to general opinion, anurans are not the most primitive vertebrates to contain muscle spindles. The superficial layer of the well-developed jaw-closing muscle (adductor mandibulae) of the primitive teleostean *Oncorhynchus masou* contains one or two very simple muscle spindles with a single intrafusal fiber (Maeda, Miyoshi, and Toh 1983). Similarly, unencapsulated sensory endings are not unique to caudates; such endings, of various morphological types, also occur in the respiratory muscles of *Cyprinus carpio* (Ballintijn and Bamford 1975), in the pelvic fin of *Raja* (Barets 1956; Fessard and Sand 1937), in the frog sartorius (Ito 1968), and in the extraocular muscles of *Girella tricuspidata* (Teleostei; Montgomery and MacDonald 1980) and various mammals (Barker 1974).

FUNCTIONAL MORPHOLOGY
Some Problems

The muscular architecture of amphibians, as well as many other amphibian systems covered in this volume, reflects and is complicated by metamorphosis. The life cycles are complex for most forms, shifting back and forth between water and air. This affects both the aquatic and terrestrial roles of these animals, not only doubling the major functional states, but introducing the concept and the complications of mechanical transitions. These are spectacularly reflected in some of the curiosities seen in adult amphibians.

The study of the way in which animals use their mechanical systems is variably called biomechanics or, better, functional morphology. For amphibians this discipline is still at a very preliminary stage with but few of the six families of caecilians, nine of urodeles, and twenty-one of anurans (Duellman and Trueb 1986) having been sampled. Also the stage reflects the substantial difficulty of working with animals that are often small and composed mostly of soft tissues. Hence the literature contains far more comparative and morphological analyses than experimental ones. More important, "hypothesis testing," in the currently fashionable pattern, may still be premature. Studies can still be justified on the basis that, because such a small fraction of the diversity has been considered, a careful sampling of the remainder is bound to generate surprising discoveries. The accounts that follow are again relatively brief and are supplemented by table 11.5. They are intended to be, not exhaustive treatments

of the topics, but stimulating samples from the experimental and natural history literature.

In interpreting functional aspects of a muscle, it is useful to consider that such ectothermic animals sometimes or even often conform to environmental circumstances, and thus must function throughout environmental ranges that would pose problems to endotherms. This is obvious for temperature; thus, the stamina of amphibians' muscles is temperature-sensitive (Feder 1986; Gatten and Clark 1989; Putnam and Bennett 1981; John-Alder, Barnhart, and Bennett 1989; see chapters 8 and 12). Moreover, the contractile properties of some frog muscles also may deteriorate in anoxia (Baldwin, Friedman, and Lillywhite 1977) and dehydration (McClanahan 1964; Gatten and Clark 1989). Although some species will accommodate relatively quickly to imposed stress, such responses have to be taken into account in these studies (see also chapters 5, 6, 8, and 12).

An important generality of amphibian systems is that they show transitional stages between the axial muscle pattern of fishes and that of amniotes (Böker 1935). Beyond the increase in relative mass of the appendicular and hyoid muscles relative to that of the axial ones (Böker 1935), amphibians shift from a fish pattern, in which the axial muscles consist of short segments reflecting segmental organization. The major trend to fusion and elongation of body wall muscles into sheets spanning multiple segments begins in amphibians (Renous in press), although it does not become common until the level of amniotes.

Ancestrally, most of the fish musculature was axial and started with blocks reflecting their origin from repetitive somites. In adults, somites are reflected in muscle units structured in parallel with the vertebral and rib units. More anteriorly, however, some of the striated muscles are organized into a branchiomeric pattern. This reflects their ancestral association with a segmented branchial basket, variants of which show up in all premetamorphic amphibians, and which provides the basis of the mandibular or hyoid systems. These branchiomeric muscles (and the extraocular muscles) derive from somitomeres rather than from hypomeric mesoderm; hence, they are fundamentally not different in origin from those of the axial-appendicular system (cf. Gans 1993).

Skeleton and Joints

The bony skeleton of Recent amphibians seems highly diverse, particularly in the smaller species in which much of the system is supported by an essentially hydrostatic cartilaginous framework and framing sheets of connective tissues. In a number of cases, closely related forms differ much more in bony architecture than in the muscular array or the connective tissues to which they attach. Some examples are seen in various anurans that have heterotopic bony processes (os tarsalia) on their hind feet; in related species, the process may be variably expressed as ossified connective tissues (Nussbaum 1982). Besides the functional aspects of ossifications, this suggests caution in using the extent of calcification as a taxonomic character.

As noted, amphibians also show wide use of hydrostatic skeletal mechanisms. The shape of larvae, the body walls and phallodeum of gymnophionans, and the corpus of the anuran

TABLE 11.5 Sample Studies of Amphibian Muscular Arrangements and Their Roles

Order	Family	Species	Reference
		Locomotion	
Limbed walking			
Caudata			Schaeffer 1941
Caudata			Sukhanov 1974
Caudata			Edwards 1976, 1977
Caudata			Peters and Goslow 1983
Undulant swimming			
Caudata			Blight 1977
Limbed swimming and jumping			
Anura			Barclay 1946
Anura			Gray and Lissmann 1946a, 1946b
Anura			Emerson and de Jongh 1980
Anura			Emerson 1979
Limbless			
Amphibia			Gans 1975
Jumping—evolution			
Anura			Gans and Parsons 1966
Jumping—trials			
Anura			Rand 1952
Anura			Rand and Rand 1966
Anura			Gans and Rosenberg 1966
Anura			Emerson 1978
Anura			Calow and Alexander 1973
Anura			Zug 1978; Zug and Altig 1978
Skittering			
Anura			Gans 1976
Toe pad function			
Anura			Emerson and Diehl 1980
Larval locomotor patterns			
Anura			Wassersug and Hoff 1985, 1989
Anura			Wassersug 1989
Larval terrestrial			
Anura			Oldham 1977
Burrowing			
Anura			Emerson 1976a
Gymnophiona			Gaymer 1971
Gymnophiona			Gans 1986
		Ventilation	
Gas exchange review			
Amphibia			Gans 1970, 1971, 1974
Amphibia			Bentley and Shield 1973
Ventilation mechanism			
Caudata			Bruner 1914
Caudata	Ambystomatidae	*Rhyacotriton olympicus*	Whitford and Hutchison 1966
Caudata	Ambystomatidae	*Ambystoma macrodactylum*	Whitford and Hutchison 1966
Caudata	Ambystomatidae	*Ambystoma maculatum*	Whitford and Hutchison 1966
Caudata	Ambystomatidae	*Ambystoma opacum*	Whitford and Hutchison 1966
Caudata	Ambystomatidae	*Ambystoma talpoideum*	Whitford and Hutchison 1966
Caudata	Ambystomatidae	*Ambystoma tigrinum*	Whitford and Hutchison 1966
Anura			Gnanamuthu 1936
Anura	Ranidae	*Rana tigrina*	Das and Srivastava 1956
Anura	Ranidae	*Rana catesbeiana*	Gans, de Jongh, and Farber 1969
Anura	Ranidae	*Rana catesbeiana*	de Jongh and Gans 1969
Anura	Ranidae	*Rana pipiens*	West and Jones 1975a
Anura	Bufonidae	*Bufo* sp.	Shinkai and Narita 1957
Anura	Ranidae	*Conraua goliath*	V. H. Hutchison pers. comm.
Caudata	Cryptobranchidae	*Cryptobranchus alleganiensis*	Guimond and Hutchison 1976
Caudata	Proteidae	*Necturus maculosus*	Guimond and Hutchison 1976
Caudata	Amphiumidae	*Amphiuma means*	Guimond and Hutchison 1976
Caudata	Amphiumidae	*Amphiuma tridactylum*	Martin and Hutchison 1979

TABLE 11.5 (*continued*)

Order	Family	Species	Reference
Caudata	Sirenidae	*Siren lacertina*	Guimond and Hutchison 1976
Caudata	Sirenidae	*Siren lacertina*	Martin and Hutchison 1979
Underwater buccal movements			
Anura			Hutchison and Whitford 1966
Narial closure			
Caudata			Bruner 1896, 1899
Anura			Gans and Pyles 1983
Caudata	Salamandridae	*Salamandrina*	Bruner 1901
Larval ventilation			
Anura		*Xenopus*	Gradwell 1971b
Anura	Ranidae	*Rana catesbeiana*	Gradwell 1972a, 1972b
Anura	Leiopelmatidae	*Ascaphus*	Gradwell 1973
		Feeding	
Review of experimental studies			
Tetrapoda			de Vree and Gans 1989
Caudata			Roth 1987
Caudata			Roth et al. 1988a
Anura			Roth et al. 1988a
Inertial feeding			
General			Gans 1969
Jaw mechanisms			
Amphibia			Olson 1961
Feeding			
Amphibia			Severtzov 1969, 1971a, 1971b, 1972
Caudata larvae			Severtzov 1969
Caudata			Regal 1966
Caudata			D. B. Wake 1982
Caudata	Plethodontidae		Lombard and Wake 1976, 1977, 1986
Caudata	Plethodontidae	*Desmognathus*	Larsen and Beneski 1988
Caudata	Salamandridae		Özeti and Wake 1969
Caudata	Salamandridae		Miller and Larsen 1989
Caudata	Ambystomatidae	*Ambystoma*	Larsen and Guthrie 1975
Caudata	Ambystomatidae	*Ambystoma*	Larsen and Guthrie 1975
Caudata	Ambystomatidae	*Ambystoma*	Reilly and Lauder 1989a
Caudata	Ambystomatidae	*Ambystoma*	Shaffer and Lauder 1985a, 1985b
Caudata	Ambystomatidae	*Ambystoma*	Lauder and Shaffer 1986
Caudata	Amphiumidae	*Amphiuma*	Erdman and Cundall 1984
Anura larvae			Severtzov 1971b
Anura	Pipidae	*Xenopus laevis*	Avila and Frye 1977
Anura	Pipidae	*Hymenochirus boettgeri*	Sokol 1969
Feeding mechanism, behavior, control neurons			
Caudata	Plethodontidae	*Hydromantes italicus*	Roth 1976
Anura	Bufonidae	*Bufo*	Takei et al. 1987
Anura	Rhinophrynidae	*Rhinophrynus*	Trueb and Gans 1983
Feeding			
Anura	Leiopelmatidae	*Ascaphus truei*	Nishikawa and Cannatella 1988
Jaw biomechanics			
Anura (parastreptostylic)			Pyles 1986
Feeding EMG			
Gymnophiona	Dermophiidae	*Dermophis mexicanus*	Bemis, Schwenk, and Wake 1983
Gymnophiona	Typhlonectidae	*Typhlonectes*	Wake 1978
Feeding phylogeny			
Gymnophiona			Nussbaum 1983
Tongue flip			
Caudata			Severtzov 1961, 1971a, 1971b
Caudata	Plethodontidae	*Bolitoglossa*	Thexton, Wake, and Wake 1977
Caudata	Plethodontidae		
Anura			Gaupp 1901
Anura			Tatarinov 1957
Anura	Ranidae	*Rana catesbeiana*	Gans 1961, 1962b

TABLE 11.5 (*continued*)

Order	Family	Species	Reference
Anura			Severtzov 1961
Anura			Regal and Gans 1976
Anura			Emerson 1978, 1979
Anura	Ranidae	*Rana hexadactyla*	Gnanamuthu 1933
Tongue flip, electric, evoked			
Anura	Bufonidae	*Bufo*	Matsushima, Satou, and Ueda 1985, 1987
Anura	Bufonidae	*Bufo marinus*	Gans and Gorniak 1982a, 1982b
Feeding on snails			
Anura			Drewes and Roth 1981
Larval feeding			
Anura			Wassersug 1972
Emitic behavior			
Anura			Naitoh, Wassersug, and Leslie 1989
		Vocalization	
Sound transmitter			
Caudata			Reed 1920
Anura	Ranidae	*Rana pipiens*	Wilczynski, Resler, and Capranica 1981b
Anura			Martin 1971
Anura	Hylidae	*Hyla a. arborea*	Schneider 1977
Anura	Bufonidae	*Bufo valliceps*	Martin and Gans 1972
Anura	Pipidae	*Xenopus borealis*	Yager 1982
Sound transmitter–androgen regulation			
Anura		*Xenopus laevis*	Sassoon and Kelley 1986
Tuning of receiver EMG			
Anura	Ranidae	*Rana catesbeiana*	Hetherington 1988a
Anura	Ranidae	*Rana catesbeiana*	Hetherington and Lombard 1983
Tuning of receiver			
Anura			Lombard and Straughan 1974
Anura			Capranica and Moffat 1975
Anura	Ranidae	*Rana catesbeiana*	Hetherington 1989
Anura	Hylidae	*Hyla regilla*	Straughan 1975
Anura	Hylidae	*Hyla cadaverina*	Straughan 1975

tongue are obvious examples. In each case, one sees tissues that become soft and lose shape under anesthesia. In the tongue, the key modifications that permit such mechanisms are spiral wrappings of collagen that resist diametric increase of the muscular mass and hence cause the tubular muscle to stiffen, rather than complying by diametric increase (Regal and Gans 1976). (As the area of sarcolemma required to define a fiber of given volume decreases with shortening, only wrapped fibers or ends of unipinnate arrays will establish internal pressures.) Hydrostatic skeletal mechanisms are common in invertebrates and also occur in various fishes; those seen in Recent species may be either primitive or derived states.

Amphibians display unusual patterns in the attachment of their muscles to the joints. The epiphyses normally consist of caps of calcified "cartilage" sitting like a thimble on top of the diaphyses. Such soft-tissue epiphyses are much more responsive to developmental changes in the degrees of freedom at joints than are the joints of amniotes, in which much of the excursion is constrained by the shape of bony condyles.

Miniaturization has clearly been important in the recent history of multiple amphibian lines (Renous and Gasc 1989; Trueb and Alberch 1985). Its evolutionary development and ontogeny have recently been characterized and discussed (Alberch 1981; Alberch and Gale 1985; Hanken 1983, 1984, 1985). In the present context, miniaturization is significant, as it may involve skeletal elements and consequently muscular attachment sites. This provides a quantum change in architectural pattern and with this a shift of the functional parameters. On the other hand, mere scaling down will not affect the moments generated, as these depend on the sarcomere pattern (Gans and de Vree 1987), rather than on muscle length (Rieppel 1985).

A set of parallel processes, possibly rare in amphibians, is enlargement, hypertrophy, and gigantism. It should affect both fiber properties and overall mechanics and hence seems an interesting topic for future analysis of the few very large amphibians.

Muscle Activities

Locomotion   Each of the three orders of surviving amphibians has a distinct set of locomotor patterns, and in each case these change at metamorphosis. Locomotion of tetrapod caudates is a variant of simple tetrapod locomotion. However, several aquatic caudates possess an elongated trunk with a paddle-shaped tail and greatly reduced limbs, and mainly propel themselves by swimming. Anurans commonly hop or jump and swim, locomotor activities propelled by simultaneous activation of the hindlimbs (Emerson 1978, 1988). However, some anurans move by patterns of alternating tetrapod footfall sequences (Barclay 1946; Gray and Lissmann 1946a, 1946b); this is the most common pattern for some arboreal species. The locomotor muscles of anurans are the most markedly modified from a general tetrapod condition; the axial mass is the most severely reduced, and most of the locomotor muscles are concentrated in the appendicular system. Caecilians show various limbless movements and can generate their own tunnels (Wake 1993). They lack major lateral ribs, and the patency of their trunk is likely maintained by muscular hydrostatic effects established by the thickened lateral walls of the trunk and the firm connection of superficial muscles and skin (Gaymer 1971). Almost all larval amphibians retain variants of undulant aquatic locomotion (Wassersug 1989; Wassersug and Hoff 1985; see chapter 16); possible differences in kinds of larval locomotion among the three major lines have not been assayed.

In caudates and caecilians, the axial musculature of the trunk can be divided into muscle segments. The large and relatively undifferentiated dorsalis trunci forms most of the epaxial muscle and is myomeric. The hypaxial trunk muscles are divided into a superficial external oblique, internal oblique, and transversus abdominis and a rectus abdominis along the ventral midline; all are myomeric in caudates, but in caecilians only external oblique and rectus abdominis are myomeric (Naylor and Nussbaum 1980). The axial musculature of the tail is not differentiated into distinct layers. The axial muscles participate in the establishment of undulant waves (Blight 1977), although some such animals can use S-start patterns in attack or C-start in escape (Webb 1978). Caudate locomotion combines limb-support patterns with the axial waves. The coordination of limb and axial bends has never been tested, although a comparative study of locomotor kinematics is available (Edwards 1976, 1977). The conceptually elegant analyses of Coghill (1914, 1916, 1924a, 1924b, 1926a, 1926b, 1926c), mapping the neuronal nature and ontogenetic changes in the central nervous system, should be reconsidered from a functional viewpoint and perhaps reviewed with the new techniques now available.

The studies of caudate body position deserve further extension in terms of limb and foot position (Schaeffer 1941; fig. 11.9). Other topics that deserve functional analyses are the use of the adhesive glands and balancers, ectodermal attachment mechanisms for the early anuran and caudate embryos (Duellman and Trueb 1986), and a specific study of limb reduction and trunk elongation in larger individuals of some caudates. Study of terrestrial locomotion (see chapter 12) will have to consider the scale and coefficients of friction, which are complicated by the adhesive properties of the moist skin on diverse substrates. We also lack experiments on foot structure, except for those associated with miniaturization, and considerations of the anuran toe pads and climbing patterns (Emerson and Diehl 1980).

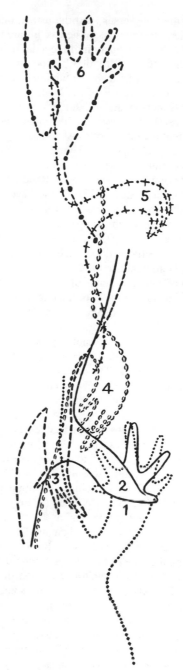

Fig. 11.9 Film tracings of the positions of the hindlimb of a caudate amphibian during propulsion (1–2) and recovery (3–6). This documents foot and ankle position of the hindlimb, but needs to be supplemented with those of hip and knee. (Reprinted, by permission, from Schaeffer 1941.)

The origin of the anuran body form has promoted multiple discussions (Green 1931; Hodler 1949; Gans and Parsons 1966; Hillenius 1976; Emerson 1982, 1984). Of interest in analysis of the locomotor pattern are the several types of shoulder girdles and the number of vertebrae. The trunk is differentiated, and the axial musculature reduced. The myomeric dorsalis trunci is divided longitudinally into medial and lateral portions (Nishi 1938); the hypaxial muscles include one oblique, the transversus, and the rectus; only the rectus retains myomeric inscriptions. Whereas this architectural pattern showing a drastic reduction of the axial muscles is often claimed to relate to the "froglike" locomotion, it may also represent a constraint of their ventilatory pattern. In swimming ranids, all the muscles of the hindlimbs are simultaneously active (Emerson and de Jongh 1980; de Jongh and Grootenboer 1989). However, the locomotor and escape patterns of different anurans vary substantially.

The ability of salamanders to jump still lacks functional analysis. In contrast, a variety of studies deal with observations of anuran jumping (Rand 1952; Rand and Rand 1966; Zug 1978; Zug and Altig 1978). These have recently been amplified by comparative anatomical analyses (Emerson 1978, 1979, 1980), and the jump of a frog has been modeled (Calow and Alexander 1973). More detailed EMG analyses of the muscular activity during the jump are forthcoming (de Jongh and Grootenboer 1989).

The origin of anuran appendicular locomotor patterns must have involved a shift in the coordinating ability from simultaneous to alternative activation of the members of girdle pairs (Gray and Lissmann 1946a, 1946b). Whereas the hindlimb activation concerns locomotion, there is also the forelimb pattern, which in males is associated with amplexus, the clasping action in mating. The diversity of ampletic patterns is astounding. The females of *Polypedates maculatus* (Anura: Rhacophoridae) can swing the hindlimbs dorsally. Thus, females clasp the males while these are on their backs and use the distal portions of the crossed appendages to beat the egg mass into a foamy nest (pers. observation). The pectoral muscles of males also respond to endocrine action, hypertrophying during the mating season. The stiffness of the arrangement may preclude a forelimb contribution to the jump and may provide a reason why anurans are precluded from elastic recovery of energy on landing from a jump. Species of *Phyllomedusa* (Hylidae) use their hind feet to coat their backs with protective wax (Blaylock, Ruibal, and Platt-Aloia 1976). The architecture of toes varies among the groups, and there is great diversity in anuran adhesive disks (Emerson and Diehl 1980). Also, anurans may dig, some entering the soil headfirst and others tailfirst (Emerson 1976a).

Swimming in anuran larvae recently has been studied by both EMG and kinematic analysis (Wassersug and Hoff 1985; chapter 16). The results suggest major taxonomic differences in locomotor patterns and disclose that mainly the distal tissues are activated in *Xenopus,* while the proximal tissues are in *Rana* (Hoff 1988; Wassersug and Hoff 1989). Larval *Xenopus* can beat their caudal tips continuously, positioning themselves in midwater. Other larvae live in flowing waters. Those occupying streams show streamlined patterns, and others are even able to move over land or climb rock faces (Oldham 1977, pers. comm.); the mechanics and distribution of this behavior deserve much further attention. Yet other larvae burrow in the substrate (Wassersug and Pyburn 1987).

Terrestrial locomotion in caecilians must overcome friction. Locomotion over the surface and within tunnels involves lateral undulation and concertina. The latter may proceed by curvature of the axial mass within the integument and integumentary muscles (Gaymer 1971). Digging involves stem

pushing, and many species appear to show specializations for tunneling by ramming their head into the tunnel end (Peter 1898; Wake 1993). It is likely that these animals show differences in muscle fiber properties and proportions along the column.

Ventilation The pharyngeal chamber of amphibians derives from the segmental gill basket of the earlier fishes, and this is reflected in the ventilatory pattern (Gans 1970, 1971; Liem 1985). The postmandibular elements tend to retain their association, and their position and movements are established by the activation of both the branchiomeric muscles and the hypobranchial slips of the axial musculature (Schaefer and Lauder 1986). However, convergence is possible, so that the homology of the elements concerned requires careful consideration (cf. Bemis 1987). The pattern generators of the brain stem maintain joint activation of serial muscles, contracting and expanding the pharyngeal volume (see chapter 7).

In Recent aquatic forms, mainly anuran larvae and perennibranchiate caudates that use muscular activation to shift water for gill ventilation, the vascularized surfaces either lie along the pharyngeal slits or represent external diverticula, of which the vascular supply branches off a single arch (see chapters 5 and 16). In each case the pumping activity tends to be based on pharyngeal distention-suction, pulling in water through the open mouth, followed by a contraction that drives a water stream out through one or more gill slits. In species with external gills, the pumping activity will swing the gills and thus produce a waving action, presumably enhancing exchange. Although the general pattern of anuran larvae has often been described, the detailed EMG of the pumping pattern has rarely been determined (Gradwell 1971a, 1971b, 1972a, 1972b, 1973). The buccal pump creates a unidirectional, continuous flow of water across the gills in a pattern modeled by Wassersug and Hoff (1979). Nothing is known about the embryonic gas exchange mechanics of species practicing direct development.

Many caudate larvae, some frog larvae, and the larvae of the caecilian *Epicrionops* (J. O'Riley, pers. comm.) swim to the surface to inspire gas bubbles through the mouth. These may be stored in or near the buccal cavity or in pulmonary diverticula. Transport remains via the bite, followed by constriction of the pharynx. Whereas muscle action has received limited attention, in small specimens the escape of the bubbles through pharyngeal slits is size-limited and may be blocked by muscular closure. In larger species, the incurrent drive involves rapid closure of the mouth and speedy contraction by action of the branchiomeric muscles.

Plethodontids and a few other terrestrial caudates (*Chioglossa:* Salamandridae; *Salamandrina:* Hynobiidae; *Rhyacotriton:* Dicamptodontidae) are lungless; most other amphibians possess lungs (Gans 1970). Lungless species rely on buccal and cutaneous oxygen uptake, a method that is also commonly used by other amphibians (Bentley and Shield 1973; see chapter 6). Recent lunged Anura and Caudata lack extensive ribs, and all amphibians lack a diaphragm; they fill their lungs by the pulsing of a buccopharyngeal force pump.

The muscular mechanism of ventilation in caudates and gymnophionans remains to be studied. The cycle was initially

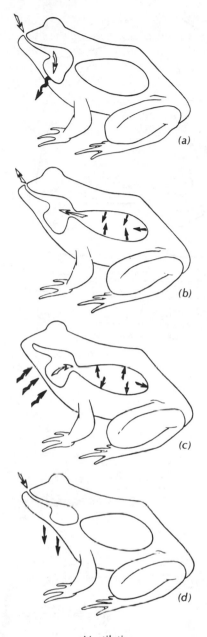

Ventilation

Fig. 11.10 The ventilation cycle of the American bullfrog, *Rana catesbeiana*, takes less than 1 s and is powered by the muscles of the floor of the mouth (*C*). These distend the elastic tissues of the lung, so that some of the muscular energy from each cycle powers the pulmonary efflux during the second phase (*B*) of the next cycle. (Reprinted, by permission, from Gans 1974.)

determined for the anuran *Rana catesbeiana* (de Jongh and Gans 1969; Gans, de Jongh, and Farber 1969) and then confirmed for *R. pipiens* (West and Jones 1975a). Three types of ventilatory movements occur. These involve two chambers (buccal and pulmonary) and the action of two valves (narial and glottal). The mouth always remains closed. Pulmonary pressure is always maintained significantly above atmospheric by smooth muscle fibers of the lungs, facilitating the expulsion of air during ventilation. The first cycles involve

rapid, rhythmic oscillations of the floor of the mouth; the nostrils remain open and the glottis closed, so that the buccal contents are flushed. At irregular intervals, there are interspersed pulmonary ventilation cycles preceded by a deeper muscle-powered depression of the pharyngeal floor (fig. 11.10). Contraction of the sternohyoid muscles pulls the hyoid posteriorly and ventrally, thus enlarging the buccal cavity just prior to a ventilation cycle. The glottis next opens, allowing the pressurized lungs to empty (bypassing the gas stored in the posterior pharynx); thereafter the nostrils wink closed and the rise of the buccal floor fills the lungs. A buccal force pump is formed by the transverse muscles of the floor of the mouth. A third set of cycles is that of the level of lung distention as multibreath inflation (deflation) cycles occur. R. M. Jones (1982) suggested (on the basis of the *Kopfkappe* experiments) that in *Bufo marinus* the narial openings only close incompletely during pulmonary ventilation cycles.

The closure of the nares has been a source of confusion. Those of caudates are supposed to be closed independently by smooth intrinsic narial muscles (Bruner 1901, 1914). Contrary to the findings of West and Jones (1975), Gans and Pyles (1983) report that anurans appear to lack intrinsic striated narial muscles capable of effecting closure. Smooth narial muscles do occur in the neighborhood of the nostrils of some anurans but are not involved in rapid closure (Bruner 1901; Gans and Pyles 1983; Gaupp 1896–1904). The mechanism for narial closure in anurans, hypothesized by Gaupp (1896–1904) and Bruner (1901), is unequivocally confirmed by experimental techniques (Shinkai and Narita 1957; *Rana*: de Jongh and Gans 1969; *Bufo*: Gans and Pyles 1983; Martin and Gans 1972). Closing involves lifting of the zone of the mandibular tips mainly by activation of the thick, spindle-shaped anterior intermandibular muscle, placed immediately posterior to the mandibular symphysis (fig. 11.11). The mento-Meckelian elements (sometimes discrete) act against the premaxillae, which rotate and press against alary cartilages, thus occluding the nostrils. The Mexican burrowing toad, *Rhinophrynus dorsalis* (Rhinophrynidae), lacks an anterior intermandibular muscle, there being a pad of dense fibrous connective tissue in its place (Tyler 1974); other variants undoubtedly occur in yet unstudied anurans. Gymnophionans have narial plugs on the tip of the tongue.

Feeding: Suck and Bite   All living amphibians are primarily carnivorous, at least as adults, and feed on living prey. (The ingestion of algal masses by some populations of *Rana tigrina* deserves further study.) In each group, the food-acquisition pattern of aquatic members involves components of the "gape-and-suck" mechanism, using pharyngeal distention shifted from ventilation (Drüner 1902; Lauder 1985b; Oezeti and Wake 1969; Wassersug and Hoff 1979). During forward attacks, suction avoids the bow wave (anterior compression due to relatively small mouth and presence of labial folds) generated during a head-on approach; coincidentally, suction sweeps along small prey positioned anterior to the stationary head. The head may be accelerated to the prey by variants of a C-start (Weihs and Webb 1983).

The functional morphology of aquatic feeding patterns has been studied experimentally (see de Vree and Gans 1989). In

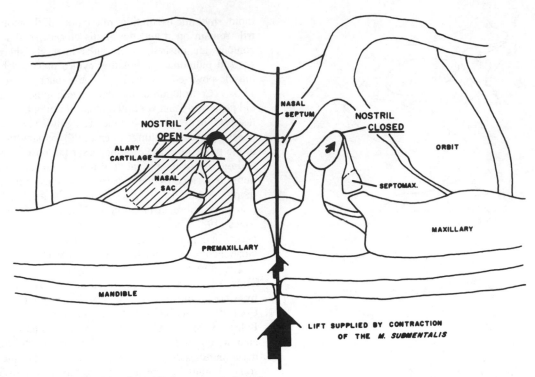

Fig. 11.11 Reconstruction of narial region of *Bufo marinus* in frontal view to illustrate the closing mechanism. Left nostril open, right nostril closed. (Reprinted, by permission, from Gans and Pyles 1983.)

larval caudates, aquatic feeding is associated with a unidirectional water flow through the buccal cavity: the distention of the oral cavity sucks water and prey into the mouth, then filters out the water posteriorly among the gill supports (Lauder and Shaffer 1985).

Opening of the mouth involves cranial elevation, accomplished with the cervical epaxial muscles. Mandibular depression involves action of the depressor mandibulae and posteroventral translation of a relatively rigid hyoid (fig. 11.12), as well as the action of the rectus cervicis muscle (= sternohyoideus, the strongest muscle associated with the hyobranchial apparatus), the hypaxial muscles, and the mandibulohyoid ligament. Coincidentally, the posteroventral rotation as well as lateral expansion of the hyobranchial apparatus distends the buccal cavity.

Maximum gape usually precedes both maximum cranial elevation and maximum hyoid depression. These events are only occasionally synchronous. The gill bars function as a dynamic resistance to water flow in the buccal cavity. Shortly after the buccal pressure drops, the gill bars start adduction. Maximum adduction is synchronous with peak gape and minimum buccal pressure, thus preventing (reverse) flow of water into the buccal cavity through the gill slits (Lauder and Shaffer 1985, 1986, 1988).

EMGs of feeding in ambystomatid caudates indicate synchronous activation of all cranial muscles—adductor mandibulae, depressor mandibulae, rectus cervicis, epaxials, hypaxials, geniohyoideus (= branchiohyoideus), intermandibularis posterior, and coracomandibularis. In contrast, the antagonistic depressor mandibulae and adductor mandibulae internus display different spike and amplitude patterns (Lau-

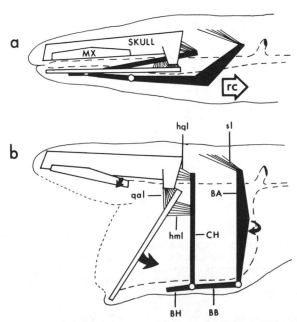

Fig. 11.12 Diagrammatic view of major excursions of the parts of the skull and hyoid during prey capture in *Amphiuma*. The hyoid acts as an open, three-bar linkage. Contraction of the rectus cervicis (*rc*) pulls the ventral region of the linkage posteriorly. Posterior or dorsal movement of the dorsal ends of the linkage is prevented by the hyoquadrate ligament (*hql*), the spiracular ligament (sl), and additional connective tissues and muscles associated with the dorsal ends of the ceratohyal (*CH*) and branchial arm (*BA*). *Long dashes* represent the midsagittal position of the buccal lining. *Short dashes* indicate the edges of the upper and lower labial lobes. *BB*, basibranchial; *BH*, basihyal complex; *hml*, hyomandibular ligament; *MX*, maxilla; *qal*, quadratoarticular ligament. (Reprinted, by permission, from Erdman and Cundall 1984.)

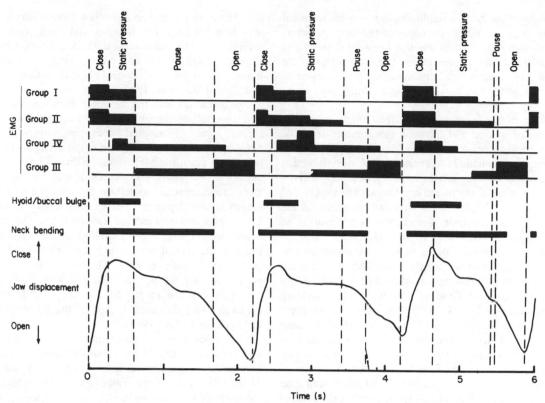

Fig. 11.13 Summary diagram of EMG activity, head and lower jaw movements during a sequence of three bites by the gymnophionan *Dermophis mexicanus*. The muscles have been divided into four groups, each showing approximately equivalent activity. The level of activity is shown by solid *blocks;* the height of each block represents relative amplitude of EMG spikes. Periods of hyoid/buccal bulging and vertical neck bending have been determined from film records. Jaw displacement (the relative position of the tip of the mandible relative to the maxillary tooth row) also was measured from the film sequences. (Reprinted, by permission, from Bemis, Schwenk, and Wake 1983).

der and Reilly 1988; Lauder and Shaffer 1985, 1986; Reilly and Lauder 1988; Shaffer and Lauder 1985a, 1985b, 1988).

The general kinematic pattern of head movement during aquatic suction feeding is similar in all larval caudates and resembles that used by ray-finned fishes and lungfishes. This may indicate that the biomechanics of aquatic prey capture are evolutionarily conservative (Lauder 1985b; Lauder and Shaffer 1985, 1988). The hyoid apparatus and cranial elevation are retained as major components of the feeding system; both facilitate opening of the mouth. However, the caudate branchial apparatus regulates water flow through the buccal cavity and is thus analogous to the fish operculum. Detailed kinematic, dynamic, and EMG analyses of the mechanism of the skull during suction feeding in ambystomatid caudates indicate profound behavioral and physiological variability in some of the parameters among individuals of the same species (Reilly and Lauder 1988; Shaffer and Lauder 1985a, 1985b). On the other hand, individual axolotls (*Ambystoma mexicanum*) do not change motor patterns during feeding on different prey (Reilly and Lauder 1989a).

Metamorphosed caudates continue to use suction feeding when in water (Özeti and Wake 1969). The pattern of skull movement does not change with metamorphosis. Aquatic adults of *Amphiuma tridactylum* (Amphiumidae) retain one pair of gill slits as spiracles (Regal 1966a) but show two types of suction feeding (kinematic analysis, Erdman and Cundall 1984). These are stationary capture, with little or no forward movement (used for small and sluggish prey), and strikes, coincident with a rapid approach (used for agile, elusive prey). During stationary capture, mouth opening is assumed to precede buccal expansion, due to sequential activation of the depressor and rectus cervicis muscles; hyoid depression then is limited. During the strike, both muscles may act synchronously as mouth opening and buccal expansion occur simultaneously. Also, the extent of buccal expansion is greater, and the lateral hyoid elements obtain a nearly vertical orientation (fig. 11.13). The spiracles open as the jaws begin to close, and the water flows unidirectionally. The jaw depressors and rectus cervicis act simultaneously during rapid strikes to increase suction velocity (Erdman and Cundall 1984).

Those caudates that do not retain gill slits at metamorphosis use a bidirectional feeding system when feeding in water. The closure of the gill openings after loss of the external gills forces the water that was sucked into the mouth to reverse direction. This increases the required pulse of positive pressure beyond the negative pressure, generated as the mouth opens, that is needed for a unidirectional system (*Ambystoma tigrinum*, Lauder and Shaffer 1986; *Ambystoma mexicanum*, Lauder and Reilly 1988). Other morphological transformations associated with metamorphosis (decrease of the buccal volume and reduction of the musculature associated with the mandibular and hyoid arches) result in an overall decrease of the levels of negative and positive buccal pressures. Operations changing flow from a unidirectional to a bidirectional mechanism decrease the effectiveness of the feeding performance, although other factors are also involved (Lauder and Reilly 1988; Reilly and Lauder 1988). The morphology of the metamorphosed hyobranchial apparatus itself is claimed to lack influence on the feeding performance (Reilly and Lauder 1988).

Free-living anuran larvae generally feed on algae, using a combination of suction and filtration (see chapter 16). The internal gills and associated peribranchial chambers allow the buccal pumping mechanism to create a respiratory flow that sucks suspended particles into the mouth. The pump is driven by cyclic activation of the paired ceratohyal cartilages (aided by the copula and hyobranchial plate). Contraction of the large orbitohyoideus muscle elevates the lateral margin of each ceratohyal and depresses its medial margin, thus expanding the buccal cavity. Contraction of the transversely oriented interhyoideus muscle, which is attached to the ventral surface of the ceratohyals, returns the latter to their resting position (de Jongh 1968; Gradwell 1971b, 1972b; Wassersug 1972; Wassersug and Hoff 1979). The resulting unidirectional water flow is maintained by an oral orifice, opening during ceratohyal depression, and a ventral velum (dorsal vela in *Xenopus*, Gradwell 1971b) between the buccal cavity and the pharynx that is moved passively by the water current. Papillae in the buccal cavity, gill filters, and mucus trap food particles (Wassersug 1972; Viertel 1985, 1986). Ciliary cushions also produce mucus (Viertel 1989) and effect subsequent transport of filtrate (mucus with food particles) to the ciliary groove and then to the esophagus (Viertel 1985, 1986). Larvae can modify their filtering and ingestion rate as a function of nutrient availability (Seale and Wassersug 1979). They regulate buccal volume, pumping rate, and efficiency of particle capture (Wassersug and Hoff 1979).

Some larvae, such as those of *Rana*, are facultative suspension feeders. They also use their keratinized mouthparts and mandibular muscles as a rasping and cutting mechanism that facilitates grazing on substrates. Their mouth is pressed against the food by action of the locomotor system. Other larvae are facultatively carnivorous or can ingest eggs (Taylor 1954; see chapter 16).

Terrestrial amphibians can bite at larger prey. The generally relatively small, pedicellate teeth will hold and may aid in tearing or cutting such objects. In some anurans (e.g., *Ceratophrys*), wiping movements of the forelimbs may facilitate tearing and manipulation of bulky prey (see chapter 13). Elongate species of caudates and gymnophionans tend to bite and spin upon their long axis, either discommoding the prey or tearing out pieces if it becomes wedged. Some aquatic species also use this method. The pedicellate bicuspid or monocuspid teeth of gymnophionans may facilitate grasping of their prey (Wake 1978), aiding the solid jaws and complex musculature (Bemis, Schwenk, and Wake 1983; De Jager 1939; Edgeworth 1935; Renous and Gans 1989; fig. 11.13).

A single experimental study reports on the feeding kinematics and EMG of the terrestrial caecilian *Dermophis mexicanus* (Bemis, Schwenk, and Wake, 1983). This species manipulates prey with a large nonprotrusible muscular tongue, which is only slightly free from the margin of its lower jaw. Hence this caecilian is a "jaw feeder" that reduces its prey with its large jaw muscles and teeth, simultaneously compressing it by constricting the buccal floor (static pressure method, Olson 1961). The prey is shifted further into the throat with the aid of esophageal peristalsis (Bemis, Schwenk, and Wake 1983; Gans 1962a).

The adductors from the temporal zone, common to all amphibians, are supplemented by the interhyoideus and longus capitis, apparently adapted for especially forceful bites. The bite then involves forces applied to the enlarged retroarticular process of the mandible, which facilitates both opening and closing of the jaws. The depressor mandibulae and dorsal trunk musculature act to depress the jaw. The relatively large longus capitis depresses the cranium at the craniovertebral kinetic joint and may increase closure force. The jaw is lifted mainly by a large pinnate interhyoideus that originates on the fascia of the ventral and lateral body wall and pulls ventrally on the retroarticular process. The buccal and hyoid muscles are active only during the static pressure phase and cause movements of the tongue to shift the food from the buccal cavity into the anterior part of the esophagus (Bemis, Schwenk, and Wake 1983).

The arrangement of the gymnophionan masticatory muscles apparently reflects the small diameter of these animals and limited sites for vertical placement of muscles (fig. 11.14). The shift of the major jaw-closing muscles beyond the temporal fossa allows the application of an increased muscular mass without increase of the cross-sectional area of the head, which would increase the cost of tunnel formation in a burrowing vertebrate (Gans 1974). The mechanical arrangement of the skull and feeding apparatus and the model of jaw adduction in caecilians thus differ from those of any other amphibians and may represent a key innovation in the evolution of caecilians (Nussbaum 1983).

Feeding: Propulsive Tongues Terrestrial "jaw feeding" amphibians must approach their prey closely before biting and must grasp and manipulate it within the mouth. Most ventilate by pulse pumping, however, which is facilitated by a wide head and a flexible buccal floor, both precluding the manipulation of food by development of a fleshy tongue or by inertial feeding (Gans 1962b). This conflict seems to have led to an experimental radiation (Gans 1990) with discrete solutions seen in some caudates and in anurans. In caudates, the solution uses hyoid linkage and reflects reduced reliance on buccal pulse pumping; in anurans, the soft tongue is generally attached to the symphyseal region and thus does not interfere with the buccal pump.

Terrestrial caudates include forms retaining a straight bite and various kinds of experimental tongue arrangements (cf. Regal 1966a). In most species the tongue can be projected. This tongue projection is assisted by movements of the entire hyoid skeleton, thus contrasting with the free tongue of almost all frogs. The functional morphology of tongue projection in terrestrial caudates has been studied from many perspectives. Early anatomical descriptions of the hyobranchial apparatus include some speculations on function (Drüner 1902; Edgeworth 1935; Francis 1934; Krogh and Tanner 1972). Many comparative studies address diversity and phy-

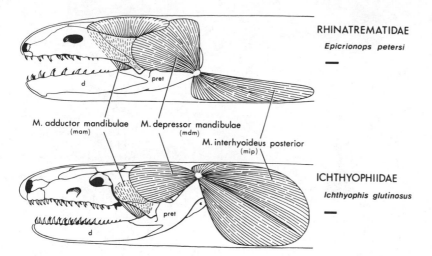

RHINATREMATIDAE

Epicrionops petersi

M. adductor mandibulae
(mam)

M. depressor mandibulae
(mdm)

M. interhyoideus posterior
(mip)

ICHTHYOPHIIDAE

Ichthyophis glutinosus

Fig. 11.14 Differences among four versions of the dual jaw-closing system of caecilians. *d*, pseudodentary; *pret*, processus retroarticularis. (Reprinted, by permission, from Nussbaum 1983.)

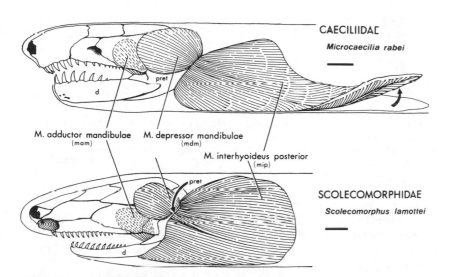

CAECILIIDAE

Microcaecilia rabei

M. adductor mandibulae
(mam)

M. depressor mandibulae
(mdm)

M. interhyoideus posterior
(mip)

SCOLECOMORPHIDAE

Scolecomorphus lamottei

logeny of the system (Lombard and Wake 1976, 1977, 1986; Özeti and Wake 1969; Regal 1966a; Roth 1976; Wake, Roth, and Wake 1983). Other feeding systems have been studied with cinematography or cineradiography (Dockx and de Vree 1986; Larsen and Beneski 1988; Larsen and Guthrie 1975; Reilly and Lauder 1988; Severtzov 1971b, 1972) and with EMG (Lauder and Shaffer 1988; Shaffer and Lauder 1988; Thexton, Wake, and Wake 1977), and data exist on topics such as the visual aiming of the strike (Luthardt and Roth 1979; Roth 1976, 1987). All these studies suggest that most, if not all, terrestrial caudates use a common pattern of prey capture, despite the profound diversity of the feeding apparatus and feeding mechanism among and within the four terrestrial families. The diversity of the caudate projection mechanism has been modeled (Lombard and Wake 1976).

The most successful radiation of tongue projection is displayed by the lungless plethodontids and especially clearly in the bolitoglossines, the most speciose subfamily (Lombard and Wake 1976; D. B. Wake 1982; Wake, Roth, and Wake 1983). In these, the hyoid skeleton is even more specialized and has been incorporated into the propulsive system; the soft

and adhesive lingual pad is attached to its distal tip (fig. 11.15). The extremely fast outward motion for a relatively great distance is generated by mechanical amplification of skeletal motions (Lombard and Wake 1976). In *Bolitoglossa,* one of the plethodontid caudates with the fastest projectile tongue, projection distance ranges between 12 and 19 mm (at 25.6°C), whereas tongue velocity ranges between 3 and 5 m·s^{-1}; hence prey capture may take less than 10 ms (Thexton, Wake, and Wake 1977).

Specializations for tongue projection in bolitoglossines, and in plethodontids in general, include posterodorsal elongation of the distal elements of the hyobranchial skeleton (epibranchials), modifications of its associated musculature, and a tendency toward freeing the tongue pad. In plethodontids, the long epibranchials (= ceratobranchials) articulate via the paired ceratobranchials 1 and 2 (= hypobranchials 1 and 2) with the basibranchial (= copula). The bolitoglossines lack a genioglossus muscle, restricting movements of the tongue pad. The tongue is projected by a pair of complex subarcualis rectus 1 muscles (Lombard and Wake 1976, 1977; Roth 1976; Thexton, Wake, and Wake 1977; Wake,

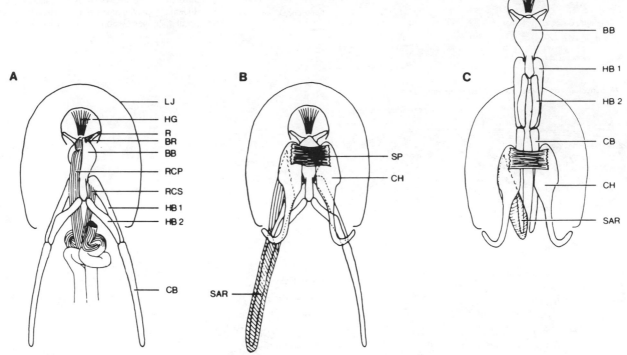

Fig. 11.15 Dorsal views of the tongue-supporting skeleton and tongue-projection muscles of the caudate *Eurycea bislineata*. Retractor muscles (*A*) and protractor muscles (*B*) are shown in rest position. Note particularly the coiled retractor and the spirally wound protractors. *C*, midway through the activation sequence. Note the folding of the posterior skeletal elements, which provides mechanical amplification of the muscular shortening. *BB*, basibranchial; *BR*, basiradial muscle; *CB*, ceratobranchial; *CH*, ceratohyal; *HB1*, hypobranchial 1; *HB2*, hypobranchial 2; *HG*, hyoglossus muscle; *LJ*, lower jaw; *R*, radial cartilage; *RCP*, rectus cervicis profundus muscle; *RCS*, rectus cervicis superficialis muscle; *SAR*, subarcualis rectus muscle; *SP*, suprapenduncular muscle. (Reprinted, by permission, from Roth et al. 1988.)

Roth, and Wake 1983) that arise from the ceratohyal cartilages in the floor of the buccal cavity and wrap around the elongated epibranchial cartilages in a complex spiral that protracts the elements upon stimulation. Retraction involves the rectus cervicis profundus, which arises on the pelvic girdle, passes among the ceratobranchials, and inserts near the anterior end of the basibranchial. The genioglossus also may help retract the tongue.

Tongue protraction of caudates is controlled via the glossopharyngeal and vagal nerves, and tongue retraction by the first and second spinal nerves (Roth and Wake 1985a; Roth et al. 1988a; Wake, Roth, and Wake 1983). Apparently, the muscles are activated nearly synchronously. In analogy to aquatic feeding, EMG reveals extensive synchrony both in onset and duration of the activity of the hyolingual protractors and retractors throughout the protraction-retraction cycle. Furthermore, the magnitude of this activity appears independent of projection distance, and mean force and duration of contact decrease with projection distance. Hence, tongue protraction-retraction may not be controlled by sensory feedback.

Coordination of tongue flipping has been modeled as a function of the characteristics of the muscles driving the system. At rest the protractors are slightly stretched, and the retractors are folded in the throat region (Lombard and Wake 1976). Hence, the protractors may be at or near optimum length during the onset of tongue projection, but as the folded retractors become stretched, the advantage gradually shifts to the retractors, finally resulting in tongue retraction. In this model, the opposing length-tension curves of protractors and retractors at any time during a protraction-retraction cycle determine the direction and timing of the movements (Thexton, Wake, and Wake 1977).

Tongue projection in other terrestrial caudates is stated to involve the same structures and mechanism as in plethodontids. Differences in projection distance result from differences in the ability of the tongue to lengthen and of the basibranchial and posterior cornua to protract. In the primitive Hynobiidae, tongue protraction is confined to some stretching of the tongue itself; its anterior edge is not protruded from the mouth (Severtzov 1971b). Ambystomatid caudates possess a geniohyoideus muscle and a relatively more elaborated tongue pad that can be protracted only slightly from the mouth (Dockx and de Vree 1986; Larsen and Guthrie 1975; Reilly and Lauder 1989a). Posterior movements of the ceratohyals are limited by their insertion on the quadrate bone (hyoquadrate and hyomandibular ligaments and fascia of depressor mandibulae muscle); anterior movements are limited by the first radials, connecting the ceratohyals with the basibranchial. The distal hyobranchial elements are short and rigid, and medial folding is limited by the slight insertion of the associated subarcualis rectus 1 (Dockx and de Vree 1986; Larsen and Guthrie 1975; Reilly and Lauder 1989a). Electrical stimulation of the hyobranchial muscles indicates that the subarcualis rectus 1 is not the only muscle effecting hyobranchial protraction of *Ambystoma tigrinum*. Tongue protraction appears to be a combination of a dorsal moment, produced by the subarcualis rectus 1, intermandibularis posterior and interhyoideus muscles (the latter two muscles raising the floor of the mouth), and a ventral moment, produced by the geniohyoideus muscle, which is strongly attached via a fascia to the basibranchial (Reilly and Lauder 1989a).

Terrestrial salamandrid caudates having a "land tongue" (*Salamandra, Chioglossa*: Salamandridae; *Salamandrina*: Hynobiidae) possess highly elaborated anterior parts of the hyobranchial apparatus, including the tongue pad, and reduced posterior parts as compared to plethodontids (Oezeti and Wake 1969). The tongue is attached at the front of the mandible by the genioglossus muscles but has a distinctly developed posterior tongue flap in most forms. The ceratobranchials 1 are fused and in line with the epibranchials. As contrasted to the condition in ambystomatid caudates, the tongue pad is flipped by projecting the basibranchial beyond the symphysis (Dockx and de Vree 1986; Severtzov 1971b). Furthermore, the flexible hyobranchium allows folding of its distal elements, resulting in ventral rotation of its tip. As in plethodontids, protractors and retractors, as well as mouth openers and closers, are active synchronously (F. de Vree pers. comm.).

In all terrestrial caudates thus far studied, skull elevation and depression appears to play a major role in the feeding mechanism (Bramble and Wake 1985; Dalrymple, Jutterbock, and La Valley 1985; Dockx and de Vree 1986; Larsen and Beneski 1988; Larsen and Guthrie 1975; Reilly and Lauder 1989a; Roth 1976; Severtzov 1971b, 1972). The kinematic pattern in part resembles that of aquatic suction feeders. In terrestrial caudates the mouth is opened in two steps. Protrusion of the tongue coincides with rapid cranial elevation, straightening the craniovertebral axis, and generally with mandibular depression. The posterior end of the mandible pivots anterodorsally around the symphysis, and the head frequently begins a surge towards the prey (Dockx and de Vree 1986; Larsen and Beneski 1988; Larsen and Guthrie 1975; Reilly and Lauder 1989a). After prey contact, most caudates further increase the gape by the same mechanism as the tongue starts to retract, apparently to facilitate entry and manipulation of incoming food. The head eventually surges further forward. Hence, maximum gape occurs during tongue retraction (Bemis and Findeis 1986; Dockx and de Vree 1986; Larsen and Beneski 1988; Larsen and Guthrie 1975; Miller and Larsen 1986). The only exception thus far is the plateau of near-constant peak gape observed in adult *Ambystoma tigrinum*, during which maximum tongue protrusion is reached (Reilly and Lauder 1989a). Peak hyobranchial depression and retraction are caudally far beyond the rest position (Dockx and de Vree 1986; Larsen and Beneski 1988). Immediately after the tongue is returned into the buccal cavity, the mouth closes by a rapid snapping motion of the cranium, generally associated with a flexion of the neck, and completion of the forward surge of the head. The mouth is closed mainly by depression of the head, coupled with very slight elevation of the lower jaw (Dockx and de Vree 1986; Larsen and Beneski 1988; Larsen and Guthrie 1975; Reilly and Lauder 1989a).

Intraoral transport and swallowing, associated with elevation and depression of the skull and posteroventral movement of the hyobranchial apparatus (seen as gular expansion), reflects less complex movements (Dockx and de Vree 1986; Larsen and Beneski 1988; Larsen and Guthrie 1975; Reilly and Lauder 1989a). Inertial feeding is sometimes used. It involves the antagonistic action of subarcualis rectus 1 and rectus cervicis superficialis muscles. Finally, the prey is forced into the esophagus by contraction of the interhyoideus posterior, which changes the configuration of the floor of the oropharyngeal cavity, and is accompanied by eye depression (Dockx and de Vree 1986; Larsen and Guthrie 1975; Severtzov 1971b).

In almost all terrestrial anurans thus far studied, the projectile tongue is separated from the hyoid system, so that the pulse-pumping capacity is not affected. In most of these species, the anterior end of the tongue is attached near the symphysis, but the posterior end is freely moveable. Some species are aglossal and display some specialized feeding patterns (Avila and Frye 1977).

The basic anuran projectile system consists of two sets of muscular tissues, the longitudinal elements intrinsic to the tongue (hyoglossus and genioglossus medialis) and a second variably transverse basal mass (genioglossus basalis and submentalis; Gans 1962b; Gans and Gorniak 1982a, 1982b; fig. 11.16). Additional facilitatory muscles include the intermandibularis posterior and interhyoideus, forming the floor of the mouth; the geniohyoideus medialis and lateralis and sternohyoideus muscles, connecting the hyoid respectively with the mandible near the symphysis and the shoulder girdle; and the petrohyoid muscles, connecting the hyoid with the prootic region (Roth et al. 1988b). Hyoglossals act to return and reposition the tongue and adherent prey. The lower jaw is composed of the variably discrete mento-Meckelian bones, the dentary and the angulospherical. The great diversity of structure of the anuran intrinsic tongue muscles has been studied extensively for taxonomic (Magimel-Pélonnier 1924; Horton 1982) and evolutionary purposes (Regal and Gans 1976; fig. 11.17). Motor innervation occurs by brain-stem and cervicospinal nerves and is similar among species studied. Tongue projection is controlled via the trigeminal and hypoglossal nerves, tongue retraction via the hypoglossus (Matesz and Szekely 1978; Matsushima, Satou, and Ueda 1986, 1987; Roth et al. 1988a; Stuesse, Cruce, and Powell 1983).

The function of this tongue projection system, seen variably in *Rana* and *Bufo,* has been studied by EMG (Gans and Gorniak 1982a, 1982b), leading to the conclusion that it represents a catapult (Regal and Gans 1976). The muscles involved are activated sequentially and at different levels during the course of the tongue flip. The tongue is propelled by the nearly simultaneous contraction of the genioglossus (basalis and medialis) and submentalis muscles. Contraction of the genioglossus medialis results in stiffening of tongue into a rod, which facilitates initial tongue propulsion as it is rotated over the symphysis by depression of its anterior end. The final phase of lingual propulsion merely results from inertial travel of the tongue pad, which is loosely attached to the genioglossus medialis. Contraction of the transversely oriented genioglossus basalis forms a wedge under the anterior part of the stiffened tongue, which in turn is lifted further by contraction of the submentalis muscle. This provides a second wedge able to transmit upward and forward momentum to the

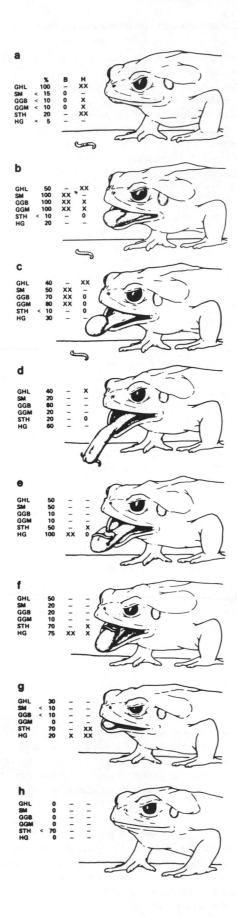

a

	%	B	H
GHL	100	–	XX
SM	< 15	0	–
GGB	< 10	0	X
GGM	< 10	0	X
STH	20	–	XX
HG	< 5	–	–

b

GHL	50	–	XX
SM	100	XX	–
GGB	100	XX	X
GGM	100	XX	X
STH	< 10	–	0
HG	20	–	X

c

GHL	40	–	XX
SM	50	XX	–
GGB	70	XX	0
GGM	80	XX	0
STH	< 10	–	–
HG	30	–	–

d

GHL	40	–	X
SM	20	–	–
GGB	60	–	–
GGM	20	–	–
STH	20	–	0
HG	60	–	–

e

GHL	50	–	–
SM	50	–	–
GGB	10	–	–
GGM	10	–	–
STH	50	–	X
HG	100	XX	0

f

GHL	50	–	–
SM	20	–	–
GGB	20	–	–
GGM	10	–	X
STH	70	–	X
HG	75	XX	X

g

GHL	30	–	–
SM	< 10	–	–
GGB	< 10	–	–
GGM	0	–	–
STH	70	–	XX
HG	20	X	XX

h

GHL	0	–	–
SM	0	–	–
GGB	0	–	–
GGM	0	–	–
STH	< 70	–	–
HG	0	–	–

Fig. 11.16 Tongue protrusion and prey capture by adult *Bufo marinus*. The illustrations represent tracings from sequences filmed at 400 frames per second (the EMG values represent means from at least ten sequences involving multiple toads.) *GHL*, geniohyoideus lateralis; *SM*, submentalis; *GGB*, genioglossus basalis; *GGM*, genioglossus medialis; *STH*, sternohyoideus; *HG*, hyoglossus. The percentages are the maximum activity observed in the muscles during 6 to 12 flips (represented as spike number × mean spike amplitude for 7-ms intervals) at positions similar to those shown. The sequence from open to closed mouth takes approximately 145 ms. Adjacent to the EMG values are code symbols indicating the values predicted by the ballista (*B*), and hyoid (*H*) hypothesis (—, no prediction; *O*, no activity; *X*, low activity; *XX*, high activity). The former hypothesis is supported.

A, toad in anticipatory position with body rotated over forelimbs. The mouth is still closed, but the lateral geniohyoid is highly active in the protrusion of the hyoid and in facilitating ventrad rotation of the mandibular tips as soon as the mouth opens. *B,* the mouth has opened, and the base of the tongue has lifted toward the symphysis. The soft tissues of the lingual pad trail the stiffened base, which is already rotating over the depressed mandibular symphysis. Throughout this phase, the submentalis, genioglossus basalis, and genioglossus medialis are highly active, while the activity in the geniohyoideus lateralis and sternohyoideus have dropped to about one-half of their previous values. *C,* the base of the tongue has now rotated 180° from its resting position to point toward the prey, extending over and beyond the depressed symphysis. The soft tissues of the lingual pad are still trailing the tip but are being catapulted toward the prey. Activity in all lingual muscles has dropped from the previous values, indicating that the peak of energy input for propulsion has passed. *D,* the soft tissues of the lingual pad have now reached their full extent and contacted the prey. (The sequence illustrated shows the initial position of the prey fairly close to the mandibular symphysis. This allows the soft distal portion to rotate ventrally beyond the stiffened lingual base, thus delineating the distal tip of the extended lingual rod by a bend in the tongue). Muscle activity has generally dropped from that in the preceding view, except for that in the hyoglossus, where it now rises. *E,* retraction has started. The distal soft tissues are first accelerated toward the mouth, apparently by the hyoglossus, which now shows maximal activity, so that they pass the stiffened lingual base, which remains beyond the mandibular symphysis. Both the genioglossus lateralis and the submentalis have increased activity, as have the sternohyoideus and hyoglossus. This is reflected in the secondary depression of the symphyseal region, which occurs at the beginning of the retraction and increases the effective gape as tongue and prey enter. *F,* while the mouth is already closing, the tip of the tongue rolls inward over the still depressed mandibular symphysis. The geniohyoideus lateralis is still active and substantial, but activity decreases in the sternohyoideus and hyoglossus. The hyoid is being retracted, although the symphysis is still slightly depressed. *G,* the tongue has almost completed its inward travel, and the hyoglossal activity has dropped sharply, although the sternohyoid remains active. *H,* the toad has now closed its mouth, and the geniohyoideus lateralis and the intrinsic lingual muscles are silent. The sternohyoid continues to be active, however, as are some of the more posterior muscles (not shown), which will be involved in swallowing and, of course, ventilation. (Reprinted, by permission, from Gans and Gorniak 1982. Copyright 1982 by the AAAS.)

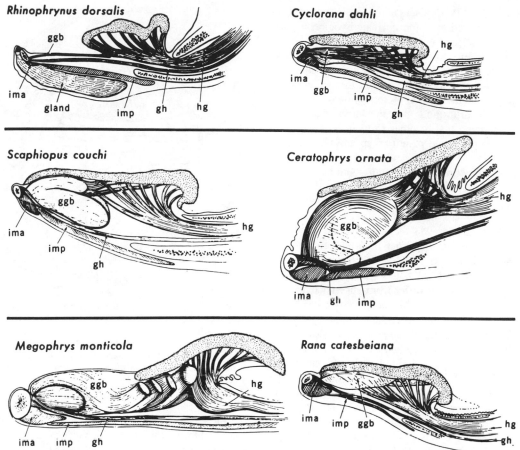

Fig. 11.17 Sagittal and parasagittal sections through the tongues of representative anurans to illustrate morphological diversity. Although diagrammatic, these views were drawn with the aid of a camera lucida. The heads point to the left. *Rhinophrynus* (Rhinophrynidae): Note the massive development of the hyoglossal retractor muscle (*hg*) and poor development of the genioglossus basalis (*ggb*) or any other potential protractors. *Cyclorana* (Hylidae): This drawing also serves to represent the condition in *Ascaphus* (Leiopelmatidae) and *Bombina* (Discoglossidae). Note particularly the diffuse organization of the *ggb*; here they are not organized so as to form a lever system. The interdigitating insertion of the protractor and retractor fibers into the tongue pad is characteristic of the tongues of all the following frogs. *Scaphiopus* (Pelobatidae): It is notable that the "wedgelike" portion of the *ggb* is relatively huge. Diffuse fascicles diverge lateral to the midline as the dorsal portions of this muscle, and are compact primarily in the small area where they join along the midline. *Ceratophrys* (Leptodactylidae): The dorsal portion of

the *ggb* is relatively huge along the midline. It branches into loose fascicles as it turns laterally to interdigitate with fascicles of the *hg* and insert into the tongue pad. Note that the basal "wings" or "wedge" of the *ggb* are primarily lateral to the midline; hence the right flap is indicated by a *dashed line* since it would be located deeper than the primary plane in view. *Megophrys* (Pelobatidae): The sagittal section illustrated passes only through a left lateral wing of the *ggb* and the stout bundles of its left posterior portion as they branch beneath the tongue pad, apparently offering structural support. Thus, one sees primarily the surface of the *ggb* and the five severed lateral portions (indicated by *heavy lines*). *Rana* (Ranidae): The compact form of the *ggb* is particularly noteworthy. Lateral fascicles from the genioglossus can be seen beneath the *hg*. *ggb*, genioglossus basalis; *gh*, geniohyoid; *hg*, hyoglossal; *ima*, intermandibularis anterior; *imp*, intermandibularis posterior. The nature of the structure labeled *gland* was not investigated. (Reprinted, by permission, from Regal and Gans 1976.)

side of the rigid genioglossus. Coincident bending and depression of the mandible (by contraction of geniohyoideus and submentalis muscles) finally results in the tongue being rotated outward over the symphysis. Contrary to the findings of Emerson (1976b, 1977), hyolingual projection in anurans is not associated with a significant displacement of the hyoid skeleton; the hyoid is fixed by the simultaneous contraction of geniohyoid and sternohyoid muscles. Tongue retraction is accomplished by the hyoglossus muscle alone, which is also the first muscle to become active. The sequence of muscle activity has been confirmed by a series of studies in which feeding was elicited by stimulation of the brain (Matsushima, Satou, and Ueda 1985, 1987; Satou et al. 1985).

More recently, the feeding pattern of multiple anurans has been studied by a change of the EMG paradigm; beyond ask-

ing which muscles are active, this asks whether the muscles are necessary for (buccal pumping and) lingual projection. The multiple analyses involve nerve tracing, deinnervation and muscle stimulation. The analyses show that the mouth opening and lingual projection actions of *Bufo marinus* (Bufonidae, Anura) involve diverse reflex actions (Nishikawa and Gans 1990, 1992). Beyond the earlier observations of morphological diversity (Regal and Gans 1972), now confirmed by experimental studies (cf. Gans, Nishikawa and Canatella 1991; Nishikawa and Roth 1991; Nishikawa and Canatella, 1991), a phylogenetic analysis (Nishikawa, O'Reilly and Canatella 1991) documents that projectile tongue systems appear to have arisen at least six times within the Anura.

Thus far, the single exception to this general scheme is the Mexican ant-eating frog, *Rhinophrynus dorsalis* (Rhinophrynidae). Its liquid-filled muscular tongue is mounted on the hyoid plate. Contraction of the intrinsic hyoglossal muscles exerts hydrostatic pressure on the fluid contents of the lingual sinus and stiffens and extends the tongue anteriorly. Coincidentally, the hyoid plate shifts forward and squeezes the lingual tip out through a palatal groove. Retraction of the tongue through the palatal groove, by retraction of the hyoid, sucks small attached arthropods into the buccal cavity. The mechanism differs from that of other frogs in its association with movements of the hyoid plate (Trueb and Gans 1983).

Vocalization   Vocalization by male anurans in breeding aggregations is a major aspect of the social behavior of amphibians (see chapters 2 and 14). The laryngeal muscles are innervated by the caudal column of the vagus (Schneichel, Walkowiak, and Schneider 1988). The larynx and associated muscles of males appear to be larger than those of females (McClelland and Wilczynski 1989b), and hormonal effects on the musculature have been noted (Sassoon and Kelley 1986). The laryngeal muscles differ from appendicular muscles and are sexually dimorphic in fine structure and fusion frequency (Manz 1975; Eichelberg and Schneider 1973, 1974; Schneider 1970). Sexually active males produce a species-specific mating call selectively to attract females. The sound is generally loud and of limited structural variability. Aroused males frequently clasp the axial region of another male (or sexually nonactive female). If it is not a receptive female, the animal clasped in amplexus emits a release signal that consists of body vibrations, some of which are associated with sound. The release call is more aperiodic than the mating call, weaker in amplitude, and shorter in duration and pulse rate. However, its sound pattern appears to be basically similar to that of the mating call. Whereas the mating and release calls are mainly associated with the breeding season, anurans in addition frequently emit miscellaneous sounds, such as calls elicited by rainfall, territorial calls, and warning and distress calls (Martin and Gans 1972).

The release sound can be elicited experimentally by axial pressure back to the forelimbs. The mechanism of release vibration and release call has been studied in the toad *Bufo valliceps* (Martin and Gans 1972), and much of what follows derives from this report. The process is associated with the pulse-pumping method of breathing but differs from it in being more complex. Release calling involves three rather than two chambers, buccal and pulmonary cavities and vocal sacs, and the action of three rather than two valves, nostrils, larynx, and slits to vocal sacs. When the animal is at rest, the three cavities are closed from each other, and the nostrils are open. The release sequence starts with the animal inflating its lungs and sometimes its buccal cavity. Then follows a train of pulsatile movements that shake the entire body and are associated with closed nostrils, swelling of the floor of the buccal cavity, and decrease in body diameter. After the third pulsation, the pulse trains may be associated with sound. Increase in sound amplitude tends to be associated with stepwise inflations of the vocal sac. After a few seconds the release sequence stops with a terminal reinflation of the lungs, and vocal and buccal sacs shrink.

The pulse trains are mainly driven by pressure pulses that are within the lung and visceral cavity and are produced by the muscles of the body wall. These increase pulmonary pres-

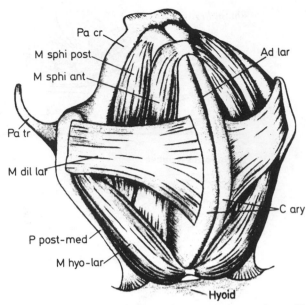

Fig. 11.18 Laryngeal musculature of a male *Hyla a. arborea* (Hylidae) *Ad lar*, aditus laryngis; *C ary*, arytenoid cartilage; *M dil lar*, laryngeal dilator muscle; *m hyo-lar*, hyolaryngeal muscle; *M sphi ant*, anterior sphincter muscle; *M sphi post*, posterior sphincter muscle; *Pa cr*, pars cricoidea of the cricotracheal cartilage; *Pa tr*, pars trachealis of the cricotracheal cartilage; *P postmed*, posteromedial process. (Reprinted, by permission, from Schneider 1970.)

sure far above the resting value, facilitating airflow from the lungs to the buccal cavity via the larynx. Between pulses, pulmonary pressure is further increased by inertia of the visceral mass, resulting in peak pulmonary pressure values several times the highest pressure during normal inflation. The body wall pump is supplemented by the buccal pump and compressor of the vocal sac. Sound emission always is associated with sudden pulmonary and buccal pressure pulses. However, the first sharp rises in pulmonary pressure usually proceed with the larynx closed, so that they are not associated with buccal pressure pulses. Inflation of the vocal sac(s) is always associated with a drop in buccal pressure.

In many anurans, the glottis is supported by a pair of triangular arytenoid cartilages, which articulate with the anterior edge of the cricoid surrounding the laryngeal chamber (fig. 11.18). The glottis may be opened by a laryngeal dilator and closed by laryngeal external, anterior, and posterior constrictors. However, elastic closing is achieved by the soft tissues lining the arytenoid cartilages.

The larynx is the primary source of sound production. It works as a self-exciting vibrator, emitting puffs of air from the continuously pressurized pulmonary air. The anatomy of the larynx passively determines the specificity of the sound. The dominant frequency of sound reflects the resonant frequency of the vocal cords. This frequency is amplitude modulated by vibrations of the arytenoid cartilages (Martin 1971). However, the laryngeal output is also modulated actively by laryngeal muscles. Before sound production, the magnitude of the pressure differential across the larynx, produced by contraction of the pulmonary compressors and buccal dilator, depends on resistance to airflow in the larynx. The larynx is kept tightly closed by simultaneous activity in both laryngeal constrictors and the dilator. Possibly the laryngeal muscles hold the larynx depressed between the posterior horns of the hyoid, so that it remains closed while pulmonary pressure builds up. The buccal dilator (sternohyoideus) pulls the hyolaryngeal apparatus posteriorly; the buccal compressors keep vocal slits closed (Martin and Gans 1972). Sound starts as the laryngeal muscles relax and the pressurized pulmonary air forces the arytenoid cartilages apart. With increase in buccal pressure, the chords vibrate and alternately dilate and occlude the orifice. The cessation of the sound is achieved by sudden contraction of the laryngeal dilator, which opens the larynx widely and deactivates the vibrators.

The vocal sacs act as resonators. In most species of all higher anuran families, these secondary vocal structures are present, for instance, one at the throat (e.g., *Hyla arborea, Rana catesbeiana, Bufo valliceps*) or two behind the lower jaw (*R. esculenta*). The sacs arise as an invagination of the gular skin and grow between the geniohyoideus and subhyoideus muscles dorsally, and submaxillaris and subhyoideus ventrally (Inger 1956). The vocal sacs open in the floor of the buccal cavity. The elongated interhyoideus is supposed to have given rise to the vocal sac compressor in most anurans. The muscle forms the anterior border of the slit-shaped connection between vocal sac and buccal cavity. During calling, the subhyoideus, attached to the interior surface of the gular pouches, is stretched by inflation. Contraction of the interhyoideus returns the air (Inger 1956).

Taxonomic studies document the enormous diversity of call types, but the diversity of their production remains largely unstudied (Martin 1971). Muscles may modify the pulmonary pressure and may actively affect the tension of components such as the vocal cords. In *Rhinophrynus* the interhyoideus is highly specialized, due to the reduction of the anterior cornua of the hyoid (Tyler 1974). A unique sheet of fibers attaches the vocal sacs to the epicoracoid cartilages of the pectoral girdle. Furthermore, the sacs are perforated by the separated distal portion of the anterior cornu.

Hearing Acoustic communications (advertisement calls) in anurans rely on the perception of higher-frequency sounds that are associated with the carrier frequency. The perception of lower frequencies, common to all amphibians, appears to fulfill several possible roles, such as detection of release calls in anurans or detection of predators and other ambient environmental sounds (Capranica and Moffat 1975; Loftus-Hills and Johnstone 1970; Lombard and Straughan 1974; Straughan 1975). Despite considerable diversity the morphology of the middle ear, the site of sound perception in caudates and anurans, exhibits several common features that are unique among vertebrates (caudates: Dunn 1941; Kingsbury and Reed 1909; Monath 1965; anurans: Eiselt 1941; Sedra and Michael 1959; Wever 1979, 1985; see also chapter 16).

In most species two cartilaginous or bony plates are present in the oval window of the otic capsule. The columella is the more anterior one and, when fully developed, has a stylar process that runs through a large middle ear cavity to connect on a superficially situated tympanum. It is homologous to the stapes of other vertebrates. The operculum lies posteriorly and lacks a homologue in any other vertebrate. A unique muscle, the opercularis muscle, is associated with the operculum in almost all caudates and anurans (fig. 11.19). The

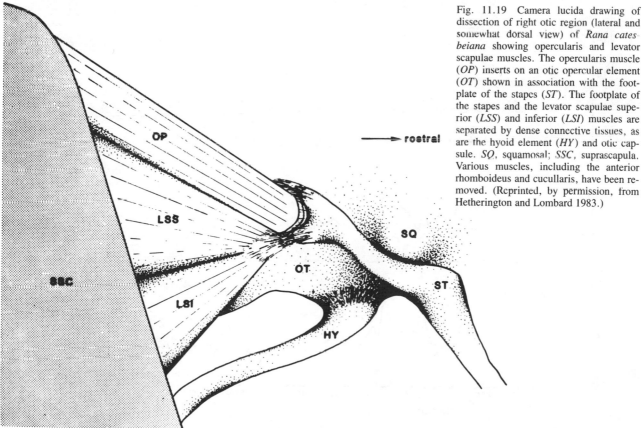

Fig. 11.19 Camera lucida drawing of dissection of right otic region (lateral and somewhat dorsal view) of *Rana catesbeiana* showing opercularis and levator scapulae muscles. The opercularis muscle (*OP*) inserts on an otic opercular element (*OT*) shown in association with the footplate of the stapes (*ST*). The footplate of the stapes and the levator scapulae superior (*LSS*) and inferior (*LSI*) muscles are separated by dense connective tissues, as are the hyoid element (*HY*) and otic capsule. *SQ*, squamosal; *SSC*, suprascapula. Various muscles, including the anterior rhomboideus and cucullaris, have been removed. (Reprinted, by permission, from Hetherington and Lombard 1983.)

muscle connects the suprascapular cartilage of the shoulder girdle with the opercular element. Several anurans and all caudates and caecilians lack a tympanum and middle ear. Furthermore, the columella may be absent or reduced in anurans and some caudates. The presence of the opercular complex sometimes is correlated with terrestriality; however, many terrestrial bufonids and leptodactylids lack the complex or have reduced components. Both operculum and opercularis muscle are absent in all obligate aquatic species (Eiselt 1941; Monath 1965). In plethodontid caudates the opercularis muscle is derived from the cucullaris muscle and hence has a branchiomeric origin (Dunn 1941). In all anurans and some caudates, the opercularis muscle represents, respectively, a portion of or the entire levator scapulae musculature, which probably is derived from cervical myotomes (Dunn 1941; Eiselt 1941). Whatever its origin, however, the opercularis appears to be analogous among amphibians.

Earlier hypotheses on the functional significance of the opercular complex suggested that the opercularis muscle may act as a couple between the forelimb and the inner ear to detect substrate vibrations (Kingsbury and Reed 1909), or that the opercularis system functions as a monitor of body position (Baker 1969; Eiselt 1941). More recent studies provide evidence that the opercularis muscle has a role in the perception of low-frequency sounds below 1,000 Hz (Lombard and Straughan 1974), as well as in substrate vibration detection via the forelimb (Hetherington and Lombard 1983). However, the precise mechanism remains unclear. Contraction of the opercularis muscle may couple the opercular plate to the columellar plate, thus shifting the frequency sensitivity of the columella-tympanum complex of the middle ear toward the lower-frequency range. Upon relaxation, decoupling of the plates allows perception of higher frequencies, up to several thousand Hz (Lombard and Straughan 1974). The tym-

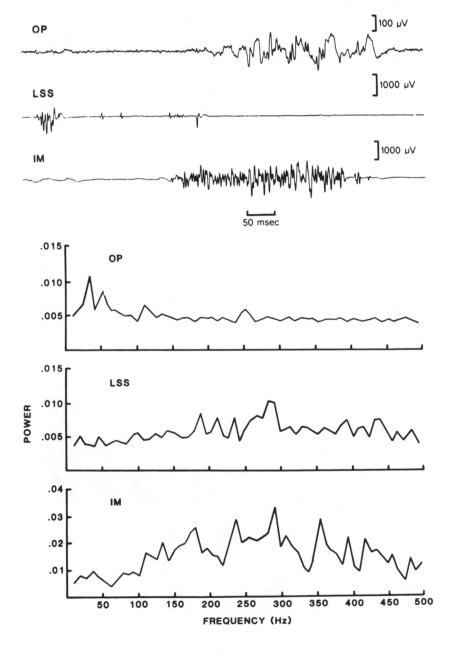

Fig. 11.20 *Top,* part of the aerial sequence of the EMG showing ventilatory muscle responses of the opercularis, levator scapulae superior, and intermandibularis muscles of *Rana catesbeiana. Bottom,* power spectra of the above EMG responses. Spectra represent plots of averages of every 6 points of 1,024-point fast Fourier transform, to improve statistical stability of peaks. (Reprinted, by permission, from Hetherington and Lombard 1983.)

panum of *Rana* is relatively unresponsive to low frequencies; this supports the classical view of a nontympanic route of low-frequency transmission (Chung, Pettigrew, and Anson 1978). However, recent experiments with selective stimuli suggest that both mechanisms may be used (Wilczynski, Resler, and Capranica 1981a).

Whatever the mechanism, the proposed opercularis function in aerial hearing and substrate vibration detection implies that the muscle is under tension for extended periods of time. EMG has indicated that the opercularis muscle maintains rhythmic, low-level activity in conditions in which aerial respiration is possible (Hetherington and Lombard 1983). The activity appears not to be actively controlled but is synchronized with respiration, occurring at twice the frequency of buccal pumping. During lung ventilation, higher-amplitude activity is superimposed on this basic rhythm. Apart from firing pattern, opercularis activity appears to differ further from that in other ventilatory muscles, in displaying a dominant low-frequency component. Histology and ultrastructural analyses of the opercularis muscle of several genera of anurans and caudates indicate that this activity may represent tonic fiber potentials (Becker and Lombard 1977; Hetherington and Lombard 1983; fig. 11.20). The majority of fibers (generally more than 50%) all have a small diameter and may be defined as tonic 5 fibers, whereas the large-diameter fibers all belong to twitch 3 fibers of Smith and Ovalle (1973). Hence, the rhythmic activity may serve to maintain a constant tension or to fluctuate tension relative to the frequency of ventilation (Hetherington and Lombard 1983), supporting the functional role of the opercularis muscle.

Miscellaneous Muscles are so ubiquitous in the body of amphibians that it is well-nigh impossible to list all of their utilizations. Defense postures (such as the *Unkenreflex*) and escape behaviors would require a chapter of their own. An example is the patterns of caudal autotomy (Wake and Dresner 1967), to which muscles contribute by posturing and moving the tail, as well as by its rupture and by its movement after separation.

Striated muscles are also involved in closing of brood pouches (del Pino 1980) and infolding the moisture-absorbing integumentary patches of some anurans (Winokur and Hillyard 1985, 1988). Most such special roles are yet to be studied.

CONCLUSION: QUESTIONS TO ASK

In many ways this overview incorporates its own conclusions. The first section derives almost entirely from detailed studies on some dozen species with minimal attention to diversity. The last section (and table 11.5) skims over some of the actions of striated muscles in facilitating some major activities of amphibians, locomotion, ventilation, feeding, vocalization, and hearing. The catalogue is hardly complete. This presentation has been designed to indicate diversity of activity and diversity of analysis. However, the data discussed here are inadequate to represent the obvious behavioral and phylogenetic diversity. The understanding of muscular function indicated in the first section has barely been applied to the most obvious questions of physiological ecology.

For most systems, we know something about the first level of activity, namely that animals perform in a particular way. Sometimes we have kinematic analyses and in a couple of cases indicators of kinematic variability. However, we generally lack combined morphometric and truly functional analyses, with the possible exception of the recent studies on one species of *Ambystoma*.

For many biological roles we have functional descriptions only of performance by particular species. Sometimes the descriptions rely heavily on morphology or on physiology, rarely on both. However, they do provide a basis for deciding which animals to use for resolving functional diversity. We have almost no studies that apply functional morphology to the performance of members of an adaptive radiation. Such experimental analyses should help us to establish the extent to which muscular arrangements, fiber patterns, and fiber physiology are adaptive and the roles they play in the organism.

Throughout, there is a need for diversity of sampling. Beyond this is a need to separate aspects that are essential for performing biological roles from aspects that permit roles to be performed but are not essential. Are the diversity of fiber types, fiber architecture, muscle mass, and muscle activation due to currently adaptive reasons, to factors associated with ontogeny (adaptation one level removed), to past adaptation and ontogeny (adaptation two levels removed), or to an array of homoplastic accidents? Comparison of the diversity among animals and experimentation with the significance of adaptive factors may help resolve such questions. We hope the sampling of analyses offered here has suggested the major discoveries yet to be made.

12 Energetics at Rest and during Locomotion

ROBERT E. GATTEN, JR., KIRK MILLER, AND ROBERT J. FULL

Amphibians are well known for their generally quiescent and inconspicuous lifestyles and for their low annual use of energy (Pough 1983). At times in their life cycle, however, most amphibians engage in increased levels of activity and energy expenditure. Short periods of intense effort may be important in escaping from predators (Blem, Steiner, and Miller 1978; Formanowicz et al. 1981). Longer intervals of sustained locomotion may be vital for reproduction (Magnusson and Windle 1988). The major purpose of this chapter is to summarize what is known about the rates at which amphibians use energy for such short-term and long-term movements, and to consider the factors that influence those rates of energy use.

Before such an assessment is possible, we must know the rate of energy use by amphibians at rest. Therefore, we first address the minimal energetic cost of living for amphibians. We then turn to the energetics of sustained locomotion and finally to the cost of brief, intense, nonsustainable movement.

In focusing on the energetics of locomotion, we intentionally exclude many topics (such as muscle biochemistry and increased respiratory and cardiovascular function) that are closely related to the ability of amphibians to use energy during exercise. We do so both out of practical necessity and because such topics are included elsewhere in this volume or because recent reviews of such topics are available. Various aspects of the energetics of amphibians at rest or during exercise have previously been reviewed by Bennett (1978, 1980a, 1984, 1985, 1986), Gatten (1985), Paladino (1985), Pough (1983), Seale (1987), Taigen (1983), and Taigen and Pough (1985).

Throughout this chapter we pay special attention to two factors, body temperature and body mass, that have an extraordinarily important influence on the energetics of amphibians. Although many authors have considered the effect of body temperature on the resting metabolic rate of amphibians (see chapter 8), no comprehensive analyses describe how temperature affects energy use during locomotion. Some authors have described the influence of body mass on the resting and/or exercise oxygen consumption of amphibians (Feder 1976a; Taigen 1983; Whitford and Hutchison 1967; and Withers and Hillman 1981); in this chapter, however, we conduct a comprehensive review of all the data that bear on this topic.

The major taxonomic groups of amphibians (anurans, apodans, and salamanders) have been separated evolutionarily for at least 250 million years (Pough 1983). Thus, extant representatives of these groups may reveal an evolutionary divergence in the cost of living in these animals. We focus on this question in our analyses of resting metabolism, the cost of sustained locomotion, and the energetics of short-term, intense exercise.

As were the editors (chapter 1) and other contributors to this book, we were struck by the strong bias of investigators towards easily obtainable species, especially those from the temperate zones of Europe and North America, where most of the research on the topic of our review has been carried out. Our analyses and conclusions are thus based on data from relatively few species. We make no attempt to correct for this bias. Throughout the chapter, we explicitly state the limits of the data; readers should consider the implications of these limits and avoid the dangers of unwarranted extrapolation beyond these limits.

In this chapter we make little direct reference to studies of the actual locomotor performance of amphibians. Such material is reviewed primarily in chapters 11, 14, and 16. However, wherever possible we include such information where it directly pertains to data on the energetic cost of movement.

Finally, it should be noted that our analyses of the energetics of locomotion pertain to data from animals moving in a laboratory setting in relatively controlled, stereotyped, and perhaps unnatural ways. In chapter 14, Pough and coauthors consider the energetic cost of locomotion and other behaviors in more natural surroundings.

We thank Mary Rutherford and the Interlibrary Loan staff of the Franklin and Marshall College Shadek-Fackenthal Library for their patience and perseverance while they filled our innumerable requests. We are grateful to Pat McCarron for assistance with preparation of the various drafts and to Malinda Longphre-Walters for assistance with proofing. We thank Mike Walton for making his unpublished data available and Stan Hillman, Paul Licht, and David Wake for critically reading portions of the manuscript. Comments from an anonymous referee improved the manuscript. The preparation of a portion of the manuscript was supported by National Science Foundation Grant DCB87-19066.

MAINTENANCE COSTS

The resting or standard metabolism of an amphibian is its minimal energetic cost for maintenance. It is the minimal energy expenditure required to sustain its life while it has the option of becoming active (i.e., it is not dormant). Because amphibians spend a large part of their daily cycle at rest, their low resting metabolic rate contributes to their low annual energy budget (Pough 1983; see also chapter 13). The resting metabolic rates of amphibians and other organisms are useful in comparing organisms of different sizes, or at different temperatures, or of different species. These comparisons have led to an important theoretical understanding of the effect of body size, temperature, and ecology on metabolic rate.

The measurement of the minimal maintenance cost requires that the conditions of measurement be rigorously controlled, because many factors affect metabolism. Obviously, the animal must be inactive and quiet. For an amphibian, body temperature must be known and carefully controlled, although the earliest workers did not always appreciate this fact. An increase in temperature, within the limits compatible with life, is associated with an increase in metabolism in amphibians and other ectotherms (Krogh 1914; Whitford 1973; chapters 8 and 9). The previous thermal history of the animal also affects its metabolic rate, so the temperature to which an amphibian is acclimated (for a period of about a week or more) affects its metabolic rate at each of a series of test temperatures (chapter 8). The pattern of the effect of acclimation temperature on metabolism, however, is variable. The time of day at which metabolism is measured affects the minimal maintenance cost of amphibians. Minimal metabolic rates taken during the time of day when the animal is normally active are usually referred to as resting metabolic rates, whereas metabolic rates measured during the time of day when the animal is normally inactive are called standard metabolic rates. Unfortunately, this usage is not universal. Further, some amphibian species have different periods of daily activity at different seasons of the year and after they achieve a certain body mass (Taigen and Pough 1981), but the daily period of activity is not known for all amphibian species, nor do all authors report the season in which measurements were taken. Some authors acclimate animals in the dark, and the coincidence of the (presumably) free-running rhythm of metabolism with the particular clock time at which measurements of metabolism were taken is not known. Interestingly, Taigen and Pough (1983) found no difference in standard and resting metabolic rates of four species of anuran amphibians. In contrast, many authors report substantial diurnal variation of oxygen consumption of amphibians (e.g., Dunlap 1969; Turney and Hutchison 1974). Independent of this, the metabolism of amphibians varies with the season of the year (Athanasiu 1900; Dolk and Postma 1927), being generally lower in the season of inactivity (winter in the case of temperate zone species) and higher in the season of greatest activity (spring; Harri and Hedenstam 1972).

Feeding also affects the metabolism of amphibians (Feder, Gibbs, Griffith, and Tsuji 1984). Most authors report resting or standard values of metabolism from animals fasted for several days prior to measurement. Further starvation, however, lowers metabolism below resting or standard values (Merkle and Hanke 1988), but amphibians kept at cooler temperatures have longer transit times for food through the gut compared with those at warmer temperatures, and should presumably be starved for longer periods. Dormancy also lowers metabolism below resting values (Loveridge and Withers 1981; Seymour 1973a; van Beurden 1980). Fromm and Johnson (1955) report, however, that feeding does not affect the rate of metabolism in several amphibian species.

Body mass has a profound effect on the metabolism of amphibians, yet many authors do not report the mass of the animals they used, or report only a range of masses. The comparison of ratios of metabolic rate to body mass, without taking actual body mass into consideration, may bias analyses (Packard and Boardman 1988). As in most organisms, increasing body mass is associated with increasing absolute but decreasing relative metabolism (metabolic rate per unit mass; Davison 1955; Smith 1925).

Our intention is to provide a complete (but not a critical) list of the published values for resting and standard metabolism of larval and adult amphibians (see Boell 1948; Feder 1981a; Salthe and Mecham 1974; and chapter 16 for reviews of the metabolism of embryonic amphibians), and to use this compilation to examine the effect of temperature and body mass on the resting metabolism of different groups of amphibians. We have compiled values for O_2 consumption, CO_2 production (when O_2 consumption was not measured simultaneously), and heat production for amphibians. When possible, original data in volume of O_2 (STPD) per unit time were used. When these data were not available, they were estimated from mass-specific rates of O_2 consumption multiplied by the mean (or median) body mass. We report minimal published values for the metabolic rates of inactive amphibians that were not dormant, if possible taken during a season when they would normally be active, and if possible when their previous thermal history was known or could be inferred. We include values from animals acclimated to a temperature within 5°C of the temperature at which measurements were taken. Other chapters in this volume deal with the effect of acclimation temperature on metabolism, seasonal effects on metabolism, rhythms of metabolism, the ratio of CO_2 production to O_2 consumption, the partitioning of O_2 consumption and CO_2 production among different gas exchangers, and the effects of dormancy, diving, nutritional state, age, sex, and altitude on the metabolism of amphibians. Our intention was originally to report data as either standard, resting, or routine metabolism (routine metabolism is used to refer to the average metabolism of a relatively inactive animal over a period of the day or the whole day), but the inconsistent use of these terms by different authors, the seasonal variation in the period of normal activity, and the many authors who do not report the time of day at which measurements were taken, made this impossible. For the sake of convenience only, we refer to all values we compiled as representing resting metabolism. Many authors report mass-specific rates of metabolism without reporting the masses of the animals they used. Although we have included these data in our compilation, we could not use them in our analyses. In the future, authors should publish this important time and size information.

Symbols and Terminology

This chapter will use the following abbreviations and expressions: $\dot{V}O_2$ is the rate of O_2 consumption in volume (STPD) consumed per unit time. $\dot{V}O_{2rest}$ refers to resting, standard, or minimal $\dot{V}O_2$. $\dot{V}O_{2ex}$ is the maximal $\dot{V}O_2$ under specific conditions of exercise. $\dot{V}O_{2max}$ is not used to denote a singular maximal $\dot{V}O_2$ because various forms of activity (e.g., calling and locomotor activity) may yield different maximal $\dot{V}O_2$'s (see chapter 14). The absolute aerobic scope is the difference of $\dot{V}O_{2ex}$ and $\dot{V}O_{2rest}$. The factorial aerobic scope is the ratio of $\dot{V}O_{2ex}$ to $\dot{V}O_{2rest}$. $\dot{V}O_{2ss}$ is the "steady-state" rate of O_2 consumption eventually attained in exercise at sustainable speeds. MAS is the maximal aerobic speed, the minimal speed at which $\dot{V}O_{2ss}$ is maximal. The $\dot{V}O_2$ (of whatever sort) is often related to body mass by the following equation: $\dot{V}O_2 = a \cdot mass^b$, where a and b ("the allometric coefficient") are constants. Taking the logarithm of both sides of the equation yields $\log \dot{V}O_2 = \log a + b \log mass$. Linear regression of log $\dot{V}O_2$ versus log mass typically yields a line with slope equal to b and a y-intercept equal to log a. The

following discussion will equate "allometric coefficient," "regression coefficient," "exponent," "b or b value," and "slope." $\dot{V}O_{2ss}$ is typically a linear function of locomotor speed, and the $\dot{V}O_{2ss}$-speed function is also characterized by its slope or regression coefficient and its y-intercept. The slope of the $\dot{V}O_{2ss}$ versus speed function is also termed the "minimal cost of transport." "Aerobic capacity" lacks a singular definition, but in general is proportional to the various measures of $\dot{V}O_2$. In experiments in which $\dot{V}O_2$ is measured as a function of PO_2 (partial pressure of O_2), the critical PO_2 is that below which $\dot{V}O_2$ declines in proportion to PO_2 and above which $\dot{V}O_2$ is independent of PO_2.

Effect of Mass and Temperature on Resting Metabolic Rates of Salamanders

Table 12.1 summarizes the data we compiled for adult amphibians. The effect of body mass on the resting metabolism of salamanders at 5°, 15°, 20°, and 25°C is illustrated in figures 12.1, 12.2, 12.3, and 12.4. Least squares linear equations were fit to log-transformed data illustrated in figures

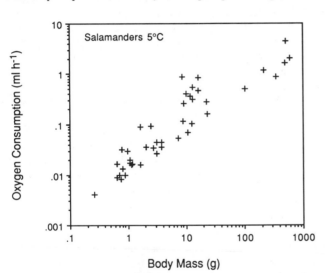

Fig. 12.1   Resting oxygen consumption as a function of body mass for salamanders between 4° and 6°C. Data from table 12.1.

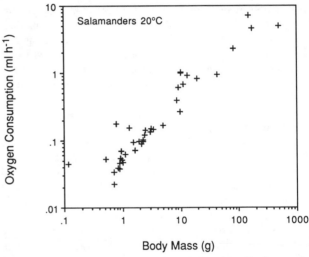

Fig. 12.3   Resting oxygen consumption as a function of body mass for salamanders between 19° and 21°C. Data from table 12.1.

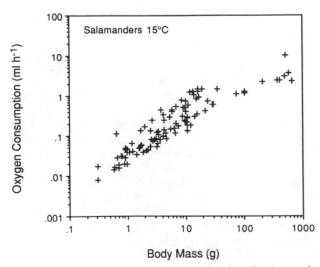

Fig. 12.2   Resting oxygen consumption as a function of body mass for salamanders between 14° and 16°C. Data from table 12.1.

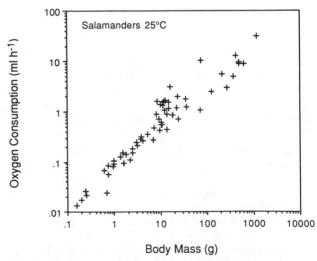

Fig. 12.4   Resting oxygen consumption as a function of body mass for salamanders between 24° and 26°C. Data from table 12.1.

TABLE 12.1 Oxygen Consumption of Adult Amphibians at Rest

	Temp. (°C)	$\dot{V}O_2$ (ml·h^{-1})	Mass (g)	$\dot{V}O_2$ (ml·g^{-1}·h^{-1})	Reference	Note
				Caudata		
Ambystomatidae						
Ambystoma gracile	15	0.6352	30.39	0.0209	Feder 1976a	
Ambystoma jeffersonianum	15	0.3158	8.92	0.0354		
Ambystoma macrodactylum	15	0.1098	3.41	0.0322		
		0.4514	3.7	0.122	Whitford and Hutchison 1966	1
Ambystoma maculatum	5	0.3157	13.1	0.0241	Whitford and Hutchison 1963	1
		0.3631	11.75	0.0309	Whitford and Hutchison 1967	
	10	0.6045	11.9	0.0508	Whitford and Hutchison 1963	1
		0.5875	11.75	0.05	Whitford and Hutchison 1967	
	15	0.3625	15.83	0.0229	Feder 1976a	
		1.3199	13.4	0.0985	Whitford and Hutchison 1963	1
		N.A.	N.A.	0.0557	Whitford and Hutchison 1965a	1
		1.2396	11.75	0.1055	Whitford and Hutchison 1967	
	20	0.0518	0.512	0.1011	Branch and Taylor 1977	2
	25	1.677	12.9	0.13	Whitford and Hutchison 1963	1
		1.544	11.75	0.1314	Whitford and Hutchison 1967	
	30	1.7183	12.9	0.1332	Whitford and Hutchison 1963	1
		1.5592	11.75	0.1327	Whitford and Hutchison 1967	
Ambystoma mexicanum	10	N.A.	N.A.	0.0414	Lenfant, Johansen, and Hanson 1970	Neotene
	20	0.9614	43.7	0.022	Gahlenbeck and Bartels 1970	Neotene
		N.A.	N.A.	0.0972	Lenfant, Johansen, and Hanson 1970	Neotene
	22	0.3195	21.3	0.015	Gahlenbeck and Bartels 1970	Artificially transformed
	30	N.A.	N.A.	0.1176	Lenfant, Johansen, and Hanson 1970	Neotene
Ambystoma opacum	14	0.0865	4.65	0.0186	Sherman and Stadlen 1986	
	15	0.464	5.8	0.08	Whitford and Hutchison 1966	1
Ambystoma talpoideum	15	0.56	7	0.08		1
Ambystoma tigrinum	5	0.276	23	0.012	Burggren and Wood 1981	
	6	0.8595	16.49	0.0521	Vernon 1897	3, 4
	10	0.8895	15	0.0593	Whitford and Hutchison 1965b	1
	15	0.138	10.78	0.0128	Feder 1976a	
		1.5484	35	0.0442	Hutchison, Turney, and Gratz 1977	
		N.A.	N.A.	0.016	Mitton, Carey, and Kocher 1986	
		1.3213	16.49	0.0801	Vernon 1897	3, 4
		1.5246	16.5	0.0924	Whitford and Hutchison 1965b	1
		N.A.	N.A.	0.049	Whitford and Sherman 1968	Axolotl
		N.A.	N.A.	0.055		
	23	2.9988	29.4	0.102	Heath 1976	
		2.6026	33.8	0.077		Neotene
	25	1.978	23	0.086	Burggren and Wood 1981	
		0.891	8.1	0.11	Gehlbach, Kimmel, and Weems 1969	
		1.7885	35	0.0511	Hutchison, Turney, and Gratz 1977	
		3.1908	16.49	0.1935	Vernon 1897	3, 4
		1.5675	14.9	0.1052	Whitford and Hutchison 1965b	1
		N.A.	N.A.	0.06	Whitford and Sherman 1968	Axolotl
		N.A.	N.A.	0.104		
Amphiumidae						
Amphiuma means	5	0.884	352	0.0025	Guimond and Hutchison 1974	
		1.65	500	0.0033	Morgan, Singh, and Fisette 1967	
	10	2.8	500	0.0056		
	15	2.531	375	0.0068	Guimond and Hutchison 1974	
		3.1	500	0.0062	Morgan, Singh, and Fisette 1967	
		2.513	408	0.0062	Ultsch 1976b	5
	18	4.875	125	0.039	Withers and Hillman 1981	
	20	2.324	83	0.028	Bentley 1975a	5
		5.05	500	0.0101	Morgan, Singh, and Fisette 1967	
	21.5	17.304	1,270	0.0136	Smith 1925	3, 6
	25	5.038	376	0.0134	Guimond and Hutchison 1974	
		9.25	500	0.0185	Morgan, Singh, and Fisette 1967	
	27	15.8	500	0.0316		
	30	35.3	500	0.0706		

TABLE 12.1 (*continued*)

	Temp. (°C)	$\dot{V}_{O_2}$ (ml·h⁻¹)	Mass (g)	$\dot{V}_{O_2}$ (ml·g⁻¹·h⁻¹)	Reference	Note
Amphiuma tridactylum	15	2.452	652	0.0038	Toews 1973	
	25	9.86	493	0.02	Preslar and Hutchison 1978	
Cryptobranchidae						
Cryptobranchus alleganiensis	5	4.4615	514	0.0087	Guimond and Hutchison 1973a	
	15	10.6595	511	0.0209		
	25	13.0792	423	0.0309		
Dicamptodontidae						
Dicamptodon ensatus	15	1.3061	101.25	0.0129	Feder 1976a	
		0.7488	24	0.0312	Wood 1972	
Rhyacotriton olympicus	15	0.2496	2.6	0.096	Whitford and Hutchison 1966	1
Plethodontidae						
Aneides ferreus	15	0.0743	2.73	0.0272	Feder 1976b	
	25	0.2118	3.2	0.0662		
Aneides flavipunctatus	15	0.1197	4.57	0.0262		
	25	0.1421	1.79	0.0794		
Aneides hardii	5	0.0301	0.97	0.031	Whitford 1968	
	10	0.0359	0.97	0.037		
	15	0.0485	0.97	0.05		
	20	0.0514	0.97	0.053		
	25	0.0912	0.97	0.094		
Aneides lugubris	15	0.1495	5.58	0.0268	Feder 1976b	
	20	0.0447	0.116	0.387	Cook 1949	6
Batrachoseps attenuatus	5	0.0166	0.65	0.0255	Feder 1976b	
	15	0.0318	0.77	0.0413		
		0.0453	0.93	0.0487	Feder 1978b	
	20	0.093	1.55	0.06	Bennett and Licht 1973	
		0.0692	0.931	0.0757	Cook 1949	6
	25	0.0838	0.74	0.1132	Feder 1976b	
		0.0802	0.93	0.0862	Feder 1978b	
Bolitoglossa franklini	15	0.055	3.18	0.0173	Feder 1976b	
Bolitoglossa morio	15	0.0445	2.09	0.0213		
Bolitoglossa occidentalis	5	0.0196	1.07	0.0183		
	15	0.0202	0.97	0.0208		
		0.0168	0.61	0.0276	Feder 1978b	
	25	0.1039	0.98	0.106	Feder 1976b	
		0.0673	0.61	0.1104	Feder 1978b	
Bolitoglossa subpalmata	5	0.0159	1.63	0.0098	Feder 1987b	
	10	0.0251	1.63	0.0154		
	15	0.0513	1.63	0.0315		
	20	0.0708	1.63	0.0434		
Chiropterotriton bromeliacia	15	0.0144	0.59	0.0244	Feder 1976b	
Desmognathus fuscus	5	0.0132	0.8	0.0165	Fitzpatrick 1971	Females
		0.0163	1.17	0.0139		Males
		0.035	2.07	0.0169	Fitzpatrick, Bristol, and Stokes 1972	
	10	0.0525	1.67	0.0314		
		0.2139	1.95	0.1097	Wood and Orr 1969	
	13	0.1935	4.5	0.043	Gatz, Crawford, and Piiper 1974a	
	15	0.0291	0.91	0.032	Fitzpatrick 1971	Females
		0.0423	1.24	0.0341		Males
		0.0584	1.7	0.0344	Fitzpatrick, Bristol, and Stokes 1972	
	16.5	0.0972	2.53	0.0384	Evans 1939	
	17	0.059	1.31	0.045		
	20	0.1022	2.26	0.0452	Beckenbach 1976	
		0.0895	2.09	0.0428		
		0.0974	1.92	0.0507	Fitzpatrick, Bristol, and Stokes 1972	
Desmognathus monticola	15	0.3078	5.4	0.057	Whitford and Hutchison 1965b	1
	20	0.1454	3.43	0.0424	Beckenbach 1976	

TABLE 12.1 (continued)

	Temp. (°C)	$\dot{V}O_2$ (ml·h⁻¹)	Mass (g)	$\dot{V}O_2$ (ml·g⁻¹·h⁻¹)	Reference	Note
Desmognathus ochrophaeus	5	0.01	0.9	0.0111	Feder 1985a	
		0.0338	2.75	0.0123	Fitzpatrick and Brown 1975	
		0.0163	1.17	0.0139	Fitzpatrick 1973a	
		0.0173	1.07	0.0162	Fitzpatrick, Bristol, and Stokes 1971	
	10	0.017	0.9	0.0189	Feder 1985a	
		0.0496	2.68	0.0185	Fitzpatrick and Brown 1975	
		0.0341	1.16	0.0294	Fitzpatrick, Bristol, and Stokes 1971	
	14	0.02	0.9	0.0222	Feder 1985a	
	15	0.1769	1.965	0.09	Bennett and Houck 1983	
		0.0822	2.56	0.0321	Fitzpatrick and Brown 1975	
		0.0423	1.24	0.0341	Fitzpatrick 1973a	
		0.0392	1.09	0.036	Fitzpatrick, Bristol, and Stokes 1971	
	17.5	0.045	0.9	0.05	Feder 1985a	
		0.051	1.4	0.0364	Feder 1985b	
		0.0427	1.6	0.0267	Feder, Gibbs, Griffith, and Tsuji 1984	
		0.082	2.5	0.0328		
	20	0.1196	2.43	0.0492	Fitzpatrick and Brown 1975	
		0.0615	1.11	0.0554	Fitzpatrick, Bristol, and Stokes 1971	
	21	0.038	0.9	0.0422	Feder 1985a	
Desmognathus quadramaculatus	5	0.1639	23.41	0.007	Feder 1976b	
		0.4723	16.4	0.0288	Whitford and Hutchison 1965b	1
		0.2646	9.25	0.0286	Whitford and Hutchison 1967	
	10	0.4444	10.1	0.044	Whitford and Hutchison 1965b	1
		0.4033	9.25	0.0436	Whitford and Hutchison 1967	
	15	0.43	22.28	0.0193	Feder 1976b	
		0.9341	16.8	0.0556	Whitford and Hutchison 1965b	1
		0.5337	9.25	0.0577	Whitford and Hutchison 1967	
	20	0.0977	2.24	0.0436	Beckenbach 1976	
		0.8267	19.36	0.0427		
		0.9323	13.3	0.0701	Whitford and Hutchison 1965b	1
		0.6216	9.25	0.0672	Whitford and Hutchison 1967	
	25	1.1866	22.82	0.052	Feder 1976b	
		1.1612	15.1	0.0769	Whitford and Hutchison 1965b	1
		0.7104	9.25	0.0768	Whitford and Hutchison 1967	
Ensatina eschscholtzi	14	0.0176	0.308	N.A.	Bradford 1984a	2
	15	0.1292	3.39	0.0381	Feder 1976b	
	25	0.3572	5.3	0.0674		
Eurycea bislineata	1	0.016	1.041	0.0153	Vernberg 1952	
	5	0.0157	1.14	0.0179	Fitzpatrick 1973b	
	10	0.0263	1.07	0.0281		
		0.0489	1.092	0.0448	Vernberg 1952	
	15	0.0494	0.93	0.0459	Fitzpatrick 1973b	
	16	0.0674	1.17	0.0576	Evans 1939	
	20	0.0539	0.93	0.0501	Fitzpatrick 1973b	
Eurycea longicauda	15	0.0504	1.57	0.0321	Feder 1976b	
Eurycea multiplicata	5	0.0088	0.64	0.0138	Brown and Fitzpatrick 1981b	
		0.0322	0.78	0.0413	McAllister and Fitzpatrick 1985	Cave-dwelling neotenes
	10	0.0093	0.63	0.0148	Brown and Fitzpatrick 1981b	
		0.0858	0.8	0.1073	McAllister and Fitzpatrick 1985	Cave-dwelling neotenes
	15	0.0155	0.71	0.0218	Brown and Fitzpatrick 1981b	
		0.1162	0.65	0.1787	McAllister and Fitzpatrick 1985	Cave-dwelling neotenes
	20	0.0391	0.84	0.0465	Brown and Fitzpatrick 1981b	
		0.1764	0.79	0.2233	McAllister and Fitzpatrick 1985	Cave-dwelling neotenes
	25	0.0555	0.73	0.076	Brown and Fitzpatrick 1981b	
Eurycea nana	25	0.0132	0.154	0.086	Norris, Grandy, and Davis 1963	
Eurycea neotenes	25	0.0258	0.243	0.106		
Eurycea pterophila?	25	0.0176	0.196	0.09		
Gyrinophilus danielsi	5	0.1035	12.78	0.0081	Feder 1976b	
	15	0.322	14.44	0.0223		
	25	0.9109	13.76	0.0662		

TABLE 12.1 (*continued*)

	Temp. (°C)	$\dot{V}O_2$ (ml·h⁻¹)	Mass (g)	$\dot{V}O_2$ (ml·g⁻¹·h⁻¹)	Reference	Note
Gyrinophilus	5	0.0531	7.28	0.0073		
porphyriticus	15	0.8874	15.3	0.058	Whitford and Hutchison 1965b	1
	15.5	0.1885	12.4	0.0152	Evans 1939	
	25	0.4858	7.36	0.066	Feder 1976b	
	15	0.1795	7.67	0.0234		
Hydromantes spp.	15	0.124	3.23	0.0384		
Plethodon cinereus	1	0.012	0.844	0.0143	Vernberg 1952	
	5	0.01	0.7	0.0143	Feder 1985a	
	10	0.015	0.7	0.0214		
		0.0323	0.862	0.0374	Vernberg 1952	
	14	0.019	0.7	0.0271	Feder 1985a	
	15	0.032	0.8	0.04	Stern and Mueller 1972	
	15.5	0.039	0.99	0.0394	Evans 1939	
	17.5	0.028	0.7	0.04	Feder 1985a	
		0.0168	0.6	0.028	Feder 1985b	
		0.03	0.9	0.0333	Feder, Gibbs, Griffith, and Tsuji 1984	
	18.5	0.0415	0.94	0.0441	Evans 1939	
	20	0.0476	1	0.0476		
		0.0451	0.89	0.0506	Vernberg 1955	6
	21	0.034	0.7	0.0486	Feder 1985a	
Plethodon dorsalis	5	0.0083	0.75	0.0111	Brown and Fitzpatrick 1981a	
	10	0.0178	0.77	0.0231		
	15	0.0293	0.66	0.0444		
	20	0.0222	0.71	0.0312		
	25	0.0239	0.69	0.0346		
Plethodon glutinosus	5	0.0443	3.75	0.0118	Feder 1976b	
	10	0.0762	3.65	0.0209	Maguire 1981	7
	14	0.2464	4.33	0.0569	Sherman and Stadlen 1986	
	15	0.1441	4.25	0.0339	Feder 1976b	
		0.1167	3.65	0.0320	Maguire 1981	7
		0.3444	4.2	0.082	Whitford and Hutchison 1965b	1
	20	0.1583	3.65	0.0434	Maguire 1981	7
		0.1671	5.01	0.0334	Vernberg 1955	6
	25	0.3237	3.91	0.0828	Feder 1976b	
Plethodon jordani	5	0.027	3.1	0.0087	Feder 1985a	
	10	0.058	3.1	0.0187		
	14	0.087	3.1	0.0281		
	15	0.0511	1.83	0.0279	Stefanski, Gatten, and Pough 1989	7
	17.5	0.109	3.1	0.0352	Feder 1985a	
		0.138	4.3	0.0321	Feder, Gibbs, Griffith, and Tsuji 1984	
		0.071	2.2	0.0323		
	21	0.148	3.1	0.0477	Feder 1985a	
	25	0.1243	1.83	0.0679	Stefanski, Gatten, and Pough 1989	7
Plethodon neomexicanus	5	0.0914	2.47	0.037	Whitford 1968	
	10	0.1186	2.47	0.048		
	15	0.1359	2.47	0.055		
	20	0.1408	2.47	0.057		
	25	0.1507	2.47	0.061		
Plethodon spp.	22	0.1859	3.25	0.0572	Withers 1980	
Pseudoeurycea belli	15	0.1882	10.94	0.0172	Feder 1976b	
	25	0.7188	24.45	0.0294		
Pseudoeurycea brunnata	15	0.0656	3.33	0.0197		
Pseudoeurycea cephalica	15	0.0354	1.45	0.0244		
Pseudoeurycea cochranae	15	0.0457	2.23	0.0205		
Pseudoeurycea gadovii	5	0.0442	3.09	0.0143		
	15	0.085	2.88	0.0295		
	25	0.2443	2.99	0.0817		
Pseudoeurycea goebeli	5	0.0359	3.78	0.0095		
	15	0.0831	3.66	0.0227		
	25	0.2842	3.73	0.0762		

TABLE 12.1 *(continued)*

	Temp. (°C)	$\dot{V}_{O_2}$ (ml·h⁻¹)	Mass (g)	$\dot{V}_{O_2}$ (ml·g⁻¹·h⁻¹)	Reference	Note
Pseudoeurycea leprosa	15	0.0556	2.46	0.0226		
Pseudoeurycea rex	15	0.0392	1.86	0.0211		
Pseudoeurycea smithii	15	0.1185	6.66	0.0178		
		0.1008	4.2	0.024	Feder 1978b	
	25	0.2617	4.2	0.0623		
Pseudotriton ruber	5	0.0681	10.81	0.0063	Feder 1976b	
	15	0.2324	10.33	0.0225		
		0.4234	5.8	0.073	Whitford and Hutchison 1965b	1
	25	0.6172	10.66	0.0579	Feder 1976b	
Thorius sp.	5	0.0041	0.26	0.0159		
	15	0.008	0.31	0.0258		
	25	0.0217	0.25	0.0867		
Proteidae						
Necturus maculosus	5	1.1684	214	0.0055	Guimond and Hutchison 1972	
		0.5095	101.9	0.005	Miller and Hutchison 1979	
	15	2.3031	206	0.0112	Guimond and Hutchison 1972	
		1.2228	101.9	0.012	Miller and Hutchison 1979	
	20	7.215	150	0.0481	Shield and Bentley 1973	
	21.5	3.8956	115	0.0339	Smith 1925	3, 6
	22	3.1488	114.5	0.0275	Bentley and Shield 1973	8
	25	5.6222	212	0.0265	Guimond and Hutchison 1972	
		2.475	125	0.0198	Ultsch 1976b	5
Salamandridae						
Molga torosa?	18.5	2.73	17.5	0.156	Buytendijk 1910	
Notophthalmus viridescens	5	0.0898	1.63	0.0551	Pitkin 1977	
		N.A.	N.A.	0.0264	Pitkin 1987	5, 9
	10	0.1993	2.43	0.082	Pitkin 1977	
	14	N.A.	N.A.	0.0568	Pitkin 1987	5,9
	15	0.0592	1.72	0.0344	Feder 1976a	
		0.1365	1.7	0.0803	Pitkin 1977	
		N.A.	N.A.	0.095	Rieck, Belli, and Blaskovics 1960	
		0.0752	1.23	0.0611	Stefanski, Gatten, and Pough 1989	Eft, 7
	20	0.135	3	0.045	Brown et al. 1955	
		0.1533	1.31	0.117	Pitkin 1977	
	21	N.A.	N.A.	0.0842	Pitkin 1987	5, 9
	25	0.125	1.35	0.0926	Ultsch 1976c	5
		0.1532	1.5	0.1021	Wakeman and Ultsch 1976	
	30	N.A.	N.A.	0.095	Rieck, Belli, and Blaskovics 1960	
Salamandra atra	10	N.A.	N.A.	0.0357	Knapp 1974	
	20	N.A.	N.A.	0.0786		
Salamandra maculosa	18.5	3.6448	28.32	0.1287	Buytendijk 1910	
Salamandra salamandra	15	1.5471	19.1	0.081	Whitford and Hutchison 1965b	1
	16	1.1273	75	0.015	Degani 1983	
		0.6238	29	0.0215		
		0.4176	10	0.0418		2
Taricha granulosa	5	0.1152	9	0.0128	Feder 1983c	
		0.5413	13.3	0.0407	Whitford and Hutchison 1965b	1
		0.4	10	0.04	Whitford and Hutchison 1967	
	10	0.745	12.5	0.0596	Whitford and Hutchison 1965b	1
		0.6	10	0.06	Whitford and Hutchison 1967	
	15	0.1601	6.56	0.0244	Feder 1976a	
		1.093	13.8	0.0792	Whitford and Hutchison 1965b	1
		0.768	10	0.0768	Whitford and Hutchison 1967	
	20	0.392	8.75	0.0448	Feder 1983c	
		1.0262	10.1	0.1016	Whitford and Hutchison 1965b	1
		1.004	10	0.1004	Whitford and Hutchison 1967	
	25	1.6398	11.9	0.1378	Whitford and Hutchison 1965b	1
		1.4	10	0.14	Whitford and Hutchison 1967	
Taricha rivularis	15	0.3011	10.83	0.0278	Feder 1976a	

TABLE 12.1 (*continued*)

	Temp. (°C)	$\dot{V}O_2$ (ml·h⁻¹)	Mass (g)	$\dot{V}O_2$ (ml·g⁻¹·h⁻¹)	Reference	Note
Taricha torosa	10	0.1797	11.23	0.016	Harlow 1978	Aquatic stage
		0.0888	9.87	0.009		Terrestrial stage
	15	0.2089	6.94	0.0301	Feder 1976a	
		0.286	10.67	0.0268	Feder 1978b	
		0.5238	9.7	0.054	Harlow 1977	Aquatic stage
		0.2425	9.7	0.025		Terrestrial stage
		0.6064	11.23	0.054	Harlow 1978	Aquatic stage
		0.2566	9.87	0.026		Terrestrial stage
Taricha torosa (*Triturus torosus*)	17	1.3514	19.7	0.0686	Taylor 1939	
Taricha torosa	20	0.685	11.23	0.061	Harlow 1978	Aquatic stage
		0.2665	9.87	0.027		Terrestrial stage
	25	0.5452	10.67	0.0511	Feder 1978b	
		1.3364	11.23	0.119	Harlow 1978	Aquatic stage
		0.4244	9.87	0.043		Terrestrial stage
		0.5555	11	0.0505	Ultsch 1976b	5
		1.0738	12.5	0.0859	Wakeman and Ultsch 1976	
Triturus alpestris	10	N.A.	N.A.	0.054	Knapp 1974	
		N.A.	N.A.	0.057	Pocrnjic 1965	
		N.A.	N.A.	0.083		Neotene
	20	N.A.	N.A.	0.13	Knapp 1974	
		N.A.	N.A.	0.112	Pocrnjic 1965	
		N.A.	N.A.	0.188		Neotene
Triturus cristatus	10	0.385	7	0.055	Eddy and McDonald 1978	
Triturus (Molge) vulgaris	6	0.863	8.75	0.0986	Vernon 1897	3, 4
Triturus vulgaris	10	N.A.	N.A.	0.1125	Pocrnjic 1965	
Triturus (Molge) vulgaris	15	0.8127	8.75	0.0929	Vernon 1897	3, 4
Triturus vulgaris	20	N.A.	N.A.	0.2161	Pocrnjic 1965	
Triturus (Molge) vulgaris	25	1.6264	8.75	0.1859	Vernon 1897	3, 4
Sirenidae						
Pseudobranchus striatus	25	0.0932	1.58	0.059	Ultsch 1974a	
		0.1116	2.19	0.0509	Ultsch 1976b	5
		0.184	2.5	0.0736	Wakeman and Ultsch 1976	
Siren intermedia	25	10.7631	74.9	0.1437	Gehlbach, Gordon, and Jordan 1973	
		0.4521	13.7	0.033	Ultsch 1974a	
		0.28	7	0.04	Ultsch 1974b	2
		0.8661	18.1	0.0479	Ultsch 1976b	
Siren lacertina	5	2.0855	601	0.0035	Guimond and Hutchison 1973b	
	15	3.8114	581	0.0066		
	20	4.6268	172	0.0269	Shield and Bentley 1973	
	22	6.6654	126	0.0529	Bentley and Shield 1973	8
	25	9.0118	628	0.0144	Guimond and Hutchison 1973b	
		1.08	73	0.0148	Ultsch 1973b	
		3.0397	269	0.0113	Ultsch 1974a	
		32.174	1,182	0.0272	Ultsch 1976a	
		1.2679	36	0.0352	Ultsch 1976b	
			Anura			
Bufonidae						
Bufo alvarius	15	11.868	150.8	0.0787	Hutchison, Whitford, and Kohl 1968	
Bufo americanus	5	0.6081	25.2	0.0241		
	15	2.0934	19	0.1102		
	20	1.377	27	0.051	Taigen and Beuchat 1984	10
		1.39	50	0.0278	Taigen and Pough 1981	
		1.38	27.03	0.0511	Taigen 1983	
		1.377	27	0.051	Taigen, Emerson, and Pough 1982	
	21.5	1.2815	11	0.1165	Smith 1925	3, 6
	23	0.0247	0.102	0.243	Lewis and Frieden 1959	2
	25	2.9371	40.4	0.0727	Gatten 1987	
		2.5873	21.1	0.1226	Hutchison, Whitford, and Kohl 1968	
Bufo boreas	5	4.0908	72.7	0.0563		
	9	N.A.	N.A.	0.046	Bishop and Gordon 1967	
	10	0.5548	40.2	0.0138	Carey 1979a	11

TABLE 12.1 (continued)

	Temp. (°C)	$\dot{V}O_2$ (ml·h⁻¹)	Mass (g)	$\dot{V}O_2$ (ml·g⁻¹·h⁻¹)	Reference	Note
		0.6244	47.3	0.0132	Carey 1979b	
		0.7283	57.8	0.0126		
	14	4.9648	46.4	0.107	Tashian and Ray 1957	
		4.484	29.5	0.152		
	15	3.8706	68.7	0.0563	Hutchison, Whitford, and Kohl 1968	
	20	1.3025	40.2	0.0324	Carey 1979a	11
		2.3177	47.3	0.049	Carey 1979b	
		1.052	57.8	0.0182		
		0.25	2.5	0.1	Lillywhite, Licht, and Chelgren 1973	2
	25	2.64	27.3	0.0967	Hillman and Withers 1979	
		5.5812	53.8	0.1037	Hutchison, Whitford, and Kohl 1968	
	30	3.0512	40.2	0.0759	Carey 1979a	11
		2.4265	47.3	0.0513	Carey 1979b	
		6.4852	57.8	0.1122		
Bufo bufo (*vulgaris*)	6	2.037	28.59	0.0713	Vernon 1897	3, 4
		1.7415	76.13	0.0229		3, 4
	15	4.8389	28.59	0.1693		3, 4
		2.8549	76.13	0.0375		3, 4
Bufo bufo	17	4.8246	43	0.1122	Jones 1967	
	20	4.901	29	0.169	Leivestad 1960	Animal restrained
		3.915	29	0.135		12, animal restrained
Bufo bufo (*vulgaris*)	25	4.5851	28.59	0.1604	Vernon 1897	3, 4
		9.64	76.13	0.1266		3, 4
Bufo calamita	20	0.511	8.67	0.0589	Taigen 1983	
		0.5046	8.7	0.058	Taigen, Emerson, and Pough 1982	
Bufo cognatus	5	1.2792	45.2	0.0283	Hutchison, Whitford, and Kohl 1968	
	10	1.979	39.58	0.05	Seymour 1973c	11
	15	3.8481	50.5	0.0762	Hutchison, Whitford, and Kohl 1968	
		N.A.	N.A.	0.131	Whitford and Meltzer 1976	2
	20	4.4725	39.58	0.113	Seymour 1973c	11
	25	2.9587	40.2	0.0736	Hutchison, Whitford, and Kohl 1968	
	30	7.2036	39.58	0.182	Seymour 1973c	11
Bufo debilis	15	0.0845	0.66	0.128	Whitford and Meltzer 1976	2
Bufo marinus	15	2.2877	101	0.0227	Feder 1982b	
		1.5515	145	0.0107	Hutchison and Kohl 1971	
		4.6276	123.8	0.0374	Hutchison, Whitford, and Kohl 1968	
Bufo (Bubo) marinus	18.5	33.15	1,200	0.0276	Buytendijk 1910	3
Bufo marinus	20	2.6088	101	0.0258	Feder 1982b	
		3.042	156	0.0195	Shield and Bentley 1973	13
	22	7.32	152.5	0.048	Bentley and Shield 1973	
		11.088	252	0.044	Withers, Hillman, Simmons, and Zygmunt 1988	
	25	3.1704	101	0.0314	Feder 1982b	
		6.3447	88.7	0.0715	Hutchison, Whitford, and Kohl 1968	
	26	N.A.	N.A.	0.0644	Smith 1974	
	30	5.7782	101	0.0572	Feder 1982b	
	35	8.2669	101	0.0819		
Bufo terrestris	5	0.6527	21.4	0.0305	Hutchison, Whitford, and Kohl 1968	
	15	1.336	16.6	0.0805		
		7.5	102	0.0735	G. C. Smith 1976	
	20	15.1	102	0.148		
	25	2.2425	19.8	0.1133	Hutchison, Whitford, and Kohl 1968	
		30.42	102	0.2982	G. C. Smith 1976	
	30	61.25	102	0.6005		
Bufo viridis	20	0.875	35	0.025	Degani and Meltzer 1988	
	25	61.502	38.2	1.61	Katz 1973b	14, acclimated to 21°C
Bufo woodhousii	10	1.2739	67.4	0.0189	Fitzpatrick and Atebara 1974	
	15	2.7255	69	0.0395		
	20	4.4129	64.8	0.0681		
	23	2.16	25.2	0.0857	Walton 1988	11
	25	2.2351	56.3	0.0397	Fitzpatrick and Atebara 1974	
		1.017	9	0.113	Maher 1967	2

TABLE 12.1 (*continued*)

	Temp. (°C)	$\dot{V}_{O_2}$ (ml·h^{-1})	Mass (g)	$\dot{V}_{O_2}$ (ml·g^{-1}·h^{-1})	Reference	Note
Dendrobatidae						
Colostethus inguinalis	20	0.1366	1.57	0.087	Taigen and Pough 1983	
	25	0.2127	1.53	0.139		
Colostethus nubicola	20	0.0314	0.28	0.112		
	25	0.0435	0.27	0.161		
Colostethus trinitatus						
(*Prostherapis*)	25	0.201	1	0.201	Tashian and Ray 1957	
Dendrobates auratus	20	0.1421	2.09	0.068	Taigen and Pough 1983	
	25	0.1593	1.77	0.09		
Phyllobates subpunctatus	15	0.108	1.5	0.072	Funkhouser and Mills 1969	9, 11
Discoglossidae						
Bombina orientalis	20	0.149	2.62	0.0569	Taigen 1983	
		0.1456	2.6	0.056	Taigen, Emerson, and Pough 1982	
Discoglossus pictus	20	1.142	30.71	0.0372	Taigen 1983	
		1.1359	30.7	0.037	Taigen, Emerson, and Pough 1982	
Hylidae						
Acris crepitans	5	0.0459	1.935	0.0888	Dunlap 1971	
	15	0.0477	1.59	0.03	Dunlap 1969	
		0.1118	1.735	0.1939	Dunlap 1971	
		0.1155	1.5	0.077	Dunlap 1972	
		0.0335	0.5	0.067		
		0.0838	1.27	0.066	Dunlap 1973	
		0.0612	0.9	0.068		
	25	0.3288	1.855	0.6099	Dunlap 1971	
		0.2535	1.5	0.169	Dunlap 1972	
		0.117	0.5	0.234		
Agalychnis callidryas	20	0.337	5.65	0.0596	Taigen 1983	
		0.3477	5.7	0.061	Taigen, Emerson, and Pough 1982	
Cyclorana platycephala						
(*platycephalus*)	15	0.5907	11	0.0537	van Beurden 1980	
Hyla arborea	18.5	2.4429	7.78	0.314	Buytendijk 1910	
Hyla arenicolor	20	0.3	3.37	0.089	Taigen 1983	
		0.3162	3.4	0.093	Taigen, Emerson, and Pough 1982	
Hyla chrysoscelis	10	0.1482	3.9	0.038	Blem, Ragan, and Scott 1986	Males
	20	0.4368	3.9	0.112		Males
		0.7056	5.47	0.129	Kamel, Marsden, and Pough 1985	
	30	1.1365	3.9	0.2914	Blem, Ragan, and Scott 1986	Males
Hyla cinerea	10	0.217	3.82	0.0568		Males
	15	0.8097	6.4	0.1265	Hutchison, Whitford, and Kohl 1968	
	20	0.5596	3.82	0.1465	Blem, Ragan, and Scott 1986	Males
	22	1.513	8.9	0.17	Muchlinski 1985	
	25	0.459	4.5	0.102	Davison 1955	
	27	0.689	5.1	0.135	Prestwich, Brugger, and Topping 1989	7
	30	0.8488	3.82	0.2222	Blem, Ragan, and Scott 1986	Males
Hyla crepitans	25	1.1484	9.9	0.116	Tashian and Ray 1957	
Hyla crucifer	14	0.1037	0.85	0.122		
	20	0.1443	1.3	0.111	Taigen and Beuchat 1984	10
		0.149	1.31	0.1137	Taigen 1983	
		0.1443	1.3	0.111	Taigen, Emerson, and Pough 1982	
		0.1265	1.15	0.11	Taigen, Wells, and Marsh 1985	
Hyla gratiosa	5	0.5281	10.2	0.0518	Hutchison, Whitford, and Kohl 1968	
	15	0.9081	10.2	0.089		
	25	1.4431	9.8	0.1473		
	29	1.321	13.9	0.095	Prestwich, Brugger, and Topping 1989	7
Hyla maxima	25	3.933	41.4	0.095	Tashian and Ray 1957	
Hyla regilla	20	0.1656	2.76	0.06	Bennett and Licht 1973	
		0.0004	2.27	0.0002	Jameson, Taylor, and Mountjoy 1970	14
	21	0.089	N.A.	N.A.	Funkhouser and Foster 1970	2
		N.A.	N.A.	0.24		2, 9
Hyla squirella	27	0.363	2.2	0.165	Prestich, Brugger, and Topping 1989	7
Hyla versicolor	5	0.5997	8.3	0.0723	Hutchison, Whitford, and Kohl 1968	
	15	0.8644	8.3	0.1042		

TABLE 12.1   (*continued*)

	Temp. (°C)	$\dot{V}_{O_2}$ (ml·h⁻¹)	Mass (g)	$\dot{V}_{O_2}$ (ml·g⁻¹·h⁻¹)	Reference	Note
	19	0.6724	8.62	0.078	Taigen and Wells 1985	
	20	0.6029	6.09	0.099	Kamel, Marsden, and Pough 1985	
	25	1.5252	7.6	0.2007	Hutchison, Whitford, and Kohl 1968	
Osteopilus septentrionalis	20	0.33	4.98	0.0663	Taigen 1983	
		0.33	5	0.066	Taigen, Emerson, and Pough 1982	
Phyllomedusa sauvagei	10	0.5075	17.5	0.029	McClanahan, Stinner, and Shoemaker 1978	15
	15	0.77	17.5	0.044		15
	25	1.8025	17.5	0.103		15
	30	2.7475	17.5	0.157		15
	35	4.1825	17.5	0.239		15
	38	6.125	17.5	0.35		15
Pseudacris nigrita	25	0.162	1	0.162	Davison 1955	
Pseudacris triseriata	5	0.0141	0.94	0.015	Dunlap 1980	
		0.1695	1.41	0.1202	Packard 1971	
	10	0.1774	1.192	0.1488	Packard and Bahr 1969	
		0.2556	1.065	0.24	Packard 1972	Acclimated to 5°C
	15	0.3015	1.34	0.225	Packard 1971	
	18.5	0.209	1.9	0.11	Pettus and Spencer 1964	13
	20	0.2687	1.125	0.2388	Packard and Bahr 1969	
		0.4836	1.056	0.458	Packard 1972	Acclimated to 25°C
	25	0.1119	0.94	0.119	Dunlap 1980	
		0.5015	1.31	0.3828	Packard 1971	
Pternohyla fodiens	20	0.514	15.13	0.034	Taigen 1983	
		0.4832	15.1	0.032	Taigen, Emerson, and Pough 1982	
Smilisca baudinii	15	1.5832	23.7	0.0668	Hutchison 1971b	4
Hyperoliidae						
Hyperolius marmoratus	20	0.0671	1	0.0671	Withers, Louw, and Nicolson 1982	
Hyperolius parallelus	20	0.0765	1	0.0765		
Hyperolius tuberilinguis	20	0.0679	1	0.0679		
Hyperolius viridiflavus	20	0.083	0.88	0.0943	Taigen 1983	
		0.0846	0.9	0.094	Taigen, Emerson, and Pough 1982	
Kassina senegalensis	20	0.228	3.02	0.0755	Taigen 1983	
		0.231	3	0.077	Taigen, Emerson, and Pough 1982	
Kassina weali	20	0.318	6.25	0.0509	Taigen 1983	
		0.3402	6.3	0.054	Taigen, Emerson, and Pough 1982	
Leptodactylidae						
Ceratophrys calcarata	25	2.967	55.5	0.0535	Hutchison, Whitford, and Kohl 1968	
	35	4.0434	58.6	0.069		
Eleutherodactylus coqui	20	0.1786	4.06	0.044	Taigen and Pough 1983	
		0.167	4.06	0.0411	Taigen 1983	
		0.1804	4.1	0.044	Taigen, Emerson, and Pough 1982	
Eleutherodactylus portoricensis	15	0.2566	3.7	0.0694	Hutchison, Whitford, and Kohl 1968	
Lepidobatrachus llanensis	25	8.5845	88.5	0.097	McClanahan, Ruibal, and Shoemaker 1983	
Leptodactylus typhonius	25	0.5865	5.1	0.115	Tashian and Ray 1957	
Odontophrynus americanus	20	0.549	15.24	0.036	Taigen 1983	
		0.5624	15.2	0.037	Taigen, Emerson, and Pough 1982	
Physalaemus pustulosus	25	0.26	1.72	0.1512	Bucher, Ryan and Bartholomew 1982	
Physalaemus pustulosus (Eupemphix)		0.3393	2.9	0.117	Tashian and Ray 1957	
Telmatobius culeus	10	1.7244	122.3	0.0141	Hutchison, Haines, and Engbretson 1976	
Telmatobius marmoratus	10	0.92	18.4	0.05	Ruiz, Rosenmann, and Veloso 1983	Cutaneous only
Microhylidae						
Gastrophryne carolinensis	20	0.103	1.94	0.0531	Taigen 1983	
		0.0988	1.9	0.052	Taigen, Emerson, and Pough 1982	
Kaloula pulchra	20	0.89	30.66	0.029	Taigen 1983	
		0.7982	30.7	0.026	Taigen, Emerson, and Pough 1982	

TABLE 12.1 *(continued)*

	Temp. (°C)	$\dot{V}O_2$ (ml·h⁻¹)	Mass (g)	$\dot{V}O_2$ (ml·g⁻¹·h⁻¹)	Reference	Note
Microhyla carolinensis	15	0.2315	3.5	0.0661	Hutchison, Whitford, and Kohl 1968	
Myobatrachidae						
Crinia parinsignifera	5	0.0398	0.653	0.061	MacNally 1981a	Males
	10	0.0501	0.597	0.084		Males
	15	0.1073	0.658	0.163		Males
	20	0.1166	0.63	0.184		Males
	25	0.1765	0.666	0.265		Males
	30	0.1709	0.452	0.378		Males
	35	0.3757	0.665	0.565		Males
Crinia signifera	5	0.041	0.683	0.06		Males
		0.0499	0.908	0.055		Females
	10	0.0593	0.69	0.086		Males
		0.0823	0.968	0.085		Females
	15	0.1078	0.638	0.169		Males
		0.1331	0.853	0.156		Females
	20	0.131	0.615	0.213		Males
	25	0.149	0.621	0.24		Males
	30	0.1761	0.485	0.363		Males
	35	0.399	0.612	0.652		Males
Pelobatidae						
Scaphiopus bombifrons	15	1.851	13.3	0.1392	Hutchison, Whitford, and Kohl 1968	
Scaphiopus couchii	10	N.A.	N.A.	0.0296	McClanahan 1967	6
	15	2.2609	26.9	0.0841	Hutchison, Whitford, and Kohl 1968	
		N.A.	N.A.	0.026	Jones 1980a	
		N.A.	N.A.	0.0311	McClanahan 1967	6
	20	N.A.	N.A.	0.0576		6
	21	1.8179	24.6	0.0739	Seymour 1973a	
	25	N.A.	N.A.	0.0656	McClanahan 1967	6
	30	N.A.	N.A.	0.081		6
	35	N.A.	N.A.	0.1296		6
Scaphiopus hammondii	15	2.2163	23.6	0.0939	Hutchison, Whitford, and Kohl 1968	
		0.2666	1.55	0.172	Whitford and Meltzer 1976	2
		0.75	10.87	0.069	Seymour 1973c	
	21	1.1466	12.74	0.09	Seymour 1973a	
Scaphiopus holbrooki	15	1.1712	14	0.0837	Hutchison, Whitford, and Kohl 1968	
Pipidae						
Xenopus laevis	15	1.6847	30.03	0.0561	Hutchison and Miller 1979a	
		2.1516	63.6	0.0338	Hutchison, Whitford, and Kohl 1968	
		1.9106	33.3	0.0574	Tsugawa 1982	3
	17	4.2277	67	0.0631	Jones 1967	
	17.3	3.834	67.3	0.057	Charles 1931	
	18	1.7901	22.1	0.081	Hillman and Withers 1981	
	20	4.5	100	0.045	Emilio and Shelton 1974	
		2.53	55	0.046	Merkle and Hanke 1988	
		3.8364	139	0.0276	Shield and Bentley 1973	
	22	5.5998	122	0.0459	Bentley and Shield 1973	8
	25	3.526	41	0.086	Emilio and Shelton 1980	4
		4.2	29.3	0.1433	Hillman and Withers 1979	
		3.824	23.9	0.16	Hillman 1978a	7
		1.6063	28.39	0.0566	Hutchison and Miller 1979a	
		3.2218	33.3	0.0968	Tsugawa 1982	3
Xenopus mulleri	17	2.5104	24	0.1046	Jones 1967	
Ranidae						
Conraua goliath	25	18.86	251	0.0751	V. H. Hutchison pers. comm.	
Occidozyga martensii (*Ooeidozyga laevis*)	15	0.4167	9.3	0.0448	Feder 1982b	
	20	0.524	9.3	0.0563		
	25	0.8872	9.3	0.0954		
	30	0.9402	9.3	0.1011		
	35	1.0779	9.3	0.1159		
Pyxicephalus adspersus	20	14.22	562.3	0.0253	Loveridge and Withers 1981	

TABLE 12.1 *(continued)*

	Temp. (°C)	$\dot{V}_{O_2}$ (ml·h^{-1})	Mass (g)	$\dot{V}_{O_2}$ (ml·g^{-1}·h^{-1})	Reference	Note
Rana arvalis	5	0.4233	17	0.0249	Mazur 1968	11
	10	0.9554	17	0.0562		11
	15	1.6337	17	0.0961		11
	20	2.8866	17	0.1698		11
	25	4.7685	17	0.2805		11
	30	7.6857	17	0.4521		11
Rana aspersa	18.5	31.6688	563	0.0563	Buytendijk 1910	3
Rana berlandieri (*pipiens*)	29	7.035	70	0.1005	May and Packer 1976	
Rana blythi	25	4.3729	88.7	0.0493	Weathers and Snyder 1977	Acclimated to 28°C
Rana cancrivora	20	1.0409	20.45	0.0509	Feder 1982b	
	25	1.5767	20.45	0.0771		
	30	2.2597	20.45	0.1105		
		1.75	12.5	0.14	Gordon and Tucker 1968	6
	35	4.1043	20.45	0.2007	Feder 1982b	
Rana catesbeiana	5	3.3638	80.9	0.0416	Hutchison, Whitford, and Kohl 1968	
		1.3171	262	0.005	Pinder 1987a	5, curarized
		10.013	646	0.0155	Weathers 1976a	
	10	0.4355	43.55	0.01	Seymour 1973c	11
	15	2.7008	47.3	0.0571	Hutchison, Whitford, and Kohl 1968	
	19	10.61	303.5	0.035	Fanslow 1961	Acclimated to 24°C
	20	5.6137	228.2	0.0246	Burggren and West 1982	
		7.2	300	0.024	Gottlieb and Jackson 1976	16
		6.9028	277.5	0.0249	Jackson and Braun 1979	3, 16
		17.4725	241	0.0725	MacKenzie and Jackson 1978	3, 16
		1.6549	43.55	0.038	Seymour 1973c	11
		33.0993	621	0.0533	Weathers 1976a	
	21.5	18.6739	503	0.0371	Smith 1925	3, 6
	22.5	7.525	175	0.043	Quinn and Burggren 1983	
	25	2.1	14	0.15	Burggren and Moalli 1984	2
		13.052	251	0.052		
		15.05	350	0.043	Davison 1955	
		25.017	269	0.093	Tazawa, Mochizuki, and Piiper 1979b	
	30	3.7889	43.55	0.087	Seymour 1973c	11
Rana chalconota	25	0.3911	4.1	0.0954	Weathers and Snyder 1977	Acclimated to 28°C
Rana clamitans	5	0.5397	31	0.0174	Vinegar and Hutchison 1965b	1
	14	1.7442	34.2	0.051	Tashian and Ray 1957	
	15	1.6085	34	0.0473	Vinegar and Hutchison 1965b	1
	21.5	2.1684	19	0.1141	Smith 1925	3, 6
	25	2.7008	32.5	0.0831	Vinegar and Hutchison 1965b	1
Rana cyanophlyctis	29	0.1729	0.142	1.215	Cherian 1962	2
		0.2157	0.294	0.7338		2
Rana erythraea	15	0.1786	19	0.0094	Feder 1982b	
	20	0.7809	19	0.0411		
	25	1.6245	19	0.0855		
	30	2.1299	19	0.1121		
	35	3.8703	19	0.2037		
Rana esculenta	6	0.8617	50.32	0.0171	Vernon 1897	3, 4
	7	0.2468	17.5	0.0141	Kayser and Schieber 1969	
		0.5887	31.2	0.0189		
	12	1.9937	28.4	0.0702	Jusiak and Poczopko 1972	
		1.91	22.15	0.0862	Jusiak 1970	
		2.1953	28.4	0.0773	Poczopko and Jusiak 1972	
	15	0.8176	28	0.0292	Kayser and Schieber 1969	
		N.A.	N.A.	0.119	Poczopko 1959–60	6
Rana esculenta?		2.5225	57.2	0.0441	Regnault and Reiset 1849	4
Rana esculenta		4.4533	50.32	0.0885	Vernon 1897	3, 4
	17	3.4488	36	0.0958	Jones 1967	
	18.5	6.327	30	0.2109	Buytendijk 1910	
		9.3612	116	0.0807		
	20	4.3941	45.3	0.097	Athanasiu 1900	
		1.3874	16.4	0.0846	Bohr 1900	

TABLE 12.1 *(continued)*

	Temp. (°C)	$\dot{V}_{O_2}$ (ml·h⁻¹)	Mass (g)	$\dot{V}_{O_2}$ (ml·g⁻¹·h⁻¹)	Reference	Note
		3.7037	28.8	0.1286	Krogh 1904	Males
	22.5	N.A.	N.A.	0.148	Locker and Weish 1966	6
	23	0.2523	15.2	0.0166	Kayser and Schieber 1969	
	24	5.988	34.5	0.1736	Jones 1972a	
	25	4.1954	50.32	0.0834	Vernon 1897	3, 4
Rana hexadactyla	29	11.9889	51.9	0.231	Cherian 1962	
		7.35	30	0.245		2
Rana magna	20	1.4022	34.2	0.041	Feder 1982b	
	30	2.8523	34.2	0.0834		
Rana mugiens?	25.3	0.0624	600	0.0001	Krehl and Soetbeer 1899	12, 14
Rana muscosa	4	0.099	13.5	0.0073	Bradford 1983	
	15	0.6061	18	0.0337		
Rana nicobariensis	25	0.2561	2.6	0.0985	Weathers and Snyder 1977	Acclimated to 28°C
Rana palustris	15	0.9412	14.7	0.064	Hutchison, Whitford, and Kohl 1968	
	21.5	3.672	36	0.102	Smith 1925	3, 6
Rana pipiens	5	0.529	33.5	0.0158	Guimond and Hutchison 1968	
		0.7025	25	0.0281	Hutchison, Whitford, and Kohl 1968	
	10	0.4907	34.8	0.0141	Carey 1979a	11
		1.6124	38.39	0.042	Seymour 1973c	11
	15	1.1528	31.8	0.0363	Guimond and Hutchison 1968	
		1.2918	25	0.0517	Hutchison, Whitford, and Kohl 1968	
		2.88	43.7	0.0659	Jones 1972b	Acclimated to 25°C
		1.625	32.5	0.05	Turney and Hutchison 1974	
	17	2.912	32	0.091	Jones 1967	
	18	N.A.	N.A.	0.036	McNabb 1969	
	19	1.68	26.5	0.0634	Fanslow 1961	Acclimated to 24°C
	20	1.5208	34.8	0.0437	Carey 1979a	11
		2.64	27.5	0.096	Maher 1967	
		3.6854	38.39	0.096	Seymour 1973c	11
		3.5476	49	0.0724	Shield and Bentley 1973	13
	21.5	2.982	33.6	0.0888	Smith 1925	3, 6
	22	3.5046	49.5	0.0708	Bentley and Shield 1973	
		3.4032	52.6	0.0647	Warren 1940	Males
	23	4.68	30	0.156	Calhoon and Angerer 1955	
	23.5	N.A.	N.A.	0.0338	Fromm and Johnson 1955	Curarized
	24	4.0	25	0.16	Fromm 1956	12
		4.69	37.1	0.1264	Jones and Mustafa 1973	Curarized
	25	3.255	35	0.093	Davison 1955	
		4.352	32	0.136	Gatten 1987	
		3.4433	35.24	0.0977	Guimond and Hutchison 1968	
		5.64	44.3	0.1273	Hillman and Withers 1979	
		3.028	25	0.1211	Hutchison, Whitford and Kohl 1968	
		3.276	42	0.078	Pinder and Burggren 1986	
		4.147	32.5	0.1276	Turney and Hutchison 1974	
	30	4.29	27.5	0.156	Calhoon 1955	4
		4.6945	34.8	0.1349	Carey 1979a	11
		N.A.	N.A.	0.107	McNabb 1969	
		5.7585	38.39	0.15	Seymour 1973c	11
Rana ridibunda	20	1.12	35	0.032	Degani and Meltzer 1988	
		23.936	35.2	0.68	Katz 1975a	
	23	4.0375	47.5	0.085	Emilio 1974	16
Rana sylvatica	5	0.4862	9	0.054	Hutchison, Whitford, and Kohl 1968	
	14	0.5896	8.8	0.067	Tashian and Ray 1957	
	15	0.7319	7.4	0.0989	Hutchison, Whitford, and Kohl 1968	
	20	1.0795	12.7	0.085	Taigen and Beuchat 1984	10
		1.098	12.67	0.0867	Taigen 1983	
		1.0795	12.7	0.085	Taigen, Emerson, and Pough 1982	
	25	0.648	6	0.108	Davison 1955	
Rana temporaria	6	1.0066	38.53	0.0261	Vernon 1897	3, 4
Rana temporaria (fusca)	9.5	1.21	44	0.0275	Athanasiu 1900	
Rana temporaria	10	N.A.	N.A.	0.0534	Harri and Hedenstam 1972	Summer animals
		N.A.	N.A.	0.0414		Winter animals
		0.8143	38	0.0214	Kayser 1940	6

TABLE 12.1   *(continued)*

	Temp. (°C)	$\dot{V}_{O_2}$ (ml·h⁻¹)	Mass (g)	$\dot{V}_{O_2}$ (ml·g⁻¹·h⁻¹)	Reference	Note
	10.4	2.332	53	0.044	Krogh 1914	
	14	0.356	30	0.0119	Bastert 1929	
	15	0.28	39	0.0072		
		2.6008	38.53	0.0675	Vernon 1897	3, 4
	15.1	0.49	35	0.014	Krogh 1914	
	17	3.3712	43	0.0784	Jones 1967	
	19	1.5831	38	0.0417	Kayser 1940	6
	19.2	2.7166	39.6	0.0686	Bohr 1900	
	20	1.58	15.8	0.1	Hill 1911	12
Rana temporaria (fusca)		5.8875	37.5	0.157	Krogh 1904	Males
Rana temporaria		1.75	25	0.07	Terroine and Delpech 1931	
	22	N.A.	N.A.	0.081	Harri 1973b	Winter animals
		N.A.	N.A.	0.142		Summer animals
		6.095	53	0.115	Krogh 1914	
	23	4.3775	42.5	0.103	Kasbohm 1967	
	24.6	3.456	21.6	0.16	Dolk and Postma 1927	
	24.8	3.9373	31.1	0.1266		
	25	N.A.	N.A.	0.117	Harri and Hedenstam 1972	Summer animals
		N.A.	N.A.	0.081		Winter animals
		7.5037	38.53	0.1948	Vernon 1897	3, 4
Rana temporaria (fusca)	26.3	2.0697	32.8	0.0631	Joel 1919	
Rana virgatipes	5	0.14	7	0.02	Holzman and McManus 1973	
	15	0.35	7	0.05		
	25	1.015	7	0.145		
Rhacophoridae						
Chiromantis petersi	25	0.729	9	0.081	Johansen et al. 1980	
		0.7952	11.2	0.071		

Gymnophiona

	Temp. (°C)	$\dot{V}_{O_2}$ (ml·h⁻¹)	Mass (g)	$\dot{V}_{O_2}$ (ml·g⁻¹·h⁻¹)	Reference	Note
Caeciliidae						
Boulengerula taitanus	20	0.3175	5	0.0635	Wood et al. 1975	
	25	0.4205	5	0.0841		
	35	0.86	5	0.172		16
Geotrypetes seraphini	20	0.0714	1.93	0.037	Bennett and Wake 1974	2
Typhlonectidae						
Typhlonectes compressicauda	20	4.52	135	0.033	Sawaya 1947	
	25	9.546	64	0.149		
	25	11.253	138	0.081		2
Typhlonectes compressicauda (compressicaudus)	25	1.442	30.62	0.0471	Gonçalves and Sawaya 1978	

Notes: Species names enclosed in parentheses are those used in the original publication. Species names followed by a question mark are of uncertain identification. Mass given in table is mean mass of animals (if given in reference cited), midpoint of mass range (if only the mass range is given in the reference cited), or a reasonable, central value of mass from studies in which oxygen consumption as a function of body mass is described by an allometric equation in the reference cited. N.A. = data not available.

[1] Metabolic rate determined on animals wearing masks (so pulmonary and cutaneous rates could be determined separately). These values may be elevated as a result.

[2] Juvenile form (an animal of adult body form but not sexually mature).

[3] Rate of CO_2 production converted to rate of O_2 consumption assuming $R = 0.8$ (Bohr 1900).

[4] Temperature acclimation regime not reported.

[5] Metabolic rate determined on animals forcibly submerged.

[6] Acclimated to (unspecified) laboratory conditions.

[7] These data were received too late to be included in the calculation of the effect of body mass on the resting rate of O_2 consumption.

[8] Metabolic rate determined in air (in this normally aquatic form).

[9] Shaken during the determination of O_2 consumption.

[10] These data were originally reported in Taigen, Emerson, and Pough (1982), and thus they were not included in the calculation of the effect of body mass on the resting rate of O_2 consumption.

[11] Acclimated to field conditions.

[12] Rate of heat production converted to O_2 consumption using 4.8 cal·(ml O_2)⁻¹ (Schmidt-Nielsen 1983).

[13] Metabolic rate determined in water (in this normally terrestrial form).

[14] These data were not included in the calculation of the effect of body mass on the resting rate of O_2 consumption.

[15] Acclimated to greenhouse conditions.

[16] Incomplete acclimation (animals were probably not at their acclimation temperature long enough to complete acclimation).

TABLE 12.2 Summary of Least Squares Regressions of log Resting Metabolic Rate (log ml·h^{-1}) versus log Body Mass (log g) of Amphibians at Various Temperatures

	Temp. (°C)	N	b	95% CI of b	log a	95% CI of log a	a	r^2
Caudata	5	43	0.81	0.71–0.92	−1.69	−1.82 to −1.57	0.020	.85
Caudata	15	100	0.81	0.74–0.88	−1.34	−1.42 to −1.27	0.045	.83
Caudata	20	39	0.80	0.71–0.89	−1.17	−1.26 to −1.08	0.068	.90
Caudata	25	61	0.80	0.74–0.86	−1.02	−1.11 to −0.94	0.095	.91
Anura	5	26	0.81	0.66–0.96	−1.31	−1.53 to −1.10	0.049	.84
Anura	15	66	0.79	0.69–0.89	−0.98	−1.11 to −0.85	0.104	.80
Anura	20	98	0.82	0.75–0.89	−0.99	−1.08 to −0.90	0.103	.86
Anura	25	71	0.84	0.78–0.90	−0.76	−0.84 to −0.68	0.174	.92
Gymnophiona	20	3	0.93		−1.30		0.050	.98
Gymnophiona	25	4	1.06		−1.18		0.067	.91
Larvae	15	34	0.78	0.72–0.84	−1.15	−1.22 to −1.09	0.070	.96
Larvae	20	71	0.65	0.55–0.75	−1.18	−1.26 to −1.10	0.066	.72
Anuran larvae	20	48	0.59	0.47–0.71	−1.13	−1.24 to −1.03	0.074	.68
Salamander larvae	20	23	0.79	0.66–0.92	−1.25	−1.36 to −1.14	0.056	.88
Larvae	25	13	0.77	0.61–0.94	−0.82	−0.95 to −0.70	0.150	.91

Notes: b and log a are the slope and intercept, respectively, of the line fitted by the equation log metabolism = log a + b log mass. The 95% confidence intervals (CI) of these values arc also included. a is the antilog of log a, corresponding to the predicted metabolic rate of a 1g animal in milliliters per hour.

12.1 to 12.4. A summary of the results of these statistical analyses is presented in table 12.2.

The slopes of the lines fitted to the log-transformed metabolic rates of salamanders at various temperatures are all very similar, ranging only from 0.80 to 0.81, with substantial areas of overlap in the 95% confidence intervals (table 12.2). These slopes are similar to those reported for the effect of body mass on the metabolism of salamanders by other authors (Feder 1976a; Ultsch 1974a; Whitford and Hutchison 1967).

Comparison of the intercepts of these lines (table 12.2) allows calculation of the temperature coefficient Q_{10}, between values determined at different temperatures. These are $Q_{10} = 2.24$ between 5° and 15°C and $Q_{10} = 2.09$ between 15° and 25°C. This means that a 10°C increase in temperature is accompanied by approximately a doubling of the rate of resting metabolism in salamanders. These values are well within the range of values of Q_{10} reported by other authors for the effect of temperature on the resting metabolism of salamanders (Brown and Fitzpatrick 1981a, 1981b; Feder 1976b; Fitzpatrick 1973b; Guimond and Hutchison 1972, 1973b, 1974; Pitkin 1977).

Effect of Mass and Temperature on Resting Metabolic Rates of Anurans

The effect of body mass on the resting metabolism of anurans at 5°, 15°, 20° (with the exception of one value; see table 12.1), and 25°C (with the exception of two values; see table 12.1) is illustrated in figures 12.5, 12.6, 12.7, and 12.8. Least squares linear equations were fit to log-transformed data illustrated in figures 12.5 to 12.8. A summary of the results of these statistical analyses is presented in table 12.2.

The slopes of the lines fitted to the log-transformed metabolic rates of anurans at various temperatures are all very similar, ranging only from 0.79 to 0.84, with substantial areas of overlap in the 95% confidence intervals (table 12.2). These slopes are similar to those reported for anurans by

other authors (Dunlap 1971; Hillman and Withers 1979; Hutchison, Whitford, and Kohl 1968; Taigen 1983; Taigen and Pough 1981; Taigen, Emerson, and Pough 1982; Tashian and Ray 1957).

The single value omitted from our analysis of the effect of body mass on resting metabolic rate of anurans at 20°C (Jameson, Taylor, and Mountjoy 1970), and the two values omitted from the analysis at 25°C (Katz 1973b; Krehl and Soetbeer 1899), represent obvious far outliers. The first, we believe, may have been reported in the wrong units (standardized residual = −7.29), the second may represent elevated metabolism because animals were active within the metabolic chambers (standardized residual = 3.31), and we cannot explain the deviation of the third from its expected value (standardized residual = −6.92).

Comparison of the intercepts of the lines estimating the effect of body mass on the resting metabolism of anurans at different temperatures (table 12.2) allows calculation of the temperature coefficient Q_{10} between values determined at different temperatures. These are $Q_{10} = 2.15$ between 5° and 15°C and $Q_{10} = 1.67$ between 15° and 25°C. These values are well within the range of values of Q_{10} reported by other authors for the effect of temperature on the resting metabolism of anurans (Carey 1979b; Dunlap 1971; Feder 1982b; Fitzpatrick and Atebara 1974; Guimond and Hutchison 1968; Jusiak 1970; Packard 1971).

Effect of Mass and Temperature on Resting Metabolic Rates of Apodans

The effect of body mass on the resting metabolism of gymnophionans at 20° and 25°C is illustrated in figures 12.9 and 12.10. Least squares linear equations were fit to log-transformed data illustrated in figures 12.9 and 12.10. A summary of the results of these statistical analyses is presented in table 12.2. These generalizations must be considered extremely tentative because of the very few available data on the metabolism of gymnophionans. They are, how-

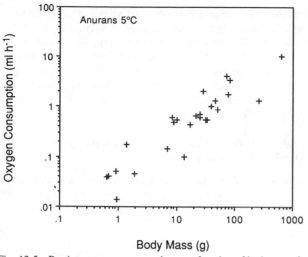

Fig. 12.5   Resting oxygen consumption as a function of body mass for anurans between 4° and 6°C. Data from table 12.1.

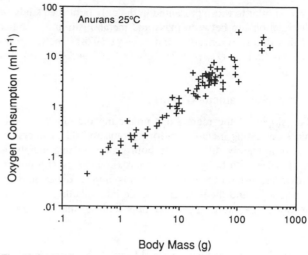

Fig. 12.8   Resting oxygen consumption as a function of body mass for anurans between 24° and 26°C. Data from table 12.1.

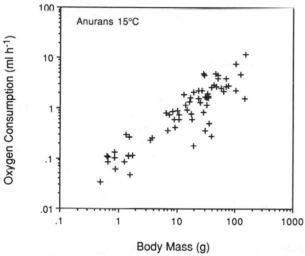

Fig. 12.6   Resting oxygen consumption as a function of body mass for anurans between 14° and 16°C. Data from table 12.1.

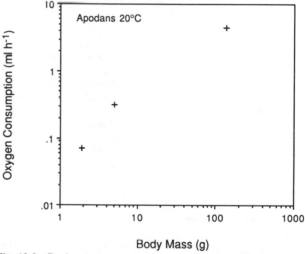

Fig. 12.9   Resting oxygen consumption as a function of body mass for apodans at 20°C. Data from table 12.1.

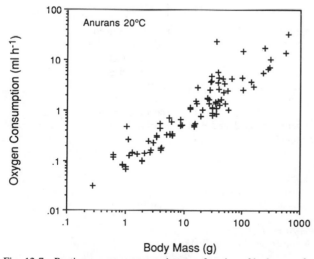

Fig. 12.7   Resting oxygen consumption as a function of body mass for anurans between 19° and 21°C. Data from table 12.1.

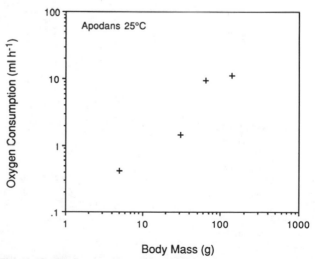

Fig. 12.10   Resting oxygen consumption as a function of body mass for apodans at 25°C. Data from table 12.1.

ever, similar to those presented in the only published study of the relationship between mass and metabolism in a member of this family (Gonçalves and Sawaya 1978). The temperature coefficient Q_{10} is 1.75 between 20° and 25°C in this group.

Comparisons among Groups

The slopes of the regressions predicting the effect of body mass on resting metabolism for anurans and salamanders are not significantly different. In both groups resting metabolic rate scales with body mass to approximately the 0.8 power. However, differences in the intercepts of these regressions are substantial, and the 95% confidence intervals do not overlap at any temperature. The intercepts indicate that the resting

metabolic rate of an "average" anuran is 1.5 (at 20°C) to 2.5 (at 5°C) times that of an "average" salamander (see also Feder 1976a). The proximate and ultimate sources of the differences in the resting metabolism of caudate and anuran amphibians are unknown. This substantial taxonomic difference in resting metabolic rate prevents us from developing equations predicting metabolic rate as a function of mass for amphibians in general.

Effect of Mass and Temperature on Resting Metabolic Rates of Larvae

A summary of the data we compiled for larval amphibians is presented in table 12.3. Our original intention was to compare analyses of data from larvae with analyses of pooled data

TABLE 12.3 Oxygen Consumption of Larval Amphibians at Rest

	Temp. (°C)	$\dot{V}_{O_2}$ (ml·h⁻¹)	Mass (g)	$\dot{V}_{O_2}$ (ml·g⁻¹·h⁻¹)	Reference	Note
					Caudata	
Ambystomatidae						
Ambystoma jeffersonianum						
(*Amblystoma*)	20	0.0317	0.241	0.1317	Helff 1927	
		0.0059	0.062	0.0955	Hopkins and Handford 1943	1
		0.024	0.46	0.0522		1
		0.0213	0.661	0.0322		1
		0.0702	1.746	0.0402		1
Ambystoma maculatum	10	0.0012	N.A.	N.A.	Kaplan 1980	Harrison stage 40
		0.0012				Harrison stage 40
		0.0018				Harrison stage 42
		0.0025				Harrison stage 43
		0.0022				Harrison stage 44
		0.0022				Harrison stage 45
		0.0016				Harrison stage 46
	20	0.0375	0.559	0.0671	Branch and Taylor 1977	
Ambystoma maculatum						
(*Amblystoma*						
punctatum)	20	0.033	0.202	0.1633	Helff 1927	
		0.0035	0.057	0.0617	Hopkins and Handford 1943	1
		0.0066	0.107	0.0617		1
		0.0094	0.184	0.0512		1
		0.0263	0.572	0.046		1
		0.0596	1.462	0.0408		1
Ambystoma maculatum	20	0.0021	N.A.	N.A.	Kaplan 1980	Harrison stage 40
		0.0022				Harrison stage 40
		0.0035				Harrison stage 42
		0.0051				Harrison stage 43
		0.0047				Harrison stage 44
		0.0047				Harrison stage 45
		0.0038				Harrison stage 46
Ambystoma maculatum (*punctatum*)	25	0.011			Boell, Greenfield, and Hille 1963	Harrison stage 46?
Ambystoma texanum (*Amblystoma microstomum*)	20	0.0584	0.175	0.3335	Helff 1927	
Ambystoma tigrinum	5	0.39	65	0.006	Burggren and Wood 1981	
	10	0.0013	N.A.	N.A.	Kaplan 1980	Harrison stage 40
Ambystoma tigrinum						
(*Amblystoma*)	20	0.028	0.25	0.1118	Helff 1927	
		0.005	0.056	0.0888	Hopkins and Handford 1943	1
		0.0289	0.358	0.0806		1
		0.0674	1.128	0.0597		1

TABLE 12.3 (*continued*)

	Temp. (°C)	$\dot{V}_{O_2}$ (ml·h⁻¹)	Mass (g)	$\dot{V}_{O_2}$ (ml·g⁻¹·h⁻¹)	Reference	Note
		0.1364	2.957	0.0461		1
		0.2138	6.065	0.0353		1
		0.2983	6.586	0.0453		1
Ambystoma tigrinum	20	0.0032	N.A.	N.A.	Kaplan 1980	Harrison stage 40
	23	0.5186	11.2	0.0463	Belehrádek and Huxley 1927	
		1.9272	13.2	0.146	Heath 1976	
	25	3.38	65	0.052	Burggren and Wood 1981	
Dicamptodontidae						
Dicamptodon ensatus	15	0.414	20	0.0207	Wood 1972	
Plethodontidae						
Gyrinophilus porphyriticus	16	0.1617	4.7	0.0344	Evans 1939	
	16.5	0.122	2.5	0.0488		
Salamandridae						
Taricha granulosa	20	0.0026	0.029	0.0886	Connon 1947	1, Harrison stage 46
Taricha rivularis	20	0.0081	0.1	0.0809		1, Harrison stage 46
Taricha torosa	20	0.0057	0.045	0.1271		1, Harrison stage 46

Anura

	Temp. (°C)	$\dot{V}_{O_2}$ (ml·h⁻¹)	Mass (g)	$\dot{V}_{O_2}$ (ml·g⁻¹·h⁻¹)	Reference	Note
Bufonidae						
Bufo americanus	23	0.0068	0.032	0.212	Lewis and Frieden 1959	
		0.0074	0.056	0.118		
		0.0146	0.104	0.1515		
		0.0198	0.138	0.145		
		0.023	0.154	0.151		
		0.0218	0.136	0.165		
		0.0226	0.124	0.185		
Bufo boreas	20	0.0028	0.01	0.2793	Sivula, Mix, and McKenzie 1972	2, Gosner stage 20
		0.0037	0.02	0.1866		2, Gosner stage 26
		0.0059	0.06	0.0979		2, Gosner stage 38
		0.0089	0.117	0.0763		2, Gosner stage 30
		0.0156	0.187	0.0833		2, Gosner stage 32
		0.0589	0.44	0.1338		2, Gosner stage 35
		0.0789	0.458	0.1722		2, Gosner stage 37
		0.1005	0.463	0.217		2, Gosner stage 40
		0.0344	0.243	0.1418		2, Gosner stage 44
		0.0159	0.126	0.1265		2, Gosner stage 45
		0.0137	0.115	0.1188		2, Gosner stage 46
Bufo bufo (vulgaris)	14.2	0.0005	0.005	0.122	Gayda 1921 (cited in Shapiro 1948)	3
	14.8	0.004	0.034	0.119		3
	14.9	0.0023	0.012	0.194		3
Bufo bufo	20	0.0076	0.078	0.0981	Guyétant, Herold, and Cudey 1981	3, Taylor and Kollros stage IX
		0.0205	0.318	0.0645		3, Taylor and Kollros stage XIII
		0.0208	0.282	0.0738		3, Taylor and Kollros stage XVII
		0.0109	0.218	0.05		3, Taylor and Kollros stage XVIII
Bufo bufo (vulgaris)	23	0.002	0.005	0.405	Fletcher and Myant 1959	2
		0.0024	0.006	0.445		2
		0.004	0.008	0.495		2
		0.0051	0.01	0.505		2
		0.0072	0.019	0.38		2
		0.01	0.027	0.37		2
		0.0111	0.042	0.265		2
		0.0212	0.071	0.3		2
		0.0238	0.085	0.28		2
Bufo terrestris	22	0.0123	0.047	0.262	Noland and Ultsch 1981	
		0.0498	0.204	0.244		
	32	0.0144	0.045	0.32		
		0.0759	0.172	0.441		
Bufo woodhousii	25	0.0443	0.31	0.1429	Feder 1982a	

TABLE 12.3 (*continued*)

	Temp. (°C)	$\dot{V}O_2$ (ml·h^{-1})	Mass (g)	$\dot{V}O_2$ (ml·g^{-1}·h^{-1})	Reference	Note
Dendrobatidae						
Phyllobates subpunctatus	15	0.0029	0.02	0.152	Funkhouser and Mills 1969	2, 4, Taylor and Kollros stage I
		0.0022	0.02	0.105		2, 4, Taylor and Kollros stage II
		0.0041	0.03	0.113		2, 4, Taylor and Kollros stage III
		0.0097	0.06	0.135		2, 4, Taylor and Kollros stage IV
		0.0128	0.1	0.124		2, 4, Taylor and Kollros stage V
		0.0145	0.12	0.132		2, 4, Taylor and Kollros stage VI
		0.0149	0.14	0.126		2, 4, Taylor and Kollros stage VII
		0.0163	0.15	0.125		2, 4, Taylor and Kollros stage VIII
		0.0183	0.16	0.126		2, 4, Taylor and Kollros stage IX
		0.0218	0.21	0.108		2, 4, Taylor and Kollros stage X
		0.0237	0.24	0.114		2, 4, Taylor and Kollros stage XI
		0.0276	0.25	0.108		2, 4, Taylor and Kollros stage XII
		0.0286	0.25	0.106		2, 4, Taylor and Kollros stage XIII
		0.0301	0.28	0.105		2, 4, Taylor and Kollros stage XIV
		0.0329	0.29	0.105		2, 4, Taylor and Kollros stage XV
		0.0342	0.31	0.107		2, 4, Taylor and Kollros stage XVI
		0.0297	0.27	0.105		2, 4, Taylor and Kollros stage XVII
		0.0303	0.27	0.106		2, 4, Taylor and Kollros stage XVIII
		0.0304	0.26	0.107		2, 4, Taylor and Kollros stage XIX
		0.0299	0.24	0.097		2, 4, Taylor and Kollros stage XX
		0.0215	0.19	0.08		2, 4, Taylor and Kollros stage XXI
		0.0204	0.19	0.086		2, 4, Taylor and Kollros stage XXII
		0.0177	0.19	0.092		2, 4, Taylor and Kollros stage XXIII
		0.0146	0.16	0.093		2, 4, Taylor and Kollros stage XXIV
		0.01	0.13	0.07		2, 4, Taylor and Kollros stage XXV
Hylidae						
Hyla regilla	21	0.0711	0.18	0.395	Funkhouser and Foster 1970	2, Taylor and Kollros stage X
		0.0856	0.276	0.3101		2, Taylor and Kollros stage XIII
		0.111	0.36	0.3083		2, Taylor and Kollros stage XV
		0.111	0.37	0.3		2, Taylor and Kollros stage XVIII
		0.101	0.306	0.3301		2, Taylor and Kollros stage XIX
		0.0856	0.3	0.2853		2, Taylor and Kollros stage XX
		0.0733	0.235	0.3119		2, Taylor and Kollros stage XXII
		0.0736	0.17	0.4329		2, Taylor and Kollros stage XXIII
		0.0583	0.17	0.3429		2, Taylor and Kollros stage XXIV
		0.0622	0.16	0.3888		2, Taylor and Kollros stage XXV
		N.A.	N.A.	0.259		2, Taylor and Kollros stage I
				0.254		2, Taylor and Kollros stage II
				0.266		2, Taylor and Kollros stage III
				0.259		2, Taylor and Kollros stage IV
				0.302		2, Taylor and Kollros stage V
				0.356		2, Taylor and Kollros stage VI
				0.329		2, Taylor and Kollros stage IX
				0.288		2, Taylor and Kollros stage XIII
				0.265		2, Taylor and Kollros stage XV
				0.293		2, Taylor and Kollros stage XVIII
				0.259		2, Taylor and Kollros stage XIX
				0.253		2, Taylor and Kollros stage XX
				0.286		2, Taylor and Kollros stage XXII
				0.316		2, Taylor and Kollros stage XXIII
				0.311		2, Taylor and Kollros stage XXIV
				0.299		2, Taylor and Kollros stage XXV
Leiopelmatidae						
Ascaphus truei	15	0.0048	0.035	0.1366	Brown 1977	
		0.0058	0.036	0.1624		
		0.0091	0.037	0.2482		
Myobatrachidae						
Limnodynastes peronii	15	0.0243	0.27	0.09	Marshall and Grigg 1980	
	25	0.0813	0.25	0.325		
Limnodynastes tasmaniensis	25	0.0704	0.163	0.4322	Panter, Chapman, and Williams 1987	1

TABLE 12.3 (*continued*)

	Temp. (°C)	$\dot{V}O_2$ (ml·h^{-1})	Mass (g)	$\dot{V}O_2$ (ml·g^{-1}·h^{-1})	Reference	Note
Pseudophryne bibronii	12	0.0018	0.057	0.0313	Bradford and Seymour 1985	1, Gosner stage 28
		0.0022	0.056	0.0393		1, Gosner stage 28
		0.0019	0.059	0.032		1, Gosner stage 28
		0.0017	0.057	0.0303		1
		0.0013	0.054	0.0245		1
		0.0011	0.053	0.0211		1
		0.0009	0.049	0.0177		1
		0.0007	0.042	0.0173		1
		0.0005	N.A.	N.A.		
Pipidae						
Hymenochirus boettgeri	25	0.012	0.093	0.1293	Feder 1982a	
Xenopus laevis	20	0.075	0.676	0.1109	Feder 1981a	
	23	0.0552	0.48	0.115	Fletcher and Myant 1959	2
		0.066	0.6	0.11		2
		0.084	0.96	0.0875		2
		0.0767	0.93	0.0825		2
		0.0817	0.86	0.095		2
		0.098	0.8	0.1225		2
	25	0.1466	1.589	0.0923	Feder 1982a	
Ranidae						
Rana berlandieri	25	0.949	3.65	0.26	Burrgren, Feder, and Pinder 1983	Cannulated
		0.2121	2.114	0.1003	Feder 1982a	
Rana catesbeiana	20	0.4759	3.6	0.1322	Burggren and West 1982	
		0.8194	5.3	0.1546		
		0.5779	4.3	0.1344		
		0.0647	6.6	0.0098	Etkin 1934	5
		0.0972	6.9	0.0141		5
		0.0959	7	0.0137		5
		0.1586	8.5	0.0187		5
		0.1063	9.2	0.0116		5
		0.1388	9.6	0.0145		5
		0.1571	10.5	0.015		5
		0.1531	10.8	0.0142		5
		0.1534	9.8	0.0157		5
		0.1401	9.3	0.0151		5
		N.A.	N.A.	0.0291	West and Burggren 1982	6, Taylor and Kollros stages XVI–XIX
	22.5	0.255	5	0.051	Quinn and Burggren 1983	
	25	0.6429	5.74	0.112	Burggren, Feder, and Pinder 1983	Cannulated
Rana clamitans	25	0.228	2.5	0.0912	Bernhardt 1934	
		0.4336	6.3	0.0688	Narins 1930	4
Rana cyanophlyctis	29	0.0875	0.113	0.778	Cherian 1962	
		0.154	0.102	1.504		
Rana esculenta	26	0.0656	0.31	0.2117	Méhes and Berde 1947	
Rana grylio	23	0.103	1.25	0.0824	Lewis and Frieden 1959	
Rana muscosa	4	0.0422	4.5	0.0094	Bradford 1983	
Rana pipiens	13	0.0265	0.68	0.039	Parker 1967	
	21	0.3322	3.65	0.091		
		0.5292	4.9	0.108		
	22	0.2189	1.394	0.157	Helff 1926	Anesthetized
		0.2195	0.942	0.233		Anesthetized
		0.2342	0.922	0.254		Anesthetized
		0.2236	0.793	0.282		Anesthetized
		0.2131	0.745	0.286		Anesthetized
		0.1748	0.662	0.264		Anesthetized
		0.1916	0.643	0.298		Anesthetized
		0.2081	0.605	0.344		Anesthetized
		0.0308	0.2	0.154	Noland and Ultsch 1981	
		0.1778	1.71	0.104		
	26	0.6747	5	0.1349	Helff and Stubblefield 1931	

TABLE 12.3 (*continued*)

	Temp. (°C)	$\dot{V}_{O_2}$ (ml·h⁻¹)	Mass (g)	$\dot{V}_{O_2}$ (ml·g⁻¹·h⁻¹)	Reference	Note
	27	0.185	1.35	0.137	Parker 1967	
	32	0.1768	0.8	0.221	Noland and Ultsch 1981	
		0.3423	1.72	0.199		
Rana temporaria	18	0.0549	0.194	0.283	Groebbels 1922	
	20	0.0024	0.014	0.1765	Guyétant, Herold, and Cudey 1981	3, Taylor and Kollros stage I
		0.0058	0.023	0.2522		3
		0.017	0.11	0.1547		3, Taylor and Kollros stage IX
		0.0237	0.293	0.081		3, Taylor and Kollros stage XIII
		0.0305	0.466	0.0653		3, Taylor and Kollros stage XVII
		0.0604	0.525	0.115		3, Taylor and Kollros stage XVIII
		0.0493	0.41	0.1201		3, Taylor and Kollros stage XIX
	22.5	0.0017	0.008	0.222	Locker and Weish 1969	0 days old
		0.0017	0.008	0.218		1 day old
		0.0036	0.013	0.282		3 days old
		0.0062	0.024	0.257		4 days old
		0.0129	0.039	0.328		6 days old
		0.0171	0.061	0.282		8 days old
		0.0244	0.114	0.214		12 days old
		0.0238	0.113	0.211		14 days old
		0.0264	0.154	0.171		20 days old
		0.0319	0.192	0.166		22 days old
		0.0349	0.234	0.149		25 days old
		0.0314	0.223	0.141		26 days old
		0.0262	0.213	0.123		29 days old
	23	0.0341	0.262	0.13	Fletcher and Myant 1959	2
		0.033	0.3	0.11		2
		0.0296	0.32	0.0925		2
		0.0441	0.333	0.1325		2
		0.0348	0.348	0.1003		2
		0.0387	0.344	0.1125		2

Notes: Species names enclosed in parentheses are those used in the original publication. Species names followed by a question mark are of uncertain identification. Mass given in table is mean mass of animals (if given in reference cited), midpoint of mass range (if only the mass range is given in the reference cited), or a reasonable, central value of mass from studies in which oxygen consumption as a function of body mass is described by an allometric equation in the reference cited. N.A. = data not available.

[1] Wet mass estimated from dry body mass using allometric equation in Feder 1981a.

[2] Shaken during the determination of O_2 consumption.

[3] Rate of heat production converted to O_2 consumption using 4.8 cal·(ml O_2)⁻¹ (Schmidt-Nielsen 1983).

[4] Acclimated to (unspecified) laboratory conditions.

[5] Animals fed immediately prior to the determination of O_2 consumption.

[6] Only O_2 consumption across the gills.

from adult amphibians, but the marked differences among orders of adult amphibians precluded the formation of those pooled models. Furthermore, the differences between adult anurans and adult salamanders led us to question the appropriateness of pooling data from larval amphibians. Data to examine this question are sufficient only from salamander and anuran larvae at 20°C. At this temperature, slopes or intercepts of the equations generated do not differ (table 12.2). The absence of differences can be attributed, at least in part, to a substantial scatter in the data (see Feder 1981a for an examination of the reasons for this scatter). Nevertheless, we feel justified in pooling metabolic data for larvae from these two amphibian orders.

The effect of body mass on the resting metabolism of larval amphibians at 15°, 20°, and 25°C is illustrated in figures 12.11, 12.12, and 12.13. Least squares linear equations were fit to log-transformed data illustrated in figures 12.11 to

12.13. A summary of the results of these statistical analyses is presented in table 12.2.

The slopes of the lines fitted to the log-transformed metabolic rates of larvae at various temperatures are all similar, ranging only from 0.65 to 0.78, with substantial areas of overlap in the 95% confidence intervals (table 12.2). These slopes are similar to those reported for anuran larvae by Feder (1982a) and calculated from data on salamander larvae in Hopkins and Handford 1943.

Comparison of the intercepts of these lines (table 12.2) allows calculation of the Q_{10} between values determined at different temperatures. $Q_{10} = 2.14$ between 15° and 25°C. This value is well within the range of values of Q_{10} reported by other authors for the effect of temperature on the resting metabolism of amphibian larvae (Feder 1985c; Kaplan 1980; Marshall and Grigg 1980; Noland and Ultsch 1981; Parker 1967).

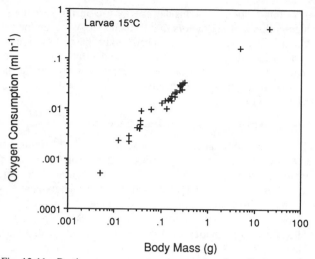

Fig. 12.11 Resting oxygen consumption as a function of body mass for larval amphibians between 14° and 16°C. Data from table 12.3.

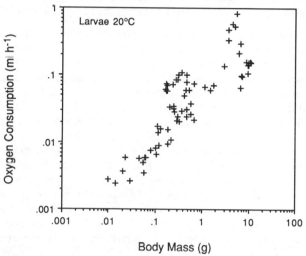

Fig. 12.12 Resting oxygen consumption as a function of body mass for larval amphibians between 19° and 21°C. Data from table 12.3.

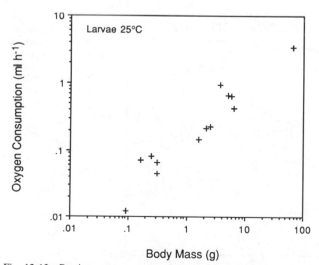

Fig. 12.13 Resting oxygen consumption as a function of body mass for larval amphibians between 24° and 26°C. Data from table 12.3.

Comparison between Larvae and Adults (Are Larvae Just Small Adults from a Metabolic Point of View?)

The 95% confidence intervals of the slopes of lines predicting the effect of body mass on the resting metabolic rates of larval amphibians at 15°, 20°, and 25°C overlap substantially with those for lines predicting the effect of body mass on the resting metabolic rates of adult salamanders at the same temperatures (table 12.2). The effect of body mass on the resting metabolism of these two groups is therefore very similar. At 15°C and (despite a small overlap of the 95% confidence intervals) 25°C, however, the intercepts of the predictive equations for larval amphibians are greater than those for caudate amphibians, suggesting that at any body mass the resting metabolic rate of an amphibian larva is about 1.5 times that of a salamander.

Anurans present a different picture. Although the slopes of the lines predicting the effect of body mass on resting metabolism of adult anurans are similar to those for larval amphibians at 15° and 25°C, at 20°C the slope for adult anurans is substantially greater than the slopes for anuran larvae or pooled amphibian larvae (table 12.2). Further, at 15°C (despite a small overlap of the 95% confidence intervals) and at 20°C, the intercepts of the predictive equations for adult anurans are greater than those for larval amphibians, suggesting that at any body mass the resting metabolic rate of an adult anuran is about 1.5 times that of an amphibian larva. Apparently the resting metabolism of larval amphibians lies between that of adult caudate and anuran amphibians, with the effect of temperature and body mass on resting metabolic rate being similar in these distinct forms.

Comparison between Amphibians and Reptiles and between Amphibians and Birds and Mammals

Similar analyses are available for the resting metabolism of other terrestrial vertebrate groups. Allometric equations predicting the effect of body mass and temperature on the resting metabolism of reptiles and the effect of body mass on the resting metabolism of birds and mammals have been published and afford us the opportunity to compare amphibian groups with these other groups.

Reptiles as a group operate at higher body temperatures than do amphibians, but the highest temperatures commonly experienced by amphibians are similar to the lowest temperatures experienced by most reptiles. At 20° and 25°C, the resting metabolism of a salamander is approximately two-thirds that of a reptile of the same size, while the resting metabolism of an anuran amphibian is approximately the same as that of a reptile of the same size (Andrews and Pough 1985; Bennett and Dawson 1976).

Mammals and birds have higher body temperatures than amphibians, and allometric equations relating the effect of body mass on resting metabolism of birds and mammals often include only data gathered when the animals were in thermal neutrality. Although these equations do not reflect the thermoregulatory cost of metabolism, they nonetheless cannot be compared directly with ours because of endotherms' higher body temperatures. We can, however, extrapolate our values at 25° to 38°C (the body temperature of most birds and mammals) assuming $Q_{10} = 2.0$. The resting metabolism of amphibians is one-thirtieth to one-tenth that of passerine and nonpasserine birds, respectively (Lasiewski and Dawson 1967), and one-fourteenth to one-eighth that of wild mammals (McNab 1988).

More and better data must be collected on the resting metabolic rates of amphibians, with the kind of control mentioned above, before the kind of detailed ecological and taxonomic analyses can be made for amphibians as have already been made for reptiles, birds, and mammals (Andrews and Pough 1985; Bennett and Harvey 1987; McNab 1980).

ENERGETICS OF SUSTAINABLE LOCOMOTION

The majority of studies on amphibian energetics have focused either on animals at rest or on those undergoing "maximal activity." In contrast, only a few studies have determined the energetic cost of submaximal, sustainable exercise. This is unfortunate from an ecological point of view, because many behaviors of amphibians (e.g., foraging, exploration, migration) appear to require submaximal exertion.

One major problem in the study of sustainable exercise has been the lack of an adequate method to control and quantify activity. A few investigators of terrestrial locomotion have overcome this difficulty by using a treadmill to characterize the relationship between the intensity of activity and the energetic cost of movement in anurans and urodeles (Else and Bennett 1987; Full 1986; Full et al. 1988; Walton and Anderson 1988). Likewise, others have used water flow chambers to study aquatic locomotion (Else and Bennett 1987; Quinn and Burggren 1983; Wassersug and Feder 1983). In these studies, amphibians exercised at controlled speeds for specified durations while O_2 consumption, net lactate production, or endurance was measured. Data collected for amphibians with such techniques can be compared directly with results from mammals, birds, lizards, and arthropods studied with similar methods.

In this section, we consider energy use during sustainable locomotion and the factors that influence it. We examine the kinetics of energy use; how speed, body mass, and temperature affect the energetics of sustained effort; the cost of transport; the contribution of anaerobic metabolism during submaximal activity; and the endurance of amphibians during such exercise.

Energy Kinetics of Submaximal Exercise

The demand for energy increases abruptly at the beginning of exercise. At the onset of exercise, the rate of O_2 transport increases along each step in the pathway, from mitochondria to respiratory surface. Increased aerobic metabolism, as estimated from environmental O_2 uptake ($\dot{V}O_2$), does not immediately match the energy demands of muscle (fig. 12.14). Therefore, the kinetics of $\dot{V}O_2$ are significant in that they indicate the (1) time required to initiate circulatory and respiratory responses, (2) rate of O_2 delivery by diffusion, (3) size of O_2 and high-energy phosphate stores, (4) type of muscle fiber activated and (5) changes in ATP, ADP, and P_i concentration, which affect mitochondrial respiration rate.

Methods and Equations for the Determination of Instantaneous Oxygen Consumption Rapid changes in $\dot{V}O_2$ during amphibian terrestrial locomotion have been successfully measured in treadmill respirometers using an electrochemical O_2 analyzer with open-flow respirometry (Full 1986; Full et al. 1988; Walton and Anderson 1988). Humidified air is drawn through the respirometer at a constant flow rate ($\dot{V}$) determined by a flow meter or flow controller. The air exiting the chamber passes through a column containing $CaSO_4$ and Ascarite to remove H_2O and CO_2 from the air, respectively. In the open-flow system, $\dot{V}O_2$ equals the difference between the rates of O_2 influx and efflux only when $\dot{V}O_2$ is constant and the system is at equilibrium. For most flow rates and respirometer volumes, single rapid changes within the respirometer will only result in a gradual change of the excurrent

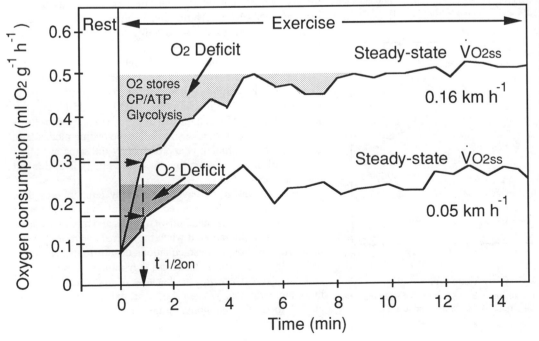

Fig. 12.14 O_2 consumption kinetics of a lungless salamander, *Plethodon jordani*, exercising at 27°C. Energetic demand of the muscles increases abruptly and creates an O_2 deficit. O_2 consumption increases to a steady state ($\dot{V}O_{2ss}$) with a time to 50% response ($t_{1/2on}$) of 1 min.

fractional O_2 concentration (F_e) towards some equilibrium concentration (F_{eq}). Rapid changes in $\dot{V}O_2$ will be dampened due to the non-steady-state conditions produced by mixing. However, F_e will change some known fraction f toward F_{eq} according to the equation

$$(1) \qquad f = 1 - e^{-\dot{V}\Delta t/V_{\text{eff}}},$$

where the time interval (Δt) and effective volume of the respirometer (V_{eff}) are known. The fractional concentration can also be represented by

$$(2) \qquad f = (F_{e_t} - F_{e_{t-1}})(F_{eq} - F_{e_{t-1}})^{-1}.$$

Solving for the equilibrium value that would eventually be attained if $\dot{V}O_2$ were held constant yields

$$(3) \qquad F_{eq} = (F_{e_t} - F_{e_{t-1}})(1 - e^{-\dot{V}\Delta t/V_{\text{eff}}})^{-1} + F_{e_{t-1}}.$$

Given two measurements separated by a brief interval and the effective volume of the chamber, F_{eq} can be calculated and substituted for F_e in the standard equation (where F_i is the fractional concentration of oxygen in the incurrent air)

$$(4) \qquad \dot{V}O_2 = \dot{V}(F_i - F_{eq})(1 - F_i)^{-1}$$

to estimate instantaneous $\dot{V}O_2$ (Bartholomew, Vleck, and Vleck 1981; Withers 1977). The effective volume used in the calculation of F_{eq} is measured from the washout kinetics of a specialized gas mixture (i.e., 20.850% O_2, balance N_2; Feder, Full, and Piiper 1988). Digital filtering is often necessary to remove noise in the O_2 concentration signal before $\dot{V}O_2$ is calculated.

Oxygen Uptake Kinetics, Steady State, and the Oxygen Deficit

Figure 12.14 shows the general pattern of $\dot{V}O_2$ kinetics. A relatively constant level of $\dot{V}O_2$ is eventually attained at submaximal speeds. These plateaus are referred to as a "steady-state" or steady-rate O_2 consumption ($\dot{V}O_{2ss}$; see Stainsby and Barclay 1970). The lag in $\dot{V}O_2$ kinetics is termed an O_2 deficit or an incursion of an O_2 debt. O_2 deficit is the difference between the theoretical abrupt rise in $\dot{V}O_2$ which should occur if a $\dot{V}O_{2ss}$ were attained instantly and the actual increase in $\dot{V}O_2$ that occurs when the animal begins to exercise at that constant, submaximal speed. One useful measure of the O_2 deficit's size, as well as $\dot{V}O_2$ kinetics, is the time required for O_2 consumption to increase halfway from the resting value to $\dot{V}O_{2ss}$, abbreviated as $t_{1/2on}$. Sluggish $\dot{V}O_2$ kinetics, long $t_{1/2on}$ times, and a large O_2 deficit may result in a greater reliance on stored O_2 or nonaerobic energy sources, such as high-energy phosphates and accelerated glycolysis.

The $\dot{V}O_2$ kinetics of amphibians at the onset of terrestrial locomotion are similar to those of mammals and lizards that ventilate lungs ($t_{1/2on}$ = 25 to 100 s; Cerretelli et al. 1979; Gleeson 1980; Marconi et al. 1982), several insects that rely on trachea ($t_{1/2on}$ = 30 to 180 s; Herreid and Full 1983), and some crabs that use gills ($t_{1/2on}$ = 50 to 150 s; Full and Herreid 1983). Amphibian $\dot{V}O_2$ kinetics are far more rapid than reported in several amphibious and terrestrial crabs ($t_{1/2on}$ = 4 to 6 min) that do not attain a $\dot{V}O_{2ss}$ during 15 min of exercise (Full and Herreid 1984; Full, Herreid, and Assad 1985; Herreid, O'Mahoney, and Full 1983). The toad *Bufo woodhousii* has slow $\dot{V}O_2$ kinetics during saltatory locomotion ($t_{1/2on}$ = 2 to 5 min); however, these animals require nearly 5 min to adjust to treadmill locomotion and are probably doing less work initially (Walton and Anderson 1988).

Surprisingly, lungless salamanders show a rapid adjustment of $\dot{V}O_2$ at the onset of exercise (Full 1986; Full et al. 1988). In lungless salamanders, $\dot{V}O_2$ attains its highest rate after 3 min of uncontrolled but intense activity (Hillman and Withers 1979; Withers 1980). In *Plethodon jordani*, $\dot{V}O_2$ increases from resting rates to a "steady state" in approximately 2 to 5 min ($t_{1/2on}$ = 100 s; fig. 12.14; Full 1986). No increase in net whole-body lactate production occurs after 20 min at slow speeds (0.05 km $\cdot$ h^{-1}). However, net whole-body lactate increases during the first 5 min at faster speeds (0.13 km $\cdot$ h^{-1}), but the net rate of production decreases as $\dot{V}O_{2ss}$ is attained. Therefore, with respect to $\dot{V}O_2$ kinetics, lunglessness does not appear to limit locomotion in salamanders. Feder, Full, and Piiper (1988) have demonstrated that cutaneous gas exchange becomes less diffusion-limited during exercise. Cutaneous gas exchange may be regulated by initiating blood flow through previously nonperfused capillaries. A rapid increase in "functional surface area" due to capillary recruitment could account for a more rapid increase in O_2 uptake.

Data on the $\dot{V}O_2$ kinetics of anurans also show that $\dot{V}O_{2ss}$ is attained after 4 to 5 min of exercise (Taigen and Beuchat 1984; Walton 1992). No net whole-body lactate production occurs at speeds below 45 to 63% of the speed where maximal O_2 uptake, abbreviated as $\dot{V}O_{2ex}$, is seen (Taigen and Beuchat 1984). Although data are limited, neither salamanders nor anurans differ from other vertebrates in $\dot{V}O_2$ kinetics (Gleeson and Bennett 1982; Seeherman et al. 1981). Therefore, $\dot{V}O_{2ss}$ can be taken to represent the energy requirement for locomotion at submaximal speeds (Full 1986).

Energy per Time

Effect of Speed of Locomotion on Steady-State Oxygen Consumption

Steady-state O_2 consumption increases linearly with speed of locomotion in frogs, toads, and salamanders (fig. 12.15). This pattern is common in terrestrial locomotion for a wide diversity of animals, including mammals and birds (Taylor, Heglund, and Maloiy 1982), lizards (Bennett 1982), insects (Herreid and Full 1983; Herreid, Full, and Prawel 1981), and crustaceans (Full 1987; Full and Herreid 1983). In mammals, curvilinear relationships have been shown to occur within a single gait, but gait transitions may mask this relationship (Hoyt and Taylor 1981). At present, data on amphibian locomotion are insufficient to quantify any possible energetic consequences of gait changes or variations in the style of locomotion (e.g., increased lateral bending of the trunk). However, $\dot{V}O_{2ss}$ of walking salamanders is significantly less than that of frogs and toads that hop (fig. 12.15).

$\dot{V}O_{2ss}$ is lower in salamanders than in anurans for at least three reasons. First, resting O_2 consumption is significantly lower in salamanders than in anurans ($F_{[1,9]}$ = 24.5, p = .001, ANCOVA with body mass as covariate; table 12.4) as has been discussed previously. However, the low $\dot{V}O_{2rest}$ alone cannot completely account for the lower $\dot{V}O_{2ss}$. Second, the y-intercept of the $\dot{V}O_{2ss}$ versus speed function is considerably higher in anurans than in salamanders ($F_{[1,10]}$ = 25.3, p = .001; table 12.4). In most vertebrates and invertebrates, the y-intercept does not extrapolate to $\dot{V}O_{2rest}$ at zero speed; it is elevated by approximately 70% of $\dot{V}O_{2rest}$ (Herreid 1981). The

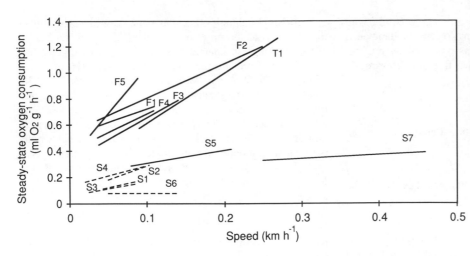

Fig. 12.15 Mass-specific steady-state O_2 consumption increases linearly with speed in frogs (*F#*), a toad (*T1*), and salamanders (*S#*). Ends of regression lines show maximal O_2 consumption and speed at maximal aerobic speed (MAS). *Solid lines* represent amphibians possessing lungs, whereas *dashed lines* represent lungless animals. Measurements were taken at 21°C except for *S1, S3,* and *S4.* y-intercept and MAS were temperature-corrected for these animals assuming a Q_{10} of 2.0. Species number designation increases with body mass. See table 12.4 for species and references.

TABLE 12.4 Steady-State Oxygen Consumption as a Function of Body Mass, Temperature, and Speed

	Mass (g)	Temp. (°C)	$\dot{V}O_{2rest}$ (ml·g⁻¹·h⁻¹)	y-Intercept (ml·g⁻¹·h⁻¹)	C_{min} or Slope (ml·g⁻¹·km⁻¹)	y-Int/ $\dot{V}O_{2rest}$	$\dot{V}O_{2ex}$ (ml·g⁻¹·h⁻¹)	$\dot{V}O_{2ex}/ \dot{V}O_{2rest}$	MAS (km·h⁻¹)	Reference
					Caudata					
Lunged										
Ambystoma laterale (S5)	4.4	21	0.101	0.2	1.04	1.98	0.42	4.2	0.200	Full et al. 1988
Ambystoma tigrinum (S7)	34.2	21	0.06	0.25	0.307	4.17	0.39	6.5	0.540	
Lungless										
Bolitoglossa subpalmata (S1)	1.5	16	0.038	0.03	1.38	0.79	0.18	4.7	0.062	R. J. Full unpublished
Desmognathus ochrophaeus (S2)	1.6	21	0.085	0.13	1.58	1.53	0.3	3.5	0.110	Full et al. 1988
Hydromantes italicus (S3)	2.5	16	0.041	0.05	1.07	1.22	0.11	2.7	0.062	R. J. Full unpublished
Plethodon jordani (S4)	4.1	27	0.14	0.1	2.3	0.71	0.46	3.3	0.160	Full 1986
Desmognathus quadramaculatus (S6)	28.0	21	0.048	0.08	−0.05	1.67	0.08	1.7	0.043	Full et al. 1988
					Anura					
Hyla crucifer (F1)	1.0	21	0.17	0.51	2.06	3.00	0.8	4.7	0.11	M. Walton unpublished
Hyla regilla (F2)	3.4	21	0.13	0.55	2.67	4.23				
Hyla versicolor (F3)	4.6	21	0.11	0.32	3.41	2.91	1.21	9.3	0.25	
Hyla cinerea (F4)	8.4	21	0.12	0.4	2.85	3.33	0.95	8.6	0.14	
Osteopilus septentrion alis (F5)	14.7	21	N.A.	0.33	6.95	N.A.	0.77 0.96	6.4	0.11 0.09	
Bufo woodhousii fowleri (T1)	25.8	21	0.13	0.22	3.87	1.69	1.17	9.0	0.27	Walton and Anderson 1988

Notes: Species are listed by increasing mass within a category. Numbers in parentheses identify species in figures 12.15 and 12.16. $\dot{V}O_{2rest}$ = average O_2 consumption of an inactive animal during 15–30 min prior to exercise; y-Intercept = the intercept of the steady-state O_2 consumption versus speed function; C_{min} = minimal cost of locomotion or the slope of the steady-state O_2 consumption versus speed function; $\dot{V}O_{2ex}$ = maximal O_2 consumption defined as that rate when an increase in speed does not result in an increase in consumption; MAS = speed at maximal O_2 consumption. N.A. = data not available.

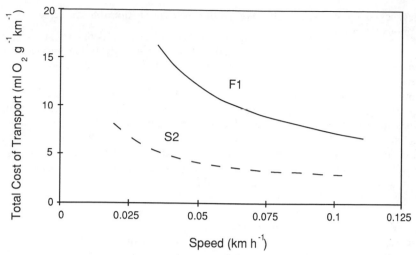

Fig. 12.16 Total cost of transport decreases toward a minimum, as a function of speed in frogs and salamanders. Example shown for *Hyla crucifer* (*F1*) and *Desmognathus ochrophaeus* (*S2*).

y-intercept of anurans constitutes a 300% increase over $\dot{V}O_{2rest}$ (Walton 1992), whereas in salamanders the increase averages 90% over their significantly lower $\dot{V}O_{2rest}$ (Full 1986; Full et al. 1988). The cause of the elevated y-intercept in anurans is unknown. Whatever the cause, the consequence for anurans is a greatly increased energetic cost, especially at low speeds. Third, in addition to a lower $\dot{V}O_{2rest}$ and y-intercept, the slope of the $\dot{V}O_{2ss}$ versus speed function (minimal cost of locomotion per distance) is significantly less in salamanders than in frogs and toads ($F_{[1,10]} = 11.1$, $p = .008$; table 12.4; see section below on energy per distance).

Effect of Body Mass on Steady-State Oxygen

Consumption Surprisingly, amphibians show no significant effect of body mass on mass-specific $\dot{V}O_{2ss}$ (table 12.4). In mammals and birds (Taylor, Heglund, and Maloiy 1982), reptiles (Bennett 1982), insects (Herreid and Full 1983), and crustaceans (Full 1987), mass-specific $\dot{V}O_{2ss}$ decreases with an increase in body mass. The most likely explanation for the absence of an effect in amphibians is an inadequate sample size (table 12.4).

Effect of Temperature on Steady-State Oxygen

Consumption No study on amphibians has directly examined the effect of temperature on steady-state O_2 consumption over a range of speeds. However, data on several species measured at a single temperature are consistent with results obtained for reptiles (Bennett and John-Alder 1984) and some insects (Herreid, Full, and Prawel 1981). The $\dot{V}O_{2ex}$, speed at maximal O_2 consumption, and y-intercept are lower for lungless plethodontid salamanders (*Hydromantes italicus* and *Bolitoglossa subpalmata*, R. J. Full unpublished) measured at 16°C compared to those at 21°C (*Desmognathus ochrophaeus;* table 12.4; Full et al. 1988). Measurements of $\dot{V}O_{2ss}$ at 16° and 21°C are much lower than those reported for another species (*Plethodon jordani*) at 27°C (Full 1986). The slope, or minimal cost of locomotion, appears to be relatively temperature-independent.

Energy per Distance

Cost of Transport as a Function of Speed The economy (energy per distance) of amphibian locomotion can be calculated from the $\dot{V}O_{2ss}$ versus speed relationship by dividing $\dot{V}O_{2ss}$ by speed. The total cost of locomotion (defined as the amount of energy required to move 1 g of animal 1 km) is a function of speed (fig. 12.16). Locomotion at low speed is less economical than moving at higher speeds. This results in a hyperbolic function. When traveling a kilometer at slow speeds, the cost to begin locomotion (y-intercept) and the maintenance cost ($\dot{V}O_{2rest}$) represent a higher percentage of the total cost than at higher speeds. At higher speeds, these components contribute less, and the cost of locomotion approaches a minimum (slope of the $\dot{V}O_{2ss}$ versus speed function).

The total cost of locomotion is higher in frogs than in salamanders (fig. 12.16). At slow speeds, the high cost to travel a given distance in frogs is due to the elevated y-intercept; this "idling" or "start-up" cost contributes more to the total when a given distance is traveled slowly. At high speeds, both frogs and salamanders approach a minimal cost. Frogs have a significantly greater minimal cost than salamanders (see next section). Moreover, frogs may not attain a minimal cost if they travel at slow speeds where the total cost per distance is elevated (fig. 12.16).

Minimal Cost of Transport as a Function of Body Mass

The minimal cost of transport (the minimal amount of energy required to move 1 g of animal 1 km, or the slope of the $\dot{V}O_{2ss}$ versus speed function) is widely used for interspecific comparisons of locomotor economy (Full 1986, 1987; Herreid and Full 1983; John-Alder, Garland, and Bennett 1986; Taylor, Schmidt-Nielsen, and Raab 1970). The mass-specific minimal cost of transport in amphibians does not vary with body mass in the narrow range of masses examined ($F_{[1,12]} = 0.74$, $p = .79$; 1 to 35 g; fig. 12.17 exploded plot; table 12.4). Body mass significantly affects the minimal cost of transport in a wide diversity of species, with small animals less economical than large animals on a mass-specific basis (fig. 12.17).

The mass-specific minimal cost of transport is significantly less in salamanders than in frogs and toads ($F_{[1,10]} = 11.1$, $p = .008$). Salamanders require less energy than frogs and toads to increase speed and also use less energy at the slowest speeds. These findings are in contrast to those for small lungless salamanders walking in a rotating-wheel respirometer; these salamanders had much greater costs than predicted for their size (Feder 1986, 1987a). This discrepancy is most likely due to the use of the rotating-wheel respirometer rather than a treadmill.

Amphibian Cost of Transport in Comparison with That of Other Animals

Amphibians show considerable variation with respect to the mass-specific minimal cost of transport (fig. 12.17). Minimal cost of transport values for frogs and toads fall both above and below the regression line for several vertebrates and invertebrates; thus, no generalizations about the minimal cost of transport for anurans can be made at this time. On the other hand, salamanders appear to have a reduced cost of transport in comparison with insects, crustaceans, and lizards: all values for salamanders fall below the regression line and approach the lower range of the data collected. The reason for the low cost is unknown. One possibility is that fundamental differences exist between salamanders and other vertebrates with regard to the muscles themselves, perhaps relating to the energy cost of force production in their slow muscles (Taylor 1985). John-Alder, Garland, and Bennett (1986) suggest a similar explanation for two lizard species similar in morphology but differing in minimal cost.

Anaerobic Metabolism during Sustainable Exercise

In amphibians, sustained exercise at levels that exceed 45 to 85% of $\dot{V}o_{2ex}$ results in net whole-body lactate production (Full 1986; Taigen and Beuchat 1984). Accumulation of lactate at submaximal levels of work (60 to 80% $\dot{V}o_{2ex}$) occurs in mammals (Nagle et al. 1970; Seeherman et al. 1981), reptiles (Gleeson 1980), and crabs (Full 1987). The submaximal work load at which blood lactate and ventilation increase is referred to as the "anaerobic threshold" (Wasserman et al. 1973; Whipp and Wasserman 1972). The "anaerobic threshold" model contends that tissue hypoxia results in the production of lactate, which enters into the blood. Lactic acid entry into the blood increases CO_2 flux. Increased CO_2 is sensed and ventilation is increased. The implications of the "anaerobic threshold" model are controversial for several reasons (Hagberg, Nagle, and Carson 1978; Hughes, Turner, and Brooks 1982). Such results do not necessarily indicate that an animal's O_2 delivery system is limited, for evidence of tissue hypoxia is lacking. Humans with a syndrome preventing lactic acid formation still demonstrate a ventilatory or "anaerobic" threshold (Hagberg et al. 1982). Blood lactate concentration will increase if blood is shunted away from

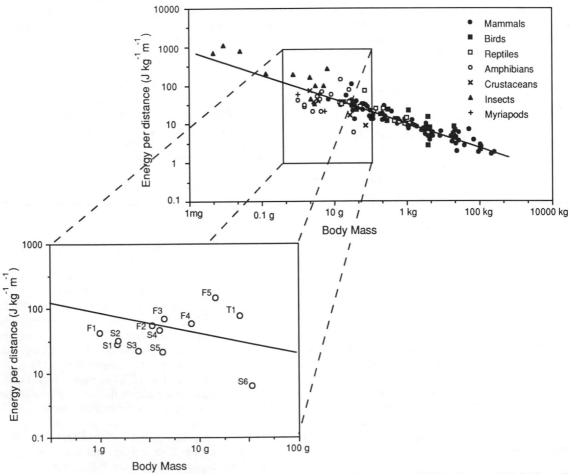

Fig. 12.17 Mass-specific minimal cost of transport decreases with body mass (C_{min} = 10.76 $M^{-0.31}$, r^2 = 0.84) in birds and mammals (Taylor, Heglund, and Maloiy 1982), reptiles (John-Alder, Garland, and Bennett 1986), crustaceans (Full 1987; Full and Herreid 1983, 1984; Herreid and Full 1983), insects (Herreid and Full 1983; Herreid, Full, and Prawel 1981; Jensen and Holm-Jensen 1980; Lighton 1985), and myriapods (R.J. Full unpublished). Exploded plot: mass-specific minimal cost of transport in frogs (F#), a toad (T1), and salamanders (S#). See table 12.4 for species and references.

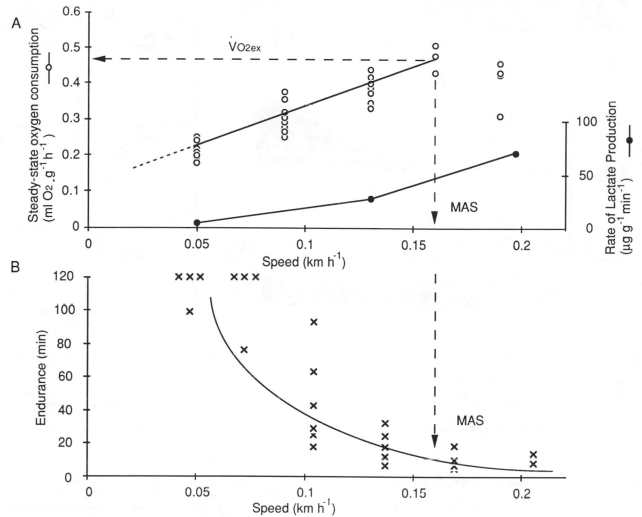

Fig. 12.18 *A*, steady-state O₂ consumption as a function of speed in *Plethodon jordani* (left ordinate) compared to the net rate of whole-body lactate production (right ordinate). Net rate of whole-body lactate production increases at submaximal speeds (0.13 km · h⁻¹; 80% V̇o₂ₑₓ). The greatest increase is shown when the speed at maximal O₂ consumption (*MAS*, maximal aerobic speed) is exceeded. *B*, endurance decreases as a function of speed. Endurance above MAS is less variable than at low speeds and is about 2 to 20 min.

organs normally removing lactate from the blood. Furthermore, to distinguish between the anaerobic energy mobilization necessary during the initial period of sustained exercise and that required during prolonged steady-state locomotion is often difficult. Until lactate kinetics (i.e., lactate production and removal) are well studied, the significance of lactate production during submaximal exercise is unclear.

During submaximal exercise in the lungless salamander, *Plethodon jordani,* most of the accelerated glycolysis occurs early in the O₂ deficit period, after which levels tend to stabilize or decrease (Full 1986). Glycolysis supplies approximately 60% of the ATP during the first 5 min of exercise at 85% V̇o₂ₑₓ, while providing only 15% during the balance of the exercise period. At speeds above the MAS (the lowest speed at which maximal O₂ consumption, V̇o₂ₑₓ, is attained), accelerated glycolysis contributes significantly, as net whole-body lactate concentration increases at a constant rate until fatigue. Thirty to forty-five percent of the ATP is derived from accelerated glycolysis throughout the exercise bout in these salamanders.

Submaximal Endurance

Endurance decreases hyperbolically as speed increases in amphibians (fig. 12.18). A similar function has been described for species of many taxa. In salamanders (Full et al. 1988), as in other species, endurance increases considerably at speeds below MAS. At the slowest submaximal speeds (20 to 30% of maximal V̇o₂ₛₛ), salamanders can exercise for over 2 h and travel over 100 m without showing signs of fatigue. Variation in endurance also increases at speeds below 50 to 80% of maximal V̇o₂ₛₛ (fig. 12.18). Endurance at submaximal speeds may depend more on the condition of the animal than endurance at speeds above MAS. These observations are consistent with the hypothesis that fatigue at submaximal speeds has a different causal agent than fatigue when sprinting.

ENERGETICS OF NONSUSTAINABLE LOCOMOTION

When amphibians engage in exercise of low to moderate intensity, their reliance on aerobic metabolism is high, their dependence on anaerobic metabolism is minimal, and their

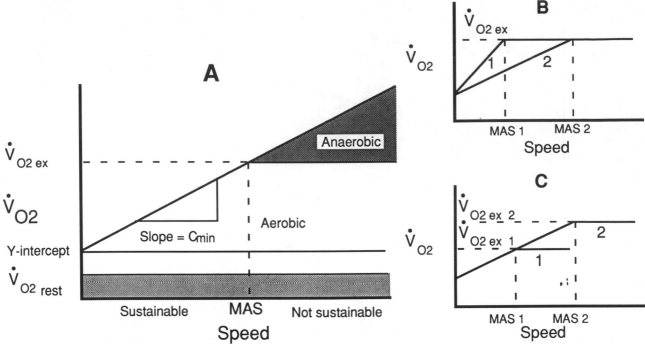

Fig. 12.19 Patterns of variation in the steady-state O_2 consumption ($\dot{V}_{O_{2ss}}$) versus speed relationship. *A*, general pattern of variation (after Bennett 1982). $\dot{V}_{O_{2rest}}$ is the O_2 consumption during the preexercise period. $\dot{V}_{O_{2ss}}$ increases linearly with speed until the speed at which maximal O_2 consumption ($\dot{V}_{O_{2ex}}$) is attained (maximal aerobic speed, *MAS*), above which faster speeds are powered anaerobically. MAS has been considered equivalent to the maximal sustainable speed (Bennett 1982). *B* and *C* show the potential effects of variations in the minimal cost of locomotion (i.e., slope) and $\dot{V}_{O_{2ex}}$. *B*, animals with an uneconomical morphology (*1*) have a greater minimal cost of locomotion than animals with an economical morphology (*2*). If $\dot{V}_{O_{2ex}}$ is similar, then *1* will have a lower MAS than *2* and therefore a lower endurance. *C*, animals with similar minimal costs of locomotion, but differing in $\dot{V}_{O_{2ex}}$. The animal with the lower $\dot{V}_{O_{2ex}}$. (*1*) will have a lower MAS and a lower endurance.

endurance is high (see above). At speeds below the maximal aerobic speed (MAS), O_2 consumption is not maximal (i.e., it has not reached $\dot{V}_{O_{2ex}}$), and locomotion can be sustained for long periods. At speeds higher than the MAS, even though O_2 consumption has peaked at $\dot{V}_{O_{2ex}}$, aerobic pathways cannot provide all the ATP needed by the active muscles, reliance on anaerobic metabolism increases, and endurance falls; such speeds are not sustainable (fig. 12.19A). Many of the behaviors of amphibians in nature, such as foraging, seem to occur at relatively low levels of exertion and thus appear to depend mainly on aerobic metabolism. On the other hand, some behaviors, such as attempts to escape from predators, may require high levels of effort. The latter type of behavior is likely to be powered in part by anaerobic metabolism and thus is likely not to be sustainable. Such a burst of high-intensity exercise often leads to fatigue and perhaps exhaustion. Depending on the intensity and duration of effort, the recovery period after such exercise may be prolonged; during this interval the animal has a reduced capacity for locomotion and is therefore vulnerable to predators. Thus, the type of behavior, the type of metabolic support for that behavior, and the consequences of that behavior have considerable ecological significance for amphibians on a daily basis.

In this section, we examine the metabolic support for nonsustainable exercise by amphibians. We consider the relationship between endurance, speed, and O_2 consumption and focus attention on the important influence of body size and temperature on metabolic support for locomotion. In addi-

tion, we discuss the many factors that influence the use of energy by amphibians during exercise. Finally, we examine the basis for fatigue, exhaustion, and recovery. In considering these topics, we have attempted to provide an ecological perspective on physiological topics.

Endurance and Speed at Maximal Oxygen Consumption

All else being equal, animals with the greatest $\dot{V}_{O_{2ex}}$ can sustain the highest speeds. However, high costs of locomotion will cause $\dot{V}_{O_{2ex}}$ to be attained at lower speeds and therefore limit endurance (fig. 12.19B). The MASs of hopping anurans (Walton 1992) are not significantly different from the speeds reported for walking salamanders (fig. 12.15; table 12.4). Although $\dot{V}_{O_{2ex}}$ is higher in anurans, so is the y-intercept and slope of the $\dot{V}_{O_{2ss}}$ versus speed function. The higher cost of locomotion results in a lower MAS, despite the higher $\dot{V}_{O_{2ex}}$. If the relationship between MAS and $\dot{V}_{O_{2ex}}$ were similar to that of salamanders, then anurans should have comparable endurance at MAS. This appears to be the case in frogs, but not in the toad *Bufo woodhousii fowleri*, which can sustain MAS for over 2 h without signs of fatigue (Walton and Anderson 1988).

If two animals have a similar metabolic cost of transport, then the animal with the greater $\dot{V}_{O_{2ex}}$ can sustain the higher speed (fig. 12.19C). Garland (1982, 1983) derived an allometric equation predicting the MAS as a function of body mass for lizards and mammals. MAS increases with body mass for both groups; however, the MAS for lizards is only

10% of that calculated for a mammal of a similar mass. Lungless salamanders attain $\dot{V}O_{2ex}$ at speeds only 20% of that of the measured speeds in lizards (Full et al. 1988; table 12.4). In contrast, two lunged salamander species show a MAS more comparable to that of lizards (fig. 12.15). Two species of lungless salamanders have a MAS that is two orders of magnitude lower than that predicted for lizards (Feder 1986, 1987b); however, these data were collected using a different apparatus, a rotating-wheel respirometer, in which work output may vary. In lungless salamanders, the relatively low $\dot{V}O_{2ex}$ is correlated with a low MAS and a modest capacity for sustained activity at fast speeds. Diffusion may very well limit gas transport and therefore endurance at these speeds. However, this conclusion must await further study of O_2 transport during exercise.

Large size may further limit cutaneous O_2 uptake in lungless salamanders by limiting skin surface area and increasing skin thickness (Czopek 1965; Ultsch 1976b; Withers 1980; Feder 1988). Even at the slowest speeds, the large lungless (plethodontid) species *Desmognathus quadramaculatus* is always at $\dot{V}O_{2ex}$. The onset of fatigue is rapid at all except the slowest speeds. Despite being only 5% as large, a lungless species of the same genus, *D. ochrophaeus*, can walk at speeds nearly twice that of *D. quadramaculatus* before attaining $\dot{V}O_{2ex}$. Results from previous studies on plethodontid salamanders exposed to hypoxia are consistent with the hypothesis that body size limits respiratory surface area and hence O_2 uptake (Ultsch 1976b; Withers 1980).

Aerobic Support of Nonsustainable Locomotion

The ATP needed to power the contractions of skeletal muscles of amphibians during movement at speeds above MAS can come from muscle stores of phosphagens, from aerobic pathways, and from anaerobic pathways. Olmsted and Harvey (1927) carried out the first known measurements of the change in O_2 consumption of an intact amphibian during muscular exercise. These authors delivered electric shocks to a frog (species unknown) at a rate of 2 Hz for 7.5 min and noted that the oxygen consumption was 3.5 times that of the frog at rest. About 1 h elapsed before O_2 uptake returned to normal. Forty-six years passed before other physiologists examined the change in O_2 consumption that accompanies muscular exercise in amphibians (Bennett and Licht 1973; Seymour 1973c), although many papers have since appeared. In this section, we review the data currently available on aerobic support of short-term, intense exercise by amphibians and also discuss how the methods employed can influence the results obtained.

Methods Used in the Measurement of Oxygen Consumption during Nonsustainable Exercise

In much of the early work on the aerobic cost of activity in amphibians, electric shocks stimulated the animals to exercise (Bennett and Licht 1973; Bennett and Wake 1974; Feder 1977; Hutchison, Turney, and Gratz 1977; Turney and Hutchison 1974; and numerous others). The advantage of such a method is that it permits repeatable, easily controlled delivery of stimulation. However, the disadvantages of using shocking to induce activity are considerable: the rate of O_2 consumption by the animal may be underestimated, the relative importance of anaerobic metabolism may be overestimated, the behavior may be abnor-

mal, O_2 transport may be impaired, and the muscles may be stimulated to contract directly by the shock (Hillman et al. 1979). In many of the early studies, workers used electrical stimulation in combination with manometry for the measurement of O_2 use. This combination can generate serious artifacts, including electrically induced heating and electrolytic reactions (Hillman et al. 1979). Furthermore, even if manual stimulation rather than shocking is used with manometry, heat production can lead to an underestimate of O_2 use by the animal (Hillman et al. 1979). In many cases, the use of shocking and manometry led to the conclusion that amphibians consume little or no O_2 during activity, but instead have maximal O_2 uptake during recovery (Bennett and Licht 1973; Bennett and Wake 1974; Feder 1977; and numerous others); this conclusion has been questioned by others who found maximal uptake during exercise rather than recovery when other methods were used (Gatten 1987; Withers 1980). For these reasons, the following analyses will, in general, omit data obtained by electrical stimulation. Because many of the data have been obtained in conjunction with electrical stimulation, the data subjected to analyses here will sometimes be limited. In those exceptional cases in which we do discuss activity of electrically stimulated animals, we will explicitly note this fact.

A few investigators have stimulated amphibians to swim by manual prodding during measurement of O_2 uptake (Hillman and Withers 1981; Pinder and Burggren 1986; Quinn and Burggren 1983; Withers and Hillman 1981). However, the most commonly used method for inducing activity is rotation of the metabolic chamber, first described by Seymour (1973c). Rotation may provoke jumping or hopping, but sometimes the animals may attempt to prop themselves in position with their limbs, and often as the animals tire, they withdraw their limbs and tumble within the rotating chamber (Gatten 1987). Such exertion in a rotating chamber certainly uses different groups of muscles from those used in normal locomotion. Both motorized and manual rotation of chambers have been used; these two variations may not result in identical rates of O_2 consumption (Walsberg 1986). However, motorized rotation and treadmill exercise yield similar values for O_2 consumption by toads (Walton and Anderson 1988).

Many authors refer to the rate of consumption of O_2 of amphibians exercising in response to stimulation as "$\dot{V}O_{2max}$." Recent work demonstrating that some male anurans may consume significantly more O_2 during calling than during exercise in a rotating chamber, however, suggests that $\dot{V}O_{2max}$ may not be an appropriate designation for rates of O_2 consumption during exercise in the laboratory (Taigen and Wells 1985; Taigen, Wells, and Marsh 1985). Hillman and his colleagues (Hillman 1982a; Hillman et al. 1985; Walsberg, Lea, and Hillman 1986; Withers and Hillman 1983, 1988) argue that each species at a given temperature has a maximal rate of O_2 use limited by the O_2 transport properties of the cardiovascular system. On the other hand, Taigen and his colleagues (Marsh and Taigen 1987; Taigen, Wells, and Marsh 1985) believe that O_2 uptake will vary for each type of activity (calling, exercise, territorial defense, mating, etc.) and that the maximal rate of O_2 use is determined by the oxidative capacity of the tissues involved, not by O_2 transport. In any case, it is clear that use of the term "$\dot{V}O_{2max}$" should be avoided unless it can be conclusively demonstrated that such a rate is the highest possible for the species. In this chapter, we use the term "$\dot{V}o_{2ex}$" to represent O_2 use during short-term, burst, nonsustainable exercise.

After the beginning of exercise, the respiratory and cardiovascular systems slowly reach their peak O_2 delivery capacity (fig. 12.14); in anurans at 22° to 25°C, this lag is about 2 to 5 min (Gatten 1987; Hillman et al. 1979). Thus, if O_2 consumption is measured by taking gas samples before exercise and after only 2 to 5 min of activity, the integrated value will not represent steady-state O_2 consumption. On the other hand, if intense exercise is prolonged, O_2 uptake may fall if the animal fatigues. A compromise is to measure $\dot{V}o_{2ex}$ during the 3 to 10 min that include the lag time as well as some time at steady-state O_2 uptake (e.g., see Kamel, Marsden, and Pough 1985; Mitton, Carey, and Kocher 1986; Stefanski, Gatten, and Pough 1989; Taigen, Emerson, and Pough 1982; Walton 1988; Withers 1980). Use of an open-flow system with calculation of instantaneous O_2 consumption, as dis-

cussed above, avoids these problems and permits determination of a steady-state value (Full 1986).

The method of stimulation and the method of measurement of O_2 consumption may have a large impact on the $\dot{V}o_2$ measured during exercise. The methods used should be carefully matched to the goals of each study. Preliminary measurements are necessary in each case to confirm the validity of the techniques for the particular species, temperature, duration, and intensity of effort. Careful reporting of the details of the methods used is necessary to allow researchers to repeat experiments or review the field.

Effects of Body Mass and Temperature on Aerobic Support of Nonsustainable Exercise

SALAMANDERS AND A CAECILIAN   Data are available for the O_2 consumption of one species of caecilian and thirty species of salamanders during non-steady-state exercise (table 12.5). The data set remaining after exclusion of results from studies

TABLE 12.5   Oxygen Consumption of Salamanders and a Caecilian during Nonsustainable Exercise

	Mass (g)	Temp. (°C)	$\dot{V}o_2$ ($ml \cdot g^{-1} \cdot h^{-1}$)	Method of Stimulation	Method of O_2 Meas.	Duration (min)	Reference
			Gymnophiona				
Geotrypetes seraphini	1.93	20	0.159[a]	Shock	Mano.	2	Bennett and Wake 1974
			Caudata				
Ambystoma gracile	22.47	5	0.054[b]	Shock	Mano.	2	Feder 1977; Feder 1978a
		15	0.090[b]				
		25	0.126[b]				
Ambystoma jeffersonianum	5.20	5	0.050[b]	Shock	Mano.	2	Feder 1977; Feder 1978a
		15	0.078[b]				
		25	0.208[b]				
Ambystoma laterale	4.4	21	0.414	Tread	E-c	20	Full et al. 1988
Ambystoma macrodactylum	2.17	5	0.067[b]	Shock	Mano.	2	Feder 1977; Feder 1978a
		15	0.135[b]				
		25	0.281[b]				
Ambystoma tigrinum	37.5	15	0.074[c]	Shock	Mano.	30	Hutchison, Turney, and Gratz 1977
		25	0.085[c]				
	N.A.	15	0.230[d]	Mot. rot.	E-c	3	Mitton, Carey, and Kocher 1986
			0.400[e]				
	34.2	21	0.410	Tread	E-c	20	Full et al., 1988
Amphiuma means	125	18	0.118	Man. prod. in water	Pol.	30	Withers and Hillman 1981
			0.142	Man. rot. in air			
Amphiuma tridactylum	493	25	0.063[b,f]	Shock in water	Mano., pol.	30	Preslar and Hutchison 1978
Aneides lugubris	5.4	23	0.70	Man. rot.	Para.	3	Hillman et al. 1979
Batrachoseps attenuatus	1.55	20	0.14[a,f,g]	Shock	Mano.	2	Bennett and Licht 1973
	0.78	5	0.100[b]	Shock	Mano.	2	Feder 1977; Feder 1978a
		15	0.175[b]				
		25	0.251[b]				
	0.93	25	0.204[b,h]	Shock	Mano.	2	Feder 1978b
	0.59	20	0.228	Stir in water	Pol.	2	Feder and Olsen 1978
	0.6	23	0.82	Man. rot.	Para.	3	Hillman et al. 1979
Bolitoglossa occidentalis	0.61	5	0.074[b]	Shock	Mano.	2	Feder 1977; Feder 1978a
		15	0.176[b]				
		25	0.222[b]				

TABLE 12.5 (continued)

	Mass (g)	Temp. (°C)	$\dot{V}_{O_2}$ (ml·g⁻¹·h⁻¹)	Method of Stimulation	Method of O_2 Meas.	Duration (min)	Reference
	0.61	25	0.174[b,h]	Shock	Mano.	2	Feder 1978b
Bolitoglossa rostrata	2.62	5	0.044[b]	Shock	Mano.	2	Feder 1977; Feder 1978a
		15	0.099[b]				
		25	0.170[b]				
Bolitoglossa subpalmata	1.71	13	0.240	Mot. rot.	E-c	15	Feder 1987b
Desmognathus ochrophaeus	2	21	0.289[i]	Prod	E-c	15	Feder 1986
	1.56	21	0.300	Tread	E-c	20	Full et al. 1988
Desmognathus quadramaculatus	17.82	5	0.033[b]	Shock	Mano.	5	Feder 1977; Feder 1978a
		15	0.076[b]				
		25	0.076[b]				
	28.0	21	0.077	Tread	E-c	20	Full et al. 1988
Ensatina eschscholtzi	3.54	5	0.053[b]	Shock	Mano.	2	Feder 1977; Feder 1978a
		15	0.111[b]				
		25	0.194[b]				
	2.1	23	0.37	Man. rot.	Para.	3	Hillman et al. 1979
Eurycea longicauda	1.24	15	0.228[b]	Shock	Mano.	2	Feder 1977; Feder 1978a
		25	0.271[b]				
Gyrinophilus porphyriticus	7.00	15	0.102[b]	Shock	Mano.	2	Feder 1977; Feder 1978a
		25	0.131[b]				
Hydromantes platycephalus	2.40	5	0.070[b]	Shock	Mano.	2	Feder 1977; Feder 1978a
		15	0.161[b]				
		25	0.240[b]				
Necturus maculosus	101.9	15	0.031[f,j]	Shock in water	Mano., pol.	30	Miller and Hutchison 1979
Notophthalmus viridescens	0.97	5	0.066[b]	Shock	Mano.	2	Feder 1977; Feder 1978a
		15	0.134[b]				
		25	0.171[b]				
	1.23	15	0.178	Man. rot.	E-c	5	Stefanski, Gatten, and Pough 1989
Plethodon glutinosus	5.12	15	0.124[b]	Shock	Mano.	2	Feder 1977; Feder 1978a
	3.83	25	0.208[b]				
	3.6	22	0.179[k]	Man. rot.	E-c	3	Withers 1980
Plethodon jordani	1.7	22	0.240[k]	Man. rot.	E-c	3	Withers 1980
	4.1	27	0.46	Tread[l]	E-c	15	Full 1986
	1.83	15	0.147	Man. prod.[m]	E-c	5	Stefanski, Gatten, and Pough 1989
		25	0.209	Man. prod.[n]			
Plethodon yonahlossee	4.7	22	0.161[k]	Man. rot.	E-c	3	Withers 1980
Pseudoeurycea belli	15.31	15	0.050[b]	Shock	Mano.	2	Feder 1977; Feder 1978a
		25	0.068[b]				
Pseudoeurycea gadovii	1.81	5	0.057[b]	Shock	Mano.	2	Feder 1977; Feder 1978a
		15	0.140[b]				
		25	0.184[b]				
Pseudoeurycea smithii	4.90	5	0.034[b]	Shock	Mano.	2	Feder 1977; Feder 1978a
		15	0.093[b]				
		25	0.134[b]				
	4.20	25	0.234[b,h]	Shock	Mano.	2	Feder 1978b
Pseudoeurycea unguidentis	2.92	5	0.051[b]	Shock	Mano.	2	Feder 1977; Feder 1978a
		15	0.118[b]				
		25	0.155[b]				

TABLE 12.5 (*continued*)

	Mass (g)	Temp. (°C)	$\dot{V}O_2$ (ml·g⁻¹·h⁻¹)	Method of Stimulation	Method of O_2 Meas.	Duration (min)	Reference
Pseudotriton ruber	11.26	15	0.091[b]	Shock	Mano.	2	Feder 1977; Feder 1978a
		25	0.116[b]				
Salamandra salamandra	7.78	15	0.135[b]	Shock	Mano.	2	Feder 1978a
Taricha torosa	10.14	5	0.029[b]	Shock	Mano.	2	Feder 1977; Feder 1978a
		15	0.083[b]				
		25	0.133[b]				
	10.67	25	0.118[b,o]	Shock	Mano.	2	Feder 1978b
	11.23	10	0.067[p]	Mot. rot.	Para.	20	Harlow 1978
		15	0.132[p]				
		20	0.203[p]				
		25	0.287[p]				
	9.87	10	0.066[q]				
		15	0.093[q]				
		20	0.120[q]				
		25	0.161[q]				

Notes: Mass shown in the table is the mean mass of animals (if given in the reference cited), midpoint of mass range (if only the mass range is given in the reference cited), or a reasonable, central value of mass from studies in which O_2 consumption as a function of body mass is described by an allometric equation in the reference cited. All measurements are for animals in air unless otherwise noted. For animals in water, value is total of O_2 consumption from air and water. Method of stimulation: Man. prod. = manual prodding; man. rot. = manual rotation of chamber; mot. rot. = motorized rotation of chamber at constant or variable rate; prod = stimulation by sliding lead weight; shock = electrical stimuli via electrodes; stir = stimulation of animal by magnetic stirring bar in water; tread = treadmill. Method of O_2 consumption measurement: e-c = electrochemical (i.e., Ametek Applied Electrochemistry Oxygen Analyzer); mano. = manometry; para. = paramagnetic; pol. = polarographic. N.A. = data not available.

[a] O_2 consumption during exercise was too low to measure. Value shown is for 2 min of exercise plus first 5 min of recovery.

[b] No increase in O_2 consumption was noted during exercise. Value shown is maximal value recorded during recovery following exercise.

[c] Value shown is O_2 consumption during exercise; however, maximal O_2 consumption occurred during the recovery period.

[d] Animals heterozygous at one of eight loci.

[e] Animals heterozygous at five of eight loci.

[f] Value shown is estimated from data in figure.

[g] Maximal O_2 consumption occurred during recovery period and is higher than value shown here.

[h] Data for animals acclimated to 22°C. Value is in ml O_2·g⁻⁰·⁶³¹·h⁻¹.

[i] Data for animals acclimated to 21°C.

[j] Data for animals acclimated to 15°C and measured at 0700.

[k] Value derived from equation relating O_2 consumption to body mass.

[l] Animals moving at 0.16 km·h⁻¹.

[m] Animals moving at 0.036 km·h⁻¹.

[n] Animals moving at 0.054 km·h⁻¹.

[o] Data for animals acclimated to 22°C. Value is in ml O_2·g⁻⁰·⁸¹⁶·h⁻¹.

[p] Data for animals in aquatic phase.

[q] Data for animals in terrestrial phase.

using shocking and manometry pertains to only fourteen species of salamanders at 10° to 27°C; however, we analyzed only the data collected at 20° to 23°C (table 12.6, fig. 12.20) to determine the effect of body mass, the presence of lungs, and the duration of exercise on $\dot{V}O_{2ex}$.

We used analysis of covariance and linear regression, with log-transformed values for O_2 consumption and body mass, to examine the data, both here and in the following section on anurans. O_2 consumption during exercise in salamanders is influenced by body mass ($F_{[1,8]} = 18.93$, $p = .0024$). When the effect of body mass is removed by the analysis of covariance, neither the presence or absence of lungs ($F_{[1,8]} = 0.96$, $p = .36$) nor the duration of exercise ($F_{[1,8]} = 0.69$, $p = .43$) influence $\dot{V}O_{2ex}$. The former result is consistent with that noted above for salamanders during steady-state exercise in which lunglessness does not appear to influence $\dot{V}O_2$ kinetics. The latter result is surprising because these animals were presumably engaged in exertion comparable to that seen at

nonsustainable speeds on treadmills. At such a level of effort, fatigue and exhaustion should set in after a few minutes, with a decline in speed and $\dot{V}O_{2ex}$. The most likely explanation is that the level of effort of experimental animals in many of the studies used in the analysis was not carefully controlled and was not consistent from study to study. In some cases, animals exhausted after only 3 min, whereas in others they continued exercise for 20 min. In the future, investigators should devote attention to the relation between intensity of effort above MAS, $\dot{V}O_{2ex}$, and endurance.

The equation relating O_2 uptake (ml · h⁻¹) to body mass (g) in salamanders (0.6 to 34 g) at 20° to 23°C is

(5) $$\dot{V}O_{2ex} = 0.41M^{0.72},$$

$r^2 = 0.66$, $N = 12$, 95% CI for $b = 0.34$ to 1.10. The slope for this relationship is indistinguishable from that for salamanders at rest at 20° or 25°C (table 12.2).

Withers (1980) measured the rate of O_2 consumption of

TABLE 12.6   Oxygen Consumption of Salamanders during Nonsustainable Exercise in Air at 20°–23°C

	Lungs	Mass (g)	Temp. (°C)	$\dot{V}_{O_{2ex}}$ (ml·h⁻¹)	Duration (min)	Reference
Ambystoma laterale	+	4.4	21	1.82	20	Full et al. 1988
Ambystoma tigrinum	+	34.2	21	14.02	20	Full et al. 1988
Aneides lugubris	−	5.4	23	3.78	3	Hillman et al. 1979
Batrachoseps attenuatus	−	0.6	23	0.49	3	Hillman et al. 1979
Desmognathus ochrophaeus	−	1.56	21	0.47	20	Full et al. 1988
		2	21	0.58	15	Feder 1986
Desmognathus quadramaculatus	−	28.0	21	2.16	20	Full et al. 1988
Ensatina eschscholtzi	−	2.1	23	0.78	3	Hillman et al. 1979
Plethodon glutinosus	−	3.6	22	0.65	3	Withers 1980
Plethodon jordani	−	1.7	22	0.41	3	Withers 1980
Plethodon yonahlossee	−	4.7	22	0.76	3	Withers 1980
Taricha torosa	+	9.87	20	1.18	20	Harlow 1978

Notes: Data from studies in which animals were stimulated to exercise by electric shocks and in which O_2 consumption was measured by manometry are excluded. Data are shown in figure 12.20.

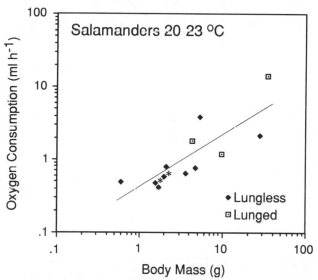

Fig. 12.20   The effect of body mass on the rate of consumption of O_2 by salamanders ($N = 11$ species) exercising at 20° to 23°C. The regression equation is $\dot{V}_{O_{2ex}} = 0.41M^{0.72}$. Data points indicated by *asterisks* are for the same species. Data from table 12.6.

exercising plethodontid salamanders, *Plethodon jordani* (mean mass = 1.7 g), *P. glutinosus* (3.6 g), and *P. yonahlossee* (4.7 g), at 22°C. The relationship between O_2 uptake and body mass is similar in all three species, and the overall interspecific exponent relating O_2 consumption to mass is 0.61, which falls within the 95% confidence interval for the exponent found above for all eleven species. Withers and Hillman (1981) analyzed the relationship between O_2 uptake during exercise and body mass in nine species of salamanders, including the three species of plethodontids mentioned above, and found the interspecific regression equation to be

$$(6) \qquad \dot{V}_{O_{2ex}} = 0.43M^{0.71},$$

$r^2 = 0.83$, $N = 9$. The exponent and intercept are indistinguishable from those reported above in equation (5).

Data are insufficient to permit generalization about the effect of temperature on O_2 consumption of exercising sala-

manders. Stefanski, Gatten, and Pough (1989) found a Q_{10} of 1.4 for $\dot{V}_{O_{2ex}}$ for *Plethodon jordani* between 15° and 25°C. Harlow (1978) determined Q_{10} values for O_2 uptake during activity by *Taricha torosa* (Salamandridae) in both the terrestrial and aquatic phases between 10° and 25°C; specimens in the terrestrial phase have a Q_{10} that varies less (1.67 to 1.98) than that of specimens in the aquatic phase (2.00 to 3.88). In the latter case, Q_{10} declines as temperature increases from 10° to 25°C.

Aerobic metabolic scope for activity is the difference between the maximal rate of O_2 uptake during exercise and the standard or resting metabolic rate, and indicates the amount of energy provided by aerobic pathways for muscular activity. Table 12.7 lists values for aerobic scope for salamanders from studies in which O_2 consumption during both rest and exercise were measured. When the data for O_2 consumption (in ml · h⁻¹) and body mass (1.5 to 34 g) at only 20° to 22°C are analyzed, the following equation results:

$$(7) \qquad \text{aerobic scope} = 0.23M^{0.75},$$

$r^2 = 0.58$, $N = 9$, 95% CI for $b = 0.18$ to 1.31.

Aerobic scope rises with temperature in *Plethodon jordani* (Q_{10} from 15° to 25°C of 1.2; Stefanski, Gatten, and Pough 1989) and in *Taricha torosa* (Q_{10} of 1.4 to 3.3, depending on the temperature range and whether animals are in the terrestrial or aquatic phase; Harlow 1978).

The ratio of $\dot{V}_{O_{2ex}}$ to $\dot{V}_{O_{2rest}}$, which indicates the factor by which O_2 consumption increases with exercise, ranges from 1.6 to 14.5 for salamanders at 20° to 22°C (table 12.7) and is not dependent on body mass ($F_{[1,6]} = 0.10$, $p = .76$) or the presence or absence of lungs ($F_{[1,6]} = 0.03$, $p = .85$). The mean value for animals at 20° to 22°C is 5.0.

ANURANS   Published data on the rate of consumption of O_2 during non-steady-state exercise are available for forty-two species of anurans (table 12.8). The data for anurans studied at 20°C without the use of shocking to induce activity or the use of manometry to measure O_2 uptake are shown in table 12.9. In the statistical analysis of the effects of body mass and duration of activity on the rate of O_2 consumption, we omitted some of the data in table 12.9 to prevent any one

TABLE 12.7 Aerobic Metabolic Scope of Salamanders

	Mass (g)	Temp. (°C)	Aerobic Scope (ml $O_2 \cdot g^{-1} \cdot h^{-1}$)	$\dot{V}O_{2ex}/\dot{V}O_{2rest}$	Reference
Ambystoma laterale	4.4	21	0.313	4.1	Full et al. 1988
Ambystoma tigrinum	N.A.	15	0.210[a]	11.5	Mitton, Carey, and Kocher 1986
			0.381[b]	21.1	
	34.2	21	0.350	6.8	Full et al. 1988
Amphiuma means	125	18	0.103[c]	3.6	Withers and Hillman 1981
Bolitoglossa subpalmata	1.67[d]	13	0.216	10.0	Feder 1987b
Desmognathus ochrophaeus	2	21[e]	0.269	14.5	Feder 1986
	1.56	21	0.215	3.5	Full et al. 1988
Desmognathus quadramaculatus	28.0	21	0.029	1.6	Full et al. 1988
Notophthalmus viridescens	1.23	15	0.117	2.9	Stefanski, Gatten, and Pough 1989
Plethodon glutinosus	3.6	22	0.123	3.2	Withers 1980
Plethodon jordani	1.7	22	0.174	3.6	Withers 1980
	1.83	15	0.120	5.3	Stefanski, Gatten, and Pough 1989
		25	0.141	3.1	
	4.1	27	0.320	3.3	Full 1986
Plethodon yonahlossee	4.7	22	0.108	3.0	Withers 1980
Taricha torosa	11.23[f]	10	0.051	4.2	Harlow 1978
		15	0.078	2.4	
		20	0.142	3.3	
		25	0.168	2.4	
	9.87[g]	10	0.057	7.3	
		15	0.067	3.6	
		20	0.093	4.4	
		25	0.118	3.7	

Notes: Data for studies in which animals were stimulated to exercise by electric shocks and in which O_2 consumption was measured by manometry are excluded. Only studies in which both $\dot{V}O_{2rest}$ and $\dot{V}O_{2ex}$ were measured are included. N.A. = data not available

[a] Animals heterozygous at one of eight loci.
[b] Animals heterozygous at five of eight loci.
[c] Manual rotation of chamber with animals in air.
[d] Mean mass of resting and exercising animals.
[e] Animals acclimated to 21°C only.
[f] Animals in aquatic phase; data not included in calculation of equation (7).
[g] Animals in terrestrial phase.

TABLE 12.8 Oxygen Consumption of Anurans during Nonsustainable Exercise

	Mass (g)	Temp. (°C)	$\dot{V}O_{2ex}$ (ml$\cdot$g$^{-1}\cdot$h^{-1})	Method of Stimulation	Method of O_2 Meas.	Duration (min)	Reference
Agalychnis callidryas	5.7	20	0.525	Mot. rot.	E-c	4	Taigen, Emerson, and Pough 1982
Bombina orientalis	2.6	20	0.473	Mot. rot.	E-c	4	Taigen, Emerson, and Pough 1982
Bufo alvarius	174.2	26	1.331[a]	Man. rot.	Para.	3	Hillman and Withers 1979
Bufo americanus	0.1[b]	20	0.685[a]	Mot. rot.	E-c	10	Taigen and Pough 1981; Pough and Kamel 1984
	30.0[c]	20	1.113[a]	Mot. rot.	E-c	10	Taigen and Pough 1981; Pough and Kamel 1984
	27.0[d]	20	1.039	Mot. rot.	E-c	4	Taigen and Beuchat 1984; Taigen, Emerson, and Pough 1982
	20.6[d]	20	1.182	Mot. rot	E-c	4	Wells and Taigen 1984
	40.4	25	0.844	Mot. rot.	E-c	4	Gatten 1987
	24	N.A.	0.56	Man. rot.	Pol.	10	Withers, Lea, Solberg, Baustian, and Hedrick 1988
Bufo boreas boreas	40.2[e]	5	0.153[f]	Mot. rot.	Para.	10	Carey 1979a
		10	0.288[f]				
		15	0.496[f]				

TABLE 12.8 (*continued*)

	Mass (g)	Temp. (°C)	$\dot{V}O_{2ex}$ (ml·g⁻¹·h⁻¹)	Method of Stimulation	Method of O₂ Meas.	Duration (min)	Reference
		20	0.776[f]				
		25	1.109[f]				
		30	1.445[f]				
	47.3[g]	5	0.130[f]	Mot. rot.	Para.	10	Carey 1979b
		10	0.246[f]				
		15	0.422[f]				
		20	0.661[f]				
		25	0.944[f]				
		30	1.230[f]				
Bufo boreas halophilus	57.8[g]	5	0.120[f]	Mot. rot.	Para.	10	Carey 1979b
		10	0.251[f]				
		15	0.465[f]				
		20	0.759[f]				
		25	1.090[f]				
		30	1.380[f]				
Bufo boreas	24.9[h]	26	1.339[a]	Man. rot.	Para.	3	Hillman and Withers 1979
Bufo calamita	8.7	20	0.779	Mot. rot.	E-c	4	Taigen, Emerson, and Pough 1982
Bufo cognatus	39.6	10	0.468	Mot. rot.	Para.	20	Seymour 1973c
		20	1.17				
		30	1.53				
	27.1	25	1.91	Man. rot.	Para.	3–5	Hillman 1976
	42.8	26	1.623[a]	Man. rot.	Para.	3	Hillman and Withers 1979
	28	20–23	1.51	Man. rot.	Pol.	3	Withers and Hillman 1983
Bufo marinus	359	15	0.54	Mot. rot.	E-c	3	Miller and Hutchison 1980
			0.66	Shock			
	266	25	1.43	Mot. rot.			
			1.45	Shock			
	223	20	0.70	Man. rot.	Pol.	3	Hillman 1987
	252	22	0.49	Man. rot.	Pol.	3	Withers, Hillman, Simmons, and Zygmunt 1988
Bufo retiformis	10.4	26	1.887[a]	Man. rot.	Para.	3	Hillman and Withers 1979
Bufo woodhousii	71.0[d]	25	1.21	Man. rot.	E-c	3	Sullivan and Walsberg 1985; G. E. Walsberg pers. comm.
			1.09			15	
	71	20	1.13	Mot. rot.	E-c	4	Walsberg 1986
			1.41	Man. rot.			
	20	22.0–23.5	1.090[a]	Mot. rot.	E-c	5	Walton 1988
	25.8	21	1.17	Tread	E-c	30	Walton and Anderson 1988
	0.017[i]	25	5.648[a]	Stir in water	Pol.	N.A.	Feder 1983a
Colostethus inguinalis	1.52	20	0.744[j]	Mot. rot.	E-c	4	Taigen and Pough 1983
		25	0.917[j]				
Colostethus nubicola	0.25	20	0.573[j]	Mot. rot.	E-c	4	Taigen and Pough 1983
		25	0.654[j]				
Dendrobates auratus	1.95	20	0.909[j]	Mot. rot.	E-c	4	Taigen and Pough 1983
	1.50	25	1.357[j]				
Discoglossus pictus	30.7	20	0.266	Mot. rot.	E-c	4	Taigen, Emerson, and Pough 1982
Eleutherodactylus coqui	4.1	20	0.291[j]	Mot. rot.	E-c	4	Taigen, Emerson, and Pough 1982; Taigen and Pough 1983
	4.94	20	0.279[k]	Mot. rot.	E-c	4	Pough et al. 1983
Gastrophryne carolinensis	1.9	20	0.814	Mot. rot.	E-c	4	Taigen, Emerson, and Pough 1982
Hyla arenicolor	3.4	20	0.835	Mot. rot.	E-c	4	Taigen, Emerson, and Pough 1982

TABLE 12.8 (*continued*)

	Mass (g)	Temp. (°C)	$\dot{V}O_{2ex}$ (ml·g⁻¹·h⁻¹)	Method of Stimulation	Method of O_2 Meas.	Duration (min)	Reference
Hyla cadaverina	3.1	23	1.25	Man. rot.	Para.	3	Hillman et al. 1979
	2.9		1.06	Shock 1 ms, 1 Hz			
	2.6		0.44	Shock 10 ms, 2 Hz			
Hyla chrysoscelis	5.47	20	0.984	Mot. rot.	E-c	4	Kamel, Marsden, and Pough 1985
Hyla cinerea	5.1	27	1.020[l]	Man. rot.	E-c	18.2	Prestwich, Brugger, and Topping 1989
Hyla crucifer	1.3[d]	20	1.043	Mot. rot.	E-c	4	Taigen and Beuchat 1984; Taigen, Emerson, and Pough 1982
	1.22[d]	19	1.10	Mot. rot.	E-c	4	Taigen, Wells, and Marsh 1985
	1.05[m]		0.91				
Hyla gratiosa	13.8	29	1.250[l]	Man. rot.	E-c	19.5	Prestwich, Brugger, and Topping 1989
Hyla regilla	2.76	20	0.27[n]	Shock	Mano.	2	Bennett and Licht 1973
	3.6	23	1.16	Man. rot.	Para.	3	Hillman et al. 1979
			0.88	Shock			
Hyla squirella	2.2	28	1.790[l]	Man. rot.	E-c	19.7	Prestwich, Brugger, and Topping 1989
Hyla versicolor	6.1	20	1.020	Mot. rot.	E-c	4	Kamel, Marsden, and Pough 1985
	8.6[d]	19.3	1.085	Mot. rot.	E-c	4	Taigen and Wells 1985
Hyperolius viridiflavus	0.9	20	0.737	Mot. rot.	E-c	4	Taigen, Emerson, and Pough 1982
Kaloula pulchra	30.7	20	0.696	Mot. rot.	E-c	4	Taigen, Emerson, and Pough 1982
Kassina senegalensis	3.0	20	0.827	Mot. rot.	E-c	4	Taigen, Emerson, and Pough 1982
Kassina weali	6.3	20	0.654	Mot. rot.	E-c	4	Taigen, Emerson, and Pough 1982
Odontophrynus americanus	15.2	20	0.578	Mot. rot.	E-c	4	Taigen, Emerson, and Pough 1982
Osteopilus septentrionalis	5.0	20	0.652	Mot. rot.	E-c	4	Taigen, Emerson, and Pough 1982
Physalaemus pustulosus	1.84[d]	25	1.82	Man. rot.	E-c	2.9	Ryan, Bartholomew, and Rand 1983
	1.51[d]		1.16			34.9	
Pternohyla fodiens	15.1	20	0.397	Mot. rot.	E-c	4	Taigen, Emerson, and Pough 1982
Pyxicephalus adspersus	400	20	0.860	Man. rot.	Pol.	5	Loveridge and Withers 1981
Rana catesbeiana	43.6	10	0.044	Mot. rot.	Para.	20	Seymour 1973c
		20	0.159				
		30	0.256				
	26	20	0.67	Mot. rot.	E-c	4	Walsberg 1986
			0.82	Man. rot.			
	15.5	18	0.28	Man. rot.	Pol.	3	Walsberg, Lea, and Hillman 1986
	403	20	0.22	Man. rot.	Pol.	3	Hillman 1987
Rana clamitans	4[b]	20	0.496[a]	Mot. rot.	E-c	4	Pough and Kamel 1984
	50[c]		0.337[a]				
Rana palustris	2[b]	20	0.600[a]	Mot. rot.	E-c	4	Pough and Kamel 1984
	20[c]		0.529[a]				
Rana pipiens	38.4	10	0.147	Mot. rot.	Para.	20	Seymour 1973c
		20	0.369				
		30	0.492				
	32.5	15	0.062[o,p]	Shock	Mano.	30	Turney and Hutchison 1974
		25	0.117[o,p]				
	50.2	25	0.54	Man. rot.	Para.	3–5	Hillman 1976
	34.8[e]	5	0.061[f]	Mot. rot.	Para.	5	Carey 1979a

TABLE 12.8 (*continued*)

	Mass (g)	Temp. (°C)	$\dot{V}O_{2ex}$ (ml·g⁻¹·h⁻¹)	Method of Stimulation	Method of O_2 Meas.	Duration (min)	Reference
		10	0.141[f]				
		15	0.284[f]				
		20	0.490[f]				
		25	0.729[f]				
		30	0.933[f]				
	42.5[h]	26	0.845[a]	Man. rot.	Para.	3	Hillman and Withers 1979
	N.A.	23	0.95[q]	Man. rot.	Para.	2–3	Hillman et al. 1979
			0.7			30	
	25.1	19	0.7	Man. rot.	Pol.	3	Hillman 1980a
	28	20–23	0.59	Man. rot.	Pol.	3	Withers and Hillman 1983
	18.5	20	0.63	Mot. rot.	E-c	4	Walsberg 1986
			0.80	Man. rot.			
	42	25	0.157	Man. prod. in water	Pol.	30–90	Pinder and Burggren 1986
	32.0	25	0.563	Mot. rot.	E-c	4	Gatten 1987
Rana sylvatica	12.7[d]	20	0.745	Mot. rot.	E-c	4	Taigen and Beuchat 1984; Taigen, Emerson, and Pough 1982
	0.5[b]	20	0.548[a]	Mot. rot.	E-c	4	Pough and Kamel 1984
	10[c]		0.541[a]				
Scaphiopus couchii	21.4	25	1.91	Man. rot.	Para.	3–5	Hillman 1976
Scaphiopus hammondii	10.9	7.5	0.286	Mot. rot.	Para.	20	Seymour 1973c
		15	0.396				
		20	0.815				
		25	0.854				
		32.5	1.41				
Xenopus laevis	36.4	25	1.33	Man. rot.	Para.	3–5	Hillman 1976
	23.9	25	1.17[q]	Man. rot.	Para.	5	Hillman 1978a
	27.7	15	0.047[o]	Shock in water	Mano., pol.	30	Hutchison and Miller 1979a
		25	0.118[o]				
	35.6[h]	26	1.340[a]	Man. rot.	Para.	3	Hillman and Withers 1979
	22.1	18	0.642	Man. prod. in water	Pol.	30	Hillman and Withers 1981
			0.722	Man. rot. in air		3	
			0.719			30	

Notes: Mass shown in the table is the mean mass of animals (if given in the reference cited), midpoint of mass range (if only the mass range is given in the reference cited), or a reasonable, central value of mass from studies in which O_2 consumption as a function of body mass is described by an allometric equation in the reference cited. All measurements are for animals in air unless otherwise noted. For animals in water, value is total of O_2 consumption from air and water. Method of stimulation: man. prod. = manual prodding; man. rot. = manual rotation of chamber; mot. rot. = motorized rotation of chamber at constant or variable rate; shock = electrical stimuli via electrodes; stir = stimulation of animal by magnetic stirring bar in water; tread = treadmill. Method of O_2 consumption measurement: e-c = electrochemical (i.e., Ametek Applied Electrochemistry Oxygen Analyzer); mano. = manometry; para. = paramagnetic; pol. = polarographic. N.A. = data not available.

[a] Value derived from equation relating O_2 consumption to body mass.

[b] Predispersal animals.

[c] Adult animals.

[d] Males only.

[e] Animals maintained under field conditions.

[f] Value derived from equation relating O_2 consumption to body temperature.

[g] Animals acclimated to 20°C.

[h] Mean mass of animals studied at rest and during exercise.

[i] Dry mass of larvae, estimated from data in figure.

[j] Data for animals measured at 1300–1500 only.

[k] Animals fully hydrated.

[l] Data not included in any statistical analyses.

[m] Nongravid females.

[n] O_2 consumption during exercise was too low to measure. Value shown here is for 2 min of exercise plus first 5 min of recovery. Maximal O_2 consumption occurred later during the recovery period. Value shown here is estimated from data in figure.

[o] Maximal O_2 consumption occurred during recovery following exercise.

[p] Data for animals measured at 1800 only.

[q] Value estimated from data in figure.

TABLE 12.9   Oxygen Consumption of Anurans during Nonsustainable Exercise in Air at 20°C

	Mass (g)	$\dot{V}_{O_{2\,ex}}$ (ml·h^{-1})	Duration (min)	Reference
Agalychnis callidryas	5.7	2.99	4	Taigen, Emerson, and Pough 1982
Bombina orientalis	2.6	1.23	4	Taigen, Emerson, and Pough 1982
Bufo americanus	30.0	33.39[a]	10	Taigen and Pough 1981; Pough and Kamel 1984
	27.0[b]	28.05	4	Taigen and Beuchat 1984; Taigen, Emerson, and Pough 1982
	20.6[b]	24.35[a]	4	Wells and Taigen 1984
Bufo boreas boreas	40.2[c]	31.20[a]	10	Carey 1979a
	47.3[d]	31.27	10	Carey 1979b
Bufo boreas halophilus	57.8[d]	43.87[a]	10	Carey 1979b
Bufo calamita	8.7	6.78	4	Taigen, Emerson, and Pough 1982
Bufo cognatus	39.6	46.33	20	Seymour 1973c
Bufo marinus	223	156.10	3	Hillman 1987
Bufo woodhousii	71	100.11[e]	4	Walsberg 1986
Colostethus inguinalis	1.52	1.13[f]	4	Taigen and Pough 1983
Colostethus nubicola	.25	0.14[f]	4	Taigen and Pough 1983
Dendrobates auratus	1.95	1.77[f]	4	Taigen and Pough 1983
Discoglossus pictus	30.7	8.17	4	Taigen, Emerson, and Pough 1982
Eleutherodactylus coqui	4.1	1.19[f]	4	Taigen, Emerson, and Pough 1982; Taigen and Pough 1983
	4.94	1.38[a,g]	4	Pough et al. 1983
Gastrophryne carolinensis	1.9	1.55	4	Taigen, Emerson, and Pough 1982
Hyla arenicolor	3.4	2.84	4	Taigen, Emerson, and Pough 1982
Hyla chrysoscelis	5.47	5.38	4	Kamel, Marsden, and Pough 1985
Hyla crucifer	1.3[b]	1.36	4	Taigen and Beuchat 1984; Taigen, Emerson, and Pough 1982
Hyla versicolor	6.1	6.22	4	Kamel, Marsden, and Pough 1985
Hyperolius viridiflavus	0.9	0.66	4	Taigen, Emerson, and Pough 1982
Kaloula pulchra	30.7	21.37	4	Taigen, Emerson, and Pough 1982
Kassina senegalensis	3.0	2.48	4	Taigen, Emerson, and Pough 1982
Kassina weali	6.3	4.12	4	Taigen, Emerson, and Pough 1982
Odontophrynus americanus	15.2	8.79	4	Taigen, Emerson, and Pough 1982
Osteopilus septentrionalis	5.0	3.26	4	Taigen, Emerson, and Pough 1982
Pternohyla fodiens	15.1	5.99	4	Taigen, Emerson, and Pough 1982
Pyxicephalus adspersus	400	344.00	5	Loveridge and Withers 1981
Rana catesbeiana	43.6	6.93	20	Seymour 1973c
	26	31.32[a,e]	4	Walsberg 1986
	403	88.66[a]	3	Hillman 1987
Rana clamitans	50	16.85	4	Pough and Kamel 1984
Rana palustris	20	10.58	4	Pough and Kamel 1984
Rana pipiens	38.4	14.17[a]	20	Seymour 1973c
	34.8[c]	17.05	5	Carey 1979a
	18.5	14.80[a,e]	4	Walsberg 1986
Rana sylvatica	12.7[b]	9.46[a]	4	Taigen and Beuchat 1984; Taigen, Emerson, and Pough 1982
	10	5.41	4	Pough and Kamel 1984
Scaphiopus hammondii	10.9	8.88	20	Seymour 1973c

Notes: Data from studies in which animals were stimulated to exercise by electric shocks and in which O$_2$ consumption was measured by manometry are excluded. Data are shown in figure 12.21.

[a] Data not included in figure 12.21, in calculation of equation (8), or in other statistical analyses, so as to avoid having any one species represented more than once.

[b] Males only.

[c] Animals maintained under field conditions.

[d] Animals acclimated to 20°C.

[e] Manual rotation of metabolic chamber.

[f] Animals measured at 1300–1500 only.

[g] Animals fully hydrated.

species from being represented more than once. O$_2$ consumption during exercise by anurans at 20°C (fig. 12.21) is influenced by mean body mass ($F_{[1,29]} = 326.52$, $p < .0001$) but not by duration of activity ($F_{[1,29]} = 0.32$, $p = .57$). The interspecific equation relating O$_2$ consumption (ml · h^{-1}) to body mass (0.25 to 400 g) in anurans at 20°C is

$$(8) \qquad \dot{V}_{O_{2ex}} = 0.69M^{0.97},$$

$r^2 = 0.92$, $N = 32$, 95% CI for $b = 0.86$ to 1.08. The exponent found here does not differ significantly from that for anurans resting at 20°C ($b = 0.82$, table 12.2) because the 95% confidence limits for the two exponents overlap.

Similar data for anurans exercising at 25°C are shown in table 12.10 and figure 12.22. Analysis of covariance on the data indicates that O$_2$ uptake during exercise at 25°C is influenced by mean body mass ($F_{[1,13]} = 532.15$, $p < .0001$) but

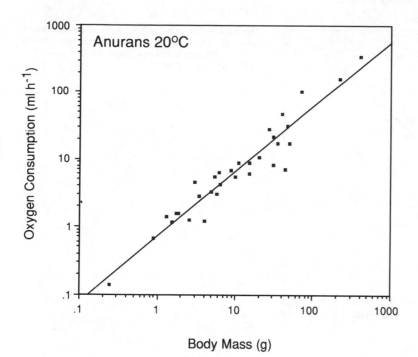

Fig. 12.21 The effect of body mass on the rate of consumption of O_2 by anurans ($N = 32$ species) exercising at 20°C. The regression equation is $\dot{V}_{O_2ex} = 0.69M^{0.97}$. Data from table 12.9.

TABLE 12.10 Oxygen Consumption of Anurans during Nonsustainable Exercise in Air at 25°C

	Mass (g)	$\dot{V}_{O_2ex}$ (ml·h⁻¹)	Duration (min)	Reference
Bufo alvarius	174.2	231.86	3	Hillman and Withers 1979
Bufo americanus	40.4	34.10	4	Gatten 1987
Bufo boreas boreas	40.2[a]	44.58[b]	10	Carey 1979a
	47.3[c]	44.65	10	Carey 1979b
Bufo boreas halophilus	57.8[c]	63.00[b]	10	Carey 1979b
Bufo boreas	24.9[d]	33.34	3	Hillman and Withers 1979
Bufo cognatus	27.1	51.76[b]	3–5	Hillman 1976
	42.8	69.46	3	Hillman and Withers 1979
Bufo marinus	266	380.38[e]	3	Miller and Hutchison 1980
Bufo retiformis	10.4	19.62	3	Hillman and Withers 1979
Bufo woodhousii	71.0[f]	85.91	3	Sullivan and Walsberg 1985; G. E. Walsberg pers. comm.
Colostethus inguinalis	1.52	1.39[g]	4	Taigen and Pough 1983
Colostethus nubicola	0.25	0.16[g]	4	Taigen and Pough 1983
Dendrobates auratus	1.50	2.04[g]	4	Taigen and Pough 1983
Physalaemus pustulosus	1.84[f]	3.35	2.9	Ryan, Bartholomew, and Rand 1983
Rana pipiens	50.2	27.11[b]	3–5	Hillman 1976
	34.8[a]	25.37	5	Carey 1979a
	42.5[d]	35.91[b]	3	Hillman and Withers 1979
	32.0	18.02[b]	4	Gatten 1987
Scaphiopus couchii	21.4	40.87	3–5	Hillman 1976
Scaphiopus hammondii	10.9	9.31	20	Seymour 1973c
Xenopus laevis	36.4	48.41[b]	3–5	Hillman 1976
	23.9	27.96[b]	5	Hillman 1978a
	35.6[d]	47.70	3	Hillman and Withers 1979

Notes: Data from studies in which animals were stimulated to exercise by electric shocks and in which O_2 consumption was measured by manometry are excluded. Data from Hillman and Withers (1979) were collected at 26°C. Data are shown in figure 12.22.

[a] Animals maintained under field conditions.
[b] Data not included in figure 12.22 or in calculation of equation (9), so as to avoid having any one species represented more than once.
[c] Animals acclimated to 20°C.
[d] Mean mass of animals studied during rest and during exercise.
[e] Motorized rotation of metabolic chamber.
[f] Males only.
[g] Data for animals measured at 1300–1500 only.

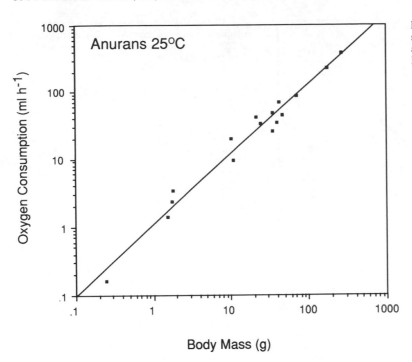

Fig. 12.22 The effect of body mass on the rate of consumption of O_2 by anurans ($N = 16$ species) exercising at 25°C. The regression equation is $\dot{V}O_{2ex} = 1.06M^{1.04}$. Data from table 12.10.

not by duration of effort ($F_{[1,13]} = 2.50$, $p = .14$, as for exercise at 20°C. The lack of an effect of duration of exercise on $\dot{V}O_{2ex}$ in anurans at both temperatures and in salamanders, as discussed above, may be due to the fact that intensity of effort was not carefully controlled in many studies and certainly varied among studies (see discussion above in section on salamanders). The equation for these data (ml · h⁻¹) for anurans ranging in mass from 0.25 to 266 g at 25°C is

$$(9) \qquad \dot{V}O_{2ex} = 1.06M^{1.04},$$

$r^2 = 0.97$, $N = 16$, 95% CI for $b = 0.94$ to 1.15. The intercepts for the equations at 20° and 25°C are different ($t_{[46]} = 5.75$, $p < .001$); however the slopes are statistically indistinguishable ($t_{[44]} = 0.97$, $p = .34$). The exponent in equation (9) is greater than that for anurans resting at 25°C ($b = 0.84$, table 12.2) because the 95% confidence limits for the slopes do not overlap. Thus, as anuran body size increases, $\dot{V}O_{2ex}$ rises faster than $\dot{V}O_{2rest}$ at 25°C. Data are insufficient to permit analysis of the effect of body mass on $\dot{V}O_{2ex}$ at other temperatures.

The slope found here for the interspecific relationship between $\dot{V}O_{2ex}$ and body mass for anurans at 20°C (0.97) does not differ from that found above for salamanders at 20° to 23°C ($b = 0.72$, eq. [5], $t_{[40]} = 1.76$, $p = .089$). However, the intercepts of these two equations do differ ($t_{[42]} = 3.23$, $p = .003$). Therefore, although body mass influences $\dot{V}O_{2ex}$ in the same way in salamanders and anurans, an anuran will have a higher $\dot{V}O_{2ex}$ than a salamander of similar size near 20°C. This finding, previously reported by Withers (1980) and Withers and Hillman (1981), indicates a major phylogenetic difference between these groups in their ability to use aerobic metabolism to support physical activity. This difference parallels that described above for resting metabolism. The comparison may be biased because the salamander sample analyzed here is heavily weighted with lungless animals (eight of eleven species). Respiratory surface area and other variables governing diffusion may limit $\dot{V}O_{2ex}$ in exclu-

sively skin-breathing salamanders, especially at large body size (Feder 1977, 1988; Full 1986; Full et al. 1988; Withers 1980). On the other hand, respiratory surface area is not the major factor limiting maximal O_2 uptake in skin- and lung-breathing anurans (Hillman 1982a; Hillman and Withers 1979; Taigen, Emerson, and Pough 1982; Withers and Hillman 1983) and may not be in all salamanders. Thus, the difference in $\dot{V}O_{2ex}$ between salamanders and anurans awaits a definitive explanation.

For eighteen species of reptiles (13 to 3,473 g) at 20°C, the allometric equation relating $\dot{V}O_{2ex}$ and body mass is ml O_2 · h⁻¹ $= 0.65$ mass$^{0.83}$ (table 3 in Bennett 1982). In comparison with salamanders at 20°C (eq. [5]), reptiles have a higher intercept but a similar exponent; thus, at any body mass, reptiles consume more O_2 during intense exercise than do salamanders. In contrast, reptiles have the same intercept as anurans but a lower exponent at 20°C (eq. [8]). As a consequence, as body size increases, the difference in aerobic metabolism during exercise between anurans and reptiles increases: at 20°C, a 25-g anuran consumes 1.7 times as much O_2 as a reptile; at 400 g, an anuran consumes 2.5 times as much. No published equation relates $\dot{V}O_{2ex}$ to mass in reptiles at 25°C, the only other temperature for which such an equation exists for anurans (eq. [9]). Given that reptiles are often active at body temperatures higher than those of active amphibians (Avery 1982; Brattstrom 1970a), reptiles are likely to have a higher $\dot{V}O_{2ex}$ than amphibians under field conditions. These gross generalizations are derived from interspecific allometric equations; as such, they should be accepted and applied with appropriate caution.

Several studies describe the intraspecific relationship between $\dot{V}O_{2ex}$ and body mass in anurans (table 12.11, fig. 12.23). The data were collected over a fairly narrow range of temperatures (20° to 26°C) with individual animals having a body mass of 0.5 to 1,030 g. The exponents (b) for intraspecific regression equations range from 0.68 to 1.02. These exponents can be compared with those for interspecific re-

TABLE 12.11   Intraspecific Variation in Oxygen Consumption as a Function of Body Mass in Anurans during Nonsustainable Exercise

	Temp. (°C)	Mass Range (g)	a	b	Reference
Bufo alvarius	26	133–234	2.23	0.90	Hillman and Withers 1979
Bufo americanus	20	0.5–40[a]	1.04	1.02	Taigen and Pough 1981
Bufo boreas	26	1–69	2.39	0.82	Hillman and Withers 1979
Bufo cognatus	26	14–89	4.15	0.75	Hillman and Withers 1979
Bufo retiformis	26	1–17	2.62	0.86	Hillman and Withers 1979
Bufo woodhousii	23	3–42	1.20	0.97	Walton 1988
Pyxicephalus adspersus	20	10–1,030	3.22	0.78	Loveridge and Withers 1981
Rana clamitans	20	7–60[a]	1.18	0.68	Pough and Kamel 1984
Rana palustris	20	3–20[a]	0.63	0.94	Pough and Kamel 1984
Rana pipiens	26	5–122	1.02	0.95	Hillman and Withers 1979
Rana sylvatica	20	2–15[a]	0.73	0.87	Pough and Kamel 1984
Xenopus laevis	26	6–105	1.44	0.98	Hillman and Withers 1979

Notes: The constants a and b given above pertain to the equation $\dot{V}_{O_2\,ex} = a\cdot mass^b$ where $\dot{V}_{O_2\,ex}$ is in ml·h^{-1} and mass is in grams. Regression lines for all species are shown in figure 12.23.

[a]Postdispersal animals only.

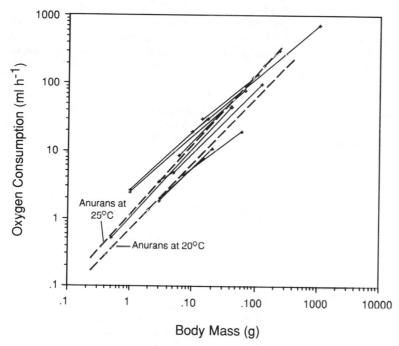

Fig. 12.23   The effect of body mass on the rate of consumption of O_2 by twelve species of anurans during exercise. Each *solid line* represents the intraspecific effect of mass at a given temperature for a species listed in table 12.11. The *dashed lines* represent the interspecific relationships shown in figs. 12.21 and 12.22.

gressions at 20° and 25°C (eqs. [8] and [9]). In four species of toads (genus *Bufo*) the intraspecific effect of body size on $\dot{V}_{O_2 ex}$ is less than in anurans in general (b for the four species falls below the 95% confidence interval for b for all anurans); in two other bufonid species, the intraspecific allometric coefficient is indistinguishable from that for all anurans. However, analyses of variance indicate that neither the intercepts nor the exponents of the twelve intraspecific regression equations vary significantly with temperature, mean mass, or genus ($p > .1$ in all analyses). Thus, no clear explanation exists for the variability in the effect of body mass on $\dot{V}_{O_2 ex}$ among species. Finally, larvae of *Bufo woodhousii* ranging from 0.005 to 0.035 g of dry mass have allometric coefficients (a and b) of 11.6 and 0.75, respectively, during induced exercise at 25°C (Feder 1983a); the large value for a is at least in part due to the use of dry mass rather than wet mass in Feder's analysis.

In early studies of aerobic support for exercise in amphibians, some species had a considerably higher aerobic capacity than others. For example, a bufonid had a much greater $\dot{V}_{O_2 ex}$

than two ranids or a hylid (Bennett and Licht 1973; Seymour 1973c). Recent data allow further analysis of variation in aerobic capacity among genera. Equation (8) reveals that $\dot{V}_{O_2 ex}$ (in ml · h^{-1}) of anurans at 20°C (the temperature at which data for the greatest number of species are available) varies with body mass with an exponent not significantly different from 1.0. Thus, expression of $\dot{V}_{O_2}$ as ml O_2 · g^{-1} · h^{-1} adequately corrects for differences in body mass among species. Mass-specific $\dot{V}_{O_2 ex}$ varies significantly among the eight families of anurans represented by more than one species in table 12.9 ($F_{[7,23]} = 2.86$, $p = .027$). Furthermore, toads of the genus *Bufo* and treefrogs of the genus *Hyla* (Hylidae) have an aerobic capacity that is more than twice that of frogs of the genus *Rana* (*Bufo*, $N = 6$, $\bar{x} = 0.960$ ml · g^{-1} · h^{-1}, SE $= 0.122$; *Hyla*, $N = 4$, $\bar{x} = 0.971$, SE $= 0.047$; *Rana*, $N = 5$, $\bar{x} = 0.411$, SE $= 0.073$). These conclusions contrast with those of a previous analysis on fewer species in which interspecific variation in aerobic capacity was attributed to locomotor mode and foraging style rather than phylogenetic position (Taigen, Emerson, and Pough 1982).

To a large extent, physiological ecologists and comparative physiologists have given insufficient attention to variation in physiological and behavioral traits among individuals of a species, and to the broader biological meaning of such differences (Bennett 1987). For example, in spite of the large number of studies reporting metabolic rates of anurans during exercise (table 12.8), only a handful consider intraspecific variation in $\dot{V}_{O_{2ex}}$. Wells and Taigen (1984) found that 90% of the variance in $\dot{V}_{O_{2ex}}$ in a group of *Bufo americanus* is due to differences among individuals, whereas only 10% of the variance can be attributed to repeated trials for the individual animals. Similar results were found by Sullivan and Walsberg (1985) and Walton (1988) for *Bufo woodhousii* and by Walsberg (1986) for *B. woodhousii*, *Rana catesbeiana*, and *R. pipiens*. The biological significance of such variation among individuals is unclear; contrary to expectation, toads with a high $\dot{V}_{O_{2ex}}$ do not have the best locomotor performance in the laboratory (Walton 1988) or in the field (Walton 1988; Wells and Taigen 1984). This absence of a correlation between physiological capacity and behavioral performance may in part be due to the fact that aerobic capacity is reached in the laboratory only when animals move at a rate ten times that of animals moving voluntarily in the field (Walton 1988; Wells and Taigen 1984); animals in nature may routinely use only a fraction of their aerobic capacity. Taigen and Pough (1985) reported a 14% difference in $\dot{V}_{O_{2ex}}$ between two populations of *Dendrobates pumilio* (Dendrobatidae); this difference in aerobic capacity is associated with interpopulational differences in color, degree of toxicity, habitat, and type, size, and number of prey items taken. The cause-and-effect relationships among these variables, however, is not clear. O_2 consumption during exercise can also vary between subspecies: *Bufo boreas halophilus* has a higher $\dot{V}_{O_{2ex}}$ than *B. b. boreas*, regardless of temperature or acclimation regime ($F_{[1,48]}$ = 12.71, $p < .0001$, reanalysis of data from Carey 1979b). Thus, some individuals of a given species of anuran may have a significantly higher aerobic capacity than others, but the advantage this might provide them during locomotion in their natural environment is not apparent (see also Wells and Taigen 1984 for lack of correlation between aerobic capacity and duration of calling and number of clasping attempts by male toads).

Temperature affects not only the resting metabolic rate of amphibians, as described above, but also the rate of O_2 consumption during strenuous exercise (table 12.12). In general, Q_{10} for $\dot{V}_{O_{2ex}}$ is above 3.0 at low temperatures (i.e., below 10°C) and falls to approximately 1.5 as temperatures approach 30°C. The relationships shown in figures 12.21 and 12.22 and described in equations (8) and (9) permit an assessment of the effect of body mass on Q_{10} between 20° and 25°C. As body size of anurans increases from 1 to 100 g, Q_{10} between 20° and 25°C rises from 2.4 to 4.5. Thus, aerobic capacity is more thermally dependent in large anurans than in small ones, at least over this relatively small but ecologically significant temperature range. The physiological basis for this difference deserves attention.

TABLE 12.12 Q_{10} for $\dot{V}_{O_{2ex}}$ and Aerobic Scope of Anurans

	Temp. Range (°C)	Q_{10} for $\dot{V}_{O_{2ex}}$	Q_{10} for Aerobic Scope	Reference
Bufo boreas[a]	5–10	3.5	3.6	Carey 1979a
	10–15	3.0	3.0	
	15–20	2.4	2.5	
	20–25	2.0	2.0	
	25–30	1.7	1.7	
Bufo cognatus	10–20	2.5	2.5	Seymour 1973c
	20–30	1.3	1.3	
Bufo marinus[b]	15–25	2.6	2.5	Miller and Hutchison 1980
Colostethus inguinalis	20–25	1.5	1.5	Taigen and Pough 1983
Colostethus nubicola	20–25	1.3	1.2	Taigen and Pough 1983
Dendrobates auratus	20–25	2.2	2.2	Taigen and Pough 1983
Rana catesbeiana	10–20	3.6	3.6	Seymour 1973c
	20–30	1.6	1.4	
Rana pipiens	10–20	2.5	2.6	Seymour 1973c
	20–30	1.3	1.3	
Rana pipiens[a]	5–10	5.3	5.7	Carey 1979a
	10–15	4.1	4.2	
	15–20	3.0	3.0	
	20–25	2.2	2.1	
	25–30	1.6	1.5	
Scaphiopus hammondii	7.5–15	1.5	2.0	Seymour 1973c
	15–20	4.2	4.6	
	20–25	1.1	1.1	
	25–32.5	2.0	1.9	
1-g anuran	20–25	2.4	1.7	Equations (8), (9), (10), and (11)
10-g anuran	20–25	3.3	2.2	
100-g anuran	20–25	4.5	2.8	

Note: Q_{10} values derived from information in tables 12.8 and 12.13.

[a] Animals maintained under field conditions.

[b] Motorized rotation of metabolic chamber.

In 1979, Bennett and Ruben proposed that thermoregulatory concerns alone are not sufficient to explain the evolution of endothermy. They hypothesized that selection may have favored a high aerobic capacity to support prolonged, high-intensity exercise and that as aerobic capacity increased, so did resting metabolism (and resting heat production). If so, species with a high $\dot{V}O_{2ex}$ should also have a high $\dot{V}O_{2rest}$. Taigen (1983) tested this hypothesis for seventeen species of anurans at 20°C and found a significant correlation between rank for $\dot{V}O_{2ex}$ and rank for $\dot{V}O_{2rest}$: the general tendency is for anurans with a high aerobic capacity also to have a high resting metabolic rate. The present data permit a more extensive test of this hypothesis for anurans at 20°C. The analysis includes data for $\dot{V}O_{2ex}$ and $\dot{V}O_{2rest}$ for the seventeen species used by Taigen as well as data from eleven other species from studies in which both $\dot{V}O_{2ex}$ and $\dot{V}O_{2rest}$ were reported. The twenty-eight species included are those listed in table 12.13 for which data are available at 20°C. Log-transformed values for $\dot{V}O_{2ex}$ and for $\dot{V}O_{2rest}$ (ml · h^{-1}) were regressed on log mass. The residuals from the two regressions were then used in a third regression. A positive correlation between the residuals for $\dot{V}O_{2ex}$ and the residuals for $\dot{V}O_{2rest}$ would indicate that species with a higher than average $\dot{V}O_{2ex}$ also have a higher than average $\dot{V}O_{2rest}$. This is indeed the case ($F_{[1,26]} = 14.26$, $p < .001$, $b = 0.74$, $r^2 = 0.35$). Thus, this more extensive analysis confirms Taigen's (1983) initial finding that for anurans at 20°C, species with a high aerobic capacity in general have a high resting metabolic rate as well. A similar relationship exists at the intraspecific level, at least in *Bufo woodhousii* (Walton 1988).

The data for $\dot{V}O_{2ex}$ of anurans can be used in conjunction with data for $\dot{V}O_{2rest}$ to calculate the aerobic metabolic scope for activity (table 12.13). Only one value for each species at 20° or 25°C was used, and aerobic scope was converted from units of ml · g^{-1} · h^{-1} to ml · h^{-1}. The values for aerobic scope at 20°C were then regressed on the values for body mass (0.25 to 400 g) to yield the following equation:

(10) $$\text{aerobic scope} = 0.62M^{0.97},$$

$r^2 = 0.90$, $N = 28$, 95% CI for $b = 0.84$ to 1.10. The corresponding equation for anurans from 0.25 to 266 g at 25°C is

(11) $$\text{aerobic scope} = 0.82M^{1.02},$$

$r^2 = 0.98$, $N = 10$, 95% CI for $b - 0.90$ to 1.14. The intercepts for these two equations for anurans differ significantly ($t_{[36]} = 2.97$, $p = .0067$), but their slopes are indistinguishable ($t_{[34]} = 0.55$, $p = .59$).

Aerobic scope can also be calculated from the general equations relating O_2 consumption to mass during rest (table 12.2) and exercise (eqs. [8] and [9]). Such a method is less precise than that used above because it does not require that each species be measured both at rest and during exercise. The equations for resting anurans at 20°C (table 12.2) and exercising anurans at 20°C (eq. [8]) predict that a 1-g anuran will have an aerobic scope of 0.59 ml O_2 · g^{-1} · h^{-1}, whereas equation (10) predicts a value of 0.62 ml · g^{-1} · h^{-1}. Similar use of the equations for anurans resting and exercising at 25°C (table 12.2 and eq. [9]) yields values of 0.89 and 0.82 ml · g^{-1} · h^{-1}, respectively.

The equation for aerobic scope as a function of body mass for anurans at 20°C (eq. [10]) can be compared with the corresponding equation for salamanders at 20° to 22°C (eq. [7]). The slopes of these equations do not differ ($t_{[33]} = 1.19$, $p = .025$), but their intercepts do ($t_{[35]} = 3.33$, $p = .0021$). For an anuran and a salamander of equal size near 20°C, the anuran will have a greater aerobic scope. This difference represents an ecologically significant divergence between salamanders and anurans in their ability to convert stored energy into muscular activity by aerobic pathways.

Values for the temperature sensitivity of aerobic scope for anurans have been summarized in table 12.12. Q_{10} values generally decline with increasing temperature and are very close to corresponding Q_{10} values for $\dot{V}O_{2ex}$ for the same animals. As body mass rises from 1 to 100 g, the thermal sensitivity of aerobic scope between 20° and 25°C increases from 1.7 to 2.8; thus a large anuran experiences a larger rise in aerobic scope with an increase in body temperature from 20° to 25°C than a small one does.

The ratio of $\dot{V}O_{2ex}$ to $\dot{V}O_{2rest}$ (the factorial aerobic scope) indicates the factor by which O_2 consumption rises with induced exercise. For twenty-nine species of anurans at 20°C, the mean value for this ratio is 12.0, with values for individual species ranging from 4.2 to 35.2 (table 12.13). In contrast, the mean value reported above for salamanders at 20° to 22°C is 5.0. Thus, anurans and salamanders differ greatly in factorial aerobic scope. The equations relating O_2 consumption to body mass in anurans at rest (table 12.2) and during exercise (eqs. [8] and [9]) can also be used to calculate this ratio. For anurans at 20°C, the factorial aerobic scope varies with mass: for a 1-g animal, the ratio is 6.7, whereas for a 100-g anuran, the value is 13.4. For anurans at 25°C, the values are 6.1 for a 1-g animal and 15.3 for a 100-g specimen. Thus, as body size increases, the factor by which O_2 consumption rises with exercise increases. This change with mass must necessarily be correlated with differences in O_2 transport and aspects of locomotor behavior. No clear pattern emerges for the change in $\dot{V}O_{2ex}/\dot{V}O_{2rest}$ as temperature changes within a species (table 12.13). Only two studies (Feder 1983a; Quinn and Burggren 1983) report the $\dot{V}O_2$ of exercising larval anurans. In these animals, $\dot{V}O_{2ex}$ is two to three times that of undisturbed individuals.

Anaerobic Support of Nonsustainable Locomotion

The increase in aerobic metabolism during locomotion by amphibians may or may not supply all of the ATP required by the muscles, depending on the intensity and duration of effort, among other factors. Use of muscle phosphagen stores and of glycolysis can be vital during some types of locomotion in some species. The first report of the use of glycolysis in amphibians during exercise was provided by Marcuse (1886), who demonstrated that frog skeletal muscle stimulated *in vitro* accumulates large amounts of lactate. The significance of glycolysis to intact amphibians during locomotion was not further elucidated until Bennett and Licht (1973) and Seymour (1973c) measured lactate accumulation in animals stimulated to jump. Since that time, many studies have clarified the relative importance of glycolysis, the use of phosphagens, and aerobic metabolism during short-

TABLE 12.13 Aerobic Metabolic Scope of Anurans

	Mass (g)	Temp. (°C)	Aerobic Scope (ml $O_2 \cdot g^{-1} \cdot h^{-1}$)	$\dot{V}O_{2ex}/\dot{V}O_{2rest}$	Reference
Agalychnis callidryas	5.7	20	0.464	8.6	Taigen, Emerson, and Pough 1982
Bombina orientalis	2.6	20	0.417	8.4	Taigen, Emerson, and Pough 1982
Bufo americanus	30.0	20	1.082	35.2	Pough and Kamel 1984; Taigen and Pough 1981
	27.0[a]	20	0.988	20.4	Taigen and Beuchat 1984; Taigen, Emerson, and Pough 1982
	40.4	25	0.778	13.0	Gatten 1987
Bufo boreas	40.2[b]	5	0.144	17.0	Carey 1979a
		10	0.275	20.9	
		15	0.474	23.5	
		20	0.744	24.0	
		25	1.060	22.4	
		30	1.370	19.0	
	24.9	26	1.239	13.4	Hillman and Withers 1979
Bufo calamita	8.7	20	0.721	13.4	Taigen, Emerson, and Pough 1982
Bufo cognatus	39.6	10	0.418	9.4	Seymour 1973c
		20	1.057	10.4	
		30	1.348	8.4	
Bufo marinus	359[c]	15	0.34	2.7	Miller and Hutchison 1980
	266[c]	25	0.85	2.5	
Bufo woodhousii	20	22.8	1.006	13.0	Walton 1988
	25.8	21	1.040	9.0	Walton and Anderson 1988
Bufo woodhousii larvae	0.017[d]	25	3.413	2.5	Feder 1983a
Colostethus inguinalis	1.52	20	0.614[e]	5.7	Taigen and Pough 1983
		25	0.758[e]	5.8	
Colostethus nubicola	0.25	20	0.438[e]	4.2	Taigen and Pough 1983
		25	0.472[e]	3.6	
Dendrobates auratus	1.95	20	0.830[e]	11.5	Taigen and Pough 1983
	1.50	25	1.242[e]	11.8	
Discoglossus pictus	30.7	20	0.229	7.2	Taigen, Emerson, and Pough 1982
Eleutherodactylus coqui	4.1	20	0.247[e]	6.6	Taigen, Emerson, and Pough 1982; Taigen and Pough 1983
	4.94	20	0.226[f]	5.3	Pough et al. 1983
Gastrophryne carolinensis	1.9	20	0.762	15.7	Taigen, Emerson, and Pough 1982
Hyla arenicolor	3.4	20	0.742	9.0	Taigen, Emerson, and Pough 1982
Hyla cinerea	5.1	27	0.885	7.6	Prestwich, Brugger, and Topping 1989
Hyla crucifer	1.3[a]	20	0.932	9.4	Taigen and Beuchat 1984; Taigen, Emerson, and Pough 1982
	1.22[a]	19	0.992	10.2	Taigen, Wells, and Marsh 1985
	1.05[g]		0.798	8.1	
Hyla chrysoscelis	5.47	20	0.855	7.6	Kamel, Marsden, and Pough 1985
Hyla gratiosa	13.9	29	1.155	13.2	Prestwich, Brugger, and Topping 1989
Hyla squirella	2.2	28	1.625	10.8	Prestwich, Brugger, and Topping 1989
Hyla versicolor	6.1	20	0.921	10.3	Kamel, Marsden, and Pough 1985
	8.6[a]	19.3	1.007	13.9	Taigen and Wells 1985
Hyperolius viridiflavus	0.9	20	0.643	7.8	Taigen, Emerson, and Pough 1982
Kaloula pulchra	30.7	20	0.670	26.8	Taigen, Emerson, and Pough 1982
Kassina senegalensis	3.0	20	0.750	10.7	Taigen, Emerson, and Pough 1982
Kassina weali	6.3	20	0.600	12.1	Taigen, Emerson, and Pough 1982
Odontophrynus americanus	15.2	20	0.541	15.6	Taigen, Emerson, and Pough 1982
Osteopilus septentrionalis	5.0	20	0.586	9.9	Taigen, Emerson, and Pough 1982
Physalaemus pustulosus	1.75[a,h]	25	1.500	5.7	Bucher, Ryan, and Bartholomew 1982; Ryan, Bartholomew, and Rand 1983
Pternohyla fodiens	15.1	20	0.365	12.4	Taigen, Emerson, and Pough 1982
Pyxicephalus adspersus	400	20	0.823	23.2	Loveridge and Withers 1981
Rana catesbeiana	43.6	10	0.034	4.4	Seymour 1973c
		20	0.121	4.2	
		30	0.169	2.9	

TABLE 12.13 (continued)

	Mass (g)	Temp. (°C)	Aerobic Scope (ml $O_2 \cdot g^{-1} \cdot h^{-1}$)	$\dot{V}O_{2ex}/\dot{V}O_{2rest}$	Reference
Rana muscosa	N.A.	4	N.A.	6.7[i]	Bradford 1983
Rana pipiens	38.4	10	0.105	3.5	Seymour 1973c
		20	0.273	3.8	
		30	0.342	3.3	
	34.8	5	0.053	7.6	Carey 1979a
		10	0.127	10.0	
		15	0.259	11.4	
		20	0.446	11.2	
		25	0.652	9.5	
		30	0.798	6.9	
	42.5	26	0.717	6.6	Hillman and Withers 1979
	32.0	25	0.435	4.4	Gatten 1987
Rana sylvatica	12.7[a]	20	0.660	8.8	Taigen and Beuchat 1984; Taigen, Emerson, and Pough 1982
Scaphiopus hammondii	10.9	7.5	0.202	3.4	Seymour 1973c
		15	0.336	6.6	
		20	0.720	8.6	
		25	0.764	9.5	
		32.5	1.244	8.5	
Xenopus laevis	23.9	25	1.00	6.9	Hillman 1978a
	35.6	26	1.195	9.2	Hillman and Withers 1979
	22.1	18	0.641[j]	8.9	Hillman and Withers 1981

Notes: Data from studies in which animals were stimulated to exercise by electric shocks and in which O_2 consumption was measured by manometry are excluded. Only studies in which both $\dot{V}O_{2rest}$ and $\dot{V}O_{2ex}$ were measured are included. N.A. = data not available.
[a] Males only.
[b] Animals maintained under field conditions.
[c] Motorized rotation of metabolic chamber.
[d] Dry mass; larvae tested in water.
[e] Data for animals measured at 1300–1500 only.
[f] Animals fully hydrated
[g] Nongravid females only.
[h] Mean mass of animals at rest (Bucher, Ryan, and Bartholomew 1982) and during 2.9 min of exercise (Ryan, Bartholomew, and Rand 1983).
[i] Value for frogs in water at sea level, extrapolated from value determined at high altitude.
[j] Animals exercised in air for 3 min.

term, intense locomotion by amphibians, as will now be discussed.

Phosphagens and Glycolysis

The cycling of cross bridges in exercising muscles requires ATP both for the release of the cross bridges from the thin filaments and for the "recocking" of the cross bridges prior to the next power stroke (Woledge, Curtin, and Homsher 1985). Although amphibian skeletal muscle does contain a store of ATP, the concentration of another phosphagen, phosphocreatine (PC), is approximately six times that of ATP (Mainwood, Worsley-Brown, and Paterson 1972). During the stimulation of isolated frog muscle to fatigue *in vitro*, the concentration of ATP does not change, but that of PC falls 83% (Mainwood, Worsley-Brown, and Paterson 1972). Only after this supply of high-energy phosphate in PC is largely depleted does glycolysis begin (Cerretelli, diPrampero, and Ambrosoli 1972; Karpatkin, Helmreich, and Cori 1964). Thus, use of PC during the early stages of muscular activity is likely to be important to amphibians. In spite of this insight gained from *in vitro* studies, measurements of the use of PC stores during exercise in intact amphibians are few. Larvae of *Rana catesbeiana* swimming vigorously for 30 s completely deplete the PC stores in their tails (Gatten, Caldwell, and Stockard 1984). Swimming *Xenopus laevis* rapidly use the PC stores in their hind-leg muscles as they

swim 1,400 cm in about 20 s (Miller and Sabol 1989). However, PC concentration changes little as the frogs cover an additional 3,850 cm in another 56 s. Swimming speed does not decline as PC is depleted. The rate of ATP production resulting from PC breakdown as the frogs swim the first 1,400 cm is approximately nine times the rate of ATP production via glycolysis. Further studies of the importance of the use of PC stores during short-term exercise in amphibians should prove rewarding.

Although ATP and PC stores within amphibian muscles can be used to power about one hundred contractions (Carey 1979a; Miller and Sabol 1989), exercise of greater duration must be powered by a combination of other anaerobic pathways and aerobic means. The only other significant anaerobic pathway involved in energy liberation during burst activity in amphibians is glycolysis: muscle glycogen is degraded and lactate accumulates, but concentrations of other metabolites such as pyruvate, succinate, and alanine change little (Bennett 1978). The significance of glycolysis during intense, nonsustainable locomotion by amphibians cannot be overemphasized: in some cases glycolysis provides over 80% of the total supply of ATP during activity (see below). What is surprising is that only recently have we begun to understand the importance of this process during exercise by amphibians (Bennett and Licht 1973; see also Gatten 1985).

Methods Used in the Measurement of Glycolysis during Nonsustainable Exercise Measurements of lactate in blood cannot accurately reflect the extent of glycolysis occurring in the entire body during exercise. In the seven species of amphibians in which muscle lactate, blood lactate, and total-body lactate concentrations have been measured simultaneously, the following relationship generally exists both before and after exercise: muscle lactate concentration > total-body lactate concentration > blood lactate concentration (Hutchison, Miller, and Gratz 1981; Hutchison and Turney 1975; Hutchison, Turney, and Gratz 1977; Miller and Hutchison 1979; Preslar and Hutchison 1978; Putnam 1979a). The slow diffusion of lactate from skeletal muscles into the blood during exercise is at least in part due to the shunting of blood to cutaneous capillaries to aid in O_2 uptake (Boutilier, McDonald, and Toews 1980). Furthermore, during recovery following exercise, the pattern of change in blood lactate does not accurately reflect the change in total-body lactate (Hutchison, Miller, and Gratz 1981; Hutchison and Turney 1975; Hutchison, Turney, and Gratz 1977; Miller and Hutchison 1979; Preslar and Hutchison 1978; Putnam 1979b; Quinn and Burggren 1983). Thus, in the analyses to follow, only data on total-body lactate concentration will be included.

To assess glycolysis during exercise, it is necessary to know the preexercise level of lactate in the body. Even minimal handling may increase the lactate level (Feder 1981a), and processing of accumulated lactate may require as much as 24 h (see below). These factors may contribute to the wide range of values reported for "resting" amphibians: *Bufo americanus*, 33 to 410 $\mu g \cdot g^{-1}$ (Gatten 1987; Hutchison and Miller 1979b); *Rana pipiens*, 73 to 447 $\mu g \cdot g^{-1}$ (Carey 1979a; Hutchison and Turney 1975); *Xenopus laevis*, 110 to 720 $\mu g \cdot g^{-1}$ (Hillman and Withers 1979; Hutchison and Miller 1979a). Some of this variability may, of course, be due to methodological differences and some may be due to the effects of temperature (see below). Nevertheless, the importance of allowing adequate time after handling, so that a minimal resting value is reached, cannot be overstressed: one study reports a *decrease* in lactate concentration from 880 to 780 $\mu g \cdot g^{-1}$ during 10 min of exercise (Baldwin, Friedman, and Lillywhite 1977).

Temperature may or may not influence resting lactate concentration in amphibians. Harlow (1978) found that resting lactate level in *Taricha torosa* (Caudata: Salamandridae) does not vary between 10° and 25°C. On the other hand, resting lactate concentration increases with temperature in both *Bufo boreas* and *Rana pipiens* (Carey 1979a; Wine 1988). Thus, it cannot be assumed that total-body lactate level is independent of temperature. If one wishes to measure the effect of temperature on glycolysis during exercise, resting lactate concentration must be determined at each temperature studied.

Stimulation by electrical shocks, one of several methods used to elicit locomotion, may simply induce escape behavior or it may directly affect muscle contraction, with concomitant effects on muscle glycolysis. Bennett and Licht (1973) found that postexercise whole-body lactate values are similar following electrical stimulation and manual stimulation in two anurans and a salamander. Likewise, Miller and Hutchison (1980) reported that electrical stimulation and motorized rotation of a metabolic chamber produce similar post exercise gastrocnemius lactate concentrations in *Bufo marinus*. However, Hillman et al. (1979) found that electrical shocking results in a postexercise lactate concentration in *Hyla cadaverina* that is twice that of individuals stimulated by manual prodding. Because of potential problems introduced by electrical shocking and because most recent investigators have used mechanical stimulation to induce activity, data from studies in which electrical stimulation was employed will not be analyzed here.

The muscles used and the pattern of movement produced will certainly be different for an amphibian moving along a linear track, jumping and righting itself in response to manual prodding, and righting itself in a rotating cylindrical chamber. Few studies evaluate the consequences of this methodological variation for lactate production. Bennett and Licht (1974) and Carey (1979a) measured lactate production at 10°, 20°, and 30°C in *Bufo boreas* (10-min duration) and *Rana pipiens* (5-min duration), the former authors using manual prodding and the latter author using motorized rotation of the metabolic chamber. The latter method, on average, elicits a rate of glycolysis 10% greater than the former. On the other hand, *R. pipiens* stimulated to jump by manual prodding accumulate lactate 39% faster than those jumping and righting themselves in a rotating metabolic chamber (Hillman 1980a). Thus, no clear pattern is evident at the moment as to which method results in the fastest rate of glycolysis. If the goal of a study is to determine the importance of glycolysis during natural locomotion, a technique that elicits normal locomotor action (such as jumping on a linear track) is preferable to one that involves less routine behaviors (such as righting responses). On the other hand, if the goal of a study is to compare the importance of aerobic and anaerobic pathways, similar methods of stimulation should be used during the measurement of $\dot{V}O_{2ex}$ and lactate accumulation.

As will be discussed below, the duration of exercise has a profound impact on the overall rate of glycolysis. Lactate accumulates most rapidly at the beginning of exercise; the overall rate of production diminishes as exercise continues. Bennett and Licht (1972) recognized this early in the study of glycolysis in ectothermic vertebrates; they defined anerobic scope as the rate of lactate production during the first 30 s of activity and anaerobic capacity as the total amount of lactate accumulated during exercise to exhaustion. The use of these terms has not been rigorous; some authors refer to anaerobic scope during a variety of intervals of exercise. In order to avoid the semantic difficulties relating to these issues, in this chapter we use "rate of lactate production" to refer to the intensity of glycolysis, with careful attention to the important influence of duration of movement on this overall rate.

Effects of Body Mass, Temperature, and Duration of Effort on Glycolytic Support of Nonsustainable Exercise In the following analyses of lactate formation, we first included body mass as one explicit independent variable among others (e.g., temperature, species, duration of activity). In every case, body size significantly affects rates of lactate formation. This in itself is not surprising; larger animals are expected to produce more lactate than smaller ones per unit time. However, in every case the allometric coefficient relating the rate of lactate production to body size is not significantly different from 1.0. In other words, the rate of lactate production per gram of animal is independent of body size. Accordingly, for simplicity's sake, we reanalyzed the effects of other variables on mass-specific rates of lactate formation. Although the reanalysis does not explicitly present any effect of body size, the foregoing effect is present in every case.

SALAMANDERS AND A CAECILIAN   Table 12.14 summarizes the data currently available on resting lactate concentration, postexercise lactate concentration, and rate of lactate formation during exercise in fifteen species of salamanders and one caecilian. Forty-two percent of the variance in the rate of lactate formation can be accounted for by variation in duration of exercise, ($F_{[1,12]} = 18.77$, $p = .0010$). However, neither temperature nor individual species explain a significant portion of the variation in the rate of lactate formation (temperature: $F_{[1,12]} = 0.85$, $p = .3743$; species: $F_{[7,12]} = 2.41$, $p =$

.0867). The strong effect of duration of exercise on the overall rate of lactate formation is shown in figure 12.24 for salamanders at 20°C only. Glycolysis proceeds rapidly in the first 30 s of exercise but occurs at a much slower pace as exercise continues.

ANURANS   Table 12.15 presents the data available for the resting lactate concentration, postexercise lactate concentration, and rate of lactate formation during exercise for adults of thirty-six species and larvae of five species of anurans. If only data from studies in which information is available on adult body mass, temperature, duration of exercise, and rate of total-body lactate formation are included, sixty-three values for adults of ten species remain. In the analysis, the dependent variable is rate of lactate formation (in μg lactate $\cdot$ $g^{-1} \cdot min^{-1}$) and the independent variables are temperature,

TABLE 12.14   Lactate Production by Salamanders and a Caecilian during Nonsustainable Exercise

	Mass (g)	Temp. (°C)	Method of Stimulation	Duration (min)	Resting Lactate ($\mu g \cdot g^{-1}$)	Post-exercise Lactate ($\mu g \cdot g^{-1}$)	Rate of Lactate Production ($\mu g \cdot g^{-1} \cdot min^{-1}$)	Reference
			Gymnophiona					
Geotrypetes seraphini	1.93	20	Man. prod.	0.5	200	530	660	Bennett and Wake 1974
				2		700	250	
				10		950	75	
			Caudata					
Ambystoma talpoideum	4.71	15	Shock	30	260	1,490	41	Hutchison and Miller 1979b
Ambystoma tigrinum	51[a]	18	Man. prod. in water	5	94	349	51	Cushman, Packard, and Boardman 1976
	23[b]				170	548	76[c]	
	35	15	Shock	2	78[d]	85[d]	4	Hutchison, Turney, and Gratz 1977
				10		95[d]	2	
				30		120[d]	1	
		25		30	71[d]	130[d]	2	
Amphiuma tridactylum	493	25	Shock in water	30	700	2,230	51	Preslar and Hutchison 1978
Aneides flavipunctatus	1.89	20	Man. prod.	0.5	83	356	546[c]	Bennett and Licht 1974
				10		1,177	109[c]	
Aneides lugubris	4.09	20	Man. prod.	0.5	201	408	414[c]	Bennett and Licht 1974
				10		841	64[c]	
Batrachoseps attenuatus	1.55	20	Man. prod. Shock	2	203	1,371	584[c]	Bennett and Licht 1973
						1,503	650	
	0.71	10	Man. prod.	0.5	190	512	644[c]	Bennett and Licht 1974
				10		1,155	97[c]	
		20		0.5	203	855	1,304[c]	
				10		1,655	145[c]	
	0.45	20	Man. prod., shock[e]	N.A.	297	1,128	N.A.	Feder and Olsen 1978
	0.93	5	Man. prod.	2	N.A.	859[f]	N.A.	Feder 1978b
						735[g]		
		15				954[f]		
						928[g]		
		25				1,356[f]		
						1,102[g]		
Bolitoglossa occidentalis	0.61	5	Man. prod.	2	N.A.	174[f]	N.A.	Feder 1978b
						147[g]		
		15				303[f]		
						318[g]		
		25				342[f]		
						362[g]		

TABLE 12.14 (continued)

	Mass (g)	Temp. (°C)	Method of Stimulation	Duration (min)	Resting Lactate ($\mu g \cdot g^{-1}$)	Post-exercise Lactate ($\mu g \cdot g^{-1}$)	Rate of Lactate Production ($\mu g \cdot g^{-1} \cdot min^{-1}$)	Reference
Cryptobranchus alleganiensis	500	25	Man. prod., shock in water	30	50[h]	365[h]	N.A.	Boutilier, McDonald, and Toews 1980
Desmognathus ochrophaeus	2.05	15	Man. prod.	5	61	795	147[c]	Bennett and Houck 1983
	2	21	Mot. rot.	15	150[d,i]	725[d,i]	38	Feder 1986
					75[d,j]	525[d,j]	30	
					100[d,k]	400[d,k]	20[c]	
Necturus maculosus	101.9	5	Shock in water	30	218	1,121	30	Miller and Hutchison 1979
		15			212	1,010	27	
Notophthalmus viridescens	1.51	20	Man. prod. in water	0.5	534	598[l]	128	Bennett and Licht 1974
				10		657[l]	12	
			Man. prod. in air	0.5		689	310[c]	
				10		828	29[c]	
Plethodon glutinosus	6.29	15	Shock	30	390	1,450	35	Hutchison and Miller 1979b
Plethodon jordani	2.1	20	Man. prod.	2	120	1,170	525[c]	Feder and Arnold 1982
	4.1	27	Tread[m]	5	157	502	69[c]	Full 1986
				11.4[e]		944	69	
	1.88	15[n]	Man. prod.	5	121	669	110[c]	Stefanski, Gatten, and Pough 1989
		25[n]			151	540	78[c]	
Pseudoeurycea smithii	4.20	5	Man. prod.	2	N.A.	314[f]	N.A.	Feder 1978b
						430[g]		
		15				402[f]		
						462[g]		
		25				516[f]		
						609[g]		
Taricha torosa	10.67	5	Man. prod.	2	N.A.	461[f]	N.A.	Feder 1978b
						561[g]		
		15				614[f]		
						501[g]		
		25				573[f]		
						546[g]		
	11.23[o]	10	Mot. rot.	20	1247[p]	1,339	5[c]	Harlow 1978
		15				2,099	43[c]	
		20				1,883	32[c]	
		25				1,726	24[c]	

Notes: Values shown are whole-body lactate concentrations unless otherwise noted. Mass shown in the table is the mean mass of animals (if given in the reference cited) or midpoint of mass range (if only the mass range is given in the reference cited). All measurements are for animals in air unless otherwise noted. Method of stimulation: man. prod. = manual prodding; mot. rot. = motorized rotation of chamber at constant or variable rate; shock = electrical stimuli via electrodes; tread = treadmill. N.A. = data not available.

[a] Neotenic animals.
[b] Transformed animals.
[c] Data used in analysis of effects of temperature and duration of exercise on rate of lactate formation.
[d] Estimated from data in figure.
[e] Animals stimulated to exercise to exhaustion.
[f] Animals acclimated to 12°C.
[g] Animals acclimated to 22°C.
[h] Blood lactate concentration in $\mu g \cdot ml^{-1}$.
[i] Animals acclimated to 5°C.
[j] Animals acclimated to 13°C.
[k] Animals acclimated to 21°C.
[l] Animals had access to air.
[m] 0.2 km·h⁻¹.
[n] Data for fully hydrated animals.
[o] Animals in aquatic phase.
[p] Resting lactate concentration did not vary with temperature.

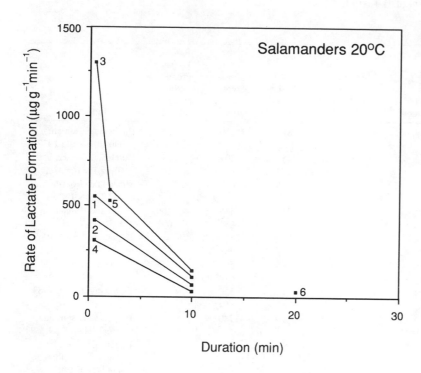

Fig. 12.24 The effect of the duration of exercise on the rate of lactate production in six species of salamanders at 20°C. Data from table 12.14. *1, Aneides flavipunctatus; 2, A. lugubris; 3, Batrachoseps attenuatus; 4, Notophthalmus viridescens; 5, Plethodon jordani;* and *6, Taricha torosa.*

TABLE 12.15   Lactate Production by Anurans during Nonsustainable Exercise

	Mass (g)	Temp. (°C)	Method of Stimulation	Duration (min)	Resting Lactate (μg·g^{-1})	Post-exercise Lactate (μg·g^{-1})	Rate of Lactate Production (μg·g^{-1}·min^{-1})	Reference
				Adults				
Agalychnis callidryas	5.7	20	Mot. rot.	4	N.A.	684	N.A.	Taigen, Emerson, and Pough 1982
Bombina orientalis	2.6	20	Mot. rot.	4	N.A.	486	N.A.	Taigen, Emerson and Pough 1982
Bufo americanus	15.78	15	Shock	30	410	890	16	Hutchison and Miller 1979b
	30	20	Man. rot.	1	200	340	140	Taigen and Pough 1981
	27.0	20	Mot. rot.	4	220	639	105	Taigen and Beuchat 1984; Taigen, Emerson, and Pough 1982
	21.3	25	Mot. rot.	4	33	514	120	Gatten 1987
	24	N.A.	Man. rot.	10	250	630	38	Withers, Lea, Solberg, Baustian, and Hedrick 1988
Bufo boreas	33.3	20	Man. prod. Shock	2	107	339 275	116 84	Bennett and Licht 1973
	22	10	Man. prod.	1 10	133	276 578	143 45	Bennett and Licht 1974
		20		1 10	107	342 655	235 55	
		30		1 10	161	521 817	360 66	
	40.2	10	Mot. rot.	10	61	560	50	Carey 1979a
		20			83	680	60	
		30			105	800	70	
	24.9	26	Man. rot.	3	160	450	97	Hillman and Withers 1979
	58.91	20	Man. prod.	15	90	650	37	Putnam 1979a
Bufo calamita	8.7	20	Mot. rot.	4	N.A.	341	N.A.	Taigen, Emerson, and Pough 1982

TABLE 12.15 *(continued)*

	Mass (g)	Temp. (°C)	Method of Stimulation	Duration (min)	Resting Lactate (μg·g^{-1})	Post-exercise Lactate (μg·g^{-1})	Rate of Lactate Production (μg·g^{-1} ·min^{-1})	Reference
Bufo marinus	N.A.	20	Mot. rot.	10	870	1,640	77	Baldwin, Friedman, and Lillywhite 1977
	N.A.	15	Shock	30	459	1,007	18	Hutchison, Miller, and Gratz 1981
		25			434	826	13	
	435	25	Man. rot.	30	36[a]	690[a]	N.A.	McDonald, Boutilier, and Toews 1980
	356	15	Mot. rot.	3	216[b]	335[b]	40[b]	Miller and Hutchison 1980
	293	25			326[b]	653[b]	109[b]	
Colostethus inguinalis	1.52	20	Mot. rot.	4	N.A.	521	N.A.	Taigen and Pough 1983
		25				503		
Colostethus nubicola	0.25	20	Mot. rot.	4	N.A.	594		Taigen and Pough 1983
		25				670		
Dendrobates auratus	1.95	20	Mot. rot.	4	N.A.	338	N.A.	Taigen and Pough 1983
	1.50	25				454		
Discoglossus pictus	30.7	20	Mot. rot.	4	N.A.	780	N.A.	Taigen, Emerson, and Pough 1982
Eleutherodactylus coqui	4.1	20	Mot. rot.	4	N.A.	884	N.A.	Taigen, Emerson, and Pough 1982; Taigen and Pough 1983
Gastrophryne carolinensis	1.9	20	Mot. rot.	4	N.A.	570	N.A.	Taigen, Emerson, and Pough 1982
Hyla arenicolor	3.4	20	Mot. rot.	4	N.A.	1,285	N.A.	Taigen, Emerson, and Pough 1982
Hyla cadaverina	3.0	23	Man. prod. Shock	3	N.A.	550 1,020	N.A.	Hillman et al. 1979
Hyla chrysoscelis	5.47	20	Mot. rot.	4	164	856	173	Kamel, Marsden, and Pough 1985
Hyla crucifer	1.3	20	Mot. rot.	4	480	966	122	Taigen and Beuchat 1984; Taigen, Emerson, and Pough 1982
	1.60	12[c]	Man. prod.	To exhaustion	37	653	N.A.	Pough and Gatten 1984
Hyla regilla	2.76	20	Man. prod. Shock	2	282	895 984	307 351	Bennett and Licht 1973
	2.61	10	Man. prod.	0.5	266	369	206	Bennett and Licht 1974
				10		946	68	
		20		0.5	282	680	796	
				10		1,266	98	
Hyla squirella	2.45	N.A.	Man. prod.	4.25	238	948	167	Prestwich, Brugger, and Topping 1989
Hyla versicolor	7.96	15	Shock	30	280	1,320	35	Hutchison and Miller 1979b
	6.09	20	Mot. rot.	4	184	629	111	Kamel, Marsden, and Pough 1985
Hyperolius viridiflavus	0.9	20	Mot. rot.	4	N.A.	1,158	N.A.	Taigen, Emerson, and Pough 1982
Kaloula pulchra	30.7	20	Mot. rot.	4	N.A.	451	N.A.	Taigen, Emerson, and Pough 1982
Kassina senegalensis	3.0	20	Mot. rot.	4	N.A.	1,064	N.A.	Taigen, Emerson, and Pough 1982
Kassina weali	6.3	20	Mot. rot.	4	N.A.	417	N.A.	Taigen, Emerson, and Pough 1982
Limnodynastes tasmaniensis	N.A.	20	Mot. rot.	10	620	920	30	Baldwin, Friedman, and Lillywhite 1977
Litoria ewingi	N.A.	20	Mot. rot.	10	880	780	−10	Baldwin, Friedman, and Lillywhite 1977
Litoria raniformis	N.A.	20	Mot. rot.	10	420	1,220	80	Baldwin, Friedman, and Lillywhite 1977

TABLE 12.15 *(continued)*

	Mass (g)	Temp. (°C)	Method of Stimulation	Duration (min)	Resting Lactate (μg·g^{-1})	Post-exercise Lactate (μg·g^{-1})	Rate of Lactate Production (μg·g^{-1}·min^{-1})	Reference
Odontophrynus americanus	15.2	20	Mot. rot.	4	N.A.	393	N.A.	Taigen, Emerson, and Pough 1982
Osteopilus septentrionalis	5.0	20	Mot. rot.	4	N.A.	1,106	N.A.	Taigen, Emerson, and Pough 1982
Physalaemus pustulosus	1.5	25	Man. rot.	34.9	320	670	20	Ryan, Bartholomew, and Rand 1983
Pternohyla fodiens	15.1	20	Mot. rot.	4	N.A.	329	N.A.	Taigen, Emerson, and Pough 1982
Rana catesbeiana	217.1	15	Shock	30	290	1,480	40	Hutchison and Miller 1979b
	384	23	Man. prod.	6	800[b]	3,100[b]	383[b]	Quinn and Burggren 1983
Rana pipiens	39.7	10	Man. prod.	0.5	93	275	364	Bennett and Licht 1974
				5		787	139	
		15		0.5	135	408	546	
				5		1,198	213	
		20		0.5	148	655	1,014	
				5		1,286	228	
		30		0.5	289	734	890	
				5		1,434	220	
	29	15	Shock	2	447	958	256	Hutchison and Turney 1975
				15		1,704	84	
				30		1,808	45	
	34.8	10	Mot. rot.	5	73	860	157	Carey 1979a
		20			124	1,290	233	
		30			175	1,500	265	
	38	21	Man. prod.	5.7[d,e]	390	1,470	189	Cummings 1979
				7.2[d,f]	420	1,320	125	
	42.5	26	Man. rot.	3	160	670	170	Hillman and Withers 1979
	63.58	20	Man. prod.	4.9[d]	160	1,230	218	Putnam 1979a
	55	20	Man. prod.	4.5	120[g]	1,620[g]	333	Putnam 1979b
	25.1	19	Man. rot.	3	N.A.	N.A.	490[b]	Hillman 1980a
			Man. prod.	To exhaustion	N.A.	N.A.	680[b]	
	18.3	25	Mot. rot.[h]	4	108	834	182	Gatten 1987
	16.5	15	Man. prod.	0.25	88	257	676	Wine 1988
				0.50		231	286	
				1.0		418	330	
				2.0		761	337	
		20		0.25	185	260	300	
				0.50		470	570	
				1.0		735	550	
				2.0		956	386	
		25		0.25	184	448	1,056	
				0.50		576	784	
				1.0		826	642	
				2.0		1,034	425	
		30		0.25	184	579	1,580	
				0.50		679	990	
				1.0		905	721	
				2.0		1,165	491	
Rana sylvatica	12.7	20	Mot. rot.	4	410	1,083	168	Taigen and Beuchat 1984; Taigen, Emerson, and Pough 1982
Scaphiopus bombifrons	12.32	15	Shock	30	320	840	17	Hutchison and Miller 1979b
Scaphiopus hammondii	10.87	20	Mot. rot.	20	64[a]	559[a]	N.A.	Seymour 1973c

TABLE 12.15 (continued)

	Mass (g)	Temp. (°C)	Method of Stimulation	Duration (min)	Resting Lactate ($\mu g \cdot g^{-1}$)	Post-exercise Lactate ($\mu g \cdot g^{-1}$)	Rate of Lactate Production ($\mu g \cdot g^{-1} \cdot min^{-1}$)	Reference
Xenopus laevis	23.9	25	Man. rot.[h]	4	400[g]	1,900[g]	375	Hillman 1978a
	35.6	26	Man. rot.	3	110	1,030	207	Hillman and Withers 1979
	27.7	15	Shock in water	30	720	2,220	50	Hutchison and Miller 1979a
		25			440	1,950	50	
	57.65	20	Man. prod. in water	8.9[d]	110	2,130	227	Putnam 1979a
	55	20	Man. prod. in water	7.5[d]	330[g]	2,210[g]	251	Putnam 1979b
	N.A.	22	Shock in water	Swam 51.5 m	910[b,e]	3,290[b,e]	N.A.	Miller and Camilliere 1981
					580[b,f]	2,540[b,f]	N.A.	
	4.94	23	Man. prod. in water	0.67	N.A.	N.A.	1,015	Miller 1983
				Larvae				
Bufo woodhousii	N.A.	25	Water current	1	640[i]	3,200[i]	2,560[i]	Feder 1983b
				20[d,j]		6,140[i]	275[i]	
Hyla gratiosa	0.88	24[k]	Man. prod. in water	0.5	253	333	160	Gatten, Caldwell, and Stockard 1984
	0.71	27[l]			300	326	52	
Rana berlandieri	N.A.	26	Man. prod. in water	0.34	450	540	265	Feder 1983a
Rana catesbeiana	9.19	20	Man. prod. in water	0.5	180	240	120	Bennett and Licht 1974
				10		667	49	
	18	23	Water current, man. prod.	9[d]	300	1,400	122	Quinn and Burggren 1983
	4.31	4[k]	Man. prod. in water	0.5	151	203	104	Gatten, Caldwell, and Stockard 1984
	2.45	15[l]			183	209	52	
Rana utricularia	1.59	4[k]	Man. prod. in water	0.5	167	199	64	Gatten, Caldwell, and Stockard 1984

Notes: Values shown are whole-body lactate concentrations unless otherwise noted. Mass shown in the table is the mean mass of animals (if given in the reference cited) or midpoint of mass range (if only the mass range is given in the reference cited). All measurements are for animals in air unless otherwise noted. Method of stimulation: man. prod. = manual prodding; man. rot. = manual rotation of chamber; mot. rot. = motorized rotation of chamber at constant or variable rate; shock = electrical stimuli via electrodes. Data in this table were used in the preparation of equations (12) to (15) and figures 12.25 and 12.26 with the following exceptions: (1) data from studies in which animals were stimulated to exercise by electric shocks were excluded, (2) only data from studies in which body mass was available were used, and (3) only whole-body lactate values were used. N.A. = data not available.

[a] Blood lactate concentration.
[b] Muscle lactate values.
[c] Mean temperature of rested and exhausted animals.
[d] Exercised to exhaustion.
[e] Untrained animals.
[f] Trained animals.
[g] Values derived from data in figure.
[h] Animals at full hydration.
[i] Values are in μg lactate $\cdot$ (g of dry mass)$^{-1}$.
[j] Midpoint of range of times to exhaustion.
[k] Animals studied in the laboratory.
[l] Animals studied in their home pond.

duration, and species. A much better fit is obtained if the $\log_{10}$ of rate of lactate formation, rather than rate, is used ($F = 30.94$ and $F = 5.77$, respectively); hereafter, the use of "rate of lactate formation" implies the use of the logarithm of this variable. Lactate production is dependent on duration of effort ($F_{[1,51]} = 106.25$, $p < .0001$), species ($F_{[9,51]} = 10.64$, $p < .0001$), and temperature ($F_{[1,51]} = 15.17$, $p = .0003$). Together, the three independent variables account for 87% of the variance in the rate of lactate production. If the two data points gathered for animals stimulated to activity for long periods (15 and 34.9 min) are excluded, the following equation relates lactate formation during exercise to duration of effort (0.25 to 10 min) and temperature (10° to 30°C) in adult anurans:

(12) $\log$ rate (μg lactate $\cdot$ g^{-1} $\cdot$ min^{-1}) = 2.411
  + 0.014 (temperature in °C) -0.087 (duration in min),

$r^2 = 0.66$, $N = 61$. This equation predicts that, in general, lactate production rises with temperature with a Q_{10} of 1.38 and falls as duration of exercise increases (fig. 12.25). An

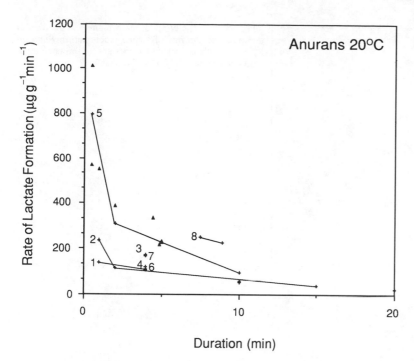

Fig. 12.25 The effect of the duration of exercise on the rate of lactate production in nine species of anurans at 20°C. Data from table 12.16. ▲, *Rana pipiens; 1, Bufo americanus; 2, B. boreas; 3, Hyla chrysosçelis; 4, H. crucifer; 5, H. regilla; 6, H. versicolor; 7, R. sylvatica; 8, Xenopus laevis.*

increase in duration of 1 min causes the overall rate of lactate formation to fall by 18%.

An "average" salamander active for 0.5 min at 20°C generates lactate at a rate of 644 μg lactate · g⁻¹ · min⁻¹ (N = 4, range = 310 to 1,304, fig. 12.24). In comparison, an "average" anuran exercising under identical conditions produces lactate at 444 μg · g⁻¹ · min⁻¹ (eq. [12]). The latter rate is only 69% of the former, but a definitive comparison must await more data on salamanders. Squamate reptiles generate lactate during exercise according to the following equation from Gatten (1985): lactate formation in μg · g⁻¹ · min⁻¹ = 780 − 281 (duration of exercise in min) + 18 (temperature in °C). This equation for squamates and equation (12) for anurans can be used to compare the rate of glycolysis during exercise in these groups. For an animal active for 1 min at 30°C, the following values result for squamates and anurans, respectively: 1,039 and 555 μg lactate · g⁻¹ · min⁻¹. In general, squamate reptiles use glycolysis during burst exercise at a rate about 1.9 times that for anurans. This ratio changes little with duration of exercise or with body temperature. Thus, glycolytic support for exercise is considerably higher in squamates than in frogs and toads. Caution should be used in applying this generality that was derived from data from many species; a given species of amphibian may well surpass a given species of reptile in glycolytic ability.

Intraspecific analysis of the effects of temperature and duration of effort on the rate of lactate accumulation during intense exercise is currently possible for only two species of anurans, *Bufo boreas* and *Rana pipiens* (see table 12.15 for data and references). In *B. boreas,* duration of effort contributes to variation in lactate formation ($F_{[1,8]} = 42.07$, $p < .0001$), but based on this sample, temperature does not ($F_{[1,8]} = 3.87$, $p = .09$). The equation for *B. boreas* active for 1 to 10 min at 10° to 30°C is

(13)   log rate (μg lactate · g⁻¹ · min⁻¹) = 2.331
                                − 0.058 (duration in min),

$r^2 = 0.79$, $N = 11$. The average rate of glycolysis declines as exercise continues at a rate of 13% min⁻¹ (versus 18% min⁻¹ for anurans in general, equation [12]). In *R. pipiens,* lactate accumulation depends on duration of exercise ($F_{[1,30]} = 81.79$, $p < 0.0001$) and temperature ($F_{[1,30]} = 13.85$, $p < .001$; fig. 12.26). The equation for leopard frogs active for 0.25 to 7.2 min at 10° to 30°C is

(14)   log rate (μg lactate · g⁻¹ · min⁻¹) = 2.520
            + 0.015 (temperature in °C) − 0.105 (duration in min),

$r^2 = 0.78$, $N = 33$. Glycolysis increases with a rise in temperature with an overall Q_{10} of 1.41 (versus 1.38 for anurans in general) and slows as exercise continues at a rate of decline of 21% min⁻¹ (versus 13% min⁻¹ for *B. boreas* and 18% min⁻¹ for an "average" anuran).

At a temperature of 20°C, an "average" anuran (eq. [12]) active for 1 min will generate lactate at 402 μg · g⁻¹ · min⁻¹ whereas comparable values for *B. boreas* (eq. [13]) and *R. pipiens* (eq. [14]) are 188 and 519 μg · g⁻¹ · min⁻¹, respectively. This analysis confirms the early observations of Bennett and Licht (1973, 1974) regarding differences in anaerobic metabolism between *Bufo* and *Rana*. However, data are insufficient for a comprehensive analysis of the variability in glycolytic ability among genera or families of anurans: at 20°C, the most commonly used temperature, and for exercise lasting 4 min, the most common duration, data exist for only five species. Taigen, Emerson, and Pough (1982) used postexercise lactate concentration, rather than rate of lactate production, in their study of the energetics of exercise in seventeen species of anurans from seven families. Their analysis indicated that lactate concentration after 4 min of activity at 20°C was not associated with taxonomic position; no family had consistently high or low values. Their results suggest caution in attempting to categorize a single genus or family as having a particular level of glycolytic capacity.

As described above, the overall Q_{10} for the rate of lactate accumulation in exercising anurans, as derived from equation

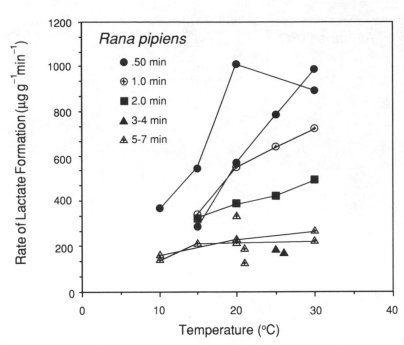

Fig. 12.26   The effect of temperature and duration of exercise on the rate of lactate production in *Rana pipiens*. Points connected by lines are for the same duration in a single study. Data from table 12.16.

(12), is 1.38. Q_{10} values for discrete temperature ranges for each species studied are shown in table 12.16. In *Bufo boreas,* the values are quite low and are consistent with the conclusion above that, after the effect of duration of exercise is removed, temperature has no influence on the rate of glycolysis. The overall Q_{10} for *Rana pipiens,* as derived from equation (14), is 1.41; individual values range below and above that average. In *B. boreas,* Q_{10} is almost constant as temperature changes from 10° to 30°C within any one period of activity; in addition, Q_{10} falls as duration increases. The latter trend is also seen in *Hyla regilla* (Hylidae). In the case of *R. pipiens,* Q_{10} usually falls as temperature increases at any duration, and often decreases with increased duration of effort. A comparison of the Q_{10} values for the rate of lactate formation during exercise in adult anurans (table 12.16) with comparable values for aerobic scope (table 12.12) reveals that the thermal sensitivity of glycolytic support for exercise is less than that of aerobic metabolism. This means that a change in body temperature will have less of an impact on the ability of an anuran to power locomotion by glycolysis than it will on its ability to generate ATP by aerobic pathways. This finding implies that glycolysis is relatively more important during intense exercise at low temperatures than at high ones, everything else remaining constant (see below).

As duration (and, presumably, distance traveled) increases, the postexercise lactate concentration also increases (table 12.15). However, few studies have directly examined the relationship between locomotor performance and glycolysis. In theory, an individual with a high anaerobic scope should be able to perform better during short-term, burst activity than an individual with a low anaerobic scope, especially in a species that is highly dependent on glycolysis for powering muscle contraction. Likewise, an individual with a high anaerobic capacity should perform better during exhaustive exercise than one with a low capacity. Such an association between physiological and behavioral indices could be tested simply by inducing individuals to exercise for a predetermined period or to exhaustion, measuring some index of

TABLE 12.16 Q_{10} for Rate of Lactate Formation in Anurans during Nonsustainable Exercise

	Duration (min)	Temp. Range (°C)	Q_{10}	Reference
Bufo boreas	1	10–20	1.6	Bennett and Licht 1974
		20–30	1.5	
	10	10–20	1.2	
		20–30	1.2	
	10	10–20	1.2	Carey 1979a
		20–30	1.2	
Hyla regilla	0.5	10–20	3.9	Bennett and Licht 1974
	10	10–20	1.4	
Rana pipiens	0.5	10–15	2.3	Bennett and Licht 1974
		15–20	3.4	
		20–30	0.9	
	5	10–15	2.3	
		15–20	1.1	
		20–30	1.0	
	5	10–20	1.5	Carey 1979a
		20–30	1.1	
	0.5	15–20	4.0	Wine 1988
		20–25	1.9	
		25–30	1.6	
	1.0	15–20	2.8	
		20–25	1.4	
		25–30	1.3	
	2.0	15–20	1.3	
		20–25	1.2	
		25–30	1.3	

Notes: Values calculated from data in table 12.15. Data from studies in which animals were stimulated to exercise by electric shocks were excluded. Only data from studies that reported whole-body lactate concentrations were used.

locomotor performance such as distance traveled, and then measuring lactate concentration. Hillman (1980a) found that time to exhaustion is significantly associated with both gastrocnemius lactate concentration and blood lactate concentration in *Rana pipiens.* Miller (1983) reported that distance swum by *Xenopus laevis* is closely associated with postexercise lactate concentration ($r^2 = 0.78$ in linear regression). Wine (1988) measured distance traveled and postexercise lactate concentration for *R. pipiens* jumping on a linear track. He found that distance traveled is strongly associated with postexercise lactate concentration ($r^2 = 0.90$), regardless of temperature. Thus, locomotor performance is clearly related to glycolytic activity in anurans. In the latter two studies, lactate production was fastest in the early stages of exercise and decreased (in a nonlinear fashion) as exercise continued. This important influence of the duration of exercise on the rate of glycolysis is seldom recognized. Additional studies of the relationship between individual performance and physiological capacity, in both short-term and exhaustive exercise, are clearly warranted. Likewise, the relationship between the duration of exercise and the rate of lactate formation deserves more attention.

Larval anurans generate lactate more slowly during intense swimming than their adult counterparts during jumping (table 12.15; see also Gatten 1985). Neither species ($N = 4$), duration of effort (0.5 to 10 min), nor temperature (4° to 27°C) influence the rate of glycolysis ($N = 9$, $p > .3$ in each case).

Total Supply of ATP during Nonsustainable Locomotion

During the first few seconds of intense exercise, amphibians substantially deplete their stores of phosphocreatine (Gatten, Caldwell, and Stockard 1984; Miller and Sabol 1989). As exercise continues, both aerobic and glycolytic pathways supply ATP for muscle contraction. Data on O_2 consumption and lactate production during exercise can be used to calculate the amount of ATP generated by aerobiosis and glycolysis, respectively (Bennett and Licht 1972). Such data are available for three species of salamanders and eight species of anurans (table 12.17). Because both aerobic scope (ml $O_2 \cdot h^{-1}$) and the rate of lactate formation during exercise (μg lactate $\cdot$ min^{-1}) vary with mass with an exponent not

TABLE 12.17 The Contribution of Aerobic Metabolism and of Glycolysis to the Total Supply of ATP during Exercise in Amphibians

	Temp. (°C)	Duration (min)	Aerobiosis (μM ATP·g^{-1})	Glycolysis (μM ATP·g^{-1})	Total (μM ATP·g^{-1})	Glycolytic Contribution (%)	Reference
			Caudata				
Desmognathus ochrophaeus[a]	21	15	19.5	5.0	24.5	20	Feder 1986
Plethodon jordani	15	5	2.9	9.2	12.1	76	Stefanski, Gatten, and
	25		3.4	6.5	9.9	66	Pough 1989
Taricha torosa[b]	10	20	4.9	1.7	6.6	26	Harlow 1978
	15		7.5	14.4	21.9	66	
	20		13.7	10.7	24.4	44	
	25		16.2	8.0	24.2	33	
			Anura				
Bufo americanus	20	4	19.1	7.0	26.1	27	Taigen and Beuchat 1984; Taigen, Emerson, and Pough 1982
	25		15.0	8.0	23.0	35	Gatten 1987
Bufo boreas	10	10	13.3	8.4	21.7	39	Carey 1979a
	20		36.0	10.0	46.0	22	
	30		66.2	11.7	77.9	15	
	26	3	18.0	4.9	22.9	21	Hillman and Withers 1979
Hyla chrysoscelis	20	4	16.5	11.6	28.1	41	Kamel, Marsden, and Pough 1985
Hyla versicolor	20	4	17.8	7.4	25.2	29	Kamel, Marsden, and Pough 1985
Physalaemus pustulosus	25	34.9	253.0	11.7	264.7	4	Bucher, Ryan and Bartholomew 1982; Ryan, Bartholomew, and Rand 1983
Rana pipiens	10	5	3.1	13.1	16.2	81	Carey 1979a
	20		10.8	19.5	30.3	64	
	30		19.3	22.1	41.4	53	
	25	4	8.4	12.2	20.6	59	Gatten 1987
	26	3	10.4	8.5	18.9	45	Hillman and Withers 1979
Rana sylvatica	20	4	12.8	11.2	24.0	47	Taigen and Beuchat 1984; Taigen, Emerson, and Pough 1982
Xenopus laevis	25	4	19.3	25.1	44.4	57	Hillman 1978a
	26	3	17.3	10.4	27.7	38	Hillman and Withers 1979

Notes: Data shown are derived from values in tables 12.7, 12.13, 12.14, and 12.15. Data included here are only those values from studies in which animals were induced to exercise by the same methods for measurement of both O_2 consumption and lactate production. Data from Full 1986 were excluded because his animals were exercising at only 85% of $\dot{V}O_{2ex}$.

[a] Animals acclimated to 21°C.
[b] Animals in aquatic phase.

different from 1.0, as demonstrated above, expression of ATP production per gram (table 12.17) adequately adjusts for differences in body mass among species. The total amount of ATP yielded by both pathways combined increases with duration of effort ($F_{[1,11]} = 14.92$, $p = .0026$) and with temperature ($F_{[1,11]} = 17.65$, $p = .0015$). In addition, the total ATP yield varies significantly among the eleven species ($F_{[10,11]} = 34.38$, $p < .0001$). When the total amount of ATP yielded is regressed on duration and temperature, the residuals for the three species of salamanders are generally negative ($\bar{x} = -33$, range $= -69$ to 14), whereas those for the eight species of anurans are generally positive ($\bar{x} = 16$, range $= -6$ to 108), suggesting that salamanders produce less ATP per gram body mass than do anurans. The effect of temperature on the total ATP yield in salamanders is unclear: in *Plethodon jordani* the total falls with a rise in temperature, but in *Taricha torosa* the total rises between 10° and 15°C and then remains virtually constant from 15° to 25°C. In both *Bufo boreas* and *Rana pipiens* a rise in temperature from 10° to 30°C results in a significant increase in the total ATP produced (table 12.17).

For the eleven species studied to date, glycolysis supplies between 4 and 81% of the total ATP derived from both aerobic and glycolytic pathways during exercise (table 12.17). The relative importance of glycolysis and aerobiosis is not dependent on temperature ($F_{[1,11]} = 4.52$, $p = .0570$) and, surprisingly, does not vary with duration ($F_{[1,11]} = 0.08$, $p = .7843$). However, the percentage of the total ATP attributable to glycosis does vary among the eleven species ($F_{[10,11]} = 3.67$, $p = .0217$). The very low value of 4% for the contribution of glycolysis is for *Physalaemus pustulosus* (Anura: Leptodactylidae) active for 35 min; for animals active for 5 min or less, glycolysis contributes an average of 49% of the total ATP. In anurans, the percentage contribution of glycolysis varies significantly among species ($F_{[7,7]} = 7.44$, $p = .0084$) and declines as temperature increases ($F_{[1,7]} = 11.78$, $p = .0109$). However, duration has no effect on the percentage contribution of glycosis in anurans alone ($F_{[1,7]} = 0.03$, $p = .8622$). The six values for percentage of contribution of glycolysis for *Rana* (45 to 81%) all exceed the six values for *Bufo* (15 to 39%), which confirms earlier conclusions regarding the relative importance of glycolysis and aerobiosis in these genera (Carey 1979a; Gatten 1987; Hillman and Withers 1979; Taigen and Beuchat 1984; Taigen, Emerson, and Pough 1982).

FACTORS THAT INFLUENCE AEROBIC AND ANAEROBIC SUPPORT FOR LOCOMOTION

As noted above, temperature and body size profoundly affect the aerobic and glycolytic support of locomotion in amphibians. In addition, aerobic capacity varies among taxonomic groups: anurans differ from salamanders in $\dot{V}o_{2rest}$, $\dot{V}o_{2ss}$, and $\dot{V}o_{2ex}$. Furthermore, interspecific differences in aerobic and glycolytic support for exercise are large. Intraspecific variation in oxidative and glycolytic metabolism during exercise has so far received little attention, but future studies will surely help to elucidate the degree, significance, and causes of differences among individuals of a single population or species. We are only beginning to gain an appreciation of how such factors as genotype, enzyme activity, developmental stage, O_2 availability, training, acclimation, and dehydration may contribute to these differences in activity metabolism. In this section, we address what is known about these topics.

Genetics and Enzymes

The heritability of physiological traits has received very little scrutiny (for review, see Arnold 1987), and only fragmentary information is available on how genetic factors influence the activity metabolism of amphibians. Szarski (1983) theorized that polyploid vertebrates should have an advantage over the diploid species from which they were derived because their metabolic rate should be depressed due to the increased nuclear volume and cell size. Kamel, Marsden, and Pough (1985) tested this hypothesis by measuring the O_2 consumption and lactate concentration of resting and exercising specimens of the diploid *Hyla chrysoscelis* (Anura: Hylidae) and its recently evolved tetraploid congener, *H. versicolor*. Contrary to the hypothesis of Szarski (1983), the species did not differ in O_2 consumption or lactate concentration at rest or during exercise. Thus, polyploidy does not seem to influence the metabolic capacity in at least one group of anurans.

Whole-animal physiological performance is influenced by the degree of heterozygosity among individuals of a species (Mitton and Grant 1984). In *Ambystoma tigrinum* (Caudata: Ambystomatidae) increasing heterozygosity at the locus for alcohol dehydrogenase is associated with a high $\dot{V}o_{2ex}$ (Mitton, Carey, and Kocher 1986). This relationship may stem in part from the influence of alcohol dehydrogenase genotype on the level of ATP in red blood cells, one determinant of hemoglobin O_2 transport (J. B. Mitton pers. comm.).

Citrate synthase is an important regulatory enzyme in the citric acid cycle and is a useful indicator of the aerobic capacity of a given tissue in amphibians (Marsh and Taigen 1987). Species with a high aerobic capacity such as *Bufo boreas* and *Xenopus laevis* have a higher level of citrate synthase activity in their hindlimb muscles (iliofibularis and triceps femoris) than a species with a low aerobic capacity, *Rana pipiens* (Putnam and Bennett 1983). Furthermore, individuals of *R. pipiens* with high gastrocnemius citrate synthase activity excel in locomotor performance (Cummings 1979). In contrast, aerobic capacity and pooled hindlimb muscle citrate synthase activity are not correlated in individual *R. catesbeiana* (Walsberg, Lea, and Hillman 1986), but this result may be due to the use of pooled thigh muscles rather than the lack of a relationship.

The activity of enzymes important in glycolysis also varies among amphibians. Although the substrate affinity and substrate inhibition characteristics of hindlimb muscle phosphofructokinase and lactate dehydrogenase do not differ between *B. boreas* and *R. pipiens*, the activities of these enzymes are twice as high in the species with the greater glycolytic capacity (*R. pipiens*) than in the species with the lower capacity (*B. boreas;* Bennett 1974). In a subsequent study, Putnam and Bennett (1983) confirmed these earlier results by showing that species with high glycolytic capacity (*R. pipiens* and *X. laevis*) have higher iliofibularis and triceps femoris lactate dehydrogenase activity than a species with low glycolytic capacity (*B. boreas*). Baldwin, Friedman, and Lillywhite (1977) found a high correlation between glycolytic capacity and hindlimb muscle phosphofructokinase activity, phosphorylase activity, and the ratio of phosphorylase to hexokinase activity in four species of Australian anurans. Surprisingly, glycolytic capacity was not correlated with lactate dehydrogenase activity or hexokinase activity alone. The interspecific relationship between aerobic and glycolytic enzyme activities and measures of whole-animal physiology (such as $\dot{V}O_{2ex}$ and the rate of lactate production) and whole-animal performance (such as distance and time to exhaustion) is a topic for investigation that should offer many exciting discoveries.

Developmental Stage

Amphibian larvae typically differ from their adult counterparts in morphological, behavioral, and ecological traits. Thus, major physiological changes must occur during the transition from larva to adult (see chapter 16 for a full discussion of this topic). Little work has focused on the metabolic changes relating to locomotion that occur during the larval stages or during metamorphosis. Hillman and Lea (1983) measured the $\dot{V}O_{2ex}$ of larval *Rana catesbeiana* in air at developmental stages 17 through 25. At the latter stage, the mass specific O_2 consumption during exercise is five times that at the earliest stage. Part of the change in $\dot{V}O_{2ex}$ is correlated with developmental changes in lung structure and function and with changes in blood O_2 transport capacity; as development proceeds during the stages examined, the lungs greatly increase their O_2 exchange capacity, and the blood becomes better able to transport O_2 (see chapter 16). However, the ontogenetic change in $\dot{V}O_{2ex}$ is not accompanied by any change in locomotor muscle citrate synthase activity; larval tail muscle has the same enzymatic activity as adult hindlimb muscle.

Some anurans, such as *Bufo americanus* and *Rana sylvatica*, have a short larval stage and metamorphose at a small body size; others, such as *R. clamitans*, have a long larval stage and metamorphose when relatively large. These different patterns of larval development are correlated with physiological and behavioral characteristics related to locomotor capacity (Pough and Kamel 1984; Taigen and Pough 1981). Juveniles of the former species exhibit a rapid increase in $\dot{V}O_{2ex}$ and in endurance as they grow to the size at which they disperse from the margins of their natal ponds. After they reach dispersal size, they show no further changes in $\dot{V}O_{2ex}$ or endurance and are identical to adults in these respects. On the other hand, juveniles of the latter species exhibit no changes in $\dot{V}O_{2ex}$ or endurance as they grow to dispersal size; their capabilities are the same as adults. A species such as *R. palustris* that has an intermediate length of larval life and an intermediate size at metamorphosis exhibits only moderate changes in capability for locomotion during the juvenile period prior to dispersal. Increases in $\dot{V}O_{2ex}$ and endurance during the early juvenile phase are correlated with adjustments in hematocrit, hemoglobin concentration, and relative heart mass (Pough and Kamel 1984; Taigen and Pough 1981).

As noted above, larval anurans have a much lower capacity for glycolysis during exercise than their adult counterparts. Furthermore, neotenic *Ambystoma tigrinum* have a lower rate of lactate production during exercise than transformed individuals (Cushman, Packard, and Boardman 1976). The difference in glycolytic capacity between anuran adults and larvae may rest in part on the fact that adult limb muscle has a significantly higher lactate dehydrogenase activity than larval tail muscle (Quinn and Burggren 1983). Glycolytic capacity reaches the adult level during metamorphosis; recently transformed *Bufo americanus* (less than 0.1 g) have the same rate of lactate production during exercise as adults (Taigen and Pough 1981). Further studies of the physiological basis for the difference in activity metabolism between larval and adult amphibians seem well justified.

Oxygen Availability

Most terrestrial amphibians never encounter hypoxic conditions. However, fossorial species, especially those that estivate in mud, may experience severe limitations in O_2 availability that will influence the metabolic machinery employed at rest and during physical exertion (see chapters 6 and 10). Aquatic species are likely to encounter hypoxic water at some stage in their life cycle (see chapter 5). The physiological effects of low environmental PO_2 are exacerbated by high temperatures, which elevate O_2 demand. In most cases a critical O_2 tension, P_c, exists for $\dot{V}O_{2ex}$; at PO_2's above P_c, $\dot{V}O_{2ex}$ is not influenced by O_2 partial pressure, but at PO_2's below the P_c, $\dot{V}O_{2ex}$ falls (usually linearly) as PO_2 declines. The P_c for $\dot{V}O_{2ex}$ of plethodontid salamanders active in air at 22°C is 110 mm Hg (Withers 1980), whereas that for *Bufo cognatus* and *Rana pipiens* active in air at 20° to 23°C is 80 mm Hg; these species are unlikely to encounter such O_2 levels on a routine basis, and thus for practical purposes their aerobic metabolism during exercise is not influenced by PO_2 (Withers and Hillman 1983). Larvae of *Bufo woodhousii* exhibit a depression of $\dot{V}O_{2ex}$ below an aquatic PO_2 of 57 mm Hg at 25°C; furthermore, the P_c is size dependent: large larvae are more susceptible to hypoxia than small ones (Feder 1983a). The stamina of anuran larvae is also depressed by hypoxia (Wassersug and Feder 1983). Adults and larvae of *Rana muscosa* overwinter in ponds at altitudes over 3,000 m; although the low water temperatures result in a low metabolic demand for O_2, the high altitude results in aquatic O_2 levels that are sufficiently low to interfere with O_2 consumption during spontaneous exercise (Bradford 1983). For frogs and larvae active under the ice, no P_c is apparent; any degree of hypoxia leads to a decline in $\dot{V}O_{2ex}$ (Bradford 1983). Hypoxia not only depresses $\dot{V}O_{2ex}$ in amphibians but also can reduce $\dot{V}O_2$ during the postexercise recovery period (Feder and Olsen 1978).

Hypoxia can also result in alterations in glycolytic energy liberation during exercise by amphibians, presumably as an indirect consequence of the direct effect of O_2 availability on aerobic pathways. Specimens of *Notophthalmus viridescens* (Caudata: Salamandridae) induced to swim without access to atmospheric air generate more lactate and exhibit poorer swimming performance than specimens that can rise to the surface to ventilate their lungs (Bennett and Licht 1974). Among anurans, individuals of *Litoria ewingi* and *L. raniformis* (Hylidae) stimulated to hop for 10 min in 100% N_2 have postactivity lactate levels higher than specimens exercising in air; however, specimens of *Limnodynastes tasmaniensis* (Myobatrachidae) have postexercise values in N_2 and in air that are statistically equivalent (Baldwin, Friedman, and Lillywhite 1977). Furthermore, hypoxia delays the processing of lactate during recovery following exercise in *Batrachoseps attenuatus* (Caudata: Plethodontidae; Feder and Olsen 1978). Before we can develop a more complete understanding of the impact of low O_2 levels on the activity metabolism of amphibians, we need field data on the degree to which amphibians in their natural habitats actually encounter hypoxic conditions.

Training

When mammals repeat a strenuous, sustained activity, they exhibit an improvement in performance in that activity resulting from numerous physiological and biochemical alterations (Shephard 1982). The first known report of the effect of training on locomotor performance in an amphibian is that of Twain (1867), who chronicled the consequences of repeated trials on a single anuran. Subsequent studies indicate that training enhances locomotor performance in *Rana pipiens* (Cummings 1979) and *Xenopus laevis* (Miller and Camilliere 1981). In the former species, training increases endurance (as measured by number of hops before exhaustion) by 35% and also increases the distance traveled and time to exhaustion. The increased locomotor performance in leopard frogs is apparently due entirely to alterations in aerobic metabolism: gastrocnemius citrate synthase activity increases 38% after training, but the conditioning does not affect glycogen depletion or lactate production during exercise (Cummings 1979). Moreover, trained frogs process accumulated lactate faster than untrained ones in the 15-min interval immediately after exercise (Cummings 1979). In *X. laevis*, training improves both sprint and endurance performance: trained frogs show a 30% decrease in the time required to sprint 1.5 m or swim 51 m (Miller and Camilliere 1981). However, in this species the biochemical alterations are significantly different from those seen in trained leopard frogs. Trained *Xenopus* accumulates less lactate than do untrained ones; experienced animals have low resting muscle glycogen stores that are not depleted during exercise, whereas untrained animals deplete their muscle glycogen during swimming (Miller and Camilliere 1981). Conditioning has no effect on muscle citrate synthase activity or heart mass (Miller and Camilliere 1981). Thus, in *R. pipiens* training appears to act on aerobic mechanisms, whereas in *X. laevis* it apparently influences the glycolytic machinery. No data exist for the effect of training on $\dot{V}o_{2ex}$ in amphibians.

Does time in captivity, during which amphibians presumably engage in little locomotor behavior, affect locomotor performance or physiology? If training improves performance, inactivity should diminish it. Untrained frogs kept in captivity for up to 7 weeks show no change in locomotor performance or in resting muscle glycogen or lactate concentration or resting whole-body lactate concentration (Cummings 1979; Miller and Camilliere 1981). Zug (1985) measured the jumping performance of nine species of anurans over a 15-day period of captivity; each animal was tested on days 1, 5, 10, and 15. Performance varied among days of captivity in eight of the nine species, but only *Bufo americanus* showed a consistent, monotonic change (decline) in jumping ability over time (Zug 1985). Zug also found that locomotor performance is highly variable from day to day for a given individual; this result

contrasts with that of Miller and Camilliere (1981), who found that individual performance (relative to other frogs) is highly consistent over time. Future studies should include appropriate controls to account for any possible change in performance (or physiology) of animals during captivity.

Acclimation

A large body of literature examines the effect of thermal acclimation on the resting metabolic rate of amphibians (see Feder 1982b; Seale 1987; chapter 8 of this volume for review). In contrast, little is known about the influence of thermal history on the energetics of amphibians during exercise. Acclimation temperature has little influence on the $\dot{V}o_{2ex}$ of either lowland or montane subspecies of *Bufo boreas* (Carey 1979b). Thermal history may or may not exert an influence on aerobic metabolism during exercise in a given species, depending on the temperature at which measurements are taken: at 13°C, cold-acclimated *Desmognathus ochrophaeus* have a higher $\dot{V}o_{2ex}$ than warm-acclimated specimens, but at 21°C, acclimation does not affect $\dot{V}o_{2ex}$ (Feder 1986). Acclimation temperature has a greater effect on O_2 consumption in temperate zone salamanders than in tropical ones during the recovery period following electrically stimulated exercise (Feder 1978b). However, thermal history does not influence lactate production during electrically stimulated exercise by four species of salamanders (Feder 1978b). On the other hand, cold-acclimated *D. ochrophaeus* generate more lactate than warm-acclimated individuals during exercise in a rotating wheel respirometer at 21°C (Feder 1986).

The influence of thermal acclimation on locomotor performance varies with the species studied, the temperature of measurement, and the particular index of locomotor performance employed. Acclimation temperature has no influence on distance traveled during exercise in *Bufo boreas* or *Rana pipiens* (Putnam and Bennett 1981), on sprint performance in *Necturus maculosus* (Caudata: Proteidae) or *Xenopus laevis* (Miller 1982), on maximal jump distance in *B. americanus* or *Pseudacris triseriata* (Hylidae; Knowles and Weigl 1990; Renaud and Stevens 1983), on the time needed to swim 37.5 m in *X. laevis* (Miller and Zoghby 1986), or on burst or endurance performance in *Ambystoma tigrinum* (Else and Bennett 1987). In a given species, the effect of acclimation on locomotor performance may vary with measurement temperature: warm-acclimated *R. pipiens* jump further than cold-acclimated specimens only at high temperatures (Renaud and Stevens 1983). Similarly, acclimation temperature influences stamina and maximal sustainable speed in *D. ochrophaeus* at 21°C but not at 13°C (Feder 1986). The effect of acclimation also varies with the measure of performance selected: *B. woodhousii* acclimated to 30°C have greater mean and maximal jump lengths than those acclimated to 20°C, but the opposite is true for mean jump frequency (Londos and Brooks 1988). Different species respond to thermal acclimation differently: warm-acclimated *B. marinus* cover a given distance more quickly than cold-acclimated ones, but the reverse is true for *R. pipiens* (Miller and Zoghby 1986). The effect of acclimation on locomotor performance in a given species may vary between different studies: for *R. pipiens*, cold acclimation may increase (Miller and Zoghby

1986) or decrease (Renaud and Stevens 1983) locomotor performance.

The effects of an acclimation regime on locomotor or other measures of whole-animal performance presumably reflect biochemical and physiological adjustments that occur during the acclimation period. However, few studies address the degree of correlation between physiological and behavioral consequences of acclimation. The influence of acclimation temperature on jumping performance in *R. pipiens* (Miller and Zoghby 1986; Renaud and Stevens 1983) cannot be attributed to acclimation-induced changes in sartorius mechanical properties (Renaud and Stevens 1984; Rome 1983) but may be related to acclimation-induced alterations in skeletal muscle oxidative enzyme activities (Ohira and Ohira 1988) or lactate dehydrogenase characteristics (Enig, Ramsay, and Eby 1976). The effect of acclimation temperature on jumping performance in *B. marinus* (Miller and Zoghby 1986) stands in contrast to the absence of an effect of acclimation temperature on iliofibularis isometric force in this species (Rees and Stephenson 1987). The absence of an effect of acclimation temperature on locomotor performance corresponds with a lack of acclimation in muscle contractile properties in *Ambystoma tigrinum* (Else and Bennett 1987). Physiological and behavioral consequences of acclimation for locomotion in *Desmognathus ochrophaeus* are not tightly coupled: at a measurement temperature of 13°C, acclimation affects $\dot{V}O_{2ex}$ but not stamina or speed; for animals at 21°C, acclimation does not influence $\dot{V}O_{2ex}$ but does influence stamina and rate of lactate accumulation (Feder 1986). Future studies should address in detail the relation between the physiological and behavioral consequences of thermal acclimation.

Dehydration

The integument of most amphibians offers little resistance to water flux (see chapters 4–6). As a consequence, many amphibians desiccate rapidly in terrestrial environments. Amphibians under natural conditions can lose (and subsequently regain) water equivalent to as much as 22% of their normal hydrated body mass during a 24-h cycle (Dole 1967; Lee 1968; Pough et al. 1983; Preest and Pough 1989). Such dehydration affects locomotor physiology and behavior. Although the resting O_2 consumption of amphibians may or may not be altered by water loss (Degani and Meltzer 1988; Gatten 1987; Hillman 1978a, Katz 1975a; Pough et al. 1983; Sherman and Stadlen 1986), O_2 use during exercise is depressed following dehydration. Loss of 20% of the body mass by evaporation of water leads to a decline in $\dot{V}O_{2ex}$ of 15% in *Bufo americanus*, 31% in *B. marinus*, 37% in *Eleutherodactylus coqui* (Anura: Leptodactylidae), 75% in *Rana catesbeiana*, 36% in *R. pipiens*, and 29% in *Xenopus laevis* (Gatten 1987; Hillman 1978a, 1987; Pough et al. 1983). In contrast with the case in anurans, loss of 15 to 20% of the body mass by dehydration results in no change in $\dot{V}O_{2ex}$ in *Plethodon jordani* and *Notophthalmus viridescens* (Stefanski, Gatten, and Pough 1989). The impact of water loss on $\dot{V}O_{2ex}$ varies among species: as dehydration proceeds from mild to severe levels, $\dot{V}O_{2ex}$ falls more steeply in *R. catesbeiana* and *R. pipiens* than in *B. americanus* and *B. marinus* (Gatten 1987; Hillman 1987). Those species of anurans with

a $\dot{V}O_{2ex}$ that is resistant to dehydration are also those with a high overall tolerance to water loss, as measured by survival during desiccation (Gatten 1987; Hillman 1980b). In general, terrestrial amphibians are more tolerant of water loss than less terrestrial ones (Farrell and MacMahon 1969; Thorson 1955; Thorson and Svihla 1943).

The underlying causes for the effect of dehydration on aerobic metabolism during exercise are fairly well understood. Loss of body water in *B. marinus* reduces CO_2 flux across the skin and imposes changes in ventilation frequency and in the use of the kidneys in acid-base balance (Boutilier et al. 1979c). Dehydration of anurans results in a decline in plasma volume and a rise in hematocrit, plasma solute concentration, and plasma colloid and total osmotic pressure (Hillman 1978a, 1978b, 1980b, 1982b, 1984; Hillman, Zygmunt, and Baustian 1987). As a consequence, cardiac output falls, mainly because of the decline in stroke volume; the arteriovenous difference in blood O_2 content increases; and the total peripheral resistance rises because of hemoconcentration and vasoconstriction (Hillman 1978a, 1987). In addition to these changes in gas exchange and cardiovascular function, dehydration also affects the contractile properties of both cardiac and skeletal muscles (Hillman 1982b, 1984). Although these numerous physiological consequences of dehydration influence $\dot{V}O_{2ex}$, they have no effect on glycolysis during exercise (Gatten 1987; Stefanski, Gatten, and Pough 1989).

When faced with desiccating conditions, amphibians exhibit behavioral changes to prevent or retard evaporative water loss (see chapter 6). These include, but are not limited to, changes in posture and aggregations of several individuals to reduce exposed surface area, burrowing, and changes in calling and feeding behavior (Bentley 1966a; Duellman and Trueb 1986; Feder 1983b; Keen 1984; McClanahan 1967; Packer 1963; Pough et al. 1983; Ray 1958; Shoemaker and Nagy 1977; Warburg 1972; Zug and Zug 1979). Such hydroregulatory behavior does not occur independently of other regulatory behaviors; rather, amphibians must engage in behavior that results in successful maintenance of many variables (Bundy and Tracy 1977). Despite attempts to prevent or retard water loss, terrestrial amphibians often dehydrate in their normal environments, with both behavioral consequences and the physiological consequences outlined above. When specimens of *Bufo boreas* and *Xenopus laevis* are placed in dry laboratory chambers, they become more active as water loss becomes more severe, presumably in an effort to locate moisture, even though the increased activity causes additional water loss (Putnam and Hillman 1977). For *B. boreas*, activity decreases only when dehydration nears the level where locomotion is impossible (Putnam and Hillman 1977). In contrast, specimens of *Desmognathus ochrophaeus* abandon foraging and retreat to moist areas at very low levels of water loss, far from the level of dehydration where locomotion becomes impaired (Feder and Londos 1984). Presumably these small salamanders act to prevent further dehydration when they experience only a small water deficit; the anurans studied by Putnam and Hillman (1977) apparently sought to do the same but had no source of moisture available.

Water loss alters both sprint performance and endurance performance of amphibians. When specimens of three species of *Eleutherodactylus* (Leptodactylidae) lose about 30% of their mass by evaporation, the distance they cover in six jumps falls by 30% (Beuchat, Pough, and Stewart 1984). Loss of only 20% of the body mass has no effect on sprint performance in four species of anurans, but loss of 30% of standard mass significantly reduces the distance covered in 30 s by *Rana pipiens* (Moore and Gatten 1989). The relevance to amphibians in nature of data from animals that have lost as much as 30% of their mass is unclear; under natural conditions, anurans routinely experience daily water loss amounting to only 10 to 22% of their mass (Dole 1967; Lee 1968; Pough et al. 1983; Preest and Pough 1989). Loss of 20% of the body mass by evaporation significantly depresses endurance performance in *B. americanus, R. clamitans,* and *R. pipiens* (Moore and Gatten 1989; Preest and Pough 1989). The severity of loss in locomotor capacity after dehydration in *B. americanus* and *R. pipiens* is closely coupled with the degree of depression of aerobic capacity following water loss in these species: after loss of 20% of the initial hydrated mass, specimens of *B. americanus* exhibit a decrease in $\dot{V}_{O_{2ex}}$ of 17% and a decline in distance traveled of 27%, whereas the corresponding values for *R. pipiens* are 38 and 36% (Gatten 1987; Moore and Gatten 1989). Comparable water loss has no effect on endurance locomotion in *B. marinus;* obviously marine toads are highly tolerant of xeric conditions (Heatwole and Newby 1972; Zug and Zug 1979). Claussen (1974) also reported that specimens of *Bufo* and *Rana* that lose more than 20% of their mass exhibit a decrease in jumping performance. Changes in plasma osmolality unrelated to changes in total body water volume can also inhibit locomotor and feeding performance of anurans (Dole, Rose, and Baxter 1985; Moore and Gatten 1989; Rose et al. 1986).

Temperature may interact with dehydration in altering locomotor performance. In two species of *Eleutherodactylus,* temperature does not influence the tolerance of sprint locomotion to water loss, but in a third species, tolerance to dehydration increases with temperature (Beuchat, Pough, and Stewart 1984). The effect of dehydration on distance traveled in 10 min by *B. americanus* is highly dependent on body temperature: a loss of 20% of the body mass reduces distance traveled by 21% at 20°C and by 57% at 30°C (Preest and Pough 1989). Future studies should be designed with the knowledge that the influence of water loss on locomotor performance (and physiological indices of locomotor capacity) can vary significantly over the range of temperatures normally encountered by amphibians in nature.

RECOVERY FOLLOWING EXERCISE AND THE PHYSIOLOGICAL BASIS FOR FATIGUE

After the end of exercise, biochemical and physiological processes eventually return to their preexercise levels. During this recovery period, the intracellular stores of phosphocreatine, glycogen, and myoglobin-bound O_2 must be replenished, and accumulated lactate and hydrogen ions must be processed, among numerous other changes (Shephard 1982). Indices of behavioral capacity, such as stamina, also return to preexercise levels during the recovery period. Despite the large number of measurements of the physiological changes during exercise in amphibians, relatively few investigators have examined the factors that determine the length of the recovery period in these animals.

Olmsted and Harvey (1927) apparently conducted the first measurements of the length of time necessary for O_2 consumption (and CO_2 production) to reach resting values following exercise in an amphibian. They electrically stimulated two frogs for 7.5 min and noted that their aerobic metabolism returned to normal in about 1 h. Following mechanically stimulated exercise in water or in air, most salamanders reach resting levels of O_2 uptake after about 1 h, although the rate of recovery is apparently influenced by body size (Feder and Olsen 1978; Harlow 1978; Withers 1980; Withers and Hillman 1981). After 10 to 20 min of exercise, *Bufo americanus* and *Scaphiopus hammondii* (Anura: Pelobatidae) reach resting $\dot{V}_{O_2}$ in 1 h (Seymour 1973c; Withers, Lea, Solberg, Baustian, and Hedrick 1988). In contrast, after 4 min of exercise, O_2 consumption of *B. americanus* and *Rana pipiens* returns to preactivity values in only 15 min (Gatten 1987). Larvae of *B. woodhousii* have rates of O_2 uptake that return to the resting level within 25 min after exercise ceases (Feder and Wassersug 1979). The duration of the recovery period for O_2 consumption depends on the species, the temperature, the intensity and duration and effort, and perhaps the body mass, among other factors. However, data are insufficient at this time to permit a statistical analysis of the relative importance of these factors.

Total-body lactate concentration returns to the resting level much more slowly than O_2 consumption following mechanically induced exercise. In salamanders, recovery of lactate level requires 4 to 6 h (Bennett and Licht 1973; Cushman, Packard, and Boardman 1976), whereas the comparable time for adult anurans is 2 to 4 h (Bennett and Licht 1973; Gatten 1987; Withers, Lea, Solberg, Baustian, and Hedrick 1988). Feder and Wassersug (1979) reported that larvae of *B. woodhousii* require only 1 min to eliminate 67% of the lactate accumulated during exhaustive exercise, whereas Quinn and Burggren (1983) found that exhausted larvae of *R. catesbeiana* require 4 h of rest to reach preexercise total-body lactate concentration. The time amphibians need to process lactate accumulated during intense exercise certainly depends on the species, the temperature, and the amount of lactate generated, among many other factors. However, the currently available data do not allow an assessment of the relative importance of these factors.

The fate of the lactate accumulated during exercise in amphibians is poorly understood. Little or no lactate is excreted via the urine or lost to the surrounding water across the gills or skin of aquatic amphibians (Cushman, Packard, and Boardman 1976; Quinn and Burggren 1983). Withers, Lea, Solberg, Baustian, and Hedrick (1988) exercised specimens of *B. americanus* for 10 min and then immediately injected them with labeled lactate and glucose. The toads oxidized less than 10% of the labeled lactate; most of the label was recovered as glycogen, protein, or lipid in skeletal muscle, liver, or skin. This situation contrasts with that of mammals that typically oxidize 55 to 90% of labeled lactate following exercise (Brooks and Gaesser 1980; Issekutz, Shaw, and Issekutz 1976). Further studies of the biochemical mechanisms active during recovery in amphibians seem warranted.

Following intense exercise, the time course of recovery of

behavioral capacity (measured as stamina or distance traveled before reexhaustion) is more similar to the time course of recovery of O_2 consumption than to that of recovery of lactate concentration. Specimens of *Batrachoseps attenuatus* induced to swim to exhaustion recover 50% of their behavioral capacity after 30 min of rest, but their total-body lactate values do not fall during that interval (Feder and Olsen 1978). The same is true of the tail musculature. Total-body lactate in these salamanders does not return to resting level until after 6 h of rest; in contrast, electrically stimulated animals reach resting O_2 consumption values after only 45 to 60 min (Bennett and Licht 1973). Bennett and Licht also found that behavioral recovery precedes removal of lactate in *Batrachoseps*. Similarly, when specimens of *Rana pipiens* are exercised to exhaustion and then allowed to rest before being exercised again, they recover their full jumping ability in 15 to 30 min (Gatten and Clark 1989), whereas their total-body lactate value does not return to resting level until after 2 h; as noted above, their O_2 consumption reaches preexercise values in 15 min (Gatten 1987). A lack of synchrony between recovery of behavioral capacity and processing of accumulated lactate has also been found in larval *B. woodhousii* (Feder 1983a). Neither dehydration nor increased plasma osmolality retards the recovery of jumping capacity in *R. pipiens* (R. E. Gatten and S. C. Gregory unpublished data; Gatten and Clark 1989).

Further evidence that lactate accumulation per se is not an adequate explanation for fatigue comes from the work of Fitts and Holloszy (1976) and Putnam (1979b), who found that recovery of contractile capacity in isolated muscles of *R. pipiens* precedes the removal of lactate from the muscles. Furthermore, Putnam (1979b) found a similar lack of correlation between elimination of muscle lactate and recovery of behavioral capacity in intact frogs. He also found that fatigue is not related to depletion of muscle glycogen or to an increase in blood lactate or hydrogen ions.

Fatigue is in some way associated with an increase in the intramuscular concentration of free hydrogen ions, derived mainly from lactic acid (Hermansen 1981). Although a rise in muscle hydrogen ion concentration has a direct inhibitory effect on some of the major regulatory enzymes involved in muscle energetics (Hermansen 1981; Shephard 1984), the major effect of increased hydrogen ion concentration seems to be indirect. Muscle acidification promotes the formation of acidified inorganic phosphorus ions such as $H_2PO_4^-$. A rise in the intramuscular concentration of this particular ion is the direct cause of fatigue in frogs (Wilkie 1986) and mammals (Nosek, Fender, and Godt 1987; Wilson et al. 1988). Such an increase seems to interfere with the force-producing step of the cross bridge cycle (Hibberd et al. 1985; Wilson et al. 1988). Additional studies using $H_2PO_4^-$ rather than lactate as an indicator of intramuscular changes should be carried out.

CONCLUSION

This chapter has tabulated, analyzed, and summarized what is known about the minimal cost of living and about the cost of sustainable and nonsustainable locomotion in amphibians. We have documented the pervasive effects of body temperature and body mass on the energetics of these animals. Perhaps the most remarkable finding of our analyses is a consistent difference between anurans and salamanders in the rate of O_2 consumption during rest, during steady-state exercise, and during burst exercise. Theoretically, salamanders could have a lower $\dot{V}O_{2rest}$ and a lower $\dot{V}O_{2ex}$ than anurans but still have the same aerobic scope. However, the data indicate otherwise: not only are the absolute levels of O_2 uptake during rest and exercise lower in salamanders than in anurans, but also the difference between these two measures, the aerobic scope, is significantly lower. Thus, the low resting metabolic rate of salamanders, which has been interpreted as an adaptation for an especially economical life style (Feder 1983b; Pough 1983), is accompanied by a low aerobic capacity and a low aerobic scope. This linkage between the intensity of metabolism during rest and during exercise at the ordinal level supports the arguments for the "aerobic capacity" model for the evolution of endothermy (Taigen 1983).

Based on the knowledge summarized here, several areas of investigation could be profitably explored in the future. Additional studies of the aerobic and glycolytic support for exercise should be attempted, but only if the degree of effort can be quantified and controlled. Measurements of the cost of locomotion should be carried out with animals moving in normal locomotor patterns using the normal locomotor muscles rather than exerting themselves in continual righting movements. Further studies of the variability of physiological and behavioral capacity among individuals of a species are greatly needed. Additional measurements of $\dot{V}O_{2rest}$ or $\dot{V}O_{2ex}$ that fail to consider underlying mechanisms or ecological factors are unnecessary. Rather, studies should explore the causal relationships among biomechanics, biochemistry, contractile properties of muscles, and the aerobic and anaerobic cost of exercise, as well as between the physiology of exercise and important ecological factors. For example, the effect of thermal acclimation at several layers of biological organization, such as enzyme activity, muscle properties, O_2 consumption, lactate production, and locomotor performance, all measured simultaneously, should be explored. All such relationships might change during metamorphosis, with training, or with water loss.

We hope this chapter will serve not only as a summary of what has been learned in the past but also as a stimulus for future studies on the energetics of amphibians.

13 Feeding and Digestion

LIS OLESEN LARSEN

This chapter presents an integrated survey of internal and external factors affecting feeding and digestion in amphibians. It focuses on the disciplines of organ and organismic physiology, behavior (as a physiological discipline reflecting the integrated function of the sensory system, the central nervous system, and the motor system), and ecology/natural history. The chapter is organized so that the natural sequence of events, from food intake to defecation, is the guiding line. The role of environmental factors has been integrated in the discussion of the natural sequence of physiological processes.

The amount of literature related to the various sections of the chapter varies enormously. The role of the visual system in feeding, based on a few species of urodeles and anurans, is massive and has been reviewed numerous times (see chapter 2). By contrast, only a single review of the physiology of the amphibian digestive system (Reeder 1964) is available.

A wide variety of external and internal factors influence food intake (fig. 13.1). The literature on laboratory mammals and human beings (see Blaxter 1989; Silverstone 1976) inspired figure 13.1, but the concepts it presents are generally applicable to most vertebrates, including amphibians, in which phases of eating (meals) are interspersed with phases of fasting (meal intervals). Such eating behavior is typical of feeding after metamorphosis. However, larvae may graze or be suspension feeders (filter feeders); embryos or larvae may feed continuously on exudates from the mother. Developmental aspects of feeding and digestion in amphibians are discussed in detail in chapter 16.

Figure 13.1 presents the relationships between environment and the animal in question from the point of view of the animal as a living entity, influenced by external and internal factors and responding in a way that figure 13.2 elaborates further. Figure 13.1 is grossly simplified and is intended as a framework for integration, discussion, and proposal of new experiments.

Table 13.1 presents a scheme of digestive organs and functions in vertebrates generally and amphibians specifically. Specific details for amphibians are extremely meager, and most information is either old or very specialized. Temperature is the best-investigated external factor. In all cases involving the autonomic nervous system, stress factors or memory of positive or negative experience may affect the function, be it peristalsis, secretion, or blood flow. However, no experimental documentation of such effects is available except for casual observations that handling will inhibit digestion (Johnson and Christiansen 1976). The necessary experiments on amphibian digestion are thus largely lacking and should be carried out after consulting the rich literature on mammals and fish.

FOOD
Food in Nature

It is not easy to generalize about types of food eaten by amphibians in nature. Porter (1972) and Duellman and Trueb (1986) cite examples of nearly all possible types of food for amphibians. The following account will add recent examples not cited in the above-mentioned books and emphasize the diversity of amphibians.

Ruibal and Thomas (1988) have published a detailed report on feeding and food of the larvae of *Lepidobatrachus laevis* (Anura: Leptodactylidae) and supplemented it with a review of larval types. Larval *L. laevis* are similar to adults in that they may eat prey of their own size and only eat prey that moves or is moved (also see chapter 16). Remarkably, they are able to eat during metamorphosis, probably because their feeding system undergoes little change.

Zimmermann and Zimmermann (1982, 1985) have observed larvae of *Dendrobates histrionicus* (Anura: Dendrobatidae) eating unfertilized eggs of the mother. Polis and Myers (1985) survey the literature on intraspecific predation, ranging from cannibalism between siblings *in utero* or between larvae, to older (larger) amphibians eating younger (smaller) ones.

Bury and Whelan (1984) extensively review the literature on food of adult *Rana catesbeiana*. Bush and Menhinick (1962) reported on the food of *Bufo woodhousii*. Oplinger

The following persons kindly provided me with recent literature: J.-P. Ewert, R. G. Jaeger, M. Feder, V. Hutchison, G. Roth, R. Ruibal, D. B. Seale, M. J. Tyler, D. Wake, M. H. Wake, E. Zimmermann, and an anonymous referee. Comments and suggestions from Martin Feder and Per Rosenkilde greatly helped me to improve the chapter. Marvalee Wake (University of California, Berkeley) provided surveys of the literature and personal observations on caecilians; I am grateful for her help.

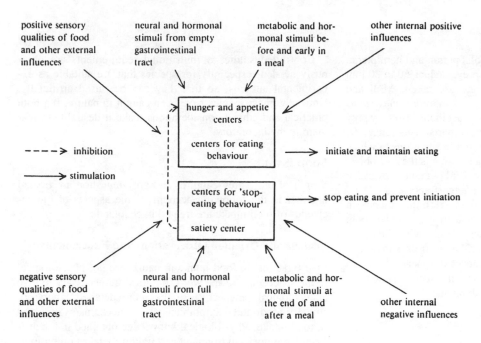

positive sensory qualities of food and other external influences

neural and hormonal stimuli from empty gastrointestinal tract

metabolic and hormonal stimuli before and early in a meal

other internal positive influences

Fig. 13.1 Survey of external and internal factors influencing food intake generally. (Reprinted, by permission, from Larsen 1984.)

- - - ► inhibition

———► stimulation

hunger and appetite centers

centers for eating behaviour

initiate and maintain eating

centers for 'stop-eating behaviour'

satiety center

stop eating and prevent initiation

negative sensory qualities of food and other external influences

neural and hormonal stimuli from full gastrointestinal tract

metabolic and hormonal stimuli at the end of and after a meal

other internal negative influences

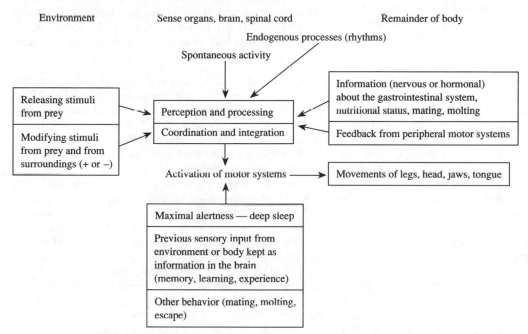

Fig. 13.2 Survey of external and internal factors influencing food intake in the toad.

Environment   Sense organs, brain, spinal cord   Remainder of body

Endogenous processes (rhythms)

Spontaneous activity

Releasing stimuli from prey

Modifying stimuli from prey and from surroundings (+ or −)

Perception and processing

Coordination and integration

Information (nervous or hormonal) about the gastrointestinal system, nutritional status, mating, molting

Feedback from peripheral motor systems

Activation of motor systems

Movements of legs, head, jaws, tongue

Maximal alertness — deep sleep

Previous sensory input from environment or body kept as information in the brain (memory, learning, experience)

Other behavior (mating, molting, escape)

TABLE 13.1 Transport, Digestion, and Absorption of Food in Amphibians

Site	Process
Mouth	Open and suck, bite, rasp or flip out tongue with sticky slime; secretion of weak amylase activity; secretion of mucus.
Pharynx	Swallow food.
Esophagus	Peristaltic movement.
Stomach (if present)	Peristaltic movement; mixing of food with digestive juice (HCl and proteases)
Intestine	Mixing of food with digestive juice from intestinal mucosa, pancreas, and bile bladder (proteases, lipases, peptidases, HCO_3^-, bile salts). Absorption by diffusion, active transport, and in some cases endocytosis (of protein).
Rectum	Reservoir until defecation; in some cases formation of a fecal sac.

(1967) has published a detailed study of food and feeding activity of *Hyla crucifer* (Anura: Hylidae).

Amphibian feeding has gained attention due to the possible use of amphibians for controlling pest animals in agriculture/ horticulture. Tyler (1982) gives a vivid description of the unintended effects of importing *Bufo marinus* to Queensland, Australia, in 1935. Schwabe (1977) discusses the possible use of *B. calamita*. One problem is that amphibians show little selectivity in food intake, so they will eat useful animals as well as pest animals.

Caecilians are opportunistic carnivores. Terrestrial forms eat a diversity of prey items that live in or on the ground cover or in the top layers of soil; aquatic and semiaquatic species forage in the substrate and take arthropod items that live on submerged objects (Wake 1978). Gut analyses of Costa Rican species (Wake 1980b, 1983) and of African taxa (M. H. Wake unpublished) show that, in order of frequency, several species of earthworms, termites, coleopteran and hemipteran larvae, ants, and occasional larger prey, such as 60 to 80 mm dermapteran and orthopteran instars, are taken. Moll and Smith (1967) reported that a large *Dermophis mexicanus* from Chiapas had eaten two lizards. Caecilians also may prey on small snakes (Wake 1983). In most parts of its range, *D. mexicanus* takes a diversity of prey, but in situations in which a single prey item is in great abundance, that is the sole object in the gut contents (Wake 1980b). Barbour and Loveridge (1928) noted that *Boulengerula boulengeri* appeared to specialize on termites and actively sought termite mounds in which to forage. Wake (1978) associated a particular tooth crown morphology in *Typhlonectes obesus* with their presumed habit of scraping coleopteran larvae from submerged logs. Even given this possible instance, it appears that most caecilians take a diversity of prey, and any specialization is a consequence of specific prey-item abundance.

Food in the Laboratory

Several parameters may be of interest in evaluating a given food type or feeding schedule: growth in body mass and length, net protein synthesis, skin condition, reproductive capacity, and resistance toward infections. The quality of the food depends not only on the content of nutrients, but also on its ability to elicit feeding and on its digestibility. Speaking about "optimal diet" necessitates a definition of what is meant by optimal with regard to the functions of the animal.

A huge amount of empirical knowledge exists and is reported in several general books on care of amphibians (e.g., Mattison 1982) or in amateur journals. Few experiments are published, however. Kaltenbach and Hagedorn (1981) have collected a list of fifty-seven published reports on the effects of various diets on amphibian metamorphosis. A few more may be added. Mohanty and Dash (1986) tested the effects of five different diets on growth and metamorphosis of larval *Rana tigrina*. Nagai, Nagai, and Nishikawa (1971) compared growth and absorption efficiency in larvae of *Bufo vulgaris* fed artificial food or larvae of their own species. Scorgie (1980) tested four different diets on growth and development of *B. bufo* larvae. Claussen and Layne (1983) fed *B. woodhousii* with mealworms, cabbage loopers, crickets, or a combination thereof. They consider mealworms superior food for promotion of growth. Modzelewski and Culley (1974) measured the growth of *R. catesbeiana* fed mosquito fish, earthworms, crickets, or combinations thereof. Rickets occurred on a diet of crickets, and muscles developed poorly on a diet of earthworms. The latter two studies, however, reported body mass but not body length and thus cannot distinguish between true growth and fat deposition (cf. Jørgensen and Wind-Larsen 1987b).

Caecilians are relatively easily maintained in the laboratory. Terrestrial taxa readily eat earthworms (*Lumbricus,* red worms, etc.; M. H. Wake unpublished). Occasional injection of a slurry of vitamins and minerals (especially calcium salts) into prey items provides additional nutrients, though the animals live for several years without such supplementation. Mealworms are not a preferred prey item. Aquatic taxa do well on a diet of 1-cm cubes of raw chicken liver placed in the water. Small caecilians eat *Tubifex.*

Controlled studies of nutritional requirements are obviously needed, especially for species that are suitable as experimental animals, so that they can be raised artificially. Until now most species have been caught in nature, but both practical and ethical considerations make it desirable to rear them in the laboratory.

FOOD INTAKE

Search of prey, prey capture, and prey ingestion are treated together in the following account. Some aspects of biomechanics of food intake are treated in chapter 11.

Ecologically Oriented Observations and Experiments

Investigations on food intake in nature are not physiological in the strict sense of the word, but they are necessary to give an ecological perspective to the more detailed laboratory studies in individual amphibians of the mechanisms involved in food intake. Physiological knowledge obtained in the artificial laboratory environment certainly only takes on biological meaning when an attempt is made to integrate it with that from data collected in nature. Ideally, the same species should be studied both in nature and in the laboratory. Fortunately, this has been done in a number of cases.

Urodeles Salamanders have been the subject of extensive and detailed investigations in nature and in the laboratory to quantify their food intake at the ecological level and their impact on forest ecosystems. Despite the small size and cryptic habits of certain salamander species, they are quantitatively important in the food web due to their great number and their energetically economic way of living (Burton and Likens 1975; Feder 1983b; Jaeger 1980a; Seale 1987; Toft 1985; see also chapters 4, 12, and 14).

Many of the more recent papers refer to "optimal foraging theory" and "feeding strategies." Speculation about evolution of feeding systems has been considerable, and interest has often centered on how amphibians can maximize net energy gain, both in food intake and digestion (see Seale 1987). In some cases the language used to describe feeding behavior indicates a conflation of proximal (physiological) and ultimate (evolutionary) explanations. For instance, it is assumed that amphibians prefer prey with high energy content that can be quickly and efficiently digested and absorbed.

Tests of the predictions of optimal foraging theory involving amphibians, whether experimental or descriptive, tend to be negative or only partially positive. This is probably because the evolutionary importance of obtaining sufficient energy (and food material of sufficient quality) for survival, growth, and reproduction has led some investigators to neglect other factors that affect food intake. These include, for example, movement, size (irrespective of energy content), and shape of prey. In a given situation, individuals may not maximize energy intake per unit time. This is not surprising, since nothing in nature is optimal in all possible regards. A more reasonable view is that in extant amphibian species, a sufficient number of males and females eat, digest, and assimilate enough food to allow survival and reproduction.

The following features of amphibians may contribute to the inapplicability of optimal foraging theory. Amphibians have a central nervous system in which key stimuli elicit motor patterns suitable for food intake (also see chapters 2 and 16). However, these key stimuli may have no direct correlation with nutritional value. By comparison with endotherms, amphibians have modest caloric and nutritional requirements and grow slowly. Thus, maximization of energy intake per unit time may be far less critical for amphibians than for endotherms. Finally, amphibians (like other organisms) evolve as entities; natural selection cannot decouple foraging from all other attributes or organismal structure and function (see the exemplary discussion by Roth and Wake 1985b, 1989).

Jaeger and his co-workers present many interesting data from investigations in nature and from experiments in the laboratory. A four-year field study of *Plethodon cinereus* (Plethodontidae) recorded the volume and number of prey in the stomach under varying conditions of rainfall and environmental temperature (Jaeger 1980a). On this basis energy budgets were calculated and evolutionary speculation made. (Their various laboratory experiments will be described below.)

Detailed investigations on feeding of *Triturus vulgaris* (Salamandridae) in nature and in the laboratory have recently been published (Nuutinen and Ranta 1986; Ranta and Nuutinen 1985; Ranta, Tjossem, and Leikola 1987). Useful comparisons are made with teleosts and other vertebrates, but not with other urodele species. Feeding behavior and food intake was investigated in males and females, after various periods of food deprivation (decreasing satiety, increasing hunger), at different times of the day and night, and using different combinations of size and color of prey (*Daphnia*). Breathing activity, swimming, and sexual activity were also studied (Nuutinen and Ranta 1986). Prey size, the ability of prey to escape or fight after being captured, and handling time were related (Nuutinen and Ranta 1986). Such studies are important because they pay attention to various qualities of the food and to aspects of physiology other than feeding.

Anurans Studies on anurans comparable to those described for urodeles have been reviewed by Toft (1980a, 1985). Toft herself performed extensive field studies and compiled and evaluated the large literature. She stresses that many factors determine the type of prey consumed and discusses how species manage to exist in the same habitat and partition food and other resources. She argues convincingly against competition as a dominant factor; many amphibian species seem to coexist peacefully. Several inspiring but undocumented reports on American anurans in the older literature are cited in Duellman and Trueb (1986). Seale (1987) gives a broad and careful review of literature on anuran food and feeding, especially seen from an energetic point of view. She pays attention to "complex life cycles" but disregards physiological complexities. Alexander (1964) reports interesting observations on feeding behavior of *Bufo marinus* in an area populated by human beings. *B. marinus* was also studied extensively by Zug and Zug (1979).

Christian (1982) made an extensive year-long investigation of the prey found in the stomachs of 346 *Pseudacris triseriata* (Hylidae). Juveniles (17 to 19 mm) have more prey in their stomachs (and thus probably eat more prey per unit time) and are less discriminatory with regard to size than smaller or larger frogs (10.5 to 17 mm, 19 to 29.8 mm). This was discussed by Christian in an evolutionary context but also makes physiological sense, given that juveniles have the largest growth potential and also the largest appetite, and a large appetite makes an animal less discriminatory. The largest frogs were caught in their breeding period, in which food intake is generally reduced or abolished. The smallest frogs cannot eat very large prey (maximal prey length was 12.6 mm) because of the size of their mouth and pharynx. Interestingly, in the laboratory the smallest frogs (10 to 13 mm) could consume prey items 9 mm long, 1.5 times larger than the largest item encountered in the stomach content in frogs from nature. Under natural conditions prey of that size is encountered but apparently not consumed. Christian's discussion of what the frogs "encounter" and how they "select" or "choose" prey is misleading, because only the frequency distribution of prey is investigated by "suction sampling"; terms like "overlook," "omit," and "deletion" with regard to small prey do not contribute to a sound understanding of the mechanisms involved in food intake. Christian does not mention that very small food items are likely to be digested first and transported away, so stomach contents do not necessarily reflect ingested food.

Labanick (1976) made a similar extensive investigation of prey availability, consumption, and selection of prey in 279 cricket frogs, *Acris crepitans* (Hylidae). As in many other juvenile or adult anurans and urodeles, prey selection was not as important as prey availability. An additional explanation for Labanick's findings, that of habitat selection, deserves attention.

Freed (1982) performed a meticulous and thought-provoking experimental analysis of prey selection in *Hyla cinerea* (Hylidae). The study is based on extensive field studies and careful observations and experiments in the laboratory. Stomach contents from 163 frogs collected in the field were analyzed and described, and compared with prey abundance estimated by traps and sweep net. These results then led to laboratory experiments with thirty-five frogs. Their feeding responses to eight top-ranked prey species plus the attractive *Musca domestica*, normally used as food in the laboratory, were studied, and the behavior of the prey species was carefully observed. This yields a detailed insight in the importance of cues eliciting food intake (the stimulus strength). Freed (1982) was unable to demonstrate diurnal changes in prey selection in the laboratory, probably reflecting the artificial laboratory conditions. In nature, diurnal variation in both predator and prey behavior is probably of great importance. One important factor may be humidity, which is rarely measured or controlled in the laboratory. Humidity should receive more attention in studies of terrestrial amphibians and of the abundance and species composition of their prey.

In studies of European anurans, especially the common toad, *Bufo bufo*, there is a tradition of careful observations in nature or under seminatural conditions in terraria or enclosures (for exemplary studies of this sort see Eibl-Eibesfeldt 1952; Eikmanns 1955; Freisling 1948; Heusser 1968a, 1969; Lescure 1965, 1982; and Schneider 1954). These observations were rarely quantified according to modern standards of scientific documentation, but they do contain a wealth of reliable information of interest to physiologists and ethologists. As an example of the careful observations, oversimplified when cited in several later papers, I have translated three extracts from Eibl-Eibesfeldt (1952, 2–4): "F-J. Buytendijk (1941) distinguishes between frogs as 'sit-and-wait' animals and toads as hunting animals. J. Freisling (1948) considers this description insufficient since frogs may hunt on the banks of a lake, and toads may sit and wait." "Between the two extreme types of hunting and 'sit-and-wait' animals our anurans show many intermediary types. A comparison shows that dominant sitting-and-waiting and dominant hunting are not valid taxonomic characters, but only ecologically based types of behavior." "During the day adult toads [*Bufo bufo*] mostly hide and sleep or sit and wait for passing prey. Only in warm rainy weather they hunt in daytime. Juveniles tend to be active at daytime. They are often seen in sunshine, on moist meadows or fields or in forests." These quotations demonstrate well the complexities of feeding in nature; individual variation and variation in environmental conditions may determine whether an amphibian hunts or sits and waits.

A paper by Grüsser and Grüsser-Cornehls (1968) forms a rare example of neurophysiologists supplementing their laboratory studies with field experiments, and then discussing them together.

Hanne Gyde Poulsen and Jan Nyholm Pedersen (unpublished) studied food intake of ten female and thirty male *Bufo bufo* in a dimly lit forest for 104 days. Larsen and Pedersen (1982) undertook complementary laboratory studies, and Jørgensen (1986b) compared feeding patterns in nature and in the laboratory. To summarize the first study, activity in the field was related to rain and temperature, with most activity between 12° and 20°C. Rainfall and the number of toads leaving their hiding places (as indicated by the disruption of glue threads across the opening of toads' retreats) were correlated. On dry nights about 30% of the toads were active. About 55% were active with up to 2 mm rain, about 70% with 2 to 10 mm rain, and about 90% with more than 10 mm rain. However, the degree of stomach filling (evaluated by palpation) was not markedly different on dry and wet nights. Prey are available even on dry nights, and thus the pattern of activity cannot be explained solely by prey availability; water or just exploration in general are alternative explanations. When individual toads could be followed, they fed 0.5–8 m from their retreat; 36% found their prey on fallen trees, 30% on live trees, and 25% on the litter. The main prey was three species of wood lice.

The amount of food in the stomachs of toads in nature could be estimated from palpated stomach contents and parallel measurements on toads fed a well-defined number of wood lice in the laboratory. An annual food intake of about 22 kcal in males of around 30 g body mass was calculated from these and other data. An independent estimate (by L. O. Larsen) based on estimates of active days, length of the feeding period, and observed feeding activity was 34 kcal—not very different from the other estimate, and not unrealistic when compared with approximate estimates of energy used, lost, or deposited.

A quantitative study comparing the diet of *Rana temporaria* in northern Finland and southern Germany gives information on the importance of geographic and seasonal variation in prey availability (Itämies and Koskela 1970).

Caecilians The literature includes few ecological observations on caecilians and no experiments on feeding. M. H. Wake (unpublished) has assessed food preferences in five different terrestrial genera by applying extracts of diverse potential prey items (and such substances as honey) to cotton swabs and holding the swabs above the entrance holes to burrows of caecilians housed in tanks in the laboratory. Not surprisingly, animals conditioned in the laboratory sought earthworm extract 95% of the time; they did not respond to other prey items. The few trials using animals new to the laboratory showed no prey preference; the animals may well have been stressed.

Physiological Experiments

Experiments in the laboratory have mainly dealt with a few anuran and urodele species, and mainly terrestrial forms. Studies of the role of vision in food intake overwhelm the literature. Other aspects of physiological mechanisms involved in food intake are sparse, and toads seem to be the only group investigated comprehensively.

Martin, Witherspoon, and Keenleyside (1974) performed the classical work establishing the relative importance in urodeles of visual, chemical, and tactile stimuli for food intake with *Notophthalmus viridescens* (Salamandridae). Visual cues from mosquito larvae were more important than the chemical cues, and tactile cues were the least important. Movement of the prey is important but not necessary. A careful study by Lindquist and Bachmann (1982) on *Ambystoma tigrinum* (Ambystomatidae) eating earthworms showed that olfactory stimuli probably function in recognition of edible prey. However, little is known about inedible prey and consequences of intake of such prey in amphibians. Jaeger and his co-workers have performed a number of well-planned experiments testing the importance of prey size, type, and density and the importance of visual versus chemical cues from the prey in *Plethodon cinereus* (Plethodontidae; David and Jaeger 1981; Jaeger and Barnard, 1981; Jaeger and Rubin 1982; Jaeger, Joseph, and Barnard 1981; Jaeger, Barnard, and Joseph 1982). The data are important but do not elucidate physiological mechanisms. Taken together with the field observations, they give a well-founded insight into the biology of feeding in this species. However, the results are discussed in an unrealistic paradigm. The concluding sentences in Jaeger and Rubin (1982) may serve as an example: "Salamanders seem to refrain from making rash judgements of prey profitabilities on the size of prey alone, as suggested in general by Hughes (1979). Instead they forgo judgements on profitabilities until they have ample information about gross caloric value v. the rate of digestion of particular prey types. Currently we state this as a hypothesis until further experiments are completed, but obviously larger prey are not judged to be necessarily better prey by salamanders." This represents a step forward in relation to previous ideas, because it takes digestion/absorption into consideration, but apparently the authors still believe that the salamander chooses its prey on the basis of knowledge about prey profitability. The following physiological experiments have a more appropriate background, both with regard to planning and interpretation.

Visual Stimuli A wealth of experiments have elucidated the role of the visual system for orientation towards prey or dummies and for snapping (see also chapter 2). They include manipulation of prey stimuli (e.g., size, shape, color, rate, direction and pattern of movement) or of the surroundings (e.g., color of the background, light intensity, other sensory information like smell and sound). Further analysis of the visual system has been at the level of the retina and other parts of the brain. Several excellent reviews of this important work have appeared: a book on urodeles by Roth (1987), chapters on anurans by Ingle (1983), Grüsser-Cornehls (1984), and Ewert (1987), and a general mathematical model (an der Heiden and Roth 1987). Increasingly sophisticated methodology is being used. For example, a recent important development has been a technique for registration of neuronal activity in freely moving toads (see Ewert 1984). This area of research has developed to a very high level of quality, but its scope is somewhat restricted. For a long time, attention has focused on higher levels of the central nervous system. A historical review of integrative functions of the brain (Jørgensen 1974a) widens this scope by citing older literature that points to the importance of the medulla oblongata and the spinal cord for motor patterns, and lately the medulla oblongata has again been investigated (Satou and Ewert 1985). This wider scope allows attempts to analyze how the central nervous system processes visual information that then activates motor activity such as approach, orientation, fixation, and snapping (Satou et al. 1985). This work provides the physiological background for the "decision" of the animal as to what to eat, whereas "optimal foraging theory" considers the evolutionary context of such "decisions." A more profitable approach to evolutionary aspects of feeding is evident in two papers by Roth and Wake (1985b) and Wake and Larson (1987). They place food-catching mechanisms and the morphological structures related to tongue protrusion (snapping) in an evolutionary perspective. The two papers represent a fine example of integrative biology, which works at all levels, from molecules to environment, includes structure and function, and pays attention to the whole life history.

Ingle and Crews (1985) thoughtfully discuss the discipline of neuroethology and broaden the scope of the aforementioned studies, which center on visual information. They stress the importance of naturalistic conditions in experimental situations, and of combining studies in the field and the laboratory. Statements about the importance of this are numerous, but few investigators actually perform such investigations.

Burghagen and Ewert (1983) and Roth and Wiggers (1983) have reexamined the old dogma that *Bufo bufo* only respond to moving prey. Burghagen and Ewert (1983) show convincingly that under certain conditions toads may respond by snapping at a nonmoving prey, provided the image moves on the retina, as when the toad walks towards the dummy or when the toad is passively moved. This corresponds to previous reports (Honigmann 1944; Kaess and Kaess 1960) that when the background moves and the prey is stationary, the toad may also respond by snapping. This can be considered a relatively simple brain process. More surprising are the observations of Roth and Wiggers (1983); they show that toads may respond by snapping at stationary dummies (especially black squares on a wall at long distance), and they describe the behavior in the following way:

> In most choice tests, toads approached the preferred stimulus directly without stopping or glancing at the other stimulus. Often the subjects sat quietly in front of and facing the stimulus for several seconds. Head movements, which are supposed to be means for localization of stationary stimuli, were observed in only two of several hundred cases. About 10% of the subjects wiped their mouth with the forelegs; most of these subjects did not respond to the stimulus afterwards. . . . The behavioral observations reported here indeed indicate that the choice between the two stimuli is done before approaching them from a distance of 30 cm. The subjects nearly always directly approached the stimulus at which they snapped afterwards without turning to the other stimulus, fixated the stimulus for several seconds, and then snapped at it. (230, 232)

Toads facing a stationary target may thus show a subtle brain function resulting either in a "decision" to go and snap or alternative behaviors such as mouth (or eye) wiping. The latter are typical of other "ambiguous" situations and have been described repeatedly (Eibl-Eibesfeldt 1952; Larsen and Sørensen 1980; Lescure 1965). Similar cases may involve obstacles, for example, jumping from a table to the floor (Larsen 1984) or passing barriers to approach prey (Collett 1982; Lock and Collett 1979). In the latter studies, toads (*Bufo bufo, B. marinus,* and *B. viridis*) seem to obey "rules" that do not necessarily take them the shortest route to the goal. They may walk with closed eyes, and the "planning" of the route seems to take place before the toads move. Recent work on activity of premotor interneurons involved in snapping (Satou et al. 1985) will probably lead to deepened understanding of these more subtle functions of the brain.

The plasticity and capacity for processing information of the amphibian brain is large (Ingle 1976). Explanations of differences between individual amphibians, and differing results obtained at different habitats in nature or in different laboratories, should consider the long-term effects of previous experience with prey. The response to a black square on a wall as described above, for instance, may necessitate previous exposure to houseflies. Luthardt and Roth (1979) provided the best documentation of this point in an experiment with *Salamandra salamandra* (Salamandridae). They raised newly metamorphosed salamanders with five types of live or dead food (moved or stationary) for up to 6 months and tested the reactions of the salamanders to various movement patterns. Salamanders tended to prefer a movement pattern similar to that of their food during postmetamorphic development, even if stationary. Roth (1987, 65–82) provides an excellent discussion of the "ontogeny of feeding behavior and the role of learning."

In approach to prey and in snapping, the ability to measure distances is important (see a recent discussion by Douglas, Collett, and Wagner 1986). From experimental brain studies, Grobstein, Comer, and Kostyk (1983) attempted to model how a frog (*Rana pipiens*) can link sensory information (vi-

TABLE 13.2   Habituation in *Bufo boreas:* Number of Snappings at Dummy Mealworm

Date	Female No. 1	2	3	Date	Male No. p1	S2	p2	p3	p5
21 August	6	15	13	2 April	15	3	17	5	7
24 August	0	>5	0	4 April	2		11	1	0
27 August	0	0	0	7 April	2		0	2	1
29 August	0	0	0	9 April	0	0	1	0	0
31 August	0	1	0	24 April	2		4	0	0
5 September	0	1?	0	22 May	3	0	0	0	0
6 September	0	0	0						
7 September	0	0	0						
13 September	0	0	0						
18 September[a]		0	0						
9 October	10	0	0						
11 October	1	5	0						
12 October	2	0	0						
16 October	0		3						
17 October		0							
7 November	1?	0	0						

Source: Reprinted, by permission, from Larsen 1984.

Note: The figures indicate number of snappings in the mealworm-dummy apparatus described by Larsen and Sørensen 1980.

[a]Cricket odor added.

sual or tactile) with the motor output, resulting in movements of the body, head, and tongue so that the prey is hit; they concluded that their model was too simple!

The ability to react to prey dummies by snapping persists at very low light intensities in at least two species of urodeles (Roth 1987) and in the toad *Bufo bufo* (Aho et al. 1988; Larsen and Pedersen 1982). In *B. bufo* the number of photons reaching the retina is so small that the question arises of how the toad distinguishes this information from spontaneous photoisomerizations. Aho et al. (1988) argue that the low temperature of Scandinavian toads at night reduces the spontaneous photoisomerization compared with that in the warmer eyes of mammals. In addition, the brain may be able to distinguish the regular movement of the image of the prey over the retina in both eyes from photoisomerizations in the retina, which will not occur in a synchronized way in the two eyes or form a regular pattern.

Caecilians probably do not rely on visual stimuli for prey identification. Their eyes are reduced, and components of accommodation and image formation are absent; some species lack lenses and some have amorphous retinas. Wake (1985a) inferred from morphology that even taxa with the most reduced eyes have the components necessary for light versus dark discrimination. Many species of caecilians come to the surface at dusk, especially in light rains, apparently to forage. This may be the sole effect of visual stimulation associated with prey capture.

Odor   Odor of the prey elicits food intake in many amphibians (see Duellman and Trueb 1986 for extensive references). In *Bufo bufo,* odor of prey only stimulates the visually elicited orientation response towards prey dummies but does not elicit the response (Ewert 1976). In *B. boreas* odor is very important, and cricket odor and mealworm odor may elicit a snapping response (see Dole, Rose, and Tachiki 1981). If the source of odor is located on a dish, the toads may snap at the dish or elsewhere. If the odor is uniformly distributed around

the toad, it may snap in any direction (L. O. Larsen pers. observation) and thus apparently wastes energy. On the other hand *B. boreas* avoids wasting energy in a situation where *B. bufo* does so. As shown in table 13.2, *B. boreas* displayed rapid and long-lasting habituation to the same dummy apparatus to which *B. bufo* do not habituate if tested for a short time every second day (Larsen and Pedersen 1982; Larsen and Sørensen 1980). The habituation in *B. boreas* seemed to be specific for the mealworm dummy (a piece of light-brown rubber tubing), because toads still snapped at live mealworms placed beneath the transparent box at the same place the dummies passed. Cricket odor, which would elicit snapping in other situations, did not break the habituation. The tendency for odor from prey to elicit snapping in *B. boreas* causes them to eat dead (nonmoving) mealworms or crickets or even meatballs, which *B. bufo* never do (Larsen 1984, pers. observation). Thus, two species as similar in behavior repertoire as *B. boreas* and *B. bufo* may differ markedly in their response to olfactory stimuli and to a dummy.

Caecilians use olfactory cues for prey detection (see Billo and Wake 1987) and possibly identification of conspecifics (Taylor 1968). The olfactory apparatus is well developed, with large olfactory sacs and vomeronasal organs (information summarized in Schmidt and Wake 1990). The relative sizes of olfactory sacs and vomeronasal organs and sensory epithelium vary among taxa (Schmidt and Wake 1990). Caecilians have an extrusible tentacle, a structure unique among vertebrates, which apparently carries odorants from the external environment to the vomeronasal organ. Billo and Wake (1987) summarize the structure and development of the tentacle and postulate its evolutionary origin. The lumen of the tentacle opens into the vomeronasal organ. The tentacle incorporates part of the "eyelid" and of the palpebral space to encompass the nasolacrimal duct. The Harderian gland lubricates the channel of the tentacle. The tentacle is retracted by the retractor tentaculi muscle, which is homologous to the retractor bulbi of the eye of other amphibians. Olfaction

TABLE 13.3 Feeding and "Drinking" in *Bufo bufo*

| | 8–9 March (22 h) | | | | | | 14–15 March (22 h) | | | | | | 15–16 March (23.5 h) | | | | | |
| | Males | | | Females | | | Males | | | Females | | | Males | | | Females | | |
Toad No.	61	57	59	62	58	60	61	57	59	62	58	60	61	57	59	62	58	60
Weight (g)	26	33	30	86	60	85												
Number of feeding periods	3	3	6	5	3	3	3	7	9	3	6	3	2	2	3	3	4	3
Time feeding (%)	8	4	15	4	7	6	6	7	30	11	12	3	3	2	6	24	8	4
Mealworms eaten (g)	3.9	1.5	0.9	2.0	3.0	3.2		14–16 March:					5.0	4.9	3.3	4.3	6.3	4.7
Number of drinking periods	1	2	1	5	2	1	2	1	3	1	1	1	2	1	2	1	2	0
Time drinking (%)	19	10	11	20	41	20	33	7	43	8	46	41	24	7	36	22	37	0
Time hidden (%)	73	82	54	66	48	72	48	81	0	79	30	53	72	86	53	53	54	96

Source: Reprinted, by permission, from Larsen 1984.

seems enhanced by a structure largely formed of components that were formerly associated with the eye in evolutionary history. The tentacle is also tactile, having such sensory structures at its tip (Fox 1985b). Odorants produce a response when introduced to caecilians (see the experiments reported above). The first indication of perception of odor is increased and rapid extrusion and retraction of the tentacles in terrestrial taxa; animals then move slowly toward the source of the odor. When food is placed in the tank of aquatic species, 1–2 min pass before the food is perceived. The animals then swim toward it, but often overshoot. M. H. Wake (unpublished) speculates that the dispersion of odorants in the water is required for perception and also creates an initially imprecise field for location of prey. Having found one piece of food, the animals locate others much more precisely.

Other Senses Knowledge about the role of other sensory systems, including taste, hearing, or touch, in food intake in adults is scattered and superficial, although more is known for larvae (see chapter 16). Himstedt, Kopp, and Schmidt (1982) showed that an electric stimulus could elicit snapping in *Ambystoma mexicanum* (Caudata: Ambystomatidae) previously stimulated by a prey dummy; sensory organs in the skin probably detect the electric stimulus. Ranta and co-workers (1990) present experimental evidence for involvement of nonvisual cues when *Triturus vulgaris* (Caudata:Salamandridae) feed on chironomid larvae hidden in the sediment, and they argue for involvement of the lateral line organs.

Time Patterns of Food Intake Few quantitative descriptions exist of patterns in time of food intake apart from those obtained in the studies of *Bufo bufo* reported below. Such knowledge is essential for planning and interpretation of experiments on, for example, hunger and satiety mechanisms.

Larsen (1984) videotaped voluntary food intake in *B. bufo*. Table 13.3 shows that the eating periods (meals) were well defined, although of irregular duration and distribution in time. Periods of water uptake were also well defined, but they showed no obvious relation to the feeding periods. Toads had thirty-one meals on the first day of observation, but only seventeen on the following day, probably because they filled their digestive tract faster than it could be emptied. Figure 13.3 shows a similar phenomenon in *B. boreas*. A 24-h break in feeding is enough to reestablish appetite. These studies

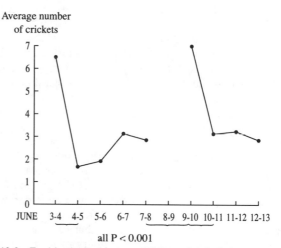

Fig. 13.3 Food intake in thirteen ad libitum–fed *Bufo boreas* males. No food for 24 h. Statistics: Student's *t*-test. *P* < .001 for all differences between dates connected with a *bracket*. (Reprinted, by permission, from Larsen 1984.)

reflect short-term regulation of food intake in relation to one or a few meals.

Individual variation in feeding and drinking activity was followed for 61 days in forty-six male *B. bufo* (Jytte Nielsen unpublished; see Larsen 1984). The toads were kept individually, and their movements were deduced from their footprints (carbon powder on filter paper). These toads were offered mealworms for 24 h once a week. Individual variation in activity was large. Some toads stopped eating after a previous feeding period of about 3 months and stayed in their shelters for up to 29 days. During such periods they slowly lost mass (mainly water), up to 31.6% of their body mass, with an average mass loss of 1.6% per day (range 1.0–2.6%, N = 12). Other toads continued to eat and visit water. None of the toads were active only when fed. The most active toad left shelter 49 days out of 61 and fed 8 out of 8 times food was offered. The least active toad left shelter 9 out of 61 days and ate 3 times.

Guha, Jørgensen, and Larsen (1980) and Jørgensen (1986b, 1989) followed long-term changes in overall food intake in *B. bufo*. A typical pattern is an initial rise in food intake, followed by a plateau and a gradual decline to a level of low or no food intake. Such a lack of food intake despite an empty stomach may be termed long-term satiety. A combination of endogenous processes related to season and to high level of fat reserves is probably responsible for long-term satiety in these experiments. The initial rise may have several explanations. Toads taken from artificial hibernation in one experiment required from 3 to more than 19 days to develop quick and efficient snapping responses (Jytte Nielsen unpublished; see Larsen 1984). Growth of the gastrointestinal tract may also be important. In frogs the mass of the gastrointestinal tract changes markedly during the year (Juszczyk, Obrzut, and Zamachowski 1966). Studies of morphology and function of the gastrointestinal tract in nature and under various experimental situations would be rewarding.

Daily rhythms in feeding activity are evident, especially in day-active or night-active species. However, experimental studies on diurnal rhythms of feeding are rare. Van Bergeijk (1967) examined "anticipatory feeding behavior" in which captive *Rana catesbeiana* gathered *before* food appeared, at a site where food was presented each working day at 1600. This behavior turned out to be a conditioned response related to the human working schedule; it did not occur during holidays. However, a careful analysis revealed a slight endogenous (circadian) rhythmicity in the behavior in relation to land/water of these frogs; around 0200 most frogs appeared on land (in the absence of food). These experiments were supplemented with further experiments with change of time and place of feeding to see how fast the frogs learned and changed their habits; the frogs were able to learn and forget and relearn. No anticipatory activity was present during relearning. In the beginning of a regular feeding schedule frogs apparently react only to food stimuli, but later they react in advance, probably because of a memory of food combined with a registration of sensory information related to the working day. Van Bergeijk's (1967) paper is a good example of careful and open-minded experimental work. It would be interesting to extend the study with observation of individual variation in feeding and learning.

Lescure (1965) reported changed food intake as a result of learning in *Bufo bufo*. This work supplements the often-cited works of Brower, Brower, and Westcott (1960), Brower and Brower (1962), and Cott (1936); like these, Lescure (1965) describes the individual variability in the modification of the behavior of the toads toward bees. Lescure also considers the varying tendency of bees to sting, and the varying interaction between individual bees and individual toads. Figure 13.4 shows that not all the toads avoided bees, but they ate at a constant level from day 4 to 9. Moreover, the time course of the food intake depended on the size of toads (fig. 13.4B). Lescure argued that the large toads avoid stings because of their forceful tongue snap. He described and discussed many details in behavior and physiology elucidating various factors in figures 13.1 and 13.2, and he showed clearly that food intake depends on a variety of external and internal factors, of which hunger or appetite is but one.

Effects of Hormones Injections of growth hormone can modify the typical pattern of food intake described above, as first shown in young *Bufo boreas* treated with two types and dosages of growth hormone (Zipser, Licht, and Bern 1969). The same phenomenon occurs in adult male *B. boreas* (Larsen 1984; Larsen and Licht 1984) treated for 7 weeks with

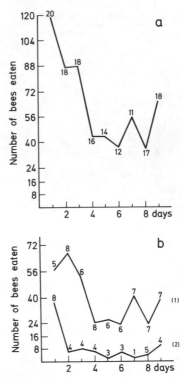

Fig. 13.4 *a*, Number of bees (*Apis mellifica*) eaten by thirty *Bufo bufo* on consecutive days. The *figures* on the curve indicate number of feeding toads. *b*, Data from the ten largest (> 10 cm) (*1*) and the ten smallest (< 9 cm) toads (*2*); otherwise as in *a*. (Redrawn from Lescure 1965.)

growth hormone, either bovine or from *Rana catesbeiana*. The bovine growth hormone had the most marked effects (fig. 13.5). The growth hormone–treated toads grew in mass and length for a longer period than control toads. The time course of events was similar to the *B. bufo* experiments, with an initial rise in food intake over the first 4 to 5 weeks and then a drop. At the same time growth leveled off in controls, but in toads treated with growth hormone, growth continued and food intake dropped less. Growth hormone improved food conversion from around 40% to around 60%. Growth hormone may exert its main effect via a counteraction of the long-term satiety otherwise seen in well-fed toads after some weeks. Jørgensen (1989) and Wind-Larsen and Jørgensen (1987) confirmed and extended these studies with regard to pattern and dosage of growth hormone in *B. bufo*.

In this connection some papers on the effect of total hypophysectomy or of ablation of its pars distalis alone are relevant. The effects reported in the literature vary from none to total abolition of food intake. Larsen and Sørensen (1980) reconciled these apparent discrepancies, by critical analysis of literature and by experiments with *B. bufo*. They concluded that the pars distalis hormones facilitate feeding behavior directly or indirectly, and that the pars distalis is necessary for normal feeding behavior in frogs and toads when the stimulus strength of the prey is weak and/or when the animal is well fed; the pars distalis is less important if the stimulus strength of the prey is high and/or the animal is starved. Nybroe, Rosenkilde, and Ryttersgaard (1985) give good examples of the variable effects of hypophysectomy and substitution therapy on food intake and the pattern of feeding

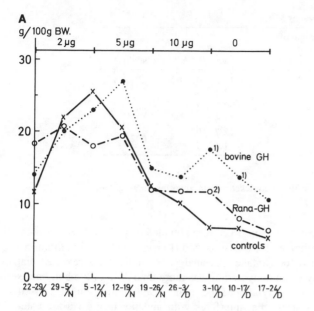

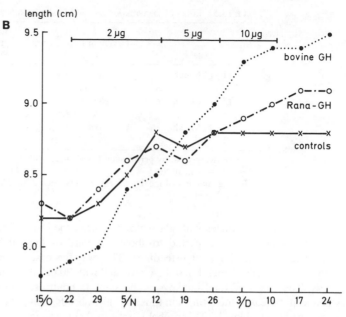

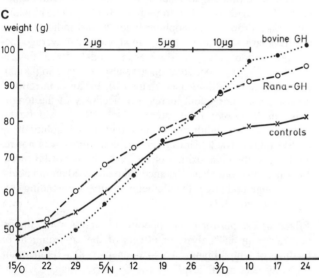

Fig. 13.5 *a*, food intake in growth hormone–treated *Bufo boreas* males (injections five times per week). Grams of food eaten each week expressed as percentage of body weight at the beginning of that week. The values indicated by *1)* and *2)* were significantly different from those of the control toads. *1), p* = .016; *2), p* = .004 (a two-tailed Mann-Whitney test). *b*, body length in growth hormone–treated *B. boreas* males. *C*, body weight in growth hormone–treated *B. boreas* males.

behavior in *Xenopus laevis*. Animals were fed kidney, liver, or heart, and it was noted that "control animals were easily disturbed and would not eat immediately when food was offered, but ate during the following 90 min. Hypophysectomized animals treated with growth hormone ate as soon as they discovered the food, but only for a short period. Untreated hypophysectomized animals ate vigourously when food was offered, but soon lost interest and surplus food left in the containers was generally not eaten" (261).

No other hormones than growth hormone have been studied with regard to effects on food intake. In view of the generally low or lacking food intake in the period of breeding, a study of the possible role of gonadotropin, prolactin, sex steroids, and interrenal steroids should be undertaken.

Effects of Stomach Filling Larsen (1984) experimentally analyzed mechanisms of short-term satiety in *Bufo boreas* by force-feeding them glass beads and testing their food intake afterwards with mealworms or crickets (table 13.4). Force-

TABLE 13.4 Food Intake in *Bufo boreas* Females after Force-feeding with Glass Beads

	No. of Tests[a]	No. of Beads	Mealworms Eaten[b], Average (Range)	Probability
Control	8	0	27.8 (0–51)	}.03
Bead-fed	8	60	9.7 (0–20)	
Control	4	0	25.5 (12–45)	}.006
Bead-fed	4	20 or 40	10.3 (3–24)	
Next day, percentage of day 1				
Control	All		103% (44–263%)	} <.002
Bead-fed	All		296% (93–667%)	

Source: Reprinted, by permission, from Larsen 1984.

Notes: Statistics: two-tailed Mann-Whitney test. Weight of toads 50–60 g.

[a] Two females in each test.

[b] Or equivalents. One cricket = 4 mealworms (in weight as well as volume).

TABLE 13.5 Effect of Dehydration on Food Intake in *Bufo boreas* Males

Date	Degree of Dehydration (Range)	Length of Feeding Period (h)	Amount Eaten[a]	Probability
11–12 March	None	4	14.3	.002
	24% (12–37)		2.1	
17–18 March	None	4	30.7	.07
	17% (14–20)		13.0	
24–25 March	None	2	12.7	.002
	25% (20–32)		1.4	

Source: Reprinted, by permission, from Larsen 1984.
Note: $N = 7$ in all tests.
[a] Average number of mealworm equivalents eaten during 2 or 4h. One cricket = 4 mealworms (in weight as well as volume).

feeding *B. boreas* females with glass beads reduced food intake in a subsequent 2-h period to about one-third of the control level (after sham force-feeding). This was the case both with 60 beads, which filled the toads, and with 20 or 40 beads. The next day food intake was the same in controls, whereas it increased three times in those fed glass beads, that is, reached control levels. This probably reflects that the food intake of controls on one day was too small to affect food intake the next day, and that the toads in the group fed glass beads had no more beads left in the stomach. They appeared as "feces" after more than 1–2 days. That toads filled with glass beads still may eat mealworms probably reflects rapid emptying of the stomach and the attractiveness of mealworms. Among the controls a majority ate intermittently for 2 h, whereas among the bead-fed toads a majority ate a little early in the feeding period and then stopped. That 20 and 40 glass beads did not cause a smaller reduction in food intake than 60 beads may reflect that the rate of stomach emptying is larger when the stomach is maximally distended than when it is not full, which may counteract the smaller distension caused by the smaller number of beads. Another possibility is that 20 beads elicits maximal sensory or hormonal output from the stomach. When a large meal is eaten voluntarily, the stimulating effect of odor and perhaps taste are probably important to make the toad continue feeding until it is full.

Enough glass beads to fill the stomach weigh about 10 g, corresponding to the mass of 80 mealworms or 20 crickets; in volume 10 g of glass beads correspond to 9 ml and 36 mealworms or 9 crickets. The latter number of prey items correspond to the size of a large meal, supporting the importance of food volume and stomach distension in satiety. In the field Livezey (1962) found twenty-one food items in the stomach of an average adult *B. boreas*. That stomach filling may be the primary regulator of the amount of prey eaten compared to other characteristics of the prey (size, color, way of moving, contrast to the background, odor, chemical composition, taste) was demonstrated in the growth hormone experiment (see above), where the toads were alternately fed mealworms and crickets. Food intake (in g) in a 24-h period did not differ with these two very different prey species.

Effects of Dehydration or High Salinity

Dehydration may limit food intake in terrestrial amphibians. Feder (1983b) reviewed the literature on the correlation between relative humidity and duration of foraging. However, little is known about the mechanisms by which dehydration affects feeding.

The data in table 13.5 were obtained from *Bufo boreas* males, dehydrated for a 24-h period (Larsen 1984). Dehydration reduced food intake. An analysis of individuals revealed that only when dehydration was more than 20% of the body mass did it clearly affect food intake. Dehydration might in itself be a stress that interferes with appetite (e.g., via the catecholamine–blood sugar–insulin complex). To examine this possibility, toads were kept on a black background, in which situation a drop in melanophore index would indicate stress (see Bagnara and Hadley 1973). In all cases the average melanophore index was a little lower in the dehydrated than in the control group. Dehydration may also increase ionic concentration in body fluids (see chapter 6). In this connection a decrease and subsequent increase in accuracy of the tongue strike in *B. boreas* is of interest (Dole, Rose, and Baxter 1985). They kept adult toads for 10 days in salt solutions up to 400 mOsm NaCl. Unfortunately, body mass was not recorded and the composition of the body fluids not followed. Not only ions, but also substances like urea and amino acids, may change and affect the elements involved in feeding (see figs. 13.1 and 13.2).

Effects of Temperature

Temperature is another very important factor in an analysis of effects of the environment on feeding of amphibians (see also chapter 8). Temperature probably acts at all levels of the body (see figs. 13.1 and 13.2), but few details are known about the most important sites of action.

Although *Bufo bufo* are stated not to feed below 7° to 8°C (Lescure 1965), they do snap at 5°C in a mealworm-dummy apparatus, although rarely and slowly (L. O. Larsen pers. observation). Temperature of course also affects the abundance and behavior of prey, which may explain the apparent discrepancy.

Surprisingly few experiments have been performed on the effect of temperature on food intake in urodeles. Merchant (1970) found that salamanders (*Plethodon cinereus:* Plethodontidae) fed ants ate about 17 to 18 cal·g⁻¹·day⁻¹ at 10° to 15°C and much less at 5°, 20°, and 25°C (about 3 to 5 cal·g⁻¹·day⁻¹) at an unspecified time of the year. These laboratory findings were compared with field data from caged salamanders in late May (15.5°C), mid-July (18.8°C), and late September (14.5°C). The field data corresponded to those expected on the basis of the laboratory data, assuming that temperature is the most important parameter for food intake. Since humidity, rain, availability of prey, and endogenous changes during the year are known to be important too, this assumption appears unrealistic. Furthermore, data from free-ranging salamanders in April, June, August, and September are far more variable than data from the laboratory and the cages, but unfortunately temperature of the environment was not reported.

More experiments used anurans. Stevens (1988a, 1988b, 1988c) carefully studied food intake in *Bufo americanus* from 5° to 35°C, investigating both effects of acute changes in temperature and thermal acclimation. In toads acclimated for 1 week, food intake was absent at 5°, maximal at 20°, and half-maximal at 35°C (1988c). Mealworms were presented on a moving track, eliminating the importance of temperature effects on prey behavior (Stevens 1988b, 1988c). This was not the case in Stevens (1988a), in which crickets were used as food; in that study the rate of acclimation at changes from 20° to 10° or from 10° to 20°C were tested and found to require days or even weeks. Since food intake is a very variable phenomenon, long-term experiments are difficult.

Lillywhite, Licht, and Chelgren (1973) studied intake of mealworms in young *Bufo boreas* at 14°, 20°, 27°, and 33°C and in a photothermal gradient for 8 weeks. Survival was poor at 33°C. Food intake was otherwise positively correlated with temperature. In the gradient the preferred body temperature was from 22° to 32°C, and food intake was initially high; food intake declined in weeks 4 to 6. The decline was correlated with a decline in growth rates and perhaps caused by inadequate access to the heat source due to crowding. When these toads were placed in two photothermal gradients, rapid growth was resumed and food intake increased. Temperature also affects food intake in *Bufo bufo* (fig. 13.6).

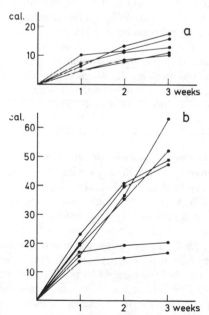

Fig. 13.6 Food intake in *Bufo bufo* fed mealworms ad libitum. *a*, At 15°C: one sexually mature female, two juveniles, and two males (14–25 g). *b*, At 30°C: three females and three males (16–19 g). The toads were kept unfed at about 21°C for 8 days before the experiment. The two toads (males) that showed decreased food intake after the first week grew in length and mass only during that week. (The experiments were performed by C. Christophersen, Lars Nielsen, Gert Lorenzen, and John Mønsted Jensen.)

Effects of Social Interactions

The ecological literature suggests competition for food and consequent establishment of feeding hierarchies. However, experiments are few (see Boice and Williams 1971; Tracy 1973), and the consequences of competition and feeding hierarchies for nutritional condition or growth are unknown. In a recent experiment toads of similar size were kept together under crowded conditions (five per cage) or singly, and fed for only 1 h each day (Larsen et al. 1990). The crowded toads ate, grew, and digested as well as the single toads but had a lower melanophore index on a black illuminated background, indicating "excitement." A feeding hierarchy does not necessarily involve aggressive behavior. With food available ad libitum, small toads may be prevented from eating by the mere presence of larger toads; when such small toads are isolated, they often start feeding and growing.

Hunger and Satiety

Hunger (appetite, motivation for eating) can be measured in a number of ways in amphibians feeding on prey animals: (1) With live prey, measurements are made of the amount eaten, the latency period, and the rate and intensity of the feeding response. (2) With prey dummies, measurements are made of orientation or snapping responses, the latter probably best reflecting the motivation for eating. Satiety is avoided, but habituation may be a problem. (3) Measurements can also be made of the willingness to neglect bad taste or to circumvent obstacles to obtain food. Such behavior has been investigated but not yet applied in studies of hunger (Mikulka, Vaughan, and Hughes 1981; Collett 1982). The emergence from retreats may reflect hunger, but other factors (e.g., thirst) may be important too.

When an amphibian does not eat when food is presented, or when it stops eating and turns or walks away from the prey, it may be sated. One problem is to exclude other factors than satiety. Before and during molting in *Bufo bufo*, food stimuli must be strong to elicit feeding (Heusser 1958b; Larsen and Pedersen 1982). Sleep will postpone feeding. Heusser (1958a) describes a sleeping natterjack toad (*B. calamita*) that registered prey odor, breathed more frequently, raised its head from the sleep posture (the same as during hibernation) with eyes still half-closed, awakened, and pursued the prey. Apart from the natural situations mentioned above, sickness or infections may cause lowered or total lack of food intake, as may distracting stimuli.

Heatwole and Heatwole (1968) performed the first experiment related to hunger and satiety in amphibians, but did not plan the experiment or discuss the data in a physiological context. They investigated the effects of increasing amount of food eaten and increasing time of food deprivation on prey selection or avoidance in *Bufo fowleri*. Although the study has serious shortcomings (with regard to selection of prey animals and toads and with regard to timing), at least it assumes that amphibians do have satiety mechanisms. Otherwise most authors describing feeding had focused on the voracious feeding of various amphibians. Heatwole and Heatwole (1968) demonstrated that the upper size threshold for prey decreased with increased food intake.

The mechanisms responsible for initiation of food intake, for its continuation, and for stopping food intake in amphibians have received surprisingly little attention apart from the glass-bead experiments reported above. The following studies are worthy of mention because they may inspire further research, although they are inconclusive with regard to physiological mechanisms. Lillywhite, Licht, and Chelgren (1973) found that juvenile *Bufo boreas* in a photothermal gradient showed a temperature preference of about 26° to 27°C when fed but preferred 15° to 20° during starvation. The authors then filled the stomach of the starved toads with glass beads, but this did not increase the preferred body temperature. P. Licht and L. O. Larsen (unpublished) measured a preferred body temperature of about 23°C in *B. boreas* but could not demonstrate any effect of food intake on it. Carey (1978b) found only small differences in preferred body temperature of fed and starved *B. boreas* adults. Experiments with other fed and starved toad species did not give clear results (H. B. Lillywhite pers. comm.), but the preferred body temperatures of juvenile plethodontid salamanders, *Pseudoeurycea smithii*, increased after feeding (Feder 1982c).

The first observation of postprandial thermophily (Lillywhite, Licht, and Chelgren 1973) was interpreted as a physiological adaptation that maximizes growth rate in juvenile toads: thermophily will increase rates of digestion and growth, which presumably will outweigh increased energy requirements for maintenance (see also chapter 9). Not all subsequent studies have been consistent with the original observation. Moreover, the idea that maximum growth rate is "optimal" or "adaptive" should not be accepted uncritically. Still, relationships between feeding and preferred body temperature deserve additional study.

Lescure (1965) described the behavior of toads deprived of food. He states that reduction of hunger is difficult to achieve, but one large toad (10 cm) that had eaten three earthworms (15 to 20 cm each) did not react to earthworms the next day. Metcalf (1921) provides a vivid description of a *Bufo fowleri* eating from 26 to 43 May beetles (*Lachnosterna ephilida*) on six consecutive evenings. The toad showed "relish" in the first 15 to 20 beetles; after that it needed "coaxing" to eat more, and when it was "tempted" further, by a beetle in front of it, it hopped away in "disgust." This description should motivate research on the mechanisms behind these signs of appetite and satiety (but serves as an unfortunate example of anthropomorphism).

The only studies of brain function in relation to hunger and satiety are observations of Ewert (1984, 392–396) in a section called "motivation determining factors." He mentions neurophysiological data ("far from a quantitative treatment") related to level of satiation, time of the day or year, and air pressure. There seems to be a total lack of brain studies in amphibians aiming at centers for hunger and satiety, for instance, in hypothalamus.

Swallowing No physiological experiments related to swallowing have been published, but Dean (1980) described swallowing (and rejection of food) in *Bufo americanus* and *B. marinus*. The presence of food or other mechanical stimulus in the mouth elicits swallowing; glass beads placed in the mouth of hungry *B. boreas* are readily swallowed (L. O. Larsen pers. observation). A hungry toad is willing to swallow; infected, sick, or severely dehydrated *B. bufo* and *B. boreas* do not swallow when force-fed and spit out the food, or vomit if the food has been pressed into their stomachs (pers. observation). Retraction of the eyes and sometimes gaping and mouth wiping accompany swallowing in toads and frogs. Naitoh, Wassersug, and Leslie (1989) describe emetic behavior in detail for three anuran species. These authors conclude that the ability to vomit appears at metamorphosis when the amphibian becomes able to swallow a bolus of food.

FATE OF FOOD IN THE DIGESTIVE TRACT

The physiology of the digestive system is treated in many surveys of amphibian biology, most recently in Duellman and Trueb 1986. The only thorough review is by Reeder (1964), and the most recent review is by Seale (1987). Herter (1936, 16–27) gives a broad, basic, and critical review of the classical literature with many interesting details.

Before going into details, it is appropriate to ask how the environment influences the digestive system. Apart from the effects of temperature and stress factors mentioned earlier, some changes in structure and function may be adaptations to the annual cycle of feeding activity in the temperate zones, with maximum activity in the feeding period and minimum activity during hibernation. Much circumstantial evidence points to these phenomena as being basically endogenous and set by long-term adaptation to climate, and now only modified by unpredictable variations in temperature, amount of prey, and so forth. As is typical of the uneven distribution of knowledge in environmental physiology, little is known about the effect of environmental factors on the digestive system.

Juszczyk, Obrzut, and Zamachowski (1966) describe important changes in the gastrointestinal tract in *Rana temporaria*. The gastrointestinal tract reaches maximum relative mass by midsummer and declines *before* hibernation. In *R. esculenta* Geuze (1971) followed the structure of the gastric mucosa during hibernation and found indications of activation *before* the end of hibernation in spite of constant low temperature. Such endogenously controlled changes probably explain the observations that frogs kept at room temperature show little appetite in wintertime, and when force-fed do not digest the food properly (Herter 1936).

Transport

When food has been swallowed, it stays in the stomach for 8–24 h, during which it mixes with gastric secretions and digestion begins (Corse and Metter 1980; Johnson and Christiansen 1976; Miller 1909; Smith and Bragg 1949). Regrettably, some papers lack precise terminology. Freed (1980) used the terms "digestive rate," "gastric digestion," "gastric clearance," and "digestive clearance time" for disappearance of ingested flies from the stomach of *Hyla cinerea* (Anura: Hylidae). He obtained the data by pumping out stomach contents every 1 or 2 h over a 17-h period; this procedure undoubtedly stressed the frogs. Rates evaluated by means of palpation or killing animals at various intervals after feeding are probably more reliable. The rate of gastric emptying is probably related to internal and external factors such as species, size and sex, nutritional condition and health of the animal, time of the year, temperature, type and amount of food, disturbing factors, and so forth. Little is known about how these factors affect the stomach.

A rich classical literature on peristalsis and tonus (see Patterson 1916; Babkin 1924) investigated the mechanisms responsible for the activity of the smooth muscle system in gastric movements. Patterson recorded contractions in the stomach with a manometer attached to a balloon surgically implanted into the stomach of *Rana catesbeiana*. During fasting for 12–14 days at room temperature, "hunger contractions" increased but tonus did not. The "hunger contractions" disappeared below 13°C and above 35°C. When the balloon was inflated in the stomach, the stomach wall widened without increasing tonus. However, few modern studies exist, and the old data are difficult to interpret, because the authors paid little attention to the frog as a species in its own right; it only served as a model for the supposedly more complex functions in human beings.

The huge capacity for expansion seen in anuran stomachs is especially conspicuous in the following two examples; both examples, interestingly enough, are correlated with very specialized types of reproduction.

Scaphiopus couchii (Pelobatidae) emerge from their burrows in the sand of the desert for perhaps only one night to eat termites (present for about half an hour) and spawn. They may consume up to 55% of their body mass, an amount of food large enough to cover energy requirements for more than a year. In laboratory investigations, a sound (or vibration) stimulus corresponding to a heavy rainfall (and thunder) could elicit emergence from dormancy (Dimmitt and Ruibal 1980a, 1980b). This is the only known example of an external factor experimentally shown to induce emergence and subsequent feeding. Interestingly, soil moisture, which was expected to be important, was not essential.

Tyler and his co-workers have studied the mechanisms involved in "gastric brooding" in two Australian frog species, *Rheobatrachus silus* and *R. vitellinus* (Myobatrachidae). Both are very rare, so only a few specimens have been studied; supplementary physiological experiments have been performed on the closely related *Limnodynastes tasmaniensis* (Myobatrachidae) or on *Bufo marinus*. *R. silus* is the better investigated of the two species and also shows the most marked changes in the structure of the stomach during the brooding period (Fanning, Tyler, and Shearman 1982; Leong, Tyler, and Shearman 1986). Although never observed directly, the female is supposed to swallow fertilized eggs or embryos and keep them in her stomach for 6 to 8 weeks (Tyler and Carter 1981). The young frogs then leave the mother, one or a few at a time. In one instance twenty-six young frogs were "born" in this way; all together they weighed 7.7 g and the mother 11.6 g. The stomach was so expanded by the small frogs that the lungs apparently were nonfunctional. The authors do not discuss whether growth of the larvae can depend solely on yolk or whether extra supplies are obtained from the mother. If the gravid mother is disturbed, she may expel the young frogs prematurely by vomiting. Tyler and his co-workers have sought a substance secreted by the larvae that might be responsible for the reversible changes in structure and function of the gastrointestinal system during brooding. They isolated prostaglandin E_2 from the aquarium water containing twenty-two early-stage larvae that were prematurely born (Tyler et al. 1983). This substance and related substances inhibit acid secretion and delay gastric emptying

in *Bufo marinus* (Tyler et al. 1983; Taylor, Tyler, and Shearman 1985a, 1985b). During brooding, remains of food stay undigested in the intestine (Fanning, Tyler, and Shearman 1982). Prostaglandin also relaxes longitudinal muscles in isolated intestinal preparations in *B. marinus* and *L. tasmaniensis* (de la Lande et al. 1984). Besides prostaglandin, unknown factors related to the presence of larvae are probably responsible for preventing the mother from food intake, from digestion of the larvae, and from transporting them out of the stomach.

Several investigators have measured the time required for food to pass through the whole digestive system (transit or passage time). The same general remarks made about stomach emptying apply here. Importantly, the feeding pattern may influence intestinal transport; frequent feeding probably stimulates the transport system more than infrequent feeding or a single meal. Passage times of single meals of live food varied between 30 h and several days at various temperatures, according to Hofer (1972; *Rana esculenta/ridibunda* and *R. temporaria*, mealworms), Carey (1976; *Bufo boreas*, ants, crickets), Merchant (1970; *Plethodon cinereus*, ants), and Jaeger and Barnard (1981; *P. cinereus*, two species of *Drosophila*).

Gossling et al. (1980) followed transport of food marked with chromium oxide and introduced into the stomach or intestine of *Rana pipiens*. In spite of the sophisticated method, the data were few and perhaps not valid because of the abnormal way of presenting the food. The data for transport in the intestine were not conclusive, but the stomach was empty after about 3 h in frogs at 21°C and after 1–12 days at 4°C. Taylor, Tyler, and Shearman (1985b) force-fed toads (*Bufo marinus*) with Tc[99]-labeled chicken liver. The data do not allow conclusions with regard to passage time; the purpose of the experiment was to demonstrate an inhibitory effect of prostaglandin on gastrointestinal transport. The authors note "a high degree of variability between individual toads" (223).

Bufo boreas males alternately fed mealworms or crickets for 24 h twice a week for 46 days delivered fecal sacs on average every 2.3 days (Larsen 1984). When feeding was stopped, fecal material sometimes accumulated in the posterior part of the intestine; the maximal interval between feeding (crickets) and defecation (with cricket remnants) was 37 days. Renewed feeding in such cases stimulated defecation. Dehydration significantly prolonged transit time in *B. boreas* males dehydrated over an 18-h period and then kept in a dehydrated state for 12 days. Transit time for toads dehydrated by 19.3% (range of 15–24%) was 8.8 days (range 7–11 days, $N = 7$), as compared to 5.8 days in controls (range 5–8 days, $N = 7$; $p = .002$) (Larsen 1984).

The digestive tract is linear in caecilians, with rare convolution of the intestine. The stomach of *Hypogeophis* is elongate and highly muscular (Oyama 1952; Werner 1941). The intestine is somewhat thinner-walled, and small and large intestinal regions are not clearly demarcated. Considerable digestion takes place before food leaves the stomach. Wings, bits of carapace, and so forth, are the only recognizable items in the intestine, and even these are rather well digested by the time material reaches the end of the intestine. A "rectum" is recognizable only as the lower intestinal region, which is usually packed with soil that had presumably been ingested by prey items previous to their seizure. The amount of time from feeding to defecation in terrestrial taxa is unknown. Fecal matter passes into the cloaca as a bolus when the muscular valve at the end of the intestine is relaxed, and a large mass (as much as 50 mm by 8 mm in an animal of 300-mm total length) accumulates before passage into the cloaca. However, in the aquatic *Typhlonectes,* defecation occurs within 2 days after feeding in the laboratory. Fecal material is formed in two to five lobes held together by a stout mucous sheath.

Digestion and Absorption

The rather large literature on digestive enzymes and other secretions involved in the function of the digestive system mostly concerns particular enzymes or organs and pays little attention to the organism as such or to the interaction with the environment. The regulation of gastric and intestinal secretion by way of the nervous system, hormones, or stimuli from the food has also received little attention.

Best investigated is the secretion of gastric juice (acid and enzymes; see Smit 1968). In *Bufo marinus,* feeding elicits a marked drop in pH within 2 h (Taylor, Tyler, and Shearman 1985a, 1985b; Taylor and Tyler 1986). Otherwise, no data elucidate this area of digestive physiology.

Both Seale (1987) and chapter 16 review the very fragmentary literature on anuran larvae. Ruibal and Thomas (1988) discuss the function of the foregut and midgut in larvae without a true stomach, and also describe larval *Lepidobatrachus laevis* (Leptodactylidae) with an "adult" stomach. Cytological data indicate that larval *Rana catesbeiana* may absorb intact protein molecules (Sugimoto, Ichikawa, and Nakamura 1981).

Reports on pancreatic and intestinal enzymes not cited in the above reviews are those by Balogun and Fisher (1970) and by Scapin and Lambert-Gardini (1979).

In general, feeding probably elicits secretion in both the stomach and the intestine. Jørgensen (1986b) showed that during large meals (>10% of body mass) of mealworms, body mass of *Bufo bufo* increased beyond the mass of the mealworms. This can be explained by secretion of digestive fluids in amounts similar to the amount of food; since the fluid is drawn from the body fluids, it must be replenished by water uptake through the skin. Dehydration may reduce the production of digestive fluids.

The efficiency of absorption (also called digestive or gross assimilation efficiency), equal to the proportion of ingested food not lost as feces, reflects the completeness with which food is digested and absorbed. This measure is an underestimate because the feces may contain substances from the body in addition to undigested food. Absorption efficiency has been measured in a number of anuran and urodele species. It generally varies between 55 and 95% and depends on the type and amount of food and on the temperature, but probably also on many other external and internal factors that have not yet been systematically investigated. Their variance may explain some apparent discrepancies, for example, with regard to the effect of temperature. Changes in blood flow or in vascularization of the gastrointestinal tract may also affect absorption. Blood flow to the gut of *Bufo marinus* increases after

voluntary ingestion of young mice (B. Dumsday and W. W. Burggren unpublished), but the effects on absorption are unknown. The absorbing surface area may show seasonal changes as mentioned previously. How absorption efficiency is related to passage time is not clear from the literature. Seale (1987) reviewed most of the relevant literature; more data are in Dimmitt and Ruibal (1980b). These data are not directly relevant for the area of environmental physiology of feeding and digestion, but they become important in energy budgets (see chapters 12 and 14 and below).

Sloughed skin may be an important component of energy budgets. G. C. Smith (1976) makes the tacit assumption that, since the molted skin is ingested, it is also digested and absorbed and therefore constitutes no loss. Smith disregards the unknown digestibility of the keratinized cells of the sloughed skin; my estimate from the appearance of feces in *Bufo bufo* would be 50%, but it has never been investigated thoroughly. Fitzpatrick (1973a), on the other hand, calculates the energy lost with shed skin not eaten on the basis of data from Merchant (1970); he assumes the annual loss to be 0.11 kcal in the salamander *Desmognathus* (Plethodontidae), compared with an annual amount of ingested calories of 2.56 kcal. Merchant's (1970) finding of so much shed skin may indicate that his salamanders were not thriving; healthy, fully metamorphosed amphibians eat sloughed skin (see Larsen 1976 for a review of molting). I have calculated the annual loss of energy in Danish *B. bufo* with shed skin, assuming no absorption, to be about 6 kcal (30 molts at 70 mg at 0.005 kcal.). If the annual food intake, as calculated from the field studies mentioned previously, is 34 kcal, absorption of 50% of the shed skins may represent about 10% of the annual energy intake.

Little is known about digestion in caecilians. Mang (1935) and recently Zylberberg (1972, 1977) have studied the glands of the mouth, and Zylberberg has done histochemistry. Many mucous glands are present, presumably involved in food transport, and many cells secrete "proteins." These are not characterized, but, given the state of prey items in the pharynx, M. H. Wake (unpublished) observes that some digestion has begun in the mouth. Again, observations indicate that extensive processing occurs in the stomach, but nothing is known of the enzymes. Bons (1986) notes the lack of esophageal glands and the presence of mucous pyloric glands and lymphoid patches along the digestive tract. The endocrine pancreas has been characterized, with comments on the exocrine, in terms of fine structure by Welsch and Storch (1972). Virtually all such studies of caecilians to date are morphological and not related directly to feeding.

Defecation

In anurans, the undigested food (especially chitinous parts from insects) together with remnants of sloughed skin eaten during the molt (especially nuptial pads) are delivered in a mucous sac formed in the posterior part of the intestine (Herter 1936). *Bufo bufo* often deposit feces in water under laboratory conditions (Ponse 1924; Heusser 1958b). When defecating, toads stretch the forelegs, and the hind legs form an *M;* toads adopt the same posture when the cloacal region is stimulated artificially (Heusser 1960). In *B. boreas* (Larsen

1984) the hind legs are pressed against the body, and the urostyle is lifted and sometimes moved up and down. In some cases the lungs are inflated or the viscera moved from side to side.

GENERAL DISCUSSION AND CONCLUSION

Figure 13.1, which is general for meal-eating vertebrates, will now be discussed in light of the previous survey of literature on amphibians. Figure 13.1 includes centers for hunger and satiety. Centers may be defined morphologically or physiologically, and it is general knowledge that the brain has many centers in the morphological sense. When it comes to function, however, the interplay between widespread neuronal networks is essential. In mammals, the most thoroughly investigated centers for hunger and satiety are located in the hypothalamus. The concept of centers of hunger and satiety has been criticized to the extent that some textbooks have stopped using these terms. These concepts are still useful, however, because they correctly reflect that lesions and stimulations in certain hypothalamic areas have dramatic effects on food intake. The trouble is that the same lesions and stimulations also may influence alertness, arousal, gastrointestinal peristalsis, secretion of growth hormone and of insulin, blood sugar, and so forth. Still, experiments similar to those performed with mammals need to be performed with amphibians, to supplement the huge effort in analysis of the visual system. For example, the method used to study the effects of advertisement calling on metabolic activity in various brain regions in the dendrobatid frog *Phyllobates tricolor* (Zimmermann and Rahmann 1987) should be applied to amphibians reacting to food stimuli. Such an analysis would be a very useful supplement to recording electrical activity in single neurons or brain areas.

When read from the left, figure 13.1 first mentions positive and negative influences from the environment, including the positive sensory qualities of the prey. A huge literature on amphibians describes these factors, among which are type and direction of movement, shape, color, contrast to background, and smell. Other positive external influences include conditions optimal for feeding behavior such as temperature and, for terrestrial amphibians, relative humidity. Negative sensory qualities of potential food items may be lack of movement, excessively large size (a predator), disturbing sound, aversive odor, or extreme temperature or humidity. Experimentalists must take care to avoid inhibiting feeding behavior by noise, movement, or other negative stimuli; techniques such as video may be valuable in this respect.

How an empty or full gastrointestinal tract may provide neural or hormonal stimuli is poorly known for amphibians. Only very simple experiments have been done. The same applies to the metabolic and hormonal stimuli present in the blood and affecting the brain before, during, and after a meal. Insulin, blood glucose, glycerol, and gastrointestinal hormones, which seem important in mammals, have not been investigated with regard to feeding behavior or food intake in amphibians. The only well-investigated hormone is growth hormone, which may counteract long-term satiety for a while.

"Other internal influences" may include (1) memory of food that tasted good or bad or caused pain (a stinging bee) or frustration (snapping at a dummy); (2) the blood pattern of hormones and metabolites typical of fatness or leanness, causing animals to react weakly or strongly to food-related stimuli; (3) the blood pattern of hormones and metabolites typical of breeding; (4) the period of molting or sleep, causing low appetite or total lack of appetite. Dehydration may reduce food intake. Finally, a genetically based endogenous circannual rhythm may occur (see Wind-Larsen and Jørgensen 1987 for a recent example). Endogenous processes may lead to physiological and morphological changes similar to those occurring when amphibians start hibernation or finish hibernation, even when external factors like temperature, food, and light are constant (see Holzapfel 1937). Growth hormone can influence endogenous processes related to food intake, growth, and fat deposition. However, extensive multiyear studies and other experiments are needed to establish circannual rhythms according to the strict definitions.

Finally, in reality the hunger and satiety centers in the brain are integrated in the whole body, which moves through the environment, senses it, and reacts to it. "Motivation" (unknown endogenous processes) drives the search for prey, and the amphibian captures prey by movements (behavioral patterns) elicited by certain key stimuli. The passing of time is also important: day and night, seasons of year, the whole life period. A biologically meaningful review might be to describe the physiology of feeding in one species throughout life, taking into consideration individual variation, various habitats, and changes throughout the day and the year. Furthermore, genetic information is important to the perspective: it influences brain function so that it can act in a preprogrammed way in reflex type of activity and can show, in an adaptive way, plasticity. Little is known of the genetic influence on brain function related to feeding behavior. Individual amphibians vary greatly in feeding behavior, but attempts to clarify the relative importance of the genome and the life history events of the individual are few. Cloned amphibians would be especially suitable to elucidate this fundamental problem. It would be interesting to know how the genome evolved in its interplay with the body and the environment.

Bufo bufo may exemplify the elements indicated in figure 13.2. A feeding sequence may be as follows: A toad leaves its hiding place and searches for food that may not be in sight when it starts out. The toad then sees prey, orients toward it, approaches it, fixates it, snaps at it, and finally swallows it. This sequence of events is probably governed by a hierarchy of brain centers and networks connecting them, influenced by stimuli from the body and from the environment. Processes in the brain probably elicit the search for food, and internal influences related to the physiological state of hunger are dominating. Environmental factors are important only as permissive factors. When a potential prey is seen, certain key stimuli, like movement and size, are processed in the brain networks. Normally only moving prey elicits snapping, and information from accommodation of the lens is used to aim the tongue precisely at the prey. Furthermore, stored information of previous experience with that type of prey or in that environment is added to the processing. The processing results in a brain activity in neuronal networks responsible for orientation, fixation, and snapping. During these movements sensory information from the muscular system and from the external senses is influencing the brain so that the inborn, fixed motor patterns may be modified in a way suited to the special circumstances. In this later part of food intake, environmental stimuli are more dominating. Swallowing comes close to being a "simple" reflex, but swallowing in amphibians may still be prevented by sensory information like bad taste or by an internal state like sickness or satiety, and instead spitting or vomiting behavior is elicited.

The most difficult task in this aspect of amphibian physiology will be to understand what takes place in the brain when the toad makes "spontaneous" movements, that is, movements lacking obvious external stimuli. In human beings such movements are most typically and convincingly seen during sleep. In toads they may occur when the toad leaves its hiding place. Often, hunger is assumed to elicit emergence. However, other "motivations" may have the same effect, as indicated by the terms "thirst," causing search for water, or "exploratory behavior" caused by "restlessness" and with no specific goal, except that a new environment may increase the chance of getting food or water or a better hiding place. Other spontaneous movements are displacement activities, like snapping, wiping the mouth, and retracting the eyes when no prey is present. Mental imagery or memory may be involved.

Finally, let us return to feeding strategies, again using *B.*
bufo as a typical example. When hungry, toads can eat voraciously because of their large, distensible stomach. The physiological background for their hunger is poorly known. They can survive without food for a long time, reflecting their slow metabolism and considerable fat stores. The unknown internal factors affecting the tendency to eat seem correlated with daily and annual rhythms to a large extent. The size of meals in ad libitum situations is related to stomach capacity, and the frequency of meals probably to the rate of stomach emptying and digestion. Growth and atrophy of the gastrointestinal tract during the year probably are important in long-term regulation of food intake. Learning plays a role in feeding, too. After metamorphosis or hibernation toads slowly learn to hit prey precisely, and learning plays a role in disregarding unsuitable moving objects as prey. The tendency to leave burrows and other hiding places is dependent on the humidity of the air and the moisture of the ground. This reflects the lack of protection against evaporation from the skin of moving toads.

An essential part of the toads' success (survival as species) is probably their extreme flexibility with regard to type of food and with regard to behavior. Individual variation is very important ecologically and evolutionarily because of its importance for differential survival and reproduction. This aspect tends to disappear in literature centering on cost/benefit analyses, models, and strategies of feeding and digestion.

14 Behavioral Energetics

F. Harvey Pough, with William E. Magnusson, Michael J. Ryan, Kentwood D. Wells, and Theodore L. Taigen

All animal activities require energy. Foraging for prey and escaping from predators are readily apparent uses of energy, as are the growth of an individual organism and the production of a brood of young. The processes that support these activities, such as movement of blood through the cardiovascular system, elimination of nitrogenous wastes by the kidney, and propagation of action potentials by nerves, also have energetic costs. How does an animal obtain this energy, and, having obtained it, how should it use the energy to best advantage?

These questions define the emerging field of behavioral energetics, and emphasize its close links to topics such as environmental physiology, optimal behavior, and life history theory. The assumption that energy limits ecological processes is a theme in most of these studies, as is the hypothesis that organisms allocate energy among compartments in a web of interactions that ultimately influence their Darwinian fitness. That is, investing energy in foraging reduces the amount of energy immediately available for growth or reproduction, but if foraging is successful, more energy is ultimately available for increasing biomass.

Two papers published during the 1940s were particularly influential in shaping the development of the broad area of physiological ecology and some of the specific topics of behavioral energetics. R. B. Cowles's and C. M. Bogert's (1944) demonstration of thermoregulation by desert lizards and snakes showed that exporting laboratory techniques to the field provided an excellent tool for understanding natural processes. Soon after, F. E. J. Fry's (1947) study of the metabolic capacities of fishes as a function of two or more simultaneously applied variables showed that experiments that attempt to duplicate the complexity of natural situations in the laboratory are another powerful method for asking questions about organisms. These methods underlie much of the current research in behavioral energetics.

Furthermore, both Cowles and Bogert (1944) and Fry (1947) emphasized the responses of individual organisms during short-term activities, such as temperature selection and acclimation, that occur in minutes, hours, or days. That focus on individuals and on discrete activities largely continues to distinguish behavioral energetics from physiology, which emphasizes processes, and from studies of behavior, in which the time frame is often a season or a generation.

Short-term activities carried out by individual organisms lend themselves to measurements of the actual energetic costs of specific behaviors. For example, how much energy is expended in capturing and eating an insect, and how much energy is subsequently realized from digesting the meal? That information can be used to formulate hypotheses about long-term phenomena, for example, about optimal diets and foraging modes or about mating systems and courtship behavior. As a result of this sequence of reasoning, studies of discrete activities—especially foraging behavior, prey selection, digestion, territorial defense, and courtship—dominate the literature of behavioral energetics (Aspey and Lustick 1983; Gittleman and Thompson 1988; Spotila 1989; Townsend and Calow 1981).

Presently a new emphasis has appeared in behavioral energetics. Attention is shifting increasingly from the description of characteristics of species to analysis of the significance of physiological variation among and within species (e.g., Feder et al. 1987). Questions are framed in the contexts of evolutionary biology and sociobiology, and investigations may employ the techniques of quantitative genetics and biophysical modeling. Arnold (1983) has described the interplay of methods needed to elucidate the relationships among behavior, energy, and fitness. The goal remains understanding how organisms work and the ecological and evolutionary consequences of variation in organismal function.

Amphibians and reptiles have been important in many studies of behavioral energetics, and their prominence in several recent reviews attests to the role they have played (Feder and Lauder 1986; Feder et al. 1987; Spotila 1989). Lizards have been the subjects of many investigations because a com-

Douglas G. Brust, Marc Hero, Catherine Loudon, and Catherine A. Toft kindly read the manuscript and made suggestions for improvements. Ulmar Grafe generously provided unpublished data. Original data reported by W. E. Magnusson are from studies supported by grants from the Brazilian Conselho Nacional de Desenvolvimento Cientifoc e Tecnologico. Unpublished data reported by K. D. Wells and T. L. Taigen were supported in part by National Science Foundation Grant BNS84-18768. Preparation of this chapter was supported by Hatch Project NY(C)-1836412.

bination of diurnal activity, conspicuous behavior, and inter- and intraspecific variation makes some species particularly suitable for field and laboratory studies (e.g., Anderson and Karasov 1981; Andrews 1984; Huey and Pianka 1981; Huey et al. 1984; Huey and Bennett 1987).

In contrast to lizards, most amphibians are nocturnal, and many are inconspicuous as well. These characteristics have hampered field studies of behavior, although the present volume attests to the enormous amount of information available concerning the physiology and ecology of amphibians. Despite the logistic difficulties of working with amphibians, two areas of their biology—feeding and reproduction—have been fruitful sources of information about relations among physiology, ecology, and behavior (summarized by Taigen and Pough 1985). These two lines of investigation have had independent origins: many of the assumptions that shaped studies of the foraging behavior of amphibians were derived from work on lizards, whereas students of amphibian mating systems and of the energetics of amphibian reproduction have drawn many of their models from work with birds. But amphibians, of course, are neither lizards nor birds, and an increasing body of evidence suggests that important aspects of their biology are unique.

This chapter reviews progress in studies of the energetic aspects of natural behaviors of amphibians, especially foraging behavior and reproduction. Other activities are no less important, but they have received little attention. As is often the case with studies that integrate laboratory and field components, gathering quantitative information about the ecology and behavior of free-ranging animals has been more difficult than making physiological measurements. The interactions of amphibian behavior, ecology, and morphology are complex, and the difficulties of designing field experiments have not been fully surmounted. Furthermore, nonenergetic factors such as the risk of predation might be important in determining the selective forces that act on individuals, but balancing energy expenditure and risk of predation is not simple because those costs are not expressed in the same units. Assessment of the ecological and evolutionary significance of metabolic characters requires synthesis of diverse aspects of organismal biology. Consequently, our treatment places as much emphasis on the ecological and behavioral context of the studies discussed as on physiological measurements.

MORPHOLOGY, PHYSIOLOGY, AND FORAGING BEHAVIOR
F. Harvey Pough and William E. Magnusson

Interspecific variation in the foraging behaviors of amphibians can be strikingly apparent even on casual observation. At a pond in the evening, toads (Bufonidae) move steadily along the shore, repeatedly flicking out their tongues to capture small prey, while frogs (Ranidae) rest in the aquatic vegetation, lunging at passing insects only at long intervals. These very different foraging behaviors are associated with interspecific variation in diet, morphology, and physiology. Furthermore, examination of independent evolutionary lineages reveals that similar combinations of behavior, morphology, and physiology have evolved repeatedly among

anurans. These convergences indicate that at least some of the characters associated with variation in foraging behavior are evolutionarily labile.

Predators have usually been divided into two categories, sit-and-wait or widely foraging, depending on their relative activity during foraging (e.g., Eckhardt 1979; Huey and Bennett 1986; Huey and Pianka 1981; Toft 1981; Webb 1984). Regal (1978, 1983) has proposed a third category, cruising foragers, for species that move frequently but at low speeds. Some authors (e.g., Magnusson et al. 1985; Pietruszka 1986; Pough 1983; Strüssmann et al. 1984; Taigen and Pough 1983) have suggested that foraging mode cannot be divided into discrete classes, but rather varies along several axes. However, Huey and Bennett (1986) defended the use of qualitative categories because in many taxa most species cluster at the ends of a movement spectrum.

Whatever the distribution of foraging modes, the predictability of associations of morphological characters and dietary habits with locomotion and metabolism suggests that interacting cause-and-effect relations may shape these aspects of the ecology and evolution of amphibians. For example, the physiological and morphological requirements of different patterns of locomotion (e.g., the lever arms, contraction velocities, and enzyme activities of limb muscles; see chapter 11) might determine what foraging modes are possible for a particular species. In turn, foraging mode and locomotor patterns might limit the range of structural habitats a species could exploit and the kinds of prey it encountered. Thus, studies of the functional morphology and physiology of amphibians may increase our understanding of the structure and evolution of ecological guilds and communities.

Morphology, Locomotion, and Diet

The ways amphibians move about are clearly associated with the ways they locate prey and the types of prey they find. Morphological specializations of the girdles and limbs are closely associated with locomotor modes, and prey capture often involves specializations of the jaws, tongue, and hyobranchial apparatus (see chapter 11). In fact, some of these anatomical features are so distinctive that they allow inferences about foraging mode when no direct behavioral information about a species is available.

Anurans Studies of anurans by Emerson and her colleagues (Emerson 1976a, 1978, 1979, 1982, 1985, 1988; Emerson and Diehl 1980; Emerson and de Jongh 1980) present the most detailed analyses of the correlations among morphology, locomotion, and foraging mode for amphibians. Pelvic morphology distinguishes anurans that jump (travel ten body lengths or more in one leap) from species that walk, hop, and burrow (Emerson 1979, 1980). The type I pelvic girdle lacks a direct ligamentous connection between the ilium and the sacrum. Instead, the lumbodorsal fascia over the sacrum is thickened and forms a ligament that extends across the pelvis from ilium to ilium. This morphology is found in swimming, walking, hopping, and burrowing frogs including pipids, pelobatids, *Rhinoderma darwinii* (Rhinodermatidae), *Bombina orientalis* (Discoglossidae), and some hylids and microhylids.

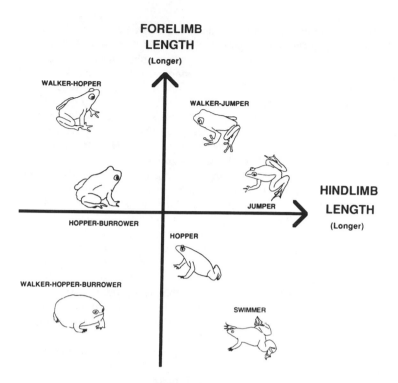

Fig. 14.1 The relation of body form and loco-motor mode to morphological characters for an-urans. (Modified from Emerson 1988.)

A second type of pelvic girdle (type IIA) is characteristic of other species of walking, hopping, and burrowing frogs (bufonids, some leptodactylids, some hylids, some microhylids, a few ranids, *Rhinophrynus dorsalis* [Rhinophrynidae], and *Discoglossus pictus* [Discoglossidae]). This pelvic morphology has a direct ligamentous attachment between the pelvic girdle and the vertebral column in addition to the superficial dorsolumbar fascia seen in type I.

A third pelvic morphology (type IIB) has been identified in jumping frogs (most ranids, some leptodactylids, *Ascaphus truei* [Leiopelmatidae], and *Dendrobates tinctorius* [Dendrobatidae]). In these species the pelvic girdle is attached to the vertebral column by a short ligament that runs from the ilium to the sacral diapophysis.

Variation in pelvic morphology appears to be the critical factor leading to differences in the amount and direction of movement at the iliosacral articulation during locomotion, because the sequence of activity of the four paired muscles surrounding the articulation is almost identical in all three types of pelvis. An anteroposterior movement of the pelvis permitted by the type I morphology increases body length by as much as 20%, probably increasing the reach of a frog during walking, climbing, and swimming. Lateral rotation of the pelvis occurs during walking by frogs with pelvic type IIA, moving the femur of the protracting limb to a more anterior position than it would occupy if the pelvis were fixed. Simultaneous lateral flexion of the vertebral column advances the contralateral forelimb. These specializations increase stride length and, provided stride rate is maintained, increase the speed of locomotion. Type IIB pelvises may store elastic energy during jumping as the pelvis flexes in a vertical plane with respect to the vertebral column.

Hindlimb lengths are the most conspicuous morphological features that distinguish among the locomotor modes of frogs

(Emerson 1978, 1988). Species with long hindlimbs are generally jumpers or swimmers, whereas species with short hindlimbs walk, run, or hop (fig. 14.1). Hindlimb muscle mass scales isometrically during ontogenetic growth, and that isometry should result in lower rates of acceleration during a jump for large individuals of a species. However, two of the three species of frogs that Emerson studied maintained constant acceleration over a range of body sizes, and she suggested that changes within the muscles during ontogeny may increase mass-specific energy production. In contrast, interspecific variation in jumping ability appears to be correlated with variation in the mass of hindlimb extensor muscles relative to total body mass. However, variation in limb lengths does not correspond directly to variation in locomotor mode: kinematic analysis of gait distinguished nine locomotor modes, but only two morphological categories (swimmer-jumpers and walker-hopper-burrowers) were distinguished by principal components analysis (Emerson 1988).

Some species of walking/hopping frogs have long forelimbs, but these are not features of all walkers (fig. 14.1), and they may be associated with unusual gaits (e.g., *Atelopus:* Bufonidae) or with the use of the forelimbs during intraspecific combat (e.g., *Dendrobates*). No simple correlation links pectoral girdle morphology and mode of locomotion: firmisternal and arciferal pectoral girdles both occur among jumping frogs and among walking/hopping types (Emerson 1983).

Many of the specializations that facilitate burrowing also enhance walking ability, and the selective pressures for walking and burrowing are difficult to separate (Emerson 1976a). Most terrestrial walking frogs are at least facultative burrowers. However, the morphological specializations that facilitate walking by most frogs permit only backward burrowing. Species that feed underground have morphological specializations of the cranium, pectoral girdle, and associated musculature that permit the use of the head as a shovel during forward burrowing.

The skull morphology of adult anurans is related to diet (Emerson 1985). Species that eat small, slow prey do not need a large gape, but they make many captures, sometimes in rapid succession at a concentration of prey, and shortening the length of a feeding cycle may be important in maximizing the number of prey that can be captured. These anurans have short jaws and the prey is captured about midway through the feeding cycle. In contrast, anurans that eat large, fast prey require a large gape, rapid tongue extension, and considerable force at closing. These species have long jaws, and prey capture occupies only the first quarter of the feeding cycle.

The genus *Bufo* is an apparent exception to these generalizations. *Bufo* eat slow, small prey, yet their jaws are relatively long (Emerson 1985). However, this anomaly may be an artifact of the presentation of dietary information as percentages of the total diet rather than as absolute values. Most species of *Bufo* are generalists, and the fact that they eat large numbers of ants and termites does not necessarily indicate that they eat small quantities of large prey (e.g., Strüssmann et al. 1984).

Study of both live and dead animals is necessary to understand morphology (e.g., Emerson 1976a, 1978, 1985). Once mechanisms are known, however, the study of preserved specimens yields much supplementary information. Ecologists and physiologists can facilitate this process by identifying and preserving their specimens and depositing them in museums, even if they do not themselves intend to study the morphological correlates of their ecological or physiological data.

Many anuran larvae are nonselective filter feeders, extracting suspended particles from the water (reviewed by Seale 1987; see chapter 16). A buccal pump formed by the paired ceratohyal cartilages in the floor of the mouth creates a flow of water that passes across the branchial food traps and gill filters. Mucus secreted on the ventral velum and on the branchial food traps is driven by cilia medially and caudally into the esophagus. Ingestion rate increases with increasing concentration of suspended particles and asymptotically approaches a maximum. At low particle concentrations larvae decrease filtering rates and perhaps produce less mucus; these mechanisms should reduce the energetic costs of feeding (Seale, Hoff, and Wassersug 1982).

Many anuran larvae employ both aerial and aquatic gas exchange (see chapter 16). Trips to the water surface for air can have direct energy costs (i.e., the cost of locomotion) as well as indirect costs (e.g., resting near the water surface and hence away from food, increased skin capillary density, increased reliance on gills for gas exchange). As predicted by that hypothesis, air-breathing larvae (*Rana pipiens*) kept in moderately hypoxic conditions grew more slowly in deep water than in shallow water (Feder and Moran 1985). Aquatic gas exchange and food capture are potentially competing functions of the buccopharyngeal region, and larval *Xenopus laevis* denied access to the surface increase buccal pumping rates while simultaneously decreasing rates of food ingestion (Feder, Seale, Boraas, Wassersug, and Gibbs 1984). The branchial food traps continue to produce mucus under these conditions, but the food and mucus are expectorated (Wassersug and Murphy 1987).

The larvae of some anurans are obligatory or opportunistic carnivores or oophages (Lannoo, Townsend, and Wassersug 1987; Wassersug 1980). Carnivorous morphs have hypertrophied jaw muscles and short guts compared to omnivorous larvae (Pomeroy 1981; Wassersug 1980). Oophagy has been reported for larvae of *Osteopilus brunneus* (Hylidae) and for larvae of three species of *Dendrobates* (Dendrobatidae; see also chapter 16). The specializations of oophagous larvae include a reduced number of denticle rows. They feed on unfertilized eggs of their own species (Lannoo, Townsend, and Wassersug 1987), and *D. pumilio* also eats conspecific larvae (Brust 1990). Cannibalistic morphs of the salamander *Ambystoma tigrinum* (Ambystomatidae) are larger than noncannibalistic individuals and have broader, flatter heads and more teeth (Collins and Cheek 1983; Lannoo and Bachman 1984a; Pierce, Mitton, and Rose 1981). Cannibalistic larvae of spadefoot toads (*Scaphiopus*: Pelobatidae) grow faster and metamorphose sooner and at larger body sizes than do omnivores (Pomeroy 1981).

Salamanders Aquatic salamanders (and the aquatic larvae of terrestrial species) use the hyobranchial apparatus to expand the buccopharyngeal region, creating a suction that draws prey into the mouth. Most aquatic salamanders have small tongues and robust hyobranchial skeletons (Özeti and Wake 1969). The mechanics of suction feeding by salamanders have been extensively studied by Lauder and his colleagues (Findeis and Bemis 1990; Lauder and Reilly 1988; Reilly and Lauder 1988, 1989a, 1989b; Shaffer and Lauder 1985a, 1985b). Some of this work was reviewed by Lauder (1985a). The ancestral feeding mechanism of terrestrial salamanders is probably illustrated by *Ambystoma* (Ambystomatidae), which combines a limited degree of tongue protrusion when feeding on land with prey capture in the jaws (Regal 1966a; Reilly and Lauder 1989a).

The best-studied morphological specializations of salamanders associated with feeding are the protrusible tongues of plethodontids (Lombard and Wake 1976, 1977, 1986; Roth 1976; Roth and Wake 1985b; Thexton, Wake, and Wake 1977; D. B. Wake 1982; Wake and Larson 1987; Wake, Roth, and Wake 1983; see also chapter 11). Evolutionary modifications of the hyoid apparatus of plethodontids have produced a high-speed projectile tongue. The morphological basis of tongue protrusion by plethodontids is entirely different from that of anurans (Roth et al. 1988a). The tongue is protruded 20 to 25 mm from the mouth in 2 to 4 ms by some species of *Bolitoglossa,* and *Hydromantes italicus* can project its tongue 45 to 50 mm in 6 to 8 ms.

Ecological aspects of these morphological specializations have not been studied. Projectile tongues probably allow specialized plethodontids to capture small or fast-moving prey, but this hypothesis has not been tested with comparative studies, and no information about interspecific variation in foraging modes is available. However, laboratory studies show that plethodontid salamanders are capable of complex feeding behavior that can maximize energy intake (but see chapter 13). Red-backed salamanders (*Plethodon cinereus*) in laboratory experiments captured large fruit flies in preference to small flies (Jaeger and Barnard 1981). The salamanders were most selective when prey were abundant and maximized net energy intake by eating large flies; they became less selective as prey density decreased. At high prey densities the salamanders used a sit-and-wait foraging mode, but switched to active searching at low prey densities. The sit-and-wait tactic was energetically less costly than active searching (estimated as 1.9×10^{-2} J · min^{-1} · g^{-1} versus 2.4×10^{-2} J · min^{-1} · g^{-1}) and also more successful (0.67 versus 0.42 flies · min^{-1}). When intruding salamanders were introduced to the feeding boxes, the resident salamanders diverted time from feeding to defense and switched from a selective to a generalized diet. As a result of these behavioral changes, the rate of energy intake was reduced by more than 50% (Jaeger, Nishikawa, and Barnard 1983).

Ecological studies of the feeding behavior of salamanders have focused on constraints on food intake imposed by physical factors (principally moisture), predators, or competition within or between species (Davic and Orr 1987; Feder and Londos 1984; Hutchison and Spriestersbach 1986a; Jaeger 1971, 1978; Jaeger, Joseph, and Barnard 1981; Keen 1982, 1984; Keen and Reed 1985; Maiorana 1978; Pauley 1978; Southerland 1986a, 1986b, 1986c; Stauffer, Gates, and Goodfellow 1983; White 1977; Wrobel, Gergits, and Jaeger 1980; Wyman and Hawksley-Lescault 1987). The low metabolic rates of salamanders (see chapter 12) allow them to suspend feeding during unfavorable periods rather than risk injury or death from desiccation, predation, or territorial encounters (Feder 1983b). Parallels between the foraging behaviors of terrestrial species of salamanders and anurans seem plausible. For example, the diurnal activity of red efts (Salamandridae) is associated with toxicity and aposematic color, as is the diurnality of dart-poison frogs (*Dendrobates* and *Phyllobates*: Dendrobatidae). Cryptically colored, palatable salamanders like *Desmognathus* (Plethodontidae) are nocturnal, as are cryptic palatable frogs like *Eleutherodactylus* (Leptodactylidae). Field studies of the foraging behavior of salamanders are lacking, however, and the parallels may not extend beyond very general similarities.

Caecilians Both terrestrial and aquatic species of caecilians are fossorial, digging burrows in the soil or in the sediments of a body of water. They capture prey with a slow approach followed by a quick grab, and a prey item may be sheared into mouth-size pieces against the walls of the burrow as the caecilian rotates about its body axis (Bemis, Schwenk, and Wake 1983; Wake 1986; Wake and Wurst 1979). Most caecilians appear to be opportunistic predators, consuming earthworms, termites, and insect pupae (Taylor 1968). *Afrocaecilia* and *Boulengerula* may specialize on termites, and *Dermophis* on earthworms (Wake 1986). Most caecilians have recurved mono- or bicuspid teeth that penetrate and hold prey (Wake and Wurst 1979). The aquatic caecilian *Typhlonectes obesus* has dilated tooth crowns and may scrape the pupae of aquatic insects from rock surfaces (Wake 1978; Wake and Wurst 1979). Caecilians have a unique form of static pressure jaw system that combines downward rotation of the skull with jaw closure to produce a strong bite while maintaining a small cross-sectional area (Bemis, Schwenk, and Wake 1983).

Foraging, Diet, and Metabolism

Mechanistic interpretations of behavior provide a conceptual basis for studies of the behavioral energetics of foraging by amphibians. This perspective is the product of two decades of investigation of interspecific variation in the exercise physiology of amphibians (see chapter 12). From its beginning in laboratory studies, behavioral energetics has expanded to incorporate ecological and phylogenetic perspectives. Laboratory and field studies are being integrated, and some experiments have measured individual variation in performance capacity and the synergistic effects of environmental parameters. Our changing perspective of amphibian activity metabolism is most clearly illustrated by a chronological summary of the hypotheses that have been tested.

Variation in the Metabolic Capacities of Amphibians Initial attempts to understand interspecific variation in the exercise physiology of amphibians focused on the modes of escape from predators employed by different species of frogs and salamanders, perhaps because escape was the behavior that physiological ecologists most often observed. These studies established that amphibians employ both aerobic and anaerobic metabolic pathways of ATP synthesis during high levels of exercise (see chapter 12 for an extensive discussion of this topic) and that the relative magnitude of the two types of metabolism varied among species (Bennett and Licht 1973, 1974). Oxygen consumption was measured during 2 to 10 min of forced activity that was induced by electrical shock or by prodding animals with a blunt probe, and whole-body lactic acid concentration was used as an index of anaerobic energy output. High rates of aerobic and low rates of anaerobic metabolism were typical of slow-moving amphibians such as toads (*Bufo boreas*) that rely on skin toxins for defense, whereas the opposite balance of metabolic pathways typified treefrogs (*Hyla regilla*: Hylidae) and grass frogs (*Rana pipiens*) that escape predators with a brief series of rapid leaps. The toads sustained their relatively low levels of activity for 10 min of exercise without apparent fatigue, whereas the treefrogs and grass frogs lost coordination or were completely exhausted in less than 5 min.

The salamanders *Batrachoseps attenuatus*, *Aneides flavipunctatus*, *A. lugubris* (all Plethodontidae), and *Notophthalmus viridescens* (Salamandridae) conformed to the pattern of anaerobic metabolism exhibited by the frogs. Two of the species (*B. attenuatus* and *A. flavipunctatus*) rely on rapid movement to escape predators: *B. attenuatus* repeatedly springs into the air from a coiled position and *A. flavipunctatus* crawls rapidly away. These species have high anaerobic metabolic capacities and are exhausted quickly during forced exercise. In contrast, *A. lugubris* stands its ground and may attack a predator; it has a low rate of lactate accumulation during exercise as does the aquatic newt *Notophthalmus viridescens*, which has dermal poison glands that secrete a potent toxin.

Reciprocal relations of energy input from aerobic and anaerobic pathways have been reported for several additional species of salamanders and anurans (Hutchison and Turney 1975; Hutchison, Turney, and Gratz 1977; Hutchison and Miller 1979a, 1979b; Miller and Hutchison 1979, 1980; Hillman and Withers 1981; Miller 1983). In general, species that rely on toxins to deter predators have low rates of lactic acid accumulation and sustain activity for long periods, whereas species that flee rapidly from predators accumulate lactic acid quickly and are soon exhausted. Caecilians and anuran larvae appear to conform to this pattern (Bennett and Wake 1974; Gatten, Caldwell, and Stockard 1984). Measurements of oxygen consumption in some of these studies as well as the initial observations of *Hyla regilla* (Anura: Hylidae), *Bufo boreas*, and *Batrachoseps attenuatus* (Bennett and Licht 1973) are compromised by the use of electrical stimulation to elicit activity (Hillman et al. 1979; see chapter 12 for a discussion of the problems with electrical stimulation), but the general patterns described for those species have been confirmed by subsequent studies using other methods of forcing animals to be active.

The apparent dichotomy in exercise physiology of amphibians based on mode of escape from predators led next to a search for mechanisms at the level of tissues and cells that would account for interspecific differences in metabolic capacity. The activities of the glycolytic enzymes phosphofructokinase and lactic dehydrogenase are higher in limb muscles of *Rana pipiens* than in those of *B. boreas*, whereas activity of the aerobic enzyme citrate synthase is greater in *B. boreas* and in *Xenopus laevis* than in *R. pipiens* (Putnam and Bennett 1983; see also Baldwin, Friedman, and Lillywhite 1977). However, the proportions of three muscle fiber types distinguished by histochemical methods (fast-twitch glycolytic, fast-twitch oxidative glycolytic, and tonic fibers) do not differ among the species (Putnam and Bennett 1983; but see also Sperry 1981). Nonetheless, contractile properties of limb muscles show variation that parallels whole-animal performance: muscles from *B. boreas* contract more slowly and accumulate less lactic acid than do muscles from *R. pipiens* or *X. laevis*.

In addition, heart ventricle mass and blood oxygen capacity are approximately correlated with rates of oxygen consumption during exercise among the anurans *B. cognatus*, *Scaphiopus couchii* (Pelobatidae), *X. laevis*, and *R. pipiens*, and experimentally induced anemia reduces the rate of oxygen consumption of *R. pipiens* during forced activity (Hillman 1976, 1980a; see also chapter 12).

Ecological Correlates of Activity Metabolism The apparently simple dichotomy of metabolic characteristics revealed by physiological studies of amphibian exercise has been challenged by ecologists and morphologists. An initial suggestion of a more complex relation between the ecology and behavior of amphibians and the relative contributions of aerobic and anaerobic metabolic pathways to high levels of activity emerged from a morphological study (Emerson 1976a). Noting the close correspondence among locomotion (walking or hopping versus jumping), fossorial activity, and the importance of ants and termites in the diet, Emerson (1976a) suggested that foraging modes provided another context in which to interpret interspecific variation in the exercise physiology of anurans. She proposed that walking and burrowing frogs have high aerobic scopes and can sustain locomotion for long periods while they search for prey, whereas jumping frogs are sit-and-wait predators. This association between foraging mode and diet presumably reflects the costs and benefits of specialization for active foraging. Emerson suggested that the major advantages of foraging compared to sit-and-wait predation are the increased probabilities of encountering prey and of locating concentrated sources of food such as termite nests. The primary direct cost of active foraging is the energetic expense of locomotion. In addition, an animal is probably more vulnerable to its own predators when it is moving than when it is still. Many widely foraging anurans are toxic and aposematically colored. These characteristics deter predators, but production and sequestration of their toxic compounds probably require energy and could expose the anuran to damage from its own toxins.

Initial field studies of foraging modes of amphibians were based largely on concepts derived from studies of lizards. Huey and Pianka (1981) proposed a network of correlations among the foraging behaviors of lizard species, what and how much they eat, the conditions under which they are exposed to predators and their methods of escape, and their patterns of energy use (table 14.1). Desert lizards figured largely in the development of these hypotheses and their subsequent extension, and the studies drew from and contributed to contemporary ideas in ecology, especially adaptation, optimality, and ecological energetics (Anderson and Karasov 1981; An-

TABLE 14.1 Postulated Correlates of Foraging Mode of Desert Lizards

	Sit and Wait	Widely Foraging
Prey type	Eat mobile prey	Eat sedentary and unpredictable (but clumped or large) prey
Volume prey captured per day	Generally low	Generally high
Daily metabolic expense (Bennett and Gorman 1979	Low	High
Types of predators	Vulnerable primarily to widely foraging predators	Vulnerable to both sit-and-wait and to widely foraging predators
Rate of encounters with predators (Salt 1967)	Probably low	Probably high
Mode of escape from predators (Toft 1980a)	Camouflage, speed, saltation	Camouflage, speed, aposematism (poisonous)
Morphology (Vitt and Congdon 1978)	Stocky (short tails)	Streamlined (generally long tails)
Probable physiological correlates (Bennett and Licht 1973; Ruben 1976a, 1976b)	Limited endurance	High endurance capacity
Relative clutch mass (Vitt and Congdon 1978)	High	Low
Sensory mode (Enders 1975; Regal 1978)	Visual primarily	Visual or chemoreceptory
Learning ability (Regal 1978)	Limited[a]	Enhanced learning and memory, larger brains

Source: Reprinted, by permission, from Huey and Pianka 1981.
[a] Unless use trapline (T. L. Poulson *pers. comm.*).

TABLE 14.2   Postulated Correlates of Foraging Mode of Tropical Leaf-Litter Anurans

	Sit and Wait	Widely Foraging
Prey type	Large, mobile prey, depend on escape as first predator defense	Small, slow-moving prey that sting or are distasteful or chitinous
Number of prey	Lower	Higher
Volume of prey	Might be the same for both modes	
Search cost	Lower[a]	Higher[b]
Handling cost:		
Capture (cost/capture)	Higher	Lower
Digestion (net)	Lower	Higher
Predator defense	Crypticity, escape detection	Skin toxins; may be aposematic
Morphology	Stocky, wide-mouthed	Slim, narrow-mouthed
Physiology (Bennett and Licht 1974)	Anaerobic; capable of large bursts of energy, tire easily	Aerobic; maintain constant but low levels of activity

Source: Reprinted, by permission, from Toft 1981.
[a]Costs may be ameliorated by physiology.

drews 1984; Huey and Bennett 1986; Huey and Pianka 1981; Huey et al. 1984; Pianka 1966, 1973, 1977, 1980; Vitt and Congdon 1978). The questions asked were (1) Do the rate and quality of prey (= energy) acquisition differ among foraging modes? (2) Does the rate of prey acquisition by a given foraging mode depend on the dispersion and quality of the prey? (3) Are foraging mode and morphology correlated? (4) Do the metabolic characteristics of an organism reflect its foraging mode? (5) Does foraging mode influence the intensity of predation or the type of predator to which an organism is exposed? The answers to all of these questions appear to be yes, and the complications derive from identifying interacting components and attempting to define cause-and-effect relations.

Field studies of the foraging behavior of amphibians have dealt exclusively with anurans. Toft (1981) described a continuum of dietary habits among leaf-litter frogs in Panama extending from species that specialize on ants and mites to species that avoid those prey. This variation in diet was associated with a continuum of foraging behaviors. At one extreme, typical sit-and-wait species (e.g., *Eleutherodactylus* [Leptodactylidae]) were characterized as stocky, wide-mouthed anurans that capture small numbers of large, mobile prey and have limited powers of endurance for locomotion, whereas at the opposite end of the spectrum widely foraging species (e.g., *Atelopus* [Bufonidae]) and *Dendrobates* [Dendrobatidae]) were slim and narrow-mouthed, captured large numbers of small sedentary prey, and were able to sustain activity for long periods. The active foragers were mostly toxic, and some were aposematically colored, whereas the sit-and-wait species had cryptic colors and patterns. The ecological correlates of foraging mode that Toft defined among leaf-litter anurans were similar to those of lizards (table 14.2).

The paradox of a relatively simple bipolarity in metabolic capacities, as suggested by studies of exercise physiology, and the more complex picture presented by multivariate ecological hypotheses prompted a broader survey than had previously been attempted of the relative contributions of aerobic and anaerobic metabolism to anuran locomotor physiology (Taigen, Emerson, and Pough 1982). Species were chosen to test the null hypothesis that exercise physiology is a phylogenetically conservative trait in anuran evolution, as

well as to examine possible correlations of aerobic and anaerobic metabolism with locomotion, habitat, and defensive behavior. The seventeen species studied revealed a broad range of combinations of aerobic and anaerobic energy input during forced locomotion (fig. 14.2), and the total energy output during activity varied among species by a factor greater than 2 (see also chapter 12). No dichotomy between predominantly aerobic and predominantly glycolytic species was evident, and Emerson and her colleagues concluded that interspecific variation in exercise physiology forms a continuum like the one Toft (1981) described for variation in behavior and diet.

Phylogenetic conservatism does not appear to explain interspecific variation in the relative importance of aerobic and anaerobic metabolism among the anurans studied, because variation among species within a genus was as large as variation among genera or families. Furthermore, predator avoidance behavior was not a good predictor of the metabolic characteristics of a species: no statistically significant patterns of normalized values of aerobic dependence were detected for active versus static predator avoidance behavior. The structural habitat occupied by a species (terrestrial versus arboreal) also failed to predict metabolic characteristics.

In contrast, aerobic dependence was correlated with mode of locomotion (walkers and hoppers > jumpers) and with foraging behavior (widely foraging > sit-and-wait). That is, species of frogs that walk or hop have high aerobic capacities, and most of these species are also widely foraging predators. These conclusions must be tentative, however, because few quantitative data are available from field observations to characterize the diet or foraging behavior of many of the species tested.

Field Studies of Foraging Behavior

The trend to more ecologically oriented interpretations of the exercise physiology of amphibians has stimulated studies in which observations of free-ranging animals in the field are combined with measurements of metabolism. The information currently available from work with anurans suggests the following generalizations about correlations among foraging behavior, diet, and metabolism: (1) The degree of foraging activity is correlated positively with aerobic metabolic capac-

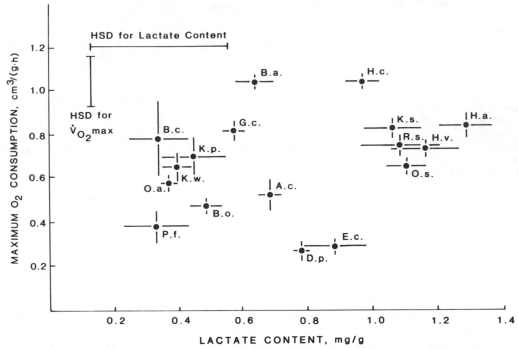

Fig. 14.2 Mass-specific rates of oxygen consumption during activity plotted on logarithmic coordinates as a function of whole-body lactate concentration following forced exercise. Points represent species means and lines show ±1 SE of the mean. The values of Tukey's honestly significant difference (HSD) for oxygen consumption and lacate concentration are shown. *A.c., Agalychnis callidryas; B.a., Bufo americanus; B.c., Bufo calamita; B.o., Bombina orientalis; D.p., Discoglossus pic-* *tus; E.c., Eleutherodactylus coqui; G.c., Gastrophryne carolinensis; H.a., Hyla arenicolor; H.c., H. crucifer; H.v., Hyperolius viridiflavus; K.p., Kaloula pulchra; K.s., Kassina senegalensis; K.w., Kassina weali; O.a., Odontophrynus americanus; O.s., Osteopilus septentrionalis; P.f., Pternohyla fodiens; R.s., Rana sylvatica.* (Reprinted, by permission, from Taigen, Emerson, and Pough 1982.)

ity and negatively with anaerobic capacity. (2) Widely foraging species capture more individual prey items than do sedentary species. (3) Widely foraging species seek out prey that occur in patches, whereas sedentary species eat prey that are found singly.

Tests of these hypotheses have focused on widely foraging species of anurans, especially dart-poison frogs in the Neotropical family Dendrobatidae. This family is a monophyletic radiation of primarily terrestrial frogs in Central and northern South American (Silverstone 1975; Myers, Daly, and Malkin 1978). Dendrobatids are diurnally active, and the behavior of individual frogs can be observed in the field. An initial analysis combined information about diet from Toft's (1981) study with metabolic measurements of three species of dendrobatid frogs and a leptodactylid (Taigen and Pough 1983). Within those species dietary electivity for ants was correlated positively with rate of oxygen consumption during locomotion and negatively with whole-body lactic acid concentration (fig. 14.3). A stepwise analysis of variance showed that electivity for ants accounted for 77% of the variation in rate of oxygen consumption and for 54% of the variation in lactate concentration.

A subsequent field study employed focal animal observations lasting from 1 to 12 h (overall average 2.9 h) of each of four species of Panamanian dendrobatid frogs (Pough and Taigen 1990). The average distance that frogs moved per hour of observation was taken as an estimate of how widely a species forages, and the predicted association was found with metabolic characteristics of the species: species that moved

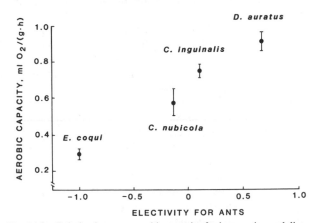

Fig. 14.3 Relation between aerobic capacity for locomotion and dietary preference for ants by *Colostethus inguinalis, C. nubicola, Dendrobates auratus,* and *Eleutherodactylus coqui.* (Reprinted, by permission, from Taigen and Pough 1985.)

long distances had high aerobic and low anaerobic capacities during laboratory measurements of locomotion (fig. 14.4). In addition, the species that moved long distances made more prey capture attempts per hour and made more captures at each feeding location than did the sedentary species.

Field Metabolic Rates Measurements of the daily energy expenditure of free-ranging animals have contributed substantially to understanding the ecological energetics of birds, mammals, lizards, and invertebrates (e.g., Karasov 1981; Nagy 1975, 1987, 1989a; Nagy and Shoemaker 1984). Un-

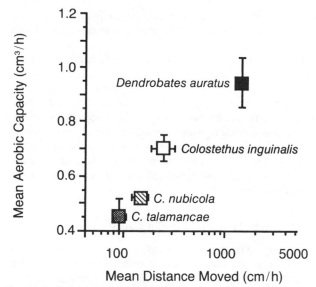

Fig. 14.4 Relation between the mean distance a species of frog moved in 1 h and the mean aerobic capacity for locomotion of the species. Aerobic capacity was calculated for an individual weighing 0.95 g, the grand mean for the sample of four species. Horizontal and vertical lines show ± 1 SE. (Reprinted, by permission, from Pough and Taigen 1990.)

fortunately, the techniques that have been successful with those animals are not well suited to use with amphibians. The most widely used method, doubly labeled water, relies on the differential rates of loss of injected isotopes of oxygen (which is lost as H_2O and as CO_2) and hydrogen (lost as H_2O only). The accuracy of these measurements depends on several assumptions about the routes and rates of movement of hydrogen and oxygen (Nagy 1983a, 1989a). In particular, the rate of water loss must be constant through time, and the animal must not take up unlabeled water from the environment. Thus, the high and variable rates of evaporative water loss and of cutaneous water uptake that are characteristic of amphibians (see chapter 6) make doubly labeled water an unsuitable method for measuring field metabolic rates of these animals.

A method that relies on measuring food intake by determining the rate of turnover of ^{22}Na (Green 1978) may have promise for measuring the field metabolic rates of terrestrial amphibians that do not have large cutaneous sodium fluxes. Knowledge of the sodium content of the diet is required, and species with a narrow range of food items that have stable exchangeable sodium contents are most suitable for this technique (Nagy 1989b). The method has been applied successfully to studies of mammals (Green 1978; Green, Anderson, and Whatley 1984; Green and Eberhard 1984; Green, Griffiths, and Newgrain 1985).

In the absence of direct methods of measuring field metabolic rates, investigators have used extrapolations from laboratory measurements of the energy expenditure during different activities combined with time budgets that estimate the amount of time that animals spend in different activities. This method can give results that correspond well with estimates of energy expenditure obtained with doubly labeled water (Buttemer et al. 1986; Goldstein 1988; Masman and Klaasen 1987; Weathers et al. 1984), but it is fraught with difficulty,

especially for cryptic animals like amphibians that are hard to observe in the field. Consequently, estimates of long-term energy expenditure must be treated cautiously, and the evaluation of specific activities in terms of their magnitude relative to an annual energy budget involves a substantial measure of uncertainty.

Individual Variation

Individual anurans vary in their locomotor and physiological capacities (Preest and Pough 1989; Taigen and Pough 1985; Walton 1988; Wells and Taigen 1984), and part of that variation is probably determined genetically (Travis 1980; Mitton, Carey, and Kocher 1986). Individual variation in metabolic capacities is stable in repeated measurements: 89% of the variation in aerobic capacity of toads (*Bufo americanus*) was attributed to differences among individuals in two measurements separated by a week (Wells and Taigen 1984). Individual variation in aerobic capacity of bullfrogs (*Rana catesbeiana*) was correlated with differences in heart ventricle mass and blood hemoglobin concentration (Walsburg, Lea, and Hillman 1986; see also chapter 12).

Learning and physical conditioning are nongenetic sources of individual variation that could potentially confound experiments. Although amphibians are probably limited to fairly stereotyped behavior (Ewert 1985), they modify their foraging behavior to increase energy gain (Jaeger and Rubin 1982). Physical training improves locomotor endurance of *Rana pipiens* and increases both endurance and sprint speed of *Xenopus laevis* (Cummings 1979; Miller and Camilliere 1981). The roles of learning and physical training in the behavior of anurans in the wild are unexplored.

An adaptationist view regards the character complexes identified by studies of anuran foraging behavior as responses to selection operating on intraspecific variation in physiological and behavioral characters that enhance the fitness of individual frogs (cf. Gans 1988). This hypothesis implies that the correlations of behavior and physiology observed in comparisons among species will also be seen in comparisons of individuals within a species. That is, if widely foraging species A captures more prey, on average, than does sedentary species B, the most widely foraging individuals of species A will capture more prey than more sedentary individuals of the species. Furthermore, for any individual of species A, effort invested in foraging should be repaid by an increase in prey captures compared to spending the same time in sedentary behavior. In turn, individual variation in capacity for active foraging should parallel individual variation in capacity for aerobically sustained locomotion: the individuals of species A with the greatest aerobic capacities to sustain locomotion should be the ones that forage most widely.

These hypotheses can be tested by analyzing individual variation in behavior and physiology. If the hypotheses are correct, that examination should yield positive correlations among distance moved, number of prey-capture attempts, and aerobic capacity for locomotion, and in fact positive correlations between distance traveled by individuals and the number of prey-capture attempts they made were observed for two species (fig. 14.5). Finding statistically significant correlations that support the predictions of the hypothesis in two of

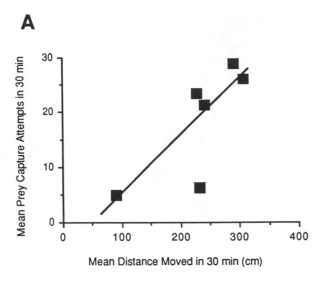

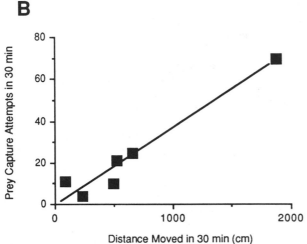

Fig. 14.5 The relation between distance moved and number of feeding attempts by individual *Dendrobates auratus*. *A*, overall mean values for six individuals followed for two or more observation periods. (Spearman rank correlation $r_s = 0.771$, $p = .05$). *B*, values for 30-min observations of *D. auratus* no. 7. (Spearman rank correlation $r_s = 0.899$, $p < .01$. The correlation remains significant when the observation at 1,876 cm is omitted: $r_s = 0.821$, $p < .05$.) (Reprinted, by permission, from Pough and Taigen 1990.)

four species is encouraging and suggests that studies that focus on the role of individual variation could be productive.

The only such study published to date tested the hypotheses that individual variation in foraging behavior of toads (*Bufo woodhousii*) is correlated with variation in prey-capture success and with physiological characteristics (Walton 1988). Toads were followed for periods of 0.25 to 1.97 h (overall average = 0.55 h) as they foraged in a beach habitat at night, and the distance they traveled was recorded. Toads that moved frequently traveled longer distances and encountered and consumed more prey than did individuals that moved less frequently. The animals were returned to the laboratory after the field observations, and aerobic capacity on a treadmill was measured for each individual. No correlation between aerobic capacity and distance moved was detected. Thus, active foraging does appear to pay off with more prey captures, but no evidence yet links individual variation in foraging behavior to individual variation in metabolic characteristics. No

studies have yet attempted to quantify individual variation in the foraging behavior, locomotion, and metabolism of salamanders or caecilians.

Free-ranging amphibians alternate periods of activity and quiescence, and long observation periods are needed to characterize the behavior of individuals. Negative results from short-term studies are probably not informative. At a minimum, records should extend over a day's activity cycle, and repeated observations over a period of days or weeks are desirable. Field enclosures may provide the most satisfactory combination of natural conditions and repeated observations of individuals, and an automated activity monitoring system would be helpful.

Multivariate Analyses of Performance

The study of metabolic capacities and behavioral performance of amphibians originated in the laboratory, and manipulative studies have long retained the traditional form of experimental biology: one parameter (usually temperature or species identity) is varied while other factors that might influence the results (e.g., humidity, feeding status, time of day) are held constant. This approach has the desirable results of isolating the effects of single factors and reducing variation, but it does not attempt to duplicate natural conditions. As the hypotheses proposed by behavioral energetics have become more sophisticated, experimental conditions that more closely approach those that animals encounter in the field have been employed to test them.

The physical environment can strongly influence the behavioral and physiological capacities of ectotherms. Free-ranging animals confront more than one environmental variable at a time, and laboratory studies that manipulate two or more variables simultaneously may provide more realistic estimates of performance under natural conditions than do single-variable studies (e.g., Fry 1947; Truchot 1988; Wheatly 1988). Two-factor interactions that have been studied in detail for amphibians include size × sex (Shine 1979), competition × predation (De Benedictis 1974; Morin 1981, 1983b), size × predation (Cronin and Travis 1986; Formanowicz 1986; Kusano, Kusano, and Miyashita 1985), sex × habitat (Keen, McManus, and Wohltman 1987; T. Lamb 1984), reproduction × daily cycles (Griffiths 1985b), pH × habitat (Freda and Dunson 1986), pH × temperature (Pough and Wilson 1977), pH × density (Cummins 1989), habitat × daily cycles (Gregory 1983), competition × habitat (Maiorana 1978; Keen 1982), temperature × habitat (Stauffer, Gates, and Goodfellow 1983), temperature × dehydration (Preest and Pough 1989), temperature × daily cycles (Smits 1984), social behavior × temperature (Gatten and Hill 1984), habitat × season (Toft 1980b) and parasitism × habitat (Pounds and Crump 1987). Three-factor interactions such as habitat × body size × temperature (Wollmuth et al. 1987), and habitat × body size × daily cycles (fig. 14.9) have also been documented.

Biophysical models predict the consequences of simultaneous variation in several environmental parameters, but translating these predictions into experimental designs is difficult. Temperature and water are probably the environmental parameters that most directly affect the physiological status of an amphibian (Tracy 1976; see also chapters 4, 6, 8, and

9). Recently three studies of metabolism and locomotion by amphibians have applied this multivariate approach with results that emphasize the utility of such investigations. The canyon treefrog of Arizona, *Hyla arenicolor* (Hylidae), rests in sunlit areas on rock outcrops during the day and undergoes

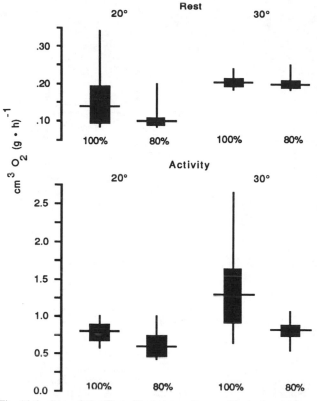

Fig. 14.6 Synergistic effect of body temperature and hydration state on oxygen consumption by *Hyla arenicolor;* only during forced locomotion at 30°C does dehydration to 80% of standard mass significantly reduce the rate of oxygen consumption. *Vertical line,* range; *horizontal line,* mean; *bar,* ±2 SE. (Data from D. G. Brust and M. R. Preest pers. comm.)

substantial dehydration. Evaporative water loss equivalent to 20% of the fully hydrated body mass had no effect on resting or activity metabolism of frogs at 20°C (fig. 14.6). At 30°C resting metabolism was again unaffected by dehydration, but oxygen consumption during activity was decreased by 36% (Brust and Preest 1988).

Three species of Puerto Rican *Eleutherodactylus* (Leptodactylidae) differed in their response to simultaneous dehydration and thermal stress in ways that appear to correspond to the conditions they may encounter in their habitats (Beuchat, Pough, and Stewart 1984). The jump distance of a lowland species, *E. antillensis,* which is found primarily in grassland habitats that are hot and often dry, was less affected by dehydration at high body temperatures than at low temperatures. In contrast, two forest-dwelling species from higher altitudes, *E. coqui* and *E. portoricensis,* were equally sensitive to dehydration at all temperatures tested.

Body temperature and hydration state had synergistic effects on the locomotor capacity of toads (*B. americanus*) in laboratory trials (Preest and Pough 1989). The distance moved in 10 min of forced locomotion decreased as the animals were dehydrated at body temperatures between 15° and 30°C (fig. 14.7): fully hydrated and slightly dehydrated toads traveled farthest at high test temperatures, whereas more severely dehydrated toads moved farthest at intermediate temperatures. The interaction of body temperature and hydration state was statistically significant, and individual toads varied in their sensitivity to those parameters.

Experiments like these that measure performance as a function of simultaneous variation in two or more environmental parameters provide information that is not available from studies of single variables. For example, the individual variation in sensitivity to the combined effects of temperature and hydration observed for American toads means that the relative performance capacities of individual toads under natural conditions cannot be predicted from laboratory measurements at a single combination of temperature and hydration; the toads that do best under cold wet conditions are not

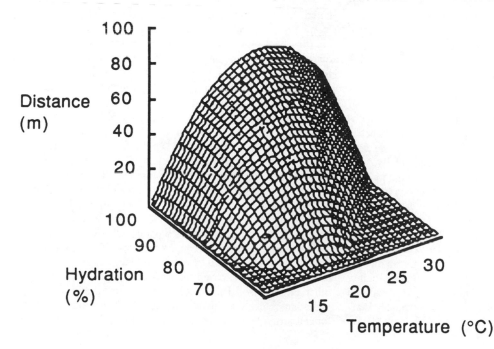

Fig. 14.7 Synergistic effect of body temperature and hydration state on the average distance moved in 10 min of forced locomotion by American toads (*Bufo americanus*). The maximum distance traveled decreased with progressively greater levels of dehydration, and the temperature yielding the maximum distance shifted downward. (Reprinted, by permission, from Preest and Pough 1989.)

necessarily the same individuals that excel when it is hot and dry. This result differs from the observation that the rank order of sprint speeds of lizards was unchanged when only temperature was varied (Huey and Dunham 1987).

Do Generalizations about Lizards Apply to Anurans?

Many of the influential ideas in the behavioral energetics of anurans were developed from studies of lizards and snakes and were subsequently applied to frogs. Is this transfer of models justified, or are frogs and other amphibians so different from squamate reptiles that similar ecological pressures produce distinct evolutionary responses? For example, Toft (1980a) noted that ant-specialist frogs are wide foragers but ant-specialist lizards are sit-and-wait foragers. Both Huey and Pianka (1981) and Toft (1981) suggested that prey type should differ among foraging modes. Huey and Pianka (1981) and Huey and Bennett (1986) suggested that widely foraging desert lizards should eat sedentary and unpredictable (but clumped or large) prey such as termites found at a nest or large scorpions. Toft (1981) suggested that widely foraging frogs eat small, slow-moving prey that are distasteful or chitinous; these were mites or ants in her sample. Termites and ants are social insects that share many characteristics of behavior and predator defense, but are they equivalent in food value? Palatability and digestibility vary among termite and ant species as well as among castes within species. Termite alates appear to be higher-quality food for anurans than are worker castes of ants (Dimmitt and Ruibal 1980b). Perhaps the sensory modalities employed by sedentary and searching anurans and lizards contribute to the differences in diet: widely foraging insectivorous lizards like *Cnemidophorus* and *Ameiva* repeatedly extend their tongues and probably locate hidden prey by olfaction, whereas anurans may be sensitive primarily to visual cues. We would expect the lizards to detect termites, which live mainly underground or in covered galleries, whereas anurans would find ants, which forage largely on the surface of the ground. It may be significant in this context that *Bufo marinus,* which is one of the few anurans known to respond readily to olfactory cues when feeding (Rossi 1983), eats large quantities of termites under some conditions (Strüssmann et al. 1984).

The foraging behaviors of frogs and lizards have been difficult to compare because techniques vary among studies and most researchers have not studied the behavior of both frogs and lizards in the field. Figure 14.8 compares the results of two studies of Brazilian anurans and lizards in which the techniques were comparable. At night, on the open sand beaches of Alter do Chao, *Bufo marinus* (Bufonidae) and *Leptodactylus ocellatus* (Leptodactylidae) forage syntopically, and they differ in their frequency of movement and in the proportion (by number) of ants in their diets (Strüssmann et al. 1984). During the daylight hours in the tropical rainforest near Manaus, four species of lizards forage sympatrically. These species also differ in their rates of movement and the proportion of ants in their diets. *Uranoscodon superciliosa* (Iguanidae) sits on tree trunks and captures prey mainly on the ground. *Kentropyx calcaratus* (Teiidae) forages mainly on the ground. *Anolis punctatus* (Iguanidae) is arboreal and forages mainly on foliage and *Plica umbra* (Iguanidae) is arboreal and forages mainly on tree trunks. As Toft (1981)

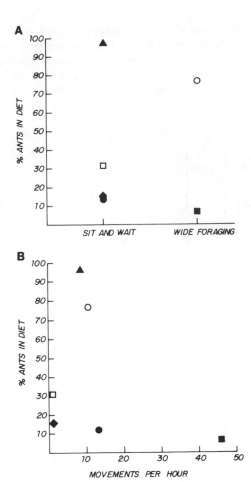

Fig. 14.8 Mean proportion of items in the diet represented by ants for the frogs *Leptodactylus ocellatus* (□), *Bufo marinus* (○), and the lizards *Uranoscodon superciliosa* (◆), *Plica umbra* (▲), *Anolis punctatus* (●), and *Kentropyx calcaratus* (■). *A,* species classified by subjective indices of foraging mode. *B,* species ordered by mean number of movements per minute. (Data for frogs are from Strüssmann et al. 1984, and data for lizards are from T. Gasnier, A. Lima and W. Magnusson in preparation.)

noted, lizards and frogs appear to differ when they are lumped into the categories sit-and-wait versus widely foraging (fig. 14.8A). However, a continuous measure such as frequency of movement shows no differences between frogs and lizards (fig. 14.8B).

The velocity of movement by amphibians is substantially lower than that of lizards; the fastest frogs travel only a tenth as far per unit time as widely foraging lizards (table 14.3). In fact, the mean velocities even of large, widely foraging anurans such as *Bufo marinus* fall within the range of velocities of sit-and-wait lizards of similar body lengths. Furthermore, the metabolic correlates of foraging mode are not exactly the same for anurans as for squamate reptiles (Taigen and Pough 1985). Widely foraging species in both groups have high aerobic capacities for locomotion, but the squamates also have high anaerobic capacities whereas widely foraging species of anurans have low anaerobic capacities. Taigen and Pough (1985) proposed two nonexclusive explanations for this divergence, one based on prey-handling behavior and the other on defense. They noted that capturing and subduing prey that is capable of quick evasive movements and prolonged struggle, as squamates often do, is quite a different

TABLE 14.3 Velocities of Movement by Free-Ranging Anurans, Salamanders, and Lizards

	Velocity (m·h⁻¹)		
	Mean Velocity[a]	Velocity Moving[b]	Reference
Anurans			
Bufo bufo	20–50		Van Gelder, Aarts, and Staal 1986
Bufo marinus	≤30		Strüssmann et al. 1984
Bufo woodhousii	18		Walton 1988
Colostethus inguinalis	2.5	144	Pough and Taigen 1990
Colostethus nubicola	0.9	57.6	Pough and Taigen 1990
Colostethus talamancae	1.5	230	Pough and Taigen 1990
Dendrobates auratus	13.6	241.2	Pough and Taigen 1990
Eleutherodactylus coqui	0.2		Pough and Taigen unpublished data
Leptodactylus ocellatus	≤20		Strüssmann et al. 1984
Salamanders			
Plethodon jordani	36–60		Madison and Shoop 1970
Lizards			Garland 1985
Insectivores and Carnivores			
Sit-and-Wait Predators			
Iguanidae			
Anolis (9 species)	3.1 ± 0.7 (N = 9)	234 (N = 1)	
Sceloporus (3 species)	5.7 ± 1.0 (N = 3)		
Phrynosoma cornutum	8.5		
Uta stansburiana	17.6		
Callisaurus draconoides	25.0		
Lacertidae			
Eremias and *Meroles* (2 species)	67.5 ± 7.0 (N = 2)	469 ± 8 (N = 2)	
Widely Foraging Predators			
Iguanidae			
Gambelia (2 species)	66.2 ± 3.2 (N = 2)		
Lacertidae			
Eremias, Ichnotropis, and *Nucras* (5 species)	341 ± 57 (N = 5)	537 ± 72 (N = 4)	
Teiidae			
Ameiva, Cnemidophorus, and *Kentropyx* (7 species)	111 ± 30 (N = 7)	397 ± 200 (N = 5)	
Helodermatidae			
Heloderma suspectum	107		
Varanidae			
Varanus (3 species)	475 (N = 1)	812 and 4,800 (N = 2)	
Herbivores and Omnivores			
Iguanidae			
Conolophus and *Dipsosaurus* (2 species)	171 ± 129 (N = 2)	1,400 ± 111 (N = 2)	
Scincidae			
Egernia and *Tiliqua* (2 species)		320 ± 50 (N = 2)	
Teiidae			
Cnemidophorus murinus	96	125	

[a] Total distance moved divided by total time observed.
[b] Distance moved divided by time actually moving.

matter from eating prey that is captured and subdued with a flick of the tongue. Lizards and snakes require anaerobic metabolic input during feeding: rates of oxygen consumption of lizards eating insects are as high as 84% of the aerobic scope, and lactic acid accumulates as they chew and swallow prey (Pough and Andrews 1985a, 1985b). Garter snakes also accumulate lactic acid as they subdue and swallow salamanders (Feder and Arnold 1982).

The difference in anaerobic capacities of squamates and anurans might also be related to differences in their defensive behaviors. Widely foraging frogs appear to be toxic and to rely on static defenses, whereas lizards do not have toxins and widely foraging species appear to escape by running, probably using anaerobic metabolism.

Do Studies of Foraging Demonstrate a Direct Relation between Energetics and Fitness?

The early prominence of studies of foraging in our understanding of the behavioral energetics of amphibians resulted partly from the momentum of similar studies of lizards and partly from the influence of dietary studies in community ecology (see reviews by Hairston 1987; Seale 1987; Toft 1985). However, hindsight suggests that this emphasis on foraging may have been misplaced in two respects. One reason to doubt that studies of foraging will yield evidence of a direct connection between energetics and fitness lies in the apparently low levels of exertion required during most foraging activities. Animals do not appear to be working near their physiological capacities during foraging, and if this is the case, natural selection may not act on exercise physiology via foraging mode.

Furthermore, foraging is a complex behavior that is interwoven with other activities, such as avoidance of predators and territorial defense, that are equally important to the fitness of an individual. The trade-offs that result from the interactions of these activities have provided a fruitful ground for ecological models, but experimentalists have not yet been able to disentangle potentially confounding influences to reveal clear-cut relations among physiology, foraging, and fitness.

Confounding Factors in the Study of Foraging Behavior

Body size is one of the most important variables affecting the life of any organism. The body sizes of amphibian species vary enormously within phylogenetic lineages and within ecological communities. Even among sympatric species of arboreal hylids, body lengths vary by sixfold (fig. 14.9). However, we know little of the effects of this variation in body size on foraging modes and diets of amphibians. Emerson (1985) used deviations from reduced-major-axis regressions to investigate correlates of head morphology in anurans independent of size. However, most studies have simply restricted comparisons to animals of similar size (e.g., Strüssmann et al. 1984) or have apparently assumed that size differences will not confound the results.

Often it is difficult to separate the effects of size, age, and reproduction (see also chapter 15). At the simplest level, the body size of a predator affects the size of the prey it eats because most amphibians (with the exception of some caecilians) do not chew their prey and hence are gape-limited, and qualitative ontogenetic changes have been recorded in diet (e.g., Christian 1982; Luthardt-Laimer 1983; Petranka 1984; Strüssmann et al. 1984), foraging efficiency (Reilly and Lauder 1988), and metabolism (Taigen and Pough 1981; Pough and Kamel 1984). K. L. Jones (1982) suggested that movement rate is proportional to size in a group of sit-and-wait arboreal *Eleutherodactylus*. Changes in foraging behavior may also be mediated by size-related changes in susceptibility to predators (e.g., Brodie and Formanowicz 1983; Cooke 1974; Cronin and Travis 1986; Crump 1984; Formanowicz 1986; Formanowicz et al. 1981; Kusano, Kusano, and Miyashita 1985).

Sexual differences in metabolism of amphibians have been reported (e.g., Fitzpatrick 1971; Taigen, Wells, and Marsh 1985), and gender may also affect habitat selection (e.g., Keen, McManus, and Wohltman 1987) and diet (e.g., T. Lamb 1984). Differences in diet and behavior of lizards have been attributed to the hypothesis that adult males are searching primarily for females, whereas adult females search for

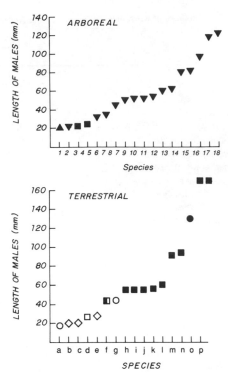

Fig. 14.9   Sizes of anurans that forage above ground (excludes microhylids and pipids) in undisturbed rainforest in Reserva Ducke, central Amazonia. Sizes are based on the largest males in the Instituto Nacional de Pesquisas da Amazónia collections or recorded by Barbara Zimmerman at the World Wildlife Fund, Minimum Critical Size of Ecosystems Project, 90 km north of Reserva Ducke. Mean sizes of males and sizes of females undoubtedly differ from those given, but the general patterns would remain the same for any index of the size of the species. *Open symbols* represent diurnal species, and *filled symbol* represent nocturnal species. The *half-filled symbol* represents a species that has been reported as being diurnally and nocturnally active. ▼, hylids; ▲, centrolenids; *squares*, leptodactylids; *circles*, bufonids; ◇, dendrobatids. Arboreal species are *1, Centrolenella oyampiensis; 2, Hyla minuta; 3, Eleutherodactylus lacrimosus; 4, Eleutherodactylus sp.; 5, H. rubra; 6, H. garbei; 7, Osteocephalus buckleyi; 8, Phyllomedusa tomopterna; 9, Phrynohyas resinifictrix; 10, Osteocephalus sp.; 11, H. granosa; 12, Phyllomedusa vaillanti; 13, H. geographica; 14, H. lanciformis; 15, O. taurinus; 16, Phyllomedusa tarsius; 17, H. boans; 18, Phyllomedusa bicolor.* Terrestrial species are *a, Dendrophryniscus minutus; b, Colostethus marchesianus; c, Colostethus sp.; d, Adenomera andreae; e, Dendrobates femoralis; f, Lithodytes lineatus; g, Bufo cf. typhonius; h, Leptodactylus fuscus; i, Eleutherodactylus fenestratus; j, Leptodactylus mystaceus; k, Leptodactylus wagneri; l, Leptodactylus rhodomystax; m, Leptodactylus stenoderma; n, B. marinus; o, Leptodactylus pentadactylus; p, Leptodactylus knudseni.*

ing primarily for females, whereas adult females search for food (Stamps 1977), and the same phenomenon may occur among amphibians. Studies of anurans are often facilitated by the aggregation of large numbers of males in or around aquatic habitats. Unfortunately, the anurans that are easiest to find are engaged in activities that may exclude or sharply modify foraging behavior (e.g., J. G. M. Robertson 1986b; Woolbright and Stewart 1987). Studies of the correlates of foraging modes of amphibians might be directed more profitably at females and perhaps juveniles.

Parental care by both male and female amphibians is common (see below), and individuals involved in parental care may give low priority to foraging (Forester 1981; Juterbock

1987; Simon 1983; Townsend, Stewart, and Pough 1984; Vaz-Ferreira and Gehrau 1975; Weygoldt 1980; Woodruff 1977; Woolbright and Stewart 1987). An extreme case of conflict between foraging and parental care is the Australian frog *Rheobatrachus silus* (Myobatrachidae), in which the stomach becomes modified as a brood pouch (Tyler and Carter 1981).

Habitat structure can affect both diet and foraging mode of amphibians. The magnitude of variation in diet within species among habitats is sometimes greater than variation among species within habitats (e.g., Strüssmann et al. 1984; Toft 1980b; White 1977). Those differences may reflect only the differences in the availability of prey from habitat to habitat, but differences in habitat structure can induce changes in foraging mode that may in turn lead to differences in diet. For example, habitat structure affects the activity of juvenile *Leptodactylus melanonotus* (Leptodactylidae). Frogs of this species were active during the day and night in a pond-edge habitat with tall vegetation, but were active only at night at an adjacent pond with low vegetation (Gregory 1983). Few species of amphibians forage syntopically, and habitat segregation is characteristic of most amphibian communities (Hairston 1987; Seale 1987; Toft 1985). One of the most difficult tasks confronting a researcher studying the foraging modes of amphibians is to ensure that habitat variability does not confound the behavioral variables being measured. Samples of the prey spectrum potentially available to a predator are an essential part of an analysis of interhabitat or interspecific variation in foraging mode and diet.

Physical characteristics of the habitat such as pH (Freda and Dunson 1986; Wyman and Hawksley-Lescault 1987), water speed (Odendaal and Bull 1980), temperature (Casterlin and Reynolds 1978; Noland and Ultsch 1981; Pauley 1978; Stauffer, Gates, and Goodfellow 1983), moisture (Keen 1984; Duellman and Trueb 1986; van Beurden 1980), salinity (Mullen and Alvarado 1976), and refuge sites (Davic and Orr 1987; Stewart and Pough 1983) may affect the distribution of amphibians and hence their access to prey. The same factors may affect the distribution of the prey species themselves (e.g., Jaeger 1978), and this aspect of the trophic biology of amphibians has been little considered in studies of foraging behavior.

Amphibians have endogenous daily and seasonal rhythms (e.g., Robertson 1976; Weathers and Snyder 1977) that can influence the results of behavioral and physiological studies. In the field, behavior always varies throughout the daily cycle. This variation has been related to predation (Gregory 1983; Holomuzki 1986; Stangel and Semlitsch 1987), thermoregulation (Hutchison and Spriestersbach 1986; Taigen and Pough 1981), or response to light levels (Hailman 1982, 1984; Hailman and Jaeger 1976; Jaeger 1981b; Jaeger and Hailman 1981; Jaeger, Hailman, and Jaeger 1976). Furthermore, characteristics of a habitat are often subject to daily and seasonal changes that may induce predictable changes in prey availability or amphibian behavior (Feder and Londos 1984; Hutchison and Spriestersbach 1986; Jaeger 1978; Keen 1984; Pough et al. 1983; Smits 1984; Smits and Crawford 1984; Toft 1980a). Complex relationships of behavior, ambient light levels, and predator vulnerability may be shown

for amphibian foraging behavior, as they have been for reproductive behavior (e.g., Nunes 1988; Ryan, Tuttle, and Rand 1982).

Predators have undoubtedly influenced the evolution of amphibian morphology and foraging strategies. They may influence the outcome of competitive interactions (e.g., Morin 1981, 1983a, 1983b; Wilbur, Morin, and Harris 1983) and select directly against certain foraging modes (Feder 1983d; Wassersug and Sperry 1977). The presence of fish predators modifies the foraging behavior of fish and salamander larvae (Stangel and Semlitsch 1987; Werner et al. 1983), and similar effects of predators on terrestrial amphibians are likely.

Inter- and intraspecific competition may determine when and where many species of amphibians forage, especially salamanders and larval anurans (Jaeger 1971; Jaeger, Joseph, and Barnard 1981; Keen 1982; Keen and Reed 1985; Odendaal, Bull, and Richards 1984; Richards 1962; Savage 1952; Southerland 1986a, 1986b, 1986c). Such interactions confound simple comparisons of diet. Indeed, Maiorana (1978) suggested that difference in diet of salamanders is an epiphenomenon attributable to habitat differences.

The effects of diseases and parasites on wild populations of vertebrates have largely been overlooked despite their probable importance (May 1983). Amphibians are susceptible to debilitation by a variety of microorganisms and parasites (reviewed by Duellman and Trueb 1986). However, studies such as those of Schall (1983), which relate infection by pathogens to reduced physiological, whole-animal, and reproductive performance, are unavailable for amphibians. Infection by pathogens might change an animal's principal motivation from foraging to thermoregulation (Hutchison and Erskine 1981; Kluger 1979), so knowledge of the health of the study animals would undoubtedly be of use in the interpretation of behavioral studies.

Is Foraging Hard Work? The prediction that the aerobic capacity of species or individuals will be correlated with behavioral characters such as mode of foraging or velocity of movement is based on the assumption that normal activity requires rates of oxygen consumption approaching the maximum aerobic scope. That assumption was a natural outgrowth of the observation that many species of frogs and salamanders are exhausted by a few minutes of forced locomotion (see chapter 12). However, natural velocities of movement by free-ranging animals appear to be substantially lower than those imposed on animals in laboratory experiments. Velocities of spontaneous movement by amphibians in the field (table 14.3) are within the range they sustain on treadmills with little increase in rate of oxygen consumption and little or no accumulation of lactic acid (Taigen and Beuchat 1984). Rates of oxygen consumption during most other natural activities are well below those elicited by forced activity in the laboratory (table 14.4).

Foraging lizards in the field also rarely reach the maximum speeds they can sustain with aerobic metabolism (Hertz, Huey, and Garland 1988). These observations suggest that the energy requirements of foraging would not be an important selective force in the evolution of the physiological characteristics of either amphibians or lizards, but if that is the

TABLE 14.4 Mass-specific Metabolic Rates and Net Cost of Activity for Selected Amphibians Engaged in Natural Behaviors and at Rest

	Activity	Temp. (°C)	Mass (g)	$\dot{V}O_{2rest}$ (ml $O_2 \cdot g^{-1} \cdot h^{-1}$)	$\dot{V}O_{2act}$ (ml $O_2 \cdot g^{-1} \cdot h^{-1}$)	Net Cost (J·h⁻¹)
Scaphiopus hammondii[a]	Burrowing	30	11.8	0.11	0.51	95
Bufo woodhousii fowleri[b]	Foraging	21	25.8	0.13	0.30[c]	85
Physalaemus pustulosus[d]	Nest building	25	1.7	0.16	0.77	20
Desmognathus ochrophaeus[e]	Aggression	15	2.0	0.07	0.11	1.6
	Courtship	15	2.0	0.07	0.10	1.2

Note: Net cost = $(\dot{V}O_{2act} - \dot{V}O_{2rest}) \times$ mass $\times$ 20.1 J·ml⁻¹ O_2. (See also table 14.10.)
[a]Seymour 1973c.
[b]Walton 1988; Walton and Anderson 1988.
[c]$\dot{V}O_2$ during foraging calculated from regression of $\dot{V}O_2$ versus speed of locomotion (Walton and Anderson 1988) and average speed of foraging toads of 0.018 km·h⁻¹ (Walton 1988).
[d]Ryan, Bartholomew, and Rand 1983.
[e]Bennett and Houck 1983.

case, what accounts for the correlations that do exist for both groups among aerobic capacity, diet, and foraging mode?

Possibly the metabolic demands of free-ranging animals are not well duplicated by laboratory studies, and the activities of free-ranging animals may require higher rates of energy input than we realize. That hypothesis is supported by two studies showing that, despite the apparently low levels of exertion by lizards under natural conditions, free-ranging lizards accumulate elevated concentrations of lactic acid. This indicates that routine locomotion, feeding, and territorial defense require rates of energy input higher than those that can be sustained aerobically (Bennett, Gleeson, and Gorman 1981; Pough and Andrews 1985b).

The use of glycolysis by amphibians in the field or in the laboratory while engaged in activities other than locomotion has received little attention. Plethodontid salamanders (*Plethodon jordani*) accumulated high concentrations of lactic acid during staged encounters with predatory snakes, and lactate concentration was correlated with the duration of an encounter (Feder and Arnold 1982). Male *Hyla crucifer* (Hylidae) captured in a breeding chorus (not necessarily individuals that had been vocalizing) had an average whole-body lactate concentration of 0.062 mg · g⁻¹. This was nearly twice that of control frogs resting in a laboratory at the same temperature and time of day (0.037 · g⁻¹; Pough and Gatten 1984). Two samples of vocalizing *H. versicolor* had whole-body lactate concentrations higher than resting levels (Taigen and Wells 1985). Lactate concentrations were higher early in the evening than later (0.225 mg · g⁻¹ versus 0.103 mg · g⁻¹), suggesting that the effort of moving to the breeding pond from daytime retreat sites may have been responsible for the accumulation of lactic acid. This hypothesis is consistent with the observation that vocalization by anurans is sustained aerobically (see below).

Alternatively, the metabolic capacities of species may not reflect the demands of day-to-day life. Instead they could be examples of excess construction (in the sense of Gans [1979] as proposed by Walton [1988]). That is, the selective forces that are important in determining metabolic capacity might be found not among the routine activities of organisms but in rare events such as defending a territory or sprinting to escape a predator. Unfortunately, phenomena of this sort are not likely to be observed often enough to provide a useful basis for testing hypotheses about the significance of interspecific

or individual variation in metabolic capacities (e.g., van Berkum, Huey, and Adams 1986).

DISCRETE ACTIVITIES AS MEASURES OF PERFORMANCE AND FITNESS

Attempts to understand the relations of physiological, behavioral, and ecological aspects of foraging mode may be frustrated by the lack of a clear link between physiological and behavioral capacities and by the complexity of the day-to-day life of an amphibian. Foraging is not a simple behavior: at a minimum an amphibian must simultaneously confront the costs and benefits of searching versus ambushing and the risks of predation during activity or concealment. Individual fitness will be related to an individual's performance in diverse and sometimes conflicting activities, and one-to-one correspondences are less likely than multivariate relationships that may shift spatially, daily, seasonally, and during the lifetime of an individual.

Correlations of physiological variation with variation in performance and fitness might be seen more clearly if we chose an energetically costly behavior that occupies an animal to the near exclusion of other activities (Pough 1989b). Sociobiologists have found it productive to concentrate on limited aspects of the biology of organisms, choosing activities in which a link between behavior and some aspects of fitness can be demonstrated (e.g., Clutton-Brock 1988). Some of the activities associated with reproduction by amphibians require high rates of energy input and exclude for a time most or all confounding behaviors. Thus, studies of the energetics of reproduction may illuminate constraints and selective forces that are associated with natural activities.

THE ENERGETICS OF REPRODUCTIVE BEHAVIOR
Kentwood D. Wells and Theodore L. Taigen

In many species of animals, sexual selection appears to favor males that maximize the repetition rate, intensity, duration, or complexity of their displays, because such signals enhance a male's ability to attract mates or retain possession of groups of females (e.g., insects: Forrest 1983; Hedrick 1986; fishes: Farr 1980; Schmale 1981; frogs: Arak 1983a; Ryan 1985b; Pallett and Passmore 1988; Wells 1988; birds: Gibson and Bradbury 1985; Höglund and Lundberg 1987; Radesäter et al. 1987; mammals: Clutton-Brock and Albon 1979; Lundberg and Gerell 1986; McComb 1987). In addition, energetically costly displays could provide females with information about variation in overall male quality that may be genetically based (Andersson 1982b; Kodric-Brown and Brown 1984; Lambrechts and Dhondt 1986; Klump and Gerhardt 1987; Reid 1987). However, physiological constraints may limit the ability of males to perform these displays (Parker 1982, 1983; Halliday 1987). Hence, the energetic costs of display behavior are of interest not only to physiologists, but to behavioral ecologists as well.

Measurements of the metabolic costs of displays are difficult to obtain, especially for large vertebrates, but indirect evidence suggests that physiological constraints limit display rates. For example, singing rates of some birds decrease at cold temperatures, possibly because thermoregulatory requirements reduce the energy available for singing (Garson and Hunter 1979; Higgins 1979; Gottlander 1987; Reid 1987). On the other hand, singing rates increase when food resources increase (Searcy 1979; Wilhelm, Comtesse, and Phlumm 1980; Davies and Lundberg 1984; Gottlander 1987; Radesäter et al. 1987; Reid 1987).

Relatively small animals such as amphibians are ideal subjects for studies of behavioral energetics because they often will perform natural activities inside metabolic chambers. Studies of anuran vocalization are particularly interesting because vocalization is a natural activity that may require rates of energy input that approach an animal's physiological limits (see above and chapter 12). Other activities, such as foraging, are supported by metabolic rates well below maximum sustainable levels (table 14.4). Laboratory measurements of physiological performance, such as maximum rate of oxygen consumption during forced exercise, can reveal significant correlations between physiology and behavior at the interspecific level (e.g., Taigen, Emerson, and Pough 1982; Taigen and Pough 1983, 1985; chapter 12), but attempts to relate individual variation in metabolic performance to behavioral performance in the field have not been very successful (Wells and Taigen 1984; Sullivan and Walsberg 1985; Walton 1988).

This section reviews the energetic costs of reproductive behavior of both urodeles and anurans, although relatively little information is available for urodeles. The focus of the discussion will be on males, because only males of most species engage in costly display behavior during the breeding season. Differences between males and females in patterns of energy use are discussed elsewhere in this chapter. After reviewing the metabolic costs of vocalization in some detail, we consider the relationship between whole-animal behavior and physiology and the morphological and biochemical features of the muscles involved in call production. Because anurans can be studied in the laboratory and the field, they provide a unique opportunity to integrate behavioral, morphological, physiological, and biochemical studies into an interdisciplinary approach to behavioral energetics, as recently advocated (Feder et al. 1987).

Costs of Reproductive Behavior of Salamanders

Terrestrial plethodontid salamanders are good examples of amphibians as low-energy systems (Pough 1983). They have

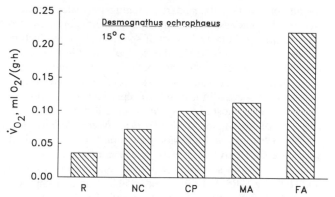

Fig. 14.10 Mean metabolic rates of *Desmognathus ochrophaeus* during natural activities. *R*, rest; *NC*, noncourting pairs; *CP*, courting pairs; *MA*, male-male aggression; *FA*, forced activity. (Resting metabolism from Fitzpatrick 1973a; forced activity from Feder 1986; all others from Bennett and Houck 1983.)

low resting metabolic rates compared to other terrestrial ectotherms (Feder 1983b; Pough 1983) and generally have very low capacities for sustained locomotor activity (Hillman et al. 1979; Withers 1980; Feder 1986, 1987b; see also chapter 12). The lives of most terrestrial plethodontids are characterized by long periods of inactivity punctuated by bouts of foraging, courtship, or aggressive behavior (Feder 1983b).

The only attempt to determine the energetic costs of reproductive behavior for a salamander is Bennett and Houck's (1983) study of the plethodontid *Desmognathus ochrophaeus*. They measured oxygen consumption of noncourting pairs of males and females, courting pairs, and pairs of males engaged in aggressive interactions. Courtship bouts lasted more than an hour on average, but metabolic rates of courting pairs were only 38% higher than those of noncourting pairs (fig. 14.10) and less than three times the resting rates of males and females measured by Fitzpatrick (1973). This is a small increase when one considers that metabolic rates of inactive salamanders may increase by as much as 77% simply as a result of feeding (Feder, Gibbs, Griffith, and Tsuji 1984). Metabolic rates of males engaged in aggressive behavior were only slightly higher. Courting and fighting pairs of *Desmognathus* did not approach levels of oxygen consumption achieved by individuals during forced exercise, which averaged six to ten times resting rates (Feder 1986; see also chapter 12).

Bennett and Houck (1983) also reported significant increases in whole-body lactate following courtship and aggressive behavior. However, lactate levels were only 10 to 30% of those found in males after forced activity. Anaerobic metabolism accounted for about 10% of ATP production during courtship or aggressive behavior. The estimated cost of an average courtship bout (1.23 h) was 2.70 J for the male and female combined, or about 1 to 2% of a salamander's daily energy intake. For comparison, a 1.2-g male *Hyla crucifer* (Anura: Hylidae) calling for an hour at 15°C would use about twenty-five times as much energy as a 2.0-g male *Desmognathus ochrophaeus* engaged in an hour of courtship at the same temperature (Taigen, Wells, and Marsh 1985). These figures do not include all possible costs of reproductive behavior for a male salamander; searching for mates, production of pheromones, and production of spermatophores also require energy. In fact, the cost of spermatophore production in this species can exceed the cost of courtship behavior (Marks and Houck 1989), but both costs are small, and it seems unlikely that males of most species of terrestrial salamanders are energy-limited in their reproductive behavior.

The urodeles most likely to have energetically costly courtship are aquatic salamandrids (*Triturus, Notophthalmus,* and *Paramesotriton*), and physiological constraints may limit their courtship activities. Newts have prolonged breeding seasons lasting from several weeks to several months (Verrell and Halliday 1985; Verrell, Halliday, and Griffiths 1986; Verrell and McCabe 1988). Breeding males of most species develop elaborate secondary sexual characters, such as bright colors and enlarged tail fins, and engage in vigorous courtship that may last up to several hours (Halliday 1974, 1975, 1976, 1977a; Verrell 1982; Sparreboom 1983, 1984a; Giacoma and Sparreboom 1987). Males of some species also engage in aggressive interactions that can lead to prolonged struggles for possession of females (Verrell 1983, 1986; Sparreboom 1984a, 1984b; Zuiderwijk and Sparreboom 1986). Although metabolic rates of courting and fighting newts have not been measured, the length and vigor of courtship and aggressive interactions suggest that such behavior is supported mainly by aerobic metabolism.

The ability of male newts to sustain courtship directly affects their success in fertilizing eggs. Males that engage in more than one courtship bout with a female and deposit more than one spermatophore are more likely to achieve fertilization than those that go through a single courtship sequence (Halliday 1976, 1977a). Displays by male *Triturus vulgaris* have a cumulative affect on female receptivity (Teyssedre and Halliday 1986). Males that deposited spermatophores for females had significantly longer courtship bouts than did unsuccessful males. The number of individual courtship acts by male *Notophthalmus viridescens* can reach several thousand per courtship bout and is positively correlated with success in transferring spermatophores (Verrell 1982). A similarly strong correlation exists for *T. cristatus* between total time spent in courtship and mating success.

Several lines of evidence suggest that physiological constraints limit these courtship activities by newts (Halliday 1987). The frequency with which male *T. vulgaris* go to the surface to breathe is directly related to their level of activity (Halliday and Worsnop 1977). Breathing frequency increases during sexual activity, and the need to breathe can significantly limit the duration of courtship bouts (Halliday and Sweatman 1976). Breathing rates increase if oxygen dissolved in the water or in the gas phase decreases, whereas breathing rates decrease when the water is aerated (Spurway and Haldane 1953; Halliday 1977b). These results do not demonstrate that newts are energy-limited during courtship, but they do suggest that metabolic rates during vigorous activity exceed levels that can be supported solely by cutaneous respiration.

Changes in body mass are not very useful for estimating depletion of energy substrates by male newts during the breeding season because adult newts typically absorb a substantial amount of water when they first enter the breeding ponds (Verrell and Halliday 1985). Most species of newts feed during the breeding season (Verrell 1985) and may increase in mass if they remain in ponds for long periods (Verrell and Halliday 1985). On the other hand, the mass of the liver and abdominal fat bodies of male *T. vulgaris* decreased during the summer breeding season and increased during the fall (Verrell, Halliday, and Griffiths 1986). The proportion of energy reserves used for production of sperm and spermatophores versus reproductive behavior has yet to be determined, but breeding males do appear to be under some energy stress. Fat body mass and carcass lipids of males of another aquatic salamander, *Amphiuma means* (Amphiumidae), decrease during the breeding season (Rose 1967), but the courtship behavior of this species is completely unknown.

Costs of Reproductive Behavior of Anurans

No urodele has a display equivalent to the loud and sustained calling of frogs and toads. That calling can be a very metabolically expensive activity has forced a revision of earlier views of amphibians as animals poorly adapted for sustained activity and heavily dependent on anaerobic metabolism (Bennett 1978; Pough 1980, 1983; Taigen and Pough 1985; see also chapter 12). The energetic costs of vocalization may stress male anurans during the breeding season. Growth rate, total body mass, and the masses of energy-storing organs may decrease during the breeding season and increase when reproductive activities cease (Jenssen 1972; Wells 1978; MacNally 1981b; Morton 1981; Woolbright 1983, 1985a; J. G. M. Robertson 1986b; Long 1987a, 1987b; Given 1988; McKay 1989). While this cycle may be due in part to reduced opportunities for foraging during the breeding season (Martof 1956; Jenssen and Klimstra 1966; Woolbright and Stewart 1987), it also may reflect the energetic cost of calling. For example, individual male *Rana virgatipes* show a negative relationship between calling rates and growth rates during the breeding season (Given 1988; see also below).

Intensity of Anuran Vocalizations The energetic cost of calling is related to both the sound power of a male's calls and the amount of time invested in calling. Therefore, a brief review of anuran call intensities and calling persistence will provide a useful background for a more detailed discussion of calling energetics. Sound pressure levels (SPL) of selected anuran species are shown in table 14.5; data for additional North American and African species were given by Gerhardt (1975) and Passmore (1981). For most species, only peak SPL measurements are available, but whenever possible, root-mean-square (RMS) values have been included as well. The latter are the measurements most appropriate for calculating total sound power (MacNally and Young 1981; Kavanagh 1987; Prestwich, Brugger, and Topping 1989), and they are also useful for comparison with other animals. Most anurans measured to date have peak SPLs exceeding 100 dB at 50 cm in front of the frog, and some are as high as 115 dB (table 14.5; Gerhardt 1975; Passmore 1981). RMS SPLs average about 10 dB lower, but the precise relationship depends on the structure of the call (Gerhardt 1975).

The acoustic energy output of these frogs is impressive compared to the songs of small birds. Mean RMS SPLs of twenty species of frogs were 84 to 100 dB ($\bar{x}$ = 91 dB) at 50

TABLE 14.5 Mean Sound Pressure Levels of the Calls of Selected Anuran Species at 50 cm in Front of the Frog

	Peak SPL (dB)		RMS SPL (dB)		
	Mean	Range	Mean	Range	Reference
Bufonidae					
Bufo americanus	106	102–109	96	91–100	Gerhardt 1975
Centrolenidae					
Centrolenella fleischmanni	100	92–104			Wells and Schwartz 1982
Hylidae					
Hyla chrysoscelis	105	101–108		88–97	Gerhardt 1975
Hyla cinerea	103	97–107	89	84–94	Gerhardt 1975
Hyla crucifer	103	100–106	94	92–97	Gerhardt 1975
Hyla ebraccata	100	96–105			Schwartz and Wells 1984
Hyla gratiosa	108	106–109	90	86–93	Gerhardt 1975
Hyla microcephala	106	101–109			Schwartz and Wells 1984
Hyla squirella	103		88	86–89	Gerhardt 1975
Hyla versicolor	109	108–113	100	99–103	Wells and Taigen 1986
Litoria ewingi	105	103–106			Harrison 1987
Litoria verreauxi	100	96–101			Harrison 1987
Hyperoliidae					
Hyperolius argus	108	105–111			Passmore 1981
Hyperolius marmoratus	104	102–105			Passmore 1981
Kassina maculata	114	112–116			Passmore 1981
Leptodactylidae					
Eleutherodactylus coqui[a]	100	96–105			Narins and Hurley 1982
Physalaemus pustulosus	90				Ryan 1985b
Myobatrachidae					
Geocrinia victoriana	94	90–97			Littlejohn and Harrison 1985
Ranidella signifera	100	98–101			Littlejohn, Harrison, and MacNally 1985
Ranidella parinsignifera	96	93–98			Littlejohn, Harrison, and MacNally 1985
Uperoleia laevigata[b]	85				Robertson 1984
Ranidae					
Rana lessonae	105				Brzoska 1982
Rana ridibunda	116				Brzoska 1982
Rana virgatipes	109	102–112			Given 1987

Note: Data for some species were calculated from measurements made at 15 or 25 cm.

[a] High-altitude population.

[b] The population referred to *U. rugosa* by Robertson (1984) was placed in *U. laevigata* by Davies and Littlejohn (1986).

cm (Gerhardt 1975). Values for seventeen species of European songbirds were 80 to 106 dB ($\bar{x}$ = 89 dB; Brackenbury 1979). Subsequent measurements of European blackbirds (90 dB) and red-winged blackbirds (97 dB) fall in the same range (Dabelsteen 1981; Brenowitz 1982). However, the birds measured by Brackenbury (1979) averaged 23 g in mass, whereas most of the frogs have masses of less than 10 g, and many species are only 1 to 2 g. No strong interspecific relationship between body size and sound intensity was apparent for frogs or birds. A tiny (1.2 g) *Hyla crucifer* (Hylidae) has an SPL of 94 dB RMS, which is similar to that of a 10-g wren (96 dB), a 20-g warbler (94 dB), or a 96-g blackbird (93 dB; Brackenbury 1979).

The frogs shown in table 14.5 also appear to be considerably louder than most insects. Some of the loudest species of insects are shown in table 14.6. The songs of some tettigoniid bush crickets and katydids reach RMS SPLs of 90 dB at 50 cm, which is about average sound intensity of North American frogs. The bladder cicada (*Cystosoma saundersii*), which is a loud insect, has an SPL of about 82 dB, lower than any of the frogs measured by Gerhardt (1975). Many insects, including the common house cricket (*Acheta domesticus*) and a

number of acridid grasshoppers, have SPLs of only 25 to 50 dB at 50 cm (Dumortier 1963). These data are not strictly comparable to measurements for frogs because they represent instantaneous sound pressure levels. Many insects have continuous trills that may last for minutes at a time. Hence, total sound power output per hour could be higher than that of many frogs, even if SPLs are equal or lower. Nevertheless, anurans do appear to have some of the loudest acoustic signals of any small terrestrial animals, and they have very high sound power outputs for their body sizes.

The data in table 14.5 do not give a complete picture of intraspecific variation in sound power of anuran vocalizations. The calls of different individuals in a population often vary in sound pressure level by 6 to 10 dB (Gerhardt 1975; Passmore 1981). An increase of 10 dB represents a tenfold increase in sound power (measured in watts), and a 6 dB increase translates to about a fourfold increase in power output. Therefore, relatively small differences in SPL could translate into substantial differences in the energetic cost of calling. Few workers have investigated sources of intraspecific variation in sound pressure levels of anuran calls. However, in some species, including *Bufo americanus* (Gerhardt

TABLE 14.6   Root-Mean-Square Sound Pressure Levels of Selected Insect Species at 50 cm Directly above the Insect

	Family	SPL at 50 cm (dB)	Reference
Ephippiger terrestris	Ephippigeridae	89	Dumortier 1963
Acheta domesticus	Gryllidae	49	Dumortier 1963
Teleogryllus commodus	Gryllidae	64	Kavanagh 1987
Gryllotalpa australis	Gryllotalpidae	79	Kavanagh 1987
Conocephalus brevipennis	Tettigoniidae	69	Bailey and Morris 1986
Neoconocephalus affinis	Tettigoniidae	87	Brush, Gain, and Greenfield 1985
Psorodontus illyricus	Tettigoniidae	69	Keuper et al. 1988
Tettigonia cantans	Tettigoniidae	81	Keuper et al. 1988
Tettigonia viridissima	Tettigoniidae	90	Keuper et al. 1988
Cystosoma saundersii	Cicadidae	82	MacNally and Young 1981

Note: All the insects are orthopterans except the cicada.

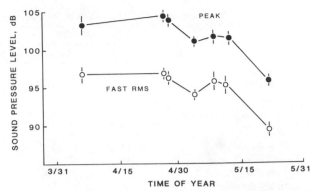

Fig. 14.11   Seasonal changes in sound pressure levels of *Hyla crucifer* calls measured at 50 cm directly in front of the frog. Data are shown as means ± 1 SE. (Unpublished data collected by K. D. Wells and T. L. Taigen in 1988.)

1975), *B. calamita* (Arak 1983a, 1983b), and *Rana virgatipes* (Given 1987), SPL is positively correlated with body size. Call SPLs also may vary seasonally as the physical condition of calling males changes. Wells and Taigen (unpublished) measured SPLs of *Hyla crucifer* throughout the breeding season and found a substantial decline toward the end of the season (Fig. 14.11). This change could have resulted from recruitment of smaller males into the population late in the season, as documented by McKay (1989), as well as the deterioration of calling muscles of males that had been in the chorus for several weeks (see discussion of muscle physiology below). In either case, the sound power of calls produced by males late in the season is much lower than that of males calling earlier in the year.

Duration of Anuran Vocalization   Frogs can be remarkably persistent in their vocalization, often calling almost continuously for several hours each night. Precise data on calling effort are difficult to obtain because most workers have been content to describe features of individual calls without recording hourly calling rates, call durations, or the number of hours of calling per night. Several measures of calling effort for both tropical and temperate zone species are shown in table 14.7. Some species have calls consisting of simple single-note calls, whereas others produce complex multinote calls that may have more than one type of note. For comparison, calling rates of most species in table 14.7 are reported as the number of individual notes per hour. The number of seconds of calling per hour was estimated from average note durations and does not include intervals between call notes. Most figures for number of hours of calling per night and total number of notes given per night are estimates based on average calling times for the chorus as a whole. Only a few investigators have monitored individual males throughout the

night to obtain precise estimates of total calling times (e.g., Ryan, Bartholomew, and Rand 1983; Wells and Taigen 1986; Grafe 1988).

Frogs vary considerably in hourly calling efforts. Some species, such as *Hyla rosenbergi* and *Ranidella signifera* (Myobatrachidae), may produce more than 7,000 call notes per hour and more than 25,000 notes per night. Others, such as *Rana virgatipes,* produce fewer than 200 notes per hour. The data in table 14.7 probably are biased toward active callers and may not be representative of frogs as a whole. All of these species call in relatively dense choruses where complex vocal interactions among males and high calling rates are common (Wells 1988). In contrast, many tropical frogs call from isolated positions in the forest, and their low calling rates suggest that energetic costs of calling are lower than costs for actively chorusing species.

Energetic Costs of Calling   Because sustained vocalization by frogs is supported almost entirely by aerobic metabolism (see discussion of anaerobic metabolism below), energetic costs can be estimated directly by measuring the metabolic rates of males calling in small chambers. This was first done with a tropical leptodactylid frog, *Physalaemus pustulosus* (Bucher, Ryan, and Bartholomew 1982), and subsequently with several other tropical and temperate zone frogs (table 14.8). In most of these studies, frogs are placed in closed metabolic chambers from which an initial air sample is drawn before the animal begins calling. After a period of vocalization by the frog, a second air sample is withdrawn, and the fractional oxygen content of the two samples is measured with an oxygen analyzer (Bucher, Ryan, and Bartholomew 1982; Taigen and Wells 1985; Taigen, Wells, and Marsh 1985; Prestwich, Brugger, and Topping 1989; Wells and Taigen 1989). Flow-through respirometry, such as that used by Lighton (1987) to measure the cost of substrate tapping in beetles, has not been attempted for frogs. However, Grafe (1988) used an open-flow system to measure carbon dioxide production by calling *Hyperolius viridiflavus* (Hyperoliidae) with an infrared gas analyzer; these data were then converted to oxygen consumption using a respiratory quotient measured in the laboratory for frogs that were not vocalizing. This procedure could introduce a substantial error if

TABLE 14.7   Estimates of Calling Effort for Selected Anuran Species

	Temp (°C)	Notes·h⁻¹	s·h⁻¹	h·night⁻¹	Notes·night⁻¹	Reference
Bufonidae						
Bufo woodhousii	20	240	360			3, 5
Centrolenidae						
Centrolenella fleischmanni	18	580	120	4	2,320	9
Hylidae						
Hyla cinerea	27	3,100	430	2–4		20
Hyla crucifer	16	4,500	500	2–4	13,500	12
Hyla ebraccata	26	2,700	270	2–4	8,100	7
Hyla gratiosa	29	3,600	650			20
Hyla microcephala	26	3,800	355	2–4	11,500	21
Hyla rosenbergi	26	7,200	430	4	28,800	1
Hyla squirella	27	6,600	1,320			20
Hyla versicolor	19	1,000	700	2–4	3,000	16
Litoria ewingi	10	2,200	450			18
Hyperoliidae						
Hyperolius marmoratus	24	3,300	330	4	13,200	8
Hyperolius viridiflavus	25	5,400[a]	330	2–4	10,000[a]	19
Leptodactylidae						
Eleutherodactylus coqui	23	1,450[b]	350	3	4,350[b]	13, 14
Physalaemus pustulosus	25	1,000[b]	400	5–7	6,000[b]	2, 4
Myobatrachidae						
Geocrinia victoriana	13	3,840	350			10
Ranidella signifera	12	7,800	940			6, 11
Uperoleia laevigata	14	1,200	580	4–5	5,400	15
Ranidae						
Rana virgatipes	26	180	20	7	1,260	17

Sources: (1) Kluge 1981; (2) Bucher, Ryan, and Bartholomew 1982; (3) Sullivan 1982b; (4) Ryan, Bartholomew, and Rand 1983; (5) Sullivan 1983; (6) MacNally 1984; (7) Wells and Schwartz 1984; (8) Dyson 1985; (9) Jacobson 1985; (10) Littlejohn and Harrison 1985; (11) Littlejohn, Harrison, and MacNally 1985; (12) Taigen, Wells, and Marsh 1985; (13) Woolbright 1985c; (14) Zelick and Narins 1985; (15) J. G. M. Robertson 1986a; (16) Wells and Taigen 1986; (17) Given 1987; (18) Harrison 1987; (19) Grafe 1988; (20) Prestwich, Brugger, and Topping 1989; (21) Wells and Taigen 1989.
[a]Measurements for frogs in the laboratory.
[b]Number of calls·h⁻¹; calls are composed of two distinct types of notes.

TABLE 14.8   Oxygen Consumption of Male Frogs during Rest, Forced Exercise, and Calling

	Temp. (°C)	V̇o₂ (ml O₂·g⁻¹·h⁻¹) Rest	Exercise	Call (avg)[a]	Call (max)[b]	Reference
Hyla cinerea	27	0.14	1.02	0.92	1.20	7
Hyla crucifer	19	0.11	1.10	1.51	1.70	4
Hyla gratiosa	29	0.10	1.25	1.22[c]	1.21[c]	7
Hyla microcephala	26	0.15		1.70	2.80	8
Hyla squirella	27	0.17	1.79	2.27[c]	2.10[c]	7
Hyla versicolor	19	0.08	1.09	1.70[c]	1.67[c]	3, 5
Hyperolius viridiflavus	25	0.13[d]	1.10[d]	1.37	1.40	6
Physalaemus pustulosus	26	0.15	1.82	0.91	1.18	1, 2
	25	0.16[e]		0.98	1.83	9

Sources: (1) Bucher, Ryan, and Bartholomew 1982; (2) Ryan, Bartholomew, and Rand 1983; (3) Taigen and Wells 1985; (4) Taigen, Wells, and Marsh 1985; (5) Wells and Taigen 1986; (6) Grafe 1988; (7) Prestwich, Brugger, and Topping 1989; (8) Wells and Taigen 1989; (9) T. L. Taigen and K. D. Wells unpublished data.
[a]Estimated metabolic rate at the average calling rate measured in the field.
[b]Highest rate for a frog calling in a metabolic chamber.
[c]Average calling rates in field exceeded those of most males calling in metabolism chambers.
[d]Data from Taigen, Emerson, and Pough 1982 adjusted to 25°C, assuming a Q_{10} of 2.0.
[e]Resting rates measured at 26°–28°C and adjusted to 25°C assuming a Q_{10} of 2.0.

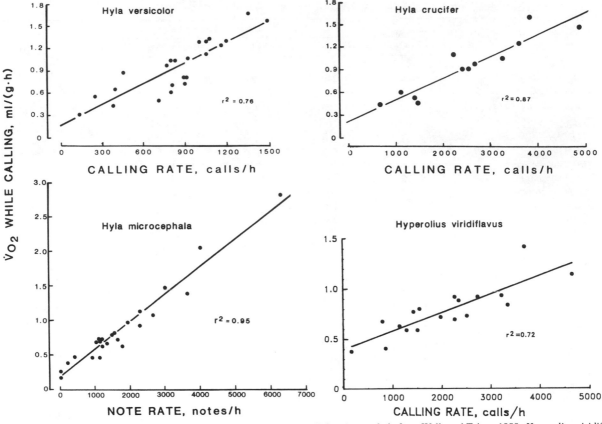

Fig. 14.12 Rate of oxygen consumption during calling in relation to calling effort for selected anurans. (*Hyla crucifer* data from Taigen, Wells, and Marsh 1985; *Hyla versicolor* from Taigen and Wells 1985; *Hyla microcephala* from Wells and Taigen 1989; *Hyperolius viridiflavus* from Grafe 1988, pers. comm.)

the metabolic substrates differ when frogs are at rest and vocalizing.

Average metabolic rates for several species of frogs at rest, while calling, and during forced exercise are given in table 14.8. Both the metabolic rate of males calling at average rates in the field and maximum rates of oxygen consumption measured for any individual calling in a metabolic chamber are included. Metabolic rates of calling frogs are very high compared to other measurements of activity metabolism in amphibians (see chapter 12). In fact, the maximum values for *Hyla microcephala* and *H. squirella* (Hylidae) at 26° to 27°C are the highest yet measured for any ectothermal vertebrate. In all of the species, the maximum rate of oxygen consumption while calling is more than ten times resting metabolism, and average levels for males in the field are six to twenty times resting rates. Maximum oxygen consumption while calling equals or exceeds maximum metabolic rates during exercise for almost all of the species. The maximum values shown in table 14.8 may be underestimates for some species, because frogs often call at higher rates in the field than in metabolic chambers. For example, male *H. versicolor* in a chorus call at rates equivalent to an oxygen consumption of 2.2 to 2.4 ml $\cdot$ g^{-1} $\cdot$ h^{-1}), or nearly thirty times resting metabolism (Wells and Taigen 1986). Clearly, oxygen consumption during forced exercise is not the maximum aerobic capacity of many anurans (Taigen and Wells 1985; see also chapter 12).

For most of the species in table 14.8, the rate of oxygen consumption while calling is a simple linear function of calling effort measured as number of notes or as number of seconds of calling per hour (fig. 14.12). For species such as *Hyla crucifer*, *Hyla microcephala*, and *Hyperolius viridiflavus*, call note duration varies little, and call rate alone explains most of the variation in oxygen consumption (Taigen, Wells, and Marsh 1985; Grafe 1988; Wells and Taigen 1989). On the other hand, *Hyla versicolor* gives relatively long trills that vary in duration, and the best predictor of oxygen consumption is the product of note rate and duration (Taigen and Wells 1985). *Physalaemus pustulosus* (Leptodactylidae) is unusual in that oxygen consumption appears to increase at an accelerating rate as calling rate increases, a pattern found in both the original data reported by Bucher, Ryan, and Bartholomew (1982) and in more recent data collected over a wider range of calling rates (fig. 14.13; Taigen and Wells unpublished). In the combined data, maximum calling rates and maximum rates of oxygen consumption are higher than those reported by Bucher, Ryan, and Bartholomew, but estimated oxygen consumption for an average calling rate in the field is similar (table 14.8; oxygen consumption based on an average calling rate of 1,200 calls $\cdot$ h^{-1}).

Bucher, Ryan, and Bartholomew (1982) reported that noncalling male frogs exposed to a chorus had metabolic rates elevated above resting levels. They suggested that this stimulated rate of oxygen consumption should be considered an additional cost of reproduction. In subsequent studies, zero-intercepts for regressions of oxygen consumption versus calling rate have been only slightly above resting levels (fig. 14.13) and within the 95% confidence intervals for resting metabolism (Taigen and Wells 1985; Taigen, Wells, and Marsh 1985; Prestwich, Brugger, and Topping 1989; Wells and Taigen 1989). Hence, stimulation by a chorus probably does not cause a significant increase in metabolic rate for most frogs. Slight elevations above daytime resting metabolism are to be expected, because inactive frogs measured at night are never as quiescent as frogs measured during the day. Furthermore, frogs that give relatively few calls are more likely to move than those calling at high rates, leading to slightly inflated values of metabolic rate at low calling rates. For example, reliable measurements of *Physalaemus pustulosus* in the field were difficult at low calling rates because most males moved during measurements (Taigen and Wells unpublished). Even if metabolic rates of noncalling frogs are slightly elevated above resting rates, the increase in oxygen consumption is trivial compared to levels achieved during sustained calling (compare figs. 14.12 and 14.13).

Social Interactions and Calling Energetics   The strong correlation between metabolic rate and calling effort in all of the species of frogs studied to date suggests that social interac-

tions that increase calling should have a strong influence on its total cost. Males of many anuran species respond to the calls of other individuals in a chorus by increasing their calling rate, call duration, or the number of notes per call (reviewed by Wells 1988). Often this behavior leads to substantial variation in calling effort among males in the same population. For example, calling efforts (seconds of calling per hour) of *Hyla microcephala* can vary by more than 300% (Wells and Taigen 1989). In dense choruses, males increase calling efforts by increasing the number of secondary click notes in their calls (Schwartz and Wells 1985; Schwartz 1986). This makes the calls more attractive to females (Schwartz 1986) but also increases the cost of calling. Males appear to conserve energy by maintaining a low calling effort when only a few males are present, but increase calling effort and energetic expenditures when competition among males is intense (Wells and Taigen 1989). Consequently, average metabolic rates of males in a chorus are only about 60% of the maximum level measured in a metabolic chamber (table 14.8).

Other anuran species do not show such a simple relationship between chorus density and energy expenditure. Male *Hyla versicolor* respond to the calls of other males by adding pulses to their calls, thereby increasing call duration (fig. 14.14; Wells and Taigen 1986; Klump and Gerhardt 1987). However, males exhibit a simultaneous decrease in calling

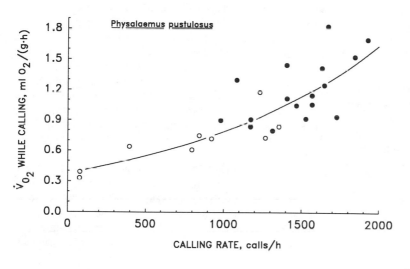

Fig. 14.13   Rate of oxygen consumption during calling in relation to calling rate for *Physalaemus pustulosus*. ○, data from Bucher, Ryan, and Bartholomew 1982. ●, unpublished data collected by T. L. Taigen and K. D. Wells in 1986. The equation is for a linear regression with a log-transformed value of rate of oxygen consumption.

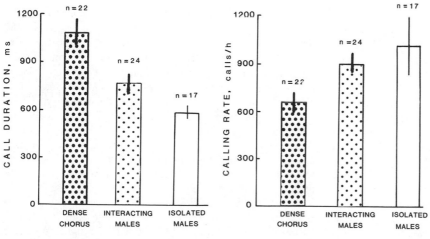

Fig. 14.14   Relation of call duration and calling rate to chorus density for *Hyla versicolor*. (Reprinted, by permission, from Wells and Taigen 1986.)

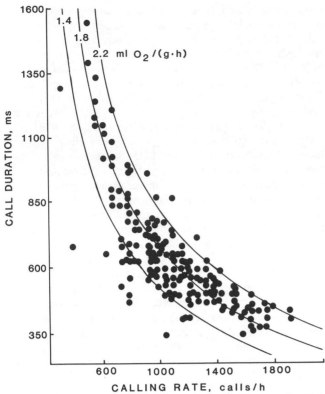

Fig. 14.15 Relation between call duration and calling rate for *Hyla versicolor. Lines* show approximate rates of oxygen consumption at different combinations of rate and duration. (Reprinted, by permission, from Wells and Taigen 1986.)

rate (fig. 14.15), resulting in a relatively constant level of calling effort regardless of chorus density. Playback experiments have shown that females prefer long calls to short calls, and high calling rates to low rates (Klump and Gerhardt 1987). More importantly, as predicted by Wells and Taigen (1986), females prefer long calls delivered at slow rates to short calls delivered at fast rates, even when total calling effort is equal (Klump and Gerhardt 1987). Therefore, males in dense choruses alter their calls in ways that enhance their attractiveness to females. However, most individuals appear to be calling near maximum sustainable levels, even when calling in isolation, and males may be unable to increase calling rate and call duration simultaneously because of energetic constraints (fig. 14.15).

The effects of social interactions on calling energetics also has been examined in *Physalaemus pustulosus.* This species has an unusual call consisting of a frequency-modulated whine note that may be combined with one or more secondary chuck notes. The latter are given simultaneously with the whine note and are not added onto the end of the call as in other species with complex multinote calls (Ryan 1985b). Males calling in low-density choruses generally give calls with relatively few chucks. In dense choruses, males call at faster rates and add more chuck notes to their calls. Females prefer high calling rates to low rates and calls with chuck notes to whines alone (Rand and Ryan 1981). Although energetic expenditures increase with increasing calling rate (fig. 14.13), there is no evidence from the data of Bucher, Ryan, and Bartholomew (1982) or the data collected by Taigen and

Wells (unpublished) that number of chucks is related to the energetic cost of calling. Probably this is because the chuck is produced by passive vibration of a fibrous mass in the airstream of the larynx, not by additional contractions of the trunk muscles (Drewry, Heyer, and Rand 1982; Ryan 1985b). Variation in the number of chuck notes appears to be mediated by risks of predation, rather than by energetic constraints (see below).

Temperature Effects Most of the frogs studied to date are tropical species or summer-breeding temperate zone species that call at body temperatures within a relatively narrow range. Consequently, variation in temperature explains little of the variation in rate of oxygen consumption while calling (Bucher, Ryan, and Bartholomew 1982; Wells and Taigen 1985; Grafe 1988; Wells and Taigen 1989). However, *Hyla crucifer* calls at a wide range of temperatures during a breeding season that can last from late March through late May. Early in the season males call at temperatures as low as 3° to 4°C, whereas late in the season temperatures can be as high as 25°C. Previous work has shown that calling rate is closely correlated with ambient temperature (Lemon and Struger 1980). However, seasonal variation complicates this relationship. Early in the breeding season, calling rates are tightly coupled with ambient temperature, and become decoupled late in the season (McKay 1989). Late-season males have lower calling rates than males calling at the same temperature earlier in the year, probably because energy reserves are depleted and the aerobic capacity of their muscles is decreased (see discussion of enzyme activities below).

Although intercepts of regressions relating oxygen consumption to calling rate change at different temperatures because of changes in resting metabolism, the relation between calling rate and metabolic rate for *H. crucifer* was essentially the same for temperatures from 5° to 23°C (fig. 14.16; T. L. Taigen and K. D. Wells unpublished). When data for all temperatures were combined into a single regression equation, calling rate explained 91% of the variation in rate of oxygen consumption. In a multiple regression analysis of oxygen consumption, calling rate explained 82% of the variance, mass explained an additional 7%, and temperature explained only 3%. Hence, temperature has relatively little effect on the energetic cost of calling independent of its effect on calling rate.

Contributions of Anaerobic Metabolism Because calling is a vigorous activity that is sustained for many hours, anaerobic pathways are unlikely to make a substantial contribution to calling metabolism. Measurements of lactate accumulation by calling frogs support this prediction. Pough and Gatten (1984) reported levels of whole-body lactate in male *Hyla crucifer* from a chorus that were double those of animals resting in the laboratory and slightly above those of noncalling males in the field. They concluded that calling animals may exceed maximum aerobic capacity and obtain some of their energy for calling through anaerobic pathways. However, whole-body lactate levels in calling frogs were less than 10% of those found in animals exercised to exhaustion and would make a trivial contribution to total ATP production. In *Hyla regilla* and *Physalaemus pustulosus,* whole-body lactate levels of calling males were not significantly different from those

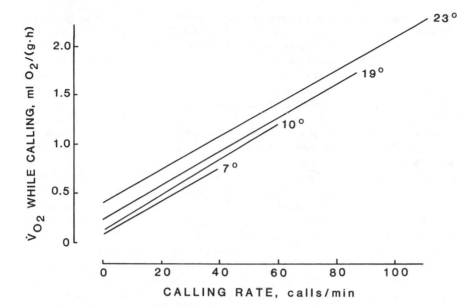

Fig. 14.16 Relation of rate of oxygen consumption to calling rate for *Hyla crucifer* at different temperatures. (T. L. Taigen and K. D. Wells unpublished data.)

TABLE 14.9 Net Cost of Calling for Eight Species of Frogs

	Temp. (°C)	Mass (g)	Net Cost of Calling[a]			Reference
			$J \cdot h^{-1}$[b]	$J \cdot g^{-1} \cdot h^{-1}$	$J \cdot min^{-1}$ calling[c]	
Hyla gratiosa	29	12.5	280	22	25.9	7
Hyla versicolor	19	8.6	280	33	24.0	3, 5
Hyla cinerea	27	5.1	80	16	11.2	7
Hyla squirella	27	2.2	93	42	4.2	7
Hyperolius viridiflavus	25	2.0	50	25	9.1	6
Physalaemus pustulosus	25	1.8	29	16	3.6	9
	26	1.7	25	15	3.8	1, 2
Hyla crucifer	19	1.2	25	21	3.0	4
Hyla microcephala	26	0.6	20	33	3.4	8, 9

Source: (1) Bucher, Ryan, and Bartholomew 1982; (2) Ryan, Bartholomew, and Rand 1983; (3) Taigen and Wells 1985; (4) Taigen, Wells, and Marsh 1985; (5) Wells and Taigen 1986; (6) Grafe 1988; (7) Prestwich, Brugger, and Topping 1989; (8) Wells and Taigen 1989; (9) T. L. Taigen and K. D. Wells unpublished data.

[a]From table 14.7.

[b]Calculated from $\dot{V}_{O_{2call}}$ (avg) and $\dot{V}_{O_{2rest}}$ in table 14.8. Hourly cost = $(\dot{V}_{O_{2call}} - \dot{V}_{O_{2rest}}) \cdot mass \cdot 20.1 \; J \cdot ml^{-1} O_2$.

[c]Cost/min of calling = hourly cost/calling effort $\cdot$ 60.

of resting animals (Whitney and Krebs 1975; Ryan, Bartholomew, and Rand 1983), and in *Hyla versicolor,* lactate levels decreased after several hours of calling (Taigen and Wells 1985). T. U. Grafe, R. Schmuck, and K. E. Linsenmair (in preparation) found high whole-body lactate levels in calling male *Hyperolius viridiflavus* (Hyperoliidae) compared to resting animals, but this was due entirely to elevation of lactate in the leg muscles. Lactate levels in the rest of the body, including the trunk muscles, was virtually identical in calling and resting frogs. Similar results were obtained by Prestwich, Brugger, and Topping (1989) with *Hyla squirella.* In summary, evidence that anaerobic metabolism makes a significant contribution to ATP production to support routine calling behavior is lacking, and anaerobic contributions generally can be ignored in calculating total energetic costs.

Total Energetic Costs of Calling

Estimates of total energetic costs of calling for eight species of frogs are given in table 14.9. These estimates are based on metabolic rates of average-size males calling at average rates in the field and do not indicate the range of variation within species. In some cases, such variation can be considerable. For example, a large *Hyla microcephala* with the highest metabolic rate measured for a calling frog would have a net cost of calling of about 38 J $\cdot$ h^{-1}, nearly double the average figure (Wells and Taigen 1989). In *H. versicolor,* the largest males in a chorus (12 g) can be 2.5 times the mass of the smallest males (5 g). If the largest and smallest males had the same calling effort, the larger individual still would have a net cost of calling 2.5 times that of the smaller male, presumably reflected in the louder calls and greater sound power output of large males.

Interspecific differences in net cost are due in part to greater sound power of larger species. For example, *Hyla versicolor* has an RMS SPL at least 15 dB higher than that of *Physalaemus pustulosus,* representing more than a thirtyfold difference in instantaneous sound power output, but the net cost of calling is only ten times higher, suggesting that *H. versicolor* is probably a more efficient caller than *P. pustulosus* (see Ryan 1985a). The exact relationship depends on the relative duration of their calls as well as instantaneous power output. Some small species, such as *H. microcephala,* have remarkably loud calls relative to their body size (table 14.5), again suggesting substantial differences among species in calling efficiency (see also Prestwich, Brugger, and Topping 1989).

Table 14.9 also shows the cost per minute of actual sound production. With the exception of *Hyperolius viridiflavus,* all of the small species (body mass = 1 to 2 g) have similar costs per minute of calling, despite major differences in the structure of their calls. *Hyla crucifer* has a simple tonelike call, while *Physalaemus pustulosus* has a much longer and more complex frequency-modulated call. *Hyla microcephala* and *H. squirella* both have rather "noisy" calls, but the former has distinct pulses in the calls, while the latter does not. Most of the differences in call structure reflect differences in the structure and action of the larynx and laryngeal muscles (Ryan 1985b; Schneider 1988), which probably contribute relatively little to total energetic costs. The power for sound production is provided by the trunk muscles, and the similarity in cost per minute of sound production may reflect similarities in trunk muscle structure and function. Nevertheless, interspecific differences in trunk muscle physiology are related to differences in calling effort (see further details below).

Vocalization Compared to Other Activities of Amphibians

Information on the energetic cost of natural activities in amphibians is very limited, but the available data indicate that calling is by far the most expensive behavior performed by these animals (tables 14.4 and 14.8). The only activity that entails rates of oxygen consumption approaching that of calling males is construction of foam nests by *Physalaemus* (table 14.10). In this species, the male uses his hind legs to kick the mucous coating around the eggs into a froth as the eggs are laid (Ryan 1985b). Metabolic rates of nest-building pairs of males and females are about five times resting rates (Ryan, Bartholomew, and Rand 1983), and the net cost of nest building is about 70 to 80% of the cost of calling (tables 14.9 and 14.10). Ryan, Bartholomew, and Rand (1983) estimated that frogs actually kick their legs only about 20% of the time, so the net cost per minute of activity would be about 1.7 J, or about 45% of the cost of a minute of sound production.

Burrowing is another vigorous activity that many species of anurans perform. Metabolic rates of burrowing spadefoot toads, *Scaphiopus hammondii* (Pelobatidae), are up to 4.5

TABLE 14.10 The Average Rate of Oxygen Consumption for Various Activities of the Frog *Physalaemus pustulosus*

Activity	$\dot{V}_{O_2}$ (mg·g^{-1}·h^{-1})
Daytime resting	0.15
Nighttime resting	0.32
Sound of chorus audible	0.40
Calling	0.58
Nesting	0.77
35-min forced activity	1.16
3-min continuous activity	1.82

Source: Data from Ryan 1985a.

times resting rates, and the net cost of an hour of burrowing for a 12-g toad is about 95 J (Seymour 1973c). The cost of calling for spadefoot toads is unknown, but in two hylids of about the same size, *Hyla gratiosa* and *H. versicolor,* the cost of calling is about three times the cost of burrowing in *Scaphiopus.* Seymour (1973c) estimated that the toads were actually burrowing only about 22% of the time, or about 13 min · h^{-1}, so the cost per minute of burrowing is approximately 7.3 J at 30°C. By comparison, a minute of sound production by *H. gratiosa* at a similar temperature costs about 25.9 J.

Other routine activities by amphibians probably are much less expensive. For example, Walton (1988) reported that foraging toads (*Bufo woodhousii fowleri*) typically move at a very slow rate ($\bar{x}$ = 0.018 km · h^{-1}). From a regression of metabolic rate versus movement speed (Walton and Anderson 1988), the estimated rate of oxygen consumption during foraging is about 2.3 times resting metabolism, yielding a net cost of 85 J · h^{-1} for a 26-g toad (table 14.4). This is a downward extrapolation from the metabolic data, because natural foraging velocities were only 20% of the lowest speed at which oxygen consumption was measured. This figure is well below maximum rates of oxygen consumption during forced exercise, indicating that toads probably do not approach their physiological limits during routine foraging (Walton 1988). The same is true of courting and fighting salamanders, which have been discussed already. Net costs of reproductive activities in *Desmognathus* (Caudata: Plethodontidae) are only about 5% of the cost of calling in a frog of similar size, and routine locomotion appears to be equally inexpensive.

Comparisons with Acoustic Insects

The only measurements of the costs of signaling behavior comparable to those for frogs are for acoustic behavior of insects (table 14.11). These include a cicada and several species of orthopterans that produce sound by stridulation, as well as the tok-tok beetle, *Psammodes striatus,* which produces sound by tapping its hard abdomen on the substrate (Lighton 1987). For the stridulating insects, the rate of oxygen consumption during calling is generally four to twenty times resting metabolism, a range similar to that found in frogs, whereas oxygen consumption during substrate tapping in the tok-tok beetle is only about 2.5 times resting rates. The figure for a cricket, *Neoconocephalus robustus,* is much lower than that frequently cited by other authors (Bucher, Ryan, and Bartholomew 1982; Kavanagh 1987) because it represents the average rate of oxygen consumption of males that called sporadically during a 4-h period in a metabolic chamber. Peak rates during actual calling are much higher (15.8 ml O$_2$ · g^{-1} · h^{-1}), or about twenty times resting rate (Stevens and Josephson 1977). However, these peak levels cannot be translated directly into hourly costs because the insects do not call continuously. Comparing the costs of calling by frogs and insects is difficult because information about calling efforts in the field is not generally available for insects.

In insects with a body mass similar to the small frogs in table 14.9, the range of variation in net cost of calling also is similar to that of the frog (10 to 90 J · h^{-1}). Differences among species reflect mainly differences in the structure and intensity of their calls. For example, the crickets *Gryllotalpa*

TABLE 14.11   Mass-specific Metabolic Rates of Selected Insects during Rest and Signaling and the Net Cost of Signaling

	Temp. (°C)	Mass (g)	$\dot{V}O_{2rest}$ (ml $O_2 \cdot$ g^{-1}h^{-1})	$\dot{V}O_{2act}$ (ml $O_2 \cdot$ g^{-1}h^{-1})	Net Cost[a] (J·h^{-1})	Reference
Cystosoma saundersii	23	1.20	0.30	6.28	150	MacNally and Young 1981
Gryllotalpa australis	23	0.87	0.42	5.30	90	Kavanagh 1987
Neoconocephalus robustus	23	0.87	0.80	4.40	65	Stevens and Josephson 1977
Anurogryllus arboreus	24	0.39	0.32	3.89	30	Prestwich and Walker 1981
Psammodes striatus	23	3.01	0.22	0.55[b]	20	Lighton 1987
Teleogryllus commodus	23	0.60	0.31	1.21	10	Kavanagh 1987
Oecanthus celerinictus	23	0.06	0.44	3.37	4	Prestwich and Walker 1981
Oecanthus quadripunctatus	23	0.06	0.48	3.82	4	Prestwich and Walker 1981

Sources: Modified from table 9 of Kavanagh 1987.

[a] Net cost = $(\dot{V}O_{2call} - \dot{V}O_{2rest}) \cdot$ mass $\cdot$ 20.8 J·ml^{-1}O_2. Values for net cost are rounded off. Prestwich and Walker (1981) used a conversion factor of 21.97 J·ml^{-1}O_2, while MacNally and Young (1981) and Kavanagh (1987) used 19.796 J·ml^{-1}O_2; the average of the two values is used here.

[b] Substrate tapping at 12,000 taps·h^{-1}.

and *Neoconocephalus* have continuously trilled calls that are relatively loud (table 14.6), whereas the cricket *Teleogryllus* is a chirping species with a much softer call. Prestwich and Walker (1981) found that interspecific differences in the cost of calling were best predicted by differences in wing-stroke rate. The cicada *Cystosoma saundersii* has a much higher net cost of calling (150 J · h^{-1}) than frogs of similar body size, such as *Hyla crucifer* (25 J · h^{-1}), even though instantaneous SPL is much lower (table 14.6). The difference is due in part to the nature of its call, which is a trill given without interruption for up to 35 min per night (MacNally and Doolan 1982). Therefore, an hour of calling by this species represents a full hour of sound production, whereas an hour of calling by *H. crucifer* entails less than one-seventh of an hour of sound production (table 14.7). Hence, the sixfold difference in cost of calling is not surprising.

Physiological and Biochemical Basis of Vocalization

High metabolic rates in vertebrates usually are associated with high levels of muscular activity, and anuran vocalization is no exception. Each call a frog produces requires a forceful muscle contraction to drive air over the vocal cords and into the vocal sac. A male *H. crucifer* calling on a warm night in the midst of a dense chorus may contract the trunk muscles twice per second for several hours each night. Some individuals may produce as many as 30,000 full contractions of the sound-producing muscles in a single evening, although a rate of 13,000 to 15,000 per night probably is more typical (table 14.7). This performance becomes even more impressive when one considers that the frogs maintain these levels of vocal activity night after night during a breeding season that may last for several weeks. Few other natural activities of ectothermal vertebrates entail such high levels of sustained muscle contraction.

These levels of activity are possible only if the muscles are endowed with the structural and biochemical features necessary for sustained rates of contraction. The next four sections will discuss how the muscles used for calling work to produce sound, the structural and biochemical characteristics associated with their function, the metabolic events that occur in these muscles during vocalization, and the ways in which

these features and processes combine to constrain the behavior of individuals in a chorus.

Muscle Activity during Vocalization   Anuran vocalization varies greatly among species in sound power output, calling effort, fundamental frequency, and pulse repetition rate. In addition, most species produce more than one type of call: advertisement calls that signal to females, aggressive calls that convey information to males, and release calls produced when two males come into direct contact (Littlejohn 1977; Wells 1977, 1988). In virtually all cases, however, sound is produced when air is moved from the thoracic cavity, across the vocal cords, and into the vocal sac. The pipids (*Pipa* and *Xenopus*) are an exception; they do not produce sound by means of a moving airstream, although sound production does involve rapid contraction of laryngeal muscles (Rabb 1960; Yager 1982; Tobias and Kelley 1987). Nothing is known about the energetics of acoustic communication in these animals.

At least two features of the mechanics of call production in anuran amphibians are clear from previous studies. First, the fundamental frequency of a call is determined mainly by the rate at which the vocal cords vibrate (Martin 1971, 1972). Second, the pressure to drive the movement of air is created by active contraction of muscles surrounding the thorax and abdomen. These consist of two broad sheets of muscle, the external oblique and the internal oblique (also known as the transverse muscle), along with the smaller rectus abdominis (Martin 1972; Martin and Gans 1972; Schneider 1988). In species with simple single-note calls, such as *Hyla crucifer*, or those that give a series of short notes (e.g., *H. microcephala*), the trunk muscles contract to produce each call note. In some species with long, amplitude-modulated (pulsed) calls, periodic contractions of the trunk muscles may be involved in producing the amplitude modulations. This has been best documented in studies of release calls in bufonids, but Martin (1972) suggested that the trunk muscles may be involved in amplitude modulation of advertisement calls in species such as *Bufo americanus*. The low rates of amplitude modulation that are characteristic of the aggressive calls of several European hylid frogs also appear to be produced by contractions of the trunk muscles (Schneider 1977, 1988). In

H. savignyi these pulses are produced even when laryngeal muscles have been removed, indicating that trunk muscles are involved (Weber 1976).

In some anurans, the laryngeal muscles are involved in active amplitude modulation of the call. For example, Schmidt (1965, 1972) demonstrated that the laryngeal dilators and constrictors are activated alternately and coincidentally with the pulses of advertisement calls of *Hyla chrysoscelis* and the release calls of *Rana pipiens*. The same mechanism appears to be responsible for amplitude modulation of the advertisement calls of several species of European hylids (Schneider 1977, 1988). In bufonids, the larynx apparently is opened passively by pulmonary gas pressure, rather than by contraction of laryngeal muscles. However, the muscles are involved in positioning the edges of the arytenoid cartilages (the major cartilage of the larynx) in the moving gas stream (Martin 1971, 1972). Vibration of these cartilages at a characteristic resonant frequency produces passive amplitude modulation that resembles the active modulation of other frogs but does not require active muscle contraction for each pulse. Species with passive amplitude modulation typically have calls consisting of a series of very short pulses, each with a very rapid onset time.

This sort of passive amplitude modulation may account for the very high pulse repetition rates of some anuran calls that appear to exceed the sustainable contraction rates of most vertebrate muscles. For example, *Hyla microcephala* produces advertisement calls with a pulse repetition rate of more than 200 pulses $\cdot$ s^{-1} and aggressive calls with rates of up to 320 pulses $\cdot$ s^{-1} (Schwartz and Wells 1985; Schwartz 1987). If these pulses were produced by active mechanisms, the muscles would be contracting at a rate approaching or perhaps exceeding the capacity of the fastest vertebrate muscles known. Most mammalian skeletal muscles are locked in completely fused tetanus by stimulation frequencies of 50 Hz or less. Even the pectoral muscles of hummingbirds during hovering flight are contracting at a rate well below the pulse repetition rate of several tropical hylids.

Structural and contractile properties indicate that the laryngeal muscles of some species of anurans are also very fast. The muscles of two species of hylids are composed almost entirely of fast oxidative fibers and have well-developed sarcoplasmic reticulum, high mitochondrial densities, and high fusion frequencies (Eichelberg and Schneider 1973, 1974; Schneider 1977, 1988; Marsh and Taigen 1987). In fact, fusion frequencies, the lowest stimulation frequency that results in full tetanic contraction, correlate with the rate of amplitude modulation in the call. The laryngeal muscles of male *Hyla arborea* have a fusion frequency of 180 to 195 Hz at 20°C (Manz 1975), which appears adequate to accommodate a pulse rate of more than 130 $\cdot$ s^{-1} at that temperature (Schneider 1977). This would be true especially if the muscles are operating in a partially fused tetanus, as occurs during stridulation in some tettigoniid grasshoppers (Josephson 1973). The laryngeal muscles of female *H. arborea* have lower fusion frequencies and would not be capable of sustaining such high rates of contraction. The fusion frequency in muscles of male *H. versicolor* is about 100 Hz (R. L. Marsh, pers. comm.), which is fast enough to accommodate the observed pulse rate of 20 $\cdot$ s^{-1}.

Although data are not available to evaluate directly the role of active muscle contraction in producing the very high pulse repetition rates of some hylid frogs, the possibility that this occurs cannot be dismissed without additional experiments, because there are vertebrate muscles with even higher fusion frequencies. Many fish produce sounds by contracting specialized muscles surrounding air-filled spaces such as the swim bladder (Schneider 1964; Cohen and Winn 1967; Daugherty and Marshall 1976; Fine 1979). Electromyographic studies of sound production have documented active contraction of the sonic muscles at frequencies up to 230 Hz at a temperature of approximately 23°C (Gainer, Kusano, and Mathewson 1965; Cohen and Winn 1967). These muscles also have extraordinarily short contraction times and high fusion frequencies (Skoglund 1961; Gainer, Kusano, and Mathewson 1965).

Structural Characteristics of Trunk Muscles The most obvious structural characteristic of the trunk muscles of male anurans is their size (table 14.12). The combined mass of the internal and external oblique muscles accounts for 7 to 15% of total body mass. Variance in the mass of the trunk muscles appears to arise from two sources: (1) variation in calling effort and (2) variation in the amount of lipid present in the muscle. *Rana virgatipes,* the species with the smallest relative muscle mass, also has the lowest calling effort. This pat-

TABLE 14.12   Comparison of Body Mass and Trunk Muscle Mass for Selected Tropical and Temperate Zone Anurans

| | Distribution | Sex | Body Mass (g) | Trunk Muscle Mass | | Reference |
				Grams	% Body Mass	
Hyla crucifer	Temperate	M	1.25	0.19	14.8	1
		F	1.05	0.04	3.3	
Hyla versicolor	Temperate	M	9.90	1.24	12.5	2
		F	6.60	0.16	2.5	
Hyla microcephala	Tropical	M	0.60	0.06	10.1	5
Hyla rubra	Tropical	M	3.35	0.32	9.7	5
Hyla ebraccata	Tropical	M	0.87	0.05	5.7	5
Physalaemus pustulosus	Tropical	M	1.64	0.12	7.3	5
Rana virgatipes	Temperate	M	8.00	0.55	6.7	3
		F	10.80	0.23	2.1	
Rana sylvatica	Temperate	M	12.17	0.39	3.2	4
Bufo americanus	Temperate	M	22.73	0.77	3.4	4

Sources: (1) Taigen, Wells, and Marsh 1985; (2) Marsh and Taigen 1987; (3) Given and McKay 1990; (4) M. T. Lawrence and T. L. Taigen unpublished data; (5) T. L. Taigen and K. D. Wells unpublished data.

tern is consistent with generalizations concerning the extent of muscle hypertrophy and muscle use. Additional data are needed to test the hypothesis that species that call at low rates have lower relative trunk muscle mass than those that call at high rates.

The presence of lipid in the muscles also contributes to the overall muscle size. Among the hylids studied to date, the species with the most northerly distribution (*Hyla crucifer*) has the largest muscles (15% of body mass). The large size of these muscles may be due in part to the presence of stored lipids that fuel calling early in the spring when few prey are available. Lipids account for 45% of the trunk muscle mass of some males at the start of the breeding season (McKay 1989) and are fully depleted after 6 weeks of calling. In contrast, male gray treefrogs (*H. versicolor*) have a lower lipid content in the trunk muscles (14% of muscle mass; Marsh and Taigen 1987), and muscle lipid content does not appear to decrease as the breeding season progresses (Walker 1989). This pattern is consistent with the seasonal timing of reproduction of gray treefrogs; males call primarily during the

months of June and July when prey are readily available. Tropical species probably rely on stored fats to fuel calling activity even less than *H. versicolor,* and the somewhat lower mass of their trunk muscles reflects this.

Biochemical Features of Trunk Muscles The biochemical characteristics of muscles involved in vocalization vary interspecifically with vocal behavior. The muscle biochemistry of species with high calling efforts and long breeding seasons is distinctive, perhaps unique, among ectothermal vertebrates. For example, the trunk muscles of male *Hyla crucifer* exhibit activities of citrate synthase (CS), a rate-limiting enzyme in the citric acid cycle, that rival those of the most oxidative endothermic muscles, including cardiac muscle of small mammals and flight muscles of passerine birds (table 14.13). Female spring peepers do not call, and their trunk muscles are not impressive in either size (3% of body mass, table 14.12) or oxidative capacity (table 14.13). In fact, the CS activity of trunk muscle of males is twenty to thirty times that of females.

TABLE 14.13 Citrate Synthase (CS) Activity in Selected Muscles of Anurans and Other Vertebrates (per Gram of Fresh Muscle)

	Sex	Muscle Type	Assay Temp. (°C)	CS Activity (μmoles· min^{-1}·g^{-1})	Reference
		Anurans			
Hyla crucifer					5, 8
Early season	M	Trunk	25	166	
Midseason	M	Trunk	20	86	
Late season	M	Trunk	25	96	
Midseason	M	Leg	20	14	
Midseason	F	Trunk	20	5	
Hyla versicolor	M	Trunk	20	79	6
	M	Larynx	20	65	
	M	Leg	20	17	
	F	Trunk	20	6	
Hyla microcephala	M	Trunk	25	119	10
	M	Leg	25	11	
Hyla ebraccata	M	Trunk	25	63	10
	M	Leg	25	24	
Rana virgatipes	M	Trunk	20	13	9
	M	Leg	20	6	
Rana sylvatica	M	Trunk	20	23	11
	M	Leg	20	12	
Rana pipiens		Leg	25	7	1, 4
Bufo boreas		Leg	25	40	4
Xenopus laevis		Leg	25	26	4
		Mammals			
Laboratory mouse		Heart	25	146	1
Laboratory rat		Heart	25	96	1
Rabbit		Heart	25	69	1
Bat		Flight	25	200	3
		Birds			
Pigeon		Pectoral	25	115	1
Sparrow		Pectoral	25	112	1
		Heart	25	120	
Catbird		Pectoral	25	200	2
Tufted duck		Pectoral	25	87	7
		Heart	25	108	

Sources: (1) Alp, Newsholme, and Zammit 1976; (2) Marsh 1981; (3) Yacoe et al. 1982; (4) Putnam and Bennett 1983; (5) Taigen, Wells, and Marsh 1985; (6) Marsh and Taigen 1987; (7) Turner and Butler 1988; (8) McKay 1989; (9) Given and McKay 1990; (10) T. L. Taigen and K. D. Wells unpublished data; (11) M. T. Lawrence and T. L. Taigen unpublished data.

The CS activity of the trunk musculature of the six anuran species for which data are available exceeds that of leg muscles. In some cases the differences are striking and appear to underlie differences in metabolic performance during calling and during exhaustive locomotor exercise (table 14.8). For example, the rate of oxygen consumption by *Hyla versicolor* during sustained calling is 60% greater than that achieved during forced locomotor exercise. CS activity in the trunk muscles of these animals is five times greater than that found in the muscles of the leg. Similar patterns are evident in other species, with trunk muscle exhibiting from two to ten times the oxidative capacity of leg muscle. These biochemical data help explain why calling frogs can achieve higher metabolic rates than frogs engaged in locomotor exercise, but they also generate new and more subtle questions concerning the nature of the interrelationships among muscle biochemistry, metabolic performance, and vocal behavior.

Not all anuran species possess vocalization muscles with extreme oxidative capacities. Trunk muscle CS activities of *Rana virgatipes* and *R. sylvatica* are not distinctive (table 14.13). Interspecific variation in muscle biochemistry appears to correlate with metabolic rates achieved during sustained vocalization (fig. 14.17). Species with high calling efforts and rates of metabolism during vocalization have high CS activities, whereas those with less active vocal behavior and lower vocalization costs have lower CS activities. Similar relationships between enzyme activities and patterns of behavior have been observed in fish (Johnston 1987). Mitochondrial density in slow muscle fibers of several species of fish correlates with swimming velocities; species with high sustained speeds have higher densities of mitochondria than species that are sedentary or only moderately active. Activities of individual enzymes also varied with interspecific differences in activity patterns.

Tissue aerobic capacity of ectothermal vertebrates can be altered by environmental temperature (Sidell 1983), and some of the extreme biochemical profiles of the vocalization muscles can be attributed to the demands imposed by high calling efforts at low ambient temperatures. This explanation is not generally acceptable because tropical anurans and temperate zone species exhibit similar CS activities for a given rate of metabolism during sustained vocalization (fig. 14.17). An important exception to this generalization may be male *Hyla crucifer* that call very early in the breeding season when air temperatures are low. Only a small subset of males call under these conditions, despite the fact that female availability is very high (McKay 1989). The ratio of females to males early in the year is approximately 1 to 2; by the end of the breeding season, it is less than 1 to 20. The trunk muscle biochemistry of male spring peepers collected early in the breeding season is strikingly different from that of males collected later in the spring. Citrate synthase activity is nearly twice as high in these males (table 14.13), suggesting that individual variation in tissue aerobic capacity may be closely correlated with differences in behavior and reproductive success. Calling activity at very low temperatures may include only those males that possess the biochemical characteristics necessary to meet the rigorous demands of sustained muscle activity under these conditions. Additional data are needed to determine the extent to which muscle biochemistry constrains the vocal behavior of individuals within a chorus and contributes to their reproductive success.

Further evidence for the distinctive nature of the vocalization muscles can be found in histochemical and morphometric analyses. The trunk muscles of *Hyla versicolor* consist 100% of fast oxidative fibers, whereas the leg muscles of these animals comprise primarily (75%) fast glycolytic fibers. Nearly 20% of the total volume of the trunk muscles is mitochondria (Marsh and Taigen 1987).

The relations between the biochemical characteristics of anuran trunk muscles and the activity patterns of the muscles are similar in many ways to those documented for other vertebrate classes (see chapter 11). The catabolic capacities of mammalian muscles can be altered by training regimes, and these physiological changes are accompanied by changes in the biochemistry and anatomy of muscles. In a similar way, the very high aerobic capacity of the pectoral muscles in small passerine birds reflects the high levels of sustained

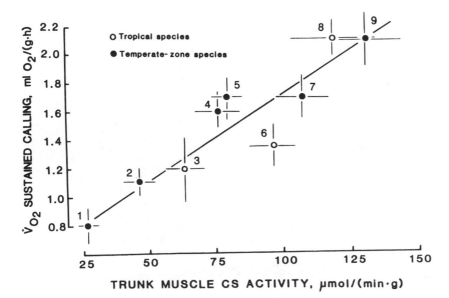

Fig. 14.17 Rate of oxygen consumption during sustained calling versus citrate synthase (CS) activity in trunk muscle. Rates of oxygen consumption were estimated from regression equations in figures 14.12, 14.13, and 14.16 using average field calling rates of males in a sustained chorus. Temperatures refer to the conditions under which metabolic performances were estimated and enzyme activities assayed. *1, Hyla crucifer*, 5°C; *2, H. crucifer*, 10°C; *3, Physalaemus pustulosus*, 25°C; *4, H. crucifer*, 15°C; *5, H. versicolor*, 20°C; *6, H. ebraccata*, 25°C; *7, H. crucifer*, 20°C; *8, H. microcephala*, 25°C; *9, H. crucifer*, 25°C.

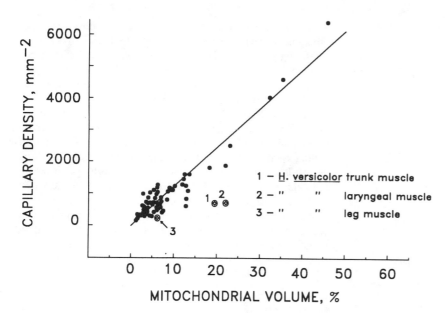

Fig. 14.18 Capillary density versus mitochondrial volume density. ●, data from a large range of mammalian species and muscle types from Hoppeler et al. 1981. ◎, data for leg, trunk, and laryngeal muscles of *Hyla versicolor* from Marsh and Taigen 1987.)

activity in these animals during flight and thermogenesis (Marsh 1981). However, anuran muscles differ structurally from those of birds and mammals in the relationship between mitochondrial density and capillary density (fig. 14.18). The leg and trunk muscles of *Hyla versicolor* have capillary densities only one-third of those found in endothermic tissue of similar mitochondrial densities. Two nonexclusive hypotheses could explain this disparity: (1) If ectothermal vertebrates possess mitochondria with intrinsically lower oxidative capacity for ATP production and oxygen consumption, the number of capillaries per unit mitochondrion would be lower than those characteristic of endotherms. (2) Alternatively, the structural features of anuran trunk muscles may reflect the thermal environment within which the muscles are active. Because mitochondrial function is likely to be affected more profoundly by changes in temperature than by oxygen delivery (at least within the tissue), it is possible to identify a temperature for every combination of mitochondrial density and capillary density for which the system can be described as maximally designed. Such a calculation can be made for *H. versicolor* muscles by assuming that the temperature of maximum efficiency in the mammalian mitochondria-capillary relationship is 37°C and by assuming that mitochondrial function in anuran muscles decreases with temperature according to normal van't Hoff kinetics ($Q_{10} = 2$; see McKay 1989). The temperature for maximum efficiency under these assumptions in *H. versicolor* muscles is 19°, 20°, and 20°C for the trunk, laryngeal, and leg muscles, respectively. These calculations agree well with the environmental conditions in which this species vocalizes. In fact, gray treefrogs rarely call at ambient temperatures below 15°C, and our field observations over the past several years indicate that the choruses are generally at their peak activity at air temperatures between 18° and 22°C (Taigen and Wells 1985; Wells and Taigen 1986). A prediction from this analysis is that species that call in warmer climates, such as tropical anurans, will have higher capillary densities per unit mitochondria than species that call and reproduce in colder climates. A test of this prediction must await further data on the relationship between mitochondrial and capillary density in anurans from very different thermal enviroments.

Substrate Oxidation The high costs of vocalization appear to be met by the oxidation of fats and carbohydrates. Fat oxidation is indicated in two ways, a decline in the amount of fat found in the trunk muscles of some species as described perviously, and high activity of enzymes involved in fatty acid oxidation (Taigen, Wells, and Marsh 1985; Marsh and Taigen 1987). Measurements of the activity of 3-hydroxyacyl-CoA dehydrogenase (HOAD), an indicator of tissue capacity for fatty acid oxidation, shows that trunk muscles of *Hyla crucifer* and *H. versicolor* rely extensively on fat oxidation to support muscle contraction during calling. These enzymatic data are consistent with observations of structural characteristics of the laryngeal and trunk muscles of *H. arborea* and *H. versicolor* in which lipid droplets are distributed through the muscle fibers, immediately adjacent to mitochondria (Eichelberg and Schneider 1973; Marsh and Taigen 1987). By comparison, the hindlimb muscles of these species are nearly devoid of lipid.

A more detailed analysis of trunk muscle enzyme profiles reveals differences among species in substrate oxidizing capacity that appear to correlate with differences in reproductive behavior. The relative capacity for fatty acid oxidation, calculated as the ratio of HOAD to CS activity, is high for temperate zone species, such as *H. crucifer* and *Rana sylvatica,* that breed early in the year when insect prey are unavailable or present only at low densities (Taigen, Wells, and Marsh 1985; M. T. Lawrence and T. L. Taigen unpublished data). Temperate zone species that breed later in the year, such as *H. versicolor* and *Bufo americanus,* have lower HOAD activities relative to the total aerobic capacity of their muscle tissue and appear to rely less on stored fats to fuel calling activity (Marsh and Taigen 1987; M. T. Lawrence and T. L. Taigen unpublished data).

Data for tropical anurans that breed when prey are readily available are largely consistent with the above pattern. *H. microcephala* and *H. ebraccata* both have trunk muscles with

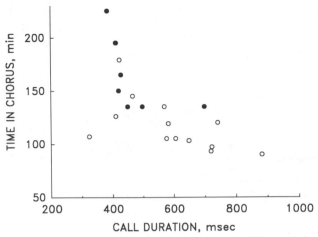

Fig. 14.19 Average duration of calls given by male *Hyla versicolor* versus the length of time the male called during an evening. Vocal behavior was assessed every 15 min. All males ceased calling of their own volition, and none was observed in amplexus at the end of the evening. Data from 2 years are shown by open and closed symbols. Correlations are significant for both years analyzed independently and when combined. (Data from Wells and Taigen 1986 and Walker 1989.)

low HOAD to CS ratios (Taigen and Wells unpublished). *Physalaemus pustulosus* is an apparent exception to this pattern; although it is a tropical species, its HOAD to CS ratio is similar to that of *H. crucifer*. However, the reproductive pattern of *P. pustulosus* consists of relatively short visits to the breeding pond, punctuated by long periods of absence during which the animals appear to be foraging in preparation for return to the chorus (Ryan 1985a). Hence, any behavior that entails a regular sequence of lipid storage and depletion might engender muscle biochemical profiles conducive to fatty acid oxidation, regardless of the thermal environment in which the behavior is performed.

Carbohydrate oxidation, especially in the form of glycogen utilization, is also important when frogs are vocalizing. Glycogen depletion has been observed in the laryngeal muscles of the discoglossid frog *Bombina bombina* (Eichelberg and Obert 1976) following 4 h of electrical stimulation, and measurements of trunk muscle glycogen content of calling *Hyla versicolor* indicate that glycogen depletion occurs during an evening of calling activity (Walker 1989). Males collected after 2 to 3 h of calling had glycogen levels in their trunk muscles that were approximately 50% of the levels found in males collected early in the evening as the chorus was forming. These results suggest that glycogen serves as a short-term energy store, perhaps undergoing a circadian cycle of depletion during a period of calling followed by replenishment the subsequent day. In fact, cessation of calling may occur when glycogen stores reach a critical low level. This hypothesis is like that describing human athletes in which depletion of intramuscular glycogen stores is associated with reduced muscle performance (Hollozsy and Booth 1976).

Variation in substrate levels may account for individual variation in patterns of activity and behavior in male *H. versicolor* (Wells and Taigen 1986). The vocal behavior of males in a dense chorus consists of long calls given at low rates, whereas males in more isolated situations produce short calls at high rates (fig. 14.14). The total calling efforts, calculated

as the product of call duration and rate, appear to be the same, as do the total energy costs (fig. 14.15). Females overwhelmingly prefer males that produce long calls at low rates (Klump and Gerhardt 1987). Wells and Taigen (1986) proposed that differential rates of glycogen depletion may account for these patterns. The vocal behavior that is most attractive to females is also the most costly in terms of the rate at which glycogen is used. This prediction is confirmed by an analysis of the length of time male *H. versicolor* spend calling each night. Individuals that produce relatively long calls at low rates remain in the chorus for shorter periods than individuals producing short calls at high rates (fig. 14.19). However, additional measurements of tissue substrate concentrations are needed to determine the degree of individual variation in patterns of substrate oxidation and the role that variation plays in constraining the behavior and reproductive success of male frogs.

COSTS OF REPRODUCTION
Michael J. Ryan

A central concern of studies of behavioral energetics is the pattern of acquisition and utilization of energy that supports reproductive behaviors. All behaviors have a physiological cost that potentially can be measured as energy expended. Animals cannot reproduce without expending energy, and measuring the energetics of reproduction has been an important endeavor of physiological ecologists (e.g., Calow 1981). A different kind of cost associated with reproduction has concerned evolutionary biologists because it is so closely tied to the measure used to quantify evolutionary effects of selection—fitness. Reproducing today has some effect on an individual's ability to reproduce in the future (e.g., Pianka and Parker 1975). Thus, costs of reproduction can be estimated in the context of physiology (energy expended) or evolution (decreased fitness). Other costs of reproductive behaviors include the time that would otherwise be spent in other important activities (e.g., foraging) and the loss of a benefit of those activities (e.g., reduced energy intake).

"Cost" often is used without definition, not always due to confusion but because, rightly or wrongly, physiological cost is thought to necessitate evolutionary cost. Presumably, on average and over sufficiently long periods of time, any energetic expenditure should decrease fitness. This assumption, for example, is central to optimal foraging theory (MacArthur and Pianka 1966; Stephens and Krebs 1986). The equality of physiological and fitness costs has not been documented in most studies, and this is a serious omission.

My purpose is to consider the costs of reproduction for amphibians, but few data are available for taxa other than anurans. Ecologists and behaviorists have employed a variety of measures of reproductive costs, and I will not attempt to catalogue all of these. Instead I will discuss why measurements of this physiological characteristic are critically important in evaluating behavioral, ecological, and evolutionary hypotheses. Of course, not all of the costs of reproduction are physiological. Indeed, the risk of predation is a conspicuous cost associated with reproductive behavior, and I will discuss how to relate physiological and behavioral costs in an evolutionary context.

Amphibians, and especially anurans, have emerged as tractable models for investigating both evolutionary and physiological aspects of reproduction (e.g., Wilczynski and Ryan 1988b). Evolutionary studies have documented relations between variance in male traits and variance in male reproductive success. Because anuran fertilization is usually external and mating behaviors are conspicuous, some studies of anuran mating systems have even estimated lifetime fitness (Howard 1979). Studies have also elucidated the relation between variation in male courtship behavior, especially vocalizations, and both male mating success (Gerhardt 1988; J. G. M. Robertson 1986a; Ryan 1980, 1983; Sullivan 1983; Wells 1988) and susceptibility to predation (Ryan, Tuttle, and Taft 1981, Tuttle and Ryan 1982). At the physiological level, measures of the number, size, and caloric content of eggs have been used to estimate energetic costs of reproduction by female amphibians (Crump and Kaplan 1979; Salthe and Duellman 1973).

In addition, reproductive behavior has a substantial physiological cost for males, and this cost has been difficult to measure in most animals. However, for most anurans the major reproductive behavior is vocalization, and Bucher, Ryan, and Bartholomew (1982) and Ryan, Bartholomew, and Rand (1983) were the first to estimate both the aerobic and anaerobic support of calling for a frog (*Physalaemus pustulosus*). These measures, which have now been made for several other anurans (described earlier this chapter), estimate energetic costs of male reproductive behavior. Reproductive behaviors can be costly in terms of survivorship because they attract predators (Tuttle and Ryan 1982), and anurans provide perhaps the best examples of the two most obvious costs associated with male courtship: energy and predation.

Energetic Costs of Reproduction

This section reviews the energetic costs of reproduction of amphibians, focusing on anurans because few data are available for salamanders and caecilians. Energetic costs incurred by both sexes have been measured or estimated, and I will consider their consequences for future reproduction. This analysis provides a basis for speculation about the potential evolutionary significance of these costs.

Female Reproduction Female amphibians devote a large amount of energy to reproduction, mostly in the form of egg production. The ability to acquire energy is assumed to be an important determinant of a female's ability to produce progeny (Pianka 1981), although this relationship has been documented for only a few species. However, most interest in variation of anuran female investment in reproduction has concerned its relation to interspecific differences in reproductive mode. At the intraspecific level, investigation of variation in reproductive investment has been restricted mostly to size-related fecundity (e.g., Howard 1979). No data yet show that variation among female anurans in any behavioral or physiological trait influences the amount of energy that can be devoted to reproduction.

The size and number of eggs produced per clutch provides an estimate of the energy devoted to reproduction by female amphibians (Salthe and Duellman 1973). Duellman and Trueb (1986) summarize such data for eighty-four species of anurans and show that clutch sizes range from 4 to 15,000 eggs.

That variation suggests a correspondingly large interspecific variation in energy investment. A more direct estimate of energy costs of female reproduction comes from measures of the caloric content of eggs. The total energy per clutch for nine species of tropical frogs varied from 1.49 kJ to 8.17 kJ, and the mass-specific energy ranged from 14.36 to 25.90 kJ · g^{-1} (Crump and Kaplan 1979). Females of larger species devoted more energy to reproduction absolutely, but not relative to body mass. Energy invested in eggs did not differ between females of species that deposit their eggs in standing water versus those that deposit their eggs in overhanging vegetation. However, the partitioning of energy differed among reproductive modes: species that deposit eggs in standing water have more and smaller eggs than species that use overhanging vegetation for oviposition sites.

These limited data indicate that physiological constraints might impose a ceiling on energy expended per clutch. To confirm this hypothesis, one would have to determine the number of clutches produced per lifetime (a difficult measure to obtain) or at least the number of clutches produced per season.

Females of the frog *Physalaemus pustulosus* partition the energy they devote to reproduction into a somatic contribution to eggs and into behaviors associated with reproduction (Ryan, Bartholomew, and Rand 1983; Ryan 1985a). Females produced an average of 234 eggs per clutch, and the average total caloric content of the clutch was 3.96 kJ (= 22.92 kJ · g^{-1}).

Female *P. pustulosus* have another energetic cost involved in reproduction—nest construction. As the female extrudes eggs from her cloaca, the male beats the jelly matrix of the egg into a foam with his hind legs. The foam nest may provide protection from desiccation if the temporary pools used by these frogs dry during periods without rain. It was not possible to measure rates of oxygen consumption of each sex during nest construction. Therefore, Ryan, Bartholomew, and Rand (1983) measured this rate for a pair of frogs and assumed that each individual expended the same amount of energy (table 14.10). This assumption probably underestimates male expenditure and overestimates female. During the approximately 1 h of nest construction, the pair expended 0.26 kJ. Aerobic metabolism is not the only source of energy for nest building; an accumulation of lactic acid indicates that some of the behavior is supported anaerobically. However, anaerobic metabolism contributes only about 4% of the total ATP yield.

Besides knowing the total amount of energy that females invest in reproduction, it would be instructive to evaluate the magnitude of this energy allocation relative to the total energy budget. This proportion, rather than total calories, might give a more accurate indication of the effects of reproductive investment on future reproduction and survivorship. Calculations for the salamander *Desmognathus ochrophaeus* (Plethodontidae) indicate that reproductive activities, which in this species include both egg production and parental care, comprise 48% of the female's energy flow (Fitzpatrick 1973a). The largest single category of energy expenditure for this species appears to be the production and care of offspring.

Females of species with extended breeding seasons may produce more than one clutch of eggs annually, and energy investment can vary substantially within a season (Crump

1974; Duellman and Trueb 1986; Davidson and Hough 1969). For example, female *P. pustulosus* exhibit a synchronous pattern of oogenesis at the beginning of the breeding season and then switch to a pattern of asynchronous oogenesis (Davidson and Hough 1969). Early in the season, when favorable breeding conditions are more predictable, clutch size is large but interclutch interval is long. As the breeding season progresses, favorable conditions become less predictable, and females have asynchronous oogenesis resulting in smaller clutches that can be deposited at shorter intervals. This mechanism may allow females to exploit favorable breeding conditions as they arise.

Partitioning the annual reproductive energy investment of a female anuran into multiple clutches could have potentially important effects on mating systems, operational sex ratios, and the intensity of sexual selection on male traits (Wade and Arnold 1980). When females partition their energy among several clutches in a season, in contrast to producing only one clutch, the breeding season is extended and the opportunity for a few males to monopolize breeding increases (Emlen and Oring 1977). This hypothesis parallels the expectation that variance in male mating success should be greater in species with prolonged breeding seasons relative to explosive breeders (Wells 1977; Woolbright 1983). Kluge (1981) and Ryan (1985a) have compared variance in male mating success for species with prolonged versus explosive breeding seasons. Contrary to expectation, the variance was not higher in species with prolonged breeding seasons.

The activity associated with choosing a mate is a potential cost of reproduction for females that is crucial to some theories of sexual selection, but it has not been documented. In many species of amphibians, especially frogs, females select mates with minimal interference from other males. For example, female *P. pustulosus* do this by moving among males in the chorus, often sitting directly in front of one male for several minutes before moving on to the other males (Ryan 1985a). This behavior occurs in other anurans such as the bullfrog, *Rana catesbeiana* (Emlen 1976; Howard 1978a), and the red-groined toadlet, *Uperoleia laevigata* (formerly *U. rugosa*), a myobatrachid (J. G. M. Robertson 1986b). The energetic cost of this behavior could affect fitness (e.g., Kirkpatrick 1987a), or it could have a trivial impact on the female's energy budget with virtually no evolutionary consequence. However, exposure to predation is likely to be a more important cost of mate selection. A chorus of males not only attracts members of the opposite sex but also advertises a resource concentration to predators (Tuttle and Ryan 1982). Both calling males and silent females increase their predation risk as they increase their time and movements at a chorus.

Mate selection by female anurans can include additional energy costs and even a risk of injury or death as a result of the behavior of conspecific males. Noncalling males of some species clasp females that are moving toward calling males, and the females struggle vigorously to escape (e.g., Sullivan 1982a). Also, unmated males of many species attempt to disrupt mated pairs (e.g., Howard and Kluge 1985). In both situations females probably expend energy while attempting to escape. The most vigorous struggles might result in substantial lactate concentrations, and some females drown (Ryan 1985a). Some of these costs of mate choice would have im-mediate evolutionary consequences, and their documentation would be worthwhile.

A significant evolutionary cost associated with exercising mate choice would have important implications for theories of sexual selection. Female preference for a male trait can result in an increase in the frequency of both the trait and the preference (Fisher 1958; Kirkpatrick 1982; Lande 1981); the phenomenon is called "runaway sexual selection." For example, assume that choosy females prefer males with long tails. If there is a heritable component to the preference and to the trait itself, choosy females will produce sons with longer tails and daughters that prefer males with longer tails. As a result the trait and the preference will become genetically correlated. The trait increases in frequency due to the preference, and, because of the genetic correlation, the preference increases in frequency as a correlated response to selection acting on the trait. The process causes the frequencies of the preference and trait to increase at an ever-accelerating rate. This process can occur even if the male trait reduces survivorship.

A critical assumption of models of runaway selection is that there is no cost to the female in exercising a choice. A recent model suggests that if there is a cost to female choice, female preference will evolve to favor the male trait that is optimum for his survival (Kirkpatrick 1987a). This prediction is an important departure from those of models that assume no cost of female preference.

Parental care can incur a reproductive cost. Only a minority of anuran species exhibit parental care, although the phenomenon is phylogenetically widespread (McDiarmid 1978), but it is more common in salamanders (Forester 1979) and occurs in caecilians, some of which also nourish the fetus with oviductal secretions (Wake 1977b). Parental care surely enhances the survivorship of immediate progeny, but at what cost to future progeny? Undoubtedly, there are energetic costs from reduced energy intake during parental care (e.g., males of the leptodactylid frog *Eleutherodactylus coqui;* Townsend 1984). These costs should be investigated systematically.

Perhaps the most interesting form of parental care among anurans is the provisioning of offspring by female dart-poison frogs, *Dendrobates pumilio* (Dendrobatidae; Brust 1990; Weygolt 1980). Females of this species carry larvae that hatch from terrestrial eggs and release them individually in small pools of water that accumulate in the leaf axils of plants. For some weeks the female returns to these sites and deposits unfertilized eggs that her larvae eat. Similar obligate oophagy has been described for the larvae of other species of frogs (see chapter 16). The costs and benefits of enhancing the survivorship of immediate offspring at the cost of future fitness invite analysis.

Male Reproduction   In general, secondary sexual characteristics associated with male reproduction appear to be costly in two ways: a physiological cost of providing energy for growth of epigamic structures and for the support of often extravagant courtship behaviors and an evolutionary cost because these characters seem to shorten the life span of their bearers.

Male amphibians, especially anurans, have structures associated with reproduction, such as the enlarged teeth of some male salamanders (Arnold 1977), the keratinized spines used in battles by gladiator frogs (Kluge 1981), and the larynxes of some male anurans that dwarf the size of the homologous structures in females (Martin 1972). Presumably the growth and maintenance of such structures require an energy expenditure that is unique to males, but these costs have not been measured.

The importance of vocalization in anuran reproduction has long been recognized (Dickerson 1906). Species-specific differences in advertisement calls (Blair 1958; Gerhardt 1988) and the neural mechanisms underlying acoustically mediated species recognition (Capranica 1976a; Fuzessery 1988; Walkowiak 1988b) have been especially important focuses in anuran biology. It is now clear that calls also exhibit variation that influences aggressive interactions among conspecific males (Davies and Halliday 1978; Wells 1988) and female choice of mates from individuals of the same population (Ryan 1980; Gerhardt 1988) or nearby populations (Ryan and Wilczynski 1988). Studies of anuran vocalization have allowed direct measurements of energy expenditure and predation risk associated with male secondary sexual characters and behaviors.

An indirect energetic cost of calling is decreased food intake (Jenssen and Klimstra 1966; Martof 1956; Ryan 1985a; Woolbright 1985c; Woolbright and Stewart 1987). Male coquís (*Eleutherodactylus coqui* [Leptodactylidae]) are smaller than females, as is true for most anurans despite demonstrations of sexual selection favoring larger male body size number of species (Shine 1979). Male coquís grew more slowly than females in the field where they engaged in their normal reproductive behavior, whereas males and females grew at the same rate in captivity where reproductive behavior was not exhibited (Woolbright 1985c; Woolbright and Stewart 1987). This observation is consistent with the hypothesis that male reproductive behavior might reduce the growth rate or ultimate adult body size in this species.

Either sex can incur a physiological cost of reproduction during parental care. Again, studies of *E. coqui* suggest that significant costs of parental care are due to decreased energy intake. Males guard eggs that are deposited terrestrially. Males guarding eggs ate less than calling males, perhaps because they did not leave the eggs to go to places where they were likely to encounter prey (Townsend 1984). Similarly, males of the frog *Cophixalus parkeri* (Microhylidae) that were brooding eggs had lower intakes, smaller fat bodies, and less carcass fat than did nonbrooding males (Simon 1983).

Does Energy Constrain Reproductive Behavior?

Evolutionary biologists have been concerned with reproductive energetics for two reasons: the amount of energy available for reproduction might influence reproductive success, and costs of mate choice by females and displaying by males have implications for hypotheses of sexual selection (e.g., Halliday 1987; Kirkpatrick 1987a; Ryan 1988b).

Energetic constraints on male reproductive behavior could be manifested in the short term or in the long term. In the short term, the amount of energy a male invests in calling might be limited by energy stores. In the long term, energy expenditure could influence the number of nights that a male

spends at the chorus. All of these factors could affect the fitness of an individual male frog. If energy does constrain male reproductive behavior, another question arises: do males perform energy-demanding behaviors to indicate their physical vigor (and perhaps their genetic quality) to females? In other words, do females rely on these behaviors to select physically and genetically superior mates?

Acoustic Energy of Vocalization Intraspecific call variation influences mate choice by females of some anuran species, and often the males that emit the most acoustic energy attract females preferentially (Gerhardt 1988). Several call variables are correlated with acoustic energy, and females may prefer calls with more components, longer duration, greater intensity, or greater repetition rate, all of which have more energy than their counterparts (i.e., fewer components, shorter duration, lower repetition rate—see Ryan 1988a, 1988b, and above). Therefore, selection might favor males that can increase the energy in the call. This could be done by increasing both the metabolic energy used for calling and the efficiency with which metabolic energy is converted to acoustic energy (Ryan 1988a, 1988b).

Selection acts on morphological and physiological aspects of calling to increase call energy content (Ryan 1988a, 1988b, and above). The transformation of metabolic energy to acoustic energy (energetic efficiency of calling) is quite low for most animals, and frogs are no exception (Ryan 1985b, 1988b; Prestwich, Brugger, and Topping 1989). The energetic efficiency of vocalization by *P. pustulosus* ranged from 0.55 to 1.2% depending upon the number of components in the call (Ryan 1985b). This value is similar to estimates for the bladder cicada (0.8%, MacNally and Young 1981), a cockerel (1.6%, Brackenbury 1977), and humans (1%, Wood 1962). Presumably, the greater the amount of energy devoted to calling, the greater the amount of acoustic energy emitted by a male. However, this relation rests on the untested assumption that individual variation in the energetic efficiency of calling is trivial.

The low efficiencies of anuran vocalization probably result from a mismatch between the dominant wavelengths used in communication and the size of the resonating and radiating structures of the animal (MacNally and Young 1981; Prestwich, Brugger, and Topping 1989; Ryan 1985b, 1986a; Wiley and Richards 1982). In general, animals use wavelengths that are too long to be either resonated or radiated at maximum efficiency. Some species probably could produce shorter wavelengths. For example, males of some species of frogs can shorten the wavelength of their call (increase the frequency) by using the laryngeal muscles to deform the shape of the larynx, thus increasing the tension and the frequency of vibration of the vocal cords (Drewry, Heyer, and Rand 1982; Martin 1972). In some species of frogs, such as *Leptodactylus albilabris* (Leptodactylidae) and *Acris crepitans* (Hylidae), males change the frequency of the call in response to social situations (Lopez et al. 1988; Wagner 1989).

Several factors may counteract any advantage of increasing the energetic efficiency of calling by producing calls with shorter wavelengths (fig. 14.20). Generally, shorter wavelengths are attenuated more rapidly than sounds of longer wavelengths. This attenuation results from heat loss through

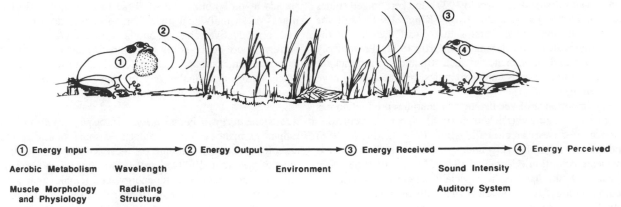

Fig. 14.20 Major factors influencing the amount of acoustic energy in the male's advertisement call that is perceived by females. (Reprinted, by permission, from Ryan 1988b.)

molecular interactions, and interference from small objects in the sound path (Marten, Quine, and Marler 1977; Morton 1975; Wiley and Richards 1982). Differential attenuation of frequencies has been demonstrated for a variety of animal sights, including frog calls (Ryan 1986a). Thus, the efficiency with which metabolic energy is converted to short wavelength acoustic energy might not be realized at the receiver because of the greater attenuation of short wavelengths.

A female's choice of mates is influenced by the energy her auditory system receives. The auditory system adds another layer of complexity because it can be differentially sensitive to frequencies (Fuzessery 1988; Zakon and Wilczynski 1988). Consequently, the sound energy perceived is not necessarily proportional to the sound energy received, and only the former influences a female's evaluation of mates. The production, transmission, reception, and perception of the acoustic energy that influences mate choice are of obvious evolutionary significance. Investigation of this problem must integrate various levels of biological investigation, including muscle biochemistry, morphology, environmental acoustics, and sensory physiology for a complete understanding of sexual selection and communication by anurans.

Energy Stores and Chorus Tenure Another short-term effect of energetics on male behavior is the degree to which available energy influences a male's ability to engage in particular activities. Vocal advertisement, as energetically expensive as it may be, is the most common behavior male anurans use to attract females. However, some males in many species may adopt noncalling behaviors (Howard 1984). Some noncalling males, referred to as satellite males, wait near calling males and attempt to intercept females as they approach calling males (e.g., Perrill, Gerhardt, and Daniels 1978). Other noncalling males actively but quietly search for females (e.g., Wells and Taigen 1984). The energetic costs of any aspect of noncalling behavior are unknown but are probably less than those of calling. Thus, the energy available to a male might dictate its choice of mating behaviors.

Some evidence supports this hypothesis: calling territorial males in a breeding chorus of *Uperoleia rugosa* (= *U. laevigata* [see Davies and Littlejohn 1986], Myobatrachidae) lost weight, whereas noncalling satellite males gained weight

(J. G. M. Robertson 1986a). A weight loss could have important fitness consequences because fighting ability is related to weight and heavier males win more encounters. MacNally (1981b) reported depletion of energy reserves during the breeding season for male *Ranidella signifera* and *R. parinsignifera* (Myobatrachidae) at the population level. He suggested a considerable expenditure of energy for reproduction, although he did not document either weight loss of individuals or correlated shifts in behavior. Small male *Rana clamitans* spend less time in territories and lose less weight during the breeding season than do large males (Wells 1977, 1978). *Rana virgatipes* provides the clearest demonstration of a trade-off between growth and calling effort (Given 1988). Small males call less than large males, and within small males calling effort and growth rate were negatively correlated after the effect of initial mass was removed.

No correlation between individual variation in physiological capacity and mating behavior has yet been demonstrated. The aerobic capacity of male *Bufo americanus* that call is the same as those that search (Wells and Taigen 1984), and the calling rates of male *B. woodhousii* are not correlated with their aerobic capacities (Sullivan and Walsberg 1985). Aerobic capacity was estimated by locomotory performance in these studies, however, and the muscles used for vocalization are anatomically and physiologically distinct from the muscles used during locomotion (see above). Consequently, measurements of the aerobic capacity for locomotion probably have little relevance to the capacity for vocalization.

Energy constraints that limit male reproductive behaviors might have long-term effects. An important determinant of male mating success is the number of nights a male spends at the breeding site (chorus tenure). This correlation has been demonstrated for *Bufo calamita* (Arak 1983a), *B. woodhousii* (B. Woodward 1982), *Hyla chrysoscelis* (Godwin and Roble 1983), *H. cinerea* (Gerhardt et al. 1987), *H. rosenbergi* (Kluge 1981), the centrolenids *Centrolenella fleischmanni* and *C. prosoblepon* (Greer and Wells 1980; Jacobson 1985), and the leptodactylid *Physalaemus pustulosus* (Ryan 1983, 1985a). Because males often do not forage at the breeding site (e.g., Ryan 1985a), energy stores might influence the number of nights an individual spends at the breeding site. Green (1990) investigated the relation between energy intake and male chorus tenure and vocalization in *P. pustulosus* by feeding one group of males and starving a second group. He measured the amount of calling by each group, released the males, and then determined which males returned to the chorus site. The starved and fed groups did not differ in the amount of calling while they were in captivity or in chorus attendance after they were released. Thus, the energy stores of these males did not influence their reproductive behavior.

Only J. G. M. Robertson's (1986a) study of *Uperoleia laevigata* and Given's (1988) study of *Rana virgatipes,* both conducted over an entire breeding season, suggest that the reproductive behaviors of male frogs are constrained by their energy stores. The other studies that have addressed this question examined species with short breeding seasons, and Green's experiments were restricted to a relatively short period in a long breeding season. Energetic constraints may operate over longer time periods.

Favorable Genes and Runaway Selection

Documentation of physiological costs of male courtship behavior has confirmed the notion of Darwin (1871) and many others that these behaviors incur serious energy expenditures that may eventually reduce the survival ability of males relative to females (Halliday 1987). One of the important questions remaining in sexual selection is why females have evolved preferences for males bearing such apparently maladaptive traits. The potential costs incurred by females in choosing males and the amount of energy invested in displays as an indicator of differences in heritable true fitness among males are important and controversial issues that need further exploration to evaluate seriously many of the hypotheses of the evolution of female mate choice.

The possibility that physiological costs of male behavior indicate heritable differences in true fitness among males has been a contentious issue in sexual selection (e.g., Kirkpatrick 1987b). Behavioral differences among males clearly can reflect differences in the amount of energy devoted to behavior. Even without evidence that these differences among males indicate differences in physiological abilities to support behavior, a number of authors have suggested that females prefer energetically expensive behaviors because they allow females to evaluate underlying genetic differences among males. This favorable genes hypothesis has been developed and advocated by several authors in slightly different contexts (e.g., Hamilton and Zuk 1982; Kodric-Brown and Brown 1984; Zahavi 1977) and applied to female call preference in *Hyla versicolor* by Klump and Gerhardt (1987).

Sexual Differences in Energy Devoted to Reproduction

Sexual differences in rates of growth, longevity, and age at first reproduction (e.g., Pianka and Parker 1975; Stearns 1976) and in the time and energy invested in parental care (e.g., Trivers 1972; Williams 1966) are of great interest in evolutionary ecology. Some of the theories proposed to explain these differences are based on differences in costs of reproduction. Energy expended for production of gametes is the primary reproductive investment for species with no parental care, and eggs contain more energy than sperm. A female has relatively few ova, whereas a male might have enough sperm to fertilize a substantial fraction of the female population. Increasing the number of mates will have little or no influence on a female's reproductive success, whereas the number of mates will be the most important determinant of a male's success. Consequently, females usually are the limiting sex and have low variance in reproductive success, whereas males are the limited sex and have a much higher variance in reproductive success. As a result, sexual selection has a more important influence on males than on females.

One important issue of parental investment theory is the degree to which the energy cost of forming gametes limits an individual's ability to reproduce. The costs of spermatogenesis (in time and energy) are not known, but sperm production is not the only reproductive cost for a male. Comparisons of energy invested in reproduction by males and females have been hampered by a difference in the form of the investment: the energy invested by females can be estimated by determining the energy content of their eggs, whereas much of the energy invested by males is used for reproductive behavior.

The energy invested in reproduction by both sexes has been estimated for only a few species of amphibians. Sexual differences in reproductive energy expenditures for *Physalaemus pustulosus* were compared by estimating the energy invested in eggs by females, in calling by males, and in nest building by both sexes. These estimates were combined with a detailed study of the phenology of both sexes throughout a breeding season. Based on average values for the amount of time males spent at the breeding site, the amount of that time they called each night, the number of times they mated and constructed nests, and the interclutch interval of females (Ryan 1985a), Ryan, Bartholomew, and Rand (1983) estimated the amount of energy devoted to reproduction by each sex (table 14.14). During an average breeding season of 152 days, males were present at the breeding site for 264 h over 44 days and mated about eight times. Females mated ten times per season. An average male expended 3.25 kJ for re-

TABLE 14.14   Total Energy Expended for Reproduction by Three Species of Ectothermal Vertebrates

	Sex	Body Mass	Breeding Season (days)	Energy (kJ)		
				Total	Total per g	Daily per g
Physalaemus pustulosus	M	1.7	259	3.25	2.19	0.008
Physalaemus pustulosus	F	1.8	259	40.96	26.43	0.102
Ranidella signifera	M	0.7	60	2.20	2.88	0.047
Ranidella parinsignifera	M	0.7	120	2.30	2.99	0.024
Uta stansburiana	M	3.3	117	21.50	8.78	0.075
First year	F	2.3	117	44.80	23.96	0.204
>1 year	F	2.7	117	45.50	21.52	0.186

Source: Data from Ryan 1985a.

production if he always called when present at the breeding site, and only 1.02 kJ if he remained silent. A female, on the other hand, invested 40.96 kJ in reproduction, mostly for egg production. Unfortunately, the annual food intake for this species was not determined.

The large difference in energy devoted to reproduction between male and female *P. pustulosus* is due to the large amount of energy invested in eggs. However, if females reproduced only once per season, they would still invest more energy in reproduction than would males. And if males were present at the breeding site on every night of the season, called on each of those nights, and nested at the same rate, they would invest 24.9 kJ per season, which is only about half that of the average female. Males of this species probably never invest more energy in reproduction than do females, because producing eggs costs much more than calling.

Nagy's (1983b) study of the lizard *Uta stansburiana* suggests a pattern of energy investment in reproduction that is similar to that of *P. pustulosus*. Female lizards expend about the same amount of energy as female *P. pustulosus* even when adjusted for differences in body mass (table 14.14). Male lizards, on the other hand, expend more energy than the male frogs after adjusting for differences in body mass. The high energy investment of male lizards results from their defending territories every day during the breeding season, whereas male frogs are present at the breeding site on only 17% of the nights. Thus, *U. stansburiana* are similar to *P. pustulosus* in that males expend much less energy in reproduction than females do.

In contrast are the reproductive energetics of the Puerto Rican leptodactylid frog *Eleutherodactylus coqui* (Woolbright 1985c). Both sexes have higher energy intakes during the wet season (July) than during the dry season (January), and in each season females acquire more energy than do males: average seasonal totals of 1.60 kJ versus 0.60 kJ during the wet season, and 0.62 kJ versus 0.26 kJ during the dry season. Female *E. coqui* expend 45.99 kJ per year, similar to the 40.96 kJ for female *P. pustulosus*. Woolbright's (1985c) estimate of the energy invested in reproduction by male coquís is extraordinarily high: 78.84 kJ per season versus 3.25 kJ for *P. pustulosus*. However, these figures include energy forfeited by not feeding during vocalization. This cost was not included in the estimate for *P. pustulosus*. Even without this cost, however, *E. coqui* males were estimated to expend 36.35 kJ per season.

The large difference between energy expended in reproduction by the males of *E. coqui* and *P. pustulosus* seems to be due to differences in male reproductive behavior. Like the lizards, male *E. coqui* do not leave the breeding site. Furthermore, they call on 50% of the nights of the breeding season. If the energetic cost of reproduction is adjusted for these differences in the number of nights at the breeding site, as well as for body mass, the expenditures are similar: 0.030 kJ · g⁻¹ · day⁻¹ for *E. coqui* and 0.043 kJ · g⁻¹ · day⁻¹ for *P. pustulosus*. Data for *Ranidella parinsignifera* and *R. signifera* (Myobatrachidae) indicate similar mass-specific daily energy expenditures for males. Like *P. pustulosus*, this is a pond-breeding species that is not always present at the breeding site. By measuring the depletion of energy reserves in males throughout the breeding season, MacNally (1981b) esti-

mated that male *R. parinsignifera* and *R. signifera* expended 2.30 kJ (0.024 kJ · g⁻¹ · day⁻¹) and 2.22 kJ (0.047 kJ · g⁻¹ · day⁻¹), respectively.

An interesting aspect of Woolbright's (1985c) study is the estimated energy expended relative to estimated energy gained. During the dry season energy gained and energy expended by females are similar, whereas during the wet season gain exceeds expenditure. Males in the dry season, on the other hand, have a balanced energy budget if they do not call and a negative energy balance if they call. In the wet season, calling results in a balanced energy budget; if males abstain from calling, their energy gain exceeds their expenditure.

These energy budgets indicate that a male's decision to call or not to call should have importance consequences for its future reproductive effort. If males call in the wet season, they must use energy that has been stored during the same season on nights when they did not call. In the dry season their energy budgets are balanced at best—there is no excess energy for storage or growth.

Predation as a Cost of Reproduction

The importance of predation in the evolution of reproductive traits was invoked by Darwin (1871) in his theory of sexual selection. The general notion is that courtship is usually ostentatious and that by engaging in courtship individuals expose themselves to an increased risk of predation. In addition, the foraging associated with accumulating energy reserves or meeting the demands of reproduction may increase the risk of predation.

Foraging and mate selection are behaviors that probably expose female amphibians to predators, but no data demonstrate that female amphibians increase their chances of survival by forsaking reproduction. The possibility of investigating this problem exists because some species of anurans, especially in the tropics, breed several times per season, so that mortality during breeding and nonbreeding cycles could be compared.

Also, the risk of predation to females could be measured as a function of the time they spend sampling males at the breeding site. Females are less conspicuous than males while at the breeding site prior to amplexus. However, the contrast of interest is not between males and females but among individuals within the sexes: do different individuals have different risks of predation as a result of their behavior at a breeding site? For example, some females spend more time than others selecting a mate; does that increase their risk of predation? Predators such as snakes, turtles, and crocodilians can be plentiful at amphibian breeding sites, and the movement of females should increase their susceptibility to those predators. It seems likely, but needs to be documented, that females are in more danger at a breeding site than away from it and that the risk increases in proportion to the time spent at the breeding site. Kirkpatrick (1987a) suggested that the most important contribution that empirical research can make to sexual selection theory is documentation of the selection forces acting on female mate choice. This goal might be achieved with some anurans.

Male anurans greatly increase their conspicuousness while advertising for mates, and the risk of predation has been mea-

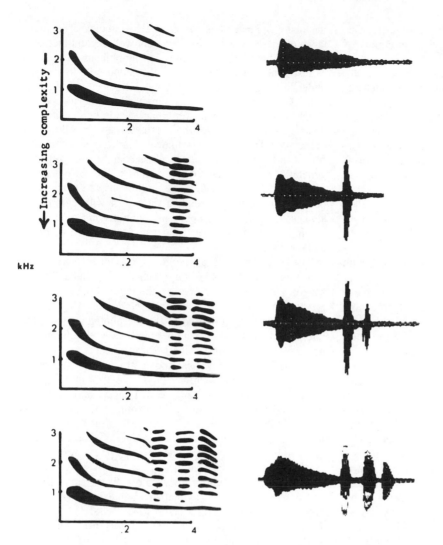

Fig. 14.21 Sonograms (*left*) and oscillograms (*right*) of the call complexity series of *Physalaemus pustulosus*. Each call contains a whine with zero (*top*) to three (*bottom*) chucks. (Reprinted, by permission, from Rand and Ryan 1981.)

sured for some species. Male bullfrogs (*Rana catesbeiana*) that defended territories in the middle of a pond were susceptible to predation by snapping turtles (Emlen 1976; Howard 1978a). Marine toads (*Bufo marinus*) have been observed to orient toward a chorus of *Physalaemus pustulosus*, apparently attracted by the calls of their potential prey (Jaeger 1976). Predators of *P. pustulosus* include a crab (*Potamocarcinus richmondi*), a snake (*Leptodeira annulata*), a leptodactylid frog (*Leptodactylus pentadactylus*), an opossum (*Philander opossum*), and a bat (*Trachops cirrhosus*; reviewed in Ryan 1985a). *Leptodactylus* and the mammals use the frogs' advertisement calls as a localization cue. Males increase their predation risk while calling, and the risk to noncalling males increases when predators are attracted to a breeding site.

Studies of predation by the bat *T. cirrhosus* on *P. pustulosus* revealed the interaction of mate attraction and predation. Male *P. pustulosus* produce a call that consists of whine and from zero to six chucks (fig. 14.21). A male calling in isolation usually produces only a whine, but males add chucks to their calls when they are in a chorus. Females are attracted to calls with only whines, but they prefer calls with chucks. Thus, by adding chucks to the call, a male can increase his ability to attract mates (Rand and Ryan 1981). Why, then, do

males not always produce the calls that are most attractive to females? Energetic cost does not limit the production of chucks: male *P. pustulosus* increase their metabolic rate severalfold while calling, but the number of chucks in the call does not appear to affect the rate of oxygen consumption (Bucher, Ryan, and Bartholomew 1982). Instead, predation by bats (*T. cirrhosus*) appears to be an important factor.

T. cirrhosus is unusual among microchiropteran bats so far studied in its ability to perceive and localize the relatively low frequencies that are characteristic of frog calls (Ryan, Tuttle, and Barclay 1983; Ryan and Tuttle 1987). *T. cirrhosus* is attracted to the calls of a variety of frog species, although they tend to avoid calls of species that are unpalatable or too large for them to eat (Tuttle and Ryan 1982). Among the many calls to which they are attracted is the simple whine (i.e., without chucks) call of *P. pustulosus*. However, *T. cirrhosus* is attracted preferentially to calls with chucks, just as female *P. pustulosus* are (Ryan, Tuttle, and Rand 1982). Thus, males vary their ability to attract mates and their predation risk in parallel when they change the number of components in the call. Male *P. pustulosus* are not completely at the mercy of the predators; they can detect and escape bats on all but the darkest nights, and they vary the intensity of their escape behavior from merely becoming silent to submerging and swimming away depending on the proximity of the bat (Tuttle, Taft, and Ryan 1982).

A chorus of calling male anurans should be especially prone to bat predation. One possible explanation for such aggregations is the selfish herd hypothesis, which suggests that the per capita risk of predation decreases with increasing size of aggregations (Hamilton 1971). This prediction is supported by observations of *P. pustulosus*: males in large choruses were less likely to be eaten than those in small choruses (Ryan, Tuttle, and Taft 1981). Furthermore, this benefit was not achieved at the cost of reduced mating success, because larger choruses attracted proportionally more females than did small choruses, and the per capita mating success of males was higher in larger choruses (Ryan 1985a; Green 1990).

Another frog, *Smilisca sila* (Hylidae), produces calls with varying numbers of components and frequently falls prey to *T. cirrhosus*. The bats are attracted preferentially to multi-component calls, and *S. sila* are able to detect an approaching bat on all but the darkest nights. In darkness, when the bats are difficult to detect, the frogs produce calls with fewer components than they do in bright light (Tuttle and Ryan 1982). The frogs also alter their calling sites, calling from the tops of exposed rocks in the middle of streams on bright nights and from under vegetation on dark nights. The frogs also call near small waterfalls that produce a broad frequency band of background noise. When given a choice, bats are attracted preferentially to calls farther from such noisy sources.

Integrating Predation Risk and Energetic Costs of Reproduction

The cost of predation to male reproductive behavior is perhaps better documented for anurans than for any other animal. However, few data indicate that exposure to predation has anything more than a short-term effect on the behavior of male anurans, that differences in predation levels within and among populations or species of anurans have caused the evolution of differences in reproductive behavior, or that predation affects the age or size structure or the degree of sexual dimorphism within populations. If this apparent absence of effects of predation is correct, studies of reproductive energetics can treat the risk of predation as a cost of reproduction that does not interact with the energetics of reproductive behavior. Experimental confirmation of that assumption would require detailed comparisons of the reproductive behaviors of individuals from populations that are known to have had different predation intensities for many generations (cf. Endler's [1980] studies of guppies). However, the apparent absence of long-term effects of predation on the activities of primary interest to physiological ecologists suggests that studies of the behavioral energetics of anuran reproduction may lead to demonstration of a link between individual variation in physiology and Darwinian fitness.

BEHAVIORAL ENERGETICS AND THE ECOLOGY OF AMPHIBIANS
F. Harvey Pough

The topics reviewed in this chapter demonstrate the contributions that investigations of amphibians can make to understanding patterns of biological variation, and they emphasize the many opportunities for integrative studies. The importance of these investigations extends well beyond increasing our understanding of the biology of amphibians, fascinating as that goal is, because these studies contribute to a general understanding of mechanics of natural selection and evolution. As Emerson (1988) has emphasized, the independent evolution of similar character complexes in unrelated phylogenetic lineages provides the best evidence for a direct role of morphological and physiological characters in determining fitness. Information about amphibians can be used to test the generality of hypotheses derived from studies of other taxa, such as lizards, and data from amphibians can generate hypotheses that can be tested in their turn with comparative studies. Even among amphibians, anurans and salamanders are independent radiations that can fruitfully be compared and contrasted.

The goal of behavioral energetics is to understand patterns in nature, and studies of amphibians have emphasized two sets of natural patterns: one in foraging and the other in reproductive behavior. Studies of the relation of foraging mode to community structure and to the morphological and physiological characteristics that are correlated with different foraging modes were among the earliest attempts to merge the perspectives of physiological and community ecologists. Examples of correlations among physiology, morphology, and foraging ecology of anurans are widespread and so familiar that we take them for granted. For example, the general body form of a frog provides a basis for an informed prediction of its behavior and diet. Furthermore, patterns of body form and diet can be extended to include exercise physiology: species that forage widely have higher capacities to sustain aerobic metabolism than sit-and-wait predators. These subjective impressions are supported by statistical analyses (Taigen, Emerson, and Pough 1982; Emerson 1985, 1988).

The emergence of intelligible patterns from descriptive studies is satisfying, but the next step in the analysis, understanding the mechanistic basis of the patterns, has so far proven intractable. We currently have little understanding of why the patterns we see in foraging biology appear so robust. Correlations are widespread, especially at the whole-animal level, and these can be extended to elements of the oxygen-transport system, but mechanistic links tracing variation in foraging behavior to variation in the structure, physiology, or biochemistry of muscle tissue are rare, especially at the level of individual variation (table 14.15). Furthermore, current evidence indicates that the normal foraging behavior of anurans does not require rates of energy input that approach the maximum values measured in laboratory tests, so no theoretical basis for the correlations can be suggested. Perhaps, as Walton (1988) has proposed, the aerobic capacities of widely foraging anurans represent excessive construction that provides a margin of safety for rare, critical events in the lives of individuals. Testing hypotheses will be difficult, as will be the search for mechanistic links between individual variation in performance and fitness during rare events. Alternatively, the observation of elevated levels of lactic acid in free-ranging animals engaged in apparently low levels of activity may indicate that extrapolation of laboratory measurements to the field is more complicated than we appreciate. In that event, mechanistic links between variation in physiology and foraging behavior might yet be demonstrated.

TABLE 14.15   Patterns of Variation in the Behavioral Energetics of Anurans

Pattern	Interspecific Comparisons	Intraspecific Comparisons
Predatory Behavior and Diet		
Ecology and behavior		
WF make more prey captures than SW.	Yes (30).	Yes (30, 54).
WF capture prey that occur in patches.	Yes (30).	Not tested.
WF travel at lower velocities than SW.	No (30).	Not tested.
WF feed on small prey.	Maybe, but spatial and seasonal variation is large (30, 46, 49, 50, 51).	Not tested.
WF are less territorial than SW.	No (30).	Not tested.
Morphology		
WF have slim bodies and small mouths.	Yes, but phylogenetic bias is large and *Bufo* is an exception (41, 50).	Not tested.
WF have short jaws.	Yes, but *Bufo* is an exception (10).	Not tested.
WF have short limbs.	Yes (11).	Not tested.
Fiber type of limb muscles parallels whole-animal performance.	Varies (25, 32, 40).	Not tested.
Physiology		
WF have greater aerobic capacity.	Yes (3, 4, 45).	No (54).
Heart mass and blood oxygen capacity parallel aerobic capacity.	Yes (20, 21).	Yes (29, 53).
Contractile properties of muscles parallel whole-animal performance.	Yes (27, 32).	Not tested.
Enzyme activities of limb muscles parallel whole-animal performance.	Varies (7, 55).	Yes (2, 3, 5, 31, 32).
Reproductive Behavior		
Ecology and Behavior		
Intensity of call is proportional to body size.	No (58).	Yes (1, 15, 17).
Loud calls are more costly.	Yes (58).	Yes (57, 58, 59).
Long or complex calls are more costly	Yes (58).	Varies (6, 36, 37, 47, 58)
Costly calls are more attractive to females.	Not applicable.	Yes (13, 24, 33).
Call characteristics are correlated with aerobic capacity for locomotion.	Not applicable.	No (44, 56).
Mating success is proportional to chorus tenure.	Not applicable.	Yes (1, 12, 14, 16, 17, 18, 19, 22, 23, 35, 39, 42, 43, 55, 58, 60).
Chorus tenure is limited by energy reserves.	Not applicable.	Varies (34, 58).
Morphology		
Mass of trunk muscles is proportional to calling effort.	Yes (47).	Yes (26, 47).
Mass of laryngeal muscles is proportional to calling effort.	Not tested.	Yes (52).
Structural properties of laryngeal muscles are correlated with calling effort.	Yes (8, 9, 28, 38).	Not tested.
Physiology		
Tetanic frequency of laryngeal muscles is proportional to pulse rate of call.	Yes (27).	Yes (27).
Metabolic substrates of calling muscles are related to reproductive behavior.	Yes (58).	Yes (48).
Enzyme activities of trunk muscles are proportional to calling effort.	Yes (26).	Yes (58).

Sources: (1) Arak 1983b; (2) Baldwin, Friedman, and Lillywhite 1977; (3) Bennett 1974; (4) Bennett, and Licht 1973; (5) Bennett and Licht 1974; (6) Bucher, Ryan, and Bartholomew 1982; (7) Cummings 1979; (8) Eichelberg and Schneider 1973; (9) Eichelberg and Schneider 1974; (10) Emerson 1985; (11) Emerson 1988; (12) Emlen 1976; (13) Forester and Czarnowsky 1985; (14) Gatz 1981; (15) Gerhardt 1975; (16) Gerhardt et al. 1987; (17) Given 1987; (18) Godwin and Roble 1983; (19) Greer and Wells 1980; (20) Hillman 1976; (21) Hillman 1980a; (22) Jacobson 1985; (23) Kluge 1981; (24) Klump and Gerhardt 1987; (25) Lannergren and Smith 1966; (26) McKay 1989; (27) Manz 1975; (28) Marsh and Taigen 1987; (29) Pough and Kamel 1984; (30) Pough and Taigen 1990; (31) Putnam 1979a; (32) Putnam and Bennett 1983; (33) Rand and Ryan 1981; (34) J.G.M. Robertson 1986a; (35) Ryan 1983; (36) Ryan 1988a; (37) Ryan 1988b; (38) Schneider 1977; (39) Sherman 1980; (40) Smith and Ovalle 1973; (41) Sperry 1981; (42) Strüssmann et al. 1984; (43) Sullivan 1982b; (44) Sullivan 1987; (45) Sullivan and Walsberg 1985; (46) Taigen, Emerson, and Pough 1982; (47) Taigen and Pough 1983; (48) Taigen and Wells 1985; (49) Taigen, Wells, and Marsh 1985; (50) Toft 1980b; (51) Toft 1980a; (52) Toft 1981; (53) Trewavas 1933; (54) Walsberg, Lea, and Hillman 1986; (55) Walton 1988; (56) Wells 1976b; (57) Wells and Taigen 1984; (58) Wells and Taigen 1989; (59) Wells and Taigen, this chapter; (60) B. Woodward 1982.

Notes: WF = widely foraging; SW = sit and wait.

However, studies of the physiological correlates of foraging mode pose a second challenge that will be difficult to meet: foraging is a diffuse activity that integrates interactions with the physical environment, such as thermoregulation and hydroregulation, with the biological activities of defending territories, finding prey, and avoiding predators. Furthermore, daily and seasonal cycles affect the behavior of the study species and of its prey and predators simultaneously; complex interactions of factors are likely to occur.

Mechanistic aspects of the significance of physiological traits in evolution are best studied in behaviors that occupy an animal to the near exclusion of other activities, especially when a mechanistic link between performance and fitness can be demonstrated (Pough 1989b). Reproductive behavior appears particularly suited to studies of this sort, especially for species in which reproduction is separated in time and space from other activities (e.g., Clutton-Brock 1988). Anurans may be uniquely suitable for these investigations because their reproductive biology is more diverse at the species level than that of any other group of vertebrates except fishes (Pough, Heiser, and McFarland 1989).

The reproductive behavior of males of some species of anurans is energetically costly, and it excludes many other activities. Furthermore, males of some species reduce food intake during the breeding season, thereby increasing the chance that energy reserves may limit costly behaviors. The risk of predation during courtship, although it is large for males of some species of anurans, does not appear to confound the interpretation of energetic costs.

Studies of the reproductive behavior of anurans have described species-level correlations between behavior and energetics that appear to reflect mechanistic relationships (table 14.15). For example, male gray treefrogs, *Hyla versicolor* (Hylidae), employ the form of vocalization that maximizes nightly calling duration when they are calling in isolation. When they call in choruses, competing with other males for the attention of females, they shift to complex and energetically expensive calls that are more attractive, but these calls exact a price measured by a reduction in the total time spent calling during an evening (figs. 14.14 and 14.15).

Similarly, the biochemical and physiological characteristics of the trunk muscles of spring peepers, *H. crucifer*, that call at low body temperatures early in the spring are different from those of males that join the chorus later in the spring when it is warmer (McKay 1989). The ratio of females to males is most favorable in early spring, so males that call

early probably obtain a disproportionately large number of matings. Studies of these frogs may provide direct evidence of a role of individual physiological variation among males in determining mating success.

The surprisingly short chorus tenures of males of many species of anurans with long breeding seasons may be another example of an energetic constant. Because vocalization is so expensive, males may leave choruses to replenish their energy stores at intervals during the season. If this is the case, the foraging abilities of an individual male (perhaps including its capacity to sustain activity at unfavorable combinations of body temperature and hydration state) might determine how quickly it could return and thus contribute directly to the total time it spent in a chorus during a year.

Although salamanders do not form choruses of vocalizing males, they may be equally useful subjects for study. Salamanders have been the focus of an enormous amount of ecological investigation (e.g., Hairston 1987), but the physiological and morphological correlates of their ecology have been less studied. The mass-specific cost of egg production by salamanders appears to be as great as that of frogs, and the brooding behavior of females of many species of plenthodontid salamanders appears to impose the same limits on feeding as described for some frogs. Many salamanders are less vagile than frogs, and they may be correspondingly more tractable for studies that use habitat manipulations to link foraging behavior to energy intake and biomass production.

Experiments that test hypotheses drawn from detailed and specific information about diverse aspects of the biology of a study species appear to be the most productive way to address questions about the processes that lead to the patterns of physiology, morphology, ecology, and behavior revealed by descriptive studies. Reliance on interpretation of correlations revealed by a posteriori analyses is an inefficient experimental design, and it is beset with pitfalls because even the limited information currently available suggests that complex interactions of the phenomena we are investigating are likely to be the rule. For example, the role of energy stores in constraining chorus attendance and calling effort by male anurans may depend on the time of year a species breeds, the length of its breeding season, and the predictability of suitable conditions. The breadth of information needed to design and interpret studies that address questions about the relations between variation in performance and fitness reaffirms the traditional importance of the mechanistic and field-oriented perspective of physiological ecology.

Part 4
Development and Reproduction

The ultimate measure of an individual's evolutionary success is its ability to develop, grow, mature, and produce viable offspring. In this context, all of the physiological systems and processes discussed previously in this book have evolved because they improve this criterion of success in various, often challenging environments. Although this criterion is singular, the means to this end are not. As introduced in chapter 1, amphibians exhibit enormous diversity in developmental and reproductive modes, and many species do not conform to the well-known life cycle of aquatic egg, aquatic larva, and metamorphosis to terrestrial adult. This final section focuses in detail on the diversity of reproductive modes as well as the complex and fascinating changes in physiology that occur during development in amphibian larvae.

Chapter 15, by Jørgensen, examines growth and reproduction. Several themes emerge from this chapter. First, amphibians cannot entirely suspend other activities in the interest of reproducing—reproduction and its energetic and regulatory demands thus put often greatly increased demands on the major physiological systems. To maximize reproductive effectiveness while minimizing reproductive physiological costs has been a major selection pressure in amphibian reproductive biology. The second theme is diversity of reproductive modes. The tremendous diversity that characterizes the "everyday" physiological processes of amphibians, as described in the preceding chapters, extends into the usually seasonal physiological activities associated with reproduction. A third major theme is the interplay between external seasonality and the internal physiological cycles of growth, fat deposition, and gametogenesis, as well as the endocrinological mechanisms that link these cycles.

Chapter 16, by Burggren and Just, examines developmental changes in physiological systems from fertilization of the egg onward. The developmental biology of amphibians has been and continues to be of particular interest to scientists for several reasons, some related to amphibian biology per se and some not. Historically, amphibian development has served as a major model for the study of vertebrate development. Such studies have usually focused on developmental features that are common to all vertebrates (or, at least, to mammals and amphibians) rather than characterize the developmental diversity within Amphibia. In any event, the development of physiological systems has not been a particular priority. Thus, many studies of amphibian development provide but meager insight into how environmental changes may alter developmental processes or whether development in amphibians has evolved to accommodate such environmental challenges. Chapter 16 emphasizes *diversity* in the physiology of developing amphibians, particularly with respect to environmental influences. Chapter 16 is the longest in the book because it revisits each of the topics of the previous chapters, describing the ontogenetic changes leading to the more familiar and more frequently studied processes of adult amphibians. It devotes particular emphasis to several new topics, including nonthyroid aspects of endocrinological development and the ontogeny of osmoregulation in amphibians.

15 Growth and Reproduction

C. Barker Jørgensen

Morphological adaptations of high phylogenetic uniformity characterize the amphibians. In the urodeles and even more so in the anurans, this uniformity combines with a functional adaptability to permit broad geographical ranges; for example, from probable origins in humid tropical climates to arctic environments, to high altitudes, and to desertlike habitats (Duellman and Trueb 1986; Vial 1973). Amphibians thus combine morphological uniformity with physiological and behavioral diversity.

Two large genera, *Rana* and *Bufo*, exemplify this high functional adaptability of fixed structural aptations (Gould and Vrba 1982). These two genera are also among the most thoroughly studied amphibian groups (see chapter 1). Knowledge of the basic life history traits of these animals, including patterns of growth, deposition, and reproduction, may provide clues to the understanding of the high adaptability of these and other amphibian genera.

Growth in the sense of increase in lean body mass begins in early embryonic life and may continue into adulthood in amphibians (see chapter 16). This review is restricted to postmetamorphic growth. At metamorphosis, amphibians acquire their final proportions, so postmetamorphic growth is approximately isometric. The primary interest in postmetamorphic growth therefore centers on the rates at which organisms increase lean body mass and the factors that control or affect rates of growth and final body size.

Besides growth, deposition of fat may contribute significantly to the amphibian body mass. Moreover, in adult female amphibians, ovaries containing complements of fully grown vitellogenic oocytes may constitute a substantial fraction of the body mass, amounting up to 20–30% or more. By contrast, the mature gonads in the males contribute only marginally to the body mass, usually less than 1%.

In budget terms, growth, fat and glycogen deposition, and gametogenesis figure together as organic production, that is, synthesis of macromolecules such as proteins, nucleic acids, lipids, and glycogen. Production depends on acquisition of food. Availability of food, as well as appetite, thus determines the level of production (see chapter 13), whereas both amounts and composition of food assimilated and the func-

tional state of the organism determine the allocation of assimilated food for the various types of production, somatic growth, deposition, and gametogenesis. This chapter aims at elucidating the complex relationships between feeding and allocation of assimilated food to growth, deposition, and vitellogenesis in amphibians within an ecological framework. A comparison of amphibian growth and reproduction as a function of climatic and other environmental conditions is hampered, however, by the lack of analyses of species outside the temperate zone, particularly in North America and Europe (see chapter 1).

PATTERNS OF GROWTH

Amphibian growth and adult body size is characteristically highly plastic and indeterminate, implying that environmental factors substantially affect the genetically fixed growth pattern. The most important environmental factors are temperature, water, and food availability, which may vary seasonally depending upon latitude and altitude of the geographical location of the habitat (see also chapters 5, 6, 8, 9, and 11–14).

Amphibian growth has been studied both in nature and in the laboratory. Growth in the laboratory may serve to assess the physiological capabilities for growth (growth potential), which may be higher than actually realized in nature. Thus, the growth rate of the high-altitude Neotropical plethodontid salamander, *Bolitoglossa subpalmata*, in its habitat in Cerro de la Muerte, Costa Rica, is remarkably lower than is typical in salamanders. When young *B. subpalmata* were kept in the laboratory at their normal temperature of about 10°C and fed *Drosophila* ad libitum, they grew about 1.3 mm·month⁻¹ in their first year. This rate is lower than for other plethodontid salamanders, but greater than the monthly growth of <0.5 mm in nature (table 15.3). In the laboratory, males matured sexually at the age of 1.5 years and females at the age of 3 years, as compared to 6 and 12 years in nature, respectively (Houck 1982; Vial 1968).

Growth rates may also be low in the laboratory, revealing difficulties in establishing optimal conditions for growth, including a proper diet. Juvenile *Bufo woodhousii* grew slowly

TABLE 15.1 Growth Rates of Juvenile Anurans in Nature

	Sex	Growth Rate (mm·month^{-1})	Time of Year	Locality	Reference
Rana clamitans		9	July	Michigan	Martof 1956
Rana pretiosa		7	July	Yellowstone Park, Wyoming	Turner 1960a, 1960b
Rana sylvatica		5–6	Jun–Sep	Minnesota	Bellis 1961
Rana erythraea	M	6	Year round	Philippines	Brown and Alcala 1970
	F	11			
Bufo bufo		5	Aug–Sep	Denmark	K.-E. Hede pers. comm.
Bufo hemiophrys	M, F	5	Autumn	Waubun Prairie, Minnesota	Breckenridge and Tester 1961
Bufo cognatus	M, F	22	May–Jun	Oklahoma	Bragg and Weese 1950
		9	Jul–mid-Aug		
		3	Mid-Aug–mid-Sep		
Bufo woodhousii		13	Summer	Connecticut	Clarke 1974
Bombina variegata		4	Summer half	Germany	Kapfberger 1984

TABLE 15.2 Growth Rates of Juvenile Anurans in the Laboratory

	Age (months)	Sex	Growth Rate (mm·month^{-1})	Reference
Rana pipiens	0–5	M, F	7	Richards and Lehmann 1980
Rana catesbeiana	0–1	M, F	27[a]	Modzelewski and Culley 1974
	1–2		14	
	2–3		8	
Bufo houstonensis	0–1	M, F	19	Quinn and Mengden 1984
	1–2		9	
	2–3		8	
	3–4		6	
	4–5		3	
Bufo boreas	0–2		15	Lillywhite, Licht, and Chelgren 1973
Bufo calamita	0–1		9	Hemmer and Kadel 1972
Bufo woodhousii	0–2		5[b]	Claussen and Layne 1983
Hyla rosenbergi	0–?		6	Kluge 1981
Hyla cinerea	?		5	Freed 1980

[a]Lengths are calculated from body mass M by means of the equation log $M(g) = -3.866 + 2.865$ log $L(mm)$ (Bruneau and Magnin 1980).
[b]Calculated from body mass by means of conversion equations in Clarke 1974.

on diets of cabbage loopers and crickets, compared with the growth rates of toads fed mealworms (Claussen and Layne 1983). But even the toads fed mealworms grew at a rate less than half that recorded from nature (Clarke 1974). Crickets were also deficient as a complete food for the bullfrog, *Rana catesbeiana,* whereas frogs fully exploited their potential for growth on a diet of mosquito fish (Modzelewski and Culley 1974).

The inferior value of crickets as food seems to be due to vitamin deficiencies, particularly of vitamin D (Modzelewski and Culley 1974). Crickets dusted with vitamin preparation supported normal growth, including rates of growth, in the frog *Rana pipiens* (Richards and Lehman 1980) and the tree-frog *Hyla rosenbergi* (Hylidae; Kluge 1981).

In *H. cinerea,* basking enhanced the rate of growth. Thus, 8-week-old juvenile frogs fed on house flies (*Musca domestica*) and with access to basking increased in length by 9.4 mm against 6.5 mm in nonbasking controls (Freed 1980).

The environmentally determined low growth rate in *Bolitoglossa subpalmata* may be exceptional. More typically,

growth rates recorded from nature agree with those obtained under optimal conditions in the laboratory. Tables 15.1 and 15.2 summarize juvenile growth rates in a number of anurans, mostly ranids and bufonids, in nature and in the laboratory. Data on rates of growth in nature are obtained from recaptured animals, marked by toe clipping. The growth rates in table 15.1 are mean growth rates during the season of maximum growth.

An initial high potential for growth that rapidly declines characterizes the postmetamorphic pattern of growth. The pattern is most clearly observed in frogs or toads raised in the laboratory (e.g., *Rana catesbeiana,* Modzelewski and Culley 1974, and *Bufo houstonensis,* Quinn and Mengden 1984), or in nature in populations that metamorphose at the beginning of the active season (e.g., *B. cognatus* in Oklahoma, Bragg and Weese 1950) or in the tropics under climatic conditions that are compatible with growth for the entire year (e.g., *R. erythraea,* Brown and Alcala 1970).

The study of rates of postmetamorphic growth as a function of body size in *R. erythraea* is based on more than 8,000 toe-clipped frogs recaptured over several years. Figure 15.1 shows the declining growth rates with increasing body size, until growth practically ceases at the onset of sexual maturation, 6–7 months after metamorphosis in the males and 9 months in the females. This pattern of growth may be typical of amphibians inhabiting humid, tropical climates. Figure 15.1 also illustrates the substantial variation in growth rate among the members of a frog population living in a constant tropical climate. Presumably, this great individual variation in growth is not environmentally imposed but is an intrinsic characteristic of amphibian growth; it also occurs in animals fed ad libitum under constant conditions in the laboratory.

In the temperate zone, growth rates vary seasonally, determined by the varying temperature and food supply. In the warm temperate zone, however, growth may be completed within one growth period, as was observed in a cohort of *Bufo cognatus* that metamorphosed in mid-May in Oklahoma and reached full size before hibernation in the fall, about 5 months after metamorphosis (Bragg and Weese 1950).

At higher latitudes, in species that metamorphose late in the active season, the high postmetamorphic potential for growth may not be exploited, as indicated by the relatively low initial growth rates of *B. hemiophrys* in Minnesota and *B. bufo* in Denmark. In the months following emergence *B.*

hemiophrys grew much faster than prior to hibernation (table 15.1).

The declining annual growth with increasing latitude may be due to declining temperatures, but the shortening of the active period may be equally or even more important.

Most studies on urodele growth rates are from populations of plethodontid salamanders in the United States and Central America (table 15.3). Maximum growth rates in these salamanders are lower than in the anurans, correlated with their smaller size. Growth rates tend to increase from north to south in the populations from the United States, and they are lowest in the newt *Triturus vulgaris* (Salamandridae) from England. All the species studied from Central America are high-altitude forms, which may affect this comparison.

Correlated with the reduced annual growth at high latitudes and altitudes is the older age at sexual maturation. This correlation has been documented by the age composition of sexually mature urodeles and anurans, as determined by counting annual growth rings in a phalange. In Scandinavia, the age at sexual maturation in *T. vulgaris* increases from 1–2 years in southeast Norway to 4–5 years in Jämtland, Sweden, the northernmost locality sampled (Dolmen 1983).

A particularly careful study of the relationship between climate and growth and age at sexual maturation was made by Hemelaar (1986, 1988) in five populations of *Bufo bufo*, geographically ranging from central Norway to southern France. The toad populations were sampled on the spawning grounds, and from the frequency distribution of age groups the age at first maturation could be estimated. Table 15.4 shows that this age varied with latitude, as well as with altitude, and that the females normally reached sexual maturation 1 year later than the males. The extremes were represented by the Dutch toad population, where the males matured at the age of 2 or 3 years and the females at the age of 3 or 4 years, and the Swiss population at an elevation of 1,850 m, with ages at first maturation of 6–9 and 8–10 years for males and females, respectively. It was previously generally assumed that amphibians matured at well-defined ages, implying well-defined growth rates of a population (Duellman and Trueb 1986; Franchi 1962; Perry and Rowlands 1962; Redshaw 1972; Sadleir 1973; Smith 1955; Tokarz 1978). The actual large variation in age at first maturation, disclosed by skeletochronological analyses (Acker, Kruse, and Krehbiel 1986; Gittins, Steeds, and Williams 1982; Hemelaar 1986; Verrell and Francillon 1986), presumably reflects the individual variation

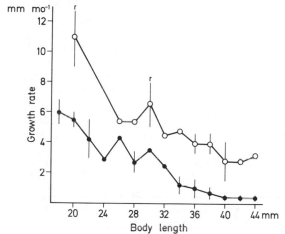

Fig. 15.1 Postmetamorphic growth rates (mm month⁻¹) as a function of body length in male (●) and female (○) frogs, *Rana erythraea*, in the Philippines. Means ± 1 SE of sample numbers of ≥4; *r*, range of three measurements. Data from Brown and Acala 1970.

TABLE 15.3 Growth Rates of Juvenile Urodeles in Nature

	Growth Rate (mm·month⁻¹)	Time of Year	Locality	Reference
Triturus vulgaris	1.3	Summer	England	Bell 1977
Plethodon cinereus	2.0	May–Aug	Maryland	Sayler 1966
	1.9	May–Aug	Tennessee	Nagel 1977
Plethodon richmondi	2.3	May–Aug		Angle 1969
Plethodon jordani	2.5	May–Jun to Jul–Aug	North Carolina	Hairston 1983
Plethodon glutinosus	2.5	Aug–Sep	Pennsylvania	Highton 1962
	2.7	Jan–May	Florida	
Bolitoglossa rostrata	1.3	Year round	Guatemala (2,515–3,000 m)	Houck 1977b
Bolitoglossa subpalmata	<0.5	Year round	Costa Rica (3,300 m)	Vial 1968
Pseudoeurycea brunnata	2.0	Jun–Aug	Guatemala (2,415–2,860 m)	Houck 1977c

TABLE 15.4   Age at Sexual Maturation in Populations of the Toad *Bufo bufo* from Different Sites in Europe

Locality	Age at Sexual Maturation (years)	
	Males	Females
Norway	4–7	6–9
Netherlands	2–3	3–4
Germany	3–4	4–5
Switzerland	6–9	8–10
France	3–5	4–7

Source: Data from Hemelaar 1986.

characteristic of rates of growth and body size in amphibians (Halliday and Verrell 1988).

The difference in age at sexual maturation among toads from various geographical locations may not arise entirely from different climatic environments, but may also be genetically fixed, determined by relationships between growth, body size, and sexual maturation that are established independently of particular climatic conditions (see below).

Growth rates may be affected by different behavior within a population, as observed in the salamander *Notophthalmus viridescens* (Salamandridae) from Massachusetts (Healy 1973). Normally, juvenile *N. viridescens* are terrestrial, but the population in Massachusetts also contains aquatic juveniles, permitting examination of the effects of aquatic and terrestrial environments on growth and sexual maturation in an amphibian population. Aquatic juveniles grew at a faster annual rate than terrestrial juveniles because the aquatic juveniles grew throughout the year, whereas growth on land was largely restricted to the summer months. Moreover, annual increments were far more variable from year to year on land than they were in the aquatic environment. The individuals became sexually mature at the same size in both habitats. Hence, the difference in growth rate results in a reduction in the age at first reproduction in the population that omits the terrestrial eft stage. The cause of the behavioral difference with regard to choice of habitat is unknown (Healy 1973).

The difference in size between the sexes in amphibians may vary from absent to striking. Typically, females are larger than males, as in 90% of 589 anuran species and 61% of 79 urodele species (Shine 1979). In some species, differences in size are correlated with different growth rates throughout postmetamorphic growth, for example, *Rana erythraea* (Brown and Alcala 1970; fig. 15.1) and *Bufo bufo* (Jørgensen 1986b). In other species, the juvenile growth rates are similar in both sexes, but females continue to grow for a longer period, for example, *R. catesbeiana* (Bruneau and Magnin 1980) and *R. temporaria* (Gibbons and McCarthy 1984).

INHERENT GROWTH RHYTHMS

Seasonal growth in temperate zone amphibians is usually interpreted in terms of environmental control, acting through varying temperature and availability of food. Indirect evidence, however, indicates that internal factors also may be involved in seasonal growth patterns. Growth requires eating, and feeding may presumably vary seasonally independently of temperature and food availability. Thus, after emergence in spring, temperate zone anurans may feed little or not at all until after breeding, for example, the frogs *Rana temporaria* (Blackith and Speight 1974; Itämies and Koskela 1970; Jastrzebski 1968; Juszczyk, Obrzut, and Zamachowski 1966; Koskela and Pasanen 1975; Victoroff 1908) and *R. pipiens* (Mizell 1965) and the toads *Bufo bufo* (Heusser 1968b, 1969; Moore 1954) and *B. canorus* (Morton 1981).

At the end of the active season, feeding may decline or stop and digestion may become deficient in a hibernator prevented from hibernating. Thus, the frog *R. temporaria* does not feed in winter and, if force-fed, digests food poorly at room temperature (Herter 1936). Obligatory hibernators from xeric regions, the spadefoot toads *Scaphiopus couchii* and *S. hammondii* (Pelobatidae) in southeast Arizona, also failed to feed and showed increased mortality at room temperature during autumn and winter (Seymour 1973a).

Heusser (1968c) states that in Switzerland the toad *B. bufo* starts hibernating during the first half of October, whatever the temperature. Also in *R. temporaria* from northern Finland, hibernation and thus feeding and growth appear determined by an inherent rhythm (Koskela and Pasanen 1974).

Experiments with toads, *B. viridis* (Jørgensen 1983) and *B. bufo* (Jørgensen 1986b, 1989), reveal the complex interactions of inherent rhythms in feeding and growth with season, photoperiod, hibernation, hormonal control, feeding schedule, and quality of food in temperate zone anurans. Such detailed investigations are currently unavailable for other anurans, urodeles, and caecilians, and thus these results are but an indication of patterns likely to be present in other forms. In *B. viridis,* experiments were performed on a cohort of 1-year-old toads collected in August and fed mealworms. As growth is isometric, the nutritional condition could be assessed by calculating the condition index (CI), that is, body mass divided by the length cubed. The pattern of growth and condition is shown in figure 15.2. All toads initially grew in length and increased in body mass, but growth practically ceased by October. Growth resumed in February–March and proceeded rapidly during the spring, subsequently to decline again. By July the toads had reached body sizes typical of adult toads from the sampling locality.

Monthly growth rates were high in August and September of the first year and then dropped to insignificant levels (fig. 15.3). Growth resumed in February and reached peak values of about $5 \text{ mm} \cdot \text{month}^{-1}$ during April. The CI initially increased until September. During the period of growth stagnation, CI tended to decrease. After growth resumed in spring, the CI again increased but with a delay. It continued to increase, however, after the rate of growth in length had begun to decline.

At constant temperature and day length and with regular access to food, growth thus gradually declined and practically stopped in the autumn at the normal time for hibernation in nature. In early spring the toads again began rapid growth, even exceeding that in the beginning of the experiment. Exposure to an artificial light regimen of 18 h light and 6 h dark from October to December did not affect the growth. This agrees with the slight effects of photoperiod on growth in the frog *Rana pipiens* (Richards and Lehman 1980). Thus, an-

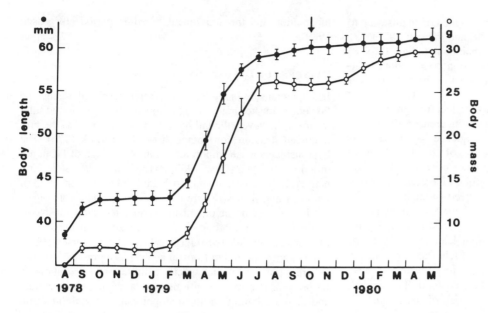

Fig. 15.2 Pattern of growth of male toads, *Bufo viridis,* over 22 months maintained at 20°C. The *arrow* indicates the development of thumb pads. ●, Body length; ○, body mass. Monthly means ±1 SEM. (Reprinted, by permission, from Jørgensen 1983.)

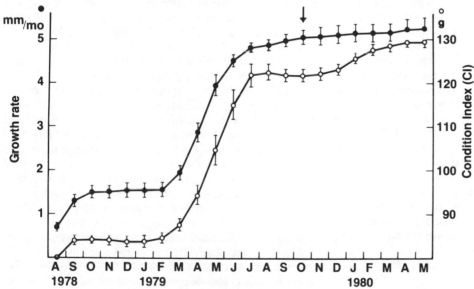

Fig. 15.3 Monthly growth rates (●) and nutritional condition (○) of toads, *Bufo viridis,* from figure 15.2.

ticipatory behavioral and physiological mechanisms adapted to the normal climatic cycle may already have become inherent in 1-year-old *Bufo viridis.*

The experiments on the second species, *B. bufo,* showed that even newly metamorphosed toadlets reduced food intake and ceased growing during the months from October to January. By January growth increased strongly, which may be interpreted as a physiological readjustment to posthibernating activity. This readjustment was strikingly revealed in the change in pattern of partitioning of food and body matter between growth in length and fat deposition. During January–February, toads grew in length independently of feeding at the expense of deposited matter, indicating internal control of growth.

Also 1-year-old *B. bufo* grew slowly when transferred to room temperature in the autumn, but in contrast to *B. viridis* this pattern did not change during prolonged exposure to a high temperature. Rapid growth was restored in 1-year-old

B. bufo only after simulated hibernation (storage at 2°C). Growth declined and ceased after periods that varied in length with the feeding level, being longer in toads fed once a week than in toads fed three times a week. A new growth period could be initiated by again exposing the toads to hibernation conditions for about half a year. Thus, hibernation is of basic importance in the annual life cycle of the toad, constituting a period during which the organism prepares for the activities of the posthibernating period, including growth (Jørgensen 1986b).

Growth depends upon circulating growth hormone (GH). The decline in feeding and discontinued growth observed in *B. bufo* in the autumn could be prevented be treating the toads with bovine GH (Wind-Larscn and Jørgensen 1987). Toads treated with daily doses of 10 μg hormone attained maximum growth rates (Jørgensen 1989). Bovine GH is thus highly potent in *B. bufo,* as in *B. marinus* and *B. boreas* (Larsen and Licht 1984; Zipser, Licht, and Bern 1969), in contrast to the bullfrog, *Rana catesbeiana*, where bovine GH in doses up to 200 μg had no effect (Farmer, Licht, and Papkoff 1977).

Treatment of toads with GH maintained high rates of feeding and growth for a longer duration than without treatment, but after some months lean growth subsided, whereas deposition continued (Jørgensen 1989). Thus GH does not qualitatively influence the sequence of feeding, growth, and deposition. This basic pattern seems inherent in the organism, but GH is required for the sequence to unfold. This unfolding is remarkably independent of the dose level of GH. At the constant dosage of 10 μg hormone injected 5 days a week, rates of food intake and growth increased over several weeks and subsequently continued at high levels for several weeks, even though the body mass of the toads increased severalfold. In *B. boreas* a dosage of 50 μg bovine GH did produce a significantly larger lean growth response than 0.3 μg of the hormone (Zipser, Licht, and Bern 1969).

In the experiments on *B. bufo*, the toads were fed mealworms dusted with vitamins as the sole food. The animals remained healthy, but they tended to deposit fat in amounts far exceeding those that normally apply in nature (fig. 15.3). Such obesity was the result not only of too much food, because it also occurred in toads kept at low rations. Figure 15.4 shows that deposition of fat predominates over protein deposition down to the lowest food intakes. The relative deposition of absorbed food as fat increases with decreasing intake, so that the fattening effect of a mealworm diet increases with decreasing rations of mealworms. A high protein catabolism, lacking adaptability to the composition of the diet, may be typical of carnivorous vertebrates (MacDonald, Rogers, and Morris 1984; Walton 1986). In toads exposed to pronounced seasonal climatic cycles, it may be considered a preadaptation (*exaptation* in the terminology of Gould and Vrba 1982). In such environments an increasing importance of protein catabolism with decreasing feeding rates tends to promote deposition of fat rather than that of protein in periods of low food availability, and thus to save the fat depots for

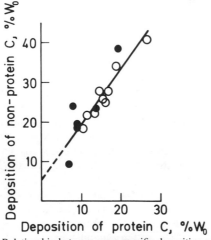

Fig. 15.4 Relationship between mass-specific deposition of protein C, expressed as a percentage of the initial body mass W_0, and deposition of nonprotein C in young female toads, *Bufo bufo*, fed mealworms for 24 h once a week (○), compared with growth rates in female toads fed similar rations distributed over 3 means (●). Inserted is the common regression line for both sets of data and its extrapolation to the y-intercept. (Reprint, by permission, from Jørgensen 1989.)

hibernation and the subsequent breeding period (Jørgensen 1989).

PATTERNS OF DEPOSITION

In amphibians, as in reptiles, fat is stored in special organs, the fat bodies, located anterior to the gonads. In plethodontid salamanders, however, the tail has taken over the role as the predominant structure for storage of fat (Fitzpatrick 1976). The liver also acts as an important organ for storage of fat in addition to glycogen (Bush 1963; Byrne and White 1975; Fitzpatrick 1976; Pasanen and Koskela 1974; Seymour 1973a). Fat-body and liver sizes are therefore good indicators of the nutritional state of the organism, as reflected in the close correlation between condition index and size of fat bodies and liver in the toad *Bufo bufo* (Jørgensen and Wind-Larsen 1987).

Fat storage occurs in tropical as well as temperate species. Whereas temperate zone species exhibit annual variations in fat-body size correlated with the annual cycle in temperature and food availability, tropical amphibians may exhibit variations in fat-body size that are comparable with those observed in temperate zone species, but with no clear annual or other pattern (Alexander 1933; Church 1960; Zug and Zug 1979). In a population of the toad *Bufo melanostictus* from Bangalore, India, the fat-body size in females varied unpredictably. At any time of the year, samples might include toads with uniformly depleted or uniformly replete fat bodies, or with fat bodies ranging from depleted to replete (table 15.5). Most of the variation in fat-body size seems to arise from local environmental conditions, but the variation is also related to the reproductive state. Fat bodies tend to be large in juvenile females and in females with ovaries in the early vitellogenic growth phase. With progressing growth of oocytes the size of the fat bodies decreases significantly. Small fat bodies prevail in toads with large oocytes and in postspawning toads. Moreover, fat bodies tend to be larger in primiparous toads as compared with the same phase of subsequent ovarian cycles (table 15.5). Seemingly, the nutritional condition prior to the first maturation is not restored before the initiation of subsequent ovarian cycles (Jørgensen, Shakuntala, and Vijayakumar 1986). An inverse relationship between ovary mass and fat-body mass is also found in the frog *Rana cyanophlyctis* from southern India (Pancharatna and Saidapur 1985) and in the salamander *Ambystoma tigrinum* (Ambystomatidae) from southern North America (Rose and Lewis 1968). Fat-body size and ovarian cycles are not correlated in other species, for example, the salamanders *Amphiuma means* (Amphiumidae) from southern Louisiana (Rose 1967) and *Taricha torosa* (Salamandridae) from California (Miller and Robbins 1954).

The size of fat bodies of amphibians inhabiting the temperate zone varies seasonally (e.g., Athanasiu and Dragoiu 1910; Du Bois 1927; Giglio-Tos 1895, 1896; Toldt 1870). It also varies greatly among individuals from the same population, even when sampled at the same time of the year (Victoroff 1908). The first thorough quantitative study of the annual variation in nutritional state, as well as the gonadal cycle, in a temperate zone amphibian was of the frog *Rana esculenta* in Switzerland (Gaule 1901).

Due to their exclusive function as depot organs, the annual rhythmic cycle in food balance of the organism is closely

TABLE 15.5 *Bufo melanostictus* Body Size, Ovary Mass, and Fat-Body Mass

Reproductive State	N	Body Mass (g)		Ovaries (% body mass)	Fat bodies (% body mass)
		Total	Without Ovaries		
Juveniles	25	39 ± 3	39 ± 3	1.1 ± 0.2	1.30 ± 0.20
Vitellogenesis					
Early growth phase	34	50 ± 3	48 ± 3	4.0 ± 0.3	1.36 ± 0.26
First ovarian cycle	24	50 ± 4			1.79 ± 0.33
Subsequent cycle(s)	10	50 ± 5			0.32 ± 0.12
Middle growth phase	40	55 ± 3	50 ± 3	9.8 ± 0.5	0.66 ± 0.14
First ovarian cycle	25	53 ± 4			0.79 ± 0.20
Subsequent cycle(s)	15	54 ± 3			0.46 ± 0.16
Late or finished growth	51	58 ± 2	46 ± 2	20.4 ± 0.6	0.27 ± 0.08
First ovarian cycle	38	59 ± 3			0.33 ± 0.11
Subsequent cycle(s)	13	56 ± 5			0.09 ± 0.06
Postspawning	18	42 ± 4	41 ± 4	2.0 ± 0.2	0.17 ± 0.06

Source: Jørgensen, Shakuntala, and Vijayakumar 1986.
Notes: Means ± SEM. Statistically significant differences: Ovaries: juveniles versus postspawning, $p < .001$. Fat bodies: early growth phase, first versus subsequent cycles, $p < .001$; early versus middle growth phase, $p < .02$; middle versus late or finished growth, $p < .05$.

TABLE 15.6 Annual Cycle of Fat-Body Mass in Some Temperate Zone Anurans

	Locality	Sex	Mean Masses of Fat Bodies (% body mass)						Reference
			Maximum	Month	Minimum	Month	Mass at Spawning	Month	
Bufo bufo	Denmark	M	1.0	Aug	0.15	Jun	0.3	Apr	Jørgensen, Larsen,
		F	ca. 1	Aug	0	May	0	Apr	and Lofts 1979
	Peking, China	M	2.3	Aug	0.05	May	0.08	Apr	Ting and Boring
		F	3.5	Aug	0.02	Jun	0.04	Apr	1940
Rana temporaria	Besançon, France	M	1.4	Oct	0.11	Apr	0.11	Apr	von Kennel 1913
		F	ca. 3	Oct–Nov	0.06	May	0.08	Apr	
	Bonn, Germany	M	0.5	Jun–Jul	0	Apr	0.05	Mar	Zepp 1923
		F	0.7	Aug	0.03	May	0.2	Mar	
	Shropshire, U.K.	F, M	0.8–0.9	Jul–Oct	0.02	May	0.04	Mar	Smith 1950
	Cracow, Poland	M	1.0	Jul–Sep	0.02	Mar	0.02	Mar	Krawczyk 1971
		F	1.3	Jul	0.03	Mar	0.03	Mar	
	Haapavesi, N. Finland	M	0.7	Sep	ca. 0.1	May	ca. 0.1	May	Pasanen and Koskela 1974
		F	0.4	Sep	0.03	May	0.03	May	
Rana esculenta	Zurich, Switzerland	M	2.0	Sep	0.12	Jun	0.12	Jun	Gaule 1901
		F	1.3	Aug–Sep	0.03	Jul	0.04	Jun	
	Bonn, Germany	M	1.2	Sep	0.13	May	0.13	May	Zepp 1923
		F	0.9	Aug	0.10	May	0.10	May	
	Cracow, Poland	M	2.3	Sep	0.08	May	0.08	May	Krawczyk 1974
		F	1.7	Oct	0.03	May	0.03	May	
Rana pipiens	U.S.	F, M	0.4	Aug	0.01	Jun	0.03	Apr	Mizell 1965

Source: Jørgensen, Larsen, and Lofts 1979.

reflected in the seasonal change in size of the fat bodies. Reasonably complete data on annual cycles in fat-body size are available for only a small number of anuran species, however (table 15.6). Comparisons of the fat-body cycles among species or among populations of the same species are difficult owing to ignorance of the time between capture and necropsy of specimens, or because of storage conditions. The recorded fat-body sizes may therefore not be representative of the populations sampled. In one instance (the frog *Rana pipiens,* Mizell 1965), the fat-body sizes recorded are obviously lower than they were in the freshly captured animals because of the treatment of the animals.

Table 15.6 shows that fat bodies generally reach their smallest size at or after the spawning period, when fat-body sizes less than 0.1% of the body mass predominate. Fat bodies of this size are practically depleted of fat (Roca et al. 1970). Other less complete studies on annual cycles in amphibian fat bodies support the view that the fat bodies in temperate zone anurans reach minimum size around the breeding time (*Bufo arenarum,* Argentina, Mazzocco 1940; *B. fowleri,* Georgia, Bush 1963), in agreement with decreased feeding until after breeding.

It is widely believed that the fat bodies in amphibians reach their maximum size in autumn at the time of hibernation, and that the fat bodies serve as an energy depot primarily during hibernation (e.g., Brown 1968; Holmes 1916). However, as shown in table 15.6, the most complete studies suggest that in populations of the toad *B. bufo* from Denmark and from

China, as well as in other temperate zone anurans, the fat bodies reach their largest size well in advance of hibernation, in agreement with the finding of declining feeding rates prior to hibernation.

Only in the northernmost populations of the frog *Rana temporaria* does the time of maximum fat-body size coincide with the start of hibernation. This may be correlated with the short duration of the feeding period and early hibernation of frogs at high latitudes. Moreover, the size reached by the fat bodies tends to be smaller in the frogs from northern Finland than in frog populations from other parts of Europe (table 15.6). In the toad *B. canorus*, living at elevations of 2,000 to 3,700 m in California, total body lipids also reached maximum at the end of the short feeding period (Morton 1981).

Thus temperate zone anurans usually begin to draw upon their energy reserves late in summer or early autumn, in advance of the hibernating period, and do not begin to accumulate energy as fat until after breeding is complete.

This annual cycle in food balance is concordant with the pattern of feeding, growth, and deposition in toads, *B. viridis* and *B. bufo*, kept at a constant high temperature in the laboratory. As mentioned, the feeding rates are not dependent solely upon the availability of food but are determined by an inherent rhythm, presumably initially synchronized with the climatic cycle of the habitat. The pattern is characterized by an initial increase in feeding rate and a concurrent increase in growth. Somatic growth gradually declines, and food is partitioned among fat depots, reflected in high condition indices and large fat bodies, before the feeding rate again declines to levels that may result in a negative food balance. The end of hibernation initiates a new feeding, growth, and deposition cycle (Jørgensen 1983, 1986b).

The large individual variation in size of fat bodies and other depots may not only reflect environmental conditions, including food availability, but may also depend upon differences in functional state of the organism. The data summarized in table 15.6 indicate that fat accumulation may differ between the sexes in sexually mature anurans, but no consistent trend is obvious, even within the same species. Thus, in populations of *R. temporaria* in France and Poland, mean fat-body size was larger in the females than in the males, whereas in Finland the reverse occurred. In Danish populations of *B. bufo* mean sizes of the fat bodies were uniform, but individual variation was more pronounced in the females than in the males.

Fat-body size in the temperate zone anurans is correlated with the functional state of the gonads, as was the case in the tropical anurans. An inverse relationship between gonadal development and size of the fat bodies was first observed in the last century in the frogs *R. esculenta* and *R. temporaria* (Ploetz 1890) and repeatedly confirmed since then (Ackermann 1949; Du Bois and Ponse 1927; Gaule 1901; Patzelt 1918). In Finland, immature males and females of *R. temporaria* possess fat bodies about twice as large as those of the sexually mature frogs prior to hibernation (Pasanen and Koskela 1974). Comparable patterns occur in *B. bufo* in Denmark (Jørgensen, Larsen, and Lofts 1979).

The above discussion on annual cycles of fat bodies in temperate zone anurans applies to species inhabiting mesic regions. However, anurans from xeric regions may exhibit similar cycles. Thus, in spadefoot toads *Scaphiopus* (Pelobatidae), from southwestern North America, the fat bodies reach their minimum size at emergence from dormancy and their maximum size when the toads enter the next period of dormancy (Jones 1980a; Long 1989; Seymour 1973a). This is in contrast to another xeric anuran from the same region, the toad *B. cognatus*, in which no clear annual cycle in fat-body size was evident (Long 1987b).

Annual cycles in fat deposition have been analyzed in few urodeles, but the anuran pattern seems to apply also to temperate zone urodeles. Maximum size of fat bodies occurs prior to hibernation and minimum size during spawning in spring or early summer, for example, in the salamandrids *Notophthalmus viridescens* in North America (Adams and Rae 1929), *Triturus vulgaris* in England (Verrell, Halliday, and Griffiths 1986), and *T. pyrrhogaster* in Japan (Tachi 1963). In *Triturus* maximum values amounted to 1–2% of the body mass, whereas minimum values might approach complete depletion of the fat bodies.

In the salamander *Amphiuma means* (Amphiumidae) from southern Louisiana, where feeding occurs throughout the year, fat-body size varies only moderately in the females. This contrasts with the pronounced annual cycle in males, in which the maximum size reaches about 4 g per 100-g lean carcass in April to July, falling to <1 g in September to November (Rose 1967).

REPRODUCTIVE MODES AND PATTERNS

The large literature dealing with reproductive modes and patterns in amphibians has been reviewed by Duellman (1978), Duellman and Trueb (1986), Lamotte and Lescure (1977), Salthe and Duellman (1973), Salthe and Mecham (1974), Taylor and Guttman (1977), and M. H. Wake (1982). Only major features and recent findings will be outlined here.

Reproductive Modes

The primitive mode of reproduction in amphibians is by means of large numbers of small eggs that are deposited in water and fertilized externally. The larvae are truly aquatic organisms until they metamorphose into the terrestrial and final stage (see chapter 16). In all three orders of amphibians, however, other reproductive modes have evolved, ranging from direct development that circumvents the aquatic larval stage, to various degrees of ovoviviparity, where the developing embryos are retained by the female or male, to viviparity where the embryos are nourished in the maternal oviducts.

The three orders vary strikingly in the extent to which derived modes of reproduction have evolved. The primitive mode predominates among the anurans, and only a few are viviparous, for example, the bufonid *Nectophrynoides occidentalis* (Xavier 1977) and the hylid *Gastrotheca riobambae* (del Pino 1989). Among salamanders only the primitive families (Cryptobranchidae and Hynobiidae) have external fertilization, and many species are direct developers, laying their eggs on land and guarding them, typical of plethodontid salamanders. A few salamandrid species, including *Salamandra*

TABLE 15.7   Allometric Relationships between Body Mass and Mass of Mature Ovaries or Number of Eggs in Ranids and Bufonids

	Locality	b^a	Reproductive Capacity	Reference
Rana nigromaculata	Japan	0.9		Kuramoto 1978
Rana japonica	Japan	1.3		Kuramoto 1978
Rana tsushimensis	Japan	1.5	M	Kuramoto 1978
Rana limnocharis	Japan	2.0		Kuramoto 1978
Rana temporaria	Denmark	1.21	M	Jørgensen 1981
Bufo bufo	Denmark	1.18	M	Jørgensen, Larsen, and Lofts 1979
Bufo viridis	Germany	1.15	N	Hemmer and Kadel 1971
		1.63	V	
	Denmark	1.16	M	Jørgensen 1984b
		1.55	M	
	Israel	1.13	M	
Bufo marinus	Panama	1.17	N	Zug and Zug 1979

Notes: M = ovarian mass; V = clutch volume; N = number of eggs.
[a] From ovary mass = a body mass^b.

atra and *S. salamandra,* are viviparous. All species of caecilians have internal fertilization. Both oviparous direct developers and viviparous species are found in the order. In the first group the females guard the clutch, which is laid on land in burrows or under vegetation. Half of the species for which the reproductive mode is known, that is, some 25 out of about 170 species, are viviparous (M. H. Wake 1982).

The total amount of yolk deposited in the ovaries during vitellogenic growth of the oocytes is correlated with the reproductive mode, the amount being highest in the species that oviposit small eggs in water. In these species, moreover, body mass and mass of the ovaries at the end of vitellogenesis are closely related. The full-grown vitellogenic oocytes constitute 90% or more of the ovarian mass, which thus is representative of the reproductive output. Its relationship to body mass can be expressed by an allometric equation: ovary mass = a Body mass^b. In anurans, ranids and bufonids, b tends to be larger than 1 (table 15.7). The species include representatives from the temperate zone and from the tropics (the toad *Bufo marinus* from the Canal Zone, Panama; Zug and Zug 1979), indicating that the reproductive capacity increases with body size, independent of climatic conditions.

The absolute reproductive output may also be independent of the climatic conditions. Thus, the mean mass of ovaries with full-grown complements of vitellogenic oocytes in 70-g female toads, *B. viridis,* from two cold temperate zone populations (Denmark) was 22 and 25% of the body mass, respectively, whereas the mean mass was 23% in a warm temperate zone population (Israel; Jørgensen 1984b).

The reproductive output may also vary between populations, however, as observed in lowland and mountain populations of the frog *Rana sylvatica* from Maryland and Virginia, respectively (Berven 1982a). The total egg volume was 7% higher in the lowland than in the mountain population. Transplantation experiments of juveniles from the lowland locality to the mountain locality and vice versa revealed that the difference was genetically fixed, and the difference was interpreted in adaptive terms.

Geographical variation in reproductive capacity is particularly well documented in European populations of the frog *R. temporaria.* In western Ireland the volume of deposited eggs amounts to about 22% of the body mass (Gibbons and McCarthy 1986, who erroneously calculated the clutch mass as the difference in weights of gravid and spent females, amounting to 36%). Weights of mature ovaries are 15–17% of the total body mass in England (Smith 1950), 12–14% in France, Germany, and Poland (Bleibtreu 1911; Gallien 1940; Krawczyk 1971; Zepp 1923), 10–13% in Denmark (Jørgensen 1981), and 10–11% in northern Finland (Koskela and Pasanen 1975). At the northern limit of distribution of the species in Sweden the mature ovaries weigh less than 10% of the body mass. Moreover, the ovarian mass amounts to 2–4% of the body mass immediately after spawning, against about 1% in more southern populations. The large mass of spent ovaries is due to the presence of a complement of follicles in early vitellogenic stages already at spawning (Elmberg 1990). Presumably, this early recruitment of oocytes to vitellogenic growth constitutes an adaptation to the climatic conditions at high latitudes and altitudes. Thus, ovarian mass in spent females tends to increase from a lowland population at Umeå, 64°N, to midaltitude (Ammarnäs) at 400 m, 66°N, to a mountain heath (Kraipe) at 800 m, 66°N (Elmberg 1990). Recruitment of small oocytes to vitellogenic growth before breeding may depend upon ovulation preceding oviposition in ranid frogs. Ovulation eliminates the inhibition that vitellogenic follicles exert on further recruitment of small oocytes to vitellogenic growth (see below). Dissociation of ovulation and oviposition in *R. temporaria* may thus constitute an exaptation for habitat expansion toward higher latitudes and altitudes in northern Scandinavia.

Variations in reproductive pattern among populations of *R. temporaria* and other anurans may thus be interpreted in adaptive terms. Part of the variation may also reflect great nonadaptive variability and plasticity in many life history traits, however, such as final body size, size at sexual maturation, and relationship between number and size of eggs, as discussed below.

In urodeles, the relative reproductive capacity mostly decreases with body mass, the value of b being lower than 1 (Danstedt 1975; Houck 1977c; Kaplan and Salthe 1979; Tilley 1968). A value of $b > 1$ has, however, been recorded in the plethodontid salamander *Gyrinophilus porphyriticus*

(Bruce 1972) and in three out of four species of *Ambystoma* (Wilbur 1977). In a fifth species, *Ambystoma annulatum* (Ambystomatidae), the relationship between egg number and body length could be described by the equation Y = 8.47 × body length (mm) − 425.6 (r^2 = 0.30; Hutcherson, Peterson, and Wilkinson 1989), indicating a value of $b < 1$ in the allometric relationship between egg number and body mass. By contrast, the linear relationship between ovarian mass and body length in the newt *Triturus vulgaris* (Salamandridae), Y(g) = 0.023 × body length (mm) − 0.75 (r^2 = 0.48) suggests an allometric coefficient (b) greater than 1. Typically, the scatter is large in data sets on urodele fecundity or reproductive capacity, and more complete data are needed.

Anurans thus resemble teleosts, in which the allometric relation of fecundity to body mass typically is described by values of $b > 1$ (Wootton 1979). This is concordant with the similar reproductive modes in teleosts and anurans, both mostly producing large numbers of small eggs, typically 1 to 2 mm in diameter, whereas urodeles produce relatively fewer but larger eggs, typically 2 to 6 mm (Duellman and Trueb 1986). The caecilians produce the largest known eggs for any amphibians, exceeding 6 mm. The number of young born in the viviparous species is not correlated with size of the female (M. H. Wake 1982).

The correlation between egg mass produced in a clutch and body size thus decreases from anurans to urodeles to caecilians, even as egg size increases. Presumably this trend is not a consequence of egg size per se, but rather a result of an increasing part of the reproductive effort being devoted to parental care. The trend culminates in the viviparous species, which, as mentioned, are exceptions among anurans and urodeles but widespread among caecilians. In viviparous species, the gestation period may be long, 11–12 months in the caecilid *Dermophis mexicanus* (Wake 1980b). The developing young in the oviducts have exhausted the yolk after 2 to 3 months of gestation at an embryonic length of 25–35 mm. At birth the young have grown to a length of 110–150 mm on the nutritive material secreted by the oviduct epithelium (see also chapter 16). Assuming isometric growth, little more than 1% of the body mass obtained is thus derived from the yolk originally present in the egg. The material secreted by the oviductal epithelium is very lipid-rich, but contains little protein (M. H. Wake 1982). This is consistent with the slow growth of the larvae in the oviducts, implying relatively high costs of maintenance.

Variability in Number and Size of Eggs Number of eggs produced is species-specific, but the actual number may vary. The variation may be genetically fixed, as observed between populations of a species, and it may be determined by the functional state of the ovaries (see below) or by environmental factors.

The variation between populations may be exemplified by the toad *Bufo viridis*, where the complements of full-grown vitellogenic oocytes in standard-sized females of 70 g amounted to about 11,000 and 15,000 in two Danish populations and 9,000 in an Israeli population (Jørgensen 1984b). As mentioned, the reproductive output in terms of egg mass was the same in the three populations. The same relative

amount of matter and energy was thus allocated to vitellogenic growth of oocytes in all the populations, but the number of oocytes that shared this ration varied. The number of oocytes recruited to vitellogenic growth was presumably genetically determined in the Danish populations of *B. viridis*, whereas much of the variation among the toads from Jerusalem was apparently phenotypic, as indicated by the large inverse variation in number and size of full-grown oocytes (Jørgensen 1984b). Such phenotypic variation in number of oocytes recruited to vitellogenic growth, and thus of final oocytes size also occurred in the frog *Rana temporaria* (Jørgensen 1981). In frogs this variation was correlated with age, the egg number decreasing and egg size increasing with age, whereas total egg volume remained constant (*R. temporaria:* Gibbons and McCarthy 1986; *R. sylvatica:* Berven 1988).

Differences in egg size among populations of amphibian species have been interpreted in evolutionary terms as adaptations of the populations to their particular environments (Kaplan 1980; Koskela and Pasanen 1975; Kozlowska 1971; Pettus and Angleton 1967; Salthe and Duellman 1973; Salthe and Mecham 1974; Takahashi and Iwasawa 1988; B. D. Woodward 1982). However, phenotypic variation in number and size of eggs within populations may equal that observed to be genetically fixed between populations. Moreover, differences that have been interpreted as adaptations to climatic factors may be equally pronounced between populations that live under presumably identical environmental conditions, for example, Danish populations of the toads *Bufo bufo* and *B. viridis* (Jørgensen, Larsen, and Lofts 1979; Jørgensen 1984b). Differences in number and size of eggs, as well as their interrelationships, may therefore reflect the great plasticity of the ovarian system that regulates these relationships (discussed below) combined with the tendency of amphibian populations to differentiate into more or less isolated demes. This tendency is particularly pronounced in Danish *B. viridis*, which typically inhabit small islets (Jørgensen 1984b). Much of the variation in number and size of eggs between amphibian populations and demes may thus have arisen from genetic drift rather than natural selection.

Number and size of eggs produced may also be influenced by environmental factors, such as food and temperature. Thus, in the toad *Bombina orientalis* (Discoglossidae), both number and size of eggs spawned was higher in females fed ad libitum than in females fed a ration corresponding to half the ad libitum intake. Toads at both feeding regimens produced more eggs at 24°C than at 16°C, but the eggs tended to be smaller at the higher temperature. Temperatures of 24° and 16°C correspond to the natural temperature variation during the breeding season (Kaplan 1987).

Reproductive Pattern

Reproductive patterns are correlated with the climatic conditions prevailing in the habitats. In equatorial habitats with a constantly warm and humid climate, amphibians may reproduce throughout the year, for example, the frog *Rana erythraea* on Borneo (Inger and Greenberg 1963) and the toad *Bufo melanostictus* in Singapore and Djakarta (Berry 1964; Church 1960).

In regions with pronounced wet and dry seasons, for example, southern India, the main breeding season for *B. melanostictus* coincides with the monsoon rains, but spawning may also occur outside this period (Jørgensen, Shakuntala, and Vijayakumar 1986). No fixed species-specific pattern seems to couple a main breeding period to the climatic conditions. Thus, in Bangalore, south India, the main breeding coincides with the height of the monsoon rains during August–October, whereas in Dharwar, 400 km northwest of Bangalore, the breeding period is June–August, in the early part of the monsoon rains (Kanamadi and Saidapur 1982).

Similarly plastic relations occur in the toad *B. regularis,* the commonest toad throughout Africa (Inger and Greenberg 1956) and probably the most studied of African amphibians other than *Xenopus laevis.* Mostly, breeding coincides with the beginning of the rainy season: in September–October in Egypt when the fields are flooded by the rising Nile (Boulenger 1880), from November to April in a dammed pool in Tanganyika (Chapman and Chapman 1958), in March in Kenya (Keith 1968), and in October in southeast Zaire (Inger and Greenberg 1956). Both in Kenya and Zaire, *B. regularis* breeds at the beginning of the heavy rains. Less well-defined breeding seasons are recorded in urban Lagos, Nigeria, where breeding coincides with the beginning and the end of the main rainy season, extending from April to July, and with the short rainy season September–October (Winston 1955). In Sierra Leone, Menzies (1963) recorded main breeding from October–December to May during the relatively dry season that follows the heavy rains, and he concluded that the very heavy rainfall, amounting to 15–20 inches per month during June–October, inhibits toad breeding.

In Panama, the population of the toad *B. marinus* inhabiting the Canal Zone breeds during the late dry season and early wet season, in contrast to a population inhabiting the more xeric Azuero Peninsula that breeds in the mid- or late wet season (Zug and Zug 1979). The authors hypothesize that "stream breeding toad populations might have been selected for dry season reproduction, because of the low flow rate of that time . . . ; whereas temporary or shallow-pond toad populations breed in the wet season when the ponds are full and stable" (11).

Other tropical amphibians exhibit breeding patterns similar to those exemplified in the bufonids. Basically, tropical amphibians are capable of breeding throughout the year. However, even slight annual variation in environmental conditions tends to establish breeding cycles. Annual variation in precipitation seems to be the main factor in inducing periodicity in breeding activity. The degree to which such periodicity is established varies among species as well as among populations of a species. The same habitat may accommodate species or populations exhibiting a range from little to pronounced annual reproductive cyclicity. The tendency toward reproductive cyclicity seems to be a basic feature of ovarian function in amphibians.

The trend toward seasonal breeding, correlated with climatic cycles in temperature and precipitation, is reinforced in the temperate zones. In mesic habitats, breeding is primarily correlated with the seasonal cycle in temperature, precipitation playing a secondary, modifying role in the timing of breed-

ing, whereas in xeric habitats, precipitation is the dominant environmental factor in controlling breeding, for example, spadefoot toads, *Scaphiopus* (Pelobatidae), throughout North America (Gosner and Black 1955; Hansen 1958; Trowbridge and Trowbridge 1937) and the frog *Microhyla carolinensis* (Microhylidae) in Oklahoma (Bragg 1950).

The remarkable adaptability in amphibian reproductive patterns is well illustrated by a species pair of leopard frogs (*Rana pipiens* complex) occurring in sympatry along the coast of western Mexico in a climate that theoretically is compatible with reproduction at any time of the year. The two populations exhibit well-defined, temporally separate breeding seasons, however, one species, *R. magnaocularis,* being a fall-winter breeder, the other, *R. forreri,* a spring-summer breeder (Frost 1983).

The seasonal synchronization of breeding increases with increasing latitude and altitude. This may be observed also within a species distributed over a wide latitudinal range, such as the toad *Bufo viridis.* Populations in Israel do not hibernate, and they may breed throughout the year, mainly correlated with the annual pattern of precipitation. *B viridis* usually breeds in temporary ponds, and breeding thus depends upon the rainy season filling the ponds. But breeding can occur outside the main breeding period if new ponds are established, for example, through watering. The Mediterranean populations of *B. viridis* may therefore be characterized as opportunistic breeders. Danish populations, in contrast, breed in a well-defined season, usually in June, correlated with a substantial rise in temperature. The toads breed in localities with permanent water, and precipitation may be of little importance (Jørgensen 1984b).

The duration of the breeding season may vary from several months to days, as in the species that breed in large aggregations, the so-called explosive breeding of some ranids and bufonids. Typically, the temperate zone explosive breeders, such as the Eurasian frog *Rana temporaria* and toad *Bufo bufo,* also breed early in the season, immediately after emergence from hibernation in the spring. Of all anurans, *R. temporaria* occurs farthest to the north, closely followed by *B. bufo* (Darlington 1957; Terhivno 1981). Explosive early breeding presumably constitutes an exaptation for penetration into habitats compatible with short active periods. Explosive breeding seems, however, not to be a climatic adaptation. Spawning aggregations comparable with those in temperate zone *B. bufo* have also been observed in populations of *B. melanostictus* in the tropics (Bangkok [Smith 1917]; Assam [McCann 1932]).

Actual spawning, including ovulation, is usually believed to be controlled exclusively by external factors (Salthe and Mecham 1974), although such factors are poorly understood. Courtship and, in anurans, amplexus are ascribed an especially important role in stimulating ovulation. Bragg (1941) observed ten species of North American anurans, including the genera *Bufo, Hyla, Scaphiopus,* and *Rana,* and he concluded that in all species ovulation occurred only when the female had been clasped by the male. Such generalization seems unwarranted, however, because in some anurans, including species studied by Bragg, ovulation may take place prior to amplexus, for example, in the hylids *Pseudacris ni-*

grita (Gosner and Rossman 1959) and *Hyla crucifer* (Oplinger 1966). In some species, ovulation seems obligatory for amplexus, for example, *Rana pipiens*, in which nonovulated females avoid amplexus by emitting a release call when clasped by males (Diakow 1978; Noble and Aronson 1942). In species that may ovulate prior to amplexus, other stimuli may serve to trigger ovulation, especially the call of the males (Gosner and Rossman 1959; Oplinger 1966). In the toad *Bufo bufo*, contact with water seems to be a major factor in eliciting ovulation (Heusser 1963, 1968b).

In cold temperate zone species, breeding may become increasingly independent of direct environmental control. At the northern limit of distribution, *Rana temporaria* may enter amplexus during hibernation without any obvious change in the environmental condition in the hibernation quarter in the mud in ice-covered rivers (Koskela and Pasanen 1974, 1975). The date of spawning correlates with mean air temperature, the date ranging from April in southern Finland to May in northern Finland (Terhivno 1988). This timing of the spawning is not only controlled by the ambient temperature, however, but governed by an internal rhythm synchronized with local environmental conditions. Thus, male and female *R. temporaria* from a northern population (64°N) spawned 5 to 17 days later than frogs from a southern population (61°N) when kept at the same temperature in spring (Harri and Koskela 1977). This inherent control of breeding has been confirmed in artificially hibernating frogs, kept in water at low temperatures and in constant darkness, under which conditions female frogs ovulated and oviposited in the absence of males (Allison 1956; Jørgensen 1984c; Juszczyk and Zamachowski 1965; Koskela and Pasanen 1975). Both ovulation and oviposition were, however, delayed in the artificially hibernating frogs. Oviposition may be more sensitive to adverse environmental conditions than is ovulation.

Ovulation before mating would seem to depend upon a means of storing the eggs prior to oviposition, which is normally coordinated with amplexus on the spawning grounds. Oviductal sections for storing have evolved in some genera, such as *Rana* and *Hyla* (Hylidae), whereas they are absent in *Bufo*, for example (Gaupp 1896–1904; Noble 1931).

In species with short breeding periods the whole complement of vitellogenic oocytes in the ovaries matures and is ovulated and spawned simultaneously (Duellman and Trueb 1986). This pattern also applies in many species with long breeding periods, and even in the tropics, for example, in the toad *B. melanostictus* (Jørgensen, Shakuntala, and Vijayakumar 1986). Spawning may also occur repeatedly, with smaller portions of vitellogenic oocytes maturing at a time. The number of spawnings may depend upon the length of the breeding season and may decrease with increasing latitude within the range of geographical distribution of a species (Duellman and Trueb 1986).

Repeated spawnings occur in several anuran families, for example, *Discoglossus pictus*, France (Knoepffler 1962), *Bombina variegata* and *B. bombina* (all Discoglossidae), Germany (Kapfberger 1984; Obert 1977), and *Dendrobates granuliferus* (Dendrobatidae), Costa Rica (Crump 1972). But repeated spawnings have also been recorded in other anuran families, for example, the leaf frog *Pachymedusa dacnicolor* (Hylidae), Texas (Iela et al. 1986), *Hyperolius viridiflavus*

(Hyperoliidae), Kenya (Richards 1977), and some ranids, *Rana esculenta*, Italy (Rastogi, Izzo-Vitiello, Di Meglio, Di Matteo, Franzese, Di Costanzo, Minucci, Iela, and Chieffi 1983), *R. catesbeiana*, Michigan (Howard 1978b), and *R. clamitans*, New York (Wells 1976a). In the ranids, only females that spawned early in the season produced a second but smaller clutch about a month later. In the laboratory, *Dendrobates auratus* females produced about ten clutches during a breeding period of about 3 months (Senfft 1936). The salamander *Pleurodeles waltl* (Salamandridae) breeds about every second month during the breeding period (Gallien 1952).

Repeated spawnings during the reproductive season may depend upon the establishment of a pool of oocytes in advanced stages of vitellogenesis, from which complements of oocytes to final vitellogenic growth and maturation may be recruited. Such a pattern of the annual ovarian cycle has been demonstrated in the clawed frog *Xenopus laevis* (E. Billeter pers. comm.).

Biannual breeding can occur within a population that normally spawns only once a year. Thus, a pair of the salamander *Triturus cristatus* (Salamandridae) that bred in April and was kept in an indoor vivarium bred again in November, laying fertile eggs (Simms 1968). The oocyte growth patterns determining monophasic and polyphasic breeding patterns are dealt with below.

Biennial Gonadal Cycles Biennial breeding has been reported in a number of amphibians, particularly among North American plethodontid salamanders, including several species of *Desmognathus* and *Plethodon* as well as the genera *Pseudotriton* and *Ensatina* (Bull and Shine 1979). In all these genera the female broods the egg clutches, which in most species are deposited on land under decaying logs and rocks, in cliff crevices, and in other hidden nesting sites.

Because of the difficulties in directly observing breeding in these species, the evidence for a biennial pattern is usually a bimodal size distribution of the largest follicles in the ovaries during the prebreeding season. Advocates of biennial ovarian cycles assume that the females with large oocytes are those that are going to breed during the next breeding season. The females with ovaries in early oocyte growth stages are assumed to be those that bred during the foregoing breeding season and which, due to low oocyte growth rates, will produce eggs ready for spawning a season ahead.

A closer inspection of the data on which biennial breeding is assumed in female plethodontids discloses, however, that the evidence for bimodal distributions of largest follicles may be inconclusive, for example, in *Plethodon jordani* (Hairston 1983), *P. wehrlei* (Hall and Stafford 1972), *P. cinereus* (Nagel 1977; Sayler 1966), *P. neomexicanus* (Reagan 1972), *P. richmondi* (Angle 1969), *P. glutinosus* (Highton 1962), *Ensatina eschscholtzi* (Stebbins 1954), *Leurognathus marmoratus* (Martof 1962), *Pseudotriton montanus* (Bruce 1975), and *Desmognathus santeetlah* (Jones 1986). Conclusive examples also exist, for example, *Plethodon vehiculum* (Peacock and Nussbaum 1973) and *Desmognathus ochrophaeus* (Organ 1961).

The breeding period must be known before drawing conclusions about biennial ovarian cycles from a bimodal size distribution of largest follicles. Often, time and duration of breeding are only imprecisely known because breeding is temporally separated from courtship and mating, and oviposition sites are hidden.

The examples listed above as inconclusive are characterized by large variation in size distribution of the largest follicles within the population, suggestive of protracted breeding periods. Tendencies towards bimodal size distributions would also arise if breeding activities have bimodal trends. Two breeding seasons a year have in fact been reported in populations of plethodontid species exhibiting bimodal ovarian patterns, for example, *Plethodon cinereus* (Davidson and Heatwole 1960) and *Desmognathus ochrophaeus* (Fitzpatrick 1973a; Tilley 1970; Tilley and Tinkle 1968). In North Carolina, *D. ochrophaeus* showed two peaks of egg laying, a summer and a winter, correlated with a bimodal size distribution of largest follicles, which was interpreted as indicating a biannual reproductive cycle (Tilley and Tinkle 1968). Tilley (1970) revised the interpretation to annual cycles, implying that about half of the females in the population lay and brood eggs during the summer and the other half during the winter. Subsequent studies were also consistent with annual breeding in *D. ochrophaeus;* however, females occasionally skip an ovarian cycle (Forester 1977; Keen and Orr 1980; Tilley 1977).

Biennial ovarian cycles in plethodontids inhabiting the temperate zone have been interpreted in energetic terms, brooding and hibernation limiting the gathering of food needed for an annual vitellogenic cycle (Highton 1962; Bull and Shine 1979). This interpretation was consistent with the findings of annual breeding pattern at the southern range of some species, for example, *Plethodon glutinosus*, which is an annual breeder in Florida (Highton 1956). Therefore, biennial ovarian cycles in females of Neotropical plethodontids, including the genera *Bolitoglossa, Pseudoeurycea,* and *Chiropterotriton,* are unexpected. Dichotomies in ovarian functional states, ova sizes, and parental behavior all imply such cycles in tropical plethodontids (Vial 1968; Houck 1977a, 1977b). As mentioned, however, the distribution of follicle sizes does not permit definitive conclusions about patterns of oviposition. Rates of vitellogenic growth of oocytes should also be known. A crucial argument for the biennial ovarian cycle in Neotropical plethodontids is a slow rate of oocyte growth. From mark-recapture data in a population of *Bolitoglossa subpalmata*, Costa Rica, Vial (1968) assumed that the period from beginning vitellogenic growth of oocytes to ovulation lasted 10 months or more. However, documentation for this assumption seems inadequate. Much higher rates of oocyte growth have been recorded from other urodeles, including plethodontids. Thus, in a population of *Eurycea multiplicata*, oocytes increased in diameter from less than 1.0 mm in July to full size of about 2.5 to 3.0 mm in November (Ireland 1976). Similar growth rates were found in *Pseudotriton montanus* (Bruce 1975).

Biennial ovarian cycles are also reported from other groups of urodeles. Thus, in *Amphiuma tridactylum* (Amphiumidae), size distribution of large follicles suggested a biennial ovarian cycle (Cagle 1948). In *Ambystoma maculatum* (Ambystomatidae), mark-recapture data of migrating animals collected at the breeding pond over 5 years indicated a very irregular breeding pattern, with an average interval between

visits to the breeding pond of 3 years in both males and females (Husting 1965). Incomplete recapture of marked individuals may have affected this result.

Irregular breeding patterns in both sexes also occur in the salamanders *Taricha torosa* and *T. rivularis* (Salamandridae). In populations in California and Oregon, about half of adult-size animals had immature gonads. The breeding or nonbreeding status was independent of the nutritional state, as both groups had equally well-developed fat bodies, amounting to 2–3% of the body mass in the males and 1–2% in the females, during the normal breeding season (Miller and Robbins 1954). Presumably, breeding in alternate seasons is not obligatory, because mark-recapture data from Oregon provided examples of animals that bred in successive years (Pimentel 1960).

Environmental control of gonadal cycles is evident in the European salamander *Triturus alpestris* (Salamandridae). Lowland populations breed annually, but those in the Alps at 1,300 m breed biennially, as evidenced from analyses of the gonadal status (Vilter and Vilter 1963). Also the females of the viviparous *Salamandra salamandra* and *S. atra* (Salamandridae) may breed at intervals of 1 or more years, depending on the elevation of the habitats in the Pyrenees and Alps (Gasser and Joly 1972; Vilter and Vilter 1960; Wunderer 1910). In high-altitude populations of *S. salamandra* from the Pyrenees, the biennial ovarian cycle has become partly a genetically fixed adaptation but is partly under direct environmental control. Thus, at an elevation of 1,000 m the ovarian cycle is biennial, and the ovaries remain immature during the year of gestation. At 550 m, however, some females initiate the next ovarian cycle during the gestation period and thus breed annually (Gasser and Joly 1972). The breeding pattern in high-altitude female *S. salamandra* is probably the best-documented example of a biennial ovarian cycle, in concert with a long gestation period and a short feeding period as an adaptation to energetical constraints.

Breeding at intervals of more than 1 year has also been reported in the females of some toads (*Bufo cognatus*: Bragg 1940; *B. americanus*: Blair 1943; and *B. bufo*: Heusser 1968c) and one frog (*Rana pretiosa*: Licht 1974; Turner 1958). However, only the data from *R. pretiosa* seem conclusive. The breeding patterns were studied by mark-recapture in a lowland population in British Columbia, and at the high elevation of 2,600 m in Yellowstone Park, Wyoming. The data are consistent with annual breeding in the lowland population but indicate breeding cycles for females of 2–3 years in the mountains, correlated with annual active periods of about 8 months and 3–4 months, respectively, in the two habitats (Licht 1974).

The Annual Cycle A resting period may follow breeding before a new ovarian cycle is initiated. Eagleson (1976) equated "resting" with "refractory." As long as evidence is lacking for a true refractory state of the reproductive system, however, the resting period is better characterized as a period of restitution of the organism. Resting periods are most evident in populations of anurans that exhibit short early spawning periods. Although early spawners may have longer resting periods than late spawners, the length of the resting period decreases with increasing latitude. Thus, the resting period in

TABLE 15.8   Resting Period between Spawning and Next Ovarian Cycle in Some Temperate Zone Anurans

	Locality	Month of Spawning	Duration of Resting Period (months)	Reference
Bufo bufo	Denmark	Apr	2–3	Jørgensen, Larsen, and Lofts 1979
	Peking, China	Apr	2–3	Ting and Boring 1940
Rana temporaria	France	Mar	3–4	Gallien 1940
	Germany	Mar	3–4	Bleibtreu 1911; Zepp 1923
	Poland	Mar	3–4	Krawczyk 1971
	England	Mar	3–4	Smith 1950
	North Scandinavia	May	0	Koskela and Pasanen 1975; Elmberg 1990
Rana arvalis	Poland	Apr	2–3	Jastrzebski 1968
Rana esculenta	Switzerland	May–Jun	1–2	Gaule 1901
	Poland	May	2	Juszczyk and Zamachowski 1973
Rana pipiens	Northeast United States	Apr	1–2	Zahl 1937
	Wisconsin	Apr–May	2–3	Mizell 1964
Rana catesbeiana	Washington	Jun–Jul	0	Byrne and White 1975
Rana nigromaculata	Peking, China	Apr	3–4	Ting and Boring 1940; Maruyama 1979

Source: Jørgensen, Larsen, and Lofts 1979.

female *Rana temporaria* is 3–4 months in middle Europe but is reduced to 0 in northern Scandinavia (table 15.8).

Ovarian quiescence after breeding in temperate zone, spring-breeding anurans and urodeles (Eagleson 1976; Ireland 1976) may be adaptive, ensuring that vitellogenesis is postponed until the energy reserves of the organism are restored. This interpretation is supported by the finding that freshly spawned female toads, *Bufo bufo,* fed in the laboratory, resume vitellogenic growth of oocytes with little delay (Jørgensen 1973b).

After breeding of several months' duration, resting before a new ovarian cycle is initiated also occurs in nonhibernating anurans inhabiting xeric regions in southern North America, for example, the microhylid *Microhyla carolinensis* (Anderson 1954) and the hylid *Acris crepitans* (Fisher and Richards 1950).

In *B. bufo* (and probably other anurans as well as urodeles), a mechanism that synchronizes the reproductive cycle with the climatic cycle restricts the time of year in which an ovarian cycle can begin. Thus, in *B. bufo* in Denmark an ovarian cycle normally does not begin later than July, ensuring that vitellogenic growth of the oocytes is complete before hibernation (Jørgensen 1975).

Both the onset of sexual maturation and subsequent ovarian cycles apparently involve an endogenous cyclicity in the reproductive system that ensures its activation at the proper time of year. This endogenous cycle is not entirely innate in *B. bufo.* If newly metamorphosed toads are kept at a high temperature and fed abundantly, they will grow quickly and become sexually mature unseasonally (Jørgensen 1986b). The seasonal cycle seems to become established during the first year of life in toads exposed to the climatic cycle. The endogenous cycle renders the reproductive system insensitive to a stimulatory environment in autumn and winter when the completion of a vitellogenic growth phase normally is impossible. Presumably, the potential for activation of the reproductive system, alternating with insensitivity of the system toward suitable external conditions, resides centrally at the level of the central nervous system–hypophysis, as discussed below.

In vertebrate reproduction, "refractoriness" refers to the phenomenon in which virtually all species of birds and many reptiles become insensitive during the breeding season to continued optimal environmental conditions (Follett 1984; Licht 1984). The refractory state prevents breeding too late in the season for the successful raising of the offspring. In *B. bufo,* and probably other cold temperate zone amphibians as well, the refractory state is not established to discontinue a seasonal breeding sequence, but it is already established in the immature organism to synchronize the onset of sexual maturation in the juvenile female toad with the climatic cycle (Jørgensen 1988b).

ALLOCATION OF MATTER AND ENERGY
Allocation to Somatic Growth and Reproduction

As mentioned, growth in amphibians is basically indeterminate, but sexual maturation is typically correlated with an abrupt decline in the rate of somatic growth in anurans (e.g., *Rana erythraea:* Brown and Alcala 1970; *R. temporaria:* Ryser 1989; *Bufo bufo:* Gittins, Steeds, and Williams 1982; Hemelaar 1986, 1988) as well as urodeles (the plethodontid *Desmognathus ochrophaeus:* Tilley 1980; the salamandrid *Triturus vulgaris:* Verrell 1987; and several Neotropical plethodontids, Houck 1977c). Halliday and Verrell (1988) review the relationship between body size and age in amphibians and reptiles. The decline in rate of somatic growth is particularly pronounced in females, in which somatic growth may approach zero concurrently with the initiation of the first ovarian cycle of vitellogenic growth of oocytes (Jørgensen 1986b). Vitellogenesis constitutes so large an investment in matter and energy that continuation of the rate of somatic growth during juvenile stages would imply a substantial increase in total production. Reduction in somatic growth at the onset of vitellogenic growth of a complement of oocytes in female amphibians may therefore be interpreted in terms of reallocation of matter and energy in the food (Iles 1974; Jørgensen 1986b). The mechanisms behind such reallocation are discussed below.

In males, sexual maturation and reduction in rate of somatic growth is less tightly coupled (Jørgensen 1986b). This is consistent with the marginal energetic cost of spermatogenesis. Moreover, the onset of sexual maturation is poorly defined in amphibian males. Spermatogenesis may start far in advance of the development of secondary sexual characters, as discussed below. Sexual maturation in the males may be defined better by the development of these characters.

Allocation to Fattening and Reproduction

The inverse relationship between mass of ovaries and fat bodies has been interpreted as indicating that the fat bodies store fat for use in vitellogenic growth of oocytes (Fitzpatrick 1976). This interpretation disregards the small size of the stores in the fat bodies compared with the amounts of fat deposited in the ovaries during vitellogenesis. (Other aspects of fat body–gonad relationships are discussed below.) By contrast, fat as well as protein stored in the tail of plethodontid salamanders may serve as a depot for vitellogenic growth of oocytes. Thus, in *Plethodon cinereus* (Plethodontidae), oocyte size is significantly correlated with tail volume, reflecting the size of the stores (Fraser 1980). In unfed *Batrachoseps attenuatus* (Plethodontidae), removal of the tail prevented the animals from becoming reproductive, unlike the controls with intact tails (Maiorana 1977). The importance of the tail for reproduction in plethodontid salamanders is consistent with completion of the reproductive state during the dry season when the animals retreat underground and do little or no feeding.

The inverse relationship between mass of ovaries and of fat bodies reflects the character of vitellogenesis and deposition as alternative processes, representing different functional states of the organism. In adult females in which an ovarian cycle has been initiated, mass is allocated to vitellogenic growth at the expense of fat bodies and other depots. Vitellogenic growth proceeds at a fixed rate above threshold levels of food intake (Jørgensen 1975). Increases in fat stores therefore depend on how much actual food intake exceeds this threshold. If temperate zone female amphibians do not initiate an ovarian cycle (e.g., because the conditions in the organism for such an event do not materialize before refractoriness), the ovaries do not compete for mass and energy in the food for the rest of the active season, and mass may be available for deposition of fat (Jørgensen 1973a). Thus, female toads that reach the size and development compatible with sexual maturation too late in the season will enter hibernation with immature ovaries, but the fat bodies may be large. The incidence of such adult-sized immature females at the time of hibernation varies, but it may be high. In *Bufo bufo* sampled just before onset of hibernation, thirty out of forty-nine adult-sized females were immature, which represents an unusually high proportion. The dichotomy in ovarian development was correlated with fat-body size. In the sexually mature females, sixteen possessed small fat bodies, up to 0.5% of the body mass, and only three had fat bodies between 0.5 and 2%. In the immature toads, only five had small fat bodies, and in eleven, fat-body masses ranged from >2 to >6% (table 15.9). In the five immature toads with reduced fat bodies, the lack of vitellogenic growth of oocytes may be due to an inferior nutritional condition that prevents the initiation of an ovarian cycle or causes atresia of vitellogenic

TABLE 15.9   The Relationship between Sexual Maturity and Fat-Body Size in a Sample of Adult-sized Female *Bufo bufo* at the Onset of Hibernation

Sexual State	N	Number of Toads in Which Fat Bodies Constitute:		
		≤0.5% Body Mass	>0.5–2% Body Mass	>2–6% Body Mass
Immature	30	5	14	11
Mature	19	16	3	0

Source: Jørgensen 1973a.

oocytes if a cycle has been initiated (Adams and Rae 1929; Jørgensen 1967; Jørgensen, Larsen, and Lofts 1979; Penhos 1952). The large fat bodies in immature toads presumably stem from the absence of vitellogenic growth in the ovaries due to environmental and/or internal factors other than food availability or feeding behavior.

A comparable instance concerns the toad *B. canorus* collected in or near the breeding pools in June (Morton 1981). As mentioned, fat bodies were small at emergence and breeding, as is normal in temperate zone amphibians and particularly this species, which lives at 2,000 to 3,700 m elevation. However, five adult-sized female toads collected at the same time about 750 m from the nearest major breeding site, and therefore presumably immature, had large fat bodies. In fact, they constituted the fattest group of toads collected at any time of the year.

GONADAL FUNCTION
Ovarian Cycle

Production of oocytes and their development into full-grown eggs in amphibians and other groups of lower vertebrates has until recently been considered a linear, sequential process. It has been assumed that ovulation of the mature follicles is followed by proliferation of oogonia and their differentiation into new follicles, whereas follicles already present in the ovaries proceed through further growth stages to establish a new complement of full-grown oocytes (Gaupp 1896–1904; Franchi, Mandl, and Zuckerman 1962; Lofts 1974; Nussbaum 1880; Smith 1955; Tokarz 1978). In temperate zone amphibians, this conception implies that the number of eggs shed during the breeding season is determined when the oocytes arise from a wave of oogonial proliferation, usually 3 years in advance of the ovulation of the full-grown follicles. However, more recent studies have not confirmed such rigid, sequential coupling of the stages from oogonial proliferation to final maturation of a complement of eggs (Jørgensen 1973b, 1984a).

Pool of Small Oocytes   Two categories of oocytes are evident in the amphibian ovary, small, gonadotropin-independent oocytes and larger, gonadotropin-dependent oocytes (Franchi 1962). The two categories differ strikingly in their patterns of growth and population dynamics, as well as in their relationships to the environment.

The number of small, nonvitellogenic oocytes increases rapidly in the ovaries of metamorphosed female amphibians. In the toad *Bufo bufo,* their number reaches a maximum by an early juvenile stage, to remain more or less constant

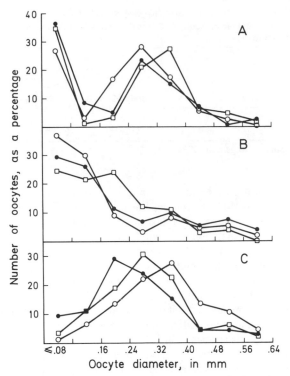

Fig. 15.5 Examples of types of size-frequency distribution of small oocytes in *Bufo bufo*. *A*, three toads in the stage of early oogenesis; *B*, three toads in the stage of late oogenesis; *C*, three toads in the resting stage. (Reprinted, by permission, from Jørgensen 1984a.)

throughout life at about 30,000 to 40,000 oocytes. This indicates that influx of oocytes to the pool balances efflux (Billeter and Jørgensen 1976). Influx of oocytes is episodic, following waves of oogenesis *sensu stricto*. An influx episode is evident from the size-frequency distribution of the small oocytes in the ovary. In the resting stage, the modal oocyte diameter is about 0.3 mm (fig. 15.5C). During an influx event, very small (<0.08 mm) oocytes proliferate (fig. 15.5A). Within a month new oocytes may grow to sizes up to 0.16 mm or more and become incorporated in the existing pool of small oocytes. An influx event is followed by a resting period, probably lasting for about 1–2 years. Oogenesis is not coordinated with ovulation or recruitment of oocytes to vitellogenic growth, and it occurs also in the ovaries of sexually immature toads (Jørgensen 1984a). Oogenic episodes are not correlated with the seasons and may also occur at low temperature, for example, in hibernating *R. temporaria* (Jørgensen 1984c).

Oogenesis proceeds synchronously in the two ovaries, indicating that the initiation of an oogenic episode is basically under systemic control, but the factors that control oogenesis are not well understood. Presumably, gonadotropin is not involved (Billeter and Jørgensen 1976; Jørgensen 1973b). The nutritional condition of the organism may be of importance (Jørgensen 1984a). Oogenesis may be provoked by unilateral ovariectomy, which in the toad caused a compensatory response that restores the normal pool size of small oocytes within about 5 months. Presumably, the mechanisms that control oogenesis and pool size of small oocytes are of a somatic-type growth control (Jørgensen, Billeter, and Poulsen 1979).

The pool of small oocytes serves as a reserve from which oocytes can be recruited to vitellogenic growth, normally at sexual maturation and after ovulation but also after atresia of a complement of vitellogenic oocytes. Even though oocytes in the pool usually amount to about five times the normal number recruited to vitellogenic growth, practically all small oocytes can become available for spontaneous recruitment, for example, by reducing the pool size by excision of ovarian mass (Vijayakumar, Jørgensen, and Kjaer 1971).

The pool of small oocytes and its mechanisms of control constitute a robust, highly dynamic system that is relatively independent of the environment. This is in striking contrast to the system that comprises growth, maturation, and ovulation of a complement of vitellogenic follicles, the ovarian cycle, which is closely linked to the environment.

Vitellogenic Phase The recruitment of a complement of small oocytes to vitellogenic growth initiates an ovarian cycle, which proceeds at a uniform rate until the oocytes are full-grown (Jørgensen 1973b, 1975; Jørgensen, Billeter, and Poulsen 1979). Vitellogenic oocyte growth is synchronous, as shown by the size-frequency distribution of the large oocytes during the growth phase in toads and frogs both from the temperate zone (*Bufo bufo, B. viridis,* and *Rana temporaria*: Jørgensen 1974b, 1984b, unpublished data; fig. 15.6) and the tropics (*B. melanostictus*: Jørgensen, Shakuntala, and Vijayakumar 1986).

Whereas synchronous growth of vitellogenic oocytes may prevail in the individual female, patterns of growth within a population vary with the environment, for example, from basically asynchrony in the tropics to more or less complete synchrony in cold temperate climates. This trend can be observed within species with a large latitudinal range of distri-

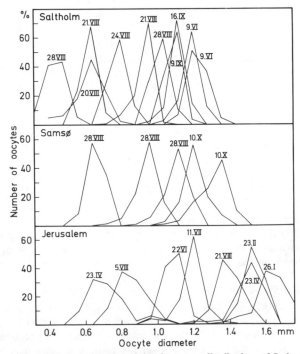

Fig. 15.6 Typical examples of size-frequency distributions of *Bufo viridis* oocytes during vitellogenic growth in populations from two Danish islets (Saltholm and Samsø) and from Jerusalem, Israel. (Reprinted, by permission, from Jørgensen 1984b.)

bution, such as the toad *B. viridis*. In Israel, ovarian cycles may proceed throughout the year, but in Denmark they proceed only in late summer and autumn (Jørgensen 1984b).

In amphibians from the cold temperate zone, the vitellogenic oocytes reach sizes required for subsequent maturation of the follicles before hibernation commences, at least in species that breed shortly after emergence from hibernation, for example, the toad *B. bufo* (Jørgensen, Larsen, and Lofts 1979) and the frog *Rana temporaria* (Jørgensen 1984c) in Denmark. This pattern of an ovarian cycle may constitute an adaptation to the low temperature prevailing during hibernation, which prevents vitellogenic growth. Thus, oocyte growth ceases in toads with ovaries still in the vitellogenic phase when exposed to 4°C, a hibernation temperature. Oocyte growth resumes at its normal rate when the toads are returned to room temperature after 2.5 months (Jørgensen, Hede, and Larsen 1978).

In species from the warm temperate zone, vitellogenic growth of oocytes may proceed during periods of estivation in the absence of feeding. Thus, both the mesic *Bufo woodhousii* and the semiarid-adapted *B. cognatus* more than doubled ovarian mass during dormancy (Long 1987a, 1987b). Also in spadefoot toads, *Scaphiopus* (Pelobatidae) Seymour (1973a) found the major part of vitellogenic growth to take place during dormancy. In contrast, Long (1989) found no change in ovarian mass during 6–7 months' dormancy in *Scaphiopus multiplicatus*. However, the large oocytes increased in diameter from 1.04 ± 0.08 (SE) to 1.38 ± 0.04 mm. Throughout the active period, volume of large oocytes is closely correlated with ovary mass, as expressed in the equation: oocyte volume (mm³) = −19.3 + 1.07 ovary mass (mg) (r^2 = 0.79), based on data from table 1 in Long's article. The relationship shows that large follicles of uniform size predominate, indicating synchronous growth of vitellogenic oocytes. The number recruited presumably varied markedly, however, from a mean of 683 in the postdormancy toads to a mean of 1,210 in the toads collected June to mid-August, when the last mating was observed. Long (1987a, 1987b, 1989) interpreted his results both in *Bufo* and *Scaphiopus* as indicating asynchronous growth of vitellogenic oocytes and ovulation of only the largest follicles, the smaller being retained as a reserve to allow for reproductive preparedness for opportunistic breeding. Also the xeric Australian anuran *Cyclorana platycephala* (Hylidae) does not release all eggs in one spawning, but stores eggs over winter to secure reproductive readiness at any time of the year (van Beurden 1979). Further studies are needed to establish the ovarian functional patterns in individual females of these xeric an-

urans, including size-frequency distributions of oocytes in individual ovaries throughout the year.

Vitellogenic oocyte growth may also continue in salamanders that spend the winter in subterranean refuges, for example, the salamandrid *Taricha torosa* (Miller and Robbins 1954) and the plethodontids *Desmognathus ochrophaeus* (Tilley and Tinkle 1968), *Plethodon richmondi* (Angle 1969), and *P. jordani* (Hairston 1983).

In temperate zone mammals, birds, reptiles, and teleost fishes, seasonal variation in day length is paramount in timing the reproductive cycle (Lamming 1984). This is in contrast to amphibians, in which the annual light cycle seems unimportant in controlling the gonadal cycles. Complete darkness has no significant effect on vitellogenic growth of oocytes in *Xenopus laevis* (Bellerby 1937) or *Rana pipiens* (Brenner and Brenner 1969). In the toad *Bufo fowleri* ovarian cycles start and proceed independently of photoperiod, ranging from 4 to 20 h (Bush 1963).

However, artificial light regimens may affect normal vitellogenic growth. Thus, female toads, *B. bufo*, exposed to photoperiods of 14 h light to 10 h dark (LD 14:10) and LD 6:18 in the spring, recruited normal complements of oocytes to vitellogenic growth. The incidence of atresia among the vitellogenic oocytes was higher than in the toads that remained at natural day lengths, and atresia was more pronounced at LD 6:18 than at LD 14:10. At the LD 6:18 regimen, recruitment was abortive in six out of eighteen toads, all oocytes degenerating immediately after commencing vitellogenic growth (table 15.10). The deficient ovarian cycles at the artificial-light regimens were not nutritionally determined, since all toads ate the same rations (K. Poulsen pers. comm.). Adverse effects of artificial light regimens on vitellogenic growth were also evident in the bullfrog, *R. catesbeiana*, where exposure to photoperiods of <8 h and >14 h enhanced atresia as compared with an LD 12:12 photoperiod (Horseman, Smith, and Culley 1978).

Growth and maintenance of vitellogenic oocytes depends upon circulating gonadotropin, and extirpation of the pars distalis of the hypophysis results in degeneration of vitellogenic stages of oocytes in both anurans and urodeles (Lofts 1974). The role of gonadotropin in the ovarian cycle could be analyzed in the toad *B. bufo* by administering human chorion gonadotropin (hCG) to females without vitellogenic oocytes. In immature females, females after breeding in the spring, nonvitellogenic females late in the season (Jørgensen 1975), and hypophysectomized females with degenerated oocytes, treatment initiated an ovarian cycle. At a constant dosage throughout, a complement of oocytes was recruited to vitel-

TABLE 15.10 Effect of Light Regimen on Vitellogenic Growth of Oocytes in *Bufo bufo*

| Light Regimen | Normal Recruitment and Growth of Vitellogenic Oocytes | | | |
	Slight Atresia	Medium Atresia	Massive Atresia	Abortive Recruitment
Daylight	20	0	0	0
14 h light, 10 h dark	13	5	0	2
6 h light, 18 h dark	3	3	6	6

Source: K. Poulsen pers. comm.

logenic growth within some weeks, after which no further recruitment occurred. The transition in the ovarian cycle from the recruitment phase to the phase of synchronous vitellogenic growth thus does not depend upon a concomitant regulation of gonadotropic activity but is presumably the result of intraovarian regulatory mechanisms in which the vitellogenic complement of oocytes inhibits further recruitment. The existence of such mechanisms is indicated by the finding that treatment with hCG, which causes recruitment to vitellogenic growth in females with ovaries that lack vitellogenic oocytes, is without effect in females with ovaries that do contain complements of vitellogenic oocytes (Jørgensen 1974b). Moreover, if a complement becomes atretic, a new complement may immediately enter the vitellogenic growth phase (Jørgensen, Hede, and Larsen 1978).

Vitellogenic growth proceeds until the normal size of fullgrown oocytes is reached, about 3 months at 20°C. Thus, the entire growth phase of an ovarian cycle may proceed at a constant level of circulating gonadotropin, supporting the concept that unknown intraovarian mechanisms regulate the normal pattern of the vitellogenic phase (Jørgensen 1975, 1982).

Maturation Phase   At hibernation, the function of the ovary of early breeders, such as *Bufo bufo* and *Rana temporaria*, presumably switches from vitellogenic growth to follicular maturation. The oocyte size attained at the onset of hibernation thus determines the actual egg size. This size is not precisely fixed but can vary with the stage in oocyte growth at hibernation. Thus, in frogs (*R. temporaria*) prematurely exposed to hibernating temperatures, follicles mature and ovulate at oocyte volumes about half the typical volume (Jørgensen 1984c). Conversely, if toads (*B. bufo*) are maintained at high temperature in the period of natural hibernation, the oocytes continue vitellogenic growth and may reach double normal volume before the oocytes die (Jørgensen, Hede, and Larsen 1978). Also, eggs were larger in laboratory-maintained frogs (*R. pipiens*) than in nature (Smalley and Nace 1983).

Exposure to low temperatures in hibernating amphibians may be an important factor in the control of the annual ovarian cycle. The importance of low temperatures may be greater in species that breed immediately after hibernation (Jørgensen, Hede, and Larsen 1978; Jørgensen 1984c). Even in early breeders, however, exposure to hibernation temperatures during winter may not be obligatory. Thus, more than half of a group of toads (*B. bufo*) that was kept during winter at about 13°C bred in March, and the eggs developed into larvae (Jørgensen, Hede, and Larsen 1978). Presumably, the significance of low temperatures in controlling the ovarian cycle may also vary with latitude within a species, but direct evidence for this assumption is lacking.

Maturation of follicles under the influence of low temperatures is slow. During maturation, sensitivity toward ovulation-inducing gonadotropin gradually increases (Rugh 1948). In the toad *B. bufo* the sensitivity to hCG increases gradually throughout hibernation (Jørgensen, Hede, and Larsen 1978). In species such as the frog *R. temporaria*, which may ovulate before emergence from hibernation, the duration of the maturation process terminating in ovulation may reflect a genetically fixed adaptation to the duration of the winter prevailing at the population's latitude. Such an assumption is supported by natural differences in timing of oviposition in nature that remain when frogs from different areas overwinter and spawn in a common environment (Koskela and Pasanen 1975).

Ovulation   Rupture of the mature follicles and extrusion of the eggs into the body cavity terminate a normal ovarian cycle. Injection of gonadotropin, for example, hCG, into mature females induces ovulation in frogs and toads (Houssay 1949; Lofts 1974). The reliability of this response led to its use for pregnancy diagnosis (Galli Mainini 1947). Presumably, the action of gonadotropin on the follicles is indirect, probably via progesterone secreted by the follicle cells. This was indicated by the finding that the injection of a specific inhibitor of 3β-hydroxysteroid dehydrogenase resulted in complete inhibition of gonadotropin-induced ovulation in the frog *R. pipiens*, whereas the effect of progesterone was unaffected (Wright 1971). Ovulation may be induced by a number of steroids, but progesterone is the most potent (Smith and Ecker 1970, 1971).

Natural ovulation is induced by a "surge" of gonadotropin in the blood, as observed in the bullfrog, *R. catesbeiana* (fig. 15.7; McCreery and Licht 1983). The hormonal control of ovulation in amphibians thus adheres to the general vertebrate pattern (see also chapter 3). Figure 15.7 also shows a concomitant peak in the blood level of progesterone, compatible with its supposed role as the hormonal inducer of ovulation.

Human Chorion Gonadotropin as Gonadotropin Agonist
In evaluating studies using a heterologous hormone, assessing its potency relative to the endogenous hormone is important. The daily dose of hCG used to sustain vitellogenesis in toads was 50 IU · 100 g^{-1} body mass, corresponding to 3.5 μg · 100 g^{-1} (Amir 1972). The hormone is only slowly eliminated; at daily injections the concentration remains at about one-fifth of initial levels for two-thirds of the time, and the hormone is distributed in 25% of the body mass (Roos and Jørgensen 1974). Accordingly, the predominating level in the circulation is approximately 30 ng · ml^{-1}. This level is at the upper end of the range of gonadotropins circulating in the blood of freshly caught female bullfrogs in the months from May to July (fig. 15.8).

The dose of hCG needed to induce ovulation in the prebreeding toads is 7 to 35 μg · 100 g^{-1} (Jørgensen, Hede, and Larsen 1978). Distributed in the extracellular space, this corresponds to initial concentrations of 400 to 2,000 ng · ml^{-1}, decreasing to about 160 to 800 ng · ml^{-1} after 4 h (Roos and Jørgensen 1974). These concentrations are within the range of those of luteinizing hormone (LH) measured in the plasma of ovulating bullfrogs (fig. 15.7). hCG and homologous gonadotropin(s) thus seem to be equipotent in sustaining the vitellogenic growth phase and in inducing ovulations. hCG, an LH analogue, is sufficient to support vitellogenic growth of the oocytes in toads with extirpated pars distalis, indicating nonspecific gonadotropin receptors on the membranes of the toad ovary follicles.

Nature of Gonadotropin Action
The nature of gonadotropin action varies with the phases of an ovarian cycle. During the vitellogenic phase a long-lasting sequential pattern of dif-

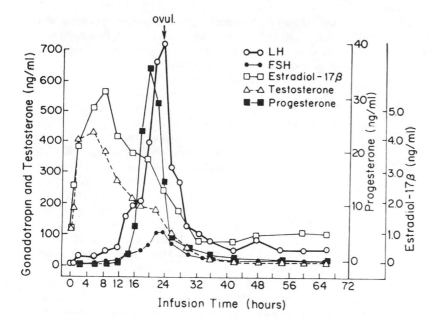

Fig. 15.7 Changes in plasma gonadotropins (luteinizing hormone [LH] and follicle-stimulating hormone [FSH]) and ovarian steroids in a preovulatory female bullfrog (*Rana catesbeiana*) infused continuously with gonadotropin-releasing hormone. The *arrow* indicates the time when ovulation was first observed. (Reprinted, by permission, from McCreery and Licht 1983.)

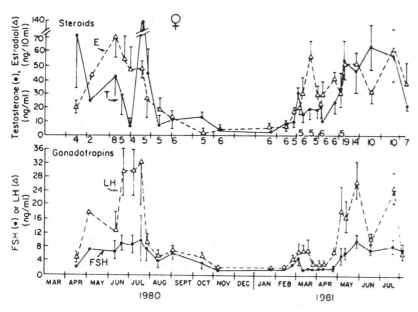

Fig. 15.8 Seasonal changes in plasma gonadotropin (luteinizing hormone [LH] and follicle-stimulating hormone [FSH]) in female bullfrogs (*Rana catesbeiana*) sampled immediately after capture in California. Means ± 1 SEM. (Reprinted, by permission, from Licht et al. 1983.)

ferentiation and growth may occur at a constant level of gonadotropin, indicating that gonadotropin plays a general permissive role, rather than a specific regulatory role during this phase. The pattern may thus be predominantly controlled by intraovarian mechanisms (Jørgensen 1974b, 1982). Such a permissive nature of gonadotropin in maintaining ovarian function may be general in vertebrates, also applying to the menstrual cycle in the mammalian female (Pohl and Knobil 1982).

A permissive role of gonadotropin eliminates the necessity of postulating a complex interplay between the ovaries and the gonadotropic system during the vitellogenic phase of an ovarian cycle. It also renders a precise regulation of gonadotropin secretion unnecessary. Above threshold levels of circulating gonadotropin, a normal vitellogenic phase may proceed independently of actual concentrations. This concept is consistent with the highly varying concentrations of gonado-

tropins in the blood of wild female bullfrogs, *R. catesbeiana*. Notably, the concentrations varied independently of the functional state of the ovaries (fig. 15.8; Licht et al. 1983).

In contrast, the ovulatory "surge" of gonadotropin seems to exert a more specific action in initiating the processes that within hours lead to the rupture of the follicular wall surrounding the oocyte and the subsequent expulsion of the oocytes. This difference in nature of gonadotropin action in the two phases of the ovarian cycle may be related to the character of the phases. The vitellogenic phase is predominantly metabolic in nature, characterized by long-lasting synthesis of vitellogenin in the liver and its subsequent incorporation in the yolk of the growing oocytes (Lofts 1984). By contrast, ovulation is an acute process in which gonadotropin specifically stimulates the follicle cells to secrete progesterone as the second step in the sequence that leads to ovulation. Common to both gonadotropin functions is their all-or-none nature. The complete processes may proceed above threshold values of circulating hormone, but actual concentrations may vary considerably (figs. 15.7 and 15.8).

The Adverse Environment The vitellogenic growth phase is very sensitive to adverse conditions of starvation and light, which may cause atresia among the vitellogenic oocytes as well as reduced rate and synchrony of growth of the surviving oocytes (*Plethodon cinereus* [Plethodontidae]: Fraser 1980; *Xenopus laevis:* Holland and Dumont 1975; Wallace 1978; *Bufo bufo:* Jørgensen 1982, 1986b). Even in well-fed toads and frogs in the laboratory, the vitellogenic growth of the oocytes tends to be less synchronous and atresia more common than in nature. The deterioration of the normal growth pattern progresses with time (Jørgensen, Hede, and Larsen 1978; Shapiro and Zwarenstein 1933; Smalley and Nace 1983). In *Xenopus laevis,* crowding affects ovarian growth more strongly than underfeeding (Alexander and Bellerby 1938). Presumably, these effects result from declining levels of circulating gonadotropin, because treatment with hCG could induce or maintain normal ovarian cycles even in toads that were emaciated from starvation (Jørgensen 1982). Transfer to the laboratory also reduces plasma gonadotropins to low levels in female *Rana catesbeiana* (Daniels and Licht 1980). As discussed below, gonadotropin secretion depends upon central nervous stimulation. An adverse environment may therefore compromise ovarian function through the nervous system.

The integrative function of the central nervous structures that maintain gonadotropin secretion at appropriate levels is more easily suspended than are the functions that control the secretion of other hypophyseal hormones such as thyrotropin and corticotropin (Jørgensen 1974a).

TESTICULAR CYCLE
Spermatogenic Patterns

Lofts (1974, 1984) has made excellent reviews of the extensive literature on testicular cycles in amphibians. Spermatogenesis is basically similar in all vertebrate classes. It starts with mitotic divisions of spermatogonia and progresses through the meiotic spermatocyte stages to the maturation stages as the spermatogenic wave, terminating in the insertion of spermatozoan bundles into the Sertoli cells. In anurans at optimal temperatures, the duration of a spermatogenic wave from the proliferation of nests of secondary spermatogonia to the maturation of spermatozoans lasts about 5 to 6 weeks (*Xenopus laevis:* Kalt 1976; *Bufo bufo:* Guha and Jørgensen 1978a; *Rana esculenta:* Rastogi, Iela, Di Meglio, Di Matteo, Minucci, and Izzo-Vitiello 1983; the hylid *Hyla japonica:* Toyoshima and Iwasawa 1984c).

During the spermatogenic wave, the stages proceed synchronously. In the young male amphibian (e.g., the toad *Bufo bufo*) when the first generation of seminiferous tubules has differentiated in the testes, spermatogenesis may begin simultaneously in all the tubules to establish a synchronous wave of spermatogenesis in the whole organ. However, as the animal grows and additional tubules differentiate, spermatogenesis becomes increasingly asynchronous, and seminiferous tubules in all stages of spermatogenesis may occur mixed in the testes (Jørgensen and Billeter 1982). In a constant environment such as the laboratory, moreover, spermatogenesis may continue throughout the year.

Asynchronous continuous spermatogenesis presumably is characteristic of anuran and perhaps other amphibian males living in constant environments, for example, in the tropics, but analyses of spermatogenesis in such regions are lacking. However, in tropical southern India where the temperature is constantly high, ranging between about 20° and 30°C, but where wet seasons alternate with dry seasons, the spermatogenic status throughout the year has been quantitatively evaluated in five species from numbers of cell nests, spermatozoan bundles, and free sperm within the seminiferous tubules. Three species show little annual variation, namely, the toad *Bufo melanostictus* (Kanamadi, Saidapur, and Nadkarni 1983; Mondal and Basu 1960; Thyagaraja and Sarkar 1971) and the frogs *Rana cyanophlyctis* (Saidapur and Kanamadi 1982; Saidapur and Nadkarni 1975a) and *R. hexadactyla* (Saidapur 1983). One species, however, the frog *R. tigrina,* shows a pronounced annual cyclicity in spermatogenesis, which discontinues during the dry season in winter and early spring (Basu and Mondal 1961; Saidapur and Kanamadi 1982; Saidapur and Nadkarni 1975b). Spermatogenesis is also cyclic in the toad *B. marinus* (Saidapur 1983).

Both the species with continuous and with cyclic spermatogenesis could be sampled in the same locality, for example, around Dharwar in southern Bombay. In *Rana tigrina* the annual cycle in spermatogenesis is correlated with estivation during the dry season, when spermatogenesis is discontinued, whereas the species with continuous cycles may be active throughout the year. Moreover, *R. tigrina* has a short breeding period of 2–3 weeks, whereas the species with continuous spermatogenesis are capable of breeding throughout the year, with a main breeding period around the monsoon rains in the autumn.

Cyclicity in spermatogenesis becomes more pronounced with increasing latitude, correlated with the climatic cycle. In the cold temperate zone, spermatogenesis ceases during hibernation, to be resumed after spermiation during breeding. But the process may remain potentially continuous, as occurs in anuran species including the European *Rana esculenta* (Galgano 1936), *R. graeca, R. latestei* (Cei 1944), *R. iberica* (Crespo and Cei 1971), the Japanese *R. catesbeiana* and *Hyla japonica* (Toyoshima and Iwasawa 1984a; Yoneyama and Iwasawa 1985), and the South American leptodactylid frogs *Pleurodema cinerea, P. tucumane,* and *P. bibronii* (Cei 1961).

In the cold temperate zones a further spermatogenic pattern has evolved in which the cyclicity is inherent and independent of the climatic cycle (van Oordt 1960). This pattern was first identified in ranid frogs from northern Europe, *R. temporaria, R. arvalis,* and *R. dalmatina* (Cei 1944; Witschi 1924). It also occurs in one South American *Pleurodema* species, *P. bufonina,* which penetrates into the high latitudes of Patagonia (Cei 1961). The pattern was analyzed in detail in *R. temporaria* (van Oordt 1956). Spermatogenesis is not resumed after breeding in early spring, but only after a lag period, even under optimal environmental conditions. Inherent cyclicity may also occur in some urodeles. Thus, whereas high temperatures induce a new spermatogenic cycle in the salamander *Plethodon cinereus* late in the quiescent period, they fail to do so early in the period, suggesting that the organism has become refractory to a stimulating environment (Werner 1969).

Environmental Control

In tropical amphibians (e.g., in the south Indian anurans with cyclic spermatogenesis), the seasons of precipitation or drought may induce the spermatogenic cycle. In the temperate zones temperature is obviously the predominant environmental factor. Low temperatures thus inhibit spermatogenesis in anurans (Nussbaum 1906b; Galgano 1936; van Oordt 1956) as well as in urodeles (Ifft 1942; Werner 1969).

Light is of little or no importance in controlling spermatogenesis. In *Rana temporaria* complete darkness during the period of spermatogenesis from April to June did not affect the spermatogenic wave (van Oordt and van Oordt 1955), nor did constant darkness or light in the newt *Notophthalmus viridescens* (Ifft 1942). Other authors report on some effects of light on the normal spermatogenic cycle. However, the effects are erratic. In *R. esculenta* complete darkness stimulated spermatid production, whereas continuous light caused degeneration of spermatocytes (Rastogi 1976; Rastogi et al. 1976). In June, daily light regimens of both LD 21:3 and LD 3:21 enhanced degeneration of spermatocytes, as compared with an LD 12:12 regimen in an experiment made in June. In September only the ultralong light period affected spermatogenesis adversely, and in November neither ultralong nor ultrashort periods had any effect (Rastogi et al. 1978). Similar erratic results occur in *Hyla japonica*: complete darkness stimulated spermatocyte production at 30°C but not at 17°C, whereas both complete darkness and continuous light stimulated differentiation into spermatids at 17°C but not at 30°C (Toyoshima and Iwasawa 1984b).

The most convincing evidence for an effect of photoperiod on spermatogenesis is from the salamander *Plethodon cinereus* (Werner 1969). Spermatogenic cycles were followed from the onset at three light regimens, LD 8:16, LD 12:12, and LD 16:8, at two temperatures, 10° and 20°C. In experiments performed in spring, longer daily periods of light accelerated spermatogenesis, particularly at the higher temperature. In winter the effect occurred only at the higher temperature. However, the effects of photoperiod were modest compared with the enhanced rates of spermatogenesis caused by the increase in temperature.

Gonadal function in the male is less dependent upon the nutritional condition of the organism than is gonadal function in female amphibians. Thus, Nussbaum (1906a) observed normal spermatogenesis in starving frogs, *Rana temporaria*, after the breeding period. In the newt *Notophthalmus viridescens*, starvation during the period of spermatogenesis in early summer was also without measurable effects (Ifft 1942). However, longer-lasting starvation affects spermatogenesis. In toads (*Bufo bufo*) starved for 10 weeks at room temperature after simulated hibernation for 6 months, spermatogenesis had progressed as in the fed controls after 1 month. But,

at the end of the experiment, the number of secondary spermatogonial cysts was strongly reduced, indicating that spermatogenesis was severely affected. The secondary spermatogonial stage is the gonadotropin-dependent stage in the spermatogenesis in toads (Guha and Jørgensen 1978b). Starvation may therefore depress spermatogenic activity by reducing the rate of gonadotropin secretion (Guha, Jørgensen, and Larsen 1980).

Juvenile Spermatogenesis

Spermatogenesis is usually identified with sexual maturity. However, in several anuran species spermatogenic waves may arise during early development before secondary sexual characters develop. Spermatogenesis in larval or newly metamorphosed frogs has been termed "prespermatogenesis" (Champy 1913; Witschi 1924) or "precocious" spermatogenesis (Iwasawa and Kobayashi 1976; Kobayashi and Iwasawa 1988; Swingle 1921), and it is stated to end with degeneration of the spermatogenic nests before completion of the spermatogenic cycle. However, in some species the juvenile spermatogenic cycle may proceed to the formation of spermatozoans with no clear difference from the adult spermatogenic cycle, for example, in frogs *Rana catesbeiana* (Swingle 1921) and *R. esculenta* (Rastogi, Iela, Di Meglio, Di Matteo, Minucci, and Izzo-Vitiello 1983) and the toads *Bufo lentiginosus* (King 1907) and *B. bufo* (Jørgensen and Billeter 1982). In *B. bufo* the early phase of tubule formation proceeds directly into the phase of normal spermatogenesis.

Gonadotropin

In adult male amphibians, normal testis function depends upon secretion of gonadotropin. This dependence may, however, develop gradually. Thus, normal spermatogenic activity occurs in hypophysectomized larvae of the frog *Alytes obstetricans* (Discoglossidae; Disclos 1970). Also, the testes of hypophysectomized juvenile toads contain almost normal numbers of secondary spermatogonial nests 2 months after surgery (Jørgensen and Billeter 1982), whereas in sexually mature toads spermatogenic activity practically ceases within 1 month after hypophysectomy (Guha and Jørgensen 1978b).

Hypophysectomy in adult male amphibians interrupts spermatogenesis, and eventually only primary spermatogonia remain in the seminiferous tubules, as observed in several species of both anurans and urodeles (see references in Guha and Jørgensen 1978b). In the frog *Rana temporaria* (van Oordt 1956) and the toad *Bufo bufo* (Guha and Jørgensen 1978b), only the premeiotic spermatogenic stages are gonadotropin-dependent. Once the stage of primary spermatocytes is reached, the remaining part of the cycle proceeds without significant degeneration of nests or cells.

In hypophysectomized male toads (*Bufo*), daily injections of 5 IU or about 3.5 μg hCG $\cdot$ 100 g^{-1} body mass maintains both high levels of spermatogenesis and interstitium function, as revealed in the full development of the secondary sex characters, the thumb pads (Guha and Jørgensen 1978a; Jørgensen 1984d). This dosage establishes a predominating level in the circulation of about 10 ng $\cdot$ ml^{-1}, which is similar to the plasma level of LH in the bullfrog male during the months from March to July (fig. 15.8). Notably, hCG acted both as a potent follicle-stimulating hormone (FSH) and LH agonist, spermatogonia and interstitium being about equally sensitive.

During the normal annual testis cycle, spermatogenesis and activity of the interstitium proceed independently, and the development of the interstitium begins only in the autumn when spermatogenesis is declining (Lofts 1964; Jørgensen, Larsen, and Lofts 1979). This pattern may be typical of cold temperate zone anurans exhibiting an annual cycle in testis function, both in species with a discontinuous and those with a potentially continuous cycle (*Rana esculenta:* Lofts 1964; *R. temporaria:* van Oordt 1960; van Oordt and Lofts 1963). Therefore, the normal annual testis cycle depends upon a temporal pattern of secretion of two gonadotropins that act on cells with higher specificities toward the endogenous gonadotropins than toward hCG (Jørgensen 1984d). In the bullfrog, *R. catesbeiana,* the action of LH on the interstitium has a high specificity. Homologous LH was potent in stimulating androgen secretion, whereas *Rana* FSH was without effect. The hormones were equipotent in stimulating spermiation, however, and LH stimulated divisions of the secondary spermatogonia in two out of three frogs. FSH was active in all of three treated frogs (Muller 1976).

Nature of Gonadotropin Action

In long-term hypophysectomized toads, *Bufo bufo,* the seminiferous tubules showed extensive histological dedifferentiation, which could be reversed by daily injections of low doses of hCG (Guha and Jørgensen 1978a). The gonadotropin agonist thus exerts trophic functions, including differentiation and development of the seminiferous tubules, stimulation of spermatogenesis, and multiplication and growth of the interstitial cells, leading to hyperplasia and hypertrophy of the tissue, as well as specific functions, including secretion of androgen from the interstitium and spermiation. The range of actions of gonadotropin in the male toad is thus comparable to that observed in the female.

Significance of Gonadotropin Levels in Blood

The long-lasting phases of vitellogenic growth, maturation of ovarian follicles, spermatogenesis, and androgen secretion of the testicular interstitium proceed at low levels of circulating gonadotropin. By contrast, ovulation and spermiation require "surges" in gonadotropin secretion, acutely increasing the circulating gonadotropin level by an order of magnitude. The significance of the different levels needed in the two phases in the gonadal cycles may be to prevent premature release of gametes and to synchronize ovulation and spermiation during actual breeding.

Central Nervous–Hypophyseal–Gonadal Axis

The relationships among the central nervous system, the hypophysis, and the gonads, as well as other peripheral organs and structures under hypophyseal control, are basically similar in all vertebrate classes (Ball 1981; Crews and Silver 1985; Fasolo, Franzoni, and Mazzi 1980; Jørgensen 1974a; Licht and Porter 1987; Peter 1983). These basic elements include a central nervous hypophysiotropic area, which communicates with the pars distalis through neurons that terminate on the capillaries in the median eminence. The transmitter substances liberated into the blood reach the adenohypophyseal cells through the portal vessels, as shown in the toad in figure 15.9.

In the female amphibian, normal ovarian function, including vitellogenic growth of oocytes and ovulation, depends upon intact vascular connections with the brain. In the toad *Bufo bufo,* ectopic transplantation of the pars distalis of the hypophysis in females bearing complements of growing vitellogenic oocytes consistently results in degeneration of the oocytes, whereas in most of the toads with the pars distalis regrafted onto the median eminence the follicles survive and continue to grow (van Dongen et al. 1966; Jørgensen 1968). The ectopically transplanted pars distalis continues to secrete gonadotropin at low levels, as indicated by abortive recruitment of oocytes to the vitellogenic growth, even after extirpation of the hypothalamic-hypophysiotropic area. Such recruitment is not seen in hypophysectomized toads (Vijayakumar, Jørgensen, and Kjaer 1971). Presumably, the level of gonadotropin needed to sustain vitellogenic growth increases with increasing size of the oocytes (Jørgensen 1968). Also, in the newt *Triturus cristatus* (Salamandridae), ectopic transplantation of the hypophysis causes degeneration of mature oocytes and prevents vitellogenic growth (Mazzi, Vellano, and Vottero 1979).

In male toads the ectopically transplanted pars distalis is capable of maintaining normal spermatogenesis, whereas the interstitium regresses (van Dongen et al. 1966). In the frog *Rana esculenta* (Rastogi and Chieffi 1972) and two salamandrid urodeles, *T. cristatus* (Mazzi 1970; Mazzi and Peyrot 1963) and *Pleurodeles waltl* (Pasteels 1960), ectopic transplantation of the pars distalis strongly reduced or abolished both spermatogenesis and function of the interstitium, which atrophied. Presumably, the transplanted pars distalis may continue to secrete gonadotropin at low levels, because in *R. esculenta* a pars distalis transplanted into a testis maintains normal spermatogenesis and causes hyperplasia of the interstitium in the vicinity of the graft (Husson 1970).

Central nervous components control hypophyseal function and mediate environmental control of gonadotropic function. Transection at various levels of the nerve tracts terminating at the median eminence indicate that in the frog *R. temporaria* the structures that maintain gonadotropin secretion during the ovarian and testicular cycles are located in the ventral posterior hypothalamus in the infundibulum. When this region is surgically isolated from the rest of the brain, the pars distalis secretes gonadotropin in amounts sufficient to maintain vitellogenic growth of oocytes in female frogs, as well as spermatogenesis and thumb pads in males. By contrast, the functions are absent in frogs in which the connections through the portal vessels are interrupted (Dierickx 1966, 1974). Frogs in which the infundibular region is isolated from the brain, however, do not ovulate. Ovulation also fails to occur in frogs with lesions in the anterior hypothalamus that destroy the preoptic nucleus. This region of the hypothalamus, which has no obvious role in the vitellogenic phase of the ovarian cycle, may thus be involved in the stimulation of go-

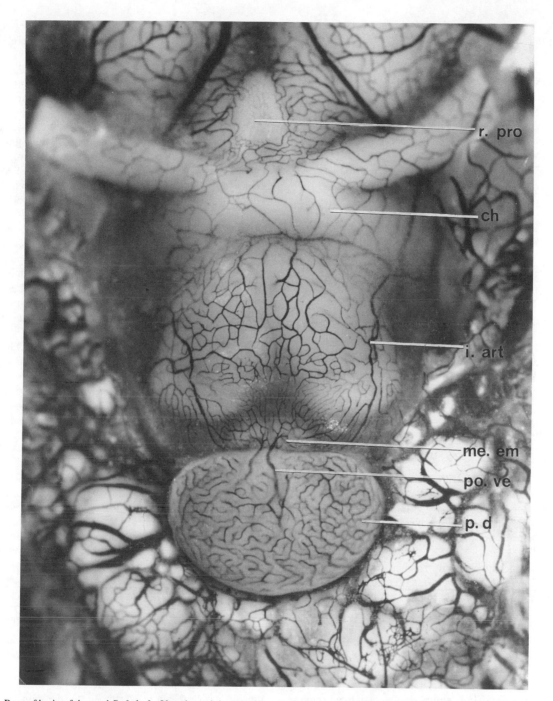

r. pro

ch

i. art

me. em

po. ve

p. d

Fig. 15.9   Base of brain of the toad *Bufo bufo*. Vessels are injected with India ink gelatin suspension. *ch*, optic chiasma; *i. art*, infundibular ar- teries; *me. em*, median eminence; *p. d*, pars distalis; *po. ve*, portal ves- sels; *r. pro*, preoptic recess. (Courtesy of K. G. Wingstrand original.)

nadotropin in amounts resulting in the ovulatory "surge" (Dierickx 1967a, 1967b). In the bullfrog, *R. catesbeiana*, graded electrical stimulation of the preoptic area causes graded release of gonadotropin (McCreery 1984), supporting this conclusion.

In the newt *Triturus cristatus*, gonadotropin secretion in amounts needed to support gonadal cycles depends upon in- tact connections to structures located more anteriorly than in anurans. Insertion of a barrier in the brain at the level of the

anterior commissure abolishes spermatogenesis and vitello- genic growth of oocytes (Mazzi 1978; Mazzi, Vellano, and Andreone 1978; Mazzi et al. 1979) and blocks oviposition (Malacarne and Giacoma 1978).

During recent years, research in central nervous–hypo- physeal–gonadal relationships in vertebrates, including am- phibians, has followed two main lines, both based on the advances made in purifying, identifying, measuring, and synthesizing peptides and steroids (see chapter 3). One line

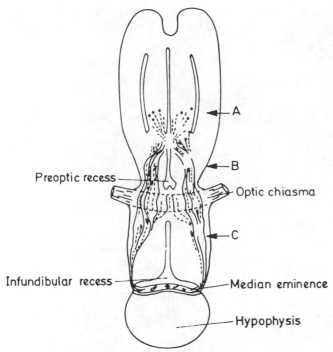

Preoptic recess

Optic chiasma

Infundibular recess

Median eminence

Hypophysis

A

B

C

Fig. 15.10 Diagram of the distribution of gonadotropin–releasing hormone (GnRH)–secretory neurons and fiber pathways in the forebrain of *Xenopus laevis*. *A,* two groups of GnRH-like cells in the septal zone of the telencephalon; *B,* GnRH-like cells on either side of the preoptic recess among the neurosecretory fibers; *C,* GnRH-like cells in the infundibulum. (From Doerr-Schott and Dubois 1975, modified by Lofts 1984. Reprinted by permission.)

is concerned with the identification and actions of the transmitter substances that control gonadotropin secretion, the gonadotropin-releasing hormones (GnRH), as well as their analogues. The other line uses immunohistochemical techniques for identifying and localizing GnRH neurons in the brain.

GnRH is a decapeptide of which five homologues have been identified in vertebrate classes (Peter 1986; Sherwood et al. 1988). Amphibian GnRH seems chemically identical with the mammalian GnRH (McCreery et al. 1982; Sherwood, Zoeller, and Moore 1986). In frogs, salmon and chicken-I GnRH were equipotent with mammalian GnRH, whereas lamprey GnRH was inactive (Licht, Porter, and Millar 1987).

Mammalian GnRH is very potent in stimulating the secretion of both FSH and LH from the hypophysis in bullfrogs (*Rana catesbeiana*). Thus, single injections into a lymph sac increased the plasma levels of the gonadotropins several hundred times (Daniels and Licht 1980).

In the newt *Triturus cristatus*, daily injections of mammalian GnRH close to a pars distalis grafted under the skin of the gular fold stimulated spermatogenesis (Mazzi et al. 1974), and in sexually mature males in winter *in situ* perfusion with mammalian GnRH stimulated spermiation and raised plasma levels of testosterone (Andreoletti et al. 1980).

Infusion experiments in preovulatory bullfrogs (*R. catesbeiana*) demonstrated the importance of GnRH stimulation to the gonadotropin "surge" needed for ovulation (McCreery and Licht 1983). Figure 15.7 shows that, with continued

infusion, the stimulation of gonadotropin secretion reached peak values concurrently with ovulation after about 24 h, after which plasma levels declined.

Ovulation seems under both inhibitory and stimulatory control. Thus, in the frog *R. temporaria*, lesions in the ventral hypothalamus caused premature ovulation in hibernating females, which could be prevented by treatment with anti-GnRH rabbit serum (Sotowska-Brochocka 1988). The inhibitory nerves involved in timing of the ovulatory gonadotropin secretion may be dopaminergic because a dopamine agonist, bromocriptine, prevented the normal posthibernatory ovulation (Sotowska-Brochocka 1988). Dopaminergic inhibitory control of ovulation may be widespread in lower vertebrates (Chang et al. 1984).

The immunohistochemical tracing of GnRH fibers in the brains of both anurans and urodeles has supported the existence of gonadotropin-regulating tracts in the ventral hypothalamus, extending to the septal zone of the telencephalon (fig. 15.10; Alpert et al. 1976; Doerr-Schott and Dubois 1975). However, immunoreactive GnRH fibers extend into the telencephalon beyond the septal region (Fujita et al. 1987; Jokura and Urano 1986).

Environmental control of annual gonadal cycles may act not only through central nervous control of gonadotropin secretion. In *Rana temporaria* in northern Europe, cyclic spermatogenesis also implies refractoriness of the germ cells toward gonadotropin in the period following breeding in early spring (van Oordt 1956, 1960; van Oordt and Lofts 1963). It is not known how this refractoriness is regulated.

Fat Body–Gonad Relations

The fat bodies are located in close proximity to the gonads. The two organs are of common embryological origin, differentiating from a peritoneal fold at the base of the mesentery, the fat bodies from the anterior end of the fold and the gonads from the posterior (Gaupp 1896–1904). The relationships between the two organs have been debated for more than 200 years, and the subject has been reviewed several times (Adams and Rae 1929; Du Bois 1927; Fitzpatrick 1976; Jørgensen 1986a; Jørgensen, Larsen, and Lofts 1979; von Kennel 1913).

Early evidence for a functional relationship between fat body and gonad was found in the inverse relationships observed in size of fat bodies and development of testes or ovaries in both anurans and urodeles. That the fat bodies specifically serve the gonads rather than the somatic tissues is supported by the reduction in fat-body size before and during breeding (Fitzpatrick 1973a; Gaule 1901; Gadow 1909; von Kennel 1912; Mauget et al. 1971). Such observations led to studies of possible effects on the gonads of excising the fat bodies. Early experiments showed no results of fat-body ablation on gonadal functioning (Aron 1924; von Kennel 1911, 1913; Ponse 1924), but subsequent investigations yielded opposite results. Adams and Rae (1929) found general degeneration of gametes in male and female newts, *Notophthalmus viridescens*, with excised fat bodies. In the salamander *Amphiuma means* (Amphiumidae), the operation prevented vitellogenic growth of oocytes (Rose 1967). Similar results occur in anurans, for example, in males of the frogs *Rana esculenta* (Chieffi et al. 1975), *R. hexadactyla* (Kasinathan, Singh, and Basu 1978) and *R. nigromaculata* (Kobayashi and Iwasawa 1984), and in females of *R. esculenta* (Pierantoni et al. 1983). In *R. cyanophlyctis*, Prasadmurthy and Saidapur (1987) observed only a transient increase in atresia of vitellogenic oocytes after fat-body excision.

Adams and Rae (1929) noticed that unilateral excision of a fat body affected gametogenesis only in the ipsilateral gonad, gametogenesis proceeding normally within the contralateral gonad, indicating a local mechanism in mediating the fat body–gonad interaction. This concept dominated subsequent studies, particularly those of Chieffi and his co-workers, who assume that the fat bodies constitute a link in the hypothalamo-hypophyseal-gonadal axis (Chieffi et al. 1975; Pierantoni et al. 1983; Rastogi, Izzo-Vitiello, Di Meglio, Di Matteo, Franzese, Di Costanzo, Minucci, Iela, and Chieffi 1983; Varriale et al. 1988).

The concept implies vascular connections between fat body and gonad of the nature of a portal circulation, which has also been suggested (Chieffi et al. 1975; Duvernoy 1844; Bargmann and von Hehn 1969). In fact, such vascularization does not exist. Gonads and fat bodies in frogs are independently vascularized (Toldt 1870; Gaupp 1896–1904). This was confirmed in the toad *Bufo bufo* in an experiment on the effects of unilateral excision of a fat body (Jørgensen 1986a). The capillary and venous blood circulations were consistently observed to constitute parallel drainage systems in the two organs, the systems meeting at the attachments of the organs to the peritoneum. These experiments removed the fat bodies in fourteen out of twenty-seven toads, leaving the ovarian circulation intact. The ovaries were in an early stage of vitellogenic growth, which proceeded normally in the absence of the neighboring fat body.

Gametogenesis may also proceed normally in the absence of contact with a fat body in the male toad (*B. bufo*). Thus, testis fragments, isolated spatially from the fat body by excision of the anterior three-fourths of the testis, exhibited compensatory growth as well as normal spermatogenesis and interstitial cell function (Guha and Jørgensen 1981).

A reverse functional relationship between gonads and fat bodies has also been suggested, based on the finding of hypertrophied fat bodies in toads and frogs with atrophic gonads (Du Bois and Ponse 1927; Patzelt 1918). Furthermore, extirpation of the pars distalis of the hypophysis, which causes atrophy of the gonads, results in hypertrophy of the fat bodies in both anurans and urodeles (Burns and Buyse 1932; Chieffi et al. 1975; Dodd and Dodd 1976; van Dongen et al. 1966; Smith 1920; Tachi 1963). However, the fat-body hypertrophy may result from lack of a hypophyseal lipid-mobilizing factor (van Dongen et al. 1966; Smith and Smith 1923; Tachi 1963).

The fact remains, as mentioned above, that fat bodies tend to be large in immature and small in mature amphibians. This inverse relationship is often interpreted in terms of competition for food energy between gonads and fat bodies. The competition concept may be misleading, because it implies restricted food resources. The inverse relationship may reflect shifts in anabolic patterns with the onset of sexual maturation, including resetting of mechanisms controlling deposition (Jørgensen, Shakuntala, and Vijayakumar 1986).

GROWTH AND REPRODUCTION INTERRELATIONSHIPS

As mentioned, growth and reproduction in amphibians, as well as in other vertebrates, tend to be mutually exclusive. Adult size, determined by the transition from the phase of rapid growth to sexual maturation, is species-specific. But size may also vary significantly among populations of a species. Hemelaar's (1986, 1988) studies of the toad *Bufo bufo* from different localities and climates provide a useful example. The relationships between age and body size showed little or no growth after sexual maturation (fig. 15.11). However, the mean lengths of the mature toads varied remarkably among the populations (table 15.11).

Size differences that vary with latitude and altitude are often interpreted in adaptational terms. In *B. bufo*, however, no correlation was obvious between adult body size and latitude or altitude. The variation in body size between the populations thus largely seems to be adaptationally "neutral." Such presumably nonadaptive differences in body size were also found in *B. viridis*, where body size might vary strongly between isolated populations inhabiting a small region of uniform climatic conditions (Jørgensen 1984a).

Body size at sexual maturation may also vary strongly within amphibian populations, as seen from the large standard deviations from the means (table 15.11 and fig. 15.11). In *B. viridis* the size of gravid females in a population in Jerusalem ranged from 66 to 104 mm, mean 79 mm (Jørgensen 1984a) and in a population of *B. melanostictus* from Bangalore from <23 to >72 g, corresponding to 60 to 90 mm (Jørgensen, Shakuntala, and Vijayakumar 1986).

Large intrapopulational variation in the body size at which the organism passes from somatic to ovarian growth may be genetically fixed, or it may reflect phenotypical adaptability. The relative importance of internal and external factors in determining the relationships between growth, size, and reproduction may be analyzed by reciprocal transplantations of juveniles among populations. Berven (1982a) made such an analysis on mountain and lowland populations of the frog *Rana sylvatica*. Mountain frogs were older and larger at sexual maturation than were lowland frogs. Transplantation experiments showed that age and size at sexual maturation are both genetically and phenotypically determined. Particularly, size remained relatively little affected by the transfer from a lowland to a mountain locality and vice versa. The transplantations did not affect the relationships between body size and number and size of eggs, as well as total egg volume, which were thus genetically fixed, the mountain population producing larger but fewer eggs than the lowland population. Total egg volume was about 7% higher in the lowland than in the mountain population.

Striking phenotypic adaptability has been demonstrated in the toad *B. bufo* in the laboratory (Jørgensen 1986b, 1988b). In females sexual maturation is defined by the first recruitment of a complement of oocytes to vitellogenic growth, in males by the first appearance of the secondary sexual character, the thumb pads. The body size at maturation varies

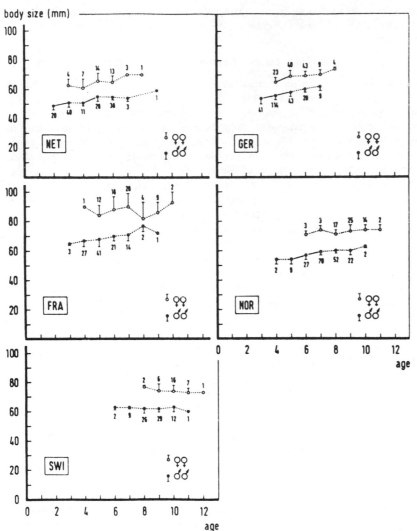

Fig. 15.11 Body length (mm ± SD) as a function of age of adult female and male toads (*Bufo bufo*) from various European populations. *Figures* indicate number of toads in the sample. *Solid lines* indicate statistically significant differences between adjacent age classes. *NET*, Netherlands; *GER*, Germany; *FRA*, France; *NOR*, Norway; *SWI*, Switzerland. (Reprinted, by permission, from Hemelaar 1986.)

TABLE 15.11 Frequency Distribution of Body Size in Toads (*Bufo bufo*) from Different Populations, Captured on Spawning Grounds

			Body Size (mm, means ± SD [N])	
Locality	Latitude	Altitude (m)	Males	Females
Norway	63°23′N	150	58.9 ± 2.9 (208)	72.1 ± 3.5 (84)
Netherlands	51°47′N	15	52.9 ± 4.0 (1,178)	64.7 ± 4.9 (205)
Germany	51°45′N	25	56.8 ± 3.7 (777)	68.4 ± 4.1 (391)
Switzerland	46°39′N	1,850	62.5 ± 2.6 (82)	73.9 ± 3.5 (34)
France	43°28′N	500	69.1 ± 4.3 (1,545)	87.4 ± 8.2 (95)

Source: Hemelaar 1986.

strongly, but in females maturation is mostly accompanied by reduced or suspended growth. This is not the case for males, in which growth in many individuals continues unabated after maturation. In females, age and growth rate are important factors in determining the body size at which maturation occurs, as was observed in juvenile toads in which growth rates were manipulated by feeding levels and by exposure to simulated hibernation (fig. 15.12). The maturational processes, including differentiation and activation of the central nervous gonadotropic system, seems to be both size- and time-depen-

dent. Thus, the fastest-growing toads reached body sizes of about 60–65 g, or 78–80 mm, before activation of the gonadotropic system, as evidenced by the initiation of an ovarian cycle, whereas the slowest-growing toads might mature at body sizes of 30 g and 62 mm or below. Maturation is controlled at the central level and not peripherally, as indicated by the recruitment of a normal-size complement of small oocytes to vitellogenic growth before final differentiation of the pool of small oocytes in the ovaries of a fast-growing toad.

Maturation was greatly accelerated under the experimental

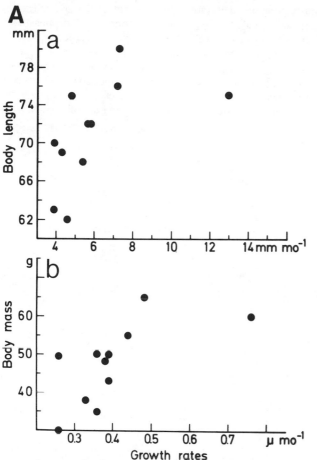

Fig. 15.12 Relationship between growth rate and body size at first maturation in female toads, *Bufo bufo,* as expressed in (*a*) body length and monthly increase in length or (*b*) body mass and monthly instantaneous growth. ●, prehibernating toads; (○), posthibernating toads; *A,* metamorphosed toads; *B,* 1-year-old toads. (Reprinted, by permission, from Jørgensen 1986b.)

conditions in the laboratory (Jørgensen 1986b, 1988b). In a group of hibernating 1-year-old toads, eleven out of thirteen females matured after 2–4 months' growth following hibernation, at an age of 2 years, or earlier than reported from any natural European population (table 15.4). The accelerated maturation resulted in adult body sizes far below those typical of the population from which the toads originated, ranging from about 50 to about 120 g (Jørgensen, Larsen, and Lofts 1979). The laboratory environment thus modified growth and sexual maturation and their interrelationship to a degree that could not have been predicted from the variation observed in nature, thus disclosing unexploited phenotypic adaptability inherent in the female population sampled.

In contrast to the female toads, the male toads reached body sizes typical of *B. bufo* males in nature.

The onset of sexual maturation in juvenile female toads is controlled not only by body size and age but also by the annual rhythm of initiation of ovarian cycles. The importance of season was indicated by the finding that juvenile female toads (about 30 g) kept at a constant light regimen (LD 12:12) and temperature (21°C) all matured sexually within 2 months after simulated hibernation, but none did so before hibernation. This difference in response toward identical and constant external conditions may be due to a direct effect of

hibernation in promoting sexual maturation or to an endogenous mechanism that synchronizes the activation of the reproductive system with the climatic cycle. Hibernation probably did not stimulate sexual maturation directly, because the toads did not mature immediately after hibernation, but only when they had reached large body sizes. Body size per se, however, did not determine the onset of maturation. All toads matured at about the same time, in June, including toads treated with GH, which had attained sizes substantially larger than those of the nontreated toads. Sexual maturation was thus correlated with calendar time and not with body size (Jørgensen 1988b).

Both growth and sexual maturation ultimately depend upon the control exerted by the central nervous hypophysiotropic system. The mechanisms coupling maturation with the suspension of growth in female amphibians may therefore imply switching from predominant stimulation of GH secretion to predominant secretion of gonadotropic hormone at the expense of GH. Intrapopulational and interpopulational variation in body size at sexual maturation may thus depend upon the response to environmental and/or internal factors of the mutual interaction between the central nervous structures controlling the secretion of GH and gonadotropin.

As mentioned, in male toads sexual maturation did not affect the rate of growth. However, growth eventually abates in males too, presumably correlated with reduced GH secretion. Juvenile males treated with ovine GH continued growing to reach sizes far in excess of those attained in nature (C. B. Jørgensen unpublished data).

In conclusion, the dynamic interplay between environment and amphibian growth, reproduction, and deposition thus varies with the functional states of the organisms constituting a population, determined by inherent cycles as well as by physiological responses to the environment. A deeper understanding of this interplay depends upon an appreciation of its basically hierarchical nature and upon the correct identification and characterization of the functional entities at the various levels of organization, complementing the more conventional approach of correlating averaged population parameters, including body size, ovary mass, and depots.

16 Developmental Changes in Physiological Systems

WARREN W. BURGGREN AND JOHN J. JUST

All vertebrates (indeed, all complex metazoans) undergo complex morphological, physiological, and biochemical transitions as they develop from a single fertilized cell into the terminal, sexually mature or "adult" form of their species. Consequently, studies of ontogenetic processes could in theory be directed toward any vertebrate taxa. While the vast literature on vertebrate development is certainly broadly based across the vertebrate classes, without doubt the amphibians have served disproportionately as models with which to probe development at levels from the macromolecular to the organismal. The anatomical literature on amphibian development is enormous (for references see Fox 1984), as is that for the endocrinological aspects of metamorphosis (Dent 1988; Rosenkilde 1985; White and Nicoll 1981) and the molecular processes of tissue growth and differentiation (Atkinson 1981; Frieden and Just 1970; Smith-Gill and Carver 1981).

Several reasons account for the pivotal position in the developmental literature that amphibians occupy. Pragmatically, amphibians are readily available, produce large numbers of offspring with considerable regularity, and have short generation times. Importantly, spawning in many species can be easily induced pharmacologically in the lab, and the fertilized eggs are easily reared. The developing embryos are usually very hardy and are the basis of most studies involving tissue transplantation or other studies requiring surgical manipulation. These features alone, though important to the developmental biologist who seeks a convenient model for studying general molecular, cellular, and systemic developmental processes, are not the compelling features from the perspective of environmental physiology. Rather, the major distinguishing character of amphibian development that has stimulated interest literally for centuries among zoologists is the combination of (1) the *magnitude* and *rapidity* of morphological and physiological changes that accompany development in most amphibians, combined with the fact that (2) these radical changes by and large occur in free-living, independent organisms where they are unobscured by a shell (as in reptiles and birds) or uterus (as in mammals).

In this chapter we discuss the physiological changes that characterize development in amphibians. Several points require particular emphasis at the outset.

1. The study of amphibians has been confined to relatively few species for many aspects of their biology (see chapter 1). For example, Wassersug and Nishikawa (1988) report that more than 80% of all citations on amphibian biology are based on just two genera—*Rana* and *Xenopus*. Rather than necessarily being "representative" amphibians, these genera are either easily reared in captivity (*Xenopus*) or are found naturally (*Rana*) in the region of the world where most amphibian biologists live (temperate Europe and North America). In fact, the species generally regarded as exceptional are often more the rule. For example, more than forty species of anurans have arboreal larvae (Lannoo, Townsend, and Wassersug 1987). The Neotropical anuran genus *Eleutherodactylus* (Leptodactylidae) is the single largest vertebrate genus, with over four hundred named species (Frost 1985), yet occupies only a miniscule fraction of the literature. The studies of physiological development discussed in this chapter clearly reflect the focus on *Rana* and *Xenopus*.

2. Our physiological knowledge of amphibian development lags far behind our understanding of the anatomy of amphibian development. Thus, by necessity many aspects of the physiological account that follows must remain incomplete (e.g., little is known about developmental changes in hemodynamics). On the other hand, considerable information is available on developmental changes in hormonal and neural regulation of physiological processes, and because much

The authors acknowledge their many colleagues and students at the University of Kentucky and the University of Massachusetts who provided critical input during the preparation of this chapter. The objective, invariably accurate criticisms offered by the senior editor of this volume, Martin Feder, were particularly useful during the revision process. John J. Just thanks his wife, Jeannette K. Just, for typing portions of the manuscript and making numerous suggestions of both an editorial and academic nature. The library staff at both the University of Kentucky and the University of Massachusetts provided invaluable help in obtaining rare published works. Warren W. Burggren acknowledges the support during the preparation of this chapter provided by NSF Operating Grant DCB 9046092.

of this information has not been reviewed before, the corresponding sections of this chapter are extensive.

3. While this volume is on *environmental* physiology and we have endeavored to emphasize environmental aspects, much of the available information on amphibian developmental physiology is of a more mechanistic nature, primarily focused on organ level rather than organismal physiology. This is particularly so in recent papers in the areas of developmental changes in amphibian endocrinology and nervous function. We felt it important nonetheless to describe this information in detail since much of it has never been reviewed, and its very nature and the questions that emerge show that additional studies must be carried out in a more environmental context.

4. Finally, although metamorphic climax is a critical and dramatic stage of development, it is only one in a long series of developmental stages between egg and adult and will not be the sole focus of this chapter. Because previous chapters have discussed primarily the physiology of sexually mature, adult forms, we will not emphasize the physiology of adults and will frequently refer the reader to earlier chapters for details of the process in adults.

DESCRIBING AMPHIBIAN DEVELOPMENT

Most investigations of amphibians examine sexually mature adults. (In fact, to facilitate physiological experimentation, usually the largest possible animals are chosen.) Normally, such studies report the mass of their subjects to enable future researchers to repeat the work or draw some comparative conclusions. Unfortunately, many studies on developmental physiology of amphibians give far too little information about the subject animals to allow comparisons. Many times authors provide data on "larvae" or "tadpoles" and compare that data to "juveniles" and "adults." These authors assume these terms are sufficient to describe developmental state—but in reality such vague descriptions provide insufficient information to allow detailed interpretation of physiological changes occurring during development. We have been painfully aware of this during the course of reviewing the literature for this chapter, and feel it important to emphasize the absolute necessity of clearly specifying developmental stages of experimental material.

Several errors are common in reporting "stages." These should be avoided because they do not accurately designate degree of development. For example, authors often refer to "limbless" anuran larvae; however, every anuran larva has microscopic limb buds upon hatching. Some authors, particularly those working on urodeles, rely on length and/or mass measurements alone to indicate metamorphic progress. Total body measurement without stages makes comparison between species nearly impossible, and even within species comparison becomes difficult if animals come from different sites with different opportunities for feeding. Many authors refer to larvae as being "premetamorphic," "prometamorphic," and "climax" animals. Unfortunately, these terms have been defined variously in the literature (Wilder 1924; Marx 1935; Taylor and Kollros 1946; Witschi 1956; Etkin

TABLE 16.1 Comparison of Larval Anuran Staging Methods

Method	Stages											
	Limb-Bud Growth					Toe Differentiation						
Gosner[a]	26	27	28	29	30	31	32	33	34	35	36	37
Terentlev[b]	25	26	26	26	26	26	26	26	26	26	26	26
Witschi[c]	25	26	26	26	26	26	27	27	27	27	27	28
Alytes obstetricans[d]	IV_1	IV_2	IV_3	IV_4	$IV_{5,6}$	IV_7	$IV_{8,9}$	$IV_{10,11}$	$IV_{12,13}$	IV_{14}	IV_{14}	IV_{14}
Bufo[e]												
Bufo bufo[f]	23	24	25	I	II	III	IV	V	VI	VII	VIII	VIII
Bufo bufo[g]	III_{10}	IV_1	IV_2	$IV_{3,4}$	IV_5	IV_6	IV_7	IV_8	IV_9	IV_9	IV_{10}	IV_{10}
Bufo melanostictus[h]	25	26	27	28, 29	30	30	31	32	33	34	35	35
Bufo regularis[i]	46	47	48, 49	50	51	52	53	54	54	55	55	56
Bufo valliceps[j]	26	27	28	29	30	31	32	33	34	35	36	37
Bufo vulgaris[k]	11	11	12	12	13	13	13	13	13	13	13	13
Nectophrynoides occidentalis[l]	I_b	I_b	I_b	I_b	I_b	I_b	I_b	I_b	I_b	II_a	II_a	II_a
Rana catesbeiana[m]			A1	A2	A3	A4	A5	A6	A7	A8	A8	A8
Rana chalconota[n]	VIII	VIII	VIII	VIII	IX	IX	IX	IX	IX	IX	IX	IX
Rana dalmatina[o]	39	40	41	42	42	43	44	45	45	46	46	47
Rana fusca[p]	18	18	19	20	21	22	22	23	23	24	24	24
Rana pipiens[q]	I	II	III	IV	V	VI	VII	VIII	IX	X	XI	XII
Rana temporaria[r]	8	9, 10	11, 12	13	13							
Rana sylvatica[s]		A1	A2	A3	A4	A5	A6	A6	A6	B	B	B
Xenopus laevis[t]	46	47, 48	49, 50	51	52	53	53	53	54	55	55	55

[a] Gosner 1960.
[b] Terentlev 1950.
[c] Witschi 1956.
[d] Cambar and Martin 1959.
[e] Schreiber 1937.
[f] Rossi 1959.
[g] Cambar and Gipouloux 1956.
[h] Khan 1965.
[i] Sedra and Michael 1961.
[j] Limbaugh and Volpe 1957.
[k] Adler 1901.
[l] Lamotte and Xavier 1972.
[m] Hammerman 1969a.
[n] Hing 1959.
[o] Cambar and Marrot 1954.
[p] Kopsch 1952.
[q] Taylor and Kollros 1946.
[r] Moser 1950.
[s] Helff and Mellicker 1941a.
[t] Nieuwkoop and Faber 1967.

1968; Dodd and Dodd 1976; Just, Kraus-Just, and Check 1981). We suggest that the terms *premetamorphic, prometamorphic,* and *climax* should be limited to certain thyroid hormone–dependent phenomena in amphibian metamorphosis (Just, Kraus-Just, and Check 1981). *Premetamorphosis* should refer to stages in amphibian metamorphosis that are independent of thyroid hormone function. Only development that will still occur after thyroidectomy should be considered *premetamorphosis.* The term *prometamorphosis* should be applied only to stages and events that are dependent on thyroid hormones. *Climax* should be used to refer only to these events that require the tremendous surge of thyroid hormones in late larval stages that is dependent on a functioning pituitary-hypothalamus axis.

Authors also commonly use vague developmental terms without any reference as to which previously established usage is being followed. Any of the more precise staging methods described below is preferable to general terms (e.g., *tadpole*). If general terms must be used, the range of stages encompassed by these terms should also be noted. Some authors use stages and attribute them to general texts on development, which contain many different staging methods, without actually giving the classification scheme being used. Finally, some authors refer to "metamorphosing" animals. What convention they are using is seldom clear, nor is what they mean by the term, but these authors usually are referring to animals in late larval stages. The terms *metamorphosing* and *metamorphosis* should be used for any and all morphological, biochemical, and physiological nonreoccur-

ing changes that occur during the entire larval life span, and not just those observed during the late larval climax stages.

We feel very strongly that researchers in amphibian developmental physiology should state as precisely and unequivocally as possible the developmental stage of the animals and the staging scheme in use, in addition to body mass. Only when such information becomes more widely available will we be able to summarize and compare data on different species or different developmental time periods.

To define development in a given species precisely and to allow comparisons between species, numerous papers describe the sequence of external morphological changes that occur during development in anurans (table 16.1) and urodeles (table 16.2). These staging methods are very simple and require only a dissecting microscope (or even a magnifying glass) to stage any amphibian larva.

In anuran larvae, the growth and differentiation of the hindlimbs usually define the earliest stages. The forelimbs may or may not be enclosed in the branchial chambers; if they are enclosed, the forelimbs erupt in late larval stages. During the final stages the tail regresses and the adult mouth forms. The first three methods of staging in table 16.1 were developed in the hope that they could be applied to all species; however, they are not necessarily more precise or more useful than those established for individual species. In fact they may be little more than a combining of suggested stages by previous authors. For example the Gosner (1960) stages (1–46) appear to combine the embryonic stages (1–25) of Shumway (1942) and the larval stages (I–XXV) of Taylor and Kollros

Stages												
Rapid Hindlimb Growth						Tail Resorption						
38	39	40	40	40	41	41	41	42	43	44	45	46
27	27	27	27	28	28	28	29	30	30	30	30	31
28	28	28	28	28	29	30	31	31	32	32	33	33
IV_{14}	IV_{15}	IV_{15}	IV_{15}	IV_{16}	IV_{16}	IV_{17}	IV_{17}	IV_{18}	IV_{19}	IV_{19}	IV_{19}	IV_{20}
1	1	1	1	1	2	2	3	4	5	6	7	8
VIII	IX	IX	X	X	XI	XI	XII	XIII	XIV	XIV	XIV	XV
IV_{11}	IV_{11}	IV_{12}	IV_{12}	IV_{13}	IV_{13}	IV_{14}	IV_{14}	IV_{15}	IV_{15}	IV_{16}	IV_{16}	IV_{17}
35	36	36	37	37	38	38	39	40	41	42	42	43
56	56	57	57	57	57	58	58	59, 60	61, 62	63, 64	65	66
37	38	38	39	40	40	41	42	43	44	45	45	46
13	13	13	13	14	14	14	14	14	15	15	15	15
II_a	II_a	II_b	II_b	II_b	II_b	III_a	III_a	III_b	III_b	III_b	III_b	IV
A9	A9	A10	A11	A12	BC	DE	FG	H	I	J	K	L
IX	IX	IX	IX	IX	IX	X	X	X	X	X	X	X
48	48	49	49	50	50	50	51	51	52	53	53	53
25	25	26	26	26	26	26	27	27	28	29	29	30
XIII	XIV	XV	XVI	XVII	XVIII	XIX	XX	XXI	XXII	XXIII	XXIV	XXV
B	C	C	C	D	D	E	FG	H	I	J	K	L
56	57	57	58	59	60	60	61	62	63	64	65	66

TABLE 16.2   Comparison of Larval Urodele Staging Methods

Method	Forelimb and Hindlimb Growth and Differentiation																	Stages
Ambystoma maculatum[a]	38	38	39	40	41	42, 43	44	45	46									
Ambystoma mexicanum[b]																		
Ambystoma tigrinum[c]																		
Hynobius nigrescens[d]	40	41	42	43	44, 45	46, 47	47, 48	49	50	51	52	53	54	55	56	57	58	59
Megalobatrachus japonicus[e]	26	26	27	27	27	27	27	28	28	28	28	28	28	28	29	29	30	30
Necturus maculosus[f]	31	31	32	32	33	33	33	33	34	34	34	34	35	35	36	36	36	37
Pleurodeles waltl[g]	34	35	36	37	38	39	40	41	42	43	44	45	46	47	48	49	50	51
Triton alpestris[h]	28	28	29	29	30													
Triton taeniatus[i]	34	35	36	37	38	39	40	41	42	43	44	45	46	47	48	49	50	51
Triturus helveticus[j]	33	34	35, 36	37	38	39, 40	41	42	43	44	45	46	46	47	48	49	50	51
Triturus pyrrhogaster[k]	23	23	23	23	24	24	24	24	25									

[a]Rugh 1962. Stages of Harrison or Leavitt, improperly referred to as *A. punctatum*.
[b]Marx 1935.
[c]Norman 1985.
[d]Usui and Hamasaki 1939.
[e]Kudo 1938.

[f]Eycleshymer and Wilson 1910.
[g]Gallien and Durocher 1957.
[h]Knight 1938.
[i]Glucksohn 1931.
[j]Gallien and Bidaud 1959.
[k]Anderson 1943.

(1946). The other seventeen entries in table 16.1 refer to staging methods developed for specific amphibian species. The various stages in different species were equated subjectively from descriptions of hindlimb development, degree of tail resorption, and development of adult mouth. We have equated the stages of a live-bearing toad (*Nectophrynoides* [Leptodactylidae] and the midwife toad (*Alytes* [Discoglossidae]) with normal free-living anuran larvae. We have not, however, attempted to equate the stages of direct-developing amphibians (*Eleutherodactylus coqui* [Leptodactylidae]; Townsend and Stewart 1985) with that of other amphibians because differences in the developmental sequences are too numerous to justify equating stages.

Staging methods for free-living urodeles including *Necturus* (Proteidae), a neotenic genus, are given in table 16.2. The youngest stages can be equated primarily on forelimb differentiation and balancer growth. The midlarval stages are equated by hindlimb development and balancer degeneration. The final larval stages are represented by various degrees of tail fin and gill regression. Unlike in anurans, mouth structure does not change suddenly during urodele larval life, because all animals in this order are predatory and carnivorous during their entire life span.

No staging methods for the embryos, larvae, or fetuses of caecilian amphibians are known to us.

Hereafter, we will abbreviate some staging schemes as follows: G, Gosner (1960); NF, Nieuwkoop and Faber 1967); and TK, Taylor and Kollros (1946). For example, TK XXV refers to a larva at Taylor and Kollros stage XXV.

In summary, the study of physiological development (indeed, all aspects of development) will advance more rapidly with the adoption of clear, explicit descriptions of developmental stage. We do not advocate any particular developmental staging scheme—just that precise, accepted schemes be used at all times.

ENDOCRINE SYSTEM

Most adult amphibians are terrestrial, yet their larvae are aquatic. Thus the two life stages clearly experience different environments. Even in species in which both adults and larvae are aquatic or both are terrestrial, a single life span will nevertheless include many anatomical, biochemical, and behavioral changes (i.e., type of food consumed, means of obtaining food, type of locomotion). The many changes in both the internal and external environments that amphibians face during their life span require changes in the integrative capacities of the animals. Indeed, the two major systems involved in integration and control, namely the endocrine and nervous systems, change greatly during metamorphosis. Chapters 2, 3, and 7 in particular discuss the nervous and endocrine systems of adults. In this chapter we describe the special changes in form and function that occur during amphibian development.

The endocrine system's involvement in metamorphosis, particularly the thyroid gland's role in causing many of the anatomical, biochemical, and physiological changes needed to occupy the new environment often inhabited by the adult, has been known for nearly a century. In the last 10 years, it has become increasingly obvious that many other endocrine

			Gill and Tail Fin Resorption						
			II	III	IV	V	VII	VII	VIII
			I	II	III	IV	V	VI	VII
60	61	62	63	64	65	66			
31	31	31	31	31	32	32	32	32	33
38–41	42–48	49							
52	53	54	55$_a$	55$_a$	55$_b$	55$_b$	55$_c$	55$_c$	56
52	53	54	55$_a$	55$_a$	55$_b$	55$_b$	55$_c$	55$_c$	56
52	53	54	55$_a$	55$_a$	55$_b$	55$_b$	55$_c$	55$_c$	56

glands change their function and therefore represent new integrative potentials during metamorphosis. In adult mammals more than a hundred hormones are involved in homeostasis. Very few of these hormones have received any experimental attention in any family of amphibians, and attempts specifically to analyze patterns associated with phylogeny or environmental adaptation have been few. Most work has focused on the hormones *controlling* metamorphosis rather than on hormones regulating such chronic phenomena as carbohydrate metabolism, ionic regulation, sexual development, and blood pressure. Not only do hormones and growth factors regulate the day-to-day functions of the immature organism, but they alter the direction of differentiation of various cells, organs, and organ systems in all classes of vertebrates. The work of Gudernatsch and of Allen (see Allen 1938) first clearly demonstrated the effect of hormones on differentiation in anuran amphibians. These and other early workers clearly showed that anuran metamorphosis requires the thyroid, the pituitary, and their hormones. Administering hormones from these two glands to young larvae induces metamorphosis prematurely. Metamorphic progress can be stopped in midlarval stages when these hormones are removed by ablations of either gland. Later work by Hanoaka (1967) proved that the hypothalamus is also required to complete metamorphosis, because surgical removal inhibits metamorphosis at early climax stages.

An endocrine gland must synthesize and release hormones to effect growth, differentiation, and homeostasis during development. The blood levels of hormones must be sufficient to cause tissue responses. These hormone levels can be con-

trolled by changes in the rate of hormone synthesis, peripheral hormone destruction, or peripheral conversion to an active hormone form. All hormones require cellular receptors located either in the cell membrane or inside the cell (usually in the nucleus) for function. In addition, the responding tissues of the organism develop proteins and other molecules linked to the receptor to help generate cellular signals (second messengers). Modulation of hormonal responsiveness during development therefore has a significant number of possible control points. Many hormones are involved in physiological regulation of larvae; typically, however, information is available on only a few of the possible modulatory points for any hormone.

Thyroid Gland

General Physiology Etkin (1968) and Kollros (1961) suggested that for normal metamorphosis, the concentration of thyroid hormones must increase continuously in the blood of larvae. This hypothesis resulted from studies of thyroidectomized and/or of hypophysectomized larvae that were induced to undergo normal metamorphosis by immersion in increasing concentrations of thyroid hormones. Just (1967, 1972) first presented proof for this hypothesis when he demonstrated that circulating levels of thyroid hormones, as measured by protein-bound iodine (PBI), increased in *R. pipiens* during larval development and that pituitary ablation decreased the blood thyroid hormone levels.

Subsequently the more specific technique of radioimmunoassay (RIA) has been used to measure thyroid hormones in blood. Some authors have questioned PBI as a valid indicator of thyroid hormone function in anurans (Regard, Taurog, and Nakashima 1978; Suzuki and Suzuki 1981). The relative concentration of thyroid hormones during metamorphosis of various species is shown in table 16.3. All authors agree that the levels of hormones are low in early larval stages, increase dramatically during climax, then drop precipitously after tail loss and remain low in the adult. Major disagreement surrounds the timing of the maximum increases and the absolute amount of hormones released. Some species show the maximum increase immediately before or after front-limb emergence (seven values, table 16.3; also *Rana clamitans*, Race and Cameron 1966; *R. ornativentris*, Suzuki and Suzuki 1985), while the latest reported surge occurs at TK XXIII (three values, table 16.3). A midclimax surge of thyroid hormones at TK XXI to XXII also occurs (eight values, table 16.3; also *R. esculenta* and *Xenopus laevis*, Schultheiss 1980b).

These apparent discrepancies about the timing of maximum thyroid hormone peak may not reflect true physiological differences, because only two of the studies cited in table 16.3 analyzed their data statistically (Just 1972; Weil 1986). In *R. pipiens* the thyroid hormone levels found in TK XIX, XX, and XXI are not statistically different (Just 1972), while in *R. clamitans* the ratio of tail length/snout-vent length and levels of tetraiodothyronine (T_4 or thyroxine) are not correlated, implying that none of the differences in hormone concentration during climax is significant in that species. Because of the paucity of statistical analyses, the exact stage of maximum hormone release is unclear, although the average

TABLE 16.3 Relative Percentage of Circulating Thyroid Hormones Present in Various Stages of Anuran Metamorphosis

	Hormone	I–V[a] 52[b]	VI–X 53–55	XI–XV 56–57	XVI 58	XVII 59	XVIII 60	XIX 60	XX 61	XXI 62
Rana catesbeiana[d]	T_4	ND[e]	ND	ND	ND	—[f]	ND	—	ND	100
	T_3	ND	ND	ND	ND	—	ND	17	100	75
Rana catesbeiana[g]	T_4	—	ND	ND	ND	ND	18	ND	24	20
	T_3	—	ND	ND	ND	ND	2	ND	21	35
Rana catesbeiana[h]	T_4	ND	ND	ND	ND	ND	ND	28	23	81
Rana catesbeiana[i]	T_4	5[j]	—	6	—	9	33	40	96	100
	T_3	14[g]	—	15	—	13	19	38	61	100
Rana clamitans[k]	T_4	—	66	47	19	43	54	54	51	78
Rana pipiens[l]	PBI	22	19	27	36	33	47	100	75	69
Xenopus borealis[m]	T_4	—	—	—	23	24	—	—	74	100
	T_3	—	—	—	ND	—	—	—	47	100
Xenopus clivii[m]	T_4	—	—	22	—	16	—	100	71	33
	T_3	—	—	2	—	25	—	50	100	10
Xenopus laevis[n]	T_4	—	1	33	51	—	—	67	68	100
	T_3	—	ND	11	24	—	—	92	100	59
Xenopus laevis[m]	T_4	—	7	32	—	52	—	67	63	100
	T_3	—	ND	11	—	22	—	100	—	67
Xenopus mulleri[m]	T_4	—	ND	ND	—	28	—	100	94	66
	T_3	—	ND	ND	—	12	—	75	56	100
All species	T_4[o]	2	11	16	16	22	21	57	58	78
All species	T_3[p]	8	1	6	7	15	7	53	69	68
All species	All[q]	7	8	13	14	20	20	58	63	73

Notes: The average hormone concentration for each stage in each species was obtained directly from tables or estimated from the figures in publications. Once the average hormone concentration per stage in each species was found, the relative concentration per stage was determined using the following calculations: (mean hormone concentration for any stage)/(maximum hormone concentration in a specific stage) · 100 = (relative percentage of circulating hormones at stage). This calculated relative percentage is presented in the table. If more than one set of data were available in one publication, the relative percentages were combined and the average presented in the table.

[a] All authors using *Rana* species used Taylor and Kollros stages (1946).

[b] All authors using *Xenopus* species used Nieuwkoop and Faber stages (1967).

[c] Froglets (Fl) are animals that have lost their tails for a year or less.

[d] Miyauchi et al. 1977.

[e] ND indicates that nondetectable levels of hormone were present in that species using the methods of the publication. The ND values were used as a 1% relative hormone concentration when the overall mean was calculated. We felt that some hormone was present and realize that this could lead to a relative underestimation of the hormone present.

[f] — indicates that no attempts were made to determine the hormone concentration at that stage for that species.

[g] Regard, Taurog, and Nakashima 1978 (combined data from fig. 2 and table 2).

[h] Mondou and Kaltenbach 1979.

[i] Suzuki and Suzuki 1981.

[j] Even when values are available for any stage, some animals in that specific stage may have had nondetectable hormone levels. Since only the actual relative percentage was used, this leads to an overestimation of the hormone present.

[k] Weil 1986.

[l] Just 1972.

[m] Buscaglia, Leloup, and Deluze 1985.

[n] Leloup and Buscaglia 1977.

[o] The relative percentages of circulating T_4 of each species for the same stage were averaged.

[p] The relative percentages of circulating T_3 of each species for the same stage were averaged.

[q] The relative percentage of circulating thyroid hormones of each species at the same stage were averaged, irrespective of the method used or type of hormone detected.

of all species suggests a maximum at about TK XXI (fig. 16.1).

Data for urodele larvae show the same trend as for anurans (table 16.4), namely that thyroid hormone levels are low in larvae before metamorphic climax. Most authors use tail fin and gill regression as indices of metamorphic climax. Sometimes circulating levels of thyroid hormone increase during climax but then decrease in the adult, and may never increase in animals that remain neotenic. As with the anuran data, most authors did not statistically analyze their data for maximum hormone concentration. Statistical analysis of the uro-

dele data showed no differences in triiodothyronine (T_3 levels during all six climax stages, and five of six climax stages do not differ in the T_4 concentrations (Norman, Carr, and Norris 1987).

Hormone concentrations are commonly below detectable levels during preclimax stages in both anuran and urodele larvae (tables 16.3 and 16.4). Perplexingly, even when the average hormone concentrations are at their maximum, individual animals may have nondetectable or low premetamorphic hormone levels at climax stages (Alberch, Gale, and Larsen 1986; Just 1972; Larras-Regard 1985; Miyauchi et al.

XXII 63	XXIII 64	XXIV 65	XXV 66	Fl[c]	Adult
—	60	53	—	—	ND
—	71	17	—	—	ND
31	100	57	18	41	31
62	87	83	71	18	ND
86	100	14	19	—	36
72	64	62	38	22	8
79	52	45	34	19	14
94	100	71	—	67	—
42	36	30	29	—	40
23	24	—	35	—	—
65	—	—	ND	—	—
—	—	21	—	—	—
—	—	—	—	—	—
76	58	44	61	—	—
29	45	11	9	—	—
77	57	50	56	—	—
39	47	11	—	—	—
—	47	16	—	—	—
—	—	ND	—	—	—
66	68	43	38	43	19
55	60	28	29	19	5
60	63	37	33	33	17

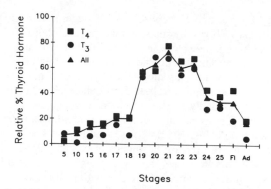

Fig. 16.1   The relative percentage of thyroid hormones in the plasma of various Anura during normal metamorphosis. The abscissa gives the Taylor-Kollros stages (Taylor and Kollros 1946), converted to Arabic numerals. Froglets (*Fl*) are animals that have lost their tails for 1 year or less, while adults (*A*) are animals older than 1 year. The data for the relative percentages are presented in table 16.3. The raw data are contained in eight publications studying thyroid hormone levels during the metamorphosis of seven species.

TABLE 16.4   Relative Percentage of Circulating Thyroid Hormones Present during Various Stages of Urodele Metamorphosis

	Hormone	Premet.[a]	Promet.	Early Climax	Mid climax[a]	Late Climax	Postmet.	Adult	Neotenic
Ambystoma gracile[b]	T_4		26		100			12	11
Ambystoma tigrinum[c]	T_4		ND[d]	21	49	100	23	47	
	T_3		12[f]	20	100	64	27	9	
Ambystoma tigrinum[e]	T_4	16		47 64	61 58	91 100			
	T_3	19		74 99	80 95	86 100			
Eurycea bislineata[f]	T_4	ND	24[g]	28	100	61	ND	ND	
	T_3	ND	32[g]	71	100	80	46	ND	
Hynobius nigrescens[h]	T_4	ND	12	25	100	74	36		
	T_3	ND	ND	ND	100	21	ND		
All species	T_4[i]	6	16	37	78	85	20	20	11
All species	T_3[i]	7	15	53	95	70	25	5	
All species	All[i]	7	15	45	86	78	22	14	11

Notes: The average hormone concentration for each stage in each species was obtained directly from tables or estimated from the figures in publications. Once the average hormone concentration per stage in each species was found, the relative concentration per stage was determined using the following calculations: (mean hormone concentration for any stage)/(maximum hormone concentration in a specific stage) · 100 = (relative percentage of circulating hormones at stage). This calculated relative percentage is presented in the table. If more than one set of data were available in one publication, the relative percentages were combined and the average presented in the table. Empty cells in the table refer to stages at which no measurements were made.

[a] All authors developed their own staging methods, and the stages for the different species may not correspond precisely.

[b] Eagleson and McKeown 1978.

[c] Larras-Regard, Taurog, and Dorris 1981.

[d] ND indicates that nondetectable levels of hormone were present in that species using the methods of the publication. The ND values were used as a 1% relative hormone concentration, when the overall mean was calculated. We felt that some hormone was present and realize that this could lead to a relative underestimation of the hormone present.

[e] Norman, Carr, and Norris 1987.

[f] Alberch, Gale, and Larsen 1986.

[g] The relative percentages of circulating T_4 of each species for the same stage were averaged.

[h] Suzuki and Suzuki 1985.

[i] Mean of all species.

1977; Mondou and Kaltenbach 1979; Regard, Taurog, and Nakashima 1978). Why some animals have low hormone levels at climax is not clear, nor is whether this occurs in all species. Many authors pooled blood from several animals, obscuring individual variation. Two hypotheses may account for these low hormone levels at climax stages. The first is that all animals suddenly release hormones during climax but destroy them just as rapidly, leading to a rapid disappearance from the blood (Just 1972). The second hypothesis is that all animals suddenly release hormones at climax. Thyroid hormone receptors in tissues rapidly sequester the released hormones, and they disappear from circulation. If and only if all tissue receptors become saturated and hormones continue to be released do the circulating hormones increase (Dodd and Dodd 1976).

Many organs and organ systems respond to these rising hormone levels. In anurans the legs and lungs grow while the tail and gill degenerate. Populations of cells change, including the red blood cells and the intestinal lining cells, while some organs (e.g., liver and skin) change only their functions, without a complete change in cell population. A complete listing of such changes is beyond the scope of the present review but has been reviewed numerous times (Fox 1984; Frieden and Just 1970; Gilbert and Frieden 1981; Hourdry and Beaumont 1985).

Frieden and his co-workers first tested the assumption that cells and organs that respond to thyroid hormones must contain thyroid hormone receptors (Kistler, Yoshizato, and Frieden 1975; Yoshizato and Frieden 1975). Thyroid hormone receptors have been found in the nuclei from cells in the tail, liver, blood cells, intestine, and kidney (Galton 1988; Jaffe 1987). The number of thyroid hormone receptors in the nucleus of cells from the tail and red blood cells increase during the early larval stages; the number of receptors peaks in early climax stages and then drops to low adult levels by the end of climax (Galton 1988; Moriya, Thomas, and Frieden 1984; Yoshizato and Frieden 1975). The number of thyroid hormone receptors in the liver nucleus does not change during development (Galton 1988). Thyroid hormones, T_4, and T_3 all can and do bind to these receptors (Galton 1988). The chemical properties of different tissue receptors in larval anurans are similar and have led to the suggestion that they may be identical in all larval anuran tissues (Jaffe 1987). In mammals, however, two or more receptors are present, even though many tissues probably have only one type of receptor (Thompson et al. 1987).

Most authors believe that the active thyroid hormone responsible for physiological action in amphibians is T_3 (Buscaglia, Leloup, and Deluze 1985; Frieden 1981; Galton 1988). T_4 is the major hormone in the thyroid gland and is released by the thyroid gland of all amphibians investigated (Buscaglia, Leloup, and Deluze 1985). When extremely low doses of high specific activity of $I^{133}-T_4$ are injected into *Xenopus laevis* larvae, the larvae convert T_4 to T_3. This conversion occurs at all stages studied, is greatest at climax stages, and declines to adult levels by the end of metamorphic climax. The skin, intestine, tail, and liver all show this type of deiodination activity (Galton 1988; Galton and Hiebert 1988). Partial inhibition of T_4 deiodination by pharmacological means (iopanoic acid) reduces the rate of metamorphosis in *X. laevis*

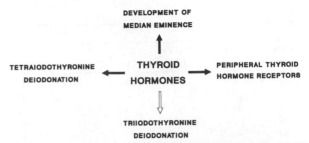

Fig. 16.2 Mechanisms by which thyroid hormones accelerate amphibian metamorphosis following thyroid hormone administration or release from the thyroid gland. The hormone stimulates (*filled arrows*) certain events while inhibiting (*open arrows*) others.

(Buscaglia, Leloup, and Deluze 1985). This conversion may not be essential for all events in metamorphosis, since some tissues in amphibian larvae are more responsive to T_4 than to T_3 (Kollros 1961). Furthermore, certain physiological responses occur only with T_4 and not with T_3 in adult amphibians (Dupré, Just, and Ritchart 1986), birds (Chandola and Bhatt 1982), and mammals (Erfurth and Hedner 1987).

Thyroid hormones have broad effects on numerous tissues and organs (Hourdry and Beaumont 1985; Fox 1984; Frieden and Just 1970; Gilbert and Frieden 1981), but accelerate metamorphosis in four particular ways (fig. 16.2). They increase the thyroid hormone receptor numbers in the peripheral tissues (Galton 1988; Moriya, Thomas, and Frieden 1984). They increase 5-monodeiodinase, the enzyme responsible for the peripheral conversions T_4 to T_3 (Buscaglia, Leloup, and Deluze 1985; Galton 1988). They may decrease $5'$-monodeiodinase, the enzyme responsible for the peripheral conversions of T_3 to $3',3$-deiodothyronine (T_2; Galton 1988). They cause the differentiation of the median eminence, the vascular bed located at the base of the brain that integrates the hypothalamus and the anterior pituitary (Etkin 1963).

Regulation of Thyroid Function Since Adler (1914) first demonstrated that pituitary ablation inhibits metamorphosis, numerous others have shown that metamorphosis requires the anterior pituitary. After hypophysectomy, larval development arrests at more advanced stages than after thyroid removal (Allen 1938; Etkin 1968; Kollros 1961). The thyroid gland seems to function independently of the pituitary during embryonic development and the first few larval stages (Hanoaka et al. 1973; Kaye 1961). After these early larval stages the pituitary becomes necessary for thyroid function. Amphibian metamorphosis arrests after hypophysectomy (Hanoaka 1967; Kollros 1961), thyroid gland function declines (Dodd and Dodd 1976; Hanoaka et al. 1973; Hourdry and Regard 1975; Kaye 1961), and circulating levels of thyroid hormones decrease (Just 1972). On the other hand, administration of thyroid-stimulating hormone (TSH, also called thyrotropin) stimulates thyroid gland function (Dodd and Dodd 1976; Larras-Regard 1985; Norman and Norris 1987; Norris, Jones, and Criley 1973; Prahlad 1968).

Considering these ablative and additive experiments in larval amphibians, most authors have simply assumed that an increased release of TSH by the anterior pituitary increases circulating levels of thyroid hormones (tables 16.3 and 16.4, fig. 16.1). Yet remarkably little information is available on this point. The basophil cell type believed to contain TSH makes its appearance in the pituitary in the early limb-bud stages after hatching at NF 52 (Kerr 1966). Granulation increases steadily until NF 58. No degranulation is evident during climax stages after maximum granulation (Kerr 1966). Bioassays for pituitary TSH in *Xenopus laevis* larvae show, however, that the levels in the pituitary change during metamorphic climax (Dodd and Dodd 1976). The pituitary levels are high immediately before forelimb emergence. There probably is a release of TSH at about the time of forelimb emergence, because the pituitary TSH levels fall. In midclimax stages the pituitary TSH levels rise again, only to decrease gradually in late climax stage to low postmetamorphic levels (Dodd and Dodd 1976). Measurement (RIA) of pituitary TSH levels in *X. laevis* indicates the absence of TSH before NF 56, an increase until midclimax stages (NF 63), and decline thereafter (Bray and Sicard 1982).

Surprisingly, *circulating* levels of TSH during metamorphosis are unknown. Eddy and Lipner (1976) injected antibodies to mammalian TSH into anuran larvae and inhibited metamorphosis, implying that circulating levels of TSH participate in regulating amphibian metamorphosis. This work furthermore suggests that using antibodies to mammalian TSH could quantify amphibian TSH. Amphibian TSH can be isolated from the pituitary of adult bullfrogs and neotenic axolotls (MacKenzie, Licht, and Papkoff 1978; Schultheiss 1980a). Therefore, amphibian-specific TSH antibodies should also permit measurement of TSH during metamorphosis. So far, neither potential method to quantify circulating TSH levels is in use.

No data are available on TSH receptors in the thyroid of metamorphosing amphibians. Circulating TSH levels may not need to change, because the TSH receptor number or receptor type on the thyroid may change during metamorphosis. Such changes could make the thyroid more receptive to TSH, causing rising thyroid hormone levels without concomitant TSH increases. Preliminary data in urodeles suggest that the thyroid gland's sensitivity to TSH changes during development (Darras and Kuhn 1983; Norman and Norris 1987; Prahlad 1968).

Pituitary transplantation studies in larvae suggest that complete metamorphic climax requires a stimulus by the hypothalamus (Etkin 1963; Voitkevich 1962). Ablation of the hypothalamus anlage at the open neural tube of the embryo results in normal growth rate, but differentiation stops in the earliest climax stages (Goos 1969; Hanoaka 1967; Voitkevich 1962). The neurons from the hypothalamus typically do not enter the anterior lobe of the pituitary but terminate in the median eminence. The median eminence contains a capillary portal system that delivers the neurosecretions from the neuronal terminals of the hypothalamus to the pituitary. This capillary bed appears at midlarval stages and matures just before climax (Etkin 1963, 1968).

The hypothalamus has four recognizable types of nerve terminals from the midclimax to adult stages of amphibian life (Belenky, Chetverukhin, and Polenov 1973a). The classification of the types is by size, location, and appearance of the secretory granules. The percentage of each individual nerve terminal type changes during larval life, and in fact, terminal development continues even after tail loss (Belenky,

Chetverukhin, and Polenov 1973b). Two of the four types of terminals (A1 and A2) become degranulated at TK XXI. Belenky and his co-workers suggest that the terminals that become degranulated contain TRH. The other two types of nerve terminals (B and C) probably contain monoaminergic compounds (e.g., dopamine, adrenaline, noradrenaline). One of these monoaminergic neuron types (B) also becomes degranulated at climax (Belenky, Chetverukhin, and Polenov 1973b). These hypothalamic monoaminergic neurons appear early in larval life and in some species even send terminals into the pars distalis of the pituitary. The amount of monoaminergic material and number of these neurons increase at the beginning of climax. They disappear in the pars distalis and do not reappear in the adult (Aronsson 1976). The role of these monoaminergic neurons in the control of TSH in amphibian metamorphosis is not understood, but dopamine can antagonize TRH responses in the pituitary gland, particularly the response of prolactin-secreting cells (Gershengorn 1985).

Shortly after the isolation, purification, and sequencing of thyrotropin-releasing hormone (TRH) from the mammalian hypothalamus in the late 1960s, TRH was found in the amphibian brain (Jackson and Reichlin 1974). Since then TRH has been found in many amphibian tissues including the pineal, hypothalamus, skin, intestinal tract, thymus, and blood (Balls et al. 1985; Jackson and Reichlin 1979; Mimhagh et al. 1987). The TRH content of various organs changes during larval life. It cannot be found in the earliest stages of development, and then it increases in all organs up to early climax stages (Balls et al. 1985; Bray and Sicard 1982; King and Millar 1981; Prasad, Wilber, and Amborski 1982). After the end of metamorphic climax, TRH decreases in the brain and intestine of *Xenopus* (Balls et al. 1985; Bray and Sicard 1982; King and Millar 1981). However, TRH continues to increase in the skin and thymus of *X. laevis* and the brain of *Rana catesbeiana*. The TRH concentrations do not decrease in the whole animal at climax and are actually highest in the adult (Balls et al. 1985; Prasad, Wilber, and Amborski 1982).

Immunohistochemical methods demonstrate TRH in several hypothalamic nuclei, the median eminence, parts of the telencephalon, and the brain stem of all larval stages and adult bullfrogs, *R. catesbeiana* (Mimhagh et al. 1987). Low levels occur in all brain regions up to midlarval stages. After midlarval stages (TK XI to XVII) TRH increases and then remains constant in the adult. The ability to synthesize TRH increases in the brain during metamorphosis, while homogenates of brain tissues in the larva have a higher TRH-degrading activity than in the adult (Prasad, Wilber, and Amborski 1982). The amount of TRH available for release by an organ at any stage is the result of both degradation and synthesis. Rates of these processes are unknown for most organs in amphibians. Therefore, the amount of TRH available for release into the circulation is unknown.

Because TRH was isolated in mammals by its ability to regulate pituitary TSH release and indirectly increase thyroid hormones, many authors have attempted to induce anuran and urodele metamorphosis by TRH administration but have failed (Darras and Kuhn 1983; Etkin and Gona 1968; Gona and Gona 1974; Jacobs, Michielsen, and Kuhn 1988; J. J. Just unpublished; Millar et al. 1983). Some claim that, as

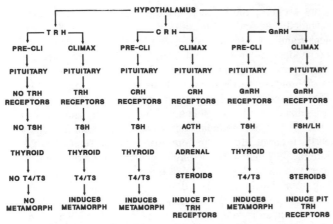

Fig. 16.3 A propsed model to explain the role of the hypothalamus in the control of metamorphosis. The model accounts for the need of the hypothalamus as well as the inability of thyrotropin-releasing hormone (TRH) to induce climax stages. We suggest that corticotropin-releasing hormone (CRH) and gonadotropin-releasing hormone (GnRH) can induce thyroid-stimulating hormone (TSH) before climax and that steroid hormones induce pituitary TRH receptors. *FSH,* follicle-stimulating hormone; *LH,* luteinizing hormone.

expected, TRH accelerates metamorphosis in anurans (abstracts by Etkin and Kim 1971; Schultheiss 1978; Shiomi et al. 1972). In adults, TRH stimulates the thyroid-pituitary axis (Darras and Kuhn 1982, 1983; Jacobs et al. 1988; Rosenkilde 1979) or produces no effect (Millar et al. 1983; Taurog et al. 1974; Vandesande and Aspeslagh 1974). Perhaps circulating levels of TRH do not change during metamorphosis (Sawin et al. 1978). TRH disappears rapidly from the plasma of adult mammals and anurans (Jackson and Reichlin 1979; Taurog et al. 1974), suggesting that TRH would not increase in general circulation during normal metamorphosis or during attempted TRH-induced metamorphosis (Balls et al. 1985). TRH levels in general circulation become high in larvae after TRH administration, however, possibly because plasma of both anuran and urodele larvae has almost no ability to destroy TRH (Taurog et al. 1974).

Because the completion of metamorphic climax requires the hypothalamus and its secretions, one might ask why TRH does not induce metamorphosis. Several explanations seem possible. (1) Not enough TRH reaches the pituitary in the animal even if TRH receptors are present. (2) TRH responsiveness and TRH receptor number in the basophilic cells in amphibian larvae change during development just as they do in the mammalian pituitary (Banerji and Prasad 1982; Walker, Coulombe, and Dussault 1980). Perhaps not enough TRH receptors exist in the amphibian pituitary when TRH is administered. (3) In mammals TRH receptors are affected by a number of hormones including TRH, T_4, estrogen, and glucocorticoids. TRH and T_4 downregulate the TRH receptors while the steroids increase the TRH receptors (Sharif 1987). All these hormones change during amphibian development, affecting the availability of TRH receptors in unknown ways. (4) Even if TRH receptors are present in the basophilic cells, many amphibians may not respond to TRH by releasing TSH. (5) TRH induces both TSH and prolactin release in larval pituitary, but these hormones counteract each other, resulting in no net increase in metamorphic rate (see below concerning

possible interaction). (6) Although mammalian TRH occurs in many amphibian organs, perhaps a unique amphibian TRH is responsible for initiating metamorphic climax. This is plausible, since a whole family of pro-TRH peptides occur in mammals (Wu, Lechan, and Jackson 1987), any one of which might act in amphibian metamorphosis. (7) Perhaps another known mammalian hypothalamic-releasing factor stimulates the pituitary-thyroid axis of larval amphibians. This possibility should be considered since both mammalian gonadotropin-releasing hormone (GnRH; Denver 1988; Jacobs, Michielsen, and Kuhn 1988) and mammalian corticotropin-releasing hormone (CRH; Denver 1988) can cause the release of TSH from the adult amphibian pituitary.

Figure 16.3 presents a possible sequence of events for hypothalamic control during development. Inherent in this scheme are numerous testable hypotheses that deserve the attention of amphibian endocrinologists.

Growth-Promoting Hormones

General Physiology Autotransplantation of the pituitary leads to gigantism of larvae, while hypophysectomized animals are smaller than normal (Etkin and Lehrer 1960), indicating that the larval pituitary contains a growth-promoting hormone under inhibitory hypothalamic control. Since Berman et al. (1964) first showed that prolactin can act as a growth factor in amphibian larvae, numerous others have confirmed this finding (see Dodd and Dodd 1976). There is less consensus about the effect of mammalian growth hormone (GH). GH is as effective or more effective than prolactin in promoting the growth of hypophysectomized larvae of *Alytes obstetricans* (Discoglossidae; Remy and Bounhiol 1965, 1966), *Rana pipiens* (Just and Kollros 1968), and *R. temporaria* (Dodd and Dodd 1976), and normal young intact *R. temporaria* (Enemar, Essvik, and Klang 1968). GH administration increases growth in postmetamorphic animals (Frye, Brown, and Snyder 1972).

For almost half a century, mammalian GH was assumed directly responsible for mammalian growth. In the 1970s it became obvious that mammalian GH causes growth by causing the liver and other organs to produce somatomedins (SMs) or insulinlike growth factors (IGFs). These SMs are the actual factors (hormones) responsible for fetal and postnatal mammalian growth (Hall and Sara 1983). SMs occur in the blood of adult amphibians (Daughaday et al. 1985; Rothstein et al. 1980; Shapiro and Pimstone 1977). No studies are available for larvae, but in developing mammals both the SM levels and the site of production may change (Hall and Sara 1983). By analogy with mammalian GH, prolactin administration to larval *R. catesbeiana* releases "synlactin" from the liver (Delidow, Baldocchi, and Nicoll 1988; Delidow et al. 1986). "Synlactin" can cause the growth of both the larval tail fin as well as the pigeon crop (Delidow, Baldocchi, and Nicoll 1988). It is not clear whether growth factors (like "synlactin" or SMs) or combinations of growth factors and pituitary hormones control all the growth-promoting effects of the two pituitary hormones (GH and prolactin).

Aside from prolactin's effect on amphibian larval growth, it also inhibits metamorphosis, as demonstrated by three different methods: prolactin administration inhibits the thyroid glands of larval amphibians, prolactin administration inhibits peripheral tissue responses to thyroid hormones, and prolactin removal accelerates metamorphosis.

Prolactin's ability to inhibit thyroid gland function is far from universal. Experiments on larval *R. catesbeiana* and *R. pipiens* (Gona 1967, 1968) and *X. laevis* (Dodd and Dodd 1976; Regard and Hourdry 1975; Regard and Mauchamp 1973) indicate that prolactin can inhibit thyroid activity, as measured by various means, including I^{131} uptake. On the other hand, experimentation with *Bufo bufo* indicates that prolactin increases iodine uptake by the thyroid gland of older larvae (Campantico, Olivero, and Peyrot 1968), while it has no effect on the earliest climax stages of *R. catesbeiana* and *R. pipiens* (Gona 1968). Our understanding of thyroid function in urodeles is no clearer. Whereas prolactin administration does not affect iodine uptake by the thyroid of neotenic *Ambystoma tigrinum* (Norris and Platt 1974), it nevertheless suppresses thyroid hormone release induced by TSH (Norris 1978). In *A. mexicanum* prolactin does not block the TSH-induced T_4 release (Darras and Kuhn 1984).

Bern, Nicoll, and Strohman (1967) and Etkin and Gona (1967) first suggested that prolactin inhibits metamorphosis at the peripheral tissue level, reporting that prolactin counteracted thyroid hormone–induced tail regression. *In vivo* prolactin administration also counteracts T_4 effects on various organs including tail, gut, gill, and pancreas in numerous anuran and urodele species (see Dodd and Dodd 1976; Dent 1988). Prolactin does not always inhibit the effects of thyroid hormones in peripheral tissues—for example, hind-leg growth (Just and Kollros 1968) or the appearance of hydrolytic enzymes in tail fins (Platt et al. 1986; Ray and Dent 1986).

If prolactin retards metamorphosis, then removal of prolactin from larvae should accelerate metamorphosis. Indeed, injection of bullfrog larvae with antibodies against bovine prolactin (Eddy and Lipner 1975) or against bullfrog prolactin (Clemons and Nicoll 1977b; Yamamoto and Kikuyama

1982a) accelerates metamorphosis. Ergot alkaloids, which are presumed to inhibit prolactin release selectively in mammals, increased metamorphic progression in neotenic *A. tigrinum* (Platt 1976) and *B. bufo japonicus* (Seki and Kikuyama 1979).

Etkin (1968) and Bern, Nicoll, and Strohman (1967) suggested a major role for prolactin during metamorphosis and also predicted changes in circulating prolactin levels. Prolactin levels should be high during early larva stages, causing larval growth, and should decrease before climax and then drop to very low levels during climax. This would allow thyroid hormones to cause the many reported effects on tissues during climax (Frieden and Just 1970). This hypothesis rested on prolactin's antimetamorphic effects, its growth-promoting capabilities, and the development of the medium eminence just before climax, when it presumably could send an inhibitory signal to suppress prolactin release.

This hypothesis appeared to find early support when bioassays found more prolactin in the pituitary of young salamanders (Norris, Jones, and Cohen 1973) and bullfrog larvae (Hsu, Yu, and Liang 1976) than in the pituitary of climax larvae of the same species. Measurements of prolactin by RIA soon provided evidence that this hypothesis is not correct. The pituitary and serum prolactin levels are low during early stages of development and increase at climax stages (fig. 16.4; Clemons and Nicoll 1977a; Yamamoto and Kikuyama 1982b; Yamamoto, Niihuma, and Kikuyama 1986). Furthermore, rates of prolactin synthesis mirror these hormone levels and are highest at climax stages (fig. 16.4b; Yamamoto, Niihuma, and Kikuyama 1986). The circulating levels of GH are also highest at metamorphic climax, when the growth rate is lowest (Clemons 1976).

Work on prolactin receptors also does not suggest that prolactin is most effective in early stages. Prolactin receptors occur in many peripheral amphibian tissues, including tail fins, kidney, gills, testes, epidermis, and liver (Carr and Jaffe

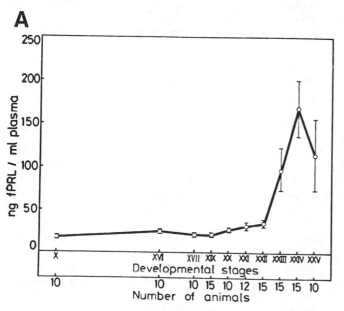

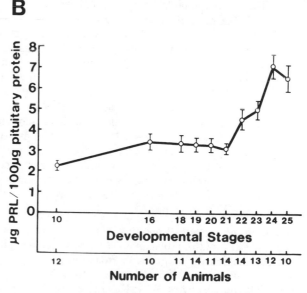

Fig. 16.4 Changes in immunoreactive prolactin (*fPRL*) level in plasma (*A*) and in pituitary protein (*B*) as a function of development in larval *Rana catesbeiana*. Staging according to Taylor and Kollros 1946. Mean values ± 1 SE are presented. (*A* reprinted, by permission, from Yamamoto and Kikuyama 1982b; *B* reprinted, by permission, from Yamamoto, Niihuma, and Kikuyama 1986.)

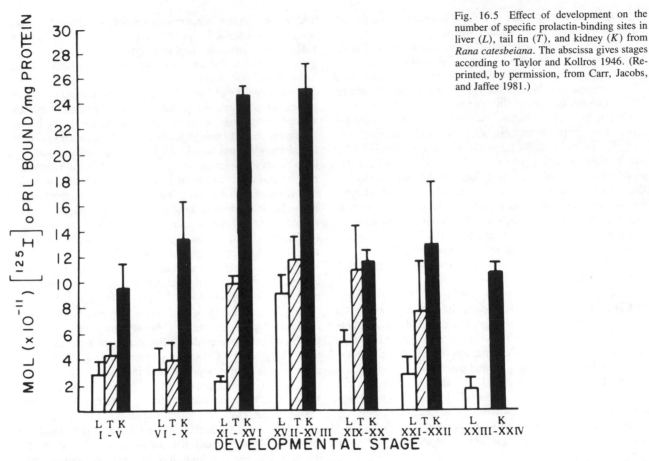

Fig. 16.5 Effect of development on the number of specific prolactin-binding sites in liver (*L*), tail fin (*T*), and kidney (*K*) from *Rana catesbeiana*. The abscissa gives stages according to Taylor and Kollros 1946. (Reprinted, by permission, from Carr, Jacobs, and Jaffee 1981.)

1980, 1981; Carr, Jacobs, and Jaffe 1981; Guardabassi et al. 1987; White 1981; White and Nicoll 1979; White and Nicoll 1981; White, Lebovic, and Nicoll 1981). Histochemical studies of the kidneys suggest that these receptors are located in specific cells, such as the proximal convoluted tubules of kidney (Gona 1982; Guardabassi, Campantico, and Pattano 1984). The number of prolactin receptors in various tissues is highest right before or at climax (fig. 16.5; Carr, Jacobs, and Jaffe 1981; White and Nicoll 1979), but receptor numbers are lower in young larvae and in animals at late climax stages.

Prolactin receptor number is under hormonal control. Thyroid hormones increase prolactin receptor number in all tissues examined (Carr, Jacobs, and Jaffe 1981; White and Nicoll 1981). In mammals prolactin administration increases the prolactin receptor number. Osmotic manipulation of amphibians (Guardabassi et al. 1987; Muccioli et al. 1989) and direct prolactin administration (Carr, Jacobs, and Jaffe 1981) yield similar results. On the other hand, White and Nicoll (1981) claim that prolactin administration "downregulates" its receptor numbers. Clearly more work is needed on the control of prolactin receptors.

Regulation of Growth-Promoting Hormone Both dopamine and TRH control prolactin release into the blood. TRH increases the release of prolactin from the adult pituitary gland both *in vitro* and *in vivo* (Clemons, Russell, and Nicoll 1979; Hall and Chadwick 1984; Kuhn et al. 1985; Seki and Kikuyama 1986). Dopamine can inhibit *in vitro* prolactin release from the pituitary (Seki and Kikuyama 1986). Thus,

both dopamine and TRH may control circulating prolactin levels in larvae. That ergot alkaloids probably decrease circulating prolactin levels in larvae (Alonso-Bedate and Delgado 1983; Platt 1976; Seki and Kikuyama 1979), thereby accelerating metamorphosis, suggests dopaminergic control. Dopamine levels in the anterior pituitary decrease during metamorphic climax, perhaps increasing circulating levels of prolactin at midclimax stages (Aronsson 1976).

Increasing levels of thyroid hormones at the beginning of climax stages (table 16.3) are necessary for the rising circulating prolactin levels in midclimax stages (Kawamura, Yamamoto, and Kikuyama 1986). The normal increase in circulating levels of prolactin seen in midclimax stages requires a pituitary-hypothalamus connection, as animals with this connection severed and animals with their pituitary autotransplanted all have low levels of circulating prolactin (Kawamura, Yamamoto, and Kikuyama 1986). In midclimax stages a releasing factor (probably TRH) produced in the brain and released into the median eminence controls prolactin release.

This would offer additional explanations to those in figure 16.3 for the lack of effect of TRH administration on metamorphic rate. Namely, TRH would increase circulating prolactin levels without increasing TSH secretion if prolactin blocks the TRH responsiveness of pituitary TSH cells. The rise in circulating prolactin levels after TRH administration may not prevent TSH release but may inhibit thyroid follicle cell responsiveness to TSH. Unfortunately, no data exist on prolactin receptors in either the thyroid or pituitary gland during amphibian metamorphosis.

The Adrenal Gland

General Physiology The administration of adrenal steroid hormones can accelerate thyroid hormone–induced metamorphosis in both anuran and urodele larvae (Bock 1938; Voitkevich 1937). The acceleration does not occur in early larvae, but animals in late developmental stages increase their developmental rate after steroid hormone administration (see Kaltenbach 1968). Many adrenal steroids (deoxycorticosterone, corticosterone, cortisol, and aldosterone) accelerate thyroid hormone–induced metamorphosis (see Kaltenbach 1968, 1985; Kikuyama et al. 1983). Thus, adrenal steroids apparently accelerate metamorphosis only when the circulating levels of thyroid hormone are high. Estrogens may also accelerate thyroid hormone–induced metamorphosis (Frieden and Naile 1955), but the sex steroids progesterone, estrogen, and testosterone are not required to accelerate metamorphosis (Kikuyama et al. 1983). These discrepancies in the action of sex steroids' effects on metamorphosis have not yet been explained.

Because both steroid pellet implantation into tail fins and *in vitro* steroid hormone administration accelerate thyroid hormone–induced tail regression, steroids function at the peripheral tissue levels. How adrenal steroids accelerate metamorphosis *in vivo* is unknown. Adrenal steroid hormones increase the number of thyroid hormone receptors in tail fins (Suzuki and Kikuyama 1983). The increase in thyroid hormone receptors requires that RNA and protein synthesis occur. This increase of receptors at the peripheral tissue levels could account for adrenal steroid accelerating metamorphosis, as could the postulated stimulation of hypothalamic TRH receptors (fig. 16.3).

Obviously, a major question is whether steroid hormone levels change in *normal* metamorphosis, which requires that the adrenal gland synthesize and release adrenal hormones. The adrenal gland in amphibians consists of two cell types, the steroidogenic cells and the chromaffin cells. These adrenal cells occur in the mesonephric kidney in adults of all three orders (Gabe 1971; Milano and Accordi 1986). The first adrenal cells appear just before hatching, at the anterior part of the kidney but not in the pronephros (Accordi and Corbellini 1986–1987, Accordi and Milano 1977; Leist et al. 1969). The number and sizes of both types of cell increase during metamorphosis. The adrenal tissue spreads from the anterior end of the mesonephros to the posterior end (Accordi and Corbellini 1986–1987; Leist et al. 1969; Rapola 1963; Setoguti et al. 1985). During climax stages the adrenal cells are located at the margin of the ventral surface of the mesonephros in both urodeles and anurans (Milano and Accordi 1986). In many species this is the permanent location of adrenal tissues, but in some species (*Rana esculenta, Bufo bufo, Hyla arborea*) a lateral shift occurs sometime after completion of metamorphic climax (Milano and Accordi 1986). The histochemistry of these cells indicates that they can produce hormones either before (Hsu, Yu, and Chen 1980) or immediately after hatching (Leist et al. 1969; Leist 1970; Rapola 1962, 1963), and their production capacities increase in all species until the earliest climax stages (Hsu, Yu, and Chen 1980; Leist et al. 1969; Leist 1970; Rapola 1962, 1963). Histochemically, the adrenal gland decreases during climax stages of *Xenopus laevis* (Leist 1970), while in *R. cates-*

beiana activity increases throughout the climax stages (Hsu, Yu, and Chen 1980).

The histological and biochemical development of the chromaffin cells has not received as much attention as the steroidogenic cells (Accordi and Corbellini 1986–1987). A few scattered chromaffin cells appear before hatching, and homogeneous dense granules appear in the first few larval stages (Accordi et al. 1975; Accordi and Milano 1977). During mid-larval stages (TK X) two types of chromaffin cells appear, as judged by different granular structure inside the cells. The so-called type I granules are presumably in the noradrenaline cells, while the type II granules are in the adrenaline cells. The granules in the noradrenaline-containing cells are about 25% larger by the end of climax than the granules in the adrenaline-containing cells. The chromaffin cells as well as the granules grow throughout the latter half of larval life. The chromaffin cells proliferate throughout larval life, with the noradrenaline cell types predominating throughout metamorphosis (Accordi and Corbellini 1986–1987; Accordi and Milano 1977). Increases in cell size and number and granular size suggest that adrenaline and noradrenaline become more available during metamorphosis. At no time during larval life does morphology indicate altered hormone release, however, and no data are available on circulating levels of adrenal medulla hormone.

In both anurans and urodeles, steroidogenic cells appear before hatching at the anterior end of the mesonephros (Accordi and Corbellini 1986–1987; Leist et al. 1969). After they appear, the new steroidogenic cells spread craniocaudally on the medial surface of the mesonephros. By the late larval stages these cells spread the entire length of the mesonephros (Accordi and Corbellini 1986–1987; Branin 1937; Certain 1961; Leist et al. 1969; Rapola 1962, 1963).

Dale (1962) and Rapola (1963) first attempted to measure steroid hormone production during the entire metamorphic period by determining the amount of excreted steroid hormones. *Rana pipiens* and *R. sylvatica* excrete hydrocortisone at very early limb-bud stages (Dale 1962), whereas *Xenopus laevis* does not excrete the first corticoid hormone until mid-larval stages (Leist 1970; Rapola 1963). Excreted hormone increases until the earliest climax stages and then decreases by midclimax stages (Dale 1962; Leist 1970; Rapola 1963). Aldosterone does not appear in the urine until midclimax stages (Dale 1962).

Levels of circulating adrenal steroids (corticosterone, cortisol, and aldosterone) have now been measured during metamorphosis in both anurans and urodeles. All authors agree that the lowest circulating levels of steroid hormones occur in early limb-bud stages (before TK XIII). During rapid hindlimb growth (TK XIV to XVIII), steroid hormone levels increase. Just as for thyroid hormones, consensus is lacking as to the stage at which circulating corticosteroid hormone levels peak. However, levels clearly peak during climax (table 16.5). Only rarely do corticosterone levels peak well before climax (TK XVII; Krug et al. 1983). Most authors do not analyze their data statistically, and some of the differences may therefore not be significant. All three hormones (corticosterone, cortisol, and aldosterone) are also present in *Ambystoma tigrinum* (Stiffler et al. 1986). Circulating levels of corticosterone in *A. tigrinum* also peak at midclimax

TABLE 16.5 Relative Percentage of Circulating Adrenal Steroid Hormones Present in Various Stages of Anuran Metamorphosis

		Stages								
	Hormone	X[a] 55[b]	XI 55	XII 55	XIII 56	XIV 57	XV 57	XVI 58	XVII 59	XVIII 60
Rana catesbeiana[c]	CRT	ND[d]	ND	ND	ND	ND	ND	ND	ND	4
Rana catesbeiana[e]	CRT	1[f]		14		43	61		100	68
Xenopus laevis[g]	CRT	33			35	31	31	27	40	
Rana catesbeiana[e]	ALD	54		54		60	86		51	63
Rana catesbeiana[h]	ALD	6						7		8
Xenopus laevis[g]	ALD			45	30		58	65	40	
Rana catesbeiana[e]	CRL[d]	11		18		23	36		45	54
All data[i]	CRT	9		7	18	25	31	14	47	36
All data[i]	ALD	30		50	30	60	72	36	46	36
All data[j]	All	18		26	22	32	46	25	46	40

Notes: The average hormone concentration for each stage in each species was obtained directly from tables or estimated from the figures in publications. Once the average hormone concentration per stage in each species was found, the relative concentration per stage was determined using the following calculations: (mean hormone concentration for any stage)/(maximum hormone concentration in a specific stage) · 100 = (relative percentage of circulating hormones at stage). This calculated relative percentage is presented in the table. If more than one set of data were available in one publication, the relative percentages were combined and the average presented in the table. Empty cells in the table refer to stages at which no measurements were made.

ALD = aldosterone; CRL = cortisol; CRT = corticosterone.

[a] All authors using *Rana* species and Taylor and Kollros stages (1946).

[b] All authors using *Xenopus* species used Nieuwkoop and Faber stages (1967).

[c] Jaffe 1981 (combined data fig. 1).

[d] ND indicates that nondetectable levels of hormone were present in that species using the methods of the publication. The ND values were used as a 1% relative hormone concentration, when the overall mean was calculated. We felt that some hormone was present and realize that this could lead to a relative underestimation of the hormone present.

[e] Krug et al. 1983.

[f] Even when values are available for any stage, some animals in that specific stage may have had nondetectable hormone levels. Since only the actual relative percentage was used, this leads to an overestimation of the hormone present.

[g] Jolivet-Jaudet and Leloup-Hatey 1984.

[h] Kikuyama, Suzuki, and Iwamuro 1986.

[i] Relative percentages of circulating T_4 of each species for the same stage were averaged.

[j] The relative percentages of circulating T_3 of each species for the same stage were averaged.

stages and decrease in late climax stages (Carr and Norris 1988).

Steroid hormones released into circulation are either free or bound to plasma proteins. Aldosterone and corticosterone bind to plasma from adult *X. laevis* (Jolivet-Jaudet and Leloup-Hatey 1986). Aldosterone does not bind to plasma of NF 57 *Xenopus*, but corticosterone does bind. The corticosterone-binding capacity of plasma in larvae is lower than that in adults. The increase in total corticosterone in *X. laevis* metamorphosis actually represents an increase in free and bound hormone concentration (table 16.6). The percentage of free hormone is 50% at midclimax stages but is less than 20% in all other stages. Young larvae and late climax stage animals have about one-third of the total hormone concentration (tables 16.5 and 16.6) and only about one-tenth of the free hormone concentration found in the midclimax stages (table 16.6). These circulating levels affect metamorphosis; inhibition of corticoid synthesis retards metamorphosis (Kikuyama et al. 1982).

Adrenal steroid hormone receptors in amphibians are poorly understood. Glucocorticoid receptors in the liver of adult *R. catesbeiana* (Woody and Jaffe 1982), *R. esculenta* (Incerpi, Luly, and Scapin 1983), and *X. laevis* (Lange and Hanke 1988; Lange, Hanke, and Morishige 1989) and in the gut and kidney of *R. catesbeiana* (Mehdi, DiBattista, and Sandor 1984) typically bind all adrenal steroids or their analogues (triamcinolone acetonide, dexamethasone, corticosterone, cortisol, aldosterone). They usually do not bind sex

TABLE 16.6 Concentration of Corticosterone in the Plasma of Larval and Adult *Xenopus laevis*

	Corticosterone Concentration[b]				
	Total	Bound		Free	
Stage[a]	(ng·ml⁻¹)	(ng·ml⁻¹)	(%)	(ng·ml⁻¹)	(%)
NF 54–58	14.2 ± 1.4	12.6	89	1.5	11
NF 59–61	21.3 ± 1.8	17.5	82	3.6	17
NF 62–63	45.8 ± 4.0	22.5	49	23.1	50
NF 64–65	17.1 ± 3.1	14.8	87	2.3	13
Adult	4.5 ± 1.5	4.5	98	0.1	1

[a] Nieuwkoop and Faber 1967.

[b] Jolivet-Jaudet and Leloup-Hatey 1986.

steroids or bind them weakly (estrogen, progesterone, testosterone). Adrenal steroid hormone binding to liver, tail fin, and intestine changes during metamorphosis in larval *R. catesbeiana* (Woody and Jaffe 1984). The number of cytosolic glucocorticoid receptors decreases in the liver and intestine during larval life, but the number of tail fin receptors does not change. In the liver, binding capacities drop after forelimb emergence (Woody and Jaffe 1984). The liver-binding capacity at TK XXIV is only about 4% of that found at TK XX and is 2% of that found in adult bullfrogs.

The control of adrenal steroid receptor numbers is not understood, but they clearly fluctuate with season, diurnal cycles, sex of animal, food availability, and developmental stage (Lange and Hanke 1988; Lange, Hanke, and Morishige

XIX 60	XX 61	XXI 62	XXII 63	XXIII 64	XXIV 65	XXV 66
5	17	77	79	79	83	
	75		71		100	
44	49	100	100	35	39	
	68		63		100	
13	17	41	100	64	55	35
75		100	48	65	85	
	68		100		63	
25	52	89	80	57	74	
44	43	71	70	65	80	35
35	52	80	80	61	75	35

1989; Woody and Jaffe 1984). Normal levels of thyroid hormones do not influence adrenal steroid hormone receptors (Lange, Hanke, and Morishige 1989; Woody and Jaffe 1984), but massive doses of thyroid hormones increase adrenal steroid hormone receptors (Lange, Hanke, and Morishige 1989).

Regulation of Adrenal Glands In mammals, the pituitary-hypothalamus axis controls glucocorticoid (cortisol), while the renin-angiotensin system controls mineral corticoids. Adrenal gland differentiation of both urodele and anuran larvae depends on the pituitary gland (Pehlemann 1962). At hatching the pituitary has cells containing adrenocorticotropic hormone (ACTH; Dodd and Dodd 1976). Hypophysectomy decreases steroid hormone synthesis, and either pituitary gland transplantations or ACTH administration restores this synthesis to normal or near-normal levels (Horn 1976; Hsu et al. 1984). ACTH causes a dose-related release by kidneys of both glucocorticoids and mineral corticoids (Maser, Janssens, and Hanke 1982). In larval *Ambystoma tigrinum*, hypophysectomy decreases circulating aldosterone concentration, while ACTH administration increases it (DeRuyter and Stiffler 1986). In larval *X. laevis*, ACTH probably increases corticosterone release, because more appears in the urine after ACTH administration.

Because circulating steroid hormones change during development (tables 16.5 and 16.6), one might predict changes in pituitary ACTH content and/or release. No direct measurements of ACTH levels in amphibians are available. The rate of steroidogenesis in hypophysectomized larvae treated with ACTH can be matched to the rate of normal adrenal steroidogenesis in control larvae, which gives an indirect measure of ACTH production. Increasing concentrations of ACTH are required to match normal steroidogenesis (Yu et al. 1985), suggesting that ACTH levels are very low in young larvae, rise during midlarval stages, and increase dramatically during climax stages. A corticotropin-releasing factor (CRF) isolated and purified from the hypothalamus can trigger release of ACTH in mammals (Vale et al. 1981). CRF has been localized in the hypothalamus of adult amphibians (Tonon et al. 1986). CRF causes ACTH secretion in adult *Rana ridibunda* (Tonon et al. 1986) but not in adult *R. pipiens* (Denver 1988). Lesions in the ventral region of the hypothalamic preoptic

nucleus in larval *X. laevis* decrease both the number of ACTH cells and the amounts of ACTH in these cells (Notenboom, Terlou, and Matem 1976), suggesting that CRF is present in amphibian larvae. However, no quantitative data are available on CRF levels during metamorphosis. The most common conclusion is that, as the median eminence matures (see above), it releases CRF, which leads to increased ACTH release and adrenal steroid hormone levels (table 16.5).

In adult amphibians, factors other than ACTH affect adrenal function, including factors that increase steroid release, namely, renin (Johnston et al. 1967), increased plasma K^+ concentration (Maser, Janssens, and Hanke 1982), angiotensin II (Hanke and Maser 1985; Lihrmann et al. 1988), arginine vasotocin (AVT), and catecholamines (Hanke and Maser 1985); and factors that inhibit steroid release, namely, elevated plasma Na^+ concentration (Maser, Janssens, and Hanke 1982). The administration of atrial natriuretic factor can inhibit the ACTH response of the adrenal, namely, the release of steroid hormones (Lihrmann et al. 1988). Although not all these factors may be involved in modulating adrenal steroid hormone release in larval amphibians, some modulators of adrenal gland function act during metamorphosis.

In bullfrog larvae, T_4 together with ACTH increases adrenal steroid synthesis more than does ACTH alone (Hsu et al. 1984). Injection of ACTH probably leads to increased steroid hormone release in larvae of *Ambystoma tigrinum* (DeRuyter and Stiffler 1986). Manipulation of the plasma ionic composition of intact larval *A. tigrinum* changes plasma levels of aldosterone and corticosterone (Stiffler et al. 1986). Because the ion effects differ (i.e., high Na^+ suppresses aldosterone while increasing corticosterone, and ACTH alone always increases adrenal steroid hormone release), some non-ACTH effect of ions on steroid hormone release may occur. The renin-angiotensin system, present in developing amphibians, is not known to affect adrenal steroids during development. In *Litoria wotjulumensis* (Anura: Hylidae), the renal renin decreases with development, while *Cyclorana longipes* (Hylidae) show no developmental change in renin content (Taylor et al. 1982).

Reproductive Glands

General Physiology In the embryo the gonads consist of two major elements, cortex and medulla, located as germinal ridges along the inner edges of the anterior mesonephros. As the genital ridges start to enlarge, the germ cells migrate into them from the presumptive endoderm in anurans and from the lateral plate mesoderm in urodeles (see Lofts 1974). During early larval development, the cortex expands when an ovary forms, while the medulla expands when a testis develops (Witschi 1956). Right after hatching (TK I–V for anurans), the ova and testes are anatomically indistinguishable. By TK V–VI ovaries are evident by the eggs within them in *Rana catesbeiana*, *R. japonica*, *R. nigromaculata*, *R. pipiens*, *Rhacophorus buergeri* (Anura: Rhacophoridae), and *X. laevis* (Hsu, Chiang, and Liang 1977; Iwasawa and Kobayashi 1976; M. Kobayashi 1975; Michibata 1973; Shirane 1984, 1986).

Both the internal and the external environment can influence the differentiation of gonads and their associated ducts (see also chapter 15). In every species tested, temperatures greater than 25°C convert all larvae into adult male animals, while temperatures less than 15°C convert all larvae to females (see Gallien 1974). Testosterone administration to various ranid species during early larval life converts all larvae to males, while it has either no effect or only a minor sexual reversal effect in all tested urodeles and in the nonranid anurans. In urodeles and nonranid anurans, estrogen administration during larval life leads to all animals becoming females, including the genetic males (see Gallien 1974). In ranid amphibians, on the other hand, high levels of estrogen cause all animals to become females, while low levels of estrogen cause all animals to become males (see Dale 1962; Gallien 1974).

The sexual reversal caused by sex steroid hormones prompts questions about the timing of sex hormone production. Enzymes involved in sex hormone production are evident histochemically in both anurans (Chieffi and Botte 1963; Hsu, Chiang, and Liang 1977) and urodeles (Collenot 1965; Collenot and Collenot 1977). Larval gonads of urodeles (Ozon 1963, 1967, 1969) and anurans (Hsu et al. 1985; Rao, Breuer, and Witschi 1968, 1969) synthesize steroids. These histochemical and steroid synthetic studies suggest that at least some genera (*Triton, Pleurodeles* [both Caudata: Salamandridae], *Rana, Xenopus*) can produce steroid hormones right after hatching and throughout larval life.

Steroidogenesis increases during development and peaks during or after climax (Hsu et al. 1985; Hsu et al. 1989; Rao, Breuer, and Witschi 1969). In the earliest larval stages, both the male and female gonads can metabolize androgens and estrogens (Rao, Breuer, and Witschi 1968), which helps explain why metabolites of androgens and estrogens appear in the excretory products of larvae during all stages of development (Dale 1962). In *Xenopus laevis* the gonads produce low levels of androst-4-ene-3,17-dione from progesterone at the beginning of climax, and conversion increases during climax stages. Neither ovaries nor testes convert progesterone to either testosterone or estrogen (Rao, Breuer, and Witschi 1968). However, the ovaries of *Rana catesbeiana* can synthesize estrogen throughout larval life (Hsu et al. 1985; Hsu et al. 1989).

Estrogen synthesis and release is three times higher at metamorphic climax (TK XXV) than at midlarval stages (TK X). After climax, estrogen biosynthesis increases dramatically (Hsu et al. 1985; Hsu et al. 1989). Circulating levels of sex steroids during larval life are unknown. Dale (1962) did show that *Rana pipiens* excrete both estrogen and androgens by TK II–VI. The excreted levels increase during larval life, peak at TK XIX, and then decrease slightly at the end of climax (Dale 1962).

Regulation of Reproductive Glands Pituitary hormones control gonadal steroid synthesis and ovulation in adult amphibians (Fortune 1983; Licht and Papkoff 1974; Papkoff, Farmer, and Licht 1976; chapters 3 and 15). Adult amphibian pituitaries contain both follicle-stimulating hormone (FSH) and luteinizing hormone (LH; Licht and Papkoff 1974; Papkoff, Farmer, and Licht 1976). However, LH but not FSH influences ovulation and steroid biosynthesis (Fortune 1983). Large dissected follicles (diameter larger than 450 μm) obtained from adult *Xenopus laevis* respond to LH by markedly increasing their steroid hormone biosynthesis. Previtellogenic follicles (diameters smaller than 450 μm) do not respond to either hormone and produce progesterone, testosterone, and estradiol (Fortune 1983).

In contrast to adults, gonads in larvae seem independent of the pituitary. Hypophysectomized larvae develop and differentiate ovaries or testes as do normal larvae until late climax stages (Hsu, Chiang, and Liang 1973; Pehlemann 1962; Smith 1916; Yoshikura 1959). *In vitro*, ovaries from bullfrog larvae and adults secrete estrogen. Pituitary extracts do not affect *in vitro* estradiol secretion up to TK XX, produce a slight nonsignificant stimulatory effect at TK XXV, and increase secretion in young and mature frogs (Hsu et al. 1989). Thus, the larval pituitary produces no gonadotropin hormones, larval gonads do not contain gonadotropin hormone receptor until very late climax stages, or both. The gonads can respond to gonadotropins, however, because mammalian gonadotropin can cause oocytes to grow in bullfrog larval ovaries (Puckett 1939). Furthermore, implanting the anterior pituitary lobe of adult frogs into larvae near climax stages changes the ultrastructure of ovaries, indicating an increase in steroidogenesis (Hsu et al. 1985). These structural studies suggest that larval gonads have gonadotropin receptors. No data are available on the gonadotropin hormones in the blood of larvae.

In mammals, GnRH is a decapeptide found in the hypothalamus, extrahypothalamic brain regions, and nonneuronal tissues. It releases both FSH and LH from the pituitary. The adult amphibian brain contains mammalian GnRH and other forms of GnRH (King and Millar 1986; Sherwood, Zoeller, and Moore 1986). The adult amphibian pituitary responds both *in vivo* and *in vitro* to a variety of GnRHs by releasing FSH and LH (Licht 1984; Licht, Porter, and Millar 1987). Mammalian GnRH occurs in the brain of larval *Xenopus laevis* (King and Millar 1981) and *Rana catesbeiana* (Crim 1984; Whalen and Crim 1985). In *X. laevis*, whole-brain GnRH content increases throughout the larval period and especially after climax (King and Millar 1981). Immunostaining for GnRH in the brain, median eminence, and pituitary of *R. catesbeiana* larvae indicates that GnRH is present in the median eminence of TK XIII. The amount of GnRH increases gradually during larval life and is greatest at climax stages (Crim 1984; Whalen and Crim 1985). A few neurons staining for GnRH appear in the anterior preoptic area at climax stages, and their numbers increase in postmetamorphic animals and adults (Crim 1984, 1987). The role of GnRH during metamorphosis has not been determined but may be involved in the control of the gonads and thyroid (fig. 16.3).

Postmetamorphic Effects of Sex Steroids

In adult amphibians, estrogen causes the liver of both males and females to produce a protein called vitellogenin. This protein is released into the blood stream and is taken up by the ovaries and incorporated into eggs as part of the yolk (see Follett and Redshaw 1974). Larval liver first responds *in vivo* to estrogen by producing vitellogenin proteins and mRNA in early-to-midclimax stages in *X. laevis* (Huber, Ryffel, and Weber 1979; Kawahara et al. 1987; May and Knowland 1980), while the liver can respond *in vitro* at earlier stages

(Knowland 1978; Skipper and Hamilton 1979; Ng, Wolffe, and Tata 1984). The ability of the liver of larval *X. laevis* to respond to estrogen seems to reside in a population of cells arising in midclimax stages (Kawahara et al. 1987). This subpopulation makes up less than 5% of the hepatocyte population at NF 62 and increases during the remainder of climax. Even in 4-month-old froglets the estrogen-responsive cells do not make up 100% of the population as they do in adults. The urodele *Pleurodeles waltl* (Salamandridae) also does not respond to estrogen administration by producing vitellogenin until the beginning of climax stages (Cayrol and Deparis 1987).

A possible explanation for the late vitellogenin production is an increase in estrogen receptor number during late climax stage. However, estrogen receptors are present in the liver before estrogen responsiveness (May and Knowland 1981). Furthermore, estrogen receptors increase gradually and steadily, while vitellogenin production increases suddenly. Increasing levels of thyroid hormones are required for estrogen to stimulate the liver to produce vitellogenin (Huber, Ryffel, and Weber 1979; May and Knowland 1980). Perhaps the late climax responsiveness is because thyroid hormones affect estrogen binding to its receptor.

Some steroids also regulate postmetamorphic sound production. Urodeles and caecilians have a limited capacity to produce sound, while anurans have complex vocal capabilities (Duellman and Trueb 1986). Among the capabilities are the males' courtship calls to attract conspecific females (chapter 14). The larynx produces these sounds with its associated muscles and cartilage. Sexes differ in the larynx, with the mass of the adult male larynx three times greater than that of the female. In males the dilator laryngeal muscle is made up of two distinct bands, while in the female it is only partially separated. In *Xenopus laevis* the larynx is structurally the same in both sexes throughout larval life. After metamorphic climax the male larynx grows and differentiates more rapidly than that of the female (Sassoon and Kelley 1986). Males and females differ by 3 months after climax, and these differences increase with postmetamorphic age. In adult male *X. laevis* an average of 31,953 muscle fibers are in the larynx, while the corresponding number in adult females is 4,726 (Sassoon and Kelley 1986).

Androgens stimulate these sexual differences in larynx size. Androgen administration accelerates male laryngeal differentiation and can cause the transformation of the larval

female larynx into a male larynx. Administration of antiandrogens prevents male-type larynx differentiation (Sassoon and Kelley 1986). Androgen receptors are present in the laryngeal muscle of both males and females. However, receptors in males are three times more numerous than in females (Segil, Silverman, and Kelley 1987). Receptors proliferate after androgen administration and decrease after androgen removal (Segil, Silverman, and Kelley 1987). At climax the androgen levels are 30 pg · ml^{-1} in both males and females (Kelley 1986). Three months after tail loss males have more androgens than the females, and by 6 months males have nine times more androgens than do females (Kelley 1986).

The motor nerves (cranial nerve IX–X) that control the laryngeal muscle come from motor neurons in the medulla (fig. 16.6; see also chapter 2). These motor neurons receive direct afferent inputs from at least three brain nuclei, including the pretrigeminal nucleus of the dorsal tegmental area of the medulla (DTAM), the inferior reticular nucleus (Ri), and the medial reticular nucleus. The DTAM receives inputs from various anterior nuclei including those located at the anterior preoptic area (APOA), the ventral striatum, and several thalamic nuclei. This system is sexually dimorphic. The male has more connections between the APOA and DTAM and between the DTAM and Ri than does the female. In addition, afferents in cranial nerves IX–X leading to the larynx are more numerous in males than in females (Kelley 1986).

Electrical stimulation of the APOA in *Rana pipiens* results in courtship calls (Schmidt 1968) and in action potentials in both the pretrigeminal nucleus of the DTAM and in the laryngeal nerve (IX–X; Schmidt 1976). In normal frogs, no neuronal correlates of calling are evident in the first 41 days following tail loss; one animal tested about 4 months after tail loss showed typical adult neuronal correlates of calling (Schmidt 1978). This implies that the neuronal circuits for calling in *R. pipiens* develop sometime between the second and fourth month after tail loss, at a time comparable to the onset of sexual dimorphism in the larynx of *Xenopus laevis*. Administration of testosterone to *R. pipiens* larvae during climax stages induces the premature appearance of neuronal correlates of calling as early as the first week after tail loss (Schmidt 1978) but not before. The developing central nervous system of *X. laevis* cannot bind androgens to any of the brain areas associated with the neuronal calling circuit until late climax stages (Gorlick and Kelley 1986). Thus, development of androgen receptors and androgen attachment to the

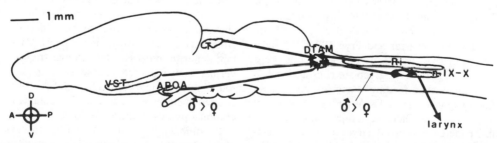

Fig. 16.6 Neural pathway for vocalization in anuran amphibians. The laryngeal motor neurons (cranial nerves IX–X) lead to muscles of the larynx and stimulate sound production. The nucleus of these nerves receives inputs from the dorsal tegmental area of the medulla (*DTAM*), as well as from the medius and inferior reticular nuclei (*Ri*). Since the DTAM receives neuronal inputs from various anterior brain structures including the thalamic nuclei (*T*), anterior preoptic area (*APOA*), and ventral striatum (*VST*), sound production may be controlled by anterior brain structures. (Reprinted, by permission, from Kelley 1986.)

receptors is necessary for the differentiation of anuran courtship calling circuits.

Pancreatic Hormones

During embryonic development the pancreas originates as a dorsal and two ventral evaginations from the anterior portion of the intestine in both urodeles (Frye 1962) and anurans (Frye 1964a). Ablation studies in urodeles have shown that the entire endocrine portion of the pancreas, the islets of Langerhans, arises from the dorsal evagination (Frye 1962). Anuran larvae contain two types of islet cells during larval life (Beaumont 1968; Hirata 1934; Janes 1938).

β-cell morphology changes throughout larval life in *Rana clamitans* (Frye 1964b), *R. pipiens* (Kaung 1981, 1983), and *R. catesbeiana* (Farrar and Hulsebus 1988). In all species before hatching a few cuboidal-shaped β-cells are interspersed among the acinar digestive cells of the pancreas. Just before hatching, α-cells containing glucagon and pancreatic polypeptides appear (Kaung 1981). After hatching (TK II) Δ-cells containing somatostatin appear (Kaung 1981). By TK V the adult type of topographical organization emerges, with the Δ-cells surrounding a core of α- and β-cells (Kaung 1981). In all species the β-cell height, insulin content per cell, and numbers of β-cells per islet increase up to metamorphic climax (TK XIX). After this maximum, β-cell volume in the pancreas decreases. The pancreas of all species is composed primarily of acinar tissue, which produces digestive enzymes, and a small amount of islet tissue, which produces hormones. During climax stages in normal and thyroid hormone–induced metamorphosis, the mass of the pancreas declines by about 80% (see Fox 1984). Relatively more acinar tissue degenerates than islet tissue, since the β-cell fraction of the total pancreas increases during climax stages (Kaung 1983).

Direct RIA measurements of insulin concentration in the embryonic pancreas of *R. catesbeiana* detect insulin before hatching (Hulsebus and Farrar 1985) and in early larval stages (TK I–IV). Insulin concentration rises in both the pancreas and serum until TK XVII, after which the levels decrease rapidly during climax stages (fig. 16.7). Ablation of the islet tissues or pancreatectomy does not influence growth and metamorphic progress of amphibian larvae (Frye 1962, 1964a). Islets of Langerhans do influence carbohydrate metabolism during the larval period, however.

Blood sugar increases during normal development and decreases slightly during climax stages (Frye 1964b; Farrar and Frye 1973; Hulsebus and Farrar 1984; Just, Sperka, and Strange 1977). Liver glycogen increases during larval life from TK I until TK XIX (Farrar and Frye 1973). At stage XIX, 8% of the wet mass of liver is glycogen, but this drops to 1.7% at stage XX–XXI. Liver glycogen rises during late larval life after animals start feeding. Pancreatectomy does not increase blood sugar levels at TK V and XXII, while at all other stages blood sugar increases. Injection of glucose into normal and pancreatectomized larvae temporarily elevates blood sugar. At all stages studied (TK V, XI, XIX, XXII, XXV, and adult) the pancreatectomized animals have higher blood sugar levels after glucose injection than do normal animals receiving glucose (Frye 1964b). These results

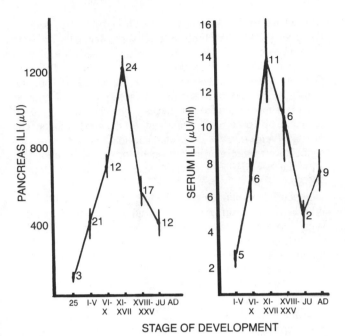

Fig. 16.7 Insulinlike immunoreactivity in the pancreas and serum of the bullfrog, *Rana catesbeiana*. Developmental periods include embryos (Shumway [1940] stage 25), larvae (TK I–XXV), and adults. The means ±1 SE are shown. The *numbers* to the right indicate the number of pancreases used or the number of pooled serum samples assayed for insulin. (Reprinted, by permission, from Hulsebus and Farrar 1985.)

suggest that the plasma insulin in larvae helps control blood glucose, while without it the blood glucose increases during both normal and stressful conditions. Glucagon administration to larval *Rana pipiens* (TK XII–XV) causes a transitory increase in blood sugar levels (3 h) while simultaneously decreasing the liver glycogen content (Farrar and Frye 1979a). No data are available on the role of the other pancreatic hormones during metamorphosis, nor are any quantitative data available on their concentration in the gland or the blood.

Endocrine Control of Pigmentation

In adult amphibians the pigments occur in three chromatophores: melanophores (black, brown, or red in color), iridophores (white or blue), and xanthophores (yellow, orange, or red; see chapter 3). The pigment in melanophores is melanin, that in xanthophores is pteridine, and those in iridophores are purines (Bagnara 1976; Frost and Robinson 1984). These chromatophores occur throughout the body, including blood vessels, peritoneum, mesentery, and skin. In the skin the chromatophores occur in both the epidermis and dermis. The epidermis contains only melanophores, which contain long thin dendritic processes that extend from the cells. The epidermal melanophores release some melanin, and the surrounding epidermal cells can engulf this pigment and become colored themselves. The dermis contains all three types of chromatophores (Bagnara 1976).

In some adult amphibians but by no means in all species or in all areas of the body, these dermal pigment cells are arranged in the so-called dermal chromatophore unit (Frost and Robinson 1984; Smith-Gill and Carver 1981). In such a unit, three types of chromatophores lie one on top of another

(Bagnara, Taylor, and Hadley 1968). The xanthophore is next to the basal lamella separating the dermis and epidermis. The iridophore is below the xanthophore, while the melanophore is below them both. Fingerlike structures extend from the melanophore over the other two chromatophores. Many adult amphibians have very distinctive patches or spots of pigments, where only one or two of the chromatophores are present in large numbers (Duellman and Trueb 1986; Frost and Robinson 1984).

These chromatophores originate from the neural crest cells in amphibian embryos (Bagnara et al. 1979; Dushane 1935). The melanophores and xanthophores develop in the embryonic stages during neural crest migration (Epperlein and Claviez 1982). When the iridophores appear is not known. In *Rana pipiens* they are present in young larvae (TK IV), decline until climax stages, and increase again at climax (Smith-Gill 1974). In *Ambystoma mexicanum*, iridophores first appear in midlarval stages and then increase (Frost and Robinson 1984). Melanophores and xanthophores increase throughout larval life in both anurans and urodeles (Frost and Robinson 1984; Pehlemann 1972; Smith-Gill 1974; Stearner 1946). The increase is most obvious in the dermal melanophores: they first appear at midlarval stages and increase by as much as tenfold before climax stages. Dermal chromatophore units form at metamorphic climax stages (Bagnara, Taylor, and Hadley 1968; Smith-Gill and Carver 1981). In *R. pipiens* the typical dark spots of the adult appear in early climax stages but form fully only after tail loss, when the dermal melanophores increase (Smith-Gill 1974). As a precursor to the adult dark spot, a lightened area develops during midlarval (TK IX–XIII) stages, brought about by fewer and less pigmented epidermal melanophores (Smith-Gill 1974). The types and amounts of pteridines synthesized by xanthophores in *Ambystoma mexicanum* and *Bombina orientalis* (Anura: Discoglossidae) change during late larval life (Frost and Robinson 1984).

Hormones control the development and distribution of pigmented cells, as well as pigment synthesis and its distribution within pigment cells. At least four hormones affect chromatophores in larvae: melanophore-stimulating hormone (MSH), melatonin, steroid hormones, and thyroid hormones. During embryonic and early larval life is a phase when larvae cannot alter their coloration in response to environmental background (Verburg–van Kemenade et al. 1984; Fox 1984). The reason for the early expanded form of the melanophores in this phase is unknown, particularly since the pituitary may not have formed yet, nor can MSH be found in the early pituitary anlage. After this phase many embryos and larvae develop the ability to contract melanophores (blanch) on white backgrounds. In *Xenopus laevis* this physiological response appears before hatching (Verburg–van Kemenade et al. 1984), while it appears after hatching in larvae of *Rana* and *Hyla* (Anura: Hylidae) and probably never appears in *Bufo* (Fox 1984).

Melanophore-Stimulating Hormone Chromatophore development depends on the pituitary, presumably because of the MSH it contains (Pehlemann 1972). The pituitary darkens larvae by enhancing the division of existing melanophores, increasing melanophore cell differentiation from the pigment

stem cells, and promoting melanin synthesis in melanophores (Pehlemann 1972). The neurointermediate lobe of amphibians synthesizes a prohormone, proopiomelanocortin (POMC), which is processed to yield three melanotropic peptides (α-MSH, des-N-α-acetyl-α-MSH and γ-3 MSH), two forms of a corticotropin-like intermediate peptide and two β-endorphin peptides (see Verburg–van Kemenade et al. 1984; see also chapter 3). Immunocytochemically MSH appears in the embryo (NF 39); a light background causes melanophore contraction. The intensity of this reaction increases during embryonic development, and before hatching all the POMC peptides can be demonstrated immunocytochemically (Verburg–van Kemenade et al. 1984).

Because melanophores increase during development and the pituitary is required for this increase, circulating levels of MSH should increase during larval life. Measurements of POMC hormone synthesis and release of its component peptides indicate that both synthesis and release increase during development until just before forelimb emergence (Verburg–van Kemenade et al. 1984). When larvae are black-background adapted, they become darker, and at the same time the rates of MSH synthesis and release increase.

Dopaminergic neurons reach the neurointermediate lobe at NF 39/40 (Terlou and van Straaten 1973), when the animals respond to white background by melanophore contraction (fig. 16.8). Dopamine inhibits the release of all POMC peptides (Verburg–van Kemenade et al. 1986). Presumably during white background adaptation larvae release dopamine, which suppresses the release of MSH, resulting in melanophore contraction.

Accordingly, a dopamine receptor agonist (apomorphine) and pituitary removal (by embryonic decapitation) cause melanophore contraction (fig. 16.8; Verburg–van Kemenade et al. 1984). Other small peptides can affect the release of MSH from the amphibian pituitary, including TRH, γ-aminobutyric acid (GABA), neuropeptide Y (NPY), CRF, and catecholamines (for detailed information see Verburg–van Kemenade, Jenks, and Houben 1987; chapter 3). This array of peptides implies that many compounds may be indirectly involved in color control of amphibian larvae during exposure to different environmental inputs.

Melatonin The pineal forms as a single dorsal vesicular evagination from the diencephalic roof and connects to the brain by a stalk. The pineal grows continuously during larval life and until the animals mature sexually (Hendrickson and Kelly 1969). During embryonic and larval life the pineal gland contains three cell types: photoreceptor, supporting cells, and neurons. The proportion of these cell types is constant during the entire larval life (Flight 1973; Hendrickson and Kelly 1969). The gross morphology of this endocrine gland changes during larval life: the lumen disappears and the whole organ flattens dorsal-ventrally. In the adult, part of the pineal complex remains extracranial (frontal organ or parietal eye), while the remainder (pineal organ proper or epiphysis) is located within the braincase like the pituitary.

The pineal also affects coloration of amphibian larvae. Pineal extracts contract melanophores (McCord and Allen 1917). When larvae are in complete darkness, the body melanophores contract. If larvae are pinealectomized, blanching

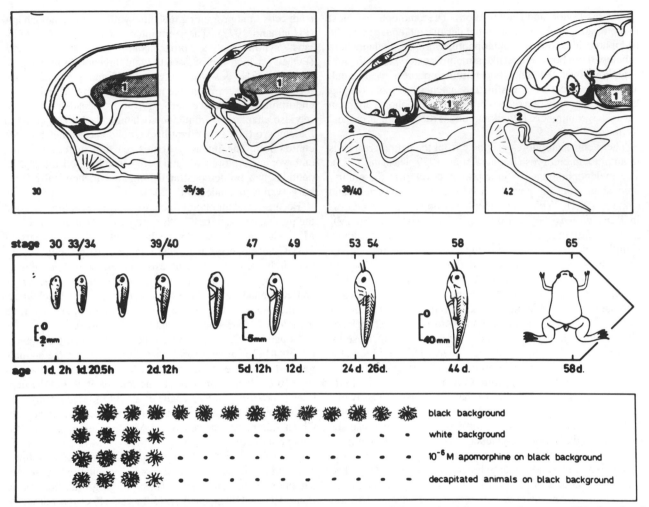

Fig. 16.8 The relationship between developmental stages, pituitary development, and melanophore appearance under different environmental conditions. *Top*, pituitary development shown in black in relation to the notochord (*1*), mouth opening (*2*), optic chiasma (*3*), pineal gland (*4*), and infundibular recess of the third ventricle (*VII*). *Middle*, the external appearance of *Xenopus laevis* larvae at various stages (NF scheme) and and ages of development. *Bottom*, the timing of melanophore appearance and its reaction to various experimental manipulations. (Reprinted, by permission, from Verburg–van Kemenade et al. 1984.)

does not occur in darkness (Bagnara 1963). When melatonin, the hormone of the pineal gland, is administered to larvae, the melanophores contract just as they do in darkness. Presumably, the larval pineal itself detects light intensity, since both larval and adult pineals contain photoreceptor cells (Bagnara 1965; Hendrickson and Kelly 1969; Flight 1973; Foster and Roberts 1982).

In both urodeles and anurans the photoreceptors of the pineal complex make synaptic connections to neurons in the pineal complex and with neural processes of extrapineal origin (Flight 1973; Korf et al. 1981). The nerves leading from the pineal complex respond to illumination by changing the frequency of firing in the pineal complex nerve (Foster and Roberts 1982; Korf et al. 1981). Photic stimulation of the pineal complex causes achromatic and chromatic responses in the nerve. Achromatic units respond by decreasing their firing rate, with the maximum decrease at a 520-nm wavelength (Foster and Roberts 1982; Korf et al. 1981). When the firing frequency of the achromatic units increases in dim light, larvae respond by increasing motor activity (Foster and Roberts 1982). This implies that the achromatic units could

help larvae escape predators who cast shadows on them. These units can also act as "dosimeters" for detection of solar radiation intensity. The chromatic units either decrease in firing rate, with the maximum decrease at 360-nm wavelength, or increase in firing rate, with the maximum increase at 520 nm. The chromatic units would allow larvae to discriminate between long and short wavelengths. Larvae could detect shifts in spectral distribution occurring during twilight and modify behavior accordingly (Korf et al. 1981).

The brain, pineal, and eyes of amphibians all contain melatonin (Baker and Hoff 1971; van de Veerdonk 1967; see also chapter 3). The amount in these structures changes little during embryonic development but decreases after hatching (NF 42) and subsequently (NF 47), eventually attaining prehatching levels (Baker 1969). Because the retina contains nearly all of the melatonin in the lateral eyes, most authors assume that the photoreceptors of the pineal complex contain its melatonin. How light influences the release of melatonin from the pineal complex is not clear; however, more melatonin is released from the pineal during darkness than during daylight in amphibians and other vertebrates (Gern and Norris 1979). Most authors assume that the blanching of larvae in darkness results from increased circulating melatonin levels. The ability of the skin to blanch in response to melatonin decreases during larval life and is not present in the adult (Bagnara 1963, 1976). No studies are available on either the number or type of MSH and/or melatonin receptors in amphibian chromatophores during ontogeny.

Other Hormones Affecting Pigmentation The skin of adult amphibians (*Rana esculenta* and *Triturus cristatus* [Caudata: Salamandridae]) has receptors for sex steroid hormones (d'Istria, Delrio, and Chieffi 1975). These steroid hormone receptors do not appear in the skin until midclimax (Chieffi, Delrio, and Valentino 1975). Steroid hormone receptors also appear late in other structures: brain, larynx, and so forth. The African reed frog, *Hyperolius viridiflavus* (Hyperoliidae), has tan stripes on its dorsal side as a juvenile froglet. Dorsally, adult females are bright green and yellow with red stripes, while males are colored like females or have brown stripes. After treatment with either estrogen or testosterone during climax stages, the dorsal surface of juvenile froglets gains the bright green and yellow coloration of the adult (Richards 1982). The sex steroid–treated animals assume the coloration of normal adult females. These changes involve all three types of chromatophores. Sex steroid hormones administered before forelimb emergence do not affect pigmentation (Richards 1982).

Finally, thyroid hormones accelerate the development of adult coloration (see Bagnara 1976). Thyroid hormone pellets placed beneath the skin of young *R. pipiens* larvae (Kollros and Kaltenbach 1952) cause normal adult spots in the skin, while the rest of the body retains its typical larval body appearance. The mechanism by which thyroid hormones bring about these changes is completely unknown.

Regulation of Calcium

Four hormones regulate plasma calcium levels in adult amphibians: three raise calcium levels, while the fourth decreases calcium levels (Bentley 1984; Clark, Kaul, and Roth 1986; D. R. Robertson 1986; chapter 3). Calcitonin, produced by the ultimobranchial bodies, is the only demonstrated hypocalcemic hormone and increases bone calcium deposition. The parathyroids produce and release parathormone, which elevates plasma calcium by mobilizing calcium from bones. Vitamin D elevates calcium levels in anurans, but its effects on urodeles and caecilians are unknown (Bentley 1984). Prolactin elevates plasma calcium levels in adult urodeles but not in adult anurans (Bentley 1984).

The ultimobranchial bodies are paired structures in caecilians (Welsch and Schubert 1975) and anurans (D. R. Robertson 1986). The ultimobranchial bodies are paired in the urodeles *Necturus maculosus* (Proteidae) and *Amphiuma means* (Amphiumidae), but in eighteen other urodele species single structures occur, located only on the left side (Wilder 1929). Histologically the ultimobranchial bodies of adult amphibians are composed of follicles, with pseudostratified cells and a lumen containing secretions (D. R. Robertson 1986).

The development of the ultimobranchial bodies has been described in fifteen species of urodeles (Baldwin 1918; Coleman and Phillips 1972; Maurer 1888; Platt 1896; Uhlenhuth and McGowan 1924; Watzka 1933; Wilder 1929) and in ten species of anurans (Boschwitz 1960b; Coleman and Phillips 1974; Coleman 1975; Greil 1905; Maurer 1888; Robertson and Swartz 1964; Saxen and Toivonen 1955; Sterba 1950; Watzka 1933). In all species the ultimobranchial bodies first appear as evaginations of the last (sixth) pharyngeal pouch. In anurans, bilateral evaginations occur, while in most urodeles a single left evagination appears. At hatching the ultimobranchial bodies are normally detached from the pharynx and are composed of simple columnar epithelial cells surrounding a follicle or a solid mass of cells. During the midlarval stages the epithelium becomes pseudostratified, the follicle increases in size, and in some species additional minor follicles develop. In late larval and climax stages secretions appear in the follicles. In *Xenopus* (Saxen and Toivonen 1955; Sterba 1950) and in *Ambystoma* (Baldwin 1918; Uhlenhuth and McGowan 1924; Wilder 1929) the ultimobranchial bodies shrink during climax. These observations led Boschwitz (1960a) to examine the role of thyroid function on ultimobranchial body development. He demonstrated that hypothyroidism expands the ultimobranchial body, while hyperthyroidism inhibits ultimobranchial development.

The parathyroids are present in all orders of amphibians. Two pairs of parathyroids are present in all anurans, most urodeles have only a single pair, and some urodeles (e.g., *Necturus*) have no parathyroids (for review see Clark, Kaul, and Roth 1986). The number in caecilians is not known (Klumpp and Eggert 1934; Welsch and Schubert 1975). Histologically the glands also vary. In urodeles they have chords of epithelial cells, while those in anurans have closely packed epithelial cells (Clark, Kaul, and Roth 1986). In anurans from the temperate zones, the parathyroid glands degenerate during winter months. In caecilians the parathyroids comprise loosely packed, irregularly shaped cells surrounded by connective tissue (Klumpp and Eggert 1934; Welsch and Schubert 1975).

Surprisingly, the development of parathyroids has been examined in only five amphibian species. In anurans the parathyroids develop from the ventral part of the third and fourth pharyngeal pouches, while in urodeles they originate from the third pharyngeal pouch (Boschwitz 1961; Maurer 1888; Saxen and Toivonen 1955). In at least one genus (*Xenopus*) the parathyroid glands grow during the entire larval period but do not lose their connection to the pharyngeal pouches until early climax stages (Saxen and Toivonen 1955).

Anuran larvae have three separate calcium deposits in the body: endolymphatic sacs, skin, and bone. They can redistribute calcium among these structures and can draw upon those deposits to control plasma calcium levels (see chapter 3 for a discussion of endocrine regulation of calcium deposition). The endolymphatic sacs develop from the sacculus of the inner ear and extend out of the auditory capsule into the dura matra before hatching (Whiteside 1922). The endolymphatic sacs extend to the hind-brain regions and contain calcium in the earliest larval stages. By midlarval stages the endolymphatic sacs have extended into the vertebral column of the body, but they never extend into the tail (Whiteside 1922). The calcium in the endolymphatic sacs is mobilized throughout larval life for deposit into the developing skeleton system (Guardabassi 1960; Pilkington and Simkiss 1966). In urodeles, the forelimbs develop before the hindlimbs, while in anurans, the forelimbs and hindlimbs develop simultaneously or the hindlimbs appear first (Saint-Aubain 1981a). The limbs typically appear before hatching, but ossification of the limb skeleton does not start until midlarval stages (TK X–XIII) in anurans (see review by Atkinson 1981; Fox 1984). Ossification of certain skull elements starts in early larval stages of both anurans and urodeles (Fox 1984; Reilly 1986, 1987; Trueb 1985). Many bones in the skull and the sternum do not ossify until late climax stages (Reilly 1986, 1987). In thirty anuran species, the skin is a third calcium storage site. However, Guardabassi and Sacerdote (1951) detected no calcium in the skin of urodeles (ten species) and caecilians (one species). These same authors examined the skin of several species of anuran larvae, always detecting calcium. This work received little attention until Baldwin and Bentley (1980) showed that the skin of larval *Rana catesbeiana* accounts for 30% of total calcium. No quantitative data are available on calcium in the skin of other larvae.

Calcium enters larvae by intestinal transport from their food and by transport across the skin and gills (Baldwin and Bentley 1980; Sasayama and Oguro 1985). Larvae daily absorb up to 0.6% of their body calcium, and total calcium in the body increases during the entire larval period (Baldwin and Bentley 1980; Oguro et al. 1980). In nonfeeding bullfrog larvae, 5% of calcium uptake is via the intestine, 25% via the skin, and the balance via the buccal epithelium and gills (Baldwin and Bentley 1980). Calcium is lost via the urine and feces and across the skin (Baldwin and Bentley 1980; Sasayama and Oguro 1982a).

Bioassays and histochemical techniques have demonstrated the presence of parathyroid hormones and calcitonin in the parathyroids and ultimobranchial bodies, respectively, of adult amphibians (Clark, Kaul, and Roth 1986; D. R. Robertson 1986; chapter 3). Although no biochemical techniques have been used to demonstrate these hormones in larval amphibian glands, physiological work suggests that they are present. Serum and coelomic fluid calcium levels increase continuously during bullfrog (*R. catesbeiana*) larval development (Oguro et al. 1975). The serum calcium levels increase steadily from about 7.5 mg · 100 ml^{-1} in young larvae (TK II) to about 11 mg · 100 ml^{-1} at the end of metamorphic climax (TK XXIV). Normal plasma calcium levels of other anuran and urodele larvae also range from 7 to 10 mg · 100 ml^{-1}. Unfortunately, many publications do not report larval stages, and whether calcium levels change during metamorphosis in all amphibian species is unknown. Throughout the metamorphic period of bullfrog larvae (TK II–XXV), parathyroidectomy reduces plasma and coelomic fluid calcium levels (Sasayama and Oguro 1975; Uchiyama and Pang 1981). No data are available on the effects of parathyroidectomy on calcium stores, nor on the effect of exogenous parathyroid hormone on plasma calcium levels in larvae or on calcium in body stores. Bovine parathyroid hormone administration does not change calcium flux in larvae (Baldwin and Bentley 1980).

Removal of ultimobranchial bodies (UBX) from bullfrog larvae (TK I–XVIII) does not affect plasma or coelomic-fluid calcium levels in animals maintained in normal tap water (Sasayama and Oguro 1976). The ultimobranchial bodies appear hyperactive in larvae maintained at high external calcium concentrations (Robertson 1971), and calcium levels are elevated in the plasma and coelomic fluid of UBX larvae (Sasayama and Oguro 1976). The rise in calcium levels after UBX can be prevented by transplantation of either larval or adult ultimobranchial bodies or by injection of calcitonin (Sasayama 1978). In UBX larvae (TK VI–XXV), calcium deposition into the endolymphatic sacs decreases (Robertson 1971; Sasayama and Oguro 1985). In addition, ossification of some chondrocranial bones, limb bones, and the otolith of the ear decreases in UBX larvae (Robertson 1971). In UBX larvae, urine calcium levels increase, possibly due to a calcitonin effect on the kidney or a secondary response to the elevated plasma calcium concentration (Sasayama and Oguro 1982a). Administration of calcitonin to UBX larvae does not influence intestinal uptake of calcium (Baldwin and Bentley 1980; Sasayama and Oguro 1985). Calcitonin administration decreases the uptake of calcium via the skin and gills in both anurans and urodeles (Baldwin and Bentley 1980; Kingsbury and Fenwick 1989).

Larvae maintained at different external concentrations of calcium maintain constant plasma calcium levels (Uchiyama and Pang 1981). Plasma calcium levels decrease 1 week after hypophysectomy irrespective of the external calcium concentration, suggesting that a hypercalcemic factor is present in the pituitary (Sasayama and Oguro 1982b; Uchiyama and Pang 1981). Injection of pituitary extracts or prolactin restores normal calcium levels in hypophysectomized larvae (Sasayama and Ogura 1982b; Uchiyama and Pang 1981). Whether prolactin decreases calcium deposits in body stores or alters calcium fluxes into or out of the larvae is not known, nor is how injection of prolactin increases plasma calcium.

Two other hormones affect calcium levels in amphibians. Vitamin D$_3$ causes plasma hypercalcemia in adult anurans, and increases calcium uptake in bullfrog larvae (Baldwin and Bentley 1980; Bentley 1984). Thyroid hormone pellets implanted into young larvae cause local bone ossification (Kaltenbach 1953).

Predictor of Transformation Time: Growth or Differentiation?

Developmental biologists typically predict climax times of amphibians based on differentiation rates (i.e., stages) rather than larval size (tables 16.1 and 16.2). Wilbur and Collins (1973) and Wilbur (1976) have predicted that body size and growth rate are most important in predicting transformation times. They suggest that larval transformation cannot occur at less than a certain minimum size. However, no endocrinological evidence exists to suggest that a minimum and/or maximum larval size is necessary for thyroid hormones to induce metamorphic climax. Smith-Gill and Berven (1979) showed that 95% of the variance in the length of the larval life can be accounted for by differentiation rates, while growth rates account for less than 50% of the variance. Thus, these findings quantitatively confirm the subjective observations of developmental biologists who view stages as the predictor of metamorphic climax.

Although body size and its rate of change cannot be used to predict transformation time, food availability and therefore growth rate could indirectly trigger endocrinological changes that may alter transformation rates (Wassersug 1986). This theory predicts that larvae excrete prostaglandins from their oral mucosa when feeding, and that these compounds retard metamorphosis (at least of the gut). When food is scarce, less mucus and prostaglandins are produced, and animals therefore metamorphose. Although larvae produce prostaglandins, the theory is incorrect, because prostaglandin administration does not affect metamorphic rate (Mobbs, King, and Wassersug 1988).

In vertebrates, the gastrointestinal tract produces many other hormones aside from prostaglandins, including cholecystokinin (Hadley 1988a). Cholecystokinin decreases food intake in mammals by affecting the satiety center in the hypothalamus (Dourish, Rycroft, and Iversen 1989). Cholecystokinin also affects the release of pituitary hormones in mammals (Vijayan, Samaon, and McCann 1979). Thus, in mammals at least one gastrointestinal hormone can affect the hypothalamus and pituitary.

The amphibian hypothalamus controls the release of anterior pituitary hormones (e.g., TSH, prolactin, ACTH), which indirectly or directly affects metamorphic rate. If food available to larvae changes the secretion rate of any of the many gastrointestinal hormones, it may affect the pituitary-hypothalamus axis and therefore metamorphosis. This type of feedback would help integrate the ecological and endocrinological view of the control of metamorphosis. Some gastrointestinal hormones change during metamorphosis, but it is not known whether food in the gastrointestinal tract affects the hormone levels. Cholecystokinin appears just after hatching and attains its highest levels in midlarval stages (NF 56), then declines during early climax (Scalise and Vigna 1988). We know of no attempts to alter metamorphic rate with any gastrointestinal hormone aside from the work with prostaglandins.

SENSORY NERVOUS SYSTEM

The sensory system changes during metamorphosis. Larvae of all stages evidently succeed in accommodating these changes, because the animals continue to react to external environmental stimuli (temperature, light, chemicals) despite ontogenetic changes in locomotor, feeding, and thermoregulatory behaviors. Whether these behavioral changes reflect only changes in peripheral sensory input and/or possible changes in central interpretation of sensory inputs is not clear. No information is available about possible changes in central interpretation and/or integration. If survival is any indication of successful integration, then the low survival rates observed during late anuran climax stages (Arnold and Wassersug 1978) suggest that peripheral-central integration may not be equally successful at all developmental stages.

Mechanoreceptors

Mechanical stimulation elicits swimming in amphibian embryos at very early stages. In NF 37/38 *Xenopus,* for example, mechanical stimulation initiates reflex body movement via touch-sensitive neurons innervating both head skin and the cement gland (Roberts 1989).

As larvae, amphibians have two different types of mechanosensory systems—the lateral line system and the ear—that help detect mechanical vibrations in their environment. These two systems develop during early embryonic neural tube stages from the closely associated anterior ectodermal placodes (Harrison 1904). Cells migrate from these placodes to form the lateral line system, while the cells remaining as the placode at the anterior (otic) end become the ear. These migratory cells give rise to the lateral line receptors and the peripheral nerves supplying the lateral line (see Lannoo and Smith 1989). Both of these systems change during development.

The lateral line system of amphibians acts physiologically as a mechanoreceptor, electroreceptor, and chemoreceptor. The lateral line system is present in all three orders of amphibians. Receptors are of two types—mechanoreceptors (neuromast organs) and electroreceptors (ampullary organs). Caecilians and urodeles have both types of receptors while anurans have only the neuromast (Fritzsch, Wahnschaffe, and Bartsch 1988). Most aquatic urodeles retain the lateral line system after metamorphosis, and in fact, the numbers of receptors increase as the animals grow (Fritzsch, Wahnschaffe, and Bartsch 1988; Lannoo 1987b). The terrestrial urodeles may lose their lateral line system during metamorphosis, or perhaps skin ectoderm covers the lateral lines at metamorphosis. Some terrestrial urodeles that return to water after their terrestrial sojourn (e.g., *Notophthalmus viridescens:* Salamandridae) regain their lateral line (Fritzsch, Wahnschaffe, and Bartsch 1988; Russell 1976). Caecilians and the majority of anurans lose their lateral lines during metamorphic climax, except for those that remain in water as adults (Fritzsch, Wahnschaffe, and Bartsch 1988; Lannoo 1987a). The latter species retain the lateral line system and show little or no degenerative changes (Fritzsch, Wahnschaffe, and Bartsch 1988). Degeneration of the anuran lateral lines begins with neuronal degeneration in the lateral line nucleus in the brain at TK XXII (fig. 16.9; Wahnschaffe, Bartsch, and Fritzsch 1987). By TK XXII the neuromast number starts to decrease (fig. 16.9), and by TK XXIV lateral line nerve degeneration begins.

Physiologically, the neuromast organs function as mechanoreceptors, while the ampullary organs are electroreceptors. With their neuromast organs, adult *Xenopus laevis* can detect pressure changes transmitted through water both in the horizontal and vertical axis and therefore can localize the source of the waves (Wilcox 1987). *X. laevis* can respond to water wave frequencies from 5 to 30 Hz and can be trained to recognize various wavelengths (Elepfandt, Seiler, and Aicher 1985). Although a wealth of anatomical studies exists on changes in neuromast organs during development, no corresponding physiological studies are available.

The ampullary organs in the axolotl *Ambystoma mexicanum* are less numerous than the mechanoreceptors. Nerves leading from the lateral line near the eye contain 120 electroreceptive units and 252 mechanoreceptive units (Münz, Claas, and Fritzsch 1984). These receptors increase their resting firing frequency (5 to 25 impulses $\cdot$ s^{-1}) in a cathodal current and decrease their resting firing rate with an anodal stimulus. These electroreceptors respond to electrical stimuli down to 5 μV $\cdot$ cm^{-1} (Münz, Claas, and Fritzsch 1984). Unfortunately these studies do not indicate any shifts in detection associated with postmetamorphic maturation (Fritzsch and Münz 1986).

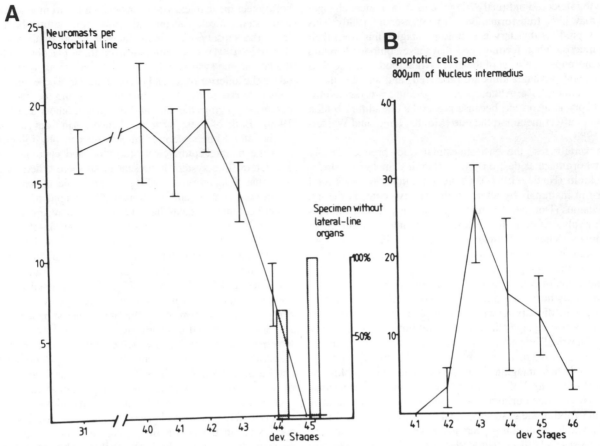

Fig. 16.9 Quantitative data on the degeneration of the anuran lateral line during development. Stages according to Gosner (1960). *A* shows the disappearance of the peripheral sensory organs, neuromasts, from one branch of the lateral line. The *bars* on the right indicate the percent- age of larvae that have lost all of their sensory organs. As the neuromasts disappear, degenerating (apoptotic) cells can be found in the lateral line nucleus of the rhombencephalic alar plate (*B*). (Reprinted, by permission, from Fritzsch, Wahnschaffe, and Bartsch 1988.)

The amphibian ear consists of three components: the inner, middle, and outer ear. The inner ear consists of the semicir- cular canals, utricles, and saccula. These inner ear structures start development before the embryo hatches, and nerve fi- bers grow into the brain near the time of hatching (Witschi 1956). Both the size of the vestibular organs of the inner ear and the number of myelinated nerve fibers that innervate them increase during development (Witschi 1956). No functional changes in vestibular organ physiology during larval devel- opment are known. Clearly, most species can recognize and maintain equilibrium posture and can respond to sound soon after hatching, and they maintain this sensitivity throughout their lifetimes. The auditory organs of amphibians consist of two evaginations from the saccula and basilar papilla. The amphibian papilla has two to ten times more hair cells and a larger number of nerve fibers than the basilar papilla (table 16.7). The total number of hair cells increases progressively with development (Alfs and Schneider 1973; Fritzsch, Wahn- schaffe, and Bartsch 1988; Li and Lewis 1974; Will and Fritzsch 1988). Studies on metamorphic changes of hair cell number or nerve fiber numbers tend to be incomplete because most authors examine only one or two stages (table 16.7).

The individual auditory nerve fibers respond to sound by generating an action potential (see chapter 2). When the fre- quency of the sound changes, the frequency of the action po-

TABLE 16.7 Numbers of Hair Cells in the Basilar and Amphibian Papillae and Their Myelinated Nerve Fibers in Larval and Adult Amphibians

		Amphibian Papilla		Basilar Papilla		
	Stage	Hair Cells	Fibers	Hair Cells	Fibers	Refer- ence
Ascaphus	Adult	172	141	85	31	1
truei		181		62		2
	Larva	81	120	39	28	1
Ichthyophis	Adult	145	79	47	20	1
kohtaoensis	Larva	99	68	30	20	1
Rana	Adult	1,165	1,548	97	392	2, 4
catesbeiana				95		3
	Larva:					
	VIII			65		3
	XVI			77		3
Xenopus	Adult	456	496		310	5
laevis	Larva:					
	54		150		179	5

Sources: (1) Fritzsch, Wahnschaffe, and Bartsch 1988. (2) Wever 1985. (3) Li and Lewis 1974. (4) Dunn 1978. (5) Will and Fritzsch 1988.

tential of that individual auditory nerve fiber also changes. Individual auditory anuran nerve fibers are tuned to a particular frequency, at which the frequency of action potentials is greatest. When the optimal frequency of nerve fibers from the auditory nerves from animals of similar body mass is plotted, three more or less distinct populations of fibers become apparent, namely, low-, mid-, and high-frequency fibers (fig. 16.10). Low- and midfrequency populations of fibers arise from the nerve fibers innervating the amphibian papilla, while the high-frequency fibers come from the basilar papilla. The population of nerve fibers that have their greatest firing rates in the midfrequency ranges also shows a suppression of firing rate with the addition of a second higher-frequency tone (fig. 16.10). Intracellular recordings of the hair cells in the adult amphibian papilla indicate an intrinsic electrical resonator with frequency oscillations of the membrane potential corresponding to frequency of the afferent nerve fibers (Pitchford and Ashmore 1987). The frequency at which the maximal response occurs decreases in all three populations of afferent nerve fibers during postmetamorphic development of bullfrogs (Shofner 1988). This shift in responsiveness sug-

gests that young froglets can hear higher-frequency tones than adults of the species. No studies are available on the responsiveness of either hair cells or afferent nerve fibers during the larval period, although all authors suggest that both structures are functional. Spaeti (1978) claims that larvae between TK VI and XX "swim" in response to sound transmitted through the ear. Unfortunately, he did not control for possible input from the lateral line system; therefore, which sensory system led to the motor output is uncertain.

Mechanical input into the inner ear changes drastically during amphibian development. In most anuran species inner ear structures have no obvious mechanical input for most of larval life. Only species with large larvae have any structure to transmit environmental vibrations to the inner ear. In large larvae a rodlike structure, the bronchial columella, passes from the round window through the dorsal aorta and attaches to the lung (*Rana clamitans* or *R. catesbeiana*: Witschi 1949, 1956; *R. temporaria*: Spaeti 1978). This arrangement suggests that the lung serves as an eardrum (Capranica 1976b; Witschi 1956). Since the bronchial columella has to date been found only in ranid larvae that can occupy deep permanent ponds, perhaps this structure actually responds to depth-related pressure changes on lungs (Witschi 1949). Certainly changes in intrapulmonary pressure can stimulate cardiorespiratory responses in anuran larvae (West and Burggren 1983; see chapter 7). Another possible function of this structure could be a sensory input for blood pressure, since the columella passes through the aorta. The tail of the larva and this structure degenerate simultaneously.

In adult anurans two mechanical systems can stimulate the inner ear by oval window movement, namely the operculum and/or the stapes (plectrum, columella). The operculum with its associated muscle develops at the time of forelimb emergence and may transmit substrate vibrations and/or aerial sound to the inner ear (fig. 16.11; Vorobyeva and Smirnov 1987; Hetherington 1988b). The development of the stapes, tympanic annulus, and tympanum is not synchronous with tail loss (fig. 16.11A–E). All three elements develop fully only in anuran species that metamorphose at a relatively large size (fig. 16.11F), while in anurans that complete metamorphosis as small froglets these structures do not develop fully until after metamorphosis (Hetherington 1988b; Witschi 1949). Once the tympanic membrane appears, it continues to enlarge as the frog grows. In *R. catesbeiana* the rates of tympanic membrane growth and body-length growth are constant, so that the ratio of the membrane to the length of the animal remains nearly constant (about one to ten; Shofner 1988). The tympanic membrane grows more rapidly than the oval window, however, so that its size relative to the oval window size increases significantly (Vorobyeva and Smirnov 1987). This relative increase of the tympanic membrane compared to the oval window enhances the efficiency of the force transfer of the middle ear and may partially explain the shift in the hearing sensitivity of anuran ears with increasing development and body size (fig. 16.10; Shofner 1988).

In urodele larvae, the stapes develop simultaneously with the round window and form completely in early larval stages. In most urodele families the stapes is partially reabsorbed or becomes immobilized during metamorphic climax, while the opercular system starts its development and becomes the only

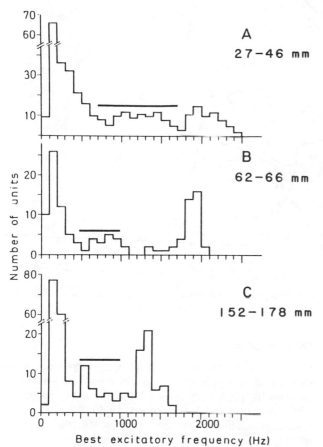

Fig. 16.10 The distribution of the greatest excitatory frequencies of the auditory nerve fibers found in three different age groups (sizes) of postmetamorphic bullfrogs, *Rana catesbeiana*, when stimulated by a broad range of auditory inputs. The distributions are shown as histograms with a 100-Hz bin width. Low- and midfrequency nerve fibers arise from the amphibian papilla, while the high-frequency nerve fibers come from the basilar papilla. The amphibian papilla midfrequency nerve fibers can be suppressed by additional sound input with a higher-frequency tone (*solid bar* above histogram). (Reprinted, by permission, from Shofner 1988.)

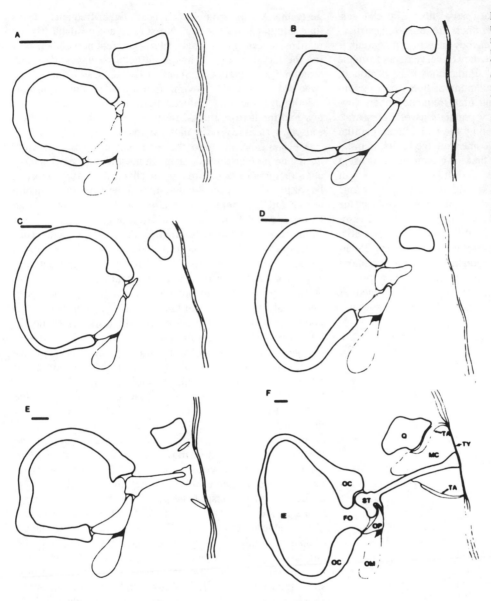

Fig. 16.11 Diagrammatic representation of structures in the right otic region of different-sized anurans at the end of metamorphosis (TK XXV). The figures show variations in middle ear development at metamorphic climax. *Scale bar* represents 0.25 mm. The snout-vent lengths for each species are A, *Bufo americanus*, 9.8 mm; B, *Hyla crucifier* (Hylidae), 10.1 mm; C, *Pseudacris triseriata* (Hylidae), 10.4 mm; D, *H. versicolor*, 17.9 mm; E, *Rana sylvatica*, 18.1 mm; F, *R. pipiens*, 25.3 mm. *FO*, fenestra ovalis; *IE*, inner ear; *MC*, middle ear cavity; *OC*, otic capsule; *OM*, opercularis muscle; *OP*, operculum; *Q*, palatoquadrate; *ST*, stapes; *TA*, tympanic annulus; *TY*, tympanum. (Reprinted, by permission, from Hetherington 1988.)

moveable middle ear element in the adult. In caecilians, an opercular system never appears; instead, the stapes appear before hatching and are present for the remainder of life (Hetherington 1988b).

The afferent inputs from the lateral line and inner ear terminate in the neuropil of the rhombencephalic alar plate (fig. 16.12; Fritzsch 1988). The ampullary receptors project to the neuropil of the nucleus dorsalis of the alar plate, while the neuromast organs project to the intermediate nucleus (fig. 16.12A). The vestibular afferents of the inner ear project to the neuropil of the nucleus ventralis. In anurans, the amphibian and basilar papillae of the inner ear send their afferents to the dorsolateral nucleus (fig. 16.12C), but this never occurs in urodeles or caecilians. This nucleus starts to develop at early limb-bud stages, and the number of cells increases dramatically before metamorphic climax and then decreases to adult levels, presumably due to death of existing neurons (Jacoby and Rubinson 1983). Since the dorsolateral nucleus changes drastically during development, the long-standing claims of Witschi (1949) about the functions of the auditory

ear during larval period need investigation with modern behavioral and physiological techniques.

Photoreceptors

Before development of the lateral eyes, amphibian larvae show sensitivity to light, which can initiate movement. In *Xenopus* the photoreceptors are located in the receptor cells within the pineal vesicle (see Roberts 1989). With further embryonic development, the eyes take on the role of photosensation.

The amphibian eye has three major components, the cornea, lens, and retina, all of which change during metamorphosis. At hatching each eye has two corneas separated by intraorbital fluid. These fluids are reabsorbed at metamorphic climax, and the two cornea fuse into a single structure (Kollros 1981). Biochemically, the lens contains many of the same crystalline proteins from embryonic stages to young froglets (Brahma, McDevitt, and Defize 1986, 1987). Morphologically and functionally, however, the lens changes during de-

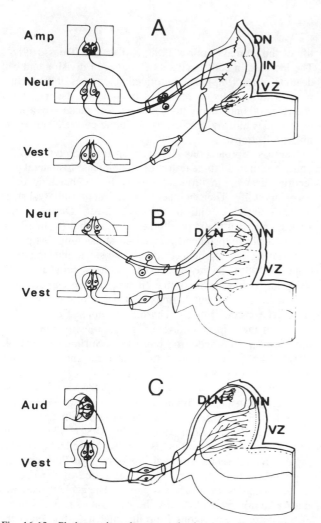

Fig. 16.12 Phylogenetic and ontogenetic changes in the alar plate and octavolateral system of *A*, urodeles and caecilians, *B*, anuran larvae, and *C*, adult anurans. *Amp*, ampullary organs; *Aud*, auditory epithelia of inner ear; *DLN*, dorsolateral nucleus; *DN*, dorsal nucleus; *IN*, intermediate nucleus; *Neur*, neuromast; *Vest*, iner ear; *VZ*, ventral zone. *Arrows* indicate dual source of neurons in DLN. (Reprinted, by permission, from Fritzsch 1988.)

velopment in those species that transform from aquatic to terrestrial habits (fig. 16.13; Sivak 1987). The lens in all aquatic amphibians, whether larva or adult, is spherical, while the diameter of the lens of terrestrial amphibians is greater than its thickness. The changes in shape of cornea and lens ensure that images form properly on the retina in both water and air.

The amphibian neural retinas contain three cell layers and two fiber layers (Roth 1987). The innermost cell layer contains the photoreceptor cells. Amphibians have four photosensitive cells, two cylindrical-shaped rods and two tapered cones (Roth 1987). Red rods, common to all vertebrates, are the predominant rod in amphibians. In addition, amphibian eyes contain a unique rod, the green rod. All amphibian eyes contain both single and double cones. The principal cone of the two double cones contains an oil droplet, while the accessory cone does not. Although the eyes of most anurans contain more rods than cones, salamanders that are nocturnal have rod-dominated retinas, while diurnal species have more cones (Donner and Reuter 1976; Roth 1987). During larval development the size of the rods and cones increases in all amphibians, but few data are available on changes in distribution of these cell types during development.

Visual pigments are located in double-membrane stacked disks at the ends of the photosensitive cells. The pigments are composed of proteins (opsins) and chromatophores. Rhodopsin, the visual red pigment, contains the chromatophore retinal 1, the aldehyde of vitamin A_1, while porphyropsin, the purple pigment, contains the chromatophore retinal 2, the aldehyde of vitamin A_2 (Wald 1981). Porphyropsin is in all aquatic amphibians whether larval or adult, while rhodopsin is only in terrestrial amphibians (table 16.8). Anurans transforming to a terrestrial adult shift from porphyropsin to rhodopsin during the time of tail loss. A shift in the spectral preference of larvae accompanies the shift in photopigments (Jaeger and Hailman 1976). Premetamorphic anuran larvae strongly prefer green light; in prometamorphic stages animals

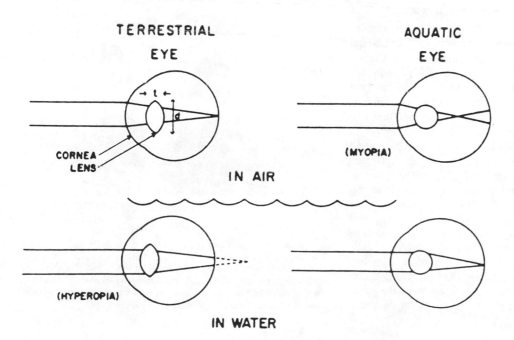

Fig. 16.13 The optical effects produced by lens shape in an aquatic and aerial environment. The eye of a terrestrial amphibian has a lens with a diameter (*d*) that is greater than its thickness (*t*), while in an aquatic amphibian the diameter and the thickness are equal. (Reprinted, by permission, from Sivak 1987.)

TABLE 16.8 The Maximal Absorption Spectra of the Visual Pigments and Their Location in Individual Photosensitive Cells of Amphibians

	Absorption Spectra (nm[a])	
Type of Cells	Terrestrial Amphibian	Aquatic Amphibian
Red rod	502[b]	523[c]
Green rod	432	438
Accessory cone	502[b]	523[c]
Principle cone	580	620
Single cone	580	620

Sources: Wald 1981; Roth 1987.

[a]The wavelength of maximum absorption by the pigment in each cell type.

[b]Porphyropsin.

[c]Rhodopsin.

choose green or blue light equally, while climax larval stages and adults prefer blue light (Jaeger and Hailman 1976).

As amphibians grow, so does the retina. Retinal growth occurs by concentric addition of cells so that the youngest cells are at the periphery. In late larval stages, more cells accrue dorsally than ventrally (Beach and Jacobson 1979b). During retinal development of most amphibians, more photoreceptor cells form than retinal ganglion cells. However, in seven species of adult plethodontid salamander, which are extremely small as adults, the ratio of retinal ganglion cells to photoreceptor approaches 1.0 (Roth, Rottluff, and Linke 1988). Presumably during growth of these plethodontid species, equal numbers of both cell types accrue (Roth, Rottluff, and Linke 1988). In anurans photoreceptor cells are at least ten times as numerous as ganglion cells. The total number of retinal ganglion cells varies in the three orders of amphibians. The greatest number occurs in anurans (300,000 to 600,000), urodeles have 25,000 to 100,000, and caecilians have about 4,000. Each ganglion cell sends its axon toward the brain as part of the optic nerve. The total number of fibers in the optic nerves varies with animal size. Less than 10% of the optic nerve fibers in all amphibians are myelinated, irrespective of body size, age, or species (Roth 1987).

The central connections of the optic nerve fibers change during amphibian development. All three orders of amphibians hatch with crossed visual projections to the contralateral optic tectum and thalamus (Fritzsch, Himstedt, and Crapon de Caprona 1985; Grobstein 1988b; Roth 1987). Contralateral visual projections to the thalamus are always sparser than and appear later than the optic tectal projections in anurans and urodeles. On the other hand, these contralateral thalamic projections are the major projections of the optic nerve in caecilians, in which tectal innervation is sparse. Although all amphibians hatch with visual projections onto the optic tectum, these retinal projections spread over the entire optic tectum gradually during larval life as the retina grows. The optic tectum contains a single layer of cells before hatching, while the adult optic tectum has nine layers: two layers composed exclusively of fibers, three layers composed of obvious cells and fibers, and about four layers composed primarily of cells (Kollros 1988). This layering of the tectum is nearly complete by midlarval stages of most anurans (Kollros 1988; Spaeti 1978). Cells in the optic tectum proliferate until midlarval stages and thereafter increase slowly, probably for the entire life of the animal (Kollros 1988; Kollros and Thiesse 1988). The increase in cells occurs by mitotic cell division and cell death (Kollros 1988). The mitotic division rates of the tectum increase drastically in the areas over which the ingrowing contralateral optic nerve fiber spreads. Cell death is restricted to the areas already reached by the optic contralateral nerve fiber projections.

Uncrossed projections also develop from the retina to the optic tectum in all three orders of amphibians. Ipsilateral projections develop in urodeles shortly before hatching or in early larval life. Their number increases until midlarval stage and then decreases until the onset of climax. During climax stages ipsilateral fibers proliferate considerably (Roth 1987). Caecilians have ipsilateral projections at hatching that proliferate during development (Fritzsch, Himstedt, and Crapon de Caprona 1985). In the Anura the ipsilateral projections develop just before metamorphic climax, and the number of fibers increases through climax and early postmetamorphic stages (Grobstein 1988b). Thyroid hormone stimulates formation of these ipsilateral retinal projections in anurans and urodeles (Hoskins and Grobstein 1985c; Stirling and Brandle 1982). The ipsilateral projections have no known developmental effects on optic tectal growth.

Developmental changes also occur in the visual neuronal connections inside the brain. In anurans and urodeles a nucleus isthmi is present in the caudal midbrain tegmentum (Grobstein 1988b; Roth 1987; Udin 1986). The nucleus isthmi receives neuronal inputs from the optic tectum on the same side and sends neuronal inputs back to the same and contralateral optic tectum. The organization of the nucleus isthmi changes during metamorphosis. The nucleus increases during larval development by the addition of neurons to the dorsal portion. The axons from the nucleus isthmi enter the tectum before climax stages and spread over the entire tectum (Udin 1986).

Lázár (1971) postulated that binocular vision requires ip-

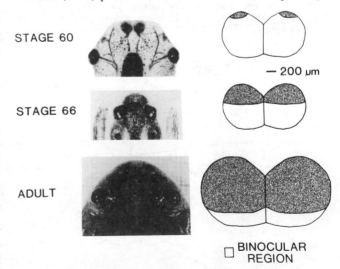

Fig. 16.14 Photographs of eye location in three developmental stages of the anuran *Xenopus laevis*, showing medial eye migration. The stages are according to Nieuwkoop and Faber, 1967. Drawings show the changes in tectal size. The *stippling* indicates the area of the tectal binocular vision. The bottom portion of the tectum area receives only monocular input. (Reprinted, by permission, from Udin 1986.)

silateral projections. Many urodeles are active predatory feeders when they hatch, and need binocular vision to capture prey (Roth 1987). Since urodeles have ipsilateral projections from both the retina and the nucleus isthmi to the optic tectum during most of the larval life, they clearly fit Lázár's postulate. Most anuran larvae have laterally placed eyes, which move medially and anteriorly (or dorsally in *Xenopus*) during metamorphic climax (fig. 16.14). After the eyes have moved medially, the muscles (i.e., superior oblique muscle) and nerves that innervate them (i.e., cranial nerves III and IV; Spaeti 1978) enlarge. Lateral eyes permit very little or no binocular vision, and central ipsilateral projections are rare or undeveloped (fig. 16.14). The ipsilateral projections begin to develop a few stages before the eyes become medially located. All the ipsilateral components increase dramatically during climax stages, permitting the animal to become active binocular predatory feeders. Even though larval caecilians have ipsilateral projections, whether these larvae have any binocular vision is unknown (Fritzsch, Himstedt, and Crapon de Caprona 1985).

Chemoreceptors

The lateral line system, taste buds, and nasal sacs are the three chemoreceptor systems of amphibians. The anatomy and mechanical and electrical receptor functions of the lateral line system are well documented (e.g., Coombs, Görner, and Münz 1989; Fritzsch and Münz 1986). However, the role of this system in chemical detection has received little attention. The lateral line system of the bullfrog larva responds to monovalent Na$^+$, K$^+$, and Ag$^+$ and divalent Sr^{2+}, Ca^{2+}, and Mg^{2+} cations by increasing the discharge in lateral line nerves (Yoshioka, Kawai, and Katsuki 1976). In adult anurans (*X. laevis*) the lateral line system responds similarly (Onoda and Katsuki 1972). Responsiveness to cations varies depending on prolactin (Blanchi, Camino, and Guardabassi 1976) and concentrations of KCl. Hypophysectomy markedly decreases this neural response. However, prolactin administration restores the control response (Blanchi, Camino, and Guardabassi 1976). Because prolactin varies during amphibian metamorphosis, the responsiveness of the lateral line to chemical stimulation should vary during ontogeny. However, such changes are yet to be documented.

Taste Chemoreceptors occur throughout the oral cavity of all amphibians, including the floor, lateral walls, and roof of the mouth. The present description concerns the structures on the floor of the mouth or on the dorsal surface of the tongue (absent in pipid frogs). These surfaces have multicellular mucous glands and two types of papillae, the filiform and fungiform papillae. The filiform papillae are very slender and highly abundant. The epithelium of the filiform papillae contains secretory epithelium and ciliated cells. The fungiform papillae are larger broad structures. Less than a thousand fungiform papillae are on the surface of anuran tongues (Jaeger and Hillman 1976). The fungiform papilla contains a single taste bud that occupies nearly its entire surface.

The taste buds of frogs are flat disks surrounded by ciliated cells with a central portion containing supporting cells and taste cells (fig. 16.15). Supporting cells contain microvilli and numerous secretory granules. They secrete a mucus that covers the entire taste bud and perhaps the entire oral cavity. Between the supporting cells the sensory cells reach the surface with thin dendritic extensions (Kinnamon 1987). The taste buds of salamanders have a distinct pore and contain at least two receptor cell types, a light and a dark cell (Cummings, Delay, and Roper 1987). These sensory cells contain three types of apical specialization. Light cells contain short unbranched microvilli as surface modifications; lightlike (intermediate) cells contain stereocilia as surface specializations, while dark cells contain long branched microvilli.

The taste receptors of adult anurans respond to stimuli applied to the tongue surface, including salts, acids, sugars, and amino acids. When chemical stimuli are applied to receptor cells, their membrane potential decreases, and the firing frequency of the glossopharyngeal nerve fibers in the tongue increases. The stimulus concentrations, the responses of the taste bud receptors, and the firing frequencies of the glossopharyngeal nerve are correlated, suggesting that concentration-dependent depolarization of the receptor cells yields information on concentration to the brain (Akaike, Noma, and Sato 1976). The response to salts varies tremendously. The threshold concentrations for NaCl, MgCl$_2$, and CaCl$_2$ are about 210 mM, 10 mM, and 0.21 mM, respectively. The receptor sites for these salts are different for each ion (Kitada 1986). The mechanisms by which the various stimuli (salt, acids, sugar, bitter, amino acids, and water) generate taste sensation differ and are beyond the scope of this review (see Teeter et al. 1987). Sodium ions, for instance, depolarize the taste buds of most amphibians. Yet amiloride (a Na$^+$ channel blocker) blocks depolarization in anurans but has no effect in urodeles (McPheeters and Roper 1985; Miyamoto, Okada, and Sato 1985). No information is available on mechanistic changes in taste bud receptor sites or receptor functions during larval development.

Otto Helff, a pioneer in amphibian developmental physiology, was the first to study the complete ontogeny of the tongue and taste bud growth in anurans (Helff and Mellicker 1941a, 1941b). All anuran larvae hatch without a tongue. However, they do contain specialized structures on the floor of the oral cavity (fig. 16.15). These structures, which have been termed "premetamorphic papillae," "premetamorphic lingual papillae," or "protuberances" (Hammerman 1969a, 1969b; Helff and Mellicker 1941a, 1941b; Nomura et al. 1979a, 1979b; Shiba et al. 1979, 1980), show clear phylogenetic variation in structure.

Premetamorphic papillae are present when larvae hatch, and they grow until about TK X–XII, after which they start decreasing in size (Hammerman 1969a; Helff and Mellicker 1941a). They contain innervated cells with microvilli projections at the oral surface, suggesting function as a chemoreceptor (Nomura et al. 1979a) or mechanoreceptor (Wassersug 1980). When premetamorphic papillae are stimulated by sucrose, ammonium chloride, and quinine hydrochloride, action potentials occur in the larval glossopharyngeal nerve (Shiba et al. 1980), proving that they can indeed function as oral chemosensory organs. The premetamorphic papillae begin to degenerate just before front legs emerge and disappear by late climax stages (Hammerman 1969a; Helff and Mellicker 1941a; Nomura 1979b; Shiba et al. 1979).

The tongue anlage of ranids appears at about TK V (Ham-

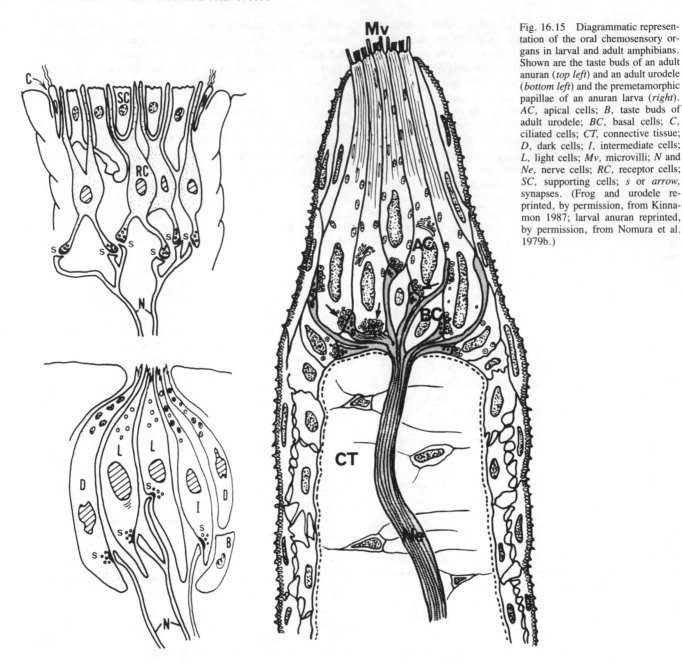

Fig. 16.15 Diagrammatic representation of the oral chemosensory organs in larval and adult amphibians. Shown are the taste buds of an adult anuran (*top left*) and an adult urodele (*bottom left*) and the premetamorphic papillae of an anuran larva (*right*). *AC*, apical cells; *B*, taste buds of adult urodele; *BC*, basal cells; *C*, ciliated cells; *CT*, connective tissue; *D*, dark cells; *I*, intermediate cells; *L*, light cells; *Mv*, microvilli; *N* and *Ne*, nerve cells; *RC*, receptor cells; *SC*, supporting cells; *s* or *arrow*, synapses. (Frog and urodele reprinted, by permission, from Kinnamon 1987; larval anuran reprinted, by permission, from Nomura et al. 1979b.)

merman 1969a; Helff and Mellicker 1941a; Spaeti 1978). Tongue size increases slowly but steadily during metamorphosis so that it doubles or triples in volume between TK X and XVIII. The tongue grows very rapidly during climax stages so that by the end of larval life tongue volume is thirty times larger than just before climax. During this rapid growth, the tongue of ranids also starts to bifurcate (TK XX). When the tongue appears, the epithelium on its dorsal surface is 2 cell layers deep. By the time climax starts, the epithelium increases to 10 to 18 cell layers deep. During climax the surface layer of epithelium decreases by 4 to 5 cell layers.

At about TK XXI the anlagen of the filiform papillae and mucous glands appear (Helff and Mellicker 1941a). By end of climax the histological appearance of filiform papillae and the multicellular mucous glands are identical to the adult structures. The anlagen of the fungiform papillae appear ear-

lier (TK XIV), and many evaginations are present over the entire dorsal surface of the tongue by TK XVIII (Hammerman 1969a; Helff and Mellicker 1941b; Rieck 1932; Spaeti 1978). By TK XVIII the anlagen push to the surface of the tongue and are distinct structures. By TK XXI primitive sensory disks with attached microvilli appear in the center of the fungiform papillae (Nomura et al. 1979a, 1979b). Cilia surround the primary sensory disk at TK XXII, and fully developed taste buds occur before tail loss is complete.

Even though *Xenopus laevis* has no tongue as an adult, it nevertheless possesses gustatory organs in the floor of its mouth. The larva starts to feed at NF 46, and by NF 47 numerous protuberances appear on the posterior floor of the mouth (Shiba et al. 1979, 1980). These protuberances start to degenerate just before forelimb emergence (NF 60). Gustatory organs similar to fungiform papillae of ranid species start appearing on the anterior surface of the oral epithelium at NF 60, and their numbers increase until midclimax NF 62. The premetamorphic protuberances completely disappear by NF 62. At NF 63 numerous microvilli appear on fungiform papillae, and by the time the tail is reabsorbed, these papillae are identical to those found in the adult *Xenopus* (Shiba et al. 1979).

Solutions of sucrose, ammonium chloride, and quinine hydrochloride applied to the floor of the larval bullfrog mouth change the firing frequency of the glossopharyngeal nerve (fig. 16.16). The responsiveness to these three stimuli changes during development (Shiba et al. 1980). The response to ammonium chloride is present from TK VI to XIX and then disappears nearly completely during midclimax stages. The response to sucrose disappears temporarily at TK XX, while the quinine hydrochloride response changes little during metamorphosis.

Because the premetamorphic papillae disappear early in climax (TK XXI) and anatomically the fungiform papillae do not appear complete until TK XXIII, these structures can serve as taste organs either during degeneration (premetamorphic papillae) or before completing development (fungiform papillae). Bullfrogs have decreased oral chemoreception during early climax stages. The decreased responsiveness during metamorphic climax may be important, because most anurans stop feeding for about three or four TK stages (XIX–XXII, J. J. Just unpublished). Chemical detection of food is therefore not necessary in early climax stages, and changes in oral musculature may make feeding impossible (Alley and Cameron 1983).

Olfaction The olfactory system has received more attention than the other two chemoreceptors in amphibians (Duellman and Trueb 1986). All orders contain a dual olfactory system:

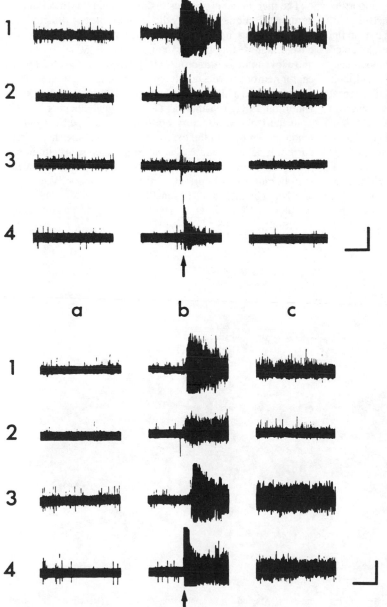

Fig. 16.16 Action potentials produced by chemical stimulation of the floor of the mouth and recorded in the glossopharyngeal nerve of larval bullfrogs, *Rana catesbeiana*. Action potentials were recorded (*a*) before application of a chemical stimulus, (*b*) at the time of chemical application (*arrow*), and (*c*) 7–10 s after chemical application. *Top panel*, four recordings showing the response to 0.02-M ammonium chloride. *Bottom panel*, four recordings showing response to 0.01-M quinine hydrochloride. *Time bar*, 1 s; *vertical bar*, 50 μV. *1, 2, 3*, and *4* correspond to developmental stages (TK) 19, 20, 21, and 22. (Reprinted, by permission, from Shiba et al. 1980.)

a principal and an accessory (Jacobson's organ or vomero-nasal organ). The principal olfactory system and its receptor cells arise from the olfactory placodes and terminate postsynaptically on the principal olfactory bulb of the telencephalon. The accessory system arises from Jacobson's organ, and its sensory epithelium forms the vomeronasal nerve and terminates in the accessory olfactory bulb of the telencephalon. Although these two organs have unique telencephalic termination points, information from the two systems reaches similar places in the brain by both ipsilateral and contralateral central connections (Kemali and Guglielmotti 1987).

The olfactory system of almost all amphibians consists of interconnected sacs with a common external opening (the nares) and an opening into the buccal cavity (the choana). The detailed cellular and physiological studies described below concern the largest of these sacs, the so-called cavan principal. In the nasal cavity the olfactory epithelium thickens from the posterior to the anterior end. The epithelium appears pseudostratified (fig. 16.17), containing supporting cells, sensory cells, and basal cells (Mackay-Sim, Breipohl, and Kremer 1987). The supporting columnar cells extend the entire thickness of the epithelial surface and have elongated nuclei located in the upper third of the cells. The bipolar sensory cells extend a slender process to the surface, and their axons pass through the epithelium to the dermis. The deepest nuclear layer belongs to the basal cells, whose apical ends do not reach the external surface. All three cell types are continuously replaced even in the adult (Mackay-Sim, Breipohl, and Kremer 1987). At the external surface the sensory cells are ciliated, while the support cells contain numerous microvilli. Numerous other surface modifications occur in the cavan principal, including the so-called respiratory surface cilia types (Breipohl et al. 1982). The epithelial surface is covered by mucus, produced by the supporting cells and the multicellular Bowman's glands, which have ducts leading to the surface.

The olfactory epithelium of adult amphibians responds to monovalent cations, divalent cations, monovalent anions, salt, acid, bitter, and many organic compounds. Different areas of the sac respond to different stimuli (Mackay-Sim and Shaman 1984). Although sac morphology differs regionally, morphological and physiological variation do not correspond. Chemical stimulation of the olfactory sac changes the electrical activity of the sensory cells, olfactory nerve, and olfactory bulb. The regional topographic specificity in the mucosa is partially maintained in the projection to the olfactory bulb (Mackay-Sim and Nathan 1984). Chemicals inducing depolarization currents in sensory cells and olfactory nerves also cause mucus secretion from the supporting cells and the multicellular Bowman's glands (Getchell et al. 1987). Basal cells do not responsed to chemical stimuli.

The membrane properties, as measured by intracellular recording techniques, are very different for the two olfactory cell types that respond to chemical stimuli. The supporting cells have a high resting membrane potential (-80 to -120 mV) and a low input resistance (10 MΩ). However, the olfactory receptor neurons have a relatively low resting potential (-40 to -60 mV) and a high input resistance (100 MΩ; Anderson and Hamilton 1987; Masukawa, Hedland, and Shepherd 1985).

In the isolated olfactory epithelium, the open current potential is 3.6 mV on the external surface and the short circuit current is 53 μA $\cdot$ cm^{-2}. The nonstimulated short circuit current occurs through an apical Na$^+$ cotransport system, while the odorant-evoked current is due to odorant-activated, passive Na$^+$ channels that are sensitive to amiloride, a Na$^+$ channel blocker (Persaud et al. 1987). It has been postulated that

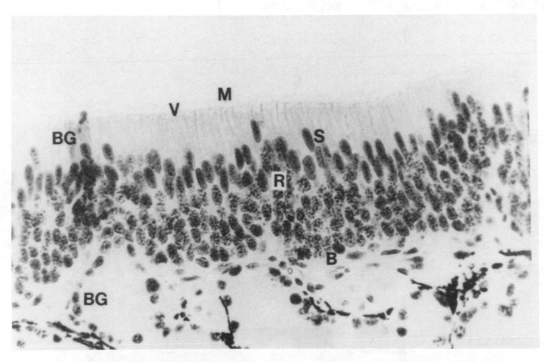

Fig. 16.17 Olfactory epithelium of the tiger slamander, *Ambystoma tigrinum*. *B*, basal cells; *BG*, Bowman's glands; *M*, mucus layer; *R*, receptor neuron cell bodies; *S*, supporting cells; *V*, vesicles of receptor neurons. Magnification approximately 400×. (Reprinted, by permission, from Masukawa, Hedlund, and Shepherd 1985.)

the Na⁺/Cl⁻ cotransporter is located in the sustentacular (supporting) cells, while the odorant-activated Na^+ channels are located in olfactory receptoneurons (Persaud et al. 1987). Both receptor and supporting cells have ouabain-sensitive (Na^+ and K^+) ATPase-linked Na^+ pumps on the basolateral membrane.

During embryonic development the olfactory epithelium begins as a thickening (olfactory placode) located anteriorly near the telencephalon. This placode includes two cell layers, one a nonnervous ectoderm and the other a thick neural ectodermal layer previously continuous with the neural plate (Klein and Graziadei 1983). The olfactory neurons and basal cells derive from the neural ectoderm layer while the supporting (sustentacular) cells and Bowman's glands arise from the nonnervous ectoderm. As the olfactory placode starts to invaginate, the ectoderm differentiates into the olfactory neurons and supporting cells. Simultaneously the olfactory neurons send large numbers of axons into the telencephalon (Klein and Graziadei 1983). The cells of the olfactory epithelium appear complete before a choanal canal forms and fuses with the gut endoderm (Cooper 1943; Klein and Graziadei 1983). The entire olfactory canal and sac system along with sensory epithelium differentiation is complete before hatching.

Additional differentiation of the olfactory system occurs after hatching. Although Bowman's glands are present in young urodele larvae, very few have ducts that extend to the epithelium surface. Three days after the completion of urodele metamorphosis, most Bowman's glands have ducts that extend to the surface and contribute to mucus secretion. Even after completion of metamorphosis, the sensory epithelium of urodeles changes. In the larva, the olfactory receptors are localized as discrete patches between nonsensory epithelium on a series of ridges and grooves, while in the sexually mature adult the receptors are organized in a flat epithelial sheet (Getchell, Rafols, and Getchell 1984; Getchell, Zielinski, and Getchell 1987). The internal nares of most anuran larvae are covered with narial flaps that degenerate after forelimb emergence (microhylids are an exception). During tail loss, ciliated grooves develop in an anterior-posterior direction from the internal nares and end at the esophageal opening (LeCluyse, Frost, and Dentler 1985). The cilia in the nasal sacs and nasal grooves help remove debris entering through the external nares and chemicals trapped in the secreted mucus of supporting cells and Bowman's glands. These cilia movements therefore ensure a more rapid detection of changes in the chemical environment.

The olfactory epithelium functions after the larval amphibians hatch. Exposure to three types of stimuli—airborne volatiles, volatile solutions, and amino acid solutions—all yield an electrophysiological response in the olfactory epithelium of both larval and adult salamanders (Arzt et al. 1986). The olfactory sacs of larval and adult salamanders differ in their response to these stimuli. When threshold values and dose-response curve variables are compared, the nonvolatile amino acids in solution are more potent stimuli for larvae, but airborne volatile compounds are a more potent stimuli for adults (fig. 16.18).

Larval amphibians use the olfactory epithelium in various

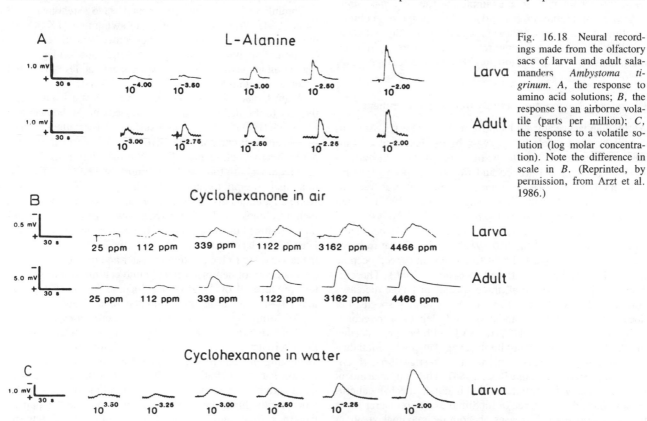

Fig. 16.18 Neural recordings made from the olfactory sacs of larval and adult salamanders *Ambystoma tigrinum*. A, the response to amino acid solutions; B, the response to an airborne volatile (parts per million); C, the response to a volatile solution (log molar concentration). Note the difference in scale in B. (Reprinted, by permission, from Arzt et al. 1986.)

ways. Anuran larvae use chemical signals to recognize and associate with siblings (Waldman 1986). Chemicals in food attract anuran larvae and stimulate gnawing (Kiseleva 1984; Kiseleva and Manteifel 1982). Both anuran and urodele larvae avoid water containing chemical compounds released by predatory fish or amphibians (Kats, Petranka, and Sih 1988; Kiseleva and Manteifel 1982; Petranka, Kats, and Sih 1987). The chemical detection of siblings and predatory fish occurs via the olfactory epithelium rather than the taste buds or the lateral line system. When the external nares are plugged, anuran larvae cannot detect siblings (Waldman 1985), and salamander larvae cannot detect predatory fish (Kats 1988). When the plugs are removed from the external nares, the larvae once again can detect the chemical cues.

MOTOR SYSTEM AND LOCOMOTION

Changes in the neural and endocrine systems allow amphibians to occupy different ecological niches at different stages of larval and adult development, to modify behavior, to maximize their growth and survival, and to move to optimal environmental conditions. Almost all anuran larvae swim to filter-feed at some early stage in development (Just, Kraus-Just, and Check 1981; see "Feeding and Digestion" below). Animals aggregate in areas of greatest food availability, unless potential predators occupy such areas or there is potential interspecific competition (Just, Kraus-Just, and Check 1981). Larvae can choose different environmental temperatures (Just, Kraus-Just, and Check 1981; Wollmuth and Crawshaw 1988; see chapter 9). For example, larvae of *Rana catesbeiana* chose higher temperatures as they progress to climax (Wollmuth and Crawshaw 1988), and increased thyroid gland function at elevated temperatures ensures a more rapid metamorphosis (Bowers, Segaloff, and Brown 1959; Dupré et al. 1986).

Changes in Locomotor Activity during Development

Amphibian larvae and adults move in different ways. Anuran, caecilian, and urodele larvae swim by oscillation of the tail, whereas frogs use limbs to swim, walk, or hop. In bottom-feeding anuran larvae (*Bufo* and *Rana*) the speed of swimming increases linearly over an average of tail beat frequencies from 4 to 16 Hz (Wassersug and Hoff 1985). When midwater-feeding larval *Xenopus* swim at six body lengths per second, however, the tail beat frequency is not correlated with swimming speed (fig. 16.19). At high tail beat frequencies (14 to 22 Hz) the tail beat frequency and speed become positively correlated (Hoff and Wassersug 1986). The efficiency of locomotion in all three species of larvae increases continuously with speed at the lower swimming speeds, but does not increase above about six body lengths per second.

In midlarval stages (TK XII–XVI) with both appreciable hindlimbs and tails, the hindlimbs extend against the tail during swimming (*X. laevis,* Hughes and Prestige 1967; *R. catesbeiana,* Stehouwer and Farel 1984). This limb placement may decrease water turbulence and maintain mechanical efficiency. Indeed, the degree of hindlimb extension increases as tail beat frequency increases, becoming maximal at about seven beats per second (Stehouwer and Farel 1984). This frequency corresponds approximately to that at which the effi-

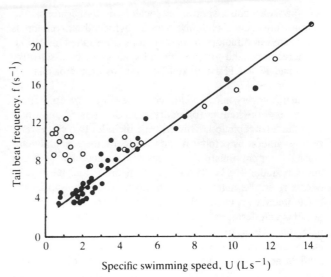

Fig. 16.19 Tail beat frequency, (f), as a function of swimming speed, U, measured as forward velocity in body lengths per second measured at the snout. ○, *Xenopus laevis;* ●, *Rana catesbeiana, R. septentrionalis, R. clamitans,* and *Bufo americanus.* (Reprinted, by permission, from Hoff and Wassersug 1986.)

ciency of swimming reaches its maximum (Wassersug and Hoff 1985). Starting at about TK XVII, animals use both limbs and tails to swim, while animals use only the limbs after TK XXII (Hughes and Prestige 1967; Stehouwer and Farel 1983). Locomotor activity of the hindlimbs during swimming varies with developmental stage (Stehouwer and Farel 1984). When the legs first aid swimming (TK XVII), the right and left legs alternate their movement to generate a "stepping" activity. "Kicking" (both right and left legs moving simultaneously for swimming) appears at TK XVIII and becomes the dominant movement by TK XXIII.

When larvae of different stages are removed from water, they try to use their hindlimbs for movement (Stehouwer and Farel 1984). On dry and rough surfaces larvae attempt hindlimb location as early as at TK XII; however, these movements are ineffective before TK XVIII. Normal adult movement on land requires both fore- and hindlimbs. At TK XX, only 25% of animals attempt to support their body with their forelimbs, while all animals display adultlike support of their body with their forelimbs by TK XXII (Stehouwer 1988). No studies have examined the mechanics of larval locomotion during the later half of larval life (e.g., the relative contribution of both the tail and leg to locomotion in water and on land).

A network of neurons arranged into central pattern generators produce all of the rhythmic locomotor activities of anurans (tail undulation, hindlimb "stepping" and/or "kicking"). Motor neurons of the isolated nervous system show rhythmic right and left alternating activity that corresponds to the alternate contractions of axial tail musculature during swimming movement (Roberts, Soffe, and Dale 1986; Stehouwer and Farel 1980, 1983; Roberts 1989). Patterned electrical activity is also evident in the lateral motor rootlets that innervate the hindlimbs. Two patterns occur: the "stepping" pattern, a right- and left-side alteration of electrical activity, and the "kicking" or jumping pattern, in which electrical activity occurs simultaneously on both sides. This central pattern generating activity corresponding to hindlimb use in larvae appears in the isolated nervous system earlier than in intact animals (Stehouwer and Farel 1983, 1984).

Spinally transected larvae and froglets show typical locomotor activity when amino acid receptors are activated by injecting N-methyl-DL-aspartate (NMDA) or D-glutamate into the spinal cord (McClellan 1986; McClellan and Farel 1985). Such spinally transected animals usually show little or no locomotor activity before amino acid injection. When the central nervous system is isolated and the brain stem is detached, this preparation shows little spontaneous electrical activity, even though "normal" locomotor electrical activity can be seen when the entire nervous system is isolated. Electrical activity begins when electrically quiescent spinal cords of larvae are exposed to these two amino acids, and this activity corresponds to the typical rhythmic activity of swimming. No such activation occurs in isolated frog spinal cords. These data suggest that the brain may use amino-acid-like neurotransmitters to activate locomotor activity in the larval spinal cord.

Developmental changes in locomotor activity in larval and adult urodeles and caecilians have not been described. One would predict maturational changes in limb movement during development in urodeles, particularly in species with aquatic larvae and terrestrial adults. The contributions of the tail to forward thrust should change during urodele metamorphic climax stages when the tail fin degenerates, even if the adults remain aquatic.

Many neuronal connections from the brain to the spinal cord occur in embryos and larvae as well as adult amphibians. These connections are to both the primary and secondary motor neurons of the spinal cord. Such spinal anatomical connections can be established before, at the time of, or after the motor neuron functions develop (van Mier 1986; Roberts 1989). The number and type of connections are beyond the scope of this review, and most important, evidence for the physiological role of most of these connections is limited. Bilateral removal of the cerebral hemispheres and/or the optic tectum greatly reduces the overall locomotor activity of larvae (fig. 16.20) but has little or no effect on a juvenile frog's overall activity (Stehouwer 1987). The decrease in locomotor activity in larvae after tectal and/or cerebral removal is not due to a generalized depression of activity. When the spinal cord of a larva is transected, nearly complete paralysis of the tail musculature occurs (McClellan and Farel 1985; Roberts, Soffe, and Dale 1986). Thus, locomotor circuits in the brain stem are needed for normal swimming, and locomotion requires no inputs from the tectum or cerebrum. However, some neuronal connections from the brain to the spinal cord contribute greatly to locomotion in larvae of numerous amphibian species.

Such a neuronal connection leads to the Mauthner cells. These neurons were first detected in fish over a century ago and are found in anuran and urodele larvae (Hughes 1959; Will 1986). However, they have not been found in caecilian larvae and in some anuran larvae (Fox 1984; Kollros 1981; Will 1986). Mauthner cells can be identified by their large size in the medulla at the level of cranial nerve VIII. Mauthner cells contain two large dendritic trees. One connects to the vestibular root of cranial nerve VIII, while the other den-

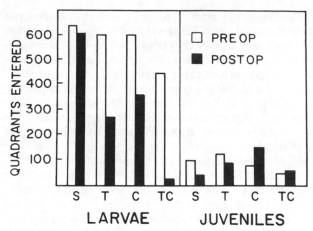

Fig. 16.20 Effects of various brain lesions on the spontaneous activity of larval and juvenile bullfrogs (*Rana catesbeiana*). Spontaneous activity of animals was measured by counting the number of new quadrants entered in a circular container during a 4-h period. Data are presented for preoperative and postoperative animals. Operations included sham operation (*S*) and removal of the optic tectum (*T*), the telencephalon (*C*), or both of these structures (*TC*). (Reprinted, by permission, from Stehouwer 1987.)

dritic tree connects to the lateral line nerve (Kimmel, Schabtach, and Kimmel 1977; Rock 1980). Each cell has one large axon that extends posteriorly and crosses over to the contralateral side of the animal in the floor of the fourth ventricle (Rock 1980). Mauthner cells in amphibians produce the startle response in the animal by causing flexion of the body, triggered by action potentials that stimulate one side of the body and inhibit the motor activity on the ipsilateral side (Rock 1980).

For many years numerous authors claimed that Mauthner cells disappeared at metamorphic climax (see Fox 1984; Kollros 1981). A recent study of various adult amphibians demonstrates their presence in the adults of numerous species. In fact, every species that contains Mauthner cells as a larva retains them as an adult (Will 1986). That some larvae do not contain Mauthner cells (*Bombina* or *Bufo bufo*) suggests that the startle response can occur without Mauthner cells, or that this behavior is not always essential. Obviously, the functions of these cells must be determined in adult terrestrial amphibians.

Changes in the Neuromotor System during Development

Regardless of how many developmental changes occur in the mode of sensory input in larvae, the motor neurons and muscles must develop sufficiently to allow the animals to respond to changes in environmental inputs. The classic work of Coghill (1929) on embryos removed from jelly coats demonstrated that during late embryonic life and early larval life locomotion is accomplished by rhythmic undulation of the tail. In fact, hatching represents a behavioral response to environmental changes and can be triggered prematurely in aquatic vertebrates by a decrease in the available environmental oxygen to the embryos (Latham and Just 1989; Petranka, Just, and Crawford 1982). Therefore all muscles and nerves for undulatory swimming movements must develop before normal hatching can occur in aquatic vertebrates.

The majority of primary motor neurons that innervate the skeletal muscles used for larval locomotion develop before any myotomes appear. Only about 20% develop after hatching (van Mier 1986). Secondary motor neurons appear after hatching and include two populations of cells in the spinal column, the medial and lateral motor column. The lateral motor column (LMC) cells innervate the limb musculature. These cells appear after hatching, become more numerous until midlarval stages, and then decrease during the latter half of larval life (Kollros 1981; van Mier 1986). The number of LMC cells stabilizes around metamorphic climax (Fox 1984; Kollros 1981; Sperry and Grobstein 1985). The medial motor column (MMC) cells innervate the trunk and neck musculature and probably appear after hatching (Flanigan 1960; the morphological changes in motor neurons associated with amphibian development are discussed in detail in chapter 11).

Skeletal muscles of amphibians arise from myotomes. The number of myotomes increases continuously in amphibian larvae even after hatching, and this contributes to body lengthening (van Mier 1986). In some species larval growth continues by the addition of myotomes, while in other species the growth of existing myotomes is responsible (Nishikawa and Wassersug 1988; Nordlander 1986). The myotomes give rise to myoblasts in which myofibrils appear even before the muscle cells become multinucleated, which occurs before embryonic hatching in all amphibians examined (Fox 1984). The size of the nucleus in multinucleated skeletal muscles decreases during the entire larval period (Boudjelida and Muntz 1987). In *Xenopus laevis* the typical multinucleated skeletal muscle cells may form in a unique amitotic fashion from a single myoblast cell, rather than in the typical vertebrate way, namely, by fusion of many individual cells (Boudjelida and Muntz 1987).

For coordinated movement, both primary and secondary motor cells must make synaptic connections with neurons centrally and muscles peripherally. About 90% of embryonic and larval muscles have a single end plate innervated by more than one motor axon (Lynch et al. 1986). These multiply innervated end plates disappear after completion of metamorphosis, and less than 20% of sexually mature frogs have multiaxonal end plates. The primary motor neurons make these peripheral neuromuscular connections to the myomeres of the tail before hatching. These neurons persist until midclimax stages, when they degenerate (Stehouwer and Farel 1980; Moody and Jacobson 1983). The secondary motor neurons of the lateral motor column make their first peripheral synaptic connection to the limb at the early limb-bud stage, and increase these synaptic muscle connections until early climax stages (Stehouwer and Farel 1983; Taylor 1943).

In terms of central connections of the motor neurons, the primary motor neurons send dendrites into the dorsal and lateral marginal zone (white matter) of the spinal cord a few hours after they make their peripheral muscle connections. The primary motor neurons develop ventral dendrites in the marginal zone before hatching (van Mier, van Rheden, and ten Donkelaar 1985). The secondary motor neurons develop dendrites after hatching and after limb-muscle innervation, and the first of these neurons extends into the dorsal marginal zone. These dendrites next extend into the dorsolateral part of the marginal zone, which is devoid of dendrites of primary motor neurons. Dendrites into the ventral marginal zone ap-

pear later from the secondary motor neurons (van Mier, van Rheden, and ten Donkelaar 1985). The primary motor neurons have most of their dendrites in the ventromedial and ventrolateral parts of the marginal zone, while dendrites of the secondary motor neurons occur predominantly in the dorsolateral and ventromedial parts of the marginal zone.

Coordinated movements require sensory inputs either directly or indirectly to both the primary and secondary motor neurons by way of interneurons. The primary motor neurons respond to tactile stimulation of the tail and body by swimming movements (Coghill 1929). These tactile stimulations activate the nonmyelinated peripheral neurites of the Rohon-Beard cells (Clarke et al. 1984; Roberts and Hayes 1977; Roberts, Soffe, and Dale 1986). Rohon-Beard cells are large segmentally arranged cells in the dorsolateral regions of the spinal cord and are easily recognizable in early tail-bud stages (fig. 16.21). Rohen-Beard cells are most numerous (200–300) at or near the time of hatching (Fox 1984; Kollros 1981). These sensory cell bodies are in the middorsal surface of the neural tube, while the primary motor cells are near the ventral surface of the neural tube (fig. 16.21). The exact circuits connecting these two cells have not been established, and the details are beyond the scope of this review but involve identified interneurons (ascending, commissural, descending, and dorsolateral) and other interneurons (see Roberts, Soffe, and Dale 1986). After hatching, the sensory cells start to de-

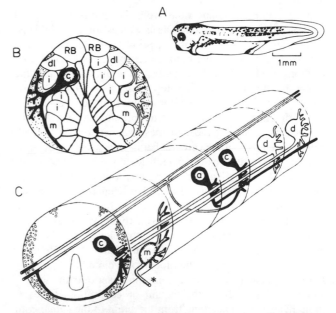

Fig. 16.21 The possible connections between sensory cells and motor neurons in the spinal cord of an embryonic *Xenopus laevis*. *A*, external body morphology of NF 37/38 embryos. *B*, Transverse section of trunk spinal cord (about 100-μm diameter). The lumen of the cord is surrounded by ependymal cells (*stippled*). The neurons in the gray matter of the spinal cord include the dorsally located sensory neurons (Rohon-Beard cells, *RB*) and the ventrally located primary motor neurons (*m*). Between these cells are found various identified interneurons (*c*, commissural; *d*, descending; *dl*, dorso-lateral), and unidentified interneurons (*i*). All neurons have axons and dendrites that extend into the white matter of the spinal cord. *C*, diagram of neurons that have action potentials during swimming. Rostral is to the right. *, the axon of the primary motor neuron that innervates the trunk and tail musculature; *a*, ascending interneuron. (Reprinted, by permission, from Roberts, Soffe, and Dale 1986.)

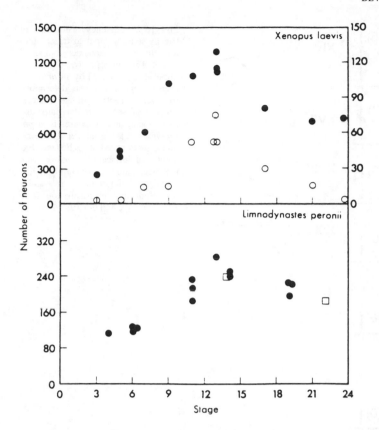

Fig. 16.22 Comparison of the total number of living neurons (●) in thoracic ganglia of *Xenopus laevis* and *Limnodynastes peroni* (Myobatrachidae) at different developmental stages (TK scheme). ○, the number of degenerating cells per day. □, number of live neurons determined by horseradish-peroxidase labeling from sensory rami. (Reprinted, by permission, from Bennett and Lai 1981.)

generate. All the Rohon-Beard cells degenerate when metamorphosis is complete; in some species degeneration is complete before the climax stages (Fox 1984; Kollros 1981).

Because the Rohon-Beard cells degenerate in all amphibians and the lateral line degenerates in many amphibians during larval life, another sensory system must arise during development to supply sensory input from the skin. This other system is the dorsal root ganglia, whose neurons arise from neural crest cells before the embryos hatch. The neurons from the dorsal root ganglia send dendrites into the limb and trunk musculature as well as into the skin, and project axons via the dorsal root horn into the neural tube (Bennett and Lai 1981; Taylor 1943). These ganglia cells project some neurons into the skin before hatching, but major neuronal outgrowth does not occur until after hatching. In fact, the limb bud of *Rana pipiens* is not innervated until early larva stages, but all major branches are visible before TK X (Taylor 1943). Sensory cell density in the ganglia (fig. 16.22) increases during early larval stages and then starts to decrease in midlarval stages (Bennett and Lai 1981; Kollros 1981).

The final number of cells in the spinal ganglia results from both cell death and cell divisions during larval development. The sensory ganglia themselves are a mosaic, with cells innervating specific regions of the body being restricted to specific ganglia (hindlimb ganglia 8–10 in Anura) or specific regions in ganglia innervating specific body parts (Bennett and Lai 1981; Taylor 1943). Sensory neurons innervating skin on the dorsal surface are in the dorsal region of the dorsal ganglion, whereas those innervating belly skin are in the ventral region of the ganglia (Bennett and Lai 1981). The sensory cells from the dorsal root ganglia innervating the skin can act both as mechanoreceptors (Baker, Corner, and Veltman 1978; Watts and French 1985) and as temperature-sensitive neurons

(Dupré et al. 1986). The sensory cells to the muscle can act as proprioceptors and/or stretch receptors (Frank and Westerfield 1983). When axons from these sensory cells enter the spinal cord, axons coming from limb musculature enter before those axons that contain cutaneous leg axons (Liuzzi, Beattie, and Bresnahan 1985; van Mier 1986). After these axons enter the spinal cord, they project to the areas where dendrites from the secondary motor neurons are located.

These anatomical connections are also evident from electrophysiological and behavioral techniques (Dupré et al. 1986; Frank and Westerfield 1983). Remarkably, the physiology of such sensory inputs changes with development. At TK XIII the conduction velocities of anterior limb nerves are about 0.2 to 0.4 m · s⁻¹, indicating that the fibers are nonmyelinated. As development progresses, conduction velocities increase to about 5 m · s⁻¹ at TK XXII and remain constant even in adults. The higher conduction velocities suggest some fibers are myelinated. Stimulation of forelimb sensory fibers at TK XIV rarely leads to stimulation of motor fibers (fig. 16.23), and synaptic connections have a long latency (25 to 45 m · s⁻¹). At TK XVII one-third of forelimb motor neurons connect to the dorsal ganglion sensory cells, and the latency of about half of these connections is short (less than 3 ms), indicating monosynaptic inputs. At TK XIX, 50% of all motor neurons showed monosynaptic connections, 86% at TK XXII, and 99% in adults (Frank and Westerfield 1983). The projections of the triceps muscle's sensory neurons to various branchial motor neurons throughout development are specific, with few aberrant connections in any larval stages (Frank and Westerfield 1983).

The dorsal cutaneous nerves of various stages of *Rana catesbeiana* contain mechanoreceptors and temperature-sensitive neurons (Dupré et al. 1986), including both cold- and

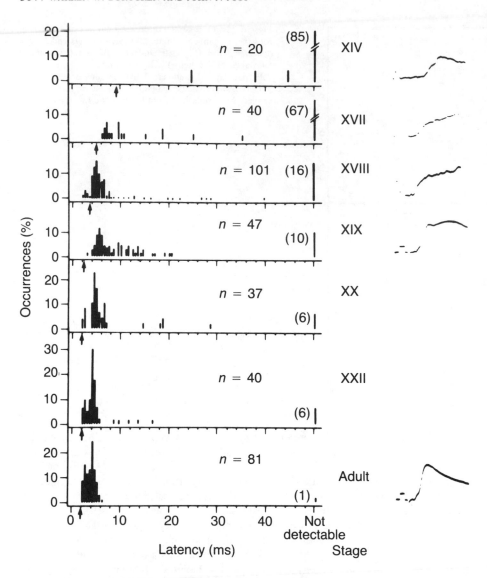

Fig. 16.23 Latency histograms of triceps sensory input to triceps motor neurons at various developmental stages. The time of arrival of sensory impulses is indicated by an *arrow* in each histogram and was determined from ventral root recordings. The percentage of sensory-motor pairs that had undetectable responses is in *parentheses; N* is the number of sensory-motor pairs tested at each stage. Examples of intracellular records from the triceps are to the right of the histograms. Calibration: 0.5 mV and 2 ms. (Reprinted, by permission, from Frank and Westerfield 1983.)

warm-sensitive neurons. The static maximum temperature increases gradually but steadily from 16°C at TK XIII to as high as 32°C at TK XXV (Dupré et al. 1986). An increase in preferred body temperature selected by larvae in a continuous thermal gradient accompanies these shifts in sensory inputs (Dupré et al. 1986; see chapter 9).

RESPIRATION AND METABOLISM

All amphibians essentially undergo "aquatic" embryonic and/or larval development before assuming (in most species) a more terrestrial existence. Since water and air differ so greatly in their physicochemical properties and thus as respiratory media (see Burggren and Roberts 1991; Dejours 1981; Scheid 1982), it is hardly surprising that development of the cardiorespiratory system closely reflects the different constraints and demands of breathing water versus breathing air.

Metabolism and Development

The pathways and rate of metabolism change qualitatively during amphibian development. Early embryonic stages have a large potential for anaerobic utilization of yolk substrate via glycolysis (Gregg 1962). Aerobic pathways progressively

dominate as embryonic development proceeds. However, even late embryos and, in some instances, posthatch larvae, can survive anoxic conditions for hours or days (Adolph 1979; Rose, Armentrout, and Roper 1971; Detwiler and Copenhaver 1940; Gregg 1960; Weigmann and Altig 1975), suggesting a considerable anaerobic capability. While many species of adult amphibians can also survive brief anoxia at 20° to 25°C or much longer at near-freezing temperature (see chapter 10), this is due to near-complete suspension of metabolism rather than use of anaerobic metabolic pathways.

The rate of aerobic metabolism changes during amphibian development. During embryonic development, as depicted in figure 16.24, O_2 consumption ($\dot{M}O_2$) is very low before folding of the neural crest, after which it increases substantially (Bialaszewicz and Bledowski 1915; Boell 1948; Brachet 1934; Gregg 1960; Hopkins and Handford 1943; Parnas and Kraskinska 1921; Wills 1936). Importantly, the total $\dot{M}O_2$ of the egg/embryo/larva is not identical to the *mass-specific* $\dot{M}O_2$. Expressing total $\dot{M}O_2$ on a per egg or per embryo basis is reasonable when comparing individuals of uniform size and developmental stage. However, descriptions of developmental changes in metabolic rate require accounting for covariation in body mass. The accurate determination of these

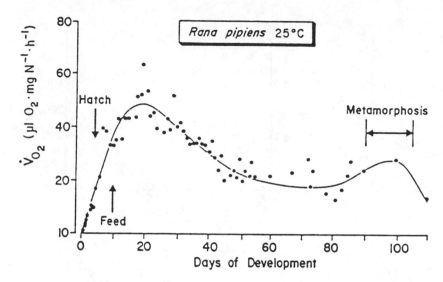

Fig. 16.24 O_2 uptake (expressed in terms of milligrams of nitrogen) as a function of development in the anuran *Rana pipiens*. (After Wills 1936.)

variables is not trivial; although measurement of $\dot{M}O_2$ in embryos in the milligram range is feasible, determination of any "body mass" is difficult. Amphibians may contain considerable quantities of "nonliving" materials, for example, large water stores in the bladder of adults, and gut contents of both larvae and adults. Particularly in early development, the largely metabolically inert lipids stored in yolk cells make up the vast majority of "body mass." Expressing mass as embryo plus yolk considerably underestimates mass-specific $\dot{M}O_2$ and may erroneously suggest greatly accelerating aerobic metabolism accompanying yolk depletion. Alternatively, dry body mass after ethanol extraction of lipid, total nitrogen content (fig. 16.24), or even total DNA might better represent the metabolically active body mass. Unfortunately, methodology is seldom uniform or validated. Determining how development influences the "true" metabolic rate of embryos (i.e., anabolically active tissue excluding nonmetabolizing energy and substrate stores) remains an important area for future exploration.

Resting and active $\dot{M}O_2$ have been measured in posthatch larval amphibians after yolk absorption but before metamorphic climax (see Burggren 1984 and Feder 1981a for reviews of the extensive literature). However, the effects of development on $\dot{M}O_2$ are less well known. A major complication is that body mass and developmental stage may not covary in many amphibian species. In *Ambystoma tigrinum*, for example, metamorphosis can occur at any body mass between 5 and 130 g (W. W. Burggren unpublished). Once larvae of the bullfrog, *R. catesbeiana*, reach 3 to 5 g, they can proceed through most of their development (including metamorphosis) with little change in body mass, though continued growth until metamorphosis is common (W. W. Burggren unpublished). The anurans *Phyllobates subpunctatus* (Dendrobatidae) and *Bufo boreas* show complex changes in body mass with development, first increasing, then decreasing immediately before metamorphic climax (fig. 16.25).

Due to either incongruence of body mass and developmental stage or consistent but complex patterns of change in amphibian larvae, intraspecific differences in $\dot{M}O_2$ between larvae of different sizes may or may not reflect development. As Feder (1981) emphasizes in his critical analysis of the literature on $\dot{M}O_2$ in amphibian larvae, mass-specific $\dot{M}O_2$ decreases with increasing body mass in almost all animals, including amphibian larvae (see also Feder 1982a). Any changes in metabolic intensity may reflect an interaction of body mass and development, if body mass changes with development.

Given this caveat about interpreting $\dot{M}O_2$ in amphibian larvae, what can be said about changes in $\dot{M}O_2$ due to *development* per se? From the relatively few published studies that present data on mass-specific $\dot{M}O_2$, body mass, and developmental stage, no consistent pattern emerges. The anurans *Phyllobates subpunctatus* (Funkhouser and Mills 1969) and *Bufo boreas* (Sivula, Mix, and McKenzie 1972) differ in patterns of change in resting $\dot{M}O_2$. In resting unrestrained *P. subpunctatus*, $\dot{M}O_2$ is independent of developmental stage until about TK XVI; that is, all of the changes in resting $\dot{M}O_2$ are solely attributable to body mass change (Feder 1982a). After stage 16, mass-specific resting $\dot{M}O_2$ decreases sharply and out of proportion to the change in body mass. In *B. boreas*, on the other hand, changes in resting $\dot{M}O_2$ in larvae of advancing age are consistent with changes predicted solely by adjustment in body mass throughout larval development (Feder 1982a). Similarly, in larvae of anurans—*Bufo woodhousii*, *Hymenochirus boettgeri* (Pipidae), and *Rana berlandieri*—all of the variation in resting $\dot{M}O_2$ of larvae is attributable to changes in body mass (Feder 1982a). In most stages of development the same is true for *Xenopus*, although in late larval development mass-specific $\dot{M}O_2$ declines.

Although body mass has a major, pervasive effect on $\dot{M}O_2$, in some species changes in $\dot{M}O_2$ relate specifically to development. These relationships may stem from the relatively intense metabolic activity associated with differentiation in early developmental stages, transfer of gas exchange from gills and skin using water toward lungs using air (water being metabolically more "expensive" to pump), and changes in physical activity associated with changes in feeding habits (see Feder 1981, 1982a for discussion). As Feder (1982a, 40) comments, "All of these possible explanations are amenable to experimental verification." Such verification is required but is yet to occur. Another unexplored area involves the ability of posthatch larvae to exploit anaerobic metabolic pathways. Temperate aquatic larvae can experience quite severe hypoxia during both summer and winter (see chapter 10),

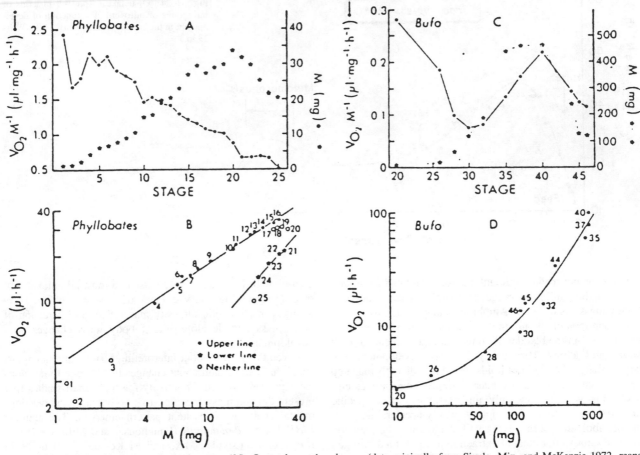

Fig. 16.25 Relationship between body dry mass (*M*), O₂ uptake, and developmental stage (Gosner 1960) in the anurans *Phyllobates subpunctatus* (Dendrobatidae; data from Funkhouser and Mills 1969) and *Bufo*

boreas (data originally from Sivula, Mix, and McKenzie 1972, reanalyzed and plotted by Feder 1982a. Reprinted, by permission.)

but little is known about whether these animals continue to extract O₂ at very low concentrations in the environment, or resort to anaerobic metabolism.

Gas Exchange Organs, Ventilation, and Development

Amphibians show probably the most complex developmental changes in respiratory organs of any of the vertebrates. This complexity arises in part because almost all amphibians of any developmental stage use more than one organ for gas exchange (some combination of gills, skin, and lungs). Additionally, many amphibian larvae and adults use a combination of air and water, which have vastly different physicochemical properties as respiratory media (see also chapters 4–6).

Initially, all amphibian embryos depend completely upon diffusional gas exchange across the body wall. In fact, cutaneous exchange of O₂ and CO₂ remains a lifelong feature of amphibians (for references see Burggren 1984; Feder and Burggren 1985a, 1985b, 1985c; chapters 5 and 6). Figure 16.26 shows changes in gas exchange partitioning between skin, gills, and lungs in larvae of the bullfrog, *Rana catesbeiana*. Throughout larval development, the skin is the single most important gas exchange organ, accounting for about 50% of CO₂ exchange and 60% of O₂ uptake. The dependence upon the skin is surprisingly constant at temperatures ranging from 15° to 33°C in both *R. catesbeiana* and *R. berlandieri*, even

though total metabolic rate increases threefold (Burggren, Feder, and Pinder 1983).

External gills appear early in embryonic development in amphibians. The role of these embryonic external gills in gas exchange is equivocal, for in most species they are little more than externalized capillary loops of relatively short length. After hatching, the external gills of the larvae of urodeles continue to differentiate into elaborate, highly vascularized respiratory structures. These gills can be ventilated by water currents generated by movement of the animal through the water (or the presence of the animal in flowing water), or by subtle movements of the gill arches generated by contraction of branchiomeric levator and depressor muscles (Guimond and Hutchison 1972, 1976; see also chapter 11). At 25°C, about 60 to 70% of both O₂ uptake and CO₂ elimination is across the gills in the neotenic urodeles *Necturus* (Proteidae) and *Siren* (Sirenidae; Guimond and Hutchison 1972, 1976). As Burggren (1984, 41) notes, however, "Data from large neotenic (paedomorphic, paedogenic) amphibians may not necessarily be typical of amphibians that undergo metamorphosis to an adult form," and experiments on early larval stages of urodeles are needed.

Anuran larvae differ from urodeles in that, shortly after hatching, internal gills located within paired branchial chambers replace the external gills, which degenerate (fig. 16.27). The development of the internal gills varies greatly among species, but no clear correlation with phylogeny or environ-

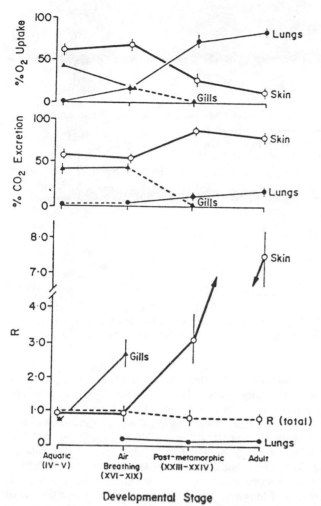

Fig. 16.26 Changes in O_2 uptake, CO_2 elimination, and the gas exchange ratio, R (CO_2 elimination/O_2 uptake), of the skin, gills, and lungs of the bullfrog, *Rana catesbeiana*, at 20°C. Taylor-Kollros stages. (Reprinted, by permission, from Burggren and West 1982.)

larval stage in *Rana catesbeiana* (Burggren and West 1982) and *R. berlandieri* (Burggren, Feder, and Pinder 1983), progressively decreasing as lung ventilation begins (fig. 16.26). In larval *R. catesbeiana* about 40% of metabolically produced CO_2 is eliminated via the gills. General branchial performance in anuran larvae is thus similar to that in fishes (see Shelton 1970). In normoxia at 10° to 25°C, buccal pumping at 70 to 100 cycles · min^{-1} produces a rhythmically oscillating pressure in the buccal cavity of 1 to 2 cm H_2O (fig. 16.28). Ventilation volume through the left and right branchial chambers combined is approximately 0.15 to 0.30 ml · g^{-1} · min^{-1} (see Burggren 1984 for references). O_2 utilization from air-saturated water flowing through the gills is about 65%.

In anuran larvae with internal gills, hypoxic water stimulates gill ventilation (see Burggren and Doyle 1986c for references), which allows larvae to maintain some branchial O_2 uptake down to a Po_2 as low as 40 mm Hg at 20°C (West and

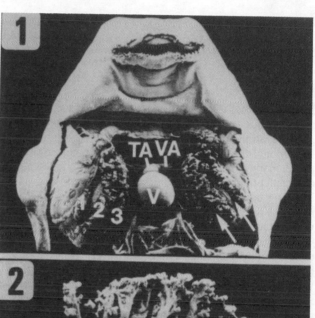

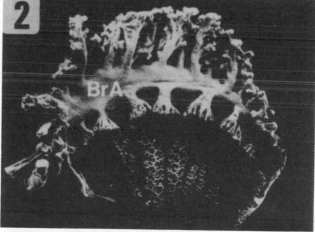

Fig. 16.27 Scanning electron micrographs of the larval branchial chambers of the anuran *Litoria ewingi* (Hylidae). *1*, anterior of the larva. Paired branchial chambers are lateral to the ventricle of the heart (*V*) and the emerging truncus arteriosus (*TA*) leading into the ventral aorta (*VA*). Water flows in the mouth and into each branchial chamber. Water from the right branchial chamber passes in a narrow channel across to the left branchial chamber, and all postbranchial water exits via a single opercular spout located on the left side of the body wall. The spaces between gill arches *1*, *2*, and *3* are indicated by *arrows*. Magnification 20 ×. *2*, lateral side of third branchial arch (*BrA*) from the larva. Magnification 30 ×. (Reprinted, by permission, from McIndoe and Smith 1984.)

ment emerges (Atkinson and Just 1975; Burggren and Mwalukoma 1983; Gradwell 1969a, 1969b; Medvedev 1937; McIndoe and Smith 1984a; Strawinski 1956; Saint-Aubain 1982a). Ranids generally have highly developed gills with extensive vascularization, while the larvae of some pipid and hylid anurans have a reduced branchial apparatus specialized for filter-feeding rather than gas exchange (Noble 1931; Wassersug and Feder 1983).

Anuran larvae use dorsoventral movements of the buccal floor to ventilate the branchial chambers by inspiring water into the buccal cavity and forcing it through the branchial cavity (Gradwell 1972a, 1972b). This mechanism is homologous with that of fishes. The regulation of gill ventilation in anuran larvae is extremely sophisticated and complex and is different from, rather than simpler than, regulation of lung ventilation in adults (see reviews by Burggren 1984; Feder 1984; also Burggren and Doyle 1986c: chapter 7). A review of the extensive literature is beyond the scope of this chapter, but several aspects deserve description. Once again, the literature reflects choice of specimens based on convenience rather than systematic or environmental representation; most measurements are on the large larvae of temperate ranids. The uptake of O_2 across the branchial surfaces depends on

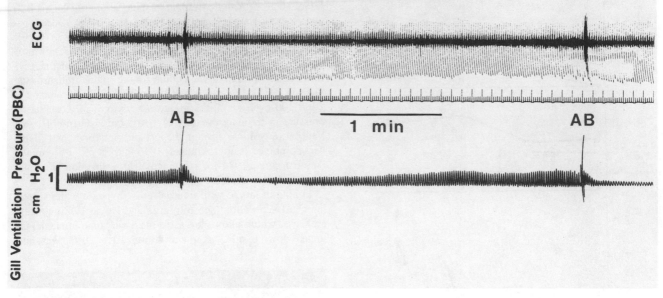

Fig. 16.28   Records of water pressures measured in buccal cavity (*bottom*) and of the ECG (*top*) in an unrestrained larva (TK XIX) of the bullfrog, *Rana catesbeiana*. Two air breaths (*AB*) occur in this record. (Reprinted, by permission, from West and Burggren 1983.)

Burggren 1982). Ventilation of the gills and lungs interact reflexly, such that an air breath depresses buccal ventilation pressures in the ensuing few minutes (fig. 16.28). West and Burggren (1983) propose a hypoxic drive to gill ventilation; the temporary increase in blood and tissue P_{O_2} following an air breath briefly reduces the branchial hypoxic drive resulting in strong buccal ventilation. Chemoreceptors and mechanoreceptors (or gas-sensitive mechanoreceptors) modifying gill ventilation occur in the lungs of anuran larvae (see below). O_2-sensitive chemoreceptors occur externally in the branchial chamber or in blood immediately downstream from the gills in larvae of the bullfrog, *R. catesbeiana,* and alter the basic gill ventilation pattern when stimulated by hypoxic or hypercapnic water (X. Jia and W. W. Burggren unpublished). Unfortunately, ventilatory responses to aquatic hypoxia in species with larvae inhabiting potentially hypoxic water have not been compared with responses from larvae from generally highly oxygenated cool water streams.

Both the internal gills of anurans and the external gills of urodeles progressively degenerate as metamorphic climax approaches. Lungs first appear in quite early larval stages, though premetamorphic lungs are structurally less complex than those of adults (Atkinson and Just 1975; Burggren and Mwalukoma 1983; Burggren 1989). Lung ventilation begins well before gill regression at metamorphic climax in most species of anurans (see Burggren 1984; Helff 1932) and urodeles (Noble 1931). Helff's (1932) early studies indicated that the lungs are not essential for life before metamorphosis in *Rana pipiens,* as also suggested for *R. catesbeiana* (Just, Gatz, and Crawford 1973). In larvae of *R. catesbeiana* the lungs account for 20% of O_2 uptake before metamorphic climax and 70 to 80% of O_2 uptake immediately afterward (fig. 16.26). Pulmonary CO_2 elimination is minimal in anuran larvae, however, as generally is the case in adult anurans (Burggren and Moalli 1984; Burggren and West 1982; Gottlieb and Jackson 1976; Jackson and Braun 1979; MacKenzie and Jackson 1978) and urodeles (Guimond and Hutchison 1976).

Ventilation of the lungs occurs at TK I (a free-swimming stage with microscopic hindlimb buds) in the anurans *Hymenochirus boettgeri* (Pipidae), *Pseudacris triseriata* (Hylidae), *X. laevis, R. berlandieri,* and *R. catesbeiana* (see Feder 1984 for references). *R. cyanophlyctis, R. pipiens,* and *Scaphiopus bombifrons* (Pelobatidae) are reported to breathe air at later stages, but as Feder (1984) indicates, this may reflect the stages that have been examined rather than the actual initiation of lung ventilation. The lungs are not ventilated until metamorphosis in some anurans such as bufonids (Feder 1983a), *Scaphiopus* (Wassersug and Seibert 1975), and megophryine pelobatid larvae. Generally, the larvae of stream-adapted anurans delay ventilation of the lungs until after metamorphic climax.

Lung ventilation begins in larvae in almost all urodeles examined. Interestingly, the frequency of lung ventilation in larvae of the tiger salamander, *Ambystoma tigrinum,* is a function not only of respiratory requirements but also of buoyancy regulation for both acquiring prey and avoiding predation (Lannoo and Bachman 1984a). Lung ventilation frequencies are greater when larvae require greater buoyancy to remain midwater to forage, while lung ventilation decreases when only benthic prey is available. Lungs of larval *Xenopus laevis* may also function as buoyancy regulators (van Bergeijk 1954), though this suggestion has never been tested. Lung gas volume of *Xenopus* larvae affects swimming stamina, presumably because swimming larvae have to overcome the buoyancy of lungs (Feder and Wassersug 1984).

Hydrostatic pressure transients in the buccal cavity of anuran larvae (West and Burggren 1983) indicate that, as in adults, lung ventilation involves compression of buccal gas to drive it through the opened glottis into the paired lungs. However, no study has focused on the complex transition of lung ventilation mechanics from primarily water-breathing anuran larvae to the air-breathing adult.

The lungs of ranid larvae contain pulmonary sense receptors responding to stretch (mechanoreceptors) (West and Burggren 1983; see also chapter 7). In *Rana catesbeiana,* stimulation of the pulmonary stretch receptors by inflation of the lung with air, N₂, or O₂ temporarily reduces gill ventilation frequency. The response is greatest when pure O₂ is injected, however, suggesting that chemoreceptors are also in the lungs or peripheral circulation. (See chapter 7 for additional information on sensory receptors modifying ventilation in anurans.)

Chronic changes in environmental O₂ availability cause major changes in the respiratory organs of developing amphibian larvae. Hypertrophy of gills and lungs occurs in both urodeles and anurans, including decreases in diffusion distance between blood and the respiratory medium as well as an increase in surface area (Babak 1907; Bond 1960; Burggren and Mwalukoma 1983; Drastich 1925; Guimond and Hutchison 1976; Preyer 1885; fig. 16.29). The skin of anuran larvae, an important site for gas exchange, also changes during chronic environmental hypoxia (Po₂ about 75 mm Hg), with the cutaneous capillaries moving closer to the surface of the skin, thereby reducing the diffusion distance between water outside the skin and blood in the capillaries (fig. 16.29).

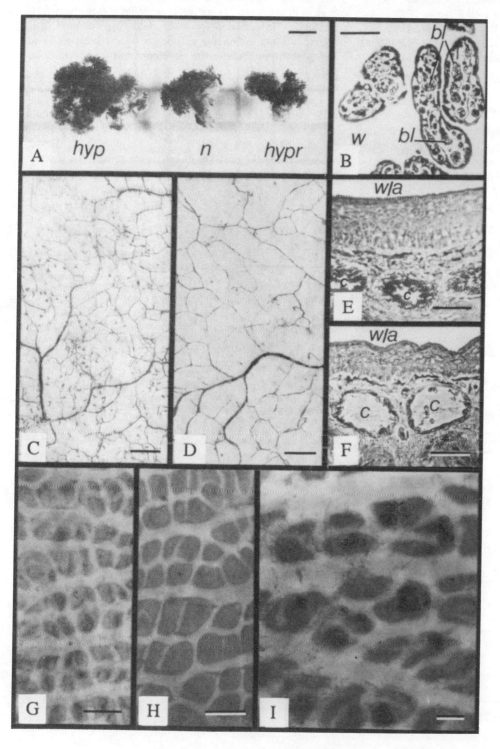

Fig. 16.29 Effects of chronic environmental hypoxia on the structure of the gas exchange organs in larval (TK XV–XX) and adult bullfrogs, *Rana catesbeiana.* Animals were raised for 28 days in experimental chambers containing both water and air. Both respiratory media had a Po₂ of approximately one-half saturation (70 mm Hg, 28 days). *A,* center gill filaments from left gill arch 5 from three 15-g larvae exposed to chronic normoxia (*n*), hypoxia (*hyp*), and hyperoxia (>350 mm Hg; *hypr*). Scale marker = 1.0 mm. *B,* cross section through gill filament. *bl,* blood channel; *w,* water. Scale marker = 10 μm. *C,* skin of tail perfused with India ink removed from larva exposed to chronic hypoxia. *D,* skin of tail perfused with India ink removed from larva exposed to chronic normoxia. Scale marker = 250 μm for *C* and *D. E,* thin section through tail of larva exposed to chronic hypoxia. *F,* thin section through tail of larva exposed to chronic normoxia. For *E* and *F:* *w/a,* water or air. Scale marker = 20 μm. *G,* internal surface of the lung of larva exposed to chronic hypoxia. *H,* internal surface of the lung of larva exposed to chronic normoxia. *I,* internal surface of the lung of adult bullfrog exposed to chronic hypoxia. Scale marker = 0.5 mm for *G–I.* (Reprinted, by permission, from Burggren and Mwalukoma 1983.)

In *R. catesbeiana* these changes occur only in larvae exposed to chronic hypoxia. Adult bullfrogs show little if any change in morphology of the skin or lungs, instead showing major adjustments in blood respiratory properties, for example hematocrit, hemoglobin concentration, and O_2 carrying capacity (Pinder and Burggren 1983).

In summary, the considerable information on metamorphic transitions in metabolism and gas exchange in amphibians shows that complex changes occur as gas exchange shifts between skin, gills, and lungs. However, most information is from just a few genera (e.g., *Rana, Ambystoma*), and metabolism and gas exchange might well differ in other larvae. Caecilians are almost entirely unknown in this respect. Viviparity in many caecilian species (chapter 15) lends particular interest to future studies of the ontogeny of gas exchange in this group.

CARDIOVASCULAR PHYSIOLOGY

The cardiovascular system of amphibian embryos is a model system for studying chordate cardiovascular development. Despite more than a century of study, two ironies emerge:

1. The vast majority of studies have been anatomical rather than physiological; the anatomy has been explained in detail for a system about which we have almost no knowledge of function.

2. Most studies have examined *embryonic* stages of amphibians; consequently, we still know relatively little about the morphological changes during larval development leading up to metamorphic climax.

As for metabolism and respiration, studies of both anatomical and physiological development have used ranid frogs and ambystomatid salamanders primarily. Although these taxa are not particularly representative of the total diversity evident in anurans and urodeles, respectively (see chapter 1), the lack of information for other amphibians dictates that, regrettably, our comments will be confined largely to *Rana* and *Ambystoma*. Studies on development of cardiovascular physiology in other amphibian taxa, inhabiting a variety of environments, are sorely needed.

The ontogenetic changes in morphology of the cardiovascular system are beyond the scope of this chapter (for details and additional references see Burggren 1984; Czopek 1957; Millard 1945; Malvin 1985b; McIndoe and Smith 1984a; Witschi 1956). Figures 16.30 and 16.31 present the essence of these changes. Vascular complexity increases in the late

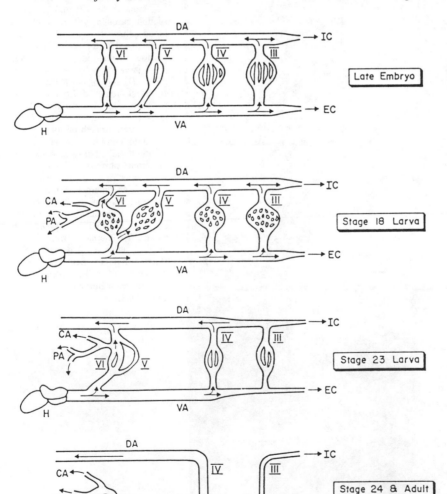

Fig. 16.30 Highly diagrammatic representation of the central circulation of the bullfrog, *Rana catesbeiana*, at four developmental stages (Taylor-Kollros). Gill arch numbers are indicated by *roman numerals*. *CA*, cutaneous artery; *DA*, dorsal artery; *EC*, external (ventral) carotid artery; *H*, heart; *IC*, internal (dorsal) carotid artery; *PA*, pulmonary artery; *PC*, pulmocutaneous arch; *SA*, systemic arch; *SP*, spiral valve; *VA*, ventral aorta. (Reprinted, by permission, from Burggren 1984 after Witschi 1956 and Just, Gatz, and Crawford 1973.)

Neotene

Adult

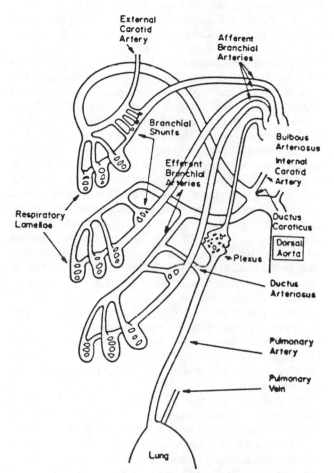

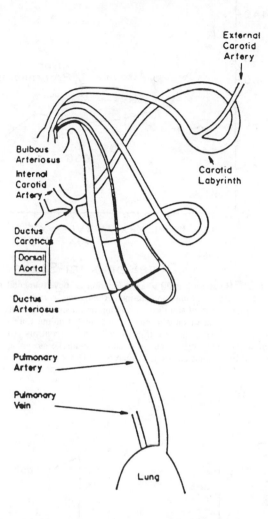

Fig. 16.31   Developmental changes in the circulation of the salamander *Ambystoma tigrinum*. (Reprinted, by permission, from Malvin 1985b.)

larval stages of both ranid frogs and ambystomatid salamanders. An arterial supply separate from the systemic arteries exists for the gills and the lungs, and also for the skin in anurans. Metamorphosis in both taxa considerably simplifies the cardiovascular system, as the branchial vessels undergo the classic chordate pattern of degeneration and reduce into the vessels supplying the head and lungs.

Cardiac Physiology

Given the generally small size of the embryonic and larval circulations of amphibians, information on cardiovascular physiology is scant. Current physiological knowledge is clustered in two areas: heart rate and its regulation and the physiology and pharmacology of blood vessels. Recent technological developments (e.g., pulsed Doppler and laser blood flow monitoring, microelectrodes for measurement of blood pressure and blood gases, respiratory mass spectrometers capable of measuring blood and tissue gases) all promise to revolutionize our ability to investigate cardiovascular physiology in amphibian larvae.

Developmental changes in heart rate and its regulation have been studied most extensively in the bullfrog, *Rana ca-*

tesbeiana (West and Burggren 1983; Burggren and Doyle 1986b, 1986c). Resting heart rate falls steeply in the early larval stages, is constant during the remainder of larval development, and then falls once more after metamorphosis (fig. 16.32). The resting heart rate of the intermediate larval stages reflects a vagus nerve tone, since treatment with atropine (a muscarinic cholinergic blocker) substantially increases heart rate. β-adrenergic tone (either from sympathetic activity or circulating catecholamines) is absent, since propranolol does not affect heart rate. The resting vagal tone disappears after metamorphosis, and in the adult the resting heart rate reflects the intrinsic (nonstimulated, noninhibited) rate of the cardiac pacemaker.

Part of this complex pattern of change in heart rate is due to change in body mass *independent of any developmental change per se*. A mature bullfrog weighs approximately 10,000 times more than a newly hatched larva. In animals of all descriptions considerable differences in heart rate usually accompany such large differences in body mass (see Schmidt-Nielsen 1984).

Developmental changes in the cholinergic and adrenergic sensitivity of the cardiac pacemaker of *R. catesbeiana* are evident both *in situ* and *in vitro*. The pacemaker's cholinergic

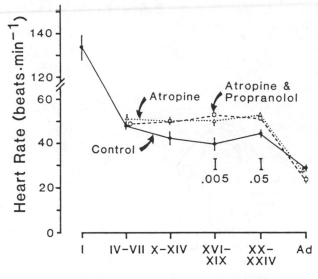

Developmental Stage

Fig. 16.32 Heart rate at 20°C as a function of developmental stage (Taylor-Kollros) in resting, unrestrained *Rana catesbeiana*. Values are means ± 1 SE. Level of significance and minimum significant difference are shown where heart rates in control and treated animals are significantly different. Animals were injected with saline (controls), atropine (a cholinergic antagonist), and propranol (a β-adrenergic antagonist). (Reprinted, by permission, from Burggren and Doyle 1986b.)

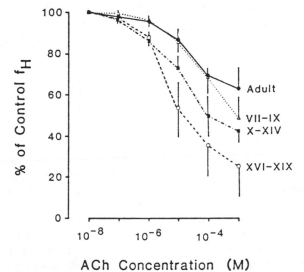

ACh Concentration (M)

Fig. 16.33 Dose-response curves for the effect of acetylcholine upon heart rate (f_H) at 20° to 22°C in three groups of larvae and in adults of the bullfrog, *Rana catesbeiana* (Taylor-Kollros stages). Mean values ± 1 SE are presented. Animals were pithed and the heart exposed, but the circulation was otherwise intact. (Reprinted, by permission, from Burggren and Doyle 1986a.)

sensitivity increases progressively during larval development, but then decreases sharply at metamorphic climax (fig. 16.33; Burggren and Doyle 1986a). Whether this change is due to a decrease in cholinergic receptors in the pacemaker cell membranes or a developmental change in cholinergic affinity of each receptor site requires further investigation. Isolated atria

and ventricles from larvae of a wide range of developmental stages and adults all begin to show chronotropic response at similar physiological doses (about 10^{-7} M) of norepinephrine, but the heart of adults requires greater doses than larval hearts for maximal stimulation (Kimmel 1990; S. Petrou, I. Walhquist, and W. Burggren unpublished).

Chronotropic responses of the heart of larval amphibians to the external and internal environment change during development, but further experiments are required. While adult anurans show a clear ventilation tachycardia, larvae do not typically show this chronotropic response (fig. 16.28). Certainly, larvae can increase heart rate, since either a pharmacological removal of the resting vagal inhibition or β-adrenergic stimulation could transiently increase heart rate. Increases in heart rate accompany both spontaneous and induced activity in both larval and adult *R. catesbeiana* (Burggren and Doyle 1986b). In larvae, lifting of vagal inhibition produces tachycardia, while in adults tachycardia is due to β-adrenergic stimulation. Environmental hypoxia down to a P_{O_2} of about 40–50 mm Hg, which often induces either bradycardia or tachycardia in adult lower vertebrates (see Jones and Milsom 1982), does not affect heart rate in larvae of either *R. catesbeiana* (Burggren and Doyle 1986b) or *Xenopus laevis* (Feder and Wassersug 1984). Heartbeat and gill ventilation are synchronous in larvae of the anurans *X. laevis, Pachymedusa dacnicolor* (Hylide), and *R. berlandieri* (Wassersug, Paul, and Feder 1981), although Burggren, Feder, and Pinder (1983) did not observe this phenomenon in *R. berlandieri* and *R. catesbeiana*.

Developmental changes in heart rate also occur in the frog *Eleutherodactylus coqui* (Leptodactylidae), which metamorphoses within the egg before hatching as a miniature adult. Heart rate, initially about 90 beats · min⁻¹ (25°C) in the tiny embryo, progressively increases to about 125 beats · min⁻¹ at hatching (fig. 16.34; Burggren, Infantino, and Townsend 1990). Thus, heart rate changes counter to the usual allometric trend. During hatching, heart rate increases to as high as 170 beats · min⁻¹ for several minutes. In dehydrated eggs, fairly common in the field in Puerto Rico, the heart rate of the animal declines.

Few measurements of cardiac output are available for larvae. Cardiac output in conscious, restrained larval *Ambystoma tigrinum* is about .10 ml · g⁻¹ · min⁻¹ at 20°C (Hoyt, Eldrigdte, and Wood 1984). In *Xenopus laevis*, mass specific cardiac output at 20-24°C increases from .078 ml · g⁻¹ · min⁻¹ at NF 40 to .284 ml · g⁻¹ · min⁻¹ at NF 51 (Hou 1992). These values are within the range reported for adult *Rana, Xenopus,* and *Amphiuma* (Caudata: Amphiumidae). Interindividual variation in cardiac output in larval *Ambystoma tigrinum* is due primarily to changes in stroke volume rather than in heart rate.

Studies using embryonic mutants of *Ambystoma mexicanum* have elucidated the basic physiology of development in amphibian cardiac pacemakers and their regulation of embryonic heart rate. "Cardiac lethal" mutants of this species show normal embryonic development of heart structure, but the cardiac pacemaker fails to depolarize spontaneously (Justus 1978, for review). Interestingly, the mutant embryos develop into larvae that hatch, swim, and survive for several days

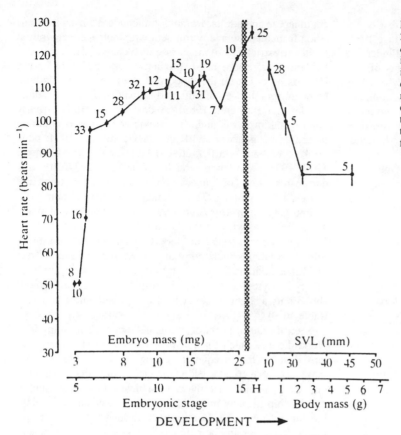

Fig. 16.34 Ontogenetic changes in heart rate at 23° to 25°C in the direct-developing Neotropical frog *Eleutherodactylus coqui* (Leptodactylidae). The *cross-hatched line* indicates the time of hatching. Mean values ± 1 SE; *numbers* indicate the number of specimens observed at each point in development. Embryonic mass and snout-vent length (SVL) measured on a different population of embryos and adults of comparable embryonic stage and body mass, respectively, are also indicated for comparison. Stages according to Townsend and Stewart 1985. (Reprinted, by permission, from Burggren, Infantino and Townsend 1990.)

without a heartbeat! Diffusion of gases, nutrients, and wastes can obviously substitute for convection in extremely small animals, and this mutant could serve as a model with which to study diffusion *in vivo*.

Physiology and Pharmacology of the Peripheral Circulation

Extensive early studies on the pharmacology of the vasculature of larval *Ambystoma* by Figge (1936) have been confirmed and expanded by Saint-Aubain (1982a) and Malvin (1985b, 1985c) using both *in situ* preparations and *in vitro* perfused segments of the circulation. The pharmacology of the branchial and pulmonary vessels in ambystomatid larvae is complex, as is the morphology of this vascular bed (fig. 16.31). Briefly, acetylcholine (or vagal stimulation) causes vasoconstriction in the branchial vessels and the pulmonary artery. Catecholamines (norepinephrine, epinephrine) dilate the respiratory vessels in the gills but do not affect the shunt vessels that bypass the respiratory surface. In contrast to Figge's (1936) early work, Malvin (1985c) reported that local alterations in CO_2 and pH do not affect the branchial circulation. Catecholamines do not affect the pulmonary artery of larval *Ambystoma*, but vagal stimulation causes vasoconstriction (Saint-Aubain 1982a), as in the adults of other amphibian species (see chapter 7). The larval forms of *Ambystoma* can alter vascular resistance (and thus blood flow) within the branchial and pulmonary circulation in response to changing respiratory needs. Either neural stimulation or changes in circulating levels of catecholamines can produce reciprocal

changes in blood flow between the pulmonary and branchial vascular beds, as in adult amphibians (Burggren 1988b; Feder and Burggren 1985a, 1985b, 1985c).

A simplification of the circulation accompanies metamorphosis in *Ambystoma* (fig. 16.31). The gills and their arches regress, and their remains give rise to the carotid vessels, while the pulmonary artery enlarges. The fraction of cardiac output perfusing the lung doubles after metamorphosis (Malvin and Heisler 1988), which is appropriate for the greater lung ventilation and dependence upon pulmonary gas exchange in the adult salamander. The physiology and pharmacology of the blood vessels of adult salamanders are less well known than are those of larvae.

Unfortunately, the small size of anuran larvae has to date precluded the same detail of pharmacological investigation as for ambystomatid larvae. *In situ* studies of perfused vascular beds in larvae of *Rana catesbeiana* have shown that catecholamines dilate the branchial vasculature in larval stages as early as TK III (Kimmel 1990). There is an extensive network of shunt vessels in the branchial vessels of larvae of the anuran *Litoria ewingi* (Hylidae; McIndoe and Smith 1984a), but they have not been characterized pharmacologically.

BLOOD, BLOOD-GAS TRANSPORT, AND ACID-BASE BALANCE
Blood

Most studies of ontogenetic transitions in blood have focused on *in vitro* blood respiratory properties and hematological aspects including types of hemoglobin, sites of erythropoiesis, erythrocyte concentration, hematocrit, and so forth (for literature reviews see Broyles 1981; Forman and Just 1981; Just, Schwager, and Weber 1977; Just et al. 1980; Pinder and Burggren 1983; see also chapter 5). Measurements of P_{50}, hematocrit, or other blood variables are available for many different amphibian species. However, relatively complete data on the developmental changes in hematology and respiratory characteristics are available primarily for the tiger salamander, *Ambystoma tigrinum*, and the bullfrog, *R. catesbeiana* (table 16.9), probably because the larvae of these species are sufficiently large to give blood samples. One of the most notable changes at metamorphosis in the bullfrog is a marked increase in blood P_{50} from around 10 mm Hg in the larva up to 35 to 40 mm Hg in the adult (fig. 16.35). This fall in O_2 affinity reflects a difference in the types of globins pres-

ent in larvae and adults. Hemoglobin changes during the transition from an aquatic environment with low O_2 concentration to the terrestrial environment (see also chapter 5).

Chronic environmental hypoxia (30 days at a P_{O_2} of 70 mm Hg) has no effect on the blood of larvae, but increases both hemoglobin (Hb)–O_2 affinity and blood O_2 capacity in adults (Pinder and Burggren 1983). A decrease in Hb-O_2 affinity upon metamorphosis under normoxic conditions is common in anurans (Aggarwal and Riggs 1969; Sullivan 1974; table 16.9), caecilians (Garlick et al. 1979; Toews and Macintyre 1977, 1978), and some urodeles (Ducibella 1974; Edwards and Justus 1969; Gahlenbeck and Bartels 1970; Hattingh and Bartels 1973; Wood 1971), although this phenomenon is apparently absent in *Ambystoma tigrinum* (Burggren and Wood 1981; Wood, Hoyt, and Burggren 1982).

A very large increase in blood O_2 capacity (two- to three-fold) also attends metamorphosis in *R. catesbeiana*. A rise in intracellular hemoglobin, rather than increased numbers of erythrocytes, mediates this response, since hematocrit shows only a slight tendency to rise as development proceeds (table 16.9).

Several other aspects of ontogenetic change in amphibian blood deserve much further investigation. First, as amphibians develop they frequently change considerably in body mass (see table 16.11). Blood characteristics, like most other physiological and anatomical variables, show an allometric relationship to body mass that may be unrelated to developmental change per se. In a study of allometry of blood respiratory properties and hematology in larvae of the salamander *Ambystoma tigrinum*, Burggren, Dupré, and Wood (1987) concluded that blood hemoglobin concentration and blood O_2 capacity showed positive allometry with body mass, while blood P_{50} scaled isometrically. Future investigations of the effects of development on respiratory properties must regard blood properties as covarying with developmental stage and body mass.

A second aspect that deserves additional study involves changes in site of erythropoesis (spleen, kidney, liver, bone marrow) and the switch between synthesis of embryonic/larval/adult hemoglobins (Broyles et al. 1981; Frangioni and Borgioli 1988). When larval metamorphosis is inhibited, adult hemoglobins still appear (Just, Schwager, and Weber 1977; Just et al. 1980). Moreover, the genes regulating larval hemoglobin stop being expressed after metamorphosis in ranid frogs, but can be re-activated in the adult during severe anemia (see Maples, Palmer, and Broyles 1986; Meints and Forehand 1977). Most experiments on this fascinating problem have proceeded from a genetic/biochemical viewpoint with the intent to probe gene function. Future experiments should examine whether the reversal of the normal ontogenetic pattern of hemoglobin switching has any physiological value in amphibians.

Blood respiratory properties and how they change with development in amphibians also need to be investigated in both a phylogenetic and environmental context. We currently have no idea of how larval blood respiratory properties vary across broad taxa, nor how they are adapted in larvae of species living in different habitats (e.g., warm, stagnant ponds compared with cool, oxygenated streams). Of course, this infor-

TABLE 16.9 Hematology and Respiratory Properties of the Blood of the Bullfrog, *Rana catesbeiana*, and the Tiger Salamander, *Ambystoma tigrinum*

	Rana catesbeiana		Ambystoma tigrinum	
	Premet. Larva	Postmet. Adult	Premet. Larva	Postmet. Adult
Hematocrit (%)	20.9	22.2	32.0	40
	17.8	23.4	32	
	19.2	27.0		
	30.9	30.0		
		23.5		
		23.8		
Hemoglobin	3.73	6.3	7.7[a]	
(g·100 ml⁻¹)	2.77	5.7		
	4.03	5.7		
		6.6		
		6.2		
ATP or NTP	7.56	3.56		2.5
(µmol·ml⁻¹ RBC)	4.2	3.38		
	6.02	1.80		
	5.98	11.0		
2,3-DPG	2.20	2.29	3.25	
(µmol·ml⁻¹ RBC)	4.1	1.79		
	0.92–2.2	3.3		
	3.13	1.10		
O₂ capacity (vol %)	2.91	5.84	6.3	
		7.15		
		9.2		
		8.02		
Bohr shift	−0.60	−0.65	−0.03	
(log P₅₀ pH⁻¹)	−0.18	−0.18	−0.08	
		−0.29		
		−0.18		
P₅₀ (mm Hg)	9.4	33	34	41
	13	37	41	40
	5.5	37	40	
		42		
		39		
Hill's coefficient (n)	2.5	2.4	2.6	
	1.8	2.5		
	2.8	1.95		
		2.8–3.0		

Sources: Data compiled from both citations and original observations reported in Pinder and Burggren 1983; Burggren and Wood 1981; and Burggren, Dupré, and Wood 1987.

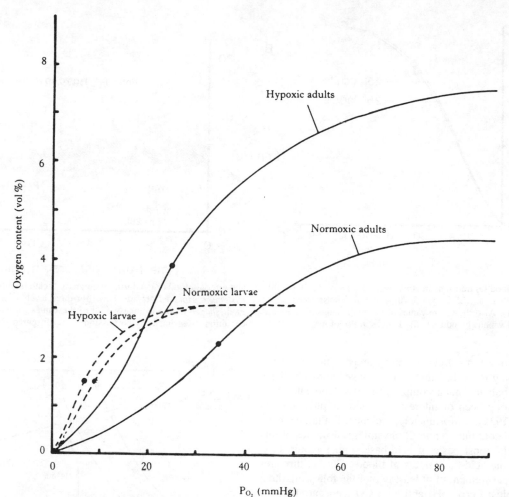

Fig. 16.35 O_2 equilibrium curves of whole blood (23°C, Pco_2 7 mm Hg) from larval and adult *Rana catesbeiana* maintained for 28 days under either normoxia (Po_2 = 150 mm Hg) or environmental hypoxia (Po_2 = 75 mm Hg). (Reprinted, by permission, from Pinder and Burgren 1983.)

mation is also largely lacking for adult amphibians (see chapter 5).

Blood-Gas Transport

Few studies have examined actual changes in blood-gas transport, especially in an environmental context. One of the largest obstacles is that interpretation of blood function from data on O_2 equilibrium curves and Hb-O_2 affinity requires *in vivo* data on arterial and venous Po_2 as well as Po_2 in the gas exchanger organ(s). Not surprisingly, such data are not yet available for the vast majority of amphibian larvae, which are small relative to the requirements of current methodologies. Because the larvae of the salamander *Ambystoma tigrinum* are very large (up to 150 g), some aspects of the ontogenetic change in *in vivo* O_2 and CO_2 transport have been investigated in this species (see also chapter 5). Although this salamander is atypical in that metamorphosis produces little change in the O_2 affinity of whole blood (fig. 16.36A), arterial blood is about 80% saturated under normoxic conditions. Estimated venous O_2 saturation in larvae is 40 to 45%, indicating substantial "venous reserve" should larvae become hypoxic. Be-

cause their aquatic environment is frequently hypoxic, the larvae of *Ambystoma tigrinum* are air breathers. Thus, a water Po_2 of 40 mm Hg, a level of environmental hypoxia severe enough to stimulate considerable increase in air-breathing frequency, has little effect on the arterial Po_2 (fig. 16.36B) and thus on the O_2 saturation of arterial blood.

Acid-Base Balance

The acid-base balance of adult amphibians is known in detail for several species, including *Rana catesbeiana, Xenopus laevis, Bufo marinus, Cryptobranchus alleganiensis* (Caudata: Cryptobranchidae), and *Amphiuma means* (Caudata: Amphiumidae; see reviews by Boutilier 1989; Shelton and Boutilier 1982; Toews and Boutilier 1986), and is discussed in detail in chapter 5. Aquatic vertebrates often regulate acid-base balance by the active transport of bicarbonate (HCO_3^-) and H^+, especially across epithelia in contact with the water (see Randall et al. 1980; Truchot 1987). Air-breathing animals, on the other hand, rely more heavily upon changes in lung ventilation to alter plasma CO_2 levels in the short term, and upon kidney excretion of ions involved in acid-base bal-

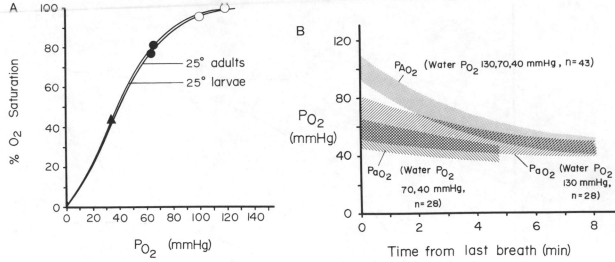

Fig. 16.36 Blood O_2 transport in *Ambystoma tigrinum*. *A*, O_2 equilibrium curves of larvae (25°C, pH 7.70) and fully transformed adults (25°C, pH 7.51). Also shown are values of Po_2 in the lungs (○), arterial blood (●), and venous blood (▲). *B*, changes in Po_2 of lung gas ($P_{A}O_2$) and arterial blood (P_aO_2) during pulmonary breath holding in larval *Ambystoma tigrinum*. Data are shown for three levels of aquatic hypoxia. Each *shaded area* encompasses all of the values for each of the stated condition. (Reprinted, by permission, from Burggren and Wood 1981.)

ance in the long term. Because many amphibians pass from water breathing to air breathing, the changes in mechanisms of acid-base balance that accompany this developmental transition have long been of interest to vertebrate physiologists (e.g., Helff 1932). Unfortunately, technical limitations have retarded (and continue to retard) physiological studies of this transition. The most basic of acid-base studies requires assessment of the acid-base status of blood. This, in turn, requires the measurement of at least two of the following three blood variables: Pco_2, pH, and total CO_2 concentration (or HCO_3^- concentration). Even the most recently developed micro techniques for such blood analysis require quantities of blood that in some larval species approach the total blood volume of the animal! Even in larger larvae, sampling the blood must not disturb the animal, for changes in blood pH follow within seconds of severe disturbance.

As a consequence of the above-mentioned limitations, acid-base studies concern but a few species with large larvae, including *R. catesbeiana* (Erasmus, Howell, and Rahn 1970; Just, Gatz, and Crawford 1973), *R. clamitans* (Helff 1932), and *Ambystoma tigrinum* (Burggren and Wood 1981). In aquatic anuran and urodele larvae depending predominantly upon gills or skin for both O_2 uptake and CO_2 elimination, the ranges of both blood Pco_2 (3 to 7 mm Hg) and blood HCO_3^- (7 to 15 mM·l^{-1}) are similar to or slightly greater than those for strictly aquatic fishes (see Truchot 1987 for references on fishes). A large increase in blood Pco_2 and HCO_3^- routinely accompanies the transition to air breathing, as shown in fig. 16.37 for *R. catesbeiana*. The rise in blood Pco_2 in animals switching from water to air breathing results from a relative hypoventilation of the lungs, and consequent accumulation of molecular CO_2 within the tissues (see Randall et al. 1980; Truchot 1987). A sharp rise in blood HCO_3^- offsets the increasing concentration of blood H^+ ions in *R. catesbeiana* during metamorphosis. Blood pH declines only slightly due to the correlative sharp rise in blood HCO_3^-;

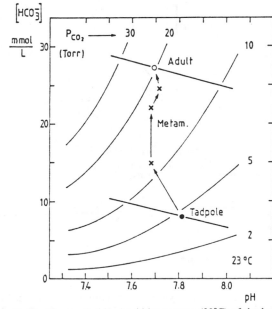

Fig. 16.37 Changes in blood acid-base status (23°C) of the bullfrog, *Rana catesbeiana*, during development from the aquatic larva to the adult, as shown in a pH-HCO_3^- (Davenport) diagram. The five developmental points on the diagram correspond to TK XVIII–XX (labeled *tadpole*), XXI–XXII, XXIII–XXIV, XXV, and adults. (Data from Just, Gatz, and Crawford 1973; redrawn by Truchot 1987. Reprinted, by permission.)

in a sense the acid-base state of adults is a partially compensated respiratory acidosis.

The acid-base status of ectothermic vertebrates is highly dependent upon body temperature. While the effects of temperature change on acid-base balance of adult amphibians have received considerable attention (see Toews and Boutilier 1986), the *combined* effects of acute temperature changes and development on acid-base balance have been examined for

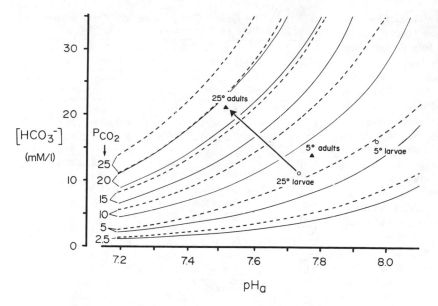

Fig. 16.38 HCO$_3^-$-pH (Davenport) diagram showing changes in acid-base state of arterial blood (pH$_a$) associated with changes in acclimation temperature and metamorphosis in the tiger slamander *Ambystoma tigrinum*. The curved lines are P$_{CO_2}$ isopleths (mm Hg), with *solid lines* representing 25°C and *dashed lines* representing 5°C. The *large arrow* indicates the changes in acid-base status that accompany metamorphosis at 25°C. (Reprinted, by permission, from Burggren and Wood 1981.)

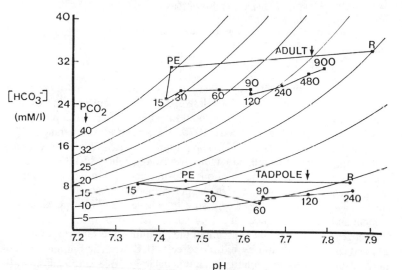

Fig. 16.39 HCO$_3^-$-pH (Davenport) diagram showing acid-base status of arterial blood in bullfrog larvae (*Rana catesbeiana*; TK VI–XVII) at rest (*R*), within 1 min after exhaustive exercise (*PE*), and at time in minutes (*numbers*) following exercise. The *curved lines* are P$_{CO_2}$ isopleths (mm Hg) calculated for 25°C. Exercise for larvae consisted of swimming for 8–10 min in a water tunnel until unable to maintain a position in the water stream. Exercise for adults consisted of being prodded to hop until exhausted. (Reprinted, by permission, from Quinn 1982.)

very few species. In the aquatic larvae of the tiger salamander *Ambystoma tigrinum* (body mass 51–79 g) maintained at 5°C with access to air, lung ventilation is rare, and almost all O$_2$ uptake is through the skin. The P$_{CO_2}$ is about 5 mm Hg, and the pH above 7.9 (fig. 16.38). With an increase to 25°C body temperature, pH falls to about 7.7, and P$_{CO_2}$ rises to above 8 mm Hg. The rise in temperature results in a "functional metamorphosis" in the sense that the warm larva relies heavily upon air breathing for O$_2$ uptake. However, that HCO$_3^-$ concentration falls rather than rises indicates that the respiratory acidosis is not compensated, at least in the time frame of these experiments (2 to 4 weeks). In adult *Ambystoma tigrinum* (body mass 12–34 g) in water with access to air, the same rise in temperature nearly doubles the HCO$_3^-$ concentration even when arterial blood pH decreases, as in larvae. At least for this species, temperature greatly affects acid-base status, and differently in larvae and adults. Although our knowledge of the effects of temperature on gas exchange in developing amphibians is considerable (e.g.,

Burggren, Feder, and Pinder 1983; chapters 5 and 6), further studies of the joint effects of acid-base balance of temperature and development are necessary.

Locomotor activity can disturb the pH of amphibians, primarily because of anaerobic metabolism during prolonged exercise in amphibians (see Toews and Boutilier 1986; chapter 12). Lactic acid is released from the active tissues, producing a severe metabolic acidosis. The developmental aspects of this physiological problem are largely unknown (Cushman, Packard, and Boardman 1976; Quinn 1982; Quinn and Burggren 1983). In *Rana catesbeiana*, swimming (larvae) or hopping (adults) to exhaustion produces a severe respiratory and metabolic acidosis (Quinn 1982; fig. 16.39). While lactate peaks in arterial blood within a few minutes of exhaustion in adults, in larvae lactate does not peak for about 30 min. The respiratory and metabolic acidosis lasts far longer in adults than in larvae, however, and lactate returns to preexercise levels more rapidly in larvae. The larvae eliminate a small (7%) proportion of the lactate produced during exhaustive exercise via the gills (80%), skin (13%), and kidneys (6%). The elimination of lactate and presumed coelimination of H$^+$ may help restore normal acid-base balance following exercise in larval *R. catesbeiana* (Quinn and Burggren 1983).

In *Ambystoma tigrinum*, adults have higher blood lactate than do neotenes immediately following exercise (Cushman, Packard, and Boardman 1976), but lactate disappearance is the same in both morphs. Lactate elimination does not appear to play a role in lactate disappearance from the body tissues in either neotenes or adults. Unfortunately, little comparison of these results can be made with those of Quinn and Burggren (1983) on larval anurans, since the latter study looked at lactate concentrations in specific compartments (blood, muscle, urine) rather than total-body lactate. More detailed studies on the interactions of exercise, acid-base disturbance, and development are justified.

In summary, the acid-base changes during developmental transitions remain a largely unexplored problem in amphibian developmental physiology. Not only is the acid-base physiology of amphibians with the common transition from aquatic larvae to air-breathing adults poorly known, but it is yet to be studied in some of the fascinating direct-developing anuran or urodele species or in viviparous caecilians. Similarly, any environmental adaptations in acid-base balance remain to be described.

ION AND WATER REGULATION

Many amphibians experience major changes in the availability of water during their development. For example, while all amphibians develop initially in fresh water (or at least in the aqueous environment of the egg), as adults many inhabit semiterrestrial or terrestrial environments where they experience varying degrees of water deprivation (see chapter 6). Even amphibians that remain fully aquatic during development have organs for water and ion exchange between environment and tissues, and these may undergo radical ontogenetic changes. Thus, it is not surprising that the various parameters and capacities associated with osmoregulation change during amphibian development.

Ion and Water Content

The water content of the amphibian embryo increases during early embryonic stages (Krogh, Schmidt-Nielsen, and Zeuthen 1938; Tuft 1961; Dunson, Packer, and Dunson 1971). By midembryonic stages 66% of the total embryonic weight is water. Water content increases continuously until it reaches 85–90% immediately after hatching (Krogh, Schmidt-Nielsen, and Zeuthen 1938; Dunson, Packer, and Dunson 1971). Water content continues to increase during the first two or three larval stages (Fletcher and Myant 1959), until it exceeds 90%. Watercontent typically decreases continuously during the larval period and is about 85% by the end of metamorphosis (table 16.10). Water content decreases during metamorphosis in anurans (*Bufo vulgaris, Rana palustris, R. temporaria, Xenopus laevis*) and urodeles (*Ambystoma punctatum;* Dempster 1930; Etkin 1932; for review see Weber 1967).

The mineral content of the larvae remains at 10% of the dry mass throughout larval life, with the balance organic

TABLE 16.10 The Relative Changes in the Body Composition of Anuran Larvae During Metamorphosis

TK Stage[a]	Rana pipiens[b] Water[e]	Rana pipiens[b] Dry wt[e,f]	Rana sylvatica[c] Water[e]	Rana sylvatica[c] Dry wt[e,f]	Xenopus laevis[d] Water[e]	Xenopus laevis[d] Dry wt[e]
V	93.1	6.9 ± 0.5	93.1 ± 0.3	6.9		
X	91.9	8.1 ± 0.3	92.0 ± 0.4	8.0	92.8	7.2
XV	89.8	9.2 ± 0.2	89.8 ± 0.3	10.2	92.0	8.0
XVI			89.6 ± 0.4	10.4	91.2	8.8
XVII			89.6 ± 0.5	10.4	90.8	9.2
XVIII			89.1 ± 0.3	10.9		
XIX			88.5 ± 0.1	11.5	89.0	11.0
XX	88.1	11.9 ± 0.6	88.1 ± 0.2	11.9	87.6	12.4
XXI	87.3	12.7 ± 0.4	87.5 ± 0.4	12.5	86.3	13.7
XXII			86.7 ± 0.2	13.3	85.0	15.0
XXIII	85.0	15.0 ± 0.6	86.6 ± 0.6	13.4	83.8	16.2
XXIV			86.4 ± 0.2	13.6	83.2	16.8
XXV	83.1	16.8 ± 0.8	87.5 ± 0.5	12.5	83.0	17.0

[a] Taylor and Kollros 1946.
[b] Just 1968.
[c] Brown, Barry, and Brown 1988.
[d] Leist 1970.
[e] Percentage relative to wet weight of larvae.
[f] ± 1 SEM.

compounds (Just 1968). Because water content of larvae decreases while the relative dry mass increases, the osmotic pressure of plasma should change during development (Alvarado and Moody 1970; Just, Sperka, and Strange 1977; Funkhouser 1977). The plasma osmotic pressure of *R. catesbeiana* gradually increases from about 180 mOsm · l^{-1} in young larvae to about 200 mOsm · l^{-1} in newly metamorphosed froglets (Just, Sperka, and Strange 1977). This shift in total osmotic pressure may have significant physiological consequences (fig. 16.40; J. J. Just unpublished observations). The osmotic pressure of the medium affects the rate of protein production by red blood cells (RBCs). The optimum osmolarity for protein production in larval RBCs is 150 mOsm · l^{-1}, while that in adult RBCs is 230 mOsm · l^{-1}. If the synthetic capacities of all new cells appearing in late larval life (i.e., RBCs, intestinal cells, skin cells, tongue- and jaw-muscle cells, urinary bladder cells, and new brain cells) respond in such a dramatic manner to osmotic pressure, then the relatively small but steady changes in plasma osmotic pressure could be far more important than previously suspected.

Not only do the *relative* amounts of water change during metamorphosis (table 16.10) but the *absolute* amounts of water also shift dramatically during metamorphosis (table 16.11). Typical anuran larvae gain mass until late larval stages (TK XVI–XVIII), after which they lose considerable mass until the tail is completely reabsorbed. Aside from the three species listed in table 16.11, for which stages and weights during metamorphosis are thoroughly characterized, other species increase body mass to a maximum before metamorphic climax (forelimb emergence in anurans or gill degeneration in urodeles), and then start losing mass (*Bufo bufo, B. boreas, B. vulgaris, Phylobates subpunctatus* [Anura: Dendrobatidae], *Rana catesbeiana, R. clamitans, R. palustris, R. pipiens, R. sylvatica, R. temporaria, Triturus crista-*

tus, *T. vulgaris* [Caudata: Salamandridae], *Xenopus laevis*), as reported by numerous authors (Adolph 1931a, 1931b; Etkin 1932; Savage 1952; Munro 1953; Fletcher and Myant 1959; background: Weber 1967; Funkhouser and Mills 1969; Sivula, Mix, and McKenzie 1972; Smith-Gill and Berven 1979). Not all of these studies determined the mass for the entire climax period; those that did observed a total wet mass loss between 40 and 60%.

During late larval stages (TK XIX–XXV) 85–90% of the wet mass is water. The relative loss of water is greater than the loss of organic material, so that the relative percentage of

organic material increases from 10 to 15% even though the absolute amount of organic compounds is decreasing. Implied, although rarely stated, is the assumption that organic-compound loss at this time represents atrophy of larval structures (tail, gills, intestine, and intestinal content). The organic compounds in these structures may be used as a caloric source when feeding ceases, during changes in the mouth and digestive tract. Some of the organic compounds may be used in the production of new cells during late larval stages (TK XX–XXV). Few studies directly examine the loss of water during metamorphic climax, and this large amount of water loss is unexplained (Brown, Barry, and Brown 1988). For example, is this loss accomplished by decreasing water uptake and/or increasing its elimination? The daily rate of water loss is clearly large. For instance, *R. catesbeiana* loses 3.96 g of water between TK XIX and XXV, a developmental change requiring approximately 21 days (Atkinson et al. 1972). Thus, these larvae lose about 190 μl of water per day, which corresponds to 1.7% of body mass per day at TK XIX to as much as 2.7% per day at TK XXV.

Osmoregulatory Capability of Larvae

In osmotic environments ranging from 10 to 15 mOsm · l^{-1}, many amphibian larvae are competent osmoregulators, but at external osmotic pressures between 200 and 300 mOsm · l^{-1} larvae become osmoconformers (fig. 16.41). For any one species, the range of osmoconformation is narrow (e.g., 200–250 or 225–275 mOsm · l^{-1}), and the larvae maintain a slightly positive plasma gradient (10 to 20 mOsm · l^{-1}) from that found in the medium. Only one species of amphibian (*Rana cancrivora*) has larvae that can survive osmotic pressures in excess of 300 mOsm · l^{-1} for extended times. Indeed, larvae of this species occur in seawater, which is hyperosmotic to their plasma. Larval *R. cancrivora* are osmoregulators at a wide range of external osmotic pressures (fig. 16.41). They are hyperosmotic, like all larvae, to about 300 mOsm · l^{-1} external concentration; above this they become hypoosmotic to their medium. These larvae appear to be the only known larval

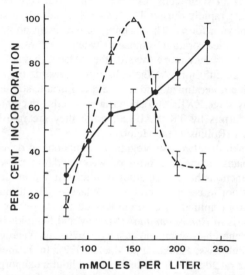

Fig. 16.40 Effects of varying the osmotic pressure of incubation media on the rate of amino acid incorporation into blood cells of *Rana catesbeiana*. The abscissa indicates osmotic pressure of the incubation meda in mmol · l^{-1}, while the ordinate gives relative rates of radioactive amino acid incorporation. The relative incorporation into blood cells at the 4-h incubation is indicated ($\triangle$, larval; $\bullet$, adult). The *vertical lines* on each point represent 1 SEM. Only one vertical line is indicated where SEs overlap, and no vertical lines indicate no deviation. (J. J. Just unpublished observations.)

TABLE 16.11   Body Composition Changes of Anuran Larvae during Metamorphosis

TK Stage[a]	Water[b] (%)	*Rana catesbeiana*[c] Wet (g)	*Rana catesbeiana*[c] Water[f] (g)	*Rana catesbeiana*[c] Dry (g)	*Rana sylvatica*[d] Wet (mg)	*Rana sylvatica*[d] Water (mg)	*Rana sylvatica*[d] Dry (mg)	*Xenopus laevis*[e] Wet (mg)	*Xenopus laevis*[e] Water (mg)	*Xenopus laevis*[e] Dry (mg)
V	93.1	6.5	6.05	0.45	199.9	186.2	13.7			
X	92.6	7.8	7.22	0.58	389.3	362.4	26.9	475	430	45
XV	90.5	10.4	9.41	0.99	629.2	565.0	64.2	590	544	46
XVI	90.4				596.4	534.7	61.7	620	560	60
XVII	90.2	11.5	10.37	1.13	640.3	572.9	67.4	667	590	77
XVIII	89.8				640.8	570.4	70.4			
XIX	88.7	11.3	10.02	1.28	598.1	529.3	68.8	560	485	75
XX	87.9				505.9	445.7	60.2	487	425	62
XXI	87.1	8.9	7.75	1.15	455.4	398.4	57.0	440	375	65
VVII	85.8				421.3	365.0	56.3	400	340	60[f]
XXIII	85.1	7.5	6.38	1.12	409.9	355.1	54.8	450	375	75

[a] Taylor and Kollros 1946.
[b] Average percentage of water from data in table 16.10.
[c] Data from Cecil and Just 1979, plus unpublished data collected in 1975 by J. J. Just from Fred's Pond referred to in Cecil and Just 1984.
[d] Data from Brown, Barry, and Brown 1988.
[e] Data from Leist 1970, fig. 3.
[f] Calculated using average water content.

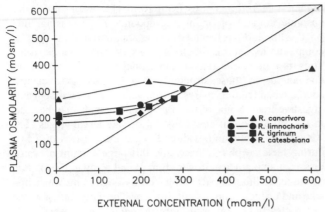

Fig. 16.41 The plasma osmotic concentration in amphibian larvae during long-term dehydration. Animals were exposed to various external salinities for 2 to 2.5 weeks. Anuran larvae (*Rana cancrivora* and *R. limnocharis:* Gorden and Tucker 1965; *R. catesbeiana:* Goldsmith and Just 1990) were all younger than TK XIX, while no stage was reported for the salamander larvae (*Ambystoma tigrinum:* Kirschner et al. 1971).

or adult amphibians who can remain hypoosmotic to their environment, just like marine telosts. How these animals accomplish this physiological feat is unknown.

Developmental Changes in Osmoregulatory Organs

Amphibians have a wide array of structures that help regulate the movement of water and ions, including the digestive tract, kidney, urinary bladder, gills, and skin. The relative contribution that each organ makes during development changes drastically; however, sometime during climax (TK XX–XXV) all of these organs are functional.

Skin The skin has received the most attention of all the osmoregulatory organs (see also chapters 5 and 6). The skin of all three amphibian orders consists of a dermis and an epidermis, and both change during development. The epidermis is ciliated during embryonic development. At hatching most ciliated epidermal cells disappear, while mitochondria-rich cells appear. In the dermis the layers of collagen increase from after hatching until midclimax stages. In late larval stages (TK XVII–XXV) the collagen in the dermis is replaced with new "adult" collagen, while the epidermis starts to synthesize keratin, which leads to the beginning of epidermal keratinization and sloughing of the epidermis (Fox 1985a, 1986). Numerous epithelial cell types change during metamorphosis (e.g., *Riesenzellen*, goblet cells, Leydig cells), although these cells are unlikely to function in osmoregulation (H. Fox 1988).

The principal osmoregulatory functions occur in the epidermal cells of the skin, while the dermis serves only as a mechanical support for the epidermis. In adults the ventral epidermis plays a larger role than the rest of the epidermis in osmoregulation (Yorio and Bentley 1977; Cree 1988b), and its development has been examined in both anurans (Rosenberg and Warburg 1978; Robinson and Heintzelman 1987) and urodeles (Warburg and Lewinson 1977). Although these species differ in some aspects of the ventral epidermis, certain generalities emerge. In adults there are four recognized layers (striatum) from the dermis to the outside surface,

namely germinativum, spinosum, granulosum, and corneum. In all three orders, these four layers are not present until late climax stages; before that, fewer layers exist. We will describe the morphological events in the skin of *Rana catesbeiana* during metamorphosis, because most of the osmoregulatory studies concern this species.

In young larvae (>TK XVIII) three cell types are in the epidermis (Robinson and Heintzelman 1987). The surface is composed of cuboidal apical cells, below which are two or three layers of large skein cells. At the interface between the epidermis and dermis is a basal cell layer. At TK XIX the apical cells begin to slough and the skein cells decrease. By TK XXII all skein cells disappear. The basal cells begin to proliferate rapidly during TK XX–XXI, and a true stratum germinativum forms. The forming cells contain no granules and are called stratum spinosum; when granules appear in these cells as they move towards the surface, they are called stratum granulosum. As the cells move towards the surface they flatten, keratinize, and form a recognizable stratum corneum by stage XXII. Mitochondria-rich cells are common in the epidermis by TK XXII, although they are rare before stage XX (Robinson and Heintzelman 1987).

The skin has two osmoregulatory functions in developing amphibians, namely, control of water and ion movement. Both functions have been studied in anuran and urodele larvae but not in caecilian embryos or larvae. The turnover of water from animal to environment decreases during metamorphosis in *Rana clamitans* (Mackay and Schmidt-Nielsen 1969; Schmidt-Nielsen and Mackay 1970) and *Xenopus laevis* (Schultheiss, Hanke, and Maetz 1972). In *X. laevis* the turnover rate decreases gradually throughout metamorphosis, while in *R. clamitans* the turnover rate remains constant until midclimax stages and then decreases suddenly until the end of climax. In *R. clamitans* larvae, both osmotic and diffusional flux rates are about 20 $\mu l \cdot g^{-1} \cdot h^{-1}$. In adults, diffusional flux rates are about 6 $\mu l \cdot g^{-1} \cdot h^{-1}$, while the osmotic flux rates are about 25 $\mu l \cdot g^{-1} \cdot h^{-1}$. Since the osmotic flux occurs through pores via bulk flow and the osmotic flux rates are four times greater than the diffusional flux, pores must be present in frog skin (Mackay and Schmidt-Nielsen 1969; Schmidt-Nielsen and Mackay 1970). Because osmotic and diffusional water fluxes do not differ significantly in preclimax larvae, few or no pores may be present initially, with their number increasing dramatically at climax.

The uptake of water in urodele larvae (*Ambystoma gracile*) is 3 μl, 11 μl, and 20 $\mu l \cdot g^{-1} \cdot h^{-1}$ at 5°, 15°, and 25°C, respectively (Parsons and Alvarado 1968). Unlike in anurans, water uptake does not decrease during metamorphosis in the urodele *A. tigrinum*. The rate of water uptake in larvae is 11 $\mu l \cdot g^{-1} \cdot h^{-1}$, while the rate in adults is 13 $\mu l \cdot g^{-1} \cdot h^{-1}$ at 14° to 16°C (Alvarado and Kirschner 1963). In *A. tigrinum* the diffusion of water into animals increases (Bentley and Baldwin 1980), while bulk flow (hydrostatic) entry decreases during metamorphosis (Galey, Wood, and Mancha 1987). These results, like those in anurans, indicate that water pores change in urodele skin during metamorphosis. Perhaps the radii of the pores decrease while the number of pores increases during *A. tigrinum* metamorphosis (Galey, Wood, and Mancha 1987).

Ion exchange across the amphibian skin can be purely passive down an electrochemical gradient, or active against the electrochemical gradient via membrane-bound proteins that consume ATP. From the response of larvae and adults to alterations in available ions in the environment, both Adolph (1927) and Krogh (1937) concluded that adults and larvae regulate ions differently. Adolph concluded that the difference disappeared during tail loss, while Krogh correctly concluded that adults could actively transport ions, while larvae lack that capability.

Transporting sodium chloride across an epithelium leads to transepithelial electrical potential (TEP) and a short-circuit current (SCC) across that epithelium, with the inside (serosa) being positive when compared to the outside (mucosa) (Ussing, Erlij, and Lassen 1974). Such TEP and SCC are present in all larval and adult urodeles examined (Alvarado and Kirschner 1963; Dietz, Kirschner, and Porter 1967; Bentley 1975b; Bentley and Baldwin 1980; Cox 1986; Brown 1988). Therefore, active transport occurs across the skin in both phases of urodele life history. The rate of active Na⁺ transport across the skin of larval urodeles is lower than that in the adult (*A. tigrinum,* Bentley and Baldwin 1980) The transport characteristics for Na⁺ or K⁺ of the larval and adult urodele skin appear the same (Bentley and Baldwin 1980; Cox 1986).

The skin of *Rana catesbeiana* larvae shows little or no TEP or SCC (fig. 16.42) until early climax stages (TK XXI–XXII), but TEP and SCC increase to nearly adult values by the end of metamorphosis (Taylor and Barker 1965b; Alvarado and Moody 1970; Cox and Alvarado 1979; Hillyard, Zeiske, and Van Driessche 1982a; Takada 1985). Administration of thyroid hormones to young intact larvae induces many changes

prematurely, including the TEP and SCC in larval skin (Taylor and Barker 1965b; Hillyard, Zeiske, and Van Driessche 1982a). Thyroid hormones applied directly to the skin during *in vitro* TEP or SCC measurements have no effect (Taylor and Barker 1965a).

Sodium transport by epithelia (including anuran skin) occurs in two separate steps across two separate membranes (Ussing, Erlij, and Lassen 1974): (1) The apical cell membranes close to the mucosal side have low permeability to K⁺ and high permeability to Na⁺ through numerous Na⁺ channels, features that are unique to transporting epithelial cells. (2) At the basal lateral cell membrane close to the serosal side, "pumps" move Na⁺ from the cell in exchange for extracellular K⁺. The "pumps" require Na⁺-K⁺–dependent ATPase. The basolateral membrane has a low permeability to Na⁺ due to few Na⁺ channels, and a high K⁺ permeability due to numerous K⁺ channels.

The skin of young anuran larvae (TK V–XX) has low levels of Na⁺-K⁺-ATPase, and these levels increase dramatically during climax stages, approaching adult levels at complete tail absorption (*R. catesbeiana:* Kawada, Taylor, and Barker 1969; Boonkoom and Alvarado 1971; Robinson and Mills 1987a; the Chilean frog, *Calyptocephalella* [now *Caudiverbera*] *caudiverbera* [Leptodactylidae]: Gonzalez, Morales, and Zambrano 1979). The Na⁺-K⁺-ATPase is located in the epidermis rather than in the dermis (Kawada, Taylor, and Barker 1969; Robertson and Mills 1987b). In the epidermis of young larvae, more of the Na⁺-K⁺-ATPase activity is in the apical cells than in any other layer (Robertson and Mills 1987b). In the skin of TK XX larvae the Na⁺-K⁺-

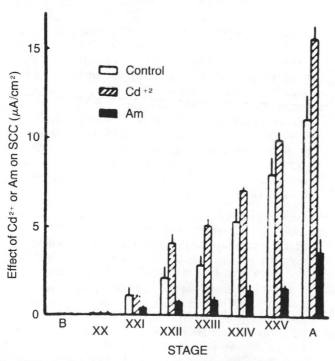
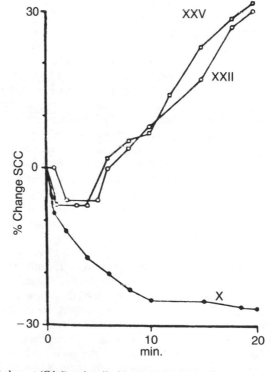

Fig. 16.42 Studies on the short-circuit current (Na⁺ transport) across the skin of metamorphosing *Rana catesbeiana. Left,* the development of transport capabilities as measured by control SCC at various stages of development. The left panel also shows epidermal applications of transitional element (Cd⁺²) and amiloride (*Am*). *Right,* the effects of epidermal application of transitional element (La⁺³) on preclimax stages (TK X) and two climax stages (TK XXII, XXV). (Left panel, data from Takada 1985; right panel, data from Alvarado and Cox 1985.)

ATPase activity is located evenly among the cellular layers, while by TK XXIII more of the Na^+-K^+-ATPase activity is found in the stratum germinativum than in any other layer (Robertson and Mills 1987b). The Na^+-K^+-ATPases in larval and adult ventral skin show similar kinetic properties, implying that the ATPase is the same during development (Robinson and Mills 1987b). The number of ATPases per epithelial cell thus apparently increases during metamorphosis.

Entry of ions at the apical surface changes during development (Cox and Alvarado 1979, 1983; Hillyard, Zeiske, and Van Driessche 1982a, 1982b; Alvarado and Cox 1985; Takada 1985; Van Driessche and Hillyard 1985). The cation channels in the apical membrane of larval skin are not specific for Na^+, while the cation channels are highly specific for Na^+ in the adult skin (Hillyard, Zeiske, and Van Driessche 1982b; Cox and Alvarado 1983). Compounds that increase Na^+ movement across the apical membrane (i.e., nystatin) increase both the SCC and the TEP across larva skin, implying an increase of sodium movement to the serosal side when the apical membrane permits more Na^+ entry (Cox and Alvarado 1979, 1983; Van Driessche and Hillyard 1985). The adult anuran skin is far less sensitive to nystatin, implying that apical entry is not as limiting in adult skin as in larval skin (Cox and Alvarado 1979, 1983; Van Driessche and Hillyard 1985). Compounds that block sodium entry across the apical membrane (e.g., amiloride) have little or no effect on TEP, SCC, and Na^+ transport in larval skin, but greatly reduce these parameters in adults (Cox and Alvarado 1979; Hillyard, Zeiske, and Van Driessche 1982a, 1982b; Takada 1985). This inhibition of TEP and SCC by amiloride develops during climax stages when the number of amiloride blockable channels increases (fig. 16.42, left).

Transition element cations (Co^{2+}, Cd^{2+}, La^{3+}) and alkaline earth divalent cations (Ba^{2+}, Ca^{2+}, Sr^{2+}, Mg^{2+}) interact in unknown ways with the apical membrane of transporting epithelia. Transition elements lead to stimulation of TEP and SCC in adult anuran skin but have inhibitory effects on larvae (fig. 16.42; Takada 1985; Alvarado and Cox 1985). The transition from inhibition to stimulation is abrupt, occurring at TK XXI (Alvarado and Cox 1985). Alkaline earths decrease the SCC in both larvae and adult skin by reducing the entry of Na^+ across channels located in the apical membrane.

The ratio of Na^+ influx to Na^+ efflux in *Rana catesbeiana* is 4 for larvae and about 5 for adults, showing a net sodium uptake across the skin throughout development (Cox and Alvarado 1979). The sodium influx in adults is 8.3 times higher than in larvae, implying that the adults are better at obtaining Na^+ from the environment than are the larvae. These differences are partially due to lower levels of Na^+-K^+-ATPase at the basal lateral membrane in larval skin. Equally important changes must occur during metamorphosis at the apical membrane. The number and specificities of the channels change during late climax stages. The recent work on the morphological transition of the ventral skin (Robinson and Heintzelman 1987) strongly suggests that the changing components of osmoregulation (i.e., increase in water pores, shift in apical membrane cation channels, and increase in Na^+-K^+-ATPase levels in basal lateral membrane) appear in a new population of cells rather than emerging in existing cells.

In adult skin, the lipid composition of membranes affects epithelial membrane permeability to ions and fluids (Yorio 1987). One study on transporting epithelium (skin and gills) has demonstrated changes in total extractable lipids during metamorphosis (Gonzalez, Morales, and Zambrano 1979). This study suggested that when one component of the transporting system (Na^+-K^+-ATPase activity) increases during metamorphosis, the membrane lipid sulfide content increases simultaneously. Clearly the isolation of the lipid and protein components of transporting membranes requires more study to understand the shifts in osmoregulatory capacity of the skin.

Gills Anuran larvae (*R. catesbeiana*) take up Na^+ and Cl^- ions across the gill chamber epithelium (Alvarado and Moody 1970; Dietz and Alvarado 1974). Before climax, the gill chamber epithelium and not the skin is the major site of Na^+ and Cl^- uptake in exchange for NH_4^+ and HCO_3^-, respectively (Dietz and Alvarado 1974). Na^+-K^+-ATPase occurs in the gills of anuran larvae (Boonkoom and Alvarado 1971; Gonzalez, Morales, and Zambrano 1979). If animals are placed in distilled water for several weeks and thereby depleted of ions, their ability to transport ions across the gills increases, as does Na^+-K^+-ATPase activity (Dietz and Alvarado 1974; Boonkoom and Alvarado 1971). Salt loading of larval anurans has the opposite effect. The gills of bullfrog larvae start to degenerate at TK XIX and completely disappear by TK XXIV (Atkinson and Just 1975). During this period the adult skin structures and functions appear. Accordingly gills should decrease their Na^+ and Cl^- uptake in late larval stages; however, TK VI and XXI do not differ in ion uptake (Dietz and Alvarado 1974). The gill Na^+-K^+-ATPase activity, however, decreases during climax stages (Gonzalez, Morales, and Zambrano 1979). No studies are available on the flux rates of water across the gills of anuran larvae.

Little information is available on the osmoregulatory function of the gills in developing urodeles. The gills of larval *Ambystoma mexicanum* can take up sodium (Dunson, Packer, and Dunson 1971), while gills of adults are the major site of ammonia excretion (Munro 1953). However, whether ammonia excretion represents an exchange of Na^+ for NH_4^+, as in anurans, is unknown (Dietz and Alvarado 1974). Neotenic urodeles (*Necturus maculosus* [Proteidae] or *Ambystoma tigrinum*) do not take up any Na^+ across their gills (Baldwin and Bentley 1982). Little water exchanges across the gills of any urodele species (Dunson, Packer, and Dunson 1971; Baldwin and Bentley 1982).

Alimentary Tract Adult anuran amphibians generally do not drink water (Overton 1904; Bentley and Yorio 1979a). When adult frogs are exposed to salt, they sometimes swallow water, which has been interpreted as drinking (Bentley and Schmidt-Nielsen 1971; Katz 1975a). However, the amount is too small to aid osmoregulation significantly (Bentley and Yorio 1979a). Adult urodeles also do not drink to osmoregulate but sometimes swallow water when exposed to high salinities (Alvarado and Kirschner 1963; Bentley 1973a; Baldwin and Bentley 1982; Licht, Feder, and Bledsoe 1975). In all cases these adult amphibians drank less than 3% of their body weight per day, which represents less than 10% of the water that animals can take up across their skin (Baldwin and Bentley 1982; Bentley and Yorio 1979a). The South American arboreal frog

(*Phyllomedusa sauvagei:* Hylidae), by contrast, takes up more water through the mouth (0.2 ml·g⁻¹·h⁻¹) than through the skin (0.05 ml·g⁻¹·h⁻¹; McClanahan and Shoemaker 1987; see also chapter 5).

Free-living amphibian larvae that inhabit fresh water should not drink water, as is the case for freshwater fish. One early study of larval urodeles (*Ambystoma tigrinum*) supports this suggestion (Alvarado and Kirschner 1963). Free-living anuran larvae that are filter feeders (see below), however, might well ingest water. Indeed, this occurs in *Rana cancrivora* at various external salinities (Gordon and Tucker 1965). Water ingested by larvae of the anuran *R. catesbeiana* in normal pond water is considerable (Alvarado and Moody 1970; Bentley and Yorio 1979a; Kobayashi et al. 1979; Baldwin and Bentley 1980; Just and Hayati 1990). Rates of ingestion range from 1.3 to 16 μl·g⁻¹·h⁻¹, with 6.62 μl·g⁻¹·h⁻¹ the average of the five studies. Thus, average preclimax *R. catesbeiana* larvae drink 0.159 ml·g⁻¹·24 h⁻¹, or about 15.9% of their body mass every day. If total osmotic uptake of water into preclimax larvae is 17 μl·g⁻¹·h⁻¹ (Schmidt-Nielsen and Mackay 1970), the ingested water would account for 38.9% of the water uptake per hour. Average water uptake from ingested water per hour is about 7.8% of the total water uptake in adult anurans (*R. pipiens, Bufo marinus,* and *Xenopus laevis;* Bentley and Yorio 1979a). We cannot tell what role this water and accompanying ions play in osmoregulation because no measurements are available on ionic and water flux across the intestine during larval life. Water ingestion decreases during climax stages (Just and Hayati 1990). If the flux rates do not change during metamorphosis, decreased water ingestion can explain the decrease in water content during climax (table 16.11).

Kidney and Bladder The external shape of the adult mesonephric kidney varies among the amphibians. The kidneys of caecilians are long and slender and extend nearly the whole length of the body cavity. The relative lengths of all urodele and anuran kidneys are shorter than those of caecilians, being shortest among anurans. Nevertheless, even in adult anurans they are three to eight times as long as wide (Duellman and Trueb 1986; Dantzler 1989). The internal renal organization is similar for all three orders, and all have a dorsally placed renal portal vein and ventral renal artery. The nephrons are drained by the ventrally placed renal vein (fig. 16.43). From 800 to 8,000 nephrons are in the two kidneys of the adult amphibians (Deyrup 1964). All nephrons contain a glomerulus, ciliated neck segment, proximal tubule, ciliated intermediate segment, and distal tubule. The distal tubule enters into the collecting duct system, which empties into the mesonephric duct, often incorrectly termed the ureter (fig. 16.43).

The renal artery sends its blood supply into the glomerulus, while the proximal tubules are supplied with blood from the renal portal veins (Deyrup 1964). Changes in whole glomerular filtration rates (GFR) result from the changes in the number of filtering glomeruli rather than in filtration rates of each nephron (Dantzler 1989). The single nephron GFR (SNGFR) of adult amphibians ranges from 12 to 18 nl·min⁻¹. The GFR of completely hydrated adults in fresh water ranges from 30 to 92 ml·kg⁻¹·h⁻¹, while during dehydration this rate decreases to 2 to 12 ml·kg⁻¹·h⁻¹ (Dantzler 1989).

Both the net filtration pressure at the glomerulus and the cilia found in various tubule segments probably propel fluid through the nephrons (Dantzler 1989). As the fluid moves through the tubules, some materials are absorbed while other compounds are secreted into the tubules. Both sodium and

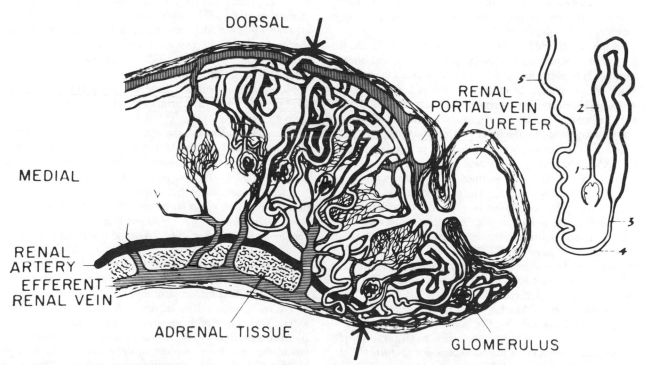

Fig. 16.43 Cross section of a frog kidney, showing its blood supply, nephrons, and ureter (mesonephric duct). *Arrows,* typical sites for micropuncture studies. The insert on the right side shows a single nephron with its various segments: *1,* neck segment; *2,* proximal tubule; *3,* intermediate segment; *4,* distal tubule; *5,* collecting tubule. (Reprinted, by permission, from Dantzler 1989.)

chloride are absorbed along the nephron; however, in amphibians most absorption (50–70%) occurs in the distal tubules and collecting duct. Potassium is secreted in the distal tubule of amphibians. Some is K^+ absorbed in the proximal tubules of anurans, but not in those of urodeles. Water is reabsorbed in the proximal tubule (15–30% of total), while the collecting tubule system absorbs about 25–45% of the water. Amino acids, glucose, and bicarbonate are absorbed, while ammonia and urates are transported into the tubules. The net result is that amphibians always produce hypoosmotic urine. The mechanisms involved in the movements across these tubules are beyond the scope of the present chapter (see Dantzler 1989 for details).

The amphibian kidney develops from mesodermal nephrotomes located between somite and lateral plates of the embryo (Fox 1963). The nephrotome gives rise to the pronephros and pronephric duct. The pronephros is made up of a number of nephrostomes or segmental ciliated openings into the coelom of the embryo. There are 24 nephrostomes in caecilians, 6–10 in urodeles, and only 6 in anurans (Fox 1963). Each nephrostome connects to a ciliated nephrostomial tubule, which leads into a coiled collecting tubule, which then enters into the pronephric duct. The pronephric duct grows posteriorly until it connects to the cloaca. Suspended from the dorsal aorta and hanging freely into the coelomic cavity are pairs of glomi, one opposite each nephrostome of the pronephros. Each glomus forms as an out-pocketing of the coelomic epithelium. Blood vessels from the dorsal aorta invade the epithelium (Fox 1963). Ultrafiltrates of the blood are presumably formed by the glomus and deposited into the coelomic cavities. The nephrostome of the pronephros transports fluids through the pronephric duct to the cloaca and thence out of the embryo. The excretory function of the pronephros starts at tail-bud stages of the embryo and is essential to prevent swelling of the embryo (Rappaport 1955).

As the pronephric duct grows posteriorly, it induces the formation of new tubules possessing a glomerulus and opening into the pronephric duct. These new tubules are the nephrons of the mesonephros; the collecting duct is now renamed the mesonephric duct. The mesonephros starts to form immediately before or right after hatching. In larvae both pronephric and mesonephric tubules function in osmoregulation (Jaffee 1954) until the pronephros degenerates in late larval stages (TK XVI; Fox 1963). The mass of mesonephros increases until TK XVIII and then declines until metamorphosis ends (J. J. Just unpublished data). The mesonephric kidney represents about 1.5% of the body mass throughout metamorphosis. The size and/or number of nephrons increases until TK XVIII and subsequently decreases as the whole animal loses mass (see table 16.11). Functional changes of the mesonephric nephron during metamorphosis are unknown.

The rates of urine formation have been measured in larval *Rana clamitans* and *R. catesbeiana* larvae (21.1 $\mu l \cdot g^{-1} \cdot h^{-1}$, Schmidt-Nielson and Mackay 1970; 6.1 $\mu l \cdot g^{-1} \cdot h^{-1}$, Brown, Murphy, and Brown 1989). The inulin clearance was reported to be 27.8 $\mu l \cdot g^{-1} \cdot h^{-1}$ for *R. catesbeiana* (Brown, Murphy, and Brown 1989) and estimated to be about 35.1 $\mu l \cdot g^{-1} \cdot h^{-1}$ for *R. clamitans* (Schmidt-Nielson and Mackay 1970). The GFR of larval *R. catesbeiana* (as measured by inulin clearance) is similar to those reported for adults (19 $\mu l \cdot g^{-1} \cdot h^{-1}$, Forster 1938; 26 $\mu l \cdot g^{-1} \cdot h^{-1}$, Long 1973). The tubules of the larval nephron thus absorb between 40% (Schmidt-Nielson and Mackay 1970) and 78% (Brown, Murphy, and Brown 1989) of the water. The site at which the nephron of larvae absorbs the water is unknown. The osmotic pressure of urine produced by hydrated larvae is hypotonic compared to the plasma in both *R. cancrivora* (Gordon and Tucker 1965) and *R. catesbeiana* (Goldsmith and Just 1990), implying that the renal tubules of larvae can absorb Na^+ and Cl^- and that the absorption rate for ions is higher than for water.

Among larval urodeles, the GFR for *Ambystoma tigrinum* is 8.3 $\mu l \cdot g^{-1} \cdot h^{-1}$ (Kirschner et al. 1971), 14.0 $\mu l \cdot g^{-1} \cdot h^{-1}$ (DeRuyter and Stiffler 1986), or 25 $\mu l \cdot g^{-1} \cdot h^{-1}$ (Alvarado and Johnson 1965). The GFR for two other species, *Ambystoma gracile* and *Dicamptodon ensatus* (Dicamptodontidae), is about 11 $\mu l \cdot g^{-1} \cdot h^{-1}$ (Stiffler and Alvarado 1974). Urine production rates are always lower than GFR. Three studies suggest that the tubules of the mesonephros reabsorb 9, 36, or 58% of the filtered water in *A. tigrinum*, while the same tubules reabsorb 25% of the water in *A. gracile*. The urine of urodele larvae living in pond water is always hypoosmotic to plasma; ions (Na^+, Cl^-, K^+) are at lower concentrations than in plasma (Alvarado and Kirschner 1963; Kirschner et al. 1971; DeRuyter and Stiffler 1986). Therefore, the nephron of urodele larval can absorb ions faster than water. Ion absorption rates exceed water absorption rates by more than 90% for Na^+ and Cl^- and 70% for K^+ (Stiffler and Alvarado 1974; DeRuyter and Stiffler 1986).

When larvae are exposed to dehydrating conditions, the osmotic pressure of the urine increases (Gordon and Tucker 1965; Kirschner et al. 1971; Stiffler and Alvarado 1974; Stiffler et al. 1986) and the rate of urine production decreases (Kirschner et al. 1971; Stiffler and Alvarado 1974; Stiffler et al. 1986). When urodele larvae are maintained in salt-depleting media, the osmotic pressure of the urine decreases, and the GFR and rate of urine production increases (Alvarado and Dietz 1970a; Stiffler et al. 1986).

Most adult amphibians have a urinary bladder (Bentley 1971a; Wake 1970). The urinary bladder of terrestrial species has a greater capacity than in aquatic species (Bentley 1971a). When water is plentiful, the mesonephric kidney forms a dilute urine, which the bladder stores until it is full. During dehydration, the bladder epithelium absorbs the stored dilute urine (Bentley 1971a; Shoemaker 1987).

Because many amphibian larvae are aquatic, however, a bladder might be of no particular use. Surprisingly, *Ambystoma tigrinum* larvae have bladders that can store urine (Alvarado and Kirschner 1963; Alvarado and Johnson 1965; Alvarado and Dietz 1970a; Kirschner et al. 1971). Larvae of 10 g normally contain about 0.1 ml urine (1% of their body weight). When the cloaca of these larvae is ligated, the urinary bladder becomes greatly distended and can contain up to 1.0 ml urine, or 10% of mass (Alvarado and Kirschner 1963). This is half of the maximum bladder capacity of adult *A. tigrinum* (Bentley 1971a). Stored urine decreases when larvae are in a hyperosmotic medium, suggesting that the bladder of *A. tigrinum* is a water reservoir during dehydration (Kirschner et al. 1971).

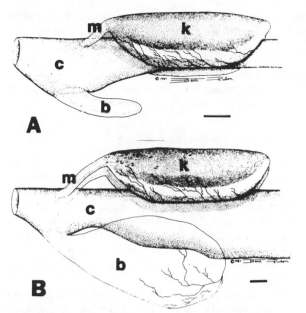

Fig. 16.44 Composite view of the relative positions and size of the excretory system of larval *Rana catesbeiana*. *A*, TK XVI; *B*, TK XXIV. Bars = 300 μm. *b*, bladder; *c*, cloaca; *k*, kidney; *m*, mesonephric duct. (Reprinted, by permission, from Powell and Just 1990.)

The bladder arises as a ventral evagination from the cloaca during midlarval life in *Xenopus laevis* (Nieuwkoop and Faber 1967) and *Rana catesbeiana* (Powell and Just 1990). No other species, anuran or urodele, has been investigated for the earliest appearance of the bladder. The bullfrog bladder never has any direct connection to the mesonephric duct, and the size of the bladder increases gradually during the entire larval life (fig. 16.44). Attempts to obtain urine by abdominal pressure in larvae are unsuccessful until TK XXIV, when on the average 30 μl of urine can be obtained. This volume represents only about 0.5% of the body mass (Goldsmith and Just 1990). The bladders of TK XXIV larvae can hold water equal to 13% of their body mass. Adults have a bladder capacity equal to about 30% of their body mass (Powell and Just 1990). Thus, the bladder increases in relative size during postmetamorphic growth. By TK XXIV, the larval bladder can respond to dehydration both *in vivo* and *in vitro* by moving water from the mucosal to the serosal side (Goldsmith and Just 1990; Powell, Just, and Jackson 1990). Thus, neither bladder nor skin of *R. catesbeiana* can participate in osmoregulation until late climax stages.

Hormonal Control of Water and Ion Movement

Larval amphibians must alter the influx and efflux of ions and/or water to keep the internal environment constant in the face of environmental fluctuations in ions and water. During metamorphosis, both the osmoregulatory organs (gills, intestine, skin, and kidney) and hormone production (steroid hormones, prolactin, antidiuretic hormone) change. During short-term environmental fluctuations, adjustments in the flux rates of either water or ions accomplish the osmoregulation in larval amphibians (fig. 16.41). These changes in fluxes most likely result from hormones.

Posterior Pituitary Hormones The posterior pituitary of adult amphibians contains two hormones, arginine vasotocin (AVT), and mesotocin (MT), both of which are cleaved from a single large neurophysin (Chauvet et al. 1988; Nojiri et al. 1987). In adult amphibians dehydration leads to an increase in circulating AVT (Nouwen and Kuhn 1983). In adults, the environmentally induced release of AVT or injection of AVT decreases renal urine production, increases water reabsorption across the urinary bladder, and increases cutaneous absorption of water. These changes result in increased mass in adult amphibians ("Brunn effect") (Bentley 1971a; Alvarado 1979; Shoemaker 1987; see also chapters 4 and 6).

The posterior pituitary contains axons that arise in cells in the caudodorsal region of the preoptic nucleus (Notenboom 1972). Neurosecretory material increases in these cells during development in larval *Xenopus laevis* (Notenboom 1972). In *Hyla regilla* (Anura: Hylidae), the axons of the cells reach the posterior pituitary by TK I and appear to contain neurosecretory granules (Smoller 1966). During larval life, neurosecretion per volume of posterior pituitary remains constant; however, the total volume of all components increases (Smoller 1966). These histological data suggest that the amount of posterior pituitary hormones increases during larval life. Antidiuretic hormones are present during larval life (Desol and Masnou 1957; Bentley and Greenwald 1970). However, hormone concentration does not increase during development and at most is only 20% of that in adults (Bentley and Greenwald 1970). Larval *X. laevis* in a hyperosmotic medium decrease granule content in the preoptic nucleus, indicating increased hormone release (Notenboom 1972). However, circulating levels of AVT have not been determined in any larval amphibians.

Administration of posterior pituitary hormones affects water retention variably in larval amphibians. Early studies suggested that AVT does not increase water content in young anuran larvae (*Bufo bufo*: Howes 1940; *Heleioporus eyrei* [Myobatrachidae]: Bentley 1959; *Alytes obstetricans* [Discoglossidae]: Delsol and Masnou 1957), while others showed that even very young animals respond to AVT by increasing mass (*Rana catesbeiana*: Alvarado and Johnson 1966; Bentley and Greenwald 1970; *R. ridibunda*: Goldenberg and Warburg 1977a). All studies agree that during climax stages larvae respond to AVT administration with a "Brunn effect." Oxytocin administration to young larvae increases mass in some species (*Heleioporus eyrei*: Bentley 1959; *R. ridibunda* and *B. viridis*: Goldenberg and Warburg 1976) but not in others (*R. catesbeiana*: Alvarado and Johnson 1966). In all anuran species studied, oxytocin administration during climax stages increases mass. Urodele larvae (*Ambystoma tigrinum* and *A. gracile*: Alvarado and Johnson 1965) increase mass after AVT but not oxytocin administration.

Few data explain the increased mass of larvae (Brunn effect) after posterior pituitary hormone administration. Vasotocin (AVT) increases the *in vitro* transfer of water across the skin of larval *R. catesbeiana* from TK III to XXIII (Bentley and Greenwald 1970). AVT has no effect on the SCC of the skin of larval *R. catesbeiana* until midclimax stages (Taylor and Barker 1965a; Cox and Alvarado 1979), indicating a lack of effect on sodium transport in the skin. AVT administration causes a net uptake of sodium by decreasing its efflux (Alvarado and Johnson 1966), suggesting a possible decrease in urinary sodium loss. AVT administration decreases urine production in larval *A. tigrinum* (Alvarado and Johnson 1965). The ability of the urinary bladder to increase the transport of water *in vitro* from the mucosa to the serosa side in response to AVT does not appear until late climax stages (Powell, Just, and Jackson 1990).

Anterior Pituitary Hormone For nearly a quarter of a century, investigators have found increased larval wet mass after chronic prolactin administration and have concluded that this represents growth (see above). Some of these long-term effects of prolactin may be due to shifts in water and ion distribution (Brown and Brown 1987). Both anuran and urodele larvae gain water 1 to 24 h after prolactin administration (Goldenberg and Warburg 1977b, 1983; Warburg and Goldenberg 1978a). Tissue water content increases after long-term prolactin administration in both anuran and urodele larvae (Platt and Christopher 1977; Brown et al. 1986), perhaps due to a decrease in urine production (Brown, Murphy, and Brown 1989).

In vitro, prolactin transiently increases the SCC of the skin of larval bullfrogs, suggesting that prolactin should cause an increase in sodium transport into the animals (Eddy and Allen 1979; Takada 1986). Long-term *in vivo* prolactin administration (2 weeks) during climax in *R. catesbeiana* either prevents the rise of the SCC or depresses its magnitude (Takada 1989), indicating that prolactin does not affect *in vivo* sodium skin transport. In fact, prolactin administration has no consistent effect on plasma sodium concentration (Brown and Brown 1987), and the effects of prolactin on sodium transport in other organs of larvae (e.g., gills, kidney, bladder) have not been investigated.

Other Hormones Aldosterone can increase plasma Na$^+$ concentration in adult and larval amphibians (Stiffler et al. 1986; see also chapter 6). The increase in plasma Na$^+$ is the result of aldosterone stimulation of sodium uptake across the skin of urodeles (Alvarado and Kirschner·1964) and anurans (Hillyard and Van Driessche 1985). Aldosterone decreases sodium loss in the urine of larval amphibians (Heney and Stiffler 1983; DeRuyter and Stiffler 1986). Unfortunately, the effects of steroids on ionic regulation were studied in only a limited number of stages. No information is available on adrenal steroid responsiveness of the gills and bladders of larval amphibians.

The possible effects of several hormones on osmotic and ionic regulation have not been examined in amphibian larvae. These include renin, angiotensin, and atrial natriuretic peptides.

FEEDING AND DIGESTION

In discussing the digestive system of amphibians, Reeder (1964, 000) comments that "for a group of such notable diversity and whose members have evolved in different lines for vast lengths of time, it is impressive that all known members of the Class Amphibia, at least as adults, are primarily carnivorous." As larvae, however, amphibians vary widely in feeding habits, from strict herbivory through omnivory to carnivory. Moreover, the manner of acquiring food, and its subsequent digestion and assimilation, is equally varied, as is discussed in detail in chapter 13. Thus, perhaps even more amazing that Reeder's (1964) observation of ubiquitous carnivory in adult amphibians is that numerous species of amphibian larvae also have arrived at this form of energy intake, as will now be discussed.

Feeding Modes: Anuran Larvae

Anuran larvae hatch with large yolk reserves and typically do not feed for several days. The larvae of a few anurans have sufficient yolk for all development and do not feed before metamorphosis. Examples are the microhylids *Kalophrynus pleurostigma* (Inger 1966), *Anodonthyla, Platypelis,* and *Plethodontohyla* (Blommers-Schlosser 1975), the leptodactylids *Eupsophus roseus* and *E. vittatus* (Formas and Vera 1980), and the bufonids *Pelophryne albotaeniata* and *P. lighti* (Inger 1954).

Most anuran larvae progressively absorb the nutrients of the embryonic yolk sac before or shortly following hatching, and species with aquatic free-living larvae have an early developmental period characterized by suspension (filter) feeding, the removal of suspended bacteria, zooplankton, phytoplankton, and organic detritus from inspired water (Seale 1987; Wassersug and Heyer 1988). Suspension feeding requires great specialization of the branchial skeleton and gills. As water from the buccal chamber passes over and through the gill arches forming the branchial basket within the branchial chamber, it encounters branchial filter plates (fig. 16.27). These filters are formed by ruffled extensions from each branchial arch and contain additional epithelial ridges that increase surface area of the filter plates. Mucus secreted from the floor of the buccal cavity and transferred to the filter plates themselves traps suspended particulate matter. The epithelium of the filter plates is ciliated, and mucus currents set up by ciliary motion sweep the trapped material into the esophagus, where it is swallowed and subsequently digested in the stomach.

The simultaneous use of the branchial apparatus of many anuran larvae for both feeding and gas exchange poses the interesting question of possible functional conflicts. Larvae of *Xenopus,* which have elaborate gill filters for suspension feeding (Wassersug 1972, 1980; Wassersug and Rosenberg 1979), decrease gill ventilation in proportion to the concentration of particles in inspired water (Seale, Hoff, and Wassersug 1982; Wassersug and Hoff 1979). Presumably, this maintains constant ingestion rates but potentially reduces the respiratory effectiveness of the gills. Indeed, *Xenopus* larvae in dense food suspensions not only reduce branchial gill ventilation, but additionally increase air breathing to compensate for the reduction of branchial gas exchange (Feder, Seale, Boraas, Wassersug, and Gibbs 1984).

Macrophagous feeding replaces suspension feeding as development proceeds in many anurans. Keratinized plates on the beaks ("lips") scrape algae, bacteria, and other material from the substrate (see Wassersug 1980 for an extensive description of the oral anatomy of anurans and list of references). In other anurans, however, suspension feeding remains the dominant or exclusive form of food acquisition until metamorphic climax. Not surprisingly, then, the development of the branchial filter plates in different species is correlated with the degree of dependence upon suspension feeding (Savage 1952; Wassersug 1980). Extremely large, well-developed filter systems are found in species using suspension feeding largely or exclusively, including the hylids *Agalychnis callidryas* and *Phyllomedusa trinitas* (Kenney 1969), most microhylids (Savage 1952, 1955), *Xenopus* (Bles 1905; Kratochwill 1933; Sterba 1950; Ueck 1967; Wassersug 1972, 1980; Wassersug and Rosenberg 1979) and free-swimming *Pipa* (Pipidae; Sokol 1977). Not only are the branchial basket and the filter plates of the gills larger in primarily suspension-feeding larvae, but generally the number of filter rows on each plate is also greater (see Wassersug 1980 for extensive discussion of this topic).

While filter feeding and macrophagous collection of primarily plant material from the substrate are the two most common modes of feeding in anuran larvae, other patterns exist and are generally associated with a reduction of the branchial basket. Several species (e.g., *Colostethus nubicola* [Dendrobatidae], *Microhyla heymonsi* [Microhylidae], *Megaphrys minor* [Pelobatidae] have larvae with dorsally upturned rather than ventrally oriented mouths. These so-called funnel-mouth larvae, which tend to live in waters free of suspended food materials, feed at the water surface on larger food particles. Anuran species with carnivorous larvae have also forgone suspension feeding. Carnivory can take many forms. *Hymenochirus* (Pipidae) and *Anotheca* (Hylidae) feed on large individual prey items, including pelagic arthropods, found in either the water column or on the substrate. Many anuran larvae are cannibalistic (Crump 1986; Noble 1931; Polis and Myers 1985; Ruibal and Thomas 1988), including the leptodactylids *Ceratophrys ornata* and *Lepidobatrachus laevis* and the hylids *Hyla pseudopuma* and *Osteopilus septentrionalis*. Marsupial frog larvae (Hylidae) apparently feed on exudates from the incubatory integument in the pouch (del Pino 1980), while fetuses of the viviparous bufonid *Nectophrynoides occidentalis* feed on exudates from the oviducts (Xavier 1973).

One of the most interesting forms of "carnivory" involves oophagy, the "cannibalistic" consumption of eggs of the same species. This practice is common in anuran species with free-living arboreal larvae, including more than a dozen species in the Hylidae, Rhacophoridae, Microhylidae, and Dendrobatidae (see Lannoo, Townsend, and Wassersug 1987 for references). As an example, the hylid *Osteopilus brunneus* develops as an arboreal larva living in water within bromeliads. In addition to laying fertilized eggs, females leave nonfertile "trophic" eggs in the bromeliad cups. The larvae feed primarily, if not solely, on these eggs, and their stomachs are modified as a storage organ to hold up to 180 eggs at a time (Lannoo, Townsend, and Wassersug 1987). Carnivorous larvae tend to have shorter guts and hypertrophied jaw muscles when compared with omnivorous or herbivorous forms (Pomeroy 1981; Wassersug 1980).

Regardless of larval feeding modes, all anuran adults are carnivorous. Few detailed observations have been made of the timing of the actual transition between food items of larvae and postmetamorphic forms. *Xenopus laevis* stops filter-feeding at NF 59 to 61, before any gross morphological

changes occur in the larval feeding structures or tail (Naitoh, Wassersug, and Leslie 1989). The earliest developmental stage at which pieces of food are ingested "in adultlike fashion" is NF 63, with true deglutition occurring at NF 63 to 64. The ontogeny of emesis (vomiting) has been described in detail for *X. laevis*, with observations on *Rana clamitans* and *R. catesbeiana* (Naitoh, Wassersug, and Leslie 1989). *Xenopus* larvae can vomit concurrent with the switch to adult feeding mode at NF 63, and the sensitivity to the emetic agent apomorphine increases sharply with further development. Essentially, emesis is an adult behavior.

With metamorphosis in most anuran species, feeding mechanisms shift to prey capture by tongue extrusion (Duellman and Trueb 1986). Completely aquatic pipid frogs (*Pipa, Xenopus, Hymenochirus*) do not develop tongues at metamorphosis and rely upon suction feeding as adults. Rapid depression of the buccal floor (as in some larval urodeles; see below) sucks water bearing food material into the mouth. The water is then expelled through the partially closed lips, with larger zooplankton retained in the mouth (Sokol 1969).

Feeding Modes: Urodele Larvae

The larvae of almost all salamanders are strictly carnivorous. After yolk sac absorption, the small larvae of *Ambystoma tigrinum* and *Notophthalmus viridescens* (Salamandridae) initially feed on zooplankton such as ostracods and cylopoid copepods (Brophy 1980). As larval body mass increases, so does larval mobility, strength, and size and number of teeth. Accordingly, the diet progressively switches to larger aquatic invertebrates (e.g., snails, aquatic insects, chironomid larvae). Some urodele larvae eat small vertebrates, especially smaller amphibian larvae including conspecifics. *Dicamptodon ensatus* (Dicamptodontidae) capture both anuran and urodele larvae, which may form up to 40% of their diet (Johnson and Schreck 1969; Metter 1963). *Ambystoma tigrinum* has a cannibalistic morph, with wider head and greater dentition (Collins and Cheek 1983; Lannoo and Bachmann 1984b; Pierce, Mitton, and Rose 1981; Rose and Armentrout 1976). Many salamander larvae also consume the eggs of fish, amphibians, and aquatic invertebrates.

Although omnivory or herbivory is rare in larval urodeles, the aquatic larvae of *Notophthalmus* and *Triturus* (Salamandridae) reportedly will feed on algae (Creed 1964; Pope 1924), and the highly coiled gut characteristic of some populations of *A. tigrinum* could predispose them towards herbivory (Tilley 1964).

The dentition of several urodeles changes during development (see Greven and Clemen 1985a, 1985b; Noble 1931; Parker and Dunn 1964). Basically, the sequence is from monocuspid undivided to monocuspid divided teeth (Greven and Clemen 1985a). At metamorphosis divided bicuspid teeth replace the larval teeth.

Methods of prey capture by aquatic larvae vary but essentially involve suction feeding. The jaws are opened and the buccal cavity is depressed, drawing in the prey item on an inward current of water (for references see Duellman and Trueb 1986). The jaws are relatively weak, and the small teeth are used primarily for holding and manipulating prey items rather than for actual capture. In salamander species with aquatic adults (or with terrestrial adults in the water temporarily for breeding purposes), suction feeding persists in the adult. In species with terrestrial adults, however, the mechanism for prey capture changes to capture by tongue projection (see Findeis and Bemis 1990 for references).

Feeding Modes: Caecilian Larvae

Like so many aspects of their biology, feeding in caecilian larvae is largely enigmatic or known in only a few species. Caecilians hatch, or are born in the case of viviparous species like *Dermophis mexicanus* (Wake 1980a) or ovoviviparous species with direct development like *Hypogeophis* and *Grandisonia* (see Duellman and Trueb 1986), in an advanced state of development relative to most anurans or urodeles. Larvae of ichthyophiid, rhinotrematid, and caeciliid caecilians, which are terrestrial as adults, differ from adults primarily in having an open opercular slit and a more extensive lateral line. The basic morphology of the cranial and hyoid bones and musculature and the oral cavity differs little from that of adults, suggesting that prey items and modes of prey capture are similar.

Adult dentition replaces the teeth of larval caecilians at hatching or birth; tooth crown morphology, tooth number, and tooth distribution all change (Wake 1976, 1977a, 1977b, 1979, 1980a, 1985b). The fetuses of many viviparous species use their teeth to scrape the maternal uterine epithelial lining and ingest the cells as an energy source. Developing fetuses remain in the oviduct for up to 11 months, but in *Dermophis mexicanus*, for example, yolk in the fetus is depleted within 2–3 months. For 8–9 months the fetuses (which may number 3–16) feed on oviductal secretions, which are primarily free amino acids and carbohydrates. In late gestation, the secretions become very lipid-rich. The ultrastructure and histochemistry of the epithelium of the oviduct have been described for pregnant *Chthonerpeton* (Welsch, Müller, and Schubert 1977). Frequent scraping of the oviduct wall by the fetus may actually stimulate cell turnover in oviductal secretory epithelium.

As adults (and we presume as larvae), caecilians differ from other anurans in that they do not use their tongue for prey capture (see Bemis, Schwenk, and Wake 1983). Instead, these strictly carnivorous animals use strong, often heavily fanged jaws to seize prey (often elongate animals like worms). To our knowledge, herbivory has not been noted in either larval or adult caecilians.

Alimentary Canal and Metamorphosis to Carnivory

As larvae almost all anurans, regardless of a microphagous or macrophagous mode of feeding, are herbivorous (with exceptions noted above), but as adults are carnivores (see also chapter 12). The morphological and physiological requirements of the digestive system of herbivores and carnivores are radically different. Because of the relative difficulty with which plant material is broken down and chemically digested, maximal nutrient uptake requires that the gut of herbivores have as large a surface area for absorption as possible (Hume 1989). In contrast, animal material is comparatively easily digested, and the gut of carnivores typically is much

shorter and consequently has much less surface area for nutrient absorption.

As a consequence of different diets, herbivorous anuran larvae and their carnivorous adults differ in the structural/functional nature of their digestive systems. The greatest dedication to herbivory occurs in the digestive system of anuran larvae. As described in detail by Fox (1984), the alimentary tract of anuran larvae consists of a foregut, midgut, and hindgut. The foregut, composed of the esophagus, the stomach, and a short ciliated region leading into the midgut, is relatively undifferentiated. The stomach is relatively undeveloped in most anurans (Barrington 1945), but near the equivalent of the cardiac portion of the stomach is a structure known as the manicotto glandulare (Lambertini 1928). This structure is absent in pelobatids and bufonids (Griffiths 1961). The function of this glandlike structure remains obscure. Possibly the stomach, including the manicotto glandulare, serves only as a storage site for food particles (Ueck 1967), and Fox (1984, 121) indicates that the foregut of anurans probably "functions partly as a temporary storage organ and also for some modest luminal digestion of food." In bullfrog larvae the extracellular digestion of protein may occur in the stomach, while actual absorption occurs in the midgut (Sugimoto, Ichikawa, and Nakamura 1981). In any event, the midgut receives digestive enzymes directly from the pancreas and liver and is a major site of extracellular digestion (Frieden and Just 1970). The liver of anuran larvae is very prominent, and in some species (e.g., *Leptobrachium montanum:* Pelobatidae) accounts for as much as one-fifth of the total volume of the animal (Nodzenski, Wassersug, and Inger 1989). The midgut is extremely long and coiled within the abdomen, providing maximal surface area for nutrient digestion (Kemp 1954). Interestingly, the size, form, and degree of abdominal "packing" of the viscera vary considerably among larvae of different species, with both overall body form and mode of life playing a role in shaping the visceral organs (Nodzenski, Wassersug, and Inger 1989).

Metamorphic changes are considerable in the gross anatomy of the gut of anuran larvae (see Duellman and Trueb 1986; Fox 1984; Frieden and Just 1970; Ohtake 1982). Most striking, of course, is the considerable shortening of the gut to reflect the carnivorous diet of postmetamorphic individuals (e.g., Hourdry and Beaumont 1985; Nodzenski, Wassersug, and Inger 1989). Some larval *Lepidobatrachus laevis* (a cannibalistic species—see above) have an "adult stomach" (Ruibal and Thomas 1988). As discussed above, the change in diet is relatively small when comparing larvae and adults of caecilians and salamanders. A pepsin-secreting stomach, required for digestion of meat, is present in salamander larvae but is absent in *Rana pipiens* larvae (Kunz 1924). The total length of the gut shortens by 25% in *Ambystoma tigrinum* (Tilley 1964), but otherwise relatively few changes in structure or function occur in salamanders and caecilians.

With respect to ultrastructure, drastic changes in the epithelial lining the entire intestinal tract accompany anuran metamorphosis. These changes begin about TK XVIII as the entire larval intestinal epithelium begins to degenerate. A completely new adult epithelial layer develops by about TK XXIII (Griffiths 1961; Bonneville 1963; Brown and Millington 1968; Hourdry and Dauca 1977). The foregut epithelium of larvae contains ciliated columnar epithelial cells as well as mucus-secreting cells. The midgut contains epithelial cells with microvilli at the surface as well as goblet cells.

The lysosomal hydrolase enzymes (acid phosphatase, aryl-sulfatase, thiolacetate esterase, β-glucuronidase, and N-ace-tyl-β-glucosaminidase) all increase in the epithelium of the midgut intestine until climax (TK XX), when the epithelium is shed into the intestinal lumen (Brown and Millington 1968; Hourdry and Dauca 1977; Kaltenbach, Wang, and Lipson 1981). The largest quantities of the lysosomal enzyme acid phosphatase are also present in the epithelial lining of the esophagus, manicotto glandulare (larval stomach), and large intestine just before the primary epithelium is shed at TK XX (Kaltenbach, Wang, and Lipson 1981). As the secondary epithelial lining of the entire gastrointestinal tract appears at TK XXI–XXV, levels of acid phosphatase are lower but still detectable (Kaltenbach, Wang, and Lipson 1981). These lysosomal enzymes may be important for nutrition if the organic and inorganic compounds of the degenerating primary epithelium are absorbed during their passage through the gut.

The larval stomach has a transmucosal potential difference (PD) across the epithelium in which the mucosal (secretory) side is negative to the serosal (nutrient) side. This gastric PD is generated by a Cl^- pump from the serosal side to the mucosal side and a Na^+ pump operating from the interior of the cell to the serosal side (Forte, Limlomwongse, and Kasebekar 1969). Between TK XX and XXII the stomachs cannot secrete HCl, while by TK XXIII about 20% of stomachs can be stimulated to produce HCl with histamine (Forte, Limlomwongse, and Kasbekar 1969; Forte, Limlomwongse, and Forte 1969a). Larval stomachs at TK XXIV and XXV produce HCl following artificial stimulation, but only 50% secrete HCl without artificial stimulation (Forte, Limlomwongse, and Kasbekar 1969; Forte, Limlomwongse, and Forte 1969b).

Digestive enzymes occur in the foregut of larvae. Little or no lipase or amylase activity is in the foregut, which has some proteolytic activity (Griffiths 1961). The proteolytic activity is only in the manicotto glandulare region of the foregut. The proteolytic activity is trypsinlike (pH optimum 8.5) and appears at the earliest larval stages. The trypsin activity starts to disappear by TK XVII and is completely gone by TK XX (Griffiths 1961). A pepsin proteolytic activity (pH optimum 2.3) appears at TK XXII (Griffiths 1961), when HCl secretion becomes possible.

The midgut contains a number of enzymes, including those that digest carbohydrates (trehalase, maltase, glucoamylase) and proteins (α-glutamic transpeptidase), but does not contain sucrase and lactase (Hourdry et al. 1979). These digestive enzymes are present in the microvilli membranes of the small intestine (Dauca et al. 1979) and can be isolated with sodium dodecyl sulfate (SDS) and electrophoresis (Dauca et al. 1981). All these enzymes increase during normal metamorphosis (Hourdry et al. 1979). However, these enzyme activities are not controlled by thyroid hormones alone, because insulin and hydrocortisone also change the levels of these enzymes in both primary and secondary intestinal epithelium (El Maraghi-Ater, Mesnard, and Hourdry 1986; Ben Brahim, Mesnard, and Hourdry 1987). Aside from the brush border

enzymes originating in the intestine, the pancreas also contributes to digestion in the midgut (Leone et al. 1976). Pancreatic lipase activity increases after hatching and is fairly constant from NF 53 until NF 63, when it declines. Lipase activity in the pancreas increases again after the completion of metamorphosis. From NF 50 to the completion of metamorphosis the amylase activity declines in *Xenopus laevis* and remains low in the adult. Surprisingly, no quantitative measurements are available on proteolytic-like activity in the pancreas, although proteinases are present in larval pancreas (Griffiths 1961; Altig et al. 1975).

Proteinases are found in the gut and pancreas (Griffiths 1961; Altig et al. 1975), and luminal protein digestion should occur. The intestinal mucosa of larval *Rana catesbeiana* (TK XII–XIV) can take up a large protein (horseradish peroxidase) by pinocytosis (Sugimoto, Ichikawa, and Nakamura 1981), after which the protein is digested intracellularly when the pinocytotic vesicles fuse with vesicles containing proteinases. Thus, anuran larval digestion is probably the result of both extracellular and intracellular digestion.

A large number of lipids, vitamins, and amino acids affect larval growth as well as metamorphic rate (see review Kaltenbach and Hagedorn 1981). Whether these nutrients are normally in the digestive tract of larval amphibians is not clear. Any nutrients in the digestive tract could come from the diet or be synthesized by bacteria living in the intestine. The intestine of larvae contains numerous enterobacteria. In one study, the intestine of thirty-four larval *R. pipiens* contained ten different enterobacteria, including *Escherichia coli* and *Hafnia alvei* in many animals. Eight other bacterial species were in less than 20% of the larvae (Hird et al. 1983).

Nutrient uptake across the foregut, midgut, and hindgut has not been studied during amphibian metamorphosis. Active transport sites in the digestive tract typically show microvilli, alkaline phosphatase activity, and ATPase activity (Bonneville 1963; Brown and Millington 1968). The epithelia of the esophagus and stomach show no alkaline phosphatase activity, suggesting that they have no potential to absorb nutrients at any stage of anuran development (Kaltenbach, Lipson, and Wang 1977). The majority of the larval midgut epithelium contains microvilli, alkaline phosphatase, and ATPase activity from hatching until early climax stages (TK XXI), when the levels decrease (Brown and Millington 1968; Ben Brahim, Mesnard, and Hourdry 1987; Kaltenbach, Lipson, and Wang 1977). In late climax stages, when the adult epithelium appears in the midgut, the enzymatic and ultrastructural indicators of transport capability reappear (Kaltenbach, Lipson, and Wang 1977). The hindgut epithelium never shows any alkaline phosphatase activity, suggesting no transport capabilities in this region (Kaltenbach, Lipson, and Wang 1977).

In summary, the ontogenetic transition in feeding is from herbivory (anuran larvae) or carnivory (urodele and caecilian larvae) to carnivory (adults of all amphibians). The morphological, physiological, and biochemical makeup of the digestive system of amphibian larvae clearly reflects these transitions. Within the broad categories of herbivory or carnivory, however, is a wide variety of diets, ranging from algae to aquatic plants in herbivorous larvae, to crabs (*Rana cancri-*

vora) and rodents in carnivorous species. The particular specializations and adaptations of the adult digestive system, and the ontogeny of these features, are largely unknown.

POSTSCRIPT

The environmental physiology of adult amphibians is fascinating, complicated, and in many respects still rather poorly understood, as evident from the previous chapters of this book. Yet adults represent but the final stage of a complex series of developmental changes beginning after fertilization of the egg. As evident from this chapter, in many (if not most) instances the physiology of the embryos and larvae is as complex or even more complex than that of adults. Our understanding of the physiology (or any other biological aspect) of any "species" is complete only when we have studied all developmental stages (see Burggren 1992). To understand physiological adaptation and evolution, study of only the adult form of bullfrogs, for example, is no more or less insightful than the study of only TK X larvae. Selection pressures continue to act on physiological processes in all developmental stages of any species or phylogenetic group.

We hope that this chapter has not only indicated the fascinating physiological changes that accompany amphibian development, but also will stimulate workers in amphibian physiology to introduce a more developmental perspective into their studies. Thus, ultimately, we may truly understand the range of environmental fluctuations that amphibian species can tolerate and survive. Until we understand all the physiological responses to the environment in all developmental stages, we cannot hope to understand why a particular species thrives or disappears from the biosphere.

Bibliography

Those who cannot remember the past are condemned to repeat it.
—George Santayana, *The Life of Reason*

The literature concerning amphibian physiology is both immense and diverse. The diversity of this literature poses a particular problem for those who wish to take best advantage of it. Relevant publications appear in the specialty journals of physiology, herpetology, neurobiology, biochemistry, endocrinology, developmental biology, and natural history; in nearly every language; and in a myriad of monographs, books, and special publications. As a result, publications relevant to investigators are unknown to them simply because each investigator is familiar with but a small portion of the literature. The editors of this volume have intentionally formatted its bibliography to address this problem. First, we have pooled all of the bibliographic entries so that any inspection of a particular citation will naturally lead the reader to other citations of a particular author. Second, at the end of each bibliographic entry is a parenthetical reference to all of the chapters that cite it. This practice, we hope, will lead the reader of a particular chapter to other contexts in which a work has been cited. Third, the editors have included some recent references that are not cited in any chapter. We hope, therefore, that this bibliography will be a useful tool for those who investigate the environmental physiology of amphibians.

Scientific names that are obsolete or are spelled incorrectly in the titles of cited publications have not been corrected in this bibliography. For example, this bibliography includes numerous references to the salamandrid salamander *Pleurodeles waltlii* [*sic*]; the correct name is *Pleurodeles waltl.* Such errors are common in the literature, and users of this bibliography should guard against them. We have attempted to use the correct spellings in the index.

Abbott, B. C., and A. J. Brady. 1964. Amphibian muscle. In *Physiology of the Amphibia*, ed. J. A. Moore, 1:329–370. New York: Academic Press. (11)

Abraham, A. 1969. *Innervation of the Heart and Blood Vessels in Vertebrates Including Man.* Toronto: Pergamon Press. (7)

Accordi, F., and F. Corbellini. 1986–1987. Morphogenesis of adrenal gland of *Triturus cristatus carnifex* during larval development and metamorphosis. *Archives d'Anatomie Microscopie et de Morphologie Expérimentale* 75:241–251. (16)

Accordi, F., L. Mastrolia, E. G. Milano, and H. Manelli. 1975. Electron microscopic observations of adrenal chromaffin cells in the frog, *Rana esculenta*, during embryonal development and metamorphosis. *Rivista di Biologica* 68:135–163. (16)

Accordi, F., and E. G. Milano. 1977. Catecholamine secreting cells in the adrenal gland of *Bufo bufo* during metamorphosis and in the adult. *General and Comparative Endocrinology* 33:187–195. (16)

Acher, R. 1990. Structure evolution and processing adaptation of neurohypophyseal hormone–neurophysin precursors. In *Progress in Comparative Endocrinology,* ed. A. Epple, C. G. Scanes, and M. H. Stetson, 1–9. New York: Wiley-Liss. (3)

Acher, R., J. Chauvet, M. T. Chauvet, and D. Crepy. 1964. Phylogenie peptides neurohypophysaires: Isolemente de la mesotocine (ileu-8-ocytocine) de la grenouille, intermédiaire entre la ser4-ileu8-ocytocine des poissons osseux et l'ocytocine des mammifères. *Biochimica et Biophysica Acta* 90:613–615. (5)

Acher, R., J. Chauvet, M. T. Lenci, and F. Morel. 1960. Présence d'une vasotocine dans la neurohypophyse de la grenouille (*Rana esculenta* L.). *Biochimica et Biophysica Acta* 42:379–380. (5)

Acker, P. M., K. C. Kruse, and E. B. Krehbiel. 1986. Aging *Bufo americanus* by skeletochronology. *Journal of Herpetology* 20:570–574. (15)

Ackerman, R. A., R. C. Seagrave, R. Dmi'el, and A. Ar. 1985. Water and heat exchange between parchment-shelled reptile eggs and their surroundings. *Copeia* 1985:703–711. (4)

Ackermann, J. 1949. The annual rhythm of the fatty metamorphosis of the liver in the frog *Rana esculenta* L. *Bulletin International del'Académie Polonaise des Sciences et des Lettres* B2:145–175. (15)

Ackrill, P., J. S. Dixon, R. Green, and S. Thomas. 1970. Effects of prolonged saline exposure on water, sodium, and urea transport and on electron-microscopical characteristics of the isolated urinary bladder of the toad *Bufo bufo. Journal of Physiology* (London) 210:73–85. (6)

Adams, A. E., and E. E. Rae. 1929. An experimental study of the fat bodies in *Triturus (Diemyctylus) viridescens. Anatomical Record* 41:181–204. (15)

Adams, W. E. 1958. *The Comparative Morphology of the Carotid Body and Carotid Sinus.* Springfield, IL: Charles C. Thomas. (7)

Adkins, W. M. 1961. A study of the role of the pineal system in amphibian behavior. *Natural History* 70:72–76. (9)

Adler, K. 1976. Extraocular photoreception in amphibians. *Photochemistry and Photobiology* 23:275–298. (2,9)

Adler, K., and D. H. Taylor. 1973. Extraocular perception of polarized light by orienting salamanders. *Journal of Comparative Physiology* 87:203–212. (9)

Adler, L. 1914. Metamorphosestudien an Batrachier-larven: 1. Exstirpation endokriner Drusen: A. Exstirpation der Hypophyse. *Wilhelm Roux's Archive für Entwicklungsmechanik der Organism* 39:21–45. (16)

Adler, W. 1901. Die Entwicklung der ausseren Korperform und des mesoderms bei *Bufo vulgaris. Internationale Monatschrift für Anatomie und Physiologie* 18:19. (16)

Adolph, E. F. 1927. Changes in the physiological regulation of body volume in *Rana pipiens* during ontogeny and metamorphosis. *Journal of Experimental Zoology.* 47:179–195. (16)

———. 1931a. Body size as a factor in the metamorphosis of tadpoles. *Biological Bulletin* 61:376–386. (16)

———. 1931b. The size of the body and the size of the environment in the growth of tadpoles. *Biological Bulletin* 61:350–375. (16)

———. 1931c. The water exchanges of frogs with and without skin. *American Journal of Physiology* 96:569–596. (6)

———. 1932. The vapor tension relations of frogs. *Biological Bulletin* 62:112–125. (4,5,6)

———. 1933. Exchanges of water in the frog. *Biological Review* 8:224–240. (5)

———. 1934. Influences of the nervous system on the intake and excretion of water by the frog. *Journal of Cellular and Comparative Physiology* 5:123–139. (6)

———. 1979. Development of dependence on oxygen in embryo salamanders. *American Journal of Physiology* 236:R282–R291. (16)

Aggarwal, S. J., and A. Riggs. 1969. The hemoglobin of the bullfrog, *Rana catesbeiana:* I. Purification, amino acid composition, and oxygen equilibria. *Journal of Comparative Chemistry* 244:2372–2383. (5,16)

Aguilar, C. E., M. A. Bisby, E. Cooper, and J. Diamond. 1973. Evidence that axoplasmic transport of trophic factors is involved in the regulation of peripheral nerve fields in salamanders. *Journal of Physiology* (London) 234:449–464. (11)

Aho, A.-C., K. Donner, C. Hydén, L. O. Larsen, and T. Reuter. 1988. Low retinal noise in animals with low body temperature allows high visual sensitivity. *Nature* 334:348–350. (2,8,13)

Aho, A.-C., K. Donner, C. Hydén, and T. Reuter. 1987. Retinal noise, the performance of retinal ganglion cells, and visual sensitivity in the dark-adapted frog. *Journal of the Optical Society of America* 4:2321–2329. (2)

Aitken, P. G., and R. R. Capranica. 1984. Auditory input to a vocal nucleus in the frog *Rana pipiens:* Hormonal and seasonal effects. *Experimental Brain Research* 57:33–39. (2)

Akaike, N., A. Noma, and M. Sato. 1976. Electrical responses in frog taste cells. *Journal of Physiology* (London) 254:87–107. (16)

Akaike, N., and M. Sato. 1976. Water response in frog taste cells. *Comparative Biochemistry and Physiology* 54A:149–156. (7)

Alberch, P. 1981. Convergence and parallelism in foot evolution in the Neotropical salamander genus *Bolitoglossa:* 1. Function. *Evolution* 35:84–100. (11)

Alberch, P., and E. A. Gale. 1985. A developmental analysis of an evolutionary trend: Digital reduction in amphibians. *Evolution* 39:8–23. (11)

Alberch, P., E. A. Gale, and P. R. Larsen. 1986. Plasma T_4 and T_3 levels naturally metamorphosing *Eurycea bislineata* (Amphibia: Plethodontidae). *General and Comparative Endocrinology* 61:153–163. (16)

Alexander, G. 1933. Seasonal variation in a tropical toad. *University of Colorado Studies* 20:195–205. (15)

Alexander, S. S., and C. W. Bellerby. 1938. Experimental studies on the sexual cycle of the South African clawed toad (*Xenopus laevis*). *Journal of Experimental Biology* 15:74–81. (10,15)

Alexander, T. R. 1964. Observations on the feeding behavior of *Bufo marinus* (Linne). *Herpetologica* 20:255–259. (13)

Alford, R. A., and M. L. Crump. 1982. Habitat partitioning among size classes of larval southern leopard frogs, *Rana utricularia*. *Copeia* 1982:367–373. (14)

Alfs, B., and H. Schneider. 1973. Vergleichend-anatomische Untersuchungen am Labyrinth zentraleuropäisher Froschlurch-Arten. *Zeitschrift für Morphologie der Tiere* 76:129–143. (16)

Allen, B. M. 1938. The endocrine control of amphibian metamorphosis. *Biological Reviews* 13:1–19. (16)

Alley, K. E., and M. D. Barnes. 1983. Birth dates of trigeminal motoneurons and metamorphic reorganization of the jaw myoneural system in frogs. *Journal of Comparative Neurology* 218:395–405. (11)

Alley, K. E., and J. A. Cameron. 1983. Turnover of anuran jaw muscles during metamorphosis. *Anatomical Record* 205:7A–8A. (11,16)

———. 1984. Cellular features of metamorphic myofiber turnover in the leopard frog. *Anatomical Record* 208:7A. (11)

Allison, J. D., and W. Wilczynski. 1989. An HRP study of pathways linking the preoptic area to auditory nuclei in *Hyla cinerea*. *Society for Neuroscience Abstracts* 15:374. (2)

Allison, R. M. 1956. Failure of enforced hibernation to inhibit breeding in the frog (*Rana temporaria*). *Nature* 177:342. (15)

Alonso-Bedate, M., and M. J. Delgado. 1983. Effects of prolactin and bromocriptine in *Discoglossus pictus* (anuran amphibian. Otth) tadpoles. *Comparative Biochemistry and Physiology* 74A:765–772. (16)

Alp, P. R., and E. A. Newsholme, and V. A. Zammit. 1976. Activities of citrate synthase and NAD$^+$-linked and NADP$^+$-linked isocitrate dehydrogenase in muscle from vertebrates and invertebrates. *Biochemical Journal* 154:689–700. (14)

Alpert L. C., J. R. Brawer, I. M. D. Jackson, and S. Reichlin. 1976. Localization of LHRH in neurons in frog brain (*Rana pipiens* and *Rana catesbeiana*). *Endocrinology* 98:910–921. (15)

Altig, R., J. P. Kelly, M. Wells, and J. Phillips. 1975. Digestive enzymes of seven species of anuran tadpoles. *Herpetologica* 31:104–108. (16)

Alvarado, R. H. 1967. The significance of grouping on water conservation in *Ambystoma*. *Copeia* 1967:667–668. (5)

———. 1972. The effects of dehydration on water and electrolytes in *Ambystoma tigrinum*. *Physiological Zoology* 45:43–53. (6)

———. 1979. Amphibians. In *Comparative Physiology of Osmoregulation in Animals*, ed. G. M. O. Maloiy, 1:261–303. New York: Academic Press. (6,16)

Alvarado, R. H., and T. C. Cox. 1985. Action of polyvalent cations on sodium transport across skin of larval and adult *Rana catesbeiana*. *Journal of Experimental Zoology* 236:127–136. (5,16)

Alvarado, R. H., and T. H. Dietz. 1970a. Effect of salt depletion on hydromineral balance in larval *Ambystoma gracile:* 1. Ionic composition. *Comparative Biochemistry and Physiology* 33:85–92. (16)

———. 1970b. Effect of salt depletion on hydromineral balance in larval *Ambystoma gracile:* 2. Kinetics of ion exchange. *Comparative Biochemistry and Physiology* 33:93–110. (5)

Alvarado, R. H., T. H. Dietz, and T. L. Mullen. 1975. Chloride transport across isolated skin of *Rana pipiens*. *American Journal of Physiology* 229:869–876. (5)

Alvarado, R. H., and S. R. Johnson. 1965. Effects of arginine vasotocin and oxytocin on sodium and water balance in *Ambystoma*. *Comparative Biochemistry and Physiology* 16:531–546. (5,16)

———. 1966. The effects of neurohypophysial hormones on water and sodium balance in larval and adult bullfrogs (*Rana catesbeiana*). *Comparative Biochemistry and Physiology* 18:549–561. (5,16)

Alvarado, R. H., and L. B. Kirschner. 1963. Osmotic and ionic regulation in *Ambystoma tigrinum*. *Comparative Biochemistry and Physiology* 10:55–67. (5,16)

———. 1964. Effect of aldosterone on sodium fluxes in larval *Ambystoma tigrinum*. *Nature* 202:922–923. (5,16)

Alvarado, R. H., and A. Moody. 1970. Sodium and chloride transport in tadpoles of the bullfrog *Rana catesbeiana*. *American Journal of Physiology* 218:1510–1516. (5,16)

Alvarado, R. H., A. M. Poole, and T. L. Mullen. 1975. Chloride balance in *Rana pipiens*. *American Journal of Physiology* 229:861–868. (5)

Alvarado, R. H., and D. F. Stiffler. 1970. The transepithelial potential difference in intact larval and adult salamanders. *Comparative Biochemistry and Physiology* 33:209–212. (5)

Amara, S. J., V. Jonas, M. G. Rosenfield, E. S. Ong, and R. M. Evans. 1982. Alternative RNA processing in calcitonin gene expression generated mRNA encoding different polypeptide products. *Nature* (London) 298:240–244. (3)

Amir, S. M. 1972. Dissociation of glycoprotein hormones. *Acta Endocrinologica* 70:21–34. (15)

Anagnostopoulos, T., and G. Planelles. 1987. Cell and luminal activities of chloride, potassium, sodium, and protons in the late distal tubule of *Necturus* kidney. *Journal of Physiology* (London) 393:73–89. (5)

an der Heiden, U., and G. Roth. 1987. Mathematical model and simulation of retina and tectum opticum of lower vertebrates. *Acta Biotheoretica* 36:179–212. (13)

Andersen, B., and H. H. Ussing. 1957. Solvent drag on nonelectrolytes during osmotic flow through isolated toad skin and its response to antidiuretic hormone. *Acta Physiologica Scandinavica* 39:228–239. (5)

Andersen, M. L. 1978. The comparative myology and osteology of the carpus and tarsus of selected anurans. Ph.D. diss., University of Kansas, Lawrence. (11)

Anderson, J. D., and R. E. Graham. 1967. Vertical migration and stratification of larval *Ambystoma*. *Copeia* 1967:371–374. (9)

Anderson, J. D., and G. K. Williamson. 1974. Nocturnal stratification in larvae of the mole salamander, *Ambystoma talpoideum*. *Herpetologica* 30:28–29. (9)

Anderson, P. A. V., and K. A. Hamilton. 1987. Intracellular recordings from isolated salamander olfactory receptor neurons. *Neuroscience* 21:167–173. (16)

Anderson, P. K. 1954. Studies in the ecology of the narrow-mouthed toad, *Microhyla carolinensis carolinensis*. *Tulane Studies in Zoology* 2:15–16. (15)

Anderson, P. L. 1943. The normal development of *Triturus pyrrhogaster*. *Anatomical Record* 86:58–69. (16)

Anderson, R. A., and W. Karasov. 1981. Contrasts in energy intake and expenditure in sit-and-wait and widely foraging lizards. *Oecologia* (Berlin) 49:67–72. (14)

Andersson, B., and Y. Zotterman. 1950. The water taste in the frog. *Acta Physiologica Scandinavica* 20:95–100. (7)

Andersson, M. 1982a. Female choice selects for extreme tail length in widow birds. *Nature* 299:818–820. (14)

———. 1982b. Sexual selection, natural selection, and quality advertisement. *Biological Journal of the Linnean Society* 17:375–393. (14)

Andreoletti, G. E., V. Mazzi, C. Vellano, and M. Sacerdote. 1980. Effects of LHRH on spermiation in the winter newt, *Triturus cristatus carnifex* (Laur.). *Monitore Zoologico Italiano*, n.s. 14:255–262. (15)

Andrews, R. M. 1979. The lizard *Corytophanes cristatus:* An extreme "sit-and-wait" predator. *Biotropica* 11:6–139. (14)

———. 1984. Energetics of sit-and-wait and widely-foraging lizard predators. In *Vertebrate Ecology and Systematics: A Tribute to Henry S. Fitch,* ed. R. A. Siegel, L. E. Hunt, J. L. Knight, L. Malaret, and N. Zuschlag, 137–144. Lawrence: University of Kansas Museum of Natural History. (14)

Andrews, R. M., and F. H. Pough. 1985. Metabolism of squamate reptiles: Allometric and ecological relationships. *Physiological Zoology* 58:214–231. (12,14)

Angaut-Petit, D., and A. Mallart. 1979. Dual innervation of end-plate sites and its consequences for neuromuscular transmission in muscles of adult *Xenopus laevis*. *Journal of Physiology* (London) 289:203–218. (11)

Angle, J. P. 1969. The reproductive cycle of the northern ravine salamander, *Plethodon richmondi richmondi,* in the Valley and Ridge Province of Pennsylvania and Maryland. *Journal of Washington Academy of Science* 59:192–202. (15)

Anthony, R., and H. Vallois. 1914. Sur la signification des éléments ventraux de la ceinture scapulaire chez les batraciens. *Bibliographica Anatomica* 24:218–276. (11)

Anzil, A. P., A. Biezer, and A. Wernig. 1984. Light and electron microscopic identification of nerve terminal sprouting and retraction in normal adult frog muscle. *Journal of Physiology* (London) 350:393–399. (11)

Appleton, A. B. 1928. The muscles and nerves of the post-axial region of the tetrapod thigh. *Journal of Anatomy* (London) 62:364–438. (11)

Arak, A. 1983a. Male-male competition and mate choice in anuran amphibians. In *Mate Choice,* ed. P. Bateson, 181–210. New York: Cambridge University Press. (14)

———. 1983b. Sexual selection by male-male competition in natterjack toad choruses. *Nature* 306:261–262. (14)

———. 1988. Sexual dimorphism in body size: A model and a test. *Evolution* 42:820–825. (14)

Arieff, A. I., R. Guisado, and V. C. Lazarowitz. 1977. Pathophysiology of hyperosmolar states. In *Disturbances in Body Fluid Osmolality,* ed. T. E. Andreoli, J. J. Grantham, and F. C. Rector, 227–250. Bethesda, MD: American Physiological Society. (6)

Ariëns-Kappers, C. U., G. C. Huber, and E. C. Crosby. 1960. *The Comparative Anatomy of the Nervous System of Vertebrates, Including Man*. New York: Hafner Publishing Company. (2)

Arnold, E. N., and J. A. Burton. 1978. *A Field Guide to the Reptiles and Amphibians of Britain and Europe*. London: Collins. (10)

Arnold, S. J. 1977. The evolution of courtship behavior in New World salamanders with a comment on Old World salamandrids. In *The Reproductive Biology of Amphibians,* ed. D. H. Taylor and S. I. Guttman, 141–183. New York: Plenum Press. (14)

———. 1982. A quantitative approach to antipredator performance: Salamander defense against snake attack. *Copeia* 1982:247–253. (14)

———. 1983. Morphology, performance, and fitness. *American Zoologist* 23:347–361. (14)

———. 1987. Genetic correlation and the evolution of physiology. In *New Directions in Ecological Physiology,* ed. M. E. Feder, A. F. Bennett, W. W. Burggren, and R. B. Huey, 189–215. New York: Cambridge University Press. (12)

Arnold, S. J., and R. J. Wassersug. 1978. Differential predation on metamorphic anurans by garter snakes (*Thamnophis*): Social behavior as a possible defense. *Ecology* 59:1014–1022. (16)

Aroesty, J., and J. F. Gross. 1970. Convection and diffusion in the microcirculation. *Microvascular Research* 2:247–267. (5)

Aron, M. 1924. Recherches morphologiques et expérimentales sur le déterminisme des caracteres sexuels mâles chez les urodèles. *Archives Biologique* (Paris) 34:1–166. (15)

Aronson, L. R., and G. K. Noble. 1945. The sexual behavior of Anura: 2. Neural mechanisms controlling mating in the leopard frog. *Bulletin of the American Museum of Natural History* 86:83–140. (2)

Aronsson, S. 1976. The ontogenesis of monoaminergic nerve fibers in the hypophysis of *Rana temporaria* with special reference to the pars distalis. *Cell and Tissue Research* 171:437–448. (16)

Arzt, A. H., W. L. Silver, J. R. Mason, and L. Clark. 1986. Olfactory responses of aquatic and terrestrial tiger salamanders to airborne and waterborne stimuli. *Journal of Comparative Physiology* 158A:479–487. (16)

Ashmore, J. F., and S. Pitchford. 1985. Evidence for electrical resonant tuning in hair cells of the frog amphibian papilla. *Journal of Physiology* (London) 336:39P. (2)

Ashton, R. E. 1975. A study of movement, home range, and winter behavior of *Desmognathus fuscus* (Rafinesque). *Journal of Herpetology* 9:85–91. (10)

Ashton, R. E., and P. S. Ashton. 1978. Movements and winter behavior of *Eurycea bislineata* (Amphibia, Urodela, Plethodontidae). *Journal of Herpetology* 12:295–298. (10)

Ask-Upmark, E. 1935. The carotid sinus and cerebral circulation. *Acta Psychiatrica et Neurologica,* suppl. 6. (7)

Asmussen, G., and A. Kiessling. 1970. Die Muskelfasersorten des Frosches: Ihre Identifikation und die Gesetzmässigkeiten ihrer Anordnung in der Skelettmuskulatur. *Acta Biologica Medica Germanica* 24:871–889. (11)

———. 1974. Characterisierung von besonderen Muskelfasergruppen in der Skeletmuskulatur des Frosches durch ihre motorische Innervation und ihre Gefässversorgung. *Acta Anatomica* 90:226–242. (11)

Aspey, W. P., and S. I. Lustick. 1983. *Behavioral Energetics*. Columbus: Ohio State University Press. (14)

Athanasiu, J. 1900. Über den Respirationswechsel des Frosches in den verschiedenen Jahreszeiten. *Archiv für die gesamte Physiologie des Menschen und der Tiere* 79:400–422. (12)

Athanasiu, J., and J. Dragoin. 1910. Die Wanderung des Fettes im Froschkörper im Verhältnis zur Jahreszeit. *Archiv für die gesamte Physiologie* 132:296–306. (15)

Atkinson, B. G. 1981. Biological basis of tissue regression and synthesis. In *Metamorphosis: A Problem in Developmental Biology,* ed. L. I. Gilbert and E. Frieden, 397–444. New York: Plenum Press. (16)

Atkinson, B. G., K. H. Atkinson, J. J. Just, and E. Frieden. 1972. DNA synthesis in *Rana catesbeiana* tadpole liver during spontaneous and triiodothyronine-induced metamorphosis. *Developmental Biology* 29:162–175. (16)

Atkinson, B. G., and J. J. Just. 1975. Biochemical and histological changes in the respiratory system of *Rana catesbeiana* during normal and induced metamorphosis. *Developmental Biology* 45:151–165. (16)

Auffenberg, W. 1959. The epaxial musculature of *Siren, Amphiuma,* and *Necturus* (Amphibia). *Bulletin of the Florida State Museum* 4:253–265. (11)

———. 1962. A review of the trunk musculature in the limbless land vertebrates. *American Zoologist* 2:183–190. (11)

Avery, R. A. 1982. Field studies in body temperatures and thermoregulation. In *Biology of the Reptilia,* vol. 12, ed. C. Gans and F. H. Pough, 93–166. New York: Academic Press. (9,12)

Avila, V. L., and P. G. Frye. 1977. Feeding behavior in the African clawed frog (*Xenopus laevis* Daudin). *Herpetologica* 33:152–161. (11)

Azuma, T., A. Binia, and M. B. Visscher. 1965. Adrenergic mechanisms in the bullfrog and turtle. *American Journal of Physiology* 209:1287–1294. (3)

Babak, E. 1907. Über die funktionelle Anpassung der ausseren Kiement bei Sauerstoffmange. *Zentralblatt für Physiologie* 21:97. (16)

Babkin, B. P. 1924. The influence of natural chemical stimuli on the movements of the frog's stomach. *Quarterly Journal of Experimental Physiology* 14:259–277. (13)

Bachmann, K. 1969. Temperature adaptations of amphibian embryos. *American Naturalist* 103:115–130. (8,9)

Backstrom, A. C., and T. Reuter. 1975. Receptive field organization of ganglion cells in the frog retina: Contributions from cones, green rods, and red rods. *Journal of Physiology* (London) 246:79–107. (2)

Bagnara, J. T. 1960. Pineal regulation of the body-lightening reaction in amphibian larvae. *Science* 132:1481–1483. (3,9)

———. 1963. The pineal and body-lightening reaction of larval amphibians. *General and Comparative Endocrinology* 3:86–100. (16)

———. 1965. Pineal regulation of body blanching in amphibian larvae. *Progress in Brain Research* 10:489–506. (16)

———. 1976. Color change. In *Physiology of the Amphibia*, ed. B. Lofts, 3:1–52. New York: Academic Press. (3,16)

———. 1983. Developmental aspects of vertebrate chromatophores. *American Zoologist* 23:465–478. (3)

———. 1987. The neural crest as a source of stem cells. In *Developmental and Evolutionary Aspects of the Neural Crest*, ed. P. Maderson, 57–87. New York: John Wiley and Sons. (3)

Bagnara, J. T., and M. E. Hadley. 1973. *Chromatophores and Color Change: The Comparative Physiology of Animal Pigmentation*. Englewood Cliffs, N.J.: Prentice Hall. (3,13)

Bagnara, J. T., J. Matsumoto, W. Ferris. S. K. Frost, W. A. Turner, Jr., T. T. Tchen, and J. D. Taylor. 1979. Common origin of pigment cells. *Science* 203:410–415. (16)

Bagnara, J. T., J. D. Taylor, and M. E. Hadley. 1968. The dermal chromatophore unit. *Journal of Cell Biology* 38:67–69. (3,16)

Bagshaw, R. J. 1985. Evolution of cardiovascular baroreceptor control. *Biological Reviews* 60:121–162. (7)

Bailey, W. J., and G. K. Morris. 1986. Confusion of phonotaxis by masking sounds in the bushcricket *Conocephalus brevipennis* (Tettigoniidae: Conocephalinae). *Ethology* 73:19–28. (14)

Baird, I. L. 1951. An anatomical study of certain salamanders of the genus *Pseudoeurycea*. *University of Kansas Science Bulletin* 34:221–265. (11)

Baker, M. C. 1969. The effects of severing the opercularis muscle on body orientation of the leopard frog, *Rana pipiens*. *Copeia* 1969:613–616. (11)

Baker, P. C. 1969. Melatonin levels in developing *Xenopus laevis*. *Comparative Biochemistry and Physiology* 28:1387–1393. (16)

Baker, P. C., and K. M. Hoff. 1971. Melatonin localization in the eyes of larval *Xenopus*. *Comparative Biochemistry and Physiology* 39A:879–881. (16)

Baker, P. C., W. B. Quay, and J. Axelrod. 1965. Development of hydroxyindole-O-methyl transferase activity in the eye and brain of the amphibian *Xenopus laevis*. *Life Sciences* 4:1981–1987. (3)

Baker, R. C., M. A. Corner, and W. A. M. Veltman. 1978. Topography of cutaneous mechanoreceptive neurons in the dorsal root ganglia of skin-grafted frogs. *Journal of Physiology* (London) 284:181–192. (16)

Bakken, G. S. 1981. A two-dimensional operative-temperature model for thermal energy management by animals. *Journal of Thermal Biology* 6:23–30. (4)

———. 1989. Influence of arboreal perch properties on the operative temperature experienced by small lizards. *Ecology* 70:922–930. (4)

Bakken, G. S., and D. M. Gates. 1975. Heat-transfer analysis of animals: Some implications for field ecology, physiology, and evolution. In *Perspectives in Biophysical Ecology*, ed. D. M. Gates and R. Schmerl, 255–290. New York: Springer-Verlag. (4)

Bakken, G. S., D. M. Gates, T. H. Strunk, and M. Kleiber. 1974. Linearized heat transfer relations in biology. *Science* 183:976–978. (4)

Bakken, G. S., W. R. Santee, and D. J. Erskine. 1985. Operative and standard operative temperature: Tools for thermal energetic studies. *American Zoologist* 25:933–944. (4)

Bakker, H. R., and S. D. Bradshaw. 1977. Effect of hypothalamic lesions on water metabolism of the toad *Bufo marinus*. *Journal of Endocrinology* 75:161–172. (5,6)

Baksi, S. N., S. M. Galli-Gallardo, and P. K. T. Pang. 1977. Vitamin D metabolism in Amphibia and fish. *Federation of the American Societies of Biology and Medicine* 36:1097. (3)

Baksi, S. N., A. D. Kenny, S. M. Galli-Gallardo, and P. K. T. Pang. 1978. Vitamin D metabolism in bullfrogs and Japanese quail: Effects

of estradiol and prolactin. *General and Comparative Endocrinology* 35:258–262. (3)

Baldwin, F. M. 1918. Pharyngeal derivatives of *Amblystoma*. *Journal of Morphology* 30:605–680. (16)

Baldwin, G. F., and P. J. Bentley. 1980. Calcium metabolism in bullfrog tadpoles (*Rana catesbeiana*). *Journal of Experimental Biology* 88:357–365. (3,5,16)

———. 1981a. Calcium exchange in two neotenic urodeles: *Necturus maculosus* and *Ambystoma tigrinum:* Role of the integument. *Comparative Biochemistry and Physiology* 70A:65–68. (3,5)

———. 1981b. A role of skin in the Ca metabolism of frogs? *Comparative Biochemistry and Physiology* 68A:181–185. (3,5)

———. 1982. Roles of the skin and gills in sodium and water exchanges in neotenic urodele amphibians. *American Journal of Physiology* 242:R94–R96. (5,16)

Baldwin, J., G. Friedman, and H. Lillywhite. 1977. Adaptation to temporary muscle anoxia in anurans: Activities of glycolytic enzymes in muscles from species differing in their ability to produce lactate during exercise. *Australian Journal of Zoology* 25:15–18. (11,12,14)

Balinsky, J. B. 1970. Nitrogen metabolism in amphibians. In *Comparative Biochemistry of Nitrogen Metabolism*, vol. 2, *The Vertebrates*, ed. J. W. Campbell, 519–637. New York: Academic Press. (5,6)

———. 1981. Adaptation of nitrogen metabolism to hyperosmotic environment in Amphibia. *Journal of Experimental Zoology* 215:335–350. (6,10)

Balinsky, J. B., S. M. Chemaly, A. E. Currin, A. R. Lee, R. L. Thompson, and D. R. Van der Westhuizen. 1976. A comparative study of enzymes of urea and uric acid metabolism in different species of Amphibia, and the adaptation to the environment of the tree frog *Chiromantis xerampelina* Peters. *Comparative Biochemistry and Physiology* 54B:549–555. (6)

Balinsky, J. B., E. L. Choritz, C. G. Coe, and G. S. van der Schans. 1967. Amino acid metabolism and urea synthesis in naturally aestivating *Xenopus laevis*. *Comparative Biochemistry and Physiology* 22:59–68. (10)

Balinsky, J. B., M. M. Cragg, and E. Baldwin. 1961. The adaptation of amphibian waste nitrogen excretion to dehydration. *Comparative Biochemistry and Physiology* 3:236–244. (5,6)

Balinsky, J. B., S. E. Dicker, and A. B. Elliott. 1972. The effect of long-term adaptation to different levels of salinity on urea synthesis and tissue amino acid concentrations in *Rana cancrivora*. *Comparative Biochemistry and Physiology* 43B:71–82. (6)

Ball, J. N. 1981. Hypothalamic control of the pars distalis in fishes, amphibians, and reptiles. *General and Comparative Endocrinology* 44:135–170. (3,15)

Ballintijn, C. M., and O. S. Bamford. 1975. Proprioceptive motor control in fish respiration. *Journal of Experimental Biology* 62:99–114. (11)

Balls, M., R. H. Clothier, J. M. Rowles, N. A. Kiteley, and G. W. Bennett. 1985. TRH distribution levels, and significance during the development of *Xenopus laevis*. In *Metamorphosis: The Eighth Symposium of the British Society for Developmental Biology*, ed. M. Balls and M. Bownes, 260–272. Oxford: Clarendon Press. (16)

Balogun, R. A., and O. Fisher. 1970. Studies on the digestive enzymes of the common African toad *Bufo regularis* Boulenger. *Comparative Biochemistry and Physiology* 33:813–820. (13)

Bamford, O. S. 1974. Oxygen reception in the rainbow trout (*Salmo gairdneri*). *Comparative Biochemistry and Physiology* 48A:69–76. (7)

Bamford, O. S., and D. R. Jones. 1974. On the initiation of apnoea and some cardiovascular responses to submergence in ducks. *Respiration Physiology* 22:199–216. (7)

Banerji, A., and C. Prasad. 1982. The postnatal development of the pituitary thyrotropin-releasing hormone receptor in male and female rats. *Endocrinology* 110:663–664. (16)

Baranska, J., and P. Wlodawer. 1969. Influence of temperature on the composition of fatty acids and on lipogenesis in frog tissues. *Comparative Biochemistry and Physiology* 28:553–570. (8,10)

Barber, B. J., and E. C. Crawford, Jr. 1977. A stochastic dual-limit hypothesis for behavioral thermoregulation in lizards. *Physiological Zoology* 50:53–60. (9)

———. 1979. Dual threshold control of peripheral thermoregulation in the lizard *Dipsosaurus dorsalis*. *Physiological Zoology* 52:250–263. (9)

Barbour, T., and A. Loveridge. 1928. A comparative study of the herpetological journal of the Uluguru and Usambara Mountains, Tanganyika Territory, with descriptions of new species. *Memoirs of the Museum of Comparative Zoology* (Harvard) 50:87–265. (13)

Barclay, D. R. 1946. The mechanics of amphibian locomotion. *Journal of Experimental Biology* 23:177–203. (11)

Barets, A. 1952. Différences dans le mode d'innervation des diverses portions du muscle lateral et leurs rapports avec la structure musculaire chez le poisson-chat. *Archives d'Anatomie Microscopique et de Morphologie Expérimentale* 41:305–331. (11)

———. 1956. Les récepteurs intra-musculaire des nageoires chez les selachiens. *Archives d'Anatomie Microscopique et de Morphologie Expérimentale* 45:254–260. (11)

Bargmann, W., and G. von Hehn. 1969. Über epithelio-retikuläre Fettorgane: Untersuchungen am Gonadenfettkörper von Amphibien. *Zeitschrift für Zellforschung* 94:1–18. (15)

Barica, J., and J. A. Mathias. 1979. Oxygen depletion and winterkill risk in small prairie lakes under extended ice cover. *Journal of the Fisheries Research Board of Canada* 36:980–986. (10)

Barker, D. 1974. The morphology of muscle receptors. In *Handbook of Sensory Physiology*, vol. 3, *Muscle Receptors*, ed. C. C. Hunt, 1–190. Berlin: Springer-Verlag. (11)

Barlet, J. P. 1982. Comparative physiology of calcitonin. In *Endocrinology of Calcium Metabolism*, ed. J. A. Parson, 235–270. New York: Raven Press. (3)

Barlow, H. B. 1956. Retinal noise and absolute threshold. *Journal of the Optical Society of America* 46:634–639. (2)

Barnawell, E. B. 1982. Central nervous system regulation of pituitary melanocyte-stimulating hormone. *Advances in Comparative Physiology and Biochemistry* 8:53–71. (3)

Barnes, M. D., and K. E. Alley. 1983. Maturation and recycling of trigeminal motoneurons in anuran larvae. *Journal of Comparative Neurology* 218:406–414. (2,11)

Barnikol, W. K. R., and O. Burkhard. 1979. The fine structure of O_2 binding in animals: *Rana esculenta*. *Pflugers Archiv* 379:R27. (5)

Barrett, A. N. 1981. A theoretical explanation of directional hearing characteristics in Amphibia. *Journal of Theoretical Biology* 93:591–596. (2)

Barrington, E. J. W. 1945. The delayed development of the stomach of the frog. *Proceedings of the Zoological Society of London* 116:1–21. (16)

Bartholomew, G. A. 1982. Physiological control of body temperature. In *Biology of the Reptilia*, vol. 12, ed. C. Gans and F. H. Pough, 167–212. New York: Academic Press. (9)

———. 1987. Interspecific comparison as a tool for physiological ecologists. In *New Directions in Ecological Physiology*, ed. M. E. Feder, A. F. Bennett, W. W. Burggren, and R. B. Huey, 11–37. Cambridge: Cambridge University Press. (1)

Bartholomew, G. A., D. Vleck, and C. M. Vleck. 1981. Instantaneous measurement of oxygen consumption during pre-flight warm-up and post-flight cooling in sphingid moths. *Journal of Experimental Biology* 90:17–32. (12)

Bartlett, G. R. 1980. Phosphate compounds in vertebrate red blood cells. *American Zoologist* 20:103–114. (16)

Bastert, C. 1929. Über die Regulierung des Sauerstoffverbrauches aus der Lunge der Frösche, im Hinblick auf ihr Tauchvermögen. *Zeitschrift für vergleichende Physiologie* 9:212–258. (12)

Bastide, F., and S. Jard. 1968. Actions de la noradrénaline et de l'oxytocine sur le transport actif de sodium et la perméabilité à l'eau de la peau de grenouille: Rôle du 3',5'-AMP cyclique. *Biochimica et Biophysica Acta* 150:113–123. (6)

Basu, S. L., and A. Mondal. 1961. The normal spermatogenetic cycle of the common Indian frog, *Rana tigrina* Daud. *Folia Biologica* 9:135–142. (15)

Baylor, D. A., B. J. Nunn, and J. F. Schnapf. 1984. The photocurrent, noise, and spectral sensitivity of rods of the monkey *Macaca fascicularis*. *Journal of Morphology* 136:469–488. (2)

Beach, D. H., and M. Jacobson. 1979a. Influences of thyroxin on cell proliferation in the retina of the clawed frog at different ages. *Journal of Comparative Neurology* 183:615–624. (2)

———. 1979b. Patterns of cell proliferation in the retina of the clawed frog during development. *Journal of Comparative Neurology* 183:603–614. (16)

Beattie, R. C. 1987. The reproductive biology of common frog (*Rana temporaria*) populations from different altitudes in northern England. *Journal of Zoology* (London) 211:387–398. (8)

Beauchat, C. A., F. H. Pough, and M. M. Stewart. 1984. Response to

simultaneous dehydration and thermal stress in three species of Puerto Rican frogs. *Journal of Comparative Physiology* 154B:579–585. (6)

Beaumont, A. 1968. Les types cellulaires dan le pancréas endocrine des larves d'amphibiens anoures. *Journal of Microscopy* 7:21a. (16)

Beauwens, R., V. Beaujeans, M. Zizi, M. Rentmeesters, and J. Crabbe. 1986. Increased chloride permeability of amphibian epithelia treated with aldosterone. *Pflugers Archiv* 407:620–624. (5)

Bebak, B. 1958. Thermal studies in the development of the grass frog *Rana temporaria* L. *Bulletin Polonaise Scientia Biologica* 6:367–369. (10)

Beckenbach, A. T. 1976. Influence of body size and temperature on the critical oxygen tension of some plethodontid salamanders. *Physiological Zoology* 48:338–347. (6,12)

Becker, R. P., and R. E. Lombard. 1977. Structural correlates of function in the "opercularis" muscle of amphibians. *Cell and Tissue Research* 175:499–522. (11)

Beddard, F. E. 1895a. On some points in the anatomy of *Pipa americana*. *Proceedings of the Zoological Society of London* 1895:827–841. (11)

———. 1895b. On the diaphragm and on the muscular anatomy of *Xenopus*, with remarks on its affinities. *Proceedings of the Zoological Society of London* 1895:841–850. (11)

———. 1907. Notes on the anatomy of a species of frog of the genus *Megalophrys*, with references to other genera of Batrachia. *Proceedings of the Zoological Society of London* 1907:324–352. (11)

———. 1908a. On the musculature and other points in the anatomy of the engystomatid frog *Breviceps verrucosus*. *Proceedings of the Zoological Society of London* 1908:11–41. (11)

———. 1908b. Some notes on the muscular and visceral anatomy of the batrachian genus *Hemisus*, with notes on the lymph-hearts of this and other genera. *Proceedings of the Zoological Society of London* 1908:894–934. (11)

Beiswenger, R. E. 1977. Diel patterns of aggregative behavior in tadpoles of *Bufo americanus*, in relation to light and temperature. *Ecology* 58:98–108. (9)

———. 1978. Responses of *Bufo* tadpoles (Amphibia, Anura, Bufonidae) to laboratory gradients of temperature. *Journal of Herpetology* 12:499–504. (9)

Beitinger, T. L., and L. C. Fitzpatrick. 1979. Physiological and ecological correlates of preferred temperature in fish. *American Zoologist* 19:319–329. (9)

Beitinger, T. L., and J. J. Magnuson. 1975. Influence of social rank and size on thermoselection behavior of bluegill (*Lepomis macrochirus*). *Journal of Fisheries Research Board of Canada* 32:2133–2136. (9)

Belehrádek, J., and J. S. Huxley. 1927. Changes in oxygen consumption during metamorphosis induced by thyroid administration in the axolotl. *Journal of Physiology* (London) 64:267–278. (12)

Belenky, M. A., V. K. Chetverukhin, and A. L. Polenov. 1973a. The hypothalamo-hypophysial system of the frog *Rana temporaria*: 1. Morphometric analysis of functional states of the median eminence. *General and Comparative Endocrinology* 21:241–249. (16)

———. 1973b. The hypothalamo-hypophysial system of the frog *Rana temporaria*: 2. Functional morphology of the external zone of the median eminence during metamorphosis. *General and Comparative Endocrinology* 21:250–261. (16)

Bell, G. 1977. The life of the smooth newt (*Triturus vulgaris*) after metamorphosis. *Ecological Monographs* 47:279–299. (15)

Bellerby, C. W. 1937. Experimental studies on the sexual cycle of the South African clawed toad (*Xenopus laevis*). *Journal of Experimental Biology* 15:82–90. (15)

Bellis, E. D. 1957. The effects of temperature on salientian breeding calls. *Copeia* 1957:85–89. (8)

———. 1961. Growth of the wood frog, *Rana sylvatica*. *Copeia* 1961:74–77. (15)

Bemis, W. E. 1987. Convergent evolution of jaw-opening muscles in lepidosirenid lungfishes and tetrapods. *Canadian Journal of Zoology* 65:2814–2817. (11)

Bemis, W. E., and E. Findeis. 1986. Tongue projection kinematics of the salamander, *Taricha torosa*. *American Zoologist* 26:83A. (11)

Bemis, W. E., K. Schwenk, and M. H. Wake. 1983. Morphology and function of the feeding apparatus in *Dermophis mexicanus* (Amphibia: Gymnophiona). *Zoological Journal of the Linnean Society* 77:75–96. (11,14,16)

Ben Brahim, O., J. Mesnard, and J. Hourdry. 1987. Hormonal control of the intestinal brush border enzyme activities in developing anuran amphibians: 2. Effects of glucocorticoids and insulin during experimental metamorphosis. *General and Comparative Endocrinology* 65:489–495. (16)

Benchetrit, G., J. Armand, and P. Dejours. 1977. Ventilatory chemoreflex drive in the tortoise, *Testudo horsfieldi. Respiration Physiology* 31:183–191. (7)

Bennett, A. F. 1974. Enzymatic correlates of activity metabolism in anuran amphibians. *American Journal of Physiology* 226:1149–1151. (12,14)

———. 1978. Activity metabolism of the lower vertebrates. *Annual Review of Physiology* 40:447–469. (4,7,12,14)

———. 1980a. The metabolic foundations of vertebrate behavior. *BioScience* 30:452–456. (9,12)

———. 1980b. The thermal dependence of lizard behavior. *Animal Behaviour* 28:752–762. (8)

———. 1982. The energetics of reptilian activity. In *Biology of the Reptilia,* vol. 13, C. Gans and F. H. Pough, 155–199. New York: Academic Press (12)

———. 1984. Thermal dependence of muscle function. *American Journal of Physiology* 247:R217–R229. (8,12)

———. 1985. Energetics and locomotion. In *Functional Vertebrate Morphology,* ed. M. Hildebrand, D. M. Bramble, K. F. Liem, and D. B. Wake, 173–184. Cambridge, MA: Harvard University Press. (12)

———. 1986. Measuring behavioral energetics. In *Predator-Prey Relationships,* ed. M. E. Feder and G. V. Lauder, 69–81. Chicago: University of Chicago Press. (12)

———. 1987. Interindividual variability: An underutilized resource. In *New Directions in Ecological Physiology,* ed. M. E. Feder, A. F. Bennett, W. W. Burggren, and R. B. Huey, 147–169. Cambridge, Cambridge University Press. (12)

Bennett, A. F., and W. R. Dawson. 1976. Metabolism. In *Biology of the Reptilia,* vol. 5, C. Gans and W. R. Dawson, 127–223. New York: Academic Press. (12)

Bennett, A. F., T. T. Gleeson, and G. C. Gorman. 1981. Anaerobic metabolism in a lizard (*Anolis bonairensis*) under natural conditions. *Physiological Zoology* 54:237–241. (14)

Bennett, A. F., and G. C. Gorman. 1979. Population density, thermal relations, and energetics of a tropical insular lizard community. *Oecologia* (Berlin) 42:339–358. (14)

Bennett, A. F., and L. D. Houck. 1983. The energetic cost of courtship and aggression in a plethodontid salamander. *Ecology* 64:979–83. (12,14)

Bennett, A. F., R. B. Huey, and H. John-Alder. 1984. Physiological correlates of natural activity and locomotor capacity in two species of lacertid lizards. *Journal of Comparative Physiology* 154B:113–118. (14)

———. 1986. Body temperature, sprint speed, and muscle contraction kinetics in lizards. *Physiologist* 29:179.

Bennett, A. F., and H. B. John-Alder. 1984. The effect of body temperature on the locomotor energetics of lizards. *Journal of Comparative Physiology* 155:21–27. (12)

Bennett, A. F., and P. Licht. 1972. Anaerobic metabolism during activity in lizards. *Journal of Comparative Physiology* 81:277–288. (12)

———. 1973. Relative contributions of anaerobic and aerobic energy production during activity in Amphibia. *Journal of Comparative Physiology* 87B:351–360. (8,12,14)

———. 1974. Anaerobic metabolism during activity in amphibians. *Comparative Biochemistry and Physiology* 48A:319–327. (8,12,14)

Bennett, A. F., and J. A. Ruben. 1979. Endothermy and activity in vertebrates. *Science* 206:649–654. (12)

Bennett, A. F., and M. H. Wake. 1974. Metabolic correlates of activity in the caecilian *Geotrypetes seraphini. Copeia* 1974:764–769. (12,14)

Bennett, M. R. 1983. Development of neuromuscular synapses. *Physiological Reviews* 63:915–1048. (11)

Bennett, M. R., and K. Lai. 1981. The development of topographical distributions of cutaneous sensory neurons in amphibian ganglia. *Developmental Biology* 86:212–223. (16)

Bennett, M. R., and A. G. Pettigrew. 1975. The formation of synapses in amphibian striated muscle during development. *Journal of Physiology* (London) 252:203–239. (11)

Bennett, P. M., and P. H. Harvey. 1987. Active and resting metabolism in birds: Allometry, phylogeny, and ecology. *Journal of Zoology* 213:327–363. (12)

Benski, J. T., Jr., E. J. Zalisko, and J. H. Larsen, Jr. 1986. Demography and migratory patterns of the eastern long-toed salamander, *Ambystoma macrodactylum columbianum. Copeia* 1986:398–408. (12)

Bentley, P. J. 1958. The effects of neurohypophysial extracts on water transfer across the wall of the isolated urinary bladder of the toad *Bufo marinus. Journal of Endocrinology* 17:201–209. (5)

———. 1959. The effects of neurohypophysial extracts on the tadpole of the frog, *Heleioporus eyrei. Endocrinology* 64:609–610. (16)

———. 1966a. Adaptations of Amphibia to arid environments. *Science* 152:619–623. (6,10,12)

———. 1966b. The physiology of the urinary bladder of Amphibia. *Biological Reviews* 41:275–316. (5,6)

———. 1969. Neurohypophyseal hormones in Amphibia: A comparison of their actions and storage. *General and Comparative Endocrinology* 13:39–44. (5)

———. 1971a. *Endocrines and Osmoregulation: A Comparative Account of the Regulation of Salt and Water in Vertebrates.* New York: Springer-Verlag. (6,16)

———. 1971b. Sodium and water movement across the urinary bladder of a urodele amphibian (the mudpuppy *Necturus maculosus*): Studies with vasotocin and aldosterone. *General and Comparative Endocrinology* 16:356–362. (5)

———. 1973a. Osmoregulation in the aquatic urodeles *Amphiuma means* (the Congo eel) and *Siren lacertina* (the mud eel): Effects of vasotocin. *General and Comparative Endocrinology* 20:386–391. (5,6,16)

———. 1973b. Role of the skin in amphibian sodium metabolism. *Science* 181:686–687. (6)

———. 1974. Actions of neurohypophyseal hormones in amphibians, reptiles, and birds. In *Handbook of Physiology,* ed. Ernst Knobil and Wilbur H. Sawyer, 4:545–563. Bethesda, MD: American Physiological Society. (6)

———. 1975a. Cutaneous respiration in the congo eel *Amphiuma means* (Amphibia: Urodela). *Comparative Biochemistry and Physiology* 50A:121–124. (12)

———. 1975b. The electrical P.D. across the integument of some neotenous urodele amphibians. *Comparative Biochemistry and Physiology* 50A:639–643. (16)

———. 1979. The vertebrate urinary bladder: Osmoregulatory and other uses. *Yale Journal of Biology and Medicine* 52:563–568. (6)

———. 1983. Urinary loss of calcium in an anuran amphibian (*Bufo marinus*) with a note on the effects of calcemic hormones. *Comparative Biochemistry and Physiology* 76B:717–719. (3)

———. 1984. Calcium metabolism in the amphibian. *Comparative Biochemistry and Physiology* 79A:1–5. (3,16)

Bentley, P. J., and G. F. Baldwin. 1980. Comparison of transcutaneous permeability in skins of larval and adult salamanders (*Ambystoma tigrinum*). *American Journal of Physiology* 239:R505–R508. (5,16)

Bentley, P. J., and L. Greenwald. 1970. Neurohypophysial function in bullfrog (*Rana catesbeiana*) tadpoles. *General and Comparative Endocrinology* 14:412–415. (16)

Bentley, P. J., and H. Heller. 1964. The action of neurohypophysial hormones on the water and sodium metabolism of urodele amphibians. *Journal of Physiology* (London) 171:434–453. (5)

———. 1965. The water-retaining action of vasotocin on the fire salamander (*Salamandra maculosus*): Role of the urinary bladder. *Journal of Physiology* (London) 181:124–129. (5)

Bentley, P. J., A. K. Lee, and A. R. Main. 1958. Comparison of dehydration and hydration of two genera of frogs (*Heleioporus* and *Neobatrachus*) that live in areas of varying aridity. *Journal of Experimental Biology* 35:677–684. (5,6)

Bentley, P. J., and A. R. Main. 1972. Zonal differences in the skin of some anuran Amphibia. *American Journal of Physiology* 223:361–363. (5,6)

Bentley, P. J., and K. Schmidt-Nielsen. 1966. Cutaneous water loss in reptiles. *Science* 151:1547–1599. (6)

———. 1971. Acute effects of sea water on frogs (*Rana pipiens*). *Comparative Biochemistry and Physiology* 40A:547–548. (6,16)

Bentley, P. J., and J. W. Shield. 1973. Respiration of some urodele and anuran Amphibia: 2. In air, role of the skin and lungs. *Comparative Biochemistry and Physiology* 46A:29–38. (11,12)

Bentley, P. J., and T. Yorio. 1977. The permeability of the skin of a neotenous urodele amphibian, the mudpuppy *Necturus maculosus*. *Journal of Physiology* (London) 265:537–547. (5)

———. 1979a. Do frogs drink? *Journal of Experimental Biology* 79: 41–46. (6,7,16)

———. 1979b. Evaporative water loss in anuran Amphibia: A comparative study. *Comparative Biochemistry and Physiology* 62A:1005–1009. (5,6)

Benyamina, M., F. Leboulenger, I. Lihrmann, C. Delarue, M. Feuilloley, and H. Vaudry. 1987. Acetylcholine stimulates steroidogenesis in isolated frog adrenal gland through muscarinic receptors: Evidence for a desensitization mechanism. *Journal of Endocrinology* 113: 339–348. (3)

Berk, M. L., and J. E. Heath. 1975a. An analysis of behavioral thermoregulation in the lizard, *Dipsosaurus dorsalis*. *Journal of Thermal Biology* 1:15–22. (9)

———. 1975b. Effects of preoptic, hypothalamic, and telencephalic lesions on thermoregulation in the lizard, *Dipsosaurus dorsalis*. *Journal of Thermal Biology* 1:65–78. (9)

Berman, D. I., A. N. Leirikh, and E. I. Mikhailova. 1984. Winter hibernation of the Siberian salamander, *Hynobius keyserlingi*. *Journal of Evolutionary Biochemistry and Physiology* 1984 (3): 323–327. In Russian with English summary. (10)

Berman, D. M., M. O. Soria, and A. Coviello. 1987. Reversed short-circuit current across isolated skin of the toad *Bufo arenarum*. *Pflugers Archiv für die gesamte Physiologie des Menschen und der Tiere* 409:616–619. (5)

Berman, R., H. A. Bern, C. S. Nicoll, and R. C. Strohman. 1964. Growth promoting effects of mammalian prolactin and growth hormone in tadpoles of *Rana catesbeiana*. *Journal of Experimental Zoology* 156:353–360. (16)

Bern, H. A. 1975. Prolactin and osmoregulation. *American Zoologist* 15:937–948. (5)

Bern, H. A., C. S. Nicoll, and R. C. Strohman. 1967. Prolactin and tadpole growth. *Proceedings of the Society of Experimental Biology and Medicine* 126:518–520. (16)

Bernhardt, H. 1934. The effect of chloretone on the oxygen consumption of amphibian larvae (*Rana clamitans*). *Physiological Zoology* 7:17–35. (12)

Berry, P. Y. 1964. The breeding patterns of seven species of Singapore Anura. *Journal of Animal Ecology* 33:227–243. (15)

———. 1966. The food and feeding habits of the torrent frog, *Amolops larutensis*. *Journal of Zoology* 149:204–214. (14)

Berssebrugge, A., J. Dempsey, and J. Skatrud. 1984. Hypoxic versus hypocapnic effects on periodic breathing during sleep. In *High Altitude and Man*, ed. J. B. West and S. Lahiri, 115–127. Bethesda, MD: American Physiological Society. (7)

Berven, K. A. 1982a. The genetic basis of altitudinal variation in the wood frog *Rana sylvatica*: 1. An experimental analysis of life history traits. *Evolution* 36:962–983. (9,15)

———. 1982b. The genetic basis of altitudinal variation in the wood frog *Rana sylvatica*: 2. An experimental analysis of larval development. *Oecologia* (Berlin) 52:360–369. (9)

———. 1988. Factors affecting variation in reproductive traits within a population of wood frogs (*Rana sylvatica*). *Copeia* 1988:605–615. (15)

Berven, K. A., D. E. Gill, and S. J. Smith-Gill. 1979. Counter-gradient selection in the green frog, *Rana clamitans*. *Evolution* 33:609–623. (8)

Best, A. C. G., and Q. Bone. 1973. The terminal neuromuscular junctions of lower chordates. *Zeitschrift für Zellforschung* 143:495–504. (11)

Beuchat, C. A., F. H. Pough, and M. M. Stewart. 1984. Response to simultaneous dehydration and thermal stress in three species of Puerto Rican frogs. *Journal of Comparative Physiology* 154B: 579–585. (9,12,14)

Bhati, D. P. S. 1955. The pectoral musculature of *Rana tigrina* Daud. and *Rana andersonii* Bouleng. *Annals of Zoology* (Agra) 1:23–78. (11)

Bialaszewicz, K., and R. Bledowski. 1915. Wpływ zapłodnienia na oddyehanie jaj. *Comptes Rendues des Séances de la Société des Sciences de Varsovie* 8:1. (16)

Biber, T. U. L., and L. J. Cruz. 1973. Effect of antidiuretic hormone on sodium uptake across outer surface of frog skin. *American Journal of Physiology* 225:912–917. (5)

Biber, T. U. L., and T. L. Mullen. 1980. Effect of external cation and anion substitutions on sodium transport in isolated frog skin. *Journal of Membrane Biology* 52:121–132. (5)

Biber, T. U. L., T. L. Mullen, and J. A. DeSimone. 1980. Effect of FeCl₃ on ion transport in isolated frog skin. *Journal of Membrane Biology* 52:133–139. (5)

Bider, J. R., and K. A. Morrison. 1981. Changes in toad (*Bufo americanus*) responses to abiotic factors at the northern limit of their distribution. *American Midland Naturalist* 106:293–304. (8,9)

Bigalke, R. 1926. Zur Myologie der Erdkröte (*Bufo vulgaris*, Laurenti). *Zeitschrift für die Anatomie und Entwicklungsgeschichte* 82:286–353. (11)

Billeter, E., and C. B. Jørgensen. 1976. Ovarian development in young toads, *Bufo bufo bufo* (L.): Effects of unilateral ovariectomy, hypophysectomy, treatment with gonadotropin (HCG), growth hormone, and prolaction, and importance of body growth. *General and Comparative Endocrinology* 29:531–544. (15)

Billo, R., and M. H. Wake. 1987. Tentacle development in *Dermophis mexicanus* (Amphibia: Gymnophiona: Caeciliidae). *Journal of Morphology* 192:101–111. (13)

Birkebak, R. C. 1966. Heat transfer in biological systems. *International Review of General and Experimental Zoology* 2:269–344. (4)

Bishop, G. H., and P. Heinbecker. 1930. Differentiation of axon types in visceral nerves by means of the potential record. *American Journal of Physiology* 94:170–200. (7)

Bishop, L. G., and M. S. Gordon. 1967. Thermal adaptation of metabolism in anuran amphibians. In *Molecular Mechanisms of Temperature Adaptation*, ed. C. L. Prosser, 263–280. Washington, DC: American Association for the Advancement of Science. (12)

Bishop, S. C. 1943. *Handbook of Salamanders*. Ithaca, NY: Comstock Publishing Associates. (10)

Bizer, J. R. 1978. Growth rates and size at metamorphosis of high elevation populations of *Ambystoma tigrinum*. *Oecologia* (Berlin) 34:175–184. (9)

Black, J. H., and J. N. Black. 1969. Postmetamorphic basking aggregations of the boreal toad, *Bufo boreas boreas*. *Canadian Field Naturalist* 83:155–156. (9)

Blackith, R. M., and M. C. D. Speight. 1974. Food and feeding habits of the frog, *Rana temporaria*, in bogland habitats of the west of Ireland. *Journal of Zoology* (London) 172:67–79. (15)

Blackshaw, S. E., and A. E. Warner. 1975. Membrane properties during myotome formation in tadpoles of *Xenopus laevis* and *Bombina bombina*. *Journal of Physiology* (London) 246:73P–74P. (11)

———. 1976. Low resistance junctions between mesoderm cells during development of trunk muscles. *Journal of Physiology* (London) 255:209–230. (11)

Blair, A. P. 1943. Population structure in toads. *American Naturalist* 77:563–568. (15)

Blair, W. F. 1958. Mating call in the speciation of anuran amphibians. *American Naturalist* 92:27–51. (14)

Blanchard, F. N. 1933. Late autumn collections and hibernating situations of the salamander *Hemidactylium scutatum* (Schlegel) in southern Michigan. *Copeia* 1933:216. (10)

Blanchi, D., E. Camino, and A. Guardabassi. 1976. Chemoreceptors of the lateral-line organs in intact, hypophysectomized, and prolactin treated hypophysectomized *Xenopus laevis* specimens. *Comparative Biochemistry and Physiology* 55A:301–307. (16)

Blatteis, C. M. 1981. Hypothalamic substances in the control of body temperature: General characteristics. *Federation Proceedings* 40: 2735–2740. (9)

Blatz, A. L. 1984. Asymmetric proton block of inward rectifier K channels in skeletal muscle. *Pflugers Archiv* 401:402–407. (7)

Blaustein, A. R., and R. K. O'Hara. 1982. Kin recognition cues in *Rana cascadae* tadpoles. *Behavioral and Neural Biology* 36:77–87. (2)

Blaxter, K. 1989. *Energy Metabolism in Animals and Man*. Cambridge: Cambridge University Press. (13)

Blaylock, L. A., R. Ruibal, and K. Platt-Aloia. 1976. Skin structure and wiping behavior of phyllomedusine frogs. *Copeia* 1976:283–295. (4,6,11)

Bleibtreu, M. 1911. Weitere Untersuchungen über das Verhalten des Glykogens im Eierstock der *Rana fusca*. *Pflugers Archiv* 141: 328–342. (15)

Blem, C. R., C. A. Ragan, and L. S. Scott. 1986. The thermal physiology of two sympatric treefrogs *Hyla cinerea* and *Hyla chrysoscelis*

(Anura, Hylidae). *Comparative Biochemistry and Physiology* 85A: 563–570. (8,12)

Blem, C. R., J. W. Steiner, and M. A. Miller. 1978. Comparison of jumping abilities of the cricket frogs *Acris gryllus* and *Acris crepitans*. *Herpetologica* 34:288–291. (12)

Bles, E. J. 1905. The life history of *Xenopus laevis*. Daud. *Transactions of the Royal Society of Edinburgh* 41:789–821. (16)

Blier, P., and H. Guderley. 1986. The enzymatic and metabolic effects of extended food deprivation in *Rana pipiens*. *Physiological Zoology* 59:230–239. (10)

Bligh, J. 1973. *Temperature Regulation in Mammals and Other Vertebrates*. New York: American Elsevier Publishing Company. (9)

Bligh, J., and K. G. Johnson. 1973. Glossary of terms for thermal physiology. *Journal of Applied Physiology* 35:941–961. (9)

Bligh, J., G. Louw, and B. A. Young. 1976. Effect of cerebroventricular administration of noradrenaline and carbachol on behavioral and autonomic thermoregulation in the monitor lizard *Varanus albigularis albigularis*. *Journal of Thermal Biology* 1:241–243. (9)

Blight, A. R. 1977. The muscular control of vertebrate swimming movements. *Biological Reviews* 52:181–218. (11)

Block, B. A. 1991. Evolutionary novelties: How fish have built a heater out of muscle. *American Zoologist* 31:726–742. (1)

Blommers-Schlosser, R. 1975. Observations on the larval development of some Malagasy frogs, with notes on their ecology and biology (Anura: Dyscophinae, Scaphiophryninae, and Cophylinae). *Beaufortia* 24:7–26. (16)

Bobka, M. S., R. G. Jaeger, and D. C. McNaught. 1981. Temperature dependent assimilation efficiencies of two species of terrestrial salamanders. *Copeia* 1981:417–421. (8,9)

Bock, K. A. 1938. Die Einwirkung von Nebennierenrindne-extrakt auf den Ablauf der Thyroxin metamorphose bei Froschlarven und beim Axolotl. *Klinische Wochenschrift* 17:1311–1314. (16)

Boell, E. J. 1948. Biochemical differentiation during amphibian development. *Annals of the New York Academy of Sciences* 49:773–800. (12,16)

Boell, E. J., P. Greenfield, and B. Hille. 1963. The respiratory function of gills in the larvae of *Amblystoma punctatum*. *Developmental Biology* 7:420–431. (12)

Bogert, C. M. 1949. Thermoregulation in reptiles, a factor in evolution. *Evolution* 3:195–211. (9)

Bohlin, R. G., and T. L. Beitinger. 1979. Heat exchange in the aquatic salamander, *Amphiuma means*. *Journal of Thermal Biology* 4: 63–67. (9)

Bohnsack, K. 1951. Temperature data on the terrestrial hibernation of the green frog, *Rana clamitans*. *Copeia* 1951:236–239. (10)

———. 1952. Terrestrial hibernation of the bullfrog, *Rana catesbeiana* Shaw. *Copeia* 1952:114. (10)

Bohr, C. 1900. Über die Haut- und Lungenatmung der Frösche. *Skandinavisches Archiv für Physiologie* 10:74–90. (12)

Boice, R., and R. C. Williams. 1971. Competitive feeding behaviour of *Rana pipiens* and *Rana clamitans*. *Animal Behaviour* 19:548–551. (13)

Böker, H. 1935. *Einführung in die vergleichende biologische Anatomie der Wirbeltiere*. Vol. 1. Jena: G. Fischer. (11)

Bonaventura, C., B. Sullivan, J. Bonaventura, and S. Bourne. 1977. Anion modulation of the negative Bohr effect of hemoglobin from a primitive amphibian. *Nature* 265:474–476. (5)

Bond, A. N. 1960. An analysis of the response of salamander gills to changes in the oxygen concentration of the medium. *Developmental Biology* 2:1–20. (16)

Bone, Q. 1966. On the function of the two types of myotomal muscle fibre in elasmobranch fish. *Journal of the Marine Biological Association of the United Kingdom* 46:321–349. (11)

Bone, Q., R. M. A. P. Ridge, and K. P. Ryan. 1976. Stretch receptors in urodele limb muscles. *Cell and Tissue Research* 165:249–266. (11)

Bonhoeffer, K., and T. Kolitat. 1958. Druckvolumendiagramm und Dehnungsreceptoren der Froschlunge. *Pflugers Archiv* 265:477–484. (7)

Bonneville, M. A. 1963. Fine structural changes in the intestinal epithelium of the bullfrog during metamorphosis. *Journal of Cell Biology* 18:579. (16)

Bons, J. 1986. Données histologiques sur le tube digestif de *Typhlo-*

nectes compressicaudus (Dumeril et Bibron, 1841) (Amphibien Apode). *Mémoire Société Zoologique de France* 43:87–91. (13)

Boonkoom, V., and R. H. Alvarado. 1971. Adenosinetriphosphatase activity in gills of larval *Rana catesbeiana*. *American Journal of Physiology* 220:1820–1824. (5,16)

Booth, D. T., and M. E. Feder. 1991. Formation of hypoxic boundary layers and their biological implications in a skin-breathing aquatic salamander, *Desmognathus quadramaculatus*. *Physiological Zoology* 64:1307–1321.

Borgia, G. 1987. A critical review of sexual selection models. In *Sexual Selection: Testing the Alternatives*, ed. J. W. Bradbury and M. B. Andersson, 55–66. New York: Wiley. (14)

Boron, W. F., and E. L. Boulpaep. 1983a. Intracellular pH regulation in the renal proximal tubule of the salamander: Basolateral HCO_3^- transport. *Journal of General Physiology* 81:53–94. (5)

———. 1983b. Intracellular pH regulation in the renal proximal tubule of the salamander: Na/H exchange. *Journal of General Physiology* 81:29–52. (5)

Boron, W. F., and A. Roos. 1976. Comparison of microelectrode, DMO, and methylamine methods for measuring intracellular pH. *American Journal of Physiology* 231:799–801. (5)

Boschwitz, D. 1960a. The influence of the hypophysis and the thyroid on the ultimobranchial body of the Anura of Israel. *Journal of Embryological Experimentation* 8:425–436. (16)

———. 1960b. The ultimobranchial body of the Anura of Israel. *Herpetologica* 16:91–100. (16)

———. 1961. The parathyroid glands of *Bufo viridis* Laurent. *Herpetologica* 17:192–199. (16)

Boschwitz, D., and H. A. Bern. 1971. Prolactin, calcitonin, and blood calcium in the toads *Bufo boreas* and *Bufo marinus*. *General and Comparative Endocrinology* 17:586–588. (3)

Bott, P. A. 1962. Micropuncture study of renal excretion of water, K^+, Na^+, and Cl^- in *Necturus*. *American Journal of Physiology* 203: 662–666. (5)

Boudjelida, H., and L. Muntz. 1987. Multinucleation during myogenesis of the myotome of *Xenopus laevis:* A qualitative study. *Development* 101:583–590. (16)

Bougeois, N. M., and J.-J. Houben. 1975. Morphogénèse primordiale du membre antérieure et ses aspects histochimiques chez le pleurodèle et l'axolotl. *Comptes Rendues Hebdomadaires des Séances de l'Académie des Sciences* (Paris) 80D:2037–2040. (11)

Boulant, J. A., and J. B. Dean. 1986. Temperature receptors in the central nervous system. *Annual Review of Physiology* 48:639–654. (9)

Boulenger, G. A. 1880. On the Palearctic and Æthiopian species of *Bufo*. *Proceedings of the Zoological Society of London* 1880: 545–574. (15)

Boulpaep, E. L. 1972. Permeability changes of the proximal tubule of *Necturus* during saline expansion. *American Journal of Physiology* 222:517–531. (5)

Boutilier, R. G. 1981. Gas exchange and transport during intermittent ventilation in the aquatic amphibian, *Xenopus laevis*. Ph.D. diss., University of East Anglia, Norwich, U.K. (5,7)

———. 1984. Characterization of the intermittent breathing pattern in *Xenopus laevis*. *Journal of Experimental Biology* 110:291–309. (5,7)

———. 1988a. Control of arrhythmic breathing in bimodal breathers: Amphibia. *Canadian Journal of Zoology* 66:6–19. (5,7)

———. 1988b. Interactions between transcutaneous ion transfer processes and carbon dioxide excretion in amphibians. *American Zoologist* 28:1009–1018. (4,5,10)

———. 1989. Diving physiology: Amphibians. In *Comparative Pulmonary Physiology: Current Concepts*, vol. 39, *Lung Biology in Health and Disease*, ed. S. C. Wood, 677–695. New York: Marcel Dekker. (5,7,16)

———. 1990a. Control and co-ordination of gas exchange in bimodal breathers. In *Vertebrate Gas Exchange: From Environment to Cell*, vol. 6, *Advances in Environmental and Comparative Physiology*, ed. R. G. Boutilier, 279–345. Berlin: Springer-Verlag. (5)

———. 1990b. Respiratory gas tensions in the environment. In *Vertebrate Gas Exchange from Environment to Cell*, vol. 6, *Advances in Environmental and Comparative Physiology*, ed. R. G. Boutilier, 1–13. Berlin: Springer-Verlag. (5)

Boutilier, R. G., M. G. Emilio, and G. Shelton. 1986. The effects of mechanical work on electrolyte and water distribution in amphibian skeletal muscle. *Journal of Experimental Biology* 120:333–350. (5,10)

Boutilier, R. G., M. L. Glass, and N. Heisler. 1986. The relative distribution of pulmocutaneous blood flow in *Rana catesbeiana:* Effects of pulmonary or cutaneous hypoxia. *Journal of Experimental Biology* 126:33–39. (5,7)

———. 1987. Blood gases, and extracellular/intracellular acid-base status as a function of temperature in the anuran amphibians *Xenopus laevis* and *Bufo marinus. Journal of Experimental Biology* 130: 13–25. (5)

Boutilier, R. G., and N. Heisler. 1988. Acid-base regulation and blood gases in the anuran amphibian, *Bufo marinus,* during environmental hypercapnia. *Journal of Experimental Biology* 134:79–98. (5,7)

Boutilier, R. G., and C. J. Lantz. 1989. The effects of forced and voluntary diving on plasma catecholamines and erythrocyte pH in the aquatic anuran, *Xenopus laevis. Experimental Biology* 48:83–88. (5)

Boutilier, R. G., D. G. McDonald, and D. P. Toews. 1980. The effects of enforced activity on ventilation, circulation, and blood acid-base balance in the aquatic gill-less urodele, *Cryptobranchus alleganiensis:* A comparison with the semiterrestrial anuran, *Bufo marinus. Journal of Experimental Biology* 84:289–302. (5,6,7,12)

Boutilier, R. G., D. J. Randall, G. Shelton, and D. P. Toews. 1979a. Acid-base relationships in the blood of the toad *Bufo marinus:* 1. The effects of environmental CO₂. *Journal of Experimental Biology* 82: 331–344. (5,7)

———. 1979b. Acid-base relationships in the blood of the toad *Bufo marinus:* 2. The effects of dehydration. *Journal of Experimental Biology* 82:345–355. (5,10)

———. 1979c. Acid-base relationships in the blood of the toad *Bufo marinus:* 3. The effects of burrowing. *Journal of Experimental Biology* 82:357–365. (5,10,12)

Boutilier, R. G., and G. Shelton. 1986a. The effects of voluntary and forced diving on ventilation, blood gases, and pH in *Xenopus laevis. Journal of Experimental Biology* 122:209–222. (5,7)

———. 1986b. Gas exchange, storage, and transport in voluntarily diving *Xenopus laevis. Journal of Experimental Biology* 126:133–155. (5,7)

———. 1986c. Respiratory properties of blood from voluntarily and forcibly submerged *Xenopus laevis. Journal of Experimental Biology* 121:185–300. (5)

Boutilier, R. G., and D. P. Toews. 1977. The effect of progressive hypoxia on respiration in the toad, *Bufo marinus. Journal of Experimental Biology* 68:99–107. (5,7)

———. 1981a. Respiratory, circulatory, and acid-base adjustments to hypercapnia in a strictly aquatic and predominantly skin breathing urodele, *Cryptobranchus alleganiensis. Respiration Physiology* 46: 177–192. (5,7)

———. 1981b. Respiratory properties of blood in a strictly aquatic and predominantly skin-breathing urodele *Cryptobranchus alleganiensis. Respiratory Physiology* 46:161–176. (5)

Bower, A., M. E. Hadley, and V. J. Hruby. 1974. Biogenic amines and control of melanophore-stimulating hormone release. *Science* 184: 70–72. (3)

Bowers, C. Y., A. Segaloff, and B. Brown. 1959. Factors affecting the thyroid gland uptake of I¹³¹ of the *Rana catesbeiana* tadpoles. *Endocrinology* 65:882–888. (16)

Bowker, R. G. 1984. Precision of thermoregulation of some African lizards. *Physiological Zoology* 57:401–412. (9)

Bowker, R. G., and O. W. Johnson. 1980. Thermoregulatory precision in three species of whiptail lizards (Lacertilia: Teiidae). *Physiological Zoology* 53:176–185. (9)

Boyd, J. D. 1933. The development and significance of the amphibian carotid body. *Journal of Anatomy* 68:154–155. (7)

Brachet, J. 1934. Etude du métabolisme de l'oeuf de grenouille *Rana fusca* au cours de développement: 1. La respiration et la glycolyse, de la segmentation à l'éclosion. *Archives de Biologie* 45:611. (16)

Brachet, J., F. Broch, A. Gaudiano, G. Petti, and M. Polizzi. 1971. Variations biochimiques et morphologiques saisonnières dans le foie de *Rana esculenta. Archives de Biologie* (Liége) 82:25–40. (10)

Brackenbury, J. H. 1977. Physiological energetics of cock-crow. *Nature* 270:433–435. (14)

———. 1979. Power capabilities of the avian sound-producing system. *Journal of Experimental Biology* 78:163–166. (14)

Bradbury, J. W., and R. M. Gibson. 1983. Leks and mate choice. In *Mate Choice,* ed. P. Bateson, 109–138. New York: Cambridge University Press. (13)

Bradford, D. F. 1983. Winterkill, oxygen relations, and energy metabolism of a submerged dormant amphibian, *Rana muscosa. Ecology* 64:1171–1183. (10,12)

———. 1984a. Physiological features of embryonic development in terrestrial-breeding plethodontid salamanders. In *Respiration and Metabolism of Embryonic Vertebrates,* ed. R. S. Seymour, 87–98. Dordrecht, Netherlands: Junk. (12)

———. 1984b. Temperature modulation in a high-elevation amphibian, *Rana muscosa. Copeia* 1984:966–976. (9)

———. 1984c. Water and osmotic balance in overwintering tadpoles and frogs, *Rana muscosa. Physiological Zoology* 57:474–480. (10)

Bradford, D. F., and R. S. Seymour. 1985. Energy conservation during the delayed-hatching period in the frog *Pseudophryne bibroni. Physiological Zoology* 58:491–496. (10,12)

Bradshaw, S. D., C. Gans, and H. Saint Girons. 1980. Behavioral thermoregulation in a pygopodid lizard, *Lialis burtonis. Copeia* 1980: 738–743. (9)

Bragg, A. N. 1940. Observations on the ecology and natural history of Anura: 1. Habits, habitat, and breeding of *Bufo cognatus* Say. *American Naturalist* 74:424–438. (15)

———. 1941. Observations on the ecology and natural history of Anura: 8. Some factors in the initiation of breeding behavior. *Turtox News* 19:10–12. (15)

———. 1944. Spadefoot toads in Oklahoma with a summary of our knowledge of the group: 1. *American Naturalist* 78:517–533. (10)

———. 1945. Spadefoot toads in Oklahoma with a summary of our knowledge of the group: 2. *American Naturalist* 79:52–72. (10)

———. 1950. Observations on *Microhyla* (Salientia: Microhylidae). *Wasmann Journal of Biology* 8:113–118. (15)

———. 1964. Mass movements resulting in aggregations of tadpoles of the plains spadefoot, some of them in response to light and temperature (Amphibia: Salientia). *Wasmann Journal of Biology* 22:299–305. (9)

Bragg, A. N., and M. Brooks. 1958. Social behavior in juveniles of *Bufo cognatus* Say. *Herpetologica* 14:141–147. (9)

Bragg, A. N., and A. O. Weese. 1950. Observations on the ecology and natural history of Anura: 14. Growth rates and age at sexual maturity of *Bufo cognatus* under natural conditions in central Oklahoma. In *Researches on the Amphibia of Oklahoma,* ed. A. N. Bragg, 47–58. Norman: University of Oklahoma Press. (15)

Brahma, S. K., D. S. McDevitt, and L. H. K. Defize. 1986. Ontogeny of the 35 K epsilon cystallin during *Rana temporaria* lens development. *Current Eye Research* 5:739–743. (16)

———. 1987. Ontogeny of A and B crystallin polypeptide during *Rana temporaria* lens development. *Experimental Eye Research* 45:253–261. (16)

Bramble, D. M., and D. B. Wake. 1985. Feeding mechanisms of lower tetrapods. In *Functional Vertebrate Morphology,* ed. M. Hildebrand, D. M. Bramble, K. F. Liem, and D. B. Wake, 230–261. Cambridge, MA: Harvard University Press. (11)

Branch, L. C. 1983. Social behavior of the tadpoles of *Phyllomedusa vaillanti. Copeia* 1983:420–428. (14)

Branch, L. C., and R. Altig. 1981. Nocturnal stratification of three species of *Ambystoma* larvae. *Copeia* 1981:870–873. (9)

Branch, L. C., and D. H. Taylor. 1977. Physiological and behavioral responses of larval spotted salamanders (*Ambystoma maculatum*) to various concentrations of oxygen. *Comparative Biochemistry and Physiology* 58A:269–274. (12)

Branin, M. L. 1937. The development of the cortical adrenal in the four-toed salamander *Hemidactylium scutatum* (Schlegel). *Journal of Morphology* 60:521–561. (16)

Brattstrom, B. H. 1962. Thermal control of aggregation behavior in tadpoles. *Herpetologica* 18:38–46. (4,9)

———. 1963. A preliminary review of the thermal requirements of amphibians. *Ecology* 44:238–255. (8,9)

———. 1965. Body temperatures of reptiles. *American Midland Naturalist* 73:376–422. (8)

———. 1968. Thermal acclimation in anuran amphibians as a function of latitude and altitude. *Comparative Biochemistry and Physiology* 24:93–111. (8,9)

————. 1970a. Amphibia. In *Comparative Physiology of Thermoregulation*, vol. 1, *Invertebrates and Nonmammalian Vertebrates*, ed. G. C. Whittow, 135–166. New York: Academic Press. (9,12)

————. 1970b. Thermal acclimation in Australian amphibians. *Comparative Biochemistry and Physiology* 35:69–103. (8,9)

————. 1979. Amphibian temperature regulation studies in the field and laboratory. *American Zoologist* 19:345–356. (4,8,9)

Brattstrom, B. H., and P. Lawrence. 1962. The rate of thermal acclimation in anuran amphibians. *Physiological Zoology* 35:148–156. (9)

Brattstrom, B. H., and J. W. Warren. 1955. Observations on the ecology and behavior of the Pacific treefrog, *Hyla regilla*. *Copeia* 1955: 181–191. (8,9)

Bray, T., and R. E. Sicard. 1982. Correlation among the changes in the levels of thyroid hormones, thyrotropin, and thyrotropin-releasing hormone during the development of *Xenopus laevis*. *Experimental Cellular Biology* 50:101–107. (16)

Breckenridge, W. J. 1944. *Reptiles and Amphibians of Minnesota*. Minneapolis: University of Minnesota Press. (10)

Breckenridge, W. J., and J. R. Tester. 1961. Growth, local movements, and hibernation of the Manitoba toad, *Bufo hemiophrys*. *Ecology* 42:637–646. (10,15)

Breipohl, W., D. Moulton, M. Ummels, and D. H. Matulionis. 1982. Spatial pattern of sensory cell terminals in the olfactory sac of the tiger salamander: 1. A scanning electron microscope study. *Journal of Anatomy* (London) 134:757–769. (16)

Brekke, D. R., S. D. Hillyard, and R. M. Winokur. 1991. Behavior associated with the water absorption response by the toad, *Bufo punctatus*. *Copeia* 1991:393–401. (6)

Brenner, F. J. 1969. The role of temperature and fat deposition in hibernation and reproduction in two species of frogs. *Herpetologica* 25: 105–113. (10)

Brenner, F. J., and P. E. Brenner. 1969. The influence of light and temperature on body fat and reproductive conditions of *Rana pipiens*. *Ohio Journal of Science* 69:305–312. (15)

Brenowitz, E. A. 1982. The active space of red-winged blackbird song. *Journal of Comparative Physiology* 147:511–522. (14)

————. 1986. Environmental influences on acoustic and electric animal communication. *Brain, Behavior, and Evolution* 28:32–42. (2)

Brenowitz, E. A., G. Rose, and R. R. Capranica. 1985. Neural correlates of temperature coupling in the vocal communication system of the gray treefrog (*Hyla versicolor*). *Brain Research* 359:364–367. (2)

Brenowitz, E. A., W. Wilczynski, and H. H. Zakon. 1984. Acoustic communication in spring peepers: Environmental and behavioral aspects. *Journal of Comparative Physiology* 155:585–592. (2)

Brett, J. R. 1952. Temperature tolerance in young Pacific salmon *Oncorhynchus*. *Journal of Fisheries Research Board of Canada* 9: 265–323. (4,9)

————. 1956. Some principles in the thermal requirements of fishes. *Quarterly Review of Biology* 31:75–87. (8)

————. 1964. The respiratory metabolism and swimming performance of young sockeye salmon. *Journal of Fisheries Research Board of Canada* 21:1183–1226. (8)

————. 1971. Energetic responses of salmon to temperature: A study of some thermal relations in the physiology and freshwater ecology of sockeye salmon (*Oncorhynchus nerka*). *American Zoologist* 11:99–113. (9)

Brett, S. S. 1980. Breathing and gas exchange in an aquatic amphibian, *Xenopus laevis*. Ph.D. diss., University of East Anglia, Norwich, U.K. (5,7)

Brett, S. S., and G. Shelton. 1979. Ventilatory mechanisms of the amphibian, *Xenopus laevis:* The role of the buccal force pump. *Journal of Experimental Biology* 80:251–269. (5)

Bridges, C. R., B. Pelster, and P. Scheid. 1985. Oxygen binding in blood of *Xenopus laevis* (Amphibia) and evidence against Root effect. *Respiration Physiology* 61:125–136. (5)

Brodie, E. D., Jr. 1981 Phenological relationships of model and mimic salamanders. *Evolution* 35:988–994. (14)

Brodie, E. D., Jr., and E. D. Brodie. 1980. Differential avoidance of mimetic salamanders by free-ranging birds. *Science* 208:181–182. (14)

Brodie, E. D., Jr., and D. R. Formanowicz. 1981a. Larvae of the predaceous diving beetle *Dytiscus verticalis* acquire an avoidance response to skin secretions of the newt *Notophthalmus viridescens*. *Herpetologica* 37:172–176. (14)

————. 1981b. Palatability and antipredator behavior of the tree frog *Hyla versicolor* to the shrew *Blarina brevicauda*. *Journal of Herpetology* 15:235–236. (14)

————. 1983. Prey size preference of predators: Differential vulnerability of larval anurans. *Herpetologica* 39:67–75. (14)

————. 1987. Antipredator mechanisms of larval anurans: Protection of palatable individuals. *Herpetologica* 43:369–373. (14)

Brodie, E. D., Jr., D. R. Formanowicz, and E. D. Brodie III. 1978. The development of noxiousness of *Bufo americanus* tadpoles to aquatic insect predators. *Herpetologica* 34:302–306. (14)

Brodie, E. D., Jr., R. A. Nussbaum, and M. DiGiovanni. 1984. Antipredator adaptations of Asian salamanders (Salamandridae). *Herpetologica* 40:56–58. (14)

Brooks, G. A., and G. A. Gaesser. 1980. End points of lactate and glucose metabolism after exhausting exercise. *Journal of Applied Physiology* 49:1057–1069. (12)

Brooks, G. R., and J. F. Sassman. 1965. Critical thermal maxima of larval and adult *Eurycea bislineata*. *Copeia* 1965:251–252. (8)

Brooks, S. P. J., and K. B. Storey. 1988. Anoxic brain function: Molecular mechanisms of metabolic depression. *Federation of European Biochemical Societies Letters* 232:214–216. (10)

————. 1989. Influence of hormones, second messengers, and pH on the expression of metabolic responses to anoxia in a marine whelk. *Journal of Experimental Biology* 145:31–43. (10)

Brooks, V. B., ed. 1981. Motor control, part 1. In *Handbook of Physiology*, sec. 1, vol. 2. Bethesda, MD: American Physiological Society. (11)

Brophy, T. E. 1980. Food habits of sympatric larval *Ambystoma tigrinum* and *Notophthalmus viridescens*. *Journal of Herpetology* 14:1–6. (16)

Broughton, R. E., and R. deRoos. 1984. Temporal effects of infused corticosterone and aldosterone on plasma glucose levels in the American bullfrog (*Rana catesbeiana*). *General and Comparative Endocrinology* 53:325–330. (3)

Brower, J. v. Z., and L. P. Brower. 1962. Experimental studies of mimicry: 6. The reaction of toads (*Bufo terrestris*) to honeybees (*Apis mellifera*) and their dronefly mimics (*Eristalis vinetorum*). *American Naturalist* 96:297–308. (13)

Brower, L. P., J. v. Z. Brower, and P. W. Westcott. 1960. Experimental studies of mimicry: 5. The reactions of toads (*Bufo terrestris*) to bumblebees (*Bombus americanorum*) and their robberfly mimics (*Mallophora bomboides*), with a discussion of aggressive mimicry. *American Naturalist* 94:343–355. (13)

Brown, A. 1972. Responses to problems of water and electrolyte balance by salamanders (genus *Aneides*) from different habitats. Ph.D. diss., University of California, Berkeley. (10)

Brown, A. C., and P. F. Millington. 1968. Electron microscope studies of phosphatases in the small intestine of *Rana temporaria* during larval development and metamorphosis. *Histochemie* 12:83–94. (16)

Brown, A. V., and L. C. Fitzpatrick. 1981a. Metabolic acclimation to temperature in the Ozark salamander *Plethodon dorsalis angusticlavius*. *Comparative Biochemistry and Physiology* 69A:499–503. (12)

————. 1981b. Thermal acclimation and metabolism in the gray-bellied salamander, *Eurycea multiplicata griseogaster* (Plethodontidae). *Comparative Biochemistry and Physiology* 69A:505–509. (12)

Brown, D., N. Fleming, and M. Balls. 1975. Hormonal control of glucose production by *Amphiuma means* liver in organ culture. *General and Comparative Endocrinology* 27:380–388. (3)

Brown, F. A., Jr., H. M. Webb, M. F. Bennett, and M. I. Sandeen. 1955. Evidence for an exogenous contribution to persistent diurnal and lunar rhythmicity under so-called constant conditions. *Biological Bulletin* 109:238–254. (12)

Brown, G. W., Jr. 1964. The metabolism of Amphibia. In *The Physiology of the Amphibia*, ed. J. A. Moore, 1–98. New York: Academic Press. (15)

Brown, H. A. 1967. High temperature tolerance of the eggs of a desert anuran, *Scaphiopus hammondii*. *Copeia* 1967:365–370. (8)

————. 1969. The heat resistance of some anuran tadpoles (Hylidae and Pelobatidae). *Copeia* 1969:138–147. (8)

————. 1975a. Embryonic temperature adaptations of the pacific treefrog, *Hyla regilla*. *Comparative Biochemistry and Physiology* 51A: 863–873. (9)

————. 1975b. Temperature and development of the tailed frog, *Ascaphus truei*. *Comparative Biochemistry and Physiology* 50A:397–405. (9)

————. 1977. Oxygen consumption of a large, cold-adapted frog egg (*Ascaphus truei* [Amphibia: Ascaphidae]). *Canadian Journal of Zoology* 55:343–348. (12)

Brown, L. E., and J. R. Brown. 1977. Comparison of environmental and body temperatures as predictions of mating call parameters of spring peepers. *American Midland Naturalist* 97:209–211. (9)

Brown, M. C. 1971. A comparison of the spindles in two different muscles of the frog. *Journal of Physiology* (London) 216:553–563. (11)

Brown, M. R. 1981. Bombesin, somatostatin, and related peptides: Actions on thermoregulation. *Federation Proceedings* 40:2765–2768. (9)

Brown, P. S., B. Barry, and S. C. Brown. 1988. Changes in absolute and proportional water content during growth and metamorphosis of *Rana sylvatica*. *Comparative Biochemistry and Physiology* 91A:189–194. (16)

Brown, P. S., and S. C. Brown. 1973. Prolactin and thyroid hormone interactions in salt and water balance in the newt *Notophthalmus viridescens*. *General and Comparative Endocrinology* 20:456–466. (5)

————. 1977. Water balance responses to dehydration and neurohypophysial peptides in the salamander, *Notophthalmus viridescens*. *General and Comparative Endocrinology* 31:189–201. (5,6)

————. 1982. Effects of hypophysectomy and prolactin on the water-balance response of the newt, *Taricha torosa*. *General and Comparative Endocrinology* 46:7–12. (5)

————. 1987. Osmoregulatory actions of prolactin and other adenophysial hormones. In *Vertebrate Endocrinology: Fundamentals and Biomedical Implications*, vol. 2, *Regulation of Water and Electrolytes*, ed. P. K. T. Pang and M. P. Schreibman, 45–84. New York: Academic Press. (16)

Brown, P. S., S. C. Brown, J. T. Bisceglio, and S. M. Lemke. 1983. Breeding condition, temperature, and the regulation of salt and water by pituitary hormones in the red-spotted newt, *Notophthalmus viridescens*. *General and Comparative Endocrinology* 51:292–302. (5)

Brown, P. S., S. C. Brown, and B. E. Frye. 1979. Effects of hypophysectomy and thyroidectomy on salt balance in the plethodontid salamanders, *Desmognathus fuscus* and *Desmognathus monticola*. *Journal of Comparative Physiology* 132:357–361. (5)

Brown, P. S., S. C. Brown, and J. L. Specker. 1984. Osmoregulatory changes during the aquatic-to-terrestrial transition in the rough-skinned newt, *Taricha granulosa*: The roles of temperature and ACTH. *General and Comparative Endocrinology* 56:130–139. (5)

Brown, P. S., S. A. Hastings, and B. E. Frye. 1977. A comparison of the water-balance response in five species of plethodontid salamanders. *Physiological Zoology* 50:203–213. (6)

Brown, P. S., A. M. Hayner, T. C. Bania, and S. C. Brown. 1985. Sensitivity and specificity of salamandrid integumental transepithelial potential to prolactin. *General and Comparative Endocrinology* 59:56–63. (5)

Brown, P. S., M. J. Murphy, and S. C. Brown. 1989. Effects of prolactin on water balance and kidney function in bullfrog tadpoles. *General and Comparative Endocrinology* 75:389–396. (16)

Brown, R. W. 1970. Measurement of water potential with thermocouple psychrometers: Construction and applications. U.S. Department of Agriculture, Intermountain Research Paper INT-80. (6)

Brown, S. C. 1988. Electrophysiology of newt skin: Effects of prolactin. *General and Comparative Endocrinology* 72:161–167. (5,16)

Brown, S. C., and P. S. Brown. 1980. Water balance in the California newt *Taricha torosa*. *American Journal of Physiology* 238:R113–118. (5,6)

Brown, S. C., P. S. Brown, and K. P. Wittig. 1981. Effects of hypophysectomy and prolactin on sodium balance in the newt, *Taricha torosa*. *General and Comparative Endocrinology* 45:256–261. (5)

Brown, S. C., E. A. Horgan, L. M. Savage, and P. S. Brown. 1986. Changes in body water and plasma constituents during bullfrog development: Effects of temperature and hormones. *Journal of Experimental Zoology* 237:25–34. (8,16)

Brown, W. C., and A. C. Alcala. 1970. Population ecology of the frog *Rana erythraea* in southern Negros, Philippines. *Copeia* 1970:611–622. (15)

Broyles, R. H. 1981. Changes in the blood during amphibian metamorphosis. In *Metamorphosis: A Problem in Developmental Biology*, ed. L. I. Gilbert and E. Frieden, 461–490. New York: Plenum Press. (16)

Broyles, R. H., G. M. Johnson, P. B. Maples, and G. R. Kindell. 1981. Two erythropoietic microenvironments and two larval red cell lines in bullfrog tadpoles. *Developmental Biology* 81:299–314. (16)

Bruce, R. C. 1972. Variation in the life cycle of the salamander *Gyrinophilus porphyriticus*. *Herpetologica* 28:230–245. (15)

————. 1975. Reproductive biology of the mud salamander, *Pseudotriton montanus*, in western South Carolina. *Copeia* 1975:129–137. (15)

Bruneau, M., and E. Magnin. 1980. Croissance, nutrition, et reproduction des ouaouarons *Rana catesbeiana* Shaw (Amphibia, Anura) des Laurentides au nord de Montréal. *Canadian Journal of Zoology* 58:175–183. (15)

Bruner, H. L. 1896. Ein neuer Muskelapparat zum Schliessen und Öffnen der Nasenlöcher bei den Salamandriden. *Anatomischer Anzeiger* 12:272–273. (11)

————. 1899. Description of new facial muscles in Anura with new observations on the nasal muscles of Salamandridae. *Anatomischer Anzeiger* 15:411–412. (11)

————. 1901. The smooth facial muscles of Anura and *Salamandrina*: A contribution to the anatomy and physiology of the respiratory mechanisms of the amphibians. *Morphologisches Jahrbuch* 29:317–364. (11)

————. 1914. The mechanism of pulmonary respiration in amphibians with gill clefts. *Morphologisches Jahrbuch* 48:63–82. (11)

Brunn, F. 1921. Beitrag zur Kenntnis der Wirkung von Hypophysenextrakten auf den Wasserhaushalt des Frosches. *Zeitschrift für die Gesamten Experimentellen Medizin* 25:170–175. (5,6)

Brunori, M., A. Bellelli, B. Giardina, S. Condo, and M. F. Perutz. 1987. Is there a Root effect in *Xenopus* hemoglobin? *Federation of European Biochemical Societies Letters* 221:161–166. (5)

Bruns, V., H. Burda, and M. J. Ryan. 1989. Ear morphology of the frog-eating bat (*Trachops cirrhosus*, Family Phylostomatidae): Apparent specializations for low-frequency hearing. *Journal of Morphology* 199:103–118. (14)

Brush, J. S., V. G. Gain, and M. D. Greenfield. 1985. Phonotaxis and aggression in the coneheaded katydid *Neoconocephalus affinis*. *Physiological Entomology* 10:23–32. (14)

Brust, D. G. 1990. Maternal brood care by *Dendrobates pumilio*: A frog that feeds its young. Ph.D. diss., Cornell University, Ithaca, NY. (14)

Brust, D. G., and M. R. Preest. 1988. The effects of temperature and hydration state on aerobic metabolism of canyon treefrogs (*Hyla arenicolor*). *American Zoologist* 28:107A. (14)

Brutsaert, W. 1975. On a derivable formula for long-wave radiation from clear skies. *Water Resources Research* 11:742–744. (4)

Brzoska, J. 1982. Vocal response of male European water frogs (*Rana esculenta* complex) to mating and territorial calls. *Behavioral Processes* 7:37–47. (14)

Brzoska, J., and H.-J. Obert. 1980. Acoustic signals influencing the hormone production of the testes in the grass frog. *Journal of Comparative Physiology* 140:25–29. (2)

Bucher, T. L., M. J. Ryan, and G. A. Bartholomew. 1982. Oxygen consumption during resting, calling, and nest building in the frog, *Physalaemus pustulosus*. *Physiological Zoology* 55:10–22. (12,14)

Buck, J. 1962. Some physical aspects of insect respiration. *Annual Review of Entomology* 7:27–56. (4)

Budtz, P. E. 1979. Epidermal structure and dynamics of the toad *Bufo bufo* deprived of the pars distalis of the pituitary gland. *Journal of Zoology* (London) 189:57–92. (3)

Bull, J. J., and R. Shine. 1979. Iteroparous animals that skip opportunities for reproduction. *American Naturalist* 114:296–303. (15)

Bundy, D., and C. R. Tracy. 1977. Behavioral response of American toads (*Bufo americanus*) to stressful thermal and hydric environments. *Herpetologica* 33:455–458. (9,12,14)

Burggren, W. W. 1984. Transition of respiratory processes during amphibian metamorphosis: From egg to adult. In *Respiration and Metabolism of Embryonic Vertebrates*, ed. R. S. Seymour, 31–53. Dordrecht, Netherlands: Junk. (16)

————. 1985. Gas exchange, metabolism, and "ventilation" in gelatinous frog egg masses. *Physiological Zoology* 58:503–514. (16)

————. 1987. Invasive and noninvasive methodologies in ecological physiology: A plea for integration. In *New Directions in Ecological Physiology,* ed. M. E. Feder, A. F. Bennett, W. W. Burggren, and R. B. Huey, 251–274. Cambridge: Cambridge University Press. (5)

———. 1988a. Cardiac design in lower vertebrates: What can phylogeny reveal about ontogeny. *Experientia* 44:919–930. (5)

———. 1988b. Role of the central circulation in regulation of cutaneous gas exchange. *American Zoologist* 28:985–998. (4,5,6,9,16)

———. 1989. Lung structure and function: Amphibians. In *Comparative Pulmonary Physiology: Current Concepts,* vol. 39, *Lung Biology in Health and Disease,* ed. S. C. Wood, 153–192. New York: Marcel Dekker. (5,6,7,16)

———. 1991. Does comparative respiratory physiology have a role in evolutionary biology (and vice versa?) In *Comparative Insights into Strategies for Gas Exchange and Metabolism,* eds. A. J. Woakes, M. K. Grieshaber, and C. R. Bridges, 1–13. Cambridge: Cambridge University Press. (1)

———. 1992. The importance of an ontogenetic perspective in physiological studies: Amphibian cardiology as a case study. In *Physiological Adaptations in Vertebrates,* ed. S. C. Wood, R. Weber, A. Hargens, and R. Millard, 235–253. New York: Marcel Dekker. (16)

Burggren, W. W., and W. E. Bemis. 1990. Studying physiological evolution: Paradigms and pitfalls. In *Evolutionary Innovations,* ed. M. H. Nitecki, 191–228. Chicago: University of Chicago Press.

Burggren, W. W., and M. Doyle. 1986a. The action of acetylcholine upon heart rate changes markedly with development in the bullfrog. *Journal of Experimental Zoology* 240:137–140. (16)

———. 1986b. Ontogeny of heart rate regulation in the bullfrog, *Rana catesbeiana. American Journal of Physiology* 251:R231–R239. (16)

———. 1986c. Ontogeny of regulation of gill and lung ventilation in the bullfrog, *Rana catesbeiana. Respiration Physiology* 66:279–291. (16)

Burggren, W. W., R. K. Dupré, and S. C. Wood. 1987. Allometry of red cell oxygen binding and hematology in larvae of the salamander, *Ambystoma tigrinum. Respiratory Physiology* 70:73–84. (16)

Burggren, W. W., and M. E. Feder. 1986. Effect of experimental ventilation of the skin on cutaneous gas exchange in the bullfrog. *Journal of Experimental Biology* 121:445–450. (4,5,6,7)

Burggren, W. W., M. E. Feder, and A. W. Pinder. 1983. Temperature and the balance between aerial and aquatic respiration in larvae of *Rana berlandieri* and *Rana catesbeiana. Physiological Zoology* 56:263–273. (5,12,16)

Burggren, W. W., R. L. Infantino, and D. S. Townsend. 1990. Developmental changes in cardiac and metabolic physiology of the direct-developing tropical frog *Eleutherodactylus coqui. Journal of Experimental Biology* 152:129–147. (16)

Burggren, W. W., and R. Moalli. 1984. "Active" regulation of cutaneous gas exchange by capillary recruitment in amphibians: Experimental evidence and a revised model for skin respiration. *Respiration Physiology* 55:379–392. (5,6,7,10,12,16)

Burggren, W. W., and A. Mwalukoma. 1983. Respiration during chronic hypoxia and hyperoxia in larval and adult bullfrogs (*Rana catesbeiana*): 1. Morphological responses of lungs, skin, and gills. *Journal of Experimental Biology* 105:191–203. (5,16)

Burggren, W. W., D. Powers, and B. R. McMahon. 1991. Respiratory functions of blood. In *Comparative Animal Physiology,* 4th ed., ed. C. L. Prosser, 437–508. New York: Wiley-Interscience. (16)

Burggren, W. W., and N. H. West. 1982. Changing respiratory importance of gills, lungs, and skin during metamorphosis in the bullfrog, *Rana catesbeiana. Respiration Physiology* 47:151–164. (5,6,7,12,16)

Burggren, W. W., and S. C. Wood. 1981. Respiration and acid-base balance in the salamander, *Ambystoma tigrinum:* Influence of temperature acclimation and metamorphosis. *Journal of Comparative Physiology* 144:241–246. (5,6,8,12,16)

Burghagen, H., and J.-P. Ewert. 1983. Influence of the background for discriminating object motion from self-induced motion in toads *Bufo bufo* (L.). *Journal of Comparative Physiology* 152:241–249. (13)

Burkard, O. 1902. Über die Periorbita der Wirbelthiere und ihre muskulösen Elemente. *Archiv für die Anatomie und Physiologie, Abteilung Anatomie,* Suppl.: 79–98. (11)

Burke, E. M., and F. H. Pough. 1976. The role of fatigue in temperature resistance of salamanders. *Journal of Thermal Biology* 1:163–167. (8)

Burke, W., and B. L. Ginsborg. 1956. The electrical properties of the slow muscle fibre membrane. *Journal of Physiology* (London) 132:586–598. (11)

Burns, R. K., and A. Buyse. 1932. Effects of hypophysectomy on the reproductive system of salamanders. *Anatomical Record* 51:333–359. (15)

Burton, A. C., and S. Yamada 1951. Relation between blood pressure and flow in human forearm. *Journal of Applied Physiology* 4:329–339. (7)

Burton, T. C. 1980. Phylogenetic and functional significance of cutaneous muscles in microhylid frogs. *Herpetologica* 36:256–264. (11)

———. 1983. The musculature of the Papuan frog *Phrynomantis stictogaster* (Anura, Microhylidae). *Journal of Morphology* 175:307–324. (11)

Burton, T. M., and G. E. Likens. 1975. Energy flow and nutrient cycling in salamander populations in the Hubbard Brook experimental forest, New Hampshire. *Ecology* 56:1068–1080. (13)

Bury, R. B., and T. G. Balgooyen. 1976. Temperature selectivity in the legless lizard, *Anniella pulchra. Copeia* 1976:152–155. (9)

Bury, R. B., and J. A. Whelan. 1984. Ecology and management of the bullfrog. U.S. Department of the Interior, Fish and Wildlife Service/Resource Publication 155:1–23. Washington, DC. (13)

Busa, W. B., and R. Nuccitelli. 1984. Metabolic regulation via intracellular pH. *American Journal of Physiology* 246:R409–R438. (10)

Buscaglia, M., J. Leloup, and A. Deluze. 1985. The role and regulation of monodeiodination of thyroxine to 3,5,3'-triiodothyronine during amphibian metamorphosis. In *Metamorphosis: The Eighth Symposium of the British Society for Developmental Biology,* ed. M. Balls and M. Bownes, 273–293. Oxford: Clarendon Press. (16)

Busch, E. 1929. Studies on the nerves of the blood vessels with special reference to periarterial sympathectomy. *Acta Pathologica et Microbiologica Scandinavica,* suppl. 2. (7)

Bush, F. M. 1963. Effects of light and temperature on the gross composition of the toad, *Bufo fowleri. Journal of Experimental Biology* 153:1–13. (15)

Bush, F. M., and E. F. Menhinick. 1962. The food of *Bufo woodhousei fowleri* Hinckley. *Herpetologica* 18:110–114. (13)

Bustard, H. R. 1967. Activity cycle and thermoregulation in the Australian gecko *Gehyra variegata. Copeia* 1967:753–758. (4)

Buttemer, W. A. 1990. Effect of temperature on evaporative water loss in the Australian tree frogs *Litoria caerulea* and *Litoria chloris. Physiological Zoology* 63:1043–1057. (6)

Buttemer, W. A., A. M. Hayworth, W. W. Weathers, and K. A. Nagy. 1986. Time-budget estimates of avian energy expenditure: Physiological and meteorological considerations. *Physiological Zoology* 59:131–149. (14)

Butterstein, G. M., and C. M. Osborn. 1968. Integumentary physiology and protein metabolism in the urodele, *Triturus viridescens. Anatomical Record* 101:678–679. (3)

Buytendijk, F. J. J. 1910. About exchange of gases in cold-blooded animals in connection with their size. *Akademie van Wetenschappen, Proceedings* 13:48–53. (12)

Byrne, J. J., and R. J. White. 1975. Cyclic changes in liver and muscle glycogen, tissue lipid, and blood glucose in a naturally occurring population of *Rana catesbeiana. Comparative Biochemistry and Physiology* 50A:709–715. (10,15)

Byrnes, E. F. 1898. Experimental studies on the development of limb-muscles in Amphibia. *Journal of Morphology* 14:103–140. (11)

Cabanac, H. P., and H. T. Hammel. 1971. Comportement thermorégulateur du lîzard *Tiliqua scincoides:* Réponses au froid. *Journal de Physiologie* 63:222–225. (9)

Cabanac, M. 1975. Temperature regulation. *Annual Review of Physiology* 37:415–439. (9)

Cabanac, M., M. Cormarèche-Leydier, and L. J. Porier. 1976. The effect of capsaicin on temperature regulation of the rat. *Pflugers Archiv* 366:217–221. (9)

Cabanac, M., H. T. Hammel, and J. D. Hardy. 1967. *Tiliqua scincoides:* Temperature sensitive units in lizard brain. *Science* 158:1050–1051. (9)

Cabanac, M., and E. Jeddi. 1971. Thermopréférendum et thermorégulation comportementale chez trois poikilothermes. *Physiology and Behavior* 7:375–380. (9)

Cabanac, M., and L. LeGuelte. 1980. Temperature regulation and prostaglandin E₁ fever in scorpions. *Journal of Physiology* (London) 303:365–370. (9)

Cagle, F. R., and P. E. Smith. 1939. A winter aggregation of *Siren intermedia* and *Triturus viridescens*. *Copeia* 1939:232–233. (10)

Cagle, R. R. 1948. Observations on a population of the salamander, *Amphiuma tridactylum* Cuvier. *Ecology* 29:479–490. (15)

Caldwell, J. P. 1986. Selection of egg deposition sites. A seasonal shift in the southern leopard frog, *Rana sphenocephala*. *Copeia* 1986:249–253. (8)

Caldwell, R. S. 1975. Observations on the winter activity of the red-backed salamander, *Plethodon cinereus*, in Indiana. *Herpetologica* 31:21–22. (10)

Caldwell, R. S., and G. S. Jones. 1973. Winter congregations of *Plethodon cinereus* in ant mounds, with notes on their food habits. *American Midland Naturalist* 90:482–485. (10)

Calhoon, T. B. 1955. Adrenal cortical extract on the oxygen consumption of propylthiouracil treated frogs. *Endocrinology* 57:70–75. (12)

Calhoon, T. B., and C. A. Angerer. 1955. Adrenal cortical extract on the oxygen consumption of normal frogs. *Physiological Zoology* 28:340–345. (12)

Callard, G. V. 1985. Estrogen synthesis and other androgen converting pathways in the vertebrate brain and pituitary. In *Current Trends in Comparative Endocrinology*, ed. B. Lofts and W. N. Holmes, 1179–1184. Hong Kong: Hong Kong University Press. (3)

Calof, A. L., R. B. Jones, and W. J. Roberts. 1981. Sympathetic modulation of mechanoreceptor sensitivity in frog skin. *Journal of Physiology* (London) 310:481–499. (7)

Calow, L. J., and R. McNeil Alexander. 1973. A mechanical analysis of a hind leg of a frog (*Rana temporaria*). *Journal of Zoology* (London) 171:293–321. (8,11)

Calow, P. 1981. Resource utilization and reproduction. In *Physiological Ecology: An Evolutionary Approach to Resource Use*, ed. C. R. Townsend and P. Calow, 245–270. Sunderland, MA: Sinauer Associates. (14)

———. 1987. Towards a definition of functional ecology. *Functional Ecology* 1:57–61. (1)

Cambar, R., and J. D. Gipouloux. 1956. Table chronologique du développement embryonnaire et larvaire du crapaud commun: *Bufo bufo* L. *Bulletin Biologique de la France et de la Belgique* 90:97–114. (16)

Cambar, R., and B. Marrot. 1954. Table chronologique du développement de la grenouille agile (*Rana dalmatina* Bon.). *Bulletin Biologique de la France et de la Belgique* 88:168–177. (16)

Cambar, R., and S. Martin. 1959. Table chronologique du développement embryonnaire et larvaire du crapaud accoucheur ("*Alytes obstetricans*" Laur.). *Actes de la société Linneenne Bordeaux* 98:3–21. (16)

Cameron, J. N. 1984. Acid-base status of fish at different temperatures. *American Journal of Physiology* 246:R452–R459. (6)

———. 1989. Acid-base homeostasis: Past and present perspectives. *Physiological Zoology* 62:845–865. (5,6)

Campantico, E., A. Guastalla, and E. Patriarca. 1985. Identification by immunofluorescence of ACTH-producing cells in the pituitary gland of the tree frog *Hyla arborea*. *General and Comparative Endocrinology* 59:192–198. (3)

Campantico, E., M. Olivero, and A. Peyrot. 1968. Accrescimento corpores e metabolismo dello iodio in larve du *Bufo bufo* trattate con prolattina: Studio con I¹²⁵. *Ricerca Scientifica* 38.980–985. (16)

Campbell, G. S. 1977. *An Introduction to Environmental Biophysics*. New York: Springer-Verlag. (4)

Campbell, J. B. 1970. Hibernacula of a population of *Bufo boreas boreas* in the Colorado front range. *Herpetologica* 26:278–282. (10)

Campbell, J. W. 1973. Nitrogen excretion. In *Comparative Animal Physiology*, 3d ed., ed. C. L. Prosser, 279–316. Philadelphia: W. B. Saunders. (5)

Campbell, J. W., J. E. Vorhaben, and D. D. Smith, Jr. 1984. Hepatic ammonia metabolism in a uricotelic tree frog *Phyllomedusa sauvagei*. *American Journal of Physiology* 246:R805–R810. (6)

———. 1987. Uricoteley: Its nature and origin during the evolution of tetrapod vertebrates. *Journal of Experimental Zoology* 243:349–363. (6)

Candelas, G. C., E. Ortiz, C. Vasqez, and L. Felix. 1961. Respiratory metabolism in tadpoles of *Leptodactylus albilabris*. *American Zoologist* 1:348. (10)

Cannatella, D. C. 1985. A phylogeny of primitive frogs (archaeobatrachians). Ph.D. diss., University of Kansas, Lawrence. (11)

Cannatella, D. C., and L. Trueb. 1988. Evolution of pipoid frogs: Intergeneric relationships of the aquatic frog family Pipidae (Anura). *Zoological Journal of the Linnaean Society* 94:1–38. (11)

Canty, A., W. R. Driedzic, and K. B. Storey. 1986. Freeze tolerance of isolated ventricle strips of the wood frog, *Rana sylvatica*. *Cryo Letters* 7:81–86. (10)

Capek, K. 1937. *War with the Newts*. Translation from Czech. London: George Allen and Unwin. (11)

Capranica, R. R. 1976a. The auditory system. In *Physiology of the Amphibia*, ed. B. Lofts, 3:443–466. New York: Academic Press. (14)

———. 1976b. Morphology and physiology of the auditory system. In *Frog Neurobiology: A Handbook*, ed. R. Llinás and W. Precht, 551–575. Berlin: Springer-Verlag. (16)

Capranica, R. R., L. S. Frishkopf, and E. Nevo. 1973. Encoding of geographic dialects in the auditory system of the cricket frog. *Science* 182:1272–1275. (2)

Capranica, R. R., and A. J. M. Moffat. 1975. Selectivity of the peripheral auditory system of spadefoot toads (*Scaphiopus couchii*) for sounds of biological significance. *Journal of Comparative Physiology* (London) 100:231–249. (11)

———. 1980. Nonlinear properties of the peripheral auditory system of anurans. In *Comparative Studies of Hearing in Vertebrates*, ed. A. N. Popper and R. R. Fay, 139–165. Berlin: Springer-Verlag. (2)

———. 1983. Neurobehavioral correlates of sound communication in anurans. In *Advances in Vertebrate Neuroethology*, ed. J.-P. Ewert, R. R. Capranica, and D. Ingle, 701–730. New York: Plenum Press. (2)

Capranica, R. R., and G. Rose. 1983. Frequency and temporal processing in the auditory system of anurans. In *Neuroethology and Behavioral Physiology*, ed. F. Huber and H. Markl, 136–152. Berlin: Springer-Verlag. (2)

Carey, C. 1976. Thermal physiology and energetics of boreal toads, *Bufo boreas boreas*. Ph.D. diss., University of Michigan, Ann Arbor. (13)

———. 1978. Factors affecting body temperatures of toads. *Oecologia* (Berlin) 35:179–219. (4,9,13)

———. 1979a. Aerobic and anaerobic energy expenditure during rest and activity in montane *Bufo b. boreas* and *Rana pipiens*. *Oecologia* (Berlin) 39:213–228. (8,12)

———. 1979b. Effect of constant and fluctuating temperatures on resting and active oxygen consumption of toads, *Bufo boreas*. *Oecologia* (Berlin) 39:201–212. (8,12)

Carey, C., and J. R. Hazel. 1984. Relation of fluctuating body temperatures and composition of membranes of desert ectotherms. *American Zoologist* 24:98A. (10)

Carlisky, N. J., V. Botbol, C. A. Garcia Argiz, A. Barrio, and V. L. Lew. 1968. Properties and subcellular distribution of ornithine cycle enzymes in amphibian kidney. *Comparative Biochemistry and Physiology* 25:835–848. (6)

Carlisky, N. J., M. Cereijido, A. Barrio, and G. Migliora. 1970. Studies on the relationship between sodium and water balance and renal mechanisms of excretion of urea in Amphibia. *Comparative Biochemistry and Physiology* 36:321–337. (5)

Carlson, A. J., and A. B. Luckhardt. 1920. Studies on the visceral sensory nervous system: 1. Lung automation and lung reflexes in the frog *Rana pipiens* and *Rana catesbeiana*. *American Journal of Physiology* 54:55–59. (7)

Carlsten, A., L. E. Ericson, O. Poupa, and S. Winell. 1983. Heart lesions in the frog at high environmental temperature. *Comparative Biochemistry and Physiology* 76A:583–591. (8)

Carlton, R. G., and R. G. Wetzel. 1985. A box corer for studying metabolism of epipelic microorganisms in sediment under in situ conditions. *Limnology and Oceanography* 30:422–426. (16)

———. 1987. Distribution and fates of oxygen in periphyton communities. *Canadian Journal of Botany* 65:1031–1037. (16)

Carman, J. B. 1955. The carotid labyrinth in *Hyla aurea*, with a note on that in *Leiopelma hochstetteri*. *Journal of Anatomy* 89:503–525. (7)

———. 1967a. The carotid labyrinth in the anuran *Breviceps mossambicus*. *Transactions of the Royal Society of New Zealand: Zoology* 10:1–15. (7)

———. 1967b. The morphology of the carotid labyrinth in *Bufo bufo* and *Leiopelma hochstetteri*. *Transactions of the Royal Society of New Zealand: Zoology* 10:71–76. (7)

Carr, F. E., P. J. Jacobs, and R. C. Jaffe. 1981. Changes in specific prolactin binding in *Rana catesbeiana* tadpole tissues during metamorphosis and following prolactin and thyroid-hormone treatment. *Molecular and Cellular Endocrinology* 23:65–76. (16)

Carr, F. E., and R. C. Jaffe. 1980. Prolactin and tadpole metamorphosis: Evidence of prolactin receptors in premetamorphic *Rana catesbeiana* liver and tail. *Molecular and Cellular Endocrinology* 17:145–155. (16)

———. 1981. Solubilization and molecular weight estimation of prolactin receptors from *Rana catesbeiana* tadpole liver and tail fin. *Endocrinology* 109:943–949. (16)

Carr, J. A., and D. O. Norris. 1988. Interrenal activity during metamorphosis of the tiger salamander *Ambystoma tigrinum*. *General and Comparative Endocrinology* 71:63–69. (16)

Carrier, D. 1989. Ventilatory action of the hypaxial muscles of the lizard *Iguana iguana:* A function of slow muscle. *Journal of Experimental Biology* 143:435–457. (11)

Carroll, R. G., and D. F. Opdyke. 1982. Evolution of angiotensin II–induced catecholamine release. *American Journal of Physiology* 243:R65–R69. (3)

Carroll, R. L., and R. Holmes. 1980. The skull and jaw musculature as guides to the ancestry of salamanders. *Zoological Journal of the Linnean Society* 68:1–40. (11)

Carstensen, H., A. C. Burgers, and C. H. Li. 1961. Demonstration of aldosterone and corticosterone as principal steroids formed in incubates of adrenals of the American bullfrog (*Rana catesbeiana*) and stimulation of their production by mammalian adrenocorticotropin. *General and Comparative Endocrinology* 1:37–50. (3)

Carter, D. B. 1979. Structure and function of the subcutaneous lymph sacs in the Anura (Amphibia). *Journal of Herpetology* 13:321–327. (5)

Casterlin, M. E., and W. W. Reynolds. 1977. Behavioral fever in anuran amphibian larvae. *Life Sciences* 20:593–596. (9)

———. 1978. Behavioral thermoregulation in *Rana pipiens* tadpoles. *Journal of Thermal Biology* 3:143–145. (9,14)

———. 1980. Diel activity and thermoregulatory behavior of a fully aquatic frog: *Xenopus laevis*. *Hydrobiologia* 75:189–191. (9)

Castrucci, A. M. de L., M. E. Hadley, and V. J. Hruby. 1984. Melanotropin bioassays: *In vitro* and *in vivo* comparisons. *General and Comparative Endocrinology* 55:104–111. (3)

Castrucci, A. M. de L., M. A. Visconti, M. E. Hadley, V. J. Hruby, N. Oshima, and R. Fujii. 1988. Melanin-concentrating hormone (MCH) control of chromatophores. In *Advances in Pigment Cell Research*, ed. J. T. Bagnara, 547–557. New York: Alan R. Liss. (3)

Catton, W. T. 1970. Mechanoreceptor function. *Physiological Reviews* 50:297–318. (7)

———. 1976. Cutaneous mechanoreceptors. In *Frog Neurobiology: A Handbook*, ed. R. Llinás and W. Precht, 629–642. Berlin: Springer-Verlag. (2)

Cayrol, C., and P. Deparis. 1987. Effects of thyroxine on the ontogeny of the vitellogenic response in *Pleurodeles waltlii* of both sexes. *Wilhelm Roux's Archives of Developmental Biology* 196:257–261. (16)

Ceccherelli, G. 1904. Sulle "terminazioni nervose a paniere" del Giacomini, nei muscoli dorsali degli anfibi anuri adulti. *Anatomischer Anzeiger* 24:428–435. (11)

Cecchi, G., F. Colomo, and V. Lombardi. 1978. Force-velocity relation in normal and nitrate-treated frog single muscle fibres during rise of tension in an isometric tetanus. *Journal of Physiology* (London) 285:257–273. (8)

Cecil, S. G., and J. J. Just. 1979. Survival rate, population density, and development of a naturally occuring anuran larvae (*Rana catesbeiana*). *Copeia* 1979:447–453. (16)

Cei, G. 1944. Analisi biogeografica e ricerche biologiche e sperimentali sal ciclo sessuale annuo delle rane rosse d'Europe. *Monitore Zoologico Italiano* 54, suppl.: 1–117. (15)

Cei, J. M. 1961. *Pleurodema bufonina* Bell, anfibio australe con ciclo spermatogenetico discontinuo autoregolato. *Archivo Zoologico Italiano* 46:167–180. (15)

Cereijido, M., and C. A. Rotunno. 1971. The effect of antidiuretic hormone on Na movement across frog skin. *Journal of Physiology* (London) 213:119–133. (5)

Cerretelli, P. D., P. E. diPrampero, and G. Ambrosoli. 1972. High-energy phosphate resynthesis from anaerobic glycolysis in frog gastrocnemius muscle. *American Journal of Physiology* 222:1021–1026. (12)

Cerretelli, P. D., D. Pendergast, W. C. Paganelli, and D. W. Rennie. 1979. Effects of specific training on $\dot{V}O_2$ on-response and early blood lactate. *Journal of Applied Physiology* 47:761–769. (12)

Certain, P. 1961. Organogénèse des formations interrénales chez le batracien urodèle *Pleurodeles waltlii* Michah. *Bulletin Biologique de la France et de la Belgique* 95:134–149. (16)

Ceusters, R., V. M. Darras, and E. R. Kuhn. 1978. Difference in thyroid function between male and female frogs (*Rana temporaria* L.) with increasing temperature. *General and Comparative Endocrinology* 36:598–603. (3)

Chaine, J. 1901. Anatomie comparée de certains muscles sushyoidiens. *Bulletin Scientifique France-Belgique* 35:1–210. (11)

———. 1903. Observations sur le muscle transverse de l'hyoïde des batraciens. *Processes-verbaux de la Société Scientifique, Bordeaux* 1902/3:111–115. (11)

Champy, C. 1913. Recherches sur la spermatogénèse des batraciens et les éléments accessoires du testicule. *Archives de Zoologie Expérimentale et Générale* 52:13–304. (15)

Chan, D. K. O. 1985. Evolution of cardiovascular function in vertebrates. In *Current Trends in Comparative Endocrinology*, ed. B. Lofts and W. N. Holmes, 985–991. Hong Kong: Hong Kong University Press. (3)

Chandola, A., and D. Bhatt. 1982. Tri-iodothyronine fails to mimic gonado-inhibitory action of thyroxine in spotted munia: Effects of injections at different times of the day. *General and Comparative Endocrinology* 48:499–503. (16)

Chang, J. P., R. E. Peter, C. S. Nahorniak, and M. Sokolowska. 1984. Effects of catecholaminergic agonists and antagonists on serum gonadotropin concentrations and ovulation in goldfish: Evidence for specificity of dopamine inhibition of gonadotropin secretion. *General and Comparative Endocrinology* 55:351–360. (15)

Chapeau, C., J. Gutkowska, P. W. Schiller, R. W. Milne, G. Thibault, R. Garcia, J. Genest, and M. Cantin. 1985. Localization of immunoreactive synthetic atrial natriuretic factor (ANF) in the heart of various animal species. *Journal of Histochemistry and Cytochemistry* 33:541–550. (3)

Chapman, B. M., and R. F. Chapman. 1958. A field study of a population of leopard toads (*Bufo regularis regularis*). *Journal of Animal Ecology* 27:265–286. (15)

Charan, D. 1971. The pelvic musculature of *Rana tigrina*. *Annals of Zoology* (Agra) 7:81–92. (11)

Charles, E. 1931. Metabolic changes associated with pigmentary effector activity and pituitary removal in *Xenopus laevis*: 1. Respiratory exchange. *Proceedings of the Royal Society of London* 107B:486–503. (12)

Chauvet, J., G. Michel, M. T. Chauvety, and R. Acher. 1988. An amphibian two-domain "big" neurophysin: Conformational homology with the mammalian MSEL-neurophysin/copeptin intermediate precursor shown by trypsin-sepharose proteolysis. *Federation of European Biochemical Societies Letters* 230:77–80. (16)

Chavin, W., K. V. Honn, and P. J. Clifford. 1978a. cAMP involvement in the control of corticosterone and aldosterone output in the adrenal of the frog (*Rana berlandieri forreri*). *General and Comparative Endocrinology* 35:445–450. (3)

———. 1978b. Prostaglandin effects upon cyclic AMP levels, corticosterone output, and aldosterone output in the adrenal of the frog *Rana berlandieri forreri*. *General and Comparative Endocrinology* 36:442–450. (3)

Cheetham, J. L., C. T. Garten, Jr., C. L. King, and M. H. Smith. 1976. Temperature tolerance and preference of immature channel catfish (*Ictalurus punctatus*). *Copeia* 1976:609–612. (9)

Chein, S., S. Usami, R. J. Dellenback, and C. A. Bryant. 1971. Comparative hemorheology: Hematological implications of species differences in blood viscosity. *Biorheology* 8:35–57. (5)

Cherian, A. 1962. Metabolism as a function of age and weight in frog. *Acta Physiologica et Pharmacologica Neerlandica* 11:443–456. (12)

Chernetski, K. E. 1964. Sympathetic enhancement of peripheral sensory input in the frog. *Journal of Neurophysiology* 27:493–515. (7)

Chester-Jones, I., and J. G. Phillips. 1987. The adrenal and interrenal glands. In *Vertebrate Endocrinology: Fundamentals and Biomedical Implications*, vol. 1, *Morphological Considerations*, ed. P. K. T. Pang and M. P. Schreibman, 319–350. New York: Academic Press. (3)

Chew, M. M., A. B. Elliott, and H. Y. Wong. 1972. Permeability of urinary bladder of *Rana cancrivora* to urea in the presence of oxytocin. *Journal of Physiology* (London) 223:757–772. (6)

Chieffi, G., and V. Botte. 1963. Osservazioni istochimiche sull'attività della steroide-B-olodeidrogenasi nell' interrenale e nelle gonadi di girihi e adulti di *Rana esculenta. Rivista di Istochimica, Normale et Patologica* 9:172–174. (16)

Chieffi, G., G. Delrio, and M. A. Valentino. 1975. Appearance of sex hormone receptor in frog (*Rana esculenta*) tadpole skin during metamorphosis. *Experientia* 31:989–990. (16)

Chieffi, G., R. K. Rastogi, L. Iela, and M. Milone. 1975. The function of fat bodies in relation to the hypothalamo-hypophyseal-gonadal axis in the frog, *Rana esculenta. Cell and Tissue Research* 161:157–165. (15)

Chinoy, N. J., and J. C. George. 1965. Cholinesterases in the pectoral muscles of some vertebrates. *Journal of Physiology* (London) 177:346–354. (11)

Chiono, M., R. S. Heller, J. J. Andazola, and C. A. Herman. 1991. Leucotriene C4 binds to receptors and has positive inotropic effects in bullfrog heart. *Journal of Pharmacology and Experimental Therapeutics* 256:1042–1048. (3)

Chitko, C. 1977. The effects of temperature and body size on the metabolic rate of the shiny salamander. *Bulletin of the New Jersey Academy of Science* 22:4. (8)

Chiu, K. W., H. Y. Lim, and P. K. T. Pang. 1988. The cardiac effects of arginine vasotocin in amphibians. *Comparative Biochemistry and Physiology* 89C:147–151. (3)

Chiu, K. W., M. Uchiyama, and P. K. T. Pang. 1983. Cardiovascular effects of bPTH-(l-34) in the frog, *Rana* sp. *Comparative Biochemistry and Physiology* 74C:99–101. (3)

Chong, G., H. Heatwole, and B. T. Firth. 1973. Panting thresholds of lizards: 2. Diel variation in the panting threshold of *Amphibolurus muricatus. Comparative Biochemistry and Physiology* 46A:827–829. (9)

Chowdhary, D. S. 1951. The carotid labyrinth of *Rana tigrina. Nature* 167:1074. (7)

Christensen, C. U. 1974a. Adaptations in the water economy of some anuran Amphibia. *Comparative Biochemistry and Physiology* 47A:1035–1049. (6)

———. 1974b. Effect of arterial perfusion on net water flux and active sodium transport across the isolated skin of *Bufo bufo bufo* (L.). *Journal of Comparative Physiology* 93:93–104. (4,6)

———. 1975a. Correlation between net water flux, osmotic concentration of the interstitial fluid, and osmotic water permeability of the isolated skin of *Bufo bufo bufo* (L.). *Journal of Comparative Physiology* 96:95–100. (6)

———. 1975b. Effects of dehydration, vasotocin, and hypertonicity on net water flux through the isolated, perfused pelvic skin of *Bufo bufo bufo* (L.). *Comparative Biochemistry and Physiology* 51A:7–10. (4,6)

Christian, K. A. 1982. Changes in the food niche during postmetamorphic ontogeny of the frog *Pseudacris triseriata. Copeia* 1982:73–80. (13,14)

Christian, K. A., C. R. Tracy, and W. P. Porter. 1983. Seasonal shifts in body temperature and use of microhabitats by Galapagos land iguanas (*Conolophus pallidus*). *Ecology* 64:463–468. (4)

———. 1984. Physiological and ecological consequences of sleeping site selection by the Galapagos land iguana (*Conolophus pallidus*). *Ecology* 65:752–758. (4)

Christiansen, J., and D. Penney. 1973. Anaerobic glycolysis and lactic acid accumulation in cold submerged *Rana pipiens. Journal of Comparative Physiology* 87:237–245. (10)

Chung, S. H., A. Pettigrew, and M. Anson. 1978. Dynamics of the amphibian middle ear. *Nature* 272:142–147. (11)

Church, G. 1960. Annual and lunar periodicity in the sexual cycle of the Javanese toad, *Bufo melanostictus* Schneider. *Zoologica* (New York Zoological Society) 45:181–188. (15)

Churchill, E. D., F. Nakazawa, and C. K. Drinker. 1927. The circulation of body fluids in the frog. *Journal of Physiology* (London) 63:304–308. (5)

Clark, N. B. 1983. Evolution of calcium regulation in lower vertebrates. *American Zoologist* 23:719–727. (3)

Clark, N. B., K. Kaul, and S. I. Roth. 1986. The parathyroid glands. In *Vertebrate Endocrinology: Fundamentals and Biomedical Implications*, vol. 1, *Morphological Considerations*, ed. P. K. T. Pang and M. P. Schreibman, 207–234. New York: Academic Press. (3,16)

Clarke, J. D. W., H. P. Hayes, S. P. Hunt, and A. Roberts. 1984. Sensory physiology, anatomy, and immunohistochemistry of Rohon-Beard neurones in embryos of *Xenopus laevis. Journal of Physiology* (London) 348:511–525. (16)

Clarke, R. D. 1974. Postmetamorphic growth rates in a natural population of Fowler's toad, *Bufo woodhousei fowleri. Canadian Journal of Zoology* 52:1489–1498. (15)

Claussen, D. L. 1969. Studies on water loss and rehydration in anurans. *Physiological Zoology* 42:1–14. (5,6)

———. 1973. The thermal relations of the tailed-frog, *Ascaphus truei,* and the Pacific treefrog, *Hyla regilla. Comparative Biochemistry and Physiology* 44A:137–153. (5,6,8,9)

———. 1974. Water balance and jumping ability in anuran amphibians. *American Zoologist* 14:1257. (12)

———. 1977. Thermal acclimation in ambystomatid salamanders. *Comparative Biochemistry and Physiology* 58A:333–340. (8)

Claussen, D. L., and J. R. Layne, Jr. 1983. Growth and survival of juvenile toads, *Bufo woodhousei,* maintained on four different diets. *Journal of Herpetology* 17:107–112. (13,15)

Clemons, G. K. 1976. Development and preliminary application of a homologous radioimmunoassay for bullfrog growth hormone. *General and Comparative Endocrinology* 30:357–363. (16)

Clemons, G. K., and C. S. Nicoll. 1977a. Development and preliminary application of a homologous radioimmunoassay for bullfrog prolactin. *General and Comparative Endocrinology* 32:531–535. (16)

———. 1977b. Effects of antisera to bullfrog prolactin and growth hormone on metamorphosis of *Rana catesbeiana* tadpoles. *General and Comparative Endocrinology* 31:495–497. (16)

Clemons, G. K., S. M. Russell, and C. S. Nicoll. 1979. Effect of mammalian thyrotropin-releasing hormone on prolactin secretion by bullfrog and adenohypophyses *in vitro. General and Comparative Endocrinology* 38:62–67. (16)

Clutton-Brock, T. H., ed. 1988. *Reproductive Success.* Chicago: University of Chicago Press. (14)

Clutton-Brock, T. H., and S. D. Albon. 1979. The roaring of red deer and the evolution of honest advertisement. *Behaviour* 69:145–170. (14)

Cochran, S. L., N. Dieringer, and W. Precht. 1984. Basic optokinetic-ocular reflex pathways in the frog. *Journal of Neuroscience* 4:43–57. (2)

Cockrum, L. 1941. Notes on *Siren intermedia. Copeia* 1941:264. (10)

Coghill, G. E. 1914. Correlated anatomical and physiological studies of the growth of the nervous system of Amphibia: 1. The afferent system of the trunk of *Amblystoma. Journal of Comparative Neurology* 24:161–233. (11)

———. 1916. Correlated anatomical and physiological studies of the growth of the nervous system of Amphibia: 2. The afferent system of the head of *Amblystoma. Journal of Comparative Neurology* 26:247–340. (11)

———. 1924a. Correlated anatomical and physiological studies of the growth of the nervous system of Amphibia: 3. The floor plate of *Amblystoma. Journal of Comparative Neurology* 37:37–69. (11)

———. 1924b. Correlated anatomical and physiological studies of the growth of the nervous system of Amphibia: 4. Rates of proliferation and differentiation in the central nervous system of *Amblystoma. Journal of Comparative Neurology* 37:71–120. (11)

———. 1926a. Correlated anatomical and physiological studies of the growth of the nervous system of Amphibia: 5. The growth of the pattern of the motor mechanism of *Amblystoma punctatum. Journal of Comparative Neurology* 40:47–94. (11)

———. 1926b. Correlated anatomical and physiological studies of the growth of the nervous system of Amphibia: 6. The mechanisms of integration of *Amblystoma punctatum. Journal of Comparative Neurology* 41:95–152. (11)

———. 1926c. Correlated anatomical and physiological studies of the growth of the nervous system of Amphibia: 7. The growth of the pattern of the association mechanism of the rhombencephalon and spinal cord of *Amblystoma punctatum. Journal of Comparative Neurology* 42:1–18. (11)

———. 1929. *Anatomy and the Problem of Behavior.* Cambridge: Cambridge University Press. (16)

Cohen, B., G. Giebisch, L. L. Hansen, U. Teuscher, and M. Wiederholt. 1984. Relationship between peritubular membrane potential and net fluid reabsorption in the distal tubule of *Amphiuma*. *Journal of Physiology* (London) 348:115–134. (5)

Cohen, M. J., and H. E. Winn. 1967. Electrophysiological observations on hearing and sound production in the fish *Porichthys notatus*. *Journal of Experimental Zoology* 165:355–370. (14)

Cohen, N. W. 1952. Comparative rates of dehydration and hydration in some California salamanders. *Ecology* 33:462–479. (6)

Cohen, P. 1980. *Recently Discovered Systems of Enzyme Regulation by Reversible Phosphorylation*. Amsterdam: Elsevier/North Holland Biomedical Press. (10)

Coleman, R. 1975. The development and fine structure of ultimobranchial glands in larval anurans: 2. *Bufo viridis*, *Hyla arborea*, and *Rana ridibunda*. *Cell Tissue Research* 164:215–232. (16)

Coleman, R., and A. D. Phillips. 1972. Ultimobranchial gland ultrastructure of larval axolotls, *Ambystoma mexicanum* Shaw, with some observations on the newt, *Pleurodeles waltlii* Micahelles. *Zeitschrift für Zellforschung und mikroskopishe Anatomie* 134:183–191. (16)

———. 1974. The development and fine structure of the ultimobranchial glands in larval *Rana temporaria* L. *Cell and Tissue Research* 148:69–82. (16)

Collenot, A. 1965. L'activité de la Δ⁵—³β-hydroxystéroïde déshydrogénasique dans le testicule de *Pleurodeles waltlii* au cours de l'ontogénèse. *General and Comparative Endocrinology* 5:669–670. (16)

Collenot, G., and A. Collenot. 1977. L'activité 3 β hydroxystéroïde déshydrogénasique dans les gonades en différenciation de *Pleurodeles waltlii* (Amphibien, Urodèle), visualisation sur coupes seriées a l'aide d'une nouvelle technique histochimique. *Journal of Embryological and Experimental Morphology* 42:29–42. (16)

Collett, T. S. 1982. Do toads plan routes? A study of the detour behavior of *Bufo viridis*. *Journal of Comparative Physiology* 146:261–271. (13)

Collins, J. P., and J. E. Cheek. 1983. Effect of food and density on development of typical and cannibalistic salamander larvae in *Ambystoma tigrinum nebulosum*. *American Zoologist* 23:77–84. (14)

Collins, J. P., and M. A. Lewis. 1979. Overwintering tadpoles and breeding season variation in the *Rana pipiens* complex in Arizona. *Southwestern Naturalist* 24:371–373. (10)

Collins, J. T. 1974. *Amphibians and Reptiles in Kansas*. Lawrence: University of Kansas Museum of Natural History. (10)

Comer, C., and P. Grobstein. 1978. Prey acquisition in atectal frogs. *Brain Research* 153:217–221. (2)

———. 1981a. Involvement of midbrain structures in tactually and visually elicited prey acquisition behavior in the frog, *Rana pipiens*. *Journal of Comparative Physiology* 142:151–160. (2)

———. 1981b. Organization of sensory inputs to the midbrain of the frog, *Rana pipiens*. *Journal of Comparative Physiology* 142:161–168. (2)

———. 1981c. Tactually elicited prey acquisition behavior in the frog, *Rana pipiens*, and a comparison with visually elicited behavior. *Journal of Comparative Physiology* 142:141–150. (2)

Commission for Thermal Physiology of the International Union of Physiological Sciences. 1987. Glossary of terms for thermal physiology, second edition. *Pflugers Archiv* 410:567–587. (8,9)

Conant, R. 1975. *A Field Guide to Reptiles and Amphibians of Eastern and Central North America*. Boston: Houghton Mifflin Company. (10)

Condo, S. G., B. Andrea, M. Brunori, M. Corda, M. G. Pellegrini, E. M. Clementi, and B. Giardina. 1989. The functional properties of amphibian hemoglobin: The case of *Salamandra salamandra* and *Hydromantes genei*. *Comparative Biochemistry and Physiology* 93A:319–325. (5)

Condo, S. G., B. Giardina, A. Bellelli, M. Lunadei, A. Ferracin, and M. Brunori. 1983. Comparative studies of hemoglobins from newts: A kinetic approach. *Comparative Biochemistry and Physiology* 74A:545–548. (5)

Condo, S. G., B. Giardini, M. Lunadei, A. Ferracin, and M. Brunori. 1981. Functional properties of hemoglobins from *Triturus cristatus*. *European Journal of Biochemistry* 120:323–327. (5)

Conklin, A. E. 1930. The formation and circulation of lymph in the frog: 1. The rate of lymph production. *American Journal of Physiology* 1:79–110. (5)

Connon, F. E. 1947. A comparative study of the respiration of normal and hybrid *Triturus* embryos and larvae. *Journal of Experimental Zoology* 105:1–24. (12)

Constantine-Paton, M., and J. J. Norden. 1986. Synapse regulation in the developing visual system. In *Development of Order in the Visual System*, ed. S. R. Hilfer and J. B. Sheffield, 1–14. Berlin: Springer-Verlag. (16)

Cook, S. F. 1949. Respiratory metabolism of certain reptiles and Amphibia. *University of California Publications in Zoology* 53:367–376. (13)

Cooke, A. S. 1974. Differential predation by newts on tadpoles. *British Journal of Herpetology* 5:386–390. (14)

———. 1982. A comparison of dates of breeding activity for the frog (*Rana temporaria*) and the toad (*Bufo bufo*) at a site in Cambridgeshire, 1971–1981. *British Journal of Herpetology* 6:202–205. (8)

Coombs, S., P. Görner, and H. Münz, eds. 1989. *The Mechanosensory Lateral Line: Neurobiology and Evolution*. New York: Springer-Verlag. (16)

Cooper, K. S. 1943. An experimental study of the development of the larval olfactory organ of *Rana pipiens* Schreber. *Journal of Experimental Zoology* 93:415–451. (16)

Cordeiro de Sousa, M. B., and A. Hoffmann. 1981. Autonomic variations caused by stimulation of the rhombencephalic visceral sensory zone in anesthetized toads. *Comparative Biochemistry and Physiology* 70C:123–127. (7)

———. 1985. Autonomic adjustments during avoidance and orienting responses induced by electrical stimulation of the central nervous system in toads (*Bufo paracnemis*). *Journal of Comparative Physiology* 155B:381–386. (7)

Cords, E. 1922. Die Hautmuskeln der Amphibien nebst Bemerkungen über Hautmuskeln im Allgemeinen. *Zoologische Jahrbücher, Abteilung für Anatomie und Ontogenie der Thiere* 42:283–326. (11)

———. 1923. Zur vergleichenden Anatomie der prävertebralen Muskulatur bei den Amphibien. *Jenaische Zeitschrift für Naturwissenschaften* 59:527–574. (11)

Cormarèche-Leydier, M. 1986. The effect of an intraperitoneal injection of capsaicin on the thermopreferendum in the frog (*Rana esculenta*). *Physiology and Behavior* 36:29–32. (9)

Corse, W. A., and D. E. Metter. 1980. Economics, adult feeding, and larval growth of *Rana catesbeiana* on a fish hatchery. *Journal of Herpetology* 14:231–238. (13)

Cortelyou, J. R. 1962. Phosphorous changes in totally parathyroidectomized *Rana pipiens*. *Endocrinology* 70:618–622. (5)

———. 1967. The effect of commercially prepared parathyroid extract on plasma and urine calcium levels in *Rana pipiens*. *General and Comparative Endocrinology* 9:234–240. (3,5)

Cortelyou, J. R., A. Hibner-Owerko, and J. Mulloy. 1960. Blood and urine calcium changes in totally parathyroidectomized *Rana pipiens*. *Endocrinology* 66:441–450. (3,5)

Cortelyou, J. R., and D. J. McWhinnie. 1967. Parathyroid glands of amphibians: 1. Parathyroid structure and function in the amphibian, with emphasis on regulation of mineral ions in body fluids. *American Zoologist* 7:843–855. (3)

Cortelyou, J. R., P. A. Quipse, and D. J. McWhinnie. 1967. Parathyroid extract effects on phosphorous metabolism in *Rana pipiens*. *General and Comparative Endocrinology* 9:76–92. (5)

Cossins, A. R. 1983. The adaptation of membrane structure and function to changes in temperature. In *Cellular Acclimatisation to Environmental Change*, ed. A. R. Cossins and P. Sheterline, 3–32. Cambridge: Cambridge University Press. (10)

Cossins, A. R., and K. Bowler. 1987. *Temperature Biology of Animals*. New York: Chapman and Hall. (9)

Costanzo, J. P., D. L. Claussen, and R. E. Lee. 1988. Natural freeze tolerance in a reptile. *Cryo Letters* 9:380–385. (10)

Costill, D. L., J. Daniels, W. Evans, W. Fink, G. Krahenbuhl, and B. Saltin. 1976. Skeletal muscle enzymes and fiber composition in male and female track athletes. *Journal of Applied Physiology* 40:149–154. (14)

Cothran, M. L., and V. H. Hutchison. 1979. Effect of melatonin on thermal selection by *Crotaphytus collaris* (Squamata: Iguanidae). *Comparative Biochemistry and Physiology* 63A:461–466. (9)

Cott, H. B. 1936. The effectiveness of protective adaptations in the hive bee, illustrated by experiments on the feeding reactions, habit formation, and memory of the common toad (*Bufo bufo bufo*). *Proceedings of Zoology Society* (London) 1:111–134. (13)

———. 1940. *Adaptive Coloration in Animals.* London: Methuen Press. (4)

Coutant, C. C. 1977. Compilation of temperature preference data. *Journal of Fisheries Research Board of Canada* 34:739–745. (9)

Couteaux, R. 1955. Localization of cholinesterase at neuromuscular junctions. *International Review of Cytology* 4:335–375. (11)

Cowles, R. B. 1940. Additional implications of reptilian sensitivity to high temperatures. *American Naturalist* 74:542–561. (9)

———. 1962. Semantics in biothermal studies. *Science* 135:670. (9)

Cowles, R. B., and C. M. Bogert. 1944. A preliminary study of the thermal requirements of desert reptiles. *Bulletin of the American Museum of Natural History* 83:261–296. (8,9,14)

Cox, D. K., and C. C. Coutant. 1981. Growth dynamics of juvenile striped bass as functions of temperature and ration. *Transactions of the American Fisheries Society* 110:226–238. (9)

Cox, T. C. 1986. Ion transport across the skin of a larval salamander. *Biochimica et Biophysica Acta* 858:142–152. (5,16)

Cox, T. C., and R. H. Alvarado. 1979. Electrical and transport characteristics of skin of larval *Rana catesbeiana. American Journal of Physiology* 237:R74–R79. (5,16)

———. 1983. Nystatin studies of the skin of larval *Rana catesbeiana. American Journal of Physiology* 244:R58–R65. (5,16)

Crabbe, J., and P. DeWeer. 1964. Action of aldosterone on the bladder and skin of the toad. *Nature* 202:298–299. (5)

Crawford, E. C., Jr. 1982. Behavioral and autonomic thermoregulation in terrestrial ectotherms. In *A Companion to Animal Physiology,* ed. C. R. Taylor, K. Johansen, and L. Bolis, 198–215. New York: Cambridge University Press. (9)

Crawshaw, L. I. 1980. Temperature regulation in vertebrates. *Annual Review of Physiology* 42:473–491. (9)

Crawshaw, L. I., and H. T. Hammel. 1971. Behavioral thermoregulation in two species of antarctic fish. *Life Sciences* 10:1009–1020. (9)

———. 1974. Behavioural regulation of internal temperature in the brown bullhead, *Ictalurus nebulosus. Comparative Biochemistry and Physiology* 47A:51–60. (9)

Crawshaw, L. I., L. P. Wollmuth, and C. S. O'Connor. 1989. Intracranial ethanol and ambient anoxia elicit selection of cooler water by goldfish. *American Journal of Physiology* 256:R133–R137. (9)

Cree, A. 1985. Water balance and nitrogen excretion in two introduced frogs (*Litoria raniformis* and *L. ewingi*). *New Zealand Journal of Zoology* 12:341–348. (6)

———. 1988a. Effects of arginine vasotocin on water-balance of three leiopelmatid frogs. *General and Comparative Endocrinology* 72:340–350. (6)

———. 1988b. Water balance responses of the hylid frog *Litoria aurea. Journal of Experimental Zoology* 247:119–125. (6,9,16)

———. 1989. Relationship between environmental conditions and nocturnal activity of the terrestrial frog, *Leiopelma archeyi. Journal of Herpetology* 23:61–68. (6)

Creed, K. 1964. A study of newts in the New Forest. *British Journal of Herpetology* 3:170–181. (16)

Crerar, M. M., E. S. David, and K. B. Storey. 1988. Electrophoretic analysis of liver glycogen phosphorylase activation in the freeze-tolerant wood frog. *Biochimica et Biophysica Acta* 971:72–84. (10)

Crespo, E. G., and J. M. Cei. 1971. L'activité spermatogénétique saisonnière de *Rana iberica* Boul. du nord de Portugal. *Arquivos do Museu Bocage* 3:37–50. (15)

Crews, D., and R. Silver. 1985. Reproductive physiology and behavior interactions in nonmammalian vertebrates. In *Handbook of Behavioral Neurobiology,* ed. N. Adler, D. Pfaff, and R. W. Goy, 7:101–182. New York: Plenum Publishing. (15)

Crim, J. W. 1984. Immunocytochemistry of luteinizing hormone–releasing hormone in brains of bullfrogs (*Rana catesbeiana*) during spontaneous metamorphosis. *Journal of Experimental Zoology* 229:327–337. (16)

———. 1987. LHRH systems in the amphibian nervous system: Comparative neuroendocrinology of development. In *The Terminal Nerve (Nervus Terminalis): Structure, Function, and Evolution,* ed. L. S. Demski and M. Schwanzel-Fukuda, Annals of New York Academy of Sciences 519, 117–127. New York: New York Academy of Sciences. (16)

Cronin, J. T., and J. Travis. 1986. Size limited predation on larval *Rana areolata* (Anura: Ranidae) by two species of backswimmer (Insecta: Hemiptera: Notonectidae). *Herpetologica* 42:171–174. (14)

Crowley, S. R. 1987. The effect of dessication upon the preferred body temperature and activity level of the lizard *Sceloporus undulatus. Copeia* 1987:25–32. (9)

Crump, M. L. 1972. Territoriality and mating behavior in *Dendrobates granuliferus* (Anura: Dendrobatidae). *Herpetologica* 28:195–198. (15)

———. 1974. Reproductive strategies in a tropical anuran community. University of Kansas Museum of Natural History Miscellaneous Publication 61. Lawrence: University of Kansas Press. (14)

———. 1984. Ontogenetic changes in vulnerability to predation in tadpoles of *Hyla pseudopuma. Herpetologica* 40:265–271. (14)

———. 1986. Cannibalism by younger tadpoles: Another hazard of metamorphosis. *Copeia* 1986:1007–1009. (16)

———. 1989a. Effect of habitat drying on developmental time and size at metamorphosis in *Hyla pseudopuma. Copeia* 1989:794–797. (16)

———. 1989b. Life history consequences of feeding versus non-feeding in facultative non-feeding toad larvae. *Oecologia* (Berlin) 78:486–489. (16)

Crump, M. L., and R. H. Kaplan. 1979. Clutch energy partitioning of tropical treefrogs. *Copeia* 1979:626–635. (14)

Cuccati, G. 1888. Sopra il distribuimento e la terminazione delle fibre nervii nei polmoni della *Rana temporaria. International Monatsschrift für Anatomy und Physiology* (Leipzig) 5:194–203. (7)

Cummings, J. W. 1979. Physiological and biochemical adaptations to training in *Rana pipiens. Journal of Comparative Physiology* 134B:345–350. (12,14)

Cummings, T. A., R. J. Delay, and S. D. Roper. 1987. Scanning and high voltage electron microscopy of taste cells in the mudpuppy, *Necturus maculosus.* In *Olfaction and Taste,* ed. S. D. Roper and J. Atema, Annals of New York Academy of Sciences 510, 247–249. New York: New York Academy of Sciences. (16)

Cummins, C. P. 1989. Interaction between the effects of pH and density on growth and development in *Rana temporaria* L. tadpoles. *Functional Ecology* 3:45–52. (14)

Cunjak, R. A. 1986. Winter habitat of northern leopard frogs, *Rana pipiens,* in a southern Ontario stream. *Canadian Journal of Zoology* 64:255–257. (10)

Cunningham, J. C., P. A. Robbins, and C. B. Wolff. 1986. Integration of respiratory responses to changes in alveolar partial pressures of CO_2 and O_2 and in arterial pH. In *Handbook of Physiology,* ed. N. S. Cherniack and J. G. Widdicombe, 2:475–528. Bethesda, MD: American Physiological Society. (7)

Cunningham, J. D. 1960. Aspects of the ecology of the Pacific slender salamander, *Batrachoseps pacificus,* in southern California. *Ecology* 41:88–99. (6)

Cunningham, J. D., and D. P. Mullally. 1956. Thermal factors in the ecology of the Pacific treefrog. *Herpetologica* 12:68–79. (9,10)

Cupp, P. V., Jr. 1980. Thermal tolerance of five salientian amphibians during development and metamorphosis. *Herpetologica* 36:234–244. (8)

Curran, P. F. 1972. Effect of silver ion on permeability properties of frog skin. *Biochimica et Biophysica Acta* 288:90–97. (5)

Cushman, J. R., G. C. Packard, and T. J. Boardman. 1976. Concentrations of lactic acid in neotenic and transformed tiger salamanders (*Ambystoma tigrinum*) before and after activity. *Journal of Comparative Physiology* 112B:273–281. (12,16)

Cuthbert, A. W. 1973. An upper limit to the number of sodium channels in frog skin epithelium. *Journal of Physiology* (London) 228:681–692. (5)

Cuthbert, A. W., E. Painter, and W. T. Prince. 1969. The effects of anions on sodium transport. *British Journal of Pharmacology* 36:97–106. (5)

Czopek, J. 1957. The vascularization of respiratory surfaces in *Ambystoma mexicanum* (Cope) in ontogeny. *Zoologica Poloniae* 8:131–149. (16)

———. 1959. Skin and lung capillaries in European common newts. *Copeia* 1959:91–96. (5)

———. 1961. Vascularization of respiratory surfaces of some Plethodontidae. *Zoologica Poloniae* 11:131–148. (5)

———. 1963. The distribution of capillaries in muscles of some Amphibia. *Studia Societa Scientifica Torunen* E7:61–98. (11)

———. 1965. Quantitative studies on the morphology of respiratory surfaces in amphibians. *Acta Anatomica* 62:296–323. (5,6,10,12)

Dabelsteen, T. 1981. The sound pressure level in the dawn song of the blackbird *Turdus merula* and a method for adjusting to the level in experimental song to the level in natural song. *Zeitschrift für Tierpsychologie* 56:137–149. (14)

Dale, E. 1962. Steroid excretion by larval frogs. *General and Comparative Endocrinology* 2:171–176. (16)

Dalrymple, G. H., J. E. Jutterbock, and A. L. La Valley. 1985. Function of the atlanto-mandibular ligaments of desmognathine salamanders. *Copeia* 1985:254–257. (11)

Daly, J. W., G. B. Brown, M. Mensah-Dwumah, and C. W. Myers. 1978. Classification of the skin alkaloids from Neotropical poisondart frogs (Dendrobatidae). *Toxicon* 16:163–188. (14)

Damstra, K. St. J. 1986. A kinetic analysis of evaporative water loss barriers. *Journal of Theoretical Biology* 121:439–448. (6)

Daniels, E., and P. Licht. 1980. Effects of gonadotropin-releasing hormone on the levels of plasma gonadotropins (FSH and LH) in the bullfrog, *Rana catesbeiana*. *General and Comparative Endocrinology* 42:455–463. (15)

Danstedt, R. T., Jr. 1975. Local geographic variation in demographic parameters and body size of *Desmognathus fuscus* (Amphibia: Plethodontidae). *Ecology* 56:1054–1067. (15)

Dantzler, W. H. 1989. *Comparative Physiology of the Vertebrate Kidney*. Berlin: Springer-Verlag. (16)

Darlington, P. J., Jr. 1957. *Zoogeography: The Geographical Distribution of Animals*. New York: Wiley. (10,15)

Darras, V. M., and E. R. Kuhn. 1982. Increased plasma levels of thyroid hormones in a frog *Rana ridibunda* following intravenous administration of TRH. *General and Comparative Endocrinology* 48:469–475. (3,16)

———. 1983. Effects of TRH, bovine TSH, and pituitary extracts on thyroidal T₄ release in *Ambystoma mexicanum*. *General and Comparative Endocrinology* 51:286–291. (16)

———. 1984. Difference of the *in vivo* responsiveness to thyrotropin stimulation between the neotenic and metamorphosed axolotl, *Ambystoma mexicanum*: Failure of prolactin to block the thyrotopin-induced thyroxine release. *General and Comparative Endocrinology* 56:321–325. (16)

Darwin, C. 1871. *The Descent of Man and Selection in Relation to Sex*. Reprint. New York: Random House. (14)

Das, S. M., and V. K. Srivastava. 1956. On the mechanism of respiration in *Rana tigrina* Daud., with a note on its respiratory muscles. *Zoologischer Anzeiger* 159:202–214. (11)

Dauca, M., J. Hourdry, J. S. Hugon, and D. Menard. 1979. Amphibian intestinal brush border membranes: 1. Isolation from *Rana catesbeiana* tadpole. *Comparative Biochemistry and Physiology* 64B:155–159. (16)

———. 1981. Amphibian intestinal brush border membranes: 3. Comparison during metamorphosis of the protein, glycoprotein, and enzyme patterns after gel electrophoretic separation of SDS-solubilized membranes. *Comparative Biochemistry and Physiology* 69B:15–22. (16)

Daughaday, W. H., M. Kapadia, C. E. Yanowi, K. Fabrick, and I. K. Mariz. 1985. Insulin-like growth factors I and II of nonmammalian sera. *General and Comparative Endocrinology* 59:316–325. (16)

Daugherty, J. L., and J. A. Marshall. 1976. The sound-producing mechanism of the croaking gourami, *Trichopsis vittatus* (Pisces, Belontidae). *Physiological Zoology* 49:141–162. (14)

Davic, R. D., and L. P. Orr. 1987. The relationship between rock density and salamander density in a mountain stream. *Herpetologica* 43:357–361. (14)

David, R. S., and R. G. Jaeger. 1981. Prey location through chemical cues by a terrestrial salamander. *Copeia* 1981:435–440. (13)

Davidson, E. H., and B. R. Hough. 1969. Synchronous oogenesis in *Engystomops pustulosus*, a Neotropic anuran suitable for laboratory studies: Localization in the embryo of RNA synthesized at the lampbrush stage. *Journal of Experimental Zoology* 172:25–48. (14)

Davidson, M., and H. Heatwole. 1960. Late summer oviposition in the salamander, *Plethodon cinereus*. *Herpetologica* 16:141–142. (15)

Davies, K., C. Donovan, C. Refino, G. Brooks, L. Packer, and P. Dallman. 1984. Distinguishing effects of anemia and muscle iron deficiency on exercise bioenergetics in the rat. *American Journal of Physiology* 246:E535–E543. (14)

Davies, K., J. Maguire, G. Brooks, P. Dallman, and L. Packer. 1982. Muscle mitochondrial bioenergenics, oxygen supply, and work capacity during dietary iron deficiency and repletion. *American Journal of Physiology* 242:E418–E427. (14)

Davies, M., and T. C. Burton. 1982. Osteology and myology of the gastric brooding frog *Rheobatrachus silus* Liem (Anura: Leptodactylidae). *Australian Journal of Zoology* 30:503–521. (11)

Davies, M., and M. J. Littlejohn. 1986. Frogs of the genus *Uperoleia* Gray (Anura: Leptodactylidae) in south-eastern Australia. *Transactions of the Royal Academy of South Australia* 109:111–143. (14)

Davies, N. B., and T. R. Halliday. 1978. Deep croaks and fighting assessment in toads. *Nature* 274:683–685. (14)

Davies, N. B., and A. Lundberg. 1984. Food distribution and a variable mating system in the dunnock (*Prunella modularis*). *Journal of Animal Ecology* 53:895–912. (14)

Davis, J. E., J. R. Spotila, and W. C. Schefler. 1980. Evaporative water loss from the American alligator, *Alligator mississippiensis*: Relative importance of respiratory and cutaneous components and the regulatory role of the skin. *Comparative Biochemistry and Physiology* 67A:439–446. (6)

Davison, J. 1955. Body weight, cell surface, and metabolic rate in anuran Amphibia. *Biological Bulletin* 109:407–419. (12)

Dawley, E. M. 1984. Recognition of individual, sex, and species odours by salamanders of the *Plethodon glutinosus–P. jordani* complex. *Animal Behaviour* 32:353–361. (2)

Dawson, T. J., and T. R. Grant. 1980. Metabolic capabilities of monotremes and the evolution of homeothermy. In *Comparative Physiology: Primitive Mammals,* ed. K. Schmidt-Nielsen, L. Bolis, and C. R. Taylor, 140–147. Cambridge: Cambridge University Press. (9)

Dawson, W. R. 1975. On the physiological significance of the preferred body temperatures of reptiles. In *Perspectives of Biophysical Ecology,* ed. D. M. Gates and R. B. Schmerl, 443–473. New York: Springer-Verlag. (9)

Dean, J. 1980. Encounters between bombardier beetles and two species of toads (*Bufo americanus, B. marinus*): Speed of prey-capture does not determine success. *Journal of Comparative Physiology* 135:41–50. (13)

De Benedictis, P. A. 1974. Intraspecific competition between tadpoles of *Rana sylvatica*. *Ecological Monographs* 44:129–151. (14)

De Boissezon, P. 1939. Le labyrinthe carotidien de la grenouille rousse adulte. *Bulletin de la Société d'Histoire Naturelle de Toulouse* 73:145–152. (7)

De Costa, J., M. Alonso-Bedate, and A. Fraile. 1979. Temperature acclimation in amphibians in lactate dehydrogenase activities and isozyme patterns in *Discoglossus pictus* tadpoles. *Acta Embryologiae Experimentalis* 1979:233–246. (8)

———. 1981. Temperature acclimation in amphibians: Changes in lactate dehydrogenase activities and isozyme patterns in several tissues from adult *Discoglossus pictus pictus*. *Comparative Biochemistry and Physiology* 70B:331–339. (8)

———. 1983. Seasonal acclimatization in anuran amphibians: Changes in lactate dehydrogenase specific activities and isozyme patterns in several tissues from a naturally occurring population of *Discoglossus pictus pictus* (Otth.). *Comparative Biochemistry and Physiology* 76B:299–307. (10)

Deeds, D. G., L. P. Sullivan, and D. J. Welling. 1978. Potassium reabsorption and secretion in the perfused bullfrog kidney. *American Journal of Physiology* 235:F26–F32. (5)

Degani, G. 1982. Amphibian tadpole interaction in a winter pond. *Hydrobiologia* 96:3–8. (8)

———. 1983. Oxygen consumption rates of *Salamandra salamandra* (L.) from different habitats. *British Journal of Herpetology* 6:281–283. (12)

———. 1984. Temperature selection in *Salamandra salamandra* (L.) larvae and juveniles from different habitats. *Biology of Behaviour* 9:175–183. (9)

Degani, G., S. Goldenberg, and M. R. Warburg. 1980. Cannibalistic phenomena in *Salamandra* larvae in certain water bodies and under experimental conditions. *Hydrobiologia* 75:123–128. (8)

Degani, G., and A. Meltzer. 1988. Oxygen consumption of a terrestrial toad (*Bufo viridis*) and semi-aquatic frog (*Rana ridibunda*). *Comparative Biochemistry and Physiology* 89A:347–349. (12)

Degani, G., N. Silanikove, and A. Shkolnik. 1984. Adaptation of the green toad (*Bufo viridis*) to terrestrial life by urea accumulation. *Comparative Biochemistry and Physiology* 77A:585–587. (6)

Degani, G., and M. R. Warburg. 1980. The response to substrate moisture of juvenile and adult *Salamandra salamandra* (L.). (Amphibia: Urodela). *Biology of Behavior* 5:281–290. (6)

———. 1984. Changes in concentrations of ions and urea in both plasma and muscle tissue in a dehydrated hylid anuran. *Comparative Biochemistry and Physiology* 77A:357–360. (6)

De Jager, E. F. J. 1939. Contributions to the cranial anatomy of the Gymnophiona: Further points regarding the cranial anatomy of the genus *Dermophis*. *Anatomischer Anzeiger* 88:193–222. (11)

de Jongh, H. J. 1968. Functional morphology of the jaw apparatus of larval and metamorphosing *Rana temporaria* L. *Netherlands Journal of Zoology* 18:1–103. (11)

de Jongh, H. J., and C. Gans. 1969. On the mechanism of respiration in the bullfrog, *Rana catesbeiana*: A reassessment. *Journal of Morphology* 127:259–290. (5,6,7,11)

de Jongh, H. J., and H. J. Grootenboer. 1989. Biomechanics of jumping in the frog. *Annals de la Société Zoologique de Belgique* (Abstracts 3d International Congress of Vertebrate Morphology) 119:63. (11)

Dejours, P. 1976. Water versus air as the respiratory medium. In *Respiration of Amphibious Vertebrates*, ed. G. M. Hughes, 1–15. New York: Academic Press. (7)

———. 1979. Respiratory controls: Oxygenation, CO_2 clearance, or acid-base equilibrium? In *Claude Bernard and the Internal Environment: A Memorial Symposium*, ed. E. D. Robin. New York: Marcel Dekker. (7)

———. 1981. *Principles of Comparative Respiratory Physiology*. Amsterdam: Elsevier/North Holland Biomedical Press. (6,7,16)

Dejours, P., W. F. Garey, and H. Rahn. 1970. Comparison of ventilatory and circulatory flow rates between animals in various physiological conditions. *Respiration Physiology* 9:108–117. (6)

de la Lande, I. S., P. E. O'Brien, D. J. C. Shearman, P. Taylor, and M. J. Tyler. 1984. On the possible role of prostaglandin E₂ in intestinal stasis in the gastric brooding frog *Rheobatrachus silus*. *Australian Journal of Experimental Biology and Medical Science* 62:317–323. (13)

DeLaney, R. G., S. Lahiri, and A. P. Fishman. 1974. Aestivation of the African lungfish *Protopterus aethiopicus*: Cardiovascular and pulmonary function. *Journal of Experimental Biology* 61:111–128. (10)

DeLaney, R. G., S. Lahiri, R. Hamilton, and A. P. Fishman. 1977. Acid-base balance and plasma composition in the aestivating lungfish (*Protopterus*). *American Journal of Physiology* 232:R10–R17. (10)

Delarue, C., F. Leboulenger, F. Homo-Delarche, M. Benyamina, I. Lirhmann, I. Perroteau, and H. Vaudry. 1986. Involvement of prostaglandins in the response of frog adrenocortical cells to muscarinic receptor activation. *Prostaglandins* 32:87–91. (3)

Delarue, C., M. C. Tonon, F. Leboulenger, S. Jégou, P. Leroux, and H. Vaudry. 1979. *In vitro* study of frog (*Rana ridibunda* Pallas) interrenal function by use of a simplified perfusion system: 2. Influence of adrenocorticotropin upon aldosterone production. *General and Comparative Endocrinology* 38:399–409. (3)

Delgado, M. J., P. Gutiérrez, and M. Alonso-Bedate. 1990. Annual ovarian cycle and plasma levels of 17β-estradiol in the frog *Rana perezi*. *Physiological Zoology* 63:373–387. (3)

Delgado, M. J., and B. Vivien-Roels. 1989. Effect of environmental temperature and photoperiod on the melatonin levels in the pineal, lateral eye, and plasma of the frog, *Rana perezi*: Importance of ocular melatonin. *General and Comparative Endocrinology* 75:46–53. (3)

Delidow, B. C., R. A. Baldocchi, and C. S. Nicoll. 1988. Evidence for hepatic involvement in the regulation of amphibian development by prolactin. *General and Comparative Endocrinology* 70:418–424. (16)

Delidow, B. C., N. Herbert, S. Steiny, and C. S. Nicoll. 1986. Secretion of prolactin-synergizing activity (synlactin) by the liver of ectothermic vertebrates *in vitro*. *Journal of Experimental Zoology* 238:147–153. (16)

del Pino, E. M. 1980. Morphology of the pouch and incubatory integument in marsupial frogs (Hylidae). *Copeia* 1980:10–17. (11,13,16)

———. 1989. Marsupial frogs. *Scientific American* 260:110–118. (15)

Delsol, M., and F. Masnou. 1957. Dosage de l'hormone antidiurétique hypophysaire et capacité réactionnelle à cette hormone chez les *Alytes obstetricans* au cours de la métamorphose. *Actes Société Linneenne de Bordeaux* 97:65–66. (16)

Delson, J. and W. G. Whitford. 1973. Adaptation of the tiger salamander, *Ambystoma tigrinum*, to arid habitats. *Comparative Biochemistry and Physiology* 46A:631–638. (6)

De Marneffe-Foulon, C. 1962. Contribution a l'étude du mechanisme et du contrôle des mouvements respiratoires chez *Rana*. *Annales de la Société Royale Zoologique de Belgique* 92:81–132. (7)

Demian, J. J., and D. H. Taylor. 1977. Photoreception and locomotor rhythm entrainment by the pineal body of the newt, *Notophthalmus viridescens* (Amphibia, Urodela, Salamandridae). *Journal of Herpetology* 11:131–139. (2,9)

Dempster, W. T. 1930. The growth of larvae of *Ambystoma punctatum* under normal conditions. *Biological Bulletin* 58:182–192. (16)

Demski, L. S., and R. G. Northcutt. 1983. The terminal nerve: A new chemosensory system in vertebrates? *Science* 220:435–437. (2)

Dent, J. N. 1987. The thyroid gland. In *Vertebrate Endocrinology: Fundamentals and Biomedical Implications*, vol. 1, *Morphological Considerations*, ed. P. K. T. Pang and M. P. Schreibman, 175–206. New York: Academic Press. (3)

———. 1988. Hormonal interaction in amphibian metamorphosis. *American Zoologist* 28:297–308. (3,16)

Denver, R. J. 1988. Several hypothalamic peptides stimulate in vitro thyrotropin secretion by pituitaries of anuran amphibians. *General and Comparative Endocrinology* 72:383–393. (16)

deRoos, R., and A. V. Parker. 1982. Nondetectable plasma glucose levels after insulin administration in the American bullfrog (*Rana catesbeiana*). *General and Comparative Endocrinology* 46:505–510. (3)

deRoos, R., and R. P. Rumpf. 1987. Plasma levels of glucose, alanine, lactate, and β-hydroxybutyrate after mammalian insulin treatment in the American bullfrog (*Rana catesbeiana*). *Journal of Experimental Zoology* 244:49–57. (3)

DeRuyter, M. L., and D. F. Stiffler. 1985. Osmotic and ionic regulation in the aquatic caecilian *Typhlonectes compressicauda* and the fossorial caecilian *Icthyophis biangularis*. *Physiologist* 28:367. (5)

———. 1986. Interrenal function in larval *Ambystoma tigrinum*: 2. Control of aldosterone secretion and electrolyte balance by ACTH. *General and Comparative Endocrinology* 62:298–305. (5,16)

———. 1988. Acid-base and electrolyte responses to low pH maintained by phosphate-citrate buffers in the bathing medium of the larval salamander *Ambystoma tigrinum*. *Canadian Journal of Zoology* 66:2383–2389. (5)

De Sousa, R. C., and A. Grosso. 1982. Osmotic water flow across the abdominal skin of the toad *Bufo marinus*: Effect of vasopressin and isoprenaline. *Journal of Physiology* (London) 329:281–296. (6)

Dettlaff, T. A. 1986. The rate of development in poikilothermic animals calculated in astronomical and relative time units. *Journal of Thermal Biology* 11:1–8. (8)

Detwiler, S. R. 1920. Experiments on the transplantation of limbs in *Ambystoma*: The formation of nerve plexuses and the function of limbs. *Journal of Experimental Zoology* 31:117–169. (11)

———. 1955. Experiments on the origin of the ventro-lateral trunk musculature in the urodele (*Ambystoma*). *Journal of Experimental Zoology* 129:45–75. (11)

Detwiler, S. R., and W. M. Copenhaver. 1940. The developmental behaviour of *Ambystoma* eggs subjected to atmospheres of low oxygen and high carbon dioxide. *American Journal of Anatomy* 66:393–410. (16)

Deuchar, E. M. 1975. *Xenopus: The South African Clawed Frog*. London: John Wiley and Sons. (11)

Deviche, P., and F. L. Moore. 1988. Steroidal control of sexual behavior in the rough-skinned newt (*Taricha granulosa*): Effects of testosterone, estradiol, and dihydratestosterone. *Hormones and Behavior* 22:26–34. (3)

De Villiers, C. G. S. 1929. The comparative anatomy of the breast-shoulder apparatus of the three aglossal anuran genera: *Xenopus*, *Pipa*, and *Hymenochirus*. *Annals of the Transvaal Museum* 13:37–69. (11)

DeVlaming, V. L., and R. B. Bury. 1970. Thermal selection in tadpoles of the tailed frog, *Ascaphus truei*. *Journal of Herpetology* 4:179–189. (9)

de Vree, F., and C. Gans. 1989. Functional morphology of the feeding mechanisms in lower tetrapods. *Fortschritte der Zoologie* 35:115–127. (11)

DeWitt, C. B. 1967. Precision of thermoregulation and its relation to environmental factors in the desert iguana, *Dipsosaurus dorsalis. Physiological Zoology* 40:49–66. (9)

DeWitt, C. B., and R. M. Friedman. 1979. Significance of skewness in ectotherm thermoregulation. *American Zoologist* 19:195–209. (9)

Deyrup, I. J. 1964. Water balance and kidney. In *Physiology of the Amphibia*, ed. J. A. Moore, 251–328. New York: Academic Press. (5,6,16)

Dhawan, B. N., R. Shuckla, and R. C. Srimal. 1982. Analysis of histamine receptors in the central thermoregulatory mechanism of *Mastomys natelensis. British Journal of Pharmacology* 75:145–149. (9)

Diakow, C. 1978. Hormonal basis for breeding behavior in female frogs: Vasotocin inhibits the release call of *Rana pipiens. Science* 199:1456–1457. (15)

Diakow, C., and A. Nemiroff. 1981. Vasotocin, prostaglandin, and female reproductive behavior in the frog, *Rana pipiens. Hormones and Behavior* 15:86–93. (2)

Diakow, C., and D. Raimondi. 1981. Physiology of *Rana pipiens* reproductive behavior: A proposed mechanism for inhibition of the release call. *American Zoologist* 21:295–304. (2)

Diamond, J. 1986. Overview: Laboratory experiments, field experiments, and natural experiments. In *Community Ecology*, ed. J. Diamond and T. J. Case, 3–22. New York: Harper and Row. (9)

Dicker, S. E., and A. B. Elliott. 1967. Water uptake by *Bufo melanostictus*, as affected by osmotic gradients, vasopressin, and temperature. *Journal of Physiology* (London) 190:359–370. (5)

———. 1970. Water uptake by the crab-eating frog *Rana cancrivora*, as affected by osmotic gradients and by neurohypophyseal hormones. *Journal of Physiology* (London) 207:119–132. (6)

Dickerson, M. C. 1906. *The Frog Book*. New York: Doubleday. (14)

Dickhoff, W. W., and D. S. Darling. 1983. Evolution of thyroid function and its control in lower vertebrates. *American Zoologist* 23:697–707. (3)

Diekamp, B., and H. C. Gerhardt. 1988. Auditory neurons selective for combinations of behaviorally relevant sound patterns. *Society for Neuroscience Abstracts* 14:90. (2)

Dierickx, K. 1966. Experimental identification of a hypothalamic gonadotropic centre. *Zeitschrift für Zellforschung* 74:53–79. (15)

———. 1967a. The function of the hypophysis without preoptic neurosecretory control. *Zeitschrift für Zellforschung* 78:114–130. (15)

———. 1967b. The gonadotropic centre of the tuber cinereum hypothalami and ovulation. *Zeitschrift für Zellforschung* 77:188–203. (15)

———. 1974. Identification of adeno-hypophysiotropic neurohormone producing neurosecretory cells in *Rana temporaria*. In *Neurosecretion: The Final Neuroendocrine Pathway*, 170–181. Sixth International Symposium on Neurosecretion, London, 1973. Berlin: Springer-Verlag. (15)

Dietz, T. H., and R. H. Alvarado. 1974. Na$^+$ and Cl$^-$ transport across gill chamber epithelium of *Rana catesbeiana* tadpoles. *American Journal of Physiology* 226:764–770. (5,16)

Dietz, T. H., B. Kirschner, and D. Porter. 1967. The roles of sodium transport and anion permeability in generating transepithelial potential differences in larval salamanders. *Journal of Experimental Biology* 46:85–96. (5,16)

Dimmitt, M. A., and R. Ruibal. 1980a. Environmental correlates of emergence in spadefoot toads (*Scaphiopus*). *Journal of Herpetology* 14:21–29. (8,13)

———. 1980b. Exploitation of food resources by spadefoot toads (*Scaphiophus*). *Copeia* 1980:854–862. (13,14)

Dingerkus, G., and L. D. Uhler. 1977. Enzyme clearing of alcian blue stained whole small vertebrates for demonstration of cartilage. *Stain Technology* 52:229–232. (11)

Dinno, M. A., and W. Nagel. 1988. Temperature dependence of transcellular and intracellular parameters of frog skin. *Progress in Clinical and Biological Research* 258:103–120. (8)

Disclos, P. 1970. Étude du développement post-embryonnaire des gonades d'un amphibien anoure: *Alytes obstetricans* Laur.; Influence de facteurs exogenes et endogenes. Ph.D. diss., University of Bordeaux, Bordeaux. (15)

d'Istria, M., F. Citarella, G. Delrio, and G. Chieffi. 1985. Role of androgens in amphibian reproduction. In *Current Trends in Comparative Endocrinology*, ed. B. Lofts and W. N. Holmes, 243–245. Hong Kong: Hong Kong University Press. (3)

d'Istria, M., G. Delrio, and G. Chieffi. 1975. Receptors for sex hormones in the skin of Amphibia. *General and Comparative Endocrinology* 26:281–283. (16)

Dobkin, D. S., R. D. Gettinger, and M. P. O'Connor. 1989. Importance of retreat site for hydration state in *Bufo marinus* during a dry rainy season. *American Zoologist* 29:88A. (6)

Dockx, P., and F. De Vree. 1986. Prey capture and intra-oral food transport in terrestrial salamanders. In *Studies in Herpetology*, ed. Z. Roček, 521–524. Proceedings of the 3d Ordinary General Meeting, Societas Europaea Herpetologica. Prague: Charles University. (11)

Dodd, J. M. 1987. The ovary. In *Vertebrate Endocrinology: Fundamentals and Biomedical Implications*, vol. 1, *Morphological Considerations*, ed. P. K. T. Pang and M. P. Schreibman, 351–397. New York: Academic Press. (3)

Dodd, M. H. I., and J. M. Dodd. 1976. The biology of metamorphosis. In *Physiology of the Amphibia*, ed. B. Lofts, 3:467–599. New York: Academic Press. (3,15,16)

Doerr-Schott, J. 1976. Immunohistochemical detection, by light and electron microscopy, of pituitary hormones in cold-blooded vertebrates: 1. Fish and amphibians. *General and Comparative Endocrinology* 28:487–512. (3)

Doerr-Schott, J., and M. P. Dubois. 1975. Localisation et identification d'un centre LH-RF dans l'encéphale du crapaud, *Bufo vulgaris* Laur. *Comptes Rendus de l'Académie de Sciences* (Paris) 280D:1285–1287. (15)

Dohm, G. L., R. L. Huston, E. W. Askew, and H. L. Fleshood. 1973. Effects of exercise, training, and diet on muscle citric acid cycle enzyme activity. *Canadian Journal of Biochemistry* 51:849–654. (14)

Dole, J. W. 1965a. Spatial relations in natural populations of the leopard frog, *Rana pipiens* Schreber, in northern Michigan. *American Midland Naturalist* 74:464–478. (4)

———. 1965b. Summer movements of adult leopard frogs, *Rana pipiens* Schreber, in northern Michigan. *Ecology* 46:236–255. (4)

———. 1967. The role of substrate moisture and dew in the water economy of leopard frogs, *Rana pipiens. Copeia* 1967:141–149. (4,6,12)

Dole, J. W., B. B. Rose, and C. F. Baxter. 1985. Hyperosmotic saline environment alters feeding behavior in the Western toad, *Bufo boreas. Copeia* 1985:645–648. (12,13)

Dole, J. W., B. B. Rose, and K. H. Tachiki. 1981. Western toads (*Bufo boreas*) learn odor of prey insects. *Herpetologica* 37:63–68. (13)

Dolk, H. E., and N. Postma. 1927. Über die Haut- und die Lungenatmung von *Rana temporaria. Zeitschrift für vergleichende Physiologie* 5:417–444. (12)

Dolmen, D. 1983. Growth and size of *Triturus vulgaris* and *T. cristatus* (Amphibia) in different parts of Norway. *Holarctic Ecology* 6:356–371. (15)

Donner, K. O. 1989. The absolute sensitivity of vision: Can a frog become a perfect detector of light-induced and dark rod events? *Physica Scripta* 39:133–140. (2)

Donner, K. O., S. Hemila, and A. Koskelainen. 1988. Temperature-dependence of rod photoresponses from the aspartate-treated retina of the frog (*Rana temporaria*). *Acta Physiologica Scandinavica* 134:535–541. (9)

Donner, K. O., and T. Reuter. 1976. Visual pigments and photoreceptor function. In *Frog Neurobiology: A Handbook*, ed. R. Llinás and W. Precht, 251–277. Berlin: Springer-Verlag. (2,16)

Dores, R. M. 1990. The proopiomelanocortin family. In *Progress in Comparative Endocrinology*, ed. A. Epple, C. G. Scanes, and M. H. Stetson, 22–27. New York: Wiley-Liss. (3)

Dores, R. M., J. C. Meza, L. M. Schenk, J. A. Carr, and D. O. Norris. 1989. Detection of adrenocorticotropin-related and α-melanocyte-stimulating hormone–related substances in the anterior pituitary of larval and adult *Ambystoma tigrinum* (Class: Amphibia). *Endocrinology* 124:1007–1016. (3)

Dores, R. M., and M. E. Rothenberg. 1987. Isolation of immunoreactive β-endorphin-related and Met-enkephalin-related peptides from the posterior pituitary of the amphibian, *Xenopus laevis. Peptides* 8:1119–1125. (3)

Dores, R. M., L. M. Schenk, and M. E. Rothenberg. 1987. Isolation of α-melanotropin from the pars intermedia of the larval amphibian, *Ambystoma tigrinum. General and Comparative Endocrinology* 68:322–330. (3)

Douglas, R. H., T. S. Collett, and H.-J. Wagner. 1986. Accommodation in anuran Amphibia and its role in depth vision. *Journal of Comparative Physiology* 158A:133–143. (13)

Dourish, C. T., W. Rycroft, and S. D. Iversen. 1989. Postponement of satiety by blockade of brain cholecystokinin (CCK-B) receptors. *Science* 245:1509–1511. (16)

Dournon, C., and C. Houillon. 1983. Genotypic sex determination and sexual inversion in *Pleurodeles:* An analysis of the offspring of temperature sex reversed genotypic females. *Comptes Rendus de l'Académie des Sciences* 296:779–782. (8)

———. 1984. Genetic demonstration of functional sex inversion in *Pleurodeles* under the effect of temperature. *Reproduction Nutrition Development* 24:361–378. (8)

———. 1985. Thermosensitivity of sexual differentiation in the newt: 100% sex reversal in genotypic females by heat treatment. *Reproduction Nutrition Development* 25:671–688. (8)

Dousa, T. P. 1974. Effects of hormones on cyclic AMP formation in kidneys of nonmammalian vertebrates. *American Journal of Physiology* 226:1193–1197. (3)

Downing, S. E., and R. W. Torrance. 1961. Vagal baroreceptors of the bullfrog. *Journal of Physiology* (London) 156:13P. (7)

Drane, C. R. 1981. The thermal conductivity of the skin of crocodilians. *Comparative Biochemistry and Physiology* 68A:107–110. (4)

Drastich, L. 1925. Über das Leben der Salamandra-Larvaen bein hohem und niedrigem Sauerstoff partialdruck. *Zeitschrift für vergleichende Physiologie* 2:632–657. (16)

Dreisig,H. 1984. Control of body temperature in shuttling ectotherms. *Journal of Thermal Biology* 9:229–233. (4,9)

Drewes, R. C., S. S. Hillman, R. W. Putnam, and O. M. Sokol. 1977. Water, nitrogen, and ion balance in the African treefrog *Chiromantis petersi,* with comments on the structure of the integument. *Journal of Comparative Physiology* 116B:257–267. (4,5,6)

Drewes, R. C., and B. Roth. 1981. Snail-eating frogs from the Ethiopian highlands: A new anuran specialization. *Zoological Journal of the Linnean Society* 73:267–287. (11)

Drewnowska, K., and T. U. L. Biber. 1988. Effect of changes in extracellular Cl⁻ on intracellular Cl⁻ activity in frog skin. *American Journal of Physiology* 254:F95–F104. (5)

Drewry, G. E., W. R. Heyer, and A. S. Rand. 1982. A functional analysis of the complex call of the frog *Physalaemus pustulosus. Copeia* 1982:636–645. (14)

Drewry, G. E., and A. S. Rand. 1983. Characteristics of an acoustic community: Puerto Rican frogs of the genus *Eleutherodactylus. Copeia* 1983:941–953. (2)

Drüner, L. 1902. Studien zur Anatomie des Zungenbein, Kiemenbogen, und Kehlkopfmuskeln der Urodelen: 1. Theil. *Zoologische Jahrbücher, Abteilung für Anatomie und Ontogenie der Thiere* 15:435–622. (11)

———. 1903. Über die Muskulatur der Visceralbogen der Urodelen. *Verhandlungen der Anatomischen Gesellschaft* 17, suppl.: 142–144. (11)

———. 1904. Studien zur Anatomie der Zungenbein-, Kiemenbogen-, und Kehlkopfmuskulatur der Urodelen: 2. Theil. *Zoologische Jahrbücher, Abteilung für Anatomie und Ontogenie der Thiere* 19:361–690. (11)

Dubecq, J. 1925. Constitution du muscle temporal chez les amphibiens urodèles: Signification morphologique de ce muscle. *Comptes Rendus de la Société Biologique* 93:1523. (11)

Du Bois, A.-M. 1927. Les corrélations physiologiques entre les glandes génitales et les corps jaunes chez les batraciens. *Revue Suisse de Zoologie* 34:499–581. (15)

Du Bois, A.-M., and K. Ponse. 1927. Hypogénitalisme chez *Rana esculenta. Comptes Rendus de la Société Biologique* 97:544. (15)

Du Bois-Reymond, E. 1848. *Untersuchungen über tierische Elektrizität.* Berlin. (5)

Ducibella, T. 1974. The occurrence of biochemical metamorphic events without anatomical metamorphosis in the axolotl. *Developmental Biology* 38:175–186. (16)

Duclaux, R., M. Fantino, and M. Cabanac. 1973. Compartement thermorégulateur chez *Rana esculenta:* Influence du réchauffement spinal. *Pflugers Archiv* 342:347–358. (9)

Duellman, W. E. 1970. *The Hylid Frogs of Middle America.* Monographs of the Museum of Natural History of the University of Kansas 1. Lawrence: University of Kansas, Museum of Natural History. (8)

———. 1978. *The Biology of an Equatorial Herpetofauna in Amazonian Ecuador.* University of Kansas Museum of Natural History, Miscellaneous Publication 65. Lawrence: University of Kansas Museum of Natural History. (15)

Duellman, W. E., and L. Trueb. 1986. *Biology of Amphibians.* New York: McGraw-Hill Book Company. (1,2,9,11,12,13,14,15,16)

Dugès, A. 1834. Recherches sur l'ostéologie et la myologie des batraciens à leurs différens âges. Paris: Bailliere. (11)

Duméril, M. A. 1849. À l'action du froid sur les grenouilles. *Annales de Science Naturale de Zoologie* 12:346. (10)

Dumortier, B. 1963. The physical characteristics of sound emissions in Arthropoda. In *Acoustic Behaviour of Animals,* ed. R. G. Busnel, 346–373. New York: Elsevier. (14)

Dumsday, B. 1990. Resting heart rate of the toad *Bufo marinus:* A longterm study of individual differences and environmental influences. *Physiological Zoology* 63:420–431.

Duncan, D. B. 1955. Multiple range and multiple F tests. *Biometrics* 11:1–42. (9)

Dunham, A. E., B. W. Grant, and K. L. Overall. 1989. Interfaces between biophysical and physiological ecology and the population ecology of terrestrial vertebrate ectotherms. *Physiological Zoology* 62:335–355. (4)

Dunlap, D. G. 1960. The comparative myology of the pelvic appendage in the Salientia. *Journal of Morphology* 106:1–76. (11)

———. 1969. Influence of temperature and duration of acclimation, time of day, sex, and body weight on metabolic rates in the hylid frog, *Acris crepitans. Comparative Biochemistry and Physiology* 31:555–570. (8,12)

———. 1971. Acutely measured metabolic rate-temperature curves in the cricket frog, *Acris crepitans. Comparative Biochemistry and Physiology* 38A:1–16. (12)

———. 1972. Latitudinal effects on metabolic rates in the cricket frog, *Acris crepitans;* Acutely measured rates in summer frogs. *Biological Bulletin* 143:332–343. (12)

———. 1973. Latitudinal effects on metabolic rates in the frog, *Acris crepitans:* Seasonal comparisons. *Biological Bulletin* 145:103–118. (10,12)

———. 1980. Comparative effects of thermal acclimation and season on metabolic compensation to temperature in the hylid frogs, *Pseudacris triseriata* and *Acris crepitans. Comparative Biochemistry and Physiology* 66A:243–249. (12)

Dunn, E. R. 1922. The sound-transmitting apparatus of salamanders and the phylogeny of the Caudata. *American Naturalist* 56:418–427. (11)

———. 1941. The "opercularis" muscle of salamanders. *Journal of Morphology* 69:207–215. (11)

Dunn, R. F. 1978. Nerve fibers of the eighth nerve and their distribution to the sensory nerve of the inner ear in the bullfrog. *Journal of Comparative Neurology* 182:621–636. (16)

Dunson, W. A., R. K. Packer, and M. K. Dunson. 1971. Ion and water balance in normal and mutant fluid imbalanced (ff) embryos of the axolotl (*Ambystoma mexicanum*). *Comparative Biochemistry and Physiology* 40A:319–337. (16)

Dupont, W., F. Leboulenger, H. Vaudry, and R. Vaillant. 1976. Regulation of aldosterone secretion in the frog *Rana esculenta* L. *General and Comparative Endocrinology* 29:51–60. (3)

Dupré, R. K., and E. C. Crawford, Jr. 1985. Control of panting in the desert iguana: Roles for peripheral temperatures and the effect of dehydration. *Journal of Experimental Zoology* 235:341–347. (9)

Dupré, R. K., J. J. Just, E. C. Crawford, Jr., and T. L. Powell. 1986. Temperature preference and responses of cutaneous temperature-sensitive neurons during bullfrog development. *Physiological Zoology* 59:254–262. (9,16)

Dupré, R. K., J. J. Just, and J. P. Ritchart. 1986. Thyroid hormones and behavioral thermoregulation by *Xenopus laevis:* Differential effects of thyroxine and triiodothyronine. *Canadian Journal of Zoology* 64:1076–1079. (9,16)

Dupré, R. K., and J. W. Petranka. 1985. Ontogeny of temperature selection in larval amphibians. *Copeia* 1985(2):462–467. (9)

Dupré, R. K., R. F. Taylor, and D. T. Frazier. 1985. Static lung compliance during the development of the bullfrog, *Rana catesbeiana. Respiration Physiology* 59:231–238. (6)

Dupré, R. K., and S. C. Wood. 1988. Behavioral temperature regulation by aquatic ectotherms during hypoxia. *Canadian Journal of Zoology* 66:2649–2652. (9)

Dushane, G. P. 1935. An experimental study of the origin of pigment cells in Amphibia. *Journal of Experimental Zoology* 72:1–31. (16)

Duvernoy, G. L. 1844. Sur l'appareil de la génération chez les males, plus particulièrement, et chez les femelles des salamandres et des tritons. *Comptes Rendus de l'Académie des Sciences* (Paris) 19: 585–600. (15)

Dyer, W. G. 1975. Parasitism as an indicator of food sources in a cave-adapted salamander habitat. *Bulletin of the Southern California Academy of Sciences* 74:72–75. (14)

Dyer, W. G., R. A. Brandon, and R. L. Price. 1980. Gastrointestinal helminths in relation to sex and age of *Desmognathus fuscus* (Green 1818) from Illinois. *Proceedings of the Helminthological Society of Washington* 47:95–99. (14)

Dyson, M. L. 1985. Aspects of social behaviours and mate choice in caged populations of painted reed frogs, *Hyperolius marmoratus*. M.S. thesis, University of the Witwatersrand, Johannesburg. (14)

Eagleson, G. W. 1976. A comparison of the life histories and growth patterns of populations of the salamander *Ambystoma gracile* (Baird) from permanent low-altitude and mountain lakes. *Canadian Journal of Zoology* 54:2098–2111. (15)

Eagleson, G. W., and B. A. McKeown. 1978a. Changes in thyroid activity of *Ambystoma gracile* (Baird) during different larval, transforming, and postmetamorphic phases. *Canadian Journal of Zoology* 56:1377–1381. (16)

———. 1978b. Factors affecting larval growth and development of laboratory-reared *Ambystoma* from the natural populations of different temperature regimes. *Biochemistry and Experimental Biology* 14:299–304. (8)

Eales, J. G. 1990. Thyroid function in poikilotherms. In *Progress in Comparative Endocrinology,* ed. A. Epple, C. G. Scanes, and M. H. Stetson, 415–420. New York: Wiley-Liss. (3)

Easton, D. P., P. S. Rutledge, and J. R. Spotila. 1987. Heat shock protein induction and induced thermal tolerance are independent in adult salamanders. *Journal of Experimental Zoology* 241:263–267. (8)

Eaton, T. H., Jr. 1937. The myology of salamanders with particular reference to *Dicamptodon ensatus* (Eschscholtz): 1. Muscles of the head. *Journal of Morphology* 60:31–72. (11)

———. 1951. Origin of tetrapod limbs. *American Midland Naturalist* 46:245–251. (11)

———. 1957. Motor areas and superficial muscle action in salamanders. *Journal of the Elisha Mitchell Scientific Society* 73:1–10. (11)

Ebbesson, S. O. E. 1976. Morphology of the spinal cord. In *Frog Neurobiology: A Handbook,* ed. R. Llinás and W. Precht, 679–706. Berlin: Springer-Verlag. (2)

———, ed. 1980. *Comparative Neurology of the Telencephalon.* New York: Plenum Press. (2)

Ecker, A. 1889. *The Anatomy of the Frog.* Trans. by G. Haslam. Oxford: Clarendon Press. (7)

Eckhardt, R. C. 1979. The adaptive syndromes of two guilds of insectivorous birds in the Colorado Rocky Mountains. *Ecological Monographs* 49:129–149. (14)

Eddy, F. B., and P. McDonald. 1978. Aquatic respiration of the crested newt *Triturus cristatus. Comparative Biochemistry and Physiology* 59A:85–88. (12)

Eddy, L. J., and R. F. Allen. 1979. Prolactin action on short circuit current in the developing tadpole skin: A comparison with ADH. *General and Comparative Physiology* 38:360–364. (5,16)

Eddy, L. J., and H. Lipner. 1975. Acceleration of thyroxine-induced metamorphosis by prolactin antiserum. *General and Comparative Endocrinology* 25:462–466. (16)

———. 1976. Amphibian metamorphosis: The role of thyrotropin-like hormone. *General and Comparative Endocrinology* 29:333–336. (16)

Edelman, A., M. Bouthier, and T. Anagnostopoulos. 1981. Chloride distribution in the proximal convoluted tubule of *Necturus* kidney. *Journal of Membrane Biology* 62:7–17. (5)

Edgeworth, F. H. 1911. On the morphology of the cranial muscles in some vertebrates. *Quarterly Journal of Microscopical Science* (London), n.s. 56:167–316. (11)

———. 1920. On the development of the hypobranchial and laryngeal muscles in Amphibia. *Journal of Anatomy* (London) 54:125–162. (11)

———. 1923. On the larval hypobranchial skeleton and musculature of *Cryptobranchus, Menopoma,* and *Ellipsoglossa. Journal of Anatomy* (London) 57:97–105. (11)

———. 1931. On the muscles used in shutting and opening the mouth. *Proceedings of the Zoological Society of London* 1931:817–818. (11)

———. 1935. *The Cranial Muscles of Vertebrates.* Cambridge: Cambridge University Press. (11)

Edgren, R. A. 1954. Factors controlling color change in the tree frog, *Hyla versicolor* Wied. *Proceedings of the Society for Experimental Biology and Medicine* 87:20–23. (9)

Edsall, J. T., and J. Wyman. 1958. *Biophysical Chemistry.* New York: Academic Press. (5)

Edwards, B. R., and T. H. Chan. 1973. Effects of adenohypophysectomy and aminoglutethimide on water and electrolyte composition of *Xenopus laevis* Daudin. *Journal of Endocrinology* 59:623–632. (5)

Edwards, J. A., and J. T. Justus. 1969. Hemoglobins of two urodeles: Changes with metamorphosis. *Proceedings of the Society for Experimental Biology and Medicine* 139:524–526. (16)

Edwards, J. L. 1976. A comparative study of locomotion in terrestrial salamanders. Ph.D. diss., University of California, Berkeley. Reprinted in *Dissertation Abstracts International* 37 (9), 1977. (11)

———. 1977. The evolution of terrestrial locomotion. In *Major Patterns in Vertebrate Evolution,* ed. M. K. Hecht, P. C. Goody, and B. M. Hecht, 553–577. New York: Plenum Press. (11)

Egeberg, J. C., and P. Rosenkilde. 1965. Iodine uptake and ultrastructure of the thyroid gland in cold-exposed toads, *Bufo bufo. General and Comparative Endocrinology* 5:673. (3)

Eggena, P. 1987. Hydroosmotic responses to short pulses of vasotocin by toad bladder. *American Journal of Physiology* 252:E705–E711. (5)

Eggermont, J. J. 1988. Mechanisms of sound localization in anurans. In *The Evolution of the Amphibian Auditory System,* ed. B. Fritzsch, M. J. Ryan, W. Wilczynski, T. E. Hetherington, and W. Walkowiak, 307–336. New York: John Wiley and Sons. (2)

Ehrenfeld, J., and F. Garcia-Romeu. 1977. Active hydrogen excretion and sodium absorption through isolated frog skin. *American Journal of Physiology* 233:F46–F54. (5)

———. 1978. Coupling between chloride absorption and base excretion in isolated skin of *Rana esculenta. American Journal of Physiology* 235:F33–F39. (5)

Ehrenfeld, J., F. Garcia-Romeu, and B. J. Harvey. 1985. Electrogenic active proton pump in *Rana esculenta* skin and its role in sodium ion transport. *Journal of Physiology* (London) 359:331–355. (5)

Ehrenfeld, J., and B. J. Harvey. 1987. Evidence for basolateral sodium/hydrogen ion exchange in frog-skin epithelium and its role in sodium transport and intracellular pH regulation. *Journal of Physiology* (London) 382:144P. (5)

Ehret, G., A. J. M. Moffat, and R. R. Capranica. 1983. Two-tone suppression in auditory nerve fibers of the green treefrog (*Hyla cinerea*). *Journal of the Acoustic Society of America* 73:2093–2095. (2)

Eibl-Eibesfeldt, I. 1952. Nahrungserwerb und Beuteschema der Erdkröte (*Bufo bufo* L.). *Behaviour* 4:1–36. (13)

Eichelberg, H., and H.-J. Obert. 1976. Fat and glycogen utilization in the larynx muscles of fire-bellied toads (*Bombina bombina* L.) during calling activity. *Cell and Tissue Research* 167:1–10. (14)

Eichelberg, H., and H. Schneider. 1973. Die Feinstruktur der Kehlkopfmuskeln des Laubfrosches, *Hyla arborea arborea* (L.) im Vergleich zu einem Skelettmuskel. *Zeitschrift für Zellforschung* 141:223–233. (11,14)

———. 1974. The fine structure of the larynx muscles in female tree frogs, *Hyla a. arborea* L. (Anura, Amphibia). *Cell and Tissue Research* 152:185–191. (11,14)

Eikmanns, K.-H. 1955. Verhaltensphysiologische Untersuchungen über den Beutefang und das Bewegungssehen der Erdkröte (*Bufo bufo* L.) *Zeitschrift für Tierpsychologie* 12:229–253. (13)

Eiselt, J. 1941. Der Musculus opercularis und die mittlere Ohrsphäre der Amphibien. *Archiv für Naturgeschichte* 10:179–270. (11)

Eldred, W. D., T. E. Finger, and J. Nolte. 1980. Central projections of the frontal organ of *Rana pipiens,* as demonstrated by the anterograde transport of horseradish peroxidase. *Cell and Tissue Research* 211:215–222. (2)

Elepfandt, A. 1982. Accuracy of taxis response to water waves in the clawed toad (*Xenopus laevis* Daudin) with intact or with lesioned lateral line system. *Journal of Comparative Physiology* 148:535–545. (2)

———. 1988a. Central organization of wave localization in the clawed frog, *Xenopus laevis:* 1. Involvement and bilateral organization of the midbrain. *Brain, Behavior, and Evolution* 31:349–357.

———. 1988b. Central organization of wave localization in the clawed frog, *Xenopus laevis:* 2. Midbrain topology for wave directions. *Brain, Behavior, and Evolution* 31:358–368.

Elepfandt, A., B. Seiler, and B. Aicher. 1985. Water wave frequency discrimination in the clawed frog *Xenopus laevis. Journal of Comparative Physiology* 157:255–261. (2,16)

Elepfandt, A., and L. Wiedemer. 1987. Lateral-line responses to water surface waves in the clawed frog, *Xenopus laevis. Journal of Comparative Physiology* 160:667–682. (2)

Elliott, A. B. 1968. Effect of adrenaline on water uptake in *Bufo. Journal of Physiology* (London) 197:87P–88P. (6)

Elliott, A. B., and M. M. Chew. 1973. Vasotocin-like activity in the plasma of the euryhaline frog (*Rana cancrivora*) after transfer from fresh water to saline. *Journal of Endocrinology* 66:427–434. (6)

El Maraghi-Ater, H., J. Mesnard, and J. Hourdry. 1986. Hormonal control of the intestinal brush border enzyme activities in developing anuran amphibians: 1. Effects of hydrocortisone and insulin during and after spontaneous metamorphosis. *General and Comparative Endocrinology* 61:53–63. (16)

Elmberg, J. 1990. Intraspecific variation in reproduction in northern anuran populations. Ph.D. diss., University of Umeå, Sweden. (15)

Els, W. J., and S. I. Helman. 1981. Vasopressin, theophylline, PGE_2, and indomethacin on active Na transport in frog skin: Studies with microelectrodes. *American Journal of Physiology* 241:F279–F288. (5)

Else, P. L., and A. F. Bennett. 1987. The thermal dependence of locomotor performance and muscle contractile function in the salamander *Ambystoma tigrinum nebulosum. Journal of Experimental Biology* 128:219–233. (8,12)

Emerson, E. T. 1905. General anatomy of *Typhlomolge rathbuni. Proceedings of the Boston Society of Natural History* 32:43–76. (11)

Emerson, S. B. 1976a. Burrowing in frogs. *Journal of Morphology* 149:437–458. (11,14)

———. 1976b. A preliminary report on the superficial throat musculature of the Microhylidae and its possible role in tongue action. *Copeia* 1976:546–551. (11)

———. 1977. Movement of the hyoid in frogs during feeding. *American Journal of Anatomy* 149:115–120. (11)

———. 1978. Allometry and jumping in frogs: Helping the twain to meet. *Evolution* 32:551–564. (11,14)

———. 1979. The ilio-sacral articulation in frogs: Form and function. *Biological Journal of the Linnean Society* 11:153–168. (11,14)

———. 1980. Muscle activity at the ilio-sacral articulation of frogs. *Journal of Morphology* 166:129–144. (11,14)

———. 1982. Frog postcranial morphology: Identification of a functional complex. *Copeia* 1982:603–613. (11,14)

———. 1983. Functional analysis of frog pectoral girdles: The epicoracoid cartilages. *Journal of Zoology* (London) 201:293–308. (14)

———. 1984. Morphological variation in frog pectoral girdles: Testing alternatives to a traditional adaptive explanation. *Evolution* 38:376–388. (11)

———. 1985. Skull shape in frogs: Correlations with diet. *Herpetologica* 41:177–188. (11,14)

———. 1988. Convergence and morphological constraint in frogs: Variation in postcranial morphology. *Fieldiana* 43:1–19. (11,14)

Emerson, S. B., and H. J. de Jongh. 1980. Muscle activity in the ilio-sacral joint in frogs. *Journal of Morphology* 166:129–144. (11,14)

Emerson, S. B., and D. Diehl. 1980. Toe pad morphology and adhesive mechanisms in frogs. *Biological Journal of the Linnean Society* 13:199–216. (11,14)

Emery, A. R., A. H. Berst, and K. Kodaira. 1972. Under-ice observations of wintering sites of leopard frogs. *Copeia* 1972:123–126. (10)

Emilio, M. G. 1974. Gas exchangers and blood gas concentrations in the frog, *Rana ridibunda. Journal of Experimental Biology* 60:901–908. (7,12)

Emilio, M. G., and G. Shelton. 1972. Factors affecting blood flow to the lungs in the amphibian, *Xenopus laevis. Journal of Experimental Biology* 56:67–77. (5,7)

———. 1974. Gas exchange and its effect on blood gas concentrations in the amphibian, *Xenopus laevis. Journal of Experimental Biology* 60:567–579. (12)

———. 1980. Carbon dioxide exchange and its effects on pH and bicarbonate equilibria in the blood of the amphibian *Xenopus laevis. Journal of Experimental Biology* 83:253–262. (5,12)

Emlen, S. T. 1976. Lek organization and mating strategies in the bullfrog. *Behavioral Ecology and Sociobiology* 1:283–313. (14)

Emlen, S. T., and L. W. Oring. 1977. Ecology, sexual selection, and the evolution of mating systems. *Science* 197:215–223. (14)

Emmel, V. E. 1924. Studies on the non-nucleated elements of the blood: 2. The occurrence and genesis of non-nucleated erythrocytes or erythroplastids in vertebrates other than mammals. *American Journal of Anatomy* 30:347–405. (5)

Enders, F. 1975. The influence of prey size, particularly in spiders with long attack distances (Araneidae, Linyphiidae, and Salticidae). *American Naturalist* 109:737–763. (14)

Endler, J. A. 1980. Natural selection on color patterns in *Poecilia reticulata. Evolution* 34:76–91. (14)

Enemar, A. 1978. Adenohypophysis and growth in tadpoles of *Rana temporaria. General and Comparative Endocrinology* 34:211–218. (16)

Enemar, A., B. Essvik, and R. Klang. 1968. Growth-promoting effects of ovine somatotropin and prolactin in tadpoles of *Rana temporaria. General and Comparative Endocrinology* 11:328–331. (16)

Engbretson, G. A., and V. H. Hutchison. 1976. Parietalectomy and thermal selection in the lizard, *Sceloporus magister. Journal of Experimental Zoology* 198:29–38. (9)

Engel, W. K., and R. L. Irwin. 1967. A histochemical-physiological correlation of frog skeletal muscle fibers. *American Journal of Physiology* 213:511–518. (11)

Enig, M., J. Ramsay, and D. Eby. 1976. Effect of temperature on pyruvate metabolism in the frog: The role of lactate dehydrogenase isozymes. *Comparative Biochemistry and Physiology* 53B:145–148. (8,12)

Ensor, D. M., and J. N. Ball. 1972. Prolactin and osmoregulation in fishes. *Federation Proceedings* 31:1615–1623. (5)

Epperlein, H. H., and M. Claviez. 1982. Formation of pigment patterns in *Triturus alpestris* embryos. *Developmental Biology* 91:497–502. (16)

Epple, A., and J. E. Brinn. 1987. Pancreatic islets. In *Vertebrate Endocrinology: Fundamentals and Biomedical Implications,* vol. 1, *Morphological Considerations,* ed. P. K. T. Pang and M. P. Schreibman, 279–317. New York: Academic Press. (3)

Erasmus, B.-E. W., B. J. Howell, and H. Rahn. 1970/71. Ontogeny of acid-base balance in the bullfrog and chicken. *Respiration Physiology* 11:46–53. (6,16)

Erdman, S., and D. Cundall. 1984. The feeding apparatus of the salamander *Amphiuma tridactylum:* Morphology and behavior. *Journal of Morphology* 181:175–204. (11)

Erfurth, E. M., and P. Hedner. 1987. Increased plasma gonadotropin levels in spontaneous hyperthyroidism reproduced by thyroxine but not by triiodothyronine administration to normal subjects. *Journal of Clinical Endocrinology and Metabolism* 64:698–703. (16)

Erlij, D., R. Certrangolo, and R. Valdez. 1965. Adrenotropic receptors in the frog. *Journal of Pharmacology and Experimental Therapeutics* 149:65–70. (3)

Erskine, D. J., and V. H. Hutchison. 1981. Melatonin and behavioral thermoregulation in the turtle, *Terrapene carolina triunguis. Physiology and Behavior* 26:991–994. (9)

———. 1982. Reduced thermal tolerance in an amphibian treated with melatonin. *Journal of Thermal Biology* 7:121–123. (8,9)

Erskine, D. J., and J. R. Spotila. 1978. Heat energy budget analysis and heat transfer in the largemouth blackbass (*Micropterus salmoides*). *Physiological Zoology* 50:157–169. (4)

Erulkar, S. D., and R. W. Soller. 1980. Interactions among lumbar motoneurons on opposite sides of the frog spinal cord: Morphological and electrophysiological studies. *Journal of Comparative Neurology* 192:473–488. (2)

Etheridge, K. 1986. Estivation in the sirenid salamanders, *Siren lacertina* (Linnaeus) and *Pseudobranchus striatus* (Le Conte). Ph.D. diss., University of Florida, Gainesville. (10)

Etkin, W. 1932. Growth and resorption phenomena in anuran metamorphosis. *Physiological Zoology* 5:275–300. (16)

———. 1934. The phenomena of anuran metamorphosis: 2. *Physiological Zoology* 7:129–148. (12)

———. 1962. Hypothalamic inhibition of the pars intermedia in the frog. *General and Comparative Endocrinology,* suppl. 2:148–159. (3)

————. 1963. Metamorphosis-activating system of the frog. *Science* 139:810–814. (16)

————. 1964. Metamorphosis. In *Physiology of the Amphibia*, ed. J. A. Moore, 1:427–468. New York: Academic Press. (3)

————. 1968. Hormonal control of metamorphosis. In *Metamorphosis: A Problem in Developmental Biology*, ed. W. Etkin and L. Gilbert, 313–348. New York: Appleton-Century-Crofts. (16)

Etkin, W., and A. G. Gona. 1967. Antagonism between prolactin and thyroid hormone in amphibian development. *Journal of Experimental Zoology* 165:249–258. (16)

————. 1968. Failure of mammalian thyrotropin-releasing factor preparation to elicit metamorphic responses in tadpoles. *Endocrinology* 82:1067–1068. (3,16)

Etkin, W., and Y. S. Kim. 1971. Effects of TRH on tadpole. *American Zoologist* 11:654. (16)

Etkin, W., and R. Lehrer. 1960. Excess growth in tadpoles after transplantation of the adenohypophysis. *Endocrinology* 67:457–466. (16)

Evans, B. K., and G. Shelton. 1984. Ventilation in *Xenopus laevis* after lung or carotid labyrinth denervation. In *First Congress of Comparative Physiology and Biochemistry*, A75, Liége, Belgium. (7)

Evans, G. 1939. Factors influencing the oxygen consumption of several species of plethodontid salamanders in aërial and aquatic media. *Ecology* 20:74–95. (12)

Ewer, R. F. 1952a. The effect of pituitrin on fluid distribution in *Bufo regularis* Reuss. *Journal of Experimental Biology* 29:173–177. (5,6)

————. 1952b. The effects of posterior pituitary extracts on water balance in *Bufo carens* and *Xenopus laevis*, together with some general considerations of anuran water economy. *Journal of Experimental Biology* 29:429–439. (6)

Ewert, J.-P. 1970. Neural mechanisms of prey-catching and avoidance behavior in the toad (*Bufo bufo* L.). *Brain, Behavior, and Evolution* 3:36–56. (2)

————. 1976. *Neuro-Ethologie: Einführung in die neuro-physiologischen Grundlagen des Verhaltens*. Berlin: Springer-Verlag. (13)

————. 1984. Tectal mechanisms that underlie prey-catching and avoidance behaviors in toads. In *Comparative Neurology of the Optic Tectum*, ed. H. Vanegas, 247–416. New York: Plenum Press. (2,13)

————. 1985. Concepts in vertebrate neuroethology. *Animal Behavior* 33:1–29. (14)

————. 1987. Neuroethology of releasing mechanisms: Preycatching in toads. *Behavioral and Brain Sciences* 10:337–405. (2,13)

Eycleshymer, A. C., and J. M. Wilson. 1910. Normal plates of the development of *Necturus maculosus*. In *Normentafeln zur Entwicklungsgeschichte der Wirbeltiere*, ed. F. Keibels, 2:1–50. Vienna: Gustav Fischer. (16)

Faber, J., and B. Zawadowska. 1988. Histochemical study of the forelimb muscles in *Rana temporaria* L. *Morphologisches Jahrbuch* 134:877–884. (11)

Fairchild, L. 1981. Mate selection and behavioral thermoregulation in Fowlers toads. *Science* 212:950–951. (8)

Fanning, J. C., M. J. Tyler, and D. J. C. Shearman. 1982. Converting a stomach to a uterus: The microscopic structure of the stomach of the gastric brooding frog *Rheobatrachus silus*. *Gastroenterology* 82:62–70. (13)

Fanslow, D. J. 1961. The relation of oxygen consumption to body weight and starvation in *Rana pipiens* and *Rana catesbeiana*. *Proceedings of the South Dakota Academy of Science* 40:103–111. (12)

Farmer, S. W., P. Licht, and H. Papkoff. 1977. Biological activity of bullfrog growth hormone in the rat and the bullfrog (*Rana catesbeiana*). *Endocrinology* 101:1145–1150. (15)

Farquhar, M. G., and G. E. Palade. 1964. Functional organization of amphibian skin. *Proceedings of the National Academy of Sciences* 51:569–577. (5)

Farr, J. A. 1980. Social behavior patterns as determinants of reproductive success in the guppy, *Poecilia reticulata* Peters (Pisces: Poeciliidae). *Behaviour* 74:38–91. (14)

Farrar, E. S., and R. K. Dupré. 1983. The role of diet in glycogen storage by juvenile bullfrogs prior to overwintering. *Comparative Biochemistry and Physiology* 75A:255–260. (10)

Farrar, E. S., and B. E. Frye. 1973. Comparison of blood glucose and liver glycogen of larval and adult frogs (*Rana pipiens*). *General and Comparative Endocrinology* 21:513–516. (16)

————. 1977. Seasonal variation in the effects of adrenaline and gluca-

gon in *Rana pipiens*. *General and Comparative Endocrinology* 33:76–81. (3,10)

————. 1979a. A comparison of adrenalin and glucagon effects on carbohydrate levels of larval and adult *Rana pipiens*. *General and Comparative Endocrinology* 39:372–380. (3,16)

————. 1979b. Factors affecting normal carbohydrate levels in *Rana pipiens*. *General and Comparative Endocrinology* 39:358–371. (3,10)

Farrar, E. S., J. J. Hulsebus. 1988. Morphometry of pancreatic B cell populations during larval growth and metamorphosis of *Rana catesbeiana*. *General and Comparative Endocrinology* 69:65–70. (16)

Farrell, M. P. 1971. Effect of temperature and photoperiod on the water economy of *Hyla crucifer*. *Herpetologica* 27:41–48. (9)

Farrell, M. P., and J. A. MacMahon. 1969. An eco-physiological study of water economy in eight species of tree frogs (Hylidae). *Herpetologica* 25:279–294. (6,12)

Fasano, S., S. Minucci, L. DiMatteo, M. D'Antonio, and R. Pierantoni. 1989. Intratesticular feedback mechanisms in the regulation of steroid profiles in the frog, *Rana esculenta*. *General and Comparative Endocrinology* 75:335–342. (3)

Fasano, S., S. Minucci, R. Pierantoni, A. Fasolo, L. DiMatteo, C. Basile, B. Varriale, and G. Chieffi. 1988. Hypothalamus-hypophysis and testicular GnRH control of gonadal activity in the frog, *Rana esculenta*: Seasonal GnRH profiles and annual variations of *in vitro* androgen output by pituitary stimulated testes. *General and Comparative Endocrinology* 70:31–40. (3)

Fasolo, A., M. F. Franzoni, and V. Mazzi. 1980. Evolution of the hypothalamo-hypophysial regulation in tetrapods. *Bolletino di Zoologica* 47, suppl.: 127–147. (15)

Fassina, G., F. Carpendo, and R. Santi. 1969. Effect of prostaglandin E₁ on isolated short circuited frog skin. *Life Sciences* 8:181–187. (5)

Fay, R. R., and A. N. Popper. 1980. Structure and function in teleost auditory systems. In *Comparative Studies of Hearing in Vertebrates*, ed. A. N. Popper and R. R. Fay, 3–42. New York: Springer-Verlag. (2)

Fedde, M. R., R. N. Gatz, H. Slama, and P. Scheid. 1974. Intrapulmonary CO_2 receptors in the duck: 1. Stimulus specificity. *Respiration Physiology* 22:115–124. (7)

Fedele, M. 1943. La innervazione del tronco arterio nei batraci anuri. *Archivio Italiano di Anatomia e di Embriologia* 48:84–119. (7)

Feder, M. E. 1976a. Lunglessness, body size, and metabolic rate in salamanders. *Physiological Zoology* 49:398–406. (1,5,6,12)

————. 1976b. Oxygen consumption and body temperature in Neotropical and temperate zone lungless salamanders (Amphibia: Plethodontidae). *Journal of Comparative Physiology* 110:197–208. (8,12)

————. 1977. Oxygen consumption and activity in salamanders: Effects of body size and lunglessness. *Journal of Experimental Zoology* 202:403–414. (6,12)

————. 1978a. Effect of temperature on post-activity oxygen consumption in lunged and lungless salamanders. *Journal of Experimental Zoology* 206:179–190. (8,12)

————. 1978b. Environmental variability and thermal acclimation in Neotropical and temperate zone salamanders. *Physiological Zoology* 51:7–16. (4,8,12)

————. 1981a. Effect of body size, trophic state, time of day, and experimental stress on oxygen consumption of anuran larvae: An experimental assessment and evaluation of the literature. *Comparative Biochemistry and Physiology* 70A:497–508. (12,16)

————. 1981b. Responses to acute aquatic hypoxia in larvae of amphibians, *Rana* and *Xenopus*. *American Zoologist* 21:928. (5)

————. 1982a. Effect of developmental stage and body size on oxygen consumption of anuran larvae: A reappraisal. *Journal of Experimental Zoology* 220:33–43. (12,16)

————. 1982b. Environmental variability and thermal acclimation of metabolism in tropical anurans. *Journal of Thermal Biology* 7:23–28. (8,12)

————. 1982c. Thermal ecology of Neotropical lungless salamanders (Amphibia: Plethodontidae): Environmental temperatures and behavioral responses. *Ecology* 63:1665–1674. (8,9,13)

————. 1983a. Effect of hypoxia and body size on the energy metabolism of lungless tadpoles, *Bufo woodhousei*, and air-breathing anuran larvae. *Journal of Experimental Zoology* 228:11–19. (5,12,16)

————. 1983b. Integrating the ecology and physiology of plethodontid salamanders. *Herpetologica* 39:291–310. (4,6,12,13,14)

————. 1983c. Metabolic and biochemical correlates of thermal acclimation in the rough-skinned newt *Taricha granulosa*. *Physiological Zoology* 56:513–521. (8,12)

————. 1983d. The relation of air breathing and locomotion to predation on tadpoles, *Rana berlandieri*, by turtles. *Physiological Zoology* 56:522–531. (14)

————. 1983e. Responses to acute aquatic hypoxia in larvae of the frog *Rana berlandieri*. *Journal of Experimental Biology* 104:79–95. (5)

————. 1984. Consequences of aerial respiration for amphibian larvae. In *Respiration and Metabolism of Embryonic Vertebrates*, ed. R. S. Seymour, 71–86. Dordrecht, Netherlands: Junk. (5,16)

————. 1985a. Acclimation to constant and variable temperatures in plethodontid salamanders: 1. Rates of oxygen consumption. *Comparative Biochemistry and Physiology* 81:673–682. (8,12)

————. 1985b. Acclimation to constant and variable temperatures in plethodontid salamanders: 2. Time course of acclimation to cool and warm temperatures. *Herpetologica* 41:241–245. (8,12)

————. 1985c. Thermal acclimation of oxygen consumption and cardiorespiratory frequencies in frog larvae. *Physiological Zoology* 58:303–311. (5,12)

————. 1986. Effect of thermal acclimation on locomotor energetics and locomotor performance in a lungless salamander, *Desmognathus ochrophaeus*. *Journal of Experimental Biology* 121:271–283. (6,8,11,12,14)

————. 1987a. The analysis of physiological diversity: The prospects for pattern documentation and general questions in ecological physiology. In *New Directions in Ecological Physiology*, ed. M. E. Feder, A. F. Bennett, W. W. Burggren, and R. B. Huey, 38–75. Cambridge: Cambridge University Press. (1)

————. 1987b. Effect of thermal acclimation on locomotor energetics and locomotor performance in a tropical salamander, *Bolitoglossa subpalmata*. *Physiological Zoology* 60:18–26. (8,12,14)

————. 1988. Exercising with and without lungs: 2. Experimental elimination of pulmonary and buccopharyngeal gas exchange in individual salamanders (*Ambystoma tigrinum*). *Journal of Experimental Biology* 138:487–497. (5,6,8,10,12)

Feder, M. E., and S. J. Arnold. 1982. Anaerobic metabolism and behavior during predatory encounters between snakes (*Thamnophis elegans*) and salamanders (*Plethodon jordani*). *Oecologia* (Berlin) 53:93–97. (12,14)

Feder, M. E., A. F. Bennett, W. W. Burggren, and R. B. Huey, eds. 1987. *New Directions in Ecological Physiology*. New York: Cambridge University Press. (1,14)

Feder, M. E., and B. Block. 1991. On the future of physiological ecology. *Functional Ecology* 5:136–144. (1)

Feder, M. E., and W. W. Burggren. 1985a. Cutaneous gas exchange in vertebrates: Design, patterns, control, and implications. *Biological Reviews* 60:1–45. (4,5,6,10,16)

————. 1985b. The regulation of cutaneous gas exchange in vertebrates. In *Circulation, Respiration, and Metabolism*, ed. R. Gilles, 101–113. Berlin: Springer-Verlag. (6,7,16)

————. 1985c. Skin-breathing in vertebrates. *Scientific American* 253:126–142. (16)

Feder, M. E., W. W. Burggren, and J. B. Graham. 1988. Introduction to the symposium: Cutaneous exchange of gases and ions. *American Zoologist* 28:941–944.

Feder, M. E., R. J. Full, and J. Piiper. 1988. Elimination kinetics of acetylene and Freon 22 in resting and active lungless salamanders. *Respiration Physiology* 72:229–240. (5,6,9,10,12)

Feder, M. E., and A. G. Gibbs. 1982. Thermal acclimation of oxygen consumption, enzyme kinetics, and lipids in salamanders. *American Zoologist* 22:962. (8)

Feder, M. E., A. G. Gibbs, G. A. Griffith, and J. Tsuji. 1984. Thermal acclimation of metabolism in salamanders: Fact or artefact? *Journal of Thermal Biology* 9:255–260. (8,12,14)

Feder, M. E., and G. V. Lauder, eds. 1986. *Predator-Prey Relationships*, Chicago: University of Chicago Press. (14)

Feder, M. E., and P. L. Londos. 1984. Hydric constraints upon foraging in a terrestrial salamander, *Desmognathus ochrophaeus* (Amphibia: Plethodontidae). *Oecologia* (Berlin) 64:413–418. (6,12,14)

Feder, M. E., and J. F. Lynch. 1982. Effects of latitude, season, elevation, and microhabitat on field body temperatures of Neotropical and temperature zone salamanders. *Ecology* 63:1657–1664. (9)

Feder, M. E., J. F. Lynch, H. B. Shaffer, and D. B. Wake. 1982. Field body temperatures of tropical and temperate zone salamanders. *Smithsonian Herpetological Information Service Publication* 52:1–23. (8,9)

Feder, M. E., and C. M. Moran. 1985. Effect of water depth on costs of aerial respiration and its alternatives in tadpoles of *Rana pipiens*. *Canadian Journal of Zoology* 63:643–648. (14)

Feder, M. E., and L. E. Olsen. 1978. Behavioral and physiological correlates of recovery from exhaustion in the lungless salamander *Batrachoseps attenuatus* (Amphibia: Plethodontidae). *Journal of Comparative Physiology* 128B:101–107. (12)

Feder, M. E., T. J. Papenfuss, and D. B. Wake. 1982. Body size and elevation in Neotropical salamanders. *Copeia* 1982:186–188.

Feder, M. E., and A. W. Pinder. 1988a. Dimensions and importance of oxygen boundary layers in cutaneous gas exchange. *American Zoologist* 28:46A. (4)

————. 1988b. Ventilation and its effect on "infinite pool" exchangers. *American Zoologist* 28:973–983. (4,5,6,7,10)

Feder, M. E., and F. H. Pough. 1975a. Increased temperature resistance produced by ionizing radiation in the newt *Notophthalmus v. viridescens*. *Copeia* 1975:658–661. (8)

————. 1975b. Temperature selection by the red-backed salamander, *Plethodon c. cinereus* (Green) (Caudata: Plethodontidae). *Comparative Biochemistry and Physiology* 50A:91–98. (8,9)

Feder, M. E., T. Robbins, and C. R. Talbot. 1991. Effect of bulk flow on cutaneous ion uptake in the bullfrog, *Rana catesbeiana*. *American Zoologist* 31:57A.

Feder, M. E., D. B. Seale, M. E. Boraas, R. J. Wassersug, and A. G. Gibbs. 1984. Functional conflicts between feeding and gas exchange in suspension-feeding tadpoles, *Xenopus laevis*. *Journal of Experimental Biology* 110:91–98. (5,14,16)

Feder, M. E., and R. J. Wassersug. 1979. Activity and energy metabolism in larvae of the toad *Bufo woodhousei*. *American Zoologist* 19:863. (12)

————. 1984. Aerial versus aquatic oxygen consumption in larvae of the clawed frog, *Xenopus laevis*. *Journal of Experimental Biology* 108:231–245. (5,16)

Feinblatt, J. D. 1982. The comparative physiology of calcium regulation in submammalian vertebrates. *Advances in Comparative Physiology and Biochemistry* 8:73–110. (3)

Feng, A. S. 1980. Directional characteristics of the acoustic receiver of the leopard frog (*Rana pipiens*): A study of eighth nerve auditory responses. *Journal of the Acoustical Society of America* 68:1107–1114. (2)

————. 1981. Directional response characteristics of single neurons in the torus semicircularis of the leopard frog (*Rana pipiens*). *Journal of Comparative Physiology* 144:419–428. (2)

————. 1982. Neck muscle innervation patterns in the northern leopard frog (*Rana p. pipiens*). *Neuroscience Letters* 29:19–23. (11)

Feng, A. S., and W. P. Shofner. 1981. Peripheral basis of sound localization in anurans: Acoustic properties of the frog's ear. *Hearing Research* 5:201–216. (2)

Ferreira, K. T. G. 1968. Anionic dependence of sodium transport in the frog skin. *Biochimica et Biophysica Acta* 150:587–598. (5)

Ferroni, E. N., and A. M. de L. Castrucci. 1987. α-MSH (melanocyte stimulating hormone) and MCH (melanin concentrating hormone) actions in *Bufo ictericus ictericus* melanophores. *Comparative Biochemistry and Physiology* 88A:15–20. (3)

Fessard, A., and A. Sand. 1937. Stretch receptors in the muscles of fishes. *Journal of Experimental Biology* 14:383–404. (11)

Fetcho, J. R. 1987. A review of the organization and evolution of motoneurons innervating the axial musculature of vertebrates. *Brain Research Reviews* 12:243–280. (11)

Figge, F. H. J. 1936. The differential reaction of the blood vessels of a branchial arch of *Ambystoma tigrinum* (Colorado axolotl): 1. The reaction to adrenalin, oxygen, and carbon dioxide. *Physiological Zoology* 9:79–101. (7,16)

Filogamo, G., and G. Gabella. 1967. The development of neuromuscular correlations in vertebrates. *Archives de Biologie* (Liége) 78:9–60. (11)

Findeis, E. K., and W. E. Bemis. 1990. Functional morphology of tongue projection in *Taricha torosa* (Urodela: Salamandridae). *Zoological Journal of the Linnean Society* 99:129–157. (14,16)

Fine, M. 1979. Sound evoked by brain stimulation in the toadfish *Opanus tau* L. *Experimental Brain Research* 35:197–212. (14)

Finkenstädt, T. 1980. Disinhibition of prey-catching in the salamander following thalamic-pretectal lesions. *Naturwissenschaften* 67:471–472. (2)

Finkenstädt, T., and J.-P. Ewert. 1983. Processing of area dimensions of visual key stimuli by tectal neurons in *Salamandra salamandra*. *Journal of Comparative Physiology* 153:85–98. (2)

Finn, A. L., J. S. Handler, and J. Orloff. 1967. Active chloride transport in the isolated toad bladder. *American Journal of Physiology* 213:179–184. (5)

Firth, B. T., and H. Heatwole. 1976. Panting thresholds of lizards: The role of the pineal complex in panting responses in the agamid, *Amphibolurus muricatus*. *General and Comparative Endocrinology* 29:388–401. (9)

Firth, B. T., R. E. Mauldin, and C. L. Ralph. 1988. The role of the pineal complex in behavioral thermoregulation in the collared lizard *Crotaphytus collaris* under seminatural conditions. *Physiological Zoology* 61:176–185. (9)

Firth, B. T., C. L. Ralph, and T. J. Boardman. 1980. Independent effects of the pineal and a bacterial pyrogen in behavioural thermoregulation in lizards. *Nature* 285:399–400. (9)

Firth, B. T., and J. S. Turner. 1982. Sensory, neural, and hormonal aspects of thermoregulation. In *Biology of the Reptilia*, vol. 12, ed. C. Gans and F. H. Pough, 213–274. New York: Academic Press. (9)

Fischer, R. U., Jr., E. A. Standora, and J. R. Spotila. 1987. Predator-induced changes in thermoregulation of bluegill, *Lepomis macrochirus*, from a thermally altered reservoir. *Canadian Journal of Fisheries and Aquatic Sciences* 44:1629–1634. (9)

Fischer, T. M. 1978. A comparison of the flow behavior of disc shaped versus elliptic red blood cells (RBC). *Blood Cells* 4:453–461. (5)

Fisher, H. T., and A. Richards. 1950. The annual ovarian cycle of *Acris crepitans* Baird. In *Research on the Amphibia of Oklahoma*, ed. A. N. Bragg, 129–142. Norman: University of Oklahoma Press. (15)

Fisher, R. A. 1958. *The Genetical Theory of Natural Selection*. 2d rev. ed. New York: Dover Press. (14)

Fitch, H. S. 1956. Temperature responses in free-living amphibians and reptiles of northeastern Kansas. *University of Kansas Publications, Museum of Natural History* 8:417–476. (8,9)

Fite, K. V., ed. 1976. *The Amphibian Visual System*. New York: Academic Press. (2)

———. 1985. The pretectal and accessory optic nuclei of fish, Amphibia, and reptiles: Theme and variations. *Brain, Behavior, and Evolution* 26:71–90. (2)

Fite, K. V., L. C. Bengston, and N. M. Montgomery. 1988. Anuran accessory optic system: Evidence for a dual organization. *Journal of Comparative Neurology* 273:377–384. (2)

Fite, K. V., R. G. Carey, and D. Vicario. 1977. Visual neurons in frog anterior thalamus. *Brain Research* 127:283–290. (2)

Fite, K. V., J. Soukup, and R. G. Carey. 1978. Wavelength discrimination in the leopard frog: A reexamination. *Brain, Behavior, and Evolution* 15:404–414. (2)

Fitts, R. H., and J. O. Holloszy. 1976. Lactate and contractile force in frog muscle during development of fatigue and recovery. *American Journal of Physiology* 231:430–433. (12)

Fitzgerrel, W., and J. C. Vanatta. 1980. Factors affecting bicarbonate secretion in the urinary bladder of *Bufo marinus*. *Comparative Biochemistry and Physiology* 66A:227–281. (5)

Fitzpatrick, L. C. 1971. Influence of sex and reproductive condition on metabolic rates in the Allegheny Mountain salamander *Desmognathus ochrophaeus*. *Comparative Biochemistry and Physiology* 40A:603–608. (12,14)

———. 1973a. Energy allocation in the Allegheny Mountain salamander, *Desmognathus ochrophaeus*. *Ecological Monographs* 43:43–58. (12,13,14,15)

———. 1973b. Influence of seasonal temperatures on the energy budget and metabolic rates of the northern two-lined salamander *Eurycea bislineata bislineata*. *Comparative Biochemistry and Physiology* 45A:807–818. (12)

———. 1976. Life history patterns of storage and utilization of lipids for energy in amphibians. *American Zoologist* 16:725–732. (10,15)

Fitzpatrick, L. C., and M. Y. Atebara. 1974. Effects of acclimation to seasonal temperatures on energy metabolism in the toad *Bufo woodhousei*. *Physiological Zoology* 47:119–129. (12)

Fitzpatrick, L. C., J. R. Bristol, and R. M. Stokes. 1971. Thermal acclimation and metabolism in the Allegheny Mountain salamander *Des-*

mognathus ochrophaeus. *Comparative Biochemistry and Physiology* 40A:681–688. (12)

———. 1972. Thermal acclimation and metabolic rates in the dusky salamander *Desmognathus fuscus*. *Comparative Biochemistry and Physiology* 41A:89–96. (12)

Fitzpatrick, L. C., and A. V. Brown. 1975. Metabolic compensation to temperature in the salamander *Desmognathus ochrophaeus* from a high elevation population. *Comparative Biochemistry and Physiology* 50A:733–737. (10,12)

Flanigan, J. J. 1960. Experiments on the development of the mesial motor column in the frog. *Journal of Comparative Neurology* 114:67–77. (16)

Fletcher, G. L., and R. T. Haedrich. 1987. Rheological properties of rainbow trout blood. *Canadian Journal of Zoology* 65:879–883. (5)

Fletcher, K., and N. B. Myant. 1959. Oxygen consumption of tadpoles during metamorphosis. *Journal of Physiology* (London) 145:353–368. (12,16)

Fletcher, N. H., and S. Thwaites. 1979. Physical models for the analysis of acoustic systems in biology. *Quarterly Review of Biophysics* 12:25–65. (2)

Flight, W. F. G. 1973. Observations on the pineal ultrastructure of the urodele, *Diemictylus viridescens*. *Koninklijke Nederlandse Akademie van Wetenshappen verhandelingen-Amsterdam* 76C:425–448. (16)

Flitney, F. W., and J. Singh. 1980. Release of prostaglandins from the isolated frog ventricle and associated changes in endogenous cyclic nucleotide levels. *Journal of Physiology* (London) 304:1–20. (3)

Flores, G., and E. Frieden. 1968. Induction and survival of hemoglobin-less and erythrocyte-less tadpoles and young bullfrogs. *Science* 159:101–103. (5)

Floyd, K., and I. C. H. Smith. 1971. The mechanical and thermal properties of frog slow muscle fibers. *Journal of Physiology* (London) 213:617–631. (11)

Floyd, R. B. 1984. Variation in temperature preference with stage of development of *Bufo marinus* larvae. *Journal of Herpetology* 18:153–158. (9)

———. 1985. Effects of photoperiod and starvation on the temperature tolerance of larvae of the giant toad, *Bufo marinus*. *Copeia* 1985:625–631. (8)

Focant, B., and M. Reznik. 1980. Comparison of the sarcoplasmic and myofibrillar proteins of twitch and tonic fibres of frog muscle (*Rana temporaria*). *European Journal of Cell Biology* 21:195–199. (11)

Foley, R. E., and J. R. Spotila. 1978. Effect of wind speed, air temperature, and body size on evaporative water loss from the turtle *Chrysemys scripta*. *Copeia* 1978:627–634. (4)

Folk, G. E., Jr. 1974. *Textbook of Environmental Physiology*. 2d ed. Philadelphia: Lea and Febinger. (9)

Follett, B. K. 1984. Birds. In *Marshall's Physiology of Reproduction*, 4th ed., ed. G. E. Lamming, 1:283–350. Edinburgh: Churchill Livingstone. (15)

Follett, B. K., and M. R. Redshaw. 1974. The physiology of vitellogenesis. In *Physiology of the Amphibia*, ed. B. Lofts, 2:219–308. New York: Academic Press. (16)

Forehand, C. J., and P. B. Farel. 1982a. Spinal cord development in anuran larvae: 1. Primary and secondary neurons. *Journal of Comparative Neurology* 209:389–394. (2)

———. 1982b. Spinal cord development in anuran larvae: 2. Ascending and descending pathways. *Journal of Comparative Neurology* 209:395–408. (2)

Forester, D. C. 1977. Comments on the female reproductive cycles and philopatry by *Desmognathus ochrophaeus* (Amphibia, Urodela, Plethodontidae). *Journal of Herpetology* 11:311–316. (15)

———. 1979. The adaptiveness of parental care in *Desmognathus ochrophaeus* (Urodela; Plethodontidae). *Copeia* 1979:332–341. (14)

———. 1981. Parental care in the salamander *Desmognathus ochrophaeus*: Female activity pattern and trophic behavior. *Journal of Herpetology* 15:29–34. (14)

Forester, D. C., and R. Czarnowsky. 1985. Sexual selection in the spring peeper, *Hyla crucifer* (Amphibia, Anura): Role of the advertisement call. *Behaviour* 92:112–128. (14)

Forman, L. J., and J. J. Just. 1981. Cellular quantification of hemoglobin transition during natural and thyroid hormone induced metamorphosis of the bullfrog, *Rana catesbeiana*. *General and Comparative Endocrinology* 44:1–20. (16)

Formanowicz, D. R. 1986. Anuran tadpole aquatic insect predator-prey interactions: Tadpole size and predator capture success. *Herpetologica* 42:367–373. (14)

Formanowicz, D. R., and E. D. Brodie, Jr. 1979. Palatability and antipredator behavior of selected *Rana* to the shrew *Blarina*. *American Midland Naturalist* 101:456–458. (14)

———. 1982. Relative palatabilities of members of a larval amphibian community. *Copeia* 1982:91–97. (14)

Formanowicz, D. R., M. M. Stewart, K. Townsend, F. H. Pough, and P. F. Brussard. 1981. Predation by giant crab spiders on the Puerto Rican frog *Eleutherodactylus coqui*. *Herpetologica* 37:125–129. (12,14)

Formas, J. R., and M. I. Vera. 1980. Reproductive patterns of *Eupsophys roseus* and *E. vittatus*. *Journal of Herpetology* 14:11–14. (16)

Forrest, T. G. 1983. Calling songs and mate choice in mole crickets. In *Orthopteran Mating Systems*, ed. D. T. Gwynne and G. K. Morris, 195–204. Boulder, CO: Westview Press. (14)

Forrester, T., and H. Schmidt. 1970. An electrophysiological investigation of the slow fibre system in the frog rectus abdominis muscle. *Journal of Physiology* (London) 207:477–491. (11)

Forster, R. P. 1938. The use of inulin and creatinine as glomerular filtrate measuring substance in the frog. *Journal of Cellular and Comparative Physiology* 12:213–222. (16)

———. 1942. The nature of the glucose reabsorptive process in the frog renal tubule: Evidence for intermittency of glomerular function in the intact animal. *Journal of Cellular and Comparative Physiology* 20:55–69. (5)

———. 1943. The effect of epinephrine upon frog renal hemodynamics in the intact animal. *American Journal of Physiology* 140:221–225. (6)

———. 1954. Active cellular transport of urea by frog renal tubules. *American Journal of Physiology* 179:372–377. (5)

Forster, R. P., B. Schmidt-Nielsen, and L. Goldstein. 1963. Relation of renal tubular transport of urea to its biosynthesis in metamorphosing tadpoles. *Journal of Cellular and Comparative Physiology* 61:239–244. (5)

Forte, G. M., L. Limlomwongse, and J. G. Forte. 1969a. The development of intracellular membranes concomitant with the appearance of HCl secretion in oxyntic cells of the metamorphosing bullfrog tadpole. *Journal of Cell Science* 4:709–727. (16)

———. 1969b. The intestinal epithelium during anuran metamorphosis. *International Review of Cytology Supplement* 5:337–385. (16)

Forte, J. G., L. Limlomwongse, and D. K. Kasbekar. 1969. Ion transport and the development of hydrogen ion secretion in the stomach of the metamorphosing bullfrog tadpole. *Journal of General Physiology* 54:76–95. (16)

Fortune, J. E. 1983. Steroid production by *Xenopus* ovarian follicles at different developmental stages. *Developmental Biology* 99:502–509. (16)

Foskett, J. K., and H. H. Ussing. 1986. Location of chloride conductance to mitochondria-rich cells in the frog skin epithelium. *Journal of Membrane Biology* 91:251–258. (5)

Foster, R. G., and A. Roberts. 1982. The pineal eye in *Xenopus laevis* embryos and larvae: A photoreceptor with a direct excitatory effect on behaviour. *Journal of Comparative Physiology* 145:413–419. (16)

Fox, H. 1963. The amphibian pronephros. *Quarterly Review of Biology* 38:1–25. (16)

———. 1984. *Amphibian Morphogenesis*. Clifton, NJ: Humana Press. (11,16)

———. 1985a. Changes in amphibian skin during larval development and metamorphosis. In *Metamorphosis: The Eighth Symposium of the British Society for Developmental Biology*, ed. M. Balls and M. Bower, 59–87. Oxford: Clarendon Press. (16)

———. 1985b. The tentacles of *Ichthyophis* (Amphibia: Caecilia) with special reference to the skin. *Journal of Zoology* (London) 205A:223–234. (13)

———. 1986. Early development of caecilian skin with special reference to the epidermis. *Journal of Herpetology* 20:154–167. (16)

———. 1988. Riesenzellen, goblet cells, Leydig cells, and the large clear cells of *Xenopus*, in the amphibian larval epidermis: Fine structure and a consideration of their homology. *Journal of Submicroscopic Cytology and Pathology* 20:437–451. (16)

Fox, J. H. 1988. Possible active space optimization by the male cricket frog, *Acris crepitans*, through adjustment of neighbor spacing. *Society for Neuroscience Abstracts* 14:88. (2)

Foxon, G. E. H. 1964. Blood and respiration. In *Physiology of the Amphibia*, ed. J. A. Moore, 151–209. New York: Academic Press. (5)

Fraenkel, G. S., and D. L. Gunn. 1940. *The Orientation of Animals: Kineses, Taxes, and Compass Reactions*. London: Oxford University Press. (9)

Fraile, B., R. Paniagua, M. C. Rodriguez, and F. J. Saez. 1989. Effects of photoperiod and temperature on spermiogenesis in marbled newts (*Triturus marmoratus marmoratus*). *Copeia* 1989:357–363. (8)

Franchi, L. L. 1962. The structure of the ovary. In *The Ovary*, ed. S. Zuckerman, 1:121–143. New York: Academic Press. (15)

Franchi, L. L., A. M. Mandl, and S. Zuckerman. 1962. The development of the ovary and the process of oogenesis. In *The Ovary*, ed. S. Zuckerman, 1:1–88. New York: Academic Press. (15)

Francis, E. T. B. 1934. *The Anatomy of the Salamander*. Oxford: Clarendon Press. (7,11)

Frangioni, G., and G. Borgioli. 1988. Sites and trend of erythropoiesis in anemic, normal, and splenectomized newts. *Journal of Experimental Zoology* 247:244–250. (16)

Frank, E., and M. Westerfield. 1983. Development of sensory-motor synapses in the spinal cord of the frog. *Journal of Physiology* (London) 343:593–616. (16)

Franks, F. 1985. *Biophysics and Biochemistry at Low Temperature*. Cambridge: Cambridge University Press. (10)

Fraser, D. F. 1980. On the environmental control of oocyte maturation in a plethodontid salamander. *Oecologia* (Berlin) 46:302–307. (15)

Fraser, S., and G. C. Grigg. 1984. Control of thermal conductance is insignificant to thermoregulation in small reptiles. *Physiological Zoology* 57:392–400. (4)

Frazier, L. W., and J. C. Vanatta. 1971. Excretion of H^+ and NH_4^+ by the urinary bladder of the acidotic toad and the effects of short-circuit current on the excretion. *Biochimica et Biophysica Acta* 241:20–29. (5)

———. 1980. Evidence that the frog skin excretes ammonia. *Comparative Biochemistry and Physiology* 66A:525–527. (5)

———. 1981. Excretion of K^+ by frog skin with rate varying with K^+ load. *Comparative Biochemistry and Physiology* 69A:157–160. (5)

Freda, J. 1986. The influence of acidic pond water on amphibians: A review. *Water, Air, and Soil Pollution* 30:439–450. (5)

Freda, J., and W. A. Dunson. 1984. Sodium balance of amphibian larvae exposed to low environmental pH. *Physiological Zoology* 57:435–443. (5)

———. 1986. Effects of low pH and other chemical variables on the local distribution of amphibians. *Copeia* 1986:454–466. (14)

Freed, A. N. 1980. An adaptive advantage of basking behavior in an anuran amphibian. *Physiological Zoology* 54:433–444. (8,9,13,15)

———. 1982. A treefrog's menu: Selection for an evening's meal. *Oecologia* (Berlin) 53:20–26. (13)

Freisling, J. 1948. Studien zur Biologie und Psychologie der Wechselkröte (*Bufo viridis* Laur.). *Österreichishe Zoologische Zentralblatt* 1:383–440. (13)

Freund, G. 1973. Hypothermia after acute ethanol and benzyl alcohol administration. *Life Sciences* 13:345–349. (9)

Frieden, E. 1961. Biochemical adaptation and anuran metamorphosis. *American Zoologist* 1:115–149. (5)

———. 1967. Thyroid hormones and the biochemistry of amphibian metamorphosis. *Recent Progress in Hormone Research* 23:139–194. (3)

———. 1981. The dual role of thyroid hormones in vertebrate development and calorigenesis. In *Metamorphosis: A Problem in Developmental Biology*, ed. L. I. Gilbert and E. Frieden, 545–563. New York: Plenum Press. (16)

Frieden, E., and J. J. Just. 1970. Hormonal responses in amphibian metamorphosis. In *Biochemical Actions of Hormones*, ed. G. Litwak, 1:1–52. New York: Academic Press. (16)

Frieden, E., and B. Naile. 1955. Biochemistry of amphibian metamorphosis: 1. Enhancement of induced metamorphosis by gluco-corticoids. *Science* 121:37–39. (16)

Friedman, R. T., R. M. Aiyawar, W. D. Hughes, and E. G. Huf. 1967. Effects of NH_4^+-ions on acid-base properties and ion movements in isolated frog skin. *Comparative Biochemistry and Physiology* 23:847–869. (5)

Fritzsch, B. 1980. Retinal projections in European Salamandridae. *Cell and Tissue Research* 213:325–341. (2)

———. 1981. The pattern of lateral-line afferents in urodeles. *Cell and Tissue Research* 218:581–594. (2)

———. 1988. Phylogenetic and ontogenetic origins of the dorsolateral auditory nucleus of anurans. In *The Evolution of the Amphibian Auditory System,* ed. B. Fritzsch, M. J. Ryan, W. Wilczynski, T. E. Hetherington, and W. Walkowiak, 561–585. New York: John Wiley and Sons. (2,16)

Fritzsch, B., W. Himstedt, and M. D. Crapon de Caprona. 1985. Visual projections in larval *Ichthyophis kohtaoensis* (Amphibia: Gymnophiona). *Developmental Brain Research* 23:201–210. (16)

Fritzsch, B., and H. Münz. 1986. Electroreception in amphibians. In *Electroreception,* ed. T. H. Bullock and W. Heiligenberg, 483–496. New York: John Wiley and Sons. (16)

Fritzsch, B., A. M. Nikundiwe, and U. Will. 1984. Projection patterns of lateral-line afferents in anurans: A comparative HRP study. *Journal of Comparative Neurology* 229:451–469. (2)

Fritzsch, B., M. J. Ryan, W. Wilczynski, T. E. Hetherington, and W. Walkowiak, eds. 1988. *The Evolution of the Amphibian Auditory System.* New York: John Wiley and Sons. (2)

Fritzsch, B., and U. Wahnschaffe. 1983. The electroreceptive ampullary organs of urodeles. *Cell and Tissue Research* 229:483–503. (2)

Fritzsch, B., U. Wahnschaffe, and U. C. Bartsch. 1988. Metamorphic changes in the octavolateralis system of amphibians. In *The Evolution of the Amphibian Auditory System,* ed. B. Fritzsch, M. J. Ryan, W. Wilczysnki, T. E. Hetherington, and W. Walkowiak, 359–376. New York: John Wiley and Sons. (2,16)

Fromm, P. O. 1956. Heat production of frogs. *Physiological Zoology* 29:234–240. (12)

Fromm, P. O., and R. E. Johnson. 1955. The respiratory metabolism of frogs as related to season. *Journal of Cellular and Comparative Physiology* 45:343–359. (10,12)

Froom, B. 1982. *Amphibians of Canada.* Toronto: McClelland and Stewart. (10)

Frost, D. R. 1985. *Amphibian Species of the World: A Taxonomic and Geographical Reference.* Lawrence, KS: Allen Press. (11,16)

Frost, J. S. 1983. Comparative feeding and breeding strategies of a sympatric pair of leopard frogs (*Rana pipiens* complex). *Journal of Experimental Zoology* 225:135–140. (15)

Frost, S. K., L. G. Epp, and S. J. Robinson. 1984. The pigmentary system of developing axolotls: 1. A biochemical and structural analysis of chromatophores in wild-type axolotls. *Journal of Embryology and Experimental Morphology* 81:105–125. (16)

Frost, S. K., and S. J. Robinson. 1984. Pigment cell differentiation in the fire bellied toad, *Bombina orientalis:* 1. Structural, chemical, and physical aspects of the adult pigment pattern. *Journal of Morphology* 179:229–242. (16)

Fry, F. E. J. 1947. Effects of the environment on animal activity. University of Toronto Studies in Biological Sciences, no. 55. Publications of the Ontario Fisheries Research Laboratory, no. 68:1–62. (4,8,9,14)

———. 1958. The experimental study of behavior in fish. *Proceedings of the Indo-Pacific Fisheries Council* 3:37–42. (9)

———. 1971. The effect of environmental factors on the physiology of fish. In *Fish Physiology,* ed. W. S. Hoar and D. R. Randall, 6:79–134. New York: Academic Press. (9)

Fry, F. E. J., J. R. Brett, and G. H. Clawson. 1942. Lethal limits of temperature for young goldfish. *Revue Canadian de Biologie* 1:50–56. (4)

Frye, B. E. 1962. Extirpation and transplantation of the pancreatic rudiments of the salamanders *Ambystoma punctatum* and *Eurycea bislineata. Anatomical Record* 144:97–107. (16)

———. 1964a. Hypertrophy of the islets of Langerhans of frog tadpoles after partial pancreatectomy. *Journal of Experimental Zoology* 158:133–140. (16)

———. 1964b. Metamorphic changes in blood sugar and the pancreatic islets of frog *Rana clamitans. Journal of Experimental Zoology* 155:215–224. (16)

Frye, B. E., P. S. Brown, and B. W. Snyder. 1972. Effects of prolactin and somatotropin on growth and metamorphosis of amphibians. *General and Comparative Endocrinology,* suppl. 3:209–218. (16)

Fujita, Y., Y. Jokura, S. Takami, and A. Urano. 1987. Effects of castration on volumes of the preoptic nucleus and the amygdala and on immunoreactivity of LH-RH fibers in the brain of the toad, *Bufo japonicus. General and Comparative Endocrinology* 68:278–285. (15)

Fukuzawa, T., and J. T. Bagnara. 1989. Control of melanoblast differentiation in Amphibia by α-melanocyte stimulating hormone, a serum melanizing factor, and a melanization inhibiting factor. *Pigment Cell Research* 2:171–181. (3)

Fukuzawa, T., and H. Ide. 1988. A ventrally-localized inhibitor of melanization in *Xenopus laevis* skin. *Developmental Biology* 129:25–36. (3)

Full, R. J. 1986. Locomotion without lungs: Energetics and performance of a lungless salamander. *American Journal of Physiology* 251:R775–R780. (5,6,12)

———. 1987. Locomotion energetics of the ghost crab: 1. Metabolic cost and endurance. *Journal of Experimental Biology* 130:137–154. (12)

Full, R. J., B. D. Anderson, C. M. Finnerty, and M. E. Feder. 1988. Exercising with and without lungs: 1. The effects of metabolic cost, maximal oxygen transport, and body size on terrestrial locomotion in salamander species. *Journal of Experimental Biology* 138:471–485. (5,6,12)

Full, R. J., and C. F. Herreid. 1983. The aerobic response to exercise of the fastest land crab. *American Journal of Physiology* 244:R530–R536. (12)

———. 1984. Fiddler crab exercise: Energetic cost of running sideways. *Journal of Experimental Biology* 109:141–161. (12)

Full, R. J., C. F. Herreid, and J. A. Assad. 1985. Energetics of the exercising wharf crab, *Sesarma cinereum. Physiological Zoology* 58:605–615. (12)

Full, R. J., D. A. Zuccarello, and A. Tullis. 1990. Effects of variation in form on the cost of terrestrial locomotion. *Journal of Experimental Biology* 150:233–246. (1)

Fung, Y. C. 1981. *Biomechanics: Mechanical Properties of Living Tissues.* New York: Springer-Verlag. (5)

———. 1984. *Biodynamics: Circulation.* New York: Springer-Verlag. (5)

Funkhouser, A. 1977. Plasma osmolarity of *Rana catesbeiana* and *Scaphiopus hammondi* tadpoles. *Herpetologica* 33:272–274. (16)

Funkhouser, A., and S. A. Foster. 1970. Oxygen uptake and thyroid activity in *Hyla regilla* tadpoles. *Herpetologica* 26:366–371. (12)

Funkhouser, A., and K. S. Mills. 1969. Oxygen consumption during spontaneous amphibian metamorphosis. *Physiological Zoology* 42:15–21. (12,16)

Funkhouser, D., and L. Goldstein. 1973. Urea response to pure osmotic stress in the aquatic toad, *Xenopus laevis. American Journal of Physiology* 224:524–529. (5,6)

Fürbringer, M. 1873. Zur vergleichenden Anatomie der Schultermuskeln: 1. Theil. *Jenaische Zeitschrift für Naturwissenschaften* 1873:237–320. (11)

———. 1874. Zur vergleichenden Anatomie der Schultermuskeln: 1. Theil. *Jenaische Zeitschrift für Naturwissenschaften* 1874:175–280. (11)

Fürlinger, F. 1930. Über einen Zusammenhang zwischen Struktur und Funktion von Skelettmuskeln bei *Rana temporaria. Zoologischer Anzeiger* 90:325–331. (11)

Furspan, P. B., J. S. K. Sham, R. L. Shew, G. Peng, and P. K. T. Pang. 1984. Cardiac actions of bovine parathyroid hormone fragment (1-34) in some lower vertebrates. *General and Comparative Endocrinology* 56:246–251. (3)

Fuzessery, Z. M. 1988. Frequency tuning in the anuran central auditory system. In *The Evolution of the Amphibian Auditory System,* ed. B. Fritzsch, M. J. Ryan, W. Wilczynski, T. E. Hetherington, and W. Walkowiak, 253–273. New York: John Wiley and Sons. (2,14)

Gabe, M. 1971. Données histologiques sur la glande surrénale d'*Ichthyophis glutinosus. Archives de Biologie* (Liége) 82:1–23. (16)

Gadow, H. 1909. *Cambridge Natural History.* Vol. 8, *Amphibia and Reptiles.* London: Macmillan. (15)

Gaehtgens, P., F. Schmidt, and G. Will. 1981. Comparative rheology of nucleated and non-nucleated red blood cells: 1. Microrheology of avian erythrocytes during capillary flow. *Pflugers Archiv* 390:278–282. (5)

Gahlenbeck, H., and H. Bartels. 1968. Temperaturadaptation der Sauerstoffaffinität des Blutes von *Rana esculenta* L. *Zeitschrift für vergleichende Physiologie* 59:232–240. (5)

———. 1970. Blood gas transport properties in gill and lung forms of the axolotl (*Ambystoma mexicanum*). *Respiration Physiology* 9:175–182. (5,12,16)

Gainer, H., K. Kusano, and R. F. Mathewson. 1965. Electrophysiological and mechanical properties of squirrelfish sound-producing muscle. *Comparative Biochemistry and Physiology* 14:661–671. (14)

Galeotti, G. 1904. Concerning the EMF which is generated at the surface of animal membranes on contact with different electrolytes. *Zeitschrift für physikalische Chemie* 49:542–562. (5)

Galey, W. R., S. C. Wood, and V. M. Mancha. 1987. Effects of metamorphosis on water permeability of skin in the salamander *Ambystoma tigrinum*. *Comparative Biochemistry and Physiology* 86A:429–432. (16)

Galgano, M. 1936. Intorno all'influenza del clima sulla spermatogenesi di *Rana esculenta*. *Archivo Italiano di Anatomia e di Embriologia* 35:511–541. (15)

Gallardo, R., P. K. T. Pang, and W. H. Sawyer. 1980. Neural influences on bullfrog renal functions. *Proceedings of the Society for Experimental Biology and Medicine* 165:233–240. (6)

Gallien, L. 1940. Recherches sur la physiologie hypophysaire dans ces relations avec les gonades et le cycle sexuel, chez la grenouille rousse, *Rana temporaria* L. *Bulletin Biologique de la France et de la Belgique* 74:1–42. (15)

———. 1952. Élevage et comportement du pleurodèle au laboratoire. *Bulletin Société Zoologique de France* 77:456–461. (15)

———. 1974. Intersexuality. In *Physiology of the Amphibia*, ed. B. Lofts, 2:523–549. New York: Academic Press. (16)

Gallien, L., and O. Bidaud. 1959. Table chronologique du développement chez *Triturus helveticus* Razoumowsky. *Bulletin de la Société Zoologique de France* 84:22–32. (16)

Gallien, L., and M. Durocher. 1957. Table chronologique du développement chez *Pleurodeles waltlii* Michah. *Bulletin Biologique de la France et de la Belgique* 91:97–114. (16)

Galli-Gallardo, S. M., P. K. T. Pang, and C. Oguro. 1979. Renal responses of the Chilean toad, *Calyptocephalella caudiverbera*, and the mudpuppy, *Necturus maculosus*, to mesotocin. *General and Comparative Endocrinology* 37:134–136. (5)

Galli Mainini, C. 1947. Ovulación del *Bufo arenarum* con gonadotrofina coriónica. *Revista de la Sociedad Argentina de Biologia* 23:299. (15)

Galton, V. A. 1980. Binding of thyroid hormones *in vivo* by hepatic nuclei of *Rana catesbeiana* tadpoles. *Endocrinology* 106:859–866. (3)

———. 1983. Thyroid hormone action in amphibian metamorphosis. In *Molecular Basis of Thyroid Hormone Action*, ed. J. H. Oppenheimer and H. H. Samuels, 445–483. New York: Academic Press. (11)

———. 1984. Putative nuclear triiodothyronine receptors in tadpole erythrocytes: Regulation of receptor number by thyroid hormones. *Endocrinology* 114:735–742. (3)

———. 1985. 3,4,3'-triiodothyronine receptors and thyroxine 5'-monodeiodinating activity in thyroid hormone-insensitive Amphibia. *General and Comparative Endocrinology* 57:465–471. (3)

———. 1988. The role of thyroid hormone in amphibian development. *American Zoologist* 28:309–318. (16)

Galton, V. A., and A. Hiebert. 1988. The ontogeny of iodothyronine 5'-monodeiodinase activity in *Rana catesbeiana* tadpoles. *Endocrinology* 122:640–645. (16)

Galton, V. A., and S. H. Ingbar. 1962. Observations on the relation between the action and the degradation of thyroid hormones as indicated by studies in the tadpoles and the frog. *Endocrinology* 70:622–632. (9)

Galton, V. A., and K. Munck. 1981. Metabolism of thyroxine in *Rana catesbeiana* tadpoles during metamorphic climax. *Endocrinology* 109:1127–1131. (3)

Galvani, L. 1791. *De Viribus Electricitatis in Motu Musculari Commentarius*. Bononiae: Instituti Scientiarum. (11)

Gans, C. 1961. A bullfrog and its prey: A look at the biomechanics of jumping. *Natural History* 70:26–37. (11)

———. 1962a. The legless tetrapod: Caecilian poses question for research. *Natural History* 71:26–27. (11)

———. 1962b. The tongue protrusion mechanism in *Rana catesbeiana*. *American Zoologist* 2:524. (11)

———. 1969. Comments on inertial feeding. *Copeia* 1969:855–857. (11)

———. 1970. Respiration in early tetrapods: The frog is a red herring. *Evolution* 24:723–724. (6,11)

———. 1971. Strategy and sequence in the evolution of the external gas exchangers of ectothermal vertebrates. *Forma et Functio* 3:66–104. (11)

———. 1973a. Locomotion and burrowing in limbless vertebrates. *Nature* 242:414–415. (11)

———. 1973b. Sound production in the Salientia: Mechanism and evolution of the emitter. *American Zoologist* 13:1179–1194. (11)

———. 1974. *Biomechanics: An Approach to Vertebrate Biology*. Philadelphia: J. B. Lippincott Company. (11)

———. 1975. Tetrapod limblessness: Evolution and functional corollaries. *American Zoologist* 15:455–467. (11)

———. 1976. The process of skittering in frogs. *Annals of Zoology* (Agra) 12:37–40. (11)

———. 1979. Momentarily excessive construction as the basis for protoadaptation. *Evolution* 33:227–233. (14)

———. 1986. Evolution of limbless squamates: Functional aspects. In *Studies in Herpetology*, ed. Z. Roček, 71–74. Proceedings of the 3d Ordinary General Meeting, Societas Europaea Herpetologica. Prague: Charles University. (11)

———. 1988. Adaptation and the form-function relation. *American Zoologist* 28:681–697. (14)

———. 1990. Adaptations and conflicts. In *Evolutionary Biology: Theory and Principles*, ed. J. Slipka, 23–31. Prague: Czechoslovakian Academy of Sciences. (11)

———. 1993. Evolution of the head. In *The Vertebrate Skull*, ed. J. Hanken and B. Hall, vol. 2. Chicago: University of Chicago Press. (Forthcoming) (11)

Gans, C., and W. J. Bock. 1965. The functional significance of muscle architecture: A theoretical analysis. *Ergebnisse der Anatomie und Entwicklungsgeschichte* 38:115–142. (11)

Gans, C., H. J. de Jongh, and J. Farber. 1969. Bullfrog (*Rana catesbeiana*) ventilation: How does the frog breathe? *Science* 163:1223–1225. (11)

Gans, C., and F. de Vree. 1987. Functional bases of fiber length and angulation in muscle. *Journal of Morphology* 192:63–85; erratum, 193:323. (11)

Gans, C., and G. C. Gorniak. 1982a. Functional morphology of lingual protrusion in marine toads (*Bufo marinus*). *American Journal of Anatomy* 163:195–222. (2,11)

———. 1982b. How does the toad flip its tongue? Test of two hypotheses. *Science* 216:1335–1337. (11)

Gans, C., G. E. Loeb, and F. de Vree. 1989. Architecture and physiological properties of the semitendinosus muscle in domestic goats. *Journal of Morphology* 199:287–297. (11)

Gans, C., Nishikawa, K. C. and Canatella, D. C. 1991. The frog *Megophrys montana*: Specialist in large prey. *American Zoologist* 31:52A.

Gans, C., and T. S. Parsons. 1966. On the origin of the jumping mechanism in frogs. *Evolution* 20:92–99. (11)

Gans, C., and R. Pyles. 1983. Narial closure in toads: Which muscles? *Respiration Physiology* 53:215–223. (7,11)

Gans, C., and H. I. Rosenberg. 1966. Numerical analysis of frog jumping. *Herpetologica* 22:209–213. (11)

Gapp, D. 1986. Hormonal control of metabolism. In *Fundamentals of Comparative Endocrinology*, ed. I. Chester-Jones, P. M. Ingleton, and J. G. Phillips, 623–660. New York: Plenum Publishing. (3)

Garcia-Romeu, F., and J. Ehrenfeld. 1975a. Chloride transport through the non-short-circuited isolated skin of *Rana esculenta*. *American Journal of Physiology* 228:845–849. (5)

———. 1975b. *In vivo* Na⁺ and Cl⁻ independent transport across the skin of *Rana esculenta*. *American Journal of Physiology* 228:839–844. (5)

Garcia-Romeu, F., A. Salibian, and S. Pezzani-Hernandez. 1969. The nature of the *in vivo* sodium and chloride uptake mechanisms through the epithelium of the Chilean frog *Calyptocephalella gayi* (Dum. et Bibr., 1841). *Journal of General Physiology* 53:816–835. (5)

Garland, H. O., and I. W. Henderson. 1975. Influence of environmental salinity on renal and adrenocortical function in the toad, *Bufo marinus*. *General and Comparative Endocrinology* 27:136–143. (6)

Garland, H. O., I. W. Henderson, and J. A. Brown. 1975. Micropuncture study of the renal responses of the urodele *Necturus maculosus* to injections of arginine vasotocin and to an anti-aldosterone compound. *Journal of Experimental Biology* 63:249–264. (5)

Garland, T. 1982. Scaling maximal running speed and maximal aerobic speed to body mass in mammals and lizards. *Physiologist* 25:388. (12)

———. 1983. The relationship between maximal running speed and maximal aerobic speed in terrestrial mammals. *Journal of Zoology* (London) 199:157–170. (12)

———. 1985. Physiological and ecological correlates of locomotory performance and body size in lizards. Ph.D. diss., University of California at Irvine. (14)

Garlick, R. L., B. J. Davis, M. Farmer, H. J. Fyhn, U. E. Fyhn, R. W. Noble, D. A. Powers, A. Riggs, and R. E. Weber. 1979. A fetal-maternal shift in the oxygen equilibrium of hemoglobin from the viviparous caecilian, *Typhlonectes compressicauda*. *Comparative Biochemistry and Physiology* 62A:239–244. (5,16)

Garson, P. J., and M. L. Hunter, Jr. 1979. Effects of temperature and time of year on the singing behaviour of wrens *Troglodytes troglodytes* and great tits *Parus major*. *Ibis* 121:481–487. (14)

Gasser, F., and J. M. J. Joly. 1972. Existence d'un cycle sexuel biennal chez la femelle de *Salamandra salamandra fastuosa* Schreiber (Urodèle, Salamandridae) a différentes altitudes dans les Pyrénées centrales: Influence des facteurs génétiques et climatiques. *Annales des Sciences Naturelles, Zoologie* (Paris) 14:427–444. (15)

Gasser, K. W., and B. T. Miller. 1986. Osmoregulation of larval blotched tiger salamanders, *Ambystoma tigrinum melanostictum*, in saline environments. *Physiological Zoology* 59:643–648. (6)

Gates, D. M. 1962. *Energy Exchange in the Biosphere*. New York: Harper and Row. (4)

———. 1980. *Biophysical Ecology*. New York: Springer-Verlag. (4)

Gates, D. M., and R. B. Schmerl. 1975. *Perspectives in Biophysical Ecology*. New York: Springer-Verlag. (4)

Gatten, R. E., Jr. 1974. Effect of nutritional status on the preferred body temperature of the turtles *Pseudemys scripta* and *Terrapene ornata*. *Copeia* 1974:165–169. (9)

———. 1985. The uses of anaerobiosis by amphibians and reptiles. *American Zoologist* 25:945–954. (12)

———. 1987. Activity metabolism of anuran amphibians: Tolerance to dehydration. *Physiological Zoology* 60:576–585. (6,12,14)

Gatten, R. E., Jr., J. P. Caldwell, and M. E. Stockard. 1984. Anaerobic metabolism during intense swimming by anuran larvae. *Herpetologica* 40:164–169. (12,14)

Gatten, R. E., Jr., and R. M. Clark. 1989. Locomotor performance of hydrated and dehydrated frogs: Recovery following exhaustive exercise. *Copeia* 1989:451–455. (11,12)

Gatten, R. E., Jr., and C. J. Hill. 1984. Social influence on thermal selection by *Hyla crucifer*. *Journal of Herpetology* 18:87–88. (9,14)

Gatz, J. 1981. Non-random mating by size in American toads, *Bufo americanus*. *Animal Behaviour* 29:1004–1012. (14)

Gatz, R. N., E. C. Crawford, Jr., and J. Piiper. 1974a. Metabolic and heart rate response of the plethodontid salamander *Desmognathus fuscus* to hypoxia. *Respiration Physiology* 20:43–49. (6,12)

———. 1974b. Respiratory properties of the blood of a lungless and gill-less salamander, *Desmognathus fuscus*. *Respiration Physiology* 20:33–41. (5,6)

———. 1975. Kinetics of inert gas equilibration in an exclusively skin-breathing salamander, *Desmognathus fuscus*. *Respiration Physiology* 24:15–29. (7)

Gatz, R. N., and J. Piiper. 1979. Anaerobic energy metabolism during severe hypoxia in the lungless salamander *Desmognathus fuscus* (Plethodontidae). *Respiration Physiology* 38:377–384. (6,10)

Gaule, J. 1901. Die Veränderungen des Froschorganismus (*R. esculenta*) während des Jahres. *Archiv für die gesamte Physiologie* 87:473–537. (15)

Gaunt, A. S., and C. Gans. 1989. Motor end-plate and myofiber arrangement in adult and newly-hatched chickens. *Annales de la Société Royale Zoologique de Belgique* (abstracts of the 3d International Congress of Vertebrate Morphology), 85. (11)

Gaunt, R., B. G. Steinetz, and J. J. Chart. 1968. Pharmacologic alteration of steroid hormone functions. *Clinical Pharmacological Therapy* 9:657–681. (5)

Gaupp, E. 1896–1904. *Anatomie des Frosches*. Ed. A. Ecker and R. Wiedersheim. Braunschweig: Vieweg und Sohn. (7,11,15)

———. 1901. Über den Muskelmechanismus bei den Bewegungen der Froschzunge. *Anatomischer Anzeiger* 19:385–396. (11)

Gayda, T. 1921. Ricerche di calorimetria: Nota 2. La produzione di calore nello sviluppo ontogenetico del *Bufo vulgaris*. *Archivo di Fisiologia* 19:211–242. (12)

Gaymer, R. 1971. New methods of locomotion in limbless terrestrial vertebrates. *Nature* 234:150–151. (11)

Gayou, D. C. 1984. Effects of temperature on the mating call of *Hyla versicolor*. *Copeia* 1984:733–738. (8)

Gehlbach, F. R., R. Gordon, and J. B. Jordan. 1973. Aestivation of the salamander, *Siren intermedia*. *American Midland Naturalist* 89:455–463. (10,12)

Gehlbach, F. R., J. R. Kimmel, and W. A. Weems. 1969. Aggregations and body water relations in tiger salamanders (*Ambystoma tigrinum*) from the Grand Canyon rims, Arizona. *Physiological Zoology* 42:173–182. (5,12)

Geise, W., and K. E. Linsenmair. 1986. Adaptations of the reed frog *Hyperolius viridiflavus* (Amphibia, Anura, Hyperoliidae) to its arid environment: 2. Some aspects of the water economy of *Hyperolius viridiflavus nitidulus* under wet and dry season conditions. *Oecologia* (Berlin) 68:542–548. (4,6)

———. 1988. Adaptations of the reed frog *Hyperolius viridiflavus* (Amphibia, Anura, Hyperoliidae) to its arid environment: 4. Ecological significance of water economy with comments on thermoregulation and energy allocation. *Oecologia* (Berlin) 77:327–338. (9)

Gerencser, G. A. 1978. Effect of prostaglandin E_1 on transmural potential difference and short-circuit current in isolated frog (*Rana catesbeiana*) skin. *Comparative Biochemistry and Physiology* 60A:199–203. (5)

Gerhardt, H. C. 1975. Sound pressure levels and radiation patterns of the vocalizations of some North American frogs and toads. *Journal of Comparative Physiology* 102:1–12. (14)

———. 1977. Temperature coupling in the vocal communication system of the tree frog. *Journal of the Acoustical Society of America* 62:S88. (8)

———. 1978. Temperature coupling in the vocal communication system of the gray tree frog, *Hyla versicolor*. *Science* 199:992–994. (2,8,9)

———. 1988. Acoustic properties used in call recognition by frogs and toads. In *The Evolution of the Amphibian Auditory System*, ed. B. Fritzsch, M. J. Ryan, W. Wilczynski, T. E. Hetherington, and W. Walkowiak, 455–483. New York: John Wiley and Sons. (2,14)

Gerhardt, H. C., R. E. Daniel, S. A. Perrill, and S. Schramm. 1987. Mating behaviour and male mating success in the green treefrog. *Animal Behaviour* 35:1490–1503. (14)

Gerhardt, H. C., and K. M. Mudry. 1980. Temperature effects on frequency preferences and mating call frequencies in the green treefrog, *Hyla cinerea* (Anura: Hylidae). *Journal of Comparative Physiology* 137:1–6. (2,8)

Gern, W. A., and D. O. Norris. 1979. Plasma melatonin in the neotenic tiger salamander (*Ambystoma tigrinum*): Effects of photoperiod and pinealectomy. *General and Comparative Endocrinology* 38:393–398. (16)

Gern, W. A., D. O. Norris, and D. Duvall. 1983. The effect of light and temperature on plasma melatonin in neotenic tiger salamanders (*Ambystoma tigrinum*). *Journal of Herpetology* 17:228–234. (9)

Gershengorn, M. C. 1985. Thyrotropin-releasing hormone action: Mechanism of calcium-mediated stimulation of prolactin secretion. In *Recent Progress in Hormone Research*, vol. 41, ed. R. O. Greep, 607–638. New York: Academic Press. (16)

Gershon, N. D., K. R. Porter, and B. L. Trus. 1985. The cytoplasmic matrix: Its volume and surface area and the diffusion of molecules through it. *Proceedings of the National Academy of Science* 82:5030–5034. (8)

Getchell, M. L., J. A. Rafols, and T. V. Getchell. 1984. Histological and histochemical studies of the secretory components of the salamander olfactory mucosa: Effects of isoproterenol and olfactory nerve section. *Anatomical Record* 208:553–565. (16)

Getchell, M. L., B. Zielinski, J. A. DeSimone, and T. V. Getchell. 1987. Odorant stimulation of secretory and neural processes in the salamander olfactory mucosa. *Journal of Comparative Physiology* 160A:155–168. (16)

Getchell, M. L., B. Zielinski, and T. V. Getchell. 1987. Ontogeny of the secretory elements in the vertebrate olfactory mucosa. In *Ontogeny of Olfaction: Principles of Olfactory Maturation in Vertebrates*, ed. W. Breipohl, 71–85. Berlin: Springer-Verlag. (16)

Geuze, J. J. 1971. Light and electron microscope observations on the gastric mucosa of the frog (*Rana esculenta*): 2. Structural alterations during hibernation. *Zeitschrift für Zellforschung* 117:103–117. (13)

Ghiara, P., L. Parente, and D. Piomelli. 1984. The cyclooxygenase pathway in the avascular heart of the frog *Rana esculenta* L. *General Pharmacology* 15:309–313. (3)

Giacoma, C., and M. Sparreboom. 1987. On the sexual behaviour of the Italian newt, *Triturus italicus* (Caudata: Salamandridae). *Bijdragen tot de Dierkunde* 57:19–30. (14)

Gibbons, M. M., and T. K. McCarthy. 1983. Age determination of frogs and toads (Amphibia, Anura) from north-western Europe. *Zoologica Scripta* 12:145–151. (15)

———. 1984. Growth, maturation and survival of frogs *Rana temporaria* L. *Holarctic Ecology* 7:419–427. (15)

———. 1986. The reproductive output of frogs *Rana temporaria* (L.)

with particular reference to body size and age. *Journal of Zoology* (London) 209A:579–593. (15)

Gibson, A. R. 1984. Multivariate analysis of lizard thermal behavior. *Copeia* 1984:267–272. (9)

Gibson, R. M., and J. W. Bradbury. 1985. Sexual selection in lekking sage grouse: Phenotypic correlates of male mating success. *Behavioral Ecology and Sociobiology* 18:117–123. (14)

Giebisch, G. 1956. Measurements of pH, chloride, and inulin concentrations in proximal tubule fluid of *Necturus*. *American Journal of Physiology* 185:171–174. (5)

———. 1961. Measurements of electrical potential differences of single nephrons of the perfused *Necturus* kidney. *Journal of General Physiology* 44:659–768. (5)

Giebisch, G., L. P. Sullivan, and G. Whittembury. 1973. Relationship between tubular net sodium reabsorption and peritubular potassium uptake in the perfused *Necturus* kidney. *Journal of Physiology* (London) 230:51–74. (5)

Giebisch, G., and E. E. Windhager. 1963. Measurement of chloride movement across single proximal tubules of *Necturus* kidney. *Journal of Physiology* (London) 204:387–391. (5)

Giglio-Tos, E. 1895. Sui corpi grassi degli anfibi. *Atti della Accademia delle Scienze di Torino* 30:853–868. (15)

———. 1896. Sur les corps gras des amphibies. *Archives Italiennes de Biologie* 25:98–100. (15)

Gil, P., and G. Barja-de-quiroga. 1988. Effect of temperature acclimation on enzymatic activities and thermal sensitivity of catalase oxygen consumption and concentration of tissue peroxidation products in *Discoglossus pictus* tadpoles. *Comparative Biochemistry Physiology* 89B:363–374. (8)

Gilbert, L. I., and E. Frieden. 1981. *Metamorphosis: A Problem in Developmental Biology.* 2d ed. New York: Plenum Press. (16)

Gilly, W. F. 1975. Slow fibers in the frog cruralis muscle. *Tissue and Cell Research* 7:203–210. (11)

Gittins, S. P. 1983. The breeding migration of the common toad (*Bufo bufo*) to a pond in mid-Wales. *Journal of Zoology London* 199:555–562. (8)

Gittins, S. P., A. G. Parker, and F. M. Slater. 1980. Population characteristics of the common toad (*Bufo bufo*) visiting a breeding site in mid-Wales. *Journal of Animal Ecology* 49:161–173. (8)

Gittins, S. P., J. E. Steeds, and R. Williams. 1982. Population age-structure of the common toad (*Bufo bufo*) at a lake in mid-Wales determined from annual growth rings in the phalanges. *British Journal of Herpetology* 6:249–252. (15)

Gittleman, J. L., and S. T. Thompson, eds. 1988. Energetics and animal behavior. *American Zoologist* 28:811–938. (14)

Given, M. F. 1987. Vocalizations and acoustic interactions of the carpenter frog, *Rana virgatipes*. *Herpetologica* 43:467–481. (14)

———. 1988. Growth rate and the cost of calling activity in male carpenter frogs, *Rana virgatipes*. *Behavioral Ecology and Sociobiology* 22:153–160. (14)

Given, M. F., and D. M. McKay. 1990. Variation in citrate synthase activity in calling muscles of carpenter frogs, *Rana virgatipes*. *Copeia* 1990:863–867. (14)

Glass, M. L., R. G. Boutilier, and N. Heisler. 1983. Ventilatory control of arterial Po$_2$ in the turtle, *Chrysemys picta bellii*: Effects of temperature and hypoxia. *Journal of Comparative Physiology* 151:145–153. (5)

Glass, M. L., W. W. Burggren, and K. Johansen. 1981. Pulmonary diffusing capacity of the bullfrog (*Rana catesbeiana*). *Acta Physiologica Scandinavica* 113:485–490. (6)

Gleeson, T. T. 1980. Metabolic recovery from exhaustive exercise by a large lizard. *Journal of Applied Physiology* 48:689–694. (12)

———. 1981. Preferred body temperatures, aerobic scope, and activity capacity in the monitor lizard, *Varanus salvator*. *Physiological Zoology* 54:423–429. (9)

Gleeson, T. T., and A. F. Bennett. 1982. Acid-base imbalance in lizards during activity and recovery. *Journal of Experimental Biology* 98:439–453. (12)

Glucksohn, S. 1931. Äussere Entwicklung der Extremitäten und Stadieneinteilung der Larvenperiode von *Triton taeniatus* Leyd. und *Triton cristatus* Laur. *Wilhelm Roux's Archiv für Entwicklungsmechanik der Organism* 125:341–405. (16)

Gnanamuthu, C. P. 1933. The anatomy of the tongue of *Rana hexadactyla*. *Records of the Indian Museum* 35:125–144. (11)

———. 1936. The respiratory mechanism of the frog. *Journal of Experimental Zoology* 74:157–165. (11)

Godwin, G. J., and S. M. Roble. 1983. Mating success in male tree-frogs, *Hyla chrysoscelis* (Anura: Hylidae). *Herpetologica* 36:318–326. (14)

Goin, C. J., O. B. Goin, and G. R. Zug. 1978. *Introduction to Herpetology.* San Francisco: W. H. Freeman and Company. (10)

Goldenberg, S., and M. R. Warburg. 1976. Changes in the response to oxytocin followed throughout ontogenesis in two anuran species. *Comparative Biochemistry and Physiology* 53C:105–113. (16)

———. 1977a. Changes in the effect of vasotocin on water balance of *Rana ridibunda*. *Comparative Biochemistry and Physiology* 57A:451–455. (5,16)

———. 1977b. Osmoregulatory effect of prolactin during ontogenesis in two anurans. *Comparative Biochemistry and Physiology* 56A:137–143. (5,16)

———. 1983. Water balance of five amphibian species at different stages and phases as affected by hypophysial hormones. *Comparative Biochemistry and Physiology* 75A:447–455. (16)

Goldsmith, J. L., and J. J. Just. 1990. The bladder and osmoregulation in *Rana catesbeiana* tadpoles and froglets. (16)

Goldstein, D. L. 1988. Estimates of daily energy expenditure in birds: The time-energy budget as an integrator of laboratory and field studies. *American Zoologist* 28:829–844. (14)

Goldstein, L. 1972. Adaptation of urea metabolism in aquatic vertebrates. In *Nitrogen Metabolism and the Environment*, ed. J. W. Campbell and L. Goldstein, 55–77. New York: Academic Press. (6)

Gollnick, P. D., R. B. Armstrong, B. Saltin, C. W. Saubert IV, W. L. Sembrowich, and R. E. Shepherd. 1973. Effect of training on enzyme activity and fiber composition of human skeletal muscle. *Journal of Applied Physiology* 34:107–111. (14)

Gollnick, P. D., R. B. Armstrong, C. W. Saubert IV, K. Piehl, and B. Saltin. 1972. Enzyme activity and fiber composition in skeletal muscle in untrained and trained men. *Journal of Applied Physiology* 33:312–319. (14)

Gona, A. G. 1967. Prolactin as a goitrogenic agent in Amphibia. *Endocrinology* 81:748–754. (16)

———. 1968. Radioiodine studies on prolactin action in tadpoles. *General and Comparative Endocrinology* 11:278–283. (16)

Gona, A. G., and O. Gona. 1974. Failure of synthetic TRF to elicit metamorphosis in frog tadpoles or red-spotted newts. *General and Comparative Endocrinology* 24:223–225. (3,16)

Gona, A. G., T. K. Pendurthi, S. Al-Rabiai, O. Gona, and S. Christakos. 1986. Immunocytochemical localization and immunological characterization of vitamin D–dependent calcium-binding protein in the bullfrog cerebellum. *Brain Behavior and Evolution* 29:176–183. (3)

Gona, O. 1982. Uptake of I^{125}-labelled prolactin by bullfrog kidney tubules: An autoradiographic study. *Journal of Endocrinology* 93:193–198. (16)

Gonçalves, A. A., and P. Sawaya. 1978. Oxygen uptake by *Typhlonectes compressicaudus* related to the body weight. *Comparative Biochemistry and Physiology* 61A:141–143. (12)

Goncharevskaya, O. A., Y. G. Monin, and Y. V. Natochin. 1986. The influence of furosemide and Co^{2+} on electrolyte and water transport in newt distal tubule and frog skin. *Pflugers Archiv* 406:557–562. (5)

Gonzales, M., M. Morales, and F. Zambrano. 1979. Sulfatide content and (Na$^+$ and K$^+$) ATPase activity of skin and gill during larval development of the Chilean frog, *Calyptocephalella caudiverbera*. *Journal of Membrane Biology* 51:347–359. (16)

Goodrich, E. S. 1930. *Studies on the Structure and Development of Vertebrates.* London: Macmillan. (5)

Goos, H. J. T. 1969. Hypothalamic neurosecretion and metamorphosis in *Xenopus laevis*: 4. The effect of extirpation of the presumed TRF cells and of a subsequent PTU treatment. *Zeitschrift für Zellforschung und mikroskopische Anatomie* 97:449–458. (16)

Göppert, E. 1894. Die Kehlkopfmuskulatur der Amphibien: Eine vergleichend-anatomische Untersuchung. *Morphologisches Jahrbuch* 22:1–78. (11)

Gorbman, A. 1964. Endocrinology of the Amphibia. In *Physiology of the Amphibia*, ed. J. A. Moore, 1:371–425. New York: Academic Press. (3)

———. 1987. Evolutionary morphology of endocrine glands. In *Vertebrate Endocrinology: Fundamentals and Biomedical Implications*, vol. 1, *Morphological Considerations*, ed. P. K. T. Pang and M. P. Schreibman, 465–477. New York: Academic Press. (3)

Gordon, A. G. 1960. Humoral influences on blood cell formation and release. In *Haemopoiesis Cell Production and Its Regulation,* ed. G. E. W. Wolstenholme and M. O'Connor, 325–362. London: J. and A. Churchill. (5)

Gordon, M. S. 1962. Osmotic regulation in the green toad (*Bufo viridis*). *Journal of Experimental Biology* 39:261–270. (6)

———. 1965. Intracellular osmoregulation in skeletal muscle during salinity adaptation in two species of toads. *Biological Bulletin* 128:218–229. (6)

Gordon, M. S., K. Schmidt-Nielsen, and H. M. Kelly. 1961. Osmotic regulation in the crab-eating frog (*Rana cancrivora*). *Journal of Experimental Biology* 38:659–678. (6)

Gordon, M. S., and V. A. Tucker. 1965. Osmotic regulation in the tadpoles of the crab-eating frog (*Rana cancrivora*). *Journal of Experimental Biology* 42:437–445. (6,16)

———. 1968. Further observations on the physiology of salinity adaptation in the crab-eating frog (*Rana cancrivora*). *Journal of Experimental Biology* 49:185–193. (12)

Gorlick, D. L., and D. B. Kelley. 1986. The ontogeny of androgen receptors in the CNS of *Xenopus laevis* frogs. *Developmental Brain Research* 26:193–200. (16)

———. 1987. Neurogenesis in the vocalization pathway of *Xenopus laevis*. *Journal of Comparative Neurology* 257:614–627. (2)

Görner, P., P. Moller, and W. Weber. 1984. Lateral-line input and stimulus localization in the African clawed toad *Xenopus* sp. *Journal of Experimental Biology* 108:315–328. (2)

Gosner, K. L. 1960. A simplified tale for staging anuran embryos and larvae with notes on identification. *Herpetologica* 16:183–190. (9, 16)

Gosner, K. L., and I. H. Black. 1955. The effects of temperature and moisture on the reproductive cycle of *Scaphiopus h. holbrooki*. *American Midland Naturalist* 54:192–203. (15)

Gosner, K. L., and D. A. Rossman. 1959. Observations on the reproductive cycle of the swamp chorus frog, *Pseudacris nigrita*. *Copeia* 1959:263–266. (15)

Gossling, J., W. J. Loesche, L. D. Ottoni, and G. W. Nace. 1980. Passage of material through the gut of hibernating *Rana pipiens* (Amphibia, Anura, Ranidae). *Journal of Herpetology* 14:407–409. (8, 13)

Gottlander, K. 1987. Variation in the song rate of the male pied flycatcher *Ficedula hypoleuca*: Causes and consequences. *Animal Behaviour* 35:1037–1043. (14)

Gottlieb, G., and D. C. Jackson. 1976. Importance of pulmonary ventilation in respiratory control in the bullfrog. *American Journal of Physiology* 230:608–613. (5, 6, 10, 12, 16)

Gould, S. J., and E. S. Vrba. 1982. Exaptation: A missing term in the science of form. *Paleobiology* 8:4–15. (15)

Gradwell, N. 1969a. The function of the internal nares of the bullfrog tadpole. *Herpetologica* 25:120–121. (16)

———. 1969b. The respiratory importance of vascularization of the tadpole operculum in *Rana catesbeiana* Shaw. *Canadian Journal of Zoology* 47:1239–1243. (16)

———. 1970. The function of the ventral velum during gill irrigation in *Rana catesbeiana*. *Canadian Journal of Zoology* 48:1179–1186. (7)

———. 1971a. *Ascaphus* tadpole: Experiments on the suction and gill irrigation mechanisms. *Canadian Journal of Zoology* 49:307–332. (7, 11)

———. 1971b. *Xenopus* tadpole: On the water pumping mechanism. *Herpetologica* 27:107–123. (11)

———. 1972a. Gill irrigation in *Rana catesbeiana*: 1. On the anatomical basis. *Canadian Journal of Zoology* 50:481–499. (11, 16)

———. 1972b. Gill irrigation in *Rana catesbeiana*: 2. On the musculoskeletal mechanism. *Canadian Journal of Zoology* 50:501–521. (11, 16)

———. 1973. On the functional morphology of suction and gill irrigation in the tadpole of *Ascaphus*, and notes on hibernation. *Herpetologica* 29:84–93. (11)

Gradwell, N., and B. Walcott. 1971. Dual functional and structural properties of the interhyoideus muscle of the bullfrog tadpole (*Rana catesbeiana*). *Journal of Experimental Zoology* 176:193. (11)

Grafe, T. U. 1988. Untersuchungen zur Fortpflanzungsbiologie und zu Lebensstrategien von *Hyperolius viridiflavus* (Amphibia, Anura, Hyperoliidae). Master's thesis, Bayerische Julius-Maximilians-Universität Würzburg, Würzburg, Germany. (14)

Graham, T. E., and V. H. Hutchison. 1977. A device for simulating twilight in studies of animal activity. *Behavioral Research Methods and Instrumentation* 99:395–396. (9)

———. 1979. Effect of temperature and photoperiod acclimatization on thermal preferences of selected freshwater turtles. *Copeia* 1979: 165–169. (9)

Grainger, J. N. R., and G. Goldspink. 1964. The effect of adaptation temperature on the properties of nerve-muscle preparations and on the performance of the frog *Rana temporaria*. *Helgolander wissenschaftlich Meeresuntersuchungen* 9:420–427. (8)

Grant, B. W., and A. E. Dunham. 1988. Thermally imposed time constraints on the activity of the desert lizard *Sceloporus merriami*. *Ecology* 69:167–176. (4)

Gray, E. G. 1957. The spindle and extrafusal innervation of a frog muscle. *Proceedings of the Royal Society of London* 146B:416–430. (11)

Gray, J. 1968. *Animal Locomotion*. London: Weidenfeld and Nicolson. (11)

Gray, J., and H. W. Lissmann. 1940. Ambulatory reflexes in spinal amphibians. *Journal of Experimental Biology* 17:237–251. (2)

———. 1946a. The coordination of limb movements in the Amphibia. *Journal of Experimental Biology* 23:133–142. (11)

———. 1946b. Further observations on the effect of de-afferentiation on the locomotory activity of amphibian limbs. *Journal of Experimental Biology* 23:121–132. (2, 11)

Green, A. J. 1990. Determinants of chorus participation and the effects of size, weight, and competition on advertisement calling in the tungara frog, *Physalaemus pustulosus* (Leptodactylidae). *Animal Behaviour* 39:620–638. (14)

Green, B. 1978. Estimation of food consumption in the dingo, *Canis familiaris dingo*, by means of ^{22}Na turnover. *Ecology* 59:207–210. (14)

Green, B., J. Anderson, and T. Whatley. 1984. Water and sodium turnover and estimated food consumption in free-living lions (*Panthera leo*) and spotted hyaenas (*Crocuta crocuta*). *Journal of Mammalogy* 65:593–599. (14)

Green, B., and I. Eberhard. 1984. Water and sodium intake and estimated food consumption in free-living eastern quolls *Dasyurus viverrinus*. *Australian Journal of Zoology* 31:871–880. (14)

Green, B., M. Griffiths, and K. Newgrain. 1985. Intake of milk by suckling echidnas (*Tachyglossus aculeatus*). *Comparative Biochemistry and Physiology* 81A:441–444. (14)

Green, F. A., C. A. Herman, R. P. Herman, H. Claesson, and M. Hamberg. 1987. Leukotrienes and related eicosanoids are produced by frog leukocytes. *Biochemical and Biophysical Research Communications* 142:309–314. (3)

Green, K., and A. J. Matty. 1963. Action of thyroxine on active transport in isolated membranes of *Bufo bufo*. *General and Comparative Endocrinology* 3:244–252. (5)

Green, M. D., and P. Lomax. 1976. Behavioural thermoregulation and neuroamines in fish (*Chromus chromus*). *Journal of Thermal Biology* 1:237–240. (9)

Green, T. L. 1931. On the pelvis of the Anura: A study in adaptation and recapitulation. *Proceedings of the Zoological Society of London* 1931:1259–1290. (11)

Greenwald, L. 1972. Sodium balance in amphibians from different habitats. *Physiological Zoology* 45:229–237. (5)

Greer, B. J., and K. D. Wells. 1980. Territorial and reproductive behavior of the tropical American frog *Centrolenella fleischmanni*. *Herpetologica* 36:318–326. (14)

Gregg, J. R. 1960. Respiratory regulation in amphibian development. *Biological Bulletin* 119:428–439. (16)

———. 1962. Anaerobic glycolysis in amphibian development. *Biological Bulletin* 123:555–561. (16)

Gregory, J. E., A. R. Luff, D. L. Morgan, and U. Proske. 1978. The stiffness of amphibian slow and twitch muscle during high-speed stretches. *Pflugers Archiv* 375:207–211. (11)

Gregory, P. T. 1983. Habitat structure affects diel activity pattern in the Neotropical frog *Leptodactylus melanotus*. *Journal of Herpetology* 17:179–181. (14)

Greil, A. 1905. Über die Anlage der Lungen sowie der ultimobranchialen (postbranchialen, suprapericardialen) Körper bei anuren Amphibien. *Anatomische Hefte, Arbeiten aus Anatomischen Instituten* (Wiesbaden) 29:455–506. (16)

Greven, H., and G. Clemen. 1985a. Metamorphosebedingte Veränderungen der Zahne und zahntragenden Knochen im Munddach von *Salamandra salamandra* (L.) (Amphibia, Urodela). *Verhandlungen der Deutschen Zoologischen Gesellschaft* 78:162. (16)

———. 1985b. Morphological studies on the mouth cavity of Urodela: 8. The teeth of the upper jaw and the palate in two *Hynobius* species (Hynobiidae: Amphibia). *Zeitschrift für zoologische Systematik und Evolutionsforschung* 23:136–147. (16)

Griffiths, D. 1980. Foraging costs and relative prey size. *American Naturalist* 116:743–752. (14)

Griffiths, I. 1963. The phylogeny of the Salientia. *Biological Reviews* 38:241–292. (11)

Griffiths, J. 1961. The form and function of the fore-gut in anuran larvae (Amphibia, Salientia) with particular reference to the manicotto glandulare. *Proceedings of the Zoological Society of London* 137:249–283. (16)

Griffiths, R. A. 1985a. Diel pattern of movement and aggregation in tadpoles of the common frog, *Rana temporaria*. *Herpetological Journal* 1:5–10. (9)

———. 1985b. Diel profile of behaviour in the smooth newt, *Triturus vulgaris* (L): An analysis of environmental clues and endogenous timing. *Animal Behaviour* 33:573–582. (14)

———. 1986. Natural environmental cues and circadian rhythms of behaviour: A perspective. *Chronobiology International* 3:247–253. (9)

Griffiths, R. A., J. M. Getliff, and V. J. Mylotte. 1988. Diel patterns of activity and vertical migration in tadpoles of the common toad, *Bufo bufo*. *Herpetological Journal* 1:223–226. (9)

Grigg, G. C., C. R. Drane, and G. P. Courtice. 1979. Time constants of heating and cooling in the eastern water dragon, *Physignathus leseurii*, and some generalizations about heating and cooling in reptiles. *Journal of Thermal Biology* 4:95–103. (4)

Grill, G., P. Granger, and K. Thurau. 1972. The renin angiotensin system of amphibians: 1. Determination of the renin content of amphibian kidneys. *Pflugers Archiv* 331:1–12. (3)

Grobbelaar, C.S. 1924. Beiträge zu einer anatomischen Monographie von *Xenopus laevis* (Daud.). *Zeitschrift der Gesellschaft für Anatomie München* 72:131–168. (11)

Grobstein, P. 1988a. Between retinotectal projection and directed movement: Topography of a sensorimotor interface. *Brain, Behavior, and Evolution* 31:34–48. (2)

———. 1988b. On beyond neuronal specificity: Problems in going from cells to networks and from networks to behavior. In *Advances in Neural and Behavioral Development*, ed. P. G. Shinkman, 3:1–58. Norwood, NJ: Ablex Publishing. (2, 16)

———. 1988c. Organization in the sensorimotor interface: A case study with increased resolution. In *Visuomotor Coordination: Amphibians, Comparisons, Models, and Robots*, ed. J.-P. Ewert and M. A. Arbib, 1–32. New York: Plenum Press. (2)

Grobstein, P., and C. Comer. 1983. The nucleus isthmi as an intertectal relay for the ipsilateral oculotectal projection in the frog, *Rana pipiens*. *Journal of Comparative Neurology* 217:54–74. (2)

Grobstein, P., C. Comer, M. Hollyday, and S. M. Archer. 1978. A crossed isthmotectal projection in *Rana pipiens* and its involvement in the ipsilateral visuotectal projection. *Brain Research* 156:117–123. (2)

Grobstein, P., C. Comer, and S. K. Kostyk. 1983. Frog prey capture behavior: Between sensory maps and directed motor output. In *Advances in Vertebrate Neuroethology*, J.-P. Ewert, R. R. Capranica, and D. J. Ingle, 331–347. New York: Plenum Press. (13)

Groebbels, F. 1922. Unzureichende Ernährung und Hormonwirkung: 2. Der Einfluß unzureichender Ernährung und Schilddrüsenfütterung auf den Sauerstoffverbrauch von Larven der *Rana temporaria*. *Zeitschrift für Biologie* 75:155–168. (12)

Grubb, J. C. 1976. Maze orientation by Mexican toads, *Bufo valliceps* (Amphibia, Anura, Bufonidae), using olfactory and configurational cues. *Journal of Herpetology* 10:97–104. (2)

Gruberg, E. R., and K. L. Grasse. 1984. Basal optic complex in the frog (*Rana pipiens*): A physiological and HRP study. *Journal of Neurophysiology* 51:998–1010. (2)

Gruberg, E. R., and J. Y. Lettvin. 1980. Anatomy and physiology of a binocular system in the frog *Rana pipiens*. *Brain Research* 192:313–325. (2)

Grüsser, O.-J., and U. Grüsser-Cornehls. 1968. Neurophysiologische Grundlagen visueller angeborener Auslösemechanismen beim Frosch. *Zeitschrift für vergleichende Physiologie* 59:1–24. (13)

Grüsser-Cornehls, U. 1984. The neurophysiology of the amphibian optic tectum. In *Comparative Neurology of the Optic Tectum*, ed. H. Vanegas, 211–245. New York: Plenum Press. (13)

Guardabassi, A. 1960. The utilization of the calcareous deposits in the endolymphatic sacs of *Bufo bufo bufo* in the mineralization of the skeleton: Investigations by means of ^{45}Ca. *Zeitschrift für Zellforschung und mikroskopische Anatomie* 51:278–282. (16)

Guardabassi, A., E. Campantico, and P. Pattano. 1984. Localization of I^{125}-labelled prolactin in the kidney of normal and subtotally hypophysectomized *Xenopus laevis* Daudin adult specimens: A preliminary report. *Anatomica Istologia Embriologia* 118:193–199. (16)

Guardabassi, A., G. Muccioli, P. Pattono, and G. Bellusi. 1987. Prolactin binding sites in *Xenopus laevis* tissues: Comparison between normal and dehydrated animals. *General and Comparative Endocrinology* 65:40–47. (16)

Guardabassi, A., and M. Sacerdote. 1951. La lamina calcificata del derma cutaneo di anfibi anuri nostrani ed sesatici. *Archivio Italiano di Anatomia e di Embriologia* 56:247–272. (16)

Guggino, W. B., R. London, E. L. Boulpaep, and G. Giebisch. 1983. Chloride transport across the basolateral cell membrane of the *Necturus* proximal tubule: Dependence on bicarbonate and sodium. *Journal of Membrane Biology* 71:227–240. (5)

Guha, K. K., and C. B. Jørgensen. 1978a. Effects of human chorionic gonadotropin and salmon gonadotropin on testis in hypophysectomized toads (*Bufo bufo bufo* L.) *General and Comparative Endocrinology* 36:371–379. (15)

———. 1978b. Effects of hypophysectomy on structure and function of testis in adult toads, *Bufo bufo bufo* (L.). *General and Comparative Endocrinology* 34:201–210. (15)

———. 1981. Growth response of testis tissue to partial castration in toads, *Bufo bufo bufo*. *Journal of Zoology* (London) 193:171–181. (15)

Guha, K. K., C. B. Jørgensen, and L. O. Larsen. 1980. Relationship between nutritional state and testis function, together with observations on patterns of feeding, in the toad, *Bufo bufo bufo*. *Journal of Zoology* (London) 192:147–155. (13, 15)

Guimond, R. W., and V. H. Hutchison. 1968. The effect of temperature and photoperiod on gas exchange in the leopard frog, *Rana pipiens*. *Comparative Biochemistry and Physiology* 27:177–195. (9, 12)

———. 1972. Pulmonary, branchial, and cutaneous gas exchange in the mudpuppy, *Necturus maculosus maculosus* (Rafinesque). *Comparative Biochemistry and Physiology* 42A:367–392. (5, 9, 10, 12, 16)

———. 1973a. Aquatic respiration: An unusual strategy in the hellbender, *Cryptobranchus alleganiensis alleganiensis* (Daudin). *Science* 182:1263–1265. (4, 5, 6, 12)

———. 1973b. Trimodal gas exchange in the large aquatic salamander, *Siren lacertina* (Linnaeus). *Comparative Biochemistry and Physiology* 46A:249–268. (5, 9, 12)

———. 1974. Aerial and aquatic respiration in the congo eel *Amphiuma means means* (Garden). *Respiration Physiology* 20:147–159. (5, 9, 12)

———. 1976. Gas exchange of the giant salamanders of North America. In *Respiration of Amphibious Vertebrates*, ed. G. M. Hughes. New York: Academic Press. (5, 7, 9, 10, 11, 16)

Gunn, D. L., and Cosway, C. A. 1938. Temperature and humidity relations of the cockroach: 5. Humidity preference of *Blatta orientalis*. *Journal of Experimental Biology* 15:555–563. (9)

Günther, P. G. 1949. Die Innervation der tetanischen und tonischen Fasern der quergestreiften Skelettmuskulatur der Wirbeltiere: 1. Die Innervation des M. sartorius und des M. iliofibularis des Frosches. *Anatomischer Anzeiger* 97:175–191. (11)

Guthe, K. F. 1981. Reptilian muscle: Fine structure and physiological parameters. In *Biology of the Reptilia*, vol. 11, ed. C. Gans and T. S. Parsons, 265–354. New York: Academic Press. (11)

Guyétant, R., J. P. Herold, and G. Cudey. 1981. Microcalorimetric measurements of energy flux in *Rana temporaria* L., and *Bufo bufo* L. tadpoles during development. *Comparative Biochemistry and Physiology* 69A:705–708. (12)

Guyton, A. C. 1976. *Textbook of Medical Physiology*. Philadelphia: W. B. Saunders. (4)

———. 1980. *Circulatory Physiology: 3. Arterial Pressure and Hypertension*. Toronto: W. B. Saunders. (7)

Haab, P. E., J. Piiper, and H. Rahn. 1960. Simple method for rapid determination of an O_2 dissociation curve of the blood. *Journal of Applied Physiology* 15:1148–1149. (5)

Haapanen, A. 1982. Breeding of the common frog (*Rana temporaria* L.). *Annales of Zoologici Fennici* 19:75–79. (8)

Habermehl, G. G. 1974. Venoms of Amphibia. In *Chemical Zoology*, ed. M. Florkin and B. T. Scheer, 10:161–183. New York: Academic Press. (14)

Hackett, J. T., S. L. Cochran, and D. L. Brown. 1979. Functional properties of afferents which synapse on the Mauthner neuron in the amphibian tadpole. *Brain Research* 176:148–152. (2)

Hackford, A. W., C. G. Gillies, and P. J. Goldblatt. 1977. Thyroxine-induced gill resorption in the axolotl (*Ambystoma mexicanum*). *Journal of Morphology* 153:479–504. (5)

Hadfield, S. 1966. Observations of body temperature and activity in the toad *Bufo woodhousei fowleri*. *Copeia* 1966:581–582. (9)

Hadley, M. E. 1988a. *Endocrinology*. 2d ed. Englewood Cliffs, NJ: Prentice Hall. (16)

———. 1988b. The melanotropic hormones. In *Endocrinology*, 159–183. Englewood Cliffs, NJ: Prentice Hall. (3)

Hadley, M. E., B. Anderson, C. B. Heward, T. K. Sawyer, and V. J. Hruby. 1981. Calcium-dependent prolonged effects on melanophores of (4-norleucine, 7-D-phenylalanine) α-melanotropin. *Science* 213:1025–1027. (3)

Hadley, M. E., A. M. de L. Castrucci, and V. J. Hruby. 1988. Melanin concentrating hormone (MCH) mechanism of action. In *Advances in Pigment Cell Research*, ed. J. T. Bagnara, 531–545. New York: Alan R. Liss. (3)

Hadley, M. E., M. D. Davis, and C. M. Morgan. 1977. Cellular control of melanocyte stimulating hormone secretion. *Frontiers in Hormone Research* 4:94–104. (3)

Hadley, M. E., and J. M. Goldman. 1970. Adrenergic receptors and geographical variation in *Rana pipiens* chromatophore response. *American Journal of Physiology* 219:72–77. (3)

Hadley, M. E., J. H. Mieyr, B. E. Martin, A. M. de L. Castrucci, V. J. Hruby, T. K. Sawyer, E. A. Powers, and K. R. Rao. 1985. Nle[4], D-Phe[7]-α-MSH: A superpotent melanotropin with prolonged action on vertebrate chromatophores. *Comparative Biochemistry and Physiology* 81A:1–6. (3)

Hagberg, J. M., E. F Coyle, J. E. Carroll, J. M. Miller, W. H. Martin, and M. H. Brooke. 1982. Exercise hyperventilation in patients with McArdle's disease. *Journal of Applied Physiology* 52:991–994. (12)

Hagberg, J. M., F. S. Nagle, and J. L. Carson. 1978. Transient O_2 uptake response at the onset of exercise. *Journal of Applied Physiology* 44:90–92. (12)

Hailman, J. P. 1982. Extremely low ambient light levels of *Ascaphus truei*. *Journal of Herpetology* 16:83–84. (14)

———. 1984. Bimodal activity of the western toad (*Bufo boreas*) in relation to ambient illumination. *Copeia* 1984:283–290. (14)

Hailman, J. P., and R. G. Jaeger. 1976. A model of phototaxis and its evaluation with anuran amphibians. *Behaviour* 56:215–249. (2, 14)

———. 1978. Phototactic responses of anuran amphibians to monochromatic stimuli of equal quantum intensity. *Animal Behaviour* 26:274–281. (2)

Haines, R. W. 1939. A revision of the extensor muscles of the forearm in tetrapods. *Journal of Anatomy* (London) 73:211–233. (11)

Hainsworth, F. R. 1981. *Animal Physiology*. Reading, MA: Addison-Wesley Publishing Company. (9)

Hairston, N. G. 1983. Growth, survival, and reproduction of *Plethodon jordani*: Trade-offs between selective pressures. *Copeia* 1983:1024–1035. (15)

———. 1987. *Community Ecology and Salamander Guilds*. New York: Cambridge University Press. (14)

———. 1989. Hard choices in ecological experimentation. *Herpetologica* 45:119–123. (9)

Hakumaki, M. O. K. 1987. Seventy years of the Bainbridge reflex. *Acta Physiologica Scandinavica* 130:177–185. (7)

Hall, F. G. 1966. Hemoglobin functions in the blood of *Bufo marinus*. *Journal of Cellular and Comparative Physiology* 68:69–74. (5)

Hall, J. C., and A. S. Feng. 1987. Evidence for parallel processing in the frog's auditory thalamus. *Journal of Comparative Neurology* 258:407–419. (2)

Hall, K., and V. R. Sara. 1983. Growth and somatomedins. *Vitamins and Hormones* 40:175–233. (16)

Hall, R. J., and D. P. Stafford. 1972. Studies in the life history of Wehrle's salamander, *Plethodon wherlei*. *Herpetologica* 28:300–309. (15)

Hall, T. R., and A. Chadwick. 1984. Effects of synthetic mammalian thyrotropin releasing hormone, somatostatin, and dopamine on the secretion of prolactin and growth hormone from amphibian and reptilian pituitary glands incubated *in vitro*. *Journal of Endocrinology* 102:175–180. (16)

Halliday, E. C., and T. J. Hugo. 1963. Photodermoplanimeter. *Journal of Applied Physiology* 18:1285. (4)

Halliday, T. R. 1974. Sexual behaviour of the smooth newt, *Triturus vulgaris* (Urodela, Salamandridae). *Journal of Herpetology* 8:277–292. (14)

———. 1975. An observational and experimental study of sexual behaviour in the smooth newt, *Triturus vulgaris* (Amphibia: Salamandridae). *Animal Behaviour* 23:291–300. (14)

———. 1976. The libidinous newt: An analysis of variations in the sexual behaviour of the male smooth newt, *Triturus vulgaris*. *Animal Behaviour* 25:39–45. (14)

———. 1977a. The courtship of European newts: An evolutionary perspective. In *The Reproductive Biology of Amphibians*, ed. D. H. Taylor and S. I. Guttman, 185–232. New York: Plenum Press. (14)

———. 1977b. The effects of experimental manipulation of breathing behaviour on the sexual behaviour of the smooth newt, *Triturus vulgaris*. *Animal Behaviour* 25:39–45. (14)

———. 1987. Physiological constraints on sexual selection. In *Sexual Selection: Testing the Alternatives*, ed. J. W. Bradbury and M. B. Andersson, 247–264. New York: Wiley. (14)

Halliday, T. R., and K. Adler, eds. 1986. *The Encyclopedia of Reptiles and Amphibians*. New York: Facts on File. (1)

Halliday, T. R., and H. P. A. Sweatman. 1976. To breathe or not to breathe: The newt's problem. *Animal Behaviour* 24:551–561. (5, 7, 14)

Halliday, T. R., and P. A. Verrell. 1988. Body size and age in amphibians and reptiles. *Journal of Herpetology* 22:253–265. (15)

Halliday, T. R., and A. Worsnop. 1977. Correlation between activity and breathing rate in the smooth newt, *Triturus vulgaris*. *Journal of Herpetology* 11:244–246. (14)

Hamasaki, D. I., and D. J. Eder. 1977. Adaptive radiation of the pineal system. In *Handbook of Sensory Physiology*, ed. F. Crescitelli, 497–548. Berlin: Springer-Verlag. (9)

Hamilton, W. D. 1971. Geometry for the selfish herd. *Journal of Theoretical Biology* 31:295–311. (14)

Hamilton, W. D., and M. Zuk. 1982. Heritable true fitness and bright birds: A role for parasites. *Science* 218:386–387. (14)

Hammel, H. T., F. T. Caldwell, and R. M. Abrams. 1967. Regulation of body temperature in the blue-tongued lizard. *Science* 156:1260–1262. (9)

Hammel, H. T., S. B. Stromme, and K. Myhre. 1969. Forebrain temperature activates behavioral thermoregulatory response in arctic sculpins. *Science* 165:83–85. (9)

Hammen, C., and V. H. Hutchison. 1962. Carbon dioxide assimilation in the symbiosis of the salamander, *Ambystoma maculatum*, and the alga, *Oophila amblystomatis*. *Life Sciences* 10:527–532. (9)

Hammerman, D. L. 1969a. The frog tongue: 1. General development and histogenesis of filiform papillae and mucous glands in *Rana catesbeiana*. *Acta Zoologica* (Stockholm) 50:11–23. (16)

———. 1969b. The frog tongue: 2. Histogenesis of fungiform papillae in *Rana catesbeiana*. *Acta Zoologica* (Stockholm) 50:25–33. (16)

———. 1969c. The frog tongue: 3. Histogenesis and regeneration following complete and partial extirpations of anlagen. *Acta Zoologica* (Stockholm) 50:215–232. (16)

Hanaoka, Y. 1967. The effects of posterior hypothalectomy upon the growth and metamorphosis of the tadpole of *Rana pipiens*. *General and Comparative Endocrinology* 8:417–431. (16)

Hanaoka, Y., and K. S. Miyashita, Y. Kondo, Y. Kobayashi, and K. Yamamoto. 1973. Morphological and functional maturation of the thyroid during early development of anuran larvae. *General and Comparative Endocrinology* 21:410–423. (16)

Handler, J. S., and A. S. Preston. 1981. Vasopressin-elicited refractoriness of the response to vasopressin in toad urinary bladder. *American Journal of Physiology* 240:F551–F557. (5)

Hanke, W. 1974. Endocrinology of Amphibia. In *Chemical Zoology*, ed.

M. Florkin and B. T. Scheer, 9:123–159. New York: Academic Press. (3)

———. 1978. The adrenal cortex of Amphibia. In *General, Comparative, and Clinical Endocrinology of the Adrenal Cortex*, ed. I. Chester-Jones and I. W. Henderson, 2:419–495. New York: Academic Press. (3)

———. 1990. Corticosteroid function: Evolutionary aspects. In *Progress in Comparative Endocrinology*, ed. A. Epple, C. G. Scanes, and M. H. Stetson, 445–452. New York: Wiley-Liss. (3)

Hanke, W., and C. Maser. 1985. Regulation of interrenal function in amphibians. In *Current Trends in Comparative Endocrinology*, ed. B. Lofts and W. N. Holmes, 447–449. Hong Kong: Hong Kong University Press. (3, 16)

Hanke, W., and U. Neumann. 1972. Carbohydrate metabolism in Amphibia. *General and Comparative Endocrinology*, suppl. 3:198–208. (3)

Hanken, J. 1983. Miniaturization and its effect on cranial morphology in plethodontid salamanders, genus *Thorius* (Amphibia, Plethodontidae): 2. The fate of the brain and sense organs and their role in skull morphogenesis and evolution. *Journal of Morphology* 177:255–268. (11)

———. 1984. Miniaturization and its effect on cranial morphology in plethodontid salamanders, genus *Thorius* (Amphibia, Plethodontidae): 1. Osteological variation. *Biological Journal of the Linnean Society* 23:55–75. (11)

———. 1985. Morphological novelty in the limb skeleton accompanies miniaturization in salamanders. *Science* 229:871–874. (11)

Hannigan, P. C., and D. B. Kelley. 1981. Male and female laryngeal motor neurons in *Xenopus laevis*. *Society for Neuroscience Abstracts* 7:269. (2)

Hansen, K. L. 1958. Breeding pattern of the eastern spadefoot toad. *Herpetologica* 14:57–67. (15)

Harkey, G. A., and R. D. Semlitsch. 1988. Effects of temperature on growth, development, and color polymorphism in the ornate chorus frog *Pseudacris ornata*. *Copeia* 1988:1001–1007. (9)

Harlow, H. J. 1977. Seasonal oxygen metabolism and cutaneous osmoregulation in the California newt, *Taricha torosa*. *Physiological Zoology* 50:231–236. (5, 12)

———. 1978. Seasonal aerobic and anaerobic metabolism at rest and during activity in the salamander *Taricha torosa*. *Comparative Biochemistry and Physiology* 61A:177–182. (12)

Harlow, J. J., S. S. Hillman, and M. Hoffman. 1976. The effect of temperature on digestive efficiency in the herbivorous lizard *Dipsosaurus dorsalis*. *Journal of Comparative Physiology* 111:1–6. (9)

Harper, R. A., and G. Stephens. 1985. Blockade of the pressor response to angiotensins I and II in the bullfrog, *Rana catesbeiana*. *General and Comparative Endocrinology* 60:227–235. (3)

Harri, M. N. E. 1973a. Neural control of temperature adaptation in *Rana temporaria*. In *Effects of Temperature on Ectothermic Organisms*, ed. W. Wieser, 35–43. Heidelberg: Springer-Verlag. (10)

———. 1973b. The rate of metabolic temperature acclimation in the frog, *Rana temporaria*. *Physiological Zoology* 46:148–156. (8, 12)

———. 1973c. Simulation of cold acclimation by repeated injections of neurotransmitters in warm-maintained frogs (*Rana temporaria*). *Annales Zoologici Fennici* 10:536–538. (10)

———. 1975. Effect of season, temperature acclimation, and starvation upon plasma FFA and glycerol levels in the frog, *Rana temporaria*, and in the toad, *Bufo bufo*. *Comparative Biochemistry and Physiology* 50B:531–534. (10)

Harri, M. N. E., and R. Hedenstam. 1972. Calorigenic effect of adrenaline and noradrenaline in the frog, *Rana temporaria*. *Comparative Biochemistry and Physiology* 41A:409–419. (9, 12)

Harri, M. N. E., and P. Koskela. 1977. Terms of spawning in southern and northern Finnish populations of the common frog, *Rana temporaria* L., under laboratory conditions. *Aquilo Series Zoology* 17:49–51. (15)

Harri, M. N. E., and E. Lindgren. 1972. Adrenergic control of carbohydrate metabolism in the frog, *Rana temporaria*. *Comparative and General Pharmacology* 3:226–234. (10)

Harri, M. N. E., and A. Talo. 1975a. Effect of season and temperature acclimation on the heart rate–temperature relationship in the frog, *Rana temporaria*. *Comparative Biochemistry and Physiology* 50A:469–472. (8)

———. 1975b. Effect of season and temperature acclimation on the heart rate–temperature relationship in the isolated frog's heart, *Rana temporaria*. *Comparative Biochemistry and Physiology* 52A:409–412. (8)

Harrison, J. D., S. P. Gittins, and F. M. Slater. 1983. The breeding migrations of smooth and palmate newts (*Triturus vulgaris* and *T. helveticus*) at a pond in mid Wales. *Journal of Zoology* (London) 199:249–258. (8)

Harrison, P. A. 1987. Vocal behaviour in the south-eastern Australian tree frogs, *Litoria ewingi* and *L. verreauxi* (Anura: Hylidae). M. S. diss., University of Melbourne, Australia. (14)

Harrison, R. G. 1904. Experimentelle Untersuchung über die Entwicklung der Sinnesorgane der Seitenlinie bei den Amphibien. *Archives für mikroskopische Anatomie* 63:35–149. (16)

Hart, C., J. Shemer, J. C. Penhos, M. A. Lesniak, J. Roth, and D. LeRoith. 1987. Frog brain and liver show evolutionary conservation of tissue-specific differences among insulin receptors. *General and Comparative Endocrinology* 68:170–178. (3)

Hartenstein, H. R., and D. F. Stiffler. 1981. Effects of mesotocin on renal function in adult salamanders. *American Zoologist* 21:912. (5)

———. 1990. Renal responses to mesotocin in adult *Ambystoma tigrinum* and *Notophthalmus viridescens*. *Experimental Biology* 48:373–377. (5)

Harvey, P. H. and G. Mace. 1982. Comparisons between taxa and adaptive trends: Problems of methodology. In *Current Problems in Sociobiology*, ed. King's College Sociobiology Group, 343–361. Cambridge: Cambridge University Press. (14)

Hasegawa, Y., T. X. Watanabe, H. Sokabe, and T. Nakajima. 1983. Chemical structure of angiotensin in the bullfrog *Rana catesbeiana*. *General and Comparative Endocrinology* 50:75–80. (3)

Hassinger, D. D. 1970. Notes on the thermal properties of frog eggs. *Herpetologica* 26:49–51. (8)

Hassinger, D. D., J. D. Anderson, and H. H. Dalrymple. 1970. The early life history and ecology of *Ambystoma tigrinum* and *Ambystoma opacum* in New Jersey. *American Midland Naturalist* 84:474–495. (9)

Hattingh, J., and H. Bartels. 1973. The oxygen affinity of axolotl blood and haemoglobin before and after metamorphosis. *Respiration Physiology* 18:1–13. (16)

Hay, E. D. 1963. The fine structure of differentiating muscle in the salamander tail. *Zeitschrift für Zellforschung* 59:6–34. (11)

Hayes, B. P. 1975. The distribution of intercellular junctions in the developing myotomes of the clawed toad. *Zeitschrift für Anatomie und Entwicklungsgeschichte* 147:345–354. (11)

Hazard, E. S. and V. H. Hutchison. 1978. Ontogenetic changes in erythrocytic organic phosphates in the bullfrog, *Rana catesbeiana*. *Journal of Experimental Zoology* 206:109–118. (5, 9, 16)

———. Distribution of acid-soluble phosphates in the erythrocytes of selected species of amphibians. *Comparative Biochemistry and Physiology* 73A:111–124. (5, 9)

Hazel, J. R. 1984. Effects of temperature on the structure and metabolism of cell membranes in fish. *American Journal of Physiology* 246:R460–R470. (10)

Healy, W. R. 1973. Life history variation and growth of juvenile *Notophthalmus viridescens* from Massachusetts. *Copeia* 1973:641–647. (15)

Heap, S. P., P. W. Watt, and G. Goldspink. 1985. Consequences of thermal change on the myofibrillar ATPase of five fresh water teleosts. *Journal of Fish Biology* 26:733–738. (8)

Hearne, S. 1911. *A Journey from Prince of Wales's Fort in Hudson's Bay to the Northern Ocean in the Years 1769, 1770, 1771, and 1772*. Toronto: Champlain Society. (10)

Heath, A. G. 1975. Behavioral thermoregulation in high altitude tiger salamanders, *Ambystoma tigrinum*. *Herpetologica* 31:84–93. (9)

———. 1976. Respiratory responses to hypoxia by *Ambystoma tigrinum* larvae, paedomorphs, and metamorphosed adults. *Comparative Biochemistry and Physiology* 55A:45–49. (12)

Heath, J. E. 1964. Reptilian thermoregulation: Evaluation of field studies. *Science* 146:784–785. (9)

———. 1965. Reptilian thermoregulation. *Science* 148:1251. (9)

———. 1970. Behavioral thermoregulation of body temperature in poikilotherms. *Physiologist* 13:399–410. (9)

Heatwole, H. 1984. Adaptations of amphibians to aridity. In *Arid Aus-*

tralia, ed. H. G. Cogger and E. E. Cameron, 177–222. Sydney: Australian Museum. (6)

Heatwole, H., and A. Heatwole. 1968. Motivational aspects of feeding behavior in toads. *Copeia* 1968:692–698. (13, 14)

Heatwole, H., and K. Lim. 1961. Relation of substrate moisture to absorption and loss of water by the salamander, *Plethodon cinereus*. *Ecology* 42:814–819. (6)

Heatwole, H., and R. C. Newby. 1972. Interaction of internal rhythm and loss of body water in influencing activity levels of amphibians. *Herpetologica* 28:156–162. (12)

Heatwole, H., F. Torres, S. B. de Austin, and A. Heatwole. 1969. Studies of anuran water balance: I. Dynamics of evaporative water loss by the coqui, *Eleutherodactylus portoricensis*. *Comparative Biochemistry and Physiology* 28:245–269. (6)

Hecht, S., S. Schlaer, and M. H. Pirenne. 1942. Energy, quanta, and vision. *Journal of General Physiology* 25:819–840. (2)

Hedges, S. B. 1986. An electrophoretic analysis of Holarctic hylid frog evolution. *Systematic Zoology* 35:1–21. (8)

Hedrick, A. V. 1986. Female preferences for male calling about duration in a field cricket. *Behavioral Ecology and Sociobiology* 19:73–77. (14)

Heiligenberg, W., C. Baker, and J. Matsubara. 1978. The jamming avoidance response in *Eigenmannia* revisited: The structure of a neuronal democracy. *Journal of Comparative Physiology* 127:267–286. (2)

Heisler, N. 1982. Intracellular and extracellular acid-base regulation in the tropical fresh-water teleost *Symbranchus marmoratus* in response to the transition from water breathing to air breathing. *Journal of Experimental Biology* 99:9–28. (5)

———. 1984. Acid-base regulation in fishes. In *Fish Physiology*, ed. W. S. Hoar and D. J. Randall, 10A:315–401. New York: Academic Press. (5)

———. 1986. Comparative aspects of acid-base regulation. In *Acid-Base Regulation in Animals*, ed. N. Heisler, 397–450. Amsterdam: Elsevier. (5, 6)

Heisler, N., G. Forcht, G. R. Ultsch, and J. F. Anderson. 1982. Acid-base regulation in response to environmental hypercapnia in two aquatic salamanders, *Siren lacertina* and *Amphiuma means*. *Respiration Physiology* 49:141–158. (5, 7)

Helff, O. M. 1926. Studies on amphibian metamorphosis: 2. The oxygen consumption of tadpoles undergoing precocious metamorphosis following treatment with thyroid and di-iodotyrosine. *Journal of Experimental Zoology* 45:69–93. (12)

———. 1927. The rate of oxygen consumption in five species of *Amblystoma* larvae. *Journal of Experimental Zoology* 49:353–361. (12)

———. 1932. Studies on amphibian metamorphosis: 10. Hydrogen ion concentration of the blood of anuran larvae during involution. *Biological Bulletin* 63:405–418. (16)

Helff, O. M., and M. C. Mellicker. 1941a. Studies on amphibian metamorphosis: 19. Development of the tongue in *Rana sylvatica*, including the histogenesis of "premetamorphic" and filiform papillae and the mucous glands. *American Journal of Anatomy* 68:339–369. (16)

———. 1941b. Studies on amphibian metamorphosis: 20. Development of the fungiform papillae of the tongue in *Rana sylvatica*. *American Journal of Anatomy* 68:371–395. (16)

Helff, O. M., and K. I. Stubblefield. 1931. The influence of oxygen tension on the oxygen consumption of *Rana pipiens* larvae. *Physiological Zoology* 4:271–286. (12)

Heller, H. C., L. I. Crawshaw, and H. T. Hammel. 1978. The thermostat of vertebrate animals. *Scientific American* 239:102–113. (9)

Heller, H. C., X. J. Musacchia, and L. C. H. Wang. 1986. *Living in the Cold: Physiological and Biochemical Adaptations*. New York: Elsevier Science Publishing. (10)

Helman, S. I., T. C. Cox, and W. Van Driessche. 1983. Hormonal control of apical membrane Na transport in epithelia: Studies with fluctuation analysis. *Journal of General Physiology* 82:210–220. (5)

Helman, S. I. and D. A. Miller. 1974. Edge damage effect on measurements of urea and sodium flux in frog skin. *American Journal of Physiology* 226:1198–1203. (5)

Helwig, J., and P. K. T. Pang. 1987. Parathyroid hormone stimulation of renal adenylate cyclase in various vertebrate species: Evidence for an effect in the frog. *Comparative Biochemistry and Physiology* 88A:349–354. (3)

Hemelaar, A. S. M. 1986. Demographic study on *Bufo bufo* L. (Anura, Amphibia) from different climates, by means of skeletochronology. Ph.D. diss., Katholie Universiteit te Nijmegen, Nijmegen, Netherlands. (15)

———. 1988. Age, growth, and other population characteristics of *Bufo bufo* from different latitudes and altitudes. *Journal of Herpetology* 22:369–388. (9, 15)

Hemmer, H., and K. Kadel. 1971. Untersuchungen zur Laichgrösse der Kreuzkröte (*Bufo calamita* Laur.) und der Wechselkröte (*Bufo viridis* Laur.). *Zoologische Beiträge* 17:327–336. (15)

———. 1972. Gewichtszustand und Wachstumsverlauf bei der Kreuzkröte (*Bufo calamita* Laur.). *Forma et Functio* 5:113–120. (15)

Henderson, R. W., T. A. Noeske-Hallin, B. I. Crother, and A. Schwartz. 1988. The diets of Hispaniolan colubrid snakes: 2. Prey species, prey size, and phylogeny. *Herpetologica* 44:55–70. (14)

Hendrickson, A. E., and D. E. Kelly. 1969. Development of the amphibian pineal organ: Cell proliferation and migration. *Anatomical Record* 165:211–228. (16)

Heney, H. W., and D. F. Stiffler. 1983. The effects of aldosterone on sodium and potassium metabolism in larval *Ambystoma tigrinum*. *General and Comparative Endocrinology* 49:122–127. (5, 16)

Hensel, H., A. Iggo, and I. Witt. 1960. A quantitative study of sensitive cutaneous thermoreceptors with C afferent fibers. *Journal of Physiology* (London) 153:113–126. (9)

Herbert, C. V., and D. C. Jackson. 1985. Temperature effects on the responses to prolonged submergence in the turtle *Chrysemys picta bellii:* 2. Metabolic rate, blood acid-base, and ionic changes, and cardiovascular function in aerated and anoxic water. *Physiological Zoology* 58:670–681. (10)

Herman, C. A. 1977. Comparative effects of epinephrine and norepinephrine on plasma glucose and hematocrit levels in the American bullfrog (*Rana catesbeiana*). *General and Comparative Endocrinology* 32:321–329. (3)

———. 1990. Prostaglandins in lower vertebrates. In *Progress in Comparative Endocrinology*, ed. A. Epple, C. S. Scanes, and M. H. Stetson, 608–613. New York: Wiley-Liss. (3)

Herman, C. A., and L. B. Brown. 1983. Effects of catecholamines and divalent cations on frog liver adenylate cyclase. *General and Comparative Endocrinology* 50:87–94. (3)

Herman, C. A., G. A. Charlton, and R. L. Cranfill. 1991. Metabolism and cardiovascular effects of leukotrienes in warm- and cold-acclimated American bullfrogs, *Rana catesbeiana*. *American Journal of Physiology* 260:R834–R838. (3)

Herman, C. A., M. Hamberg, and E. Granström. 1987. Quantitative determination of prostaglandins E_1, E_2, and E_3 in frog tissue. *Journal of Chromatography* 394:353–362. (3)

Herman, C. A., R. S. Heller, and R. P. Herman. 1990. Leukotriene metabolism and action in amphibians: A model system. *Journal of Experimental Zoology*, suppl. 4:150–153. (3)

Herman, C. A., M. M. McCloskey, and K. Doolittle. 1982. Prostaglandins of the one, two, and three series affect blood pressure in the American bullfrog, *Rana catesbeiana*. *General and Comparative Endocrinology* 48:491–498. (3)

Herman, C. A., and P. L. Mata. 1985. Catecholamine effects on blood pressure and heart rate in warm- and cold-acclimated American bullfrogs (*Rana catesbeiana*). *General and Comparative Endocrinology* 59:434–441. (3)

Herman, C. A., D. O. Robleto, P. L. Mata, and R. S. Heller. 1986. Cardiovascular effects of catecholamines at 12° in the American bullfrog, *Rana catesbeiana*. *Journal of Experimental Zoology* 240:17–23. (3)

Herman, C. A., D. O. Robleto, P. L. Mata, and M. D. Lujan. 1986. Attenuated cardiovascular effects of prostaglandin I_2 and prostaglandin F_2 in cold-acclimated American bullfrogs, *Rana catesbeiana*. *Journal of Experimental Zoology* 238:167–174. (3)

Herman, C. A., D. O. Robleto, S. L. Reitmeyer, L. A. Martinez, and R. P. Herman. 1988. Cardiovascular effects of leukotrienes in bullfrogs. *Biomedica Biochemica Acta* 47:S178–S181. (3)

Herman, C. A., and E. J. Sandoval. 1983. Catecholamine effects on blood pressure and heart rate in the American bullfrog, *Rana catesbeiana*. *General and Comparative Endocrinology* 52:142–148. (3, 7, 8)

Herman, R. P., R. S. Heller, C. M. Canavan, and C. A. Herman. 1988.

Leukotriene C₄ action and metabolism in the isolated perfused bullfrog heart. *Canadian Journal of Physiology and Pharmacology* 66: 980–984. (3)

Hermansen, L. 1981. Effect of metabolic changes on force generation in skeletal muscle during maximal exercise. In *Human Muscle Fatigue: Physiological Mechanisms*, ed. R. Porter and J. Whelan, 75–88. London: Pitman Medical. (12)

Herreid, C. F. 1981. Energetics of pedestrian arthropods. In *Locomotion and Energetics in Arthropods*, ed. C. F. Herreid and C. R. Fourtner, 491–526. New York: Plenum Press. (12)

Herreid, C. F., and R. J. Full. 1983. Cockroaches on a treadmill: Aerobic running. *Journal of Insect Physiology* 30:395–403. (12)

Herreid, C. F., R. J. Full, and D. A. Prawel. 1981. Energetics of cockroach locomotion. *Journal of Experimental Biology* 94:189–202. (12)

Herreid, C. F., and S. Kinney. 1966. Survival of Alaskan wood frog (*Rana sylvatica*) larvae. *Ecology* 47:1039–1041. (9)

———. 1967. Temperature and development of the wood frog, *Rana sylvatica*, in Alaska. *Ecology* 48:579–590. (8, 9)

Herreid, C. F., P. J. O'Mahoney, and R. J. Full. 1983. Locomotion in land crabs: Respiratory and cardiac response of *Gecarcinus lateralis*. *Comparative Biochemistry and Physiology* 74A:117–124. (12)

Herrera, F. C., G. Whittembury, and J. A. Planchart. 1963. Effect of insulin on short-circuit current across isolated frog skin in the presence of calcium and magnesium. *Biochimica et Biophysica Acta* 66:170–172. (5)

Herter, K. 1926. Thermotaxis und Hydrotaxis bei Tieren. *Bethes Handbuch für normal und pathologische Physiologie* 11:173–180. (9)

———. 1936. Die Physiologie der Amphibien. In *Handbuch der Zoologie*, ed. W. Kükenthal, 6:1–252. Berlin: Gruyter. (13, 15)

Hertz, P. E. 1979. Sensitivity to high temperature in three West Indian grass anoles (Sauria, Iguanidae), with a review of heat sensitivity in the genus *Anolis*. *Comparative Biochemistry and Physiology* 63A: 217–222. (9)

Hertz, P. E., and R. B. Huey. 1981. Compensation for altitudinal changes in the thermal environment by some *Anolis* lizards on Hispaniola. *Ecology* 62:515–521. (9)

Hertz, P. E., R. B. Huey, and T. Garland, Jr. 1988. Time budgets, thermoregulation, and maximal locomotor performance: Are reptiles olympians or boy scouts? *American Zoologist* 28:927–938. (9, 14)

Hertz, P. E., R. B. Huey, and E. Nevo. 1983. Homage to Santa Anita: Thermal sensitivity of sprint speed in agamid lizards. *Evolution* 37:1075–1084. (8)

Hess, A. 1960. The structure of extrafusal muscle fibers in the frog and their innervation studied by the cholinesterase technique. *American Journal of Anatomy* 107:129–151. (11)

———. 1967. The structure of vertebrate slow and twitch muscle fibers. *Investigative Ophthalmology* 6:217–228. (11)

———. 1970. Vertebrate slow muscle fibers. *Physiological Reviews* 50:40–62. (11)

Hetherington, T. E. 1981. Morphology of the pineal organ in the salamander *Ensatina eschscholtzi*. *Journal of Morphology* 169:191–206. (2)

———. 1985. The role of the opercularis muscle in seismic sensitivity in the bullfrog *Rana catesbeiana*. *Journal of Experimental Zoology* 235:27–34. (2)

———. 1988a. Biomechanics of vibration reception in the bullfrog, *Rana catesbeiana*. *Journal of Comparative Physiology* 163:43–52. (2, 11)

———. 1988b. Metamorphic changes in the middle ear. In *The Evolution of the Amphibian Auditory System*, ed. B. Fritzsch, M. J. Ryan, W. Wilczynski, T. E. Hetherington, and W. Walkowiak, 339–357. New York: John Wiley and Sons. (2, 16)

———. 1989. Effect of the amphibian opercularis muscle on auditory response. *Fortschrifte der Zoologie* 35:356–359. (11)

Hetherington, T. E., A. P. Jaslow, and R. E. Lombard. 1986. Comparative morphology of the amphibian opercularis muscle: 1. General design features and functional interpretation. *Journal of Morphology* 190:43–61. (2)

Hetherington, T. E., and R. E. Lombard. 1983. Electromyography of the opercularis muscle of *Rana catesbeiana*: An amphibian tonic muscle. *Journal of Morphology* 175:17–26. (11)

Heusser, H. 1958a. Zum geruchlichen Beutefinden und Gähnen der Kreuzkröte (*Bufo calamita* Laur.). *Zeischrift für Tierpsychologie* 15:94–98. (13)

———. 1958b. Zum Häutungesverhalten von Amphibien. *Revue Suisse de Zoologie* 65:793–823. (13)

———. 1960. Instinkterscheinungen an Kröten, unter besonderer Berücksichtigung des Fortpflanzungsinstinktes der Erdkröte (*Bufo bufo* L.). *Zeitschrift für Tierpsychologie* 17:67–81. (13)

———. 1963. Die Ovulation des Erdkrötenweibchens im Rahmen der Verhaltensorganisation von *Bufo bufo* L. *Revue Suisse de Zoologie* 70:741–758. (15)

———. 1968a. Die Lebensweise der Erdkröte, *Bufo bufo* (L.): Der Magenfüllungsgrad in Abhängigkeit von Jagdstimmung und Wetter. *Sitzungsberichte der Gesellschaft Naturforschender Freunde* (Berlin) 8:148–156. (13, 15)

———. 1968b. Die Lebensweise der Erdkröte, *Bufo bufo* (L.): Laichzeit: Umstimmung, Ovulation, Verhalten. *Vierteljahrsschrift der naturforschenden Gesellschaft* (Zürich) 113:257–289. (15)

———. 1968c. Die Lebensweise der Erdkröte *Bufo bufo* (L.).: Wanderungen und Sommerquartiere. *Revue Suisse de Zoologie* 75:927–982. (15)

———. 1969. Die Lebensweise der Erdkröte, *Bufo bufo* (L.). Nahrungsaufnahme und Pigmentierung der Daumenschwielen im Jahreslauf. *Biologisches Zentralblatt* 88:457–467. (13, 15)

Hevesy, G. V., E. Hofer, and A. Krogh. 1935. The permeability of the skin of frogs to water as determined by D₂O and H₂O. *Skandinavisches Archiv für Physiologie* 72:199–214. (5)

Heward, C. B., and M. E. Hadley. 1975. Structure-activity relationships of melatonin and related indolamines. *Life Sciences* 17:1167–1178. (3)

Hews, D. K., and A. R. Blaustein. 1985. An investigation of the alarm response in *Bufo boreas* and *Rana cascadae* tadpoles. *Behavioral and Neural Biology* 43:47–57. (2)

Heyer, W. R. 1973. Ecological interactions of frog larvae at a seasonal tropical location in Thailand. *Journal of Herpetology* 7:337–361. (14)

———. 1974. Niche movements of frog larvae from a seasonal tropical location in Thailand. *Ecology* 55:651–656. (14)

———. 1976. Studies in larval amphibian habitat partitioning. *Smithsonian Contributions in Zoology* 242:1–27. (14)

Heymans, C., and E. Neil. 1958. *Reflexogenic Areas of the Cardiovascular System*. London: J. A. Churchill. (7)

Hibberd, M. G., J. A. Dantzig, D. R. Trentham, and Y. E. Goldman. 1985. Phosphate release and force generation in skeletal muscle fibers. *Science* 228:1317–1319. (12)

Hicks, G. H. and D. F. Stiffler. 1980. The effects of temperature and hypercapnia on acid-base status of larval *Ambystoma tigrinum*. *Federation Proceedings* 39:1060. (5)

———. 1984. Patterns of acid-base regulation in urodele amphibians in response to variations in environmental temperature. *Comparative Biochemistry and Physiology* 77A:693–697. (5)

Hicks, J. W., and S. C. Wood. 1985. Temperature regulation in lizards: Effects of hypoxia. *American Journal of Physiology* 248:R595–R600. (9)

———. 1989. Oxygen homeostasis in lower vertebrates: The impact of external and internal hypoxia. In *Comparative Pulmonary Physiology: Current Concepts*, vol. 39, *Lung Biology in Health and Disease*, ed. S. C. Wood, 311–341. New York: Marcel Dekker. (5)

Higgens, R. M. 1979. Temperature-related variation in the duration of morning song of the song thrush, *Turdus ericetorium*. *Ibis* 121: 333–335. (14)

Highton, R. 1956. The life history of the slimy salamander, *Plethodon glutinosus*, in Florida. *Copeia* 1956:75–93. (15)

———. 1962. Geographic variation in the life history of the slimy salamander. *Copeia* 1962:597–613. (15)

Hildebrand, M. 1968. *Anatomical Preparations*. Berkeley: University of California Press. (11)

Hildebrand, M., D. M. Bramble, K. F. Liem, and D. B. Wake, eds. 1985. *Functional Vertebrate Morphology*. Cambridge, MA: Harvard University Press. (11)

Hill, A. V. 1911. The total energy exchanges of intact cold-blooded animals at rest. *Journal of Physiology* (London) 43:379–394. (10, 12)

———. 1938. The heat of shortening and the dynamic constants of muscle. *Proceedings of the Royal Society of London* 126B:136–195. (8, 11)

Hill, L. G., G. D. Schnell, and J. Pigg. 1975. Thermal acclimation and temperature selection in sunfishes (*Lepomis*, Centrarchidae). *Southwestern Naturalist* 20:177–184. (9)

Hill, V. 1970. *First and Last Experiments in Muscle Mechanics*. Cambridge: Cambridge University Press. (11)

Hillenius, D. 1976. On the origin of the anuran body-form (Amphibia: Anura). *Beaufortia* 25:63–76. (11)

Hillery, C. M., and P. M. Narins. 1984. Neurophysiological evidence for a traveling wave in the amphibian inner ear. *Science* 225:1037–1039. (2)

Hillman, S. S. 1974. The effect of arginine vasopressin on water and sodium balance in the urodele amphibian *Aneides lugubris*. *General and Comparative Physiology* 24:74–82. (5)

———. 1976. Cardiovascular correlates of maximal oxygen consumption rates in anuran amphibians. *Journal of Comparative Physiology* 109B:199–207. (12, 14)

———. 1978a. The roles of oxygen delivery and electrolyte levels in the dehydrational death of *Xenopus laevis*. *Journal of Comparative Physiology* 128B:169–175. (6, 12)

———. 1978b. Some effects of dehydration on internal distributions of water and solutes in *Xenopus laevis*. *Comparative Biochemistry and Physiology* 61A:303–307. (6, 12)

———. 1980a. The effect of anemia on metabolic performance in the frog, *Rana pipiens*. *Journal of Experimental Zoology* 211:107–111. (12, 14)

———. 1980b. Physiological correlates of differential dehydration tolerance in anuran amphibians. *Copeia* 1980:125–129. (6, 12)

———. 1982a. The effects of DL-propranolol on exercise heart rate and maximal rates of oxygen consumption in *Scaphiopus intermontanus*. *Experientia* 38:940–941. (12)

———. 1982b. The effects of *in vivo* and *in vitro* hyperosmolality on skeletal muscle performance in the amphibians *Rana pipiens* and *Scaphiopus couchii*. *Comparative Biochemistry and Physiology* 73A:709–712. (6, 10, 12)

———. 1984. Inotropic influence of dehydration and hyperosmolal solutions on amphibian cardiac muscle. *Journal of Comparative Physiology* 154:325–328. (6, 12)

———. 1987. Dehydrational effects on cardiovascular and metabolic capacity in two amphibians. *Physiological Zoology* 60:608–613. (6, 12, 14)

———. 1988. Dehydrational effects on brain and cerebrospinal fluid electrolytes in two amphibians. *Physiological Zoology* 61:254–259. (6, 10)

Hillman, S. S., and M. S. Lea. 1983. Aerial activity oxygen consumption during metamorphosis of the bullfrog, *Rana catesbeiana*. *Copeia* 1983:407–410. (12)

Hillman, S. S., V. H. Shoemaker, R. Putnam, and P. C. Withers. 1979. Reassessment of aerobic metabolism in amphibians during activity. *Journal of Comparative Physiology* 129B:309–313. (12, 14)

Hillman, S. S., and P. C. Withers. 1979. An analysis of respiratory surface area as a limit to activity metabolism in anurans. *Canadian Journal of Zoology* 57:2100–2105. (6, 12, 14)

———. 1981. Aerobic contributions to sustained activity metabolism in *Xenopus laevis*. *Comparative Biochemistry and Physiology* 69A:605–606. (12, 14)

———. 1988. The hemodynamic consequences of hemorrhage and hypernatremia in two amphibians. *Journal of Comparative Physiology* 157:807–812. (6)

Hillman, S. S., P. C. Withers, M. S. Hedrick, and P. B. Kimmel. 1985. The effects of erythrocythemia on blood viscosity, maximal systemic oxygen transport capacity, and maximal rates of oxygen consumption in an amphibian. *Journal of Comparative Physiology* 155B:577–581. (6, 12)

Hillman, S. S., A. Zygmunt, and M. Baustian. 1987. Transcapillary fluid forces during dehydration in two amphibians. *Physiological Zoology* 60:339–345. (6, 12)

Hillyard, S. D. 1975. The role of antidiuretic hormone in the water economy of the spadefoot toad, *Scaphiopus couchi*. *Physiological Zoology* 48:242–251. (6)

———. 1976a. The movement of soil water across the isolated amphibian skin. *Copeia* 1976:314–320. (6)

———. 1976b. Variation in the effects of antidiuretic hormone on the isolated skin of the toad, *Scaphiopus couchi*. *Journal of Experimental Zoology* 195:199–206. (6)

———. 1979. The effect of isoproterenol on the anuran water balance response. *Comparative Biochemistry and Physiology* 62C:93–95. (6)

Hillyard, S. D., D. Brekke, and R. M. Winokur. 1987. Behavior associated with substrate moisture absorption by the toad, *Bufo punctatus*. *American Zoologist* 27:4A. (6)

Hillyard, S. D., and W. Van Driessche. 1985. Ontogeny of aldosterone stimulation of short-circuit current of larval bullfrogs. *Physiologist* 28:309. (16)

Hillyard, S. D., W. Zeiske, and W. Van Driessche. 1982a. A fluctuation analysis of the study of the development of amiloride sensitive Na$^+$ transport in the skin of larval bullfrogs (*Rana catesbeiana*). *Biochimica et Biophysica Acta* 692:455–461. (16)

———. 1982b. Poorly selective cation channels in the skin of the larval frog (stage ≤ XIX). *Pflugers Archiv* 394:287–293. (16)

Hilton, W. A. 1956. Eye muscles of salamanders. *Herpetologica* 12:273–276. (11)

Himstedt, W. 1973. Die spektrale Empfindlichkeit von *Triturus alpestris* (Amphibia, Urodela) wahrend des Wasser- und Landlebens. *Pflugers Archiv* 341:7–14. (2)

Himstedt, W., A. Helas, and T. J. Sommer. 1981. Projection of color coding retinal neurons in urodele amphibians. *Brain, Behavior, and Evolution* 18:19–32. (2)

Himstedt, W., J. Kopp, and W. Schmidt. 1982. Electroreception guides feeding behaviour in amphibians. *Naturwissenschaften* 69:552–553. (13)

Himstedt, W., and G. Roth. 1980. Neuronal responses in the tectum opticum of *Salamandra* to visual prey stimuli. *Journal of Comparative Physiology* 135:251–257. (2)

Hing, L. K. 1959. The breeding habits and development of *Rana chalconota* (Schleg.) (Amphibia). *Treubia* (Indonesia) 25:89–111. (16)

Hinton, D. E., L. C. Stoner, M. Burg, and B. F. Trump. 1982. Heterogeneity in the distal nephron of the salamander (*Ambystoma tigrinum*): A correlated structure function study of isolated tubule segments. *Anatomical Record* 204:21–32. (5)

Hirano, M., and L. C. Rome. 1984. Jumping performance of frogs (*Rana pipiens*) as a function of muscle temperature. *Journal of Experimental Biology* 108:429–439. (8, 9)

Hirata, K. 1934. On the histogenesis of the Island of Langerhans in *Rana japonica* (Gunther). *Science Reports of Tohoku Imperial University*, 4th series 9:159–182. (16)

Hird, D. W., S. L. Diesch, R. G. McKinnell, E. Gorham, F. B. Martin, C. A. Meadows, and M. Gasiorowski. 1983. Enterobacteriaceae and *Aeromonas hydrophila* in Minnesota frogs and tadpoles (*Rana pipiens*). *Applied and Environmental Microbiology* 46:1423–1425. (16)

Hitzig, B. M., and D. C. Jackson. 1978. Central chemical control of ventilation in the unanaesthetized turtle. *American Journal of Physiology* 235:R257–R264. (6, 7)

Hitzig, B. M., and E. E. Nattie. 1982. Acid-base stress and central chemical control of ventilation in turtles. *Journal of Applied Physiology* 53:1365–1370. (7)

Ho, S. M., P. Mak, A. R. Salhanick, G. J. Heiserman, and I. P. Callard. 1985. Steroid hormone receptors in subavian species. In *Current Trends in Comparative Endocrinology*, ed. B. Lofts and W. N. Holmes, 747–750. Hong Kong: Hong Kong University Press. (3)

Hochachka, P. W., and M. Guppy. 1987. *Metabolic Arrest and the Control of Biological Time*. Cambridge: Harvard University Press. (5, 10)

Hochachka, P. W., and G. N. Somero. 1984. *Biochemical Adaptation*. Princeton, NJ: Princeton University Press. (5, 8, 10)

Hock, R. J. 1964. Animals in high altitudes: Reptiles and amphibians. In *Handbook of Physiology, sec. 4, Adaptation to the Environment*, ed. D. B. Dill, 841–842. Bethesda, MD: American Physiological Society. (6)

———. 1967. Temperature effect on breeding of the toad, *Bufo variegatus*, in southern Chile. *Copeia* 1967:227–230. (8)

Hodler, F. 1949. Untersuchungen über die Entwicklung von Sacralwirbel und Urostyl bei den Anuren: Ein Beitrag zur Deutung des anuren Amphibientypus. *Review Suisse de Zoologie* 56:748–790. (11)

Hofbauer, K. 1934. Untersuchungen an der Rumpfmuskulatur einiger urodeler Amphibien. *Biologia Generalis* 10:403–416. (11)

Hofer, R. 1972. Einfluss von Temperatur Photoperiode und Jahreszeiten auf Verdauung und Atmung zweier Froscharten: *Rana ridibunda* (bzw, *Rana esculenta*) und *Rana temporaria*. *Zoologische Jahrbücher, Abteilung für allgemeine Zoologie und Physiologie der Tiere* 76:507–530. (9, 13)

Hofer, R., H. Ladurner, A. Gattringer, and W. Wieser. 1975. Relationship between the temperature preferenda of fishes, amphibians, and reptiles, and the substrate affinities of their trypsins. *Journal of Comparative Physiology* 99:345–355. (9)

Hoff, K. 1988. Locomotion in tadpoles. Ph.D. diss., Dalhousie University, Halifax, Nova Scotia. (11)

Hoff, K., and R. J. Wassersug. 1986. The kinematics of swimming in larvae of the clawed frog, *Xenopus laevis*. *Journal of Experimental Biology* 122:1–12. (16)

Hoff, K. S., and S. D. Hillyard. 1991. Angiotensin II stimulates cutaneous drinking in a toad, *Bufo punctatus:* A new perspective on the evolution of thirst in terrestrial vertebrates. *Physiological Zoology*. 64:1165–1172. (6)

Hoffman, A., and M. B. Cordeiro de Sousa. 1982. Cardiovascular reflexes in conscious toads. *Journal of the Autonomic Nervous System* 5:345–355. (7)

Hoffman, J., U. Eliath, and U. Katz. 1988. *Bufo viridis:* Physiological responses to osmotic stress (burrowing and salt acclimation). *Israel Journal of Zoology* 35:103–104. (6)

Hoffmann, A. 1985. Interaction of bilateral baroreceptor signals in conscious toads. *Brazilian Journal of Medical and Biological Research* (São Paulo) 18:55–60. (7)

Höglund, J., and A. Lundberg. 1987. Sexual selection in a monomorphic lek-breeding bird: Correlates of male mating success in the great snipe *Gallinago media*. *Behavioral Ecology and Sociobiology* 21:211–216. (14)

Holland, C. A., and J. N. Dumont. 1975. Oogenesis in *Xenopus laevis* (Daudin): 4. Effects of gonadotropin, estrogen, and starvation on endocytosis in developing oocytes. *Cell and Tissue Research* 162:177–184. (15)

Holland, R. A. B., and R. E. Forster. 1966. The effect of size of red cells on the kinetics of their oxygen uptake. *Journal of General Physiology* 49:727–742. (5)

Holloszy, J. O., and F. W. Booth. 1976. Biochemical adaptations to endurance exercise in muscle. *Annual Review of Physiology* 38:273–291. (14)

Holloway, J. A., C. F. Ramsundar, and L. E. Wright. 1976. Excitability and functional organization of cutaneous tactile units of the bullfrog (*R. catesbeiana*). *Journal of Neuroscience Research* 2:261–270. (2)

Holmes, E. B. 1975. A reconsideration of the phylogeny of the tetrapod heart. *Journal of Morphology* 147:209–228. (5)

Holmes, S. J. 1916. *The Biology of Frogs*. New York: Macmillan. (15)

———. 1932. *The Biology of the Frog*. Boston: Macmillan. (10)

Holomuzki, J. R. 1986. Predator avoidance and diel patterns of microhabitat use by larval tiger salamanders. *Ecology* 67:737–748. (9, 14)

Holomuzki, J. R., and J. P. Collins. 1983. Diel movement of larvae of the tiger salamander, *Ambystoma tigrinum nebulosum*. *Journal of Herpetology* 17:276–278. (9)

Holtfreter, J. 1965. Differentiation of striated muscle cells "in vitro." *American Zoologist* 5:719. (11)

Holzapfel, R. A. 1937. The cyclic character of hibernation in frogs. *Quarterly Review of Biology* 12:65–84. (10, 13)

Holzman, N., and J. J. McManus. 1973. Effects of acclimation on metabolic rate and thermal tolerance in the carpenter frog, *Rana vergatipes* [*sic*]. *Comparative Biochemistry and Physiology* 45A:833–842. (10, 12)

Honigmann, H. 1944. The visual perception of movement by toads. *Proceedings of the Royal Society of London* 132B:291–307. (13)

Hopkins, H. S., and S. W. Handford. 1943. Respiratory metabolism during development in two species of *Amblystoma*. *Journal of Experimental Biology* 93:403–414. (12, 16)

Hoppe, D. M. 1979. The influence of color on behavioral thermoregulation and hydroregulation. In *The Behavioral Significance of Color*, ed. E. H. Burtt, Jr., 37–68. New York: Garland Press. (9)

Hoppeler, H., O. Mathieu, R. Krauer, H. Claassen, R. B. Armstrong, and E. R. Weibel. 1981. Design of the mammalian respiratory system: 6. Distribution of mitochondria and capillaries in various muscles. *Respiration Physiology* 44:87–111. (14)

Horn, J. 1976. The stimulatory effect of hypothalamic and mesencephalic tissues on the interrenal of tadpoles of *Xenopus laevis* Daudin. *General and Comparative Endocrinology* 29:175–189. (16)

Horne, E. A., and R. G. Jaeger. 1988. Territorial pheromones of female red-backed salamanders. *Ethology* 78:143–152. (2)

Horseman, N. D., C. A. Smith, and D. D. Culley, Jr. 1978. Effects of age and photoperiod on ovary size and condition in bullfrogs (*Rana catesbeiana* Shaw) (Amphibia, Anura, Ranidae). *Journal of Herpetology* 12:287–290. (15)

Horton, P. 1977. The tongue musculature of Australian frogs. B.S. thesis, University of Adelaide. (11)

———. 1982. The diversity and systematic significance of anuran tongue musculature. *Copeia* 1982:595–602. (11)

Hoskins, S. G., and P. Grobstein. 1985a. Development of the ipsilateral retinothalamic projection in the frog *Xenopus laevis:* 1. Retinal distribution of ipsilaterally projecting cells in normal and experimentally manipulated animals. *Journal of Neuroscience* 5:911–919. (2)

———. 1985b. Development of the ipsilateral retinothalamic projection in the frog *Xenopus laevis:* 2. Ingrowth of optic fibers and production of ipsilaterally projecting retinal ganglion cells. *Journal of Neuroscience* 5:920–929. (2)

———. 1985c. Development of the ipsilateral retinothalamic projection in the frog *Xenopus laevis:* 3. The role of thyroxine. *Journal of Neuroscience* 5:930–940. (2, 16)

Hou, P.-C. L. 1992. Development of hemodynamic regulation in larvae of the African clawed toad, *Xenopus laevis*. Ph.D. diss., University of Massachusetts, Amherst. (16)

Houck, L. D. 1977a. Life history patterns and reproductive biology of Neotropical salamanders. In *The Reproductive Biology of Amphibians*, ed. D. H. Taylor and S. I. Guttman, 43–72. New York: Plenum Press. (15)

———. 1977b. Reproductive biology of a Neotropical salamander, *Bolitoglossa rostrata*. *Copeia* 1977:70–83. (15)

———. 1977c. Reproductive patterns in Neotropical salamanders. Ph.D. diss., University of California, Berkeley. (15)

———. 1982. Growth rates and age at maturity for the plethodontid salamander *Bolitoglossa subpalmata*. *Copeia* 1982:474–478. (15)

Hourdry, J., and A. Beaumont. 1985. *Les métamorphoses des amphibiens*. Paris: Fondation Singer-Polignac et Masson. (16)

Hourdry, J. J. G. Chabot, D. Menard, and J. S. Hugon. 1979. Intestinal brush border enzyme activities in developing amphibian *Rana catesbeiana*. *Comparative Biochemistry and Physiology* 69A:121–1125. (16)

Hourdry, J., and M. Dauca. 1977. Cytological and cytochemical changes in the intestinal epithelium during anuran metamorphosis. *International Review of Cytology*, suppl. 5:337–385. (16)

Hourdry, J., and E. Regard. 1975. Mesure relative de la quantité d'iode décelable dans la colloïde des follicules thyroïdiens chez la larvae du Xénope, par spectrométrie des rayons X: Effets de l'hypophysectomie et de l'administration de TSH. *General and Comparative Endocrinology* 27:277–288. (16)

Houssay, B. A. 1949. Hypophyseal functions in the toad *Bufo arenarum* Hensel. *Quarterly Review of Biology* 24:1–27. (3, 15)

Howard, J. H., R. L. Wallace, and J. R. Stauffer, Jr. 1983. Critical thermal maxima in populations of *Ambystoma macrodactylum* from different elevations. *Journal of Herpetology* 17:400–402. (8)

Howard, K., and D. M. Ensor. 1975. Effect of prolactin on sodium transport across frog skin in vitro. *Journal of Endocrinology* 67:56–57. (5)

Howard, R. D. 1978a. The evolution of mating strategies in bullfrogs, *Rana catesbeiana*. *Evolution* 32:850–871. (14)

———. 1978b. The influence of male-defended oviposition sites on early embryo mortality in bullfrogs. *Ecology* 59:789–798. (15)

———. 1979. Estimating reproductive success in natural populations. *American Naturalist* 14:221–231. (14)

———. 1984. Alternative mating behaviors of young male bullfrogs. *American Zoologist* 24:397–406. (14)

———. 1988. Reproductive success in two species of anurans. In *Reproductive Success*, ed. T. H. Clutton-Brock, 99–113. Chicago: University of Chicago Press. (14)

Howard, R. D., and A. G. Kluge. 1985. Proximate mechanisms of sexual selection in wood frogs. *Evolution* 39:260–277. (14)

Howell, A. B. 1936. Phylogeny of the distal musculature of the pectoral appendage. *Journal of Morphology* 60:287–315. (11)

Howell, B. J. 1970. Acid-base balance in transition from water breathing to air breathing. *Federation Proceedings* 29:1130–1134. (5)

Howell, B. J., F. W. Baumgardner, K. Bondi, and H. Rahn. 1970. Acid-base balance in cold-blooded vertebrates as a function of body temperature. *American Journal of Physiology* 218:600–606. (5, 6, 9)

Howell, B. J., and H. Rahn. 1976. Regulation of acid-base balance in reptiles. In *Biology of the Reptilia,* vol. 5, C. Gans and W. R. Dawson, 335–363. New York: Academic Press. (6)

Howes, B. N. 1940. The response of the water regulation mechanism of development stages of the common toad, *Bufo bufo* L., to treatment with extracts of the posterior lobe of the pituitary body. *Journal of Experimental Biology* 17:128–138. (16)

Hoyle, G. 1983. *Muscles and Their Neural Control.* New York: Wiley-Interscience. (11)

Hoyt, D. F., and C. R. Taylor. 1981. Gait and the energetics of locomotion in horses. *Nature* 292:239–240. (12)

Hoyt, R. W., M. Eldridge, and S. C. Wood. 1984. Noninvasive pulsed Doppler determination of cardiac output in an unanesthetized neotenic salamander, *Ambystoma tigrinum. Journal of Experimental Zoology* 230:491–493. (16)

Hruby, V. J., B. C. Wilkes, M. E. Hadley, F. Al-Obeidi, T. K. Sawyer, D. J. Stapes, A. E. deVaux, O. Dym, A. M. de L. Castrucci, M. F. Hintz, J. P. Riehm, and K. R. Rao. 1987. α-melanotropin: The minimal active sequence in the frog skin bioassay. *Journal of Medicinal Chemistry* 30:2126–2130. (3)

Hsu, C. Y., L. Chang, H. Ku, and M. Lu. 1985. *In vitro* estradiol synthesis and secretion by tadpole ovaries of different developmental stages. *General and Comparative Endocrinology* 57:393–396. (16)

Hsu, C. Y., C. H. Chiang, and H. M. Liang. 1973. Effect of hypophysectomy on sex transformation in frog tadpoles. *Endocrinology Japan* 20:391–396. (16)

———. 1977. A histochemical study on the development of hydroxysteroid dehydrogenases in tadpole ovaries. *General and Comparative Endocrinology* 32:272–278. (16)

Hsu, C. Y., M. H. Lu, H. T. Huang, and H. M. Liang. 1985. The correlation of fine structure with endocrine function of ovarian follicle cells in tadpoles. *General and Comparative Endocrinology* 56:77–87. (16)

Hsu, C. Y., N. W. Yu, L. T. Chang, H. H. Ku, and M. H. Lu. 1989. Estradiol secretion by the ovarian tissue, in response to hypophyseal stimulation during ontogenesis of the bullfrog. *General and Comparative Endocrinology* 74:161–164. (3, 5, 8, 16)

Hsu, C. Y., N. W. Yu, and S. J. Chen. 1980. Development of Δ5-3β-hydroxysteroid dehydrogenase activity in the interrenal gland of *Rana catesbeiana. General and Comparative Endocrinology* 42:167–170. (16)

Hsu, C. Y., N. W. Yu, and H. M. Liang. 1976. The changes of growth activities in pituitaries of tadpoles at different metamorphic stages. *General and Comparative Endocrinology* 26:424–431. (16)

Hsu, C. Y., N. W. Yu, C. M. Pi, S. J. Chen, and C. C. Ruan. 1984. Hormonal regulation of development of the internal activity of Δ5-3β-hydroxysteroid dehydrogenase in bullfrog tadpoles. *Journal of Experimental Zoology* 232:73–78. (16)

Hubbard, G. M., and P. Licht. 1986. *In vitro* ovarian responses to pulsatile and continuous gonadotropin administration on steroid secretion and oocyte maturation in the frogs, *Rana pipiens* and *Rana catesbeiana. General and Comparative Endocrinology* 61:417–423. (3)

Huber, S., G. U. Ryffel, and R. Weber. 1979. Thyroid hormone induces competence for oestrogen-dependent vitellogenin synthesis in developing *Xenopus* larvae. *Nature* 278:65–67. (16)

Huey, R. B. 1978. Latitudinal pattern of between-altitude faunal similarity: Mountains might be "higher" in the tropics. *American Naturalist* 112:225–229. (8)

———. 1982. Temperature, physiology, and the ecology of reptiles. In *Biology of the Reptilia,* vol. 12, ed. C. Gans and F. H. Pough, 25–91. New York: Academic Press. (8, 9)

Huey, R. B., and A. F. Bennett. 1986. A comparative approach to field and laboratory studies in evolutionary biology. In *Predator-Prey Relationships,* ed. M. E. Feder and G. V. Lauder, 82–98. Chicago: University of Chicago Press. (14)

———. 1987. Phylogenetic studies of coadaptation: Preferred temperatures versus optimal performance temperatures of lizards. *Evolution* 41:1098–1115. (8, 14)

Huey, R. B., A. F. Bennett, H. John-Alder, and K. A. Nagy. 1984. Locomotor capacity and foraging behaviour of Kalahari lacertid lizards. *Animal Behaviour* 32:41–50. (14)

Huey, R. B., and A. E. Dunham. 1987. Repeatability of locomotor performance in natural populations of the lizard *Sceloporus merriami. Evolution* 41:1116–1120. (14)

Huey, R. B., P. H. Niewiarowski, J. Kaufmann, and J. C. Herron. 1989. Thermal biology of nocturnal ectotherms: Is sprint performance of geckos maximal at lower body temperatures? *Physiological Zoology* 62:488–504. (9)

Huey, R. B., and E. R. Pianka. 1981. Ecological consequences of foraging mode. *Ecology* 62:991–999. (14)

Huey, R. B., and R. D. Stevenson. 1979. Integrating thermal physiology and ecology of ectotherms: A discussion of approaches. *American Zoologist* 19:357–366. (8, 14)

Huf, E. G. 1936. Über aktiven Wasser- und Salztransport durch die Froschhaut. *Pflugers Archiv* 237:143–166. (5)

Hughes, A. 1959. Studies on embryonic and larval development in Amphibia: 1. The embryology of *Eleutherodactylus ricordii,* with special reference to the spinal cord. *Journal of Embryology and Experimental Morphology* 7:22–38. (16)

———. 1976. Metamorphic changes in the brain and spinal cord. In *Frog Neurobiology: A Handbook,* ed. R. Llinás and W. Precht, 856–863. Berlin: Springer-Verlag. (2)

Hughes, A. F., and M. C. Prestige. 1967. Development of behavior in the hindlimb of *Xenopus laevis. Journal of Zoology* 152:347–359. (16)

Hughes, E. F., S. C. Turner, and G. A. Brooks. 1982. Effects of glycogen depletion and pedaling speed on "anaerobic threshold." *Journal of Applied Physiology* 52:1598–1607. (12)

Hughes, G. M., and G. S. Vergara. 1978. Static pressure-volume curves for the lung of the frog (*Rana pipiens*). *Journal of Experimental Biology* 76:149–165. (6)

Hulsebus, J. J., and E. S. Farrar. 1985. Insulin-like immunoreactivity in serum and pancreas of metamorphosing tadpoles. *General and Comparative Endocrinology* 58:114–119. (16)

Hulsebus, J. J., E. S. Farrar, and L. B. Tabataba. In press. Purification and amino acid sequence of bullfrog (*Rana catesbeiana*) insulin. *General and Comparative Endocrinology.* (3)

Hume, I. D. 1989. Optimal digestive strategies in mammalian herbivores. *Physiological Zoology* 62:1145–1163. (16)

Humphry, G. M. 1871. The muscles and nerves of the *Cryptobranchus japonicus. Journal of Anatomy and Physiology* (London) 6:1–61. (11)

Hurlbert, S. H. 1984. Pseudoreplication and the design of ecological field experiments. *Ecological Monographs* 54:187–211. (14)

Husson, A. 1970. Activité gonadotrope de l'hypophyse greffée dans le testicule chez la grenouille verte (*Rana esculenta*). *Comptes Rendus de la Société Biologique* 164:2180–2182. (15)

Husting, E. L. 1965. Survival and breeding structure in a population of *Ambystoma maculatum. Copeia* 1965:352–362. (15)

Hutcherson, J. E., C. L. Peterson, and R. F. Wilkinson. 1989. Reproductive and larval biology of *Ambystoma annulatum. Journal of Herpetology* 23:181–183. (15)

Hutchison, V. H. 1958. The distribution and ecology of the cave salamander, *Eurycea lucifuga. Ecological Monographs* 28:1–20. (9)

———. 1961. Critical thermal maxima in salamanders. *Physiological Zoology* 34:92–125. (8, 9)

———. 1971a. Herpetological expedition to Colombia. In *National Geographic Research Reports for 1965,* ed. P. H. Dehser, 113–122. Washington, DC: National Geographic Society. (9)

———. 1971b. Oxygen consumption: Part 4. Amphibians. In *Respiration and Circulation,* ed. P. L. Altman and D. S. Dittmer, 481–485. Bethesda, MD: Biological Handbooks, Federation of American Societies for Experimental Biology. (12)

———. 1976. Factors influencing thermal tolerances of individual organisms. In *Thermal Ecology,* ed. G. W. Esch and R. W. McFarlane, 10–26. Oak Ridge, TN: U.S. National Technical Information Service. (9)

———. 1979. Thermoregulation. in *Turtles: Perspectives and Research,* ed. M. Harless and H. Morlock, 207–228. New York: John Wiley and Sons. (9)

———. 1980. The concept of critical thermal maximum. *American Journal of Physiology* 237:R367–R368. (9)

———. 1981. Pharmacological studies on behavioral thermoregulation in the salamander, *Necturus maculosus. Journal of Thermal Biology* 6:331–339. (9)

———. 1982. Physiological ecology of telmatobiid frogs of Lake Titicaca. *National Geographic Research Reports* 14:357–361. (9)

Hutchison, V. H., J. J. Black, and D. Erskine. 1979. Melatonin and chlorpromazine: Thermal selection in the mudpuppy, *Necturus maculosus*. *Life Sciences* 25:527–530. (9)

Hutchison, V. H., and M. J. Dady. 1964. The viability of *Rana pipiens* and *Bufo terrestris* submerged at different temperatures. *Herpetologica* 20:149–162. (9, 10)

Hutchison, V. H., G. A. Engbretson, and L. D. Turney. 1973. Thermal acclimation and tolerance in the hellbender, *Cryptobranchus alleganiensis*. *Copeia* 1973:805–807. (9)

Hutchison, V. H., and D. J. Erskine. 1981. Thermal selection and prostaglandin E₁ fever in the salamander *Necturus maculosus*. *Herpetologica* 37:195–198. (9, 14)

Hutchison, V. H., and M. R. Ferrance. 1970. Thermal tolerances of *Rana pipiens* acclimated to daily temperature cycles. *Herpetologica* 26:1–8. (9)

Hutchison, V. H., H. B. Haines, and G. A. Engbretson. 1976. Aquatic life at high altitude: Respiratory adaptations in the Lake Titicaca frog, *Telmatobius culeus*. *Respiration Physiology* 27:115–129. (4, 5, 9, 12)

Hutchison, V. H., and C. S. Hammen. 1958. Oxygen utilization in the symbiosis of embryos of the salamander, *Ambystoma maculatum*, and the alga, *Oophila ambystomatis*. *Biological Bulletin* 115:483–489. (9)

Hutchison, V. H., and E. S. Hazard. 1984. Erythrocytic phosphates: Diel and seasonal cycles in the frog, *Rana berlandieri*. *Comparative Biochemistry and Physiology* 79A:533–538. (9)

Hutchison, V. H., and L. G. Hill. 1976. Thermal selection in the hellbender, *Cryptobranchus alleganiensis*, and the mudpuppy, *Necturus maculosus*. *Herpetologica* 32:327–331. (8, 9)

———. 1977. Thermal selection of bullfrog tadpoles (*Rana catesbeiana*) at different stages of development and acclimation temperatures. *Journal of Thermal Biology* 3:57–60. (9)

Hutchison, V. H., and M. A. Kohl. 1971. The effect of photoperiod on daily rhythms of oxygen consumption in the tropical toad, *Bufo marinus*. *Zeitschrift für vergleichende Physiologie* 75:367–382. (9, 12)

Hutchison, V. H., and R. J. Kosh. 1965. The effect of photoperiod on the critical thermal maxima of painted turtles, *Chrysemys picta*. *Herpetologica* 20:233–238. (9)

———. 1974. Thermoregulatory function of the parietal eye in the lizard *Anolis carolinensis*. *Oecologia* (Berlin) 16:173–177. (9)

Hutchison, V. H., and J. L. Larimer. 1960. Reflectivity of the integuments of some lizards from different habitats. *Ecology* 41:199–209. (9)

Hutchison, V. H., and J. D. Maness. 1979. The role of behavior in temperature acclimation and tolerance in ectotherms. *American Zoologist* 19:367–384. (8, 9)

Hutchison, V. H., and K. Miller. 1979a. Aerobic and anaerobic contributions to sustained activity in *Xenopus laevis*. *Respiration Physiology* 38:93–103. (5, 9, 12, 14)

———. 1979b. Anaerobic capacity of amphibians. *Comparative Biochemistry and Physiology* 63A:213–216. (9, 12, 14)

Hutchison, V. H., K. Miller, and R. K. Gratz. 1981. The anaerobic contribution to sustained activity in the giant toad *Bufo marinus*. *Comparative Biochemistry and Physiology* 69A:693–696. (9, 12)

Hutchison, V. H., and K. Murphy. 1985. Behavioral thermoregulation in the salamander *Necturus maculosus* after heat shock. *Comparative Biochemistry and Physiology*. 82A:391–394. (9)

Hutchison, V. H., and J. P. Ritchart. 1988. Annual cycle of thermal tolerance in the salamander *Necturus maculosus*. *Journal of Herpetology* 23:73–76. (9)

Hutchison, V. H., and S. Rowlan. 1975. Thermal acclimation and tolerance in the mudpuppy, *Necturus maculosus*. *Journal of Herpetology* 9:367–368. (9)

Hutchison, V. H., and K. K. Spriestersbach. 1986a. Diel and seasonal cycles of activity and behavioral thermoregulation in the salamander *Necturus maculosus*. *Copeia* 1986:612–618. (9, 14)

———. 1986b. Histamine receptors: Behavioral thermoregulation in the salamander *Necturus maculosus*. *Comparative Biochemistry and Physiology* 85C:199–206. (9)

Hutchison, V. H., and H. Szarski. 1965. The number of erythrocytes in some amphibians and reptiles. *Copeia* 1965:373–375. (9)

Hutchison, V. H., and L. D. Turney. 1975. Glucose and lactate concentrations during activity in the leopard frog, *Rana pipiens*. *Journal of Comparative Physiology* 99:287–295. (9, 12, 14)

Hutchison, V. H., L. D. Turney, and R. K. Gratz. 1977. Aerobic and anaerobic metabolism during activity in the salamander *Ambystoma tigrinum*. *Physiological Zoology* 50:189–202. (9, 12, 14)

Hutchison, V. H., and W. G. Whitford. 1966. Survival and underwater buccal movements in submerged amphibians. *Herpetologica* 22:122–127. (9, 10, 11)

Hutchison, V. H., W. G. Whitford, and M. A. Kohl. 1968. The relation of body size and surface area to gas exchange in anurans. *Physiological Zoology* 41:65–85. (5, 6, 9, 10, 12)

Ide, H., I. Kawazoe, and H. Kawauchi. 1985. Fish melanin-concentrating hormone disperses melanin in amphibian melanophores. *General and Comparative Endocrinology* 58:486–490. (3)

Iela, L., R. K. Rastogi, G. Delrio, and J. T. Bagnara. 1986. Reproduction in the Mexican leaf frog, *Pachymedusa dacnicolor*: 3. The female. *General and Comparative Endocrinology* 63:381–392. (3, 15)

Ifft, J. D. 1942. The effect of environmental factors on the sperm cycle of *Triturus viridescens*. *Biological Bulletin* 83:111–128. (15)

Iga, T., and J. T. Bagnara. 1975. An analysis of color change in the leaf frog, *Agalychnis dacnicolor*. *Journal of Zoology* (London) 192:331–341. (9)

Ihle, J. E. W., P. N. van Kampen, H. F. Nierstrasz, and J. Versluys. 1927. *Vergleichende Anatomie der Wirbeltiere*. Berlin: Springer-Verlag. (11)

Iles, T. D. 1974. The tactics and strategy of growth in fishes. In *Sea Fisheries Research*, ed. F. R. Harden Jones, 331–345. London: Elek Science. (15)

Incerpi, S., P. Luly, and S. Scapin. 1983. Glucocorticoid receptor of frog (*Rana esculenta*) liver. *Comparative Biochemistry and Physiology* 75B:645–648. (16)

Infantino, R. L. 1991. Ontogeny of ventilatory regulation in the bullfrog *Rana catesbeiana*. Ph.D. diss., University of Massachusetts, Amherst. (16)

Inger, R. F. 1954. Systematics and zoogeography of Philippine Amphibia. *Fieldiana: Zoology* 33:181–531. (16)

———. 1956. Morphology and development of the vocal sac apparatus in the African clawed frog *Rana* (*Ptychadena*) *porosissima* Steindachner. *Journal of Morphology* 99:57–72. (11)

———. 1966. The systematics and zoogeography of the Amphibia of Borneo. *Fieldiana: Zoology* 52:1–402. (16)

———. 1986. Diets of tadpoles living in a Bornean rain forest. *Alytes* 5:153–164. (14)

Inger, R. F., and B. Greenberg. 1956. Morphology and seasonal development of sex characters in two sympatric African toads. *Journal of Morphology* 99:549–574. (15)

———. 1963. The annual reproductive pattern of the frog *Rana erythraea* in Sarawak. *Physiological Zoology* 36:21–33. (15)

Ingle, D. 1970. Visuomotor functions of the frog optic tectum. *Brain, Behavior, and Evolution* 3:57–71. (2)

———. 1973. Disinhibition of tectal neurons by pretectal lesions in the frog. *Science* 180:422–424. (2)

———. 1976. Behavioral correlates of central visual function in anurans. In *Frog Neurobiology: A Handbook*, ed. R. Llinás, and W. Precht, 435–451. Berlin: Springer-Verlag. (13)

———. 1977. Detection of stationary objects by frogs (*Rana pipiens*) after ablation of optic tectum. *Journal of Comparative and Physiological Psychology* 91:1359–1364. (2)

———. 1980. Some effects of pretectum lesions on the frog's detection of stationary objects. *Behavioral Brain Research* 1:139–163. (2)

———. 1983. Brain mechanisms of visual localization in frogs and toads. In *Advances in Vertebrate Neuroethology*, ed. J.-P. Ewert, R. R. Capranica, and D. Ingle, 177–226. New York: Plenum Press. (2, 13)

Ingle, D., and D. Crews. 1985. Vertebrate neuroethology: Definitions and paradigms. *Annual Review of Neuroscience* 8:457–494. (13)

Inoue, I. 1978. Reflex discharges in the hypoglossal nerve elicited by stimulating parts of the frog's tongue. *Journal of Kyushu Dental Science* 32:119–131. (7)

Ireland, M. P. 1973. Studies on the adaptation of *Xenopus laevis* to hyperosmotic media. *Comparative Biochemistry and Physiology* 46A:469–476. (6)

Ireland, P. H. 1976. Reproduction and larval development of the gray-bellied salamander *Eurycea multiplicata griseogaster. Herpetologica* 32:233–238. (15)

Irish, J. M., and W. H. Dantzler. 1976. PAH transport and fluid absorption by isolated perfused frog proximal renal tubules. *American Journal of Physiology* 230:1509–1516. (5)

Isayama, S. 1924. Über die Strimung der Lymph bei den Amphibien. *Zeitschrift für Biologie* 82:90–100. (5)

Ishida, S. 1954. The so-called carotic body of the Amphibia. *Igaku Kenkyuu* 24:1024–1050. (7)

Ishii, K., K. Honda, and K. Ishii. 1966. The function of the carotid labyrinth in the toad. *Tohoku Journal of Experimental Medicine* 88:103–116. (6, 7)

Ishii, K., and K. Ishii. 1967. Adrenergic transmission of the carotid chemoreceptor impulses in the toad. *Tohoku Journal of Experimental Medicine* 91:119–128. (7)

———. 1970. Efferent innervation to the chemoreceptor of the carotid labyrinth of the toad. *Tohoku Journal of Experimental Medicine* 102:113–119. (7)

———. 1973. Fiber composition and derivation of afferent and efferent nerve fibers in the carotid nerve innervating the carotid labyrinth of the toad. *Tohoku Journal of Experimental Medicine* 109:323–337. (7)

———. 1976. The chemoreceptors of amphibians. In *Morphology and Mechanisms of Chemoreceptors*, ed. A. S. Paintal, 265–274. Delhi: Vallabhbhai Patel Chest Institute. (7)

———. 1978. A reflexogenic area for controlling blood pressure in the toad *Bufo vulgaris formosa. Japanese Journal of Physiology* 28:423–431. (7)

Ishii, K., K. Ishii, dn K. Honda. 1966. Evidence for adrenergic transmission of the carotid chemoreceptor impulses in the toad. *Nature* 210:1057–1058. (7)

Ishii, K., K. Ishii, and T. Kusakabe. 1985a. Chemo- and baroreceptor innervation of the aortic trunk of the toad *Bufo vulgaris. Respiration Physiology* 60:365–375. (7)

———. 1985b. Electrophysiological aspects of reflexogenic area in the chelonian, *Geoclemmys reevesii. Respiration Physiology* 59:45–54. (7)

Ishii, K., and T. Oosaki. 1966. Electron microscopy of the chemoreceptor cells of the carotid labyrinth of the toad. *Nature* 212:1499–1500. (7)

———. 1969. Fine structure of the chemoreceptor cell in the amphibian carotid labyrinth. *Journal of Anatomy* 104:263–280. (7)

Ishii, S. 1990. Evolution of gonadotropins in vertebrates. In *Progress in Comparative Endocrinology*, ed. A. Epple, C. G. Scanes, and M. H. Stetson, 40–46. New York: Wiley-Liss. (3)

Ishii, S., and K. Kubokawa. 1985. Adaptation of vertebrate gonadotropin receptors to environmental temperature. In *Current Trends in Comparative Endocrinology*, ed. B. Lofts and W. N. Holmes, 751–754. Hong Kong: Hong Kong University Press. (3)

Issekutz, B., Jr., W. A. S. Shaw, and A. C. Issekutz. 1976. Lactate metabolism in resting and exercising dogs. *Journal of Applied Physiology* 40:312–319. (12)

Itämies, J., and P. Koskela. 1970. On the diet of the common frog (*Rana temporaria* L.). *Aguilo* (Zoology) 10:53–60. (13, 15)

Ito, F. 1968. Functional properties of leaf-like muscle receptors in the frog sartorius muscle. *Japanese Journal of Physiology* 18:590–600. (11)

Ito, F., K. Toyama, and R. Ito. 1964. A comparative study on structure and function between the extrafusal receptor and the spindle receptor in the frog. *Japanese Journal of Physiology* 14:12–33. (11)

Iwasawa, H., and M. Kobayashi. 1976. Development of the testis of the frog *Rana nigromaculata* with special reference to germ cell maturation. *Copeia* 1976:461–467. (15, 16)

Jackson, D. C. 1978a. Respiratory and CO_2 conductance: Temperature effects in a turtle and a frog. *Respiration Physiology* 33:103–114. (6, 10)

———. 1978b. Respiratory control in air-breathing ectotherms. In *Regulation of Ventilation and Gas Exchange*, ed. D. G. Davies and C. D. Barnes, 93–130. New York: Academic Press. (5, 7)

———. 1987a. Assigning priorities among interacting physiological systems. In *New Directions in Ecological Physiology*, ed. M. E. Feder, A. F. Bennett, W. W. Burggren, and R. B. Huey, 310–327. Cambridge: Cambridge University Press. (1)

———. 1987b. How do amphibians breathe both water and air? In *Comparative Physiology: Life in Water and on Land*, ed. P. Dejours, L. Bolis, C. R. Taylor, and E. R. Weibel, 49–58. Padua: Liviana Press. (6)

Jackson, D. C., and B. A. Braun. 1979. Respiratory control in bullfrogs: Cutaneous versus pulmonary response to selective CO_2 exposure. *Journal of Comparative Physiology* 129:339–342. (5, 6, 7, 12, 16)

Jackson, D. C., and N. Heisler. 1983. Intracellular and extracellular acid-base and electrolyte status of submerged anoxic turtles at 3°C. *Respiration Physiology* 53:187–201. (10)

Jackson, D. C., C. V. Herbert, and G. R. Ultsch. 1984. The comparative physiology of diving in North American freshwater turtles: 2. Plasma ion balance during prolonged anoxia. *Physiological Zoology* 57:632–640. (10)

Jackson, D. C., and H. Silverblatt. 1974. Respiration and acid-base status of turtles following experimental dives. *American Journal of Physiology* 226:903–909. (6)

Jackson, D. C., and G. R. Ultsch. 1982. Long-term submergence at 3°C of the turtle, *Chrysemys picta bellii*, in normoxic and severely hypoxic water: 2. Extracellular ionic responses to extreme lactic acidosis. *Journal of Experimental Biology* 96:29–43. (10)

Jackson, I. M. D., and S. Reichlin. 1974. Thyrotropin-releasing hormone (TRH): Distribution in hypothalamic and extrahypothalamic brain tissues of mammalian and submammalian chordates. *Endocrinology* 95:854–862. (16)

———. 1979. Thyrotropin-releasing hormone in the blood of the frog, *Rana pipiens*: Its nature and possible derivation from regional localizations in the skin. *Endocrinology* 104:1814–1821. (3, 16)

Jackson, I. M. D., R. Saperstein, and S. Reichlin. 1977. Thyrotropin-releasing hormone (TRH) in pineal and hypothalamus of the frog: Effect of season and illumination. *Endocrinology* 100:97–100. (3)

Jacobs, G. F. M., M. P. Goyvaerts, G. Vandorpe, A. M. L. Quaghebeur, and E. R. Kuhn. 1988. Luteinizing hormone-releasing hormone as a potent stimulator of the thyroidal axis in ranid frogs. *General and Comparative Endocrinology* 70:274–283. (3, 16)

Jacobs, G. F. M., R. P. A. Michielsen, and E. R. Kuhn. 1988. Thyroxine and triiodothyronine in plasma and thyroids in the neotenic and metamorphosed axolotl *Ambystoma mexicanum*: Influence of TRH injections. *General and Comparative Endocrinology* 70:145–151. (3, 16)

Jacobson, S. K. 1985. Reproductive behavior and male mating success in two species of glass frogs (Centrolenidae). *Herpetologica* 41:396–404. (14)

Jacoby, J., and K. Rubinson. 1983. The acoustic and lateral line nuclei are distinct in the premetamorphic frog, *Rana catesbeiana. Journal of Comparative Neurology* 216:152–161. (2, 16)

Jaeger, C. B., and D. E. Hillman. 1976. Morphology of gustatory organs. In *Frog Neurobiology: A Handbook*, ed. R. Llinś and W. Precht, 588–606. Berlin: Springer-Verlag. (16)

Jaeger, R. G. 1971. Competitive exclusion as a factor influencing the distribution of two species of terrestrial salamanders. *Ecology* 54:632–637. (14)

———. 1976. A possible prey-call window in anuran auditory processing. *Copeia* 1976:833–834. (14)

———. 1978. Plant climbing by salamanders: Periodic availability of plant-dwelling prey. *Copeia* 1978:686–691. (4, 6, 14)

———. 1980a. Fluctuations in prey availability and food limitation for a terrestrial salamander. *Oecologia* (Berlin) 44:335–341. (13)

———. 1980b. Microhabitats of a terrestrial forest salamander. *Copeia* 1980:265–268. (4, 6)

———. 1981a. Dear enemy recognition and the costs of aggression between salamanders. *American Naturalist* 117:962–974. (4)

———. 1981b. Foraging in optimum light as a niche dimension for Neotropical frogs. *National Geographic Society Research Reports* 13:297–302. (14)

Jaeger, R. G., and D. E. Barnard. 1981. Foraging tactics of a terrestrial salamander: Choice of diet in structurally simple environments. *American Naturalist* 117:639–644. (13, 14)

Jaeger, R. G., D. E.Barnard, and R. G. Joseph. 1982. Foraging tactics of a terrestrial salamander: Assessing prey density. *American Naturalist* 119:885–890. (13)

Jaeger, R. G., and J. P. Hailman. 1976. Ontogenetic shift of spectral phototactic preferences in anuran tadpoles. *Journal of Comparative Physiology and Psychology* 10:930–945. (2, 9, 16)

————. 1981. Activity of Neotropical frogs in relation to ambient light. *Biotropica* 13:59–65. (14)

Jaeger, R. G., J. P. Hailman, and L. S. Jaeger. 1976. Bimodal daily activity of a Panamanian dendrobatid frog, *Colostethus nubicola,* in relation to light. *Herpetologica* 32:77–81. (14)

Jaeger, R. G., R. G. Joseph, and D. Barnard. 1981. Foraging tactics of a terrestrial salamander: Sustained yield in territories. *Animal Behaviour* 29:1100–1105. (13, 14)

Jaeger, R. G., K. C. B. Nishikawa, and D. E. Barnard. 1983. Foraging tactics of a terrestrial salamander: Costs of territorial defense. *Animal Behaviour* 31:191–198. (14)

Jaeger, R. G., and A. M. Rubin. 1982. Foraging tactics of a terrestrial salamander: Judging prey profitability. *Journal of Animal Ecology* 51:167–176. (13, 14)

Jaffe, R. C. 1981. Plasma concentration of corticosterone during *Rana catesbeiana* tadpole metamorphosis. *General and Comparative Endocrinology* 44:314–318. (16)

————. 1987. Physiochemical properties of the triiodothyronine nuclear receptor from tadpole liver, intestine, and tail fin. *Molecular and Cellular Endocrinology* 52:137–142. (16)

Jaffee, O. C. 1954. Phenol red transport in the pronephros and mesonephros of the developing frog (*Rana pipiens*). *Journal of Cellular and Comparative Physiology* 44:347–361. (16)

James, F. C., and W. P. Porter. 1979. Behavior-microclimate relationships in the African rainbow lizard, *Agama agama. Copeia* 1979:585–593. (9)

Jameson, D. L., W. Taylor, and J. Mountjoy. 1970. Metabolic and morphological adaptation to heterogeneous environments by the Pacific tree toad, *Hyla regilla. Evolution* 24:75–89. (12)

Jan, L. Y., and Y. N. Jan. 1981. Role of LHRH-like peptide as a neurotransmitter in sympathetic ganglia of the frog. *Federation Proceedings* 40:2560–2564. (3)

Janes, R. G. 1938. Studies on the amphibian digestive system: 3. The origin and development of pancreatic islands in certain species of Anura. *Journal of Morphology* 62:375–391. (16)

Janssens, P. A. 1970. The evolution of corticosteroid function. *Steroidologia* 1:308–320. (3)

Janssens, P. A., A. G. Caine, and J. E. Dixon. 1983. Hormonal control of glycogenolysis and the mechanism of action of adrenaline in amphibian liver *in vitro. General and Comparative Endocrinology* 49:477–484. (3)

————. 1985. The mechanism for adrenergic control of glycogenolysis in *Ambystoma mexicanum:* An *in vitro* study. In *Current Trends in Comparative Endocrinology,* ed. B. Lofts and W. N. Holmes, 1103–1105. Hong Kong: Hong Kong University Press. (3)

Janssens, P. A., and P. P. Cohen. 1968. Biosynthesis of urea in the estivating African lungfish and in *Xenopus laevis* under conditions of water-shortage. *Comparative Biochemistry and Physiology* 24:887–898. (10)

Janssens, P. A., and F. Maher. 1986. Glucagon and insulin regulate *in vitro* hepatic glycogenolysis in the axolotl *Ambystoma mexicanum* via changes in tissue cyclic AMP concentration. *General and Comparative Endocrinology* 61:64–70. (3)

Janzen, D. H. 1967. Why mountain passes are higher in the tropics. *American Naturalist* 101:233–249. (8)

Jard, S., and F. Morel. 1963. Actions of vasotocin and some of its analogues on salt and water excretion by the frog. *American Journal of Physiology* 204:222–226. (5)

Jaslow, A. P., T. E. Hetherington, and R. E. Lombard. 1988. Structure and function of the amphibian middle ear. In *The Evolution of the Amphibian Auditory System,* ed. B. Fritzsch, M. J. Ryan, W. Wilczynski, T. E. Hetherington, and W. Walkowiak, 69–91. New York: John Wiley and Sons. (2)

Jastrzebski, M. 1968. Morphological changes in the reproductive organs of the female marsh frog (*Rana arvalis* Nilss.) in the yearly cycle. *Acta Biologica Cracoviensia* (Zoology) 11:9–19. (15)

Jayne, B. C., A. F. Bennett, and G. V. Lauder. 1988. Effects of temperature on muscle activity during lizard locomotion. *American Zoologist* 28:15A. (8)

————. 1990. Muscle recruitment during terrestrial locomotion: How speed and temperature affect fibre type use in a lizard. *Journal of Experimental Biology* 152:101–128. (8)

Jégou, S., M. C. Tonon, P. Leroux, C. Delarue, R. Leboulenger, G. Pelletier, J. Cote, N. Ling, and H. Vaudry. 1983. Immunological

characterization of endorphins, adrenocorticotropin, and melanotropins in frog hypothalamus. *General and Comparative Endocrinology* 51:246–254. (3)

Jenks, B. G., G. J. M. Martens, H. P. M. van Helden, and A. P. van Overbeeke. 1985. Biosynthesis and release of melanotropins and related peptides by the pars intermedia in *Xenopus laevis.* In *Current Trends in Comparative Endocrinology,* ed. B. Lofts and W. N. Holmes, 149–153. Hong Kong: Hong Kong University Press. (3)

Jensen, D. W. 1972. The effect of temperature on transmission at the neuro-muscular junction of the sartorius muscle of *Rana pipiens. Comparative Biochemistry and Physiology* 41A:685–695. (8)

Jensen, T. F., and I. Holm-Jensen. 1980. Energetic cost of running in workers of three ant species *Formica fusca* L., *Formica rufa* L., and *Camponotus herculaneaus* L. (Hymenoptera, Formicidae). *Journal of Comparative Physiology* 137:151–156. (12)

Jenssen, T. A. 1972. Seasonal organ weights of the green frog, *Rana clamitans* (Anura, Ranidae), under natural conditions. *Transactions of the Illinois State Academy of Science* 65:15–24. (14)

Jenssen, T. A., and W. D. Klimstra. 1966. Food habits of the green frog, *Rana clamitans,* in southern Illinois. *American Midland Naturalist* 76:169–182. (14)

Jia, X. 1992. Chemoreceptor modulation of gill ventilation in the larval bullfrog *Rana catesbeiana.* Ph.d. diss., University of Massachusetts, Amherst. (16)

Jobling, M. 1981. Temperature tolerance and the final preferendum: Rapid methods for the assessment of optimum growth temperatures. *Journal of Fish Biology* 19:439–455. (9)

Joel, A. 1919. Über den Einfluss der Temperatur auf den Sauerstoffverbrauch wechselwarmer Tiere. *Hoppe-Seyler's Zeitschrift für physiologische Chemie* 107:231–263. (12)

Johansen, K. 1963. Cardiovascular dynamics in the amphibian, *Amphiuma tridactylum* Cuvier. *Acta Physiologica Scandinavica* 60, suppl. 217:1–82. (5,7)

————. 1985. A phylogenetic overview of cardiovascular shunts. In *Cardiovascular Shunts: Phylogenetic, Ontogenetic, and Clinical Aspects,* ed. K. Johansen and W. W. Burggren, 17–32. Copenhagen: Munksgaard. (5)

Johansen, K., and W. W. Burggren, eds. 1985. *Cardiovascular Shunts: Phylogenetic, Ontogenetic, and Clinical Aspects.* Copenhagen: Munksgaard. (1)

Johansen, K., and A. S. F. Ditadi. 1966. Double circulation in the giant toad, *Bufo paracnemis. Physiological Zoology* 39:140–150. (5)

Johansen, K., and C. Lenfant. 1972. A comparative approach to the adaptability of O_2-Hb affinity. In *Oxygen Affinity and Red Cell Acid-Base Status,* Proceedings of Alfred Benzon Symposium 4, ed. M. Rørth and P. Astrup, 750–780. Copenhagen: Munksgaard. (5,16)

Johansen, K., C. Lenfant, and D. Hanson. 1970. Phylogenetic development of pulmonary circulation. *Federation Proceedings* 29:1135–1140. (5)

Johansen, K., G. Lykkeboe, S. Kornerup, and G. M. O. Maloiy. 1980. Temperature insensitive O_2 binding in blood of the tree frog *Chiromantis petersi. Journal of Comparative Physiology* 136B:71–76. (5,12)

Johansen, K., and R. E. Weber. 1976. On the adaptability of haemoglobin function to environmental conditions. In *Perspectives in Experimental Biology,* vol. 1, *Zoology and Botany,* ed. P. Spencer-Davis and N. Sunderland, 219–234. New York: Pergamon. (6)

John-Alder, H. B., M. C. Barnhart, and A. F. Bennett. 1989. Thermal sensitivity of swimming performance and muscle contraction in northern and southern populations of tree frogs (*Hyla crucifer*). *Journal of Experimental Biology* 142:357–372. (8,9,11)

John-Alder, H. B., and A. F. Bennett. 1981. Thermal dependence of endurance and locomotory energetics in a lizard. *American Journal of Physiology* 241:R342–R349. (12)

————. 1987. Thermal adaptations of lizard muscle function. *Journal of Comparative Physiology* 157B:241–252. (8)

John-Alder, H. B., T. Garland, and A. F. Bennett. 1986. Locomotory capacities, oxygen consumption, and the cost of locomotion of the shingle-back lizard (*Trachydosaurus rugosus*). *Physiological Zoology* 59:523–531. (12)

John-Alder, H. B., P. J. Morin, and S. Lawler. 1988. Thermal physiology, phenology, and distribution of treefrogs. *American Naturalist* 132:506–520. (8)

Johnson, B. K., and J. L. Christiansen. 1976. The food and food habits of Blanchard's cricket frog *Acris crepitans blanchardi* (Amphibia, Anura, Hylidae), in Iowa. *Journal of Herpetology* 10:63–74. (13)

Johnson, C. R. 1971a. Thermal relations and water balance in the day frog, *Taudactylus diurnus,* from an Australian rain forest. *Australian Journal of Zoology* 19:35–39. (9)

————. 1971b. Thermal relations in some southern and eastern Australian anurans. *Proceedings of the Royal Society of Queensland* 82: 87–94. (9)

————. 1972. Thermal relations and daily variation in the thermal tolerance in *Bufo marinus. Journal of Herpetology* 6:35–38. (9)

Johnson, C. R., and C. B. Schreck. 1969. Food and feeding of larval *Dicamptodon ensatus* from California. *American Midland Naturalist* 81:280–281. (16)

Johnson, T. R. 1987. *The Amphibians and Reptiles of Missouri.* Jefferson City: Missouri Department of Conservation. (10)

Johnston, C. E., J. O. Davis, F. S. Wright, and S. S. Howards. 1967. Effects of renin and ACTH on adrenal steroid secretion in the American bullfrog. *American Journal of Physiology* 213:393–399. (3,16)

Johnston, I. A. 1987. Respiratory characteristics of muscle fibres in a fish (*Chaenocephalus aceratus*) that lacks haem pigments. *Journal of Experimental Biology* 133:415–428. (14)

Johnston, I. A., B. D. Sidell, and W. R. Driedzic. 1985. Force-velocity characteristics and metabolism of carp muscle fibers following temperature acclimation. *Journal of Experimental Biology* 119:239–249. (8)

Jokumsen, A., and R. E. Weber. 1980. Haemoglobin-oxygen binding properties in the blood of *Xenopus laevis,* with special reference to the influences of aestivation and of temperature and salinity acclimation. *Journal of Experimental Biology* 86:19–37. (5,10)

Jokura, Y., and A. Urano. 1985. An immunohistochemical study of seasonal changes in luteinizing hormone-releasing hormone and vasotocin in the forebrain and neurohypophysis of the toad, *Bufo japonicus. General and Comparative Endocrinology* 59:238–245. (3)

————. 1986. Extrahypothalamic projection of luteinizing hormone-releasing hormone fibers in the brain of the toad, *Bufo japonicus. General and Comparative Endocrinology* 62:80–88. (15)

Jolivet-Jaudet, G., and J. Leloup-Hatey. 1984. Variations in aldosterone and corticosterone plasma levels during metamorphosis in *Xenopus laevis* tadpoles. *General and Comparative Endocrinology* 56:59–65. (16)

————. 1986. Corticosteroid binding in plasma of *Xenopus laevis:* Modifications during metamorphosis and growth. *Journal of Steroid Biochemistry* 25:343–350. (16)

Jones, D. R. 1967. Oxygen consumption and heart rate of several species of anuran Amphibia during submergence. *Comparative Biochemistry and Physiology* 20:691–707. (12)

————. 1970. Experiments on amphibian respiratory and circulatory systems. *Experiments in Physiology and Biochemistry* 3:233–293. (7)

————. 1972a. Anaerobiosis and the oxygen debt in an anuran amphibian, *Rana esculenta* (L.). *Journal of Comparative Physiology* 77: 356–382. (5,7,12)

————. 1972b. The effect of thermal acclimation on heart rate and oxygen consumption of frogs during submergence. *Comparative Biochemistry and Physiology* 41A:97–104. (12)

————. 1983. Ontogeny and phylogeny of the oxygen response. *Proceedings of the Physiological Society of New Zealand* 3:79–81. (7)

Jones, D. R., and C. Chu. 1988. Effect of denervation of carotid labyrinths on breathing in unrestrained *Xenopus laevis. Respiration Physiology* 73:243–256. (7)

Jones, D. R., and W. K. Milsom. 1982. Peripheral receptors affecting breathing and cardiovascular function in non-mammalian vertebrates. *Journal of Experimental Biology* 100:59–91. (6,7,16)

————. 1986. Control of breathing in ectothermic vertebrates. In *Handbook of Physiology,* ed. A. P. Fishman, N. S. Cherniak, J. G. Widdecombe, and S. R. Geiger, 2:857–909. Bethesda MD: American Physiological Society. (7)

Jones, D. R., and T. Mustafa. 1973. The lactacid oxygen debt in frogs after one hour's apnoea in air. *Journal of Comparative Physiology* 85:15–24. (12)

Jones, D. R., and G. Shelton. 1964. Factors influencing heart rate and submergence in the frog. *Journal of Experimental Biology* 41:417–431. (7)

Jones, E. I. 1933. Observations on the pectoral muscles of Amphibia Salientia. *Annals and Magazine of Natural History,* series 10, 12: 403–420. (11)

Jones, K. L. 1982. Prey patterns and trophic niche overlap in four species of Caribbean frogs. In *Herpetological Communities,* ed. N. J. Scott, 49–55. Fish and Wildlife Service Report 13. Washington, DC: United States Department of the Interior.

Jones, P. L., and B. D. Sidell. 1982. Metabolic responses of striped bass *Morone saxatilis* to temperature acclimation: Alterations in metabolic carbon sources and distributions of fiber types in locomotory muscle. *Journal of Experimental Zoology* 219:163–171. (8)

Jones, R. L. 1986. Reproductive biology of *Desmognathus fuscus* and *Desmognathus santeetlah* in Unicoi Mountains. *Herpetologica* 42: 323–334. (15)

Jones, R. M. 1978. Rapid pelvic water uptake in *Scaphiopus couchi* toadlets. *Physiological Zoology* 51:51–55. (5)

————. 1980a. Metabolic consequences of accelerated urea synthesis during seasonal dormancy of spadefoot toads, *Scaphiopus couchi* and *Scaphiopus multiplicatus. Journal of Experimental Zoology* 212: 255–267. (6,10,12,15)

————. 1980b. Nitrogen excretion by *Scaphiopus* tadpoles in ephemeral ponds. *Physiological Zoology* 53:26–31. (6)

————. 1982. How toads breathe: Control of air flow to and from the lungs by the nares in *Bufo marinus. Respiration Physiology* 49:251–265. (5,6,7,10)

Jones, R. M., and S. S. Hillman. 1978. Salinity adaptation in the salamander *Batrachoseps. Journal of Experimental Biology* 76:1–10. (6)

Jordan, H. E. 1938. Comparative hematology. In *Handbook of Hematology,* ed. H. Downey, 699–862. London: Hamish Hamilton. (5)

Jørgensen, B. B., and N. P. Revsbech. 1985. Diffusive boundary layers and the oxygen uptake of sediments and detritus. *Limnology and Oceanography* 30:111–122. (10)

Jørgensen, C. B. 1950. Osmotic regulation in the frog, *Rana esculenta,* at low temperatures. *Acta Physiologica Scandinavica* 20:46–55. (10)

————. 1967. Influence of nutritional state on oocyte growth in the toad ovary. *General and Comparative Endocrinology* 9:462. (15)

————. 1968. Gonadotropic function of the autotransplanted pituitary gland in the female toad *Bufo bufo* (L.). *Archives d'Anatomie, d'Histologie, et d'Embryologie Normales et Expérimentales* 51:357–361. (15)

————. 1970. Hypothalamic control of hypophyseal function in anurans. In *The Hypothalamus,* ed. L. Martini, M. Motta, and F. Fraschini, 649–661. New York: Academic Press. (15)

————. 1973a. Mechanisms regulating ovarian function in amphibians (toads). In *The Development and Maturation of the Ovary and Its Functions,* ed. H. Peters, 133–151. Amsterdam: Excerpta Medica. (15)

————. 1973b. Pattern of recruitment of oocytes to second growth phase in normal toads, and in hypophysectomized toads, *Bufo bufo bufo* (L.), treated with gonadotropin (hCG). *General and Comparative Endocrinology* 21:152–159. (15)

————. 1974a. Integrative functions of the brain. In *Physiology of Amphibia,* ed. B. Lofts, 2:1–51. New York: Academic Press. (2,13,15)

————. 1974b. Mechanisms regulating ovarian cycle in the toad *Bufo bufo bufo* (L.): Role of presence of second growth phase oocytes in controlling recruitment from pool of first growth phase oocytes. *General and Comparative Endocrinology* 23:170–177. (15)

————. 1975. Factors controlling the annual ovarian cycle in the toad *Bufo bufo bufo* (L.). *General and Comparative Endocrinology* 25: 264–273. (15)

————. 1981. Ovarian cycle in a temperate zone frog, *Rana temporaria,* with special reference to factors determining number and size of eggs. *Journal of Zoology* (London) 195:449–458. (15)

————. 1982. Factors controlling the ovarian cycle in a temperate zone anuran, the toad *Bufo bufo:* Food uptake, nutritional state, and gonadotropin. *Journal of Experimental Zoology* 224:437–443. (15)

————. 1983. Pattern of growth in a temperate zone anuran (*Bufo viridis* Laur.). *Journal of Experimental Zoology* 227:433–439. (15)

————. 1984a. Dynamics of oogenesis in a lower vertebrate, the toad *Bufo bufo. Acta Zoologica* (Stockholm) 65:179–185. (15)

————. 1984b. Ovarian functional patterns in Baltic and Mediterranean populations of a temperate zone anuran, the toad *Bufo viridis. Oikos* 43:309–321. (15)

————. 1984c. Relations between hibernation and ovarian functions in a temperate zone frog, *Rana temporaria. Acta Zoologica* (Stockholm) 65:239–247. (10,15)

————. 1984d. Testis function in the toad *Bufo bufo* (L.) (Amphibia,

Anura) at organ and subunit levels. *Videnskabelige Meddelelser fra Dansk Naturhistorisk Forening* 145:117–130. (15)

———. 1986a. Effect of fat body excision in female *Bufo bufo* on the ipsilateral ovary, with a discussion of fat body–gonad relationships. *Acta Zoologica* (Stockholm) 67:5–10. (15)

———. 1986b. External and internal control of patterns of feeding, growth, and gonadal function of a temperate zone anuran, the toad *Bufo bufo. Journal of Zoology* (London) 210A:211–241. (10,13,15)

———. 1988a. Nature of moulting control in amphibian: Effects of cortisol implants in toads *Bufo bufo. General and Comparative Endocrinology* 71:29–35. (3)

———. 1988b. The role of endogenous factors in seasonal maturation in temperate zone female toads, *Bufo bufo. Journal of Herpetology* 22:295–300. (10,15)

———. 1989. Pattern of growth and fattening in young toads *Bufo bufo* fed mealworms: Effects of growth hormone and feeding regimen. *Copeia* 1989:124–128. (10,13,15)

Jørgensen, C. B., and E. Billeter. 1982. Growth, differentiation, and function of the testes in the toad *Bufo bufo bufo* (L.), with special reference to regulatory capacities: Effects of unilateral castration, hypophysectomy, and excision of Bidder's organs. *Journal of Experimental Zoology* 221:225–236. (15)

Jørgensen, C. B., E. Billeter, and K. Poulsen. 1979. Effects of unilateral ovariectomy on growth of oocytes in the ovaries of adult toads (*Bufo bufo bufo* L.). *Biology of Reproduction* 20:346–354. (15)

Jørgensen, C. B., K. Brems, and P. Geckler. 1978. Volume and osmotic regulation in the toad *Bufo bufo bufo* (L.) at low temperature, with special reference to amphibian hibernation. In *Osmotic and Volume Regulation*, ed. C. B. Jørgensen and E. Skadhauge, 62–75. Proceedings of Alfred Benzon Symposium 9. Copenhagen: Munksgaard. (10)

Jørgensen, C. B., K.-E. Hede, and L. O. Larsen. 1978. Environmental control of annual ovarian cycle in the toad *Bufo bufo bufo* L.: Role of temperature. In *Environmental Endocrinology*, ed. I. Assenmacher and D. S. Farner, 28–36. Berlin: Springer-Verlag. (10,15)

Jørgensen, C. B., and L. O. Larsen. 1961. Molting and its hormonal control in toads. *General and Comparative Endocrinology* 1:145–153. (3)

———. 1964. Further observations on molting and its hormonal control in *Bufo bufo* (L.). *General and Comparative Endocrinology* 4:389–400. (3)

Jørgensen, C. B., L. O. Larsen, and B. Lofts. 1979. Annual cycles of fat bodies and gonads in the toad *Bufo bufo bufo* (L.), compared with cycles in other temperate zone anurans. *Det Kongelige Danske Videnskabernes Selskab Biologiske Skrifter* 22.1–37. (15)

Jørgensen, C. B., L. O. Larsen, and P. Rosenkilde. 1965. Hormonal dependency of molting in amphibians: Effect of radiothyroidectomy in the toad *Bufo bufo* (L.). *General and Comparative Endocrinology* 5:248–251. (3)

Jørgensen, C. B., H. Levi, and H. H. Ussing. 1947. On the influence of the neurohypophyseal principles on the sodium metabolism in the axolotl (*Ambystoma mexicanum*). *Acta Physiologica Scandinavica* 12:350–371. (5)

Jørgensen, C. B., H. Levi, and K. Zerahn. 1954. On active uptake of sodium and chloride ions in anurans. *Acta Physiologica Scandinavica* 30:178–190. (5)

Jørgensen, C. B., and P. Rosenkilde. 1956. Relative effectiveness of dehydration and neurohypophysial extracts in enhancing water absorption in toads and frogs. *Biological Bulletin* 110:306–309. (6)

Jørgensen, C. B., P. Rosenkilde, and K. G. Wingstrand. 1969. Role of the preoptic-neurohypophysial system in the water economy of the toad *Bufo bufo* (L.). *General and Comparative Endocrinology* 12:91–98. (6)

Jørgensen, C. B., K. Shakuntala, and S. Vijayakumar. 1986. Body size, reproduction, and growth in a tropical toad, *Bufo melanostictus,* with a comparison of ovarian cycles in tropical and temperate zone anurans. *Oikos* 46:379–389. (15)

Jørgensen, C. B., and H. Wind-Larsen. 1987a. Allocation of matter in the body of growing toads, *Bufo bufo:* Components of "condition." *Acta Zoologica* (Stockholm) 68:57–64. (15)

———. 1987b. Energetics of growth in a temperate zone toad *Bufo bufo:* Effects of growth hormone. *Acta Zoologica* (Stockholm) 68:107–113. (13)

Jørgensen, C. B., K. G. Wingstrand, and P. Rosenkilde. 1956. Neurohypophysis and water metabolism in the toad *Bufo bufo* (L.). *Endocrinology* 59:601–610. (6)

Josephson, R. K. 1973. Contraction kinetics of fast muscles used in singing by a katydid. *Journal of Experimental Biology* 59:781–801. (14)

Jouffroy, F. In press. Appendicular muscle. In *Traité de Zoologie,* ed. P.-P. Grassé. Paris: Masson. (11)

Juacaba, S. F., R. G. McKinnell, W. H. Hanson, and D. Tarin. 1987. Vascular dissemination of tumour cells in relation to temperature-dependent metastasis in frogs. *Journal of the National Cancer Institute* 78:259–264. (8)

Jungreis, A. M. 1970. The effects of long-term starvation and acclimation temperature on glucose regulation and nitrogen anabolism in the frog, *R. pipiens:* 2. Summer animals. *Comparative Biochemistry and Physiology* 32:433–444. (10)

Jungreis, A. M., and A. B. Hooper. 1970. The effects of long-term starvation and acclimation temperature on glucose regulation and nitrogen anabolism in the frog, *R. pipiens:* 1. Winter animals. *Comparative Biochemistry and Physiology* 32:417–432. (10)

Jungreis, A. M., and J. W. Johnston. 1979. Urea production in *Rana pipiens:* Effect of dehydration and aldosterone administration. *Comparative Biochemistry and Physiology* 64A:59–66. (3)

Jusiak, R. 1970. The metabolic rate of the intact frog (*Rana esculenta* L.) and its isolated tissues at different ambient temperatures. *Bulletin de l'Académie Polonaise des Sciences Série des Sciences Biologiques* 18:493–496. (12)

Jusiak, R., and P. Poczopko. 1972. A comparison of the effect of temperature on metabolic rate of tissue slices of the mouse and the frog. *Bulletin de l'Académie Polonaise des Sciences Série des Sciences Biologiques* 20:523–529. (12)

Just, J. J. 1967. The plasma protein-bound iodine (PBI) concentration of *Rana pipiens* larvae. *American Zoologist* 7:719. (16)

———. 1968. Thyroid hormone and protein concentration in plasma and pericardial fluid of metamorphosing anuran tadpoles. Ph.D. diss., University of Iowa, Iowa City. (16)

———. 1972. Protein-bound iodine and protein concentration in plasma and pericardial fluid of metamorphosing anuran tadpoles. *Physiological Zoology* 45:143–152. (16)

Just, J. J., R. N. Gatz, and E. C. Crawford. 1973. Changes in respiratory functions during metamorphosis of the bullfrog, *Rana catesbeiana. Respiration Physiology* 17:276–282. (6,16)

Just, J. J., and L. Hayati. 1990. Water ingestion rates during metamorphosis of bullfrog tadpoles, *Rana catesbeiana.* Unpublished manuscript. (16)

Just, J. J., and J. J. Kollros. 1968. Effects of hypophysectomy, thyroxine, and pituitary hormones on growth of *Rana pipiens* larvae. *American Zoologist* 8:762. (16)

Just, J. J., J. Kraus-Just, and D. A. Check. 1981. Survey of chordate metamorphosis. In *Metamorphosis: A Problem in Developmental Biology,* 2d ed., ed. L. I. Gilbert and E. Frieden, 265–326. New York: Plenum Press. (16)

Just, J. J., J. Schwager, and R. Weber. 1977. Hemoglobin transition in relation to metamorphosis in normal and isogenic *Xenopus. Wilhelm Roux's Archives of Developmental Biology* 183:307–323. (16)

Just, J. J., J. Schwager, R. Weber, H. Fey, and H. Pfister. 1980. Immunological analysis of hemoglobin transition during metamorphosis of normal and isogenic *Xenopus. Wilhelm Roux's Archives of Developmental Biology* 188:75–80. (16)

Just, J. J., and R. Sperka. 1977. The effects of whole body radiation on survival and erythropoiesis of *Rana catesbeiana* tadpoles. *Radiation Research* 69:258–266. (16)

Just, J. J., R. Sperka, and S. Strange. 1977. A quantitative analysis of plasma osmotic pressure during metamorphosis of bullfrog, *Rana catesbeiana. Experientia* 33:1503–1504. (16)

Justis, C. S., and D. H. Taylor. 1976. Extraocular photoreception and compass orientation in larval bullfrogs, *Rana catesbeiana. Copeia* 1976:98–105. (9)

Justus, J. T. 1978. The cardiac mutant: An overview. *American Zoologist* 18:321–326. (16)

Juszczyk, W., K. Obrzut, and W. Zamachowski. 1966. Morphological changes in the alimentary canal of the common frog (*Rana temporaria* L.) in the annual cycle. *Acta Biologica Cracoviensia* (Zoology) 9:239–246. (13,15)

Juszczyk, W., and W. Zamachowski. 1965. Terms of ovulation and oviposition of the grass frog (*Rana temporaria* L.) under conditions of an artificial and prolonged hibernation. *Acta Biologica Cracoviensia* (Zoology) 8:211–223. (15)

———. 1973. Morphological changes in the reproductive organs of the female edible frog (*Rana esculenta* L.) in the annual cycle. *Acta Biologica Cracoviensia* (Zoology) 16:167–178. (15)

Juterbock, J. E. 1987. The nesting behavior of the dusky salamander, *Desmognathus fuscus*: 2. Nest site tenacity and disturbance. *Herpetologica* 43:361–368. (14)

Kaess, W., and F. Kaess. 1960. Perception of apparent motion in the common toad. *Science* 132:953. (13)

Kalt, M. R. 1976. Morphology and kinetics of spermatogenesis in *Xenopus laevis*. *Journal of Experimental Zoology* 195:393–408. (15)

Kaltenbach, J. C. 1953. Local action of thyroxine in amphibian metamorphoses: 1. Local metamorphosis in *Rana pipiens* larvae effected by thyroxine-cholesterol implants. *Journal of Experimental Zoology* 122:21–39. (16)

———. 1968. Nature of hormone action in amphibian metamorphosis. In *Metamorphosis: A Problem in Developmental Biology*, ed. W. Etkin and L. I. Gilbert, 399–441. New York: Appleton-Century-Crofts. (16)

———. 1985. Amphibian metamorphosis: Influence of thyroid and steroid hormones. In *Current Trends in Comparative Endocrinology*, ed. B. Lofts and W. N. Holmes, 533–534. Hong Kong: Hong Kong University Press. (16)

Kaltenbach, J. C., and H. H. Hagedorn. 1981. Effects of nutrition on metamorphosis. In *CRC Handbook of Nutritional Requirements in a Functional Context*, vol. 1, *Development and Conditions of Physiologic Stress*, ed. M. Rechcigl, 81–96. Boca Raton, FL: CRC Press. (13,16)

Kaltenbach, J. C., M. J. Lipson, and C. H. K. Wang. 1977. Histochemical study of the amphibian digestive tract during normal and thyroxine-induced metamorphosis: 1. Alkaline phosphatase. *Journal of Experimental Zoology* 202:103–120. (16)

Kaltenbach, J. C., C. H. K. Wang, and M. J. Lipson. 1981. Histochemical study of the amphibian digestive tract during normal and thyroxine-induced metamorphosis: 2. Acid phosphatase. *Journal of Experimental Zoology* 216:247–259. (16)

Kamel, S., J. E. Marsden, and F. H. Pough. 1985. Diploid and tetraploid grey treefrogs (*Hyla chrysoscelis* and *Hyla versicolor*) have similar metabolic rates. *Comparative Biochemistry and Physiology* 82A: 217–220. (12)

Kanamadi, R. D., and S. K. Saidapur. 1982. Pattern of ovarian activity in the Indian toad *Bufo melanostictus* (Schn.). *Proceedings of the Indian Natural Science Academy* B48:307–316. (15)

Kanamadi, R. D., S. K. Saidapur, and V. B. Nadkarni. 1983. Pattern of testicular activity in the toad, *Bufo melanostictus*. *Biological Bulletin, India* 5:10–19. (15)

Kapfberger, D. 1984. Untersuchungen zu Populationsaufbau, Wachstum, und Ortsbeziehungen der Gelbauchunke, *Bombina variegata variegata* (Linnaeus, 1758). *Zoologischer Anzeiger* 212:105–116. (15)

Kaplan, R. H. 1980. Ontogenetic energetics in *Ambystoma*. *Physiological Zoology* 53:43–56. (12,15)

———. 1987. Developmental plasticity and maternal effects of reproductive characteristics in the frog, *Bombina orientalis*. *Oecologia* (Berlin) 71:273–279. (15)

Kaplan, R. H., and S. N. Salthe. 1979. The allometry of reproduction: An empirical view in salamanders. *American Naturalist* 113:671–689. (15)

Karasov, W. H. 1981. Daily energy expenditure and the cost of activity in free-living mammals. *Oecologia* (Berlin) 51:253–259. (14)

Karlstrom, E. L. 1962. The toad genus *Bufo* in the Sierra Nevada of California. *University of California Publications in Zoology* 61: 1–104. (9)

Karnovsky, M. J., and L. Roots. 1964. A "direct-coloring" thiocholine method for cholinesterases. *Journal of Histochemistry and Cytochemistry* 12:219–221. (11)

Karpatkin, S., E. Helmreich, and C. F. Cori. 1964. Regulation of glycolysis in muscle: 2. Effect of stimulation and epinephrine in isolated frog sartorius muscle. *Journal of Biological Chemistry* 239:3139–3145. (12)

Kasbohm, P. 1967. Der Einfluss des Lichtes auf die Temperaturadaptation bei *Rana temporaria*. *Helgolander wissenschaftliche Meeresuntersuchungen* 16:157–178. (12)

Kasinathan, S., A. G. Singh, and S. L. Basu. 1978. Fatbodies and spermatogenesis in South Indian green frog *Rana hexadactyla* Lesson. *Bolletino di Zoologica* 45:15–22. (15)

Kats, L. B. 1988. The detection of certain predators via olfaction by

small-mouth salamander larvae *Ambystoma texanum*. *Behavioral and Neural Biology* 50:126–131. (16)

Kats, L. B., J. W. Petranka, and A. Sih. 1988. Antipredator defenses and the persistence of amphibian larvae with fishes. *Ecology* 69: 1865–1870. (16)

Katte, O., and K. P. Hoffman. 1980. Direction-specific neurons in the pretectum of the frog (*Rana esculenta*). *Journal of Comparative Physiology* 140:53–57. (2)

Katz, B. 1949. The efferent regulation of the muscle spindle of the frog. *Journal of Experimental Biology* 26:201–217. (11)

———. 1961. The terminations of the afferent nerve fibres in the muscle spindle of the frog. *Philosophical Transactions of the Royal Society* 243B:221–240. (11)

Katz, U. 1973a. Sodium transport across toad epithelia: Different responses of skin and urinary bladder to salinity adaptation. *Pflugers Archir* 343:185–188. (6)

———. 1973b. Studies on the adaptation of the toad *Bufo viridis* to high salinities: Oxygen consumption, plasma concentration, and water content of the tissues. *Journal of Experimental Biology* 58:785–796. (6,12)

———. 1975a. NaCl adaptation in *Rana ridibunda* and a comparison with the euryhaline toad *Bufo viridis*. *Journal of Experimental Biology* 63:763–773. (12,16)

———. 1975b. Salt induced changes in sodium transport across the skin of the euryhaline toad *Bufo viridis*. *Journal of Physiology* (London) 247:537–550. (6)

———. 1978. Ionic and volume regulation in selected tissues of the euryhaline toad *Bufo viridis*. In *Osmotic and Volume Regulation*, ed. C. B. Jørgensen and E. Skadhauge, 457–469. Copenhagen: Munksgaard. (6)

———. 1981. The effect of salt adaptation and amiloride on the *in vivo* acid-base status of the euryhaline toad *Bufo viridis*. *Journal of Experimental Biology* 93:93–99. (5)

———. 1986. The role of amphibian epidermis in osmoregulation and its adaptive response to changing environment. In *Biology of the Integument*, vol. 2, *Vertebrates*, ed. J. Bereiter-Hahn, A. G. Matoltsy, and K. S. Richards, 472–498. Berlin: Springer-Verlag. (5)

———. 1989. Strategies of adaptation to osmotic stress in anuran Amphibia under salt and burrowing conditions. *Comparative Biochemistry and Physiology* 93A:499–503. (6)

Katz, U., G. Degani, and S. Gabbay. 1984. Acclimation of the euryhaline toad *Bufo viridis* to hyperosmotic solution (NaCl, urea, and mannitol). *Journal of Experimental Biology* 108:403–409. (6)

Katz, U., and S. Gabbay. 1986. Water retention and plasma and urine composition in toads (*Bufo viridis* Laur.) under burrowing conditions. *Journal of Comparative Physiology* 156B:735–740. (6,10)

Katz, U., and R. Graham. 1980. Water relations in the toad (*Bufo viridis*) and a comparison with the frog (*Rana ridibunda*). *Comparative Biochemistry and Physiology* 67A:245–251. (5)

Katz, U., W. Van Driessche, and C. Scheffey. 1985. The role of mitochondria-rich cells in the chloride current conductance across toad skins. *Biology of the Cell* 55:245–249. (5)

Kaul, R., and V. H. Shoemaker. 1989. Control of thermoregulatory evaporation in the waterproof treefrog *Chiromantis xerampelina*. *Journal of Comparative Physiology* 158B:643–649. (4,6,9)

Kaung, H. C. 1981. Immunocytochemical localization of pancreatic endocrine cells in frog embryos and young larvae. *General and Comparative Endocrinology* 45:204–211. (16)

———. 1983. Changes of pancreatic beta cell population during larval development of *Rana pipiens*. *General and Comparative Endocrinology* 49:50–56. (16)

Kavanagh, M. W. 1987. The efficiency of sound production in two cricket species, *Gryllotalpa australis* and *Teleogryllus commodus* (Orthoptera: Grylloidea). *Journal of Experimental Biology* 130:107–119. (14)

Kawada, J., R. E. Taylor, and S. B. Barker. 1969. Measurement of Na-K-ATPase in the separated epidermis of *Rana catesbeiana* frogs and tadpoles. *Comparative Biochemistry and Physiology* 30:963–975. (12)

Kawahara, A., S. Kohara, Y. Sugimoto, and M. Amano. 1987. A change of the hepatocyte population is responsible for the progressive increase of vitellogenin synthetic capacity at and after metamorphosis of *Xenopus laevis*. *Developmental Biology* 122:139–145. (16)

Kawamura, K., K. Yamamoto, and S. Kikuyama. 1986. Effects of thyroid hormone, stalk section, and transplantation of the pituitary gland on plasma prolactin levels at metamorphic climax in *Rana catesbeiana*. *General and Comparative Endocrinology* 64:129–135. (16)

Kayama, T. 1985. Shear rate and orientation of erythrocytes in pulmonary microvessels of bullfrogs. *Biorheology* 22:379–384. (5)

Kaye, N. W. 1961. Interrelationships of the thyroid and pituitary in embryonic and premetamorphic stages of the frog *Rana pipiens*. *General and Comparative Endocrinology* 1:1–19. (16)

Kayser, C. 1940. Le quotient respiratoire chez quelques espèces poikilothermes. *Annales de Physiologie et de Physicochimie Biologiques* 16:1–68. (12)

Kayser, C., and J.-P. Schieber. 1969. Le rythme nychthéméral de la consommation d'oxygène chez la grenouille (*Rana esculenta*). *Archives des Sciences Physiologiques* 23:365–382. (12)

Keddy-Hector, A. C., W. Wilczynski, and M. J. Ryan. 1989. Intraspecific variation in the tuning of female cricketfrogs. *American Zoologist* 29:16A. (2)

Keen, W. H. 1979. Feeding and activity patterns in the salamander *Desmognathus ochrophaeus* (Amphibia, Urodela, Plethodontidae). *Journal of Herpetology* 13:461–467. (4,6)

———. 1982. Habitat selection and interspecific competition in two species of plethodontid salamanders. *Ecology* 63:94–102. (4,14)

———. 1984. Influence of moisture on the activity of a plethodontid salamander. *Copeia* 1984:684–688. (12,14)

Keen, W. H., M. G. McManus, and M. Wohltman. 1987. Cover site recognition and sex differences in cover site use by the salamander, *Desmognathus fuscus*. *Journal of Herpetology* 21:363–365. (14)

Keen, W. H., and L. P. Orr. 1980. Reproductive cycle, growth, and maturation of northern female *Desmognathus ochrophaeus*. *Journal of Herpetology* 14:7–10. (15)

Keen, W. H., and R. W. Reed. 1985. Territorial defense of escape and feeding sites by a plethodontid salamander. *Animal Behaviour* 33:1119–1123. (14)

Keen, W. H., and E. E. Schroeder. 1975. Temperature selection and tolerance in three species of *Ambystoma* larvae. *Copeia* 1975:523–530. (8,9)

Keen, W. H., J. Travis, and J. Julianna. 1984. Larval growth in three sympatric *Ambystoma* salamander species: Species differences and the effects of temperature. *Canadian Journal of Zoology* 62:1043–1047. (8)

Keith, R. 1968. A new species of *Bufo* from Africa, with comments on the toads of the *Bufo regularis* complex. *American Museum Novitates* 2345:1–22. (15)

Kelley, D. B. 1980. Auditory and vocal nuclei in the frog brain concentrate sex hormones. *Science* 207:553–555. (2)

———. 1981. Localization of androgen-concentrating cells in the brain of *Xenopus laevis*: Autoradiography with ³H-dihydrotestosterone. *Journal of Comparative Neurology* 199:221–231. (2)

———. 1986. Neuroeffectors for vocalization in *Xenopus laevis*: Hormonal regulation of sexual dimorphism. *Journal of Neurobiology* 17:231–248. (2,16)

Kelley, D. B., R. S. Bockman, and A. Weintraub. 1987. Prostaglandin regulation of reproductive behaviors in female *Xenopus laevis*: Sources and target sites. In *Advances in Prostaglandin, Thromboxane, and Leukotriene Research*, vol. 17B, ed. B. Samuelsson, 1133–1135. New York: Raven Press. (3)

Kelley, D. B., S. Fenstemaker, P. Hannigan, and S. Shih. 1988. Sex differences in the motor nucleus of cranial nerve IX–X in *Xenopus laevis*: A quantitative Golgi study. *Journal of Neurobiology* 19:413–429. (2)

Kellogg, R. L., and J. J. Gift. 1983. Relationship between optimum temperatures for growth and preferred temperatures for the young of four fish species. *Transactions of the American Fisheries Society* 112:424–430. (9)

Kelly, D. A., and K. B. Storey. 1988. Organ-specific control of glycolysis in the anoxic turtle. *American Journal of Physiology* 255:R774–R779. (10)

Kemali, M., and V. Guglielmotti. 1987. A horseradish peroxidase study of the olfactory system of the frog, *Rana esculenta*. *Journal of Comparative Neurology* 263:400–417. (2,16)

Kemp, N. E. 1954. Development of intestinal coiling in anuran larvae. *Journal of Experimental Zoology* 116:259–288. (16)

Kenney, J. S. 1969. Feeding mechanisms in anuran larvae. *Journal of Zoology* (London) 157:225–246. (16)

Kern, D. M. 1960. The hydration of carbon dioxide. *Journal of Chemical Education* 37:14–23. (5)

Kerr, T. 1966. The development of the pituitary in *Xenopus laevis* Daudin. *General and Comparative Endocrinology* 6:303–311. (16)

Kerstetter, T. H., and L. B. Kirschner. 1971. The role of the hypothalamo-neurohypophysial system in maintaining hydromineral balance in larval salamanders (*Ambystoma tigrinum*). *Comparative Biochemistry and Physiology* 40A:373–384. (5)

Kesteven, H. L. 1944. The evolution of the skull and cephalic muscles, a comparative study of their development and adult morphology: Part 2. The Amphibia. *Memoirs of the Australian Museum* 8:133–236. (11)

Keuper, A., S. Wiedemann, K. Kalmring, and D. Kaminski. 1988. Sound production and sound emission in seven species of European tettigoniids: Part 1. The different parameters of the song: Their relation to the morphology of the bushcricket. *Bioacoustics* 1:31–48. (14)

Khalsa, B. D. S., J. M. Goldinger, and S. K. Hong. 1984. Renal transport of various organic anions in *Necturus*. *Journal of Comparative Physiology* 154B:119–123. (5)

Khan, M. S. 1965. A normal table of *Bufo melanostictus* Schneider. *Biologica Lahore* 2:1–39. (16)

Kharlamova, O. M. 1976. Concentration function of the frog gallbladder at differing temperatures. *Fiziologicheskii Zhurnal SSRR* 22:823–825. (8)

Khuri, R. N., G. A. Goldstein, D. L. Maude, C. Edmonds, and A. K. Solomon. 1963. Single proximal tubules of *Necturus*: 8. Na and K determinations by glass electrodes. *American Journal of Physiology* 204:743–748. (5)

Khuri, R. N., J. J. Hajjar, S. A. Anulian, K. Bogharian, A. Kalloghlian, and H. Bizri. 1972. Intracellular potassium in cells of the proximal tubule of *Necturus maculosus*. *Pflugers Archiv* 338:73–80. (5)

Kicliter, E. 1979. Some telencephalic connections in the frog, *Rana pipiens*. *Journal of Comparative Neurology* 185:75–86. (2)

Kicliter, E., and S. O. E. Ebbesson. 1976. Organization of the "nonolfactory" telencephalon. In *Frog Neurobiology: A Handbook*, ed. R. Llinás and W. Precht, 946–972. Berlin: Springer-Verlag. (2)

Kicliter, E., C. J. Kay, and Y. M. Chino. 1981. Spectral opponency of on-type ganglion cells and the blue preference of *Rana pipiens*. *Brain Research* 210:103–113. (2)

Kiessling, A. 1964. Die Acetylcholinempfindlichkeit der Muskelfasern im Tonusbundel des *M. iliofibularis* des Frosches. *Archiv für die gesamte Physiologie* 280:189–192. (14)

Kikuyama, S., K. Niki, M. Mayumi, and K. Kawamura. 1982. Retardation of thyroxine-induced metamorphosis by amphenone B in toad tadpoles. *Endocrinology Japan* 29:659–662. (16)

Kikuyama, S., K. Niki, M. Mayumi, R. Shibayama, M. Nishikawa, and N. Shintake. 1983. Studies on corticoid action on the toad tadpole tail *in vitro*. *General and Comparative Endocrinology* 52:395–399. (16)

Kikuyama, S., M. R. Suzuki, and S. Iwamuro. 1986. Elevation of plasma aldosterone levels of tadpoles at metamorphic climax. *General and Comparative Endocrinology* 63:186–190. (16)

Kilarski, W., and J. Bigaj. 1969. Organisation and fine structure of extraocular muscles in *Carassius* and *Rana*. *Zeitschrift für Zellforschung und mikroskopische Anatomie* 94:194–204. (11)

Kimmel, C. B., E. Schabtach, and R. J. Kimmel. 1977. Developmental interactions in the growth and branching of the lateral dendrite of Mauthner cell (*Ambystoma mexicanum*). *Developmental Biology* 55:244–259. (16)

Kimmel, P. 1990. Ontogeny of cardiovascular control mechanisms in the bullfrog, *Rana catesbeiana*. Ph.D. diss., University of Massachusetts, Amherst. (16)

King, H. D. 1907. The spermatogenesis of *Bufo lentiginosus*. *American Journal of Anatomy* 7:345–387. (15)

King, J. A., and R. P. Millar. 1979. Hypothalamic luteinizing hormone-releasing hormone content in relation to the seasonal reproductive cycle of *Xenopus laevis*. *General and Comparative Endocrinology* 39:309–312. (7)

———. 1980. Comparative aspects of luteinizing hormone-releasing hormone structure and function in vertebrate phylogeny. *Endocrinology* 106:707–717. (3)

———. 1981. TRH, GH-RIH, and LH-RH in metamorphosing *Xenopus laevis*. *General and Comparative Endocrinology* 44:20–27. (16)

———. 1986. Identification of His[5], Try[7], Try[8]–GnRH (chicken GnRH II) in amphibian brain. *Peptides* 7:827–834. (16)

———. 1990. Genealogy of the GnRH family. In *Progress in Comparative Endocrinology,* ed. A. Epple, C. G. Scanes, and M. H. Stetson, 45–59. New York: Wiley-Liss. (3)

Kingsbury, B. F., and H. D. Reed. 1909. The columella auris in Amphibia: Second contribution. *Journal of Morphology* 20:549–628. (11)

Kingsbury, D. L., and J. C. Fenwick. 1989. The effect of eel calcitonin on calcium influx and plasma ion levels in axolotls, *Ambystoma mexicanum. General and Comparative Endocrinology* 75:135–138. (3,16)

Kingsley, J. S. 1902. The cranial nerves of *Amphiuma. Tufts College Studies* 7:293–321. (7)

Kinnamon, J. C. 1987. Organization and innervation of taste bud. In *Neurobiology of Taste and Smell,* ed. T. E. Finger and W. L. Silver, 277–297. New York: John Wiley and Sons. (16)

Kinter, W. B. 1959. Renal tubular transport of diodrast-I[131] and PAH in *Necturus:* Evidence for simultaneous reabsorption and secretion. *American Journal of Physiology* 196:1141–1149. (5)

Kirkpatrick, M. 1982. Sexual selection and the evolution of female choice. *Evolution* 36:1–12. (14)

———. 1987a. The evolutionary forces acting on female mating preferences in polygynous animals. In *Sexual Selection: Testing the Alternatives,* ed. J. W. Bradbury and M. B. Andersson, 67–82. New York: Wiley. (14)

———. 1987b. Sexual selection by female choice in polygynous animals. *Annual Review of Ecology and Systematics* 18:43–70. (14)

Kirschner, L. B. 1970. The study of NaCl transport in aquatic animals. *American Zoologist* 10:365–376. (5)

———. 1983. Sodium chloride absorption across the body surface: Frog skins and other epithelia. *American Journal of Physiology* 244:R429–R443. (5)

———. 1988. Basis for apparent saturation kinetics of Na[+] influx in freshwater hyperregulators. *American Journal of Physiology* 254:R984–R988. (5)

Kirschner, L. B., L. Greenwald, and T. H. Kerstetter. 1973. Effect of amiloride on sodium transport across surfaces of freshwater animals. *American Journal of Physiology* 224:832–837. (5)

Kirschner, L. B., T. H. Kerstetter, D. Porter, and R. H. Alvarado. 1971. Adaptation of larval *Ambystoma tigrinum* to concentrated environments. *American Journal of Physiology* 220:1814–1819. (5,6,16)

Kiseleva, E. I. 1984. Responses of behavioral reactions in the *Rana temporaria* tadpoles to chemical stimuli under the conditions of pretreatment. *Zoologicheskii Zhurnal* 63:1046–1054. (16)

Kiseleva, E. I., and Y. B. Manteifel. 1982. Behavioral reactions of *Bufo bufo* and *Rana temporaria* tadpoles to chemical stimuli. *Zoologicheskii Zhurnal* 61:1669–1681. (16)

Kistler, A., K. Yoshizato, and E. Frieden. 1975. Binding of thyroxine and triiodothyronine by nuclei of isolated tadpole liver cells. *Endocrinology* 97:1036–1042. (16)

Kitada, Y. 1986. Salt taste responses in the frog glossopharyngeal nerve: Different receptor sites for Mg[2+] and Na[+]. *Brain Research* 380:172–175. (16)

Klein, S. L., and D. P. C. Graziadei. 1983. The differentiation of the olfactory placode in *Xenopus laevis:* A light and electron microscope study. *Journal of Comparative Neurology* 217:17–30. (16)

Kline, L. W., T. Kaneko, K. W. Chiu, S. Harvey, and P. K. T. Pang. 1988. Calcitonin gene-related peptide in the bullfrog *Rana catesbeiana:* Localization and vascular actions. *General and Comparative Endocrinology* 72:123–129. (3)

Kluge, A. G. 1981. The life history, social organization, and parental behavior of the gladiator frog *Hyla rosenbergi* Boulenger, a nest-building gladiator frog. *Miscellaneous Publications of the University of Michigan Museum of Zoology* 160:1–170. (14,15)

Kluger, J. J., R. S. Tarr, and J. E. Heath. 1973. Posterior hypothalamic lesions and disturbances in behavioral thermoregulation. *Physiological Zoology* 46:79–84. (9)

Kluger, M. J. 1977. Fever in the frog *Hyla cinerea. Journal of Thermal Biology* 2:79–88. (9)

———. 1979. Fever in ectotherms: Evolutionary implications. *American Zoologist* 19:295–304. (9,14)

Klump, G. M., and H. C. Gerhardt. 1987. Use of non-arbitrary acoustic criteria in mate choice by female gray tree frogs. *Nature* 326:286–288. (14)

Klumpp, W., and B. Eggert. 1934. Die Schildrüse und die branchiogenen Organe von *Ichthyophis glutinosus* L. *Zeitschrift für Wissenschaftliche Zoologie* 146:329–381. (16)

Knapp, W. 1974. Die jahreszeitliche Steuerung der Atmung in Abhängigkeit von Akklimationstemperatur und Experimentaltemperatur bei *Triturus alpestris* Laur. und *Salamandra atra* Laur. (Amphibia). *Oecologia* (Berlin) 15:353–374. (9,12)

Knight, F. C. E. 1938. Die Entwicklung von *Triton alpestris* bei verschiedenen Temperaturen, mit Normentafel. *Wilhelm Roux's Archives für Entwicklungsmechanik der Organismen* 137:461–473. (16)

Knoepffler, L.-P. 1962. Contribution a l'étude de genre *Discoglossus* (Amphibiens, Anoures). *Vie et Milieu* 13:1–94. (15)

Knowland, J. 1978. Induction of vitellogenin synthesis in *Xenopus laevis* tadpoles. *Differentiation* 12:47–51. (16)

Knowles, T. W., and P. D. Weigl. 1990. Thermal dependence of anuran burst locomotor performance. *Copeia* 1990:796–802. (12)

Kobayashi, H. H., H. Uemura, M. Wada, and Y. Takei. 1979. Ecological adaptation of angiotensin II: Induced thirst mechanism in tetrapods. *General and Comparative Endocrinology* 38:93–104. (16)

Kobayashi, I., and H. Iwasawa. 1984. Effects of fat body excision on testicular ultrastructure in young frogs of *Rana nigromaculata. Zoological Science* (Japan) 1:972. (15)

Kobayashi, M. 1975. Sexual and bilateral differences in germ-cell numbers in the course of the gonadal development of *Rana nigromaculata. Zoology Magazine* 84:109–114. (16)

Kobayashi, S. 1975. Ultrastructure of the synapses on the chief cell of the carotid body: A comparative study. In *The Peripheral Arterial Chemoreceptors,* ed. M. J. Purves, 25–40. Cambridge: Cambridge University Press. (6,7)

Kobayashi, T., and H. Iwasawa. 1988. Dynamics of precocious spermatogenesis in *Rana nigromaculata. Copeia* 1988:1067–1071. (15)

Kobelt, F., and K. E. Linsenmair. 1986. Adaptation of the reed frog *Hyperolius viridiflavus* (Amphibia, Anura, Hyperoliidae) to its arid environment. *Oecologia* (Berlin) 68:533–541. (4,6,9)

Koch, E. 1931. *Die reflektorische Silbsteurung des Dreislaufs.* Leipzig: Steinkopff. (7)

Kodric-Brown, A., and J. H. Brown. 1984. Truth in advertising: The kinds of traits favored by sexual selection. *American Naturalist* 124:309–323. (14)

Koefoed-Johnson, V., and H. H. Ussing. 1952. The origin of the short-circuit current in the adrenaline-stimulated frog skin. *Acta Physiologica Scandinavica* 27:38–48. (5)

———. 1953. The contribution of diffusion and flow to the passage of D_2O through living membranes. *Acta Physiologica Scandinavica* 17:38–43. (5)

———. 1958. The nature of the frog skin potential. *Acta Physiologica Scandinavica* 42:298–308. (5)

Koft, H. W. 1976. Histological, histochemical, and electron microscopical studies on the nervous apparatus of the pineal organ in the tiger salamander, *Ambystoma tigrinum. Cell and Tissue Research* 174:475–497. (2)

Koketsu, K. 1951. Impulses from receptors in the tongue of the frog. *Kyushu Memoirs of Medical Sciences* (Fukuoka, Japan) 2:53–61. (7)

Kokoros, J. J., and R. G. Northcutt. 1977. Telencephalic efferents of the tiger salamander *Ambystoma tigrinum tigrinim* (Green). *Journal of Comparative Neurology* 173:613–628. (2)

Kolatat, T., K. Kramer, and N. Muhl. 1957. Über die Aktivität sensibler Herzherven des Frosches und ihre Beziehungen zur Herzdynamik. *Pflugers Archiv* 264:127–144. (7)

Kollros, J. J. 1961. Mechanisms of amphibian metamorphosis: Hormones. *American Zoologist* 1:107–114. (16)

———. 1981. Transitions in the nervous system during amphibian metamorphosis. In *Metamorphosis: A Problem in Developmental Biology,* 2d ed., ed. L. I. Gilbert and E. Frieden, 445–459. New York: Plenum Press. (16)

———. 1988. Toward an understanding of tectal development in frogs. In *Developmental Neurobiology of the Frog,* ed. E. D. Pollack and H. D. Bibb, 207–229. New York: Alan R. Liss. (16)

Kollros, J. J., and J. C. Kaltenbach. 1952. Local metamorphosis of larval skin of *Rana pipiens. Physiological Zoology* 25:163–170. (16)

Kollros, J. J., and M. L. Thiesse. 1988. Control of tectal cell number during larval development in *Rana pipiens. Journal of Comparative Neurology* 278:430–445. (16)

Kontani, H., and R. Koshiura. 1981a. Action of divalent cations on the mechanoreceptor of isolated frog heart. *Nippon Yakurigaku Zasshi* 77:177–185. English abstract. (7)

———. 1981b. Recording of pulmonary afferent activities from receptors in the perfused lung preparation of bullfrog and effects of drugs on the afferent activities. *Japanese Journal of Pharmacology* 31:967–974. (7)

———. 1983. Effects of local anesthetics, tetrodotoxin, aconitine, and verapamil on the mechanoreceptors of isolated frog heart. *Japanese Journal of Pharmacology* 33:503–513. (7)

Kopsch, F. 1952. *Die Entwicklung des braunen Grasfrosches* Rana fusca *Roesel: Dargestellt in der Art der Normentaflen zur Entwicklungsgeschichte der Wirbelthiere*. Stuttgart: George Thieme Verlag. (16)

Kordylewski, L. 1986. Differentiation of tail and trunk musculature in the tadpoles of *Xenopus laevis*. *Zeitschrift für Mikroskopisch-anatomische Forschung* (Leipzig) 100:767–789. (11)

Kordylewski, L., and J. Gruszka. 1986. Changes of motor innervation pattern in musculus longissimus dorsi of *Xenopus laevis* at metamorphosis. *Zeitschrift für Mikroskopisch-anatomische Forschung* (Leipzig) 100:790–813. (11)

Korf, H.-W., and A. Oksche. 1987. The pineal organ. In *Vertebrate Endocrinology: Fundamentals and Biomedical Implications*, vol. 1, *Morphological Considerations*, ed. P. K. T. Pang and M. P. Schreibman, 105–145. New York: Academic Press. (3)

Korf, H.-W., R. Liesner, H. Meissl, and A. Kirk. 1981. Pineal complex of the clawed toad, *Xenopus laevis* Daud.: Structure and function. *Cell and Tissue Research* 216:113–130. (16)

Koskela, P., and S. Pasanen. 1974. The wintering of the common frog, *Rana temporaria* L., in northern Finland. *Aquilo* (Zoology) 15:1–17. (10,15)

———. 1975. The reproductive biology of the female common frog, *Rana temporaria* L., in northern Finland. *Aquila* (Zoology) 16:1–12. (15)

Kostyk, S. A., and P. Grobstein. 1982. Visual orienting deficits in frogs with various unilateral lesions. *Behavioral Brain Research* 6:379–388. (2)

Kowalewski, L. 1979. Hibernation periods of amphibians in the Krakow-Czestochowa upland. *Przeglad Zoologiczny* 23:153–158. In Polish. (10)

Kowalski, G. J., and J. W. Mitchell. 1976. Heat transfer from spheres in the naturally turbulent outdoor environment. *American Society of Mechanical Engineers Papers* 75-WA/HT-57. (4)

Koyama, H., E. R. Lewis, E. L. Leverenz, and R. A. Baird. 1982. Acute seismic sensitivity in the bullfrog ear. *Brain Research* 250:168–172. (2)

Kozlowska, M. 1971. Differences in the reproductive biology of mountain and lowland common frogs, *Rana temporaria* L. *Acta Biologica Cracoviensia* (Zoology) 14:17–32. (15)

Krakauer, T. 1970. Tolerance limits of the toad, *Bufo marinus*, in south Florida. *Comparative Biochemistry and Physiology* 33:15–26. (6,9)

Kramer, D. L. 1988. The behavioral ecology of air breathing by aquatic animals. *Canadian Journal of Zoology* 66:89–94. (5,7)

Kratochwill, K. 1933. Zur Morphologie und Physiologie der Nahrungsaufnahme der Froschlarven. *Zeitschrift für Wissenschaftliche Zoologie* 144:421–468. (16)

Krauhs, J. M. 1979. Structure of rat aortic baroreceptors and their relationship to connective tissue. *Journal of Neurocytology* 8:401–414. (7)

Krawczyk, S. 1971. Changes in the lipid and water content in some organs of the common frog (*Rana temporaria* L.) in the annual cycle. *Acta Biologica Cracoviensia* (Zoology) 14:211–237. (15)

———. 1974. Annual cycle of changes in lipid and water content of some organs of the edible frog (*Rana esculenta* L.). *Folia Biologica* Kraków 22:309–326. (15)

Krehl, L., and F. Soetbeer. 1899. Untersuchungen über die Wärmeökonomie der poikilothermen Wirbelthiere. *Pflugers Archiv* 77:611–638. (12)

Kreith, F. 1973. *Principles of Heat Transfer*. New York: Intext Press. (4)

Krogh, A. 1904. On the cutaneous and pulmonary respiration of the frog. *Skandinavisches Archiv für Physiologie* 15:328–419. (12)

———. 1914. The quantitative relation between temperature and standard metabolism in animals. *Internationale Zeitschrift für physikalisch-chemie Biologie* 1:491–508. (12)

———. 1919. The rate of diffusion of gasses through animal tissues with some remarks on the coefficient of invasion. *Journal of Physiology* (London) 52:391. (8)

———. 1937. Osmotic regulation in the frog (*Rana esculenta*) by active absorption of chloride ions. *Skandinavisches Archiv für Physiologie* 76:60–73. (4,5,16)

———. 1938. The active absorption of ions in some freshwater animals. *Zeitschrift für vergleichende Physiologie* 25:335–350. (5)

Krogh, A., K. Schmidt-Nielsen, and E. Zeuthen. 1938. The osmotic behaviour of frog eggs and young tadpoles. *Zeitschrift für vergleichende Physiologie* 26:230–238. (16)

Krogh, J. E., and W. W. Tanner. 1972. The hyobranchium and throat myology of adult Ambystomidae of the United States and northern Mexico. *Brigham Young University Science Bulletin, Biological Series* 16:1–69. (11)

Krug, E. C., K. V. Honn, J. Battista, and C. S. Nicoll. 1983. Corticosteroids in serum of *Rana catesbeiana* during development and metamorphosis. *General and Comparative Endocrinology* 52:232–241. (5,16)

Krüger, P. 1929. Über einen möglichen Zusammenhang zwischen Struktur, Funktion, und chemischer Beschaffenheit der Muskeln. *Biologisches Zentralblatt* 49:616. (11)

———. 1949. Die Innervation der tetanischen und tonischen Fasern der quergestreiften Skelettmuskulatur der Wirbeltiere. *Anatomischer Anzeiger* 97:169–175. (11)

———. 1950. Die Grundlagen des Tetanus und Tonus der quergestreiften Skelettmuskelfasern der Wirbeltiere. *Experientia* 6:75–80. (11)

———. 1952. *Tetanus und Tonus der quergestreiften Skelettmuskeln der Wirbeltiere und des Menschen*. Leipzig: Akademische Verlagsgesellschaft. (11)

Kruhoffer, M., M. L. Glass, A. S. Abe, and K. Johansen. 1987. Control of breathing in an amphibian *Bufo paracnemis:* Effects of temperature and hypoxia. *Respiration Physiology* 69:267–275. (5,6,7)

Kruse, K. C., and M. G. Francis. 1977. A predation deterrent in larvae of the bullfrog, *Rana catesbeiana*. *Transactions of the American Fisheries Society* 106:248–252. (14)

Kruse, K. C., and B. M. Stone. 1984. Largemouth bass (*Micropterus salmonoides*) learn to avoid feeding on toad (*Bufo*) tadpoles. *Animal Behaviour* 32:1035–1039. (14)

Kudo, T. 1938. Normentafel zur Entwicklungsgeschichte des Japanischen Riesensalamanders (*Megalobatrachus japonicus* Temminck). In *Normentafel zur Entwicklungsgeschichte der Wirbeltiere*, ed. F. Keibelis, 16:1–98. Jena: Gustav Fischer. (16)

Kuffler, D. P. 1986. Accurate reinnervation of motor end plates after disruption of sheath cells and muscle fibers. *Journal of Comparative Neurology* 250:228–235. (11)

Kuffler, S. W., and R. W. Gerard. 1947. The small-nerve motor system to skeletal muscle. *Journal of Neurophysiology* 10:383–394. (11)

Kuffler, S. W., and E. M. Vaughan Williams. 1953a. Properties of the "slow" skeletal muscle fibres of the frog. *Journal of Physiology* (London) 121:318–334. (11)

———. 1953b. Small-nerve junction potentials: The distribution of small motor nerves to frog skeletal muscle, and the membrane characteristics of the fibres they innervate. *Journal of Physiology* (London) 121:289–317. (11)

Kuhlenbeck, H. 1973. *The Central Nervous System of Vertebrates*. Vol. 3. Part 2. *Overall Morphologic Pattern: 3. Cranial or Cerebral Nerves and the Head Problem*. New York: Academic Press. (7)

Kuhlmann, W. D., and M. R. Fedde. 1979. Intrapulmonary receptors in the bullfrog: Sensitivity to CO_2. *Journal of Comparative Physiology* 132A:69–75. (6,7)

Kuhn, E. R., V. M. Darras, and T. M. Verlinden. 1985. Annual variations of thyroid reactivity following thyrotropin stimulation and circulating levels of thyroid hormones in the frog *Rana ridibunda*. *General and Comparative Endocrinology* 57:266–273. (3)

Kuhn, E. R., S. Kikuyama, K. Yamamoto, and W. M. Darras. 1985. *In vivo* release of prolactin in *Rana ridibunda* following an intravenous injection of thyrotropin-releasing hormone. *General and Comparative Endocrinology* 60:86–89. (3,16)

Kumai, T. 1981. Reflex response of the hypoglossal nerve induced by chemical stimulation of the tongue and electrical stimulation of the glossopharyngeal nerve in the frog. *Japanese Journal of Physiology* 31:625–637. (7)

Kuno, Y. 1914. Einige Beobachtungen über den Blutdruck des Frosches. *Pflugers Archiv* 158:1–18. (7)

Kunz, A. 1924. Anatomical and physiological changes in the digestive system during metamorphosis in *Rana pipiens* and *Ambystoma tigrinum*. *Journal of Morphology* 38:581–598. (16)

Kuramoto, M. 1975. Embryonic temperature adaptation in development rate of frogs. *Physiological Zoology* 48:360–366. (8,9)

———. 1978. Correlations of quantitative parameters of fecundity in amphibians. *Evolution* 32:287–296. (15)

———. 1981. Relationships between number, size, and shape of red blood cells in amphibians. *Comparative Biochemistry and Physiology* 69A:771–775. (5)

Kusakabe, T., K. Ishii, and K. Ishii. 1987. A possible role of the glomus cell in controlling vascular tone of the carotid labyrinth in *Xenopus laevis*. *Tohoku Journal of Experimental Medicine* 151:395–408. (7)

Kusano, T., H. Kusano, and K. Miyashita. 1985. Size-related cannibalism among larval *Hynobius nebulosus*. *Copeia* 1985:472–476. (14)

Labanick, G. M. 1976. Prey availability, consumption, and selection in the cricket frog *Acris crepitans* (Amphibia, Anura, Hylidae). *Journal of Herpetology* 10:293–298. (13)

———. 1984. Anti-predator effectiveness of autotomized tails of the salamander *Desmognathus ochrophaeus*. *Herpetologica* 40:110–118. (14)

Lagerspetz, K. Y. H. 1977. Effect of temperature acclimation on the microsomal ATPases of the frog brain. *Journal of Thermal Biology* 2:27–30. (8)

Lagerspetz, K. Y. H., M. N. E. Harri, and R. Okslahti. 1974. The role of the thyroid in the temperature acclimation of the oxidative metabolism in the frog *Rana temporaria*. *General and Comparative Endocrinology* 22:169–176. (10)

Lagerspetz, K. Y. H., and A. Laine. 1984. Fluidity of epidermal cell membranes and thermal acclimation of sodium transport in frog skin. *Molecular Physiology* 6:211–220. (8,10)

Lagerspetz, K. Y. H., and M. Skytta. 1979. Temperature compensation of sodium transport and ATPase activity in frog skin. *Acta Physiologica Scandinavica* 106:151–158. (8)

Lahiri, S., K. Maret, and M. G. Sherpa. 1983. Dependance of high altitude sleep apnea on ventilatory sensitivity to hypoxia. *Respiration Physiology* 52:281–301. (7)

Lahiri, S., N. Smatresk, M. Pokorski, P. Barnard, and A. Mokashi. 1983. Efferent inhibition of carotid body chemoreception in chronically hypoxic cats. *American Journal of Physiology* 245:R678–R683. (7)

Lamb, T. 1984. The influence of sex and breeding condition on microhabitat selection and diet in the pig frog *Rana grylio*. *American Midland Naturalist* 111:311–318. (14)

Lamb, T. D. 1984. Effects of temperature changes on toad rod photocurrents. *Journal of Physiology* (London) 346:557–578. (9)

Lambertini, G. 1928. Il manicotto glandulare di *Rana esculenta*. *Ricerche di Morfologia* (Rome) 9:71–88. (16)

Lambrechts, M., and A. A. Dhondt. 1986. Male quality, reproduction, and survival in the great tit (*Parus major*). *Behavioral Ecology and Sociobiology* 19:57–63. (14)

Lamers, A. P. M., A. M. Stadhouders, A. A. J. Verhofstad, and A. M. Michelakis. 1985. Immunoelectron microscope localization of renin in the juxtaglomerular cells of the amphibian *Bufo bufo*. *General and Comparative Endocrinology* 60:380–389. (3)

Lamming, G. E., ed. 1984. *Marshall's Physiology of Reproduction*. 4th ed. Vol. 1. Edinburgh: Churchill Livingstone. (15)

Lamotte, M., and J. Lescure. 1977. Tendances adaptives à l'affranchissement du milieu aquatique chez les amphibiens anoures. *La Terre et la Vie* 2:225–311. (15)

Lamotte, M., and F. Xavier. 1972. Recherches sur le développement embryonnaire de *Nectophrynoides occidentalis* Angel, amphibien anoure vivipare: 1. Les principaux traits morphologiques et biométriques du développement. *Annales d'Embryologie et de Morphogénèse* 5:315–340. (16)

Lande, R. 1981. Models of speciation by sexual selection of polygenic characters. *Proceedings of the National Academy of Sciences* 78:3721–3725. (14)

Lang, J. W. 1979. Thermophilic response of the American alligator and the American crocodile to feeding. *Copeia* 1979:48–59. (9)

Lange, C. B., and W. Hanke. 1988. Corticosteroid receptors in liver cytosol of the clawed toad, *Xenopus laevis*: Daily and seasonal variations. *General and Comparative Endocrinology* 71:141–152. (3,16)

Lange, C. B., W. Hanke, and W. K. Morishige. 1989. Corticosteroid receptors in liver cytosol of the clawed toad, *Xenopus laevis*: Influence of thyroid and ovarian hormones. *General and Comparative Endocrinology* 73:485–497. (16)

Langille, B. L., and B. Crisp. 1980. Temperature dependence of blood viscosity in frogs and turtles: Effect on heat exchange with environment. *American Journal of Physiology* 239:R248–R253. (9)

Langille, B. L., and D. R. Jones. 1977. Dynamics of blood flow through the hearts and arterial systems of anuran Amphibia. *Journal of Experimental Biology* 68:1–18. (7)

Lännergren, J. 1978. The force-velocity relation of isolated twitch and slow muscle fibres of *Xenopus laevis*. *Journal of Physiology* (London) 283:501–521. (11)

———. 1979. An intermediate type of muscle fiber in *Xenopus laevis*. *Nature* 279:254–256. (11)

Lännergren, J., P. Lindblom, and B. Johansson. 1982. Contractile properties of two varieties of twitch muscle fibres in *Xenopus laevis*. *Acta Physiologica Scandinavica* 114:523–535. (11)

Lännergren, J., and R. S. Smith. 1966. Types of muscle fibres in toad skeletal muscle. *Acta Physiologica Scandinavica* 68:263–274. (11,14)

Lannoo, M. J. 1987a. Neuromast topography in anuran amphibians. *Journal of Morphology* 191:115–129. (16)

———. 1987b. Neuromast topography in urodele amphibians. *Journal of Morphology* 191:247–263. (16)

Lannoo, M. J., and M. D. Bachmann. 1984a. Aspects of cannibalistic morphs in a population of *Ambystoma t. tigrinum* larvae. *American Midland Naturalist* 112:103–110. (14,16)

———. 1984b. On flotation and air breathing in *Ambystoma tigrinum* larvae: Stimuli for and the relationship between these behaviors. *Canadian Journal of Zoology* 62:15–18. (7,16)

Lannoo, M. J., and S. C. Smith. 1989. The lateral line system. In *Developmental Biology of the Axolotl*, ed. J. B. Armstrong and G. M. Malacinski, 176–186. New York: Oxford University Press. (16)

Lannoo, M. J., D. S. Townsend, and R. J. Wassersug. 1987. Larval life in the leaves: Arboreal tadpole types, with special attention to the morphology, ecology, and behavior of the oophagous *Osteopilus brunneus* (Hylidae) larvae. *Fieldiana: Zoology* 38:1–31. (14,16)

Lapennas, G. N. 1983. The magnitude of the Bohr coefficient: Optimal for oxygen delivery. *Respiration Physiology* 54:161–172. (5)

Lara, R., and M. A. Arbib. 1985. A model of neural mechanisms responsible for pattern recognition and stimulus specific habituation in toads. *Biological Cybernetics* 51:223–237. (2)

Larionov, N. P., L. N. Medvedev, and S. A. Khramenko. 1978. Effect of ambient temperature on sodium-potassium-ATPase from frog myocardium. *Biokhimiya* 43:653–655. (8)

Larras-Regard, E. 1985. Hormonal determination of neoteny in facultative neotonic urodeles. In *Metamorphosis: The Eighth Symposium of the British Society for Developmental Biology*, ed. M. Balls and M. Bownes, 294–312. Oxford: Clarendon Press. (16)

Larras-Regard, E., A. Taurog, and M. Dorris. 1981. Plasma T_4 and T_3 levels in *Ambystoma tigrinum* at various stages of metamorphosis. *General and Comparative Endocrinology* 43:443–450. (16)

Larsen, E. H. 1988. NaCl transport in amphibian skin. In *Advances in Comparative and Environmental Physiology*, ed. R. Greger, 189–248. Berlin: Springer-Verlag. (5)

Larsen, J. H., and J. T. Beneski. 1988. Quantitative analysis of feeding kinematics in dusky salamanders (*Desmognathus*). *Canadian Journal of Zoology* 66:1309–1317. (11)

Larsen, J. H., Jr., J. T. Beneski, and D. B. Wake. 1989. Hyolingual feeding systems of the Plethodontidae: Comparative kinematics of prey capture by salamanders with free and attached tongues. *Journal of Experimental Zoology* 252:25–33. (11)

Larsen, J. H., Jr., and D. J. Guthrie. 1975. The feeding mechanism of terrestrial tiger salamanders (*Ambystoma tigrinum melanostictum* Baird). *Journal of Morphology* 147:137–154. (11)

Larsen, L. O. 1976. Physiology of molting. In *Physiology of the Amphibians*, ed. B. Lofts, 3:53–100. New York: Academic Press. (3,13)

———. 1984. Feeding in adult toads: Physiology, behaviour, ecology. *Videnskabelige Meddelelser fra Dansk Naturhistorisk Forening* 145:97–116. (13)

Larsen, L. O., M. B. Christiansen, T. Due, S. Hastrup, C. Kapel, M. Sciuto, and A. M. Wulff. 1990. Crowding in toads: Are crowded toads stressed or not? *Fortschritte der Zoologie* 38:271–277. (13)

Larsen, L. O., and P. Licht. 1984. The effects of growth hormone (GH) on food intake and growth in adult toads (*Bufo boreas*). *General and Comparative Endocrinology* 53:474. (13,15)

Larsen, L. O., and J. N. Pedersen. 1982. The snapping response of the toad *Bufo bufo* towards prey dummies at very low light intensities. *Amphibia-Reptilia* 2:321–327. (13)

Larsen, L. O., and J. E. Sørensen. 1980. Feeding experiments in the toad *Bufo bufo bufo* (L.): Effects of extirpation of pars distalis of the pituitary gland on feeding behavior. *General and Comparative Endocrinology* 40:291–296. (13)

Lasiewski, R. C., and G. A. Bartholomew. 1969. Condensation as a mechanism for water gain in nocturnal desert poikilotherms. *Copeia* 1969:405–407. (4)

Lasiewski, R. C., and W. R. Dawson. 1967. A re-examination of the relation between standard metabolic rate and body weight in birds. *Condor* 69:13–23. (12)

Latham, K. E., and J. J. Just. 1989. Oxygen availability provides a signal for hatching in the rainbow trout (*Salmo gairdneri*) embryo. *Canadian Journal of Fisheries and Aquatic Sciences* 46:55–58. (16)

Lauder, G. V. 1985a. Aquatic feeding in lower vertebrates. In *Functional Vertebrate Morphology*, ed. M. Hildebrand, D. M. Bramble, K. F. Liem, and D. B. Wake, 210–229, 397–399. Cambridge, MA: Harvard University Press. (14)

———. 1985b. Functional morphology of the feeding mechanism in lower vertebrates. In *Functional Morphology of Vertebrates*, ed. H.-R. Duncker and G. Fleischer, 179–188. New York: Springer-Verlag. (11)

Lauder, G. V., and S. M. Reilly. 1988. Functional design of the feeding mechanism in salamanders: Causal bases of ontogenetic changes in function. *Journal of Experimental Biology* 134:219–233. (11,14)

Lauder, G. V., and H. B. Shaffer. 1985. Functional morphology of the feeding mechanism in aquatic ambystomatid salamanders. *Journal of Morphology* 185:297–326. (11)

———. 1986. Functional design of the feeding mechanism in lower vertebrates: Unidirectional and bidirectional flow systems in the tiger salamander. *Zoological Journal of the Linnean Society* 88:277–290. (11)

———. 1988. Ontogeny of functional design in tiger salamanders (*Ambystoma tigrinum*): Are motor patterns conserved during major morphological transformations? *Journal of Morphology* 197:249–268. (11)

———. 1993. Design and feeding systems in aquatic vertebrates: Major patterns and their evolutionary interpretations. In *The Vertebrate Skull*, ed. J. Hanken and B. Hall, vol. 3. Chicago: University of Chicago Press. (Forthcoming) (11)

Laudien, H. 1973. Animals: 4. Activity, behavior, etc. In *Temperature and Life*, ed. H. Precht, J. Christophersen, H. Hensel, and W. Larcher, 441–502. New York: Springer-Verlag. (9)

Lawson, R. 1965. The anatomy of *Hypogeophis rostratus* (Amphibia: Apoda or Gymnophiona): 2. The musculature. *Proceedings of the University of Newcastle upon Tyne Philosophical Society* 1:52–63. (11)

Layne, J. R., and D. L. Claussen. 1982. Seasonal variation in the thermal acclimation of critical thermal maxima (CTMax) and minima (CTMin) in the salamander *Eurycea bislineata*. *Journal of Thermal Biology* 7:29–34. (8)

———. 1987. Time courses of thermal acclimation for critical thermal minima in salamanders. *Comparative Biochemistry Physiology* 87:895–898. (8)

Layne, J. R., and R. E. Lee. 1987. Freeze tolerance and the dynamics of ice formation in wood frogs (*Rana sylvatica*) from southern Ohio. *Canadian Journal of Zoology* 65:2062–2065. (10)

Layne, J. R., and M. A. Romano. 1985. Critical thermal minima of *Hyla chrysoscelis*, *Hyla cinerea*, *Hyla gratiosa* and natural hybrids *H. cinera* × *H. gratiosa*. *Herpetologica* 41:216–221. (8)

Lázár, G. 1971. The projections of the retinal quadrants of the optic centers in the frog: A terminal degeneration study. *Acta Morphologica Academiae Scientiarium Hungaricae* 19:325–334. (16)

———. 1984. Structure and connections of the frog optic tectum. In *Comparative Neurology of the Optic Tectum*, ed. H. Vanegas, 185–210. New York: Plenum Press. (2)

Leaf, A. 1967. Membrane effects of antidiuretic hormone. *American Journal of Medicine* 42:745–756. (6)

Leaf, A., J. Anderson, and L. B. Page. 1958. Active sodium transport

by the isolated bladder. *Journal of General Physiology* 41:657–688. (5)

Leboulenger, F., C. Delarue, A. Belanger, I. Perroteau, P. Netchitaïlo, P. Leroux, S. Jégou, M. C. Tonon, and H. Vaudry. 1982. Direct radioimmunoassay for plasma corticosterone and aldosterone in frog: 1. Validation of the methods and evidence for daily rhythms in a natural environment. *General and Comparative Endocrinology* 46:521–532. (3)

Leboulenger, F., C. Delarue, M. C. Tonon, S. Jégou, and H. Vaudry. 1978. In vitro study of frog (*Rana ridibunda* Pallas) interrenal function by use of a simplified perfusion system: 1. Influence of adrenocorticotropin upon corticosterone release. *General and Comparative Endocrinology* 36:327–338. (3)

Leboulenger, F., P. Leroux, C. Delarue, M. C. Tonon, Y. Charnay, P. M. Dubois, D. H. Coy, and H. Vaudry. 1983. Co-localization of vasoactive intestinal peptide (VIP) and enkephalins of chromaffin cells of the adrenal gland of Amphibia: Stimulation of corticosteroid production by VIP. *Life Sciences* 32:375–383. (3)

Leboulenger, F., I. Perroteau, P. Netchitaïlo, I. Lihrmann, P. Leroux, C. Delarue, D. H. Coy, and H. Vaudry. 1984. Action of vasoactive intestinal peptide (VIP) on amphibian adrenocortical function in vitro. *Peptides* 4:299–303. (3)

LeCluyse, E. L., S. K. Frost, and W. Dentler. 1985. Development and ciliation of the palate in two frogs, *Bombina* and *Xenopus*: A comparative study. *Tissue and Cell* 17:853–864. (16)

Lee, A. K. 1968. Water economy of the burrowing frog, *Heleioporus eyrei* (Gray). *Copeia* 1968:741–745. (6,10,12)

Lee, A. K., and E. H. Mercer. 1967. Cocoon surrounding desert-dwelling frogs. *Science* 157:87–88. (4,6,10)

Lee, A. R., M. Silove, U. Katz, and J. B. Balinsky. 1982. Urea cycle enzymes and glutamate dehydrogenase in *Xenopus laevis* and *Bufo viridis* adapted to high salinity. *Journal of Experimental Zoology* 221:169–172. (6,10)

LeFevre, M. E. 1974. Correlation of tissue water content with lymphatic structure in toad and turtle bladders. *Comparative Biochemistry and Physiology* 47A:79–82. (5)

Leffler, C. W., R. C. Hanson, and E. G. Schneider. 1980. Effects of prostaglandins and prostaglandin precursors on the arterial pressure of the bullfrog, *Rana catesbeiana*. *Comparative Biochemistry and Physiology* 66C:199–202. (3)

Leist, K. H. 1970. Die Bedeutung des Adenohypophysen-interrenal-systems für den Osmomineral-haushalt des Krallenfrosches (*Xenopus laevis* Daudin) in Verlauf der Metamorphose. *Zoologische Jahrbücher Abteilung für Allgemeine Zoologie und Physiologie der Tiere* 75:375–401. (16)

Leist, K. H., K. Bergerhoff, F. W. Pehlemann, and W. Hanke. 1969. Histophysiologische Untersuchungen der Entwicklung des interrenal Organs beim Krallenfrosch (*Xenopus laevis* Daudin). *Zeitschrift für Zellforschung und mikroskopische Anatomie* 93:105–125. (16)

Leivestad, H. 1960. The effect of prolonged submersion on the metabolism and the heart rate in the toad (*Bufo bufo*). *Arbok for Univsitetet i Bergen Matematisk-Naturvitenskapelig Serie* 5:1–15. (10,12)

Leloup, J., and M. Buscaglia. 1977. La triiodothyronine, hormone de la métamorphose des amphibiens. *Comptes Rendus de l'Académie des Sciences* (Paris) 284D:2261–2263. (16)

Lemon, R. E., and J. Struger. 1980. Acoustic entrainment to randomly generated calls by the frog, *Hyla crucifer*. *Journal of the Acoustical Society of America* 67:2090–2095. (14)

Lenfant, C., and K. Johansen. 1967. Respiratory adaptations in selected amphibians. *Respiration Physiology* 2:247–260. (5,6,16)

Lenfant, C., K. Johansen, and D. Hanson. 1970. Bimodal gas exchange and ventilation-perfusion relationship in lower vertebrates. *Federation Proceedings* 29:1124–1129. (5,12)

Lentz, T. L. 1970. Development of the neuromuscular junction: 2. Cytological and cytochemical studies on the neuromuscular junction of dedifferentiating muscle in the regenerating limb of the newt *Triturus*. *Journal of Cell Biology* 47:423–436. (11)

Leone, F., S. Lambert-Gardini, C. Sartori, and S. Scapin. 1976. Ultrastructural analysis of some functional aspects of *Xenopus laevis* pancreas during development and metamorphosis. *Journal of Embryology and Experimental Morphology* 36:711–724. (16)

Leong, A. S.-Y., M. J. Tyler, and D. J. C. Shearman. 1986. Gastric brooding: A new form in a recently discovered Australian frog of the genus *Rheobatrachus*. *Australian Journal of Zoology* 34:205–209. (13)

Lerner, A. B., J. D. Case, Y. Takahashi, T. H. Lee, and W. Mori. 1958. Isolation of melatonin, the pineal gland factor that lightens melanocytes. *Journal of the American Chemical Society* 80:2587. (3)

Leroux, P., M. C. Tonon, P. Saulot, S. Jegou, and H. Vaudry. 1983. *In vitro* study of frog (*Rana ridibunda* Pallas) neurointermediate lobe secretion by use of a simplified perfusion system: 2. Lack of action of thyroxine on TRH-induced α-MSH secretion. *General and Comparative Endocrinology* 51:323–328. (3)

Lescure, J. 1965. L'alimentation et le comportement de prédation chez *Bufo bufo* (Linnaeus, 1758). Ph.D. diss., Faculté des Sciences, Paris. (13)

———. 1982. Le comportement alimentaire. In *Traité de Zoologie: Amphibiens 2*, ed. P. P. Grassé, 215–222. Paris: Masson. (13)

Letinsky, M. S. 1974. The development of nerve-muscle junctions in *Rana catesbeiana* tadpoles. *Developmental Biology* 40:129–153. (11)

Letinsky, M. S., and P. A. Decino. 1980. Histological staining of pre- and postsynaptic components of amphibian neuromuscular junctions. *Journal of Neurocytology* 9:305–320. (11)

Letinsky, M. S., and K. Morrison-Graham. 1980. Structure of developing frog neuromuscular junctions. *Journal of Neurocytology* 9:321–342. (11)

Lettvin, J. Y., H. R. Maturana, W. S. McCulloch, and W. H. Pitts. 1959. What the frog's eye tells the frog's brain. *Proceedings of the Institute of Radio Engineers* 47:1940–1951. (2)

Leusen, I. R. 1954. Chemosensitivity of the respiratory center: Influence of CO_2 in the cerebral ventricles on respiration. *American Journal of Physiology* 176:39–44. (6)

Levine, S. D., M. Jacoby, and A. Finkelstein. 1984a. The water permeability of the toad urinary bladder: 1. Permeability of barriers in series with the luminal membrane. *Journal of General Physiology* 83:529–541. (5)

———. 1984b. The water permeability of the toad urinary bladder: 2. The value of $p_f/p_d(w)$ for the antidiuretic hormone-induced water permeation pathway. *Journal of General Physiology* 83:543–561. (5)

Levinsky, N. G., and W. H. Sawyer. 1953. Significance of the neurohypophysis in regulation of fluid balance in the frog. *Proceedings of the Society for Experimental Biology and Medicine* 82:272–274. (6)

Levitt, J. 1980. *Responses of Plants to Environmental Stresses*. New York: Academic Press. (10)

Lewis, E. J. C., and E. Frieden. 1959. Biochemistry of amphibian metamorphosis: Effect of triiodothyronine, thyroxin, and dinitrophenol on the respiration of the tadpole. *Endocrinology* 65:273–282. (12)

Lewis, E. R. 1981a. Evolution of inner-ear auditory apparatus in the frog. *Brain Research* 219:149–155. (2)

———. 1981b. Suggested evolution of tonotopic organization in the frog amphibian papilla. *Neuroscience Letters* 21:131–136. (2)

———. 1984. On the frog amphibian papilla. *Scanning Electron Microscopy* 1984:1899–1913. (2)

Lewis, E. R., R. A. Baird, E. L. Leverenz, and H. Koyama. 1982. Inner ear: Dye injection reveals peripheral origins of specific sensitivities. *Science* 215:1641–1643. (2)

Lewis, E. R., E. L. Leverenz, and H. Koyama. 1982. The tonotopic organization of the bullfrog amphibian papilla, an auditory organ lacking a basilar membrane. *Journal of Comparative Physiology* 145:437–445. (2)

Lewis, E. R., and R. E. Lombard. 1988. The amphibian inner ear. In *The Evolution of the Amphibian Auditory System*, ed. B. Fritzsch, M. J. Ryan, W. Wilczynski, T. E. Hetherington, and W. Walkowiak, 93–123. New York: John Wiley and Sons. (2)

Lewis, P. R. 1958. A simultaneous coupling azo-dye technique suitable for whole mounts. *Quarterly Journal of Microscopical Science* 99:67–71. (11)

Lewis, P. R., and A. F. W. Hughes. 1960. Patterns of myo-neural junctions and cholinesterase activity in the muscles of tadpoles of *Xenopus laevis*. *Quarterly Journal of Microscopical Science* 101:55–67. (11)

Lewis, S. A., D. C. Eaton, C. Claussen, and J. M. Diamond. 1977. Nystatin as a probe for investigating the electrical properties of a tight epithelium. *Journal of General Physiology* 70:427–440. (5)

Lewis, W. H. 1910. The relation of the myotomes to the ventrolateral musculature and to the anterior limbs in *Amblystoma*. *Anatomical Record* 4:183–190. (11)

Li, C. W., and E. R. Lewis. 1974. Morphogenesis of auditory receptor epithelia in the bullfrog. *Scanning Electron Microscope Symposium* 3:792–797. (16)

Licht, L. E. 1971. Breeding habits and embryonic thermal requirements of the frogs, *Rana aurora aurora* and *Rana pretiosa pretiosa*, in the Pacific Northwest. *Ecology* 52:116–124. (9)

———. 1974. Survival of embryos, tadpoles, and adults of the frogs *Rana aurora aurora* and *Rana pretiosa pretiosa* sympatric in southwestern British Columbia. *Canadian Journal of Zoology* 52:613–627. (15)

Licht, P. 1968. Response of the thermal preferendum and heat resistance to thermal acclimation under different photoperiods in the lizard *Anolis carolinensis*. *American Midland Naturalist* 79:149–158. (9)

———. 1979. Reproductive endocrinology of reptiles and amphibians: Gonadotropins. *Annual Reviews of Physiology* 41:337–351. (3)

———. 1983. Evolutionary divergence in the structure and function of pituitary gonadotropins of tetrapod vertebrates. *American Zoologist* 23:672–683. (3)

———. 1984. Reptiles. In *Marshall's Physiology of Reproduction*, 4th ed., vol. 1, ed. G. E. Lamming, 206–282. Edinburgh: Churchill Livingstone. (15)

———. 1986. Suitability of the mammalian model in comparative reproductive endocrinology. In *Comparative Endocrinology, Development and Directions*, ed. C. L. Ralph, 95–114. New York: Alan R. Liss. (3)

Licht, P., and A. G. Brown. 1967. Behavioral thermoregulation and its role in the ecology of the red-bellied newt *Taricha rivularis*. *Ecology* 47:598–611. (9)

Licht, P., W. R. Dawson, V. H. Shoemaker, and A. R. Main. 1966. Observations on the thermal relations of western Australian lizards. *Copeia* 1966:97–110. (9)

Licht, P., M. E. Feder, and S. Bledsoe. 1975. Salinity tolerance and osmoregulation in the salamander *Batrachoseps*. *Journal of Comparative Physiology* 102:123–134. (6,16)

Licht, P., B. R. McCreery, R. Barnes, and R. Pang. 1983. Seasonal and stress related changes in plasma gonadotropins, sex steroids, and corticosterone in the bullfrog, *Rana catesbeiana*. *General and Comparative Endocrinology* 50:124–145. (3,15)

Licht, P., R. Millar, J. A. King, B. R. McCreery, M. T. Mendonça, A. Bona-Gallo, and B. Lofts. 1984. The effects of chicken and mammalian gonadotropin-releasing hormones (GnRH) on *in vivo* pituitary gonadotropin release in amphibians and reptiles. *General and Comparative Endocrinology* 54:89–96. (16)

Licht, P., and H. Papkoff. 1974. Separation of two distinct gonadotropins from the pituitary gland of the bullfrog *Rana catesbeiana*. *Endocrinology* 94:1587–1595. (16)

Licht, P., and D. A. Porter. 1987. Role of gonadotropin-releasing hormone in regulation of gonadotropin secretion from amphibian and reptile pituitaries. In *Hormones and Reproduction in Fishes, Amphibians, and Reptiles*, ed. D. O. Norris and R. E. Jones, 61–85. New York: Plenum Press. (15)

Licht, P., D. Porter, and R. P. Millar. 1987. Specificity of amphibian and reptilian pituitaries for various forms of gonadotropin releasing hormones *in vitro*. *General and Comparative Endocrinology* 66:248–255. (3,15,16)

Licht, P., M. J. Ryan, and R. Barnes. 1985. Changes in hormone levels in relation to breeding behavior in male bullfrogs (*Rana catesbeiana*) at the individual and population levels. *General and Comparative Endocrinology* 58:270–279. (3)

Liebman, P. A., and G. Entine. 1968. Visual pigments of frog and tadpole (*Rana pipiens*). *Vision Research* 8:761–775. (2)

Liem, K. F. 1985. Ventilation. In *Functional Vertebrate Morphology*, ed. M. Hildebrand, D. M. Bramble, K. F. Liem and D. B. Wake, 185–209. Cambridge, MA: Harvard University Press. (11)

Lighton, J. R. B. 1985. Minimum cost of transport and ventilatory patterns in three African beetles. *Physiological Zoology* 58:390–399. (12)

———. 1987. Cost of tokking: The energetics of substrate communication in the tok-tok beetle, *Psammodes striatus*. *Journal of Comparative Physiology* 157B:11–20. (14)

Lihrmann, I., P. Netchitailo, M. Feuilloley, M. Cantin, C. Delarue, F. Leboulenger, A. DeLean, and H. Vaudry. 1988. Effect of atrial natriuretic factor on corticosteroid production by perfused frog interrenal studies. *General and Comparative Endocrinology* 71:55–62. (3,16)

Likens, G. E., and F. H. Bormann. 1974. Acid rain: A serious regional environmental problem. *Science* 184:1176–1179. (5)

Lillo, R. S. 1980a. Heart rate and blood pressure in bullfrogs during prolonged maintenance in water at low temperature. *Comparative Biochemistry and Physiology* 65A:251–253. (10)

———. 1980b. Localization of chemoreceptors which may cause diving bradycardia in bullfrogs. *Canadian Journal of Zoology* 58:931–936. (7)

Lillywhite, H. B. 1970. Behavioral temperature regulation in the bullfrog. *Copeia* 1970:158–168. (9)

———. 1971a. Temperature selection by the bullfrog *Rana catesbeiana*. *Comparative Biochemistry and Physiology* 40A:213–227. (9)

———. 1971b. Thermal modulation of cutaneous mucus discharge as a determinant of evaporative water loss in the frog, *Rana catesbeiana*. *Zeitschrift für vergleichende Physiologie* 73:84–104. (4,6,9)

———. 1975. Physiological correlates of basking in amphibians. *Comparative Biochemistry and Physiology* 52A:323–330. (4,9)

———. 1987. Temperature, energetics, and physiological ecology. In *Snakes: Ecology and Evolutionary Biology*, ed. R. A. Seigel, J. T. Collins, and S. S. Novak, 422–477. New York: Macmillan. (9)

Lillywhite, H. B., and P. Licht. 1974. Movement of water over toad skin: Functional role of epidermal sculpturing. *Copeia* 1974:165–171. (6)

———. 1975. A comparative study of integumentary mucous secretions in amphibians. *Comparative Biochemistry and Physiology* 51A:937–941. (4)

Lillywhite, H. B., P. Licht, and P. Chelgren. 1973. The role of behavioral thermoregulation in the growth energetics of the toad, *Bufo boreas*. *Ecology* 54:375–383. (8,9,12,13,14,15)

Lillywhite, H. B., and P. F. A. Maderson. 1982. Skin structure and permeability. In *Biology of the Reptilia*, vol. 12, ed. C. Gans and F. H. Pough, 397–442. New York: Academic Press. (4)

———. 1988. The structure and permeability of integument. *American Zoologist* 28:945–962. (4)

Lillywhite, H. B., and R. J. Wassersug. 1974. Comments on a postmetamorphic aggregate of *Bufo boreas*. *Copeia* 1974:984–986. (9)

Lima, A. A. M., N. C. Meirelles, L. P. S. Airoldi, and A. Foccsi. 1985. Allosteric effect of protons and adenosine triphosphate on hemoglobins from aquatic Amphibia. *Journal of Comparative Physiology* 155:353–355. (5)

Limbaugh, B. A., and E. P. Volpe. 1957. Early development of the Gulf Coast toad *Bufo valliceps* Wiegmann. *American Museum Novitates* 1842:1–32. (16)

Limeses, C. E. 1963. La musculatura del muslo en las especies del género *Lepidobatrachus* (Anura: Ceratophrynidae). *Physis* 24:205–218. (11)

———. 1964. La musculatura del muslo en los ceratofrínidos y formas afines: Con un análisis crítico sobre la significacion de los characteres miológicos en la sistemática de los anuros superiores. *Contribuciones Cientificas, Seria Zoologica, Universidad de Buenos Aires* 1:193–245. (11)

———. 1965. La musculatura mandibular en los ceratofrínidos y formas afines (Anura: Ceratophrynidae). *Physis* 25:41–58. (11)

Lindemann, B. 1977. Steady-state kinetics of a floating receptor model for the inhibition of sodium uptake by sodium in frog skin. In *Renal Function*, ed. G. Giebisch and E. F. Purcell, 110–131. New York: Josiah Macy Jr. Foundation. (5)

Lindinger, M. I. 1984. Fine structure of the abdominal epidermis of the adult mudpuppy, *Necturus maculosus* (Rafinesque). *Cell and Tissue Research* 238:395–405. (5)

Lindquist, S. B., and M. D. Bachmann. 1982. The role of visual and olfactory cues in the prey catching behavior of the tiger salamander *Ambystoma tigrinum*. *Copeia* 1982:81–90. (13)

List, R. J. 1951. *Smithsonian Meteorological Tables*. 6th rev. ed. Washington, DC: Smithsonian Institution Press. (4,9)

Littleford, R. A., W. F. Keller, and N. E. Phillips. 1947. Studies on the vital limits of water loss in the plethodontid salamanders. *Ecology* 28:440–447. (6)

Littlejohn, M. J. 1977. Long-range acoustic communication in anurans: An integrated and evolutionary approach. In *The Reproductive Biology of Amphibians*, ed. D. H. Taylor and S. I. Guttman, 263–294. New York: Plenum Press. (14)

Littlejohn, M. J., and P. A. Harrison. 1985. The functional significance of the diphasic advertisement call of *Geocrinia victoriana* (Anura: Leptodactylidac). *Behavioral Ecology and Sociobiology* 16:363–373. (14)

Littlejohn, M. J., P. A. Harrison, and R. C. MacNally. 1985. Interspecific acoustic interactions in sympatric populations of *Ranidella signifera* and *R. parinsignifera* (Anura: Leptodactylidae). In *Biology of Australasian Frogs and Reptiles*, ed. G. Grigg, R. Shine, and H. Ehmann, 287–296. Chipping Norton, NSW, Australia: Surey Beatty and Sons. (14)

Liuzzi, F. J., M. S. Beattie, and J. C. Bresnahan. 1985. The development of the relationship between dorsal root afferents and motoneurons in the larval bullfrog spinal cord. *Brain Research Bulletin* 14:377–392. (16)

Livezey, R. L. 1962. Food of adult and juvenile *Bufo boreas* Exsul. *Herpetologica* 17:267–268. (13)

Llinás, R., and W. Precht. 1976. *Frog Neurobiology: A Handbook*. Berlin: Springer-Verlag. (11)

Lock, A., and T. Collett. 1979. A toad's devious approach to its prey: A study of some complex uses of depth vision. *Journal of Comparative Physiology* 131:179–189. (13)

Locker, A., and P. Weish. 1966. Quantitative aspects of cold-adaptation and its thyroxine model in cold- and warm-blooded animals. *Helgolander wissenschaftliche Meeresuntersuchungen* 14:503–513. (12)

———. 1969. Beziehungen zwischen Sauerstoffverbrauch, Wachstum, und Körpergrösse während der Larvenentwicklung und Metamorphose von *Rana temporaria*. *Biologisches Zentralblatt* 88:497–507. (12)

Lodi, G., M. Biciotti, and B. Viotto. 1982. Cutaneous osmoregulation in *Triturus cristatus carnifex* (Laur.) (Urodela). *General and Comparative Endocrinology* 46:452–457. (5)

Loeb, G. E., and C. Gans. 1986. *Electromyography for Experimentalists*. Chicago: University of Chicago Press. (11)

Loewi, O. 1921. Concerning the humoral transmissability of nerve heart actions. *Pflugers Archiv* 189:239–242. (1)

Lofts, B. 1964. Seasonal changes in the functional activity of the interstitial and spermatogenetic tissues of the green frog, *Rana esculenta*. *General and Comparative Endocrinology* 4:550–562. (15)

———. 1974. Reproduction. In *Physiology of the Amphibia*, ed. B. Lofts, 2:107–218. New York: Academic Press. (15,16)

———, ed. 1974–76. *Physiology of the Amphibia*. Vols. 2, 3. New York: Academic Press. (1)

———. 1984. Amphibians. In *Marshall's Physiology of Reproduction*, 4th ed., vol. 1, ed. G. E. Lamming, 127–205. Edinburgh: Churchill Livingstone. (3,15)

Loftus-Hills, J. J., and B. M. Johnstone. 1970. Auditory function, communication, and brain-evoked response in anuran amphibians. *Journal of the Acoustical Society of America* 47:1131–1138. (11)

Logier, E. B. S. 1952. *The Frogs, Toads, and Salamanders of Eastern Canada*. Toronto: Clarke, Irwin and Company. (10)

Lomax, P., J. G. Bajorek, W. A. Chesarek, and R. R. J. Chafee. 1980. Ethanol-induced hypothermia in the rat. *Pharmacology* 21:288–294. (9)

Lombard, R. E., and J. R. Bolt. 1979. Evolution of the tetrapod ear: An analysis and reinterpretation. *Biological Journal of the Linnean Society* 11:19–76. (2)

———. 1988. Evolution of the stapes in paleozoic tetrapods: Conservative and radical hypotheses. In *The Evolution of the Amphibian Auditory System*, ed. B. Fritzsch, M. J. Ryan, W. Wilczynski, T. E. Hetherington, and W. Walkowiak, 37–67. New York: John Wiley and Sons. (2)

Lombard, R. E., and I. R. Straughan. 1974. Functional aspects of anuran middle ear structures. *Journal of Experimental Biology* 61:71–93. (2,11)

Lombard, R. E., and D. B. Wake. 1976. Tongue evolution in the lungless salamanders, family Plethodontidae: 1. Introduction, theory, and a general model of dynamics. *Journal of Morphology* 148:265–286. (11,14)

———. 1977. Tongue evolution in the lungless salamanders, family Plethodontidae: 2. Functional and evolutionary diversity. *Journal of Morphology* 153:39–80. (11,14)

———. 1986. Tongue evolution in the lungless salamanders, family Plethodontidae: 4. Phylogeny of plethodontid salamanders and the evolution of feeding dynamics. *Systematic Zoology* 35:532–551. (11,14)

Lombroso, U. 1913. The reflex inhibition of the heart during reflex respiratory inhibition in various animals. *Zeitschrift für Biologie* 61:517–538. (7)

Londos, P. L., and R. J. Brooks. 1988. Effect of temperature acclimation on locomotory performance curves in the toad, *Bufo woodhousii woodhousii*. *Copeia* 1988:26–32. (8,9,12)

Long, D. R. 1987a. A comparison of energy substrates and reproductive patterns of two anurans, *Acris crepitans* and *Bufo woodhousei*. *Comparative Biochemistry and Physiology* 87A:81–91. (14,15)

———. 1987b. Reproductive and lipid patterns of a semiarid-adapted anuran, *Bufo cognatus*. *Texas Journal of Science* 39:3–13. (14,15)

———. 1989. Energetics and reproduction in female *Scaphiopus multiplicatus* from western Texas. *Journal of Herpetology* 23:176–179. (15)

Long, S. 1982. Renal electrolyte handling, acid-base status, and urinary acidification in *Bufo marinus*. *American Journal of Physiology* 243:F60–F66. (5)

Long, W. S. 1973. Renal handling of urea in *Rana catesbeiana*. *American Journal of Physiology* 224:482–490. (5,16)

Lonnerholm, G., and Y. Ridderstrale. 1974. Distribution of carbonic anhydrase in the frog nephron. *Acta Physiologica Scandinavica* 90:764–778. (5)

Lopes, A. G., A. W. Siebens, G. Giebisch, and W. F. Boron. 1987. Electrogenic Na/HCO_3 cotransport across basolateral membrane of isolated perfused *Necturus* proximal tubule. *American Journal of Physiology* 253:F340–F350. (5)

Lopes, O. U., and J. F. Palmer. 1976. Proposed respiratory "gating" mechanism for cardiac slowing. *Nature* 264:454–456. (7)

Lopez, P. T., P. M. Narins, E. R. Lewis, and S. W. Moore. 1988. Acoustically induced call modification in the white-lipped frog *Leptodactylus albilabris*. *Animal Behaviour* 36:1295–1308. (14)

Lote, C. J., J. B. Rider, and S. Thomas. 1974. The effect of prostaglandin E₁ on the short circuit current and sodium, potassium, chloride, and calcium movements across isolated frog (*Rana temporaria*) skin. *Pflugers Archiv* 352:145–153. (5)

Lotshaw, D. P. 1977. Temperature adaptation and effects of thermal acclimation in *Rana sylvatica* and *Rana catesbeiana*. *Comparative Biochemistry and Physiology* 56A:287–294. (10)

Love, T. J. 1968. *Radiation Heat Transfer*. Columbus, OH: Merrill Press. (4)

Loveridge, J. P. 1970. Observations on nitrogenous excretion and water relations of *Chiromantis xerampelina* (Amphibia, Anura). *Arnoldia* 5:1–6. (4,6)

———. 1976. Strategies of water conservation in southern African frogs. *Zoologica Africana* 11:319–333. (6)

Loveridge, J. P., and G. Crayé. 1979. Cocoon formation in two species of southern African frogs. *South African Journal of Science* 75:18–20. (4,6)

Loveridge, J. P., and P. C. Withers. 1981. Metabolism and water balance of active and cocooned African bullfrogs *Pyxicephalus adspersus*. *Physiological Zoology* 54:203–214. (10,12)

Lowe, D. A. 1986. Organization of lateral line and auditory areas in the midbrain of *Xenopus laevis*. *Journal of Comparative Neurology* 245:498–513. (2)

Lowenstein, W. R. 1956. Modulation of cutaneous mechanoreceptors by sympathetic stimulation. *Journal of Physiology* (London) 132:40–60. (7)

Lozar, J., C. Laguerie, and J. P. Couderc. 1975. Diffusivité de l'acide benzoique dans l'eau: Influence de la température. *Canadian Journal of Chemical Engineering* 53:200–203. (8)

Lubosch, W. 1913. Die Kaumuskulatur der Amphibien, vergleichen mit dem der Sauropsiden und Säugetiere. *Verhandlungen der Anatomischen Gesellschaft* 27:67–76; *Anatomischer Anzeiger* 44 (Ergänzungsheft). (11)

———. 1914. Vergleichende Anatomie der Kaumuskeln der Wirbeltiere, in fünf Teilen: 1. Die Kaumuskeln der Amphibien. *Jenaische Zeitschrift für Naturwissenschaften* 53:51–188. (11)

Lucas, E. A., and A. W. Reynolds. 1967. Temperature selection by amphibian larvae. *Physiological Zoology* 40:159–171. (9)

Luckhardt, A. B., and A. J. Carlson. 1921. Studies on the visceral sensory nervous system: 8. On the presence of vasomotor fibres in the vagus nerve to the pulmonary vessels of the amphibian and the reptilian lung. *American Journal of Physiology* 56:72–112. (7)

Ludens, H. J., and D. D. Fanestil. 1972. Acidification of urine by the isolated urinary bladder of the toad. *American Journal of Physiology* 223:1338–1344. (5)

———. 1974. Aldosterone stimulation of acidification of urine by isolated urinary bladder of the Colombian toad. *American Journal of Physiology* 226:1321–1326. (5)

Luff, A. R., and U. Proske. 1976. Properties of motor units of the frog sartorius muscle. *Journal of Physiology* (London) 258:673–685. (11)

———. 1979. Properties of motor units of the frog iliofibularis muscle. *American Journal of Physiology* 236:C35–C40. (8,11)

Lundberg, K., and R. Gerrell. 1986. Territorial advertisement and mate attraction in the bat *Pipistrellus pipistrellus*. *Ethology* 71:115–124. (14)

Luthardt, G., and G. Roth. 1979. The influence of prey experience on movement pattern preference in *Salamandra salamandra* (L.). *Zeitschrift für Tierpsychologie* 51:252–259. (11,13)

———. 1983. The interaction of the visual and the olfactory systems on guiding prey catching behaviour in *Salamandra salamandra* (L.). *Behaviour* 83:69–79. (2)

Luthardt-Laimer, G. 1983. Ontogeny of preferences to visual stimulus parameters in salamanders. *Journal of Herpetology* 17:221–227. (14)

Luther, A. 1914. Über die vom *N. trigeminus* versorgte Muskulatur der Amphibien mit einem vergleichenden Ausblick über der Adductor mandibulae der Gnathostomen und einen Beitrag zum Verständnis der Organisation der Anurenlarven. *Acta Societa Scientifica Fennica* 44:1–151. (11)

Lutz, B. R., and L. C. Wyman. 1932. The evolution of a carotid sinus reflex and the origin of vagal tone. *Science* 75:590–591. (7)

Lutz, P. L., M. Rosenthal, and T. J. Sick. 1985. Living without oxygen: Turtle brain as a model of anaerobic metabolism. *Molecular Physiology* 8:411–425. (10)

Lykkeboe, G., and K. Johansen. 1978. An O_2-Hb "paradox" in frog blood? (n-values exceeding 4.0). *Respiration Physiology* 35:119–127. (5)

Lynch, K. 1983. Structure of the *rectus abdominis* muscle in frog larvae and postmetamorphic juveniles. *Anatomical Record* 205:115A. (11)

———. 1984. Growth and metamorphosis of the *rectus abdominis* muscle in *Rana pipiens*. *Journal of Morphology* 182:317–337. (11)

Lynch, K., and C. D. Harris. 1984. Metamorphosis of the *rectus abdominis* muscle in *Rana pipiens*. *Anatomical Record* 208:106A. (11)

Lynch, K., M. J. Homer, C. D. Harris, and J. Morrissey. 1986. An ultrastructural comparison of neuromuscular junctions in normal and developmentally arrested *Rana pipiens* larvae: Limited maturation in the absence of metamorphosis. *American Journal of Anatomy* 176:83–95. (16)

Lysenko, S., and J. E. Gillis. 1980. The effect of ingestive status on the thermoregulatory behavior of *Thamnophis sirtalis sirtalis* and *Thamnophis sirtalis parietalis*. *Journal of Herpetology* 14:155–159. (9)

McAllister, C. T., and L. C. Fitzpatrick. 1985. Thermal acclimation and oxygen consumption rates in neotenic grey-bellied salamanders, *Eurycea multiplicata griseogaster* (Plethodontidae), from an Arkansas cave. *Journal of Thermal Biology* 10:1–4. (8,12)

MacArthur, D. L., and J. W. T. Dandy. 1982. Physiological aspects of overwintering in the boreal chorus frog (*Pseudacris triseriata maculata*). *Comparative Biochemistry and Physiology* 72A:137–141. (10)

MacArthur, R. H., and E. R. Pianka. 1966. On the optimal use of a patchy environment. *American Naturalist* 100:603–609. (14)

McBean, R., and L. Goldstein. 1970a. Accelerated synthesis of urea in *Xenopus laevis* during osmotic stress. *American Journal of Physiology* 219:1124–1130. (6)

———. 1970b. Renal function during osmotic stress in the aquatic toad *Xenopus laevis*. *American Journal of Physiology* 219:1115–1123. (5,6,10)

McCann, C. 1932. Notes on Indian batrachians. *Journal of Bombay Natural History Society* 36:152–180. (15)

McCauley, R. W. 1977. Laboratory methods for determining temperature preference. *Journal of Fisheries Research Board of Canada* 34:749–752. (9)

McClanahan, L. L. 1964. Osmotic tolerance of the muscles of two desert inhabiting toads, *Bufo cognatus* and *Scaphiopus couchi*. *Comparative Biochemistry and Physiology* 12:501–508. (10,11)

———. 1967. Adaptations of the spadefoot toad, *Scaphiopus couchi*, to desert environments. *Comparative Biochemistry and Physiology* 20:73–99. (6,9,10,12)

———. 1972. Changes in body fluids of burrowed spadefoot toads as a function of soil water potential. *Copeia* 1972:209–216. (6,10)

McClanahan, L. L., and R. Baldwin. 1969. Rate of water uptake through the integument of the desert toad, *Bufo punctatus*. *Comparative Biochemistry and Physiology* 28:381–389. (6)

McClanahan, L. L., R. Ruibal, and V. H. Shoemaker. 1983. Rate of cocoon formation and its physiological correlates in a ceratophryd frog. *Physiological Zoology* 56:430–435. (3,6,10,12)

McClanahan, L. L., and V. H. Shoemaker. 1987. Behavior and thermal relations of the arboreal frog *Phyllomedusa sauvagei*. *National Geographic Research* 3:11–21. (6,9,16)

McClanahan, L. L., V. H. Shoemaker, and R. Ruibal. 1976. Structure and function of the cocoon of a ceratophryd frog. *Copeia* 1976: 179–185. (4,6,10)

McClanahan, L. L., J. N. Stinner, and V. H. Shoemaker. 1978. Skin lipids, water loss, and energy metabolism in a South American tree frog (*Phyllomedusa sauvagei*). *Physiological Zoology* 51:179–187. (4,6,12)

McClellan, A. D. 1986. Command systems for initiating locomotion in fish and amphibians: Parallels to initiation systems in mammals. In *Neurobiology of Vertebrate Locomotion*, ed. S. Grillner, P. S. G. Stein, D. G. Stuart, H. Forssberg, and R. M. Herman, 3–20. Wenner-Gren International Symposium Series no. 45. London: Macmillan. (16)

McClellan, A. D., and P. B. Farel. 1985. Pharmacological activation of locomotor patterns in larval and adult frog spinal cords. *Brain Research* 332:119–130. (16)

McClelland, B. E., and W. Wilczynski. 1989a. Release call characteristics of male and female *Rana pipiens*. *Copeia* 1989:1041–1045. (2)

———. 1989b. Sexually dimorphic laryngeal morphology in *Rana pipiens pipiens*. *Journal of Morphology* 201:293–299. (2,11)

McClelland, B. E., W. Wilczynski, and M. J. Ryan. 1988a. Mating call characteristics and laryngeal morphology in two populations of *Acris crepitans*. *Society for Neuroscience Abstracts* 14:90. (2)

———. 1988b. Mating call dominant frequency and ear morphology in two populations of *Acris crepitans*. *American Zoologist* 28: 179A. (2)

McComb, K. 1987. Roaring by red deer stags advances the date of oestrus in hinds. *Nature* 330:648–649. (14)

McCord, C. P., and F. P. Allen. 1917. Evidences associating pineal gland function with alterations of pigmentation. *Journal of Experimental Zoology* 23:207–224. (16)

McCreery, B. R. 1984. Pituitary gonadotropin release by graded electrical stimulation of the preoptic area in the male bullfrog, *Rana catesbeiana*. *General and Comparative Endocrinology* 55:367–372. (15)

McCreery, B. R., and P. Licht. 1983. Induced ovulation and changes in pituitary responsiveness to continuous infusion of gonadotropin-releasing hormone (GnRH) during the ovarian cycle in the bullfrog, *Rana catesbeiana*. *Biology of Reproduction* 29:863–871. (15)

———. 1984. Effect of gonadectomy and sex steroids on pituitary gonadotropin release and response to gonadotropin-releasing hormone (GnRH) agonist in the bullfrog, *Rana catesbeiana*. *General and Comparative Endocrinology* 54:283–296. (3)

McCreery, B. R., P. Licht, R. Barnes, J. E. Rivier, and W. W. Vale. 1982. Actions of agonistic and antagonistic analogs of gonadotropin-releasing hormone (Gn-RH) in the bullfrog *Rana catesbeiana*. *General and Comparative Endocrinology* 46:511–520. (15)

McCutcheon, F. H. 1936. Hemoglobin function during the life history of the bullfrog. *Journal of Cellular and Comparative Physiology* 8:63–81. (5)

McCutcheon, F. H., and F. G. Hall. 1937. Hemoglobin in the Amphibia. *Journal of Cellular and Comparative Physiology* 9:191–197. (5)

McDiarmid, R. W. 1978. Evolution of parental care in frogs. In *The Development of Behavior: Comparative and Evolutionary Aspects*, ed. G. M. Burghardt and M. Bekoff, 127–147. New York: STMP Press. (14)

McDiarmid, R. W., and M. S. Foster. 1987. Cocoon formation in another hylid frog, *Smilisca baudinii*. *Journal of Herpetology* 21: 352–355. (6)

McDonald, D. G., R. G. Boutilier, and D. P. Toews. 1980. The effects of enforced activity on ventilation, circulation, and blood acid-base balance in the semi-terrestrial anuran, *Bufo marinus*. *Journal of Experimental Biology* 84:273–287. (5,7,12)

McDonald, D. G., J. L. Ozog, and B. P. Simons. 1984. The influence of low pH environments on ion regulation in the larval stages of the anuran amphibian, *Rana clamitans*. *Canadian Journal of Zoology* 62:2171–2177. (5)

Macdonald, J. A., and J. C. Montgomery. 1982. Thermal limits of neuromuscular function in an Antarctic fish. *Journal of Comparative Physiology* 147B:237–250. (8)

MacDonald, M. L., Q. R. Rogers, and J. G. Morris. 1984. Nutrition of the domestic cat, a mammalian carnivore. *Annual Review of Nutrition* 4:521–562. (15)

Macedo, H. de. 1960. Vergleichende Untersuchungen an Arten der Gattung *Telmatobius* (Amphibia, Anura). *Zeitschrift für wissenschaftliche Zoologie Abteilung* 163:355–396. (4)

McGregor, J. H., and W. R. Teska. 1989. Olfaction as an orienting mechanism in migrating *Ambystoma maculatum*. *Copeia* 1989:779–781. (2)

McIndoe, R., and D. G. Smith. 1984a. Functional morphology of gills in larval amphibians. In *Respiration and Metabolism of Embryonic Vertebrates*, ed. R. S. Seymour, 55–69. Dordrecht, Netherlands: Junk. (16)

———. 1984b. Functional anatomy of the internal gills of the tadpole of *Litoria ewingii* [Anura, Hylidae]. *Zoomorphology* 104:280–291.

Macintyre, D. H., and D. P. Toews. 1976. The mechanics of lung ventilation and the effects of hypercapnia on respiration in *Bufo marinus*. *Canadian Journal of Zoology* 54:1364–1374. (5,6,7)

Mackay, B., A. L. Muir, and A. Peters. 1960. Observations on the terminal innervation of segmental muscle fibres in Amphibia. *Acta Anatomica* 40:1–12. (11)

Mackay, C. W., and B. Schmidt-Nielsen. 1969. Osmotic and diffusional water permeability in tadpoles and frogs *Rana clamitans*. *Bulletin Mount Desert Island Laboratory* 9:26–27. (16)

McKay, D. M. 1989. Seasonal variation in calling behavior and muscle biochemistry in spring peepers (*Hyla crucifer*). M.S. diss., University of Connecticut, Storrs. (14)

Mackay-Sim, A., W. Breipohl, and M. Kremer. 1987. Cell dynamics in the olfactory epithelium of the tiger salamander: A morphometric analysis. *Experimental Brain Research* 60:1–10. (16)

Mackay-Sim, A., and M. H. Nathan. 1984. The projection from the olfactory epithelium to the olfactory bulb in the salamander *Ambystoma tigrinum*. *Anatomy and Embryology* 170:93–97. (16)

Mackay-Sim, A., and P. Shaman. 1984. Topographic coding of odorant quality is maintained at different concentrations in the salamander olfactory epithelium. *Brain Research* 297:207–216. (16)

McKean, T. A. 1969. A linear approximation of the transfer function of pulmonary mechanoreceptors in the frog. *Journal of Applied Physiology* 27:775–781. (7)

MacKenzie, D. S., and P. Licht. 1984. Studies on the specificity of thyroid response to pituitary glycoprotein hormones. *General and Comparative Endocrinology* 56:156–166. (3)

MacKenzie, D. S., P. Licht, and H. Papkoff. 1978. Thyrotropin from amphibian (*Rana catesbeiana*) pituitaries and evidence for heterothyrotropic activity of bullfrog luteinizing hormone in reptiles. *General and Comparative Endocrinology* 36:566–574. (3,16)

MacKenzie, J. A., and D. C. Jackson. 1978. The effect of temperature on cutaneous CO_2 loss and conductance in the bullfrog. *Respiration Physiology* 32:313–323. (5,6,10,12,16)

MacKnight, A. D. C., D. R. DiBona, and A. Leaf. 1980. Sodium transport across toad urinary bladder: A model "tight" epithelium. *Physiological Review* 60:615–713. (5)

McLaren, I. A., and J. M. Cooley. 1972. Temperature adaptation of embryonic development rate among frogs. *Physiological Zoology* 45:223–228. (8,9)

McMurrich, J. P. 1903a. The phylogeny of the forearm flexors. *American Journal of Anatomy* 2:177–209. (11)

———. 1903b. The phylogeny of the palmar musculature. *American Journal of Anatomy* 2:463–500. (11)

———. 1904. The phylogeny of the crural flexors. *American Journal of Anatomy* 4:33–76. (11)

McNab, B. K. 1978. The evolution of endothermy in the phylogeny of mammals. *American Naturalist* 112:1–21. (4)

———. 1980. Food habits, energetics, and the population biology of mammals. *American Naturalist* 116:106–124. (12)

———. 1988. Complications inherent in scaling the basal rate of metabolism in mammals. *Quarterly Review of Biology* 63:25–54. (12)

McNabb, R. A. 1969. The effects of thyroxine on glycogen stores and oxygen consumption in the leopard frog, *Rana pipiens*. *General and Comparative Endocrinology* 12:276–281. (9,12)

MacNally, R. C. 1981a. An analysis of factors affecting metabolic rates of two species of *Ranidella* (Anura). *Comparative Biochemistry and Physiology* 69A:731–737. (12)

———. 1981b. On the reproductive energetics of chorusing males: Energy depletion, restoration, and growth for two sympatric species of *Ranidella* (Anura). *Oecologia* (Berlin) 51:181–188. (14)

———. 1984. On the reproductive energetics of chorusing males: Costs and patterns of call production in two sympatric species of *Ranidella* (Anura). *Oikos* 42:82–91. (14)

MacNally, R. C., and J. M. Doolan. 1982. Comparative reproductive energetics of the sexes in the cicada *Cystosoma saundersii*. *Oikos* 39:179–186. (14)

MacNally, R. C., and D. Young. 1981. Song energetics of the bladder cicada, *Cystosoma saundersii*. *Journal of Experimental Biology* 90: 185–196. (14)

McNeil, S. A. 1989. The role of the lymphatic system in water balance processes in the toad *Bufo marinus* (L.). B.S. thesis, Acadia University, Wolfville, Nova Scotia. (5)

McPheeters, M., and S. D. Roper. 1985. Amiloride does not block taste transduction in the mudpuppy, *Necturus maculosus*. *Chemical Senses* 10:341–352. (16)

Madison, D. M., and C. R. Shoop. 1970. Homing behavior, orientation, and home range of salamanders tagged with tantalum-182. *Science* 168:1484–1487. (14)

Maeda, N., S. Miyoshi, and H. Toh. 1983. First observation of a muscle spindle in fish. *Nature* 302:61–62. (11)

Magherini, P. C., W. Precht, and P. C. Schwindt. 1976. Evidence for electronic coupling between motor neurons in the *in situ* spinal cord. *Journal of Neurophysiology* 39:474–483. (2)

Magimel-Pélonnier, O.-L. 1924. La langue des amphibiens. Thesis, Faculté des Sciences, Paris. (11)

Maginniss, L. A., Y. K. Song, and R. B. Reeves. 1980. Oxygen equilibria of ectotherm blood containing multiple hemoglobins. *Respiration Physiology* 42:329–343. (5,16)

Maginniss, L. A., S. S. Tapper, and L. S. Miller. 1983. Effect of chronic cold and submergence on blood oxygen transport in the turtle, *Chrysemys picta*. *Respiration Physiology* 53:15–29. (10)

Magnuson, J. J., L. B. Crowder, and P. A. Medvick. 1979. Temperature as an ecological resource. *American Zoologist* 19:331–343. (4)

Magnusson, W. E., L. J. de Paiva, R. M. de Rocha, C. R. Franke, L. A. Kasper, and A. P. Lima. 1985. The correlates of foraging mode in a community of Brazilian lizards. *Herpetologica* 41:324–332. (14)

Magnusson, W. E., and J. Windle. 1988. Marathon swimming to egg-laying sites by *Bufo granulosus*. *Journal of Herpetology* 22:235–236. (12)

Maguire, C. C. 1981. *Plethodon glutinosus* metabolism: Applicability to natural populations. *Journal of Herpetology* 15:127–132. (12)

Mahany, T. M., and R. H. Parsons. 1978. Circulatory effects on osmotic water exchange in *Rana pipiens*. *American Journal of Physiology* 234:R172–R177. (4,5,6,10)

Maher, M. J. 1967. Response to thyroxine as a function of environmental temperature in the toad, *Bufo woodhousii*, and the frog, *Rana pipiens*. *Copeia* 1967:361–365. (9,12)

Mahler, M. 1978. Diffusion and consumption of oxygen in resting frog sartorius. *Journal of General Physiology* 71:533–577. (8)

Mahoney, J. J., and V. H. Hutchison. 1969. Photoperiod acclimation and 24-hour variations in the critical thermal maxima of a tropical and temperate frog. *Oecologica* (Berlin) 2:143–161. (8)

Main, A. R. 1968. Ecology, systematics, and evolution of Australian frogs. In *Advances in Ecological Research*, vol. 5, ed. J. B. Cragg, 37–86. New York: Academic Press. (10)

Main, A. R., and P. J. Bentley. 1964. Water relations of Australian burrowing frogs and tree frogs. *Ecology* 45:379–382. (6,10)

Main, A. R., M. J. Littlejohn, and A. K. Lee. 1959. Ecology of Australian frogs. In *Biogeography and Ecology in Australia*, ed. A. Keast, R. L. Crocker, and C. S. Christian, 396–411. Monographs in Biology 8. The Hague: Junk. (10)

Mainwood, G. W., P. Worsley-Brown, and R. A. Paterson. 1972. The metabolic changes in frog sartorius muscles during recovery from fatigue at different external bicarbonate concentrations. *Canadian Journal of Physiology and Pharmacology* 50:143–155. (12)

Maiorana, V. C. 1977. Tail autotomy: Functional conflicts and their resolution by a salamander. *Nature* 265:533–535. (14,15)

———. 1978. Difference in diet as an epiphenomenon: Space regulates salamanders. *Canadian Journal of Zoology* 56:1017–1025. (14)

Malacarne, G., and R. Cortass. 1983. Sexual selection in the crested newt. *Animal Behaviour* 31:1256–1257. (14)

Malacarne, G., and C. Giacoma. 1978. Lesions to the CNS and ovariectomy in *Triturus cristatus carnifex* Laur: Effects on sexual behaviour. *Atti della Accademia delle Scienze di Torino* 112:49–61. (15)

Malan, A., T. L. Wilson, and R. B. Reeves. 1976. Intracellular pH in cold-blooded vertebrates as a function of body temperature. *Respiration Physiology* 28:29–47. (5)

Malvin, G. M. 1985a. Adrenoceptor types in the respiratory vasculature of the salamander gill. *Journal of Comparative Physiology* 155B:591–596. (5,7)

———. 1985b. Cardiovascular shunting during amphibian metamorphosis. In *Cardiovascular Shunts: Ontogenetic, Phylogenetic, and Clinical Aspects*, ed. K. Johansen and W. W. Burggren, 163–178. Copenhagen: Munksgaard. (5,7,16)

———. 1985c. Vascular resistance and vasoactivity of gills and pulmonary artery of the salamander, *Ambystoma tigrinum*. *Journal of Comparative Physiology* 155B:241–249. (5,7,16)

———. 1988. Microvascular regulation of cutaneous gas exchange in amphibians. *American Zoologist* 28:999–1007. (5,6,7,9)

———. 1989. Gill structure and function: Amphibian larvae. In *Comparative Pulmonary Physiology: Current Concepts*, vol. 39, *Lung Biology in Health and Disease*, ed. S. C. Wood, 121–151. New York: Marcel Dekker. (5)

Malvin, G. M., and R. G. Boutilier. 1985. Ventilation-perfusion relationships in Amphibia. In *Circulation, Respiration, and Metabolism*, ed. R. Gilles, 114–124. Berlin: Springer-Verlag. (5)

Malvin, G. M., and N. Heisler. 1988. Blood flow patterns in the salamander *Ambystoma tigrinum*, before, during, and after metamorphosis. *Journal of Experimental Biology* 137:53–74. (7,16)

Malvin, G. M., and M. P. Hlastala. 1986a. Effects of lung volume and O_2 and CO_2 content on cutaneous gas exchange in frogs. *American Journal of Physiology* 251:R941–R946. (5,6,7)

———. 1986b. Regulation of cutaneous gas exchange by environmental O_2 and CO_2 in the frog. *Respiration Physiology* 65:99–111. (5,6,7)

———. 1989. Effects of environmental O_2 on blood flow and diffusing capacity in amphibian skin. *Respiration Physiology* 76:229–242. (6)

Malvin, G. M., S. C. Wood, and C. Reidel. 1989. Behavioral hypothermia in dehydrated toads. *FASEB Journal* 3:A234. (9)

Man, J. G. de. 1873. *Vergelijkende myologische en neurologische studien over amphibien en vogels.* Leiden: S. C. van Doesburgh. (11)

———. 1874–75. Myologie comparée de l'extrémité postérieure chez les amphibiens. *Nederländisches Archiv für Zoologie* 2:53–88. (11)

Mandelbrot, B. B. 1967. How long is the coast of Britain? Statistical self-similarity and fractional dimension. *Science* 156:636–638. (14)

Maness, J., and V. H. Hutchison. 1980. Acute adjustment of thermal tolerance in vertebrate ectotherms following exposure to critical thermal maxima. *Journal of Thermal Biology* 5:225–233. (9)

Mang, A. 1935. Beiträge zur Kenntnis der Gymnophionen: 22. Über die Drüsen der Haut und der Mundhöhle von *Hypogeophis. Morphologisches Jahrbuch* 75:295–314. (13)

Manion, J. J., and L. Cory. 1952. Winter kill of *Rana pipiens* in shallow ponds. *Herpetologica* 8:32. (10)

Manis, M. L., and D. L. Claussen. 1986. Environmental and genetic influences on the thermal physiology of *Rana sylvatica*. *Journal of Thermal Biology* 11:31–36. (8)

Manteuffel, G., J. Kopp, and W. Himstedt. 1986. The amphibian optokinetic after nystagmus: Properties and comparative analysis in various species. *Behavioral and Brain Research* 28:186–197. (2)

Manteuffel, G., J. Petersen, and W. Himstedt. 1983. Optic nystagomogen centers in the European fire salamander (*Salamandra salamandra*). *Zoologische Jahrbuch Physiologie* 87:113–125. (2)

Manz, R. 1975. Die Fusionsfrequenzen der Kehlkopfmuskeln und eines Beinmuskels in Abhängigkeit von der Temperatur bei europäischen Froschlurchen (Anura). *Zoologische Jahrbücher, Abteilung für Allgemeine Zoologie und Physiologie der Tiere* 79:221–245. (11,14)

Maples, P. B., J. C. Palmer, and R. H. Broyles. 1986. *In vivo* regulation of hemoglobin phenotypes of developing *Rana catesbeiana*. *Developmental Biology* 117:337–341. (16)

Marconi, C. D., D. Pendergast, P. Selyk, D. W. Rennie, and P. Cerretelli. 1982. Dynamical and steady-state metabolic changes in running dogs. *Respiration Physiology* 50:93–110. (12)

Marcuse, W. 1886. Über die Bildung von Milchsaure bei der Thätigkeit des Muskels und ihr weiteres Schicksal im Organismus. *Pflugers Archiv* 39:425–448. (12)

Margules, D. L., B. Goldman, and A. Finck. 1979. Hibernation: An opioid dependent state? *Brain Research Bulletin* 4:721–724. (10)

Marian, M. P., and T. J. Pandian. 1985. Effect of temperature on development, growth, and bioenergetics of the bullfrog tadpole *Rana tigrina*. *Journal of Thermal Biology* 10:157–162. (8)

Marks, S. B., and L. D. Houck. 1989. Partial cost of spermatophore production in the salamander *Desmognathus ochrophaeus*. *Journal of Herpetology* 23:81–84. (14)

Marsh, R. L. 1981. Catabolic enzyme activities in relation to premigratory fattening and muscle hypertrophy in the gray catbird (*Dumetella corolinensis*). *Journal of Comparative Physiology* 141B:417–423. (14)

Marsh, R. L., and A. F. Bennett. 1985. Thermal dependence of isotonic contractile properties of skeletal muscle and sprint performance of the lizard *Dipsosaurus dorsalis*. *Journal of Comparative Physiology* 155B:541–551. (8)

———. 1986a. Thermal dependence of contractile properties of skeletal muscle from the lizard *Sceloporus occidentalis* with comments on methods of fitting and comparing force-velocity curves. *Journal of Experimental Biology* 126:63–77. (8)

———. 1986b. Thermal dependence of sprint performance of the lizard *Sceloporus occidentalis*. *Journal of Experimental Biology* 126:79–87. (8)

Marsh, R. L., and T. L. Taigen. 1987. Properties enhancing aerobic capacity of calling muscles in gray tree frogs, *Hyla versicolor*. *American Journal of Physiology* 252:R786–R793. (12,14)

Marshall, A. M. 1928. *The Frog*. 12th ed. Ed. H. G. Newth. London: Macmillan and Company. (7)

Marshall, E., and G. C. Grigg. 1980. Lack of metabolic acclimation to different thermal histories by tadpoles of *Limnodynastes peroni* (Anura: Leptodactylidae). *Physiological Zoology* 53:1–7. (12)

Marshall, E. K., Jr., and M. M. Crane. 1924. The secretory function of the renal tubules. *American Journal of Physiology* 70:465–488. (5)

Marten, K., D. Quine, and P. Marler. 1977. Sound transmission and its significance for animal vocalization: 2. Tropical habitats. *Behavioral Ecology and Sociobiology* 2:291–302. (14)

Martens, G. J. M., B. G. Jenks, and A. P. van Overbeeke. 1981. N alpha-acetylation is linked to alpha-MSH release from pars intermedia of the amphibian pituitary gland. *Nature* 94:558–560. (3)

Martens, G. J. M., F. Soeterik, B. G. Jenks, and A. P. van Overbeeke. 1983. *In vivo* biosynthesis of melanotropins and related peptides in the pars intermedia of *Xenopus laevis*. *General and Comparative Endocrinology* 49:73–80. (3)

Martin, A. A., and A. K. Cooper. 1972. The ecology of terrestrial anuran eggs, genus *Crinia* (Leptodactylidae). *Copeia* 1972:162–168. (10)

Martin, J. B., N. B. Witherspoon, and M. H. A. Keenleyside. 1974. Analysis of feeding behavior in the newt *Notophthalmus viridescens*. *Canadian Journal of Zoology* 52:277–281. (13)

Martin, K. M., and V. H. Hutchison. 1979. Ventilatory activity in *Amphiuma tridactylum* and *Siren lacertina* (Amphibia, Caudata). *Journal of Herpetology* 13:427–434. (9,11)

Martin, W. F. 1971. Mechanics of sound production in toads in the genus *Bufo*: Passive elements. *Journal of Experimental Zoology* 176:273–294. (11,14)

———. 1972. Evolution of vocalization in the genus *Bufo*. In *Evolution of the Genus Bufo*, ed. W. F. Blair, 279–309. Austin: University of Texas Press. (2,14)

Martin, W. F., and C. Gans. 1972. Muscular control of the vocal tract during release signaling in the toad *Bufo valliceps*. *Journal of Morphology* 137:1–28. (11,14)

Martof, B. S. 1956. Growth and development of the green frog, *Rana clamitans*, under natural conditions. *American Midland Naturalist* 55:101–117. (14,15)

———. 1962. Some aspects of the life history and ecology of the salamander *Leurognathus*. *American Midland Naturalist* 67:1–35. (15)

Marusic, E., R. Martinez, and J. Torretti. 1966. Unresponsiveness of the adult toad to thyroxine administration. *Proceedings of the Society for Experimental Biology and Medicine* 122:164–167. (9)

Maruyama, K. 1979. Seasonal cycles in organ weights and lipid levels of the frog, *Rana nigromaculata*. *Annotationes Zoologicae Japonenses* 52:18–27. (15)

Marx, L. 1935. Bedingungen für die Metamorphose des Axolotls. *Ergebnisse der Biologie* 11:246–334. (16)

Maser, C., K. Hittler, and W. Hanke. 1980. External induction of changes of corticosterone level in Amphibia. *General and Comparative Endocrinology* 40:335. (3)

Maser, C., P. A. Janssens, and W. Hanke. 1982. Stimulation of interrenal secretion in Amphibia: 1. Direct effects of electrolyte concentration on steroid release. *General and Comparative Endocrinology* 47:458–466. (16)

Masino, T., and P. Grobstein. 1989a. The organization of descending tectofugal pathways underlying orienting in the frog, *Rana pipiens*: 1. Lateralization, parcellation, and an intermediate spatial representation. *Experimental Brain Research* 75:227–244. (2)

———. 1989b. The organization of descending tectofugal pathways underlying orienting in the frog, *Rana pipiens*: 2. Evidence for the involvement of a tecto-tegmento-spinal pathway. *Experimental Brain Research* 75:245–264. (2)

Masman, D., and M. Klaasen. 1987. Energy expenditure during free flight in trained and free-living kestrels, *Falco tinnunculus*. *Auk* 104:603–616. (14)

Mastro, A. M., M. A. Babich, W. D. Taylor, and A. D. Keith. 1984. Diffusion of a small molecule in the cytoplasm of mammalian cells. *Proceedings of the National Academy of Sciences* 81:3414–3418. (8)

Mastrolia, L. 1985. Comparative cytological and cytochemical aspects of adrenal chromaffin cells in frogs. In *Current Trends in Comparative Endocrinology*, ed. B. Lofts and W. N. Holmes, 1011–1012. Hong Kong: Hong Kong University Press. (3)

Masukawa, L. M., B. Hedland, and G. M. Shepherd. 1985. Electrophysiological properties of identified cells in the *in vitro* olfactory epithelium of the tiger salamander. *Journal of Neuroscience* 5:128–135. (16)

Matesz, C., and G. Szekely. 1978. The motor column and sensory projections of the branchial cranial nerves in the frog. *Journal of Comparative Neurology* 178:157–176. (11)

Mather, V., and M. Hines. 1934. Studies in the innervation of skeletal muscle: 5. The limb muscles of the newt, *Triturus torosus*. *American Journal of Anatomy* 54:177–196. (11)

Mathur, D., R. M. Schutsky, E. J. Purdy, Jr., and C. A. Silver. 1981. Similarities in acute temperature preferences of freshwater fishes. *Transactions of the American Fisheries Society* 110:1–13. (9)

———. 1983. Similarities in avoidance temperatures of freshwater fishes. *Canadian Journal of Fisheries and Aquatic Sciences* 40:2144–2152. (9)

Mathur, D., and C. A. Silver. 1980. Statistical problems in studies of temperature preference of fishes. *Canadian Journal of Fisheries and Aquatic Sciences* 37:733–737. (9)

Matsui, M. 1985. Male release call characteristics of Japanese toads. *Contributions of the Biological Laboratory of Kyoto University* 27:111–120. (8)

Matsushima, T., M. Satou, and K. Ueda. 1985. An electromyographic analysis of electrically-evoked prey-catching behavior by means of stimuli applied to the optic tectum in the Japanese toad. *Neuroscience Research* 3:154–161. (2,11)

———. 1986. Glossopharyngeal and tectal influences on tongue-muscle motoneurons in the Japanese toad. *Brain Research* 365:198–203. (2,11)

———. 1987. Direct contact between glossopharyngeal afferent terminals and hypoglossal motoneurons revealed by double labelling with cobaltic lysine and horseradish peroxidase in the Japanese toad. *Neuroscience Letters* 80:241–245. (11)

Matthews, P. B. C. 1964. Muscle spindles and their motor control. *Physiological Reviews* 44:219–288. (11)

Mattison, C. 1982. *The Care of Reptiles and Amphibians in Captivity*. Poole, Dorset, England: Blandford Press. (13)

Maturana, H. R., J. Y. Lettvin, W. S. McCulloch, and W. H. Pitts. 1960. Anatomy and physiology of vision in the frog (*Rana pipiens*). *Journal of General Physiology* 43:129–175. (2)

Mauget, C., R. Cambar, A. Maurice, and J. Baraud. 1971. Observations sur les variations cycliques annuelles des corps adipeux chez l'adulte de grenouille verte (*Rana esculenta*). *Compte Rendus de l'Académie des Sciences* (Paris), series D 273:2603–2605. (15)

Mauer, F. 1888. Schilddrüse, Thymus, und Kiemenreste der Amphibien. *Morphologisches Jahrbuch* 13:296–382. (16)

———. 1891. Der Aufbau und die Entwicklung der ventralen Rumpf-muskulatur bei den urodelen Amphibien und deren Beziehung zu den gleichen Muskeln der Selachier und Teleostier. *Morphologisches Jahrbuch* 18:76–179. (11)

———. 1895. Die ventrale Rumpfmuskulatur der anuren Amphibien. *Morphologisches Jahrbuch* 22:225–263. (11)

———. 1911. Die ventrale Rumpfmuskulature von *Menobranchus, Menopoma,* und *Amphiuma,* vergleichen mit den gleichen Muskeln anderer Urodelen. *Jenaische Zeitschrift für Naturwissenschaften* 47:1–42. (11)

Mautz, W. J. 1982. Patterns of evaporative water loss. In *Biology of the Reptilia,* vol. 12, ed. C. Gans and F. H. Pough, 443–481. New York: Academic Press. (4)

May, F. E. B., and J. Knowland. 1980. The role of thyroxine in the transition of vitellogenin synthesis from noninducibility to inducibility during metamorphosis in *Xenopus laevis. Developmental Biology* 77:419–430. (16)

———. 1981. Oestrogen receptor levels and vitellogenin synthesis during development of *Xenopus laevis. Nature* 292:853–855. (16)

May, R. M. 1983. Parasitic infections as regulators of animal populations. *American Scientist* 71:36–45. (14)

May, T. W., and R. K. Packer. 1976. Thyroid hormones stimulate *in vivo* oxygen consumption of adult *Rana pipiens berlandieri* at high environmental temperatures. *General and Comparative Endocrinology* 30:525–527. (12)

Mayhew, W. W. 1962. *Scaphiopus couchi* in California's Colorado desert. *Herpetologica* 18:153–161. (10)

———. 1965. Adaptations of the amphibian, *Scaphiopus couchi,* to desert conditions. *American Midland Naturalist* 74:95–109. (4,6,10)

———. 1968. Biology of desert amphibians and reptiles. In *Desert Biology,* ed. G. W. Brown, Jr., 195–356. New York: Academic Press. (10)

Maynard Smith, J. 1987. Sexual selection: A classification of models. In *Sexual Selection: Testing the Alternatives,* ed. J. W. Bradbury and M. B. Andersson, 9–20. New York: Wiley. (14)

Mazin, A. L., and T. A. Detlaf. 1985. Dependence of the duration of one mitotic cycle during synchronous cleavage divisions on temperature in four species of the genus *Rana. Ontogeny* 16:382–388. (8)

Mazur, T. 1968. Costs of maintenance in *Rana arvalis* Nilss. at different ambient temperatures. *Ekologia Polska,* series A 16:699–704. (12)

Mazzi, V. 1970. The hypothalamus as a thermodependent neuroendocrine center in urodeles. In *The Hypothalamus,* ed. L. Martini, M. Motta, and F. Fraschini, 663–676. New York: Academic Press. (15)

———. 1978. Effects on spermatogenesis of permanent lesions to the rostral preoptic area in the crested newt (*Triturus cristatus carnifex* Laur.). *General and Comparative Endocrinology* 34:247–250. (15)

Mazzi, V., and A. Peyrot. 1963. Osservazioni preliminari sulle attitudini funzionali di autotrapianti eterotopici ipofisari nel tritone crestato. *Monitore Zoologico Italiano* 71:124–130. (15)

Mazzi, V., C. Vellano, and C. Andreone. 1978. Effects of permanent lesions to the rostral preoptic area on ovogenesis in the newt *Triturus cristatus carnifex* (Laur.). *Monitore Zoologico Italiano,* n.s. 12:253–256. (15)

Mazzi, V., C. Vellano, D. Colucci, and A. Merlo. 1974. Gonadotropin stimulation by chronic administration of synthetic luteinizing hormone–releasing hormone in hypophysectomized pituitary grafted male newts. *General and Comparative Endocrinology* 24:1–9. (15)

Mazzi, V., C. Vellano, C. Vaccarino, and F. Scaranari. 1979. Further observations on the effects elicited by permanent lesions to the rostral preoptica area on the testis of the newt (*Triturus cristatus carnifex* Laur.). *Atti della Accademia delle Scienze di Torino* 113:473–477. (15)

Mazzi, V., C. Vellano, and V. Vottero. 1979. Changes in the ovary of *Triturus cristatus* female specimens bearing a long-term ectopic pituitary autograft. *Estratto dagli Atti della Accademia delle Scienze di Torino* 113:49–52. (15)

Mazzocco, P. 1940. Variaciones estacionales del peso y composición de los cuerpos adiposos del sapo *Bufo arenarum* Hensel. *Revista de la Sociedad Argentina de Biologia* 16:129–138. (15)

MbangKollo, D., and R. deRoos. 1983. Comparative effects of epinephrine, norepinephrine, and a gentle handling stress on plasma lactate, glucose, and hematocrit levels in the American bullfrog (*Rana catesbeiana*). *General and Comparative Endocrinology* 49:167–175. (3)

Meban, C. 1973. The pneumocytes in the lung of *Xenopus laevis. Journal of Anatomy* 114:235–244. (5)

Medvedev, L. 1937. The vessels of the caudal fin in amphibian larvae and their respiratory function. *Zoologicheskii Zhurnal* 16:393–403. (16)

Medvick, V. A., J. J. Magnuson and S. Sharr. 1981. Behavioral thermoregulation and social interaction of a bluegill (*Lepomis macrochirus*). *Copeia* 1981:9–13. (9)

Megela, A. L., and R. R. Capranica. 1982. Differential patterns of physiological masking in the anuran auditory nerve. *Journal of the Acoustic Society of America* 71:641–645. (2)

Mehdi, A. Z., J. A. DiBattista, and T. Sandor. 1984. Glucocorticoid receptors of the American bullfrog (*Rana catesbeiana*). *General and Comparative Endocrinology* 53:475. (16)

Méhes, J., and B. Berde. 1947. Vergleichende Untersuchungen über Metamorphose- und Stoffwechselwirkungen von Thyroxine und α-Dinitrophenol auf Kaulquappen. *Zeitschrift für Vitamin-, Hormon-, und Fermentforschung* 1:408–423. (12)

Meints, R. H., and Forehand, C. 1977. Hemoglobin switching in the frog, *Rana pipiens* and *Rana catesbeiana:* The effect of hemorrhage on transition from adult to tadpole hemoglobin patterns. *Comparative Biochemistry and Physiology* 58A:265–268. (16)

Meldrin, J. W., and J. J. Gift. 1971. Temperature preference, avoidance, and shock experiments with estuarine fishes. *Ichthyological Associates Bulletin* 7:1–76. (9)

Mendes, E. G. 1945. Contribuicao para a fisiologica dos sistemas respiratorio e circulatoria de *Siphonops annulatus* (Amphibia: Gymnophiona). *Boletim de Faculdade de Filosofia, Ciencias, e Letras, Universidade de São Paulo* 1945:25–64. (5)

Mendonça, M. T., P. Licht, M. J. Ryan, and R. Barnes. 1985. Changes in hormone levels in relation to breeding behavior in male bullfrogs (*Rana catesbeiana*) at the individual and population levels. *General and Comparative Endocrinology* 58:270–279. (2)

Menzies, J. I. 1963. The climate of Bo, Sierra Leone, and the breeding behavior of the toad, *Bufo regularis. Journal of West African Science Association* 8:60–73. (15)

Merchant, H. C. 1970. Estimated energy budget of the red-backed salamander *Plethodon cinereus.* Ph.D. diss., Rutgers University, New Brunswick, NJ. (13)

Merkle, S., and W. Hanke. 1988. Long-term starvation in *Xenopus laevis* Daudin: 1. Effects on general metabolism. *Comparative Biochemistry and Physiology* 89B:719–739. (12)

Metcalf, Z. P. 1921. The food capacity of the toad. *Copeia* 1921:81–82. (13)

Metter, D. E. 1963. Stomach contents of Idaho larval *Dicamptodon. Copeia* 1963:435–436. (16)

Meyer, F. 1927. Versuche über Blutdruckzugler beim Frosch. *Pflugers Archiv* 215:545–552. (7)

Meyer, R. A., G. A. Dudley, and R. L. Terjung. 1980. Ammonia and IMP in different skeletal muscle fibres after exercise in rats. *Journal of Applied Physiology* 49:1037–1041. (5)

Meyers, R. S., and J. Felsher. 1976. Continuous recording and quantification of selective blood distribution in the amphibian *Rana catesbeiana. Comparative Biochemistry and Physiology* 54A:359–363. (5)

Michael, P. 1981. A normal table of early development in relation to rearing temperature. *Development Growth and Differentiation* 23:149–156. (8)

Michibata, H. 1973. Sex differentiation of the gonad in the frog, *Rhacophorus buergeri. Zoology Magazine* 82:16–23. (16)

Middler, S. A., C. R. Kleeman, and E. Edwards. 1968a. The influence of hypovolemia and curarization on the reabsorption of water from the intact urinary bladder of the toad, *Bufo marinus. Comparative Biochemistry and Physiology* 25:335–341. (6)

———. 1968b. Lymph mobilization following acute blood loss in the toad, *Bufo marinus. Comparative Biochemistry and Physiology* 24:343–353. (5,6)

———. 1968c. The role of the urinary bladder in salt and water metabolism of the toad, *Bufo marinus. Comparative Biochemistry and Physiology* 26:57–68. (6)

Middler, S. A., C. R. Kleeman, E. Edwards, and D. Brody. 1969. Effect of adenohypophysectomy on salt and water metabolism of the toad *Bufo marinus* with studies on hormonal replacement. *General and Comparative Endocrinology* 12:290–304. (5)

Mikulka, P., P. Vaughan, and J. Hughes. 1981. Lithium chloride–prey aversion in the toad (*Bufo americanus*). *Behavioral and Neural Biology* 33:220–229. (13)

Milano, E. G., and F. Accordi. 1986. Evolutionary trends in adrenal gland of anurans and urodeles. *Journal of Morphology* 189:249–259. (16)

Miledi, R., and O. D. Uchitel. 1984. A study of the submaxillaris muscle of the frog. *Journal of Physiology* (London) 350:279–291. (11)

Millar, R. P., S. Nicolson, J. A. King, and G. N. Louw. 1983. Functional significance of TRH in metamorphosing and adult anurans. In *Thyrotropin-Releasing Hormone*, ed. E. C. Griffiths and G. W. Bennett, 217–227. New York: Raven Press. (16)

Millard, N. 1945. The development of the arterial system of *Xenopus laevis*, including experiments on the destruction of larval aortic arches. *Transactions of the Royal Society of South Africa* 30:217–234. (16)

Millard, R. W., and R. Moalli. 1980. Baroreflex sensitivity in an amphibian *Rana catesbeiana*, and a reptilian, *Pseudemys scripta elegans*. *Journal of Experimental Zoology* 213:283–288. (7)

Miller, B. T., and J. H. Larsen. 1986. Feeding habits of metamorphosed *Ambystoma tigrinum melanostictum* in ponds of high pH (> 9). *Great Basin Naturalist* 46:299–301. (11)

———. 1989. Feeding performance in aquatic postmetamorphic newts (Urodela: Salamandridae): Are bidirectional flow systems necessarily inefficient? *Canadian Journal of Zoology* 67:2414–2421. (11)

Miller, D. A., M. L. Standish, and A. E. Thurman. 1968. Effects of temperature on water and electrolyte balance in the frog. *Physiological Zoology* 41:500–506. (10)

Miller, K. 1982. Effect of temperature on sprint performance in the frog *Xenopus laevis* and the salamander *Necturus maculosus*. *Copeia* 1982:695–698. (8,9,12,14)

———. 1983. The role of lactate production in the metabolic support of locomotion by clawed frogs, *Xenopus laevis*. *Physiological Zoology* 56:550–584. (12,14)

Miller, K., and J. J. Camilliere. 1981. Physical training improves swimming performance of the African clawed frog, *Xenopus laevis*. *Herpetologica* 37:1–10. (12,14)

Miller, K., and V. H. Hutchison. 1979. Activity metabolism in the mudpuppy, *Necturus maculosus*. *Physiological Zoology* 52:22–37. (5,9,12,14)

———. 1980. Aerobic and anaerobic scope for activity in the giant toad, *Bufo marinus*. *Physiological Zoology* 53:170–175. (9,12,14)

Miller, K., and G. C. Packard. 1977. An altitudinal cline in critical thermal maxima of chorus frogs (*Pseudacris triseriata*). *American Naturalist* 111:267–277. (8)

Miller, K., and J. L. Sabol. 1989. The role of phosphocreatine breakdown in the metabolic support of locomotion by clawed frogs, *Xenopus laevis*. *Comparative Biochemistry and Physiology* 93B:251–254. (12)

Miller, K., and G. M. Zoghby. 1983. Thermal acclimation of locomotor performance in anuran amphibians. *American Zoologist* 23:916. (8)

———. 1986. Thermal acclimation of locomotor performance in anuran amphibians. *Canadian Journal of Zoology* 64:1956–1960. (12)

Miller, L. K., and P. J. Dehlinger. 1969. Neuromuscular function at low temperatures in frogs from cold and warm climates. *Comparative Biochemistry and Physiology* 28:915–921. (10)

Miller, M. R., and M. E. Robbins. 1954. The reproductive cycle in *Taricha torosa* (*Triturus torosus*). *Journal of Experimental Zoology* 125:415–443. (15)

Miller, N. 1909. The American toad (*Bufo lentiginosus americanus*, LeConte): A study in dynamic biology. *American Naturalist* 43:641–668. (13)

Mills, J. W., S. A. Ernst, and D. R. DiBona. 1977. Localization of Na⁺-pump sites in frog skin. *Journal of Cell Biology* 73:88–110. (5)

Milone, M., L. Iela, V. Esposito, R. K. Rastogi, and G. Chieffi. 1978. Annual variations in the total lipid and protein content of the liver, fat body, ovary, and plasma of the female frog (*Rana esculenta* L.). *Journal of Endocrinology* 78:165–169. (10)

Milsom, W. K. 1989. Comparative aspects of vertebrate pulmonary mechanics. In *Comparative Pulmonary Physiology: Current Concepts*, vol. 39, *Lung Biology in Health and Disease*, ed. S. C. Wood, 587–619. New York: Marcel Dekker. (6)

Milsom, W. K., and D. R. Jones. 1977. Carbon dioxide sensitivity of pulmonary receptors in the frog. *Experientia* 33:1167–1168. (6,7)

Mimhagh, K. M., J. L. Bolaffi, N. M. Montgomery, and J. C. Kalten-

bach. 1987. Thyrotropin-releasing hormone (TRH): Immunohistochemical distribution in tadpole and frog brain. *General and Comparative Endocrinology* 66:394–404. (16)

Miner, R. W. 1925. The pectoral limb of *Eryops* and other primitive tetrapods. *Bulletin of the American Museum of Natural History* 517:145–312. (11)

Mitchell, G. S., B. A. Cross, T. Hiramoto, and P. Scheid. 1980. Effects of intrapulmonary CO_2 and airway pressure on phrenic activity and pulmonary stretch receptor discharge in dogs. *Respiration Physiology* 41:29–48. (7)

Mitchell, J. W. 1976. Heat transfer from spheres and other animal forms. *Biophysical Journal* 16:561–569. (4,6)

Mitton, J. B., C. Carey, and T. D. Kocher. 1986. The relation of enzyme heterozygosity to standard and active oxygen consumption and body size of tiger salamanders, *Ambystoma tigrinum*. *Physiological Zoology* 59:574–582. (12,14)

Mitton, J. B., and M. C. Grant. 1984. Associations among protein heterozygosity, growth rate, and developmental stability. *Annual Review of Ecology and Systematics* 15:479–499. (12)

Mivart, S. G. 1869. Notes on the myology of *Menopoma alleghaniense*. *Proceedings of the Zoological Society of London* 1869:254–271. (11)

Miyamoto, T., Y. Okada, and T. Sato. 1985. Response of frog taste cells to salt stimuli. *Chemical Senses* 10:129–130. (16)

Miyauchi, H., F. T. LaRochelle, Jr., M. Suzuki, M. Freeman, and E. Frieden. 1977. Studies on thyroid hormones and their binding in bullfrog tadpole plasma during metamorphosis. *General and Comparative Endocrinology* 33:254–266. (16)

Mizell, S. 1964. Seasonal differences in spermatogenesis and oogenesis in *Rana pipiens*. *Nature* 202:875–876. (15)

———. 1965. Seasonal changes in energy reserves in the common frog, *Rana pipiens*. *Journal of Cellular and Comparative Physiology* 66:251–258. (10,15)

Moalli, R., R. S. Meyers, D. C. Jackson, and R. W. Millard. 1980. Skin circulation in the frog, *Rana catesbeiana*, distribution and dynamics. *Respiration Physiology* 40:137–148. (7)

Moalli, R., R. S. Meyers, G. R. Ultsch, and D. C. Jackson. 1981. Acid-base balance and temperature in a predominantly skin-breathing salamander, *Cryptobranchus alleganiensis*. *Respiration Physiology* 43:1–11. (5,6)

Mobbs, I. G., U. A. King, and R. J. Wassersug. 1988. Prostaglandin E₂ does not inhibit metamorphosis of tadpole tails in tissue culture. *Experimental Biology* 47:151–154. (16)

Modzelewski, E. H., and D. D. Culley, Jr. 1974. Growth responses of the bullfrog, *Rana catesbeiana*, fed various live foods. *Herpetologica* 30:396–405. (13,15)

Moerland, T. S., and B. D. Sidell. 1986. Contractile responses to temperature in the locomotory musculature of striped bass, *Morone saxatilis*. *Journal of Experimental Zoology* 240:25–33. (8)

Moermond, T. C. 1979. Habitat constraints on the behavior, morphology, and community structure of *Anolis* lizards. *Ecology* 60:152–164. (14)

Moffat, A. J. M., and R. R. Capranica. 1976a. Auditory sensitivity of the saccule in the American toad (*Bufo americanus*). *Journal of Comparative Physiology* 105:1–8. (2)

———. 1976b. Effects of temperature on the response properties of auditory nerve fibers in the American toad *Bufo americanus*. *Journal of the Acoustical Society of America* 60, suppl. 1:80. (8)

Mohanty, S. N., and M. C. Dash. 1986. Effects of diet and aeration on the growth and metamorphosis of *Rana tigrina* tadpoles. *Aquaculture* 51:89–96. (13)

Moll, E. O., and J. M. Legler. 1971. The life history of a Neotropical slider turtle, *Pseudemys scripta* (Schoepff), in Panama. *Bulletin of the Los Angeles City Museum of Natural History and Science* 11:1–102. (9)

Moll, E. O., and H. M. Smith. 1967. Lizards in the diet of an American caecilian. *Natural History Miscellany of the Chicago Academy of Science* 187:1–2. (13)

Molony, V. 1974. Classification of vagal afferents firing in phase with breathing in *Gallus domesticus*. *Respiration Physiology* 22:57–76. (7)

Monath T. 1965. The opercular apparatus of salamanders. *Journal of Morphology* 116:149–170. (11)

Mondal, A., and S. L. Basu. 1960. Spermatogenetic cycle in *Bufo melanostictus* Schneid. *Indian Journal of Physiology and Allied Sciences* 14:43–46. (15)

Mondou, P. M., and J. C. Kaltenbach. 1979. Thyroxine concentrations in blood serum and pericardial fluid of metamorphosing tadpoles and of adult frogs. *General and Comparative Endocrinology* 39: 343–349. (16)

Monteith, J. L. 1973. *Principles of Environmental Physics*. London: Edward Arnold. (4)

Montgomery, H., and J. A. Pierce. 1937. The site of acidification of the urine within the renal tubule in Amphibia. *American Journal of Physiology* 118:144–152. (5)

Montgomery, J. C., and J. A. MacDonald. 1980. Stretch receptors in the eye muscles of a teleost fish. *Experientia* 36:1176–1177. (11)

Montgomery, N., K. V. Fite, and L. Bengston. 1981. The accessory optic system of *Rana pipiens:* Neuroanatomical connections and intrinsic organization. *Journal of Comparative Neurology* 203:595–612. (2)

Montgomery, N., K. V. Fite, M. Taylor, and L. Bengston. 1982. Neural correlates of optokinetic nystagmus in the mesencephalon of *Rana pipiens. Brain, Behavior, and Evolution* 21:137–150. (2)

Moody, S. A., and M. Jacobson. 1983. Compartmental relationship between primary spinal motoneurons and somatic muscle fiber that they first innervate. *Journal of Neuroscience* 3:1670–1682. (16)

Moore, F. L., and P. Deviche. 1988. Neuroendocrine processing of environmental information in amphibians. In *Processing of Environmental Information in Vertebrates*, ed. M. H. Stetson, 19–45. New York: Springer-Verlag. (3)

Moore, F. L., and L. J. Miller. 1984. Stress-induced inhibition of sexual behavior: Cortisone inhibits courtship behaviors of a male amphibian (*Taricha granulosa*). *Hormones and Behavior* 18:400–410. (3)

Moore, F. L., and C. H. Muller. 1977. Androgens and male-mating behavior in rough-skinned newts, *Taricha granulosa. Hormones and Behavior* 9:309–320. (3)

Moore, F. L., L. Muske, and C. R. Propper. 1987. Regulation of reproductive behaviors in amphibians by LHRH. *Annals of the New York Academy of Sciences* 519:108–116. (3)

Moore, F. R., and R. E. Gatten, Jr. 1989. Locomotor performance of hydrated, dehydrated, and osmotically stressed anuran amphibians. *Herpetologica* 45:101–110. (12)

Moore, H. J. 1954. Some observations on the migration of the toad (*Bufo bufo bufo*). *British Journal of Herpetology* 1:194–224. (15)

Moore, J. A. 1939. Temperature tolerance and rates of development in the eggs of Amphibia. *Ecology* 20:459–478. (8)

———. 1940. Adaptative differences in the egg membranes of frogs. *American Naturalist* 74:89–93. (8)

———. 1949a. Geographic variation of adaptive characters in *Rana pipiens* Schreber. *Evolution* 3:1–24. (8)

———. 1949b. Patterns of evolution in the genus *Rana*. In *Genetics, Paleontology, and Evolution*, ed. G. L. Jepsen, E. Mayr, and G. G. Simpson, 315–338. Princeton, NJ: Princeton University Press. (9)

———. 1952. An analytical study of the geographic distribution of *Rana septemtrionalis. American Naturalist* 86:5–22. (8)

———, ed. 1964. *Physiology of the Amphibia*. New York: Academic Press. (1)

Moore, R. G., and B. A. Moore. 1980. Observations on the body temperature and activity in the red-spotted toad, *Bufo punctatus. Copeia* 1980:362–363. (9)

Moore, S. W., E. R. Lewis, P. M. Narins, and P. T. Lopez. 1989. The call-timing algorithm of the white-lipped frog *Leptodactylus albilabris. Journal of Comparative Physiology* 164:309–319. (2)

Morgan, D. L., and U. Proske. 1984. Vertebrate slow muscle: Its structure, pattern of innervation, and mechanical properties. *Physiological Reviews* 64:103–169. (11)

Morgan, L. R., R. Singh, and R. J. Fisette. 1967. Relationship of oxygen consumption and cytochrome oxidase–succinic dehydrogenase activities in *Amphiuma means. Comparative Biochemistry and Physiology* 20:343–349. (12)

Morgareidge, K. R., and H. T. Hammel. 1975. Evaporative water loss in box turtles: Effects of rostral brainstem and other temperatures. *Science* 187:366–368. (9)

Morin, P. J. 1981. Predatory salamanders reverse the outcome of competition among three species of anuran tadpoles. *Science* 212:1284–1286. (14)

———. 1983a. Competitive and predatory interactions in natural and experimental populations of *Notophthalmus viridescens dorsalis* and *Ambystoma tigrinum. Copeia* 1983:628–639. (14)

———. 1983b. Predation, competition, and the composition of larval anuran guilds. *Ecological Monographs* 53:119–138. (14)

———. 1987. Predation, breeding asynchrony, and the outcome of competition among tree frog tadpoles. *Ecology* 68:675–683. (8)

Moriya, T. 1979. Effect of temperature on embryonic and post-embryonic development of the salamander. *Low Temperature Science* 37B:113–116. (8)

Moriya, T., and Y. Miyashita. 1989. Melanophore dispersion in northern amphibian larva induced by exposure to cold. *Journal of Experimental Zoology* 250:349–353. (9)

Moriya, T., C. R. Thomas, and E. Frieden. 1984. Increase in 3,5,3'-triiodothyronine (T$_3$)–binding sites in tadpole erythrocyte nuclei during spontaneous and T$_3$-induced metamorphosis. *Endocrinology* 114:170–175. (16)

Morpurgo, G., P. A. Battaglia, and T. Leggio. 1970. Negative Bohr effect in newt hemolysates and its regulation. *Nature* 225:76–77. (5)

Morris, J. L. 1983. Effects of renal nerve stimulation on vascular resistance in the toad kidney. *Naunyn-Schmiedeberg's Archives of Pharmacology* 323:335–340. (6)

Morris, J. L., and I. L. Gibbins. 1983. Innervation of the renal vasculature of the toad (*Bufo marinus*). *Cell and Tissue Research* 231:357–376. (6)

Morton, E. S. 1975. Ecological sources of selection on avian sounds. *American Naturalist* 109:17–34. (14)

Morton, M. L. 1981. Seasonal changes in total body lipid and liver weight in the Yosemite toad. *Copeia* 1981:234–238. (10,14,15)

Moser, H. 1950. Ein Beitrag zur Analyse der Thyroxineinwirkung im Haulquappenversuch und zur Frage nach dem Zustandekommen der Frühbereitschaft des Metamorphose-Reaktionssystems. *Revue Suisse de Zoologie*, suppl. 2, 57:1–144. (16)

Moss, B., and V. M. Ingram. 1968. Hemoglobin synthesis during amphibian metamorphosis: 1. Chemical studies on the hemoglobins from the larval and adult stages of *Rana catesbeiana. Journal of Molecular Biology* 32:481–492. (5)

Moulton, J. M., A. Jurand, and H. Fox. 1968. A cytological study of Mauthner's cells in *Xenopus laevis* and *Rana temporaria* during metamorphosis. *Journal of Embryology and Experimental Morphology* 19:415–431. (2)

Muccioli, G., A. Guardabassi, P. Pattoni, and E. Genazzani. 1989. Further study on the changes in the concentration of prolactin-binding sites in different organs of *Xenopus laevis* male and female, kept under dry conditions and then returned to water. *General and Comparative Endocrinology* 74:411–417. (16)

Muchlinski, A. E. 1985. The energetic cost of the fever response in three species of ectothermic vertebrates. *Comparative Biochemistry and Physiology* 81A:577–579. (12)

Muchmore, W. B. 1962. Increase in numbers of nuclei in striated muscle fibers. *American Zoologist* 2:542–543. (11)

———. 1965. Mitoses in developing myotomes of *A. maculatum. American Zoologist* 5:721. (11)

Mudry, K. M., and R. R. Capranica. 1980. Evoked auditory activity within the telencephalon of the bullfrog (*Rana catesbeiana*). *Brain Research* 182:303–311. (2)

———. 1987. Correlation between auditory evoked responses in the thalamus and species-specific call characteristics: 1. *Rana catesbeiana* (Anura: Ranidae). *Journal of Comparative Physiology* 160:477–489. (2)

Mudry, K. M., M. Constantine-Paton, and R. R. Capranica. 1977. Auditory sensitivity of the diencephalon of the leopard frog *Rana p. pipiens. Journal of Comparative Physiology* 114:1–13. (2)

Mueller, C. F. 1970. Temperature acclimation in two species of *Sceloporus. Herpetologica* 26:83–85. (9)

Mullally, D. P. 1952. Habits and minimum temperatures of the toad *Bufo boreas halophilus. Copeia* 1952:274–276. (9,10)

Mullally, D. P., and J. D. Cunningham. 1956. Aspects of the thermal ecology of the Yosemite toad. *Herpetologica* 12:57–67. (9)

Mullen, T. L., and R. H. Alvarado. 1976. Osmotic and ionic regulation in amphibians. *Physiological Zoology* 49:11–23. (5,6,14)

Mullen, T. L., M. Kashgarian, D. Biemesderfer, G. H. Giebisch, and T. U. L. Biber. 1976. Ion transport and structure of urinary bladder epithelium of *Amphiuma. American Journal of Physiology* 231:501–508. (5)

Muller, C. 1976. Steroidogenesis and spermatogenesis in the male bullfrog, *Rana catesbeiana*. Ph.D. diss., University of California, Berkeley. (15)

Muller, J. 1832. On the existence of four distinct hearts, having regular pulsations, connected with the lymphatic system in certain amphibious animals. *Philosophical Transactions of the Royal Society* 1833: 1–89. (5)

Munro, A. F. 1953. The ammonia and urea excretion of different species of Amphibia during their development and metamorphosis. *Biochemical Journal* 54:29–36. (16)

Muntz, L. 1975. Myogenesis in the trunk and leg during development of the tadpole of *Xenopus laevis* (Daudin 1802). *Journal of Embryology and Experimental Morphology* 33:757–774. (11)

Muntz, W. R. A. 1962a. Effectiveness of different colors of light in releasing positive phototactic behavior of frogs, and a possible function of the retinal projection to the diencephalon. *Journal of Neurophysiology* 25:712–720. (2)

———. 1962b. Microelectrode recordings from the diencephalon of the frog (*Rana pipiens*) and a blue-sensitive system. *Journal of Neurophysiology* 25:699–711. (2)

Münz, H., B. Claas, and B. Fritzsch. 1982. Electrophysiological evidence of electroreception in the axolotl *Siredon mexicanum*. *Neuroscience Letters* 28:107–111. (2)

———. 1984. Electroreceptive and mechanoreceptive units in the lateral line of the axolotl *Ambystoma mexicanum*. *Journal of Comparative Physiology* 154:33–44. (2,16)

Murith, D. 1981. Examples of the close relationships between the mode of transmission of some parasites and the niche of the host amphibian. *Monitore Zoologico Italiano*, n.s., suppl. 15:359–365. (14)

Muske, L. E., and F. L. Moore. 1987. Luteinizing hormone–releasing hormone–immunoreactive neurons in the amphibian brain are distributed along the course of the nervus terminalis. *Annals of the New York Academy of Sciences* 519:433–446. (3)

———. 1988. The nervus terminalis in amphibians: Anatomy, chemistry, and relationship with the hypothalamic gonadotropin-releasing hormone system. *Brain, Behavior, and Evolution* 32:141–150. (2)

Mutatori, G. 1932. L'innervazione del glomo carotico studiata sperimentalmente. *Bollettino Societa Italiana Biologia Sperimentale* (Naples) 7:1143–1145. (7)

Myers, C. W., and J. W. Daly. 1976. Preliminary evaluation of skin toxins and vocalizations in taxonomic and evolutionary studies of poison-dart frogs (Dendrobatidae). *Bulletin of the American Museum of Natural History* 157:173–262. (14)

Myers, C. W., J. W. Daly, and B. Malkin. 1978. A dangerously toxic new frog (*Phyllobates*) used by the Emberá Indians of western Colombia, with discussion of blowgun fabrication and dart poisoning. *Bulletin of the American Museum of Natural History* 161:307–366. (14)

Myers, R. D., and W. L. Veale. 1971. The role of sodium and calcium ions in the hypothalamus in the control of body temperature of the anaesthetized cat. *Journal of Physiology* (London) 212:411–430. (9)

Myers, R. D., and T. L. Yaksh. 1971. Thermoregulation around a new "set-point" established by altering the ratios of sodium to calcium ions within the hypothalamus. *Journal of Physiology* (London) 218:509–533. (9)

Myhre, K., M. Cabanac, and G. Myhre. 1977. Fever and behavioral temperature regulation in the frog, *Rana esculenta*. *Acta Physiologica Scandinavica* 101:219–229. (9)

Myhre, K., and H. T. Hammel. 1969. Behavioral regulation in the lizard *Tiliqua scincoides*. *American Journal of Physiology* 217:1490–1495. (9)

Nagahama, Y. 1987. Testes. In *Vertebrate Endocrinology: Fundamentals and Biomedical Implications*, vol. 1, *Morphological Considerations*, ed. P. K. T. Pang and M. P. Schreibman, 399–437. New York: Academic Press. (3)

Nagai, M., and M. Iriki. 1985. Cardiovascular responses of the bullfrog (*Rana catesbeiana*) to thermal stimulation of the spinal cord. *Comparative Biochemistry and Physiology* 82A:77–81. (9)

———. 1986. Characteristics of cardiovascular responses of the bullfrog (*Rana catesbeiana*) to thermal stimulation of the spinal cord. *Journal of Comparative Physiology* 156B:611–616. (9)

Nagai, Y., S. Nagai, and T. Nishikawa. 1971. The nutritional efficiency of cannibalism and an artificial feed for the growth of tadpoles of Japanese toad (*Bufo vulgaris* sp.). *Agricultural Biology and Chemistry* 35:697–703. (13)

Nagano, H., H. Itoh, and R. Shukuya. 1975. Seasonal variation in hepatic phosphoenolpyruvate carboxykinase activity of the bullfrog,

Rana catesbeiana. *Comparative Biochemistry and Physiology* 51B: 255–256. (10)

Nagel, J. W. 1977. Life history of the red-backed salamander, *Plethodon cinereus*, in northeastern Tennessee. *Herpetologica* 33:13–18. (15)

Nagel, W. 1980. Rheogenic sodium transport in a tight epithelium, the amphibian skin. *Journal of Physiology* (London) 302:281–295. (5)

Nagel, W., and J. Crabbe. 1980. Mechanism of action of aldosterone on active sodium transport across frog skin. *Pflugers Archiv* 385: 181–187. (5)

Nagel, W., and X. Hirschmann. 1980. K⁺ permeability of the outer border of the frog skin (*R. temporaria*). *Journal of Membrane Biology* 52:107–113. (5)

Nagle, F., D. Robinhold, E. Howley, J. Daniels, G. Baptisa, and K. Stoedefalke. 1970. Lactic acid accumulation during running at submaximal aerobic demands. *Medicine and Science in Sports* 2: 182–186. (12)

Nagy, K. A. 1975. Water and energy budgets of free-living animals: Measurement using isotopically labeled water. In *Environmental Physiology of Desert Organisms*, ed. N. F. Hadley, 227–245. Stroudsburg, PA: Dowden, Hutchinson, and Ross. (14)

———. 1983a. The doubly labeled water (^{3}HH^{18}O) method: A guide to its use. University of California at Los Angeles Publication 12-1417. (14)

———. 1983b. Ecological energetics of a lizard. In *Lizard Ecology: Studies of a Model Organism*, ed. R. B. Huey, E. R. Pianka, and T. W. Schoener, 24–54. Cambridge, MA: Harvard University Press. (14)

———. 1987. Field metabolic rate and food requirement scaling in mammals and birds. *Ecological Monographs* 57:111–128. (14)

———. 1989a. Doubly-labeled water studies of vertebrate physiological ecology. In *Stable Isotopes in Ecological Research*, ed. P. W. Rundel, J. R. Ehleringer, and K. A. Nagy, 270–287. New York: Springer-Verlag. (14)

———. 1989b. Field bioenergetics: Accuracy of models and methods. *Physiological Zoology* 62:237–252. (14)

Nagy, K. A., and C. C. Peterson. 1988. Scaling of water flux rate in animals. *University of California Publications in Zoology* 120:1–172. (5)

Nagy, K. A., and V. H. Shoemaker. 1984. Field energetics and food consumption of the Galapagos marine iguana, *Amblyrhynchus cristatus*. *Physiological Zoology* 57:281–290. (14)

Naitoh, T., R. J. Wassersug, and R. A. Leslie. 1989. The physiology, morphology, and ontogeny of emetic behavior in anuran amphibians. *Physiological Zoology* 62:819–843. (11,13,16)

Narins, P. M., and R. R. Capranica. 1976. Sexual differences in the auditory system of the tree frog *Eleutherodactylus coqui*. *Science* 192:378–380. (2)

Narins, P. M., G. Ehret, and J. Tautz. 1988. Accessory pathway for sound transfer in a Neotropical frog. *Proceedings of the National Academy of Science* 85:1508–1512. (2)

Narins, P. M., and D. D. Hurley. 1982. The relationship between call intensity and function in the Puerto Rican coquí (Leptodactylidae). *Herpetologica* 38:287–295. (14)

Narins, P. M., and E. R. Lewis. 1985. The vertebrate ear as an exquisite seismic sensor. *Journal of the Acoustical Society of America* 76:1384–1387. (2)

Narins, P. M., and S. L. Smith. 1986. Clinal variation in anuran advertisement calls: Basis for acoustic isolation? *Behavioral Ecology and Sociobiology* 19:135–141. (2)

Narins, P. M., and R. Zelick. 1988. The effects of noise on auditory processing and behavior in amphibians. In *The Evolution of the Amphibian Auditory System*, ed. B. Fritzsch, M. J. Ryan, W. Wilczynski, T. E. Hetherington, and W. Walkowiak, 511–536. New York: John Wiley and Sons. (2)

Narins, S. A. 1930. A quantitative study of the effect of chloroform on oxygen consumption on the tadpole (*Rana clamitans*). *Physiological Zoology* 3:519–538. (12)

Nartsissova, O. V. 1977. Influence of environmental temperature on pigment migration in cells of the retinal epithelium of common frog tadpoles. *Vestnik Moskovskogo Universiteta Seriya XVI Biologiya* 2:32–38. (8)

Nasledov, G. A. 1969. On the cholinoreception of a tonic muscle fiber. *Journal of Evolutionary Biochemistry and Physiology* (USSR) 5: 398–404. (11)

Nasledov, G. A., and S. Thesleff. 1974. Denervation changes in frog skeletal muscle. *Acta Physiologica Scandinavica* 90:370–380. (11)

Naujoks-Manteuffel, C., and G. Manteuffel. 1986. Internuclear connections between the pretectum and accessory optic system in *Salamandra salamandra*. *Cell and Tissue Research* 243:595–602. (2)

Navar, L. G., D. J. Marsh, R. E. Blantz, J. Hall, and D. W. Ploth. 1982. Intrinsic control of renal hemodynamics. *Federation Proceedings* 41:3022–3030. (5)

Naylor, B. G. 1978. The systematics of fossil and recent salamanders (Amphibia: Caudata): With special reference to the vertebral column and trunk musculature. Ph.D. diss., University of Alberta, Edmonton. (11)

Naylor, B. G., and R. A. Nussbaum. 1980. The trunk musculature of caecilians (Amphibia: Gymnophiona). *Journal of Morphology* 166:259–273. (11)

Neary, T. J. 1984. Anterior thalamic nucleus projections to the dorsal pallium in ranid frogs. *Neuroscience Letters* 51:213–218. (2)

———. 1988. Forebrain auditory pathways in ranid frogs. In *The Evolution of the Amphibian Auditory System*, ed. B. Fritzsch, M. J. Ryan, W. Wilczynski, T. E. Hetherington, and W. Walkowiak, 233–252. New York: John Wiley and Sons. (2)

Neary, T. J., and R. G. Northcutt. 1983. Nuclear organization of the bullfrog diencephalon. *Journal of Comparative Neurology* 213:262–278. (2)

Neary, T. J., and W. Wilczynski. 1977. Ascending thalamic projections from the obex region in ranid frogs. *Brain Research* 138:529–533. (2)

———. 1980. Descending inputs to the optic tectum in ranid frogs. *Society for Neuroscience Abstracts* 6:629. (2)

———. 1986. Auditory pathways to the hypothalamus in ranid frogs. *Neuroscience Letters* 71:142–146. (2)

Neil, E., and R. G. O'Regan. 1971. The effects of electrical stimulation of the distal end of the cut sinus and aortic nerves on peripheral arterial chemoreceptor activity in the cat. *Journal of Physiology* (London) 215:15–32. (7)

Neil, E., L. Strom, and Y. Zotterman. 1950. Action potential studies of afferent fibres in the IXth and Xth cranial nerves of the frog. *Acta Physiologica Scandinavica* 20:338–350. (7)

Neill, W. H., J. J. Magnuson, and G. G. Chipman. 1972. Behavioral thermoregulation by fishes: A new experimental approach. *Science* 176:1443–1445. (9)

Nel, P. S. 1941. Some aspects of the thigh musculature of certain microranid genera. *Annals of the University of Stellenbosch* 19A:1–15. (11)

Nelson, D. O., and C. L. Prosser. 1979. Effect of preoptic lesions on behavioral thermoregulation of green sunfish, *Lepomis cyanellus*, and of goldfish, *Carassius auratus*. *Journal of Comparative Physiology* 129:193–197. (9)

———. 1981. Temperature-sensitive units in the preoptic region of the sunfish. *American Journal of Physiology* 241:R259–R263. (9)

Netchitaïlo, P., M. Feuilloley, I. Lihrmann, F. Leboulenger, J. Gutkowska, M. Cantin, G. Pelletier, and H. Vaudry. 1988. Distribution of atrial natriuretic factor (ANF)–like immunoreactivity in the brain of the frog *Rana ridibunda*. *Canadian Journal of Physiology and Pharmacology* 66:262–269. (3)

Netchitaïlo, P., M. Feuilloley, G. Pelletier, M. Cantin, A. DeLéan, F. Leboulenger, and H. Vaudry. 1986. Localization and characterization of atrial natriuretic factor (ANF)–like peptide in the frog atrium. *Peptides* 7:573–579. (3)

Netchitaïlo, P., M. Feuilloley, G. Pelletier, A. DeLéan, H. Ong, M. Cantin, J. Gutkowska, F. Leboulenger, and H. Vaudry. 1988. Localization and identification of immunoreactive atrial natriuretic factor (ANF) in the frog ventricle. *Peptides* 9:1–6. (3)

Neuman, V. K., L. Quevedo, and J. Concha. 1986. Effect of progesterone on the sodium transporting mechanism of isolated toad skin. *Cellular and Molecular Biology* 32:685–690. (5)

Neuwirth, M., J. W. Daly, C. W. Myers, and L. W. Tice. 1979. Morphology of the granular secretory glands in skin of poison-dart frogs (*Dendrobatidae*). *Tissue and Cell* 11:755–771. (14)

Nevo, E., and R. R. Capranica. 1985. Evolutionary origin of ethological reproductive isolation in cricket frogs, *Acris*. *Evolutionary Biology* 19:147–214. (2)

Ng, W. C., A. P. Wolffe, and J. R. Tata. 1984. Unequal activation by estrogen of individual *Xenopus* vitellogenin genes during development. *Developmental Biology* 102:238–247. (16)

Nichol, J., F. Girling, W. Jerrald, E. B. Claxton, and A. C. Burton. 1951. Fundamental instability of the small blood vessels and critical closing pressures in vascular beds. *American Journal of Physiology* 164:330–334. (7)

Nielsen, R. 1979. A 3 to 2 coupling of the Na-K pump responsible for transepithelial Na transport in frog skin disclosed by the effect of Ba. *Acta Physiologica Scandinavica* 107:189–191. (5)

———. 1984. Active transepithelial potassium transport in frog skin via specific potassium channels in the apical membrane. *Acta Physiologica Scandinavica* 120:287–296. (5)

Nieuwenhuys, R. 1964. Comparative anatomy of the spinal cord. *Progress in Brain Research* 11:1–57. (2)

Nieuwkoop, P. D., and J. Faber. 1967. *Normal table of Xenopus laevis*. Amsterdam: North-Holland. (3,16)

Niijima, A. 1970. Experimental studies on the afferent innervation of the toad's heart. *Japanese Journal of Physiology* 20:527–539. (7)

Nikinmaa, M. 1990. *Vertebrate Red Blood Cells*. Berlin: Springer-Verlag. (5)

Nilsson, S. 1978. Sympathetic innervation of the spleen of the cane toad, *Bufo marinus*. *Comparative Biochemistry and Physiology* 61C:133–149. (5)

Nishi, S. 1916. Zur vergleichenden Anatomie der eigentlichen (genuinen) Rückenmuskeln: Spino-dorsale Muskeln der tetrapoden Wirbeltiere. *Morphologisches Jahrbuch* 50:167–318. (11)

———. 1925. Pri la génerala diferencigô de l'trunkomuskularo: 2. Diferencigô de l'trunkomuskularo céamfibioj, reptilioj, kaj mamuloj. *Okajimas Folia Anatomica Japonica* (Tokyo) 3:1–10. (11)

———. 1938. Muskeln des Rumpfes. In *Handbuch der Vergleichenden Anatomie der Wirbeltiere*, ed. L. Bolk, E. Göppert, E. Kallius, and W. Lubosch, 5:351–466. Berlin and Vienna: Urban and Schwarzenberg. (11)

Nishi, Y., and K. I. Ibamoto. 1969. Model skin temperature: An index of thermal sensation in cold, warm, and humid environments. *Transactions of the American Society of Heating, Refrigeration, and Air Conditioning Engineers* 75:94. (4)

Nishikawa, K. 1987. Staining peripheral nerves with Sudan black B: Progressive vs. regressive methods. *Copeia* 1987:489–491. (11)

Nishikawa, K., and D. C. Cannatella. 1988. Kinematics of feeding behavior in *Ascaphus truei*. *American Zoologist* 28:116A. (11)

Nishikawa, K., and D. C. Canatella. 1991. Kinematics of prey capture in the tailed frog, *Ascaphis truei*. *Zoological Journal of the Linnean Society* 103:286–307. (11)

Nishikawa, K., and C. Gans. 1990. Neuromuscular control of prey capture in the marine toad, *Bufo marinus*. *American Zoologist* 30:141A. (11)

———. 1992. The role of hypoglossal sensory feedback during feeding in the marine toad, *Bufo marinus*. *Journal of Experimental Zoology*, in press. (11)

Nishikawa, K. C., J. C. O'Reilly, and D. C. Canatella. 1991. Biomechanical and behavioral transitions in the evolution of frog feeding. *American Zoologist* 31:52A. (11)

Nishikawa, K. C., and G. Roth. 1991. The mechanism of tongue protraction during prey capture in the frog *Discoglossus pictus*. *Journal of Experimental Biology* 159:217–234. (11)

Nishikawa, K., and R. Wassersug. 1988. Morphology of the caudal spinal cord in *Rana* (Ranidae) and *Xenopus* (Pipidae). *Journal of Comparative Physiology* 269:193–202. (11,16)

———. 1989. Evolution of spinal nerve number in anuran larvae. *Brain, Behavior, and Evolution* 33:15–24. (2)

Nishimura, H. 1980. Evolution of the renin-angiotensin system. In *Evolution of Vertebrate Endocrine Systems*, ed. P. K. T. Pang and A. Epple, 373–404. Lubbock: Texas Tech Press. (3)

Nissanov, J., and R. C. Eaton. 1989. Reticulospinal control of rapid escape turning in fishes. *American Zoologist* 29:103–121. (2)

Noble, G. K. 1922. The phylogeny of the Salientia: 1. The osteology and the thigh musculature: Their bearing on classification and phylogeny. *Bulletin of the American Museum of Natural History* 46:1–78. (11)

———. 1931. *The Biology of Amphibia*. New York: MacGraw-Hill. (1,4,5,11,15,16)

Noble, G. K., and L. R. Aronson. 1942. The sexual behavior of Anura: 1. The normal mating pattern of *Rana pipiens*. *Bulletin of the American Museum for Natural History* 80:127–142. (15)

Nodzenski, E., R. J. Wassersug, and R. F. Inger. Developmental differences in visceral morphology of megophryine pelobatid tadpoles in relation to their body form and mode of life. *Biological Journal of the Linnean Society* 38:369–388. (16)

Nojiri, H., I. Ishida, E. Miyashita, M. Sato, A. Urano, and T. Deguchi. 1987. Cloning and sequence analysis of cDNAs for neurohypophysial hormones vasotocin and mesotocin for the hypothalamus of toad, *Bufo japonicus*. *Proceedings of the National Academy of Science* 84:3034–3046. (16)

Noland, R., and G. R. Ultsch. 1981. The roles of temperature and dissolved oxygen in microhabitat selection by the tadpoles of a frog (*Rana pipiens*) and a toad (*Bufo terrestris*). *Copeia* 1981:645–652. (5,9,12,14)

Nomura, S., Y. Shiba, Y. Muneoka, and Y. Kanno. 1979a. Developmental changes of premetamorphosis and fungiform papillae of the frog (*Rana japonica*) during metamorphosis: A scanning electron microscopy. *Hiroshima Journal of Medical Science* 28:79–86. (16)

———. 1979b. A scanning and transmission electron microscope study of the premetamorphic papillae: Possible chemoreceptive organs in the oral cavity of anuran tadpoles (*Rana japonica*). *Archivum Histologicum Japonicum* 42:507–516. (16)

Nordlander, R. H. 1986. Motoneurons of the tail of young *Xenopus* tadpoles. *Journal of Comparative Neurology* 253:403–413. (16)

Norman, M. F. 1985. A practical method of staging metamorphosis in the tiger salamander *Ambystoma tigrinum*. *Anatomical Record* 211:102–109. (16)

Norman, M. F., J. A. Carr, and D. O. Norris. 1987. Adenohypophysial-thyroid activity of the tiger salamander *Ambystoma tigrinum*, as a function of metamorphosis and captivity. *Journal of Experimental Zoology* 242:55–66. (16)

Norman, M. F., and D. O. Norris. 1987. Effects of metamorphosis and captivity on the *in vitro* sensitivity of thyroid glands from the tiger salamander, *Ambystoma tigrinum*, to bovine thyrotropin. *General and Comparative Endocrinology* 67:77–84. (16)

Norris, B. C., S. M. Palacios, J. B. Concha, and M. T. Chiang. 1988. Fenoterol stimulation of sodium transport in the isolated toad skin: A beta adrenergic effect. *General Pharmacology* 19:97–102. (5)

Norris, D. O. 1978. Hormonal and environmental factors involved in the determination of neoteny in urodeles. In *Comparative Endocrinology,* ed. P. J. Gaillard and H. H. Boer, 109–112. Amsterdam: Elsevier/North-Holland. (16)

———. 1983. Evolution of endocrine regulation of metamorphosis in lower vertebrates. *American Zoologist* 23:709–718. (3)

Norris, D. O., D. Duvall, K. Greendale, and W. A. Gern. 1977. Thyroid function in pre- and post-spawning neotenic tiger salamanders (*Ambystoma tigrinum*). *General and Comparative Endocrinology* 33:512–517. (3)

Norris, D. O., R. E. Jones, and D. C. Cohen. 1973. Effects of mammalian gonadotropins (LH, FSH, HCG) and gonadal steroids on TSH-induced metamorphosis of *Ambystoma tigrinum* (Amphibia: Caudata). *General and Comparative Endocrinology* 20:467–473. (16)

Norris, D. O., R. E. Jones, and B. B. Criley. 1973. Pituitary prolactin levels in larval, neotenic, and metamorphosed salamanders (*Ambystoma tigrinum*). *General and Comparative Endocrinology* 20:437–442. (16)

Norris, D. O., and J. E. Platt. T_3 and T_4 induced rates of metamorphosis in immature and sexually mature larvae of *Ambystoma tigrinum* (Amphibia: Caudata). *Journal of Experimental Zoology* 189:303–310. (16)

Norris, H. W. 1908. The cranial nerves of *Amphiuma means. Journal of Comparative Neurology* 18:527–568. (7)

Norris, W. E., Jr., P. A. Grandy, and W. K. Davis. 1963. Comparative studies of the oxygen consumption of three species of neotenic salamanders as influenced by temperature, body size, and oxygen tension. *Biological Bulletin* 125:523–533. (12)

Northcutt, R. G. 1974. Some histochemical observations on the telencephalon of the bullfrog, *Rana catesbeiana* Shaw. *Journal of Comparative Neurology* 157:379–390. (2)

———. 1981. Evolution of the telencephalon in nonmammals. *Annual Review of Neuroscience* 4:301–350. (2)

Northcutt, R. G., and E. Kicliter. 1980. Organization of the amphibian telencephalon. In *Comparative Neurology of the Telencephalon*, ed. S. O. E. Ebbesson, 203–255. New York: Plenum Press. (2)

Northcutt, R. G., T. J. Neary, and D. G. Senn. 1978. Observations on the brain of the coelacanth *Latimeria chalumnae*: External anatomy and quantitative analysis. *Journal of Morphology* 155:181–192. (2)

Northcutt, R. G., and W. Plassmann. 1989. Electrosensory activity in the telencephalon of the axolotl. *Neuroscience Letters* 99:79–84. (2)

Northcutt, R. G., and G. J. Royce. 1975. Olfactory bulb projections in the bullfrog *Rana catesbeiana*. *Journal of Morphology* 145:251–268. (2)

Nosek, T. M., K. Y. Fender, and R. E. Godt. 1987. It is diprotonated inorganic phosphate that depresses force in skinned skeletal muscle fibers. *Science* 236:191–193. (12)

Notenboom, C. D. 1972. The reaction of the preoptic nucleus of *Xenopus laevis* tadpoles to osmotic stimulation: A fluorescence microscopical investigation. *Zeitschrift für Zellforschung und mikroskopische Anatomie* 134:383–402. (16)

Notenboom, C. D., M. Terlou, and M. L. Matem. 1976. Evidence for corticotropin releasing factor synthesis in the preoptic nucleus of *Xenopus laevis* tadpole: A preliminary report based on lesion experiments. *Cell and Tissue Research* 169:23–31. (16)

Nouwen, E. J., and E. R. Kühn. 1983. Radioimmunoassay of arginine vasotocin and mesotocin in serum of the frog *Rana ridibunda*. *General and Comparative Endocrinology* 50:242–251. (3,6,16)

Novales, R. R. 1983. Cellular aspects of hormonally controlled pigment translocations within chromatophores of poikilothermic vertebrates. *American Zoologist* 23:559–568. (3)

Nunes, V. S. 1988. Vocalizations of treefrogs (*Smilisca sila*) in response to bat predation. *Herpetologica* 44:8–10. (14)

Nussbaum, M. 1880. Zur Differenzierung des Geschlechts im Tierreich. *Archiv für die mikroskopische Anatomie* 18:1. (15)

———. 1906a. Fortgesetzte Untersuchungen über den Einfluss des Hungers auf die Entwicklung der männlichen Geschlechtsorgane der *Rana fusca. Anatomischer Anzeiger* 29:315–316. (15)

———. 1906b. Über den Einfluss der Jahreszeit, des Alters, und der Ernährung auf die Form der Hoden und Hodenzellen der Batrachier. *Archiv für die mikroskopische Anatomie* 68:1–121. (15)

Nussbaum, R. A. 1982. Heterotopic bones in the hindlimbs of frogs of the families Pipidae, Ranidae, and Sooglossidae. *Herpetologica* 38:312–320. (11)

———. 1983. The evolution of a unique dual jaw-closing mechanism in caecilians (Amphibia: Gymnophiona) and its bearing on caecilian ancestry. *Journal of Zoology* (London) 199:545–554. (11)

Nussbaum, R. A., and B. G. Naylor. 1982. Variation in the trunk musculature in caecilians (Amphibia: Gymnophiona). *Journal of Zoology* (London) 198:383–398. (11)

Nuutinen, V., and E. Ranta. 1986. Size-selective predation on zooplankton by the smooth newt, *Triturus vulgaris*. *Oikos* 47:83–91. (13)

Nybroe, O., P. Rosenkilde, and L. Ryttersgaard. 1985. Effects of hypophysectomy and substitution with growth hormone, prolactin, and thyroxine on growth and deposition in juvenile frogs, *Xenopus laevis*. *General and Comparative Endocrinology* 57:257–265. (3,13)

Obal, F., Jr., G. Benedek, A. Jansco-Gabor, and F. Obal. 1979. Salivary cooling, escape reaction, and heat pain in capsaicin-sensitized rats. *Pflugers Archiv* 382:249–254. (9)

Oberleithner, H., W. Guggino, and G. Giebisch. 1983a. The effect of furosemide on luminal sodium, chloride, and potassium transport in the early distal tubule of *Amphiuma* kidney: Effects of potassium transport. *Pflugers Archiv* 396:27–33. (5)

———. 1983b. Potassium transport in the early distal tubule of *Amphiuma* kidney: Effects of potassium adaptation. *Pflugers Archiv* 396:185–191. (5)

———. 1985. Resistance properties of the diluting segment of *Amphiuma* kidney: Influence of K^+ adaption. *Journal of Membrane Biology* 88:139–147. (5)

Oberleithner, H., F. Lang, R. Greger, W. Wang, and G. Giebisch. 1983. Effect of luminal potassium on cellular activity in the early distal tubule of *Amphiuma* kidney. *Pflugers Archiv* 396:34–40. (5)

Oberleithner, H., F. Lang, G. Messner, and W. Wang. 1984. Mechanism of hydrogen ion transport in the diluting segment of frog kidney. *Pflugers Archiv* 402:272–280. (5)

Oberleithner, H., F. Lang, W. Wang, and G. Giebisch. 1982. Effects of inhibition of chloride transport on intracellular sodium activity in distal amphibian nephron. *Pflugers Archiv* 394:55–60. (5)

Oberleithner, H., F. Lang, W. Wang, G. Messner, and P. Deetjen. 1983. Evidence for an amiloride sensitive Na^+ pathway in the amphibian diluting segment induced by K^+ adaptation. *Pflugers Archiv* 399:166–172. (5)

Obert, H.-J. 1977. Hormonal influences on calling and reproductive behavior in anurans. In *The Reproductive Biology of Amphibians*, ed. D. H. Taylor and S. I. Guttman, 357–366. New York: Plenum Press. (15)

O'Connor, C. S., L. I. Crawshaw, R. C. Bedichek, and J. C. Crabbe. 1988. The effect of ethanol on temperature selection in the goldfish, *Carassius auratus*. *Pharmacology, Biochemistry, and Behavior* 29: 243–248. (9)

O'Connor, M. P. 1989. Thermoregulation in anuran amphibians: Physiology, biophysics, and ecology. Ph.D. diss., Colorado State University, Fort Collins. (4)

Odendaal, F. J., and C. M. Bull. 1980. Influence of water speed on tadpoles of *Ranidella signifera* and *R. riparia* (Anura: Leptodactylidae). *Australian Journal of Zoology* 28:79–82. (14)

Odendaal, F. J., C. M. Bull, and S. J. Richards. 1984. Interactions during feeding between tadpoles of *Ranidella signifera* and *R. riparia*. *Journal of Herpetology* 18:489–492. (14)

Oeltgen, P. R., J. W. Walsh, S. R. Hamann, D. C. Randall, W. A. Spurrier, and R. D. Myers. 1982. Hibernation "trigger": Opioid-like inhibitory action on brain function of the monkey. *Pharmacological Biochemistry and Behaviour* 17:1271–1274. (10)

Ogata, T. 1958. A histochemical study of the red and white muscle fibers: Part 1. Activity of the succinoxydase system in muscle fibers. *Acta Medica Okayama* 12:216–227. (11)

Ogawa, H., K. Morimoto, and Y. Yamashita. 1981. Physiological characteristics of low threshold mechanoreceptor afferent units innervating frog skin. *Quarterly Journal of Experimental Physiology* 66: 105–116. (7)

Ogawa, H., Y. Yamashita, T. Nomura, and K. Tanigushi. 1984. Discharge patterns of the slowly adapting mechanoreceptor afferent units innervating the non-warty skin of the frog. *Japanese Journal of Physiology* 34:255–267. (7)

Oglivy, C. S., and A. B. DuBois. 1982. Effect of tilting on blood pressure and interstitial fluid pressures of bluefish and smooth dogfish. *American Journal of Physiology* 242:R70–R76. (7)

Oguro, C. 1973. Parathyroid gland and serum calcium concentrations in the giant salamander, *Megalobatrachus davidianus*. *General and Comparative Endocrinology* 21:565–568. (3)

Oguro, C., K. Nagai, H. Tarui, and Y. Sasayama. 1981. Hypocalcemic factor in the ultimobranchial gland of the frog *Rana rugosa*. *Comparative Biochemistry and Physiology* 68A:95–97. (3)

Oguro, C., and Y. Sasayama. 1978. Function of the parathyroid gland in serum calcium regulation in the newt, *Tylototriton andersoni* Boulenger. *General and Comparative Endocrinology* 35:10–15. (3)

———. 1985. Endocrinology of hypocalcemic regulation in anuran amphibians. In *Current Trends in Comparative Endocrinology*, ed. B. Lofts and W. N. Holmes, 839–841. Hong Kong: Hong Kong University Press. (3)

Oguro, C., Y. Sasayama, H. Ikadai, and H. Yoshizawa. 1975. Changes in calcium concentration of serum and coelomic fluid of the bullfrog, *Rana catesbeiana*, during larval development and metamorphosis. *Development, Growth, and Differentiation* 17:71–76. (16)

Oguro, C., Y. Sasayama, H. Nambu, and T. O. Ando. 1980. Calcium content in the salamander, *Hynobius nigrescens*, during development and metamorphosis. *Comparative and Biochemical Physiology* 67A: 523–526. (16)

Oguro, C., H. Tarui, and Y. Sasayama. 1983. Hypocalcemic potency of the ultimobranchial gland in some urodelan amphibians. *General and Comparative Endocrinology* 51:272–277. (3)

Oguro, C., and M. Uchiyama. 1975. Control of serum calcium concentration by parathyroid gland in two species of urodele amphibians. *General and Comparative Endocrinology* 27:531–537. (3)

Ohira, M., and Y. Ohira. 1988. Effects of exposure to cold on metabolic characteristics in gastrocnemius muscle of frog (*Rana pipiens*). *Journal of Physiology* (London) 395:589–595. (12)

Ohtake, S.-I. 1982. Ultrastructure of larval stomach in *Rana japonica*. *Bulletin of the Liberal Arts and Science Course, Nihon University School of Medicine* 10:1–7. (16)

Oken, D. E., and M. Weise. 1978. Micropuncture studies of the transport of individual amino acids by the *Necturus* proximal tubule. *Kidney International* 13:445–451. (5)

Oldham, R. S. 1977. Terrestrial locomotion in two species of amphibian larva. *Journal of Zoology* (London) 181:285–295. (11)

Oliver, J. A. 1955. *The Natural History of North American Amphibians and Reptiles*. Princeton, NJ: D. Van Nostrand Company. (10)

Olmsted, J. M. D., and J. M. Harvey. 1927. The respiratory exchange in frogs during muscular exercise and after injection of insulin. *American Journal of Physiology* 78:28–33. (12)

Olson, E. C. 1961. Jaw mechanisms: Rhipidistians, amphibians, reptiles. *American Zoologist* 1:205–215. (11)

Onoda, N., and Y. Katsuki. 1972. Chemoreception of the lateral line organ of an aquatic amphibian, *Xenopus laevis*. *Japanese Journal of Physiology* 221:87–102. (16)

Opdam, P., M. Kemali, and R. Nieuwenhuys. 1976. Topological analysis of the brainstem of the frogs *Rana esculenta* and *Rana catesbeiana*. *Journal of Comparative Neurology* 165:307–331. (2)

Opdam, P., and R. Nieuwenhuys. 1976. Topological analysis of the brainstem of the axolotl *Ambystoma mexicanum*. *Journal of Comparative Neurology* 165:285–306. (2)

Oplinger, C. S. 1966. Sex ratio, reproductive cycles, and time of ovulation in *Hyla crucifer crucifer* Wied. *Herpetologica* 22:276–283. (15)

———. 1967. Food habits and feeding activity of recently transformed and adult *Hyla crucifer crucifer* Wied. *Herpetologica* 23:209–217. (13)

Organ, J. A. 1961. Studies on the local distribution, life history, and population dynamics of the salamander genus *Desmognathus* in Virginia. *Ecological Monographs* 31:189–220. (15)

Orkand, P. M., R. K. Orkand, and M. W. Cohen. 1978. Distribution of acetylcholine receptors on *Xenopus* slow muscle fibres determined by alpha-bungarotoxin binding. *Neuroscience* 3:435–446. (11)

Orkand, R. K. 1963. A further study of electrical responses in slow and twitch muscle fibres of the frog. *Journal of Physiology* (London) 167:181–191. (11)

Orr, P. R. 1955. Heat death: 2. Differential response of entire animal (*Rana pipiens*) and several organ systems. *Physiological Zoology* 28:294–302. (8)

Osborne, J. L., and R. E. Burger. 1974. Intrapulmonary chemoreceptors in *Gallus domesticus*. *Respiration Physiology* 22:77–85. (7)

Ott, M., N. Heisler, and G. R. Ultsch. 1980. A re-evaluation of the relationship between temperature and the critical oxygen tension in freshwater fishes. *Comparative Biochemistry and Physiology* 67A: 337–340. (10)

Overton, E. 1904. Neununddreissig Thesen über die Wasserökonomie der Amphibien und osmotischen Eigenschaften der Amphibienhaut. *Verhandlungen der Physikalisch-medizinischen Gesellschaft zu Würzburg* 36:277–295. (5,16)

Oyama, J. 1952. Microscopical study of the visceral organs of Gymnophiona: *H. rostratus*. *Kumamoto Journal of Science* 1B:117–125. (13)

Özeti, N., and D. B. Wake. 1969. The morphology and evolution of the tongue and associated structures in salamanders and newts (family Salamandridae). *Copeia* 1969:91–123. (11,14)

Ozon, R. 1963. Analyse *in vivo* du métabolisme des oestrogens au cous de la différenciation sexuelle chez le triton *Pleurodeles waltlii* Mich. *Comptes Rendus de l'Académie des Sciences* (Paris) 257:2332–2335. (16)

———. 1967. Synthèse *in vitro* des hormones stéroïdes dans le testicule et l'ovaire de l'amphibien urodèle *Pleurodeles waltlii* Mich. *General and Comparative Endocrinology* 8:214–227. (16)

———. 1969. Steroid biosynthesis in larval and embryonic gonads of lower vertebrates. *General and Comparative Endocrinology*, suppl. 2:135–140. (16)

Pace, A. E. 1974. Systematic and biological studies of the leopard frogs (*Rana pipiens* complex) of the United States. *Miscellaneous Publications of the Museum of Zoology, University of Michigan* 148: 1–140. (8)

Packard, G. C. 1971. Oxygen consumption of montane and piedmont chorus frogs (*Pseudacris triseriata*): A study of evolutionary temperature compensation. *Physiological Zoology* 44:90–97. (12)

———. 1972. Inverse compensation for temperature in oxygen consumption of the hylid frog *Pseudacris triseriata*. *Physiological Zoology* 45:270–275. (10,12)

Packard, G. C., and T. G. Bahr. 1969. Montane and piedmont chorus frogs (*Pseudacris triseriata*): Metabolic rate as a function of temperature. *Experientia* 25:1212–1213. (12)

Packard, G. C., and T. J. Boardman. 1988. The misuse of ratios, indices, and percentages in ecophysiological research. *Physiological Zoology* 61:1–9. (12)

Packard, G. C., and M. J. Packard. 1975. The influence of acclimation temperature on the metabolic response of frog tissue to thyroxine administration *in vivo*. *General and Comparative Endocrinology* 27:162–168. (3)

———. 1988. The physiological ecology of reptilian eggs and embryos. In *Biology of the Reptilia*, vol. 16, ed. C. Gans and R. B. Huey, 523–605. New York: Alan R. Liss. (8)

Packer, W. C. 1963. Dehydration, hydration, and burrowing behavior in *Heleioporus eyrei* (Gray) (Leptodactylidae). *Ecology* 44:643–651. (6,10,12)

Page, S. G. 1965. A comparison of the fine structures of frog slow and twitch muscle fibres. *Journal of Cell Biology* 26:447–497. (11)

———. 1966. Intrafusal muscle fibers in the frog. *Journal of Microscopy* 5:101–104. (11)

Paladino, F. V. 1985. Temperature effects on locomotion and activity bioenergetics of amphibians, reptiles, and birds. *American Zoologist* 25:965–972. (9,12)

Pallett, J. R., and N. I. Passmore. 1988. The significance of multi-note advertisement calls in the reed frog, *Hyperolius tuberlinguis*. *Bioacoustics* 1:13–23. (14)

Pancak, M. K., and D. H. Taylor. 1983. Seasonal and daily corticosterone rhythms in American toads, *Bufo americanus*. *General and Comparative Endocrinology* 50:490–497. (3)

Pancharatna, M., and S. K. Saidapur. 1985. Ovarian cycle in the frog *Rana cyanophlyctis*: A quantitative study of follicular kinetics in relation to body mass, oviduct, and fat body cycles. *Journal of Morphology* 186:135–147. (15)

Pandian, T. J., and M. P. Marian. 1985. Time and energy costs of metamorphosis in the Indian bullfrog, *Rana tigrina*. *Copeia* 1985:653–662. (8)

Pang, P. K. T. 1977. Osmoregulatory functions of neurohypophysial hormones in fishes and amphibians. *American Zoologist* 17:739–749. (5,6)

———. 1981. Pituitary and prolactin influences on calcium regulation in the mudpuppy, *Necturus maculosus*. *General and Comparative Endocrinology* 44:524–529. (3)

Pang, P. K. T., S. M. Galli-Gallardo, N. Collie, and W. H. Sawyer. 1980. Renal and peripheral vascular responsiveness to arginine vasotocin in the bullfrog, *Rana catesbeiana*. *American Journal of Physiology* 239:R156–R160. (5,6)

Pang, P. K. T., A. D. Kenny, and C. Oguro. 1980. Evolution of endocrine control of calcium regulation. In *Evolution of Vertebrate Endocrine Systems*, ed. P. K. T. Pang and A. Epple, 323–356. Lubbock: Texas Tech Press. (3)

Pang, P. K. T., and W. H. Sawyer. 1974. Effects of prolactin on hypophysectomized mudpuppies *Necturus maculosus*. *American Journal of Physiology* 226:458–462. (5)

———. 1978. Renal and vascular responses of the bullfrog (*Rana catesbeiana*) to mesotocin. *American Journal of Physiology* 235:F151–F155. (5,6)

Pang, P. K. T., M. Uchiyama, and W. H. Sawyer. 1982. Endocrine and neural control of amphibian renal functions. *Federation Proceedings of the American Societies for Experimental Biology* 41:2365–2370. (6)

Pang, P. K. T., M. Yang, C. Oguro, J. G. Phillips, and J. A. Yee. 1980. Hypotensive actions of parathyroid hormone preparations in vertebrates. *General and Comparative Endocrinology* 41:135–138. (3)

Pang, S. F., S. Y. W. Shui, and S. F. Tse. 1985. Effect of photic manipulation on the level of melatonin in the retinas of frogs (*Rana tigrina regulosa*). *General and Comparative Endocrinology* 58:464–470. (3)

Panter, H. C., J. E. Chapman, and A. R. Williams. 1987. Effect of radiation and trophic state on oxygen consumption of tadpoles of the frog *Limnodynastes tasmaniensis*. *Comparative Biochemistry and Physiology* 88A:373–375. (12)

Paolucci, M., and V. Botte. 1988. Estradiol-binding molecules in the hepatocytes of the female water frog, *Rana esculenta*, and plasma estradiol and vitellogenin levels during the reproductive cycle. *General and Comparative Endocrinology* 70:466–476. (3)

Papkoff, H., S. W. Farmer, and P. Licht. 1976. Isolation and characterization of luteinizing hormone from amphibian (*Rana catesbeiana*) pituitaries. *Life Science* 18:245–250. (16)

Parker, G. A. 1982. Phenotype limited evolutionarily stable strategies. In *Current Problems in Sociobiology*, ed. King's College Sociobiology Group, 173–201. Cambridge: Cambridge University Press. (14)

———. 1983. Mate quality and mating decisions. In *Mate Choice*, ed. P. Bateson, 141–164. Cambridge: Cambridge University Press. (14)

Parker, G. E. 1967. The influence of temperature and thyroxine on oxygen consumption in *Rana pipiens* tadpoles. *Copeia* 1967:610–616. (9,12)

Parker, H. W., and E. R. Dunn. 1964. Dentitional metamorphosis in the amphibians. *Copeia* 1964:75–86. (16)

Parnas, J. K., and Z. Kraskinska. 1921. Über den Stoffwechsel der Amphibienlarven. *Biochemische Zeitschrift* 116:108. (16)

Parsons, R. H., and R. H. Alvarado. 1968. Effect of temperature on water and ion balance in larval *Ambystoma gracile*. *Comparative Biochemistry and Physiology* 24:61–72. (16)

Parsons, R. H., R. Brady, B. Goddard, and D. Kernan. 1978. Seasonal effects on osmotic permeability of *Rana pipiens in vivo* and *in vitro*. *Journal of Experimental Zoology* 204:347–352. (5)

Parsons, R. H., and F. Mobin. 1989. Regional osmotic water flow in Amphibia: Effect of dehydration. *American Zoologist* 29:103A. (6)

Parsons, R. H., L. M. Thorn, S. M. Salerno, and S. Petronis. 1990. Salt load effects on osmotic water flow, tritiated water diffusion, and the cardiovascular system in *Rana pipiens* and *Rana catesbeiana*. *Physiological Zoology* 63:571–586. (6)

Parzefall, J., J. P. Durand, and B. Richard. 1980. Chemical communication in *Necturus maculosus* and its cave-living relative *Proteus anguinus* (Proteidae, Urodela). *Zeitschrift für Tierpsychologie* 53:133–138. (2)

Pasanen, S. 1977. Seasonal variations in certain enzyme activities in the common frog, *Rana temporaria* L., under natural and experimental conditions. *Comparative Biochemistry and Physiology* 56B:163–167. (10)

———. 1979. The isoenzymes of lactic dehydrogenase in some tissues of the wintering common frog during warm acclimation. *Joensuun Korkeakorlun Julk Sar* 0:1–4. (8)

Pasanen, S., and P. Koskela. 1974. Seasonal and age variation in the metabolism of the common frog, *Rana temporaria* L., in northern Finland. *Comparative Biochemistry and Physiology* 47A:635–654. (10,15)

Pashkova, I. M. 1985. Seasonal changes in the heat resistance of *Bufo viridis* and its muscles and of contractile muscle models. *Journal of Thermal Biology* 10:105–108. (8)

Pasquier, D. A., M. A. Cannata, and J. H. Tramezzani. 1980. Central connections of the toad neural lobe as shown by retrograde neuronal labeling: Classical and new connections. *Brain Research* 195:37–45. (2)

Passmore, M. I. 1981. Sound levels of mating calls of some African frogs. *Herpetologica* 37:166–171. (14)

Passmore, M. I., and M. Malherbe. 1985. High nocturnal body temperature in the painted reed frog (*Hyperolius marmoratus*). *Herpetologica* 41:212–215. (9)

Pasteels, J. L., Jr., 1960. Étude expérimentale des différentes catégories d'éléments chromophiles de l'hypophyse adulte de *Pleurodeles waltlii*, de leur fonction, et de leur contrôle par l'hypothalamus. *Archives de Biologie* 71:409–471. (15)

Patterson, T. L. 1916. Contributions to the physiology of the stomach: 36. The physiology of the gastric hunger contractions in the Amphibia and the Reptilia: Comparative studies: 1. *American Journal of Physiology* 42:56–88. (13)

Pattle, R. E., C. Schock, J. M. Creasey, and G. M. Hughes. 1977. Surpellic films, lung surfactant, and their cellular origin in newt, caecelian, and frog. *Journal of Zoology* (London) 182:125–136. (6)

Patton, P., and P. Grobstein. 1986. Forebrain modulation of orienting circuitry in the frog: Involvement of the striatum. *Society for Neuroscience Abstracts* 12:106. (2)

Patzelt, V. 1918. Über verschiedene Missbildungen beim Frosch, zugleich ein Betrag zur Histologie und Entwicklungsgeschichte des Urogenitalapparates. *Wilhelm Roux's Archiv für Entwicklungsmechanik der Organismen* 44:256–290. (15)

Pauley, T. K. 1978. Temperature and insolation as factors regulating the partitioning of habitats of two sympatric *Plethodon* species. *Proceedings of the West Virginia Academy of Sciences* 50:77–84. (14)

Paulson, B. K., and V. H. Hutchison. 1987a. Blood changes in *Bufo cognatus* following heat stress. *Comparative Biochemistry and Physiology* 87A:461–466. (9)

————. 1987b. Origin for the stimulus for muscular spasms at the critical thermal maximum in anurans. *Copeia* 1987:810–813. (8,9)

Pawlowska, I. A. 1980. Effect of temperature on the embryonic development of *Bombina variegata*. *Zoologica Poloniae* 27:397–408. (8)

————. 1985. The effect of temperature during embryonic development on the structure of the vertebral column of *Xenopus*. *Zoologica Poloniae* 32:211–222. (8)

Peachey, L. D. 1961. Structure and function of slow striated muscle. In *Biophysics of Physiological and Pharmacological Actions*, ed. A. M. Shanes, 391–411. Washington, DC: American Association for the Advancement of Science. (11)

————. 1968. Muscle. *Annual Review of Physiology* 30:401–429. (11)

————. 1983. Skeletal muscle. In *Handbook of Physiology*, sec. 10, ed. L. D. Peachey. Bethesda, MD: American Physiological Society. (11)

Peachey, L. D., and A. F. Huxley. 1962. Structural identification of twitch and slow striated muscle fibers of the frog. *Journal of Cell Biology* 13:177–180. (11)

Peachey, L. D., and H. Rasmussen. 1961. Structure of the toad's urinary bladder as related to its physiology. *Journal of Biophysics and Biochemical Cytology* 10:529–533. (6)

Peacock, R. L., and R. A. Nussbaum. 1973. Reproductive biology and population structure of the western red-backed salamander, *Plethodon vehiculum* (Cooper). *Journal of Herpetology* 7:215–224. (15)

Pearson, O. P. 1954. Habits of the lizard *Liolaemus multiformis multiformis* at high altitudes in southern Peru. *Copeia* 1954:111–116. (9)

Pearson, O. P., and D. F. Bradford. 1976. Thermoregulation of lizards and toads at high altitudes in Peru. *Copeia* 1976:155–170. (9)

Pehlemann, F. W. 1962. Experimentelle Untersuchungen zur Determination und Differenzierung der Hypophyse bei Anuren (*Pelobates fuscus, Rana esculenta*). *Wilhelm Roux's Archiv für Entwicklungsmechanik der Organismen* 153:551–602. (16)

————. 1972. Regulation of differentiation and cell division of melanophores in *Xenopus laevis* larvae. In *Pigmentation: Its Genesis and Biologic Control*, ed. V. Riley, 295–305. New York: Appleton-Century-Crofts. (16)

Penhos, J. C. 1952. Papel de los cuerpos grasos del *Bufo arenarum* Hensel. *Revista de la Sociedad Argentina de Biologia* 28:213–219. (15)

Penhos, J. C., and E. Ramey. 1973. Studies on the endocrine pancreas of amphibians and reptiles. *American Zoologist* 13:667–698. (3)

Penman, H. L. 1958. Natural evaporation from open water, bare soils, and grass. *Proceedings of the Royal Society of London* 193:120–140. (4)

Penney, D. G. 1987. Frogs and turtles: Different ectotherm overwintering strategies. *Comparative Biochemistry and Physiology* 86A:609–615. (10)

Perrill, S. A., H. C. Gerhardt, and R. Daniels. 1978. Sexual parasitism in the green treefrog (*Hyla cinerea*). *Science* 200:1179–1180. (14)

Perrin, A. 1892a. Contributions à l'étude de la myologie comparée du membre postérieur chez un certain nombre de batraciens et de sauriens. *Bulletin Scientifique de la France et de la Belgique* 24:372–540. (11)

————. 1892b. Muscles du pied chez la *Salamandra maculosa* et le *Siredon pisciformis*. *Bulletin de la Société Philomatique* (Paris) 3:118–124. (11)

————. 1899. Contribution à l'étude de la myologie et de l'ostéologie comparée du membre antérieur chez un certain nombre de batraciens et de sauriens. *Bulletin Scientifique de la France et de la Belgique* 32:220–82. (11)

Perroteau, I., P. Netchitailo, F. Homo-Delarche, C. Delarue, I. L. Lihrmann, F. Leboulenger, and H. Vaudry. 1984. Role of exogenous and endogenous prostaglandins in steroidogenesis by isolated frog interrenal gland: Evidence for dissociation in adrenocorticotropin and angiotensin action. *Endocrinology* 115:1765–1773. (3)

Perry, J. S., and I. W. Rowlands. 1962. The ovarian cycle in vertebrates. In *The Ovary*, ed. S. Zuckerman, 1:275–309. New York: Academic Press. (15)

Persaud, K. C., J. A. DeSimone, M. L. Getchell, G. L. Heck, and T. V. Getchell. 1987. Ion transport across the olfactory mucosa: The basal and odorant-stimulated states. *Biochimica et Biophysica Acta* 902:65–79. (16)

Persson, B. E. 1981. Dynamics of glomerular ultrafiltration in *Amphiuma means*. *Pflugers Archiv* 391:135–140. (5)

Persson, B. E., and D. J. Marsh. 1987. GFR regulation and flow-dependent electrophysiology of early distal tubule in *Amphiuma*. *American Journal of Physiology* 253:F263–F268. (5)

Persson, B. E., and A. E. G. Persson. 1981. The existence of a tubulo-glomerular feedback mechanism in the *Amphiuma* nephron. *Pflugers Archiv* 392:129–134. (5)

————. 1983. Acidification in the distal tubule of the *Amphiuma* kidney. *Acta Physiologica Scandinavica* 117:343. (5)

Perutz, M. F., and M. Brunori. 1982. Stereochemistry of cooperative effects in fish and amphibian hemoglobins. *Nature* 299:421–426. (5)

Peter, J. B., R. J. Barnard, V. R. Edgerton, C. A. Gillespie, and K. E. Stempel. 1972. Metabolic profiles of three fiber types of skeletal-muscle in guinea pigs and rabbits. *Biochemistry* 11:2627–2633. (11)

Peter, K. 1898. Die Entwicklung und funktionelle Gestaltung des Schädels von *Ichthyophis glutinosus*. *Morphologisches Jahrbuch* 25:1–78. (11)

Peter, R. E. 1983. Evolution of neurohormonal regulation of reproduction in lower vertebrates. *American Zoologist* 23:685–695. (15)

————. 1986. Structure-activity studies on gonadotropin-releasing hormone in teleosts, amphibians, reptiles, and mammals. In *Comparative Endocrinology: Developments and Directions*, ed. C. L. Ralph, 75–93. New York: Alan R. Liss. (15)

————. 1987. Vertebrate neurohormonal systems. In *Vertebrate Endocrinology: Fundamentals and Biomedical Implications*, vol. 1, *Morphological Considerations*, ed. P. K. T. Pang and M. P. Schreibman, 57–104. New York: Academic Press. (3)

Peters, R. H., and K. Wassenberg. 1983. The effect of body size on animal abundance. *Oecologia* (Berlin) 60:89–96. (14)

Peters, S. E., and G. E. Goslow. 1983. From salamanders to mammals: Continuity in musculoskeletal function during locomotion. *Brain, Behavior and Evolution* 22:191–197. (11)

Peterson, C. R. 1987. Daily variation in the body temperatures of free-ranging garter snakes. *Ecology* 68:160–169. (4,9)

Peterson, E. H. 1989. Motorpool organization of vertebrate axial muscles. *American Zoologist* 29:123–137. (2)

Petranka, J. W. 1979. The effects of severe winter weather on *Plethodon dorsalis* and *Plethodon richmondi* populations in central Kentucky. *Journal of Herpetology* 13:369–371. (10)

————. 1984. Ontogeny of the diet and feeding behavior of *Eurycea bislineata* larvae. *Journal of Herpetology* 18:48–55. (14)

Petranka, J. W., J. J. Just, and E. C. Crawford. 1982. Hatching of amphibian embryos: The physiological trigger. *Science* 217:257–259. (16)

Petranka, J. W., L. B. Kats, and A. Sih. 1987. Predator-prey interactions among fish and larval amphibians: Use of chemical cues to detect predatory fish. *Animal Behaviour* 35:420–425. (16)

Petriella, S., J. C. Reboreda, M. Otero, and E. T. Segura. 1989. Antidiuretic responses to osmotic cutaneous stimulation in the toad, *Bufo arenarum*. *Journal of Comparative Physiology* 159B:91–95. (6)

Pettus, D., and G. M. Angleton. 1967. Comparative reproductive biology of montane and piedmont chorus frogs. *Evolution* 21:500–507. (15)

Pettus, D., and A. W. Spencer. 1964. Size and metabolic differences in *Pseudacris triseriata* (Anura) from different elevations. *Southwestern Naturalist* 9:20–26. (12)

Pianka, E. R. 1966. Convexity, desert lizards, and spatial heterogeneity. *Ecology* 47:1055–1059. (14)

————. 1973. The structure of lizard communities. *Annual Review of Ecology and Systematics* 4:53–74. (14)

————. 1977. Reptilian species diversity. In *Biology of the Reptilia*, vol. 7, ed. C. Gans and D. W. Tinkle, 1–34. New York: Academic Press. (14)

————. 1980. Guild structure in desert lizards. *Oikos* 35:194–201. (14)

————. 1981. Resource acquisition and allocation among animals. In *Physiological Ecology: An Evolutionary Approach to Resource Use*, ed. C. R. Townsend and P. Calow, 300–314. Sunderland, MA: Sinauer Associates. (14)

————. 1986. *Ecology and Natural History of Desert Lizards*. Princeton, NJ: Princeton University Press. (14)

Pianka, E. R., and W. S. Parker. 1975. Age-specific reproductive tactics. *American Naturalist* 109:453–64. (14)

Piatt, J. 1935. A comparative study of the hyobranchial apparatus and throat musculature of the Plethodontidae. *Journal of Morphology* 57:213–251. (11)

————. 1938. Morphogenesis of the cranial muscles of *Ambystoma punctatum*. *Journal of Morphology* 63:531–587. (11)

————. 1939. Correct terminology in salamander myology: 1. Intrinsic gill musculature. *Copeia* 1939:220–224. (11)

————. 1940. Correct terminology in salamander myology: 2. Transverse ventral throat musculature. *Copeia* 1940:9–14. (11)

Pierantoni, R., L. Iela, G. Delrio, and R. K. Rastogi. 1984. Seasonal plasma sex steroid levels in the female *Rana esculenta*. *General and Comparative Endocrinology* 53:126–134. (3)

Pierantoni, R., B. Varriale, S. Minucci, L. Di Matteo, S. Fasano, M. D'Antonio, and G. Chieffi. 1986. Regulation of androgen production by frog *Rana esculenta* testes: An *in vitro* study on the effects exerted by estradiol, 5-dihydrotestosterone, testosterone, melatonin, and serotonin. *General and Comparative Endocrinology* 64:405–410. (3)

Pierantoni, R., B. Varriale, C. Simeoli, L. Di Matteo, M. Milone, R. K. Rastogi, and G. Chieffi. 1983. Fat body and autumn recrudescence of the ovary in *Rana esculenta*. *Comparative Biochemistry and Physiology* 76A:31–35. (15)

Pierce, B. A., J. B. Mitton, and F. L. Rose. 1981. Allozyme variation among large, small, and cannibal morphs of the tiger salamander inhabiting the Llano Estacado of west Texas. *Copeia* 1981:590–595. (14,16)

Pietruszka, R. D. 1986. Search tactics of desert lizards: How polarized are they? *Animal Behaviour* 34:1742–1758. (14)

Piiper, J. 1988. Models for cutaneous gas exchange and transport. *American Zoologist* 28:963–972. (4,5,6)

Piiper, J., R. N. Gatz, and E. C. Crawford. 1976. Gas transport characteristics in an exclusively skin-breathing salamander, *Desmognathus fuscus* (Plethodontidae). In *Respiration of Amphibious Vertebrates*, ed. G. M. Hughes, 339–356. New York: Academic Press. (5,6,7,10)

Piiper, J., and P. Scheid. 1975. Gas transport efficacy of gill, lungs, and skin: Theory and experimental data. *Respiration Physiology* 23:209–221. (6,7)

Pilc, A., and J. Z. Nowak. 1980. The influence of 4-methylhistamine, an agonist of histamine H_2-receptors, on body temperature in rats. *Neuropharmacology* 19:773–775. (9)

Pilkington, J. B., and K. Simkiss. 1966. The mobilization of the calcium carbonate deposits in the endolymphatic sacs of metamorphosing frogs. *Journal of Experimental Biology* 45:329–341. (3,16)

Pimentel, R. A. 1960. Inter- and intrahabitat movements of the rough-skinned newt, *Taricha torosa granulosa* (Skilton). *American Midland Naturalist* 63:470–496. (15)

Pinder, A. W. 1985. Respiratory physiology of two amphibians, *Rana pipiens* and *Rana catesbeiana*. Ph.D. diss., University of Massachusetts, Amherst. (10)

————. 1987a. Cutaneous diffusing capacity increases during hypoxia in cold submerged bullfrogs (*Rana catesbeiana*). *Respiration Physiology* 70:85–95. (5,6,10,12)

————. 1987b. The diffusion boundary layer can limit O_2 uptake in submerged bullfrogs (5°C). *American Zoologist* 24:9A. (4,10)

Pinder, A. W., and W. W. Burggren. 1983. Respiration during chronic hypoxia and hyperoxia in larval and adult bullfrogs (*Rana catesbeiana*): 2. Changes in respiratory properties of whole blood. *Journal of Experimental Biology* 105:205–229. (5,10,16)

————. 1986. Ventilation and partitioning of oxygen uptake in the frog *Rana pipiens*: Effects of hypoxia and activity. *Journal of Experimental Biology* 126:453–468. (5,6,12)

Pinder, A. W., D. Clemens, and M. E. Feder. 1990. An isolated perfused frog skin preparation for the study of gas exchange. In *Oxygen Transport to Tissue*, ed. J. Piiper and M. Meyer, 12:719–724. New York: Plenum Press. (6)

————. 1991. Gas exchange in isolated perfused frog skin as a function of perfusion rate. *Respiration Physiology*. 85:1–14. (6,10)

Pinder, A. W., and M. E. Feder. 1990. Effect of boundary layers on cutaneous gas exchange. *Journal of Experimental Biology*. 154:67–80. (7,10)

Pitchford, S., and J. L. Ashmore. 1987. An electrical resonance in hair cells of the amphibian papilla of the frog *Rana temporaria*. *Hearing Research* 27:75–83. (16)

Pitkin, R. B. 1977. Effects of temperature on respiration of *Notophthalmus viridescens*, the red-spotted newt. *Comparative Biochemistry and Physiology* 57A:413–416. (12)

————. 1978. Effects of temperature on nitrogen excretion of the red-spotted newt. *American Zoologist* 18:671. (8)

————. 1987. Anemia and cutaneous gas exchange in adult aquatic red-spotted newts. *Notophthalmus viridescens viridescens*. *Journal of Herpetology* 21:1–5. (12)

Plassmann, W. 1980. Central neuronal pathways in the lateral line system of *Xenopus laevis*. *Journal of Comparative Physiology* 136:203–213. (2)

Platt, J. B. 1896. The development of the thyroid gland and of the suprapericardial bodies in *Necturus*. *Anatomischer Anzeiger* 11:557–567. (16)

Platt, J. E. 1976. The effects of ergocornine on tail height, spontaneous and T_4 induced metamorphosis, and thyroidal uptake of radioiodide in neotenic *Ambystoma tigrinum*. *General and Comparative Endocrinology* 28:71–81. (16)

Platt, J. E., G. B. Brown, S. A. Erwin, and K. T. McKinley. 1986. Antagonistic effects of prolactin and oxytocin on tail fin regression and acid phosphatase activity in metamorphosing *Ambystoma tigrinum*. *General and Comparative Endocrinology* 61:376–382. (16)

Platt, J. E., and M. A. Christopher. 1977. Effects of prolactin on the water and sodium content of larval tissue from neotenic and metamorphosing *Ambystoma tigrinum*. *General and Comparative Endocrinology* 31:243–248. (16)

Plaxton, W. C., and K. B. Storey. 1986. Glycolytic enzyme binding and metabolic control in anaerobiosis. *Journal of Comparative Physiology* 156:635–640. (10)

Ploetz, A. J. 1890. Die Vorgänge in den Froschhoden unter den Einfluss der Jahreszeit. *Archiv für Anatomie und Physiologie, physiologische Abteilung*, suppl. 1890:1–32. (15)

Pocrnjic, Z. 1965. The influence of thermal adaptation on the oxygen consumption of the newt (*Triturus vulgaris*). *Archives of Biological Sciences* (English translation of *Archiv Bioloskih Nauka*) 17:139–148. (12)

Poczopko, P. 1958. The influence of an atmosphere enriched in CO_2 and O_2 on the skin capillaries of the edible frog (*Rana esculenta* L.). *Studia Societatis Scientiarum Torunensis, Section E, Zoologia* 4:23–28. (7)

————. 1959–1960. Respiratory exchange in *Rana esculenta* L. in different respiratory media. *Zoologica Poloniae* 10:45–55. (7,12)

————. 1980. Relations of metabolic rate and body temperature. In *Comparative Physiology: Primitive Mammals*, ed. K. Schmidt-Nielsen, L. Bolis, and C. R. Taylor, 155–162. Cambridge: Cambridge University Press. (9)

Poczopko, P., and R. Jusiak. 1972. The effect of ambient temperature and season on total and tissue metabolism of the frog (*Rana esculenta* L.). *Bulletin de l'Académie Polonaise des Sciences Série des Sciences Biologiques* 20:437–441. (12)

Pohl, C. R., and E. Knobil. 1982. The role of the central nervous system in the control of ovarian function in higher primates. *Annual Reviews of Physiology* 44:583–593. (15)

Polis, G. A., and C. A. Myers. 1985. A survey of intraspecific predation among reptiles and amphibians. *Journal of Herpetology* 19:99–107. (13,16)

Pollack, E. D., and H. D. Bibb, eds. 1988. *Neurology and Neurobiology*. Vol. 44, *Developmental Neurobiology of the Frog*. New York: Alan R. Liss. (11)

Pomeroy, L. V. 1981. Developmental polymorphism in the tadpoles of the spadefoot toad, *Scaphiopus multiplicatus*. Ph.D. diss., University of California, Riverside. (14,16)

Ponse, K. 1924. L'organe de Bidder et le déterminisme des caractères sexuels secondaires du crapaud (*Bufo vulgaris* L.). *Revue Suisse de Zoologie* 31:177–336. (13,15)

Pope, C. H. 1924. Notes on North Carolina salamanders with special reference to the egg-laying habits of *Leurognathus* and *Desmognathus*. *American Museum Novitates* 153:1–15. (16)

————. 1944. *Amphibians and Reptiles of the Chicago Area*. Chicago: Chicago Natural History Museum. (10)

Porter, K. R. 1972. *Herpetology*. Philadelphia: Saunders. (1,4,9,13)

Porter, W. P. 1989. New animal models and experiments for calculating growth potentials at different elevations. *Physiological Zoology* 62:286–313. (1)

Porter, W. P., and D. M. Gates. 1969. Thermodynamic equilibria of animals with environment. *Ecological Monographs* 39:245–270. (4)

Porter, W. P., and F. C. James. 1979. Behavioral implications of mechanistic ecology: 2. The African rainbow lizard, *Agama agama*. *Copeia* 1979:594–619. (4)

Porter, W. P., J. W. Mitchell, W. A. Beckman, and C. B. DeWitt. 1973. Behavioral implications of mechanistic ecology: Thermal and behavioral modeling of desert ectotherms and their microenvironments. *Oecologia* (Berlin) 13:1–54. (4)

Porter, W. P., J. W. Mitchell, W. A. Beckman, and C. R. Tracy. 1975. Environmental constraints on some predator-prey interactions. In *Perspectives of Biophysical Ecology,* ed. D. M. Gates and R. Schmerl, 347–363. New York: Springer-Verlag. (4)

Porter, W. P., and C. R. Tracy. 1974. Modeling the effects of temperature changes on the ecology of the garter snake and leopard frog. In *Thermal Ecology,* ed. J. W. Gibbons and R. R. Scharitz, 594–609. Technical Information Center, Office of Information Services, U.S. Atomic Energy Commission, Oak Ridge, TN. (4)

———. 1983. Biophysical analyses of energetics, time-space utilization, and distributional limits. In *Lizard Ecology: Studies of a Model Organism,* ed. R. B. Huey, E. R. Pianka, and T. W. Schoener, 55–83. Cambridge, MA: Harvard University Press. (4)

Pough, F. H. 1974a. Natural daily temperature acclimation of eastern red efts, *Notophthalmus v. viridescens* (Rafinesque) (Amphibia: Caudata). *Comparative Biochemistry and Physiology* 47A:71–78. (8,14)

———. 1974b. Preface to facsimile reprint of "A preliminary study of the thermal requirements of desert reptiles," by R. B. Cowles and C. M. Bogert. Milwaukee, WI: Society for the Study of Amphibians and Reptiles. (9)

———. 1976. The effect of temperature on oxygen capacity of reptile blood. *Physiological Zoology* 49:141–151. (9)

———. 1980. The advantages of ectothermy for tetrapods. *American Naturalist* 115:92–112. (1,9,14)

———. 1983. Amphibians and reptiles as low-energy systems. In *Behavioral Energetics: The Cost of Survival in Vertebrates,* ed. W. P. Aspey and S. I. Lustick, 141–188. Columbus: Ohio State University Press. (1,9,12,14)

———. 1989a. Amphibians: A rich source of biological diversity. In *Nonmammalian Animal Models for Biomedical Research,* ed. A. D. Woodhead, 245–277. Boca Raton: CRC Press. (1)

———. 1989b. Organismal performance and Darwinian fitness: Approaches and interpretations. *Physiological Zoology* 62:199–236. (1,14)

Pough, F. H., and R. M. Andrews. 1985a. Energy costs of subduing and swallowing prey for a lizard. *Ecology* 66:1525–1533. (14)

———. 1985b. Use of anaerobic metabolism by free-ranging lizards. *Physiological Zoology* 58:205–213. (14)

Pough, F. H., and C. Gans. 1982. The vocabulary of reptilian thermoregulation. In *Biology of the Reptilia,* vol. 12, ed. C. Gans and F. H. Pough, 17–24. New York: Academic Press. (9)

Pough, F. H., and R. E. Gatten, Jr. 1984. The use of anaerobic metabolism by frogs in a breeding chorus. *Comparative Biochemistry and Physiology* 78A:337–340. (12,14)

Pough, F. H., J. B. Heiser, and W. N. McFarland. 1989. *Vertebrate Life.* 3d ed. New York: Macmillan. (1,14)

Pough, F. H., and S. Kamel. 1984. Post-metamorphic change in activity metabolism of anurans in relation to life history. *Oecologia* (Berlin) 65:138–144. (12,14)

Pough, F. H., M. M. Stewart, and R. G. Thomas. 1977. Physiological basis of habitat partitioning in Jamaican *Eleutherodactylus. Oecologia* (Berlin) 27:285–293. (9)

Pough, F. H., and T. L. Taigen. 1990. Metabolic correlates of the foraging and social behaviour of dart-poison frogs. *Animal Behaviour* 38:145–155. (14)

Pough, F. H., T. L. Taigen, M. M. Stewart, and P. F. Brussard. 1983. Behavioral modification of evaporative water loss by a Puerto Rican frog. *Ecology* 64:244–252. (4,6,12,14)

Pough, F. H., and R. E. Wilson. 1970. Natural daily temperature stress, dehydration, and acclimation in juvenile *Ambystoma maculatum* (Shaw) (Amphibia: Caudata). *Physiological Zoology* 43:194–205. (8,14)

———. 1977. Acid precipitation and reproductive success of *Ambystoma* salamanders. *Water, Air, and Soil Pollution* 7:307–316. (14)

Pounds, J. A., and M. L. Crump. 1987. Harlequin frogs along a tropical montane stream: Aggregation and the risk of predation by frog-eating flies. *Biotropica* 19:306–309. (14)

Powell, T. L., and J. J. Just. 1990. Development of the urinary bladder in tadpoles of *Rana catesbeiana* (Anura: Ranidae) during normal and induced metamorphosis. Unpublished manuscript. (16)

Powell, T. L., J. J. Just, and B. A. Jackson. 1990. Physiology of developing urinary bladder in tadpoles of *Rana catesbeiana.* Unpublished manuscript. (16)

Poynton, J. C. 1964. The Amphibia of Southern Africa. *Annals of the Natal Museum* 17:1–334. (6,10)

Prahlad, K. V. 1968. Induced metamorphosis, rectification of a genetic disability by thyroid hormone in the Mexican axolotl *Siredon mexicanum. General and Comparative Endocrinology* 11:21–30. (16)

Prasad, C., J. F. Wilber, and R. L. Amborski. 1982. Thyrotropin-releasing hormone: Its distribution and metabolism during development in bullfrog (*Rana catesbeiana*). *Developmental Neuroscience* 5:293–297. (16)

Prasadmurthy, Y. S., and S. K. Saidapur. 1987. Role of fat bodies in oocyte growth and recruitment in the frog *Rana cyanophlyctis* (Schn.). *Journal of Experimental Zoology* 243:153–162. (15)

Precht, H. 1958. Theory of temperature adaptation in cold-blooded animals. In *Physiological Adaptation,* ed. C. L. Prosser, 50–78. Washington, DC: American Physiological Society. (8)

Precht, H., J. Christophersen, H. Hensel, and W. Larcher. 1973. *Temperature and Life.* New York: Springer-Verlag. (8,9)

Precht, H., H. Laudien, and B. Havsteen. 1973. Animals: 2. The normal temperature range. In *Temperature and Life,* ed. H. Precht, J. Christophersen, H. Hensel, and W. Larcher, 302–399. New York: Springer-Verlag. (9)

Preest, M. R., and F. H. Pough. 1989. Interactive effects of body temperature and hydration state on locomotor performance of the toad *Bufo americanus. Functional Ecology* 3:693–699. (12,14)

Preslar, A. J., and V. H. Hutchison. 1978. Energetics for activity in the salamander, *Amphiuma tridactylum. Journal of Comparative Physiology* 128B:139–146. (9,12)

Prestwich, K. N., K. E. Brugger, and M. Topping. 1989. Energy and communication in three species of hylid frogs: Power input, power output, and efficiency. *Journal of Experimental Biology* 144:53–80. (12,14)

Prestwich, K. N., and T. J. Walker. 1981. Energetics of singing in crickets: Effect of temperature in three trilling species (Orthoptera: Gryllidae). *Journal of Comparative Physiology* 143:199–212. (14)

Preyer, W. 1885. *Specielle Physiologie des Embryo.* Leipzig: Grieben. (16)

Prosser, C. L. 1973a. *Comparative Animal Physiology.* 3d ed. Philadelphia: W. B. Saunders. (4,8,10)

———. 1973b. Water: Osmotic balance: Hormonal regulation. In *Comparative Animal Physiology,* 3d ed., ed. C. L. Prosser, 1–78. Philadelphia: W. B. Saunders. (4)

———. 1986. *Adaptational Biology.* New York: Wiley. (1,4,6,8)

Prothero, J., and A. C. Burton. 1961. The physics of blood flow in capillaries: 1. The nature of the motion. *Biophysical Journal* 1:567–579. (5)

Pruett, S. J., D. F. Hoyt, and D. F. Stiffler. 1991. The allometry of osmotic and ionic regulation in Amphibia with emphasis on intraspecific scaling in the larval *Ambystoma tigrinum. Physiological Zoology.* 64:1173–1199. (5)

Pruett, S. J., and D. F. Stiffler. 1987. Scaling of osmotic and ionic regulatory transport in Amphibia. *Physiologist* 30:137. (5)

Puckett, W. O. 1939. Some reactions of the gonads of *Rana catesbeiana* tadpoles to injections of mammalian hormonal substances. *Journal of Experimental Zoology* 8:23–65. (16)

Purves, D. 1988. *Body and Brain.* Cambridge, MA: Harvard University Press. (2)

Putnam, J. L. 1975. Septation in the ventricle of the heart of *Siren intermedia. Copeia* 1975:773–774. (5)

———. 1977. Anatomy of the heart of Amphibia: 1. *Siren lacertina. Copeia* 1977:476–488. (5)

Putnam, J. L., and J. F. Dunn. 1978. Septation in the ventricle of the heart of *Necturus maculosus. Herpetologica* 34:292–297. (5)

Putnam, J. L., and D. L. Kelly. 1978. A new interpretation of interatrial septation in the lungless salamander, *Plethodon glutinosus. Copeia* 1978:251–254. (5)

Putnam, J. L., and J. B. Parkerson, Jr. 1978. Anatomy of the heart of *Cryptobranchus alleganiensis. ASB Bulletin* 25:92. (5)

Putnam, J. L., and B. N. Sebastian. 1977. The fifth aortic arch in *Amphiuma,* a new discovery. *Copeia* 1977:600–601. (5)

Putnam, R. W. 1979a. The basis for differences in lactic acid content after activity in different species of anuran amphibians. *Physiological Zoology* 52:509–519. (12,14)

———. 1979b. The role of lactic acid accumulation in muscle fatigue of two species of anurans, *Xenopus laevis* and *Rana pipiens*. *Journal of Experimental Biology* 82:35–51. (12)

Putnam, R. W., and A. F. Bennett. 1981. Thermal dependence of behavioural performance of anuran amphibians. *Animal Behaviour* 29:502–509. (9,11,12,14)

———. 1983. Histochemical, enzymatic, and contractile properties of skeletal muscles of three anuran amphibians. *American Journal of Physiology* 244:R558–R567. (11,12,14)

Putnam, R. W., and S. S. Hillman. 1977. Activity responses of anurans to dehydration. *Copeia* 1977:746–749. (12)

Pyles, R. A. 1986. An hypothesis of jaw biomechanics for parastreptostylic anurans. *American Zoologist* 26:64A. (11)

Quinn, D. E. 1982. The exercise physiology of *Rana catesbeiana* during recovery from exercise to exhaustion. Ph.D. diss., University of Massachusetts, Amherst. (16)

Quinn, D. E., and W. W. Burggren. 1983. Lactate production, tissue distribution, and elimination following exhaustive exercise in larval and adult bullfrogs, *Rana catesbeiana*. *Physiological Zoology* 56:597–613. (12,16)

Quinn, H. R., and G. Mengden. 1984. Reproduction and growth of *Bufo houstonensis* (Bufonidae). *Southwestern Naturalist* 29:189–195. (15)

Rabb, G. B. 1960. On the unique sound production of the Surinam toad (*Pipa pipa*). *Copeia* 1960:368–369. (14)

Race, J., and J. Cameron. 1966. A method for the detection of the thyroid hormones in the plasma of amphibian larvae by thin layer chromatography. *American Zoologist* 6:302. (16)

Radesäter, T., S. Jakobsson, N. Andbjer, A. Bylin, and K. Nyström. 1987. Song rate and pair formation in the willow warbler, *Phylloscopus trochilus*. *Animal Behaviour* 35:1645–1651. (14)

Rahman, M. S., and K. B. Storey. 1988. Role of covalent modification in the control of glycolytic enzymes in response to environmental anoxia in goldfish. *Journal of Comparative Physiology* 157:813–820. (10)

Rahn, H. 1966. Aquatic gas exchange theory. *Respiration Physiology* 1:1–12. (6)

———. 1967. Gas transport from the environment to the cell. In *Development of the Lung*, ed. A.V. S. de Reuck and R. Porter, 3–23. London: Churchill. (5,6,7)

Rahn, H., and B. J. Howell. 1976. Bimodal gas exchange. In *Respiration of Amphibious Vertebrates*, ed. G. M. Hughes, 271–285. New York: Academic Press. (5,6)

Rahn, H., and R. B. Reeves. 1980. Protons, proteins, and Claude Bernard's "Fixité du milieu intérieur." In *Colloque Claude Bernard* (Fondation Singer-Polignac), 263–272. Paris: Masson Cie. (5)

Rahn, H., O. D. Wangensteen, and L. E. Farhi. 1971. Convection and diffusion gas exchange in air or water. *Respiration Physiology* 12:1–6. (4)

Rajerison, R. M., M. Montegut, S. Jard, and F. Morel. 1972. The isolated frog skin epithelium: Presence of α and β adrenergic receptors regulating active sodium transport and water permeability. *Pflugers Archiv* 332:313–331. (5)

Ralin, D. B., and J. S. Rogers. 1972. Aspects of tolerance to desiccation in *Acris crepitans* and *Pseudacris streckeri*. *Copeia* 1972:519–524. (6)

Ralph, C. L. 1983. Evolution of pineal control of endocrine function in lower vertebrates. *American Zoologist* 23:597–605. (3)

Ralph, C. L., B. T. Firth, and J. S. Turner. 1979. The role of the pineal body in ectotherm thermoregulation. *American Zoologist* 19:273–293. (9)

Ramaswami, L. S. 1943. An account of the chondrocranium of *Rana afghana* and *Megalophrys*, with a description of the masticatory musculature of some tadpoles. *Proceedings of the National Institute of Science* (India) 9:43–58. (11)

Rand, A. S. 1950. Leopard frogs in caves in winter. *Copeia* 1950:324. (10)

———. 1952. Jumping ability of certain anurans with notes on endurance. *Copeia* 1952:15–20. (11)

———. 1988. An overview of anuran acoustic communication. In *The Evolution of the Amphibian Auditory System*, ed. B. Fritzsch, M. J. Ryan, W. Wilczynski, T. E. Hetherington, and W. Walkowiak, 415–431. New York: John Wiley and Sons. (2)

Rand, A. S., and P. Rand. 1966. The relation of size and distance jumped in *Bufo marinus*. *Herpetologica* 22:206–209. (11)

Rand, A. S., and M. J. Ryan. 1981. The adaptive significance of a complex vocal repertoire in a Neotropical frog. *Zeitschrift für Tierpsychologie* 57:209–14. (14)

Randall, D. G., W. W. Burggren, A. P. Farrell, and M. S. Haswell. 1980. *The Evolution of Air Breathing in Vertebrates*. Cambridge: Cambridge University Press. (5,16)

Randall, D. J. 1990. Control and co-ordination of gas exchange in water breathers. In *Vertebrate Gas Exchange: From Environment to Cell*, vol. 6, *Advances in Comparative and Environmental Physiology*, ed. R. G. Boutilier, 253–278. Berlin: Springer-Verlag. (5)

Randall, D. J., and P. A. Wright. 1989. The interaction between carbon dioxide and ammonia excretion and water pH in fish. *Canadian Journal of Zoology* 67:2936–2942. (5)

Ranta, E., J. McManus, and N. Leikola. 1990. Non-visual detection of prey patches by the smooth newt (*Triturus vulgaris*). *Journal of Herpetology* 24:202–204. (13)

Ranta, E., and V. Nuutinen. 1985. Foraging by the smooth newt (*Triturus vulgaris*) on zooplankton: Functional responses and diet choice. *Journal of Animal Ecology* 54:275–293. (13)

Ranta, E., S. F. Tjossem, and N. Leikola. 1987. Female-male activity and zooplankton foraging by the smooth newt (*Triturus vulgaris*). *Annales Zoologici Fennici* 24:79–88. (13)

Rao, G. S., H. Breuer, and E. Witschi. 1968. Metabolism of oestradiol-17β by male and female larvae of *Xenopus laevis*. *Experientia* 24:1258. (16)

———. 1969. *In vitro* conversion of 17α-hydroxy progesterone to androstenedione by mashed gonads from metamorphic stages of *Xenopus laevis*. *General and Comparative Endocrinology* 12:119–123. (16)

Rapola, J. 1962. Development of the amphibian adrenal cortex: Morphological and physiological studies on *Xenopus laevis* (Daudin). *Annales Medicinae Experimentalis et Biologiae Fenniae*, series A Biology 1:1–81. (16)

Rapola, L. 1963. The adrenal cortex and metamorphosis of *Xenopus laevis* Daudin. *General and Comparative Endocrinology* 3:412–421. (16)

Rapoport, S., and G. M. Guest. 1941. Distribution of acid-soluble phosphorus in the blood cells of various vertebrates. *Journal of Biological Chemistry* 138:269–282. (5)

Rappaport, R. 1955. The initiation of pronephric function in *Rana pipiens*. *Journal of Experimental Zoology* 128:481–488. (16)

Rastogi, R. K. 1976. Seasonal cycle in anuran (Amphibia) testis: The endocrine and environmental controls. *Bolletino di Zoologica* 43:151–172. (15)

Rastogi, R. K., and G. Chieffi. 1972. Hypothalamic control of the hypophyseal gonadotropic function in the adult male green frog, *Rana esculenta*. *Journal of Experimental Zoology* 131:263–270. (15)

Rastogi, R. K., and L. Iela. 1980. Steroidogenesis and spermatogenesis in anuran Amphibia: A brief survey. In *Steroids and Their Mechanism of Action in Nonmammalian Vertebrates*, ed. G. Delrio and J. Brachet, 131–146. New York: Raven Press. (3)

Rastogi, R. K., L. Iela, G. Delrio, and J. T. Bagnara. 1986. Reproduction in the Mexican leaf frog, *Pachymedusa dacnicolor*: 2. The male. *General and Comparative Endocrinology* 62:23–35. (3)

Rastogi, R. K., L. Iela, G. Delrio, M. Di Meglio, A. Russo, and G. Chieffi. 1978. Environmental influence on testicular activity in the green frog, *Rana esculenta*. *Journal of Experimental Zoology* 206:49–64. (15)

Rastogi, R. K., L. Iela, M. Di Meglio, L. Di Matteo, S. Minucci, and I. Izzo-Vitiello. 1983. Initiation and kinetic profiles of spermatogenesis in the frog, *Rana esculenta* (Amphibia). *Journal of Zoology* (London) 201:515–525. (15)

Rastogi, R. K., L. Iela, P. K. Saxena, and G. Chieffi. 1976. The control of spermatogenesis in the green frog, *Rana esculenta*. *Journal of Experimental Zoology* 196:151–166. (15)

Rastogi, R. K., I. Izzo-Vitiello, M. Di Meglio, L. Di Matteo, R. Franzese, M. G. Di Costanzo, S. Minucci, L. Iela, and G. Chieffi. 1983. Ovarian activity and reproduction in the frog, *Rana esculenta*. *Journal of Zoology* (London) 200:233–247. (15)

Ray, C. 1958. Vital limits and rates of desiccation in salamanders. *Ecology* 39:75–83. (6,12)

Ray, L. B., and J. N. Dent. 1986. Observations on the interaction of prolactin and thyroxine in the tail of the bullfrog tadpole. *General and Comparative Endocrinology* 64:44–51. (16)

Reagan, D. P. 1972. Ecology and distribution of the Jemez Mountains salamander, *Plethodon neomexicanus. Copeia* 1972:486–492. (15)

Reboreda, J. C., and E. T. Segura. 1989. Water balance effects of systemic and intracerebroventricular administration of angiotensin II in the toad *Bufo arenarum. Comparative Biochemistry and Physiology* 93A:505–509. (6)

Redshaw, M. R. 1972. The hormonal control of the amphibian ovary. *American Zoologist* 12:289–306. (15)

Reed, H. D. 1920. The morphology of the sound-transmitting apparatus in caudate Amphibia and its phylogenetic significance. *Journal of Morphology* 33:325–275. (11)

Reeder, W. G. 1964. The digestive system. In *Physiology of the Amphibia,* ed. J. A. Moore, 99–149. New York: Academic Press. (13,16)

Rees, B. B., and D. G. Stephenson. 1987. Thermal dependence of maximum Ca^{2+}-activated force in skinned muscle fibres of the toad *Bufo marinus* acclimated at different temperatures. *Journal of Experimental Biology* 129:309–327. (12)

Reese, A. M. 1906. Anatomy of *Cryptobranchus alleganiensis. American Naturalist* 40:287–326. (5)

Reeves, R. B. 1972. An imidazole alphastat hypothesis for vertebrate acid-base regulation: Tissue carbon dioxide content and body temperature in bullfrogs. *Respiration Physiology* 14:219–236. (5,6)

———. 1977. The interaction of body temperature and acid-base balance in ectothermic vertebrates. *Annual Review of Physiology* 39:559–586. (6)

Regal, P. J. 1966a. Feeding specializations and the classification of terrestrial salamanders. *Evolution* 20:392–407. (11,14)

———. 1966b. Thermophilic response following feeding in certain reptiles. *Copeia* 1966:588–590. (9)

———. 1967. Voluntary hypothermia in reptiles. *Science* 155:1551–1553. (9)

———. 1971. Long-term studies with operant conditioning techniques of temperature regulation patterns in reptiles. *Journal de Physiologie* (Paris) 63:403–406. (9)

———. 1978. Behavioral differences between reptiles and mammals: An analysis of activity and mental capabilities. In *Behavior and Neurobiology of Lizards,* ed. N. Greenberg and P. D. MacLean, 183–202. Publication (ADM) 77-491. Washington, DC: Department of Health, Education, and Welfare. (14)

———. 1983. The adaptive zone and the behavior of lizards. In *Lizard Ecology: Studies of a Model Organism,* ed. R. B. Huey, E. R. Pianka and T. W. Schoener, 105–118. Cambridge, MA: Harvard University Press. (14)

Regal, P. J., and C. Gans. 1976. Functional aspects of the evolution of frog tongues. *Evolution* 30:718–734. (11,14)

Regard, E., and J. Hourdry. 1975. Modifications structurelles des cellules thyroidiennes chez la larve du Xénope traitée par la prolactine ovine: Incidences sur le métabolisme de l'iode. *Journal de Microscopie et de Biologie Cellulaire* 22:39–54. (16)

Regard, E., and J. Mauchamp. 1973. Activité peroxydasique dans la glande thyroide du Xénope au cours du développement larvaire: Corrélations avec l'organification de l'iodure et controle thyréotrope. *Journal de Microscopie* (Paris) 18:291–306. (16)

Regard, E., A. Taurog, and T. Nakashima. 1978. Plasma thyroxine and triiodothyronine levels in spontaneously metamorphosing *Rana catesbeiana* tadpoles and in adult anuran Amphibia. *Endocrinology* 102:674–684. (16)

Regnault, H. V., and J. Reiset. 1849. Recherches sur la respiration des diverses classes des animaux. *Annales de Chimie et de Physique* 26:299–542. (12)

Rehfeld, J. F., N. Goltermann, L. I. Larson, P. M. Emson, and C. M. Lee. 1979. Gastrin and cholecystokinin in central peripheral neurons. *Federation Proceedings* 38:2325–2329. (9)

Reichling, H. 1957. Transpiration und Vorzugstemperatur mitteleuropäischer Reptilien und Amphibien. *Zoologische Jahrbücher, Abteilung für allgemeine Zoologie und Physiologie der Tiere* 67:1–64. (9)

Reid, M. L. 1987. Costliness and reliability in the singing vigour of Ipswich sparrows. *Animal Behaviour* 35:1735–1743. (14)

Reilly, S. M. 1986. Ontogeny of cranial ossification in the eastern newt, *Notophthalmus viridescens* (Caudata: Salamandridae) and its relationship to metamorphosis and neoteny. *Journal of Morphology* 188:315–326. (16)

———. 1987. Ontogeny of the hyobranchial apparatus in the salamanders *Ambystoma talpoideum* (Ambystomatidae) and *Notophthalmus*

viridescens (Salamandridae): The ecological morphology of two neotenic strategies. *Journal of Morphology* 191:205–214. (16)

Reilly, S. M., and G. V. Lauder. 1988. Ontogeny of aquatic feeding performance in the eastern newt, *Notophthalmus viridescens* (Salamandridae). *Copeia* 1988:87–91. (11,14)

———. 1989a. Kinetics of tongue projection in *Ambystoma tigrinum:* Quantitative kinematics, muscle function, and evolutionary hypothesis. *Journal of Morphology* 199:223–243. (11,14)

———. 1989b. Physiological bases of feeding behaviour in salamanders: Do motor patterns vary with prey type? *Journal of Experimental Biology* 141:343–358. (11,14)

Reis, J. O. 1989. The meaning of developmental time: A metric for comparative embryology. *American Naturalist* 134:170–189. (16)

Remy, C., and J. J. Bounhiol. 1965. Croissance exagerée des têtards de crapau d'accoucheur entiers au prives de leur hypophyse et subissant un traitement par la prolactine. *Comptes Rendus des Sciences de la Société de Biologie* 159:1532–1535. (16)

———. 1966. Gigantisme expérimental obtenu par intervention chirurgicale et traitments hormonaux chez le têtard du crapaud accoucheur. *Annales d'Endocrinology* (Paris) 27:377–382. (16)

Renaud, J. M., and E. D. Stevens. 1983. The extent of long-term temperature compensation for jumping distance in the frog, *Rana pipiens,* and the toad, *Bufo americanus. Canadian Journal of Zoology* 61:1284–1287. (8,9,12)

———. 1984. The extent of short-term and long-term compensation to temperature shown by frog and toad sartorius muscle. *Journal of Experimental Biology* 108:57–75. (8,12)

Reno, H. W., F. R. Gehlbach, and R. A. Turner. 1972. Skin and aestivational cocoon of the aquatic amphibian, *Siren intermedia* Le Conte. *Copeia* 1972:625–631. (6,10)

Renous, S. In press. Axial musculature. In *Traité de Zoologie,* ed. P.-P. Grassé. Paris: Masson. (11)

Renous, S., and J. P. Gasc. 1989. Effects of miniaturization in *Microcaecilia unicolor* (Amphibia, Gymnophiona). *Annales de la Société Royale Zoologique de Belgique* (Abstracts 3d International Congress of Vertebrate Morphology) 119:10. (11)

Rettig, G., and G. Roth. 1982. Afferent visual projections in three species of lungless salamanders (family Plethodontidae). *Neuroscience Letters* 31:221–224. (14)

Reuter, H. 1987. Modulation of ion channels by phosphorylation and second messengers. *News in Physiological Sciences* 2:168–171. (10)

Reuter, T., and K. Virtanen. 1976. Color discrimination mechanisms in the retina of the toad (*Bufo bufo*). *Journal of Comparative Physiology* 109:337–343. (2)

Reutter, J. M., and C. E. Herdendorf. 1976. Thermal discharge from a nuclear power plant: Predicted effects on Lake Erie fish. *Ohio Journal of Science* 76:39–45. (9)

Rey, P. 1937. *Recherches expérimentelles sur l'economie de l'eau chez les batraciens.* Lons-le-Saunier: Declume. (10)

Reynolds, W. W. 1977a. Fish orientation behavior: An electronic device for studying simultaneous responses to two variables. *Journal of Fisheries Research Board of Canada* 34:300–304. (9)

———. 1977b. Temperature as a proximate factor in orientation behavior. *Journal of Fisheries Research Board of Canada* 34:734–739. (9)

———. 1978. The final thermal preferendum of fishes: Shuttling behavior and acclimation overshoot. *Hydrobiologia* 57:123–124. (9)

Reynolds, W. W., and M. E. Casterlin. 1976. Thermal preferenda and behavioral thermoregulation in three centrarchid fishes. In *Thermal Ecology,* eds. G. W. Esch, and R. W. McFarlane, 185–190. Oak Ridge, TN: U.S. National Technical Information Center. (9)

———. 1978. Complementarity of thermoregulatory rhythms in *Micropterus salmoides* and *M. dolomieui. Hydrobiologica* 60:89–91. (9)

———. 1979. Behavioral thermoregulation and the "final preferendum" paradigm. *American Zoologist* 19:211–224. (9)

Reynolds, W. W., M. E. Casterlin, and J. B. Covert. 1980. Behaviorally mediated fever in aquatic ectotherms. In *Fever,* ed. J. M. Lipton, 207–212. New York: Raven Press. (9)

Reynolds, W. W., M. E. Casterlin, and R. E. Spieler. 1982. Thyroxine: Effect on behavioral thermoregulation in fishes. *Canadian Journal of Zoology* 60:926–928. (9)

Reynolds, W. W., R. W. McCauley, M. E. Casterlin, and L. I. Crawshaw. 1976. Body temperatures of behaviorally thermoregulating largemouth blackbass (*Micropterus salmoides*). *Comparative Biochemistry and Physiology* 54A:461–463. (9)

Rheinlaender, J., W. Walkowiak, and H. C. Gerhardt. 1981. Directional hearing in the green treefrog: A variable mechanism? *Naturwissenschaften* 67:430–431. (2)

Ribbing, L. 1907. Die distale Armmuskulatur der Amphibien, Reptilien, und Säugetiere. *Zoologische Jahrbücher, Abteilung für Anatomie und Ontogenie der Thiere* 23:587–682. (11)

———. 1909. Die Unterschenkel- und Fussmuskulatur der Tetrapoden und ihr Verhalten zur der entsprechenden Arm- und Handmuskulatur. *Lund Universitetets Arsskrift*, N.F. 5:1–158. (11)

———. 1938. Die Muskeln und Nerven der Extremitäten. In *Handbuch der vergleichenden Anatomie der Wirbeltiere*, ed. L. Bolk, E. Göppert, E. Kallius, and W. Lubosch, 5:543–656. Berlin and Vienna: Urban and Schwarzenberg. (11)

Richards, A. N., and C. F. Schmidt. 1925. A description of the glomerular circulation in the frog's kidney and observations concerning the action of adrenalin and various other substances upon it. *American Journal of Physiology* 71:178–208. (6)

Richards, C. M. 1962. The control of tadpole growth by alga-like cells. *Physiological Zoology* 35:285–296. (14)

———. 1977. Reproductive potential under laboratory conditions of *Hyperolius viridiflavus* (Amphibia, Anura, Hyperoliidae), a Kenyan reed frog. *Journal of Herpetology* 11:426–428. (15)

———. 1982. The alteration of chromatophore expression by sex hormones in the Kenyan reed frog, *Hyperolius viridiflavus*. *General and Comparative Endocrinology* 46:59–67. (16)

Richards, C. M., and G. C. Lehman. 1980. Photoperiod stimulation of growth in postmetamorphic *Rana pipiens*. *Copeia* 1980:147–149. (15)

Rick, R., A. Dorge, E. von Arnim, and K. Thurau. 1978. Electron microprobe analysis of frog skin epithelium: Evidence for a syncytial sodium transport compartment. *Journal of Membrane Biology* 39:313–331. (5)

Rick, R., C. Roloff, A. Dorge, F. X. Beck, and K. Thurau. 1984. Intracellular electrolyte concentrations in the frog skin epithelium: Effect of vasopressin and dependence on the Na concentration in the bathing media. *Journal of Membrane Biology* 78:129–145. (5)

Ridge, R. M. A. P., and A. T. Thomson. 1980a. Electrical responses of muscle fibres in a small foot muscle of *Xenopus laevis*. *Journal of Physiology* (London) 306:41–49. (11)

———. 1980b. Polyneural innervation: Mechanical properties of overlapping motor units in a small foot muscle of *Xenopus laevis*. *Journal of Physiology* (London) 306:29–39. (11)

———. 1980c. Properties of motor units in a small foot muscle of *Xenopus laevis*. *Journal of Physiology* (London) 306:17–27. (11)

Rieck, A. F., J. A. Belli, and M. E. Blaskovics. 1960. Oxygen consumption of whole animal and tissues in temperature acclimated amphibians. *Proceedings of the Society for Experimental Biology and Medicine* 103:436–439. (12)

Rieck, W. 1932. Die Entwicklung des Mundhöhlenepithels der Anuren. *Zoologische Jahrbücher, Abteilung für Anatomie und Ontogenie der Tiere* 55:603–646. (16)

Riedel, C., and S. Wood. 1988. Effects of hypercapnia and hypoxia on temperature of the toad, *Bufo marinus*. *FASEB Journal* 2:A500. (9)

Rieppel, O. 1985. Miniaturization of the tetrapod head: Muscle fibre length as a limiting factor. In *Konstruktionsprinzipien lebender und ausgestorbener Reptilien*, 121–137. Sonderforschungsbereich 230 "Natürliche Konstruktionen." Tubingen: Universität Tübingen Institut für Geologie und Paläontologie. (11)

Riggs, A. 1951. The metamorphosis of hemoglobin in the bullfrog. *Journal of General Physiology* 35:23–40. (5,16)

———. 1988. The Bohr effect. *Annual Review of Physiology* 50:181–204. (5)

Riggs, D. S. 1970. *The Mathematical Approach to Physiological Problems*. Cambridge, MA: MIT Press. (8)

Ritchart, J. P., and V. H. Hutchison. 1986. The effects of ATP and cAMP on the thermal tolerance of the mudpuppy, *Necturus maculosus*. *Journal of Thermal Biology* 11:47–51. (9)

Ritland, R. M. 1955. Studies on the post-cranial morphology of *Ascaphus truei*: 2. Myology. *Journal of Morphology* 97:215–282. (11)

Roberts, A. 1989. The neurons that control axial movements in a frog embryo. *American Zoologist* 29:53–63. (2,11,16)

Roberts, A., and B. P. Hayes. 1977. The anatomy and function of free

nerve endings in an amphibian skin sensory system. *Proceedings of the Royal Society of London* 196B:415–429. (16)

Roberts, A., S. R. Soffe, and N. Dale. 1986. Spinal interneurones and swimming in frog embryos. In *Neurobiology of Vertebrate Locomotion*, ed. S. Grillner, P. S. G. Stein, D. G. Stuart, H. Forssberg, and R. M. Herman, 279–306. Wenner-Gren Center International Symposium Series 45. London: Macmillan. (16)

Robertson, D. R. 1968. The ultimobranchial body in *Rana pipiens*: 4. Hypercalcemia and glandular hypertrophy. *Zeitschrift für Zellforschung und mikroskopische Anatomie* 85:441–452. (3)

———. 1969. The ultimobranchial body of *Rana pipiens*: 8. Effects of extirpation upon calcium distribution and bone cell types. *General and Comparative Endocrinology* 12:479–490. (3)

———. 1970. The ultimobranchial body in *Rana pipiens*: 9. Response to increased dietary calcium: Evidence of possible physiological function. *Endocrinology* 87:1041–1050. (3)

———. 1971. Cytological and physiological activity of the ultimobranchial glands in the premetamorphic anuran *Rana catesbeiana*. *General and Comparative Endocrinology* 16:329–341. (3,16)

———. 1975. Effects of the ultimobranchial and parathyroid glands and vitamins D_2, D_3, and dihydrotachysterol₂ on blood calcium and intestinal calcium transport. *Endocrinology* 96:934–940. (3)

———. 1976. Diurnal and lunar periodicity of intestinal calcium in the frog, *Rana pipiens*. *Comparative Biochemistry and Physiology* 54A:225–231. (14)

———. 1977. The annual pattern of plasma calcium in the frog and the seasonal effect of ultimobranchialectomy and parathyroidectomy. *General and Comparative Endocrinology* 33:336–343. (3)

———. 1978. Diurnal variations in the influence of the ultimobranchial glands on calcium homeostasis in the frog, *Rana pipiens*. *Journal of Endocrinology* 79:167–187. (3)

———. 1981. A competitive inhibition enzyme-linked immunosorbant assay for frog. *General and Comparative Endocrinology* 45:12–20. (3)

———. 1986. Plasma ionic calcium regulation by anuran parathyroid glands. *Comparative Biochemistry and Physiology* 85A:359–364. (3,16)

———. 1987a. Plasma immunoreactive calcitonin in the frog (*Rana pipiens*). *Comparative Biochemistry and Physiology* 88A:701–704. (3)

———. 1987b. The ultimobranchial body. In *Vertebrate Endocrinology: Fundamentals and Biomedical Implications*, vol. 1, *Morphological Considerations*, ed. P. K. T. Pang and M. P. Schreibman, 235–259. New York: Academic Press. (3,16)

———. 1988. Immunohistochemical and morphometric analysis of calcitonin distribution in anuran ultimobranchial glands. *General and Comparative Endocrinology* 71:349–358. (3)

Robertson, D. R., and G. E. Swartz. 1964. The development of the ultimobranchial body in the frog *Pseudacris nigrita triseriata*. *Transactions of the American Microscopical Society* 83:330–337. (16)

Robertson, J. G. M. 1984. Acoustic spacing by breeding males of *Uperoleia rugosa* (Anura: Leptodactylidae). *Zeitschrift für Tierpsychologie* 64:283–297. (2,14)

———. 1986a. Female choice, male strategies, and the role of vocalizations in *Uperoleia rugosa*. *Animal Behaviour* 34:773–784. (14)

———. 1986b. Male territoriality, fighting, and assessment of fighting ability in the Australian frog *Uperoleia rugosa*. *Animal Behaviour* 34:763–772. (14)

Robertson, S. L., and E. N. Smith. 1982. Evaporative water loss in the spiny soft-shelled turtle *Trionyx spiniferus*. *Physiological Zoology* 55:124–129. (6)

Robin, E. D. 1962. Relationship between temperature and plasma pH and carbon dioxide tension in the turtle. *Nature* (London) 195:249–251. (5,6)

Robinson, D. H., and M. B. Heintzelman. 1987. Morphology of ventral epidermis of *Rana catesbeiana* during metamorphosis. *Anatomical Record* 217:305–317. (16)

Robinson, D. H., and J. W. Mills. 1987a. Ouabain binding in tadpole ventral skin: 1. Kinetics and effect on intracellular ions. *American Journal of Physiology* 253:R402–R409. (5,16)

———. 1987b. Ouabain binding in tadpole ventral skin: 2. Localization of Na⁺ pump sites. *American Journal of Physiology* 253:R410–R417. (5,16)

Robleto, D. O., S. L. Reitmeyer, and C. A. Herman. 1988. Cardiac inotropic effects of leukotriene C_4 and prostaglandin I_2 in the unanesthetized American bullfrog, *Rana catesbeiana. Canadian Journal of Physiology and Pharmacology* 66:233–238. (3)

Roca, A., A. Maurice, J. Baraud, C. Maugé, and R. Cambar. 1970. Étude des lipides du corps adipeux de *Rana esculenta. Compte Rendus de l'Académie des Sciences* (Paris), series D, 270:1278–1281. (15)

Rock, M. K. 1980. Functional properties of Mauthner cell in the tadpole *Rana catesbeiana. Journal of Neurophysiology* 44:135–150. (2,16)

Roddie, I. C. 1983. Circulation to the skin and adipose tissue. In *Handbook of Physiology*, ed. J. T. Shepherd and F. M. Abboud, 3:285–317. Bethesda, MD: American Physiological Society. (7)

Rogers, D. C. 1964. Possible baroreceptor nerve endings in the vicinity of the amphibian carotid labyrinth. *Acta Anatomica* (Basel) 57:253–266. (7)

———. 1966. A histological and histochemical study of the carotid labyrinth in the anuran amphibians, *Bufo marinus, Hyla aurea*, and *Neobatrachus pictus. Acta Anatomica* (Basel) 63:249–280. (7)

———. 1973. The significance of the amphibian carotid labyrinth in the evolution of the carotid body. *Zeitschrift für zoologische Systematik und Evolutionsforschung* 12:226–237. (7)

Rogers, D. C., and C. J. Haller. 1978. Innervation and cytochemistry of the neuroepithelial bodies in the ciliated epithelium of the toad lung (*Bufo marinus*). *Cell and Tissue Research* 195:395–410. (7)

Rohrbach, J. W., and D. F. Stiffler. 1987. Blood-gas, acid-base, and electrolyte responses to exercise in larval *Ambystoma tigrinum. Journal of Experimental Zoology* 244:39–47. (5)

Rome, L. C. 1982. The energetic cost of running with different muscle temperatures in savannah monitor lizards. *Journal of Experimental Biology* 97:411–426. (8)

———. 1983. The effect of long-term exposure to different temperatures on the mechanical performance of frog muscle. *Physiological Zoology* 56:33–40. (8,11,12)

———. 1986. The influence of temperature on muscle and locomotory performance. In *Living in the Cold: Physiological and Biochemical Adaptations*, ed. H. C. Heller, X. J. Musacchia, and L. C. H. Wang, 485–495. New York: Elsevier Science Publishing. (8)

———. 1990. The influence of temperature on muscle recruitment and function in vivo. *American Journal of Physiology* 259:R210–R222. (8)

Rome, L. C., R. P. Funke, and R. M. Alexander. 1990. The influence of temperature on muscle velocity and sustained performance in swimming carp. *Journal of Experimental Biology* 154:163–178. (8)

Rome, L. C., R. P. Funke, R. M. Alexander, G. Lutz, H. Aldridge, F. Scott, and M. Freadman. 1988. Why animals have different muscle fibre types. *Nature* 355:824–827. (8)

Rome, L. C., and M. J. Kushmerick. 1983. The energetic cost of generating isometric force as a function of temperature in isolated frog muscle. *American Journal of Physiology* 244:C100–C109. (8)

Rome, L. C., P. T. Loughna, and G. Goldspink. 1984. Muscle fiber recruitment as a function of swim speed and muscle temperature in carp. *American Journal of Physiology* 247:R272–R279. (8)

———. 1985. Temperature acclimation improves sustained swimming performance at low temperatures in carp. *Science* 228:194–196. (8)

Rome, L. C., and A. A. Sosnicki. 1990. The influence of temperature on mechanics of red muscle in carp. *Journal of Physiology* (London) 427:151–169. (8)

Romer, A. S. 1924. Pectoral limb musculature and shoulder-girdle structure in fish and tetrapods. *Anatomical Record* 27:119–143. (11)

———. 1971. *The Vertebrate Body*. 4th ed. Philadelphia: W. B. Saunders. (2)

Romspert, A. P. 1976. Osmoregulation of the African clawed frog, *Xenopus laevis*, in hypersaline media. *Comparative Biochemistry and Physiology* 54A:207–210. (6)

Ronan, M. C., and R. G. Northcutt. 1979. Afferent and efferent connections of the bullfrog medial pallium. *Society for Neuroscience Abstracts* 5:146. (2)

Roos, A., and W. F. Boron. 1981. Intracellular pH. *Physiological Review* 61:296–434. (5)

Roos, J., and C. B. Jørgensen. 1974. Rates of disappearance from blood and biological potencies of mammalian gonadotropins (hCG and ovine LH) in the toad *Bufo bufo bufo* (L.). *General and Comparative Endocrinology* 23:432–437. (15)

Rose, B. B., C. F. Baxter, J. W. Dole, K. H. Tachiki, and R. A. Baldwin. 1986. Abnormal feeding behavior of western toads (*Bufo bo-*

reas) kept in a hyperosmotic environment: 1. A quantitative behavioral analysis as related to cerebral amino acid concentrations. *Pharmacology, Biochemistry, and Behavior* 24:1315–1321. (12)

Rose, C. W. 1966. *Agricultural Physics*. London: Pergamon Press. (4)

Rose, F. L. 1967. Seasonal changes in lipid levels of the salamander *Amphiuma means. Copeia* 1967:662–666. (14,15)

Rose, F. L., and D. Armentrout. 1976. Adaptive strategies of *Ambystoma tigrinum* (Green) inhabiting the Llano Estacado of west Texas. *Journal of Animal Ecology* 45:713–729. (16)

Rose, F. L., D. Armentrout, and P. Roper. 1971. Physiological responses of paedogenic *Ambystoma tigrinum* to acute anoxia. *Herpetologica* 17:101–107. (16)

Rose, F. L., and H. L. Lewis. 1968. Changes in weight and free fat concentration of fat bodies of paedogenic *Ambystoma tigrinum* during vitellogenesis. *Comparative Biochemistry and Physiology* 26:149–154. (15)

Rose, G. J., E. A. Brenowitz, and R. R. Capranica. 1985. Species specificity and temperature dependency of temporal processing by the auditory midbrain of two species of treefrogs. *Journal of Comparative Physiology* 157:763–769. (2)

Rose, G. J., and R. R. Capranica. 1984. Processing amplitude-modulated sounds by the auditory midbrain of two species of toads: Matched temporal filters. *Journal of Comparative Physiology* 154:211–219. (2)

Rose, G. J., M. Kawasaki, and W. Heiligenberg. 1988. "Recognition units" at the top of a neuronal hierarchy? *Journal of Comparative Physiology* 162:759–772. (2)

Rose, G. J., and W. Wilczynski. 1984. The anuran superficial reticular nucleus: Evidence for homology with nuclei of the lateral lemniscus. *Brain Research* 304:170–172. (2)

Rose, W. 1962. *The Reptiles and Amphibians of Southern Africa*. Cape Town: Maskew Miller. (10)

Rosen, S., and N. J. Friedley. 1973. Carbonic anhydrase activity in *Rana pipiens* skin: Biochemical and histochemical analysis. *Histochemie* 36:1–4. (5)

Rosenberg, M., and M. R. Warburg. 1978. Changes in structure of ventral epidermis of *Rana ridibunda* during metamorphosis. *Cell and Tissue Research* 195:111–122. (16)

Rosenberg, N. J. 1974. *Microclimate: The Biological Environment*. New York: John Wiley and Sons. (4)

Rosenbloom, A. A., and D. A. Fisher. 1974. Radioimmunoassay of arginine vasotocin. *Endocrinology* 95:1726–1732. (5)

Rosenkilde, P. 1979. The thyroid hormones in Amphibia. In *Hormones and Evolution*, ed. E. J. W. Barrington, 437–491. New York: Academic Press. (3,16)

———. 1982. The role of thyroid hormones in adult amphibians. In *Phylogenetic Aspects of Thyroid Hormone Actions*, vol. 19, ed. Institute of Endocrinology, Gumma University, 91–106. Gumma Symposium on Endocrinology. Tokyo: Center for Academic Publications. (3)

———. 1985. The role of hormones in the regulation of amphibian metamorphosis. In *Metamorphosis: The Eighth Symposium of the British Society for Developmental Biology*, ed. M. Balls and M. Bownes, 221–259. Oxford: Clarendon Press. (16)

Rosenthal, E. J., and R. deRoos. 1985. Elevation of plasma glucose, alanine, and urea levels by mammalian ACTH in the American bullfrog (*Rana catesbeiana*). *General and Comparative Endocrinology* 59:199–209. (3)

Rosenthal, G. M. 1957. The role of moisture and temperature in the local distribution of the plethodontid salamander *Aneides lugubris. University of California Publications in Zoology* 54:371–420. (9)

Rosenzweig, M. R., and A. L. Leiman. 1989. *Physiological Psychology*. 2d ed. New York: Random House. (2)

Rosoff, C. J., G. F. Baldwin, and P. J. Bentley. 1983. Active transport of calcium across the urinary bladder and colon of the toad *Bufo marinus. American Journal of Physiology* 245:R91–R94. (5)

Rosoff, L., R. Zeldin, E. Hew, and A. Aberman. 1980. Changes in blood P_{50}: Effects on oxygen delivery when arterial hypoxemia is due to shunting. *Chest* 77:142–146. (5)

Rosse, W. F., T. Waldmann, and E. Hull. 1963. Factors stimulating erythropoiesis in frogs. *Blood* 22:66–72. (5)

Rossi, A. 1959. Tavole cronologiche dello sviluppo embrionale e larvale del *Bufo bufo* (L.). *Monitore Zoologico Italiano* 66:133–149. (16)

Rossi, J. V. 1983. The use of olfactory cues by *Bufo marinus*. *Journal of Herpetology* 17:72–73. (14)

Roth, G. 1976. Experimental analysis of prey catching behavior of *Hydromantes italicus* Dunn (Amphibia, Plethodontidae). *Journal of Comparative Physiology* 109:47–58. (2,11,14)

———. 1982. Responses in the optic tectum of the salamander *Hydromantes italicus* to moving prey stimuli. *Experimental Brain Research* 45:386–392. (2)

———. 1987. *Visual Behavior in Salamanders*. Berlin: Springer-Verlag. (2,11,13,16)

Roth, G., and M. Jordan. 1982. Response characteristics and stratification of tectal neurons in the toad *Bufo bufo* L. *Experimental Brain Research* 45:393–398. (2)

Roth, G., K. Nishikawa, U. Dicke, and D. B. Wake. 1988a. Funktionsmorphologie und neuronale Kontrolle des Beutefangs bei Salamandern und Fröschen: Gemeinsamkeiten und Alternativen. *Verhandlungen der Deutsche Zoologische Gesellschaft* 81:59–75. (11,14)

———. 1988b. Topography and cytoarchitecture of the motor nuclei in the brainstem of salamanders. *Journal of Comparative Physiology* 278:181–194. (2,11)

Roth, G., B. Rottluff, and R. Linke. 1988. Miniaturisation, genome site, and the origin of functional constraints in the visual system of salamanders. *Naturwissenschaften* 75:297–304. (16)

Roth, G., and D. B. Wake. 1985a. The structure of brainstem and cervical spinal cord in lungless salamanders (family Plethodontidae) and its relation to feeding. *Journal of Comparative Neurology* 241:99–110. (2,11)

———. 1985b. Trends in functional morphology and sensorimotor control of feeding behavior in salamanders: An example of the role of internal dynamics in evolution. *Acta Biotheoretica* 34:175–192. (13,14)

———. 1989. Conservatism and innovation in the evolution of feeding in vertebrates. In *Complex Organismal Functions: Integration and Evolution in Vertebrates*, ed. D. B. Wake and G. Roth, 7–21. Dahlem Konferenzen. Chichester: John Wiley. (13)

Roth, G., and W. Wiggers. 1983. Responses of the toad *Bufo bufo* (L.) to stationary prey stimuli. *Zeitschrift für Tierpsychologie* 61:225–234. (13)

Roth, J. J. 1973. Vascular supply to the ventral pelvic region of anurans as related to water balance. *Journal of Morphology* 140:443–460. (6)

Rothstein, H., J. H. Hayden, S. R. Gordon, and A. Weinsieder. 1980. Somatomedin C: Restoration *in vivo* of cycle traverse in Golgi blocked cells of hypophysectomized animals. *Science* 208:410–412. (16)

Rouf, M. A. 1969. Hematology of the leopard frog *Rana pipiens*. *Copeia* 1969:682–687. (5)

Roughgarden, J., W. P. Porter, and D. Heckel. 1981. Resource partitioning of space and its relationship to body temperature in *Anolis* populations. *Oecologia* (Berlin) 50:256–264. (4)

Rouse, H. 1938. *Fluid Mechanics for Hydraulic Engineers*. Reprinted 1961. New York: Dover Publications. (4)

Ruben, J. A. 1976a. Aerobic and anaerobic metabolism during activity in snakes. *Journal of Comparative Physiology* 109:147–157. (14)

———. 1976b. Correlation of enzyme activity, muscle myoglobin concentration, and lung morphology with activity metabolism in snakes. *Journal of Experimental Zoology* 197:313–319. (14)

Rubinson, K. 1968. Projections of the tectum opticum of the frog. *Brain, Behavior, and Evolution* 1:529–561. (2,7)

Rudolph, D. C. 1978. Aspects of the larval ecology of five plethodontid salamanders of the western Ozarks. *American Midland Naturalist* 100:141–159. (9)

Rugh, R. 1948. *Experimental Embryology*. Minneapolis: Burgess Publishing Company. (15)

———. 1962. *Experimental Embryology: Techniques and Procedures*. 3d ed. Minneapolis: Burgess Publishing Company. (16)

Rühmekorf, E. 1958a. Beiträge zur Ökologie mitteleuropäischer Salientia: 1. Abhängigkeit der Laichabgabe von Aussenfaktoren. *Zeitschrift für Morphologie und Ökologie der Tiere* 47:1–19. (8)

———. 1958b. Beiträge zur Ökologie mitteleuropäischer Salientia: 2. Temperaturwahl der Larven. *Zeitschrift für Morphologie und Ökologie der Tiere* 47:20–36. (9)

Ruibal, R. 1955. A study of altitudinal races in *Rana pipiens*. *Evolution* 9:322–338. (8)

———. 1962. The adaptive value of bladder water in the toad, *Bufo cognatus*. *Physiological Zoology* 35:218–223. (6,10)

Ruibal, R., and S. Hillman. 1981. Cocoon structure and function in the burrowing hylid frog, *Pternohyla fodiens*. *Journal of Herpetology* 15:403–408. (3,6)

Ruibal, R., L. Tevis, Jr., and V. Roig. 1969. The terrestrial ecology of the spadefoot toad *Scaphiopus hammondii*. *Copeia* 1969:571–584. (6,10)

Ruibal, R., and E. Thomas. 1988. The obligate carnivorous larvae of the frog, *Lepidobatrachus laevis* (Leptodactylidae). *Copeia* 1988:591–604. (13,16)

Ruiz, G., M. Rosenmann, and A. Veloso. 1983. Respiratory and hematological adaptations to high altitude in *Telmatobius* frogs from the Chilean Andes. *Comparative Biochemistry and Physiology* 76A:109–113. (5,12)

Russell, I. J. 1976. Amphibian lateral line receptors. In *Frog Neurobiology: A Handbook*, ed. R. Llinás and W. Precht, 513–550. Berlin: Springer-Verlag. (2,16)

Rutledge, P. S., D. P. Easton, and J. C. Near. N.d. A population of north temperate salamanders (*Eurycea bislineata*) naturally experiences unexpectedly warm microhabitat temperatures. Unpublished manuscript. (8)

Rutledge, P. S., D. P. Easton, and J. R. Spotila. 1987. Heat shock proteins from lungless salamanders. *Comparative Biochemistry and Physiology* 88B:13–18. (8)

Rutledge, P. S., J. R. Spotila, and D. P. Easton. 1987. Heat hardening in response to two types of heat shock in the lungless salamanders. *Journal of Thermal Biology* 12:235–241. (8)

Ryan, M. J. 1978. A thermal property of the *Rana catesbeiana* (Amphibia, Anura, Ranidae) egg mass. *Journal of Herpetology* 12:247–248. (8)

———. 1980. Female mate choice in a Neotropical frog. *Science* 209:523–525. (14)

———. 1983. Sexual selection and communication in a Neotropical frog, *Physalaemus pustulosus*. *Evolution* 37:261–272. (14)

———. 1985a. Energetic efficiency of vocalization by the frog *Physalaemus pustulosus*. *Journal of Experimental Biology* 116:47–52. (14)

———. 1985b. *The Tungara Frog: A Study in Sexual Selection and Communication*. Chicago: University of Chicago Press. (2,14)

———. 1986a. Environmental bioacoustics: Evaluation of a commonly used experimental design. *Animal Behaviour* 34:931–933. (14)

———. 1986b. Factors influencing the evolution of acoustic communication: Biological constraints. *Brain, Behavior, and Evolution* 28:70–82. (2,14)

———. 1986c. Neuroanatomy influences speciation rates in anurans. *Proceedings of the National Academy of Science* 83:1379–1382. (2)

———. 1986d. Synchronized calling in a treefrog (*Smilisca sila*). *Brain, Behavior, and Evolution* 29:196–206. (2)

———. 1988a. Constraints and patterns in the evolution of anuran communication. In *The Evolution of the Amphibian Auditory System*, ed. B. Fritzsch, M. J. Ryan, W. Wilczynski, T. E. Hetherington, and W. Walkowiak, 637–677. New York: John Wiley and Sons. (2,14)

———. 1988b. Energy, calling, and selection. *American Zoologist* 28:885–898. (14)

Ryan, M. J., G. A. Bartholomew, and A. S. Rand. 1983. Energetics of reproduction in a Neotropical frog, *Physalaemus pustulosus*. *Ecology* 64:1456–1462. (12,14)

Ryan, M. J., and M. D. Tuttle. 1987. The roles of prey-generated sound, vision, and echolocation in prey localization by the African bat *Cardioderma cor*. *Journal of Comparative Physiology* 161A:59–66. (14)

Ryan, M. J., M. D. Tuttle, and R. M. R. Barclay. 1983. Behavioral responses of the frog-eating bat to sonic frequencies. *Journal of Comparative Physiology* 150:413–418. (14)

Ryan, M. J., M. D. Tuttle, and A. S. Rand. 1982. Bat predation and sexual advertisement in a Neotropical frog. *American Naturalist* 119:136–139. (14)

Ryan, M. J., M. D. Tuttle, and L. K. Taft. 1981. The costs and benefits of frog chorusing behavior. *Behavioral Ecology and Sociobiology* 8:273–278. (14)

Ryan, M. J., and W. Wilczynski. 1988. Coevolution of sender and receiver: Effect on local mate preference in cricket frogs. *Science* 240:1786–1788. (2,14)

Rylkoff, H. 1924. Die Entwicklung der Schultermuskeln bei urodelen Amphibien. *Zeitschrift für wissenschaftliche Zoologie* 122:116–171. (11)

Ryser, J. 1989. Weight loss, reproductive output, and the cost of reproduction in the common frog, *Rana temporaria*. *Oecologia* (Berlin) 78:264–268. (15)

Sadleir, R. M. F. S. 1973. *The Reproduction of Vertebrates*. New York: Academic Press. (15)

Saidapur, S. K. 1983. Patterns of testicular activity in Indian amphibians. *Indian Review of the Life Sciences* 3:157–184. (15)

Saidapur, S. K., and R. D. Kanamadi. 1982. A comparative study of spermatogenetic cycle in *Rana cyanophlyctis* (Schn.) and *Rana tigrina* (Daud.). *Biological Bulletin* (India) 4:110–113. (15)

Saidapur, S. K., and V. B. Nadkarni. 1975a. The annual testicular cycle and its relation to thumb pad structure in the frog, *Rana cyanophlyctis* (Schn.). *Journal of Animal Morphology and Physiology* 22:140–147. (15)

———. 1975b. Seasonal variation in the structure and function of testis and thumb pad in the frog *Rana tigrina* (Daud.). *Indian Journal of Experimental Biology* 13:432–438. (15)

Saint-Aubain, M. L. de. 1981a. Amphibian limb ontogeny and its bearing on the phylogeny of the group. *Zeitschrift für zoologische Systematik und Evolutionsforschung* 19:175–194. (16)

———. 1981b. Shunts in the gill filament in tadpoles of *Rana temporaria* and *Bufo bufo* (Amphibia, Anura). *Journal of Experimental Zoology* 217:143–145. (7)

———. 1982a. The morphology of amphibian skin before and after metamorphosis. *Zoomorphology* 100:55–63. (5,16)

———. 1982b. Vagal control of pulmonary blood flow in *Ambystoma mexicanum*. *Journal of Experimental Zoology* 221:155–158. (7,16)

Saint-Aubain, M. L. de, and K. Wingstrand. 1979. A sphincter in the pulmonary artery of the frog *Rana temporaria* and its influence on blood flow in skin and lungs. *Acta Zoologica* (Stockholm) 60:163–172. (5)

Sakakibara, Y. 1978. Localization of CO_2 sensor related to the inhibition of the bullfrog respiration. *Japanese Journal of Physiology* 28:721–735. (7)

Salibian, A., S. Pezzani-Hernandez, and F. Garcia-Romeu. 1968. *In vivo* ionic exchange through the skin of the South American frog, *Leptodactylus ocellatus*. *Comparative Biochemistry and Physiology* 25:311–317. (5)

Salisbury, F., and C. Ross. 1969. *Plant Physiology*. Belmont, CA: Wadsworth Publishing. (4)

Salt, G. W. 1967. Predation in an experimental protozoan population (*Woodruffia-Paramecium*). *Ecological Monographs* 37:113–144. (14)

Salthe, S. N., and W. E. Duellman. 1973. Quantitative constraints associated with reproductive mode in anurans. In *The Evolutionary Biology of Anurans*, ed. J. L. Vial, 229–249. Columbia: University of Missouri Press. (14,15)

Salthe, S. N., and J. S. Mecham. 1974. Reproductive and courtship patterns. In *Physiology of the Amphibia*, ed. B. Lofts, 2:309–521. New York: Academic Press. (12,15)

Santiagio, T. V., and N. H. Edelman. 1976. Mechanism of the ventilatory response to carbon monoxide. *Journal of Clinical Investigation* 57:977–986. (7)

Sasaki, F. 1974. Histochemical and ultrastructural studies of tail muscles in the anuran tadpole. *Acta Histochemica Cytochemica* 7:239–256. (11)

———. 1977. Histochemical and biochemical investigation of the tail muscle of anuran tadpoles during metamorphosis. *Acta Histochemica Cytochemica* 10:413–425. (11)

Sasaki, F., and K. Watanabe. 1983. Tail muscle hydrolases during metamorphosis of the anuran tadpole: 1. Histochemical studies. *Histochemistry* 78:11–20. (11)

Sasayama, Y. 1978. Effects of implantation of the ultimobranchial glands and the administration of synthetic salmon calcitonin on serum Ca concentration in ultimobranchialectomized bullfrog tadpoles. *General and Comparative Endocrinology* 34:229–233. (16)

Sasayama, Y., and N. B. Clark. 1984. Renal handling of phosphate, calcium, sodium, and potassium in intact and parathyroidectomized *Rana pipiens*. *Journal of Experimental Zoology* 229:197–203. (3,5)

Sasayama, Y., and C. Oguro. 1975. Effects of parathyroidectomy on calcium and sodium concentrations of serum and coelemic fluid in bullfrog tadpoles. *Journal of Experimental Zoology* 192:293–298. (3,16)

———. 1976. Effects of ultimobranchialectomy on calcium and sodium concentrations of serum and coelomic fluid in bullfrog tadpoles under high calcium and high sodium environment. *Comparative Biochemistry and Physiology* 55A:35–37. (3,16)

———. 1982a. Effects of hypophysectomy and replacement therapy with pituitary homogenates or ovine prolactin on serum calcium, sodium, and magnesium concentrations in bullfrog tadpoles. *General and Comparative Endocrinology* 46:75–80. (3,16)

———. 1982b. Urine calcium concentration in bullfrog tadpoles kept in tap water or high calcium environment with special reference to ultimobranchialectomy. *Comparative and Biochemical Physiology* 71A:309–311. (16)

———. 1985. The role of the ultimobranchial glands on Ca balance in bullfrog tadpoles. In *Current Trends in Comparative Endocrinology*, eds. B. Lofts and W. N. Holmes, 837–838. Hong Kong: Hong Kong University Press. (3,16)

SAS Institute. 1982. *SAS User's Guide: Statistics*. Cary, NC: SAS Institute. (9)

Sassoon, D. A., G. E. Gray, and D. B. Kelley. 1987. Androgen regulation of muscle fiber type in the sexually dimorphic larynx of *Xenopus laevis*. *Journal of Neuroscience* 7:3198–3206. (2)

Sassoon, D. A., and D. B. Kelley. 1986. The sexually dimorphic larynx of *Xenopus laevis*: Development and androgen regulation. *American Journal of Anatomy* 177:457–472. (2,11,16)

Satinoff, E. 1978. Neural organization and evolution of thermal regulation in mammals. *Science* 201:16–22. (9)

———. 1980. Independence of behavioral and autonomic thermoregulatory responses. In *Neural Mechanism of Goal-Directed Behavior and Learning*, ed. R. F. Thompson, L. H. Hicks, and V. B. Shvyrokov, 189–196. New York: Academic Press. (9)

Satou, M., and J.-P. Ewert. 1985. The antidromic activation of tectal neurons by electrical stimuli applied to the caudal medulla oblongata in the toad *Bufo bufo* L. *Journal of Comparative Physiology* 157:739–748. (2,13)

Satou, M., T. Matsushima, H. Takeuchi, and K. Ueda. 1985. Tongue-muscle-controlling neurons in the Japanese toad, *Bufo japonicus*: Topography, morphology, and neuronal pathways, from the "snapping-evoking" area in the optic tectum. *Journal of Comparative Physiology* 157A:717–737. (2,11,13)

Saunders, R. L., and A. M. Sutterlin. 1971. Cardiac and respiratory responses to hypoxia in the sea raven, *Hemitripterus americanus*, and an investigation of possible control mechanisms. *Journal of the Fisheries Research Board of Canada* 28:491–503. (7)

Savage, R. M. 1952. Ecological and anatomical observations on some species of anuran tadpoles. *Proceedings of the Zoological Society of London* 122:467–514. (14,16)

———. 1955. The ingestive, digestive, and respiratory systems of the microhylid tadpole, *Hypopachus aguae*. *Copeia* 1955:120–127. (16)

———. 1961. *The Ecology and Life History of the Common Frog*. London: Sir Isaac Pitman and Sons. (10)

Sawaya, P. 1947. Metabolismo respiratório de anfíbio Gymnophiona, *Typhlonectes compressicauda*. *Boletim da Faculdade de Filosofia, Ciências, e Letras Universidade de São Paulo Serie Zoologia* 12:51–56. (5,12)

Sawin, C. T., J. L. Bolaffi, I. P. Callard, P. Bacharach, and I. M. D. Jackson. 1978. Induced metamorphosis in *Ambystoma mexicanum*: Lack of effect of triiodothyronine on tissue or blood levels of thyrotropin-releasing hormone (TRH). *General and Comparative Endocrinology* 36:427–432. (16)

Sawyer, T. K., V. J. Hruby, M. E. Hadley, and M. H. Engel. 1983. α-melanocyte stimulating hormone: Chemical nature and mechanism of action. *American Zoologist* 23:529–540. (3)

Sawyer, W. H. 1951. Effect of posterior pituitary extracts on urine formation and glomerular circulation in the frog. *American Journal of Physiology* 164:457–466. (3)

———. 1957. Increased renal reabsorption of osmotically free water by the toad (*Bufo marinus*) in response to neurohypophysial hormones. *American Journal of Physiology* 189:564–568. (5,6)

Sawyer, W. H., R. H. Munsick, and H. B. van Dyke. 1961. Evidence for the presence of arginine vasotocin (8-arginine oxytocin) and oxytocin in neurohypophyseal extracts from amphibians and reptiles. *General and Comparative Endocrinology* 1:30–36. (3)

Sawyer, W. H., and P. K. T. Pang. 1975. Endocrine adaptation to osmotic requirements of the environment: Endocrine factors in osmoregulation by lungfishes and amphibians. *General and Comparative Endocrinology* 25:224–229. (6)

———. 1987. Endocrine osmoregulation and vertebrate evolution. In *Vertebrate Endocrinology: Fundamentals and Biomedical Implications*, vol. 2, *Regulation of Water and Electrolytes*, ed. P. K. T. Pang and M. P. Schreibman, 203–305. New York: Academic Press. (3)

Saxen, L., and S. Toivonen. 1955. The development of the ultimobranchial body in *Xenopus laevis* Daudin and its relation to the thyroid gland and epithelial bodies. *Journal of Embryological and Experimental Morphology* 3:376–384. (16)

Saxena, P. K. 1967. The cranial nerves of the mud-eel *Amphipnous cuchia* (Ham.). *Acta Anatomica* (Basel) 68:306–320. (7)

Sayler, A. 1966. The reproductive ecology of the red-backed salamander, *Plethodon cinereus*, in Maryland. *Copeia* 1966:183–193. (15)

Scalia, F. 1976a. The optic pathway of the frog: Nuclear organization and connections. In *Frog Neurobiology: A Handbook*, ed. R. Llinás and W. Precht, 386–406. Berlin: Springer-Verlag. (2)

———. 1976b. Structure of the olfactory and accessory olfactory systems. In *Frog Neurobiology: A Handbook*, ed. R. Llinás and W. Precht, 213–233. Berlin: Springer-Verlag. (2)

Scalise, F. W., and S. R. Vigna. 1988. Temporal pattern of appearance and distribution of cholecystokinin-like peptides during development in *Xenopus laevis*. *General and Comparative Endocrinology* 72:303–311. (16)

Scapin, S., and S. Lambert-Gardini. 1979. Digestive enzymes in the exocrine pancreas of the frog *Rana esculenta*. *Comparative Biochemistry and Physiology* 62A:691–697. (13)

Schaefer, S. A., and G. V. Lauder. 1986. Historical transformation of functional design: Evolutionary morphology of feeding mechanisms in loricarioid catfishes. *Systematic Zoology* 35:489–508. (11)

Schaeffer, B. 1941. The morphological and functional evolution of the tarsus in amphibians and reptiles. *Bulletin of the American Museum of Natural History* 78:395–472. (11)

Schaeffer, H. J., U. Schmidt, J. Brzoska, and L. Hubl. 1978. Temperature dependence of visual fusion frequency in *Rana lessonae*. *Behavioral Processes* 3:259–264. (8)

Schall, J. J. 1983. Lizard malaria: Parasite-host ecology. In *Lizard Ecology: Studies of a Model Organism*, ed. R. B. Huey, E. R. Pianka, and T. W. Schoener, 84–100. Cambridge, MA: Harvard University Press. (14)

Schatzmann, H. J., E. E. Windhager, and A. K. Soloman. 1958. Single proximal tubules of the *Necturus* kidney: 2. Effect of 2,4-dinitrophenol and ouabain on water reabsorption. *American Journal of Physiology* 195:570–574. (5)

Schauble, M. K., and M. R. Nentwig. 1974. Temperature and prolactin as control factors in newt forelimb regeneration. *Journal of Experimental Zoology* 187:335–344. (8)

Scheid, P. 1982. A model for comparing gas-exchange systems in vertebrates. In *A Companion to Animal Physiology*, ed. C. R. Taylor, K. Johansen, and L. Bolis, 1–16. Cambridge: Cambridge University Press. (16)

Schindelmeiser, J. 1985. The influence of exogenous factors on the metamorphosis of *Salamandra*. *Zoologischer Anzeiger* 214:273–284. (8)

Schlaghecke, R., and V. Blum. 1978a. Seasonal variations in fat body metabolism of the green frog, *Rana esculenta* (L.). *Experientia* 34:1019–1020. (10)

———. 1978b. Seasonal variations in liver metabolism of the green frog, *Rana esculenta* (L.). *Experientia* 34:456–457. (10)

———. 1981. Seasonal variation in serum and pancreatic concentrations of insulin and glucagon in the frog *Rana esculenta*. *General and Comparative Endocrinology* 43:470–483. (3)

Schlisio, V. W., K. Jürss, and L. Spannhof. 1973. Osmo- und Ionenregulation von *Xenopus laevis* Daud. nach Adaptation in verschiedenen osmotisch wirksamen Losungen: 1. Toleranz und Wasserhaushalt. *Zoologische Jahrbücher, Abteilung für allgemeine Zoologie und Physiologie der Tiere* 77:275–290. (6)

Schamlbruch, H. 1985. Skeletal muscle. In *Handbook of Microscopic Anatomy*, ed. A. Oksche and L. Vollrath, 2:i–xi, 1–441. Berlin: Springer-Verlag. (11)

Schmale, M. C. 1981. Sexual selection and reproductive success in males of the bicolor damselfish, *Eupomacentrus partitus* (Pisces: Pomacentridae). *Animal Behaviour* 29:1172–1184. (14)

Schmid, W. D. 1965. Some aspects of the water economies of nine species of amphibians. *Ecology* 46:261–269. (5,6,10)

———. 1982. Survival of frogs at low temperature. *Science* 215:697–698. (10)

Schmid-Shonbein, H., and P. Gaehtgens. 1981. What is red cell deformability. *Scandinavian Journal of Clinical and Laboratory Investigation* 41:13–26. (5)

Schmidt, A., C. Naujoks-Manteuffel, and G. Roth. 1988. Olfactory and vomeronasal projections and the pathway of the *nervus terminalis* in ten species of salamanders. *Cell and Tissue Research* 251:45–50. (2)

Schmidt, A., and M. H. Wake. 1990. Olfactory and vomeronasal systems of caecilians (Amphibia: Gymnophiona). *Journal of Morphology* 205:255–268. (13)

Schmidt, R. S. 1965. Larynx control and call production in frogs. *Copeia* 1965:143–147. (14)

———. 1968. Preoptic activation of frog mating behaviour. *Behaviour* 30:239–257. (16)

———. 1972. Action of the intrinsic laryngeal muscles during release calling in leopard frog. *Journal of Experimental Zoology* 181:233–244. (14)

———. 1973. Central mechanisms of frog calling. *American Zoologist* 13:1169–1177. (2)

———. 1974a. Neural correlates of frog calling: Independence from peripheral feedback. *Journal of Comparative Physiology* 88:321–333. (2)

———. 1974b. Neural correlates of frog calling: Trigeminal tegmentum. *Journal of Comparative Physiology* 92:229–254. (2)

———. 1976. Neural correlates of frog calling: Isolated brainstem. *Journal of Comparative Physiology* 108:99–113. (16)

———. 1978. Neural correlates of frog calling: Circum-metamorphic calling in leopard frog. *Journal of Comparative Physiology* 126:49–56. (16)

———. 1984a. Mating call phonotaxis in the female American toad: Induction by hormones. *General and Comparative Endocrinology* 55:150–156. (3)

———. 1984b. Neural correlates of frog calling: Preoptic area trigger of "mating calling." *Journal of Comparative Physiology* 154:847–853. (2)

———. 1988. Mating calling phonotaxis in female American toads: Lesions of central auditory system. *Brain, Behavior, and Evolution* 32:119–128. (2)

Schmidt-Nielsen, B., and R. P. Forster. 1954. The effect of dehydration and low temperature on renal function in the bullfrog. *Journal of Cellular and Comparative Physiology* 44:233–246. (5,6,10)

Schmidt-Nielsen, B., and W. C. Mackay. 1970. Osmotic and diffusional water permeability in metamorphosing *Rana clamitans* tadpoles. *Bulletin of the Mount Desert Island Laboratory* 10:71–75. (10)

Schmidt-Nielsen, B., and C. R. Schrauger. 1963. Handling of urea and related compounds by the renal tubules of the frog. *American Journal of Physiology* 205:483–488. (5)

Schmidt-Nielsen, K. 1983. *Animal Physiology: Adaptation and Environment*. Cambridge: Cambridge University Press. (9,10,12)

———. 1984. *Scaling: Why Is Animal Size So Important?* Cambridge: Cambridge University Press. (16)

Schmidt-Nielsen, K., and P. Lee. 1962. Kidney function in the crab-eating frog (*Rana cancrivora*). *Journal of Experimental Biology* 39:167–177. (5,6)

Schmuck, R., F. Kobelt, and K. E. Linsenmair. 1988. Adaptations of the reed frog *Hyperolius viridiflavus* (Amphibia, Anura, Hyperoliidae) to its arid environment: 5. Iridophores and nitrogen metabolism. *Journal of Comparative Physiology* 158B:537–546. (6,9)

Schmuck, R., and K. E. Linsenmair. 1988. Adaptations of the reed frog *Hyperolius viridiflavus* (Amphibia, Anura, Hyperoliidae) to its arid environment: 3. Aspects of nitrogen metabolism and osmoregulation in the reed frog, *Hyperolius viridiflavus taeniatus*, with special reference to the role of iridophores. *Oecologia* (Berlin) 75:354–361. (6,9)

Schneichel, W., W. Walkowiak, and H. Schneider. 1988. Motorische und prämotorische Ansteuerung der Kehlkopfmuskeln beim Grasfrosch. *Verhandlungen der Deutschen Zoologischen Gesellschaft* (Bielefeld) 1988:213–214. (11)

Schneider, D. 1954. Beitrag zu einer Analyse des Beute- und Fluchtverhaltens einheimischer Anuren. *Biologisches Zentralblatt* 73:225–282. (13)

Schneider, H. 1964. Physiologische und morphologische Untersuchungen zur Bioakustik der Tigerfische (Pisces, Theraponidae). *Zeitschrift für vergleichende Physiologie* 47:493–558. (14)

———. 1970. Morphologie des Larynx von *Hyla a. arborea* (L.) und *Hyla meridionalis* Boettger (Amphibia, Anura). *Zeitschrift für die Morphologie der Tiere* 66:299–309. (11)

———. 1977. Acoustic behavior and physiology of vocalization in the European tree frog, *Hyla arborea* (L.). In *The Reproductive Biology of Amphibians,* ed. D. H. Taylor and S. I. Guttman, 295–336. New York: Plenum Press. (11,14)

———. 1988. Peripheral and central mechanisms of vocalization. In *The Evolution of the Amphibian Auditory System,* ed. B. Fritzsch, M. J. Ryan, W. Wilczynski, T. E. Hetherington, and W. Walkowiak, 537–558. New York: John Wiley and Son. (2,14)

Schneider, H., and J. Brzoska. 1981. Release calls of the central European water frogs. *Zoologischer Anzeiger* 206:189–202. (8)

Schneider, H., and T. S. Sofianidou. 1985. The mating call of *Rana ridibunda* in northern Greece as compared with those of Yugoslavian and Israeli populations. *Zoologischer Anzeiger* 214:309–319. (8)

Schneider, H., H. G. Tunner, and W. Hoedl. 1979. The mating call of *Rana lessonae. Zoologischer Anzeiger* 202:20–28. (8)

Schneider, W. 1975. Chloride transport in isolated skin of *Rana esculenta. Pflugers Archiv* 355:107–124. (5)

Schoener, T. W. 1971. Theory of feeding strategies. *Annual Review of Ecology and Systematics* 2:369–403. (14)

Schoffeniels, E. 1955. Influence du pH sur le transport actif de sodium à travers la peau de grenouille. *Archives Internationales de Physiologie et de Biochimie* 63:513–530. (5)

Schreiber, G. 1937. La definizione degli stadi della metamorfosi del *Bufo. Atti della Accademia Nazionale dei Lincei Rendi Conti Classe di Science Fisiche, Matematiche, e Naturali* 25:342–348. (16)

Schreibman, M. P. 1987. Pituitary gland. In *Vertebrate Endocrinology: Fundamentals and Biomedical Implications,* vol. 1, *Morphological Considerations,* ed. P. K. T. Pang and M. P. Schreibman, 11–55. New York: Academic Press. (3)

Schreiner, D. S., S. S. Jande, and D. E. Lawson. 1985. Target cells of vitamin D in the vertebrate retina. *Acta Anatomica* (Basel) 121:153–162. (3)

Schultheiss, H. 1978. Influence of purified amphibian pituitary hormones, pituitary grafts and TRH in thyroid activity and metamorphosis. In *Comparative Endocrinology,* ed. P. J. Gaillard and H. H. Boer, 75. Amsterdam: Elsevier/North-Holland. (16)

———. 1980a. Isolation of pituitary proteins from Mexican axolotls (*Ambystoma mexicanum* Cope) by polyacrylamide gel electrophoresis. *Journal of Experimental Zoology* 213:351–358. (16)

———. 1980b. T₃ and T₄ concentrations during metamorphosis of *Xenopus laevis* and *Rana esculenta* and in the neotenic Mexican axolotl. *General and Comparative Endocrinology* 40:372. (16)

Schultheiss, H., W. Hanke, and J. Maetz. 1972. Hormonal regulation of the skin diffusional permeability to water during development and metamorphosis of *Xenopus laevis* Daudin. *General and Comparative Endocrinology* 18:400–404. (5,16)

Schumacher, G. H. 1958a. Ein Beitrag zur Kaumuskulatur der Amphibien: Untersuchungen an *Cryptobranchus japonicus. Anatomischer Anzeiger* 105:361–378. (11)

———. 1958b. Zur Morphologie des Mundbodens der Urodelen: Untersuchungen an *Cryptobranchus japonicus. Morphologisches Jahrbuch* 99:344–371. (11)

Schurg-Pfeiffer, E., and J.-P. Ewert. 1981. Investigation of neurons involved in the analysis of gestalt prey features in the frog *Rana temporaria. Journal of Comparative Physiology* 141:139–152. (2)

Schwabe, H. W. 1977. Studien zur potentiellen Landwirdschaftlichen Bedeutung der Kreuzkröte (*Bufo calamita* Laur.) im Rhein-Main-Gebiet. *Zeitschrift für angewandte Zoologie* 64:331–351. (13)

Schwalm, P. A., P. H. Starrett, and R. W. McDiarmid. 1977. Infrared reflectance in leaf-sitting Neotropical frogs. *Science* 196:1225–1227. (4,9)

Schwartz, J. J. 1986. Male calling behavior and female choice in the Neotropical treefrog *Hyla microcephala. Ethology* 73:116–127. (2,14)

———. 1987. The importance of spectral and temporal properties in species and call recognition in a Neotropical treefrog with a complex vocal repertoire. *Animal Behaviour* 35:340–347. (14)

Schwartz, J. J., and K. D. Wells. 1984. Interspecific acoustic interactions of the Neotropical treefrog *Hyla ebraccata. Behavioral Ecology and Sociobiology* 14:211–224. (14)

———. 1985. Intra- and interspecific vocal behavior of the Neotropical treefrog *Hyla microcephala. Copeia* 1985:27–38. (14)

Scorgie, H. R. A. 1980. Growth and development of tadpoles of the common toad *Bufo bufo* Linnaeus on different foods. *British Journal of Herpetology* 6:41–43. (13)

Scott, J. R., C. R. Tracy, and D. Pettus. 1982. A biophysical analysis of daily and seasonal utilization of climate space by a montane snake. *Ecology* 63:482–493. (4)

Seale, D. B. 1980. Influence of amphibian larvae on primary production, nutrient flux, and competition in a pond ecosystem. *Ecology* 61:1531–1550. (14)

———. 1982. Physical factors influencing oviposition by the woodfrog, *Rana sylvatica,* in Pennsylvania. *Copeia* 1982:627–635. (8)

———. 1987. Amphibia. In *Animal Energetics,* vol. 2, ed. P. J. Vernberg and T. J. Pandian, 467–552. New York: Academic Press. (9,12,13,14,16)

Seale, D. B., and N. Beckvar. 1980. The comparative ability of anuran larvae (genera *Hyla, Bufo,* and *Rana*) to ingest blue-green algae. *Copeia* 1980:495–503. (14)

Seale, D. B., K. Hoff, and R. Wassersug. 1982. *Xenopus laevis* larvae (Amphibia: Anura) as model suspension feeders. *Hydrobiologia* 87:161–169. (5,14,16)

Seale, D. B., and R. J. Wassersug. 1979. Suspension feeding dynamics of anuran larvae related to their functional morphology. *Oecologia* (Berlin) 39:259–272. (11,14)

Searcy, W. A. 1979. Sexual selection and male body size in male red-winged blackbirds. *Evolution* 33:649–661. (14)

Sedra, S. N. 1950. The metamorphosis of the jaws and their muscles in the toad, *Bufo regularis* Reuss, correlated with changes in the animal's feeding habits. *Proceedings of the Zoological Society of London* 120:405–449. (11)

Sedra, S. N., and M. I. Michael. 1959. The ontogenesis of the sound conducting apparatus of the Egyptian toad *Bufo regularis* Reuss, with a review of this apparatus in the Salientia. *Journal of Morphology* 104:359–373. (11)

———. 1961. Normal table of the Egyptian toad, *Bufo regularis* Reuss, with an addendum on the standardization of the stages considered in previous publications. *Csekaslovenska Morfologie* 9:331–351. (16)

Seeherman, H. J., C. R. Taylor, G. M. O. Maloiy, and R. B. Armstrong. 1981. Design of the mammalian respiratory system: Measuring maximum aerobic capacity. *Respiration Physiology* 44:11–24. (12)

Segil, N., L. Silverman, and D. B. Kelley. 1987. Androgen-binding levels in sexually dimorphic muscle of *Xenopus laevis. General and Comparative Endocrinology* 66:95–101. (16)

Segura, E. T. 1979. Pressure and heart rate responses to raised carotid pressure in the toad. *American Journal of Physiology* 237:H639–H643. (7)

Segura, E. T., U. C. Bandsholm, and A. Bronstein. 1982. Role of the CNS in the control of the water economy of the toad *Bufo arenarum* Hensel: 2. Adrenergic control of water uptake across the skin. *Journal of Comparative Physiology* 146B:101–106. (5,6)

Segura, E. T., U. C. Bandsholm, A. Bronstein, and D. Woscoboinik. 1982. Role of the CNS in the control of the water economy of the toad *Bufo arenarum* Hensel: 1. Effects of handling, brain lesions, anaesthesia, and reversible coma upon water uptake, urine production, and overall water balance. *Journal of Comparative Physiology* 146B:95–100. (5,6)

Segura, E. T., A. Bronstein, and N. A. Schmajuk. 1981. Effect of breathing upon blood pressure and heart rate in the toad, *Bufo arenarum* Hensel. *Journal of Comparative Physiology* 143:223–227. (7)

Segura, E. T., and S. D'Agostino. 1964. Seasonal variations of blood pressure, vasomotor reactivity, and plasmatic catecholamines in the toad. *Acta Physiologica Latinoamericana* 14:231–237. (7)

Segura, E. T., J. C. Reboreda, A. Skorka, M. E. Cuello, and S. Petriella. 1984. Role of the CNS in the control of the water economy of the toad *Bufo arenarum* Hensel: 3. Skin permeability increases to raised osmotic pressure of the external "millieu." *Journal of Comparative Physiology* 154B:573–578. (2)

Segura, E. T., A. Varsavsky, and S. Petriella. 1987. Effects of temperature and general anesthesia on the water gain and the inulin space of the brain of a toad. *Comparative Biochemistry Physiology* 88C: 331–334. (8)

Seibel, R. V. 1970. Variables affecting the critical thermal maximum of the leopard frog *Rana pipiens* Schreber. *Herpetologica* 26:208–213. (9)

Seibert, E. A., H. B. Lillywhite, and R. J. Wassersug. 1974. Cranial coossification in frogs: Relationship to rate of evaporative water loss. *Physiological Zoology* 47:261–265. (6)

Seiter, P., H. Schultheiss, and W. Hanke. 1978. Osmotic stress and excretion of ammonia and urea in *Xenopus laevis*. *Comparative Biochemistry and Physiology* 61A:571–576. (6)

Seki, T., and S. Kikuyama. 1979. Effects of ergocornine and reserpine on metamorphosis in *Bufo bufo japonicus* tadpoles. *Endocrinology Japan* 26:675–678. (16)

———. 1986. Effect of thyrotropin-releasing hormone and dopamine on the *in vitro* secretion of prolactin by the bullfrog pituitary gland. *General and Comparative Endocrinology* 61:197–202. (16)

Semlitsch, R. D. 1985a. Analysis of climatic factors influencing migrations of the salamander *Ambystoma talpoideum*. *Copeia* 1985:477–489. (8)

———. 1985b. Reproductive strategy of a facultatively paedomorphic salamander *Ambystoma talpoideum*. *Oecologia* (Berlin) 65:305–313. (10)

Senfft, W. 1936. Das Brutgeschäft des Baumsteigerfrosches (*Dendrobates auratus* Girard) in Gefangenschaft. *Zoologische Garten* 8:122–136. (15)

Seppanen, E. D., R. G. McKinnell, D. Tarin, L. A. Rollinssmith, and W. Hanson. 1984. Temperature-dependent dissociation of Lucké renal adenocarcinoma cells. *Differentiation* 26:227–230. (8)

Serbeniuk, T. S. V., and I. E. Gurskaia. 1986. Stretch receptors of the lungs in the frog, *Rana temporaria* (in Russian). *Zhurnal Evoliutsionnoi Biokhimii i Fiziologii* 22:548–554. (7)

———. 1987. Role of the pulmonary mechanoreceptor apparatus in molding the natural respiration of the frog *Rana temporaria* (in Russian). *Zhurnal Evoliutsionnoi Biokhimii i Fiziologii* 23:502–508. (7)

Setoguti, T., M. Shin, Y. Inone, H. Matsumura, H.-S. Chen. 1985. Ultrastructural changes in development and aging of the interrenal cell of the salamander, *Hynobius nebulosus*. *Archivum Histologicum Japonicum* 48:199–211. (16)

Severtzov, A. S. 1961. Mechanism of protrusion of the tongue in tailless amphibians (in Russian). *Doklady Akademie Nauk* (USSR), Series Biology 140:256–259. In translation series, 140 (1962): 830–832. (11)

———. 1969. Food seizing mechanisms in anuran larvae. *Doklady Akademie Nauk* (USSR), Series Biology, translation, 187:530–532. (11)

———. 1971a. Food-seizing mechanisms in Urodela larvae. *Proceedings of the Academy of Sciences USSR* 197:341–344. (11)

———. 1971b. The mechanisms of food capture in tailed amphibians (in Russian). *Doklady Akademie Nauk* (USSR), Series Biology, 154:34–37. Translation in *Proceedings of the Academy of Sciences USSR* 197:185–187. (11)

———. 1972. Mechanism of movements of the sublingual system and possible causes for reduction of lungs in Urodela (in Russian). *Zoological Zhurnal* 51:94–112. (11)

Sewertzov, A. N. 1907. Studien über die Entwicklung der Nerven, Muskeln, und des Skelettes der Extremitäten der niederen Tetrapoden: Beiträge zur einer Theorie der pentadactylen Extremität der Wirbeltiere. *Bulletin de la Société Impériale des Naturalistes de Moscow*, n.s. 21:1–432. (11)

Seymour, R. S. 1972. Behavioral thermoregulation by juvenile green toads, *Bufo debilis*. *Copeia* 1972:572–575. (6,8,9)

———. 1973a. Energy metabolism of dormant spadefoot toads (*Scaphiopus*). *Copeia* 1973:435–445. (10,12,15)

———. 1973b. Gas exchange in spadefoot toads beneath the ground. *Copeia* 1973:452–460. (10)

———. 1973c. Physiological correlates of forced activity and burrowing in the spadefoot toad, *Scaphiopus hammondii*. *Copeia* 1973:103–115. (12,14)

———. 1982. Physiological adaptations to aquatic life. In *Biology of the Reptilia*, vol. 13, ed. C. Gans and F. H. Pough, 1–51. New York: Academic Press. (5)

Seymour, R. S., and A. K. Lee. 1974. Physiological adaptations of an-

uran amphibians to aridity: Australian prospects. *Australian Zoologist* 18:53–65. (10)

Shaffer, H. B., and G. V. Lauder. 1985a. Aquatic prey capture in ambystomatid salamanders: Patterns of variation in muscle activity. *Journal of Morphology* 183:273–284. (11,14)

———. 1985b. Patterns of variation in aquatic ambystomatid salamanders: Kinematics of the feeding system. *Evolution* 39:83–92. (11,14)

———. 1988. The ontogeny of functional design: Metamorphosis of feeding behaviour in the tiger salamander (*Ambystoma tigrinum*). *Journal of Zoology* (London) 216:437–454. (11)

Sham, J. S. K., A. D. Kenny, and P. K. T. Pang. 1984. Cardiac actions and structural-activity relationship of parathyroid hormone on isolated frog atrium. *General and Comparative Endocrinology* 55:373–377. (3)

Shamarina, N. M. 1962. Electric response of "tonic" muscle fibres of the frog skeletal musculature. *Nature* 193:783–784. (11)

Shannon, P., and D. L. Kramer. 1988. Water depth alters respiratory behaviour of *Xenopus laevis*. *Journal of Experimental Biology* 137:597–602. (5,7)

Shapiro, B., and B. L. Pimstone. 1977. A phylogenetic study of sulphation factor activity in 26 species. *Journal of Endocrinology* 74:129–135. (16)

Shapiro, H. 1948. Heat production of different cells. *Tabulae Biologicae* 19:1–29. (12)

Shapiro, H. A., and H. Zwarenstein. 1933. Metabolic changes associated with endocrine activity and reproductive cycle in *Xenopus laevis*. *Journal of Experimental Biology* 10:186–195. (15)

Share, L., and H. H. Ussing. 1965. Effect of potassium on the movement of water across the isolated amphibian skin. *Acta Physiologica Scandinavica* 64:109–118. (5)

Sharif, N. A. 1987. Adaptive changes in brain and pituitary TRH receptors: Effects of lesions, kindling hormones, drugs, and other factors. *Medical Science Research* 15:223–237. (16)

Shelton, G. 1970. The effect of lung ventilation on blood flow to the lungs and body of the amphibian, *Xenopus laevis*. *Respiration Physiology* 9:183–196. (5,7,16)

———. 1976. Gas exchange, pulmonary blood supply, and the partially divided amphibian heart. In *Perspectives in Experimental Biology*, ed. P. Spencer Davies, 247–259. Oxford: Pergamon. (5)

———. 1985. Functional and evolutionary significance of cardiovascular shunts in the Amphibia. In *Cardiovascular Shunts: Phylogenetic, Ontogenetic, and Clinical Aspects*, ed. K. Johansen and W. W. Burggren, 100–116. Copenhagen: Munksgaard. (5,7)

Shelton, G., and R. G. Boutilier. 1982. Apnoea in amphibians and reptiles. *Journal of Experimental Biology* 100:245–273. (5,6,7,16)

Shelton, G., and P. C. Croghan. 1988. Gas exchange and its control in non-steady-state systems: The consequences of evolution from water to air breathing in the vertebrates. *Canadian Journal of Zoology* 66:109–123. (7)

Shelton, G., D. R. Jones, and W. K. Milsom. 1986. Control of breathing in ectothermic vertebrates. In *Handbook of Physiology*, ed. N. S. Cherniack and J. G. Widdicombe, 2:857–909. Bethesda, MD: American Physiological Society. (5,6,7)

Shephard, R. J. 1982. *Physiology and Biochemistry of Exercise*. New York: Praeger Publishers. (12)

———. 1984. *Biochemistry of Physical Activity*. Springfield, IL: C. C. Thomas. (12)

Shepherd, G. M., and D. Ottoson. 1965. Response of the isolated muscle spindle to different rates of stretching. *Cold Spring Harbor Symposia in Quantitative Biology* 30:95–103. (11)

Sherman, C. K. 1980. A comparison of the natural history and mating systems of two anurans: Yosemite toads (*Bufo canorus*) and black toads (*Bufo exsul*). Ph.D. diss., University of Michigan, Ann Arbor. (14)

Sherman, E., and S. G. Stadien. 1986. The effect of dehydration on rehydration and metabolic rate in a lunged and a lungless salamander. *Comparative Biochemistry and Physiology* 85A:483–487. (12)

Sherwood, N. M., J. C. Wingfield, G. F. Ball, and A. M. Duffy. 1988. Identity of gonadotropin-releasing hormone in passerine birds: Comparison of GnRH in song sparrow (*Melospiza melodia*) and starling (*Sturnus vulgaris*) with five vertebrate GnRHs. *General and Comparative Endocrinology* 69:341–351. (15)

Sherwood, N. M., R. T. Zoeller, and F. L. Moore. 1986. Multiple forms of gonadotropin-releasing hormone in amphibian brains. *General and Comparative Endocrinology* 61:313–322. (3,15,16)

Shiba, Y., H. Sumomogi, S. Nomura, Y. Muneoka, and Y. Kanno. 1979. Structures of gustatory organs of *Xenopus laevis* during metamorphosis. *Journal of the Hiroshima University Dental Society* 11:236–242. (16)

———. 1980. Oral chemoreceptor organs of bullfrog tadpoles during metamorphosis. *Development, Growth, and Differentiation* 22:209–217. (16)

Shield, J. W., and P. J. Bentley. 1973. Respiration of some urodele and anuran Amphibia: 1. In water, role of the skin and gills. *Comparative Biochemistry and Physiology* 46A:17–28. (12)

Shindo, T., and K. R. Spring. 1981. Chloride movement across the basolateral membrane of proximal tubule cells. *Journal of Membrane Biology* 58:35–42. (5)

Shine, R. 1979. Sexual size selection and sexual dimorphism in the Amphibia. *Copeia* 1979:297–306. (14,15)

Shinkai, K., and T. Narita. 1957. Electromyographical studies on toad respiratory movements. *Nagoya Journal of Medical Science* 19:1–6. (11)

Shinn, E. A., and J. W. Dole. 1978. Evidence for a role for olfactory cues in the feeding response of leopard frogs, *Rana pipiens. Herpetologica* 34:167–172. (2)

Shiomi, K., T. Hachiya, M. Yoshimura, T. Miyazaki, and Y. Ochi. 1972. Effect of synthetic TRH (thyrotropin releasing hormone) on tadpole metamorphosis. *Folia Endocrinology Japan* 48:670–673. (16)

Shirane, T. 1984. Regulation of gonadal differentiation in frogs derived from UV-irradiated eggs. *Zoological Sciences* 1:281–289. (16)

———. 1986. A new, early, morphological indication of sex differentiation in Anura, *Rana japonica* and *R. nigromacula. Journal of Experimental Zoology* 240:113–118. (16)

Shoemaker, V. H. 1964a. The effects of dehydration on electrolyte concentrations in a toad, *Bufo marinus. Comparative Biochemistry and Physiology* 13:261–271. (6)

———. 1964b. Physiological effects of water deprivation in a toad, *Bufo marinus.* Ph.D. thesis, University of Michigan, Ann Arbor. (6)

———. 1987. Osmoregulation in amphibians. In *Comparative Physiology: Life in Water and on Land*, ed. P. Dejours, L. Bolis, C. R. Taylor, and E. R. Weibel, 109–120. Padua: Liviana Press. (16)

———. 1988. Physiological ecology of amphibians in arid environments. *Journal of Arid Environments* 14:145–153. (9)

Shoemaker, V. H., M. A. Baker, and J. P. Loveridge. 1989. Effect of water balance on thermoregulation in waterproof frogs (*Chiromantis* and *Phyllomedusa*). *Physiological Zoology* 62:133–146. (9)

Shoemaker, V. H., D. Balding, R. Ruibal, and L. L. McClanahan. 1972. Uricotelism and low evaporative water loss in a South American frog. *Science* 175:1018–1020. (4,6)

Shoemaker, V. H., and P. E. Bickler. 1979. Kidney and bladder function in a uricotelic treefrog (*Phyllomedusa sauvagei*). *Journal of Comparative Physiology* 133:211–218. (6)

Shoemaker, V. H., and L. L. McClanahan. 1975. Evaporative water loss, nitrogen excretion, and osmoregulation in phyllomedusine frogs. *Journal of Comparative Physiology* 100:331–345. (4,5,6)

———. 1980. Nitrogen excretion and water balance in amphibians of Borneo. *Copeia* 1980:446–451. (6)

Shoemaker, V. H., L. L. McClanahan, and R. Ruibal. 1969. Seasonal changes in body fluids in a field population of spadefoot toads. *Copeia* 1969:585–591. (6,10)

Shoemaker, V. H., L. L. McClanahan, P. C. Withers, S. S. Hillman, and R. C. Drewes. 1987. Thermoregulatory response to heat in the waterproof frogs *Phyllomedusa* and *Chiromantis. Physiological Zoology* 60:365–372. (4,6,9)

Shoemaker, V. H., and K. A. Nagy. 1977. Osmoregulation in amphibians and reptiles. *Annual Review of Physiology* 39:449–471. (6,10,12)

Shoemaker, V. H., and H. Waring. 1968. Effect of hypothalamic lesions on the water-balance response of a toad (*Bufo marinus*). *Comparative Biochemistry and Physiology* 24:47–54. (6)

Shofner, W. P. 1988. Postmetamorphic changes in the auditory system. In *The Evolution of the Amphibian Auditory System*, ed. B. Fritzsch, M. J. Ryan, W. Wilcynski, T. E. Hetherington, and W. Walkowiak, 377–392. New York: John Wiley and Sons. (2,16)

Shpun, S., and U. Katz. 1988. Urea transport across the isolated urinary bladder of the green toad *Bufo viridis:* Adaptation to NaCl solutions. *Israel Journal of Zoology* 35:104. (6)

Shukla, V. N., and D. P. S. Bhati. 1973. The pectoral musculature of *Uperodon systoma* (Schn.). *Annals of Zoology* (Agra) 9:95–118. (11)

Shuldiner, A. R., C. Bennett, E. A. Robinson, and J. Roth. 1989. Isolation and characterization of two different insulins from an amphibian *Xenopus laevis. Endocrinology* 125:469–477. (3)

Shumway, W. 1940. Stages in the normal development of *Rana pipiens. Anatomical Record* 78:139–148. (16)

Sibly, R. M., and P. Calow. 1986. *Physiological Ecology of Animals: An Evolutionary Approach.* Oxford: Blackwell Scientific Publications. (1)

Sidell, B. D. 1980. Responses of goldfish (*Carassius auratus* L.) muscle to acclimation temperature: Alterations in biochemistry and proportions of different fiber types. *Physiological Zoology* 53:98–107. (8)

———. 1983. Cellular acclimatisation to environmental change by quantitative alterations in enzymes and organelles. In *Cellular Acclimatisation to Environmental Change*, ed. A. R. Cossins and P. Sheterline, 103–120. Cambridge: Cambridge University Press. (14)

Sidell, B. D., and J. R. Hazel. 1987. Temperature affects the diffusion of small molecules through cytosol of fish muscle. *Journal of Experimental Biology* 129:191–203. (8)

Sidell, B. D., and I. A. Johnston. 1985. Thermal sensitivity of contractile function in chain pickerel, *Esox niger. Canadian Journal of Zoology* 63:811–816. (8)

Sidell, B. D., I. A. Johnston, T. S. Moerland, and G. Goldspink. 1983. The eurythermal myofibrillar protein complex of the mummichog (*Fundulus heteroclitus*): Adaptation to a fluctuating thermal environment. *Journal of Comparative Physiology* 153B:167–173. (8)

Sievert, L. M. 1989. Postprandial temperature selection in *Crotaphytus collaris. Copeia* 1989:983–989. (9)

Sievert, L. M., and V. H. Hutchison. 1988. Light versus heat: Thermoregulatory behavior in a nocturnal lizard (*Gekko gecko*). *Herpetologica* 44:266–273. (9)

———. 1989. Influences of season, time of day, light, and sex on the thermoregulatory behavior of *Crotaphytus collaris. Journal of Thermal Biology* 14:159–165. (9)

Sillman, A. J., D. A. Bolnick, E. W. Clinite, and K. S. Rudert. 1978. The effect of temperature on rapid dark adaptation in bullfrog photoreceptors, a difference between rods and cones. *Vision Research* 18:1375–1380. (8)

Silver, M. L. 1942. The motoneurons of the spinal cord of the frog. *Journal of Comparative Neurology* 77:1–39. (11)

Silverstone, P. A. 1975. A revision of the poison-arrow frogs of the genus *Dendrobates* Wagler. *Natural History Museum of Los Angeles County Science Bulletin* 21:1–55. (14)

Silverstone, T. 1976. *Appetite and Food Intake: Report of the Dahlem Workshop on Appetite and Food Intake.* Berlin: Abakon Verlagsgesellschaft. (13)

Simkiss, K. 1968. Calcium and carbonate metabolism in the frog (*Rana temporaria*) during respiratory acidosis. *American Journal of Physiology* 214:627–634. (5,10)

Simmons, A. M. 1988. Masking patterns in the bullfrog (*Rana catesbeiana*): 1. Behavioral effects. *Journal of the Acoustic Society of America* 83:1087–1092. (2)

Simms, C. 1968. Crested newt, *Triturus cristatus* Laurentius, double brooded in an indoor vivarium. *British Journal of Herpetology* 4:43. (15)

Simon, M. P. 1983. The ecology of parental care in a terrestrial breeding frog from New Guinea. *Behavioral Ecology and Sociobiology* 14:61–67. (14)

Simpson, H. B., M. L. Tobias, and D. B. Kelley. 1986. Origin and identification of fibers in the cranial nerve IX–X complex of *Xenopus laevis:* Lucifer yellow backfills *in vitro. Journal of Comparative Neurology* 244:430–444. (2)

Sinsch, U. 1984. Thermal influences on the habitat preference and the diurnal activity in three European *Rana* species. *Oecologia* (Berlin) 64:125–131. (9)

———. 1989. Behavioral thermoregulation of the Andean toad (*Bufo spinulosus*) at high altitude. *Oecologia* (Berlin) 80:32–38. (9)

Sisson, J. E., and B. D. Sidell. 1987. Effects of thermal acclimation on muscle fiber recruitment of swimming striped bass (*Morone saxatilis*). *Physiological Zoology* 60:310–320. (8)

Sivak, J. G. 1987. Optics of amphibious eyes in vertebrates. In *Sensory*

Biology of Aquatic Animals, ed. J. Atema, R. R. Fay, J. Popper, and W. N. Tavolga, 467–485. New York: Springer-Verlag. (16)

Sivula, J. C., M. C. Mix, and D. S. McKenzie. 1972. Oxygen consumption of Bufo boreas boreas tadpoles during various developmental stages of metamorphosis. Herpetologica 28:309–313. (12,16)

Skipper, J. K., and T. H. Hamilton. 1979. Xenopus liver: Ontogeny of oestrogen responsiveness. Science 206:693–695. (16)

Skoglund, C. R. 1961. Functional analysis of swim-bladder muscles engaged in sound production in the toadfish. Journal of Biophysics and Cytology 10:187–200. (14)

Slatyer, R. O. 1967. Plant-Water Relationships. New York: Academic Press. (6)

Small, J. V., and H. G. Davies. 1970. The haemoglobin in the condensed chromatin of mature amphibian erythrocytes: Further study. Journal of Cell Science 7:15–33. (5)

Smalley, K. N., and G. W. Nace. 1983. Vitellogenic cycles in laboratory-maintained females of the leopard frog, Rana pipiens. Journal of Experimental Zoology 226:211–219. (15)

Smatresk, N. J., and A. Smits. 1989. Evidence for central chemoreceptor control of ventilation in Bufo marinus. American Zoologist 29:58A. (6)

———. 1991. Effects of central and peripheral chemoreceptor stimulation on ventilation in the marine toad, Bufo marinus. Respiration Physiology 83:223–238. (7)

Smit, H. 1968. Gastric secretion in the lower vertebrates and birds. In Handbook of Physiology, sec. 6, ed. C. F. Code, 2791–2805. Bethesda, MD: American Physiological Society. (13)

Smith, A. U. 1958. The resistance of animals to cooling and freezing. Biological Reviews 33:197–253. (10)

Smith, C. C., and A. N. Bragg. 1949. Observations on the ecology and natural history of Anura: 8. Food and feeding habits of the common species of toads in Oklahoma. Ecology 30:333–349. (13)

Smith, C. L. 1950. Seasonal changes in blood sugar, fat body, liver glycogen, and gonads in the common frog, Rana temporaria. Journal of Experimental Biology 26:412–429. (10,15)

———. 1955. Reproduction in female Amphibia. Memoirs of the Society of Endocrinology 4:39–56. (15)

Smith, D. D., Jr., and J. W. Campbell. 1988. Distribution of glutamine synthetase and carbamyl-phosphate synthetase I in vertebrate liver. Proceedings of the National Academy of Science 85:160–164. (6)

Smith, D. G. 1974. Insensitivity of toad carbon dioxide exchange to acetazolamide. Comparative Biochemistry and Physiology 48A:337–341. (5,12)

———. 1976. The innervation of the cutaneous artery in the toad (Bufo marinus). General Pharmacology 7:405–409. (5,7)

———. 1978. Evidence for pulmonary vasoconstriction during hypercapnia in the toad Bufo marinus. Canadian Journal of Zoology 56:1530–1534. (7)

Smith, D. G., P. J. Berger, and B. K. Evans. 1981. Baroreceptor control of heart rate in the conscious toad, Bufo marinus. American Journal of Physiology 241:R307–R311. (7)

Smith, D. G., and L. Rapson. 1977. Differences in pulmonary microvascular anatomy between Bufo marinus and Xenopus laevis. Cell and Tissue Research 178:1–15. (5)

Smith, D. G., D. C. Rogers, J. Chainley-Campbell, and G. R. Campbell. 1981. The mechanism of blood flow redistribution within the carotid labyrinth of the toad, Bufo marinus. Journal of Experimental Zoology 216:387–394. (7)

Smith, F. M., and D. R. Jones. 1982. The effect of changes in blood oxygen-carrying capacity on ventilation volume in the rainbow trout (Salmo gairdneri). Journal of Experimental Biology 97:325–334. (7)

Smith, G. C. 1976. Ecological energetics of three species of ectothermic vertebrates. Ecology 57:252–264. (12,13)

Smith, H. M. 1925. Cell size and metabolic activity in Amphibia. Biological Bulletin 48:347–378. (12)

Smith, H. W. 1931. Observations on the African lungfish Protopterus aethiopicus, and on evolution from water to land environments. Ecology 12:164–181. (10)

Smith, L. D., and R. E. Ecker. 1970. Regulatory processes in the maturation and early cleavage of amphibian eggs. In Current Topics in Developmental Biology, ed. A. A. Moscona and A. Monroy, 5:1–38. New York: Academic Press. (15)

———. 1971. The interaction of steroids with Rana pipiens oocytes in the induction of maturation. Developmental Biology 25:232–247. (15)

Smith, M. 1951. The British Amphibians and Reptiles. London: Collins. (10)

Smith, M. A. 1917. On tadpoles from Siam. Journal of the Natural History Society of Siam 2:261–275. (15)

Smith, P. E. 1916. The effect of hypophysectomy in the early embryo upon growth and development of the frog. Anatomical Records 11:57–64. (16)

———. 1920. The pigmentary, growth, and endocrine disturbances induced in the anuran tadpole by the early ablation of the pars buccalis of the hypophysis. American Anatomical Memoirs 11:1–151. (15)

Smith, P. E., and I. B. Smith. 1923. The function of the lobes of the hypophysis as indicated by replacement therapy with different portions of the ox gland. Endocrinology 7:579–591. (15)

Smith, R. S. 1964a. Activity of intrafusal muscle fibres in muscle spindles of Xenopus laevis. Acta Physiologica Scandinavica 60:223–239. (11)

———. 1964b. Contraction in intrafusal muscle fibres of Xenopus laevis following stimulation of their motor nerves. Acta Physiologica Scandinavica 62:195–208. (11)

Smith, R. S., G. Blinston, and W. K. Ovalle. 1973. Skeletomotor and fusimotor organization in amphibians. In Control of Posture and Locomotion, ed. R. B. Stein, K. G. Pearson, R. S. Smith, and J. B. Redford, 105–118. New York: Plenum Press. (11)

Smith, R. S., and J. Lännergren. 1968. Types of motor units in the skeletal muscle of Xenopus laevis. Nature 217:281–283. (11)

Smith, R. S., and W. K. Ovalle. 1973. Varieties of fast and slow extrafusal muscle fibres in amphibian hind limb muscles. Journal of Anatomy (London) 116:1–24. (11,14)

Smith, V. D. E., and C. M. Jackson. 1931. The changes during desiccation and rehydration in the body and organs of the leopard frog (Rana pipiens). Biological Bulletin 60:80–93. (6)

Smith-Gill, S. J. 1974. Morphogenesis of the dorsal pigmentary pattern in wild-type and mutant Rana pipiens. Developmental Biology 37:153–170. (16)

Smith-Gill, S. J., and K. A. Berven. 1979. Predicting amphibian metamorphosis. American Naturalist 113:563–585. (9,16)

Smith-Gill, S. J., and V. Carver. 1981. Biochemical characterization of organ differentiation and maturation. In Metamorphosis: A Problem in Developmental Biology, 2d ed., ed. L. I. Gilbert and E. Frieden, 491–544. New York: Plenum Press. (16)

Smits, A. W. 1984. Activity patterns and thermal biology of the toad Bufo boreas halophilus. Copeia 1984:689–696. (9,14)

Smits, A. W., and D. L. Crawford. 1984. Emergence of toads to activity, a statistical analysis of contributing cues. Copeia 1984:696–701. (8,14)

Smits, A. W., N. H. West, and W. W. Burggren. 1986. Pulmonary fluid balance following pulmocutaneous baroreceptor denervation in the toad. Journal of Applied Physiology 61:331–337. (7)

Smoller, C. G. 1966. Ultrastructural studies on the developing neurohypophysis of the Pacific treefrog, Hyla regilla. General and Comparative Endocrinology 7:44–73. (16)

Smyth, D. H. 1939. The central and reflex control of respiration in the frog. Journal of Physiology (London) 95:305–327. (6,7)

Snell, E. S., and E. Atkins. 1968. The mechanisms of fever. In The Biological Basis of Medicine, ed. E. E. Bittar and N. Bittar, 397–419. New York: Academic Press. (9)

Snyder, G. K. 1971. Influence of temperature and hematocrit on blood viscosity. American Journal of Physiology 220:1667–1672. (9)

Snyder, G. K., and W. W. Weathers. 1975. Temperature adaptations in amphibians. American Naturalist 109:93–101. (8,9)

Soboslai, G. B., M. McTigue, and M. W. Weiner. 1977. Mechanism of active chloride transport by urinary bladder of the Colombian toad. American Journal of Physiology 235:F421–F427. (5)

Soeda, H., and F. Sakudo. 1988. Characteristics of the water response across the dorsal epithelium of frog tongue. Comparative Biochemistry and Physiology 89A:683–691. (7)

Sokol, O. M. 1969. Feeding in the pipid frog Hymenochirus boettgeri (Tornier). Herpetologica 25:9–24. (11,16)

———. 1977. The free swimming Pipa larvae, with a review of pipid larvae and pipid phylogeny (Anura: Pipidae). Journal of Morphology 154:357–426. (16)

Sommerkamp, H. 1928. Das Substrat der Dauerverkürzung am Froschmuskel: Physiologische und pharmakologische Sonderstellung bestimmter Muskelfasern. Archiv für experimentelle Pathologie und Pharmakologie 128:99–115. (11)

Sonnhof, U., D. W. Richter, and R. Taughner. 1977. Electronic coupling between frog spinal motoneurons: An electrophysiological and morphological study. *Brain Research* 138:197–215. (2)

Sotowska-Brochocka, J. 1988. The stimulatory and inhibitory role of the hypothalamus in the regulation of ovulation in grass frog, *Rana temporaria* L. *General and Comparative Endocrinology* 70:83–90. (15)

Southerland, M. T. 1986a. Behavioral interactions among four species of the salamander genus *Desmognathus*. *Ecology* 67:175–181. (14)

———. 1986b. Behavioral niche expansion in *Desmognathus fuscus* (Amphibia: Caudata: Plethodontidae). *Copeia* 1986:235–237. (14)

———. 1986c. Coexistence of three congeneric salamanders: The importance of habitat and body size. *Ecology* 67:721–728. (14)

Spaeti, U. 1978. Development of the sensory system in the larval and metamorphosing European grass frog (*Rana temporaria*). *Journal Hirnforshung* 19:543–575. (16)

Sparreboom, M. 1983. On the sexual behaviour of *Paramesotriton caudopunctatus* (Liu & Hu) (Amphibia: Caudata: Salamandridae). *Amphibia-Reptilia* 4:25–33. (14)

———. 1984a. Gedrag en voortplanting van de wrattensalamanders *Paramesotriton hongkongensis* en *P. chinesis*: 1. *Lacerta* 43:7–14. (14)

———. 1984b. Gedrag en voortplanting van de wrattensalamanders *Paramesotriton hongkongensis* en *P. chinesis*: 2. *Lacerta* 43:28–35. (14)

Speit, G. 1980. Effects of temperature on sister chromatid exchanges. *Human Genetics* 55:333–336. (8)

Sperry, D. G. 1981. Fiber type composition and postmetamorphic growth of anuran hindlimb muscles. *Journal of Morphology* 170:321–345. (11,14)

———. 1987. Relationship between natural variations in motoneuron number and body size in *Xenopus laevis*: A test for size matching. *Journal of Comparative Neurology* 264:250–267. (11)

———. 1988. The origin of interindividual variation in motoneuron number in the lumbar lateral motor column of *Xenopus laevis*. In *Neurology and Neurobiology*, vol. 44, *Developmental Neurobiology of the Frog*, ed. E. D. Pollack and H. D. Bibb, 29–51. New York: Alan R. Liss. (11)

Sperry, D. G., and P. Grobstein. 1985. Regulation of neuron numbers in *Xenopus laevis*: Effects of hormonal manipulation altering size at metamorphosis. *Journal of Comparative Neurology* 232:287–298. (11,16)

Spight, T. M. 1967a. Evaporation from toads and water surfaces. *Nature* 214:835–836. (6)

———. 1967b. The water economy of salamanders: Exchange of water with the soil. *Biological Bulletin* 132:126–132. (6)

———. 1968. The water economy of salamanders: Evaporative water loss. *Physiological Zoology* 41:195–203. (5,6)

Spotila, J. R. 1972. Role of temperature and water in the ecology of lungless salamanders. *Ecological Monographs* 42:95–125. (4,6,9)

———. 1980. Constraints of body size and environment on the temperature regulation of dinosaurs. In *A Cold Look at Warm-Blooded Dinosaurs*, ed. R. D. K. Thomas and E. C. Olson, 233–252. American Association for the Advancement of Sciences Symposium 28. Boulder, CO: Westview Press. (4)

———. 1989. Constraints of bioenergetics on animal population dynamics: An introduction to the symposium. *Physiological Zoology* 62:195–198. (1,14)

Spotila, J. R., and E. N. Berman. 1976. Determination of skin resistance and the role of the skin in controlling water loss in amphibians and reptiles. *Comparative Biochemistry and Physiology* 55A:407–411. (4,6)

Spotila, J. R., P. W. Lommen, G. S. Bakken, and D. M. Gates. 1973. A mathematical model for body temperatures of large reptiles: Implications for dinosaur ecology. *American Naturalist* 107:391–404. (4)

Spotila, J. R., O. H. Soule, and D. M. Gates. 1972. The biophysical ecology of the alligator: Heat energy budgets and climate spaces. *Ecology* 53:1094–1102. (4)

Spotila, J. R., and E. A. Standora. 1985. Environmental constraints on the thermal energetics of sea turtles. *Copeia* 1985:694–702. (4)

Spotila, J. R., E. A. Standora, D. P. Easton, and P. S. Rutledge. 1989. Bioenergetics, behavior, and resource partitioning in stressed habitats: Biophysical and molecular approaches. *Physiological Zoology* 62:253–285. (1)

Spotila, J. R., C. J. Weinheimer, and C. V. Paganelli. 1981. Shell resis-

tance and evaporative water loss from bird eggs: Effects of wind speeds and egg size. *Physiological Zoology* 54:195–202. (4)

Spray, D. C. 1974. Characteristics, specificity, and efferent control of frog cutaneous cold receptors. *Journal of Physiology* (London) 237:15–38. (9)

———. 1975. Effect of reduced acclimation temperature on responses of frog cold receptors. *Comparative Biochemistry and Physiology* 50A:391–395. (9)

———. 1976. Pain and temperature receptors of anurans. In *Frog Neurobiology: A Handbook*, ed. R. Llinás and W. Precht, 607–628. Berlin: Springer-Verlag. (2,9)

Spray, D. C., and S. H. Galansky. 1975. Effects of cholinergic agonists and antagonists on frog cold receptor activity. *Comparative Biochemistry and Physiology* 50C:97–103. (9)

Spring, K. R. 1973. A parallel path model for *Necturus* proximal tubule. *Journal of Membrane Biology* 13:323–352. (5)

Spring, K. R., and G. Kimura. 1978. Chloride reabsorption by renal proximal tubules of *Necturus*. *Journal of Membrane Biology* 38:233–254. (5)

Spring, K. R., and C. V. Paganelli. 1972. Sodium flux in *Necturus* proximal tubule under voltage clamp. *Journal of General Physiology* 60:181–201. (5)

Spurway, H., and J. B. S. Haldane. 1953. The comparative ethology of vertebrate breathing: 1. Breathing in newts, with a general survey. *Behaviour* 6:8–34. (7,14)

Srivastav, A. K., and L. Rani. 1989. Influence of calcitonin administration on serum calcium and inorganic phosphate level of the frog, *Rana tigrina*. *General and Comparative Endocrinology* 74:14–17. (3)

Stainsby, W. N., and J. K. Barclay. 1970. O_2 deficit, steady level O_2 uptake, and O_2 uptake for recovery. *Medicine and Science in Sports* 2:177–181. (12)

Stamatoyannopoulos, G., A. J. Bellingham, and C. Lenfant. 1971. Abnormal hemoglobins with high and low oxygen affinity. *Annual Review of Medicine* 22:221–234. (5)

Stamps, J. A. 1977. Social behavior and spacing patterns in lizards. In *Biology of the Reptilia*, vol. 7, ed. C. Gans and D. W. Tinkle, 265–334. New York: Academic Press. (14)

Stangel, P. W., and R. D. Semlitsch. 1987. Experimental analysis of predation on the diel vertical migrations of a larval salamander. *Canadian Journal of Zoology* 65:1554–1558. (9,14)

Stanton, B. 1988. Electroneutral NaCl transport by distal tubule: Evidence for Na^+/H^+-Cl^-/HCO_3^- exchange. *American Journal of Physiology* 254:F80–F86. (5)

Stanton, B., D. Biemsderfer, D. Stetson, M. Kashgarian, and G. Giebisch. 1984. Cellular ultrastructure of *Amphiuma* distal nephron: Effects of exposure to potassium. *American Journal of Physiology* 247:C204–C216. (5)

Stanton, B., A. Omerovic, B. Koeppen, and G. Giebisch. 1987. Electroneutral H^+ secretion in distal tubule of *Amphiuma*. *American Journal of Physiology* 252:F691–F699. (5)

Stark-Vancs, V., P. B. Bell, and V. H. Hutchison. 1984. Morphological and pharmacological bases for pulmonary function in *Amphiuma tridactylum*. *Cell and Tissue Research* 238:1–12. (9)

Starrett, P. H. 1973. Evolutionary patterns in larval morphology. In *The Evolutionary Biology of Anurans*, ed. J. L. Vial, 251–271. Columbia: University of Missouri Press. (14)

Stauffer, J. R., Jr., J. E. Gates, and W. L. Goodfellow. 1983. Preferred temperature of two sympatric *Ambystoma* larvae: A proximate factor in niche segregation? *Copeia* 1983:1001–1005. (9,14)

Stearnet, S. P. 1946. Pigmentation studies in salamanders, with special reference to the changes at metamorphosis. *Physiological Zoology* 19:375–403. (16)

Stearns, S. C. 1976. Life history tactics: A review of the ideas. *Quarterly Review of Biology* 51:3–47. (14)

Stebbins, R. C. 1954. Natural history of the salamanders of the plethodontid genus *Ensatina*. *University of California Publications in Zoology* 54:47–123. (15)

———. 1960. Effects of pinealectomy in the western fence lizard, *Sceloporus occidentalis*. *Copeia* 1960:276–283. (9)

———. 1966. *A Field Guide to Western Reptiles and Amphibians*. Boston: Houghton Mifflin Company. (10)

Steele, W. K., and G. N. Louw. 1988. Caecilians exhibit cutaneous respiration and high evaporative water loss. *South African Journal of Zoology* 23:134–135. (9)

Stefanelli, A. 1951. The Mauthnerian apparatus in Icthyopsida: Its nature and function and correlated problems of neurohistogenesis. *Quarterly Review of Biology* 26:17–34. (2)

Stefano, F. J. E., and A. O. Donoso. 1964. Hypophyso-adrenal regulation of moulting in the toad. *General and Comparative Endocrinology* 4:473–480. (3)

Stefanski, M., R. E. Gatten, Jr., and F. H. Pough. 1989. Activity metabolism of salamanders: Tolerance to dehydration. *Journal of Herpetology* 23:45–50. (12)

Stehouwer, D. J. 1987. The effect of tectotomy and decerebration on spontaneous and elicited behavior of tadpoles and juvenile frog. *Behavioral Neurosciences* 101:378–384. (16)

———. 1988. Metamorphosis of behavior in the bullfrog (*Rana catesbeiana*). *Developmental Psychobiology* 21:383–395. (16)

Stehouwer, D. J., and P. B. Farel. 1980. Central and peripheral controls of swimming in anuran larvae. *Brain Research* 195:323–335. (2,16)

———. 1981. Sensory interactions with a central motor program in anuran larvae. *Brain Research* 218:131–140. (2)

———. 1983. Development of hindlimb locomotor activity in the bullfrog (*Rana catesbeiana*) studied *in vitro*. *Science* 219:516–518. (2,16)

———. 1984. Development of hindlimb locomotor behavior in the frog. *Developmental Psychobiology* 17:217–232. (16)

Stene-Larsen, G., and K. B. Helle. 1978. Cardiac adrenoceptors in the frog. *Comparative Biochemistry and Physiology* 60C:165–173. (3)

Stephens, D. W., and J. R. Krebs. 1986. *Foraging Theory*. Princeton, NJ: Princeton University Press. (14)

Stephens, N., and N. Holder. 1985. A horseradish peroxidase study of motoneuron pools of the forelimb and hindlimb musculature of the axolotl. *Proceedings of the Royal Society of London* 224B:325–339. (11)

Sterba, G. 1950. Über die morphologischen und histogenetischen Thymusprobleme bei *Xenopus laevis* Daudin nebst einigen Bermerkungen über die Morphologie der Kaulquappen. *Abhandlungen der Sachsischen Akademie der Wissenschaften zu Leipzig: Mathematisch-naturwissenschaftliche Klasse* 44:1–54. (16)

Stern, S. L., and C. F. Mueller. 1972. Diurnal variation in the oxygen consumption of *Plethodon cinereus*. *American Midland Naturalist* 88:502–506. (12)

Stevens, E. D. 1979. The effect of temperature of tail beat frequency of fish swimming at constant velocity. *Canadian Journal of Zoology* 57:1628–1635. (8)

———. 1988a. Acclimation temperature markedly alters the motivation to feed in the toad *Bufo americanus*. *Journal of Thermal Biology* 13:73–78. (8,9,13)

———. 1988b. The effect of acclimation temperature on feeding performance in the toad *Bufo americanus*. *Comparative Biochemistry and Physiology* 89A:131–135. (13)

———. 1988c. Feeding performance of toads at different acclimation temperatures. *Canadian Journal of Zoology* 66:537–539. (8,9,13)

Stevens, E. D., and R. K. Josephson. 1977. Metabolic rate and body temperature in singing katydids. *Physiological Zoology* 50:31–42. (14)

Stevens, E. D., and J. M. McLeese. 1984. Why bluefin tunas have warm tummies: Temperature effect on trypsin and chymotrypsin. *American Journal of Physiology* 246:487–494. (8)

Stevenson, R. D. 1985a. Body size and limits to the daily range of body temperature in terrestrial ectotherms. *American Naturalist* 125:102–112. (4)

———. 1985b. The relative importance of behavioral and physiological adjustments controlling body temperature in terrestrial ectotherms. *American Naturalist* 126:362–386. (4)

Steward, J. W. 1969. *The Tailed Amphibians of Europe*. New York: Taplinger Publishing Company. (10)

Stewart, M. M., and F. H. Pough. 1983. Population density of tropical forest frogs: Relation to retreat sites. *Science* 221:570–572. (14)

Stieff, C. L., and J. C. Kaltenbach. 1986. Immunofluorescent detection and localization of thyroxine in blood of adult amphibians. *General and Comparative Endocrinology* 64:419–427. (3)

Stiffler, D. F. 1981. The effects of mesotocin on renal function in hypophysectomized *Ambystoma tigrinum* larvae. *General and Comparative Endocrinology* 45:49–55. (5)

———. 1988. Cutaneous exchange of ions in lower vertebrates. *American Zoologist* 28:1019–1029. (4,5,10)

Stiffler, D. F., and R. H. Alvarado. 1974. Renal function in response to reduced osmotic load in larval salamanders. *American Journal of Physiology* 226:1243–1249. (5,6,16)

———. 1980. Renal regulation of electrolytes in two species of ambystomatid salamanders. *Copeia* 1980:918–921. (5)

Stiffler, D. F., B. J. Atkins, L. D. Burt, and S. C. Roach. 1982. Control of renal function in larval *Ambystoma tigrinum*. *Journal of Comparative Physiology* 149:91–97. (5)

Stiffler, D. F., M. L. DeRuyter, P. B. Hanson, and M. Marshall. 1986. Interrenal function in larval *Ambystoma tigrinum*: 1. Responses to alterations in external electrolyte concentrations. *General and Comparative Endocrinology* 62:290–297. (5,16)

Stiffler, D. F., M. L. DeRuyter, and C. R. Talbot. 1990. Osmotic and ionic regulation in aquatic and terrestrial caecilians. *Physiological Zoology* 63:649–668. (5)

Stiffler, D. F., C. T. Hawk, and B. C. Fowler. 1980. Renal excretion of urea in the salamander, *Ambystoma tigrinum*. *Journal of Experimental Zoology* 213:205–212. (5)

Stiffler, D. F., S. C. Roach, and S. J. Pruett. 1984. A comparison of the responses of the amphibian kidney to mesotocin, isotocin, and oxytocin. *Physiological Zoology* 57:63–69. (5)

Stiffler, D. F., S. L. Ryan, and R. A. Mushkot. 1987. Interactions between acid-base balance and cutaneous ion transport in larval *Ambystoma tigrinum* (Amphibia: Caudata) in response to hypercapnia. *Journal of Experimental Biology* 130:389–404. (5)

Stiffler, D. F., B. L. Tufts, and D. P. Toews. 1983. Acid-base and ionic balance in *Ambystoma tigrinum* and *Necturus maculosus* during hypercapnia. *American Journal of Physiology* 245:R689–R694. (5)

Stille, W. T. 1951. The nocturnal amphibian fauna of the southern Lake Michigan beach. *Ecology* 33:149–162. (6)

———. 1958. The water absorption response of an anuran. *Copeia* 1958:217–218. (6)

Stinner, J. N. 1987. Thermal dependence of air convection requirement and blood gases in the snake *Coluber constrictor*. *American Zoologist* 27:41–47. (6)

Stinner, J. N., and V. H. Shoemaker. 1987. Cutaneous gas exchange and low evaporative water loss in the frogs *Phyllomedusa sauvagei* and *Chiromantis xerampelina*. *Journal of Comparative Physiology* 157B:423–427. (4,6)

Stirling, R. V., and K. Brandle. 1982. Expansion of the visual projection to the tectum of axolotls during metamorphosis. *Developmental Brain Research* 5:343–345. (16)

Stoner, L. C. 1977. Isolated, perfused amphibian renal tubules: The diluting segment. *American Journal of Physiology* 233:F438–F444. (5)

Storey, J. M., and K. B. Storey. 1985a. Freeze tolerance in the grey tree frog, *Hyla versicolor*. *Canadian Journal of Zoology* 63:49–54. (10)

———. 1985b. Triggering of cryoprotectant synthesis by the initiation of ice nucleation in the freeze tolerant frog, *Rana sylvatica*. *Journal of Comparative Physiology* 156B:191–195. (10)

Storey, K. B. 1984. Freeze tolerance in the frog, *Rana sylvatica*. *Experientia* 40:1261–1262. (10)

———. 1985a. Freeze tolerance in terrestrial frogs. *Cryo Letters* 6:115–134. (10)

———. 1985b. A re-evaluation of the Pasteur effect: New mechanisms in anaerobic metabolism. *Molecular Physiology* 8:439–461. (10)

———. 1987a. Glycolysis and the regulation of cryoprotectant synthesis in liver of the freeze tolerant wood frog. *Journal of Comparative Physiology* 157B:373–380. (10)

———. 1987b. Organ-specific metabolism during freezing and thawing in a freeze tolerant frog. *American Journal of Physiology* 253:R292–R297. (10)

———. 1988. Suspended animation: The molecular basis of metabolic depression. *Canadian Journal of Zoology* 66:124–132. (10)

———. 1990. Life in a frozen state: Adaptive strategies for natural freeze tolerance in amphibians and reptiles. *American Journal of Physiology* 258:R559–R568. (10)

Storey, K. B., and J. M. Storey. 1984. Biochemical adaptation for freezing tolerance in the wood frog, *Rana sylvatica*. *Journal of Comparative Physiology* 155B:29–36. (10)

———. 1986a. Freeze tolerance and intolerance as strategies of winter survival in terrestrially-hibernating amphibians. *Comparative Biochemistry and Physiology* 83A:613–617. (10)

———. 1986b. Freeze tolerant frogs: Cryoprotectants and tissue metabolism during freeze/thaw cycles. *Canadian Journal of Zoology* 64:49–56. (10)

———. 1987. Persistence of freeze tolerance in terrestrially hibernating frogs after spring emergence. *Copeia* 1987:720–726. (10)

———. 1988. Freeze tolerance in animals. *Physiological Reviews* 68:27–84. (10)

———. 1990. Facultative metabolic rate depression: Molecular regulation and biochemical adaptation in anaerobiosis, hibernation, and estivation. *Quarterly Review of Biology* 65:145–174. (10)

Storey, K. B., J. M. Storey, S. P. J. Brooks, T. A. Churchill, and R. J. Brooks. 1988. Hatchling turtles survive freezing during winter hibernation. *Proceedings of the National Academy of Sciences* 85:8350–8354. (10)

Straughan, I. R. 1975. An analysis of the mechanisms of mating call discrimination in the frogs *Hyla regilla* and *H. cadaverina*. *Copeia* 1975:415–424. (11)

Straus, E., and R. S. Yalow. 1979. Gastrointestinal peptides in the brain. *Federation Proceedings* 28:2320–2324. (9)

Strawinski, S. 1956. Vascularization of respiratory surfaces in ontogeny of the edible frog, *Rana esculenta*. *Zoologica Poloniae* 7:327–365. (16)

Streeter, V. L., and E. B. Wylie. 1975. *Fluid Mechanics*. New York: McGraw-Hill. (4)

Strübing, H. 1954. Über Vorzugstemperaturen von Amphibien. *Zeitschrift für Morphologie und Ökologie der Tiere* 43:357–386. (9)

Strüssmann, C., M. B. R. do Vale, M. H. Meneghini, and W. E. Magnusson. 1984. Diet and foraging mode in *Bufo marinus* and *Leptodactylus ocellatus*. *Journal of Herpetology* 18:138–146. (14)

Stuart, L. C. 1951. The distributional implications of temperature and hemoglobin values in the toads *Bufo marinus* (Linnaeus) and *Bufo bocourti* Brocchi. *Copeia* 1951:220–229. (9)

Stuesse, S. L., W. L. R. Cruce, and K. S. Powell. 1983. Afferent and efferent components of the hypoglossal nerve in the grass frog, *Rana pipiens*. *Journal of Comparative Physiology* 217:432–439. (11)

Sugimoto, K., Y. Ichikawa, and I. Nakamura. 1981. Absorption of protein molecules by the small intestine of the bullfrog tadpole *Rana catesbeiana*. *Journal of Experimental Zoology* 215:53–62. (13,16)

Sukhanov, V. B. 1974. *General System of Symmetrical Locomotion of Terrestrial Vertebrates and Some Features of Movement of Lower Tetrapods*. New Delhi: Amerind Publishing Company. (11)

Sullivan, B. 1974. Amphibian hemoglobins. In *Chemical Zoology*, ed. M. Florkin, and B. T. Scheer, 9:77–122. New York: Academic Press. (16)

Sullivan, B. K. 1982a. Sexual selection in Woodhouse's toad (*Bufo woodhousei*): 1. Chorus organization. *Animal Behaviour* 30:680–686. (14)

———. 1982b. Significance of size, temperature, and call attributes to sexual selection in *Bufo woodhousei australis*. *Journal of Herpetology* 16:103–106. (8,14)

———. 1983. Sexual selection in Woodhouse's toad (*Bufo woodhousei*): 2. Female choice. *Animal Behaviour* 31:1011–1017. (14)

———. 1984a. Advertisement call variation and observations on breeding behavior of *Bufo debilis* and *B. punctatus*. *Journal of Herpetology* 18:406–411. (8,9)

———. 1984b. Size dimorphism in anurans: A comment. *American Naturalist* 123:721–724. (14)

———. 1987. Sexual selection in Woodhouse's toad (*Bufo woodhousei*): 3. Seasonal variation in male mating success. *Animal Behaviour* 35:912–919. (14)

Sullivan, B. K., and M. J. Leek. 1987. Acoustic communication in Woodhouse's toad (*Bufo woodhousei*): 2. Response of females to variation in spectral and temporal components of advertisement calls. *Behaviour* 103:16–26. (2)

Sullivan, B. K., and G. E. Walsberg. 1985. Call rate and aerobic capacity in Woodhouse's toad (*Bufo woodhousei*). *Herpetologica* 41:404–407. (12,14)

Sullivan, W. J. 1968. Electrical potential differences across distal renal tubules of *Amphiuma*. *American Journal of Physiology* 214:1096–1103. (5)

Sulze, W. 1942. Über die physiologische Bedeutung des Kalksackchenapparates der Amphibien. *Archiv für die Gesamte Physiologie* 246:250–257. (5)

Suzuki, M. R., and S. Kikuyama. 1983. Corticoids augment nuclear binding capacity for triiodothyronine in bullfrog tadpole tail fins. *General and Comparative Endocrinology* 52:272–278. (3,16)

Suzuki, S., and M. Suzuki. 1981. Changes in thyroidal and plasma iodine compounds during and after metamorphosis of the bullfrog, *Rana catesbeiana*. *General and Comparative Endocrinology* 45:74–81. (16)

———. 1985. Plasma thyroxine and triiodothyronine levels during and after metamorphosis of *Rana ornativentris* and *Hynobius nigrescens*. In *Current Trends in Comparative Endocrinology*, ed. B. Lofts and W. N. Holmes, 545–546. Hong Kong: Hong Kong University Press. (16)

Svelto, M., C. Casavola, G. Valenti, and C. Lippe. 1982. Phloretin sensitive active urea absorption in frog skin. *Pflugers Archiv* 394:226–229. (5)

Swan, H., F. G. Reinhard, D. L. Caprio, and C. L. Schatte. 1981. Hypometabolic brain peptide from vertebrates capable of torpor. *Cryobiology* 18:598–602. (10)

Swan, L. W. 1952. Some environmental conditions influencing life at high altitudes. *Ecology* 33:109–111. (9)

Swanson, R. E. 1956. Creatinine secretion by the frog renal tubule. *American Journal of Physiology* 184:529–534. (5)

Swihart, R. K., N. A. Slade, and B. J. Bergstrom. 1988. Relating body size to the rate of home range use in mammals. *Ecology* 69:393–399. (14)

Swingle, W. W. 1921. The germ cells of Anurans: 1. The male sexual cycle of *Rana catesbeiana* larvae. *Journal of Experimental Zoology* 32:235–331. (15)

Szarski, H. 1964. The structure of respiratory organs in relation to body size in Amphibia. *Evolution* 18:118–126. (6)

———. 1983. Cell size and the concept of wasteful and frugal evolutionary strategies. *Journal of Theoretical Biology* 105:201–209. (12)

Tachi, C. 1963. Seasonal variations in the fat body and possible role of hypophysial factors in regulation of fat mobilization in the Japanese newt, *Triturus pyrrhogaster*. *Annotationes Zoologicae Japonenses* 36:7–13. (15)

Taglietti, V., and C. Casella. 1966. Stretch receptors stimulation in frog's lungs. *Pflugers Archiv* 292:297–308. (7)

———. 1968. Deflation receptors in frog's lungs. *Pflugers Archiv* 304:81–89. (7)

Taigen, T. L. 1983. Activity metabolism of anuran amphibians: Implications for the origin of endothermy. *American Naturalist* 121:94–109. (12)

Taigen, T. L., and C. A. Beuchat. 1984. Anaerobic threshold of anuran amphibians. *Physiological Zoology* 57:641–647. (12,14)

Taigen, T. L., S. B. Emerson, and F. H. Pough. 1982. Ecological correlates of anuran exercise. *Oecologia* (Berlin) 52:49–56. (12,14)

Taigen, T. L., and F. H. Pough. 1981. Activity metabolism of the toad (*Bufo americanus*): Ecological consequences of ontogenetic change. *Journal of Comparative Physiology* 144B:247–252. (12,14)

———. 1983. Prey preference, foraging behavior, and the metabolic characteristics of frogs. *American Naturalist* 122:509–520. (12,14)

———. 1985. Metabolic correlates of anuran behavior. *American Zoologist* 25:987–997. (12,14)

Taigen, T. L., and K. D. Wells. 1985. Energetics of vocalizations by an anuran amphibian. *Journal of Comparative Physiology* 155:163–170. (12,14)

Taigen, T. L., K. D. Wells, and R. L. Marsh. 1985. The enzymatic basis of high metabolic rates in calling frogs. *Physiological Zoology* 58:719–726. (11,12,14)

Takada, M. 1985. Differentiation of the active sodium transport system during metamorphosis in *Rana catesbeiana* skin in relation to cadmium and amiloride induced responses. *Japanese Journal of Physiology* 35:525–534. (16)

———. 1986. The short-term effect of prolactin on the active Na transport system of the tadpole skin during metamorphosis. *Comparative Biochemistry and Physiology* 85A:755–759. (5,16)

———. 1989. Effect of prolactin on the active Na transport across *Rana catesbeiana* skin during metamorphosis. *General and Comparative Endocrinology* 73:318–324. (16)

Takada, M., and Hara, K. 1988. T$_3$-induced differentiation of the electromotive force related to active Na transport across the skin of the neotenous urodele, *Ambystoma mexicanum*. *Comparative Biochemistry and Physiology* 89A:157–161. (5)

Takahashi, H., and H. Iwasawa. 1988. Interpopulation variations in clutch size and egg size in the Japanese salamander, *Hynobius nigrescens*. *Zoological Science* 5:1073–1081. (15)

Takei, K., Y. Oka, M. Satou, and K. Ueda. 1987. Distribution of motoneurons involved in the prey-catching behavior in the Japanese toad, *Bufo japonicus*. *Brain Research* 4:395–400. (11)

Takeuchi, N. 1958. The effect of temperature on the neuromuscular junction of the frog. *Japanese Journal of Physiology* 8:391–404. (8)

Takisawa, A., Y. Shimura, and K. Kaneko. 1976. Metamorphic changes in anuran muscles following thyroxine treatment. *Okajimas Folia Anatomica Japonica* (Tokyo) 53:253–278. (11)

Takisawa, A., and Y. Sunaga. 1951. Über die Entwicklung des *M. depressor mandibulae* bei Anuren im Laufe der Metamorphose. *Okajimas Folia Anatomica Japonica* (Tokyo) 23:273–293. (11)

Talbot, C. R., and M. E. Feder. 1989. Regional variation in cutaneous gas exchange in the bullfrog. *American Zoologist* 29:56A. (6)

Talesara, C. L., and V. Mala. 1978. A comparative study of histochemical profile of pectoralis and gastrocnemius muscles of the frog *Rana tigrina*, the lizards *Hemidactylus flaviviridis* and *Uromastix hardwickii*, and the turtle *Lissemys punctata*. *Indian Journal of Experimental Biology* 16:561–564. (11)

Tanaka, S., M. K. Park, H. Takikawa, and K. Wakabayashi. 1985. Comparative studies on the electric nature of amphibian gonadotropin. *General and Comparative Endocrinology* 59:110–119. (3)

Tanner, G. A. 1967. Micropuncture study of PAH and diodrast transport in *Necturus* kidney. *American Journal of Physiology* 212:1341–1346. (5)

Tanner, G. A., P. K. Carmines, and W. B. Kinter. 1979. Excretion of phenol red by the *Necturus* kidney. *American Journal of Physiology* 236:F442–F447. (5)

Tanner, G. A., and W. B. Kinter. 1966. Reabsorption and secretion of p-aminohippurate and diodrast in *Necturus* kidney. *American Journal of Physiology* 210:221–231. (5)

Tanner, W. W. 1952. A comparative study of the throat musculature in the Plethodontidae of Mexico and Central America. *University of Kansas Science Bulletin* 34:583–677. (11)

Tasaki, I., and K. Mitzutani. 1944. Comparative studies on the activities of the muscle evoked by two kinds of motor nerve fibres: 1. Myographic studies. *Japanese Journal of Medical Science and Biophysics* 10:237–244. (11)

Tashian, R. E., and C. Ray. 1957. The relation of oxygen consumption to temperature in some tropical, temperate, and boreal anuran amphibians. *Zoologica* 42:63–68. (12)

Tatarinov, L. P. 1957. Tongue movement mechanisms in tailless Amphibia. *Comptes Rendus de l'Académie des Sciences de l'URSS* 116:916–918. (11)

Taubenhaus, M., I. B. Fritz, and J. V. Morton. 1956. *In vitro* effects of steroids upon electrolyte transfer through frog skin. *Endocrinology* 59:458–462. (5)

Taurog, A., C. Oliver, R. L. Eskay, J. C. Porter, and J. M. McKenzie. 1974. The role of TRH in the neoteny of the Mexican axolotl (*Ambystoma mexicanum*). *General and Comparative Endocrinology* 24:267–279. (16)

Taxi, J. 1976. Morphology of the autonomic nervous system. In *Frog Neurobiology: A Handbook*, ed. R. Llinás and W. Precht, 93–150. Berlin: Springer-Verlag. (7)

Taylor, A. C. 1939. The effect of athyroidism and hyperthyroidism on the oxygen consumption of the adult salamander. *Journal of Experimental Zoology* 81:135–146. (12)

———. 1943. Development of the innervation pattern in the limb bud of the frog. *Anatomical Record* 87:379–413. (16)

Taylor, A. C., and J. Kollros. 1946. Stages in the normal development of *Rana pipiens* larvae. *Anatomical Reviews* 94:7–23. (5,6,7,16)

Taylor, C. R. 1985. Force development during sustained locomotion: A determinant of gait, speed, and metabolic power. *Journal of Experimental Biology* 115:253–262. (12)

Taylor, C. R., N. C. Heglund, T. A. McMahon, and T. R. Looney. 1980. The energetic cost of generating muscular force during running. *Journal of Experimental Biology* 86:9–18. (8)

Taylor, C. R., N. C. Heglund, and G. M. O. Maloiy. 1982. Energetics and mechanics of terrestrial locomotion: 1. Metabolic energy consumption as a function of speed and body size in birds and mammals. *Journal of Experimental Biology* 97:1–21. (12)

Taylor, C. R., K. Schmidt-Nielsen, and J. L. Raab. 1970. Scaling of energetic cost to body size in mammals. *American Journal of Physiology* 219:1104–1107. (12)

Taylor, C. R., and E. R. Weibel. 1981. Design of the mammalian respiratory system: 1. Problem and strategy. *Respiration Physiology* 44:1–10. (5)

Taylor, D. H., and K. Adler. 1978. The pineal body: Site of extraocular perception of celestial cues for orientation in the tiger salamander (*Ambystoma tigrinum*). *Journal of Comparative Physiology* 124:357–361. (9)

Taylor, D. H., and S. I. Guttman, eds. 1977. *The Reproductive Biology of Amphibians*. New York: Plenum Press. (15)

Taylor, E. H. 1954. Frog-egg-eating tadpoles of *Anotheca coronata* (Stejneger) (Salienta, Hylidae). *University of Kansas Science Bulletin* 36:589–596. (11)

———. 1968. *The Caecilians of the World: A Taxonomic Review*. Lawrence: University of Kansas Press. (11,13,14)

Taylor, P., C. G. Scroop, M. J. Tyler, and M. Davies. 1982. An ontogenetic and interspecific study of the renin-angiotensin system in Australian anuran Amphibia. *Comparative Biochemical Physiology* 73A:187–191. (16)

Taylor, P. M., and M. J. Tyler. 1986. Pepsin in the toad *Bufo marinus*. *Comparative Biochemistry and Physiology* 84A:669–672. (13)

Taylor, P. M., M. J. Tyler, and D. J. C. Shearman. 1985a. Gastric acid secretion in the toad *Bufo marinus* with the description of a new technique for *in vivo* monitoring. *Comparative Biochemistry and Physiology* 81A:325–327. (13)

———. 1985b. Gastric emptying and intestinal transit in *Bufo marinus* and the actions of E prostaglandins. *Australian Journal of Experimental Biology and Medical Science* 63:223–230. (13)

Taylor, R. E., Jr., and S. B. Barker. 1965a. Thyroxine and sodium transport by anuran membranes. *Journal of Endocrinology* 31:175–176. (16)

———. 1965b. Transepidermal potential differences: Development in anuran larvae. *Science* 148:12–13. (5,16)

———. 1967. Absence of an *in vitro* thyroxine effect on oxygen consumption and sodium or water transport by anuran skin and bladder. *General and Comparative Endocrinology* 9:129–134. (5)

Taylor, S., and D. Ewer. 1956. Moulting in the Anura: The normal moulting cycle of *Bufo regularis* Reuss. *Proceedings of the Royal Society of London* 127:435–440. (3)

Tazawa, H., M. Mochizuki, and J. Piiper. 1979a. Blood oxygen dissociation curve in the frogs *Rana catesbeiana* and *Rana brevipoda*. *Journal of Comparative Physiology* 129:111–114. (5,16)

———. 1979b. Respiratory gas transport by the incompletely separated double circulation in the bullfrog, *Rana catesbeiana*. *Respiration Physiology* 36:77–95. (5,12)

Tchau, S., and Y.-L. Wang. 1963. Hibernation, a critical factor in the maturation of the ovule of the toad *Bufo bufo asiaticus*. *Scientia Sinica* 12:1161–1164. (10)

Teeter, J. M., M. Funakoshi, S. Kurihara, S. Roper, T. Suto, and K. Tonosaki. 1987. Generation of taste cell potential. *Chemical Senses* 12:217–234. (16)

Templeton, J. R. 1970. Reptiles. In *Comparative Physiology of Thermoregulation*, vol. 1, *Invertebrates and Nonmammalian Vertebrates*, ed. G. C. Whittow, 167–222. New York: Academic Press. (9)

———. 1971. Peripheral and central control of panting in the desert iguana, *Dipsosaurus dorsalis*. *Journal of Physiology* (Paris) 63:439–442. (9)

ten Donkelaar, H. J., and R. de Boer–van Huizen. 1982. Observations on the development of descending pathways from the brainstem to the spinal cord in the clawed toad *Xenopus laevis*. *Anatomy and Embryology* 163:461–473. (2)

ten Donkelaar, H. J., R. de Boer–van Huizen, F. T. M. Schouten, and S. J. H. Eggen. 1981. Cells of origin of descending pathways to the spinal cord in the clawed toad (*Xenopus laevis*). *Neuroscience* 6:2297–2312. (2)

Tenney, S. M. 1979. A synopsis of breathing mechanisms. In *Evolution of Respiratory Processes: A Comparative Approach*, vol. 13, *Lung Biology in Health and Disease*, ed. S. C. Wood and C. Lenfant, 51–106. New York: Marcel Dekker. (6)

Tenney, S. M., and T. W. Lamb. 1965. Physiological consequences of hypoventilation and hyperventilation. In *Handbook of Physiology: Respiration*, ed. W. O. Fenn and H. Rahn, 2:979–1010. Washington, DC: American Physiological Society. (7)

Tenney, S. M., and J. B. Tenney. 1970. Quantitative morphology of cold-blooded lungs: Amphibia and Reptilia. *Respiration Physiology* 9:197–215. (6)

Tercafs, R. R. 1966. Chromatophores and permeability characteristics of frog skin. *Comparative Biochemistry and Physiology* 17:937–951. (9)

Terentlev, P. V. 1950. *The Frog*. Moscow: Sovetskaya Nauka. (16)

Terhivno, J. 1981. Provisional atlas and population status of the Finnish amphibian and reptile species with reference to their range in northern Europe. *Annales Zoologici Fennici* 18:139–164. (15)

———. 1988. Phenology of spawning for the common frog (*Rana temporaria* L.) in Finland from 1846 to 1986. *Annales Zoologici Fennici* 25:165–175. (15)

Terlou, M., and H. W. M. van Straaten. 1973. The development of a hypothalamic monoaminergic system for the regulation of the pars intermedia activity in *Xenopus laevis*. *Zeitschrift für Zellforschung und mikroskopische Anatomie* 143:229–238. (16)

Terroine, E. F., and G. Delpech. 1931. La loi des surfaces et les vertébrés poikilothermes. *Annales de Physiologie* 7:341–379. (12)

Tester, J. R., A. Parker, and D. B. Siniff. 1965. Experimental studies on habitat preference and thermoregulation of *Bufo americanus, B. hemiophrys*, and *B. cognatus*. *Journal of the Minnesota Academy of Science* 33:27–32. (9)

Teulon, J., and T. Anagnostopoulos. 1982. The electrical profile of the distal tubule in *Triturus* kidney. *Pflugers Archiv* 395:138–144. (5)

Teyssedre, C., and T. Halliday. 1986. Cumulative effect of male's display in the sexual behaviour of the smooth newt *Triturus vulgaris* (Urodela, Salamandridae). *Ethology* 71:89–102. (14)

Thexton, A. J., D. B. Wake, and M. H. Wake. 1977. Tongue function in the salamander *Bolitoglossa occidentalis*. *Archives of Oral Biology* 22:361–366. (11,14)

Thillart, G. van den. 1982. Adaptations of fish energy metabolism to hypoxia and anoxia. *Molecular Physiology* 2:49–61. (10)

Thompson, C. C., C. Weinberger, R. Lebo, and R. M. Evans. 1987. Identification of a novel thyroid hormone receptor expressed in the mammalian central nervous system. *Science* 237:1610–1614. (16)

Thoren, P. 1981. Characteristics and reflex effects of aortic baroreceptors with non-medullated afferents in rabbit and rat. *Advances in Physiological Science* 9:85–94. (7)

Thorson, T. B. 1955. The relationship of water economy to terrestrialism in amphibians. *Ecology* 36:100–116. (6,10,12)

———. 1964. The partitioning of body water in Amphibia. *Physiological Zoology* 37:395–399. (5)

Thorson, T. B., and A. Svihla. 1943. Correlation of the habitats of amphibians with their ability to survive the loss of body water. *Ecology* 24:374–381. (6,12)

Thurmond, W., W. Kloas, and W. Hanke. 1986a. Circadian rhythms of interrenal activity in *Xenopus laevis*. *General and Comparative Endocrinology* 61:260–271. (3)

———. 1986b. The distribution of interrenal stimulating activity in the brain of *Xenopus laevis*. *General and Comparative Endocrinology* 63:117–124. (3)

Thyagaraja, B. S., and H. B. D. Sarkar. 1971. Male reproductive cycle in the toad *Bufo melanostictus* Schn. *Science Journal of the Mysore University* 24:27–36. (15)

Tiegs, D. W. 1953. Innervation of voluntary muscle. *Physiological Reviews* 33:90–144. (11)

Tilley, S. G. 1964. A quantitative study of the shrinkage in the digestive tract of the tiger salamander (*Ambystoma tigrinum* Green) during metamorphosis. *Journal of the Ohio Herpetological Society* 4:81–85. (16)

———. 1968. Size-fecundity relationships and their evolutionary implications in five desmognathine salamanders. *Evolution* 22:806–816. (15)

———. 1970. Aspects of the reproductive and population ecology of *Desmognathus ochrophaeus* in the southern Appalachian Mountains. Ph.D. diss., University of Michigan, Ann Arbor. (15)

———. 1977. Studies of life histories and reproduction in North American plethodontid salamanders. In *The Reproductive Biology of Amphibians*, ed. D. H. Taylor and S. I. Guttman, 1–41. New York: Plenum Press. (15)

———. 1980. Life histories and comparative demography of two salamander populations. *Copeia* 1980:806–821. (15)

Tilley, S. G., and D. W. Tinkle. 1968. A reinterpretation of the reproductive cycle and demography of the salamander *Desmognathus ochrophaeus*. *Copeia* 1968:299–303. (15)

Ting, H.-P., and A. M. Boring. 1940. The seasonal cycle in the reproductive organs of the Chinese toad *Bufo bufo* and the pond frog. *Rana nigromaculata*. *Peking Natural History Bulletin* 14:49–80. (15)

Tinkle, D. W. 1967. The life and demography of the side-blotched lizard, *Uta stansburiana*. *Miscellaneous Publications, Museum of Zoology, University of Michigan* 132:1–182. (9)

Tobias, M. L., and D. B. Kelley. 1987. Vocalization by a sexually dimorphic isolated larynx: Peripheral constraints on behavioral expression. *Journal of Neuroscience* 7:3191–3197. (14)

Toews, D. P. 1971. Factors affecting the onset and termination of ventilation in the salamander, *Amphiuma tridactylum*. *Canadian Journal of Zoology* 49:1231–1237. (5,7)

———. 1973. Oxygen consumption in *Amphiuma tridactylum*. *Canadian Journal of Zoology* 51:664–666. (12)

Toews, D. P., and R. G. Boutilier. 1986. Acid-base regulation in the Amphibia. In *Acid-Base Regulation in Animals*, ed. N. Heisler, 265–308. Amsterdam: Elsevier. (5,6,10,16)

Toews, D. P., R. G. Boutilier, L. Todd, and N. Fuller. 1978. Carbonic anhydrase in the Amphibia. *Comparative Biochemistry and Physiology* 59A:211–213. (5)

Toews, D. P., and N. Heisler. 1982. The effects of hypercapnia on intracellular and extracellular acid-base status in the toad, *Bufo marinus*. *Journal of Experimental Biology* 97:79–86. (5)

Toews, D. P., and S. Kirby. 1985. The ventilatory and acid-base physiology of the toad, *Bufo marinus*, during exposure to environmental hyperoxia. *Respiration Physiology* 59:225–230. (7)

Toews, D. P., and D. Macintyre. 1977. Blood respiratory properties of a viviparous amphibian. *Nature* 266:464–465. (5,16)

———. 1978. Respiration and circulation in an apodan amphibian. *Canadian Journal of Zoology* 56:998–1004. (5,16)

Toews, D. P., M. Mallet, and L. MacLatchy. 1989. Renal responses to continuous and short-pulse infusion of arginine vasotocin in the toad *Bufo marinus*. *Journal of Experimental Biology* 142:177–189. (5)

Toews, D. P., G. Shelton, and D. J. Randall. 1971. Gas tensions in the lungs and major blood vessels of the urodele amphibian, *Amphiuma tridactylum*. *Journal of Experimental Biology* 55:47–61. (5)

Toews, D. P., and D. F. Stiffler. 1989. The role of the amphibian kidney and bladder in the regulation of acid-base relevant ions. *Canadian Journal of Zoology* 67:3064–3069. (5)

———. 1990. Compensation of progressive hypercapnia in the toad *Bufo marinus* and the bullfrog *Rana catesbeiana*. *Journal of Experimental Biology* 148:293–302. (5)

Toft, C. A. 1980a. Feeding ecology of thirteen syntopic species of anurans in a seasonal tropical environment. *Oecologia* (Berlin) 45:131–141. (13,14)

———. 1980b. Seasonal variation in populations of Panamanian litter frogs and their prey: A comparison of wetter and drier sites. *Oecologia* (Berlin) 47:34–38. (14)

———. 1981. Feeding ecology of Panamanian litter anurans: Patterns in diet and foraging mode. *Journal of Herpetology* 15:139–144. (14)

———. 1982. Community structure of litter anurans in a tropical forest, Makoku, Gabon: A preliminary analysis in the minor dry season. *Revue d'Écologie* (la Terre et la Vie) 36:223–232. (14)

———. 1985. Resource partitioning in amphibians and reptiles. *Copeia* 1985:1–21. (13,14)

Tokarz, R. R. 1978. Oogonial proliferation, oogenesis, and folliculogenesis in nonmammalian vertebrates. In *The Vertebrate Ovary*, ed. R. E. Jones, 145–179. New York: Plenum Press. (15)

Toldt, C. 1870. Beiträge zur Histologie und Physiologie des Fettgewebes. *Sitzungsberichte der Akademie der Wissenschaften in Wien, Mathematisch-naturwissenschaftliche Klasse* 62:445–467. (15)

Tomlinson, R. W. S., and A. W. Wood. 1976. Catecholamine-induced changes in ion transport in short-circuit frog skin and the effect of β-blockade. *Journal of Physiology* (London) 257:515–530. (5)

Tomori, Z., and J. B. Widdicombe. 1969. Muscular, bronchomotor, and cardiovascular effects elicited by mechanical stimulation of the respiratory tract. *Journal of Physiology* (London) 200:25–49. (7)

Tonon, M. C., A. Burlet, M. Lauber, P. Cuet, S. Jégou, L. Grouteux, N. Ling, and H. Vaudry. 1985. Immunohistochemical localization and radioimmunoassay of corticotropin-releasing factor in the forebrain and hypophysis of the frog *Rana ridibunda*. *Neuroendocrinology* 40:109–119. (16)

Tonon, M. C., P. Cuet, M. Lamacz, S. Jégou, J. Cote, L. Gouteux, N. Ling, G. Pelletier, and H. Vaudry. 1986. Comparative effects of corticotropin-releasing factor, arginine vasopressin, and related neuropeptides on the secretion of ACTH and α-MSH by frog anterior pituitary cells and neurointermediate lobes *in vitro*. *General and Comparative Endocrinology* 61:438–445. (16)

Tonon, M. C., F. Leboulenger, C. Delarue, S. Jégou, J. Fresel, P. Leroux, and H. Vaudry. 1980. TRH as MSH-releasing factor in the frog. In *Biochemical Endocrinology: Synthesis and Release of Adenohypophyseal Hormones*, ed. M. Jutisz and K. McKerns, 731–751. New York: Plenum Press. (3)

Tonon, M. C., P. Leroux, S. Jégou, P. Saulot, C. Delarue, P. Leboulenger, I. Perroteau, P. Netchitaïlo, G. Pelletier, and H. Vaudry. 1985. Control of amphibian alpha melanotropin (α-MSH) release by catecholamines and thyroliberin (TSH). In *Current Trends in Comparative Endocrinology*, ed. B. Lofts and W. N. Holmes, 91–93. Hong Kong: Hong Kong University Press. (3)

Tonon, M. C., P. Leroux, M. E. Stoeckel, S. Jégou, G. Pelletier, and H. Vaudry. 1983. Catecholaminergic control of α-melanocyte-stimulating hormone (α-MSH) release by frog neurointermediate lobes *in vitro*. *Endocrinology* 112:133–141. (3)

Totland, G. K. 1976a. Histological and histochemical studies of segmental muscle in the axolotl *Ambystoma mexicanum* Shaw (Amphibia: Urodela). *Norwegian Journal of Zoology* 24:79–90. (11)

———. 1976b. Three muscle fibre types in the axial muscle of axolotl (*Ambystoma mexicanum* Shaw). A quantitative light- and electron microscopic study. *Cell and Tissue Research* 168:65–78. (11)

Townsend, C. R., and P. Calow, eds. 1981. *Physiological Ecology: An Evolutionary Approach to Resource Use*. Sunderland, MA: Sinauer Associates. (14)

Townsend, D. S. 1984. The adaptive significance of male parental care in a Neotropical frog. Ph.D. diss., State University of New York, Albany. (14)

Townsend, D. S., and M. M. Stewart. 1985. Direct development in *Eleutherodactylus coqui* (Anura: Leptodactylidae): A staging table. *Copeia* 1985:423–436. (16)

———. 1986a. Courtship and mating behavior of a Puerto Rican frog, *Eleutherodactylus coqui*. *Herpetologica* 42:165–170. (11)

———. 1986b. The effect of temperature on the direct development in a terrestrial breeding Neotropical frog. *Copeia* 1986:520–523. (8)

Townsend, D. S., M. M. Stewart, and F. H. Pough. 1984. Male parental care and its adaptive significance in a Neotropical frog. *Animal Behaviour* 32:421–431. (14)

Toyoshima, S., and H. Iwasawa. 1984a. Annual dynamics of germ cells in male *Hyla japonica*. *Herpetologica* 40:308–313. (15)

———. 1984b. Changes in the effect of light-cycles on spermatogenetic activity by temperature in late autumn frogs of *Hyla japonica*. *Science Reports of Niigata University*, series D (Biology) 21:9–13. (15)

———. 1984c. An estimate of spermatogenous duration in the tree frog *Hyla japonica*. *Science Reports of Niigata University*, series D (Biology) 21:1–8. (15)

Tracy, C. R. 1973. Observations on social behavior in immature California toads (*Bufo boreas*) during feeding. *Copeia* 1973:342–345. (13)

———. 1975. Water and energy relations of terrestrial amphibians: Insights from mechanistic modeling. In *Perspectives of Biophysical Ecology*, ed. D. M. Gates and R. B. Schmerl, 325–346. New York: Springer-Verlag. (4,9)

———. 1976. A model of the dynamic exchange of water and energy between a terrestrial amphibian and its environment. *Ecological Monographs* 46:293–326. (4,6,9,14)

———. 1979a. Emissivity: A little explored variable: Discussion. In *The Behavioral Significance of Color*, ed. E. H. Burtt, Jr., 28–32. New York: Garland Press. (4)

———. 1979b. Further thoughts on anuran thermoregulation: Discussion. In *The Behavioral Significance of Color*, ed. E. H. Burtt, Jr., 63–67. New York: Garland Press. (8,9)

———. 1982. Biophysical modeling in reptilian physiology and ecology. In *Biology of the Reptilia*, vol. 12, ed. C. Gans and F. H. Pough, 275–321. New York: Academic Press. (4)

Tracy, C. R., and K. A. Christian. 1986. Ecological relations among space, time, and thermal niche axes. *Ecology* 67:609–615. (4)

Tracy, C. R., and W. L. Rubink. 1978. The role of dehydration and antidiuretic hormone on water exchange in *Rana pipiens*. *Comparative Biochemistry and Physiology* 61A:559–562. (4)

Tracy, C. R., and P. R. Sotherland. 1979. Boundary layers of bird eggs: Do they ever constitute a significant barrier to water loss? *Physiological Zoology* 52:63–66. (4)

Tracy, C. R., J. S. Turner, and R. B. Huey. 1986. A biophysical analysis of possible thermoregulatory adaptations in sailed pelycosaurs. In *The Ecology and Biology of Mammal-like Reptiles*, ed. N. Hotton III, P. D. MacLean, J. J. Roth, and E. C. Roth, 195–206. Washington, DC: Smithsonian Institution Press. (4)

Tracy, C. R., F. H. van Berkum, J. S. Tsuji, R. D. Stevenson, J. A. Nelson, B. M. Barnes, and R. B. Huey. 1984. Errors resulting from linear approximations in energy balance equations. *Journal of Thermal Biology* 9:261–264. (4)

Tracy, C. R., W. R. Welch, and W. P. Porter. 1980. *Properties of Air: A Manual for Use in Biophysical Ecology*. Technical Report 1, Madison: University of Wisconsin. (4,6,8)

Travis, J. 1980. Genetic variation for larval specific growth rate in the frog *Hyla gratiosa*. *Growth* 44:167–181. (14)

Treilhou-Lahille, F., A. Jullienne, M. Aziz, A. Beaumont, and M. S. Moukhtar. 1984. Ultrastructural localization of immunoreactive calcitonin in the two cell types of the ultimobranchial gland of the common toad (*Bufo bufo* L.). *General and Comparative Endocrinology* 53:241–251. (3)

Tretjakoff, D. 1906. Der Musculus protractor lentis im Urodelenauge. *Anatomischer Anzeiger* 28:25–32. (11)

Trewavas, E. 1933. The hyoid and larynx of the Anura. *Philosophical Transactions of the Royal Society* (London) 58:719–726. (14)

Tripathi, S., and E. L. Boulpaep. 1988. Cell membrane water permeabilities and streaming currents in *Ambystoma* proximal tubule. *American Journal of Physiology* 255:F188–F203. (5)

Tripp, J. B., and S. Lustick. 1974. The effects of heating and cooling in water on the heart rate of the bullfrog. *Comparative Biochemistry and Physiology* 48A:547–554. (9)

Trivers, R. L. 1972. Parental investment and sexual selection. In *Sexual Selection and the Descent of Man*, ed. B. Campbell, 136–179. Chicago: Aldine. (14)

Trowbridge, A. H., and M. S. Trowbridge. 1937. Notes on the cleavage rate of *Scaphiopus bombifrons* (Cope), with additional remarks on certain aspects of its life history. *American Naturalist* 71:460–480. (15)

Truchot, J.-P. 1987. *Comparative Aspects of Extracellular Acid-Base Balance*. Berlin: Springer-Verlag. (16)

———. 1988. Problems of acid-base balance in rapidly changing intertidal environments. *American Zoologist* 28:55–64. (14)

Trueb, L. 1985. Summary of osteocranial development in anurans on the sequence of cranial ossification in *Rhinophrynus dorsalis* (Anura; Pipoidea: Rhinophrynidae). *South American Journal of Science* 81:181–185. (16)

Trueb, L., and P. Alberch. 1985. Miniaturization and the anuran skull: A case study of heterochrony. In *International Symposium on Vertebrate Morphology*, ed. H. R. Duncker and G. Fleischer, Fortschritte der Zoologie, 30:113. Stuttgart: Gustav Fischer. (11)

Trueb, L., and C. Gans. 1983. Feeding specializations of the Mexican burrowing toad, *Rhinophrynus dorsalis* (Anura: Rhinophrynidae). *Journal of Zoology* 199:198–208. (11,14)

Tsin, A. T. C., and D. D. Beatty. 1980. Visual pigments and vitamin A in the adult bullfrog. *Experimental Eye Research* 30:143–154. (8)

Tsugawa, K. 1976. Direct adaptation of cells to temperature: Similar changes of LDH isozyme patterns by *in vitro* and *in situ* adaptations in *Xenopus laevis*. *Comparative Biochemistry and Physiology* 55B:259–263. (8)

———. 1980. Thermal dependence in kinetic properties of lactate dehydrogenase from the African clawed toad, *Xenopus laevis*. *Comparative Biochemistry and Physiology* 66B:459–466. (8)

———. 1982. Effects of cold acclimation on the standard metabolic rate and osmotic fragility of erythrocytes in an aquatic Anura, *Xenopus laevis*. *Comparative Biochemistry and Physiology* 73A:431–436. (8,12)

Tucker, V. L., and V. H. Huxley. 1987. Multiplicative response of capillary water transfer to abluminal and luminal O_2 lack. *Physiologist* 30:217. (10)

Tuft, P. 1961. Role of water-regulating mechanisms in amphibian morphogenesis: A quantitative hypothesis. *Nature* 192:1049–1051. (16)

Tufts, B. L., D. C. Mense, and D. J. Randall. 1987. The effects of forced activity on circulating catecholamines and pH and water content of erythrocytes in the toad. *Journal of Experimental Biology* 128:411–418. (5)

Tufts, B. L., M. Nikinmaa, J. F. Steffensen, and D. J. Randall. 1987. Ion exchange mechanisms on the erythrocyte membrane of the aquatic salamander, *Amphiuma tridactylum*. *Journal of Experimental Biology* 133:329–338. (5)

Tufts, B. L., and D. P. Toews. 1985. Partitioning of regulatory sites in *Bufo marinus* during hypercapnia. *Journal of Experimental Biology* 119:199–209. (5,10)

———. 1986. Renal function and acid-base balance in the toad *Bufo marinus* during short-term dehydration. *Canadian Journal of Zoology* 64:1054–1057. (5,6,10)

Turner, D. L., and P. J. Butler. 1988. The aerobic capacity of locomotory muscles in the tufted duck, *Aythya fuligula*. *Journal of Experimental Biology* 135:445–460. (14)

Turner, F. B. 1958. Life-history of the western spotted frog in Yellowstone National Park. *Herpetologica* 14:96–100. (15)

———. 1960a. Population structure and dynamics of the western spotted frog, *Rana p. pretiosa* Baird and Girard, in Yellowstone Park, Wyoming. *Ecological Monographs* 30:251–278. (15)

———. 1960b. Postmetamorphic growth in anurans. *American Midland Naturalist* 64:327–338. (15)

Turner, J. S. 1987. On the transient temperatures of ectotherms. *Journal of Thermal Biology* 12:207–214. (4)

Turner, J. S., and C. R. Tracy. 1985. Body size and the control of heat exchange in alligators. *Journal of Thermal Biology* 10:9–11. (4)

———. 1986. Body size, homeothermy, and the control of heat exchange in mammal-like reptiles. In *The Ecology and Biology of Mammal-like Reptiles,* ed. N. Hotton III, P. D. MacLean, J. J. Roth, and E. C. Roth, 185–194. Washington, DC: Smithsonian Institution Press. (4)

Turner, R. J. 1988. Amphibians. In *Vertebrate Blood Cells,* ed. A. F. Rowley and N. A. Ratcliffe, 129–209. Cambridge: Cambridge University Press. (5)

Turney, L. D., and V. H. Hutchison. 1974. Metabolic scope, oxygen debt, and the diurnal oxygen consumption cycle of the leopard frog, *Rana pipiens*. *Comparative Biochemistry and Physiology* 49A:583–601. (9,12)

Tuttle, M. D., and M. J. Ryan. 1982. Bat predation and the evolution of anuran vocalizations. *Science* 214:677–678. (14)

Tuttle, M. D., L. K. Taft, and M. J. Ryan. 1981. Acoustical location of calling frogs by *Philander* opossums. *Biotropica* 13:233–234. (14)

———. 1982. Evasive behaviour of a frog in response to bat predation. *Animal Behaviour* 30:393–397. (14)

Twain, M. 1867. *The Celebrated Jumping Frog of Calavaras County, and Other Sketches*. New York: C. H. Webb. (12)

Tyler, M. J. 1971a. Observations on anuran myo-integumental attachments associated with the vocal sac apparatus. *Journal of Natural History* 5:225–231. (11)

———. 1971b. The phylogenetic significance of vocal sac structure in hylid frogs. *University of Kansas Publications, Museum of Natural History* 19:316–360. (11)

———. 1974. Superficial mandibular musculature and vocal sac structure of the Mexican burrowing toad, *Rhinophrynus dorsalis*. *Herpetologica* 30:313–316. (11)

———. 1982. *Frogs*. Australian Naturalist Library. Sydney: William Collins. (13)

Tyler, M. J., and D. B. Carter. 1981. Oral birth of the young of the gastric brooding frog *Rheobatrachus silus*. *Animal Behaviour* 29:280–282. (13,14)

Tyler, M. J., D. J. C. Shearman, R. Franco, P. O'Brien, R. F. Seamark, and R. Kelly. 1983. Inhibition of gastric acid secretion in the gastric brooding frog *Rheobatrachus silus*. *Science* 220:609–610. (13)

Uchiyama, M., and P. K. T. Pang. 1981. Endocrine influence on hypercalcemic regulation in bullfrog tadpoles. *General and Comparative Endocrinology* 44:428–435. (3,16)

———. 1985. Renal and vascular responses to AVT and its antagonistic analog (KB IV-24) in the lungfish, mudpuppy, and bullfrog. In *Current Trends in Comparative Endocrinology,* ed. B. Lofts and W. N. Holmes, 929–932. Hong Kong: Hong Kong University Press. (3)

Udin, S. B. 1986. The development of the map from the nucleus isthmi: The influence of visual experience on the formation of orderly connections in the visual system. In *Development of Order in the Visual System,* ed. S. R. Hilfer and J. B. Sheffield, 15–34. Berlin: Springer-Verlag. (16)

Ueck, M. 1967. Der Manicotto glandular ("Drusenmagen") der Anurenlarve in Bau, Funktion, und Beziehung zur Gesamtranges des Darmes: Eine mikroskopisch-anatomische, histochemische, und

elektronenoptische Studie an der omnivoren und mikrophagen Larve von *Xenopus laevis* und der carnivoren und makrophagen Larve von *Hymenochirus boettgeri* (Anura, Pipidae). *Zeitschrift für wissenschaftliche Zoologie* 176:173–270. (16)

Uhlenhuth, E., and F. McGowan. 1924. The growth of the thyroid and post-branchial body of the salamander, *Ambystoma opacum*. *Journal of General Physiology* 6:597–602. (16)

Uhrik, B., and H. Schmidt. 1973. Distribution of slow muscle fibres in the frog rectus abdominis muscle: An electron microscopical investigation. *Pflugers Archiv* 340:361–366. (11)

Ultsch, G. R. 1973a. The effects of water hyacinths (*Eichhornia crassipes*) on the microenvironment of aquatic communities. *Archiv für Hydrobiologie* (Stuttgart) 72:460–473. (7)

———. 1973b. A theoretical and experimental investigation of the relationships between metabolic rate, body size, and oxygen exchange capacity. *Respiration Physiology* 18:143–160. (10,12)

———. 1974a. Gas exchange and metabolism in the Sirenidae (Amphibia: Caudata): 1. Oxygen consumption of submerged sirenids as a function of body size and respiratory surface area. *Comparative Biochemistry and Physiology* 47A:485–498. (5,6,10,12)

———. 1974b. *In vivo* permeability coefficient to oxygen of the skin of *Siren intermedia*. *American Journal of Physiology* 226:1219–1220. (12)

———. 1976a. Ecophysiological studies of some metabolic and respiratory adaptations of sirenid salamanders. In *Respiration of Amphibious Vertebrates,* ed. G. M. Hughes, 287–312. New York: Academic Press. (5,12)

———. 1976b. Respiratory surface area as a factor controlling the standard rate of O_2 consumption of aquatic salamanders. *Respiration Physiology* 26:357–369. (10,12)

Ultsch, G. R., and D. S. Anthony. 1973. The role of the aquatic exchange of carbon dioxide in the ecology of the water hyacinth (*Eichhornia crassipes*). *Florida Scientist* (Orlando) 36:16–22. (7)

Ultsch, G. R., C. V. Herbert, and D. C. Jackson. 1984. The comparative physiology of diving in North American freshwater turtles: 1. Submergence tolerance, gas exchange, and acid-base balance. *Physiological Zoology* 57:620–631. (10)

Uranga, J., and W. H. Sawyer. 1960. Renal responses of the bullfrog to oxytocin, arginine-vasotocin, and frog neurohypophysial extract. *American Journal of Physiology* 198:1287–1290. (5)

Urano, A., and A. Gorbman. 1981. Effects of pituitary hormonal treatment on responsiveness of anterior preoptic neurons in male leopard frogs, *Rana pipiens*. *Journal of Comparative Physiology* 141:163–171. (2)

Ushakov, B. P., and I. M. Pashkova. 1986. Population analysis of thermal responses: Changes in the rate of development of salamander larvae. *Journal of Thermal Biology* 11:167–173. (8)

Ussing, H. H. 1949. The active ion transport through the isolated frog skin in the light of tracer studies. *Acta Physiologica Scandinavica* 17:1–37. (5)

———. 1982. Volume regulation in frog skin epithelium. *Acta Physiologica Scandinavica* 114:363–369. (5)

Ussing, H. H., D. Erlij, and U. Lassen. 1974. Transport pathways in biological membranes. *Annual Review of Physiology* 36:17–49. (16)

Ussing, H. H., and E. E. Windhager. 1964. Nature of shunt path and active sodium transport path through frog skin epithelium. *Acta Physiologica Scandinavica* 61:484–504. (5)

Ussing, H. H., and K. Zerahn. 1951. Active transport of sodium as the source of electric current in the short-circuited isolated frog skin. *Acta Physiologica Scandinavica* 23:110–127. (5)

Usui, M., and Hamasaki, M. 1939. Tafeln zur Entwicklungeschichte von *Hynobius nigrescens* Stejneger. *Zoological Magazine* (Tokyo) 51:195–206. (16)

Uwa, H., Y. Watanabe, Y. Sakakura, S. Asai, and H. Shiono. 1981. Estimation of the spring emergence of the toad *Bufo bufo* using underground temperature. *Zoological Magazine* (Tokyo) 90:157–163. (8)

Valdivieso, D., and J. R. Tamsitt. 1974. Thermal relations of the Neotropical frog *Hyla labialis* (Anura: Hylidae). *Royal Ontario Museum Life Sciences Occasional Papers* 26:1–10. (9)

Vale, W., J. Spiess, C. Rivier, and J. Rivier. 1981. Characterization of a 41-residue ovine hypothalamic peptide that stimulates secretion of corticotropin and β-endorphin. *Science* 213:1394–1397. (16)

Vanatta, J. C., and L. W. Frazier. 1981. The epithelium of *Rana pipiens* excretes H$^+$ and NH$_4$$^+$ in acidosis and HCO$_3$$^-$ in alkalosis. *Comparative Biochemistry and Physiology* 68A:511–513. (5)

———. 1982. The uptake of glucose by the skin of *Rana pipiens*. *Comparative Biochemistry and Physiology* 72A:603–606. (5)

van Bergeijk, W. A. 1954. Hydrostatic balancing mechanism of *Xenopus* larvae. *Journal of the Acoustic Society of America* 31:1340–1347. (16)

———. 1967. Anticipatory feeding behaviour in the bullfrog (*Rana catesbeiana*). *Animal Behaviour* 15:231–238. (13)

van Berkum, F. H. 1986. Evolutionary patterns of the thermal sensitivity of sprint speed in *Anolis* lizards. *Evolution* 40:594–604. (8,9)

van Berkum, F. H., R. B. Huey, and B. A. Adams. 1986. Physiological consequences of thermoregulation in a tropical lizard (*Ameiva festiva*). *Physiological Zoology* 59:464–472. (14)

van Berkum, F. H., F. H. Pough, M. M. Stewart, and P. F. Brussard. 1982. Altitudinal and interspecific differences in the rehydration abilities of Puerto Rican frogs (*Eleutherodactylus*). *Physiological Zoology* 55:130–136. (6,14)

van Beurden, E. K. 1979. Gamete development in relation to season, moisture, energy reserve, and size in the Australian water-holding frog *Cyclorana platycephalus*. *Herpetologica* 35:370–374. (15)

———. 1980. Energy metabolism of dormant Australian water-holding frogs (*Cyclorana platycephalus*). *Copeia* 1980:787–799. (10,12,14)

———. 1984. Survival strategies of the Australian water-holding frog, *Cyclorana platycephalus*. In *Arid Australia*, ed. H. G. Cogger and E. E. Cameron, 223–234. Sydney: Australian Museum. (6)

Van der Heiden, U., and G. Roth. 1987. Mathematical model and simulation of retina and tectum opticum of lower vertebrates. *Acta Biotheoretica* 36:179–212. (13)

Vandesande, F., and M. R. Aspeslagh. 1974. Failure of the thyrotropin-releasing hormone to increase I^{125} uptake by the thyroid in *Rana temporaria*. *General and Comparative Endocrinology* 23:355–356. (16)

van de Veerdonk, F. C. G. 1967. Demonstration of melatonin in Amphibia. *Current Medical Biology* 1:175–177. (16)

van de Veerdonk, F. C. G., and E. Brouwer. 1973. Role of calcium and prostaglandin (PGE$_1$) in the MSH-induced activation of adenylate cyclase in *Xenopus laevis*. *Biochemical and Biophysical Research Communications* 52:130–136. (3)

van Dongen, W. J., C. B. Jørgensen, L. O. Larsen, P. Rosenkilde, B. Lofts, and P. G. W. J. van Oordt. 1966. Function and cytology of the normal and autotransplanted pars distalis of the hypophysis in the toad *Bufo Bufo* (L.). *General and Comparative Endocrinology* 6:491–518. (15)

Van Driessche, W., and S. D. Hillyard. 1985. Quinidine blockage of K$^+$ channels in basolateral membrane of the larval bullfrog skin. *Pflugers Archiv* 405:577–582. (16)

van Gelder, J. J., H. M. J. Aarts, and H. W. M. Staal. 1986. Routes and speed of migrating toads (*Bufo bufo*): A telemetric study. *Herpetological Journal* 1:111–114. (14)

van Mier, P. 1986. The development of the motor system in the clawed toad, *Xenopus laevis*. Ph.D. diss., CIP Data Koninklijke Bibliotheek den Haag. (16)

van Mier, P., R. van Rheden, and H. J. ten Donkelaar. 1985. The development of the dendritic organization of primary and secondary motoneurons in the spinal cord of *Xenopus laevis*. *Anatomical Embryology* 172:311–324. (16)

van Oordt, G. J., and P. G. W. J. van Oordt. 1955. The regulation of spermatogenesis in the frog. *Memoirs of the Society for Endocrinology* 4:25–38. (15)

van Oordt, P. G. W. J. 1956. Regulation of the spermatogenetic cycle in the common frog (*Rana temporaria*). Arnhem, Netherlands: G. W. van der Wiel and Company. (15)

———. 1960. The influence of internal and external factors in the regulation of the spermatogenetic cycle in Amphibia. *Symposia of the Zoological Society of London* 2:29–52. (15)

van Oordt, P. G. W. J., and B. Lofts. 1963. The effects of high temperature on gonadotrophin secretion in the male common frog (*Rana temporaria*) during autumn. *Journal of Endocrinology* 27:137–146. (15)

Van Slyke, D. D. 1922. On the measurement of buffer values and on the relationship of buffer value to the dissociation constant of the buffer and the concentration and the reaction of the buffer system. *Journal of Biological Chemistry* 52:525–570. (5)

Van Vliet, B. N., and N. H. West. 1986. Cardiovascular responses to electrical stimulation of the recurrent laryngeal nerve in conscious toads (*Bufo marinus*). *Journal of Comparative Physiology* 156B:363–375. (7)

———. 1987a. Chronic (16 day) effects of pulmocutaneous arterial baroreceptor denervation on blood pressure and heart rate of conscious toads. *Journal of Physiology* (London) 394:36P. (7)

———. 1987b. Response characteristics of pulmocutaneous arterial baroreceptors in the toad, *Bufo marinus*. *Journal of Physiology* (London) 388:55–70. (7)

———. 1987c. Responses to circulatory pressures, and conduction velocity of pulmocutaneous baroreceptors in *Bufo marinus*. *Journal of Physiology* (London) 388:41–53. (7)

———. 1989. Cardiovascular responses to denervation of pulmocutaneous baroreceptors in toads. *American Journal of Physiology* 256:R946–R954. (7)

———. 1992. Functional characteristics of arterial chemoreceptors in an amphibian (*Bufo marinus*). *Respiration Physiology*, in press. (7)

van Zoest, I. D., P. S. Heijmen, P. M. J. M. Cruijsen, and B. G. Jenks. 1989. Dynamics of background adaptation in *Xenopus laevis*: Role of catecholamines and melanophore-stimulating hormone. *General and Comparative Endocrinology* 76:19–28. (3)

Varanda, W. A., and F. Lacaz-Vieira. 1979. Transient potassium fluxes in toad skin. *Journal of Membrane Biology* 49:199–233. (5)

Varma, M. M. 1977. Ultrastructural evidence for aldosterone- and corticosterone-secreting cells in the adrenocortical tissue of the American bullfrog (*Rana catesbeiana*). *General and Comparative Endocrinology* 33:61–75. (3)

Varriale, B., R. Pierantoni, L. Di Matteo, S. Minucci, M. Milone, and G. Chieffi. 1988. Relationship between estradiol-17β seasonal profile and annual vitellogenin content of liver, fat body, plasma, and ovary in the frog (*Rana esculenta*). *General and Comparative Endocrinology* 69:328–334. (15)

Vaz-Ferreira, R., and A. Gehrau. 1975. Comportamiento epimeletico de la rana comun, *Leptodactylus ocellatus* (L.) (Amphibia, Leptodactylidae): 1. Atencion de la cria y actividades alimentarias y agresivas relacionadas. *Physis* 34:1–14. (14)

Verburg-van Kemenade, B. M. L., B. G. Jenks, A. J. H. M. Houben. 1987. 3. Regulation of cyclic-AMP synthesis in amphibian melanotrope cells through catecholamine and GABA receptors. *Life Sciences* 40:1859–1867. (16)

Verburg-van Kemenade, B. M. L., B. G. Jenks, F. J. A. Lenssen, and H. Vaudry. 1987. Characterization of γ-aminobutyric acid receptors in the neurointermediate lobe of the amphibian *Xenopus laevis*. *Endocrinology* 120:622–628. (3)

Verburg-van Kemenade, B. M. L., B. G. Jenks, and A. P. van Overbeeke. 1986. Regulation of melanotropin release from the pars intermedia of the amphibian *Xenopus laevis*: Evaluation of the involvement of serotonergic, cholinergic, or adrenergic receptor mechanisms. *General and Comparative Endocrinology* 63:471–480. (3)

Verburg-van Kemenade, B. M. L., M. C. Tonon, B. G. Jenks, and H. Vaudry. 1986. Characteristics of receptors for dopamine in the pars intermedia of the amphibian *Xenopus laevis*. *Neuroendocrinology* 44:446–456. (16)

Verburg-van Kemenade, B. M. L., P. H. G. M. Willems, B. G. Jenks, and A. P. van Overbeeke. 1984. The development of the pars intermedia and its role in the regulation of dermal melanophores in the larvae of the amphibian, *Xenopus laevis*. *General and Comparative Endocrinology* 55:54–65. (3,16)

Vernberg, F. J. 1952. The oxygen consumption of two species of salamanders at different seasons of the year. *Physiological Zoology* 25:243–249. (12)

———. 1953. Hibernation studies of two species of salamanders, *Plethodon cinereus cinereus* and *Eurycea bislineata bislineata*. *Ecology* 34:55–62. (10)

———. 1955. Correlation of physiological and behavioral indexes of activity in the study of *Plethodon cinereus* (Green) and *Plethodon glutinosus* (Green). *American Midland Naturalist* 54:382–393. (12)

Vernon, H. M. 1897. The relation of the respiratory exchange of cold-blooded animals to temperature: Part 2. *Journal of Physiology* (London) 21:443–496. (12)

Verrell, P. A. 1982. The sexual behaviour of the red-spotted newt, *Notophthalmus viridescens* (Amphibia: Urodela: Salamandridae). *Animal Behaviour* 30:1224–1236. (14)

———. 1983. The influence of the ambient sex ratio and inter-male competition on the sexual behavior of the red-spotted newt, *Notoph-*

thalmus viridescens (Amphibia: Urodela: Salamandridae). *Behavioral Ecology and Socibiology* 13:307–313 (14)

———. 1985. Feeding in adult smooth newts (*Triturus vulgaris*), with particular emphasis on prey changes in the aquatic phase. *Amphibia-Reptilia* 6:133–136. (14)

———. 1986. Wrestling in the red-spotted newt (*Notophthalmus viridescens*): Resource value and contestant asymmetry determine contest duration and outcome. *Animal Behaviour* 34:398–402. (14)

———. 1987. Growth in the smooth newt (*Triturus vulgaris*) during the aquatic phase of the annual cycle. *Herpetological Journal* 1:137–140. (15)

———. 1989. The sexual strategies of natural populations of newts and salamanders. *Herpetologica* 45:265–282. (14)

Verrell, P. A., and H. Francillon. 1986. Body size, age, and reproduction in the smooth newt, *Triturus vulgaris*. *Journal of Zoology* (London) 210A:89–100. (15)

Verrell, P. A., and T. R. Halliday. 1985. Reproductive dynamics of a population of smooth newts, *Triturus vulgaris*, in southern England. *Herpetologica* 41:386–395. (14)

Verrell, P. A., T. R. Halliday, and M. L. Griffiths. 1986. The annual reproductive cycle of the smooth newt (*Triturus vulgaris*) in England. *Journal of Zoology* (London) 210A:101–119. (14,15)

Verrell, P. A., and N. McCabe. 1988. Field observations of the sexual behaviour of the smooth newt, *Triturus vulgaris vulgaris* (Amphibia: Salamandridae). *Journal of Zoology* (London) 214A:533–545. (14)

Veseley, D. L., and M. E. Hadley. 1979. Ionic requirements for melanophore stimulating hormone (MSH) action on melanophores. *Comparative Biochemistry and Physiology* 62A:501–508. (3)

Vial, J. L. 1968. The ecology of the tropical salamander, *Bolitoglossa subpalmata*, in Costa Rica. *Revista de Biologia Tropical* 15:13–115. (15)

———. ed. 1973. *The Evolutionary Biology of the Anurans*. Columbia: University of Missouri Press. (15)

Victoroff, K. 1908. Zur Kenntniss der Veränderungen des Fettgewebes beim Fröschen während des Winterschlafes. *Archiv der gesamte Physiologie* 125:230–236. (15)

Viertel, B. 1985. The filter apparatus of *Rana temporaria* and *Bufo bufo* larvae (Amphibia, Anura). *Zoomorphology* 105:345–355. (11)

———. 1986. The filter apparatus of *Xenopus laevis*, *Bombina variegata*, and *Bufo calamita* (Amphibia, Anura): A comparison of different larval types. *Zoologische Jahrbücher, Abteilung für Anatomie und Ontogenie der Tiere* 115:425–452. (11)

———. 1989. The filter apparatus of anuran larvae: Aspects of the filtering mechanism. *Fortschritte der Zoologie* 35:526–533. (11)

Vigna, S. R. 1987. Gastrointestinal tract. In *Vertebrate Endocrinology: Fundamentals and Biomedical Implications*, vol. 1, *Morphological Considerations*, ed. P. K. T. Pang and M. P. Schreibman, 261–278. New York: Academic Press. (3)

Vijayakumar, S., C. B. Jørgensen, and K. Kjaer. 1971. Regulation of ovarian cycle in the toad *Bufo bufo bufo* (L.): Effects of autografting pars distalis of the hypophysis, of extirpating gonadotropic hypothalamic region, and of partial ovariectomy. *General and Comparative Endocrinology* 17:432–443. (15)

Vijayan, E., W. K. Samaon, and S. M. McCann. 1979. *In vivo* and *in vitro* effects of cholecystokinin on gonadotropin, prolactin, growth hormone, and thyrotropin release in the rat. *Brain Research* 172:295–302. (16)

Vilter, V., and A. Vilter. 1960. Sur la gestation de la salamandre noire des Alpes, la *Salamandra atra* Laur. *Comptes Rendus de la Société de Biologie* 154:290–294. (15)

———. 1963. Mise en évidence d'un cycle reproducteur biennal chez le triton alpestre de montagne. *Comptes Rendus de la Société de Biologie* 157:464–469. (15)

Vincent, S., and A. T. Cameron. 1919–1920. A note on an inhibitory respiratory reflex in the frog and some other animals. *Journal of Comparative Neurology* 31:283–292. (7)

Vinegar, A., and V. H. Hutchison. 1965a. The effect of photoperiod on the critical thermal maxima of painted turtles, *Chrysemys picta*. *Herpetologica* 20:233–238. (9)

———. 1965b. Pulmonary and cutaneous gas exchange in the green frog, *Rana clamitans*. *Zoologica* 50:47–53. (12)

Vitalis, T. Z. 1988. Breathing in frogs: The mechanism of ventilation and gas exchange in *Rana pipiens*. Ph.D. diss., University of East Anglia, Norwich, England. (6)

Vitt, L. J., and J. D. Congdon. 1978. Body shape, reproductive effort, and relative clutch mass in lizards: Resolution of a paradox. *American Naturalist* 112:595–608. (14)

Vogel, S. 1981. *Life in Moving Fluids: The Physical Biology of Flow*. Princeton, NJ: Princeton University Press. (4)

Voitkevich, A. A. 1937. Besitzt die Rinden- und Markschicht der Nebenniere von Säugetieren eine metamorphogene Eigenschaft. *Zoologische Jahrbücher, Abteilung allgemeine Zoologie und Physiologie der Tiere* 58:11. (16)

———. 1962. Neurosecretory control of the amphibian metamorphosis. *General and Comparative Endocrinology*, suppl. 1:133–147. (16)

Volpe, E. P. 1953. Embryonic temperature adaptations and relationships in toads. *Physiological Zoology* 26:344–354. (8)

———. 1957. Embryonic temperature tolerance and rate of development of *Bufo valliceps*. *Physiological Zoology* 30:164–175. (8)

Vondersaar, M. E., and D. F. Stiffler. 1989. Renal function in urodele amphibians: A comparison of strictly aquatic and amphibious species, with observations on the effects of anesthesia. *Comparative Biochemistry and Physiology* 94A:243–248. (5)

von Euler, C. 1986. Brain stem mechanisms for generation and control of breathing pattern. In *Handbook of Physiology*, ed. A. P. Fishman, 3:1–67. Bethesda, MD: American Physiological Society. (7)

von Kennel, P. 1911. Les corps adipolymphoïdes de quelques batraciens. *Compte Rendus de l'Académie des Sciences* (Paris) 152:1352–1354. (15)

———. 1912. Les corps adipolymphoïdes des batraciens. *Compte Rendus de l'Académie des Sciences* (Paris) 154:1378–1380. (15)

———. 1913. Les corps adipolymphoïdes des batraciens. *Annales des Sciences Naturales Zoologie* 17:219–254. (15)

Vorobyeva, E., and S. Smirnov. 1987. Characteristic features in the formation of anuran sound-conducting systems. *Journal of Morphology* 192:1–11. (16)

Voute, C. L., and W. Meier. 1978. The mitochondria-rich cell of frog skin as hormone sensitive "shunt path." *Membrane Biology* 40:141–165. (5)

Voute, C. L., and H. H. Ussing. 1970. The morphological aspects of shunt-path in the epithelium of the frog skin (*R. temporaria*). *Experimental Cell Research* 61:133–140. (5)

Wachholder, K. 1930a. Untersuchungen über "tonische" und "nicht tonische" Wirbeltiermuskeln: 2. Mitteilung: Acetylcholin- und tiegelsche Contractur in ihre Beziehungen zueinander und zur tetanischen Kontraktionsform: Die Plastizität der beiden Muskelarten. *Pflugers Archiv* 226:255–273. (11)

———. 1930b. Untersuchungen über "tonische" und "nicht tonische" Wirbeltiermuskeln: 3. Mitteilung: Verschiedenes Verhalten bei ermüdender Reizung. *Pflugers Archiv* 226:274–291. (11)

Wachholder, K., and J. F. von Ledebur. 1930. Untersuchungen über "tonische" und "nicht tonische" Wirbeltiermuskeln: 1. Mitteilung: Die Umklammerungshaltung des Frosches und die Schutzhaltung der Schildkröte: Ihre spezifische Nachahmung durch muskuläre Acetylcholinwirkung. *Pflugers Archiv* 225:627–642. (11)

Wada, M., and A. Gorbman. 1977. Relation of mode of administration of testosterone to evocation of male sex behavior in frogs. *Hormones and Behavior* 8:310–319. (2)

Wade, M., and S. J. Arnold. 1980. The intensity of sexual selection in relation to male sexual behaviour, female choice, and sperm precedence. *Animal Behaviour* 28:446–61. (14)

Wagner, W. E., Jr. 1989. Social correlates of variation in male calling behavior in Blanchard's cricket frog, *Acris crepitans blanchardi*. *Ethology* 82:27–45. (2,9)

———. 1989. Fighting, assessment, and frequency alteration in Blanchard's cricket frog. *Behavioral Ecology and Sociobiology* 25:429–436. (14)

Wahlqvist, I., and G. Campbell. 1988. Autonomic influences on heart rate and blood pressure in the toad, *Bufo marinus*, at rest and during exercise. *Journal of Experimental Biology* 134:377–396. (7)

Wahnschaffe, U., U. Bartsch, and B. Fritzsch. 1987. Metamorphic changes within the lateral line system of Anura. *Anatomical Embryology* 73:431–442. (16)

Wahnschaffe, U., B. Fritzsch, and W. Himstedt. 1985. The fine structure of the lateral-line organs of larval *Icthyophis* (Amphibia: Gymnophiona). *Journal of Morphology* 186:369–377. (2)

Wake, D. B. 1966. Comparative osteology and evolution of the lungless salamanders, family Plethodontidae. *Memoirs of the Southern California Academy of Sciences* 4:1–111. (11)

———. 1982. Functional and developmental constraints and opportunities in the evolution of feeding systems in urodeles. In *Environmental Adaptation and Evolution*, ed. D. Mossakowski and G. Roth, 51–66. Stuttgart: Gustav Fischer. (11,14)

Wake, D. B., and I. G. Dresner. 1967. Functional morphology and evolution of tail autonomy in salamanders. *Journal of Morphology* 122:265–306. (11)

Wake, D. B., and A. Larson. 1987. Multidimensional analysis of an evolving lineage. *Science* 238:42–48. (13,14)

Wake, D. B., and J. F. Lynch. 1976. The distribution, ecology, and evolutionary history of plethodontid salamanders in tropical America. *Natural History Museum of Los Angeles County Scientific Bulletin* 25:1–65. (8)

Wake, D. B., K. C. Nishikawa, U. Dicke, and G. Roth. 1988. Organization of the motor nuclei in the cervical cord of salamanders. *Journal of Comparative Neurology* 278:195–208. (2,11)

Wake, D. B., G. Roth, and M. H. Wake. 1983. Tongue evolution in lungless salamanders, family Plethodontidae: 3. Patterns of peripheral innervation. *Journal of Morphology* 178:207–224. (11,14)

Wake, M. H. 1970. Evolutionary morphology of the caecilian urogenital system: 4. The bladder. *Herpetologica* 26:120–128. (16)

———. 1976. The development and replacement of teeth in viviparous caecilians. *Journal of Morphology* 148:33–64. (13,16)

———. 1977a. Fetal maintenance and its evolutionary significance in the Amphibia: Gymnophiona. *Journal of Herpetology* 11:379–386. (13,16)

———. 1977b. The reproductive biology of caecilians: An evolutionary perspective. In *The Reproductive Biology of Amphibians*, ed. D. H. Taylor and S. I. Guttman, 73–101. New York: Plenum Press. (13,14,16)

———. 1978. Ontogeny of *Typhlonectes obesus*, with emphasis on dentition and feeding. *Papeis Avulsos Zoologia* 12:1–13. (11,13,14)

———. 1979. Fetal tooth development and adult replacement: Fields versus clones. *American Zoologist* 19:1013. (13,16)

———. 1980a. Fetal tooth development and adult replacement in *Dermophis mexicanus* (Amphibia: Gymnophiona): Fields versus clones. *Journal of Morphology* 166:203–216. (13,16)

———. 1980b. Reproduction, growth, and population structure of the caecilian *Dermophis mexicanus*. *Herpetologica* 36:244–256. (13,15,16)

———. 1982. Diversity within a framework of constraints: Amphibian reproductive modes. In *Environmental Adaptation and Evolution*, ed. D. Mossakowski and G. Roth, 87–106. Stuttgart: Gustav Fischer. (15)

———. 1983. *Gymnopsis multiplicata* Peters, *Dermophis mexicanus* (Dumeril and Bibron), and *Dermophis parviceps* (Dunn) (Caecilians). In *Costa Rican Natural History*, ed. D. H. Janzen, 400–401. Chicago: University of Chicago Press. (13)

———. 1985a. The comparative morphology and evolution of the eyes of caecilians (Amphibia: Gymnophiona). *Zoomorphology* 105:277–295. (13)

———. 1985b. Oviduct structure and function in non-mammalian vertebrates. *Fortschritte der Zoologie* 30:427–435. (13,16)

———. 1986. Caecilians. In *The Encyclopedia of Reptiles and Amphibians*, ed. T. R. Halliday and K. Adler, 16–17. New York: Facts on File. (14)

———. 1993. The skull as a locomotor organ. In *The Vertebrate Skull*, ed. J. Hanken and B. Hall, vol. 3. Chicago: University of Chicago Press. (Forthcoming) (11)

Wake, M. H., and G. Z. Wurst. 1979. Tooth crown morphology in caecilians (Amphibia: Gymnophiona). *Journal of Morphology* 159:331–342. (14)

Wakeman, J. M., and G. R. Ultsch. 1976. The effects of dissolved O$_2$ and CO$_2$ on metabolism and gas-exchange partitioning in aquatic salamanders. *Physiological Zoology* 48:348–359. (12)

Wald, G. 1981. Metamorphosis: An overview. In *Metamorphosis: A Problem in Developmental Biology*, 2d ed., ed. L. I. Gilbert and E. Frieden, 1–39. New York: Plenum Press. (16)

Waldman, B. 1985. Olfactory basis of kin recognition in toad tadpoles. *Journal of Comparative Physiology* 156A:565–577. (16)

———. 1986. Chemical ecology of kin recognition in anuran amphibians in chemical signals in vertebrates: 4. In *Ecology, Evolution, and Comparative Biology*, ed. D. Duvall, D. Muller-Schwarze, and R. M. Silverstein, 1–18. New York: Plenum Press. (16)

———. 1988. The ecology of kin recognition. *Annual Review of Ecology and Systematics* 19:543–571. (2)

Waldschmidt, S. 1980. Orientation to the sun by the iguanid lizards *Uta stansburiana* and *Sceloporus undulatus:* Hourly and monthly variations. *Copeia* 1980:458–462. (4)

Waldschmidt, S., and C. R. Tracy. 1983. Interactions between a lizard and its thermal environment: Implications for sprint performance and space utilization in the lizard *Uta stansburiana*. *Ecology* 64:476–484. (4,9)

Walker, A. M. 1940. Ammonia formation in the amphibian kidney. *American Journal of Physiology* 131:187–194. (5)

Walker, A. M., and C. L. Hudson. 1937. The role of the tubule in the excretion of urea by the amphibian kidney. *American Journal of Physiology* 118:153–166. (5)

Walker, P., P. Coulombe, and J. H. Dussault. 1980. Effects of triiodothyronine on thyrotropin-releasing hormone–induced thyrotropin release in the neonatal rat. *Endocrinology* 107:1731–1737. (16)

Walker, R. F., and W. G. Whitford. 1970. Soil water absorption capabilities in selected species of anurans. *Herpetologica* 26:411–418. (6)

Walker, S. L. 1989. The effect of substrate depletion on the calling behavior of the gray treefrog. M.S. thesis, University of Connecticut, Storrs. (14)

Walkowiak, W. 1980. Sensitivity range and temperature dependence of hearing in the grass frog. *Behavioral Processes* 5:363–372. (8)

———. 1988a. Central temporal coding. In *The Evolution of the Amphibian Auditory System*, ed. B. Fritzsch, M. J. Ryan, W. Wilczynski, T. E. Hetherington, and W. Walkowiak, 275–294. New York: John Wiley and Sons. (2)

———. 1988b. Neuroethology of anuran call recognition. In *The Evolution of the Amphibian Auditory System*, ed. B. Fritzsch, M. J. Ryan, W. Wilczynski, T. E. Hetherington, and W. Walkowiak, 485–509. New York: John Wiley and Sons. (2,14)

———. 1988c. Two auditory filter systems determine the calling behavior of the fire-bellied toad: A behavioral and neurophysiological characterization. *Journal of Comparative Physiology* 164:31–41. (2)

Walkowiak, W., R. R. Capranica, and H. Schneider. 1981. A comparative study of auditory sensitivity in the genus *Bufo* (Amphibia). *Behavioural Processes* 6:223–237. (2)

Wallace, R. A. 1978. Oocyte growth in nonmammalian vertebrates. In *The Vertebrate Ovary*, ed. R. E. Jones, 469–502. New York: Plenum Press. (15)

Walsberg, G. E. 1986. Comparison of two techniques for estimating the maximum aerobic capacity of amphibians. *Herpetologica* 42:389–394. (12)

Walsberg, G. E., M. S. Lea, and S. S. Hillman. 1986. Individual variation in maximum aerobic capacity: Cardiovascular and enzymatic correlates in *Rana catesbeiana*. *Journal of Experimental Zoology* 239:1–5. (12,14)

Walter, F. 1887. Das Visceralskelett und seine Muskulatur bei den einheimischen Amphibien und Reptilien. *Jenaische Zeitschrift für Naturwissenschaften* 21:1–45. (11)

Walton, M. 1988. Relationships among metabolic, locomotory, and field measures of organismal performance in the Fowler's toad (*Bufo woodhousei fowleri*). *Physiological Zoology* 61:107–118. (12,14)

———. 1992. Physiology and phylogeny: The evolution of locomotor energetics in hylid frogs. *American Naturalist*, in press.

Walton, M., and B. D. Anderson. 1988. The aerobic cost of saltatory locomotion in the Fowler's toad (*Bufo woodhousei fowleri*). *Journal of Experimental Biology* 136:273–288. (8,12,14)

Walton, M. J. 1986. Metabolic effects of feeding a high protein/low carbohydrate diet as compared to a low protein/high carbohydrate diet to rainbow trout *Salmo gairdneri*. *Fish Physiology and Biochemistry* 1.7–15. (15)

Wang, L. C. H., D. Belke, M. L. Jourdan, T. F. Lee, J. Westly, and F. Nurnberger. 1988. The "hibernation induction trigger": Specificity and validity of bioassay using the 13-lined ground squirrel. *Cryobiology* 25:355–362. (10)

Wang, W., P. Dietl, and H. Oberleithner. 1987. Evidence for Na$^+$ dependent rheogenic HCO$_3^-$ transport in fused cells of frog distal tubules. *Pflugers Archiv* 408:291–299. (5)

Warburg, M. R. 1965. Studies on the water economy of some Australian frogs. *Australian Journal of Zoology* 13:317–330. (5)

———. 1967. On thermal and water balance of three central Australian frogs. *Comparative Biochemistry and Physiology* 20:27–43. (6)

———. 1972. Water economy and thermal balance of Israeli and Australian Amphibia from xeric habitats. *Symposium of Zoological Society* (London) 31:79–111. (6,12)

Warburg, M. R., and G. Degani. 1979. Evaporative water loss and uptake in juvenile and adult *Salamandra salamandra* (L.) (Amphibia: Urodela). *Comparative Biochemistry and Physiology* 62A:1071–1075. (5,8)

Warburg, M. R., and S. Goldenberg. 1978a. The changes in osmoregulatory effects of prolactin during the life cycle of two urodeles. *Comparative Biochemistry and Physiology* 61A:321–324. (16)

———. 1978b. Effect of oxytocin and vasotocin on water balance in two urodeles followed throughout their life cycle. *Comparative Biochemistry and Physiology* 60A:113–116. (5)

Warburg, M. R., and D. Lewinson. 1977. Ultrastructure of epidermis of *Salamandra salamandra* followed throughout ontogenesis. *Cell and Tissue Research* 181:369–393. (16)

Warren, M. R. 1940. Studies on the effect of experimental hyperthyroidism on the adult frog, *Rana pipiens*, Schreber. *Journal of Experimental Zoology* 83:127–159. (12)

Wasserman, K., B. J. Whipp, S. N. Koyal, and W. L. Beaver. 1973. Anaerobic threshold and respiratory gas exchange during exercise. *Journal of Applied Physiology* 35:236–243. (12)

Wassersug, R. J. 1971. On the comparative palatability of some dry-season tadpoles from Costa Rica. *American Midland Naturalist* 86:101–109. (14)

———. 1972. The mechanism of ultraplanktonic entrapment in anuran larvae. *Journal of Morphology* 137:279–288. (11,16)

———. 1973. Aspects of social behavior in anuran larvae. In *The Evolutionary Biology of the Anurans*, ed. J. L. Vial, 273–297. Columbia: University of Missouri Press. (9)

———. 1980. *Internal Oral Features of Larvae from Eight Anuran Families: Functional, Systematic, Evolutionary, and Ecological Considerations*. University of Kansas Museum of Natural History Miscellaneous Publication 68. Lawrence: University of Kansas Press. (14,16)

———. 1986. How does a tadpole know when to metamorphose? A theory linking environmental and hormonal cues. *Journal of Theoretical Biology* 118:171–181. (16)

———. 1989. Locomotion in amphibian larvae, or "why aren't tadpoles built like fishes?" *American Zoologist* 29:65–84. (2,11,14)

Wassersug, R. J., and M. E. Feder. 1983. The effects of aquatic oxygen concentration, body size, and respiratory behaviour on the stamina of obligate aquatic (*Bufo americanus*) and facultative air-breathing (*Xenopus laevis* and *Rana berlandieri*) anuran larvae. *Journal of Experimental Biology* 105:173–190. (5,12,16)

Wassersug, R. J., and R. Heyer. 1988. A survey of internal oral features of leptodactyloid larvae (Amphibia: Anura). *Smithsonian Contributions to Zoology* 457:1–99. (13,16)

Wassersug, R. J., and K. Hoff. 1979. A comparative study of the buccal pumping mechanism of tadpoles. *Biological Journal of the Linnean Society* 12:225–259. (11,16)

———. 1985. The kinematics of swimming in anuran larvae. *Journal of Experimental Biology* 119:1–30. (11,14,16)

———. 1989. The implications of shape and metamorphosis for drag forces on anuran larvae. *Annals de la Société Royale Zoologique de Belgique* (Abstracts 3d International Congress of Vertebrate Morphology) 119:62–63. (11)

Wassersug, R. J., and A. M. Murphy. 1987. Aerial respiration facilitates growth in suspension-feeding anuran larvae (*Xenopus laevis*). *Experimental Biology* 46:141–147. (14,16)

Wassersug, R. J., and K. Nishikawa. 1988. Functional morphology of the caudal spinal cord in *Rana* (Ranidae) and *Xenopus* (Pipidae). *Journal of Comparative Neurology* 269:193–202. (1,16)

Wassersug, R. J., R. D. Paul, and M. E. Feder. 1981. Cardio-respiratory synchrony in anuran larvae (*Xenopus laevis, Pachymedusa dacnicolor,* and *Rana berlandieri*). *Comparative Biochemistry and Physiology* 70A:329–334. (16)

Wassersug, R. J., and W. F. Pyburn. 1987. The biology of the Pe-ret′ toad, *Otophryne robusta* (Microhylidae), with special consideration of its fossorial larva and systematic relationships. *Zoological Journal of the Linnaean Society* 91:137–169. (11)

Wassersug, R. J., and K. Rosenberg. 1979. Surface anatomy of branchial food traps of tadpoles: A comparative study. *Journal of Morphology* 159:393–426. (16)

Wassersug, R. J., and E. A. Seibert. 1975. Behavioral responses of amphibian larvae to variation in dissolved oxygen. *Copeia* 1975:86–103. (5,14,16)

Wassersug, R. J., and D. G. Sperry. 1977. The relationship of locomotion to differential predation on *Pseudacris triseriata* (Anura: Hylidae). *Ecology* 58:830–839. (14)

Watanabe, K., and F. Sasaki. 1974. Ultrastructural changes in the tail muscles of anuran tadpoles during metamorphosis. *Cell and Tissue Research* 155:321–336. (11)

Watanabe, K., F. Sasaki, H. Takahama, and H. Iseki. 1980. Histogenesis and distribution of red and white muscle fibres of urodelan larvae. *Journal of Anatomy* (London) 130:83–96. (11)

Watlington, C. O. 1968. Effect of catecholamines and adrenergic blockade on sodium transport in isolated frog skin. *American Journal of Physiology* 214:1001–1007. (5)

Watlington, C. O., P. K. Burke, and H. L. Estep. 1968. Calcium flux in isolated frog skin: The effect of parathyroid substances. *Proceedings of the Society for Experimental Biology and Medicine* 128:853–856. (5)

Watt, K. W. K., T. Maruyama, and A. Riggs. 1980. Hemoglobins of the tadpole of the bullfrog, *Rana catesbeiana*: Amino acid sequence of the β chain of a major component. *Journal of Biological Chemistry* 255:3294–3301. (5)

Watt, K. W. K., and A. Riggs. 1975. Hemoglobins of the tadpole of the bullfrog, *Rana catesbeiana*: Structure and function of the isolated components. *Journal of Biological Chemistry* 250:5934–5944. (5)

Watteville, Baron A. de. 1875. A description of the cerebral and spinal nerves of *Rana esculenta*. *Journal of Anatomy* 9:145–162. (7)

Watts, R. E., and A. S. French. 1985. Sensory transduction in dorsal cutaneous mechanoreceptor of the frog, *Rana pipiens*. *Journal of Comparative Physiology* 157A:657–665. (16)

Watzka, M. 1933. Vergleichende Untersuchungen über den ultimobranchialen Korper. *Zeitschrift für mikroskopisch-anatomische Forschung* 34:485–433. (16)

Weast, R. C. 1987. *Handbook of Chemistry and Physics*. 68th ed. Boca Raton, FL: CRC Press. (4)

Weathers, W. W. 1976a. Influence of temperature acclimation on oxygen consumption, haemodynamics, and oxygen transport in bullfrogs. *Australian Journal of Zoology* 24:321–330. (12)

———. 1976b. Influence of temperature on the optimal hematocrit of the bullfrog, *Rana catesbeiana*. *Journal of Comparative Physiology* 109:173–183. (6,9)

Weathers, W. W., W. A. Buttemer, A. M. Hayworth, and K. A. Nagy. 1984. An evaluation of time-budget estimates of daily energy expenditure in birds. *Auk* 101:459–472. (14)

Weathers, W. W., and G. K. Snyder. 1977. Relation of oxygen consumption to temperature and time of day in tropical anuran amphibians. *Australian Journal of Zoology* 25:19–24. (12,14)

Webb, P. W. 1975. Hydrodynamics and energetics of fish propulsion. *Bulletin of the Fish Research Board of Canada* 190:1–159. (8)

———. 1978. Fast-start performance and body form in seven species of teleost fish. *Journal of Experimental Biology* 74:211–216. (8,11)

———. 1984. Body form, locomotion, and foraging in aquatic vertebrates. *American Zoologist* 24:107–120. (14)

Webb, R. G. 1969. Survival adaptations of tiger salamanders (*Ambystoma tigrinum*) in the Chihuahuan desert. In *Physiological Systems in Semiarid Environments*, ed. C. C. Hoff and M. C. Riedesel, 143–147. Albuquerque: University of New Mexico Press. (10)

Weber, E. 1976. Die Veranderung der Paarungs- und Revierrufe von *Hyla savignyi* Audouin (Anura) nach Ausschaltung von Kehlkopfmuskeln. *Bonner Zoologische Beitrage* 27:87–97. (14)

Weber, R. 1967. Biochemistry of amphibian metamorphosis. In *Biochemistry of Animal Development*, vol. 2, *Biochemical Control Mechanisms and Adaptations in Development*, ed. R. Weber, 227–301. New York: Academic Press. (16)

Weber, R. E., and F. B. Jensen. 1988. Functional adaptations in hemoglobins from ectothermic vertebrates. *Annual Review of Physiology* 50:161–179. (5)

Weber, R. E., R. M. G. Wells, and J. E. Rossetti. 1985. Adaptations to neoteny in the salamander, *Necturus maculosus*: Blood respiratory properties and interactive effects of pH, temperature, and ATP on hemoglobin oxygenation. *Comparative Biochemistry and Physiology* 80A:495–501. (5)

Weerasuriya, A., and J.-P. Ewert. 1981. Prey-selective neurons in the toad's optic tectum and sensorimotor interfacing: HRP studies and recording experiments. *Journal of Comparative Physiology* 144A: 429–434. (2,11)

Weibel, E. R. 1972. Morphometric estimation of pulmonary diffusion capacity: 5. Comparative morphometry of alveolar lungs. *Respiration Physiology* 14:26–43. (5)

Weigmann, D. L., and R. Altig. 1975. Anaerobic glycolysis in two larval amphibians. *Journal of Herpetology* 9:355–357. (16)

Weigt, M., P. Dietl, S. Silbernagl, and H. Oberleithner. 1987. Activation of luminal Na$^+$/H$^+$ exchange in distal nephron of frog kidney. An early response to aldosterone. *Pflugers Archiv* 48:609–614. (5)

Weihs, D., and P. W. Webb. 1983. Optimization of locomotion. In *Fish Biomechanics*, ed. P. W. Webb, and D. Weihs, 339–371. New York: Praeger. (11)

Weil, M. R. 1986. Changes in plasma thyroxine levels during and after spontaneous metamorphosis in a natural population of the green frog, *Rana clamitans*. *General and Comparative Endocrinology* 62:8–12. (16)

Weiner, I. M. 1973. Transport of weak acids and bases. In *Handbook of Physiology*, sec. 8, ed. J. Orloff and R. W. Berliner, 521–554. Bethesda, MD: American Physiological Society. (5)

Weiner, M. W. 1980. The effects of bicarbonate and hydroxyl ions on chloride transport by toad bladders. *Biochimica et Biophysica Acta* 596:292–301. (5)

Weissberg, J., and U. Katz. 1975. Effects of osmolarity and salinity adaptation on cellular composition and on potassium uptake of erythrocytes from the euryhaline toad *Bufo viridis*. *Comparative Biochemistry and Physiology* 52A:165–169. (6)

Wells, K. D. 1976a. Multiple egg clutches in the green frog (*Rana clamitans*). *Herpetologica* 32:85–87. (15)

———. 1976b. Territorial behavior of the green frog (*Rana clamitans*). Ph.D. diss., Cornell University, Ithaca, NY. (14)

———. 1977. The social behavior of anuran amphibians. *Animal Behaviour* 25:666–693. (2,14)

———. 1978. Territoriality in the green frog (*Rana clamitans*): Vocalizations and aggressive behaviour. *Animal Behaviour* 26:1051–1063. (14)

———. 1988. The effect of social interactions on anuran vocal behavior. In *The Evolution of the Amphibian Auditory System*, ed. B. Fritzsch, M. J. Ryan, W. Wilczynski, T. E. Hetherington, and W. Walkowiak, 433–454. New York: John Wiley and Sons. (2,14)

Wells, K. D., and J. J. Schwartz. 1982. The effect of vegetation on the propagation of calls in the Neotropical frog *Centrolenella fleischmanni*. *Herpetologica* 38:449–455. (14)

———. 1984. Vocal communication in a Neotropical treefrog, *Hyla ebraccata*: Advertisement calls. *Animal Behaviour* 32:405–420. (14)

Wells, K. D., and T. L. Taigen. 1984. Reproductive behavior and aerobic capacities of male American toads (*Bufo americanus*): Is behavior constrained by physiology? *Herpetologica* 40:292–298. (12,14)

———. 1986. The effect of social interactions on calling energetics in the gray treefrog (*Hyla versicolor*). *Behavioral Ecology and Sociobiology* 19:9–18. (14)

———. 1989. Calling energetics of a Neotropical treefrog, *Hyla microcephala*. *Behavioral Ecology and Sociobiology* 25:13–22. (14)

Wells, R. M. G. 1990. Hemoglobin physiology in vertebrate animals: A cautionary approach to adaptationist thinking. In *Vertebrate Gas Exchange: From Environment to Cell*, vol. 6, *Advances in Environmental and Comparative Physiology*, ed. R. G. Boutilier, 143–161. Heidelberg: Springer-Verlag. (5)

Welsch, U., W. Müller, and C. Schubert. 1977. Elektronenmikroskopische und histochemische Beobachtungen zur Fortpflanzungsbiologie vivparer Gymnophionen (*Chthonerpeton indistinctum*). *Zoologisches Jahrbuch der Anatomie* 97:532–549. (13,16)

Welsch, U., and C. Schubert. 1975. Observations on the fine structure, enzyme histochemistry, and innervation of the parathyroid gland and ultimobranchial body of *Chthonerpeton indistinction* (Gymnophiona, Amphibia). *Cell and Tissue Research* 4:105–119. (16)

Welsch, U., and V. Storch. 1972. The fine structure of the endocrine pancreatic cells of *Ichthyophis kohtaoensis* (Gymnophiona, Amphibia). *Archivum Histologicum Japonicum* 34:73–85. (13)

Werner, E. E., J. F. Gilliam, D. J. Hall, and G. G. Mittlebach. 1983.

An experimental test of the effects of predation risk on habitat use in fish. *Ecology* 64:1540–1548. (14)

Werner, F. 1936. Apoda. In *Handbuch der Zoologie*, ed. W. Kükenthal, 6:143–208. Berlin: Grutyer. (13)

Werner, J. K. 1969. Temperature-photoperiod effects on spermatogenesis in the salamander *Plethodon cinereus*. *Copeia* 1969:592–602. (15)

Wernig, A., A. P. Anzil, A. Bieser, and U. Schwartz. 1981. Abandoned synaptic sites in muscles of normal adult frog. *Neuroscience Letters* 23:105–110. (11)

Wernig, A., M. Pécot-Dechavassine, and H. Stöver. 1980. Sprouting and regression of the nerve at the frog neuromuscular junction in normal conditions and after prolonged paralysis with curare. *Journal of Neurocytology* 9:277–303. (11)

West, J. B. 1974. *Respiratory Physiology: The Essentials*. Baltimore: Williams and Wilkins. (4)

———. 1977. *Pulmonary Pathophysiology*. Baltimore: Williams and Wilkins. (4)

———. 1984. *Respiratory Physiology: The Essentials*. 3d ed. Baltimore: Williams and Wilkins. (7)

West, N. H., and W. W. Burggren. 1982. Gill and lung ventilatory responses to steady-state aquatic hypoxia and hyperoxia in the bullfrog tadpole. *Respiration Physiology* 47:165–176. (5,7,12,16)

———. 1983. Reflex interactions between aerial and aquatic gas exchange organs in the larval bullfrog. *American Journal of Physiology* 244:R770–R777. (5,7,16)

———. 1984. Control of pulmonary and cutaneous blood flow in the toad, *Bufo marinus*. *American Journal of Physiology* 247:R884–R894. (5,7)

West, N. H., and D. R. Jones. 1975a. Breathing movements in the frog *Rana pipiens*: 1. The mechanical events associated with lung and buccal ventilation. *Canadian Journal of Zoology* 53:332–344. (5,6,7,11)

———. 1975b. Breathing movements in the frog *Rana pipiens*: 2. The power output and efficiency of breathing. *Canadian Journal of Zoology* 53:345–353. (6)

———. 1976. The initiation of diving apnoea in the frog *Rana pipiens*. *Journal of Experimental Biology* 64:25–38. (7)

West, N. H., Z. L. Topor, and B. N. Van Vliet. 1987. Hypoxemic threshold for lung ventilation in the toad. *Respiration Physiology* 70:377–390. (7)

West, N. H., and B. N. Van Vliet. 1983. Open-loop analysis of the pulmocutaneous baroreflex in the toad *Bufo marinus*. *American Journal of Physiology* 245:R642–R650. (7)

West Eberhard, M. J. 1985. Sexual selection, competitive communication, and species-specific signals in insects. In *Insect Communication*, ed. T. Lewis, 283–324. New York: Academic Press. (14)

Wetzel, D. M., U. L. Haerter, and D. B. Kelley. 1985. A proposed neural pathway for vocalization in South African clawed frogs, *Xenopus laevis*. *Journal of Comparative Physiology* 157:749–761. (2)

Wetzel, D. M., and D. B. Kelley. 1983. Androgen and gonadotropin effects on male mate calls in South African clawed frogs, *Xenopus laevis*. *Hormones and Behavior* 17:388–404. (2)

Wever, E. G. 1979. Middle ear muscles of the frog. *Proceedings of the National Academy of Sciences* 76:3031–3033. (11)

———. 1985. *The Amphibian Ear*. Princeton, NJ: Princeton University Press. (11,16)

Weygoldt, P. 1980. Complex brood care and reproductive behavior in captive poison-dart frogs, *Dendrobates pumilia* O. Schmidt. *Behavioral Ecology and Sociobiology* 7:329–332. (14)

Whalen, R., and J. W. Crim. 1985. Immunocytochemistry of luteinizing hormone–releasing hormone during spontaneous and thyroxine-induced metamorphosis of bullfrogs. *Journal of Experimental Zoology* 234:131–144. (16)

Wheatly, M. G. 1988. Integrated responses to salinity fluctuation. *American Zoologist* 28:65–77. (14)

Whipp, B. J., and K. Wasserman. 1972. Oxygen uptake kinetics for various intensities of constant-load work. *Journal of Applied Physiology* 33:351–356. (12)

White, A. W., and C. S. Nicoll. 1979. Prolactin receptors in *Rana catesbeiana* during development and metamorphosis. *Science* 204:851–853. (16)

White, B. A. 1981. Occurrence and binding affinity of prolactin receptors in amphibian tissues. *General and Comparative Endocrinology* 45:153–161. (16)

White, B. A., G. S. Lebovic, and C. S. Nicoll. 1981. Prolactin inhibits the induction of its own renal receptors in *Rana catesbeiana* tadpoles. *General and Comparative Endocrinology* 43:30–38. (16)

White, B. A., and C. S. Nicoll. 1981. Hormonal control of amphibian metamorphosis. In *Metamorphosis: A Problem in Developmental Biology*, 2d ed., ed. L. I. Gilbert and E. Frieden, 363–396. New York: Plenum Press. (9,16)

White, F. M. 1984. *Heat Transfer*. Reading, MA: Addison-Wesley. (4)

White, F. N. 1989. Carbon dioxide homeostasis. In *Comparative Pulmonary Physiology: Current Concepts*, ed. S. C. Wood, 439–466. New York: Marcel Dekker. (5)

White, F. N., and G. Somero. 1982. Acid-base regulation and phospholipid adaptations to temperature: Time courses and physiological significance of modifying the milieu for protein function. *Physiological Reviews* 62:40–90 (6)

White, R. L. 1977. Prey selection by the rough-skinned newt (*Taricha granulosa*) in two pond types. *Northwest Scientist* 51:114–118. (14)

Whitehead, P. J., J. T. Puckridge, C. M. Leigh, and R. S. Seymour. 1989. Effect of temperature on jump performance of the frog *Limnodynastes tasmaniensis*. *Physiological Zoology* 62:937–949. (8,9)

Whiteside, B. 1922. Development of the saccus endolymphaticus in *Rana temporaria* Linne. *American Journal of Anatomy* 30:231–266. (16)

Whitford, W. G. 1968. Physiological responses to temperature and desiccation in the endemic New Mexico plethodontids, *Plethodon neomexicanus* and *Aneides hardii*. *Copeia* 1968:247–251. (12)

———. 1969. Heart rate and changes in body fluids in aestivating toads from xeric habitats. In *Physiological Systems in Semiarid Environments*, ed. C. C. Hoff and M. C. Riedesel. Albuquerque: University of New Mexico Press. (10)

———. 1973. The effects of temperature on respiration in the Amphibia. *American Zoologist* 13:505–512. (8,12)

Whitford, W. G., and V. H. Hutchison. 1963. Cutaneous and pulmonary gas exchange in the spotted salamander, *Ambystoma maculatum*. *Biological Bulletin* 124:344–354. (9,12)

———. 1965a. Effect of photoperiod on pulmonary and cutaneous respiration in the spotted salamander, *Ambystoma maculatum*. *Copeia* 1965:53–58. (9,12)

———. 1965b. Gas exchange in salamanders. *Physiological Zoology* 38:228–242. (6,9,10,12)

———. 1966. Cutaneous and pulmonary gas exchange in ambystomatid salamanders. *Copeia* 1966:573–577. (9,11,12)

———. 1967. Body size and metabolic rate in salamanders. *Physiological Zoology* 40:127–133. (5,9,10,12)

Whitford, W. G., and M. Massey. 1970. Responses of a population of *Ambystoma tigrinum* to thermal and oxygen gradients. *Herpetologica* 26:372–376. (9)

Whitford, W. G., and K. H. Meltzer. 1976. Changes in O_2 consumption, body water, and lipid in burrowed desert juvenile anurans. *Herpetologica* 32:23–25. (12)

Whitford, W. G., and R. E. Sherman. 1968. Aerial and aquatic respiration in axolotl and transformed *Ambystoma tigrinum*. *Herpetologica* 24:233–237. (12)

Whitford, W. G., and A. Vinegar. 1966. Homing, survivorship, and overwintering of larvae in spotted salamanders, *Ambystoma maculatum*. *Copeia* 1966:515–519. (10)

Whitney, C. L., and J. R. Krebs. 1975. Mate selection in Pacific tree frogs. *Nature* 255:325–326. (14)

Whittembury, G., and E. E. Windhager. 1961. Electrical potential difference measurements in perfused single proximal tubules of *Necturus* kidney. *Journal of General Physiology* 44:679–687. (5)

Wicht, H., and W. Himstedt. 1986. Two thalamo-telencephalic pathways in a urodele, *Triturus alpestris*. *Neuroscience Letters* 68:90–94. (2)

———. 1988. Topological and connectional analysis of the dorsal thalamus of *Triturus alpestris* (Amphibia, Urodela, Salamandridae). *Journal of Comparative Neurology* 267:545–561. (2)

Wiederholt, M., W. J. Sullivan, and G. Giebisch. 1971. Transport of potassium and sodium across single distal tubules of *Amphiuma*. *Journal of General Physiology* 57:495–529. (5)

Wiedersheim, R. 1875. *Salamandrina perspicillata* und *Geotriton fuscus*: Versuch einer vergleichenden Anatomie der Salamandriden mit besonderer Berücksichtigung der Skelet-Verhältnisse. Genoa: Institut der Sordo-Muti. (11)

———. 1879. *Die Anatomie der Gymnophionen*. Jena: Gustav Fischer. (11)

Wieser, W. 1973. Temperature relations of ectotherms. In *Effects of Temperature on Ectothermic Organisms: Ecological Implications and Mechanisms of Compensation*, ed. W. Wieser, 1–24. New York: Springer-Verlag. (9)

Wilbrandt, W. 1938. Electrical potential differences across the wall of kidney tubules of *Necturus*. *Journal of Cellular and Comparative Physiology* 11:425–432. (5)

Wilbur, H. M. 1976. Density-dependent aspects of metamorphosis in *Ambystoma* and *Rana sylvatica*. *Ecology* 57:1289–1296. (16)

———. 1977. Propagule size, number, and dispersion pattern in *Ambystoma* and *Asclepias*. *American Naturalist* 111:43–68. (15)

———. 1989. In defense of tanks. *Herpetologica* 45:122–123. (9)

Wilbur, H. M., and R. A. Alford. 1985. Priority effects in experimental pond communities: Responses of *Hyla* to *Bufo* and *Rana*. *Ecology* 66:1106–1114. (8)

Wilbur, H. M., and J. P. Collins. 1973. Ecological aspects of amphibian metamorphosis. *Science* 182:1305–1314. (9,16)

Wilbur, H. M., P. J. Morin, and R. N. Harris. 1983. Salamander predation and the structure of experimental communities: Anuran responses. *Ecology* 64:1423–1429. (14)

Wilcox, R. S. 1987. Surface wave reception in invertebrates and vertebrates. In *Sensory Biology of Aquatic Animals*, ed. J. Atema, R. R. Fay, J. Popper, and W. N. Tavolga, 648–663. New York: Springer-Verlag. (16)

Wilczynski, W. 1981. Afferents to the midbrain auditory center in the bullfrog, *Rana catesbeiana*. *Journal of Comparative Neurology* 198:3421–433. (2)

———. 1986. Sexual differences in neural tuning and their effect on active space. *Brain, Behavior, and Evolution* 28:83–94. (2)

———. 1988. Brainstem auditory pathways in anuran amphibians. In *The Evolution of the Amphibian Auditory System*, ed. B. Fritzsch, M. J. Ryan, W. Wilczynski, T. E. Hetherington, and W. Walkowiak, 209–231. New York: John Wiley and Sons. (2)

Wilczynski, W., and J. D. Allison. 1989. Acoustic modulation of neural activity in the hypothalamus of the leopard frog. *Brain, Behavior, and Evolution* 33:317–324. (2)

Wilczynski, W., and E. A. Brenowitz. 1988. Acoustic cues mediate inter-male spacing in a Neotropical frog. *Animal Behaviour* 36:1054–1063. (2)

Wilczynski, W., and R. R. Capranica. 1984. The auditory system of anuran amphibians. *Progress in Neurobiology* 22:1–38. (2)

Wilczynski, W., J. L. Knoll, H. B. Anderson, S. A. Castner, and R. E. Wilcox. 1989. Testosterone effects on motor behaviors and dopamine binding in *Rana pipiens*. *Society for Neuroscience Abstracts* 15:620. (2)

Wilczynski, W., and R. G. Northcutt. 1977. Afferents to the optic tectum of the leopard frog: An HRP study. *Journal of Comparative Neurology* 173:219–230. (2)

———. 1983a. Connections of the bullfrog striatum: Afferent organization. *Journal of Comparative Neurology* 214:321–332. (2)

———. 1983b. Connections of the bullfrog striatum: Efferent projections. Journal of Comparative Neurology 214:333–343. (2)

Wilczynski, W., C. Resler, and R. R. Capranica. 1981a. A study of the mechanism underlying the directional sensitivity of the anuran ear. *Society for Neuroscience Abstracts* 7:147. (2)

———. 1981b. Tympanic and extratympanic sound transmission in the leopard frog, *Rana pipiens*. *Journal of the Acoustical Society of America* 70:S93. (11)

———. 1987. Tympanic and extratympanic sound transmission in the leopard frog. *Journal of Comparative Neurology* 161:659–669. (2)

Wilczynski, W., and M. J. Ryan. 1987. Microgeographic variation in the acoustic communication system of the cricket frog. *Society for Neuroscience Abstracts* 13:869. (2)

———. 1988a. The allometry of acoustic communication in *Acris crepitans*. *American Zoologist* 28:178A. (2)

———. 1988b. The amphibian auditory system as a model for neurobiology, behavior, and evolution. In *The Evolution of the Amphibian Auditory System*, ed. B. Fritzsch, M. J. Ryan, W. Wilczynski, T. E. Hetherington, and W. Walkowiak, 3–12. New York: John Wiley and Sons. (2,14)

Wilczynski, W., H. H. Zakon, and E. A. Brenowitz. 1984. Acoustic communication in spring peepers: Call characteristics and neurophysiological aspects. *Journal of Comparative Physiology* 155:577–584. (2)

Wilder, H. H. 1908. The limb muscles of *Necturus,* and their bearing upon the question of limb homology. *Science,* n.s. 27:493–494. (11)

Wilder, I. W. 1924. The relation of growth to metamorphosis in *Eurycea bislineata* (Green). *Journal of Experimental Zoology* 40:1–112. (16)

Wilder, M. C. 1929. The significance of the ultimobranchial body: A comparative study of its occurrence in urodeles. *Journal of Morphology* 47:383–933. (16)

Wiley, E. O. 1979. Ventral gill arch muscles and the interrelationships of gnathostomes, with a new classification of the Vertebrata. *Zoological Journal of the Linnean Society* 67:149–179. (11)

Wiley, R. H., and D. G. Richards. 1982. Adaptations for acoustic communication in birds: Sound transmission and signal detection. In *Acoustic Communication in Birds,* ed. D. E. Kroodsma and E. H. Miller, 1:113–181. New York: Academic Press. (14)

Wilhelm, K. H., H. Comtesse, and W. Phlumm. 1980. Zur Abhängigkeit des Gesangs von Nahrungsangebot beim Gelbbauchnektarvogel (*Nectarina venusta*). *Zeitschrift für Tierpsychologie* 54:185–202. (14)

Wilhoft, D. C., and J. D. Anderson. 1960. Effect of acclimation on the preferred body temperature of the lizard, *Sceloporus occidentalis.* *Science* 131:610–611. (9)

Wilkes, B. C., V. J. Hruby, A. M. de L. Castrucci, W. C. Sherbrooke, and M. E. Hadley. 1984. Synthesis of a cyclic melanotropic peptide exhibiting both melanin concentrating and dispersing activities. *Science* 224:1111–1113. (3)

Wilkie, D. R. 1986. Muscular fatigue: Effects of hydrogen ions and inorganic phosphate. *Federation Proceedings* 45:2921–2923. (12)

Will, U. 1986. Mauthner neurons survive metamorphosis in anurans: A comparative HRP study on the cytoarchitecture of Mauthner neurons in amphibians. *Journal of Comparative Neurology* 244:111–120. (2,16)

———. 1988. Organization and projections of the area octavolateralis in amphibians. In *The Evolution of the Amphibian Auditory System,* ed. B. Fritzsch, M. J. Ryan, W. Wilczynski, T. E. Hetherington, and W. Walkowiak, 185–208. New York: John Wiley and Sons. (2)

Will, U., and B. Fritzsch. 1988. The eighth nerve of amphibians: Peripheral and central distribution. In *The Evolution of the Amphibian Auditory System,* ed. B. Fritzsch, M. J. Ryan, W. Wilcynski, T. E. Hetherington, and W. Walkowiak, 159–183. New York: John Wiley and Sons. (2,16)

Willem, V. 1920. Observations sur la respiration des amphibiens. *Bulletin de l'Académie Royale de Belgique* 6:298–314. (7)

Williams, G. C. 1966. *Adaptation and Natural Selection: A Critique of Some Current Evolutionary Thought.* Princeton, NJ: Princeton University Press. (14)

Willis, Y. L., D. L. Moyle, and T. S. Baskett. 1956. Emergence, breeding, hibernation, movements, and transformation of the bullfrog, *Rana catesbeiana,* in Missouri. *Copeia* 1956:30–41. (10)

Wills, I. A. 1936. The respiratory rate of developing amphibians with special reference to sex differentiation. *Journal of Experimental Zoology* 73:481–510. (16)

Willumsen, N. J., and E. H. Larsen. 1985. Passive Cl⁻ currents in toad skin: Potential dependence and relation to mitochondria-rich cell density. In *Transport Processes, Iono- and Osmoregulation,* ed. R. Gilles and M. Bailhen, 20–63. Berlin: Springer-Verlag. (5)

Wilson, J. R., K. K. McCully, D. M. Mancini, B. Boden, and B. Chance. 1988. Relationship of muscular fatigue to pH and diprotonated Pᵢ in humans: A ³¹P-NMR study. *Journal of Applied Physiology* 64:2333–2339. (12)

Wilson, J. X. 1984. The renin-angiotensin system in nonmammalian vertebrates. *Endocrine Reviews* 5:45–61. (3)

Wilson, J. X., K. J. Saleh, E. D. Armogan, and E. J. Jaworska. 1987. Catecholamine and blood pressure regulation by gonadotropin-releasing hormone analogs in amphibians. *Canadian Journal of Physiology and Pharmacology* 65:2379–2385. (7)

Wilson, J. X., B. N. Van Vliet, and N. H. West. 1984. Gonadotropin-releasing hormone increases plasma catecholamines and blood pressure in toads. *Neuroendocrinology* 39:437–441. (7)

Windhager, E. E., G. Whittembury, D. E. Oken, H. J. Schatzmann, and A. K. Soloman. 1959. Single proximal tubules of the *Necturus* kidney: 3. Dependence of H₂O movement on NaCl concentration. *American Journal of Physiology* 197:313–318. (5)

Wind-Larsen, H., and C. B. Jørgensen. 1987. Hormonal control of seasonal growth in a temperate zone toad *Bufo bufo. Acta Zoologica* (Stockholm) 68:49–56. (10,13,15)

Wine, R. N. 1988. The effect of temperature on the anaerobic support of locomotion in *Anolis carolinensis* and *Rana pipiens.* M.A. thesis, University of North Carolina, Greensboro. (12)

Winer, B. J. 1971. *Statistical Principles in Experimental Design.* 2d ed. New York: McGraw-Hill. (9)

Winklebauer, R. 1989. Development of the lateral line system in *Xenopus. Progress in Neurobiology* 32:181–206. (16)

Winokur, R. M., and S. D. Hillyard. 1985. Cutaneous musculature associated with pelvic "seat patch" in bufonid anurans. *American Zoologist* 25:131A. (6,11)

———. 1988. Integumentary muscle attachments to the pelvic skin of anurans. *American Zoologist* 28:194A. (11)

Winston, R. M. 1955. Identification and ecology of the toad *Bufo regularis. Copeia* 1955:293–302. (15)

Wintrobe, M. M. 1933. Variations in the size and hemoglobin content of erythrocytes in the blood of various vertebrates. *Folia Haematologie* (Leipzig) 51:32. (5)

Wirsig, C. R., and T. V. Getchell. 1986. Amphibian terminal nerve: Distribution revealed by LHRH and AChE markers. *Brain Research* 385:10–21. (2)

Wischnitzer, S. 1972. *Atlas and Dissection Guide for Comparative Anatomy,* 2d ed. San Francisco: Freeman. (5)

Wisniewski, P. J., L. M. Paull, and F. M. Slater. 1981. The effects of temperature on the breeding migration and spawning of the common toad (*Bufo bufo*). *British Journal of Herpetology* 6:119–121. (8)

Withers, P. C. 1977. Measurement of V̇o₂, V̇co₂, and evaporative water loss with a flow-through mask. *Journal of Applied Physiology* 42:120–123. (12)

———. 1978. Acid-base regulation as a function of body temperature in ectothermic toads, a heliothermic lizard, and a heterothermic mammal. *Journal of Thermal Biology* 3:163–171. (10)

———. 1980. Oxygen consumption of plethodontid salamanders during rest, activity, and recovery. *Copeia* 1980:781–787. (6,12,14)

Withers, P. C., and J. D. Campbell. 1985. Effects of environmental cost on thermoregulation in the desert iguana. *Physiological Zoology* 58:329–339. (9)

Withers, P. C., and S. S. Hillman. 1981. Oxygen consumption of *Amphiuma means* during forced activity and recovery. *Comparative Biochemistry and Physiology* 69A:141–144. (12,14)

———. 1983. The effects of hypoxia on pulmonary function and maximal rates of oxygen consumption in two anuran amphibians. *Journal of Comparative Physiology* 152B:125–129. (6,12)

———. 1988. A steady-state model of maximal oxygen and carbon dioxide transport in anuran amphibians. *Journal of Applied Physiology* 64:860–868. (6,12)

Withers, P. C., S. S. Hillman, and R. C. Drewes. 1984. Evaporative water loss and skin lipids of anuran amphibians. *Journal of Experimental Zoology* 232:11–17. (4,6)

Withers, P. C., S. S. Hillman, R. C. Drewes, and O. M. Sokol. 1982. Water loss and nitrogen excretion in sharp-nosed reed frogs (*Hyperolius nasutus:* Anura, Hyperoliidae). *Journal of Experimental Biology* 97:335–343. (4,6)

Withers, P. C., S. S. Hillman, L. A. Simmons, and A. C. Zygmunt. 1988. Cardiovascular adjustments to enforced activity in the anuran amphibian, *Bufo marinus. Comparative Biochemistry and Physiology* 89A:45–49. (12)

Withers, P. C., M. Lea, T. C. Solberg, M. Baustian, and M. Hedrick. 1988. Metabolic fates of lactate during recovery from activity in an anuran amphibian, *Bufo americanus. Journal of Experimental Zoology* 246:236–243. (12)

Withers, P. C., G. Louw, and S. Nicolson. 1982. Water loss, oxygen consumption, and colour change in "waterproof" reed frogs (*Hyperolius*). *South African Journal of Science* 78:30–32. (6,9,12)

Witschi, E. 1924. Die Entwicklung der Keimzellen der *Rana temporaria* L.: 1. Urkeimzellen und Spermatogenese. *Zeitschrift für Zellforschung und Gewebelehre* 1:523. (15)

———. 1949. The larval ear of the frog and its transformation during metamorphosis. *Zeitschrift für Naturforschung* 4B:230–242. (16)

———. 1956. *Development of Vertebrates.* Philadelphia: W. B. Saunders. (2,16)

Wittig, K. P., and S. C. Brown. 1977. Sodium balance in the newt,

Notophthalmus viridescens. Comparative Biochemistry and Physiology 58A:49–52. (6)

Wittle, L. W. 1984. Effects of hypophysectomy and prolactin on calcium regulation in the red-spotted newt, *Notophthalmus viridescens. General and Comparative Endocrinology* 54:181–187. (3)

Wittle, L. W., and J. Dent. 1979. Effects of parathyroidectomy and parathyroid extracts on levels of calcium and phosphate in the blood and urine of the red-spotted newt. *General and Comparative Endocrinology* 37:428–439. (3,5)

Wittouck, P. J. 1975. Influence de la composition saline du milieu sur la concentration ionique du sérum chez l'axolotl, intact et hypophysectomise: Effet de lat prolactine. *General and Comparative Endocrinology* 27:169–178. (5)

Wojcieszyn, J. W., R. A. Schlegel, E.-S. Wu, and K. A. Jacobson. 1981. Diffusion of injected macromolecules within the cytoplasm of living cells. *Proceedings of the National Academy of Sciences* 78:4407–4410. (8)

Wolanczyk, J. P., K. B. Storey, and J. G. Baust. 1989. Ice nucleating activity in the blood of the freeze tolerant frog *Rana sylvatica. Cryobiology* 27:328–335. (10)

Woledge, R. C. 1968. The energetics of tortoise muscle. *Journal of Physiology* (London) 197:685–707. (8)

Woledge, R. C., N. A. Curtin, and E. Homsher. 1985. *Energetic Aspects of Muscle Contraction.* London: Academic Press. (12)

Wollmuth, L. P., and L. I. Crawshaw. 1988. The effect of development and season on temperature selection in bullfrog tadpoles. *Physiological Zoology* 61:461–469. (9,16)

Wollmuth, L. P., L. I. Crawshaw, R. B. Forbes, and D. A. Grahn. 1987. Temperature selection during development in a montane anuran species, *Rana cascadae. Physiological Zoology* 60:472–480. (9,14)

Wollmuth, L. P., L. I. Crawshaw, and H. Panayiotides-Djaferis. 1987. Thermoregulatory effects of intracranial norepinephrine injections in goldfish. *American Journal of Physiology* 253:R821–R826. (9)

Wollmuth, L. P., L. I. Crawshaw, and R. N. Rausch. 1988. Adrenoceptors and temperature regulation in goldfish. *American Journal of Physiology* 255:R600–R604. (9)

Wood, A. 1962. *The Physics of Music.* London: Methuen. (14)

Wood, C. M., R. S. Munger, and D. P. Toews. 1989. Ammonia, urea, and H+ distribution and the evolution of ureotelism in amphibians. *Journal of Experimental Biology* 144:215–233. (5)

Wood, C. M., and G. Shelton. 1980. Cardiovascular dynamics and adrenergic responses of the rainbow trout *in vivo. Journal of Experimental Biology* 87:271–284. (7)

Wood, S. C. 1971. Effects of metamorphosis on blood respiratory properties and erythrocyte adenosine triphosphate level of the salamander *Dicamptodon ensatus* (Eschscholtz). *Respiration Physiology* 12:53–65. (5,16)

———. 1972. Metabolic rate of larval and adult Pacific giant salamanders, *Dicamptodon ensatus* (Eschscholtz). *Copeia* 1972:177–179. (12)

———. 1982. The effect of oxygen affinity on arterial Po₂ in animals with central vascular shunts. *Journal of Applied Physiology* 53:1360–1364. (5)

———. 1984. Cardiovascular shunts and oxygen transport in lower vertebrates. *American Journal of Physiology* 247:R3–R14. (5,10)

Wood, S. C., and J. W. Hicks. 1985. Oxygen homeostasis in vertebrates with cardiovascular shunts. In *Cardiovascular Shunts: Phylogenetic, Ontogenetic, and Clinical Aspects,* ed. K. Johansen and W. W. Burggren, 354–366. Copenhagen: Munksgaard. (5,9)

Wood, S. C., J. W. Hicks, and R. K. Dupré. 1987. Hypoxic reptiles: Blood gases, body temperature, and control of breathing. *American Zoologist* 27:21–29. (9)

Wood, S. C., R. W. Hoyt, and W. W. Burggren. 1982. Control of hemoglobin function in the salamander, *Ambystom tigrinum. Molecular Physiology* 2:263–272. (5,16)

Wood, S. C., and C. Lenfant. 1979. Oxygen transport and oxygen delivery. In *Evolution of Respiratory Processes: A Comparative Approach,* vol. 12, *Lung Biology in Health and Disease,* ed. S. C. Wood, and C. Lenfant, 193–223. New York: Marcel Dekker. (5)

———. 1987. Phylogeny of the gas-exchange system: Red cell function. In *Handbook of Physiology,* sec. 3, ed. L. E. Farhi and S. M. Tenney, 4:131–146. Bethesda, MD: American Physiological Society. (5)

Wood, S. C., G. M. Malvin, and C. Reidel. 1989. Effect of hematocrit on behavioral temperature regulation of the toad, *Bufo marinus. FASEB Journal* 3:A234. (9)

Wood, S. C., and L. P. Orr. 1969. Effects of photoperiod and size on the oxygen consumption of the dusky salamander *Desmognathus fuscus. Ohio Journal of Science* 69:121–125. (12)

Wood, S. C., R. E. Weber, G. M. O. Maloiy, and K. Johansen. 1975. Oxygen uptake and blood respiratory properties of the caecilian *Boulengerula titanus. Respiration Physiology* 24:355–363. (6,12)

Woodruff, D. S. 1977. Male postmating brooding behavior in three Australian *Pseudophryne* (Anura: Leptodactylidae). *Herpetologica* 33:296–303. (14)

Woodward, B. 1982. Male persistence and mating success in Woodhouse's toad. *Ecology* 63:583–585. (14)

Woodward, B. D. 1982. Local intraspecific variation in clutch parameters in the spotted salamander (*Ambystoma maculatum*). *Copeia* 1982:157–160. (15)

Woody, C. J., and R. C. Jaffe. 1982. Partial characterization of frog (*Rana catesbeiana*) hepatic glucocorticoid receptor. *General and Comparative Endocrinology* 47:28–35. (16)

———. 1984. Binding of dexamethasone by hepatic, intestine, and tail-fin cytosol in *Rana catesbeiana* tadpoles during spontaneous and triiodothyronine-induced metamorphosis. *General and Comparative Endocrinology* 54:194–202. (16)

Woolbright, L. L. 1983. Sexual selection and size dimorphism in anuran Amphibia. *American Naturalist* 1221:110–119. (14)

———. 1985a. Anuran size dimorphism: A reply to Sullivan. *American Naturalist* 125:741–743. (14)

———. 1985b. Patterns of nocturnal movement and calling by the tropical frog *Eleutherodactylus coqui. Herpetologica* 41:1–9. (14)

———. 1985c. Sexual dimorphism in body size of the subtropical frog, *Eleutherodactylus coqui.* Ph.D. diss., State University of New York, Albany. (14)

Woolbright, L. L., and M. M. Stewart. 1987. Foraging success of the tropical frog, *Eleutherodactylus coqui:* The cost of calling. *Copeia* 1987:69–75. (14)

Wootton, J. R. 1979. Energy costs of egg production and environmental determinants of fecundity in teleost fishes. *Symposia of the Zoological Society of London* 44:133–160. (15)

Wright, A. H., and Wright, A. A. 1949. *Handbook of Frogs and Toads.* Ithaca, NY: Comstock Publishing Associates. (10)

Wright, P. A. 1971. 3-keto-μ4-steroid: Requirement for ovulation in *Rana pipiens. General and Comparative Endocrinology* 16:511–515. (15)

Wright, P. A., D. J. Randall, and C. M. Wood. 1988. The distribution of ammonia and H+ between tissue compartments in lemon sole (*Parophys vetulus*) at rest, during hypercapnia, and following exercise. *Journal of Experimental Biology* 136:149–175. (5)

Wright, P. A., and C. M. Wood. 1988. Muscle ammonia stores are not determined by pH gradients. *Fish Physiology and Biochemistry* 5:159–162. (5)

Wrobel, W. F., W. F. Gergits, and R. G. Jaeger. 1980. An experimental study of interference competition among terrestrial salamanders. *Ecology* 61:1034–1039. (14)

Wu, P., R. M. Lechan, and I. M. D. Jackson. 1987. Identification and characterization of thyrotropin-releasing hormone precursor peptides in the rat brain. *Endocrinology* 121:108–115. (16)

Wunderer, H. 1910. Die Entwicklung der äussern Körperform des Alpensalamanders (*Salamandra atra* Laur.). *Zoologische Jahrbücher* 29:367–414. (15)

Wygoda, M. 1984. Low cutaneous evaporative water loss in arboreal frogs. *Physiological Zoology* 57:329–337. (4,6)

———. 1988a. Adaptive control of water loss resistance in an arboreal frog. *Herpetologica* 44:251–257. (4,6,9)

———. 1988b. A comparative study of time constants of cooling in green tree frogs (*Hyla cinerea*) and southern leopard frogs (*Rana sphenocephala*). *Herpetologica* 44:261–265. (4)

———. 1989a. Body temperatures in arboreal and nonarboreal anuran amphibians: Differential effects of a small change in water vapor density. *Journal of Thermal Biology* 14:293–242. (9)

———. 1989b. A comparative study of heating rates in arboreal and nonarboreal frogs. *Journal of Herpetology* 23:141–145. (6,9)

Wylie, S. R. 1981. Effects of basking on the biology of the canyon treefrog *Hyla arenicolor.* Ph.D. diss., Arizona State University, Tempe. (4)

Wyman, J. 1852. Anatomy of the nervous system of *Rana pipiens. Smithsonian Contributions to Knowledge* 5, article 4. (7)

Wyman, R. L., and D. S. Hawksley-Lescault. 1987. Soil acidity affects distribution, behavior, and physiology of the salamander *Plethodon cinereus*. *Ecology* 68:1819–1827. (14)

Xavier, F. 1973. Le cycle des voies génitales femelles de *Nectophrynoides occidentalis* Angel amphibien anoure vivipare. *Zeitschrift für Zellforschung* 140:509–534. (13,16)

———. 1977. An exceptional reproductive strategy in Anura: *Nectophrynoides occidentalis* Angel (Bufonidae), an example of adaptation to terrestrial life by viviparity. In *Major Patterns in Vertebrate Evolution*, ed. M. K. Hecht, P. C. Goody, and B. M. Hecht, 545–552. New York: Plenum Press. (15)

Yacoe, M. E., J. W. Cummings, P. Myers, and G. K. Creighton. 1982. Muscle enzyme profile, diet, and flight in South American bats. *American Journal of Physiology* 242:R189–R194. (14)

Yager, D. 1982. A novel mechanism for underwater sound production in *Xenopus borealis*. *American Zoologist* 22:887. (11,14)

Yamaguchi, K., K. D. Jurgens. H. Bartels, and J. Piiper. 1987. Oxygen transfer properties and dimensions of red blood cells in high altitude camelids, dromedary camel, and goat. *Journal of Comparative Physiology* 157B:1–9. (5)

Yamaguchi, K., K. D. Jurgens, H. Bartels, P. Scheid, and J. Piiper. 1988. Dependence of O$_2$ transfer conductance of red blood cells on cellular dimensions. In *Oxygen Transport to Tissue X*, ed. T. K. Goldstick and D. F. Bruley, 571–578. New York: Plenum Publishing. (5)

Yamamoto, K., and S. Kikuyama. 1982a. Effect of prolactin antiserum on growth and resorption of tadpole tail. *Endocrinology Japonica* 29:81–85. (16)

———. 1982b. Radioimmunoassay of prolactin in plasma of bullfrog tadpoles. *Endocrinology Japonica* 29:159–167. (16)

Yamamoto, K., K. Niihuma, and S. Kikuyama. 1986. Synthesis and storage of prolactin in the pituitary gland of bullfrog tadpoles during metamorphosis. *General and Comparative Endocrinology* 62:247–253. (16)

Yancey, P. H., and G. N. Somero. 1979. Counteraction of urea destabilization of protein structure by methylamine osmoregulatory compounds of elasmobranch fishes. *Biochemical Journal* 183:317–323. (10)

———. 1980. Methylamine osmoregulatory solutes of elasmobranch fishes counteract urea inhibition of enzymes. *Journal of Experimental Zoology* 212:205–213. (10)

Yokota, S. D., S. Benyajati, and W. H. Dantzler. 1985. Comparative aspects of glomerular filtration in vertebrates. *Renal Physiology* 8:193–221. (5,6)

Yokota, S. D., and S. S. Hillman. 1984. Adrenergic control of anuran cutaneous hydroosmotic response. *General and Comparative Endocrinology* 53:309–314. (5,6)

Yoneyama, H., and H. Iwasawa. 1985. Annual changes in the testis and accessory sex organs of the bullfrog *Rana catesbeiana*. *Zoological Science* 2:229–237. (15)

Yorio, T. 1987. Membrane lipids and their significance for ion and fluid transport. In *Comparative Physiology of Environmental Adaptations*, ed. L. Kirsch and B. Lahlou, 148–157. Basel: S. Karger. (16)

Yorio, T., and P. J. Bentley. 1977. Asymmetrical permeability of the integument of tree frogs (Hylidae). *Journal of Experimental Biology* 67:197–204. (6,16)

———. 1978a. The permeability of the skin of the aquatic anuran *Xenopus laevis* (Pipidae). *Journal of Experimental Biology* 72:285–289. (5)

———. 1978b. Stimulation of the short-circuit current (sodium transport) across the skin of the frog (*Rana pipiens*) by corticosteroids: Structure-activity relationships. *Journal of Endocrinology* 79:283–290. (6)

Yoshikura, M. 1959. The action of the pituitary in sex differentiation and sex reversal in amphibians: 2. Effect of high temperature on gonads of hypophysectomized frog larvae. *Kumamoto Journal of Science* 2B:69–101. (16)

Yoshimura, H., M. Yata, M. Yuasa, and R. A. Wolbach. 1961. Renal regulation of acid-base balance in the bullfrog. *American Journal of Physiology* 201:980–986. (5)

Yoshioka, T., K. Kawai, and Y. Katsuki. 1976. The receptive mechanism of various metallic ions in the lateral-line organ of the tadpoles of *Rana catesbeiana*. *Japanese Journal of Physiology* 26:441–453. (16)

Yoshizato, K., and E. Frieden. 1975. Increase in binding capacity for

triiodothyronine in tadpole tail nuclei during metamorphosis. *Nature* 254:705–706. (16)

Yovanof, S., and A. S. Feng. 1983. Effects of estradiol on auditory evoked responses from the frog's auditory midbrain. *Neuroscience Letters* 36:291–297. (2)

Ypey, D. L. 1975. Effects of muscle length and stimulus frequency on neuromuscular transmission in the frog. Ph.D. diss., University of Leiden, Netherlands. (11)

———. 1978. A topographical study of the distribution of end-plates in the cutaneous pectoris, sartorius, and gastrocnemius of the frog. *Journal of Morphology* 155:327–348. (11)

Yu, N. Y., C. Y. Hsu, H. H. Ku, and H. C. Wang. 1985. The development of ACTH-like substance during tadpole metamorphosis. *General and Comparative Endocrinology* 57:72–76. (16)

Yucha, C. B., and L. C. Stoner. 1986. Bicarbonate transport by amphibian nephron. *American Journal of Physiology* 251:F865–F872. (5)

———. 1987. Bicarbonate transport by initial collecting tubule of aquatic- and land-phase Amphibia. *American Journal of Physiology* 253:F310–F317. (5)

Zadunaisky, J. A., O. A. Candia, and D. J. Chiarandini. 1963. The origin of the short circuit current in the isolated skin of the South American frog *Leptodactylus ocellatus*. *Journal of General Physiology* 47:393–402. (5)

Zadunaisky, J. A., and M. A. Lande. 1972. Calcium content and exchange in amphibian skin and its isolated epithelium. *American Journal of Physiology* 222:1309–1315. (5)

Zahavi, A. 1977. The cost of honesty (further remarks on the handicap principle). *Journal of Theoretical Biology* 67:603–605. (14)

Zahl, P. A. 1937. Cytologische Untersuchungen über die Hypophysis cerebri des weiblichen Frosches: Unter besonderer Berücksichtung der Fortpflanzungstätigkeit. *Zeitschrift der mikroskopische und anatomische Forschung* 42:303–361. (15)

Zakon, H. H., and W. Wilczynski. 1988. The physiology of the anuran eighth nerve. In *The Evolution of the Amphibian Auditory System*, ed. B. Fritzsch, M. J. Ryan, W. Wilczynski, T. E. Hetherington, and W. Walkowiak, 125–155. New York: John Wiley and Sons. (2,14)

Zavenella, T. 1985. Environmental temperature and metastatic spread of melanoma in the crested newt. *Cancer Letters* 27:171–180. (8)

Zeiske, W., and W. Van Driessche. 1979. Saturable K$^+$ pathway across outer border of frog skin (*Rana temporaria*): Kinetics and inhibition by Cs and other cations. *Journal of Membrane Biology* 47:77–96. (5)

Zclick, R. D. 1986. Jamming avoidance in electric fish and frogs: Strategies of signal oscillator timing. *Brain, Behavior, and Evolution* 28:60–69. (2)

Zelick, R. D., and P. M. Narins. 1982. Analysis of acoustically evoked call suppression behaviour in a Neotropical frog. *Animal Behaviour* 30:728–733. (2)

———. 1985. Characterization of the advertisement call oscillator in the frog *Eleutherodactylus coqui*. *Journal of Comparative Physiology* 156:223–230. (2,14)

Zepp, P. 1923. Beiträge zur vergleichenden Untersuchungen der heimischen Froscharten. *Zeitschrift für Anatomie und Entwicklungsgeschichte* 69:84–180. (15)

Zetler, G. 1982. Cholecystokinin octapeptide, caerulein, and caerulein analogues: Effects on thermoregulation in the mouse. *Neuropharmacology* 21:795–801. (9)

Ziegler, T. W., J. H. Ludens, and D. D. Fanestil. 1974. Role of carbonic anhydrase in urinary acidification by the toad bladder. *American Journal of Physiology* 277:1132–1138. (5)

Zimmerman, B. L., and J. P. Bogart. 1984. Vocalizations of primary forest frog species in the central Amazon. *Acta Amazonica* 14:473–519. (14)

Zimmerman, L. C., and C. R. Tracy. 1989. Interactions between the environment and ectothermy and herbivory in reptiles. *Physiological Zoology* 62:374–409. (4)

Zimmermann, E., and H. Rahmann. 1987. Acoustic communication in the poison-arrow frog *Phyllobates tricolor*: Advertisement calls and their effects on behavior and metabolic brain activity of recipients. *Journal of Comparative Physiology* 160A:693–702. (13)

Zimmermann, E., and H. Zimmermann. 1982. Soziale Interaktionen, Brutpflege, und Zucht des Pfeilgiftfrosches *Dendrobates histrionicus* (Amphibia: Salientia: Dendrobatidae). *Salamandra* 18:150–167. (13)

———. 1985. Brutpflegestrategien bei Pfeilgiftfröschen (*Dendrobatidae*). *Verhandlungen der Deutschen Zoologischen Gesellschaft* 78: 220. (13)

Zipser, R. D., P. Licht, and H. A. Bern. 1969. Comparative effects of mammalian prolactin and growth hormone on growth in the toads *Bufo boreas* and *Bufo marinus*. *General and Comparative Endocrinology* 13:382–391. (13,15)

Ziyadeh, F. N., E. Kelepouris, and Z. S. Agus. 1986. Relationships between calcium and chloride transport in frog skin. *American Journal of Physiology* 251:F647–F654. (5)

Ziyadeh, F. N., E. Kelepouris, M. M. Civan, and Z. S. Agus. 1985. cAMP- and β-adrenergic-stimulated chloride-dependent Ca^{2+} secretion in frog skin. *American Journal of Physiology* 249:F713–F722. (5)

Zoeller, R. T., and F. L. Moore. 1985. Seasonal changes in luteinizing hormone–releasing hormone concentrations in microdissected brain regions of male rough-skinned newts (*Taricha granulosa*). *General and Comparative Endocrinology* 58:222–230. (3)

———. 1986. Correlation between immunoreactive vasotocin in optic tectum and seasonal changes in reproductive behaviors of male rough-skinned newts. *Hormones and Behavior* 20:148–154. (3)

———. 1988. Brain arginine vasotocin concentrations related to sexual behaviors and hydromineral balance in an amphibian. *Hormones and Behavior* 22:66–75. (3)

Zotterman, Y. 1949. The response of frog taste fibers to the application of pure water. *Acta Physiologica Scandinavica* 18:181–189. (7)

Zucker, A. 1980. Procedural and anatomical considerations of the determination of cutaneous water loss in squamate reptiles. *Copeia* 1980: 425–439. (4)

Zug, G. R. 1978. Anuran locomotion: Structure and function: 2. Jumping performance of semiaquatic, terrestrial, and arboreal frogs. *Smithsonian Contributions to Zoology* 276:1–31. (11)

———. 1985. Anuran locomotion: Fatigue and jumping performance. *Herpetologica* 41:188–194. (12,14)

Zug, G. R., and R. Altig. 1978. Anuran locomotion: Structure and function: The jumping forces of frogs. *Journal of the Washington Academy of Science* 8:144–147. (11)

Zug, G. R., and P. B. Zug. 1979. The marine toad, *Bufo marinus:* A natural history resume of native populations. *Smithsonian Contributions to Zoology* 284:1–58. (9,12,13,15)

Zuiderwijk, A., and M. Sparreboom. 1986. Territorial behaviour in crested newt *Triturus cristatus* and marbled newt *T. marmoratus* (Amphibia, Urodela). *Bijdragen tot de Dierkunde* 56:205–213. (14)

Zweifel, R. G. 1957. Studies on the critical thermal maxima of salamanders. *Ecology* 38:64–69. (8)

———. 1959. Effect of temperature on call of the frog, *Bombina variegata*. *Copeia* 1959:322–327. (8)

———. 1968a. Effects of temperature, body size, and hybridization on mating calls of toads, *Bufo a. americanus* and *Bufo woodhousii fowleri*. *Copeia* 1968:269–284. (2,8)

———. 1986b. Reproductive biology of anurans of the arid Southwest, with emphasis on adaptation of embryos to temperature. *Bulletin of the American Museum of Natural History* 140:1–64. (8)

———. 1977. Upper thermal tolerances of anuran embryos in relation to stage of development and breeding habits. *American Museum Novitates* 2617:1–21. (8)

Zylberberg, L. 1972. Données histologiques sur les glandes linguales d'*Ichthyophis glutinosus* (L.) (Batracien, Gymnophione). *Archives d'Anatomie Microscopie* 61:227–242. (13)

———. 1977. Histochemistry and ultrastructure of amphibian lingual glands and phylogenetic relations. *Histological Journal* 9:505–520. (13)

Contributors

George S. Bakken
Department of Life Sciences
Indiana State University
Terre Haute, Indiana 47809

Robert G. Boutilier
Department of Zoology
University of Cambridge
Downing Street
Cambridge CB2 3EJ
United Kingdom

Warren Burggren
Department of Biological Sciences
University of Nevada
4505 Maryland Parkway
Las Vegas, Nevada 89154-4004

Greet De Gueldre
Department of Zoology
University of Antwerp (UIA)
Universiteitplein 1
B-2610 Antwerp-Wilrijk
Belgium

R. Keith Dupré
Deceased

Martin E. Feder
Department of Organismal Biology and Anatomy
University of Chicago
1025 East 57th Street
Chicago, Illinois 60637-1574

Robert J. Full
Department of Integrative Biology
University of California, Berkeley
Berkeley, California 94720

Carl Gans
Department of Biology
2127 Kraus Natural Sciences Building
University of Michigan
Ann Arbor, Michigan 48109-1048

Robert E. Gatten, Jr.
Department of Biology
University of North Carolina at Greensboro
Greensboro, North Carolina 27412

Ceil A. Herman
Department of Biology
New Mexico State University
Las Cruces, New Mexico 88003

Stanley S. Hillman
Department of Biology
Portland State University
Portland, Oregon 97207-0751

Stanley D. Hillyard
Department of Biological Sciences
University of Nevada
4505 Maryland Parkway
Las Vegas, Nevada 89154-4004

Victor H. Hutchison
Department of Zoology
University of Oklahoma
Norman, Oklahoma 73019

Donald C. Jackson
Division of Biological and Medical Science
Brown University
Providence, Rhode Island 02912

Henry B. John-Alder
Department of Biological Sciences
Rutgers University
Post Office Box 1059
Piscataway, New Jersey 08855

C. Barker Jørgensen
Zoophysiological Laboratory A
August Krogh Institute
Universitetsparken 13
DK-2100 Copenhagen Ø
Denmark

John J. Just
Comparative Physiology Group
School of Biological Sciences
University of Kentucky
Lexington, Kentucky 40506

Lis Olesen Larsen
Zoophysiological Laboratory A
August Krogh Institute
Universitetsparken 13
DK-2100 Copenhagen Ø
Denmark

Lon L. McClanahan
Department of Biology
California State University
Fullerton, California 92634

William E. Magnusson
Departamento de Ecologia
Instituto Nacional de Pesquisas Amazônia
Caixa Postal 478
69011 Manaus Amazonas
Brasil

Kirk Miller
Department of Biology
Franklin and Marshall College
Lancaster, Pennsylvania 17604

Michael P. O'Connor
Department of Bioscience and Biotechnology
Drexel University
Philadelphia, Pennsylvania 19104
and
Savannah River Ecology Laboratory
Drawer E
Aiken, South Carolina 29801

Alan W. Pinder
Biology Department
Dalhousie University
Halifax, Nova Scotia B3H 4J1
Canada

F. Harvey Pough
Laboratory of Functional Ecology
Section of Ecology and Systematics
Corson Hall
Cornell University
Ithaca, New York 14853-2701

Lawrence C. Rome
Department of Biology
University of Pennsylvania
Leidy Laboratories
Philadelphia, Pennsylvania 19104

Michael J. Ryan
Department of Zoology
University of Texas
Austin, Texas 78712-1064

Vaughan H. Shoemaker
Department of Biology
University of California
Riverside, California 92521

James R. Spotila
Department of Bioscience and Biotechnology
Drexel University
Philadelphia, Pennsylvania 19104
and
Savannah River Ecology Laboratory
Drawer E
Aiken, South Carolina 29801

E. Don Stevens
Department of Zoology
University of Guelph
Guelph, Ontario N1G 2W1
Canada

Daniel F. Stiffler
Biological Sciences Department
California State Polytechnic University
Pomona, California 91768

Kenneth B. Storey
Institute of Biochemistry
Department of Biology
Carleton University
Ottawa, Ontario K1S 5B6
Canada

Theodore L. Taigen
Department of Ecology and Evolutionary Biology
Box U-43
Room TLS 312
University of Connecticut
Storrs, Connecticut 06268

Daniel P. Toews
Department of Biology
Acadia University
Wolfville, Nova Scotia B0P 1X0
Canada

Gordon R. Ultsch
Department of Biology
University of Alabama
Tuscaloosa, Alabama 35487

Bruce N. Van Vliet
Department of Physiology and Biophysics
University of Mississippi Medical Center
Jackson, Mississippi 39216–4505

Kentwood D. Wells
Department of Ecology and Evolutionary Biology
Box U-43
Room TLS 312
University of Connecticut
Storrs, Connecticut 06268

Nigel H. West
Department of Physiology
University of Saskatchewan
Saskatoon, Saskatchewan S7N 0W0
Canada

Walter Wilczynski
Department of Psychology and Institute for Neuroscience
University of Texas
Austin, Texas 78712

Philip C. Withers
Department of Zoology
University of Western Australia
Nedlands, Western Australia 6009
Australia

Mark L. Wygoda
Department of Biological and Environmental Science
McNeese State University
Lake Charles, Louisiana 70609

Systematic Index

Subject Index

637